# SMITH AND ROBERSON'S

# BUSINESS LAW

## *Eleventh Edition*

**RICHARD A. MANN**

Professor of Business Law
The University of North Carolina at Chapel Hill
Member of the North Carolina Bar

**BARRY S. ROBERTS**

Professor of Business Law
The University of North Carolina at Chapel Hill
Member of the North Carolina and Pennsylvania Bars

**WEST** WEST LEGAL STUDIES IN BUSINESS
Thomson Learning™

Australia • Canada • Denmark • Japan • Mexico • New Zealand • Philippines
Puerto Rico • Singapore • South Africa • Spain • United Kingdom • United States

Vice President/Publisher: Jack W. Calhoun
Senior Acquisitions Editor: Rob Dewey
Acquisitions Editor: Scott D. Person
Developmental Editors: Bob Sandman, Mary H. Draper
Marketing Manager: Michael Worls
Production Editor: Deanna R. Quinn
Manufacturing Coordinator: Georgina Calderon
Internal Design: Adapted by Ellen Pettengell, Ellen Pettengell Design, Chicago, IL
Cover Design: Kim Torbeck, Imbue Design, Cincinnati, OH
Production House: DPS Associates, Inc.
SGML Management Services and Composition: Texterity Inc.
Printer: West Group

Printed in the United States of America

2  3  4  5  02  01  00  99

For more information contact West Legal Studies in Business, South-Western College Publishing, 5101 Madison Road, Cincinnati, Ohio, 45227 or find us on the Internet at http://www.westbuslaw.com

**For permission to use material from this text or product, contact us by**
· **telephone: 1-800-730-2214**
· **fax: 1-800-730-2215**
· **web: http://www.thomsonrights.com**

**Library of Congress Cataloging-in-Publication Data**
Mann, Richard A.
    Smith and Roberson's business law. -- 11th ed. / Richard A. Mann, Barry S. Roberts.
        p.    cm.
    Includes index.
    ISBN 0-324-00195-9 (hc. : alk. paper)
    1. Commercial law--United States.  2. Business law--United States.
  I. Roberts, Barry S.  II. Smith, Len Young, 1901-1993. Business law.  III. Title.  IV. Title: Business law.
  KF888.S554  2000
  346.7307--dc21                                                                                    99-27528

This book is printed on acid-free paper.

# About the Authors

**Richard A. Mann** received a B.S. in Mathematics from the University of North Carolina at Chapel Hill and a J.D. from Yale Law School. He is currently professor of Business Law at the Kenan-Flagler School of Business Administration, University of North Carolina at Chapel Hill and is past president of the Southeastern Regional Business Law Association. He is a member of Who's Who in American Law, Outstanding Young Men of America, and the North Carolina Bar.

Professor Mann has written extensively on a number of legal topics including bankruptcy, sales, secured transactions, real property, insurance law, and business associations. He has received the *American Business Law Journal* award both for the best article and for the best comment. He has served as a reviewer and staff editor for the *American Business Law Journal.* He teaches in several executive education programs and is a founder, managing director, and instructor in the Carolina CPA Review. He is a co-author of *Essentials of Businesss Law (Sixth Edition), Business Law and the Regulation of Business (Sixth Edition),* and *Contemporary Business Law (First Edition).*

**Barry S. Roberts** received a B.S. in Business Administration from Pennsylvania State University, a J.D. from the University of Pennsylvania, and an LL.M. from Harvard Law School. He served as a judicial clerk for the Pennsylvania Supreme Court prior to practicing law in Pittsburgh. Barry Roberts is currently Professor of Business Law at the Kenan-Flagler School of Business Administration, University of North Carolina at Chapel Hill. He is a member of Who's Who in American Law, Outstanding Young Men in America, and the North Carolina and Pennsylvania Bars.

Professor Roberts has written numerous articles on such topics as antitrust, products liability, constitutional law, banking law, employment law, and business associations. He has been a reviewer and staff editor for the *American Business Law Journal.* Professor Roberts is a founder, managing director and instructor in the Carolina CPA Review. He is a co-author of *Essentials of Businesss Law (Sixth Edition), Business Law and the Regulation of Business (Sixth Edition),* and *Contemporary Business Law (First Edition).*

# Contents in Brief

# Contents

Contents

# Preface

The format of the Eleventh Edition is basically the same as that of the ten prior editions, in that each chapter contains narrative text, cases consisting of selected court decisions, and problems.

## Topical Coverage

This text is designed for use in business law and legal environment courses generally offered in universities, colleges, and schools of business and commerce. By reason of the broad coverage and variety of the material, instructors may readily adapt this volume to specially designed courses in business law by assigning and emphasizing different combinations of the subject matter. The text covers all topics included in the CPA exam.

Emphasis has been placed upon the regulatory environment of business law: the first eight chapters introduce the legal environment of business, and Part Nine (Chapters 40 through 47) addresses government regulation of business.

## New to This Edition

Almost every chapter now has an end-of-chapter INTERNET question that leads the student to the rich resources of the World Wide Web to obtain additional knowledge about the law. One caveat for students is that they should examine the reliability and currency of the information found; not all of it is current or accurate. In the Uniform Commercial Code Sales chapters (Chapters 21 through 25), we have added extensive references to Leases of Goods. In these chapters we have also included substantial coverage of the United Nations Convention on Contracts for the International Sales of Goods (CISG). In the first partnership chapter (Chapter 31), we have added a section describing the most important

factors to consider in choosing a form of business association and a brief explanation of how the various forms of business associations differ with respect to these factors.

## Improved Readability

To improve readability, all unnecessary "legalese" has been omitted while necessary legal terms have been printed in boldface and clearly defined, explained, and illustrated. The text is enriched by numerous illustrative hypothetical and case examples which help students relate the material to real-life experiences. The end-of-chapter cases are cross-referenced in the text, as are related topics covered in other chapters.

## Case Treatment

From long classroom experience, we are of the opinion that fundamental legal principles can be learned more effectively from text and case materials having at least a degree of human interest. Accordingly, we have included a large number of recent cases. Landmark cases, on the other hand, have not been neglected. All have been carefully edited to preserve the actual language of the court and to show the essential facts of the case, the issue or issues involved, the decision of the court, and the reason for its decision.

## Illustrations

In this text, we have used more than 140 classroom-tested figures, charts, and diagrams. The diagrams help the student conceptualize the many abstract concepts in the law; the charts not only summarize prior discussions but also help to illustrate relationships among legal rules. In addition, each chapter has a summary in the form of an annotated outline of the entire chapter, including key terms.

## End-of-Chapter Materials

Classroom-proven problems appear at the end of chapters to test the student's understanding of major concepts. We have used the problems, many of which are taken from reported court decisions, and consider them excellent stimulants to classroom discussion. Students, in turn, have found the problems helpful in enabling them to apply the basic rules of law to factual situations. In addition to the problems, which readily suggest other and related problems to the inquiring, analytical mind, we have included discussion questions to provide students another opportunity to assess their comprehension of the material.

## Appendices

The text contains comprehensive appendices, including the Constitution of the United States (Appendix A); the Uniform Commercial Code (Appendix B); the Uniform Partnership Act (Appendix C); and the Revised Model Business Corporation Act (Appendix D). A comprehensive Dictionary of Legal Terms appears in Appendix E.

## Pedagogical Benefits

Classroom use and study of this book should provide for the student the following benefits and skills:

1. Perception and appreciation of the scope, extent, and importance of the law.
2. Basic knowledge of the fundamental concepts, principles, and rules of law that apply to business transactions.
3. Knowledge of the function and operation of courts and governmental administrative agencies.
4. Ability to recognize the potential legal problems which may arise in a doubtful or complicated situation, and the necessity of consulting a lawyer and obtaining competent professional legal advice.
5. Development of analytical skills and reasoning power.

## *SUPPLEMENTAL MATERIALS*

**Instructor's Manual,** by Richard Mann and Barry Roberts with Beth Woods, is perforated and three-hole punched. It includes:

- part opening ethics questions, suggested activities, and research projects
- chapter lecture outlines
- answers to problems and discussion questions

- briefs to cases page-referenced to the book
- suggested case questions for students
- recommendations for use of transparency acetates
- supplemental lectures

**Test Bank,** by Michelle Rehwinkel at Tallahassee Community College of Florida, comes in a separate volume and includes approximately seventy-five test questions per chapter—thirty-five true/false, thirty-five multiple choice, and five short essay.

**Thomson Learning Testing Tools**™ allows instructors to create, edit, store, and print exams. Instructors may add and edit questions directly on screen, plus choose how they are arranged; randomly, by type, or in the order you specify. Available to qualified adopters.

**PowerPoint**™ **Presentation Slides** give easy customization of transparency concepts to complement lectures.

## *STUDENT SUPPLEMENTS*

**Study Guide,** by Dennis Hower and Peter Kahn of the University of Minnesota, provides for each chapter a brief statement of purpose; chapter objectives; key terms; and true/false, multiple choice, and short essay questions. Each part has a sample examination. The study guide also includes a CPA exam business law review.

**WESTLAW**®. Ten free hours of WESTLAW are available to qualified adopters. WESTLAW provides instant access to one of the largest law libraries in the world. Consult with your local West representative for more information.

**Contracts: An Interactive Guide** and **UCC Article 2 Sales: An Interactive Guide.** These software packages supplement the study of contract law and UCC Article 2 sales. Cases are presented and then followed by three to four multiple choice items. Consult with your local West representative for more information.

**You Be the Judge Software.** An easy-to-use program designed to further enhance students' understanding of the law by presenting them with new cases and asking them to resolve the issue. Consult with your local West representative for more information.

## *ACKNOWLEDGMENTS*

We express gratitude to the following professors for their helpful comments:

- Richard Dalebout, Brigham Young University
- Craig Disbrow, Plymouth State College, New Hampshire

- Edward Eramus, State University of New York–Brockport
- Jay Ersling, University of St. Thomas, Minnesota
- Mary C. Keifer, Ohio University
- Edward M. Kissling, Ocean County College, New Jersey
- L.K. O'Drudy, Jr., University of Virginia
- Scott A. White, University of Wisconsin

We are also grateful to those who provided us with comments regarding recent editions of the book: Mark Altieri, Cleveland State University; Albert Anderson, Mount Aloysius College; Albert Andrews, Jr., University of Minnesota; Lois Yoder Beier, Kent State University; Robert Bing, William Paterson College; Joell Bjorke, Winona State University; William N. Bockanic, John Carroll University; Donald Boren, Bowling Green State University; Joe Boucher, University of Wisconsin–Madison; L. Brooks, Nichols College; Nicolaus Bruns, Jr., Lake Forest Graduate School of Management; Thomas J. Canavan, Long Island University–C. W. Post Campus; Donald Cantwell, University of Texas–Arlington; John P. Carnasiotis, University of Missouri; Albert L. Carter, Jr., University of the District of Columbia; Richard R. Clark, University of the District of Columbia; Mitchell F. Crusto, Washington University–St. Louis; Arthur S. Davis, Long Island University; William Day, Cleveland State University; Alex DeVience, Jr., DePaul University; William G. Elliott, Saginaw Valley State University; Kurt Erickson, South West Michigan College; Joe W. Fowler, Oklahoma State University–Stillwater; Karla H. Fox, University of Connecticut; Stanley Fuchs, Fordham University; Nathan T. Garrett, Esq., North Carolina Central University; Michael J. Garrison, North Dakota State University; Sue Gragiano, Bowling Green State University; James Granito, Youngstown State University; Donald Haley, Cleveland State University; James V. Harrison, St. Peter's State College; Edward J. Hartman, St. Ambrose University; Frances J. Hill, University of Wisconsin–Whitewater; Telford F. Hollman, University of Northern Iowa–Cedar Falls; Georgia L. Holmes, Mankato State University; James Holzinger, Muhlenberg College; Norman Hope, Tabor College; Sarah H. Hudwig, Mary Baldwin College; Theresa Johnson, Cleveland State University; Marilee Jones-Confield, California State University–Long Beach; Al Joyner, Eastern Illinois University; Mary C. Keifer, Ohio University; Randall Kilbourne, Northwestern State University; Barbara Kirkpatrick, Virginia Intermont College; Louise Knight, Bucknell University; Duane R. Lambert, California State University–Hayward; Andrew Liput, Felician College; Sarah H. Ludwig, Mary Baldwin College; Richard Luke, Ricks College; Pat Maroney, Florida State University; Michael A. Mass, American University; Cheryl Massingale, University of Tennessee–Knoxville; Greg K. McCann, Stetson University; Bruce McClain, Cleveland State University; Ann L. McClure, Fort Hays State University; Charles R. McGuire, Illinois State University; Herbert McLaughlin, Bryant College; James Molloy, University of Wisconsin–Whitewater; Donald Nelson, University of Denver; Carol L. Nielsen, Bemidji State University; Richard Paxton, San Diego Community College; James L. Porter, University of New Mexico; Elinor Rahm, Central Missouri State University; Samuel H. Ramsay, Jr., Bryant College; Lor K. Harris Ransom, Caldwell College; Richard E. Regan, St. John Fisher College; Roger Reinsch, Emporia State University; L. Reppert, Marymount University; Caroline Rider, Marist College; George Roe, University of Illinois–Chicago; Stanford Rosenberg, La Roche College; Tim Rueth, Marquette University; Carol Wahle Smith, Central Florida Community College; Janis Stamm, Edinboro University of Pennsylvania; Al Stauber, Florida State University; David Steele, University of Wisconsin–Eau Claire; Peter Strohm, Georgian Court College; Al Talarczyk, Edgewood College; Kevin M. Teeven, Bradley University; Robert J. Tepper, University of New Mexico; Leonard Tripodi, St. Joseph's College; Charles H. Walker, University of Mississippi; Peter M. Wasemiller, Fresno Pacific College; David Webster, University of South Florida–Tampa; E. Marshall Wick, Gallaudet University; Wells J. Wright, University of Minnesota; and James B. Zimarowski, University of Notre Dame.

We express our thanks and deep appreciation to Peggy Pickard and Dana Lewandowski for administrative assistance. For their support we extend our thanks to Karlene Fogelin Knebel and Joanne Erwick Roberts. And we are grateful to Texterity Inc.; Crystal Chapin of DPS; and Rob Dewey, Bob Sandman, and Deanna Quinn of West Legal Studies in Business for their invaluable assistance and cooperation in connection with the preparation of this text.

This text is dedicated to our children Lilli-Marie Knebel Mann, Justin Erwick Roberts, and Matthew Charles Roberts.

*Richard A. Mann*
*Barry S. Roberts*

# Table of Cases

Cases in *italic* are the principal cases included at the ends of the chapters.
References are to pages.

# Table of Illustrations

# The Legal Environment of Business

# CHAPTER 1

# Introduction to Law

Law concerns the relations of individuals with one another as such relations affect the social and economic order. It is both the product of civilization and the means by which civilization is maintained. As such, law reflects the social, economic, political, religious, and moral philosophy of society. The laws of the United States influence the lives of every U.S. citizen. At the same time, the laws of each State influence the lives of its citizens and the lives of many noncitizens as well. The rights and duties of all individuals, as well as the safety and security of all people and their property, depend upon the law.

The law is pervasive. It interacts with and influences the political, economic, and social systems of every civilized society. It permits, forbids, and/or regulates practically every known human activity and affects all persons either directly or indirectly. Law is, in part, prohibitory: certain acts must not be committed. For example, one must not steal; one must not murder. Law is also partly mandatory: certain acts must be done or be done in a prescribed way. Taxes must be paid; corporations must make and file certain reports with State authorities; traffic must keep to the right. Finally, law is permissive: individuals may choose to perform or not to perform certain acts. Thus, one may or may not enter into a contract; one may or may not dispose of one's estate by will.

Because the areas of law are so highly interrelated, an individual who intends to study the several branches of law known collectively as business law should first consider the nature, classification, and sources of law as a whole. This enables the student not only to comprehend better any given branch of law but also to understand its relation to other areas of law.

## NATURE OF LAW

The law has evolved slowly, and it will continue to change. It is not a pure science based upon unchanging and universal truths. Rather, it results from a continuous effort to balance, through a workable set of rules, the individual and group rights of a society. In *The Common Law,* Oliver Wendell Holmes writes,

The life of the law has not been logic; it has been experience. The felt necessities of the time, the prevalent moral and political theories, avowed or unconscious, even the prejudices which judges share with their fellowmen, have had a good deal more to do than the syllogism in determining the rules by which men should be governed. The law embodies the story of a nation's development through many centuries, and it cannot be dealt with as if it contained only the axioms and corollaries of a book of mathematics.

## Definition of Law

A fundamental but difficult question regarding law is this: What is it? Numerous philosophers and jurists (legal scholars) have attempted to define it. American jurists and Supreme Court Justices Oliver Wendell Holmes and Benjamin Cardozo defined law as predictions of the way that a court will decide specific legal questions. Blackstone, an English jurist, on the other hand, defined law as "a rule of civil conduct prescribed by the supreme power in a state, commanding what is right, and prohibiting what is wrong." Similarly, Austin, a nineteenth-century English jurist, defined law as a general command that a state or sovereign makes to those who are subject to its authority by laying down a course of action enforced by judicial or administrative tribunals.

Because of its great complexity, many legal scholars have attempted to explain the law by outlining its essential characteristics. Roscoe Pound, a distinguished American jurist and former dean of the Harvard Law School, described law as having multiple meanings:

First, we may mean the legal order, that is, the régime of ordering human activities and relations through systematic application of the force of politically organized society, or through social pressure in such a society backed by such force. We use the term "law" in this sense when we speak of "respect for law" or for the "end of law."

Second, we may mean the aggregate of laws or legal precepts; the body of authoritative grounds of judicial and administrative action established in such a society. We may mean the body of received and established materials on which judicial and administrative determinations proceed. We use the term in this sense when we speak of "systems of law" or of "justice according to law."

Third, we may mean what Mr. Justice Cardozo has happily styled "the judicial process." We may mean the process of determining controversies, whether as it actually takes place, or as the public, the jurists, and the practitioners in the courts hold it ought to take place.

## Functions of Law

At a general level the primary function of law is to maintain stability in the social, political, and economic system while simultaneously permitting change. The law accomplishes this basic function by performing a number of specific functions, among them dispute resolution, protection of property, and preservation of the state.

Disputes, which inevitably arise in a society as complex and interdependent as ours, may involve criminal matters, such as theft, or noncriminal matters, such as an automobile accident. Because disputes threaten the stability of society, the law has established an elaborate and evolving set of rules to resolve them. In addition, the legal system has instituted societal remedies, usually administered by the courts, in place of private remedies such as revenge.

The recognition of private ownership of property is fundamental to our economic system, based as it is upon the exchange of goods and services among privately held units of consumption. Therefore, a second crucial function of law is to protect the owner's use of property and to facilitate voluntary agreements (called contracts) regarding exchanges of property and services. Accordingly, a significant portion of law, as well as this text, involves property and its disposition, including the law of property, contracts, sales, commercial paper, and business associations.

A third essential function of the law is preservation of the state. In our system, law ensures that changes in leadership and the political structure are brought about by political actions such as elections, legislation, and referenda, rather than by revolution, sedition, and rebellion.

## Legal Sanctions

A primary function of the legal system is to make sure that legal rules are enforced. **Sanctions** are the means by which the law enforces the decisions of the courts. Without sanctions, laws would be ineffectual and unenforceable.

An example of a sanction in a civil (noncriminal) case is the seizure and sale of the property of a debtor who fails to pay a court-ordered obligation, called a judgment. Moreover, under certain circumstances a court may enforce its order by finding an offender in contempt and sentencing him to jail until he obeys the court's order. In criminal cases, the principal sanctions are the imposition of a fine, imprisonment, and capital punishment.

## Law and Morals

Although moral and ethical concepts greatly influence the law, morals and law are not the same. They may be considered as two intersecting circles, as shown in Figure 1–1. The more darkly shaded area common to both circles includes the vast body of ideas that are both moral and legal. For instance, "Thou shall not kill" and "Thou shall not steal" are both moral precepts and legal constraints.

On the other hand, that part of the legal circle which does not intersect the morality circle includes many rules of law that are completely unrelated to morals, such as the rules stating that you must drive on the right side of the road and that you must register before you can vote. Likewise, the portion of the morality circle which does not intersect the legal circle includes moral precepts not enforced by law, such as the moral prohibition against silently standing by and watching a blind man walk off a cliff or foreclosing a poor widow's mortgage.

◆ *See Figure 1–1*

## Law and Justice

Law and justice represent separate and distinct concepts. Without law, however, there can be no justice. Although justice has at least as many definitions as law does, justice may be defined as fair, equitable, and impartial treatment of the competing interests and desires of individuals and groups with due regard for the common good.

On the other hand, law is no guarantee of justice. Some of history's most monstrous acts have been committed pursuant to "law." For example, the Nazis acted "legally" under German law during the 1930s and 1940s.

FIGURE 1–1 Law and Morals

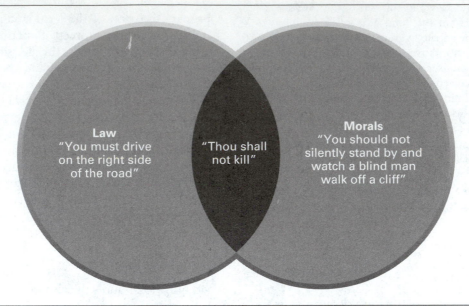

Totalitarian societies often have shaped formal legal systems around the atrocities they have sanctioned.

## CLASSIFICATION OF LAW

Because the subject is vast, classifying the law into categories is helpful. Though a number of classifications are possible, the most useful categories are (1) substantive and procedural, (2) public and private, and (3) civil and criminal.

Basic to understanding these classifications are the terms *right* and *duty*. A **right** is the capacity of a person, with the aid of the law, to require another person or persons to perform, or to refrain from performing, a certain act. Thus, if Alice sells and delivers goods to Bob for the agreed price of $500 payable at a certain date, Alice has the capability, with the aid of the courts, of enforcing the payment by Bob of the $500. A **duty** is the obligation the law imposes upon a person to perform, or to refrain from performing, a certain act. Duty and right are correlatives: no right can rest upon one person without a corresponding duty resting upon some other person or, in some cases, upon all other persons.

◆ *See Figure 1–2*

### Substantive and Procedural Law

**Substantive law** creates, defines, and regulates legal rights and duties. Thus, the rules of contract law that determine when a binding contract is formed are rules of substantive law. This book is principally concerned with substantive law. On the other hand, **procedural law** establishes the rules for enforcing those rights that exist by reason of substantive law. Thus, procedural law defines the method by which one may obtain a remedy in court.

### Public and Private Law

**Public law** is the branch of substantive law that deals with the government's rights and powers in its political or sovereign capacity and in its relation to individuals or groups. Public law consists of constitutional, administrative, and criminal law. **Private law** is that part of substantive law governing individuals and legal entities (such as corporations) in their relations with one another. Business law is primarily private law.

### Civil and Criminal Law

The **civil law** defines duties the violation of which constitutes a wrong against the party injured by the violation. In contrast, the **criminal law** establishes duties the violation of which is a wrong against the whole community. Civil law is a part of private law, whereas criminal law is a part of public law. (The term *civil law* should be distinguished from the concept of a civil law *system*, which is discussed later in this chapter.) In a civil action the injured party **sues** to recover **compensation** for the damage and injury he has sustained as a result of the defendant's wrongful conduct. The party bringing a civil action (the **plaintiff**) has the burden of proof, which he

**FIGURE 1–2** Classification of Law

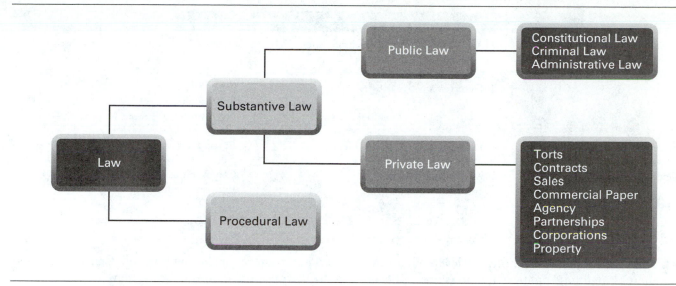

must sustain by a **preponderance** (greater weight) of the evidence. Whereas the purpose of criminal law is to punish the wrongdoer, the purpose of civil law is to compensate the injured party. The principal forms of relief the civil law provides are a judgment for money damages and a decree ordering the defendant to perform a specified act or to desist from specified conduct.

A crime is any act or omission that public law prohibits in the interest of protecting the public and that the government makes punishable in a judicial proceeding brought (**prosecuted**) by it. The government must prove criminal guilt **beyond a reasonable doubt,** which is a significantly higher burden of proof than that required in a civil action. The government prohibits and punishes crimes upon the ground of public policy, which may include the safeguarding of the government itself, human life, or private property. Additional purposes of the criminal law include deterrence and rehabilitation.

◆ *See Figure 1–3*

## SOURCES OF LAW

The sources of law in the U.S. legal system are the Federal and State constitutions, Federal treaties, interstate compacts, Federal and State statutes and executive orders, the ordinances of countless local municipal governments, the rules and regulations of Federal and State administrative agencies, and an ever-increasing volume of reported Federal and State court decisions.

The *supreme law* of the land is the United States Constitution. The Constitution provides that Federal statutes and treaties shall be the supreme law of the land. Federal legislation and treaties are, therefore, paramount to State constitutions and statutes. Federal legislation is of great significance as a source of law. Other Federal actions having the force of law are executive orders of the president and rules and regulations of Federal administrative officials, agencies, and commissions. The Federal courts also contribute considerably to the body of law in the United States.

The same pattern exists in every State. The paramount law of each State is contained in its written constitution. (Although a State constitution cannot deprive citizens of Federal constitutional rights, it can guarantee rights beyond those provided in the U.S. Constitution.) Subordinate to the State constitution are the statutes that the State's legislature enacts and the case law that its judiciary develops. Likewise, State administrative agencies issue rules and regulations having the force of law, as do executive orders promulgated by the State's governor. In addition, cities, towns, and villages have limited legislative powers within their respective municipal areas to pass ordinances and resolutions.

◆ *See Figure 1–4*

## Constitutional Law

A **constitution**—the fundamental law of a particular level of government—establishes the governmental

FIGURE 1–3 Comparison of Civil and Criminal Law

| | Civil Law | Criminal Law |
|---|---|---|
| **Commencement of Action** | Aggrieved individual (plaintiff) sues | State or Federal government prosecutes |
| **Purpose** | Compensation<br>Deterrence | Punishment<br>Deterrence<br>Rehabilitation<br>Preservation of peace |
| **Burden of Proof** | Preponderance of the evidence | Beyond a reasonable doubt |
| **Principal Sanctions** | Monetary damages<br>Equitable remedies | Capital punishment<br>Imprisonment<br>Fines |

structure and allocates power among the levels of government, thereby defining political relationships. One of the fundamental principles on which our government is founded is that of separation of powers. As detailed in our Constitution, this means that the government consists of three distinct and independent branches: the Federal judiciary, the Congress, and the Executive branch.

A constitution also restricts the powers of government and specifies the rights and liberties of the people. For example, the Constitution of the United States not only specifically states what rights and authority are vested in the national government but also specifically enumerates certain rights and liberties of the people. Moreover, the Ninth Amendment to the U.S. Constitution makes it clear that this enumeration of rights does not in any way deny or limit other rights that the people retain.

All other law in the United States is subordinate to the Federal Constitution. No law, Federal or State, is valid if it violates the Federal Constitution. Under the principle of **judicial review,** the Supreme Court of the United States determines the constitutionality of *all* laws.

## Judicial Law

The U.S. legal system is a **common law system,** first developed in England. It relies heavily on the judiciary as a source of law and on the adversary system for the adjudication of disputes. In an **adversary system** the parties, not the court, must initiate and conduct litigation. This approach is based upon the belief that the truth is more likely to emerge from the investigation and presentation of evidence by two opposing parties, both motivated by self-interest, than from judicial investigation motivated only by official duty. Other English-speaking countries, including England, Canada, and Australia, also use the common law system.

In distinct contrast to the common law system are civil law systems, which are based on Roman law. **Civil law systems** depend on comprehensive legislative enactments (called codes) and an inquisitorial method of adjudication. In the **inquisitorial system,** the judiciary initiates litigation, investigates pertinent facts, and conducts the presentation of evidence. The civil law system prevails in most of Europe, Scotland, the State of Louisiana, the province of Quebec, Latin America, and parts of Africa and Asia.

*Common Law*　The courts in common law systems have developed a body of law, known as "case law," "judge-made law," or "common law," that serves as precedent for determining later controversies. In this sense, common law is distinguished from other sources of law such as legislation and administrative rulings.

To evolve steadily and predictably, the common law has developed by application of *stare decisis.* Under the principle of **stare decisis** (to stand by the decisions), courts, in deciding cases, adhere to and rely on rules of law that they or superior courts announced and applied in prior decisions involving similar cases. Judicial decisions thus have two uses: to determine with finality the case currently being decided and to indicate how the courts will decide similar cases in the future. *Stare decisis* does not, however, preclude courts from correcting erroneous decisions or from choosing among conflicting precedents. Thus, the doctrine allows sufficient flexibility for the common law to change.

The strength of the common law is its ability to adapt to change without losing its sense of direction. As Justice Cardozo said, "The inn that shelters for the night is not

**FIGURE 1—4**  Hierarchy of Law

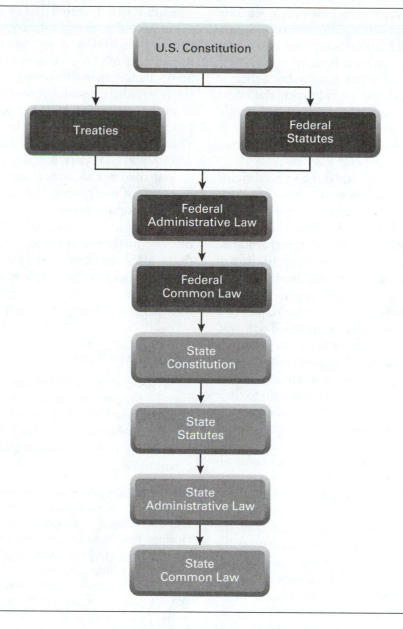

the journey's end. The law, like the traveler, must be ready for the morrow. It must have a principle of growth."

***Equity*** As the common law developed in England, it became overly rigid and beset with technicalities. Consequently, in many cases the courts provided no remedies because the judges insisted that a claim must fall within one of the recognized forms of action. Moreover, courts of common law could provide only limited remedies; the principal type of relief obtainable was a money judgment.

Consequently, individuals who could not obtain adequate relief from monetary awards began to petition the king directly for justice. He, in turn, came to delegate these petitions to his chancellor.

Gradually, there evolved a supplementary system of judicial relief for those who had no adequate remedy at common law. This new system, called **equity,** was administered by a court of chancery presided over by a chancellor. The chancellor, deciding cases on "equity and good conscience," afforded relief in many instances where common law judges had refused to act or where the remedy at law was inadequate. Thus, two systems of law administered by different tribunals developed side by side: the common law courts and the courts of equity.

An important difference between law and equity was that the chancellor could issue a **decree,** or order, compelling a defendant to do or refrain from doing a specific act. A defendant who did not comply with the order could be held in contempt of court and punished by fine or imprisonment. This power of compulsion available in a court of equity opened the door to many needed remedies not available in a court of common law.

Equity jurisdiction, in some cases, recognized rights that were enforceable at common law but for which equity provided more effective remedies. For example, in a court of equity, for breach of a land contract the buyer could obtain a decree of **specific performance** commanding the defendant seller to perform his part of the contract by transferring title to the land. Another powerful and effective remedy available only in the courts of equity was the **injunction,** a court order requiring a party to do or refrain from doing a specified act. Still another remedy not available elsewhere was **reformation,** where, upon the ground of mutual mistake, contracting parties could bring an action to reform or change the language of a written agreement to conform to their actual intentions. Finally, an action for **rescission** of a contract allowed a party to invalidate a contract under certain circumstances.

Although courts of equity provided remedies not available in courts of law, they granted such remedies only at their discretion, not as a matter of right. The courts exercised this discretion according to the general legal principles, or **maxims,** that they formulated over the years. A few of these familiar maxims of equity are the following: Equity will not suffer a wrong to be without a remedy. Equity regards the substance rather than the form. Equity abhors a forfeiture. Equity delights to do justice and not by halves. He who comes into equity must come with clean hands. He who seeks equity must do equity.

In nearly every jurisdiction in the United States, courts of common law and courts of equity have united to form a single court that administers both systems of law. Vestiges of the old division remain, however. For example, the right to a trial by jury applies only to actions at law but not under Federal law and in almost every State to suits filed in equity.

***Restatements of Law***   The common law of the United States results from the independent decisions of the State and Federal courts. The rapid increase in the number of

decisions by these courts led to the establishment of the American Law Institute (ALI) in 1923. The ALI was composed of a distinguished group of lawyers, judges, and law teachers who set out to prepare "an orderly restatement of the general common law of the United States, including in that term not only the law developed solely by judicial decision, but also the law that has grown from the application by the courts of statutes that were generally enacted and were in force for many years." Wolkin, "Restatements of the Law: Origin, Preparation, Availability," 21 *Ohio B.A.Rept.* 663 (1940).

Regarded as the authoritative statement of the common law of the United States, the Restatements cover many important areas of the common law, including torts, contracts, agency, property, and trusts. Although not law in themselves, they are highly persuasive and frequently have been used by courts in support of their opinions. Because they state much of the common law concisely and clearly, relevant portions of the Restatements are frequently relied upon in this book.

## Legislative Law

Since the end of the nineteenth century, legislation has become the primary source of new law and ordered social change in the United States. The annual volume of legislative law is enormous. Justice Felix Frankfurter's remarks to the New York City Bar in 1947 are even more appropriate today:

Inevitably the work of the Supreme Court reflects the great shift in the center of gravity of law-making. Broadly speaking, the number of cases disposed of by opinions has not changed from term to term. But even as late as 1875 more than 40 percent of the controversies before the Court were common-law litigation, fifty years later only 5 percent, while today cases not resting on statutes are reduced almost to zero. It is therefore accurate to say that courts have ceased to be the primary makers of law in the sense in which they "legislated" the common law. It is certainly true of the Supreme Court that almost every case has a statute at its heart or close to it.

This modern emphasis upon legislative or statutory law has occurred because common law, which develops evolutionarily and haphazardly, is not well suited for making drastic or comprehensive changes. Moreover, courts tend to be hesitant about overruling prior decisions, whereas legislatures frequently repeal prior enactments. In addition, legislatures are independent and able to choose the issues they wish to address, while courts may deal only with issues that arise in actual cases. As a result, legislatures are better equipped to make the dramatic, sweeping, and relatively rapid changes in the law that enable it to respond to numerous and vast technological, social, and economic innovations.

While some business law topics, such as contracts, agency, property, and trusts, still are governed principally by the common law, most areas of commercial law have become largely statutory, including partnerships, corporations, sales, commercial paper, secured transactions, insurance, securities regulation, antitrust, and bankruptcy. Because most States enacted statutes dealing with these branches of commercial law, a great diversity developed among the States and hampered the conduct of commerce on a national scale. The increased need for greater uniformity led to the formation of the National Conference of Commissioners on Uniform State Laws to prepare legislation that would reduce the conflicts among State laws.

The most successful example is the **Uniform Commercial Code** (UCC), which was prepared under the joint sponsorship and direction of the National Conference of Commissioners on Uniform State Laws and the American Law Institute. (The entire Official Text of the Code is set forth in Appendix B of this book.) All fifty States (although Louisiana has adopted only part of it), the District of Columbia, and the Virgin Islands have adopted the UCC. The underlying purposes and policies of the Code are to

1. simplify, clarify, and modernize the law governing commercial transactions;
2. permit the continued expansion of commercial practices through custom, usage, and agreement of the parties; and
3. make uniform the law among the various jurisdictions.

Other uniform laws include the Uniform Partnership Act, the Uniform Limited Partnership Act, the Model Business Corporation Act, and the Uniform Probate Code.

*Treaties*  A treaty is an agreement between or among independent nations. Article II of the U.S. Constitution authorizes the President to enter into treaties with the advice and consent of the Senate, "providing two thirds of the Senators present concur."

Only the Federal government, not the States, may enter into treaties. A treaty signed by the President and approved by the Senate has the legal force of a Federal statute. Accordingly, a Federal treaty may supersede a prior Federal statute, while a Federal statute may supersede a prior treaty. Like statutes, treaties are subordinate to the Federal Constitution and subject to judicial review.

*Executive Orders*  In addition to his executive functions, the President of the United States also has authority to issue laws, which are called **executive orders.** Typically, Federal legislation specifically delegates this authority. An executive order may amend, revoke, or supersede a prior executive order. An example of an executive order is the one issued by President Johnson in 1965 prohibiting discrimination by Federal contractors on the basis of race, color, sex, religion, or national origin in employment on any work the contractor performed during the period of the Federal contract.

State governors enjoy comparable authority to issue executive orders.

## Administrative Law

**Administrative law** is the branch of public law that is created by administrative agencies in the form of rules, regulations, orders, and decisions to carry out the regulatory powers and duties of those agencies. Administrative functions and activities concern matters of national safety, welfare, and convenience, including the establishment and maintenance of military forces, police, citizenship and naturalization, taxation, coinage of money, elections, environmental protection, the regulation of transportation, interstate highways, waterways, television, radio, trade and commerce, and, in general, public health, safety, and welfare.

To accommodate the increasing complexity of the social, economic, and industrial life of the nation, the scope of administrative law has expanded enormously. Justice Jackson stated that "the rise of administrative bodies has been the most significant legal trend of the last century, and perhaps more values today are affected by their decisions than by those of all the courts, review of administrative decisions apart." *Federal Trade Commission v. Ruberoid Co.*, 343 U.S. 470 (1952). This is evidenced by the great increase in the number and activities of Federal government boards, commissions, and other agencies. Certainly, agencies create more legal rules and adjudicate more controversies than all the legislatures and courts combined.

## LEGAL ANALYSIS

Decisions in State trial courts generally are not reported or published. The precedent a trial court sets is not sufficiently weighty to warrant permanent reporting. Except in New York and a few other States where selected trial court opinions are published, decisions in trial courts are simply filed in the office of the clerk of the court, where they are available for public inspection. Decisions of State courts of appeals are published in consecutively numbered volumes called "reports." Court decisions are found in the official State reports of most States. In addition, West Publishing Company publishes State reports in a regional reporter, called the National Reporter System, which comprises the following: Atlantic (A. or A.2d); South Eastern (S.E. or S.E.2d); South Western (S.W. or S.W.2d); New York Supplement (N.Y.S. or N.Y.S.2d); North Western (N.W. or N.W.2d); North Eastern (N.E. or N.E.2d); Southern (So. or So.2d); and Pacific (P. or P.2d). A number of States no longer publish official reports and have designated a commercial reporter as the authoritative source of State case law. After they are published, these opinions, or "cases," are referred to ("cited") by giving the name of the case, the volume, name, and page of the official State report, if any, in which it is published; the volume, name, and page of the particular set and series of the National Reporter System; and the volume, name, and page of any other selected case series. For instance, *Lefkowitz v. Great Minneapolis Surplus Store, Inc.*, 251 Minn. 188, 86 N.W.2d 689 (1957) indicates that the opinion in this case may be found in Volume 251 of the official Minnesota Reports at page 188; and in Volume 86 of the North Western Reporter, Second Series, at page 689.

The decisions of courts in the Federal system are found in a number of reports. Federal District Court opinions appear in the Federal Supplement (F.Supp.). Decisions of the U.S. Court of Appeals are found in the Federal Reporter (Fed., F.2d, or F.3d), while the U.S. Supreme Court's opinions are published in the United States Supreme Court Reports (U.S.), Supreme Court Reporter (S.Ct.), and Lawyers Edition (L.Ed.).

In reading the title of a case, such as "*Jones v. Brown*," the "v." or "vs." means "versus" or "against." In the trial court, Jones is the **plaintiff,** the person who filed the suit, and Brown is the **defendant,** the person against whom the suit was brought. When a case is appealed, some, but not all, courts of appeal place the name of the party who appeals, or the **appellant,** first, so that "*Jones v. Brown*" in the trial court becomes, if Brown loses and becomes the appellant, "*Brown v. Jones*" in the appellate court. But because some appellate courts retain the trial court order of names, determining from the title itself who was the plaintiff and who was the defendant is not always possible. The student must read the facts of each case carefully and clearly identify each party in her mind to understand the discussion by the appellate court. In a criminal case the caption in the trial court will first designate the prosecuting governmental unit and then will indicate the defendant, as in "*State v. Jones*" or "*Commonwealth v. Brown*."

The study of reported cases requires the student to understand and apply legal analysis. Normally, the reported opinion in a case sets forth (a) the essential facts, the nature of the action, the parties, what happened to bring about the controversy, what happened in the lower court, and what pleadings are material to the issues; (b) the issues of law or fact; (c) the legal principles involved; (d) the application of these principles; and (e) the decision.

A serviceable method by which students may analyze and brief cases after reading and comprehending the opinion is to write a brief containing the following:

1. the facts of the case
2. the issue or question involved
3. the decision of the court
4. the reasons for the decision

By way of example, the edited case of *Ryan v. Friesenhahn* is presented after the chapter summary and then briefed using the suggested format.

 *See Case 1–1*

# Chapter Summary

| Nature of Law | **Definition of Law** "a rule of civil conduct prescribed by the supreme power in a state, commanding what is right, and prohibiting what is wrong" (Blackstone) <br> **Functions of Law** to maintain stability in the social, political, and economic system through dispute resolution, protection of property, and the preservation of the state, while simultaneously permitting ordered change |
| --- | --- |

**Legal Sanctions** are means by which the law enforces the decisions of the courts
**Law and Morals** are different but overlapping; law provides sanctions, while morals do not
**Law and Justice** are separate and distinct concepts; justice is the fair, equitable, and impartial treatment of competing interests with due regard for the common good

## Classification of Law

**Substantive and Procedural Law**
- *Substantive Law* law creating rights and duties
- *Procedural Law* rules for enforcing substantive law

**Public and Private Law**
- *Public Law* law dealing with the relationship between government and individuals
- *Private Law* law governing the relationships among individuals and legal entities

**Civil and Criminal Law**
- *Civil Law* law dealing with rights and duties the violation of which constitutes a wrong against an individual or other legal entity
- *Criminal Law* law establishing duties which, if violated, constitute a wrong against the entire community

## Sources of Law

**Constitutional Law** fundamental law of a government establishing its powers and limitations

**Judicial Law**
- *Common Law* body of law developed by the courts that serves as precedent for determination of later controversies
- *Equity* body of law based upon principles distinct from common law and providing remedies not available at law

**Legislative Law** statutes adopted by legislative bodies
- *Treaties* agreements between or among independent nations
- *Executive Orders* laws issued by the president or by the governor of a State

**Administrative Law** body of law created by administrative agencies to carry out their regulatory powers and duties

---

 # Case

### CASE 1–1
## *RYAN v. FRIESENHAHN*
Court of Appeals of Texas, 1995
911 S.W.2d 113

RICKHOFF, J.
This is an appeal from a take-nothing summary judgment granted the defendants in a social host liability case. Appellants' seventeen-year-old daughter was killed in a single-car accident after leaving appellees' party in an intoxicated condition. While we hold that the appellants were denied an opportunity to amend their pleadings, we also find that their pleadings stated a cause of action for negligence and negligence per se. We reverse and remand.

Todd Friesenhahn, son of Nancy and Frederick Friesenhahn, held an "open invitation" party at his parents' home that encouraged guests to bring "bring your own bottle." Sabrina Ryan attended the party, became intoxicated, and was involved in a fatal accident after she left the event. According to the Ryans' petition, Nancy and Frederick Friesenhahn were aware of this activity and of Sabrina's condition.

Sandra and Stephen Ryan, acting in their individual and representative capacities, sued the Friesenhahns for

wrongful death, negligence, and gross negligence.
* * *

* * *

**a. The Petition** The Ryans pled, in their third amended petition, that Todd Friesenhahn planned a "beer bust" that was advertised by posting general invitations in the community for a party to be held on the "Friesenhahn Property." The invitation was open and general and invited persons to "B.Y.O.B." (bring your own bottle). According to the petition, the Friesenhahns had actual or constructive notice of the party and the conduct of the minors in "possessing, exchanging, and consuming alcoholic beverages."

The Ryans alleged that Friesenhahns were negligent in (1) allowing the party to be held on the Friesenhahn property; (2) directly or indirectly inviting Sabrina to the party; (3) allowing the party to continue on their property "after they knew that minors were in fact possessing, exchanging, and consuming alcohol"; (4) failing "to provide for the proper conduct at the party"; (5) allowing Sabrina to become intoxicated and failing to "secure proper attention and treatment"; (6) and allowing Sabrina to leave the Friesenhahn property while driving a motor vehicle in an intoxicated state. * * *

**b. Negligence Per Se** Accepting the petition's allegations as true, the Friesenhahns were aware that minors possessed and consumed alcohol on their property and specifically allowed Sabrina to become intoxicated. The Texas Alcoholic Beverage Code provides that one commits an offense if, with criminal negligence, he "makes available an alcoholic beverage to a minor." [Citation.] The exception for serving alcohol to a minor applies only to the minor's adult parent. [Citation.]

An unexcused violation of a statute constitutes negligence per se if the injured party is a member of the class protected by the statute. [Citation.] The Alcoholic Beverage Code was designed to protect the general public and minors in particular and must be liberally construed. [Citation.] We conclude that Sabrina is a member of the class protected by the Code.

In viewing the Ryans' allegations in the light most favorable to them, we find that they stated a cause of action against the Friesenhahns for the violation of the Alcoholic Beverage Code.

**c. Common Law Negligence** The elements of negligence include (1) a legal duty owed by one person to another; (2) breach of that duty; and (3) damages proximately caused by the breach. [Citation.] To determine whether a common law duty exists, we must consider several factors, including risk, foreseeabillity, and likelihood of injury weighed against the social utility of the defendant's conduct, the magnitude of the burden of guarding against the injury and consequences of placing that burden on the defendant. [Citation.] We may also consider whether one party has superior knowledge of the risk, and whether one party has the right to control the actor whose conduct precipitated the harm. [Citation.]

As the Supreme Court in [citation] explained, there are two practical reasons for not imposing a third-party duty on social hosts who provide alcohol to adult guests: first, the host cannot reasonably know the extent of his guests' alcohol consumption level; second, the host cannot reasonably be expected to control his guests' conduct. [Citation.] The Tyler court in [citation] relied on these principles in holding that a minor "had no common law duty to avoid making alcohol available to an intoxicated guest [another minor] who he knew would be driving." [Citation.]

We disagree with the Tyler court because the rationale expressed [by the Supreme Court] in [citation] does not apply to the relationship between minors, or adults and minors. The adult social host need not estimate the extent of a minor's alcohol consumption because serving minors any amount of alcohol is a criminal offense. [Citation.] Furthermore, the social host may control the minor, with whom there is a special relationship, analogous to that of parent-child. [Citation.]

* * *

As this case demonstrates, serving minors alcohol creates a risk of injury or death. Under the pled facts, a jury could find that the Friesenhahns, as the adult social hosts, allowed open invitations to a beer bust at their house and they could foresee, or reasonably should have foreseen, that the only means of arriving at their property would be by privately operated vehicles; once there, the most likely means of departure would be by the same means. That adults have superior knowledge of the risk of drinking should be apparent from the legislature's decision to allow persons to become adults on their eighteenth birthday for all purposes but the consumption of alcohol. [Citations.]

While one adult has no general duty to control the behavior of another adult, one would hope that adults would exercise special diligence in supervising minors—even during a simple swimming pool party involving potentially dangerous but legal activities. We may have no special duty to watch one adult to be sure he can swim, but it would be ill-advised to turn loose young children without insuring they can swim. When the "party" is for the purpose of engaging in dangerous and illicit activity, the consumption of alcohol by minors, adults certainly have a greater duty of care. [Citation.]

* * * Accordingly, we find that the Ryans' petition stated a common-law cause of action.

* * *

We reverse and remand the trial court's summary judgment.

## BRIEF OF RYAN V. FRIESENHAHN

### I. Facts

Todd Friesenhahn, son of Nancy and Frederick Friesenhahn, held an open invitation party at his parents' home that encouraged guests to bring their own bottle. Sabrina Ryan attended the party, became intoxicated, and was involved in a fatal accident after she left the party. Sandra and Stephen Ryan, Sabrina's parents, sued the Friesenhahns for negligence, alleging that the Friesenhahns were aware of underage drinking at the party and of Sabrina's condition when she left the party. The trial court granted summary judgment for the Friesenhahns.

### II. Issue

Is a social host who serves alcoholic beverages to a minor liable in negligence for harm suffered by the minor as a result of the minor's intoxication?

### III. Decision

In favor of the Ryans. Summary judgment reversed and case remanded to the trial court.

### IV. Reasons

Accepting the Ryans' allegations as true, the Friesenhahns were aware that minors possessed and consumed alcohol on their property and specifically allowed Sabrina to become intoxicated. The Texas Alcoholic Beverage Code provides that a person commits an offense if, with criminal negligence, he "makes available an alcoholic beverage to a minor." A violation of a statute constitutes negligence *per se* if the injured party is a member of the class protected by the statute. Since the Alcoholic Beverage Code was designed to protect the general public and minors in particular, Sabrina is a member of the class protected by the Code. Therefore, we find that the Ryans stated a cause of action against the Friesenhahns for the violation of the Alcoholic Beverage Code.

In considering common-law negligence as a basis for social host liability, the Texas Supreme Court has held that there are two practical reasons for not imposing a third-party duty on social hosts who provide alcohol to adult guests: first, the host cannot reasonably know the extent of his guests' alcohol consumption level; second, the host cannot reasonably be expected to control his guests' conduct. However, this rationale does not apply where the guest is a minor. The adult social host need not estimate the extent of a minor's alcohol consumption because serving minors any amount of alcohol is a criminal offense. Furthermore, the social host may control the minor, with whom there is a special relationship, analogous to that of parent-child.

# Questions

1. Identify and describe the basic functions of law.
2. Distinguish between law and justice.
3. Distinguish between law and morals.
4. Define and discuss substantive and procedural law.
5. Distinguish between public and private law.
6. Distinguish between civil and criminal law.
7. Identify and describe the sources of law.
8. Distinguish between law and equity.
9. Explain the principle of *stare decisis*.
10. Identify and define four remedies available in equity.

 **Internet Exercise** Find for the Federal government and for your State examples of the following sources of law: (a) constitutional law, (b) judicial law, (c) legislative law, and (d) administrative law. (If such information on your State is not available, choose another State.)

# CHAPTER 2

# Business Ethics and the Social Responsibility of Business

Business ethics is a subset of ethics: there is no special set of ethical principles that applies only to the world of business. Immoral acts are immoral, whether or not a businessperson has committed them. But before a behavior, in business or elsewhere, is judged immoral, special attention must be accorded the circumstances surrounding it. For example, suppose a company discovers a new cost-effective technology that enables it to outperform its competitors. Few would condemn the company for using the technology even if it put one or more competitors out of business. After all, the economic benefits derived from the new technology would seem to so outweigh the social costs of unemployment that it would be difficult to conclude that the business acted immorally.

On the other hand, unethical business practices date from the very beginning of business and continue today. As one court stated in connection with a securities fraud,

Since the time to which the memory of man runneth not to the contrary, the human animal has been full of cunning and guile. Many of the schemes and artifices have been so sophisticated as almost to defy belief. But the ordinary run of those willing and able to take unfair advantage of others are mere apprentices in the art when compared with the manipulations thought up by those connected in one way or another with transactions in securities.

In the last decade, the almost daily reporting of business wrongs has included, among countless others, insider trading, the Beech-Nut adulterated apple juice scandal, the Bhopal disaster, the Dalkon Shield tragedy, and the savings and loan industry depredations.

Ethics can be broadly defined as the study of what is right or good for human beings. It pursues the questions of what people ought to do, what goals they should pursue. In *Business Ethics,* 2d ed., Richard T. DeGeorge provides the following explanation of ethics:

*Ethics* in general can be defined as a systematic attempt, through the use of reason, to make sense of our individual and social moral experience, in such a way as to determine the rules that ought to govern human conduct and the values worth pursuing in life. The attempt is systematic and therefore goes beyond what each reflective person tends to do in his daily life in making sense of his moral experience, organizing it, and attempting to make it coherent and unified. Because it uses reason and not revelation, ethics can be distinguished from a religious or theological approach to morality. Insofar as it attempts to ascertain what rules and values *ought* to be followed and pursued, ethics can be distinguished from anthropology, psychology, and sociology. Those disciplines describe how people behave, but they usually do not prescribe how they should or ought to behave. Ethics concerns itself with human conduct, taken here to mean human activity that is done knowingly and, to a large extent, willingly. It does not concern itself with automatic responses, or with, for example, actions done in one's sleep or under hypnosis.

**Business ethics,** as a branch of applied ethics, is the study and determination of what is right and good in business settings. Business ethics seeks to understand the moral issues that arise from business practices, institutions, and decision making and their relationship to generalized human values. Unlike the law, analyses of ethics have no central authority, such as courts or legislatures, upon which to rely; nor do they have clear-cut, universal standards. Despite these inherent limitations, making meaningful ethical judgments is still possible. To improve ethical decision making, it is important to understand how others have approached the task.

Some examples of the many ethics questions confronting business may help to clarify the definition of business ethics. In the employment relationship, countless ethical issues arise regarding the safety and compensation of workers, their civil rights (such as equal treatment, privacy, and freedom from sexual harassment), and the legitimacy of whistle-blowing. In the relationship between business and its customers, ethical issues permeate marketing techniques, product safety, and consumer protection. The relationship between business and its owners bristles with ethical questions involving corporate governance, shareholder voting, and management's duties to the shareholders. The relationship among competing businesses involves numerous ethical matters, including efforts to promote fair competition over the temptation of collusive conduct. The interaction between business and society at large has additional ethical dimensions: pollution of the physical environment, commitment to the community's economic and social infrastructure, and the depletion of natural resources. At the international level, these issues not only recur but couple themselves to additional ones, such as bribery of foreign officials, exploitation of less-developed countries, and conflicts among differing cultures and value systems.

In resolving the ethical issues raised by business conduct, it is helpful to use a seeing-knowing-doing model. First, the decision maker should *see* (identify) the ethical issues involved in the proposed conduct, including the ethical implications of the various available options. Second, the decision maker should *know* (resolve) what to do by choosing the best option. Finally, the decision maker should *do* (implement) the chosen option by developing implementing strategies.

This chapter first surveys the most prominent ethical theories, then examines ethical standards in business, and concludes by exploring the ethical responsibilities of business.

 *See Case 2–1*

# LAW VERSUS ETHICS

As discussed in Chapter 1, the law is strongly affected by moral concepts, but law and morality are not the same. Although it is tempting to say that "if it's legal, it's moral," such a proposition is inaccurate and generally too simplistic. For example, it would seem gravely immoral to stand by silently while a blind man walks off a cliff if one could prevent the fall by shouting a warning, even though one is under no legal obligation to do so. Similarly, moral questions arise concerning "legal" business practices, such as failing to fulfill a promise that is not legally binding; exporting products banned in the United States to third world countries, where they are not prohibited; manufacturing and selling tobacco or alcohol products; or slaughtering baby seals for fur coats. The mere fact that these practices may be legal does not prevent them from being challenged on moral grounds.

Just as it is possible for legal acts to be immoral, it is equally possible for illegal acts to seem morally preferable

to following the law. It is, for example, the moral conviction of the great majority of people that those who sheltered Jews in violation of Nazi edicts during World War II and those who committed acts of civil disobedience in the 1950s and 1960s to challenge racist segregation laws in the United States were acting properly and that the laws themselves were immoral.

 *See Case 2–2*

# ETHICAL THEORIES

Philosophers have sought for centuries to develop dependable universal methods for making ethical judgments. In earlier times, some thinkers analogized the discovery of ethical principles with the derivation of mathematical proofs. They asserted that people could discover fundamental ethical rules by applying careful reasoning *a priori*. (*A priori* reasoning is based on theory rather than experimentation and deductively draws conclusions from cause to effect and from generalizations to particular instances.) In more recent times, many philosophers have concluded that although careful reasoning and deep thought assist substantially in moral reasoning, experience reveals that the complexities of the world defeat most attempts to fashion precise, *a priori* guidelines. Nevertheless, reviewing the most significant ethical theories can help to analyze issues of business ethics.

## Ethical Fundamentalism

Under **ethical fundamentalism,** or absolutism, individuals look to a central authority or set of rules to guide them in ethical decision making. Some look to the Bible; others look to the Koran or the writings of Karl Marx or to any number of living or deceased prophets. The essential characteristic of this approach is a reliance upon a central repository of wisdom. In some cases, such reliance is total. In others, it occurs to a lesser degree: followers of a religion or a spiritual leader may believe that all members of the group have an obligation to assess moral dilemmas independently, according to each person's understanding of the dictates of certain fundamental principles.

## Ethical Relativism

**Ethical relativism** is a doctrine asserting that individuals must judge actions by what they feel is right or wrong for themselves. It holds that both parties to a disagreement regarding a moral question are correct, because morality is relative. While ethical relativism promotes open-mindedness and tolerance, it has limitations. If each person's actions are always correct for that person, then his behavior is, by definition, moral, and no one can truly criticize it. If a child abuser truly felt it right to molest children, a relativist would accept the proposition that the child abuser was acting properly. As almost no one would accept the proposition that child abuse could ever be ethical, few can truly claim to be relativists. Once a person concludes that criticizing or punishing behavior is, in some cases, appropriate, he abandons ethical relativism and faces the task of developing a broader ethical methodology.

Although bearing a surface resemblance to ethical relativism, situational ethics actually differs substantially. **Situational ethics** holds that developing precise guidelines for navigating ethical dilemmas is difficult because real-life decision making is so complex. To judge the morality of someone's behavior, the person judging must actually put herself in the other person's shoes to understand what motivated the other to choose a particular course of action. In this respect, situational ethics shares with ethical relativism the notion that we must judge actions from the perspective of the person who actually made the judgment. From that point on, however, the two approaches differ dramatically. Ethical relativism passes no judgment on what a person did other than to determine that he truly believed the decision was right for him. Much more judgmental, situational ethics insists that once a decision has been viewed from the actor's perspective, a judgment can be made as to whether or not her action was ethical. Situational ethics does not cede the ultimate judgment of propriety to the actor; rather, it insists that another evaluate the actor's decision or act from the perspective of a person in the actor's shoes.

## Utilitarianism

**Utilitarianism** is a doctrine that assesses good and evil in terms of the consequences of actions. Those actions that produce the greatest net pleasure compared with the net pain are better in a moral sense than those that produce less net pleasure. As Jeremy Bentham, one of the most influential proponents of utilitarianism, proclaimed, a good or moral act is one that results in "the greatest happiness for the greatest number."

The two major forms of utilitarianism are act utilitarianism and rule utilitarianism. **Act utilitarianism** assesses each separate act according to whether it maximizes pleasure over pain. For example, if telling a lie in a particular situation produces more overall pleasure than pain, then an act utilitarian would support lying as the moral thing to do. Rule utilitarians, disturbed by the unpredictability of act utilitarianism and by its potential for abuse, follow a different approach by holding that general rules must be established and followed even though, in some instances, following rules may produce less overall pleasure than not following them. In applying utilitarian principles to developing rules, **rule utilitarianism** thus supports rules that on balance produce the greatest satisfaction. Determining whether telling a lie in a given instance would produce greater pleasure than telling the truth is less important to the rule utilitarian than deciding if a general practice of lying would maximize society's pleasure. If lying would not maximize pleasure generally, then one should follow a rule of not lying, even though telling a lie occasionally would produce greater pleasure than would telling the truth.

Utilitarian notions underlie cost-benefit analysis, an analytical tool used by many business and government managers today. **Cost-benefit analysis** first quantifies in monetary terms and then compares the direct and indirect costs and benefits of program alternatives for meeting a specified objective. Cost-benefit analysis seeks the greatest economic efficiency, given the underlying notion that acts achieving the greatest output at the least cost promote the greatest marginal happiness over less efficient acts, other things being equal.

The primary purpose of cost-benefit analysis is to choose from alternative courses of action the program that maximizes society's wealth. For example, based on cost-benefit analysis, an auto designer might choose to devote more effort to perfecting a highly expensive air bag that would save hundreds of lives and prevent thousands of disabling injuries than to developing an improved car hood latching mechanism that would produce a less favorable cost-benefit ratio.

The chief criticism of utilitarianism is that in some important instances it ignores justice. A number of situations would maximize the pleasure of the majority at great social cost to a minority. Under a strict utilitarian approach, it would, for example, be ethical to compel a few citizens to undergo painful, even fatal medical tests to develop cures for the rest of the world. For most people, however, such action would be unacceptable. Another major criticism of utilitarianism is that measuring pleasure and pain in the fashion its supporters advocate is extremely difficult, if not impossible.

## Deontology

**Deontological** theories (from the Greek word *deon,* meaning "duty" or "obligation") address the practical problems of utilitarianism by holding that certain underlying principles are right or wrong regardless of calculations regarding pleasure or pain. Deontologists believe that actions cannot be measured simply by their results but must be judged by means and motives as well.

Our criminal laws apply deontological reasoning. Knowing that John shot and killed Marvin is not enough to tell us how to judge John's act. We must know whether John shot Marvin in anger, self-defense, or by mistake. Although under any of these motives Marvin is just as dead, we judge John quite differently depending on the mental process that we believe led him to commit the act. Similarly, deontologists judge the morality of acts not so much by their consequences but by the motives that lead to them. To act morally, a person not only must achieve just results but also must employ the proper means.

The best-known deontological theory was proffered by the eighteenth-century philosopher Immanuel Kant. Kant asserted what he called the **categorical imperative,** which has been summarized by Bowie and Duska in *Business Ethics,* 2d ed., as follows:

1. Act only according to that maxim by which you can, at the same time, will that it should become a universal law.
2. Act as never to treat another human being merely as a means to an end.

Thus, for an action to be moral, it (1) must possess the potential to be made a consistently applied universal law and (2) must respect the autonomy and rationality of all human beings and avoid treating them as an expedient. That is, one should avoid doing anything that he or she would not have everyone do in a similar situation. For example, you should not lie to colleagues unless you support the right of all colleagues to lie to one another. Similarly, you should not cheat others unless you advocate everyone's right to cheat. We apply Kantian reasoning when we challenge someone's behavior by asking, What if everybody acted that way?

Under Kant's approach, it would be improper to assert a principle to which one claimed personal exception, such as insisting that it was acceptable for you to cheat but not for anyone else to do so. Because everyone would then insist on similar rules by which to except themselves, this principle could not be universalized.

Kant's philosophy also rejects notions of the end justifying the means. To Kant, every person is an end in himself or herself and deserves respect simply because of his or her humanity. Thus, any sacrifice of a person for the greater good of society would be unacceptable to Kant.

In many respects, Kant's categorical imperative is a variation of the Golden Rule. Like the Golden Rule, the categorical imperative reflects the idea that people are, to a certain extent, self-centered. As one writer on business ethics notes, this is what makes the Golden Rule so effective:

> It is precisely this self-centeredness of the Golden Rule that makes it so valuable, and so widely acknowledged, as a guide. To inquire of yourself, "How would I feel in the other fellow's place?" is an elegantly simple and reliable method of focusing in on the "right" thing to do. The Golden Rule works not in spite of selfishness, but because of it. Tuleja, *Beyond the Bottom Line.*

As does every theory, Kantian ethics has its critics. Just as deontologists criticize utilitarians for excessive pragmatism and flexible moral guidelines, utilitarians and others criticize deontologists for rigidity and excessive formalism. For example, if one inflexibly adopts as a rule to tell the truth, one ignores situations in which lying might well be justified. A person hiding a terrified wife from her angry, abusive husband would seem to be acting morally by falsely denying that the wife is at the person's house. Yet, a deontologist, feeling bound to tell the truth, might ignore the consequences of truthfulness, tell the husband where his wife is, and create the possibility of a terrible tragedy. Less dramatically, one wonders whether the world would effect a higher ethical code by regarding as immoral "white lies" concerning friends' appearance, clothing, or choice of spouse.

## Social Ethics Theories

Social ethics theories assert that special obligations arise from the social nature of human beings. Such theories focus not only on each person's obligations to other members of society, but also on the individual's rights and obligations within society. For example, **social egalitarians** believe that society should provide all persons with equal amounts of goods and services regardless of the contribution each makes to increase society's wealth.

Two other ethics theories have received widespread attention in recent years. One is the theory of **distributive justice** proposed by Harvard philosopher John Rawls, which seeks to analyze the type of society that people in a "natural state" would establish if they could not determine in advance whether they would be talented, rich, healthy, or ambitious, relative to other members of society. According to Rawls, the society contemplated through this "veil of ignorance" should be given precedence in terms of development because it considers the needs and rights of all its members. Rawls did not argue, however, that such a society would be strictly egalitarian. That would unfairly penalize those who turned out to be the most talented and ambitious. Instead, Rawls suggested that such a society would stress equality of opportunity, not of results. On the other hand, Rawls stressed that society would pay heed to the least advantaged to ensure that they did not suffer unduly and that they enjoyed society's benefits. To Rawls, society must be premised on justice. Everyone is entitled to her fair share in society, a fairness all must work to guarantee.

In contrast to Rawls, another Harvard philosopher, Robert Nozick, stressed liberty, not justice, as the most important obligation that society owes its members. **Libertarians** stress market outcomes as the basis for distributing society's rewards. Only to the extent that one meets the demands of the market does one deserve society's benefits. Libertarians oppose interference by society in their lives as long as they do not violate the rules of the marketplace; that is, as long as they do not cheat others and as long as they honestly disclose the nature of their transactions with others. The fact that some end up with fortunes while others accumulate little simply proves that some can play in the market effectively while others cannot. To libertarians, this is not unjust. What is unjust to them is any attempt by society to take wealth earned by citizens and then distribute it to those who did not earn it.

These theories and others (e.g., Marxism) judge society in moral terms by its organization and by its method of distributing goods and services. They demonstrate the difficulty of ethical decision making in the context of a social organization: behavior that is consistently ethical from individual to individual may not necessarily produce a just society.

## Other Theories

The preceding theories do not exhaust the possible approaches to evaluating ethical behavior, but represent the most commonly cited theories advanced over the years. Several other theories also deserve mention. **Intuitionism** holds that a rational person possesses inherent powers to assess the correctness of actions. Though an individual may refine and strengthen these powers, they are just as basic to humanity as our instincts for survival and self-defense. Just as some people are better artists

or musicians, some people have more insight into ethical behavior than others. Consistent with intuitionism is the **good persons** philosophy, which declares that individuals who wish to act morally should seek out and emulate those who always seem to know the right choice in any given situation and who always seem to do the right thing. One variation of these ethical approaches is the **"Television Test,"** which directs us to imagine that every ethical decision we make is being broadcast on nationwide television. Adherents of this approach believe an appropriate decision is one we would be comfortable broadcasting on television for all to witness.

## ETHICAL STANDARDS IN BUSINESS

This section will explore the application of the theories of ethical behavior to the world of business.

## Choosing an Ethical System

In their efforts to resolve the moral dilemmas facing humanity, philosophers and other thinkers have struggled for years to refine the various systems discussed above. No one ethical system is completely precise, however, and each tends occasionally to produce unacceptable prescriptions for action. But to say that a system has limits is not to say it is useless. On the contrary, many such systems provide insight into ethical decision making and help us formulate issues and resolve moral dilemmas. Furthermore, concluding that moral standards are difficult to articulate and that the boundaries are imprecise is not the same as concluding that moral standards are unnecessary or nonexistent.

Research by noted psychologist Lawrence Kohlberg provides insight into ethical decision making and lends credibility to the notion that moral growth, like physical growth, is part of the human condition. Kohlberg observed that people progress through stages of moral development according to two major variables: age and education. During the first level—the **preconventional level**—a child's conduct is a reaction to the fear of punishment and, later, to the pleasure of reward. Although people who operate at this level may behave in a moral manner, they do so without understanding why their behavior is moral. The rules are imposed upon them. During adolescence—Kohlberg's **conventional level**—people conform their behavior to meet the expectations of groups, such as family, peers, and eventually society. The motivation for conformity is loyalty, affection, and trust. Most adults operate at this level. According to Kohlberg, some people reach the third level—the **post-conventional level**—where they accept and conform to moral principles because they understand *why* the principles are right and binding. At this level, moral principles are voluntarily internalized, not externally imposed. Moreover, individuals at this stage develop their own universal ethical principles, and even question the laws and values that society and others have adopted.

Kohlberg believed that these stages are sequential and that not all people reach the third, or even the second, stage. He therefore argued that exploring ways of enabling people to develop to the advanced stage of post-conventional thought was essential to the study of ethics. Other psychologists assert that individuals do not pass from stage to stage but rather function in all three stages simultaneously.

Whatever the source of our ethical approach, we cannot avoid facing moral dilemmas that challenge us to recognize and to do the right thing. Moreover, for those who plan business careers, such dilemmas will necessarily have implications for many others: employees, shareholders, suppliers, customers, and society at large.

◆ *See Figure 2–1*

## Corporations as Moral Agents

Because corporations are not persons but artificial entities created by the State, it is not obvious whether they can or should be held morally accountable. As Lord Chancellor Thurlow lamented two hundred years ago, "A company has no body to kick and no soul to damn, and by God, it ought to have both." Clearly, individuals within corporations can be held morally responsible, but the corporate entity presents unique problems.

Commentators are divided on the issue. Some, like philosopher Manuel Velasquez, insist that only people can engage in behavior that can be judged in moral terms. Opponents of this view, like philosophers Kenneth Goodpaster and John Matthews, Jr., concede that corporations are not persons in any literal sense but insist that the attributes of responsibility inherent in corporations are sufficient in number to permit judging corporate behavior from a moral perspective.

## ETHICAL RESPONSIBILITIES OF BUSINESS

Many people assert that the only responsibility of business is to maximize profit and that this obligation overrides any other ethical or social responsibility. Although our economic system of modified capitalism is based on the pursuit of self-interest, it contains components to check this motivation of greed. Our system has always recognized the need for some form of regulation, whether it be the "invisible hand" of competition, the self-regulation of business, or government regulation.

## Regulation of Business

As explained and justified by Adam Smith in *The Wealth of Nations* (1776), the capitalistic system is composed of six "institutions": economic motivation, private productive property, free enterprise, free markets, competition, and limited government. Economic motivation assumes that a person who receives an economic return for his effort will work harder; therefore, the economic system should provide greater economic rewards for those who work harder. Private productive property, the means by which economic motivation is exercised, permits individuals to innovate and produce while securing to them the fruits of their efforts. Jack Behrman, a professor of business ethics, has described how the four other institutions combine with these two to bring about industrialized capitalism:

Free enterprise permits the combination of properties so people can do things together that they can't do alone. Free enterprise means a capitalistic combination of factors of production under decisions of free individuals. Free enterprise is the group expression of the use of private property, and it

FIGURE 2–1 Kohlberg's Stages of Moral Development

| Levels | Perspective | Justification |
| --- | --- | --- |
| **Preconventional (Childhood)** | Self | Punishment/Reward |
| **Conventional (Adolescent)** | Group | Group Norms |
| **Postconventional (Adult)** | Universal | Moral Principles |

permits greater efficiency in an industrial setting through variation in the levels and kinds of production.

. . . The free market operates to equate supply and demand—supply reflecting the ability and willingness to offer certain goods or services, and demand reflecting the consumer's ability and willingness to pay. Price is adjusted to include the maximum number of *both* bids and offers. The market, therefore, is *the* decisionmaking mechanism outside of the firm. It is the *means* by which basic decisions are made about the use of resources, and all factors are supposed to respond to it, however they wish.

. . . Just in case it doesn't work out that way, there is one more institution—the *Government*—which is supposed to set rules and provide protection for the society and its members. That's all, said Smith, that it should do: it should set the rules, enforce them, and stand aside. J. Behrman, *Discourses on Ethics and Business* (1981), 25–29.

As long as all these constituent institutions continue to exist and operate in a balanced manner, the factors of production—land, capital, and labor—combine to produce an efficient allocation of resources for individual consumers and for the economy as a whole. To achieve this outcome, however, Smith's model requires the satisfaction of several conditions: "standardized products, numerous firms in markets, each firm with a small share and unable by its actions alone to exert significant influence over price, no barriers to entry, and output carried to the point where each seller's marginal cost equals the going market price." E. Singer, *Antitrust Economics and Legal Analysis* (1981), 2.

History has demonstrated that the actual operation of the economy has satisfied almost none of these assumptions. More specifically, the actual competitive process falls considerably short of the classic economic model of perfect competition:

Competitive industries are never perfectly competitive in this sense. Many of the resources they employ cannot be shifted to other employments without substantial cost and delay. The allocation of those resources, as between industries or as to relative proportions within a single industry, is unlikely to have been made in a way that affords the best possible expenditure of economic effort. Information is incomplete, motivation confused, and decision therefore ill informed and often unwise. Variations in efficiency are not directly reflected in variations of profit. Success is derived in large part from competitive selling efforts, which in the aggregate may be wasteful, and from differentiation of products, which may be undertaken partly by methods designed to impair the opportunity of the buyer to compare quality and price. C. Edwards, *Maintaining Competition* (1964), 7.

In addition to capitalism's failure to allocate resources efficiently, it cannot be relied on to achieve all of the social and public policy objectives a pluralistic democracy requires. For example, the free enterprise model simply does not comprehend or address equitable distribution of wealth, national defense, conservation of natural resources, full employment, stability in economic cycles, protection against economic dislocations, health and safety, social security, and other important social and economic goals. Because the "invisible hand" and self-regulation by business have failed not only to preserve the competitive process in our economic system but also to achieve social goals extrinsic to the efficient allocation of resources, governmental intervention in business has become increasingly common. Such intervention attempts to (1) regulate both "legal" monopolies, such as those conferred by law through copyrights, patents, and trade symbols, and "natural" monopolies such as utilities, transportation, and communications; (2) preserve competition by correcting imperfections in the market system; (3) protect specific groups, especially labor and agriculture, from failures of the marketplace; and (4) promote other social goals. Successful government regulation involves a delicate balance between regulations that attempt to preserve competition and those that attempt to advance other social objectives. The latter should not undermine the basic competitive processes that provide an efficient allocation of economic resources.

## Corporate Governance

In addition to the broad demands of maintaining a competitive and fair marketplace, another factor demanding the ethical and social responsibility of business is the sheer size and power of individual corporations. The five thousand largest U.S. firms currently produce more than half of the nation's gross national product. Statutorily, their economic power should be delegated by the shareholders to the board of directors, who in turn appoint the officers of the corporation.

In reality, this legal image is virtually a myth. In nearly every large American business corporation, there exists a management autocracy. One man—variously titled the President, or the Chairman of the Board, or the Chief Executive Officer—or a small coterie of men rule the corporation. Far from being chosen by the directors to run the corporation, this chief executive or executive clique chooses the board of directors and, with the acquiescence of the board, controls the corporation. R. Nader, M. Green, and J. Seligman, *Taming the Giant Corporation* (1976), 75–76.

In a classic study published in 1932, Adolf Berle and Gardner Means concluded that significant amounts of economic power had been concentrated in a relatively few large corporations, that the ownership of these corporations had become widely dispersed, and that the shareholders had become far removed from active participation in management. Since their original study, these trends have steadily continued. The five hundred largest U.S. industrial corporations have combined sales of approximately $2 trillion, profits of $100 billion, assets over $1 trillion, and more than fifteen million employees.

Thus, vast amounts of wealth and power are controlled by a small number of corporations, which are in turn controlled by a small group of corporate officers. In fact, the separation of ownership and control has widened so far that Myles Mace, a leading scholar in this area, describes how one board of directors was so reluctant to discharge ineffective management that "the leadership of the [chief executive] was so unsatisfactory that even his mother thought he ought [to be removed] for the good of the company . . . before the board [of directors] reluctantly moved." Testimony before the Securities and Exchange Commission, 30 September 1977.

These developments raise social, policy, and ethical issues about the governance of large, publicly owned corporations. Many observers insist that companies playing such an important role in economic life should have a responsibility to undertake projects that benefit society in ways that go beyond mere financial efficiency in producing goods and services. In some instances, the idea of corporate obligation comes from industrialists themselves. Andrew Carnegie, for example, advocated philanthropy throughout his life and contributed much of his fortune to educational and social causes.

## Arguments against Social Responsibility

Among the arguments opposing business involvement in socially responsible activities are profitability, unfairness, accountability, and expertise.

*Profitability* As economist Milton Friedman and others have argued, businesses are artificial entities established to permit people to engage in profit-making, not social, activities. Without profits, they assert, there is little reason for a corporation to exist and no real way to measure the effectiveness of corporate activities. Businesses are not organized to engage in social activities; they are structured to produce goods and services for which they receive money. Their social obligation is to return as much of this money to their direct stakeholders as possible. In a free market with significant competition,

the selfish pursuits of corporations will lead to maximizing output, minimizing costs, and establishing fair prices. All other concerns distract companies and interfere with achieving these goals.

*Unfairness* Whenever companies stray from their designated role of profit-maker, they take unfair advantage of company employees and shareholders. For example, a company may support the arts or education or spend excess funds on health and safety; however, these funds rightfully belong to the shareholders or employees. The company's decision to disburse these funds to others who may well be less deserving than the shareholders and employees is unfair. Furthermore, consumers can express their desires through the marketplace, and shareholders and employees can decide independently if they wish to make charitable contributions. In most cases, senior management consults the board of directors about supporting social concerns but does not seek the approval of the company's major stakeholders. Thus, these shareholders are effectively disenfranchised from actions that reduce their benefits from the corporation.

*Accountability* Corporations, as previously noted, are private institutions that are subject to a lower standard of accountability than are public bodies. Accordingly, a company may decide to support a wide range of social causes and yet submit to little public scrutiny. But a substantial potential for abuse exists in such cases. For one thing, a company could provide funding for causes its employees or shareholders do not support. It could also provide money "with strings attached," thereby controlling the recipients' agendas for less than socially beneficial purposes. For example, a drug company that contributes to a consumer group might implicitly or explicitly condition its assistance on the group's agreement never to criticize the company or the drug industry.

This lack of accountability warrants particular concern because of the enormous power corporations wield in modern society. Many large companies, like General Motors or IBM, generate and spend more money in a year than all but a handful of the world's countries. If these companies suddenly began to vigorously pursue their own social agendas, their influence might well rival, and perhaps undermine, that of their own governments. In a country like the United States, founded on the principles of limited government and the balance of powers, too much corporate involvement in social affairs might well present substantial problems. Without clear guidelines and accountability, the corporate pursuit of socially responsible behavior might well distort the entire process of governance.

There is a clear alternative to corporations engaging in socially responsible action. If society wishes to increase the resources devoted to needy causes, it has the power to do so. Let corporations seek profits without the burden of a social agenda, let the consumers vote in the marketplace for the products and services they desire, and let the government tax a portion of corporate profits for socially beneficial causes.

*Expertise*   Even though a corporation has an expertise in producing and selling its product, it may not possess a talent for recognizing or managing socially useful activities. Corporations become successful in the market because they can identify and meet customers' needs. Nothing suggests that this talent spills over into nonbusiness arenas. In fact, critics of corporate engagement in social activities worry that corporations will prove unable to distinguish the true needs of society from their own narrow self-interest.

## Arguments in Favor of Social Responsibility

First, it should be recognized that even business critics acknowledge that the prime responsibility of business is to make a reasonable return on its investment by producing a quality product at a reasonable price. They do not suggest that business entities be charitable institutions. They do assert, however, that business has certain obligations beyond making a profit or not harming society. Critics contend that business must help to resolve societal problems, and they offer a number of arguments in support of their position.

*The Social Contract*   Society creates corporations and accords them a special social status, including the grant of limited liability, which insulates the owners from liability for debts the organization incurs. Supporters of social roles for corporations assert that limited liability and other rights granted to companies carry a responsibility: corporations, just like other members of society, must contribute to its betterment. Therefore, companies owe a moral debt to society to contribute to its overall well-being. Society needs a host of improvements, such as pollution control, safe products, a free marketplace, quality education, cures for illness, and freedom from crime. Corporations can help in each of these areas. Granted, deciding which social needs deserve corporate attention is difficult; however, this challenge does not lessen a

company's obligation to choose a cause. Corporate America cannot ignore the multitude of pressing needs that still remain, despite the efforts of government and private charities.

A derivative of the social contract theory is the stakeholder model for the societal role of the business corporation. Under the **stakeholder model** a corporation has fiduciary responsibilities to all of its stakeholders, not just its stockholders. Historically, the stockholder model for the role of business has been the norm. Under this theory, a corporation is viewed as private property owned by and for the benefit of its owners—the stockholders of the corporation. (For a full discussion of this legal model, see Chapter 36.) The stakeholder model, on the other hand, holds that corporations are responsible to society at large and more directly, to all those constituencies on which it depends for its survival. Thus, it is argued that a corporation should be managed for the benefit of all of its stakeholders—stockholders, employees, customers, suppliers, and managers, as well as the local communities in which it operates. Compare Figure 2–2 with Figure 36–1.

◆ *See Figure 2–2*

*Less Government Regulation*   According to another argument in favor of corporate social responsibility, the more responsibly companies act, the less regulation the government must provide. This idea, if accurate, would likely appeal to those corporations that typically view regulation with distaste, perceiving it as a crude and expensive way of achieving social goals. To them, regulation often imposes inappropriate, overly broad rules that hamper productivity and require extensive recordkeeping procedures to document compliance. If companies can use more flexible, voluntary methods of meeting a social norm such as pollution control, then government will be less tempted to legislate norms.

The argument can be taken further. Not only does anticipatory corporate action lessen the likelihood of government regulation, but social involvement by companies creates a climate of trust and respect that reduces the overall inclination of government to interfere in company business. For example, a government agency is much more likely to show some leniency toward a socially responsible company than toward one that ignores social plights.

*Long-Run Profits*   Perhaps the most persuasive argument in favor of corporate involvement in social causes is that such involvement actually makes good business

FIGURE 2–2  The Stakeholder Model

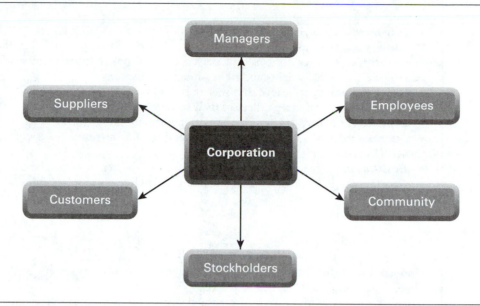

sense. Consumers often support good corporate images and avoid bad ones. For example, consumers generally prefer to patronize stores with "easy return" policies. Even though such policies are not required by law, companies institute them because they create goodwill—an intangible though indispensable asset for ensuring repeat customers. In the long run, enhanced goodwill often leads to stronger profits. Moreover, corporate actions to improve the well-being of their communities make these communities more attractive to citizens and more profitable for business.

# Chapter Summary

| Definitions | **Ethics**  study of what is right or good for human beings<br>**Business Ethics**  study of what is right and good in a business setting |
|---|---|

| Ethical Theories | **Ethical Fundamentalism**  individuals look to a central authority or set of rules to guide them in ethical decision making<br>**Ethical Relativism**  actions must be judged by what individuals subjectively feel is right or wrong for themselves<br>**Situational Ethics**  one must judge a person's actions by first putting oneself in the actor's situation<br>**Utilitarianism**  moral actions are those that produce the greatest net pleasure compared with net pain<br>• *Act Utilitarianism*  assesses each separate act according to whether it maximizes pleasure over pain<br>• *Rule Utilitarianism*  supports rules that on balance produce the greatest pleasure for society |
|---|---|

- *Cost-Benefit Analysis* quantifies the benefits and costs of alternatives

**Deontology**  actions must be judged by their motives and means as well as their results

**Social Ethics Theories**  focus is on a person's obligations to other members in society and also on the individual's rights and obligations within society

- *Social Egalitarians* believe that society should provide all its members with equal amounts of goods and services regardless of their relative contributions
- *Distributive Justice* stresses equality of opportunity rather than results
- *Libertarians* stress market outcomes as the basis for distributing society's rewards

**Other Theories**

- *Intuitionism* a rational person possesses inherent power to assess the correctness of actions
- *Good Person* individuals should seek out and emulate good role models

## Ethical Standards in Business

**Choosing an Ethical System**  Kohlberg's stages of moral development is a widely accepted model (See Figure 2–1)

**Corporations as Moral Agents**  because a corporation is a statutorily created entity, it is not clear whether it should be held morally responsible

## Ethical Responsibilities of Business

**Regulation of Business**  governmental regulation has been necessary because all the conditions for perfect competition have not been satisfied and free competition cannot by itself achieve other societal objectives

**Corporate Governance**  vast amounts of wealth and power have become concentrated in a small number of corporations, which are in turn controlled by a small group of corporate officers

**Arguments against Social Responsibility**

- *Profitability* because corporations are artificial entities established for profit-making activities, their only social obligation should be to return as much money as possible to shareholders
- *Unfairness* whenever corporations engage in social activities such as supporting the arts or education, they divert funds rightfully belonging to shareholders and/or employees to unrelated third parties
- *Accountability* a corporation is subject to less public accountability than public bodies are
- *Expertise* although a corporation may have a high level of expertise in selling its goods and services, there is absolutely no guarantee that any promotion of social activities will be carried on with the same degree of competence

**Arguments in Favor of Social Responsibility**

- *The Social Contract* because society allows for the creation of corporations and gives them special rights, including a grant of limited liability, corporations owe a responsibility to our society
- *Less Government Regulation* by taking a more proactive role in addressing society's problems, corporations create a climate of trust and respect that has the effect of reducing government regulation
- *Long-Run Profits* corporate involvement in social causes creates goodwill, which simply makes good business sense

# Cases

Throughout this book the authors have included cases dealing with ethical or social issues. Every chapter has at least one case relating to ethical or social issues; in a number of chapters, all of the cases discuss these issues.

---

## CASE 2–1
### Business Ethics
### *A. H. ROBINS: DALKON SHIELD SETTLEMENT APPROVAL*
U.S. District Court, Minnesota, 1984

LORD, J.

Mr. Robins [President of A. H. Robins], Mr. Forrest [vice president and general counsel], and Dr. Lunsford [vice president for research and development]: After months of reflection, study, and cogitation—and no small amount of prayer—I have concluded that it is perfectly appropriate to make this statement, which will constitute my plea to you to seek new horizons in corporate consciousness and a new sense of personal responsibility for the activities of those who work under you in the name of the A. H. Robins Company.

It is not enough to say, "I did not know," "It was not me," "Look elsewhere." Time and again, each of you has used this kind of argument in refusing to acknowledge your responsibility and in pretending to the world that the chief officers and directors of your gigantic multinational corporation have no responsibility for its acts and omissions.

Today as you sit here attempting once more to extricate yourselves from the legal consequences of your acts, none of you has faced up to the fact that more than 9000 women claim they gave up part of their womanhood so that your company might prosper. It has been alleged that others gave their lives so you might prosper. And there stand behind them legions more who have been injured but who have not sought relief in the courts of this land.

I dread to think what would have been the consequences if your victims had been men rather than women—women, who seem, through some quirk of our society's mores, to be expected to suffer pain, shame, and humiliation.

If one poor young man were, without authority or consent, to inflict such damage upon one woman, he would be jailed for a good portion of the rest of his life. Yet your company, without warning to women, invaded their bodies by the millions and caused them injuries by the thousands. And when the time came for these women to make their claims against your company, you attacked their characters. You inquired into their sexual practices and into the identity of their sex partners. You ruined families and reputations and careers in order to intimidate those who would raise their voices against you. You introduced issues that had no relationship to the fact that you had planted in the bodies of these women instruments of death, of mutilation, of disease.

Gentlemen, you state that your company has suffered enough, that the infliction of further punishment in the form of punitive damages would cause harm to your business, would punish innocent shareholders, and could conceivably depress your profits to the point where you could not survive as a competitor in this industry. When the poor and downtrodden commit crimes, they too plead that these are crimes of survival and that they should be excused for illegal acts that helped them escape desperate economic straits. On a few occasions when these excuses are made and remorseful defendants promise to mend their ways, courts will give heed to such pleas. But no court will heed the plea when the individual denies the wrongful nature of his deeds and gives no indication that he will mend his ways. Your company, in the face of overwhelming evidence, denies its guilt and continues its monstrous mischief.

Mr. Forrest, you have told me that you are working with members of the Congress of the United States to find a way of forgiving you from punitive damages that might otherwise be imposed. Yet the profits of your company continue to mount. Your last financial report boasts of new records for sales and earnings, with a profit of more than $58 million in 1983. And, insofar as this court has been able to determine, you three men and your company are still engaged in a course of wrongdoing. Until your company indicates that it is willing to cease and desist this deception and to seek out and advise the victims, your remonstrances to Congress and to the courts are indeed hollow and cynical. The company has not suffered, nor have you men personally. You are collectively being enriched by millions of dollars each year. There is no evidence that your company has suffered any penalty from these litigations. In fact, the evidence is to the contrary.

The case law suggests that the purpose of punitive damages is to make an award that will punish a defendant for his wrongdoing. Punishment has traditionally involved the principles of revenge, rehabilitation, and deterrence. There is no evidence I have been able to find in my review of these cases to indicate that any of these objectives has been accomplished.

Mr. Robins, Mr. Forrest, Dr. Lunsford: You have not been rehabilitated. Under your direction, your company has continued to allow women, tens of thousands of them, to wear this device—a deadly depth charge in their wombs, ready to explode at any time. Your attorney denies that tens of thousands of these devices are still in women's bodies. But I submit to you that he has no more basis for denying the accusation than the plaintiffs have for stating it as truth. We simply do not know how many women are still wearing these devices because your company is not willing to find out. The only conceivable reasons that you have not recalled this product are that it would hurt your balance sheet and alert women who have already been harmed that you be liable for their injuries. You have taken the bottom line as your guiding beacon and the low road as your route. That is corporate irresponsibility at its meanest. Rehabilitation involves an admission of guilt, a certain contrition, an acknowledgment of wrongdoing, and a resolution to take a new course toward a better life. I find none of this in you or your corporation. Confession is good for the soul, gentlemen. Face up to your misdeeds. Acknowledge the personal responsibility you have for the activities of those who work under you. Rectify this evil situation. Warn the potential victims and recompense those who have already been harmed.

Mr. Robins, Mr. Forrest, Dr. Lunsford: I see little in the history of this case that would deter others. The policy of delay and obfuscation practiced by your lawyers in courts throughout this country has made it possible for you and your insurance company to put off the payment of these claims for such a long period that the interest you earned in the interim covers the cost of these cases. You, in essence, pay nothing out of your own pockets to settle these cases. What corporate officials could learn a lesson from this? The only lesson they might learn is that it pays to delay compensating victims and to intimidate, harass, and shame the injured parties.

Your company seeks to segment and fragment the litigation of these cases nationwide. The courts of this country are burdened with more than 3000 Dalkon Shield cases. The sheer number of claims and the dilatory tactics used by your company's attorneys clog court calendars and consume vast amounts of judicial and jury time. Your company settles those cases out of court in which it finds itself in an uncomfortable position, a handy device for avoiding any proceeding that would give continuity or cohesiveness to this nationwide problem. The decision as to which cases are brought to trial rests almost solely at the whim and discretion of the A. H. Robins Company. In order to guarantee that no plaintiff or group of plaintiffs mounts a sustained assault upon your system of evasion and avoidance, you have time after time demanded that, as the price of settling a case, able lawyers agree not to bring a Dalkon Shield case again and not to help less experienced lawyers with cases against your company.

Another of your callous legal tactics is to force women of little means to withstand the onslaughts of your well-financed attorneys. You target your worst tactics at the meek and the poor.

If this court had the authority, I would order your company to make an effort to locate each and every woman who still wears this device and recall your product. But this court does not. I must therefore resort to moral persuasion and a personal appeal to each of you. Mr. Robins, Mr. Forrest, and Dr. Lunsford: You are the people with the power to recall. You are the corporate conscience.

Please, in the name of humanity, lift your eyes above the bottom line. You, the men in charge, must surely have hearts and souls and consciences.

Please, gentlemen, give consideration to tracing down the victims and sparing them the agony that will surely be theirs.

---

## CASE 2–2
## Law versus Ethics
### *McGANN v. H & H MUSIC COMPANY*
United States Court of Appeals, Fifth Circuit, 1991
946 F.2d 401

GARWOOD, J.

Plaintiff-appellant John McGann (McGann) filed this suit under . . . the Employee Retirement Income Security Act of 1974, [citation] (ERISA), against defendants-appellees H & H Music Company (H & H Music), Brook Mays Music Company (Brook Mays) and General American Life Insurance Company (General American) (collectively defendants) claiming that they discriminated against McGann, an employee of H & H Music, by reducing benefits available to H & H Music's group medical plan beneficiaries for treatment for acquired immune deficiency syndrome (AIDS) and related illnesses. The district court granted defendants' motion for summary judgment on the ground that an employer has an absolute right to alter the terms of medical coverage available to plan beneficiaries. [Citation]. We affirm.

McGann, an employee of H & H Music, discovered that he was afflicted with AIDS in December 1987. Soon thereafter, McGann submitted his first claims for reimbursement under H & H Music's group medical plan, provided through Brook Mays, the plan administrator, and issued by General American, the plan insurer, and informed his employer that he had AIDS. McGann met with officials of H & H Music in March 1988, at which time they discussed McGann's illness. Before the change in the terms of the plan, it provided for lifetime medical benefits of up to $1,000,000 to all employees.

In July 1988, H & H Music informed its employees that, effective August 1, 1988, changes would be made in their medical coverage. These changes included, but were not limited to, limitation of benefits payable for AIDS-related claims to a life-time maximum of $5,000. No limitation was placed on any other catastrophic illness. H & H Music became self-insured under the new plan and General American became the plan's administrator. By January 1990, McGann had exhausted the $5,000 limit on coverage for his illness.

* * *

McGann's allegations show no promised benefit, for there is nothing to indicate that defendants ever promised that the $1,000,000 coverage limit was permanent.

The H & H Music plan expressly provides: "Termination or Amendment of Plan: The Plan Sponsor may terminate or amend the Plan at any time or terminate any benefit under the Plan at any time." There is no allegation or evidence that any oral or written representations were made to McGann that the $1,000,000 coverage limit would never be lowered. Defendants broke no promise to McGann. The continued availability of the $1,000,000 limit was not a right to which McGann may have become entitled. . . .

McGann appears to contend that the reduction in AIDS benefits alone supports an inference of specific intent to retaliate against him or to interfere with his future exercise of rights. . . . McGann characterizes as evidence of an individualized intent to discriminate the fact that AIDS was the only catastrophic illness to which the $5,000 limit was applied and the fact that McGann was the only employee known to have AIDS. He contends that if defendants reduced AIDS coverage because they learned of McGann's illness through his exercising of his rights . . . by filing claims, the coverage reduction therefore could be "retaliation" for McGann's filing of the claims. Under McGann's theory, any reduction in employee benefits would be impermissibly discriminatory if motivated by a desire to avoid the anticipated costs of continuing to provide coverage for a particular beneficiary. McGann would find an implied promise not to discriminate for this purpose; it is the breaking of this promise that McGann appears to contend constitutes interference with a future entitlement.

* * *

McGann effectively contends that section 510 was intended to prohibit any discrimination in the alteration of an employee benefits plan that results in an identifiable employee or group of employees being treated differently from other employees.

* * *

The Supreme Court has observed in dictum: "ERISA does not mandate that employers provide any particular benefits, and does not itself proscribe discrimination in the provision of employee benefits." [Citations.] To interpret "discrimination" broadly to include defendants' conduct would clearly conflict with Congress's intent that employers remain free to create, modify and terminate the terms and conditions of employee benefits plans without governmental interference.

* * *

As persuasively explained by the Second Circuit, the policy of allowing employers freedom to amend or eliminate employee benefits is particularly compelling with respect to medical plans:

"With regard to an employer's right to change medical plans, Congress evidenced its recognition of the need for flexibility in rejecting the automatic vesting of welfare plans. Automatic vesting was rejected because the costs of such plans are subject to fluctuating and unpredictable variables. Actuarial decisions concerning fixed annuities are based on fairly stable data, and vesting is appropriate. In contrast, medical insurance must take account of inflation, changes in medical practice and technology, and increases in the costs of treatment independent of inflation. These unstable variables prevent accurate predictions of future needs and costs." [Citation.]

* * *

McGann's claim cannot be reconciled with the well-settled principle that Congress did not intend that ERISA circumscribe employers' control over the content of benefits plans they offered to their employees. * * *

* * * ERISA does not broadly prevent an employer from "discriminating" in the creation, alteration or termination of employee benefits plans; thus, evidence of such intentional discrimination cannot alone sustain a claim. * * * It does not prohibit an employer from electing not to cover or continue to cover AIDS, while covering or continuing to cover other catastrophic illnesses, even though the employer's decision in this respect may stem from some "prejudice" against AIDS or its victims generally. The same, of course, is true of any other disease and its victims. That sort of "discrimination" is simply not addressed by [ERISA]. Under [ERISA], the asserted discrimination is illegal only if it is motivated by a desire to retaliate against an employee or to deprive an employee of an existing right to which he may become entitled. The district court's decision to grant summary judgment to defendants therefore was proper. Its judgment is accordingly

Affirmed.

---

 # Questions

1. Describe the differences between law and ethics.
2. List and contrast the various ethical theories.
3. Describe cost-benefit analysis and explain when it should be used and when it should be avoided.

4. Explain Kohlberg's stages of moral development.
5. Explain the ethical responsibilities of business.

---

 # Problems

1. You have an employee who has a chemical imbalance in the brain that causes him to be severely emotionally unstable. The medication that is available to treat this schizophrenic condition is extremely powerful and decreases the taker's life span by one to two years for every year that the user takes it. You know that his doctors and family believe that it is in his best interest to take the medication. What course of action should you follow?
2. You have an employee from another country who is very shy. After a time, you notice that the quality of her performance is deteriorating rapidly. You find an appropriate time to speak with her and determine that she is extremely distraught. She informs you that her family has arranged a marriage for her and that she refuses to obey their contract. She further informs

you that she is contemplating suicide. Two weeks later, with her poor performance continuing, you determine that she is on the verge of a nervous breakdown; once again she informs you that she is going to commit suicide. What should you do? Consider further that you can petition a court to have her involuntarily committed to a mental hospital. You know, however, that her family would consider such a commitment an extreme insult and that they might seek retribution. Does this prospect alter your decision?
3. You receive a telephone call from a company you never do business with requesting a reference on one of your employees, Mary Sunshine. You believe that Mary is generally incompetent and would be delighted to see her take another job. You give her a glowing reference. Is this right? Explain.

**4.** You have just received a report suggesting that a chemical your company uses in its manufacturing process is very dangerous. You have not read the report, but you are generally aware of its contents. You believe that the chemical can be replaced fairly easily, but that if word gets out, panic may set in among employees and community members. A reporter asks if you have seen the report, and you say no. Is your behavior right or wrong? Explain.

**5.** Joe Jones, your neighbor and friend, and you bought lottery tickets at the corner drugstore. While watching the lottery drawing on TV with you that night, Joe leaps from the couch, waves his lottery ticket, and shouts, "I've got the winning number!" Suddenly, he clutches his chest, keels over, and dies on the spot. You are the only living person who knows that Joe, not you, bought the winning ticket. If you substitute his ticket for yours, no one will know of the switch, and you will be $10 million richer. Joe's only living relative is a rich aunt whom he despised. Will you switch his ticket for yours? Explain.

**6.** Omega, Inc., a publicly held corporation, has assets of $100 million and annual earnings in the range of $13 to $15 million. Omega owns three aluminum plants, which are profitable, and one plastics plant, which is losing $4 million a year. The plastics plant shows no sign of ever becoming profitable because of its very high operating costs, and there is no evidence that the plant and the underlying real estate will increase in value. Omega decides to sell the plastics plant. The only bidder for the plant is Gold, who intends to use the plant for a new purpose, to introduce automation, and to replace all current employees. Would it be ethical for Omega to turn down Gold's bid and keep the plastics plant operating indefinitely, for the purpose of preserving the employees' jobs? Explain.

**7.** You are the sales manager of a two-year-old electronics firm. At times, the firm has seemed to be on the brink of failure but recently has begun to be profitable. In large part, the profitability is due to the aggressive and talented sales force you have recruited. Two months ago, you hired Alice North, an honors graduate from State University who decided that she was tired of the research department and wanted to try sales.

Almost immediately after you send Alice out for training with Brad West, your best salesperson, he begins reporting to you an unexpected turn of events. According to Brad, "Alice is terrific: she's confident, smooth, and persistent. Unfortunately, a lot of our buyers are good old boys who just aren't comfortable around young, bright women. Just last week, Hiram Jones, one of our biggest customers, told me that he simply won't continue to do business with 'young chicks' who think they invented the world. It's not that Alice is a know-it-all. She's not. It's just that these guys like to booze it up a bit, tell some off-color jokes, and then get down to business. Alice doesn't drink, and although she never objects to the jokes, it's clear she thinks they're offensive." Brad believes that several potential deals have fallen through "because the mood just wasn't right with Alice there." Brad adds, "I don't like a lot of these guys' styles myself, but I go along to make the sales. I just don't think Alice is going to make it."

When you call Alice in to discuss the situation, she concedes the accuracy of Brad's report but indicates that she's not to blame and insists that she be kept on the job. You feel committed to equal opportunity but don't want to jeopardize your company's ability to survive. What should you do?

**8.** Major Company subcontracted the development of part of a large technology system to Start-up Company, a small corporation specializing in custom computer systems. The contract, which was a major breakthrough for Start-up Company and crucial to its future, provided for an initial development fee and subsequent progress payments, as well as a final date for completion.

Start-up Company provided Major Company with periodic reports indicating that everything was on schedule. After several months, however, the status reports stopped coming, and the company missed delivery of the schematics, the second major milestone. As an in-house technical consultant for Major Company, you visit Start-up Company and find not only that they are far behind schedule but that they had lied about their previous progress. Moreover, you determine that this slippage has put the schedule for the entire project in jeopardy. The cause of Start-up's slippage was the removal of personnel from your project to work on short-term contracts to obtain money to meet the weekly payroll.

Your company decides that you should stay at Start-up Company to monitor their work and to assist in the design of the project. After six weeks and some progress, Start-up is still way behind their delivery dates. Nonetheless, you are now familiar enough with the project to complete it in-house with Major's personnel.

Start-up is still experiencing severe cash flow problems and repeatedly requests payment from Major. But your CEO, furious with Start-up's lies and deceptions, wishes to "bury" Start-up and finish the project using Major Company's internal resources. She knows that withholding payment to Start-up will put them out of business. What do you do? Explain.

**9.** A customer requests certain sophisticated tests on equipment he purchased from your factory. Such tests are very expensive and must be performed by a third party. The equipment meets all of the industry standards but shows anomalies which can not be explained.

Though the problem appears to be minor, you decide to inspect the unit to try to understand the test data—a very expensive and time-consuming process. You inform the customer of this decision. A problem is found, but it is minor and highly unlikely ever to cause the unit to fail. Rebuilding the equipment would be very expensive and time-consuming; moreover, notifying the customer that you are planning to rebuild the unit would also put your overall manufacturing procedures in question. What should you do—fix it, ship it, inform the customer?

**10.** (a)   You are a project manager for a company making a major proposal to a Middle Eastern country. Your major competition is from Japan. Your local agent, who is closely tied to a very influential sheik, would receive a 5 percent commission if the proposal were accepted. Near the date for decision, the agent asks you for $150,000 to grease the skids so that your proposal is accepted. What do you do?

(b)   What if, after you say no, the agent goes to your vice president, who provides the money? What do you do?

(c)   Your overseas operation learns that most other foreign companies in this Middle Eastern location bolster their business by exchanging currency on the gray market. You discover that your division is twice as profitable as budgeted due to the amount of domestic currency you have received on the gray market. What do you do?

**Internet Exercise**  Find and identify some Web sites pertaining to business ethics that contain (a) political, social, or economic bias; (b) codes of conduct for companies, associations, or users; and (c) other significant material.

# Legal Process

As discussed in Chapter 1, substantive law establishes the rights and duties of individuals and other legal entities while procedural law determines the means by which these rights are asserted. Procedural law attempts to accomplish two competing objectives: (1) to be fair and impartial and (2) to operate efficiently. The judicial process in the United States represents a balance between these two objectives as well as a commitment to the adversary system.

The first part of this chapter describes the structure and function of the Federal and State court systems. The second part deals with jurisdiction; the third part discusses civil dispute resolution, including the procedure in civil lawsuits.

## THE COURT SYSTEM

Courts are impartial tribunals (seats of judgment) established by governmental bodies to settle disputes. A court may render a binding decision only when it has jurisdiction over the dispute and the parties to that dispute; that is, when it has a right to hear and make a judgment in a case. The United States has a dual court system: The Federal government has its own independent system, as does each of the fifty States plus the District of Columbia.

### *THE FEDERAL COURTS*

Article III of the U.S. Constitution states that the judicial power of the United States shall be vested in one Supreme Court and such lower courts as Congress may establish. Congress has established a lower Federal court system consisting of a number of special courts, district courts, and courts of appeals. The Federal court system is staffed by judges who receive lifetime appointments

from the President, subject to confirmation by the Senate.

◆ *See Figure 3–1*

### District Courts

The district courts are the general trial courts in the Federal system. Most cases begin in a district court, and it is here that issues of fact are decided. The district court is generally presided over by *one* judge, although in certain cases three judges preside. In a few cases, an appeal from a judgment or decree of a district court is taken directly to the Supreme Court. In most cases, however, appeals go to the Circuit Court of Appeals of the appropriate circuit, the decision of which is, in most cases, final.

Congress has established judicial districts, each of which is located entirely in a particular State. All States have at least one district, while certain States contain more than one. For instance, New York has four districts, Illinois has three, and Wisconsin has two, while a number of less populated States comprise a single district.

◆ *See Figure 3–2*

### Courts of Appeals

Congress has established twelve judicial circuits (eleven numbered circuits plus the D.C. Circuit), each having a court known as the Court of Appeals, which primarily hears appeals from the district courts located within its circuit. In addition, these courts review decisions of many administrative agencies, the Tax Court, and the Bankruptcy Court. Congress has also established the U.S. Court of Appeals for the Federal Circuit, which is discussed below in the section on "Special Courts." The United States Courts of Appeals generally hear cases in

**FIGURE 3–1** Federal Judicial System

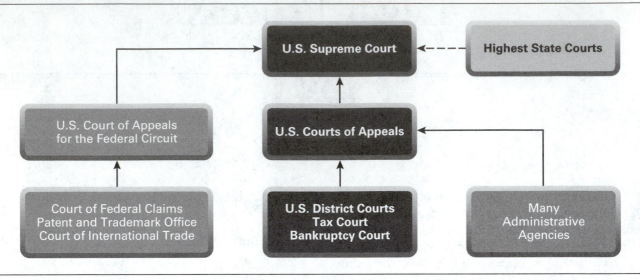

panels of *three* judges, although in some instances all of the judges of the circuit will sit *en banc* to decide a case.

The function of appellate courts is to examine the record of a case on appeal and to determine if the trial court committed prejudicial error. If so, the appellate court will **reverse** or **modify** the judgment and if necessary **remand** it (send it back) to the lower court for further proceeding. If no prejudicial error exists, the appellate court will **affirm** the decision of the lower court.

◆ *See Figure 3–2*

## The Supreme Court

The nation's highest tribunal is the United States Supreme Court, which consists of nine justices (a Chief Justice and eight Associate Justices) who sit as a group in Washington, D.C. A quorum consists of any six justices. In certain types of cases the U.S. Supreme Court has original jurisdiction (the right to hear a case first). The Court's principal function, nonetheless, is to review decisions of the Federal Courts of Appeals and, in some instances, those of the highest State courts or other tribunals. Cases reach the Supreme Court under its appellate jurisdiction by one of two routes. Very few come by way of **appeal by right**—cases the Court must hear should a party request the review. In 1988, Congress enacted legislation that almost completely eliminated the right to appeal to the U.S. Supreme Court.

The second way in which the Supreme Court may review a decision of a lower court is by the discretionary **writ of certiorari,** which requires a lower court to produce the records of a case it has tried. Now almost all cases reaching the Supreme Court come to it by means of writs of *certiorari*. The Court uses the writ as a device to choose the cases it wishes to hear. The Court grants writs for cases involving a Federal question of substantial importance or a conflict in the decisions of the U.S. Circuit Courts of Appeals. Only a small percentage of the petitions to the Supreme Court for review by *certiorari* are granted, however. The vote of four justices is required to grant a writ.

## Special Courts

The special courts in the Federal judicial system include the U.S. Court of Federal Claims, the U.S. Tax Court, the U.S. Bankruptcy Courts, and the U.S. Court of Appeals for the Federal Circuit. These courts have jurisdiction over particular areas. The U.S. Court of Federal Claims hears claims against the United States. The U.S. Tax Court has jurisdiction over certain cases involving Federal taxes. The U.S. Bankruptcy Courts hear and decide certain matters under the Federal Bankruptcy Act, subject to review by the U.S. District Court. The U.S. Court of Appeals for the Federal Circuit reviews decisions of the Court of Federal Claims, the Patent and Trademark Office, patent cases decided by the U.S. District Court, the United States Court of International Trade, the Merit Systems Protection Board, and the U.S. Court of Veterans Appeals.

**FIGURE 3–2** District and Circuit Courts of the United States

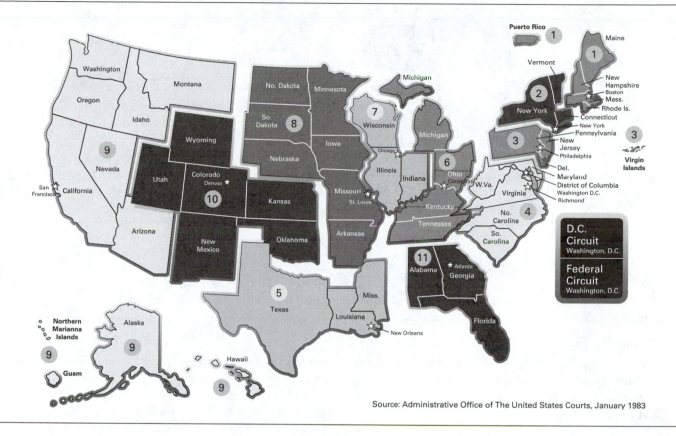

Source: Administrative Office of The United States Courts, January 1983

## STATE COURTS

Each of the fifty States and the District of Columbia has its own court system. In most States the voters elect judges for a stated term.

◆ *See Figure 3–3*

### Inferior Trial Courts

At the bottom of the State court system are the inferior trial courts, which decide the least serious criminal and civil matters. Usually, inferior trial courts do not keep a complete written record of trial proceedings. Such courts, which are referred to as municipal courts, justice of the peace courts, or traffic courts, hear minor criminal cases such as traffic offenses. They also conduct preliminary hearings in more serious criminal cases.

**Small claims courts** are inferior trial courts which hear civil cases involving a limited amount of money. Usually there is no jury, the procedure is informal, and neither side employs an attorney. An appeal from small claims court is taken to the trial court of general jurisdiction, where a new trial (called a trial *de novo*), in which the small claims court's decision is given no weight, is begun.

### Trial Courts

Each State has trial courts of general jurisdiction, which may be called county, district, superior, circuit, or common pleas courts. (In New York the trial court is called the Supreme Court.) These courts do not have a dollar limitation on their jurisdiction in civil cases and hear all criminal cases other than minor offenses. Unlike the inferior trial courts, these trial courts of general jurisdiction maintain formal records of their proceedings as procedural safeguards.

### Special Courts

Many States have special courts that have jurisdiction over particular areas. For example, many States have probate courts with jurisdiction over the administration of

**FIGURE 3–3** State Court System

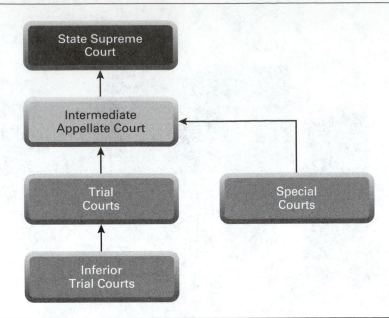

wills and estates. Many States also have family courts, which have jurisdiction over divorce and child custody cases. Appeals from these special courts go to the general State appellate courts.

## Appellate Courts

At the summit of the State court system is the State's court of last resort, a reviewing court generally called the Supreme Court of the State. Except for those cases in which review by the U.S. Supreme Court is available, the decision of the highest State tribunal is final. Most States also have created intermediate appellate courts to handle the large volume of cases seeking review. Review by such a court is usually by right. Further review is in most cases at the highest court's discretion.

## JURISDICTION

**Jurisdiction** means the power or authority of a court to hear and decide a given case. To resolve a lawsuit, a court must have two kinds of jurisdiction. The first is subject matter jurisdiction. Where a court lacks jurisdiction over the subject matter of a case, no action it takes in the case will have legal effect.

The second kind of jurisdiction is over the parties to a lawsuit. This jurisdiction is required for the court to render an enforceable judgment that affects the rights and duties of the parties to the lawsuit. A court usually may obtain jurisdiction over the defendant if she lives and is present in the court's territory or the transaction giving rise to the case has a substantial connection to the court's territory. The court obtains jurisdiction over the plaintiff when he voluntarily submits to the court's power by filing a complaint with the court.

## SUBJECT MATTER JURISDICTION

**Subject matter jurisdiction** refers to the authority of a particular court to adjudicate a controversy of a particular kind. Federal courts have *limited* subject matter jurisdiction, as set forth in the U.S. Constitution, Article III, Section 2. State courts have jurisdiction over *all* matters that the Constitution or Congress has not given exclusively to the Federal courts or expressly denied the State courts.

### Federal Jurisdiction

The Federal courts have, to the exclusion of the State courts, subject matter jurisdiction over some areas. Such jurisdiction is called **exclusive Federal jurisdiction.** Federal jurisdiction is exclusive only if Congress so provides, either explicitly or implicitly. If Congress does not so provide and the area is one over which Federal courts have subject matter jurisdiction, they share this jurisdiction with the State courts. Such jurisdiction is known as **concurrent Federal jurisdiction.**

*Exclusive Federal Jurisdiction* The Federal courts have exclusive jurisdiction over Federal criminal prosecutions; admiralty, bankruptcy, antitrust, patent, trademark and copyright cases; suits against the United States; and cases arising under certain Federal statutes that expressly provide for exclusive Federal jurisdiction.

*Concurrent Federal Jurisdiction* There are two types of concurrent Federal jurisdiction: Federal question jurisdiction and diversity jurisdiction. The first arises whenever there is a Federal question over which the Federal courts do not have exclusive jurisdiction. A **Federal question** is any case arising under the Constitution, statutes, or treaties of the United States. For a case to be treated as "arising under" Federal law, either Federal law must create the plaintiff's cause of action or the plaintiff's right to relief must depend upon the resolution of a substantial question of Federal law in dispute between the parties. There is no minimum dollar requirement in Federal question cases.

Diversity jurisdiction arises where there is "diversity of citizenship" and the amount in controversy exceeds $75,000. Then private litigants may bring an action in a Federal district court or a State court. **Diversity of citizenship** exists (1) when the plaintiffs are all citizens of a State or States different from the State or States of which the defendants are citizens; (2) when a foreign country brings an action against citizens of the United States; or (3) when the controversy is between citizens of the United States and citizens of a foreign country. The citizenship of an individual litigant is the State in which the litigant resides or is domiciled, whereas that of a corporate litigant is both the State of incorporation and the State in which its principal place of business is located. For example, if the amount in controversy exceeds $75,000, then diversity of citizenship jurisdiction would be satisfied if Ada, a citizen of California, sues Bob, a citizen of Idaho. If, however, Carol, a citizen of Virginia, and Dianne, a citizen of North Carolina, sue Evan, a citizen of Georgia, and Farley, a citizen of North Carolina, diversity of citizenship would not exist because both Dianne, a plaintiff, and Farley, a defendant, are citizens of North Carolina.

The $75,000 jurisdictional requirement is satisfied if the plaintiff makes a good faith claim to the amount in the complaint, unless it is clear to a legal certainty that the claim does not exceed the required amount.

 *See Case 3–1*

When a Federal district court hears a case solely under diversity of citizenship jurisdiction, no Federal question is involved, and, accordingly, the Federal court must apply substantive State law. The conflict of laws rules of the State in which the district court is located determine which State's substantive law the court will use. (Conflict of laws is discussed below.) Federal courts apply Federal procedural rules in diversity cases.

In any case involving concurrent jurisdiction, the plaintiff has the choice of bringing the action in either an appropriate Federal court or State court. If the plaintiff brings the case in a State court, however, the defendant usually may have it *removed* (shifted) to a Federal court for the district in which the State court is located.

## State Jurisdiction

*Exclusive State Jurisdiction* The State courts have exclusive jurisdiction over *all other matters* not granted to the Federal courts in the Constitution or by Congress. Accordingly, exclusive State jurisdiction would include cases involving diversity of citizenship where the amount in controversy is $75,000 or less. In addition, the State courts have exclusive jurisdiction over all cases to which Federal judicial power does not reach. These matters include, but are by no means limited to, property, torts, contract, agency, commercial transactions, and most crimes.

◆ *See Figure 3–4*

*Choice of Law in State Courts* A court in one State may be a proper forum for a case even though some or all of the relevant events occurred in another State. For example, a California plaintiff may sue a Washington defendant in Washington over a car accident that occurred in Oregon. Because of Oregon's connections to the accident, Washington may choose, under its **conflict of laws** rules, to apply the substantive law of Oregon. Conflict of laws rules vary from State to State.

 *See Case 3–1*

## *Stare Decisis* in the Dual Court System

The doctrine of *stare decisis* presents certain problems when there are two parallel court systems. Consequently, in the United States, *stare decisis* functions approximately as follows:

**FIGURE 3–4** Federal and State Jurisdiction

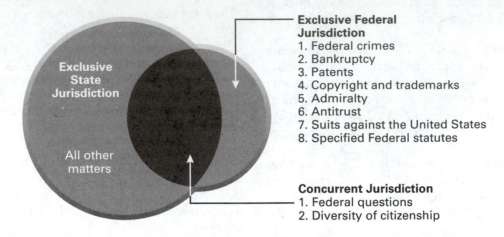

**Exclusive State Jurisdiction**

All other matters

**Exclusive Federal Jurisdiction**
1. Federal crimes
2. Bankruptcy
3. Patents
4. Copyright and trademarks
5. Admiralty
6. Antitrust
7. Suits against the United States
8. Specified Federal statutes

**Concurrent Jurisdiction**
1. Federal questions
2. Diversity of citizenship

1. The United States Supreme Court has never held itself to be bound rigidly by its own decisions, and lower Federal courts and State courts have followed that course with respect to their own decisions.

2. A decision of the U.S. Supreme Court on a Federal question is binding on all other courts, Federal or State.

3. On a Federal question, although a decision of a Federal court other than the Supreme Court may be persuasive in a State court, the decision is not binding.

4. A decision of a State court may be persuasive in the Federal courts, but it is not binding except where Federal jurisdiction is based on diversity of citizenship. In such a case the Federal courts must apply State law as determined by the highest State tribunal.

5. Decisions of the Federal courts (other than the U.S. Supreme Court) are not binding upon other Federal courts of equal or inferior rank, unless the latter owe obedience to the deciding court. For example, a decision of the Fifth Circuit Court of Appeals binds district courts in the fifth circuit but binds no other Federal court.

6. A decision of a State court is binding upon all courts inferior to it in its jurisdiction. Thus, the decision of the supreme court in a State binds all other courts in that State.

7. A decision of a State court is not binding on courts in other States except where the latter courts are required, under their conflict of laws rules, to apply the law of the former State as determined by the highest court in that State. For example, if a North Carolina court is required to apply Virginia law, it must follow decisions of the Virginia Supreme Court.

◆ *See Figure 3–5*

# JURISDICTION OVER THE PARTIES

The second essential type of jurisdiction a court must have is the power to bind the parties involved in the dispute. A court may meet the requirements for this type of jurisdiction, called **jurisdiction over the parties,** in any of three ways: (1) *in personam* jurisdiction, (2) *in rem* jurisdiction, or (3) attachment jurisdiction. In addition, the exercise of jurisdiction must satisfy the constitutionally imposed requirements of due process: reasonable notification and a reasonable opportunity to be heard. Moreover, the court's exercise of jurisdiction is valid under the Due Process Clause of the U.S. Constitution only if the defendant has minimum contacts with the State sufficient to prevent the court's assertion of jurisdiction from offending "traditional notions of fair play and substantial justice." For a court constitutionally to assert jurisdiction over a defendant, the defendant must have engaged in either purposeful acts in the State or acts outside the State that are of such a nature that the defendant could reasonably foresee being sued in that State. This overriding limitation on jurisdictional power is imposed upon the Federal and State courts through the U.S. Constitution, as discussed more fully in Chapter 4.

What notice is due depends on several factors but generally must be "notice reasonably calculated, under the circumstances, to apprise interested parties of the

**FIGURE 3–5** *Stare Decisis* in the Dual Court System

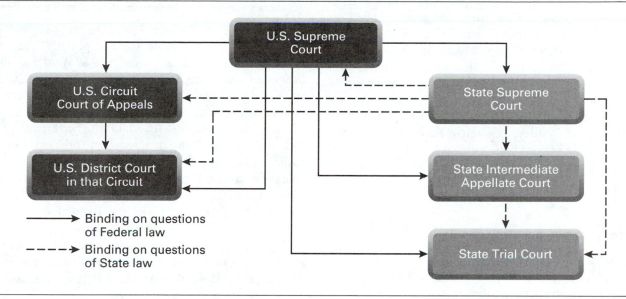

## *In Personam* Jurisdiction

*In personam* jurisdiction, or **personal jurisdiction,** is jurisdiction of a court over the parties to a lawsuit, in contrast to jurisdiction over their property. A court obtains *in personam* jurisdiction over a person either (1) by serving process on the party within the State in which the court is located or (2) by reasonable notification to a party outside the State in those instances where a "long-arm statute" applies. To *serve process* means to deliver a summons, which is an order to respond to a complaint lodged against a party. (The terms *summons* and *complaint* are explained more fully later in this chapter.)

Personal jurisdiction may be obtained by personally serving a person within a State if that person is domiciled in that State. The U.S. Supreme Court has held that a State may exercise personal jurisdiction over a nonresident defendant who is temporarily present if the defendant is personally served in that State. Personal jurisdiction may also arise from a party's consent. For example, parties to a contract may agree that any dispute concerning that contract will be subject to the jurisdiction of a specific court.

Most States have adopted **long-arm statutes** to expand their jurisdictional reach beyond those persons who may be personally served within the State. These statutes allow courts to obtain jurisdiction over nonresident defendants whose contacts with the State in which the court is located are such that the exercise of jurisdiction does not offend traditional notions of fair play and substantial justice. The typical long-arm statute permits a court to exercise jurisdiction over a defendant, even though process is served beyond its borders, if the defendant (1) has committed a tort (civil wrong) within the State, (2) owns property within the State and that property is the subject matter of the lawsuit, (3) has entered into a contract within the State, or (4) has transacted business within the State and that business is the subject matter of the lawsuit.

## *In Rem* Jurisdiction

Courts in a State have the jurisdiction to adjudicate claims to property situated within the State if the plaintiff gives those persons who have an interest in the property reasonable notice and an opportunity to be heard. Such jurisdiction over property is called ***in rem*** jurisdiction, from the Latin word *res,* which means "thing." For example, if Carpenter and Miller are involved in a lawsuit over property located in Kansas, then an appropriate court in Kansas would have *in rem* jurisdiction to adjudicate claims with respect to this property so long as both parties are given notice of the lawsuit and a reasonable opportunity to contest the claim.

pendency of the action and afford them the opportunity to present their objections."

*See Case 3–2*

## Attachment Jurisdiction

Attachment jurisdiction, or **quasi *in rem*** jurisdiction, is jurisdiction over property rather than over a person. Attachment jurisdiction is invoked by seizing the defendant's property located within the State to obtain payment of a claim against the defendant that is *unrelated* to the property seized. For example, Allen, a resident of Ohio, has obtained a valid judgment in the amount of $20,000 against Bradley, a citizen of Kentucky. Allen can attach Bradley's automobile, which is located in Ohio, to satisfy his court judgment against Bradley.

◆ *See Figure 3–6*

## Venue

Venue, which often is confused with jurisdiction, concerns the geographical area in which a lawsuit *should* be brought. The purpose of venue is to regulate the distribution of cases within a specific court system and to identify a convenient forum. In the Federal court system, venue determines the district or districts in a given State in which a suit may be brought. State rules of venue typically require that a suit be initiated in a county where one of the defendants resides. In matters involving real estate, most venue rules require that a suit be initiated in the county where the property is situated. A defendant may, however, object to the venue for various reasons.

# CIVIL DISPUTE RESOLUTION

As mentioned in Chapter 1, one of the primary functions of law is to provide for the peaceful resolution of disputes. Accordingly, our legal system has established an elaborate set of governmental mechanisms to settle disputes. The most prominent of these is judicial dispute resolution, called *litigation*. The rules of civil procedure, discussed in the first part of this section, govern judicial resolution of civil disputes. Judicial resolution of criminal cases is governed by the rules of criminal procedure, which are covered in Chapter 6. Dispute resolution by administrative agencies, which is also very common, is discussed in Chapter 5.

As an alternative to governmental dispute resolution, several nongovernmental methods of dispute resolution, such as arbitration, have developed. These are discussed in the second part of this section.

## *CIVIL PROCEDURE*

Civil disputes that enter the judicial system must follow the rules of civil procedure. These rules are designed to resolve the dispute justly, promptly, and inexpensively.

To acquaint the student with civil procedure, it will be helpful to carry a hypothetical action through the trial court to the highest court of review in the State.

**FIGURE 3–6** Jurisdiction

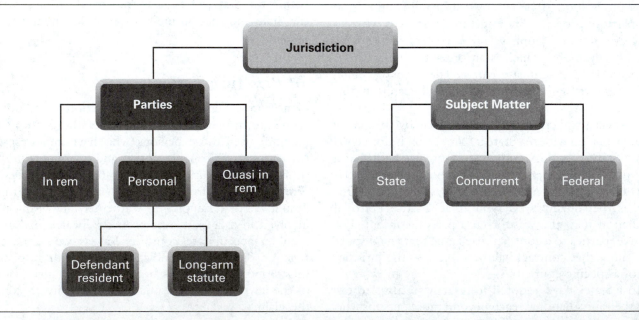

Although there are technical differences in trial and appellate procedure among State and Federal courts, the following illustration will provide a general understanding of the trial and appeal of cases. Assume that Pam Pederson, a pedestrian, while crossing a street in Chicago, is struck by an automobile driven by David Dryden. Pederson suffers serious personal injuries, incurs heavy medical and hospital expenses, and is unable to work for several months. Pederson desires that Dryden pay her for the loss and damages she sustained. After attempts at settlement fail, Pederson brings an action at law against Dryden. Pederson is the plaintiff, and Dryden the defendant. Each is represented by a lawyer. Let us follow the progress of the case.

## The Pleadings

The **pleadings** are a series of responsive, formal, written statements in which each side to a lawsuit states its claims and defenses. The purpose of pleadings is to give notice and to establish the issues of fact and law that the parties dispute. An "issue of fact" is a dispute between the parties regarding the events that gave rise to the lawsuit. In contrast, an "issue of law" is a dispute between the parties as to what legal rules apply to these facts. Issues of fact are decided by the jury, or by the judge when there is no jury, whereas issues of law are decided by the judge.

*Complaint and Summons* A lawsuit commences when Pederson, the plaintiff, files with the clerk of the trial court a **complaint** against Dryden which contains (1) a statement of the claim and supporting facts showing that she is entitled to relief and (2) a demand for that relief. Pederson's complaint alleges that while exercising due and reasonable care for her own safety, she was struck by Dryden's automobile, which was negligently being driven by Dryden, causing her personal injuries and damages of $50,000, for which Pederson requests judgment.

Once the plaintiff has filed a complaint, the clerk issues a **summons** to be served upon the defendant to notify him that a suit has been brought against him. If the defendant has contacts with the State sufficient to show that the State's assertion of jurisdiction over him is constitutional, proper service of the summons establishes the court's jurisdiction over the person of the defendant. The sheriff of the county or a deputy sheriff serves a summons and a copy of the complaint upon Dryden, the defendant, commanding him to file his appearance and answer with the clerk of the court within a specific time, usually thirty days from the date the summons was served. A number of States permit the server to leave a copy of the summons at the defendant's home with a person of "suitable age and discretion." Most long-arm statutes allow service of the summons to be sent to out-of-state defendants by registered mail. If the defendant is a corporation, the statutes typically authorize actual service to the company's general or managing agent. When direct methods of notifying the defendant are unavailable, service by publication may be allowed.

*Responses to Complaint* At this point Dryden has several options. If he fails to respond at all, a **default judgment** will be entered against him for the relief the court determines in a hearing. He may make **pretrial motions** contesting the court's jurisdiction over him or asserting that the action is barred by the statute of limitations, which requires suits to be brought within a specified time. Dryden also may move that the complaint be made more definite and certain, or that the complaint be dismissed for failure to state a claim upon which the court may grant relief. Such a motion, sometimes called a **demurrer**, essentially asserts that even if all of Pederson's allegations were true, she still would not be entitled to the relief she seeks, and that, therefore, there is no need for a trial of the facts. The court rules on this motion as a matter of law. If it rules in favor of the defendant, the plaintiff may appeal the ruling.

If he does not make any pretrial motions, or if they are denied, Dryden will respond to the complaint by filing an **answer,** which may contain admissions, denials, affirmative defenses, and counterclaims. Thus, Dryden might answer the complaint by denying its allegations of negligence and stating, on the other hand, that he, Dryden, was driving his car at a low speed and with reasonable care (a **denial**) when his car struck Pederson (an **admission**), who had dashed across the street in front of Dryden's car without looking in any direction to see whether cars or other vehicles were approaching; that, accordingly, Pederson's injuries were caused by her own negligence (an **affirmative defense**) and that, therefore, she should not be permitted to recover any damages. Dryden might further state that Pederson caused damages to his car and request a judgment for $2,000 (a **counterclaim**). These pleadings create an issue of fact regarding whether Pederson or Dryden, or both, failed to exercise due and reasonable care under the circumstances and were thus negligent and liable for their carelessness.

If the defendant counterclaims, the plaintiff must respond by a **reply,** which may also contain admissions, denials, or affirmative defenses.

## Pretrial Procedure

*Judgment on Pleadings* After the pleadings, either party may move for **judgment on the pleadings,** which requests the judge to rule as a matter of law whether the facts as alleged in the pleadings, which for the purpose of the motion are taken to be as the nonmoving party alleges them, form a sufficient basis to warrant granting the requested relief.

*Discovery* In preparation for trial and even before completion of the pleadings stage, each party has the right to obtain relevant evidence, or information that may lead to evidence, from the other party. This procedure is known as **discovery.** It includes (1) pretrial **depositions** consisting of sworn testimony, taken out of court, of the opposing party or other witnesses; (2) sworn answers by the opposing party to **written interrogatories;** (3) **production** of documents and physical objects in the possession of the opposing party; (4) a relevant court-ordered physical and/or mental **examination,** by a physician, of the opposing party; and (5) admissions of facts set forth in a **request for admissions** submitted to the opposing party. By properly using discovery, each party may become fully informed of relevant evidence and avoid surprise at trial. Another purpose of this procedure is to encourage and facilitate settlements by providing both parties with as much relevant information as possible.

*Pretrial Conference* Also furthering these objectives is the pretrial conference between the judge and the attorneys representing the parties. The basic purposes of the **pretrial conference** are (1) to simplify the issues in dispute by amending the pleadings, admitting or stipulating facts, and limiting the number of expert witnesses; and (2) to encourage settlement of the dispute without trial. (More than 90 percent of all cases are settled before going to trial.) If no settlement occurs, the judge will enter a pretrial order containing all of the amendments, stipulations, admissions, and other matters agreed to during the pretrial conference. The order supersedes the pleadings and controls the remainder of the trial.

*Summary Judgment* The evidence disclosed by discovery may be so clear that a trial to determine the facts becomes unnecessary. Thus, after discovery, either party may move for a summary judgment, which requests the judge to rule that, because there are no issues of fact to be determined by trial, the party thus moving should prevail as a matter of law. A **summary judgment** is a

binding determination on the merits made by the judge before a trial.

 *See Case 3–3*

## Trial

In all Federal civil cases at common law involving more than $20, the U.S. Constitution guarantees the right to a jury trial. In addition, nearly every State constitution provides a similar right. Under Federal law and in almost all States, jury trials are *not* available in equity cases. Even in cases where a jury trial is available, the parties may waive (choose not to have) a trial by jury. When a trial is conducted without a jury, the judge serves as the fact finder and will make separate findings of fact and conclusions of law. When a trial is conducted with a jury, the judge determines issues of law and the jury determines questions of fact.

*Jury Selection* Assuming a timely demand for a jury has been made, the trial begins with the selection of a jury. The jury selection process involves a **voir dire,** an examination by the parties' attorneys (or, in some courts, by the judge) of the potential jurors. Each party may make an unlimited number of **challenges for cause,** which prevent a prospective juror from serving if the juror is biased or cannot be fair and impartial. In addition, each party has a limited number of **peremptory challenges,** which allow the party to disqualify a prospective juror without showing cause. The Supreme Court has held that the U.S. Constitution prohibits discrimination in jury selection on the basis of race or gender.

*Conduct of Trial* After the jury has been selected, both attorneys make an **opening statement** concerning the facts that they expect to prove in the trial. The plaintiff and her witnesses then testify upon **direct examination** by the plaintiff's attorney. Each is then subject to **cross-examination** by the defendant's attorney. Thus, in our hypothetical case, the plaintiff and her witnesses testify that the traffic light at the street intersection where Pederson was struck was green for traffic in the direction in which Pederson was crossing but changed to yellow when she was about one-third of the way across the street.

During the trial the judge rules on the admission and exclusion of evidence. If the judge does not allow certain evidence to be introduced or certain testimony to be given, the attorney may preserve the question of admissibility for review on appeal by making an **offer of proof.** The law does not regard the offer of proof as evidence, and the offer, which consists of oral statements of counsel or witnesses showing for the record the substance of the evidence which the judge has ruled inadmissible, is not heard by the jury.

After cross-examination, followed by redirect examination of each of her witnesses, Pederson rests her case. At this point, Dryden may move for a directed verdict in his favor. A **directed verdict** is a binding determination on the merits made by the judge after a trial but before the jury renders a verdict. If the judge concludes that the evidence introduced by the plaintiff, which is assumed for the purposes of the motion to be true, would not be sufficient for the jury to find in favor of the plaintiff, then the judge will grant the directed verdict in favor of the defendant. In some States, the judge will deny the motion for a directed verdict if there is *any* evidence on which the jury might possibly render a verdict for the plaintiff. If a directed verdict is reversed on appeal, a new trial is necessary.

If the judge denies the motion for a directed verdict, the defendant then has the opportunity to present evidence. The defendant and his witnesses testify that Dryden was driving his car at a low speed when it struck Pederson and that Dryden at the time had the green light at the intersection. After the defendant has presented his evidence and both parties have rested (concluded), either party may move for a directed verdict. By this motion the party contends that the evidence is so clear that reasonable persons could not differ as to the outcome of the case. If the judge grants the motion for a directed verdict, he takes the case away from the jury and enters a judgment for the party making the motion.

If the judge denies the motion, the plaintiff's attorney makes a **closing argument** to the jury, reviewing the evidence and urging a verdict in favor of Pederson. Dryden's attorney then makes a closing argument, summarizing the evidence and urging a verdict in favor of Dryden. Pederson's attorney is permitted to make a short argument in rebuttal.

*Jury Instructions* The attorneys previously have tendered written **jury instructions** on the applicable law to the trial judge, who gives to the jury those instructions he approves and denies those he considers incorrect. The judge also may give the jury instructions of his own. These instructions (called "charges" in some States) advise the jury of the particular rules of law that apply to the facts the jury determines from the evidence.

*Verdict* The jury then retires to the jury room to deliberate and to reach a **general verdict** in favor of one party or the other. If it finds the issues in favor of the defendant,

its verdict is that the defendant is not liable. If, however, it finds the issues for the plaintiff and against the defendant, its verdict will hold the defendant liable and will specify the amount of the plaintiff's damages. In this case, the jury found that Pederson's damages were $35,000. Upon returning to the jury box, the foreman either announces the verdict or hands it in written form to the clerk to give to the judge, who reads the general verdict in open court. In some jurisdictions, the jury must reach a **special verdict** by making specific written findings on each factual issue. The judge then applies the law to these findings and renders a judgment.

*Motions Challenging the Verdict* The unsuccessful party may then file a written motion for a new trial or for judgment notwithstanding the verdict. The judge may grant a **motion for a new trial** if (1) the judge committed prejudicial error during the trial, (2) the verdict is against the weight of the evidence, (3) the damages are excessive, or (4) the trial was not fair. The judge has the discretion to grant a motion for a new trial (on grounds 1, 3, or 4 above) even if substantial evidence supports the verdict. On the other hand, he must deny the motion for judgment notwithstanding the verdict (also called a judgment n.o.v.) if any substantial evidence supports the verdict. This motion is similar to a motion for a directed verdict, only it is made after the jury's verdict. To grant the **motion for judgment notwithstanding the verdict,** the judge must decide that the evidence is so clear that reasonable people could not differ as to the outcome of the case. If the judge denies the motions for a new trial or for a judgment notwithstanding the verdict, he enters **judgment on the verdict** for $35,000 in favor of Pederson.

## Appeal

The purpose of an appeal is to determine whether the trial court committed prejudicial error. As a general rule, an appellate court reviews only errors of law. Errors of law include the judge's decisions to admit or exclude evidence; the judge's instructions to the jury; and the judge's actions in denying or granting a motion for a demurrer, a summary judgment, a directed verdict, or a judgment notwithstanding the verdict. Appellate courts review errors of law *de novo.* An appellate court will reverse errors of fact only if they are so clearly erroneous that the court considers them to constitute an error of law.

Assume that Dryden directs his attorney to appeal. The attorney files a notice of appeal with the clerk of the trial court within the prescribed time. Later, Dryden, as appellant, files in the reviewing court the record on appeal, which contains the pleadings, transcript of the testimony, rulings by the judge on motions made by the parties, arguments of counsel, jury instructions, the verdict, posttrial motions, and the judgment from which the appeal is taken. In States having an intermediate court of appeals, such court will usually be the reviewing court. In States having no intermediate courts of appeal, a party may appeal directly from the trial court to the State supreme court.

Dryden, as appellant, is required to prepare a condensation of the record, known as an abstract, or pertinent excerpts from the record, which he files with the reviewing court together with a brief and argument. His **brief** contains a statement of the facts, the issues, the rulings by the trial court which Dryden contends are erroneous and prejudicial, grounds for reversal of the judgment, a statement of the applicable law, and arguments on his behalf. Pederson, the appellee, files an answering brief and argument. Dryden may, but is not required to, file a reply brief. The case is now ready for consideration by the reviewing court.

The appellate court does not hear any evidence; rather, it decides the case upon the record, abstracts, and briefs. After **oral argument** by the attorneys, if the court elects to hear one, the court then takes the case under advisement and makes a decision based upon majority rule, after which the court prepares a written opinion containing the reasons for its decision, the applicable rules of law, and its judgment. The judgment may **affirm** the judgment of the trial court, or, if the appellate court finds that reversible error was committed, the judgment may be **reversed,** or the case may be **reversed and remanded** for a new trial. In some instances the appellate court will affirm the lower court's decision in part and reverse it in part. The losing party may file a petition for rehearing, which is usually denied.

If the reviewing court is an intermediate appellate court, the party losing in that court may decide to seek a reversal of its judgment by filing within a prescribed time a notice of appeal, if the appeal is by right, or a petition for leave to appeal to the State supreme court, if the appeal is by discretion. This petition corresponds to a petition for a writ of *certiorari* in the U.S. Supreme Court. The party winning in the appellate court may file an answer to the petition for leave to appeal. If the petition is granted, or if the appeal is by right, the record is certified to the supreme court, where each party files a new brief and argument. Oral argument may be held, and the case is taken under advisement. If the supreme court concludes that the judgment of the appellate court is correct, it affirms. If it decides otherwise, it reverses the judgment of the appellate court and enters a reversal or an order of remand. The unsuccessful party may again file a petition for a rehearing, which is likely to be denied. Barring the remote possibility of an application for still further review by the U.S. Supreme Court, the case either has reached its termination or, upon remand, is about to start its second journey through the courts, beginning, as it did originally, in the trial court.

## Enforcement

If Dryden does not appeal, or if the reviewing court affirms the judgment if he does appeal, and Dryden does not pay the judgment, the task of enforcement remains. Pederson must request the clerk to issue a **writ of execution,** demanding payment of the judgment, which is served by the sheriff upon the defendant. If the writ is returned "unsatisfied," Pederson may post bond or other security and order a levy on and sale of specific nonexempt property belonging to Dryden, which is then seized by the sheriff, advertised for sale, and sold at public sale under the writ of execution. If the proceeds of the sale do not produce sufficient funds to pay the judgment, plaintiff Pederson's attorney may institute a supplementary proceeding in an attempt to locate money or other property belonging to Dryden. In an attempt to collect the judgment, Pederson's attorney also may proceed by **garnishment** against Dryden's employer to collect from Dryden's wages or against a bank in which Dryden has an account.

If Pederson cannot satisfy the judgment with Dryden's property located within Illinois (the State where the judgment was obtained), Pederson will have to bring an action on the original judgment in other States where Dryden owns property. Because the U.S. Constitution requires each State to accord judgments of other States **full faith and credit,** Pederson will be able to obtain a local judgment that may be enforced by the methods described above.

◆ *See Figure 3–7*

## ALTERNATIVE DISPUTE RESOLUTION

Litigation is complex, time-consuming, and expensive. Furthermore, court adjudications involve long delays, lack special expertise in substantive areas, and provide

**FIGURE 3–7** Stages in Civil Procedure

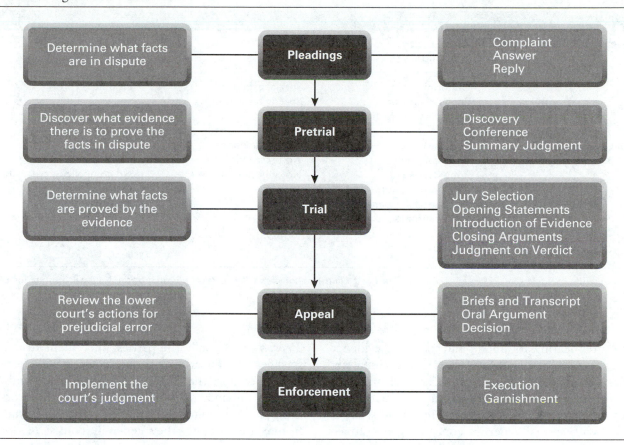

only a limited range of remedies. In addition, the litigation process offers little opportunity for compromise and often causes or exacerbates animosity between the disputants. Consequently, in an attempt to overcome some of the disadvantages of litigation, several nonjudicial methods of dealing with disputes have developed. The most important of these alternatives to litigation is arbitration. Others include conciliation, mediation, "minitrials," and summary jury trials.

The various techniques differ in a number of ways, including (1) whether the process is voluntary, (2) whether the process is binding, (3) whether the disputants represent themselves or are represented by attorneys, (4) whether the decision is made by the disputants or by a third party, (5) whether the procedure used is formal or informal, and (6) whether the basis for the decision is law or some other criterion.

Which method of civil dispute resolution—litigation or one of the nongovernmental methods—is better for a particular dispute depends on several factors, including the financial circumstances of the disputants, the nature

of their relationship (commercial or personal, ongoing or limited), and the urgency of their need for a quick resolution. Alternative dispute resolution methods are especially suitable where privacy, speed, preservation of continuing relations, and control over the process—including the flexibility to compromise—are important to the parties. Nevertheless, the disadvantages of using alternative dispute mechanisms may make court adjudication more appropriate. For example, except for arbitration, only courts can compel participation and provide a binding resolution. In addition, only courts can establish precedents and create public duties. Furthermore, the courts provide greater due process protections and uniformity of outcome. Finally, the courts are independent of the disputants and are publicly funded.

◆ *See Figure 3–8*

## Arbitration

In **arbitration,** the parties select a neutral third person or persons (the arbitrator[s]) who render(s) a binding

**FIGURE 3—8** Comparison of Adjudication, Arbitration, and Mediation/Conciliation

|  | Court Adjudication | Arbitration | Mediation/Conciliation |
|---|---|---|---|
| **Advantages** | Binding | Binding | Preserves relations |
|  | Public norms | Parties control process | Parties control process |
|  | Precedents | Privacy | Privacy |
|  | Uniformity | Special expertise | Flexible |
|  | Publicly funded | Speedy resolution |  |
|  | Compels participation |  |  |
| **Disadvantages** | Expensive | No public norms | Not binding |
|  | Time-consuming | No precedent | Lacks finality |
|  | Long delays | No uniformity | No compelled participation |
|  | Limited remedies |  | No precedent |
|  | Lacks special expertise |  | No uniformity |
|  | No compromise |  |  |
|  | Disrupts relationships |  |  |
|  | Publicity |  |  |

Source: Adapted from Table 4 of *Report of the Ad Hoc Panel on Dispute Resolution and Public Policy,* prepared by the National Institute for Dispute Resolution.

decision after hearing arguments and reviewing evidence. Because the presentation of the case is less formal and the rules of evidence are more relaxed, arbitration usually takes less time and costs less than litigation. Moreover, in many arbitration cases the parties are able to select an arbitrator with special expertise concerning the subject of the dispute. Thus, the quality of the arbitrator's decision may be higher than that available through the court system. In addition, arbitration normally is conducted in private, which enables the parties to avoid unwanted publicity. Arbitration is commonly used in commercial and labor management disputes.

*Types of Arbitration* Arbitration is of two basic types—consensual, which is by far the most common, and compulsory. **Consensual arbitration** occurs whenever the parties to a dispute agree to submit the controversy to arbitration. They may do this in advance by agreeing in their contract that disputes arising out of the contract will be resolved by arbitration. Or, after a dispute arises, they may agree to submit the dispute to arbitration. In either instance, such agreements are enforceable under the Federal Arbitration Act and statutes in more than forty States. The great majority of these States have adopted the Uniform Arbitration Act. In **compulsory arbitration,** which is relatively infrequent, a Federal or State statute requires arbitration for specific types of disputes, such as those involving public employees like police officers, teachers, and firefighters.

*Procedure* Usually the parties' agreement to arbitrate specifies how the arbitrator or arbitrators will be chosen. If it does not, the Federal Arbitration Act and State statutes provide methods for selecting arbitrators. Although the requirements for arbitration hearings vary from State to State, they generally consist of opening statements, case presentation, and closing statements. Case presentations may include witnesses, documentation, and site inspections. The parties may cross-examine witnesses and the parties may be represented by attorneys.

The decision of the arbitrator, called an **award,** is binding on the parties. Nevertheless, it is subject to very limited judicial review. Historically, the courts were unfriendly to arbitration; now, however, they favor the procedure.

*International Arbitration* Arbitration is a commonly used means for resolving international disputes. The United Nations Committee on International Trade Law (UNCITRAL) and the International Chamber of Commerce have promulgated arbitration rules which have won broad international adherence. The Federal Arbitration Act has provisions implementing the United Nations Convention on the Recognition and Enforcement of Foreign Arbitral Awards. A number of States have enacted laws specifically governing international arbitration; some of the statutes have been based on the Model Law on International Arbitration drafted by UNCITRAL.

*Court-Annexed Arbitration* A growing number of Federal and State courts have adopted court-annexed arbitration in civil cases where the parties seek limited amounts of damages. The arbitrators are usually attorneys. Appeal from this type of *nonbinding* arbitration is by trial *de novo*.

Many States have enacted statutes requiring the arbitration of medical malpractice disputes. Some States provide for mandatory nonbinding arbitration before bringing a case to court. Other States provide for voluntary but binding arbitration agreements which patients sign before receiving medical treatment.

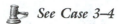 *See Case 3–4*

## Conciliation

**Conciliation** is a nonbinding, informal process in which the disputing parties select a neutral third party (the conciliator) who attempts to help them reach a mutually acceptable agreement. The duties of the conciliator include improving communications, explaining issues, scheduling meetings, discussing differences of opinion, and serving as an intermediary between the parties when they are unwilling to meet.

## Mediation

**Mediation** is a process in which a neutral third party (the mediator) selected by the disputants helps them to resolve their disagreement. In addition to employing conciliation techniques to improve communications, the mediator, unlike the conciliator, proposes possible solutions for the parties to consider. Like the conciliator, the mediator lacks the power to render a binding decision. Mediation has become commonly used by the judicial system in such tribunals as small claims courts, housing courts, family courts, and neighborhood justice centers.

Sometimes the techniques of arbitration and mediation are combined in a procedure called "med-arb." In med-arb, the neutral third party serves first as a mediator. If all issues are not resolved through such mediation, she then serves as an arbitrator authorized to render a binding decision on the remaining issues.

## Mini-Trial

A mini-trial is a structured settlement process that combines elements of negotiation, mediation, and trials. Mini-trials are most commonly used when both disputants are corporations. In a mini-trial, attorneys for the two corporations conduct limited discovery and then present evidence to a panel consisting of managers from each company, as well as a neutral third party, who may be a retired judge or other attorney. After the lawyers complete their presentations, the managers try to negotiate a settlement without the attorneys. The managers may consult the third party on how a court might resolve the issues in dispute.

## Summary Jury Trial

A summary jury trial is a mock trial in which the parties present their case to an advisory jury. Though not binding, the jury's verdict does influence the negotiations in which the parties must participate following the mock trial. If the parties do not reach a settlement, they may have a full trial *de novo*.

## Negotiation

Negotiation is a consensual bargaining process in which the parties attempt to reach an agreement resolving their dispute. Negotiation differs from other methods of alternate dispute resolution in that there are no third parties involved.

---

 # Chapter Summary

## The Court System

| **Federal Courts** | **District Courts** trial courts of general jurisdiction that can hear and decide most legal controversies in the Federal system |
| --- | --- |
| | **Courts of Appeals** hear appeals from the district courts and review orders of certain administrative agencies |

**The Supreme Court**  nation's highest court, whose principal function is to review decisions of the Federal Courts of Appeals and the highest State courts
**Special Courts**  have jurisdiction over cases in a particular area of Federal law and include the U.S. Court of Federal Claims, the U.S. Tax Court, the U.S. Bankruptcy Courts, and the U.S. Court of Appeals for the Federal Circuit

## State Courts

**Inferior Trial Courts**  hear minor criminal cases, such as traffic offenses, and civil cases involving small amounts of money; conduct preliminary hearings in more serious criminal cases
**Trial Courts**  have general jurisdiction over civil and criminal cases
**Special Courts**  trial courts, such as probate courts and family courts, having jurisdiction over a particular area of State law
**Appellate Courts**  include one or two levels; the highest court's decisions are final except in those cases reviewed by the U.S. Supreme Court

# Jurisdiction

## Subject Matter Jurisdiction

**Definition**  authority of a court to decide a particular kind of case
**Federal Jurisdiction**
- *Exclusive Federal Jurisdiction*  Federal courts have sole jurisdiction over Federal crimes, bankruptcy, antitrust, patent, trademark, copyright, and other specified cases
- *Concurrent Federal Jurisdiction*  authority of more than one court to hear the same case; State and Federal courts have concurrent jurisdiction over (1) Federal question cases (cases arising under the Constitution, statutes, or treaties of the United States) that do not involve exclusive Federal jurisdiction and (2) diversity of citizenship cases involving more than $75,000

**State Jurisdiction**  State courts have exclusive jurisdiction over all matters to which the Federal judicial power does not reach

## Jurisdiction over the Parties

**Definition**  the power of a court to bind the parties to a suit
*In Personam* **Jurisdiction**  jurisdiction based upon claims against a person, in contrast to jurisdiction over the person's property
*In Rem* **Jurisdiction**  jurisdiction based on claims against property
**Attachment Jurisdiction**  jurisdiction over a defendant's property to obtain payment of a claim not related to the property
**Venue**  geographical area in which a lawsuit should be brought

# Civil Dispute Resolution

**Civil Procedure**

**The Pleadings** a series of statements that give notice and establish the issues of fact and law presented and disputed
- *Complaint* initial pleading by the plaintiff stating his case
- *Summons* notice given to inform a person of a lawsuit against her
- *Answer* defendant's pleading in response to the plaintiff's complaint
- *Reply* plaintiff's pleading in response to the defendant's answer

**Pretrial Procedure** process requiring the parties to disclose what evidence is available to prove the disputed facts; designed to encourage settlement of cases or to make the trial more efficient
- *Judgment on Pleadings* a final ruling in favor of one party by the judge based on the pleadings
- *Discovery* right of each party to obtain evidence from the other party
- *Pretrial Conference* a conference between the judge and the attorneys to simplify the issues in dispute and to attempt to settle the dispute without trial
- *Summary Judgment* final ruling by the judge in favor of one party based on the evidence disclosed by discovery

**Trial** determines the facts and the outcome of the case
- *Jury Selection* each party has an unlimited number of challenges for cause and a limited number of peremptory challenges
- *Conduct of Trial* consists of opening statements by attorneys, direct and cross-examination of witnesses, and closing arguments
- *Jury Instructions* judge gives the jury the particular rules of law that apply to the case
- *Verdict* the jury's decision based on those facts the jury determines the evidence proves
- *Motions Challenging the Verdict* include motions for a new trial and a motion for judgment notwithstanding the verdict

**Appeal** determines whether the trial court committed prejudicial error

**Enforcement** plaintiff with an unpaid judgment may resort to a writ of execution to have the sheriff seize property of the defendants and to garnishment to collect money owed to the defendant by a third party

**Alternative Dispute Resolution**

**Arbitration** a nonjudicial proceeding in which a neutral party selected by the disputants renders a binding decision (award)

**Conciliation** a nonbinding process in which a third party acts as an intermediary between the disputing parties

**Mediation** a nonbinding process in which a third party acts as an intermediary between the disputing parties and proposes solutions for them to consider

**Mini-Trial** a nonbinding process in which attorneys for the disputing parties (typically corporations) present evidence to managers of the disputing parties and a neutral third party, after which the managers attempt to negotiate a settlement in consultation with the third party

**Summary Jury Trial** mock trial followed by negotiations

**Negotiation** consensual bargaining process in which the parties attempt to reach an agreement resolving their dispute without the involvement of third parties

# Cases

Concurrent Federal Jurisdiction/Choice of Law
## *RAM PRODUCTS CO., INC. v. CHAUNCEY*
United States District Court, N.D. Indiana, South Bend Division, 1997
967 F.Supp. 1071

SHARP, C. J.

[Defendant, Warren C. Chauncey (Chauncey), is an Indiana resident, who briefly held the position of Vice President of Sales and Marketing while employed at RAM Products. He is fifty-nine years old and has been in the plastics industry for twenty-five years. Defendant, Replex Plastics (Replex), is an Ohio Corporation now employing Chauncey in a management position. Plaintiff, RAM Products (RAM), a Michigan corporation, and Replex are both in the plastics industry. The employment contract in controversy was entered into between Chauncey and RAM in St Joseph County, Michigan on November 18, 1991 and contained a clause prohibiting former employees from competing against RAM for a period of one year after termination of employment with RAM. On December 3, 1996, Chauncey was released from his employment at RAM and soon after began employment with Replex.

The plaintiff contends that this was a breach of its former employment contract's covenant not to compete, that Chauncey has converted and continues to convert RAM's property and trade secrets, and that he has made derogatory remarks regarding RAM to its customers and the general public. The plaintiff argues that Chauncey's breach of contract causes irreparable harm to it through the disclosure of confidential information, the loss of client confidence, loss of goodwill, and loss of business reputation. The plaintiff seeks a preliminary injunction requiring Chauncey to cease his employment with Replex until the one year time period required by the contract has expired, an injunction restraining Chauncey from working for any other competitor during the one year period, and damages originally in the amount of $50,000. The defendant Chauncey asserts that he is not violating his former employment contract, that the contract is void due to RAM's failure to perform certain provisions of the contract, that the non-competition clause is overly-broad and unenforceable, and that he has not disclosed any trade secrets or confidential information.]

The court heard oral argument regarding the issues on February 5, 1997, at which time the court directed the parties to brief the issues. Subsequently, the parties entered into settlement negotiations with the Magistrate and requested several extensions for the filing of their briefs. The settlement conferences were ultimately unsuccessful. On March 18, 1997 the court received the parties' briefs addressing the preliminary injunction. At that time, the court expressed serious reservations regarding jurisdictional issues and requested the parties to supplement the record by briefing those issues. [Court's footnote: Specifically, the court questioned the amount in controversy. Plaintiff's complaint alleged an amount of $50,000. At the time plaintiff filed, the increased jurisdictional amount of $75,000 was required, as the amendment to 28 U.S.C. § 1332 [the diversity jurisdiction statute] became effective on January 16, 1997. Additionally, the complaint contained only unsupported allegations of potential lost profits and sales. Plaintiff has since filed an amended complaint and a brief on the jurisdictional issue.]

This court has subject matter jurisdiction over this case pursuant to [citation], as amended October 19, 1996, because the matter in controversy exceeds the sum or value of $75,000 and is between citizens of different states. [Court's footnote: While this court still has concerns regarding the amount of actual damages attributable to defendant, the court finds that plaintiff has alleged sufficient facts to proceed with the case. However, close attention should be given to [citation], which authorizes cost to be assessed against the plaintiff where the recovery is less than the jurisdictional amount. It has been this court's practice to do such.] * * *

If the right of recovery is uncertain, the doubt should be resolved, for jurisdictional purposes, in favor of the subjective good faith of the plaintiff. [Citation.]. Moreover, even where those allegations leave "grave doubt about the likelihood of a recovery of the requisite amount, dismissal is not warranted." [Citation.]

Applying this rationale, this court resolves the jurisdictional conflict in favor of Plaintiff. [Only] if it appears to a legal certainty that the plaintiff cannot recover the jurisdictional amount will the case be dismissed for want of jurisdiction. [Citation.]

This action is based on an employment contract with no express choice of law provision. * * * Therefore, prior to determining the merits of plaintiff's request for an injunction, this court must determine which state's law applies to the substantive contract issues.

As a rule, a court in a diversity case must apply the substantive law of the forum in which it sits, [*Erie v. Tomkins*, citation], including that pertaining to choice of law. [Citation.] Therefore, if the laws of more than one jurisdiction arguably are in issue, *Erie* requires the federal court to apply the choice of law rules of the state in which it sits. [Citation.]. Accordingly, this court will apply Indiana's choice of law rules in making its determination of which state's law governs the substantive issues.

The characterization of the nature of an action bears upon the choice-of-law question. The present action arises from a breach of contract claim. Formerly, in contract cases, Indiana courts applied the law of the state in which the alleged contract was made or was to be performed. [Citation.] The focus upon performance, in most instances, resulted in application of the law where the breach took place. That rule was modified, however, to allow application of the law of the state with the most significant contacts to the subject matter of the litigation, regardless of the place of the breach. [Citation.] The test requires that a court analyze "all acts of the parties touching the transaction in relation to the several states involved" and apply "the law of the state with which the facts are in most intimate contact." [Citation.] * * * Applying the above principles this court now considers the relevant factors to determine whether Michigan or Indiana substantive law applies to the claims at issue.

Indiana maintains at least some interest in the present action. Defendant Chauncey is an Indiana resident. Indiana has an interest in protecting its citizens' rights to earn a livelihood. [Citation.] Furthermore, Indiana's public policy disfavors non-competition clauses. [Citation.] In addition, both the plaintiff, RAM, and one of the defendants, Replex, transact business in Indiana. Indiana has an economic interest in the ability of companies to conduct business there. Certainly, the final resolution of the case may have some economic impact on Indiana.

In determining the state where the facts are in "most intimate contact" the court notes that defendant RAM is a Michigan corporation. Additionally, both RAM and Replex transact business in Michigan. Similar to Indiana, Michigan has an interest in protecting its corporations and in protecting the ability of companies to conduct business in the state. As a result, Michigan also has an economic interest in this case. Furthermore, while there is no indication of where the negotiations for this contract occurred, the "home office" for which Chauncey worked was located in Michigan. In addition, the employment agreement in question was formed in Michigan. Moreover, Michigan public policy and statutes favor non-competition covenants as long as they are reasonable. [Citation.]

Based on the above facts, this court finds that the balance of factors tips slightly in favor of Michigan's interests, therefore, this court will apply Michigan law to resolve the substantive contract issues.

---

## CASE 3–2
### Jurisdiction
# *WORLD-WIDE VOLKSWAGEN CORP. v. WOODSON*

Supreme Court of the United States, 1980
444 U.S. 286, 100 S.Ct. 559, 62 L.Ed.2d 490

WHITE, J.
The issue before us is whether, consistently with the Due Process Clause of the Fourteenth Amendment, an Oklahoma court may exercise *in personam* jurisdiction over a nonresident automobile retailer and its wholesale distributor in a products-liability action, when the defendants' only connection with Oklahoma is the fact that an automobile sold in New York to New York residents became involved in an accident in Oklahoma.

Respondents Harry and Kay Robinson purchased a new Audi automobile from petitioner Seaway Volkswagen, Inc. (Seaway), in Massena, N.Y., in 1976. The following year the Robinson family, who resided in New York, left that State for a new home in Arizona. As they passed through the State of Oklahoma, another car struck their Audi in the rear, causing a fire which severely burned Kay Robinson and her two children.

The Robinsons subsequently brought a products-liability action in the District Court for Creek County, Okla., claiming that their injuries resulted from defective design and placement of the Audi's gas tank and fuel system. They joined as defendants the automobile's manufacturer, Audi NSU Auto Union Aktiengesellschaft (Audi); its importer, Volkswagen of America, Inc. (Volkswagen); its regional distributor, petitioner World-Wide Volkswagen Corp. (World-Wide); and its retail dealer, petitioner Seaway. Seaway and World-Wide entered special appearances, claiming that Oklahoma's exercise of jurisdiction over them would offend the limitations on the State's jurisdiction imposed by the Due Process Clause of the Fourteenth Amendment.

The facts presented to the District Court showed that World-Wide is incorporated and has its business office in New York. It distributes vehicles, parts, and accessories, under contract with Volkswagen, to retail dealers in New York, New Jersey, and Connecticut. Seaway, one of these retail dealers, is incorporated and has its place of business in New York. Insofar as the record reveals, Seaway and World-Wide are fully independent corporations whose relations with each other and with Volkswagen and Audi are contractual only. Respondents adduced no evidence that either World-Wide or Seaway does any business in Oklahoma, ships or sells any products to or in that State, has an agent to receive process there, or purchases advertisements in any media calculated to reach Oklahoma. In fact, as respondents' counsel conceded at oral argument, [citation], there was no showing that any automobile sold by World-Wide or Seaway has ever entered Oklahoma with the single exception of the vehicle involved in the present case.

\* \* \*

The Supreme Court of Oklahoma [held] that personal jurisdiction over petitioners was authorized by Oklahoma's "long-arm" statute, [citation]. \* \* \*

\* \* \*

The Due Process Clause of the Fourteenth Amendment limits the power of a state court to render a valid personal judgment against a nonresident defendant. [Citation.] A judgment rendered in violation of due process is void in the rendering State and is not entitled to full faith and credit elsewhere. [Citation.] Due process requires that the defendant be given adequate notice of the suit, [citation], and be subject to the personal jurisdiction of the court, [citation]. In the present case, it is not contended that notice was inade-

quate; the only question is whether these particular petitioners were subject to the jurisdiction of the Oklahoma courts.

As has long been settled, and as we reaffirm today, a state court may exercise personal jurisdiction over a nonresident defendant only so long as there exist "minimum contacts" between the defendant and the forum State. [Citation.] The concept of minimum contacts, in turn, can be seen to perform two related, but distinguishable, functions. It protects the defendant against the burdens of litigating in a distant or inconvenient forum. And it acts to ensure that the States, through their courts, do not reach out beyond the limits imposed on them by their status as coequal sovereigns in a federal system.

The protection against inconvenient litigation is typically described in terms of "reasonableness" or "fairness." We have said that the defendant's contacts with the forum State must be such that maintenance of the suit "does not offend 'traditional notions of fair play and substantial justice.'" [Citation.] The relationship between the defendant and the forum must be such that it is "reasonable . . . to require the corporation to defend the particular suit which is brought there." [Citation.] Implicit in this emphasis on reasonableness is the understanding that the burden on the defendant, while always a primary concern, will in an appropriate case be considered in light of other relevant factors, including the forum State's interest in adjudicating the dispute, [citation]; the plaintiff's interest in obtaining convenient and effective relief, [citation], at least when that interest is not adequately protected by the plaintiff's power to choose the forum, [citation]; the interstate judicial system's interest in obtaining the most efficient resolution of controversies; and the shared interest of the several States in furthering fundamental substantive social policies, [citation].

\* \* \*

Thus, the Due Process Clause "does not contemplate that a state may make binding a judgment *in personam* against an individual or corporate defendant with which the state has no contacts, ties, or relations." [Citation.]

\* \* \*

Applying these principles to the case at hand, we find in the record before us a total absence of those affiliating circumstances that are a necessary predicate to any exercise of state-court jurisdiction. Petitioners carry on no activity whatsoever in Oklahoma. They close no sales and perform no services there. They avail themselves of none of the privileges and benefits of Oklahoma law. They solicit no business there either through salespersons or through advertising reasonably calculated to reach the

State. Nor does the record show that they regularly sell cars at wholesale or retail to Oklahoma customers or residents or that they indirectly, through others, serve or seek to serve the Oklahoma market. In short, respondents seek to base jurisdiction on one, isolated occurrence and whatever inferences can be drawn therefrom: the fortuitous circumstance that a single Audi automobile, sold in New York to New York residents, happened to suffer an accident while passing through Oklahoma.

* * *

Because we find that petitioners have no "contacts, ties, or relations" with the State of Oklahoma, [citation], the judgment of the Supreme Court of Oklahoma is Reversed.

---

## CASE 3–3
### Pretrial Procedure: Summary Judgment
### *PARKER v. TWENTIETH CENTURY—FOX FILM CORP.*

Supreme Court of California, 1970
3 Cal.3d 176, 89 Cal.Rptr. 737, 474 P.2d 689

BURKE, J.
Defendant Twentieth Century-Fox Film Corporation appeals from a summary judgment granting to plaintiff [Shirley MacLaine Parker] the recovery of agreed compensation under a written contract for her services as an actress in a motion picture. As will appear, we have concluded that the trial court correctly ruled in plaintiff's favor and that the judgment should be affirmed.

Plaintiff is well known as an actress, and in the contract between plaintiff and defendant is sometimes referred to as the "Artist." Under the contract, dated August 6, 1965, plaintiff was to play the female lead in defendant's contemplated production of a motion picture entitled "Bloomer Girl." The contract provided that defendant would pay plaintiff a minimum "guaranteed compensation" of $53,571.42 per week for 14 weeks commencing May 23, 1966, for a total of $750,000. Prior to May 1966 defendant decided not to produce the picture and by a letter dated April 4, 1966, it notified plaintiff of that decision and that it would not "comply with our obligations to you under" the written contract.

By the same letter and with the professed purpose "to avoid any damage to you," defendant instead offered to employ plaintiff as the leading actress in another film tentatively entitled "Big Country, Big Man" (hereinafter, "Big Country"). The compensation offered was identical, as were 31 of the 34 numbered provisions or articles of the original contract. Unlike "Bloomer Girl," however, which was to have been a musical production, "Big Country" was a dramatic "western type" movie. "Bloomer Girl" was to have been filmed in California; "Big Country" was to be produced in Australia. Also, certain terms in the proffered contract varied from those of the original. Plaintiff was given one week within which to accept; she did not and the offer lapsed. Plaintiff then commenced this action seeking recovery of the agreed guaranteed compensation.

The complaint sets forth two causes of action. The first is for money due under the contract; the second, based upon the same allegations as the first, is for damages resulting from defendant's breach of contract. Defendant in its answer admits the existence and validity of the contract, that plaintiff complied with all the conditions, covenants and promises and stood ready to complete the performance, and that defendant breached and "anticipatorily repudiated" the contract. It denies, however, that any money is due to plaintiff either under the contract or as a result of its breach, and pleads as an affirmative defense to both causes of action plaintiff's allegedly deliberate failure to mitigate damages, asserting that she unreasonably refused to accept its offer of the leading role in "Big Country."

Plaintiff moved for summary judgment under Code of Civil Procedure section 437c, the motion was granted, and summary judgment for $750,000 plus interest was entered in plaintiff's favor. This appeal by defendant followed.

The familiar rules are that the matter to be determined by the trial court on a motion for summary judgment is whether facts have been presented which give rise to a triable factual issue. The court may not pass upon the issue itself. Summary judgment is proper only if the affidavits or declarations in support of the moving party would be sufficient to sustain a judgment in his favor and his opponent does not by affidavit show facts sufficient to present a triable issue of fact. The affidavits of the moving party are strictly construed, and doubts as to the propriety of summary judgment should be resolved against granting the motion. Such summary procedure is drastic and should be used with caution so that it does not become a substitute for the open trial method of determining facts. The moving party cannot depend upon allegations in his own pleadings to cure deficient affidavits, nor can his adversary rely upon his own pleadings in lieu or in support of affidavits in opposition to a motion; however, a party can rely on his adversary's pleadings to establish facts not contained in his own affidavits. [Citations.] Also, the court may consider facts stipulated to by the parties and facts which are properly the subject of judicial notice. [Citations.]

* * *

Applying the foregoing rules to the record in the present case, with all intendments in favor of the party opposing the summary judgment motion—here, defendant—it is clear that the trial court correctly ruled that plaintiff's failure to accept defendant's tendered substitute employment could not be applied in mitigation of damages because the offer of the "Big Country" lead was of employment both different and inferior, and that no factual dispute was presented on that issue. The mere circumstance that "Bloomer Girl" was to be a musical review calling upon plaintiff's talents as a dancer as well as an actress, and was to be produced in the City of Los Angeles, whereas "Big Country" was a straight dramatic role in a "Western Type" story taking place in an opal mine in Australia, demonstrates the difference in kind between the two employments; the female lead as a dramatic actress in a western style motion picture can by no stretch of imagination be considered the equivalent of or substantially similar to the lead in a song-and-dance production.

Additionally, the substitute "Big Country" offer proposed to eliminate or impair the director and screenplay approvals accorded to plaintiff under the original "Bloomer Girl" contract . . . and thus constituted an offer of inferior employment. No expertise or judicial notice is required in order to hold that the deprivation or infringement of an employee's rights held under an original employment contract converts the available "other employment" relied upon by the employer to mitigate damages, into inferior employment which the employee need not seek or accept. [Citation.]

Statements found in affidavits submitted by defendant in opposition to plaintiff's summary judgment motion, to the effect that the "Big Country" offer was not of employment different from or inferior to that under the "Bloomer Girl" contract, merely repeat the allegations of defendant's answer to the complaint in this action, constitute only conclusionary assertions with respect to undisputed facts, and do not give rise to a triable factual issue so as to defeat the motion for summary judgment. [Citations.]

* * *

The judgment is affirmed.

---

## CASE 3–4
## Arbitration

## *ALLIED-BRUCE TERMINIX COMPANIES, INC. v. DOBSON*

Supreme Court of the United States, 1995
513 U.S. 265, 115 S.Ct. 834, 130 L.Ed.2d 753

BREYER, J.

This case concerns the reach of §2 of the Federal Arbitration Act. That section makes enforceable a written arbitration provision in "a contract *evidencing* a transaction *involving* commerce." [Citation.] Should we read this phrase broadly, extending the Act's reach to the limits of Congress' Commerce Clause power? Or, do the two underscored words—"involving" and "evidencing"—significantly restrict the Act's application? We conclude that the broader reading of the Act is the correct one; and we reverse a State Supreme Court judgment to the contrary.

I

In August 1987 Steven Gwin, a respondent, who owned a house in Birmingham, Alabama, bought a lifetime "Termite Protection Plan" (Plan) from the local office of Allied-Bruce Terminix Companies, a franchise of Terminix International Company. In the Plan, Allied-Bruce promised "to protect" Gwin's house "against the attack of subterranean termites," to reinspect periodically, to provide any "further treatment found necessary," and to repair, up to $100,000, damage caused by new termite infestations. [Citation.] Terminix International "guarantee[d] the fulfillment of the terms" of the Plan.

[Citation.] The Plan's contract document provided in writing that "any controversy or claim . . . arising out of or relating to the interpretation, performance or breach of any provision of this agreement shall be settled exclusively by arbitration." [Citation.]

In the Spring of 1991 Mr. and Mrs. Gwin, wishing to sell their house to Mr. and Mrs. Dobson, had Allied-Bruce reinspect the house. They obtained a clean bill of health. But, no sooner had they sold the house and transferred the Termite Protection Plan to Mr. and Mrs. Dobson than the Dobsons found the house swarming with termites. Allied-Bruce attempted to treat and repair the house, but the Dobsons found Allied-Bruce's efforts inadequate. They therefore sued the Gwins, and (along with the Gwins, who cross-claimed) also sued Allied-Bruce and Terminix in Alabama state court. Allied-Bruce and Terminix, pointing to the Plan's arbitration clause and §2 of the Federal Arbitration Act, immediately asked the court for a stay, to allow arbitration to proceed. The court denied the stay. Allied-Bruce and Terminix appealed.

The Supreme Court of Alabama upheld the denial of the stay on the basis of a state statute, [citation], making written, predispute arbitration agreements invalid and "unenforceable." [Citation.] To reach this conclusion, the court had to find that the Federal Arbitration Act, which preempts conflicting state law, did not apply to the termite contract. It made just that finding. The court considered the federal Act inapplicable because the connection between the termite contract and interstate commerce was too slight. In the court's view, the Act applies to a contract only if "'at the time [the parties entered into the contract] and accepted the arbitration clause, they contemplated substantial interstate activity.'" [Citation.] Despite some interstate activities (e.g., Allied-Bruce, like Terminix, is a multistate firm and shipped treatment and repair material from out of state), the court found that the parties "contemplated" a transaction that was primarily local and not "substantially" interstate.

Several state courts and federal district courts, like the Supreme Court of Alabama, have interpreted the Act's language as requiring the parties to a contract to have "contemplated" an interstate commerce connection. [Citation.] Several federal appellate courts, however, have interpreted the same language differently, as reaching to the limits of Congress' Commerce Clause power. [Citation.] We granted certiorari to resolve this conflict, [citation], and, as we said, we conclude that the broader reading of the statute is the right one.

## II

Before we can reach the main issues in this case, we must set forth three items of legal background.

First, the basic purpose of the Federal Arbitration Act is to overcome courts' refusals to enforce agreements to arbitrate. [Citation.] The origins of those refusals apparently lie in "'ancient times,'" when the English courts fought "'for extension of jurisdiction—all of them being opposed to anything that would altogether deprive every one of them of jurisdiction.'" [Citation.] American courts initially followed English practice, perhaps just "'stand[ing] . . . upon the antiquity of the rule'" prohibiting arbitration clause enforcement, rather than "'upon its excellence or reason.'" [Citation.] Regardless, when Congress passed the Arbitration Act in 1925, it was "motivated, first and foremost, by a . . . desire" to change this antiarbitration rule. [Citation.] It intended courts to "enforce [arbitration] agreements into which parties had entered," [citation], and to "place such agreements 'upon the same footing as other contracts.'" [Citation.]

Second, some initially assumed that the Federal Arbitration Act represented an exercise of Congress' Article III power to "ordain and establish" federal courts, U.S. Const., Art. III, §1. [Citation.] In 1967, however, this Court held that the Act "is based upon and confined to the incontestable federal foundations of 'control over interstate commerce and over admiralty.'" [Citation.]

* * *

Third, the holding in [citation] led to a further question. Did Congress intend the Act also to apply in state courts? Did the Federal Arbitration Act pre-empt conflicting state antiarbitration law, or could state courts apply their antiarbitration rules in cases before them, thereby reaching results different from those reached in otherwise similar federal diversity cases? In *Southland Corp. v. Keating*, this Court decided that Congress would not have wanted state and federal courts to reach different outcomes about the validity of arbitration in similar cases. The Court concluded that the Federal Arbitration Act pre-empts state law; and it held that state courts cannot apply state statutes that invalidate arbitration agreements. [Citation.]

* * *

We therefore proceed to the basic interpretive questions aware that we are interpreting an Act that seeks broadly to overcome judicial hostility to arbitration agreements and that applies in both federal and state courts. We must decide in this case whether that Act used language about interstate commerce that nonetheless limits the Act's application, thereby carving out an important statutory niche in which a State remains free to apply its antiarbitration law or policy. We conclude that it does not.

## III

The Federal Arbitration Act, §2, provides that a written provision in any maritime transaction or

a contract evidencing a transaction involving commerce to settle by arbitration a controversy thereafter arising out of such contract or transaction . . . shall be valid, irrevocable, and enforceable, save upon such grounds as exist at law or in equity for the revocation of any contract. [Citation.]

The initial interpretive question focuses upon the words "involving commerce." These words are broader than the often-found words of art "in commerce." They therefore cover more than "'only persons or activities within the flow of interstate commerce.'" [Citations.] * * *

After examining the statute's language, background, and structure, we conclude that the word "involving" is broad and is indeed the functional equivalent of "affecting." * * *

Further, this Court has previously described the Act's reach expansively as coinciding with that of the Commerce Clause. * * *

Finally, a broad interpretation of this language is consistent with the Act's basic purpose, to put arbitration provisions on "the same footing" as a contract's other terms. * * *

* * *

## IV

Section 2 applies where there is "contract *evidencing a transaction* involving commerce." [Citation.] The second interpretive question focuses on the underscored words. Does "evidencing a transaction" mean only that the transaction (that the contract "evidences") must turn out, in fact, to have involved interstate commerce? Or, does it mean more?

Many years ago, Second Circuit Chief Judge Lumbard said that the phrase meant considerably more. He wrote:

The significant question . . . is not whether, in carrying out the terms of the contract, the parties did cross state lines, but whether, at the time they entered into it and accepted the arbitration clause, they contemplated substantial interstate activity. * * *

The Supreme Court of Alabama, and several other courts, have followed this view, known as the "contemplation of the parties" test. [Citation.]

We find the interpretive choice difficult, but for several reasons we conclude that the first interpretation ("commerce in fact") is more faithful to the statute than the second ("contemplation of the parties"). * * *

* * *

Finally, we note that an amicus curiae argues for an "objective" ("reasonable person" oriented) version of the "contemplation of the parties" test on the ground that such an interpretation would better protect consumers asked to sign form contracts by businesses. We agree that Congress, when enacting this law, had the needs of consumers, as well as others, in mind. [Citation] (the Act, by avoiding "the delay and expense of litigation," will appeal "to big business and little business alike, . . . corporate interests [and] . . . individuals"). Indeed, arbitration's advantages often would seem helpful to individuals, say, complaining about a product, who need a less expensive alternative to litigation. See, [citation] ("The advantages of arbitration are many: it is usually cheaper and faster than litigation; it can have simpler procedural and evidentiary rules; it normally minimizes hostility and is less disruptive of ongoing and future business dealings among the parties; it is often more flexible in regard to scheduling of times and places of hearings and discovery devices . . ."). And, according to the American Arbitration Association (also an amicus here), more than one-third of its claims involve amounts below $10,000, while another third involve claims of $10,000 to $50,000 (with an average processing time of less than six months). [Citation.]

We are uncertain, however, just how the "objective" version of the "contemplation" test would help consumers. Sometimes, of course, it would permit, say, a consumer with potentially large damage claims, to disavow a contract's arbitration provision and proceed in court. But, if so, it would equally permit, say, local business entities to disavow a contract's arbitration provisions, thereby leaving the typical consumer who has only a small damage claim (who seeks, say, the value of only a defective refrigerator or television set) without any remedy but a court remedy, the costs and delays of which could eat up the value of an eventual small recovery.

In any event, §2 gives States a method for protecting consumers against unfair pressure to agree to a contract with an unwanted arbitration provision. States may regulate contracts, including arbitration clauses, under general contract law principles and they may invalidate an arbitration clause "upon such grounds as exist at law or in equity for the revocation of any contract." [Citation.] What States may not do is decide that a contract is fair enough to enforce all its basic terms (price, service, credit), but not fair enough to enforce its arbitration clause. The Act makes any such state policy unlawful, for that kind of policy would place arbitration clauses on an unequal "footing," directly contrary to the Act's language and Congress's intent. [Citation.]

For these reasons, we accept the "commerce in fact" interpretation, reading the Act's language as insisting that the "transaction" in fact "involve" interstate commerce, even if the parties did not contemplate an interstate commerce connection.

## V

The parties do not contest that the transaction in this case, in fact, involved interstate commerce. In addition to the multistate nature of Terminix and Allied-Bruce, the termite-treating and house-repairing material used by Allied-Bruce in its (allegedly inadequate) efforts to carry out the terms of the Plan, came from outside Alabama.

Consequently, the judgment of the Supreme Court of Alabama is reversed and the case is remanded for further proceedings consistent with this opinion.

It is so ordered.

---

# Questions

1.  List and describe the courts in the Federal court system and in a typical State court system.
2.  Distinguish between appeal by right and writ of *certiorari*.
3.  Distinguish between subject matter jurisdiction and jurisdiction over the parties.
4.  Distinguish between exclusive and concurrent Federal jurisdiction. Identify the two types of Federal concurrent jurisdiction.
5.  Define and describe a typical long-arm statute.
6.  List and distinguish among the three types of jurisdiction over the parties.
7.  Describe the purpose of pleadings.
8.  List and explain the various stages of a civil proceeding.
9.  Compare and contrast the following: demurrer, judgment on the pleadings, summary judgment, directed verdict, and judgment notwithstanding the verdict.
10. Compare and contrast litigation, arbitration, conciliation, and mediation.

---

# Problems

1.  On June 15, a newspaper columnist predicted that the coast of State X would be flooded on the following September 1. Relying on this pronouncement, Gullible quit his job and sold his property at a loss so as not to be financially ruined. When the flooding did not occur, Gullible sued the columnist in a State X court for damages. The court dismissed the case for failure to state a cause of action under applicable State law. On appeal, the State X Supreme Court upheld the lower court. Three months after this ruling, the State Y Supreme Court heard an appeal in which a lower court had ruled that a reader could sue a columnist for falsely predicting flooding.
    (a)   Must the State Y Supreme Court follow the ruling of the State X Supreme Court as a matter of *stare decisis*?
    (b)   Should the State Y lower court have followed the ruling of the State X Supreme Court until the State Y Supreme Court issued a ruling on the issue?
    (c)   Once the State X Supreme Court issued its ruling, could the U.S. Supreme Court overrule the State X Supreme Court?
    (d)   If the State Y Supreme Court and the State X Supreme Court rule in exactly opposite ways, must the U.S. Supreme Court resolve the conflict between the two courts?

2.  State Senator Bowdler convinced the legislature of State Z to pass a law requiring all professors to submit their class notes and transparencies to a board of censors to be sure that no "lewd" materials were presented to students at State universities. Professor Rabelais would like to challenge this law as being violative of his First Amendment rights under the U.S. Constitution.
    (a)   May Professor Rabelais challenge this law in the State Z courts?
    (b)   May Professor Rabelais challenge this law in a Federal district court?

3.  While driving his car in Virginia, Carpe Diem, a resident of North Carolina, struck Butt, a resident of Alaska. As a result of the accident, Butt suffered more than $60,000 in medical expenses. Butt would like to know, if he personally serves the proper papers to Diem, whether he can obtain jurisdiction against Diem for damages in the following courts:
    (a)   Alaska State trial court
    (b)   Federal Circuit Court of Appeals for the Ninth Circuit (includes Alaska)
    (c)   Virginia State trial court
    (d)   Virginia Federal district court

(e)   Federal Circuit Court of Appeals for the Fourth Circuit (includes Virginia and North Carolina)

(f)   Virginia equity court

(g)   North Carolina State trial court

4.   Sam Simpleton, a resident of Kansas, and Nellie Naive, a resident of Missouri, each bought $85,000 in stock at local offices in their home States from Evil Stockbrokers, Inc. ("Evil"), a business incorporated in Delaware with its principal place of business in Kansas. Both Simpleton and Naive believe that they were cheated by Evil Stockbrokers and would like to sue Evil for fraud. Assuming that no Federal question is at issue, assess the accuracy of the following statements:

(a)   Simpleton can sue Evil in a Kansas State trial court.

(b)   Simpleton can sue Evil in a Federal district court in Kansas.

(c)   Naive can sue Evil in a Missouri State trial court.

(d)   Naive can sue Evil in a Federal district court in Missouri.

5.   The Supreme Court of State A ruled that, under the law of State A, pit bull owners must either keep their dogs fenced or pay damages to anyone bitten by the dogs. Assess the accuracy of the following statements:

(a)   It is likely that the U.S. Supreme Court would issue a writ of *certiorari* in the "pit bull" case.

(b)   If a case similar to the "pit bull" case were to come before the Supreme Court of State B in the future, the doctrine of *stare decisis* would leave the court no choice but to rule the same way as the "pit bull" case.

6.   The Supreme Court of State G decided that the U.S. Constitution requires professors to warn students of their right to remain silent before questioning the students about cheating. This ruling directly conflicts with a decision of the Federal Court of Appeals for the circuit which includes State G.

(a)   Must the Federal Circuit Court of Appeals withdraw its ruling?

(b)   Must the Supreme Court of State G withdraw its ruling?

7.   Thomas Clements brought an action to recover damages for breach of warranty against defendant, Signa Corporation. (A warranty is an obligation that the seller of goods assumes with respect to the quality of the goods sold.) Clements had purchased a motorboat from Barney's Sporting Goods, an Illinois corporation. The boat was manufactured by Signa Corporation, an Indiana corporation with its principal place of business in Decatur, Indiana. Signa has no office in Illinois and no agent authorized to do business on its behalf within Illinois. Clements saw Signa's boats on display at the Chicago Boat Show. In addition, literature on Signa's boats was distributed at the Chicago Boat Show. Several boating magazines, delivered to Clements in Illinois, contained advertisements for Signa's boats. Clements also had seen Signa's boats on display at Barney's Sporting Goods Store in Palatine, Illinois, where he eventually purchased the boat. A written warranty issued by Signa was delivered to Clements in Illinois. Although Signa was served with a summons, it failed to enter an appearance in

this case. The court entered a default order and, subsequently, a judgment of $6,220 against Signa. Signa appealed. Decision?

8.   Mariana Deutsch worked as a knitwear mender and attended a school for beauticians. The sink in her apartment collapsed on her foot, fracturing her big toe and making it painful for her to stand. She claims that as a consequence of the injury she was compelled to abandon her plans to become a beautician because that job requires long periods of standing. She also asserts that she was unable to work at her current job for a month. She filed a tort claim against Hewes Street Realty for negligence in failing properly to maintain the sink. She brought the suit in Federal district court, claiming damages of $25,000. Her medical expenses and actual loss of salary were less than $1,500; the rest of her alleged damages were for loss of future earnings as a beautician. Hewes Street moved to dismiss the suit on the basis that Deutsch's claim fell short of the jurisdictional requirement, which then was $10,000, and that the Federal court therefore lacked subject matter jurisdiction over her claim. Decision?

9.   Vette sued Aetna under a fire insurance policy. Aetna moved for summary judgment on the basis that the pleadings and discovered evidence showed a lack of an insurable interest in Vette. (An "insurable interest" exists where the insured derives a monetary benefit or advantage from the preservation or continued existence of the property or would sustain an economic loss from its destruction.) Aetna provided ample evidence to infer that Vette had no insurable interest in the contents of the burned building. Vette also provided sufficient evidence to put in dispute this factual issue. The trial court granted the motion for summary judgment. Vette appealed. Decision?

10.   Mark Womer and Brian Perry were members of the United States Navy and were stationed in Newport, Rhode Island. On April 10, 1978, Womer allowed Perry to borrow his automobile so that Perry could visit his family in New Hampshire. Later that day, while operating Womer's vehicle, Perry was involved in an accident in Manchester, New Hampshire. As a result of the accident, Tzannetos Tavoularis was injured. Tavoularis brought this action against Womer in a New Hampshire superior court, contending that Womer was negligent in lending the automobile to Perry when he knew or should have known that Perry did not have a valid driver's license. Womer sought to dismiss the action on the ground that the New Hampshire courts lacked jurisdiction over him, citing the following facts: (1) he lived and worked in Georgia; (2) he had no relatives in New Hampshire; (3) he neither owned property nor possessed investments in New Hampshire; and (4) he had never conducted business in New Hampshire. Decision?

11.   Kenneth Thomas brought suit against his former employer, Kidder, Peabody & Company, and two of its employees, Barclay Perry and James Johnston, in a dispute over commissions on sales of securities. When he applied to work at Kidder, Peabody, Thomas had filled out a form, which contained an arbitration agreement clause. Thomas had also registered with

the New York Stock Exchange (NYSE). Rule 347 of the NYSE provides that any controversy between a registered representative and a member company shall be settled by arbitration. Kidder, Peabody is a member of the NYSE. Thomas refused to arbitrate, relying on Section 229 of the California Labor Code which provides that actions for the collection of wages may be maintained "without regard to the existence of any private agreement to arbitrate." Perry and Johnston filed a petition in a California State court to compel arbitration under Section 2 of the Federal Arbitration Act. Decision?

**WWW** **Internet Exercise** Find information about the structure and operations of (a) the Federal court system and (2) your own State's court system. (If such information about your State is not available, choose another State.)

# CHAPTER 4

# Constitutional Law

As mentioned in Chapter 1, public law is that branch of substantive law which deals with the rights and powers of government in its political or governing capacity and in its relation to individuals or groups. Public law consists of constitutional law, administrative law, and criminal law. The first is discussed in this chapter; Chapter 5 addresses administrative law, and Chapter 6 covers criminal law.

As the fundamental and organic law of particular jurisdictions, constitutions serve a number of critical functions. They are the supreme law of their respective jurisdictions. In addition, they establish the structure of and allocate power among the various levels of government. They also impose restrictions upon the powers of government and enumerate the rights and liberties of the people.

The Constitution of the United States (reprinted in Appendix A) was adopted on September 17, 1787, by representatives of the thirteen newly created States. Its purpose is stated in the preamble:

We the People of the United States, in Order to form a more perfect Union, establish Justice, insure domestic Tranquility, provide for the common defence, promote the general Welfare, and secure the Blessings of Liberty to ourselves and our Posterity, do ordain and establish this Constitution for the United States of America.

Although the framers of the U.S. Constitution enumerated precisely what rights and authority were vested in the new national government, they considered it unnecessary to list those liberties the people were to reserve for themselves. As Alexander Hamilton, a coauthor of *The Federalist,* explained, "Here in strictness the people surrender nothing; and as they retain everything, they have no need of particular reservations." Nonetheless, during the State conventions to ratify the Constitution, people expressed fear that the Federal government might abuse its powers. To calm these concerns, the first

Congress approved ten amendments to the U.S. Constitution, now known as the Bill of Rights, which were adopted on December 15, 1791.

The Bill of Rights restricts the powers and authority of the Federal government and establishes many of the civil and political rights enjoyed in the United States, including the right to due process of law and freedoms of speech, press, religion, assembly, and petition. Although the Bill of Rights does not apply directly to the States, the Supreme Court has held that the Fourteenth Amendment incorporates most of the principal guarantees of the Bill of Rights, thus making them applicable to the States.

This chapter will discuss constitutional law as it applies to business and commerce. It will begin by surveying some of the basic principles of constitutional law. Then it will examine the allocation of power between the Federal and State governments with respect to the regulation of business. Finally, it will discuss the constitutional restrictions on the power of government to regulate business.

## BASIC PRINCIPLES OF CONSTITUTIONAL LAW

The delegates to the constitutional convention desired a stronger national government but feared the accumulation of governmental power in the hands of one person or group. These two concerns underlie several principles basic to the U.S. Constitution: federalism, federal supremacy, judicial review, and separation of powers. An additional basic principle of constitutional law is state action.

### Federalism

Federalism is the division of governing power between the Federal government and the States. The U.S. Constitution enumerates the powers of the Federal government and specifically reserves to the States or the people the powers it does not expressly delegate to the Federal government. Accordingly, the Federal government is a government of enumerated, or limited, powers; and a specified power must authorize each of its acts. The doctrine of enumerated powers does not, however, significantly limit the Federal government because a number of the enumerated powers, in particular the power to regulate interstate and foreign commerce, have been broadly interpreted.

Furthermore, the Constitution grants Congress not only specified powers but the power "[t]o make all Laws which shall be necessary and proper for carrying into Execution the foregoing Powers, and all other Powers vested by this Constitution in the Government of the United States, or in any Department or Officer thereof." In the Supreme Court's view, the "necessary and proper" clause enables Congress to legislate in areas not mentioned in the list of enumerated powers as long as such legislation reasonably relates to some enumerated power. As Chief Justice John Marshall noted in the landmark case of *McCulloch v. Maryland*, 17 U.S. (4 Wheat.) 316 (1819), "[l]et the end be legitimate, let it be within the scope of the constitution, and all means which are appropriate, which are plainly adapted to that end, which are not prohibited, but consist with the letter and spirit of the constitution, are constitutional."

## Federal Supremacy and Preemption

Although under our Federalist system the States retain significant powers, the **supremacy clause** of the U.S. Constitution provides that within its own sphere, Federal law is supreme and State law must, in case of conflict, yield. Accordingly, any State constitutional provision or law that conflicts with the U.S. Constitution or valid Federal laws or treaties is unconstitutional and may not be given effect. In *McCulloch v. Maryland*, Chief Justice Marshall stated, "This great principle is, that the Constitution and the laws made in pursuance thereof are supreme; that they control the Constitution and laws of the respective states, and cannot be controlled by them."

Under the supremacy clause, whenever Congress enacts legislation within its constitutional powers, the Federal action **preempts** (overrides) any conflicting State legislation. Even a State regulation that is not obviously in conflict must give way if Congress clearly has intended that its enactment should preempt the field. In such an instance, nonconflicting State legislation would be prohibited. This intent may be expressly stated in the legislation or inferred from the pervasiveness of the Federal regulation, the need for uniformity, or the danger of conflict between concurrent Federal and State regulation.

When Congress has not intended to displace all State legislation, then nonconflicting State legislation is permitted. When Congress has not acted, the fact that it has the power to act does not prevent the States from acting. Until Congress exercises its power to preempt, State regulation is permitted.

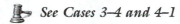 *See Cases 3–4 and 4–1*

## Judicial Review

**Judicial review** describes the process by which the courts examine governmental actions to determine whether they conform to the U.S. Constitution. If governmental action violates the U.S. Constitution, under judicial review the courts will invalidate that action. Judicial review extends to legislation, acts of the executive branch, and the decisions of inferior courts. Such review scrutinizes actions of both the Federal and State governments and applies to both the same standards of constitutionality. The U.S. Supreme Court is the final authority as to the constitutionality of any Federal and State law. The U.S. Constitution does not expressly provide for judicial review, but in 1803 Chief Justice John Marshall, speaking for the Court, declared the existence of such authority in the landmark case of *Marbury v. Madison*, 5 U.S. (1 Cranch) 137 (1803).

## Separation of Powers

Another fundamental principle on which our government is founded is that of separation of powers. The U.S. Constitution vests power in three distinct and independent branches of government: the executive, legislative, and judicial branches. The doctrine of separation of powers prevents excessive power from concentrating in any group or branch of government. Basically, the legislative branch is granted the power to make the law, the executive branch to enforce the law, and the judicial branch to interpret the law. The separation of powers is not complete, however, and in some instances two or more branches share power. For example, the executive branch has veto power over legislation enacted by Congress; the legislative branch must approve many executive appointments; and the judicial branch may declare both legislation and executive actions unconstitutional. Nevertheless, shared powers usually operate as checks and balances on the power of the branches sharing them.

◆ *See Figure 4–1*

## State Action

Most of the protections provided by the U.S. Constitution and its amendments apply only to Federal or State governmental action, collectively referred to as state action. Only the Thirteenth Amendment, which abolishes slavery or involuntary servitude, applies to the actions of private individuals. By statute, however, the government may extend to private activity some or all of the protections that guard against state action. **State action** includes any actions of the Federal and State governments, as well as their subdivisions, such as city or county governments and agencies. For example, when a legislature, executive officer, or court takes some official action against an individual, state action has occurred.

In addition, action taken by private citizens may constitute state action if the State exercised coercive power over the challenged private action or encouraged the action significantly. For example, the Supreme Court found state action when the Supreme Court of Missouri ordered a lower court to enforce an agreement among white property owners that prohibited the transfer of their property to nonwhites. *Shelley v. Kraemer*, 334 U.S. 1 (1948). Moreover, if "private" individuals or entities engage in public functions, their actions may be considered state action subject to constitutional limitations. For example, in *Marsh v. Alabama*, 326 U.S. 501 (1946), the

Supreme Court held that a company town was subject to the First Amendment because the State had allowed the company to exercise all of the public functions and activities usually conducted by a town government. Since that case, the Supreme Court has been less willing to find state action based upon the performance of public functions by private entities; the Court now limits such findings to functions "traditionally exclusively reserved to the State." For instance, in *Jackson v. Metropolitan Edison Co.*, 419 U.S. 345 (1974), the Court held that a privately owned electric utility was *not* subject to the due process clause, even though the State had granted the utility a monopoly, because operating a utility is not state action. In reaching this conclusion, the Court held that the fact that the State could have operated its own utilities did not make the activity of providing electric services state action.

⚖ *See Case 4–2*

## POWERS OF GOVERNMENT

As previously stated, the U.S. Constitution created a Federal government of enumerated powers. Moreover, as the Tenth Amendment declares, "[t]he powers not delegated to the United States by the Constitution, nor prohibited by it to the States, are reserved to the States respectively, or to the people." Consequently, legislation Congress enacts must be based on a specified power granted to the Federal government by the Constitution or be reasonably necessary for carrying out an enumerated power.

**FIGURE 4–1**  Separation of Powers: Checks and Balances

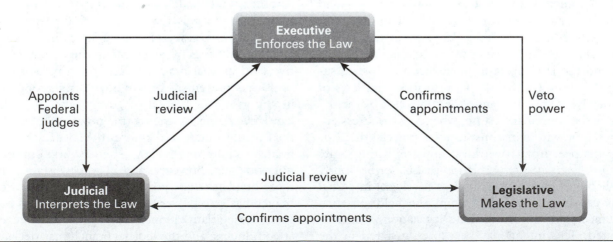

Some governmental powers may be exercised only by the Federal government. These exclusive Federal powers include the power to establish laws regarding bankruptcy, to establish post offices, to grant patents and copyrights, to coin currency, to wage war, and to enter into treaties. Other governmental powers are concurrent and may be exercised by both the Federal government and the States. Concurrent powers include taxation, spending, and the exercise of police power (regulation of the public health, safety, and welfare).

This part of the chapter examines the sources and extent of the powers of the Federal government—as well as the residual power of the States—to regulate business and commerce.

## Federal Commerce Power

The U.S. Constitution provides that "[t]he Congress shall have Power . . . To regulate Commerce with foreign Nations, and among the several States. . . ." Article I, Section 8. This commerce clause has two important effects: (1) it provides the Federal government with a broad source of power for regulating the economy and (2) it restricts State regulations that obstruct or unduly burden interstate commerce. As the U.S. Supreme Court has stated, "The Clause is both a prolific sourc[e] of national power and an equally prolific source of conflict with legislation of the state[s]." This section will discuss the first of these effects; the next section will discuss the second effect.

The U.S. Supreme Court interprets the commerce clause as granting virtually complete power to Congress to regulate the economy and business. A court may invalidate legislation enacted under the commerce clause only if it is clear either (1) that there is no rational basis for a congressional finding that the regulated activity affects interstate commerce or (2) that there is no reasonable connection between the selected regulatory means and the asserted ends.

Because of the broad and permissive interpretation of the commerce power, Congress currently regulates a vast range of activities. Many of the activities discussed in this text are regulated by the Federal government through its exercise of the commerce power, including Federal crimes, consumer warranties and credit transactions, electronic funds transfers, trademarks, unfair trade practices, other consumer transactions, residential real estate transactions, consumer and employee safety, labor relations, civil rights in employment, transactions in securities, and environmental protection.

*See Case 3–4*

## State Regulation of Commerce

The commerce clause, as previously discussed, specifically grants to Congress the power to regulate commerce among the States. In addition to acting as a broad source of Federal power, the clause also implicitly restricts the States' power to regulate activities if the result obstructs or unduly burdens interstate commerce.

***Regulations*** The Supreme Court ultimately decides the extent to which State regulation may affect interstate commerce. In doing so, the Court weighs and balances several factors: (1) the necessity and importance of the State regulation, (2) the burden it imposes upon interstate commerce, and (3) the extent to which it discriminates against interstate commerce in favor of local concerns. The application of these factors involves case-by-case analysis. In general, where a State statute regulates evenhandedly to accomplish a legitimate State interest and its effects on interstate commerce are only incidental, the Court will uphold the statute unless the burden imposed on interstate commerce is excessive compared with the local benefits. The Court will uphold a discriminatory regulation only if no other reasonable method of achieving a legitimate local interest exists.

 *See Case 4–3*

***Taxation*** The commerce clause, in conjunction with the import-export clause, also limits the power of the States to tax. The import-export clause provides: "No State shall, without the Consent of the Congress, lay any Imposts or Duties on Imports or Exports." Article I, Section 10. Together, the commerce clause and the import-export clause exempt from State taxation goods that have entered the stream of commerce, whether they are interstate or foreign, imports or exports. The purpose of this immunity is to protect goods in commerce from both discriminatory and cumulative State taxes. Once the goods enter the stream of interstate or foreign commerce, the power of the State to tax ceases and does not resume until the goods are delivered to the purchaser or the owner terminates the movement of the goods through commerce.

The due process clause of the Fourteenth Amendment also restricts the power of States to tax. Under the due process clause, for a State tax to be constitutional, sufficient nexus must exist between the State and the person, thing, or activity to be taxed.

## Federal Fiscal Powers

The Federal government exerts a dominating influence over the national economy through its control of financial matters. Much of this impact, as previously discussed, results from the exercise of its regulatory powers under the commerce clause. In addition, the government derives substantial influence from powers that are independent of the commerce clause. These include (1) the power to tax, (2) the power to spend, (3) the power to borrow and coin money, and (4) the power of eminent domain.

**Taxation**   The Federal government's power to tax, although extremely broad, is subject to three major limitations: (1) direct taxes other than income taxes must be apportioned among the States, (2) all custom duties and excise taxes must be uniform throughout the United States, and (3) no duties may be levied upon exports from any State.

Besides raising revenues, taxes also have regulatory and socioeconomic effects. For example, import taxes and custom duties can protect domestic industry from foreign competition. Graduated or progressive tax rates and exemptions may further social policies seeking to redistribute wealth. Tax credits encourage investment in favored enterprises, to the disadvantage of unfavored ones. The Court will uphold a tax that does more than just raise revenue "so long as the motive of Congress and the effect of its legislative action are to secure revenue for the benefit of the general government. . . ." *J.W. Hampton Co. v. United States*, 276 U.S. 394 (1928).

**Spending Power**   The Constitution authorizes the Federal government to pay debts and to spend for the common defense and general welfare of the United States. Article I, Section 8. The spending power of Congress, which is extremely broad, will be upheld so long as it does not violate a specific constitutional limitation upon Federal power.

Furthermore, through its spending power, Congress may accomplish indirectly what it may not do directly. For example, in *South Dakota v. Dole*, 483 U.S. 203 (1987), the Supreme Court held that Congress could condition a State's receipt of Federal highway funds on that State's mandating twenty-one as the minimum drinking age, even though the Twenty-first Amendment grants the States significant powers with respect to alcohol consumption within their respective borders. As the Court noted, "Constitutional limitations on Congress when exercising its spending power are less exacting than those on its authority to regulate directly."

**Borrowing and Coining Money**   The U.S. Constitution also grants Congress the power to borrow money on the credit of the United States and to coin money. Article I, Section 8. These two powers have enabled the Federal government to establish a national banking system, the Federal Reserve System, and specialized Federal lending programs such as the Federal Land Bank. Through these and other institutions and agencies, the Federal government wields extensive control over national fiscal and monetary policies and exerts considerable influence over interest rates, the money supply, and foreign exchange rates.

**Eminent Domain**   The government's power to take private property for public use, known as the power of **eminent domain,** is recognized as one of the inherent powers of government in the U.S. Constitution and in the constitutions of the States. Nonetheless, the power is carefully limited. The Fifth Amendment to the Constitution contains a "takings clause" that specifies that "nor shall private property be taken for public use, without just compensation." Although this amendment applies only to the Federal government, the Supreme Court has held that the takings clause is incorporated through the Fourteenth Amendment and is therefore applicable to the States. Moreover, similar or identical provisions are found in State constitutions.

As the language of the takings clause indicates, the taking must be for a public use. Public use has been held to be synonymous with public purpose. Thus, private entities such as railroads and housing authorities may use the government's power of eminent domain so long as the entity's use of the property benefits the public. When the government or a private entity properly takes property under the power of eminent domain, the owners of the property must receive just compensation, which has been interpreted as the fair market value of the property.

The Supreme Court has held that the takings clause requires just compensation only if a governmental taking actually occurs, not if governmental regulation only reduces the value of property. If, however, a regulation deprives the owner of all economic use of property, then a taking has occurred. Eminent domain is discussed further in Chapter 51.

◆ *See Figure 4–2*

**FIGURE 4-2** Powers of Government

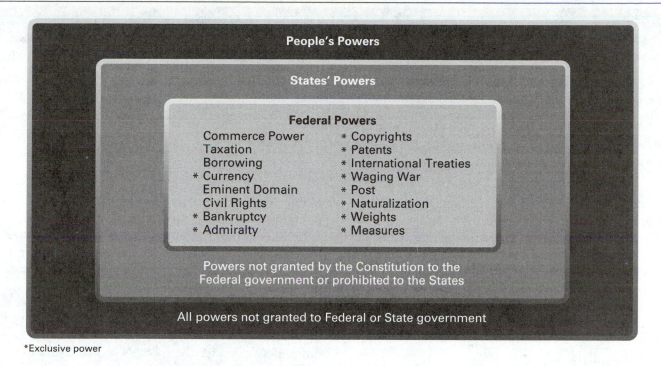

People's Powers

States' Powers

**Federal Powers**

| | |
|---|---|
| Commerce Power | * Copyrights |
| Taxation | * Patents |
| Borrowing | * International Treaties |
| * Currency | * Waging War |
| Eminent Domain | * Post |
| Civil Rights | * Naturalization |
| * Bankruptcy | * Weights |
| * Admiralty | * Measures |

Powers not granted by the Constitution to the
Federal government or prohibited to the States

All powers not granted to Federal or State government

*Exclusive power

## LIMITATIONS ON GOVERNMENT

The Constitution of the United States grants certain enumerated powers to the Federal government while reserving other powers, without enumeration, to the States. The Constitution and its amendments, however, impose limits on the powers of both the Federal government and the States. This part of the chapter will discuss those limitations most applicable to business: (1) the contract clause, (2) the First Amendment, (3) due process, and (4) equal protection. The first of these—the contract clause—applies only to the actions of State governments, whereas the other three apply to both the Federal government and the States.

None of these restrictions operates as an absolute limitation but instead triggers scrutiny by the courts to determine whether the governmental power exercised encroaches impermissibly upon the interest the Constitution protects. The U.S. Supreme Court has used different levels of scrutiny, depending on the interest affected and the nature of the governmental action. Although the Court has differentiated levels of scrutiny most thoroughly in the area of equal protection, such differentiation also occurs in other areas, including substantive due process and protection of free speech.

The least rigorous level of scrutiny is the **rational relationship test**, which requires that governmental action conceivably bear some rational relationship to a legitimate governmental interest that the governmental action proposes to further. The most exacting level of scrutiny is the **strict scrutiny test**, which requires that the governmental action be necessary to promote a compelling governmental interest. Finally, under the **intermediate test,** the governmental action must have a substantial relationship to an important governmental objective. These standards will be more fully explained below.

◆ *See Figure 4-3*

## Contract Clause

Article I, Section 10, of the Constitution provides: "No State shall . . . pass any . . . Law impairing the Obligation of Contracts. . . ." The Supreme Court has used this clause to restrict States from retroactively modifying public charters and private contracts. For example, the contract clause protects against impairing the charter of a corporation formed under a State incorporation statute. Although the contract clause does not apply to the

**FIGURE 4–3** Limitations on Government

| Test/Interest | Equal Protection | Substantive Due Process | Free Speech |
|---|---|---|---|
| Strict Scrutiny | Fundamental Rights Suspect Classifications | Fundamental Rights | Protected Noncommercial Speech |
| Intermediate | Gender Legitimacy | | Commercial Speech |
| Rational Relationship | Economic Regulation | Economic Regulation | Nonprotected Speech |

Federal government, due process limits the Federal government's power to impair contracts.

Moreover, the Supreme Court has held that the contract clause does not preclude the States from exercising eminent domain or their police powers. As the Supreme Court stated, "No legislature can bargain away the public health or the public morals." *Stone v. Mississippi*, 101 U.S. (11 Otto) 814 (1879).

## First Amendment

The First Amendment states:

Congress shall make no law respecting an establishment of religion, or prohibiting the free exercise thereof; or abridging the freedom of speech, or of the press; or the right of the people peaceably to assemble, and to petition the Government for a redress of grievances.

The First Amendment's protection of free speech is not absolute. Some forms of speech, such as obscenity, receive no protection. Most forms of speech, however, are protected by the strict or exacting scrutiny standard, which requires the existence of a compelling and legitimate state interest to justify a restriction of speech. In furthering such an interest the state must use means that least restrict free speech. This section will examine the application of the First Amendment's guarantee of free speech to (1) corporate political speech, (2) commercial speech, and (3) defamation.

 *See Case 4–4*

***Corporate Political Speech*** Freedom of speech is indispensable to the discovery and spread of political truth; indeed, "the best test of truth is the power of the thought to get itself accepted in the competition of the market." *Abrams v. United States*, 250 U.S. 616 (1919) (Holmes's dissent). To promote this competition of ideas, the First Amendment's guarantee of free speech applies not only

to individuals but also to corporations. Accordingly, corporations may not be prohibited from speaking out on political issues. For example, in *First National Bank v. Bellotti*, 435 U.S. 765 (1978), the Supreme Court held unconstitutional a Massachusetts criminal statute that prohibited banks and business corporations from making contributions and expenditures with regard to most referenda issues. The Court in *Bellotti* held that if speech is otherwise protected, the fact that the speaker is a corporation does not alter the speech's protected status.

The Supreme Court retreated somewhat from its holding in *Bellotti* when it upheld a State statute prohibiting corporations, except media corporations, from using general treasury funds to make independent expenditures in elections for public office but permitting such expenditures from segregated funds used solely for political purposes. The Court held that the statute did not violate the First Amendment because the burden on corporations' exercise of political expression was justified by a compelling State interest in preventing corruption in the political arena: "the corrosive and distorting effects of immense aggregations of wealth that are accumulated with the help of the corporate form and that have little or no correlation to the public's support for the corporations' political ideas." The Court held that the statute was sufficiently narrowly tailored because it "is precisely targeted to eliminate the distortion caused by corporate spending while also allowing corporations to express their political views" by making expenditures through segregated funds. *Austin v. Michigan Chamber of Commerce*, 494 U.S. 652 (1990).

***Commercial Speech*** Commercial speech is expression related to the economic interests of the speaker and her audience, such as advertisements for a product or service. Since the mid-1970s, U.S. Supreme Court decisions have eliminated the doctrine that commercial speech is wholly outside the protection of the First Amendment. Instead, the Court has established the principle that speech proposing a commercial transaction is entitled to protection which, though extensive, is less considerable than that accorded political speech. Protection is accorded commercial speech because of the interest such communication holds for the advertiser, consumer, and general public. Advertising and similar messages convey important information for the proper and efficient distribution of resources in our free market system. At the same time, commercial speech is less valuable and less vulnerable than other varieties of speech and therefore does not merit complete First Amendment protection.

In commercial speech cases, a four-part analysis has developed. First, the court must determine whether the expression is protected by the First Amendment. For commercial speech to come within that provision, such speech, at the least, must concern lawful activity and not be misleading. Second, the court must determine whether the asserted governmental interest is substantial. If both inquiries yield positive answers, then, third, the court must determine if the regulation directly advances the governmental interest asserted and, fourth, whether or not the regulation is more extensive than is necessary to serve that interest. The Supreme Court recently held that governmental restrictions of commercial speech need not be absolutely the least severe so long as they are "narrowly tailored" to achieve the governmental objective.

Because the constitutional protection extended to commercial speech is based on the informational function of advertising, governments may regulate or suppress commercial messages that do not accurately inform the public about lawful activity. "The government may ban forms of communication more likely to deceive the public than to inform it, or commercial speech related to illegal activity." *Central Hudson Gas and Electric Corp. v. Public Service Commission*, 447 U.S. 557 (1980). Therefore, governmental regulation of false and misleading advertising is permissible under the First Amendment.

**Defamation** Defamation is a civil wrong or tort that consists of disgracing or diminishing a person's reputation through the communication of a false statement. An example would be the publication of a false statement that a person had committed a crime or had a loathsome disease. For further discussion of defamation, see Chapter 7.

Because defamation involves a communication, it receives the protection extended to speech by the First Amendment. Moreover, the case of *New York Times Co. v. Sullivan*, 376 U.S. 254 (1964), held that a public official who was defamed in regard to his conduct, fitness, or role as public official could not recover in a defamation action unless the statement was made with *actual malice*, which requires clear and convincing proof that the defendant had knowledge of the falsity of the communication or acted in reckless disregard of its truth or falsity. This restriction upon the right to recover for defamation is based on "a profound national commitment to the principle that debate on public issues should be uninhibited, robust and wide-open, and that it may well include vehement, caustic and sometimes unpleasantly sharp attacks on government and public officials." The communication may deal with the official's qualifications for and his performance in office, which would likely include most aspects of character and public conduct.

In addition, the Supreme Court has extended the same rule to public figures and candidates for public office. Though the Court has not precisely defined the term *public figure*, examples of persons held to be public figures have included a well-known football coach of a State university and a retired army general who had taken a prominent and controversial position regarding racial segregation. In *Gertz v. Robert Welch, Inc.*, 418 U.S. 323 (1974), the Court explained:

For the most part [public figures are] those who attain this status [by assuming] roles of especial prominence in the affairs of society. Some occupy positions of such persuasive power and influence that they are deemed public figures for all purposes. More commonly, those classed as public figures have thrust themselves to the forefront of particular public controversies in order to influence the resolution of the issues involved.

Thus, the public official or public figure must prove that the defendant published the defamatory and false comment about him with knowledge or in reckless disregard of the comment's falsity and its defamatory character. In a defamation suit brought by a private person (one who is neither a public official nor a public figure) against a member of the news media, the plaintiff must prove that the defendant published the defamatory and false comment with malice *or* negligence. In contrast, where a private person brings suit against a defendant who is *not* a member of the news media, the Court has yet to determine if the plaintiff must prove anything beyond the fact that a defamatory statement has been made.

## Due Process

The Fifth and Fourteenth Amendments prohibit the Federal and State governments, respectively, from depriving any person of life, liberty, or property without due process of law. Due process has two different aspects: *substantive* due process and *procedural* due process. As discussed in Chapter 1, substantive law creates, defines, or regulates legal rights, whereas procedural law establishes the rules for enforcing those rights. Accordingly, **substantive due process** concerns the compatibility of a law or governmental action with fundamental constitutional rights such as free speech. In contrast, **procedural due process** involves the review of the decision-making process that enforces substantive laws and results in depriving a person of life, liberty, or property.

*Substantive Due Process* Substantive due process, which involves a court's determination of whether a particular governmental action is compatible with individual liberties, addresses the constitutionality of the substance of a legal rule, not the fairness of the process by which the rule is applied. From 1885 until 1937, the Supreme Court viewed substantive due process as authorization to act as a "super legislature," invalidating any law it considered unwise. Since 1937, the Court has abandoned this approach and no longer overturns legislation affecting economic and social interests, so long as the legislation relates rationally to legitimate governmental objectives.

Nonetheless, the Court will carefully scrutinize legislation that affects the fundamental rights of individuals under the Constitution to determine if such legislation is necessary to promote a compelling or overriding state interest. Included among the fundamental rights that trigger the strict scrutiny standard of substantive due process are (1) the First Amendment rights of freedom of speech, religion, press, peaceful assembly, and petition; (2) the right to engage in interstate travel; (3) the right to vote; (4) the right to privacy; and (5) the right to marry.

*Procedural Due Process* Procedural due process pertains to the governmental decision-making process that results in depriving a person of life, liberty, or property. As the Supreme Court has interpreted procedural due process, the government is required to provide an individual with a fair procedure if, but only if, the person faces deprivation of life, liberty, or property. When governmental action adversely affects an individual but does not deny life, liberty, or property, the government is not required to give the person any hearing at all.

**Liberty,** for the purposes of procedural due process, generally includes the ability of individuals to engage in freedom of action and choice regarding their personal lives. Any significant physical restraint constitutes a deprivation of liberty which requires procedural safeguards. The most important and common examples of proceedings involving deprivation of liberty are criminal proceedings, discussed more fully in Chapter 6. In addition, civil proceedings that result in depriving a person of freedom of action are subject to the requirements of procedural due process. Liberty also includes an individual's right to engage in the fundamental rights described above.

**Property,** for the purposes of procedural due process, includes not only all forms of real and personal property but also certain entitlements conferred by the government, such as social security payments and food stamps. In *Logan v. Zimmerman Brush Co.*, 455 U.S. 422 (1982), the Supreme Court stated, "The hallmark of property . . . is an individual entitlement grounded in state law, which cannot be removed except 'for cause.'" Under this interpretation of property, the Court has, for example, found protected property interests in high school education, when attendance is required; welfare benefits, when the individual has previously been found to meet the statutory requirements; social security payments; and a driver's license. On the other hand, if a public employee's job is terminable at any time, he has no property interest in his employment; accordingly, he may lose his job without any procedural due process protections.

When applicable, procedural due process requires that the procedure be fundamentally fair and impartial in resolving the factual and legal basis for the governmental actions that result in the deprivation of life, liberty, or property. The Supreme Court generally considers three factors in determining which procedures are required: the importance of the individual interest involved; the adequacy of the existing procedural protections and the probable value, if any, of additional safeguards; and the governmental interest in fiscal and administrative efficiency.

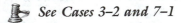 *See Cases 3–2 and 7–1*

## Equal Protection

The Fourteenth Amendment states that "nor shall any State . . . deny to any person within its jurisdiction the equal protection of the laws." Although this amendment applies only to the actions of State governments, the Supreme Court has interpreted the due process clause of the Fifth Amendment to subject Federal actions to the same standards of review. Basically, the guarantee of equal protection requires that government action provides similar treatment for similarly situated persons. Since 1937, when the Supreme Court abandoned substantive due process as a critical check on legislation, the equal protection guarantee has become the most important constitutional concept protecting individual rights.

When governmental action involves the classification of people, the equal protection guarantee comes into play. In determining whether governmental action satisfies the equal protection guarantee, the Supreme Court uses one of three standards of review, depending on the nature of the right involved: (1) the rational relationship test, (2) the strict scrutiny test, or (3) the intermediate test.

*Rational Relationship Test*   The rational relationship test, which applies to economic regulation, requires that the classification conceivably bear some rational relationship to a legitimate governmental interest that the classification proposes to further. Under this standard of review, governmental action is permitted to attack part of the evil to which the action is addressed. Moreover, there is a strong presumption that the action is constitutional. Therefore, the courts will overturn the governmental action only if clear and convincing evidence shows that there is no reasonable basis justifying the action.

*Strict Scrutiny Test*   The strict scrutiny test is far more exacting than the rational relationship test. Under this test, the courts do not defer to the government; rather, they independently determine whether a classification of persons is constitutionally permissible. This determination requires that the classification be necessary to promote a compelling or overriding governmental interest.

The strict scrutiny test is applied when governmental action affects fundamental rights or involves suspect classifications. Fundamental rights include most of the provisions of the Bill of Rights and some other rights, such as interstate travel, voting, and access to criminal justice. Suspect classifications include those made on the basis of race or national origin. A classic and important example of strict scrutiny applied to classifications based upon race is the 1954 school desegregation case, *Brown v. Board of Education of Topeka*, 347 U.S. 483, in which the Supreme Court ruled that segregated public school systems violated the equal protection guarantee. Subsequently, the Court has invalidated segregation in public beaches, buses, parks, public golf courses, and courtroom seating.

 *See Case 4–5*

*Intermediate Test*   An intermediate test applies to government action based on gender and legitimacy. Under this test, the classification must have a substantial relationship to an important governmental objective. The intermediate standard eliminates the strong presumption of constitutionality to which the rational relationship test adheres.

For example, in *Orr v. Orr*, 440 U.S. 268 (1979), the Court invalidated an Alabama law that allowed courts to grant alimony awards only from husbands to wives and not from wives to husbands. Similarly, in *Reed v. Reed*, 404 U.S. 71 (1971), where an Idaho statute gave preference to males over females in qualifying for selection as administrators of estates, the Court invalidated the statute because the preference did not bear a fair and substantial relationship to any legitimate legislative objective. More recently, the Court invalidated a State university's (Virginia Military Institute) admission policy excluding all women. *U.S. v. Virginia*, 518 U.S. 515 (1996). On the other hand, not all legislation based upon gender is invalid. For example, the Court has upheld a California statutory rape law which imposed penalties only upon males, as well as the Federal military selective service act, which exempted women from registering for the draft.

 # Chapter Summary

| **Basic Principles** | **Federalism**  the division of governing power between the Federal government and the States<br>**Federal Supremacy**  Federal law takes precedence over conflicting State law<br>**Federal Preemption**  right of the Federal government to regulate matters within its power to the exclusion of regulation by the States |
| --- | --- |

**Judicial Review** examination of governmental actions to determine whether they conform to the U.S. Constitution

**Separation of Powers** allocation of powers among executive, legislative, and judicial branches of government

**State Action** actions of governments to which constitutional provisions apply

## Powers of Government

**Federal Commerce Power** exclusive power of the Federal government to regulate commerce with other nations and among the States

**State Regulation of Commerce** the commerce clause of the Constitution restricts the States' power to regulate activities if the result obstructs interstate commerce

**Federal Fiscal Powers**

- *Taxation and Spending* the Constitution grants Congress broad powers to tax and spend; such powers are important to Federal regulation of the economy
- *Borrowing and Coining Money* enables the Federal government to establish a national banking system and to control national fiscal and monetary policy
- *Eminent Domain* the government's power to take private property for public use with the payment of just compensation

## Limitations on Government

**Contract Clause** restricts States from retroactively modifying contracts

**Freedom of Speech** First Amendment protects most speech by using a strict scrutiny standard

- *Corporate Political Speech* First Amendment protects a corporation's right to speak out on political issues
- *Commercial Speech* expression related to the economic interests of the speaker and its audience; such expression receives a lesser degree of protection
- *Defamation* a tort consisting of a false communication that injures a person's reputation; such a communication receives limited constitutional protection

**Due Process** Fifth and Fourteenth Amendments prohibit the Federal and State governments from depriving any person of life, liberty, or property without due process of law

- *Substantive Due Process* determination of whether a particular governmental action is compatible with individual liberties
- *Procedural Due Process* requires the governmental decision-making process to be fair and impartial if it deprives a person of life, liberty, or property

**Equal Protection** requires that similarly situated persons be treated similarly by governmental actions

- *Rational Relationship Test* standard of review used to determine whether economic regulation satisfies the equal protection guarantee
- *Strict Scrutiny Test* exacting standard of review applicable to regulation affecting a fundamental right or involving a suspect classification
- *Intermediate Test* standard of review applicable to regulation based on gender and legitimacy

# Cases

## CASE 4–1
### Federal Preemption
## *SILKWOOD v. KERR-McGEE CORPORATION*
Supreme Court of the United States, 1984
464 U.S. 238, 104 S.Ct. 615, 78 L.Ed.2d 443

**WHITE, J.**

This case requires us to determine whether a state-authorized award of punitive damages arising out of the escape of plutonium from a federally-licensed nuclear facility is preempted either because it falls within that forbidden field or because it conflicts with some other aspect of the Atomic Energy Act.

Karen Silkwood was a laboratory analyst for Kerr-McKee at its Cimmaron plant near Crescent, Oklahoma. The plant fabricated plutonium fuel pins for use as reactor fuel in nuclear power plants. Accordingly, the plant was subject to licensing and regulation by the Nuclear Regulatory Commission (NRC) pursuant to the Atomic Energy Act. [Citation.]

During a three-day period of November 1974, Silkwood was contaminated by plutonium from the Cimmaron plant. On November 5, Silkwood was grinding and polishing plutonium samples, utilizing glove boxes designed for that purpose. In accordance with established procedures, she checked her hands for contamination when she withdrew them from the glove box. When some contamination was detected, a more extensive check was performed. A monitoring device revealed contamination on Silkwood's left hand, right wrist, upper arm, neck, hair, and nostrils. She was immediately decontaminated, and at the end of her shift, the monitors detected no contamination. However, she was given urine and fecal kits and was instructed to collect samples in order to check for plutonium discharge.

The next day, Silkwood arrived at the plant and began doing paperwork in the laboratory. Upon leaving the laboratory, Silkwood monitored herself and again discovered surface contamination. Once again, she was decontaminated.

On the third day, November 7, Silkwood was monitored upon her arrival at the plant. High levels of contamination were detected. Four urine samples and one fecal sample submitted that morning were also highly contaminated. Suspecting that the contamination had spread to areas outside the plant, the company directed a decontamination squad to accompany Silkwood to her apartment. Silkwood's roommate, who was also an employee at the plant, was awakened and monitored. She was also contaminated, although to a lesser degree than Silkwood. The squad then monitored the apartment, finding contamination in several rooms, with especially high levels in the bathroom, the kitchen, and Silkwood's bedroom.

The contamination level in Silkwood's apartment was such that many of her personal belongings had to be destroyed. Silkwood herself was sent to the Los Alamos Scientific Laboratory to determine the extent of contamination in her vital body organs. She returned to work on November 13. That night, she was killed in an unrelated automobile accident. [Citation.]

Bill Silkwood, Karen's father, brought the present diversity action in his capacity as administrator of her estate. The action was based on common law tort principles under Oklahoma law and was designed to recover for the contamination injuries to Karen's person and property. Kerr-McGee stipulated that the plutonium which caused the contamination came from its plant, and the jury expressly rejected Kerr-McGee's allegation that Silkwood had intentionally removed the plutonium from the plant in an effort to embarrass the company. However, there were no other specific findings of fact with respect to the cause of the contamination.

\* \* \*

The jury returned a verdict in favor of Silkwood, finding actual damages of $505,000 ($500,000 for personal injuries and $5,000 for property damage) and punitive damages of $10,000,000. The trial court entered judgment against Kerr-McGee in that amount.

\* \* \*

. . . [Upon appeal the Court of Appeals for the Tenth Circuit] held that because of the federal statutes regulating the Kerr-McGee plant, "punitive damages may not be awarded in this case," [citation].

\* \* \*

Silkwood appealed, seeking review of the Court of Appeals' ruling with respect to the punitive damages award. \* \* \*

\* \* \*

As we recently observed in *Pacific Gas & Electric Co. v. State Energy Resources Conservation & Development Comm'n*, [citation], state law can be preempted in either of two general ways. If Congress evidences an intent to occupy a given field, any state law falling within that field is preempted. [Citations.] If Congress has not entirely displaced state regulation over the matter in question, state law is still preempted to the extent it actually conflicts with federal law, that is, when it is impossible to comply with both state and federal law, [citation], or where the state law stands as an obstacle to the accomplishment of the full purposes and objectives of Congress, [citation]. Kerr-McGee contends that the award in this case is invalid under either analysis. We consider each of these contentions in turn.

In *Pacific Gas & Electric*, an examination of the statutory scheme and legislative history of the Atomic Energy Act convinced us that "Congress . . . intended that the federal government regulate the radiological safety aspects involved . . . in the construction and operation of a nuclear plant." [Citation.] Thus, we concluded that "the federal government has occupied the entire field of nuclear safety concerns, except the limited powers expressly ceded to the states." [Citation.]

* * *

Congress' decision to prohibit the states from regulating the safety aspects of nuclear development was premised on its belief that the Commission was more qualified to determine what type of safety standards should be enacted in this complex area. As Congress was informed by the AEC, the 1959 legislation provided for continued federal control over the more hazardous materials because "the technical safety considerations are of such complexity that it is not likely that any State would be prepared to deal with them during the foreseeable future." [Citation.] If there were nothing more, this concern over the states' inability to formulate effective standards and the foreclosure of the states from conditioning the operation of nuclear plants on compliance with state-imposed safety standards arguably would disallow resort to state-law remedies by those suffering injuries from radiation in a nuclear plant. There is, however, ample evidence that Congress had no intention of forbidding the states from providing such remedies.

Indeed, there is no indication that Congress even seriously considered precluding the use of such remedies either when it enacted the Atomic Energy Act in 1954 and/or when it amended it in 1959. This silence takes on added significance in light of Congress' failure to provide any federal remedy for persons injured by such conduct. It is difficult to believe that Congress would,

without comment, remove all means of judicial recourse for those injured by illegal conduct. [Citation.]

More importantly, the only congressional discussion concerning the relationship between the Atomic Energy Act and state tort remedies indicates that Congress assumed that such remedies would be available. After the 1954 law was enacted, private companies contemplating entry into the nuclear industry expressed concern over potentially bankrupting state-law suits arising out of a nuclear incident. As a result, in 1957 Congress passed the Price-Anderson Act, an amendment to the Atomic Energy Act. [Citation.] That Act established an indemnification scheme under which operators of licensed nuclear facilities could be required to obtain up to $60 million in private financial protection against such suits. The government would then provide indemnification for the next $500 million of liability, and the resulting $560 million would be the limit of liability for any one nuclear incident.

Although the Price-Anderson Act does not apply to the present situation, the discussion preceding its enactment and subsequent amendment indicates that Congress assumed that persons injured by nuclear accidents were free to utilize existing state tort law remedies.

* * *

The belief that the NRC's exclusive authority to set safety standards did not foreclose the use of state tort remedies was reaffirmed when the Price-Anderson Act was amended in 1966. The 1966 amendment was designed to respond to concerns about the adequacy of state law remedies.

* * *

* * * Indeed, the entire discussion surrounding the 1966 amendment was premised on the assumption that state remedies were available notwithstanding the NRC's exclusive regulatory authority. * * *

* * *

In sum, it is clear that in enacting and amending the Price-Anderson Act, Congress assumed that state-law remedies, in whatever form they might take, were available to those injured by nuclear incidents. This was so even though it was well aware of the NRC's exclusive authority to regulate safety matters. No doubt there is tension between the conclusion that safety regulation is the exclusive concern of the federal law and the conclusion that a state may nevertheless award damages based on its own law of liability. But as we understand what was done over the years in the legislation concerning nuclear energy, Congress intended to stand by both concepts and to tolerate whatever tension there was between them. We can do no less. It may be that the award of damages based on the state law of negligence or strict liability is regulatory in the sense that a nuclear plant will be threatened with damages liability if it does not conform to state standards, but that regulatory consequence was something that Congress was quite willing to accept.

We do not suggest that there could never be an instance in which the federal law would preempt the recovery of damages based on state law. But insofar as damages for radiation injuries are concerned, preemption should not be judged on the basis that the federal government has so completely occupied the field of safety that state remedies are foreclosed but on whether there is an irrec-

oncilable conflict between the federal and state standards or whether the imposition of a state standard in a damages action would frustrate the objectives of the federal law. We perceive no such conflict or frustration in the circumstances of this case.

\* \* \*

We conclude that the award of punitive damages in this case is not preempted by federal law.

\* \* \*

\* \* \* The judgment of the Court of Appeals with respect to punitive damages is therefore reversed, and the case is remanded to the Court of Appeals for proceedings consistent with this opinion.

---

## CASE 4–2
## State Action
# NATIONAL COLLEGIATE ATHLETICS ASS'N. v. TARKANIAN

Supreme Court of the United States, 1988
488 U.S. 179, 109 S.Ct. 454, 102 L.Ed.2d 469

STEVENS, J.
When he became head basketball coach at University of Nevada, Las Vegas (UNLV) in 1973, Jerry Tarkanian inherited a team with a mediocre 14–14 record. [Citation.] Four years later the team won 29 out of 32 games and placed third in the championship tournament sponsored by the National Collegiate Athletic Association (NCAA), to which UNLV belongs. [Citation.]

Yet in September 1977 UNLV informed Tarkanian that it was going to suspend him. No dissatisfaction with Tarkanian, once described as "the 'winningest' active basketball coach," [citation], motivated his suspension. Rather, the impetus was a report by the NCAA detailing 38 violations of NCAA rules by UNLV personnel, including 10 involving Tarkanian. The NCAA had placed the University's basketball team on probation for two years and ordered UNLV to show cause why the NCAA should not impose further penalties unless UNLV severed all ties during the probation between its intercollegiate athletic program and Tarkanian.

Facing demotion and a drastic cut in pay, Tarkanian brought suit in Nevada state court, alleging that he had been deprived of his Fourteenth Amendment due process rights in violation of 42 U.S.C. § 1983. [That section provides in part: "Every person who, under color of any statute, ordinance, regulation, custom, or usage, of any State or Territory or the District of Columbia, subjects, or causes to be subjected, any citizen of the United States or other person within the jurisdiction thereof to the

deprivation of any rights, privileges, or immunities secured by the Constitution and laws, shall be liable to the party injured in an action at law, suit in equity, or other proper proceeding for redress."] Ultimately Tarkanian obtained injunctive relief and an award of attorney's fees against both UNLV and the NCAA. [Citation.] NCAA's liability may be upheld only if its participation in the events that led to Tarkanian's suspension constituted "state action" prohibited by the Fourteenth Amendment and were performed "under color of" state law within the meaning of § 1983.

\* \* \*

Embedded in our Fourteenth Amendment jurisprudence is a dichotomy between state action, which is subject to scrutiny under the Amendment's Due Process Clause, and private conduct, against which the Amendment affords no shield, no matter how unfair that conduct may be. [Citations.] As a general matter the protections of the Fourteenth Amendment do not extend to "private conduct abridging individual rights." [Citation.]

"Careful adherence to the 'state action' requirement preserves an area of individual freedom by limiting the reach of federal law" and avoids the imposition of responsibility on a State for conduct it could not control.

\* \* \*

In this case Tarkanian argues that the NCAA was a state actor because it misused power that it possessed by virtue of state law. He claims specifically that UNLV delegated its own functions to the NCAA, clothing the Association with authority both to adopt rules governing UNLV's athletic programs and to enforce those rules on behalf of UNLV. Similarly, the Nevada Supreme Court held that UNLV had delegated its authority over personnel decisions to the NCAA. Therefore, the court reasoned, the two entities acted jointly to deprive Tarkanian of liberty and property interests, making the NCAA as well as UNLV a state actor.

* * *

This case uniquely mirrors the traditional state action case. Here the final act challenged by Tarkanian—his suspension—was committed by UNLV. A state university without question is a state actor. When it decides to impose a serious disciplinary sanction upon one of its tenured employees, it must comply with the terms of the Due Process Clause of the Fourteenth Amendment to the Federal Constitution. [Citations.] Thus when UNLV notified Tarkanian that he was being separated from all relations with the University's basketball program, it acted under color of state law within the meaning of 42 U.S.C. § 1983.

The mirror image presented in this case requires us to step through an analytical looking glass to resolve it. Clearly UNLV's conduct was influenced by the rules and recommendations of the NCAA, the private party. But it was UNLV, the state entity, that actually suspended Tarkanian. Thus the question is not whether UNLV participated to a critical extent in the NCAA's activities, but whether UNLV's actions in compliance with the NCAA rules and recommendations turned the NCAA's conduct into state action.

We examine first the relationship between UNLV and the NCAA regarding the NCAA's rulemaking. UNLV is among the NCAA's members and participated in promulgating the Association's rules; it must be assumed, therefore, that Nevada had some impact on the NCAA's policy determinations. Yet the NCAA's several hundred other public and private member institutions each similarly affected those policies. Those institutions, the vast majority of which were located in States other than Nevada, did not act under color of Nevada law. It necessarily follows that the source of the legislation adopted by the NCAA is not Nevada but the collective membership, speaking through an organization that is independent of any particular State.

State action nonetheless might lie if UNLV, by embracing the NCAA's rules, transformed them into state rules and the NCAA into a state actor. [Citation.] UNLV engaged in state action when it adopted the NCAA's rules to govern its own behavior, but that would be true even if UNLV had taken no part in the promulgation of those rules. * * * UNLV retained the authority to withdraw from the NCAA and establish its own standards. The University alternatively could have stayed in the Association and worked through the Association's legislative process to amend rules or standards it deemed harsh, unfair, or unwieldy. Neither UNLV's decision to adopt the NCAA's standards nor its minor role in their formulation is a sufficient reason for concluding that the NCAA was acting under color of Nevada law when it promulgated standards governing athlete recruitment, eligibility, and academic performance.

Tarkanian further asserts that the NCAA's investigation, enforcement proceedings, and consequent recommendations constituted state action because they resulted from a delegation of power by UNLV. UNLV, as an NCAA member, subscribed to the statement in the Association's bylaws that NCAA "enforcement procedures are an essential part of the intercollegiate athletic program of each member institution." [Citation.] It is, of course, true that a state may delegate authority to a private party and thereby make that party a state actor. * * * But UNLV delegated no power to the NCAA to take specific action against any University employee. The commitment by UNLV to adhere to NCAA enforcement procedures was enforceable only by sanctions that the NCAA might impose on UNLV itself.

* * *

The NCAA enjoyed no governmental powers to facilitate its investigation. It had no power to subpoena witnesses, to impose contempt sanctions, or to assert sovereign authority over any individual. Its greatest authority was to threaten sanctions against UNLV, with the ultimate sanction being expulsion of the University from membership. Contrary to the premise of the Nevada Supreme Court's opinion, the NCAA did not—indeed, could not—directly discipline Tarkanian or any other state university employee. The express terms of the Confidential Report did not demand the suspension unconditionally; rather, it requested "the University . . . to show cause" why the NCAA should not impose additional penalties if UNLV declines to suspend Tarkanian. [Citation.] Even the University's vice president acknowledged that the Report gave the University options other than suspension: UNLV could have retained Tarkanian and risked additional sanctions, perhaps even expulsion from the NCAA, or it could have withdrawn voluntarily from the Association.

Finally, Tarkanian argues that the power of the NCAA is so great that the UNLV had no practical alternative to compliance with its demands. We are not at all sure this is true, but even if we assume that a private monopolist can impose its will on a state agency by a threatened refusal to deal with it, it does not follow that such a private party is therefore acting under color of state law. [Citation.]

In final analysis the question is whether "the conduct allegedly causing the deprivation of a federal right [can] be fairly attributable to the State." [Citation.] It would be ironic indeed to conclude that the NCAA's imposition of sanctions against UNLV—sanctions that UNLV and its counsel, including the Attorney General

of Nevada, steadfastly opposed during protracted adversary proceedings—is fairly attributable to the State of Nevada. It would be more appropriate to conclude that UNLV has conducted its athletic program under color of the policies adopted by the NCAA, rather than that those policies were developed and enforced under color of Nevada law.

The judgment of the Nevada Supreme Court is reversed and the case is remanded to that court for further proceedings not inconsistent with this opinion.

It is so ordered.

---

## CASE 4–3
## State Regulation of Commerce
### CHEMICAL WASTE MANAGEMENT, INC. v. HUNT
Supreme Court of the United States, 1992
504 U.S. 334, 112 S.Ct. 2009, 119 L.Ed.2d 121

WHITE, J.

Alabama imposes a hazardous waste disposal fee on hazardous wastes generated outside the State and disposed of at a commercial facility in Alabama. The fee does not apply to such waste having a source in Alabama. The Alabama Supreme Court held that this differential treatment does not violate the Commerce Clause. We reverse.

## I

Petitioner, Chemical Waste Management, Inc., a Delaware corporation with its principal place of business in Oak Brook, Illinois, owns and operates one of the Nation's oldest commercial hazardous waste land disposal facilities, located in Emelle, Alabama. Opened in 1977 and acquired by petitioner in 1978, the Emelle facility is a hazardous waste treatment, storage, and disposal facility operating pursuant to permits issued by the Environmental Protection Agency (EPA) under the Resource Conservation and Recovery Act of 1976 (RCRA), [citation], and the Toxic Substances Control Act, [citation], and by the State of Alabama under [citation]. Alabama is 1 of only 16 States that have commercial hazardous waste landfills, and the Emelle facility is the largest of the 21 landfills of this kind located in these 16 States. [Citation.]

The parties do not dispute that the wastes and substances being landfilled at the Emelle facility "include

substances that are inherently dangerous to human health and safety and to the environment. Such waste consists of ignitable, corrosive, toxic and reactive wastes which contain poisonous and cancer-causing chemicals and which can cause birth defects, genetic damage, blindness, crippling and death." [Citation.] Increasing amounts of out-of-state hazardous wastes are shipped to the Emelle facility for permanent storage each year. From 1985 through 1989, the tonnage of hazardous waste received per year has more than doubled, increasing from 341,000 tons in 1985 to 788,000 tons by 1989. Of this, up to 90% of the tonnage permanently buried each year is shipped in from other States.

Against this backdrop Alabama enacted Act No. 90–326 (the Act). [Citation.] Among other provisions, the Act includes a "cap" that generally limits the amount of hazardous wastes or substances that may be disposed of in any 1-year period, and the amount of hazardous waste disposed of during the first year under the Act's new fees becomes the permanent ceiling in subsequent years. [Citation.] The cap applies to commercial facilities that dispose of over 100,000 tons of hazardous wastes or substances per year, but only the Emelle facility, as the only commercial facility operating within Alabama, meets this description. The Act also imposes a "base fee" of $25.60 per ton on all hazardous wastes and substances disposed of at commercial facilities, to be paid by the operator of the facility. [Citation.] Finally, the Act imposes the "additional fee" at issue here, which states in full:

"For waste and substances which are generated outside of Alabama and disposed of at a commercial site for the disposal of hazardous waste or hazardous substances in Alabama, an additional fee shall be levied at the rate of $72.00 per ton." [Citation.]

Petitioner filed suit in state court requesting declaratory relief against the respondents and seeking to enjoin enforcement of the Act. In addition to state law claims, petitioner contended that the Act violated the Commerce, Due Process, and Equal Protection Clauses of the United States Constitution, and was preempted by various federal statutes. The Trial Court declared the base fee and the cap provisions of the Act to be valid and constitutional; but, finding the only basis for the additional fee to be the origin of the waste, the Trial Court declared it to be in violation of the Commerce Clause. [Citation.] Both sides appealed. The Alabama Supreme Court affirmed the rulings concerning the base fee and cap provisions but reversed the decision regarding the additional fee. The court held that the fee at issue advanced legitimate local purposes that could not be adequately served by reasonable nondiscriminatory alternatives and was therefore valid under the Commerce Clause. [Citation.]

Chemical Waste Management, Inc., petitioned for writ of certiorari, challenging all aspects of the Act. Because of the importance of the federal question and the likelihood that it had been decided in a way conflicting with applicable decisions of this Court, [citation], we granted certiorari limited to petitioner's Commerce Clause challenge to the additional fee. [Citation.] We now reverse.

# II

No State may attempt to isolate itself from a problem common to the several States by raising barriers to the free flow of interstate trade. * * * The Court has consistently found parochial legislation . . . to be constitutionally invalid, whether the ultimate aim of the legislation was to assure a steady supply of milk by erecting barriers to allegedly ruinous outside competition, [citation]; or to create jobs by keeping industry within the State, [citation]; or to preserve the State's financial resources from depletion by fencing out indigent immigrants, [citations]. To this list may be added cases striking down a tax discriminating against interstate commerce, even where such tax was designed to encourage the use of ethanol and thereby reduce harmful exhaust emissions, [citation], or to support inspection of foreign cement to ensure structural integrity, [citation]. For in all of these cases, "a presumably legitimate goal was sought to be achieved by the illegitimate means of isolating the State from the national economy." [Citation.]

The Act's additional fee facially discriminates against hazardous waste generated in States other than Alabama, and the Act overall has plainly discouraged the full operation of petitioner's Emelle facility. Such burdensome taxes imposed on interstate commerce alone are generally forbidden: "[A] State may not tax a transaction or incident more heavily when it crosses state lines than when it occurs entirely within the State." [Citations.] Once a state tax is found to discriminate against out-of-state commerce, it is typically struck down without further inquiry. [Citations.]

The State, however, argues that the additional fee imposed on out-of-state hazardous waste serves legitimate local purposes related to its citizens' health and safety. Because the additional fee discriminates both on its face and in practical effect, the burden falls on the State "to justify it both in terms of the local benefits flowing from the statute and the unavailability of nondiscriminatory alternatives adequate to preserve the local interests at stake." [Citations.] "At a minimum such facial discrimination invokes the strictest scrutiny of any purported legitimate local purpose and of the absence of nondiscriminatory alternatives." [Citation.]

The State's argument here does not significantly differ from the Alabama Supreme Court's conclusions on the legitimate local purposes of the additional fee imposed, which were:

"The Additional Fee serves these legitimate local purposes that cannot be adequately served by reasonable nondiscriminatory alternatives: (1) protection of the health and safety of the citizens of Alabama from toxic substances; (2) conservation of the environment and the state's natural resources; (3) provision for compensatory revenue for the costs and burdens that out-of-state waste generators impose by dumping their hazardous waste in Alabama; (4) reduction of the overall flow of wastes traveling on the state's highways, which flow creates a great risk to the health and safety of the state's citizens." [Citation.]

[Citation.] These may all be legitimate local interests, and petitioner has not attacked them. But only rhetoric, and not explanation, emerges as to why Alabama targets only interstate hazardous waste to meet these goals. As found by the Trial Court, "[a]lthough the Legislature imposed an additional fee of $72.00 per ton on waste generated outside Alabama, there is absolutely no evidence before this Court that waste generated outside Alabama is more dangerous than waste generated in Alabama. The Court finds under the facts of this case that the only basis for the additional fee is the origin of the waste." [Citation.] In the face of such findings, invalidity under the Commerce Clause necessarily follows, for "whatever [Alabama's] ultimate purpose, it may not be accomplished by discriminating against articles of commerce coming from outside the State unless there is some reason, apart from their origin, to treat them differently." [Citations.] The burden is on the State to show that "the discrimination is demonstrably justified by a valid factor unrelated to economic protectionism," [citation], and it has not carried this burden. [Citation.]

Ultimately, the State's concern focuses on the volume of the waste entering the Emelle facility. Less discriminatory alternatives, however, are available to alleviate this concern, not the least of which are a generally applicable per-ton additional fee on all hazardous waste disposed of within Alabama, [citation], or a per-mile tax on all vehicles transporting hazardous waste across Alabama roads, [citation], or an evenhanded cap on the total tonnage landfilled at Emelle, [citation], which would curtail volume from all sources. To the extent Alabama's concern touches environmental conservation and the health and safety of its citizens, such concern does not vary with the point of origin of the waste, and it remains within the State's power to monitor and regulate more closely the transportation and disposal of all hazardous waste within its borders. Even with the possible future financial and environmental risks to be borne by Alabama, such risks likewise do not vary with the waste's State of origin in a way allowing foreign, but not local, waste to be burdened. In sum, we find the additional fee to be "an obvious effort to saddle those outside the State" with most of the burden of slowing the flow of waste into the Emelle facility. [Citation.] "That legislative effort is clearly impermissible under the Commerce Clause of the Constitution." [Citation.]

* * *

## III

The decision of the Alabama Supreme Court is reversed, and the cause remanded for proceedings not inconsistent with this opinion, including consideration of the appropriate relief to petitioner. [Citations.]

So ordered.

---

## CASE 4–4
### First Amendment
## RENO v. AMERICAN CIVIL LIBERTIES UNION

Supreme Court of the United States, 1997
521 U.S. 844, 117 S.Ct. 2329, 138 L.Ed.2d 874

STEVENS, J.
At issue is the constitutionality of two statutory provisions enacted to protect minors from "indecent" and "patently offensive" communications on the Internet. Notwithstanding the legitimacy and importance of the congressional goal of protecting children from harmful materials, we agree with the three-judge District Court that the statute abridges "the freedom of speech" protected by the First Amendment.

## I

The District Court made extensive findings of fact, most of which were based on a detailed stipulation prepared by the parties. [Citation.] The findings describe the character and the dimensions of the Internet, the availability of sexually explicit material in that medium, and the problems confronting age verification for recipients of Internet communications. Because those findings provide the underpinnings for the legal issues, we begin with a summary of the undisputed facts.

The Internet is an international network of interconnected computers. * * *

The Internet has experienced "extraordinary growth." The number of "host" computers—those that store information and relay communications—increased from about 300 in 1981 to approximately 9,400,000 by the time of the trial in 1996. Roughly 60% of these hosts are located in the United States. About 40 million people used the Internet at the time of trial, a number that is expected to mushroom to 200 million by 1999.

Individuals can obtain access to the Internet from many different sources, generally hosts themselves or entities with a host affiliation. Most colleges and universities provide access for their students and faculty; many corporations provide their employees with access through an office network; many communities and local libraries provide free access; and an increasing number of storefront "computer coffee shops" provide access for a small hourly fee. Several major national "online services" such as America Online, CompuServe, the Microsoft Network, and Prodigy offer access to their own extensive proprietary networks as well as a link to the much larger resources of the Internet. These commercial online services had almost 12 million individual subscribers at the time of trial.

Anyone with access to the Internet may take advantage of a wide variety of communication and information retrieval methods. These methods are constantly evolving and difficult to categorize precisely. But, as presently constituted, those most relevant to this case are electronic mail ("e-mail"), automatic mailing list services ("mail exploders," sometimes referred to as "listservs"), "newsgroups," "chat rooms," and the "World Wide Web." All of these methods can be used to transmit text; most can transmit sound, pictures, and moving video images. Taken together, these tools constitute a unique medium—known to its users as "cyberspace"—located in no particular geographical location but available to anyone, anywhere in the world, with access to the Internet.

* * *

The best known category of communication over the Internet is the World Wide Web, which allows users to search for and retrieve information stored in remote computers, as well as, in some cases, to communicate back to designated sites. In concrete terms, the Web consists of a vast number of documents stored in different computers all over the world. Some of these documents are simply files containing information. However, more elaborate documents, commonly known as Web "pages," are also prevalent. Each has its own address—"rather like a telephone number." Web pages frequently contain information and sometimes allow the viewer to communicate with the page's (or "site's") author. They generally also contain "links" to other documents created by that site's author or to other (generally) related sites. Typically, the links are either blue or underlined text—sometimes images.

Navigating the Web is relatively straightforward. A user may either type the address of a known page or enter one or more keywords into a commercial "search engine" in an effort to locate sites on a subject of interest. A particular Web page may contain the information

sought by the "surfer," or, through its links, it may be an avenue to other documents located anywhere on the Internet. Users generally explore a given Web page, or move to another, by clicking a computer "mouse" on one of the page's icons or links. Access to most Web pages is freely available, but some allow access only to those who have purchased the right from a commercial provider. The Web is thus comparable, from the readers' viewpoint, to both a vast library including millions of readily available and indexed publications and a sprawling mall offering goods and services.

From the publishers' point of view, it constitutes a vast platform from which to address and hear from a world-wide audience of millions of readers, viewers, researchers, and buyers. Any person or organization with a computer connected to the Internet can "publish" information. Publishers include government agencies, educational institutions, commercial entities, advocacy groups, and individuals. Publishers may either make their material available to the entire pool of Internet users, or confine access to a selected group, such as those willing to pay for the privilege. "No single organization controls any membership in the Web, nor is there any centralized point from which individual Web sites or services can be blocked from the Web."

* * *

Some of the communications over the Internet that originate in foreign countries are also sexually explicit.

Though such material is widely available, users seldom encounter such content accidentally. "A document's title or a description of the document will usually appear before the document itself . . . and in many cases the user will receive detailed information about a site's content before he or she need take the step to access the document. Almost all sexually explicit images are preceded by warnings as to the content." For that reason, the "odds are slim" that a user would enter a sexually explicit site by accident. Unlike communications received by radio or television, "the receipt of information on the Internet requires a series of affirmative steps more deliberate and directed than merely turning a dial. A child requires some sophistication and some ability to read to retrieve material and thereby to use the Internet unattended."

* * *

In sum, the District Court found: "Even if credit card verification or adult password verification were implemented, the Government presented no testimony as to how such systems could ensure that the user of the password or credit card is in fact over 18. The burdens imposed by credit card verification and adult password verification systems make them effectively unavailable to a substantial number of Internet content providers." [Citation.]

## II

The Telecommunications Act of 1996, [citation], was an unusually important legislative enactment. * * * Title V—known as the "Communications Decency Act of 1996" (CDA)—contains provisions that were either added in executive committee after the hearings were concluded or as amendments offered during floor debate on the legislation. An amendment offered in the Senate was the source of the two statutory provisions challenged in this case. They are informally described as the "indecent transmission" provision and the "patently offensive display" provision.

The first, 47 U.S.C.A. § 223(a), prohibits the knowing transmission of obscene or indecent messages to any recipient under 18 years of age. * * *
The second provision, § 223(d), prohibits the knowing sending or displaying of patently offensive messages in a manner that is available to a person under 18 years of age. * * *

The breadth of these prohibitions is qualified by two affirmative defenses. See § 223(e)(5). One covers those who take "good faith, reasonable, effective, and appropriate actions" to restrict access by minors to the prohibited communications. § 223(e)(5)(A). The other covers those who restrict access to covered material by requiring certain designated forms of age proof, such as a verified credit card or an adult identification number or code. § 223(e)(5)(B).

## III

On February 8, 1996, immediately after the President signed the statute, 20 plaintiffs filed suit against the Attorney General of the United States and the Department of Justice challenging the constitutionality of §§ 223(a)(1) and 223(d). A week later, based on his conclusion that the term "indecent" was too vague to provide the basis for a criminal prosecution, District Judge Buckwalter entered a temporary restraining order against enforcement of § 223(a)(1)(B)(ii) insofar as it applies to indecent communications. A second suit was then filed by 27 additional plaintiffs, the two cases were consolidated, and a three-judge District Court was convened pursuant to § 561 of the Act. After an evidentiary hearing, that Court entered a preliminary injunction

against enforcement of both of the challenged provisions. Each of the three judges wrote a separate opinion, but their judgment was unanimous.

* * *

## V

In [citation], we observed that "[e]ach medium of expression . . . may present its own problems." Thus, some of our cases have recognized special justifications for regulation of the broadcast media that are not applicable to other speakers, see [citations]. In these cases, the Court relied on the history of extensive government regulation of the broadcast medium, [citation]; the scarcity of available frequencies at its inception, [citation]; and its "invasive" nature, [citation].

Those factors are not present in cyberspace. Neither before nor after the enactment of the CDA have the vast democratic fora of the Internet been subject to the type of government supervision and regulation that has attended the broadcast industry. Moreover, the Internet is not as "invasive" as radio or television. The District Court specifically found that "[c]ommunications over the Internet do not 'invade' an individual's home or appear on one's computer screen unbidden. Users seldom encounter content 'by accident.'" [Citation.] It also found that "[a]lmost all sexually explicit images are preceded by warnings as to the content," and cited testimony that "'odds are slim' that a user would come across a sexually explicit sight by accident." [Citation.]

* * *

Finally, unlike the conditions that prevailed when Congress first authorized regulation of the broadcast spectrum, the Internet can hardly be considered a "scarce" expressive commodity. It provides relatively unlimited, low-cost capacity for communication of all kinds. The Government estimates that "[a]s many as 40 million people use the Internet today, and that figure is expected to grow to 200 million by 1999." This dynamic, multi-faceted category of communication includes not only traditional print and news services, but also audio, video, and still images, as well as interactive, real-time dialogue. Through the use of chat rooms, any person with a phone line can become a town crier with a voice that resonates farther than it could from any soapbox. Through the use of Web pages, mail exploders, and newsgroups, the same individual can become a pamphleteer. As the District Court found, "the content on the Internet is as diverse as human thought." [Citation.] We agree with its conclusion that our cases provide no basis for qualifying the level of First Amendment scrutiny that should be applied to this medium.

# VI

Regardless of whether the CDA is so vague that it violates the Fifth Amendment, the many ambiguities concerning the scope of its coverage render it problematic for purposes of the First Amendment. For instance, each of the two parts of the CDA uses a different linguistic form. The first uses the word "indecent," 47 U.S.C.A. § 223(a), while the second speaks of material that "in context, depicts or describes, in terms patently offensive as measured by contemporary community standards, sexual or excretory activities or organs," § 223(d). Given the absence of a definition of either term, this difference in language will provoke uncertainty among speakers about how the two standards relate to each other and just what they mean. * * *

The vagueness of the CDA is a matter of special concern for two reasons. First, the CDA is a content-based regulation of speech. The vagueness of such a regulation raises special First Amendment concerns because of its obvious chilling effect on free speech. [Citation.] Second, the CDA is a criminal statute. In addition to the opprobrium and stigma of a criminal conviction, the CDA threatens violators with penalties including up to two years in prison for each act of violation. The severity of criminal sanctions may well cause speakers to remain silent rather than communicate even arguably unlawful words, ideas, and images. [Citation.] As a practical matter, this increased deterrent effect, coupled with the "risk of discriminatory enforcement" of vague regulations, poses greater First Amendment concerns than those implicated by the civil regulation reviewed in [citation].

The Government argues that the statute is no more vague than the obscenity standard this Court established in *Miller v. California*, [citation]. But that is not so. In *Miller*, this Court reviewed a criminal conviction against a commercial vendor who mailed brochures containing pictures of sexually explicit activities to individuals who had not requested such materials. [Citation.] Having struggled for some time to establish a definition of obscenity, we set forth in *Miller* the test for obscenity that controls to this day:

"(a) whether the average person, applying contemporary community standards would find that the work, taken as a whole, appeals to the prurient interest; (b) whether the work depicts or describes, in a patently offensive way, sexual conduct specifically defined by the applicable state law; and

(c) whether the work, taken as a whole, lacks serious literary, artistic, political, or scientific value." [Citation.]

* * *

In contrast to *Miller* and our other previous cases, the CDA thus presents a greater threat of censoring speech that, in fact, falls outside the statute's scope. Given the vague contours of the coverage of the statute, it unquestionably silences some speakers whose messages would be entitled to constitutional protection. That danger provides further reason for insisting that the statute not be overly broad. The CDA's burden on protected speech cannot be justified if it could be avoided by a more carefully drafted statute.

# VII

We are persuaded that the CDA lacks the precision that the First Amendment requires when a statute regulates the content of speech. In order to deny minors access to potentially harmful speech, the CDA effectively suppresses a large amount of speech that adults have a constitutional right to receive and to address to one another. That burden on adult speech is unacceptable if less restrictive alternatives would be at least as effective in achieving the legitimate purpose that the statute was enacted to serve.

In evaluating the free speech rights of adults, we have made it perfectly clear that "[s]exual expression which is indecent but not obscene is protected by the First Amendment" [Citation.] See also [citation] ("[W]here obscenity is not involved, we have consistently held that the fact that protected speech may be offensive to some does not justify its suppression"). Indeed, [citation] itself admonished that "the fact that society may find speech offensive is not a sufficient reason for suppressing it." [Citation.]

It is true that we have repeatedly recognized the governmental interest in protecting children from harmful materials. [Citation.] But that interest does not justify an unnecessarily broad suppression of speech addressed to adults. As we have explained, the Government may not "reduc[e] the adult population . . . to . . . only what is fit for children." [Citation.] "[R]egardless of the strength of the government's interest" in protecting children, "[t]he level of discourse reaching a mailbox simply cannot be limited to that which would be suitable for a sandbox." [Citation.]

* * *

We agree with the District Court's conclusion that the CDA places an unacceptably heavy burden on protected speech, and that the defenses do not constitute the sort of "narrow tailoring" that will save an otherwise patently invalid unconstitutional provision. In [citation], we remarked that the speech restriction at issue there amounted to "'burn[ing] the house to roast the pig.'" The CDA, casting a far darker shadow over free speech, threatens to torch a large segment of the Internet community.

* * *

For the foregoing reasons, the judgment of the district court is affirmed.

---

## CASE 4–5
### Equal Protection
## *BROWN v. BOARD OF EDUCATION OF TOPEKA*
Supreme Court of the United States, 1954
347 U.S. 483, 74 S.Ct. 686, 98 L.Ed. 873

WARREN, C. J.

These cases come to us from the States of Kansas, South Carolina, Virginia, and Delaware. They are premised on different facts and different local conditions, but a common legal question justifies their consideration together in this consolidated opinion.

In each of the cases, minors of the Negro race, through their legal representatives, seek the aid of the courts in obtaining admission to the public schools of their community on a nonsegregated basis. In each instance, they have been denied admission to schools attended by white children under laws requiring or permitting segregation according to race. This segregation was alleged to deprive the plaintiffs of the equal protection of the laws under the Fourteenth Amendment. In each of the cases other than the Delaware case, a three-judge federal district court denied relief to the plaintiffs on the so-called "separate but equal" doctrine announced by this Court in *Plessy v. Ferguson*, [citation]. Under that doctrine, equality of treatment is accorded when the races are provided substantially equal facilities, even though these facilities be separate. In the Delaware case, the Supreme Court of Delaware adhered to that doctrine, but ordered that the plaintiffs be admitted to the white schools because of their superiority to the Negro schools.

The plaintiffs contend that segregated public schools are not "equal" and cannot be made "equal" and that hence they are deprived of the equal protection of the laws. Because of the obvious importance of the question presented, the Court took jurisdiction. * * *

Reargument was largely devoted to the circumstances surrounding the adoption of the Fourteenth Amendment in 1868. It covered exhaustively consideration of the Amendment in Congress, ratification by the states, then existing practices in racial segregation, and the views of proponents and opponents of the Amendment. This discussion and our own investigation convince us that, although these sources cast some light, it is not enough to resolve the problem with which we are faced. At best, they are inconclusive. The most avid proponents of the post-War Amendments undoubtedly intended them to remove all legal distinctions among "all persons born or naturalized in the United States." Their opponents, just as certainly, were antagonistic to both the letter and the spirit of the Amendments and wished them to have the most limited effect. What others in Congress and the state legislatures had in mind cannot be determined with any degree of certainty.

An additional reason for the inconclusive nature of the Amendment's history, with respect to segregated schools, is the status of public education at that time. In the South, the movement toward free common schools, supported by general taxation, had not yet taken hold. Education of white children was largely in the hands of private groups. Education of Negroes was almost nonexistent, and practically all of the race were illiterate. In fact, any education of Negroes was forbidden by law in some states. Today, in contrast, many Negroes have achieved outstanding success in the arts and sciences as well as in the business and professional world. It is true that public school education at the time of the Amendment had advanced further in the North, but the effect of the Amendment on Northern States was generally ignored in the congressional debates. Even in the North, the conditions of public education did not approximate those existing today. The curriculum was usually rudimentary; ungraded schools were common in rural areas; the school term was but three months a year in many states; and compulsory school attendance was virtually unknown. As a consequence, it is not surprising that there should be so little in the history of the Fourteenth Amendment relating to its intended effect on public education.

In the first cases in this Court construing the Fourteenth Amendment, decided shortly after its adoption, the Court interpreted it as proscribing all state-imposed discriminations against the Negro race. The doctrine of "separate but equal" did not make its appearance in this Court until 1896 in the case of *Plessy v. Ferguson*, involving not education but transportation. American courts have since labored with the doctrine for over half a century. In this Court, there have been six cases involving the "separate but equal" doctrine in the field of public education. . . . In none of these cases was it necessary to reexamine the doctrine to grant relief to the Negro plaintiff. And in *Sweatt v. Painter*, [citation], the Court expressly reserved decision on the question whether *Plessy v. Ferguson* should be held inapplicable to public education.

In the instant cases, that question is directly presented. Here, unlike *Sweatt v. Painter*, there are findings below that the Negro and white schools involved have been equalized, or are being equalized, with respect to buildings, curricula, qualifications and salaries of teachers, and other "tangible" factors. Our decision, therefore, cannot turn on merely a comparison of these tangible factors in the Negro and white schools involved in each of the cases. We must look instead to the effect of segregation itself on public education.

\* \* \*

Today, education is perhaps the most important function of state and local governments. Compulsory school attendance laws and the great expenditures for education both demonstrate our recognition of the importance of education to our democratic society. It is required in the performance of our most basic public responsibilities, even service in the armed forces. It is the very foundation of good citizenship. Today it is a principal instrument in awakening the child to cultural values, in preparing him for later professional training, and in helping him to adjust normally to his environment. In these days, it is doubtful that any child may reasonably be expected to succeed in life if he is denied the opportunity of an education. Such an opportunity, where the state has undertaken to provide it, is a right which must be made available to all on equal terms.

We come then to the question presented: Does segregation of children in public schools solely on the basis of race, even though the physical facilities and other "tangible" factors may be equal, deprive the children of the minority group of equal educational opportunities? We believe that it does.

In *Sweatt v. Painter*, [citation], in finding that a segregated law school for Negroes could not provide them equal educational opportunities, this Court relied in large part on "those qualities which are incapable of objective measurement but which make for greatness in a law school." In *McLaurin v. Oklahoma State Regents*, [citation], the Court in requiring that a Negro admitted to a white graduate school be treated like all other students, again resorted to intangible considerations: ". . . his ability to study, to engage in discussions and exchange views with other students, and, in general, to learn his profession." Such considerations apply with added force to children in grade and high schools. To separate them from others of similar age and qualifications solely because of their race generates a feeling of inferiority as to their status in the community that may affect their hearts and minds in a way unlikely ever to be undone. The effect of this separation on their educational opportunities was well stated by a finding in the Kansas case by a court which nevertheless felt compelled to rule against the Negro plaintiffs:

Segregation of white and colored children in public schools has a detrimental effect upon the colored children. The impact is greater when it has the sanction of the law, for the policy of separating the races is usually interpreted as denoting the inferiority of the Negro group. A sense of inferiority affects the motivation of a child to learn. Segregation with the sanction of law, therefore, has a tendency to (retard) the educational and mental development of Negro children and to deprive them of some of the benefits they would receive in a racial(ly) integrated school system.

Whatever may have been the extent of psychological knowledge at the time of *Plessy v. Ferguson*, this finding is amply supported by modern authority. Any language in *Plessy v. Ferguson* contrary to this finding is rejected.

We conclude that in the field of public education the doctrine of "separate but equal" has no place. Separate educational facilities are inherently unequal. Therefore, we hold that the plaintiffs and others similarly situated for whom the actions have been brought are, by reason of the segregation complained of, deprived of the equal protection of the laws guaranteed by the Fourteenth Amendment. This disposition makes unnecessary any discussion whether such segregation also violates the Due Process Clause of the Fourteenth Amendment.

# Questions

1. List and distinguish the basic principles of constitutional law.

2. Describe the sources and extent of the power of the Federal and State governments to regulate business and commerce.

3. Distinguish the three levels of scrutiny used by the courts to determine the constitutionality of governmental action.

4. Explain the effect of the First Amendment upon (a) corporate political speech, (b) commercial speech, and (c) defamation.

5. Explain the difference between substantive and procedural due process.

# Problems

1. In May, Patricia Allen left her automobile on the shoulder of a road in the city of Erewhon after the car stopped running. A member of the Erewhon city police department came upon the car later that day and placed on it a sticker which stated that unless the car were moved, it would be towed. After a week the car had not been removed, and the police department authorized Baldwin Auto Wrecking Co. to tow it away and store it on its property. Allen was told by a friend that her car was at Baldwin's. Allen asked Baldwin to allow her to take possession of her car, but Baldwin refused to relinquish the car until the $70 towing fee was paid. Allen could not afford to pay the fee, and the car remained at Baldwin's for six weeks. At that time, Baldwin requested that the police department issue a permit to dispose of the automobile. After the police department tried unsuccessfully to telephone Allen, the department issued the permit. In late July, Baldwin destroyed the automobile. Allen brings an action against the city and Baldwin for damages for loss of the vehicle, arguing that she was denied due process. Decision?

2. In 1967, large oil reserves were discovered in the Prudhoe Bay area of Alaska. As a result, State revenues increased from $124 million in 1969 to $3.7 billion in 1981. In 1980, the State legislature enacted a dividend program that would distribute annually a portion of these earnings to the State's adult residents. Under the plan, each citizen eighteen years of age or older receives one unit for each year of residency subsequent to 1959, the year Alaska became a State. Crawford, a resident since 1978, brings suit challenging the dividend distribution plan as violative of the equal protection guarantee. Decision?

3. Maryland enacted a statute prohibiting any producer or refiner of petroleum products from operating retail service stations within the State. The statute also required that any producer or refiner discontinue operating its company-owned retail service stations. Approximately 3,800 retail service stations in Maryland sell more than twenty different brands of gasoline. However, no petroleum products are produced or refined in Maryland; and only 5 percent of the total number of retailers are operated by a producer or refiner. Maryland enacted the statute because a survey conducted by the State comptroller indicated that gasoline stations operated by producers or refiners had received preferential treatment during periods of gasoline shortage. Seven major producers and refiners bring an action challenging the statute on the ground that it discriminated against interstate commerce in violation of the commerce clause of the U.S. Constitution. Decision?

4. The Federal Aviation Act of 1958 provides that "the United States of America is declared to possess and exercise complete and exclusive national sovereignty in the airspace of the United States." The city of Orion adopted an ordinance which makes it unlawful for jet aircraft to take off from its airport between 11:00 P.M. of one day and 7:00 A.M. of the next day. Jordan Airlines, Inc., is adversely affected by this ordinance and brings suit challenging it under the supremacy clause of the U.S. Constitution. Decision?

5. The Public Service Commission of State X issued a regulation completely banning all advertising that "promotes the use of electricity" by any electric utility company in State X. The commission issued the order to conserve energy. Central Electric Corporation of State X challenges the order in the State courts, arguing that the commission has restrained commercial speech in violation of the First Amendment. Decision?

6. E–Z–Rest Motel is a motel with 216 rooms located in the center of a large city in State Y. It is readily accessible from two interstate highways and three major State highways. The motel solicits patronage from outside of State Y through various national advertising media, including magazines of national circulation. It accepts convention trade from outside State Y, and approximately 75 percent of its registered guests are from out of State Y. An action under the Federal Civil Rights Act of 1964 has been brought against E–Z–Rest Motel alleging that the motel discriminates on the basis of race and color. The motel contends that the statute cannot be applied to it because it is not engaged in interstate commerce. Decision?

7. State Z enacted a Private Pension Benefits Protection Act requiring private employers with 100 or more employees to pay a pension funding charge upon terminating a pension plan or closing an office in State Z. Acme Steel Company closed its offices in State Z, whereupon the State assessed the company

$185,000 under the vesting provisions of the act. Acme challenged the constitutionality of the act under the contract clause (Article I, Section 10) of the U.S. Constitution. Decision?

8. A State statute empowered public school principals to suspend students for up to ten days without any notice or hearing. A student who was suspended for ten days challenges the constitutionality of his suspension on the ground that he was denied due process. Decision?

9. Iowa enacted a statute prohibiting the use of sixty-five-foot double trailer truck combinations. All of the other midwestern and western States permit such trucks to be used on their roads. Consolidated Freightways is adversely affected by this statute and brings suit against Iowa, alleging that the statute violates the commerce clause. Decision?

10. Metropolitan Edison Company is a privately owned and operated Pennsylvania corporation subject to extensive regulation by the Pennsylvania Public Utility Commission. Under a provision of its general tariff filed with the commission, Edison had the right to discontinue electric service to any customer on reasonable notice of nonpayment of bills. Catherine Jackson had been receiving electricity from Metropolitan Edison when her account was terminated in 1970 because of her delinquency in payments. Edison later opened a new account for her residence in the name of James Dodson, another occupant of Jackson's residence. In August 1971, Dodson moved away and no further payments were made to the account. Finally, in October 1971, Edison disconnected Jackson's service without any prior notice. Jackson brought suit claiming that her electric service could not be terminated without notice and a hearing. She further argued that such action, allowed by a provision of Edison's tariff filed with the commission, constituted "state action" depriving her of property in violation of the Fourteenth Amendment's guarantee of due process of law. Decision?

11. In the fall of 1971, Miss Horowitz was admitted as an advanced medical student at the University of Missouri–Kansas City. During the spring of 1972, several faculty members expressed dissatisfaction with Miss Horowitz's clinical performance, noting that it was below that of her peers, that she was erratic in attendance at her clinical sessions, and that she lacked a critical concern for personal hygiene. Upon the recommendation of the school's Council on Evaluation, she was advanced to her second and final year on a probationary basis.

After subsequent unfavorable reviews during her second year and a negative evaluation of her performance by seven practicing physicians, the council recommended that Miss Horowitz be dismissed from the school for her failure to meet academic standards. The decision was approved by the dean and later affirmed by the provost after an appeal by Miss Horowitz. She brought suit against the school's Board of Curators, claiming that her dismissal violated her right to procedural due process under the Fourteenth Amendment and deprived her of "liberty" by substantially impairing her opportunities to continue her medical education or to return to employment in a medically related field. The trial court found for the defendant, but the appellate court reversed. The Board of Curators appealed. Decision?

12. CompuServe Incorporated ("CompuServe") is one of the major national commercial online services. It operates a computer communication service through a proprietary nationwide computer network. In addition to allowing access to the content available on its own network, CompuServe also provides its subscribers with a link to the much larger resources of the Internet. This allows its subscribers to send and receive electronic messages, known as "e-mail," by the Internet. Cyber Promotions, Inc. is in the business of sending unsolicited e-mail advertisements on behalf of itself and its clients to hundreds of thousands of Internet users, many of whom are CompuServe subscribers. CompuServe has notified Cyber Promotions that it is prohibited from using CompuServe's computer equipment to process and store the unsolicited e-mail and has requested that Cyber Promotions terminate the practice. Instead, Cyber Promotions has sent an increasing volume of e-mail solicitations to CompuServe subscribers. CompuServe has attempted to employ technological means to block the flow of Cyber Promotions e-mail transmissions, but to no avail. CompuServe seeks an injunction preventing Cyber Promotions from sending unsolicited advertisements to CompuServe subscribers. In response, Cyber Promotions argues that it has the right to continue to send unsolicited commercial e-mail to CompuServe's computer systems under the First Amendment to the U.S. Constitution. Decision?

**WWW** **Internet Exercise** Find your State's constitution and compare its protection of individual rights with that of the U.S. Constitution. (If your State's constitution is not available, choose another State.)

# CHAPTER 5

# Administrative Law

Administrative law is the branch of public law that is created by administrative agencies in the form of rules, regulations, orders, and decisions to carry out the regulatory powers and duties of those agencies. **Administrative agencies** are governmental entities—other than courts and legislatures—having authority to affect the rights of private parties through their operations. Such agencies, often referred to as commissions, boards, departments, administrations, government corporations, bureaus, or offices, regulate a vast array of important matters involving national safety, welfare, and convenience. For instance, Federal administrative agencies are charged with responsibility for national security, citizenship and naturalization, law enforcement, taxation, currency, elections, environmental protection, consumer protection, regulation of transportation, telecommunications, labor relations, trade, commerce, and securities markets, as well as providing health and social services.

Because of the increasing complexity of the social, economic, and industrial life of the nation, the scope of administrative law has expanded enormously. Justice Jackson stated that "the rise of administrative bodies has been the most significant legal trend of the last century, and perhaps more values today are affected by their decisions than by those of all the courts, review of administrative decisions apart." *Federal Trade Commission v. Ruberoid Co.*, 343 U.S. 470 (1952). This observation is even more true today, as evidenced by the dramatic increase in the number and activities of Federal government boards, commissions, and other agencies. Certainly, agencies create more legal rules and adjudicate more controversies than all the legislatures and courts combined.

State agencies also play a significant role in the functioning of our society. Among the more important State boards and commissions are those that supervise and regulate banking, insurance, communications, transpor-

tation, public utilities, pollution control, and workers' compensation.

Countless administrative agencies establish much of the Federal, State, and local law in this country. These agencies, which many label the "fourth branch of government," possess tremendous power and have long been criticized as being "in reality miniature independent governments . . . [which are] a haphazard deposit of irresponsible agencies. . . ." 1937 Presidential Task Force Report.

Despite the criticism against them, these agencies clearly play a significant and necessary role in our society. Administrative agencies relieve legislatures of the impossible burden of fashioning legislation that deals with every detail of a specific problem. As a result, Congress can enact legislation, such as the Federal Trade Commission Act, which prohibits unfair and deceptive trade practices, without having to define such practices specifically or to anticipate all the particular problems that may arise. Instead, Congress may enact an **enabling statute** that creates an agency—in this example, the Federal Trade Commission—to which it can delegate the power to issue rules, regulations, and guidelines to carry out the statutory mandate. In addition, the establishment of separate, specialized bodies enables administrative agencies to be staffed by individuals with expertise in the field being regulated. Administrative agencies can thus develop the knowledge and devote the time necessary to provide continuous and flexible solutions to evolving regulatory problems.

This chapter will focus on Federal administrative agencies, which can be classified as either independent or executive. Executive agencies are those housed within the executive branch of government, whereas independent agencies are not. Many Federal agencies are discussed in other parts of this text. More specifically, the Federal Trade Commission (FTC) and the Justice Department are discussed in Chapter 41; the FTC and the Consumer

Product Safety Commission in Chapter 42; the Department of Labor, the National Labor Relations Board (NLRB), and the Equal Employment Opportunity Commission (EEOC) in Chapter 43; the Securities and Exchange Commission (SEC) in Chapters 44 and 45; and the Environmental Protection Agency (EPA) in Chapter 46.

# OPERATION OF ADMINISTRATIVE AGENCIES

Most administrative agencies perform three basic functions: (1) rulemaking, (2) enforcement, and (3) adjudication. The term **administrative process** refers to the activities in which administrative agencies engage while carrying out their rulemaking, enforcement, and adjudicative functions. Administrative agencies exercise powers that the Constitution has allocated to the three separate branches of government. More specifically, agencies exercise legislative power when they make rules, executive power when they enforce their enabling statutes and their rules, and judicial power when they adjudicate disputes. This concentration of power has raised questions regarding the propriety of having the same bodies which establish the rules also act as prosecutors and judges in determining whether those rules have been violated. To address this issue and bring about certain additional procedural reforms, Congress enacted the Administrative Procedure Act (APA) in 1946.

## Rulemaking

Rulemaking is the process by which an administrative agency enacts or promulgates rules of law. Under the APA, a rule is "the whole or a part of an agency statement of general or particular applicability and future effect designed to implement, interpret, or process law or policy." Section 551(4). Once promulgated, rules are applicable to all parties. Moreover, the rulemaking process notifies all parties that the agency is considering the impending rule and provides concerned individuals with an opportunity to be heard. Administrative agencies promulgate three types of rules: legislative rules, interpretative rules, and procedural rules.

***Legislative Rules*** Legislative rules, often called *regulations*, are in effect "administrative statutes." **Legislative rules** are those issued by an agency that is able, under a legislative delegation of power, to make rules having the force and effect of law. For example, the FTC has

rulemaking power with which to elaborate upon its enabling statute's prohibition of unfair or deceptive acts or practices. Legislative rules, which are immediately binding, generally receive greater deference from reviewing courts than do interpretative rules.

Legislative rules have the force of law if they are constitutional, within the power granted to the agency by the legislature, and issued according to proper procedure. To be constitutional, regulations must not violate any provisions of the U.S. Constitution, such as due process or equal protection. In addition, they may not involve an unconstitutional delegation of legislative power from the legislature to the agency. To be constitutionally permissible, the enabling statute granting power to an agency must establish reasonable standards to guide the agency in implementing the statute. Statutes have met this requirement through language such as "to prohibit unfair methods of competition," "fair and equitable," "public interest, convenience, and necessity," and other equally broad expressions. In any event, an agency may not exceed the actual authority granted by its enabling statute.

Legislative rules must be promulgated in accordance with the procedural requirements of the APA, although the enabling statute may impose more stringent requirements. Most legislative rules are issued in accordance with the **informal rulemaking** procedures of the APA, which require that the agency provide the following:

1. prior notice of a proposed rule, usually by publication in the *Federal Register*;
2. an opportunity for interested parties to participate in the rulemaking; and
3. publication of a final draft containing a concise general statement of the rule's basis and purpose at least thirty days before its effective date. Section 553.

In some instances the enabling statute requires that an agency make certain rules only after providing the opportunity for a hearing. This formal rulemaking procedure, which is far more complex than the informal procedures, is governed by the same APA provisions that govern an adjudication, discussed below. In **formal rulemaking,** when an agency makes rules, it must consider the record of the trial-type agency hearing and include a statement of "findings and conclusions, and the reasons or basis therefore, on all the material issues of fact, law, or discretion presented on the record." Section 557(c).

Some enabling statutes direct that the agency, in making rules, follow certain procedures more formal than those the agency uses in informal rulemaking but do not compel the full hearing that formal rulemaking requires. This intermediate procedure, known as **hybrid rulemaking**, results from combining the informal procedures of the APA with additional procedures specified by the enabling statute. For example, an agency may be required to conduct a legislative-type hearing (formal) that permits no cross-examination (informal).

In 1990 Congress enacted the Negotiated Rulemaking Act to encourage the involvement of affected parties in the initial stages of the policy-making process prior to the publication of notice of a proposed rule. The Act authorizes agencies to use negotiated rulemaking but does not require it. If an agency decides to use negotiated rulemaking, the affected parties and the agency develop an agreement and offer it to the agency. If accepted, the agreement becomes a basis for the proposed regulation, which is then published for comment.

 *See Cases 5–1 and 5–2*

***Interpretative Rules*** Interpretative rules are agency-issued statements that explain how the agency construes its governing statute. For instance, the Securities and Exchange Commission "renders administrative interpretations of the law and regulations thereunder to members of the public, prospective registrants and others, to help them decide legal questions about the application of the law and the regulations to particular situations and to aid them in complying with the law." *The Work of the SEC* (1980).

Interpretative rules, which are exempt from the APA's procedural requirements of notice and comment, are not automatically binding on private parties the agency regulates or on the courts, although they are given substantial weight. As the Supreme Court has stated, "The weight of such [an interpretative rule] in a particular case will depend upon the thoroughness evident in its consideration, the validity of its reasoning, its consistency with earlier and later pronouncements, and all those factors which give it power to persuade. . . ." *Skidmore v. Swift & Co.*, 323 U.S. 134 (1944).

***Procedural Rules*** Procedural rules are also exempt from the notice and comment requirements of the APA and are not law. These rules establish rules of conduct for practice before the agency, identify an agency's organization, and describe its method of operation. For example, the Securities and Exchange Commission's Rules of Practice deal with such matters as who may appear before the commission; business hours and notice of proceedings and hearings; settlements, agreements, and conferences; the presentation of evidence and taking of depositions and interrogatories; and the review of hearings.

## Enforcement

Agencies also investigate to determine whether certain conduct has violated the statute or the agency's legislative rules. In carrying out this executive function, the agencies traditionally have been accorded great discretion to compel the disclosure of information, subject to constitutional limitations. These limitations require that (1) the investigation be authorized by law and undertaken for a legitimate purpose, (2) the information sought be relevant, (3) the demand for information be sufficiently specific and not unreasonably burdensome, and (4) the information sought not be privileged.

The following explains some of the investigative and enforcement functions of the Securities and Exchange Commission:

Most of the Commission's investigations are conducted privately. Facts are developed to the fullest extent possible through informal inquiry, interviewing witnesses, examining brokerage records and other documents, reviewing and trading data, and similar means. The Commission is empowered to issue subpoenas requiring sworn testimony and the production of books, records, and other documents pertinent to the subject matter under investigation. In the event of refusal to respond to a subpoena, the Commission may apply to a Federal court for an order compelling obedience. *The Work of the SEC* (1986).

## Adjudication

After concluding an investigation, the agency may use informal or formal methods to resolve the matter. Because the caseload of administrative agencies is vast, far greater than that of the judicial system, agencies adjudicate most matters informally. Informal procedures include advising, negotiating, and settling. In 1990 Congress enacted the Administrative Dispute Resolution Act to authorize and encourage Federal agencies to use mediation, conciliation, arbitration, and other techniques for the prompt and informal resolution of disputes. The act does not, however, require agencies to use alternative dispute resolution, and the affected parties must consent to its use.

The formal procedure by which an agency resolves a matter (called **adjudication**) involves finding facts, applying legal rules to the facts, and formulating orders.

An **order** "means the whole or a part of a final disposition, whether affirmative, negative, injunctive or declaratory in form, of an agency." APA Section 551(6). In essence an administrative trial, adjudication is used when required by the enabling statute.

The procedures the administrative agencies employ to adjudicate cases are nearly as varied as the agencies themselves. Nevertheless, the APA does establish certain mandatory standards for those Federal agencies the act covers. For example, under the act, an agency must give notice of a hearing. The APA also requires that the agency give all interested parties the opportunity to submit and consider "facts, arguments, offers of settlement, or proposals of adjustment." Section 554(c). In many cases this involves testimony and cross-examination of witnesses. If no settlement is reached, a hearing must be held.

The hearing is presided over by an administrative law judge (ALJ) and is prosecuted by the agency. The agency appoints ALJs through a professional merit selection system and may remove them only for good cause. There are more than twice as many administrative law judges as there are Federal judges. Hearings never use juries; thus, the agency serves as both the prosecutor and decision-maker. To reduce the potential for a conflict of interest, the APA provides for a separation of functions between those agency members engaged in investigation and prosecution from those involved in decision making. Section 544(d).

Oral and documentary evidence may be introduced by either party, and the agency must base all sanctions, rules, and orders upon "consideration of the whole record or those parts cited by a party and supported by and in accordance with the reliable, probative, and substantial evidence." Section 556(d). All decisions must include a statement of findings of fact and conclusions of law and the reasons or bases for them, as well as a statement of the appropriate rule, order, sanction, or relief.

If authorized to do so by law and within its delegated jurisdiction, an agency may impose in its orders sanctions such as penalties; fines; the seizure of property; the assessment of damages, restitution, compensation, or fees; and the requirement, revocation, or suspension of a license. Sections 551(10) and 558(b). In most instances orders are final unless appealed, and failure to comply with an order subjects the party to a statutory penalty. If the order is appealed, the governing body of the agency may decide the case *de novo*. Section 557(b). Thus, the agency may hear additional evidence and arguments in deciding whether to revise the findings and conclusions made in the initial decision.

Although administrative adjudications mirror to a large extent the procedures of judicial trials, the two differ substantially:

Agency hearings, especially those dealing with rulemaking, often tend to produce evidence of general conditions as distinguished from facts relating solely to the respondent. Administrative agencies in rulemaking and occasionally in formal adversarial adjudications more consciously formulate policy than do courts. Consequently, administrative adjudications may require that the administrative law judge consider more consciously the impact of his decision upon the public interest as well as upon the particular respondent. . . . An administrative hearing is tried to an *administrative law judge* and never to a *jury*. Since many of the rules governing the admission of proof in judicial trials are designed to protect the jury from unreliable and possibly confusing evidence, it has long been asserted that such rules need not be applied at all or with the same vigor in proceedings solely before an administrative law judge. . . . Consequently, the technical common law rules governing the admissibility of evidence have generally been abandoned by administrative agencies. *McCormick on Evidence,* 4th ed., Section 350, p. 605.

## LIMITS ON ADMINISTRATIVE AGENCIES

An important and fundamental part of administrative law is the limits judicial review imposes upon the activities of administrative agencies. On matters of policy, however, courts are not supposed to substitute their judgment for that of an agency. Additional limitations arise from the legislature and the executive branch, which, unlike the judiciary, may address the wisdom and correctness of an agency's decision or action. Moreover, legally required disclosure of agency actions provides further protection for the public.

◆ *See Figure 5–1*

### Judicial Review

As discussed in Chapter 4, judicial review describes the process by which the courts examine governmental action. Judicial review, which is available unless a statute precludes such review or the agency action is committed to agency discretion by law, acts as a control or check on a particular rule or order of an administrative agency. Section 701.

***General Requirements*** Parties seeking to challenge agency action must have standing and must have exhausted their administrative remedies. Standing requires

**FIGURE 5–1**  Limits on Administrative Agencies

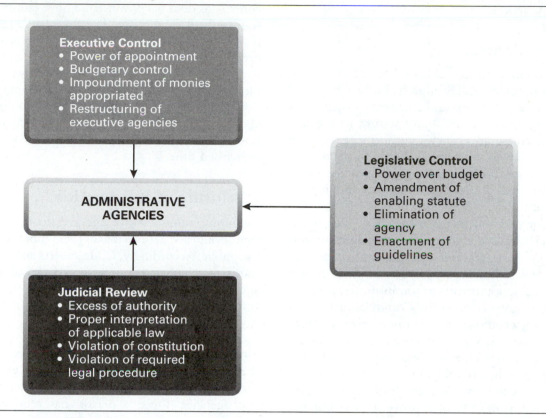

that the agency action injure the party in fact and that the party assert an interest that is in the "zone of interests to be protected or regulated by the statute in question." Judicial review is ordinarily available only for *final* agency action. Section 704. Accordingly, if a party seeks review while an agency proceeding is in progress, a court will usually dismiss the action because the party has failed to exhaust his administrative remedies.

In exercising judicial review the court may decide either to compel agency action unlawfully withheld or to set aside impermissible agency action. In making its determination the court must review the whole record and may set aside agency action only if the error is prejudicial.

*See Case 5–3*

*Questions of Law*  When conducting a review, a court decides all relevant questions of law, interprets constitutional and statutory provisions, and determines the meaning or applicability of the terms of an agency action. This review of questions of law includes determining whether the agency has (1) exceeded its authority, (2) properly interpreted the applicable law, (3) violated

any constitutional provision, or (4) acted contrary to the procedural requirements of the law.

*Questions of Fact*  When reviewing factual determinations, the courts use one of three different standards. Where informal rulemaking or informal adjudication has occurred, the standard generally is the **arbitrary and capricious** test, which requires only that the agency had a rational basis for reaching its decision. Where an agency has held a formal hearing, the substantial evidence test usually applies. It also applies to informal or hybrid rulemaking, if the enabling statute so requires. The **substantial evidence** test requires that the agency support its conclusions with "such relevant evidence as a reasonable mind might accept as adequate to support a conclusion." *Consolidated Edison Co. v. NLRB*, 305 U.S. 197 (1938). Finally, in rare instances the reviewing court may apply the **unwarranted by the facts** standard, which permits the court to try the facts *de novo*. This strict review is available only when the enabling statute so provides, when the agency has conducted an adjudication with inadequate fact-finding procedures, or when issues that were not before the agency are raised in a proceeding to enforce nonadjudicative agency action.

## Legislative Control

The legislature may exercise control over administrative agencies in various ways. Through its budgetary power, it may greatly restrict or expand an agency's operations. Congress may amend an enabling statute to increase, modify, or decrease an agency's authority. Even more drastically, it may completely eliminate an agency. Or Congress may establish general guidelines to govern agency action, as it did by enacting the Administrative Procedure Act. Moreover, it may reverse or change an agency rule or decision through specific legislation. In addition, each house of Congress has oversight committees that review the operations of administrative agencies. Finally, the Senate has the power of confirmation over some high-level appointments to administrative agencies.

In 1996 Congress enacted the Congressional Review Act, which subjects most rules to a new, extensive form of legislative control. With limited exceptions, the Act requires agencies to submit newly adopted rules to each house of Congress before they can take effect. If the rule is a major rule, it does not become final until Congress has had an opportunity to disapprove it. A **major rule** is any rule that the Office of Management and Budget (OMB) finds has resulted in or is likely to result in (1) an annual effect on the economy of at least $100 million, (2) a major increase in costs or prices, or (3) a significant adverse effect on competition, employment, investment, productivity, innovation, or international competitiveness of U.S. enterprises. If the rule is not a major rule it takes effect as it otherwise would have after its submission to Congress and it is subject to possible disapproval by Congress. All rules covered by the Act shall not take effect if Congress adopts a joint resolution of disapproval. The President may veto the joint resolution, but Congress may then vote to override the veto. A rule that has been disapproved is treated as though it had never taken effect.

## Control by Executive Branch

By virtue of his power to appoint and remove their chief administrators, the President has significant control over administrative agencies housed within the executive branch. With respect to independent agencies, however, the President has less control because commissioners serve for a fixed term that is staggered with the President's term of office. Nevertheless, his power to appoint agency chairs and to fill vacancies confers considerable control, as does his power to remove commissioners for statutorily defined cause. The President's central role in the budgeting process of agencies also enables him to exert great control over agency policy and operations. Even more extreme is the President's power to impound monies appropriated to an agency by Congress. In addition, the President may radically alter, combine, or even abolish agencies of the executive branch unless either house of Congress disapproves such an action within a prescribed time.

## Disclosure of Information

Requiring administrative agencies to disclose information about their actions makes them more accountable to the public. Accordingly, Congress has enacted disclosure statutes to enhance public and political oversight of agency activities. These statutes include the Freedom of Information Act and the Government in the Sunshine Act.

***Freedom of Information Act*** First enacted in 1966, the Freedom of Information Act (FOIA) gives the public access to most records in the files of Federal administrative agencies. Once a person has requested files, an agency must indicate within ten working days whether it intends to comply with the request and must within a reasonable time respond to the request. The agency may charge a fee for providing the records.

The FOIA permits agencies to deny access to nine categories of records: (1) records specifically authorized in the interest of national defense or foreign policy to be kept secret; (2) records that relate solely to the internal personnel rules and practices of an agency; (3) records specifically exempted by statute from disclosure; (4) trade secrets and commercial or financial information that is privileged or confidential; (5) inter- or intra-agency memorandums; (6) personnel and medical files the disclosure of which would constitute a clearly unwarranted invasion of personal privacy; (7) investigatory records compiled for law enforcement purposes; (8) records that relate to the regulation or supervision of financial institutions; and (9) certain geological and geophysical information and data.

The Electronic Freedom of Information Act Amendments of 1996 require agencies to provide public access to information in an electronic format. Agencies must, within one year after their creation, make records available by computer telecommunications or other electronic means.

***Government in the Sunshine Act*** The Government in the Sunshine Act requires meetings of many Federal agencies to be open to the public. This act applies to multimember bodies whose members the President appoints with the advice and consent of the Senate, such as the Securities and Exchange Commission, the Federal Trade Commission, the Federal Communications Commission, the Consumer Product Safety Commission, and the Commodity Futures Trading Commission. The act does not cover executive agencies such as the Environmental Protection Agency, the Food and Drug Administration, and the National Highway Safety Administration.

Agencies generally may close meetings on the same grounds on which they may refuse disclosure of records under the Freedom of Information Act. In addition, agencies such as the SEC and the Federal Reserve Board may close meetings to protect information the disclosure of which would lead to financial speculation or endanger the stability of financial institutions. The Sunshine Act also permits agencies to close meetings that concern agency participation in pending or anticipated litigation.

# Chapter Summary

| Operation of Administrative Agencies | **Rulemaking** process by which an administrative agency promulgates rules of law<br>• *Legislative Rules* substantive rules issued by an administrative agency under the authority delegated to it by the legislature<br>• *Interpretative Rules* statements issued by an administrative agency indicating how it construes its governing statute<br>• *Procedural Rules* rules issued by an administrative agency establishing its organization, method of operation, and rules of conduct for practice before it<br>**Enforcement** process by which agencies determine whether their rules have been violated<br>**Adjudication** formal methods by which an agency resolves disputes |
|---|---|
| Limits on Administrative Agencies | **Judicial Review** acts as a control or check by a court on a particular rule or order of an administrative agency<br>**Legislative Control** includes control over the agency's budget and enabling statute<br>**Control by Executive Branch** includes the President's power to appoint members of the agency<br>**Disclosure of Information** congressionally required public disclosure enhances oversight of agency activities |

# Cases

## CASE 5–1
### Legislative Rules
### *DIERSEN v. CHICAGO CAR EXCHANGE*
United States Court of Appeals, Seventh Circuit, 1997
110 F.3d 481

COFFEY, C. J.
David Diersen filed a complaint against the Chicago Car Exchange ("CCE"), an automobile dealership, alleging that the CCE fraudulently furnished him an inaccurate odometer reading when it sold him a 1968 Dodge Charger, in violation of the Vehicle Information and

Cost Savings Act ("the Odometer Act" or "the Act"). [Citation.] The Odometer Act requires all persons transferring a motor vehicle to give an accurate, written odometer reading to the purchaser or recipient of the transferred vehicle. Under the Act, those who disclose an inaccurate odometer reading with the intent to defraud are subject to a private cause of action by the transferee and may be held liable for treble damages or $1500, whichever is greater. [Citation.] The district court granted the defendant's motion for summary judgment, relying upon a regulation promulgated by the National Highway Traffic Safety Administration ("NHTSA") which purports to exempt vehicles that are at least ten years old (such as the one Diersen purchased from the CCE) from the Act's odometer disclosure requirements. [Citation.] Because we hold that the NHTSA exceeded the scope of its statutory authority when it created this exemption for older cars, we reverse that portion of the district court opinion which relies upon the NHTSA regulation as a ground for ruling in favor of the CCE. We affirm the grant of summary judgment on other grounds.

On July 23, 1994, Diersen purchased a 1968 Dodge "Charger R/T" from the CCE for $16,790. The CCE provided Diersen with a written odometer disclosure statement, as required under the Act, stating that the actual mileage of the vehicle was 22,633. * * *

The CCE had purchased the vehicle in question from an individual named Joseph Slaski, who certified to the CCE that the mileage on the car was approximately 22,600 miles and stated that the vehicle had but one prior owner. After acquiring the vehicle but before selling it to Diersen, the CCE inspected the car visually, test-drove the car, and looked at the car's engine. The CCE concluded that the car was in good condition and did not suspect that the odometer reading was inaccurate.

Diersen, after purchasing the Charger, conducted an extensive investigation into the car's title history and discovered that the vehicle had previously been described in title documents as having mileage of 75,000. * * *

Before Diersen filed this lawsuit, the CCE offered to have Diersen return the car for a complete refund. Diersen refused this offer and decided instead to sue the CCE for fraud under the Act.

In response to Diersen's claim of odometer fraud, the CCE brought a motion for summary judgment, which the district court granted on the basis of a regulation, promulgated by the NHTSA, which purported to exempt cars ten years old or older (such as the 1968 Dodge Charger) from the disclosure requirements of the Act. Following the entry of summary judgment on December

27, 1995, Diersen filed a motion to amend his complaint, pursuant to [citation]. He sought leave to amend his complaint so that he could include additional defendants, incorporate new factual material, and advance a new argument that the NHTSA regulation exempting older vehicles was invalid as a matter of law. Diersen's motion to amend was denied January 12, 1996, without a written opinion. Diersen then filed a motion for reconsideration of the court's summary judgment order, arguing that (1) the older-car exemption created by the NHTSA lacked any basis in the Act and was therefore invalid, or alternatively, (2) newly discovered facts demonstrated that the CCE knew of the exemption for older cars but waived that exemption, thus admitting that it was bound by the odometer disclosure requirements of the Act. The court denied Diersen's motion to reconsider on February 15, 1996, after both parties had submitted memoranda on the issues raised by Diersen.

\* \* \*

The Act provides, in relevant part:

**(a)** Written disclosure requirements—
**(1)** Under regulations prescribed by the Secretary of Transportation, a person transferring ownership of a motor vehicle shall give the transferee a written disclosure—
   **(A)** of the cumulative mileage registered by the odometer; or
   **(B)** that the mileage is unknown if the transferor knows that the mileage registered by the odometer is incorrect.
**(2)** A person making a written disclosure required by a regulation prescribed under paragraph (1) of this subsection may not make a false statement in the disclosure.

\* \* \*

**(4)** The regulations prescribed by the Secretary shall provide the way in which information is disclosed and retained under this section.

[Citation.] * * * The Odometer Act provides for a private cause of action against a person who violates the Act with the "intent to defraud," the violator being liable for three times the actual damages or $1500, whichever is greater. [Citation.]

In 1988, the Secretary of Transportation ("Secretary") promulgated, through the NHTSA, a regulation which purported to exempt vehicles "ten years old or older" from the disclosure requirements of the Act. [Citation.]

\* \* \*

We begin our analysis of the NHTSA regulation by observing that the text of the Act does not, either explicitly or implicitly, exempt any class of motor vehicles from its odometer disclosure requirements. Nor does the statutory definition of "motor vehicle" provide a basis for the exemption promulgated by the NHTSA. Moreover, Congress has actually circumscribed the extent to which the Secretary may interpret the Act by limiting the NHTSA's regulatory authority to the promulgation of mere procedural or logistical rules. See [citation] ("The regulations prescribed by the Secretary shall provide the way in which [the odometer] information is disclosed and retained."). The CCE argues, without reference to any specific language in the Act, that Congress expressly delegated to the Secretary the authority to create the older car exemption. We disagree. Congress directed the Secretary to promulgate rules providing for procedural adherence to the Act, but it did not authorize—either explicitly or implicitly—the creation of exemptions to the law.

The CCE argues that in considering the validity of the NHTSA regulation, we must defer to the NHTSA's interpretation of the Act, because the NHTSA is the agency charged with administering the Act and thus has familiarity and expertise that we do not possess. We do defer to an administrative agency's reasonable construction of a statute if (as is not the case here) the statute is silent or ambiguous. On the other hand, "[i]f the intent of Congress is clear, that is the end of the matter; for the court, as well as the agency must give effect to the unambiguously expressed intent of Congress." *Chevron, U.S.A., Inc. v. Natural Resources Defense Council, Inc.* [citation]. Because the text of the Odometer Act does not even suggest—much less explicitly state—a legislative intent to exempt entire classes of vehicles from the disclosure requirements of the Act, we hold that the regulation is invalid and that the district court erred in relying upon this exemption when it granted summary judgment to the CCE.

Our holding is in accord with a number of decisions by other courts on a closely analogous issue: whether the NHTSA exceeded its statutory authority in promulgating an exemption to the odometer disclosure requirements of the Odometer Act for so-called "heavy trucks" (i.e., trucks with a gross weight in excess of 16,000 pounds). [Citation.] A number of courts, including the Court of Appeals for the Ninth Circuit, have held that the NHTSA's "heavy truck" exemption, like the older-car exemption, has no basis in the text of the Odometer Act and represents an invalid exercise of regulatory authority. [Citations.] The principle behind these cases also applies to the exemption for older cars. That principle is that "legislative power rests in Congress and . . . the will of Congress as unambiguously expressed in a properly

enacted statute cannot be amended or altered by regulation. . . . [A] regulation to the extent it is in direct variance with an unambiguous statutory provision is void." [Citation.]

Our holding that the older-car exemption is invalid also comports with the broad purposes of the Act, which are "to prohibit tampering with motor vehicle odometers; and to provide safeguards to protect purchasers in the sale of motor vehicles with altered or reset odometers." [Citation.] There is nothing in this statement of purpose to suggest that the purchasers of older vehicles are less deserving of protection than consumers who buy newer vehicles. The statutory statement of purpose, read concomitantly with the language of the Act (which, to reiterate, does not specify any exemptions) establishes that Congress intended to protect all purchasers of motor vehicles from odometer tampering.

Finally, we observe that the Act provides for the levying of civil and criminal fines against violators at the discretion of the NHTSA. [Citation.] In the exercise of prosecutorial discretion, the NHTSA may opt to conserve its resources by declining to prosecute certain classes of vehicles (e.g., those cases involving older vehicles). However, the NHTSA does not, without statutory authority, have jurisdiction to tell victims of odometer fraud that they are without a remedy if the car they purchased was ten or more years old. This effectively removes a cause of action that Congress has unambiguously provided to all victims of odometer fraud, regardless of the age of the vehicle being purchased. As one member of this panel observed at oral argument, the regulation issued by the NHTSA, in effect, repeals a portion of the statute. There may be good policy reasons for exempting older vehicles from the requirements of the Act, but that determination is legislative in nature and is properly made by Congress, and not by regulatory fiat. [Citation] ("[R]ationality is not enough. The Secretary need[s] Authority.").

To summarize, we hold that the NHTSA regulation is invalid. This means that the odometer disclosure requirements of the Act apply regardless of the age of the vehicle, and thus the defendant may be held liable under the Act if, when it sold the 1968 Charger to Diersen, it provided an inaccurate odometer disclosure statement with the intent to defraud Diersen.

Although we agree with Diersen that the NHTSA regulation is invalid, this does not end our inquiry, for the CCE argues that it is entitled to summary judgment even if the odometer disclosure requirements of the Act do apply to the sale of the 1968 Dodge Charger. In order to succeed on his claim of odometer fraud, Diersen must demonstrate two essential elements: (1) a violation of the Act's odometer disclosure requirements (i.e., the providing of an inaccurate odometer reading), and (2) an intent to defraud. [Citation.] Our review of the summary judgment record persuades us that a rational trier of fact could not find in Diersen's favor as to the second element (intent to defraud); therefore, we affirm the entry of summary judgment in the defendant's favor.

---

## CASE 5–2
### Legislative Rules: Required Notice
## *TENNESSEE GAS PIPELINE COMPANY v.*
## *FEDERAL ENERGY REGULATORY COMMISSION*
United States Court of Appeals, D.C. Circuit, 1992
969 F.2d 1141

BUCKLEY, J.

This case concerns an interim rule issued by the Federal Energy Regulatory Commission requiring advance notice and disclosure by natural gas pipeline companies of the construction of new facilities or the replacement of existing ones. The Commission promulgated the interim rule without the notice and opportunity for comment required by the Administrative Procedure Act. It claimed that the rule fell within the "good cause" exception of the Act because (1) it is an interim measure, and (2) it is needed in order to avoid the environmental damage that might otherwise occur if pipelines accelerated construction and replacement activities to avoid the requirements of a final rule. Despite the minimal reach of the interim rule, we conclude that the Commission failed to provide a sufficient basis for invoking the good cause exception.

### I. Background

Section 2.55(b) of the Federal Energy Regulatory Commission's regulations permits a natural gas pipeline company to replace existing facilities without prior authorization pursuant to section 7(c) of the Natural Gas Act, [citation]. Section 284.3(c) of the regulations provides automatic authorization for the construction of facilities to be used for the transportation of natural gas pursuant to section 311 of the Natural Gas Policy Act of 1978, [citation].

On August 2, 1990, the Commission issued an interim rule as well as a Notice of Proposed Rulemaking ("NOPR") for a final rule. [Citation.] The interim rule requires interstate natural gas pipelines to provide the Commission with thirty days' advance notice of any replacement of existing facilities under section 2.55(b) and of the construction of new facilities pursuant to section 284.3(c). In the case of new construction, the rule requires that the notification include: (1) a brief description of the facilities; (2) evidence of compliance with the environmental conditions of [citation]; (3) a map showing the location of the facilities; and (4) a description of the procedures to be used for erosion control, revegetation and maintenance, and stream and wetland crossings. [Citation.] When existing facilities are to be replaced, the rule requires the notification to include items (1), (3), and (4) above. [Citation.] The agency estimated that compilation of this information would take approximately four hours per notice. [Citation.]

\* \* \*

In response, Tennessee filed the instant petition for review.

### II. Analysis

Section 553 of the Administrative Procedure Act requires agencies to provide notice of a rule thirty days before it becomes effective and to give the public an opportunity to comment on it. [Citation.] An exception exists, however, for cases when the agency for good cause finds . . . that notice and public procedure thereon are impracticable, unnecessary, or contrary to the public interest. [Citation.] Despite the broad nature of this language, our cases make clear that the good cause exception is to be "narrowly construed and only reluctantly countenanced." [Citation.] It is "not [an] escape clause that may be arbitrarily utilized at the agency's whim." [Citation.] "Rather, use of the exception by administrative agencies should be limited to emergency situations; furthermore, the grounds justifying the agency's use of the exception should be incorporated within the published rule." [Citation.]

The Commission offers two justifications for invoking the exception: (1) the interim nature of the rule; and

(2) the fear of damage to the environment that might result from a rush to avoid the mandates of a final rule. We have held that "[t]he interim status of the challenged rule is a significant factor" in the good cause analysis. [Citation.] We have also indicated that the less expansive the interim rule, the less the need for public comment. [Citation.]

The interim rule, as clarified, amounts to little more than a request for advance notice. The interim rule does not purport to implement any previously unused authority to police pipeline companies based on the notifications. Moreover, the Commission has indicated that compliance requires only a few hours. And while Tennessee complains that it cannot tell "what repairs will be needed, the lengths of lines that will need replacement, or the cost of such replacements until after the contractor has . . . tested the line in the field," [citation], the Commission's clarification of the rule indicates that in such circumstances, the agency will allow pipelines to simply list the facilities it intends to inspect and provide a good faith estimate of the repairs that might be necessary. The rule does not prevent the immediate replacement of pipeline facilities for safety reasons, and it provides for waivers where the requirements are unduly burdensome.

Nevertheless, our cases instruct that "the limited nature of the rule cannot in itself justify a failure to follow notice and comment procedures." [Citations.] Were the opposite true, agencies could issue interim rules of limited effect for any plausible reason, irrespective of the degree of urgency. Should this be allowed, the good cause exception would soon swallow the notice and comment rule.

Therefore, we turn to the Commission's contention that the interim rule is needed to prevent the environmental damage that might result from a speedup in construction and replacement as pipeline companies seek to avoid the unknown burdens of a final rule. At bottom, this justification rests on the regulator's prediction of the regulateds' reaction to a proposed rulemaking. This justification entails a degree of speculation by the agency. We are hesitant to discount such forecasts, as they "necessarily involve deductions based on expert knowledge of the Agency." [Citation.] Nevertheless, at a minimum, an agency must indicate the basis for its prediction so that the reviewing court may be in a position to determine whether it acted reasonably. In all cases, a court must "satisfy itself that the agency explains the facts and policy concerns it relies on and that, given these, a reasonable person could have made the judgment the agency did." [Citation.]

Here, the Commission has provided little factual basis for its belief that pipelines will seek to avoid its future rule by rushing new construction and replacements with attendant damage to the environment. * * *

* * *

FERC's experience with this interim rule underscores the value of public participation in rule-making. As industry comments have made clear, a scrupulous compliance with the rule could have resulted in costly interruptions in pipeline replacement operations. The clarifications the Commission has had to issue in order to make the rule workable illustrate the wisdom of the APA's requirement that an agency have the benefit of informed comment before it issues regulations that have the force of law. The Commission has failed to demonstrate sufficient cause for setting aside these important safeguards.

## III. Conclusion

FERC has claimed good cause without offering any evidence, beyond its asserted expertise, as to why the public interest is served by the immediate implementation of the interim rule. Accordingly, the petition is granted and the interim rule vacated.

So ordered.

---

CASE 5–3
# Judicial Review: Standing
## *LUJAN v. DEFENDERS OF WILDLIFE*
Supreme Court of the United States, 1992
504 U.S. 555, 112 S.Ct. 2130, 119 L.Ed. 2d 351

SCALIA, J.
This case involves a challenge to a rule promulgated by the Secretary of the Interior interpreting § 7 of the Endangered Species Act of 1973 (ESA), [citation], in such fashion as to render it applicable only to actions within the United States or on the high seas. The prelimi-

nary issue, and the only one we reach, is whether the respondents here, plaintiffs below, have standing to seek judicial review of the rule.

\* \* \*

Over the years, our cases have established that the irreducible constitutional minimum of standing contains three elements: First, the plaintiff must have suffered an "injury in fact"—an invasion of a legally-protected interest which is (a) concrete and particularized, [citations] and (b) "actual or imminent, not 'conjectural' or 'hypothetical,'" [citations]. Second, there must be a causal connection between the injury and the conduct complained of—the injury has to be "fairly . . . trace-[able] to the challenged action of the defendant, and not . . . th[e] result [of] the independent action of some third party not before the court." [Citation.] Third, it must be "likely," as opposed to merely "speculative," that the injury will be "redressed by a favorable decision." [Citation.]

The party invoking federal jurisdiction bears the burden of establishing these elements. \* \* \* When the suit is one challenging the legality of government action or inaction, the nature and extent of facts that must be averred (at the summary judgment stage) or proved (at the trial stage) in order to establish standing depends considerably upon whether the plaintiff is himself an object of the action (or forgone action) at issue. If he is, there is ordinarily little question that the action or inaction has caused him injury, and that a judgment preventing or requiring the action will redress it. When, however, as in this case, a plaintiff's asserted injury arises from the government's allegedly unlawful regulation (or lack of regulation) of someone else, much more is needed. In that circumstance, causation and redressability ordinarily hinge on the response of the regulated (or regulable) third party to the government action or inaction—and perhaps on the response of others as well. The existence of one or more of the essential elements of standing "depends on the unfettered choices made by independent actors not before the courts and whose exercise of broad and legitimate discretion the courts cannot presume either to control or to predict," [citation] and it becomes the burden of the plaintiff to adduce facts showing that those choices have been or will be made in such manner as to produce causation and permit redressability of injury. [Citation.] Thus, when the plaintiff is not himself the object of the government action or inaction he challenges, standing is not precluded, but it is ordinarily "substantially more difficult" to establish. [Citation.]

We think the Court of Appeals failed to apply the foregoing principles in denying the Secretary's motion for summary judgment. Respondents had not made the requisite demonstration of (at least) injury and redressability.

Respondents' claim to injury is that the lack of consultation with respect to certain funded activities abroad "increas[es] the rate of extinction of endangered and threatened species." [Citation.] Of course, the desire to use or observe an animal species, even for purely aesthetic purposes, is undeniably a cognizable interest for purpose of standing. [Citation.] "But the 'injury in fact' test requires more than an injury to a cognizable interest. It requires that the party seeking review be himself among the injured." To survive the Secretary's summary judgment motion, respondents had to submit affidavits or other evidence showing, through specific facts, not only that listed species were in fact being threatened by funded activities abroad, but also that one or more of respondents' members would thereby be "directly" affected apart from their "'special interest' in th[e] subject." [Citations.]

With respect to this aspect of the case, the Court of Appeals focused on the affidavits of two Defenders' members—Joyce Kelly and Amy Skilbred. Ms. Kelly stated that she traveled to Egypt in 1986 and "observed the traditional habitat of the endangered Nile crocodile there and intend[s] to do so again, and hope[s] to observe the crocodile directly," and that she "will suffer harm in fact as a result of [the] American . . . role . . . in overseeing the rehabilitation of the Aswan High Dam on the Nile . . . and [in] develop [ing] . . . Egypt's . . . Master Water Plan." Ms. Skilbred averred that she traveled to Sri Lanka in 1981 and "observed th[e] habitat" of "endangered species such as the Asian elephant and the leopard" at what is now the site of the Mahaweli Project funded by the Agency for International Development (AID), although she "was unable to see any of the endangered species;" "this development project," she continued, "will seriously reduce endangered, threatened, and endemic species habitat including areas that I visited . . . [, which] may severely shorten the future of these species;" that threat, she concluded, harmed her because she "intend[s] to return to Sri Lanka in the future and hope[s] to be more fortunate in spotting at least the endangered elephant and leopard." [Citation.] When Ms. Skilbred was asked at a subsequent deposition if and when she had any plans to return to Sri Lanka, she reiterated that "I intend to go back to Sri Lanka," but confessed that she had no current plans: "I don't know [when]. There is a civil war going on right now. I don't know. Not next year, I will say. In the future." [Citation.]

We shall assume for the sake of argument that these affidavits contain facts showing that certain agency-funded projects threaten listed species—though that is questionable. They plainly contain no facts, however, showing how damage to the species will produce "imminent" injury to Mss. Kelly and Skilbred. That the women "had visited" the areas of the projects before the projects commenced proves nothing. As we have said in a related context, "'[p]ast exposure to illegal conduct does not in itself show a present case or controversy regarding injunctive relief . . . if unaccompanied by any continuing, present adverse effects.'" [Citation.] And the affiants' profession of an "inten[t]" to return to the places they had visited before—where they will presumably, this time, be deprived of the opportunity to observe animals of the endangered species—is simply not enough. Such "some day" intentions—without any description of concrete plans, or indeed even any specification of when the some day will be—do not support a finding of the "actual or imminent" injury that our cases require. [Citation.]

Besides relying upon the Kelly and Skilbred affidavits, respondents propose a series of novel standing theories. The first, inelegantly styled "ecosystem nexus," proposes that any person who uses any part of a "contiguous ecosystem" adversely affected by a funded activity has standing even if the activity is located a great distance away. This approach, as the Court of Appeals correctly observed, is inconsistent with our opinion in National Wildlife Federation, which held that a plaintiff claiming injury from environmental damage must use the area affected by the challenged activity and not an area roughly "in the vicinity" of it. [Citation.] It makes no difference that the general-purpose section of the ESA states that the Act was intended in part "to provide a means whereby the ecosystems upon which endangered species and threatened species depend may be conserved," [citation]. To say that the Act protects ecosystems is not to say that the Act creates (if it were possible) rights of action in persons who have not been injured in fact, that is, persons who use portions of an ecosystem not perceptibly affected by the unlawful action in question.

Respondents' other theories are called, alas, the "animal nexus" approach, whereby anyone who has an interest in studying or seeing the endangered animals anywhere on the globe has standing; and the "vocational nexus" approach, under which anyone with a professional interest in such animals can sue. Under these theories, anyone who goes to see Asian elephants in the Bronx Zoo, and anyone who is a keeper of Asian elephants in the Bronx Zoo, has standing to sue because the Director of AID did not consult with the Secretary regarding the AID-funded project in Sri Lanka. This is beyond all reason. Standing is not "an ingenious academic exercise in the conceivable," [citation], but as we have said requires, at the summary judgment stage, a factual showing of perceptible harm. It is clear that the person who observes or works with a particular animal threatened by a federal decision is facing perceptible harm, since the very subject of his interest will no longer exist. It is even plausible—though it goes to the outermost limit of plausibility—to think that a person who observes or works with animals of a particular species in the very area of the world where that species is threatened by a federal decision is facing such harm, since some animals that might have been the subject of his interest will no longer exist, [citation]. It goes beyond the limit, however, and into pure speculation and fantasy, to say that anyone who observes or works with an endangered species, anywhere in the world, is appreciably harmed by a single project affecting some portion of that species with which he has no more specific connection.

* * *

We hold that respondents lack standing to bring this action and that the Court of Appeals erred in denying the summary judgment motion filed by the United States. The opinion of the Court of Appeals is hereby reversed, and the cause remanded for proceedings consistent with this opinion.

It is so ordered.

---

 # Questions

1. List and explain the three basic functions of administrative agencies.
2. List and distinguish between the three types of rules promulgated by administrative agencies.
3. Explain the difference between formal and informal methods of adjudication.
4. Identify and explain (a) the questions of law determined by a court in conducting a review of a rule or order of an

administrative agency and (b) the three standards of judicial review of factual determinations made by administrative agencies.
5. Describe the limitations imposed on administrative agencies by the legislative branch, the executive branch, and the legally required disclosure of information.

# Problems

**1.** In 1942, Congress passed the Emergency Price Control Act in the interest of national defense and security. The stated purpose of the act was "to stabilize prices and to prevent speculative, unwarranted and abnormal increases in prices and rents. . . ." The act established the Office of Price Administration, which was authorized to establish maximum prices and rents that were to be "generally fair and equitable and [were to] effectuate the purposes of this Act." Convicted for selling beef at prices in excess of those set by the agency, Stark appeals on the ground that the act unconstitutionally delegated to the agency the legislative power of Congress to control prices. Decision?

**2.** The Secretary of Commerce (Secretary) published notice in the *Federal Register* inviting comments regarding flammability standards for mattresses. Statistical data were compiled, consultant studies were conducted, and 75 groups submitted comments. The Secretary then determined that all mattresses, including crib mattresses, must pass a cigarette test, consisting of bringing a mattress in contact with a burning cigarette. Bunny Bear, Inc. now challenges the cigarette flammability test, asserting that the standard was not shown to be applicable to crib mattresses, because "infants and young children obviously do not smoke." The Secretary, according to Bunny Bear, has not satisfied the burden of proof justifying the inclusion of crib mattresses within this general safety standard. Decision?

**3.** National Airport in Washington, D.C., is one of the busiest and most crowded airports in the nation. Accordingly, the Federal Aviation Administration (FAA) has restricted the number of commercial landing and takeoff slots at National to 40 per hour. Allocation of the slots among the air carriers serving National had been by voluntary agreement through an airline scheduling committee (ASC). When a new carrier, New York Air, requested 20 slots during peak hours, National's ASC was unable to agree on a slot allocation schedule. The FAA invited public comment as a means to solve the slot allocation dilemma. The FAA then issued Special Federal Aviation Regulation 43 (SFAR 43) based on public comments and a proposal made at the last National ASC meeting, thereby decreasing the number of slots held by current carriers and shifting some slots to less desirable times. SFAR 43 also granted 18 slots to New York Air. Northwest Airlines seeks judicial review of SFAR 43, claiming that it is arbitrary, capricious, and not a product of reasoned decision making, and that it capriciously favors the Washington–New York market as well as the carrier, New York Air. Decision?

**4.** Bachowski was defeated in a United Steelworkers of America union election. After exhausting his union remedies, Bachowski filed a complaint with Secretary of Labor Dunlop. Bachowski invoked the Labor-Management Reporting and Disclosure Act, which required Dunlop to investigate the complaint and determine whether to bring a court action to set aside

the election. Dunlop decided such action was unwarranted. Bachowski then filed an action in District Court to have Dunlop's decision declared arbitrary and capricious and to order Dunlop to file suit to set aside the election. The District Court dismissed the action, claiming a lack of authority to review Dunlop's discretionary decision. The Court of Appeals reversed and remanded, saying that Dunlop's decision, which was a final order by an administrative agency, was subject to judicial review under the Administrative Procedure Act. Dunlop maintains that judicial review is inappropriate in these circumstances and petitions to the U.S. Supreme Court. Decision?

**5.** The Federal Crop Insurance Corporation (FCIC) was created as a wholly government-owned corporation to insure wheat producers against unavoidable crop failure. As required by law, the FCIC published in the *Federal Register* conditions for crop insurance. Specifically, the FCIC published that spring wheat reseeded on winter wheat acreage was ineligible for coverage. When farmer Merrill applied for insurance on his wheat crop, he informed the local FCIC agent that 400 of his 460 acres of spring wheat were reseeded on the winter wheat acreage. The agent advised Merrill that his entire crop was insurable. When drought destroyed Merrill's wheat, Merrill tried to collect the insurance, but the FCIC refused to pay, asserting that Merrill is bound by the notice provided by publication of the regulation in the *Federal Register*. Decision?

**6.** David Fenster, president and part owner of Utica Packing Company, was convicted of bribing a meat inspector. After an administrative hearing filed by the U.S. Department of Agriculture (USDA), the administrative law judge ordered withdrawal of inspection services from Utica. Upon judicial review of this decision, the court ordered Davis, the judicial officer for the USDA, to consider several mitigating circumstances. For example, there had been improper conduct by the inspectors, virulent anti-Semitic remarks by an inspector (Fenster is a Jewish survivor of the Holocaust), Fenster's serious health problems, and the fact that, despite the bribe, the Utica plant was clean. Davis ruled to reinstate inspection services to Utica. The USDA moved for reconsideration and replaced judicial officer Davis with Franke, who, unlike Davis, had no judicial background, could be fired at will, and who was assigned a legal adviser who worked with the prosecutors in the case. Fenster claims this violates his Fifth Amendment due process rights. The USDA responds that separation of investigative, prosecutorial, and adjudicative functions is relaxed in an administrative setting. Decision?

**7.** The Department of Energy (DOE) issued a subpoena requesting information regarding purchases, sales, exchanges, and other transactions in crude oil from Phoenix Petroleum Company (Phoenix). The aim of the DOE audit was to uncover violations of the Emergency Petroleum Allocation Act of 1973 (EPAA), which provided for summary, or expedited, enforcement of DOE decisions. However, after the subpoena was issued, but before Phoenix had responded, the EPAA expired. Furthermore, during this time, the President of the United States had ordered deregulation of DOE price and allocation controls. Using the summary enforcement provisions of the now defunct EPAA, the DOE sues to enforce the subpoena. Phoenix argues that because the EPAA has expired, the DOE lacks the authority either to issue the subpoena or to use the summary enforcement provisions. Decision?

**8.** In May 1976, the Federal Communications Commission issued rules requiring cable television systems of a designated size (1) to develop a minimum 20-channel capacity by 1986, (2) to make available on a first-come, nondiscriminatory basis certain channels for access by third parties, and (3) to furnish equipment and facilities for such access. The purpose of these rules was to ensure public access to cable systems. Midwest Video Corporation claimed that the access rules exceeded the Commission's jurisdiction granted it by the Communications Act of 1934, because the rules infringe upon the cable systems' journalistic freedom by in effect treating the cable operators as "common carriers." A common carrier is one that "makes a public offering to provide [communication facilities] whereby all members of the public who choose to employ such facilities may communicate or transmit. . . ." The Commission contended that its expansive mandate under the Communications Act to supervise and regulate broadcasting encompassed the access rules because they were intended to promote these broad objectives. Decision?

WWW **Internet Exercise** Find and explore several Federal administrative agencies to learn about their (a) organization, (b) purpose, and (c) operations.

# CHAPTER 6

# Criminal Law

As discussed in Chapter 1, the civil law defines duties the violation of which constitutes a wrong against the injured party. The criminal law, on the other hand, establishes duties the violation of which is a societal wrong against the whole community. Civil law is a part of private law, whereas criminal law is a part of public law. In a civil action, the injured party sues to recover compensation for the damage and injury that he has sustained as a result of the defendant's wrongful conduct. The party bringing a civil action (the plaintiff) has the burden of proof, which he must sustain by a preponderance (greater weight) of the evidence. The purpose of the civil law is to compensate the injured party.

Criminal law, by comparison, is designed to prevent harm to society by defining criminal conduct and establishing punishment for such conduct. In a criminal case, the defendant is prosecuted by the government, which must prove the defendant's guilt beyond a reasonable doubt, a burden of proof significantly higher than that required in a civil action. Moreover, under our legal system, guilt is never presumed. Indeed, the law presumes the innocence of the accused, and the defendant's failure to testify in her own defense does not affect this presumption. The government still has the burden of affirmatively proving the guilt of the accused beyond a reasonable doubt.

Of course, the same conduct may, and often does, constitute both a crime and a tort, which is a civil wrong. (Torts are discussed in Chapters 7 and 8.) But an act may be criminal without being tortious; by the same token, an act may be a tort but not a crime.

Because of the increasing use of criminal sanctions to enforce governmental regulation of business, criminal law is an essential part of business law. Moreover, businesses sustain considerable loss as victims of criminal actions. Accordingly, this chapter covers the general principles of criminal law and criminal procedure as well as specific crimes relevant to business.

## NATURE OF CRIMES

A **crime** is any act or omission forbidden by public law in the interest of protecting society and made punishable by the government in a judicial proceeding brought by it. Punishment for criminal conduct includes fines, imprisonment, probation, and death. In addition, some States and the Federal government have enacted victim indemnification statutes which establish funds, financed by criminal fines, to provide indemnification in limited amounts to victims of criminal activity. Crimes are prohibited and punished on grounds of public policy, which may include the protection and safeguarding of government (as in treason), human life (as in murder), or private property (as in larceny). Additional purposes of the criminal law include deterrence, rehabilitation, and retribution.

Historically, criminal law was primarily common law. Today, however, criminal law is almost exclusively statutory. All States have enacted comprehensive criminal law statutes (or codes) covering most, if not all, common law crimes. Moreover, these statutes have made the number of crimes defined in criminal law far greater than the number of crimes defined under common law. Some codes expressly limit crimes to those included in the codes, thus abolishing common law crimes. Nonetheless, some States do not statutorily define all of their crimes; their courts, therefore, must rely on the common law definitions. Because there are no Federal common law crimes, all Federal crimes are statutory.

Within recent times the scope of criminal law has increased greatly. The scope of traditional criminal conduct has been expanded by numerous regulations and laws which contain criminal penalties pertaining to nearly every phase of modern living. Typical examples in the field of business law are those laws concerning the licensing and conduct of a business, antitrust laws, and the laws governing the sales of securities.

## Essential Elements

In general, a crime consists of two elements: (1) the wrongful or overt act (***actus reus***) and (2) the criminal intent (***mens rea***). For example, to support a larceny conviction it is not enough to show that the defendant stole another's goods; it must also be established that he intended to steal the goods. Conversely, criminal intent without an overt act is not a crime. For instance, Ann decides to rob the neighborhood grocery store and then really "live it up." Without more, Ann has committed no crime.

*Actus reus* refers to all the nonmental elements of a crime, including the physical act that must be performed, the consequences of that act, and the circumstances under which it must be performed. The *actus reus* required for specific crimes will be discussed later in this chapter.

*Mens rea,* or mental fault, refers to the mental element of a crime. Most common law and some statutory crimes require subjective fault, other crimes require objective fault, while some statutory crimes require no fault at all. The American Law Institute's Model Penal Code and most modern criminal statutes recognize three possible types of **subjective fault:** purposeful, knowing, and reckless. A person acts *purposely* or *intentionally* if his conscious object is to engage in the prohibited conduct or to cause the prohibited result. Thus, if Arthur, with the desire to kill Donna, shoots his rifle at Donna, who is seemingly out of gunshot range, and in fact does kill her, Arthur had the purpose or intent to kill Donna. If Benjamin, desiring to poison Paula, places a toxic chemical in the water cooler in Paula's office and unwittingly poisons Gail and Victor, Benjamin will be found to have purposefully killed Gail and Victor because Benjamin's intent to kill Paula is transferred to Gail and Victor, regardless of Benjamin's feelings toward Gail and Victor.

A person acts *knowingly* if he is aware that his conduct is of a prohibited type or that a prohibited consequence is practically certain to result. A person acts *recklessly* if he consciously disregards a substantial and unjustifiable risk (1) that his conduct is prohibited or (2) that it will cause a prohibited result.

**Objective fault** involves a gross deviation from the standard of care that a reasonable person would observe under the circumstances. Criminal statutes refer to objective fault by such terms as *carelessness* or *negligence*. Such conduct occurs when a person *should* be aware of a substantial and unjustifiable risk that his conduct is prohibited or will cause a prohibited result. Examples of crimes requiring objective fault are involuntary manslaughter (negligently causing the death of another), carelessly driving an automobile, and, in some States, issuing a bad check.

Many regulatory statutes have totally dispensed with the mental element of a crime by imposing criminal liability without fault. Without regard to the care that a person exercises, criminal **liability without fault** makes it a crime for a person to commit a specified act or to bring about a certain result. Statutory crimes imposing liability without fault include the sale of adulterated food and the sale of alcoholic beverages to a minor. Most of these crimes involve regulatory statutes dealing with health and safety and impose only fines for violations.

◆ *See Figure 6–1*

⚖ *See Case 6–1*

## Classification

Historically, crimes were classified *mala in se* (wrongs in themselves or morally wrong, such as murder) or *mala prohibita* (not morally wrong but declared wrongful by

**FIGURE 6–1** Degrees of Mental Fault

| Type | Fault Required | Examples |
| --- | --- | --- |
| **Subjective Fault** | Purposeful<br>Knowing<br>Reckless | Larceny<br>Embezzlement |
| **Objective Fault** | Negligent<br>Careless | Careless driving<br>Issuing bad checks (some States) |
| **Liability Without Fault** | None | Sale of alcohol to a minor<br>Sale of adulterated food |

law, such as the prohibition against making a U-turn). From the standpoint of the seriousness of the offense, a crime is also classified as a **felony** (any crime punishable by death or imprisonment in the penitentiary) or as a **misdemeanor** (any crime punishable by a fine or imprisonment in a local jail).

## Vicarious Liability

Vicarious liability is liability imposed upon one person for the acts of another. Employers are vicariously liable for any authorized criminal act of their employees if the employer directed, participated in, or approved of the act. For example, if an employer directs an employee to fix prices with the employer's competitors, and the employee does so, both the employer and employee have criminally violated the Sherman Antitrust Act. On the other hand, employers are ordinarily not liable for the unauthorized criminal acts of their employees. As previously discussed, most crimes require mental fault; this element is absent, so far as criminal responsibility of the employer is concerned, where the employee's criminal act was not authorized.

Employers nonetheless may be subject to a criminal penalty for the unauthorized act of a manager acting in the scope of employment. Moreover, employers may be criminally liable under liability without fault statutes for certain unauthorized acts of their employees, whether those employees are managerial or not. For example, many States have statutes that punish "every person who by himself or his employee or agent sells anything at short weight," or "whoever sells liquor to a minor and any sale by an employee shall be deemed the act of the employer as well."

## Liability of the Corporation

Historically, corporations were not held criminally liable because, under the traditional view, a corporation could not possess the requisite criminal intent and, therefore, was incapable of committing a crime. The dramatic growth in size and importance of corporations changed this view. Under the modern approach, a corporation may be liable for violation of statutes imposing liability without fault. In addition, a corporation may be liable where the offense is perpetrated by a high corporate officer or the board of directors. The Model Penal Code provides that a corporation may be convicted of a criminal offense for the conduct of its employees if

1. the legislative purpose of the statute defining the offense is to impose liability on corporations and the conduct is within the scope of the [employee's] office or employment;
2. the offense consists of an omission to discharge a specific, affirmative duty imposed upon corporations by law; or
3. the offense was authorized, requested, commanded, performed, or recklessly tolerated by the board of directors or by a high managerial agent of the corporation.

Punishment of a corporation for crimes is necessarily by fine, not imprisonment. Nonetheless, individuals bearing responsibility for the criminal act face fines, imprisonment, or both. The Model Penal Code provides that the corporate agent having primary responsibility for the discharge of the duty imposed by law on the corporation is as accountable for a reckless omission to perform the required act as though the duty were imposed by law directly upon him.

On November 1, 1991, the Federal Organizational Corporate Sentencing Guidelines took effect. The overall purpose of the guidelines is to impose sanctions that will provide just punishment and adequate deterrence. To that end, the guidelines mandate corporations to formulate and implement compliance programs reasonably designed to prevent potential legal violations by the corporation and its employees.

The guidelines provide for a base fine for each criminal offense, calculated by one of the following: (a) the amount listed in the guidelines' offense-level fine table (fines range from $5,000 to $72.5 million), (b) the pecuniary gain to the organization, or (c) the pecuniary loss as a result of the offense, to the extent that the loss was intentionally, knowingly, or recklessly caused. In addition, restitution is available to victims whenever possible. In the most extreme case, a corporation's charter can be revoked. If a corporation successfully adopts and implements an adequate compliance program, the corporate fine can be reduced to as little as 5 percent of the scheduled fine. On the other hand, if a company does not have a proper program in place, the fine can be multiplied by up to four times.

An adequate compliance program should include the following:

1. a written code of conduct,
2. assignment of a senior corporate official to be responsible for the overall compliance program,
3. effective communication of the program to all employees and agents,

4. ongoing monitoring of the program,
5. proper delegation of program-related authority within the organization,
6. disciplinary measures appropriate to enforce the program, and
7. periodic reviews of the program.

## WHITE-COLLAR CRIME

White-collar crime has been defined in various ways. The Justice Department defines it as nonviolent crime involving deceit, corruption, or breach of trust. It also has been defined to include crimes committed by individuals—such as embezzlement and forgery—as well as crimes committed on behalf of a corporation—such as commercial bribery, product safety and health crimes, false advertising, and antitrust violations. A less precise definition is crime "committed by a person of respectability and high social status in the course of his occupation," while a more narrow definition identifies white-collar crime as fraud or deceit practiced through misrepresentation to gain an unfair advantage. Regardless of its definition, such crime costs society billions of dollars; estimates range from $40 billion to more than $200 billion per year. Historically, prosecution of white-collar crime was de-emphasized because such crime was not considered violent. Now, however, many contend that white-collar crime often inflicts violence but does so impersonally. For example, unsafe products cause injury and death to consumers while unsafe working conditions cause injury and death to employees. Indeed, many contend that white-collar criminals should receive stiff prison sentences due to the magnitude of their crimes.

### Computer Crime

One special type of white-collar crime is **computer crime,** which involves the use of a computer to steal money or services, to remove personal or business information, and to tamper with information. Computer crimes can be broken down into five general categories: (1) theft of computer hardware, software, or secrets; (2) unauthorized use of computer services; (3) theft of money by computer; (4) vandalism of computer hardware or software; and (5) theft of computer data.

Detecting crimes involving computers is extremely difficult. In addition, many businesses, loath to imply that their security is lax, often do not report computer crimes. Nonetheless, losses due to computer crimes are estimated to be in the tens of billions of dollars. Moreover, given society's ever-increasing dependence upon computers, this type of crime will in all likelihood continue to increase.

Computer crimes already have become commonplace. Examples abound: software piracy (the unauthorized copying of copyrighted software) is now so widespread that an estimated two out of every three copies of software are illegally obtained. A computer consultant hired by Security Pacific Bank wrongfully transferred $10 million from the bank to his own Swiss bank account. Six employees stole TRW's credit-rating data and offered to repair poor credit ratings for a fee. Disgruntled or discharged employees have used computer programs to destroy company software.

As a consequence, enterprises are spending large sums of money to increase computer security. In addition, nearly all 50 States have enacted computer crime laws, though the Federal government, despite numerous attempts, has yet to pass comprehensive legislation prohibiting computer crime. The absence of such legislation has been defended on three grounds: (1) computer crime is not unique and can be addressed under existing criminal law statutes, (2) State legislation can deal with the problem, and (3) writing effective legislation is difficult. Congress has, however, enacted specific legislation (the Counterfeit Access Device and Computer Fraud and Abuse Act) making it a Federal crime to (a) gain unauthorized access to a computer used by the government, by a financial institution, or in interstate or foreign commerce or communication; (b) cause damage, without authorization, to a computer; (c) traffic in the interstate distribution of computer passwords with the intent to defraud; or (d) extort money or other items of value by means of threats to cause damage to a computer.

### Racketeer Influenced and Corrupt Organizations Act (RICO)

The Racketeer Influenced and Corrupt Organizations Act (RICO) was enacted in 1970 with the stated purpose of terminating the infiltration of organized crime into legitimate business. The act subjects to severe civil and criminal penalties enterprises that engage in a pattern of racketeering, defined as the commission of two or more predicate acts within a period of ten years. A "predicate act" is any of several criminal offenses listed in RICO. Included are nine major categories of State crimes and and more than thirty Federal crimes, such as murder, kidnapping, arson, extortion, drug dealing, securities fraud, mail fraud, and bribery. The most controversial issue concerning RICO is its application to businesses that are not engaged in organized crime but that do meet the "pattern of racketeering" test under the Act. Criminal conviction under the law may result in a prison term of up to 20 years plus a fine of up to $25,000 per violation. In addition, businesses will forfeit any property obtained due to a RICO violation, and individuals harmed by RICO violations may invoke the statute's civil remedies, which include treble damages and attorneys' fees.

Other areas of Federal law that impose both civil and criminal penalties include bankruptcy (Chapter 39), antitrust (Chapter 41), securities regulation (Chapter 44), and environmental regulation (Chapter 46).

# CRIMES AGAINST BUSINESS

Criminal offenses against property greatly affect businesses, amounting to losses in the hundreds of billions of dollars each year. This section covers the following crimes against property: (1) larceny, (2) embezzlement, (3) false pretenses, (4) robbery, (5) burglary, (6) extortion and bribery, (7) forgery, and (8) bad checks.

## Larceny

The crime of **larceny** is the (1) trespassory (2) taking and (3) carrying away of (4) personal property (5) of another (6) with the intent to deprive the victim permanently of the goods. All six elements must be present for the crime to exist. Thus, if Barbara pays Larry $5,000 for an automobile that Larry agrees to deliver the following week, and Larry does not do so, Larry is *not* guilty of larceny because he has not trespassed on Barbara's property. Larry has not taken anything from Barbara; he has simply refused to turn the automobile over to her. Larceny applies only when a person takes personal property from another without the other's consent. Here, Barbara voluntarily paid the money to Larry, who has not committed larceny but who may have obtained the $5,000 by false pretenses (which is discussed later). Likewise, if Carol takes Dan's 1968 automobile without Dan's permission, intending to use it for a joyride and to then return it to Dan, Carol has not committed larceny because she did not intend to deprive Dan permanently of the automobile. (Nevertheless, Carol has committed the crime of unauthorized use of an automobile.) On the other hand, if Carol left Dan's 1968 car in a junkyard after the joyride, she most likely would be held to have committed a larceny because of the high risk that her action would permanently deprive Dan of the car. See

*People v. Olivo* for a discussion of whether a person may be convicted of larceny for shoplifting if he is arrested before leaving the store.

 *See Case 6–2*

## Embezzlement

**Embezzlement** is the fraudulent conversion of another's property by one who was in lawful possession of it. A **conversion** is any act that seriously interferes with the owner's rights in the property, such as exhausting the resources of the property, selling it, giving it away, or refusing to return it to its rightful owner. This statutory crime was first enacted in response to a 1799 English case in which a bank employee was found not guilty of larceny for taking money given to him for deposit in the bank because the money had been voluntarily handed to him. Thus, embezzlement is a crime intended to prevent individuals who are lawfully in possession of another's property from taking such property for their own use.

The key distinction between larceny and embezzlement, therefore, is whether the thief is in lawful possession of the property. While both crimes involve the misuse of another's property, in larceny the thief unlawfully possesses the property, whereas in embezzlement the thief possesses it lawfully. A second distinction between larceny and embezzlement is that, unlike larceny, embezzlement does not require the intent to deprive the owner permanently of his property. Nonetheless, to constitute an embezzlement, an act must interfere significantly with the owner's rights to the property.

## False Pretenses

Obtaining property by **false pretenses,** like embezzlement, is a crime addressed by statutes enacted to close a loophole in the requirements for larceny. False pretenses is the crime of obtaining title to property of another by making materially false representations of an existing fact, with knowledge of their falsity and with the intent to defraud. Larceny does not cover this situation because here the victim voluntarily transfers the property to the thief. For example, a con artist who goes door to door and collects money by saying he is selling stereo equipment, when he is not, is committing the crime of false pretenses. The test of deception is *subjective:* if the victim is actually deceived, the test is satisfied even though a reasonable person would not have been deceived by the defendant's lies. Therefore, the victim's gullibility or lack of due care is no defense.

Many courts hold that a false statement of intention, such as a promise, does not constitute false pretenses. In addition, a false expression of opinion regarding value is usually not considered a misrepresentation of fact and thus will not suffice for false pretenses.

Other specialized crimes that are similar to false pretenses include mail, wire, and bank fraud as well as securities fraud. **Mail fraud,** unlike the crime of false pretenses, does not require the victim to be actually defrauded; it simply requires the defendant to use the mails (or private carrier) to carry out a scheme that attempts to defraud others. Due to its breadth and ease of use, mail fraud has been employed extensively by Federal prosecutors. The **wire fraud** statute prohibits the transmittal by wire, radio, or television in interstate or foreign commerce of any information with the intent to defraud. The Federal statute prohibiting **bank fraud** makes it a crime knowingly to execute or attempt to execute a scheme to defraud a financial institution or to obtain by false pretenses funds under the control or custody of a financial institution. Securities fraud is discussed in Chapter 44.

## Robbery

Under the common law as well as most statutes, **robbery** is a larceny with the additional elements that (1) the property is taken directly from the victim or in the immediate presence of the victim and (2) the act is accomplished through either force or the threat of force which need not be against the person from whom the property is taken. For example, a robber threatens Sam, saying that unless Sam opens his employer's safe, the robber will shoot Maria. Moreover, the victim's presence may be actual or constructive. *Constructive presence* means that the defendant's actual or threatened force prevents the victim from being present. For example, if the robber knocks the victim unconscious or ties her up, the victim is considered constructively present.

Many laws distinguish between simple robbery and aggravated robbery. Robbery can be aggravated by any of several factors, including (1) the use of a deadly weapon; (2) the robber's intent to kill or to kill if faced with resistance; (3) serious bodily injury to the victim; *or* (4) commission of the crime by two or more persons.

## Burglary

At common law, **burglary** was defined as breaking and entering the dwelling of another at night with the intent to commit a felony. Many modern statutes differ from the common law definition by requiring merely that there be (1) an entry (2) into a building (3) with the intent to commit a felony in the building. Thus, these statutory definitions omit three elements of the common law crime: the building need not be a dwelling house, the entry need not be at night, and the entry need not be a technical breaking. Nonetheless, so greatly do the modern statutes vary (except for the idea that each contains some, but not all, of the common law elements) that generalization is nearly impossible.

## Extortion and Bribery

Although frequently confused, extortion and bribery are two distinct crimes. **Extortion,** or blackmail as it is sometimes called, is generally held to be the making of threats for the purpose of obtaining money or property. For example, Lindsey tells Jason that unless he pays her $10,000, she will tell Jason's customers that he was once arrested for disturbing the peace. Lindsey has committed the crime of extortion. In a few jurisdictions, however, the crime of extortion occurs only if the defendant actually causes the victim to give up money or property.

**Bribery,** on the other hand, is the act of offering money or property to a public official to influence the official's decision. The crime of bribery is committed when the illegal offer is made, whether accepted or not. Thus, if Andrea offered Edward, the mayor of New Town, a 20-percent interest in Andrea's planned real estate development if Edward would use his influence to have the development proposal approved, Andrea would be guilty of criminal bribery. In contrast, if Edward had threatened Andrea that unless he received a 20-percent interest in Andrea's development he would use his influence to prevent the approval of the development, Edward would be guilty of criminal extortion. Bribery of foreign officials is covered by the Foreign Corrupt Practices Act, discussed in Chapter 44.

Some jurisdictions have gone beyond traditional bribery law by adopting statutes that make commercial bribery illegal. **Commercial bribery** is the use of bribery to acquire new business, obtain secret information or processes, or receive kickbacks.

## Forgery

**Forgery** is the intentional falsification or false making of a document with the intent to defraud. Accordingly, if William prepares a false certificate of title to a stolen automobile, he is guilty of forgery. Likewise, if an individual alters some receipts to increase her income tax deductions, she has committed the crime of forgery. The most common type of forgery is the signing of another's name to a financial document.

## Bad Checks

A statutory crime that has some relation to both forgery and false pretenses is the passing of **bad checks**—that is, writing a check on an account containing funds insufficient to cover the check. All jurisdictions have now enacted laws making it a crime to issue bad checks; however, these statutes vary greatly from jurisdiction to jurisdiction. Most jurisdictions simply require that the check be issued; they do not require that the issuer receive anything in return for the check. Also, although most jurisdictions require that the defendant issue a check with knowledge that she does not have enough money to cover the check, the Model Penal Code and a number of States provide that knowledge is presumed if the issuer had no account at the bank or if the check was not paid for lack of funds and the issuer failed to pay the check within ten days.

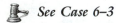 *See Case 6-3*

# DEFENSES TO CRIMES

Even though a defendant is found to have committed a criminal act, he will not be convicted if he has a valid defense. The defenses most relevant to white-collar crimes and crimes against business include defense of property, duress, mistake of fact, and entrapment. In some instances, a defense proves the absence of a required element of the crime; other defenses provide a justification or excuse that bars criminal liability.

## Defense of Person or Property

Individuals may use reasonable force to protect their property. This defense enables a person to commit, without any criminal liability, what the law would otherwise consider the crime of assault, battery, manslaughter, or murder. Under the majority rule, deadly force is *never* reasonable to safeguard property, because life is deemed more important than the protection of property. For this reason, individuals cannot use a deadly mechanical device, such as a spring gun, to protect their property. If, however, the defender's use of reasonable force in protecting his property is met with an attack upon his person, then he may use deadly force if the attack threatens him with death or serious bodily harm.

## Duress

A person who is threatened with immediate, serious bodily harm to himself or another unless he engages in criminal activity has the valid defense of **duress** (sometimes referred to as compulsion or coercion) to criminal conduct other than murder. For example, Ann threatens to kill Ben if he does not assist her in committing larceny. Ben complies. Because of duress, he would not be guilty of the larceny.

## Mistake of Fact

If a person reasonably believes the facts surrounding his conduct to be such that his conduct would not constitute a crime, then the law will treat the facts as he reasonably believes them to be. Accordingly, an honest and reasonable **mistake of fact** will justify the defendant's conduct. For example, if Ann gets into a car that she reasonably believes to be hers—the car is the same color, model, and year as hers, is parked in the same parking lot, and is started by her key—she will be relieved of criminal responsibility for taking Ben's automobile.

## Entrapment

The defense of **entrapment** arises when a law enforcement official induces a person to commit a crime when that person would not have done so without the persuasion of the police official. The rationale behind the rule which applies only to government officials and agents, not to private individuals, is to prevent law enforcement officials from provoking crime and from engaging in reprehensible conduct.

# CRIMINAL PROCEDURE

Each of the States and the Federal government have procedures for initiating and coordinating criminal prosecutions. In addition, the first ten amendments to the U.S. Constitution, called the Bill of Rights, guarantee many defenses and rights of an accused. The Fourth Amendment prohibits unreasonable searches and seizures to obtain incriminating evidence. The Fifth Amendment requires indictment for capital crimes by a grand jury, prevents double jeopardy and self-incrimination, and prohibits deprivation of life or liberty without due process of law. The Sixth Amendment requires that an accused receive a speedy and public trial by an impartial jury and that he be informed of the nature of the accusation, be confronted with the witnesses who testify against him, be given the power to obtain witnesses in his favor, and have the right to competent counsel for his defense. The Eighth Amendment prohibits excessive bail, excessive fines, and cruel or unusual punishment.

Most State constitutions have similar provisions to protect the rights of accused persons. In addition, the Fourteenth Amendment prohibits State governments from depriving any person of life, liberty, or property without due process of law. Moreover, the U.S. Supreme Court has held that most of the Constitutional protections just discussed apply to the States through the operation of the Fourteenth Amendment.

Although the details of criminal process differ in various jurisdictions, the process retains several common objectives. In every jurisdiction, the primary purpose of the process is to enforce the criminal law, but this purpose must be accomplished within the limitations imposed by other goals. These goals include advancing an adversary system of adjudication, requiring the government to bear the burden of proof, minimizing erroneous convictions, minimizing the burdens of defense, respecting individual dignity, maintaining the appearance of fairness, and achieving equality in the administration of the process.

We will first discuss the steps in a criminal prosecution; we will then focus on the major Constitutional protections for the accused in our system of criminal justice.

◆ *See Figure 6–2*

## Steps in Criminal Prosecution

Although the particulars of criminal procedure vary from State to State, the following provides a basic overview.

After arrest, the accused is booked and appears (first appearance) before a magistrate, commissioner, or justice of the peace, where formal notice of the charges is given, the accused is advised of his rights, and bail is set. Next, a **preliminary hearing** is held to determine whether there is probable cause to believe the defendant is the one who committed the crime. The defendant is entitled to be represented by counsel.

If the magistrate concludes that probable cause exists, she will bind the case over to the next stage, which is either an indictment or information, depending upon the jurisdiction. The Federal system and some States require indictments for all felony prosecutions (unless waived by the defendant), while the other States permit but do not mandate indictments. A grand jury, which is not bound by the magistrate's decision at the preliminary hearing, issues an **indictment,** or true bill, if it finds sufficient evidence to justify a trial on the charge brought. Unlike the preliminary hearing, the grand jury does not hear evidence from the defendant, nor does the defendant appear before the grand jury. A grand jury traditionally consisted of not less than sixteen and not more than twenty-three people. Today, many States use a smaller grand jury, not infrequently composed of twelve members. An **information,** by comparison, is a formal accusation of a crime brought by a prosecuting officer, not a grand jury. Such a procedure is used in misdemeanor cases and in some felony cases in those States that do not require indictments. The indictment or information at times precedes the actual arrest.

At the **arraignment,** the defendant is brought before the trial court, where he is informed of the charge against

FIGURE 6–2 Constitutional Protection for the Criminal Defendant

| Amendment | Protection Conferred |
|---|---|
| Fourth | Freedom from unreasonable search and seizure |
| Fifth | Due process<br>Right to indictment by grand jury for capital crimes*<br>Freedom from double jeopardy<br>Freedom from self-incrimination |
| Sixth | Right to speedy, public trial by jury<br>Right to be informed of accusations<br>Right to confront witnesses<br>Right to present witnesses<br>Right to competent counsel |
| Eighth | Freedom from excessive bail<br>Freedom from cruel and unusual punishment |

*This right has *not* been applied to the States through the Fourteenth Amendment.

him and where he enters his plea. The arraignment must be held promptly after the indictment or information has been filed. If his plea is "not guilty," the defendant must stand trial. He is entitled to a jury trial for all felonies and for misdemeanors punishable by more than six months imprisonment. Most States also permit a defendant to request a jury trial for lesser misdemeanors. If the defendant chooses, however, he may have his guilt or innocence determined by the court sitting without a jury, which is called a "bench trial."

A criminal trial is somewhat similar to a civil trial, but with some significant differences: (1) the defendant is presumed innocent, (2) the burden of proof on the prosecution is to prove criminal guilt beyond a reasonable doubt, and (3) the defendant is not required to testify. The trial begins with the selection of the jury and the opening statements by the prosecutor and the attorney for the defense. The prosecution presents evidence first; then the defendant presents his. At the conclusion of the testimony, closing statements are made, and the jury, instructed as to the applicable law, retires to arrive at a verdict. If the verdict is "not guilty," the case is over. The State has no right to appeal from an acquittal; and the accused, having been placed in "jeopardy," cannot be tried a second time for the same offense. If the verdict is "guilty," the judge will enter a judgment of conviction and set the case for sentencing. The defendant may make a motion for a new trial, asserting that prejudicial error occurred at his original trial, necessitating a retrial of the case. He may also appeal to a reviewing court, alleging error by the trial court and asking for either his discharge or a remandment of the case for a new trial.

## Fourth Amendment

The Fourth Amendment, which protects all individuals against unreasonable searches and seizures, is designed to safeguard the privacy and security of individuals against arbitrary invasions by government officials. Although the Fourth Amendment by its terms applies only to acts of the Federal government, the Fourteenth Amendment makes it applicable to State government action as well.

When evidence has been obtained in violation of the Fourth Amendment, the general rule prohibits the introduction of the illegally seized evidence at trial. The purpose of this **exclusionary rule** is to discourage illegal police conduct and to protect individual liberty, not to hinder the search for the truth. In *Weeks v. United States*, 232 U.S. 383 (1914), the United States Supreme Court ruled,

If letters and private documents can thus be seized and held and used in evidence against a citizen accused of an offense, the protection of the Fourth Amendment declaring his right to be secure against such searches and seizures is of no value, and, so far as those thus placed and concerned, might as well be stricken from the Constitution. The efforts of the courts and their officials to bring the guilty to punishment, praiseworthy as they are, are not to be aided by the sacrifice of those great principles established by years of endeavor and suffering which have resulted in their embodiment in the fundamental law of the land.

Nonetheless, in recent years the U.S. Supreme Court has limited the exclusionary rule.

To obtain a warrant to search a particular person, place, or thing, a law enforcement official must demonstrate to a magistrate that he has probable cause to believe that the search will reveal evidence of criminal activity. **Probable cause** means "[t]he task of the issuing magistrate is simply to make a practical, common-sense decision whether, given all the circumstances set forth . . . before him, . . ., there is a fair probability that contraband or evidence of a crime will be found in a particular place." *Illinois v. Gates*, 462 U.S. 213 (1983).

Even though the Fourth Amendment requires that a search and seizure generally be made after a valid search warrant has been obtained, in some instances a search warrant is not necessary. For example, it has been held that a warrant is not necessary where (1) there is hot pursuit of a fugitive, (2) the subject voluntarily consents to the search, (3) an emergency requires such action, (4) there has been a lawful arrest, (5) evidence of a crime is in plain view of the law enforcement officer, or (6) delay would significantly obstruct the investigation.

## Fifth Amendment

The Fifth Amendment protects persons against self-incrimination, double jeopardy, and being charged with a capital or infamous crime except by grand jury indictment.

The prohibitions against self-incrimination and double jeopardy also apply to the States through the Due Process Clause of the Fourteenth Amendment; the grand jury clause, however, does not.

The privilege against self-incrimination extends only to testimonial evidence, not to physical evidence. The Fifth Amendment "privilege protects an accused only from being compelled to testify against himself, or otherwise provide the State with evidence of a testimonial or communicative nature." *Schmerber v. California*, 384 U.S. 757 (1966). Therefore, a person can be forced to stand in a lineup for identification purposes, provide a handwriting sample, or take a blood test. Most significantly, the Fifth Amendment does not protect the records of a business entity such as a corporation or partnership; it applies only to papers of individuals. Moreover, the Fifth Amendment does not prohibit examination of an individual's business records as long as the individual is not compelled to testify against himself.

The Fifth Amendment and the Fourteenth Amendment also guarantee due process of law, which is basically the requirement of a fair trial. Every person is entitled to have the charges or complaints against him made publicly and in writing, whether in civil or criminal proceedings, and to receive the opportunity to defend himself against those charges. In criminal prosecutions, due process includes the right to counsel; to confront and cross-examine adverse witnesses; to testify in one's own behalf, if desired; to produce witnesses and offer other evidence; and to be free from any and all prejudicial conduct and statements.

## Sixth Amendment

The Sixth Amendment specifies that the Federal government shall provide the accused with a speedy and public trial by an impartial jury, inform her of the nature and cause of the accusation, confront her with the witnesses against her, have compulsory process for obtaining witnesses in her favor, and allow her to obtain the assistance of counsel for her defense. The Fourteenth Amendment extends these guarantees to the States.

The Supreme Court has explained the purpose of guaranteeing the right to a trial by jury as follows: "[T]he purpose of trial by jury is to prevent oppression by the Government by providing a safeguard against the corrupt or overzealous prosecutor and against the compliant, biased, or eccentric judge. . . . [T]he essential factors of a jury trial obviously lie in the interposition between the accused and his accuser of the common sense judgment of a group of laymen." *Apodaca v. Oregon*, 406 U.S. 404 (1972). Nevertheless, a defendant may forgo her right to a jury trial.

Historically, juries consisted of twelve jurors, but the Federal courts and the courts of certain States have since reduced the number to six. Noting no observable difference between the results reached by a jury of twelve and those reached by a jury of six, nor any evidence to suggest that a jury of twelve is more advantageous to a defendant, the Supreme Court has held that the use of a six-member jury in a criminal case does not violate a defendant's right to a jury trial under the Sixth Amendment. The jury need only be large enough "to promote group deliberation, free from outside attempts at intimidation, and to provide a fair possibility for obtaining a representative cross section of the community." Moreover, State court jury verdicts need not be unanimous, provided the vote is sufficient to ensure adequate deliberations. Thus, the Supreme Court has upheld jury votes of 11–1, 10–2, and 9–3 but rejected as insufficient a 5–1 vote.

 # Chapter Summary

| **Nature of Crimes** | **Definition** any act or omission forbidden by public law<br>**Essential Elements**<br>• *Actus Reus* wrongful or overt act<br>• *Mens Rea* criminal intent or mental fault<br>**Classification**<br>• *Felony* a serious crime<br>• *Misdemeanor* a less serious crime<br>**Vicarious Liability** liability imposed for acts of employees if the employer directed, participated in, or approved of the acts<br>**Liability of a Corporation** under certain circumstances a corporation may be convicted of crimes and punished by fines |
| --- | --- |

## White-Collar Crime

**Definition**  nonviolent crime involving deceit, corruption, or breach of trust
**Computer Crime**  use of a computer to commit a crime
**Racketeer Influenced and Corrupt Organizations Act (RICO)**  federal law intended to stop organized crime from infiltrating legitimate businesses

## Crimes Against Business

**Larceny**  trespassory taking and carrying away of personal property of another with the intent to deprive the victim permanently of the property
**Embezzlement**  taking of another's property by a person who was in lawful possession of the property
**False Pretenses**  obtaining title to property of another by means of representation one knows to be materially false; made with intent to defraud
**Robbery**  committing larceny with the use or threat of force
**Burglary**  under most modern statutes, an entry into a building with the intent to commit a felony
**Extortion**  making threats to obtain money or property
**Bribery**  offering money or property to a public official to influence the official's decision
**Forgery**  intentional falsification of a document to defraud
**Bad Checks**  knowingly issuing a check without funds sufficient to cover the check

## Defenses to Crimes

**Defense of Person or Property**  individuals may use reasonable force to protect themselves, other individuals, and their property
**Duress**  coercion by threat of serious bodily harm; a defense to criminal conduct other than murder
**Mistake of Fact**  honest and reasonable belief that conduct is not criminal
**Entrapment**  inducement by a law enforcement official to commit a crime

## Criminal Procedure

**Steps in Criminal Prosecution**  generally include arrest, booking, formal notice of charges, preliminary hearing to determine probable cause, indictment or information, arraignment, and trial
**Fourth Amendment**  protects individuals against unreasonable searches and seizures
**Fifth Amendment**  protects persons against self-incrimination, double jeopardy, and being charged with a capital crime except by grand jury indictment
**Sixth Amendment**  provides the accused with the right to a speedy and public trial, the opportunity to confront witnesses, process for obtaining witnesses, and the right to counsel

# Cases

### CASE 6–1
## Essential Elements
## *JOHNSON v. FLORIDA*
Supreme Court of Florida, 1992
597 So.2d 798

PER CURIAM.

\* \* \*

We . . . phrase the question as follows:

May a defendant be separately convicted and sentenced for grand theft of cash and grand theft of a firearm accomplished by means of snatching a purse that contained both cash and a firearm when the defendant did not know the nature of the purse's contents?

\* \* \* We answer the . . . question in the negative and remand for further proceedings.

Raymond Johnson was convicted and sentenced for the crimes of burglary of a conveyance, grand theft of property (i.e., cash and payroll checks), and grand theft of a firearm. All of these crimes allegedly were committed when Johnson snatched a purse left in an unattended car at a gas station. That purse contained both money and a firearm, among other items. A filling station attendant identified Johnson as the man he had seen near the victim's car immediately before and after the snatching. An eye witness saw Johnson fleeing the scene.

The theft occurred when Johnson wrongfully took the property of another. He did this in one swift motion. The degree of the crime of theft depends on what was taken. Because of the value of the property, his crime was a third-degree felony. Because part of the goods he took was a firearm, his crime additionally is defined as a third-degree felony. [Citation.] We conclude that the value of the goods or the taking of a firearm merely defines the degree of the felony and does not constitute separate crimes. A separate crime occurs only when there are separate distinct acts of seizing the property of another.

We recognize that our views herein appear to be contrary to State v. Getz, [citation], wherein we upheld a third-degree felony conviction for the taking of a gun and a petit theft conviction for the taking of a calculator when both takings occurred during a household burglary. In Getz, however, there was a separate intent and act to take each item. In this case there was one intent and one act of taking the handbag. Had the gun been picked up separately from the taking of the handbag, Getz would allow separate convictions. However, . . . Getz . . . should [not] apply where an enclosed bag and its contents are the subject of the theft in one swift action. Accordingly, there could be only one theft conviction in this case.

\* \* \*

### CASE 6–2
## Larceny
## *PEOPLE v. OLIVO*
Court of Appeals of New York, 1981
52 N.Y.2d 309, 438 N.Y.S.2d 242, 420 N.E.2d 40

COOKE, C.J.

[This case presents] a recurring question in this era of the self-service store which has never been resolved by this court: may a person be convicted of larceny for shoplifting if the person is caught with goods while still inside the store? For reasons outlined below, it is concluded that a larceny conviction may be sustained, in certain situations, even though the shoplifter was apprehended before leaving the store.

In *People v. Olivo*, defendant was observed by a security guard in the hardware area of a department store. Initially conversing with another person, defendant began to look around furtively when his acquaintance departed. The security agent continued to observe and saw defendant assume a crouching position, take a set of wrenches and secrete it in his clothes. After again looking around, defendant began walking toward an exit, passing a number of cash registers en route. When defendant did not stop to pay for the merchandise, the officer accosted him a few feet from the exit. In response to the guard's inquiry, [defendant] denied having the wrenches, but as he proceeded to the security office, defendant removed the wrenches and placed them under his jacket. At trial, defendant testified that he had placed the tools under his arm and was on line at a cashier when apprehended. The jury returned a verdict of guilty on the charge of . . . larceny. The conviction was affirmed by Appellate Term.

* * *

The primary issue * * * is whether the evidence, viewed in the light most favorable to the prosecution, was sufficient to establish the elements of larceny as defined by the Penal Law. To resolve this common question, the development of the common-law crime of larceny and its evolution into modern statutory form must be briefly traced.

Larceny at common law was defined as a trespassory taking and carrying away of the property of another with intent to steal it. The early common-law courts apparently viewed larceny as defending society against breach of the peace, rather than protecting individual property rights, and therefore placed heavy emphasis upon the requirement of a *trespassory taking* [citation]. Thus, a person such as a bailee who had rightfully obtained possession of property from its owner could not be guilty of larceny [citation]. The result was that the crime of larceny was quite narrow in scope.

Gradually, the courts began to expand the reach of the offense, initially by subtle alterations in the common-law concept of possession [citation]. Thus, for instance, it became a general rule that goods entrusted to an employee were not deemed to be in his possession, but were only considered to be in his custody, so long as he remained on the employer's premises [citation]. And, in the case of [citation], it was held that a shop owner retained legal possession of merchandise being examined by a prospective customer until the actual sale was made. In these situations, the employee and the customer would not have been guilty of larceny if they had first obtained lawful possession of the property from the owner. By holding that they had not acquired possession, but merely custody, the court was able to sustain a larceny conviction.

As the reach of larceny expanded, the intent element of the crime became of increasing importance, while the requirement of a trespassory taking became less significant. As a result, the bar against convicting a person who had initially obtained lawful possession of property faded * * *.

Later cases went even further, often ignoring the fact that a defendant had initially obtained possession lawfully, and instead focused upon his later intent. The crime of larceny then encompassed, not only situations where the defendant initially obtained property by a trespassory taking, but many situations where an individual, possessing the requisite intent, exercised control over property inconsistent with the continued rights of the owner. During this evolutionary process, the purpose served by the crime of larceny obviously shifted from protecting society's peace to general protection of property rights.

Modern penal statutes generally have incorporated these developments under a unified definition of larceny [citation]. Case law, too, now tends to focus upon the actor's intent and the exercise of dominion and control over the property [citation]. * * *

This evolution is particularly relevant to thefts occurring in modern self-service stores. In stores of that type, customers are impliedly invited to examine, try on, and carry about the merchandise on display. Thus in a sense, the owner has consented to the customer's possession of the goods for a limited purpose. That the owner has consented to that possession does not, however, preclude a conviction for larceny. If the customer exercises dominion and control wholly inconsistent with the continued rights of the owner, and the other elements of the crime are present, a larceny has occurred. Such conduct on the part of a customer satisfies the "taking" element of the crime.

It is this element that forms the core of the controversy in these cases. The defendants argue, in essence, that the crime is not established, as a matter of law, unless there is evidence that the customer departed the shop without paying for the merchandise.

Although this court has not addressed the issue, case law from other jurisdictions seems unanimous in holding that a shoplifter need not leave the store to be guilty of larceny. This is because a shopper may treat merchandise in a manner inconsistent with the owner's continued rights—and in a manner not in accord with that of prospective purchaser—without actually walking out of the store. Indeed, depending upon the circumstances of each case, a variety of conduct may be sufficient to allow the trier of fact to find a taking. * * *

In many cases, it will be particularly relevant that defendant concealed the goods under clothing or in a container. Such conduct is not generally expected in a self-service store and may in a proper case be deemed an exercise of dominion and control inconsistent with the store's continued rights. Other furtive or unusual behavior on the part of the defendant should also be weighed. Thus, if the defendant surveys the area while secreting the merchandise or abandoned his or her own property in exchange for the concealed goods, this may evince larcenous rather than innocent behavior. Relevant too is the customer's proximity to or movement towards one of the store's exits. Certainly it is highly probative of guilt that the customer was in possession of secreted goods just a few short steps from the door or moving in that direction. Finally, possession of a known shoplifting device actually used to conceal merchandise, such as a specially designed outer garment or false bottomed carrying case, would be all but decisive.

Of course, in a particular case, any one or any combination of these factors may take on special significance. And there may be other considerations, not now identified, which should be examined. So long as it bears upon the principal issue—whether the shopper exercised control wholly inconsistent with the owner's continued rights—any attending circumstance is relevant and may be taken into account.

\* \* \*

Accordingly, . . . the order of the Appellate Term should be affirmed.

---

## CASE 6–3
## Bad Checks
### *STATE v. KELM*
Superior Court of New Jersey, 1996
289 N.J. Super. 55, 672 A.2d 1261

BILDER, J.

Following a jury trial defendant was found guilty of issuing a bad check, N.J.S.A. 2C:21–5, . . . She was sentenced to concurrent custodial terms of four years consecutive to any sentence imposed by the State of Delaware for violation of probation. \* \* \*

The State's evidence depicted the following account. In early February 1991, through a local attorney, defendant sought a short term loan of a few thousand dollars which she said she needed to complete an escrow for an absent buyer in a real estate transaction in which defendant was the broker. Based on information obtained from the attorney, Ms. Joan Williams, believing the amount to be $2500, agreed to meet with defendant to make such a loan. When the parties met on February 10, 1991, Ms. Williams was told by defendant that she was involved in a real estate deal for a manufacturing plant and that she would lose a real estate commission if she did not obtain sufficient money to complete an escrow, the buyer she represented being out of town and unavailable. She said she needed $6000 and would repay the loan either from a reimbursement from the buyer or from commissions from a Florida sale. On that day Ms. Williams loaned defendant $6000, in the form of a check for $3500 and $2500 in cash. Five days later, on February 15, 1991, she went to the attorney's office and found an envelope addressed to her which contained a check from the defendant for $6000. Later that day in a phone conversation, defendant requested Ms. Williams to delay depositing the check to permit uncollected funds to clear. The following week Ms. Williams learned the check was uncollectible. There followed assurances from defendant and unsuccessful efforts to obtain money from the drawee bank [defendant's bank]. Finally Ms. Williams went to the police and was advised to deposit the check and let it be dishonored. When it was returned with a notation that it should not be presented again, that no account was on file, Ms. Williams filed a criminal complaint against defendant. Records of the bank, testified to at trial, showed that defendant's account had negative balances from February 10, 1991 until it was closed on March 8, 1991.

For her part defendant admitted the making and delivery of the check for $6000 but claimed it was delivered on February 10, 1991 and had been post-dated. She denied any intention to defraud Ms. Williams.

\* \* \*

# I

The principal issue on appeal is whether an intent to defraud the victim is an element of N.J.S.A. 2C:21–5 [issuing a bad check]. Defendant contends that the issuance of a post-dated check cannot be found to be a violation of the criminal statute and that proof of an intent to defraud is required for a conviction. In support of that defendant relies heavily on a predecessor bad check statute, N.J.S.A. 2A:111–15, and case law interpreting that former law.

N.J.S.A. 2C:21–5, in pertinent part, reads as follows:

A person who issues or passes a check or similar sight order for the payment of money, knowing that it will not be honored by the drawee, commits an offense * * * . For the purposes of this section as well as in any prosecution for theft committed by means of a bad check, an issuer is presumed to know that the check or money order (other than a post-dated check or order) would not be paid, if:

* * *

(b) Payment was refused by the drawee for lack of funds, upon presentation within 30 days after issue, and the issuer failed to make good within 10 days after receiving notice of that refusal or after notice has been sent to the issuer's last known address. Notice of refusal may be given to the issuer orally or in writing in any reasonable manner by that person.

Defendant's reliance on N.J.S.A. 2A:111–15 [the old bad check statute] is misplaced. The need to show that the check was drawn "with intent to defraud" was specifically set forth in the statute. N.J.S.A. 2C:21–5 does not contain any such requirement, merely knowledge at the time the check is issued or passed that it will not be honored by the drawee. Cases involving the requirement of an intent to defraud under the old statute are irrelevant.

Defendant's contention that the statute's reference to a post-dated check exempts such checks from its operation is similarly without merit. This provision merely excludes post-dated checks from the statutory presumption of knowledge that the check will not be paid. When the instrument is post-dated the presumption is inapplicable; the State must show that the drawer knew at the time the post-dated check was drawn that it would not be honored on the later date when presented.

In his charge the trial judge instructed the jury:

The State must prove the following elements beyond a reasonable doubt in order to convict the defendant under this [bad check] count. The State must prove that the defendant knowingly issued or passed the check for the payment of money and, two, that the defendant knew at the time that she issued or passed the check that it would not be honored by the drawee. Two things must occur at the same time: the defendant knowingly passed the check for the payment of the money and knew at the time she gave the check over to Mrs. Williams that it would not be honored by the bank.

* * *

There is some argument that has been made that the testimony allows you and compels you to infer that there was a post-dated check situation. It is for you to determine when this particular check was issued; was it issued on the 15th, the date it was dated, or was it issued on the 10th? You should examine the evidence carefully to determine whether or not you can make such an inference. If you do come to the conclusion that the check was issued on the 10th, that is that it is a post-dated check, then the element that the defendant knew that it would not be honored by the bank requires proof, again beyond a reasonable doubt, that the defendant knew at the time the check was issued that it would not be honored in the future on the 15th. So if you come to that determination, that check was issued on the 10th, the State must prove that the defendant knew on the 10th that the check would not be honored on the 15th. Now, the State is not required to prove under the statute that there was any intent to defraud; the State need only prove that the defendant knew that the check would not be honored in the future.

We are satisfied the jury was correctly instructed by this charge.

---

# Questions

1.   Discuss criminal intent and the various degrees of mental fault.
2.   Identify the significant features of white-collar crimes.
3.   List and define the offenses against property.

4.   Discuss the defenses of duress, mistake of fact, entrapment, and defense of property.
5.   List and explain the constitutional amendments affecting criminal procedure.

---

# Problems

1.   Sam said to Carol, "Kim is going to sell me a good used car next Monday and then I'll deliver it to you in exchange for your microcomputer, but I'd like to have the computer now." Relying on this statement, Carol delivered the computer to Sam. Sam knew Kim had no car, and would have none in the future, and he had no such arrangement with her. The

appointed time of exchange passed, and Sam failed to deliver the car to Carol. Has a crime been committed? Discuss.

**2.** Sara, a lawyer, drew a deed for Robert by which Robert was to convey land to Rick. The deed was correct in every detail. Robert examined and verbally approved it but did not sign it. Sara erased Rick's name and substituted her own. Robert signed the deed with all required legal formalities without noticing the change. Was Sara guilty of forgery? Discuss.

**3.** Ann took Bonnie's watch before Bonnie was aware of the theft. Bonnie discovered her loss immediately and pursued Ann. Ann pointed a loaded pistol at Bonnie, who, in fear of being shot, allowed Ann to escape. Was Ann guilty of robbery? Of any other crime?

**4.** Jones and Wilson were on trial, separately, for larceny of a $1,000 bearer bond (payable to the holder of the bond, not a named individual) issued by Brown, Inc. The Commonwealth's evidence showed that the owner of the bond had dropped it accidentally in the street enclosed in an envelope bearing his name and address; that Jones found the envelope with the bond in it; that Jones could neither read nor write; that Jones presented the envelope and bond to Wilson, an educated man, and asked Wilson what he should do with it; that Wilson told Jones that the finder of lost property becomes the owner of it; that Wilson told Jones that the bond was worth $100 but that the money could only be collected at the issuer's home office; that Jones then handed the bond to Wilson, who redeemed it at the corporation's home office and received $1,000; that Wilson gave Jones $100 of the proceeds. What rulings?

**5.** Truck drivers for a hauling company, while loading a desk, found a $100 bill that had fallen out of the desk. They agreed to get it exchanged for small bills and divide the proceeds. En route to a bank, one of them changed his mind and refused to proceed with the scheme, whereupon the other pulled a knife and demanded the bill. A police officer intervened. It turned out that the bill was counterfeit money. What crimes have been committed?

**6.** Peter, an undercover police agent, was trying to locate a laboratory where it was believed that methamphetamine, or "speed"—a controlled substance—was being manufactured illegally. Peter went to Mary's home and said that he represented a large organization that was interested in obtaining methamphetamine. Peter offered to supply a necessary ingredient for the manufacture of the drug, which was very difficult to obtain, in return for one-half of the drug produced. Mary agreed and processed the chemical given to her by Peter in Peter's presence. Later, Peter returned with a search warrant and arrested Mary. Charged with various narcotics law violations, Mary asserted the defense of entrapment. Decision?

**7.** The police obtained a search warrant based on an affidavit that contained the following allegations: (a) Donald was seen crossing a State line on four occasions during a five-day period and going to a particular apartment; (b) telephone records disclosed that the apartment had two telephones; (c) Donald had a reputation as a bookmaker and as an associate of gamblers; and (d) the FBI was informed by a "confidential reliable informant" that Donald was conducting gambling operations. When a search was made based on the warrant, evidence was obtained that resulted in Donald's conviction of violating certain gambling laws. Donald challenged the constitutionality of the search warrant. Decision?

**8.** A national bank was robbed by a man with a small strip of tape on each side of his face. An indictment was returned against David. David was then arrested, and counsel was appointed to represent him. Two weeks later, without notice to David's lawyer, an FBI agent arranged to have the two bank employees observe a lineup, including David and five or six other prisoners. Each person in the lineup wore strips of tape, as had the robber, and each was directed to repeat the words "Put the money in the bag," as had the robber. Both of the bank employees identified David as the robber. At David's trial he was again identified by the two, in the courtroom, and the prior lineup identification was elicited on cross-examination by David's counsel. David's counsel moved the court either to grant a judgment of acquittal or alternatively to strike the courtroom identifications on the grounds that the lineup had violated David's Fifth Amendment privilege against self-incrimination and his Sixth Amendment right to counsel. Decision?

**9.** Waronek owned and operated a trucking rig, transporting goods for L.T.L. Perishables, Inc., of St. Paul, Minnesota. He accepted an offer to haul a trailer load of beef from Illini Beef Packers, Inc., in Joslin, Illinois, to Midtown Packing Company in New York City. After his truck was loaded with ninety-five forequarters and ninety-five hindquarters of beef in Joslin, Waronek drove north to his home in Watertown, Wisconsin, rather than east to New York. While in Watertown, he asked employees of the Royal Meat Company to butcher and prepare four hindquarters of beef—two for himself and two for his friends. He also offered to sell ten hindquarters to one employee of the company at an alarmingly reduced rate. The suspicious employee contacted the authorities, who told him to proceed with the deal. When Waronek arrived in New York with his load short nineteen hindquarters, Waronek telephoned L.T.L. Perishables in St. Paul. He notified them "that he was short nineteen hindquarters, that he knew where the beef went, and that he would make good on it out of future settlements." L.T.L. told him to contact the New York police, but he failed to do so. Shortly thereafter, he was arrested by the Federal Bureau of Investigation and indicted for the embezzlement of goods moving in interstate commerce. Decision?

**10.** Four separate cases involving similar fact situations were consolidated as they presented the same constitutional question. In each case, police officers, detectives, or prosecuting attorneys took a defendant into custody and interrogated him in a police station to obtain a confession. In none of these cases did the officials fully and effectively advise the defendant of his rights at the outset of the interrogation. Police interrogations produced oral admissions of guilt from each defendant, as well as signed statements from three of them, which were used to convict them at their trials. The defendants appeal, arguing that the officials should have warned them of their constitutional rights and the consequences of waiving them before the questionings began. It was contended that to permit any statements obtained without such a warning violated their Fifth Amendment privilege against self-incrimination. Decision?

11.   The Racketeer Influenced and Corrupt Organizations Act (RICO) is directed at "racketeering activity"—defined to encompass acts indictable under specific Federal criminal provisions, including mail and wire fraud. Petitioner corporation, Sedima, which had entered into a joint business venture with respondent company, Imrex, and which believed that it was being cheated by alleged overbilling, filed suit in District Court, asserting RICO claims against respondent company and two of its officers (also respondents) based on predicate acts of mail and wire fraud. The court dismissed the RICO counts for failure to state a claim. The Court of Appeals affirmed, holding that under RICO a plaintiff must allege a "racketeering injury"—an injury "caused by an activity which RICO was designed to deter," not just an injury occurring as a result of the predicate acts themselves. Decision?

12.   Officer Cyril Rombach of the Burbank Police Department, an experienced and well-trained narcotics officer, applied for a warrant to search several residences and automobiles for cocaine, methaqualone, and other narcotics. Rombach supported his application with information given to another police officer by a confidential informant of unproven reliability. He also based the warrant application on his own observations made during an extensive investigation: known drug offenders visiting the residences and leaving with small packages as well as a suspicious trip to Miami by two of the suspects. A state superior court judge issued a search warrant to Rombach based on this information. Rombach's searches netted large quantities of drugs and other evidence, which produced indictments of several suspects on charges of conspiracy to possess and distribute cocaine. The defendants moved to suppress the evidence on the grounds that the search warrant was defective in that Rombach had failed to establish the informant's credibility and that the information provided by the informant about the suspect's criminal activity was fatally stale. The district court declared that the search lacked probable cause, that the warrant was invalid, and that the obtained evidence must be excluded from the prosecution's case under the Fourth Amendment's exclusionary rule. The Court of Appeals for the Ninth Circuit affirmed. Decision?

**WWW** **Internet Exercise**  Find and review (a) the Bureau of Justice's data concerning the rates of burglary, theft, and motor vehicle theft for the last five years, and (b) information about computer crime and its trend.

# CHAPTER 7

# Intentional Torts

All forms of civil liability are either (1) voluntarily assumed, as by contract, or (2) involuntarily assumed, as imposed by law. Tort liability is of the second type. Tort law gives persons redress from civil wrongs or injuries to their person, property, and economic interests. The law of torts has three principal objectives: (1) to compensate persons who sustain harm or loss resulting from another's conduct, (2) to place the cost of that compensation only on those parties who should bear it, and (3) to prevent future harms and losses. The law of torts therefore reallocates losses caused by human misconduct. In general, a tort is committed when

1. a duty owed by one person to another
2. is breached and
3. proximately causes
4. injury or damage to the owner of a legally protected interest.

The law of torts is not static: when necessary and appropriate, it affords relief against novel forms of misconduct. Over the past decade, the courts have expanded tort law by recognizing new torts to provide additional protection for personal, dignitary, property, and economic interests.

At the same time, State legislatures and, to a lesser extent, courts have actively assessed the need for **tort reform**. In general, tort reform has focused on limiting liability by restricting damages or narrowing claims. The majority of States have enacted at least one piece of legislation that falls into the broad category of tort reform, but these States have enacted different changes or different combinations of changes affecting specific aspects of tort law. Approaches to tort reform that have been taken at the State level include:

1. Laws that address specific types of claims; for example, limits on medical malpractice awards or on the liability of providers of alcohol.

2. Laws abolishing joint and several liability or limiting the application of this rule. Where joint and several liability is abolished, each one of the several defendants is liable only for his share of the plaintiff's damages.

3. Laws adding defenses to certain types of tort actions.

4. Laws capping noneconomic damages—so-called pain and suffering awards.

5. Laws to abolish or limit punitive damages, or to raise the standard of proof beyond the preponderance of the evidence.

6. Laws aimed at attorneys' fees; for example, laws that directly regulate contingent fees.

Each person is legally responsible for the damages his tortious conduct proximately causes. Moreover, as discussed in Chapter 20, businesses that conduct their business activities through employees are also liable for the torts their employees commit in the course of employment. The tort liability of employers makes the study of tort law essential to business managers.

Injuries may be inflicted intentionally, negligently, or without fault (strict liability). This chapter will discuss intentional torts; the following chapter will cover negligence and strict liability.

The same conduct may, and often does, constitute both a crime and a tort. An example would be an assault and battery committed by Johnson against West. For the commission of this crime, the State may take appropriate action against Johnson. In addition, however, Johnson has violated West's right to be secure in his person and so has committed a tort against West, who may, regardless of the criminal action by the State against Johnson, bring a civil action against Johnson for damages. On the other hand, an act may be criminal without being tortious, and, by the same token, an act may be a tort but not a crime.

In a tort action, the injured party *sues* to recover *compensation* for the injury sustained as a result of the defendant's wrongful conduct. The primary purpose of tort law, unlike criminal law, is to compensate the injured party, not to punish the wrongdoer. In certain cases, however, courts may award **punitive** or exemplary damages, which are damages over and above the amount necessary to compensate the plaintiff. Where the defendant's tortious conduct has been intentional and outrageous, exhibiting "malice" or a fraudulent or evil motive, most courts permit a jury to award punitive damages. The allowance of punitive damages is designed to deter others from similar conduct by punishing and making an example of the defendant.

Tort law is primarily common law. The Restatement of Torts provides an orderly presentation of this law. From 1934 to 1939, The American Law Institute adopted and promulgated the first Restatement. Since then, the Restatement has served as a vital force in shaping the law of torts. Between 1965 and 1978, the institute adopted and promulgated a revised edition of the Restatement of Torts which supersedes the First Restatement. This text will refer to the revised Restatement simply as the Restatement.

 *See Case 7–1*

## INTENT

Intent, as used in tort law, does not require a hostile or evil motive; rather, the term denotes either that the actor desires to cause the consequences of his act *or* that he believes that those consequences are substantially certain to result from it. Restatement, Section 8A.

The following examples illustrate the definition of intent: (1) If A fires a gun in the middle of the Mojave Desert, he intends to fire the gun; but when the bullet hits B, who is in the desert without A's knowledge, A does not intend that result. (2) A throws a bomb into B's office to kill B. A knows that C is in B's office and that the bomb is substantially certain to injure C, although A has no desire to harm C. A, nonetheless, is liable to C for any injury caused C. A's intent to injure B is *transferred* to C.

Infants (persons who have not reached the age of majority) are held liable for their intentional torts. The infant's age and knowledge, however, are critical in determining whether the infant had sufficient intelligence to form the requisite intent. Incompetents, like infants, are generally held liable for their intentional torts.

A number of established and specifically named torts protect an individual from various intentional interferences with his person, dignity, property, and economic interests. Because the law of torts is dynamic, new forms of relief continue to develop. To guide the courts in determining when they should impose liability for intentionally inflicted harm that does not fall within the requirements of an established tort, Section 870 of the Restatement provides a general catchall intentional tort:

One who intentionally causes injury to another is subject to liability to the other for that injury, if his conduct is generally culpable and not justifiable under the circumstances. This liability may be imposed although the actor's conduct does not come within a traditional category of tort liability.

This section also provides a unifying principle both for long-established torts and for those that have developed more recently.

◆ *See Figure 7–1*

## HARM TO THE PERSON

The law provides protection against intentional harm to the person. The primary interests protected by these torts are freedom from bodily contact (by the tort of battery), freedom from apprehension (assault), freedom from confinement (false imprisonment), and freedom from mental distress (infliction of emotional distress). Generally, intentional torts to the person entitle the injured party to recover damages for bodily harm, emotional distress, loss or impairment of earning capacity, reasonable medical expenses, and harm the tortious conduct caused to property or business.

### Battery

**Battery** is an intentional infliction of harmful or offensive bodily contact. It may consist of contact causing serious injury, such as a gunshot wound or a blow to the head with a club. Or it may involve contact causing little or no physical injury, such as knocking a hat off of a person's head or flicking a glove in another's face. Bodily contact is offensive if it would offend a reasonable person's sense of dignity, even if the defendant intended the conduct only as a joke or a compliment. Restatement, Section 19. For instance, kissing another without permission would constitute a battery. Bodily contact may be accomplished by the use of objects, such as Arthur's throwing a rock at Bea with the intention of hitting her. If the rock hits Bea or any other person, Arthur has committed a battery. Nonetheless, in a densely populated society one cannot expect complete freedom from personal contact with others. Accordingly, neither casually bumping into another in a congested area nor gently tapping that other

**FIGURE 7–1** Intent

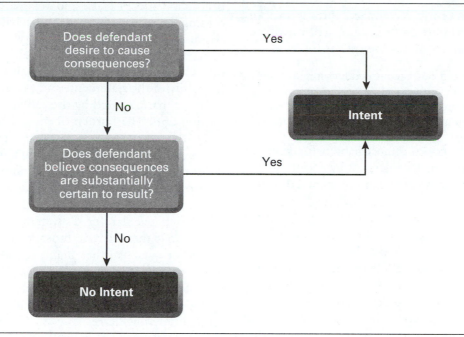

on the shoulder to get her attention would constitute a battery.

## Assault

**Assault** is intentional conduct by one person directed at another which places the other in apprehension of immediate bodily harm or offensive contact. It is usually committed immediately preceding a battery, but if the intended battery fails, the assault remains. Assault is principally a mental rather than a physical intrusion. Accordingly, damages for assault may include compensation for fright and humiliation. The person in danger of immediate bodily harm must have *knowledge* of the danger and be apprehensive of its imminent threat to his safety. For example, if Joan aims a loaded gun at Kelly's back but Pat subdues her before Kelly becomes aware of the danger, Joan has not committed an assault upon Kelly.

Historically, it has been said that words alone do not constitute an assault. Nonetheless, spoken words must be taken in context, and if as taken cause apprehension, these spoken words will constitute an assault. On the other hand, words sometimes will negate an apparent threat so that there is no assault. This does not mean that a defendant can avoid liability for an assault by making his threat conditional. The threat "If you do not give me your book, I will break your arm" constitutes an assault.

## False Imprisonment

The tort of **false imprisonment,** or false arrest, is the intentional confining of a person against her will within fixed boundaries if the person is conscious of the confinement or is harmed by it. Merely obstructing a person's freedom of movement is not false imprisonment so long as a reasonable alternative exit is available. False imprisonment may be brought about by physical force, by the threat of physical force (both express and implied), by physical barriers, or by force directed against the plaintiff's property. For instance, an individual who remains in a store after his wallet is confiscated or who remains on a train after the conductor refuses to allow her suitcase to be removed are both examples of false imprisonment through the use of force against personal property. Damages for false imprisonment may include compensation for loss of time, physical discomfort, inconvenience, physical illness, and mental suffering.

Merchants occasionally encounter potential liability for false imprisonment when they seek to question a suspected shoplifter. A merchant who detains an innocent person may face a lawsuit for false imprisonment. Nonetheless, most States have statutes protecting the merchant, provided she detains the suspect upon probable cause, in a reasonable manner, and for not more than a reasonable time.

 *See Case 7–2*

## Infliction of Emotional Distress

One of the more recently recognized torts is that of intentional *or reckless* infliction of emotional distress. The Restatement, Section 46, states the rule as follows:

One who by extreme and outrageous conduct intentionally or recklessly causes severe emotional distress to another is subject to liability for such emotional distress, and if bodily harm to the other results from it, for such bodily harm.

Under this tort, the courts impose liability for conduct exceeding all bounds usually tolerated by society when such conduct intentionally causes serious mental distress. Many courts allow recovery even in the absence of physical injury. This cause of action does not protect a person from abusive language or rudeness, but rather from atrocious, intolerable conduct beyond all bounds of decency. Examples of this tort would include leading to a person's home, when he is present, a noisy demonstrating mob yelling threats to lynch him unless he leaves town, or placing a rattlesnake in another's bed as a practical joke. Other examples would include sexual harassment on the job and outrageous, prolonged bullying tactics employed by creditors or collection agencies attempting to collect a debt or by insurance adjusters trying to force a settlement of an insurance claim.

 *See Case 7–2*

# HARM TO THE RIGHT OF DIGNITY

The law also protects a person against intentional harm to his right of dignity. This protection includes a person's reputation, privacy, and right to freedom from unjustifiable litigation.

## Defamation

The tort of **defamation** is a false communication that injures a person's reputation by disgracing him and diminishing the respect in which he is held. An example would be the publication of a false statement that a person had committed a crime or had a loathsome disease. In *Beckman v. Dunn*, 276 Pa.Super. 527, 419 A.2d 583 (1980), the court stated,

A communication is defamatory if it tends to harm the reputation of another so as to lower him in the estimation of the community or deter third persons from associating or dealing with him, and necessarily involves the idea of disgrace.

*Elements of Defamation*   The elements of a defamation action are (1) a false and defamatory statement concerning another, (2) an unprivileged publication (communication) to a third party, (3) in some cases, depending on the status of the defendant, some degree of fault on her part in knowing or failing to ascertain the falsity of the statement, and (4) in some cases, proof of special harm caused by the publication. Restatement, Section 558. The burden of proof is on the plaintiff to prove the falsity of the defamatory statement.

If a defamatory communication is handwritten, typewritten, printed, pictorial, or in another medium with like communicative power, such as a television or radio broadcast, it is designated **libel.** If it is spoken or oral, it is designated **slander.** Restatement, Sections 568 and 568A. In either case, it must be communicated to a person or persons other than the one who is defamed, a process referred to as *publication*. If Maurice hands or mails to Pierre a defamatory letter he has written about Pierre's character, this is not a publication, as it is intended only for Pierre.

Any living person, as well as corporations, partnerships, and unincorporated associations, may be defamed. Restatement, Sections 561 and 562. Unless a statute provides otherwise, no action may be brought for defamation of a deceased person. Restatement, Section 560.

A significant new trend affecting business has been the bringing of defamation suits against former employers by discharged employees. It has been reported that such suits comprise approximately one-third of all defamation lawsuits.

 *See Case 7–3*

*Defenses to Defamation*   Truth and privilege are defenses to defamation. In most States, **truth** is a complete defense without regard to the purpose or intent in publishing the defamation. By comparison, the courts grant **privilege** as an immunity from tort liability when the defendant's conduct furthers a societal interest of greater importance than the injury inflicted upon the plaintiff. Three types of **privileges** apply to defamation: absolute, conditional, and constitutional.

Like the defense of truth, **absolute privilege** protects the defendant regardless of his motive or intent. This type of privilege, which has been confined to those few situations where public policy clearly favors complete freedom of speech, includes (1) statements made by participants in a judicial proceeding regarding that proceeding; (2) statements made by members of Congress on the floor of Congress; (3) statements made by certain executive branch officers in the discharge of their governmental duties; and (4) statements regarding a third party made between spouses when they are alone.

Qualified or **conditional privilege** depends upon proper use of the privilege. A person has conditional privilege to publish defamatory matter to protect his own legitimate interests or, in some cases, the interests of another. Conditional privilege also extends to many communications in which the publisher and the recipient have a common interest, such as in letters of reference. A publisher who acts in an excessive manner, without probable cause, or for an improper purpose forfeits conditional privilege.

The First Amendment to the U.S. Constitution guarantees freedom of speech and freedom of the press. The U.S. Supreme Court has applied these rights to the law of defamation by extending a form of **constitutional privilege** to defamatory and false statements regarding public officials or public figures so long as it is done without malice. Restatement, Section 580A. For these purposes, *malice* is not ill will but clear and convincing proof of the publisher's knowledge of falsity or reckless disregard of the truth. Thus, under constitutional privilege the public official or public figure must prove that the defendant published the defamatory and false comment with knowledge or in reckless disregard of the comment's falsity and its defamatory character.

In a defamation suit brought by a private person (one who is neither a public official nor a public figure) against a member of the news media, the plaintiff must prove that the defendant published the defamatory and false comment with malice *or* negligence. Where a private person brings suit against a defendant who is *not* a member of the news media, however, it is currently unresolved whether the plaintiff must prove anything beyond the fact that a false and defamatory statement has been made.

## Invasion of Privacy

The invasion of a person's right to privacy actually consists of four distinct torts: (1) appropriation of a person's name or likeness; (2) unreasonable intrusion upon the seclusion of another; (3) unreasonable public disclosure of private facts; or (4) unreasonable publicity which places another in a false light in the public eye. Restatement, Section 652A.

It is entirely possible and not uncommon for a person to invade another's right of privacy in a manner entailing two or more of these related torts. For example, Cindy forces her way into Ozzie's hospital room, takes a photograph of Ozzie, and publishes it to promote Cindy's

cure for Ozzie's illness along with false statements about Ozzie that a reasonable person would consider highly objectionable. Ozzie would be entitled to recover on any or all of the four torts comprising invasion of privacy.

*Appropriation*  Appropriation is the unauthorized use of the plaintiff's name or likeness for the defendant's benefit, as, for example, in promoting or advertising a product or service. Restatement, Section 652C. The tort of appropriation, also known as the **right of publicity**, seeks to protect the individual's right to the exclusive use of his identity. In the example above, Cindy's use of Ozzie's photograph to promote Cindy's business constitutes the tort of appropriation.

 *See Case 7–4*

*Intrusion*  Intrusion is the unreasonable and highly offensive interference with the solitude or seclusion of another. Restatement, Section 652B. Such unreasonable interference would include improper entry into another's dwelling, unauthorized eavesdropping upon another's private conversations, and unauthorized examination of another's private papers and records. The intrusion must be offensive or objectionable to a reasonable person and must involve matters which are private. Thus, there is no liability if the defendant examines public records or observes the plaintiff in a public place. This form of invasion of privacy is committed once the intrusion occurs, as publicity is not required.

*Public Disclosure of Private Facts*  Under the tort of public disclosure of private facts, the courts impose liability for publicity given to private information about another if the matter made public would be highly offensive and objectionable to a reasonable person. Like intrusion, this tort applies only to private, not public, information regarding an individual; unlike intrusion, it requires publicity. Under the Restatement, the publicity required differs in degree from the "publication" required under the law of defamation. This tort requires that private facts be communicated to the public at large or that they become public knowledge, whereas publication of a defamatory statement need only be made to a single third party. Section 652D, Comment a. Some courts, however, have allowed recovery where the disclosure was made to only one person. Thus, under the Restatement approach, Kathy, a creditor of Gary, will not invade Gary's privacy by writing a letter to Gary's employer to inform the employer of Gary's failure to pay a debt, but Kathy would be liable if she posted in the window of her store a statement that Gary will not pay the debt he owes to her. Also, unlike defamation, this tort applies to truthful private information if the matter published would be offensive and objectionable to a reasonable person of ordinary sensibilities.

*False Light* The tort of false light imposes liability for publicity that places another in a false light that is highly offensive if the defendant *knew* or acted in *reckless disregard* of the fact that the matter publicized was false. Restatement, Section 652E. For example, Linda includes Keith's name and photograph in a public "rogues' gallery" of convicted criminals. Because Keith has never been convicted of any crime, Linda is liable to him for placing him in a false light. Other examples include publicly and falsely attributing to a person an opinion, statement, or written work, as well as the unauthorized use of a person's name on a petition or on a complaint in a lawsuit.

Like defamation, the matter must be untrue; unlike defamation, it must be "publicized," not merely "published." Restatement, Section 652D, Comment a. Although the matter must be objectionable to a reasonable person, it need not be defamatory. In many instances, the same facts will give rise to actions both for defamation and for false light.

*Defenses* The defenses of absolute, conditional, and constitutional privilege apply to publication of any matter that is an invasion of privacy to the same extent that such defenses apply to defamation.

## Misuse of Legal Procedure

Three torts comprise the misuse of legal procedure: malicious prosecution, wrongful civil proceedings, and abuse of process. Each protects an individual from being subjected to unjustifiable litigation. Malicious prosecution and wrongful civil proceedings impose liability for damages caused by improperly brought proceedings, including harm to reputation, credit, or standing; emotional distress; and the expenses incurred in defending against the wrongfully brought lawsuit. Abuse of process is a tort consisting of the use of a legal proceeding (criminal or civil) to accomplish a purpose for which the proceeding is not designed. It applies even when there is probable cause or when the plaintiff or prosecution succeeds in the litigation.

# HARM TO PROPERTY

The law also provides protection against invasions of a person's interests in property. Intentional harm to property includes the torts of (1) trespass to real property, (2) nuisance, (3) trespass to personal property, and (4) conversion.

## Real Property

**Real property** is land and anything attached to it, such as buildings, trees, and minerals. The law protects the possessor's rights to the exclusive use and quiet enjoyment of the land. Accordingly, damages for harm to land include compensation for the resulting diminution in the value of the land, the loss of use of the land, and the discomfort caused to the possessor of the land. Restatement, Section 929.

*Trespass* Section 158 of the Restatement provides:

One is subject to liability to another for trespass, irrespective of whether he thereby causes harm to any legally protected interest of the other, if he intentionally

**(a)** enters land in the possession of the other, or causes a thing or a third person to do so, or
**(b)** remains on the land, or
**(c)** fails to remove from the land a thing which he is under a duty to remove.

It is no defense that the intruder acted under the mistaken belief of law or fact that he was not trespassing. If the intruder intended to be upon the particular property, his reasonable belief that he owned the land or had permission to enter upon the land is irrelevant. Restatement, Section 164. An intruder is not liable if his own actions do not cause his presence on the land of another. For example, if Carol throws Ralph onto Tim's land, Ralph is not liable to Tim for trespass, although Carol is.

A trespass may be committed on, beneath, or above the surface of the land, although the law regards the upper air, above a prescribed minimum altitude for flight, as a public highway. Therefore, no aerial trespass occurs unless the aircraft enters into the lower reaches of the airspace and substantially interferes with the landowner's use and enjoyment. Restatement, Section 159.

*Nuisance* A nuisance is a nontrespassory invasion of another's interest in the private use and enjoyment of land. Restatement, Section 821D. In contrast to trespass, nuisance does not require interference with another's right to exclusive possession of land, but rather imposes liability for significant and unreasonable harm to another's use or enjoyment of land. Examples of nuisances include the emission of unpleasant odors, smoke, dust, or gas, as well as the pollution of a stream, pond, or underground water supply. In one case, a computer's serious disturbance of a television retailer's signal reception was considered a nuisance.

## Personal Property

**Personal property,** or chattel, is any type of property other than an interest in land. The law protects a number of interests in the possession of personal property, including an interest in the property's physical condition and usability, an interest in the retention of possession, and an interest in its availability for future use.

*Trespass*   Trespass to personal property consists of the intentional dispossession or unauthorized use of the personal property of another. Though the interference with the right to exclusive use and possession may be direct or indirect, liability is limited to instances in which the trespasser (a) dispossesses the other of the property; (b) substantially impairs the condition, quality, or value of the property; (c) deprives the possessor of the use of the property for a substantial time; or (d) causes harm to the possessor or to some person or thing in which the possessor has a legally protected interest. Restatement, Section 218. For example, Albert parks his car in front of his house. Ronald pushes Albert's car around the corner. Albert subsequently looks for his car but cannot find it for several hours. Ronald is liable to Albert for trespass.

*Conversion*   Conversion is an intentional exercise of dominion or control over another's personal property which so seriously interferes with the other's right of control as to justly require the payment of full value for the property. Restatement, Section 222A. Thus, all conversions are trespasses, but not all trespasses are conversions.

Conversion may consist of the intentional destruction of personal property or the use of property in an unauthorized manner. For example, Ken entrusts an automobile to Barbara, a dealer, for sale. After she drives the car 8,000 miles on her own business, Barbara is liable to Ken for conversion. On the other hand, in the example in which Ronald pushed Albert's car around the corner, Ronald would *not* be liable to Albert for conversion. Moreover, a person who buys stolen property is liable to the rightful owner for conversion even if the buyer

acquires the property in good faith and without knowledge that it was stolen. Restatement, Section 229.

## *HARM TO ECONOMIC INTERESTS*

Economic interests comprise a fourth set of interests the law protects against intentional interference. Economic or pecuniary interests include a person's existing and prospective contractual relations, a person's business reputation, a person's name and likeness (previously discussed under the section titled "Appropriation"), and a person's freedom from deception. Business torts—those torts that protect a person's economic interests—are discussed in this section under the following headings: (1) interference with contractual relations, (2) disparagement, and (3) fraudulent misrepresentation.

## Interference with Contractual Relations

To conduct business it is necessary to establish trade relations with employees, suppliers, and customers. Though these relations may or may not be contractual, those that are, or are capable of being established by contract, receive legal protection against interference. Section 766 of the Restatement provides:

One who intentionally and improperly interferes with the performance of a contract (except a contract to marry) between another and a third person by inducing or otherwise causing the third person not to perform the contract, is subject to liability to the other for the pecuniary loss resulting to the other from the failure of the third person to perform the contract.

The law imposes similar liability for intentional and improper interference with another's prospective contractual relation, such as a lease renewal or financing for construction. Restatement, Section 766B.

In either case, the rule requires that a person act with the purpose or motive of interfering with another's contract or with the knowledge that such interference is substantially certain to occur as a natural consequence of her actions. The interference may be by threats or by prevention through the use of physical force. Frequently, interference is accomplished through inducement, such as the offer of a better contract. For instance, Edgar may offer Doris, an employee of Frank, a yearly salary of $5,000 per year more than the contractual arrangement between Doris and Frank. If Edgar is aware that a contract exists between Doris and Frank and of the fact that his offer to Doris will interfere with that contract, then

Edgar is liable to Frank for intentional interference with contractual relations.

To be distinguished is the situation where the contract may be terminated at will or where the contractual relation is only prospective. In these cases, competition is a proper basis for interference; for if one party is pursuing a contractual relation, others also are free to pursue a similar arrangement. For example, Amos and Brenda are competing distributors of transistors. Amos induces Carter, a prospective customer of Brenda, to buy transistors from Amos instead of Brenda. Amos has no liability to Brenda because his interference with Brenda's prospective contract with Carter is justified on the basis of competition, so long as Amos does not use predatory means such as physical violence, fraud, civil suits, or criminal prosecution to persuade Carter to deal with him.

Damages for interference with contractual relations include the pecuniary loss of the benefits of the contract, consequential losses caused by the interference, and emotional distress or actual harm to reputation. Restatement, Section 774A. In one case, Pennzoil had orally entered into a contract to merge with Getty Oil. Before the merger was consummated, however, Texaco induced Getty to merge with Texaco instead. Pennzoil sued Texaco for tortious interference with the merger contract and was awarded $7.53 billion in compensatory damages and $3 billion in punitive damages. *Texaco, Inc. v. Pennzoil, Co.*, 729 S.W.2d 768 (1987).

## Disparagement

The tort of **disparagement** or injurious falsehood imposes liability upon a person who publishes a false statement that results in harm to another's interests which have pecuniary value, if the publisher knows that the statement is false or acts in reckless disregard of its truth or falsity. This tort most commonly involves false statements that the publisher intends to cast doubt upon the title or quality of another's property or products. Thus, Adam, while contemplating the purchase of merchandise that belongs to Barry, reads a newspaper advertisement in which Carol falsely asserts she owns the merchandise. Carol has disparaged Barry's property in the goods. Similarly, Marlene, knowing her statement to be false, tells Lionel that Matthew, an importer of wood, does not deal in mahogany. As a result, Lionel, who had intended to buy mahogany from Matthew, buys it elsewhere. Marlene is liable to Matthew for disparagement.

Absolute, conditional, and constitutional privileges apply to the same extent to the tort of disparagement as they do to defamation. In addition, a competitor has conditional privilege to compare her products favorably with those of a rival, even though she does not believe that her products are superior. No privilege applies, however, if the comparison contains false assertions of specific unfavorable facts about the competitor's property. For example, a manufacturer who advertises that his goods are the best in the market, even though he knows that a competitor's product is better, is not liable for disparagement. If he goes further, however, by falsely stating that his product is better because his competitor uses shoddy materials, then his disparagement would no longer be privileged, and he would be liable to his competitor for disparagement.

The pecuniary loss an injured person may recover is that which directly and immediately results from impairment of the marketability of the property disparaged. The injured party also may recover damages for expenses necessary to counteract the false publication, including litigation expenses, the cost of notifying customers, and the cost of publishing denials. Thus, Ursula publishes in a magazine an untrue statement that cranberries grown during the current season in a particular area are unwholesome. Shortly thereafter, the business of Victor, a jobber who has contracted to buy the entire output of cranberries grown in this area, falls off by 50 percent. If no other facts account for this decrease in his business, Victor is entitled to recover the amount of his loss from Ursula, plus the expenses necessary to counteract the misinformation published.

## Fraudulent Misrepresentation

With respect to intentional, or fraudulent, misrepresentation, Section 525 of the Restatement provides:

One who fraudulently makes a misrepresentation of fact, opinion, intention, or law for the purpose of inducing another to act or to refrain from action in reliance upon it, is subject to liability to the other in deceit for pecuniary loss caused to him by his justifiable reliance upon the misrepresentation.

For example, Smith represents to Jones that a tract of land in Texas is located in an area where oil drilling had recently commenced. Smith makes this statement knowing it to be false. In reliance upon the statement, Jones purchases the land from Smith, who is liable to Jones for fraudulent misrepresentation. Although fraudulent misrepresentation is a tort action, it is closely connected with contractual negotiations; the effects of such misrepresentation on assent to a contract are discussed in Chapter 11.

◆ *See Figure 7–2*

## DEFENSES TO INTENTIONAL TORTS

Even though the defendant has intentionally invaded the interests of the plaintiff, the defendant will not be liable if such conduct was privileged. A defendant's conduct is privileged if it furthers an interest of such social importance that the law confers immunity from tort liability for the damage the conduct causes to others. Examples of privilege include self-defense, defense of property, and defense of others. In addition, the plaintiff's consent to the defendant's conduct is a defense to intentional torts.

### Consent

If one consents to conduct resulting in damage or harm to his own person, dignity, property, or economic interests, no liability will generally attach to the intentional infliction of injury. **Consent,** which signifies that one is willing for an act to occur, negates the wrongfulness of the act. A person may manifest consent expressly or impliedly, by words or by conduct.

Consent must be given by an individual with capacity to do so. Consent given by a minor, mental incompetent, or intoxicated individual is invalid if he is not capable of appreciating the nature, extent, or probable consequences of the conduct to which he has consented. Consent is not effective if given under duress, by which one constrains another's will by compelling that other to give consent unwillingly.

### Privilege

A person who would otherwise be liable for a tort is *not* liable if he acts pursuant to and within the limits of a privilege. Restatement, Section 890. Conditional privileges, as discussed in the section on defamation, depend upon proper use of the privilege. Absolute privilege, on the other hand, protects the defendant regardless of his purpose. Examples of absolute privilege include untrue, defamatory statements made by participants during the course of judicial proceedings, by legislators, by certain governmental executives, and between spouses. Absolute

**FIGURE 7–2** Intentional Torts

| Interest Protected | Tort |
|---|---|
| **Person** | |
| Freedom from contact | Battery |
| Freedom from apprehension | Assault |
| Freedom of movement | False imprisonment |
| Freedom from distress | Infliction of emotional distress |
| **Dignity** | |
| Reputation | Defamation |
| Privacy | Appropriation |
| | Intrusion |
| | Public disclosure of private facts |
| | False light |
| Freedom from wrongful legal actions | Misuse of legal procedure |
| **Property** | |
| Real | Trespass |
| | Nuisance |
| Personal | Trespass |
| | Conversion |
| **Economic** | |
| Contracts | Interference with contractual rights |
| Goodwill | Disparagement |
| Freedom from deception | Fraudulent misrepresentation |

immunity also protects a public prosecutor from civil liability for malicious prosecution.

One conditional privilege—self-defense—entitles an individual to injure another's person without the other's consent. The law created the privilege of **self-defense** to enable an individual to protect himself against tortious interference. By virtue of this privilege an individual may inflict or impose what would otherwise constitute battery, assault, or false imprisonment.

Section 63 of the Restatement provides:

An actor is privileged to use reasonable force, not intended or likely to cause death or serious bodily harm, to defend himself against unprivileged harmful or offensive contact or other bodily harm which he reasonably believes that another is about to inflict intentionally upon him.

The privilege of self-defense exists whether or not the danger actually exists, provided that the defendant reasonably believed self-defense was necessary. The reasonableness of the defendant's actions is based upon what a person of average courage would have thought under the circumstances. A possessor of property is also permitted to use reasonable force, not intended or likely to cause death or serious bodily harm, to protect his real and personal property.

# Chapter Summary

## Harm to the Person

**Battery** intentional infliction of harmful or offensive bodily contact
**Assault** intentional infliction of apprehension of immediate bodily harm or offensive contact
**False Imprisonment** intentional confining of a person against her will
**Infliction of Emotional Distress** extreme and outrageous conduct intentionally or recklessly causing severe emotional distress

## Harm to the Right of Dignity

**Defamation** false communication that injures a person's reputation
- *Libel* written or electronically transmitted defamation
- *Slander* spoken defamation
- *Defenses* truth, absolute privilege, conditional privilege, and constitutional privilege are defenses to a defamation action

**Invasion of Privacy**
- *Appropriation* unauthorized use of a person's identity
- *Intrusion* unreasonable and offensive interference with the seclusion of another
- *Public Disclosure of Private Facts* offensive publicity of private information
- *False Light* offensive and false publicity about another

**Misuse of Legal Procedure** torts that protect an individual from unjustifiable litigation

## Harm to Property

**Real Property** land and anything attached to it
- *Trespass* wrongfully entering on land of another
- *Nuisance* a nontrespassory interference with another's use and enjoyment of land

**Personal Property** any property other than land
- *Trespass* an intentional taking or use of another's personal property
- *Conversion* intentional exercise of control over another's personal property

| Harm to Economic Interests | **Interference with Contractual Relations** intentionally causing one of the parties to a contract not to perform |
|---|---|
| | **Disparagement** publication of false statements about another's property or products |
| | **Fraudulent Misrepresentation** a false statement, made with knowledge of its falsity, intended to induce another to act |

| Defenses to Intentional Torts | **Consent** a person may not recover for injury to which he willingly and knowingly consents |
|---|---|
| | **Self-Defense** a person may take appropriate action to prevent harm to himself where time does not allow resort to the law |

 # Cases

### CASE 7–1
### Punitive Damages
## *BMW OF NORTH AMERICA, INC. v. GORE*
Supreme Court of the United States, 1996
517 U.S. 559, 116 S.Ct. 1589, 134 L.Ed.2d 809

STEVENS, J.

The Due Process Clause of the Fourteenth Amendment prohibits a State from imposing a "'grossly excessive'" punishment on a tortfeasor. [Citation.] The wrongdoing involved in this case was the decision by a national distributor of automobiles not to advise its dealers, and hence their customers, of predelivery damage to new cars when the cost of repair amounted to less than 3 percent of the car's suggested retail price. The question presented is whether a $2 million punitive damages award to the purchaser of one of these cars exceeds the constitutional limit.

### I

In January 1990, Dr. Ira Gore, Jr. (respondent), purchased a black BMW sports sedan for $40,750.88 from an authorized BMW dealer in Birmingham, Alabama. After driving the car for approximately nine months, and without noticing any flaws in its appearance, Dr. Gore took the car to "Slick Finish," an independent detailer, to make it look "'snazzier than it normally would appear.'" [Citation.] Mr. Slick, the proprietor, detected evidence that the car had been repainted. Convinced that he had been cheated, Dr. Gore brought suit against petitioner

BMW of North America (BMW), the American distributor of BMW automobiles. Dr. Gore alleged, *inter alia,* that the failure to disclose that the car had been repainted constituted suppression of a material fact. The complaint prayed for $500,000 in compensatory and punitive damages, and costs.

At trial, BMW acknowledged that it had adopted a nationwide policy in 1983 concerning cars that were damaged in the course of manufacture or transportation. If the cost of repairing the damage exceeded 3 percent of the car's suggested retail price, the car was placed in company service for a period of time and then sold as used. If the repair cost did not exceed 3 percent of the suggested retail price, however, the car was sold as new without advising the dealer that any repairs had been made. Because the $601.37 cost of repainting Dr. Gore's car was only about 1.5 percent of its suggested retail price, BMW did not disclose the damage or repair to the Birmingham dealer. Dr. Gore asserted that his repainted car was worth less than a car that had not been refinished. To prove his actual damages of $4,000, he relied on the testimony of a former BMW dealer, who estimated that the value of a repainted BMW was approximately 10 percent less than the value of a new car that had not been damaged and repaired. To support his claim for punitive damages, Dr. Gore introduced evidence that since 1983 BMW had sold 983 refinished cars as new, including 14 in Alabama, without disclosing that the cars had been repainted before sale at a cost of more than $300 per vehicle. Using the actual damage estimate of $4,000 per vehicle, Dr. Gore argued that a punitive award of $4 million would provide an appropriate penalty for selling approximately 1,000 cars for more than they were worth.

In defense of its disclosure policy, BMW argued that is was under no obligation to disclose repairs of minor damage to new cars and that Dr. Gore's car was as good as a car with the original factory finish. It disputed Dr. Gore's assertion that the value of the car was impaired by the repainting and argued that this good-faith belief made a punitive award inappropriate. BMW also maintained that transactions in jurisdictions other than Alabama had no relevance to Dr. Gore's claim.

The jury returned a verdict finding BMW liable for compensatory damages of $4,000. In addition, the jury assessed $4 million in punitive damages, based on a determination that the disclosure policy constituted "gross, oppressive or malicious" fraud.

BMW filed a post-trial motion to set aside the punitive damages award. The company introduced evidence to establish that its nondisclosure policy was consistent with the laws of roughly 25 States defining the disclosure obligations of automobile manufacturers, distributors, and dealers. The most stringent of these statutes required disclosure of repairs costing more than 3 percent of the suggested retail price; none mandated disclosure of less costly repairs. Relying on these statutes, BMW contended that its conduct was lawful in these States and therefore could not provide the basis for an award of punitive damages.

* * *

The trial judge denied BMW's post-trial motion, holding, *inter alia,* that the award was not excessive. On appeal, the Alabama Supreme Court also rejected BMW's claim that the award exceeded the constitutionally permissible amount. [Citation.] * * *

The Alabama Supreme Court did, however, rule in BMW's favor on one critical point: The court found that the jury improperly computed the amount of punitive damages by multiplying Dr. Gore's compensatory damages by the number of similar sales in other jurisdictions. [Citation.] Having found the verdict tainted, the court held that "a constitutionally reasonable punitive damages award in this case is $2,000,000," [citation], and therefore ordered a remittitur in that amount. The court's discussion of the amount of its remitted award expressly disclaimed any reliance on "acts that occurred in other

jurisdictions"; instead, the court explained that it had used a "comparative analysis" that considered Alabama cases, "along with cases from other jurisdictions, involving the sale of an automobile where the seller misrepresented the condition of the vehicle and the jury awarded punitive damages to the purchaser." [Citation.]

Because we believed that a review of this case would help to illuminate "the character of the standard that will identify constitutionally excessive awards" of punitive damages, [citation], we granted certiorari, [citation].

## II

Punitive damages may properly be imposed to further a State's legitimate interest in punishing unlawful conduct and deterring its repetition. [Citations.] In our federal system, States necessarily have considerable flexibility in determining the level of punitive damages that they will allow in different classes of cases and in any particular case. Most States that authorize exemplary damages afford the jury similar latitude, requiring only that the damages awarded be reasonably necessary to vindicate the State's legitimate interests in punishment and deterrence. [Citations.] Only when an award can fairly be categorized as "grossly excessive" in relation to these interests does it enter the zone of arbitrariness that violates the Due Process Clause of the Fourteenth Amendment. [Citation.] For that reason, the federal excessiveness inquiry appropriately begins with an identification of the state interests that a punitive award is designed to serve. We therefore focus our attention first on the scope of Alabama's legitimate interests in punishing BMW and deterring it from future misconduct.

No one doubts that a State may protect its citizens by prohibiting deceptive trade practices and by requiring automobile distributors to disclose presale repairs that affect the value of a new car. But the States need not, and in fact do not, provide such protection in a uniform manner.

* * *

We think it follows from these principles of state sovereignty and comity that a State may not impose economic sanctions on violators of its laws with the intent of changing the tortfeasors' lawful conduct in other States. * * * Alabama may insist that BMW adhere to a particular disclosure policy in that State. Alabama does not have the power, however, to punish BMW for conduct that was lawful where it occurred and that had no impact on Alabama or its residents. Nor may Alabama impose sanctions on BMW in order to deter conduct that is lawful in other jurisdictions.

* * * The Alabama Supreme Court therefore properly eschewed reliance on BMW's out-of-state conduct, [citation], and based its remitted award solely on conduct that occurred within Alabama. The award must be analyzed in the light of the same conduct, with consideration given only to the interests of Alabama consumers, rather than those of the entire Nation. When the scope of the interest in punishment and deterrence that an Alabama court may appropriately consider is properly limited, it is apparent—for reasons that we shall now address—that this award is grossly excessive.

## III

Elementary notions of fairness enshrined in our constitutional jurisprudence dictate that a person receive fair notice not only of the conduct that will subject him to punishment but also of the severity of the penalty that a State may impose. Three guideposts, each of which indicates that BMW did not receive adequate notice of the magnitude of the sanction that Alabama might impose for adhering to the nondisclosure policy adopted in 1983, lead us to the conclusion that the $2 million award against BMW is grossly excessive: the degree of reprehensibility of the nondisclosure; the disparity between the harm or potential harm suffered by Dr. Gore and his punitive damages award; and the difference between this remedy and the civil penalties authorized or imposed in comparable cases. We discuss these considerations in turn.

### Degree of Reprehensibility

Perhaps the most important indicium of the reasonableness of a punitive damages award is the degree of reprehensibility of the defendant's conduct. As the Court stated nearly 150 years ago, exemplary damages imposed on a defendant should reflect "the enormity of his offense." [Citation.] This principle reflects the accepted view that some wrongs are more blameworthy than others. Thus, we have said that "nonviolent crimes are less serious than crimes marked by violence or the threat of violence." [Citation.] Similarly, "trickery and deceit," [citation], are more reprehensible than negligence.

* * *

In this case, none of the aggravating factors associated with particularly reprehensible conduct is present. The harm BMW inflicted on Dr. Gore was purely economic in nature. The presale refinishing of the car had no effect on its performance or safety features, or even its appearance for at least nine months after his purchase. BMW's conduct evinced no indifference to or reckless disregard for the health and safety of others. To be sure, infliction of economic injury, especially when done intentionally through affirmative acts of misconduct, [citation], or when the target is financially vulnerable, can warrant a substantial penalty. But this observation does not convert all acts that cause economic harm into torts that are sufficiently reprehensible to justify a significant sanction in addition to compensatory damages.

* * *

Finally, the record in this case discloses no deliberate false statements, acts of affirmative misconduct, or concealment of evidence of improper motive, [citation]. We accept, of course, the jury's finding that BMW suppressed a material fact which Alabama law obligated it to communicate to prospective purchasers of repainted cars in that State. But the omission of a material fact may be less reprehensible than a deliberate false statement, particularly when there is a good-faith basis for believing that no duty to disclose exists.

That conduct is sufficiently reprehensible to give rise to tort liability, and even a modest award of exemplary damages, does not establish the high degree of culpability that warrants a substantial punitive damages award. Because this case exhibits none of the circumstances ordinarily associated with egregiously improper conduct, we are persuaded that BMW's conduct was not sufficiently reprehensible to warrant imposition of a $2 million exemplary damages award.

### Ratio

The second and perhaps most commonly cited indicium of an unreasonable or excessive punitive damages award is its ratio to the actual harm inflicted on the plaintiff. [Citation.] The principle that exemplary damages must bear a "reasonable relationship" to compensatory damages has a long pedigree. Scholars have identified a number of early English statutes authorizing the award of multiple damages for particular wrongs. Some 65 different enactments during the period between 1275 and 1753 provided for double, treble, or quadruple damages. Our decisions in [citations] endorsed the proposition that a comparison between the compensatory award and the punitive award is significant.

In [citation] we concluded that even though a punitive damages award of "more than 4 times the amount of compensatory damages," might be "close to the line," it did not "cross the line into the area of constitutional impropriety." [Citation], following dicta in [citation], refined this analysis by confirming that the proper inquiry is "'whether there is a reasonable relationship between the punitive damages award and the harm likely to result from the defendant's conduct as well as the harm that actually has occurred.'" [Citation.] Thus, in upholding the $10 million award in [citation], we relied on the difference between that figure and the harm to the victim that would have ensued if the tortious plan had succeeded. That difference suggested that the relevant ratio was not more than 10 to 1.

The $2 million in punitive damages awarded to Dr. Gore by the Alabama Supreme Court is 500 times the amount of his actual harm as determined by the jury. Moreover, there is no suggestion that Dr. Gore or any other BMW purchaser was threatened with any additional potential harm by BMW's nondisclosure policy. The disparity in this case is thus dramatically greater than those considered in [citations].

Of course, we have consistently rejected the notion that the constitutional line is marked by a simple mathematical formula, even one that compares actual and potential damages to the punitive award. [Citation.] Indeed, low awards of compensatory damages may properly support a higher ratio than high compensatory awards, if, for example, a particularly egregious act has resulted in only a small amount of economic damages. A higher ratio may also be justified in cases in which the injury is hard to detect or the monetary value of noneconomic harm might have been difficult to determine. * * * In most cases, the ratio will be within a constitutionally acceptable range, and remittitur will not be justified on this basis. When the ratio is a breathtaking 500 to 1, however, the award must surely "raise a suspicious judicial eyebrow." [Citation.]

## Sanctions for Comparable Misconduct

Comparing the punitive damages award and the civil or criminal penalties that could be imposed for comparable misconduct provides a third indicium of excessiveness. As JUSTICE O'CONNOR has correctly observed, a reviewing court engaged in determining whether an award of punitive damages is excessive should "accord 'substantial deference' to legislative judgments concerning appropriate sanctions for the conduct at issue." [Citation.] In [citation], the Court noted that although the exemplary award was "much in excess of the fine that could be imposed," imprisonment was also authorized in the criminal context. In this case the $2 million economic sanction imposed on BMW is substantially greater than the statutory fines available in Alabama and elsewhere for similar malfeasance.

The maximum civil penalty authorized by the Alabama Legislature for a violation of its Deceptive Trade Practices Act is $2,000; other States authorize more severe sanctions, with the maxima ranging from $5,000 to $10,000. * * *

* * *

The judgment is reversed, and the case is remanded for further proceedings not inconsistent with this opinion. It is so ordered.

---

## CASE 7–2
### False Imprisonment, Infliction of Emotional Distress
### *MITCHELL v. WALMART STORES, INC.*
Court of Appeals of Georgia, 1996
223 Ga.App. 328, 477 S.E.2d 631

McMurray, J.

Plaintiff Edith Mitchell brought this tort action against defendant Walmart Stores, Inc. alleging intentional and negligent infliction of emotional distress arising out of a July 18, 1995, incident whereby plaintiff was forcibly stopped as she exited defendant's store. A guard allegedly grabbed plaintiff's shopping bag and commanded her to come with him. Plaintiff was "subjected to a lengthy, unreasonable, and humiliating search[, . . . which search] produced no evidence of stolen property but revealed the presence of a security code unit still attached to one of Plaintiff's purchased items." The complaint further alleged the intentional torts of assault, battery, and false imprisonment. * * *

After discovery, defendant moved for summary judgment on the basis of OCGA § 51–7–60, supporting its motion with the following undisputed facts: Plaintiff, accompanied by her 13-year-old daughter, went through the checkout and purchased several items, including a television remote control, at defendant's store. As she exited, plaintiff passed through an electronic antitheft device. The alarm sounded. Plaintiff "wasn't going to stop because [she] knew [she] didn't have nothing in [her] pocketbook or in [her] bag." Robert Canady, employed by defendant as a "people greeter" and security guard, forcibly stopped plaintiff at the exit. Mr. Canady "grabbed [plaintiff's] bag and told [her] to step back inside[, . . . that she] had something in [the] bag. So [plaintiff] stepped back inside." This security guard removed every item plaintiff had just purchased and ran it through the security gate. Plaintiff affirmed that "one of the items still had a security code thing on it." An employee named Brenda "told [plaintiff] it could have been that [security code unit], that she [Brenda] forgot to pull it off [at the cash register]." When the security guard finished examining the contents of plaintiff's bag, "he put it on the checkout. . . ." This examination of her bag took ten or fifteen minutes. Plaintiff then "reached over there and got it and went over to the snack bar and [sat] there." The security guard never touched plaintiff or her daughter and never threatened to touch either of them. No employee of defendant ever told plaintiff she could not leave, once her bag had been checked. Plaintiff never asked to leave but felt like she could not leave. Although plaintiff told an assistant manager that "'[she] need[ed] to see the manager,' [the assistant] said, 'he won't come.'" Plaintiff knew of no circumstances indicating that the detection device was not working properly. Plaintiff was never threatened with arrest. Nevertheless, plaintiff described the security guard's actions in her affidavit as "gruff, loud, rude behavior."

Plaintiff opposed summary judgment, arguing that jury questions remain as to whether the manner and length of her detention were reasonable under OCGA § 51–7–60. The trial court granted defendant's motion, and this appeal followed.

OCGA § 51–7–60 (1) and (2) provides: "Whenever the owner or operator of a mercantile establishment . . . detains, arrests, or causes to be detained or arrested any person reasonably thought to be engaged in shoplifting . . . , no recovery [for false arrest or false imprisonment] shall be had by the plaintiff . . . where it is established by competent evidence . . . [t]hat the plaintiff . . . behaved in such manner as to cause a [person] of reasonable prudence to believe that the plaintiff . . . was committing the offense of [theft by] shoplifting, as defined by Code Section 16–8–14; or . . . [t]hat the manner of the detention or arrest and the length of time during which such plaintiff was detained was under all the circumstances reasonable."

"In the case of a mercantile establishment utilizing an antishoplifting or inventory control device, the automatic activation of the device as a result of a person exiting the establishment or a protected area within the establishment shall constitute reasonable cause for the detention of the person so exiting. . . ." OCGA § 51–7–61(b). Nevertheless, "[e]ach detention shall be made only in a reasonable manner and only for a reasonable period of time sufficient for any inquiry into the circumstances surrounding the activation of the device." Id.

In the case *sub judice* [before this court], assuming that defendant's agent was in fact gruff and rude as he forcibly halted her, it is nevertheless undisputed that this was done solely in response to the alarm of the antitheft device. Accordingly, probable cause was established for that forcible stop, and plaintiff's claims for false arrest are without merit. "[I]t makes no difference to 'reasonable cause' whether or not negligence on the part of [Walmart's] employee in failing to deactivate the special tag on the [remote control plaintiff purchased] set the device off. What matters is whether the method and time of detention were reasonable within the statutory limitations. Defendant's right to detain is lawful once the device is automatically activated." [Citation.]

Plaintiff was subjected to a ten- or fifteen-minute "detention" in the open, during which the items in plaintiff's shopping bag were individually tested for the presence of the electronic antitheft sensor and after which plaintiff's bag was returned to her and she was free to leave. This procedure was perfectly reasonable. [Citation.] The manner of plaintiff's detention, whereby defendant's employee never placed a hand on plaintiff's person but only took her shopping bag, and during which plaintiff was never accused of theft, also was reasonable. Naturally, plaintiff was mortified by this episode because she knew she had properly paid for all of her items. Nevertheless, "causing embarrassment is not the same as unlawful imprisonment.[Citation.]" [Citation.] In the case *sub judice*, there is no evidence that the length of time and the manner of plaintiff's detention were anything but reasonable. [Citation.] Consequently, the defendant mercantile establishment is entitled to the immunity afforded by OCGA § 51–7–60. Similarly, "there was no [unlawful] restraint either by force or fear here, as is necessary to recover [for false imprisonment] under OCGA § 51–7–20. [Citation.]" [Citation.] It follows that the trial court correctly granted defendant's motion for summary judgment.

---

## CASE 7–3
## Defamation
## *FRANK B. HALL & CO., INC. v. BUCK*

Court of Appeals of Texas, Fourteenth District, 1984
678 S.W.2d 612

JUNELL, J.

Larry W. Buck (Buck or appellee) sued his former employer, Frank B. Hall & Co. (Hall or appellant), for damages for defamation of character, . . . By unanimous verdict, a jury found damages for . . . defamation of character and exemplary damages. The court entered judgment for appellee for $1,905,000.00 in damages, plus interest, attorney's fees and costs of court. For the reasons set forth below we affirm.

Appellee, an established salesman in the insurance business, was approached in the spring of 1976 by a representative of Hall with a prospective job offer. Appellee was then an executive vice-president of the insurance firm of Alexander & Alexander, and in the previous year he generated approximately $550,000.00 in commissions for the firm. He was the top producer in Alexander's Houston office and was ranked nationally among the top five salesmen for Alexander. After several meetings, Buck accepted Hall's offer of employment and began working for Hall on June 1, 1976. Hall agreed to pay Buck an annual salary of $80,000.00 plus additional compensation equal to seven and one-half percent of net retained commissions for each year to a maximum commission of $600,000.00, plus fringe benefits. The agreement was to be for a three year period. Several Alexander employees followed Buck to Hall's office. During the next several months Buck generated substantial commission income for Hall and succeeded in bringing several major accounts to the firm.

In October, 1976, Mendel Kaliff, then president of Frank B. Hall & Co. of Texas, held a meeting with Buck and Lester Eckert, Hall's office manager and a former Alexander employee. Kaliff informed Buck his salary was being reduced to $65,000.00 and that Hall was eliminating Buck's incentive and profit sharing benefits. Kaliff told Buck these measures were being taken because of Buck's failure to produce sufficient income for Hall. However, Kaliff added that if Buck could generate $400,000.00 net commission income by June 1, 1977, his salary and benefits would be reinstated retroactively.

On March 31, 1977, at another impromptu meeting, Kaliff and Eckert abruptly fired Buck and instructed him not to return to Hall's offices. Buck sought employment with several other insurance firms, but his efforts were fruitless. Distraught at having lost his job and being unable to find suitable employment in the insurance business, Buck hired an investigator, Lloyd Barber, in an attempt to discover Hall's true reasons for firing him. This suit is based upon statements made by Hall employees to Lloyd Barber and to Charles Burton, a prospective employer, and upon a note written by Virginia Hilley, a Hall employee. Appellant brings eighty points of error, which will be grouped in thirteen categories.

* * *

Lloyd Barber contacted Mendel Kaliff, Lester Eckert and Virginia Hilley and told them that he was an investigator, Buck was being considered for a position of trust and responsibility, and Barber was seeking information about Buck's employment with Frank B. Hall & Co. Barber testified that he had interviewed Kaliff, Eckert and Hilley on separate occasions in September and October of 1977, and had tape-recorded the conversations. Appellee introduced into evidence Barber's properly authenticated investigative reports, which were based on these taped interviews. The report shows Kaliff remarked several times that Buck was untrustworthy, and not always entirely truthful; he said Buck was disruptive, paranoid, hostile and was guilty of padding his expense account. Kaliff said he had locked Buck out of his office and had not trusted him to return. He charged that Buck had promised things he could not deliver. Eckert told Barber that Buck was horrible in a business sense, irrational, ruthless, and disliked by office personnel. He described Buck as a "classical sociopath," who would verbally abuse and embarrass Hall employees. Eckert said Buck had stolen files and records from Alexander & Alexander. He called Buck "a zero," "a Jekyll and Hyde person" who was "lacking in compucture (sic) or scruples."

Virginia Hilley told Barber that Buck could have been charged with theft for materials he brought with him to Hall from Alexander & Alexander.

Any act wherein the defamatory matter is intentionally or negligently communicated to a third person is a publication. In the case of slander, the act is usually the speaking of the words. Restatement (Second) Torts § 577 comment a (1977). There is ample support in the record to show that these individuals intentionally communicated disparaging remarks to a third person. The jury was instructed that "Publication means to communicate defamatory words to some third person in such a way that he understands the words to be defamatory. A statement is not published if it was authorized, invited or procured by Buck and if Buck knew in advance the contents of the invited communication." In response to special issues, the jury found that the slanderous statements were made and published to Barber.

Hall argues that Buck could and should have expected Hall's employees to give their opinion of Buck when requested to do so. Hall is correct in stating that a plaintiff may not recover for a publication to which he has consented, or which he has authorized, procured or invited, [citation]; and it may be true that Buck could assume that Hall's employees would give their opinion when asked they do so. However, there is nothing in the record to indicate that Buck knew Hall's employees would defame him when Barber made the inquiries. The accusations made by Kaliff, Eckert and Hilley were not mere expressions of opinion but were false and derogatory statements of fact.

* * *

A defamer cannot escape liability by showing that, although he desired to defame the plaintiff, he did not desire to defame him to the person to whom he in fact intentionally published the defamatory communication. The publication is complete although the publisher is mistaken as to the identity of the person to whom the publication is made. Restatement (Second) of Torts § 577 comment 1 (1977). Likewise, communication to an agent of the person defamed is a publication, unless the communication is invited by the person defamed or his agent. Restatement § 577 comment e. We have already determined that the evidence is sufficient to show

that Buck did not know what Kaliff, Eckert or Hilley would say and that he did not procure the defamatory statements to create a lawsuit. Thus, the fact that Barber may have been acting at Buck's request is not fatal to Buck's cause of action. There is absolutely no proof that Barber induced Kaliff, Eckert or Hilley to make any of the defamatory comments.

* * *

When an ambiguity exists, a fact issue is presented. The court, by submission of proper fact issues, should let the jury render its verdict on whether the statements were fairly susceptible to the construction placed thereon by the plaintiff. [Citation.] Here, the jury found (1) Eckert made a statement calculated to convey that Buck had been terminated because of serious misconduct; (2) the statement was slanderous or libelous; (3) the statement was made with malice; (4) the statement was published; and (5) damage directly resulted from the statement. The jury also found the statements were not substantially true. The jury thus determined that these statements, which were capable of a defamatory meaning, were understood as such by Burton.

* * *

We hold that the evidence supports the award of actual damages and the amount awarded is not manifestly unjust. Furthermore, in responding to the issue on exemplary damages, the jury was instructed that exemplary damages must be based on a finding that Hall "acted with ill will, bad intent, malice or gross disregard to the rights of Buck." Although there is no fixed ratio between exemplary and actual damages, exemplary damages must be reasonably apportioned to the actual damages sustained. [Citation.] Because of the actual damages [$605,000] and the abundant evidence of malice, we hold that the award of punitive damages [$1,300,000] was not unreasonable. * * *

The judgment of the trial court is affirmed.

---

## CASE 7–4
### Appropriation
# WHITE v. SAMSUNG ELECTRONICS AMERICA, INC.
United States Court of Appeals, Ninth Circuit, 1992
971 F.2d 1395

GOODWIN, J.
This case involves a promotional "fame and fortune" dispute. In running a particular advertisement without Vanna White's permission, defendants Samsung Elec-

tronics America, Inc. (Samsung) and David Deutsch Associates, Inc. (Deutsch) attempted to capitalize on White's fame to enhance their fortune. White sued, alleging infringement of various intellectual property rights, but the district court granted summary judgment in favor of the defendants. We affirm in part, reverse in part, and remand.

Plaintiff Vanna White is the hostess of "Wheel of Fortune," one of the most popular game shows in television history. An estimated forty million people watch the program daily. Capitalizing on the fame which her participation in the show has bestowed on her, White markets her identity to various advertisers.

The dispute in this case arose out of a series of advertisements prepared for Samsung by Deutsch. The series ran in at least half a dozen publications with widespread, and in some cases national, circulation. Each of the advertisements in the series followed the same theme. Each depicted a current item from popular culture and a Samsung electronic product. Each was set in the twenty-first century and conveyed the message that the Samsung product would still be in use by that time. By hypothesizing outrageous future outcomes for the cultural items, the ads created humorous effects. For example, one lampooned current popular notions of an unhealthy diet by depicting a raw steak with the caption: "Revealed to be health food, 2010 A.D." Another depicted irreverent "news"-show host Morton Downey Jr. in front of an American flag with the caption: "Presidential candidate. 2008 A.D."

The advertisement which prompted the current dispute was for Samsung videocassette recorders (VCRs). The ad depicted a robot, dressed in a wig, gown, and jewelry which Deutsch consciously selected to resemble White's hair and dress. The robot was posed next to a game board which is instantly recognizable as the Wheel of Fortune game show set, in a stance for which White is famous. The caption of the ad read: "Longestrunning game show. 2012 A.D." Defendants referred to the ad as the "Vanna White" ad. Unlike the other celebrities used in the campaign, White neither consented to the ads nor was she paid.

Following the circulation of the robot ad, White sued Samsung and Deutsch in federal district court under: * * * the California common law right of publicity; * * * . The district court granted summary judgment against White on each of her claims. White now appeals.

* * *

White . . . argues that the district court erred in granting summary judgment to defendants on White's common law right of publicity claim. In *Eastwood v. Superior Court*, [citation], the California court of appeal stated that the common law right of publicity cause of action "may be pleaded by alleging (1) the defendant's use of the plaintiff's identity; (2) the appropriation of plaintiff's name or likeness to defendant's advantage, commercially or otherwise; (3) lack of consent, and (4) resulting injury." [Citation.] The district court dismissed White's claim for failure to satisfy *Eastwood*'s second prong, reasoning that defendants had not appropriated White's "name or likeness" with their robot ad. We agree that the robot ad did not make use of White's name or likeness. However, the common law right of publicity is not so confined.

The *Eastwood* court did not hold that the right of publicity cause of action could be pleaded only by alleging an appropriation of name or likeness. *Eastwood* involved an unauthorized use of photographs of Clint Eastwood and of his name. Accordingly, the *Eastwood* court had no occasion to consider the extent beyond the use of name or likeness to which the right of publicity reaches. That court held only that the right of publicity cause of action "may be" pleaded by alleging, *inter alia*, appropriation of name or likeness, not that the action may be pleaded only in those terms.

The "name or likeness" formulation referred to in *Eastwood* originated not as an element of the right of publicity cause of action, but as a description of the types of cases in which the cause of action had been recognized. The source of this formulation is Prosser, *Privacy*, 48 Cal.L.Rev. 383, 401–07 (1960), one of the earliest and most enduring articulations of the common law right of publicity cause of action. In looking at the case law to that point, Prosser recognized that right of publicity cases involved one of two basic factual scenarios: name appropriation, and picture or other likeness appropriation. [Citation.]

Even though Prosser focused on appropriations of name or likeness in discussing the right of publicity, he noted that "[i]t is not impossible that there might be appropriation of the plaintiff's identity, as by impersonation, without use of either his name or his likeness, and that this would be an invasion of his right of privacy." [Citation.] At the time Prosser wrote, he noted however, that "[n]o such case appears to have arisen." [Citation.]

Since Prosser's early formulation, the case law has borne out his insight that the right of publicity is not limited to the appropriation of name or likeness. In *Motschenbacher v. R.J. Reynolds Tobacco Co.*, [citation], the defendant had used a photograph of the plaintiff's race car in a television commercial. Although the plaintiff appeared driving the car in the photograph, his features were not visible. Even though the defendant had not appropriated the plaintiff's name or likeness, this court held that plaintiff's California right of publicity claim should reach the jury.

In *Midler*, this court held that, even though the defendants had not used Midler's name or likeness, Midler had stated a claim for violation of her California common law right of publicity because "the defendants . . . for their own profit in selling their product did appropriate part of her identity" by using a Midler sound-alike. [Citation.]

In *Carson v. Here's Johnny Portable Toilets, Inc.*, [citation], the defendant had marketed portable toilets under the brand name "Here's Johnny"—Johnny Carson's signature "Tonight Show" introduction—without Carson's permission. The district court had dismissed Carson's Michigan common law right of publicity claim because the defendants had not used Carson's "name or likeness." [Citation.] In reversing the district court, the sixth circuit found "the district court's conception of the right of publicity . . . too narrow" and held that the right was implicated because the defendant had appropriated Carson's identity by using, *inter alia,* the phrase "Here's Johnny." [Citation.]

These cases teach not only that the common law right of publicity reaches means of appropriation other than name or likeness, but that the specific means of appropriation are relevant only for determining whether the defendant has in fact appropriated the plaintiff's identity. The right of publicity does not require that appropriations of identity be accomplished through particular means to be actionable. It is noteworthy that the *Midler* and *Carson* defendants not only avoided using the plaintiff's name or likeness, but they also avoided appropriating the celebrity's voice, signature, and photograph. The photograph in *Motschenbacher* did include the plaintiff, but because the plaintiff was not visible the driver could have been an actor or dummy and the analysis in the case would have been the same.

Although the defendants in these cases avoided the most obvious means of appropriating the plaintiffs' identities, each of their actions directly implicated the commercial interests which the right of publicity is designed to protect. As the *Carson* court explained,

[t]he right of publicity has developed to protect the commercial interest of celebrities in their identities. The theory of the right is that a celebrity's identity can be valuable in the promotion of products, and the celebrity has an interest that may be protected from the unauthorized commercial exploitation of that identity . . . If the celebrity's identity is commercially exploited, there has been an invasion of his right whether or not his "name or likeness" is used.

[Citation.] It is not important how the defendant has appropriated the plaintiff's identity, but whether the defendant has done so. *Motschenbacher, Midler,* and *Carson* teach the impossibility of treating the right of publicity as guarding only against a laundry list of specific means of appropriating identity. A rule which says that the right of publicity can be infringed only through the use of nine different methods of appropriating identity merely challenges the clever advertising strategist to come up with the tenth.

Indeed, if we treated the means of appropriation as dispositive in our analysis of the right of publicity, we would not only weaken the right but effectively eviscerate it. The right would fail to protect those plaintiffs most in need of its protection. Advertisers use celebrities to promote their products. The more popular the celebrity, the greater the number of people who recognize her, and the greater the visibility for the product. The identities of the most popular celebrities are not only the most attractive for advertisers, but also the easiest to evoke without resorting to obvious means such as name, likeness, or voice.

Consider a hypothetical advertisement which depicts a mechanical robot with male features, an African-American complexion, and a bald head. The robot is wearing black hightop Air Jordan basketball sneakers, and a red basketball uniform with black trim, baggy shorts, and the number 23 (though not revealing "Bulls" or "Jordan" lettering). The ad depicts the robot dunking a basketball one-handed, stiff-armed, legs extended like open scissors, and tongue hanging out. Now envision that this ad is run on television during professional basketball games. Considered individually, the robot's physical attributes, its dress, and its stance tell us little. Taken together, they lead to the only conclusion that any sports viewer who has registered a discernible pulse in the past five years would reach: the ad is about Michael Jordan.

Viewed separately, the individual aspects of the advertisement in the present case say little. Viewed together, they leave little doubt about the celebrity the ad is meant to depict. The female-shaped robot is wearing a long gown, blond wig, and large jewelry. Vanna White dresses exactly like this at times, but so do many other women. The robot is in the process of turning a block letter on a game-board. Vanna White dresses like this while turning letters on a game-board but perhaps similarly attired Scrabble-playing women do this as well. The robot is standing on what looks to be the Wheel of Fortune game show set. Vanna White dresses like this, turns letters, and does this on the Wheel of Fortune game show. She is the only one. Indeed, defendants themselves referred to their ad as the "Vanna White" ad. We are not surprised.

Television and other media create marketable celebrity identity value. Considerable energy and ingenuity are expended by those who have achieved celebrity value to exploit it for profit. The law protects the celebrity's sole right to exploit this value whether the celebrity has achieved her fame out of rare ability, dumb luck, or a combination thereof. We decline Samsung and Deutsch's invitation to permit the evisceration of the common law right of publicity through means as facile as those in this case. Because White has alleged facts showing that Samsung and Deutsch had appropriated her identity, the district court erred by rejecting, on summary judgment, White's common law right of publicity claim.

---

 # Questions

**1.** Identify and define the torts that protect against intentional harm to personal rights.

**2.** Explain the application of the various privileges to defamation suits and how they are affected by whether the plaintiff is (a) a public figure, (b) a public official, or (c) a private person.

**3.** Distinguish the four torts comprising invasion of privacy.

**4.** Identify and describe the torts that protect against harm to property.

**5.** Distinguish by example among interference with contractual relations, disparagement, and fraudulent misrepresentation.

---

# Problems

**1.** The Penguin intentionally hits Batman with his umbrella. Batman, stunned by the blow, falls backwards, knocking Robin down. Robin's leg is broken in the fall, and he cries out, "Holy broken bat bones! My leg is broken." Who, if anyone, is liable to Robin? Why?

**2.** CEO was convinced by his employee, M. Ploy, that a coworker, A. Cused, had been stealing money from the company. At lunch that day in the company cafeteria, CEO discharges Cused from her employment, accuses her of stealing from the company, searches through her purse over her objections, and finally forcibly escorts her to his office to await the arrival of the police, which he has his secretary summon. Cused is indicted for embezzlement but subsequently is acquitted upon establishing her innocence. What rights, if any, does Cused have against CEO?

**3.** Ralph kisses Edith while she is asleep but does not waken or harm her. Edith sues Ralph for battery. Decision?

**4.** Claude, a creditor seeking to collect a debt, calls on Dianne and demands payment in a rude and insolent manner. When Dianne says that she cannot pay, Claude calls Dianne a deadbeat and says that he will never trust her again. Is Claude liable to Dianne? If so, for what tort?

**5.** Lana, a ten-year-old child, is run over by a car negligently driven by Mitchel. Lana, at the time of the accident, was acting reasonably and without negligence. Clark, a newspaper reporter, photographs Lana while she is lying in the street in great pain. Two years later, Perry, the publisher of a newspaper, prints Clark's picture of Lana in his newspaper as a lead to an article concerning the negligence of children. The caption under the picture reads: "They ask to be killed." Lana, who has recovered from the accident, brings suit against Clark and Perry. What result?

**6.** In 1963 the *Saturday Evening Post* featured an article entitled "The Story of a College Football Fix," characterized in the subtitle as "A Shocking Report of How Wally Butts and Bear Bryant Rigged a Game Last Fall." Butts was athletic director of the University of Georgia, and Bryant was head coach of the University of Alabama. The article was based on a claim by one George Burnett that he had accidentally overheard a long-distance telephone conversation between Butts and Bryant in the course of which Butts divulged information on plays Georgia would use in the upcoming game against Alabama. The writer assigned to the story by the *Post* was not a football expert, did not interview either Butts or Bryant, and did not personally see the notes Burnett had made of the telephone conversation. Butts admitted that he had a long-distance telephone conversation with Bryant but denied that any advance information on prospective football plays was given. Butts brought a libel suit against the *Post*. Decision?

**7.** Joan, a patient confined in a hospital, has a rare disease that is of great interest to the public. Carol, a television reporter, requests Joan to consent to an interview. Joan refuses, but Carol, nonetheless, enters Joan's room over her objection and photographs her. Joan brings a suit against Carol. Decision?

**8.** Owner has a place on his land where he piles trash. The pile has been there for three months. John, a neighbor of Owner and without Owner's consent or knowledge, throws trash onto the trashpile. Owner learns that John has done this and sues him. What tort, if any, has John committed?

9.   Chris leaves her car parked in front of a store. There are no signs that say Chris cannot park there. The store owner, however, needs the car moved to enable a delivery truck to unload. He releases the brake and pushes Chris's car three or four feet, doing no harm to the car. Chris returns and sees that her car has been moved and is very angry. She threatens to sue the store owner for trespass to her personal property. Can she recover?

10.   Carr borrowed John's brand new Ford Escort for the purpose of going to the store. He told John he would be right back. Carr then decided, however, to go to the beach while he had the car. Can John recover from Carr the value of the automobile? If so, for what tort?

11.   Marcia Samms, a respectable married woman, claimed that David Eccles had repeatedly and persistently called her at various hours, including late at night, from May to December, soliciting her to have illicit sexual relations with him. She also claimed that on one occasion Eccles came over to her residence to again solicit sex and indecently exposed himself to her. Mrs. Samms had never encouraged Eccles but had continuously repulsed his "insulting, indecent, and obscene" proposals. She brought suit against Eccles, claiming she suffered great anxiety and fear for her personal safety and severe emotional distress, demanding actual and punitive damages. Decision?

12.   National Bond and Investment Company sent two of its employees to repossess Whithorn's car after he failed to complete the payments. The two repossessors located Whithorn while he was driving his car. They followed him and hailed him down to make the repossession. Whithorn refused to abandon his car and demanded evidence of their authority. The two repossessors became impatient and called a wrecker. They ordered the driver of the wrecker to hook Whithorn's car and move it down the street while Whithorn was still inside the vehicle. Whithorn started the car and tried to escape, but the wrecker lifted the car off the road and progressed seventy-five to one hundred feet until Whithorn managed to stall the wrecker. Whithorn sued National Bond for false imprisonment. Decision?

13.   In March 1975 William Proxmire, a United States senator from Wisconsin, initiated the "Golden Fleece of the Month Award" to publicize what he believed to be wasteful government spending. The second of these awards was given to the Federal agencies that had for seven years funded Dr. Hutchinson's research on stress levels in animals. The award was made in a speech Proxmire gave in the Senate; the text was also incorporated into an advance press release that was sent to 275 members of the national news media. Proxmire also referred to the research in two subsequent newsletters sent to 100,000 constituents and during a television interview. Hutchinson then brought this action alleging defamation resulting in personal and economic injury. Decision?

14.   Capune was attempting a trip from New York to Florida on an eighteen-foot-long paddleboard. The trip was being covered by various media to gain publicity for Capune and certain products he endorsed. By water, Capune approached a pier owned by Robbins, who had posted signs prohibiting surfing and swimming around the pier. Capune was unaware of these notices and attempted to continue his journey by passing under the pier. Robbins ran up yelling and threw two bottles at Capune. Capune was frightened and tried to maneuver his paddleboard to go around the pier. Robbins then threw a third bottle that hit Capune in the head. Capune had to be helped out of the water and taken to the hospital. He suffered a physical wound which required twenty-four sutures and, as a result, had to discontinue his trip. Capune brought suit in tort against Robbins. Is Robbins liable? If so, for which tort or torts?

15.   Ralph Nader, who has been a critic of General Motors for several years, claims that when General Motors learned that Nader was about to publish a book entitled *Unsafe at Any Speed*, criticizing one of its automobiles, it decided to conduct a campaign of intimidation against him. Specifically, Nader claims that GMC (1) conducted a series of interviews with Nader's acquaintances, questioning them about his political, social, racial, and religious views; (2) kept him under surveillance in public places for an unreasonable length of time; (3) caused him to be accosted by women for the purpose of entrapping him into illicit relationships; (4) made threatening, harassing, and obnoxious telephone calls to him; (5) tapped his telephone and eavesdropped by means of mechanical and electronic equipment on his private conversations with others; and (6) conducted a "continuing" and harassing investigation of him. Nader brought suit against GMC for invasion of privacy. Which, if any, of the alleged actions would constitute invasion of privacy?

16.   Bill Kinsey was charged with murdering his wife while working for the Peace Corps in Tanzania. After waiting six months in jail he was acquitted at a trial that attracted wide publicity. Five years later, while a graduate student at Stanford University, Kinsey had a brief affair with Mary Macur. He abruptly ended the affair by telling Macur he would no longer be seeing her because another woman, Sally Allen, was coming from England to live with him. A few months later, Kinsey and Allen moved to Africa and were subsequently married. Soon after Bill ended their affair, Macur began a letter writing campaign designed to expose Bill and his mistreatment of her. Macur sent several letters to both Bill and Sally Kinsey, their former spouses, their parents, their neighbors, their parents' neighbors, members of Bill's dissertation committee, other faculty, and the president of Stanford University. The letters contained statements accusing Bill of murdering his first wife, spending six months in jail for the crime, being a rapist, and other questionable behavior. The Kinseys brought an action for invasion of privacy, seeking damages and a permanent injunction. Decision?

17.   The Brineys (defendants) owned a large farm on which was located an abandoned farmhouse. For a ten-year period the house had been the subject of several trespassings and housebreakings. In an attempt to stop the intrusions, Briney boarded up the windows and doors and posted "no trespassing" signs. After one break-in, however, Briney set a spring

gun in a bedroom. It was placed over the bedroom window so that the gun could not be seen from outside, and no warning of its presence was posted. The gun was set to hit an intruder in the legs. Briney loaded the gun with a live shell, but he claimed that he did not intend to injure anyone.

Katko (plaintiff) and a friend, McDonough, had broken into the abandoned farmhouse on an earlier occasion to steal old bottles and fruit jars for their antique collection. They returned for a second time after the spring gun had been set, and Katko was seriously wounded in the leg when the gun discharged as he entered the bedroom. He then brought this action for damages. Decision?

**18.** Plaintiff, John W. Carson, was the host and star of "The Tonight Show," a well-known television program broadcast by the National Broadcasting Company. Carson also appears as an entertainer in nightclubs and theaters around the country. From the time he began hosting "The Tonight Show" in 1962, he had been introduced on the show each night with the phrase "Here's Johnny." The phrase "Here's Johnny" is still generally associated with Carson by a substantial segment of the television viewing public. In 1967, Carson began authorizing use of this phrase by outside business ventures.

Defendant, Here's Johnny Portable Toilets, Inc., is a Michigan corporation engaged in the business of renting and selling "Here's Johnny" portable toilets. Defendant's founder was aware at the time he formed the corporation that "Here's Johnny" was the introductory slogan for Carson on "The Tonight Show." He indicated that he coupled the phrase with a second one, "The World's Foremost Commodian," to make "a good play on a phrase." Carson brought suit for invasion of privacy. The trial court dismissed Carson's claim, and he appealed. Decision?

**19.** Susan Jungclaus Peterson was a twenty-one-year-old student at Moorhead State University who had lived most of her life on her family farm in Minnesota. Though Susan was a dean's list student during her first year, her academic performance declined after she became deeply involved in an international religious cult organization known locally as The Way of Minnesota, Inc. The cult demanded an enormous psychological and monetary commitment from Susan. Near the end of her junior year, her parents became alarmed by the changes in Susan's physical and mental well-being and concluded that she had been "reduced to a condition of psychological bondage by The Way." They sought help from Kathy Mills, a self-styled "deprogrammer" of minds brainwashed by cults.

On May 24, 1976, Norman Jungclaus, Susan's father, picked up Susan at Moorhead State. Instead of returning home, they went to the residence of Veronica Morgel, where Kathy Mills attempted to deprogram Susan. For the first few days of her stay, Susan was unwilling to discuss her involvement. She lay curled in a fetal position in her bedroom, plugging her ears and hysterically screaming and crying while her father pleaded with her to listen. By the third day, however, Susan's demeanor changed completely. She became friendly and vivacious and communicated with her father. Susan also went roller skating and played softball at a nearby park over the following weekend. She spent the next week in Columbus, Ohio, with a former cult member who had shared her experiences of the previous week. While in Columbus, she spoke daily by telephone with her fiancé, a member of The Way, who begged her to return to the cult. Susan expressed the desire to get her fiancé out of the organization, but a meeting between them could not be arranged outside the presence of other members of The Way. Her parents attempted to persuade Susan to sign an agreement releasing them from liability for their actions, but Susan refused. After nearly sixteen days of "deprogramming" Susan left the Morgel residence and returned to her fiancé and The Way. Upon the direction of The Way ministry, she brought this action against her parents for false imprisonment. Susan appealed from the trial court's judgment in favor of her parents. Decision?

**20.** Debra Agis was a waitress in a restaurant owned by the Howard Johnson Company. On May 23, 1975, Roger Dionne, manager of the restaurant, called a meeting of all waitresses at which he informed them that "there was some stealing going on." Dionne also stated that the identity of the party or parties responsible was not known and that he would begin firing all waitresses in alphabetical order until the guilty party or parties were detected. He then fired Debra Agis, who allegedly "became greatly upset, began to cry, sustained emotional distress, mental anguish, and loss of wages and earnings." Mrs. Agis brought this complaint against the Howard Johnson Company and Roger Dionne, alleging that the defendants acted recklessly and outrageously, intending to cause emotional distress and anguish. The defendants argued that damages for emotional distress are not recoverable unless physical injury occurs as a result of the distress. The judge dismissed the complaint, and Mrs. Agis appealed. Decision?

**WWW** **Internet Exercise** Find information about punitive damages and review the proposed Model Punitive Damages Act.

# CHAPTER 8

# Negligence and Strict Liability

Whereas intentional torts deal with conduct that has a substantial certainty of causing harm, negligence involves conduct that creates an unreasonable risk of harm. The basis of liability for negligence is the failure to exercise reasonable care, under given circumstances, for the safety of another person or his property, which failure proximately causes injury to such person or damage to his property, or both. Thus, if the driver of an automobile intentionally runs down a person, she has committed the intentional tort of battery. If, on the other hand, the driver hits and injures a person while driving without reasonable regard for the safety of others, she is negligent.

Strict liability is not based upon the negligence or intent of the defendant but rather upon the nature of the activity in which he is engaging. Under this doctrine, defendants who engage in certain activities, such as keeping animals or maintaining abnormally dangerous conditions, are held liable for the injuries they cause, even if they have exercised the utmost care. The law imposes this liability to effect a just reallocation of loss, given that the defendant engaged in the activity for his own benefit and is in a better position to manage, by insurance or otherwise, the risk inherent in the activity.

## NEGLIGENCE

The Restatement defines negligence as "conduct which falls below the standard established by law for the protection of others against unreasonable risk of harm." Restatement, Section 282. The standard established by law is the conduct of a reasonable person acting prudently and with due care under the circumstances. The general rule is that a person is under a duty to all others at all times to exercise reasonable care for the safety of the others' person and property. This rule is subject to certain exceptions, however, which are discussed below.

Except when strict liability applies, a person is not liable for injury caused to another by an unavoidable accident—an unintended occurrence that the exercise of reasonable care could not have prevented. Thus, no liability results from the loss of control of an automobile because the driver suddenly and unforeseeably suffers a heart attack, stroke, or fainting spell. If, however, the driver had warning of the imminent heart attack or other infirmity, it would be negligent for him to drive at all.

An action for negligence consists of three elements, each of which the plaintiff must prove:

1. **Breach of duty of care:** that a legal duty required the defendant to conform to the standard of conduct established for the protection of others, and that the defendant failed to conform to that standard;
2. **Proximate cause:** that the defendant's failure to conform to the required standard of conduct proximately caused the injury and harm the plaintiff sustained; and
3. **Injury:** that the injury and harm is of a type protected against negligent interference, or conduct.

## *BREACH OF DUTY OF CARE*

Negligence consists of conduct that creates an unreasonable risk of harm. In determining whether a given risk of harm was unreasonable, the law considers the following factors: (1) the probability that the harm will occur, (2) the gravity or seriousness of the resulting harm, (3) the social utility of the conduct creating the risk, and (4) the cost of taking precautions that would have reduced the risk. Thus, the standard of conduct, which is the basis for the law of negligence, is usually determined by a cost-benefit analysis.

### Reasonable Person Standard

The duty of care imposed by law is measured by the degree of carefulness that a reasonable person would exercise in a given situation. The reasonable person is a fictitious individual who is always careful and prudent and never negligent. What the judge or jury determines a reasonable person would have done in light of the facts disclosed by the evidence in a particular case sets the standard of conduct for that case. The reasonable person standard is thus external and *objective,* as described by Justice Holmes:

If, for instance, a man is born hasty and awkward, is always hurting himself or his neighbors, no doubt his congenital defects will be allowed for in the courts of Heaven, but his slips are no less troublesome to his neighbors than if they sprang from guilty neglect. His neighbors accordingly require him, at his peril, to come up to their standard, and the courts which they establish decline to take his personal equation into account. Holmes, *The Common Law.*

*Children* The standard of conduct to which a child must conform to avoid being negligent is that of a reasonable person of like age, intelligence, and experience under like circumstances. Restatement, Section 283A. For example, Alice, a five-year-old girl, was walking with her father on the crowded sidewalk along Main Street when he told her that he was going to take her to Disneyworld for her birthday next week. Upon hearing the news, Alice became so excited that she began to jump up and down and run around. During this fit of exuberance, Alice accidentally ran into and knocked down an elderly woman who was passing by. Alice's liability, if any, would be determined by whether a reasonable five-year-old person of like age, intelligence, and experience under like circumstances would have the capacity and judgment to understand the increased risk her enthusiastic display of joy caused to others.

The law applies an individualized test because children do not possess the judgment, intelligence, knowledge, and experience of adults. Moreover, children as a general rule do not engage in activities entailing high risk to others, and their conduct normally does not involve a potential for harm as great as that of adult conduct. A child who engages in an adult activity, however, such as flying an airplane or driving a boat or car, is held in about half the States to the standard of care applicable to adults. Finally, some States modify this individualized test by holding that under a minimum age, most commonly the age of seven, a child is incapable of committing a negligent act.

*Physical Disability* If a person is ill or otherwise physically disabled, the standard of conduct to which he must conform to avoid being negligent is that of a reasonable person having a like disability. Thus, a blind man must act as a reasonable man who is blind, and a woman with multiple sclerosis must act as a reasonable woman with multiple sclerosis.

*Mental Deficiency* The law does not allow for the insanity, voluntary intoxication, or other mental deficiency (in terms, for example, of intelligence, judgment, memory, or emotional stability) of the defendant in a negligence case; rather, the defendant is held to the standard of conduct of a reasonable person who is *not* insane, intoxicated, or mentally deficient, even though the defendant is, in fact, incapable of conforming to the standard. Thus, an adult with the mental acumen of a six-year-old will be held liable for his negligent conduct if he fails to act as carefully as a reasonable adult of normal intelligence. In this case the law may demand more of the individual than his mental limitations permit him to accomplish.

*Superior Skill or Knowledge* Persons who are qualified and who practice a profession or trade that calls for special skill and expertise are required to exercise that care and skill which members in good standing of their profession or trade normally possess. This standard applies to such professionals as physicians, surgeons, dentists, attorneys, pharmacists, architects, accountants, and engineers and to those who perform skilled trades, such as airline pilots, electricians, carpenters, and plumbers. A member of a profession or skilled trade who possesses greater skill than that common to the profession or trade is required to exercise that skill.

*Emergencies* An emergency is a sudden and unexpected event that calls for immediate action and permits no time for deliberation. In determining whether a defendant's conduct is reasonable, the law takes into consideration the fact that he was at the time confronted with a sudden emergency. Restatement, Section 296. The standard is still that of a reasonable person under the circumstances—the emergency is simply part of the circumstances. If, however, the defendant's own negligent or tortious conduct created the emergency, he is liable for the consequences of this conduct even if he acted reasonably in the resulting emergency situation.

*Violation of Statute* The reasonable person standard of conduct may be established by legislation. Restatement, Section 285. Some statutes expressly impose civil liability upon violators. Absent such a provision, courts may adopt the requirements of the statute as the standard of conduct if the statute is intended to protect a class of persons, which includes the plaintiff, against the particular hazard and kind of harm that resulted.

If the statute is found to be applicable, the majority of the courts hold that an unexcused violation is **negligence** *per se;* that is, the violation conclusively constitutes negligent conduct. In a minority of States, the violation is considered merely to be evidence of negligence. In either event, the plaintiff must also prove legal causation and injury.

For example, a statute enacted to protect employees from injuries requires that all factory elevators be equipped with specified safety devices. Arthur, an employee in Freya's factory, and Carlos, a business visitor to the factory, are injured when the elevator falls because the safety devices have not been installed. The court may adopt the statute as a standard of conduct as to Arthur and hold Freya negligent *per se* to Arthur, but not as to Carlos, because Arthur, not Carlos, is within the class of persons the statute is intended to protect. Carlos would

have to establish that a reasonable person in the position of Freya under the circumstances would have installed the safety device.

On the other hand, compliance with a legislative enactment or administrative regulation does not prevent a finding of negligence if a reasonable person would have taken additional precautions. Restatement, Section 288C. For instance, driving at the speed limit may not constitute due care when traffic or road conditions require a lower speed. Legislative or administrative rules normally establish *minimum* standards.

◆ *See Figure 8–1*

 *See Case 1–1*

## Duty to Act

Except in special circumstances, no one is required to aid another in peril. As Prosser has stated, "The law has persistently refused to recognize the moral obligation of

**FIGURE 8–1** Negligence and Negligence *Per Se*

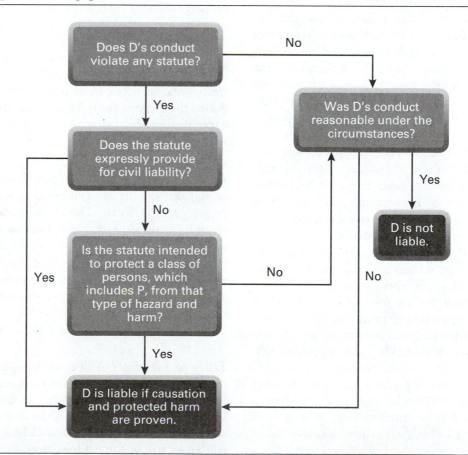

common decency and common humanity, to come to the aid of another human being who is in danger, even though the outcome is to cost him his life." For example, Toni, an adult standing at the edge of a steep cliff, observes a baby carriage with a crying infant in it slowly rolling toward the edge and certain doom. Toni could easily prevent the baby's fall at no risk to her own safety. Nonetheless, Toni does nothing, and the baby falls to his death. Toni is under no legal duty to act and, therefore, incurs no liability for failing to do so.

Section 314 of the Restatement reflects this position: "The fact that the actor realizes or should realize that action on his part is necessary for another's aid or protection does not of itself impose upon him a duty to take such action." Nonetheless, special relations between the parties may impose a duty upon the defendant to aid or protect the other. Thus, if in the example above, Toni were the baby's mother or baby-sitter, Toni would be under a duty to act and would therefore be liable for not taking action. The special relations giving rise to the duty to aid or protect another include common carrier—passenger, innkeeper—guest, employer—employee, and parent—child. Restatement, Sections 314A and 314B.

The law also imposes a duty of affirmative action upon those whose conduct, whether tortious or innocent, has injured another and left him helpless and in danger of further harm. For example, Dale drives her car into Bob, rendering him unconscious. Dale leaves Bob lying in the middle of the road, where he is run over by a second car driven by Chen. Dale is liable to Bob for the additional injuries inflicted by Chen. Moreover, a person voluntarily coming to the assistance of another in need of aid incurs a duty to exercise care. In such an instance, the actor is liable if his failure to exercise reasonable care increases the risk of harm, causes harm, or leaves the other in a worse position. For example, Ann finds Ben drunk and stumbling along a dark sidewalk. Ann leads Ben halfway up a steep and unguarded stairway, where she abandons him. Ben attempts to climb the stairs but trips and falls, suffering serious injury. Ann is liable to Ben for having left him in a worse position.

A parent is not liable for the torts of his minor child simply because of the parental relationship. Where, however, the parent authorizes, encourages, or participates in the tort of his child, or ratifies it by knowingly participating in its benefits, he is liable. So, also, tort liability may be attributed to parents, just as it may be to all other persons, on the grounds of negligence, as where a parent places a dangerous instrumentality, such as a gun or knife, in the hands of a child, who thereby causes injury to another. For example,

A is informed that his six-year-old child is shooting at a target in the street with a .22 rifle, in a manner which endangers the safety of those using the street. A fails to take the rifle away from the child, or to take any other action. The child unintentionally shoots B, a pedestrian, in the leg. A is subject to liability to B. Restatement, Section 316, Illustration 1.

 *See Case 8-1*

## Duties of Possessors of Land

The right of possessors of land to use that land for their own benefit and enjoyment is limited by their duty to do so in a reasonable manner; that is, by the use of their land, they cannot cause unreasonable risks of harm to others. Liability for breach of this obligation may arise from conduct in any of the three areas of torts discussed in this and the preceding chapter: intentional harm, negligence, or strict liability. Most of these cases fall within the classification of negligence.

In conducting activities on her land the possessor of land is required to exercise reasonable care to protect others who are not on her property. For example, a property owner who constructs a factory on her premises must take reasonable care that it is not unreasonably dangerous to people off the site.

The duty of a possessor of land to persons who come upon the land depends on whether those persons are trespassers, licensees, or invitees. A few States have abandoned these distinctions, however, and simply apply ordinary negligence principles of foreseeable risk and reasonable care.

***Duty to Trespassers*** A trespasser is a person who enters or remains on the land of another without permission or privilege to do so. The lawful possessor of the land is not liable to adult trespassers for her failure to maintain the land in a reasonably safe condition. Nonetheless, trespassers are not criminals, and the lawful possessor is not free to inflict intentional injury on them. Moreover, some courts have held that upon discovering the presence of trespassers on her land, the lawful possessor is required to exercise reasonable care for their safety.

***Duty to Licensees*** A licensee is a person who is privileged to enter or remain upon land only by virtue of the lawful possessor's consent. Restatement, Section 330. Licensees include members of the possessor's household, social guests, and salespersons calling at private homes. A licensee will become a trespasser, however, if he enters a portion of the land to which he is not invited or remains upon the land after his invitation has expired.

The possessor, who owes a higher duty of care to licensees than to trespassers, must warn a licensee of dangerous activities and conditions of which the possessor has knowledge and which the licensee does not and is not likely to discover. A licensee who is not warned may recover if the activity or dangerous condition resulted from the possessor's failure to exercise reasonable care to protect him from the danger. Restatement, Section 342. To illustrate: Jose invites a friend, Julia, to his place in the country at eight o'clock on a winter evening. Jose knows that a bridge in his driveway is in a dangerous condition that is not noticeable in the dark. Jose does not inform Julia of this fact. The bridge gives way under Julia's car, causing serious harm to Julia. Jose is liable to Julia.

Some States have extended to licensees the same protection traditionally accorded invitees. A number of States have included social guests in the invitee category.

*Duty to Invitees* An invitee is either a public invitee or a business visitor. Restatement, Section 332. A **public invitee** is a person invited to enter or remain on land as a member of the public for a purpose for which the land is held open to the public. Such invitees include those who use public parks, beaches, or swimming pools, as well as those who use governmental facilities, such as a post office or office of the Recorder of Deeds, where business with the public is transacted openly. A **business visitor** is a person invited to enter or remain on the premises for a purpose directly or indirectly concerning business dealings with the possessor of the land, such as one who enters a store or a tradesperson who enters a residence to make repairs.

With respect to the condition of the premises, the possessor of land is under a duty to exercise reasonable care to protect invitees against dangerous conditions they are unlikely to discover. This liability extends not only to those conditions of which the possessor knows but also to those of which he reasonably should know. Restatement, Section 343. For example, at the front of Tilson's supermarket is a large, glass front door that is well lit and plainly visible. Johnson, a customer, nonetheless mistakes the glass for an open doorway and walks into it, injuring himself. Tilson is not liable to Johnson. If, on the other hand, the glass was difficult to see and a person might foreseeably mistake the glass for an open doorway, then Tilson would be liable to Johnson if Johnson crashed into the glass while exercising reasonable care.

◆ *See Figure 8–2*

⚖ *See Case 8–2*

## Res Ipsa Loquitur

A rule has developed that permits the jury to infer both negligent conduct and causation from the mere occurrence of certain types of events. This rule, called *res ipsa*

**FIGURE 8–2** Duties of Possessors of Land

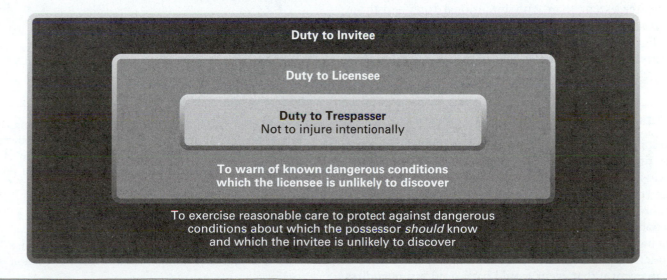

Duty to Invitee

Duty to Licensee

**Duty to Trespasser**
Not to injure intentionally

**To warn of known dangerous conditions
which the licensee is unlikely to discover**

To exercise reasonable care to protect against dangerous
conditions about which the possessor *should* know
and which the invitee is unlikely to discover

*loquitur,* meaning "the thing speaks for itself," applies when the event is of a kind that ordinarily would not occur in the absence of negligence and the evidence sufficiently eliminates other possible causes. Section 328D of the Restatement provides as follows:

(1) It may be inferred that harm suffered by the plaintiff is caused by negligence of the defendant when
   (a) the event is of a kind which ordinarily does not occur in the absence of negligence;
   (b) other responsible causes, including the conduct of the plaintiff and third persons, are sufficiently eliminated by the evidence; and
   (c) the indicated negligence is within the scope of the defendant's duty to the plaintiff.

For example, Abrams rents a room in Brown's motel. During the night a large piece of plaster falls from the ceiling and injures Abrams. In the absence of other evidence, the jury may infer that the harm resulted from Brown's negligence in permitting the plaster to become defective. Brown is permitted, however, to introduce evidence to contradict the inference of negligence.

## PROXIMATE CAUSE

Liability for the negligent conduct of a defendant requires not only that the conduct in fact caused injury to the plaintiff, but also that it was the proximate cause of the injury. Most simply expressed, proximate cause consists of the judicial limitations imposed upon a person's liability for the consequences of his or her negligence. As a matter of social policy, legal responsibility has not been permitted to follow all the consequences of a negligent act. Responsibility has been limited—to a greater extent than with intentional torts—to those persons and results that are closely connected with the negligent conduct. Moreover, in strict liability cases the courts impose a narrower rule of proximate cause than they do in negligence cases.

### Causation in Fact

To support a finding that the defendant's negligence was the proximate cause of the plaintiff's injury, it is first necessary that the defendant's conduct was the cause in fact (that is, the *actual cause*) of the injury. A widely applied test for causation in fact is the **but for rule:** A person's conduct is a cause of an event if the event would not have occurred *but for* the person's negligent conduct. Under this test, an act or omission to act is *not* a cause of an event if that event would have occurred regardless

of the act or omission. For instance, Arnold fails to erect a barrier around an excavation. Doyle is driving a truck when its accelerator becomes stuck, and he and the truck plummet into the excavation. Arnold's negligence is not a cause in fact of Doyle's death if the runaway truck would have crashed through the barrier that Arnold could have erected. Similarly, the failure to install a proper fire escape on a hotel is not the cause in fact of the death of a person who is suffocated by smoke while sleeping in bed during a hotel fire.

The but for rule, however, is not useful where two or more forces, each of which is sufficient to bring about the harm in question, are active. For example, Wilson and Hart negligently set fires that combine to destroy Kennedy's property. Either fire would have destroyed the property. Under the but for rule, either Wilson or Hart, or both, could argue that the fire caused by the other would have destroyed the property and that he, therefore, is not liable. The **substantial factor** test addresses this problem by stating that negligent conduct is a legal cause of harm to another if the conduct is a substantial factor in bringing about the harm. Restatement, Section 431. Under this test the conduct of both Wilson and Hart would be found to be a cause in fact of the destruction of Kennedy's property.

### Limitations on Causation in Fact

As a matter of policy, the law imposes limitations on the causal connection between the defendant's negligence and the plaintiff's injury. Two of the principal factors that are taken into consideration in determining such limitations are (a) unforeseeable consequences and (b) superseding cause.

*Unforeseeable Consequences* Determining the liability of a negligent defendant for unforeseeable consequences has proved to be troublesome and controversial. The Restatement and a majority of the courts have adopted the following position:

(1) If the actor's conduct is a substantial factor in bringing about harm to another, the fact that the actor neither foresaw nor should have foreseen the extent of the harm or the manner in which it occurred does not prevent him from being liable.
(2) The actor's conduct may be held not to be a legal cause of harm to another where after the event and looking back from the harm to the actor's negligent conduct, it appears to the court highly extraordinary that it should have brought about the harm. Section 435.

Even if the defendant's negligent conduct is a cause in fact of harm to the plaintiff, the conduct is not a proximate cause unless the defendant reasonably could have anticipated injuring the plaintiff or a class of persons to which the plaintiff belongs. Restatement, Section 281, Comment c. Proximate cause involves recognizing the risk of harm to the plaintiff individually or to a class of persons of which the plaintiff is a member.

For example, Albert, while negligently driving an automobile, collides with a car carrying dynamite. Albert is unaware of the contents of the other car and has no reason to know about them. The collision causes the dynamite to explode, shattering glass in a building a block away. The shattered glass injures Betsy, who is inside the building. The explosion also injures Calvin, who is walking on the sidewalk near the collision. Albert would be liable to Calvin because Albert should have realized that his negligent driving might result in a collision that would endanger pedestrians nearby, and the fact that the actual harm resulted in an unforeseeable manner does not affect his liability. Betsy, however, was beyond the zone of danger, and Albert, accordingly, is not liable to Betsy. Albert's negligent driving is not deemed to be the "proximate cause" of Betsy's injury because, looking from the harm back to Albert's negligence, it appears highly extraordinary that Albert's conduct should have brought about the harm to Betsy.

◆ *See Figure 8–3*

⚖ *See Case 8–3*

*Superseding Cause* An intervening cause is an event or act that occurs after the defendant's negligent conduct and, together with the defendant's negligence, causes the plaintiff's harm. If the intervening cause is deemed a superseding cause, then it relieves the defendant of liability for harm to the plaintiff caused in fact by both the defendant's negligence and the intervening event or act. For example, Adams negligently leaves in a public sidewalk an excavation without a fence or warning lights, into which Bogues falls at night. Darkness is an intervening, but not a superseding, cause of harm to Bogues because it is a normal consequence of the situation caused by Adams's negligence. Therefore, Adams is liable to Bogues. In contrast, if Adams negligently leaves an excavation in a public sidewalk into which Carson intentionally hurls Bogues, Adams is not liable to Bogues because Carson's conduct is a superseding cause that relieves Adams of liability.

An intervening cause that is a foreseeable or normal consequence of the defendant's negligence is not a superseding cause. Thus, a person who negligently places another in imminent danger is liable for the injury sustained by a third-party rescuer who attempts to aid the imperiled victim. The same is true of attempts by the endangered person to escape the peril, as, for example, when a person swerves off the road to avoid a head-on collision with an automobile driven negligently on the wrong side of the road. It is commonly held that a negligent defendant is liable for the results of necessary medical treatment of the injured party, even if the treatment itself is negligent.

**FIGURE 8–3** Proximate Cause

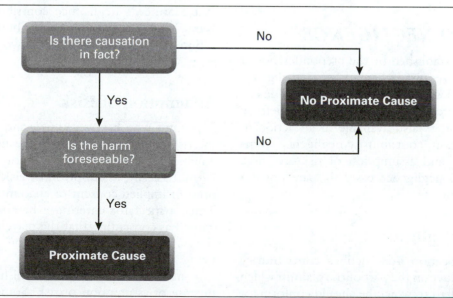

## INJURY

The plaintiff must prove that the defendant's negligent conduct proximately caused harm to a legally protected interest. Certain interests receive little or no protection against such conduct, while others receive full protection. The courts determine the extent of protection for a particular interest as a matter of law on the basis of social policy and expediency. For example, negligent conduct that is the proximate cause of harmful contact with the person of another is actionable. Thus, if Bob negligently runs into Julie, a pedestrian, who is carefully crossing the street, Bob is liable for physical injuries Julie sustains as a result of the collision. On the other hand, if Bob's careless conduct causes only offensive contact with Julie's person, Bob is not liable because Julie did not sustain harm to a legally protected interest.

The courts traditionally have been reluctant to allow recovery for negligently inflicted emotional distress. Nevertheless, this view has changed gradually during this century, and the majority of courts now hold a person liable for negligently causing emotional distress if bodily harm—such as a heart attack—results from the distress. Restatement, Section 436. In the great majority of States, a defendant is not liable for negligent conduct resulting solely in emotional disturbance. Restatement, Section 436A. A few courts, however, have recently allowed recovery of damages for negligently inflicted emotional distress even in the absence of resultant physical harm.

Most courts do not award damages for mental distress suffered by those who have witnessed injury to a closely related person caused by the negligence of another. A number of courts, however, recently have done so.

## DEFENSES TO NEGLIGENCE

A plaintiff who has established by the preponderance of the evidence all the required elements of a negligence action may, nevertheless, be denied recovery if the defendant proves a valid defense. As a general rule, any defense to an intentional tort is also available in an action in negligence. In addition, contributory negligence, comparative negligence, and assumption of risk are three defenses available in negligence cases that are not defenses to intentional torts.

### Contributory Negligence

The Restatement, Section 463, defines **contributory negligence** as "conduct on the part of the plaintiff which falls below the standard to which he should conform for his own protection, and which is a legally contributing cause co-operating with the negligence of the defendant in bringing about the plaintiff's harm." In those few States where it is still recognized, the contributory negligence of the plaintiff, whether slight or extensive, prevents him from recovering *any* damages from the defendant.

Notwithstanding the contributory negligence of the plaintiff, if the defendant had a **last clear chance** to avoid injury to the plaintiff but did not avail himself of such chance, the plaintiff's contributory negligence does not bar his recovery of damages. Restatement, Section 479.

### Comparative Negligence

The harshness of the contributory negligence doctrine has caused all but a few States to reject its all-or-nothing rule and to substitute the doctrine of comparative negligence. Under **comparative negligence,** the law apportions damages between the parties in proportion to the degree of fault or negligence found against them. For instance, Matthew negligently drives his automobile into Nancy, who is crossing against the light. Nancy sustains damages in the amount of $10,000 and sues Matthew. If the trier of fact determines that Matthew's negligence contributed 70 percent to Nancy's injury and that Nancy's contributory negligence contributed 30 percent to her injury, then Nancy would recover $7,000.

Most States that have adopted the doctrine of comparative negligence have enacted statutes that permit the plaintiff no recovery if her contributory negligence was "as great as" or "greater than" that of the defendant. Thus, in the example above, if the trier of fact determined that Matthew's negligence contributed 40 percent to Nancy's injury and Nancy's contributory negligence contributed 60 percent, then Nancy would recover nothing from Matthew.

### Assumption of Risk

A plaintiff who has *voluntarily* and *knowingly* assumed the risk of harm arising from the negligent or reckless conduct of the defendant cannot recover from such harm. Basically, **assumption of risk** is the plaintiff's express or implied consent to encounter a known danger. Thus, a spectator entering a baseball park may be regarded as consenting that the players may proceed with the game without taking precautions to protect him from being hit by the ball.

A number of States have abolished or modified the defense of assumption of risk. Some have merged one or all of the types of assumption of risk into their comparative negligence or comparative fault systems.

◆ *See Figure 8–4*

⚖ *See Case 8–4*

## STRICT LIABILITY

In some instances, people may be held liable for injuries they have caused even though they have not acted intentionally or negligently. Such liability is called strict liability, absolute liability, or liability without fault. The law has determined that because certain types of otherwise

socially desirable activities pose sufficiently high risks of harm regardless of how carefully they are conducted, those who perform these activities should bear the cost of any harm they cause. The doctrine of strict liability is not predicated upon any particular fault of the defendant, but rather upon the nature of the activity in which he is engaging.

## *ACTIVITIES GIVING RISE TO STRICT LIABILITY*

The following activities giving rise to strict liability will be discussed in this section: (1) activities that are, in themselves, abnormally dangerous, (2) the keeping of

**FIGURE 8–4** Defenses to a Negligence Action

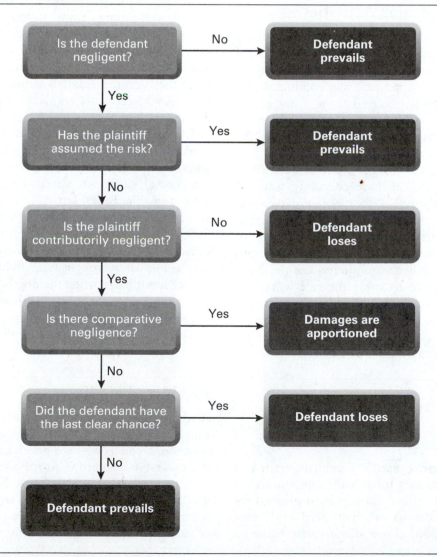

animals, and (3) selling defective, unreasonably dangerous products. In addition, strict liability is imposed upon other activities. All States have enacted workers' compensation statutes that make employers liable to employees for injuries arising out of the course of employment. Because the law imposes this liability without regard to the employer's negligence, it is a form of strict liability. Workers' compensation is discussed in Chapter 43. Moreover, the liability imposed upon an employer for torts that employees commit in the scope of their employment is a type of strict liability, as discussed in Chapter 20. Additional instances of strict liability include carriers and innkeepers (Chapter 49), innocent misrepresentation (Chapter 11), and some violations of the securities laws (Chapter 44).

## Abnormally Dangerous Activities

The law imposes strict liability for harm resulting from extraordinary, unusual, abnormal, or exceptional activities, as determined in light of the place, time, and manner in which the activity was conducted. An **abnormally dangerous activity** is one that (1) necessarily involves a high risk of serious harm to the person and/or chattels of others, which risk the exercise of reasonable care cannot eliminate, *and* (2) is not a matter of common usage. Activities to which the rule has been applied include collecting water in such quantity and location as to make it dangerous; storing explosives or flammable liquids in large quantities; blasting or pile driving; crop dusting; drilling for or refining oil in populated areas; and emitting noxious gases or fumes into a settled community. On the other hand, courts have refused to apply the rule where the activity is a "natural" use of the land, such as drilling for oil in the oil fields of Texas, collecting water in a stock watering tank, or transmitting gas through a gas pipe or electricity through electric wiring.

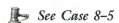 *See Case 8–5*

## Keeping of Animals

Strict liability for harm caused by animals existed at common law and continues today with some modification. As a general rule, those who possess animals for their own purposes do so at their peril and must protect against the harm those animals may cause to people and property.

*Trespassing Animals* Keepers of animals are generally held liable for any damage their animals cause by trespassing on the property of another. There are three exceptions to this rule: (1) keepers of cats and dogs are liable only for negligence, although statutes in many States have imposed strict liability for all damages caused by dogs; (2) keepers of animals are not strictly liable if those animals stray from a highway on which they are being lawfully driven, although the owner may be liable for negligence if he fails to properly control them; and (3) keepers of farm animals, typically cattle, in some western States are not strictly liable for harm caused by their trespassing animals that are allowed to graze freely.

*Nontrespassing Animals* Keepers of wild animals are strictly liable for harm caused by such animals, whether they are trespassing or not. **Wild animals** are defined as those that, in the particular region in which they are kept, are known to be likely to inflict serious damage and cannot be considered safe, no matter how domesticated they become. Animals included in this category are bears, lions, elephants, monkeys, tigers, wolves, zebras, deer, and raccoons.

**Domestic animals** are those that are traditionally devoted to the service of humankind and that as a class are considered safe. Examples of domestic animals are dogs, cats, horses, cattle, and sheep. Keepers of domestic animals are liable if they knew, or should have known, of an animal's dangerous propensity. Restatement, Section 509. The animal's dangerous propensity must be the cause of the harm. For example, merely because he knows that a dog has a propensity to fight with other dogs, a keeper is not liable when the dog bites a human. On the other hand, a person whose 150-pound sheepdog has a propensity to jump enthusiastically on visitors would be liable for any damage caused by the dog's playfulness.

## Products Liability

A recent and important trend in the law is the imposition of a limited form of strict liability upon manufacturers and merchants who sell goods in a *defective condition* unreasonably dangerous to the user or consumer. Restatement, Section 402A. Such liability, imposed regardless of the seller's due care, applies to all merchant sellers. Nearly all States have adopted some version of strict products liability. This topic is covered in Chapter 24.

## *DEFENSES TO STRICT LIABILITY*

This section will discuss the availability in a strict liability action of the following defenses: (1) contributory negligence, (2) comparative negligence, and (3) assumption of risk.

### Contributory Negligence

Because the strict liability of one who carries on an abnormally dangerous activity, keeps animals, or sells products is not based on his negligence, the ordinary contributory negligence of the plaintiff is not a defense to such liability. In imposing strict liability, the law places on the defendant the full responsibility for preventing harm. For example, Adrian negligently fails to observe a sign on a highway warning of a blasting operation conducted by Benjamin. As a result, Adrian is injured by these operations; nonetheless, he may recover from Benjamin.

### Comparative Negligence

Despite the rationale that disallows contributory negligence as a defense to strict liability, some States apply the doctrine of comparative negligence to some types of strict liability, in particular, to products liability.

### Assumption of Risk

Voluntary assumption of risk is a defense to an action based upon strict liability. If the owner of an automobile knowingly and voluntarily parks the vehicle in a blasting zone, he may not recover for harm to his automobile. The assumption of risk, however, must be voluntary. For example, the possessor of land located near a blasting operation is not required to move away; she may, in fact, recover for harm she suffers because of the operation.

---

 # Chapter Summary

## Negligence

| Breach of Duty of Care | **Definition of Negligence**  conduct that falls below the standard established by law for the protection of others against unreasonable risk of harm |
|---|---|
| | **Reasonable Person Standard**  degree of care that a reasonable person would exercise in a given situation |
| | • *Children* must conform to conduct of a reasonable person of like age, intelligence, and experience |
| | • *Physical Disability* a disabled person's conduct must conform to that of a reasonable person under like disability |
| | • *Mental Deficiency* a mentally deficient person is held to the reasonable person standard |
| | • *Superior Skill or Knowledge* professionals must exercise the same care and skill normally possessed by members of their professions |
| | • *Emergencies* the reasonable person standard applies, but the emergency is considered part of the circumstances |
| | • *Violation of Statute* if the statute applies, the violation is negligence *per se* |
| | **Duty to Act**  except in special circumstances, no one is required to aid another in peril |
| | **Duties of Possessors of Land** |
| | • *Duty to Trespassers* not to injure intentionally |
| | • *Duty to Licensees* to warn of known dangerous conditions licensees are unlikely to discover for themselves |
| | • *Duty to Invitees* to exercise reasonable care to protect invitees against dangerous conditions possessor should know of but invitees are unlikely to discover |
| | **Res Ipsa Loquitur**  permits the jury to infer both negligent conduct and causation |

| **Proximate Cause** | **Causation in Fact** the defendant's conduct was the actual cause of, or a substantial factor in causing, the injury<br>**Limitations on Causation in Fact**<br>• *Unforeseeable Consequences* no liability if defendant could not reasonably have anticipated injuring the plaintiff or a class of persons to which the plaintiff belongs<br>• *Superseding Cause* an intervening act that relieves the defendant of liability |
| :--- | :--- |
| **Injury** | **Harm to Legally Protected Interest** courts determine which interests are protected from negligent interference<br>**Burden of Proof** plaintiff must prove that defendant's negligent conduct caused harm to a legally protected interest |
| **Defenses to Negligence** | **Contributory Negligence** failure of a plaintiff to exercise reasonable care for his own protection, which in a few States prevents the plaintiff from recovering anything<br>**Comparative Negligence** damages are divided between the parties in proportion to their degree of negligence; applies in almost all States<br>**Assumption of Risk** plaintiff's express or implied consent to encounter a known danger |

# Strict Liability

| **Activities Giving Rise to Strict Liability** | **Definition of Strict Liability** liability for nonintentional and nonnegligent conduct<br>**Abnormally Dangerous Activities** involve a high degree of serious harm and are not matters of common usage<br>**Keeping of Animals** strict liability is imposed for wild animals and usually for trespassing domestic animals<br>**Products Liability** imposed upon manufacturers and merchants who sell goods in a defective condition unreasonably dangerous to the user or consumer |
| :--- | :--- |
| **Defenses to Strict Liability** | **Contributory Negligence** is *not* a defense to strict liability<br>**Comparative Negligence** most States apply this doctrine to products liability cases<br>**Assumption of Risk** is a defense to an action based upon strict liability |

# Cases

## CASE 8–1
## Duty to Act
### *SOLDANO v. O'DANIELS*
California Court of Appeal, Fifth District, 1983
141 Cal. App.3d 443, 190 Cal. Rptr. 310

**ANDREEN, J.**

Does a business establishment incur liability for wrongful death if it denies use of its telephone to a good samaritan who explains an emergency situation occurring without and wishes to call the police?

This appeal follows a judgment of dismissal of the second cause of action of a complaint for wrongful death upon a motion for summary judgment. The motion was supported only by a declaration of defense counsel. Both briefs on appeal adopt the defense averments:

This action arises out of a shooting death occurring on August 9, 1977. Plaintiff's father [Darrell Soldano] was shot and killed by one Rudolph Villanueva on that date at defendant's Happy Jack's Saloon. This defendant owns and operates the Circle Inn which is an eating establishment located across the street from Happy Jack's. Plaintiff's second cause of action against this defendant is one for negligence.

Plaintiff alleges that on the date of the shooting, a patron of Happy Jack's Saloon came into the Circle Inn and informed a Circle Inn employee that a man had been threatened at Happy Jack's. He requested the employee either call the police or allow him to use the Circle Inn phone to call the police. That employee allegedly refused to call the police and allegedly refused to allow the patron to use the phone to make his own call. Plaintiff alleges that the actions of the Circle Inn employee were a breach of the legal duty that the Circle Inn owed to the decedent.

We were advised at oral argument that the employee was the defendant's bartender. The state of the record is unsatisfactory in that it does not disclose the physical location of the telephone—whether on the bar, in a private office behind a closed door or elsewhere. The only factual matter before the trial court was a verified statement of the defense attorney which set forth those facts quoted above. Following normal rules applicable to motions for summary judgment, we strictly construe the defense affidavit. [Citation.] Accordingly, we assume the telephone was not in a private office but in a position where it could be used by a patron without inconvenience to the defendant or his guests. We also assume the call was a local one and would not result in expense to defendant.

There is a distinction, well rooted in the common law, between action and nonaction. [Citation.] It has found its way into the prestigious Restatement Second of Torts (hereafter cited as "Restatement"), which provides in section 314:

The fact that the actor realizes or should realize that action on his part is necessary for another's aid or protection does not of itself impose upon him a duty to take such action.

\* \* \*

Defendant argues that the request that its employee call the police is a request that it *do* something. He points to the established rule that one who has not created a peril ordinarily does not have a duty to take affirmative action to assist an imperiled person. [Citation.] It is urged that the alternative request of the patron from Happy Jack's Saloon that he be allowed to use defendant's telephone so that he personally could make the call is again a request that the defendant do something—assist another to give aid. Defendant points out that the Restatement sections which impose liability for negligent interference with a third person giving aid to another do not impose the additional duty to *aid* the good samaritan.

The refusal of the law to recognize the moral obligation of one to aid another when he is in peril and when such aid may be given without danger and at little cost in effort has been roundly criticized. Prosser describes the case law sanctioning such inaction as a "refus[al] to recognize the moral obligation of common decency and common humanity" and characterizes some of these decisions as "shocking in the extreme. . . . Such decisions are revolting to any moral sense. They have been denounced with vigor by legal writers." [Citation.] A similar rule has been termed "morally questionable" by our Supreme Court. [Citation.]

\* \* \*

As noted in [citation], the courts have increased the instances in which affirmative duties are imposed not by direct rejection of the common law rule, but by expanding the list of special relationships which will justify departure from that rule. * * *

* * *

Section 314A of the Restatement lists other special relationships which create a duty to render aid, such as that of a common carrier to its passengers, an innkeeper to his guest, possessors of land who hold it open to the public, or one who has a custodial relationship to another. A duty may be created by an undertaking to give assistance. [Citation.]

Here there was no special relationship between the defendant and the deceased. It would be stretching the concept beyond recognition to assert there was a relationship between the defendant and the patron from Happy Jack's Saloon who wished to summon aid. But this does not end the matter.

It is time to re-examine the common law rule of nonliability for nonfeasance in the special circumstances of the instant case.

* * *

We turn now to the concept of duty in a tort case. The [California] Supreme Court has identified certain factors to be considered in determining whether a duty is owed to third persons. These factors include:

the foreseeability of harm to the plaintiff, the degree of certainty that the plaintiff suffered injury, the closeness of the connection between the defendant's conduct and the injury suffered, the moral blame attached to the defendant's conduct, the policy of preventing future harm, the extent of the burden to the defendant and consequences to the community of imposing a duty to exercise care with resulting liability for breach, and the availability, cost, and prevalence of insurance for the risk involved. [Citation.]

We examine those factors in reference to this case. (1) The harm to the decedent was abundantly foreseeable; it was imminent. The employee was expressly told that a man had been threatened. The employee was a bartender. As such he knew it is foreseeable that some people who drink alcohol in the milieu of a bar setting are prone to violence. (2) The certainty of decedent's injury is undisputed. (3) There is arguably a close connection between the employee's conduct and the injury: the patron wanted to use the phone to summon the police to intervene. The employee's refusal to allow the use of the phone prevented this anticipated intervention. If permitted to go to trial, the plaintiff may be able to show that the probable response time of the police would have been shorter than the time between the prohibited telephone call and the fatal shot. (4) The employee's

conduct displayed a disregard for human life that can be characterized as morally wrong: he was callously indifferent to the possibility that Darrell Soldano would die as the result of his refusal to allow a person to use the telephone. Under the circumstances before us the bartender's burden was minimal and exposed him to no risk: all he had to do was allow the use of the telephone. It would have cost him or his employer nothing. It could have saved a life. (5) Finding a duty in these circumstances would promote a policy of preventing future harm. A citizen would not be required to summon the police but would be required, in circumstances such as those before us, not to impede another who has chosen to summon aid. (6) We have no information on the question of the availability, cost, and prevalence of insurance for the risk, but note that the liability which is sought to be imposed here is that of employee negligence, which is covered by many insurance policies. (7) The extent of the burden on the defendant was minimal, as noted.

The consequences to the community of imposing a duty, the remaining factor mentioned in [citation] is termed "the administrative factor" by Professor Green in his analysis of determining whether a duty exists in a given case. [Citation.] The administrative factor is simply the pragmatic concern of fashioning a workable rule and the impact of such a rule on the judicial machinery. It is the policy of major concern in this case.

* * *

Many citizens simply "don't want to get involved." No rule should be adopted which would require a citizen to open up his or her house to a stranger so that the latter may use the telephone to call for emergency assistance. As Mrs. Alexander in Anthony Burgess' *A Clockwork Orange* learned to her horror, such an action may be fraught with danger. It does not follow, however, that use of a telephone in a public portion of a business should be refused for a legitimate emergency call. Imposing liability for such a refusal would not subject innocent citizens to possible attack by the "good samaritan," for it would be limited to an establishment open to the public during times when it is open to business, and to places within the establishment ordinarily accessible to the public. Nor would a stranger's mere assertion that an "emergency" situation is occurring create the duty to utilize an accessible telephone because the duty would arise if and only if it were clearly conveyed that there exists an imminent danger of physical harm. [Citation.]

Such a holding would not involve difficulties in proof, overburden the courts or unduly hamper self-determination or enterprise.

A business establishment such as the Circle Inn is open for profit. The owner encourages the public to enter, for his earnings depend on it. A telephone is a necessary adjunct to such a place. It is not unusual in such circumstances for patrons to use the telephone to call a taxicab or family member.

We acknowledge that defendant contracted for the use of his telephone, and its use is a species of property. But if it exists in a public place as defined above, there is no privacy or ownership interest in it such that the owner should be permitted to interfere with a good faith attempt to use it by a third person to come to the aid of another.

* * *

We conclude that the bartender owed a duty to the plaintiff's decedent to permit the patron from Happy Jack's to place a call to the police or to place the call himself.

It bears emphasizing that the duty in this case does not require that one must go to the aid of another. That is not the issue here. The employee was not the good samaritan intent on aiding another. The patron was.

It would not be appropriate to await legislative action in this area. The rule was fashioned in the common law tradition, as were the exceptions to the rule. [Citation.] To the extent this opinion expands the reach of section 327 of the Restatement, it represents logical and needed growth, the hallmark of the common law. It does not involve the sacrifice of other respectable interests.

The courts have a special responsibility to reshape, refine and guide legal doctrine they have created. * * *

* * *

The possible imposition of liability on the defendant in this case is not a global change in the law. It is but a slight departure from the "morally questionable" rule of nonliability for inaction absent a special relationship. It is one of the predicted "inroads upon the older rule." (Rest.2d Torts, *supra,* § 314, com. c.§ 314, com. c.) It is a logical extension of Restatement Section 327 which imposes liability for negligent interference with a third person who the defendant knows is attempting to render necessary aid. However small it may be, it is a step which should be taken.

We conclude there are sufficient justiciable issues to permit the case to go to trial and therefore reverse.

---

**CASE 8–2**
## Duty to Invitees
### *YANIA v. BIGAN*
Supreme Court of Pennsylvania, 1959
397 Pa. 316, 155 A.2d 343

JONES, J.

A bizarre and most unusual circumstance provides the background of this appeal.

On September 25, 1957 John E. Bigan was engaged in a coal strip-mining operation in Shade Township, Somerset County. On the property being stripped were large cuts or trenches created by Bigan when he removed the earthen overburden for the purpose of removing the coal underneath. One cut contained water 8 to 10 feet in depth with side walls or embankments 16 to 18 feet in height; at this cut Bigan had installed a pump to remove the water.

At approximately 4 PM on that date, Joseph F. Yania, the operator of another coal strip-mining operation, and one Boyd M. Ross went upon Bigan's property for the purpose of discussing a business matter with Bigan, and, while there, were asked by Bigan to aid him in starting the pump. Ross and Bigan entered the cut and stood at the point where the pump was located. Yania stood at the top of one of the cut's side walls and then jumped from the side wall—a height of 16 to 18 feet—into the water and was drowned.

Yania's widow, in her own right and on behalf of her three children, instituted wrongful death and survival actions against Bigan contending Bigan was responsible for Yania's death.

* * *

The complaint avers negligence in the following manner: (1) "The death by drowning of . . . (Yania) was caused entirely by the acts of (Bigan) . . . in *urging, enticing, taunting and inveigling* (Yania) to jump into the water, which (Bigan) knew or ought to have known was of a depth of 8 to 10 feet and dangerous to the life of anyone who would jump therein"; (2) ". . . (Bigan) violated his obligations to a business invitee in not having his premises reasonably safe, and not warning his business invitee of a dangerous condition and to the contrary urged, induced and inveigled (Yania) into a dangerous position and a dangerous act, whereby (Yania) came to his death"; (3) "After (Yania) was in the water, a highly dangerous position, having been induced and inveigled therein by (Bigan), (Bigan) failed and neglected to take reasonable steps and action to protect or assist (Yania) or extradite (Yania) from the dangerous position in which (Bigan) had placed him". Summarized, Bigan stands charged with three-fold negligence: (1) by urging, enticing, taunting and inveigling Yania to jump into the water; (2) by failing to warn Yania of a dangerous condition on the land, i.e. the cut wherein lay 8 to 10 feet of water; (3) by failing to go to Yania's rescue after he had jumped into the water.

* * *

The complaint does not allege that Yania slipped or that he was pushed or that Bigan made any *physical* impact upon Yania. On the contrary, the only inference deducible from the facts alleged in the complaint is that Bigan, by the employment of cajolery and inveiglement, caused such a *mental* impact on Yania that the latter was deprived of his volition and freedom of choice and placed under a compulsion to jump into the water. Had Yania been a child of tender years or a person mentally deficient then it is conceivable that taunting and enticement could constitute actionable negligence if it resulted in harm. However, to contend that such conduct directed to an adult in full possession of all his mental faculties constitutes actionable negligence is not only without precedent but completely without merit. * * *
* * * Yania was a business invitee in that he entered upon the land for a common business purpose for the mutual benefit of Bigan and himself (Restatement, Torts, § 332; [citation.]) As possessor of the land, Bigan would become subject to liability to Yania for any physical harm caused by any artificial or natural condition upon the land (1) if, and only if, Bigan knew or could have discovered the condition which, if known to him he should have realized involved an unreasonable risk of harm to Yania, (2) if Bigan had no reason to believe Yania would discover the condition or realize the risk of harm and (3) if he invited or permitted Yania to enter upon the land without exercising reasonable care to make the condition reasonably safe or give adequate warning to enable him to avoid the harm. [Citations.] The inapplicability of this rule of liability to the instant facts is readily apparent.

The *only* condition on Bigan's land which could possibly have contributed in any manner to Yania's death was the water-filled cut with its high embankment. Of this condition there was neither concealment nor failure to warn, but, on the contrary, the complaint specifically avers that Bigan not only requested Yania and Boyd to assist him in starting the pump to remove the water from the cut but "led" them to the cut itself. If this cut possessed any potentiality of danger, such a condition was as obvious and apparent to Yania as to Bigan, both coal strip-mine operators. Under the circumstances herein depicted Bigan could not be held liable in this respect.

Lastly, it is urged that Bigan failed to take the necessary steps to rescue Yania from the water. The mere fact that Bigan saw Yania in a position of peril in the water imposed upon him no legal, although a moral, obligation or duty to go to his rescue unless Bigan was legally responsible, in whole or in part, for placing Yania in the perilous position. Restatement, Torts, § 314. [Citations.] . . . The complaint does not aver any facts which impose upon Bigan legal responsibility for placing Yania in the dangerous position in the water and, absent such legal responsibility, the law imposes on Bigan no duty of rescue.

* * *

Recognizing that the deceased Yania is entitled to the benefit of the presumption that he was exercising due care and extending to appellant the benefit of every well pleaded fact in this complaint and the fair inferences arising therefrom, yet we can reach but one conclusion: that Yania, a reasonable and prudent adult in full possession of all his mental faculties, undertook to perform an act which he knew or should have known was attended with more or less peril and it was the performance of that act and not any conduct upon Bigan's part which caused his unfortunate death.

## CASE 8–3
## Proximate Cause
### PALSGRAF v. LONG ISLAND RAILROAD CO.
Court of Appeals of New York, 1928
248 N.Y. 339, 162 N.E. 99

**CARDOZO, C.J.**

Plaintiff was standing on a platform of defendant's railroad after buying a ticket to go to Rockaway Beach. A train stopped at the station, bound for another place. Two men ran forward to catch it. One of the men reached the platform of the car without mishap, though the train was already moving. The other man, carrying a package, jumped aboard the car, but seemed unsteady as if about to fall. A guard on the car, who had held the door open, reached forward to help him in, and another guard on the platform pushed him from behind. In this act, the package was dislodged, and fell upon the rails. It was a package of small size, about fifteen inches long, and was covered by a newspaper. In fact it contained fireworks, but there was nothing in its appearance to give notice of its contents. The fireworks when they fell exploded. The shock of the explosion threw down some scales at the other end of the platform many feet away. The scales struck the plaintiff, causing injuries for which she sues.

The conduct of the defendant's guard, if a wrong in its relation to the holder of the package, was not a wrong in its relation to the plaintiff, standing far away. Relatively to her it was not negligence at all. Nothing in the situation gave notice that the falling package had in it the potency of peril to persons thus removed. Negligence is not actionable unless it involves the invasion of a legally protected interest, the violation of a right. "Proof of negligence in the air, so to speak, will not do." [Citations.] "Negligence is the absence of care, according to the circumstances." [Citations.]

\* \* \*

If no hazard was apparent to the eye of ordinary vigilance, an act innocent and harmless, at least to outward seeming, with reference to her, did not take to itself the quality of a tort because it happened to be a wrong, though apparently not one involving the risk of bodily insecurity, with reference to someone else. "In every instance, before negligence can be predicated of a given act, back of the act must be sought and found a duty to the individual complaining, the observance of which would have averted or avoided the injury." [Citations.]

\* \* \*

A different conclusion will involve us, and swiftly too, in a maze of contradictions. A guard stumbles over a package which has been left upon a platform. It seems to be a bundle of newspapers. It turns out to be a can of dynamite. To the eye of ordinary vigilance, the bundle is abandoned waste, which may be kicked or trod on with impunity. Is a passenger at the other end of the platform protected by the law against the unsuspected hazard concealed beneath the waste? If not, is the result to be any different, so far as the distant passenger is concerned, when the guard stumbles over a valise which a truckman or a porter has left upon the walk? The passenger far away, if the victim of a wrong at all, has a cause of action, not derivative, but original and primary. His claim to be protected against invasion of his bodily security is neither greater nor less because the act resulting in the invasion is a wrong to another far removed. In this case, the rights that are said to have been violated, the interests said to have been invaded, are not even of the same order. The man was not injured in his person nor even put in danger. The purpose of the act, as well as its effect, was to make his person safe. If there was a wrong to him at all, which may very well be doubted, it was a wrong to a property interest only, the safety of his package. Out of this wrong to property, which threatened injury to nothing else, there has passed, we are told, to the plaintiff by derivation or succession a right of action for the invasion of an interest of another order, the right to bodily security. The diversity of interests emphasizes the futility of the effort to build the plaintiff's right upon the basis of a wrong to someone else. . . . One who jostles one's neighbor in a crowd does not invade the rights of others standing at the outer fringe when the unintended contact casts a bomb upon the ground. The wrongdoer as to them is the man who carries the bomb, not the one who explodes it without suspicion of the danger. Life will have to be made over, and human nature transformed, before prevision so extravagant can be accepted as the norm of conduct, the customary standard to which behavior must conform.

\* \* \*

The judgment of the Appellate Division and that of the Trial Term should be reversed, and the complaint dismissed, with costs in all courts.

## CASE 8–4
# Assumption of Risk and Contributory Negligence
# *DUKAT v. LEISERV, INC.*
Court of Appeal of Nebraska, 1998
6 Neb.App. 905, 578 N.W.2d 486

SIEVERS, J.

## Introduction

We consider whether a jury should be instructed on the defense of assumption of risk when (1) the plaintiff slips and falls on an icy sidewalk outside of a bowling alley, (2) the property owner admits that the sidewalk was the only way in and out of the bowling alley, and (3) the injured plaintiff had prior knowledge of the sidewalk's icy condition.

## Factual Background

Rebecca S. Dukat arrived at Mockingbird Lanes, a bowling alley in Omaha, Nebraska, at approximately 6 PM on Wednesday, February 2, 1994, to bowl in her league game. Witnesses described the night of February 2 as cold, with some recalling that there had been sleet and snow during the day, and others testifying that they had no memory of any precipitation. However, all the witnesses who were asked about the conditions of the bowling alley's parking lot and adjacent sidewalk agreed that they were snow and ice covered.

Dukat proceeded to walk into the bowling alley on the only sidewalk provided in and out of the building. She testified that she noticed the sidewalk was icy. After bowling three games and drinking three beers, Dukat exited the bowling alley at approximately 9 PM. She retraced her steps on the same sidewalk. The sidewalk was still ice covered and in a condition which, according to Frank Jameson, general manager of Mockingbird Lanes, was "unacceptable" if the bowling alley were open to customers. As Dukat proceeded along the sidewalk to her car, she slipped, attempted to catch herself by reaching toward a car, and fell. She suffered a fracture of both bones in her left ankle as well as a ruptured ligament.

## Procedural Background

Dukat sued Leiserv, Inc., doing business as Mockingbird Lanes in Omaha, and Brunswick Corporation, the parent company of Leiserv, in the district court for Douglas County, Nebraska. Dukat alleged that Leiserv and Brunswick were negligent in failing to keep the sidewalk in a reasonably safe condition, in failing to warn her of a dangerous condition, and in failing to take adequate and reasonable measures to protect her.

Leiserv and Brunswick alleged two affirmative defenses: (1) Dukat was contributorily negligent (a) in failing to maintain a proper lookout and take notice of the condition of the sidewalk and (b) in consuming alcohol to the extent that it impaired her ability to walk and to take reasonable precautions, and (2) Dukat had assumed the risk of injury.

\* \* \*

The jury trial proceeded as scheduled on September 5, 6, and 9, 1996. At the end of Dukat's evidence, the court granted Brunswick's motion for a directed verdict on the ground that there was no evidence of Brunswick's responsibility or control over the employees of Mockingbird Lanes.

\* \* \*

On September 9, 1996, the jury returned a general verdict for Leiserv. After her motion for new trial was overruled, Dukat appealed to this court.

\* \* \*

## Analysis

**Assumption of Risk.** Before the defense of assumption of risk may be submitted to a jury, the defendant has the burden to establish the elements of assumption of risk, which are that the plaintiff knew of the danger, understood the danger, and voluntarily exposed himself or herself to the danger which proximately caused the plaintiff's injury. [Citation.] Dukat argues that Leiserv failed to meet its burden of establishing the elements of assumption of risk. Specifically, she argues that Leiserv failed to prove that she knew, understood, and voluntarily exposed herself to the danger of walking unassisted on an icy sidewalk. Dukat's argument focuses primarily on the "voluntary" element of assumption of risk. She maintains that because the sidewalk was the only route into and out of the bowling alley, she did not "voluntarily" expose herself to the danger, rather, according to Nebraska case law, she merely "encountered" it.

Leiserv maintains that Dukat "knew full well that the sidewalk and parking lot were icy," because on her way into the bowling alley she had noticed the sidewalk was slippery. Leiserv contends that Dukat voluntarily exposed herself to the danger when she failed to (1) ask someone to assist her to her car or (2) tell a Mockingbird Lanes employee about the icy conditions and that the sidewalk needed sand or "ice melt."

The standard to be applied in determining whether a plaintiff has assumed the risk of injury is a subjective one based upon the particular facts and circumstances of the event. [Citation.] The subjective standard involves what "'the particular plaintiff in fact sees, knows, understands and appreciates. In this it differs from the objective standard which is applied to contributory negligence.'" [Citation.] If one who knows and comprehends the danger chooses to expose himself or herself thereto, even though the choice is not negligent, he or she will be deemed to have assumed the risk of injury and be precluded from recovery. [Citations.] Thus, it was Leiserv's burden to show that Dukat knowingly and voluntarily exposed herself to the risk of walking on the sidewalk, but a subjective standard is employed.

\* \* \*

In [citation], \* \* \* [the plaintiff] argued that the court should have given the following instruction: "'A plaintiff does not assume a risk of harm unless he or she voluntarily accepts the risk. A plaintiff's acceptance of a risk is not voluntary if the defendant's conduct has left plaintiff no reasonable alternative course of conduct in order to avert harm to plaintiff.'" [Citation.] The court, finding that [the plaintiff's] proposed instruction should have been given, stated:

"'(1) A plaintiff does not assume a risk of harm unless he voluntarily accepts the risk. (2) The plaintiff's acceptance of a risk is not voluntary if the defendant's tortious conduct has left him no reasonable alternative course of conduct in order to (a) avert harm to himself or another, or (b) exercise or protect a right or privilege of which the defendant has no right to deprive him.'" [Citation], quoting the Restatement [(Second) of Torts] § 496E [(1965)].

\* \* \*

The doctrine of a safer choice as used in [citation] and as illustrated by § 496E suggests something other than retreat from where a person needs to be or wants to be. \* \* \* To further amplify our point, we quote two illustrations from the Restatement, supra, comment d. at 579:

8. A illegally carries on blasting operations next to the public highway. B, approaching in a car, ignores a conspicuous warning sign and a flagman who tries to stop him and informs him that there will be a delay of five minutes. B insists upon proceeding along the highway, and is injured by the blasting. B assumes the risk.
9. The A City clears the snow and ice from the sidewalk on one side of the street, leaving the sidewalk on the other side covered with ice, slippery, and visibly dangerous. B, having a free choice of either side, and fully understanding the risk, elects to walk on the icy sidewalk, slips, and is injured. B assumes the risk.

In each illustration, there is a reasonable safe choice readily available, and one which allows the "traveler" to reach his or her destination. When the "traveler" rejects the safe and reasonable choice, then there is assumption of risk. That the defendant must introduce evidence of an alternative safe route or course of conduct is supported by [citation], where the Supreme Court of Minnesota, in rejecting the applicability of assumption of risk, approvingly quoted the trial court's reasoning that "'no evidence was introduced to show alternative routes to the meat market which were safer than the route selected by plaintiff.'" \* \* \*

\* \* \*

## Contributory Negligence

\* \* \*

A plaintiff is contributorily negligent if (1) the plaintiff fails to protect himself or herself from injury; (2) the plaintiff's conduct concurs and cooperates with the defendant's actionable negligence; and (3) the plaintiff's conduct contributes to the plaintiff's injuries as a proximate cause. [Citation.] Contributory negligence is an affirmative defense which must be proved by the party asserting such defense. [Citation.] The distinction between assumption of risk and contributory negligence presents a difference which prevents interchangeable use of those defenses in a negligence action. [Citation.]

The Supreme Court of Nebraska has frequently held: "Where different minds may reasonably draw different conclusions or inferences from the evidence adduced concerning the issues of negligence or contributory negligence and the degree thereof when one is compared with the other, such issues must be submitted to the jury." [Citations.]

Minds could reasonably differ on the evidence introduced with respect to Dukat's contributory negligence.

It is a permissible inference from the record that the ice alone would not have caused the accident. It is clear from Dukat's testimony that she knew of the icy condition of the sidewalk as she entered the bowling alley and despite this knowledge may have done things a reasonably careful person might not have done. For example, the evidence shows that Dukat drank three beers while she was at the bowling alley and that she did not recall eating dinner that night. Dukat also decided to navigate the same icy path she had come in on without asking the assistance of one of her friends who remained inside the bowling alley. A reasonable person might also have asked management to spread an ice-melting substance on the sidewalk and delayed their departure.

Thus, reasonable minds could arrive at the conclusion that Dukat did not act as a reasonable person in one or more ways and that the slip and fall were contributed to by her own negligence. The trial court, therefore, was correct in submitting to the jury the question of Dukat's contributory negligence.

* * *

## Conclusion

In view of our determination that the district court committed reversible error by submitting the defense of assumption of risk, the judgment of the district court is reversed, and the cause is remanded to the district court for a new trial.

---

### CASE 8–5
## Abnormally Dangerous Activities
## *KLEIN v. PYRODYNE CORPORATION*
Supreme Court of Washington, 1991
117 Wash.2d 1, 810 P.2d 917

GUY, J.
The plaintiffs in this case are persons injured when an aerial shell at a public fireworks exhibition went astray and exploded near them. The defendant is the pyrotechnic company hired to set up and discharge the fireworks. The issue before this court is whether pyrotechnicians are strictly liable for damages caused by fireworks displays. We hold that they are.

Defendant Pyrodyne Corporation (Pyrodyne) is a general contractor for aerial fireworks at public fireworks displays. Pyrodyne contracted to procure fireworks, to provide pyrotechnic operators, and to display the fireworks at the Western Washington State Fairgrounds in Puyallup, Washington on July 4, 1987. All operators of the fireworks display were Pyrodyne employees acting within the scope of their employment duties.

As required by Washington statute, Pyrodyne purchased a $1,000,000 insurance policy prior to the fireworks show. The policy provided $1,000,000 coverage for each occurrence of bodily injury or property damage liability. Plaintiffs allege that Pyrodyne failed to carry out a number of the other statutory and regulatory requirements in preparing for and setting off the fireworks. For example, they allege that Pyrodyne failed to properly bury the mortar tubes prior to detonation, failed to provide a diagram of the display and surrounding environment to the local government, failed to provide crowd control monitors, and failed to keep the invitees at the mandated safe distance.

During the fireworks display, one of the 5-inch mortars was knocked into a horizontal position. From this position a shell inside was ignited and discharged. The shell flew 500 feet in a trajectory parallel to the earth and exploded near the crowd of onlookers. Plaintiffs Danny and Marion Klein were injured by the explosion. Mr. Klein's clothing was set on fire, and he suffered facial burns and serious injury to his eyes.

The parties provide conflicting explanations of the cause of the improper horizontal discharge of the shell. Pyrodyne argues that the accident was caused by a 5-inch shell detonating in its aboveground mortar tube without ever leaving the ground. Pyrodyne asserts that this detonation caused another mortar tube to be knocked over, ignited, and shot off horizontally. In contrast, the Kleins contend that the misdirected shell resulted because Pyrodyne's employees improperly set up the display. They further note that because all of the evidence exploded, there is no means of proving the cause of the misfire.

The Kleins brought suit against Pyrodyne under theories of products liability and strict liability. Pyrodyne filed a motion for summary judgment, which the trial court granted as to the products liability claim. The trial court denied Pyrodyne's summary judgment motion regarding the Kleins' strict liability claim, holding that Pyrodyne was strictly liable without fault and ordering summary judgment in favor of the Kleins on the issue of liability. Pyrodyne appealed the order of partial summary judgment to the Court of Appeals, which certified the case to this court. Pyrodyne is appealing solely as to the trial court's holding that strict liability is the appropriate standard of liability for pyrotechnicians. A strict liability claim against pyrotechnicians for damages caused by fireworks displays presents a case of first impression in Washington.

## Analysis

**Fireworks Displays as Abnormally Dangerous Activities**   The Kleins contend that strict liability is the appropriate standard to determine the culpability of Pyrodyne because Pyrodyne was participating in an abnormally dangerous activity. * * *

The modern doctrine of strict liability for abnormally dangerous activities derives from *Fletcher v. Rylands*, [citation], in which the defendant's reservoir flooded mine shafts on the plaintiff's adjoining land. *Rylands v. Fletcher* has come to stand for the rule that "the defendant will be liable when he damages another by a thing or activity unduly dangerous and inappropriate to the place where it is maintained, in the light of the character of that place and its surroundings." [Citation.]

The basic principle of *Rylands v. Fletcher* has been accepted by the Restatement (Second) of Torts (1977). [Citation.] Section 519 of the Restatement provides that any party carrying on an "abnormally dangerous activity" is strictly liable for ensuing damages. The test for what constitutes such an activity is stated in section 520 of the Restatement. Both Restatement sections have been adopted by this court, and determination of whether an activity is an "abnormally dangerous activity" is a question of law. [Citations.]

Section 520 of the Restatement lists six factors that are to be considered in determining whether an activity is "abnormally dangerous." The factors are as follows: (a) existence of a high degree of risk of some harm to the person, land or chattels of others; (b) likelihood that the harm that results from it will be great; (c) inability to eliminate the risk by the exercise of reasonable care; (d) extent to which the activity is not a matter of common usage; (e) inappropriateness of the activity to the place where it is carried on; and (f) extent to which its value to the community is outweighed by its dangerous attributes. Restatement (Second) of Torts § 520 (1977). As we previously recognized in [citation], the comments to section 520 explain how these factors should be evaluated: Any one of them is not necessarily sufficient of itself in a particular case, and ordinarily several of them will be required for strict liability. On the other hand, it is not necessary that each of them be present, especially if others weigh heavily. Because of the interplay of these various factors, it is not possible to reduce abnormally dangerous activities to any definition. The essential question is whether the risk created is so unusual, either because of its magnitude or because of the circumstances surrounding it, as to justify the imposition of strict liability for the harm that results from it, even though it is carried on with all reasonable care. Restatement (Second) of Torts § 520, comment f (1977). Examination of these factors persuades us that fireworks displays are abnormally dangerous activities justifying the imposition of strict liability.

We find that the factors stated in clauses (a), (b), and (c) are all present in the case of fireworks displays. Any time a person ignites aerial shells or rockets with the intention of sending them aloft to explode in the presence of large crowds of people, a high risk of serious personal injury or property damage is created. That risk arises because of the possibility that a shell or rocket will malfunction or be misdirected. Furthermore, no matter how much care pyrotechnicians exercise, they cannot entirely eliminate the high risk inherent in setting off powerful explosives such as fireworks near crowds.

* * *

The factors stated in clauses (a), (b), and (c) together, and sometimes one of them alone, express what is commonly meant by saying an activity is ultrahazardous. Restatement (Second) of Torts § 520, comment h (1977). As the Restatement explains, however, "[l]iability for abnormally dangerous activities is not . . . a matter of these three factors alone, and those stated in Clauses (d), (e), and (f) must still be taken into account." Restatement (Second) of Torts § 520, comment h (1977); [citation].

The factor expressed in clause (d) concerns the extent to which the activity is not a matter "of common usage." The Restatement explains that "[a]n activity is a matter of common usage if it is customarily carried on by the great mass of mankind or by many people in the community." Restatement (Second) of Torts § 520, comment i (1977). As examples of activities that are not matters of common usage, the Restatement comments offer driving a tank, blasting, the manufacture, storage, transportation, and use of high explosives, and drilling for oil. The deciding characteristic is that few persons engage in these activities. Likewise, relatively few persons conduct public fireworks displays. Therefore, presenting public fireworks displays is not a matter of common usage.

\* \* \*

The factor stated in clause (e) requires analysis of the appropriateness of the activity to the place where it was carried on. In this case, the fireworks display was conducted at the Puyallup Fairgrounds. Although some locations—such as over water—may be safer, the Puyallup Fairgrounds is an appropriate place for a fireworks show because the audience can be seated at a reasonable distance from the display. Therefore, the clause (e) factor is not present in this case.

The factor stated in clause (f) requires analysis of the extent to which the value of fireworks to the community outweighs its dangerous attributes. We do not find that this factor is present here. This country has a long-standing tradition of fireworks on the 4th of July. That tradition suggests that we as a society have decided that the value of fireworks on the day celebrating our national independence and unity outweighs the risks of injuries and damage.

In sum, we find that setting off public fireworks displays satisfies four of the six conditions under the Restatement test; that is, it is an activity that is not "of common usage" and that presents an ineliminably high risk of serious bodily injury or property damage. We therefore hold that conducting public fireworks displays is an abnormally dangerous activity justifying the imposition of strict liability.

\* \* \*

**Public Policy and Strict Liability for Fireworks Displays** Policy considerations also support imposing strict liability on pyrotechnicians for damages caused by their public fireworks displays, although such considerations are not alone sufficient to justify that conclusion.

Most basic is the question as to who should bear the loss when an innocent person suffers injury through the nonculpable but abnormally dangerous activities of another. In the case of public fireworks displays, fairness weighs in favor of requiring the pyrotechnicians who present the displays to bear the loss rather than the unfortunate spectators who suffer the injuries. In addition, [t]he rule of strict liability rests not only upon the ultimate idea of rectifying a wrong and putting the burden where it should belong as a matter of abstract justice, that is, upon the one of the two innocent parties whose acts instigated or made the harm possible, but it also rests on problems of proof: One of these common features is that the person harmed would encounter a difficult problem of proof if some other standard of liability were applied. For example, the disasters caused by those who engage in abnormally dangerous or extra-hazardous activities frequently destroy all evidence of what in fact occurred, other than that the activity was being carried on. Certainly this is true with explosions of dynamite, large quantities of gasoline, or other explosives. [Citation.] In the present case, all evidence was destroyed as to what caused the misfire of the shell that injured the Kleins. Therefore, the problem of proof this case presents for the plaintiffs also supports imposing strict liability on Pyrodyne.

\* \* \*

## Conclusion

We hold that Pyrodyne Corporation is strictly liable for all damages suffered as a result of the July 1987 fireworks display. Detonating fireworks displays constitutes an abnormally dangerous activity warranting strict liability. Public policy also supports this conclusion. \* \* \* This establishes the standard of strict liability for pyrotechnicians. Therefore, we affirm the decision of the trial court.

---

 # Questions

1.   List and briefly describe the three required elements of an action for negligence.

2.   Explain the duty of care that is imposed upon (a) adults, (b) children, (c) persons with a physical disability, (d) persons with a mental deficiency, (e) persons with superior knowledge, and (f) persons acting in an emergency.

3.   Differentiate among the duties that possessors of land owe to trespassers, licensees, and invitees.

4.   Identify the defenses that are available to a tort action in negligence and those that are available to a tort action in strict liability.

5.   Identify and discuss those activities giving rise to a tort action in strict liability.

# Problems

**1.** A statute requiring railroads to fence their tracks is construed as intended solely to prevent animals that stray onto the right-of-way from being hit by trains. B & A Railroad Company fails to fence its tracks. Two of Calvin's cows wander onto the track. Nellie is hit by a train. Elsie is poisoned by weeds growing beside the track. For which cow(s), if any, is B & A Railroad Company liable to Calvin? Why?

**2.** Martha invites John to come to lunch. Though she knows that her private road is dangerous to travel, having been guttered by recent rains, Martha doesn't warn John of the condition, reasonably believing that he will notice the gutters and exercise sufficient care. While John is driving over, his attention is diverted from the road by the screaming of his child, who has been stung by a bee. He fails to notice the condition of the road, hits a gutter, and skids into a tree. If John is not contributorily negligent, is Martha liable to John?

**3.** Nathan is run over by a car and left lying in the street. Sam, seeing Nathan's helpless state, places him in his car for the purpose of taking him to the hospital. Sam drives negligently into a ditch, causing additional injury to Nathan. Is Sam liable to Nathan?

**4.** Led Foot drives his car carelessly into another car. The second car contains dynamite, which Led had no way of knowing. The collision causes an explosion which shatters a window of a building half a block away on another street. The flying glass inflicts serious cuts on Sally, who is working at a desk near the window. The explosion also harms Vic, who is walking on the sidewalk near the point of the collision. Toward whom is Led Foot negligent?

**5.** A statute requires all vessels traveling on the Great Lakes to provide lifeboats. One of Winston Steamship Company's boats is sent out of port without a lifeboat. Perry, a sailor, falls overboard in a storm so strong that had there been a lifeboat, it could not have been launched. Perry drowns. Is Winston liable to Perry's estate?

**6.** Lionel is negligently driving an automobile at excessive speed. Reginald's negligently driven car crosses the center line of the highway and scrapes the side of Lionel's car, damaging its fenders. As a result, Lionel loses control of his car, which goes into the ditch. Lionel's car is wrecked, and Lionel suffers personal injuries. What, if anything, can Lionel recover?

**7.** (a) Ellen, the owner of a baseball park, is under a duty to the entering public to provide a reasonably sufficient number of screened seats to protect those who desire such protection against the risk of being hit by batted balls. Ellen fails to do so. Frank, a customer entering the park, is unable to find a screened seat and, although fully aware of the risk, sits in an unscreened seat. Frank is struck and injured by a batted ball. Is Ellen liable?

(b) Gretchen, Frank's wife, has just arrived from Germany and is viewing baseball for the first time. Without asking any questions, she follows Frank to a seat. After the batted ball hits Frank, it caroms into Gretchen, injuring her. Is Ellen liable to Gretchen?

**8.** Negligent in failing to give warning of the approach of its train to a crossing, CC Railroad thereby endangers Larry, a blind man who is about to cross. Mildred, a bystander, in a reasonable effort to save Larry, rushes onto the track to push Larry out of danger. Although Mildred acts as carefully as possible, she is struck and injured by the train.

   (a) Can Mildred recover from Larry?

   (b) Can Mildred recover from CC Railroad?

**9.** Vance was served liquor while he was an intoxicated patron of the Clear Air Force Station Non-Commissioned Officers' Club. He later injured himself as a result of his intoxication. An Alaska State statute makes it a crime to give or to sell liquor to intoxicated persons. Vance has brought an action seeking damages for the injuries he suffered, arguing that the United States was negligent *per se* by its employee's violation of the statute. Decision?

**10.** Timothy keeps a pet chimpanzee, which is thoroughly tamed and accustomed to playing with its owner's children. The chimpanzee escapes, despite every precaution to keep it upon its owner's premises. It approaches a group of children. Wanda, the mother of one of the children, erroneously thinking the chimpanzee is about to attack the children, rushes to her child's assistance. In her hurry and excitement, she stumbles and falls, breaking her leg. Can Wanda recover for her personal injuries?

**11.** Hawkins slipped and fell on a puddle of water just inside the automatic door to the H. E. Butt Grocery Company's store. The water had been tracked into the store by customers and blown through the door by a strong wind. The store manager was aware of the puddle and had mopped it up several times earlier in the day. Still, no signs had been placed to warn store patrons of the danger. Hawkins brought an action to recover damages for injuries sustained in the fall. Decision?

**12.** Escola, a waitress, was injured when a bottle of Coca-Cola exploded in her hand while she was putting it into the restaurant's cooler. The bottle came from a shipment that had remained under the counter for thirty-six hours after being delivered by the bottling company. The bottler had subjected the bottle to the method of testing for defects commonly used in the industry, and there is no evidence that Escola or anyone else did anything to damage the bottle between its delivery and the explosion. Escola brought an action against the bottler for damages. As she is unable to show any specific acts of negligence on its part, she seeks to rely on the doctrine of *res ipsa loquitur*. Decision?

**13.** Hunn injured herself when she slipped and fell on a loose plank while walking down some steps that the hotel had repaired the day before. The night before, while entering the hotel, she had noticed that the steps were dangerous, and although she knew from her earlier stays at the hotel that another exit was available, she chose that morning to leave via the dangerous steps. The hotel was aware of the hazard, as one of the other guests who had fallen that night had reported his accident to the desk clerk then on duty. Still, there were no cautionary signs on the steps to warn of the danger, and they were not roped off or otherwise excluded from use. Hunn brought an action against the hotel for injuries she sustained as a result of her fall. Decision?

14.    Fredericks, a hotel owner, had a dog named "Sport" that he had trained as a watchdog. When Vincent Zarek, a guest at the hotel, leaned over to pet the dog, it bit him. Although Sport had never bitten anyone before, Fredericks was aware of the dog's violent tendencies and, therefore, did not allow it to roam around the hotel alone. Vincent brought an action for injuries sustained when the dog bit him. Decision?

15.    An unidentified man was held up by two thugs in an alley in Manhattan. When the thieves departed with his possessions, the man quickly gave chase. He had almost caught one when the thief managed to force his way into an empty taxicab stopped at a traffic light. The cab was owned by the Peerless Transport Company. The thief pointed his gun at the driver's head and ordered him to drive on. The driver started to follow the directions while closely pursued by a posse of good citizens, but then suddenly jammed on the brakes and jumped out of the car to safety. The thief also jumped out, but the car traveled on, injuring Mrs. Cordas and her two children. The Cordases then brought an action for damages, claiming that the cab driver was negligent in jumping to safety and leaving the moving vehicle uncontrolled. Decision?

16.    A foul ball struck Marie Uzdavines on the head while she was watching the Metropolitan Baseball Club ("The Mets") play the Philadelphia Phillies at "The Mets" home stadium in New York. The ball came through a hole in a screen designed to protect spectators sitting behind home plate. The screen contained several holes that had been repaired with baling wire lighter in weight than the wire used in the original screen. Although the manager of the stadium makes no formal inspections of the screen, his employees do try to repair the holes as they find them. Weather conditions, rust deterioration, and baseballs hitting the screen are the chief causes of these holes. The owner of the stadium, the city of New York, leases the stadium to "The Mets" and replaces the entire screen every two years. Uzdavines sued "The Mets" for negligence under the doctrine of *res ipsa loquitur*. Decision?

17.    Two-year-old David Allen was bitten by Joseph Whitehead's dog while he was playing on the porch at the Allen residence. Allen suffered facial cuts, a severed muscle in his left eye, a hole in his left ear, and scarring over his forehead. Through his father, David sued Whitehead, claiming that, as owner, Whitehead is responsible for his dog's actions. Whitehead admitted that (1) the dog was large, mean-looking, and frequently barked at neighbors; (2) the dog was allowed to roam wild; and (3) the dog frequently chased and barked at cars. He stated, however, that (1) the dog was friendly and often played with his and neighbors' children; (2) he had not received previous complaints about the dog; (3) the dog was neither aggressive nor threatening; and (4) the dog had never bitten anyone before this incident. Decision?

18.    Larry VanEgdom, in an intoxicated state, bought alcoholic beverages from the Hudson Municipal Liquor Store in Hudson, South Dakota. Immediately following the purchase, VanEgdom, while driving a car, struck and killed Guy William Ludwig, who was stopped on his motorcycle at a stop sign. Lela Walz, as special administrator of Ludwig's estate, brought an action against the city of Hudson, which operated the liquor store, for the wrongful death of Ludwig. Walz alleged that the store employee was negligent in selling intoxicating beverages to VanEgdom when he knew or could have observed that VanEgdom was drunk. The trial court dismissed the action, and Walz appealed. Decision?

19.    The *MacGilvray Shiras* was a ship owned by the Kinsman Transit Company. During the winter months, when Lake Erie was frozen, the ship and others moored at docks on the Buffalo River. As oftentimes happened, one night an ice jam disintegrated upstream, sending large chunks of ice downstream. Chunks of ice began to pile up against the *Shiras*, which at that time was without power and manned only by a shipman. The ship broke loose when a negligently constructed "deadman" to which one mooring cable was attached pulled out of the ground. The "deadman" was operated by Continental Grain Company. The ship began moving down the S-shaped river stern first and struck another ship, the *Tewksbury*. The *Tewksbury* also broke loose from its mooring, and the two ships floated down the river together. Although the crew manning the Michigan Avenue Bridge downstream had been notified of the runaway ships, they failed to raise the bridge in time to avoid a collision because of a mix-up in the shift changeover. As a result, both ships crashed into the bridge and were wedged against the bank of the river. The two vessels substantially dammed the flow of the river, causing ice and water to back up and flood installations as far as three miles upstream. The injured parties brought this action for damages against Kinsman, Continental, and the city of Buffalo. The trial court found the three defendants liable, and they appealed from that decree. Decision?

20.    Carolyn Falgout accompanied William Wardlaw as a social guest to Wardlaw's brother's camp. After both parties had consumed intoxicating beverages, Falgout walked onto a pier that was then only partially completed. Wardlaw had requested that she not go on the pier. Falgout said, "Don't tell me what to do," and proceeded to walk on the pier. Wardlaw then asked her not to walk past the completed portion of the pier. She ignored his warnings and walked to the pier's end. When returning to the shore, Falgout got her shoe caught between the boards. She fell, hanging by her foot, with her head and arms in the water. Wardlaw rescued Falgout, who had seriously injured her knee and leg. She sued Wardlaw for negligence and subsequently appealed from the trial court's judgment for Wardlaw. Decision?

**WWW**    **Internet Exercise** Find and review information about tort reform.

# PART TWO

# Contracts

# CHAPTER 9

# Introduction to Contracts

It is impossible to overestimate the importance of contracts in the field of business. Every business, whether large or small, must enter into contracts with its employees, its suppliers, and its customers to conduct its business operations. Contract law is, therefore, an important subject for the business manager. Contract law is also basic to other fields of law treated in other parts of this book, such as agency, partnerships, corporations, sales of personal property, commercial paper, and secured transactions.

Even the most common transaction may involve a multitude of contracts. For example, in a typical contract for the sale of land, the seller promises to transfer title to the land, and the buyer promises to pay an agreed-upon purchase price. In addition, the seller may promise to pay certain taxes or assessments; the buyer may promise to assume a mortgage on the property or may promise to pay the purchase price to a creditor of the seller. If attorneys represent the parties, they very likely do so on a contractual basis. If the seller deposits the proceeds of the sale in a bank, he enters into a contract with the bank. If the buyer leases the property, he enters into a contract with the tenant. When one of the parties leaves his car in a parking lot to attend to any of these matters, he assumes a contractual relationship with the proprietor of the lot. In short, nearly every business transaction is based upon contract and the expectations the agreed-upon promises create. Knowing the legal requirements for making binding contracts is, therefore, essential.

## DEVELOPMENT OF THE LAW OF CONTRACTS

That law arises from social necessity is clearly true of the law of contracts. The vast and complicated institution of business can be conducted efficiently and successfully only upon the certainty that promises will be fulfilled. Business must be assured not only of supplies of raw materials or manufactured goods, but of labor, management, capital, and insurance as well. Common experience has shown that promises based solely on personal honesty or integrity do not have the reliability essential to business. Hence the development of the law of contracts, which is the law of enforceable promises.

Contract law, like law as a whole, is not static. It has undergone—and is still undergoing—enormous changes. In the nineteenth century virtually absolute autonomy in forming contracts was the rule. The law imposed contract liability only where the parties strictly complied with the required formalities. The same principle also dictated that once a contract was formed it should be enforced according to its terms and that neither party should be lightly excused from performance.

During the twentieth century, contract law has experienced tremendous changes. As will be discussed in the next ten chapters, many of the formalities of contract formation have been relaxed. Today, the law usually recognizes contractual obligations whenever the parties manifest an intent to be bound. In addition, an increasing number of promises are now enforced in certain circumstances, even though they do not comply strictly with the basic requirements of a contract. While in the past contract liability was absolute and escape from liability, once assumed, was rare, presently the law allows a party to be excused from contractual duties where fraud, duress, undue influence, mistake, unconscionability, or impossibility is present. The law has expanded the previous century's narrow view of contract damages to grant equitable remedies and restitution as remedies for breach of contract. The older doctrine of privity of contract, which sharply restricted which parties could enforce contract rights, has given way to the current view that permits intended third-party beneficiaries to sue in their own right.

In brief, the twentieth century has left its mark on contract law by limiting the absolute freedom of contract and, at the same time, by relaxing the requirements of contract formation. Accordingly, it is now considerably easier to get into a contract and correspondingly less difficult to get out of one.

## Common Law

Contracts are primarily governed by State common law. An orderly presentation of this law is found in the Restatements of the Law of Contracts. The American Law Institute adopted and promulgated the first Restatement on May 6, 1932. On May 17, 1979, the institute adopted and promulgated a revised edition of the Restatement—the Restatement, Second, Contracts—which will be referred to as the Restatement. Regarded as a valuable authoritative reference work for more than sixty years, the Restatements have been extensively relied upon and quoted in reported judicial opinions.

## The Uniform Commercial Code

The sale of personal property forms a substantial portion of commercial activity. Article 2 of the Uniform Commercial Code (the Code, or UCC) governs sales in all States except Louisiana. (The UCC is set forth in Appendix B of this text.) A **sale** consists in the passing of title to goods from a seller to a buyer for a price. Section 2–106. A contract for sale includes both a present sale of goods and a contract to sell goods at a future time. Section 2–106. The Code essentially defines goods as movable personal property. Section 2–105(1). **Personal property** is any type of property other than an interest in real property (land). For example, the purchase of a television set, automobile, or textbook is considered a sale of goods. All such transactions are governed by Article 2 of the Code, but, where the Code has not specifically modified general contract law, the common law of contracts continues to apply. Section 1–103. In other words, the law of sales is a specialized part of the general law of contracts, and the law of contracts governs unless specifically displaced by the Code.

◆ *See Figure 9–1*

 *See Case 21–1*

## Types of Contracts Outside the Code

General contract law governs all contracts outside the scope of the Code. Such contracts play a significant role in commercial activities. For example, the Code does *not* apply to employment contracts, service contracts, insurance contracts, contracts involving **real property** (land and anything attached to it, including buildings), and contracts for the sale of intangibles such as patents and copyrights. These transactions continue to be governed by general contract law.

 *See Case 9–1*

## *DEFINITION OF A CONTRACT*

A **contract** is a set of promises that the courts will enforce. Section 1 of the Restatement more precisely defines a contract as "a promise or a set of promises for the breach

**FIGURE 9–1** Law Governing Contracts

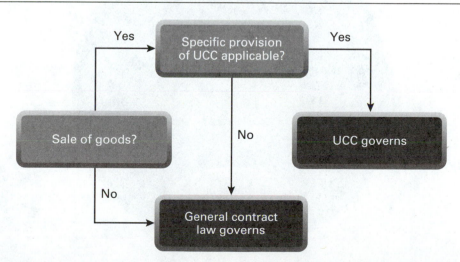

of which the law gives a remedy, or the performance of which the law in some way recognizes as a duty." The Restatement provides further insight by defining a **promise** as "a manifestation of the intention to act or refrain from acting in a specified way." Restatement, Section 2.

Those promises that meet all of the essential requirements of a binding contract are contractual and will be enforced. All other promises are not contractual, and usually no legal remedy is available for a **breach** (a failure to perform properly) of these promises. The remedies provided for breach of contract (discussed in Chapter 18) include compensatory damages, equitable remedies, reliance damages, and restitution. Thus, a promise may be contractual (and therefore binding) or noncontractual. In other words, all contracts are promises, but not all promises are contracts.

◆ *See Figure 9–2*

 *See Case 9–2*

## REQUIREMENTS OF A CONTRACT

The four basic requirements of a contract are as follows:

1. **Mutual Assent.** The parties to a contract must manifest by words or conduct that they have agreed to enter into a contract. The usual method of showing mutual assent is by offer and acceptance.

2. **Consideration.** Each party to a contract must intentionally exchange a legal benefit or incur a legal detriment as an inducement to the other party to make a return exchange.

3. **Legality of Object.** The purpose of a contract must not be criminal, tortious, or otherwise against public policy.

4. **Capacity.** The parties to a contract must have contractual capacity. Certain persons, such as those adjudicated (judicially declared) incompetent, have no legal capacity to contract, while others, such as minors, incompetent persons, and intoxicated persons, have limited capacity to contract. All others have full contractual capacity.

In addition, though occasionally a contract must be evidenced by a writing to be enforceable, in most cases an oral contract is binding and enforceable. If all of these essentials are present, the promise is contractual and legally binding. If any is absent, however, the promise is noncontractual. These requirements will be separately considered in succeeding chapters.

◆ *See Figure 9–3*

 *See Case 9–2*

**FIGURE 9–2** Contractual and Noncontractual Promises

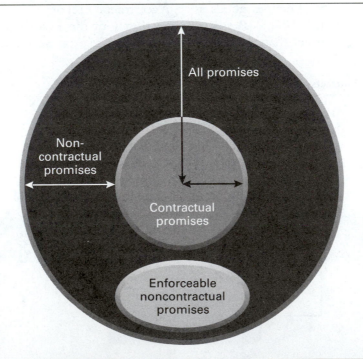

**FIGURE 9–3**  Validity of Agreements

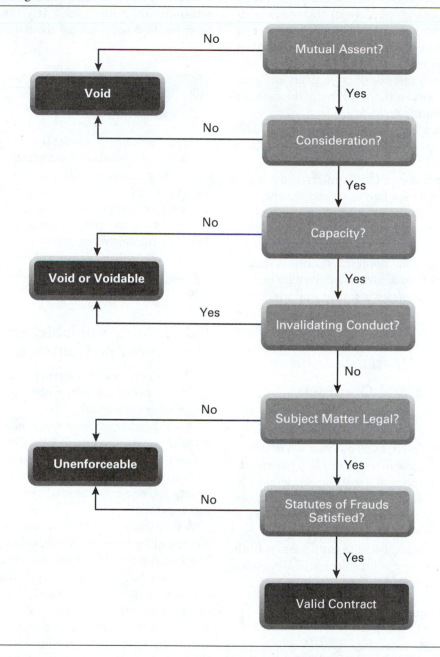

## CLASSIFICATION OF CONTRACTS

Contracts can be classified according to various characteristics, such as method of formation, content, and legal effect. The standard classifications are (1) express or implied contracts; (2) unilateral or bilateral contracts; (3) valid, void, voidable, or unenforceable contracts; (4) executed or executory contracts; and (5) formal or informal contracts. These classifications are not mutually exclusive. For example, a contract may be express, bilateral, valid, executory, and informal.

### Express and Implied Contracts

Parties to a contract may indicate their assent either by express language or by conduct that implies such willingness. Thus, a contract may be (1) entirely oral; (2) partly oral and partly written; (3) entirely written; (4) partly oral or written and partly implied from the conduct of the parties; and (5) wholly implied from the conduct of the parties. The first three are known as express contracts, and the last two as implied contracts. Both express and implied contracts are genuine contracts, equally enforceable. The difference between them is merely the manner in which the parties manifest assent.

An **express contract** is therefore one in which the parties have manifested their agreement by oral or written language, or both.

An **implied contract** is one that is inferred from the parties' conduct, not from spoken or written words. Implied contracts are also called implied in fact contracts. Thus, if Elizabeth orders and receives a meal in Bill's restaurant, a promise is implied on Elizabeth's part to pay Bill the price stated in the menu or, if none is stated, Bill's customary price. Likewise, when a passenger boards a bus, a wholly implied contract is formed by which the passenger undertakes to pay the customary fare and the bus company undertakes to provide the passenger transportation.

## Unilateral and Bilateral Contracts

In the typical contractual transaction, each party makes at least one promise. For example, if Ali says to Ben, "If you promise to mow my lawn, I will pay you ten dollars," and Ben agrees to mow Ali's lawn, Ali and Ben have made mutual promises, each undertaking to do something in exchange for the promise of the other. When a contract comes into existence by the exchange of promises, each party is under a duty to the other. This kind of contract is called a **bilateral contract,** because each party is both a *promisor* (a person making a promise) and a *promisee* (the person to whom a promise is made).

But suppose that only one of the parties makes a promise. Ali says to Ben, "If you will mow my lawn, I will pay you ten dollars." A contract will be formed when Ben has finished mowing the lawn and not before. At that time, Ali becomes contractually obligated to pay ten dollars to Ben. Ali's offer was in exchange for Ben's act of mowing the lawn, not for his promise to mow it.

Because he never made a promise to mow the lawn, Ben was under no duty to mow it. This is a **unilateral contract** because only one of the parties made a promise.

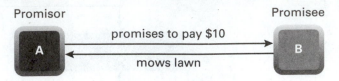

Thus, whereas a bilateral contract results from the exchange of a promise for a return promise, a unilateral contract results from the exchange of a promise either for an act or for a forbearance (refraining) from acting. If a contract is not clearly unilateral or bilateral, the courts presume that the parties intended a bilateral contract. Thus, in the above example, if Ali says to Ben, "I will pay you ten dollars if you will mow my lawn," and Ben replies, "OK, I will mow your lawn," a bilateral contract is formed.

## Valid, Void, Voidable, and Unenforceable Contracts

By definition, a **valid contract** is one that meets all of the requirements of a binding contract. It is an enforceable promise or agreement.

A **void contract** is an agreement that does not meet all of the requirements of a binding contract. Thus, it is no contract at all; it is merely a promise or agreement having no legal effect. An example of a void agreement is an agreement entered into by an adjudicated incompetent.

A voidable contract, on the other hand, is not wholly lacking in legal effect. A **voidable contract** is a contract, but because of the manner in which it was formed or a lack of capacity of a party to it, the law permits one or more of the parties to avoid the legal duties the contract creates. Restatement, Section 7. If the contract is avoided, both parties are relieved of their legal duties under the agreement. For instance, through intentional misrepresentation of a material fact (*fraud*), Thomas induces Regina to enter into a contract. Regina may, upon discovery of the fraud, notify Thomas that by reason of the misrepresentation she will not perform her promise, and the law will support Regina. Though not void, the contract induced by fraud is voidable at the election of Regina, the defrauded party. Thomas, the fraudulent party, has no such election. If Regina elects to avoid the contract, Thomas will be released from his promise under the agreement, although he may be liable under tort law for damages for fraud.

A contract that is neither void nor voidable may, nonetheless, be unenforceable. An **unenforceable contract** is one for the breach of which the law provides no remedy. Restatement, Section 8. For example, a contract may be unenforceable because of a failure to satisfy the requirements of the Statute of Frauds, which requires certain kinds of contracts to be evidenced by a writing to be enforceable. Also, the running of the time within which a suit may be filed, as provided in the Statute of Limitations, bars the right to bring a lawsuit for breach of contract. After that period has run, the contract is referred to as unenforceable, rather than void or voidable.

## Executed and Executory Contracts

The terms *executed* and *executory* pertain to the state of performance of a contract. A contract fully performed by all of the parties to it is an **executed contract.** Strictly, an executed contract is in the present tense no contract, as all duties under it have been performed; but it is useful to have a term for a completed contract. (The word *executed* is also used to mean "signed," as in to execute or sign a certain document.)

The term **executory,** which means "unperformed," applies to situations where one or more promises by any party to the contract are as yet unperformed or where the contract is wholly unperformed by one or more of the parties. Thus, David and Carla make a contract under which David is to sell and deliver certain goods to Carla in ten days and Carla is to pay the agreed price in thirty days. Prior to the delivery of the goods by David on the tenth day, the contract is wholly executory. Upon David's delivery of the goods to Carla, the contract is executed as to David and executory as to Carla. When Carla duly pays for the goods, the contract is wholly executed and thereby completely fulfilled.

## Formal and Informal Contracts

A **formal contract** depends upon a particular form, or mode of expression, for its legal existence. For example, at common law a promise under seal (a particular symbol that serves to authenticate an instrument) is enforceable without anything more. Another formal contract is a negotiable instrument, such as a check, which has certain legal attributes resulting solely from the special form in which it is made. A letter of credit (a promise to honor drafts or other demands for payment) is also a formal contract. Recognizances, or formal acknowledgments of

indebtedness made in court, are another example of formal contracts. All other contracts, whether oral or written, are simple or **informal contracts,** as they do not depend upon formality for their legal validity.

## PROMISSORY ESTOPPEL

As a general rule, promises are unenforceable if they do not meet all the requirements of a contract. Nevertheless, to avoid injustice, in certain circumstances the courts enforce noncontractual promises under the doctrine of promissory estoppel. A noncontractual promise is enforceable when it is made under circumstances that should lead the promisor reasonably to expect that the promise would induce the promisee to take definite and substantial action or forbearance in reliance on the promise, and the promisee does take such action or forbearance. See **Figure 9–2.** Section 90 of the Restatement provides:

A promise which the promisor should reasonably expect to induce action or forbearance on the part of the promisee or a third person and which does induce such action or forbearance is binding if injustice can be avoided only by enforcement of the promise. The remedy granted for breach may be limited as justice requires.

For example, Gordon promises Constance not to foreclose for a period of six months on a mortgage Gordon owns on Constance's land. Constance then expends $100,000 to construct a building on the land. His promise not to foreclose is binding on Gordon under the doctrine of promissory estoppel.

◆ *See Figure 9–4*

⚖ *See Case 9–3*

## QUASI CONTRACTS

In addition to implied in fact contracts, there are implied in law, or quasi, contracts, which were not included in the foregoing classification of contracts because a quasi (meaning "as if") contract is not a contract at all. The term *quasi contract* is used because the remedy granted for quasi contract is similar to one of the remedies available for breach of contract.

A quasi contract is *not* a contract because it is based on neither an express nor an implied promise. A **contract implied in law** or **quasi contract** is an obligation imposed by law to avoid injustice. For example, Anna by mistake delivers to Robert a plain, unaddressed envelope containing $100 intended for Claudia. Robert is under

**FIGURE 9–4**  Contracts, Promissory Estoppel, and Quasi Contracts

|  | Contract | Promissory Estoppel | Quasi Contract |
|---|---|---|---|
| **Type of Promise** | Contractual | Noncontractual | None<br>Void<br>Unenforceable<br>Invalidated |
| **Requirements** | All of the essential elements of a contract | Detrimental and justifiable reliance | Benefit conferred and knowingly accepted |
| **Remedies** | Equitable<br>Compensatory<br>Reliance<br>Restitution | Promise enforced to the extent necessary to avoid injustice | Reasonable value of benefit conferred |

no contractual obligation to return it. However, Anna is permitted to recover the $100 from Robert. The law imposes a quasi-contractual obligation upon Robert to prevent his unjust enrichment at Anna's expense. The elements of such a recovery are (1) a benefit conferred upon the defendant (Robert) by the plaintiff (Anna); (2) an appreciation or knowledge by the defendant (Robert) of the benefit; and (3) acceptance or retention by the defendant (Robert) of the benefit under circumstances rendering inequitable the defendant's (Robert's) retention of the benefit without compensating the plaintiff for its value.

One court has summarized the doctrine of quasi contract as follows:

Quasi contracts are not contracts at all, although they give rise to obligations more akin to those stemming from contract than from tort. The contract is a mere fiction, a form imposed in order to adapt the case to a given remedy. . . . Briefly stated, a quasi-contractual obligation is one imposed by law where there has been no agreement or expression of assent, by word or act, on the part of either party involved. The law creates it, regardless of the intention of the parties, to assure a just and equitable result. *Bradkin v. Leverton,* 26 N.Y.2d 192, 309 N.Y.S.2d 192, 257 N.E.2d 643 (1970).

Not infrequently, courts use quasi contracts to provide a remedy when the parties have entered into a void contract, an unenforceable contract, or a voidable contract that is avoided. In such a case, the law of quasi contracts will determine the recovery permitted for any performance rendered by the parties under the invalid, unenforceable, or invalidated agreement.

◆ *See Figure 9–4*

 *See Case 9–4*

# Chapter Summary

| **Law of Contracts** | **Definition of Contract** a binding agreement that the courts will enforce<br>**Common Law** most contracts are governed primarily by State common law, including contracts involving employment, services, insurance, real property (land and anything attached to it), patents, and copyrights<br>**Uniform Commercial Code** Article 2 of the UCC governs the sales of goods<br>• *Sale* the transfer of title from seller to buyer<br>• *Goods* tangible personal property (personal property is all property other than an interest in land) |
|---|---|

| **Requirements of a Contract** | **Mutual Assent** the parties to a contract must manifest by words or conduct that they have agreed to enter into a contract |
| | **Consideration** each party to a contract must intentionally exchange a legal benefit or incur a legal detriment as an inducement to the other party to make a return exchange |
| | **Legality of Object** the purpose of a contract must not be criminal, tortious, or otherwise against public policy |
| | **Capacity** the parties to a contract must have contractual capacity |

| **Classification of Contracts** | **Express and Implied Contracts** |
| | • *Express Contract* an agreement that is stated in words, either orally or in writing |
| | • *Implied in Fact Contract* a contract in which the agreement of the parties is inferred from their conduct |
| | **Bilateral and Unilateral Contracts** |
| | • *Bilateral Contract* a contract in which both parties exchange promises |
| | • *Unilateral Contract* a contract in which only one party makes a promise |
| | **Valid, Void, Voidable, and Unenforceable Contracts** |
| | • *Valid Contract* one that meets all of the requirements of a binding contract |
| | • *Void Contract* no contract at all; without legal effect |
| | • *Voidable Contract* a contract capable of being made void |
| | • *Unenforceable Contract* a contract for the breach of which the law provides no remedy |
| | **Executed and Executory Contracts** |
| | • *Executed Contract* a contract that has been fully performed by all of the parties |
| | • *Executory Contract* a contract that has yet to be fully performed |
| | **Formal and Informal Contracts** |
| | • *Formal Contract* an agreement that is legally binding because of its particular form or mode of expression |
| | • *Informal Contracts* all contracts other than formal contracts |

| **Promissory Estoppel** | **Definition** a doctrine enforcing *some* noncontractual promises |
| | **Requirements** a promise made under circumstances that should lead the promisor reasonably to expect that the promise would induce the promisee to take definite and substantial action, and the promisee does take such action |
| | **Remedy** a court will enforce the promise to the extent necessary to avoid injustice |

| **Quasi Contracts** | **Definition** an obligation not based on contract that is imposed to avoid injustice |
| | **Requirements** a court will impose a quasi contract when (1) the plaintiff confers a benefit upon the defendant, (2) the defendant knows or appreciates the benefit, and (3) the defendant's retention of the benefit is inequitable |
| | **Remedy** the plaintiff recovers the reasonable value of the benefit she conferred upon the defendant |

# Cases

### CASE 9–1
## Contracts Outside the Code
### *INSUL-MARK MIDWEST, INC. v. MODERN MATERIALS, INC.*
Supreme Court of Indiana, 1993
612 N.E.2d 550

SHEPARD, C. J.
[Insul-Mark is the marketing arm of Kor-It Sales, Inc. Kor-It manufactures roofing fasteners and Insul-Mark distributes them nationwide. In late 1985, Kor-It contracted with Modern Materials, Inc. to have large volumes of screws coated with a rust-proofing agent. The contract specified that the coated screws must pass a standard industry test and that Kor-It would pay according to the pound and length of the screws coated. Kor-It had received numerous complaints from customers that the coated screws were rusting, but Modern Materials unsuccessfully attempted to remedy the problem. Kor-It terminated its relationship with Modern Materials and brought suit for the deficient coating. Modern Materials counterclaimed for the labor and materials it had furnished to Kor-It. The trial court held that the contract (1) was for performance of a service, (2) not governed by the U.C.C., (3) governed by the common law of contracts, and (4) therefore barred by a two year statute of limitations. Insul-Mark appealed to the Court of Appeals, which transferred the case to the Supreme Court of Indiana to resolve conflicting authority in the Court of Appeals.]

**Applicability of the U.C.C.** The Sales chapter of the Indiana U.C.C., [citation], "applies to transactions in goods," unless the context otherwise requires. [UCC§] 2–102. The code defines goods as "all things (including specially manufactured goods) which are movable at the time of identification to the contract for sale." [UCC§] 2–105(1). An agreement solely for the performance of services is not subject to the sales provisions of the U.C.C. [Citation.]

Many modern commercial transactions cannot be classified as transactions purely for goods or for services, but are "mixed," involving both goods and services. [Citation.] The coating transactions in this case between Kor-It and Modern Materials are indeed "mixed," involving both goods (the coating material) and services (the application of coating). Kor-It did not purchase the coating material directly from Modern Materials, but

provided Modern Materials its screws for application of coating (a service).

Given that the transaction is "mixed," we must determine whether it falls within the U.C.C., or falls outside of the code and is thus governed by the common law. The Indiana Court of Appeals has formulated and applied tests for determining the applicability of the U.C.C. to mixed transactions. In [citation], the Second District adopted the "predominant thrust" test. The Third District also applied the predominant thrust test in this case to conclude that the code does not apply to the transactions between Kor-It and Modern Materials because the thrust of the transactions was predominantly for services. [Citation.]

Under the predominant thrust test, the applicability of the U.C.C. to a mixed transaction is determined by considering whether the transaction's "predominant factor, [its] thrust, [its] purpose, reasonably stated, is the rendition of service, with goods incidentally involved (e.g., contract with artist for painting) or is a transaction of sale, with labor incidentally involved (e.g., installation of a water heater in a bathroom)." [Citation.]

\* \* \*

\* \* \* Under the predominant thrust test, courts look to the agreement between the parties to determine their understanding about the predominant purpose of the contract. In focusing on the goals of the contracting parties, the predominant thrust approach preserves parties' expectations regarding their agreement.

\* \* \*

To determine whether the predominant thrust of a mixed contract is to provide services or goods, one first looks to the language of the contract, [citation], in light of the situation of the parties and the surrounding circumstances. [Citation.] Specifically, one looks to the terms describing the performance required of the parties, and the words used to describe the relationship between the parties.

Beyond the contractual terms themselves, one looks to the circumstances of the parties, and the primary reason they entered into the contract. [Citation.] One also considers the final product the purchaser bargained to receive, and whether it may be described as a good or a service.

Finally, one examines the costs involved for the goods and services, and whether the purchase was charged only for a good, or a price based on both goods and services. If the cost of the goods is but a small portion of the overall contract price, such fact would increase the likelihood that the services portion predominates. [Citation.]

### Is This Case Goods or Services?

* * *

We hold that the thrust of the agreement between Kor-It and Modern Materials was predominantly for performance of a service. Kor-It's main purpose in entering into the coating transaction was to improve the rust-resistance of its screws. Its specifications regarding rust-resistance related to the quality of its screws after application of a fluorocarbon coating material, and not to the quality of the coating material by itself. Kor-It bargained for a service which would improve the durability of its screws. It hired Modern Materials based on the company's promise that the "Process 300/400 when applied to your metal . . . fasteners will exceed 30 Kesternick [sic] cycles with less than 10% red rust."

* * *

Kor-It neither specified nor involved itself in the decision-making regarding which coating material Modern Materials would apply to the screws. The record demonstrates that Kor-It's only concern was with the finished product, i.e., the finished, rust-proofed, screws.

The performance Kor-It contracted to obtain was the transformation of its screws from a noncoated form to a coated form with enhanced rust-resistance. Modern Materials' complex multi-step application process was the crucial element completing this transformation. The transfer of the coating material, a good, in the process was incidental to the larger service.

Particularly revealing is the pricing method Modern Materials used for the coating. Kor-It was charged not by the gallon for the coating, as Modern Materials was charged by its coating supplier. Instead, it was charged by the pound of screws coated. If the coating material itself were the predominant thrust of the contract, presumably Kor-It would have paid a price based on the gallons of coating used. Charging instead by the pound of screws coated appears to tie the price to the cost of processing such an amount of screws.

Keeping in mind the uniformity policies underlying the U.C.C. when we hold that the thrust of the coating transaction was predominantly for services, we note that our holding is in line with closely analogous mixed transaction cases from other jurisdictions. For example, in [citation], the Supreme Court of Oklahoma found to be a predominantly service transaction an arrangement whereby a purchaser sent its crankshafts to a company which chrome-plated the shafts and returned them. Similarly, courts in various jurisdictions have held that arrangements for application of pesticides and herbicides are predominantly service transactions. [Citations.] Finally, in [citation], the court concluded that an agreement to strip and apply an acrylic finish to a floor was predominantly a service contract. * * *

Based upon the facts of this case as well as the well-reasoned conclusions of other courts, we hold as a matter of law that the thrust of the coating agreement between Kor-It and Modern Materials was predominantly for the performance of services. The U.C.C. does not apply to the transaction, and the parties' dispute is therefore governed by our common law.

---

### CASE 9–2
## Definition and Requirements of a Contract
## *STEINBERG v. CHICAGO MEDICAL SCHOOL*

Illinois Court of Appeals, 1976
41 Ill.App.3d 804, 354 N.E.2d 586

DEMPSEY, J.

In December 1973 the plaintiff, Robert Steinberg, applied for admission to the defendant, the Chicago Medical School, as a first-year student for the academic year 1974–75 and paid an application fee of $15. The Chicago Medical School is a private, not-for-profit educational institution, incorporated in the State of Illinois. His application for admission was rejected and Steinberg filed a[n] . . . action against the school, claiming that it had failed to evaluate his application . . . according to the academic entrance criteria printed in the school's bulletin. Specifically, his complaint alleged that the school's decision to accept or reject a particular applicant for the first-year class was primarily based on such nonacademic considerations as the prospective student's familial relationship to members of the school's faculty and to members of its board of trustees, and the ability of the applicant or his family to pledge or make payment of large sums of money to the school. The complaint further alleged that, by using such unpublished criteria to evaluate applicants, the school had breached the contract which Steinberg contended was created when the school accepted his application fee.

\* \* \*

The defendant filed a motion to dismiss, arguing that the complaint failed to state a cause of action because no contract came into existence during its transaction with Steinberg inasmuch as the school's informational publication did not constitute a valid offer. The trial court sustained [ruled in favor of] the motion to dismiss and Steinberg appeals from this order.

\* \* \*

A contract is an agreement between competent parties, based upon a consideration sufficient in law, to do or not do a particular thing. It is a promise or a set of promises for the breach of which the law gives a remedy, or the performance of which the law in some way recognizes as a duty. [Citation.] A contract's essential requirements are: competent parties, valid subject matter, legal consideration, mutuality of obligation and mutuality of agreement. Generally, parties may contract in any situation where there is no legal prohibition, since the law acts by restraint and not by conferring rights. [Citation.] However, it is basic contract law that in order for a contract to be binding the terms of the contract must be reasonably certain and definite. [Citation.]

A contract, in order to be legally binding, must be based on consideration. [Citation.] Consideration has been defined to consist of some right, interest, profit or benefit accruing to one party or some forbearance, disadvantage, detriment, loss or responsibility given, suffered, or undertaken by the other. [Citation.] Money is a valuable consideration and its transfer or payment or promises to pay it or the benefit from the right to its use, will support a contract.

In forming a contract, it is required that both parties assent to the same thing in the same sense [citation] and that their minds meet on the essential terms and conditions. [Citation.] Furthermore, the mutual consent essential to the formation of a contract must be gathered from the language employed by the parties or manifested by their words or acts. The intention of the parties gives character to the transaction, and if either party contracts in good faith he is entitled to the benefit of his contract no matter what may have been the secret purpose or intention of the other party. [Citation.]

Steinberg contends that the Chicago Medical School's informational brochure constituted an invitation to make an offer; that his subsequent application and the submission of his $15 fee to the school amounted to an offer; that the school's voluntary reception of his fee constituted an acceptance and because of these events a contract was created between the school and himself. He contends that the school was duty bound under the terms of the contract to evaluate his application according to its stated standards and that the deviation from these standards not only breached the contract, but amounted to an arbitrary selection which constituted a violation of due process and equal protection. He concludes that such a breach did in fact take place each and every time during the past ten years that the school evaluated applicants according to their relationship to the school's faculty members or members of its board of trustees, or in accordance with their ability to make or pledge large sums of money to the school. Finally, he asserts that he is a member and a proper representative of the class that has been damaged by the school's practice.

The school counters that no contract came into being because informational brochures, such as its bulletin, do not constitute offers, but are construed by the courts to be general proposals to consider, examine and negotiate. The school points out that this doctrine has been specifically applied in Illinois to university informational publications.

\* \* \*

We agree with Steinberg's position. We believe that he and the school entered into an enforceable contract; that the school's obligation under the contract was stated in the school's bulletin in a definitive manner and that by accepting his application fee—a valuable consideration—the school bound itself to fulfill its promises. Steinberg accepted the school's promises in good faith and he was entitled to have his application judged according to the school's stated criteria.

\* \* \*

[Reversed and remanded.]

---

## CASE 9–3
### Promissory Estoppel
# *GORHAM v. BENSON OPTICAL*

Court of Appeals of Minnesota, 1995
539 N.W.2d 798

**DAVIES, J.**

Appellant contends the district court erred in dismissing his claims for breach of contract, promissory estoppel, and fraud that arose from termination of an at-will employment contract. We affirm summary judgment on the fraud and breach of contract claims, but reverse summary judgment on the promissory estoppel claim and remand for further proceedings.

### Facts

In early September 1993, appellant Carl Gorham received a phone call from Ed Iwinski about a job opportunity with respondent Benson Optical. At that time, Gorham earned $38,000 annually working as a store manager for LensCrafters, but indicated he was interested in employment with Benson Optical. Iwinski, who apparently had been offered the job of chief operating officer (COO) for Benson Optical, told Gorham that he was not yet part of the decision-making process on hiring, but would forward Gorham's name to Benson Optical. The next day, Benson Optical's eastern regional manager, Sue Opahle, called Gorham to schedule an interview for an area manager position.

On September 15, 1993, Opahle interviewed Gorham in Chicago. During this interview, Gorham came to believe that Iwinski was effectively Opahle's boss and the COO at Benson Optical.

On September 18, Gorham called Opahle to inquire about the status of his application. Opahle offered him the job of area manager for half of North Carolina and some stores in Florida and Kentucky. She offered him a $50,000 annual salary and discussed relocation. Opahle described the terms of employment over the phone and promised to send a confirming letter and employee packet in two days. Gorham told Opahle that he accepted the position provisionally, and, if he changed his mind, he would notify her within two days. Otherwise, he would give LensCrafters his notice of termination.

When Gorham did not receive the packet on September 20, he called Benson Optical to inquire. Someone in the office called Gorham back, said the packet was in the mail, and reassured him that the deal was finalized

so he could give LensCrafters notice. On September 21, Gorham gave LensCrafters his two-week notice of resignation. LensCrafters attempted to keep Gorham in its employment with an offer of a raise, but Gorham declined.

When Gorham received the packet a few days later, it contained two shortcomings, which he called to Benson's attention. Gorham received a corrected letter, which asked that he sign and return it as acceptance of the terms of employment. Gorham signed this letter, but never returned it because he had started having reservations about his employment with Benson Optical.

On about September 30, Iwinski informed Benson Optical's vice president of human resources, Fran Scibora, that he was declining the COO position. Scibora, Opahle, and Benson Optical's chief financial officer, Dominic Sblendorio, immediately contacted Gorham and three other new employees who had been recommended by Iwinski, asking for their reactions to the fact that Iwinski would not be working for Benson Optical. Gorham responded that Iwinski's absence did not change his decision to accept the job. When Gorham asked if Iwinski's departure affected Gorham's job, Scibora assured him that it would not.

Gorham's last day of work for LensCrafters was October 1. On October 3, he flew to Minneapolis for Benson Optical's national sales meeting. On October 4, Scibora, Opahle, and Sblendorio met with Gorham for what they called a "getting to know you" meeting. At the meeting they asked him for the completed employee forms they had sent him; Gorham turned in all the forms except the acceptance letter. The meeting then turned into another interview in which they reviewed Gorham's skills and aptitudes. Scibora finally told Gorham that he did not possess the skills necessary for the area manager position. Gorham had the clear impression that he had been or would be terminated.

This group also met with and terminated three other employees whom Opahle had hired at Iwinski's suggestion. In a letter to Gorham dated October 15, Benson Optical explained that it had terminated his position because Iwinski had declined the job as COO, because of a "change [in] the requirements of the Area Manager's position" and because Gorham's "skills and abilities did not satisfy the requirements for the new direction in which the company is going."

Gorham brought this action claiming breach of contract, fraud, promissory estoppel, and defamation. The district court granted Benson Optical's motion for summary judgment on all claims. Gorham appeals the breach of contract, promissory estoppel, and fraud claims.

* * *

## Analysis

**I. Contract** A party may manifest acceptance of an agreement by written or spoken words, or by conduct and actions. [Citation.] The record establishes that a contract existed here before October 4 because, even though Gorham did not return the acceptance letter to Benson Optical, he demonstrated his acceptance by verbally agreeing to take the job, resigning his former employment, flying to Chicago at his own expense, and reporting for the sales meeting on October 3. He also admitted that, at that time, he considered himself hired.

The hiring letter, however, fell short as a matter of law of guaranteeing Gorham employment for 90 days as he claims. The relevant statement merely informed Gorham that he needed to produce in 90 days or face termination. Because the contract was at-will and there are no issues of fact as to its terms, the district court properly granted summary judgment on Gorham's breach of contract claim.

**II. Promissory Estoppel** Gorham alternatively contends that the district court erred in granting summary judgment for Benson Optical on the promissory estoppel claim. We agree.

The elements of promissory estoppel are:

A promise which the promisor should reasonably expect to induce action or forbearance * * * on the part of the promisee and which does induce such action or forbearance is binding if injustice can be avoided only by enforcement of the promise.

Restatement of Contracts § 90 (1932), [citation]. [Court's footnote: This provision has remained substantially the same in Restatement (Second) of Contracts § 90 (1981).]

Respondents argue that promissory estoppel is not available when a contract exists. This is true (but with one exception). [Citation.] In *Grouse*, however, the supreme

court in effect found an exception to this rule. The exception applies when the contract is of a type that provides no basis for a contract recovery, i.e., an at-will employment contract. [Citation.] Then there is no bar to a promissory estoppel claim.

In *Grouse*, the supreme court applied the doctrine of promissory estoppel to facts very similar to the present case and allowed the plaintiff to recover reliance damages. There, a pharmacy offered a pharmacist a job and, after the pharmacist accepted, resigned his current position, and declined another job offer, the pharmacy hired someone else. * * *

* * *

Significant to this case, the *Grouse* court stated, in dictum: "[U]nder appropriate circumstances we believe section 90 [of the Restatement] would apply even after employment has begun." [Citation.] Gorham presents the specific hypothetical situation the *Grouse* court's dictum addressed—a short time actually on the job. And, independent of the hypothetical and like Grouse himself, Gorham relied on the promise of a new job when he quit his job with LensCrafters and declined any renegotiations with them. Gorham came to Minneapolis to begin work on October 4, believing that he had been hired. Within a day, Benson Optical terminated him. These facts show Gorham's reasonable reliance on Benson Optical's promise of employment, his declining any other job in deference to his new job with Benson Optical, and the injustice to him when, on his first day of "employment," he went through a hostile re-interview process that led to his immediate termination.

We see no relevant difference between Gorham, who reported to the national sales meeting on his first day of employment, and Grouse, who was denied even one day on the job. Both men relied to their detriment on the promise of a new job, only to discover that the opportunity had disintegrated before they ever actually started working. Neither man had a "good faith opportunity to perform his duties." [Citation.] Given these facts, Gorham's claim fits squarely within the spirit of *Grouse* and is entitled to the benefit of promissory estoppel leading to reliance damages.

* * *

The district court erred when it granted summary judgment against Gorham's promissory estoppel claim.

## Decision

* * * The doctrine of promissory estoppel allows Gorham to recover good faith reliance damages when Benson Optical terminated him on his first day of employment,

after Gorham had detrimentally and reasonably relied on the promise of new employment. Summary judgment on the promissory estoppel claim is reversed and remanded for further proceedings.

---

## CASE 9–4
## Quasi Contracts
### *WEICHERT CO. REALTORS v. RYAN*
Supreme Court of New Jersey, 1992
128 N.J. 427, 608 A.2d 280

STEIN, J.

Plaintiff, Weichert Co. Realtors (Weichert), sought damages from defendants, Thomas Ryan and Jay Saunders, based on defendants' failure to pay Weichert for brokerage services rendered by William Tackaberry, a Weichert employee. Weichert based its claim on defendants' alleged breach of contract, or, in the alternative, on a theory of quantum meruit. The Appellate Division upheld the trial court's determination that Weichert was entitled to recover damages for breach of contract. We granted defendants' petition for certification, [citation], and now modify the judgment of the Appellate Division, remanding for a new trial limited to the issue of damages.

In late March 1987, Socrates Kyritsis, a property owner, met with Robert Olpp, the manager of Weichert's Chatham office, and Tackaberry, a real estate agent in that office, and told them he wished to sell the "William Pitt property" for $3,000,000, with the sales commission to be paid by the buyer. Shortly after that meeting, Tackaberry telephoned Ryan, a local developer, and informed him that he knew of a property that Ryan and Saunders, his partner, might be interested in purchasing. Tackaberry also stated that the purchaser would have to pay Weichert a ten percent commission. Ryan indicated that he was interested in knowing more about the property, and Tackaberry disclosed the property's identity and the seller's proposed price. Ryan ended the conversation by agreeing to meet with Tackaberry to obtain more information.

As a result of his telephone conversation with Ryan, Tackaberry met with Kyritsis to acquire information concerning the property's current leases, income, expenses, and concerning plans for its eventual development. Tackaberry also collected tax and zoning documents relevant to the property. In a face-to-face meeting held on April 4th, Tackaberry gave Ryan the data and information he had procured. Tackaberry began that meeting by presenting Ryan with a letter dated April 3, 1987, that stated in part, "As compensation for this information * * * there will be a ten percent finders fee to be paid by your group upon successfully completing and closing of title." Ryan testified that he had refused Tackaberry's request that he sign the letter, and had explained to Tackaberry that he needed more information about the property before he could commit to the broker's fee, and therefore they would discuss that fee later. Tackaberry, however, testified that he had not asked Ryan to sign the letter, although on cross-examination he admitted that he had been intent on memorializing the agreement in writing. According to Tackaberry, after Ryan had read the letter, he had indicated only that he was concerned about the method and timing of the commission payment. Tackaberry did not pursue that point, apparently assuming that the parties would resolve that issue at a later date. Ryan ended the meeting by instructing Tackaberry to arrange a meeting between Ryan and Kyritsis. Ryan took the letter and the information with him, and later used the information to evaluate the project.

On April 7th, Ryan and his attorney met with Kyritsis to discuss the sale of the property. Although Ryan initially refused to allow Tackaberry to attend that meeting, he relented when Tackaberry insisted. Before the meeting began, Tackaberry offered unsolicited advice concerning how to negotiate effectively with Kyritsis. The meeting was successful, and afterwards Ryan instructed his attorney to prepare a draft contract for the purchase of the William Pitt property for $3,000,000. At that time Ryan informed Tackaberry that he had discussed the commission issue with Saunders, and they both agreed that ten percent was too much to pay for Tackaberry's services. Tackaberry insisted that Ryan had already agreed to pay ten percent. After some discussion the two parted without resolving the issue.

* * *

Throughout May, Tackaberry continued his efforts to obtain a written agreement. During that time, Ryan and Saunders offered to pay him a $75,000 commission on an installment basis as they developed the property. Tackaberry refused to consider anything less than ten percent. * * *

The trial court found that Ryan and Saunders had contracted to pay Tackaberry a $300,000 broker's fee. * * *

The Appellate Division affirmed . . . , finding that Ryan had entered into a binding agreement with Weichert when he had availed himself of Tackaberry's services knowing that the broker expected a ten percent commission. * * *

We consider two issues: whether Ryan and Tackaberry entered into an enforceable agreement, and, if not, whether Weichert is entitled to recover the reasonable value of Tackaberry's services on a theory of quantum meruit. A contract arises from offer and acceptance, and must be sufficiently definite "that the performance to be rendered by each party can be ascertained with reasonable certainty." [Citations.] Thus, if parties agree on essential terms and manifest an intention to be bound by those terms, they have created an enforceable contract. [Citations.] Where the parties do not agree to one or more essential terms, however, courts generally hold that the agreement is unenforceable. [Citations.]

We have held that "[i]t is requisite that there be an unqualified acceptance to conclude the manifestation of assent." [Citations.] * * *

In some circumstances, however, courts will allow recovery even though the parties' words and actions are insufficient to manifest an intention to agree to the proffered terms. Recovery based on quasi-contract, sometimes referred to as a contract implied-in-law, "is wholly unlike an express or implied-in-fact contract in that it is 'imposed by the law for the purpose of bringing about justice without reference to the intention of the parties.'" [Citations.] ("In the case of actual contracts, the agreement defines the duty, while in the case of quasi-contracts the duty defines the contract.") Courts generally allow recovery in quasi-contract when one party has conferred a benefit on another, and the circumstances are such that to deny recovery would be unjust. See, e.g., [citation]; Restatement of Restitution § 53 (1937). Quasi-contractual liability "rests on the equitable principle that a person shall not be allowed to enrich himself unjustly at the expense of another." [Citation.]

Applying that principle, courts have allowed quasi-contractual recovery for services rendered when a party confers a benefit with a reasonable expectation of payment. [Citations.] That type of quasi-contractual recovery is known as quantum meruit ("as much as he deserves"), and entitles the performing party to recoup the reasonable value of services rendered. [Citations.]

Accordingly, a broker seeking recovery on a theory of quantum meruit must establish that the services were performed with an expectation that the beneficiary would pay for them, and under circumstances that should have put the beneficiary on notice that the plaintiff expected to be paid. [Citation.] Courts have allowed brokers to recover in quantum meruit when a principal accepts a broker's services but the contract proves unenforceable for lack of agreement on essential terms—for instance, the amount of the broker's commission. [Citations.] Thus, a broker who makes a sufficient showing can recover fees for services rendered even absent express or implied agreement concerning the amount of the fee.

Application of the foregoing principles to the transaction between Weichert and Ryan demonstrates that the record is insufficient to support a finding that Tackaberry and Ryan mutually manifested assent to the essential terms of the contract. First, Ryan never expressly assented to the terms of Tackaberry's offer. Although Ryan expressed interest in learning more about the Pitt property during the initial March phone call, neither his expression of interest nor his agreement to meet with Tackaberry to learn more about the transaction was sufficient to establish the "unqualified acceptance" necessary to manifest express assent. [Citation.] Moreover, Ryan refused to agree to the ten-percent figure during the April 4th meeting, and thereafter consistently rejected that term. Thus, the parties never formed an express contract.

* * *

Although the trial court concluded that the proofs were sufficient to establish agreement to pay the full commission, the court made no findings of fact inconsistent with the evidence of Ryan's rejection of the ten percent commission. In our view, the circumstances surrounding their negotiations did not justify Tackaberry's belief that Ryan had assented to the terms of his offer.

* * *

The record clearly establishes, however, that Tackaberry is entitled to recover in quantum meruit for the reasonable value of his services. The trial court's factual finding that Tackaberry was the procuring cause of the sale is supported by substantial evidence. Further, the proofs adduced at trial firmly establish that Tackaberry furnished Ryan with information about the Pitt property with an expectation that Ryan would pay a brokerage fee, and Ryan himself admitted throughout the trial that he had always intended to compensate Tackaberry for his services. Given those circumstances, to deny Tackaberry compensation for services rendered would unjustly enrich Ryan and Saunders. [Citation.]

Accordingly, we remand to the Law Division to determine the reasonable value of Tackaberry's services. By remanding, we do not imply that the reasonable value of Tackaberry's services is less than ten percent of the purchase price, nor do we imply any view concerning the value of such services. The commission amount should be determined on the basis of proofs tending to show the reasonable value of Tackaberry's services, including evidence of customary brokers' fees for similar transactions. [Citations.]

We modify the judgment of the Appellate Division and remand to the Law Division to determine the amount of plaintiff's recovery based on principles of quantum meruit.

---

# Questions

1. Distinguish between contracts that are covered by the Uniform Commercial Code and those covered by common law.
2. List the requirements of a contract.
3. Distinguish among (a) express and implied contracts, (b) unilateral and bilateral contracts, (c) valid, void, voidable, and unenforceable contracts, (d) executed and executory contracts, and (e) formal and informal contracts.
4. Explain the doctrine of promissory estoppel.
5. Identify the three elements of an enforceable quasi contract and explain how it differs from a contract.

---

# Problems

1. Owen telephones an order to Hillary's store for certain goods, which Hillary delivers to Owen. Neither party says anything about the price or payment terms. What are the legal obligations of Owen and Hillary?
2. Minth is the owner of the Hiawatha Supper Club, which he leased during 1972 and 1973 to Piekarski. During the period of the lease, Piekarski contracted with Puttkammer for the resurfacing of the access and service areas of the supper club. The work, including labor and materials, had a reasonable value of $2,540, but Puttkammer was never paid because Piekarski went bankrupt. Puttkammer brought an action against Minth to recover the amount owed to him by Piekarski. Decision?
3. Jonathan writes to Willa, stating "I'll pay you $150 if you reseed my lawn." Willa reseeds Jonathan's lawn as requested. Has a contract been formed? If so, what kind?
4. Calvin uses fraud to induce Maria to promise to pay money in return for goods he has delivered to her. Has a contract been formed? If so, what kind? What are the rights of Calvin and Maria?
5. Anna is about to buy a house on a hill. Prior to the purchase she obtains a promise from Betty, the owner of the adjacent property, that Betty will not build any structure that would block Anna's view. In reliance on this promise Anna buys the house. Is Betty's promise binding? Why or why not?
6. Mary Dobos was admitted to Boca Raton Community Hospital in serious condition with an abdominal aneurysm. The hospital called upon Nursing Care Services, Inc., to provide around-the-clock nursing services for Mrs. Dobos. She received two weeks of in-hospital care, forty-eight hours of postrelease care, and two weeks of at-home care. The total bill was $3,723.90. Mrs. Dobos refused to pay, and Nursing Care

Services, Inc., brought an action to recover. Mrs. Dobos maintained that she was not obligated to render payment in that she never signed a written contract, nor did she orally agree to be liable for the services. The necessity for the services, reasonableness of the fee, and competency of the nurses were undisputed. After Mrs. Dobos admitted that she or her daughter authorized the forty-eight hours of postrelease care, the trial court ordered compensation of $248 for that period. It did not allow payment of the balance, and Nursing Care Services, Inc., appealed. Decision?
7. St. Charles Drilling Co. contracted with Osterholt to install a well and water system that would produce a specified quantity of water. The water system failed to meet its warranted capacity, and Osterholt sued for breach of contract. Does the UCC apply to this contract?
8. On March 4, 1970, Helvey brought suit against REMC for breach of implied and express warranties. He alleged that REMC furnished electricity in excess of 135 volts to Helvey's home, damaging his 110-volt household appliances. This incident occurred on January 10, 1966. In defense, REMC pleads that the Uniform Commercial Code's Article 2 statute of limitations of four years has passed, thereby barring Helvey's suit. Helvey argues that providing electrical energy is not a transaction in goods under the UCC but rather a furnishing of services that would make applicable the general contract six-year statute of limitations. Decision?
9. In April 1980 Jack Duran, president of Colorado Carpet Installation, Inc., began negotiations with Fred and Zuma Palermo for the sale and installation of carpeting, carpet padding, tile, and vinyl floor covering in their home. Duran drew up a written proposal that referred to Colorado Carpet as "the seller" and to the Palermos as "the customer." The proposal

listed the quantity, unit cost, and total price of each item to be installed. The total price of the job was $4,777.75. Although labor was expressly included in this figure, Duran estimated the total labor cost at $926. Mrs. Palermo orally accepted Duran's written proposal soon after he submitted it to her. After Colorado Carpet delivered the tile to the Palermo home, however, Mrs. Palermo had a disagreement with Colorado Carpet's tile man and arranged for another contractor to perform the job. Colorado Carpet brought an action against the Palermos for breach of contract. The trial court determined that the agreement between Colorado Carpet and the Palermos constituted a service contract for the performance of labor, not a contract for the sale of goods, and thus did not have to be in writing to be enforceable. The court of appeals reversed the decision, finding that the agreement was a contract for the sale of goods and was unenforceable under the "writing" requirement of the statute of frauds section of the Uniform Commercial Code. Decision?

10. On November 1, 1986, the Kansas City Post Office Employees Credit Union merged into the Kansas City Telephone Employees Credit Union to form the Communications Credit Union (Credit Union). Systems Design and Management Information (SDMI) develops computer software programs for credit unions, using Burroughs (now Unisys) hardware. SDMI and Burroughs together offered to sell to Credit Union both a software package, called the Generic System, and Burroughs hardware. In November 1986, a demonstration of the software was held at SDMI's offices, and the Credit Union agreed to purchase the Generic System software. This agreement was oral. After Credit Union was converted to the SDMI Generic System, major problems with the system immediately became apparent.

SDMI filed suit against Credit Union to recover the outstanding contract price for the software. Credit Union counterclaimed for damages based upon breach of contract and negligent and fraudulent misrepresentation. The trial court entered judgment in favor of Credit Union on SDMI's claim and for SDMI on Credit Union's counterclaim. Both parties appealed. On its appeal, SDMI argued that the Uniform Commercial Code (UCC) should have governed this case because computer software is "goods" under the UCC Decision?

11. Richardson hired J. C. Flood Company, a plumbing contractor, to correct a stoppage in the sewer line of her house. The plumbing company's "snake" device, used to clear the line leading to the main sewer, became caught in the underground line. To release it, the company excavated a portion of the sewer line in Richardson's backyard. In the process, the company discovered numerous leaks in a rusty, defective water pipe that ran parallel with the sewer line. To meet public regulations, the water pipe, of a type no longer approved for such service, had to be replaced either then or later, when the yard would have to be redug for such purpose. The plumbing company proceeded to repair the water pipe. Though Richardson inspected the company's work daily and did not express any objection to the extra work involved in replacing the water pipe, she refused to pay any part of the total bill after the company completed the entire operation. J. C. Flood Company then sued Richardson for the costs of labor and material it had furnished. Richardson argued that she only requested correction of a sewer obstruction and had never agreed to the replacement of the water pipe. She appealed from a trial court judgment against her for costs of labor and materials. Decision?

**WWW** **Internet Exercise** Find several samples of contracts.

# CHAPTER 10

# Mutual Assent

Although each of the requirements for forming a contract is essential to its existence, mutual assent is so basic that frequently a contract is referred to as the agreement between the parties. The Restatement, Section 3, provides this definition: "An agreement is a manifestation of mutual assent on the part of two or more parties." Enforcing the contract means enforcing the agreement; indeed, the agreement between the parties is the very core of the contract.

The manner in which parties usually show mutual assent is by **offer** and **acceptance**. One party makes a proposal (offer) by words or conduct to the other party, who agrees by words or conduct to the proposal (acceptance). A contractual agreement always involves either a promise exchanged for a promise (*bilateral contract*) or a promise exchanged for an act or forbearance to act (*unilateral contract*), as manifested by what the parties communicate to one another.

An implied contract may be formed by conduct. Thus, though there may be no definite offer and acceptance, or definite acceptance of an offer, a contract exists if both parties have acted in a manner that manifests (indicates) a recognition by each of them of the existence of a contract. It may be impossible to determine the exact moment at which a contract was made.

To form the contract, the parties must manifest their agreement objectively. The important thing is what the parties indicate to one another by spoken or written words or by conduct. The law applies an **objective standard** and is, therefore, concerned only with the assent, agreement, or intention of a party as it reasonably appears from his words or actions. The law of contracts is not concerned with what a party may have actually thought or the meaning that he intended to convey, even if his subjective understanding or intention differed from the meaning he objectively indicated by word or conduct. For example, if Leslie seemingly offers to sell to Sam her Chevrolet automobile but intends to offer and believes that she is offering her Ford automobile, and Sam accepts the offer, reasonably believing it was for the Chevrolet, a contract has been formed for the sale of the Chevrolet. Subjectively, there is no agreement as to the subject matter, but objectively there is a manifestation of agreement, and the objective manifestation is binding.

The Code's treatment of mutual assent is covered in greater detail in Chapter 21.

## OFFER

An offer is a definite proposal or undertaking made by one person to another which manifests a willingness to enter into a bargain. The person making the proposal is the **offeror**. The person to whom it is made is the **offeree.** Upon receipt, the offer confers on the offeree the power of acceptance, by which the offeree expresses her willingness to comply with the terms of the offer.

The communication of an offer to an offeree does not of itself confer any rights or impose any duties on either of the parties. The offeror, by making his offer, simply confers upon the offeree the power to create a contract by accepting the offer. Until the offeree exercises this power, the outstanding offer creates neither rights nor liabilities.

An offer may take several forms: (1) It may propose a promise for a promise. (This is an offer to enter into a bilateral contract.) An example is an offer to sell and deliver goods in thirty days in return for the promise to pay a stipulated amount upon delivery of the goods. If the offeree accepts this offer, the resulting contract consists of the parties' mutual promises, each made in exchange for the other. (2) An offer may be a promise for an act. (This is an offer to enter into a unilateral contract.) A common example is an offer of a reward for certain information or for the return of lost property. The offeree can accept such an offer only by the performance of the act requested. (3) An offer may be in the form of an act for a promise. (This is an offer to enter into an "inverted" unilateral contract.) For example, Maria offers the stated price to a clerk in a theater ticket office and asks for a ticket for a certain performance. The clerk can accept this offer of an act only by delivery of the requested ticket, which amounts, in effect, to the theater owner's promise to admit Maria to the designated performance.

## ESSENTIALS OF AN OFFER

An offer need not take any particular form to have legal validity. To be effective, however, it must (1) be communicated to the offeree, (2) manifest an intent to enter into a contract, and (3) be sufficiently definite and certain. If these essentials are present, an offer that has not terminated gives the offeree the power to form a contract by accepting the offer.

### Communication

To have the mutual assent required to form a contract, the offeree must have knowledge of the offer; he cannot agree to something of which he has no knowledge. Accordingly, the offeror must communicate the offer, in an intended manner, to the offeree.

For example, Andy signs a letter containing an offer to Bonnie and leaves it on top of the desk in his office. Later that day, Bonnie, without prearrangement, goes to Andy's office, discovers that Andy is away, notices the letter on his desk, reads it, and writes on it an acceptance which she dates and signs. No contract is formed because the offer never became effective; Andy never communicated it to Bonnie. If Andy had mailed the letter, and it had gone astray in the mail, the offer would likewise never have become effective.

Not only must the offer be communicated to the offeree, but the communication must also be made or authorized by the offeror. For instance, if Joanne tells Karlene that she plans to offer Larry $600 for his piano, and Karlene promptly informs Larry of this proposal, no offer has been made. There was no authorized communication of any offer by Joanne to Larry. By the same token, if Lance should offer to sell his diamond ring to Ed, an acceptance of this offer by Dianne would not be effective, because Lance made the offer to Ed, not to Dianne.

An offer need not be stated or communicated by words. Conduct from which a reasonable person may infer a proposal in return for either an act or a promise amounts to an offer.

An offer may be made to the general public. No person, however, can accept such an offer until and unless he has knowledge that the offer exists. For example, if a person, without knowing of an advertised reward for information leading to the return of a lost watch, gives information that leads to its return, he is not entitled to the reward. His act was not an acceptance of the offer because he could not accept something of which he had no knowledge.

### Intent

To have legal effect an offer must manifest an intent to enter into a contract. The intent of an offer is determined objectively from the words or conduct of the parties. The meaning of either party's manifestation is based upon what a reasonable person in the other party's position would have believed. The courts sometimes consider subjective intention in interpreting the parties' communications (the interpretation of contracts is discussed in Chapter 16).

Occasionally, a person exercises her sense of humor by speaking or writing words that—taken literally and without regard to context or surrounding circumstances—a promisee could construe as an offer. The promisor intends the promise as a joke, however, and the promisee as a reasonable person should understand it to be such. Therefore, it is not an offer. Because the person to whom it is made realizes or should realize that it is not made in earnest, it should not create a reasonable expectation in his mind. No contractual intent exists on the part of the promisor, and the promisee is or reasonably ought to be aware of that fact. If, however, the intended jest is so successful that the promisee as a reasonable person under all the circumstances believes that the joke is in fact an offer, and so believing accepts, the objective standard applies and the parties have entered into a contract.

A promise made under obvious excitement or emotional strain is likewise not an offer. For example, Charlotte, after having her month-old Cadillac break down for the third time in two days, screams in disgust, "I will sell this car to anyone for $10.00!" Lisa hears Charlotte and hands her a ten-dollar bill. Under the circumstances, Charlotte's statement was not an offer, if a reasonable person in Lisa's position would have recognized it merely as an overwrought, nonbinding utterance.

It is important to distinguish language that constitutes an offer from that which merely solicits or invites offers. Such proposals, although made in earnest, lack intent and are therefore not deemed offers. As a result, a purported acceptance does not bring about a contract but operates only as an offer to accept. These proposals include preliminary negotiations, advertisements, and auctions.

 *See Case 10–1*

**Preliminary Negotiations** If a communication creates in the mind of a reasonable person in the position of the offeree an expectation that his acceptance will conclude a contract, then the communication is an offer. If it does not, then the communication is a preliminary negotiation. Initial communications between potential parties to a contract often take the form of preliminary negotiations, through which the parties either request or supply the terms of an offer that may or may not be given. A statement that may indicate a willingness to make an offer is not in itself an offer. If Terri writes to Susan, "Will you buy my automobile for $3,000?" and Susan replies "Yes," no contract exists. Terri has not made an offer to sell her automobile to Susan for $3,000. The offeror must manifest an intent to enter into a contract, not merely a willingness to enter into negotiation.

**Advertisements** Merchants desire to sell their merchandise and thus are interested in informing potential customers about the goods, the terms of sale, and the price. But if they make widespread promises to sell to each person on their mailing list, the number of acceptances and resulting contracts might conceivably exceed their ability to perform. Consequently, a merchant might refrain from making offers by merely announcing that he has goods for sale, describing the goods, and quoting prices. He is simply inviting his customers and, in the case of published advertisements, the public, to make offers to him to buy the goods. His advertisements, circulars, quotation sheets, and merchandise displays are *not* offers because (1) they do not contain a promise and (2) they leave unexpressed many terms that would be necessary to the making of a contract. Accordingly, his customers' responses are not acceptances because he has made no offer to sell.

Nonetheless, a seller is not free to advertise goods at one price and then raise the price once demand has been stimulated. Although, as far as contract law is concerned, the seller has made no offer, such conduct is prohibited by the Federal Trade Commission as well as by legislation in many States. (See Chapter 42.)

Moreover, in some circumstances a public announcement or advertisement may constitute an offer if the advertisement or announcement contains a definite promise of something in exchange for something else and

confers a power of acceptance upon a specified person or class of persons. The typical offer of a reward is an example of a definite offer, as was shown in *Lefkowitz v. Great Minneapolis Surplus Store, Inc.* In this case, the court held that a newspaper advertisement was an offer because it contained a promise of performance in definite terms in return for a requested act.

 *See Case 10–2*

**Auction Sales** The auctioneer at an auction sale does *not* make offers to sell the property that is being auctioned but invites offers to buy. The classic statement by the auctioneer is, "How much am I offered?" The persons attending the auction may make progressively higher bids for the property, and each bid or statement of a price or a figure is an offer to buy at that figure. If the auctioneer indicates acceptance of a bid, customarily by letting fall the hammer in her hand, a contract results. A bidder is free to withdraw his bid at any time prior to its acceptance. The auctioneer is likewise free to withdraw the goods from sale *unless* the sale is advertised or announced to be without reserve.

If the auction sale is advertised or announced in explicit terms to be **without reserve,** the auctioneer may not withdraw an article or lot put up for sale unless no bid is made within a reasonable time. Unless so advertised or announced, the sale is with reserve. A bidder at either type of sale may retract his bid at any time prior to acceptance by the auctioneer. Such retraction, however, does not revive any previous bid.

## Definiteness

The terms of a contract, all of which the offer usually contains, must be reasonably certain so as to provide a court with a basis for determining the existence of a breach and for giving an appropriate remedy. Restatement, Section 33. It is a fundamental policy that contracts should be made by the parties and not by the courts; accordingly, remedies for breach must have their basis in the parties' contract.

However, where the parties have intended to form a contract, the courts will attempt to find a basis for granting a remedy. Missing terms may be supplied by course of dealing, usage of trade, or inference. Thus, uncertainty as to incidental matters will seldom be fatal so long as the parties intended to form a contract. Nevertheless, the more terms the parties leave open, the less likely it is that they have intended to form a contract. Because of the great variety of contracts, the terms essential to all contracts cannot be stated. In most cases, however, material terms would include the subject matter, price, quantity, quality, terms of payment, and duration.

**Open Terms** With respect to agreements for the sale of goods, the Code provides standards by which omitted terms may be determined, provided the parties intended to enter into a binding contract. The Code provides missing terms in a number of instances, where, for example, the contract fails to specify the price, the time or place of delivery, or payment terms. Sections 2–204(3), 2–305, 2–308, 2–309, and 2–310. The Restatement, Section 34, has adopted an approach similar to the Code's in supplying terms the parties have omitted from their contract.

Under the Code, an offer for the purchase or sale of goods may leave open particulars of performance to be specified by one of the parties. Any such specification must be made in good faith and within limits set by commercial reasonableness. Section 2–311(1). **Good faith** is defined as honesty in fact in the conduct or transaction concerned. Section 1–201(19). **Commercial reasonableness** is a standard determined in terms of the business judgment of reasonable persons familiar with the practices customary in the type of transaction involved and in terms of the facts and circumstances of the case.

If the price is to be fixed otherwise than by agreement and is not so fixed through the fault of one of the parties, the other party has an option to treat the contract as cancelled or to fix a reasonable price in good faith for the goods. However, where the parties intend not to be bound unless the price is fixed or agreed upon as provided in the agreement, and it is not so fixed or agreed upon, the Code provides in accordance with the parties' intent that no contractual liability exists. In such case the seller must refund to the buyer any portion of the price she has received, and the buyer must return the goods to the seller or, if unable to do so, pay the reasonable value of the goods. Section 2–305(4).

**Output and Requirements Contracts** A buyer's agreement to purchase the entire output of a seller's factory for a stated period, or a seller's agreement to supply a buyer with all his requirements for certain goods, may appear to lack definiteness and mutuality of obligation. Such an agreement does not specify the exact quantity of goods; moreover, the seller may have some control over her output and the buyer over his requirements. Nonetheless, under the Code and the Restatement such

agreements are enforceable by the application of an objective standard based upon the good faith of both parties. Thus, a seller who operated her factory for eight hours a day before entering an output agreement cannot operate her factory twenty-four hours a day and insist that the buyer take all of the output. Nor can the buyer expand his business abnormally and insist that the seller still supply all of his requirements.

## DURATION OF OFFERS

An offer confers upon the offeree a power of acceptance, which continues until the offer terminates. The ways in which an offer may be terminated, *other than by acceptance,* are through (1) lapse of time; (2) revocation; (3) rejection; (4) counteroffer; (5) death or incompetency of the offeror or offeree; (6) destruction of the subject matter to which the offer relates; and (7) subsequent illegality of the type of contract the offer proposes.

### Lapse of Time

The offeror may specify the time within which the offer is to be accepted, just as he may specify any other term or condition in the offer. He may require that the offeree accept the offer immediately or within a specified period, such as a week or ten days. Unless otherwise terminated, the offer remains open for the **specified** period. Upon the expiration of that time, the offer no longer exists and cannot be accepted. Any subsequent purported acceptance will serve as a new offer.

If the offer states no time within which the offeree must accept, the offer will terminate after a **reasonable** time. Determining a "reasonable" period of time is a question of fact, depending on the nature of the contract proposed, the usages of business, and other circumstances of the case (including whether the offer was communicated by electronic means). Restatement, Section 41. For instance, an offer to sell a perishable good would be open for a far shorter time than an offer to sell undeveloped real estate.

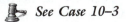 *See Case 10–3*

### Revocation

An offeror generally may withdraw an offer at any time before it has been accepted, even though he has definitely promised to keep it open for a stated time. To be effective, notice of revocation of the offer must actually reach the offeree before she has accepted. If the offeror originally promises that the offer will be open for thirty days, but after five days wishes to terminate it, he may do so merely by giving the offeree notice that he is withdrawing the offer. Notice, which may be given by any means of communication, effectively terminates the offer when **received** by the offeree. A very few states, however, have adopted a rule that treats revocations the same as acceptances thus making them effective upon dispatch. An offeror, however, may revoke an offer made to the general public only by giving to the revocation publicity equivalent to that given the offer.

Notice of revocation may be communicated indirectly to the offeree through reasonably reliable information from a third person that the offeror has disposed of the goods which he has offered for sale or has otherwise placed himself in a position which indicates an unwillingness or inability to perform the promise contained in the offer. Restatement, Section 43. For example, Jane offers to sell her portable television set to Bruce and tells Bruce that he has ten days in which to accept. One week later, Bruce observes the television set in Carl's house and is informed that Carl had purchased it from Jane. The next day Bruce sends to Jane an acceptance of the offer. There is no contract, because Jane's offer was effectively revoked when Bruce learned of Jane's inability to sell the television set to him because she had sold it to Carl.

Certain limitations, however, restrict the offeror's power to revoke the offer at any time prior to its acceptance. These limitations apply to the following five situations.

🔨 *See Case 10–4*

**Option Contracts** An **option** is a contract by which the offeror is bound to hold open an offer for a specified period of time. It must comply with all of the requirements of a contract, including *consideration* being given to the offeror by the offeree. (Consideration is discussed in Chapter 12.) For example, if Ann, in return for the payment of $500 to her by Bobby, grants Bobby an option, exercisable at any time within thirty days, to buy Blackacre at a price of $80,000, Ann's offer is irrevocable. Ann is legally bound to keep the offer open for thirty days, and any communication by Ann to Bobby giving notice of withdrawal of the offer is ineffective. Bobby is not bound to accept the offer, but the option contract entitles him to thirty days in which to accept.

**Firm Offers under the Code** The Code provides that a *merchant* is bound to keep an offer to buy or sell **goods** open for a stated period (or, if no time is stated, for

a reasonable time) not exceeding three months, if the merchant gives assurance in a **signed writing** that the offer will be held open. Section 2–205. The Code, therefore, makes a merchant's written promise not to revoke an offer for a stated period enforceable even though no consideration is given the offeror for that promise. A **merchant** is defined as a person (1) who is a dealer in goods of a given kind, (2) who by his occupation holds himself out as having knowledge or skill peculiar to the goods or practices involved, or (3) who employs an agent or broker whom he holds out as having such knowledge or skill. Section 2–104.

**Statutory Irrevocability** Certain offers, such as bids made to the State, municipality, or other governmental body for the construction of a building or some other public work, are made irrevocable by statute. Another example is preincorporation stock subscription agreements, which are irrevocable for a period of six months under many State incorporation statutes. See Section 6.20 of the Model Business Corporation Act (Appendix D).

**Irrevocable Offers of Unilateral Contracts** Where an offer contemplates a unilateral contract, that is, a promise for an act, injustice to the offeree may result if revocation is permitted after the offeree has started to perform the act requested in the offer and has substantially but not completely accomplished it. Traditionally, such an offer is not accepted and no contract is formed until the offeree has *completed* the requested act. By simply commencing performance, the offeree does not bind himself to complete performance; nor, historically, did he bind the offeror to keep the offer open. Thus, the offeror could revoke the offer at any time prior to the offeree's completion of performance. For example, Linda offers Tom $300 if Tom will climb to the top of the flagpole in the center of campus. Tom commences his ascent, and when he is five feet from the top, Linda yells to him, "I revoke."

The Restatement deals with this problem by providing that where the performance of the requested act necessarily requires the offeree to expend time and effort, the offeror is obligated not to revoke the offer for a reasonable time. This obligation arises when the offeree begins performance. If, however, the offeror does not know of the offeree's performance and has no adequate means of learning of it within a reasonable time, the offeree must exercise reasonable diligence to notify the offeror of the performance.

*Promissory Estoppel* As discussed in the previous chapter, a noncontractual promise may be enforced when it is made under circumstances that should lead the promisor reasonably to expect that the promise will induce the promisee to take action in reliance on it. This doctrine has been used in some cases to prevent an offeror from revoking an offer prior to its acceptance. The Restatement provides the following rule:

> An offer which the offeror should reasonably expect to induce action or forbearance of a substantial character on the part of the offeree before acceptance and which does induce such action or forbearance is binding as an option contract to the extent necessary to avoid injustice. Restatement, Section 87(2).

Thus, Ramanan Plumbing Co. submits a written offer for plumbing work to be used by Resolute Building Co. as part of Resolute's bid as a general contractor. Ramanan knows that Resolute is relying on Ramanan's bid, and in fact Resolute submits Ramanan's name as the plumbing subcontractor in the bid. Ramanan's offer is irrevocable until Resolute has a reasonable opportunity to notify Ramanan that Resolute's bid has been accepted.

## Rejection

An offeree is at liberty to accept or reject the offer as he sees fit. If the offeree decides not to accept it, he is not required to reject it formally but may simply wait until the offer terminates by the lapse of time. Through a **rejection** of an offer, the offeree manifests his unwillingness to accept. A communicated rejection terminates the power of acceptance. From the effective moment of rejection, which is the **receipt** of the rejection by the offeror, the offeree may no longer accept the offer. Rejection by the offeree may consist of express language or may be implied from language or from conduct.

## Counteroffer

A **counteroffer** is a counterproposal from the offeree to the offeror that indicates a willingness to contract but upon terms or conditions different from those contained in the offer. It is not an unequivocal acceptance of the original offer and, by indicating an unwillingness to agree to the terms of the offer, it operates as a rejection. It also operates as a new offer. For instance, assume that Jordan writes Chris a letter stating that he will sell to Chris a secondhand color television set for $300. Chris replies that she will pay Jordan $250 for the set. This is a counteroffer which, upon **receipt** by Jordan, terminates

the original offer. Jordan may, if he wishes, accept the counteroffer and thereby create a contract for $250. If, on the other hand, Chris states in her reply that she wishes to consider the $300 offer but is willing to pay $250 at once for the set, she is making a counteroffer which does *not* terminate Jordan's original offer. In the first instance, after making the $250 counteroffer, Chris may not accept the $300 offer. In the second instance she may do so, as the manner in which she stated the counteroffer did not indicate an unwillingness to accept the original offer, and Chris therefore did not terminate it. In addition, a mere inquiry about the possibility of obtaining different or new terms is not a counteroffer and does not terminate the offer.

Another common type of counteroffer is the **conditional acceptance,** which purports to accept the offer but expressly makes the acceptance conditional upon the offeror's assent to additional or different terms. Nonetheless, it is a counteroffer and terminates the original offer. The Code's treatment of acceptances containing terms that vary from the offer are discussed later in this chapter.

 *See Case 10–5*

## Death or Incompetency

The death or incompetency of either the offeror or the offeree ordinarily terminates an offer. Upon his death or incompetency the offeror no longer has the legal capacity to enter into a contract; thus, all his outstanding offers are terminated. Death or incompetency of the offeree likewise terminates the offer, because an ordinary offer is not assignable (transferable) and may be accepted only by the person to whom it was made. When the offeree dies or ceases to have legal capability to enter into a contract, no one else has the power to accept the offer. Therefore, the offer terminates.

The death or incompetency of the offeror or offeree, however, does *not* terminate an offer contained in an option.

## Destruction of Subject Matter

Destruction of the specific subject matter of an offer terminates the offer. The impossibility of performance prevents a contract from being consummated and thus terminates all outstanding offers with respect to the destroyed property. Suppose that Martina, owning a Buick automobile, offers to sell the car to Worthy and allows Worthy five days in which to accept. Three days later the car is destroyed by fire. On the following day, Worthy, without knowledge of the car's destruction, notifies Martina that he accepts her offer. There is no contract. Martina's offer was terminated by the destruction of the car.

## Subsequent Illegality

One of the four essential requirements of a contract, as previously mentioned, is legality of purpose or subject matter. If performance of a valid contract is subsequently made illegal, the obligations of both parties under the contract are discharged. Illegality taking effect after the making of an offer but prior to acceptance has the same effect: the offer is legally terminated.

# ACCEPTANCE

The acceptance of an offer is essential to the formation of a contract. Once an acceptance has been given, the contract is formed. An acceptance can only be made by an offeree. Acceptance of an offer for a bilateral contract requires some overt act by which the offeree manifests his assent to the terms of the offer, such as speaking or sending a letter, a telegram, or other explicit or implicit communication to the offeror. If the offer is for a unilateral contract, the offeree may refrain from acting as requested or may signify acceptance through performance of the requested act with the intention of accepting. For example, if Joy publishes an offer of a reward to anyone who returns the diamond ring which she has lost (a unilateral contract offer), and Steven, with knowledge of the offer, finds and returns the ring to Joy, Steven has accepted the offer. If, however, Steven returns the ring to Joy but in doing so disclaims the reward and says that he does not accept the offer, there is no contract. Without the intention of accepting the offer, merely doing the act requested by the offeror is not sufficient to form a contract.

A late or defective acceptance does not create a contract. After the offer has expired, it cannot be validly accepted. A late or defective acceptance, however, does manifest the offeree's willingness to enter into a contract and therefore constitutes a new offer. To create a contract based upon this offer, the original offeror must accept the new offer by manifesting his assent.

# COMMUNICATION OF ACCEPTANCE

## General Rule

Because acceptance manifests the offeree's assent to the offer, the offeree must communicate this acceptance to the offeror. This is the rule as to all offers to enter into bilateral contracts. In the case of an offer to enter into a unilateral contract, however, notice of acceptance to the offeror is usually not required. If, however, the offeree in a unilateral contract has reason to know that the offeror has no adequate means of learning of the performance with reasonable promptness and certainty, then the offeree must make reasonable efforts to notify the offeror of acceptance or lose the right to enforce the contract. Restatement, Section 54.

## Silence as Acceptance

An offeree is generally under no legal duty to reply to an offer. Silence or inaction, therefore, does *not* indicate acceptance of the offer. By custom, usage, or course of dealing, however, silence or inaction by the offeree may operate as an acceptance.

Thus, the silence or inaction of an offeree who fails to reply to an offer operates as an acceptance and causes a contract to be formed where by previous dealings the offeree has given the offeror reason to understand that the offeree will accept all offers unless the offeree sends notice to the contrary. Another example of silence operating as an acceptance occurs when the prospective member of a mail-order club agrees that his failure to return a notification card rejecting offered goods will constitute his acceptance of the club's offer to sell the goods.

Furthermore, if an offeror sends unordered or unsolicited merchandise to a person stating that she may purchase the goods at a specified price and that the offer will be deemed to have been accepted unless the goods are returned within a stated period of time, the offer is one for an inverted unilateral contract (i.e., an act for a promise). This practice led to abuse, however, which has prompted the Federal government as well as most States to enact statutes which provide that in such cases the offeree-recipient of the goods may keep them as a gift and is under no obligation either to return them or to pay for them.

## Effective Moment

As previously discussed, an offer, a revocation, a rejection, and a counteroffer are effective when they are *received*. An acceptance, on the other hand, is generally effective upon **dispatch**. This is true unless the offer specifically provides otherwise, the offeree uses an unauthorized means of communication, or the acceptance follows a prior rejection.

 *See Case 10–4*

*Stipulated Provisions in the Offer*  If the offer specifically stipulates the means of communication the offeree is to use, the acceptance, to be effective, must conform to that specification. Thus, if an offer states that acceptance must be made by registered mail, any purported acceptance not made by registered mail would be ineffective. Moreover, the rule that an acceptance is effective when dispatched or sent does not apply where the offer provides that the offeror must receive the acceptance. If the offeror states that a reply must be received by a certain date or that he must hear from the offeree or uses other language indicating that the acceptance must be received by him, the effective moment of the acceptance is when the offeror receives it, not when the offeree sends or dispatches it.

*Authorized Means*  Historically, an authorized means of communication was the means the offeror expressly authorized in the offer, or, if none was authorized, it was the means the offeror used. For example, if in reply to an offer by mail, the offeree places in the mail a letter of acceptance properly stamped and addressed to the offeror, a contract is formed at the time and place that the offeree mails the letter. This assumes, of course, that the offer at that time was open and had not been terminated by any of the methods previously discussed. The reason for this rule is that the offeror, by using the mail, impliedly authorized the offeree to use the same method of communication. It is immaterial if the letter of acceptance goes astray in the mails and is never received.

The Restatement, Section 30, and the Code, Section 2–206(1)(a), both now provide that where the language in the offer or the circumstances do not otherwise indicate, an offer to make a contract shall be construed as authorizing acceptance in any **reasonable** manner. These provisions are intended to allow flexibility of response and the ability to keep pace with new modes of communication.

*Unauthorized Means*  When the offeree uses an unauthorized method of communication, the traditional rule is that acceptance is effective when and if received by the offeror, provided that he receives it within the time during which the authorized means would have arrived. The Restatement, Section 67, provides that if these conditions are met, the effective time for the acceptance relates back to the moment of dispatch.

*Acceptance Following a Prior Rejection*  An acceptance sent after a prior rejection is not effective when sent by the offeree, but is only effective when and if the offeror **receives** it before he receives the rejection. Thus, when an acceptance follows a prior rejection, the first communication to be received by the offeror is the effective one. For example, Anna in New York sends by mail to Fritz in San Francisco an offer that is expressly stated to be open for one week. On the fourth day, Fritz sends to Anna by mail a letter of rejection that is delivered on the morning of the sixth day. At noon on the fifth day, however, Fritz had dispatched a telegram of acceptance that is received by Anna before the close of business on that day. A contract was formed when Anna received Fritz's telegram of acceptance, as it was received before the letter of rejection.

◆  *See Figure 10–1*

**FIGURE 10–1**  Offer and Acceptance

| | Time Effective | Effect |
|---|---|---|
| **Communications by Offeror** | | |
| • Offer | Received by offeree | Creates power to form a contract |
| • Revocation | Received by offeree | Terminates offer |
| | | |
| **Communications by Offeree** | | |
| • Rejection | Received by offeror | Terminates offer |
| • Counteroffer | Received by offeror | Terminates offer |
| • Acceptance | Sent by offeree | Forms a contract |
| • Acceptance after prior rejection | Received by offeror | If received before rejection, forms a contract |

## VARIANT ACCEPTANCES

A variant acceptance—one that contains terms different from or additional to those in the offer—receives distinctly different treatment under the common law and the Code.

### Common Law

An acceptance must be *positive* and *unequivocal*. In that it may not change, add to, subtract from, or qualify in any way the provisions of the offer, it must be the **mirror image** of the offer. Any communication by the offeree which attempts to modify the offer is not an acceptance but is a counteroffer, which does not create a contract.

### Code

The Code modifies the common law "mirror image" rule, by which the acceptance cannot vary or deviate from the terms of the offer. This modification is necessitated by the realities of modern business practices. A vast number of business transactions use standardized business forms. For example, a merchant buyer sends to a merchant seller on the buyer's order form a purchase order for 1,000 dozen cotton shirts at $60.00 per dozen with delivery by October 1 at the buyer's place of business. On the reverse side of this standard form are twenty-five numbered paragraphs containing provisions generally favorable to the buyer. When the seller receives the buyer's order, he agrees to the quantity, price, and delivery terms and sends to the buyer on his acceptance form an unequivocal acceptance of the offer. However, on the back of his acceptance form, the seller has thirty-two numbered paragraphs generally favorable to himself and in significant conflict with the buyer's form. Under the common law's *mirror image* rule, no contract would exist, for the seller has not accepted unequivocally all the material terms of the buyer's offer.

The Code in Section 2–207 attempts to alleviate this **battle of the forms** by focusing upon the intent of the parties. If the offeree expressly makes her acceptance conditioned upon assent to the additional or different terms, no contract is formed. If the offeree does not expressly make her acceptance conditional upon the offeror's assent to the additional or different terms, a contract is formed. The issue then becomes whether the offeree's different or additional terms become part of the contract. If both offeror and offeree are merchants, such *additional* terms may become part of the contract, provided they do not materially alter the agreement and are not objected to either in the offer itself or within a reasonable period of time. If both parties are not merchants or if the additional terms materially alter the offer, then the additional terms are merely construed as proposals to the contract. *Different* terms proposed by the offeree will not become part of the contract unless the offeror accepts them. The courts are divided over what terms a contract includes when those terms differ or conflict. Some courts hold that the offeror's terms govern; other courts, holding that the terms cancel each other out, look to the Code to provide the missing terms. Some states follow a third alternative and apply the additional terms test to different terms. (See **Figure 21–4** in Chapter 21.)

To apply Section 2–207 to the example above: because both parties are merchants and the acceptance was not conditional upon assent to the additional or different terms, (1) the contract will be formed without the seller's different terms unless the buyer specifically accepts them, (2) the contract will be formed without the seller's additional terms unless (a) the buyer specifically accepts them or (b) they do not materially alter the offer and the buyer does not object, and (3) depending upon the jurisdiction, either (a) the *buyer's* conflicting terms are included in the contract or (b) the Code provides the missing terms, as the conflicting terms cancel each other out, or (c) the additional terms test is applied.

 # Chapter Summary

## Offer

| Essentials of an Offer | **Definition** indication of willingness to enter into a contract<br>**Communication** offeree must have knowledge of the offer and the offer must be made by the offeror to the offeree |
| --- | --- |

**Intent**  determined by an objective standard of what a reasonable offeree would have believed

**Definiteness**  offer's terms must be clear enough to provide a court with a basis for giving an appropriate remedy

## Duration of Offers

**Lapse of Time**  offer remains open for the time period specified or, if no time is stated, for a reasonable period of time

**Revocation**  generally, an offer may be terminated at any time before it is accepted, subject to the following exceptions

* *Option Contract*  contract that binds offeror to keep an offer open for a specified time
* *Firm Offer*  a merchant's irrevocable offer to sell or buy goods in a signed writing ensures that the offer will not be terminated for up to three months
* *Statutory Irrevocability*  offer made irrevocable by statute
* *Irrevocable Offer of Unilateral Contract*  a unilateral offer may not be revoked for a reasonable time after performance is begun
* *Promissory Estoppel*  noncontractual promise that binds the promisor because she should reasonably expect that the promise will induce the promisee (offeree) to take action in reliance on it

**Rejection**  refusal to accept an offer terminates the power of acceptance

**Counteroffer**  counterproposal to an offer that generally terminates the original offer

**Death or Incompetency**  of either the offeror or the offeree terminates the offer

**Destruction of Subject Matter**  of an offer terminates the offer

**Subsequent Illegality**  of the purpose or subject matter of the offer terminates the offer

# Acceptance of Offer

## Requirements

**Definition**  positive and unequivocal expression of a willingness to enter into a contract on the terms of the offer

**Mirror Image Rule**  except as modified by the Code, an acceptance cannot deviate from the terms of the offer

## Communication of Acceptance

**General Rule**  acceptance effective upon dispatch unless the offer specifically provides otherwise or the offeree uses an unauthorized means of communication

**Stipulated Provisions in the Offer**  the communication of acceptance must conform to the specification in the offer

**Authorized Means**  the Restatement and the Code provide that unless the offer provides otherwise, acceptance is authorized to be in any reasonable manner

**Unauthorized Means**  acceptance effective when received, provided that it is received within the time within which the authorized means would have arrived

**Acceptance Following a Prior Rejection**  first communication received by the offeror is effective

**Defective Acceptance**  does not create a contract but serves as a new offer

# Cases

### CASE 10–1
## Objective Standard
## *CITY OF EVERETT v. ESTATE OF SUMSTAD*
Supreme Court of Washington, 1981
95 Wn.2d 853, 631 P.2d 366

**DOLLIVER, J.**

The City of Everett commenced an . . . action against the seller (the Sumstad Estate) and the buyer (Al and Rosemary Mitchell) of a safe to determine who is entitled to a sum of money found in the safe. Both the Estate and the Mitchells moved for summary judgment. The trial court entered summary judgment in favor of the Estate. The Court of Appeals affirmed. [Citation.]

Petitioners, Mr. and Mrs. Mitchell, are the proprietors of a small secondhand store. On August 12, 1978, the Mitchells attended Alexander's Auction, where they frequently had shopped to obtain merchandise for their own use and for use as inventory in their business. At the auction the Mitchells purchased a used safe with an inside compartment for $50. As they were told by the auctioneer when they purchased the safe, the Mitchells found that the inside compartment of the safe was locked. The safe was part of the Sumstad Estate.

Several days after the auction, the Mitchells took the safe to a locksmith to have the locked compartment opened. The locksmith found $32,207 inside. The Everett Police Department, notified by the locksmith, impounded the money.

. . . The issue is whether there was in fact a sale of the safe and its unknown contents at the auction. In contrast to the Court of Appeals, we find that there was.

A sale is a consensual transaction. The subject matter which passes is to be determined by the intent of the parties as revealed by the terms of their agreement in light of the surrounding circumstances. [Citation.] The objective manifestation theory of contracts, which is followed in this state [citation] lays stress on the outward manifestation of assent made by each party to the other. The subjective intention of the parties is irrelevant.

A contract has, strictly speaking, nothing to do with the personal, or individual, intent of the parties. A contract is an obligation attached by the mere force of law to certain acts of the parties, usually words, which ordinarily accompany and represent a known intent. If, however, it were proved by twenty bishops that either party, when he used the words, intended something else than the usual meaning which the law imposes upon them, he would still be held, unless there were some mutual mistake, or something else of the sort. [Citation.]

As stated in *Washington Shoe Mfg. Co. v. Duke* [citation]

The apparent mutual assent of the parties, essential to the formation of a contract, must be gathered from their outward expressions and acts, and not from an unexpressed intention.

The inquiry, then, is into the outward manifestations of intent by a party to enter into a contract. We impute an intention corresponding to the reasonable meaning of a person's words and acts. [Citation.] If the offeror, judged by a reasonable standard manifests an intention to agree in regard to the matter in question, that agreement is established. [Citation.]

\* \* \*

In the case before us, . . . the Mitchells were aware of the rule of the auction that all sales were final. Furthermore, the auctioneer made no statement reserving rights to any contents of the safe to the estate. Under these circumstances, we hold reasonable persons would conclude that the auctioneer manifested an objective intent to sell the safe and its contents and that the parties mutually assented to enter into that sale of the safe and the contents of the locked compartment.

\* \* \*

This matter is remanded to the trial court for entry of the summary judgment in favor of the Mitchells.

## CASE 10–2
### Invitations Seeking Offers
## *LEFKOWITZ v. GREAT MINNEAPOLIS SURPLUS STORE, INC.*

Supreme Court of Minnesota, 1957
251 Minn. 188, 86 N.W.2d 689

MURPHY, J.

This is an appeal from an order of . . . judgment award-[ing] the plaintiff the sum of $138.50 as damages for breach of contract.

This case grows out of the alleged refusal of the defendant to sell to the plaintiff a certain fur piece which it had offered for sale in a newspaper advertisement. It appears from the record that on April 6, 1956, the defendant published the following advertisement in a Minneapolis newspaper:

> Saturday 9 AM Sharp
> 3 Brand New
> Fur Coats
> Worth to $100.00
> First Come First Served
> $1 Each

On April 13, the defendant again published an advertisement in the same newspaper as follows:

> Saturday 9 AM
> 2 Brand New Pastel
> Mink 3–Skin Scarfs
> Selling for $89.50
> Out they go
> Saturday. Each . . . $1.00
> 1 Black Lapin Stole
> Beautiful,
> worth $139.50 . . . $1.00
> First Come First Served

The record supports the findings of the court that on each of the Saturdays following the publication of the above-described ads the plaintiff was the first to present himself at the appropriate counter in the defendant's store and on each occasion demanded the coat and the stole so advertised and indicated his readiness to pay the sale price of $1. On both occasions, the defendant refused to sell the merchandise to the plaintiff, stating on the first occasion that by a "house rule" the offer was intended for women only and sales would not be made to men, and on the second visit that plaintiff knew defendant's house rules. . . .

The defendant contends that a newspaper advertisement offering items of merchandise for sale at a named price is a "unilateral offer" which may be withdrawn without notice. He relies upon authorities which hold that, where an advertiser publishes in a newspaper that he has a certain quantity or quality of goods which he wants to dispose of at certain prices and on certain terms, such advertisements are not offers which become contracts as soon as any person to whose notice they may come signifies his acceptance by notifying the other that he will take a certain quantity of them. Such advertisements have been construed as an invitation for an offer of sale on the terms stated, which offer, when received, may be accepted or rejected and which therefore does not become a contract of sale until accepted by the seller; and until a contract has been so made, the seller may modify or revoke such prices or terms. [Citations.] . . .

On the facts before us we are concerned with whether the advertisement constituted an offer, and, if so, whether the plaintiff's conduct constituted an acceptance.

* * *

The test of whether a binding obligation may originate in advertisements addressed to the general public is "whether the facts show that some performance was promised in positive terms in return for something requested."

* * *

Whether in any individual instance a newspaper advertisement is an offer rather than an invitation to make an offer depends on the legal intention of the parties and the surrounding circumstances. [Citations.] We are of the view on the facts before us that the offer by the defendant of the sale . . . was clear, definite, and explicit, and left nothing open for negotiation. The plaintiff, having successfully managed to be the first one to appear at the seller's place of business to be served, as requested by the advertisement, and having offered the stated purchase price of the article, was entitled to performance on the part of the defendant. We think the trial court was correct in holding that there was in the conduct of the parties a sufficient mutuality of obligation to constitute a contract of sale.

* * *

Affirmed.

CASE 10–3
## Duration of Offers/Objective Manifestation
### *NEWMAN v. SCHIFF*
United States Court of Appeals, Eighth Circuit, 1985
778 F.2d 460

BRIGHT, J.

John A. Newman, an attorney practicing law in St. Louis, Missouri, brought this action against Irwin Schiff of Hamden, Connecticut, alleging breach of contract. Newman claimed that Schiff had made a public offer of reward to anyone who could cite any section of the Internal Revenue Code that says an individual is required to file an income tax return. Newman asserted that he accepted Schiff's offer, and that Schiff breached the contract by failing to pay him the reward. The district court ruled in favor of Schiff by finding that Newman's acceptance was not timely, and Newman appeals. We affirm the judgment of the district court.

\* \* \*

Irwin Schiff is a self-styled "tax rebel," who has made a career and substantial profits out of his tax protest activities. Schiff's basic contention is that the federal income tax is a voluntary tax which no one is required to pay. \* \* \*

On February 7, 1983, Irwin Schiff appeared live on CBS News Nightwatch (Nightwatch), a nighttime television program with a viewer participation format. Schiff was interviewed by host Karen Stone from approximately 3:00 AM to 4:00 AM Eastern Time. The words "Nightwatch Phone-In" and telephone number (212) 955–9555 were flashed on the screen periodically during Schiff's appearance. In addition, Ms. Stone repeated the telephone number and encouraged viewers to call and speak directly with Schiff on the air.

During the course of the Nightwatch program, Schiff repeated his long-standing position that, "there is nothing in the Internal Revenue Code which I have here, which says anybody is legally required to pay the tax." Following a discussion of his rationale for that conclusion, Schiff stated: "If anybody calls this show—I have the Code—and cites any section of this Code that says an individual is required to file a tax return, I will pay them $100,000."

Newman did not see Schiff's live appearance on Nightwatch. He did, however, see a two-minute taped segment of the original Nightwatch interview that was rebroadcast several hours later on the CBS Morning News. The CBS Morning News rebroadcast included Schiff's reward proposal.

Newman felt certain that Schiff's statements regarding the Internal Revenue Code were incorrect. Upon arriving at work that day, he researched the issue and located several sections of the Code that to his satisfaction demonstrated the mandatory nature of the federal income tax system. The next day Newman telephoned CBS Morning News and cited . . . provisions of the Internal Revenue Code as authority for his position that individuals are required to pay federal income tax. [Citation.] Newman placed his call to (212) 975–4321, the number given him by the long distance operator for CBS in New York. He then reduced this conversation to writing and sent it to the CBS Morning News. Newman's letter stated that it represented "performance of the consideration requested by Mr. Schiff in exchange for his promise to pay $100,000."

\* \* \*

On April 20, 1983, Schiff wrote to Newman and stated that: "[y]our letter to Mr. O'Regan at CBS Morning News was forwarded to me. I did make an offer on the February 7, 1983 news (which was actually part of an interview conducted earlier in the week)." Schiff said, however, that Newman had not properly accepted his offer for both substantive and procedural reasons.

Newman then sued Schiff in federal district court for breach of contract. The district court decided that: (1) Schiff intended for his offer to remain open only until the conclusion of the live Nightwatch broadcast; (2) the rebroadcast on CBS Morning News did not renew or extend Schiff's offer; and therefore (3) Newman's acceptance of the offer was untimely.

\* \* \*

**A. The Requirement of Mutual Assent**  It is a basic legal principle that mutual assent is necessary for the formation of a contract. A significant doctrinal struggle in the development of contract law revolved around whether it was a party's actual or apparent assent that was necessary. This was a struggle between subjective and objective theorists. The subjectivists looked to actual assent. Both parties had to actually assent to an agreement for there to be a contract. External acts were merely necessary evidence to prove or disprove the requisite state of mind. The familiar cliche was that a contract required a "meeting of the minds" of the parties. [Citation.] The objectivists, on the other hand, looked to apparent assent. The expression of mutual assent, and not the assent itself, was the essential element in the formation of a contract. * * *

By the end of the nineteenth century the objective approach to the mutual assent requirement had become predominant, and courts continue to use it today. [Citation.]

* * *

**B. The Mechanics of Mutual Assent: Offer and Acceptance** Courts determine whether the parties expressed their assent to a contract by analyzing their agreement process in terms of offer and acceptance. An offer is the "manifestation of willingness to enter into a bargain, so made as to justify another person in understanding that his assent to that bargain is invited and will conclude it." [Citations.]

The present case concerns a special type of offer: an offer for a reward. . . . [C]ourts have enforced public offers to pay rewards.

* * *

**1. The Nightwatch Offer** In the present case, Schiff's statement on Nightwatch that he would pay $100,000 to anyone who called the show and cited any section of the Internal Revenue Code "that says an individual is required to file a tax return" constituted a valid offer for a reward. In our view, if anyone had called the show and cited the code sections that Newman produced, a contract would have been formed and Schiff would have been obligated to pay the $100,000 reward, for his bluff would have been properly called.

**2. The CBS Morning News Rebroadcast** Newman, however, never saw the live CBS Nightwatch program upon which Schiff appeared and this lawsuit is not predicated on Schiff's Nightwatch offer. Newman saw the CBS Morning News rebroadcast of Schiff's Nightwatch appearance. This rebroadcast served not to renew or extend Schiff's offer, but rather only to inform viewers that Schiff had made an offer on Nightwatch. The rebroadcast constituted a newsreport and not a renewal of the original offer. An offeror is the master of his offer and it is clear that Schiff by his words, "If anybody calls this show * * *," limited his offer in time to remain open only until the conclusion of the live Nightwatch broadcast. A reasonable person listening to the news rebroadcast could not conclude that the above language—"calls this show"—constituted a new offer; rather than what it actually was, a newsreport of the offer previously made, which had already expired.

* * *

We affirm the judgment of the district court for the reasons discussed above.

Although Newman has not "won" his lawsuit in the traditional sense of recovering a reward that he sought, he has accomplished an important goal in the public interest of unmasking the "blatant nonsense" dispensed by Schiff. * * *

* * *

---

**CASE 10–4**

Revocation/Option Contracts/Acceptance

### FIRST DEVELOPMENT CORPORATION OF KENTUCKY v. MARTIN MARIETTA CORPORATION

United States Court of Appeals, Sixth Circuit, 1992
959 F.2d 617

**PER CURIAM.**
Appellants Martin Marietta Corporation (Martin Marietta) and Harmony Land Development Company (Harmony Land) have appealed from a judgment of the district court in this diversity case permanently enjoining Martin Marietta from selling a 15-acre parcel of riverfront real property to Harmony Land and Ordering Martin Marietta to convey the said parcel to First Development Corporation of Kentucky (FDCK), the plaintiff below.

On May 9, 1988, Martin Marietta entered into a 365-day exclusive listing agreement with Coldwell Banker, a real estate brokerage firm, to sell the property here in controversy for $750,000. Coldwell Banker designated Don Gilmour (Gilmour) as its account agent.

On August 16, 1988, FDCK, through its president Sam Pollitt (Pollitt), a sophisticated real estate broker and developer, submitted an offer to purchase the parcel for $300,000. The offer was submitted on a standard Louisville Board of Realtors form, and [contained numerous conditions in favor of the purchaser].

\* \* \*

The offer to purchase was accompanied by an earnest money deposit evidenced by a $1,000 check payable to Coldwell Banker. The deposit was fully refundable if transfer of title to FDCK was not completed for any reason except FDCK's failure to perform, as distinguished from a nonrefundable payment to a seller as consideration for an option to purchase realty within a specified period. The check was not negotiated and ultimately returned to FDCK on or about September 26 or 27 of 1988.

The offer to purchase was to expire on August 24, 1988 at 6:00 o'clock PM.

FDCK's proposal was essentially a 7 1/2-month free option to purchase the 15 acres of land, during which period Martin Marietta was foreclosed from disposing of the property to any other interested buyer. Both the purchase price and satisfaction of the open-ended conditions incorporated into the offer to purchase were contingent upon FDCK's unilateral approval and satisfaction and were totally unacceptable to Martin Marietta, and it permitted the offer to expire without response.

Immediately subsequent to the expiration of FDCK's offer to purchase, Pollitt prevailed upon Gilmour to seek a counteroffer from Martin Marietta.

In an effort to accommodate Pollitt, Gilmour persuaded Martin Marietta to reconsider the sale price of the land.

In a letter dated September 7, 1988 addressed to Gilmour, Martin Marietta agreed to sell the acreage on the following unconditional terms:

1.  purchase price—$550,000 cash;
2.  earnest money—$20,000;
3.  Martin Marietta to retain the option of closing the sale during December 1988 or January 1989; and
4.  the counteroffer to remain open for thirty days from September 7, 1988.

Upon receipt of the letter on September 7, Gilmour immediately communicated its contents to Pollitt by telephone. Pollitt received a copy of the letter from Gilmour on or about September 12, 1988. He initiated no further inquiries or action concerning the property until September 20, 1988 when Gilmour advised him that negotiations for the sale of the property to Harmony Landing were about to be concluded.

Harmony Landing had initiated the purchase of the property directly with Paxton Badham, in-house legal counsel for Martin Marietta in Raleigh, North Carolina, within days of FDCK's expired offer. Bill Harvey (Harvey), president of Harmony Landing, owned and was developing a 5-acre parcel of real property contiguous to Martin Marietta's land as a private marina and yacht club. Harvey, through a series of telephone conversations with Badham, had agreed to pay Martin Marietta a nonrefundable consideration of $10,000 for an initial 60-day option to purchase the property. During this period, he intended to obtain permits from the Oldham County Planning and Zoning Commission to deposit excavation fill from his marina upon the Martin Marietta land. Upon obtaining the permits, Harvey would pay Martin Marietta an additional nonrefundable $40,000 as consideration for an additional ten-month extension of the option. Harmony Landing had 12 months from the original date of the option within which to purchase the property for an additional $500,000. Upon the exercise of the option to purchase the land, the $50,000 advanced as consideration for the options would be applied to the sale price of $550,000.00.

Badham drafted a contract incorporating the terms of the agreement. An executed copy was delivered to Harvey by Federal Express on Monday, September 19, 1988. Upon receipt of the executed contract, Harvey telephoned Badham, who approved various suggested insignificant modifications of the agreement. Harvey executed the amended contract, attached a check for $10,000 and mailed it to Badham by overnight Federal Express on either September 21 or 22. Badham received the executed contract and the $10,000 on or about September 22 or 23, 1988.

On September 21, Gilmour, who was not current with the fast-track negotiations between Harvey and Badham, advised Pollitt of Harvey's interest in acquiring the Martin Marietta land. Pollitt remained noncommittal concerning the negotiations and communicated no further interest in the property during that telephone conversation. Pollitt testified that after talking with Gilmour on September 21, he visited the 15-acre Martin Marietta riverfront property at 4:00 PM with his partner Dike Gregory and their engineer Phil Bills of Sayback and Wilson Consulting Engineers. During the meeting, according to Pollitt, he, Bills and Gregory walked the property and discussed various studies that had been conducted and arrived at a decision to accept the September 7, 1988 offer from Martin Marietta.

Pollitt testified further that he did not convey FDCK's decision to accept Martin Marietta's offer of September

7 to Gilmour after the meeting. He testified that after the meeting on the riverfront site, he returned to his office and immediately consulted his attorneys, Brown, Todd and Heyburn, "regarding a contract for the acceptance of this offer [the Martin Marietta offer of September 7.]" The discussion included the necessity for zoning changes, the acquisition of building permits, requirements for on-site septic systems, availability of water, electricity and all other utilities that would be servicing the site—essentially, all of the conditions that had been incorporated into his expired original offer to purchase dated August 16.

He further indicated that, after concluding his conversation with his lawyers, he typed an acceptance on the bottom of the Martin Marietta letter of September 7, 1981 and signed it; that he physically attached the executed letter "acceptance" to the two-page form Louisville Board of Realtors standard purchase agreement dated 8/16/88, together with a check in the amount of $20,000 payable to Coldwell Banker. He inserted the documents into an envelope that he placed into his desk drawer. (Significantly, Pollitt did not include in the envelope a copy of the $1,000 check which had accompanied the offer that expired on August 24, 1988.) He made no effort to convey FDCK's acceptance to Gilmour. Pollitt further testified that on the morning of September 22, he placed the envelope and its contents into his Executive Office Suite's mail depository for meter stamping and delivery to the U.S. Postal Service pickup which occurred between 4:30 and 5:15 PM each day. Again, he made no effort to advise Gilmour of his purported acceptance.

As previously indicated, he returned a Gilmour telephone call at 2:30 PM on September 22, during which time the following material colloquy occurred:

* * *

After Gilmour had advised Pollitt that Martin Marietta had executed an option to sell the property to Harmony Landing, Pollitt responded:

A. Don, we've got a problem. First Development Corporation has already accepted the counter offer, which was given to them by Martin Marietta;
Q. That is, did you tell him at that point in time that you had accepted the contract?
A. Yes sir.
Q. At that point in time, had you delivered to him a $20,000 check?
A. No sir.
Q. Had you delivered to him a contract of any kind that had been . . .
A. No.

* * *

Q. It's your testimony you had not put it in the mail at that point in time, is that correct?
A. My—are you talking about the U.S. mail?
Q. Yes sir.
A. No sir.

Under Kentucky law, an offer must be accepted "before any intimation is received that offer is withdrawn," [citation]; express notice or use of the word "revoke" is not necessary to revoke an offer. An offer is revoked when the offeree learns of acts by the offeror that are inconsistent with the continuance of the offer or that imply that the offer has been revoked. [Citation.] It is obvious from the context of Pollitt's testimony in relating the above conversation, coupled with his conversation with Gilmour on September 21, that Pollitt knew that the "accepted" option agreement between Martin Marietta and Harmony Land was an option to purchase the riverfront land. He knew that the land was no longer available and off the market.

* * *

Recognizing that FDCK's initial conditional offer to purchase the riverfront property expired on August 24, 1988, the district court nevertheless concluded that the refundable earnest money evidenced by the $1,000 check, payable to and in the possession of Coldwell Banker during the period of this controversy, was, by operation of law, converted into consideration for a 30-day irrevocable option in favor of FDCK to purchase the riverfront property in accordance with the terms of Martin Marietta's letter of September 7, 1988.

* * *

In Kentucky, "It is well settled that an option [to purchase real property] is not binding as a contract where there is no consideration unless it is accepted within the time limit and before the offer is withdrawn." [Citations.]

Initially, this court must determine if the Martin Marietta letter of September 7, 1988 and FDCK's purported acceptance constituted an irrevocable option supported by consideration to purchase the riverfront property within thirty days from September 7. The answer is contingent upon the legal significance of FDCK's refundable $1,000 earnest money evidenced by the check payable to Coldwell Banker which was attached to FDCK's initial offer of 8/16/88 to purchase the Martin Marietta property.

Neither the plaintiffs' complaint nor Pollitt's testimony disclosed an affirmative allegation that the $1,000 check, which accompanied the August 16, 1988 original offer to purchase, was consideration for an irrevocable

30-day option to accept Martin Marietta's offer of September 7, 1988. * * *

* * *

We think it is clear that there was no monetary consideration to support the option contract here involved. There was no money paid for the option itself.

* * *

Having concluded that FDCK did not have a 30-day irrevocable option within which to accept Martin Marietta's September 7 offer to sell the land in controversy, this court must decide if FDCK had, in fact and in law, accepted the Martin Marietta offer to sell its property before it, FDCK, knew that the land was no longer available and had been taken off the market.

* * *

Kentucky law embraces the "mail box rule" as defined in the Restatement (Second) of Contracts, section 63(a), which provides that an acceptance of a contract becomes effective when it is "put out of the offeree's possession." Comment e to section 63(a) provides that "communication by means of the offeree's employee is excluded; the employee's possession is treated as that of the employer." Restatement (Second) of Contracts s 63(a) cmt. e. Simply stated, the Kentucky rule, adopting the pronouncements of the Restatement, provides that: "Ordinarily an offer may be accepted by mailing acceptance, properly stamped and addressed."

In the instant case, Pollitt conceded that the envelope containing FDCK's acceptance was placed into the mail depository manned by his employees for stamp metering and delivery to the U.S. Postal Service. The envelope, however, never left his possession or control as evidenced by his effortless retrieval of the documents from the office mail drop after he became aware of the option in favor of Harmony Land to purchase the property. At that point in time, the envelope had not been stamp metered. He thereafter hand-delivered the envelope and its contents to Gilmour, who accepted it at 4:15 PM on September 22. This was approximately one hour and forty-five minutes after he knew the property was off the market.
* * *

Accordingly, it is the considered opinion of this court that FDCK had not accepted Martin Marietta's offer to sell the riverfront property dated September 7, 1988 before it knew through Pollitt that the land was no longer available and had been taken off the market. The district court's contrary resolution is clearly erroneous both in fact and law.

* * *

It is the decision of this court that the trial court's decision is REVERSED and the case is REMANDED with instructions to dissolve the restraining order heretofore issued and to enter judgment not inconsistent with this opinion.

---

## CASE 10–5
## Counteroffer
### GIANNETTI v. CORNILLIE

Court of Appeals of Michigan, 1994
204 Mich.App. 234, 514 N.W.2d 221

HOOD, J.
Defendants were the copersonal representatives of their mother's estate. In that capacity, they listed her home for sale with a real estate agent. Plaintiffs [Patrick and Anne Giannetti] offered $155,000 for the home and submitted a $2,500 deposit. Defendants counteroffered to sell the home for $160,000.

Upon receiving the counteroffer, plaintiffs orally inquired whether certain items could be included with the home. Defendants declined. Plaintiffs then purportedly accepted the counteroffer, but changed the mortgage amount from $124,000 to $128,000 and initialed the change. The real estate agent did not submit this modification for defendants' approval, but, rather, told defendants that plaintiffs had accepted their counteroffer.

Defendants signed all the necessary . . . papers for the sale of the property. However, before the closing, defendants sought to rescind the deal. Plaintiffs declined and sued for specific performance.

Defendants' main argument is that the trial court clearly erred in finding that there was a contract where defendants never agreed to plaintiffs' change in the mortgage amount. We reluctantly agree.

As argued by defendants, "[a]n offer is a unilateral declaration of intention, and is not a contract. A contract is made when both parties have executed or accepted it, and not before. A counterproposition is not an acceptance." [Citations.] An acceptance must be "unambiguous and in strict conformance with an offer." [Citation.] "'[A] proposal to accept, or an acceptance, upon terms varying from those offered, is a rejection of the offer, and puts an end to the negotiation, unless the party who made the original offer renews it, or assents to the modification suggested.'" [Citation.] Thus, "'[a]ny material departure from the terms of an offer invalidates the offer as made and results in a counter proposition, which, unless accepted, cannot be enforced.'" [Citation.]

Plaintiffs argue that the modification of the mortgage amount did not vitiate their purported acceptance because the mortgage amount, unlike the purchase price, was not a material term of the contract. We disagree.

* * *

In other words, before the change, plaintiffs were obligated to buy the property if they obtained a mortgage for $124,000; after the change, no obligation to buy arose unless they obtained a $128,000 mortgage. Thus, the modification had the legal effect of widening the door through which plaintiffs could escape the contract and it was therefore material. [Citation.]

* * *

Reversed.

---

# Questions

1. Identify the three essentials of an offer and discuss briefly the requirements associated with each.
2. Identify and discuss briefly seven ways by which an offer may be terminated other than by acceptance.
3. Compare briefly the traditional and modern theories of definiteness of acceptance of an offer as shown by the common law "mirror image" rule and by the rule of the Uniform Commercial Code.
4. Discuss the five situations limiting an offeror's right to revoke her offer.
5. Explain the various rules that determine when an acceptance takes effect.

---

# Problems

1. Ames, seeking business for his lawn maintenance firm, posted the following notice in the meeting room of the Antlers, a local lodge: "To the members of the Antlers—Special this month. I will resod your lawn for two dollars per square foot using Fairway brand sod. This offer expires July 15."

The notice also included Ames's name, address, and signature and specified that the acceptance was to be in writing.

Bates, a member of the Antlers, and Cramer, the janitor, read the notice and became interested. Bates wrote a letter to Ames saying he would accept the offer if Ames would use Putting Green brand sod. Ames received this letter July 14 and wrote to Bates saying he would not use Putting Green sod. Bates received Ames's letter on July 16 and promptly wrote Ames that he would accept Fairway sod. Cramer wrote to Ames on July 10, saying he accepted Ames's offer.

By July 15, Ames had found more profitable ventures and refused to resod either lawn at the specified price. Bates and Cramer brought an appropriate action against Ames for breach of contract. Decisions as to the respective claims of Bates and Cramer?

2. Garvey owned four speedboats named *Porpoise, Priscilla, Providence,* and *Prudence.* On April 2, Garvey made written offers to sell the four boats in the order named for $4,200 each to Caldwell, Meens, Smith, and Braxton, respectively, allowing ten days for acceptance. In which, if any, of the following four situations described was a contract formed?

(a) Five days later, Caldwell received notice from Garvey that he had contracted to sell *Porpoise* to Montgomery. The next day, April 8, Caldwell notified Garvey that he accepted Garvey's offer.

(b) On the third day, April 5, Meens mailed a rejection to Garvey which reached Garvey on the morning of the fifth day. But at 10:00 AM on the fourth day, Meens sent an acceptance by telegram to Garvey, who received it at noon on the same day.

(c) Smith, on April 3, replied that she was interested in buying *Providence* but declared the price asked appeared slightly excessive and wondered if, perhaps, Garvey would be willing to sell the boat for $3,900. Five days later, having received no reply from Garvey, Smith, by letter, accepted Garvey's offer and enclosed a certified check for $4,200.

(d) Braxton was accidentally killed in an automobile accident on April 9. The following day, the executor of Braxton's estate mailed an acceptance of Garvey's offer to Garvey.

3. Alpha Rolling Mill Corporation, by letter dated June 8, offered to sell Brooklyn Railroad Company 2,000 to 5,000 tons of fifty-pound iron rails upon certain specified terms, adding that, if the offer was accepted, Alpha Corporation would expect to be notified prior to June 20. Brooklyn Company, on June 16, by telegram, referring to Alpha Corporation's offer of June 8, directed Alpha Corporation to enter an order for 1,200 tons of fifty-pound iron rails on the terms specified.

The same day, June 16, Brooklyn Company, by letter to Alpha Corporation, confirmed the telegram. On June 18, Alpha Corporation, by telegram, declined to fill the order. Brooklyn Company, on June 19, telegraphed Alpha Corporation: "Please enter an order for 2,000 tons rails as per your letter of the eighth. Please forward written contract. Reply." In reply to Brooklyn Company's repeated inquiries regarding whether the order for 2,000 tons of rails had been entered, Alpha denied the existence of any contract between Brooklyn Company and itself. Thereafter, Brooklyn Company sued Alpha Corporation for breach of contract. Decision?

**4.**   On April 8, Burchette received a telephone call from Bleluck, a truck dealer, who told Burchette that a new model truck in which Burchette was interested would arrive in one week. Although Bleluck initially wanted $10,500, the conversation ended after Bleluck agreed to sell and Burchette agreed to purchase the truck for $10,000, with a $1,000 down payment and the balance upon delivery. The next day, Burchette sent Bleluck a check for $1,000, which Bleluck promptly cashed.

One week later, when Burchette called Bleluck and inquired about the truck, Bleluck informed Burchette he had several prospects looking at the truck and would not sell for less than $10,500. The following day, Bleluck sent Burchette a properly executed check for $1,000 with the following notation thereon: "Return of down payment on sale of truck."

After notifying Bleluck that she will not cash the check, Burchette sues Bleluck for damages. Decision?

**5.**   On November 15, I. Sellit, a manufacturer of crystalware, mailed to Benny Buyer a letter stating that Sellit would sell to Buyer 100 crystal "A" goblets at $100 per goblet and that "the offer would remain open for fifteen (15) days." On November 18, Sellit, noticing the sudden rise in the price of crystal "A" goblets, decided to withdraw her offer to Buyer and so notified Buyer. Buyer chose to ignore Sellit's letter of revocation and gleefully watched as the price of crystal "A" goblets continued to skyrocket. On November 30, Buyer mailed to Sellit a letter accepting Sellit's offer to sell the goblets. The letter was received by Sellit on December 4. Buyer demands delivery of the goblets. What result?

**6.**   On May 1, Melforth Realty Company offered to sell Greenacre to Dallas, Inc., for $1,000,000. The offer was made by telegraph and stated that the offer would expire on May 15. Dallas decided to purchase the property and sent a registered letter to Melforth on May 10, accepting the offer. Due to unexplained delays in the postal service, Melforth did not receive the letter until May 22. Melforth wishes to sell Greenacre to another buyer, who is offering $1,200,000 for the tract of land. Has a contract resulted between Melforth and Dallas?

**7.**   Rowe advertised in newspapers of wide circulation and otherwise made known that she would pay $5,000 for a complete set consisting of ten volumes of certain rare books. Ford, not knowing of the offer, gave Rowe all but one of the set of rare books as a Christmas present. Ford later learned of the offer, obtained the one remaining book, tendered it to Rowe, and demanded the $5,000. Rowe refused to pay. Is Ford entitled to the $5,000?

**8.**   Scott, manufacturer of a carbonated beverage, entered into a contract with Otis, owner of a baseball park, whereby Otis rented to Scott a large signboard on top of the center field wall. The contract provided that Otis should letter the sign as Scott desired and would change the lettering from time to time within forty-eight hours after receipt of written request from Scott. As directed by Scott, the signboard originally stated in large letters that Scott would pay $100 to any ballplayer hitting a home run over the sign.

In the first game of the season, Hume, the best hitter in the league, hit one home run over the sign. Scott immediately served written notice on Otis instructing Otis to replace the offer on the signboard with an offer to pay fifty dollars to every pitcher who pitched a no-hit game in the park. A week after receipt of Scott's letter, Otis had not changed the wording on the sign. On that day, Perry, a pitcher for a scheduled game, pitched a no-hit game while Todd, one of his teammates, hit a home run over Scott's sign.

Scott refuses to pay any of the three players. What are the rights of Scott, Hume, Perry, and Todd?

**9.**   Barnes accepted Clark's offer to sell to him a portion of Clark's coin collection. Clark forgot that his prized $20 gold piece at the time of the offer and acceptance was included in the portion which he offered to sell to Barnes. Clark did not intend to include the gold piece in the sale. Barnes, at the time of inspecting the offered portion of the collection, and prior to accepting the offer, saw the gold piece. Is Barnes entitled to the $20 gold piece?

**10.**   Small, admiring Jasper's watch, asked Jasper where and at what price he had purchased it. Jasper replied, "I bought it at West Watch Shop about two years ago for around $85, but I am not certain as to that." Small then said, "Those fellows at West are good people and always sell good watches. I'll buy that watch from you." Jasper replied, "It's a deal." The next morning Small telephoned Jasper and said he had changed his mind and did not wish to buy the watch.

Jasper sued Small for breach of contract. In defense, Small has pleaded that he made no enforceable contract with Jasper (a) because the parties did not agree on the price to be paid for the watch, and (b) because the parties did not agree on the place and time of delivery of the watch to Small. Are either, or both, of these defenses good?

**11.**   Jeff says to Brenda, "I offer to sell you my IBM PC for $900." Brenda replies, "If you do not hear otherwise from me by Thursday, I have accepted your offer." Jeff agrees and does not hear from Brenda by Thursday. Does a contract exist between Jeff and Brenda? Explain.

**12.**   On November 19, 1949, Hoover Motor Express Company sent to Clements Paper Company a written offer to purchase certain real estate. Sometime in December, Clements authorized Williams to accept. Williams, however, attempted to bargain with Hoover to obtain a better deal, specifically that Clements would retain easements on the property. In a telephone conversation on January 13, 1950, Williams first told Hoover of his plan to obtain the easements. Hoover replied, "Well, I don't know if we are ready. We have not decided, we might not want to go through with it." On January 20, Clements sent a written acceptance of Hoover's offer. Hoover refused to buy, claiming it had revoked its offer through the January 13 phone conversation. Clements then brought suit to compel the sale or obtain damages. Decision?

13.    Walker leased a small lot to Keith for ten years at $100 a month, with a right for Keith to extend the lease for another ten-year term under the same terms except as to rent. The renewal option provided:

Rental will be fixed in such amount as shall actually be agreed upon by the lessors and the lessee with the monthly rental fixed on the comparative basis of rental values as of the date of the renewal with rental values at this time reflected by the comparative business conditions of the two periods.

Keith sought to exercise the renewal right and, when the parties were unable to agree on the rent, brought suit against Walker. Who prevails? Why?

14.    The Brewers contracted to purchase Dower House from McAfee. Then, several weeks before the May 7 settlement date for the purchase of the house, the two parties began to negotiate for the sale of certain items of furniture in the house. On April 30, McAfee sent the Brewers a letter containing a list of the furnishings to be purchased at specified prices; a payment schedule, including a request for a $3,000 payment, due on acceptance; and a clause reading, "If the above is satisfactory, please sign and return one copy with the first payment."

On June 3, the Brewers sent a letter to McAfee stating that enclosed was a $3,000 check; that the original contract had been misplaced and could another be furnished; that they planned to move into Dower House on June 12; and that they wished the red desk to be included in the contract. McAfee then sent a letter dated June 8 to the Brewers, listing the items of furniture purchased.

The Brewers moved into Dower House in the middle of June. Soon after they moved in, they tried to contact McAfee at his office to tell him that there had been a misunderstanding relating to their purchase of the listed items. They then refused to pay him any more money, and he brought this action to recover the balance outstanding. Decision?

15.    The Thoelkes were owners of real property located in Orange County, which the Morrisons agreed to purchase. The Morrisons signed a contract for the sale of that property and mailed it to the Thoelkes in Texas on November 26. The next day the Thoelkes executed the contract and placed it in the mail addressed to the Morrisons' attorney in Florida. After the executed contract was mailed but before it was received in Florida, the Thoelkes called the Morrisons' attorney in Florida and attempted to repudiate the contract. Decision?

16.    On December 20, 1952, Lucy and Zehmer met while having drinks in a restaurant. During the course of their conversation, Lucy apparently offered to buy Zehmer's 471.6-acre farm for $50,000 cash. Although Zehmer claims that he thought the offer was made in jest, he wrote the following on the back of a pad: "We hereby agree to sell to W. O. Lucy the Ferguson Farm complete for $50,000, title satisfactory to buyer." Zehmer then signed the writing and induced his wife Ida to do the same. She claims, however, that she signed only after Zehmer assured her that it was only a joke. Finally, Zehmer claims that he was "high as a Georgia pine" at the time but admits that he was not too drunk to make a valid contract. Decision?

17.    On July 31, Lee Calan Imports advertised a used Volvo station wagon for sale in the *Chicago Sun-Times*. As part of the information for the advertisement, Lee Calan Imports instructed the newspaper to print the price of the car as $1,795. However, due to a mistake made by the newspaper, without any fault on the part of Lee Calan Imports, the printed ad listed the price of the car as $1,095. After reading the ad and then examining the car, O'Brien told a Lee Calan Imports salesperson that he wanted to purchase the car for the advertised price of $1,095. Calan Imports refuses to sell the car to O'Brien for $1,095. Is there a contract? If so, for what price?

18.    On May 20 cattle rancher Oliver visited his neighbor Southworth, telling him, "I know you're interested in buying the land I'm selling." Southworth replied, "Yes, I do want to buy that land, especially as it adjoins my property." Although the two men did not discuss the price, Oliver told Southworth he would determine the value of the property and send that information to him, so that Southworth would have "notice" of what Oliver "wanted for the land." On June 13, Southworth called Oliver to ask if he still planned to sell the land. Oliver answered, "Yes, and I should have the value of the land determined soon." On June 17, Oliver sent a letter to Southworth listing a price quotation of $324,000. Southworth then responded to Oliver by letter on June 21, stating that he accepted Oliver's offer. However, on June 24 Oliver wrote back to Southworth, saying, "There has never been a firm offer to sell, and there is no enforceable contract between us." Oliver maintains that a price quotation alone is not an offer. Southworth claims a valid contract has been made. Who wins? Discuss.

19.    On December 23, 1977, Wyman, a lawyer representing First National Bank & Trust (defendant), wrote to Zeller (plaintiff) stating that he had been instructed to offer a building to Zeller for sale at a price of $240,000. Zeller had previously expressed an interest in purchasing the building for $240,000. The letter also set forth details concerning interest rates and loan fees.

After receiving the letter, Zeller instructed his attorney, Jamma, to send Wyman a written counteroffer of $230,000 with varying interest and loan arrangements. Jamma sent the written counteroffer as instructed on January 10. On the same day, Jamma telephoned Wyman and informed him of the counteroffer. Jamma then tried to telegraph acceptance of the original offer to Wyman. When Wyman refused to sell the property to him, Zeller brought this action to seek enforcement of the alleged contract. The trial court entered summary judgment against Zeller, and he appealed. Decision?

**Internet Exercise** Compare the provisions governing offer and acceptance contained in the United Nations Convention on Contracts for the International Sale of Goods (Vienna, 1980) with those of the U.S. common law of contracts.

# CHAPTER 11

# Conduct Invalidating Assent

The preceding chapter considered one of the essential requirements of a contract, namely, the objective manifestation of mutual assent by each party to the other. In addition to requiring that the offer and acceptance be satisfied, the law demands that the agreement be voluntary and knowing. An agreement which does not meet both of these requirements is either voidable or void. This chapter deals with situations in which the consent manifested by one of the parties to the contract is not effective because it was not knowingly and voluntarily given. These situations are considered under the headings of duress, undue influence, fraud, nonfraudulent misrepresentation, and mistake.

## *DURESS*

A person should not be held to an agreement into which she has not entered voluntarily. Accordingly, the law will not enforce any contract induced by **duress,** which in general is any wrongful act or threat that overcomes the free will of a party.

### Physical Compulsion

There are two basic types of duress. The first occurs when one party compels another to manifest assent to a contract through actual **physical force,** such as pointing a gun at a person or taking a person's hand and compelling him to sign a written contract. This type of duress, while extremely rare, renders the agreement **void.** Restatement, Section 174(1).

### Improper Threats

The second type of duress involves the use of **improper threats** or acts, *including economic and social coercion,* to compel a person to enter into a contract. The threat

may be explicit or may be inferred from words or conduct; in either case, it must leave the victim with no reasonable alternative. This type of duress makes the contract **voidable** at the option of the coerced party. Restatement, Section 175(2). For example, if Lance, a landlord, induces Tamara, an infirm, bedridden tenant, to enter into a new lease on the same apartment at a greatly increased rent by wrongfully threatening to terminate Tamara's lease and evict her, Tamara can escape or *avoid* the new lease by reason of the duress exerted upon her.

With respect to the second and more common type of duress, the fact that the act or threat would not affect a person of average strength and intelligence is not determinative if it places the particular person in fear and induces him to perform an action against his will. The test is *subjective,* and the question is, did the threat actually induce assent on the part of the person claiming to be the victim of duress? Threats that would suffice to induce assent by one person may not suffice to induce assent by another. All circumstances must be considered, including the age, background, and relationship of the parties. Restatement, Section 175. Indeed, as comment c to this section of the Restatement states,

Persons of a weak or cowardly nature are the very ones that need protection; the courageous can usually protect themselves. Timid and inexperienced persons are particularly subject to threats, and it does not lie in the mouths of the unscrupulous to excuse their imposition on such persons on the ground of their victims' infirmities.

Ordinarily, the acts or threats constituting duress are themselves crimes or torts. But this is not true in all cases. The acts need not be criminal or tortious to be *wrongful;* they merely need to be contrary to public policy or morally reprehensible. For example, if the threat involves a breach of a contractual duty of good faith and fair dealing or the use of the civil process in bad faith, it is improper.

Moreover, the courts have generally held that contracts induced by threats of criminal prosecution are voidable, regardless of whether the coerced party had committed an unlawful act. Likewise, threatening the criminal prosecution of a near relative, such as a son or husband, is duress, regardless of the guilt or innocence of the relative.

To be distinguished from such threats of prosecution are threats to resort to ordinary civil remedies to recover a debt due from another. Threatening to bring a civil suit against an individual to recover a debt is not wrongful. What is prohibited is threatening to bring a civil suit when bringing such a suit would be abuse of process.

 *See Case 11–1*

# UNDUE INFLUENCE

Undue influence is the unfair persuasion of a person by a party generally in a dominant position based upon a **confidential relationship.** The law very carefully scrutinizes contracts between those in a relationship of trust and confidence that is likely to permit one party to take unfair advantage of the other. Examples are the relationships of guardian-ward, trustee-beneficiary, principal-agent, spouses to each other, parent-child, attorney-client, physician-patient, and clergy-parishioner.

A transaction induced by unfair influence on the part of the dominant party is **voidable.** The ultimate question in undue influence cases is whether the dominant party induced the transaction by influencing a freely exercised and competent judgment or by dominating the mind or emotions of a submissive party. The weakness or dependence of the person persuaded is a strong indicator of the fairness or unfairness of the persuasion. For example, Ronald, a person without business experience, has for years relied in business matters on the advice of Nancy, who is experienced in business. Nancy, without making any false representations of fact, induces Ronald to enter into a contract with Nancy's confederate, George, that is disadvantageous to Ronald, as both Nancy and George know. The transaction is voidable on the grounds of undue influence.

Undue influence, as previously mentioned, generally arises in the context of relationships in which one person is in a position of dominance, or is likely to be. Where such a relationship exists at the time of the transaction, and it appears that the dominant party has gained at the other party's expense, the transaction is presumed to be voidable. For example, in a legally challenged contract between a guardian and his ward, the law presumes that advantage was taken by the guardian. It is, therefore, incumbent upon the guardian to rebut this presumption. Important factors in determining whether a contract is fair are (1) whether the dominant party made full disclosure of all relevant information known to him, (2) whether the consideration was adequate, and (3) whether the dependent party received competent and independent advice before completing the transaction. Without limitation, in every situation in which a confidential relationship exists, the dominant party is held to utmost good faith in his dealings with the other.

 *See Case 11–2*

# FRAUD

Another factor affecting the validity of consent given by a contracting party is fraud, which prevents assent from being knowingly given. There are two distinct types of fraud: fraud in the execution and fraud in the inducement.

## Fraud in the Execution

**Fraud in the execution,** which is extremely rare, consists of a misrepresentation that deceives the defrauded person as to the very nature of the contract. Such fraud occurs when a person does not know, or does not have reasonable opportunity to know, the character or essence of a proposed contract because the other party misrepresents its character or essential terms. Fraud in the execution renders the transaction **void.**

For example, Abigail delivers a package to Boris, requests that Boris sign a receipt for it, holds out a simple printed form headed "Receipt," and indicates the line on which Boris is to sign. This line, which to Boris appears to be the bottom line of the receipt, is actually the signature line of a promissory note cleverly concealed underneath the receipt. Boris signs where directed without knowing that he is signing a note. This is fraud in the execution. The note is void and of no legal effect because Boris has not actually given his assent, even though his signature is genuine and appears to manifest his assent to the terms of the note. The nature of Abigail's fraud precluded consent to the signing of the note because it prevented Boris from reasonably knowing what he was signing.

## Fraud in the Inducement

**Fraud in the inducement,** generally referred to as fraud or deceit, is an intentional misrepresentation of material fact by one party to the other, who consents to enter into a contract in justifiable reliance upon the misrepresentation. Fraud in the inducement renders the contract **voidable** by the defrauded party. For example, Ada, in offering to sell her dog to Ben, tells Ben that the dog won first prize in its class in a recent national dog show. In fact, the dog had not even been entered in the show. Nonetheless, Ada's statement induces Ben to accept the offer and pay a high price for the dog. A contract exists, but it is voidable by Ben because of Ada's fraud, which induced his assent.

The requisites for fraud in the inducement are:

1. a false representation
2. of a fact
3. that is material and
4. made with knowledge of its falsity and the intention to deceive (*scienter*) and
5. which representation is justifiably relied upon.

*False Representation* A basic element of fraud is a false representation or misrepresentation, that is, an assertion not in accord with the facts, made through positive statement or conduct that misleads. **Concealment** is an action intended or known to be likely to keep another from learning of a fact of which he would otherwise have learned. Active concealment is a form of misrepresentation that can form the basis for fraud, as where a seller puts heavy oil or grease in a car engine to conceal a knock. Truth may be suppressed by concealment as much as by misrepresentation.

Expressly denying knowledge of a fact which a party knows to exist is a misrepresentation if it leads the other party to believe that the facts do not exist or cannot be discovered. Moreover, a statement of misleading half-truth is considered the equivalent of a false representation.

As a general rule, **silence** or nondisclosure alone does *not* amount to fraud. A seller generally is not obligated to tell a purchaser everything he knows about the subject of a sale. Thus, it is not fraud when a buyer possesses advantageous information about the seller's property, of which he knows the seller to be ignorant, and does not disclose such information to the seller. Likewise, a buyer is under no duty to inform a seller of the greater value or other advantages of his property. Assume that Sid owns a farm which, as a farm, is worth $10,000. Brenda knows that there is oil under Sid's farm and knows that Sid is ignorant of this fact. Brenda, without disclosing this information to Sid, makes an offer to Sid to buy the farm for $10,000. Sid accepts the offer, and a contract

is duly made. Sid, on later learning the facts, can do nothing about the matter, either at law or in equity. As one case puts it, "a purchaser is not bound by our laws to make the man he buys from as wise as himself."

Although nondisclosure usually does not constitute a misrepresentation, in certain situations it does. One such situation arises when (1) a person fails to disclose a fact known to him, (2) he knows that the disclosure of that fact would correct a mistake of the other party as to a basic assumption on which that party is making the contract, and (3) nondisclosure of the fact amounts to a failure to act in a good faith and in accordance with reasonable standards of fair dealing. Restatement, Section 161. Accordingly, if the property at issue in the contract possesses a substantial latent (hidden) defect, one that the buyer would not discover by an ordinary examination, the seller may be obliged to reveal it. Suppose, for example, that Judith owns a valuable horse, which Judith knows is suffering from a disease only a competent veterinary surgeon might detect. Judith offers to sell this horse to Curt, but does not inform Curt about the condition of the horse. Curt makes a reasonable examination of the horse and, finding it in apparently normal condition, purchases it from Judith. Curt, on later discovering the disease in question, can have the sale set aside. Judith's silence, under the circumstances, was a misrepresentation.

There are other situations in which the law imposes a duty of disclosure. For example, one may have a duty of disclosure because of prior representations, innocently made before entering into the contract, which are later discovered to be untrue. Another instance in which silence may constitute fraud is a transaction involving a fiduciary. A **fiduciary** is a person in a confidential relationship who owes a duty of trust, loyalty, and confidence to another. For example, an agent owes a fiduciary duty to his principal, as does a trustee to the beneficiary of a trust and a partner to her copartners. A fiduciary may not deal at *arm's length* but rather owes a duty to make full disclosure of all relevant facts when entering into a transaction with the other party to the relationship. In contrast, in most everyday business or market transactions, the parties are said to deal at "arm's length," meaning that they deal with each other on equal terms.

*Fact* The basic element of fraud is the misrepresentation of a material fact. A **fact** is an event that actually took place or a thing that actually exists. Suppose that Dale induces Mike to purchase shares in a company unknown to Mike at a price of $100 per share by representing that she had paid $150 per share for them during the preceding year, when in fact she had paid only $50. This representation of a past event is a misrepresentation of fact.

Actionable fraud rarely can be based upon what is merely a statement of opinion. A representation is one of **opinion** if it expresses only the uncertain belief of the representer as to the existence of a fact or his judgment as to quality, value, authenticity, or other matters of judgment.

The line between fact and opinion is not an easy one to draw and in close cases presents an issue for the jury. The solution will often turn upon the superior knowledge of the person making the statement and the information available to the other party. Thus, if Dale said to Mike that the shares were "a good investment," she is merely stating her opinion, and in the usual case Mike ought to regard it as no more than that. Other common examples of opinion are statements of value, such as "This is the best car for the money in town" or "This deluxe model will give you twice the wear of a cheaper model." Such exaggerations and commendations of articles offered for sale are to be expected from dealers, who are merely puffing their wares with sales talk. If, however, the representer is a professional advising a client, the courts are more likely to regard as actionable an untrue statement of opinion. When the person expressing the opinion is one who holds himself out as having expert knowledge, the tendency is to grant relief to those who have sustained loss through reasonable reliance upon the expert evaluation.

Also to be distinguished from a representation of fact is a **prediction** of the future. Predictions, which are similar to opinions in that no one can know with certainty what will happen in the future, normally are not regarded as factual statements. Likewise, promissory statements ordinarily do not constitute a basis of fraud, as a breach of promise does not necessarily indicate that the promise was fraudulently made. A promise that the promisor, at the time of making, had no intention of keeping, however, is a misrepresentation of fact. Most courts take the position that a misrepresented state of mind "is as much a fact as the state of a person's digestion." *Edgington v. Fitzmaurice*, 29 Ch.D. 459 (1885). If a dealer promises, "I will service this machine free for the next year," but at the time has no intention of doing so, his conduct is actionable if the other elements of fraud are present.

Historically, courts held that representations of **law** were not statements of fact but rather of opinion. The present trend is to recognize that a statement of law may have either the effect of a statement of fact or a statement of opinion. Restatement, Torts, Section 545. For ex-

ample, a statement of law asserting that a particular statute has been enacted or repealed has the effect of a statement of fact. On the other hand, a statement as to the legal consequences of a particular set of facts is a statement of opinion. Nonetheless, such a statement may imply that the facts known to the maker are consistent with the legal conclusion stated. For example, an assertion that a company has the legal right to do business in a State may include the assurance that the company has taken all the steps required to be duly qualified. Moreover, a statement by one who is learned in the law, such as a practicing attorney, may be considered a statement of fact.

**See Case 11–3**

**Materiality**   In addition to being a misrepresentation of fact, a misrepresentation also must be material. A misrepresentation is **material** if (1) it would be likely to induce a reasonable person to manifest his assent or (2) the maker knows that it would be likely to induce the recipient to do so. Restatement, Section 162. In the sale of a racehorse, whether a certain jockey rode the horse in its most recent race may not be material, but its running time for the race probably would be. The Restatement of Contracts provides that a contract justifiably induced by a misrepresentation is voidable if the misrepresentation is either fraudulent *or* material. Therefore, a fraudulent misrepresentation does not have to be material for the recipient to obtain rescission, but it must be material if she is to recover damages. Restatement, Section 164; Restatement, Torts, Section 538.

**See Case 11–4**

**Knowledge of Falsity and Intention to Deceive**   To establish fraud, the misrepresentation must have been known by the one making it to be false and must have been made with an intent to deceive. This element of fraud is known as **scienter.** Knowledge of falsity can consist of (a) actual knowledge, (b) lack of belief in the statement's truthfulness, or (c) reckless indifference as to its truthfulness.

**Justifiable Reliance**   A person is not entitled to relief unless he has justifiably relied upon the misrepresentation. If the misrepresentation in no way influenced the complaining party's decision, he must abide by the terms of the contract. He is not deceived if he does not rely. Justifiable reliance requires that the misrepresentation contribute substantially to the misled party's decision to enter into the contract. If the complaining party knew or it was obvious that the defendant's representation was untrue, but he still entered into the contract, he has not justifiably relied. Moreover, where the misrepresentation is fraudulent, the party who relies on it is entitled to relief even though he does not investigate the statement or is contributorily negligent in relying on it. Restatement, Torts, Sections 540, 545A. Not knowing or discovering the facts before making a contract does not constitute unjustified reliance unless it amounts to a failure to act in good faith and in accordance with reasonable standards of fair dealing. Restatement, Section 172. Thus, most courts will not allow a person who concocts a deliberate and elaborate scheme to defraud—one that the defrauded party should readily detect—to argue that the defrauded party did not justifiably rely upon the misrepresentation.

## NONFRAUDULENT MISREPRESENTATION

Nonfraudulent misrepresentation is a material, false statement that induces another to rely justifiably but is made without *scienter*.

**Negligent misrepresentation** is a false representation that is made without due care in ascertaining its truthfulness. **Innocent misrepresentation** is a false representation made without knowledge of its falsity but with due care. To obtain relief for nonfraudulent misrepresentation, all of the other elements of fraud must be present *and* the misrepresentation must be material. The remedies that may be available for nonfraudulent misrepresentation are rescission and damages (see Chapter 18).

## MISTAKE

A **mistake** is a belief that is not in accord with the facts. Where the mistaken facts relate to the basis of the parties' agreement, the law permits the adversely affected party to avoid or reform the contract under certain circumstances. But because permitting avoidance for mistake undermines the objective approach to mutual assent, the law has experienced considerable difficulty in specifying those circumstances that justify permitting the subjective matter of mistake to invalidate an otherwise objectively satisfactory agreement. As a result, establishing clear rules to govern the effect of mistake has proven elusive.

The Restatement and modern cases treat mistakes of law in existence at the time of making a contract no differently than mistakes of fact. For example, Susan contracts to sell a parcel of land to James with the mutual understanding that James will build an apartment house on the land. Both Susan and James believe that such a building is lawful. Unknown to them, however, the town in which the land is located had enacted an ordinance precluding such use of the land three days before they entered into the contract. This mistake of law, which the courts would treat as a mistake of fact, would lead to the consequences discussed below.

### Mutual Mistake

**Mutual mistake** occurs when *both* parties are mistaken as to the same set of facts. If the mistake relates to a basic assumption on which the contract is made and has a material effect on the agreed exchange, then it is **voidable** by the adversely affected party unless he bears the risk of the mistake. Restatement, Section 152.

Usually, market conditions and the financial situation of the parties are not considered basic assumptions. Thus, if Gail contracts to purchase Pete's automobile under the belief that she can sell it at a profit to Jesse, she is not excused from liability if she is mistaken in this belief. Nor can she rescind the agreement simply because she was mistaken as to her estimate of what the automobile was worth. These are the ordinary risks of business, and courts do not undertake to relieve against them. But suppose that the parties contract upon the assumption that the automobile is a 1993 Cadillac with fifteen thousand miles of use, when in fact the engine is that of a cheaper model and has been run in excess of fifty thousand miles. Here, a court would likely allow a rescission because of mutual mistake of a material fact. Another example of mutual mistake of fact was presented in a California case where a noted violinist purchased two violins from a collector for $8,000, the bill of sale reading, "I have on this date sold to Mr. Efrem Zimbalist one Joseph Guarnerius violin and one Stradivarius violin dated 1717." Actually, unknown to either party, neither violin was genuine. Taken together they were worth no more than $300. The sale was voidable by the purchaser for mutual mistake. In a New Zealand case, the plaintiff purchased a "stud bull" at an auction. There were no express warranties as to "sex, condition, or otherwise." Actually, the bull was sterile. Rescission was allowed, the court observing that it was a "bull in name only."

 *See Case 11–5*

## Unilateral Mistake

Unilateral mistake occurs when only one of the parties is mistaken. Courts have been hesitant to grant relief for unilateral mistake even though it relates to a basic assumption on which the party entered into the contract and has a material effect on the agreed exchange. Nevertheless, relief will be granted where the nonmistaken party knows, or reasonably should know, that such a mistake has been made (palpable unilateral mistake) or where the mistake was caused by the fault of the nonmistaken party. For example, suppose a building contractor makes a serious error in his computations and as a result submits a bid on a job that is one-half the amount it should be. If the other party knows that he made such an error, or reasonably should have known, she cannot, as a general rule, take advantage of the other's mistake by accepting the offer. In addition, many courts and the Restatement allow rescission where the effect of the unilateral mistake makes enforcement of the contract unconscionable. Section 153.

## Assumption of Risk of Mistake

A party who has undertaken to bear the risk of a mistake will be unable to avoid the contract, even though the mistake (which may be either mutual or unilateral) would otherwise have permitted her to do so. This allocation of risk may occur by agreement of the parties. For instance, a ship at sea may be sold "lost or not lost." In such case the buyer is liable whether the ship was lost or not lost at the time the contract was made. There is no mistake; instead, there is a conscious allocation of risk.

Conscious ignorance may serve to allocate the risk of mistake when the parties recognize that they have limited knowledge of the facts. For example, the Supreme Court of Wisconsin refused to set aside the sale of a stone for which the purchaser paid one dollar, but which was subsequently discovered to be an uncut diamond valued at $700. The parties did not know at the time of sale what the stone was and knew they did not know. Each consciously assumed the risk that the value might be more or less than the selling price.

## Effect of Fault upon Mistake

The Restatement provides that a mistaken party's fault in not knowing or discovering a fact before making a contract does not prevent him from avoiding the contract "unless his fault amounts to a failure to act in good faith and in accordance with reasonable standards of fair dealing." Restatement, Section 157. This rule does not, however, apply to a failure to read a contract. As a general proposition, a party is held to what she signs. Her signature authenticates the writing, and she cannot repudiate that which she has voluntarily approved. Generally, one who assents to a writing is presumed to know its contents and cannot escape being bound by its terms merely by contending that she did not read them; her assent is deemed to cover unknown as well as known terms. Restatement, Section 157, Comment b.

## Mistake in Meaning of Terms

Somewhat related to mistakes of facts is the situation in which the parties misunderstand the meaning of one another's manifestations of mutual assent. A famous case involving this problem is *Raffles v. Wichelhaus*, 2 Hurlstone & Coltman 906 (1864), popularly known as the "*Peerless* Case." A contract of purchase was made for 125 bales of cotton to arrive on the *Peerless* from Bombay. It happened, however, that there were two ships by the name of *Peerless*, each sailing from Bombay, one in October and the other in December. The buyer had in mind the ship that sailed in October, while the seller reasonably believed the agreement referred to the *Peerless* sailing in December. Neither party was at fault, but both believed in good faith that a different ship was intended. The English court held that no contract existed. The Restatement, Section 20, is in accord.

There is no manifestation of mutual assent where the parties attach materially different meanings to their manifestations and neither party knows or has reason to know the meaning attached by the other. If blame can be ascribed to either party, however, that party will be held responsible. Thus, if the seller knew of two ships by the name of *Peerless* sailing from Bombay, then he would be at fault, and the contract would be for the ship sailing in October as the buyer expected. If neither party is to blame or both are to blame, there is no contract at all; that is, the agreement is void.

# Chapter Summary

**Duress**

**Definition** wrongful act or threat that overcomes the free will of a party
**Physical Compulsion** coercion involving physical force renders the agreement void
**Improper Threats** improper threats or acts, including economic and social coercion, render the contract voidable

**Undue Influence**

**Definition** taking unfair advantage of a person by reason of a dominant position based on a confidential relationship
**Effect** renders a contract voidable

**Fraud**

**Fraud in the Execution** a misrepresentation that deceives the other party as to the nature of a document evidencing the contract renders the agreement void
**Fraud in the Inducement** renders the agreement voidable if the following elements are present:
- *False Representation* positive statement or conduct that misleads
- *Fact* an event that occurred or thing that exists
- *Materiality* of substantial importance
- *Knowledge of Falsity and Intention to Deceive* called *scienter* and includes (a) actual knowledge, (b) lack of belief in statement's truthfulness, or (c) reckless indifference to its truthfulness
- *Justifiable Reliance* a defrauded party is reasonably influenced by the misrepresentation

**Nonfraudulent Misrepresentation**

**Negligent Misrepresentation** misrepresentation made without due care in ascertaining its truthfulness; renders agreement voidable
**Innocent Misrepresentation** misrepresentation made without knowledge of its falsity but with due care; renders contract voidable

**Mistake**

**Definition** an understanding that is not in accord with existing fact
**Mutual Mistake** both parties have a common but erroneous belief forming the basis of the contract; renders the contract voidable by either party
**Unilateral Mistake** courts are unlikely to grant relief unless the error is known or should be known by the nonmistaken party
**Assumption of Risk** a party may assume the risk of a mistake
**Effect of Fault upon Mistake** not a bar to avoidance unless the fault amounts to a failure to act in good faith

# Cases

## CASE 11–1
## Duress
# *JOHNSON v. INTERNATIONAL BUSINESS MACHINES CORPORATION*

United States District Court, N.D. California, 1995
891 F. Supp. 522

INFANTE, J.

## I. Introduction and Background

Plaintiff Ronald D. Johnson is a former employee of defendant International Business Machines Corporation ("IBM") who was laid off from his position at one of IBM's San Jose divisions in late 1993 and early 1994. He asserts federal race and age discrimination claims, as well as several supplemental state law claims, in connection with his discharge.

Johnson also purports to represent an uncertified class of similarly situated former IBM employees, all of whom signed a written release of legal claims against and covenant-not-to-sue IBM in consideration for enhanced severance benefits. The Second Amended Complaint, assert[s] that the uncertified class was subjected to . . . economic duress . . . at the time each signed the release and covenant-not-to-sue because of their distress at losing their jobs and the uncertain Silicon Valley job market. [The claim] seek[s] rescission of the release and covenant-not-to-sue. . . .

\* \* \*

## II. Findings of Fact

\* \* \*

Johnson started working at IBM's San Jose facility, the Storage Systems Division ("SSD"), in 1974 and remained continuously employed by IBM until he was laid off effective January 27, 1994.

\* \* \*

On October 28, 1993, IBM announced a Storage Systems Division Resource Reduction Program ("SSRP"). Johnson was notified by his manager, Paul Pederson, that he had been designated a "surplus employee" and would be involuntarily laid-off effective December 31, 1993. Johnson was given a packet of materials describing the SSRP and escorted by Pederson from the SSD facility.

\* \* \*

The SSRP provided that employees who were designated as surplus personnel were eligible to receive certain benefits, including outplacement assistance, career counseling, job retraining, and an enhanced "separation allowance."

Under the terms of the SSRP, all employees who were designated as surplus were eligible to receive, at IBM's discretion, a separation allowance of two week's pay. The SSRP also provided that, in consideration of the execution of a General Release and Covenant Not to Sue (the "Release"), surplus employees could receive an enhanced separation allowance of one week's pay for each six months of accumulated service, up to a maximum of twenty-six weeks pay. The enhanced separation allowance was the only of several separation benefits conditioned on signing the Release.

The SSRP also provided that by November 5, 1993, surplus employees could apply for alternate, generally lower-paying, positions in the SSD manufacturing area. Some of the manufacturing positions were sedentary, and it was not a condition of obtaining a manufacturing position that an employee release IBM from liability in connection with his discharge from his previous position. Eighty-nine designated surplus employees applied for manufacturing positions, and each was offered a position by the end of November 1993. Fifty-nine of these accepted the position, while the remaining thirty opted to instead sign the Release and receive enhanced severance benefits. Johnson, however, never applied for a manufacturing position at SSD.

\* \* \*

From October 28, 1993 through at least the end of January 1994, Johnson was emotionally upset about being laid-off, was concerned about his financial situation and believed that he had been designated a surplus employee because of his race. He did not seek professional counseling during this period and was not mentally-incapacitated by a depressive disorder.

Johnson suffers from a rare skin condition, known as pachyonychia congenita, which becomes exacerbated when he is under stress. The dermatological affliction, during pronounced periods, causes soreness and callousing of Johnson's hands and feet, and he encounters discomfort in walking. From October 28, 1993 through at least the end of January 1994, Johnson's skin condition was exacerbated and flared-up due to stress related to his being laid-off. However, Johnson has never at any time been immobilized or incapacitated by his skin condition.

* * *

In the meantime, on January 4, 1994, Johnson consulted with Robert Baker, an attorney whom he had located in the "yellow pages" of the local telephone directory. The purpose of the consultation regarded Johnson's potential claims against IBM. The attorney . . . told Johnson that if he signed the Release, he would have difficulty pursuing his discrimination charges.

On January 24, 1994, Johnson was examined by Denise Clement, M.D., an IBM physician. Dr. Clement observed callousing of Johnson's hands and feet, tenderness in his heels, and purplish discoloration of his toes. She noticed, nonetheless, that Johnson was able to walk "normally." Dr. Clement observed that Johnson was coherent, articulate and cooperative. He understood the questions posed to him and was able to make judgments. Dr. Clement concluded that Johnson was capable of searching for and performing sedentary work which did not require extensive walking or standing.

On January 27, 1994, at IBM's personnel office in San Jose, Johnson signed the Release, which he had read and understood. He received a check dated December 28, 1993 representing 26 weeks of separation pay, the maximum permitted under SSRP. The gross amount of the check was $19,852.64; with deductions, the net amount was $13,700.86.

The Release pertinently provides:

"IBM ADVISES YOU TO CONSULT AN ATTORNEY BEFORE YOU SIGN THIS RELEASE.

"If you feel that you are being coerced to sign this General Release and Covenant Not to Sue (hereinafter 'Release'), that your signing would for any reason not be voluntary, or you believe the process by which you have been offered this Release or the payment in exchange for this Release is discriminatory, you are encouraged to discuss this with your manager, the SSRP Project Office or Human Resources before signing this Release. After reviewing the Release with your personal attorney, you may discuss concerns you have with your manager, or your personal attorney can contact IBM legal counsel at your location. You should thoroughly review and understand the effects of the Release before signing it.

"In exchange for the sums and benefits which you will receive pursuant to the terms of the San Jose Storage Systems Division Resource Reduction Program (SSRP), (Ronald Johnson) (hereinafter 'you') agree to release International Business Machines Corporation (hereinafter 'IBM') and its benefits plans from all claims, demands, actions or liabilities you may have against IBM of whatever kind, including but not limited to those that are related to your employment with IBM, the termination of that employment, or other severance payments. . . .

* * *

"You agree that you will never institute a claim of any kind against IBM, or those associated with IBM, including but not limited to, claims related to your employment with IBM or the termination of that employment or other severance payments. . . . If you violate this Release by suing IBM . . ., you agree that you will pay all costs and expenses of defending against the suit incurred by IBM . . ., including reasonable attorney's fees."

(Emphasis in original.)

At no time between October 28, 1993 and January 27, 1994 did Johnson discuss the terms of the Release with IBM personnel. Nor did anyone from IBM ever urge, instruct, or apply any pressure whatsoever upon him, to sign the Release.

Had Johnson not signed the Release, at IBM's discretion, he would have received a separation allowance representing only two weeks pay, in a gross amount of $1,527.20, less deductions. Whether or not he signed the Release, Johnson would have been involuntarily terminated by IBM.

Johnson's job with IBM paid him roughly $40,000 annually at the time he was laid off and was his only source of income. Johnson had credit cards and other credit lines of roughly $18,000 available to him.

Johnson jointly owns a home in San Jose with his retired and disabled father. The household expenses are roughly $2000 per month. Johnson has a live-in girlfriend, Maxine Stokely, who, except for sporadic grocery purchases, does not contribute toward these expenses.

* * *

## III. Conclusions of Law

* * *

Parties to a contract must freely and mutually consent to its terms. [Citation.] If consent to a contract is not freely given, the contract may be rescinded by the parties. [Citation.] "An apparent consent is not real or free when obtained through duress. . . ." [Citation.]

**A. 6th Cause of Action for Economic Duress**   "Under California law, economic duress can serve as a basis for invalidating a release or waiver." [Citation].

Economic duress . . . "come[s] into play upon the doing of a wrongful act which is sufficiently coercive to cause a reasonably prudent person faced with no reasonable alternative to succumb to the perpetrator's pressure." [Citations.]

* * *

In order to establish his claim for economic duress, Johnson was required to prove by a preponderance of evidence the following elements: (i) IBM engaged in a sufficiently coercive wrongful act such that; (ii) a reasonably prudent person in Johnson's economic position would have had no reasonable alternative but to succumb to IBM's coercion; (iii) IBM knew of Johnson's economic vulnerability; and (iv) IBM's coercive wrongful act actually caused or induced Johnson to endorse the Release.

### i. Coercive Wrongful Act Element

The "wrongful act need not be in the nature of a tort or crime." [Citation.] However, "[m]erely being put to a voluntary choice of perfectly legitimate alternatives is the antithesis of duress . . . Encouragement is a far cry from coercion or denial of choice." [Citation.]

IBM did not commit a "wrongful act" by designating Johnson a surplus employee or by requiring that he choose between (a) accepting a lower-paying manufacturing job with IBM, (b) accepting two weeks severance, at IBM's discretion, or (c) accepting a twenty-six weeks enhanced severance package with additional health and job-placement benefits in consideration for signing the Release.

* * *

### ii. Reasonable Alternatives Element

"[A] reasonably prudent person subject to [a wrongful] act may have no reasonable alternative but to succumb when the only other alternative is bankruptcy or financial ruin." [Citation.] In determining whether a reasonable alternative was available, courts employ an objective test dependent on the circumstances of each case. [Citation.]

When he signed the Release, on January 27, 1995, Johnson was not facing imminent bankruptcy or financial ruin. Regardless of what he may subjectively have believed, Johnson had objectively reasonable alternatives to signing the Release. The employment market for computer programmers in Silicon Valley during this period was such that Johnson could have found substitute employment as a computer programmer in the two-month period between October 28 and December 31, 1993, during which he was still being paid by IBM. His skin condition and state of mind did not prevent him from seeking alternative employment during this period.

Alternatively, Johnson could have applied for transfer to a sedentary manufacturing job with IBM at a reduced income. Johnson was capable of performing a sedentary manufacturing job notwithstanding his skin condition and the income from such a position, although substantially reduced, would have been sufficient to forestall "financial ruin."

* * *

### iii. Knowledge of Plight Element

A defendant's "knowledge" of the plaintiff's economic exigencies is a necessary component of liability for economic duress. [Citation.]

IBM had no knowledge of Johnson's particular economic circumstances nor of any peculiar economic vulnerability he had.

### iv. Causation Element

Finally, the defendant's wrongful, coercive act "must induce the assent of the coerced party." [Citations.]

Johnson's decision to endorse the Release, instead of availing himself of other reasonable alternatives, was his own, made knowingly and freely after receiving advice of counsel, and was not caused by any untoward action on the part of IBM.

At the time he endorsed the Release, on January 27, 1994, Johnson was not subject to economic duress.

* * *

## IV. Order

Accordingly, IT IS HEREBY ORDERED that defendant IBM is entitled to judgment on plaintiff Johnson's [economic duress claim] and dismissal of all other claims in the Second Amended Complaint.

---

## CASE 11–2
## Undue Influence
### *REA v. PAULSON*
Court of Appeals of Oregon, 1994
131 Or. App. 743, 887 P.2d 355

**BUTTLER, J.**

Plaintiff (Ken Rea), as personal representative of his mother's estate, brought this action to set aside a deed from his mother to defendant Paulson (Larry), a son of decedent by a second marriage, and a deed from Larry to defendant Brady executed after this action had been commenced. Brady, in turn, filed a cross-claim against Larry for damages in the event plaintiff prevailed in setting aside the deed to him. The trial court, sitting in equity, found in favor of plaintiff on his complaint, and in favor of Brady on her cross-complaint. Brady, alone, appeals from the resulting judgment.

\* \* \*

Decedent died on January 31, 1988, leaving four children: Ken, Donald, Barbara and Larry. She had purchased a home in Rainier, the property that is the subject of this lawsuit, in 1983, for $21,300. At that time, she had a will that she had executed in 1967, leaving all of her property to her four children in equal shares. That will was never changed. After she moved into the house in Rainier, Ken and his wife, and Barbara and Don, helped decedent, who suffered from arthritis in both hands, renal failure, congestive heart failure and diabetes, as a result of which she had trouble getting around and, during the last part of her life, used an electric cart. She was taking several medications, \* \* \*, and was receiving insulin daily and dialysis an average of three times a week. Although there is no evidence that she was mentally incompetent, the medications and treatments made her drowsy, tired and depressed, and caused mood swings. It is undisputed that she was dependent on the help of others in her daily living.

Larry was not in the Rainier area when his mother moved there and did not visit her. The other children and her neighbor helped her. The other children re-roofed the house for her, picked fruit and stored it and mowed the lawn; her daughter helped her with her finances and had a joint account with her, which the daughter never used. All of those children visited her frequently, and at least one of them saw her every day. Decedent expressed concern about losing the house because of her medical bills, and suggested that she put the house in Ken's name; he and Barbara looked into the situation and concluded that it was not necessary, and so advised their mother. At some point, it is not clear when, Larry was told by state welfare authorities, as Ken and Barbara had learned, that so long as his mother maintained her house as her primary residence and was not receiving Medicaid, she was not in danger of losing her house to the state. There is no evidence that decedent was receiving Medicaid, although she did receive Social Security benefits and Medicare.

Some time in early 1987, Larry and his then girl-friend (later his wife) moved in with decedent and took over her care. Larry expressed his concern to his mother that the state might take her house. Not long thereafter, Larry rented a house in Longview in his name and persuaded his mother to move in with him, his girlfriend and her child. After decedent moved to Longview, she rented her house in Rainier; the rent was used to maintain the house in Longview. At that time decedent had a savings account with approximately $2,000 in it; Larry held his mother's power of attorney. At the time of her death in January, 1988, that account was exhausted, although her medical expenses were being paid by Medicare. Larry admitted that he used some of that money to buy a bicycle and a guitar. He had also used her credit card, on which there was a substantial balance after her death, which he did not pay. He said that that debt "died with his mother." On numerous occasions, Larry expressed to his mother his concern that the state would take her house if she kept it in her name. She was fearful of that, in spite of what she had been told by Ken and Barbara. Larry told her that they were wrong, and frequently urged her to make up her mind "about the deed."

Decedent was hospitalized three times during 1987: February 13 to 18, August 2 to 10 and November 11 to 30. She was in a nursing home following her first hospitalization and again shortly before her death.

Finally, on September 30, 1987, Larry suggested to his mother that they go to a title company in Rainier to get a deed. He took her, along with his then wife and her child, to the title company where he obtained a statutory form of warranty deed and filled it out in his handwriting, using the property description provided by the title company. For no explained reason, he then drove to Longview to a notary public, where decedent signed the deed after the notary explained to her that when she signed it she would be giving up all of her rights in the property. Larry then had it recorded on October 22, 1987. He did not mention it to any of his half-brothers or -sister until two months later when he boasted of it to his half-sister.

Clearly, decedent had trust and confidence in Larry and was completely dependent on him in her daily life. He helped her with her finances and held her power of attorney. She was unable to write checks; Larry wrote them for her, and "she signed them as best she could." She was unable to come and go as she wished; after she moved in with Larry, she depended on him to take her places. Because Larry made it clear to decedent's other children that they were not welcome in his home, he succeeded in driving a wedge between them and their mother, with whom they had had a very close relationship until he appeared on the scene and took control of her life. He did not advise them of her death. We conclude that there was a confidential relationship between decedent and Larry and that, under the circumstances, he held a position of dominance over her; he was, literally, in the driver's seat. [Citation.]

Although one who claims that another has asserted undue influence has the burden to prove it, an inference of undue influence arises when, in addition to a confidential relationship, there are suspicious circumstances. [Citation.] That inference, if unexplained, may be sufficient, although the burden of proof remains with the one asserting undue influence. [Citation.] Circumstances that give rise to suspicions of undue influence are set out in [citation], and several are present here. Larry took his mother to the title company in St. Helens, where he procured the deed, filled it out in his own handwriting and then took his mother to Longview, where she signed it before a notary public. He not only procured the deed, he also participated in its preparation. Although he contends that it was his mother's idea, if it was, it was the result of his having persuaded her that she would lose the house if she did not deed the property to him, and of his repeatedly telling her to make up her mind "about the deed." At that time, Larry knew that the state would not take her home away from her as long as it was her primary residence, even if she was receiving Medicaid. Therefore, his persistence in raising the question was false, and he knew it was false. He did not argue that, because the Rainier house was no longer her primary residence, there was a risk that the state would take it. That argument would have been disingenuous, given that it was he who had suggested that she rent her house and move in with him.

Another important factor is the absence of independent advice. Although Ken and Barbara had advised decedent long before the deed was executed that she would not lose her house to the state if she maintained it in her name instead of deeding it to Ken, as she was contemplating at the time, Larry had persuaded her that Ken was wrong and that she should deed it to him. Under the circumstances, independent advice was essential, and Larry breached his fiduciary duty to her by not seeing to it that she get independent advice.

We also consider the change in attitude of decedent toward her other children after Larry took charge of his mother. Larry conceded that he had little good to say to his mother about his half-brothers and -sister. More than that, the record shows that he told them that they were not welcome at his home, and that when Barbara tried to call her mother on the telephone, he would get on another line to interfere with the call. As a result, the relations between decedent and her other children deteriorated after Larry took over the care of their mother.

We have no reason to doubt that decedent was grateful to Larry for his having helped her during her final days, or that she loved him. However, the circumstances leading up to the conveyance, and the preparation and signing of the deed, lead us to conclude that it was the product of undue influence exerted by Larry on his mother.

\* \* \*

Affirmed.

# CASE 11–3
## Fraud: False Representation of Fact
# *VOKES v. ARTHUR MURRAY, INC.*

Florida Court of Appeals, 1968
212 So.2d 906

**PIERCE, J.**

[Audrey E. Vokes, plaintiff, appeals from a final order dismissing her complaint, for failure to state a cause of action.]

Defendant Arthur Murray, Inc., a corporation, authorizes the operation throughout the nation of dancing schools under the name of "Arthur Murray School of Dancing" through local franchised operators, one of whom was defendant J.P. Davenport whose dancing establishment was in Clearwater.

Plaintiff Mrs. Audrey E. Vokes, a widow of 51 years and without family, had a yen to be "an accomplished dancer" with the hopes of finding "new interest in life." So, on February 10, 1961, a dubious fate, with the assist of a motivated acquaintance, procured her to attend a "dance party" at Davenport's "School of Dancing" where she whiled away the pleasant hours, sometimes in a private room, absorbing his accomplished sales technique, during which her grace and poise were elaborated upon and her rosy future as "an excellent dancer" was painted for her in vivid and glowing colors. As an incident to this interlude, he sold her eight 1/2-hour dance lessons to be utilized within one calendar month therefrom, for the sum of $14.50 cash in hand paid, obviously a baited "come-on."

Thus she embarked upon an almost endless pursuit of the terpsichorean art during which, over a period of less than sixteen months, she was sold fourteen "dance courses" totalling in the aggregate 2,302 hours of dancing lessons for a total cash outlay of $31,090.45, all at Davenport's dance emporium.

\* \* \*

These dance lesson contracts and the monetary consideration therefor of over $31,000 were procured from her by means and methods of Davenport and his associates which went beyond the unsavory, yet legally permissible, perimeter of "sales puffing" and intruded well into the forbidden area of undue influence, the suggestion of falsehood, the suppression of truth, and the free exercise of rational judgment, if what plaintiff alleged in her complaint was true. From the time of her first contact with the dancing school in February, 1961, she was influenced unwittingly by a constant and continuous barrage of flattery, false praise, excessive compliments, and panegyric encomiums, to such extent that it would be not only inequitable, but unconscionable, for a court exercising inherent chancery power to allow such contracts to stand.

She was incessantly subjected to overreaching blandishment and cajolery. She was assured she had "grace and poise"; that she was "rapidly improving and developing in her dancing skill"; that the additional lessons would "make her a beautiful dancer, capable of dancing with the most accomplished dancers"; that she was "rapidly progressing in the development of her dancing skill and gracefulness"; etc. She was given "dance aptitude tests" for the ostensible purpose of "determining" the number of remaining hours of instruction needed by her from time to time.

At one point she was sold 545 additional hours of dancing lessons to be entitled to the award of the "Bronze Medal" signifying that she had reached "the Bronze Standard," a supposed designation of dance achievement by students of Arthur Murray, Inc.

Later she was sold an additional 926 hours in order to gain the "Silver Medal," indicating she had reached "the Silver Standard," at a cost of $12,501.35.

At one point, while she still had to her credit about 900 unused hours of instructions, she was induced to purchase an additional 24 hours of lessons to participate in a trip to Miami at her own expense, where she would be "given the opportunity to dance with members of the Miami Studio."

She was induced at another point to purchase an additional 126 hours of lessons in order to be not only eligible for the Miami trip but also to become "a life member of the Arthur Murray Studio," carrying with it certain dubious emoluments, at a further cost of $1,752.30.

At another point, while she still had over 1,000 unused hours of instruction she was induced to buy 151 additional hours at a cost of $2,049.00 to be eligible for a "Student Trip to Trinidad," at her own expense as she later learned.

Also, when she still had more than 1,000 unused hours to her credit, she was prevailed upon to purchase an additional 347 hours at a cost of $4,235.74 to qualify her to receive a "Gold Medal" for achievement, indicating she had advanced to "the Gold Standard."

On another occasion, while she still had over 1,200 unused hours, she was induced to buy an additional 175 hours of instruction at a cost of $2,472.75, to be eligible "to take a trip to Mexico."

Finally, sandwiched in between other lesser sales promotions, she was influenced to buy an additional 481 hours of instruction at a cost of $6,523.81 in order to "be classified as a Gold Bar Member, the ultimate achievement of the dancing studio."

All the foregoing sales promotions, illustrative of the entire fourteen separate contracts, were procured by defendant Davenport and Arthur Murray, Inc., by false representations to her that she was improving in her dancing ability, that she had excellent potential, that she was responding to instructions in dancing grace, and that they were developing her into a beautiful dancer, whereas in truth and in fact she did not develop in her dancing ability, she had no "dance aptitude," and in fact had difficulty in "hearing the musical beat." The complaint alleged that such representations to her "were in fact false and known by the defendant to be false and contrary to the plaintiff's true ability, the truth of plaintiff's ability being fully known to the defendants, but withheld from the plaintiff for the sole and specific intent to deceive and defraud the plaintiff and to induce her in the purchasing of additional hours of dance lessons." It was averred that the lessons were sold to her "in total disregard to the true physical, rhythm, and mental ability of the plaintiff." In other words, while she first exulted that she was entering the "spring of her life," she finally was awakened to the fact there was "spring" neither in her life nor in her feet.

\* \* \*

It is true that "generally a misrepresentation, to be actionable, must be one of fact rather than of opinion." [Citation.] But this rule has significant qualifications, applicable here. . . . As stated by Judge Allen of this court [citation]: "A statement of a party having . . . superior knowledge may be regarded as a statement of fact although it would be considered as opinion if the parties were dealing on equal terms."

It could be reasonably supposed here that defendants had "superior knowledge" as to whether plaintiff had "dance potential" and as to whether she was noticeably improving in the art of terpsichore. And it would be a reasonable inference from the undenied averments of the complaint that the flowery eulogiums heaped upon her by defendants as a prelude to her contracting for 1,944 additional hours of instruction in order to attain the rank of the Bronze Standard, thence to the bracket of the Silver Standard, thence to the class of the Gold Bar Standard, and finally to the crowning plateau of a Life Member of the Studio, proceeded as much or more from the urge to "ring the cash register" as from any honest or realistic appraisal of her dancing prowess or a factual representation of her progress.

Even in contractual situations where a party to a transaction owes no duty to disclose facts within his knowledge or to answer inquiries respecting such facts, the law is if he undertakes to do so he must disclose the *whole truth*. [Citations.] From the face of the complaint, it should have been reasonably apparent to defendants that her vast outlay of cash for the many hundreds of additional hours of instruction was not justified by her slow and awkward progress, which she would have been made well aware of if they had spoken the "whole truth."

\* \* \*

Reversed.

---

## CASE 11–4
## Fraud: Materiality
### *REED v. KING*

California Court of Appeals, 1983
145 Cal.App.3d 261, 193 Cal.Rptr. 130

BLEASE, J.
In the sale of a house, must the seller disclose it was the site of a multiple murder?

Dorris Reed purchased a house from Robert King. Neither King nor his real estate agents (the other named defendants) told Reed that a woman and her four children were murdered there 10 years earlier. However, it seems "truth will come to light; murder cannot be hid long." (Shakespeare, Merchant of Venice, act II, scene II.) Reed learned of the gruesome episode from a neighbor after the sale. She sues seeking rescission and damages. King and the real estate agent defendants successfully demurred to her first amended complaint for failure to state a cause of action. Reed appeals the ensuing judgment of dismissal. We will reverse the judgment.

＊ ＊ ＊ King and his real estate agent knew about the murders and knew the event materially affected the market value of the house when they listed it for sale. They represented to Reed the premises were in good condition and fit for an "elderly lady" living alone. They did not disclose the fact of the murders. At some point King asked a neighbor not to inform Reed of that event. Nonetheless, after Reed moved in neighbors informed her no one was interested in purchasing the house because of the stigma. Reed paid $76,000, but the house is only worth $65,000 because of its past.

＊ ＊ ＊

Does Reed's pleading state a cause of action? Concealed within this question is the nettlesome problem of the duty of disclosure of blemishes on real property which are not physical defects or legal impairments to use.

Reed seeks to state a cause of action sounding in contract, i.e., rescission, or in tort, i.e., deceit. In either event her allegations must reveal a fraud. [Citation.] "The elements of actual fraud, whether as the basis of the remedy in contract or tort, may be stated as follows: There must be (1) a *false representation* or concealment of a material fact (or, in some cases, an opinion) susceptible of knowledge, (2) made with *knowledge* of its falsity or without sufficient knowledge on the subject to warrant a representation, (3) with the *intent* to induce the person to whom it is made to act upon it; and such person must (4) act in *reliance* upon the representation (5) to his *damage*." (Original italics.) [Citation.]

The trial court perceived the defect in Reed's complaint to be a failure to allege concealment of a material fact. . . .

Concealment is a term of art which includes mere nondisclosure when a party has a duty to disclose. [Citation.] Rest.2d Contracts, § 161; Rest.2d Torts, § 551; Reed's complaint reveals only nondisclosure despite the allegation King asked a neighbor to hold his peace. There is no allegation the attempt at suppression was a cause in fact of Reed's ignorance. (See Rest.2d Contracts, §§ 160, 162–164; Rest.2d Torts, § 550; Rest., Restitution, § 9.) Accordingly, the critical question is: does the seller have a duty to disclose here? Resolution of this question depends on the materiality of the fact of the murders.

In general, a seller of real property has a duty to disclose: "where the seller knows of facts *materially* affecting the value or desirability of the property which are known or accessible only to him and also knows that such facts are not known to, or within the reach of the diligent attention and observation of the buyer, the seller is under a duty to disclose them to the buyer. [Citation.] This broad statement of duty has led one commentator to conclude: "The ancient maxim *caveat emptor* ('let the buyer beware') has little or no application to California real estate transactions." [Citation.]

Whether information "is of sufficient materiality to affect the value or desirability of the property . . . depends on the facts of the particular case." [Citation.] Materiality "is a question of law, and is part of the concept of right to rely or justifiable reliance." [Citation.] ＊ ＊ ＊ Three considerations bear on this legal conclusion; the gravity of the harm inflicted by nondisclosure; the fairness of imposing a duty of discovery on the buyer as an alternative to compelling disclosure, and the impact on the stability of contracts if rescission is permitted.

Numerous cases have found nondisclosure of physical defects and legal impediments to use of real property are material. [Citation.] However, to our knowledge, no prior real estate sale case has faced an issue of nondisclosure of the kind presented here.

＊ ＊ ＊

The murder of innocents is highly unusual in its potential for so disturbing buyers they may be unable to reside in a home where it has occurred. This fact may foreseeably deprive a buyer of the intended use of the purchase. Murder is not such a common occurrence that *buyers* should be charged with anticipating and discovering this disquieting possibility. Accordingly, the fact is not one for which a duty of inquiry and discovery can sensibly be imposed upon the buyer.

Reed alleges the fact of the murders has a quantifiable effect on the market value of the premises. We cannot say this allegation is inherently wrong and, in the pleading posture of the case, we assume it to be true. If information known or accessible only to the seller has a significant and measurable effect on market value and, as is alleged here, the seller is aware of this effect, we see no principled basis for making the duty to disclose turn upon the character of the information. Physical usefulness is not and never has been the sole criterion of valuation. ＊ ＊ ＊

Reputation and history can have a significant effect on the value of realty. "George Washington slept here" is worth something, however physically inconsequential that consideration may be. Illrepute or "bad will" conversely may depress the value of property. ＊ ＊ ＊

Whether Reed will be able to prove her allegation the decade-old multiple murder has a significant effect on market value we cannot determine. If she is able to do so by competent evidence she is entitled to a favorable ruling on the issues of materiality and duty to disclose. Her demonstration of objective tangible harm would still the concern that permitting her to go forward will open the floodgates to rescission on subjective and idiosyncratic grounds.

* * *

The judgment is reversed.

---

## CASE 11–5
## Mistake
# WILKIN v. 1ST SOURCE BANK
Court of Appeals of Indiana, 1990
548 N.E.2d 170

HOFFMAN, J.

Respondents-appellants Terrence G. Wilkin and Antoinette H. Wilkin (the Wilkins) appeal from the judgment of the St. Joseph Probate Court in favor of petitioner-appellee 1st Source Bank (Bank). The Bank, as personal representative of the estate of Olga Mestrovic, had filed a petition to determine title to eight drawings and a plaster sculpture owned by Olga Mestrovic at the time of her death but in the possession of the Wilkins at the time the petition was filed. The probate court determined that the drawings and sculpture were the property of the estate, and the court ordered the Wilkins to return the items to the Bank.

* * *

Olga Mestrovic died on August 31, 1984. Her last will and testament was admitted to probate on September 6, 1984, and the Bank was appointed personal representative of the estate.

At the time of her death, Olga Mestrovic was the owner of a large number of works of art created by her husband, Ivan Mestrovic, an internationally known sculptor and artist. By the terms of Olga's will, all the works of art created by her husband and not specifically devised were to be sold and the proceeds distributed to members of the Mestrovic family.

Also included in the estate of Olga Mestrovic was certain real property. In March of 1985, the Bank entered into an agreement to sell the real estate to the Wilkins. The agreement of purchase and sale made no mention of any works of art, although it did provide for the sale of such personal property as the stove, refrigerator, dishwasher, drapes, curtains, sconces and French doors in the attic.

Immediately after closing on the real estate, the Wilkins complained that the premises were left in a cluttered condition and would require substantial cleaning effort. The Bank, through its trust officer, proposed two options: the Bank could retain a rubbish removal service to clean the property or the Wilkins could clean the premises and keep any items of personal property they wanted. The Wilkins opted to clean the property themselves. At the time arrangements were made concerning the cluttered condition of the real property, neither the Bank nor the Wilkins suspected that any works of art remained on the premises.

During their clean-up efforts, the Wilkins found eight drawings apparently created by Ivan Mestrovic. They also found a plaster sculpture of the figure of Christ with three small children. The Wilkins claimed ownership of the works of art, based upon their agreement with the Bank that if they cleaned the real property then they could keep such personal property as they desired.

The probate court ruled that there was no agreement for the purchase, sale or other disposition of the eight drawings and plaster sculpture. According to the lower court, there was no meeting of the minds, because neither party knew of the existence of the works of art.

* * *

Mutual assent is a prerequisite to the creation of a contract. [Citation.] Where both parties share a common assumption about a vital fact upon which they based their bargain, and that assumption is false, the transaction may be avoided if because of the mistake a quite different exchange of values occurs from the exchange of values contemplated by the parties. [Citation.] * * *

The necessity of mutual assent, or "meeting of the minds," is illustrated in the classic case of *Sherwood v. Walker* (1887), [citation]. The owners of a blooded cow indicated to the purchaser that the cow was barren. The purchaser also appeared to believe that the cow was barren. Consequently, a bargain was made to sell at a price per pound at which the cow would have brought approximately $80.00. Before delivery, it was discovered that the cow was with calf and that she was, therefore, worth from $750.00 to $1,000.00. The court ruled that the transaction was voidable: "[T]he mistake was not of the mere quality of the animal, but went to the very nature of the thing. A barren cow is substantially a different creature than a breeding one. There is as much difference between them . . . as there is between an ox and a cow. . . ." [Citation.]

Like the parties in *Sherwood*, the parties in the instant case shared a common presupposition as to the existence of certain facts which proved false. The Bank and the Wilkins considered the real estate which the Wilkins had purchased to be cluttered with items of personal property variously characterized as "junk," "stuff" or "trash." Neither party suspected that works of art created by Ivan Mestrovic remained on the premises.

As in *Sherwood*, one party experienced an unexpected, unbargained-for gain, while the other party experienced an unexpected, unbargained-for loss. Because the Bank and the Wilkins did not know that the eight drawings and the plaster sculpture were included in the items of personalty that cluttered the real property, the discovery

of those works of art by the Wilkins was unexpected. The resultant gain to the Wilkins and loss to the Bank were not contemplated by the parties when the Bank agreed that the Wilkins could clean the premises and keep such personal property as they wished.

The following commentary on *Sherwood* is equally applicable to the case at bar: "Here the buyer sought to retain a gain that was produced, not by a subsequent change in circumstances, nor by the favorable resolution of known uncertainties when the contract was made, but by the presence of facts quite different from those on which the parties based their bargain." [Citation.] The probate court properly concluded that there was no agreement for the purchase, sale or other disposition of the eight drawings and plaster sculpture, because there was no meeting of the minds.

The judgment of the St. Joseph Probate Court is affirmed.

# Questions

**1.** Identify the types of duress and discuss the legal effect of each.

**2.** Identify the types of fraud and the elements that must be shown to establish the existence of each.

**3.** Discuss undue influence and identify some of the situations giving rise to a confidential relationship.

**4.** Identify and discuss the situations involving voidable mistakes.

**5.** Define the two types of nonfraudulent misrepresentation.

# Problems

**1.** Anita and Barry were negotiating, and Anita's attorney prepared a long and carefully drawn contract, which was given to Barry for examination. Five days later and prior to its execution, Barry's eyes became so infected that it was impossible for him to read. Ten days thereafter and during the continuance of the illness, Anita called upon Barry and urged him to sign the contract, telling him that time was running out. Barry signed the contract despite the fact he was unable to read it. In a subsequent action by Anita, Barry claimed that the contract was not binding upon him because it was impossible for him to read and he did not know what it contained prior to his signing it. Decision?

**2.** (a) Johnson tells Davis that he paid $150,000 for his farm in 1984, and that he believes it is worth twice that at the present time. Relying upon these statements, Davis buys the farm from Johnson for $225,000. Johnson did pay $150,000 for the farm in 1984, but its value has increased only slightly, and it is presently not worth $300,000. On discovering this,

Davis offers to reconvey the farm to Johnson and sues for the return of his $225,000. Result?

(b) Modify the facts in (a) by assuming that Johnson had paid $100,000 for the property in 1984. What result?

**3.** On September 1, Adams in Portland, Oregon, wrote a letter to Brown in New York City, offering to sell to Brown one thousand tons of chromite at $48 per ton, to be shipped by *S.S. Malabar* sailing from Portland, Oregon, to New York City via the Panama Canal. Upon receiving the letter on September 5, Brown immediately mailed to Adams a letter stating that she accepted the offer. There were two ships by the name of *S.S. Malabar* sailing from Portland to New York City via the Panama Canal, one sailing in October and the other sailing in December. At the time of mailing her letter of acceptance Brown knew of both sailings and further knew that Adams knew only of the December sailing. Is there a contract? If so, to which *S.S. Malabar* does it relate?

4. Adler owes Panessi, a police captain, $500. Adler threatens that unless Panessi discharges him from the debt, Adler will disclose the fact that Panessi has on several occasions become highly intoxicated and has been seen in the company of certain disreputable persons. Panessi, induced by fear that such a disclosure would cost him his position or in any event lead to social disgrace, gives Adler a release but subsequently sues to set it aside and recover on his claim. Decision?

5. Harris owned a farm that was worth about $600 per acre. By false representations of fact, Harris induced Pringle to buy the farm at $1,500 per acre. Shortly after taking possession of the farm, Pringle discovered oil under the land. Harris, on learning this, sues to have the sale set aside on the ground that it was voidable because of fraud. Decision?

6. On February 2, Phillips induced Miller to purchase from her fifty shares of stock in the XYZ Corporation for $10,000, representing that the actual book value of each share was $200. A certificate for fifty shares was delivered to Miller. On February 16, Miller discovered that the book value on February 2 was only $50 per share. Thereafter, Miller sues Phillips. Decision?

7. Doris mistakenly accused Peter's son, Steven, of negligently burning down her barn. Peter believed that his son was guilty of the wrong and that he, Peter, was personally liable for the damage, as Steven was only fifteen years old. Upon demand made by Doris, Peter paid Doris $2,500 for the damage to her barn. After making this payment, Peter learned that his son had not caused the burning of Doris's barn and was in no way responsible for its burning. Peter then sued Doris to recover the $2,500 he had paid her. Decision?

8. Jones, a farmer, found an odd-looking stone in his fields. He went to Smith, the town jeweler, and asked him what he thought it was. Smith said he did not know but thought it might be a ruby. Jones asked Smith what he would pay for it, and Smith said $200, whereupon Jones sold it to Smith for $200. The stone turned out to be an uncut diamond worth $3,000. Jones brought an action against Smith to recover the stone. On trial, it was proved that Smith actually did not know the stone was a diamond when he bought it, but he thought it might be a ruby. Decision?

9. Decedent Judith Johnson, a bedridden, lonely woman of eighty-six years, owned outright Greenacre, her ancestral estate. Ficky, her physician and friend, visited her weekly and was held in the highest regard by Johnson. Johnson was extremely fearful of suffering and depended upon Ficky to ease her anxiety and pain. Several months before her death, she deeded Greenacre to Ficky for $5,000. The fair market value of Greenacre at this time was $125,000. Johnson was survived by two children and six grandchildren. Johnson's children challenged the validity of the deed. Decision?

10. Dorothy and John Huffschneider listed their house and lot for sale with C. B. Property. The asking price was $165,000, and the owners told C. B. that the size of the property was 6.8 acres. Dean Olson, a salesman for C. B., advertised the property in local newspapers as consisting of six acres. James and Jean Holcomb signed a contract to purchase the property through Olson after first inspecting the property with Olson and being assured by Olson that the property was at least 6.6 acres. The Holcombs never asked for or received a copy of the survey. In actuality, the lot was only 4.6 acres. The Holcombs now seek to rescind the contract. Decision?

11. In February, Gardner, a schoolteacher with no experience in running a tavern, entered into a contract to purchase for $40,000 the Punjab Tavern from Meiling. The contract was contingent upon Gardner's obtaining a five-year lease for the tavern's premises and a liquor license from the State. Prior to the formation of the contract, Meiling had made no representations to Gardner concerning the gross income of the tavern. Approximately three months after the contract was signed, Gardner and Meiling met with an inspector from the Oregon Liquor Control Commission (OLCC) to discuss transfer of the liquor license. Meiling reported to the agent, in Gardner's presence, that the tavern's gross income figures for February, March, and April were $5,710, $4,918, and $5,009, respectively. The OLCC granted the required license, the transaction was closed, and Gardner took possession on June 10. After discovering that the tavern's income was very low and that the tavern had very few female patrons, Gardner contacted Meiling's bookkeeping service and learned that the actual gross income for those three months had been approximately $1,400 to $2,000. Gardner then sued for rescission of the contract. Decision?

12. Christine Boyd was designated as the beneficiary of a life insurance policy issued by Aetna Life Insurance Company on the life of Christine's husband, Jimmie Boyd. The policy insured against Jimmie's permanent total disability and also provided for a death benefit to be paid on Jimmie's death.

Several years after the policy was issued, Jimmie and Christine separated. Jimmie began to travel extensively, and Christine therefore was unable to keep track of his whereabouts or his state of health. Jimmie, however, continued to pay the premiums on the policy until Christine tried to cash in the policy to alleviate her financial distress. A loan had previously been made on the policy, however, leaving its cash surrender value, and thus the amount that Christine received, at only $4.19. Shortly thereafter, Christine learned that Jimmie had been permanently and totally disabled before the surrender of the policy. Aetna also was unaware of Jimmie's condition, and Christine requested that the surrendered policy be reinstated and that the disability payments be made. Jimmie died soon thereafter, and Christine then requested that Aetna pay the death benefit. Decision?

13. Plaintiff, Gibson, entered into negotiation with W. S. May, president of Home Folks Mobile Home Plaza, Inc., to buy Home Plaza Corporation. Plaintiff visited the mobile home park on several occasions, at which time he noted the occupancy, visually inspected the sewer and water systems, and asked May numerous questions concerning the condition of the business. Plaintiff, however, never requested to see the books, nor did May try to conceal them. May admits making the following representations to the plaintiff: (1) the water and

sewer systems were in good condition and no major short-term expenditures would be needed; (2) the park realized a 40 percent profit on natural gas sold to tenants; and (3) usual park vacancy was 5 percent. In addition, May gave plaintiff the park's accountant-prepared income statement, which showed a net income of $38,220 for the last eight months. Based on these figures, plaintiff projected an annual net profit of $57,331.20. Upon being asked whether this figure accurately represented income of the business for the last three years, May stated by letter that indeed it did.

Plaintiff purchased the park for $275,000. Shortly thereafter, plaintiff spent $5,384 repairing the well and septic systems. By the time plaintiff sold the park three years later, he had expended $7,531 on the wells and $8,125 on the septic systems. Furthermore, in the first year, park occupancy was nowhere near 95 percent. Even after raising rent and the charges for natural gas, plaintiff still operated at a deficit.

Plaintiff sued defendant, alleging that May, on behalf of defendant, made false and fraudulent statements on which plaintiff relied when he purchased the park. Defendant moved for summary judgment. Decision?

**14.** Columbia University brought suit against Jacobsen on two notes signed by him and his parents, representing the balance of tuition he owed the University. Jacobsen counterclaimed for money damages due to Columbia's deceit or fraudulent misrepresentation. Jacobsen argues that Columbia fraudulently misrepresented that it would teach wisdom, truth, character, enlightenment, and similar virtues and qualities. He specifically cites as support the Columbia motto: *"in lumine tuo videbimus lumen"* ("In your light we shall see light"); the inscription over the college chapel: "Wisdom dwelleth in the heart of him that hath understanding"; and various excerpts from its brochures, catalogues, and a convocation address made by the University's president. Jacobsen, a senior who was not graduated because of poor scholastic standing, claims that the University's failure to meet its promises made through these quotations constituted fraudulent misrepresentation or deceit. Decision?

**15.** Frank Berryessa stole funds from his employer, the Eccles Hotel Company. His father, W. S. Berryessa, learned of his son's trouble and, thinking the amount involved was about $2,000, gave the hotel a promissory note for $2,186 to cover the shortage. In return, the hotel agreed not to publicize the incident or notify the bonding company. (A bonding company is an insurer that is paid a premium for agreeing to reimburse an employer for thefts by an employee.) Before this note became due, however, the hotel discovered that Frank had actually misappropriated $6,865. The hotel then notified its bonding company, Great American Indemnity Company, to collect the entire loss. W. S. Berryessa claims that the agent for Great American told him that unless he paid them $2,000 in cash and signed a note for the remaining $4,865, Frank would be prosecuted. Berryessa agreed, signed the note, and gave the agent a cashier's check for $1,500 and a personal check for $500. He requested that the agent not cash the

personal check for about a month. Subsequently, Great American sued Berryessa on the note. He defends against the note on the grounds of duress and counterclaims for the return of the $1,500 and the cancellation of the uncashed $500 check. Decision?

**16.** Jane Francois married Victor H. Francois in 1984. At the time of the marriage, Victor was a fifty-year-old bachelor living with his elderly mother, and Jane was a thirty-year-old, twice-divorced mother of two. Victor had a relatively secure financial portfolio; Jane, on the other hand, brought no money or property to the marriage.

The marriage deteriorated quickly over the next couple of years, with disputes centered on financial matters. During this period, Jane systematically gained a joint interest in and took control of most of Victor's assets. Then, in September of 1987, Jane contracted Harold Monoson, an attorney, to draw up divorce papers. Victor was unaware of Jane's decision until he was taken to Monoson's office, where Monoson presented for Victor's signature a "Property Settlement and Separation Agreement." Monoson told Victor that he would need an attorney, but Jane vetoed Victor's choice. Monoson then asked another lawyer, Gregory Ball, to come into the office. Ball read the agreement and strenuously advised Victor not to sign it because it would commit him to financial suicide. The agreement transferred most of Victor's remaining assets to Jane. Victor, however, signed it because Jane and Monoson persuaded him that it was the only way that his marriage could be saved. In October of 1988, Jane informed Victor that she had sold most of his former property and that she was leaving him permanently. Victor brought this action to have the agreement set aside as a result of undue influence. Decision?

**17.** Iverson owned Iverson Motor Company, an enterprise engaged in the repair as well as the sale of Oldsmobile, Rambler, and International Harvester Scout automobiles. Forty percent of the business's sales volume and net earnings came from the Oldsmobile franchise.

Whipp contracted to buy Iverson Motors, which Iverson said included the Oldsmobile franchise. After the sale, however, General Motors refused to transfer the franchise to Whipp. Whipp then returned the property to Iverson and brought this action seeking rescission of the contract. Decision?

**18.** On February 10, Mrs. Sunderhaus purchased a diamond ring from Perel & Lowenstein for $6,990. She was told by the company's salesperson that the ring was worth its purchase price, and she also received at that time a written guarantee from the company attesting to the diamond's value, style, and trade-in value. When Mrs. Sunderhaus went to trade the ring for another, however, she was told by two jewelers that the ring was valued at $3,000 and $3,500, respectively. Mrs. Sunderhaus knew little about the value of diamonds and claims to have relied on the oral representation of the Perel & Lowenstein's salesperson and the written representation as to the ring's value. She seeks rescission of the contract or damages in the amount of the sales price over the ring's value. Decision?

19.   Division West Chinchilla Ranch advertised on television that a five-figure income could be earned by raising chinchillas with an investment of only $3.75 per animal per year and only thirty minutes of maintenance per day. The minimum investment was $2,150 for one male and six female chinchillas. Division West represented to plaintiffs that chinchilla ranching would be easy and that no experience was required to make ranching profitable. Plaintiffs, who had no experience raising chinchillas, each invested $2,150 or more to purchase Division's chinchillas and supplies. After three years without earning a profit, plaintiffs sue Division for fraud. Decision?

20.   William Schmalz entered into an employment contract with Hardy Salt Company. The contract granted Schmalz six months' severance pay for involuntary termination but none for voluntary separation or termination for cause. Schmalz was asked to resign from his employment. He was informed that if he did not resign, he would be fired for alleged misconduct. When Schmalz turned in his letter of resignation, he signed a release prohibiting him from suing his former employer as a consequence of his employment. Schmalz consulted an attorney before signing the release and upon signing it received $4,583.00 (one month's salary) in consideration. Schmalz now sues his former employer for the severance pay, claiming that he signed the release under duress. Decision?

21.   Beginning in 1971, Treasure Salvors and the State of Florida entered into a series of four annual contracts governing the salvage of the *Nuestra Senora de Atocha*. The *Atocha* is a Spanish galleon that sank in 1622, carrying a treasure now worth well over $250 million. Both parties had contracted under the impression that the seabed on which the *Atocha* lay was land owned by Florida. Treasure Salvors agreed to relinquish 25 percent of the items recovered in return for the right to salvage on State lands. In accordance with these contracts, Treasure Salvors delivered to Florida its share of the salvaged artifacts. In 1975, the United States Supreme Court held that the part of the continental shelf on which the *Atocha* was resting had *never* been owned by Florida. Treasure Salvors then brought suit to rescind the contracts and to recover the artifacts it had delivered to the State of Florida. Florida appealed from a judgment in favor of Treasure Salvors. Decision?

22.   International Underwater Contractors, Inc. (IUC), entered into a written contract with New England Telephone and Telegraph Company (NET) to assemble and install certain conduits under the Mystic River for a lump sum price of $149,680. Delays caused by NET forced IUC's work to be performed in the winter months instead of during the summer as originally bid, and as a result a major change had to be made in the system from that specified in the contract. NET repeatedly assured IUC that it would pay the cost if IUC would complete the work. The change cost IUC an additional $811,810.73; nevertheless, it signed a release settling the claim for a total sum of $575,000. IUC, which at the time was in financial trouble, now seeks to recover the balance due, arguing that the signed release is not binding because it was signed under economic duress. Summary judgment was entered in favor of NET. Decision?

23.   Conrad Schaneman was a Russian immigrant who could neither read nor write the English language. In 1975 Conrad deeded (conveyed) a farm he owned to his eldest son, Laurence, for $23,500, which was the original purchase price of the property in 1945. The value of the farm in 1975 was between $145,000 and $160,000. At the time he executed the deed, Conrad was an eighty-two-year-old invalid, severely ill, and completely dependent on others for his personal needs. He weighed between 325 and 350 pounds, had difficulty breathing, could not walk more than fifteen feet, and needed a special jackhoist to get in and out of the bathtub. Conrad enjoyed a long-standing, confidential relationship with Laurence, who was his principal adviser and handled Conrad's business affairs. Laurence also obtained a power of attorney from Conrad and made himself a joint owner of Conrad's bank account and $20,000 certificate of deposit. Conrad brought this suit to cancel the deed, claiming it was the result of Laurence's undue influence. The district court found that the deed was executed as a result of undue influence, set aside the deed, and granted title to Conrad. Laurence appealed. Decision?

**Internet Exercise** Find information for businesses and consumers about avoiding and detecting fraud and scams (including online, credit card, and telemarketing).

# CHAPTER 12

# Consideration

Consideration is the primary—but not the only—basis for the enforcement of promises in our legal system. Consideration is the inducement to make a promise enforceable. The doctrine of consideration ensures that promises are enforced only where the parties have exchanged something of value in the eye of the law. Gratuitous (gift) promises, accordingly, are legally enforceable only under certain circumstances, which are discussed later in the chapter.

Consideration, or that which is exchanged for a promise, is present only when the parties intend an exchange. The consideration exchanged for the promise may be an act, a forbearance to act, or a promise to do either of these. In like manner, Section 71 of the Restatement defines consideration for a promise as (a) an act other than a promise, (b) a forbearance, (c) the creation, modification, or destruction of a legal relation, or (d) a return promise if any of these are bargained for and given in exchange for the promise.

Thus, consideration comprises two basic elements: (1) legal sufficiency (something of value) and (2) bargained-for exchange. Both must be present to satisfy the requirement of consideration. The consideration may be given to the promisor or to some other person; likewise, it may be given by the promisee or by some other person.

## LEGAL SUFFICIENCY

To be legally sufficient, the consideration exchanged for the promise must be either a legal detriment to the promisee *or* a legal benefit to the promisor. In other words, in return for the promise, the promisor must receive or the promisee must give something of legal value.

**Legal detriment** means (1) the doing (or undertaking to do) that which the promisee was under no prior legal obligation to do *or* (2) the refraining from doing (or the undertaking to refrain from doing) that which he was previously under no legal obligation to refrain from doing. On the other hand, **legal benefit** means the obtaining by the promisor of that which he had no prior legal right to obtain. Most, if not all, cases involving legal detriment to the promisee also will involve a legal benefit to the promisor. Nonetheless, the presence of **either** is sufficient.

➤ *See Case 12–1*

## Adequacy

Legal sufficiency has nothing to do with adequacy of consideration. Restatement, Section 79. The subject matter that the parties agree to exchange does not need to have the same or equal value; rather, the law will regard consideration as adequate if the parties have freely agreed to the exchange. The requirement of legally sufficient consideration is, therefore, not at all concerned with whether the bargain was good or bad, or whether one party received disproportionately more or less than what he gave or promised in exchange. Such facts, however, may be relevant to the availability of certain defenses (such as fraud, duress, or undue influence) or certain remedies (such as specific performance). The requirement of legally sufficient consideration is simply (1) that the parties have agreed to an exchange and (2) that, with respect to each party, the subject matter exchanged, or promised in exchange, either imposed a legal detriment upon the promisee or conferred a legal benefit upon the promisor. If the purported consideration is clearly without value, however, such that the transaction is a sham, many courts would hold that consideration is lacking.

## Unilateral Contracts

In a unilateral contract, a promise is exchanged for a completed act or a forbearance to act. Because only one promise exists, one party is the promisor and the other party is the promisee. For example, A promises to pay B $1,500 if B paints A's house. B paints A's house.

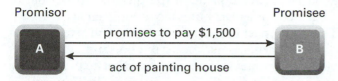

For A's promise to be binding, it must be supported by consideration consisting of either a legal detriment to B, the promisee, or a legal benefit to A, the promisor. B's having painted the house is a legal detriment to B, the promisee, because she was under no prior legal duty to paint A's house. Also, B's painting A's house is a legal benefit to A, the promisor, because A had no prior legal right to have his house painted by B.

A unilateral contract may also consist of a promise exchanged for a forbearance. To illustrate, A negligently injures B, for which B may recover damages in a tort action. A promises to pay B $5,000 if B forbears from bringing suit. B accepts by not filing suit.

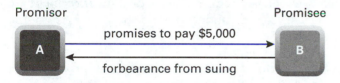

A's promise to pay B $5,000 is binding because it is supported by consideration: B, the promisee, has incurred a legal detriment by refraining from bringing suit, which he was under no prior legal obligation to refrain from doing. A, the promisor, has received a legal benefit because she had no prior legal right to B's forbearance from bringing suit.

 *See Case 12–2*

## Bilateral Contracts

In a bilateral contract, the parties exchange promises. Thus, each party is *both* a promisor and a promisee. For example, if A promises to purchase an automobile from B for $15,000 and B promises to sell the automobile to A for $15,000, the following relationship exists:

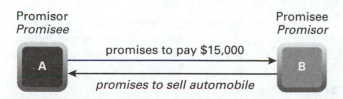

**A's promise** to pay B $15,000 is binding and therefore enforceable by B, if that promise is supported by legal consideration, which may consist of either a legal detriment to B, the promisee, or a legal benefit to A, the promisor. B's promise to sell A the automobile is a legal detriment to B because he was under no prior legal duty to sell the automobile to A. Moreover, B's promise is also a legal benefit to A because A had no prior legal right to that automobile. Consequently, A's promise to pay $15,000 to B is supported by consideration and is enforceable.

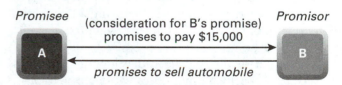

For **B's promise** to sell the automobile to A to be binding, it likewise must be supported by consideration, which may be either a legal detriment to A, the promisee, or a legal benefit to B, the promisor. A's promise to pay B $15,000 is a legal detriment to A because he was under no prior legal duty to pay $15,000 to B. At the same time, A's promise is also a legal benefit to B because B had no prior legal right to the $15,000. Thus, B's promise to sell the automobile is supported by consideration and is enforceable.

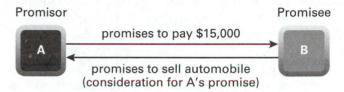

To summarize, for A's promise to B to be binding, B must support the promise with legally sufficient consideration, which requires that the promise A receives in exchange from B provide either a legal benefit to A (the promisor) or a legal detriment to B (the promisee). A, in turn, must support B's return promise with consideration for that promise to be binding on B.

Thus, in a bilateral contract each promise is the consideration for the other, a relationship that has been referred to as **mutuality of obligation.** A general consequence of mutuality of obligation is that each promisor in a bilateral contract must be bound, or neither is bound.

 *See Case 12–1*

## Illusory Promises

Words of promise that make the performance of the purported promisor entirely optional constitute no promise at all. Consequently, they cannot serve as consideration. In this section, such illusory promises will be distinguished from promises that impose obligations of performance upon the promisor and thus can be legally sufficient consideration.

An **illusory promise** is a statement that is in the form of a promise but imposes no obligation upon the maker of the statement. An illusory promise is not consideration for a return promise. Thus, a statement committing the promisor to purchase such quantity of goods as she may "desire," "want," or "wish to buy" is an illusory promise because its performance is entirely optional. For example, a statement by which Ames, Inc. offers to sell to Barnes Co. as many barrels of oil as Barnes shall choose at $40 per barrel represents lack of consideration: Barnes may wish or desire to buy none of the oil, yet in buying none it would fulfill its promise. An offer containing such a promise, although accepted by the offeree, does not create a contract because the promise is illusory—performance by Barnes is entirely optional, and the offer places no constraint upon its freedom. Barnes is not bound to do anything, nor can Ames reasonably expect to receive any performance. Thus, Barnes, by its promise, suffers no legal detriment and confers no legal benefit. Consequently, Barnes's promise does not provide legally sufficient consideration for Ames's promise; thus, Ames's promise is not binding upon Ames.

Many courts have transformed otherwise illusory promises into actual promises by implying an obligation of good faith or fair dealing. Under this approach, courts have held to be nonillusory a promise "to spend such time as he personally sees fit in developing" a business and a clause "specifying that leases 'satisfactory' to plaintiff must be secured before he would be bound to perform."

*Output and Requirements Contracts* A seller's agreement to sell her entire production to a particular purchaser is called an **output contract.** It affords the seller an ensured market for her product. Conversely, a **requirements contract,** or a purchaser's agreement to buy from a particular seller all the materials of a particular kind he needs, ensures the buyer of a ready source of inventory or supplies. These contracts may or may not be accompanied by an estimate of the quantity to be sold or to be purchased. Nevertheless, these promises are not illusory. The buyer under a requirements contract does not promise to buy as much as she desires to buy but, rather, to buy as much as she *needs*. Similarly, under an output contract the seller promises to sell to the buyer the seller's entire production, not merely as much as the seller desires.

Furthermore, the Code, Section 2–306(1), imposes a good faith limitation upon the quantity to be sold or purchased under an output or requirements contract. Thus, a contract of this type involves such actual output or requirements as may occur in good faith, except that no quantity unreasonably disproportionate to any stated estimate or, in the absence of a stated estimate, to any normal prior output or requirements may be tendered or demanded. Therefore, after contracting to sell to Adler, Inc. its entire output, Benevito Company cannot increase its production from one eight-hour shift per day to three eight-hour shifts per day.

*Exclusive Dealing Contracts* Where a manufacturer of goods grants an exclusive right to a distributor to sell its products in a designated territory, unless otherwise agreed, the manufacturer is under an implied obligation to use its best efforts to supply the goods, and the distributor must use his best efforts to promote their sale. U.C.C. Section 2–306(2). The obligations that arise upon acceptance of an **exclusive dealing agreement** are sufficient consideration to bind both parties to the contract.

*Conditional Promises* A conditional promise is a promise the performance of which depends upon the happening or nonhappening of an event not certain to occur (the condition). A conditional promise is sufficient consideration *unless* the promisor knows at the time of making the promise that the condition cannot occur. Restatement, Section 76.

Thus, if Debbie offers to pay John $8,000 for John's automobile, provided that Debbie receives such amount as an inheritance from the estate of her deceased uncle, and John accepts the offer, the duty of Debbie to pay $8,000 to John is *conditioned* upon her receiving $8,000 from her deceased uncle's estate. The consideration moving from John to Debbie is the promise to transfer title to the automobile. The consideration moving from Debbie to John is the promise of $8,000 subject to the condition.

## Preexisting Obligation

The law does not regard the performance of, or the promise to perform, a preexisting legal duty, public or private, as either a legal detriment to the party under the prior legal obligation or a benefit to the other party. A **public duty** does not arise out of a contract; rather, it is imposed upon members of society by force of the common law or by statute. As illustrated in the law of torts, public duty includes the duty not to commit an assault, battery, false imprisonment, or defamation. The criminal law also imposes numerous public duties. Thus, if Cleon promises to pay Spike, the village ruffian, $100 not to abuse him physically, Cleon's promise is unenforceable because both tort and criminal law impose on Spike a preexisting public obligation to refrain from so acting.

By virtue of their public office, public officials, such as the mayor of a city, members of a city council, police officers, and firefighters, are under a preexisting obligation to perform their duties.

The performance of, or the promise to perform, a **preexisting contractual duty,** a duty the terms of which are neither doubtful nor the subject of honest dispute, is also legally insufficient consideration because the doing of what one is legally bound to do is neither a detriment to the promisee nor a benefit to the promisor. For example, Leigh and Associates employs Jason for one year at a salary of $2,000 per month and at the end of six months promises Jason that, in addition to the salary, it will pay him $3,000 if he remains on the job for the remainder of the period originally agreed upon. Leigh's promise is not binding because Jason's promise does not constitute legally sufficient consideration. If Jason's duties were changed in nature or amount, however, Leigh's promise would be binding because Jason's new duties are a legal detriment.

 *See Case 12–3*

### Modification of a Preexisting Contract

A modification of a contract occurs when the parties to the contract mutually agree to change one or more of its terms. Under the common law, a modification of an existing contract must be supported by mutual consideration to be enforceable. In other words, the modification must be supported by some new consideration beyond that which is already owing (thus, there must be a separate and distinct modification contract). For example, Fred and Jodie agree that Fred shall put in a gravel driveway for Jodie at a cost of $2,000. Subsequently, Jodie agrees to pay an additional $1,000 if Fred will blacktop the driveway. Because Fred was not bound by the original contract to provide blacktopping, he would incur a legal detriment in doing so and is therefore entitled to the additional $1,000.

The Code has modified the common law rule for contract modification by providing that the parties can effectively modify a contract for the sale of goods without new consideration, though the Comments to this section make the modification subject to the requirement of good faith. Moreover, the Restatement has moved toward this position by providing that a modification of an executory contract is binding if it is fair and equitable in light of surrounding facts that the parties did not anticipate when the contract was made. Restatement, Section 89. A few States have followed the Code's rule by statutorily providing that the parties need provide no new consideration when modifying any contract. These States vary, however, as to whether the modification must be in writing and whether the original contract must be executory.

 *See Case 12–4*

### Substituted Contracts

A substituted contract results when the parties to a contract mutually agree to rescind their original contract and enter into a new one. This situation involves separate contracts: the original contract, the agreement of rescission, and the substitute contract. Substituted contracts are perfectly valid, allowing the parties effectively to discharge the original contract and to impose obligations under the new one. The rescission is binding in that each party, by giving up his rights under the original contract, has provided consideration to the other, as long as each party still has rights under the original contract. Where the rescission and new agreement are simultaneous, the effect is the same as a contractual modification. The Restatement takes the position that the substitute contract is *not* binding unless it is fair and equitable in view of circumstances the parties did not anticipate when they made the original contract. Section 89, Comment b.

### Settlement of a Liquidated Debt

A **liquidated debt** is an obligation the existence or amount of which is undisputed. Under the common law, the partial payment of a sum of money in consideration of a promise to discharge a fully matured, undisputed debt is legally *insufficient* to support the promise of discharge. To illustrate, assume that Pamela owes Julie $100, and in consideration of Pamela's paying Julie $50, Julie agrees to discharge the debt. In a subsequent suit by Julie against Pamela to recover the remaining $50, at common law Julie is entitled to judgment for $50 on the ground that Julie's promise of discharge is not binding because Pamela's payment of $50 was no legal detriment to the promisee, Pamela, as she was under a *preexisting legal obligation* to pay that much and more. Consequently, the consideration for Julie's promise of discharge was legally insufficient, and Julie is not bound on her promise. If, however, Julie had accepted from Pamela any new or different consideration, such as the sum of $40 and a fountain pen worth $10 or less, or even the fountain pen with no payment of money, in full satisfaction of the $100 debt, the consideration moving from Pamela would be legally sufficient inasmuch as Pamela was under no legal obligation to give a fountain pen to Julie. In this example, consideration would also exist if Julie had agreed to accept $50 *before* the debt became due, in full satisfaction of the debt. Pamela was under no legal obligation to pay any of the debt before its due date. Consequently, Pamela's early payment would represent a legal detriment to Pamela as well as a legal benefit to Julie. The law is not concerned with the amount of the discount, as that is simply a question of adequacy for the courts to decide. Likewise, Pamela's payment of a lesser amount on the due date at an agreed-upon different place of payment would be legally sufficient consideration. The Restatement requires that the new consideration "differs from what was required by the duty in a way which reflects more than a pretense of bargain." Section 73.

### Settlement of an Unliquidated Debt
An **unliquidated debt** is an obligation disputed as to either its existence or its amount. A promise to settle a validly disputed claim in exchange for an agreed payment or other performance is supported by consideration. Where the dispute is based upon contentions which are nonmeritorious or not made in good faith, however, the debtor's surrender of such a claim is no legal detriment to the claimant. The Restatement adopts a different position by providing that the settlement of a claim that proves invalid is consideration if at the time of the settlement (1) the claimant honestly believed that the claim was valid or (2) the claim was in fact doubtful because of uncertainty as to the facts or the law. Section 74.

For example, where a person has requested professional services from an accountant or a lawyer and the parties reached no agreement with respect to the amount of the fee to be charged, the accountant or lawyer is entitled to receive from her client a reasonable fee for the services rendered. As no definite amount has been agreed upon, the client's obligation is uncertain; nevertheless, his legal obligation is to pay the reasonable worth of the services performed. When the accountant or lawyer sends the client a bill for services rendered, even though the amount stated in the bill is an estimate of the reasonable value of the services, the debt does not become undisputed until and unless the client agrees to pay the amount of the bill. If the client honestly disputes the amount that is owing and tenders in full settlement an amount less than the bill, acceptance of the lesser amount by the creditor discharges the debt. Thus, if Ted sends to Betty, an accountant, a check for $120 in payment of his debt to Betty for services rendered, which services Ted considered worthless but for which Betty billed Ted $600, Betty's acceptance of the check releases Ted from any further liability. Ted has given up his right to dispute the billing further, while Betty has forfeited her right to further collection. Thus, there is mutuality of consideration.

 *See Case 12–2*

## BARGAINED-FOR EXCHANGE

The central idea behind consideration is that the parties have intentionally entered into a bargained exchange with one another and have given to each other something in exchange for a promise or performance. "A performance or return promise is bargained for if it is sought by the promisor in exchange for his promise and is given by the promisee in exchange for that promise." Restatement, Section 71. Thus, a promise to give someone a birthday present is without consideration, as the promisor received nothing in exchange for his promise of a present.

### Past Consideration

Consideration is the inducement for a promise or performance. The element of bargained-for exchange is absent where a promise is given for a past transaction. Therefore, unbargained-for past events are not consideration, despite their designation as "past consideration." A promise made on account of something that the promisee has already done is not enforceable. For example, Noel gives emergency care to Tim's adult son while the son is ill. Tim subsequently promises to pay Noel for her services, but his promise is not binding because there is no bargained-for exchange.

### Third Parties

Consideration to support a promise may be given to a person other than the promisor if the promisor bargains for that exchange. For example, A promises to pay B $15 if B delivers a specified book to C.

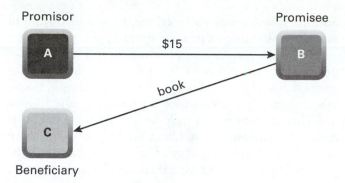

A's promise is binding because B incurred a legal detriment by delivering the book to C, as B was under no prior legal obligation to do so, and A had no prior legal right to have the book given to C. A and B have bargained for A to pay B $15 in return for B's delivering to C the book. A's promise to pay $15 is also consideration for B's promise to give the book to C.

Conversely, consideration may be given by some person other than the promisee. For example, A promises to pay B $25 in return for D's promise to give A a radio.

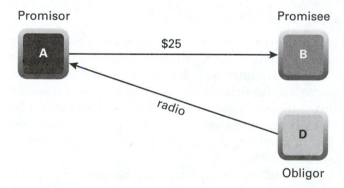

A's promise to pay $25 to B is consideration for D's promise to give A a radio and vice versa.

## CONTRACTS WITHOUT CONSIDERATION

Certain transactions are enforceable even though they are not supported by consideration. Such transactions include (1) promises to perform prior unenforceable obligations, (2) promises which induce detrimental reliance (promissory estoppel), (3) promises made under seal, and (4) promises made enforceable by statute.

### Promises to Perform Prior Unenforceable Obligations

In certain circumstances the courts will enforce new promises to perform an obligation that originally was not

enforceable or has become unenforceable by operation of law. These situations include promises to pay debts barred by the statute of limitations, debts discharged in bankruptcy, and voidable obligations. In addition, as previously indicated, some courts will enforce promises to pay moral obligations.

***Promise to Pay Debt Barred by the Statute of Limitations*** Every State has a statute of limitations, which provides that legal actions must be initiated within a prescribed period after the right to bring the action arose. Actions not commenced within the specified time period, which varies among the States and also with the nature of the legal action, will be dismissed.

An exception to the past consideration rule extends to promises to pay all or part of a contractual or quasi-contractual debt barred by the statute of limitations. The new promise is binding according to its terms without consideration for a second statutory period. Any recovery under the new promise is limited to the terms contained in the new promise. Most States require that new promises falling under this rule, except those indicated by part payment, be in writing to be enforceable.

***Promise to Pay Debt Discharged in Bankruptcy*** Another exception to the requirement that consideration be given in exchange for a promise to make it binding is a promise to pay a debt that has been discharged in bankruptcy. Restatement, Section 83. The Bankruptcy Act, however, imposes a number of requirements before a promise to pay a debt discharged in bankruptcy may be enforced. These requirements are discussed in Chapter 39.

***Voidable Promises*** Another promise that is enforceable without new consideration is a new promise to perform a voidable obligation that has not previously been avoided. Restatement, Section 85. The power of avoidance may be based on lack of capacity, fraud, misrepresentation, duress, undue influence, or mistake. For instance, a promise to perform an antecedent obligation made by a minor upon reaching the age of majority is enforceable without new consideration. To be enforceable, the promise itself must not be voidable. For example, if the new promise is made without knowledge of the original fraud or by a minor before reaching the age of majority, then the new promise is not enforceable.

***Moral Obligation*** Under the common law, a promise made to satisfy a preexisting moral obligation is made for past consideration and therefore is unenforceable for lack of consideration. Instances involving such obligations include promises to pay for board and lodging previously furnished to a needy relative of the promisor, promises to pay debts owed by a relative, and an employer's promises to pay a completely disabled former employee a sum of money in addition to an award the employee has received under a workers' compensation statute. Although in many cases the moral obligation may be strong by reason of the particular facts and circumstances, no liability generally attaches to the promise.

The Restatement and a minority of States give considerable recognition to moral obligations as consideration. The Restatement provides that a promise made for "a benefit previously received by the promisor from the promisee is binding to the extent necessary to prevent injustice." Section 86. For instance, Tim's subsequent promise to Noel to reimburse her for the expenses she incurred in rendering emergency services to Tim's son is binding even though it is not supported by new consideration.

The Restatement also provides for enforcement of a moral obligation when a person promises to pay for a mistakenly conferred benefit. For example, Pam hires Elizabeth to pave her driveway, and Elizabeth mistakenly paves Chuck's driveway next door. Chuck subsequently promises to pay Pam $1,000 for the benefit conferred. Under the Restatement, Chuck's promise to pay the $1,000 is binding.

## Promissory Estoppel

As discussed in Chapter 9, in certain circumstances where detrimental reliance has occurred, the courts will enforce noncontractual promises under the doctrine of promissory estoppel. When applicable, the doctrine makes gratuitous promises enforceable to the extent necessary to avoid injustice. The doctrine applies when a promise that the promisor reasonably should expect to induce detrimental reliance does induce such action or forbearance.

Promissory estoppel does not mean that every gratuitous promise is binding simply because it is followed by a change of position on the part of the promisee. To create liability, the promisee must make the change of position in justifiable reliance on the promise. For example, Smith promises to Barclay not to foreclose on a mortgage Smith holds on Barclay's factory for a period of six months. In justifiable reliance on Smith's promise, Barclay expends $900,000 on expanding the factory.

Smith's promise not to foreclose is binding on Smith under the doctrine of promissory estoppel.

The most common application of the doctrine of promissory estoppel is to charitable subscriptions. Numerous churches, memorials, college buildings, hospitals, and other structures used for religious, educational, and charitable purposes have been built with the assistance of contributions fulfilling pledges or promises to contribute to particular worthwhile causes. Although the pledgor regards herself as making a gift for a charitable purpose and gift promises generally are not enforceable, the courts tend to enforce charitable subscription promises. Numerous reasons and theories have been advanced in support of liability: the most accepted argues that the subscription has induced a change of position by the promisee (the church, school, or charitable organization) in reliance on the promise. The Restatement, moreover, has relaxed the reliance requirement for charitable subscriptions so that actual reliance need not be shown; the probability of reliance is sufficient.

## Promises Made Under Seal

Under the common law, when a person desired to bind himself by bond, deed, or solemn promise, he executed his promise under seal. He did not have to sign the document, his delivery of a document to which he had affixed his seal being sufficient. No consideration for his promise was necessary. In some States the courts still hold a promise under seal to be binding without consideration.

Nevertheless, most States have abolished by statute the distinction between contracts under seal and written unsealed contracts. In these States, the seal is no longer recognized as a substitute for consideration. The Code has also adopted this position, specifically eliminating the use of seals in contracts for the sale of goods.

## Promises Made Enforceable by Statute

Some gratuitous promises that would otherwise be unenforceable have been made binding by statute. Most significant among these are (1) contract modifications, (2) renunciations, and (3) irrevocable offers.

*Contract Modifications*   As mentioned previously, the Uniform Commercial Code has abandoned the common law rule requiring that a modification of an existing contract be supported by consideration to be valid. The Code provides that a contract for the sale of goods can be effectively modified without new consideration, provided the modification is made in good faith. Section 2–209.

**Renunciation** Under the Code, Section 1–107, any claim or right arising out of an alleged breach of contract can be discharged in whole or in part without consideration by a written waiver or renunciation signed and delivered by the aggrieved party.

**Irrevocable Offers** Under the Code, a *firm offer*, a written offer signed by a merchant offeror promising to keep open an offer to buy or sell goods, is not revocable for lack of consideration during the time stated, not to exceed three months, or if no time is stated, for a reasonable time. Section 2–205.

# Chapter Summary

| **Consideration** | **Definition** the inducement to enter into a contract<br>**Elements** legal sufficiency and bargained-for exchange |
|---|---|

| **Legal Sufficiency** | **Definition** consists of either a benefit to the promisor or a detriment to the promisee<br>• *Legal Benefit* obtaining something to which one had no prior legal right<br>• *Legal Detriment* doing an act one is not legally obligated to do or not doing an act that one has a legal right to do<br>**Adequacy** not required where the parties have freely agreed to the exchange<br>**Illusory Promise** promise that imposes no obligation on the promisor; the following promises are *not* illusory:<br>• *Output Contract* agreement to sell all of one's production to a single buyer<br>• *Requirements Contract* agreement to buy all of one's needs from a single producer<br>• *Exclusive Dealing Contract* grant to a franchisee or licensee by a manufacturer of the sole right to sell goods in a defined market<br>• *Conditional Promise* one where the obligations are contingent upon the occurrence of a stated event<br>**Preexisting Public Obligations** public duties such as those imposed by tort or criminal law are neither a legal detriment nor a legal benefit<br>**Preexisting Contractual Obligation** performance of a preexisting contractual duty is not consideration<br>• *Modification of a Preexisting Contract* under the common law a modification of a preexisting contract must be supported by mutual consideration; under the Code a contract can be modified without new consideration<br>• *Substituted Contracts* the parties agree to rescind their original contract and to enter into a new one; rescission and new contract are supported by consideration<br>• *Settlement of an Undisputed Debt* payment of a lesser sum of money to discharge an undisputed debt (one whose existence or amount is not contested) does not constitute legally sufficient consideration<br>• *Settlement of a Disputed Debt* payment of a lesser sum of money to discharge a disputed debt (one whose existence or amount is contested) is legally sufficient consideration |
|---|---|

| **Bargained-For Exchange** | **Definition** a mutually agreed-upon exchange<br>**Past Consideration** an act done before the contract is made is not consideration |
|---|---|

| Contracts without Consideration | **Promises to Perform Prior Unenforceable Obligations** |
|---|---|

**Contracts without Consideration**

**Promises to Perform Prior Unenforceable Obligations**
- *Promise to Pay Debt Barred by the Statute of Limitations* a new promise by the debtor to pay the debt renews the running of the statute for a second statutory period
- *Promise to Pay Debt Discharged in Bankruptcy* may be enforceable without consideration
- *Voidable Promises* a new promise to perform a voidable obligation that has not been previously avoided is enforceable
- *Moral Obligation* a promise made to satisfy a preexisting moral obligation is generally unenforceable for lack of consideration

**Promissory Estoppel** doctrine that prohibits a party from denying her promise when the promisee takes action or forbearance to his detriment reasonably based upon the promise

**Promises under Seal** where still recognized, the seal acts as a substitute for consideration

**Promises Made Enforceable by Statute** some gratuitous promises have been made enforceable by statute; the Code makes enforceable (1) contract modifications, (2) renunciations, and (3) firm offers

 **Cases**

### CASE 12–1
## Legal Sufficiency
## *PEARSALL v. ALEXANDER*
District of Columbia Court of Appeals, 1990
572 A2d 113

NEWMAN, J.

In what must be a common development wherever there are state-sponsored lotteries, this is the story of two friends who split the price of a ticket only to have the ticket win and split their friendship.

Harold Pearsall appeals from the dismissal of his complaint against Joe Alexander, in which Pearsall claimed breach of an agreement to share the proceeds of a winning D.C. Lottery ticket worth $20,000. The trial court found that such an agreement did, in fact, exist, but determined that the agreement was invalid under § 1 of the Statute of Anne [a statute outlawing certain forms of wagering or gaming], as enacted in D.C. Code §16–1701 [citation]. We conclude that the trial court erred in applying § 16–1701 to the Pearsall-Alexander agreement and, therefore, we reverse and remand with instructions to enter judgment for the appellant.

## I

Harold Pearsall and Joe Alexander were friends for over twenty-five years. About twice a week they would get together after work, when Alexander would meet Pearsall at the Takoma Metro station in his car. The pair would then proceed to a liquor store, where they would purchase what the two liked to refer to as a "package"—a half-pint of vodka, orange juice, two cups, and two lottery tickets—before repairing to Alexander's home. There they would "scratch" the lottery tickets, drink screwdrivers, and watch television. On occasion these lottery tickets would yield modest rewards of two or three dollars, which the pair would then "plow back" into the purchase of additional lottery tickets. According to Pearsall, the two had been sharing D.C. Lottery tickets in this fashion since the Lottery began.

On the evening of December 16, 1982, Pearsall and Alexander visited the liquor store twice, buying their normal "package" on each occasion. The first package was purchased when the pair stopped at the liquor store on the way to Alexander's home from the Metro station. Pearsall went into the store alone, and when he returned to the car, he said to Alexander, in reference to the tickets, "Are you in on it?" Alexander said "Yes." When Pearsall asked Alexander for his half of the purchase price of the tickets, Alexander replied that he had no money. When they reached Alexander's home, Alexander, expressing his anxiety that Pearsall might lose the tickets, demanded that Pearsall produce them, snatched them from Pearsall's hand, and "scratched" them, only to find that both were worthless.

At about 8:00 PM that same evening, Alexander, who apparently had come by some funds of his own, returned to the liquor store and bought a second "package." This time Pearsall, who had been offended by Alexander's conduct earlier in taking both tickets, snatched the two tickets from Alexander and announced that he would be the one to "scratch" them. Intending only to bring what he regarded as Alexander's childish behavior to Alexander's attention, Pearsall immediately relented and gave over one of the tickets to Alexander. Each man then "scratched" one of the tickets. Pearsall's ticket proved worthless; Alexander's was a $20,000 winner.

Alexander became very excited about the ticket and began calling friends to announce the good news. Fearing that Alexander might lose the ticket, Pearsall told Alexander to sign his name on the back of the ticket. Subsequently, Alexander cashed in the ticket and received the winnings; but, when Pearsall asked for his share, Alexander refused to give Pearsall anything.

Pearsall brought suit against Alexander, claiming breach of an agreement to share the proceeds of the winning ticket. * * *

The trial court dismissed Pearsall's complaint on the public policy grounds raised by Alexander, finding that the enforcement of contracts arising from gaming transactions is barred by the Statute of Anne, as enacted in D.C. Code § 16–1701, even when such contracts concern legalized gambling. * * *

[The court then held that the agreement involved in this case was not a gaming contract as defined in the statute.] * * *

## III

The record supports the trial court's finding that an agreement existed between Pearsall and Alexander to share equally in the proceeds of the winning ticket at issue.

The conduct of the two men on the evening of December 16, 1982, when the ticket was purchased, clearly demonstrates a meeting of the minds. After purchasing the first pair of tickets, Pearsall asked Alexander if he was "in on it." Not only did Alexander give his verbal assent, but later, when the two reached Alexander's home, Alexander, who had contributed nothing to the purchase price of the tickets, snatched *both* tickets from Pearsall and anxiously "scratched" them. It is evident from this that Alexander considered himself "in on" an agreement to share in the fortunes of the tickets purchased by his friend. It is equally clear that in giving over tickets he had purchased, Pearsall gave his assent to the agreement he had proposed earlier in the car. Moreover, this conduct took place within the context of a long-standing pattern of similar conduct, analogous to a "course of conduct" as described in the Uniform Commercial Code, which included their practice of "plowing back" small returns from winning tickets into the purchase of additional tickets.

It is also clear to us that, by exchanging mutual promises to share in the proceeds of winning tickets, adequate consideration was given by both parties. An exchange of promises is consideration, so long as it is bargained-for. [Citation.] Moreover, consideration may consist of detriment to the promisee. [Citation.] The giving over of one-half of the proceeds of a winning ticket would be a detriment to either man. Therefore, Pearsall's promise to share, as expressed in his question to Alexander, "Are you in on it?" induced a detriment in Alexander. Likewise, Alexander's promise to share, as contained in his assent, induced a detriment in Pearsall.

* * *

## IV

In conclusion, we find that there was a valid, enforceable agreement between Pearsall and Alexander to share in the proceeds of the $20,000 ticket purchased by Alexander on the evening of December 16, 1982. Therefore, we reverse and remand with instructions to enter judgment in favor of the appellant.

Reversed and remanded.

---

## CASE 12–2
## Legal Sufficiency/Settlement of an Unliquidated Debt
### *MATHIS v. ST. ALEXIS HOSPITAL*
Court of Appeals of Ohio, Cuyahoga County, 1994
99 Ohio App.3d 159, 650 N.E.2d 141

NAHRA, J.

In this consolidated appeal, Rodney D. Mathis, as administrator of the estate of Mary Mathis et al., plaintiffs-appellants, challenge the trial court's grant of summary judgment in a wrongful death action filed in connection with the death of Mary Mathis. Rodney Mathis filed a wrongful death action against St. Alexis Hospital and several of its physicians, including Keyhan Mobasseri, M.D., defendants-appellees. Mathis also filed a medical malpractice action against Mobasseri. The two cases were consolidated by the trial court. Because of a previously executed covenant not to sue, the trial court granted summary judgment in the wrongful death action against all defendants except Mobasseri, who was not a party to the covenant not to sue. * * * Mathis assigns the following error for review:

"The trial court erred in granting summary judgment to defendants-appellees, finding that plaintiffs-appellants' promise not to sue defendants-appellees, for which promise plaintiffs-appellants received no benefit and defendants-appellees incurred no detriment, was an enforceable contract supported by adequate consideration."

After reviewing the record and the arguments of the parties, we affirm the decision of the trial court. The apposite facts follow.

On June 6, 1990, Mary Mathis died of a ruptured aortic dissection at St. Alexis Hospital. She had been admitted to the emergency room the previous day after complaining of acute abdominal pain and paralysis of her legs.

On May 29, 1991, Mary Mathis' son and daughter, Rodney and Donna (hereinafter referred to as "Mathis"), filed a wrongful death action against St. Alexis Hospital and several of the physicians who treated Mary Mathis. Several weeks before trial, an expert consulted by Mathis notified the trial court and Mathis' counsel that, in his opinion, Mary Mathis' death was not proximately caused by the negligence of the physicians. Shortly thereafter, Mathis voluntarily dismissed the wrongful death action.

On October 1, 1992, Mathis and St. Alexis Hospital entered into a covenant not to sue. The agreement was signed by Rodney and Donna Mathis, as well as their attorney J. Norman Stark. Mathis agreed not to pursue any claims against St. Alexis or its employees arising from the medical care of Mary Mathis. St. Alexis agreed not to seek attorney fees and costs incurred in the defense of the voluntarily dismissed wrongful death action. The covenant not to sue contained the following language:

"NOW, THEREFORE, in consideration of the forbearance of St. Alexis Hospital Medical Center not seeking attorney fees and costs which have been expended in defending this action, namely Rodney D. Mathis, etc., Plaintiff v. St. Alexis Association, Inc., et al., Defendants, Cuyahoga County Common Pleas Court, Case No. 211807, which is hereby acknowledged, these parties, Mathis, through the covenant herein recited shall cease and desist from suing or pursuing any claims against St. Alexis Hospital Medical Center herein, arising from the medical care and treatment afforded to Mary J. Mathis, Deceased, by St. Alexis Hospital Medical Center, including its employees, nurses and house physicians, and this agreement and settlement covers and encompasses all such medical care and treatment rendered by St. Alexis Hospital Medical Center without restriction as to time and place."

On September 22, 1993, Mathis filed a medical malpractice action against Dr. Keyhan Mobasseri in connection with Mary Mathis' death. Mathis sought $25,000 in damages. On September 24, 1993, Mathis filed a wrongful death action against St. Alexis Hospital, Dr. Keyhan Mobasseri, Joseph Smith, D.O., and F.A. Greicius, M.D. & Associates, Inc. Mathis sought two million dollars in damages. In his complaint, Mathis asked the court to rescind the covenant not to sue. Mathis argued that, since St. Alexis was not entitled to recover attorney fees and costs from Mathis in connection with the prior action, there was no consideration for the covenant not to sue.

* * *

On December 30, 1993, St. Alexis . . . filed its own motion seeking summary judgment. St. Alexis claimed there was consideration for the covenant not to sue and that it should be upheld. Citing R.C. 2323.51, St. Alexis argued that an award of attorney fees may be made against a party, his counsel, or both. St. Alexis claimed Mathis engaged in frivolous conduct in the prior case by pursuing the earlier case without any expert medical testimony indicating that negligence by the defendants proximately caused Mary Mathis' death. Consequently, St. Alexis claimed, it had a reasonable belief in the validity of its claim for sanctions for frivolous conduct.

* * * On April 8, 1994, the trial court granted summary judgment for the defendants.

* * *

Mathis argued that the covenant not to sue was unsupported by sufficient consideration and was, consequently, non-binding. However, St. Alexis argued that the consideration for the covenant not to sue was St. Alexis' agreement not to file a motion for attorney fees incurred in the defense of Mathis' previously dismissed action.

A covenant not to sue is governed by the same principles as a contract and must meet all requirements for a valid contract, including consideration. [Citation.] A promise not to prosecute a valid claim may be valuable consideration, where the promisor has the right to sue on the claim and the claim is valid. [Citation.]

Mathis argued that St. Alexis did not have a valid claim for sanctions against the plaintiffs. Mathis argued that any sanctions award should have been against Mathis' attorney. Mathis argued that since St. Alexis had no claim against Mathis, St. Alexis' promise to forbear prosecution of its claim was not sufficient consideration for Mathis' promise not to sue St. Alexis for medical negligence.

St. Alexis' proposed claim for sanctions was under * * * R.C. 2323.51.

* * *

R.C. 2323.51 provides:

"(B) (1) * * * [A]t any time prior to the commencement of the trial in a civil action or within twenty-one days after the entry of judgment in a civil action, the court may award reasonable attorney's fees to any party to that action adversely affected by frivolous conduct."

According[ly] . . ., sanctions could have been awarded against Mathis. Mathis argued that St. Alexis has not shown that Mathis engaged in any frivolous conduct. However, we must note that the standard for evaluating the validity of the forborne claim is a subjective one. [Citation.] A promise to forbear pursuit of a legal claim can be sufficient consideration to support a contract when the promisor has a good faith belief in the validity of the claim. [Citation.]

"The modern trend of authority is to move still further away from an objective view of the actual validity of the surrendered claim and to focus primarily on whether the claimant's subjective belief in its legitimacy is honest and sincere; the only remnants of an objective standard are that the asserted claim must not be 'frivolous, vexatious, or unlawful' and that asserted good faith belief 'would affront the intelligence of ordinary and reasonable layman.' Compared to the first cases on the subject, the most recent ones clearly require a minimal degree of objective certainty in the existent validity of the surrendered claim." [Citation.]

We find that St. Alexis sufficiently asserted a good faith belief in the validity of its sanctions claim. In its motion for summary judgment and brief in opposition to Mathis' motion for summary judgment, St. Alexis asserted that its belief in the validity of its sanctions claim was based on Mathis' complete failure to produce any expert testimony on the issue of proximate cause. The only expert testimony presented on the issue indicated that St. Alexis' actions did not proximately cause Mary Mathis' death. St. Alexis' belief in the validity of its sanctions claim was reasonable. * * *

Because St. Alexis went forward with sufficient evidence of a valid covenant not to sue, and Mathis failed to raise any triable issues with respect to its validity, the trial court properly granted summary judgment for St. Alexis.

Judgment affirmed.

---

## CASE 12–3
## Preexisting Obligation
### DENNEY v. REPPERT
Court of Appeals of Kentucky, 1968
432 S.W.2d 647

MYRE, SPECIAL COMMISSIONER.
The sole question presented in this case is which of several claimants is entitled to an award for information leading to the apprehension and conviction of certain bank robbers.

* * *

On June 12th or 13th, 1963, three armed men entered the First State Bank, Eubank, Kentucky, and with a display of arms and threats robbed the bank of over $30,000. Later in the day they were apprehended by

State Policemen Garret Godby, Johnny Simms, and Tilford Reppert, placed under arrest, and the entire loot was recovered. Later all of the prisoners were convicted and Garret Godby, Johnny Simms, and Tilford Reppert appeared as witnesses at the trial.

The First State Bank of Eubank was a member of the Kentucky Bankers Association which provided and advertised a reward of $500.00 for the arrest and conviction of each bank robber. Hence the outstanding reward for the three bank robbers was $1,500.00. Many became claimants for the reward and the Kentucky State Bankers Association, being unable to determine the merits of the claims for the reward, asked the circuit court to determine the merits of the various claims and to adjudge who was entitled to receive the reward or share in it. All of the claimants were made defendants in the action.

At the time of the robbery the claimants Murrell Denney, Joyce Buis, Rebecca McCollum, and Jewell Snyder were employees of the First State Bank of Eubank and came out of the grueling situation with great credit and glory. Each one of them deserves approbation and an accolade. They were vigilant in disclosing to the public and the peace officers the details of the crime, and in describing the culprits, and giving all the information that they possessed that would be useful in capturing the robbers. Undoubtedly, they performed a great service. It is in the evidence that the claimant Murrell Denney was conspicuous and energetic in his efforts to make known the robbery, to acquaint the officers as to the personal appearance of the criminals, and to give other pertinent facts.

The first question for determination is whether the employees of the robbed bank are eligible to receive or share in the reward. The great weight of authority answers in the negative. *In Re Waggoner* [citation] states the rule thusly:

To the general rule that, when a reward is offered to the general public for the performance of some specified act, such reward may be claimed by any person who performs such act, is the exception of agents, employees, and public officials who are acting within the scope of their employment or official duties. . . .

Or, as the rule was set forth in *Forsythe v. Murnane et al.,* [citation]:

. . . The defendant Delaney is and during all the times herein mentioned has been, employed by defendant Great Northern Railway Company . . . and by virtue of such employment it was his duty to do and perform all the things that were done and performed by him in the matter of the arrest, identification, and prosecution. . . .

It is clear that defendant Delaney is not, in view of . . . his contractual relations and the duties in the premises . . . entitled to any part of the reward. . . .

In *Stacy v. President, etc., of State Bank of Ill.* [citation] it was held that a director of a bank was not entitled to share in the reward offered by the bank for the arrest of a robber because it was his duty as a director to further the best interests of the bank, and apprehending one who had robbed the bank was in the best interest of the bank. [Citations.]

At the time of the robbery the claimants Murrell Denney, Joyce Buis, Rebecca McCollum, and Jewell Snyder were employees of the First State Bank of Eubank. They were under duty to protect and conserve the resources and moneys of the bank, and safeguard every interest of the institution furnishing them employment. Each of these employees exhibited great courage and cool bravery, in a time of stress and danger. The community and the county have recompensed them in commendation, admiration, and high praise, and the world looks on them as heroes. But in making known the robbery and assisting in acquainting the public and the officers with details of the crime and with identification of the robbers, they performed a duty to the bank and the public, for which they cannot claim a reward.

The claims of Corbin Reynolds, Julia Reynolds, Alvie Reynolds, and Gene Reynolds also must fail. According to their statements they gave valuable information to the arresting officers. However, they did not follow the procedure as set forth in the offer of reward in that they never filed a claim with the Kentucky Bankers Association. It is well established that a claimant of a reward must comply with the terms and conditions of the offer of reward. [Citation.]

State Policemen Garret Godby, Johnny Simms, and Tilford Reppert made the arrest of the bank robbers and captured the stolen money. All participated in the prosecution. At the time of the arrest, it was the duty of the state policemen to apprehend the criminals. Under the law they cannot claim or share in the reward and they are interposing no claim to it.

This leaves the defendant, Tilford Reppert the sole eligible claimant. The record shows that at the time of the arrest he was a deputy sheriff in Rockcastle County, but the arrest and recovery of the stolen money took place in Pulaski County. He was out of his jurisdiction, and was thus under no legal duty to make the arrest, and is thus eligible to claim and receive the reward. In *Kentucky Bankers Ass'n et al. v. Cassady* [citation], it was said:

It is . . . well established that a public officer with the authority of the law to make an arrest may accept an offer of reward or compensation for acts or services performed outside of his bailiwick or not within the scope of his official duties. . . .

The claimant Tilford Reppert was present with Garret Godby and Johnny Simms at the time of the arrest and all cooperated in its consummation. The claimant Tilford Reppert personally recovered the stolen money. He recovered $2,000.00 more than the bank records show was stolen. This record does not reveal what became of the $2,000.00 excess.

It is manifest from the record that Tilford Reppert is the only claimant qualified and eligible to receive the reward. Therefore, it is the judgment of the circuit court that he is entitled to receive payment of the $1,500.00 reward now deposited with the clerk of this court.

The judgment is affirmed.

---

## CASE 12–4
### Modification of a Preexisting Contract
# GROSS v. DIEHL SPECIALTIES INTERNATIONAL, INC.

Missouri Court of Appeals, 1989
776 S.W.2d 879

SMITH, J.

Plaintiff [Gross] appeals from a jury verdict and resultant judgment for defendant in a breach of employment contract case. . . .

Plaintiff was employed under a fifteen year employment contract originally executed in 1977 between plaintiff and defendant. Defendant, at that time called Dairy Specialties, Inc., was a company in the business of formulating ingredients to produce non-dairy products for use by customers allergic to cow's milk. The owner of the company, Harry Schenberg, had produced such a product but the formulation was unable to withstand pasteurization by the customers to whom it was sold for processing and packaging for retail distribution. Schenberg requested plaintiff's technical assistance in formulating the product, Vitamite, for commercial usage. Plaintiff successfully reformulated the product for that usage.

Thereafter, on August 24, 1977, plaintiff and defendant corporation entered into an employment contract employing plaintiff as general manager of defendant for fifteen years. Compensation was established at $14,400 annually plus cost of living increases. In addition, when 10% of defendant's gross profits exceeded the annual salary, plaintiff would receive an additional amount of compensation equal to the difference between his compensation and 10% of the gross profits for such year. On top of that plaintiff was to receive a royalty for the use of each of his inventions and formulae of 1% of the selling price of all of the products produced by defendant using one or more of plaintiff's inventions or formulae during the term of the agreement. That amount was increased to 2% of the selling price following the term of the agreement. The contract further provided that during the term of the agreement the inventions and formulae would be owned equally by plaintiff and defendant and that following the term of the agreement the ownership would revert to plaintiff. During the term of the agreement defendant had exclusive rights to use of the inventions and formulae and after the term of agreement a non-exclusive right of use.

At the time of the execution of the contract, sales had risen from virtually nothing in 1976 to $750,000 annually from sales of Vitamite and a chocolate flavored product formulated by plaintiff called Chocolite. Schenberg was in declining health and in 1982 desired to sell his company. At that time yearly sales were $7,500,000. Schenberg sold the company to the Diehl family enterprises for 3 million dollars.

Prior to sale Diehl insisted that a new contract between plaintiff and defendant be executed or Diehl would substantially reduce the amount to be paid for defendant. A new contract was executed August 24, 1982. It reduced the expressed term of the contract to 10 years, which provided the same expiration date as the prior contract. It maintained the same base salary of $14,400 effective September 1982, thereby eliminating any cost of living increases incurred since the original contract. The 10% of gross profit provision remained the same. The new contract provided that plaintiff's inventions and formulae were exclusively owned by defendant during the term of the contract and after its termination. The 1% royalty during the term of the agreement remained the same, but no royalties were provided for after the term of the agreement. No other changes were made in the agreement. Plaintiff received no compensation for executing the new contract. He was not a party to the sale of the company by Schenberg and received nothing tangible from that sale.

After the sale plaintiff was given the title and responsibilities of president of defendant with additional duties but no additional compensation. In 1983 and 1984 the business of the company declined severely and in October 1984, plaintiff's employment with defendant was terminated by defendant. This suit followed.

* * *

We turn now to the [trial] court's holding that the 1982 agreement was the operative contract. Plaintiff contends this holding is erroneous because there existed no consideration for the 1982 agreement. We agree. A modification of a contract constitutes the making of a new contract and such new contract must be supported by consideration. [Citation.] Where a contract has not been fully performed at the time of the new agreement, the substitution of a new provision, resulting in a modification of the obligations on both sides, for a provision in the old contract still unperformed is sufficient consideration for the new contract. [Citation.] While consideration may consist of either a detriment to the promisee or a benefit to the promisor, a promise to carry out an already existing contractual duty does not constitute consideration. [Citation.]

Under the 1982 contract defendant assumed no detriment it did not already have. The term of the contract expired on the same date under both contracts. Defendant undertook no greater obligations than it already had. Plaintiff on the other hand received less than he had under the original contract. His base pay was reduced back to its amount in 1977 despite the provision in the 1977 contract for cost of living adjustments. He lost his equal ownership in his formulae during the term of the agreement and his exclusive ownership after the termination of the agreement. He lost all royalties after termination of the agreement and the right to use and license the formulae subject to defendant's right to non-exclusive use upon payment of royalties. In exchange for nothing, defendant acquired exclusive ownership of the formulae during and after the agreement, eliminated royalties after the agreement terminated, turned its non-exclusive use after termination into exclusive use and control, and achieved a reduction in plaintiff's base salary. Defendant did no more than promise to carry out an already existing contractual duty. There was no consideration for the 1982 agreement.

Defendant asserts that consideration flowed to plaintiff because the purchase of defendant by the Diehls might not have occurred without the agreement and the purchase provided plaintiff with continued employment and a financially viable employer. There is no evidence to support this contention. Plaintiff had continued employment with the same employer under the 1977 agreement. Nothing in the 1982 agreement provided for any additional financial protection to plaintiff. The essence of defendant's position is that Schenberg received more from his sale of the company because of the new agreement than he would have without it. We have difficulty converting Schenberg's windfall into a benefit to plaintiff.

The trial court erred in holding that the 1982 contract was the operative contract. * * * That erroneous ruling . . . requires us to reverse the judgment [on Count II and Count III] and remand for further proceedings to determine the formulae for which plaintiff is entitled to royalties from defendant and the amount thereof.

We must also remand [to determine the amount of compensation to which the plaintiff was entitled under the 1977 contract].

 # Questions

1. Define consideration and what is meant by legal sufficiency.

2. Discuss illusory promises, output contracts, requirements contracts, exclusive dealing contracts, and conditional contracts.

3. Explain whether preexisting public and contractual obligations satisfy the legal requirement of consideration.

4. Explain the concept of bargained-for exchange. Is this element present with past consideration or third-party beneficiaries? Explain.

5. Identify and discuss those contracts that are enforceable even though they are not supported by consideration.

# Problems

**1.** In consideration of $800 paid to him by Joyce, Hill gave Joyce a written option to purchase his house for $80,000 on or before April 1. Prior to April 1, Hill verbally agreed to extend the option until July 1. On May 18, Hill, known to Joyce, sold the house to Gray, who was ignorant of the unrecorded option. Joyce brought suit against Hill. Decision?

**2.**   (a)   Ann owed $500 to Barry for services Barry rendered to Ann. The debt was due June 30, 1991. In March 1992, the debt was still unpaid. Barry was in urgent need of ready cash and told Ann that if she would pay $150 of the debt at once, Barry would release her from the balance. Ann paid $150 and stated to Barry that all claims had been paid in full. In August 1992, Barry demanded the unpaid balance and subsequently sued Ann for $350. Decision?

(b)   Modify the facts in (a) by assuming that Barry gave Ann a written receipt stating that all claims had been paid in full. Result?

(c)   Modify the facts in (a) by assuming that Ann owed Barry the $500 on Ann's purchase of a motorcycle from Barry. Result?

**3.**   (a)   Judy orally promises her daughter, Liza, that she will give her a tract of land for her home. Liza, as intended by Judy, gives up her homestead and takes possession of the land. Liza lives there for six months and starts construction of a home. Is Judy bound to convey the real estate?

(b)   Ralph, knowing that his son, Ed, desires to purchase a tract of land, promises to give him the $25,000 he needs for the purchase. Ed, relying on this promise, buys an option on the tract of land. Ralph now seeks to rescind his promise. Decision?

**4.** George owed Keith $800 on a personal loan. Neither the amount of the debt nor George's liability to pay the $800 was disputed. Keith had also rendered services as a carpenter to George without any agreement as to the price to be paid. When the work was completed, an honest and reasonable difference of opinion developed between George and Keith with respect to the value of Keith's services. Upon receiving from Keith a bill of $600 for the carpentry services, George mailed in a properly stamped and addressed envelope his check for $800 to Keith. In an accompanying letter, George stated that the enclosed check was in full settlement of both claims. Keith indorsed and cashed the check. Thereafter, Keith unsuccessfully sought to collect from George an alleged unpaid balance of $600. Keith then sued George for $600. Decision?

**5.** The Snyder Mfg. Co., being a large user of coal, entered into separate contracts with several coal companies. In each contract it was agreed that the coal company would supply coal during the year 1999 in such amounts as the manufacturing company might desire to order, at a price of $49 per ton. In February 1999, the Snyder Company ordered 1,000 tons of coal from Union Coal Company, one of the contracting parties.

Union Coal Company delivered 500 tons of the order and then notified Snyder Company that no more deliveries would be made and that it denied any obligation under the contract. In an action by Union Coal to collect $49 per ton for the 500 tons of coal delivered, Snyder files a counterclaim, claiming damages of $1,500 for failure to deliver the additional 500 tons of the order and damages of $4,000 for breach of agreement to deliver coal during the balance of the year. Decision?

**6.** On February 5, Devon entered into a written agreement with Gordon whereby Gordon agreed to drill a well on Devon's property for the sum of $5,000 and to complete the well on or before April 15. Before entering into the contract, Gordon made test borings and had satisfied himself as to the character of the subsurface. After two days of drilling, Gordon struck hard rock. On February 17, Gordon removed his equipment and advised Devon that the project had proved unprofitable and that he would not continue. On March 17, Devon went to Gordon and told Gordon that he would assume the risk of the enterprise and would pay Gordon $100 for each day required to drill the well, as compensation for labor, the use of Gordon's equipment, and Gordon's services in supervising the work, provided Gordon would furnish certain special equipment designed to cut through hard rock. Gordon said that the proposal was satisfactory. The work was continued by Gordon and completed in an additional fifty-eight days. Upon completion of the work, Devon failed to pay, and Gordon brought an action to recover $5,800. Devon answered that he had never become obligated to pay $100 a day and filed a counterclaim for damages in the amount of $500 for the month's delay based on an alleged breach of contract by Gordon. Decision?

**7.** Discuss and explain whether there is valid consideration for each of the following promises:

(a)   A and B entered into a contract for the purchase and sale of goods. A subsequently promised to pay a higher price for the goods when B refused to deliver at the contract price.

(b)   A promised in writing to pay a debt, which was due from B to C, on C's agreement to extend the time of payment for one year.

(c)   A executed a promissory note to her son, B, solely in consideration of past services rendered to A by B, for which there had been no agreement or request to pay.

**8.** Alan purchased shoes from Barbara on open account. Barbara sent Alan a bill for $10,000. Alan wrote back that 200 pairs of the shoes were defective and offered to pay $6,000 and give Barbara his promissory note for $1,000. Barbara accepted the offer, and Alan sent his check for $6,000 and his note, in accordance with the agreement. Barbara cashed the check, collected on the note, and one month later sued Alan for $3,000. Decision?

9.    Nancy owed Sharon $1,500, but Sharon did not initiate a lawsuit to collect the debt within the time prescribed by the statute of limitations. Nevertheless, Nancy promises Sharon that she will pay the barred debt. Thereafter, Nancy refuses to pay. Sharon brings suit to collect on this new promise. Decision?

10.    Anthony lends money to Frank. Frank dies without having paid the loan. Frank's widow, Carol, promises Anthony to repay the loan. Upon Carol's refusal to pay the loan, Anthony brings suit against Carol for payment of the loan. Decision?

11.    The parties entered into an oral contract in June 1969, under which plaintiff agreed to construct a building for defendant on a time and materials basis, at a maximum cost of $56,146, plus sales tax and extras ordered by defendant. When the building was 90 percent completed, defendant told plaintiff he was unhappy with the whole job as "the thing just wasn't being run right." The parties then on October 17 signed a written agreement lowering the maximum cost to $52,000 plus sales tax. Plaintiff thereafter completed the building at a cost of $64,155. The maximum under the June oral agreement, plus extras and sales tax, totalled $61,040. Defendant contended that he was obligated to pay only the lower maximum fixed by the October 17 agreement. Decision?

12.    Taylor assaulted his wife, who then took refuge in Ms. Harrington's house. The next day, Mr. Taylor entered the house and began another assault on his wife, who knocked him down and, while he was lying on the floor, attempted to cut his head open or decapitate him with an axe. Harrington intervened to stop the bloodshed, and the axe, as it was descending, fell upon her hand, mutilating it badly, but sparing Taylor his life. Afterwards, Taylor orally promised to compensate Harrington for her injury. He paid a small sum but nothing more. Harrington sued to enforce Taylor's promise. Decision?

13.    Jonnel Enterprises, Inc., contracted to construct a student dormitory at Clarion State College. On May 6, Jonnel entered into a written agreement with Graham and Long as electrical contractors to perform the electrical work and to supply materials for the dormitory. The contract price was $70,544.66. Graham and Long claim that they believed the May 6 agreement obligated them to perform the electrical work on only one wing of the building, but that three or four days after work was started, a second wing of the building was found to be in need of wiring. At that time Graham and Long informed Jonnel that they would not wire both wings of the building under the present contract, so a new contract was orally agreed upon by the parties. Under the new contract Graham and Long were obligated to wire both wings and were to be paid only $65,000, but they were relieved of the obligations to supply entrances and a heating system. Graham and Long resumed their work, and Jonnel made seven of the eight progress payments called for. When Jonnel did not pay the final payment, Graham and Long brought this action. Jonnel claims that the May 6 contract is controlling. Decision?

14.    Baker entered into an oral agreement with Healey, the State distributor of Ballantine & Sons liquor products, that Ballantine would supply Baker with its products on demand and that Baker would have the exclusive agency for Ballantine within a certain area of Connecticut. Shortly thereafter the agreement was modified to give Baker the right to terminate at will. Eight months later, when Ballantine & Sons revoked its agency, Baker sued to enforce the oral agreement. Decision?

15.    PLM, Inc. entered into an oral agreement with Quaintance Associates, an executive "headhunter" service, for the recruitment of qualified candidates to be employed by PLM. As agreed, PLM's obligation to pay Quaintance did not depend on PLM's actually hiring a qualified candidate presented by Quaintance. After several months Quaintance sent a letter to PLM, admitting that it had so far failed to produce a suitable candidate, but included a bill for $9,806.61, covering fees and expenses. PLM responded that Quaintance's services were only worth $6,060.48, and that payment of the lesser amount was the only fair way to handle the dispute. Accordingly, PLM enclosed a check for $6,060.48, writing on the back of the check "IN FULL PAYMENT OF ANY CLAIMS QUAINTANCE HAS AGAINST PLM, INC." Quaintance cashed the check and then sued PLM for the remaining $3,746.13. Decision?

16.    Red Owl Stores told the Hoffman family that, upon the payment of approximately $18,000, a grocery store franchise would be built for them in a new location. Upon the advice of Red Owl, the Hoffmans bought a small grocery store in their hometown in order to get management experience. After the Hoffmans operated at a profit for three months, Red Owl advised them to sell the small grocery, assuring them that Red Owl would find them a larger store elsewhere. Although selling at that point would cost them much profit, the Hoffmans followed Red Owl's directions. In addition, to raise the money required for the deal, the Hoffmans sold their bakery business in their hometown. The Hoffmans also sold their house, and moved to a new home in the city where their new store was to be located. Red Owl then informed the Hoffmans that it would take $24,100, not $18,000, to complete the deal. The family scrambled to find the additional funds. However, when told by Red Owl that it would now cost them $34,000 to get their new franchise, the Hoffmans decided to sue instead. Decision?

17.    Plaintiff, Brenner, entered into a contract with the defendant, Little Red School House, Ltd., which stated that in return for a nonrefundable tuition of $1,080 Brenner's son could attend defendant's school for a year. When Brenner's ex-wife refused to enroll their son, plaintiff sought and received a verbal promise of a refund. Defendant now refuses to refund plaintiff's money for lack of consideration. Decision?

18.    Ben Collins was a full professor with tenure at Wisconsin State University in 1996. In March 1996 Parsons College, in an attempt to lure Dr. Collins from Wisconsin State, offered him a written contract promising him the rank of full professor with tenure and a salary of $55,000 for the 1996–97 academic year. The contract further provided that the College would increase his salary by $2,000 each year for the next five years.

In return, Collins was to teach two trimesters of the academic year beginning in October 1996. In addition, the contract stipulated, by reference to the College's faculty bylaws, that tenured professors could only be dismissed for just cause and after written charges were filed with the Professional Problems Committee. The two parties signed the contract, and Collins resigned his position at Wisconsin State.

In February 1998, the College tendered a different contract to Collins to cover the following year. This contract reduced his salary to $45,000 with no provision for annual increments, but left his rank of full professor intact. It also required that Collins waive any and all rights or claims existing under any previous employment contracts with the College. Collins refused to sign this new contract and Parsons College soon notified him that he would not be employed the following year. The College did not give any grounds for his dismissal; nor did it file charges with the Professional Problems Committee. As a result, Collins was forced to take a teaching position at the University of North Dakota at a substantially reduced salary. He sued to recover the difference between the salary Parsons College promised him until 2001 and the amount he earned. The trial court ruled in favor of Parsons College, and Collins appealed. Decision?

**19.** Anna Feinberg began working for the Pfeiffer Company in 1950 at age 17. By 1987 she had attained the position of bookkeeper, office manager, and assistant treasurer. In appreciation for her skill, dedication, and long years of service, the Pfeiffer Board of Directors resolved to increase Feinberg's monthly salary to $1,400 and to create for her a retirement plan. The plan allowed that Feinberg would be given the privilege of retiring from active duty at any time she chose and that she would receive retirement pay of $700 per month, although the Board expressed the hope that Feinberg would continue to serve the company for many years. Feinberg, however, chose to retire two years later, in 1989. The Pfeiffer Company paid Feinberg her retirement pay until 1996. The company discontinued payments, alleging that no contract had been made by the Board of Directors as there had been no consideration paid by Feinberg, and that the resolution was merely a promise to make a gift. Feinberg sued. Decision?

WWW **Internet Exercise** Find several contracts and determine what consideration is given by the parties.

# CHAPTER 13

# Illegal Bargains

An essential requirement of a binding promise or agreement is legality of objective. When the formation or performance of an agreement is criminal, tortious, or otherwise contrary to public policy, the agreement is illegal and **unenforceable** (as opposed to being void). The law does not provide a remedy for the breach of an unenforceable agreement and thus "leaves the parties where it finds them." It is preferable to use the term *illegal bargain* or *illegal agreement* rather than *illegal contract,* because the word *contract,* by definition, denotes a legal and enforceable agreement. The illegal bargain is made unenforceable (1) to discourage such undesirable conduct and (2) to preclude the inappropriate use of the judicial process in carrying out such socially undesirable bargains.

The Restatement avoids defining the term *illegal bargain,* instead focusing upon whether public policy should bar enforcement of the agreement. By relying upon the concept of public policy, the Restatement provides the courts with greater flexibility in determining the enforceability of questioned agreements by weighing the strength of legally recognized policies against the effect that declaring a particular bargain to be against public policy would have on the contracting parties and on the public.

This chapter will discuss (a) agreements in violation of a statute, (b) agreements contrary to public policy, and (c) the effect of illegality upon agreements.

## VIOLATIONS OF STATUTES

The courts will not enforce an agreement declared illegal by statute. For example, wagering or gambling contracts are specifically declared unenforceable in most States. In addition, an agreement to violate a statute prohibiting crimes, such as murder, robbery, embezzlement, forgery, and price fixing, is unenforceable. Likewise, an agreement that is induced by criminal conduct will not

be enforced. For example, if Alice enters into an agreement with Brent Co. through the bribing of Brent Co.'s purchasing agent, the agreement would be unenforceable.

## Licensing Statutes

Every jurisdiction has laws requiring a license for those who engage in certain trades, professions, or businesses. Common examples are licensing statutes which apply to lawyers, doctors, dentists, accountants, brokers, plumbers, and contractors. Some licensing statutes mandate schooling and/or examination, while others require only financial responsibility and/or good moral character. Whether or not a person may recover for services rendered if he has failed to comply with a licensing requirement depends upon the terms or type of licensing statute. This rule pertains only to the rights of the unlicensed party to enforce the obligations of the other party.

The statute itself may expressly provide that an unlicensed person engaged in a business or profession for which a license is required shall not recover for services rendered. Absent such statutory provision, the courts commonly distinguish between those statutes or ordinances that are **regulatory** in character and those that are enacted merely to raise **revenue** through the issuance of licenses. If the statute is regulatory, a person cannot recover for professional services unless he has the required license, as long as the public policy behind the regulatory purpose clearly outweighs the person's interest in being paid for his services. Restatement, Section 181. Some courts have gone further by balancing the penalty the unlicensed party suffers against the benefit the other party receives. In contrast, if the law is for revenue purposes only, agreements for such services are enforceable.

A regulatory license, including those issued under statutes prescribing standards for those wishing to practice law or medicine, is a measure designed to protect the public against unqualified persons. A revenue license, on the other hand, does not seek to protect against incompetent or unqualified practitioners but simply to furnish revenue. An example is a statute requiring a license of plumbers but not establishing standards of competence for those who seek to follow the trade. The courts regard such legislation as a taxing measure lacking any expression of legislative intent to preclude unlicensed plumbers from enforcing their business contracts.

## Gambling Statutes

In a **wager** the parties stipulate that one shall win and the other lose depending upon the outcome of an event in which their sole "interest" arises from the possibility of such gain or loss. All States have legislation pertaining to gambling or wagering, and U.S. courts generally refuse to recognize the enforceability of a gambling agreement. Thus, if Arnold makes a bet with Bernice on the outcome of a ball game, the agreement is unenforceable by either party. Some States, however, now permit certain kinds of regulated gambling. Wagering conducted by governmental agencies, principally State-operated lotteries, has come to constitute an increasingly important source of public revenues.

To be distinguished from wagers are ordinary insurance contracts in which the insured, having an "insurable interest" (discussed in Chapter 48), pays a certain sum of money or premium in exchange for an insurance company's promise to pay a larger amount upon the occurrence of some event, such as a fire, which causes loss to the insured. Here, the agreement compensates for loss under an existing risk; it does not create an entirely new risk. In a wager, the parties contemplate gain through mere chance, whereas in an insurance contract they seek to distribute possible loss. Furthermore, most games at fast-food restaurants and grocery store drawings have been upheld because the participants need not make a purchase to be eligible for the prize.

## Usury Statutes

A **usury statute** is a law establishing a maximum rate of permissible interest for which a lender and borrower of money may contract. Though, historically, every State had a usury law, a recent trend has been to limit or relax usury statutes. The maximum rates permitted vary greatly from State to State and among types of transactions. These statutes typically are general in their application,

although certain specified types of transactions are exempted. For example, numerous States impose no limit on the rate of interest that may be charged on loans to corporations. Furthermore, some States permit the parties to contract for any rate of interest on loans made to individual proprietorships or partnerships for the purpose of carrying on a business.

In addition to the exceptions accorded certain designated types of borrowers, a number of States have exempted specific lenders. For example, the majority of the States have enacted installment loan laws, which permit eligible lenders a return on installment loans that is higher than the applicable general interest statute would permit. These *specific* lender usury statutes, which have all but eliminated general usury statutes, vary greatly but generally have included small consumer loans, corporate loans, loans by small lenders, real estate mortgages, and numerous other transactions.

For a transaction to be usurious, courts usually require evidence of the following factors: (a) a loan or forbearance (b) of money (c) which is repayable absolutely and in all events (d) for which an interest charge is exacted in excess of the interest rate allowed by law. Transactions that are really loans may not be clothed with the trappings of a sale for the purpose of avoiding the usury laws.

*See Case 13–1*

The legal effect to be given a usurious loan varies from State to State. In a few States, the lender forfeits both principal and interest. In some jurisdictions, the lender can recover the principal but forfeits all interest. In other States, only that portion of interest exceeding the permitted maximum is forfeited. In several States, the amount forfeited is a multiple (double or treble) of the interest charged. Disposition of usurious interest already paid also varies. Some States do not allow any recovery of usurious interest paid; others allow recovery of such interest or a multiple of it.

## Sunday Statutes

In the absence of a statutory prohibition, the common law does not prohibit entering into contracts on Sunday. Some States, however, have legislation, referred to as **Blue Laws,** modifying this common law rule and prohibiting certain types of commercial activity on Sunday. Even in a State which prohibits contracts on Sunday, a court nonetheless will enforce a subsequent weekday ratification of a loan made on Sunday or a promise to pay for goods sold and delivered on Sunday. In addition,

Blue Laws usually do not apply to activities of "necessity" and "charity."

## VIOLATIONS OF PUBLIC POLICY

The reach of a statute may extend beyond its language. Sometimes, the courts, by analogy, use the statute and the policy it seeks to serve as a guide in determining the private contract rights of one harmed by a violation of the statute. In addition, the courts must frequently articulate the "public policy" of the State without significant help from statutory sources. This judicially declared public policy is very broad in scope, it often being said that agreements having "a tendency to be injurious to the public or the public good" are contrary to public policy. Thus, the term *public policy* eludes precise definition. Contracts raising questions of public policy include agreements that (1) restrain trade, (2) exempt or exculpate a party from liability for his own tortious conduct, (3) are unconscionable, (4) involve tortious conduct, (5) tend to obstruct the administration of justice, (6) tend to corrupt public officials or impair the legislative process, or (7) impair family relationships. This section will focus on the first four of these types of agreements.

### Common Law Restraint of Trade

A **restraint of trade** is any contract or agreement that eliminates or tends to eliminate competition or otherwise obstructs trade or commerce. One type of restraint is a **covenant not to compete,** which is an agreement to refrain from entering into a competing trade, profession, or business.

An agreement to refrain from a particular trade, profession, or business is enforceable if (1) the purpose of the restraint is to protect a property interest of the promisee and (2) the restraint is no more extensive than is reasonably necessary to protect that interest. Restraints typically arise in two situations: the sale of a business and employment contracts.

*Sale of a Business* As part of an agreement to sell a business, the seller frequently promises not to compete in that particular type of business in a *defined area* for a stated *time*. To protect the business's goodwill (an asset that the buyer has purchased), the buyer must be allowed to enforce such a covenant (promise) by the seller not to compete with the purchaser within reasonable limitations. Most litigation on this subject has involved the requirement that the restraint be no greater than is

reasonably necessary. Whether the restraint is reasonable or not depends on the geographic area it covers, the time period for which it is to be effective, and the hardship it imposes on the promisor and the public.

For example, the promise of a person selling a service station business in Detroit not to enter the service station business in Michigan for the next twenty-five years is unreasonable, both as to area and time. The business interest to be protected would not include the entire State, so it is not necessary to the protection of the purchaser that the seller be prevented from engaging in the service station business in the entire State or perhaps, for that matter, in the entire city of Detroit. Limiting the area to the neighborhood in which the station is located or to a radius of a few miles would probably be adequate.

The same type of inquiry must be made about time limitations. In the sale of a service station, a twenty-five-year ban on competition from the seller would be unreasonable; a one-year ban probably would not. The court, in determining what is reasonable under particular circumstances, must consider each case on its own facts.

*Employment Contracts* Salespeople, management personnel, and other employees frequently are required to sign employment contracts prohibiting them from competing with their employers during their time of employment and for some additional stated period after termination. The same is also frequently true among corporations or partnerships involving professionals, such as accountants, lawyers, investment brokers, stockbrokers, or doctors. Although the courts readily enforce a covenant not to compete during the period of employment, the promise not to compete after termination is subjected to an even stricter test of reasonableness than that applied to noncompetition promises included in a contract for the sale of a business. One reason for this is that the employer is in a stronger bargaining position than the employee.

A court order enjoining a former employee from competing in a described territory for a stated time is the usual method by which an employer seeks to enforce the employee's promise not to compete. Before granting such injunctions, the courts insist that the employer demonstrate that the restriction is *necessary* to protect his legitimate interests, such as trade secrets or customer lists. Because issuing the injunction may place the employee out of work, the courts must carefully balance the public policy favoring the employer's right to protect his business interests against the public policy favoring full opportunity for individuals to gain employment.

Thus, one court has held unreasonable a covenant in a contract requiring a travel agency employee, after termination of her employment, to refrain from engaging in a like business in any capacity in either of two named towns or within a sixty-mile radius of those towns for two years. There was no indication that the employee had enough influence over customers to cause them to move their business to her new agency, nor was it shown that any trade secrets were involved. *United Travel Service, Inc. v. Weber*, 108 Ill.App.2d 353, 247 N.E.2d 801 (1969). Instead of refusing to enforce an unreasonable covenant, some courts, considering the action justifiable under the circumstances of the case, will reform the agreement to make it reasonable and enforceable.

 *See Case 13–2*

## Exculpatory Clauses

Some contracts contain an **exculpatory clause** that excuses one party from liability for her own tortious conduct. The courts generally agree that exculpatory clauses relieving a person from tort liability for harm caused intentionally or recklessly are unenforceable as violating public policy. On the other hand, exculpatory clauses that excuse a party from liability for harm caused by negligent conduct are scrutinized carefully by the courts, which often require that the clause be conspicuously placed in the contract and clearly written. Accordingly, an exculpatory clause on the reverse side of a parking lot claim check, which attempts to relieve the parking lot operator of liability for negligently damaging the customer's automobile, will generally be held unenforceable as against public policy.

The Restatement provides that exculpatory clauses excusing negligent conduct are unenforceable on grounds of public policy if they exempt (1) an employer from liability to an employee, (2) a public service business (such as a common carrier) from liability to a customer, or (3) a person from liability to a party who is a member of a protected class. Restatement, Section 195.

A similar rule applies to a contractual provision unreasonably exempting a party from the legal consequences of a misrepresentation. Restatement, Section 196. Such a term is unenforceable on the grounds of public policy with respect to both fraudulent and nonfraudulent misrepresentations.

Further, where the superior bargaining position of one party has enabled him to impose upon the other party such a provision, the courts are inclined to nullify the provision. Such a situation may arise in residential leases exempting a landlord from liability for his negligence. Moreover, an exculpatory clause may be unenforceable for unconscionability.

 *See Case 13–3*

## Unconscionable Contracts

The court may scrutinize every contract of sale to determine whether it is, in its commercial setting, purpose, and effect, **unconscionable.** The court may refuse to enforce an unconscionable contract in its entirety or any part it finds to be unconscionable. Section 2–302 of the UCC provides:

If the court as a matter of law finds the contract or any clause of the contract to have been unconscionable at the time it was made the court may refuse to enforce the contract, or it may enforce the remainder of the contract without the unconscionable clause, or it may so limit the application of any unconscionable clause as to avoid any unconscionable result.

Similarly, Section 208 of the Restatement provides:

If a contract or term thereof is unconscionable at the time the contract is made a court may refuse to enforce the contract, or may enforce the remainder of the contract without the unconscionable term, or may so limit the application of any unconscionable term as to avoid any unconscionable result.

Neither the Code nor the Restatement defines the word *unconscionable;* however, the *New Webster's Dictionary* (Deluxe Encyclopedic Edition) defines the term as "contrary to the dictates of conscience; unscrupulous or unprincipled; exceeding that which is reasonable or customary; inordinate, unjustifiable."

The doctrine of unconscionability has been justified on the basis that it permits the courts to resolve issues of unfairness explicitly as regards that unfairness without recourse to formalistic rules or legal fictions. In policing contracts for fairness, the courts have again demonstrated their willingness to limit freedom of contract to protect the less advantaged from overreaching by dominant contracting parties. The doctrine of unconscionability has evolved through its application by the courts to include both procedural and substantive unconscionability.

**Procedural unconscionability** involves scrutiny for the presence of "bargaining naughtiness." In other words, was the negotiation process fair, or were there procedural irregularities, such as burying important terms of the agreement in fine print or obscuring the true meaning of the contract with impenetrable legal jargon?

**Substantive unconscionability,** which involves the actual terms of the contract, consists of oppressive or grossly unfair provisions, such as an exorbitant price or an unfair exclusion or limitation of contractual remedies. An all-too-common example is that involving a necessitous buyer in an unequal bargaining position with a seller, who consequently obtains an exorbitant price for his product or service. In one case, a court held unconscionable a price of $749 ($920 on time) for a vacuum cleaner that cost the seller $140. In another case the buyers, welfare recipients, purchased by time payment contract a home freezer unit for $900 which, when added to time credit charges, credit life insurance, credit property insurance, and sales tax, amounted to $1,235. The purchase resulted from a visit to the buyer's home by a salesman representing Your Shop At Home Service, Inc.; the maximum retail value of the freezer unit at time of purchase was $300. The court held the contract unconscionable and reformed it by reducing the price to the total payment ($620) the buyers had managed to make.

Closely akin to the concept of unconscionability is the doctrine of contracts of adhesion. A standard-form contract prepared by one party, an **adhesion contract** generally involves the preparer's offering the other party the contract on a "take-it-or-leave-it" basis. Such contracts are not automatically unenforceable but are subject to greater scrutiny for procedural or substantive unconscionability.

 *See Case 13–4*

## Tortious Conduct

"A promise to commit a tort or to induce the commission of a tort is unenforceable on grounds of public policy." Restatement, Section 192. The courts will not permit contract law to violate the law of torts. Any agreement attempting to do so is considered contrary to public policy. For example, Andrew and Barlow Co. enter into an agreement under which Andrew promises Barlow that in return for $5,000 he will disparage the product of Barlow Co.'s competitor Cosmo, Inc. in order to provide Barlow Co. with a competitive advantage. Andrew's promise is to commit the tort of disparagement and is unenforceable as contrary to public policy.

## EFFECT OF ILLEGALITY

As a general rule, illegal contracts are unenforceable. In a few instances, however, one of the parties may be permitted to enforce all or part of the contract; whereas, under other circumstances, the courts will allow one party to recover in restitution for his performance of the illegal contract.

## General Rule: Unenforceability

In most cases when an agreement is illegal, neither party can successfully sue the other for breach or recover for any performance rendered. Whichever party is plaintiff is immaterial to the courts. As is frequently said in these cases, the court will leave the parties where it finds them.

## Exceptions

The courts recognize several exceptions to the general rule regarding the effect of illegality on a contract and may, after considering the circumstances surrounding a particular contract, grant relief to one of the parties, though not to the other. The following sections will consider these exceptions.

***Party Withdrawing before Performance*** A party to an illegal agreement may, prior to performance, withdraw from the transaction and recover whatever she has contributed, if the party has not engaged in serious misconduct. Restatement, Section 199. A common example is recovery of money left with a stakeholder pursuant to a wager before it is paid over to the winner.

***Party Protected by Statute*** Sometimes an agreement is illegal because it violates a statute designed to protect persons in the position of one of the parties. For example, State "Blue Sky Laws" prohibiting the sale of unregistered securities are designed primarily for the protection of investors. In such case, even though there is an unlawful agreement, the statute usually expressly gives the purchaser the right to rescind the sale and recover the money paid.

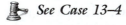 *See Case 13–4*

***Party Not Equally at Fault*** Where one of the parties is less at fault than the other, he will be allowed to recover payments made or property transferred. Restatement, Section 198. For example, this exception would apply where one party induces the other to enter into an illegal bargain through fraud, duress, or undue influence.

***Excusable Ignorance*** An agreement that appears on its face to be entirely permissible may, nevertheless, be illegal by reason of facts and circumstances of which one of the parties is completely unaware. For example, a man and woman make mutual promises to marry, but unknown to the woman, the man is already married. This is an agreement to commit the crime of bigamy, and the marriage, if entered into, is void. In such case the courts permit the party who is ignorant of the illegality to maintain a lawsuit against the other party for damages.

A party may also be excused for ignorance of relatively minor legislation. Restatement, Section 180. For instance, Jones and Old South Building Co. enter into a contract to build a factory that contains specifications in violation of the town's building ordinance. Jones did not know of the violation and had no reason to know. Old South's promise to build would not be rendered unen-

forceable on grounds of public policy, and Jones would have a claim against Old South for damages for breach of contract.

***Partial Illegality***   A contract may be partly unlawful and partly lawful. The courts view such a contract in one of two ways. First, the partial illegality may be held to taint the entire contract with illegality, so that it is wholly unenforceable. Second, it may be possible to separate the illegal from the legal part, in which case the court will hold the illegal part unenforceable but will enforce the legal part. For example, if a contract contains an illegal covenant not to compete, the covenant will not be enforced, though the rest of the contract may be.

---

 # Chapter Summary

| **Violations of Statutes** | **General Rule**  the courts will not enforce agreements declared illegal by statute |
|---|---|
| | **Licensing Statutes**  require formal authorization to engage in certain trades, professions, or businesses |
| | • *Regulatory License* licensing statute that is intended to protect the public against unqualified persons; an unlicensed person may not recover for services she has performed |
| | • *Revenue License* licensing statute that seeks to raise money; an unlicensed person may recover for services he has performed |
| | **Gambling Statutes**  prohibit wagers, which are agreements that one party will win and the other lose depending upon the outcome of an event in which their only interest is the gain or loss |
| | **Usury Statutes**  establish a maximum rate of interest |
| | **Sunday Statutes**  prohibition of certain types of commercial activity on Sunday (also called Blue Laws) |

| **Violations of Public Policy** | **Common Law Restraint of Trade**  unreasonable restraints of trade are not enforceable |
|---|---|
| | • *Sale of a Business* the promise by the seller of a business not to compete in that particular business in a reasonable geographic area for a reasonable period of time is enforceable |
| | • *Employment Contracts* an employment contract prohibiting an employee from competing with his employer for a reasonable period following termination is enforceable provided the restriction is necessary to protect legitimate interests of the employer |
| | **Exculpatory Clauses**  the courts generally disapprove of contractual provisions excusing a party from liability for her own tortious conduct |
| | **Unconscionable Contracts**  unfair or unduly harsh agreements are not enforceable |
| | • *Procedural Unconscionability* unfair or irregular bargaining |
| | • *Substantive Unconscionability* oppressive or grossly unfair contractual terms |
| | **Tortious Conduct**  an agreement that requires a person to commit a tort is unenforceable |
| | **Corrupting Public Officials**  agreements that corrupt public officials are not enforceable |

## Effect of Illegality

**Unenforceability** neither party may recover under an illegal agreement where both parties are *in pari delicto* (in equal fault)

**Exceptions** permit one party to recover payments
- *Party Withdrawing before Performance*
- *Party Protected by Statute*
- *Party Not Equally at Fault*
- *Excusable Ignorance*
- *Partial Illegality*

 # Cases

### CASE 13–1
### Usury
### *DUNNAM v. BURNS*
Court of Appeals of Texas, El Paso, 1995
901 S.W.2d 628

BARAJAS, J.

Louis Dunnam [defendant/appellant] appeals a judgment holding him liable to Appellee [plaintiff] for payment of a promissory note. Appellant and Steve Oualline jointly borrowed $35,000 from Appellee and agreed to repay the principal plus $5,000 on a date certain. After Appellant defaulted on the loan, Appellee sued to recover. Appellant defended by claiming the loan was usurious. We reverse the judgment of the trial court and remand this cause to it for further proceedings.

The four-sentence instrument that memorializes Appellant's indebtedness to Appellee is, in Appellant's words, not a model of drafting precision. * * * [The note] was drafted by Appellant and reflects that Appellant borrowed $35,000, and agreed to "pay the entire balance plus $5,000 by 2/23/89," six months after he borrowed it.

Appellant attacks the judgment of the trial court in two points of error, claiming that the trial court erred by refusing to submit his usury defense to the jury and by holding that he was personally obligated on the note which he signed.

* * *

In his first point of error, Appellant claims the trial court erred by refusing to submit his usury defense to the jury. Usury is interest in excess of the amount permitted by law. [Citation.] Interest is compensation for the use or forbearance of money. [Citation.] For most transactions between private persons, the maximum allowable rate of interest is 18 percent if the parties agree on a rate of interest [citation], and 6 percent if they do not, [citation]. Usurious contracts are against public policy, [citation] and persons who contract for or collect usurious interest are subject to penalties that may exceed the total value of the contract, [citation].

We must initially determine whether the $5,000 additional sum contained in the promissory note constitutes interest. Interest need not be denominated interest. [Citation.] When money is advanced in exchange for an obligation to repay the advance plus an additional amount, the added amount is interest that may not exceed the statutory maximum. [Citations.] The foregoing principles instruct that Appellant's absolute obligation to pay $5,000 in addition to the principal renders the additional amount interest.

Appellee does not contest that the $5,000 is interest. Neither does he claim that the amount of interest was not usurious, although we note that the promissory note effectively charges a 28.57 percent interest rate, which exceeds even the highest rate permitted by statute [citation] (permitting 28 percent interest on certain transactions). He argues, rather, that he did not "charge" such interest because the instrument was drafted by Appellant and because Appellee was actually interested in collecting only the principal amount. In so arguing, Appellee misapprehends the significance of his intent and of the identity of the drafter of the promissory note.

A document that contains an absolute obligation to repay a loan together with interest in excess of the amount permitted by statute is usurious on its face.

[Citations.] "It is not the lender's subjective intent to charge usury that makes a loan usurious, but rather his intent to make the bargain that was made." [Citations.]. The specific intent of the lender is immaterial because it is presumed to be reflected in the document he signs. [Citations.] Further, "once the agreed terms have been reduced to writing in the form of a compulsory contract, the test of alleged usury is not concerned with which party might have originated the alleged[ly] usurious provisions." [Citations.]

The foregoing principles foreclose Appellee's arguments. The drafter of the usurious promissory note is simply irrelevant. * * * The instrument embodies a usurious transaction, and Appellee, as the lender, contracted for usurious interest. Appellant's first point of error is sustained.

---

## CASE 13–2
### Restraint of Trade
# INSULATION CORPORATION OF AMERICA v. BROBSTON
Superior Court of Pennsylvania, 1995
446 Pa. Super 520, 667 A.2d 729

KELLY, J.

In this opinion, we are called on to determine whether the enforcement of a two-year, three hundred mile "non-competition" covenant contained in an employment contract is reasonable where the former employee was terminated for poor performance and the employer's proprietary business information was already protected under injunctive enforcement of a "non-disclosure" covenant of the same agreement. Under such circumstances, we hold that the modified two-year time restriction imposed upon the former employee is both broader than necessary to protect the employer's business interests and unduly oppressive on the former employee. * * *

This appeal involves a challenge to the trial court's grant of a preliminary injunction in favor of appellee, Insulation Corporation of America ("ICA"), enforcing the terms of "non-disclosure" and "non-competition" restrictive covenants contained in a post-employment agreement between ICA and appellant, Richard Brobston ("Brobston"). The pertinent facts and procedural history of this case are as follows. ICA is a corporation engaged in the manufacture and sale of polystyrene packaging, roofing and insulation products. Brobston was hired by ICA in October, 1982. At the time, Brobston was forty-seven years old, had worked in the insulation industry since 1977, and began his employment without a written contract. His initial position was territory sales manager. In 1986, he was promoted to national account manager. In 1990, he was promoted to general manager.

In July, 1992, ICA decided to expand its product line from commodity or "anyone can do" products into more specialized products through the utilization of a computer-assisted design (CAD) system. Prior to purchasing the CAD system, ICA required that Brobston and certain other employees sign employment contracts which contained restrictive covenants or be terminated. On July 24, 1992, Brobston signed the proffered employment contract, which contained the following pertinent terms:

* * *

WHEREAS, Employer is about to purchase equipment and computer software to design and cut Employer's products with the assistance of computer assisted design (CAD), and the resulting system requires extensive knowledge and training; and

WHEREAS, Employer finds it necessary and essential to give specialized education and training to certain employees; and

WHEREAS, Employee will be the recipient of information with respect to the operation of the CAD system, including requirements, design, setup, pricing and operation, and, also, the identity of customers of Employer, and Employer's sources of leads for and methods of obtaining new business, and information and training with respect to various techniques, procedures, equipment, designs, drawings, plans, engineering or test data, customer and supplier lists, cost records and other information used or developed by Employer in carrying out Employer's business; and

* * *

4. The Employee during the term of employment under this Agreement will have access to and become familiar with various trade secrets, consisting of formulas, patterns, devises, secret inventions, processes, sales, earnings, finances and compilations of information, records and specifications and all other concerns of the Employer, which are owned by the Employer and which are regularly used in the operation of the business of the Employer. The Employee shall not disclose any of the aforesaid trade secrets, directly or indirectly, nor use them in

any way, either during the term of this Agreement or at any time thereafter, except as required by the Employer in the course of the Employee's employment for the Employer.

5. On the termination of Employee's employment, for whatever reason whatsoever, the Employee shall not, directly or indirectly, within three hundred (300) miles of Allentown, Pennsylvania, enter into or engage generally in direct competition with the Employer in the business of manufacturing and/or selling expanded polystyrene insulation or packaging either as an individual on Employee's own or as a partner or joint venturer, or as an employee or agent for any person, or as an officer, director, or shareholder or otherwise for a period of three (3) years after the date of termination of Employee's employment hereunder.

The purported consideration for Brobston's agreement to be bound was a $2,000.00 increase in his base salary and proprietary information concerning the CAD system, customers and pricing. In October, 1992, Brobston became vice president of special products, which included responsibility for sales of CAD system products and the commodity products. Over the course of the next year, Brobston failed to properly file sales call and expense account reports. Further, Brobston failed to make a satisfactory number of overnight sales calls. Finally, of the fourteen accounts in his territory, only three showed growth; the others showed either flat or decreasing sales. On August 13, 1993, ICA terminated Brobston's employment. On December 8, 1993, Brobston was hired by Foam Plastics of New England, a competitor of ICA, who was aware of the existence of ICA's restrictive covenants. On December 17, 1993, ICA sought injunctive relief against Brobston, and filed a petition in equity to enforce the employment agreement by enjoining him from disclosing proprietary information about ICA, and by restraining him from competing with ICA. The trial court issued a temporary restraining order on that day, and a preliminary injunction hearing followed on December 23, 1993. Brobston was placed on leave without pay by his new employer.

Following the preliminary injunction hearing, the trial court granted ICA's petition for a preliminary injunction and enjoined Brobston from disclosing ICA's trade secrets and from competing with ICA within three hundred miles of Allentown, Pennsylvania for a period of two years from the date of Brobston's termination.

\* \* \*

Appellant contends that the "non-relationship" covenant is wholly unenforceable as it bears no reasonable relationship to the protection of ICA. The trial court,

on the other hand, concluded that enforcement of the restrictive covenants was necessary to protect ICA's legitimate business interests. Based on the following reasoning, we cannot agree.

\* \* \*

In order for a "non-competition" covenant to be enforceable, it must relate to a contract for employment, be supported by adequate consideration and be reasonably limited in both time and territory. [Citations.] More specifically, where a restrictive covenant has been entered into between an employer and its employee, our courts have permitted the enforcement of post-employment restraints only where they are ancillary to an employment relationship between the parties, the restrictions are reasonably necessary to protect the employer, and the restrictions are reasonably limited in duration and geographic extent. [Citations.]

In order for a restrictive covenant entered into subsequent to the commencement of the employee's service to be "ancillary," it must be supported by new consideration, which can be in the form of a corresponding benefit or a beneficial change in employment status. [Citations.] Brobston's $2,000.00 annual raise and change of employment status from "at-will" to a written year-to-year term upon signing the agreement was adequate consideration for Brobston's promise not to compete. [Citation.]

The salient issue for our determination is whether enforcement of the "non-competition" covenant under these circumstances is reasonable. Post-employment restrictive covenants are subject to a more stringent test of reasonableness than covenants ancillary to the sale of a business. [Citation.] This heightened scrutiny stems from a historical reluctance on the part of our courts to enforce any contracts in restraint of free trade, particularly where they restrain an individual from earning a living at his trade. [Citations.] This close scrutiny also stems from our recognition of the inherently unequal bargaining positions of employer and employee when entering into such agreements. [Citation.] \* \* \*

Generally, our determination of reasonableness of time and territory has involved a weighing of competing interests—that of the employer's need for protection—against the hardship of the restriction to be imposed upon the employee. [Citations.]

\* \* \*

Instantly, the record discloses that Brobston, a ten year employee, was privy to certain confidential corporate information such as overhead costs, profit margin, dealer discounts, customer pricing, marketing strategy and customer contract terms. Information of this nature was entitled to be protected by ICA under paragraph four, the "non-disclosure" covenant of the employment contract. [Citations.] However, the record evidence also reveals that Brobston was terminated because he failed to do his job to increase sales. Brobston was terminated for failing to take overnight sales trips to develop business and for failing to report sales calls and expenses. Thus, he was fired for failing to promote his employer's interests. It is this factor that was not properly considered by the trial court that merits further scrutiny of the trial court's decision to enforce the "non-competition" covenant.

* * * Where an employee is terminated by his employer on the grounds that he has failed to promote the employer's legitimate business interests, it clearly suggests an implicit decision on the part of the employer that its business interests are best promoted without the employee in its service. The employer who fires an employee for failing to perform in a manner that promotes the employer's business interests deems the employee worthless. Once such a determination is made by the employer, the need to protect itself from the former employee is diminished by the fact that the employee's worth to the corporation is presumably insignificant. Under such circumstances, we conclude that it is unreasonable as a matter of law to permit the employer to retain unfettered control over that which it has effectively discarded as worthless to its legitimate business interests.

Moreover, our review of the preamble to the employment contract discloses that ICA's ostensible purpose in requiring Brobston to enter into that agreement was to protect the new CAD technology it planned to acquire in order to create for itself a niche market and obtain a competitive advantage over other insulation suppliers by producing a "more specialized higher margin product." The record reveals, however, that Brobston was never given the "extensive knowledge and training" necessary to operate the CAD system. His testimony that he never received the training went unrebutted. Rather, shortly after he signed the contract, Brobston was given a new position in order to cover a sales territory for a retiring sales representative.

Thus, Brobston was left with a $2,000.00 annual increase, but no working knowledge of the CAD system and its processes. Brobston admittedly possessed confidential customer sales and profit margin information that related to the system. A close reading of the contract reveals that information of this nature was adequately addressed by the "non-disclosure" covenant of paragraph five. ICA sought and received injunctive enforcement of both that covenant and the "non-competition" covenant of paragraph five. Because we are of the opinion that ICA properly sought and was granted equitable relief

via-a-vis the confidential information, the trial court's enforcement of the non-competition covenant would be unnecessary to protect its interests and be unfairly oppressive to Brobston's ability to earn a living.

It bears noting that there is a significant factual distinction between the hardship imposed by the enforcement of a restrictive covenant on an employee who voluntarily leaves his employer and that imposed upon an employee who is terminated for failing to do his job. The salesman discharged for poor sales performance cannot reasonably be perceived to pose the same competitive threat to his employer's business interests as the salesman whose performance is not questioned, but who voluntarily resigns to join another business in direct competition with the employer.

* * *

In an Ohio case cited by our Supreme Court [citations] the factors that have been considered by courts when determining the harshness and oppression of enforcement of post-employment restrictive covenants as follows:

Matters considered

"In treating undue harshness and oppression, the courts . . . focus a great deal of attention on such inquiries as: What is the situation of employee and his family? What is employee's capacity? Is employee handicapped or disabled in any way? What effect will the restraint have on employee's life? Will it deprive him of opportunity of supporting himself and his family in reasonable comfort? Will it force him to give up the work for which he is best trained or be expatriated? What are business conditions? Is there prevailing unemployment? Was the employment terminable at employer's will? Did employee work for employer a very brief time? What were the circumstances of termination of the employment? Did the termination constitute a breach of contract by employer? If not a breach, was it unreasonable? What is the character and extent of consideration to employee?"

* * *

[W]e are of the opinion that injunctive enforcement of the "non-disclosure" clause provides the relief necessary to protect ICA's legitimate business interests. * * * Similarly, here, to impose an additional burden on Mr. Brobston under these circumstances would tip the balance of reasonableness away from the protection of ICA's legitimate business interests and into the realm of undue oppression upon his ability to earn a living. Therefore, under these circumstances, we hold that the trial court's enforcement of the instant "non-competition" covenant constitutes palpable error. [Citation.]

* * *

## CASE 13–3
## Exculpatory Clauses
# HENRIOULLE v. MARIN VENTURES, INC.

Supreme Court of California, 1978
20 Cal.3d 512, 143 Cal.Rptr. 247, 573 P.2d 465

BIRD, C.J.

Appellant, John Henrioulle, seeks to set aside orders of the superior court granting his landlord, respondent Marin Ventures, Inc., a judgment notwithstanding the jury's verdict and a new trial. Appellant contends that the exculpatory clause in his lease could not relieve the landlord of liability for the personal injuries appellant sustained in a fall on a common stairway in the apartment building. This court agrees.

* * *

From the record, it appears that on April 3, 1974, appellant entered into a lease agreement with respondent for an apartment in San Rafael, California. At that time, appellant was an unemployed widower with two children who received public assistance in the form of a rent subsidy from the Marin County Department of Social Services. There was also evidence of a shortage of housing accommodations for persons of low income in Marin County.

The printed form lease agreement which appellant signed contained the following exculpatory clause: "INDEMNIFICATION: Owner shall not be liable for any damage or injury to Tenant, or any other person, or to any property, occurring on the premises, or any part thereof, or in the common areas thereof, and Tenant agrees to hold Owner harmless from any claims for damages no matter how caused."

On May 22, 1974, appellant fractured his wrist when he tripped over a rock on a common stairway in the apartment building. At the time of the accident the landlord had been having difficulty keeping the common areas of the apartment building clean. An on-site manager, whose duties included keeping these areas clean, had proven unsatisfactory and had been terminated in the month prior to the accident. The landlord had also employed an additional person to do maintenance work, but he had worked only a few hours at the apartment building in the month preceding the accident.

* * *

In *Tunkl v. Regents of the University of California*, [citation], this court held invalid a clause in a hospital admission form which released the hospital from liability for future negligence. This court noted that although courts have made "diverse" interpretations of [California] Civil Code section 1668, which invalidates contracts which exempt one from responsibility for certain wilful or negligent acts, all the decisions were in accord that exculpatory clauses affecting the public interest are invalid. [Citation.]

In *Tunkl*, six criteria are used to identify the kind of agreement in which an exculpatory clause is invalid as contrary to public policy. "(1) It concerns a business of a type generally thought suitable for public regulation. (2) The party seeking exculpation is engaged in performing a service of great importance to the public, which is often a matter of practical necessity for some members of the public. (3) The party holds himself out as willing to perform this service for any member of the public who seeks it, or at least any member coming within certain established standards. (4) As a result of the essential nature of the service, in the economic setting of the transaction, the party invoking exculpation possesses a decisive advantage of bargaining strength against any member of the public who seeks his services. (5) In exercising a superior bargaining power, the party confronts the public with a standardized adhesion contract of exculpation, and makes no provision whereby a purchaser may pay additional fees and obtain protection against negligence. (6) Finally, as a result of the transaction, the person or property of the purchaser is placed under the control of the seller, subject to the risk of carelessness by the seller or his agents." [Citation.]

The transaction before this court, a residential rental agreement, meets the *Tunkl* criteria.

* * *

In holding that exculpatory clauses in residential leases violate public policy, this court joins an increasing number of jurisdictions. [Citations.]

* * *

The orders of the superior court granting respondent's motions for judgment notwithstanding the jury's verdict and a new trial are reversed, and the cause is remanded with direction to enter judgment for appellant on the verdict.

---

### CASE 13–4
## Unconscionable Contracts
# *WILLIAMS v. WALKER-THOMAS FURNITURE CO.*
Court of Appeals, District of Columbia, 1965
350 F.2d 445

---

**WRIGHT, C.J.**

Appellee, Walker-Thomas Furniture Company, operates a retail furniture store in the District of Columbia. During the period from 1957 to 1962 each appellant in these cases purchased a number of household items from Walker-Thomas, for which payment was to be made in installments. The terms of each purchase were contained in a printed form contract which set forth the value of the purchased item and purported to lease the item to appellant for a stipulated monthly rent payment. The contract then provided, in substance, that title would remain in Walker-Thomas until the total of all the monthly payments made equaled the stated value of the item, at which time appellants could take title. In the event of a default in the payment of any monthly installment, Walker-Thomas could repossess the item.

The contract further provided that "the amount of each periodical installment payment to be made by [purchaser] to the Company under this present lease shall be inclusive of and not in addition to the amount of each installment payment to be made by [purchaser] under such prior leases, bills, or accounts; *and all payments now and hereafter made by [purchaser] shall be credited pro rata on all outstanding leases, bills, and accounts* due the Company by [purchaser] at the time each such payment is made." (Emphasis added.) The effect of this rather obscure provision was to keep a balance due on every item purchased until the balance due on all items, whenever purchased, was liquidated. As a result, the debt incurred at the time of purchase of each item was secured by the right to repossess all the items previously purchased by the same purchaser, and each new item purchased automatically became subject to a security interest arising out of the previous dealings.

On May 12, 1962, appellant Thorne purchased an item described as a Daveno, three tables, and two lamps, having total stated value of $391.10. Shortly thereafter, he defaulted on his monthly payments and appellee sought to replevy all the items purchased since the first transaction in 1958. Similarly, on April 7, 1962, appellant Williams bought a stereo set of stated value of $514.95. She too defaulted shortly thereafter, and appellee sought to replevy all the items purchased since

December 1957. The Court of General Sessions granted judgment for appellee. The District of Columbia Court of Appeals affirmed, and we granted appellants' motion for leave to appeal to this court.

Appellants' principal contention, rejected by both the trial and the appellate courts . . ., is that these contracts, or at least some of them, are unconscionable and, hence, not enforceable. * * *

Unconscionability has generally been recognized to include an absence of meaningful choice on the part of one of the parties together with contract terms which are unreasonably favorable to the other party. Whether a meaningful choice is present in a particular case can only be determined by consideration of all the circumstances surrounding the transaction. In many cases the meaningfulness of the choice is negated by a gross inequality of bargaining power. The manner in which the contract was entered is also relevant to this consideration. Did each party to the contract, considering his obvious education or lack of it, have a reasonable opportunity to understand the terms of the contract, or were the important terms hidden in a maze of fine print and minimized by deceptive sales practices? Ordinarily, one who signs an agreement without full knowledge of its terms might be held to assume the risk that he has entered a one-sided bargain. But when a party of little bargaining power, and hence little real choice, signs a commercially unreasonable contract with little or no knowledge of its terms, it is hardly likely that his consent, or even an objective manifestation of his consent, was ever given to all the terms. In such a case the usual rule that the terms of the agreement are not to be questioned should be abandoned and the court should consider whether the terms of the contract are so unfair that enforcement should be withheld.

In determining reasonableness or fairness, the primary concern must be with the terms of the contract considered in light of the circumstances existing when the contract was made. The test is not simple, nor can it be mechanically applied. The terms are to be considered "in the light of the general commercial background and the commercial needs of the particular trade or case." Corbin suggests the test as being whether the terms are "so extreme as to appear unconscionable according to the mores and business practices of the time and place." [Citation.] We think this formulation correctly states the test to be applied in those cases where no meaningful choice was exercised upon entering the contract.

Because the trial court and the appellate court did not feel that enforcement could be refused, no findings were made on the possible unconscionability of the contracts in these cases. Since the record is not sufficient for our deciding the issue as a matter of law, the cases must be remanded to the trial court for further proceedings.

Reversed and remanded.

---

 # Questions

1. Identify and explain the types of contracts that may violate a statute, and distinguish between the two types of licensing statutes.

2. Describe when a covenant not to compete will be enforced, and discuss the two situations in which these types of covenants most frequently arise.

3. Explain when exculpatory agreements, agreements involving the commission of a tort, and agreements involving public officials will be held to be illegal.

4. Distinguish between procedural and substantive unconscionability.

5. Explain the usual effects of illegality and the major exceptions to this rule.

---

# Problems

1. Johnson and Wilson were the principal shareholders in XYZ Corporation, located in the city of Jonesville, Wisconsin. This corporation was engaged in the business of manufacturing paper novelties, which were sold over a wide area in the Midwest. The corporation was also in the business of binding books. Johnson purchased Wilson's shares of the XYZ Corporation and, in consideration thereof, Wilson agreed that for a period of two years he would not (a) manufacture or sell in Wisconsin any paper novelties of any kind that would compete with those sold by the XYZ Corporation or (b) engage in the bookbinding business in the city of Jonesville. Discuss the validity and effect, if any, of this agreement.

2. Wilkins, a resident of and licensed by the State of Texas as a certified public accountant, rendered service in his professional capacity in Louisiana to Coverton Cosmetics Company. He was not registered as a certified public accountant in Louisiana. His service under his contract with the cosmetics company was not the only occasion on which he had practiced his profession in that State. The company denied liability and refused to pay him, relying upon a Louisiana statute declaring it unlawful for any person to perform or offer to perform services as a CPA for compensation until he has been registered by the designated agency of the State and holds an unrevoked registration card. Provision is made for issuance of a certificate as a CPA without examination to any applicant who holds a valid unrevoked certificate as a CPA under the laws of any other State. The statute provides further that rendition of services of the character performed by Wilkins, without registration, is a misdemeanor punishable by a fine or imprisonment in the county jail, or both. Wilkins brought an action against Coverton seeking to recover a fee in the amount of $1,500 as the reasonable value of his services. Decision?

3. Michael is interested in promoting the passage of a bill in the State legislature. He agrees with Christy, an attorney, to pay Christy for her services in drawing up the required bill, procuring its introduction in the legislature, and making an argument for its passage before the legislative committee to which it will be referred. Christy renders these services. Subsequently, upon Michael's refusal to pay her, Christy sues Michael for damage for breach of contract. Decision?

4. Anthony promises to pay McCarthy $10,000 if McCarthy reveals to the public that Washington is a Communist. Washington is not a Communist and never has been. McCarthy successfully persuades the media to report that Washington is a Communist and now seeks to recover the $10,000 from Anthony, who refuses to pay. McCarthy initiates a lawsuit against Anthony. What result?

5. The Dear Corporation was engaged in the business of making and selling harvesting machines. It sold everything pertaining to its business to the ABC Company, agreeing "not again to go into the manufacture of harvesting machines anywhere in the United States." The seller, which had national and international goodwill in its business, now begins the manufacture of such machines contrary to its agreement. Should the court enjoin it?

6. Charles Leigh, engaged in the industrial laundry business in Central City, employed Tim Close, previously employed in the home laundry business, as a route salesperson on July 1.

Leigh rents linens and industrial uniforms to commercial customers; the soiled linens and uniforms are picked up at regular intervals by route drivers and replaced with clean ones. Every employee is assigned a list of customers. The contract of employment stated that in consideration of being employed, upon termination of his employment, Close would not "directly or indirectly engage in the linen supply business or any competitive business within Central City, Illinois, for a period of one year from the date when his employment under this contract ceases." On May 10 of the following year, Leigh terminated Close's employment for valid reasons. Thereafter, Close accepted employment with Ajax Linen Service, a direct competitor of Leigh in Central City. He commenced soliciting former customers whom he had called on for Leigh and obtained some of them as customers for Ajax.

Leigh brings an action to enforce the provisions of the contract. Decision?

7. On July 5, 1992, Barbara and Kitty entered into a bet on the outcome of the 1992 presidential election. On January 28, 1993, Barbara, who bet on the winner, approached Kitty, seeking to collect the $3,000 Kitty had wagered. Kitty paid Barbara the wager but now seeks to recover the funds from Barbara. Result?

8. Carl, a salesman for Smith, comes to Benson's home and sells him a complete set of "gourmet cooking utensils" that are worth approximately $300. Benson, an eighty-year-old man living alone in a one-room efficiency apartment, signs a contract to buy the utensils for $1,450, plus a credit charge of $145, and to make payment in ten equal monthly installments. Three weeks after Carl leaves with the signed contract, Benson decides he cannot afford the cooking utensils and has no use for them. What can Benson do? Explain.

9. Consider the same facts as in problem 8, but assume that the price was $350. Benson, nevertheless, wishes to avoid the contract based on the allegation that Carl befriended and tricked him into the purchase. Decision?

10. Adrian rents a bicycle from Barbara. The bicycle rental contract Adrian signed provides that Barbara is not liable for any injury to the renter caused by any defect in the bicycle or the negligence of Barbara. Injured when she is involved in an accident due to Barbara's improper maintenance of the bicycle, Adrian sues Barbara for her damages. Decision?

11. Merrill Lynch employed Post and Maney as account executives beginning on April 20, 1984, and May 15, 1986, respectively. Both men elected to be paid a salary and to participate in the firm's pension and profit-sharing plans rather than take a straight commission. Merrill Lynch terminated the employment of both Post and Maney on August 30, 1999. On September 4, 1999, both began working for Bache & Company, a competitor of Merrill Lynch. Merrill Lynch then informed them that all of their rights in the company-funded pension plan had been forfeited pursuant to a provision of the plan that permitted forfeiture in the event an employee directly or indirectly competed with the firm. Decision?

12. Tovar applied for the position of resident physician in Paxton Community Memorial Hospital. The hospital examined his background and licensing and assured him that he was qualified for the position. Relying upon the hospital's promise of permanent employment, Tovar resigned from his job and began work at the hospital. He was discharged two weeks later, however, because he did not hold a license to practice medicine in Illinois as required by State law. He had taken the examination but had never passed it. Tovar claims that the hospital promised him a position of permanent employment and that by discharging him it breached their employment contract. Decision?

13. Carolyn Murphy, a welfare recipient with four minor children, responded to an advertisement that offered the opportunity to purchase televisions without a deposit or credit history. She entered into a rent-to-own contract for a twenty-five-inch console color television set that required seventy-eight weekly payments of $16 (a total of $1,248, which was two and one-half times the retail value of the set). Under the contract, the renter could terminate the agreement by returning the television and forfeiting any payments already made. After Murphy had paid $436 on the television, she read a newspaper article criticizing the lease plan. She stopped payment and sued the television company. The television company has attempted to take possession of the set. Decision?

14. Albert Bennett, an amateur cyclist, participated in a bicycle race conducted by the United States Cycling Federation. During the race, Bennett was hit by an automobile. He claims that employees of the Federation improperly allowed the car onto the course. The Federation claims that it cannot be held liable to Bennett because Bennett signed a release exculpating the Federation from responsibility for any personal injury resulting from his participation in the race. Decision?

15. In February, Brady contracted to construct a house for Fulghum for $106,850. Brady began construction on March 13. Neither during the negotiation of this contract nor when he began performance was Brady licensed as a general contractor as required by North Carolina law. Brady was awarded his builder's license on October 22, having passed the examination on his second attempt. At that time, he had completed two-thirds of the work on Fulghum's house. Fulghum paid Brady $104,000. Brady brought suit, seeking an additional $2,850 on the original contract and $28,926 for "additions and changes" Fulghum requested during construction. The trial court entered summary judgment in favor of Fulghum on the basis of the contractor's noncompliance with statutory licensing requirements. Brady then appealed to the North Carolina Court of Appeals, which affirmed, concluding that the contractor had not "substantially" complied with licensing requirements. Brady now appeals to the Supreme Court of North Carolina. Decision?

16. Abramowitz obtained a one-year mortgage loan from Barnett Bank for $400,000 at 9 percent interest with a 1 percent "point" or service fee. The maximum lawful rate of interest on such a loan is 10 percent. The bank deducted the

$4,000 service fee from the loan proceeds, actually disbursing only $396,000 to Abramowitz. During the one-year term of his loan, Abramowitz was charged and he paid $36,347.78 in interest. He claims the loan was usurious because the $4,000 "service fee" plus the $36,347 interest charge exceeded the 10 percent limit on total interest. Abramowitz appealed from a judgment denying him any relief. Decision?

17.   In 1964 Michelle Marvin and actor Lee Marvin began living together, holding themselves out to the general public as man and wife without actually being married. The two orally agreed that while they lived together they would share equally any and all property and earnings accumulated as a result of their individual and combined efforts. In addition, Michelle promised to render her services as "companion, homemaker, housekeeper and cook" to Lee. Shortly thereafter, she gave up her lucrative career as an entertainer in order to devote her full time to being Lee's companion, homemaker, housekeeper, and cook. In return he agreed to provide for all of her financial support and needs for the rest of her life. In 1970, Lee compelled Michelle to leave his household but continued to provide for her support. In late 1971, however, he refused to provide further support. Michelle sued to recover support payments and half of their accumulated property. Lee contends that their agreement is so closely related to the supposed "immoral" character of their relationship that its enforcement would violate public policy. The trial court granted Lee's motion for judgment on the pleadings. Decision?

**WWW** **Internet Exercise** Find and review information on lotteries, including which States have them and how the proceeds are used.

# CHAPTER 14

# Contractual Capacity

A binding promise or agreement requires that the parties to the agreement have contractual capacity. Everyone is regarded as having such capacity unless the law for reasons of public policy holds that the individual lacks such capacity. This essential ingredient of a contract will be discussed by considering those classes and conditions of persons who are legally limited in their capacity to contract: (1) minors, (2) incompetent persons, and (3) intoxicated persons.

## MINORS

A **minor,** also called an infant, is a person who has not attained the age of legal majority. At common law, a minor was a person who was under twenty-one years of age. Today the age of majority has been changed in nearly all jurisdictions by statute, usually to age eighteen. Almost without exception, a minor's contract, whether executory or executed, is **voidable** at his or his guardian's option. Restatement, Section 14. Even an "emancipated" minor, one who because of marriage or other reason is no longer subject to strict parental control, may avoid contractual liability in most jurisdictions. Consequently, businesspeople deal at their peril with minors and in situations of consequence generally require an adult to cosign or guarantee the performance of the contract. Nevertheless, most States recognize special categories of contracts that cannot be avoided (such as student loans or contracts for medical care) or that have a lower age for capacity (such as bank account, marriage, and insurance contracts).

### Liability on Contracts

A minor's contract is not entirely void and of no legal effect; rather, it is *voidable* at the minor's option. The exercise of this power of avoidance, called a **disaffirmance,** ordinarily releases the minor from any liability on the contract. On the other hand, after the minor becomes of age, she may choose to adopt or **ratify** the contract, in which case she surrenders her power of avoidance and becomes bound.

***Disaffirmance*** As previously stated, a minor's contract is voidable at his or his guardian's option, conferring upon him a power to avoid liability. He, or in some jurisdictions his guardian, may, through words or conduct manifesting an intention not to abide by the contract, exercise the power to disaffirm.

In general, a minor's disaffirmance must come either during his minority or within a reasonable time after he reaches majority, as long as he has not already ratified the contract. In most States, defining a reasonable time depends upon such circumstances as the nature of the transaction, whether either party has caused the delay, and the extent to which either party has been injured by the delay. Some States, however, statutorily prescribe a time period, generally one year, in which the minor may disaffirm the contract.

A notable exception is that a sale of land by a minor cannot be disaffirmed until after he reaches his majority. But must he disaffirm immediately upon becoming an adult? In the case of a sale of land, there is a strong precedent that the minor may wait until the period of the statute of limitations has expired, if the sale involves no questions of fairness and equity.

Disaffirmance may be either *express* or *implied*. No particular form of words is essential, so long as they show an intention not to be bound. This intention also may be manifested by acts or by conduct. For example, a minor agrees to sell property to Alice and then sells that property to Brian. The sale to Brian would constitute a disaffirmance of the contract with Alice.

A troublesome yet important problem in this area, upon which the courts are not in agreement, pertains to the minor's duty upon disaffirmance. The majority hold that the minor must return any property he has received from the other party, provided he has it in his possession at the time of disaffirmance. Nothing more is required. If the minor disaffirms the purchase of an automobile and the vehicle has been wrecked, he need only return the wrecked vehicle. Other States require at least the payment of a reasonable amount for the use of the property or the amount of its depreciation while in the hands of the minor. A few States, either by statute or court ruling, recognize a duty upon the part of the minor to make *restitution,* that is, return an equivalent of what has been received in order to place the seller in approximately the same position she would have occupied had the sale not occurred.

Finally, can a minor disaffirm and recover property that his buyer has transferred to a good faith purchaser for value? Traditionally, the minor could avoid the contract and recover the property, despite the fact that the third person gave value for it and had no notice of the minority. Thus, in the case of the sale of real estate, a minor may rescind her deed of conveyance even against a good faith purchaser of the land who did not know of the minority. Regarding the sale of goods, however, this principle has been changed by Section 2–403 of the UCC, which provides that a person with voidable title (e.g., the person buying goods from a minor) has power to transfer valid title to a good faith purchaser for value. For example, a minor sells his car to an individual who resells it to a used car dealership, a good faith purchaser for value. The used car dealer would acquire legal title even though he bought the car from a seller who had only voidable title.

 *See Case 14–1*

**Ratification** A minor has the option of ratifying a contract after reaching the age of majority. Ratification makes the contract binding *ab initio* (from the beginning). That is, the result is the same as if the contract had been valid and binding from its inception. Ratification, once effected, is final and cannot be withdrawn. Further, it must be in total, validating the entire contract. The minor can ratify the contract only as a whole, both as to burdens and benefits. He cannot, for example, ratify so as to retain the consideration he received and escape payment or other performance on his part, nor can he retain part of the contract and disaffirm the rest.

Ratification may be express, implied from conduct, or represent the failure to make a timely disaffirmance. Suppose that a minor makes a contract to buy property from an adult. The contract is voidable by the minor,

and she can escape liability. But suppose that after reaching her majority, she promises to go through with the purchase. Because she has *expressly* ratified the contract she entered when she was a minor, her promise is binding, and the adult can recover for breach upon her failure to perform. In the absence of a statutory provision to the contrary, an express ratification may be oral.

Note that a minor has no power to ratify a contract while he remains a minor. A ratification cannot be based on words or conduct occurring while a minor is still underage, for his ratification at that time would be no more effective than his original contractual promise. The ratification must take place after the individual has acquired contractual capacity by attaining his majority.

Ratification, as previously stated, need not be express; it may be *implied* from the minor's conduct. Suppose that the minor, after attaining her majority, uses the property involved in the contract, undertakes to sell it to someone else, or performs some other act showing an intention to affirm the contract. She may not thereafter disaffirm the contract but is bound by it. Perhaps the most common form of implied ratification occurs when a minor, after attaining her majority, continues to use the property which she purchased as a minor. This use is obviously inconsistent with the nonexistence of the contract, and whether the contract is performed or still partly executory, it will amount to a ratification and prevent a disaffirmance by the minor. Simply keeping the goods for an unreasonable time after attaining majority also has been construed as a ratification. Although the courts are divided on the issue, payments by the minor upon reaching majority, either on principal or interest or on the purchase price of goods, have been held to amount to a ratification. Some courts require additional evidence of an intention to abide by the contract, such as an express promise to that effect or the actual use of the subject matter of the contract.

 *See Case 14–2*

## Liability for Necessaries

Contractual incapacity does not excuse a minor from an obligation to pay for necessaries, those things that suitably and reasonably supply his personal needs, such as food, shelter, medicine, and clothing. Even here, however, the minor is liable not for the agreed price but for the *reasonable* value of the items furnished. Recovery is based on quasi contract. Thus, if a clothier sells a minor a suit that the minor needs, the clothier can successfully sue the minor. The clothier's recovery is limited, however, to the reasonable value of the suit, even if this amount is much less than the agreed-upon selling price.

Defining "necessaries" is a difficult problem. In general, the States regard as **necessary** those things that the minor needs to maintain himself in his particular station in life. Items necessary for subsistence and health, such as food, lodging, clothing, medicine, and medical services, are obviously included. But other less essential items, such as textbooks, school instruction, and legal advice, may be included as well. Further, many States enlarge the concept of necessaries to include articles of property and services that a minor needs to earn the money required to provide the necessities of life for himself and his dependents. Nevertheless, many States limit necessaries to items that are not provided to the minor. Thus, if a minor's guardian provides her with an adequate wardrobe, a blouse the minor purchased would *not* be considered a necessity. In addition, a minor is not liable for anything on the ground that it is necessary unless it has been actually furnished to him and used or consumed by him. In other words, a minor may disaffirm his executory contracts for necessaries and refuse to accept the clothing, lodging, or other items or services.

Ordinarily, luxury items such as cameras, tape recorders, stereo equipment, television sets, and motorboats seldom qualify as necessaries. Whether automobiles and trucks are necessaries has caused considerable controversy, but some courts have recognized that under certain circumstances an automobile may be necessary when it is used by the minor for his business activities.

 *See Case 14–3*

## Liability for Misrepresentation of Age

The States do not agree on whether a minor who has fraudulently misrepresented her age when entering into contract has the power to disaffirm. Suppose a contracting minor says that she is eighteen years of age (or twenty-one if that is the year of attaining majority) and actually looks that old or even older. By the prevailing view in this country, the minor may nevertheless disaffirm the contract. Some States, however, prohibit disaffirmance if a minor misrepresents her age and the adult party, in good faith, reasonably relied upon the misrepresentation. Other States not following the majority rule either (a) require the minor to restore the other party to the position she occupied before the making of the contract or (b) allow the defrauded party to recover damages against the minor in tort.

## Liability for Tort Connected with Contract

It is well settled that minors are generally liable for their torts. There is, however, a legal doctrine providing that if a tort and a contract are so "interwoven" that the court must enforce the contract to enforce the tort action, the minor is not liable in tort. Thus, if a minor rents an automobile from an adult, he enters into a contractual relationship obliging him to exercise reasonable care and diligence to protect the property from injury. By negligently damaging the automobile, he breaches that contractual undertaking. But his contractual immunity protects him from an action by the adult based on the contract. Can the adult nonetheless recover damages on a tort theory? By the majority view, he cannot. For, it is reasoned, a tort recovery would, in effect, be an enforcement of the contract and would defeat the protection that contract law affords the minor.

A different result arises, however, when the minor departs from the terms of the agreement, as by using a rental automobile for an unauthorized purpose and in so doing negligently causing damage to the automobile. In that event, most courts would hold that the tort is independent, and the adult can collect from the minor. Such a situation would not involve the breach of a contractual duty, but rather the commission of a tort while performing an activity completely beyond the scope of the rental agreement.

## *INCOMPETENT PERSONS*

This section discusses the contract status of incompetent persons who are under court-appointed guardianship and those who are not adjudicated incompetents.

## Person under Guardianship

If a person is under guardianship by court order, her contracts are **void** and of no legal effect. Restatement, Section 13. A *guardian* is appointed by a court, generally under the terms of a statute, to control and preserve the property of a person (the *ward*) whose impaired capacity prevents her from managing her own property. Nevertheless, a party dealing with an individual under guardianship may be able to recover the fair value of any necessaries provided to the incompetent. Moreover, the contracts of the ward may be ratified by her guardian or by herself upon termination of the guardianship.

 *See Case 14–4*

## Mental Illness or Defect

A contract is a consensual transaction; therefore, for a contract to be valid, it is necessary that the parties have a certain level of mental capacity. If a person lacks such capacity (is mentally incompetent), he may avoid liability under the agreement (because the contract is **voidable**).

Under the traditional, cognitive ability test, a person who is lacking in sufficient mental capacity to enter into a contract is one unable to comprehend the subject of the contract, its nature, and probable consequences. To avoid the contract, he need not be proved permanently incompetent; but his mental defect must be something more than a weakness of intellect or a lack of average intelligence. In short, a person is competent unless he is unable to understand the nature and effect of his act in entering a contract. Restatement, Section 15. In this situation, the incompetent may disaffirm the contract even if the other party did not know or had no reason to know of the incompetent's mental condition.

A second type of mental incompetence recognized by the Restatement and some States is a mental condition that impairs a person's ability to act in a reasonable manner. Section 15. In other words, the person understands what he is doing but cannot control his behavior in order to act in a reasonable and rational way. If the contract he enters is entirely executory or grossly unfair, it is voidable. If, however, the contract is executed, fair, and the competent party had no reason to suspect the incompetency of the other, the incompetent must restore the competent party to the *status quo* by returning the consideration he has received or its equivalent in money. If restoration to the *status quo* is impossible, avoidance will depend upon the equities of the situation.

Like minors and persons under guardianship, an incompetent person is liable for necessaries furnished him on the principle of quasi contract, the amount of recovery being the reasonable value of the goods or services. Moreover, an incompetent person may ratify or disaffirm his voidable contracts when he becomes competent or during a lucid period.

## INTOXICATED PERSONS

A person may avoid any contract that he enters into if the other party has reason to know that, because of intoxication, he is unable either to understand the nature and consequences of his actions or to act in a reasonable manner. Restatement, Section 16. Such contracts are voidable, although they may be ratified when the intoxicated person regains his capacity. Slight intoxication will not destroy one's contractual capacity, but neither is it essential that one be so drunk as to be totally without reason or understanding.

The effect of intoxication on contractual capacity is similar to that accorded contracts that are voidable because of the second type of incompetency, although the courts are even more strict with contracts a party enters while intoxicated, given the idea that the condition is voluntary. The courts, therefore, require that the intoxicated person on regaining his capacity must act promptly to disaffirm and must generally offer to restore the consideration received. Individuals who are taking prescribed medication or who are involuntarily intoxicated are treated the same as those who are incompetent under the cognitive ability test. As with incompetent persons, intoxicated persons are liable in quasi contract for necessaries furnished them during their incapacity.

Figure 14–1 illustrates the various types of contractual incapacities and the resulting effects.

◆ *See Figure 14–1*

⚖ *See Case 14–4*

**FIGURE 14–1** Contractual Incapacity

| Incapacity | Effect |
| --- | --- |
| Minority | Voidable |
| Mental illness or defect | Voidable |
| Guardianship for incompetency | Void |
| Intoxication | Voidable |

# Chapter Summary

| **Minors** | **Definition** persons who are under the age of majority (usually 18 years)<br>**Liability on Contracts** a minor's contracts are voidable at the minor's option<br>• *Disaffirmance* avoidance of the contract; may be done during minority and for a reasonable time after reaching majority<br>• *Ratification* affirmation of the entire contract; may be done upon reaching majority<br>**Liability for Necessaries** a minor is liable for the reasonable value of necessary items (those that reasonably supply a person's needs)<br>**Liability for Misrepresentation of Age** prevailing view is that a minor may disaffirm the contract<br>**Liability for Tort Connected with Contract** if a tort and a contract are so intertwined that to enforce the tort the court must enforce the contract, the minor is not liable in tort |
|---|---|
| **Incompetent and Intoxicated Persons** | **Person under Guardianship** contracts made by a person placed under guardianship by court order are void<br>**Mental Illness or Defect** a contract entered into by a mentally incompetent person (one who is unable to understand the nature and consequences of his acts) is voidable<br>**Intoxicated Persons** a contract entered into by an intoxicated person (one who cannot understand the nature and consequence of her actions) is voidable |

# Cases

### CASE 14–1
## Minors: Disaffirmance
### *DODSON v. SHRADER*
Supreme Court of Tennessee, 1992
824 S.W.2d 545

O'BRIEN, J.

This is an action to disaffirm the contract of a minor for the purchase of a pick-up truck and for a refund of the purchase price. The issue is whether the minor is entitled to a full refund of the money he paid or whether the seller is entitled to a setoff for the decrease in value of the pick-up truck while it was in the possession of the minor.

In early April of 1987, Joseph Eugene Dodson, then 16 years of age, purchased a used 1984 pick-up truck from Burns and Mary Shrader. The Shraders owned and operated Shrader's Auto Sales in Columbia, Tennessee. Dodson paid $4,900 in cash for the truck, using money he borrowed from his girlfriend's grandmother. At the time of the purchase there was no inquiry by the Shraders, and no misrepresentation by Mr. Dodson, concerning his minority. However, Mr. Shrader did testify that at the time he believed Mr. Dodson to be 18 or 19 years of age.

In December 1987, nine (9) months after the date of purchase, the truck began to develop mechanical problems. A mechanic diagnosed the problem as a burnt valve, but could not be certain without inspecting the valves inside the engine. Mr. Dodson did not want, or did not have the money, to effect these repairs. He continued to drive the truck despite the mechanical problems. One month later, in January, the truck's engine "blew up" and the truck became inoperable.

Mr. Dodson parked the vehicle in the front yard at his parents' home where he lived. He contacted the Shraders to rescind the purchase of the truck and requested a full refund. The Shraders refused to accept the tender of the truck or to give Mr. Dodson the refund requested.

Mr. Dodson then filed an action . . . seeking to rescind the contract and recover the amount paid for the truck. * * * Before the circuit court could hear the case, the truck, while parked in Dodson's front yard, was struck on the left front fender by a hit-and-run driver. At the time of the circuit court trial, according to Shrader, the truck was worth only $500 due to the damage to the engine and the left front fender.

The case was heard in the circuit court in November 1988. The trial judge, based on previous common-law decisions and, under the doctrine of stare decisis reluctantly granted the rescission. The Shraders were ordered, upon tender and delivery of the truck, to reimburse the $4,900 purchase price to Mr. Dodson. The Shraders appealed.

The Court of Appeals . . . affirmed; . . . .

The earliest recorded case in this State, on the issue involved, appears to be in *Wheaton v. East*, [citation] (1833). In pronouncing the rule to apply governing infant's contracts, the court said: We do not perceive that any general rule, as to contracts which are void and voidable, can be stated with more precision than . . . this: "that when the court can pronounce the contract to be to the infant's prejudice, it is void, and when to his benefit, as for necessaries, it is good; and when the contract is of any uncertain nature, as to benefit or prejudice, it is voidable only, at the election of the infant.". . .

The law on the subject of the protection of infant's rights has been slow to evolve. However, in *Human v. Hartsell*, [citation] (1940) the Court of Appeals noted:

* * * the modern rule that contracts of infants are not void but only voidable and subject to be disaffirmed by the minor either before or after attaining majority appears to have been favored. Under this rule the efforts of early authorities to classify contracts as beneficial or harmful and determine whether they are void or only voidable upon the basis of such classification are abandoned in favor of permitting the infant himself when he has become of age to determine what contracts are and what are not to his interest and liking. * * *

As noted by the Court of Appeals, the rule in Tennessee, as modified, is in accord with the majority rule on the issue among our sister states. This rule is based upon the underlying purpose of the "infancy doctrine" which is to protect minors from their lack of judgment and "from squandering their wealth through improvident contracts with crafty adults who would take advantage of them in the marketplace." [Citation.]

There is, however, a modern trend among the states, either by judicial action or by statute, in the approach to the problem of balancing the rights of minors against those of innocent merchants. As a result, two (2) minority rules have developed which allow the other party to a contract with a minor to refund less than the full consideration paid in the event of rescission.

The first of these minority rules is called the "Benefit Rule." [Citations.] The rule holds that, upon rescission, recovery of the full purchase price is subject to a deduction for the minor's use of the merchandise. This rule recognizes that the traditional rule in regard to necessaries has been extended so far as to hold an infant bound by his contracts, where he failed to restore what he has received under them to the extent of the benefit actually derived by him from what he has received from the other party to the transaction. [Citations.]

The other minority rule holds that the minor's recovery of the full purchase price is subject to a deduction for the minor's "use" of the consideration he or she received under the contract, or for the "depreciation" or "deterioration" of the consideration in his or her possession. [Citations.]

* * * At a time when we see young persons between 18 and 21 years of age demanding and assuming more responsibilities in their daily lives; when we see such persons emancipated, married, and raising families; when we see such persons charged with the responsibility for committing crimes; when we see such persons being sued in tort claims for acts of negligence; when we see such persons subject to military service; when we see such persons engaged in business and acting in almost all other respects as an adult, it seems timely to re-examine the case law pertaining to contractual rights and responsibilities of infants to see if the law as pronounced and applied by the courts should be redefined.

* * *

We state the rule to be followed hereafter, in reference to a contract of a minor, to be where the minor has not been overreached in any way, and there has been no undue influence, and the contract is a fair and reasonable one, and the minor has actually paid money on the purchase price, and taken and used the article purchased, that he ought not to be permitted to recover the amount actually paid, without allowing the vendor of the goods reasonable compensation for the use of, depreciation, and willful or negligent damage to the article purchased, while in his hands. If there has been any fraud or imposition on the part of the seller or if the contract is unfair, or any unfair advantage has been taken of the minor inducing him to make the purchase, then the rule does not apply. Whether there has been such an overreaching on the part of the seller, and the fair market value of the property returned, would always, in any case, be a question for the trier of fact. This rule will fully and fairly protect the minor against injustice or imposition, and at the same time it will be fair to a business person who has dealt with such minor in good faith.

This rule is best adapted to modern conditions under which minors are permitted to, and do in fact, transact a great deal of business for themselves, long before they have reached the age of legal majority. * * *

* * *

We note that in this case, some nine (9) months after the date of purchase, the truck purchased by the plaintiff began to develop mechanical problems. Plaintiff was informed of the probable nature of the difficulty which apparently involved internal problems in the engine. He continued to drive the vehicle until the engine "blew up" and the truck became inoperable. Whether or not this involved gross negligence or intentional conduct on his part is a matter for determination at the trial level. It is not possible to determine from this record whether a counterclaim for tortious damage to the vehicle was asserted. After the first tender of the vehicle was made by plaintiff, and refused by the defendant, the truck was damaged by a hit-and-run driver while parked on plaintiff's property. The amount of that damage and the liability for that amount between the purchaser and the vendor, as well as the fair market value of the vehicle at the time of tender, is also an issue for the trier of fact.

The case is remanded to the trial court for further proceedings in accordance with this judgment.

---

## CASE 14–2
## Minors: Ratification
### *FLETCHER v. MARSHALL*
Appellate Court of Illinois, Second District, 1994
260 Ill.App.3d 673, 198 Ill.Dec. 494, 632 N.E.2d 1105

**BOWMAN, J.**
After a bench trial, the trial court entered a judgment in favor of defendant, John E. Marshall III. Plaintiff, Kirsten Fletcher, appeals, claiming that the trial court erroneously found that defendant was not liable for rent that plaintiff paid on defendant's behalf because defendant was a minor when he signed the lease and therefore was not bound by the lease. We reverse and remand.

Plaintiff's small claims complaint alleged that "defendant is indebted to plaintiff in the sum of $2,500 plus court costs for contribution toward rent." Plaintiff attached to the complaint a copy of a lease dated April 29, 1991, and signed by plaintiff and defendant. The lease states that plaintiff and defendant agreed to rent an apartment in Mundelein for $525 per month. The lease term was July 1, 1991, to June 30, 1992.

At the trial, plaintiff testified that, early in 1991, she and defendant were in high school and were dating. Defendant's parents ejected him from their home shortly after defendant completed high school, and defendant moved in with plaintiff and her parents. Plaintiff and defendant decided to rent an apartment and share the expenses. Plaintiff testified that she and defendant paid an additional one-half month's rent and moved into the apartment before the commencement of the lease term. Although plaintiff paid her half of the rent, plaintiff's mother paid some of the bills and purchased groceries for plaintiff and defendant on occasions when plaintiff and defendant could not afford to do so on their own.

Defendant took advantage of an opportunity to attend college and moved out of the apartment after "a couple of months." Plaintiff continued to live in the apartment and paid the entire rent amount for the remaining 10 months of the lease term.

Defendant testified that he signed the lease on April 29, 1991, and that he was 17 years old on that date. Plaintiff claimed that, although the apartment complex manager typed the lease on April 29, defendant did not sign the lease until June 30, 1991, after defendant's eighteenth birthday.

Plaintiff's mother (Mrs. Fletcher) explained that the lease remained in her possession, unsigned, until June 30, 1991, one day prior to the commencement of the lease term. She also explained that she opened a bank account in her name. The parties deposited their paychecks into this account, and Mrs. Fletcher made the rent payments on their behalf. Mrs. Fletcher testified that defendant moved out of the apartment on August 15, 1991, while defendant claimed he moved out on August 2.

Defendant testified that he made rent payments. He also paid at least part of the security deposit, although the record does not reveal the date of this payment. He moved out of the apartment because he and plaintiff were not getting along and because he had an opportunity to attend college. Defendant's father testified that defendant turned 18 on May 30, 1991.

The trial court ruled in favor of defendant, finding that defendant signed the lease before his eighteenth birthday. Plaintiff moved for reconsideration of the ruling, arguing that defendant could not disaffirm the lease because the lease was a contract for necessaries and, alternatively, that defendant ratified the contract after he turned 18. * * *

Plaintiff's sole argument on appeal is that, although defendant was a minor when he signed the lease, he ratified the lease after attaining majority by taking possession of the premises and paying rent. * * *

A contract of a minor is not void *ab initio*, but merely voidable at the election of the minor upon his attaining majority. [Citations.] After attaining majority, a person may either disaffirm or ratify a contract that he entered into while he was still a minor. [Citation.]

A contract of a minor is deemed ratified if the minor fails to disaffirm it within a reasonable time after attaining majority. [Citations.] Also, a minor ratifies a contract if, after becoming of age, he "does any distinct and decisive act clearly showing an intention to affirm [the contract]." [Citation.] Once a person ratifies such a contract, he cannot thereafter avoid his obligations under it. [Citation.]

* * *

In the instant case, it is undisputed that, about two weeks after becoming 18 years of age, defendant moved into the apartment and paid rent. There is no evidence indicating that, at this time, defendant did not intend to be bound under the lease. He lived in the apartment for about 1 1/2 months and never took any action before moving out evidencing an intention to disaffirm the lease.

* * * Here, there is no evidence on record that could give rise to a reasonable inference that defendant's acts of moving into the apartment, living there for 1 1/2 months, and making rent payments constituted anything other than an unequivocal ratification of the lease. Because he had already ratified the lease, his later attempt to disaffirm it by moving out of the apartment and refusing to make further payments was of no effect. [Citation.] Accordingly, we conclude that the trial court's judgment was against the manifest weight of the evidence. Defendant remained liable for the rent for the remainder of the lease term and is therefore liable to plaintiff for the rent payments she made on defendant's behalf.

---

## CASE 14–3
## Minors: Liability for Necessaries
### *GASTONIA PERSONNEL CORP. v. ROGERS*
Supreme Court of North Carolina, 1970
276 N.C. 279, 172 S.E.2d 19

**BOBBITT, C.J.**
[Rogers (defendant) was a nineteen-year-old (the age of majority being twenty-one) high school graduate pursuing a civil engineering degree when he learned that his wife was expecting a child. As a result he quit school and sought assistance from Gastonia Personnel Corporation (plaintiff) in finding a job. Rogers signed a contract with the employment agency providing that he would pay the agency a service charge if it obtained suitable employment for him. The employment agency found him such a job, but Rogers refused to pay the service charge asserting that he was a minor when he signed the contract. Plaintiff sued to recover the agreed upon service charge from Rogers.]

Under the common law, persons, whether male or female, are classified and referred to as *infants* until they attain the age of twenty-one years. [Citations.]

"By the fifteenth century it seems to have been well settled that an infant's bargain was in general void at his election (that is voidable), and also that he was liable for necessaries." [Citation.]

An early commentary on the common law, after the general statement that contracts made by persons (infants) before attaining the age of twenty-one "may be avoided," sets forth "some exceptions out of this generality," to wit: "*An infant may bind himself to pay for his necessary meat, drinke, apparell, necessary physicke, and such other necessaries,* and likewise for his good teaching or instruction, whereby he may profit himself afterwards." [Citations.] . . . If the infant married, "necessaries" included necessary food and clothing for his wife and child. [Citation.]

In accordance with this ancient rule of the common law, this Court has held an infant's contract, unless for "necessaries" or unless authorized by statute, is voidable by the infant, at his election, and may be disaffirmed during infancy or upon attaining the age of twenty-one. [Citations.]

\* \* \*

In general, our prior decisions are to the effect that the "necessaries" of an infant, his wife and child, include only such necessities of life as food, clothing, shelter, medical attention, etc. In our view, the concept of "necessities" should be enlarged to include such articles of property and such services as are reasonably necessary to enable the infant to earn the money required to provide the necessities of life for himself and those who are legally dependent upon him.

The evidence before us tends to show that defendant, when he contracted with plaintiff, was nineteen years of age, emancipated, married, a high school graduate, within "a quarter or 22 hours" of obtaining his degree in applied science, and capable of holding a job at a starting annual salary of $4,784.00. To hold, as a matter of law, that such a person cannot obligate himself to pay for services rendered him in obtaining employment suitable to his ability, education, and specialized training, enabling him to provide the necessities of life for himself, his wife and his expected child, would place him and others similarly situated under a serious economic handicap.

In the effort to protect "older minors" from improvident or unfair contracts, the law should not deny to them the opportunity and right to obligate themselves for articles of property or services which are reasonably necessary to enable them to provide for the proper support of themselves and their dependents. The minor should be held liable for the reasonable value of articles of property or services received pursuant to such contract.

Applying the foregoing legal principles, which modify *pro tanto* the ancient rule of the common law, we hold that the evidence offered by plaintiff was sufficient for submission to the jury for its determination of issues substantially as indicated below.

To establish liability, plaintiff must satisfy the jury by the greater weight of the evidence that defendant's contract with plaintiff was an appropriate and reasonable means for defendant to obtain suitable employment. If this issue is answered in plaintiff's favor, plaintiff must then establish by the greater weight of the evidence the reasonable value of the services received by defendant pursuant to the contract. Thus, plaintiff's recovery, if any, cannot exceed the reasonable value of its services to defendant.

[Judgment for plaintiff awarding a new trial in accordance with legal principles stated in this opinion.]

---

## CASE 14–4
### Intoxicated Persons/Incompetent Persons
### *FIRST STATE BANK OF SINAI v. HYLAND*
Supreme Court of South Dakota, 1987
399 N.W.2d 894

HENDERSON, J.

Plaintiff-appellant First State Bank of Sinai (Bank) sued defendant-appellee Mervin Hyland (Mervin) seeking to hold him responsible for payment on a promissory note which he cosigned. . . . [T]he circuit court entered . . . judgment holding Mervin not liable for the note's payment. Bank appeals, advocating that the court erred when it ruled that

1. Mervin was incompetent to transact business when he signed the note;
2. Mervin's obligation to Bank was void; and
3. Mervin did not subsequently accept/ratify the obligation.

\* \* \*

On March 10, 1981, Randy Hyland (Randy) and William Buck (Buck), acting for Bank, executed two promissory notes. One note was for $6,800 and the other note was for $3,000. Both notes became due on September 19, 1981.

The notes remained unpaid on their due date and Bank sent notice to Randy informing him of the delinquencies. On October 20, 1981, Randy came to the Bank and met with Buck. Buck explained to Randy that the notes were past due. Randy requested an extension. Buck agreed, but on the condition that Randy's father, Mervin, act as cosigner. One $9,800 promissory note dated October 20, 1981 (the two notes of $6,800 and $3,000 were combined) was created. Randy was given the note for the purpose of obtaining his father's signature. According to Randy, Mervin signed the note on October 20 or 21, 1981.

Mervin had transacted business with Bank since 1974. Previously, he executed approximately 60 promissory notes with Bank. Mervin was apparently a good customer and paid all of his notes on time. Buck testified that he knew Mervin drank, but that he was unaware of any alcohol-related problems.

Randy returned to the Bank about one week later. Mervin had properly signed the note. In Buck's presence, Randy signed the note, which had an April 20, 1982 due date.

On April 20, 1982, the note was unpaid. Buck notified Randy of the overdue note. On May 5, 1982, Randy appeared at the Bank. He brought a blank check signed by Mervin with which the interest on the note was to be paid. Randy filled in the check amount at the Bank for $899.18 (the amount of interest owing). Randy also requested that the note be extended. Buck agreed, but required Mervin's signature as a prerequisite to any extension. A two-month note for $9,800 with a due date of July 2, 1982, was prepared and given to Randy.

Randy did not secure his father's signature on the two-month note, and Mervin testified that he refused to sign that note. On June 22, 1982, Randy filed for bankruptcy which later resulted in the total discharge of his obligation on the note.

On July 14, 1982, Buck sent a letter to Randy and Mervin informing them of Bank's intention to look to Mervin for the note's payment. On December 19, 1982, Bank filed suit against Mervin, requesting $9,800 principal and interest at the rate of 17% until judgment was entered. Mervin answered on January 14, 1983. His defense hinged upon the assertion that he was incapacitated through the use of liquor when he signed the note. He claimed he had no recollection of the note, did not remember seeing it, discussing it with his son, or signing it.

Randy testified that when he brought the note home to his father, the latter was drunk and in bed. Mervin then rose from his bed, walked into the kitchen, and signed the note. Later, Randy returned to the Bank with the signed note.

The record reveals that Mervin was drinking heavily from late summer through early winter of 1981. During this period, Mervin's wife and son accepted responsibilities for managing the farm. Mervin's family testified that his bouts with liquor left him weak, unconcerned with regard to family and business matters, uncooperative, and uncommunicative. When Mervin was drinking, he spent most of his time at home, in bed.

Mervin's problems with alcohol have five times resulted in his involuntary commitment to hospitals. Two of those commitments occurred near the period of the October 1981 note. On September 10, 1981, Mervin was involuntarily committed to the Human Services Center at Yankton. He was released on September 19, 1981. On November 20, 1981, he was involuntarily committed to River Park at Pierre.

Between the periods of his commitments, September 19, 1981 until November 20, 1981, Mervin did transact some business himself. * * *

A trial was held on October 4, 1985. Mervin was found to be entirely without understanding (as a result of alcohol consumption) when he signed the October 20, 1981 promissory note. The court pointed to Mervin's lack of personal care and nonparticipation in family life and farming business as support for finding the contractual relationship between the parties void at its inception. It was further held that Bank had failed to show Mervin's subsequent ratification of the contract. Bank appeals.

* * *

Historically, the void contract concept has been applied to nullify agreements made by mental incompetents who have contracted . . . after a judicial determination of incapacity had been entered. [Citations.] * * *

Mervin had numerous and prolonged problems stemming from his inability to handle alcohol. However, he was not judicially declared incompetent during the note's signing.

* * *

Contractual obligations incurred by intoxicated persons may be voidable. [Citation.] Voidable contracts (contracts other than those entered into following a judicial determination of incapacity) . . . may be rescinded by the previously disabled party. [Citation.] However, disaffirmance must be prompt, upon the recovery of the intoxicated party's mental abilities, and upon his notice of the agreement, if he had forgotten it. [Citation.] * * *

A voidable contract may also be ratified by the party who had contracted while disabled. Upon ratification, the contract becomes a fully valid legal obligation. [Citation.] Ratification can either be express or implied by conduct. [Citations.] In addition, failure of a party to disaffirm a contract over a period of time may, by itself, ripen into a ratification, especially if rescission will result in prejudice to the other party. [Citations.]

Mervin received both verbal notice from Randy and written notice from Bank on or about April 27, 1982, that the note was overdue. On May 5, 1982, Mervin paid the interest owing with a check which Randy delivered to

Bank. This by itself could amount to ratification through conduct. If Mervin wished to avoid the contract, he should have then exercised his right of rescission. We find it impossible to believe that Mervin paid almost $900 in interest without, in his own mind, accepting responsibility for the note. His assertion that paying interest on the note relieved his obligation is equally untenable in light of his numerous past experiences with promissory notes.

\* \* \*

We conclude that Mervin's obligation to Bank is not void. . . . Mervin's obligation on the note was voidable and his subsequent failure to disaffirm (lack of rescission) and his payment of interest (ratification) then transformed the voidable contract into one that is fully binding upon him.

We reverse and remand.

---

# Questions

1. Define a necessary and explain how it affects the contracts of a minor.
2. How and when may a minor ratify a contract?
3. What is the liability of a minor who disaffirms a contract?
4. Distinguish between the legal capacity of a person under guardianship and a mentally incompetent person who is not under guardianship.
5. What is the rule governing an intoxicated person's capacity to enter into a contract?

---

# Problems

1. Michael, a minor, operates a one-man automobile repair shop. Anderson, having heard of Michael's good work on other cars, takes her car to Michael's shop for a thorough engine overhaul. Michael, while overhauling Anderson's engine, carelessly fits an unsuitable piston ring on one of the pistons, with the result that Anderson's engine is seriously damaged. Michael offers to return the sum which Anderson paid him for his work, but refuses to make good the damage. Anderson sues Michael in tort for the damage to her engine. Decision?

2. (a) On March 20, Andy Small became seventeen years old, but he appeared to be at least twenty-one. On April 1, he moved into a rooming house in Chicago where he orally agreed to pay the landlady $300 a month for room and board, payable at the end of each month.

(b) On April 4, he went to Honest Hal's Carfeteria and signed a contract to buy a used car on credit with a small down payment. He made no representation as to his age, but Honest Hal represented the car to be in A–1 condition, which it subsequently turned out not to be.

(c) On April 7, Andy sold and conveyed to Adam Smith a parcel of real estate which he owned.

On April 30, he refused to pay his landlady for his room and board for the month of April; he returned the car to Honest Hal and demanded a refund of his down payment; and he demanded that Adam Smith reconvey the land although the purchase price, which Andy received in cash, had been spent in riotous living. Decisions as to each claim?

3. Jones, a minor, owned a 1999 automobile. She traded it to Stone for a 2000 car. Jones went on a three-week trip and found that the 2000 car was not as good as the 1999 car. She asked Stone to return the 1999 car but was told that it had been sold to Tate. Jones thereupon sued Tate for the return of the 1999 car. Decision?

4. On May 7, Roy, a minor, a resident of Smithton, purchased an automobile from Royal Motors, Inc., for $12,750 in cash. On the same day, he bought a motor scooter from Marks, also a minor, for $750 and paid him in full. On June 5, two days before attaining his majority, Roy disaffirmed the contracts and offered to return the car and the motor scooter to the respective sellers. Royal Motors and Marks each refused the offers. On June 16, Roy brought separate appropriate actions against Royal Motors and Marks to recover the purchase price of the car and the motor scooter. By agreement on July 30, Royal Motors accepted the automobile. Royal then filed a counterclaim against Roy for the reasonable rental value of the car between June 5 and July 30. The car was not damaged during this period. Royal knew that Roy lived twenty-five miles from his place of employment in Smithton and that he would probably drive the car, as he did, to provide himself transportation. Decision as to (a) Roy's action against Royal Motors, Inc., and its counterclaim against Roy; (b) Roy's action against Marks?

5. George Jones on October 1, being then a minor, entered into a contract with Johnson Motor Company, a dealer in automobiles, to buy a car for $10,850. He paid $1,100 down and, under the agreement, was to make monthly payments thereafter of $325 each. After making the first payment on November 1, he failed to make any more payments. Although Jones was seventeen years old at the time he made the contract, he represented to the company that he was twenty-one years

old because he was afraid that if the company knew his real age, it would not sell the car to him. His appearance was that of a man of twenty-one years of age. On December 15, the company repossessed the car under the terms provided in the contract. At that time, the car had been damaged and was in need of repairs. On December 20, George Jones became of age and at once disaffirmed the contract and demanded the return of the $1,425 he had paid on it. On refusal of the company to do so, George Jones brought an action to recover the $1,425, and the company set up a counterclaim for $1,500 for expenses it incurred in repairing the car. Decision?

6. Rebecca entered into a written contract to sell certain real estate to Mary, a minor, for $80,000, payable $4,000 on the execution of the contract and $800 on the first day of each month thereafter until paid. Mary paid the $4,000 down payment and eight monthly installments before attaining her majority. Thereafter, Mary made two additional monthly payments and caused the contract to be recorded in the county where the real estate was located. Mary was then advised by her attorney that the contract was voidable. After being so advised, Mary immediately tendered the contract to Rebecca, together with a deed reconveying all of Mary's interest in the property to Rebecca. Also, Mary demanded that Rebecca return the money she had paid under the contract. Rebecca refused the tender and declined to repay any portion of the money paid to her by Mary. Mary then brought an action to cancel the contract and recover the amount paid to Rebecca. Decision?

7. Anita sold and delivered an automobile to Marvin, a minor. Marvin, during his minority, returned the automobile to Anita, saying that he disaffirmed the sale. Anita accepted the automobile and said she would return the purchase price to Marvin the next day. Later in the day, Marvin changed his mind, took the automobile without Anita's knowledge, and sold it to Chris. Anita had not returned the purchase price when Marvin took the car. On what theory, if any, can Anita recover from Marvin? Explain.

8. Ira, who in 1998 had been found innocent of a criminal offense because of insanity, was released from a hospital for the criminally insane during the summer of 1999 and since that time has been a reputable and well-respected citizen and businessperson. On February 1, 2000, Ira and Shirley entered into a contract in which Ira would sell his farm to Shirley for $100,000. Ira now seeks to void the contract. Shirley insists that Ira is fully competent and has no right to avoid the contract. Who will prevail? Why?

9. Daniel, while under the influence of alcohol, agreed to sell his 1995 automobile to Belinda for $8,000. The next morning, when Belinda went to Daniel's house with the $8,000 in cash, Daniel stated that he did not remember the transaction but that "a deal is a deal." One week after completing the sale, Daniel decides that he wishes to avoid the contract. What result?

10. Langstraat, age seventeen, owned a motorcycle that he insured against liability with Midwest Mutual Insurance Company. He signed a notice of rejection attached to the policy indicating that he did not desire to purchase uninsured motorists' coverage from the insurance company. Later he was involved in an accident with another motorcycle owned and operated by a party who was uninsured. Langstraat now seeks to recover from the insurance company, asserting that his rejection was not a valid rejection because he is a minor. Decision?

11. G.A.S. married his wife, S.I.S., on January 19, 1957. He began to suffer mental health problems in 1970, during which year he was hospitalized at the Delaware State Hospital for eight weeks. Similar illnesses occurred in 1972 and the early part of 1974, with G.A.S. suffering from such symptoms as paranoia and loss of a sense of reality. In early 1975, G.A.S. was still committed to the Delaware State Hospital, attending a regular job during the day and returning to the hospital at night. During this time, he entered into a separation agreement prepared by his wife's attorney. G.A.S., however, never spoke with the attorney about the contents of the agreement; nor did he read it prior to signing. Moreover, G.A.S. was not independently represented by counsel when he executed this agreement. G.A.S. brings this action to disaffirm the separation agreement. Decision?

12. A fifteen-year-old minor was employed by Midway Toyota, Inc., of Great Falls, Montana. On August 18, 1997, the minor, while engaged in lifting heavy objects, injured his lower back. In October 1997 he underwent surgery to remove a herniated disk. Midway Toyota paid him the appropriate amount of temporary total disability payments ($53.36 per week) from August 18, 1997, through November 15, 1998. In February 1999 a final settlement was reached for 150 weeks of permanent partial disability benefits totaling $6,136.40. Tom Mazurek represented Midway Toyota in the negotiations leading to the agreement and negotiated directly with the minor and his mother, Hermoine Parrent. The final settlement agreement was signed by the minor only. Mrs. Parrent, who was present at the time, did not object to the signing, but neither she nor anyone else of "legal guardian status" co-signed the agreement. The minor later sought to disaffirm the agreement and reopen his workers' compensation case. The workers' compensation court denied his petition, holding that Mrs. Parrent "participated fully in consideration of the offered final settlement and . . . ratified and approved it on behalf of her ward . . . to the same legal effect as if she had actually signed [it]. . . ." The minor appealed. Decision?

13. Rose, a minor, bought a new Buick Riviera from Sheehan Buick. Seven months later, while still a minor, he attempted to disaffirm the purchase. Sheehan Buick refused to accept the return of the car or to refund the purchase price. Rose, at the time of the purchase, gave all the appearance of being of legal age. The car had been used by him to carry on his school, business, and social activities. Decision?

14. L. D. Robertson bought a pickup truck from King and Julian, doing business as the Julian Pontiac Company. Robertson, at the time of purchase, was seventeen years old, living at home with his parents, and driving his father's truck around

the county to different construction jobs. According to the sales contract, he traded in a passenger car for the truck and was given $723 credit toward the truck's $1,743 purchase price, agreeing to pay the remainder in monthly installments. After he paid the first month's installment, the truck caught fire and was rendered useless. The insurance agent, upon finding that Robertson was a minor, refused to deal with him. Consequently, Robertson sued to exercise his right as a minor to rescind the contract and to recover the purchase price he had already paid ($723 credit for the car plus the one month's installment). The defendants argue that Robertson, even as a minor, cannot rescind the contract as it was for a necessary item. Decision?

15.   Haydocy Pontiac sold Jennifer Lee an automobile for $1,552, of which $1,402 was financed with a note and security agreement. At the time of the sale Lee, age twenty, represented to Haydocy that she was twenty-one years old, the age of majority, and capable of contracting. After receiving the car, Lee allowed John Roberts to take possession of it. Roberts took the car and has not returned. Lee has failed to make any further payments on the car. Haydocy has sued to recover on the note. Lee disaffirms the contract, claiming that she was too young to enter into a valid contract. Decision?

16.   Carol White ordered a $225 pair of contact lenses through an optometrist. White, an emancipated minor, paid $100 by check and agreed to pay the remaining $125 at a later time. The doctor ordered the lenses, incurring a debt of $110. After the lenses were ordered, White called to cancel her order and stopped payment on the $100 check. The lenses could be used by no one but White. The doctor sued White for the value of the lenses. Decision?

17.   Williamson, her mortgage in default, was threatened with foreclosure on her home. She decided to sell the house. The Matthewses learned of this and contacted her about the matter. Williamson claims that she offered to sell her equity for $17,000 and that the Matthewses agreed to pay off the mortgage. The Matthewses contend that the asking price was $1,700. On September 27, the parties signed a contract of sale, which stated the purchase price to be $1,800 (an increase of $100 to account for furniture in the house) plus the unpaid balance of the mortgage. The parties met again on October 10 to sign the deed. Later that day, Williamson, concerned that she had not received her full $17,000 consideration, contacted an attorney. On October 12, Williamson filed for injunctive relief, seeking to set aside the sale based upon inadequate consideration and mental weakness due to intoxication. Decision?

18.   Halbman, a minor, purchased a 1968 Oldsmobile from Lemke for $1,250. Under the terms of the contract, Halbman would pay $1,000 down and the balance in $25 weekly installments. Upon making the down payment, Halbman received possession of the car, but Lemke retained the title until the balance was paid. After Halbman had made his first four payments, a connecting rod in the car's engine broke. Lemke denied responsibility, but offered to help Halbman repair it if Halbman would provide the parts. Halbman, however, placed the car in a garage where the repairs cost $637.40. Halbman never paid the repair bill.

Hoping to avoid any liability for the vehicle, Lemke transferred title to Halbman even though Halbman never paid the balance owed. Halbman returned the title with a letter disaffirming the contract and demanded return of the money paid. Lemke refused. Because the repair bill remained unpaid, the garage removed the car's engine and transmission and towed the body to Halbman's father's house. Vandalism during the period of storage rendered the car unsalvageable. Several times Halbman requested Lemke to remove the car. Lemke refused. Halbman sued Lemke for the return of his consideration, and Lemke countersued for the amount still owed on the contract. Decision?

19.   On June 11, Chagnon bought a 1995 Buick from Keser for $9950. Chagnon, who was then a twenty-year-old minor, obtained the contract by falsely advising Keser that he was over twenty-one years old, the age of majority. On September 25, two months and four days after his twenty-first birthday, Chagnon disaffirmed the contract and, ten days later, returned the Buick to Keser. He then brought suit to recover the money he had paid for the automobile. Keser counterclaimed that he suffered damages as the direct result of Chagnon's false representation of his age. A trial was had to the court, sitting without a jury, all of which culminated in a judgment in favor of Chagnon against Keser in the sum of $6557.80. This particular sum was arrived at by the trial court in the following manner: the trial court found that Chagnon initially purchased the Buick for the sum of $9950 and that he was entitled to the return of his $9950; and then, by way of setoff, the trial court subtracted from the $9950 the sum of $3392.20, apparently representing the difference between the purchase price paid for the vehicle and the reasonable value of the Buick on October 5, the date when the Edsel was returned to Keser. Decision?

**WWW**  **Internet Exercise**  Find and review information on (a) laws governing the employment of minors, (b) gifts to minors, and (c) the Uniform Guardianship and Protective Proceedings Act.

# CHAPTER 15

# Contracts in Writing

An **oral** contract, that is, one not written, is in every way as enforceable as a written contract unless otherwise provided by statute. Although most contracts are not required to be in writing to be enforceable, it is highly desirable that significant contracts be written. Written contracts avoid the numerous problems that proving the terms of oral contracts inevitably involves. The process of setting down the contractual terms in a written document also tends to clarify the terms and to reveal problems the parties might not otherwise foresee. Moreover, the terms of a written contract do not change over time, while the parties' recollections of the terms might.

When the parties do reduce their agreement to a complete and final written expression, the law (under the parol evidence rule) honors this document by not allowing the parties to introduce any evidence in a lawsuit that would alter, modify, or vary the terms of the written contract. Nevertheless, the parties may differ as to the proper or intended meaning of language contained in the written agreement where such language is ambiguous or susceptible to different interpretations. To ascertain the proper meaning requires an interpretation, or construction, of the contract. The rules of construction permit the parties to introduce evidence to resolve ambiguity and to show the meaning of the language employed and the sense in which both parties used it.

This chapter will examine (1) the types of contracts that must be in writing to be enforceable, (2) the parol evidence rule, and (3) the rules of contractual interpretation.

## STATUTE OF FRAUDS

The statute of frauds requires that certain designated types of contracts be evidenced by a writing to be enforceable. The original statute became law in 1677, when the English Parliament adopted "An Act for Prevention of Frauds and Perjuries," commonly referred to as the statute of frauds. From the early days of U.S. history practically every State had and continues to have a statute of frauds patterned upon the original English statute.

The statute of frauds has no relation whatever to any kind of fraud practiced in the making of contracts. The common law rules relating to such fraud are discussed in Chapter 11. The purpose of the statute is to prevent perjured testimony in court from creating fraud in the proof of certain oral contracts, which purpose the statute accomplishes by requiring that certain contracts be evidenced by a signed writing. On the other hand, the statute does not prevent the performance of oral contracts if the parties are willing to perform. In brief, the statute relates only to the proof or evidence of a contract. It has nothing to do with the circumstances surrounding the making of a contract or with a contract's validity.

## CONTRACTS WITHIN THE STATUTE OF FRAUDS

Many more types of contracts are *not* subject to the statute of frauds than are subject to it. Most oral contracts, as previously indicated, are as enforceable and valid as a written contract. If, however, a given contract is subject to the statute of frauds, the contract is said to be **within** the statute; to be enforceable, it must comply with the statute's requirements. All other types of contracts are said to be "not within" or "outside" the statute and need not comply with its requirements to be enforceable.

The following kinds of contracts are within the original English statute and remain within most State statutes; compliance requires a writing signed by the party to be charged (the party against whom the contract is to be enforced).

1. Promises to answer for the duty of another
2. Promises of an executor or administrator to answer personally for a duty of the decedent whose funds he is administering
3. Agreements upon consideration of marriage
4. Agreements for the transfer of an interest in land
5. Agreements not to be performed within one year

A sixth type of contract within the statute applied to contracts for the sale of goods. Section 2–201 of the UCC now governs the enforceability of contracts of this kind.

The various provisions of the statute of frauds apply independently. Accordingly, a contract for the sale of an interest in land may also be a contract in consideration of marriage, a contract not to be performed in one year, *and* a contract for the sale of goods.

In addition to those contracts specified in the original statute, most States require that other contracts be evidenced by a writing as well; for example, a contract to make a will, to authorize an agent to sell or purchase real estate, or to pay a commission to a real estate broker. Moreover, the UCC requires that a contract for the sale of securities, contracts creating certain types of security interests, and contracts for the sale of other personal property for more than $5,000 also be in writing.

## Suretyship Provision

The **suretyship** provision applies to a contractual promise by a **surety** (*promisor*) to a **creditor** (*promisee*) to perform the duties or obligations of a third person (**principal debtor**) if the principal debtor does not perform. Thus, if a mother tells a merchant to extend $1,000 worth of credit to her son and says, "If he doesn't pay, I will," the promise must be in writing to be enforceable. The factual situation can be reduced to the simple statement "If X doesn't pay, I will." The promise is said to be **collateral,** in that the promisor is not primarily liable. The mother does not promise to pay in any event; her promise is to pay only if the one primarily obligated, her son, defaults.

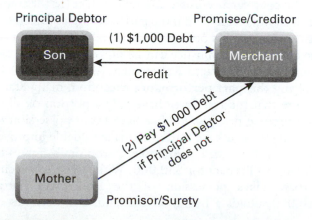

The rule applies only to cases involving three parties and two contracts. The primary contract, between the principal debtor and the creditor, creates the indebtedness. The collateral contract is made by the third person (surety) directly with the creditor, whereby the surety promises to pay the debt to the creditor in case the principal debtor fails to do so. For a complete discussion of suretyship see Chapter 38.

*Original Promise* If the promisor makes an **original promise** by undertaking to become primarily liable, then the statute of frauds does not apply. For example, a father tells a merchant to deliver certain items to his daughter and says, "I will pay $400 for them." The father is not promising to answer for the debt of another; rather, he is making the debt his own. It is to the father, and the father alone, that the merchant extends credit; only from the father may the creditor seek payment. The statute of frauds does not apply, and the promise may be oral.

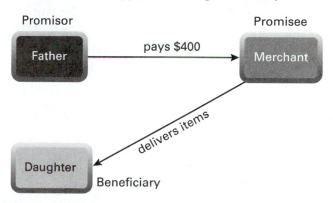

See Case 15–1

*Main Purpose Doctrine* The courts have developed an exception to the suretyship provision based on the purpose or object of the promisor, called the "main purpose doctrine" or "leading object rule." Where the object or purpose of the promisor is to obtain an economic benefit for himself, the promise is *not* within the statute. Restatement, Section 116. The expected benefit to the surety "must be such as to justify the conclusion that his main purpose in making the promise is to advance his own interest." Restatement, Section 116, Comment b. The fact that the surety received consideration for his promise or that he might receive a slight and indirect advantage is insufficient to bring the promise within the main purpose doctrine.

Suppose that a supply company has refused to furnish materials upon the credit of a building contractor. Facing a possible slowdown in the construction of his building, the owner of the land promises the supplier that if he will extend credit to the contractor, the owner will pay if the contractor does not. Here, the primary purpose of the promisor is to serve his own economic interest, even though the performance of the promise would discharge the duty of another. The intent to benefit the contractor is at most incidental, and courts will uphold oral promises of this type.

***Promise Made to Debtor***  The suretyship provision has been interpreted not to include promises made to a debtor. For example, D owes a debt to C. S promises D that she will pay D's debt in return for valid consideration from D. Because S made the promise to the debtor (D), not the creditor, the promise may be oral. The promise is not a collateral promise to pay C if D fails to pay and thus is not a promise to discharge the obligation of another.

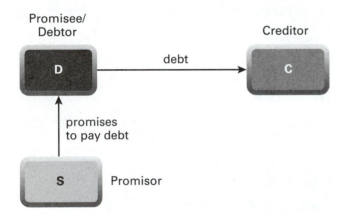

## Executor-Administrator Provision

The executor-administrator provision applies to the contractual promises of an executor of a decedent's will, or to those of the administrator of his estate if the decedent dies without a will, to answer personally for a duty of the decedent. An **executor** or **administrator** is a person appointed by a court to carry on, subject to order of court, the administration of the estate of a deceased person. If the will of a decedent nominates a certain person as executor, the court customarily appoints that person. (For a more detailed discussion of executors and administrators, see Chapter 52.) If an executor or administrator promises to pay personally a debt of the decedent, the promise must be in writing to be enforceable. For example, Brian, who is Ann's son and executor of her will, recognizing that Ann's estate will not provide funds sufficient to pay all of her debts, orally promises Curtis, one of Ann's creditors, that he, Brian, will personally pay

all of his mother's creditors in full in return for valid consideration from Curtis. Brian's oral promise is not enforceable. This provision does not apply to promises to pay debts of the deceased out of assets of the estate.

The executor-administrator provision is thus a specific application of the suretyship provision. Accordingly, the exceptions to the suretyship provision apply to this provision as well.

## Marriage Provision

The notable feature of the marriage provision is that it does *not* apply to mutual promises to marry. The provision applies only if a promise to marry is made in consideration for some promise other than a reciprocal promise to marry. Restatement, Section 124. If, for example, Greg and Betsy each orally promise and agree to marry each other, their agreement is not within the statute and is a binding contract between them. If, however, Greg promises to convey title to a certain farm to Betsy if she accepts his proposal of marriage, their agreement would fall within the statute of frauds.

## Land Contract Provision

The land contract provision covers promises to transfer "any interest in land," which includes any right, privilege, power, or immunity in real property. Restatement, Section 125. Thus, all promises to transfer, buy, or pay for an interest in land, including ownership interests, leases, mortgages, options, and easements, are within the provision.

The land contract provision does not include contracts to transfer an interest in personal property. It also does not cover short-term leases, which by statute in most States are those for one year or less; contracts to build a building on a piece of land; contracts to do work on the land; or contracts to insure a building on the land.

The courts may enforce an oral contract for the transfer of an interest in land if the party seeking enforcement has so changed his position in reasonable reliance upon the contract that injustice can be prevented only by enforcing the contract. Restatement, Section 129. In applying this **part performance** exception, many States require that the transferee have paid a portion or all of the purchase price *and* either have taken possession of the real estate or have started to make valuable improvements on the land. For example, Aaron orally agrees to sell land to Barbara for $30,000. With Aaron's consent, Barbara takes possession of the land, pays Aaron $10,000, builds a house on the land, and occupies it.

Several years later, Aaron repudiates the contract. The courts will enforce the contract against Aaron. On the other hand, the courts will not enforce the promise unless equity so demands.

An oral promise by a purchaser is also enforceable if the seller fully performs by conveying the property to the purchaser. As previously indicated, however, payment of part or all of the price is not sufficient in itself to remove the contract from the scope of the statute.

## One-Year Provision

The statute of frauds requires all contracts that *cannot* be fully performed within one year of their making to be in writing. Restatement, Section 130.

***The Possibility Test***   To determine whether a contract can be performed within a year, the courts ask whether it is *possible* to complete its performance within a year. The **possibility test** does not ask whether the agreement is likely to be performed within one year from the date it was formed; nor does it ask whether the parties think that performance will be within the year. The enforceability of the contract depends not on probabilities or on the actuality of subsequent events but on whether the terms of the contract make it possible for performance to occur within one year. For example, an oral contract between Alice and Bill for Alice to build a bridge, which should reasonably take three years, is enforceable if it is possible, although extremely unlikely and difficult, for Alice to perform the contract in one year. Similarly, if Alice agrees to employ Bill for life, this contract also is not within the statute of frauds. Given the possibility that Bill may die within the year (in which case the contract would be completely performed), the contract is therefore one that is *fully performable* within a year. Contracts of indefinite duration are likewise excluded from the provision. On the other hand, an oral contract to employ another person for thirteen months could not possibly be performed within a year and is unenforceable.

 *See Case 15–2*

***Computation of Time***   The year runs from the time the agreement is made, not from the time when the performance is to begin. For example, on January 1, 2000, A orally hires B to work for eleven months starting on May 1, 2000. That contract will be fully performed on March 31, 2001, which is more than one year after January 1, 2000, the date the contract was made. Consequently, it is *within* the statute of frauds and unenforceable as it is oral.

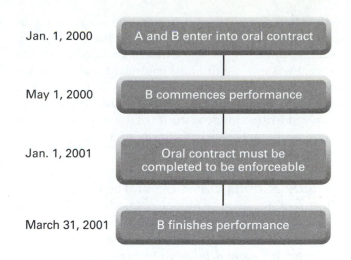

| | |
|---|---|
| Jan. 1, 2000 | A and B enter into oral contract |
| May 1, 2000 | B commences performance |
| Jan. 1, 2001 | Oral contract must be completed to be enforceable |
| March 31, 2001 | B finishes performance |

Similarly, a contract for a year's performance, which is to begin three days after the date on which the contract is made, is within the statute and, if oral, is unenforceable. If, however, the performance is to begin the following day or, under the terms of the agreement, could have begun the following day, the contract is not within the statute and need not be in writing, as the one year's performance would be completed on the anniversary date of the making of the contract.

***Full Performance by One Party***   Where one party to a contract has fully performed, most courts hold that the promise of the other party is enforceable, even though by its terms the performance of the contract was not possible within the period of a year. Restatement, Section 130. For example, Vince borrows $4,800 from Julie, orally promising to pay Julie $4,800 in three annual installments of $1,600. Vince's promise is enforceable, notwithstanding the one-year provision, because Julie has fully performed by making the loan.

## Sales of Goods

The original statute of frauds, which applied to contracts for the sale of goods, has been used as a prototype for the UCC Article 2 statute of frauds provision. Section 2–201 of the UCC provides that a contract for the sale of goods for the price of **$500 or more** is not enforceable unless there is some writing sufficient to indicate that the parties have made a contract for sale. **Goods,** as previously indicated, are defined as movable personal property. Section 2–105(1). The definition expressly includes growing crops and unborn animals.

*Admission* The Code permits an oral contract for the sale of goods to be enforced against a party who in his pleading, testimony, or otherwise in court admits that a contract was made, but limits enforcement to the quantity of goods so admitted. Section 2–201(3)(b). The language "otherwise in court" may include pretrial deposition and written interrogatories of the defendant. Some courts now apply this exception to other statute of frauds provisions.

*Specially Manufactured Goods* The Code permits a seller to enforce an oral contract for goods specially manufactured for a buyer, but only if evidence indicates that the goods were made for the buyer and the seller can show that he made a *substantial beginning* of their manufacture prior to receiving any notice of repudiation. Section 2–201(3)(a). If goods manufactured on special order are nonetheless readily marketable in the ordinary course of the seller's business, this exception does not apply.

For example, if Jim brings an action against Robin alleging breach of an oral contract under which Robin agreed to purchase from Jim three million balloons with Robin's trademark imprinted on them at a price of $30,000, the action is not subject to the defense of the statute of frauds unless Robin can show (1) that the balloons are suitable for sale to other buyers, which is highly improbable in view of the trademark, or (2) that Jim received notice of repudiation before he had made a substantial start on the production of the balloons or had otherwise substantially committed himself to procuring them.

*Delivery or Payment and Acceptance* Prior to the Code, delivery and acceptance of part of the goods or payment of part of the price made the entire oral contract enforceable against the buyer who had received part delivery or against the seller who had received part payment. Under the Code, such "partial performance" validates the contract only for the goods that have been accepted or for which payment has been accepted. Section 2–201(3)(c). To illustrate, Johnson orally agrees to buy 1,000 watches from Barnes for $15,000. Barnes delivers 300 watches to Johnson, who receives and accepts the watches. The oral contract is enforceable to the extent of 300 watches ($4,500)—those received and accepted—but is unenforceable to the extent of 700 watches ($10,500).

But what if the contract, such as one for the sale of an automobile, is indivisible so that the making of part payment creates only a choice between not enforcing the contract or enforcing it as a whole? Presently, authority is divided on this issue, although the better rule appears to be that such part payment and acceptance makes the entire contract enforceable.

Figure 15–1 summarizes the contracts within and the exceptions to the statute of frauds.

◆ *See Figure 15–1*

**FIGURE 15–1** The Statute of Frauds

| Contracts Within the Statute of Frauds | Exceptions |
|---|---|
| **Suretyship—a promise to answer for the duty of another** | • Main purpose rule<br>• Original promise<br>• Promise made to debtor |
| **Executor-Administrator—a promise to answer personally for debt of decedent** | • Main purpose rule<br>• Original promise<br>• Promise made to debtor |
| **Agreements made upon consideration of marriage** | • Mutual promises to marry |
| **Agreements for the transfer of an interest in land** | • Part performance plus detrimental reliance<br>• Seller conveys property |
| **Agreements not to be performed within one year** | • Full performance by one party<br>• Possibility of performance within one year |
| **Sale of goods for $500 or more** | • Admission<br>• Specially manufactured goods<br>• Delivery or payment and acceptance |

## Modification or Rescission of Contracts within the Statute of Frauds

Oral contracts modifying previously existing contracts are unenforceable if the resulting contract is within the statute of frauds. The reverse is also true: an oral modification of a prior contract is enforceable if the new contract is not within the statute. Thus, examples of unenforceable oral contractual modifications include an oral promise to guarantee additional duties of another, an oral agreement to substitute different land for that described in the original contract, and an oral agreement to extend an employee's contract for six months to a total of two years. On the other hand, an oral agreement to modify an employee's contract from two years to six months at a higher salary is not within the statute of frauds and is enforceable.

By extension, an oral rescission is effective and discharges all unperformed duties under the original contract. For example, Linda and Donald enter into a written contract of employment for a two-year term. Later they orally agree to rescind the contract. The oral agreement is effective, and the written contract is rescinded. Where, however, land has been transferred, an agreement to rescind the transaction constitutes a contract to retransfer the land and is within the statute of frauds.

Under the UCC, the decisive point is the contract price *after* the modification. Section 2–209(3). If the parties enter into an oral contract to sell for $450 a motorcycle to be delivered to the buyer and later, prior to delivery, orally agree that the seller shall paint the motorcycle and install new tires and that the buyer shall pay a price of $550, the modified contract is unenforceable. Conversely, if the parties have a written contract for the sale of 200 bushels of wheat at a price of $4 per bushel and later orally agree to decrease the quantity to 100 bushels at the same price per bushel, the agreement, as modified, is for a total price of $400 and thus is enforceable.

## COMPLIANCE WITH THE STATUTE OF FRAUDS

Even though a contract is within the statute of frauds, a sufficient *writing* or *memorandum* may justify its enforcement. The writing need not be in any specific form, nor be an attempt by the parties to enter into a binding contract, nor represent their entire agreement: it need only comply with the requirements of the statute of frauds.

### General Contracts Provisions

The English statute of frauds and most modern statutes of frauds require that the agreement be evidenced by a writing to be enforceable. The note or memorandum, which may be formal or informal, must:

1. specify the parties to the contract;
2. specify with reasonable certainty the subject matter and the essential terms of the unperformed promises; and
3. be signed by the party to be charged or by his agent.

The statute's purpose in requiring a writing is to ensure that the parties have entered into a contract. The writing, therefore, need not exist at the time of the litigation; showing that the memorandum once existed is sufficient.

The memorandum may be a receipt, a check, or a telegram. It may be such that the parties themselves view it as having no legal significance whatever, as, for example, a personal letter between the parties, an interdepartmental communication, an advertisement, or the record books of a business. The writing need not have been delivered to the party who seeks to take advantage of it, and it may even contain a repudiation of the oral agreement. For example, Adrian and Joseph enter into an oral agreement that Adrian will sell Blackacre to Joseph for $5,000. Adrian subsequently receives a better offer and sends Joseph a signed letter, which begins by reciting all the material terms of the oral agreement. The letter concludes, "Since my agreement to sell Blackacre to you for $5,000 was oral, I am not bound by my promise. I have since received a better offer and will accept that one." Adrian's letter constitutes a sufficient memorandum for Joseph to enforce Adrian's promise to sell Blackacre. It should be recognized that because Joseph did not sign the memorandum, the writing does not bind him. Thus, a contract may be enforceable against only one of the parties.

The "signature" may be initials or may even be typewritten or printed, so long as the party intended it to authenticate the writing. Furthermore, the signature need not be at the bottom of the page or at the customary place for a signature.

The memorandum may consist of *several* papers or documents, none of which would be sufficient by itself. The several memoranda, however, must together satisfy all of the requirements of a writing to comply with the statute of frauds and must clearly indicate that they relate to the same transaction. Restatement, Section 132. The latter requirement can be satisfied if (1) the writings are physically attached, (2) the writings refer to each other, or (3) an examination of the writings shows them to be in reference to each other.

 *See Case 15–3*

## Sale of Goods

The statute of frauds provision under Article 2 is more liberal. For a sale of goods, Section 2–201 of the Code requires merely some writing

1. sufficient to indicate that a contract has been made between the parties;
2. specifying the quantity of goods to be sold; and
3. signed by the party against whom enforcement is sought or by her authorized agent or broker.

The writing is sufficient even if it omits or incorrectly states an agreed-upon term; however, where the quantity term is misstated, the contract can be enforced only to the extent of the quantity stated in the writing.

As with general contracts, several related documents may satisfy the writing requirement. Moreover, the signature again may be by initials or even typewritten or printed, so long as the party intended thereby to authenticate the writing.

In addition, the Code provides relief to a merchant who, within a reasonable time after entering into the oral contract, confirms the contract for the sale of goods by a letter or signed writing to the other party if he too is a merchant. As between **merchants,** the **written confirmation,** if sufficient against the sender, is also sufficient against the recipient unless he gives written notice of his objection within ten days after receiving the confirmation. Section 2–201(2). This means that if these requirements have been met, the recipient of the writing is in the same position he would have assumed by signing it; and the confirmation, therefore, is enforceable against him.

For example, Brown Co. and ATM Industries enter into an oral contract which provides that ATM will deliver twelve thousand shirts to Brown at $6 per shirt. Brown sends a letter to ATM acknowledging the agreement. The letter, containing the quantity term but not the price, is signed by Brown's president and is mailed to ATM's vice president for sales. Brown was bound by the contract once its authorized agent signs the letter; ATM cannot raise the defense of the statute of frauds if ATM does not object to the letter within ten days after receiving it. Therefore, it is extremely important for merchants to examine their mail carefully and promptly to make certain that any written confirmations conform to

their understanding of their outstanding contractual agreements.

## EFFECT OF NONCOMPLIANCE

The English statute provided that "no action shall be brought" upon a contract to which the statute of frauds applied *and* which did not comply with its requirements. The Code, by comparison, states that the contract "is not enforceable by way of action or defense." Despite the difference in language the basic legal effect is the same: a contracting party has a defense to an action by the other party to enforce an oral contract that is within the statute and that does not comply with its requirements. In short, the oral contract is **unenforceable.**

For example, if Tia, a painter, and James, a homeowner, make an oral contract under which James is to give Tia a certain tract of land in return for her painting his house, the contract is unenforceable under the statute of frauds. It is a contract for the sale of an interest in land. Either party can repudiate and has a defense to an action by the other to enforce the contract.

### Full Performance

After all the promises of an oral contract have been performed by all the parties, the statute of frauds no longer applies. Accordingly, neither party can have the contract set aside on the ground that it should have been in writing. The purpose of the statute is not to prohibit the performance of oral contracts but simply to exclude oral evidence of contracts within its provisions. Courts, in other words, will not "unscramble" a fully performed contract merely because it was not in writing. In short, the statute applies to executory contracts only.

### Restitution

A party to a contract that is unenforceable because of the statute of frauds may have, nonetheless, acted in reliance upon the contract. In such a case the party may recover in restitution the benefits he conferred upon the other in relying upon the unenforceable contract. Thus, if Wilton makes an oral contract to furnish services to Rochelle that are not to be performed within a year and Rochelle discharges Wilton after three months, Wilton may recover as restitution the value of the services he rendered during the three months. Most courts require, however, that the party seeking restitution not be in default.

## Promissory Estoppel

A growing number of courts have used the doctrine of promissory estoppel to displace the requirement of a writing by enforcing oral contracts within the statute of frauds where the party seeking enforcement has reasonably and foreseeably relied upon a promise in such a way that injustice can be avoided only by enforcing the promise. Restatement, Section 139. This section is essentially identical to Section 90 of the Restatement, which, as discussed in Chapter 12, dispenses with the requirement of consideration, although the comments to Section 139 state that "the requirement of consideration is more easily displaced than the requirement of a writing." The remedy granted is limited, as justice requires, and depends upon such factors as the availability of other remedies; the foreseeability, reasonableness, and substantiality of the reliance; and the extent to which reliance corroborates evidence of the promise.

# PAROL EVIDENCE RULE

A contract reduced to writing and signed by the parties is frequently the result of many conversations, conferences, proposals, counterproposals, letters, and memoranda and sometimes is the product of negotiations conducted, or partly conducted, by agents of the parties. Any given stage in the negotiations may have produced tentative agreements that were superseded (or regarded as such by one of the parties) by subsequent negotiations. Offers may have been made and withdrawn, either expressly or by implication, or forgotten in the give-and-take of negotiations. Ultimately, though, the parties prepare and sign a final draft of the written contract, which may or may not include all of the points that were discussed and agreed upon during the negotiations. By signing the agreement, however, the parties have declared it to be their contract; and the terms it contains represent the contract they have made. As a rule of substantive law, neither party is later permitted to show that the contract they made differs from the terms and provisions that appear in the written agreement. This rule, which also applies to wills and deeds, is called the parol evidence rule.

## THE RULE

When a contract is expressed in a writing that is intended to be the complete and final expression of the rights and duties of the parties, parol evidence of *prior* oral or written negotiations or agreements of the parties, or their *contemporaneous* oral agreements that vary or change the written contract, are not admissible. The word *parol* means literally "speech" or "words." The term **parol evidence** refers to any evidence, whether oral or in writing, which is outside the written contract and not incorporated into it either directly or by reference.

The parol evidence rule applies only to an *integrated* contract; that is, one contained in a certain writing or writings to which the parties have assented as the statement of the complete agreement or contract between them. When a contract is thus integrated, the courts will not permit parol evidence of any prior or contemporaneous agreement to vary, change, alter, or modify any of the terms or provisions of the written contract. Restatement, Section 213.

A writing may contain a **merger clause,** which states that the writing is intended to be the complete and final expression of the agreement between the parties. Most courts consider a merger clause to be conclusive proof of an integrated contract, while a few courts view a merger clause only as evidence of an integrated contract.

The reason for the parol evidence rule is that the parties, by reducing their entire agreement to writing, are regarded as having intended the writing that they signed to include the whole of their agreement. The terms and provisions contained in the writing are there because the parties intended them to be there. Conversely, any provision not in the writing is regarded as having been omitted because the parties intended that it should not be a part of their contract. In safeguarding the contract as made by the parties, the rule excluding evidence that would tend to change, alter, vary, or modify the terms of a written agreement applies to all integrated written contracts and deals with what terms are part of the contract. The rule differs from the statute of frauds, which governs what contracts must be evidenced by a writing to be enforceable.

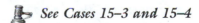 *See Cases 15–3 and 15–4*

## SITUATIONS TO WHICH THE RULE DOES NOT APPLY

The parol evidence rule, in spite of its name, is neither an exclusionary rule of evidence nor a rule of construction or interpretation; rather, it is a rule of substantive law that defines the limits of a contract. Bearing this in mind, as well as the reason underlying the rule, it should be clear that the rule does **not** apply to any of the following:

1. A contract that is *partly written* and partly oral; that is, one in which the parties do not intend the writing to be their entire agreement.
2. A clerical or *typographical error* that obviously does not represent the agreement of the parties. Where, for example, a written contract for the services of a skilled mining engineer provides that his rate of compensation is to be $7 per day, a court of equity would permit reformation (correction) of the contract to rectify the mistake upon a showing that both parties intended the rate to be $700 per day.
3. Evidence showing the lack of *contractual capacity* of one of the parties, such as proof of minority, intoxication, or mental incompetency. Such evidence would not tend to vary, change, or alter any of the terms of the written agreement, but rather would show that the written agreement was voidable or void.
4. A *defense* of fraud, misrepresentation, duress, undue influence, mistake, illegality, or unconscionability. Though evidence establishing any of these defenses would not purport to vary, change, or alter any of the terms of the written agreement, it would show such agreement to be voidable, void, or unenforceable.
5. A *condition precedent* to which the parties agreed orally at the time they executed the written agreement and to which they made the entire agreement subject. Again, such evidence does not tend to vary, alter, or change any of the terms of the agreement, but rather shows whether the entire written agreement, unchanged and unaltered, ever became effective. For example, if John signs a subscription agreement to buy stock in a corporation to be formed and delivers the agreement to Thompson with the mutual understanding that it is not to be binding unless the other persons financially responsible under it shall each agree to buy at least an equivalent amount of such stock, John is permitted to show by parol evidence this condition.
6. A *subsequent mutual rescission or modification* of the written contract. Parol evidence of a later agreement does not tend to show that the integrated writing did not represent the contract between the parties at the time it was made. Parties to an existing contract, whether written or oral, may agree to change the terms of their contract as they see fit, or to cancel it completely, if they so desire.
7. Parol evidence is admissible to explain *ambiguous* terms in the contract. To enforce a contract, it is necessary to understand its intended meaning. Nevertheless, such interpretation is not to alter, change, or vary the terms of the contract.
8. The rule does not prevent a party from proving the existence of a separate, distinct contract between the same parties.

## SUPPLEMENTAL EVIDENCE

Although a written agreement may not be contradicted by evidence of a prior agreement or of a contemporaneous agreement, under the Restatement, Section 216, and the Code, Section 2–202, a written contract may be explained or supplemented by (1) course of dealing between the parties, (2) usage of trade, (3) course of performance, or (4) evidence of consistent additional terms, unless the parties intended the writing to be a complete and exclusive statement of their agreement.

A **course of dealing** is a sequence of previous conduct between the parties under an agreement that the court reasonably may regard as establishing a common basis of understanding for interpreting their expressions and other conduct.

A **usage of trade** is a practice or method of dealing, regularly observed and followed in a place, vocation, or trade.

**Course of performance** refers to the manner and extent to which the respective parties to a contract have accepted without objection successive tenders of performance by the other party.

The Restatement and the Code permit *supplemental consistent evidence* to be introduced into a court proceeding, but only if it does not contradict a term or terms of the original agreement and would probably not have been included in the original contract.

Figure 15–2 illustrates the parol evidence rule.

◆ *See Figure 15–2*

## INTERPRETATION OF CONTRACTS

Although the written words or language in which the parties embodied their agreement or contract may not be changed by parol evidence, the ascertainment (determination) of the meaning to be given the written language is outside the scope of the parol evidence rule. Though written words embody the terms of the contract, words are but symbols. If their meaning is unclear, the courts may clarify this meaning by applying rules of interpretation or construction and by using extrinsic (external) evidence, where necessary.

The Restatement, Section 200, defines **interpretation** as the ascertainment of the meaning of a promise or

**FIGURE 15–2** Parol Evidence Rule

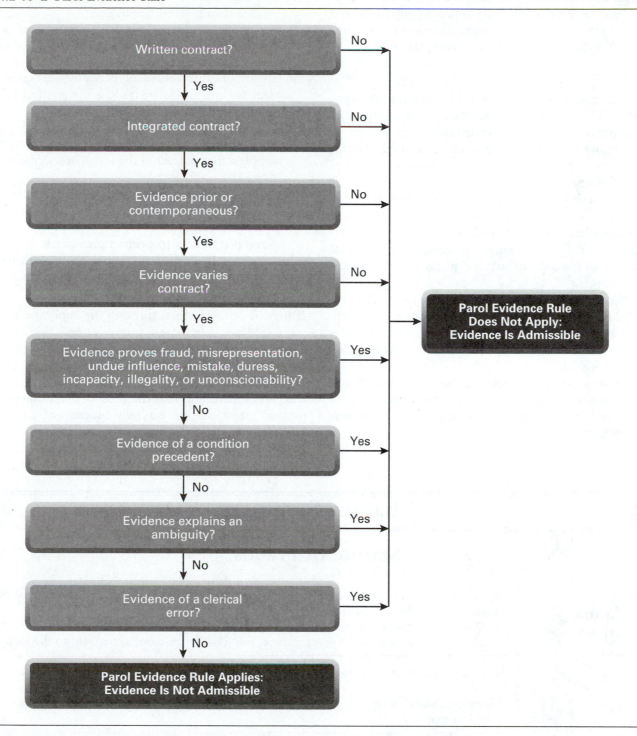

agreement or a term of the promise or agreement. Where the language in a contract is unambiguous, the courts will not accept extrinsic evidence tending to show a meaning different from that which the words clearly convey. Its function being to interpret and construe written contracts and documents, the court adopts rules of interpretation to apply a legal standard to the words contained in the agreement. The courts will attempt to interpret a contract in accordance with the intent of the parties. If the subjective intent of the parties fails to provide a clear interpretation, the courts will make an objective interpretation. Among the rules that aid interpretation are the following:

1. Words and other conduct are interpreted in the light of all the circumstances, and the principal purpose of the parties, if ascertainable, is given great weight.
2. A writing is interpreted as a whole, and all writings that are part of the same transaction are interpreted together.
3. Unless a different intention is manifested, language that has a commonly accepted meaning is interpreted in accordance with that meaning.
4. Unless a different intention is manifested, technical terms and words of art are given their technical meanings.
5. Wherever reasonable, the manifestations of intention of the parties to a promise or agreement are interpreted as consistent with each other and with any relevant course of performance, course of dealing, or usage of trade.
6. An interpretation that gives a reasonable, lawful, and effective meaning to all the terms is preferred over an interpretation that leaves a part unreasonable, unlawful, or of no effect.
7. Specific terms and exact terms are given greater weight than general language.
8. Separately negotiated or added terms are given greater weight than standardized terms or other terms not separately negotiated.
9. Express terms, course of performance, course of dealing, and usage of trade are weighted in that order.
10. Where a term or promise has several possible meanings, it will be interpreted against the party who supplied the contract or the term. Restatement, Sections 201, 202, and 203.
11. Where written provisions are inconsistent with typed or printed provisions, the written provision is given preference. Likewise, typed provisions are given preferences to printed provisions.
12. If the amount payable is set forth in both figures and words and the amounts differ, the words control the figures.

It may be observed that, through the application of the parol evidence rule (where properly applicable) and the above rules of interpretation and construction, the law not only enforces a contract but, in so doing, exercises great care that the contract being enforced is the one the parties made and that the sense and meaning of the parties' intentions are carefully ascertained and given effect.

 # Chapter Summary

## Statute of Frauds

| Contracts within the Statute of Frauds | **Rule** contracts within the statute of frauds must be evidenced by a writing to be enforceable <br> **Suretyship Provision** applies to promises to pay the debts of others <br> • *Promise Must Be Collateral* promisor must be secondarily, not primarily, liable <br> • *Main Purpose Doctrine* if primary object is to provide an economic benefit to the surety, then the promise is not within the statute <br> **Executor-Administrator Provision** applies to promises to answer personally for duties of decedents <br> **Marriage Provision** applies to promises made in consideration of marriage but not to mutual promises to marry <br> **Land Contract Provision** applies to promises to transfer any rights, privileges, powers, or immunities in real property <br> **One-Year Provision** applies to contracts that cannot be performed within one year <br> • *The Possibility Test* the criterion is whether it is possible, not likely, for the agreement to be performed within one year <br> • *Computation of Time* the year runs from the time the agreement is made |

- *Full Performance by One Party* makes the promise of the other party enforceable under majority view

**Sales of Goods**  a contract for the sale of goods for the price of $500 or more must be evidenced by a writing to be enforceable

- *Admission* an admission in pleadings, testimony, or otherwise in court makes the contract enforceable for the quantity of goods admitted
- *Specially Manufactured Goods* an oral contract for specially manufactured goods is enforceable
- *Delivery or Payment and Acceptance* validates the contract only for the goods that have been accepted or for which payment has been accepted

**Modification or Rescission of Contracts within the Statute of Frauds**  oral contracts modifying existing contracts are unenforceable if the resulting contract is within the statute of frauds

**Methods of Compliance**

**General Contract Law**  the writing or writings must
- specify the parties to the contract
- specify the subject matter and essential terms
- be signed by the party to be charged or by her agent

**Sale of Goods**  provides a general method of compliance for all parties and an additional one for merchants
- *Writing or Writings Must* (1) be sufficient to indicate that a contract has been made between the parties, (2) be signed by the party against whom enforcement is sought or by her authorized agent, and (3) specify the quantity of goods to be sold
- *Written Confirmation* between merchants, a written confirmation that is sufficient against the sender is also sufficient against the recipient unless the recipient gives written notice of his objection within ten days

**Effect of Noncompliance**

**Oral Contract within Statute of Frauds**  is unenforceable

**Full Performance**  statute does not apply to executed contracts

**Restitution**  is available in quasi contract for benefits conferred in reliance on the oral contract

**Promissory Estoppel**  oral contracts will be enforced where the party seeking enforcement has reasonably and justifiably relied on the promise and the court can avoid injustice only by enforcement

# Parol Evidence Rule and Interpretation of Contracts

**Parol Evidence Rule**

**Statement of Rule**  when parties express a contract in a writing that they intend to be the complete and final expression of their rights and duties, evidence of their prior oral or written negotiations or agreements of their contemporaneous oral agreements that vary or change the written contract are not admissible

**Situations to Which the Rule Does Not Apply**
- a contract that is not an integrated document
- correction of a typographical error
- showing that a contract was void or voidable
- showing whether a condition has in fact occurred
- showing a subsequent mutual rescission or modification of the contract

**Supplemental Evidence** may be admitted
- *Course of Dealing* previous conduct between the parties
- *Usage of Trade* practice engaged in by the trade or industry
- *Course of Performance* conduct between the parties concerning performance of the particular contract
- *Supplemental Consistent Evidence*

| | |
|---|---|
| **Interpretation of Contracts** | **Definition** the ascertainment of the meaning of a promise or agreement or a term of the promise or agreement<br>**Rules of Interpretation** include these:<br>• all the circumstances are considered and the principal purpose of the parties is given great weight<br>• a writing is interpreted as a whole<br>• commonly accepted meanings are used unless the parties manifest a different intention<br>• wherever possible, the intentions of the parties are interpreted as consistent with each other and with course of performance, course of dealing, or usage of trade<br>• technical terms are given their technical meaning<br>• specific terms are given greater weight than general language<br>• separately negotiated terms are given greater weight than standardized terms or those not separately negotiated<br>• the order for interpretation is express terms, course of performance, course of dealing, and usage of trade<br>• where a term has several possible meanings, the term will be interpreted against the party who supplied the contract or term<br>• written provisions are given preference over typed or printed provisions, and typed provisions are given preference over printed provisions<br>• if an amount is set forth in both words and figures and they differ, words control figures |

 # Cases

## CASE 15–1
## Original Promise
### *CARTER v. ALLSTATE INSURANCE COMPANY*

Court of Appeals of Texas, Houston (1st Dist.), 1997
962 S.W.2d 268

TAFT, J.

Appellants [plaintiffs], Jesse Carter and Jesse Thomas, had an auto accident with Allstate's insured. * * *

Appellants' car collided with Allstate's insured's car on November 5, 1993. Appellants hired attorney Joseph Onwuteaka to represent them in their claim for injuries from the automobile collision. On April 11, 1994, Mr. Onwuteaka sent a demand letter for settlement of appellants' claims to Allstate's adjustor, Gracie Weatherly. Mr. Onwuteaka claims Ms. Weatherly made, and he accepted, oral settlement agreements on behalf of appellants. When Allstate did not honor the agreements, appellants filed suit on May 30, 1995, for breach of contract.

Allstate filed for summary judgment based on [the] Statute of Frauds * * * On October 5, 1995, the trial court granted summary judgment without stating a particular basis.

* * *

[T]he appellants contend the alleged oral agreement is not governed by the Statute of Frauds. Allstate claims the Statute of Frauds is applicable to the alleged agreement as "a promise by another person to answer for the debt, default, or miscarriage of another person." [Citation.] This provision of the Statute of Frauds is commonly referred to as the "suretyship provision." [Citation.]

One test for determining whether a promise to pay the debt of another is within or without the Statute of Frauds is whether the promisor is a surety, only secondarily liable, or has accepted primary responsibility for the debt. [Citations.] If the party is primarily liable, its promise to pay a debt is not required to be in writing by the Statute of Frauds [Citation.] However, if the party is a surety, the promise to pay the debt of a third party is required to be in writing. [Citation.]

If Allstate were merely a surety, its obligation would have been to pay its insured's debt upon default by its insured. However, as an insurer, Allstate contracted with its insured to assume responsibility for the liability of its insured, at least to the limits of the insurance policy. By Allstate's oral promise to settle, it was settling not only its insured's potential liability but its own possible obligation to pay and its own duty to defend its insured. The oral promise to settle was an original undertaking, not a promise to answer for the debt of the insured. Therefore, the suretyship provision of the Statute of Frauds does not apply to Allstate's promise to settle. [Citation.]

We reverse the trial court's summary judgment and remand for further proceedings.

---

## CASE 15–2
### One-Year Provision
## *PRICE v. MERCURY SUPPLY CO., INC.*
Court of Appeals of Tennessee, 1984
682 S.W.2d 924

KOCH, J.

Mr. Richard P. Price was discharged from his position as vice president in charge of sales for Mercury Supply Company, Inc. He filed this action against his former employers alleging breach of an oral employment contract. * * * [T]he Chancery Court . . . granted the defendants' motion for a summary judgment. * * * This appeal follows. For the reasons stated herein, we hold that the defendants were entitled to a summary judgment based upon the undisputed facts presented in this record.

* * *

For many years prior to 1970, Mr. Leonard Weil operated a business known as Mercury Supply Company. This business sold cleaning materials and janitorial supplies in the Nashville and Middle Tennessee area. Mr. Weil had complete charge of the business, although his wife was a nominal partner.

In July, 1970, Mr. Price applied for and obtained a job as a salesman with Mercury Supply Company. On July 6, 1970, Mr. Price and Mr. Weil signed a written employment contract of indefinite duration which could be cancelled by either party for any reason upon fifteen days notice. Under this contract, Mr. Price was employed as a salesman, and his compensation consisted of a straight weekly salary as well as a commission based on

the sales he actually made. This contract specifically provided that Mr. Price's compensation could be altered from time to time without affecting the validity of the rest of the contract.

The company prospered during the years immediately after 1970. * * * In accordance with the contract, Mr. Price received annual salary increases in recognition of his performance.

In August, 1972, Mr. Price was given the title of sales coordinator. While he was still acting as a salesman, he also took on the responsibility to hire and train other salesmen. Later, in 1973, Mr. Price's title was changed to sales manager. His duties were still the same as they had been when he was the company's sales coordinator. Again, as permitted by the 1970 employment contract, the basis for Mr. Price's salary was changed so that in addition to his weekly salary and commissions based upon his personal sales, Mr. Price was entitled to receive an annual bonus based upon the company's annual profits as contained in the annual profit and loss statement. On June 30, 1974, Mr. Price received his first such bonus.

* * *

In March, 1975, Mr. Price's title was changed to vice president for sales. There was no change in his compensation at that time. His duties remained the same as they had been when he was sales manager and sales coordinator.

\* \* \*

[In 1977] both parties agree that they were experiencing difficulties. Mr. Weil went so far as to hire an industrial psychologist to help resolve these problems. In September, 1978, in the presence of this psychologist, Mr. Weil told Mr. Price that his performance was not satisfactory and gave him an ultimatum that if the situation did not improve, Mr. Price would be discharged.

The relationship between the two did not improve. Following a disagreement in February, 1981, concerning the manner in which Mr. Price conducted a sales meeting, Mr. Weil called Mr. Price into his office on March 2, 1981, and discharged him. \* \* \*

The linchpin of Mr. Price's entire claim is his assertion that on March 5, 1975, the parties entered into a valid oral employment contract wherein Mr. Price was hired as the vice president for sales of Mercury Supply Company for the rest of his life or until he retired. If this contract is found not to exist or to be unenforceable, then Mr. Price has no basis for relief because as an employee-at-will, he could be discharged at any time for any reason upon receiving fifteen days notice.

After reviewing the proof, the trial court found that the oral contract allegedly entered into on March 5, 1975 was barred by . . . the provision of Tennessee's statute of frauds providing that no action shall be brought on a contract "which is not to be performed within the space of one (1) year from the making thereof" unless the contract itself is in writing and signed by the party to be charged. Relying upon [citation], the trial court found that the oral employment contract was unenforceable because Mr. Price's retirement would take place beyond one year from the making of the contract.

We disagree with the trial court's legal conclusion in this regard.

A defense predicated upon the statute of frauds must, of necessity, presume that the parties had an agreement but that [the statute of frauds] renders this agreement unenforceable because it is one of those species of agreements required to be in writing: Tennessee's version of the statute of frauds, [citation], was originally enacted in 1801. Like those existing in all other states except Louisiana, Tennessee's statute of frauds is patterned after the English Statute of Frauds and Perjuries enacted in 1677. Its purpose is to prevent frauds based upon oral testimony and to deter the formation of contracts based upon loose statements or innuendoes long after witnesses have become unavailable or when memories of the pre-

cise agreement have been dimmed by the passage of time. [Citations.]

The portion of the statute of frauds at issue in this case, [citation] which proscribes oral contracts not to be performed in one year from the time they are made is generally referred to as the *infra annum* provision. Of all the provisions of the statute of frauds, it is generally construed very narrowly by the courts, [citation], because courts generally attempt to give effect to contracts rather than defeating them. Accordingly, our courts have declined to construe a contract to require performance over more than one year if to do so would render the contract unenforceable because of the statute of frauds. [Citation.]

\* \* \* It is now well-settled that the determination concerning whether a particular agreement is included within the statute of frauds depends upon the terms of the agreement itself and the intentions of the parties at the precise moment the contract is made. [Citations.]

\* \* \*

The Tennessee Supreme Court has specifically held that an oral employment contract for an unspecified term is not subject to the statute of frauds because it is capable of complete, *bona fide* performance within one year of its making should the employee die within that time. [Citations.] \* \* \*

This is in accord with the view expressed by most courts and commentators. Succinctly stated, the majority rule is that an oral employment contract for an indefinite term that can be terminated at any time at the will of the parties is not within the statute of frauds because it is capable of being fully performed within one year either through the employee's death or by either party's decision to terminate the contract. [Citations.]

When the disputed facts in this case are viewed in light of these precedents, it is clear that any oral contract between Mr. Price and Mercury Supply Company, if indeed there is a contract, would not be barred by the statute of frauds. Mr. Price himself stated that the term of this contract would be for life or until he decided to retire. Thus, it could be performed within one year because Mr. Price could have died or could have elected to retire within a year after the alleged contract was made. The fact that neither contingency occurred is not sufficient to bring the agreement within [the statute of frauds].

However, even if Mr. Price is able to avoid the statute of frauds, he will not necessarily be able to recover for a breach of contract unless he can show that a contract existed. The normal rules of contracts must still apply even if an agreement does not come within the statute of frauds. [Citation.]

* * *

Thus, even if this Court were to agree with Mr. Price's premise that an oral contract was formed on March 5, 1975, the undisputed facts in this record require the legal conclusion that this contract was not breached when Mr. Price was discharged because he was an employee-at-will. Thus, the defendants could discharge Mr. Price at any time without breaching the contract.

## CASE 15–3
## Writing/Parol Evidence
## *ESTATE OF JACKSON v. DEVENYNS*
Supreme Court of Wyoming, 1995
892 P.2d 786

GOLDEN, J.

Appellants, personal representatives of the estate of George Herbert Jackson, appeal the probate court's order of conveyance in favor of appellees. Appellants claim a writing signed by George Jackson purporting to sell seventy-nine acres, reserve approximately one acre, and sell machinery is unenforceable because the agreement does not sufficiently describe the property as required by . . . the statute of frauds. Following appellees' petition . . ., the probate court determined the writing satisfied the statute of frauds, was enforceable, and ordered the estate's personal representatives to perform the contract.

We hold the agreement's property description is insufficient to meet the requirements of the statute of frauds and reverse the order of conveyance.

* * *

## Facts

On February 9, 1993, George Jackson (Jackson) and his neighbors, Karen and Steve Devenyns (Devenyns), drafted and signed a document which reads as follows:

George Jackson agrees to sell 79 acres and machinery to Steve and Karen Devenyns for $120,000.00

1. 2 annual down payments of 12,500 starting in _____93 $75000.00 will be carried for 13 years at 7% interest payable in yearly payments starting 1995.
2. On the seventh year 2001 20,000.00 will be added to the balance of the mortgage payable at 7% interest.
3. George has complete right to farm 79 acres for 3 yrs or less. He pays all water & farming expenses for the first year. Devenyns splits farming and water for 2-3rd yr. but can have hay
4. Devenyns begins paying taxes in 93 for 79 acres.
5. George has right to use 9 acres for 6 yrs and at the end of the 6th year the $20,000 is added to mortgage.
6. As far as mineral rights each party will retain 50% of mineral rights with any leasing to be done by mutual consent.
7. Pumphouse and waterline remain property of George and he shall have easement to pumphouse.
8. Devenyns agree [] not to sell 9 acres which contains pumphouse at least until after place is paid for—15 years.

George want[s] to keep yard intact which is area 66' × 114' as well as area around house approximately 1.3 acres 168' × 325'.

Devenyns ha[ve] first option to buy on property

George will provide title insurance and survey house and approximately 1.3 acre from total. This survey can be done within 5 months.

These matters were discussed by both parties on 2/9/93 and agreed upon

Steve Devenyns
George H. Jackson

Jackson died on May 8, 1993. After the attorney for Jackson's estate refused the Devenyns' request to honor the contract, the Devenyns petitioned for an order of conveyance. . . .

The estate objected to the petition, contending the property description did not comply with the statute of frauds' requirement that the document itself sufficiently describe the property to be conveyed. The estate filed a motion . . ., objecting to proposed testimony as violative of the parol evidence rule, the statute of frauds, . . . However, the probate court heard testimony from witnesses for the Devenyns and considered parol evidence to determine whether the document satisfied the statute of frauds.

* * *

From parol evidence, the probate court determined that Jackson had used words of ownership referring to the eighty acres of real property he owned in Park County, Wyoming, and that Jackson did not own any other real property in the world. The probate court further found that Jackson had conveyed his seventy-nine acre farm, but had reserved out an approximate one acre parcel containing Jackson's house and yard. The probate court held that the reserved one acre could be satisfactorily determined by a surveyor using the dimensions found on page two of the agreement, and the sketch found on page three, as well as from assistance of witnesses who testified at the hearing that they could point out the specific area based on conversations with Jackson. The probate court held the agreement was enforceable and ordered conveyance by the estate to the Devenyns. This appeal followed.

## Discussion

### 1. Statute of Frauds

* * *

A written memorandum purporting to convey real estate must sufficiently describe the property so as to comply with the requirements of the statute of frauds and permit specific performance. [Citation.] Wyoming [statute of frauds] states:

(a) In the following cases every agreement shall be void [unenforceable in most states] unless such agreement, or some note or memorandum thereof be in writing, and subscribed by the party to be charged therewith:

* * *

(v) Every agreement or contract for the sale of real estate, or the lease thereof, for more than one (1) year[.]

The question of what constitutes a memorandum sufficient to satisfy the statute of frauds is set forth in Restatement (Second) of Contracts, § 131 (1979) as follows:

§ 131. General Requisites of a Memorandum
Unless additional requirements are prescribed by the particular statute, a contract within the Statute of Frauds is enforceable if it is evidenced by any writing, signed by or on behalf of the party to be charged, which

(a) reasonably identifies the subject matter of the contract,
(b) is sufficient to indicate that a contract with respect thereto has been made between the parties or offered by the signer to the other party, and
(c) states with reasonable certainty the essential terms of the unperformed promises in the contract.

* * * This Court's decision in [citation] concluded that a valid contract to convey land must expressly contain a description of the land, certain in itself or capable of being rendered certain by reference to an extrinsic source which the writing itself designates. [Citation.] Noland expressly prohibited supplying the writing's essential provisions by inferences or presumptions deduced from oral testimony. [Citation.]

**2. Parol Evidence** The parties both recognize that the central issue is the adequacy of the property description supplied in the agreement to satisfy the statute of frauds. The estate contends the probate court improperly relied upon parol evidence in deciding the document had sufficiently described Jackson's property in satisfaction of the statute of frauds. The general rule for Wyoming is that parol evidence is admissible to identify described property, but parol evidence may not supply a portion of the description. [Citation.]

This writing insufficiently describes the property it purports to convey, to reserve, and for which it grants an option to purchase. All three of these land transactions fall under the statute of frauds and each must be sufficiently definite in description to satisfy the statute of frauds or, as a matter of law, the contract is void because an essential term has been omitted. [Citation.] We also note that if the description of the property reserved out of the tract to be conveyed is indefinite and uncertain, then the general description of the land to be conveyed is indefinite and the entire conveyance must fail. [Citation.]

* * *

Nevertheless, the Devenyns urge the writing's use of words such as "remain," "retain," and "keep" was correctly found by the probate court to indicate that Jackson was selling property he owned at that time and that these words are a "key" or "index finger" which, under Noland, permits parol evidence that Jackson only owned this property in all of the world and, therefore, the location of conveyed property is described. However, Noland determined that Wyoming required greater certainty in the description provided by the writing before extrinsic evidence is permitted to supplement. [Citation.] * * *

When a writing only states the total acreage without any description of the location of the land involved, the statute of frauds' requirement that the subject matter be reasonably certain is not satisfied and the contract is void. [Citation.] Without the prohibited supplied inference of ownership, the present description only provides the total acreage, does not provide any certainty that this particular tract was intended to be conveyed and, consequently, is too uncertain to be enforced. [Citations.]

The descriptions for the property reserved and for the option also fail to satisfy the statute of frauds. The reserved property boundaries can only be ascertained by witnesses actually directing a surveyor on-site according to the witnesses' memory of Jackson's boundary description. Parol evidence cannot supply a portion of the description. [Citation.] The option granted in the document does not provide any description at all, leaving unclear for what property an option was granted.

## Conclusion

The parol evidence received in this case reveals that fraud is not a concern and leaves no doubt as to the identity of the property involved, but the property was not described in the agreement and the agreement cannot be enforced. The legislative policy justifying the statute of frauds requires this Court to test not what the parties to the contract know, but what they put in the contract as the description. A description cannot be supplied by parol proof because that allows in the harm which the statute was intended to prevent. The probate court erred as a matter of law in accepting parol evidence to describe the land.

In view of our decision that the contract is unenforceable under the statute of frauds, . . . [t]he order of conveyance is reversed.

---

## CASE 15–4
## Parol Evidence
### *LEITZ v. THORSON*
Court of Appeals of Oregon, 1992
113 Or. App. 557, 833 P.2d 343

EDMONDS, J.
Defendant appeals from a judgment for breach of contract and fraud. * * * We affirm.

Plaintiffs leased commercial space from defendant to open a florist shop. After the lease was executed, plaintiffs learned that they could not place another freestanding sign along the highway to advertise the business, because the Deschutes County Code allows only one freestanding sign on the property. A freestanding sign advertising a business owned in part by defendant was already in place. Plaintiffs filed this action and alleged that defendant had breached the lease by failing to provide them with space in the complex for which a freestanding sign could be erected. Paragraph 16 of the lease provides, in part: "Tenant shall not erect or install any signs or advertising media or door lettering or placards visible from outside the leased premises with out [sic] the previous written consent of the Landlord."

During trial, plaintiffs sought to introduce evidence that, before the lease was executed, defendant told them that they could have a freestanding sign. Defendant objected to the testimony on the basis that proving the alleged oral agreement would violate the Parol Evidence Rule. [Citation.] The court admitted the testimony.

Defendant argues that the trial court erred by holding that the Parol Evidence Rule does not bar plaintiffs' testimony that defendant had orally agreed that they could have a freestanding sign. * * * The rule is a rule of integration. It prohibits oral evidence of those aspects of the bargain that the parties intended to memorialize in the writing. [Citation.] If the parties did not intend the writing to represent their entire agreement, the agreement is only partially integrated, and prior consistent additional terms not evidenced by the writing may still form part of the entire agreement. [Citation.] An oral agreement is not integrated in a contemporaneous writing if it is not inconsistent with the written agreement and is "such an agreement as might naturally be made as a separate agreement by parties situated as were parties to the written contract." [Citation.]

Our review is to determine whether the trial court's conclusion that the lease is not a fully integrated agreement is supported by the evidence. [Citation.] We start with a presumption that the writing is intended to be a complete integration. [Citation.] The integration clause in this lease is an indication that the lease was intended to be a complete integration, but it is not conclusive. [Citation.] Oral admissions of a party may be probative of whether the agreement is integrated. [Citation.]

Defendant testified that the written form that he had used for the lease was not drafted to be used specifically for this property. Although the lease required attachment of exhibits, he admitted that no exhibits were attached to the lease. He conceded that he told plaintiffs that they could have a sign and that he did not require his written consent, despite the words in paragraph 16 of the lease. He admitted that, during the lease negotiations, the parties had discussed plaintiffs' renovations. He said that he did not require those plans to be in writing, even though the lease required his written consent before alterations, additions or installations on the premises. Defendant also testified: "Usually our detail comes later, after they've, you know, gotten their lease signed, and they're—they get it figured out, and they measure and come up with information on saying: well, this is what we're going to do."

There was evidence to support the trial court's conclusion that the parties did not intend the written lease to reflect their entire agreement, thereby overcoming the presumption of integration.

The next question is whether a separate oral agreement to allow a freestanding sign was inconsistent with the written lease. Although defendant admitted that he told plaintiffs they could have a sign, he disputes whether he told them that the sign could be "freestanding." No provision of the lease prohibits a freestanding sign. The disputed parol evidence was not inconsistent with the written agreement.

\* \* \*

There is evidence to support the trial court's finding that the parties did not intend the written lease to be their complete agreement, that the oral agreement is not inconsistent with the written agreement and that the oral agreement would have been made naturally as a separate agreement. The trial court did not err.

Affirmed.

---

  # Questions

1.  Identify and discuss the five types of general contracts covered by the statute of frauds and the contracts covered by the UCC statute of frauds' provisions.
2.  Describe the writing that is required to satisfy the statute of frauds under general contract law and the UCC.

3.  Identify and discuss the other methods of complying with the statute of frauds under general contract law and the UCC.
4.  Explain the parol evidence rule and identify the situations to which the rule does not apply.
5.  Discuss the rule that aids in the interpretation of a contract.

---

  # Problems

1.  Rafferty was the principal shareholder in Continental Corporation, and, as a result, he received the lion's share of Continental's dividends. Continental Corporation was eager to close an important deal for iron ore products to use in its business. A written contract was on the desk of Stage Corporation for the sale of the iron ore to Continental. Stage Corporation, however, was cautious about signing the contract; and it did not sign until Rafferty called Stage Corporation on the telephone and stated that if Continental Corporation did not pay for the ore, he would. Business reversals struck Continental Corporation, and it failed. Stage Corporation sues Rafferty. What defense, if any, has Rafferty? Decision?
2.  Green was the owner of a large department store. On Wednesday, January 26, he talked to Smith and said, "I will hire you as sales manager in my store for one year at a salary of $28,000; you are to begin work next Monday." Smith accepted and started work on Monday, January 31. At the end of three months, Green discharged Smith. On May 15, Smith brings an action against Green to recover the unpaid portion of the $28,000 salary. Decision?

3.  Rowe was admitted to the hospital suffering from a critical illness. He was given emergency treatment and later underwent surgery. On at least four occasions, Rowe's two sons discussed with the hospital the payment for services it was to render. The first of these four conversations took place the day after Rowe was admitted. The sons informed the treating physician that their father had no financial means but that they themselves would pay for such services. During the other conversations, the sons authorized whatever treatment their father needed, assuring the hospital that they would pay for the services. After Rowe's discharge, Dr. Peterson brought this action against the sons to recover the unpaid bill for the services rendered to their father. Decision?
4.  Ames, Bell, Cain, and Dole each orally ordered color television sets from Marvel Electronics Company, which accepted the orders. Ames's set was to be specially designed and encased in an ebony cabinet. Bell, Cain, and Dole ordered standard sets described as "Alpha Omega Theatre." The price of Ames's set was $1,800, and the sets ordered by Bell, Cain, and Dole were $700 each. Bell paid the company $75 to apply

on his purchase; Ames, Cain, and Dole paid nothing. The next day, Marvel sent Ames, Bell, Cain, and Dole written confirmations captioned "Purchase Memorandum," numbered 12345, 12346, 12347, and 12348, respectively, containing the essential terms of the oral agreements. Each memorandum was sent in duplicate with the request that one copy be signed and returned to the company. None of the four purchasers returned a signed copy. Ames promptly sent the company a repudiation of the oral contract, which it received before beginning manufacture of the set for Ames or making commitments to carry out the contract. Cain sent the company a letter reading in part, "Referring to your Contract No. 12347, please be advised I have canceled this contract. Yours truly, (Signed) Cain." The four television sets were duly tendered by Marvel to Ames, Bell, Cain, and Dole, all of whom refused to accept delivery. Marvel brings four separate actions against Ames, Bell, Cain, and Dole for breach of contract.

Decide each claim.

**5.** Moriarity and Holmes enter into an oral contract by which Moriarity promises to sell and Holmes promises to buy Blackacre for $10,000. Moriarity repudiates the contract by writing a letter to Holmes in which she states accurately the terms of the bargain, but adds "our agreement was oral. It, therefore, is not binding upon me, and I shall not carry it out." Thereafter, Holmes sues Moriarity for specific performance of the contract. Moriarity interposes the defense of the statute of frauds, arguing that the contract is within the statute and, hence, unenforceable. Decision?

**6.** On March 1, Lucas called Craig on the telephone and offered to pay him $90,000 for a house and lot which Craig owned. Craig accepted the offer immediately on the telephone. Later in the same day, Lucas told Annabelle that if she would marry him, he would convey to her the property he then owned which was the subject of the earlier agreement. On March 2, Lucas called Penelope and offered her $15,000 if she would work for him for the year commencing March 15, and she agreed. Lucas and Annabelle were married on June 25. By this time, Craig had refused to convey the house to Lucas. Thereafter, Lucas renounced his promise to convey the property to Annabelle. Penelope, who had been working for Lucas, was discharged without cause on July 5; Annabelle left Lucas and instituted divorce proceedings.

What rights, if any, have (a) Lucas against Craig for his failure to convey the property; (b) Annabelle against Lucas for failure to convey the house to her; (c) Penelope against Lucas for discharging her before the end of the agreed term of employment?

**7.** Clay orally promises Trent to sell him five crops of potatoes to be grown on Blackacre, a farm in Minnesota, and Trent promises to pay a stated price for them on delivery. Is the contract enforceable?

**8.** Grant leased an apartment to Epstein for the term May 1, 1998, to April 30, 1999, at $550 a month "payable in advance on the first day of each and every month of said term." At the time the lease was signed, Epstein told Grant that he received his salary on the tenth of the month and that he would be unable to pay the rent before that date each month. Grant replied that would be satisfactory. On June 2, due to Epstein's not having paid the June rent, Grant sued Epstein for such rent. At the trial, Epstein offered to prove the oral agreement as to the date of payment each month. Decision?

**9.** Rachel bought a car from the Beautiful Used Car Agency under a written contract. She purchased the car in reliance on Beautiful's agent's oral representations that it had never been in a wreck and could be driven at least two thousand miles without adding oil. Thereafter, Rachel discovered that the car had, in fact, been previously wrecked and rebuilt, that it used excessive quantities of oil, and that Beautiful's agent was aware of these facts when the car was sold. Rachel brings an action to rescind the contract and recover the purchase price. Beautiful objects to the introduction of oral testimony concerning representations of its agent, contending that the written contract alone governed the rights of the parties. Decision on the objection?

**10.** In a contract drawn up by Booke Company, it agreed to sell and Yermack Contracting Company agreed to buy wood shingles at $6.50. After the shingles were delivered and used, Booke Company billed Yermack Company at $6.50 per bunch of 900 shingles. Yermack Company refused to pay because it thought the contract meant $6.50 per thousand shingles. Booke Company brought action to recover on the basis of $6.50 per bunch. The evidence showed that there was no applicable custom or usage in the trade and that each party held its belief in good faith. Decision?

**11.** Halsey, a widower, was living without family or housekeeper in his house in Howell, New York. Burns and his wife claim that Halsey invited them to give up their house and business in Andover, New York, to live in his house and care for him. In return, they allege, he promised them the house and its furniture upon his death. Acting upon this proposal, the Burnses left Andover, moved into Halsey's house, and cared for him until he died five months later. No deed, will, or memorandum exists to authenticate Halsey's promise. McCormick, the administrator of the estate, claims the oral promise is unenforceable under the statute of frauds. Decision?

**12.** Amos orally agrees to hire Elizabeth for an eight-month trial period. Elizabeth performs the job magnificently, and after several weeks Amos orally offers Elizabeth a six-month extension at a salary increase of 20 percent. Elizabeth accepts the offer. At the end of the eight-month trial period, Amos discharges Elizabeth, who brings suit against Amos for breach of contract. Is Amos liable? Why?

**13.** Ethel Greenberg acquired the ownership of the Carlyle Hotel on Miami Beach. Having had little experience in the hotel business, she asked Miller to participate in and counsel her operation of the hotel, which he did. He claims that because his efforts produced a substantial profit, Ethel made an oral agreement for the continuation of his services. Miller alleges that in return for his services, Ethel promised to marry him and to share the net income resulting from the operation of the hotel. Miller maintains that he rendered his services to Ethel in reliance upon her promises. The couple planned to wed in the fall, but Ethel, due to physical illness, decided not to marry. Miller sued for damages for Ethel's breach of their agreement. Decision?

14. Dean was hired on February 12, as a sales manager of the Co-op Dairy for a minimum period of one year with the dairy agreeing to pay his moving expenses. By February 26, Dean had signed a lease, moved his family from Oklahoma to Arizona, and reported for work. After he worked for a few days, he was fired. Dean then brought this action against the dairy for his salary for the year, less what he was paid. The dairy argues that the statute of frauds bars enforcement of the oral contract because the contract was not to be performed within one year. Decision?

15. Alice solicited an offer from Robett Manufacturing Company to manufacture certain clothing that Alice intended to supply to the government. Alice contends that in a telephone conversation Robett made an oral offer that she immediately accepted. She then received the following letter from Robett, which, she claims, confirmed their agreement:

Confirming our telephone conversation, we are pleased to offer the 3,500 shirts at $4.00 each and the trousers at $3.80 each with delivery approximately ninety days after receipt of order. We will try to cut this to sixty days if at all possible.

This, of course, as quoted f.o.b. Atlanta and the order will not be subject to cancellation, domestic pack only.

Thanking you for the opportunity to offer these garments, we are

Very truly yours,
ROBETT MANUFACTURING CO., INC.

Alice sued to enforce this agreement. Decision?

16. David and Nancy Songer planned to travel outside the United States and wanted to acquire medical insurance prior to departure. They spoke with an agent of Continental who requested that Nancy Songer undergo a medical examination based on a statement that she had a heart murmur. She promptly complied, and the Songers later met with the agent to complete the application. David Songer signed the application and tendered a check for the first six months' premium. The Songers also claim that the agent stated that a "binder" was in effect such that policy coverage was available immediately. The agent subsequently denied making this statement, relying, instead, on a clause in the contract that required home office acceptance. The Songers left the United States and sixty days later inquired as to the status of their application. At approximately the same time, Continental denied the application and sent a refund to the Songers. Nancy Songer was then severely injured in an automobile accident. When Continental refused to honor the policy, the Songers claimed that the oral representation constituted part of the contract due to the vagueness of the policy "acceptance" language. The trial court heard evidence regarding the oral representations. Decision?

17. Yokel, a grower of soybeans, had sold soybeans to Campbell Grain and Seed Company and other grain companies in the past. Campbell entered into an oral contract with Yokel to purchase soybeans from him. Promptly after entering into the oral contract, Campbell signed and mailed to Yokel a written confirmation of the oral agreement. Yokel received the written confirmation but neither signed it nor objected to its content. Campbell now brings this action against Yokel for breach of contract upon Yokel's failure to deliver the soybeans. The trial court ruled in favor of the defendant, Yokel, on the ground that the defendant is not a "merchant" within the meaning of the Code. Decision?

18. Presti claims that he reached an oral agreement with Wilson by telephone in October 1999 to buy a horse for $60,000. Presti asserts that he sent Wilson a bill of sale and a postdated check, which Wilson retained. Presti also claims that Wilson told him that he wished not to consummate the transaction until January 1, 2000, for tax reasons. The check was neither deposited nor negotiated. Wilson denies that he ever agreed to sell the horse or that he received the check and bill of sale from Presti. Presti's claim is supported by a copy of his check stub and by the affidavit of his executive assistant, who says that he monitored the telephone call and prepared and mailed both the bill of sale and the check. Wilson argues that the statute of frauds governs this transaction, and because there was no writing, the contract claim is barred. Decision?

19. Louie E. Brown worked for the Phelps Dodge Corporation under an oral contract for approximately twenty-three years. In 1997, he was suspended from work for unauthorized possession of company property. In 1998, Phelps Dodge fired Brown after discovering that he was using company property without permission and building a trailer on company time. Brown sued Phelps Dodge for benefits under an unemployment benefit plan. According to the plan, "in order to be eligible for unemployment benefits, a laid-off employee must: (1) Have completed 2 or more years of continuous service with the company, and (2) Have been laid off from work because the company had determined that work was not available for him." The trial court held that the wording of the second condition was ambiguous and should be construed against Phelps Dodge, the party who chose the wording. A reading of the entire contract, however, indicates that the plan was not intended to apply to someone who was fired for cause. Decision?

20. Katz offered to purchase land from Joiner, and, after negotiating the terms, Joiner accepted. On October 13, over the telephone, both parties agreed to extend the time period for completing and mailing the written contract until October 20. Although the original paperwork deadline in the offer was October 14, Katz stated he had inserted that provision "for my purpose only." All other provisions of the contract remained unchanged. Accordingly, Joiner completed the contract and mailed it on October 20. Immediately after, however, Joiner sent Katz a telegram stating that "I have signed and returned contract, but have changed my mind. Do not wish to sell property." Joiner now claims an oral modification of a contract

within the statute of frauds is unenforceable. Katz counters that the modification is not material and therefore does not affect the underlying contract. Decision?

**21.** When Mr. McClam died, he left the family farm, heavily mortgaged, to his wife and children. To save the farm from foreclosure, Mrs. McClam planned to use insurance proceeds and her savings to pay off the debts. She was unwilling to do so, however, unless she had full ownership of the property. Mrs. McClam wrote her daughter, stating that the daughter should deed over her interest in the family farm to her mother and promising that all the children would inherit the farm equally upon their mother's death. The letter further explained that if foreclosure occurred, each child would receive very little, but if they complied with their mother's plan, each would eventually receive a valuable property interest upon her death. Finally, the letter stated that all the other children had agreed to this plan. Consequently, the daughter also agreed. Years later, Mrs. McClam tries to convey the farm to her son Donald. The daughter challenges, arguing that the mother is contractually bound to convey the land equally to all of the children. Donald says this was an oral agreement to sell land and is unenforceable. The daughter argues that the letter satisfies the statute of frauds, making the contract enforceable. Who gets the farm? Explain.

**22.** Butler Brothers Building Company sublet all of the work in a highway construction contract to Ganley Brothers, Inc. Soon thereafter, Ganley brought this action against Butler for fraud in the inducement of the contract. The contract, however, provided: "The contractor [Ganley] has examined the said contracts . . ., knows all the requirements, and is not relying upon any statement made by the company in respect thereto." Decision?

**23.** The defendant, Shane Quadri, contacted Don Hoffman, an employee of defendant Al J. Hoffman & Co., to procure car insurance. Later, Quadri's car was stolen on October 25 or 26. Quadri contacted Hoffman, who arranged with Budget Rent-a-Car, a plaintiff in this case, for a rental car for Quadri until his car was recovered. Hoffman authorized Budget Rent-a-Car to bill the Hoffman Agency. Later, when the stolen car was recovered, Hoffman telephoned plaintiff, Goodyear, and arranged to have four new tires put on Quadri's car to replace those damaged during the theft. The plaintiffs (Budget and Goodyear) sued the defendants (Quadri and Hoffman) for payment for the car rental and tires. Judgment was entered in favor of Budget and Goodyear against defendant Hoffman but in favor of Quadri. Decision.

**24.** Stuart Studio, an art studio, prepared a new catalog for the National School of Heavy Equipment, a school run by Gilbert and Donald Shaw. When the artwork was virtually finished, Gilbert Shaw requested Stuart Studio to purchase and supervise the printing of 25,000 catalogs. Shaw told the art studio that payment of the printing costs would be made within ten days after billing and that if the "National School would not pay the full total that he would stand good for the entire bill." Shaw was chairman of the board of directors of the school, and he owned 100 percent of its voting stock and 49 percent of its nonvoting stock. The school became bankrupt, and Stuart Studio was unable to recover the sum from the school. Stuart Studio then brought this action against Shaw on the basis of his promise to pay the bill. The trial court granted Shaw's motion for a directed verdict, and Stuart Studio brought this appeal. Decision?

**25.** Thomson Printing Company is a buyer and seller of used machinery. On April 10, the president of the company, James Thomson, went to the surplus machinery department of B.F. Goodrich Company in Akron, Ohio, to examine some used equipment that was for sale. Thomson discussed the sale, including a price of $9,000, with Ingram Meyers, a Goodrich employee and agent. Four days later, on April 14, Thomson sent a purchase order to confirm the oral contract for purchase of the machinery and a partial payment of $1,000 to Goodrich in Akron. The purchase order contained Thomson Printing's name, address, and telephone number, as well as certain information about the purchase, but did not specifically mention Meyers or the surplus equipment department. Goodrich sent copies of the documents to a number of its divisions, but Meyers never learned of the confirmation until weeks later, by which time the equipment had been sold to another party. Thomson Printing brought suit against Goodrich for breach of contract. Goodrich claimed that no contract had existed and that at any rate the alleged oral contract could not be enforced because of the statute of frauds. The district court found the contract unenforceable, and Thomson Printing appealed. Decision?

**WWW** **Internet Exercise** Determine whether the United Nations Convention on Contracts for the International Sale of Goods (Vienna, 1980) contains a writing requirement.

# CHAPTER 16

# Third Parties to Contracts

Whereas prior chapters considered contractual situations essentially involving only two parties, this chapter deals with the rights or duties of third parties, namely, persons who are not parties to the contract but who have a right to, or an obligation for, its performance. These rights and duties arise either by (1) an assignment of the rights of a party to the contract, (2) a delegation of the duties of a party to the contract, or (3) the express terms of a contract entered into for the benefit of a third person. In an assignment or delegation, the third party's rights or duties arise after the contract is made, whereas in the third situation the third-party beneficiary's rights arise at the time the contract was formed. We will consider these three situations in that order.

## ASSIGNMENT OF RIGHTS

Every contract creates both rights and duties. A person who owes a duty under a contract is an **obligor,** while a person to whom a contractual duty is owed is an **obligee.** For instance, Ann promises to sell to Bart an automobile for which Bart promises to pay $10,000 in monthly installments over the next three years. Ann's right under the contract is to receive payment from Bart, whereas Ann's duty is to deliver the automobile. Bart's right is to receive the automobile; his duty is to pay for it.

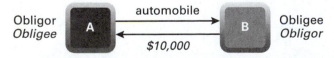

An **assignment of rights** is the voluntary transfer to a third party of the rights arising from the contract. In the above example, if Ann were to transfer her right under the contract (the installment payments due from Bart) to Clark for $8,500 in cash, this would constitute a valid assignment of rights. In this case, Ann would be

the **assignor,** Clark would be the **assignee,** and Bart would be the **obligor.**

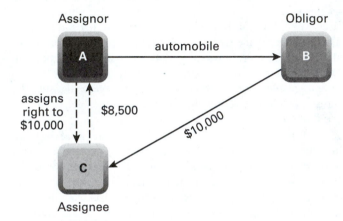

An effective assignment terminates the assignor's right to receive performance by the obligor. After an assignment, only the assignee has a right to the obligor's performance.

On the other hand, if Ann and Doris agree that Doris should deliver the automobile to Bart, this would constitute a delegation, not an assignment, of duties between Ann and Doris. A **delegation of duties** is a transfer to a third party of a contractual obligation. In this instance, Ann would be the **delegator,** Doris would be the **delegatee,** and Bart would be the **obligee.** Delegations of duties are discussed later in this chapter.

### Law Governing Assignments

The law governing assignments arises principally from the common law of contracts, Article 2 of the UCC, and Article 9 of the UCC. Article 2 applies to assignments of rights under a contract for the sale of goods. Article 9 covers all assignments made to secure the performance of an obligation *and* all assignments involving rights to payment for goods sold or leased or for services rendered.

## Requirements of an Assignment

The Restatement defines an assignment of a right as a "manifestation of the assignor's intention to transfer it by virtue of which the assignor's right to performance by the obligor is extinguished in whole or in part and the assignee acquires a right to such performance." Section 317(1). No special form or particular words are necessary to create an assignment. Any words that fairly indicate an intention to make the assignee the owner of the right are sufficient. For instance, Eve delivers to Harold a writing addressed to Mary stating, "Pay Harold for his own use $1,000 out of the amount you owe me." This writing is a legally sufficient assignment. Restatement, Section 325, Illustration 1.

Unless otherwise provided by statute, an assignment may be oral. The UCC imposes a writing requirement on all assignments beyond $5,000. Section 1–206. In addition, Article 9 requires certain assignments to be in writing.

Consideration is not required for an effective assignment. Consequently, gratuitous assignments are valid and enforceable. By giving value for the assignment, the assignee manifests his assent to the assignment as part of the bargained-for exchange. On the other hand, when the assignment is gratuitous, the assignee's assent is not always required. Any assignee who has not assented to an assignment may, however, disclaim the assignment within a reasonable time after learning of its existence and terms. Restatement, Section 327. No particular formality is required for the disclaimer, which renders the assignment inoperative from the beginning.

***Revocability of Assignments***  When the assignee gives consideration in exchange for an assignment, a contract exists between the assignor and the assignee. Consequently, the assignor may not revoke the assignment without the assignee's assent. A gratuitous assignment, in contrast, is revocable by the assignor and is terminated by her death, incapacity, or subsequent assignment of the right, unless she has made an effective delivery of the assignment to the assignee by transferring a deed or other document evidencing the right, such as a stock certificate or savings passbook. Delivery may also consist of physically delivering a signed, written assignment of the contract right.

A gratuitous assignment is also rendered irrevocable if, prior to the attempted revocation, the donee-assignee receives payment of the claim from the obligor, obtains a judgment against the obligor, or obtains a new contract with the obligor. For example, Nancy owes Howard $50,000. Howard signs a written statement granting Paul a gratuitous assignment of his rights from Nancy but dies prior to delivering to Paul the signed, written assignment of the contract right. The assignment is terminated and therefore ineffective. On the other hand, had Howard delivered the signed, written assignment to Paul before he died, the assignment would have been effective and irrevocable.

***Partial Assignments***  A partial assignment is a transfer of a portion of the contractual rights to one or more assignees. Although partial assignments were not enforceable at early common law, such assignments now are permitted and are enforceable. The obligor, however, may require all the parties entitled to the promised performance to litigate the matter in one action, thus ensuring that all parties are present and thereby avoiding the undue hardship of multiple lawsuits. For example, Jack owes Richard $2,500. Richard assigns $1,000 to Mildred. Neither Richard nor Mildred can maintain an action against Jack if Jack objects, unless the other is joined in the lawsuit against Jack.

## Rights That Are Assignable

As a general rule, most contract rights, including rights under an option contract, are assignable. The most common contractual right that may be assigned is the right to the payment of money, such as an account receivable or interest due or to be paid. The right to property other than money, such as goods or land, is also frequently assignable.

## Rights That Are Not Assignable

To protect the obligor or the public interest, some contract rights are not assignable. These nonassignable contract rights include those that (1) materially change the obligor's duty or materially increase the risk or burden upon the obligor, (2) transfer highly personal contract rights, (3) are validly prohibited by the contract, or (4) are prohibited by statute or public policy. Restatement, Section 317(2).

***Assignments That Materially Increase the Duty, Risk, or Burden***  An assignment is ineffective where performance by the obligor to the assignee would differ materially from her performance to the assignor; that is, where the assignment would significantly change the nature or extent of the obligor's duty. Thus, an automobile liability insurance policy issued to Alex is not assignable by Alex to Betty. The risk assumed by the insurance company was liability for Alex's negligent operation of the automobile. Liability for operation of the same automobile by Betty would be a risk entirely different from the one that the insurance company had assumed. Similarly, Alex would not be allowed to assign to Cynthia, the owner of a twenty-five-room mansion, his contractual right to have Betty paint his small, two-bedroom house. Clearly, such an assignment would materially increase Betty's duty of performance. By comparison, the right to receive monthly payments under a contract may be assigned; for mailing the check to the assignee costs no more than mailing it to the assignor. Moreover, if a contract explicitly provides that it may be assigned, then rights under it are assignable even if the assignment would change the duty, risk, or burden of performance on the obligor. Restatement, Section 323(1).

***Assignments of Personal Rights*** Where the rights under a contract are highly personal, in that they are limited to the person of the obligee, such rights are not assignable. An extreme example of such a contract is an agreement of two persons to marry one another. The prospective groom obviously cannot transfer to some third party the prospective bride's promise to marry him. A more typical example of a contract involving personal rights would be a contract between a teacher and a school. The teacher could not assign to another teacher her right to a faculty position. Similarly, a student who is awarded a scholarship cannot assign his right to some other person.

 *See Case 16–1*

***Express Prohibition against Assignment*** Contract terms prohibiting assignment of rights under the contract are strictly construed. Moreover, most courts interpret a general prohibition against assignments as a mere promise not to assign. As a consequence, the prohibition, if violated, gives the obligor a right to damages for breach of the terms forbidding assignment but does *not* render the assignment ineffective.

Section 322(1) of the Restatement provides that, unless circumstances indicate the contrary, a contract term prohibiting assignment of the contract bars only the delegation to the assignee (delegatee) of the assignor's (delegator's) duty of performance, not the assignment of rights. Thus, Abe and Bill contract for the sale of land by Bill to Abe for $30,000 and provide in their contract that Abe may not assign his rights under it. Abe pays Bill $30,000 and thereby fully performs his obligations under the contract. Abe then assigns his rights to Cheryl, who is entitled to receive the land from Bill (the obligor) despite the contractual prohibition of assignment.

UCC Section 2–210(2) provides that a right to damages for breach of the whole contract or a right arising out of the assignor's due performance of his entire obligation can be assigned despite a contractual provision to the contrary. UCC Section 2–210(3) provides that, unless circumstances indicate the contrary, a contract term prohibiting assignment of the contract bars only the delegation to the assignee (delegatee) of the assignor's (delegator's) duty of performance, not the assignment of rights. UCC Section 9–318(4) makes ineffective any term in a contract prohibiting the assignment of any right to payment for goods sold or leased or for services rendered.

 *See Case 16–2*

***Assignments Prohibited by Law*** Various Federal and State statutes, as well as public policy, prohibit or regulate the assignment of certain types of contract rights. For instance, assignments of future wages are subject to statutes, some of which prohibit such assignments altogether while others require them to be in writing and subject to certain restrictions. Moreover, an assignment that violates public policy will be unenforceable even in the absence of a prohibiting statute.

## Rights of the Assignee

***Obtains Rights of Assignor*** The general rule is that an assignee **stands in the shoes** of the assignor. He acquires the rights of the assignor, but no new or additional rights, and takes the assigned rights with all of the defenses, defects, and infirmities to which they would be subject, were the assignor to bring an action against the obligor. Thus, in an action brought by the assignee against the obligor, the obligor may plead fraud, duress, undue influence, failure of consideration, breach of contract, or any other defense against the assignor arising out of the original contract. The obligor also may assert rights of setoff or counterclaim arising against the assignor out of entirely separate matters, provided they arose prior to his receiving notice of the assignment.

The Code permits the buyer under a contract of sale to agree as part of the contract that he will not assert against an assignee any claim or defense that the buyer may have against the seller if the assignee takes the assignment for value and in good faith. UCC Section 9–206. Such a provision in an agreement renders the seller's rights more marketable. The Federal Trade Commission, however, has invalidated such waiver of defense provisions in consumer credit transactions. This rule is discussed more fully in Chapter 28. Most States also have statutes protecting buyers in consumer transactions by prohibiting waiver of defenses.

*Notice* To be valid, notice of an assignment does not have to be given to the obligor. Nonetheless, giving such notice is advisable because an assignee will lose his rights against an obligor who pays the assignor without notice of the assignment: to compel an obligor to pay a claim a second time, when she was not notified that a new party was entitled to payment would be unfair. For example, Donald owes Gary $1,000 due on September 1. Gary assigns the debt to Paula on August 1, but neither he nor Paula informs Donald. On September 1, Donald pays Gary. Donald is fully discharged from his obligation, whereas Gary is liable for $1,000 to Paula. On the other hand, if Paula had given notice of the assignment to Donald before September 1 and Donald had paid Gary nevertheless, Paula would then have the right to recover the $1,000 from either Donald or Gary.

Furthermore, notice cuts off any defenses based on subsequent agreements between the obligor and assignor. Moreover, as already indicated, notice precludes subsequent setoffs and counterclaims of the obligor that arise out of entirely separate matters.

## Implied Warranties of Assignor

An **implied warranty** is an obligation imposed by law upon the transfer of property or contract rights. In the absence of an express intention to the contrary, an assignor who receives value makes the following implied warranties to the assignee with respect to the assigned right:

1. that he will do nothing to defeat or impair the assignment;
2. that the assigned right actually exists and is subject to no limitations or defenses other than those stated or apparent at the time of the assignment;
3. that any writing evidencing the right delivered to the assignee or exhibited to him as an inducement to accept the assignment is genuine and what it purports to be; and

4. that the assignor has no knowledge of any fact that would impair the value of the assignment.

Thus, Eric has a right against Julia and assigns it for value to Gwen. Later, Eric gives Julia a release. Gwen may recover damages from Eric for breach of the first implied warranty.

## Express Warranties of Assignor

An **express warranty** is an explicitly made contractual promise regarding property or contract rights transferred. The assignor is further bound by any express warranties he makes to the assignee with respect to the right assigned. The assignor does not, however, guarantee that the obligor will pay the assigned debt or otherwise perform, unless such a guarantee is explicitly stated.

## Successive Assignments of the Same Right

The owner of a right could conceivably make successive assignments of the same claim to different persons. Assume that B owes A $1,000. On June 1, A for value assigns the debt to C. Thereafter, on June 15, A assigns it to D, who in good faith gives value and has no knowledge of the prior assignment by A to C. If the assignment is subject to Article 9, then that article's priority rules will control, as discussed in Chapter 38. Otherwise, the priority is determined by the common law. The majority rule in the United States is that the **first assignee in point of time** (here, C) prevails over subsequent assignees. By comparison, in England and in a minority of the States, the first assignee to notify the obligor prevails.

The Restatement adopts a third view: a prior assignee is entitled to the assigned right and its proceeds to the exclusion of a subsequent assignee, *except* where the prior assignment is revocable or voidable by the assignor or where the subsequent assignee in good faith and without knowledge of the prior assignment gives value and obtains one of the following: (1) payment or satisfaction of the obligor's duty, (2) a judgment against the obligor, (3) a new contract with the obligor, or (4) possession of a writing of a type customarily accepted as a symbol or evidence of the right assigned. Restatement, Section 342.

## DELEGATION OF DUTIES

As indicated earlier, contractual **duties** are *not* assignable, but their performance generally may be *delegated* to a third person. A **delegation of duties** is a transfer of a contractual obligation to a third party. For example, A promises to sell B a new automobile, for which B promises to pay $10,000 by monthly installments over the next three years. If A and D agree that D should deliver the automobile to B, this would not constitute an assignment but would be a delegation of duties between A and D. In this instance, A would be the **delegator,** D would be the **delegatee,** and B would be the **obligee.**

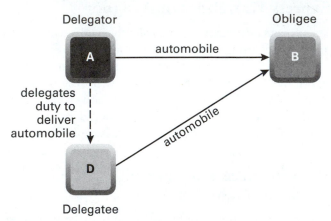

Delegator                                    Obligee

delegates
duty to
deliver
automobile

Delegatee

A delegation of duty does not extinguish the delegator's obligation to perform, because A remains liable to B. When the delegatee accepts, or assumes, the delegated duty, both the delegator and delegatee are held liable to the obligee for performance of the contractual duty.

## Delegable Duties

Although contractual duties generally are delegable, a delegation will not be permitted if

1. the nature of the duties is personal in that the obligee has a substantial interest in having the delegator perform the contract;
2. the performance is expressly made nondelegable; or
3. the delegation is prohibited by statute or public policy.

Restatement, Section 318 and UCC Section 2–210. The courts will examine a delegation more closely than an assignment because a delegation compels the nondelegating party to the contract (the obligee) to receive performance from a party with whom she has not dealt.

For example, a schoolteacher may not delegate her performance to another teacher, even if the substitute is equally competent; for this is a contract that is personal in nature. In the frequently quoted words of an English case: "You have a right to the benefit you contemplate from the character, credit and substance of the person with whom you contract." On the other hand, under a

contract in which performance involves no peculiar or special skill and in which no personal trust or confidence is involved, the party may delegate the performance of his duty. For example, the duty to pay money, to deliver fungible goods such as corn, or to mow a lawn is usually delegable.

 *See Case 16–3*

## Duties of the Parties

Even when permitted, a delegation of a duty to a third person still leaves the delegator bound to perform. If the delegator desires to be discharged of the duty, she is allowed to enter into an agreement by which she obtains the consent of the obligee to substitute a third person (the delegatee) in her place. This is a **novation,** whereby the delegator is discharged and the third party becomes directly bound upon his promise to the obligee.

Though a delegation authorizes a third party to perform a duty for the delegator, a delegatee becomes liable for performance only if he assents to perform the delegated duties. Thus, if Frank owes a duty to Grace, and Frank delegates that duty to Henry, Henry is not obligated to either Frank or Grace to perform the duty unless Henry agrees to do so. Nevertheless, if Henry promises either Frank (the delegator) or Grace (the obligee) that he will perform Frank's duty, Henry is said to have **assumed the delegated duty** and becomes liable to both Frank and Grace for nonperformance. Accordingly, when duties are both delegated and assumed, both the delegator and the delegatee are liable to the obligee for proper performance of the original contractual duty. The delegatee's promise to perform creates contract rights in the obligee who may bring an action against the delegatee as a third party beneficiary of the contract between the delegator and the delegatee. (Third-party contracts are discussed later in this chapter.)

The question of whether a delegatee has assumed delegated duties frequently arises in the following ambiguous situation: Marty and Carol agree to an assignment of Marty's contract with Bob. The Code clearly resolves this ambiguity by providing that, unless the language or circumstances indicate the contrary, an assignment of "the contract," or of "all my rights under the contract," or an assignment in similar general terms is an assignment of rights *and* a delegation of performance of the assignor's duties; its acceptance by the assignee constitutes a promise by her to perform those duties. Section 2–210(4). The Restatement, Section 328, has also adopted this position. For example, Cooper Oil Co. has a contract to deliver oil to Halsey. Cooper Oil Co. delivers to Lowell Oil Co. a writing assigning to Lowell Oil Co. "all Cooper Oil Co.'s rights under the contract." Lowell Oil Co. is under a duty to Halsey to deliver the oil called for by the contract, and Cooper Oil Co. is liable to Halsey if Lowell Oil Co. does not perform. It should also be recalled that the Restatement and the Code provide that a clause prohibiting an assignment of "the contract" is to be construed as barring only the delegation to the assignee (delegatee) of the assignor's (delegator's) performance, unless the circumstances indicate the contrary.

## THIRD-PARTY BENEFICIARY CONTRACTS

A contract in which a party (the **promisor**) promises to render a certain performance not to the other party (the **promisee**) but to a third person (the **beneficiary**) is called a third-party beneficiary contract. The third person is not a party to the contract but is merely a beneficiary of it. Such contracts may be divided into two types: (1) intended beneficiary and (2) incidental beneficiary. An **intended beneficiary** is intended by the two parties to the contract (the promisor and promisee) to receive a benefit from the performance of their agreement. Accordingly, the courts generally enforce intended beneficiary third-party contracts. For example, Abbott promises Baldwin to deliver an automobile to Carson if Baldwin promises to pay $10,000. Carson is the intended beneficiary.

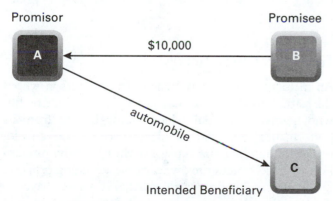

Promisor — A

Promisee — B

$10,000

automobile

Intended Beneficiary — C

In an **incidental beneficiary** contract, the third party is not intended to receive a benefit under the contract. Accordingly, courts do not enforce the third party's right to the benefits of the contract. For example, Abbott promises to purchase and deliver to Baldwin an automobile for $10,000. In all probability, Abbott would acquire

the automobile from Davis. Davis would be an incidental beneficiary.

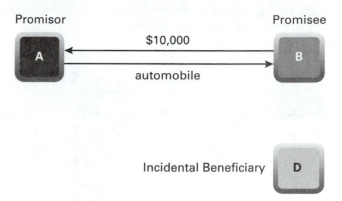

Promisor — A

Promisee — B

$10,000

automobile

Incidental Beneficiary — D

## Intended Beneficiary

Unless otherwise agreed between the promisor and promisee, a beneficiary of a promise is an intended beneficiary if the parties intended this to be the result of their agreement. Restatement, Section 302. Thus, there are two types of intended beneficiaries: (1) donee beneficiaries and (2) creditor beneficiaries.

***Donee Beneficiary*** A third party is an **intended donee beneficiary** if the promisee's purpose in bargaining for and obtaining the agreement with the promisor is to make a gift to the beneficiary. The ordinary life insurance policy illustrates this type of contract. The insured (the promisee) makes a contract with an insurance company (the promisor) that promises, in consideration of premiums paid to it by the insured, to pay upon the death of the insured a stated sum of money to the named beneficiary, who is an intended donee beneficiary.

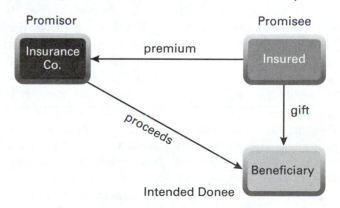

Promisor — Insurance Co.

Promisee — Insured

premium

proceeds

gift

Beneficiary

Intended Donee

***Creditor Beneficiary*** A third person is also an intended beneficiary if the promisee intends the performance of the promise to satisfy a legal duty he owes to the beneficiary, who is a creditor of the promisee. The contract involves consideration moving from the promisee to the promisor in exchange for the promisor's engaging to pay a debt or to discharge an obligation the promisee owes to the third person.

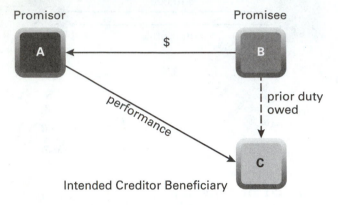

Promisor · Promisee

$

A → B

performance

prior duty owed

C

Intended Creditor Beneficiary

To illustrate, in a contract for the sale by Wesley of his business to Susan, Susan promises Wesley that she will pay all of his outstanding business debts, as listed in the contract. Here, Wesley's creditors are creditor beneficiaries. Similarly, in the classic *Lawrence v. Fox*, 20 N.Y. 268 (1859), Holly loaned Fox $300 in consideration for Fox's promise to pay that sum to Lawrence, a creditor of Holly. Fox failed to pay Lawrence, who sued Fox for the $300. The court held for Lawrence, who was permitted to recover as a third-party creditor beneficiary to the contract between Holly and Fox.

***Rights of Intended Beneficiary*** An intended *donee* beneficiary may enforce the contract only against the promisor. He cannot maintain an action against the promisee, as the promisee was under no legal obligation to him. An intended *creditor* beneficiary, however, may enforce the contract against either or both parties. If Willard owes Lola $500, and Julie contracts with Willard to pay this debt to Lola, Willard is not thereby relieved of his liability to Lola. If Julie breaks the contract, Lola, as a creditor beneficiary, may sue her. In addition, Lola may sue Willard as her debtor. If Lola should obtain judgments against both Julie and Willard, she is, of course, entitled to collect only one judgment. If Lola recovers against Willard, Willard has a right of reimbursement from Julie, the promisor. Restatement, Section 310.

In an action by the intended beneficiary of a third-party contract to enforce the promise, the promisor may assert any defense that would be available to him if the action had been brought by the promisee. The rights of the third party are based upon the promisor's contract with the promisee. Thus, the promisor may assert the

absence of mutual assent or consideration, lack of capacity, fraud, mistake, and the like against the intended beneficiary.

 *See Case 16–4*

***Vesting of Rights*** A contract for the benefit of an intended beneficiary confers upon that beneficiary rights that she may enforce. Until these rights **vest** (take effect), however, the promisor and promisee may, by later agreement, vary or completely discharge them. The States vary considerably as to when vesting occurs. Some hold that vesting takes place immediately upon the making of the contract. In others, vesting occurs when the third party learns of the contract and assents to it. In another group of States, vesting requires the third party to change his position in reliance upon the promise made for his benefit. The Restatement has adopted the following position: If the contract between the promisor and promisee provides that they may not vary its terms without the consent of the beneficiary, such a provision is effective. Otherwise, the parties to the contract may rescind or vary the contract unless the intended beneficiary (1) has brought an action upon the promise, (2) has changed her position in reliance upon it, or (3) has assented to the promise at the request of the promisor or promisee. Restatement, Section 311.

On the other hand, the promisor and promisee may provide that the benefits will *never* vest. For example, Mildred purchases an insurance policy on her own life, naming her husband as beneficiary. Her policy, as such policies commonly do, reserves to Mildred the right to change the beneficiary or even to cancel the policy entirely.

## Incidental Beneficiary

An incidental third-party beneficiary is a person whom the parties to a contract did not intend to benefit but who nevertheless would derive some benefit from its performance. For instance, a contract to raze an old, unsightly building and replace it with a costly, modern house would benefit the owner of the adjoining property by increasing his property's value. He would have no rights under the contract, however, as the benefit to him would be unintended and incidental.

A third person who may benefit incidentally from the performance of a contract to which he is not a party has no rights under the contract. Neither the promisee nor the promisor intended that the third person benefit. Assume that for a stated consideration George promises

Kathy that he will purchase and deliver to Kathy a brand-new Sony television of the latest model. Kathy performs. George does not. As an incidental beneficiary, Cosmos Appliances, Inc., the local exclusive Sony dealer, has no rights under the contract, although performance by George would produce a sale from which Cosmos would benefit.

---

 # Chapter Summary

| | |
|---|---|
| **Assignment of Rights** | **Definition of Assignment** voluntary transfer to a third party of the rights arising from a contract so that the assignor's right to performance is extinguished<br>• *Assignor* party making an assignment<br>• *Assignee* party to whom contract rights are assigned<br>• *Obligor* party owing a duty to the assignor under the original contract<br>• *Obligee* party to whom a duty of performance is owed under a contract<br>**Requirements of an Assignment** include intent but not consideration<br>• *Revocability of Assignment* when the assignee gives consideration the assignor may not revoke the assignment without the assignee's consent<br>• *Partial Assignment* transfer of a portion of contractual rights to one or more assignees<br>**Assignability** most contract rights are assignable, *except*<br>• assignments that materially increase the duty, risk, or burden upon the obligor<br>• assignments of personal rights<br>• assignments expressly forbidden by the contract<br>• assignments prohibited by law<br>**Rights of Assignee** the assignee stands in the shoes of the assignor<br>• *Defenses of Obligor* may be asserted against the assignee<br>• *Notice* is not required but is advisable<br>**Implied Warranty** obligation imposed by law upon the assignor of a contract right<br>**Express Warranty** explicitly made contractual promise regarding contract rights transferred<br>**Successive Assignments** the majority rule is that the first assignee in point of time prevails over later assignees; minority rule is that the first assignee to notify the obligor prevails |
| **Delegation of Duties** | **Definition of Delegation** transfer to a third party of a contractual obligation<br>• *Delegator* party delegating his duty to a third party<br>• *Delegatee* third party to whom the delegator's duty is delegated<br>• *Obligee* party to whom a duty of performance is owed by the delegator and delegatee<br>**Delegability** most contract duties may be delegated, *except*<br>• duties that are personal<br>• duties that are expressly nondelegable<br>• duties whose delegation is prohibited by statute or public policy<br>**Duties of Parties**<br>• *Delegation* delegator is still bound to perform original obligation<br>• *Novation* contract, to which the obligee is a party, substituting a new promisor for an existing promisor, who is consequently no longer liable on the original contract and is not liable as a delegator |

| **Third-Party Beneficiary Contracts** | **Definition** a contract in which one party promises to render a performance to a third person (the beneficiary) <br> **Intended Beneficiaries** third parties intended by the two contracting parties to receive a benefit from their contract <br> • *Donee Beneficiary* a third party intended to receive a benefit from the contract as a gift <br> • *Creditor Beneficiary* a third person intended to receive a benefit from the agreement to satisfy a legal duty owed to her <br> • *Rights of Intended Beneficiaries* an intended donee beneficiary may enforce the contract against the promisor; an intended creditor beneficiary may enforce the contract against either or both the promisor and the promisee <br> • *Vesting of Rights* if the beneficiary's rights vest, the promisor and promisee may not thereafter vary or discharge these vested rights <br> **Incidental Beneficiary** third party whom the two parties to the contract have no intention of benefiting by their contract and who acquires no rights under the contract |
| --- | --- |

 **Cases**

### CASE 16–1
### Rights That Are Not Assignable: Personal Rights
### *REISER v. DAYTON COUNTRY CLUB COMPANY*
United States Court of Appeals, Sixth Circuit, 1992
972 F.2d 689

JOINER, J.

In this case we are asked to review an order barring a trustee in bankruptcy under Chapter 7 from assuming and assigning a golf membership in a country club as an executory contract, pursuant to section 365 of the Bankruptcy Code. [Citation.]

The Dayton Country Club is an organization, in the form of a corporation, consisting of several hundred individuals who have joined together for recreation and entertainment. Its shares of stock may be held only by the members of the club and may not be accumulated in any substantial amount by one member.

The club offers social events, dining facilities, tennis courts, a swimming pool, and a golf course. It became apparent over a period of time that each of these diverse programs could be enjoyed to full advantage by a different number of members. For example, since there was only one 18-hole golf course available, and because of the nature of the game, the maximum number of members eligible to play golf needed to be limited in order to make the playing of the game enjoyable to those playing. There was no need to so limit the number of members who could use the tennis courts, the pool, the restaurants, or who could enjoy the social events of the club. The club

developed within its membership a special membership category for those who had full golfing privileges. This category was limited to 375 members. Detailed rules, procedures, and practices were developed to ensure the fair selection of golfing members. These rules, procedures, and practices define how this additional privilege is allocated, how the number of members is maintained at 375, how vacancies occur, how they are filled, and what additional fees are charged.

The record reflects that members of the club are entitled to play, eat, and socialize in all activities of the club except golf. If, in addition to these activities, a member desires to play golf, he or she asks to become a golfing member in one of several golf membership categories. When he or she makes this request, an additional substantial fee is paid to the club and the individual is placed on a waiting list. At the time the record was made in this case, there were about 70 persons on that list. When a vacancy occurs because of a failure to pay dues or a resignation, the first person on the waiting list is given the option to become a golfing member by paying an additional substantial fee. Upon becoming a golfing member, the monthly dues also increase substantially. If the person at the top of the waiting list declines the membership, then that person is placed at the bottom of the list and the next person on the list is given the opportunity to become a golfing member. There is no provision for any person to assign or sell the golf membership to any other person or for any person to become a golfing member in any other way except in two intimate and personal situations dealt with in discrete ways. When the death of a golfing member occurs, a spouse (who had been enjoying the hospitality of the club) may take the deceased member's place. If a divorce occurs, the member may designate his or her spouse as the golfing member. The club also has a program to encourage the younger generation of member families to become golfing members. Golfing members are permitted also to invite guests. Through its membership committee, the club makes the rules and establishes the procedures to describe whom among its larger membership list may be golfing members.

The nature of the golf membership within the overall club membership is the heart of this case. We are not dealing with the right to be a member of the club and there is nothing in this case relating to laws and social policies against discrimination. The issues in this case relate solely to the rights, duties, and privileges of the club and its members arising from the club's effort to provide golfing privileges to some but not all of its members, and the effect of the bankruptcy laws upon that effort.

This matter involves appeals from separate orders entered in the bankruptcies of debtors Magness and Redman, both of whom were golfing members of the Dayton Country Club. The trustee in bankruptcy sought to assume and assign, through sale, the rights under these memberships to (1) members on the waiting list, (2) other club members, or (3) the general public, provided that the purchaser first obtains membership in the Dayton Country Club. In other words, the trustee seeks to increase the value of the bankruptcy estate by taking value for and assigning to others a relationship between the bankrupt and the club. The assignment would be to the detriment of other club members who had paid for and acquired the right to become golfing members in due course. The question is whether the trustee has the right to make the assignment.

The arrangement between the members of the club, including Magness and Redman, and the Dayton Country Club, is a complex one involving rights, privileges, and duties, all of which are bound up in what is loosely called the contract for "full golf membership." At the least, this contract involves (1) an executed portion, the achievement of "full golf membership," and the payment of the nonrefundable fee the club charges for that membership in accordance with the rules, procedures, and practices prescribed by the club; (2) the rights of other

club members to apply for golf membership as set out in the rules, procedures, and practices of the club; (3) the rights of those in the club who have applied for and have been accepted and have made substantial payments for full golf membership; (4) the obligation of the members to pay monthly dues; and (5) the obligation of the club to provide recreational facilities called for in its charter and bylaws. In other words, this contract between the debtors and the club and others is neither a simple contract to buy and sell a product or a service nor is it a lease.

Not only is it appropriate to cast these complex relationships in terms of both executed and executory contracts, it is not inappropriate to think of these contracts as creating a type of property interest. The full golf membership and the rights that come from that relationship with the club can be described as a property right of that member, the parameters of which are defined by the rules, procedures, and practices of the club. These rules, procedures, and practices, and therefore the extent of the members' property interest, do not extend to any right on the members' part to pass on the membership to others, except in the two situations described above (death or divorce). The persons on the waiting list also can be described as having a type of property interest in the relationship described in their contracts with the club. Theirs is a lesser interest than that of the full golfing members, but a real one nonetheless. They have paid the club for the right to be considered in the numbered order on the list to become full golfing members as vacancies occur. They, like the full golfing members, have a status defined by the various rules, procedures, and practices pertaining to filling the membership roster.

The bankruptcy courts found, and the district court affirmed, that the full golf memberships are executory contracts under § 365 of the Bankruptcy Code. [Citation.] Section 365(f)(1) of the Bankruptcy Code provides that executory contracts may be assigned notwithstanding non-assignment provisions in the contract or the law * * *

Section 365(c)(1) contains an exception to section 365(f)'s bar to enforcement of non-assignment provisions:

(c) The trustee may not assume or assign any executory contract or unexpired lease of the debtor, whether or not such contract or lease prohibits or restricts assignment of rights or delegation of duties, if—

(1) (A) applicable law excuses a party, other than the debtor, to such contract or lease from accepting performance from or rendering performance to an entity other than the debtor or the debtor in possession, whether or not

such contract or lease prohibits or restricts assignment of rights or delegation of duties; and

(B) such party does not consent to such assumption or assignment. . . . [Citation.]

The bankruptcy courts found that the trustee was barred from assigning the full golf memberships by Ohio law under § 365(c). The courts concluded that the club's rules were, in effect, anti-assignment provisions, and that Ohio law excused the club from accepting performance by others. The court thus gave effect to the provisions. * * *

The trustee appealed these rulings to the district court. * * *

The district court affirmed the order barring assignment of Magness' full golf membership on the basis of the bankruptcy court's reasoning, and observed as well that the case did not involve "the legal equivalent of a long-term commercial lease" but rather "a noncommercial dispute over the possession of a valuable membership in a recreational and social club."

The trustee then appealed to this court * * * . We conclude that the decision of the district court was correct * * * . We now affirm.

* * *

As stated earlier in this opinion, the contracts involve complex issues and multiple parties: the members of the club, in having an orderly procedure for the selection of full golfing members; the club itself, in demonstrating to all who would become members that there is a predictable and orderly method of filling vacancies in the golfing roster; and more particularly, persons on the waiting list who have deposited substantial sums of money based on

an expectation and a developed procedure that in due course they, in turn, would become full golfing members.

If the trustee is permitted to assume and assign the full golf membership, the club would be required to breach its agreement with the persons on the waiting list, each of whom has contractual rights with the club. It would require the club to accept performance from and render performance to a person other than the debtor. * * *

* * *

The contracts creating the complex relationships among the parties and others are not in any way commercial. They create personal relationships among individuals who play golf, who are waiting to play golf, who eat together, swim and play together. They are personal contracts and Ohio law does not permit the assignment of personal contracts. [Citation.]

So-called personal contracts, or contracts in which the personality of one of the parties is material, are not assignable. Whether the personality of one or both parties is material depends on the intention of the parties, as shown by the language which they have used, and upon the nature of the contract.

The claim that the assignment will be made only to those who are already members of the club is not relevant. "Nor would the fact that a particular person it attempted to designate [assign] was personally unexceptionable affect the nature of the contract." [Citation.]

Therefore, we believe that the trustee's motion to assign the full golf membership should be denied. We reach this conclusion because the arrangements for filling vacancies proscribe assignment, the club did not consent to the assignment and sale, and applicable law excuses the club from accepting performance from or rendering performance to a person other than the debtor.

---

## CASE 16–2
### Express Prohibition of Assignment
### *ALDANA v. COLONIAL PALMS PLAZA, INC.*
District Court of Appeal of Florida, Third District, 1991
591 So.2d 953

PER CURIAM.
The appellant, Robert Aldana, appeals an adverse summary judgment in favor of appellee, Colonial Palms Plaza, Inc. and an order awarding Colonial Palms Plaza, Inc. attorney's fees pursuant to the offer of judgment rule. We reverse.

Colonial Palms Plaza, Inc. [Landlord], entered into a lease agreement with Abby's Cakes On Dixie, Inc.

[Tenant] for commercial space in a shopping center. The lease included a provision in which Landlord agreed to pay Tenant a construction allowance of up to $11,250 after Tenant satisfactorily completed certain improvements to the rented premises.

Prior to the completion of the improvements, Tenant assigned its right to receive the first $8,000 of the construction allowance to Robert Aldana [Assignee]. In return, Assignee loaned Tenant $8,000 to finance the construction. Assignee recorded the assignment and sent notice to the assignment by certified mail to Landlord.

When Tenant completed the improvements to the rented premises, Landlord ignored the assignment and paid Tenant the construction allowance. Assignee sued Landlord for the money due pursuant to the assignment. The trial court granted Landlord's motion for summary judgment. The trial court also awarded Landlord attorney's fees pursuant to the offer of judgment rule, [citation], and costs pursuant to [citation].

Landlord relies on an anti-assignment clause in the lease agreement to argue that the assignment was void and unenforceable. The clause states in part:

TENANT agrees not to assign, mortgage, pledge, or encumber this Lease, in whole or in part, or to sublet the whole or any part of the DEMISED PREMISES, or to permit the use of the whole or any part of the DEMISED PREMISES by any licensee or concessionaire, without first obtaining the prior, specific written consent of LANDLORD at LANDLORD'S sole discretion. . . . Any such assignment, encumbrance or subletting without such consent shall be void and shall at LANDLORD'S option constitute a default.

\* \* \*

Assignee argues . . . that under ordinary contract principles, the lease provision at issue here does not prevent the assignment of the right to receive contractual payments. We agree.

So far as pertinent here, the lease provides that "TENANT agrees not to assign . . . this Lease, in whole or in part. . . ." Tenant did not assign the lease, but instead assigned a right to receive the construction allowance.

The law in this area is summarized in Restatement (Second) of Contracts, § 322(1), as follows:

Unless the circumstances indicate the contrary, a contract term prohibiting assignment of "the contract" bars only the delegation to an assignee of the performance by the assignor of a duty or condition.

As a rule of construction, in other words, a prohibition against assignment of the contract (or in this case, the lease) will prevent assignment of contractual duties, but does not prevent assignment of the right to receive payments due—unless the circumstances indicate the contrary. [Citations.]

Landlord was given notice of the assignment. Delivery of the notice of the assignment to the debtor fixes accountability of the debtor to the assignee. [Citation.] Therefore, Landlord was bound by the assignment. [Citation.] The trial court improperly granted final summary judgment in favor of Landlord and the judgment must be reversed. Consequently, the trial court's award of attorney's fees and costs to Landlord must also be reversed. The cause is remanded for further proceedings consistent herewith.

Reversed and remanded.

---

## CASE 16–3
### Delegation of Duties
## *MACKE COMPANY v. PIZZA OF GAITHERSBURG, INC.*

Court of Appeals of Maryland, 1970
259 Md. 479, 270 A.2d 645

SINGLEY, J.

The appellees and defendants below, Pizza of Gaithersburg, Inc.; Pizzeria, Inc.; The Pizza Pie Corp., Inc.; and Pizza Oven, Inc., four corporations under the common ownership of Sidney Ansell, Thomas S. Sherwood, and Eugene Early and the same individuals as partners or proprietors (the Pizza Shops) operated at six locations in Montgomery and Prince George's Counties. The appellees had arranged to have installed in each of their locations cold drink vending machines owned by Virginia Coffee Service, Inc., and on 30 December 1966, this arrangement was formalized at five of the locations, by contracts for terms of one year, automatically renewable for a like term in the absence of 30 days' written notice.

A similar contract for the sixth location, operated by Pizza of Gaithersburg, Inc., was entered into on 25 July 1967.

On 30 December 1967, Virginia's assets were purchased by The Macke Company (Macke) and the six contracts were assigned to Macke by Virginia. In January, 1968, the Pizza Shops attempted to terminate the five contracts having the December anniversary date, and in February, the contract which had the July anniversary date.

Macke brought suit in the Circuit Court for Montgomery County against each of the Pizza Shops for damages for breach of contract. From judgments for the defendants, Macke has appealed.

* * *

In the absence of a contrary provision—and there was none here—rights and duties under an executory bilateral contract may be assigned and delegated, subject to the exception that duties under a contract to provide personal services may never be delegated, nor rights be assigned under a contract where *delectus personae* [choice of person] was an ingredient of the bargain. [Citations.] *Crane Ice Cream Co. v. Terminal Freezing & Heating Co.*, [citation], held that the right of an individual to purchase ice under a contract which by its terms reflected a knowledge of the individual's needs and reliance on his credit and responsibility could not be assigned to the corporation which purchased his business. In [citation], our predecessors held that an advertising agency could not delegate its duties under a contract which had been entered into by an advertiser who had relied on the agency's skill, judgment and taste.

The six machines were placed on the appellees' premises under a printed "Agreement-Contract" which identified the "customer," gave its place of business, described the vending machine, and * * *

We cannot regard the agreements as contracts for personal services. They were either a license or concession granted Virginia by the appellees, or a lease of a portion of the appellees' premises, with Virginia agreeing to pay a percentage of gross sales as a license or concession fee or as rent, [citations], and were assignable by Virginia unless they imposed on Virginia duties of a personal or unique character which could not be delegated, [citation].

The appellees earnestly argue that they had dealt with Macke before and had chosen Virginia because they preferred the way it conducted its business. Specifically, they say that service was more personalized, since the president of Virginia kept the machines in working order, that commissions were paid in cash, and that Virginia permitted them to keep keys to the machines so that minor adjustments could be made when needed. Even if we assume all this to be true, the agreements with Virginia were silent as to the details of the working arrangements and contained only a provision requiring Virginia to "install . . . the above listed equipment and . . . maintain the equipment in good operating order and stocked with merchandise." We think the Supreme Court of California put the problem of personal service in proper focus a century ago when it upheld the assignment of a contract to grade a San Francisco street:

All painters do not paint portraits like Sir Joshua Reynolds, nor landscapes like Claude Lorraine, nor do all writers write dramas like Shakespeare or fiction like Dickens. Rare genius and extraordinary skill are not transferable, and contracts for their employment are therefore personal, and cannot be assigned. But rare genius and extraordinary skill are not indispensable to the workmanlike digging down of a sand hill or the filling up of a depression to a given level, or the construction of brick sewers with manholes and covers, and contracts for such work are not personal, and may be assigned. [Citation.]

. . . Moreover, the difference between the service the Pizza Shops happened to be getting from Virginia and what they expected to get from Macke did not mount up to such a material change in the performance of obligations under the agreements as would justify the appellees' refusal to recognize the assignment, [citation].

* * *

* * * Modern authorities . . . hold that, absent provision to the contrary, a duty may be delegated, as distinguished from a right which can be assigned, and that the promisee cannot rescind, if the quality of the performance remains materially the same. * * *

As we see it, the delegation of duty by Virginia to Macke was entirely permissible under the terms of the agreements.

* * *

[Judgment reversed.]

---

## CASE 16–4
### Rights of Intended Beneficiary
# *LOCKWOOD v. STANDARD & POOR'S CORPORATION*
Appellate Court of Illinois, First District, Sixth Division, 1997
224 Ill.Dec. 570, 682  N.E.2d 131

THEIS, J.

Plaintiff, Rick Lockwood (Lockwood), appeals from the order of the circuit court dismissing with prejudice his second-amended complaint. On behalf of himself and other similarly situated options investors, Lockwood sued defendant, Standard & Poor's Corporation

(Standard & Poor's), for breach of contract * * * Lockwood alleged that he and other options investors suffered lost profits on certain options contracts because Standard & Poor's failed to correct a closing stock index value. The trial court granted Standard & Poor's motion to dismiss. On appeal, Lockwood contends the trial court erred in granting dismissal. Specifically, Lockwood argues that his second-amended complaint states a cause of action: (1) for breach of contract because options investors are third-party beneficiaries of the license agreement between Standard & Poor's and the Chicago Board Options Exchange * * * For the following reasons, we affirm.

* * *

Standard & Poor's compiles and publishes two composite stock indexes, the "S & P 100" and the "S & P 500" (collectively the S & P indexes). The S & P indexes are weighted indexes of common stocks primarily listed for trading on the New York Stock Exchange (NYSE). Standard & Poor's licenses its S & P indexes to the Chicago Board Options Exchange (CBOE) to allow the trading of securities options contracts (S & P index options) based on the S & P indexes (the license agreement). According to the rules promulgated by the CBOE regulating the trading of index options, Standard & Poor's is designated the "reporting authority" and, thus, "the official source for calculating and disseminating the current value" of the S & P 100 and S & P 500 indexes. [Citation.] As stated by the reporting authority, the closing index value "shall be the last index value reported on a business day." [Citation.]

S & P index options are settled by the Options Clearing Corporation (OCC). The exercise settlement values for S & P index options are the closing index values for the S & P 100 and S & P 500 stock market indexes as reported by Standard & Poor's to OCC following the close of trading on the day of exercise. S & P index options expire at 11:59 PM Eastern Time on the Saturday immediately following the third Friday of the expiration month. All times specified in Lockwood's complaint are to Eastern Standard Time.

In his complaint, Lockwood alleges that at approximately 4:12 PM on Friday, December 15, 1989, the last trading day prior to expiration of the December 1989 S & P index options contracts, the NYSE erroneously reported a closing price for Ford Motor Company common stock. Ford Motor Company was one of the composite stocks in both the S & P 100 and S & P 500. At approximately 4:13 PM, Standard & Poor's calculated and disseminated closing index values for the S & P 100 and S & P 500 stock market indexes based on the erroneous price for Ford stock. The NYSE reported a corrected closing price for Ford Motor at approximately 4:18 PM. Standard & Poor's corrected the values of the S & P 100 and S & P 500 stock market indexes the following Monday, December 18, 1989.

In the meantime, however, OCC automatically settled all expiring S & P index options according to the expiration date of Saturday, December 16, 1989. OCC used the uncorrected closing index values to settle all expiring S & P index options. Due to the error, Lockwood alleges that the S & P 100 index was overstated by 0.15 and he lost $105. Lockwood claims investors in S & P 500 index options suffered similar losses. Lockwood states that, according to OCC Rules, an option settlement is irrevocable once completed.

Lockwood thus filed a class action on behalf of "all holders of long put options and all sellers of short call options on the S & P 100 or S & P 500 * * * which were settled based on the closing index values for December 15, 1989 as reported by Standard & Poor's." Count I of the second-amended complaint claimed that the options holders could recover in contract as third-party beneficiaries of the license agreement between Standard & Poor's and the CBOE. * * *

* * *

Lockwood's first allegation is that options investors, via their settlement agent the OCC, are third-party beneficiaries of the license agreement between Standard & Poor's and the CBOE because the license agreement makes OCC "a special recipient" of prompt notice of daily "closing index values." While Illinois law governs this suit generally, the parties acknowledge that interpretation of the license agreement is governed by the law of New York. Relying on the Restatement (Second) of Contracts, the New York Court of Appeals has explained that an intended third-party beneficiary may enforce a contract if he is the only party who can recover if the promisor breaches the contract or if the contract language indicates an intention to permit enforcement by the third party. [Citation.]

Here, nothing in the express language of the license agreement indicates an intention to create a third-party beneficiary. Indeed, paragraph 15(a) explains that the "Agreement is solely and exclusively between the parties as presently constituted and shall not be assigned or transferred." Paragraph 15(b) provides that the "Agreement constitutes the entire agreement of the parties hereto with respect to its subject matter and may be amended or modified only by a writing signed by duly authorized officers of both parties. * * * There are no oral or written collateral representations, agreements, or understandings except as provided herein." These exclusivity and integration clauses do not evidence an intent to confer a third-party benefit. Because the license agreement intends to be wholly integrated, we do not look to extrinsic evidence of Lockwood's status. [Citation.]

Moreover, mere mention in the license agreement of the OCC as a "special recipient of closing index values" does not vault Lockwood into third-party beneficiary status. Even assuming that OCC acts as a settlement agent for options investors, retention of a third party to assist in the performance by the promisee does not mean that such third parties are intended beneficiaries of the main contract. [Citation.]

Lockwood's claim that he is the only party who can recover if the promisor breaches the agreement is likewise erroneous. Standard & Poor's and the CBOE are the only contracting parties and the CBOE can easily enforce its rights under the license agreement. In addition, paragraph 12(d) of the agreement precludes recovery of consequential damages, including lost profits, arising out of the license agreement. Thus, the express terms of the agreement indicate that the type of recovery Lockwood seeks was specifically excluded under the license agreement.

In sum, Lockwood is not an intended third-party beneficiary of the license agreement. By its express language, the license agreement intends to confine the agreement to Standard & Poor's and the CBOE. Lockwood and the other options investors clearly were not intended beneficiaries via their "agent" the OCC. We agree with the trial court that Lockwood does not have standing to sue for a breach of the terms of the license agreement.

Regardless, even if Lockwood were an intended third-party beneficiary to the agreement, his rights would be derivative and "subject to the same defenses as are available to the contracting party." [Citation.] Thus, while the license agreement does contain a warranty by Standard & Poor's to correct promptly errors brought to its attention, the agreement also expressly disclaims any guarantee of "the accuracy and/or the completeness of any of the S & P Indexes or any data included therein." And again, the license agreement precludes recovery of consequential damages, including lost profits. Even if Lockwood did have standing, by its very terms, the license agreement would preclude Lockwood's recovery for lost profits.

# Questions

1. Distinguish between an assignment of rights and a delegation of duties.
2. Identify (a) the requirements of an assignment of contract rights and (b) those rights that are not assignable.
3. Identify those situations in which a delegation of duties is not permitted.

4. Distinguish between an intended beneficiary and an incidental beneficiary.
5. Explain when the rights of an intended beneficiary vest.

# Problems

1. On December 1, Euphonia, a famous singer, contracted with Boito to sing at Boito's theatre on December 31 for a fee of $25,000 to be paid immediately after the performance.

   (a) Euphonia, for value received, assigns this fee to Carter.

   (b) Euphonia, for value received, assigns this contract to sing to Dumont, an equally famous singer.

   (c) Boito sells his theatre to Edmund and assigns his contract with Euphonia to Edmund.

State the effect of each of these assignments.

2. The Smooth Paving Company entered into a paving contract with the city of Chicago. The contract contained the

clause "contractor shall be liable for all damages to buildings resulting from the work performed." In the process of construction, one of the bulldozers of the Smooth Paving Company struck and broke a gas main, causing an explosion and a fire that destroyed the house of John Puff. Puff brought an appropriate action against the Smooth Paving Company to recover damages for the loss of his house. Decision?

3. Anne, who was unemployed, registered with the Speedy Employment Agency. A contract was then made under which Anne, in consideration of such position as the Agency would obtain for her, agreed to pay the Agency one-half of her first month's salary. The contract also contained an assignment by

Anne to the Agency of one-half of her first month's salary. Two weeks later, the Agency obtained a permanent position for Anne with the Bostwick Co. at a monthly salary of $900. The agency also notified Bostwick of the assignment by Anne. At the end of the first month, Bostwick paid Anne her salary in full. Anne then quit and disappeared. The Agency now sues Bostwick Co. for $450 under the assignment. Decision?

**4.** Georgia purchased an option on Blackacre from Pamela for $1,000. The option contract contained a provision by which Georgia promised not to assign the option contract without Pamela's permission. Georgia, without Pamela's permission, assigns the contract to Michael. Michael seeks to exercise the option, and Pamela refuses to sell Blackacre to him. Decision?

**5.** Julia contracts to sell to Hayden, an ice cream manufacturer, the amount of ice Hayden may need in his business for the ensuing three years to the extent of not more than 250 tons a week at a stated price per ton. Hayden makes a corresponding promise to Julia to buy such an amount of ice. Hayden sells his ice cream plant to Clark and assigns to Clark all Hayden's rights under the contract with Julia. Upon learning of the sale, Julia refuses to furnish ice to Clark. Clark sues Julia for damages. Decision?

**6.** Brown enters into a written contract with Ideal Insurance Company under which, in consideration of her payment of the premiums, the insurance company promises to pay XYZ College the face amount of the policy, $100,000, on Brown's death. Brown pays the premiums until her death. Thereafter, XYZ College makes demand for the $100,000, which the insurance company refuses to pay upon the ground that XYZ College was not a party to the contract. Decision?

**7.** Grant and Debbie enter into a contract binding Grant personally to do some delicate cabinetwork. Grant assigns his rights and delegates performance of his duties to Clarence.

(a) On being informed of this, Debbie agrees with Clarence, in consideration of Clarence's promise to do the work, that Debbie will accept Clarence's work, if properly done, instead of the performance promised by Grant. Later, without cause, Debbie refuses to allow Clarence to proceed with the work, though Clarence is ready to do so, and makes demand on Grant that Grant perform. Grant refuses. Can Clarence recover damages from Debbie? Can Debbie recover from Grant?

(b) Instead, assume that Debbie refuses to permit Clarence to do the work, employs another carpenter, and brings an action against Grant, claiming as damages the difference between the contract price and the cost to employ the other carpenter. Decision?

**8.** Rebecca owes Lewis $2,500 due on November 1. On August 15, Lewis assigns this right for value received to Julia, who gives notice on September 10 of the assignment to Rebecca. On August 25, Lewis assigns the same right to Wayne, who in good faith gives value and has no prior knowledge of the assignment by Lewis to Julia. Wayne gives Rebecca notice of the assignment on August 30. What are the rights and obligations of Rebecca, Lewis, Julia, and Wayne?

**9.** Lisa hired Jay in the spring, as she had for many years, to set out in beds the flowers Lisa had grown in her greenhouses during the winter. The work was to be done in Lisa's absence for $300. Jay became ill the day after Lisa departed and requested his friend, Curtis, to set out the flowers, promising to pay Curtis $250 when Jay received his payment. Curtis agreed. Upon completion of the planting, an agent of Lisa's, who had authority to dispense the money, paid Jay, and Jay paid Curtis. Within two days it became obvious that the planting was a disaster. Everything set out by Curtis had died of water rot because he had operated Lisa's automatic watering system improperly.

May Lisa recover damages from Curtis? May she recover damages from Jay? If so, does Jay have an action against Curtis?

**10.** Caleb, operator of a window-washing business, dictated a letter to his secretary addressed to Apartments, Inc. stating, "I will wash the windows of your apartment buildings at $4.10 per window to be paid upon completion of the work." The secretary typed the letter, signed Caleb's name, and mailed it to Apartments, Inc. Apartments, Inc. replied, "Accept your offer."

Caleb wrote back, "I will wash them during the week commencing July 10 and direct you to pay the money you will owe me to my son, Bernie. I am giving it to him as a wedding present." Caleb sent a signed copy of the letter to Bernie.

Caleb washed the windows during the time stated and demanded payment to him of $8,200 (2,000 windows at $4.10 each), informing Apartments, Inc. that he had changed his mind about having the money paid to Bernie.

What are the rights of the parties?

**11.** McDonald's granted to Copeland a franchise in Omaha, Nebraska. In a separate letter, it also granted him a right of first refusal for future franchises to be developed in the Omaha-Council Bluffs area. Copeland then sold all rights in his six McDonald's franchises to Schupack. When McDonald's offered a new franchise in the Omaha area to someone other than Schupack, Schupack attempted to exercise the right of first refusal. McDonald's would not recognize the right in Schupack, claiming that it was personal to Copeland and, therefore, nonassignable without its consent. Schupack brought an action for specific performance, requiring McDonald's to accord him the right of first refusal. Decision?

**12.** In 1952, the estate of George Bernard Shaw granted to Gabriel Pascal Enterprises, Limited, the exclusive rights to produce a musical play and a motion picture based on Shaw's play *Pygmalion*. The agreement contained a provision terminating the license if Gabriel Pascal Enterprises did not arrange for well-known composers, such as Lerner and Loewe, to write the musical and produce it within a specified time. George Pascal, owner of 98 percent of the Gabriel Pascal Enterprise's stock, attempted to meet these requirements but died in July 1954 before negotiations had been completed. In February 1954, however, while the license had two years yet to run, Pascal sent a letter to Kingman, his executive secretary, granting to her certain percentages of his share of the profits from the expected stage and screen productions of *Pygmalion*. Subsequently, Pascal's estate arranged for the writing and production of the highly successful *My Fair Lady,* based on Shaw's *Pygmalion.* Kingman then sued to enforce Pascal's gift assignment of the future royalties. Decision?

**13.**   Northwest Airlines leased space in the terminal building at the Portland Airport from the Port of Portland. Crosetti entered into a contract with the Port to furnish janitorial services for the building, which required Crosetti to keep the floor clean, to indemnify the Port against loss due to claims or lawsuits based upon Crosetti's failure to perform, and to provide public liability insurance for the Port and Crosetti. A patron of the building who was injured by a fall caused by a foreign substance on the floor at Northwest's ticket counter brought suit for damages against Northwest, the Port, and Crosetti. Upon settlement of this suit, Northwest sued Crosetti to recover the amount of its contribution to the settlement and other expenses on the grounds that Northwest was a third-party beneficiary of Crosetti's contract with the Port to keep the floors clean and, therefore, within the protection of Crosetti's indemnification agreement. Decision?

**14.**   Tompkins-Beckwith, as the contractor on a construction project, entered into a subcontract with a division of Air Metal Industries. Air Metal procured American Fire and Casualty Company to be surety on certain bonds in connection with contracts it was performing for Tompkins-Beckwith and others. As security for these bonds, on January 3, 1962, Air Metal executed an assignment to American Fire of all accounts receivable under the Tompkins-Beckwith subcontract. On November 26, 1962, Boulevard National Bank lent money to Air Metal. To secure the loans, Air Metal purported to assign to the bank certain accounts receivable it had under its subcontract with Tompkins-Beckwith.

In June 1963, Air Metal defaulted on various contracts bonded by American Fire. On July 1, 1963, American Fire served formal notice on Tompkins-Beckwith of Air Metal's assignment. Tompkins-Beckwith acknowledged the assignment and agreed to pay. In August 1963, Boulevard National Bank notified Tompkins-Beckwith of its assignment. Tompkins-Beckwith refused to recognize the bank's claim and, instead, paid all remaining funds that had accrued to Air Metal to American Fire. The bank then sued to enforce its claim under Air Metal's assignment. Decision?

**15.**   The International Association of Machinists (the union) was the bargaining agent for the employees of Powder Power Tool Corporation. On August 24, 1953, the union and the corporation executed a collective bargaining agreement providing for retroactively increased wage rates for the corporation's employees effective as of April 1, 1953. Three employees who were working for Powder before and for several months after April 1, 1953, but who were not employed by the corporation when the agreement was executed on August 24, 1953, were paid to the time their employment terminated at the old wage scale. The three employees assigned their claims to Springer, who brought this action against the corporation for the extra wages. Decision?

**16.**   In March 1962, Adrian Saylor sold government bonds owned exclusively by him and with $6,450 of the proceeds opened a savings account in a bank in the name of "Mr. or Mrs. Adrian M. Saylor." In June 1963, Saylor deposited the additional sum of $2,132 of his own money in the account. There were no other deposits and no withdrawals prior to Saylor's death in May 1964. Is the balance of the account on Saylor's death payable wholly to Adrian Saylor's estate, wholly to his widow, or half to each?

**17.**   Linda King was found liable to Charlotte Clement as the result of an automobile accident. King, who was insolvent at the time, declared bankruptcy and directed her attorney, Prestwich, to list Clement as an unsecured creditor. The attorney failed to carry out this duty, and consequently King sued him for legal malpractice. When Clement pursued her judgment against King, she received a written assignment of King's legal malpractice claim against Prestwich. Clement has attempted to bring the claim, but Prestwich alleges that a claim for legal malpractice is not assignable. Decision?

**18.**   Rensselaer Water Company contracted with the city of Rensselaer to provide water to the city for use in homes, public buildings, industry, and fire hydrants. During the term of the contract a building caught fire. The fire spread to a nearby warehouse and destroyed it and its contents. The water company knew of the fire but failed to supply adequate water pressure at the fire hydrant to extinguish the fire. The warehouse owner sued the water company for failure to fulfill its contract with the city. Decision?

**19.**   While under contract to play professional basketball for the Philadelphia 76ers, Billy Cunningham negotiated a three-year contract with the Carolina Cougars, another professional basketball team. The contract with the Cougars was to begin at the expiration of the contract with the 76ers. In addition to a signing bonus of $125,000, Cunningham was to receive under the new contract a salary of $100,000 for the first year, $110,000 for the second, and $120,000 for the third. The contract also stated that Cunningham "had special, exceptional and unique knowledge, skill and ability as a basketball player" and that Cunningham therefore agreed the Cougars could enjoin him from playing basketball for any other team for the term of the contract. In addition, the contract contained a clause prohibiting its assignment to another club without Cunningham's consent. In 1971 the ownership of the Cougars changed, and Cunningham's contract was assigned to Munchak Corporation, the new owners, without his consent. When Cunningham refused to play for the Cougars, Munchak Corporation sought to enjoin his playing for any other team. Cunningham asserts that his contract was not assignable. The trial court denied injunctive relief and Munchak appealed. Decision?

**20.**   Pauline Brown was shot and seriously injured by an unknown assailant in the parking lot of National Supermarkets. Pauline and George Brown brought a negligence action against National, Sentry Security Agency, and T. G. Watkins, a security guard and Sentry employee. Sentry had a security contract with National. The Browns maintained that the defendants have a legal duty to protect National's customers both in the store and in the parking lot, and that this duty was breached. The defendants denied this allegation and were granted summary judgment by the trial court. The Browns appealed. Decision?

21.  On April 1, 1980, members of Local 100, Transport Workers Union of America (TWU) began an 11-day mass transit strike that paralyzed the life and commerce of the city of New York. Plaintiffs are engaged in the practice of law as a profession, maintaining offices in Manhattan. Plaintiffs sue both individually and on behalf of all other professional and business entities (the class) that were damaged as a consequence of the defendants' willful disruption of the service provided by the public transportation system of the City of New York. The law firm sought to recover as a third-party beneficiary of the collective bargaining agreement between the union and New York City. The agreement contains a no-strike clause and states that the TWU agreed to cooperate with the city to provide a safe, efficient, and dependable mass transit system. As a member of the public which depends on the public transit system and which employs dozens of persons who need the public transit system to get to and from work, plaintiffs argue that they are within the class of persons for whose benefit the TWU has promised to provide "dependable transportation service." Decision?

**WWW** **Internet Exercise**  Find a sample of one of the following: (a) an assignment of a contract, (b) a delegation of a contractual duty, or (c) a third-party beneficiary contract.

# CHAPTER 17

# Performance, Breach, and Discharge

The subject of discharge of contracts concerns the termination of contractual duties. In earlier chapters we have seen how parties may become bound to a contract. It is also important to know how a person may become unbound from a contract. For although contractual promises are made for a purpose, and the parties reasonably expect this purpose to be fulfilled by performance, performance of a contractual duty is only one method of discharge.

Whatever causes a binding promise to cease to be binding constitutes a discharge of the contract. In general, there are four kinds of discharge: (1) performance by the parties, (2) material breach by one or both of the parties, (3) agreement of the parties, and (4) operation of law. Moreover, many contractual promises are not absolute promises to perform but rather are conditional; that is, they are dependent upon the happening or nonhappening of a specific event. After a discussion of conditions, the four kinds of discharge will be covered.

A fundamental difference exists between the breach or nonperformance of a contractual promise and the failure or nonhappening of a condition. A breach of contract subjects the promisor to liability. It may or may not, depending upon its materiality, excuse nonperformance by the nonbreaching party of his duty under the contract. The happening or nonhappening of a condition, on the other hand, either prevents a party from acquiring a right to performance by the other party or deprives him of such a right, but subjects neither party to any liability.

Conditions may be classified by *how* they are imposed: express conditions, implied-in-fact conditions, or implied-in-law conditions (also called constructive conditions). They also may be classified by *when* they affect a duty of performance: conditions concurrent, conditions precedent, or conditions subsequent. These two ways of classifying conditions are not mutually exclusive; for example, a condition may be constructive and concurrent or express and precedent.

## CONDITIONS

A **condition** is an event whose happening or nonhappening affects a duty of performance under a contract. Some conditions must be satisfied before any duty to perform arises; others terminate the duty to perform; still others either limit or modify the duty to perform. A promisor inserts conditions into a contract for her protection and benefit. Furthermore, the more conditions to which a promise is subject, the less content the promise has. For example, a promise to pay $8,000, provided that such sum is realized from the sale of an automobile, provided the automobile is sold within sixty days, and provided that the automobile, which has been stolen, can be found, is clearly different from, and worth considerably less than, an unconditional promise by the same promisor to pay $8,000.

## Express Condition

An **express condition** is explicitly set forth in language. No particular form of words is necessary to create an express condition, so long as the event to which the performance of the promise is made subject is clearly expressed. An express condition is usually preceded by such words as "provided that," "on condition that," "if," "while," "after," "upon," or "as soon as."

The basic rule applied to express conditions is that they must be fully and literally performed before the conditional duty to perform arises. Where application of the full and literal performance test would result in a forfeiture, however, the courts usually apply to the completed portion of the condition a *substantial satisfaction* test, as discussed later in this chapter under the section titled "Substantial Performance."

*Satisfaction of a Contracting Party* The parties to a contract may agree that performance by one of them will be to the **satisfaction** of the other, who will not be obligated to pay for such performance unless he is satisfied. This is an express condition to the duty to pay for the performance. Assume that tailor Melissa contracts to make a suit of clothes to Brent's satisfaction, and that Brent promises to pay Melissa $350 for the suit if he is satisfied with it when completed. Melissa completes the suit using materials ordered by Brent. Though the suit fits Brent beautifully, he tells Melissa that he is not satisfied with it and refuses to accept or pay for it. If Brent's dissatisfaction is honest and in good faith, even if it is unreasonable, Melissa is not entitled to recover $350 or any amount from Brent by reason of the nonhappening of the express condition. Where satisfaction relates to a matter of personal taste, opinion, or judgment, the law applies the **subjective satisfaction** standard: if the promisor in good faith is dissatisfied, the condition has not occurred.

If the contract does not clearly indicate that satisfaction is subjective, or if the performance contracted for relates to mechanical fitness or utility, the law assumes an **objective satisfaction** standard. For example, the objective standard would apply to the sale of a building or standard goods, such as steel, coal, or grain. In such cases, the question would not be whether the promisor was actually satisfied with the performance by the other party but whether, as a reasonable person, he ought to be satisfied.

 *See Case 17–1*

*Satisfaction of a Third Party* A contract may condition the duty to accept and pay for the performance of the other party upon the approval of a third party. For example, building contracts commonly provide that before the owner is required to pay, the builder shall furnish a certificate of the architect stating that the building has been constructed according to the plans and specifications. For although the owner is paying for the building, not for the certificate, he must have both the building and the certificate before he is obligated to pay. The duty of payment was made expressly conditional upon the presentation of the certificate.

## Implied-in-Fact Conditions

**Implied-in-fact conditions** are similar to express conditions, in that they must fully and literally occur and in that the parties understand them to be part of the agreement. They differ in that they are not stated in express language; rather, they are necessarily inferred from the terms of the contract, the nature of the transaction, or the conduct of the parties. Thus, if Fernando, for $750, contracts to paint Peggy's house any color Peggy desires, it is necessarily implied in fact that Peggy will inform Fernando of the desired color before Fernando begins to paint. The notification of choice of color is an implied-in-fact condition, an operative event that must occur before Fernando is subject to the duty of painting the house.

## Implied-in-Law Conditions

An **implied-in-law condition,** or a **constructive condition,** is imposed by law to accomplish a just and fair result. It differs from an express condition and an implied-in-fact condition in two ways: (1) it is not contained in the language of the contract or necessarily inferred from the contract, and (2) it need only be substantially performed. For example, Melinda contracts to sell a certain tract of land to Kelly for $18,000, but the contract is silent as to the time of delivery of the deed and payment of the price. The law will imply that the respective performances are not independent of one another; consequently, the courts will treat the promises as mutually dependent and will therefore hold that a delivery or tender of the deed by Melinda to Kelly is a condition to Kelly's duty to pay the price. Conversely, Melinda's duty to deliver the deed to Kelly is conditioned upon the payment or tender of $18,000 by Kelly to Melinda. If the contract specifies a sale on credit, however, giving Kelly thirty days after delivery of the deed within which to pay the price, these conditions are not implied by law because the parties have expressly agreed to make their respective duties of performance independent of each other.

## Concurrent Conditions

**Concurrent conditions** occur when the mutual duties of performances are to take place simultaneously. As indicated in the previous section, in the absence of an agreement to the contrary, the law assumes that the respective performances under a contract are concurrent conditions.

## Conditions Precedent

A **condition precedent** is an event that must occur before performance under a contract is due. For instance, if Gail is to deliver shoes to Mike on June 1, with Mike's duty to pay for the shoes on July 15, Gail's delivery of the shoes is a condition precedent to Mike's performance. Similarly, if Seymour promises to buy Edna's land for $50,000, provided Seymour can obtain financing in the amount of $40,000 at 10 percent interest or less for thirty years within sixty days of signing the contract, Seymour's obtaining the specified financing is a condition precedent to his duty. If the condition is satisfied, Seymour is bound to perform; if it is not, he is not so bound. Seymour, however, is under an implied-in-law duty to use his best efforts to obtain financing under these terms.

## Conditions Subsequent

A **condition subsequent** is an event that terminates an existing duty. For example, where goods are sold under terms of "sale or return," the buyer has the right to return the goods to the seller within a stated period but is under an immediate duty to pay the price unless she and the seller have agreed upon credit. A return of the goods, which operates as a condition subsequent, terminates the duty to pay the price. Conditions subsequent occur very infrequently in contract law, while conditions precedent are quite common.

## *DISCHARGE BY PERFORMANCE*

Discharge by performance is undoubtedly the most frequent method of discharging a contractual duty. If a promisor exactly performs his duty under the contract, he is no longer subject to that duty.

Every contract imposes upon each party a duty of good faith and fair dealing in its performance and its enforcement. Restatement, Section 205. As discussed in Chapter 21, the UCC imposes a comparable duty. Section 1–203.

**Tender** is an offer by one party—who is ready, willing, and able to perform—to the other party to perform his obligation according to the terms of the contract. Under a bilateral contract, the refusal or rejection of a tender of performance may be treated as a repudiation that excuses or discharges the tendering party from further duty of performance under the contract. For example, on the due date of contractual performance, George arrives at Thelma's house prepared to do plumbing work under their contract. Thelma, however, refuses to allow George to enter the premises. George is therefore discharged from performing the contract and has a legal claim against Thelma for material breach.

If a debtor owes money on several accounts and tenders to his creditor less than the total amounts due, the debtor has the right to designate the account or debt to which the payment is to be applied, and the creditor must accept this direction. If the debtor does not direct the application of the payment, the creditor may apply it to any account owing to him by the debtor or distribute it among several such accounts.

## *DISCHARGE BY BREACH*

**Breach** of contract is the unexcused failure of a party to perform her promise. While breach of contract always gives rise to a cause of action for damages by the aggrieved (injured) party, it may have a more important effect: an uncured (uncorrected) *material* breach by one party operates as an excuse for nonperformance by the other party and discharges the aggrieved party from any further duty under the contract. If, on the other hand, the breach is not material, the aggrieved party is not discharged from the contract, although she may recover money damages. Under the Code, *any* deviation discharges the aggrieved party.

## Material Breach

An unjustified failure to perform *substantially* the obligations promised in a contract constitutes a **material breach.** The key is whether, despite the breach, the aggrieved party obtained substantially what he bargained for or whether the breach significantly impaired his rights under the contract. A material breach discharges the aggrieved party from his duty of performance. For instance, Esta orders a custom made, tailored suit from Stuart to be made of wool; but Stuart instead makes the suit of cotton. Assuming that the labor component of this contract predominates and thus the contract is not considered a sale of goods, Stuart has materially breached the contract. Consequently, Esta not only is discharged from her duty to pay for the suit but may also recover money damages from Stuart due to his breach.

Although there are no clear-cut rules as to what constitutes a material breach, the Restatement, Section 241, lists a number of relevant factors:

In determining whether a failure to render or to offer performance is material, the following circumstances are significant:

(a) the extent to which the injured party will be deprived of the benefit which he reasonably expected;

(b) the extent to which the injured party can be adequately compensated for the part of that benefit of which he will be deprived;

(c) the extent to which the party failing to perform or to offer to perform will suffer forfeiture;

(d) the likelihood that the party failing to perform or to offer to perform will cure his failure, taking account of all the circumstances including any reasonable assurances;

(e) the extent to which the behavior of the party failing to perform or to offer to perform comports with standards of good faith and fair dealing.

An *intentional* breach of contract is generally held to be material. Moreover, a failure to perform a promise promptly is a material breach if **"time is of the essence,"** that is, if the parties have clearly indicated that a failure to perform by the stated time is material; otherwise, the aggrieved party may recover damages only for the loss caused by the delay. Finally, the parties to a contract may, within limits, specify what breaches are to be considered material.

*Prevention of Performance* One party's substantial interference with or **prevention of performance** by the other generally constitutes a material breach that discharges the other party to the contract. For instance, Craig prevents an architect from giving Maud a certificate that is a condition to Craig's liability to pay Maud a certain sum of money. Craig may not then use Maud's failure to produce a certificate as an excuse for his nonpayment. Likewise, if Harold has contracted to grow a certain crop for Rafael, and Rafael plows the field and destroys the seedlings after Harold has planted the seed, his interference with Harold's performance discharges Harold from his duty under the contract. It does not, however, discharge Rafael from his duty under the contract.

*Perfect Tender Rule* The Code greatly alters the common law doctrine of material breach by adopting what is known as the **perfect tender rule.** This rule, which is discussed more fully in Chapter 22, essentially provides that *any* deviation from the promised performance in a sales contract under the Code constitutes a material breach of the contract and discharges the aggrieved party from his duty of performance. Thus, if a seller of camera accessories delivers to a buyer ninety-nine of the hundred ordered pieces, or ninety-nine correct accessories and one incorrect accessory, the buyer may rightfully reject the improper delivery.

## Substantial Performance

If a party substantially, but not completely, performs her obligations under a contract, the common law generally will allow her to obtain the other party's performance, less any damages caused by the partial performance. Thus, in the specially ordered suit illustration discussed in the previous section, if Stuart, the tailor, used the correct fabric but improperly used black buttons instead of blue, Stuart would be permitted to collect from Esta the contract price of the suit less the damage, if any, caused to Esta by the substitution of the wrongly colored buttons. The doctrine of substantial performance assumes particular importance in the construction industry in cases where a structure is built on the aggrieved party's land. Consider the following: Kent Construction Co. builds a $300,000 house for Martha but deviates from the specifications, causing Martha $10,000 in damages. If this breach were considered material, then Martha would not have to pay for the house that is now on her land. This would clearly constitute an unjust forfeiture on Kent's part. Therefore, because Kent's performance is substantial, the courts would probably not deem the breach material. As a result, Kent would be able to collect $290,000 from Martha.

 *See Case 17–2*

## Anticipatory Repudiation

A breach of contract, as previously discussed, is a failure to perform the terms of a contract. Although it is logically and physically impossible to fail to perform a duty before the date on which that performance is due, a party nonetheless may announce before the due date that she will not perform, or she may commit an act that makes her unable to perform. Either act repudiates the contract, which notifies the other party that a breach is imminent. Such repudiation before the performance date fixed by the contract is called an **anticipatory repudiation.** The courts, as shown in the leading case of *Hochster v. De La Tour*, view it as a breach that discharges the nonrepudiating party's duty to perform and permits her to bring suit immediately. Nonetheless, the nonbreaching party may wait until the time the performance is due, to see if the repudiator will retract his repudiation and perform his contractual duties. If the repudiator does perform, then there is a discharge by performance; if he does not perform, there is a material breach.

 *See Case 17–3*

## Material Alteration of Written Contract

An unauthorized alteration or change of any of the material terms or provisions of a written contract or document is a discharge of the entire contract. To be a discharge, the alteration must be material and fraudulent and must be the act of a party to the contract or someone acting on his behalf. An alteration is material if it would vary any party's legal relations with the maker of the alteration or would adversely affect that party's legal relations with a third person. Restatement, Section 286. An unauthorized change in the terms of a written contract by a person who is not a party to the contract does not discharge the contract.

## DISCHARGE BY AGREEMENT OF THE PARTIES

The parties to a contract may by agreement discharge each other from performance under the contract. They may do this by rescission, substituted contract, accord and satisfaction, or novation.

## Mutual Rescission

A **mutual rescission** is an agreement between the parties to terminate their respective duties under the contract. Literally a contract to end a contract, it must contain all the essentials of a contract. In rescinding an executory, bilateral contract, each party furnishes consideration in giving up his rights under the contract in exchange for the other party's relinquishment of his rights under the contract. Where one party has already fully performed, a mutual rescission may not be binding at common law because of lack of consideration.

## Substituted Contract

A **substituted contract** is a new contract accepted by both parties in satisfaction of their duties under the original contract. Restatement, Section 279. A substituted contract immediately discharges the original duty and imposes new obligations. For example, the Restatement, Section 279, gives the following illustration:

A and B make a contract under which A promises to build on a designated spot a building, for which B promises to pay $100,000. Later, before this contract is performed, A and B make a new contract under which A is to build on the same spot a different building, for which B is to pay $200,000. The new contract is a substituted contract and

the duties of A and B under the original contract are discharged.

## Accord and Satisfaction

An **accord** is a contract by which an obligee promises to accept a stated performance in satisfaction of the obligor's existing contractual duty. Restatement, Section 281. The performance of the accord is called a **satisfaction,** and it discharges the original duty. Thus, if Ted owes Alan $500 and the parties agree that Ted shall paint Alan's house in satisfaction of the debt, the agreement is an accord. The debt, however, is not discharged until Ted performs the accord by painting Alan's house.

 *See Case 17–4*

## Novation

A **novation** is a substituted contract that involves an agreement among *three* parties to substitute a new promisee for the existing promisee, or to replace the existing promisor with a new one. Restatement, Section 280. A novation discharges the old obligation by creating a new contract in which there is either a new promisee or a new promisor. Thus, if B owes A $500, and A, B, and C agree that C will pay the debt and B will be discharged, the novation is the substitution of the new promisor C for B. Alternatively, if the three parties agree that B will pay $500 to D instead of to A, the novation is the substitution of a new promisee (D for A). In each instance, the debt B owes to A is discharged.

## DISCHARGE BY OPERATION OF LAW

This chapter has considered various ways by which contractual duties may be discharged. In all of these cases, the discharge resulted from the action of one or both of the parties to the contract. This section examines discharge brought about by the operation of law.

## Impossibility

"Contract liability is strict liability . . . [and an] obligor is therefore liable for breach of contract even if he is without fault and even if circumstances have made the contract more burdensome or less desirable than he had anticipated." Restatement, Introductory Note to Chapter 11. Historically, the common law excused a party from contractual duties for **objective impossibility**; that is, where no one could render the performance. If, by comparison, a particular contracting party is unable to perform because, for instance, of financial inability or lack of competence, this **subjective impossibility** does not excuse the promisor from liability for breach of contract. For example, the Christys entered into a written contract to purchase an apartment house from Pilkinton for $30,000. Pilkinton tendered a deed to the property and demanded payment of the unpaid balance of $29,000 due on the purchase price. Because of a decline in their used car business, the Christys, who did not possess and could not borrow the unpaid balance, asserted that it was impossible for them to perform their contract. The court held for Pilkinton, identifying a distinction between objective impossibility, which amounts to saying, "the thing cannot be done," and subjective impossibility—"I cannot do it." The latter, which is illustrated by a promisor's financial inability to pay, does not discharge the contractual duty. *Christy v. Pilkinton*, 224 Ark. 407, 273 S.W.2d 533 (1954).

The **death** or **incapacity** of a person who has contracted to render *personal services* discharges his contractual duty due to objective impossibility. Restatement, Section 262. For example, a singer unable to perform a contractual engagement because of a severe cold is excused from performance, as is a pianist or violinist who is unable to perform because of a hand injury.

**Destruction of Subject Matter** Destruction of the subject matter or of the agreed-upon means of performance of a contract, without the fault of the promisor, is also excusable impossibility. "Subject matter" here means specific subject matter. Suppose that Alice contracts to sell to Gary five office chairs at an agreed price. Alice has 100 of these chairs in stock, out of which she expects to deliver five to Gary. Before she can do so, fire destroys the entire 100 chairs. Though not at fault, Alice is not excused from performance. This was not a contract for the sale of specific goods; consequently, Alice could perform the contract by delivering to Gary any five chairs of the kind and grade specified in the contract. Her failure to do so will render her liable to Gary for breach of contract. Suppose, now, that Alice and Gary make a contract for Alice to manufacture these five chairs in her factory but that prior to their manufacture, fire destroys the factory. Again, Alice is not at fault. Although the chairs are available from other manufacturers, the destruction of the factory discharges Alice's duty to deliver the chairs. Suppose further that Alice and Gary enter into a contract under which Alice is to sell to Gary the particular desk that she uses in her private office. This desk, and no other, is the specific subject matter of the contract. If, before the sale is completed, this desk is destroyed by fire without Alice's fault, it is then impossible for Alice to perform. The contract is therefore discharged.

**Subsequent Illegality** If the performance of a contract which was legal when formed becomes illegal or impractical by reason of a subsequently enacted law, the duty of performance is discharged. Restatement, Section 264. For example, Jill contracts to sell and deliver to Fred ten cases of a certain whiskey each month for one year. A subsequent prohibition law makes the manufacture, transportation, or sale of intoxicating liquor unlawful. The contractual duties that Jill has yet to perform are discharged.

**Frustration of Purpose** Where, after a contract is made, a party's principal purpose is substantially frustrated without his fault by the occurrence of an event the nonoccurrence of which was a basic assumption on which the contract was made, his remaining duties to render performance are discharged, unless the party has assumed the risk. Restatement, Second 265. This rule developed from the so-called coronation cases. When, upon the death of his mother, Queen Victoria, Edward VII became King of England, impressive coronation ceremonies were planned, including a procession along a designated route through certain streets in London. Owners and lessees of buildings along the route made contracts to permit the use of rooms with a view on the date scheduled for the procession. The King, however, became ill, and the procession did not take place. The purpose for using the rooms having failed, the rooms were not used. Numerous suits were filed, some by landowners seeking to hold the would-be viewers liable on their promises, and some by the would-be viewers seeking to recover money they paid in advance for the rooms. The principle involved was novel, but from these cases evolved the **frustration of purpose doctrine,** under which a contract is discharged if supervening circumstances make impossible the fulfillment of the purpose that both parties had in mind, unless one of the parties has contractually assumed that risk.

**Commercial Impracticability** The Restatement, Section 261, and the Code, Section 2–615, have relaxed the traditional test of objective impossibility by providing that performance need not be actually or literally impossible, but that commercial impracticability will excuse nonperformance. This does not mean mere hardship or an unexpectedly excessive cost of performance. A party will be discharged from performing his duty only when a supervening event not caused by his fault makes his performance impracticable. Moreover, the nonoccurrence of the subsequent event must have been a "basic assumption" both parties made when entering into the contract, neither party having assumed the risk that the event would occur. Commercial impracticability could include "a severe shortage of raw materials or of supplies due to a contingency such as war, embargo, local crop failure, unforeseen shutdown of major sources of supply or the like, which either causes a marked increase in cost or altogether prevents the seller from securing supplies necessary to his performance. . . ." UCC Section 2–615, Comment 4.

 *See Case 17–5*

## Bankruptcy

Bankruptcy is a discharge of a contractual duty by operation of law available to a debtor who, by compliance with the requirements of the Bankruptcy Code, obtains an order of discharge by the bankruptcy court. It is applicable only to obligations that the Code provides are dischargeable in bankruptcy. The subject of bankruptcy is treated in Chapter 39.

## Statute of Limitations

At common law a plaintiff was not subject to any time limitation within which to bring an action. Now, however, all States have statutes providing such a limitation. The majority of courts hold that the running of the period of the statute of limitations does not operate to discharge the obligation, but only to bar the creditor's right to bring an action.

◆ *See Figure 17–1*

**FIGURE 17–1** Discharge of Contracts

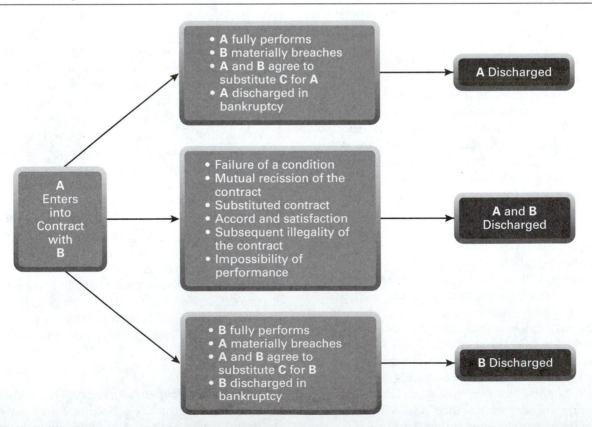

# Chapter Summary

| | |
|---|---|
| **Conditions** | **Definition of a Condition** an event whose happening or nonhappening affects a duty of performance<br>**Express Condition** contingency explicitly set forth in language<br>• *Satisfaction* express condition making performance contingent upon one party's approval of the other's performance<br>• *Subjective Satisfaction* approval based upon a party's honestly held opinion<br>• *Objective Satisfaction* approval based upon whether a reasonable person would be satisfied<br>**Implied-in-Fact Conditions** contingency understood by the parties to be part of the agreement, though not expressed<br>**Implied-in-Law Conditions** contingency not contained in the language of the contract but imposed by law; also called a constructive condition<br>**Concurrent Conditions** conditions that are to take place at the same time<br>**Conditions Precedent** an event that must or must not occur before performance is due<br>**Conditions Subsequent** an event that terminates a duty of performance |
| **Discharge by Performance** | **Discharge** termination of a contractual duty<br>**Performance** fulfillment of a contractual obligation resulting in a discharge |
| **Discharge by Breach** | **Definition of Breach** a wrongful failure to perform the terms of a contract that gives rise to a right to damages by the injured party<br>**Material Breach** nonperformance that significantly impairs the injured party's rights under the contract and discharges the injured party from any further duty under the contract<br>• *Prevention of Performance* one party's substantial interference with or prevention of performance by the other; constitutes a material breach and discharges the other party to the contract<br>• *Perfect Tender Rule* standard under the UCC that a seller's performance under a sales contract must strictly comply with contractual duties and that any deviation discharges the injured party<br>**Substantial Performance** performance that is incomplete but that does not defeat the purpose of the contract; does not discharge the injured party but entitles him to damages<br>**Anticipatory Repudiation** an inability or refusal to perform, before performance is due, that is treated as a breach, allowing the nonrepudiating party to bring suit immediately<br>**Material Alteration** a material and fraudulent alteration of a written contract by a party to the contract; discharges the entire contract |
| **Discharge by Agreement of the Parties** | **Mutual Rescission** an agreement between the parties to terminate their respective duties under the contract<br>**Substituted Contract** a new contract accepted by both parties in satisfaction of the parties' duties under the original contract<br>**Accord and Satisfaction** substituted duty under a contract (accord) and the discharge of the prior contractual obligation by performance of the new duty (satisfaction)<br>**Novation** a substituted contract involving a new third-party promisor or promisee |

## Discharge by Operation of Law

**Impossibility** performance of contract cannot be done
- *Subjective Impossibility* the promisor—but not all promisors—cannot perform; does not discharge the promisor
- *Objective Impossibility* no promisor is able to perform; generally discharges the promisor
- *Destruction of Subject Matter* will discharge contract if it occurs without the promisor's fault
- *Subsequent Illegality* if performance becomes illegal or impractical as a result of a change in the law, the duty of performance is discharged
- *Frustration of Purpose* principal purpose of a contract cannot be fulfilled because of a subsequent event
- *Commercial Impracticability* where performance can be accomplished only under unforeseen and unjust hardship, the contract is discharged under the Code and the Restatement

**Bankruptcy** discharge available to a debtor who obtains an order of discharge by the bankruptcy court

**Statute of Limitations** after the statute of limitations has run, the debt is not discharged, but the creditor cannot maintain an action against the debtor

# Cases

### CASE 17–1
## Express Conditions: Satisfaction
## *KOHLER v. LESLIE HINDMAN, INC.*
United States Court of Appeals, Seventh Circuit, 1996
80 F.3d 1181

CUDAHY, J.

An artist once produced a painting now called "The Plains of Meudon." For a while, the parties in this case thought that the artist was Theodore Rousseau, a prominent member of the Barbizon school, and that the painting was quite valuable. With this idea in mind, the Kohlers consigned the painting to Leslie Hindman, Inc., an auction house, and Richard Thune bought it at auction for $90,000 on the condition that it was, in fact, a Rousseau. It was not. The parties then pursued a lawsuit in the district court to determine who would get stuck with it. Upon a motion for summary judgment, the district court held that, as a matter of law, the contracts between the parties required that the Kohlers keep the painting. The Kohlers contend that the district court erred in its interpretation of the contracts, and they appeal. We affirm.

### Background

The Kohlers inherited the painting from their mother, Dorothy Dings Kohler, in 1989. Two years later, they decided to sell it along with some other artwork from their mother's estate, and they contacted Leslie Hindman Auctioneers (Hindman, Inc.). After arranging for the inspection of the artwork, Leslie Hindman, president of her eponymous auction house, met with the Kohlers and discussed the terms by which her company would sell it at auction. Hindman, Inc. and the Kohlers then entered into a consignment agreement which made the company the Kohlers' agent for the auction sale.

Among other things, the consignment agreement defined the scope of Hindman, Inc.'s authority as agent. Two aspects of that authority concern us here. First, Hindman, Inc. was obliged to sell the painting according to the conditions of sale spelled out in the auction catalog. Those conditions provided that neither the consignors nor Hindman, Inc. made any warranties of authenticity. Indeed, the conditions emphasized that "[a]ll lots are sold 'AS IS,'" and one provision of the conditions asserted that "[n]o statement anywhere, whether oral or written, shall be deemed" to be a warranty of authenticity. The conditions also provided that Hindman, Inc. would insure that title to all lots passed with the fall of the auctioneer's hammer. In addition to these prescriptions, another provision of the consignment agreement gave the company extensive and exclusive discretionary authority to cancel sales. In Paragraph 14 of the consignment agreement, Hindman, Inc. declared that

We are authorized as your agent to accept the return and rescind the sale of any [p]roperty if we at any time in our sole discretion determine that the offering for sale of any [p]roperty has subjected us and/or you to any liability under a warranty of authenticity.

Along with the other artwork from the Dorothy Dings Kohler estate, Hindman, Inc. listed the painting in its auction catalog, noting that the painting was, in its best judgment, by Rousseau. Hindman, Inc. also displayed the painting at a pre-auction showing where Thune's agent, Simon Parkes, saw it and developed some doubts about its authenticity. He expressed those doubts to his principal and to Scot Campbell, an employee of Hindman, Inc. Campbell relayed Parkes' suspicions to Ms. Hindman, who was soon in touch with Thune. Thune was still interested in the painting, but he wanted to have it authenticated before committing to its purchase. Unable to obtain an authoritative opinion about its authenticity before the auction, Ms. Hindman and Thune made a verbal agreement that Thune could return the painting within approximately thirty days of the auction if he was the successful bidder and if an expert then determined that Rousseau had not painted it. Neither Ms. Hindman nor anyone else at Hindman, Inc. told the Kohlers about the questions concerning the painting or about the side agreement between Thune and Hindman, Inc.

At the auction on October 13, 1991, Thune prevailed in the bidding with a high bid of $90,000, and he took possession of the painting without paying. He then sent it to an expert in Paris who decided that it was not a Rousseau. Thune returned the painting to Hindman, Inc. in March 1992.

The Kohlers sued both Hindman, Inc. and Thune. They claimed that Hindman, Inc. had breached the consignment agreement with them * * * They also claimed that they had an implied contract with Thune himself for the painting, and that Thune had breached that contract by failing to pay the $90,000. * * *

* * * The district court ruled that Hindman, Inc. and Thune were entitled to judgment on all of the Kohlers' claims against them. The Kohlers appeal that ruling.

## Discussion

* * *

Indeed, all of the Kohlers' claims depend upon how the consignment agreement defined the scope of Hindman,

Inc.'s authority as the Kohlers' agent. If Hindman, Inc. acted at all times within its authority, the Kohlers cannot prevail on any of their claims. Defining the scope of that authority requires an interpretation of the consignment agreement.

* * *

The district court focused on Paragraph 14 of the consignment agreement, which authorized Hindman, Inc. to rescind a sale when the company, in its "sole discretion," determined that it or its consignor was subject to liability under a warranty of authenticity. The district court concluded that this grant of discretion allowed Hindman, Inc. to rescind a sale whenever it perceived the threat of such liability, notwithstanding the auction catalog's emphatic disclaimers. In the district court's reading of the consignment agreement, once the questions about the authenticity of the painting arose, Hindman, Inc. had open-ended authority to avoid a lawsuit arising from a claim under a warranty of authenticity. Hindman, Inc. had the power to rescind or to make a conditional promise to rescind in side agreements with prospective buyers. The district court noted that such a side agreement was equivalent to a warranty of authenticity and would constitute a technical breach of Hindman, Inc.'s promise to adhere to the conditions of sale. But the district court reasoned that making a conditional promise to rescind was not a material breach because it was consistent with the exercise of the company's sole discretion to rescind.

* * *

Determining the extent of Hindman, Inc.'s authority to rescind is difficult. The Kohlers' brief suggests a powerful argument: a holding that Hindman, Inc. had unlimited authority to rescind would undermine most of the specified limitations on the other aspects of the auctioneer's authority. Because Illinois law requires that contracts be interpreted so that all of their provisions be given effect, we cannot conclude that Paragraph 14 vitiates the rest of the consignment agreement. [Citation.] But neither can we ignore that paragraph's reference to "sole discretion." Therefore, we must determine the limits of the discretion that emerged from the consignment agreement.

Interpretation would be easier if we could find a customary meaning for "sole discretion" as used in auctioneers' consignment agreements. Unfortunately, our research has not revealed any Illinois case law on this point. But the ruling of a federal district court in New York can give us some guidance. In [citation], that court considered the extent of an auctioneer's authority under a consignment agreement with a provision like Paragraph

14. The district court there found that such a contract provision is highly analogous to a satisfaction clause (typically conditioning one party's performance on that party's satisfaction with the other party's performance). [Citation.] Through a satisfaction clause, a party's exercise of judgment or discretion is a condition for its duty to perform. [Citations.] Because satisfaction clauses involve the same principles of contract law as apply here, we will treat Paragraph 14 as a satisfaction clause.

Illinois courts have developed rules for interpreting satisfaction clauses that require a classification. Thus, satisfaction clauses in Illinois come in two categories: those that make the exercise of discretion purely subjective and those that require the exercise of discretion according to objective factors. [Citations.] The first category includes satisfaction clauses invoking the feelings, taste or judgment of the party exercising discretion. [Citations.] When a satisfaction clause conveys this sort of subjective discretion, it does not, however, remove all limitations on the exercise of discretion. The party that has the right to act according to its personal judgment or within its sole discretion must still act in good faith. [Citation.]

On the other hand, a satisfaction clause may fall into the second category when it involves matters susceptible to objective evaluation; mechanical utility is a stereotype of such matters. [Citations.] When objective considerations control the exercise of discretion, the party to be satisfied must exercise its authority in a just and reasonable way. [Citation.]

These rules do not apply easily to Paragraph 14. By giving Hindman, Inc. "sole discretion," this provision suggests that the consignment agreement had defined Hindman, Inc.'s authority subjectively. The consignment agreement did not define any objective criteria that would control Hindman, Inc.'s exercise of judgment. Nevertheless, the object of Hindman, Inc.'s discretion was not a purely subjective phenomenon like taste or feeling. Rather, Hindman, Inc. had to evaluate risk, and demanding such an evaluation impliedly invoked rational analysis. The Kohlers were not giving Hindman, Inc. a contract right to emulate Chicken Little. Viewing all of these conditions together, the grant of "sole discretion" to assess risk is somewhat ambiguous as between objective and subjective satisfaction.

Ultimately, for lack of objective criteria, we must conclude that Hindman, Inc.'s exercise of its authority is bounded only by its satisfaction as limited, of course, by good faith. The principal factor leading us to this conclusion is the agreement's use of the phrase "sole discretion." This phrase denotes subjectivity. Moreover, this conclusion corresponds with the theoretical understanding of contract bargaining. The consignment agreement made the interests of the Kohlers and Hindman, Inc. largely coincident. The Kohlers and Hindman, Inc. would each profit most from the same set of circumstances, namely the sale of the painting for the highest possible price. Given this identity of interests, the Kohlers could trust Hindman, Inc.'s subjective decision-making. For the purposes of analyzing the risk of liability, Hindman, Inc. and the Kohlers had the same perspective. Therefore, the Kohlers did not have to hold Hindman, Inc. to some external standard as a means of making the auctioneer's interests coincide with its own. At least in theory, it would be rational for the Kohlers to accept Hindman, Inc.'s good-faith subjective judgments as part of a bargain. Because the language of the contract clearly implies that the Kohlers did trust Hindman, Inc.'s subjective judgment, we conclude the consignment agreement held the auctioneer to a subjective standard.

Hindman, Inc.'s actions towards Thune, before and after the auction, meet the standard of good faith. The Kohlers contend that the side agreement and the subsequent rescission were entirely self-interested acts. In making this contention, they emphasize that no-one in the auction house informed them of the doubts about the painting's authenticity or about the negotiations with Thune. They seem to think that this lack of disclosure reflects a consciousness of guilt, or perhaps more precisely, a consciousness of pure self-interest. This contention, however, defies the logic of the consignment agreement. The consignment agreement created one overriding interest that was identical for both the Kohlers and Hindman, Inc. Therefore, anything that Hindman, Inc. did for itself, it apparently also did for the Kohlers.

It is true that the parties' interests were opposed in one respect: under Paragraph 10 of the consignment agreement, the Kohlers would have to pay Hindman, Inc. 20% of the auctioneer's most recent pre-sale estimate and the auctioneer's expenses if the Kohlers withdrew the painting from sale on account of doubts about its authenticity. Thus, Hindman, Inc. had some interest in promoting withdrawal because it could profit at the Kohlers' expense if doubts about the painting became so widespread that its sale at auction were no longer feasible. With respect to this interest, however, Hindman, Inc. apparently acted selflessly. Telling the Kohlers about Thune's doubts before the sale might have actually advanced Hindman, Inc.'s interests because the information might have given the Kohlers an incentive to withdraw. And even if the Kohlers had not decided to withdraw, the side agreement might still have been their best option. Under the side agreement, Hindman, Inc. maintained Thune's incentive to bid as if the painting were really a Rousseau; therefore it maximized the chances of a lucrative result for the auction. This was indeed an act of good faith, and it was made within the limits of Hindman, Inc.'s authority under the consignment agreement. The district court correctly ruled that Hindman, Inc. had not breached the consignment agreement.

* * * Finally, the Kohlers cannot claim that they have a implied agreement with Thune for the sale of the painting at $90,000. Such a implied contract would exist only if the side agreement were invalid. Because Hindman, Inc. made the side agreement within the scope of its authority, that agreement is valid, and it protects Thune from the Kohlers' reach.

For these reasons, the judgment of the district court is affirmed.

* * *

---

## CASE 17–2
## Breach/Substantial Performance
### *MOUNTAIN RESTAURANT CORPORATION v.*
### *PARKCENTER MALL ASSOCIATES*
Court of Appeals of Idaho, 1992
122 Idaho 261, 833 P.2d 119

SILAK, J.
This appeal involves the question whether a shopping mall landlord's failure to provide the number of parking spaces specified in a commercial lease constitutes a material breach of that lease. Following a court trial, the district court found that the landlord had breached the contract, but that the breach was not material and that the tenant was not entitled to a rescission of the lease. Both parties have appealed. For the reasons explained below, we affirm the district court's ruling that the landlord breached the lease but that the breach was not a material breach. * * *

* * *
Mountain Restaurant Corporation (Mountain Restaurant) leased commercial space in the ParkCenter Mall to operate a restaurant called Zac's Grill. The space was leased from ParkCenter Associates (ParkCenter), an Idaho joint venture. * * *

The lease was to run for a period of seven years. Article V(A) of the lease contract specified that there would be 500 parking spaces at the mall:

Parking: Lessor shall at all times during the term of this Lease including any extension or renewal thereof, maintain a general shopping center upon the property upon which the leased premises are located, which shopping center shall always have as a part thereof, or upon premises immediately contiguous or adjacent thereto, a parking area to furnish parking space without charge to all customers of the shopping center seeking parking, so that there shall be maintained at all times a minimum of 500 parking spaces to be used in the manner further described by this paragraph.

In the course of developing the mall, ParkCenter entered into two agreements which affected the amount of parking at the mall. The first agreement was a parking easement, dated May 16, 1985, which permitted customers of the ParkCenter Mall to park in the Lake Pointe Office Center parking lot which was located to the north of ParkCenter Mall across Mallard Drive. ParkCenter had to obtain this additional parking because there were only 373 on-site parking spaces, which is approximately 25% fewer than is required by the Boise City Building Code. The easement provided 181 additional parking spaces; however, these spaces were available only on weekday evenings after 5:00 PM and on weekends.

The second agreement was a Cross-Covenant and Easement Agreement, dated November 7, 1986. This agreement was between ParkCenter and the ParkCenter Pointe Owners Association. It prohibited ParkCenter Mall customers from parking in the spaces on the west side of the mall. Compliance with the terms of the cross-covenant agreement was a specific condition imposed by the City of Boise when it issued the conditional use permit and building permit for the construction of the mall. Though ParkCenter entered into both of these agreements before it signed the lease contract with Clune, it did not provide copies of either of these agreements to him at the time the lease was signed. There is conflicting testimony regarding the question whether Clune had seen a different site development plan, which showed the parking available at Lake Pointe Center, prior to signing the lease.

In preparing to open Zac's Grill, Clune obtained bank loans and invested a substantial amount of money in finishing the interior of the restaurant space and in installing equipment. Zac's Grill was to be a fast-service lunch restaurant with a moderately priced menu. Clune had been in the restaurant business for several years and successfully operated a fast-service lunch deli in a different area of Boise. The peak period for this type of fast-service lunch restaurant is the noon hour. Clune anticipated "turning over" the tables twice during the noon lunch hour.

Zac's Grill opened on September 1, 1988. There were immediate problems with parking due to construction vehicles and mall employees parking in the areas other than the designed employee parking area. Nevertheless, Zac's Grill operated successfully until the Lake Pointe Center Office Building opened and the parking in that lot was restricted. Two other restaurants opened in the north end of ParkCenter Mall in the fall of 1988. TCBY opened two weeks after Zac's grill and Ducks' Bar and Grill opened in early December. All three restaurants were then competing for a limited number of parking spaces. The parking closest to Zac's would become full between noon and 12:30 PM each weekday. After that, the lunch traffic would decline precipitously. The evidence also showed, however, that parking was always available at other areas of the mall parking lot.

During the trial, Clune presented testimony from several former customers that they had had difficulty finding a parking place during the lunch hour and had, at times, driven through the parking lot and gone on to someplace else for lunch. Clune himself kept notes in his desk diary on the status of the parking situation. A summary of these notes was admitted as Plaintiff's Exhibit 7; Clune testified that the summary reflected an every day situation and that the lack of available parking was not limited to the specific instances listed on the summary.

Clune informed ParkCenter on several occasions that there were problems due to the lack of adequate parking. The lack of customers caused cash flow problems. Clune stopped making rental payments to ParkCenter. In an attempt to make up for the loss of lunch-time business, Clune bought a delivery truck and started delivering lunch orders outside of the restaurant. Finally, he closed the restaurant and vacated the leased premises on December 20, 1989. At that time, Clune owed ParkCenter approximately $12,000 in unpaid rent.

Mountain Restaurant filed an action for rescission of the lease contract and ParkCenter filed a counterclaim for rent that had accrued before and after Mountain Restaurant vacated the premises. Following a court trial, the district court found that ParkCenter had breached the lease, but that the breach was not a material breach. Consequently, the district court declined to grant a rescission of the contract. The district court concluded that ParkCenter was entitled to collect rent for the time that Mountain Restaurant occupied the premises, but that no rent could be recovered for the period after Mountain Restaurant vacated the premises because of ParkCenter's failure to mitigate damages. The district court found that neither party had totally prevailed, and declined to award attorney fees. ParkCenter's claim for costs pursuant to [citation] was also denied. These appeals followed.

* * *

A material breach of contract is a breach so substantial and fundamental that it defeats the object of the parties in entering into the contract. [Citations.] A material breach affects the substantive rights of the parties and a rescission of the contract may be ordered. [Citation.] Rescission is not warranted where the breach is incidental and subordinate to the main purpose of the contract. [Citation.] There is no material breach of contract where substantial performance has been rendered. [Citation.] "Substantial performance is performance which despite deviation or omission provides the important and essential benefits of the contract to the promisee." [Citation.]

Whether a breach of contract is material is a question of fact. [Citations.] * * *

In its memorandum decision, the district court found a breach of contract by ParkCenter, which is not challenged by ParkCenter on cross-appeal. The district court concluded that ParkCenter expressly agreed to provide a minimum of 500 parking spaces either on the shopping center property itself, or "immediately contiguous or adjacent thereto." The district court found that only 387 parking spaces were actually on the shopping center property but that ParkCenter had arranged for enough additional parking spaces across Mallard Drive to provide for more than the required 500 spaces. In the district court's opinion, these additional spaces were in sufficiently close proximity to meet the definition of "contiguous" or "adjacent." The district court found a breach of contract, however, in the fact that the additional parking spaces across Mallard Drive were provided only after 5:00 PM on weekdays and on weekends. The limitation on parking availability, which would limit the number of spaces to 387 during normal business hours on weekdays, did not comply, the court found, with the unequivocal language of the lease by which ParkCenter agreed "[t]hat there shall be maintained at all times a minimum of 500 parking spaces. . . ."

As to the materiality of the breach, which resulted in only 387 spaces being available during normal weekday business hours, including the lunch hour, the district court held that the deviation from the terms of the contract was immaterial, based on a review of the evidence. The district court found that there was always parking available on the shopping center property. * * *

* * *

As an additional ground for reversal, Mountain Restaurant argues that the district court should have applied a test which would focus upon whether Mountain Restaurant would have entered into the lease if it had known that parking was to be provided across Mallard Drive as opposed to on the west side of the shopping center, and that the parking hours for certain parking areas would be restricted, [citation]. Mountain Restaurant appears to suggest that if one party to a contract subjectively considers a certain term to be material, that the court must so find. * * * It is well established that materiality is a question of fact for the trial court, which must review and weigh often conflicting evidence concerning materiality. We thus reject the proffered subjective test of materiality. * * *

The balance of Mountain Restaurant's argument consists of challenging the factual basis for the district court's conclusion of an immaterial breach. Mountain Restaurant argues that the location of parking was very important because in a lunch-oriented business customers will not walk very far from their cars to a restaurant. The specific location of parking for Mountain Restaurant's customers was not stated in the lease. Rather, the relevant lease provision, Article V(A), provided that the lessee shall "at all times have a non exclusive and non revokable right, together with the other tenants and occupants of . . . the shopping center, to use the parking area . . . for itself, its customers and employees." Although Mountain Restaurant may have believed that it was extremely important to its business to have parking available right next to its location, the lease did not so provide. Thus, the fact that spaces in close proximity to the restaurant were generally not available during the lunch hour does not provide support for the claim that there was a material breach of the lease because the lease simply did not provide that parking in that area would be reserved for Mountain Restaurant's customers.

* * *

* * * The district court's determination is supported by substantial evidence and is affirmed.

---

## CASE 17–3
## Anticipatory Breach
### *HOCHSTER v. DE LA TOUR*
Queen's Bench of England, 1853
2 Ellis and Blackburn Reports 678

LORD CAMPBELL, C.J.

[On April 12, 1852, Hochster contracted with De La Tour to serve as a guide for De La Tour on his three-month trip to Europe, beginning on June 1 at an agreed-upon salary. On May 11, De La Tour notified Hochster that he would not need Hochster's services. He also refused to pay Hochster any compensation. Hochster brings this action to recover damages for breach of contract.]

On this motion . . . the question arises, Whether, if there be an agreement between A. and B., whereby B. engages to employ A. on and from a future day for a given period of time, to travel with him into a foreign country as a [guide], and to start with him in that capacity on that day, A. being to receive a monthly salary during the continuance of such service, B. may, before the day, refuse to perform the agreement and break and renounce it, so as to entitle A. before the day to commence an action against B. to recover damages for breach of the agreement; A. having been ready and willing to perform it, till it was broken and renounced by B.

* * *

If the plaintiff has no remedy for breach of the contract unless he treats the contract as in force, and acts upon it down to the 1st June, 1852, it follows that, till then, he must enter into no employment which will interfere with his promise "to start with the defendant on such travels on the day and year" and that he must then be properly equipped in all respects as a [guide] for a three months' tour on the continent of Europe. But it is surely much more rational, and more for the benefit of both parties, that, after the renunciation of the agreement by the defendant, the plaintiff should be at liberty to consider himself absolved from any future performance of it, retaining his right to sue for any damage he has suffered from the breach of it. Thus, instead of remaining idle and laying out money in preparations which must be useless, he is at liberty to seek service under another employer, which would go in mitigation of the damages to which he would otherwise be entitled for a breach of the contract. It seems strange that the defendant after renouncing the contract, and absolutely declaring that he will never act under it, should be permitted to object that

faith is given to his assertion, and that an opportunity is not left to him of changing his mind. * * *

* * * The man who wrongfully renounces a contract into which he has deliberately entered cannot justly complain if he is immediately sued for a compensation in damage by the man whom he has injured: and it seems reasonable to allow an option to the injured party, either to sue immediately, or to wait till the time when the act was to be done, still holding it as prospectively binding for the exercise of this option, which may be advantageous to the innocent party, and cannot be prejudicial to the wrongdoer.

Judgment for plaintiff.

---

## CASE 17–4
## Accord and Satisfaction
### *ENGLAND v. HORBACH*
Court of Appeals of Utah, 1995
905 P.2d 301

BILLINGS, J.

Plaintiff, Lan C. England, appeals from the trial court's dismissal of his complaint and judgment in favor of defendant, Eugene Horbach. Plaintiff contends the trial court erred when it held the parties' accord and satisfaction was unenforceable. We agree and therefore reverse and remand.

### Facts

In late 1989 or early 1990, plaintiff and defendant entered into a contract whereby defendant agreed to purchase 258,363 shares of Medicode stock from plaintiff. The parties agreed the purchase price would be $2.75 per share, resulting in a total purchase price of $710,498.25. At trial, plaintiff testified and defendant did not dispute, that the purchase money was to be paid within the first quarter of 1990. Defendant made periodic payments on the stock at least through September 1990.

In May 1991, at defendant's request, the parties met to finalize the stock purchase. At this time, plaintiff still retained the stock certificates and believed defendant owed additional money on the original purchase agreement. Plaintiff also believed defendant had breached the original stock purchase agreement by failing to pay the entire amount within the agreed time. At the May meeting, plaintiff informed defendant that at least $25,000 was still owing under the original purchase

agreement. Defendant did not dispute that amount. The parties then reached an agreement whereby defendant agreed to remit to plaintiff an additional $25,000 and hold in trust two percent of the Medicode stock for plaintiff. In return, plaintiff agreed to immediately transfer to defendant the stock certificates and to forego his right to sue for defendant's breach of the original agreement.

At trial, both parties agreed that plaintiff would not have transferred the stock certificates to defendant had the second agreement not been entered into. Further, both plaintiff and defendant testified that at the May meeting both believed that money was still owing under the original contract.

In December 1992, pursuant to the second agreement, plaintiff made a demand for the two percent Medicode stock that defendant was purportedly holding in trust for him. Defendant, however, refused to produce the stock, contending that the two percent agreement was meant only to secure defendant's payment of the additional $25,000. Plaintiff therefore sued defendant for breach of the two percent agreement. Prior to trial, defendant discovered additional business records which defendant claimed documented that, before entering into the second agreement, he had actually overpaid plaintiff for the purchase of the Medicode stock.

A bench trial was held on March 22, 1994. The court ruled that plaintiff could not enforce the second agreement as an accord and satisfaction because it was not supported by consideration and because it was based upon a mutual mistake that defendant owed additional money on the original agreement. The trial court therefore dismissed plaintiff's complaint and entered judgment in favor of defendant based upon his "counterclaim" alleging that, at the time the second agreement was entered, defendant had already overpaid plaintiff for the Medicode stock.

## Accord and Satisfaction

It is settled that

[a]n accord and satisfaction arises when the parties to a contract mutually agree that a performance different than that required by the original contract will be made in substitution of the performance originally agreed upon and that the substituted agreement calling for a different performance will discharge the obligation created under the original agreement.

[Citation.] Moreover, for an accord and satisfaction to have any legal effect, the elements of a contract, including consideration, must be present. [Citation.] The elements of an accord and satisfaction include: (i) a bona fide dispute [or uncertainty] over an unliquidated amount; (ii) a payment tendered in full settlement of the entire dispute; and (iii) an acceptance of the payment. [Citation.]

*A. Consideration*   In its first claim of error, plaintiff contends the trial court erred when it concluded the second agreement did not constitute an accord and satisfaction because there was no consideration to support that agreement. In Utah, it is clear that consideration for an accord may consist of a compromise of a bona fide dispute or uncertainty as to the amount actually owing. [Citations.] Moreover, "[i]t is not necessary for the dispute [or uncertainty] to be well-founded so long as it is in good faith." [Citations.]

Thus, if the parties in good faith believe there is a disputed or uncertain claim, mere settlement of the amount due and acceptance of that amount constitutes the consideration necessary to support the contract. [Citations.]

In the instant case, plaintiff received several checks from defendant in partial satisfaction of the original agreement over a nine month period. Plaintiff believed defendant still owed between $25,000 and $75,000 on the original purchase agreement. When the parties met at defendant's request in May 1991, plaintiff informed defendant of the amount he believed was then due and offered to settle the original contract for an additional $25,000 and two percent of the Medicode stock. Defendant did not dispute this claim, as he was equally unsure of the amount then owing on the original purchase agreement. Rather, he accepted the proposal in the interest of resolving the matter.

At that meeting, defendant was interested in getting the stock certificates and plaintiff was interested in getting paid the full purchase price. Although unfounded, plaintiff asserted in good faith that he believed additional money was still owing. Defendant accepted this representation without dispute and accepted plaintiff's resolution proposal. The May 1991 agreement reflects the parties' good faith bargain regarding an uncertain claim. We conclude the trial court erred when it determined the second agreement was not supported by consideration and was therefore unenforceable.

*B. Mutual Mistake*   Plaintiff further claims the trial court erred when it held that because neither party was aware that defendant had already paid the original purchase agreement in full, a mutual mistake of fact precluded the enforcement of the accord and satisfaction.

An accord and satisfaction based upon a mutual mistake as to a material fact can be rescinded by either party. [Citations.] "'A mutual mistake occurs when both parties, at the time of contracting, share a misconception about a basic assumption or vital fact upon which they based their bargain.'" [Citation.] Thus, an accord and satisfaction may be rescinded where there is a mutual mistake as to the bargain giving rise to the accord.

Accepting the facts as found by the trial court, at the May 1991 meeting, the parties were indeed mistaken that additional money was owed under the original agreement. However, this mistake did not go to the terms of the parties' accord; rather, it merely demonstrates their accord was indeed a compromise of a bona fide dispute which was not necessarily well-founded, but was made in good faith. [Citation.]

In the instant case, both parties were uncertain as to the amount that remained owing on the original contract when they entered into their agreement. Although mistaken as to whether money was then owing, the parties were clearly not mistaken as to the agreement they reached to compromise a good faith, though mistaken, claim. The accord and satisfaction accurately reflects the intent of the parties at the time it was entered. There was therefore no mistake regarding a basic assumption underlying the accord and satisfaction, thus, it is not void. [Court's footnote: To illustrate the difference between a bona fide uncertainty which is compromised by an accord and satisfaction from a mutual mistake going to the essence of the accord, the following example is helpful. If, in this case, the parties had agreed to exchange $25,000 for 258,363 shares of stock which both parties believed was transferable and it was then discovered the stock was not transferable, a mutual mistake as to the essence of the accord and satisfaction would be present. Under such a scenario, the mistake—that the stock was transferable—goes directly to a basic assumption underlying the substitute agreement and therefore constitutes a mutual mistake which voids that agreement. In the instant case, the parties were mistaken as to facts relevant to the original contract—whether money was then due and owing—not as to a term underlying the accord and satisfaction.]

Because we conclude the trial court erred when it held the accord and satisfaction unenforceable for lack of consideration and because we conclude the agreement was not founded upon a mutual mistake of fact, we reverse and remand for further action consistent with this opinion.

---

## CASE 17–5
## Impossibility
# NORTHERN CORP. v. CHUGACH ELECTRICAL ASSOCIATION

Supreme Court of Alaska, 1974
518 P.2d 76

BOOCHEVER, J.

[Northern Corporation entered into a contract with Chugach in August 1966 to repair and upgrade the upstream face of Cooper Lake Dam in Alaska. The contract required Northern to obtain rock from a quarry site at the opposite end of the lake and to transport the rock to the dam during the winter across the ice on the lake. In December 1966, Northern cleared the road on the ice to permit deeper freezing, but thereafter water overflowed on the ice, preventing the use of the road. Northern complained of the unsafe condition of the lake ice, but Chugach insisted on performance. In March 1967, one of Northern's loaded trucks broke through the ice and sank. Northern continued to encounter difficulties and ceased operations with the approval of Chugach. On January 8, 1968, Chugach notified Northern that it would be in default unless all rock was hauled by April 1. After two more trucks broke through the ice, causing the deaths of the drivers, Northern ceased operations and notified Chugach that it would make no more attempts to haul across the lake. Northern advised Chugach it considered the contract terminated for impossibility of performance and commenced suit to recover the cost incurred in attempting to complete the contract.]

* * *

The focal question is whether the . . . contract was impossible of performance. The September 27, 1966 directive specified that the rock was to be transported "across Cooper Lake to the dam site when such lake is frozen to a sufficient depth to permit heavy vehicle traffic thereon," and . . . specified that the hauling to the dam site would be done during the winter of 1966–67. It is therefore clear that the parties contemplated that the rock would be transported across the frozen lake by truck. Northern's repeated efforts to perform the contract by this method during the winter of 1966–67 and subsequently in February 1968, culminating in the tragic loss of life, abundantly support the trial court's findings that the contract was impossible of performance by this method.

Chugach contends, however, that Northern was nevertheless bound to perform, and that it could have used means other than hauling by truck across the ice to transport the rock. The answer to Chugach's contention is that . . . the parties contemplated that the rock would be hauled by truck once the ice froze to a sufficient depth to support the weight of the vehicles. The specification of this particular method of performance presupposed the existence of ice frozen to the requisite depth. Since this expectation of the parties was never fulfilled, and since the provisions relating to the means of performance was clearly material, Northern's duty to perform was discharged by reason of impossibility.

There is an additional reason for our holding that Northern's duty to perform was discharged because of impossibility. It is true that in order for a defendant to prevail under the original common law doctrine of impossibility, he had to show that no one else could have performed the contract. However, this harsh rule has gradually been eroded, and the Restatement of Contracts has departed from the early common law rule by recognizing the principle of "commercial impracticability." Under this doctrine, a party is discharged from his contract obligations, even if it is technically possible to perform them, if the costs of performance would be so disproportionate to that reasonably contemplated by the parties as to make the contract totally impractical in a commercial sense. . . . Removed from the strictures of the common law, "impossibility" in its modern context has become a coat of many colors, including among its hues the point argued here—namely, impossibility predicated upon "commercial impracticability." This concept—which finds expression both in case law . . . and in other authorities . . . is grounded upon the assumption that in legal contemplation something is impracticable when it can only be done at an excessive and unreasonable cost. As stated in *Transatlantic Financing Corp. v. United States* [citation]

. . . The doctrine ultimately represents the ever-shifting line, drawn by courts hopefully responsive to commercial practices and mores, at which the community's interest in having contracts enforced according to their terms is outweighed by the commercial senselessness of requiring performance. . . .

\* \* \*

In the case before us the detailed opinion of the trial court clearly indicates that the appropriate standard was followed. There is ample evidence to support its findings that "[t]he ice haul method of transporting riprap ultimately selected was within the contemplation of the parties and was part of the basis of the agreement which ultimately resulted in amendment No. 1 in October 1966," and that that method was not commercially feasible within the financial parameters of the contract. We affirm the court's conclusion that the contract was impossible of performance.

\* \* \*

# Questions

1. Identify and distinguish among the various types of conditions.
2. Distinguish between full performance and tender of performance.
3. Explain the difference between material breach and substantial performance. Explain how the UCC perfect tender rule differs.

4. Distinguish among a mutual rescission, substituted contract, accord and satisfaction, and novation.
5. Identify and discuss the ways discharge may be brought about by operation of law.

# Problems

1. A–1 Roofing Co. entered into a written contract with Jaffe to put a new roof on the latter's residence for $1,800, using a specified type of roofing, and to complete the job without unreasonable delay. A–1 undertook the work within a week thereafter, but when all the roofing material was at the site and the labor 50 percent completed, the premises were totally destroyed by fire caused by lightning. A–1 submitted a bill to Jaffe for $1,200 for materials furnished and labor performed up to the time of the destruction of the premises. Jaffe refused to pay the bill, and A–1 sued Jaffe. Decision?
2. By contract dated January 5, Rebecca agreed to sell to Nancy, and Nancy agreed to buy from Rebecca, a certain parcel of land then zoned commercial. The specific intent of Nancy, which was known to Rebecca, was to erect a storage plant on the land; and the contract stated that the agreement was conditioned upon Nancy's ability to construct such a plant

upon the land. The closing date for the transaction was set for April 1. On February 15, the city council rezoned the land from commercial to residential, which precluded the erection of the storage plant. As the closing date drew near, Nancy made it known to Rebecca that she did not intend to go through with the purchase because the land could no longer be used as intended. On April 1, Rebecca tendered the deed to Nancy, who refused to pay Rebecca the agreed purchase price. Rebecca brought an action against Nancy for breach of their contract. Decision?
3. The Perfection Produce Company entered into a written contract with Hiram Hodges for the purchase of 300 tons of potatoes to be grown on Hodge's farm in Maine at a stipulated price per ton. Although the land would ordinarily produce 1,000 tons and the planting and cultivation were properly done, Hodges was able to deliver only 100 tons because of a

partial crop failure owing to an unprecedented drought. Hodges sued the produce company to recover an unpaid balance of the agreed price for 100 tons of potatoes. The produce company, by an appropriate counterclaim against Hodges, sought damages for his failure to deliver the additional 200 tons. Decision?

4.   On November 23, Sylvia agreed to sell to Barnett her Pontiac automobile for $7,000, delivery and payment to be made on December 1. On November 26, Barnett informed Sylvia that he wished to rescind the contract and would pay Sylvia $350 if Sylvia agreed. She agreed and took the $350 cash. On December 1, Barnett tendered to Sylvia $6,650 and demanded that she deliver the automobile. Sylvia refused and Barnett initiated a lawsuit. Decision?

5.   Webster, Inc. dealt in automobile accessories at wholesale. Although he manufactured a few items in his own factory, among them windshield wipers, Webster purchased most of his supplies from a large number of other manufacturers. In January, Webster entered into a written contract to sell Hunter 2,000 windshield wipers for $4,900, delivery to be made June 1. In April, Webster's factory burned to the ground, and Webster failed to make delivery on June 1. Hunter, forced to buy windshield wipers elsewhere at a higher price, brings an action against Webster for breach of contract. Decision?

6.   Erwick Construction Company contracted to build a house for Charles. The specifications called for the use of Karlene Pipe for all plumbing. Erwick, however, got a better price on Boynton Pipe and substituted the equally good Boynton Pipe for Karlene Pipe. Upon inspection, Charles discovered the change, and he now refuses to make the final payment. The contract price was for $200,000, and the final payment is $20,000. Erwick now brings suit seeking the $20,000. Decision?

7.   Green owed White $3,500, which was due and payable on June 1. White owed Brown $3,500, which was due and payable on August 1. On May 25, White received a letter signed by Green stating, "If you will cancel my debt to you, in the amount of $3,500, I will pay, on the due date, the debt you owe Brown, in the amount of $3,500." On May 28, Green received a letter signed by White stating, "I received your letter and agree to the proposals recited therein. You may consider your debt to me canceled as of the date of this letter." On June 1, White, needing money to pay his income taxes, made a demand upon Green to pay him the $3,500 due on that date. Is Green obligated to pay the money demanded by White?

8.   By written contract Ames agreed to build a house on Bowen's lot for $65,000, commencing within ninety days of the date of the contract. Prior to the date for beginning construction, Ames informed Bowen that he was repudiating the contract and would not perform. Bowen refused to accept the repudiation and demanded fulfillment of the contract. Eighty days after the date of the contract, Bowen entered into a new contract with Curd for $62,000. The next day, without knowledge or notice of Bowen's contract with Curd, Ames began construction. Bowen ordered Ames from the premises and refused to allow him to continue. Ames sued Bowen for damages. Decision?

9.   Judy agreed in writing to work for Northern Enterprises, Inc. for three years as Superintendent of Northern's manufacturing establishment and to devote herself entirely to the business, giving it her whole time, attention, and skill, for which she was to receive $24,000 per annum, in monthly installments of $2,000. Judy worked and was paid for the first twelve months, when, through no fault of her own or Northern's, she was arrested and imprisoned for one month. It became imperative for Northern to employ another, and it treated the contract with Judy as breached and abandoned, refusing to permit Judy to resume work upon her release from jail. What rights, if any, does Judy have under the contract?

10.   The Park Plaza Hotel awarded its valet and laundry concession to Larson for a three-year term. The contract contained the following provision: "It is distinctly understood and agreed that the services to be rendered by Larson shall meet with the approval of the Park Plaza Hotel, which shall be the sole judge of the sufficiency and propriety of the services." After seven months, the hotel gave a month's notice to discontinue services based on the failure of the services to meet its approval. Larson brought an action against the hotel, alleging that its dissatisfaction was unreasonable. The hotel defended upon the ground that subjective or personal satisfaction may be the sole justification for termination of the contract. Decision?

11.   Schlosser entered into an agreement to purchase a cooperative apartment from Flynn Company. The written agreement contained the following provision:

This entire agreement is conditioned on Purchaser's being approved for occupancy by the board of directors of the Cooperative. In the event approval of the Purchaser shall be denied, this agreement shall thereafter be of no further force or effect.

When Schlosser unilaterally revoked her "offer," Flynn sued for breach of contract. Schlosser claims the approval provision was a condition precedent to the existence of a binding contract and, thus, she was free to revoke. Decision?

12.   Jacobs, owner of a farm, entered into a contract with Earl Walker in which Walker agreed to paint the buildings on the farm. Walker purchased the paint from Jones. Before the work was completed, Jacobs ordered Walker to stop because she was dissatisfied with the results. Jones and Walker made offers to complete the job, but Jacobs declined to permit Walker to fulfill his contract. Jones and Walker bring an action against Jacobs for breach of contract. Decision?

13.   On August 20, 1981, Hildebrand entered into a written contract with the city of Douglasville whereby he was to serve as community development project engineer for three years at an "annual fee" of $19,000. This salary figure could be changed without affecting the other terms of the contract. One of the provisions for termination of the contract was written notice by either party to the other at any time at least ninety days prior to the intended date of termination. The contract listed a number of services and duties Hildebrand was to perform

for the city, among which were (1) keeping the community development director (Hildebrand's supervisor) informed at all times of his whereabouts and how he could be contacted and (2) attending meetings at which his presence was requested. On September 20, 1983, by which time Hildebrand's annual fee had risen to $1,915.83 per month, the city fired Hildebrand effective immediately, citing "certain material breaches . . . of the . . . agreement." Hildebrand sued the mayor and city for breach of his employment contract, seeking damages in the amount of $5,747.49 because of the city's failure to give him ninety days' notice prior to termination. The city contended that Hildebrand repeatedly violated the terms and conditions of the contract. The city specifically charged that he did not attend the necessary meetings although requested to do so and seldom if ever kept his supervisor informed of his whereabouts and how he could be contacted. The trial court granted summary judgment to Hildebrand, and the city appealed.

14. Walker & Co. contracted to provide a sign for Harrison to place above his dry cleaning business. According to the contract, Harrison would lease the sign from Walker, making monthly payments for thirty-six months. In return, Walker agreed to maintain and service the sign at its own expense. Walker installed the sign in July 1953, and Harrison made the first rental payment. Shortly thereafter, someone hit the sign with a tomato. Harrison also claims he discovered rust on its chrome and little spider webs in its corners. Harrison repeatedly called Walker for the maintenance work promised under the contract, but Walker did not respond. Harrison then telegraphed Walker that due to Walker's failure to perform the maintenance services, he held Walker in material breach of the contract. Decision?

15. Barta entered into a written contract to buy the K&K Pharmacy, located in the local shopping center. Included in the contract was a provision stating that "this Agreement shall be contingent upon Buyer's ability to obtain a new lease from Landlord for the premises presently occupied by Seller. In the event Buyer is unable to obtain a lease satisfactory to Buyer, this Agreement shall be null and void." Barta planned to sell "high traffic" grocery items such as bread, milk, and coffee to attract customers to his drugstore. A grocery store in the local shopping center, however, held the exclusive right to sell grocery items. Barta, therefore, could not obtain a leasing agreement meeting his approval. When Barta refused to close the sale, K&K Pharmacy sued him for breach of contract. Decision?

16. Victor Packing Co. (Victor) contracted to supply Sun Maid Raisin Growers 1,800 tons of raisins from the current year's crop. After delivering 1,190 tons of raisins by August, Victor refused to supply any more. Although Victor had until the end of the crop season to ship the remaining 610 tons of raisins, Sun Maid treated Victor's repeated refusals to ship any more raisins as a repudiation of the contract. To prevent breaching its own contracts, Sun Maid went into the marketplace to "cover" and bought the raisins it needed. Unfortunately, between the time Victor refused delivery and Sun Maid entered the market, disastrous rains had caused the price of raisins to skyrocket. May Sun Maid recover from Victor the difference between the contract price and the market price before the end of the current crop year?

17. In May 1976, Watts was awarded a construction contract, based on its low bid, by the Cullman County Commission. The contract provided that it would not become effective until approved by the State director of the Farmers Home Administration. In September construction still had not been authorized, and Watts wrote to the County Commission requesting a 5 percent price increase to reflect seasonal and inflationary price increases. The County Commission countered with an offer of 3.5 percent. Watts then wrote the commission, insisting on a 5 percent increase and stating that if this was not agreeable, it was withdrawing its original bid. The commission obtained another company to perform the project, and on October 14, 1976, informed Watts that it had accepted the withdrawal of the bid. Watts sued for breach of contract. The trial court granted the county's motion for summary judgment. Decision?

18. K & G Construction Co. was the owner of and the general contractor for a housing subdivision project. Harris contracted with the company to do excavating and earth-moving work on the project. Certain provisions of the contract stated that (1) K & G was to make monthly progress payments to Harris; (2) no such payments were to be made until Harris obtained liability insurance; and (3) all of Harris's work on the project must be performed in a workmanlike manner. On August 9, a bulldozer operator, working for Harris, drove too close to one of K & G's houses, causing the collapse of a wall and other damage. When Harris and his insurance carrier denied liability and refused to pay for the damage, K & G refused to make the August monthly progress payment. Harris, nonetheless, continued to work on the project until mid-September, when the excavator ceased its operations due to K & G's refusal to make the progress payment. K & G had another excavator finish the job at an added cost of $450. It then sued Harris for the bulldozer damage, alleging negligence, and also for the $450 damages for breach of contract. Harris claims that K & G defaulted first, having no legal right to refuse the August progress payment. The trial court entered judgment for Harris, and K & G appealed. Decision?

**WWW** **Internet Question** Compare the provisions governing performance and breach of contract contained in the Principles of European Contract Law with the provisions of the U.S. common law.

# CHAPTER 18

# Remedies

When one party to a contract breaches the contract by failing to perform his contractual duties, the law provides a remedy for the injured party. Although the primary objective of contract remedies is to compensate the injured party for the loss resulting from the breach, it is impossible for any remedy to equal the promised performance. To an injured party a court can give as relief what it regards as an equivalent of the promised performance.

This chapter will examine the most common judicial remedies available for breach of contract: (1) monetary damages, (2) the equitable remedies of specific performance and injunction, and (3) restitution. Sales of goods are governed by Article 2 of the Uniform Commercial Code, which provides specialized remedies that are discussed in Chapter 25.

## INTERESTS PROTECTED BY CONTRACT REMEDIES

Contract remedies are available to protect one or more of the following interests of the injured party:

1. the **expectation interest,** which is his interest in having the benefit of his bargain by being put in a position as good as the one he would have occupied had the contract been performed;
2. the **reliance interest,** which is his interest in being reimbursed for loss caused by reliance on the contract by being put in a position as good as the one he would have been in had the contract not been made; or
3. the **restitution interest,** which is his interest in having restored to him any benefit that he has conferred on the other party. Restatement, Section 344.

The expectation interest is protected by the contract remedies of compensatory damages, specific performance, and injunction. The reliance interest is protected by the contractual remedy of reliance damages, while the restitution interest is protected by the contractual remedy of restitution.

## MONETARY DAMAGES

A judgment awarding monetary damages is the most frequently granted judicial remedy for breach of contract. Monetary damages, however, will be awarded only for losses that are foreseeable, established with reasonable certainty, and unavoidable. The equitable remedies discussed in this chapter are discretionary and are available only if monetary damages are inadequate.

### Compensatory Damages

The right to recover compensatory money damages for breach of contract is always available to the injured party. Restatement, Section 346. The purpose in allowing **compensatory damages** is to place the injured party in a position as good as the one she would have occupied had the other party performed under the contract. Because these damages are intended to protect the injured party's expectation interest, or the value he expected to derive from the contract, the amount of compensatory damages is generally computed as follows:

> Loss of value
> + Incidental damages
> + Consequential damages
> − Loss or cost avoided by injured party
> Compensatory damages

*Loss of Value* In general, **loss of value** is the *difference between the value of the promised performance* of the breaching party *and the value of the actual performance* rendered by the breaching party.

Value of promised performance
– Value of actual performance
Loss of value

If the breaching party renders no performance at all, then the loss of value is the value of the promised performance. If defective or partial performance is rendered, the loss of value is the difference between the value that the full performance would have had and the value of the performance actually rendered. Thus, where there has been a breach of warranty, the injured party may recover the difference between the value the goods would have had, if they had been as warranted, and the value of the goods in the condition in which the buyer received them. To illustrate, Victor sells an automobile to Joan and expressly warrants that it will get forty-five miles per gallon, but the automobile gets only twenty miles per gallon. The automobile would have been worth $8,000 had it been as warranted, but it is worth only $6,000 as delivered. Joan would recover $2,000 in damages for loss of value.

In addition to loss of value, the injured party may also recover for all other losses actually suffered, subject to the limitation of foreseeability discussed below. These damages include incidental and consequential damages.

*Incidental Damages*   **Incidental damages** are damages that arise directly out of the breach, such as costs incurred to acquire the nondelivered performance from some other source. For example, Agnes employs Benton for nine months for $20,000 to supervise construction of a factory, but fires him without cause after three weeks. Benton, who spends $350 in reasonable fees attempting to find comparable employment, may recover $350 in incidental damages, in addition to any other actual loss he may suffer.

*Consequential Damages*   **Consequential damages** include lost profits and injury to person or property resulting from defective performance. Thus, if Tracy leases to Sean a defective machine that causes him $4,000 in property damage and $12,000 in personal injuries, Sean may recover, in addition to damages for loss of value and incidental damages, $16,000 as consequential damages.

*Expenses Saved*   The recovery by the injured party, however, is reduced by any cost or loss she has avoided by not having to perform. For example, Clinton agrees to build a hotel for Debra for $1,250,000 by September 1. Clinton breaches by not completing construction until October 1. As a consequence, Debra loses revenues for

one month in the amount of $10,000 but saves operating expenses of $6,000. She therefore may recover damages for $4,000. Similarly, in a contract in which the injured party has not fully performed, the injured party's recovery is reduced by the value to him of the performance he promised but did not render. For example, Clinton agrees to convey land to Debra in return for Debra's promise to work for Clinton for two years, but she repudiates the contract before Clinton has conveyed the land. Clinton's recovery for loss from Debra is reduced by the value to Clinton of the land.

## Nominal Damages

An action to recover damages for breach of contract may be maintained even though the plaintiff has not sustained or cannot prove any injury or loss resulting from the breach. Restatement, Section 346. In such a case he will be permitted to recover **nominal damages**—a small sum fixed without regard to the amount of loss. For example, Edward contracts to sell and deliver goods to Florence for $1,000. Edward refuses to deliver the goods as agreed, and so breaks the contract. Florence, however, is able to purchase goods of the same kind and quality elsewhere for $1,000 without incurring any incidental damages. As a result, although Edward has violated Florence's rights under the contract, Florence has suffered no actual loss. Consequently, if Florence, as she may, should sue Edward for breach of contract, she would recover a judgment for nominal damages only. Nominal damages are also available where loss is actually sustained but cannot be proved with reasonable certainty.

## Reliance Damages

As an alternative to compensatory damages, the injured party may seek reimbursement for foreseeable loss caused by his reliance upon the contract. The purpose of **reliance damages** is to place the injured party in a position as good as the one he would have held, had the contract *not been made*. Reliance damages include expenses incurred in preparing to perform, in actually performing, or in forgoing opportunities to enter into other contracts. An injured party may prefer damages for reliance to compensatory damages when he is unable to establish his lost profits with reasonable certainty or when the contract is itself unprofitable. For example, Donald agrees to sell his retail store to Gary, who spends $50,000 acquiring inventory and fixtures. Donald then repudiates the contract, and Gary sells the inventory and fixtures for $35,000. Neither party can establish with reasonable certainty what profit Gary would have made; Gary, therefore, may recover from Donald as damages the loss of $15,000 he sustained on the sale of the inventory and fixtures plus any other costs he incurred in entering into the contract.

## Damages for Misrepresentation

The basic remedy for misrepresentation is rescission (avoidance) of the contract, though when appropriate, the courts also will require restitution. At common law, an alternative remedy to rescission is a suit for damages. The Code liberalizes the common law by not restricting a defrauded party to an election of remedies; that is, the injured party may both rescind the contract by restoring the other party to the *status quo* and recover damages or obtain any other remedy available under the Code. UCC Section 2–721. In most States, the measure of damages for misrepresentation depends upon whether the misrepresentation was fraudulent or nonfraudulent.

*Fraud*  A party induced by fraud to enter into a contract may recover general damages in a tort action. A minority of States allows the injured party to recover, under the **"out-of-pocket"** rule, general damages equal to the difference between the value of what she has received and the value of what she has given for it. The great majority of States, however, under the **"benefit-of-the-bargain"** rule, permits the intentionally defrauded party to recover general damages that are equal to the difference between the value of what she has received and the value of the fraudulent party's performance as represented. The Restatement of Torts provides the fraudulently injured party with the option of either out-of-pocket or benefit-of-the-bargain damages. Section 549. To illustrate, Emily intentionally misrepresents the capabilities of a printing press and thereby induces Melissa to purchase the machine for $20,000. The value of the press as delivered is $14,000, but if the machine had performed as represented, it would be worth $24,000. Under the out-of-pocket rule, Melissa would recover $6,000, whereas under the benefit-of-the-bargain rule, she would recover $10,000.

In addition to a recovery of general damages under one of the measures just discussed, consequential damages may be recovered to the extent they are proved with reasonable certainty and to the extent they do not duplicate general damages. Moreover, where the fraud is gross, oppressive, or aggravated, punitive damages are permitted.

*Nonfraudulent Misrepresentation*  Where the misrepresentation is negligent, the deceived party may recover general damages, under the out-of-pocket measure, and consequential damages. Restatement of Torts, Section 552B. Some States, however, permit the recovery of general damages under the benefit-of-the-bargain measure for negligent misrepresentation. Where the misrepresentation is neither fraudulent nor negligent, however, the Restatement limits damages to the out-of-pocket measure. Section 552C.

## Punitive Damages

**Punitive damages** are monetary damages in addition to compensatory damages awarded to a plaintiff in certain situations involving willful, wanton, or malicious conduct. Their purpose is to punish the defendant and thus discourage him and others from similar wrongful conduct. The purpose of allowing contract damages, on the other hand, is to compensate the plaintiff for the loss that he has sustained because of the defendant's breach of contract. Accordingly, the Restatement provides that punitive damages are *not* recoverable for a breach of contract unless the conduct constituting the breach is also a tort for which the plaintiff may recover punitive damages. Restatement, Section 355.

## Liquidated Damages

A contract may contain a **liquidated damages** provision by which the parties agree in advance to the damages to be paid in event of a breach. Such a provision will be enforced if it amounts to a reasonable forecast of the loss that may or does result from the breach. If, however, the sum agreed upon as liquidated damages bears no reasonable relationship to the amount of probable loss that may or does result from breach, it is unenforceable as a penalty. (A penalty is a contractual provision designed to deter a party from breaching her contract and to punish her for doing so.) Restatement, Section 356, Comment a states,

The parties to a contract may effectively provide in advance the damages that are to be payable in the event of breach as long as the provision does not disregard the principle of compensation. The enforcement of such provisions for liquidated damages saves the time of courts, juries, parties and witnesses and reduces the expense of litigation. This is especially important if the amount in controversy is small. However, the parties to a contract are not free to provide a penalty for its breach. The central objective behind the system of contract remedies is compensatory, not punitive.

By examining the substance of the provision, the nature of the contract, and the extent of probable harm to the promisee that a breach may reasonably be expected to cause, the courts will determine whether the agreed amount is proper as liquidated damages or unenforceable as a penalty. If a liquidated damage provision is not enforceable, the injured party nevertheless is entitled to the ordinary remedies for breach of contract.

To illustrate, Reliable Construction Company contracts with Equerry to build a grandstand at Equerry's racecourse at a cost of $1,330,000, to have it completed by a certain date, and to pay Equerry, as liquidated damages, $1,000 per day for every day's delay beyond that date in completing the grandstand. The stipulated sum for delay is liquidated damages and not a penalty because the amount is reasonable. If, instead, the sum stipulated had been $10,000 per day, it would obviously have been unreasonable and therefore a penalty. Provisions for liquidated damages are sometimes found in contracts for the sale of a business, in which the seller agrees not to reenter the same business within a reasonable geographic area and time period. Actual damages resulting from the seller's breach of his agreement would ordinarily be difficult to ascertain, and the sum stipulated, if reasonable, would be enforced as liquidated damages.

 *See Case 18–1*

## Limitations on Damages

To accomplish the basic purposes of contract remedies, the law imposes the limitations of foreseeability, certainty, and mitigation upon monetary damages. These limitations are intended to ensure that damages can be taken into account at the time of contracting, that damages are compensatory and not speculative, and that damages do not include loss that could have been avoided by reasonable efforts.

***Foreseeability of Damages*** A contracting party is generally expected to consider foreseeable risks when entering into the contract. Therefore, compensatory or reliance damages are recoverable only for loss that the party in breach had reason to foresee as a *probable* result of such breach when the contract was made; conversely, the breaching party is not liable for loss that was not foreseeable when the parties entered into the contract. The test of foreseeability is *objective*, based upon what the breaching party had reason to foresee. Loss may be deemed foreseeable as a probable result of a breach by following from the breach (a) in the ordinary course of

events or (b) as a result of special circumstances, beyond the ordinary course of events, which the party in breach had reason to know. Restatement, Section 351(2). Moreover, "[a] court may limit damages for foreseeable loss by excluding recovery for loss of profits, by allowing recovery only for loss incurred in reliance, or otherwise if it concludes that in the circumstances justice so requires in order to avoid disproportionate compensation." Restatement, Section 351(3).

The leading case on the subject of foreseeability of damages is *Hadley v. Baxendale*, decided in England in 1854. In this case, the plaintiffs operated a flour mill at Gloucester. Their mill was compelled to cease operating because of a broken crankshaft attached to the steam engine that furnished power to the mill. It was necessary to send the broken shaft to a foundry located at Greenwich so that a new shaft could be made. The plaintiffs delivered the broken shaft to the defendants, who were common carriers, for immediate transportation from Gloucester to Greenwich, but did not inform the defendants that operation of the mill had ceased because of the nonfunctioning crankshaft. The defendants received the shaft, collected the freight charges in advance, and promised to deliver the shaft for repairs the following day. The defendants, however, did not make delivery as promised; as a result, the mill did not resume operations for several days, causing the plaintiffs to lose profitable sales. The defendants contended that the loss of profits was too remote, and therefore unforeseeable, to be recoverable. Nonetheless, the jury, in awarding damages to the plaintiffs, was permitted to take into consideration the loss of these profits. The appellate court reversed the decision and ordered a new trial on the ground that the plaintiffs had never communicated to the defendants the special circumstances that caused the loss of profits, namely, the continued stoppage of the mill while awaiting the return of the repaired crankshaft. A common carrier, the court reasoned, would not reasonably have foreseen that the plaintiffs' mill would be shut down as a result of delay in transporting the broken crankshaft.

On the other hand, if the defendants in *Hadley v. Baxendale* had been informed that the shaft was necessary for the operation of the mill, or otherwise had reason to know this fact, they would be liable for the plaintiffs' loss of profit during that period of the shutdown caused by their delay. Under these circumstances, the loss would be the "foreseeable" and "natural" result of the breach.

Should a plaintiff's expected profit be extraordinarily large the general rule is that the breaching party will be liable for such special loss only if he had reason to know of it. In any event, the plaintiff may recover for any ordinary loss resulting from the breach. Thus, if Madeline breaches a contract with Jane, causing Jane, due to special circumstances, $10,000 in damages where ordinarily such a breach would only result in $6,000 in damages, Madeline would be liable to Jane for $6,000, not $10,000, provided that Madeline was unaware of the special circumstances causing Jane the unusually large loss.

***Certainty of Damages*** Damages are not recoverable for loss beyond an amount that the injured party can establish with reasonable certainty. Restatement, Section 352. If the injured party cannot prove a particular element of her loss with reasonable certainty, she nevertheless will be entitled to recover the portion of her loss that she can prove with reasonable certainty. The certainty requirement creates the greatest challenge for plaintiffs seeking to recover consequential damages for lost profits on related transactions. Those attempting to prove lost profits caused by breach of a contract to produce a sporting event or to publish a new book experience similar difficulties.

***Mitigation of Damages*** Under the doctrine of mitigation of damages, the injured party may not recover damages for loss that he could have avoided with reasonable effort and without undue risk, burden, or humiliation. Restatement, Section 350. Thus, if James is under a contract to manufacture goods for Kathy, and Kathy repudiates the contract after James has commenced performance, James will not be allowed to recover for losses he sustains by continuing to manufacture the goods, if to do so would increase the amount of damages. The amount of loss that James could reasonably have avoided is deducted from the amount that would otherwise be recoverable as damages. On the other hand, if the goods were almost completed when Kathy repudiated the contract, completing the goods might mitigate the damages, because the finished goods may be resalable whereas the unfinished goods may not. UCC Section 2–704(2).

Similarly, if Harvey contracts to work for Olivia for one year for a weekly salary and is wrongfully discharged by Olivia after two months, Harvey must use reasonable efforts to mitigate his damages by seeking other employment. If, after such efforts, he cannot obtain other employment of the same general character, he is entitled to recover full pay for the contract period that he is unemployed. He is not obliged to accept a radically different type of employment or to accept work at a distant place. For example, a person employed as a schoolteacher or accountant who is wrongfully discharged is not obliged, in order to mitigate damages, to accept available employment as a chauffeur or truck driver. On the other hand, if Harvey made no attempt to find substitute employment, his damages would be reduced by the wages he reasonably could have earned had he accepted available comparable employment.

 *See Case 3–3*

# REMEDIES IN EQUITY

At times, damages based on the expectation interest, reliance interest, or restitution interest will not adequately compensate an injured party. In these cases, equitable relief in the form of specific performance or an injunction may be available to protect the injured party's interest.

The remedies of specific performance and an injunction are not a matter of right but rest in the discretion of the court. Consequently, they will not be granted where:

1. there is an adequate remedy at law;
2. it is impossible to enforce them, as where the seller has already conveyed the subject matter of the contract to an innocent third person;
3. the terms of the contract are unfair;
4. the consideration is grossly inadequate;
5. the contract is tainted with fraud, duress, undue influence, mistake, or unfair practices;
6. the terms of the contract are not sufficiently certain; or
7. the relief would cause unreasonable hardship.

A court may grant specific performance or an injunction despite a provision for liquidated damages. Restatement, Section 361. Moreover, a court will grant specific performance or an injunction even though a term of the contract prohibits equitable relief, if denying such relief would cause unreasonable hardship to the injured party. Restatement, Section 364(2).

Another equitable remedy is **reformation,** a process whereby the court "rewrites" or "corrects" a written contract to make it conform to the true agreement of the parties. The purpose of reformation is not to make a new contract for the parties but rather to express adequately the contract they have made for themselves. The remedy of reformation is granted when the parties agree on a contract but write it in a way that inaccurately reflects their actual agreement. For example, Acme Insurance Co. and Bell agree that for good consideration Acme will issue an annuity paying $500 per month. Through a clerical error, the annuity policy is issued for

$50 per month. A court of equity, upon satisfactory proof of the mistake, will reform the policy to provide for the correct amount—$500 per month. In addition, as discussed in Chapter 13, where a covenant not to compete is unreasonable, some courts will reform the agreement to make it reasonable and enforceable.

## Specific Performance

**Specific performance** is an equitable remedy that compels the defaulting party to perform her contractual obligations. Ordinarily, where a seller breaches her contract for the sale of personal property, the buyer has a sufficient remedy at law. If, however, the **personal property** contracted for is rare or unique, this remedy is inadequate. Examples of such property would include a famous painting or statue, an original manuscript or a rare edition of a book, a patent, a copyright, shares of stock in a closely held corporation, or an heirloom. Articles of this kind cannot be purchased elsewhere. Accordingly, should the seller breach her contract for the sale of any such article, money damages will not adequately compensate the buyer. Consequently, in these instances, the buyer may avail herself of the equitable remedy of specific performance.

Although courts of equity will grant specific performance in connection with contracts for the sale of personal property only in exceptional circumstances, they will always grant it in cases involving breach of contract for the sale of **real property.** The reason for this is that every parcel of land is considered unique. Consequently, if the seller refuses to convey title to the real estate contracted for, the buyer may seek the aid of a court of equity to compel the seller to convey the title. Most courts of equity will likewise compel the buyer in a real estate contract to perform at the suit of the seller.

Courts of equity will not grant specific performance of contracts for personal services. In the first place, enforcing such a decree may be difficult if not impossible. In the second place, it is against the policy of the courts to force one person to work for or to serve another against his will, even though the person has contracted to do so, in that such enforcement would closely resemble involuntary servitude. For example, if Carmen, an accomplished concert pianist, agrees to appear at a certain time and place to play a specified program for Rudolf, a court would not issue a decree of specific performance upon her refusal to appear.

 *See Case 18–2*

## Injunctions

The **injunction,** as used as a contract remedy, is a formal court order enjoining (commanding) a person to refrain from doing a specific act or to cease engaging in specified conduct. A court of equity, at its discretion, may grant an injunction against breach of a contractual duty where damages for a breach would be inadequate. For example, Clint enters into a written contract to give Janice the right of first refusal on a tract of land he owns. Clint, however, subsequently offers the land to Blake without first offering it to Janice. A court of equity may properly enjoin Clint from selling the land to Blake. Similarly, valid covenants not to compete may be enforced by an injunction.

An employee's promise of exclusive personal services may be enforced by an injunction against serving another employer as long as the probable result will not be to deprive the employee of other reasonable means of making a living. Restatement, Section 367. Suppose, for example, that Allan makes a contract with Marlene, a famous singer, under which Marlene agrees to sing at Allan's theater on certain dates for an agreed fee. Before the date of the first performance, Marlene makes a contract with Craig to sing for Craig at his theater on the same dates. Although, as already discussed, Allan cannot secure specific performance of his contract by Marlene, a court of equity will, on suit by Allan against Marlene, issue an injunction against her, ordering her not to sing for Craig.

Where the services contracted for are not unusual or extraordinary, the injured party cannot obtain injunctive relief. His only remedy is an action at law for damages.

 *See Case 18–3*

## RESTITUTION

One remedy that may be available to a party to a contract is restitution. **Restitution** is the act of returning to the aggrieved party the consideration, or its value, which he gave to the other party. The purpose of restitution is to restore the injured party to the position he occupied before the contract was made. Therefore, the party seeking restitution must return what he has received from the other party.

Restitution is available in several contractual situations: (1) as an alternative remedy for a party injured by breach; (2) for a party in default; (3) for a party who may not enforce a contract because of the statute of frauds; and (4) for a party wishing to rescind (avoid) a voidable contract.

## Party Injured by Breach

A party is entitled to restitution if the other party totally breaches the contract by nonperformance or repudiation. Restatement, Section 373. For example, Benedict agrees to sell land to Beatrice for $60,000. After Beatrice makes a partial payment of $15,000, Benedict wrongfully refuses to transfer title. As an alternative to damages or specific performance, Beatrice may recover the $15,000 in restitution.

## Party in Default

Where a party, after having partly performed, commits a breach by nonperformance or repudiation that discharges the other party's duty to perform, the party in default is entitled to restitution for any benefit she has conferred in excess of the loss she has caused by her breach. Restatement, Section 374. For example, Nathan agrees to sell land to Lilly for $60,000, and Lilly makes a partial payment of $15,000. Lilly then repudiates the contract. Nathan sells the land to Murray in good faith for $55,000. Lilly may recover from Nathan in restitution the part payment of the $15,000 *less* the $5,000 damages Nathan sustained because of Lilly's breach, which equals $10,000.

## Statute of Frauds

A party to a contract that is unenforceable because of the statute of frauds may, nonetheless, have acted in reliance upon the contract. In such a case, that party may recover in restitution the benefits she conferred upon the other in relying upon the unenforceable contract. In most States, the party seeking restitution must not be in default. Thus, if Wilton makes an oral contract to furnish services to Rochelle that are not to be performed within a year, and Rochelle discharges Wilton after three months, Wilton may recover as restitution the value of the services he rendered during the three months.

## Voidable Contracts

A party who has rescinded or avoided a contract for lack of capacity, duress, undue influence, fraud in the inducement, nonfraudulent misrepresentation, or mistake is entitled to restitution for any benefit he has conferred upon the other party. Restatement, Section 376. For example, Samuel fraudulently induces Edith to sell land for $60,000. Samuel pays the purchase price, and Edith conveys the land. Discovering the fraud, Edith may

disaffirm the contract and recover the land as restitution. Generally, the party seeking restitution must return any benefit that he has received under the agreement; however, as discussed in Chapter 14 (which deals with contractual capacity), this is not always the case.

◆ *See Figure 18–1*

## *LIMITATIONS ON REMEDIES*

### Election of Remedies

If a party injured by a breach of contract has more than one remedy available to him, his manifesting a choice of one of them, such as bringing suit, does not prevent him from seeking another remedy unless the remedies are inconsistent and the other party materially changes his position in reliance on the manifestation. Restatement, Section 378. For example, a party who seeks specific performance, an injunction, or restitution may be entitled to incidental damages for delay in performance. Damages for *total breach*, however, are inconsistent with the remedies of specific performance, injunction, and restitution. Likewise, the remedy of specific performance or an injunction is inconsistent with that of restitution.

With respect to contracts for the sale of goods, the Code rejects any doctrine of election of remedies. Thus, the remedies it provides are essentially cumulative, including all of the available remedies for breach. Whether one remedy precludes another depends on the facts of the individual case. UCC Section 2–703, Comment 1.

 *See Case 18–4*

### Loss of Power of Avoidance

A party with a power of avoidance for lack of capacity, duress, undue influence, fraud, misrepresentation, or mistake may lose that power if (1) she affirms the contract; (2) she delays unreasonably in exercising the power of disaffirmance; or (3) the rights of third parties intervene.

*Affirmance* A party who has the power to avoid a contract for lack of capacity, duress, undue influence, fraud in the inducement, nonfraudulent misrepresentation, or mistake will lose that power by affirming the contract. Affirmance occurs where the party, with full knowledge of the facts, either declares his intention to proceed with the contract or takes some other action from which such intention may reasonably be inferred. Thus, suppose that Pam was induced to purchase a ring

**FIGURE 18–1**  Contract Remedies

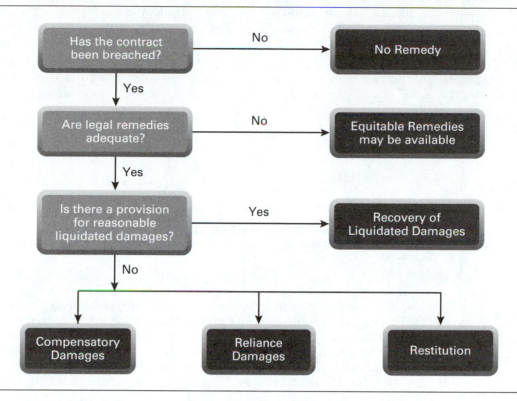

from Sally through Sally's fraudulent misrepresentation. If, after learning the truth, Pam undertakes to sell the ring to Janet or else does something that is consistent only with her ownership of the ring, she may no longer rescind the transaction with Sally. In the case of incapacity, duress, or undue influence, affirmance is effective only after the circumstances that made the contract voidable cease to exist. Where there has been fraudulent misrepresentation, the defrauded party may affirm only after he knows of the misrepresentation. If the misrepresentation is nonfraudulent or a mistake is involved, the defrauded or mistaken party may affirm only after he knows or should know of the misrepresentation or mistake.

**Delay**  The power of avoidance may be lost if the party who has the power does not rescind within a reasonable time after the circumstances that made the contract voidable have ceased to exist. Determining a reasonable time depends upon all the circumstances, including the extent to which the delay enables the party with the power of avoidance to speculate at the other party's risk. To illustrate, a defrauded purchaser of stock cannot wait unduly to see if the market price or value of the stock appreciates sufficiently to justify retaining the stock.

**Rights of Third Parties**  The intervening rights of third parties further limit the power of avoidance and the accompanying right to restitution. If A transfers property to B in a transaction that is voidable by A, and B sells the property to C (a good faith purchaser for value) before A exercises her power of avoidance, A will lose the right to recover the property.

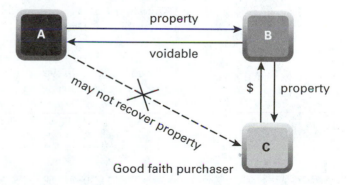

Good faith purchaser

Thus, if C, a third party who is a good faith purchaser, acquires an interest in the subject matter of the contract before A has elected to rescind, no rescission is permitted. Because the transaction is voidable, B acquires a voidable title to the property. Upon a sale of the property by B to C, who is a purchaser in good faith and for value, C obtains good title and is allowed to retain the property. As both A and C are innocent, the law will not disturb the title held by C, the good faith purchaser. In this case, as in all cases where rescission is not available, A's only recourse is against B.

The one notable exception to this rule is the situation involving a sale, *other than a sale of goods,* by a minor who subsequently wishes to avoid the transaction, in which the property has been retransferred to a good faith purchaser. Under this special rule, a good faith purchaser is deprived of the protection generally provided such third parties. Therefore, the third party in a transaction not involving goods, real property being the primary example, is no more protected from the minor's disaffirmance than is the person dealing directly with the minor.

 # Chapter Summary

**Monetary Damages**

**Compensatory Damages** contract damages placing the injured party in a position as good as the one he would have held had the other party performed; equals loss of value minus loss avoided by injured party plus incidental damages plus consequential damages
- *Loss of Value* value of promised performance minus value of actual performance
- *Expenses Saved* loss or costs the injured party avoids by not having to perform
- *Incidental Damages* damages arising directly out of a breach of contract
- *Consequential Damages* damages not arising directly out of a breach but arising as a foreseeable result of the breach

**Nominal Damages** a small sum awarded where a contract has been breached but the loss is negligible or unproved

**Reliance Damages** contract damages placing the injured party in as good a position as she would have been in had the contract not been made

**Damages for Misrepresentation**
- *Benefit-of-the-Bargain Damages* difference between the value of the fraudulent party's performance as represented and the value the defrauded party received
- *Out-of-Pocket Damages* difference between the value given and the value received

**Punitive Damages** are generally *not* recoverable for breach of contract

**Liquidated Damages** reasonable damages agreed to in advance by the parties to a contract

**Limitations on Damages**
- *Foreseeability of Damages* potential loss that the party now in default had reason to know of when the contract was made
- *Certainty of Damages* damages are not recoverable beyond an amount that can be established with reasonable certainty
- *Mitigation of Damages* injured party may not recover damages for loss he could have avoided by reasonable effort

**Remedies in Equity**

**Availability** only where there is no adequate remedy at law

**Types**
- *Specific Performance* court decree ordering breaching party to render promised performance
- *Injunction* court order prohibiting a party from doing a specific act
- *Reformation* court order correcting a written contract to conform with the original intent of the contracting parties

| Restitution | **Definition of Restitution** restoration of the injured party to the position she was in before the contract was made<br>**Availability**<br>• *Party Injured by Breach* if the other party totally breaches the contract by nonperformance or repudiation<br>• *Party in Default* for any benefit conferred in excess of the loss caused by the breach<br>• *Statute of Frauds* where a contract is unenforceable because of the statute of frauds, a party may recover the benefits conferred on the other party in reliance on the contract<br>• *Voidable Contracts* a party who has avoided a contract is entitled to restitution for any benefit conferred on the other party |
| --- | --- |

| Limitations on Remedies | **Election of Remedies** if remedies are not inconsistent, a party injured by a breach of contract may seek more than one<br>**Loss of Power of Avoidance** a party with the power to avoid a contract may lose that power by<br>• affirming the contract<br>• delaying unreasonably in exercising the power of avoidance<br>• being subordinated to the intervening rights of third parties |
| --- | --- |

 **Cases**

## CASE 18–1
## Liquidated Damages
### *WATSON v. INGRAM*
Supreme Court of Washington, 1994
124 Wash.2d 845, 881 P.2d 247

JOHNSON, J.

Petitioner, a buyer under a residential real estate purchase and sale agreement, seeks to recover $15,000 in earnest money he paid into escrow. At issue is whether the earnest money agreement is enforceable as liquidated damages. More specifically, this case involves the test used to determine the enforceability of liquidated damages provisions in real estate purchase and sale agreements. The trial court enforced the agreement, finding it was a reasonable estimate of anticipated harm as of the date of contract formation. The Court of Appeals affirmed, likewise evaluating the provision as of the date of contract formation. Petitioner contends the seller suffered no actual damage and the courts below erred by not evaluating the liquidated damages provision as of the date of trial. We affirm.

## Facts

In the summer of 1990, Wayne Watson offered to buy James Ingram's Bellingham home for $350,000, with a $5,001 earnest money deposit. Watson's offer stipulated the agreement would be contingent upon the sale of Watson's Blaine, Washington, condominium. Ingram rejected Watson's offer, but made a counteroffer, which included a sale price of $355,000, and which eliminated the condominium sale contingency.

Watson accepted Ingram's counteroffer. On August 5, 1990, Watson and Ingram entered into a purchase and sale agreement according to the terms of Ingram's counteroffer. Under the agreement, the entire amount of the purchase price was due in cash on or before December 3, 1990. The agreement provided that Ingram would, at his expense, finish remodeling an office in the house, install a sprinkler system in the front yard, and paint the fence. The agreement required Watson to pay a $15,000 earnest money deposit into escrow at Kelstrup Realty, and provided that "[i]n the event of default by Buyer, earnest money shall be forfeited to Seller as liquidated damages, unless Seller elects to seek actual damages or specific performance." Lastly, the agreement contained a provision entitled "BUYER'S REPRESENTATIONS," which stated, "Buyer represents that buyer has sufficient funds available to close this sale in accordance with this agreement, and is not relying on any contingent source of funds unless otherwise set forth in this agreement."

On September 11, 1990, Watson attempted to assume Ingram's $209,200 outstanding mortgage on the house. On October 18, 1990, the bank approved Watson's application conditioned upon Watson's obtaining approximately $116,050 of his own money for closing. Watson rejected the bank's terms and attempted to secure financing elsewhere.

On November 10, 1990, Watson sent a written proposal to Ingram seeking to modify the original agreement. The proposed modification would have allowed Watson to defer paying $54,000 of the $355,000 sale price for between 6 and 12 months after the scheduled December closing date. In exchange, Ingram would receive a second lien position on certain real estate Watson owned.

According to Ingram, the November 10 proposal was the first time he realized Watson did not have financing readily available for the purchase of the house. Ingram notified Watson on November 12, 1990, that he would not agree to modify the original agreement and intended to strictly enforce its terms. Ingram was involved in a child custody suit in California and wanted to move to that state as soon as possible.

On November 11, 1990, Ingram accepted a $380,000 "backup" offer on the house from Jamie and Sandro Catracchia. The Catracchia-Ingram agreement provided for a $10,000 earnest money deposit, which would become nonrefundable after December 3, 1990, the closing date of the Watson-Ingram agreement.

On November 14, 1990, Watson contacted a mortgage broker to apply for a new loan to finance the purchase of the house. The broker obtained a commitment from an "unnamed source" to loan Watson $266,250. December 3, 1990, the scheduled closing date, the broker notified Ingram and his agent of the loan commitment and, at Watson's request, asked Ingram to extend the closing date so Watson could finalize the financing arrangements.

However, the broker refused to disclose the name of the person or institution that had allegedly committed for the $266,250 loan. In addition, the loan commitment contained several contingencies that had to be met by Watson before the loan would actually be made. One of the contingencies was that Watson would "evidence receipt of funds from income reserve balance of $88,864.56." There was no evidence that Watson had the additional funds. Again Ingram refused to grant Watson an extension and the sale was not completed.

The sale to the Catracchias also failed. Ingram sued the Catracchias to recover the earnest money deposit. Ingram and the Catracchias settled, splitting the deposit. In September 1991, Ingram finally sold the house to a third party for $355,000, the same price that Watson had agreed to pay in December 1990.

Ingram and Watson each sought to recover Watson's $15,000 earnest money held in escrow. On December 4, 1990, Ingram wrote to Kelstrup Realty, indicating he was entitled to the $15,000 earnest money in escrow because Watson had defaulted. In January 1991, Watson filed this action to recover the earnest money, alleging it amounted to a penalty and Ingram had suffered no actual damages. Watson also alleged Ingram acted in bad faith by refusing to extend the closing date.

The trial court found the earnest money "was clearly intended by both parties to be nonrefundable" if Watson defaulted and determined $15,000 was "a reasonable forecast by [Ingram and Watson] of damages that would be incurred by [Ingram] if [Watson] failed to complete the purchase." The court entered judgment in favor of Ingram for the amount of the earnest money plus interest. The court also awarded Ingram his attorney fees pursuant to the parties' agreement. The Court of Appeals, Division One, affirmed. Watson now appeals to this court.

## Analysis

This case presents a single issue for review: whether the parties' contract provision requiring Watson to forfeit a $15,000 nonrefundable earnest money deposit is enforceable as liquidated damages. Liquidated damages clauses are favored in Washington, and courts will uphold them if the sums involved do not amount to a penalty or are otherwise unlawful. [Citation.] To determine whether liquidated damages clauses are enforceable, Washington courts have applied a 2-part test from the Restatement of Contracts § 339, at 552 (1932). Liquidated damages clauses are upheld if the following two factors are satisfied:

First, the amount fixed must be a reasonable forecast of just compensation for the harm that is caused by the breach. Second, the harm must be such that it is incapable or very difficult of ascertainment.

[Citation.]

The question before this court is whether this test is to be applied as of the time of contract formation (prospectively) or as of the time of trial (retrospectively). We have previously held, the "[r]easonableness of the forecast will be judged as of the time the contract was entered." [Citations.] Likewise, in the decision below, the Watson court adopted the time of contract formation as the proper timeframe. [Citation.]

* * *

We agree with the Watson court and adopt the date of contract formation as the proper timeframe for evaluating the Restatement test. The prospective approach concentrates on whether the liquidated sum represents a reasonable prediction of the harm to the seller if the buyer breaches the agreement, and ignores actual damages except as evidence of the reasonableness of the estimate of potential damage.

We believe this approach better fulfills the underlying purposes of liquidated damages clauses and gives greater weight to the parties' expectations. Liquidated damages permit parties to allocate business and litigation risks. Even if the estimates of damages are not exact, parties can allocate and quantify those risks and can negotiate adjustments to the contract price in light of the allocated risks. Under the prospective approach, courts will enforce the parties' allocation of risk so long as the forecasts appear reasonable when made. [Citations.]

In addition to permitting parties to allocate risks, liquidated damages provisions lend certainty to the parties' agreements and permit parties to resolve disputes efficiently in the event of a breach. Rather than litigating the amount of actual damages, the nonbreaching party must only establish the reasonableness of the agreement. The prospective approach permits parties to rely on their stipulated amounts without having to precisely establish damages at trial. In contrast, if the reasonableness of the amount is judged retrospectively, against the damage actually suffered, the "parties must fully litigate (at great expense and delay) that which they sought not to litigate." [Citation.]

Petitioner argues the prospective approach treats buyers unfairly because it permits sellers to retain earnest money deposits even when the seller suffers no actual damage, and this violates the principle that contract damages should be compensatory only. He further contends that by evaluating parties' liquidated damages agreements against actual damages established at trial, courts can most effectively determine whether such agreements were reasonable and fair.

We disagree. As this court has previously explained, "[w]e are loathe to interfere with the rights of parties to contract as they please between themselves . . .". [Citation.] It is not the role of the court to enforce contracts so as to produce the most equitable result. The parties themselves know best what motivations and considerations influenced their bargaining, and, while, "[t]he bargain may be an unfortunate one for the delinquent party, . . . it is not the duty of courts of common law to relieve parties from the consequences of their own improvidence . . ." [Citation.]

The retrospective approach fails to give proper weight to the parties' negotiations. At the time of contract formation, unpredictable market fluctuations and variations in possible breaches make it nearly impossible for contracting parties to predict "precisely or within a narrow range the amount of damages that would flow from breach." [Citation.] However, against this backdrop of uncertainty, the negotiated liquidated damages sum represents the parties' best estimate of the value of the breach and permits the parties to allocate and incorporate these risks in their negotiations. Under the prospective approach, a court will uphold the parties' agreed upon liquidated sum so long as the amount represents a reasonable attempt to compensate the nonbreaching party. On the other hand, if the reasonableness of a liquidated damages provision is evaluated under a retrospective approach, the parties cannot confidently rely on their agreement because the liquidated sum will not be enforced if, at trial, it is not a close approximation of the damage suffered or if no actual damages are proved.

Having adopted the date of contract formation as the proper timeframe for evaluating the Restatement test, the Restatement's second requirement loses independent significance. The central inquiry is whether the specified liquidated damages were reasonable at the time of contract formation. The reasonableness of liquidated damages is not determined retroactively by their correspondence with actual damages, but by reference to the prospective difficulty of estimating the possible damages that would flow from a breach. The prospective difficulty of estimating possible damages is merely an element of the court's inquiry into the reasonableness of a liquidated damages provision. The greater the prospective difficulty of estimating possible damages, the greater the range of reasonableness used in assessing a liquidated damages provision. See [citation];

Restatement (Second) of Contracts § 356, cmt. b, at 157 (1981) (the greater the difficulty of establishing the amount of loss, the easier it is to show a liquidated damages provision is reasonable).

We also agree with the Court of Appeals that in the context of real estate agreements, a requirement that damages be difficult to prove at trial would undermine the very purposes of the liquidated damage provision: "certainty, assurance that the contract will be performed, and avoidance of litigation." [Citation.] It would "encourage litigation in virtually every case in which the sale did not close, regardless of whether the earnest money deposit was a reasonable estimate of the seller's damages." [Citation.]

In sum, so long as the agreed upon earnest money agreement, viewed prospectively, is a reasonable prediction of potential damage suffered by the seller, the agreement should be enforced "without regard to the retrospective calculation of actual damages or the ease with which they may be proved." [Citation.] The prospective difficulty of estimating potential damage is a factor to be used in assessing the reasonableness of the earnest money agreement.

Applying this reasonableness test prospectively to the Watson-Ingram agreement, we find the liquidated damages clause valid and enforceable. First, evaluating the agreement as of the time of contract formation, we find the liquidated sum was a reasonable forecast of just compensation for the harm that is caused by the breach.

[Citation.] The $15,000 earnest money deposit represented several variables, including the value of the improvements Ingram was required to make under the contract, fluctuations in the real estate market, and lost value of the use of the net sale proceeds prior to the eventual sale of the property. [Citation.] Each of these variables represents a significant potential loss to Ingram in the event of a breach by Watson. In addition, Ingram was specifically interested in a quick sale because he was attempting to relocate to California as soon as possible. The liquidated sum may have, in part, reflected the personal cost to Ingram of a delay in the sale date. Under these circumstances we find $15,000 is not an unreasonable estimate of possible harm to Ingram in the event of a breach by Watson.

We likewise find Ingram's potential damages were difficult to ascertain at the time of contracting; the parties could not know what delays might ensue, what might occur in the real estate market, or how a failed sale might affect Ingram's plans. Real estate purchase and sales agreements are precisely the type of contracts that are amenable to liquidated damages provision.

Under these facts, we hold the $15,000 earnest money agreement was a reasonable estimate of Ingram's potential damages in the event of a breach. Because Ingram is the prevailing party on appeal, he is entitled to reasonable attorney fees and costs pursuant to the parties' agreement.

The decision of the Court of Appeals is affirmed.

---

## CASE 18–2
### Specific Performance
# *TAMARIND LITHOGRAPHY WORKSHOP v. SANDERS*

Court of Appeal of California, Second District, 1983
143 Cal.App.3d 571, 193 Cal.Rptr. 409

STEPHENS, J.
The essence of this appeal concerns the question of whether an award of damages is an adequate remedy at law in lieu of specific performance for the breach of an agreement to give screen credits. Our saga traces its origin to March of 1969, at which time appellant, and cross-complainant below, Terry Sanders (hereinafter "Sanders" or "appellant"), agreed in writing to write, direct and produce a motion picture on the subject of lithography for respondent, Tamarind Lithography Workshop, Inc. (hereinafter referred to as "Tamarind" or "respondent").

Pursuant to the terms of the agreement, the film was shot during the summer of 1969, wherein Sanders directed the film according to an outline/treatment of his authorship, and acted as production manager by personally hiring and supervising personnel comprising the film crew. Additionally, Sanders exercised both artistic control over the mixing of the sound track and overall editing of the picture.

After completion, the film, now titled the "Four Stones for Kanemitsu," was screened by Tamarind at its tenth anniversary celebration on April 28, 1970. Thereafter, a dispute arose between the parties concerning their respective rights and obligations under the original 1969 agreement. Litigation ensued and in January 1973 the matter went to trial. Prior to the entry of judgment, the parties entered into a written settlement agreement, which became the premise for the instant action. Specifically, this April 30, 1973, agreement provided that Sanders would be entitled to a screen credit entitled "A Film by Terry Sanders."

Tamarind did not comply with its expressed obligation pursuant to that agreement, in that it failed to include Sanders' screen credits in the prints it distributed. As a result a situation developed wherein Tamarind and co-defendant Wayne filed suit for declaratory relief, damages due to breach of contract, emotional distress, defamation and fraud.

Sanders cross-complained, seeking damages for Tamarind's breach of contract, declaratory relief, specific performance of the contract to give Sanders screen credits, and defamation. Both causes were consolidated and brought to trial on May 31, 1977. A jury was impaneled for purposes of determining damage issues and decided that Tamarind had breached the agreement and awarded Sanders $25,000 in damages.

The remaining claims for declaratory and injunctive relief were tried by the court. The court made findings that Tamarind had sole ownership rights in the film, that "both June Wayne and Terry Sanders were each creative producers of the film, that Sanders shall have the right to modify the prints in his personal possession to include his credits." All other prayers for relief were denied.

It is from the denial of appellant's request for specific performance upon which appellant predicates this appeal.

* * *

The availability of the remedy of specific performance is premised upon well established requisites. These requisites include: A showing by plaintiff of (1) the inadequacy of his legal remedy; (2) an underlying contract that is both reasonable and supported by adequate consideration; (3) the existence of a mutuality of remedies; (4) contractual terms which are sufficiently definite to enable the court to know what it is to enforce; and (5) a substantial similarity of the requested performance to that promised in the contract. [Citation.]

It is manifest that the legal remedies available to Sanders for harm resulting from the future exhibition of the film are inadequate as a matter of law. The primary reasons are twofold: (1) that an accurate assessment of damages would be far too difficult and require much speculation, and (2) that any future exhibitions might be deemed to be a continuous breach of contract and thereby create the danger of an untold number of lawsuits.

There is no doubt that the exhibition of a film, which is favorably received by its critics and the public at large, can result in valuable advertising or publicity for the artists responsible for that film's making. Likewise, it is unquestionable that the nonappearance of an artist's name or likeness in the form of screen credit on a successful film can result in a loss of that valuable publicity. However, whether that loss of publicity is measurable dollarwise is quite another matter.

By its very nature, public acclaim is unique and very difficult, if not sometimes impossible, to quantify in monetary terms. Indeed, courts confronted with the dilemma of estimating damages in this area have been less than uniform in their disposition of same. Nevertheless, it is clear that any award of damages for the loss of publicity is contingent upon those damages being reasonably certain, specific, and unspeculative. [Citation.]

* * *

Accordingly, where the jury in the matter sub judice was fully apprised of the favorable recognition Sanders' film received from the Academy of Motion Picture Arts and Sciences, the Los Angeles International Film Festival, and public television, and further, where they were made privy to an assessment of the value of said exposure by three experts, it was reasonable for the jury to award monetary damages for that ascertainable loss of publicity. However, pecuniary compensation for Sanders' future harm is not a fully adequate remedy. [Citation.]

We return to the remaining requisites for Sanders' entitlement to specific performance. The need for our finding the contract to be reasonable and supported by adequate consideration is obviated by the jury's determination of respondent's breach of that contract. The requisite of mutuality of remedy has been satisfied in that Sanders had fully performed his obligations pursuant to the agreement (i.e., release of all claims of copyright to the film and dismissal of his then pending action against respondents). [Citation.] Similarly, we find the terms of the agreement sufficiently definite to permit enforcement of the respondent's performance as promised.

In the present case it should be obvious that specific performance through injunctive relief can remedy the dilemma posed by the somewhat ambiguous jury verdict. The injunction disposes of the problem of future damages, in that full compliance by Tamarind moots the issue. Of course, violation of the injunction by Tamarind would raise new problems, but the court has numerous options for dealing with the situation and should choose the one best suited to the particular violation.

In conclusion, the record shows that the appellant is entitled to relief consisting of the damages recovered, and an injunction against future injury.

---

## CASE 18–3
### Injunctions
# MADISON SQUARE GARDEN CORP., ILL. v. CARNERA
United States Court of Appeals, Second Circuit, 1931
52 F.2d 47

**CHASE, J.**
Suit by plaintiff, Madison Square Garden Corporation, against Primo Carnera, defendant. From an order granting an injunction against defendant, defendant appeals.

On January 13, 1931, the plaintiff and defendant by their duly authorized agents entered into the following agreement in writing:

1. Carnera agrees that he will render services as a boxer in his next contest (which contest, hereinafter called the "First Contest," shall be with the winner of the proposed Schmeling-Stribling contest, or, if the same is drawn, shall be with Schmeling, and shall be deemed to be a contest for the heavyweight championship title; provided, however, that, in the event of the inability of the Garden to cause Schmeling or Stribling, as the case may be, to perform the terms of his agreement with the Garden calling for such contest, the Garden shall be without further liability to Carnera) exclusively under the auspices of the Garden, in the United States of America, or the Dominion of Canada, at such time, not, however, later than midnight of September 30, 1931, as the Garden may direct. . . .

9. Carnera shall not, pending the holding of the First Contest, render services as a boxer in any major boxing contest, without the written permission of the Garden in each case had and obtained. A major contest is understood to be one with Sharkey, Baer, Campolo, Godfrey, or like grade heavyweights, or heavyweights who shall have beaten any of the above subsequent to the date hereof. If in any boxing contest engaged in by Carnera prior to the holding of the First Contest, he shall lose the same, the Garden shall at its option, to be exercised by a two weeks' notice to Carnera in writing, be without further liability under the terms of this agreement to Carnera. Carnera shall not render services during the continuance of the option referred to in paragraph 8 hereof for any person, firm or corporation other than the Garden. Carnera shall, however, at all times be permitted to engage in sparring exhibitions in which no decision is rendered and in which the heavyweight championship

title is not at stake, and in which Carnera boxes not more than four rounds with any one opponent. . . .

Thereafter the defendant, without the permission of the plaintiff, written or otherwise, made a contract to engage in a boxing contest with the Sharkey mentioned in paragraph 9 of the agreement above quoted, and by the terms thereof the contest was to take place before the first contest mentioned in the defendant's contract with the plaintiff was to be held.

The plaintiff then brought this suit to restrain the defendant from carrying out his contract to box Sharkey, and obtained the preliminary injunction order, from which this appeal was taken. Jurisdiction is based on diversity of citizenship and the required amount is involved.

The District Court has found on affidavits which adequately show it that the defendant's services are unique and extraordinary. A negative covenant in a contract for such personal services is enforceable by injunction where the damages for a breach are incapable of ascertainment. [Citations.]

The defendant points to what is claimed to be lack of consideration for his negative promise, in that the contract is inequitable and contains no agreement to employ him. It is true that there is no promise in so many words to employ the defendant to box in a contest with Stribling or Schmeling, but the agreement read as a whole binds the plaintiff to do just that, providing either Stribling or Schmeling becomes the contestant as the result of the match between them and can be induced to box the defendant. The defendant has agreed to "render services as a boxer" for the plaintiff exclusively, and the plaintiff has agreed to pay him a definite percentage of the gate receipts as his compensation for so doing. The promise to employ the defendant to enable him to earn the compensation agreed upon is implied to the same force and effect as though expressly stated. . . . [Citations.]

As we have seen, the contract is valid and enforceable. It contains a restrictive covenant which may be given effect. Whether a preliminary injunction shall be issued under such circumstances rests in the sound discretion of the court. [Citations.] The District Court, in its discretion, did issue the preliminary injunction and required the plaintiff as a condition upon its issuance to secure its own performance of the contract in suit with a bond for $25,000 and to give a bond in the sum of $35,000 to pay the defendant such damages as he may sustain by reason of the injunction. Such an order is clearly not an abuse of discretion.

Order affirmed.

---

## CASE 18–4
### Election of Remedies
### HEAD & SEEMANN, INC. v. GREGG
Court of Appeals of Wisconsin, 1981
104 Wis.2d 156, 311 N.W.2d 667

**Voss, P. J.**

Bettye Gregg fraudulently induced Head & Seemann, Inc. to sell her a home in Brookfield. She occupied the home for five months but was subsequently ejected by a court order. In the action on the claim from which this appeal comes, Head & Seemann sought damages for the five months lost use of the property. At issue was whether a defrauded party who obtains rescission and restitution of real estate may also recover rental value and out-of-pocket expenses for the period of lost possession. The trial court held that the election of remedies doctrine barred an additional action for rental value and out-of-pocket expenses. Because we do not believe that rescission and an action for damages are inconsistent remedies, we reverse.

Defendant Bettye J. Gregg offered to buy a Brookfield home from plaintiff corporation. She represented, verbally and in writing, that she had $15,000 to $20,000 of equity in another home and would pay this amount to plaintiff after selling the other home. She knew, however, that she had no such equity. Relying on these intentionally fraudulent representations, plaintiff accepted defendant's offer to buy, and the parties entered into a land contract. After taking occupancy, defendant failed to make any of the contract payments. Plaintiff's investigation then revealed the fraud.

* * *

Plaintiff contends that it is entitled to recover for the lost use of the property and out-of-pocket expenses during defendant's possession of the property. It contends that recovery for these items, in addition to the rescission and return of the real estate, is necessary to restore plaintiff to his status before the fraud and execution of the contract. Since these "damages" would only restore plaintiff to its previous position and would not give plaintiff the purchase price or the benefit of the bargain, plaintiff argues that the remedies are not inconsistent, and the doctrine of election of remedies should not be applied. We agree.

The election of remedies doctrine is an equitable principle barring one from maintaining inconsistent theories or forms of relief. [Citation.] Its underlying purpose is to prevent double recovery for the same wrong. [Citations.] * * *

The classic application of the election of remedies doctrine is that a defrauded party has the election of either rescission or affirming the contract and seeking damages. [Citation.] The choice is forced with respect to alternative theories in a single lawsuit because of inconsistency of both rescinding and affirming the contract. [Citation.]

Thus, it superficially appears that if a claimant chooses to seek rescission, he may not sue for damages. But the word "damages," like the label "election of remedies," impedes rather than aids the inquiry into the types of relief appropriate in a given case. Rescission is always coupled with restitution: the parties return the money, property or other benefits so as to restore each other to the position they were in prior to the transaction. In the case of fraud or misrepresentation, the victim has the priority of restoration, and if a loss must be borne, the wrongdoer bears it. [Citation.]

This case presents a crucial question dealing with the nature of restitution. At issue is whether restitution to a rescinding fraud victim includes everything he has reasonably paid out or given up in the transaction or only includes what the other party has actually received.

* * *

Many . . . cases recognize that "disaffirmance" of damages [rescission] only rules out "expectation" damages—the benefit of the bargain—and distinguish restitutionary "damages."

Damages for restitution are different from damages for breach of contract; and the former are permissible to restore the plaintiff to his former position when rescission is granted because of fraud. [Citation.] Several other states allow the recovery of restitutionary damages along with rescission when fraud or misrepresentation is the cause of the claim. [Citations.] We believe that restitutionary damages conform with the purpose of rescission, which is to put the defrauded party back in as good a position as he occupied before entering the contract. Consequently, we hold that such damages may be awarded along with rescission.

[Citation.] In equity, the court makes the calculated adjustments necessary to do complete justice. If complete justice requires that damages be awarded with the rescission, the court will award them. [Citations.]

Two clear forms of restitutionary awards are recoverable when coupled with rescission: The first is "reasonable expenditures in reliance on the bargain."

[Citations.] The second is the rent or use value of the real estate during the other's possession. [Citations.]

Even in situations where the buyer is defrauded and entitled to the rescission, he or she must ordinarily pay rental value to the seller. This provides *a fortiori* support for the above authorities. [Citations.]

In the instant case, plaintiff seeks rental value and incidental expenses as part of restitution, items clearly recoverable under the great weight of authority. We believe that [citation] recognized the position that rescission and restorative damages are consistent remedies which work together to restore the injured party to his precontract position. For this reason, restorative damages, which in this case is rent, should be allowed in addition to rescission. The two are not inconsistent remedies.

Order reversed.

---

# Questions

1.  Explain how compensatory and reliance damages are computed.
2.  Define
    (a)  nominal damages,
    (b)  incidental damages,
    (c)  consequential damages,
    (d)  foreseeability of damages,
    (e)  punitive damages,
    (f)  liquidated damages, and
    (g)  mitigation of damages.

3.  Define the various types of equitable relief and discuss when the courts will grant such relief.
4.  Explain how restitutionary damages are computed and identify the situations in which restitution is available as a contractual remedy.
5.  Identify and explain the limitations on contractual remedies.

---

# Problems

1.  Edward contracted to buy 1,000 barrels of sugar from Marcia. Marcia failed to deliver, and because Edward could not buy any sugar in the market, he was compelled to shut down his candy factory.
    (a)    What damages is Edward entitled to recover?
    (b)    Would it make any difference if Edward had told Marcia that he wanted the sugar to make candies for the Christmas trade and that he had accepted contracts for delivery by certain dates?
2.  Daniel agreed to erect an apartment building for Steven for $2 million and that Daniel would suffer a deduction of $2,000 per day for every day of delay. Daniel was twenty days late in finishing the job, losing ten days because of a strike and ten days because the material suppliers were late in furnishing materials. Daniel claims that he is entitled to payment in full

(a) because the agreement as to $2,000 a day is a penalty and (b) because Steven has not shown that he has sustained any damage. Discuss each contention and decide.
3.  Sharon contracted with Jane, a shirtmaker, for 1,000 shirts for men. Jane manufactured and delivered 500 shirts, which were paid for by Sharon. At the same time, Sharon notified Jane that she could not use or dispose of the other 500 shirts and directed Jane not to manufacture any more under the contract. Nevertheless, Jane proceeded to make up the other 500 shirts and tendered them to Sharon. Sharon refused to accept the shirts, and Jane then sued for the purchase price. Decision?
4.  Stuart contracts to act in a comedy for Charlotte and to comply with all theater regulations for four seasons. Charlotte promises to pay Stuart $800 for each performance and to allow

Stuart one benefit performance each season. It is expressly agreed that "Stuart shall not be employed in any other production for the period of the contract." During the first year of the contract, Stuart and Charlotte have a terrible quarrel. Thereafter, Stuart signs a contract to perform in Elaine's production and ceases performing for Charlotte. Charlotte seeks (a) to prevent Stuart from performing for Elaine and (b) to require Stuart to perform his contract with Charlotte. What result?

5.   Louis leased a building to Pam for five years at a rental of $1,000 per month, commencing July 1, 1995, Pam depositing $10,000 as security for performance of all her promises in the lease, which was to be retained by Louis in case of any breach on Pam's part, otherwise to be applied in payment of rent for the last ten months of the term of the lease. Pam defaulted in the payment of rent for the months of May and June 2000. After proper notice to Pam of the termination of the lease for nonpayment of rent, Louis sued Pam for possession of the building and recovered a judgment for possession. Thereafter, Pam sued Louis to recover the $10,000 less the amount of rent due Louis for May and June 2000. Decision?

6.   (a)   Mary and Anne enter into a written agreement under which Mary agrees to sell and Anne agrees to buy for $10 per share 100 shares of the 300 shares outstanding of the capital stock of the Infinitesimal Steel Corporation, whose shares are not listed on any exchange and are closely held. Mary refuses to deliver when tendered the $1,000, and Anne sues in equity for specific performance, tendering the $1,000. Decision?

(b)   Modifying (a) above, assume that the subject matter of the agreement is stock of the United States Steel Corporation, which is traded on the New York Stock Exchange. Decision?

(c)   Modifying (a) above, assume that the subject matter of the agreement is undeveloped farmland of little commercial value. Decision?

7.   On March 1, Joseph sold to Sandra fifty acres of land in Oregon, which Joseph at the time represented to be fine black loam, high, dry, and free of stumps. Sandra paid Joseph the agreed price of $40,000 and took from him a deed to the land. Subsequently discovering that the land was low, swampy, and not entirely free of stumps, Sandra nevertheless undertook to convert the greater part of the land into cranberry bogs. After one year of cranberry culture, Sandra became entirely dissatisfied, tendered the land back to Joseph, and demanded from Joseph the return of the $40,000. Upon Joseph's refusal to repay the money, Sandra brings an action against him to recover the $40,000. What judgment?

8.   James contracts to make repairs to Betty's building in return for Betty's promise to pay $12,000 upon completion of the repairs. After partially completing the repairs, James is unable to continue. Betty hires another builder, who completes the repairs for $5,000. The building's value to Betty has increased by $10,000 as a result of the repairs by James, but Betty has lost $500 in rents because of the delay caused by

James's breach. James sues Betty. How much, if any, may James recover in restitution from Betty?

9.   Linda induced Sally to enter into a purchase of a stereo amplifier by intentionally misrepresenting the power output to be sixty watts at rated distortion when in fact the unit delivered only twenty watts. Sally paid $450 for the amplifier. Amplifiers producing twenty watts generally sell for $200, whereas amplifiers producing sixty watts generally sell for $550. Sally decides to keep the amplifier and sue for damages. How much may Sally recover in damages from Linda?

10.   Virginia induced Charles to sell his boat to her by misrepresentation of material fact upon which Charles reasonably relied. Virginia promptly sold the boat to Donald, who paid fair value for it and knew nothing concerning the transaction between Virginia and Charles. Upon discovering the misrepresentation, Charles seeks to recover the boat. What are Charles's rights against Virginia and Donald?

11.   Felch was employed as a member of the faculty of Findlay College on a continuing basis. He was dismissed by action of the president and board of trustees, who did not comply with a contractual provision for dismissal that requires a hearing. Felch requested the court to enjoin Findlay College to continue Felch as a member of the faculty and to pay him the salary agreed upon. Decision?

12.   Copenhaver, the owner of a laundry business, contracted with Berryman, the owner of a large apartment complex, to allow Copenhaver to own and operate the laundry facilities within the apartment complex. Berryman subsequently terminated the five-year contract with Copenhaver with forty-seven months remaining. Within six months, Copenhaver placed the equipment into use in other locations. He then filed suit, claiming that he was entitled to conduct the laundry operations for an additional forty-seven months and that through such operations he would have earned a profit of $13,886.58, after deducting Berryman's share of the gross receipts and other operating expenses. Decision?

13.   Billy Williams Builders and Developers (Williams) entered into a contract with Hillerich under which Williams agreed to sell to Hillerich a certain lot and to construct on it a house according to submitted plans and specifications. The house built by Williams was defectively constructed. Hillerich brought suit for specific performance of the contract and for damages resulting from the defective construction and delay in performance. Williams argued that Hillerich was not entitled to have both specific performance and damages for breach of the contract because the remedies were inconsistent and Hillerich had to elect one or the other. Decision?

14.   Developers under a plan approved by the city of Rye had constructed six luxury cooperative apartment buildings and were to construct six more. In order to obtain certificates of occupancy for the six completed buildings, the developers were required to post a bond with the city to ensure completion of the remaining buildings. The developers posted a $100,000 bond upon which the defendant, Public Service Mutual Insurance Company, as guarantor or surety, agreed to pay $200 for

each day after April 1, 1971, that the remaining buildings were not completed. Following the April deadline, more than 500 days passed without completion of the buildings. The city sued the developers and the insurance company to recover $100,000 on the bond. Decision?

15. Kerr Steamship Company sent a telegram to the Philippines through the Radio Corporation of America. The telegram, which contained instructions for loading cargo on one of Kerr's ships, was mislaid and never delivered. Consequently, the ship was improperly loaded and the cargo was lost. Kerr sued the Radio Corporation for $6,675.29 in profits lost on the cargo because of the Radio Corporation's failure to deliver the telegram. Decision?

16. El Dorado Tire Company fired Bill Ballard, a sales executive. Ballard had a five-year contract with El Dorado but was fired after only two years of employment. Ballard sued El Dorado for breach of contract. El Dorado claims that any damages due to breach of the contract should be mitigated because of Ballard's failure to seek other employment after he was fired. Decision?

17. California and Hawaiian Sugar Company (C and H) is an agricultural cooperative in the business of growing sugarcane in Hawaii and transporting the raw sugar to its refinery in California for processing. Because of the seasonal nature of the sugarcane crop, availability of ships to transport the raw sugar immediately after harvest is imperative. In 1979, C and H lost the services of the shipping company it previously used. To fill the void, C and H decided to build its own ship, a Macababoo, which had two components, a tug and a barge. C and H contracted with Halter Marine to build the tug and with Sun Ship to build the barge. In finalizing the contract for construction of the barge, both C and H and Sun Ship were represented by senior management and by legal counsel. The resulting contract called for a liquidated damages payment of $17,000 per day that delivery of the completed barge was delayed. Delivery of both the barge and the tug were significantly delayed. Sun Ship paid the $17,000 per day liquidated damages amount and then sued to recover it, claiming that without the liquidated damages provision, C and H's legal remedy for money damages would have been significantly less than that paid by Sun Ship pursuant to the liquidated damages provision. The trial court found in favor of C and H, upholding the validity of the liquidated damages provision. Sun Ship appealed, claiming that the liquidated damages provision was invalid as a penalty because Halter Marine was also significantly late in delivery of the tug, without which the barge was useless to C and H. Decision?

WWW **Internet Exercise** Compare the provisions governing remedies for breach of contract contained in the Principles of European Contract Law with the provisions of the U.S. common law.

# CHAPTER 19

# Relationship of Principal and Agent

By using agents, one person (the principal) may enter into any number of business transactions as though he had personally carried them out, thus multiplying and expanding his business activities. The law of agency, like the law of contracts, is basic to almost every other branch of business law. Practically every type of contract or business transaction can be created or conducted through an agent. Therefore, the place and importance of agency in the practical conduct and operation of business cannot be overemphasized.

This is particularly true in the case of partnerships and corporations. Partnership is founded on the agency of the partners. Each partner is an agent of the partnership and, as such, has the authority to represent and bind the partnership in all usual transactions pertaining to the partnership's business. A corporation, being an artificial legal entity, must function through the agency of its officers and employees. Thus, practically and legally, agency is an integral part of partnerships and corporations. In addition, sole proprietors also may employ agents in the operations of their business. Business, therefore, is very largely conducted not by owners themselves but by their representatives or agents.

The law of agency divides broadly into two main and somewhat overlapping parts: the internal and the external. An agent functions as an agent by dealing with third persons, thereby establishing legal relations between the principal and those third persons. These relations, which constitute the external part of agency law, are discussed in the next chapter. This chapter will cover the internal relationship between principal and agent, including the nature of agency, the creation of an agency, the duties of agent to principal, the duties of principal to agent, and the termination of agency.

Agency is primarily governed by State common law. An orderly presentation of this law is found in the Restatement of the Law of Agency. Regarded as a valuable authoritative reference work, the Restatement is extensively cited and quoted in reported judicial opinions.

## NATURE OF AGENCY

**Agency** is a relationship between two persons, known as principal and agent, through which the agent is authorized to act for and on behalf of the principal. Restatement, Section 1. An agent, therefore, is one who represents another, the principal, in business dealings with a third person; the operation of agency therefore involves three persons: the principal, the agent, and a third person. In dealing with a third person, the agent acts for and in the name and place of the principal, who, along with the third person, is, if properly entered into, a party to the transaction, which is usually contractual. When the agent is dealing with the third person, the principal, in legal effect, is present in the person of the agent; and the result of the agent's functioning is exactly the same as if the principal had dealt directly with the third person. If, moreover, the existence and identity of the principal are disclosed, the agent acts not as a party but simply as an intermediary.

Within the scope of the authority granted to her by her principal, the agent may negotiate the terms of contracts with others and bind her principal to such contracts. In addition, the negligence of an agent who is an employee in conducting the business of her principal exposes the principal to tort liability for injury and loss suffered by third persons. The old maxim *"Qui facit per alium, facit per se"* (Who acts through another, acts himself) accurately describes the relationship between principal and agent. The rights and liabilities of the parties where an agent enters into a contract with a third party or commits a tort against a third party are discussed in the next chapter.

### Scope of Agency Purposes

As a general rule, a person may do through an agent whatever business activity he may accomplish personally.

Conversely, whatever he cannot legally do himself, he cannot authorize another to do for him. Thus, a person may not validly authorize another to commit an illegal act or crime. Any such agreement is illegal and therefore unenforceable. Restatement, Section 19. Also, a person may not appoint an agent to perform acts that are so personal that their performance may not be delegated to another, as in the case of a contract for personal services. Restatement, Section 17. For example, Howard, a painter, contracts to paint a portrait of Doris. But Howard has one of his students execute the painting and tenders it to Doris. This is not a valid tender because the duty to paint Doris's portrait is not delegable.

## Other Legal Relations

Two other legal relationships overlap with agency: employer-employee and principal-independent contractor. In the **employment relationship** (historically referred to as the master-servant relationship), the employer has the right to *control* the physical conduct of the employee. Restatement, Section 2. In contrast, a person who engages an **independent contractor** to do a specific job does not have the right to control the conduct and activities of the independent contractor in the performance of his contract. Restatement, Section 2(3). The latter simply contracts to do a job and is free to choose the method and manner in which to perform it. For example, a full-time chauffeur is an employee, whereas a taxicab driver hired to carry a person to the airport is an independent contractor engaged by the passenger.

In determining whether a person acting for another is an employee or an independent contractor, the courts consider several factors listed in Section 220 of the Restatement:

(a) the extent of control which, by the agreement, the master may exercise over the details of the work;
(b) whether or not the one employed is engaged in a distinct occupation or business;
(c) the kind of occupation, with reference to whether, in the locality, the work is usually done under the direction of the employer or by a specialist without supervision;
(d) the skill required in the particular occupation;
(e) whether the employer or the workman supplies the instrumentalities, tools, and the place of work for the person doing the work;
(f) the length of time for which the person is employed;
(g) the method of payment, whether by the time or by the job;

(h) whether or not the work is a part of the regular business of the employer;
(i) whether or not the parties believe they are creating the relation of master and servant; and
(j) whether the principal is or is not in business.

Although all employees are agents, not all agents are employees. Agents who are not employees are independent contractors. For instance, an attorney retained to handle a particular transaction would be an independent contractor-agent regarding that particular transaction. Other examples are auctioneers, brokers, and factors. Finally, not all independent contractors are agents. For example, the taxicab driver in the example above is not an agent. Likewise, if Pam hires Bill to build a stone wall around her property, Bill is an independent contractor who is not an agent.

The distinction between employee and independent contractor has several important legal consequences. For example, as discussed in the next chapter, a principal is liable for the torts committed by an employee within the scope of his employment but ordinarily is not liable for torts committed by an independent contractor. In addition, the obligations of a principal under numerous Federal and State statutes apply only to agents who are employees. Examples of these statutes are the Social Security Act, the National Labor Relations Act, and Workers' Compensation Acts. These and other statutory enactments affecting the employment relationship are discussed in Chapter 43.

*See Case 19–1*

## CREATION OF AGENCY

Agency is a **consensual** relationship that the principal and agent may form by contract *or* agreement. The Restatement provides that "[a]n agency relation exists only if there has been a manifestation by the principal to the agent that the agent may act on his account, and consent by the agent so to act." Section 15. Thus, whether an agency relationship has been created is determined by an *objective* test. If the principal requests another to act for him with respect to a matter and indicates that the other is to act without further communication, and the other consents to act, the relation of principal and agent exists. For example, Paula writes to Austin, a factor whose business is purchasing goods for others, telling him to select described goods and ship them at once to Paula. Before answering Paula's letter, Austin does as directed, charging the goods to Paula. He is authorized to do this because an agency relationship exists between Paula and Austin.

The relationship of principal and agent is consensual and not necessarily contractual; therefore, it may exist without consideration. Restatement, Section 16. An agency created without consideration is a **gratuitous agency.** The power of a gratuitous agent to affect the principal's relations with third persons is the same as that of a paid agent, and his liabilities to and rights against third persons also are the same. Nonetheless, agency by contract, the most usual method of creating the relationship, must satisfy all the requirements of a contract.

In some circumstances a person is held liable as a principal, even though no actual agency has been created. Called **agency by estoppel,** apparent agency, or ostensible agency, this liability arises when (1) a person (P) intentionally or negligently causes a belief that another person (A) has authority to act on P's behalf, (2) a third person (T) reasonably and in good faith relies on the appearances created by P, and (3) T changes her position in reliance on A's apparent authority. Restatement, Section 8B. When these requirements are met, P is liable to T for the loss T suffered by changing her position.

 *See Case 19–2*

## Formalities

As a general rule, a contract of agency requires no particular formality. Usually the contract is express or inferred from the conduct of the principal. In some cases, however, the contract must be in writing. For example, the appointment of an agent for a period of more than a year comes within the one-year clause of the statute of frauds and thus must be in writing to be enforceable. In some States, the authority of an agent to sell land must be stated in a writing signed by the principal.

A **power of attorney** is a formal appointment of an agent, who is known as an attorney in fact. Under a power of attorney, a principal may, for example, appoint an agent not only to execute a contract for the sale of the principal's real estate, but also to execute the deed conveying title to the real estate to the third party.

## Capacity

The capacity to be a principal, and thus to act through an agent, depends upon the capacity of the principal to do the act herself. For example, contracts entered into by a minor or an incompetent not under a guardianship are voidable. Consequently, the appointment of an agent by a minor or an incompetent not under a guardianship—and any resulting contracts—are voidable, regardless of the agent's contractual capacity.

Any person, including individuals, corporations, partnerships, and other associations, has the capacity to act as an agent. Restatement, Section 21. Because the act of the agent is considered the act of the principal, the incapacity of an agent to bind himself by contract does not disqualify him from making a contract that is binding on his principal. Although the contract of agency may be voidable, an authorized contract between the principal and the third person who dealt with the agent is valid. Nonetheless, some mental capacity is necessary in an agent; therefore, minors and mental incompetents may not have the capacity to act as agents in certain situations.

# DUTIES OF AGENT TO PRINCIPAL

As the principal-agent relationship ordinarily is created by contract, the duties of the agent to the principal are determined primarily by the provisions of the contract. In addition to these contractual duties, the agent is subject to various other duties imposed by law, unless the parties agree otherwise. Restatement, Section 376. Normally, a principal bases the selection of an agent on the agent's ability, skill, and integrity. Moreover, the principal not only authorizes and empowers the agent to bind him on contracts with third persons, but frequently places the agent in possession of his money and other property. As a result, the agent is in a position, either through negligence or dishonesty, to injure the principal. Accordingly, an agent as a **fiduciary** (a person in a position of trust and confidence) owes his principal the duties of obedience, diligence, and loyalty; the duty to inform; and the duty to provide an accounting. Moreover, the agent "is subject to liability for loss caused to the principal by any breach of duty." Restatement, Section 401.

A gratuitous agent is subject to the same duty of loyalty that is imposed upon a paid agent and is liable to the principal for the harm he causes by his careless performance. Although the lack of consideration usually places a gratuitous agent under no duty to perform for the principal, such an agent may be liable to the principal for failing to perform a promise on which the principal has relied.

## Duty of Obedience

The duty of obedience requires the agent to act in the principal's affairs only as authorized by the principal and to obey all reasonable instructions and directions of the principal. Restatement, Sections 383 and 385. An agent is not, however, under a duty to follow orders to perform illegal or unethical acts, such as misrepresenting the quality of his principal's goods or those of a competitor. Still, he may be subject to liability to his principal for breach of the duty of obedience (1) because he entered into an unauthorized contract for which his principal is liable, (2) because he has improperly delegated his authority, or (3) because he has committed a tort for which the principal is liable. Thus, an agent who sells on credit in violation of his principal's explicit instructions has breached the duty of obedience and is liable to the principal for any amounts the purchaser does not pay. Moreover, an agent who breaches his duty of obedience loses his right to compensation. Restatement, Section 469.

## Duty of Diligence

A paid agent must act with reasonable care and skill in performing the work for which she is employed. She must also exercise any special skill that she may have. Restatement, Section 379. By failing to exercise the required care and skill, she is liable to the principal for any resulting loss. For example, Peg appoints Alvin as her agent to sell goods in markets where the highest price can be obtained. Although by carefully obtaining information he could have obtained a higher price in a nearby market, Alvin sells goods in a glutted market, receiving only a low price. Consequently, he is liable to Peg for breach of the duty of diligence.

 *See Case 19–3*

## Duty to Inform

An agent must use reasonable efforts to provide the principal with information relevant to the affairs entrusted to her and that, as the agent knows or should know, the principal would desire to have. Restatement, Section 381. The rule of agency providing that notice to an agent is notice to his principal makes this duty imperative. Examples of information that an agent is under a duty to communicate to his principal include the following: that a customer of the principal has become insolvent; that a debtor of the principal has become insolvent; that a partner of a firm with which the principal has previously dealt, and with which the principal or agent is about to deal, has withdrawn from the firm; or that property which

the principal has authorized the agent to sell at a specified price can be sold at a higher price.

 *See Case 19–3*

## Duty to Account

The agent is under a duty to maintain and provide the principal with a true and complete account of money or other property that the agent has received or expended on the principal's behalf. Restatement, Section 382. An agent also must keep the principal's property separate from his own.

## Fiduciary Duty

A fiduciary duty arises out of a relationship of trust and confidence. A duty imposed by law, an agent owes it to his principal and an employee to his employer. A trustee also owes it to a beneficiary of a trust, an officer or director of a corporation to the corporation and its shareholders, and a lawyer to his clients. Fiduciary duties are not limited to these situations but exist in every relationship where the law authorizes one person to place trust and confidence in another.

The **fiduciary duty** is one of utmost loyalty and good faith. Although it occurs under many circumstances involving principals and their agents, the fiduciary duty arises most frequently in the following situations.

***Conflicts of Interest*** An agent must act solely in the interest of his principal, not in his own interest or in the interest of another. In addition, an agent may not represent his principal in any transaction in which the agent has a personal interest. Nor may he act on behalf of adverse parties to a transaction without both principals' approval to the dual agency. An agent may take a position that conflicts with the interest of his principal only if the principal, with full knowledge of all of the facts, consents. For example, A, an agent of P who desires to purchase land, agrees with C, who represents B, a seller of land, that A and C will endeavor to effect a transaction between their principals and will pool their commissions. A and C have committed a breach of fiduciary duty to P and B.

The courts closely scrutinize transactions between an agent and her principal. Because the agent may not deal at arm's length with her principal, she thus owes her principal a duty of full disclosure of all relevant facts that affect the transaction. Moreover, the transaction must be fair. Thus, an agent who is employed to buy may not buy from himself without the principal's consent.

Restatement, Section 389. For example, Penny employs Albert to purchase for her a site suitable for a shopping center. Albert owns such a site and sells it to Penny at the fair market value, but does not disclose to Penny that he had owned the land. Penny may rescind the transaction. An agent who is employed to sell may not become the purchaser nor may he act as agent for the purchaser without the consent of the principal. The agent's loyalty must be undivided, and he must devote his actions exclusively to represent and promote the interests of his principal.

*See Case 19–4*

***Duty Not to Compete*** An agent cannot compete with his principal or act on behalf of a competitor. After the agency terminates, however, unless otherwise agreed, the agent may compete with his former principal. The courts will enforce by injunction a contractual agreement by the agent not to compete after the agency terminates if the restriction is reasonable as to time and place and is necessary to protect the principal's legitimate interest. Contractual agreements not to compete are discussed in Chapter 13.

***Confidential Information*** An agent may not use or disclose confidential information obtained in the course of the agency for his own benefit or contrary to the interest of his principal. Confidential information is information that, if disclosed, would harm the principal's business or that has a value because it is not generally known. Such information includes unique business methods, trade secrets, business plans, and customer lists. An agent may, however, reveal confidential information that the principal is committing, or is about to commit, a crime.

Once the agency terminates, unless otherwise agreed, the agent may not use or disclose to third persons confidential information. The agent may, however, utilize the skills, knowledge, and general information she acquired during the agency relationship. Restatement, Section 396.

***Duty to Account for Financial Benefits*** Unless otherwise agreed, an agent is accountable to the principal for any financial benefit she has received as a direct result of transactions conducted on behalf of the principal. Such benefits would include bribes, kickbacks, and gifts. Moreover, an agent may not profit secretly from any transaction subject to the agency. All profits belong to the principal, to whom the agent must account. Thus, if an agent, authorized to sell certain property of his principal for $1,000, sells it for $1,500, he may not secretly pocket the additional $500. Further, suppose Peabody employs real estate broker Anderson to sell his land for a commission of 6 percent of the sale price. Anderson, knowing that Peabody is willing to sell for $20,000, agrees secretly with a prospective buyer who is willing to pay $22,000 for the land that he will endeavor to obtain Peabody's consent to sell for $20,000, in which event the buyer will pay Anderson $1,000, or one-half of the amount that the buyer believes she is saving on the price. The broker has violated his fiduciary duty and must pay to Peabody the secret profit of $1,000. Furthermore, Anderson loses the right to any commission on the transaction.

***Principal's Remedies*** An agent who violates his fiduciary duty is liable to his principal for breach of contract, in tort for losses caused, and in restitution for profits he made or property he received in breach of the fiduciary duty. Moreover, he loses the right to compensation. Restatement, Section 469. The principal may avoid a transaction in which the agent breached his fiduciary duty, even though the principal suffered no loss. A breach of fiduciary duty may also constitute just cause for discharge of the agent.

# DUTIES OF PRINCIPAL TO AGENT

Although both principal and agent have rights and duties arising out of the agency relationship, more emphasis is placed on the duties of the agent. This is necessarily so because of the nature of the agency relationship. First, the acts and services to be performed, both under the agency contract and as may be required by law, are to be performed mostly by the agent. Second, the agent is a fiduciary and as such is subject to the duties discussed earlier. Nonetheless, an agent has certain rights against the principal, both under the contract and by the operation of law. Correlative to these rights are certain duties, based in contract and tort law, that the principal owes to the agent.

◆ *See Figure 19–1*

## Contractual Duties

The contractual duties owed by a principal to an agent are the duties of compensation, reimbursement, and indemnification; each may be excluded or modified by agreement between the principal and agent. Although a

FIGURE 19–1 Duties of Principal and Agent

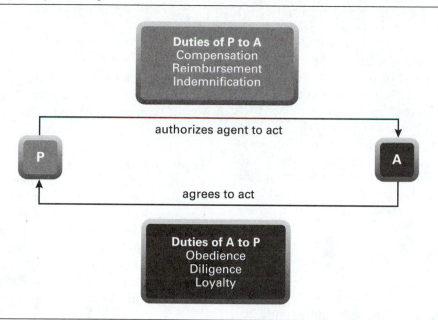

gratuitous agent is not owed a duty of compensation, she is entitled to reimbursement and indemnification.

As with any party to a contract, a principal is under a duty to perform his part of the contract according to its terms. The most important duty of the principal, from the standpoint of the agent, is to compensate the agent as specified in the contract. It is also the duty of the principal not to terminate the agency wrongfully. Whether the principal must furnish the agent with the means of employment or the opportunity for work will depend upon the particular case. For example, a principal who employs an agent to sell his goods must supply the agent with conforming goods, whereas in other cases, the agent must create his own opportunity for work, as in the case of a broker employed to procure a buyer for his principal's house. How far, if at all, the principal must assist or cooperate with the agent will depend on the particular agency. Usually, cooperation on the part of the principal is more necessary where the agent's compensation is contingent upon the success of his efforts than where the agent is paid a fixed salary regularly over a period of permanent employment.

*Compensation* A principal has a duty to compensate her agent unless the agent has agreed to serve gratuitously. If the agreement does not specify a definite compensation, a principal is under a duty to pay the reasonable value of the authorized services her agent has performed. Restatement, Section 443. An agent loses the right to compensation by (1) breaching the duty of obedience, (2) breaching the duty of loyalty, or (3) willfully and deliberately breaching the agency contract. Furthermore, an agent whose compensation depends upon her accomplishing a specific result is entitled to the agreed compensation only if she achieves the result within the time specified or within a reasonable time, if no time is stated. A common example is a listing agreement between a seller and a real estate broker providing for a commission to the broker if he finds a buyer ready, willing, and able to buy the property on the terms specified in the agreement. A principal also has a duty to maintain and provide to the agent a true and complete account of the money or property due to her.

*Reimbursement* A principal is under a duty to reimburse his agent for authorized payments the agent makes on the principal's behalf and for authorized expenses the agent incurs. Restatement, Section 438. For example, an agent who reasonably and properly pays a fire insurance premium for the protection of her principal's property is entitled to reimbursement for the payment. "The authority to pay money to third persons on account of the principal or to incur liabilities in the course of the principal's business may be created by specific directions or may be the result of the course of business between the principal and the agent, or of the customs of the business in which the agent is engaged for the principal." Section 439, Comment c.

***Indemnification*** The principal is under a duty to indemnify the agent for losses the agent incurred or suffered while acting as directed by the principal in a transaction that is neither illegal nor known by the agent to be wrongful. Restatement, Sections 438 and 439. To indemnify is to make good or pay a loss. Suppose that Perry, the principal, has in his possession goods belonging to Margot. Perry directs Alma, his agent, to sell these goods. Alma, believing Perry to be the owner, sells the goods to Turner. Margot then sues Alma for the conversion of her goods and recovers a judgment, which Alma pays to Margot. Alma is entitled to payment from Perry for her loss, including the amount she reasonably expended in defense of the action brought by Margot.

 *See Case 19–3*

## Tort Duties

A principal owes to any agent the same duties under tort law that the principal owes to all parties. Restatement, Section 470. Moreover, a principal is under a duty to disclose to an agent risks of which the principal knows or should know, if the principal should realize that the agent is unaware of such risks in the agency. For instance, in directing his agent to collect rent from a tenant who is known to have assaulted rent collectors, the principal has a duty to warn the agent of the risk involved.

Where the agent is an employee, the principal owes the agent additional duties. Among these is the duty to provide reasonably safe conditions of employment and to warn the employee of any unreasonable risk involved in the employment. An employer is also liable to her employees for injury caused by the negligence of other employees and of other agents doing work for her. The tort duties an employer owes to an employee are discussed more fully in Chapter 43.

## TERMINATION OF AGENCY

Because the authority of an agent is based upon the consent of the principal, the agency is terminated when such consent is withdrawn or otherwise ceases to exist. Upon termination of the agency, the agent's actual authority ends; and he is not entitled to compensation for services subsequently rendered, although his fiduciary duties may continue. As discussed in the next chapter, in some situations apparent authority also terminates, whereas in others apparent authority continues until a third party has knowledge or notice of the termination

of agency. Termination may take place by the acts of the parties or by operation of law.

## Acts of the Parties

Termination by the acts of the parties may occur by the provisions of the original agreement, by the subsequent acts of both principal and agent, or by the subsequent act of either one of them.

***Lapse of Time*** Authority conferred upon an agent for a specified time terminates when that period expires. If no time is specified, authority terminates at the end of a reasonable period. Restatement, Section 105. For example, Palmer authorizes Avery to sell a tract of land for him. After ten years pass without communication between Palmer and Avery, though Avery purports to have sold the tract, his authorization has terminated due to lapse of time.

***Fulfillment of Purpose*** The authority of an agent to perform a specific act or to accomplish a particular result terminates when the agent performs the act or accomplishes the result. Restatement, Section 106. Thus, if Porter authorizes Alford to sell or lease Alford's land, Alford's authority terminates when he leases the land to Taft; he may not thereafter sell or lease the land without receiving new authorization.

***Mutual Agreement of the Parties*** The agency relationship is created by agreement and may be terminated at any time by mutual agreement of the principal and the agent.

***Revocation of Authority*** A principal may revoke an agent's authority at any time. Restatement, Section 119. If, however, such revocation constitutes a breach of contract, the agent may recover damages from the principal. For example, Patrick, in consideration of Alice's agreement to advertise and give her best energies to the sale of Patrick's property, Blackacre, grants to Alice "a power of attorney, irrevocable for one year." Alice advertises and spends time trying to sell Blackacre. At the end of three months, Patrick informs Alice that he is revoking the power of attorney. Although her authority is terminated, Alice may recover damages from Patrick. Restatement, Section 118, Illustration 1. Nonetheless, where the agent has seriously breached the agency contract, willfully disobeyed, or violated the fiduciary duty, the principal is not liable for revocation. In addition, a principal ordinarily may revoke a gratuitous agency without liability to the agent.

 *See Case 19–5*

**Renunciation by the Agent** The agent also has the power to end the agency by notice to the principal that she renounces the authority given her. If the parties have contracted for the agency to continue for a specified time, an unjustified renunciation prior to the expiration of that time is a breach of contract. If the agency is gratuitous, however, the agent ordinarily may renounce it without liability to the principal.

## Operation of Law

The occurrence of certain events will automatically terminate an agency relationship by the operation of law. These events either make it impossible for the agent to perform or unlikely that the principal would want the agent to act. As a matter of law, the occurrence of any of the following events ordinarily terminates agency.

**Bankruptcy** Bankruptcy is a Federal court proceeding that affords relief to financially troubled debtors. The filing of a petition in bankruptcy, which initiates the proceedings, usually terminates all the debtor's existing agency relationships. The trustee in bankruptcy, however, may assume an executory contract of agency unless under State law the contract is not assignable. If the credit standing of the agent is important to the agency relationship, the relationship will terminate upon the bankruptcy of the agent. Restatement, Section 113. Thus, Arnold is appointed by Pacific Securities, Inc., an investment house, to act as its agent in advising Pacific's local clients as to investments. When Arnold becomes bankrupt, he is no longer authorized to act for Pacific.

**Death** The death of the principal terminates the authority of the agent. For example, Polk employs Allison to sell Polk's line of goods under a contract specifying Allison's commission and the one-year period for which the employment is to continue. When, without Allison's knowledge, Polk dies, Allison no longer has authority to sell Polk's goods, even though the contract specified that she would be employed for one year. The death of Polk, the principal, terminated the authority of the agent and voided the contract. Similarly, the authority given to an agent by a principal is strictly personal, and the agent's death terminates the agency.

**Incapacity** Incapacity of the principal that occurs after the formation of the agency terminates the agent's authority. To illustrate, Powell authorizes Anna to sell in the next ten months an apartment complex for not less than $2 million. Without Anna's knowledge, Powell is adjudicated incompetent two months later. Anna's authority to sell the apartment complex is terminated. Likewise, the subsequent incapacity of an agent to perform the acts authorized by the principal terminates the agent's authority.

Almost all of the States have statutes providing for a **durable power of attorney**. If made in compliance with one of these statutes, an appointment of an agent survives the incapacity of the principal.

**Change in Business Conditions** Notice or knowledge of a change in the value of the subject matter, or of a change in business conditions from which the agent should reasonably infer that the principal would not wish the agent to exercise the authority given him, terminates an agent's authority. Restatement, Section 109. Thus, Patricia authorizes Aaron to sell her eighty acres of farmland for $800 per acre. Subsequently, oil is discovered on nearby land, which causes Patricia's land to increase greatly in value. Because Aaron knows of this, but Patricia does not, Aaron's authority to sell the land is terminated.

**Loss or Destruction of Subject Matter** Where the authority of the agent relates to a specific subject matter that becomes lost or is destroyed, her authority is thereby terminated. Depending on the agreement between the principal and the agent, authority terminates either immediately or only when the agent has notice of the loss or destruction. For example, Paul authorizes Allan to make a contract for the sale of Paul's residence. The next week, as Allan is aware, the residence burns completely. Allan's authority is terminated.

**Disloyalty of Agent** If an agent, without the knowledge of her principal, acquires interests adverse to those of the principal or otherwise breaches her duty of loyalty to the principal, her authority to act on behalf of the principal is terminated. Restatement, Section 112. Thus, Parker employs Agnes, a realtor, to sell Parker's land. Unknown to Parker, Agnes has been authorized by Trent to purchase this land from Parker. Consequently, Agnes is not authorized to sell the land to Trent.

**Change in Law** A change in the law that takes place after the employment of the agent and that makes the performance of the authorized act illegal or criminal terminates the authority of the agent. Restatement, Section 116. Thus, Pablo directs his agent, Arp, to ship young elm trees from State X to State Y. To control elm disease, State X establishes a quarantine upon the shipment of elm trees into any other State, making any such shipment punishable by fine. Arp's authority to ship the elm trees is terminated.

*Outbreak of War* Where the outbreak of war places the principal and agent in the position of alien enemies, the authority of the agent is terminated because its exercise is illegal. Otherwise, the outbreak of war of which the agent has notice terminates his authority if conditions are so changed that the agent should infer that the principal would not consent to further exercise of the authority. Restatement, Section 115.

## Irrevocable Agencies

In the foregoing discussion of the various ways in which the authority of an agent may be terminated, the agency relationship was assumed to be the ordinary one in which the agent has no security interest in the power conferred upon him by the principal. Where the **agency is coupled with an interest** of the agent in the subject matter, as, for example, where the agent has advanced funds on behalf of the principal and his power to act is given as security for the loan, the principal may *not* revoke the authority of the agent. In addition, neither the incapacity nor bankruptcy of the principal terminates the authority or the power of the agent. Nor will the death of the principal terminate the agency, unless the duty for which the security was given terminates with the death of the principal. Restatement, Section 139.

# Chapter Summary

**Nature of Agency**

**Definition of Agency** relationship authorizing one party (the agent) to act for and on behalf of the other party (the principal)
**Scope of Agency Purposes** generally, whatever business activity a person may accomplish personally he may do through an agent
**Other Legal Relations**
- *Employment Relationship* one in which the employer has the right to control the physical conduct of the employee
- *Independent Contractor* a person who contracts with another to do a particular job and who is not subject to the control of the other

**Creation of Agency**

**Formalities** though agency is a consensual relationship that may be formed by contract or agreement between the principal and agent, agency may exist without consideration
- *Requirements* no particular formality usually is required in a contract of agency, although appointments of agents for a period of more than one year must be in writing
- *Power of Attorney* written, formal appointment of an agent
**Capacity**
- *Principal* if the principal is a minor or an incompetent not under a guardianship, his appointment of another to act as an agent is voidable
- *Agent* any person may act as an agent, as the act of the agent is considered the act of the principal

| **Duties of Agent to Principal** | **Duty of Obedience** an agent must act in the principal's affairs only as authorized by the principal and must obey all reasonable instructions and directions<br>**Duty of Diligence** an agent must act with reasonable care and skill in performing the work for which he is employed<br>**Duty to Inform** an agent must use reasonable efforts to give the principal information relevant to the affairs entrusted to her<br>**Duty to Account** an agent must maintain and provide the principal with a true and complete account of money or other property that the agent has received or expended on behalf of the principal<br>**Fiduciary Duty** an agent owes a duty of utmost loyalty and good faith to the principal<br>• *Conflicts of Interest*<br>• *Duty Not to Compete*<br>• *Confidential Information*<br>• *Duty to Account for Financial Benefits* |
|---|---|
| **Duties of Principal to Agent** | **Contractual Duties**<br>• *Compensation* a principal must compensate the agent as specified in the contract, or for the reasonable value of the services provided, if no amount is specified<br>• *Reimbursement* the principal must pay back to the agent authorized payments the agent has made on the principal's behalf<br>• *Indemnification* the principal must pay the agent for losses the agent incurred while acting as directed by the principal<br>**Tort Duties** include the duty to provide an employee with reasonably safe conditions of employment and to warn the employee of any unreasonable risk involved in the employment |
| **Termination of Agency** | **Acts of the Parties**<br>• *Lapse of Time*<br>• *Fulfillment of Purpose*<br>• *Mutual Agreement of the Parties*<br>• *Revocation of Authority*<br>• *Renunciation by the Agent*<br>**Operation of Law**<br>• *Bankruptcy* the bankruptcy of the principal usually terminates all of the principal's agency relationships; if the credit of the agent is important to the agency relationship, the relationship will be terminated by the bankruptcy of the agent<br>• *Death* of either the principal or the agent<br>• *Incapacity* of either the principal or the agent<br>• *Change in Circumstances*<br>• *Loss or Destruction of the Subject Matter*<br>• *Disloyalty of Agent*<br>• *Change in Law*<br>• *Outbreak of War*<br>**Irrevocable Agencies** an agency coupled with an interest is irrevocable and occurs where the agent has a security interest in the subject matter of the agency |

# Cases

### CASE 19–1
## Other Legal Relations: Employment versus Independent Contractor
## *JAEGER v. WESTERN RIVERS FLY FISHER*
United States District Court, District of Utah, 1994
855 F.Supp. 1217

SAM, J.
A review of the record reveals the following summary of undisputed, material facts. Western, operating under license of the U.S. Forest Service, is an "outfitter," a corporation in the business of arranging fishing expeditions on the Green River. Defendant Michael D. Petragallo is licensed by the Forest Service as a guide to conduct fishing expeditions but cannot do so by himself as the Forest Service only licenses outfitters to float patrons down the Green River. Western and several other licensed outfitters contact Petragallo to guide clients on fishing trips. Because the Forest Service licenses only outfitters to sponsor fishing expeditions, every guide must display on the boat and vehicle he uses the insignia of the outfitter sponsoring the particular trip. Western has classified the river into different sections for purposes of such fishing trips and, based upon Forest Service regulations, may suggest to clients areas in which to fish. Petragallo may agree or refuse to take individuals Western refers to him, and Western does not restrict him from guiding expeditions for other outfitters. Western pays Petragallo a certain sum per fishing trip, does not make any deductions from his compensation, supplies him with a 1099 independent contractor tax form, and the Internal Revenue Service has determined that Western is properly treating him and other river guides it hires as independent contractors, for tax purposes. Petragallo's responsibilities include: transporting patrons to the Green River, using his own boat for fishing trips, providing food and overnight needs for patrons, assisting patrons in fly fishing, and transporting them from the river to their vehicles.

Prior to May 1992, Robert McMaster contacted Western and arranged for a fishing trip for himself and two others. Plaintiff was a member of McMaster's fishing party. McMaster paid Western, which set the price for the trip, and Western planned the itinerary for the McMaster party, rented fishing rods to them, arranged for Petragallo to be their guide, and set a meeting place and time for Petragallo to meet them in Dutch John, Utah. When Petragallo met the McMaster party, he answered affirmatively when plaintiff asked him if he worked for Western. Petragallo provided his own vehicle and boat and supplied the food, equipment, and gasoline for the trip. Both the vehicle and the boat had signs bearing Western's identification and logo. While driving the McMaster party back to Dutch John at the conclusion of the fishing trip, Petragallo lost control of his vehicle when he swerved to miss a deer in the road, injuring plaintiff.

Plaintiff brought suit against Western, Petragallo, and others. Western now moves for summary judgment, arguing that, because Petragallo is an independent contractor and was never its employee, it is not liable, as a matter of law, for Petragallo's acts in causing plaintiff's injuries.

\* \* \*

Plaintiff . . . argues Petragallo was Western's employee, and, thus, Western is liable for Petragallo's actions under the doctrine of respondant superior. Western contends Petragallo is an independent contractor for whose conduct Western is not liable. [Citations] . . . (generally, employer who hires independent contractor is not liable for independent contractor's negligence to third party).

The Utah Supreme Court distinguished between an employee and an independent contractor in [citation]. In general,

[a]n employee is one who is hired and paid a salary, a wage, or at a fixed rate, to perform the employer's work as directed by the employer and who is subject to a comparatively high degree of control in performing those duties. In contrast, an independent contractor is one who is engaged to do some particular project or piece of work, usually for a set total sum, who may do the job in his own way, subject to only minimal restrictions or controls and is responsible only for its satisfactory completion.

[Citations.] Factors a court may consider in determining the nature of the relationship include:

(1) whatever covenants or agreements exist concerning the right of direction and control over the employee, whether express or implied; (2) the right to hire and fire; (3) the

method of payment, i.e., whether in wages or fees, as compared to payment for a complete job or project; and (4) the furnishing of the equipment.

[Citations.] The court has placed varying significance upon the factor of control. [Court's footnote: * * * ("While the elements of control by the employer and the intent of the parties are the most important ones, none of the factors separately is controlling. It is from consideration of all of them together that determination is to be made whether the relationship is in essence that of employer-employee or of independent contractor.")]

The Utah Supreme Court has identified differences between employment and independent contractor relationships. For example, in [citation], a truck driver was found to be an employee because the truck he operated was registered in a corporate name and had a corporate sign on it, he had to obtain approval from a corporate supervisor before driving a load, he was obligated to haul loads as instructed and check in with a dispatcher at various times en route, he was directed as to how many miles per month the truck should be operated, and he was required to drive five miles per hour under the speed limit. In [citation], a dry wall applicator had employee status because he was "shown what services were to be performed, not allowed to commence work on his first appearance, directed where to stack the dry wall and to use care in protecting the floor, furnished a protective covering and a ladder and paid at an hourly rate." [Citation.]

In contrast, in [citation], the Utah Supreme Court affirmed a ruling by the Industrial Commission that the plaintiff was an independent contractor. The court noted the plaintiff had an oral agreement with the defendant to install roof shingles periodically on homes the defendant was constructing. The plaintiff billed the defendant monthly, and the defendant made no withholding deductions from the plaintiff's compensation. The plaintiff supplied his own tools, used his discretion in establishing his own work schedule, and worked on any house he chose, whether being built by the defendant or others. [Citation.] Despite the fact that the defendant supplied the plaintiff with shingles and nails and directed the plaintiff in the manner and timing of the installation, the court concluded the defendant did not maintain sufficient supervision or control over the plaintiff for the plaintiff to be considered an employee. [Citation.] Rather, the plaintiff was an independent contractor. [Citations.]

In the instant case, the record reveals Western: advertises fishing expeditions, sets the prices, and collects a deposit from patrons; may suggest fishing areas to patrons; may create an itinerary; engages guides such as Petragallo to conduct a particular trip for a set amount without withholding taxes; sets a meeting time and place for Petragallo and patrons; provides signs for Petragallo's vehicle and boat in compliance with Forest Service regulations; and may rent fishing rods and clothing to patrons. Western also holds the license under which Petragallo and other river guides must operate, pursuant to Forest Service requirements.

Once Western sets up a fishing trip and engages Petragallo for a certain sum as a guide, Petragallo: buys food for himself and patrons for the fishing trip, may provide transportation to and from the river, uses his own vehicle and boat, supplies his own fishing equipment, and uses his expertise in floating patrons to fishing areas and assisting them in fly fishing.

The court cannot say these facts, relative to whether Petragallo is Western's employee or an independent contractor, point to a single conclusion only. On the one hand, the facts suggest Petragallo is an independent contractor. Western engages Petragallo to guide particular fishing trips, for a set sum, allowing him to conduct the trips in his own discretion. Petragallo may even choose to refuse to guide patrons Western has referred to him. Western's actions appear to involve setting up the parameters of a fishing trip and place "only minimal restrictions or controls" upon Petragallo. [Citation.] Also, Western and Petragallo seem to operate as if Petragallo were an independent contractor, as Western has the right to hire Petragallo or any other available guide as it sees fit, pays him per trip, expects him to furnish his own equipment, and treats him as an independent contractor for tax purposes. Moreover, although Petragallo must operate under Western's license, as required by the Forest Service, Western does not control through its license the manner in which Petragallo conducts fishing trips. Apparently, once Western sets up a fishing trip and engages Petragallo as a guide, it relies upon and expects Petragallo to use his own discretion in doing everything else to ensure patrons have an enjoyable experience, including using his own expertise, vehicle, boat, and equipment. [Citation.] Finally, because Forest Service licensing regulations prohibit an individual river guide from conducting tours unless sponsored by an outfitter, it may be argued that, if Petragallo is subject to any control, it is by the Forest Service, not Western.

However, on the other hand, the facts may indicate Petragallo is an employee. It is actually a judgment call as to how much control Western has over Petragallo through its advertising and arranging of fishing expeditions. Although Petragallo may refuse to guide patrons, Western apparently contacts Petragallo only after it has planned the fishing trip, without involving him, and may provide him with a set itinerary. Also, Forest Service licensing regulations place Western in a position of having the ultimate right to control Petragallo's work as, without solicitations from Western and other outfitters, Petragallo would be prohibited completely from conducting fishing expeditions.

In applying the above factors and standards, the court concludes a determination of the nature of Petragallo's relationship with Western is a factual issue inappropriate for summary judgment. Accordingly, the court denies Western's motion for summary judgment on this issue.

---

## CASE 19–2
### Creation of Agency
## *MILLER v. McDONALD'S CORPORATION*
Court of Appeals of Oregon, 1997
150 Or.App. 274, 945 P.2d 1107

WARREN, J.
Plaintiff seeks damages from defendant McDonald's Corporation for injuries that she suffered when she bit into a heart-shaped sapphire stone while eating a Big Mac sandwich that she had purchased at a McDonald's restaurant in Tigard. The trial court granted summary judgment to defendant on the ground that it did not own or operate the restaurant; rather, the owner and operator was a non-party, 3K Restaurants (3K), that held a franchise from defendant. Plaintiff appeals, and we reverse.

Most of the relevant facts are not in dispute. * * * 3K owned and operated the restaurant under a License Agreement (the Agreement) with defendant that required it to operate in a manner consistent with the "McDonald's System." The Agreement described that system as including proprietary rights in trade names, service marks and trade marks, as well as "designs and color schemes for restaurant buildings, signs, equipment layouts, formulas and specifications for certain food products, methods of inventory and operation control, bookkeeping and accounting, and manuals covering business practices and policies."

The manuals contain "detailed information relating to operation of the Restaurant," including food formulas and specifications, methods of inventory control, bookkeeping procedures, business practices, and other management, advertising, and personnel policies. 3K, as the licensee, agreed to adopt and exclusively use the formulas, methods, and policies contained in the manuals, including any subsequent modifications, and to use only advertising and promotional materials that defendant either provided or approved in advance in writing.

The Agreement described the way in which 3K was to operate the restaurant in considerable detail. It expressly required 3K to operate in compliance with defendant's prescribed standards, policies, practices, and procedures, including serving only food and beverage products that defendant designated. 3K had to follow defendant's specifications and blueprints for the equipment and layout of the restaurant, including adopting subsequent reasonable changes that defendant made, and to maintain the restaurant building in compliance with defendant's standards. 3K could not make any changes in the basic design of the building without defendant's approval.

The Agreement required 3K to keep the restaurant open during the hours that defendant prescribed, including maintaining adequate supplies and employing adequate personnel to operate at maximum capacity and efficiency during those hours. 3K also had to keep the restaurant similar in appearance to all other McDonald's restaurants. 3K's employees had to wear McDonald's uniforms, to have a neat and clean appearance, and to provide competent and courteous service. 3K could use only containers and other packaging that bore McDonald's trademarks. The ingredients for the foods and beverages had to meet defendant's standards, and 3K had to use "only those methods of food handling and preparation that [defendant] may designate from time to time." In order to obtain the franchise, 3K had to represent that the franchisee had worked at a McDonald's restaurant; the Agreement did not distinguish in this respect between a company-run or a franchised restaurant. The manuals gave further details that expanded on many of these requirements.

In order to ensure conformity with the standards described in the Agreement, defendant periodically sent field consultants to the restaurant to inspect its operations. 3K trained its employees in accordance with defendant's materials and recommendations and sent some of them to training programs that defendant administered. Failure to comply with the agreed standards could result in loss of the franchise.

Despite these detailed instructions, the Agreement provided that 3K was not an agent of defendant for any purpose. Rather, it was an independent contractor and was responsible for all obligations and liabilities, including claims based on injury, illness, or death, directly or indirectly resulting from the operation of the restaurant.

Plaintiff went to the restaurant under the assumption that defendant owned, controlled, and managed it. So far as she could tell, the restaurant's appearance was similar to that of other McDonald's restaurants that she had patronized. Nothing disclosed to her that any entity other than defendant was involved in its operation. The only signs that were visible and obvious to the public had the name "McDonald's," the employees wore uniforms with McDonald's insignia, and the menu was the same that plaintiff had seen in other McDonald's restaurants. The general appearance of the restaurant and the food products that it sold were similar to the restaurants and products that plaintiff had seen in national print and television advertising that defendant had run. To the best of plaintiff's knowledge, only McDonald's sells Big Mac hamburgers.

In short, plaintiff testified, she went to the Tigard McDonald's because she relied on defendant's reputation and because she wanted to obtain the same quality of service, standard of care in food preparation, and general attention to detail that she had previously enjoyed at other McDonald's restaurants.

Under these facts, 3K would be directly liable for any injuries that plaintiff suffered as a result of the restaurant's negligence. The issue on summary judgment is whether there is evidence that would permit a jury to find defendant vicariously liable for those injuries because of its relationship with 3K. Plaintiff asserts two theories of vicarious liability, actual agency and apparent agency. We hold that there is sufficient evidence to raise a jury issue under both theories. We first discuss actual agency.

The kind of actual agency relationship that would make defendant vicariously liable for 3K's negligence requires that defendant have the right to control the method by which 3K performed its obligations under the Agreement. The common context for that test is a normal master-servant (or employer-employee) relationship. [Citations.] The relationship between two business entities is not precisely an employment relationship, but the Oregon Supreme Court, in common with most if not all other courts that have considered the issue, has applied the right to control test for vicarious liability in that context as well. [Citation.] We therefore apply that test to this case.

* * *

A number of other courts have applied the right to control test to a franchise relationship. The Delaware Supreme Court, in [citation], stated the test as it applies to that context:

If, in practical effect, the franchise agreement goes beyond the stage of setting standards, and allocates to the franchisor the right to exercise control over the daily operations of the franchise, an agency relationship exists. [Citation.]

This statement expresses the general direction that courts have taken and is consistent with the Supreme Court's discussion in [citation]. We therefore adopt it for the purposes of this case.

* * *

* * * we believe that a jury could find that defendant retained sufficient control over 3K's daily operations that an actual agency relationship existed. The Agreement did not simply set standards that 3K had to meet. Rather, it required 3K to use the precise methods that defendant established, both in the Agreement and in the detailed manuals that the Agreement incorporated. Those methods included the ways in which 3K was to handle and prepare food. Defendant enforced the use of those methods by regularly sending inspectors and by its retained power to cancel the Agreement. That evidence would support a finding that defendant had the right to control the way in which 3K performed at least food handling and preparation. In her complaint, plaintiff alleges that 3K's deficiencies in those functions resulted in the sapphire being in the Big Mac and thereby caused her injuries. Thus, as in [citation], there is evidence that defendant had the right to control 3K in the precise part of its business that allegedly resulted in plaintiff's injuries. That is sufficient to raise an issue of actual agency.

Plaintiff next asserts that defendant is vicariously liable for 3K's alleged negligence because 3K was defendant's apparent agent. The relevant standard is in Restatement (Second) of Agency, § 267, which we adopted in [citation]:

One who represents that another is his servant or other agent and thereby causes a third person justifiably to rely upon the care or skill of such apparent agent is subject to liability to the third person for harm caused by the lack of care or skill of the one appearing to be a servant or other agent as if he were such. [Citation.]

We have not applied § 267 to a franchisor/franchisee situation, but courts in a number of other jurisdictions have done so in ways that we find instructive. In most cases the courts have found that there was a jury issue of apparent agency. The crucial issues are whether the putative principal held the third party out as an agent and whether the plaintiff relied on that holding out.

* * *

In this case * * * there is an issue of fact about whether defendant held 3K out as its agent. Everything about the appearance and operation of the Tigard McDonald's identified it with defendant and with the common image for all McDonald's restaurants that defendant has worked to create through national advertising, common signs and uniforms, common menus, common appearance, and common standards. The possible existence of a sign identifying 3K as the operator does not alter the conclusion that there is an issue of apparent agency for the jury. There are issues of fact of whether that sign was sufficiently visible to the public, in light of plaintiff's apparent failure to see it, and of whether one sign by itself is sufficient to remove the impression that defendant created through all of the other indicia of its control that it, and 3K under the requirements that defendant imposed, presented to the public.

Defendant does not seriously dispute that a jury could find that it held 3K out as its agent. Rather, it argues that there is insufficient evidence that plaintiff justifiably relied on that holding out. It argues that it is not sufficient for her to prove that she went to the Tigard McDonald's because it was a McDonald's restaurant. Rather, she also had to prove that she went to it because she believed that McDonald's Corporation operated both it and the other McDonald's restaurants that she had previously patronized. * * *

* * *

* * * in this case plaintiff testified that she relied on the general reputation of McDonald's in patronizing the Tigard restaurant and in her expectation of the quality of the food and service that she would receive. Especially in light of defendant's efforts to create a public perception of a common McDonald's system at all McDonald's restaurants, whoever operated them, a jury could find that plaintiff's reliance was objectively reasonable. The trial court erred in granting summary judgment on the apparent agency theory.

Reversed and remanded.

---

## CASE 19–3
### Duty of Diligence
### F.W. MYERS & COMPANY v. HUNTER FARMS
Supreme Court of Iowa, 1982
319 N.W.2d 186

LARSON, J.

Hunter Farms was involved in farming in Greene County, and in the sale of chemicals to other farmers. It sought to obtain a large supply of Sencor, a farm herbicide not then readily available in the area, for resale. In response to its newspaper advertisement, Hunter was contacted by Petrolia Grain & Feed Company of Petrolia, Canada, which offered to fill Hunter's order for Sencor. A representative of Petrolia's supplier contacted an "import specialist" with the United States Customs Service to determine the import duty. The specialist advised it the rate would be five percent but the final rate could only be determined upon an examination of the herbicide at the time of importation. This information was forwarded to Hunter, which continued negotiations to purchase the Sencor and retained Myers [an import broker] to assist in moving it through customs, which Myers did.

The "qualified" opinion of the customs specialist was later rescinded; customs determined there were chemicals in the herbicide, not listed on its label, which would increase the duty from approximately $30,000 to over $128,000. Myers, fearing a forfeiture of its security bond for the duty, paid the additional amount under protest and sought indemnity from Hunter. Hunter, however, refused to pay, arguing Myers had breached its duty of care as an import broker in failing to advise Hunter the five-percent duty rate was only tentative and was subject to being increased. This action was then brought by Myers, which contended it was not retained to give advice to Hunter, especially since it was never informed Hunter was a neophyte in the import business. It averred its duties as an import broker were merely to prepare the forms for importation and satisfy the bonding requirements; advice on matters of importation would be given only if requested. The trial court found Myers did not breach its duty of care to Hunter.

The right of indemnity under such circumstances is clear: If one is compelled to pay sums which another ought to pay, he is entitled to indemnity. [Citations.] Although Hunter does not challenge the general right of an agent to indemnity under such circumstances, it claims Myers had breached a concomitant duty of disclosure, thus precluding its recovery.

An agent is required to exercise such skill as is required to accomplish the object of his employment. If he fails to exercise reasonable care, diligence, and judgment under the circumstances, he is liable to his principal for any loss or damage resulting. [Citation.] Thus,

[u]nless otherwise agreed, a paid agent is subject to a duty to the principal to act with standard care and with the skill which is standard in the locality for the kind of work which he is employed to perform and, in addition, to exercise any special skill that he has.

*Restatement (Second) of Agency,* § 379(1), at 177 (1958).

We believe there was substantial evidence, [citation], to support the trial court's finding there was no breach of duty by Myers. Evidence was presented that the standard of care for import brokers did not include a special duty to render advice to the importer unless requested to do so. Expert testimony showed such brokers are basically involved in drafting the necessary papers, arranging for the necessary bonds, and actual forwarding of the duty payment. There was no evidence of a request to advise Hunter on import law, nor was there any evidence Myers was advised that Hunter was new in the import business.

Hunter contends, however, Myers had a special duty of disclosure to advise Hunter the five-percent figure was advisory or only an estimate. It claims the trial court erred in failing to recognize and apply such duty of care.

The scope of an agent's duty to disclose is explained by the *Restatement* in this manner:

Unless otherwise agreed, an agent is subject to a duty to use reasonable efforts to give his principal information which is relevant to affairs entrusted to him and which, as the agent has notice, the principal would desire to have and which can be communicated without violating a superior duty to a third person.

*Restatement, supra* § 381, at 182. This standard requires that the agent have notice the principal would desire to have the relevant information. In this case there was evidence the open-ended nature of an initial duty assessment was widely known and understood by importers. Myers was never informed of the need to convey this information to Hunter which, it could reasonably presume, possessed the fundamental knowledge of an importer. Myers was never advised of Hunter's lack of experience in the business, nor was it aware of the problem in labeling the herbicide which caused the increase in the duty charged. Absent knowledge of Hunter's special need for advice and of the circumstances which might give rise to the additional importation fees, there was no special duty on Myers to advise Hunter of the tentative nature of the assessment. Accordingly, it was not error for the trial court to refuse to recognize such a duty.

Affirmed.

---

## CASE 19–4
### Fiduciary Duty
# *DETROIT LIONS, INC. v. ARGOVITZ*
United States District Court, Eastern District of Michigan, 1984
580 F.Supp. 542

DEMASCIO, J.
The plot for this Saturday afternoon serial began when Billy Sims, having signed a contract with the Houston Gamblers on July 1, 1983, signed a second contract with the Detroit Lions on December 16, 1983. On December 18, 1983, the Detroit Lions, Inc. (Lions) and Billy R. Sims filed a complaint in the Oakland County Circuit Court seeking a judicial determination that the July 1, 1983, contract between Sims and the Houston Gamblers, Inc. (Gamblers) is invalid because the defendant Jerry Argovitz (Argovitz) breached his fiduciary duty when negotiating the Gamblers' contract and because the contract was otherwise tainted by fraud and misrepresentation. * * *

For the reasons that follow, we have concluded that Argovitz's breach of his fiduciary duty during negotiations for the Gamblers' contract was so pronounced, so egregious, that to deny recision would be unconscionable.

Sometime in February or March 1983, Argovitz told Sims that he had applied for a Houston franchise in the newly formed United States Football League (USFL). In May 1983, Sims attended a press conference in Houston at which Argovitz announced that his application for a franchise had been approved. The evidence persuades us that Sims did not know the extent of Argovitz's interest in the Gamblers. He did not know the amount of Argovitz's original investment, or that Argovitz was obligated for 29 percent of a $1.5 million letter of credit, or that Argovitz was the president of the Gamblers' Corporation at an annual salary of $275,000 and 5 percent [of] the yearly cash flow. The defendants could not justifiably expect Sims to comprehend the ramifications of Argovitz's interest in the Gamblers or the manner in which that interest would create an untenable conflict of interest, a conflict that would inevitably breach Argovitz's fiduciary duty to Sims. Argovitz knew, or should have known, that he could not act as Sims' agent under any circumstances when dealing with the Gamblers. Even the USFL Constitution itself prohibits a holder of any interest in a member club from acting "as the contracting agent or representative for any player."

Pending the approval of his application for a USFL franchise in Houston, Argovitz continued his negotiations with the Lions on behalf of Sims. On April 5, 1983, Argovitz offered Sims' services to the Lions for $6 million over a four-year period. The offer included a demand for a $1 million interest-free loan to be repaid over 10 years, and for skill and injury guarantees for three years. The Lions quickly responded with a counter offer on April 7, 1983, in the face amount of $1.5 million over a five-year period with additional incentives not relevant here. The negotiating process was working. The Lions were trying to determine what Argovitz really believed the market value for Sims really was. On May 3, 1983, with his Gamblers franchise assured, Argovitz significantly reduced his offer to the Lions. He now offered Sims to the Lions for $3 million over a four-year period, one-half of the amount of his April 5, 1983, offer. Argovitz's May 3rd offer included a demand for $50,000 to permit Sims to purchase an annuity. Argovitz also dropped his previous demand for skill guarantees. The May 10, 1983 offer submitted by the Lions brought the parties much closer.

On May 30, 1983, Argovitz asked for $3.5 million over a five-year period. This offer included an interest-free loan and injury protection insurance but made no demand for skill guarantees. The May 30 offer now requested $400,000 to allow Sims to purchase an annuity. On June 1, 1983, Argovitz and the Lions were only $500,000 apart. We find that the negotiations between the Lions and Argovitz were progressing normally, not laterally as Argovitz represented to Sims. The Lions were not "dragging their feet." . . . The evidence establishes that on June 22, 1983, the Lions and Argovitz were very close to reaching an agreement on the value of Sims' services.

Apparently, in the midst of his negotiations with the Lions and with his Gamblers' franchise in hand, Argovitz decided that he would seek an offer from the Gamblers. Mr. Bernard Lerner, one of Argovitz's partners in the Gamblers agreed to negotiate a contract with Sims. Since Lerner admitted that he had no knowledge whatsoever about football, we must infer that Argovitz at the very least told Lerner the amount of money required to sign Sims and further pressed upon Lerner the Gamblers' absolute need to obtain Sims' services. In the Gamblers' organization, only Argovitz knew the value of Sims' services and how critical it was for the Gamblers to obtain Sims. In Argovitz's words, Sims would make the Gamblers' franchise.

On June 29, 1983, at Lerner's behest, Sims and his wife went to Houston to negotiate with a team that was partially owned by his own agent. When Sims arrived in Houston, he believed that the Lions organization was not negotiating in good faith; that it was not really interested in his services. His ego was bruised and his emotional outlook toward the Lions was visible to Burrough and Argovitz. Clearly, virtually all the information that Sims had up to that date came from Argovitz. . . . The negotiations began on the morning of June 30, 1983, and ended that afternoon. At the morning meeting, Lerner offered Sims a $3.5 million five-year contract, which included three years of skill and injury guarantees. The offer included a $500,000 loan at an interest rate of 1 percent over prime. It was from this loan that Argovitz planned to receive the $100,000 balance of his fee for acting as an agent in negotiating a contract with his own team. Burrough testified that Sims would have accepted that offer on the spot because he was finally receiving the guarantee that he had been requesting from the Lions, guarantees that Argovitz dropped without too much quarrel. Argovitz and Burrough took Sims and his wife into another room to discuss the offer. Argovitz did tell Sims that he thought the Lions would match the Gamblers' financial package and asked Sims whether he (Argovitz) should telephone the Lions. But, it is clear from the evidence that neither Sims nor Burrough believed that the Lions would match the offer. . . . Sims . . . agreed to become a Gambler on the terms offered. At that moment, Argovitz irreparably breached his fiduciary duty. As agent for Sims he had the duty to telephone the Lions, receive its final offer, and present the terms of both offers to Sims. Then and only then could it be said that Sims made an intelligent and knowing decision to accept the Gamblers' offer.

During these negotiations at the Gamblers' office, Mr. Nash of the Lions telephoned Argovitz, but even though Argovitz was at his office, he declined to accept the telephone call. Argovitz tried to return Nash's call after Sims had accepted the Gamblers' offer, but it was after 5 PM and Nash had left for the July 4th weekend. When he declined to accept Mr. Nash's call, Argovitz's breach of his fiduciary duty became even more pronounced.

* * *

During the evening of June 30, 1983, Burrough struggled with the fact that they had not presented the Gamblers' offer to the Lions. He knew, as does the court, that Argovitz now had the wedge that he needed to bring finality to the Lions' negotiations. Burrough was acutely aware of the fact that Sims' actions were emotionally motivated and realized that the responsibility for Sims' future rested with him. We view with some disdain the fact that Argovitz had, in effect, delegated his entire fiduciary responsibility on the eve of his principal's most important career decision. On July 1, 1983, it was Lerner who gave lip service to Argovitz's conspicuous conflict of interest. It was Lerner, not Argovitz, who advised Sims that Argovitz's position with the Gamblers presented a conflict of interest and that Sims could, if he wished, obtain an attorney or another agent. Argovitz, upon whom Sims had relied for the past four years, was not even there. Burrough, conscious of Sims' emotional responses, never advised Sims to wait until he had talked with the Lions before making a final decision. Argovitz's conflict of interest and self-dealing put him in the position where he would not even use the wedge he now had to negotiate with the Lions, a wedge that is the dream of every agent. Two expert witnesses testified that an agent should telephone a team that he has been negotiating with once he has an offer in hand. . . . The evidence here convinces us that Argovitz's negotiations with the Lions were ongoing and it had not made its final offer. Argovitz did not follow the common practice described by both expert witnesses. He did not do this because he knew that the Lions would not leave Sims without a contract and he further knew that if he made that type of call Sims would be lost to the Gamblers, a team he owned.

On November 12, 1983, when Sims was in Houston for the Lions game with the Houston Oilers, Argovitz asked Sims to come to his home and sign certain papers. He represented to Sims that certain papers of his contract had been mistakenly overlooked and now needed to be signed. Included among those papers he asked Sims to sign was a waiver of any claim that Sims might have against Argovitz for his blatant breach of his fiduciary duty brought on by his glaring conflict of interest. Sims did not receive independent advice with regard to the wisdom of signing such a waiver. Despite having sold his agency business in September, Argovitz did not even tell Sims' new agent of his intention to have Sims sign a waiver. Nevertheless, Sims, an unsophisticated young man, signed the waiver. This is another example of the questionable conduct on the part of Argovitz who still had business management obligations to Sims. In spite of his fiduciary relationship he had Sims sign a waiver without advising him to obtain independent counseling.

* * *

The relationship between a principal and agent is fiduciary in nature, and as such imposes a duty of loyalty, good faith, and fair and honest dealing on the agent. [Citation.]

A fiduciary relationship arises not only from a formal principal-agent relationship, but also from informal relationships of trust and confidence. [Citations.]

In light of the express agency agreement, and the relationship between Sims and Argovitz, Argovitz clearly owed Sims the fiduciary duties of an agent at all times relevant to this lawsuit.

An agent's duty of loyalty requires that he not have a personal stake that conflicts with the principal's interest in a transaction in which he represents his principal. As stated in [citation]:

(T)he principal is entitled to the best efforts and unbiased judgment of his agent. . . . (T)he law denies the right of an agent to assume any relationship that is antagonistic to his duty to his principal, and it has many times been held that the agent cannot be both buyer and seller at the same time nor connect his own interests with property involved in his dealings as an agent for another.

A fiduciary violates the prohibition against self-dealing not only by dealing with himself on his principal's behalf, but also by dealing on his principal's behalf with a third party in which he has an interest, such as a partnership in which he is a member. * * *

Where an agent has an interest adverse to that of his principal in a transaction in which he purports to act on behalf of his principal, the transaction is voidable by the principal unless the agent disclosed all material facts within the agent's knowledge that might affect the principal's judgment. [Citation.]

The mere fact that the contract is fair to the principal does not deny the principal the right to rescind the contract when it was negotiated by an agent in violation of the prohibition against self-dealing. * * *

Once it has been shown that an agent had an interest in a transaction involving his principal antagonistic to the principal's interest, fraud on the part of the agent is presumed. The burden of proof then rests upon the agent to show that his principal had full knowledge, not only of the fact that the agent was interested, but also of every material fact known to the agent which might affect the principal and that having such knowledge, the principal freely consented to the transaction.

It is not sufficient for the agent merely to inform the principal that he has an interest that conflicts with the principal's interest. Rather, he must inform the principal "of all facts that come to his knowledge that are or may be material or which might affect his principal's rights or interests or influence the action he takes." [Citation.]

Argovitz clearly had a personal interest in signing Sims with the Gamblers that was adverse to Sims' interest—he

had an ownership interest in the Gamblers and thus would profit if the Gamblers were profitable, and would incur substantial personal liabilities should the Gamblers not be financially successful. Since this showing has been made, fraud on Argovitz's part is presumed, and the Gamblers' contract must be rescinded unless Argovitz has shown by a preponderance of the evidence that he informed Sims of every material fact that might have influenced Sims' decision whether or not to sign the Gamblers' contract.

We conclude that Argovitz has failed to show by a preponderance of the evidence either: 1) that he informed Sims of the [material] facts, or 2) that these facts would not have influenced Sims' decision whether to sign the Gamblers' contract. * * *

As a court sitting in equity, we conclude that recision is the appropriate remedy. We are dismayed by Argovitz's egregious conduct. The careless fashion in which Argovitz went about ascertaining the highest price for Sims' service convinces us of the wisdom of the maxim: no man can faithfully serve two masters whose interests are in conflict.

Judgment will be entered for the plaintiffs rescinding the Gamblers' contract with Sims.

---

**CASE 19–5**
# Termination of Agency by Revocation
## HILGENDORF v. HAGUE
Supreme Court of Iowa, 1980
293 N.W.2d 272

UHLENHOPP, J.
[Harvey Hilgendorf was a licensed real estate broker acting as the agent of the Hagues in the sale of eighty acres of farmland. The Hagues, however, terminated Hilgendorf's agency before the expiration of the listing contract when they encountered financial difficulties and decided to liquidate their entire holdings of land at one time. Hilgendorf brought this action for breach of the listing contract. The Hagues maintain that Hilgendorf's duty of loyalty requires him to give up the listing contract.]

* * *

Since agency is a consensual relationship, a principal has *power* to terminate an agency which is not coupled with an interest [where the agent has an ownership interest in the subject matter of the agency], although the contract is for a period which has not expired.

Ordinarily the agent's authority thereupon ceases. Absent some legal ground, however, the principal does not have a *right* to terminate an unexpired agency contract, and may subject himself to damages by doing so. [Citations.]

The whole question regarding liability here turns on whether the Hagues had a legal ground for terminating Hilgendorf's agency before the expiration of the year. All agree that they had power to terminate, but they contend they also had a right to do so. They say PCA [Hagues' principal creditor] would not renew their loan, they had to sell the 80 acres in addition to their other land, and the best way to sell the 80 acres was with the 160 acres. Did these circumstances give them a "right" to terminate the listing contract they had signed and cast on Hilgendorf a "duty" to give up his listing contract as a matter of an agent's loyalty to his principal?

The Hagues appear to confuse the two roles an agent occupies. In performing agency functions for the principal an agent does indeed occupy a fiduciary position, and his duty of loyalty requires him to place the principal's interest first. Restatement (Second) of Agency § 387. But in the contract of agency itself between the agent and principal, neither of the parties is acting for the other; each is acting for himself.

This case involves the latter role. * * *

* * *

Several circumstances are given in the texts as grounds for terminating fixed-term agencies, but coming upon hard times is not among them. [Citations.] We agree with the trial court that the Hagues did not have a right to terminate the one-year listing contract . . . and that Hilgendorf did not have a duty to give up his listing contract.

* * *

Hague terminated the listing on August 13, 1976. Since Hague had the power to do so, Hilgendorf no longer had authority to sell the . . . parcel. For that reason, he cannot recover a commission *as such*, although he thereafter and within the year produced a ready, willing, and able buyer for the price in the listing. Nonetheless, since Hague breached the listing agreement by terminating it, Hilgendorf can recover damages. [Citation.]

The question here relates to the *measure* of damages Hilgendorf is entitled to *recover*. The editors state the measure thus in [citation]:

The courts generally support the principle that a broker whose employment or authority is wrongfully revoked may consider his contract of employment as rescinded and sue for damages, in which event he is entitled to have his recovery include the value of the services he has already rendered, his disbursements, and *such prospective profits as he can establish would have been his but for such revocation.* . . .

* * *

Where as here the principal terminates an exclusive listing within the term, the agent may endeavor to show that he would, but for the termination have sold the property within the unexpired period at the listed price. If he is successful in his proof, his lost profits are ordinarily measured by the commission he would have earned. He does not recover the commission itself, but his damages are measured by the commission. As stated in section 445 of the Restatement, Comment *a*:

If the principal, in breach of contract, prevents the agent from accomplishing the result upon which the agreed compensation is conditioned, the agent is entitled to damages for such breach or, as an alternative, the fair value of his services in attempting to accomplish it. The amount of recovery for damages in such a case is not the specified compensation as such, but the damages which the agent suffers by reason of the breach of contract. *Such damages may coincide in amount with the agreed compensation*; if, however, the agent would have had to incur further expense in order to earn such compensation, and these expenses have been saved to him, he is entitled only to a sum equal to the agreed compensation minus the expenses he has thereby saved. (Emphasis added.)

* * *

Here Hilgendorf proceeded on the damage issue by showing "the gains prevented" by Hague's breach of the listing contract. He established beyond question that he would have sold the . . . parcel for the full asking price within the listing period. His lost profit was the offered price times the six percent commission rate, and this is the amount the trial court allowed him.

We agree with the trial court's decision.
Affirmed.

---

 # Questions

1. Distinguish among the following relationships: (a) agency, (b) employment, and (c) independent contractor.
2. Discuss the requirements for creating an agency relationship.
3. Discuss the duties owed by an agent to her principal.
4. Discuss the duties owed by a principal to his agent.
5. Identify the ways in which an agency relationship may be terminated.

---

 # Problems

1. Parker, the owner of certain unimproved real estate in Chicago, employed Adams, a real estate agent, to sell the property for a price of $25,000 or more and agreed to pay Adams a commission of 6 percent for making a sale. Adams negotiated with Turner, who was interested in the property and willing to pay as much as $28,000 for it. Adams made an

agreement with Turner that if Adams could obtain Parker's signature to a contract to sell the property to Turner for $25,000, Turner would pay Adams a bonus of $1,000. Adams prepared and Parker and Turner signed a contract for the sale of the property to Turner for $25,000. Turner refuses to pay Adams the $1,000 as promised. Parker refuses to pay Adams the 6 percent commission. In an action by Adams against Parker and Turner, what judgment?

2.   Perry employed Alice to sell a parcel of real estate at a fixed price without knowledge that David had previously employed Alice to purchase the same property for him. Perry gave Alice no discretion as to price or terms, and Alice entered into a contract of sale with David upon the exact terms authorized by Perry. After accepting a partial payment, Perry discovered that Alice was employed by David and brought an action to rescind. David resisted on the ground that Perry had suffered no damage for the reason that Alice had been given no discretion and the sale was made upon the exact basis authorized by Perry. Decision?

3.   Packer owned and operated a fruit cannery in Southton, Illinois. He stored a substantial amount of finished canned goods in a warehouse in East St. Louis, Illinois, owned and operated by Alden, in order to have goods readily available for the St. Louis market. On March 1, he had 10,000 cans of peaches and 5,000 cans of apples in storage with Alden. On the day named, he borrowed $5,000 from Alden, giving Alden his promissory note for this amount due June 1 together with a letter authorizing Alden, in the event the note was not paid at maturity, to sell any or all of his goods in storage, pay the indebtedness, and account to him for any surplus. Packer died on June 2 without having paid the note. On June 8, Alden told Taylor, a wholesale food distributor, that he had for sale as agent of the owner 10,000 cans of peaches and 5,000 cans of apples. Taylor said he would take the peaches and would decide later about the apples. A contract for the sale of 10,000 cans of peaches for $6,000 was thereupon signed "Alden, agent for Packer, seller; Taylor, buyer." Both Alden and Taylor knew of the death of Packer. Delivery of the peaches and payment were made on June 10. On June 11, Alden and Taylor signed a similar contract covering the 5,000 cans of apples, delivery and payment to be made June 30. On June 23, Packer's executor, having learned of these contracts, wrote Alden and Taylor stating that Alden had no authority to make the contracts, demanding that Taylor return the peaches, and directing Alden not to deliver the apples. Discuss the correctness of the contentions of Packer's executor.

4.   Green, a licensed real estate broker in Illinois, and Jones, also an Illinois resident, while both were in New York, signed a contract whereby Green agreed to endeavor to find a buyer for certain Illinois real estate owned by Jones, who agreed to pay Green a commission of $10,000 in the event of a sale. Green found a buyer, a resident of New York, to whom the land was sold. Thereafter, when Jones refused to pay the commission, Green commenced an action in Illinois to recover it. Jones defended on the sole ground that the brokerage contract was unenforceable because Green was not a licensed real estate broker in New York. Relevant provisions of the applicable New York statute forbid any person from holding himself out or acting temporarily as a real estate broker or salesperson without first procuring a license. A violation is declared to be a misdemeanor, and the commission of a single prohibited act is a violation for which the statute provides a penalty. For whom should judgment be rendered?

5.   Palmer made a valid contract with Ames under which Ames was to sell Palmer's goods on commission from January 1 to June 30. Ames made satisfactory sales up to May 15 and was then about to close an unusually large order when Palmer suddenly and without notice revoked Ames's authority to sell. Can Ames continue to sell Palmer's goods during the unexpired term of her contract?

6.   Piedmont Electric Co. gave a list of delinquent accounts to Alexander, an employee, with instructions to discontinue electric service to delinquent customers. Among those listed was Todd Hatchery, which was then in the process of hatching chickens in a large, electrically heated incubator. Todd Hatchery told Alexander that it did not consider its account delinquent, but Alexander nevertheless cut the wires leading to the hatchery. Subsequently, Todd Hatchery recovered a judgment of $5,000 in an action brought against Alexander for the loss resulting from the interruption of the incubation process. Alexander has paid the judgment and brings a cause of action against Piedmont Electric Co. Decision?

7.   In October 1991, Black, the owner of the Grand Opera House, and Harvey entered into a written agreement leasing the Opera House to Harvey for five years at a rental of $30,000 per year. Harvey engaged Day as manager of the theatre at a salary of $175 per week plus 10 percent of the profits. One of Day's duties was to determine the amount of money taken in each night and, after deducting expenses, to divide the profits between Harvey and the manager of the particular attraction which was playing at the theatre. In September 1996, Day went to Black and offered to rent the opera house from Black at a rental of $37,500 per year, whereupon Black entered into a lease with Day for five years at this figure. When Harvey learned of and objected to this transaction, Day offered to assign the lease to him for $60,000 per year. Harvey refused and brought an appropriate action seeking to have Day declared a trustee of the opera house lease on behalf of Harvey. Decision?

8.   Timothy retains Cynthia, an attorney, to bring a lawsuit upon a valid claim against Vincent. Cynthia fails to make herself aware of recently enacted legislation that shortens the statute of limitations for this type of legal action, and, consequently, she files the complaint after the statute of limitations has run. As a result, the lawsuit is dismissed. What rights, if any, does Timothy have against Cynthia?

9.   Wilson engages Ruth to sell Wilson's antique walnut chest to Harold for $2,500. The next day, Ruth learns that Sandy is willing to pay $3,000 for Wilson's chest. Ruth nevertheless sells the chest to Harold. Wilson then discovers these facts. What are Wilson's rights, if any, against Ruth?

**10.** Morris, a salesperson for Acme, Inc., a manufacturer of household appliances, receives a commission on all sales made and no further compensation. He drives his own automobile, pays his own expenses, and calls on whom he pleases. While driving to make a call on a potential customer, Morris negligently collides with Hudson, who sues (a) Acme and (b) Morris. Who should be held liable?

**11.** Sierra Pacific Industries purchased various areas of timber and six other pieces of real property, including a ten-acre parcel on which five duplexes and two single-family units were located. Sierra Pacific requested the assistance of Joseph Carter, a licensed real estate broker, in selling the nontimberland properties. It commissioned him to sell the property for an asking price of $85,000, of which Sierra Pacific would receive $80,000 and Carter would receive $5,000 as a commission. Unable to find a prospective buyer, Carter finally sold the property to his daughter and son-in-law for $85,000 and retained the $5,000 commission without informing Sierra Pacific of his relationship to the buyers. After learning of these facts, Sierra Pacific brought an action for breach of fiduciary duty against Carter. Decision?

**12.** Murphy, while a guest at a motel operated by the Betsy-Len Motor Hotel Corporation, sustained injuries from a fall allegedly caused by negligence in maintaining the premises. At that time, Betsy-Len was under a license agreement with Holiday Inns, Inc. The license contained provisions permitting Holiday Inns to regulate the architectural style of the buildings as well as the type and style of the furnishings and equipment. The contract, however, did not grant Holiday Inns the power to control the day-to-day operations of Betsy-Len's motel, to fix customer rates, or to demand a share of the profits. Betsy-Len could hire and fire its employees, determine wages and working conditions, supervise the employee work routine, and discipline its employees. In return, Betsy-Len used the trade name, "Holiday Inns," and paid a fee for use of the license and Holiday Inns's national advertising. Murphy sued Holiday Inns, claiming Betsy-Len was its agent. Decision?

**13.** Tube Art was involved in moving a reader board sign to a new location. Tube Art's service manager and another employee went to the proposed site and took photographs and measurements. Later, a Tube Art employee laid out the exact size and location for the excavation by marking a four-by-four-foot-square on the asphalt surface with yellow paint. The dimensions of the hole, including its depth of six feet, were indicated with spray paint inside the square. After the layout was painted on the asphalt, Tube Art engaged a backhoe operator, Richard F. Redford, to dig the hole. Redford began digging in the early evening hours at the location designated by Tube Art. At approximately 9:30 PM, the bucket of Redford's backhoe struck a small natural gas pipeline. After examining the pipe and finding no indication of a break or leak, he concluded that the line was not in use and left the site. Shortly before 2:00 AM on the following day, an explosion and fire occurred in the building serviced by that gas pipeline. As a result, two people in the building were killed, and most of its contents were destroyed.

Massey and his associates, as tenants of the building, brought an action against Tube Art and Richard Redford for the total destruction of drawings, plan, sketches, prototype machine components, castings, and other work products. The trial court entered judgment on a jury verdict awarding $143,000 in damages to Massey. Tube Art appealed. Decision?

**14.** On May 1, 1982, Brian Hanson sustained a paralyzing injury while playing in a lacrosse match between Ohio State University and Ashland University. Hanson had interceded in a fight between one of his teammates and an Ashland player, William Kynast. Hanson grabbed Kynast in a bear hug, but Kynast threw Hanson off his back. Hanson's head struck the ground, resulting in serious injuries. An ambulance was summoned, and after several delays Hanson was transported to a local hospital where he underwent surgery. Doctors determined that Hanson suffered a compression fracture of his sixth spinal vertebrae. Hanson, now an incomplete quadriplegic, subsequently filed suit against William Kynast and Ashland University, maintaining that because Kynast was acting as the agent of Ashland, the university was therefore liable for Kynast's alleged wrongful acts under the doctrine of *respondeat superior*. Decision?

**15.** Tony Wilson was a member of Troop 392 of the Boy Scouts of America (BSA) and of the St. Louis Area Council (Council). On September 23, 1988, Tony went on a trip with the troop to Fort Leonard Wood, Missouri. Five adult volunteer leaders accompanied the troop. The troop stayed in a building which had thirty-foot aluminum pipes stacked next to it. At approximately 10:00 PM, Tony and other scouts were outside the building, and the leaders were inside. Tony and two other scouts picked up a pipe and raised it so that it came into contact with 7200-volt power lines that ran over the building. All three scouts were electrocuted, and Tony died.

His parents brought a suit for wrongful death against the Council, claiming that the volunteer leaders were agents or servants of the Council and that it was vicariously liable for their negligence. The Council filed a motion for summary judgment, arguing as follows: The BSA chartered local councils in certain areas, and councils in turn granted charters to local sponsors such as schools, churches, or civic organizations. Local councils did not administer the scouting program for the sponsor, did not select volunteers, did not prescribe training for volunteers, and did not direct or control the activities of troops. Troops were not required to get permission from local councils before participating in an activity. The trial court granted summary judgment for the Council. Decision?

**WWW Internet Exercise** Compare the formation and termination of an agency relationship under the Convention on Agency in the International Sale of Goods (Geneva, 17 February 1983) with formation and termination under the U.S. common law.

# CHAPTER 20

# Relationship with Third Parties

The purpose of an agency relationship is to allow the principal to extend his business activities by authorizing agents to enter into contracts with third persons on the principal's behalf. Accordingly, it is important that the law balance the competing interests of principals and third persons. The principal wants to be liable *only* for those contracts he actually authorizes the agent to make for him. The third party, on the other hand, wishes the principal bound on *all* contracts that the agent negotiates on the principal's behalf. As this chapter discusses, the law has adopted an intermediate outcome: the principal and the third party are bound to those contracts the principal *actually* authorizes *plus* those the principal has *apparently* authorized.

While pursuing her principal's business, an agent may tortiously injure third parties, who then may seek to hold the principal personally liable. Under what circumstances should the principal be held liable? Similar questions arise concerning a principal's criminal liability for an agent's violation of the criminal law. The law of agency has established rules to determine when the principal is liable for the torts and crimes his agents commit. These rules are discussed in this chapter.

Finally, what liability to the third party should the agent incur, and what rights should she acquire against the third party? Usually, the agent has no liability for, or rights under, the contracts she makes on behalf of her principal. As discussed in this chapter, however, in some situations the agent has contractually created obligations or rights or both.

## RELATIONSHIP OF PRINCIPAL AND THIRD PERSONS

This section will first consider the contract liability of the principal; then it will examine the principal's potential tort liability.

## CONTRACT LIABILITY OF THE PRINCIPAL

The **power** of an agent is his ability to change the legal status of his principal. An agent having either actual or apparent authority has the power to bind his principal. Thus, whenever an agent, acting within his authority, makes a contract for his principal, he creates new rights or liabilities for his principal, thereby changing his principal's legal status. This power of an agent to act for his principal in business transactions is the basis of agency.

A principal's contract liability also depends upon whether the principal is disclosed, partially disclosed, or undisclosed. The principal is a **disclosed principal** if at the time of a transaction an agent conducts, the other party has notice that the agent is acting for a principal and also has notice of the principal's identity. The principal is a **partially disclosed principal** if at the time of the transaction, the other party has notice that the agent is or may be acting for a principal but has no notice of the principal's identity. The principal is an **undisclosed principal** if the other party has no notice that the agent is acting for a principal. Restatement, Section 4.

### Types of Authority

Authority is of two basic types: actual and apparent. **Actual authority** depends upon consent that the principal manifests to the agent. It may be either express or implied. In either case, such authority is binding and confers upon the agent both the power and the right to create or affect the principal's legal relations with third persons. Where the principal is undisclosed, an agent acting with actual authority in making the contract will contractually bind the principal and the third party unless the terms of the contract exclude the principal from being a party or unless the agent fraudulently conceals the principal's existence from the third party.

**Apparent authority** is based upon acts or conduct of the principal that lead a third person to believe that the agent has actual authority, upon which belief the third person *justifiably* relies. This manifestation, which confers upon the agent the power to create a legal relationship between the principal and a third party, may consist of words or actions of the principal as well as other facts and circumstances that induce the third person reasonably to rely upon the existence of an agency relationship.

*Actual Express Authority* The express authority of an agent, found in the spoken or written words the principal communicates to the agent, is actual authority stated in language directing or instructing the agent to do something specific. Thus, if Perkins, orally or in writing, requests his agent Abbott to sell Perkins's automobile for $6,500, Abbott's authority to sell the car for this sum is actual and express.

 *See Case 17–1*

*Actual Implied Authority* Implied authority is not found in express or explicit words of the principal but is inferred from words or conduct that the principal manifests to the agent, who has implied authority to do that which she reasonably infers the principal desires her to do, in light of the principal's manifestations to her and all other facts she knows or should know. Restatement, Section 33. Implied authority may arise from customs and usages of the principal's business. In addition, the authority granted to an agent to accomplish a particular purpose necessarily includes the authority to employ the means reasonably required to accomplish it. Restatement, Section 35. For example, Pearson authorizes Arlington to manage her eighty-two-unit apartment complex but says nothing about expenses. In order to manage the building, Arlington must employ a janitor, purchase fuel for heating, and arrange for ordinary maintenance. Even though Pearson has not expressly granted him the authority to incur such expenses, Arlington may, because such expenses are necessary to proper apartment management, infer the authority to incur them from the express authority to manage the building.

Unless otherwise agreed, the authority to make a contract is inferred from the authority to conduct a transaction, if the making of such a contract is incidental to the transaction, usually accompanies such a transaction, or is reasonably necessary to accomplish it. Restatement, Section 50. Thus, Paragon, Inc. appoints Astor as the general manager of Paragon's manufacturing business. Astor's authority is interpreted as including authority to make contracts for the employment of necessary employees. On the

other hand, suppose Paige employs Arthur, a real estate broker, to find a purchaser for her residence at a stated price. Arthur has no authority to contract for its sale.

General authority to manage or operate a business for a principal confers implied authority upon the agent to buy and sell property for the principal to the extent usual and customary in such operation; to make contracts which are incidental to the business, are usually made in it, or are reasonably necessary in conducting it; to employ, supervise, or discharge employees; to receive payment due the principal and to pay debts due from the principal arising out of the business enterprise; and to direct the ordinary operations of the business. Restatement, Section 73.

◆ *See Figure 20–1*

*Apparent Authority* Apparent authority is power arising from words or conduct of a disclosed or partially disclosed principal that, when manifested to third persons, reasonably induce them to rely upon the assumption that actual authority exists. Restatement, Sections 27 and 159. Apparent authority confers upon the agent, or supposed agent, the power to bind the disclosed or partially disclosed principal in contracts with third persons and precludes the principal from denying the existence of actual authority. Thus, when authority is apparent but not actual, the disclosed or partially disclosed principal is nonetheless bound by the act of the agent. By exceeding his actual authority, however, the agent violates his duty of obedience and is liable to the principal for any loss the principal suffers as a result of the agent's acting beyond his actual authority.

For example, Peter writes a letter to Alice authorizing her to sell his automobile and sends a copy of the letter to Thomas, a prospective purchaser. On the following day, Peter writes a letter to Alice revoking the authority to sell the car but does not send a copy of the second letter to Thomas, who is not otherwise informed of the revocation. Although Alice has no actual authority to sell the car, she continues to have apparent authority with respect to Thomas. Or suppose that Arlene, in the presence of Polly, tells Thad that Arlene is Polly's agent to buy lumber. Although this statement is not true, Polly does not deny it, as she easily could. Thad, in reliance upon the statement, ships lumber to Polly on Arlene's order. Polly is obligated to pay for the lumber because Arlene had apparent authority to act on Polly's behalf. This apparent authority of Arlene exists only with respect to Thad. If Arlene were to give David an order for a shipment of lumber to Polly, David would be unable to

FIGURE 20–1  Contract Liability of Disclosed Principal

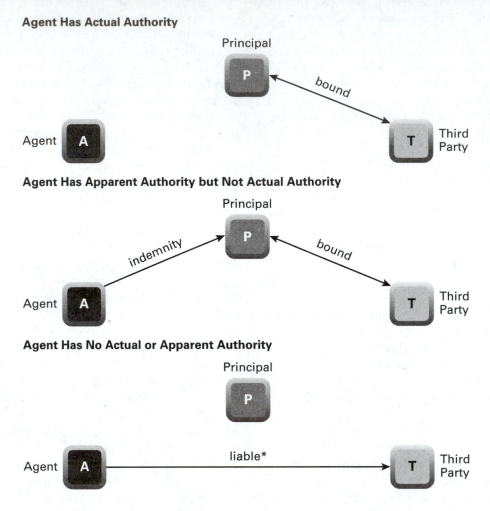

**Agent Has Actual Authority**

**Agent Has Apparent Authority but Not Actual Authority**

**Agent Has No Actual or Apparent Authority**

*Agent is liable for breach of implied warranty of authority or misrepresentation, as discussed later in this chapter.

hold Polly liable. Arlene would have had neither actual authority nor, as to David, apparent authority.

Because apparent authority is the power resulting from acts that appear to the third party to be authorized by the principal, apparent authority cannot exist where the principal is undisclosed. Nor can apparent authority exist where the third party knows that the agent has no actual authority.

◆ *See Figures 20–2 and 20–3*

 *See Case 20–1*

## Delegation of Authority

Because the appointment of an agent reflects the principal's confidence in and reliance upon the agent's personal skill, integrity, and other qualifications, the agent ordinarily has no power to delegate her authority to a subagent. Restatement, Section 18.

Nonetheless, in certain situations it is clear that the principal intended to permit the agent to delegate the authority granted to her. Such an intention may be gathered from the express authorization of the principal, the character of the business, the usages of trade, or the prior conduct of the parties. Restatement, Sections 78–81. For example, if a check is deposited in a bank for collection at a distant place, the bank is impliedly authorized to employ another bank at the place of payment.

If an agent is authorized to appoint or select other persons, called **subagents,** to perform or assist in the performance of the agent's duties, the acts of the subagent are

**FIGURE 20–2**  Contract Liability of Partially Disclosed Principal

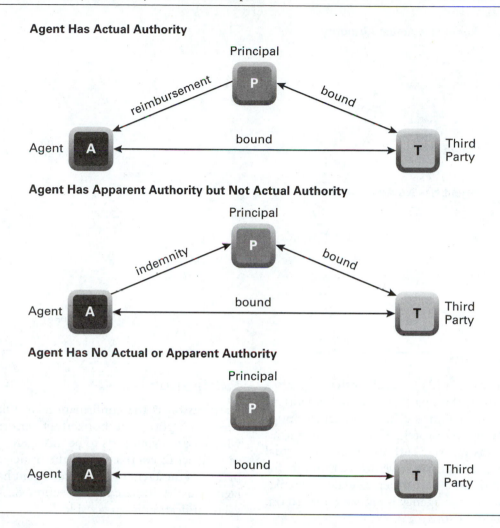

**Agent Has Actual Authority**

**Agent Has Apparent Authority but Not Actual Authority**

**Agent Has No Actual or Apparent Authority**

as binding on the principal as those performed by the agent. As an agent of both the principal and the agent, the subagent owes a fiduciary duty to both.

If an agent having no authority to delegate her authority does so nevertheless, the acts of the subagent do not impose upon the principal any obligations or liability to third persons. Likewise, the principal acquires no rights against such third persons.

## Effect of Termination of Agency on Authority

When an agency terminates, the agent's *actual authority* ceases. When the termination is by the death or incapacity of the principal or agent, the agent's *apparent authority* also expires, as notice of such termination to third persons is not required. Thus, in a case where Thomas,

a tenant of the principal, Plato, paid rent to Plato's agent, Augustus, in ignorance of Plato's death, and Augustus failed to account for the payment, Thomas is liable to Plato's estate for payment of the amount of the rent. The same holds where the performance of an authorized transaction is rendered impossible, such as where the subject matter of the transaction is destroyed or the transaction is made illegal. Restatement, Section 124. The bankruptcy of the principal terminates without notice the power of an agent to affect the principal's property that has passed to the bankruptcy trustee.

In other cases, apparent authority continues until the third party has actual knowledge or receives actual notice, if that third party is one (1) with whom the agent had previously dealt on credit, (2) to whom the agent has been specially accredited, or (3) with whom the agent has begun to deal, as the principal should know.

**FIGURE 20–3**  Contract Liability of Undisclosed Principal

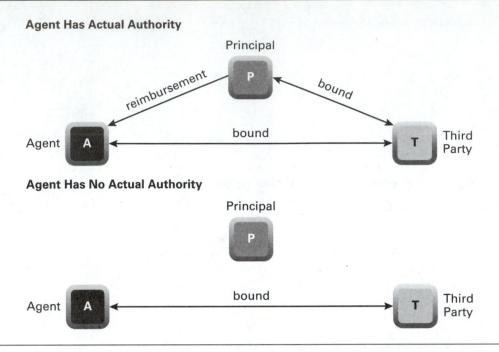

**Agent Has Actual Authority**

**Agent Has No Actual Authority**

---

Restatement, Section 136(2). **Actual notice** requires a communication to the third party, either oral or written. If notice is given by mail, it is effective as actual notice upon delivery, not upon dispatch. All other third parties as to whom there was apparent authority must have actual knowledge or be given **constructive notice** through, for example, publication in a newspaper of general circulation in the area where the agency is regularly carried on. Restatement, Section 136(3).

To illustrate: Alfred is the general agent of Pace, who carries on business in Chicago. Carol knows of the agency but has never dealt with Alfred. Daphne sells goods on credit to Alfred, as the agent of Pace. Pace revokes Alfred's authority and publishes a statement to that effect in a newspaper of general circulation published in Chicago. Carol does not see the statement and deals with Alfred in accordance with and in reliance upon the former agency. Daphne, who also does not see the statement and has no knowledge of the revocation, sells more goods to Alfred, as the agent of Pace. Because Pace has given sufficient notice of revocation as to Carol, Alfred's apparent authority has terminated with respect to Carol. On the other hand, Pace has not given sufficient notice of revocation as to Daphne; consequently, Pace is bound to Daphne by the contract of sale that Alfred made on Pace's behalf.

◆ *See Figure 20–4*

## Ratification

**Ratification** is the confirmation or affirmance by one person of a prior unauthorized act performed by another who is, or who purports to be, his agent. The ratification of such act or contract binds the principal and the third party as if the agent or purported agent had been authorized initially. Restatement, Section 82. Once made, a valid ratification is irrevocable.

***Requirements of Ratification*** Ratification may relate to acts that have exceeded the authority granted to an agent, as well as to acts that a person without any authority performs on behalf of an alleged principal. Nonetheless, for the act to may be ratified, the actor must have indicated to the third person that he was acting on a principal's behalf. There can be no ratification by an undisclosed principal. Thus Archie, without any authority, contracts to sell to Tina an automobile belonging to Pierce. Archie states that the auto is his. Tina promises to pay $5,500 for the automobile. Pierce subsequently learns of the agreement and affirms. Pierce's affirmation of Archie's action would *not* be a ratification because Archie did not purport to act on Pierce's behalf.

To effect a ratification, the principal, with knowledge of all material facts concerning the transaction, must manifest an intent to do so. Restatement, Section 91. The principal does not need to communicate this intent,

**FIGURE 20–4**  Termination of Apparent Authority

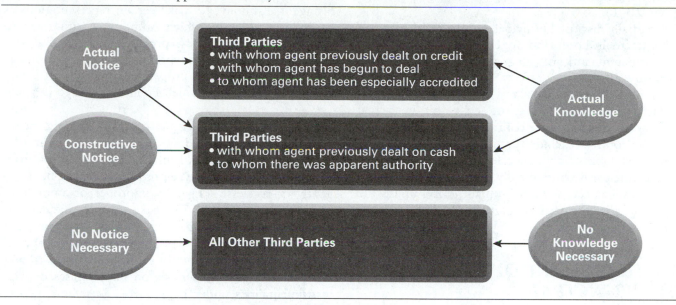

which may be manifested by express language or implied from her conduct, either to the purported agent or to the third person. Thus, if Amanda, without authority, contracts in Penelope's name for the purchase of goods from Tate on credit, and Penelope, having learned of Amanda's unauthorized act, accepts the goods from Tate, she thereby impliedly ratifies the contract and is bound on it. In any event, the principal must ratify the entire act or contract. Restatement, Section 96.

To be effective, ratification must occur before the third person gives notice of his withdrawal to the principal or agent. Restatement, Section 88. If the affirmance of a transaction occurs when the situation has so materially changed that it would be inequitable to subject the third party to liability, the third party may elect to avoid liability. For example, Alex has no authority, but, purporting to act for Penny, contracts to sell Penny's house to Taylor. The next day, the house burns down. Penny then affirms. Taylor is not bound. Moreover, the power to ratify is terminated by the death or loss of capacity of the third party and by the lapse of a reasonable time.

Finally, for ratification to be effective, the purported principal must have been in existence when the act was done. For example, a promoter of a corporation not yet in existence may enter into contracts on behalf of the corporation. In the vast majority of States, however, the corporation cannot ratify these acts because it did not exist when the contracts were made. In contrast, the principal may ratify a contract that is voidable because of the principal's incapacity after the incapacity is removed.

Thus, after she reaches majority, a principal who is a minor may ratify an unauthorized contract made on her behalf.

***Effect of Ratification*** Ratification is equivalent to prior authority, which means that the effect of ratification is substantially the same as the purported agent's having been duly authorized when she performed the act. The respective rights, duties, and remedies of the principal and the third party are the same as if the agent had originally possessed due authority. Both the principal and the agent are in the same position as they would have been if the principal had authorized the act originally. The agent is entitled to her due compensation and, moreover, is freed from liability to the principal for acting as his agent without authority or for exceeding her authority, as the case may be. Between the agent and the third party, the agent is released from any liability she may have to the third party by reason of her having induced the third party to enter into the contract without the principal's authority.

## Fundamental Rules of Contractual Liability

The following rules summarize the contractual relations between the principal and the third party:

1. A disclosed principal and the third party are contractually bound if the agent acts within her actual or

apparent authority in making the contract (see **Figure 20–1**).

2. A partially disclosed principal and the third party are contractually bound if the agent acts within her actual or apparent authority in making the contract (see **Figure 20–2**).

3. An undisclosed principal and the third party are contractually bound if the agent acts within her actual authority in making the contract unless (a) the terms of the contract exclude the principal or (b) his existence is fraudulently concealed (see **Figure 20–3**).

4. No principal is contractually bound to a third party if the agent acts without any authority, unless the principal is disclosed or partially disclosed and he ratifies the contract.

## TORT LIABILITY OF THE PRINCIPAL

In addition to being contractually liable to third persons, a principal may be liable in tort to third persons because of the acts of her agent. Tort liability may arise directly or indirectly (vicariously) from authorized or unauthorized acts of an agent. Also, a principal is liable for the unauthorized torts an agent commits in connection with a transaction that the purported principal, with full knowledge of the tort, subsequently ratifies. Restatement, Section 218. Cases involving unauthorized but ratified torts are extremely rare. Of course, in all of these situations the wrongdoing agent is personally liable to the injured persons because he committed the tort.

◆ *See Figure 20–5*

### Direct Liability of Principal

A principal is liable for his own tortious conduct involving the use of agents. Such liability primarily arises in one of two ways. First, a principal is directly liable in damages for harm resulting from his directing an agent to commit a tort. Second, the principal is directly liable if he fails to exercise care in employing competent agents.

*Authorized Acts of Agent* A principal who authorizes his agent to commit a tortious act with respect to the property or person of another is liable for the injury or loss that person sustains. Restatement, Section 212. The authorized act is that of the principal. Thus, if Phillip directs his agent, Anthony, to enter upon Clark's land and cut timber, which neither Phillip nor Anthony has any right to do, the cutting of the timber is a trespass,

and Phillip is liable to Clark. Or, suppose Phillip instructs his agent, Anthony, to make certain representations as to Phillip's property, which Anthony is authorized to sell. Phillip knows these representations are false, but Anthony does not. Such representations by Anthony to Dryden, who buys the property in reliance on them, constitute a deceit for which Phillip is liable to Dryden.

*Unauthorized Acts of Agent* A principal who negligently or recklessly conducts activities through an employee or other agent is liable for harm resulting from such conduct. Specifically, a principal is liable if he negligently or recklessly (1) gives improper or ambiguous instructions, (2) fails to make proper regulations, (3) employs improper persons as agents, (4) provides improper instruments, tools, or materials to agents, (5) supervises the activities of agents, or (6) fails to prevent tortious acts by persons on his premises or with instrumentalities under his control. Restatement, Section 213.

The liability of a principal under this provision—called **negligent hiring**—arises when the principal does not exercise proper care in selecting an agent for the job to be done. For example, if Patricia lends to her employee, Art, a company car with which to run a business errand knowing that Art is incapable of driving the vehicle, Patricia would be liable for her own negligence to anyone injured through Art's unsafe driving. The negligent hiring doctrine has also been used to impose liability on a principal for intentional torts committed by an agent against customers of the principal or members of the public, where the principal either knew or should have known that the agent was violent or aggressive.

 *See Case 20–2*

### Vicarious Liability of Principal for Unauthorized Acts of Agent

The liability of a principal for the unauthorized torts of an agent depends primarily on whether the agent is an employee or not. An employee is an agent whose physical conduct in the performance of services for the principal–employer is controlled by the principal or is subject to the principal's right to control. By comparison, an agent whose physical conduct is not controlled by, or subject to the control of, the principal is an independent contractor, not an employee. The general rule is that a principal is not liable for physical harm caused by the tortious conduct of an agent who is an independent contractor if the principal did not intend or authorize the result or

**FIGURE 20–5**  Tort Liability

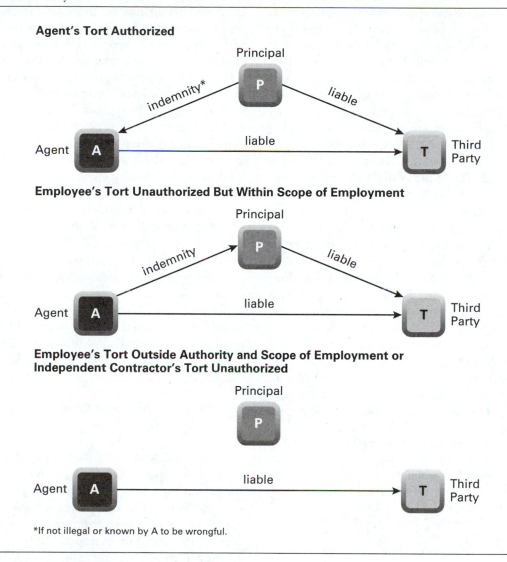

**Agent's Tort Authorized**

Principal

indemnity*

liable

Agent   A   liable   T   Third Party

**Employee's Tort Unauthorized But Within Scope of Employment**

Principal

indemnity

liable

Agent   A   liable   T   Third Party

**Employee's Tort Outside Authority and Scope of Employment or Independent Contractor's Tort Unauthorized**

Principal

Agent   A   liable   T   Third Party

*If not illegal or known by A to be wrongful.

the manner of performance. Restatement, Section 250. Conversely, a principal is liable for an unauthorized tort committed by an employee in the course of his employment. Restatement, Sections 216 and 219.

On the other hand, the liability of a principal whose agent makes an unauthorized yet tortious **misrepresentation** does not depend upon whether the agent is an employee. Rather, the principal is liable for loss caused to another who relies upon a tortious representation made by an agent (whether an employee or an independent contractor) if the representation is apparently authorized. Restatement, Section 257. For example, Pillsbury engages Adams as an agent to sell some land. While negotiating with Trent, Adams states that a stream running through the property has not overflowed its

banks during the past ten years. Adams knows that this is false. In reliance upon this false statement, Trent purchases the land. Pillsbury is liable to Trent for fraudulent misrepresentation.

***Respondeat Superior***  An employer may be liable for an unauthorized tort committed by his employee, even one that is in flagrant disobedience of his instructions, if the employee committed the tort in the course of his employment. This form of employer liability without fault is based upon the doctrine of *respondeat superior* (let the superior respond). The rationale of this doctrine is that a person who conducts his business activities through the use of employees should be liable for their tortious conduct in carrying out those activities. It does not matter how carefully the employer selected the employee, if in fact the latter tortiously injures a third person while engaged in the employer's business. Moreover, an undisclosed principal–employer is liable for the torts committed by her employee within the scope of employment. Restatement, Section 222.

The liability of the principal under *respondeat superior* is vicarious or derivative and depends upon proof of wrongdoing by the employee *in the course of his employment*. Restatement, Section 219. Frequently both principal and employee are joined as defendants in the same suit. Because the liability of the employer is based upon the employee's tortious conduct, if the employee is not held liable, the principal is not liable either. A principal who is held liable for her employee's tort has a right of **indemnification** against the employee, or the right to be reimbursed for the amount that she was required to pay as a result of the employee's wrongful act. Frequently, however, an employee is unable to reimburse his employer, who then must bear the brunt of the liability.

The wrongful act of the employee must be connected with his employment and within its scope if the principal is to be held liable for injuries or damage resulting to third persons. Section 228 of the Restatement provides a general rule for determining whether the conduct of an employee ("servant") is within the scope of employment:

(1) Conduct of a servant is within the scope of employment if, but only if:
    (a) it is of the kind he is employed to perform;
    (b) it occurs substantially within the authorized time and space limits;
    (c) it is actuated, at least in part, by a purpose to serve the master [employer]; and
    (d) if force is intentionally used by the servant against another, the use of force is not unexpectable by the master.
(2) Conduct of a servant is not within the scope of employment if it is different in kind from that authorized, far beyond the authorized time or space limits, or too little actuated by a purpose to serve the master.

For example, Eugene, while delivering gasoline for Packer Oil Co., lights his pipe and negligently throws the blazing match into a pool of gasoline that has dripped onto the ground during the delivery. The gasoline ignites, burning Ray's filling station. Packer is subject to liability for the resulting harm because the negligence of the employee who delivered the gasoline relates directly to the manner in which he handled the goods in his custody. But if a chauffeur, while driving his employer's car on an errand for his employer, suddenly decides to shoot his pistol at pedestrians for target practice, the employer would not be liable to the pedestrians. This willful and intentional misconduct is not related to the performance of the services for which the chauffeur was employed, nor is it expectable by the employer.

To further illustrate, if Page employs Earl to deliver merchandise to Page's customers in a given city, and while driving a delivery truck to or from a place of delivery Earl negligently causes the truck to hit and injure Fred, Page is liable to Fred for the injuries he sustains. But if, after making the scheduled deliveries, Earl drives the truck to a neighboring city to visit a friend and while so doing negligently causes the truck to hit and injure Dottie, Page is not liable. In the latter case, Earl is said to be on a "frolic of his own." By using the truck to accomplish his own purposes, not those of his employer, he has deviated from the purpose of his employment.

A principal may be held liable for the intentional torts of his employee if the commission of the tort is so reasonably connected with the employment as to be within its scope. For example, a principal would be liable if his employee were to make fraudulent statements about the products she is selling, defame a competitor, or disparage the competitor's product.

 *See Cases 20–3 and 20–4*

***Torts of Independent Contractor***  As previously indicated, an independent contractor is not the employee of the person for whom he is performing work or rendering services. Hence, the doctrine of *respondeat superior* generally does not apply to torts committed by an independent contractor. For example, Parnell authorizes Bob, his broker, to sell land for him. Parnell, Teresa, and Bob meet in Teresa's office, where Bob arranges the sale to Teresa. While Bob is preparing the deed for Parnell to sign, he negligently knocks over an inkstand and ruins a valuable rug belonging to Teresa. Bob, but not Parnell, is liable to Teresa. Similarly, Patty employs Igor, a roofer, as an independent contractor to repair her roof. Igor drops a hammer upon Wanda, a pedestrian walking by on the public sidewalk. Igor, but not Patty, is liable to Wanda.

Nonetheless, the principal may be *directly* liable if she fails to exercise reasonable care in selecting an independent contractor. For example, Melanie employs Gordon, whom she knows to be an alcoholic, as an independent contractor to repair her roof. Gordon attempts the repairs while heavily intoxicated and negligently drops a fifty-pound bundle of shingles upon Eric, a pedestrian walking on the sidewalk. Both Gordon and Melanie are liable to Eric.

Moreover, under some circumstances a principal will be *vicariously* liable for torts committed by a carefully selected independent contractor. Certain duties imposed by law are nondelegable, and a person may not escape the consequences of their nonperformance by having entrusted them to an independent contractor. For example, a landowner who permits an independent contractor to maintain a dangerous condition on his premises, such as an excavation, neither surrounded by a guardrail nor lit at night, adjoining a public sidewalk is liable to a member of the public who is injured by falling into the excavation.

A principal is also vicariously liable for an independent contractor's negligent conduct in carrying on an ultrahazardous activity, such as using fire or high explosives. Finally, a principal is vicariously liable if an independent contractor negligently conducts an inherently dangerous activity, such as excavating a public road, demolishing a building, or spraying crops.

## *CRIMINAL LIABILITY OF THE PRINCIPAL*

A principal is liable for the authorized criminal acts of his agents only if the principal directed, participated in, or approved of the acts. For example, if an agent, at his principal's direction or with his principal's knowledge, fixes prices with the principal's competitors, both the agent and the principal have criminally violated the antitrust laws. Otherwise, a principal ordinarily is not liable for the unauthorized criminal acts of his agents. One of the elements of a crime is mental fault, and this element is absent, so far as the criminal responsibility of the principal is concerned, where the principal did not authorize the agent's act.

An employer may, nevertheless, be subject to a criminal penalty for the act of an advisory or managerial person acting in the scope of employment. Restatement, Section 217D, Comment d. Moreover, an employer may be criminally liable under liability without fault statutes for certain unauthorized acts of an employee, whether the employee is managerial or not. These statutes, which usually are regulatory, do not require mental fault. For example, many States have statutes that punish "every person who by himself or his employee or agent sells anything at short weight," or "whoever sells liquor to a minor and any sale by an employee shall be deemed the act of the employer as well." Another example is a statute

prohibiting the sale of unwholesome or adulterated food. See Chapter 6 for a more detailed discussion of this topic.

# RELATIONSHIP OF AGENT AND THIRD PERSONS

The function of an agent is to assist in the conduct of the principal's business by carrying out his orders. Generally, the agent acquires no rights against third parties and likewise incurs no liabilities to them. There are, however, several exceptions to this general proposition. In certain instances, an agent may become personally liable to the third party for contracts she made on behalf of her principal. In some of these situations, the agent also may acquire rights against the third party. In addition, an agent who commits a tort is personally liable to the injured third party. These circumstances involving the personal liability of an agent, as well as those in which an agent may acquire rights against third persons, will be covered in this section.

## *CONTRACT LIABILITY OF AGENT*

The agent normally is not a party to the contract he makes with a third person on behalf of a disclosed principal. An agent who exceeds his actual and apparent authority, however, may be personally liable to the third party. In addition, an agent acting for a disclosed principal may become liable if he expressly assumes liability on the contract. When an agent enters into a contract on behalf of a partially disclosed principal or an undisclosed principal, the agent becomes personally liable to the third party on the contract. Furthermore, an agent who knowingly enters into a contract on behalf of a nonexistent or incompetent principal is personally liable to the third party on that contract.

### Disclosed Principal

As explained earlier, an agent acts for a disclosed principal when, at the time of the transaction, the other party has notice both of the fact that the agent is acting for a principal and of the principal's identity. The agent is not normally a party to the contract she makes with a third person on behalf of a disclosed principal. The third person is on notice that he is transacting business with an agent who is acting for an identified principal and that the agent is not personally undertaking to perform the contract but is simply negotiating on behalf of her principal. The resulting contract, if within the agent's actual authority, is between the third person and the principal, and the agent ordinarily incurs no liability on the contract to either party. Restatement, Section 320. Thus, Angela, who has actual authority to sell circuit boards manufactured by Pinter, writes to Toni, "On behalf of Pinter, I offer to sell you 5,000 circuit boards for $15,000." Toni accepts; consequently, a contract exists between Toni and Pinter. Angela is not a party to that contract and has no liability to Pinter or Toni. This is also true of unauthorized contracts that are subsequently ratified by the principal. If, however, the agent has apparent authority but no actual authority, he has no liability to the third party but is liable to the principal for any loss he causes by exceeding his actual authority.

◆ *See Figure 20–1*

***Unauthorized Contracts***   If an agent exceeds his actual *and* apparent authority, the principal is not bound. The fact that the principal is not bound does not, however, make the agent a party to the contract. The agent's liability, if any, arises from express or implied representations about his authority that he makes to the third party. For example, an agent may **expressly warrant** that he has authority by stating that he has authority and that he will be personally liable to the third party if he does not in fact have the authority to bind his principal.

Moreover, a person who undertakes to make a contract on behalf of another gives an **implied warranty** that he is in fact authorized to make the contract on behalf of the party whom he purports to represent. If the agent does not have authority to bind the principal, the agent is liable to the third party for damages unless the principal ratifies the contract or the third party knew that the agent was unauthorized. No implied warranty exists, however, if the contract expressly provides that the agent shall not be responsible for any lack of authority or if the agent, acting in good faith, discloses to the third person all of the facts upon which his authority rests. For example, agent Larson has received an ambiguous letter of instruction from his principal, Dan. Larson shows it to Carol, stating that it represents all of the authority that he has to act, and both Larson and Carol rely upon its sufficiency. Larson has made no implied or express warranty of his authority to Carol.

If a purported agent **misrepresents** to a third person that he has authority to make a contract on behalf of a principal whom he has no power to bind, he is liable in a tort action to the third person for the loss she sustained

in reliance upon the misrepresentation. If the third party knows, however, that the representation is false, then the agent is not liable.

***Agent Assumes Liability***   An agent may agree to become liable on a contract between the principal and the third party (1) by making the contract in her own name, (2) by co-making the contract with the principal, or (3) by guaranteeing that the principal will perform the contract between the third party and the principal. In each situation, the agent's liability is separate unless the parties agree otherwise. Therefore, the third party may sue the agent separately without joining the principal and may obtain a judgment against either the principal or the agent or both. If the principal satisfies the judgment, the agent is discharged. If the agent pays the judgment, he usually will have a right of reimbursement from the principal. This right is based upon the principles of suretyship, discussed in Chapter 38.

## Partially Disclosed Principal

An agent, as previously discussed, acts for a partially disclosed principal if the third party has notice that the agent is acting for a principal but has no notice of the principal's identity. The use of a partially disclosed principal may be helpful where, for example, the third party might inflate the price of property he was selling if he knew the principal's identity. Partial disclosure also may occur inadvertently, when the agent fails through neglect to inform the third party of the principal's identity.

Unless otherwise agreed, an agent making a contract for a partially disclosed principal is a party to the contract. Restatement, Section 321. For example, Ashley writes to Terrence offering to sell a rare painting on behalf of its owner, who wishes to remain unknown. Terrence accepts. Ashley is a party to the contract.

Whether the particular transaction is authorized or not, an agent for a partially disclosed principal is liable on the contract to the third party. If the agent is actually authorized to make the contract, then both the agent and the partially disclosed principal are liable. In any event, the agent is separately liable, and the third party may sue her individually without joining the principal and may obtain a judgment against either the principal or the agent or both. If the principal satisfies the judgment, the agent is discharged. If the agent pays the judgment, he has the right to be reimbursed by the principal.

◆ *See Figure 20–2*

 *See Case 20–5*

## Undisclosed Principal

An agent acts for an undisclosed principal when she appears to be acting in her own behalf and the third person with whom she is dealing has no knowledge that she is acting as an agent. The principal has instructed the agent to conceal not only the principal's identity but also the agency relationship. Such concealment can also occur if the agent simply neglects to disclose the existence and identity of her principal. Thus, the third person is dealing with the agent as though she were a principal.

The agent is personally liable upon a contract she enters into with a third person on behalf of an undisclosed principal, unless the third person, after discovering the existence and identity of the principal, elects to hold the principal to the contract. The agent is liable because the third person has relied upon the agent individually and has accepted the agent's personal undertaking to perform the contract. Obviously, where the principal is undisclosed, the third person does not know of the interest of anyone in the contract other than that of himself and the agent.

After the third person has learned of the identity of the undisclosed principal, he may hold either the principal or the agent to performance of the contract, but not both; and his choice, once made, binds him irrevocably. Nevertheless, to avoid the possibility that evidence at trial will fail to establish the agency relationship, the third person may bring suit against both the principal and agent. In most States, this act of bringing suit and proceeding to trial against both is not an election, but before the entry of any judgment, the third person is compelled to make an election because he is not entitled to a judgment against both. A judgment against the agent by a third party who knows the identity of the previously undisclosed principal discharges the liability of the principal. Restatement, Section 210. In this case, the agent would have the right to be reimbursed by the principal. If, however, the third party obtains a judgment against the agent before learning the principal's identity, the principal is not discharged. Finally, the agent is discharged from liability if the third party gets a judgment against the principal. Restatement, Section 337.

◆ *See Figure 20–3*

 *See Case 20–5*

## Nonexistent Principal

A person who purports to act as agent for a principal, whom both the agent and the third party know to be non-existent or wholly incompetent, is personally liable on a contract entered into with a third person on behalf of such a principal. Restatement, Section 326. For example, a promoter of a corporation who enters into contracts with third persons in the name of a corporation yet to be organized is personally liable on such contracts. Not yet in existence, and therefore unable to authorize the contracts, the corporation is not liable. If, after coming into existence, the corporation affirmatively adopts a preincorporation contract made on its behalf, it, in addition to the promoter, becomes bound. If the corporation enters into a new contract with such a third person, however, the prior contract between the promoter and the third person is discharged, and the liability of the promoter is terminated. This is a novation. See **Figure 34–1** in Chapter 34.

## Incompetent Principal

An agent who makes a contract for a disclosed principal whose contracts are voidable for lack of contractual capacity is *not* liable to the third party. Restatement, Section 332. There are two exceptions to this rule: (1) if the agent warrants or represents that the principal has capacity or (2) if the agent has reason to know both of the principal's lack of capacity and of the third party's ignorance of that incapacity.

## *TORT LIABILITY OF AGENT*

An agent is personally liable for his tortious acts that injure third persons, whether the principal authorizes such acts or not and whether or not the principal may also be liable. Restatement, Section 343. For example, an agent is personally liable if he converts the goods of a third person to his principal's use. An agent is also liable for making representations that he knows to be fraudulent to a third person who in reliance sustains a loss.

## *RIGHTS OF AGENT AGAINST THIRD PERSON*

An agent who makes a contract with a third person on behalf of a disclosed principal usually has no right of action against the third person for breach of contract. Restatement, Section 363. The agent is not a party to the contract. An agent for a disclosed principal may sue on the contract, however, if it provides that the agent is a party to the contract. Furthermore, an agent for an undisclosed principal or a partially disclosed principal may maintain in her own name an action against the third person for breach of contract. Restatement, Section 364.

# Chapter Summary

## Principal and Third Persons

**Contract Liability of Principal**

**Types of Principals**
- *Disclosed Principal* principal whose existence and identity are known
- *Partially Disclosed Principal* principal whose existence is known but whose identity is not known
- *Undisclosed Principal* principal whose existence and identity are not known

**Authority** power of an agent to change the legal status of the principal
- *Actual Authority* power conferred upon the agent by actual consent given by the principal
- *Actual Express Authority* actual authority derived from written or spoken words of the principal
- *Actual Implied Authority* actual authority inferred from words or conduct manifested to the agent by the principal
- *Apparent Authority* power conferred upon the agent by acts or conduct of the principal that reasonably lead a third party to believe that the agent has such power

**Delegation of Authority** is usually not permitted unless expressly or impliedly authorized by the principal; if the agent is authorized to appoint other subagents, the acts of these subagents are as binding on the principal as those of the agent

**Effect of Termination of Agency on Authority** ends actual authority
- *Termination by Operation of Law* apparent authority also ends without notice to third parties
- *Termination by Act of Parties* apparent authority ends when third parties have actual knowledge or when appropriate notice is given to third parties: actual notice must be given to third parties with whom the agent has previously dealt on credit, has been specially accredited, or has begun to deal; all other third parties as to whom there was apparent authority need be given only constructive notice

**Ratification** affirmation by one person of a prior unauthorized act that another has done as her agent or as her purported agent

**Fundamental Rules of Contractual Liability**
- *Disclosed Principal* is contractually bound with the third party if the agent acts within her actual or apparent authority in making the contract
- *Partially Disclosed Principal* is contractually bound with the third party if the agent acts within her actual or apparent authority in making the contract
- *Undisclosed Principal* is contractually bound with the third party if the agent acts within her actual authority in making the contract

**Tort Liability of Principal**

**Direct Liability of Principal** a principal is liable for his own tortious conduct involving the use of agents
- *Authorized Acts of Agent* a principal is liable for torts she authorizes another to commit
- *Unauthorized Acts of Agent* a principal is liable for failing to exercise care in employing agents whose unauthorized acts cause harm

**Vicarious Liability of Principal for Unauthorized Acts of Agent**
- *Respondeat Superior* an employer is liable for unauthorized torts committed by an employee in the course of his employment
- *Independent Contractor* a principal is usually not liable for the unauthorized torts of an independent contractor

| **Criminal Liability of Principal** | **Authorized Acts** the principal is liable if he directed, participated in, or approved the criminal acts of his agents<br>**Unauthorized Acts** the principal may be liable either for a criminal act of a managerial person or under liability without fault statutes |
| --- | --- |

## Agent and Third Persons

| **Contract Liability of Agent** | **Disclosed Principals** the agent is not normally a party to the contract she makes with a third person if she is authorized or if the principal ratifies an unauthorized contract<br>• *Unauthorized Contracts* if an agent exceeds her actual and apparent authority, the principal is not bound but the agent may be liable for breach of warranty or for misrepresentation<br>• *Agent Assumes Liability* an agent may agree to become liable on a contract between the principal and the third party<br>**Partially Disclosed Principal** an agent who acts for a partially disclosed principal is a party to the contract with the third party unless otherwise agreed<br>**Undisclosed Principal** an agent who acts for an undisclosed principal is personally liable on the contract to the third party<br>**Nonexistent or Incompetent Principal** a person who purports to act as an agent for a principal whom both the agent and the third party know to be nonexistent or wholly incompetent is personally liable on a contract entered into with a third person on behalf of such a principal |
| --- | --- |

| **Tort Liability of Agent** | **Authorized Acts** the agent is liable to the third party for his own torts<br>**Unauthorized Acts** the agent is liable to the third party for his own torts |
| --- | --- |

| **Rights of Agent** | **Disclosed Principal** the agent usually has no rights against the third party<br>**Partially Disclosed Principal** the agent may enforce the contract against the third party<br>**Undisclosed Principal** the agent may enforce the contract against the third party |
| --- | --- |

# Cases

### CASE 20–1
## Types of Authority
### *SCHOENBERGER v. CHICAGO TRANSIT AUTHORITY*

Appellate Court of Illinois, First District, First Division, 1980
84 Ill.App.3d 1132, 39 Ill.Dec. 941, 405 N.E.2d 1076

CAMPBELL, J.
The plaintiff, James Schoenberger, brought a small claims action pro se in the Municipal Department of the circuit court of Cook County against the defendant, Chicago Transit Authority (hereinafter C.T.A.) to recover contract damages. The trial court ruled in favor of the defendant and against the plaintiff. The plaintiff appeals from this judgment. At issue is whether the C.T.A. may be held liable under agency principles of a promise allegedly made by an employee of the C.T.A.

to the plaintiff at the time that he was hired to the effect that he would receive a $500 increase in salary within a specified period of time. We affirm.

Schoenberger was employed by the C.T.A. from August 16, 1976, to October, 1976, at a salary of $19,300. The facts surrounding his employment with the C.T.A. are controverted. The plaintiff's position at the trial was that he took the job with the C.T.A. at a salary of $19,300 upon the condition that he would receive a $500 salary increase, above and beyond any merit raises, within a year. Schoenberger testified at trial that, after filling out a job application and undergoing an initial interview with a C.T.A. Placement Department interviewer, he met several times with Frank ZuChristian, who was in charge of recruiting for the Data Center. At one of the meetings with ZuChristian, the Director of Data Center Operations, John Bonner, was present. At the third meeting held between ZuChristian and the plaintiff, ZuChristian informed the plaintiff that he desired to employ him at $19,800 and that he was making a recommendation to this effect. Schoenberger told ZuChristian that he would accept the offer. ZuChristian informed him that a formal offer would come from the Placement Department within a few days. However, when the offer was made, the salary was stated at $19,300. Schoenberger did not accept the offer immediately. Rather, he called ZuChristian for an explanation of the salary difference. After making inquiries, ZuChristian informed Schoenberger that a clerical error had been made and that it would take a number of weeks to have the necessary paperwork reapproved because several people were on vacation. To expedite matters, ZuChristian suggested Schoenberger take the job at the $19,300 figure and that he would see that the $500 would be made up to him at the April, 1976, October, 1976, or at the latest, the April, 1977, performance and salary review. The $500 increase was to be prospective and not retroactive in nature. John Hogan, the head of the Data Center, was aware of this promise, ZuChristian informed Schoenberger. Because the defendant was found to be ineligible for the October, 1976 performance evaluation and the April, 1976 review was cancelled, the April, 1977 evaluation was the first evaluation at which the issue of the salary increase was raised. When the increase was not given at that time, the plaintiff resigned and filed this suit.

* * *

The trial court, after hearing the evidence and reviewing the exhibits, ruled in favor of the defendant. The trial court ruled: (1) that it was inconceivable that the plaintiff thought ZuChristian had final authority in regard to employment contracts; and (2) that it was not shown that a commitment or promise was made to the plaintiff by an authorized agent of the C.T.A.

* * *

The main question before us is whether ZuChristian, acting as an agent of the C.T.A., orally contracted with Schoenberger for $500 in compensation in addition to his $19,300 salary. The authority of an agent may only come from the principal and it is therefore necessary to trace the source of an agent's authority to some word or act of the alleged principal. [Citations.] The authority to bind a principal will not be presumed, but rather, the person alleging authority must prove its source unless the act of the agent has been ratified. [Citations.] Moreover, the authority must be founded upon some word or act of the principal, not on the acts or words of the agent. [Citations.]

* * * Both Hogan and Bonner, ZuChristian's superiors, testified that ZuChristian had no actual authority to either make an offer of a specific salary to Schoenberger or to make any promise of additional compensation. Furthermore, ZuChristian's testimony corroborated the testimony that he lacked the authority to make formal offers. From this evidence, it is clear that the trial court properly determined that ZuChristian lacked the actual authority to bind the C.T.A. for the additional $500 in compensation to Schoenberger.

Nor can it be said that the C.T.A. clothed ZuChristian with the apparent authority to make Schoenberger a promise of compensation over and above that formally offered by the Placement Department. The general rule to consider in determining whether an agent is acting within the apparent authority of his principal was stated in [citation] in this way:

Apparent authority in an agent is such authority as the principal knowingly permits the agent to assume or which he holds his agent out as possessing—it is such authority as a reasonably prudent man, exercising diligence and discretion, in view of the principal's conduct, would naturally suppose the agent to possess.

* * *

Here, Schoenberger's initial contact with the C.T.A. was with the Placement Department where he filled out an application and had his first interview. There is no evidence that the C.T.A. did anything to permit ZuChristian to assume authority nor did they do anything to hold him out as having the authority to hire and set salaries. ZuChristian was not at a management level in the C.T.A. nor did his job title of Principal Communications Analyst suggest otherwise. The mere fact that he was allowed to interview prospective employees does not establish that the C.T.A. held him out as possessing the authority to hire employees or set salaries. Moreover, ZuChristian did inform Schoenberger that the formal offer of employment would be made by the Placement Department.

\* \* \*

Our final inquiry concerns the plaintiff's contention that irrespective of ZuChristian's actual or apparent authority, the C.T.A. is bound by ZuChristian's promise because it ratified his acts. Ratification may be express or inferred and occurs where "the principal, with knowledge of the material facts of the unauthorized transaction, takes a position inconsistent with nonaffirmation of the transaction." [Citations.] Ratification is the equivalent to an original authorization and confirms that which was originally unauthorized. [Citation.] Ratification occurs where a principal attempts to seek or retain the benefits of the transaction. [Citations.]

Upon review of the evidence, we are not convinced that the C.T.A. acted to ratify ZuChristian's promise. According to Bonner's testimony, when he took over the supervision of ZuChristian's group in the fall of 1976 and was told of the promise, he immediately informed ZuChristian that the promise was unauthorized and consequently would not be honored. Subsequently, he informed Schoenberger of this same fact. Mere delay in telling Schoenberger does not, as the plaintiff contends, establish the C.T.A.'s intent to ratify. [Citations.]

\* \* \*

For the reasons we have indicated, the judgment of the circuit court of Cook County granting judgment in favor of the defendant, C.T.A., is affirmed.

---

### CASE 20–2
## Direct Liability of Principal: Negligent Hiring
### *CONNES v. MOLALLA TRANSPORT SYSTEM, INC.*
Supreme Court of Colorado, 1992
831 P.2d 1316

QUINN, J.

[Terry Taylor was an employee of Molalla Transport. In hiring Taylor, Molalla followed its standard hiring procedure, which includes a personal interview with each applicant and requires the applicant to fill out an extensive job application form and to produce a current driver's license and a medical examiner's certificate. Molalla also contacts prior employers and other references about the applicant's qualifications and conducts an investigation of the applicant's driving record in the state where the applicant obtained the driver's license. Although applicants are asked whether they have been convicted of a crime, Molalla does not conduct an independent investigation to determine whether an applicant has been convicted of a crime. Approximately three months after Taylor began working for Molalla, he was assigned to transport freight from Kansas to Oregon. While traveling through Colorado, Taylor left the highway and drove by a hotel where Grace Connes was working as a night clerk. Observing that Connes was alone in the lobby, Taylor pulled his truck into the parking lot and entered the lobby. Once inside, Taylor sexually assaulted Connes at knifepoint. Although Taylor denied any prior criminal convictions on his application and during his interview, police and court records obtained since these events show that Taylor had been convicted of three felonies in Colorado and had been issued three citations for lewd conduct and another citation for simple assault in Seattle, Washington.

Connes sued Molalla on the theory of negligent hiring, claiming that Molalla knew or should have known that Taylor would come into contact with members of the public, that Molalla had a duty to hire and retain high quality employees so as not to endanger members of the public, and that Molalla had breached its duty by failing to investigate fully and adequately Taylor's criminal background. The district court granted Molalla's motion for summary judgment. The Court of Appeals upheld the lower court's ruling, holding that Molalla had no legal duty to investigate the non-vehicular criminal record of its driver prior to hiring him as an employee. Connes appealed.]

\* \* \*

## II

The elements of a negligence claim consist of the existence of a legal duty by the defendant to the plaintiff, breach of that duty by the defendant, injury to the plaintiff, and a sufficient causal relationship between the defendant's breach and the plaintiff's injuries. [Citations.] A negligence claim will fail if it is predicated on circumstances for which the law imposes no duty of care upon the defendant. [Citations.] "A court's conclusion that a duty does or does not exist is 'an expression of the sum total of those considerations of policy which lead the law to say that the plaintiff is [or is not] entitled to protection.'" [Citations.]

The initial question in any negligence action, therefore, is whether the defendant owed a legal duty to protect the plaintiff against injury. The issue of legal duty is a question of law to be determined by the court. [Citations.]

A duty of reasonable care arises when there is a foreseeable risk of injury to others from a defendant's failure to take protective action to prevent the injury. [Citation.] While foreseeability is a prime factor in the duty calculus, a court also must weigh other factors, including the social utility of the defendant's conduct, the magnitude of the burden of guarding against the harm caused to the plaintiff, the practical consequences of placing such a burden on the defendant, and any additional elements disclosed by the particular circumstances of the case. [Citations.] "No one factor is controlling, and the question of whether a duty should be imposed in a particular case is essentially one of fairness under contemporary standards—whether reasonable persons would recognize a duty and agree that it exists." [Citation.]

The tort of negligent hiring is based on the principle that a person conducting an activity through employees is subject to liability for harm resulting from negligent conduct "in the employment of improper persons or instrumentalities in work involving risk of harm to others." Restatement (Second) of Agency § 213(b) (1958). This principle of liability is not based on the rule of agency but rather on the law of torts. In [citation], the New Jersey Supreme Court offered the following distinction between the tort of negligent hiring and the agency doctrine of vicarious liability based on the rule of *respondeat superior*:

Thus, the tort of negligent hiring addresses the risk created by exposing members of the public to a potentially dangerous individual, while the doctrine of *respondeat superior* is based on the theory that the employee is the agent or is acting for the employer. Therefore the scope of employment limitation on liability which is part of the *respondeat superior* doctrine is not implicit in the wrong of negligent hiring.

Accordingly, the negligent hiring theory has been used to impose liability in cases where the employee commits an intentional tort, an action almost invariably outside the scope of employment, against the customer of a particular employer or other member of the public, where the employer either knew or should have known that the employee was violent or aggressive, or that the employee might engage in injurious conduct toward third persons.

Several jurisdictions, in addition to New Jersey, have recognized the tort of negligent hiring, e.g., [Alaska, Arizona, Connecticut, Florida, Georgia, Iowa, Kansas, Maryland, Minnesota, Mississippi, Missouri, New Mexico, and Rhode Island], and we now join those jurisdictions in formally recognizing this cause of action.

In recognizing the tort of negligent hiring, we emphasize that an employer is not an insurer for violent acts committed by an employee against a third person. On the contrary, liability is predicated on the employer's hiring of a person under circumstances antecedently giving the employer reason to believe that the person, by reason of some attribute of character or prior conduct, would create an undue risk of harm to others in carrying out his or her employment responsibilities. See Restatement (Second) of Agency § 213, comment d. The scope of the employer's duty in exercising reasonable care in a hiring decision will depend largely on the anticipated degree of contact which the employee will have with other persons in performing his or her employment duties.

Where the employment calls for minimum contact between the employee and other persons, there may be no reason for an employer to conduct any investigation of the applicant's background beyond obtaining past employment information and personal data during the initial interview. [Citation.] * * *

* * *

We endorse the proposition that where an employer hires a person for a job requiring frequent contact with members of the public, or involving close contact with particular persons as a result of a special relationship between such persons and the employer, the employer's duty of reasonable care is not satisfied by a mere review of personal data disclosed by the applicant on a job application form or during a personal interview. However, in the absence of circumstances antecedently giving the employer reason to believe that the job applicant, by reason of some attribute of character or prior conduct, would constitute an undue risk of harm to members of the public with whom the applicant will be in frequent contact or to particular persons standing in a special relationship to the employer and with whom the applicant will have close contact, we decline to impose upon the employer his duty to obtain and review official records of an applicant's criminal history. To impose such a requirement would mean that an employer would be obligated to seek out and evaluate official police and perhaps court records from every jurisdiction in which a job applicant had any significant contact. We have serious doubts whether such a task could be effectively achieved. Even if it could, there would remain the significant problem of interpreting the records and relating them in a practical way to the job in question. Accordingly, in the absence of circumstances antecedently giving the employer reason to believe that a job applicant, by reason of some attribute of character or prior conduct, would constitute an undue risk of harm to members of the public with whom the applicant will be in frequent contact or to particular persons who stand in a special relationship to the employer and with whom the applicant will be in close contact, the employer's duty of reasonable care does not extend to searching for and reviewing official records of a job applicant's criminal history.

## III

In the instant case, we agree with the court of appeals' determination that Molalla had no duty to conduct an independent investigation into Taylor's non-vehicular criminal background before hiring him as a long-haul driver. Molalla had no reason to foresee that its hiring of Taylor under the circumstances of this case would create a risk that Taylor would sexually assault or otherwise endanger a member of the public by engaging in violent conduct. To be sure, Molalla had a duty to use reasonable care in hiring a safe driver who would not create a danger to the public in carrying out the duties of the job. Far from requiring frequent contact with members of the public or involving close contact with persons having a special relationship with the employer, Taylor's duties were restricted to the hauling of freight on interstate highways and, as such, involved only incidental contact with third persons having no special relationship to Molalla or to Taylor. After checking on Taylor's driving record and contacting some of his references, Molalla had no reason to believe that Taylor would not be a safe driver or a dependable employee. In addition, Molalla specifically instructed its drivers to stay on the interstate highways and, except for an emergency, to stop only in order to service the truck and to eat and to sleep. It further directed its drivers to sleep in the sleeping compartment behind the driver's seat of the truck at rest areas or truck stops located along the interstate highway system. Furthermore, Molalla required Taylor to fill out a job application and to submit to a personal interview. Taylor stated on the application form and at the interview that he had never been convicted of a crime. Nothing in the hiring process gave Molalla reason to foresee that Taylor would pose an unreasonable risk of harm to members of the public with whom he might have incidental contact during the performance of his duties. In addition to the unforeseeability of the risk of harm, other factors weigh in favor of not imposing on Molalla a legal duty to conduct an independent investigation into Taylor's non-vehicular criminal history under the circumstances of this case. Molalla not only is engaged in a legitimate interstate freight-transportation service, but also, as part of its operations, provides a useful service in employing drivers on the basis of their safe driving record and their dependability in delivering their loads and caring for the valuable equipment entrusted to them.

We accordingly hold that Molalla, in hiring Taylor as a long-haul truck driver, had no legal duty to conduct an independent investigation into Taylor's non-vehicular criminal background in order to protect a member of the public, such as Connes, from a sexual assault committed by Taylor in the course of making a long-haul trip over the interstate highway system. The judgment of the court of appeals is affirmed.

---

## CASE 20–3
### Tort Liability of Principal
# CLOVER v. SNOWBIRD SKI RESORT
Supreme Court of Utah, 1991
808 P.2d 1037

HALL, C.J.
Plaintiff Margaret Clover sought to recover damages for injuries sustained as the result of a ski accident in which Chris Zulliger, an employee of defendant Snowbird Corporation ("Snowbird"), collided with her. From the entry of summary judgment in favor of defendants, Clover appeals.

* * * At the time of the accident, Chris Zulliger was employed by Snowbird as a chef at the Plaza Restaurant. Zulliger was supervised by his father, Hans Zulliger, who

was the head chef at both the Plaza, which was located at the base of the resort, and the Mid-Gad Restaurant, which was located halfway to the top of the mountain. Zulliger was instructed by his father to make periodic trips to the Mid-Gad to monitor its operations. Prior to the accident, the Zulligers had made several inspection trips to the restaurant. On at least one occasion, Zulliger was paid for such a trip. He also had several conversations with Peter Mandler, the manager of the Plaza and Mid-Gad Restaurants, during which Mandler directed him to make periodic stops at the Mid-Gad to monitor operations.

On December 5, 1985, the date of the accident, Zulliger was scheduled to begin work at the Plaza Restaurant at 3 PM. Prior to beginning work, he had planned to go skiing with Barney Norman, who was also employed as a chef at the Plaza. Snowbird preferred that their employees know how to ski because it made it easier for them to get to and from work. As part of the compensation for their employment, both Zulliger and Norman received season ski passes. On the morning of the accident, Mandler asked Zulliger to inspect the operation of the Mid-Gad prior to beginning work at the Plaza.

Zulliger and Norman stopped at the Mid-Gad in the middle of their first run. At the restaurant, they had a snack, inspected the kitchen, and talked to the personnel for approximately fifteen to twenty minutes. Zulliger and Norman then skied four runs before heading down the mountain to begin work. On their final run, Zulliger and Norman took a route that was often taken by Snowbird employees to travel from the top of the mountain to the Plaza. About midway down the mountain, at a point above the Mid-Gad, Zulliger decided to take a jump off a crest on the side of an intermediate run. He had taken this jump many times before. A skier moving relatively quickly is able to become airborne at that point because of the steep drop off on the downhill side of the crest. Due to this drop off, it is impossible for skiers above the crest to see skiers below the crest. The jump was well known to Snowbird. In fact, the Snowbird ski patrol often instructed people not to jump off the crest. There was also a sign instructing skiers to ski slowly at this point in the run. Zulliger, however, ignored the sign and skied over the crest at a significant speed. Clover, who had just entered the same ski run from a point below the crest, either had stopped or was traveling slowly below the crest. When Zulliger went over the jump, he collided with Clover, who was hit in the head and severely injured.

Clover brought claims against Zulliger and Snowbird, alleging that (1) Zulliger's reckless skiing was a proximate cause of her injuries, (2) Snowbird is liable for Zulliger's negligence because at the time of the collision, he was acting within the scope of his employment, * * *. Zulliger settled separately with Clover. Under two separate motions for summary judgment, the trial judge dismissed Clover's claims against Snowbird [because] as a matter of law, Zulliger was not acting within the scope of his employment at the time of the collision * * *.

Under the doctrine of *respondeat superior*, employers are held vicariously liable for the torts their employees commit when the employees are acting within the scope of their employment. Clover's respondeat superior claim was dismissed on the ground that as a matter of law, Zulliger's actions at the time of the accident were not within the scope of his employment. * * *

In [*Birkner v. Salt Lake County*], we observed that the Utah cases that have addressed the issue of whether an employee's actions, as a matter of law, are within or without the scope of employment have focused on three criteria. "First, an employee's conduct must be of the general kind the employee is employed to perform. . . . In other words, the employee must be about the employer's business and the duties assigned by the employer, as opposed to being wholly involved in a personal endeavor." Second, the employee's conduct must occur substantially within the hours and ordinary spatial boundaries of the employment. "Third, the employee's conduct must be motivated at least in part, by the purpose of serving the employer's interest." * * *

In applying the *Birkner* criteria to the facts in the instant case, it is important to note that if Zulliger had returned to the Plaza Restaurant immediately after he inspected the operations at the Mid-Gad Restaurant, there would be ample evidence to support the conclusion that on his return trip Zulliger's actions were within the scope of his employment. There is evidence that it was part of Zulliger's job to monitor the operations at the Mid-Gad and that he was directed to monitor the operations on the day of the accident. There is also evidence that Snowbird intended Zulliger to use the ski lifts and the ski runs on his trips to the Mid-Gad. It is clear, therefore, that Zulliger's actions could be considered to "be of the general kind that the employee is employed to perform." It is also clear that there would be evidence that Zulliger's actions occurred within the hours and normal spatial boundaries of his employment. Zulliger was expected to monitor the operations at the Mid-Gad during the time the lifts were operating and when he was not working as a chef at the Plaza. Furthermore, throughout the trip he would have been on his employer's premises. Finally, it is clear that Zulliger's actions in monitoring the operations at the Mid-Gad, per his employer's instructions, could be considered "motivated, at least in part, by the purpose of serving the employer's interest."

The difficulty, of course, arises from the fact that Zulliger did not return to the Plaza after he finished inspecting the facilities at the Mid-Gad. Rather, he skied four more runs and rode the lift to the top of the mountain before he began his return to the base. Snowbird claims that this fact shows that Zulliger's primary purpose for skiing on the day of the accident was for his own pleasure and that therefore, as a matter of law, he was not acting within the scope of his employment. * * * In situations where the scope of employment issue concerns an employee's trip, a useful test in determining if the transaction of business is purely incidental to a personal motive is "whether the trip is one which would have required the employer to send another employee over the same route or to perform the same function if the trip had not been made."

* * * [T]he activity of inspecting the Mid-Gad necessitates travel to the restaurant. Furthermore, there is evidence that the manager of both the Mid-Gad and the Plaza wanted an employee to inspect the restaurant and report back by 3 PM. If Zulliger had not inspected the restaurant, it would have been necessary to send a second employee to accomplish the same purpose. Furthermore, the second employee would have most likely used the ski lifts and ski runs in traveling to and from the restaurant.

There is ample evidence that there was a predominant business purpose for Zulliger's trip to the Mid-Gad. Therefore, this case is better analyzed under our decisions dealing with situations where an employee has taken a personal detour in the process of carrying out his duties. This court has decided several cases in which employees deviated from their duties for wholly personal reasons and then, after resuming their duties, were involved in accidents. In situations where the detour was such a substantial diversion from the employee's duties that it constituted an abandonment of employment, we held that the employee, as a matter of law, was acting outside the scope of employment. However, in situations where reasonable minds could differ on whether the detour constituted a slight deviation from the employee's duties or an abandonment of employment, we have left the question for the jury.

Under the circumstances of the instant case, it is entirely possible for a jury to reasonably believe that at the time of the accident, Zulliger had resumed his employment and that Zulliger's deviation was not substantial enough to constitute a total abandonment of employment. First, a jury could reasonably believe that by beginning his return to the base of the mountain to begin his duties as a chef and to report to Mandler concerning his observations at the Mid-Gad, Zulliger had resumed his employment. * * *

Second, a jury could reasonably believe that Zulliger's actions in taking four ski runs and returning to the top of the mountain do not constitute a complete abandonment of employment. It is important to note that by taking these ski runs, Zulliger was not disregarding his employer's directions. * * * In the instant case, far from directing its employees not to ski at the resort, Snowbird issued its employees season ski passes as part of their compensation.

These two factors, along with other circumstances—such as, throughout the day Zulliger was on Snowbird's property, there was no specific time set for inspecting the restaurant, and the act of skiing was the method used by Snowbird employees to travel among the different locations of the resort—constitute sufficient evidence for a jury to conclude that Zulliger, at the time of the accident, was acting within the scope of his employment.

* * *

In light of the genuine issues of material fact in regard to each of Clover's claims, summary judgment was inappropriate.

Reversed and remanded for further proceedings.

---

## CASE 20–4
## Tort Liability of Principal
### RUBIN v. YELLOW CAB CO.

Appellate Court of Illinois, First District, Fifth Division, 1987
154 Ill.App.3d 336, 107 Ill.Dec. 450, 507 N.E.2d 114

LORENZ, J.
Plaintiff was driving on one of the city's streets when he inadvertently obstructed the path of a taxi, causing the latter to swerve and come into contact with plaintiff's vehicle. Angered by plaintiff's sudden blocking of his traffic lane, defendant driver proceeded to exit his cab,

approach plaintiff and strike him about the head and shoulder with a metal pipe.

Plaintiff subsequently filed suit against Robert C. Ball ("Ball"), the cab driver, and Yellow Cab Company ("Yellow Cab"), the owner of the taxi, to recover damages for bodily injuries sustained as a result of the altercation. On defendant Yellow Cab's motion, the trial court dismissed seven of nine counts included in plaintiff's fourth amended complaint for failure to state a cause of action. * * *

We initially consider whether the subject complaint states a cause of action under the doctrine of *respondeat superior*.

It is well established that an employer may be held liable for the negligent, willful, malicious or criminal acts of its employees where such acts are committed in the course of employment and in furtherance of the business of the employer. [Citation.] However, where the acts complained of are committed solely for the benefit of the employee, the employer will not be held liable to an injured third party. [Citation.]

* * *

While we accept the principles stated in the cases primarily relied on by plaintiff, their factual inappositeness makes their application improper in the resolution of the instant case. [Citations], all present situations in which bartenders or bouncers endeavored to maintain order or protect the property of their employees. The nature of a bartender's or bouncer's job makes the use of force during the course of his employment highly probable. A cab driver, on the other hand, is basically relegated to transporting individuals from one destination to another and, as such, it is unlikely that he will undertake to attack a person that is neither a passenger nor is connected with the cab company. In [citation], an employee holding the position of office manager in a finance company

mistakenly shot plaintiff while in the pursuit of robbers. Likewise, the court found the employee to have acted within his managerial capacity and in accordance with his duty to protect the property and business of his employer.

The assault on plaintiff in the instant case amounted to a deviation from the conduct generally associated with the enterprise of cab driving. Accordingly, we find the facts before us to be more akin to those in *Webb by Harris v. Jewel Companies, Inc.*, [citation] and *Awe v. Striker*, [citation]. In *Webb by Harris*, plaintiff sought to hold Jewel liable for a sexual assault committed by one of its security guards. This court held at that time that it was impossible to interpret such act as one undertaken for the purpose of furthering Jewel's business. Similarly, plaintiff in *Awe* sought to hold the operators of a carnival liable for the battery committed on his person by several employees. Upon losing a carnival game, plaintiff had complained to the employees of crookedness and threatened to notify the Sheriff. Angered by the threats, the employees proceeded to jump on plaintiff and beat him with their fists and a hammer. In dismissing the counts brought under the doctrine of *respondeat superior* for failure to state a cause of action, the court held that since the game played by plaintiff had been completed and the carnival employees had performed the duties for which they had been hired, the subsequent attack was outside the scope and not in furtherance of their employment.

As Ball's assault on plaintiff was clearly not an act undertaken to further Yellow Cab's business but rather one propelled singularly by anger and frustration, the trial court properly dismissed Count IX of plaintiff's fourth amended complaint for failure to state a cause of action under the doctrine of *respondeat superior*.

* * *

The judgment of the trial court is affirmed.

---

## CASE 20–5
### Undisclosed or Partially Disclosed Principal
### *VAN D. COSTAS, INC. v. ROSENBERG*
District Court of Appeal of Florida, Second District, 1983
432 So.2d 656

GRIMES, J.
This is an appeal from a final judgment denying appellant's claims for mechanic's lien foreclosure and breach of contract.

Gilbert Rosenberg owned a parcel of real property on Siesta Key upon which the Magic Moment Restaurant

was located. Seascape Restaurants, Inc., operated the restaurant and paid a monthly rental to Rosenberg for use of the property. Gilbert Rosenberg, his son Jeff Rosenberg, and Chris Moore each owned one third of Seascape. Jeff was president of Seascape and Moore was vice president, and the two of them operated the restaurant.

Gilbert was not an officer of the corporation and was not actively involved in the management of the restaurant.

In November of 1980, appellant's president, Van D. Costas, met with Gilbert and Jeff to discuss the creation of a "magical entrance" for the restaurant. The following month, appellant entered into a contract to remodel the entrance. Jeff Rosenberg signed the contract on a line under which appeared "Jeff Rosenberg, The Magic Moment." After the work commenced, the parties became involved in a dispute over performance and payment, and appellant filed a claim of lien on the real estate. Appellant thereafter sued Gilbert to foreclose the lien and in a second count of the complaint sued Jeff Rosenberg for breach of contract. Jeff counter-claimed for damages for faulty performance and other relief. Following a trial, the court entered a final judgment against the appellant which stated in pertinent part:

. . . On the claim against Jeff Rosenberg, individually, the contract was addressed to "The Magic Moment Restaurant." It was drawn on plaintiff's stationery and referred to "Subject: Design and Creation of Mystical Entrance to 'The Magic Moment Restaurant.'" Under the prepared signature line for defendant's signature was typed "Jeff Rosenberg, The Magic Moment." Jeff Rosenberg signed his name on the line provided. Obviously he signed for "The Magic Moment," and there is no dispute that the plaintiff knew he was contracting with "The Magic Moment Restaurant." Plaintiff did testify that he thought the Rosenbergs owned the restaurant. However, there is also no dispute that the business was owned by Seascape Restaurants, Inc. who were doing business under the trade name of "The Magic Moment Restaurant." Under all these circumstances, there is no individual responsibility and the proper party to this suit, as to both claims and counterclaims, is Seascape Restaurants, Inc.

\* \* \*

Appellant bases its claim against Jeff upon the contention that he signed the contract as agent for an undisclosed principal. It is well settled that where one enters into a contract as agent for an undisclosed principal, he may be held individually liable on the contract. [Citations.] The extent to which an agent must make disclosure of his principal in order to avoid personal liability is explained in 3 Am.Jur.2d *Agency* § 320 (1962):

In order for an agent to avoid personal liability on a contract negotiated in his principal's behalf, he must disclose not only that he is an agent but also the identity of his principal, regardless of whether the third person might have known that the agent was acting in a representative capacity. It is not the third person's duty to seek out the identity of the principal; rather, the duty to disclose the identity of the

principal is on the agent. The disclosure of an agency is not complete for the purpose of relieving the agent from personal liability unless it embraces the name of the principal; without that, the party dealing with the agent may understand that he intended to pledge his personal liability and responsibility in support of the contract and for its performance. Furthermore, the use of a trade name is not necessarily a sufficient disclosure of the identity of the principal and the fact of agency so as to protect the agent against personal liability.

Section 321 of the Restatement (Second) of the Law of Agency (1957) discusses the liability of the agent under circumstances in which it appears that he is acting for someone else but the identity of his principal is unknown to the other party.

§ 321. Principal Partially Disclosed
Unless otherwise agreed, a person purporting to make a contract with another for a partially disclosed principal is a party to the contract.
Comment:
   a. A principal is a partially disclosed principal when, at the time of making the contract in question, the other party thereto has notice that the agent is acting for a principal but has no notice of the principal's identity. See § 4. The fact that, to the knowledge of the agent, the other party does not know the identity of the principal is of great weight in ascribing to the other party the intention to hold the agent liable either solely, or as a surety or co-promisor with the principal. The inference of an understanding that the agent is a party to the contract exists unless the agent gives such complete information concerning his principal's identity that he can be readily distinguished. If the other party has no reasonable means of ascertaining the principal, the inference is almost irresistible and prevails in the absence of an agreement to the contrary.

Restatement (Second) of Agency § 321, at 70.

In view of the contractual reference to the Magic Moment trade name, the annotation at 150 A.L.R. 1303 (1944) entitled "Use of trade name in connection with contract executed by agent as sufficient disclosure of agency or principal to protect agent against personal liability" is directly on point. The annotator points out that with the possible exception of a single decision, all of the prior cases on the subject have held that the use of a trade name is not a sufficient disclosure of the identity of the principal so as to eliminate the liability of the agent.

\* \* \*

Of course, if the contracting party knows the identity of the principal for whom the agent purports to act, the principal is deemed to be disclosed. [Citation.] A dispute concerning such knowledge presents an issue of fact.

[Citation.] Here, however, nothing indicates that appellant had ever heard of Seascape at the time the contract was signed. Subsequent knowledge of the true principal is irrelevant where performance of an indivisible contract has commenced. [Citation.] The trial court emphasized that Costas drafted the contract. However, it was not incumbent upon him to ferret out the record ownership of the Magic Moment when he had every reason to believe that one of the owners was signing the contract. Jeff knew that the owner was Seascape, and he had it within his power to avoid personal liability by properly disclosing his principal. Since there is no evidence that the appellant knew or should have known the true principal, the law holds Jeff legally responsible.

That portion of the judgment exonerating Jeff Rosenberg from liability is reversed, and the case is remanded for further proceedings. Since Jeff's counterclaim was also dismissed on the premise that only Seascape was bound on the contract, this ruling must also be reversed. If Jeff can be held personally liable on the contract, he also has a right to prosecute a claim for breach of that contract or for other relief which relates to the contract. In all other respects, the judgment is affirmed.

# Questions

1. Distinguish among actual express authority, actual implied authority, and apparent authority.

2. Discuss the contractual liability of the principal, agent, and third party when the principal is (a) disclosed, (b) partially disclosed, and (c) undisclosed.

3. Explain how apparent authority is terminated and distinguish between actual and constructive notice.

4. Discuss the tort liability of a principal for the (a) authorized acts of agents, (b) unauthorized acts of employees, and (c) unauthorized acts of independent contractors.

5. Discuss the criminal liability of a principal for the acts of agents.

# Problems

1. Alice was Peter's traveling salesperson and was also authorized to collect accounts. Before the agreed termination of the agency, Peter wrongfully discharged Alice. Alice then called on Tom, an old customer, and collected an account from Tom. She also called on Laura, a new prospect, as Peter's agent, secured a large order, collected the price of the order, sent the order to Peter, and disappeared with the collections. Peter delivered the goods to Laura per the order.

    (a)   Peter sues Tom for his account. Decision?

    (b)   Peter sues Laura for the agreed price of the goods. Decision?

2. Paula instructed Alvin, her agent, to purchase a quantity of hides. Alvin ordered the hides from Ted in his own (Alvin's) name and delivered the hides to Paula. Ted, learning later that Paula was the principal, sends the bill to Paula, who refuses to pay Ted. Ted sues Paula and Alvin. Decision?

3. Stan sold goods to Bill in good faith, believing him to be a principal. Bill in fact was acting as agent for Nancy and was within the scope of his authority. The goods were charged to Bill, and on his refusal to pay, Stan sued Bill for the purchase price. While this action was pending, Stan learned of Bill's relationship with Nancy. Nevertheless, thirty days after learning of that relationship, Stan obtained judgment against Bill and had an execution issued that was never satisfied. Three months after rendition of the judgment, Stan sued Nancy for the purchase price of the goods. Decision?

4. Green Grocery Company employed Jones as its manager. Jones was given authority by Green Company to purchase supplies and goods for resale and had conducted business for several years with Brown Distributing Company. Although her purchases previously had been limited to groceries, Jones contacted Brown Distributing Company and had it deliver a color television set to her house, informing Brown Company the set was to be used in promotional advertising to increase Green Grocery Company's business. The advertising did not develop, and Jones disappeared from the area, taking the television set with her. Brown Company sued Green Company for the purchase price of the set. Decision?

5. Stone was the agent authorized to sell stock of the Turner Company at $10 per share and was authorized in case of sale to fill in the blanks in the certificates with the name of the purchaser, the number of shares, and the date of sale. He sold 100 shares to Barrie, and without the knowledge or consent of the company and without reporting to the company, he endorsed the back of the certificate as follows:

"It is hereby agreed that Turner Company shall, at the end of three years after the date, repurchase the stock at $11 per share on thirty days' notice. Turner Company, by Stone."

After three years, demand was made on Turner Company to repurchase. The company refused the demand and repudiated the agreement on the ground that the agent had no authority to make the agreement for repurchase. Barrie sued Turner Company. Decision?

6. Helper, a delivery boy for Gunn, delivered two heavy packages of groceries to Reed's porch. As instructed by Gunn, Helper rang the bell to let Reed know the groceries had arrived. Mrs. Reed came to the door and asked Helper if he would deliver the groceries into the kitchen because the bags were heavy. Helper did so, and upon leaving he observed Mrs. Reed having difficulty in moving a cabinet in the dining room. He undertook to assist her, but being more interested in watching Mrs. Reed than the cabinet, he failed to observe a small, valuable antique table, which he smashed into with the cabinet and totally destroyed. Does Reed have a cause of action against Gunn for the value of the destroyed antique?

7. Driver picked up Friend to accompany him on an out-of-town delivery for his employer, Speedy Service. A "No Riders" sign was prominently displayed on the windshield of the truck, and Driver violated specific instructions of his employer by permitting an unauthorized person to ride in the vehicle. While discussing a planned fishing trip with Friend, Driver ran a red light and collided with an automobile driven by Motorist. Both Friend and Motorist were injured. Is Speedy Service liable to either Friend or Motorist for the injuries they sustained?

8. Cook's Department Store advertises that it maintains in its store a barber shop managed by Hunter. Actually, Hunter is not an employee of the store but merely rents space in it. While shaving Jordon in the barber shop, Hunter negligently puts a deep gash into one of Jordon's ears, requiring ten stitches. Jordon sues Cook's Department Store for damages. Decision?

9. The following contract was executed on August 22:

Ray agrees to sell and Shaw, the representative of Todd and acting on his behalf, agrees to buy 10,000 pounds of 0.32 × 1 5/8 stainless steel strip type 410.

(signed) Ray
(signed) Shaw

On August 26, Ray informs Shaw and Todd that the contract was in reality signed by him as agent for Upson. What are the rights of Ray, Shaw, Todd, and Upson in the event of a breach of the contract?

10. Harris, owner of certain land known as Red Bank, mailed a letter to Byron, a real estate broker in City X, stating, "I have been thinking of selling Red Bank. I have never met you, but a friend has advised me that you are an industrious and honest real estate broker. I therefore employ you to find a purchaser for Red Bank at a price of $35,000." Ten days after receiving the letter, Byron mailed the following reply to Harris: "Acting pursuant to your recent letter requesting me to find a purchaser for Red Bank, this is to advise that I have sold the property to Sims for $35,000. I enclose your copy of the contract of sale signed by Sims. Your name was signed to the contract by me as your agent." Is Harris obligated to convey Red Bank to Sims?

11. While crossing a public highway in the city, Joel was struck by a horse-drawn cart driven by Morison's agent. The agent was traveling between Burton Crescent Mews and Finchley on his employer's business and was not supposed to go into the city at all. Apparently, the agent was on a detour to visit a friend when the accident occurred. Joel brought this action against Morison for the injuries sustained as a result of the agent's negligence. Morison argues that he is not liable for his agent's negligence because the agent had strayed from his assigned path. Decision?

12. Serges is the owner of a retail meat marketing business. His managing agent borrowed $3,500 from David on Serges's behalf, for use in Serges's business. Serges paid $200 on the alleged loan and on several other occasions told David that the full balance owed would eventually be paid. He then disclaimed liability on the debt, asserting that he had not authorized his agent to enter into the loan agreement. David brought this action to collect on the loan. Decision?

13. Sherwood negligently ran into the rear of Austen's car, which was stopped at a stoplight. As a result, Austen received bodily injuries and her car was damaged. Sherwood, arts editor for the *Mississippi Press Register,* was en route from a Louis Armstrong concert he had covered for the newspaper. When the accident occurred he was on his way to spend the night at a friend's house. Austen sued Sherwood and—under the doctrine of *respondeat superior*—Sherwood's employer, the *Mississippi Press Register*. Decision?

14. Aretta J. Parkinson owned a 200-acre farm. Prior to her death on December 23, 1976, Parkinson deeded a one-eighth undivided interest in the farm to each of her eight children as tenants in common. On January 15, 1977, one of the daughters, Roma Funk, approached Barbara Bradshaw about selling the Parkinson farm. They orally agreed to a selling price of $33,000. After this meeting, Funk contacted Bryant Hansen, a real estate broker, to assist her in completing the transaction. Hansen prepared an earnest money agreement that was signed by the Bradshaws but by none of the Parkinson children. Hansen also prepared warranty deeds, which were signed by three of the children. Several of the children subsequently refused to convey their interests in the farm to the Bradshaws. The Bradshaws brought an action against the defendants, seeking specific performance of the oral contract of sale. The trial court ruled for the Bradshaws, finding that the defendants ratified the oral contract by their knowledge of and failure to repudiate it. The defendants appealed. Decision?

15. Raymond Zukaitis was a physician practicing medicine in Douglas County, Nebraska. Aetna issued a policy of professional liability insurance to Zukaitis through its agent, the Ed Larsen Insurance Agency. The policy covered the period from August 31, 1969, through August of the following year. On August 7, 1971, Dr. Zukaitis received a written notification of a claim for malpractice that occurred on September 27, 1969. Dr. Zukaitis notified the Ed Larsen

Insurance Agency immediately and forwarded the written claim to them. The claim was then mistakenly referred to St. Paul Fire and Marine Insurance Company, the company that currently insured Dr. Zukaitis. Apparently without notice to Dr. Zukaitis, the agency contract between Larsen and Aetna had been canceled on August 1, 1970, and St. Paul had replaced Aetna as the insurance carrier. However, when St. Paul discovered it was not the carrier on the date of the alleged wrongdoing, it notified Aetna and withdrew from Dr. Zukaitis's defense. Aetna also refused to represent Dr. Zukaitis, contending that it was relieved of its obligation to

Dr. Zukaitis because he had not notified Aetna immediately of the claim. Dr. Zukaitis then secured his own attorney to defend against the malpractice claim and brought this action against Aetna to recover attorney's fees and other expenses incurred in the defense. The trial court found for Aetna, and Dr. Zukaitis appealed. Decision?

**Internet Exercise** Compare the rules determining the authority of agents and the liability of principals for acts of agents under the Convention on Agency in the International Sale of Goods (Geneva, 17 February 1983) with the rules under the U.S. common law.

# PART FOUR

# Sales

# CHAPTER 21

# Introduction to Sales and Leases

Sales are the most common and important of all commercial transactions. In an exchange economy such as ours, sales are the essential means by which the various units of production exchange their outputs, thereby providing the opportunity for specialization and enhanced productivity. An advanced, complex, industrialized economy with highly coordinated manufacturing and distribution systems requires a reliable mechanism for ensuring that *future* exchanges can be entered into today and fulfilled at a later time. Because practically everyone in our economy is a purchaser of both durable and consumable goods, the manufacture and distribution of goods involve numerous sales transactions. The law of sales establishes a framework in which these present and future exchanges may take place in a predictable, certain, and orderly fashion with a minimum of transaction costs.

Until the early 1900s, sales transactions were completely governed by general contract law. In 1906, the Uniform Sales Act was promulgated and eventually adopted by thirty-six States. By the end of the 1930s, however, dissatisfaction with this and other uniform commercial statutes brought about the development of the Uniform Commercial Code (UCC). Article 2 of the Code deals with transactions in sales and has been adopted in all of the States (except Louisiana) plus the District of Columbia and the Virgin Islands. The UCC appears in Appendix B.

Leases of personal property, which are of great economic significance, exceed $100 billion annually. Leases range from a consumer's renting an automobile or a lawn mower to a Fortune 500 corporation's leasing heavy industrial machinery. Despite the frequent and widespread use of personal property leases, the law governing these transactions had been patched together from the common law of personal property, real estate leasing law, and the UCC (Articles 2 and 9). Although containing several applicable provisions, the UCC did not directly relate to leases. Some courts have held, nevertheless, that the UCC is applicable to leases of goods because a lease is a transaction in goods; other courts have refused to apply the Code to leases because actual title to the goods never passed. Still other courts have applied the Code to lease by analogy. Even in States where Article 2 was extended to leases, which provisions were to be applied remained unclear. In any event, no unified or uniform statutory law governed leases of personal property for most of the twentieth century.

To fill this void, the drafters of the Code approved Article 2A—Leases in 1987 and subsequently amended the Article in 1990. An analogue of Article 2, the new Article adopts many of the rules contained in Article 2. Article 2A is an attempt to codify in one statute all the rules governing the leasing of personal property. Two States (Florida and South Dakota) have enacted the 1987 version of Article 2A while more than forty other States and the District of Columbia have adopted the 1990 version.

This section of the book covers both the sale and the lease of goods. All of the chapters will cover Article 2A in addition to Article 2 by stating the Article 2A section number wherever Article 2A's provision is either identical or essentially the same as the Article 2 provision. Where Article 2A significantly deviates from Article 2, both rules will generally be discussed. This chapter will discuss the nature and formation of sales and lease contracts as well as the fundamental principles of Article 2 and Article 2A.

## NATURE OF SALES AND LEASES

The law of sales, which governs contracts involving the sale of goods, is a specialized branch of both the law of contracts (discussed previously in Chapters 9–18) and the law of personal property (discussed later in Chapter 49). This section will cover the definition of sales and lease contracts and the fundamentals of Article 2 and Article 2A.

◆ *See Figure 21–1*

# DEFINITIONS

## Goods

**Goods** are essentially defined as movable, tangible personal property. For example, the purchase of a bicycle, CD player, or this textbook is considered a sale of goods. "Goods" also include the unborn young of animals, growing crops, and, if removed by the seller, timber, minerals, or a building attached to real property. Section 2–105(1). Under Article 2A, minerals cannot be leased prior to their extraction. Section 2A–103(1)(h).

## Sale

The Code defines a **sale** as the transfer of title to goods from seller to buyer for a price. Section 2–106. The price can be money, other goods, real estate, or services.

## Lease

Article 2A defines a lease of goods as a "transfer of the right to possession and use of goods for a term in return for consideration, but . . . retention or creation of a security interest is not a lease." Section 2A–103(1)(j). A transaction within this definition of a lease is governed by Article 2A, but if the transaction is a security interest disguised as a lease, it is governed by Article 9. Categorizing a transaction as a lease has significant implications not only for the parties to the lease but for third parties as well. If the transaction is deemed to be a lease, then the residual interest in the goods belongs to the lessor, who need not file publicly to protect this interest. On the other hand, if the transaction is a security interest, then the provisions of Article 9 regarding enforceability, perfection, priority, and remedies apply (see Chapter 38).

*Consumer Leases*  Article 2A affords special treatment for consumer leases. The definition of a consumer lease requires that (1) the transaction meet the definition of a lease under Article 2A; (2) the lessor be regularly engaged in the business of leasing *or* selling goods; (3) the lessee be an individual, not an organization; (4) the lessee take the lease interest primarily for a personal, family, or household purpose; and (5) the total payments under the lease do not exceed $25,000. Section 2A–103(1)(e). Although consumer protection for lease transactions is primarily left to other State and Federal law, Article 2A does contain a number of provisions that apply to consumer leases and that may *not* be varied by agreement of the parties.

*Finance Leases*  A finance lease is a special type of lease transaction generally involving three parties instead of two. Whereas in the typical lease situation the lessor also supplies the goods, in a finance lease arrangement the lessor and the supplier are separate parties. The lessor's

**FIGURE 21–1**  Law of Sales and Leases

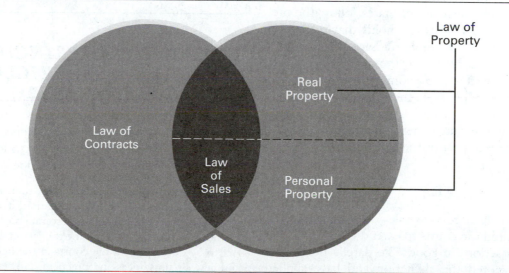

primary function in a finance lease is to provide financing to the lessee for a lease of goods provided by the supplier. For example, under a finance lease arrangement a manufacturer supplies goods pursuant to the lessee's instructions or specifications. The party functioning as the lessor will then either purchase those goods from the supplier or act as the prime lessee in leasing them from the supplier. In turn, the lessor will lease or sublease the goods to the lessee. Comment g to Section 2A–103. Because the finance lessor functions merely as a source of credit, she typically will have no special expertise as to the goods. Due to the limited role the finance lessor usually plays, Article 2A treats finance leases differently from ordinary leases.

 *See Case 21–1*

## Governing Law

Though sales transactions are governed by Article 2 of the Code, general contract law continues to apply where the Code has not specifically modified such law. In other words, the law of sales is a specialized part of the general law of contracts, and the law of contracts continues to govern unless specifically displaced by the Code.

General contract law also continues to govern all contracts outside the scope of the Code. Transactions not within the scope of Article 2 include employment contracts, service contracts, insurance contracts, contracts involving real property, and contracts for the sale of intangibles such as stocks, bonds, patents, and copyrights. For an illustration of the relationship between the law of sales and the general law of contracts see Figure 9–1. In determining whether a contract containing both a sale of goods and a service is a UCC contract or a general contract, the majority of States follow the predominant purpose test. This test holds that if the predominant purpose of the whole transaction is a sale of goods, then Article 2 applies to the entire transaction. If, on the other hand, the predominant purpose is the non-good or service portion, then Article 2 does not apply at all. A few States apply Article 2 to the goods part of a transaction and general contract law to the non-goods or service part of the transaction.

◆ *See Figure 9–1*

 *See Cases 21–2 and 9–1*

Although Article 2 governs sales, the drafters of the Article have invited the courts to extend Code principles to nonsale transactions in goods. To date, a number of courts have accepted this invitation and have applied

Code provisions by analogy to other transactions in goods not expressly included within the Act, most frequently to leases and bailments. The Code has also greatly influenced the revision of the Restatement, Second, Contracts which, as previously discussed, has great effect upon all contracts.

Although lease transactions are governed by Article 2A of the Code, general contract law continues to apply where the Code has not specifically modified such law. In other words, the law of leases is a specialized part of the general law of contracts, and the law of contracts continues to govern unless specifically displaced by the Code.

## CISG

*The United Nations Convention on Contracts for the International Sale of Goods (CISG), which has been ratified by the United States and more than forty other countries, governs all contracts for the international sales of goods between parties located in different nations that have ratified the CISG. Because treaties are Federal law, the CISG supersedes the UCC in any situation to which either could apply. The CISG includes provisions dealing with interpretation, trade usage, contract formation, obligations and remedies of sellers and buyers, and risk of loss. Parties to an international sales contract may, however, expressly exclude CISG governance from their contract. The CISG specifically excludes sales of (1) goods bought for personal, family, or household use; (2) ships or aircraft; and (3) electricity. In addition, it does not apply to contracts in which the primary obligation of the party furnishing the goods consists of supplying labor or services.*

## *FUNDAMENTAL PRINCIPLES OF ARTICLE 2 AND ARTICLE 2A*

The purpose of Article 2 is to modernize, clarify, simplify, and make uniform the law of sales. Furthermore, the Article is to be interpreted in accordance with these underlying principles and not according to some abstraction such as the passage of title. The Code

is drawn to provide flexibility so that, since it is intended to be a semi-permanent piece of legislation, it will provide its own machinery for expansion of commercial practices. It is intended to make it possible for the law embodied in this Act to be developed by the courts in the light of unforeseen and new circumstances and practices. However, the proper construction of the Act requires that its interpretation and application be limited to its reason. Section 1–102, Comment 1.

This open-ended drafting includes the following fundamental concepts.

---

## CISG

*The CISG only governs the formation of the contract of sales and the rights and obligations of the seller and buyer arising from such contract. It does not cover the validity of the contract or any of its provisions. In addition, one of the purposes of the CISG is to promote uniformity of the law of sales.*

---

## Good Faith

All parties who enter into a contract or duty within the scope of the Code must perform their obligations in good faith. The Code defines **good faith** as "honesty in fact in the conduct or transaction concerned." Section 1–201(19). For a merchant (defined below), good faith also requires the observance of reasonable commercial standards of fair dealing in the trade. Section 2–103(1)(b); Section 2A–103(3). For instance, if the parties agree that the seller is to set the price term, the seller must establish the price in good faith.

---

## CISG

*The CISG is also designed to promote the observation of good faith in international trade.*

---

## Unconscionability

The court may scrutinize every contract of sale to determine whether in its commercial setting, purpose, and effect it is unconscionable. The court may refuse to enforce an unconscionable contract or any part of it found to be unconscionable or may limit its application to prevent an unconscionable result. Section 2–302. Though the Code itself does not define *unconscionable*, the *New Webster's Dictionary* (Deluxe Encyclopedic Edition) defines the term as "contrary to the dictates of conscience; unscrupulous or unprincipled; exceeding that which is reasonable or customary; inordinate, unjustifiable."

The Code denies or limits enforcement of an unconscionable contract for the sale of goods to promote fairness and decency and to correct harshness or oppression in contracts resulting from inequality in the bargaining positions of the parties.

The doctrine of unconscionability has been justified on the basis that it permits the courts to resolve issues of unfairness explicitly on that basis without recourse to formalistic rules or legal fictions. In policing contracts for fairness, the courts have again demonstrated their willingness to limit freedom of contract to protect the less advantaged from overreaching by dominant contracting parties. Accordingly, most cases concerning unconscionability have involved low-income consumers.

The doctrine of unconscionability has evolved through its application by the courts to include both procedural and substantive unconscionability. **Procedural unconscionability** involves scrutiny for the presence of "bargaining naughtiness." In other words, was the negotiation process fair? Or were there procedural irregularities such as burying important terms of the agreement in fine print or obscuring the true meaning of the contract with impenetrable legal jargon?

In checking for **substantive unconscionability,** the court examines the actual terms of the contract for oppressive or grossly unfair provisions such as an exorbitant price or an unfair exclusion or limitation of contractual remedies. An all-too-common example places a necessitous buyer in an unequal bargaining position with a seller who consequently obtains an exorbitant price for his product or service. In one case, a price of $749 ($920 on timepayments) for a vacuum cleaner that cost the seller $140 was held unconscionable. In another case, the buyers, welfare recipients, purchased by time payment contract a home freezer unit for $900 plus time credit charges, credit life insurance, credit property insurance, and sales tax for a total price of $1,235. The maximum retail value of the freezer unit at the time of purchase was $300. The court held the contract unconscionable and reformed it by changing the price to the total payment ($620) the buyers had managed to make. *Jones v. Star Credit Corp.*, 59 Misc.2d 189, 298 N.Y.S.2d 264 (1969).

As to leases, Article 2A provides that a court faced with an unconscionable contract or clause may refuse to enforce either the entire contract or just the unconscionable clause, or may limit the application of the unconscionable clause to avoid an unconscionable result. This is similar to Article 2's treatment of unconscionable clauses in sales contracts. A lessee under a consumer lease, however, is provided with additional protection against unconscionability. In the case of a consumer lease, if a court as a matter of law finds that any part of the lease contract has been induced by unconscionable conduct, the court is expressly empowered to grant appropriate relief. Section 2A–108(2). The same is true when unconscionable conduct occurs in the collection of a claim arising from a consumer lease contract. The explicit availability of relief for consumers subjected to unconscionable conduct (procedural unconscionability)—in addition to a provision regarding unconscionable contracts (substantive unconscionability)—represents a departure from Article 2. An additional remedy that Article 2A provides for consumers is the award of attorneys' fees. If the court finds unconscionability with respect to a consumer lease, it shall award reasonable attorneys' fees to the lessee. Section 2A–108(4)(a).

 *See Cases 21–3 and 13–4*

## Expansion of Commercial Practices

An underlying policy of the Code is "to permit the continued expansion of commercial practices through custom, usage and agreement of the parties." Section 1–102(2)(b). In particular, the Code emphasizes the course of dealings and the usage of trade in interpreting agreements.

A **course of dealing** is a sequence of previous conduct between the parties that may fairly be regarded as establishing a common basis of understanding for interpreting their expressions and agreement. Section 1–205(1). For example, Plaza, a sugar company, enters into a written agreement with Brown, a grower of sugar beets, by which Brown agrees to raise and deliver and Plaza agrees to purchase specified quantities of beets during the coming season. No price is fixed. The agreement is on a standard form used by Plaza for Brown and many other growers in prior years. Plaza's practice is to pay all growers uniformly according to a formula based on Plaza's established accounting system. Unless otherwise agreed, the established pricing pattern is part of the agreement between Plaza and Brown as a course of dealing.

A **usage of trade** is a practice or method of dealing regularly observed and followed in a place, vocation, or trade. Section 1–205(2). To illustrate: Tamara contracts to sell Seth one thousand feet of San Domingo mahogany. By usage of dealers in mahogany, known to Tamara and Seth, good mahogany of a certain density is known as San Domingo mahogany, though it does not come from San Domingo. Unless otherwise agreed, the usage is part of the contract.

---

## CISG

*The parties are bound by any usage or practices that they have agreed to or established between themselves. In addition, the parties are considered, unless otherwise agreed, to be bound by any usage of international trade that is widely known and regularly observed in the particular trade.*

---

## Sales by and between Merchants

The Code establishes separate rules that apply to transactions transpiring between merchants or involving a merchant as a party. A **merchant** is defined as a person who (1) is a dealer in the type of goods the transaction involves, (2) by his occupation holds himself out as having knowledge or skill peculiar to the goods or practices involved, or (3) employs an agent or broker whom he holds out as having such knowledge or skill. Section 2–104(1); Section 2A–103(3). These rules exact a higher standard of conduct from merchants because of their knowledge of trade and commerce and because merchants as a class generally set these standards for themselves. The most significant of these merchant rules are listed in Figure 21–2.

◆ *See Figure 21–2*

## Liberal Administration of Remedies

Section 1–106 of the Code provides that its remedies shall be liberally administered to place the aggrieved party in a position as good as the one she would have occupied, had the defaulting party fully performed. The Code states clearly, however, that remedies are limited to compensation and do not include consequential or punitive damages, unless specifically provided by the Code. Nevertheless, the Code provides that even in cases where it does not expressly provide a remedy for a right or obligation, the courts should provide an appropriate remedy. Remedies are discussed in Chapter 25.

## Freedom of Contract

Most of the Code's provisions are not mandatory but permit the parties by agreement to vary or displace them altogether. The parties may not, however, disclaim by

FIGURE 21–2   Selected Rules Applicable to Merchants

| Section of UCC | Merchant Rules | Chapter in Text Where Discussed |
| --- | --- | --- |
| 2–103(1)(b), 2–103(3) | Good faith | 21 |
| 2–201 | Confirmation of oral contracts | 15, 21 |
| 2–205, 2A–205 | Firm offers | 10, 21 |
| 2–207(2) | Battle of the forms | 10, 21 |
| 2–312(3), 2A–211(2) | Warranty against infringement | 24 |
| 2–314(1), 2A–212 | Warranty of merchantability | 24 |
| 2–327(1)(c) | Sales on approval | 23 |
| 2–402(2) | Retention of possession of goods by seller | 23 |
| 2–403(2), 2A–304(2), 2A–305(2) | Entrusting of goods | 23 |
| 2–509(3), 2A–219(2)(c) | Risk of loss | 23 |
| 2–603(1), 2A–511(1) | Duties after rightful rejection | 22 |

agreement the obligations of good faith, diligence, reasonableness, and care the Code prescribes, though they may by agreement determine the standards by which to measure the performance of these obligations, so long as such standards are not obviously unreasonable. Section 1–102(3). Through this approach, the Code not only maximizes freedom of contract but also permits the continued expansion of commercial practices through private agreement.

## Validation and Preservation of Sales Contracts

One of the requirements of commercial law is the establishment of rules that determine when an agreement is valid. The Code approaches this requirement by minimizing formal requisites and attempting to preserve agreements whenever the parties manifest an intent to enter into a contract.

## FORMATION OF SALES AND LEASE CONTRACTS

The Code's basic approach to validation is to recognize contracts whenever the parties manifest such an *intent*. This is so whether or not the parties can identify a precise moment at which the contract was formed. Section 2–204(2); Section 2A–204(2).

As already noted, the law of sales and leases is a subset of the general law of contracts and is governed by general contract law unless particular provisions of the Code displace the general law. Although the Code leaves most issues of contract formation to general contract law, it has modified the general law of contract formation in several significant respects. These modifications serve to modernize contract law, to relax the validation requirements of contract formation, and to promote fairness.

## MANIFESTATION OF MUTUAL ASSENT

For a contract to exist, there must be an objective manifestation of mutual assent: an offer and an acceptance. This section examines the UCC rules that affect offers and acceptances.

### Definiteness of an Offer

At common law, the terms of a contract were required to be definite and complete. The Code has rejected the strict approach of the common law by recognizing an agreement as valid, despite missing terms, if there is any reasonably certain basis for granting a remedy. Accordingly, the Code provides that even a contract from which one or more terms have been omitted need not fail for indefiniteness. Section 2–204(3); Section 2A–204(3). The Code provides standards by which the courts may ascertain and supply omitted essential terms, provided the parties intended to enter into a binding agreement. Nevertheless, the more terms the parties leave open, the less likely their intent to enter into a binding contract. Article 2A generally does not provide the same gap-filling provisions.

**Open Price**  The parties may enter into a contract for the sale of goods even though they have reached no agreement on the price (that is, left open the price term). Under the Code, the price is reasonable at the time for delivery where the agreement (1) says nothing as to price, (2) provides that the parties shall agree later as to the price and they fail to so agree, or (3) fixes the price in terms of some agreed market or other standard as set by a third person or agency, and the price is not so set. Section 2–305(1). An agreement that the price is to be fixed by the seller or buyer means that it must be fixed in good faith.

**Open Delivery**  Unless otherwise agreed, the place of delivery is the seller's place of business. Moreover, in the absence of specific instructions, the delivery must be made within a reasonable time and in a single delivery. Section 2–308.

**Open Quantity: Output and Requirement Contracts**  A buyer's agreement to purchase a seller's entire output for a stated period, or a seller's agreement to fulfill a buyer's need for certain goods used in her business operations, may appear to lack definiteness and mutuality of obligation. In neither case do the parties specify the exact quantity of goods, and the seller and the buyer may have some control over their respective output and requirements. Nonetheless, such agreements are enforceable by the application of an objective standard based upon the good faith of both parties, and the quantities may not be disproportionate to any stated estimate or the prior output or requirements. Section 2–306(1). For example, the seller cannot operate his factory twenty-four hours a day and insist that the buyer take all of the output when the seller operated the factory only eight hours a day at the time the agreement was made. Nor can the buyer unilaterally triple the size of her business and insist that the seller supply all of her requirements.

*See Case 21–3*

**Other Open Terms**  The Code further provides rules, where the parties do not agree, as to the terms of payment, the duration of the contract, and the particulars of performance. Sections 2–310, 2–309, 2–307, 2–311.

## Irrevocable Offers

An offeror generally may withdraw an offer at any time prior to its acceptance. To be effective, notice of revocation must reach the offeree before he has accepted the offer.

An **option** is a *contract* by which the offeror is bound to hold open an offer for a specified time. It must comply with all the requirements of a contract, including consideration. Option contracts apply to all types of contracts, including those for sales of goods.

The Code has made certain offers—called **firm offers**—irrevocable without any consideration being given for the promise to keep the offer open. The Code provides that a merchant who gives assurance in a signed writing that an offer will be held open is bound to keep the offer open for a maximum of three months. Section 2–205; Section 2A–205. The Code, therefore, makes a merchant's written promise not to revoke an offer for a stated time enforceable even though no consideration is given the merchant–offeror for that promise.

For example, Ben's Brewery approached Flora Flooring, Inc. to purchase tile for Ben's floor. Ben's employees would install the tile after it was delivered by Flora. On June 6, Flora sent Ben a written, signed offer to provide the tile according to Ben's specifications for $26,000 and promised that "the offer will remain open until July 17." Flora is bound by her firm offer to keep the offer open until July 17. The result would differ, however, if Flora had merely stated that the "offer terminates on July 17" or that "the offer will terminate if not accepted on or before July 17." In both of these instances, there is no assurance to keep the offer open: because it is not a firm offer, Flora could revoke it at any time prior to Ben's acceptance.

Any firm offer on a form supplied by the offeree must be separately signed by the offeror.

## Variant Acceptances

The realities of modern business practices have necessitated the modification by the Code of the common law's **"mirror image"** rule, by which the acceptance cannot vary or deviate from the terms of the offer. A vast number of business transactions use standardized business forms, resulting in what has been termed the **battle of the forms.** For example, a merchant buyer sends to the merchant seller on the buyer's order form a purchase order for 1,000 dozen cotton shirts at $60 per dozen with delivery by October 1 at the buyer's place of business. On the reverse side of this standard form are twenty-five numbered paragraphs containing provisions generally favorable to the buyer. When the seller receives the buyer's order, he sends to the buyer an unequivocal acceptance of the offer on his acceptance form. Although the seller agrees to the buyer's quantity, price, and delivery terms, on the back of the form the seller utilizes in sending his unequivocal acceptance to the buyer are thirty-two numbered paragraphs generally favorable to the seller and in significant conflict with the buyer's form. Under the common law's "mirror image" rule, no contract would exist, for the seller has not in fact accepted unequivocally all of the material terms of the buyer's offer.

By comparison, Section 2–207 of the Code addresses variant acceptances by providing:

(1) A definite and seasonable expression of acceptance or a written confirmation which is sent within a reasonable time operates as an acceptance even though it states terms additional to or different from those offered or agreed upon, unless acceptance is expressly made conditional on assent to the additional or different terms.

(2) The additional terms are to be construed as proposals for addition to the contract. Between merchants such terms become part of the contract unless:
   (a) the offer expressly limits acceptance to the terms of the offer;
   (b) they materially alter it; or
   (c) notification of objection to them has already been given or is given within a reasonable time after notice of them is received.

(3) Conduct by both parties which recognizes the existence of a contract is sufficient to establish a contract for sale although the writings of the parties do not otherwise establish a contract. In such case the terms of the particular contract consist of those terms on which the writings of the parties agree, together with any supplementary terms incorporated under any other provisions of this Act.

Thus, the Code attempts to settle the battle of the forms by focusing upon the intent of the parties. If the

offeree expressly makes his acceptance conditioned upon the offeror's assent to the additional or different terms, no contract is formed. If the offeree does not expressly make his acceptance conditional upon such assent, a contract is formed. The issue then becomes whether the offeree's different or additional terms should become part of the contract. If both offeror and offeree are merchants, **additional** terms (terms the offeree proposed for the contract for the first time) will become part of the contract, provided they do not materially alter the agreement and are not objected to either in the offer itself or within a reasonable time. If either of the parties is not a merchant, or if the additional terms materially alter the offer, then the terms are merely construed as proposals for addition to the contract. **Different** terms (terms that contradict terms of the offer) proposed by the offeree also will generally not become part of the contract unless specifically accepted by the offeror. The courts are divided over what terms are included when the terms conflict. The majority of courts hold that the terms cancel each other out and look to the Code to provide the missing terms; other courts hold that the offeror's terms govern. Some States follow a third alternative and apply the additional terms test to different terms.

Applying Section 2–207 to the example above: because both parties are merchants and the seller did not condition his acceptance upon the buyer's assent to the additional or different terms, (1) the contract will be formed without the *seller's different terms* unless the buyer specifically accepts them; (2) the contract will be formed without the *seller's additional terms* unless (a) the buyer specifically accepts or (b) the additional terms do not materially alter the offer and the buyer does not object to them; and (3) depending upon the jurisdiction, either (a) the conflicting (different) terms cancel each other out and the Code provides the missing terms or (b) the buyer's conflicting terms are included in the contract or (c) the additional terms test is applied.

## CISG

*A reply to an offer that contains additions, limitations, or other modifications is a counteroffer that rejects the original offer. Nevertheless, a purported acceptance that contains additional or different terms acts as an acceptance if the terms do not materially alter the contract unless the offeror objects to the change. Changes in price, payment, quality, quantity, place and time of delivery, terms of delivery, liability of the parties, and settlement of a dispute are always considered to be material alterations.*

---

Finally, subsection 3 of 2–207 deals with those situations in which the writings do not form a contract but the conduct of the parties recognizes the existence of one. For instance, Ernest makes an offer to Gwen, who replies with a conditional acceptance. Although no contract has been formed, Gwen ships the ordered goods and Ernest accepts the goods. Subsection 3 provides that in this instance the contract consists of the written terms to which both parties agreed together with supplementary provisions of the Code.

◆ *See Figure 21–3*

🔨 *See Case 21–4*

## Manner of Acceptance

As with the common law, the offeror may specify the manner in which the offer must be accepted. If the offeror does not and the circumstances do not otherwise clearly indicate, an offer to make a contract invites acceptance in any manner and by any medium reasonable under the circumstances. Section 2–206(1)(a); Section 2A–206(1). The Code, therefore, allows flexibility of response and the ability to keep pace with new modes of communication.

An offer to buy goods for prompt or current shipment may be accepted either by a prompt promise to ship or by prompt shipment. Section 2–206(1)(b). Acceptance by performance requires notice within a reasonable time, or the offer may be treated as lapsed. Section 2–206(2); Section 2A–206(2).

## Auctions

The Code provides that if an auction sale is advertised or announced in explicit terms to be **without reserve,** the auctioneer may not withdraw the article put up for sale unless no bid is made within a reasonable time. Unless the sale is advertised as being without reserve, the sale is **with reserve,** and the auctioneer may withdraw the goods at any time until he announces completion of the sale. Whether the sale is with or without reserve, a bidder may retract his bid at any time prior to acceptance by the auctioneer. Such retraction does not, however, revive any previous bid. Section 2–328.

If the auctioneer knowingly receives a bid by or on behalf of the seller, and notice has not been given that the seller reserves the right to bid at the auction sale, the bidder

to whom the goods are sold can either avoid the sale or take the goods at the price of the last good faith bid.

---

## CISG

*The CISG does not apply to sales by auctions.*

---

## CONSIDERATION

The Code has abandoned the common law rule requiring that a modification of an existing contract be supported by consideration to be valid. The Code provides that a contract for the sale of goods can be effectively modified without new consideration, provided the modification is made in good faith. Section 2–209(1); Section 2A–208(1).

In addition, (1) any claim of right arising out of an alleged breach of contract can be discharged in whole or in part without consideration by a written waiver or renunciation signed and delivered by the aggrieved party, Section 1–107; and (2) as previously noted, a firm offer is not revocable for lack of consideration.

---

## CISG

*Consideration is not needed to modify a contract.*

---

## FORM OF THE CONTRACT

### Statute of Frauds

The original statute of frauds, which applied to contracts for the sale of goods, has been used as a prototype for the Article 2 statute of frauds provision. Section 2–201 of the Code provides that a contract for the sale of goods costing *$500 or more* is not enforceable unless there is some writing sufficient to evidence the existence of a contract between the parties ($1,000 or more for leases, Section 2A–201).

---

## CISG

*A contract need not be evidenced by a writing, unless one of the parties has her place of business in a country that provides otherwise.*

---

**FIGURE 21-3** Battle of the Forms

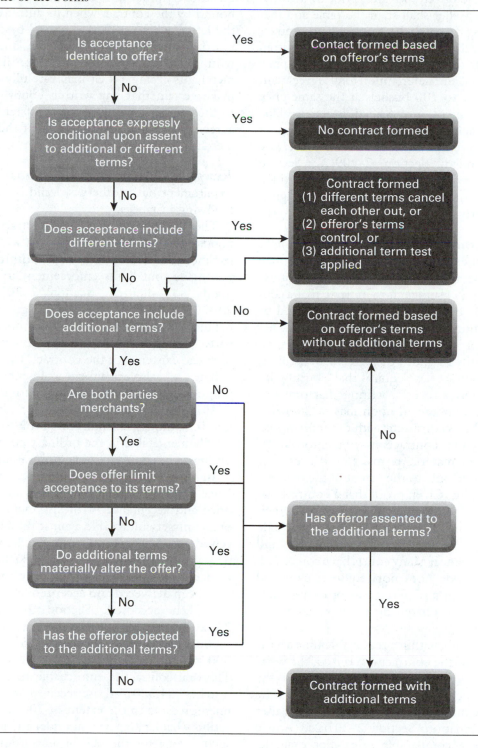

---

***Modification of Contracts*** An agreement modifying a contract must be evidenced by a writing if the resulting contract is within the statute of frauds. Section 2–209(3) (Article 2A omits this provision). Conversely, if a contract that was previously within the statute of frauds is modified so as to no longer fall within it, the modification is enforceable even if it is oral. Thus, if the parties enter into an oral contract to sell for $450 a dining room table to be delivered to the buyer and later, prior to delivery, orally agree that the seller shall stain the table and that the buyer shall pay a price of $550, the modified contract is unenforceable. In contrast, if the parties have a written contract for the sale of 150 bushels of wheat at a price of $4.50 per bushel and later, upon oral agreement, decrease the quantity to 100 bushels at the same price per bushel, the agreement, as modified, is enforceable.

A signed agreement that requires modifications or rescissions to be in a signed writing cannot be otherwise modified or rescinded. Section 2–209(2); Section 2A–208(2). If this requirement is on a form provided by a merchant, the other party must separately sign it unless the other party is a merchant.

*Written Compliance* The statute of frauds compliance provisions under the Code are more liberal than the rules under general contract law. The Code requires merely some writing (1) sufficient to indicate that a contract has been made between the parties, (2) signed by the party against whom enforcement is sought or by her authorized agent or broker, that (3) includes a term specifying the quantity of goods the agreement involves. Whereas general contract law requires that a writing include all essential terms, even a writing that omits or incorrectly states a term agreed upon may be sufficient under the Code. This is consistent with other provisions of the Code stating that contracts may be enforced despite the omission of material terms. Nevertheless, the contract is enforceable only to the extent of the quantity set forth in the writing. Given proof that a contract was intended and a signed writing describing the goods, their quantity, and the names of the parties, under the Code the court can supply omitted terms such as price and particulars of performance. Many courts have concluded, however, that the Code does not require a clear and precise quantity term in a requirements or output contract. Moreover, several related documents may satisfy the writing requirement.

Between merchants, if within a reasonable time a writing in confirmation of the contract is received, the **written merchant confirmation,** if sufficient against the sender, is also sufficient against the recipient unless he gives written notice of his objection within ten days after receiving the confirmation. Section 2–201(2). (Article 2A does not have a comparable rule). For example, Brown Co. and ATM Industries enter into an oral contract providing that ATM will deliver one thousand dozen shirts to Brown at $6 per shirt. The next day, Brown sends to ATM a letter signed by Brown's president confirming the agreement. The letter contains the quantity term but does not mention the price. Brown is bound by the contract when its authorized agent sends the letter, whereas ATM is bound by the oral contract ten days after receiving the letter, unless it objects in writing within that time. Therefore, it is essential that merchants examine their mail carefully and promptly to make certain that any written confirmations conform to their understanding of their outstanding contractual agreements. Where one or both of the parties is not a merchant, however, this rule does not apply.

*Exceptions* A contract that does not satisfy the writing requirement but is otherwise valid is enforceable in the following instances.

The Code permits an oral contract for the sale of goods to be enforced against a party who in his pleading, testimony, or otherwise in court **admits** that a contract was made, but limits enforcement to the quantity of goods so admitted. Section 2–201(3)(b); Section 2A–201(4)(b). This provision recognizes that the policy behind the statute of frauds does not apply when the party seeking to avoid the oral contract admits under oath the existence of the contract.

The Code also permits enforcement of an oral contract for goods **specially manufactured** for the buyer. Section 2–201(3)(a); Section 2A–201(4)(a). Nevertheless, if the goods, although manufactured on special order, are readily marketable in the ordinary course of the seller's business, the contract is not enforceable unless in writing.

In most States, prior to the Code, delivery and acceptance of part of the goods or payment of part of the price and acceptance of the payment made the entire oral contract enforceable against the buyer who had received part delivery or against the seller who had received part payment. Under the Code such "partial performance" validates the contract only for the goods that have been **delivered and accepted** or for which **payment** has been **accepted**. Section 2–201(3)(c); Section 2A–201(4)(c). To illustrate, Debra orally agrees to buy 1,000 watches from Brian for $15,000. Brian delivers 300 watches to Debra, who receives and accepts them. The oral contract is enforceable to the extent of 300 watches ($4,500)—those received and accepted—but is unenforceable to the extent of 700 watches ($10,500).

But what if part payment under an indivisible contract, such as one for the sale of an automobile, presents a choice between not enforcing the contract or enforcing it as a whole? Presently, there is a division of authority on this issue, although the better rule appears to be that such part payment and acceptance makes the entire contract enforceable.

## Parol Evidence

Contractual terms that the parties set forth in a writing which they intend as a final expression of their agreement may not be contradicted by evidence of any prior agreement or of a contemporaneous agreement. Nevertheless, under the Code, the terms may be explained or supplemented by (1) course of dealing, usage of trade, or course of performance; and (2) evidence of consistent additional terms, unless the writing was intended as the complete and exclusive statement of the terms of the agreement. Section 2–202; Section 2A–202.

### CISG

*The CISG permits a court to consider all relevant circumstances of the agreement, including the negotiations, any course of performance between the parties, trade usages, and any subsequent conduct.*

For a comparison of general contract law and the law governing sales and leases of goods, see Figure 21–4.

◆ *See Figure 21–4*

**FIGURE 21–4** Contract Law Compared with Law of Sales

| Section of UCC | Contract Law | Law of Sales/Leases |
|---|---|---|
| **Definiteness** | Contract must include all material terms. | Open terms permitted if parties intend to make a contract. Section 2–204; 2A–204. |
| **Counteroffers** | Acceptance must be a mirror image of offer. Counteroffer and conditional acceptance are rejections. | Battle of forms. Section 2–207. See Figure 21–3. |
| **Modification of Contract** | Consideration is required. | Consideration is not required. Section 2–209; 2A–208. |
| **Irrevocable Offers** | Options. | Options. Firm offers up to three months binding without consideration. Section 2–205; 2A–205. |
| **Statute of Frauds** | Writing must include all material terms. | Writing must include quantity term. Specially manufactured goods. Confirmation by merchants. Delivery or payment and acceptance. Admissions. Section 2–201; 2A–201 (except merchant confirmation). |

# Chapter Summary

# Nature of Sales and Leases

| Definitions | **Goods** movable personal property<br>**Sale** transfer of title to goods from seller to buyer for a price<br>**Lease** a transfer of right to possession and use of goods in return for consideration<br>• *Consumer Leases* leases by a merchant to an individual who leases for personal, family, or household purposes for no more than $25,000 |
|---|---|

- *Fianance Leases* special type of lease transaction generally involving three parties: the lessor, the supplier, and the lessee

**Governing Law**
- *Sales Transactions* governed by Article 2 of the Code, but where general contract law has not been specifically modified by the Code, general contract law continues to apply
- *Lease Transactions* governed by Article 2A of the Code, but where general contract law has not been specifically modified by the Code, general contract law continues to apply
- *Transactions outside the Code* include employment contracts, service contracts, insurance contracts, contracts involving real property, and contracts for the sale of intangibles

| **Fundamental Principles of Article 2 and Article 2A** | **Purpose** to modernize, clarify, simplify, and make uniform the law of sales and leases<br>**Good Faith** the Code requires all sales and lease contracts to be performed in good faith, which means honesty in fact in the conduct or transaction concerned; in the case of a merchant, it also includes the observance of reasonable commercial standards<br>**Unconscionability** a court may refuse to enforce an unconscionable contract or any part of a contract found to be unconscionable<br>• *Procedural Unconscionability* unfairness of the bargaining process<br>• *Substantive Unconscionability* oppressive or grossly unfair contractual provisions<br>**Expansion of Commercial Practices**<br>• *Course of Dealing* a sequence of previous conduct between the parties establishing a common basis for interpreting their agreement<br>• *Usage of Trade* a practice or method of dealing regularly observed and followed in a place, vocation, or trade<br>• *Sales by and between Merchants* the Code establishes separate rules that apply to transactions between merchants or involving a merchant (a dealer in goods or a person who by his occupation holds himself out as having knowledge or skill peculiar to the goods or practice involved, or who employs an agent or broker whom he holds out as having such knowledge or skill)<br>**Liberal Administration of Remedies**<br>**Freedom of Contract** most provisions of the Code may be varied by agreement<br>**Validation and Preservation of Sales Contract** the Code reduces formal requisites to the bare minimum and attempts to preserve agreements whenever the parties manifest an intention to enter into a contract |
| --- | --- |

# Formation of Sales and Lease Contracts

| **Manifestation of Mutual Assent** | **Definiteness of an Offer** the Code provides that a sales or lease contract does not fail for indefiniteness even though one or more terms may have been omitted; the Code provides standards by which missing essential terms may be supplied for sales of goods<br>**Irrevocable Offers**<br>• *Option* a contract to hold open an offer<br>• *Firm Offer* a signed writing by a merchant to hold open an offer for the purchase or sale of goods for a maximum of three months<br>**Variant Acceptances** the inclusion of different or additional terms in an acceptance is addressed by focusing on the intent of the parties<br>**Manner of Acceptance** an acceptance can be made in any reasonable manner and is effective upon dispatch |
| --- | --- |

| **Consideration** | **Contractual Modifications** the Code provides that a contract for the sale or lease of goods may be modified without new consideration if the modification is made in good faith<br>**Firm Offers** are not revocable for lack of consideration |
| --- | --- |

| **Form of the Contract** | **Statute of Frauds** sale of goods costing $500 or more (or lease of goods for $1,000 or more) must be evidenced by a signed writing to be enforceable<br>• *Written Compliance* the Code requires some writing or writings sufficient to indicate that a contract has been made between the parties, signed by the party against whom enforcement is sought or by her authorized agent or broker, and including a term specifying the quantity of goods<br>• *Alternative Methods of Compliance* written confirmation between merchants, admission, specially manufactured goods, and delivery or payment and acceptance<br>**Parol Evidence** contractual terms that are set forth in a writing intended by the parties as a final expression of their agreement may not be contradicted by evidence of any prior agreement or of a contemporaneous oral agreement, but such terms may be explained or supplemented by course of dealing, usage of trade, course of performance, or consistent additional evidence |
| --- | --- |

# Cases

### CASE 21–1
## Finance Leases
## *CARTER v. TOKAI FINANCIAL SERVICES, INC.*
Court of Appeals of Georgia, 1998
231 Ga.App. 755, 500 S.E.2d 638

**BLACKBURN, J.**

Tokai Financial Services, Inc. brought suit against Randy P. Carter for monies owed under Carter's guaranty of a telephone equipment lease agreement. The trial court granted summary judgment to Tokai, and Carter appeals.

\* \* \*

On January 3, 1996, Tokai's predecessor in interest, Mitel Financial, entered into a "Master Equipment Lease Agreement" (Agreement) with Applied Radiological Control, Inc. (ARC) for the lease of certain telephone equipment valued at $42,000. Carter personally guaranteed ARC's obligations under the Agreement. ARC made four rental payments and then defaulted on its obligations as of June 1, 1996. Thereafter, Tokai repossessed the telephone equipment and sold it for $5,900. \* \* \* Tokai then brought this suit against Carter, and the trial court awarded Tokai $56,765.74.

1. In his first enumeration of error, Carter contends the Agreement is a "finance agreement" rather than a true lease. \* \* \*

As an initial matter, we note that Paragraph 13 of the Agreement states that each lease contemplated therein is a finance lease as defined by Article 2A of the UCC. "A 'finance lease' involves three parties—the lessee/business, the finance lessor, and the equipment supplier. The lessee/business selects the equipment and negotiates particularized modifications with the equipment supplier. Instead of purchasing the equipment from the supplier, the lessee/business has a finance lessor purchase the selected equipment, and then leases the equipment from the finance lessor." [Citation.]

Carter contends, nonetheless, that the true intent of the parties was to enter into a security agreement. "Whether a transaction creates a lease or security interest is determined by the facts of each case; however, a transaction creates a security interest if the consideration the lessee is to pay the lessor for the right to possession and use of the goods is an obligation for the term of the lease not subject to termination by the lessee, and (a) [t]he original term of the lease is equal to or greater than the remaining economic life of the goods, (b) [t]he lessee is bound to renew the lease for the remaining economic life of the goods or is bound to become the owner of the goods, (c) [t]he lessee has an option to renew the lease for the remaining economic life of the goods for no additional consideration or nominal additional consideration upon compliance with the lease agreement, or (d) [t]he lessee has an option to become the owner of the goods for no additional consideration or nominal additional consideration upon compliance with the lease agreement." [UCC]1–201(37).

Here, the Agreement's initial term was for five years, ARC was not required to renew the lease or purchase the telephone equipment at the end of the term, and ARC did not have the option to renew the lease or purchase the property at the end of the term for nominal consideration. Therefore, the Agreement does not fit within the definition of a secured transaction provided by [UCC]1–201(37).

Furthermore, "it is commonly held that the 'best test' for determining the intent of an agreement which provides for an option to buy is a comparison of the option price with the market value of the equipment at the time the option is to be exercised. Such a comparison shows whether the lessee is paying actual value acquiring the property at a substantially lower price. . . . If, upon

compliance with the terms of the 'lease,' the lessee has an option to become the owner of the property for no additional or for a nominal consideration, the lease is deemed to be intended for security. [Citations.] ARC was given the option to purchase the telephone equipment in this case at the end of the lease term for its fair market value. "Additional consideration is not nominal if . . . when the option to become the owner of the goods is granted to the lessee the price is stated to be the fair market value of the goods determined at the time the option is to be performed." [UCC § 1–201(37)(x).] Accordingly, the agreement in this case must be considered a true lease, not a secured transaction. As a result, the procedural safeguards of Article 9 of the UCC are inapplicable to the matter at hand, and Carter's claims under this enumeration must fail. [Citations.]

\* \* \*

"In Georgia, all lease contracts for 'goods,' including finance leases, first made or first effective on or after July 1, 1993, are governed by Article 2A of the Uniform Commercial Code. [Citations.] The Agreement was entered into by the parties on January 3, 1996; therefore, it is subject to Article 2A of the UCC . . .

\* \* \*

Judgment reversed.

---

## CASE 21–2
## Governing Law
### *PITTSLEY v. HOUSER*
Idaho Court of Appeals, 1994
875 P2d 232

SWANSTROM, J.

\* \* \*

## Facts and Procedural Background

In September of 1988, Jane Pittsley contracted with Hilton Contract Carpet Co. (Hilton) for the installation of carpet in her home. The total contract price was $4,402. Hilton paid the installers $700 to put the carpet in Pittsley's home. Following installation, Pittsley complained to Hilton that some seams were visible, that gaps appeared, that the carpet did not lay flat in all areas, and it failed to reach the wall in certain locations. Although Hilton made various attempts to fix the installation, by

attempting to stretch the carpet and other methods, Pittsley was not satisfied with the work. Eventually, Pittsley refused any further efforts to fix the carpet. Pittsley initially paid Hilton $3,500 on the contract, but refused to pay the remaining balance of $902.

Pittsley later filed suit, seeking rescission of the contract, return of the $3,500 and incidental damages. Hilton answered and counterclaimed for the balance remaining on the contract. The matter was heard by a magistrate sitting without a jury. The magistrate found that there were defects in the installation and that the carpet had been installed in an unworkmanlike manner. The magistrate also found that there was a lack of evidence on damages. The trial was continued to allow the parties to procure evidence on the amount of damages incurred by Pittsley. Following this continuance, Pittsley did not introduce any further evidence of damages, though witnesses for Hilton estimated repair costs at $250.

Although Pittsley had asked for rescission of the contract and a refund of her money, the magistrate determined that rescission, as an equitable remedy, was only available when one party committed a breach so material that it destroyed the entire purpose of the contract. Because the only estimate of damages was for $250, the magistrate ruled rescission would not be a proper remedy. Instead, the magistrate awarded Pittsley $250 damages plus $150 she expended in moving furniture prior to Hilton's attempt to repair the carpet. On the counterclaim, the magistrate awarded Hilton the $902 remaining on the contract. Additionally, both parties had requested attorney fees in the action. The magistrate determined that both parties had prevailed and therefore awarded both parties their attorney fees.

Following this decision, Pittsley appealed to the district court, claiming that the transaction involved was governed by the Idaho Uniform Commercial Code (UCC), [citation]. Pittsley argued that if the UCC had been properly applied, a different result would have been reached. The district court agreed with Pittsley's argument, reversing and remanding the case to the magistrate to make additional findings of fact and to apply the UCC to the transaction. * * *

Hilton now appeals the decision of the district court. * * * Even if application of the UCC was properly raised, Hilton argues that there were no defects in the goods that were the subject of the transaction, only in the installation, making application of the UCC inappropriate. * * *

## Analysis

* * *

The single question upon which this appeal depends is whether the UCC is applicable to the subject transaction. If the underlying transaction involved the sale of "goods," then the UCC would apply. If the transaction did not involve goods, but rather was for services, then application of the UCC would be erroneous.

Idaho Code § 2–105(1) defines "goods" as "all things (including specially manufactured goods) which are movable at the time of identification to the contract for sale. . . ." Although there is little dispute that carpets are "goods," the transaction in this case also involved installation, a service. Such hybrid transactions, involving both goods and services, raise difficult questions about the applicability of the UCC. Two lines of authority have emerged to deal with such situations.

The first line of authority, and the majority position, utilizes the "predominant factor" test. The Ninth Circuit, applying the Idaho Uniform Commercial Code to the subject transaction, restated the predominant factor test as:

The test for inclusion or exclusion is not whether they are mixed, but, granting that they are mixed, whether their predominant factor, their thrust, their purpose, reasonably stated, is the rendition of service, with goods incidentally involved (e.g., contract with artist for painting) or is a transaction of sale, with labor incidentally involved (e.g., installation of a water heater in a bathroom).

[Citations.] This test essentially involves consideration of the contract in its entirety, applying the UCC to the entire contract or not at all.

The second line of authority, which Hilton urges us to adopt, allows the contract to be severed into different parts, applying the UCC to the goods involved in the contract, but not to the nongoods involved, including services as well as other nongoods assets and property. Thus, an action focusing on defects or problems with the goods themselves would be covered by the UCC, while a suit based on the service provided or some other nongoods aspect would not be covered by the UCC. * * *

We believe the predominant factor test is the more prudent rule. Severing contracts into various parts, attempting to label each as goods or nongoods and applying different law to each separate part clearly contravenes the UCC's declared purpose "to simplify, clarify and modernize the law governing commercial transactions." § 1–102(2)(a). As the Supreme Court of Tennessee suggested in [citation], such a rule would, in many contexts, present "difficult and in some instances insurmountable problems of proof in segregating assets and determining their respective values at the time of the original contract and at the time of resale, in order to apply two different measures of damages."

Applying the predominant factor test to the case before us, we conclude that the UCC was applicable to the subject transaction. The record indicates that the contract between the parties called for "165 yds Masterpiece No. 2122—Installed" for a price of $4319.50. There was an additional charge for removing the existing carpet. The record indicates that Hilton paid the installers $700 for the work done in laying Pittsley's carpet. It appears that Pittsley entered into this contract for the purpose of obtaining carpet of a certain quality and color. It does not appear that the installation, either who would provide it or the nature of the work, was a factor in inducing Pittsley to choose Hilton as the carpet supplier. On these facts, we conclude that the sale of the carpet was the predominant factor in the contract, with the installation being merely incidental to the purchase. Therefore, in failing to consider the UCC, the magistrate did not apply the correct legal principles to the facts as found. We must therefore vacate the judgment and remand for further findings of fact and application of the UCC to the subject transaction.

---

## CASE 21–3
### Unconscionability
# CONSTRUCTION ASSOCIATES, INC. v. FARGO WATER EQUIPMENT CO.
North Dakota Supreme Court, 1989
446 N.W.2d 237

ERICKSTAD, J.

Johns-Manville Sales Corporation (J-M) appealed from a district court judgment entered upon a jury verdict finding it liable for $140,000 in damages for defective pipe. We affirm.

In 1977 Construction Associates, Inc., was the successful bidder to construct a water supply line for the city of Breckenridge, Minnesota. Construction Associates purchased from Fargo Water Equipment (Fargo Water) a large supply of polyvinyl chloride (PVC) pipe manufactured by J-M. The Breckenridge pipeline was completed during the summer of 1978.

The line eventually developed numerous leaks. J-M sent a technical field specialist to Breckenridge in August 1978. On his recommendation, the line was pumped to a high pressure using a fire engine in an attempt to set the rubber gaskets in the joints. This temporarily remedied the problem, but additional leaks soon occurred. Fargo Water recommended repairs using bell clamps, which Construction Associates attempted without success. Finally, Construction Associates repaired the leaks as they were discovered by removing the defective joints and replacing them with stainless steel sleeves. At the time of trial in 1981, seventy leaks had been discovered and repaired.

Construction Associates brought this action against J-M and Fargo Water, asserting that the pipe was defective and that the defects caused the leaks in the Breckenridge line. * * * The jury awarded Construction Associates $140,000 for its expenses in repairing the line against J-M * * * J-M appealed.

* * *

J-M asserts that the trial court erred in concluding that a clause limiting the remedies available upon breach of its warranty and specifically excluding liability for consequential damages was unconscionable.

Construction Associates purchased the pipe from Fargo Water, and at the time of contracting had no direct contact with J-M. J-M shipped the pipe directly to the job site in Breckenridge. Included with each shipment of pipe was an installation guide, which expressly stated that it was "written especially for the installer and those who direct the actual handling and installation of Johns-Manville PVC Pressure Rated Pipe." On page three of the installation guide J-M expressly warranted the pipe to be free from defects in workmanship and materials. A limitation of liability clause was also included:

Limitation of Liability

It is expressly understood and agreed that the limit of J-M's liability shall be the resupply of a like quantity of non-defective Product and that J-M shall have no such liability except where the damage or claim results solely from breach of J-M's warranty. It is also agreed that J-M shall not be liable for any incidental, consequential or other damages for any alleged negligence, breach of warranty, strict liability, or any other theory, other than the limited liability set forth above.

The first sentence of the clause is essentially a limitation of remedies. The second sentence is a specific exclusion of consequential or incidental damages.

J-M asserted the provisions of the clause as a defense, arguing that it could only be held liable for replacement of defective pipe. The trial court determined that the limitation of remedies and exclusion of damages were unconscionable and therefore unenforceable. * * *

[U.C.C. § 2–719] specifically allows the parties to an agreement to limit the remedies available upon breach and to exclude consequential damages:

* * *

By its terms, § 2–302 [unconscionable contract or clause] applies to any clause of the contract. Courts thus have construed §§ 2–302 and 2–719 together in holding that a general limitation of remedies clause, including those limiting liability to repair or replacement, may be subject to unconscionability analysis under the Code. [Citations.]

The determination whether a particular contractual provision is unconscionable is a question of law for the court. [Citations.] The court is to look at the contract from the perspective of the time it was entered into, without the benefit of hindsight. * * *

Courts and commentators have generally viewed the Code's unconscionability provisions within a two-pronged framework: procedural unconscionability, which encompasses factors relating to unfair surprise, oppression, and inequality of bargaining power, and substantive unconscionability, which focuses upon the harshness or one-sidedness of the contractual provision in question. [Citations.]

**A. *Procedural Unconscionability*** We initially note that this case presents a commercial, rather than a consumer, transaction. Although courts have generally been more reluctant to find unconscionability in purely commercial settings, [citation], under appropriate circumstances a contractual provision may be found unconscionable even in a commercial setting. [Citations.]

* * *

The circumstances presented in this case demonstrate a substantial inequality in bargaining power between J-M and Construction Associates. Construction Associates is a relatively small local construction firm, while J-M is part of an enormous, highly diversified, international conglomerate. The limitation of remedies and exclusion of damages were part of a pre-printed installation guide included with all shipments of J-M Pipe. J-M has continually stressed on appeal that those limitations and exclusions are included in all of its brochures and guides. It is obvious that there is no room for bargaining or negotiation as to the warranty provisions.

We also note that the facts in this case demonstrate an actual lack of negotiation coupled with elements of unfair surprise. * * *

To be a part of the bargain, a provision limiting the defendant's liability must, unless incorporated into the contract through prior course of dealings or trade usage, have been bargained for, brought to the purchaser's attention or be conspicuous. . . . If not, the seller has no reasonable expectation that the remedy was being so restricted and the restriction cannot be said to be part of the agreement of the parties. . . . Nor does the mere fact that both parties are businessmen justify the utilization of unfair surprise to the detriment of one of the parties since the Code specifically provides for the recovery of consequential damages and an individual should be able to rely on their existence in the absence of being informed to the contrary either directly or constructively through prior course of dealings or trade usage. * * *

The limitations and exclusions clause in this case can hardly be described as "bargained for." The clauses were included on page three of a pre-printed installation guide expressly directed to the worker in the field, rather than to officers of Construction Associates. Construction Associates was not apprised at the time of contracting that their remedies under the Code were being limited or excluded. It would be within J-M's control to do so by, for example, requiring its dealers to accept orders for pipe only upon a J-M form which included the limitations and exclusions and which required the purchaser's signature. Clearly an element of procedural unconscionability is present where through a pre-printed guide which was not provided to Construction Associates (and then only to field workers) until long after the sales contract had been finalized.

**B. *Substantive Unconscionability*** Substantive unconscionability focuses upon the harshness of the particular contractual terms:

Substantive unconscionability concerns the question whether the terms themselves are commercially reasonable. . . . While the Code permits the limitation of remedies, it must be remembered that it disfavors them and specifically provides for their deletion if they would act to deprive a contracting party of reasonable protection against a breach. . . . The Code (§ 1–106(1)) specifically provides that the remedies provided by it shall be liberally construed to the end that the aggrieved party may be put in as good a position as if the other party had fully performed. Frank's Maintenance & Engineering, Inc. v. C.A. Roberts Co. [citation].

Similarly, the Official Comment to § 2–719 of the Code stresses that contractual provisions which would deprive a party of "minimum adequate remedies" for breach will not be enforced:

* * *

The clause at issue here would limit Construction Associates' remedy for J-M's breach to a like quantity of replacement pipe, with no recovery of consequential damages. Construction Associates argues, with support in the evidence, that replacement pipe is not used when making repairs to leaking joints on a completed underground water pipeline. Because the accepted method of repair is to cut out the leaking joint and repair it with a stainless steel sleeve, Construction Associates argues, the replacement pipe would be useless in effecting repairs upon the line. The trial court determined that J-M's limited remedy "amount[ed] to nothing whatsoever."

\* \* \*

Numerous courts, in a variety of commercial and consumer contexts, have held limitations and exclusions unconscionable when they leave the non-breaching party with no effective remedy. [Citations.] This is particularly true where the defect in the product is latent, so that the buyer is unable to discover the defect until additional damages are incurred. [Citations.] In this case, Construction Associates did not discover the defects until the pipe was assembled and placed underground.

The concept of unconscionability must necessarily be applied in a flexible manner, taking into consideration all of the facts and circumstances of a particular case. [Citation.] The circumstances of this case demonstrate elements of procedural and substantive unconscionability which, when viewed in totality, adequately support the trial court's conclusion that the clause limiting remedies and excluding consequential damages was unconscionable under the relevant statutory provisions. \* \* \*

The judgment of the district court is affirmed.

---

## CASE 21–4
## Variant Acceptances: Battle of the Forms
### *McJUNKIN CORP. v. MECHANICALS, INC.*
United States Court of Appeals, Sixth Circuit, 1989
888 F.2d 481

ENGEL, J.

This conflict requires a court to declare a victor in a classic Uniform Commercial Code "Battle of the Forms" under ... U.C.C. § [2–207]. We must determine whether, under the facts here, a liability limitation contained in an acknowledgment form of Appellee Alaskan Copper Companies precludes Appellant McJunkin Corporation from recovering damages after Alaskan sold it defective goods.

The problem underlying any "battle of the forms" is that parties engaged in commerce have failed to incorporate into one formal, signed contract the explicit terms of their contractual relationship. Instead, each has been content to rely upon standard terms which each has included in its purchase orders or acknowledgments, terms which often conflict with those in the other party's documents. Usually, these standard terms mean little, for a contract looks to its fulfillment and rarely anticipates its breach. Hope springs eternal in the commercial world and expectations are usually, but not always, realized. It is only when the good faith expectations of the parties are frustrated that the legal obligations and rights of the parties must be precisely determined. This case presents a situation typical in any battle of the forms: it is not that the parties' forms have said too little, but rather that they have said too much yet have expressly agreed upon too little.

Generally, where parties engaged in commerce enjoy parity in bargaining power, the Code acknowledges the parties' autonomy and recognizes the parties' right to agree upon contractual terms which might otherwise violate the Code, including liability limitations. [Citation.] \* \* \*

Nevertheless, under the facts of this case, we find that Alaskan's liability limitation is inoperative. While we find that Alaskan and McJunkin had a contract, we find that the contract existed by virtue of the parties' conduct, not by virtue of the exchange of forms. Under Ohio Rev. Code [§ 2–207(3)], the contract thus incorporated only those terms upon which both parties' standardized forms agreed; the liability limitation not being a term in McJunkin's purchase order, it did not bind McJunkin and thus limit recovery.

Emery Industries (Emery), a division of National Distillers & Chemical Corporation (National Distillers), a Virginia corporation, operates a chemical plant in Cincinnati, Ohio. On April 4, 1983, Emery contracted with Mechanicals, Inc. (Mechanicals), an Ohio corporation, for installation of a pipe system designed to carry chemicals and fatty acids under high pressure and temperature. The system required stainless steel "stub ends" (used to connect pipe segments), which Mechanicals ordered from McJunkin Corporation (McJunkin), a West Virginia corporation. McJunkin in turn ordered the stub ends from the Alaskan Copper Companies, Inc. (Alaskan) on April 27, 1983, after an agent of McJunkin had discussed the issue with an agent of Alaskan.

In a purchase order issued to Alaskan, McJunkin set out the following conditions of sale:

1. By acknowledging receipt of this order or by supplying products described herein, Seller agrees to the terms and conditions set forth herein.

* * *

5. Seller will certify that the goods and/or services delivered pursuant to this purchase order were produced and/or performed in compliance with all applicable laws, regulations, and Executive Orders.

6. Buyer takes exception to and hereby objects to all hold harmless and indemnity provisions, either express or implied, which may be set forth in Seller's acceptance that seek to impose liability upon Buyer. PLEASE ACKNOWLEDGE RECEIPT OF THIS ORDER IMMEDIATELY, ADVISING EARLIEST SHIPPING DATE.

On April 29, Alaskan shipped the stub ends directly to Mechanicals. On May 4, Alaskan then sent McJunkin an acknowledgment of the order, which contained terms and conditions of sale different from those in McJunkin's purchase order. In pertinent part, the acknowledgment provided:

6. Disclaimer of warranty. SELLER MAKES NO WARRANTY OF ANY KIND, EXPRESS OR IMPLIED (INCLUDING NO WARRANTY OF MERCHANTABILITY, FITNESS FOR PARTICULAR PURPOSE USAGE OR TRADE) TO ANY PERSON OR ENTITY WITH REGARD TO THE GOODS OR SERVICES COVERED HEREBY AND FORBIDS PURCHASER TO REPRESENT OTHERWISE TO ANYONE WITH WHICH IT DEALS.

7. Defects, Inspection, Notification.
   (a) Purchaser must inspect the goods at its expense within ten (10) days of the receipt thereof and notify Seller of any claimed defect shortage or inaccuracy therein within ten (10) days thereafter or it shall be held to have waived its rights to such remedy thereof or recovery thereupon from Seller.

   * * *

   (b) NO GOODS SHALL BE DEEMED DEFECTIVE IF THE ALLEGED DEFECT IS DISCOVERABLE ONLY BY INSPECTION MEANS MORE STRINGENT THAN THOSE REQUESTED BY PURCHASER IN CONNECTION WITH THE PLACING OF ITS ORDER.

8. Exclusivity of Remedy, Limitation of Damages. THE SOLE AND EXCLUSIVE REMEDY FOR DEFECTIVE GOODS OR SERVICES SHALL BE AT SELLER'S OPTION REPAIR REPLACEMENT OR REFUND OF PURCHASE PRICE. SELLER SHALL NOT BE LIABLE UNDER ANY CIRCUMSTANCES INCLUDING BUT NOT LIMITED TO ANY CLAIM FOR BREACH OF WARRANTY (EXPRESS OR IMPLIED) TORT (INCLUDING NEGLIGENCE OR STRICT LIABILITY) FOR ANY INCIDENTAL, CONTINGENT SPECIAL OR CONSEQUENTIAL DAMAGES ARISING FROM OR OUT OF THE GOODS OR SERVICES PURCHASED HEREUNDER INCLUDING BUT NOT LIMITED TO NO LIABILITY FOR LOSS OF PROFITS OR REVENUE, LOSS OF USE OF GOODS OR SERVICES OR OTHER ITEMS TO BE FURNISHED TO PURCHASER HEREUNDER, COST OF CAPITAL, COST OF SUBSTITUTE EQUIPMENT, ADDITIONAL COSTS INCURRED BY PURCHASER AT THE PLANT OR IN THE FIELD (WHETHER BY WAY OF CORRECTION OR OTHERWISE) OR CLAIMS OF PURCHASER'S CUSTOMERS OR OTHER THIRD PARTIES FOR DAMAGES. . . .

* * *

20. Acceptance. SELLER'S ACCEPTANCE OF THIS CONTRACT IS EXPRESSLY CONDITIONED ON PURCHASER'S ASSENT TO ALL OF THE FOREGOING STANDARD CONDITIONS OF SALE
   (a) Any additional or different terms or conditions which may appear in any communication from Purchaser are hereby objected to and shall not be effective or binding unless specifically recognized and assented to in writing by Seller's President, Vice President or authorized representative and no such additional or different terms or conditions in any printed form of Purchaser shall become part of this contract despite Seller's acceptance of the contract unless such acceptance so specifically recognizes and assents to their inclusion.
   (b) If purchaser objects to any of the terms stated herein Purchaser shall advise Seller in writing of the particular objection within ten (10) days of the date hereof or shall be held to have waived its objections.

(emphasis in original)

The stub ends were delivered to Mechanicals in several shipments throughout the course of five months. Accompanying each shipment was a document reciting the same limitation of remedies appearing on Alaskan's initial acknowledgment. Apparently McJunkin never objected to any of the terms contained in any of Alaskan's documents.

After the stub ends were installed, they were tested and many were found to leak. Emery then sent samples of the leaking stub ends to an independent research laboratory, which concluded that they were defective. Mechanicals removed and replaced them. In the course of replacing the defective stub ends, Emery had to remove and replace insulation around the defective piping and had to close its plant for several days. Mechanicals also incurred substantial labor costs in addition to the cost of replacement materials.

On September 5, 1984, McJunkin filed a complaint in the United States District Court for the Southern District of Ohio, alleging that Mechanicals had failed to pay $26,141.88 owed on account for the stub ends supplied by McJunkin. Mechanicals filed an answer and counterclaim against McJunkin, alleging $93,586.13 in damages resulting from Mechanicals' replacement and repair of the defective stub ends supplied by McJunkin. On November 5, 1984, McJunkin filed a third-party complaint against Alaskan, alleging that Alaskan was liable for any damages incurred by Mechanicals as a result of the defective stub ends.

* * * The . . . complaints then proceeded to a jury trial, with the jury finding: McJunkin liable to Mechanicals for $87,000 for having supplied defective stub ends; and Mechanicals liable to McJunkin for $19,000 for failure to pay its account. The jury likewise found that Alaskan had provided McJunkin defective stub ends, for which McJunkin could recover the cost of replacement. The jury also held, however, that McJunkin had failed to give Alaskan an opportunity to replace the defective stub ends. On September 8, 1986, the district court entered: (1) a $68,000 judgment for Mechanicals against McJunkin ($87,000 in damages minus $19,000 owed McJunkin on its account); and (2) a $6,479.23 judgment for McJunkin against Alaskan for the cost of replacement stub ends.

Both McJunkin and Alaskan then moved for judgment notwithstanding the verdict. The district court denied McJunkin's motion, holding that McJunkin was bound by the terms of sale in Alaskan's acknowledgment and shipping materials. However, the district court granted Alaskan's motion for judgment n.o.v., holding that McJunkin's failure to allow Alaskan to replace or repair the defective stub ends (in accordance with Alaskan's terms of sale) constituted a waiver of McJunkin's contractual rights, thereby relieving Alaskan of any liability for the defective stub ends. McJunkin appeals.

* * *

To determine the contractual obligations of McJunkin and Alaskan, we consider both the parties' actions and the forms exchanged, viewing the totality of circumstances surrounding the transaction. [Citation.] We must determine: (1) whether McJunkin and Alaskan assumed any contractual obligations; (2) how such obligations arose; and (3) the nature of those obligations.

There are several possible interpretations of Alaskan's and McJunkin's contractual relationship. First, by shipping the stub ends, Alaskan accepted McJunkin's offer (made in McJunkin's purchase order) and therefore was bound by the terms of McJunkin's offer, with any remedy limitation contained in Alaskan's acknowledgment being excluded from the contract. Second, McJunkin's acquiescence to the shipments and failure to object to the terms in the acknowledgment constituted an acceptance of Alaskan's terms contained in the acknowledgment, thereby giving effect to Alaskan's remedy limitation under Ohio Rev.Code § [2–207(2)(C)]. Third, Alaskan's acknowledgment was a seasonable, yet conditional, response to McJunkin's purchase order, thereby vitiating formation of a contract based upon the forms alone, although the conduct of the parties may have established a contract under Ohio Rev.Code § 2–207(3). We now address these contentions.

* * *

First, Alaskan's shipment of stub ends prior to acknowledgment might be considered an acceptance upon McJunkin's terms alone. * * * Nevertheless, although Alaskan's acknowledgment was sent five days after the initial shipment, we hold that the more reasonable interpretation of the parties' actions is that Alaskan, through its shipment and transmission of an acknowledgment within a few short days, did not intend to bind itself to McJunkin's terms, but instead sought to incorporate its own terms into a contract with McJunkin. * * *

[Secondly,] [i]t is urged that McJunkin's failure to object to the remedy limitation [in Alaskan's acknowledgment forms] indicates that McJunkin accepted that limitation. § [2–207(2)(C)] (additional or different terms become part of contract between merchants unless objection made within reasonable time). Although Alaskan's contract terms might indicate that McJunkin's failure to object within a reasonable time constituted McJunkin's acceptance of Alaskan's terms, we find that McJunkin did not accept Alaskan's terms. McJunkin never explicitly accepted the terms of Alaskan's acknowledgment. Given McJunkin's silence in the face of Alaskan's acknowledgment, McJunkin was not bound by those terms. [Citations.]

Instead, under Ohio Rev.Code § 2–207(1), a seasonable expression of acceptance, such as that made by Alaskan, does not create a contract based upon the terms contained in the forms if "acceptance is expressly made conditional on assent to the additional or different terms." It is clear that Alaskan's acknowledgment expressly conditioned Alaskan's acceptance upon McJunkin's assent to Alaskan's terms of sale: * * *

However, although we find that no contract was created by virtue of the exchanged document, "A contract for sale of goods may be made in any manner sufficient to show agreement, *including conduct* by both parties which recognizes the existence of such contract." Ohio Rev.Code § [2–207(1)]. Moreover, under Ohio Rev. Code § 2–207(3), "Conduct by both parties which recognizes the existence of a contract is sufficient to establish a contract for sale although the writings of the parties do not otherwise establish a contract. In such case the terms of the particular contract consist of those terms on which the writings of the parties agree, together with any supplementary terms incorporated under any other provisions of [Article 2]."

Abundantly clear from McJunkin's and Alaskan's actions is that they had entered a contract within the meaning of Ohio Rev.Code §§ [2–207(1) & 2–207(3)]. Alaskan sent numerous shipments of stub ends, and McJunkin paid for them before they were shipped directly to Mechanicals. Indeed, both Alaskan and McJunkin do not dispute that they had contracted; instead, they disagree about who should be obligated to bear the loss for the defective stub ends. We can thus say with confidence that McJunkin's and Alaskan's course of conduct established a contract enforceable under Ohio law.

Under Ohio Rev.Code § [2–207(3)], the terms of McJunkin's and Alaskan's contract "consist of those terms on which the writings of the parties agree, together with any supplementary terms incorporated under any other provisions of [Article 2]." Because the remedy limitation was contained only in Alaskan's form and not agreed upon by both parties' documents, Alaskan's remedy limitation did not bind McJunkin, and, contrary to the district court judgment, Alaskan could not take advantage of this provision.

[We conclude] that the remedy limitation was unenforceable.

\* \* \*

Accordingly, we VACATE the judgment of the district court and REMAND for further proceedings consistent with this opinion.

---

 **Questions**

1. Distinguish a sale and a lease from other kinds of transactions that affect goods.
2. Identify and discuss the fundamental principles of Article 2 and Article 2A.
3. Discuss the significant changes Article 2 and Article 2A have made in the need for an offer to include all material terms.

4. Distinguish between the common law's mirror image rule and the Uniform Commercial Code's (UCC's) provisions for dealing with variant acceptances.
5. Discuss (a) the UCC's approach to the requirement that certain contracts must be in writing and (b) the alternative methods of compliance.

---

 **Problems**

1. Adams orders one thousand widgets at $5 per widget from International Widget to be delivered within sixty days. After the contract is consummated and signed, Adams requests that International deliver the widgets within thirty days rather than sixty days. International agrees. Is the contractual modification binding?
2. In question 1, what effect, if any, would the following telegram have?

International Widget:
   In accordance with our agreement of this date you will deliver the 1,000 previously ordered widgets within thirty days. Thank you for your cooperation in this matter.

                                     (signed) Adams

3. Browne & Assoc., a San Francisco company, orders from U.S. Electronics, a New York company, ten thousand electronic units. Browne & Assoc.'s order form provides that any dispute would be resolved by an arbitration panel located in San Francisco. U.S. Electronics executes and delivers to Browne & Assoc. its acknowledgment form, which accepts the order and contains the following provision: "All disputes will be resolved by the State courts of New York." A dispute arises concerning the workmanship of the parts, and Browne & Assoc. wishes the case to be arbitrated in San Francisco. What result?

4. Explain how the result in problem 3 might change if the U.S. Electronics form contained any of the following provisions:

   (a) "The seller's acceptance of the purchase order to which this acknowledgment responds is expressly made conditional on the buyer's assent to any or different terms contained in this acknowledgment."

   (b) "The seller's acceptance of the purchase order is subject to the terms and conditions on the face and reverse side hereof and which the buyer accepts by accepting the goods described herein."

   (c) "The seller's terms govern this agreement—this acknowledgment merely constitutes a counteroffer."

5. Reinfort executed a written contract with Bylinski to purchase an assorted collection of shoes for $3,000. A week before the agreed shipment date, Bylinski called Reinfort and said, "We cannot deliver at $3,000; unless you agree to pay $4,000,

we will cancel the order." After considerable discussion, Reinfort agreed to pay $4,000 if Bylinski would ship as agreed in the contract. After the shoes had been delivered and accepted by Reinfort, Reinfort refused to pay $4,000 and insisted on paying only $3,000. Decision?

6.  On November 23, Acorn, a dress manufacturer, mailed to Bowman a written and signed offer to sell one thousand sundresses at $50 per dress. The offer stated that it would "remain open for ten days" and that it could "not be withdrawn prior to that date."

Two days later, Acorn, noting a sudden increase in the price of sundresses, changed his mind. Acorn therefore sent Bowman a letter revoking the offer. The letter was sent on November 25 and received by Bowman on November 28.

Bowman chose to disregard the letter of November 25; instead, she happily continued to watch the price of sundresses rise. On December 1, Bowman sent a letter accepting the original offer. The letter, however, was not received by Acorn until December 9, due to a delay in the mails.

Bowman has demanded delivery of the goods according to the terms of the offer of November 23, but Acorn has refused. Decision?

7.  Henry and Wilma, an elderly immigrant couple, agreed to purchase from Brown a refrigerator with fair market value of $450 for twenty-five monthly installments of $60 per month. Henry and Wilma now wish to void the contract, asserting that they did not realize the exorbitant price they were paying. Result?

8.  Courts Distributors needed two hundred compact refrigerators on a rush basis. It contacted Eastinghouse Corporation, a manufacturer of refrigerators. Eastinghouse said it would take some time to quote a price on an order of that size. Courts replied, "Send the refrigerators immediately and bill us later." The refrigerators were delivered three days later, and the invoice ten days after that. The invoice price was $140,000. Courts believes that the wholesale market price of the refrigerators is only $120,000. Discuss.

9.  While adjusting a television antenna beside his mobile home and underneath a high-voltage electric transmission wire, Prince received an electric shock resulting in personal injury. He claims the high-voltage electric current jumped from the transmission wire to the antenna. The wire, which carried some 7,200 volts of electricity, did not serve his mobile home but ran directly above it. Prince sued the Navarro County Electric Co-Op, the owner and operator of the wire, for breach of implied warranty of merchantability under the Uniform Commercial Code. He contends that the Code's implied warranty of merchantability extends to the container of a product—in this instance the wiring—and that the escape of the current shows that the wiring was unfit for its purpose of transporting electricity. The electric company argues that the electricity passing through the transmission wire was not being sold to Prince and that, therefore, there was no sale of goods to Prince. Decision?

10.  HMT, already in the business of marketing agricultural products, decided to try its hand at marketing potatoes for processing. Nine months before the potato harvest, HMT contracted to supply Bell Brand with 100,000 sacks of potatoes. At harvest time, Bell Brand would only accept 60,000 sacks. HMT sues for breach of contract. Bell Brand argues that custom and usage in marketing processing potatoes allows buyers to give *estimates* in contracts, not fixed quantities, because the contracts are established so far in advance. HMT responds that the quantity term in the contract was definite and unambiguous. Can custom and trade usage be used to interpret an unambiguous contract? Discuss.

11.  Schreiner, a cotton farmer, agreed over the telephone to sell 150 bales of cotton to Loeb & Co. Schreiner had sold cotton to Loeb & Co. for the past five years. Written confirmation of the date, parties, price, and conditions was mailed to Schreiner, who did not respond to the confirmation in any way. Four months later, when the price of cotton had doubled, Loeb & Co. sought to enforce the contract. Is the contract enforceable?

12.  American Sand & Gravel Inc. agreed to sell sand to Clark at a special discount if 20,000 to 25,000 tons were ordered. The discount price was 45¢ per ton, compared with the normal price of 55¢ per ton. Two years later, Clark orders, and receives, 1,600 tons of sand from American Sand & Gravel. Clark refuses to pay more then 45¢ per ton. American Sand & Gravel sues for the remaining 10¢ per ton. Decision?

13.  In September 1973, Auburn Plastics (defendant) submitted price quotations to CBS (plaintiff) for the manufacture of eight cavity molds to be used in making parts for CBS's toys. Each quotation specified that the offer would not be binding unless accepted within fifteen days. Furthermore, CBS would be subject to an additional 30 percent charge for engineering services upon delivery of the molds. In December 1973 and January 1974, CBS sent detailed purchase orders to Auburn Plastics for cavity molds. The purchase order forms stated that CBS reserved the right to remove the molds from Auburn Plastics without an additional or "withdrawal" charge. Auburn Plastics acknowledged the purchase order and stated that the sale would be subject to all conditions contained in the price quotation. CBS paid Auburn for the molds, and Auburn began to fabricate toy parts from the molds for CBS. Later, Auburn announced a price increase, and CBS demanded delivery of the molds. Auburn refused to deliver the molds unless CBS paid the additional charge for engineering services. CBS claimed that the contract did not provide for a withdrawal charge. Decision?

14.  Terminal Grain Corporation brought an action against Glen Freeman, a farmer, to recover damages for breach of an oral contract to deliver grain. According to the company, Freeman orally agreed to two sales of wheat to Terminal Grain of 4,000 bushels each at $1.65 1/2 per bushel and $1.71 per bushel, respectively. Dwayne Maher, merchandising manager of Terminal Grain, sent two written confirmations of the agreements to Freeman, who never made any written

objections to the confirmations. After the first transaction had occurred, the price of wheat rose to between $2.25 and $2.30 per bushel, and Freeman refused to deliver the remaining 4,000 bushels at the agreed-upon price. Freeman denies entering into any agreement to sell the second 4,000 bushels of wheat to Terminal Grain but admits that he received the two written confirmations sent by Maher. Decision?

15. Frank's Maintenance and Engineering, Inc., orally ordered steel tubing from C.A. Roberts Co. for use in the manufacture of motorcycle front fork tubes. Because these front fork tubes bear the bulk of the weight of a motorcycle, the steel used must be of high quality. Roberts Co. sent an acknowledgment with conditions of sale including one that limited consequential damages and restricted remedies available upon breach by requiring claims for defective equipment to be promptly made upon receipt. The conditions were located on the back of the acknowledgment. The legend "conditions of sale on reverse side" was stamped over so that on first appearance it read "No conditions of sale on reverse side." Roberts delivered the order in December 1975. The steel had no visible defects; however, when Frank's Maintenance began using the steel in its manufacture in the summer of 1976, it discovered that the steel was pitted and cracked beyond repair. Frank's Maintenance informed Roberts Co. of the defects, revoked its acceptance of the steel, and sued for breach of warranty of merchantability. Decision?

16. Dorton, as a representative for The Carpet Mart, purchased carpets from Collins & Aikman that were supposedly manufactured of 100 percent Kodel polyester fiber but were, in fact, made of cheaper and inferior fibers. Dorton then brought suit for compensatory and punitive damages against Collins & Aikman for its fraud, deceit, and misrepresentation in the sale of the carpets. Collins & Aikman moved for a stay pending arbitration, claiming that Dorton was bound to an arbitration agreement printed on the reverse side of Collins & Aikman's printed sales acknowledgment form. A provision printed on the face of the acknowledgment form stated that its acceptance was "subject to all of the terms and conditions on the face and reverse side thereof, including arbitration, all of which are accepted by buyer." Holding that there existed no binding arbitration agreement between the parties, the district court denied the stay. Collins & Aikman appealed. Decision?

17. Defendant, Gray Communications, desired to build a television tower. After a number of negotiation sessions conducted by telephone between the Defendant and Plaintiff, Kline Iron, the parties allegedly reached an oral agreement under which the Plaintiff would build a tower for the Defendant for a total price of $1,485,368. A few days later, Plaintiff sent a written document, referred to as a proposal, for execution by Defendant. The Proposal indicated that it had been prepared for immediate acceptance by Defendant and that prior to formal acceptance by Defendant it could be modified or withdrawn without notice. A few days later, without having executed the Proposal, Defendant advised Plaintiff that a competitor had provided a lower bid for construction of the tower. Defendant requested that Plaintiff explain its higher bid price, which Plaintiff failed to do. Defendant then advised Plaintiff by letter that it would not be retained to construct the tower. Plaintiff then commenced suit alleging breach of an oral contract, asserting that the oral agreement was enforceable because the common law of contracts, not the UCC, governed the transaction and that under the common law a writing is not necessary to cover this type of transaction. Even if the transaction was subject to the UCC, Plaintiff alternatively argued, the contract was within the UCC "merchant's exception." Decision?

18. Due to high gasoline prices, American Bakeries Company (ABC) considered converting its fleet of more than 3,000 vehicles to a much less expensive propane fuel system. After negotiations with Empire Gas Corporation (Empire), ABC signed a contract for approximately three thousand converter units, "more or less depending upon requirements of Buyer," as well as agreeing to buy all propane to be used for four years from Empire. Without giving any reasons, however, ABC never ordered any converter units or propane from Empire, having apparently decided not to convert its vehicles. Empire brought suit against ABC, and won a jury award of $3,254,963, representing lost profits on 2,242 converter units and the propane that would have been consumed during the contract period. ABC appealed. Decision?

**WWW** **Internet Exercise** Compare the provisions governing the formation of sales contracts under the United Nations Convention on Contracts for the International Sale of Goods (Vienna, 1980) with the provisions of Article 2 of the Uniform Commercial Code.

# CHAPTER 22

# Performance

Performance is the process of discharging contractual obligations by carrying out those obligations according to the terms of the contract. The basic obligation of the seller in a contract for the sale of goods is to transfer and deliver goods that conform to the terms of the contract. The basic obligation of the buyer is to accept and pay for conforming goods in accordance with the contract. The basic obligation of the lessor is to transfer possession of the goods for the lease term, and that of the lessee is to pay the agreed rent. Section 2A–103(1)(j). Unless the parties have agreed otherwise, a tender (offer) of performance by one party is a condition to performance by the other party. A contract of sale also requires that each party not impair the other party's expectation of having the contract performed.

The obligations of the parties are determined by their contractual agreement. For example, the contract of sale may expressly provide that the seller must deliver the goods before receiving payment of the price or that the buyer must pay the price before receiving the goods. If the contract does not sufficiently cover the particulars of performance, these terms will be supplied by the Code, common law, course of dealing, usage of trade, and course of performance. (Article 2A provides only a few gap-fillers.) In all events, both parties to the sales contract must perform their contractual obligations in good faith.

This chapter will examine the performance obligations of the seller and the buyer as well as the contractual obligations that apply to both of them.

## PERFORMANCE BY THE SELLER

Tender of conforming goods by the seller entitles him to acceptance of them by the buyer and to payment of the contractually agreed-upon price. Nonetheless, the rights of the parties may be otherwise fixed by the terms of the contract. For example, if the seller has agreed to sell goods on sixty or ninety days' credit, he is required to perform his part of the contract before the buyer performs.

**Tender** of delivery requires that the seller put and hold goods that conform to the contract at the buyer's disposition and that he give the buyer reasonable notification to enable her to take delivery. Section 2–503. Tender must also be made at a reasonable time and be kept open for a reasonable period. For example, Robert agrees to sell Barbara a sound system composed of a CD player, receiver, tape deck, and two speakers. Each component is specified by manufacturer and model number, and delivery is to be at Robert's store. Robert obtains the ordered equipment in accordance with the contractual specifications and notifies Barbara that she may pick up the system at her convenience. Robert has now tendered and thus has performed his obligations under the sales contract: he holds goods that conform to the contract, he has reasonably placed them at the buyer's disposal, and he has notified the buyer of their readiness.

---

## CISG

*As specified by the contract and the CISG, the seller must deliver the goods, hand over any documents relating to them, and transfer the property in the goods.*

---

## Time and Manner of Tender

Tender must be at a *reasonable* time, and the goods tendered must be kept available for the period reasonably necessary to enable the buyer to take possession of them. Unless otherwise agreed, the buyer must furnish facilities reasonably suited to the receipt of the goods tendered by the seller. Section 2–503.

If the terms of the contract do not fix a definite time for delivery, the seller is allowed a reasonable time after entering into the contract within which to tender the goods to the buyer. Likewise, the buyer has a reasonable time within which to accept delivery. What length of time is reasonable depends upon the facts and circumstances of each case. If the goods can be delivered immediately, a reasonable time would be very short. Where the goods must be constructed or manufactured, however, "reasonable" would take into account the usual length of time required to make the goods.

A contract may not be performed piecemeal or in installments unless the parties specifically agree. If such performance is not so specified, all of the goods the contract specifies must be tendered in a single delivery, and payment is due on such tender.

## Place of Tender

If the contract does not specify the place for delivery of the goods, the place for delivery is the *seller's place of business* or, if he has none, his residence. The seller must hold the goods for the buyer's disposition and notify her that the goods are being held for her to pick up. Section 2–308(a). If the contract is for the sale of identified goods that the parties know at the time of making the contract are located neither at the seller's place of business nor at his residence, the *location* of the goods is then the place for delivery. Section 2–308. For example, George, a boat builder in Chicago, contracts to sell to Chris a certain yacht that both parties know is anchored at Milwaukee. The place of delivery would be Milwaukee. On the other hand, if the contract provides that George shall overhaul the motor at his shipyard in Chicago, George would have to return the yacht to Chicago, and the place of delivery would be George's Chicago shipyard.

### CISG

*If a date is fixed by or determinable from the contract, the seller must deliver the goods on that date; if no date is fixed, the seller must deliver the goods within a reasonable time after the conclusion of the contract.*

The parties frequently agree expressly upon the place of tender, typically by using one of various *delivery terms*. These terms specify whether the contract is a shipment or destination contract and determine the place where the seller must tender delivery of the goods.

### CISG

*Unless the seller is required to deliver the goods at any other particular place, his obligation to deliver consists of placing the goods at the buyer's disposal at the place where the seller had his place of business at the time of the conclusion of the contract. If the contract relates to specific goods and at the time of the conclusion of the contract the parties knew that the goods were at a particular place, the seller's obligation is to place the goods at the buyer's disposal at that place.*

**Shipment Contracts** The delivery terms *F.O.B. place of shipment, F.A.S. port of shipment, C.I.F.,* and *C. & F.* are all "shipment contracts." Under a shipment contract, the seller is required or authorized to send the goods to the buyer, but the contract does not obligate her to deliver them at a particular destination. In these cases, the seller's tender of performance occurs at the point of shipment, provided the seller meets certain specified conditions designed to protect the interests of the absent buyer. A contract is assumed to be a shipment contract unless otherwise indicated.

The initials "F.O.B." and "F.A.S." mean "free on board" and "free alongside," respectively. Under the Code, these are delivery terms, even though they are used only in connection with a stated price. Section 2–319(1)(a). A contract providing that the sale is **F.O.B. place of shipment** or **F.A.S. port of shipment** is a shipment contract. For example, Linda, whose place of business is in New York, enters into a contract with Holly, the buyer, who is located in San Francisco. The contract calls for delivery of the goods F.O.B. New York. This would be a shipment contract. Under a **C.I.F.** ("cost, insurance, and freight") contract, in consideration for an agreed unit price for the goods, the seller agrees to pay all costs of transportation, insurance, and freight to the destination. The amount of the agreed unit price of the goods will, of course, reflect these costs. By comparison, under a **C. & F.** contract, the seller would pay "cost and freight." The unit price in such a contract is understandably less than in a C.I.F. contract as the C. & F. contract does not include the cost of insurance.

Under a shipment contract, the seller is required to (1) deliver the goods to a carrier; (2) make a contract for their transportation that is reasonable given the nature of the goods and other circumstances; (3) obtain and promptly deliver or tender to the buyer any document necessary to enable the buyer to obtain possession of the goods from the carrier; and (4) promptly notify the buyer of the shipment. Section 2–504. Failing either to make a proper contract for transportation or to notify the buyer of the shipment is a ground for rejection *only* if material loss or delay results. Section 2–504.

---

## CISG

*If the seller is not bound to deliver the goods at any other particular place and if the contract of sale involves carriage of the goods, his obligation to deliver consists of handing the goods over to the first carrier for delivery to the buyer.*

---

***Destination Contracts*** The delivery terms *F.O.B. city of buyer*, *ex-ship*, and *no arrival, no sale* are destination contracts. Because a destination contract requires the seller to tender delivery of conforming goods at a specified destination, the seller must place the goods at the buyer's disposition and give the buyer reasonable notice to enable him to take delivery. In addition, if the destination contract involves documents of title, the seller must tender the necessary documents. Section 2–503.

Where the contract provides that the sale is **F.O.B. place of destination,** the seller must at his own expense and risk transport the goods to that place and there tender delivery of them to the buyer. Section 2–319(1)(b). For example, if the buyer is in Boston and the seller is in Chicago, a contract providing F.O.B Boston is a destination contract under which the seller must tender the goods at the designated place in Boston at his own expense and risk. A contract that provides for delivery **"ex-ship,"** or from the ship, is also a destination contract, requiring the seller to unload the goods from the carrier at the named destination. Finally, where the contract contains the terms **"no arrival, no sale,"** the title and risk of loss do not pass to the buyer until the seller makes a tender of the goods after they arrive at their destination. The major significance of the "no arrival, no sale" term is that it excuses the seller from any liability to the buyer for the goods' failure to arrive, unless the seller has caused their nonarrival.

***Goods Held by Bailee*** Where goods are in the possession of a bailee and are to be delivered without being moved, in most instances the seller may either tender to the buyer a document of title or obtain an acknowledgment by the bailee of the buyer's right to possess the goods. Section 2–503(4). This acknowledgment permits the buyer to obtain the goods directly from the bailee.

◆ *See Figure 22–1*

## Perfect Tender Rule

The Code imposes upon the seller the obligation to conform her tender of goods *exactly* to the requirements of the contract. The seller's tender cannot deviate in any way from the terms of the contract. Thus, a buyer may rightfully reject the delivery of 110 dozen shirts under an agreement calling for delivery of 100 dozen shirts. The size or extent of the breach does not affect the right to reject.

If the goods or the tender of delivery fail in any respect to conform to the contract, the buyer may (1) reject the whole lot, (2) accept the whole lot, or (3) accept any commercial unit or units and reject the rest. Section 2–601; Section 2A–509(1). A **commercial unit** means such a unit of goods as by commercial usage is a single unit and which, if divided, would be materially impaired in character or value. A commercial unit may be a single item (such as a machine), a set of articles (such as a suite of furniture or an assortment of sizes), a quantity (such as a bale, gross, or carload), or any other unit treated in use or in the relevant market as a whole. Section 2–105(6); Section 2A–103(1)(c).

---

## CISG

*The CISG does not follow the perfect tender rule. The buyer may declare the contract avoided only if the failure by the seller to perform any of his obligations under the contract or the CISG amounts to a fundamental breach of contract. A breach of contract committed by one of the parties is fundamental if it results in such detriment to the other party as substantially to deprive him of what he is entitled to expect under the contract, unless the party in breach did not foresee and a reasonable person would not have foreseen such a result.*

---

The buyer's right to reject the goods upon the seller's failure to comply with the perfect tender rule is subject to three basic qualifications: (1) agreement between the parties limiting the buyer's right to reject nonconforming goods, (2) cure by the seller, and (3) the existence of an installment contract. In addition, as previously discussed, the perfect tender rule does not apply to a seller's breach

**FIGURE 22–1**   Tender of Performance by Seller

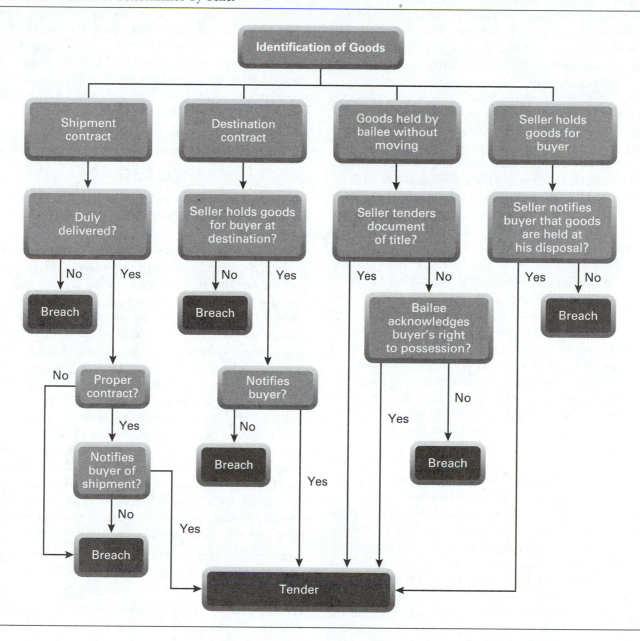

of her obligation under a shipment contract to make a proper contract for transportation or to give proper notice of the shipment. A failure to perform either of these obligations is a ground for rejection only if material loss or delay results. Section 2–504.

 *See Case 22–1*

***Agreement by the Parties***   The parties may contractually agree to limit the operation of the perfect tender rule. For example, they may agree that the seller shall

have the right to repair or replace any defective parts or goods. Such contractual limitations are discussed in Chapter 25.

***Cure by the Seller***   The Code recognizes two situations in which a seller may cure or correct a nonconforming tender of goods. This relaxation of the seller's obligation to make a perfect tender gives the seller an opportunity to make either a second delivery or a substitute tender. Whereas the first opportunity for cure occurs when the time for performance under the contract has not expired, the second opportunity is available after the time for performance has expired, but only if the seller had reasonable grounds to believe that the nonconforming tender would be acceptable to the buyer, with or without monetary adjustment.

Where the buyer refuses to accept a tender of goods that do not conform to the contract, the seller, by acting promptly and within the time allowed for performance, may make a proper tender or delivery of conforming goods and thereby cure his defective tender or performance. Section 2–508(1); Section 2A–513(1). Upon notice of the buyer's rightful rejection, the seller must first give the buyer reasonable notice of her intention to cure the defect and then must make a proper tender according to the *original* contract. This rule, which predates the Code, is fair to both parties. It gives the seller the full contractual period in which to perform while causing no harm to the buyer, who receives full performance within the time agreed to in the contract. For example, Conroy is to deliver to Elizabeth twenty-five blue shirts and fifty white shirts by October 15. On October 1, Conroy delivers twenty-nine blue shirts and forty-six white shirts, which Elizabeth rejects as not conforming to the contract. Elizabeth notifies Conroy of her rejection and the reasons for it. Conroy has until October 15 to cure the defect by making a perfect tender, provided he seasonably notifies Elizabeth of his intention to do so.

The Code also provides the seller an opportunity after the time for performance has expired to cure a nonconforming tender, which the seller had reasonable grounds to believe would be acceptable to the buyer, with or without money allowance. Section 2–508(2); Section 2A–513(2). This Code-created opportunity to cure a nonconforming tender after the date set for performance is conditioned on the seller's satisfying the following requirements: (1) the seller had reasonable grounds for believing that the nonconforming tender would be acceptable to the buyer, (2) the seller, after being informed of the buyer's rightful rejection, seasonably notifies the buyer of his intention to cure the defect, and (3) the seller cures the defect within a reasonable time. The principal difficulty in applying this rule is whether or not the first requirement has been satisfied.

For example, Vanessa orders from Gary a model 110X S.C.A. television to be delivered on January 20. The 110X is unavailable, but Gary can obtain last year's model of the same television, a model 110, which lists for 5 percent less than the 110X. On January 20, Gary delivers to Vanessa the 110 at a discount price of 10 percent less than the contract price for the 110X. Vanessa rejects the substituted television set. Gary, who promptly notifies Vanessa that he will obtain and deliver a model 110X, will most likely have a reasonable time beyond the January 20 deadline in which to deliver the 110X television set to Vanessa, because under these facts Gary appeared to have reasonable grounds to believe the model 110 would be acceptable with the money allowance.

## CISG

*The seller may cure any deficiency in goods delivered before the date for delivery, provided that the exercise of this right does not cause the buyer unreasonable inconvenience or unreasonable expense. However, the buyer retains any right to claim damages as provided for in the CISG. If the seller does not perform on time, the buyer may fix an additional period of time of reasonable length for performance by the seller of his obligations. Unless the seller notifies the buyer that he will not perform within the period so fixed, the buyer may not, during that period, resort to any remedy for breach of contract. However, the buyer retains any right he may have to claim damages for delay in performance. If the seller does not deliver the goods within the additional period of time, the buyer may declare the contract avoided.*

*The seller may, even after the date for delivery, cure a defective performance, if he can do so without unreasonable delay and without causing the buyer unreasonable inconvenience. However, the buyer retains any right to claim damages. If the seller notifies the buyer of his intent to cure and the buyer does not respond within a reasonable time, the seller may perform within the time indicated in the notice.*

See Case 22–2

***Installment Contracts***   Unless the parties have otherwise agreed, the buyer does not have to pay any part of the price of the goods until the seller has delivered or tendered the entire quantity specified in the contract. Section 2–307. An installment contract is an instance in which the parties have otherwise agreed. It expressly provides for delivery of the goods in separate lots or installments and usually provides for payment of the price in installments. If the contract is silent about payment, the Code provides that the price, if it can be apportioned, may be demanded for each lot. Section 2–307.

The buyer may reject any nonconforming installment if the nonconformity *substantially* impairs the value of that installment and cannot be cured. Section 2–612(2);

Section 2A–510(1). When, however, the installment substantially impairs the value of the installment but not the value of the entire contract, the buyer cannot reject the installment if the seller gives adequate assurance of the installment's cure. Section 2–612(2); Section 2A–510(1). Whenever the nonconformity or default with respect to one or more of the installments substantially impairs the value of the *whole contract,* however, the buyer can treat the breach as a breach of the whole contract. Section 2–612(3); Section 2A–510(2).

## CISG

*When a contract calls for delivery of goods by installments, if the seller's failure to perform any of his obligations with respect to any installment constitutes a fundamental breach of contract with respect to that installment, the buyer may declare the contract avoided with respect to that installment. A buyer who declares the contract avoided with respect to any delivery may, at the same time, declare it avoided with respect to deliveries already made or to future deliveries if, by reason of their interdependence, those deliveries could not be used for the purpose contemplated by the parties at the time of the conclusion of the contract. If the seller's failure to perform any of his obligations with respect to any installment gives the buyer good grounds to conclude that a fundamental breach of contract will occur with respect to future installments, he may declare the contract avoided for the future, provided that he does so within a reasonable time.*

## PERFORMANCE BY THE BUYER

The buyer is obligated to accept conforming goods and to pay for them according to the contract terms. Section 2–301; Section 2A–103(1)(j). Payment or tender of payment by the buyer, unless otherwise agreed, is a condition to the seller's duty to tender and to complete delivery. Section 2–507(1).

The buyer is not obliged to accept a tender or delivery of goods that do not conform to the contract. Upon determining that the tender or delivery is nonconforming, the buyer has three choices. He may (1) reject all of the goods, (2) accept all of the goods, or (3) accept any commercial unit or units of the goods and reject the rest. Section 2–601; Section

2A–509(1). The buyer must pay the contract rate for the commercial units he accepts.

## CISG

*The buyer must pay the price for the goods and take delivery of them as required by the contract and the CISG.*

 *See Case 22–3*

## Inspection

Unless the parties otherwise agree, the buyer has a right to inspect the goods before payment or acceptance. Section 2–513(1). (Section 2A–515(1) provides for the right to inspect before acceptance). This **inspection** enables him to ascertain whether the goods tendered or delivered conform to the contract. If the contract requires payment before acceptance (where, for example, the contract provides for shipment C.O.D. [collect on delivery]), payment must be made prior to inspection unless the nonconformity appears without inspection. Section 2–512. Payment, however, in such a case is *not* an acceptance of the goods and impairs neither the buyer's right to inspect nor any of his remedies.

The buyer, allowed a reasonable time in which to inspect the goods, may lose the right to reject or revoke acceptance of nonconforming goods by failing to inspect them in a timely manner. The expenses of inspection must be borne by the buyer but may be recovered from the seller if the goods do not conform and are rejected. Section 2–513(2); Section 2A–520(1).

## CISG

*The buyer is not bound to pay the price until he has had an opportunity to examine the goods, unless the parties have agreed otherwise. The buyer must examine the goods within as short a period of time as is practicable in the circumstances. Unless the buyer has a reasonable excuse, he loses the right to rely on a lack of conformity of the goods if he does not give notice to the seller of the nonconformity within a reasonable time after he has discovered it or ought to have discovered it.*

## Rejection

**Rejection** is a manifestation by the buyer of his unwillingness to become owner of the goods. It must be made within a reasonable time after the goods have been tendered or delivered and is not effective unless the buyer seasonably notifies the seller. Section 2–602(1); Section 2A–509(2).

The rejection of tendered or delivered goods may be rightful or wrongful, depending on whether the goods conform to the contract. The buyer's rejection of nonconforming goods or tender is rightful under the perfect tender rule. Nonetheless, if the buyer refuses a tender of goods or rejects it as nonconforming without disclosing to the seller the nature of the defect, she may not assert such defect as an excuse for not accepting the goods or as a breach of contract by the seller if the defect is curable. Section 2–605(1); Section 2A–514(1).

After the buyer has rejected the goods, any attempt she makes to exercise ownership of the goods is wrongful as against the seller. (Because the lessor retains title in a lease, this does not apply to leases.) If the buyer has possession of the rejected goods but does not have a security interest in them, she is obliged to hold them with reasonable care for a time sufficient to permit the seller to remove them. Section 2–602(2)(b); Section 2A–512(1). The buyer who is not a merchant is under no further obligation with regard to goods rightfully rejected. Section 2–602(2); Section 2A–512(1)(c). If the seller gives no instructions within a reasonable time after notification of rejection, the buyer may (1) store the goods for the seller's account, (2) reship them to the seller, or (3) resell them for the seller's account. Such action is not an acceptance or conversion of the goods. Section 2–604; Section 2A–511(2). A *merchant* buyer of goods who has rightfully rejected them has additional duties: she is obligated to follow reasonable instructions from the seller with respect to the disposition of the goods in her possession or control when the seller has no agent or business at the place of rejection. Section 2–603(1); Section 2A–511(1). If the merchant buyer receives no instructions from the seller within a reasonable time after giving notice of the rejection, and the rejected goods are perishable or threaten to decline in value speedily, she is obligated to make reasonable efforts to sell them for the seller's account. Section 2–603(1); Section 2A–511(1).

When the buyer sells the rejected goods, she is entitled to reimbursement for the reasonable expenses of caring for and selling them and a reasonable selling commission not to exceed 10 percent of the gross proceeds. Section 2–603(2); Section 2A–511(2).

---

## CISG

*If the goods do not conform to the contract and the nonconformity constitutes a fundamental breach of contract, the buyer may require delivery of substitute goods.*

 *See Case 22–3*

## Acceptance

**Acceptance** of goods means a willingness by the buyer to become the owner of the goods tendered or delivered to him by the seller. Acceptance of the goods, which includes overt acts or conduct manifesting such willingness, precludes any subsequent rejection of the goods. Section 2–607(2); Section 2A–516(2). Acceptance may be indicated by express words, by the presumed intention of the buyer through his failure to act, or by conduct of the buyer that is inconsistent with the seller's ownership of the goods. More specifically, acceptance occurs when the buyer, after a reasonable opportunity to inspect the goods, (1) signifies to the seller that the goods conform to the contract, (2) signifies to the seller that he will take the goods or retain them in spite of their nonconformity to the contract, or (3) fails to make an effective rejection of the goods. Section 2–606(1); Section 2A–515(1).

Acceptance, as previously noted, of any part of a commercial unit is acceptance of the entire unit. Section 2–606(2); Section 2A–515(2). Although the buyer must pay at the contract rate for those commercial units he accepts, he is entitled, after giving the seller timely notice of the breach, to recover from the seller or to deduct from the purchase price the amount of damages for nonconformity of the commercial units he has accepted and for nondelivery of the commercial units he has rejected. Sections 2–714 and 2–717; Sections 2A–516(1) and 2A–508(6) (except for finance leases in some situations). For example, Nancy agrees to deliver to Paul 500 lightbulbs of 100 watts each for $300 and 1,000 lightbulbs of 60 watts each for $500. Nancy delivers on time, but the shipment contains only 400 of the 100-watt bulbs and 750 of the 60-watt bulbs. If Paul accepts the shipment, he must pay Nancy $240 for the 100-watt bulbs accepted and $375 for the 60-watt bulbs accepted, less the amount of damages Nancy's nonconforming delivery caused him.

When goods are rejected by the buyer, the burden is on the seller to establish their conformity to the contract; but the burden is on the buyer to establish any breach of contract (including warranty) with regard to goods accepted. Section 2–607(4); Section 2A–516(3)(c).

## Revocation of Acceptance

A buyer might accept defective goods either because discovering the defect by inspection was difficult or because the buyer reasonably assumed that the seller would correct the defect. In either instance the buyer may revoke his acceptance of the goods if the uncorrected defect substantially impairs the value of the goods to him. With respect to the goods, **revocation of acceptance** gives the buyer rights and duties that are the same as if he had rejected them. Section 2–608(3); Section 2A–517(5).

More specifically, the buyer may revoke his acceptance of goods that do not conform to the contract when such nonconformity *substantially* impairs the value of the goods to him, provided that his acceptance was (1) premised on the reasonable assumption that the seller would cure the nonconformity, and it was not seasonally cured; or (2) made without discovery of the nonconformity, and such acceptance was reasonably induced by the difficulty of discovery before acceptance or by the seller's assurances. Section 2–608(1); Section 2A–517(1).

Revocation of acceptance is not effective until notification is given to the seller. This must be done within a reasonable time after the buyer discovers or should have discovered the grounds for revocation and before the goods have undergone any substantial change not caused by their own defects. Section 2–608(2); Section 2A–517(4).

 *See Case 22–4*

## Obligation of Payment

The terms of the contract may expressly state the time and place at which the buyer is obligated to pay for the goods. If so, these terms are controlling. Thus, if the buyer has agreed to pay either the seller or a carrier for the goods in advance of delivery, his duty to pay is not conditioned upon performance or a tender of performance by the seller. Furthermore, where the sale is on credit, the buyer is not obligated to pay for the goods when he receives them, as the credit provision in the contract will control the time of payment. Unless the parties agree otherwise, payment is due at the time and place at which the buyer is to receive

the goods, even though the place of shipment is the place of delivery. Section 2–310(a). This rule is understandable in view of the buyer's right, in the absence of agreement to the contrary, to inspect the goods before being obliged to pay for them.

Tender of payment in the ordinary course of business is sufficient when made by any means or in any manner current, such as a check, unless the seller demands cash and allows the buyer a reasonable time within which to obtain it. Payment by personal check is defeated as between seller and buyer, however, if the check is not paid when the seller attempts to cash it. Section 2–511(3).

---

## CISG

*Unless the buyer is bound to pay the price at any other specific time, he must pay it when the seller places either the goods or documents controlling their disposition at the buyer's disposal in accordance with the contract and the CISG. The seller may make such payment a condition for handing over the goods or documents. If the buyer is not bound to pay the price at any other particular place, he must pay it to the seller: (a) at the seller's place of business; or (b) if the payment is to be made against the handing over of the goods or of documents, at the place where the handing over takes place.*

---

◆ *See Figure 22–2*

## OBLIGATIONS OF BOTH PARTIES

Contracts for the sale of goods necessarily involve risks concerning future events that may or may not occur. In some instances, the parties explicitly allocate these risks; in most instances, they do not. The Code contains three sections that allocate these risks when the parties fail to do so. Each provision, when applicable, relieves the parties from the obligation of full performance under the sales contract. The first section deals with casualty to identified goods, the second with the nonhappening of presupposed conditions, and the third with substituted performance.

Related to the subject of whether the Code will excuse performance is the question of whether both parties are able and willing to perform. Should one party seem unwilling or unable, the Code allows the other party to seek reasonable assurance of the potentially defaulting party's willingness and ability to perform. In addition, if one of the parties clearly indicates an unwillingness or inability to perform, the Code protects the other party.

**FIGURE 22–2** Performance by the Buyer

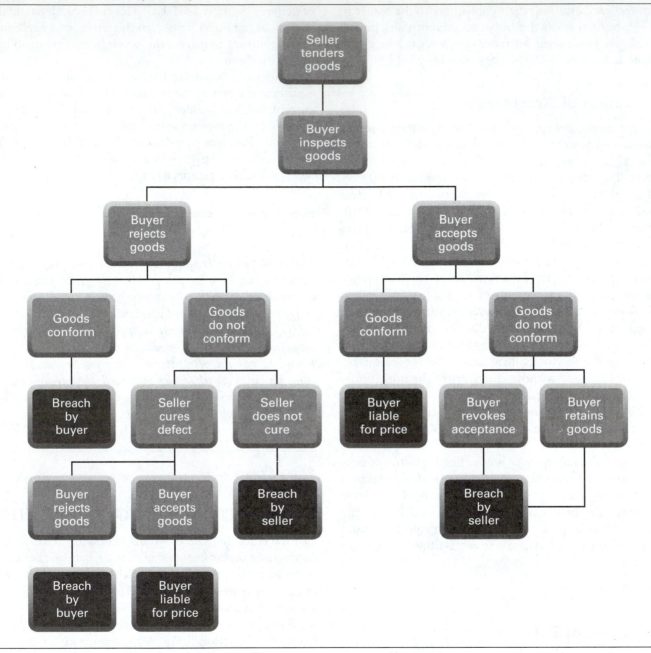

## Casualty to Identified Goods

If goods are destroyed before an offer to sell or buy them is accepted, the offer is terminated by general contract law. But what if the goods are destroyed after the sales contract is formed? The rules for the passage of risk of loss (as discussed in Chapter 23) apply with one exception: if the contract is for goods that are identified when the contract was made, and these goods are totally lost or damaged, without fault of either party, *before* the risk of loss passes to the buyer, the contract is avoided. Section 2–613(a); Section 2A–221(a). This means that each party is excused from his performance obligation under the contract: the seller is no longer obligated to deliver and the buyer need not pay the price.

In the case of a partial destruction or deterioration of the goods, the buyer may avoid the contract or may accept the goods with due allowance or deduction from the contract price sufficient to account for the deterioration or deficiency. Section 2–613(b); Section 2A–221(b) (except in a finance lease that is not a consumer lease). Thus, Adams agrees to sell to Taylor a specific lot of wheat containing 1,000 bushels at a price of $4 per bushel. Without the fault of Adams or Taylor, fire destroys 300 bushels of the wheat. Taylor does not have to take the remaining 700 bushels of wheat, but he has the option to do so upon paying $2,800, the price of 700 bushels.

If the destruction or casualty to the goods, whether total or partial, occurs *after* risk of loss has passed to the buyer, the buyer has no option but must pay the entire contract price of the goods.

## Nonhappening of Presupposed Condition

The ability to perform a contract for the sale of goods is subject to a number of possible hazards, such as strikes, lockouts, the unforeseen shutdown of supply sources, or the loss of a plant or machinery by fire or other casualty. Ordinarily such difficulties do not operate as an excuse on the ground of impossibility of performance, unless the contract expressly so provides. Both parties may have understood when they made the contract, however, that its performance depended upon the existence of certain facilities or that the purpose of the contract and the value of performance depended entirely upon the happening of a specific future event. In such a case, the seller is excused from her duty of performance upon the nonoccurrence of presupposed conditions which were a basic assumption of the contract, unless the seller has expressly assumed the risk. Section 2–615(a); Section 2A–405(a). Although the nonhappening of presupposed conditions may relieve the seller of her contractual duty, if the contingency affects only a part of the seller's capacity to perform, she must, to the extent of her remaining capacity, allocate delivery and production in a fair and reasonable manner among her customers. Section 2–615(b); Section 2A–405(b).

Central to the Code's approach to impossibility is the concept of **commercial impracticability,** through which the Code will excuse performance that, while not actually or literally impossible, is commercially impracticable. This, however, requires more than mere hardship or increased cost of performance. For a party to be discharged, performance must be rendered impracticable as a result of an unforeseen supervening event not within the contemplation of the parties at the time of contracting. Moreover, the nonoccurrence of the event must have been a "basic assumption" that both parties made when entering into the contract.

Increased production cost alone does not excuse performance by the seller, nor does a collapse of the market for the goods excuse the buyer. But a party to a contract for the sale of programs for a scheduled but subsequently canceled yacht regatta, or for the sale of tin horns for export, which become subject to embargo, or for the production of goods at a designated factory that suffers extensive fire damage would be excused from performance on the basis of commercial impracticability.

## CISG

*A party is not liable for a failure to perform any of his obligations if he proves that the failure was due to an impediment beyond his control and that he could not reasonably be expected to have taken the impediment into account at the time of contracting or to have avoided or overcome it or its consequences.*

 *See Case 17–5*

## Substituted Performance

The Code provides that where neither party is at fault and the agreed manner of delivering the goods becomes commercially impracticable, as by the failure of loading or unloading facilities or the unavailability of an agreed type of carrier, a substituted manner of performance, if commercially reasonable, must be tendered and accepted. Section 2–614(1); Section 2A–404(1). Where a practical alternative or substitute exists, the Code excuses neither seller nor buyer on the ground that delivery in the express manner provided in the contract is impossible.

## Right to Adequate Assurance of Performance

A contract of sale also requires that each party not impair the other party's expectation of having the contract performed. While the essential purpose of a contract is actual performance, an important feature of such performance is a secure and continuing sense that performance will occur when due. If, after contracting but before the time for performance, either the willingness or ability of a party to perform is put in doubt, the other party is threatened with the loss of a substantial part of what he has bargained for. Therefore, when reasonable grounds for insecurity arise regarding either party's performance, the other party may demand written assurance and suspend his own performance until he receives that assurance. The failure to provide adequate assurance of performance within a reasonable time not exceeding thirty days constitutes a repudiation of the contract. Section 2–609; Section 2A–401.

---

## CISG

*A party may suspend the performance of his obligations if, after the conclusion of the contract, it becomes apparent that the other party will not perform a substantial part of his obligations. A party suspending performance must immediately notify the other party of the suspension and must continue with performance if the other party provides adequate assurance of his performance.*

---

 *See Case 22–1*

## Right to Cooperation

Where one party's cooperation is necessary to the agreed performance but is not timely forthcoming, the other party is excused with regard to any resulting delay in her own performance. The nonbreaching party either may proceed to perform in any reasonable manner or, if the time for her performance has occurred, may treat the other's failure to cooperate as a breach. In either event,

the nonbreaching party has access to any other remedies the Code may provide, as discussed in Chapter 25.

## Anticipatory Repudiation

While a repudiation is a clear indication by either party that he is unwilling or unable to perform his obligations under the contract, an **anticipatory repudiation** is a repudiation made *before* the time to perform occurs. It may occur by express communication or by the repudiating party's taking an action that makes performance impossible, such as selling unique goods to a third party. A repudiation also may result from a party's failure to give timely assurance of performance after a justifiable demand. If an anticipatory repudiation substantially impairs the value of the contract, the aggrieved party may (1) await performance for a commercially reasonable time or (2) resort to any remedy for breach. In either case, he may suspend his own performance. Section 2–610; Section 2A–402. The repudiating party may retract his anticipatory repudiation and thereby reinstate the contract unless the aggrieved party has canceled the contract, materially changed his position, or otherwise indicated that she considers the anticipatory repudiation final. Section 2–611; Section 2A–403.

---

## CISG

*If prior to the date for performance of the contract it is clear that one of the parties will commit a fundamental breach of contract, the other party may declare the contract avoided.*

---

 *See Case 22–1*

---

    # Chapter Summary   

| Performance by the Seller | **Tender of Delivery** the seller makes available to the buyer goods conforming to the contract and so notifies the buyer |
| --- | --- |
| | • *Buyer* is obligated to accept conforming goods |
| | • *Seller* is entitled to receive payment of the contract price |
| | **Time of Tender** tender must be made at a reasonable time and kept open for a reasonable period of time |

**Place of Tender**  if none is specified, place for delivery is the seller's place of business or, if he has no such place, his residence

- *Shipment Contracts*  seller is required to tender delivery of the goods to a carrier for delivery to buyer; shipment terms include the following: *F.O.B. place of shipment, F.A.S. port of shipment, C.I.F., C. & F.*
- *Destination Contracts*  seller is required to tender delivery of the goods at a named destination; destination terms include the following: *F.O.B. place of destination; ex-ship; no arrival, no sale*
- *Goods Held by Bailee*  seller must either tender to the buyer a document of title or obtain an acknowledgment from the bailee

**Perfect Tender Rule**  the seller's tender of performance must conform exactly to the contract, subject to the following qualifications:

- *Agreement by the Parties*  the parties may contractually limit the operation of the perfect tender rule
- *Cure by the Seller*  when the time for performance under the contract has not expired or when the seller has shipped nonconforming goods in the belief that the nonconforming tender would be acceptable, a seller may cure or correct her nonconforming tender
- *Installment Contracts*  when the contract calls for the goods to be delivered in separate lots, the buyer may reject a nonconforming installment if it substantially impairs the value of that installment and cannot be cured; but if nonconformity or default of one or more of the installments substantially impairs the value of the whole contract, the buyer can treat the breach as a breach of the whole contract

## Performance by the Buyer

**Inspection**  unless otherwise agreed, the buyer has a reasonable time in which to inspect the goods before payment or acceptance to determine whether they conform

**Rejection**  buyer's manifestation of unwillingness to become the owner of the goods; must be made within a reasonable time after the goods have been tendered or delivered and gives the buyer the right to (1) reject all of the goods, (2) accept all of the goods, or (3) accept any commercial unit(s) and reject the rest

**Acceptance**  buyer's express or implied manifestation of willingness to become the owner of the goods

**Revocation of Acceptance**  rescission of buyer's acceptance of the goods if nonconformity of the goods substantially impairs their value, provided that the acceptance was (1) premised on the assumption that the nonconformity would be cured by the seller and it was not, or (2) the nonconformity was an undiscovered hidden defect

**Obligation of Payment**  in the absence of an agreement, payment is due at the time and place the buyer is to receive the goods

## Obligations of Both Parties

**Casualty to Identified Goods**  if the contract is for goods that were identified when the contract was made and those goods are totally lost or damaged without fault of either party and before the risk of loss has passed to the buyer, the contract is avoided

**Nonhappening of Presupposed Condition**  the seller is excused from the duty of performance on the nonoccurrence of presupposed conditions that were a basic assumption of the contract, unless the seller has expressly assumed the risk

**Substituted Performance**  where neither party is at fault and the agreed manner of goods becomes commercially impracticable, a substituted manner of performance must be tendered and accepted

**Right to Adequate Assurance of Performance** when reasonable grounds for insecurity arise regarding either party's performance, the other party may demand written assurance and suspend his own performance until he receives that assurance

**Right to Cooperation** where one party's required cooperation is untimely, the other party is excused from any resulting delay in her own performance

**Anticipatory Repudiation** if either party clearly indicates an unwillingness or inability to perform before the performance is due, the other party may await performance for a reasonable time or resort to any remedy for breach

---

 # Cases

## CASE 22–1
### Perfect Tender Rule; Adequate Assurance; Anticipatory Repudiation
### *ALASKA PACIFIC TRADING CO. v. EAGON FOREST PRODUCTS, INC.*
Court of Appeals of Washington, Division 1, 1997
85 Wash.App. 354, 933 P.2d 417

AGID, J.

### Facts

ALPAC and Eagon are both corporations engaged in importing and exporting raw logs. In April 1993, Setsuo Kimura, ALPAC's president, and C.K. Ahn, Eagon's vice president, entered into a contract under which ALPAC would ship about 15,000 cubic meters of logs from Argentina to Korea between the end of July and the end of August 1993. Eagon agreed to purchase the logs. In the next few months, the market for logs began to soften, making the contract less attractive to Eagon. ALPAC became concerned that Eagon would try to cancel the contract. Kimura and Ahn began a series of meetings and letters, apparently in an effort to assure ALPAC that Eagon would purchase the logs.

At Eagon, the home office was troubled by the drop in timber prices and initially withheld approval of the shipment. Ahn sent numerous internal memoranda to the home office to the effect that the corporation may not wish to go through with the deal, given the drop in timber prices, but that accepting the logs was "inevitable" under the contract. On August 30, Ahn sent a letter to the home office stating that he would attempt to avoid acceptance of the logs, but that it would be difficult and suggesting that they hold ALPAC responsible for shipment delay.

On August 23, Eagon received a faxed latter from ALPAC suggesting that the price and volume of the contract be reduced. Eagon did not respond to the fax. During a business meeting soon after, Kimura asked Ahn whether he intended to accept the logs. Ahn admitted that he was having trouble getting approval. Kimura thereafter believed that Eagon would not accept the shipment.

ALPAC eventually canceled the vessel that it had reserved for the logs because it believed that Eagon was canceling the contract. The logs were not loaded or shipped by August 31, 1993, but Ahn and Kimura continued to discuss the contract into September. On September 7, Ahn told Kimura that he would continue to try to convince headquarters to accept the delivery. Ahn also indicated that he did not want Kimura to sell the logs to another buyer. The same day, Ahn sent a letter to Eagon's head office indicating that "the situation of our supplier is extremely grave" and that Eagon should consider accepting the shipment in September or October.

By September 27, ALPAC had not shipped the logs. It sent a final letter to Eagon stating that Eagon had breached the contract because it failed to take delivery of the logs. Eagon's president, L.R. Haan, responded to the letter, stating that there was "no contract" because ALPAC's breach excused Eagon's performance. ALPAC filed a complaint for breach of contract in King County Superior Court. Eagon brought a motion for summary judgment, arguing that it did not breach, but that ALPAC breached by failing to deliver the logs. The trial court granted the motion and dismissed ALPAC's claims. ALPAC's motion for reconsideration was denied.

# Discussion

ALPAC appeals from the trial court's order granting Eagon's motion for summary judgment.

\* \* \*

**ALPAC Breached by Failing to Timely Deliver Logs**  ALPAC's first contention is that it did not breach the contract by failing to timely deliver the logs because time of delivery was not a material term of the contract. ALPAC relies on common law contract cases to support its position that, when the parties have not indicated that time is of the essence, late delivery is not a material breach which excuses the buyer's duty to accept the goods. [Citations.] However, as a contract for the sale of goods, this contract is governed by the Uniform Commercial Code, Article II (UCC II) which replaced the common law doctrine of material breach, on which ALPAC relies, with the "perfect tender" rule. Under this rule, "if the goods or the tender of delivery fail in any respect to conform to the contract, the buyer may . . . reject the whole." [U.C.C. §] 2–601(a). Both the plain language of the rule and the official comments clearly state that, if the tender of the goods differs from the terms of the contract in any way, the seller breaches the contract and the buyer is released from its duty to accept the goods. [Citation.] ALPAC does not dispute that the contract specified a date for shipment or that the logs were not shipped by that date. Thus, under the applicable "perfect tender" rule, ALPAC breached its duty under the contract and released Eagon from its duty to accept the logs.

**Parties Did Not Waive or Modify Delivery Date**  ALPAC next contends that, even if failure to timely deliver is a breach, the parties modified the delivery date or Eagon waived timely delivery. The UCC II changed the common law of contracts to eliminate the need for consideration in contract modifications but did not otherwise alter the common law. [U.C.C. §] 2–209(1). Mutual assent is still required and one party may not unilaterally modify a contract. [Citation.] ALPAC argues that Eagon agreed to modify the delivery date because it did not object to ALPAC's proposed changes in the amount and delivery time. It asserts that, if Eagon had not been silent during the discussions about the contract, the logs would have been shipped. Because the law requires mutual assent, Eagon's mere silence is not sufficient to establish a material issue of fact about modification.

ALPAC also argues that Eagon waived the shipping date because it failed to comment on its passage and continued to discuss the contract after the shipping date had passed. \* \* \*

If both parties to a contract allow the reasonable time for delivery to pass without complaint, a court may infer that the parties have extended the time for performance. [Citation.] Ahn and Kimura continued to negotiate until September 7, at least a week after the shipment date. Thus, Eagon may initially have waived the original shipment date as negotiations continued. However, by the end of September, when they exchanged their final correspondence, ALPAC still had not shipped the logs. Thus, even if the parties did waive the original date, ALPAC still had a duty to deliver the logs within a reasonable time. Its failure to ship the logs for an additional 20 days, while the price of logs continued to drop, was unreasonable and a breach.

**ALPAC Did Not Request Assurances**  ALPAC's third contention is that summary judgment was inappropriate because a material factual issue exists about whether it requested assurances from Eagon and Eagon failed to respond. The UCC II provides that:

A contract for sale imposes an obligation on each party that the other's expectation of receiving due performance will not be impaired. When reasonable grounds for insecurity arise with respect to the performance of either party the other may in writing demand adequate assurance of due performance and until he receives such assurance may if commercially reasonable suspend any performance for which he has not already received the agreed return.

[U.C.C. §] 2–609(1). ALPAC argues both that written requests are not necessary and that it provided a written request for assurance.

Washington courts have not directly determined whether a 2–609 demand for assurances must be in writing, or whether an oral request is sufficient, \* \* \* Other courts have recognized that the demand for assurances must be made in writing, absent "a pattern of interaction which demonstrat[es] a clear understanding between the parties that suspension of the demanding party's performance was the alternative, if its concerns were not adequately addressed by the other party." \* \* \* ALPAC relies on these cases to support its proposition that no written demand was needed in this case. It points out that Ahn had trouble getting approval from the Eagon home office and that Eagon knew it would lose money if the deal was completed.

Here, while Ahn had some idea that Kimura and ALPAC were concerned about the status of the contract, he did not understand that ALPAC would withhold performance as a result. * * * ALPAC's concerns were not sufficiently clear to instruct Eagon that ALPAC would be withholding performance. Eagon and ALPAC each made assumptions about the other's performance under the contract, but neither clearly expressed a need for assurance. If we were to hold that, in every case where a contract becomes less favorable for one party, general discussions between the parties can be considered requests for assurances, we would defeat the purpose of 2–609. That section requires a clear demand so that all parties are aware that, absent assurances, the demanding party will withhold performance. An ambiguous communication is not sufficient. [Citations.]

In the alternative, ALPAC argues that it did provide a written request for assurances in the fax from Kimura to Eagon dated August 23, 1993 which stated:

As we discussed, we would send a vessel to ship approx. 24-45,000 M3 of Argentina logs around mid part of Sept., 93.

I understand, and recognize your troubles to sell, and concerns about Korean market at this time. Therefore, as a seller, I (ALPAC) will offer you to reduce volume and price . . . We have approx. 21,000 M3 of logs around port of Campana, Argentina, now. Therefore, I hope you can find times to check logs with me toward end of August to early Sept., 93.Pls let me know by return fax when is the best time to go over there. Tks, Kimura.

* * * The written demand for assurances under [U.C.C. §] 2–609 must generally be clear and unequivocal. * * * While the parties here both knew that the contract was no longer favorable to Eagon, there is no showing that Eagon would not perform, or that ALPAC expressed its belief that Eagon would not perform. The letter Kimura sent to Ahn stated only that ALPAC was willing to negotiate new terms for the contract, not that

it believed Eagon would not perform. Therefore, neither the parties' interactions nor their correspondence rose to the level of a demand for assurances.

**Eagon Did Not Repudiate**  ALPAC's final contention is that Eagon repudiated the contract prior to the delivery date. It argues that Eagon's concern about the drop in log prices and its difficulty in getting final approval from its head office were sufficient to present a material factual issue about whether Eagon intended to accept the logs. * * *

"An intent to repudiate may be expressly asserted or circumstantially manifested by conduct." [Citation.] However communicated, a court will not infer repudiation from "doubtful and indefinite statements that performance may or may not take place." [Citation.] Rather, the anticipatory breach must be a clear and positive statement or action that expresses an intention not to perform the contract. Id.

ALPAC argues that Kimura's refusal to go to Argentina to see the logs and Ahn's statements that Eagon would be losing money if it accepted delivery of the logs support its position that Eagon repudiated the contract. However, Kimura testified that Ahn never stated that he would not accept the cargo. Rather, Kimura assumed that the problems with approval from the home office were the equivalent of an inability or unwillingness to accept the cargo. Washington courts have refused to hold that a communication between contracting parties that raises doubt as to the ability or willingness of one party to perform, but is not an outward denial, is a repudiation of the contract. [Citation.] Therefore, as a matter of law, neither Eagon's expressed unhappiness about the drop in timber prices nor its problems completing the contract rise to the level of repudiation.

Affirmed.

---

## CASE 22–2
## Cure by the Seller
### *WILSON v. SCAMPOLI*
United States Court of Appeals, District of Columbia Circuit, 1967
228 A.2d 848

MYERS, J.

This is an appeal from an order of the trial court granting rescission of a sales contract for a color television set and directing the return of the purchase price plus interest and costs.

Appellee purchased the set in question on November 4, 1965, paying the total purchase price in cash. The transaction was evidenced by a sales ticket showing the price paid and guaranteeing ninety days' free service and replacement of any defective tube and parts for a period of one year. Two days after purchase the set was delivered and uncrated, the antennae adjusted and the set plugged into an electrical outlet to "cook out." When the set was turned on, however, it did not function properly, the picture having a reddish tinge. Appellant's delivery man advised the buyer's daughter, Mrs. Kolley, that it was not his duty to tune in or adjust the color but that a service representative would shortly call at her house for that purpose. After the departure of the delivery men, Mrs. Kolley unplugged the set and did not use it.

On November 8, 1965, a service representative arrived, and after spending an hour in an effort to eliminate the red cast from the picture advised Mrs. Kolley that he would have to remove the chassis from the cabinet and take it to the shop as he could not determine the cause of the difficulty from his examination at the house. He also made a written memorandum of his service call, noting that the television "Needs Shop Work (Red Screen)." Mrs. Kolley refused to allow the chassis to be removed, asserting she did not want a "repaired" set but another "brand new" set. Later she demanded the return of the purchase price, although retaining the set. Appellant refused to refund the purchase price, but renewed his offer to adjust, repair, or if the set could not be made to function properly, to replace it. Ultimately, appellee instituted this suit against appellant seeking a refund of the purchase price. After a trial, the court ruled that "under the facts and circumstances the complaint is justified. Under the equity powers of the Court I will order the parties put back in their original status, let the $675 be returned, and the set returned to the defendant."

Appellant does not contest the jurisdiction of the trial court to order rescission in a proper case, but contends the trial judge erred in holding that rescission here was appropriate. He argues that he was always willing to comply with the terms of the sale either by correcting the malfunction by minor repairs or, in the event the set could not be made thereby properly operative, by replacement; that as he was denied the opportunity to try to correct the difficulty, he did not breach the contract of sale or any warranty thereunder, expressed or implied. [U.C.C. §] 2–508 provides:

(1) Where any tender or delivery by the seller is rejected because non-conforming and the time for performance has not yet expired, the seller may seasonably notify the buyer of his intention to cure and may then within the contract time make a conforming delivery.

(2) Where the buyer rejects a non-conforming tender which the seller had reasonable grounds to believe would be acceptable with or without money allowance the seller may if he seasonably notifies the buyer have a further reasonable time to substitute a conforming tender.

A retail dealer would certainly expect and have reasonable grounds to believe that merchandise like color television sets, new and delivered as crated at the factory, would be acceptable as delivered and that, if defective in some way, he would have the right to substitute a conforming tender. The question then resolves itself to whether the dealer may conform his tender by adjustment or minor repair or whether he must conform by substituting brand new merchandise. The problem seems to be one of first impression in other jurisdictions adopting the Uniform Commercial Code as well as in the District of Columbia.

* * *

While these cases provide no mandate to require the buyer to accept patchwork goods or substantially repaired articles in lieu of flawless merchandise, they do indicate that minor repairs or reasonable adjustments are frequently the means by which an imperfect tender may be cured. In discussing the analogous question of defective title, it has been stated that:

The seller, then, should be able to cure [the defect] under subsection 2–508(2) in those cases in which he can do so without subjecting the buyer to any great inconvenience, risk, or loss. [Citations.]

Removal of a television chassis for a short period of time in order to determine the cause of color malfunction and ascertain the extent of adjustment or correction needed to effect full operational efficiency presents no great inconvenience to the buyer. In the instant case, [Scampoli's] expert witness testified that this was not infrequently necessary with new televisions. Should the set be defective in workmanship or parts, the loss would be upon the manufacturer who warranted it free from mechanical defect. Here the adamant refusal of Mrs. Kolley . . . to allow inspection essential to the determination of the cause of the excessive red tinge to the picture defeated any effort by the seller to provide timely repair or even replacement of the set if the difficulty could not be corrected. The cause of the defect might have been minor and easily adjusted or it may have been substantial and required replacement by another new set—but the seller was never given an adequate opportunity to make a determination.

We do not hold that appellant [Scampoli] has no liability to appellee [Wilson], but as he was denied access and a reasonable opportunity to repair, appellee has not shown a breach of warranty entitling him either to a brand new set or to rescission. We therefore reverse the judgment of the trial court granting rescission and directing the return of the purchase price of the set.

Reversed.

---

## CASE 22–3
## Performance by the Buyer
## *FURLONG v. ALPHA CHI OMEGA SORORITY*
Bowling Green County Municipal Court, 1993
73 Ohio Misc.2d 26, 657 N.E.2d 866

BACHMAN, J.

[Alpha Chi Omega (AXO) entered into an oral contract with Furlong to buy 168 "custom designed" sweaters for the Midnight Masquerade III. The purchase price of $3,612 was to be paid as follows: $2,000 down payment when the contract was made and $1,612 upon delivery. During phone conversations with Furlong, Emily, the AXO social chairperson, described the design to be imprinted on the sweater. She also specified the colors to be used in the lettering (hunter green on top of maroon outlined in navy blue) and the color of the mask design (hunter green). Furlong promised to have a third party imprint the sweaters as specified. Furlong later sent to Emily a sweater with maroon letters to show her the color. He then sent her a fax illustrating the sweater design with arrows indicating where each of the three colors was to appear. On the day before delivery was due, Argento, Furlong's supplier, requested design changes which Furlong approved without the consent of AXO. These changes included: deleting the navy blue outline, reducing the number of colors from three to two, changing the maroon lettering to red, and changing the color of the masks from hunter green to red. Upon delivery, AXO gave a check to Furlong's agent for the balance of the purchase price. Later that day, Emily inspected the sweaters and screamed her dismay at the design changes. AXO immediately stopped payment on the check. Amy, the president of AXO, phoned Furlong stating that the sweaters were not what AXO had ordered. She gave the specifics as to why the sweaters were not as ordered and offered to return them. Furlong refused but offered to reduce the unit price of the sweaters if AXO agreed to accept them. AXO refused this offer. Furlong then filed suit against AXO for the unpaid portion of the sweaters' purchase price ($1,612) and AXO counterclaimed for return of the down payment ($2,000).]

Furlong and Emily created an express warranty by * * * affirmation of fact (his initial phone calls); by sample (the maroon sweater); by description (the fax). This express warranty became part of the contract. Each of the three methods of showing the express warranty was not in conflict with the other two methods, and thus they are consistent and cumulative [U.C.C. § 2–317], and constitute the warranty.

The design was a "dickered" aspect of the individual bargain and went clearly to the essence of that bargain [U.C.C. § 2–313]; Official Comment 1 to UCC 2–313). Thus, the express warranty was that the sweaters would be in accordance with the above design (including types of colors for the letters and the mask, and the number of colors for the same). Further, the express warranty became part of the contract.

* * *

Furlong's obligation as the seller was to transfer and deliver the goods in accordance with the contract. AXO's obligation was to accept and pay in accordance with that contract [U.C.C. § 2–301]. We will now discuss whether it legally did so.

* * *

The sweaters did not conform to the contract (specifically, the express warranty in the contract). Thus (in the words of the statute), the sweaters did "fail in any respect to conform to the contract." Actually, the sweaters failed in at least five respects [U.C.C. § 2–601]. Further, not only did they "fail in any respect," they failed in a substantial respect. In either event, they were a nonconforming tender of goods [U.C.C. § 2–601].

* * *

AXO, as the buyer, had the right to inspect the boxes of sweaters before payment or acceptance [U.C.C. § 2–513]. AXO did so at a reasonable time and place, and in a reasonable manner, on the same day that Furlong had sent the sweaters and AXO had received them [U.C.C. § 2–513]. AXO's purpose of inspection had (in the words of the statute) "to do with the buyer's check-up on whether the seller's performance is in accordance with a contract previously made * * * ." (Official Comment 9 to UCC 2–513.)

* * *

According to the statute, "if the goods * * * fail in any respect to conform to the contract, the buyer may: (A) reject the whole * * * [.]" [U.C.C. § 2–601]. As concluded above, the sweaters were nonconforming goods. Therefore, Furlong breached the contract, and AXO had the right to reject the goods (sweaters).

* * *

One [section of the] statute provides: "Rejection of goods must be within a reasonable time after their delivery * * * . It is ineffective unless the buyer seasonably notifies the seller." [U.C.C. § 2–602(1)]. AXO did what this statute requires.

That statute further provides: "[I]f the buyer has before rejection taken physical possession of goods * * * , he is under a duty after rejection to hold them with reasonable care at the seller's disposition for a time sufficient to permit the seller to remove them[.]" [U.C.C. § 2–602(2)(b).] AXO had done this, too.

Another [section of the] statute provides: "The buyer's failure to state in connection with rejection a particular defect * * * precludes him from relying on the unstated defect to justify rejection or to establish breach[.]" [U.C.C. § 2–605(1).] AXO did enough to avoid the effect of this statute also.

* * *

Thus, AXO never had an acceptance of the sweaters (as the term "acceptance" is legally defined) [U.C.C. § 2–606]. That is, AXO never did any of the following (per the statute): (1) signified to Furlong that the sweaters were conforming or that AXO would take or retain the sweaters in spite of their non-conformity; (2) failed to make an effective rejection of the sweaters; (3) did any act inconsistent with Furlong's ownership. [U.C.C. § 2–606.]

* * *

As concluded above, AXO rightfully rejected the sweaters, after having paid part of the purchase price: namely $2,000. AXO is entitled to cancel the contract and to recover the partial payment of the purchase price [U.C.C. § 2–711].

* * *

The court will prepare, file, and serve a judgment entry as follows: dismissing with prejudice Furlong's claim against all defendants; . . . granting AXO's counterclaim (for $2,000, plus ten percent per annum postjudgment interest and costs).

* * *

Judgment accordingly.

---

## CASE 22–4
## Revocation of Acceptance
### IN RE STEM
Alabama Supreme Court, 1990
571 So.2d 1112

KENNEDY, J.

William Stem filed an action against Gary Braden, seeking to rescind a contract for the sale of an automobile and to obtain the return of the purchase price plus interest. The trial court granted Stem that relief, but the Court of Civil Appeals reversed the trial court's judgment.

On February 26, 1987, Stem purchased a used automobile from Braden for $6,600. Braden indicated to Stem that, to the best of his knowledge, the car had not been wrecked and that the car was in good condition. Less than a week after purchasing the car, Stem discovered a disconnected plug that, when it was connected, caused the oil sensor warning light on the dashboard to glow. When Stem had the automobile examined because of the disconnected plug, the mechanics who examined the automobile discovered problems with the automobile that Stem did not realize existed. Among other problems, the mechanics discovered that the automobile was composed of the front end of a 1979 BMW and the rear end of a 1975 BMW. On March 10, 1987, Stem sent Braden a letter informing him that Stem refused the automobile and that he intended to rescind the sale. Further investigation revealed that the front half of the automobile actually had been driven 170,000 miles; Stem thought this automobile had 70,000 miles.

The trial court, after hearing ore tenus [oral] evidence, ordered Braden to pay Stem $6,600, an amount equal to the purchase price, plus interest of $726.

* * *

The Court of Civil Appeals reversed the trial court's judgment. That court stated that Stem, after he sent the letter refusing the automobile and attempting to rescind the sale, drove the automobile for 7 months and nearly 9,000 miles before commencing this action. The court then held that that use constituted an "acceptance" under [U.C.C.] § 2–606, which precluded Stem from receiving the relief the trial court granted:

We find that the use of the automobile by the buyer, subsequent to his attempted rescission, constituted an acceptance under [U.C.C. § 2–606]. Such acts were clearly inconsistent with the seller's ownership of the automobile as would be the case if the buyer's revocation had been effectual. Therefore, we find that the remedy of rescission sought by the buyer is not available to him.

Because there are numerous grounds for rescission of a contract, we do not agree that if Stem accepted the automobile then rescission necessarily was "not available," as the Court of Civil Appeals implies. That court, however, did address whether Stem revoked his acceptance of the automobile, which is the starting point for a proper analysis of this case.

Revocation of acceptance of goods is addressed by [U.C.C.] § 2–608, which provides:

(1) The buyer may revoke his acceptance of a lot or commercial unit whose nonconformity substantially impairs its value to him if he has accepted it:
   (a) On the reasonable assumption that its nonconformity would be cured and it has not been seasonably cured; or
   (b) Without discovery of such nonconformity if his acceptance was reasonably induced either by the difficulty of discovery before acceptance or by the seller's assurances.
(2) Revocation of acceptance must occur within a reasonable time after the buyer discovers or should have discovered the ground for it and before any substantial change in condition of the goods which is not caused by their own defects. It is not effective until the buyer notifies the seller of it.
(3) A buyer who so revokes has the same rights and duties with regard to the goods involved as if he had rejected them.

The Official Comments to that provision provide additional information concerning the provision:

1. . . . [T]he buyer is no longer required to elect between revocation of acceptance and recovery of damages for breach. Both are now available to him. The nonalternative character of the two remedies is stressed by the terms used in the present section. The section no longer

speaks of 'rescission,' a term capable of ambiguous application either to transfer of title to the goods or to the contract of sale and susceptible also of confusion with cancellation for cause of an executed or executory portion of the contract. The remedy under this section is instead referred to simply as 'revocation of acceptance' of goods tendered under a contract for sale and involves no suggestion of 'election' of any sort.

2. Revocation of acceptance is possible only where the nonconformity substantially impairs the value of the goods to the buyer. For this purpose the test is not what the seller had reason to know at the time of contracting; the question is whether the nonconformity is such as will in fact cause a substantial impairment of value to the buyer though the seller had no advance knowledge as to buyer's particular circumstances.

The record would support a finding by the trial court that Stem revoked his acceptance of the automobile pursuant to [U.C.C.] § 2–608. The trial court could properly have determined that Stem's acceptance of the automobile had been reasonably induced by Braden's assurances. The record indicates that the vehicle had been previously involved in at least one accident, that the vehicle was composed of two welded-together halves of other vehicles, that the speedometer had been disconnected for three and one-half months while Braden owned the car, that the vehicle had 100,000 more miles on its front half than Stem thought it had, and that the mileage on the back half was not known for certain. Although the trial court permissibly could have considered Stem's use of the car as evidence that its value was not substantially impaired, [citation], it was not compelled to do so. Accordingly, the trial court could have determined that the automobile's nonconformities substantially impaired its value to Stem. There is no substantial dispute either that Stem's revocation occurred within a reasonable time or that Stem properly notified Braden, and the trial court could have found that Stem revoked his acceptance within a reasonable time and that he met the notice requirements of [U.C.C.] § 2–608.

When Stem revoked his acceptance, he had the same rights and duties with regard to the automobile that he would have had had he rejected it. [U.C.C.] § 2–608(3). Section 2–602 addresses the manner and effect of rejection, and § 2–602(2)(a) provides that "after rejection any exercise of ownership by the buyer with respect to any commercial unit is wrongful as against the seller." Accordingly, although Stem revoked his acceptance, his continued use of the automobile was "wrongful" against Braden. There is no definition of "wrongful" as it is used in § 2–602(2)(a), either in statutes or in Alabama case law, to explain the consequences of Stem's continued use of the vehicle.

\* \* \*

Sections 2–602 and 2–606 through –608 are derived from the Uniform Commercial Code and, accordingly, many states have enacted similar provisions into statutory law. A review of the case law construing similar provisions indicates that the Court of Civil Appeals' treatment of the issue of Stem's use of the automobile only in terms of acceptance of the automobile is inappropriately simple. Many cases involve extensive use of automobiles and motor homes after revocation; the cases emphasize the practical consideration that an individual who buys an automobile or a motor home may very well be unable, without extraordinary financial difficulty, to tender the automobile or motor home and do without it until the litigation concerning it is completed. [Citations.] These courts . . . held that continued use after revocation was "wrongful" but did not constitute acceptance.

With uniformity, the courts have held that the "wrongful" use entitles the seller to prove the reasonable value of the buyer's use and to recover that amount as a setoff, and many courts have awarded setoffs in circumstances similar to those of the present case. [Citations.]

The Colorado Court of Appeals in [citation] used the following rationale to explain the setoff:

\* \* \*

There is no specific provision in the Uniform Commercial Code for an offset award of damages for wrongful use by the buyer. However, [U.C.C. §] 1–103, provides that:

"Unless displaced by the particular provision of this chapter, the principles of law and equity, including the law merchant and the law relative to capacity to contract, principal and agent, estoppel, fraud, misrepresentation, duress, coercion, mistake, bankruptcy, or other validating or invalidating cause shall supplement its provisions."

We recognize that the general rule is that where a buyer is entitled to rescind the sale and elects to do so, the buyer shall thereafter be deemed to hold the goods as a bailee for the seller. [Citations.] Thus, if the buyer uses the goods while he holds them as a bailee, he becomes liable for the value of that use. [Citation.] This reasoning is consistent with the Uniform Commercial Code, and, in the instant case, is consistent with the principles of law and equity which the Code provides for as supplementary to its provisions. [Citation.]

\* \* \*

The ruling of the Colorado court is sound, and we accept its rationale. Additionally, we note that if Stem had exercised any of his options available under Alabama's commercial code concerning storing or returning the vehicle, he would have been put in the position of doing without a vehicle for transporting his child, which was one of the primary purposes for which he bought the vehicle, until trial of this case or else he would have been required to purchase or lease an additional suitable vehicle. Under these circumstances Stem's continued use of the automobile was not an act of continued use that constituted an acceptance of ownership after revocation. [Citation.]

The judgment of the Court of Civil Appeals is due to be reversed and the cause remanded. The trial court is directed to determine any appropriate setoff in a manner consistent with this opinion.

Reversed and remanded with instructions.

---

  # Questions

1. Explain the requirements of tender of delivery with respect to time, manner, and place of delivery.
2. Explain the perfect tender rule and the three limitations upon it.
3. Explain when the buyer has the right to reject the goods and what obligations the buyer has upon rejection.
4. Discuss the buyer's right to revoke acceptance.
5. Identify and discuss the excuses for nonperformance.

---

  # Problems

1. Tammie contracted with Kristine to manufacture, sell, and deliver to Kristine and put in running order a certain machine. Once Tammie had set up the machine and put it in running order, however, Kristine found it unsatisfactory and notified Tammie that she rejected the machine. She continued to use it for three months but continually complained of its defective condition. At the end of the three months she notified Tammie to come and get it. Has Kristine lost her right (a) to reject the machine? (b) to revoke acceptance of the machine?

**2.** Smith, having contracted to sell to Beyer thirty tons of described fertilizer, shipped to Beyer by carrier thirty tons of fertilizer which he stated conformed to the contract. Nothing was stated in the contract as to time of payment, but Smith demanded payment as a condition of handing over the fertilizer to Beyer. Beyer refused to pay unless he were given the opportunity to inspect the fertilizer. Smith sues Beyer for breach of contract. Decision?

**3.** Benny and Sheree entered into a contract for the sale of one hundred barrels of flour. No mention was made of any place of delivery. Thereafter, Sheree demanded that Benny deliver the flour at her place of business, and Benny demanded that Sheree come and take the flour from his place of business. Neither party acceded to the demand of the other. Has either one a right of action against the other?

**4.** Johnson, a manufacturer of air conditioning units, made a written contract with Maxwell to sell to Maxwell forty units at a price of $200 each and to deliver them at a certain apartment building owned by Maxwell for installation by Maxwell. Upon the arrival of Johnson's truck for delivery at the apartment building, Maxwell examined the units on the truck, counted only thirty units, and asked the driver if this was the total delivery. The driver replied that it was as far as he knew. Maxwell told the driver that she would not accept delivery of the units. The next day Johnson telephoned Maxwell and inquired why delivery was refused. Maxwell stated that the units on the truck were not what she ordered; that she ordered forty units, that only thirty were tendered, and that she was going to buy air conditioning units elsewhere. In an action by Johnson against Maxwell for breach of contract, Maxwell defends upon the ground that the tender of thirty units was improper, as the contract called for delivery of forty units. Is this a valid defense?

**5.** Edwin sells a sofa to Jack for $800. Edwin and Jack both know that the sofa is in Edwin's warehouse, located approximately ten miles from Jack's home. The contract does not specify the place of delivery, and Jack insists that the place of delivery is either his house or Edwin's store. Is Jack correct?

**6.** On November 4, Kim contracted to sell to Lynn 500 sacks of flour at $4 each to be shipped to Lynn in November. On November 27, Kim shipped the flour. By December 5, when the car arrived, containing only 450 sacks, the market price of flour had fallen. The usual time required for shipment was five to twelve days. Lynn refused to accept delivery or to pay. Kim shipped fifty more sacks of flour, which arrived December 10. Lynn refused delivery. Kim resold the flour for $3 per sack. What are Kim's rights against Lynn?

**7.** Farley and Trudy enter into a written contract whereby Farley agrees to sell and Trudy agrees to buy 6,000 bushels of wheat at $3.75 per bushel, deliverable at the rate of 1,000 bushels a month commencing June 1, the price for each installment being payable ten days after delivery thereof. Although Farley delivered and received payment for the June installment, he defaulted by failing to deliver the July and August installments. By August 15, the market price of wheat had increased to $4 per bushel. Trudy thereupon entered into a contract with Albert to purchase 5,000 bushels of wheat at $4 per bushel deliverable over the ensuing four months. In late September, the market price of wheat commenced to decline and by December 1 was $3.25 per bushel. Trudy brings an action against Farley for breach of contract. Decision?

**8.** Bain ordered from Marcum a carload of lumber, which he intended to use in the construction of small boats for the U.S. Navy pursuant to contract. The order specified that the lumber was to be free from knots, wormholes, and defects. The lumber was shipped, and immediately upon receipt Bain looked into the door of the fully loaded car, ascertained that there was a full carload of lumber, and acknowledged to Marcum that the carload had been received. On the same day Bain moved the car to his private siding and sent to Marcum full payment in accordance with the terms of the order.

A day later, the car was moved to the work area and unloaded in the presence of the navy inspector, who refused to allow three-fourths of it to be used because of excessive knots and wormholes in the lumber. Bain then informed Marcum that he was rejecting the order and requested refund of the payment and directions on disposition of the lumber. Marcum replied that because Bain had accepted the order and unloaded it, he was not entitled to return of the purchase price. Bain thereupon brought an action against Marcum to recover the purchase price. Decision?

**9.** Plaintiff, a seller of milk, had for ten years bid on contracts to supply milk to defendant school district and had supplied milk to other school districts in the area. On June 15, 1987, plaintiff contracted to supply defendant's requirements of milk for the school year 1987–88, at a price of $.0759 per half pint. The price of raw milk delivered from the farm had been for years controlled by the U.S. Department of Agriculture. On June 15, 1987, the department's administrator for the New York–New Jersey area had mandated a price for raw milk of $8.03 per hundredweight. By December 1987, the mandated price had been raised to $9.31 per hundredweight, an increase of nearly 20 percent. If required to complete deliveries at the contract price, plaintiff would lose $7,350.55 on its contract with defendant and would face similar losses on contracts with two other school districts. Plaintiff sued for a judgment that its performance had become impracticable through unforeseen events, particularly unanticipated grain crop failures and the huge amounts of grain sold to Russia in mid–1987. Decision?

**10.** In April, F. W. Lang Company purchased an ice cream freezer and refrigeration compressor unit from Fleet for $2,160. Although the parties agreed to a written installment contract providing for an $850 down payment and eighteen installment payments, Lang made only one $200 payment upon receipt of the goods. One year later, Lang moved to a new location and took the equipment along without notifying Fleet. Two years after the sale, Lang disconnected the compressor from the freezer and used it to operate an air conditioner. Lang continued to use the compressor for that purpose until the sheriff seized the equipment and returned it to Fleet pursuant to a court order. Fleet then sold the equipment for $500 in what both parties conceded was a fair sale. Lang then brought an action charging that the equipment was defective and unusable for its intended purpose and sought to recover the down payment and expenses incurred in repairing the equipment. Fleet counterclaimed for the balance due under the installment contract less the proceeds from the sale. Decision?

11.   Deborah McCullough bought a new car from Bill Swad Chrysler-Plymouth, Inc. The car was protected by both a limited warranty and an extended warranty. McCullough immediately encountered problems with the automobile's brakes, transmission, and air conditioning and discovered a number of cosmetic defects as well. She returned the car to Swad for repairs, but Swad did not fix the brakes properly or perform any of the cosmetic work. Moreover, new problems appeared with respect to the car's steering mechanism. McCullough returned the car twice more for repairs, but on each occasion, old problems persisted and new ones emerged. After the engine abruptly shut off on a short trip away from home and the brakes again failed on a more extensive excursion, McCullough presented Swad with a list of thirty-two of the car's defects and demanded their correction. When Swad failed to remedy more than a few of the problems, McCullough wrote a letter to Swad calling for rescission of the purchase agreement and a refund of the purchase price and offering to return the car upon receipt of shipping instructions from Swad. Swad did not respond to the letter, and McCullough brought an action against Swad. She continued to operate the vehicle until the time of trial, some seventeen and one-half months (and 23,000 miles) later. Decision?

12.   On March 17, Peckham bought a new car from Larsen Chevrolet for $6,400.85. During the first one and one-half months after the purchase, Peckham discovered that the car's hood was dented, its gas tank contained no baffles, its emergency brake was inoperable, the car did not have a jack or a spare tire, and neither the clock nor the speedometer worked. Larsen claimed that Peckham knew of the defects at the time of the purchase. Peckham, on the other hand, claimed that despite his repeated efforts the defects were not repaired until June 11. Then, on July 15, the car's dashboard caught fire, leaving the car's interior damaged and the car itself inoperable. Peckham then returned to Larsen Chevrolet and told Larsen that he had to repair the car at his own expense or that he, Peckham, would either rescind the contract or demand a new automobile. Peckham also claimed that at the end of their conversation he notified Larsen Chevrolet that he was electing to rescind the contract and demanded the return of the purchase price. Larsen denied having received that oral notification. On October 12, Peckham sent a written notice of rescission to Larsen. Decision?

13.   Joc Oil bought a cargo of fuel oil for resale. The certificate from the foreign refinery stated the sulphur content of the oil was 0.5 percent. Joc Oil entered into a written contract with Con Ed for the sale of this oil. The contract specified a sulphur content of 0.5 percent. Joc Oil knew, however, that Con Ed was authorized to buy and burn oil of up to 1 percent sulphur content and that Con Ed often bought and mixed oils of varying contents to stay within this limit. The oil under contract was delivered to Con Ed, but independent testing revealed a sulphur content of 0.92 percent. Con Ed promptly rejected the nonconforming shipment. Joc Oil immediately offered to substitute a conforming shipment of oil, although the time for performance had expired after the first shipment of oil. Con Ed refused to accept the substituted shipment. Joc Oil sues Con Ed for breach of contract. Judgment?

14.   Plaintiff West German wine producer and exporter contracted to ship 620 cases of wine to the defendant distributor in North Carolina. The contract was silent as to the shipment destination. During the next several months, defendant called repeatedly to find out the status of the shipment. Later, without notifying defendant, plaintiff delivered the wine to a shipping line in Rotterdam, destined for Wilmington, N.C. The ship and the wine were lost at sea en route to Wilmington. When defendant refused to pay on the contract, plaintiff sued. Decision?

15.   Can-Key Industries, Inc., manufactured a turkey-hatching unit, which it sold to Industrial Leasing Corporation (ILC), which leased it to Rose-A-Linda Turkey Farms. ILC conditioned its obligation to pay on Rose-A-Linda's acceptance of the equipment. Rose-A-Linda indicated its dissatisfaction with the equipment, and ILC refused to perform its obligations under the contract. Can-Key then brought suit against ILC for breach of contract. It argued that Rose-A-Linda accepted the equipment, as it used it for fifteen months between March 1976 and May 1977. ILC contended that the equipment was unacceptable and asked that it be removed. It claimed that Can-Key refused and failed to instruct Rose-A-Linda to refrain from using the equipment. Therefore, ILC argued, Rose-A-Linda effectively rejected the turkey-hatching unit, relieving ILC of its contractual obligations. Decision?

16.   Frederick Manufacturing Corp. ordered 500 dozen units of Import Traders' rubber pads for $2,580. The order indicated that the pads should be "as soft as possible." Import Traders delivered the rubber pads to Frederick Manufacturing on November 19, 1981. Frederick failed to inspect the goods upon delivery, even though the parties recognized that there might be a problem with the softness. Frederick finally complained about the nonconformity of the pads in April 1982, when Import Traders requested the contract price for the goods. Import Traders then sued Frederick to recover the contract price. Decision?

17.   Moulton Cavity & Mold Inc. agreed to manufacture twenty-six innersole molds to be purchased by Lyn-Flex. Moulton delivered the twenty-six molds to Lyn-Flex after Lyn-Flex allegedly approved the sample molds. However, Lyn-Flex rejected the molds, claiming that the molds did not satisfy the specifications exactly, and denied that it had ever approved the sample molds. Moulton then sued, contending that Lyn-Flex wrongfully rejected the molds. Lyn-Flex, arguing that the

Code's perfect tender rule permitted its rejection of the imperfect molds, regardless of Moulton's substantial performance, appealed from a judgment entered by the trial court in favor of Moulton. Decision?

**18.** Neptune Research & Development, Inc. (the buyer), which manufactured solar-operated valves used in scientific instruments, saw advertised in a trade journal a hole-drilling machine with a very high degree of accuracy, manufactured and sold by Teknics Industrial Systems, Inc. (the seller). As the machine's specifications met the buyer's needs, the buyer contacted the seller in late March and ordered one of the machines to be delivered in mid-June. There was no "time-of-the-essence" clause in the contract.

Although the buyer made several calls to the seller throughout the month of June, the seller never delivered the machine and never gave the buyer any reasons for the nondelivery. By late August, the buyer desperately needed the machine. The buyer went to the seller's place of business to examine the machine and discovered that the still-unbuilt machine had been redesigned, omitting a particular feature that the buyer had wanted. Nonetheless, the buyer agreed to take the machine, and the seller promised that it would be ready on September 5. The seller also agreed to call the buyer on September 3 to give the buyer two days to arrange for transportation of the machine.

The seller failed to telephone the buyer on September 3 as agreed. On September 4 the buyer called the seller to find out the status of the machine, and was told by the seller that "under no circumstances" could the seller have the machine ready by September 5. At this point, the buyer notified the seller that the order was canceled. One hour later, still on September 4, the seller called the buyer, retracted its earlier statement, and indicated that the machine would be ready by the agreed September 5 date. The buyer sued for the return of its $3,000 deposit. Decision?

WWW **Internet Exercise** Compare the performance obligations of the seller and buyer under the United Nations Convention on Contracts for the International Sale of Goods (Vienna, 1980) with their obligations under Article 2 of the Uniform Commercial Code.

# Transfer of Title and Risk of Loss

Historically, title governed nearly every aspect of the rights and duties of the buyer and seller arising out of a sales contract. In an attempt to add greater precision and certainty to sales contracts, the Uniform Commercial Code has abandoned the common law's reliance upon title. Instead, the Code approaches each legal issue arising out of a sales contract on its own merits and provides separate and specific rules to control the various transactional situations. This chapter covers the Code's approach to the transfer of title and other property rights, the passage of risk of loss, and the transfer of goods sold in bulk.

## *TRANSFER OF TITLE*

As previously stated, a sale of goods is defined as the transfer of title from the seller to the buyer for a price. Section 2–106. Transfer of title is, therefore, fundamental to a sale of goods. Title, however, cannot pass under a contract for sale until existing goods have been identified as those to which the contract refers. Section 2–401(1). Future goods (goods that are not both existing and identified) cannot constitute a present sale. Section 2–105. If the buyer rejects the goods, whether justifiably or not, title reverts to the seller. Section 2–401(4).

In a lease title does not pass. Instead, the lessee obtains the right to possess and use the goods for a period of time in return for consideration. Section 2A–103(1)(j).

## Identification

After formation of the contract, the seller normally takes steps to obtain, manufacture, prepare, or select goods with which to fulfill her obligation under the contract. At some stage in the process the seller will have identified existing goods which she intends to ship, deliver, or hold for the buyer. Identification may be made by either the seller or the buyer and can be made at any time and in any manner agreed upon by the parties. In the absence of explicit agreement, **identification** takes place as provided in Section 2–501(1) (Section 2A–217 contains similar, but not identical, provisions):

1. upon the making of the contract if it is for goods already existing and identified;
2. if the contract is for all other future goods, when the seller ships, marks, or otherwise designates existing goods as those to which the contract refers; or
3. if the contract is (a) for crops to be grown within twelve months or at the time of the next normal harvest, when the crops are planted or start growing, or (b) for the offspring of animals to be born within twelve months, when the young animals are conceived.

To illustrate, suppose Barringer contracts to purchase a particular Buick automobile from Stevenson's car lot. Identification occurs as soon as the contract is entered into. If, however, Barringer agrees to purchase a television set from Stevenson, whose storeroom is filled with such televisions, identification will not occur until either Barringer or Stevenson selects a particular television to fulfill the contract.

If the goods are **fungible** (the equivalent of any other unit), identification of a share of undivided goods occurs when the contract is entered into. Thus, if Barringer agrees to purchase 1,000 gallons of gasoline from Stevenson, who owns a 5,000-gallon tank of gasoline, identification occurs as soon as the contract is formed.

*Insurable Interest* For a contract or policy of insurance to be valid, the insured must have an insurable interest in the subject matter (see Chapter 48). At common law only a person with title or a lien (a legal claim of a creditor on property) could insure his interest in specific goods. The Code extends this right to a buyer's interest in goods that have been identified as goods to which the contract refers. Section 2–501(1); Section 2A–218(1). This **special property interest** of the buyer enables her to purchase insurance protection on goods that she does not presently own but that she will own upon delivery by the seller.

So long as he has title to them or any security interest in them, the seller also has an insurable interest in the goods. Section 2–501(2). Nothing prevents both seller and buyer from simultaneously carrying insurance on goods in which they both have a property interest, whether it be title, a security interest, or a special property interest. In a lease, the lessor retains an insurable interest in the goods until an option to buy, if included in the lease, has been exercised by the lessee. Section 2A–218(3).

*Security Interest* The Code defines a security interest as an interest in personal property or fixtures that ensures payment or performance of an obligation. Section 1–201(37). Any reservation by the seller of title to goods delivered to the buyer is limited in effect to a reservation of a security interest. Section 2–401(1). As mentioned above, the seller retains an insurable interest in goods for which he holds title or any security interest. Section 2–501(2). Security interests in goods are governed by Article 9 of the Code (discussed in Chapter 38).

## Passage of Title

Title passes when the parties *intend* it to pass, provided the goods are in existence and have been identified. Where the parties have no explicit agreement as to transfer of title, the Code provides rules that determine when title passes to the buyer. Section 2–401.

*Physical Movement of the Goods* When delivery is to be made by moving the goods, title passes at the time and place the seller completes his performance with reference to delivery of the goods. Section 2–401(2). When and where delivery occurs depends on whether the contract is a shipment contract or a destination contract.

A **shipment contract** requires or authorizes the seller to send the goods to the buyer but does not require the seller to deliver them to a particular destination. Under a shipment contract, title passes to the buyer at the time and place that the seller *delivers* the goods to the carrier for shipment to the buyer.

A **destination contract** requires the seller to deliver the goods to a particular destination. Under a destination contract, title passes to the buyer upon *tender* of the goods at that destination. **Tender,** as discussed in Chapter 22, requires that the seller (1) put and hold conforming goods at the buyer's disposition, (2) give the buyer reasonable notice that the goods are available, and (3) keep the goods available for a reasonable time. Section 2–503.

 *See Case 23–1*

*No Movement of the Goods* When delivery is to be made without moving the goods, unless otherwise agreed, title passes (1) upon delivery of a document of title, if the contract calls for delivery of such document (documents of title are documents that evidence a right to receive specified goods—they are discussed more fully in Chapter 49); or (2) at the time and place of contracting, if the goods at the time have been identified and no documents are to be delivered. Section 2–401(3). Where the goods are not identified at the time of contracting, title passes when the goods are identified.

For a summary of passage of title in the absence of an agreement by the parties, see Figure 23–1.

◆ *See Figure 23–1*

## Power to Transfer Title

It is important to understand under what circumstances a seller has the right or power to transfer title to a buyer. If the seller is the rightful owner of goods or is authorized to sell the goods for the rightful owner, then the seller has the **right** to transfer title. But when a seller is in possession of goods that he neither owns nor has authority to sell, then the sale is not rightful. In some situations, however, these unauthorized sellers may have the **power** to transfer good title to certain buyers. This section pertains to such sales by a person in possession of goods that he neither owns nor has authority to sell.

The fundamental rule of property law protecting existing ownership of goods is the starting point for any discussion of a sale of goods by a nonowner. A basic tenet of the law is that a purchaser of goods obtains such title as his transferor had or had power to transfer, and the Code expressly so states. Section 2–403; Sections 2A–304 and 2A–305. Likewise, the purchaser of a limited interest in goods acquires rights only to the extent of the interest that he purchased. By the same token, no one can transfer what he does not have. A purported sale by a thief or finder or ordinary bailee of goods does not transfer title to the purchaser.

The principal reason underlying the policy of the law in protecting existing ownership of goods is that a person

**FIGURE 23–1**   Passage of Title in Absence of Agreement by Parties

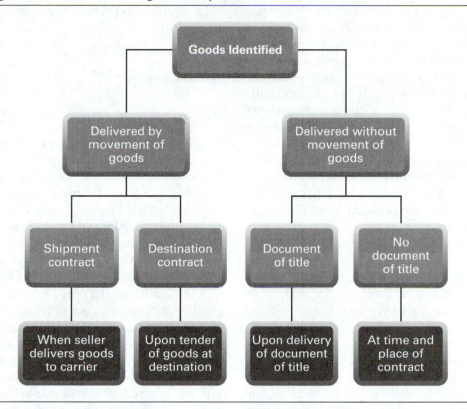

should not be required to retain possession at all times of all the goods that he owns in order to maintain his ownership of them. Incidental to the ownership of goods is the owner's freedom to make a bailment of his goods as desired; the mere possession of goods by a bailee does not authorize the bailee to sell them.

A second policy, one concerning the protection of the good faith purchaser, conflicts with the policy protecting existing ownership of goods. Protecting the expectations of good faith transactions in goods is of paramount importance in trade and commerce. To encourage and make safe good faith acquisitions of goods, *bona fide* (good faith) purchasers for value must be protected under certain circumstances. **A good faith purchaser** is defined as one who acts honestly, gives value, and takes the goods without notice or knowledge of any defect in the title of his transferor.

***Void and Voidable Title to Goods*** A **void title** is no title. A person claiming ownership of goods by an agreement that is void obtains no title to the goods. Thus, a thief or a finder of goods or a person who acquires goods from someone under physical duress or under guardianship has no title to them and can transfer none.

A **voidable title** is one acquired under circumstances that permit the former owner to rescind the transfer and revest herself with title, as in the case of mistake, common duress, undue influence, fraud in the inducement, misrepresentation, mistake, or sale by a person without contractual capacity (other than an individual under guardianship). In these situations, the buyer has acquired legal title to the goods, which may be divested by action of the seller. If, however, before the seller has rescinded the transfer of title, the buyer were to resell the goods to a good faith purchaser for value, the right of rescission in the seller is cut off, and the good faith purchaser for value acquires good title. The Code defines good faith as "honesty in fact in the conduct or transaction concerned" and value to include a consideration sufficient to support a simple contract. Section 1–201.

The distinction between a void and voidable title is, therefore, extremely important in determining the rights of good faith purchasers of goods. The good faith purchaser for value always believes that she is buying the goods from the owner or from one with authority to sell. Otherwise she would not be acting in good faith. In each situation, the party selling the goods appears to be the owner whether his title is valid, void, or voidable.

Given a transaction involving two innocent persons—the true owner and the good faith purchaser for value, who have done nothing wrong—the law will not disturb the *legal title* but will rule in favor of the one who has it. Thus, where A transfers possession of goods to B under such circumstances that B acquires no title or a void title, and B thereafter sells the goods to C, a good faith purchaser for value, B has nothing except possession to transfer to C. In a lawsuit between A and C involving the right to the goods, A will win because she has the legal title. C's only recourse is against B for breach of warranty of title, discussed in Chapter 24.

If, however, B acquired voidable title from A and resold the goods to C, in a suit between A and C over the goods, C would win. In this case, B had title, although it was voidable, which she transferred to the good faith purchaser for value. The title thus acquired by C will be protected. The voidable title in B, which is title until it has been avoided, may not be avoided after transfer to a good faith purchaser. A's only recourse is against B for restitution or damages.

The Code has enlarged this common law doctrine by providing that a good faith purchaser for value obtains valid title from one possessing voidable title even if that person obtained voidable title by (1) fraud as to her identity; (2) exchange for a subsequently dishonored check; (3) an agreement that the transaction was to be a cash sale, and the sale price has not been paid; or (4) criminal fraud punishable as larceny. Section 2–403(1); (Sections 2A–304 and 2A–305 are similar).

In addition, the Code has expanded the rights of good faith purchasers with respect to sales by **minors.** While the common law permitted a minor seller of goods to disaffirm the sale and to recover the goods from a third person who had purchased them in good faith from the party who acquired the goods from the minor, the Code

has changed this rule by no longer permitting a minor seller of goods to prevail over a good faith purchaser for value. Section 2–403.

◆  *See Figures 23–2 and 23–3*

  *See Case 23–2*

## Entrusting of Goods to a Merchant

Frequently, an owner of goods **entrusts** (transfers possession of) the goods to a bailee for resale, repair, cleaning, or some other use. In some instances, the bailee violates this entrusting by selling the goods to a third party. Although the "true" owner has a right of recourse against the bailee for the value of the goods, what right, if any, should the true owner of the goods have against the third party? Once again the law must balance the right of ownership against the rights of market transactions.

The Code takes the position of protecting a buyer of goods in the ordinary course of business from a merchant who deals in goods of the kind involved in the sale, where the owner has entrusted possession of the goods to the merchant. The Code defines **buyer in ordinary course of business** as a person who in good faith and without knowledge that the sale to him violates the ownership rights or security interest of another buys the goods in the ordinary course of business from a person, other than a pawnbroker, in the business of selling goods of that kind. Section 1–201(9). Because the merchant who deals in goods of that kind is cloaked with the appearance of ownership or apparent authority to sell, the Code seeks to protect the innocent third-party purchaser. Any such entrusting of possession bestows upon the merchant the power to transfer all rights of the entruster to a buyer in the ordinary course of business. Section 2–403(2); (Sections 2A–304(2) and 2A–305(2) are

**FIGURE 23–2** Void Title

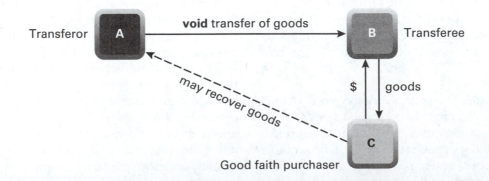

**FIGURE 23–3** Voidable Title

similar). For example, A brings her stereo for repair to B, who also sells both new and used stereo equipment. C purchases A's stereo from B in the ordinary course of business. The Code protects the rights of C and defeats the rights of A. A's only recourse is against B.

The Code, however, does not go so far as to protect the buyer in the ordinary course of business from a merchant to whom a thief, a finder, or a completely unauthorized person has entrusted the goods. It merely grants the buyer in the ordinary course of business the rights of the entruster.

Where a buyer of goods to whom title has passed leaves the seller in possession of the goods, the buyer has "entrusted the goods" to the seller. Section 2–403(3). If that seller is a merchant and resells and delivers the goods to another buyer in the ordinary course of business, this second buyer acquires good title to the goods. Thus, Marianne sells certain goods to Martin, who pays the price but allows possession to remain with Marianne. Marianne thereafter sells the same goods to Carla, a buyer in the ordinary course of business. Carla takes delivery of the goods. Martin does not have any rights against Carla or to the goods. Martin's only remedy is against Marianne.

◆ *See Figure 23–4*

⚖ *See Case 23–3*

## RISK OF LOSS

Risk of loss, as the term is used in the law of sales, addresses the question of allocation of loss between seller and buyer where the goods have been damaged, destroyed, or lost *without the fault* of either the seller or the buyer. If the loss is placed on the buyer, he is under a duty to pay the price for the goods even though they were damaged or he never received them. If loss is placed upon the seller, he has no right to recover the purchase price from the buyer and is usually liable to the buyer for damages for nondelivery unless he tenders a performance in replacement of the lost or destroyed goods.

**FIGURE 23–4** Entrusting of Goods to a Merchant

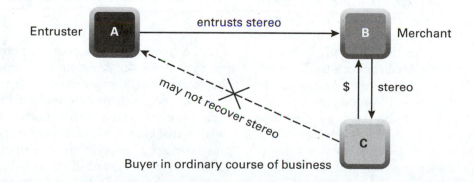

## CISG

*Loss of or damage to the goods after the risk of loss has passed to the buyer does not discharge the buyer from his obligation to pay the purchase price.*

In determining which party carries the risk of loss, the Code provides definite rules for specific situations, a sharp departure from the common law concept of risk of loss, which was determined by ownership of the goods and which depended upon the transfer of title. The transactional approach under the Code is necessarily detailed and for this reason is probably more understandable and meaningful than the common law's reliance upon the abstract concept of title. The Code has adopted rules for determining the risk of loss in the absence of breach separate from those that apply where the sales contract has been breached.

Except in a finance lease, risk of loss is retained by the lessor and does not pass to the lessee. 2A–219(1). In a finance lease, risk of loss passes to the lessee.

## Risk of Loss Where There Is a Breach

Where one party breaches the contract, the Code places the risk of loss on the breaching party. Nevertheless, where the nonbreaching party is in control of the goods, the Code places the risk of loss on him to the extent of his insurance coverage.

***Breach by the Seller*** If the seller ships nonconforming goods to the buyer, the risk of loss remains on the seller until the buyer has accepted the goods or the seller has remedied the defect. Section 2–510(1); Section 2A–220(1)(a).

Where the buyer has accepted nonconforming goods, and thereafter by timely notice to the seller rightfully revokes his acceptance (discussed in Chapter 22), he may treat the risk of loss, to the extent of any deficiency in his effective insurance coverage, as resting from the beginning on the seller. Section 2–510(2); Section 2A–220(1)(b). For example, Heidi delivers to Gary nonconforming goods, which Gary accepts. Subsequently, Gary discovers a hidden defect in the goods and rightfully revokes his prior acceptance. If the goods are destroyed through no fault of either party, and Gary has insured the goods for 60 percent of their fair market value of $10,000, then the insurance company will cover $6,000 of the loss and Heidi will bear the remainder of the loss,

or $4,000. Had the buyer's insurance coverage been $10,000, the seller would not bear any of the loss.

***Breach by the Buyer*** Where conforming goods have been identified to a contract that the buyer repudiates or breaches before risk of loss has passed to him, the seller may treat the risk of loss as resting on the buyer "for a commercially reasonable time" to the extent of any deficiency in the seller's effective insurance coverage. Section 2–510(3); Section 2A–220(2). For example, Susan agrees to sell 40,000 pounds of plastic resin to Bernie, F.O.B. Bernie's factory, delivery by March 1. On February 1, Bernie wrongfully repudiates the contract by telephoning Susan and telling her that he does not want the resin. Susan immediately seeks another buyer, but before she is able to locate one, and within a commercially reasonable time, the resin is destroyed by a fire through no fault of Susan's. The fair market value of the resin is $35,000. Because Susan's insurance covers only $15,000 of the loss, Bernie is liable for $20,000.

## Risk of Loss in Absence of a Breach

Where there is no breach of contract, the parties may by agreement allocate the risk of loss. Where there is no breach, and the parties have not otherwise agreed, the Code places the risk of loss, for the most part, upon the party who is more likely to have greater control over the goods, is more likely to insure the goods, or is better able to prevent their loss.

***Agreement of the Parties*** The parties, by agreement, not only may shift the allocation of risk of loss but also may divide the risk between them. Section 2–303. Such agreement is controlling. Thus, the parties may agree, for example, that the seller shall retain the risk of loss even though the buyer is in possession of the goods or has title to them. Or the agreement may provide that the buyer bears 60 percent of the risk and the seller bears 40 percent.

***Trial Sales*** Some sales are made with the understanding that the buyer can return the goods even though they conform to the contract. Such trial sales permit a buyer to try goods to determine if she wishes to keep them or to try to resell them. The Code recognizes two types of trial sales, a sale on approval and a sale or return, and provides a test for distinguishing between them: unless otherwise agreed, if the goods are delivered primarily for the buyer's use, the transaction is a sale on approval; if they are delivered primarily for resale by the buyer, it is a sale or return. Section 2–326(1).

In a **sale on approval,** possession of, but not title to, the goods is transferred to the buyer for a stated time or, if no time is stated, for a reasonable time, during which the buyer may use the goods to determine whether she wishes to buy them. Both title and risk of loss remain with the *seller* until the buyer approves, or accepts, the goods. Section 2–327(1)(a). Until acceptance by the buyer, the sale is a bailment with an option to purchase.

Although use of the goods consistent with the purpose of approval is not acceptance, the buyer's failure to notify the seller within a reasonable time of her election to return the goods *is* an acceptance. The buyer also may manifest approval by exercising over the goods any dominion or control that is inconsistent with the seller's ownership. Upon approval, title and risk of loss passes to the buyer, who then becomes liable to the seller for the purchase price of the goods. If the buyer elects to return the goods and so notifies the seller, the return is at the seller's risk and expense.

In a **sale or return,** the goods are sold and delivered to the buyer with an option to return them to the seller. The risk of loss is on the *buyer,* who also has title until she revests it in the seller by returning the goods. The return of the goods is at the buyer's risk and expense.

A **consignment** is a delivery of possession of personal property to an agent for sale by the agent. Under the Code, a sale on consignment is regarded as a sale or return. Therefore, creditors of the consignee (the agent who receives the merchandise for sale) prevail over the consignor and may obtain possession of the consigned goods, provided the consignee maintains a place of business where he deals in goods of the kind involved under a name other than the name of the consignor. Nevertheless, under Section 2–326(3) the consignor will prevail if he (a) complies with applicable State law requiring a consignor's interest to be evidenced by a sign, (b) establishes that the consignee is generally known by his creditors to be substantially engaged in selling the goods of others, or (c) complies with the filing provisions of Article 9 (Secured Transactions). Section 2–326(3).

*Contracts Involving Carriers* Sales contracts frequently contain terms that indicate the agreement of the parties as to delivery by a carrier. These terms identify the contract as a shipment contract or a destination contract and, by implication, indicate when the risk of loss will pass. If the contract does not require the seller to deliver the goods to a particular destination but merely to the carrier **(a shipment contract),** risk of loss passes

to the buyer upon *delivery* of the goods to the common carrier. If the seller is required to deliver them to a particular destination **(a destination contract),** risk of loss passes to the buyer at destination upon *tender* of the goods to the buyer. Section 2–509(1); Section 2A–219(2)(a).

---

## CISG

*If the sales contract involves the carriage of the goods and the seller is not obligated to hand them over at a particular destination, the risk of loss passes to the buyer when the goods are handed over to the first carrier. If the contract requires the seller to deliver the goods to a carrier at a particular destination, the risk of loss passes when the goods are handed over to the carrier at that place.*

---

*Pestana v. Karinol* deals with the question of when the risk of loss passes between parties whose contract makes no specific provision and contains no delivery term. The case demonstrates that if the contract is not clearly a destination contract or a shipment contract, the law assumes that it is a shipment contract.

 *See Case 23–4*

## Goods in Possession of Bailee

In some sales, the goods, at the time the contract is made, are held by a bailee and are to be delivered without being moved. For instance, a seller may contract with a buyer to sell grain which is located in a grain elevator and which the buyer intends to leave in the same elevator. In such situations, Sections 2–509(2) and 2A–219(2)(b) provide that the risk of loss passes to the buyer when one of the following occurs:

1. If a negotiable document of title (discussed in Chapter 49) is involved, the risk of loss passes upon the buyer's receipt of the document.
2. If a nonnegotiable document of title is involved, the risk passes when the document is tendered to the buyer.
3. If no documents of title are employed, risk passes upon either (a) the seller's tender to the buyer of written directions to the bailee to deliver the goods to the buyer or (b) the bailee's acknowledgment of the buyer's right to possession of the goods.

In situations 2 and 3(a), if the buyer seasonably objects, the risk of loss remains upon the seller until the buyer has had a reasonable time to present the document or direction to the bailee.

## CISG

*If the buyer is bound to take over the goods at a place other than the seller's place of business, the risk of loss passes when the buyer is aware of the fact that the goods are placed at her disposal at that location.*

## All Other Sales

If the buyer possesses the goods when the contract is formed, risk of loss passes to the buyer at that time. Section 2–509(3); Section 2A–219(2)(c).

All other sales not involving breach are covered by Section 2–509(3). This catchall provision applies when the buyer picks up the goods at the seller's place of business or when the seller delivers the goods using her own transportation. In these cases, risk of loss depends on whether or not the seller is a merchant. If the seller is a **merchant,** risk of loss passes to the buyer upon the buyer's *receipt* of the goods. If the seller is **not a merchant**, it passes on *tender* of the goods from the seller to the buyer. Section 2–509(3); Section 2A–219(2)(c). The policy behind this rule is that so long as the merchant seller is making delivery at her place of business or with her own vehicle, she continues to control the goods and can be expected to insure them. The buyer, on the other hand, has no control over the goods and is not likely to have insurance on them.

Suppose Belinda goes to Sidney's furniture store, selects a particular set of dining room furniture, and pays Sidney the agreed price of $800 for it upon Sidney's agreement to stain the set a darker color and deliver it. Sidney stains the furniture and notifies Belinda that he will deliver it the following day. That night, the furniture is accidentally destroyed by fire. Belinda can recover from Sidney the $800 payment. The risk of loss is on seller Sidney as he is a merchant and the goods were not received by Belinda but were only tendered to her.

## CISG

*If the sales contract does not involve the carriage of the goods, the risk of loss passes to the buyer when he takes over the goods, or, if the buyer does not take over the goods in due time, from the time when the goods are placed at his disposal.*

On the other hand, suppose Georgia, an accountant, prior to moving to a different city, contracts to sell her household furniture to Nina for $3,000. Though Georgia notifies Nina that the furniture is available for her to pick up, Nina delays picking up the furniture for several days. In the interim, the furniture is stolen from Georgia's residence without her fault. Georgia may recover from Nina the $3,000 purchase price. The risk of loss is on the buyer (Nina), as the seller is not a merchant and tender is sufficient to transfer the risk.

◆ *See Figure 23–5*

⚖ *See Case 23–5*

## SALES OF GOODS IN BULK

Because a debtor may secretly liquidate all or a major part of his tangible assets by a bulk sale and conceal or divert the proceeds of the sale without paying his creditors, creditors have an obvious interest in a merchant's bulk disposal of his merchandise made not in the ordinary course of business. The central purpose of bulk sales law is to deter two common forms of commercial fraud, namely (1) when the merchant, owing debts, sells out his stock in trade to a friend for a low price, pays his creditors less than he owes them, and hopes to come back into the business "through the back door" sometime in the future; and (2) when the merchant, owing debts, sells out his stock in trade to anyone for any price, pockets the proceeds, and disappears without paying his creditors.

Article 6 of the Code, which applies to such sales, defines a **bulk transfer** as "any transfer in bulk and not in the ordinary course of the transferor's business of a major part of the materials, supplies, merchandise or other inventory." Section 6–102. The transfer of a substantial part of equipment is a bulk transfer only if made in connection with a bulk transfer of inventory. Those subject to Article 6 of the Code are merchants whose principal business is the sale of merchandise from stock, including those who manufacture what they sell.

In 1988, the National Conference of Commissioners on Uniform State Laws and the American Law Institute jointly issued a recommendation stating "that changes in the business and legal contexts in which sales are

**FIGURE 23–5** Passage of Risk of Loss in Absence of Breach

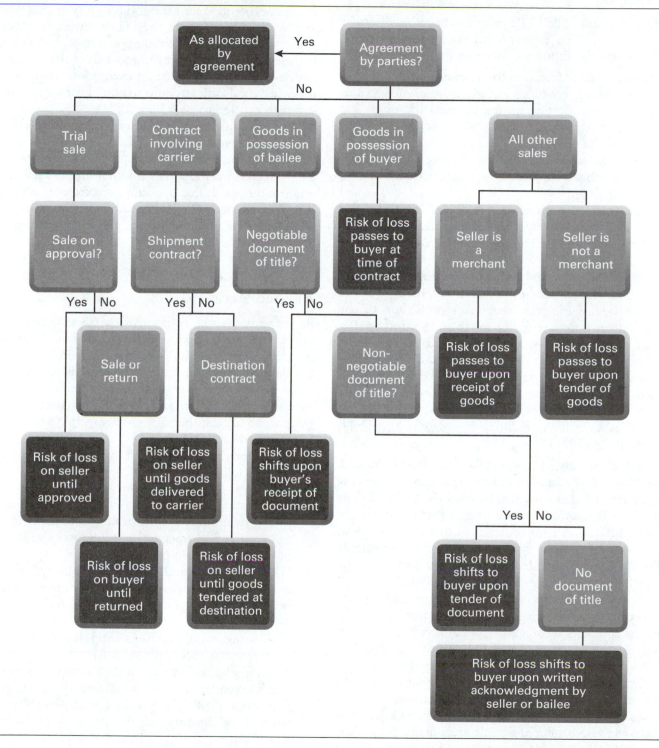

conducted have made regulation of bulk sales unnecessary." They, therefore, recommended the repeal of Article 6 or, for those States that felt the need to continue the regulation of bulk sales, the adoption of a revised Article 6 designed to afford better protection to creditors while minimizing the obstacles to good faith transactions. More than half of the States have repealed Article 6; while only a few States have adopted Revised Article 6.

# Article 6

***Requirements***   The Code provides that a bulk transfer of assets is ineffective against any creditor of the transferor, unless the following four requirements are met:

1. The transferor furnishes to the transferee a sworn list of his existing creditors, including those whose claims are disputed, stating names, business addresses, and amounts due and owing, when known. Section 6–104(1)(a).
2. The transferor and transferee prepare a schedule or list of the property being transferred. Section 6–104(1)(b).
3. The transferee preserves the list of creditors and schedule of property for six months and permits inspection by any creditor of the transferor. Section 6–104(1)(c).
4. The transferee gives notice of the proposed transfer in bulk to each creditor of the transferor at least ten days before the transferee takes possession of the goods or makes payment for them. Section 6–105. This notice must specify (a) that a bulk transfer is about to be made; (b) the names and business addresses of the transferor and transferee; and (c) whether all debts of the transferor are to be paid in full as a result of the transaction, and if so, the address to which creditors should send their bills. Section 6–107(1).

If all of the above steps are taken, the transfer in bulk complies with the statute, and the transferee acquires the goods free of claims of the transferor's creditors. The transferor is responsible for ensuring that the sworn list of his creditors is complete and accurate; nevertheless, errors or omissions in this list do not impair the validity of the bulk transfer unless the transferee has knowledge of such errors or omissions. Section 6–104(3).

Certain transfers in bulk (including transfers by way of security, transfers in settlement of a lien or security interest, and sales by executors, administrators, receivers, trustees in bankruptcy, or any public officer under judicial process) are exempt and need not comply with Article 6.

The Code also has special provisions with respect to auction sales of goods that represent a transfer in bulk not in the ordinary course of the transferor's business where the goods offered for sale are a major part of the materials, supplies, merchandise, or inventory used in the business.

***Failure to Comply***   Should a bulk transfer fail to comply with the requirements of Article 6, the goods in the transferee's possession continue to be subject to the claims of unpaid creditors of the transferor. These creditors may proceed against the goods by levy or attachment and by sheriff's sale, or by causing the involuntary bankruptcy of the transferor and the appointment of a trustee in bankruptcy to take over the goods from the transferee. Article 6 does not provide an exemption from liability for either good faith attempts to comply or for situations in which no creditor was injured.

Where the title of the transferee is subject to the defect of noncompliance with the Code, a purchaser of the goods from the transferee who pays value in good faith and who takes the property without notice of such defect acquires the goods free of claim of the transferor's creditors. A purchaser who pays no value or who takes them with notice of noncompliance, however, acquires the goods subject to the creditors' claims.

# Revised Article 6

As previously noted, revised Article 6 was promulgated in response to the perceived inadequacy of the existing Article 6. More specifically, compliance with the existing Article 6 is time-consuming and expensive, especially when the seller has a large number of creditors; and the Article, which applies to transferors even in the absence of evidence to suggest that they are engaged in a fraudulent transfer, is over-inclusive.

The major changes reflected in the revised Article 6 include the following:

1. The buyer is subject to the Article only when he has notice, or should have had notice, that the seller will not continue to operate the same or a similar type of business. Section 6–102(1)(c).
2. When the seller is indebted to two hundred or more persons, the buyer may give notice by filing and need not send individual notices. Sections 6–105(2) and 6–104(2).
3. The notice requirement is extended from ten to forty-five days. Section 6–105(5).
4. A buyer who makes a good faith attempt to comply with the requirements of the Article, or who in good faith does not believe the Article applies to him, is relieved of liability for noncompliance. Section 6–107(3).
5. A buyer's failure to comply with the requirements of the Article does not render the sale void or otherwise affect the buyer's title to the goods, but the buyer's liability is limited to the damages caused by the noncompliance. Section 6–107(1)(b).

# Chapter Summary

| | |
|---|---|
| **Transfer of Title** | **Identification** designation of specific goods as goods to which the contract of sale refers |

**Transfer of Title**

**Identification** designation of specific goods as goods to which the contract of sale refers
- *Insurable Interest* buyer obtains an insurable interest and specific remedies in the goods by the identification of existing goods as goods to which the contract of sale refers
- *Security Interest* an interest in personal property or fixtures that ensures payment or performance of an obligation

**Passage of Title** title passes when the parties intend it to pass; when the parties do not specifically agree, the Code provides rules to determine when title passes
- *Physical Movement of the Goods* when delivery is to be made by moving the goods, title passes at the time and place where the seller completes his performance with reference to delivery
- *No Movement of the Goods*

**Power to Transfer Title** the purchaser of goods obtains such title as her transferor either has or had the power to transfer; however, to encourage and make secure good faith acquisitions of goods, it is necessary to protect certain third parties under certain circumstances
- *Void Title* no title can be transferred
- *Voidable Title* the good faith purchaser acquires good title
- *Entrusting of Goods to a Merchant* buyers in the ordinary course of business acquire good title when buying from merchants

**Risk of Loss**

**Definition** allocation of loss between seller and buyer where the goods have been damaged, destroyed, or lost without the fault of either party

**Risk of Loss Where There Is a Breach**
- *Breach by the Seller* if the seller ships to the buyer goods that do not conform to the contract, the risk of loss remains on the seller until the buyer has accepted the goods or until the seller has remedied the defect
- *Breach by the Buyer* the seller may treat the risk of loss as resting on the buyer for a commercially reasonable time to the extent of any deficiency in the seller's effective insurance coverage

**Risk of Loss in Absence of a Breach**
- *Agreement of the Parties* the parties may by agreement allocate the risk of loss
- *Trial Sales* unless otherwise agreed, if the goods are delivered primarily for the buyer's use, the transaction is a sale on approval (risk of loss remains with the seller until "approval" or acceptance of the goods by the buyer); if they are delivered primarily for resale by the buyer, it is a sale or return (the risk of loss is on the buyer until she returns the goods)
- *Contracts Involving Carriers* in shipment contracts, the seller bears the risk of loss and expense until the goods are delivered to the carrier for shipment; in destination contracts, the seller bears the risk of loss and expense until tender of the goods at a particular destination
- *Goods in Possession of Bailee*
- *All Other Sales* for merchant seller, risk of loss passes to buyer on the buyer's receipt of the goods; for nonmerchant seller, risk of loss passes to buyer upon tender of goods

**Bulk Sales**

**Definition** a transfer, not in the ordinary course of the transferor's business, of a major part of his inventory

**Requirements of Article 6** transfer is ineffective against any creditor of the transferor, unless certain requirements are met

# Cases

### CASE 23–1
### Transfer of Title
## *PITTSBURGH INDUSTRIAL FURNACE COMPANY v.*
## *UNIVERSAL CONSOLIDATED COMPANIES, INC.*

United States District Court, W.D. Pennsylvania, 1991
789 F.Supp. 184

LEE, J.

Defendant, Trustcorp Financing Services, Inc. ("TFSI") . . ., has moved this Court for an Order granting summary judgment. Central to the disposition of defendant's Motion are the rights of TFSI as a secured party and the rights of Pittsburgh Industrial Furnace Company ("Pifcom"), an unpaid seller of goods, and the passage of title to goods under the Uniform Commercial Code. See U.C.C. § 2–319; U.C.C. § 2–401.

## Background

During 1988, Universal Consolidated Company ("Universal"), entered into negotiations with the China Metallurgical Import and Export Corporation ("CMIEC"), Tianjin branch, People's Republic of China, to provide seven lines of reengineered and rebuilt new and used equipment for a cold rolling steel mill. The project required, in part, that Universal provide twelve batch anneal furnaces. These furnaces needed to be designed and constructed.

The plaintiff, Pifcom entered into an agreement ("contract") with Universal Consolidated Company ("Universal") on January 25, 1989, whereby it agreed to provide engineering, equipment and materials necessary to construct the twelve batch anneal furnaces for the Tianjin Steel Mill.

The contract provided for Pifcom to receive $955,000 in four installments. Under its terms, Universal paid Pifcom a down payment of $95,000 plus two progress payments of $100,000 each. The balance of $660,000 was due upon shipment.

Pifcom performed its part of the contract in that it provided the appropriate engineering and shipped or caused to be shipped the required equipment and materials which it subcontracted with other suppliers to provide.

Pifcom directed the suppliers to ship their materials and equipment to EMPE, Inc., located in Beaver, Pennsylvania. EMPE is Universal's engineering consultant, which was responsible for refurbishing used equipment as well as accumulating and storing most of the equipment that was ultimately to be shipped to China.

Pursuant to the contract, the materials and equipment were to be shipped "FOB Points of Shipment." In accordance with Pifcom's directives, the suppliers shipped the materials and equipment to EMPE, Inc.

In September of 1989, CMIEC informed Universal that it was terminating its contract. On October 5, 1989, Universal informed Pifcom that CMIEC did not intend to proceed and requested Pifcom to suspend its performance.

As of the date Pifcom received this letter, most of the equipment and materials had already been delivered at EMPE facilities. The balance of materials and equipment not yet received had already been placed in shipment.

Thereafter, Pifcom took no steps to stop delivery of the remaining equipment or to reclaim the materials and equipment which had already been shipped to EMPE until December 8, 1989, when Pifcom's counsel wrote EMPE and instructed it to stop any delivery of equipment and materials to Universal.

\* \* \*

Pifcom asserts that it never intended to have the title to the goods pass until it was paid and claims that it had an understanding with EMPE that EMPE would act as a bailee in storing the goods for Pifcom after shipment.

***TFSI: The Secured Party*** TFSI provided financing for the Universal/CMIEC project and extended Universal a $6.5 million line of credit to enable it to purchase the necessary equipment and materials, to develop the necessary engineering for the project, and to refurbish the used equipment to be sold to CMIEC.

\* \* \*

After CMIEC canceled its agreement with Universal, and after Universal suspended its performance, TFSI declared its loan in default because it appeared that Universal would be unable to pay TFSI the amounts advanced to it under the credit security agreement.

Thereafter, in January through March of 1990, TFSI repossessed the materials and equipment located principally at EMPE, Inc., in which it asserts Universal had granted it a security interest. The items repossessed included the materials and equipment necessary for the batch anneal furnaces which had been supplied by or on behalf of Pifcom pursuant to its contract with Universal.

* * *

**Discussion**  Section 2–401 of the Uniform Commercial Code deals with the concept of "title" and the time title passes.

* * *

Under plaintiff's contract with Universal, all of the materials and equipment were to be shipped "FOB points of shipment." Under U.C.C. § 2–319 when the provision in the contract is "FOB place of shipment," the seller must bear the risk and expense of putting the goods in the possession of an independent carrier at the seller's location. U.C.C. § 2–319(1)(a).

The seller must choose a reasonable carrier, make a proper contract for the transportation of the goods in relation to the nature of the goods, obtain and promptly deliver any appropriate documents such as bills of lading that the buyer requires to obtain the goods, and promptly notify the buyer of shipment. U.C.C. § 2–504.

Once the goods are delivered to the carrier, the seller has given up possession of the goods under U.C.C. § 2–401 and title passes to the buyer because the seller's performance with reference to the physical delivery of the goods is completed. [Citations.]

Plaintiff's claim that it entered into an oral agreement which modified the original terms of the parties' contract is unsupported.

* * *

If plaintiff were to retain an interest in the goods after shipment or delivery to Universal, such reservation is limited to the reservation of a security interest. [Citation.] As we have stated earlier, plaintiff failed to obtain and perfect a security interest in the equipment and materials it shipped. See U.C.C. § 9–203.

* * *

[W]e are satisfied that [plaintiff's position] . . . falls well short of refuting two critical elements of defendant's Motion: (1) that plaintiff performed by delivering the equipment and materials to Universal according to the terms of its contract and (2) the legal consequences of those deliveries which flows directly from the contract language resulted in the proper repossession by TFSI of collateral held by Universal.

We find there is no substantial question of material fact as to when title to the property in issue passed under the Uniform Commercial Code. Nor do we find there can be any challenge to the rights of TFSI as a secured lender. Accordingly, defendant's Motions for Summary Judgment will be GRANTED.

---

## CASE 23–2
# Void and Voidable Title to Goods
## *ROBINSON v. DURHAM*
Alabama Court of Civil Appeals, 1988
537 So.2d 966

WRIGHT, J.

Ronald Robinson, Wyman Robinson, and Friendly Discount Auto Sales (appellants) appeal from the granting of summary judgment in favor of appellee Mike Durham (Durham).

The facts material to this appeal and dispositive of this case are undisputed. Appellants, who are in car sales, purchased a 1968 Chevrolet Camaro. At the time of the purchase, a female transferred to the appellants tag receipts in her name and in the name of the previous owner. Wyman Robinson then registered the automobile

in his name. In September 1986 Durham purchased the automobile from appellants, and all prior documentation was transferred to him. Shortly thereafter, the F.B.I. seized the automobile. The automobile had been reported stolen in Florida. It was subsequently returned to the original owner.

Durham filed a suit against appellants alleging fraud, breach of contract, and breach of warranty. Durham moved for summary judgment against appellants on all counts. The trial court granted Durham's motion on the count alleging that appellants made a statement to

Durham as true without knowledge of its truth and on the issue of breach of warranty of title. Durham was awarded $5,200, the amount he paid for the car. Appellants appeal.

Appellants assert that the grant of summary judgment was in error because there was "a scintilla of evidence, if not substantial evidence" from which the trial court could have concluded that appellants held good title "or at least voidable title" on the automobile, thereby conveying actual title to Durham at the time of the purchase.

Appellants' argument is without merit. It is unequivocable that "a person who has stolen goods of another cannot pass title thereto to another, whether such other knew, or did not know, that the goods were stolen." [Citations.] A thief gets only void title and without more cannot pass any title to a subsequent purchaser, even a good faith purchaser. [Citation.] It is undisputed that the automobile had been stolen. Therefore, at the time of purchase appellants obtained no title. In other words, the title was void. Appellants could not convey good title to Durham; therefore, the subsequent sale to Durham constituted a breach of warranty of good title.

Relying on § 2–403(1), [U.C.C.], appellants contend that they at least acquired a voidable title when they purchased the automobile. Section 2–403 recognizes that a person with voidable title has power to transfer a good title to a good faith purchaser for value. Voidable title can only arise from a voluntary transfer, and the rightful owner must assent to the transfer. "A possessor of goods does not have voidable title unless the true owner has consented to the transfer of title to him." [Citation.] In this case the rightful owner did not consent or assent to the transfer of the automobile. Appellants obtained no title. * * *

Affirmed. All the Judges concur.

---

## CASE 23–3
## Entrusting of Goods to a Merchant
## *HEINRICH v. TITUS–WILL SALES, INC.*

Court of Appeals of Washington, Division 2, 1994
73 Wash. App. 147, 868 P.2d 169

SEINFELD, J.
Titus–Will Ford Sales, Inc. appeals a judgment for replevin [repossession] of a 1990 Ford pickup truck that Titus–Will had previously sold to dealer/broker James Wilson. Upon consideration of the entrustment provisions of the Uniform Commercial Code, we agree that Titus–Will must bear the burden of loss of payment for the vehicle. Accordingly, we affirm the judgment in favor of Michael Heinrich, a third party bona fide purchaser for value.

In 1989 Michael Heinrich wished to buy a particular model new Ford pickup truck. James Wilson held himself out as a dealer/broker, licensed to buy and sell vehicles. Heinrich retained Wilson to make the purchase, but did not direct Wilson to any particular automobile dealer. Unbeknownst to Heinrich, Wilson had lost his Washington vehicle dealer license the previous year.

Wilson negotiated with Tutus–Will for the purchase of a Ford pickup truck with Heinrich's desired options. Titus–Will had been involved in hundreds of transactions with Wilson over the years and also was unaware that Wilson was no longer licensed to act as a vehicle dealer.

Heinrich made two initial payments to Wilson: an $1,800 down payment and a $3,000 payment when Titus–Will ordered the truck. Wilson gave Heinrich a receipt using a "Used Car Wholesale Purchase Order" that displayed Wilson's alleged vehicle dealer license number. Wilson then ordered the truck from Titus–Will, using his own check to make a $7,000 down payment. The purchase order indicated the truck was being sold to Wilson. "Dealer" was written in the space on the form for tax. Wilson told the Titus–Will salesman handling the sale that he was ordering the truck for resale.

On October 13, 1989, Wilson told Heinrich the truck was ready for delivery. Heinrich paid Wilson $15,549.55 as final payment, including tax and license fees. Wilson gave Heinrich a copy of the purchase order and of an options checklist with corresponding prices. These documents indicated that Wilson was buying the truck from Titus–Will. The Titus–Will salesman had signed off on the options list; Wilson marked it "paid in full" and signed it after Heinrich paid him. On the same day, at Wilson's behest, Heinrich signed a Washington application for motor vehicle title.

Wilson agreed to deliver the truck to Heinrich at Titus–Will on Saturday, October 21, 1989. He arranged with a Titus–Will salesman to deliver a check on the morning of October 21 to a clerk in the Titus–Will office and, in return, to receive the truck keys and paperwork. The clerk accepted Wilson's check for $11,288.00, post-dated to Monday, October 23, 1989, and delivered Wilson a packet containing the keys to the truck, the owner's manual, an odometer disclosure statement, and a warranty card. The odometer statement, which Wilson and the Titus–Will salesman signed, showed Wilson as the transferor. Titus–Will did not fill out the warranty card with the name and address of the purchaser because the sale appeared to be dealer to dealer, with the warranty to benefit the ultimate purchaser.

* * *

Wilson immediately taped Heinrich's application for title in the rear window of the truck that was parked on the Titus–Will lot. When Heinrich arrived, Wilson gave him the keys and documents and Heinrich drove off in the truck.

Wilson's check did not clear. Titus–Will demanded return of the truck. On November 6, Wilson picked up the truck from Heinrich, telling him he would have Titus–Will make certain repairs under the warranty. Wilson returned the truck to Titus–Will.

On November 9, 1989, Wilson admitted to Heinrich that he did not have funds to cover his check to Titus–Will and that Titus–Will would not release the truck without payment. Heinrich then asked Titus–Will for the truck; it refused. By a pretrial arrangement, Heinrich regained possession of, but not clear title to, the truck on April 1, 1990.

Heinrich sued Titus–Will and Wilson, seeking replevin of the truck and damages for his loss of use. Heinrich obtained a default order against Wilson. After a bench trial, the court awarded Heinrich title to the truck and $3,050 in damages for loss of its use.

On appeal, Titus–Will argues that the trial court erroneously applied the entrustment doctrine of [UCC] 2–403; * * *

## The Entrustment Doctrine

[UCC] 2–403(2) and (3) contain the entrustment provisions of the Uniform Commercial Code (UCC).

* * *

To prevail under this statute, Heinrich must show 1) Titus–Will "entrusted" the truck to Wilson and, thus, empowered Wilson subsequently to transfer all rights of Titus–Will in the truck to Heinrich; 2) Wilson was a merchant dealing in automobiles; and 3) Heinrich bought the truck from Wilson as a "buyer in ordinary course of business." [Citations.]

Three general policies support [§] 2–403(2), the UCC provision placing the risk of loss on the entruster. First, it protects the innocent buyer who, based on his observation of goods in the possession of a merchant of those goods, believes that the merchant has legal title to the goods and can, therefore, pass title in the goods to another. [Citation.] The statute carries forward the pre-Uniform Commercial Code law of estoppel under which an owner, who clothes a merchant with apparent ownership of or authority to sell goods, is estopped from denying such authority as against one buying the goods from the merchant in good faith. [Citations.]

Secondly, the entrustment clause reflects the idea that the entruster is in a better position than the innocent buyer to protect against the risk that an intermediary merchant will not pay for or not deliver the goods. [Citations.]

Thirdly, the entrustment clause facilitates the flow of commerce by allowing purchasers to rely on a merchant's apparent legal right to sell the goods. [Citations.] Without the safeguards of the entrustment provision, a prudent buyer would have to delay the finalization of any sizeable sales transaction for the time necessary to research the merchant's ownership rights to the goods.

*A. Entrusting*   The UCC definition of "entrusting," contained in 2–403(3), is broad. [Citation.] The statute declares that "any delivery and any acquiescence in retention of possession" constitutes entrustment. 2–403(3). A person can entrust goods to a merchant by a variety of methods, such as consigning them, creating a bailment, taking a security interest in inventory, leaving them with the merchant after purchase, and delivering them for purposes of repair. [Citations.] A sale can also constitute an entrustment when some aspect of the transaction remains incomplete. [Citations.]

Titus–Will properly concedes that it entrusted the truck to Wilson. However, it argues Wilson was not a merchant and Heinrich was not a buyer in ordinary course. Further, Titus–Will contends that the timing of the entrusting deprived Wilson of the power to transfer its rights.

**B. Merchant**  Titus–Will argues that Wilson was not a merchant because he had no inventory. However, it is not necessary to possess an inventory to fit within the broad statutory definition of merchant. Article 2 of the UCC defines (in part) "merchant" as "a person who deals in goods of the kind or otherwise by his occupation holds himself out as having knowledge or skill peculiar to the practices or goods involved in the transaction." 2–104(1). Wilson was a merchant who dealt in automobiles; he held himself out as a dealer in automobiles and appeared to be a dealer in automobiles. Both parties treated him as one. Titus–Will processed all the documents as it would for a dealer and understood that Wilson was buying the truck for resale.

Titus–Will also argues that Wilson was not a merchant because he did not have a vehicle dealer license. However, the UCC does not require proper state licensing for merchant status. 2–104(1), 2–403(2). ＊ ＊ ＊

**C. Buyer in Ordinary Course**  There is also substantial evidence that Heinrich was a "buyer in ordinary course of business" although the trial court referred to him as a "good faith purchaser for value." A buyer in ordinary course of business is

a person who in good faith and without knowledge that the sale to him is in violation of the ownership rights or security interest of a third party in the goods buys in ordinary course from a person in the business of selling goods of that kind[.] 1–201(9). "Buying" includes receiving goods . . . under a pre-existing contract for sale." 1–201(9). Good faith is "honesty in fact in the conduct or transaction concerned." 1–201(19).

The amount of the consideration is significant as evidence of good faith. [Citation.] Heinrich gave substantial value for the truck, more than Wilson agreed to pay Titus–Will. Nor did Heinrich know or have a basis to believe that Wilson's sale and delivery of the truck to him violated Titus–Will's ownership or security interest rights. There was no showing that Heinrich acted other than in good faith. ＊ ＊ ＊ Wilson's illegal and fraudulent activity does not taint Heinrich's status as a buyer under 2–403(2). When Heinrich accepted delivery after previously paying Wilson, Heinrich was "buying" as defined by 1–201(9).

**D. Timing of Entrustment**  Titus–Will also argues that the UCC entrustment provisions should not apply because it entrusted the truck to Wilson *after* Heinrich had completely paid Wilson. This is an issue of first impression in this jurisdiction.

Before the completion of the Wilson–Heinrich sales transaction, Titus–Will entrusted Wilson not only with the truck, but also with the signed odometer disclosure statement, the owner's manual, the warranty card, and the keys. By doing so, Titus–Will clothed Wilson with additional indicia of ownership and with the apparent authority to transfer an ownership interest in the truck. It also enabled Wilson to complete the sales transaction. 2–401(2) ("Unless otherwise explicitly agreed title passes to the buyer at the time and place at which the seller completes his performance with reference to the physical delivery of the goods"). In addition, the entrustment allowed Wilson to continue to deceive Heinrich from October 21, 1989, the date of delivery of possession, to November 9, 1989, when Wilson finally admitted the truth. We believe that under these circumstances, application of the entrustment doctrine, 2–403(2), furthers the policy of protecting the buyer who relies on the merchant's apparent legal ability to sell goods in the merchant's possession.

The second rationale for the entrustment doctrine also supports its application here. Titus–Will, in the business of selling cars, was in a better position than Heinrich to protect itself against another dealer/broker who might fail to pay for the goods. It could have insured against the loss, and it could have adopted preventive procedures. ＊ ＊ ＊

The third rationale for the entrustment doctrine focuses on the flow of commerce. Here we consider the potential impact on commercial transactions of requiring purchasers to research their dealer/broker's legal title before accepting possession of the goods. Although the record contains no evidence on this issue, it seems obvious that this requirement would inevitably cause some delay. [Citation.]

Requiring the entruster to retain the burden of risk, even when the entrustment occurs after a third party purchaser gives value, supports the policies underlying the entrustment doctrine. ＊ ＊ ＊ The trial court did not err in applying the entrustment doctrine and granting replevin.

＊ ＊ ＊

We affirm the trial court's judgment.

## CASE 23–4
### Shipment Contracts
### *PESTANA v. KARINOL CORP.*
District Court of Appeals of Florida, Third District, 1979
367 So.2d 1096

HUBBART, J.

This is an action for damages based on a contract for the sale of goods. The defendant seller and others prevailed in this action after a non-jury trial in the Circuit Court for the Eleventh Judicial Circuit of Florida. The plaintiff buyer appeals.

The central issue presented for review is whether a contract for the sale of goods, which stipulates the place where the goods sold are to be sent by carrier but contains (a) no explicit provisions allocating the risk of loss while the goods are in the possession of the carrier and (b) no delivery terms such as F.O.B. place of destination, is a shipment contract or a destination contract under the Uniform Commercial Code. We hold that such a contract, without more, constitutes a shipment contract wherein the risk of loss passes to the buyer when the seller duly delivers the goods to the carrier under a reasonable contract of carriage for shipment to the buyer. Accordingly, we affirm.

The critical facts of this case are substantially undisputed. On March 4, 1975, Nahim Amar B. (the plaintiff Pedro P. Pestana's decedent herein) who was a resident of Mexico entered into a contract through his authorized representative with the Karinol Corporation (the defendant herein) which is an exporting company licensed to do business in Florida and operating out of Miami. The terms of this contract were embodied in a one-page invoice written in Spanish and prepared by the defendant Karinol. By the terms of this contract, the plaintiff's Amar agreed to purchase 64 electronic watches from the defendant Karinol for $6,006. A notation was printed at the bottom of the contract which, translated into English, reads as follows: "Please send the merchandise in cardboard boxes duly strapped with metal bands via air parcel post to Chetumal. Documents to Banco de Commercio De Quintano Roo S.A." There were no provisions in the contract which specifically allocated the risk of loss on the goods sold while in the possession of the carrier; there were also no F.O.B., F.A.S., C.I.F. or C. & F. terms contained in the contract. See [U.C.C. §§ 2–319, 2–320]. A 25% downpayment on the purchase price of the goods sold was made prior to shipment.

On April 11, 1975, there is sufficient evidence, although disputed, that the defendant Karinol delivered the watches in two cartons to its agent American International Freight Forwarders, Inc. (the second defendant herein) for forwarding to the plaintiff's decedent Amar. The defendant American insured the two cartons with Fidelity & Casualty Company of New York (the third defendant herein) naming the defendant Karinol as the insured. The defendant American as freight forwarder strapped the cartons in question with metal bands and delivered them to TACA International Airlines consigned to one Bernard Smith, a representative of the plaintiff's decedent, in Belize City, Belize, Central America. The shipment was arranged by Karinol in this manner in accord with a prior understanding between the parties as there were no direct flights from Miami, Florida to Chetumal, Mexico. Mr. Smith was to take custody of the goods on behalf of the plaintiff's decedent in Belize and arrange for their transport by truck to the plaintiff's decedent Amar in Chetumal, Mexico.

On April 15, 1975, the cartons arrived by air in Belize City and were stored by the airline in the customs and air freight cargo room. Mr. Smith was duly notified and thereupon the plaintiff's decedent made payment on the balance due under the contract to the defendant Karinol. On May 2, 1975, Mr. Smith took custody of the cartons after a certain delay was experienced in transferring the cartons to a customs warehouse. Either on that day or shortly thereafter, the cartons were opened by Mr. Smith and customs officials as was required for clearance prior to the truck shipment to Chetumal, Mexico. There were no watches contained in the cartons. The defendant Karinol and its insurance carrier the defendant Fidelity were duly notified, but both eventually refused to make good on the loss.

\* \* \*

There are two types of sales contracts under Florida's Uniform Commercial Code wherein a carrier is used to transport the goods sold: a shipment contract and a destination contract. A shipment contract is considered the normal contract in which the seller is required to send the subject goods by carrier to the buyer but is not required to guarantee delivery thereof at a particular destination.

Under a shipment contract, the seller, unless otherwise agreed, must: (1) put the goods sold in the possession of a carrier and make a contract for their transportation as may be reasonable having regard for the nature of the goods and other attendant circumstances, (2) obtain and promptly deliver or tender in due form any document necessary to enable the buyer to obtain possession of the goods or otherwise required by the agreement or by usage of the trade, and (3) promptly notify the buyer of the shipment. On a shipment contract, the risk of loss passes to the buyer when the goods sold are duly delivered to the carrier for shipment to the buyer. [Citations.]

A destination contract, on the other hand, is considered the variant contract in which the seller specifically agrees to deliver the goods sold to the buyer at a particular destination and to bear the risk of loss of the goods until tender of delivery. This can be accomplished by express provision in the sales contract to that effect or by the use of delivery terms such as F.O.B. (place of destination). Under a destination contract, the seller is required to tender delivery of the goods sold to the buyer at the place of destination. The risk of loss under such a contract passes to the buyer when the goods sold are duly tendered to the buyer at the place of destination while in the possession of the carrier so as to enable the buyer to take delivery. The parties must explicitly agree to a destination contract; otherwise the contract will be considered a shipment contract. [Citations.]

Where the risk of loss falls on the seller at the time the goods sold are lost or destroyed, the seller is liable in damages to the buyer for non-delivery unless the seller tenders a performance in replacement for the lost or destroyed goods. On the other hand, where the risk of loss falls on the buyer at the time the goods sold are lost or destroyed, the buyer is liable to the seller for the purchase price of the goods sold. [Citation.]

In the instant case, we deal with the normal shipment contract involving the sale of goods. The defendant Karinol pursuant to this contract agreed to send the goods sold, a shipment of watches, to the plaintiff's decedent in Chetumal, Mexico. There was no specific provision in the contract between the parties which allocated the risk of loss on the goods sold while in transit. In addition, there were no delivery terms such as F.O.B. Chetumal contained in the contract.

* * *

The plaintiff Pestana contends, however, that the contract herein is a destination contract in which the risk of loss on the goods sold did not pass until delivery on such goods had been tendered to him at Chetumal, Mexico—an event which never occurred. He relies for this position on the notation at the bottom of the contract between the parties which provides that the goods were to be sent to Chetumal, Mexico. We cannot agree. A "send to" or "ship to" term is a part of every contract involving the sale of goods where carriage is contemplated and has no significance in determining whether the contract is a shipment or destination contract for risk of loss purposes. [Citations.] As such, the "send to" term contained in this contract cannot, without more, convert this into a destination contract.

It therefore follows that the risk of loss in this case shifted to the plaintiff's decedent as buyer when the defendant Karinol as seller duly delivered the goods to the defendant freight forwarder American under a reasonable contract of carriage for shipment to the plaintiff's decedent in Chetumal, Mexico. The defendant Karinol, its agent the defendant American, and its insurer the defendant Fidelity could not be held liable to the plaintiff in this action. The trial court properly entered judgment in favor of all the defendants herein.

Affirmed.

---

## CASE 23–5
### Risk of Loss: Seller Not a Merchant
### *MARTIN v. MELLAND'S INC.*
Supreme Court of North Dakota, 1979
283 N.W.2d 76

ERICKSTAD, C. J.

The narrow issue on this appeal is who should bear the loss of a truck and an attached haystack mover that was destroyed by fire while in the possession of the plaintiff, Israel Martin (Martin), but after certificate of title had

been delivered to the defendant, Melland's Inc. (Melland's). The destroyed haymoving unit was to be used as a trade-in for a new haymoving unit that Martin ultimately purchased from Melland's. Martin appeals from a district court judgment dated September 28,

1978, that dismissed his action on the merits after it found that at the time of its destruction Martin was the owner of the unit pursuant to [Section 2–401 U.C.C.]. We hold that Section 2–401 is inapplicable to this case, but we affirm the district court judgment on the grounds that risk of loss had not passed to Melland's pursuant to [Section 2–509 U.C.C.].

On June 11, 1974, Martin entered into a written agreement with Melland's, a farm implement dealer, to purchase a truck and attached haystack mover for the total purchase price of $35,389. Martin was given a trade-in allowance of $17,389 on his old unit, leaving a balance owing of $18,000 plus sales tax of $720 or a total balance of $18,720. The agreement provided that Martin "mail or bring title" to the old unit to Melland's "this week." Martin mailed the certificate of title to Melland's pursuant to the agreement, but he was allowed to retain the use and possession of the old unit "until they had the new one ready." The new unit was not expected to be ready for two to three months because it required certain modifications. During this interim period, Melland's performed minor repairs to the trade-in unit on two occasions without charging Martin for the repairs.

Fire destroyed the truck and the haymoving unit in early August, 1974, while Martin was moving hay. The parties did not have any agreement regarding insurance or risk of loss on the unit and Martin's insurance on the trade-in unit had lapsed. Melland's refused Martin's demand for his new unit and Martin brought this suit. The parties subsequently entered into an agreement by which Martin purchased the new unit, but they reserved their rights in any lawsuit arising out of the prior incident.

The district court found "that although the Plaintiff [Martin] executed the title to the . . . [haymoving unit], he did not relinquish possession of the same and therefore the Plaintiff was the owner of said truck at the time the fire occurred pursuant to Section 2–401."

Martin argues that the district court erroneously applied Section 2–401, regarding passage of title, to this case and that Section 2–509, which deals with risk of loss in the absence of breach, should have been applied instead. Martin argues further that title (apparently pursuant to Section 2–401) and risk of loss passed to Melland's and the property was then merely bailed back to Martin who held it as a bailee. Martin submits that this is supported by the fact that Melland's performed minor repairs on the old unit following the passage of title without charging Martin for the repairs. Melland's responds that Section 2–401(2), governs this case and that

the district court's determination of the issue should be affirmed.

One of the hallmarks of the pre-Code law of sales was its emphasis on the concept of title. The location of title was used to determine, among other things, risk of loss, insurable interest, place and time for measuring damages, and the applicable law in an interstate transaction. This single title or "lump" title concept proved unsatisfactory because of the different policy considerations involved in each of the situations that title was made to govern. Furthermore, the concept of single title did not reflect modern commercial practices, *i.e.,* although the single title concept worked well for "cash-on-the-barrelhead sales," the introduction of deferred payments, security agreements, financing from third parties, or delivery by carrier required a fluid concept of title with bits and pieces held by all parties to the transaction.

Thus the concept of title under the U.C.C. is of decreased importance.

\* \* \*

No longer is the question of title of any importance in determining whether a buyer or seller bears the risk of loss. [Citation.]

\* \* \*

Thus, the question in this case is not answered by a determination of the location of title, but by the risk of loss provisions in [§ 2–509 U.C.C.]. Before addressing the risk of loss question in conjunction with [§ 2–509 U.C.C.], it is necessary to determine the posture of the parties with regard to the trade-in unit, *i.e.,* who is the buyer and the seller and how are the responsibilities allocated. It is clear that a barter or trade-in is considered a sale and is therefore subject to the Uniform Commercial Code. [Citations.] It is also clear that the party who owns the trade-in is considered the seller. [§ 2–304 U.C.C.], provides that the "price can be made payable in money or otherwise. If it is payable in whole or in part in goods each party is a seller of the goods which he is to transfer." [Citations.]

Martin argues that he had already sold the trade-in unit to Melland's and, although he retained possession, he did so in the capacity of a bailee (apparently pursuant to [§ 2–509(2) U.C.C.]). White and Summers in their hornbook on the Uniform Commercial Code argue that the seller who retains possession should not be considered bailee within Section 2–509.

\* \* \*

The courts that have addressed this issue have agreed with White and Summers. [Citations.]

It is undisputed that the contract did not require or authorize shipment by carrier pursuant to Section [2–509(1)]; therefore, the residue section, subsection 3, is applicable:

In any case not within subsection 1 or 2, the risk of loss passes to the buyer on his receipt of the goods if the seller is a merchant; otherwise the risk passes to the buyer on tender of delivery.

Martin admits that he is not a merchant; therefore, it is necessary to determine if Martin tendered delivery of the trade-in unit to Melland's. * * *

It is clear that the trade-in unit was not tendered to Melland's in this case. The parties agreed that Martin would keep the old unit "until they had the new one ready."

* * *

We hold that Martin did not tender delivery of the trade-in truck and haystack mover to Melland's pursuant to [§ 2–509 U.C.C.]; consequently, Martin must bear the loss.

We affirm the district court judgment.

---

# Questions

1. Explain the relative importance of title under the common law and Article 2.
2. Distinguish between a shipment contract and a destination contract. When does title and risk of loss pass under each?
3. When does the seller have a right or power to transfer title? When is the transfer void or voidable? By whom? Against whom?

4. Discuss the rules covering (a) risk of loss in the absence of a breach, and (b) risk of loss when there is a breach.
5. What is a bulk transfer? When is it effective? What does revised Article 6 attempt to accomplish?

---

# Problems

1. Stein, a mechanic, and Beal, a life insurance agent, entered into a written contract for the sale of Stein's tractor to Beal for $2,800 cash. It was agreed that Stein would tune the motor on the tractor. Stein fulfilled this obligation and on the night of July 1 telephoned Beal that the tractor was ready to be picked up upon Beal's making payment. Beal responded, "I'll be there in the morning with the money." On the next morning, however, Beal was approached by an insurance prospect and decided to get the tractor at a later date. On the night of July 2, the tractor was destroyed by fire of unknown origin. Neither Stein nor Beal had any fire insurance. Who must bear the loss?

2. Regan received a letter from Chase, the material portion of which stated: "Chase hereby places an order with you for fifty cases of Red Top Tomatoes, ship them C.O.D." Promptly upon receipt of the letter Regan shipped the tomatoes to Chase. While en route, the railroad car carrying the tomatoes was wrecked. Upon Chase's refusal to pay for the tomatoes, Regan commenced an action to recover the purchase price. Chase defended on the ground that as the shipment was C.O.D., neither title to the tomatoes nor risk of loss passed until their delivery to Chase. Decision?

3. On May 10, the Apple Company, acting through one Brown, entered into a contract with Crane for the installation of a milking machine at Crane's farm. Following the enumeration of the articles to be furnished, together with the price of each article, the written contract provided: "This outfit is subject to thirty days' free trial and is to be installed about June 1." Within thirty days after installation the entire outfit, excepting a double utility unit, was destroyed by fire through no fault of Crane. The Apple Company sued Crane to recover the value of the articles destroyed. Decision?

4. Brown, located in Knoxville, contracted to buy sixty cases of Lovely Brand canned corn from Clark in Toledo at a contract price of $600. Pursuant to the contract, Clark selected and set aside sixty cases of Lovely Brand canned corn and tagged them "For Brown." The contract required Clark to ship the corn to Brown via T Railroad, F.O.B. Toledo. Before Clark delivered the corn to the railroad, the sixty cases were stolen from Clark's warehouse.

   (a) Who is liable for the loss of the sixty cases of corn, Brown or Clark?

   (b) Suppose Clark had delivered the corn to the railroad in Toledo. After the corn had been loaded on a freight car, but before the train left the yard, the car was broken open and its contents, including the corn, stolen. As between Brown and Clark, who is liable for the loss?

(c)   Would your answer in question (b) be the same if this was an F.O.B. Knoxville contract, all other facts remaining the same?

5.   Gardner owned a quantity of corn which was contained in a corncrib located on Gardner's farm. On March 12, Gardner wrote a letter to Bassett stating that he would sell to Bassett all of the corn in this crib, which he estimated at between 900 and 1,000 bushels, for $5.60 per bushel. Bassett received this letter on March 13 and immediately wrote and mailed on the same day a letter to Gardner stating that he would buy the corn. The corncrib and its contents were accidentally destroyed by fire which broke out about 3 AM on March 14.

(a)   What are the rights of the parties?

(b)   What difference, if any, in result if Gardner were a merchant?

6.   Anita, a New York dealer, purchased twenty-five barrels of specially graded and packed apples from a producer at Hood River, Oregon. She then resold the apples to Benji under a contract which specified an agreed price on delivery at Benji's place of business in New York. The apples were shipped to Anita from Oregon but, through no fault of either Anita or Benji, were totally destroyed before reaching New York. Does any liability rest upon Anita?

7.   Smith was approached by a man who introduced himself as Brown of Brown & Co. Brown was not known to Smith, but Smith asked Dun & Bradstreet for a credit report and obtained a very favorable report on Brown. He thereupon sold Brown some expensive gems and billed Brown & Co. "Brown" turned out to be a clever jewel thief, who later sold the gems to Brown & Co. for valuable consideration. Brown & Co. was unaware of "Brown's" transaction with Smith. Smith sued Brown & Co. for either the return of the gems or the price as billed to Brown & Co. Decision?

8.   Charlotte, the owner of a new Cadillac automobile, agreed to loan the car to Ellen for the month of February while she (Charlotte) went to Florida for a winter vacation. It was understood that Ellen, who was a small-town Cadillac dealer, would merely place Charlotte's car in her showroom for exhibition and sales promotion purposes. While Charlotte was away, Ellen sold the car to Robert. Upon Charlotte's return from Florida, she sued to recover the car from Robert. Decision?

9.   Brilles offered to sell his used automobile to Nevarro for $2,600 cash. Nevarro agreed to buy the car, gave Brilles a check for $2,600, and drove away in the car. The next day Nevarro sold the car for $3,000 to Hough, a *bona fide* purchaser. The $2,600 check was returned to Brilles by the bank in which he had deposited it because of insufficient funds in Nevarro's account. Brilles brings an action against Hough to recover the automobile. What judgment?

10.   Yount told Lewis he wished to buy Lewis's automobile. He drove the car for about ten minutes, returned to Lewis, stated he wanted to take the automobile to show it to his wife, and then left with the automobile and never returned. Yount sold the automobile in another State to Turner and gave him a bill of sale. Lewis sued Turner to recover the automobile. Decision?

11.   On February 7, Pillsbury purchased eight thousand bushels of wheat from Landis. The wheat was being stored at the Greensville Grain Company. Pillsbury also intended to store the wheat with Greensville. On February 10, the wheat was destroyed. Landis demands payment for the wheat from Pillsbury. Who prevails? Who has title? Who has the risk of loss? Explain.

12.   Johnson, who owned a hardware store, was indebted to Hutchinson, one of her suppliers. Johnson sold her business to Lockhart, one of Johnson's previous competitors, who combined the inventory from Johnson's store with his own and moved them to a new, larger store. Hutchinson claims that Lockhart must pay Johnson's debt because the sale of the business had been made without complying with the requirements of the bulk sales law. Decision?

13.   Seller had manufactured 40,000 pounds of plastic resin pellets specially for the buyer, who agreed to accept them at the rate of 1,000 pounds per day upon his issuance of shipping instructions. Despite numerous requests by the seller, the buyer issued no such instructions. On August 18, the seller, after warehousing the goods for forty days, demanded by letter that the buyer issue instructions. The buyer agreed to issue them beginning August 20 but never did. On September 22, a fire destroyed the seller's plant containing the goods, which were not covered by insurance. Who bears the risk of loss? Why?

14.   Harrison, a men's clothing retailer located in Westport, Connecticut, ordered merchandise from Ninth Street East, Ltd., a Los Angeles-based clothing manufacturer. Ninth Street delivered the merchandise to Denver-Chicago Trucking Company in Los Angeles and then sent four invoices to Harrison that bore the notation "F.O.B. Los Angeles." Denver subsequently transferred the merchandise to a connecting carrier, Old Colony Transportation Company, for final delivery to Harrison's Westport store. When Old Colony tried to deliver the merchandise, Harrison's wife asked the truck driver to deliver the boxes inside the store, but the driver refused. The dispute remained unresolved, and the truck departed with Old Colony still in possession of the goods. Harrison then notified Ninth Street by letter of the nondelivery, but Ninth Street was unable to locate the shipment. Ninth Street then sought to recover the contract purchase price from Harrison. Harrison refused, contending that risk of loss remained with Ninth Street because of its refusal to deliver the merchandise to Harrison's place of business. Decision?

15.   United Road Machinery Company, a dealer in heavy road equipment (including truck scales supplied by Thurman Scale Company), received a telephone call on July 21 from James Durham, an officer of Consolidated Coal Company, seeking to acquire truck scales for his coal mining operation. United and Consolidated entered into a twenty-four-month lease-purchase arrangement. United then notified Thurman that Consolidated would take possession of the scales directly. United paid for the scales and Consolidated took possession

of them, but the latter never signed and returned the contract papers forwarded to it by United. Consolidated also never made any of the rental payments ($608/month) due under the lease. On September 20, Consolidated, through its officer Durham, sold the scales to Kentucky Mobile Homes for $8,500. Kentucky's president, Ethard Jasper, checked the county records prior to the purchase and found no lien or encumbrance on the title; likewise, he denied knowledge of the dispute between Consolidated and United. On September 22, Kentucky sold the scales to Clyde Jasper, individually, for $8,500. His search also failed to disclose any lien on the title to the scales, and he denied knowledge of the dispute between Consolidated and United. United brought suit to recover the scales from Jasper. Decision?

**16.** McCoy, an Oklahoma cattle dealer, orally agreed with Chandler, a Texas cattle broker, to ship cattle to a New Mexico feedlot for delivery to Chandler. The agreement was for six lots of cattle valued at $119,000. After McCoy delivered the cattle, he presented invoices to Chandler which described the cattle and set forth the sales price. McCoy then demanded payment, which Chandler refused. Unknown to McCoy, Chandler had obtained a loan from First National Bank and pledged the subject cattle as collateral. The bank had no knowledge of any interest that McCoy may have had in the cattle. McCoy sued to recover the cattle. The bank counterclaimed that it had a perfected security interest in the cattle that was superior to any interest of McCoy's. The trial court ruled in favor of the bank, and McCoy appeals. Decision?

**17.** Porter, the owner of an art collection, engaged in a number of art transactions with Harold Von Maker, who used, among other names, that of Peter Wertz. Porter permitted Von Maker to have temporarily a painting by Maurice Utrillo, *Chateau de Lion-sur-Mer,* and to hang it in his home until he decided whether to purchase it. A few months later, Porter sought the return of the Utrillo painting but was unable to reach Von Maker. Porter subsequently discovered that he was not dealing with the "real" Peter Wertz but with Harold Von Maker, a man with an extensive criminal record, including a conviction for defrauding the Chase Manhattan Bank. When Porter finally reached him, Von Maker claimed that the Utrillo was on consignment with a client. Von Maker then agreed in writing either to return the painting to Porter within ninety days or to make compensation for it. At the time he entered this agreement, Von Maker had already sold the painting. He had used the real Peter Wertz, a delicatessen employee and acquaintance, to effect the sale of the Utrillo to Feigen for $20,000. Feigen, an art dealer, then sold the painting to Brenner, and it is now somewhere in Venezuela. Porter brought suit against Feigen and the others involved to recover possession of either the Utrillo or its value. Decision?

**18.** Home Indemnity, an insurance company, paid one of its insureds after the theft of his car. The car reappeared in another State and was sold to Michael Schrier for $4,300 by a used car dealer. The dealer promised to give Mr. Schrier a certificate of title. One month later the car was seized by the police on behalf of Home Indemnity. Mr. Schrier sued for the return of the car and won. Home Indemnity seeks reversal of that decision and possession of the car. Decision?

**19.** Fred Lane, who sells boats, motors, and trailers, sold a boat, motor, and trailer to John Willis in exchange for a check for $6,285. The check was not honored when Lane attempted to use the funds. Willis subsequently left the boat, motor, and trailer with John Garrett, who sold the items to Jimmy Honeycutt for $2,500. Honeycutt, surprised at how inexpensive the boat was, considering its quality, did not know where Garrett had obtained the boat, but he had dealt with Garrett before and described him as a "sly businessman." Garrett did not sell boats; normally, he sold fishing tackle and provisions. Honeycutt also received a forged certificate for the boat, on which he had observed Garrett forge the purported owner's signature. Lane sues Honeycutt for return of the boat, motor, and trailer. Decision?

**20.** Mike Moses purchased a mobile home, including installation, from Gary Newman. Newman delivered the home to Moses's lot. Upon inspection of the home, Moses's fiancée found a broken window and water pipe. Moses also had not received keys to the front door. Before Newman corrected these problems, a windstorm destroyed the home. Moses sued Newman for loss of the home. Decision?

**WWW Internet Exercise** Compare the provisions governing risk of loss contained in the United Nations Convention on Contracts for the International Sale of Goods (Vienna, 1980) with those of Article 2 of the Uniform Commercial Code.

# CHAPTER 24

# Products Liability: Warranties and Strict Liability in Tort

This chapter considers the liability of manufacturers and sellers of goods to buyers, users, consumers, and bystanders for damages caused by defective products. The rapidly expanding development of case law has established products liability as a distinct field of law that combines and enforces rules and principles of contracts, sales, negligence, strict liability in tort, and statutory law.

One reason for the expansion of this liability is the modern method of distributing goods. Today, retailers serve principally as conduits of prepackaged goods that are widely advertised by the manufacturer or distributor. This has brought about the extension of product liability coverage to include manufacturers and other parties along the chain of distribution. The extension of product liability to manufacturers, however, has not lessened the liability of the retailer to his immediate purchaser. Rather, it has broadened the base of liability through the development and application of new principles of law.

Currently, the entire area of products liability has attracted a great deal of public attention. According to the U.S. Consumer Product Safety Commission, thirty-six million Americans are injured each year in consumer product-related accidents. Of those injured, twenty-eight thousand die while many others are permanently disabled. The resultant cost of maintaining product liability insurance has skyrocketed, causing great concern in the business community. In response to the clamor over this insurance crisis, more than forty States have revised their tort laws to make successful product liability lawsuits more difficult to bring.

The liability of manufacturers and other sellers of goods for a defective product, or for its failure to perform adequately, may be based upon one or more of the following: (1) negligence, (2) misrepresentation, (3) violation of statutory duty, (4) warranty, and (5) strict liability in tort. The first three causes of actions have been covered in Chapters 8 and 11. This chapter will explore the last two.

## WARRANTIES

A **warranty** creates a duty on the part of the seller that the goods she sells will conform to certain qualities, characteristics, or conditions. A seller, however, is not required to warrant the goods; and, in general, she may, by appropriate words, disclaim, exclude, negate, or modify a particular warranty or even all warranties.

In bringing a warranty action, the buyer must prove that (1) a warranty existed, (2) the warranty has been breached, (3) the breach of the warranty proximately caused the loss suffered, and (4) notice of the breach was given to the seller. The seller has the burden of proving defenses based on the buyer's conduct. If the seller breaches his warranty, the buyer may reject or revoke acceptance of the goods. Moreover, whether he has accepted or rejected the goods, the buyer may recover a judgment against the seller for damages. Harm for which damages are recoverable include personal injury, damage to property, and economic loss. Economic loss most commonly involves damages for loss of bargain and consequential damages for lost profits. (Damages for breach of warranty are discussed in the next chapter.) This section will examine the various types of warranties as well as the obstacles to a cause of action for breach of warranty.

## *TYPES OF WARRANTIES*

A warranty may arise out of the mere existence of a sale (a warranty of title), any affirmation of fact or promise made by the seller to the buyer (an express warranty), or the circumstances under which the sale is made (an implied warranty). In a contract for the sale of goods, it is possible to have all three types of warranties. All warranties are construed as consistent with each other and cumulative, unless such a construction is unreasonable.

Article 2A carries over the warranty provisions of Article 2 with relatively minor revision to reflect differences in style, leasing terminology, or leasing practices. The creation of express warranties and, except for finance leases, the imposition of the implied warranties of merchantability and fitness for a particular purpose are virtually identical to their Article 2 analogues. Article 2 and Article 2A diverge somewhat in their treatment of the warranties of title and infringement as well as in their provisions for the exclusion and modification of warranties.

## Warranty of Title

Under the Code's warranty of title, the seller implicitly warrants (1) that the title conveyed is good and its transfer rightful and (2) that the goods have no security interest or other lien (a claim on property by another for payment of debt) of which the buyer was not aware at the time of purchase. Section 2–312(1). In a lease, title does not transfer to the lessee. Accordingly, Article 2A's analogous provision protects the lessee's right to possession and use of the goods from the claims of other parties arising from an act or omission of the lessor. Section 2A–211(1).

For example, Iris acquires goods from Sherman in a transaction that is void and then sells the goods to Brenda. Sherman brings an action against Brenda and recovers the goods. Iris has breached the warranty of title: because she did not have good title to the goods, her transfer of the goods to Brenda was not rightful. Accordingly, Iris is liable to Brenda for damages.

The Code does *not* label the warranty of title as an implied warranty, even though it arises from the sale and not from any particular words or conduct. Consequently, the Code's general disclaimer provision for implied warranties does not apply to a warranty of title, which instead is subject to its own disclaimer provision. Nevertheless, a seller of goods does implicitly warrant title to those goods.

A seller who is a merchant makes an additional warranty in sales of goods of the kind in which he regularly deals: that such goods shall be delivered free of the rightful claim of any third person that the goods infringe (use without authorization) upon any existing patent. Section 2–312(3); Section 2A–211(2).

## Express Warranties

An express warranty is an explicit undertaking by the seller with respect to the quality, description, condition, or performability of the goods. The undertaking may consist of an affirmation of fact or a promise that relates to the goods, a description of the goods, or a sample or model of the goods. In each of these instances, the undertaking must become or be made part of the basis of the bargain in order for an express warranty to be created. The seller need not, however, have a specific intention to make a warranty or use formal words such as "warrant" or "guarantee." Moreover, to be liable for a breach of express warranty a seller need not know that she has made a false statement; the seller may be acting in good faith. For example, if John mistakenly asserts to Sam that a rope will easily support 300 pounds and Sam is injured when the rope breaks while supporting only 200 pounds, John is liable for breach of an express warranty.

***Creation*** The seller can create an express warranty either orally or in writing. One of the ways in which an express warranty can be created is through an **affirmation of fact** or a **promise** relating to the goods that becomes part of the basis of the bargain. Section 2–313(1)(a); Section 2A–210(1)(a). The statement can be in regard to the quality, condition, capacity, performability, or safety of the goods. For example, a statement made by a seller that an automobile will get 42 miles to the gallon of gasoline or that a camera has automatic focus is an express warranty.

The Code further provides that a statement affirming the **value** of the goods or purporting merely to be the seller's **opinion** or recommendation of the goods does not create a warranty. Section 2–313(2); Section 2A–210(2). Such statements are not factual and do not deceive the ordinary buyer, who accepts them merely as opinions or as puffery (sales talk). For example, a statement by a salesperson that "this is one terrific deal" would likely be considered puffery. On the other hand, a statement that "this car gets 30 miles to the gallon" would be considered an express warranty, given its specificity. A statement of value may be an express warranty, however, where the seller states the price at which the goods were purchased from a former owner, or where she gives market figures relating to sales of similar goods. As statements of events, not mere opinions, these are statements of facts; and the seller is liable for breach of warranty if they are untrue. Moreover, although a statement of opinion by the seller is not ordinarily a warranty, if the seller is an expert and gives her opinion as such, she may be liable for breach of warranty. Thus, if an art expert states that a certain painting is a genuine Rembrandt, and this becomes part of the basis of the bargain, then the expert warrants the accuracy of her professional opinion.

An express warranty also can be created by the use of a **description** of the goods that becomes part of the basis of the bargain. Section 2–313(1)(b); Section 2A–210(1)(b). Under such a warranty, the seller expressly warrants that the goods shall conform to the description. Examples include statements regarding a particular brand or type of goods, technical specifications, and blueprints.

The use of a **sample** or model is another means of creating an express warranty. Section 2–313(1)(c); Section 2A–210 (1)(c). If a sample or model is part of the basis of the bargain, the seller expressly warrants that the entire lot of goods sold shall conform to the sample or model. A sample is a good drawn from the bulk of goods comprising the subject matter of the sale. A model, by comparison, is offered for inspection when the subject matter is not at hand; it is not drawn from the bulk. Section 2–313, Comment 6.

---

## CISG

*The seller must deliver goods which conform to quality and description required by the contract. In addition, the goods must possess the qualities of any sample or model used by the seller.*

---

***Basis of Bargain*** The Code does not require that the buyer rely on the affirmations, promises, descriptions, samples, or models the seller makes or uses but only that they constitute a part of the basis of the bargain. If they are part of the buyer's assumption underlying the sale, then reliance by the buyer is presumed. Some courts merely require that the buyer know of the affirmation or promise for it to be presumed to be part of the basis of the bargain. Relaxing the reliance requirement more often forces sellers to live up to their express warranties than does a rule requiring reliance.

Because they may constitute part of the basis of the bargain just as much as statements in advertisements or catalogs would, statements or promises the seller makes to the buyer prior to the sale may be express warranties. Furthermore, under the Code, statements or promises made by the seller subsequent to the contract of sale may become express warranties even though no new consideration is given. Sections 2–209(1) and 2A–208(1) provide that an agreement modifying a sale

or lease needs no consideration to be binding. Thus, a statement, promise, or assurance with respect to the goods that the seller makes to the buyer at the time of delivery may be considered a binding modification of the prior contract of sale and held to be an express warranty basic to the bargain.

 *See Cases 24–1 and 24–2*

## Implied Warranties

An implied warranty, unlike an express warranty, is not found in the language of the sales contract or in a specific affirmation or promise by the seller. Instead, an **implied warranty** is an obligation imposed by operation of law upon the transfer of property or contract rights. This warranty, which arises out of the circumstances under which the parties enter into their contract, depends on factors such as the type of contract or sale entered into, the seller's merchant or non-merchant status, the conduct of the parties, and the applicability of other statutes. The law has developed implied warranties not as something to which the parties must agree but as a departure from the early rule of *caveat emptor*.

***Merchantability*** At early common law, a seller was not held to any implied warranty as to the quality of goods. Under the Code, however, a **merchant seller** impliedly warrants the merchantability of goods that are of the kind in which she deals. The implied warranty of **merchantability** provides that the goods are reasonably fit for the ordinary purposes for which they are used, pass without objection in the trade under the contract description, and are of fair, average quality. Section 2–314; Section 2A–212. Because the warranty arises as a matter of law, the buyer does not need to prove that she relied on the warranty or that the warranty formed a basis of the bargain. The warranty applies automatically unless disclaimed by the seller. The official Comments to the Code further provide that a contract for the sale of secondhand goods "involves only such obligation as is appropriate to such goods for that is their description."

The Code in Sections 2–314(3) and 2A–212(3) expressly provides that implied warranties may arise from course of dealing or usage of trade. Thus, where the seller of a new automobile failed to lubricate it before delivery to the buyer, and the evidence established that it was the regular custom and usage of new car dealers to do so, the seller was held liable to the buyer for the resulting damages to the automobile in an action for breach of implied warranty.

The Code further provides that the serving for value of food or drink to be consumed on the premises or elsewhere is a sale. Section 2–314(1). Where a nonedible substance in food causes an injury, however, an implied warranty may not exist if the substance is natural to the food. A minority of jurisdictions distinguish between natural objects in food, such as fish bones in fish, and foreign objects such as a pebble, a piece of wire, or glass. The modern and majority test is the reasonable expectation of the consumer. That a substance is natural to a product in one stage of preparation does not necessarily imply that the consumer will reasonably anticipate or expect it to be in the final product.

 *See Case 24–2*

## CISG

*The seller must deliver goods, unless otherwise agreed, which are fit for any particular purpose expressly or impliedly made known to the seller by the buyer, except, where the buyer did not rely on the seller's skill and judgment where it was unreasonable for the buyer to rely on the seller.*

***Fitness for Particular Purpose***   Unlike the warranty of merchantability, the implied warranty of fitness for a particular purpose applies to *any* seller, whether he is a merchant or not. The **implied warranty of fitness for a particular purpose** arises if at the time of sale the seller had reason to know the buyer's particular purpose and that the buyer was relying upon the seller's skill and judgment to select suitable goods. Section 2–315; Section 2A–213.

The implied warranty of fitness for a particular purpose does not require any specific statement by the seller. Rather, the warranty requires only that the seller know that the buyer is relying on the seller's expertise in selecting a product for the buyer's specific purpose. The buyer need not specifically inform the seller of her particular purpose; it is sufficient if the seller has reason to know it. On the other hand, the implied warranty of fitness for a particular purpose would not arise if the buyer were to insist on a particular product and the seller simply conveyed it to her.

In contrast to the implied warranty of merchantability, the implied warranty of fitness for a particular purpose pertains to the *specific* purpose of the goods. The courts disagree whether an ordinary purpose of goods can be a particular purpose. Goods that are fit for ordinary purposes, and therefore are merchantable, may nonetheless be unfit for a particular purpose. A particular purpose may be a specific use or relate to a special situation in which the buyer intends to use the goods. Thus, if Miller has reason to know that Levine is purchasing a pair of shoes for mountain climbing and that Levine is relying upon Miller's judgment to furnish shoes suitable for this purpose, an implied warranty of fitness for a particular purpose would arise in this sale. If Miller sold Levine shoes suitable only for ordinary walking purposes, Miller would breach this implied warranty. Likewise, a buyer indicates to a seller that she needs a stamping machine to stamp 10,000 packages in an eight-hour period and that she relies on the seller to select an appropriate machine. By selecting the machine, the seller impliedly warrants that the machine selected will stamp 10,000 packages in an eight-hour period.

**Reliance** is therefore required for this warranty, unlike an express warranty, which requires only that the affirmation meet the broad "basis of the bargain" test, or the implied warranty of merchantability, which requires no proof of reliance. In order to prevail in a case involving an implied warranty of fitness for a particular purpose, the buyer must be able to demonstrate specifically that she relied on the seller's skill or judgment in selecting or furnishing suitable goods.

 *See Case 24–2*

## CISG

*The seller must deliver goods, unless otherwise agreed, which are fit for the purposes for which goods of the same description would ordinarily be used.*

## *OBSTACLES TO WARRANTY ACTIONS*

In certain respects, warranty claims offer injured persons many advantages. Generally, a plaintiff need only establish the existence and breach of a warranty, an injury resulting from the breach, and the giving of notice in order to recover in a warranty action. This makes warranty claims easier to bring than negligence cases, which require the plaintiff to show that the defendant failed to act with due care—often a difficult task. Nonetheless, a number of technical obstacles limit the effectiveness of warranty as a basis for recovery. These include disclaimers of warranties, limitations or modifications of warranties, privity, notice of breach, and the conduct of the plaintiff. These obstacles vary considerably from jurisdiction to jurisdiction.

## Disclaimer of Warranties

The Code calls for a reasonable construction of words or conduct to **disclaim** (negate) or limit warranties. Section 2–316; Section 2A–214. The Code makes clear that the seller should not rely on a time-honored formula of words and expect to obtain a disclaimer that may go unnoticed by the buyer. To be effective, disclaimers must be positive, explicit, unequivocal, and conspicuous.

*Express Exclusions* A **warranty of title** may be excluded only by specific language or by certain circumstances, including judicial sales or sales by sheriffs, executors, or foreclosing lienors. Section 2–312(2); Section 2A–214(4). In the latter cases the seller is manifestly offering to sell only such right or title as he or a third person might have in the goods, as it is apparent that the goods are not the property of the person selling them.

In general, a seller cannot provide an **express warranty** and then disclaim it. A seller can avoid making an express warranty, however, by carefully refraining from making any promise or affirmation of fact relating to the goods, refraining from making a description of the goods, or refraining from using a sample or model. Section 2–313; Section 2A–210. A seller also may be able to negate an express warranty by *clear, specific, unambiguous* language. The Code, however, provides that words or conduct relevant to the creation of an express warranty and words or conduct negating a warranty shall be construed wherever reasonable as consistent with each other and that a negation or limitation is inoperative to the extent that such construction is unreasonable. Section 2–316; Section 2A–214. For example, a seller and a buyer enter into a written contract for the sale of a camera in which the seller warrants that the camera being sold is free of defects. This express warranty renders inoperative another provision in the contract that attempts to disclaim liability for any repairs necessitated by defects in the camera. The inconsistency between the two contractual provisions makes the disclaimer ineffective. Moreover, if the seller's disclaimer attempts to negate "all express warranties," this general disclaimer would be ineffective against the specific express warranty providing that the camera is free of defects. Finally, oral warranties made prior to the execution of a written agreement that contains an express disclaimer are subject to the parol evidence rule. Thus, as discussed in Chapter 15, if the parties intend the written contract to be the final and complete statement of the agreement between them, oral evidence of warranties that contradict the terms of the written contract is inadmissible.

To exclude an **implied warranty of merchantability,** the language of disclaimer must mention merchantability and, in the case of a writing, must be *conspicuous.* Section 2–316(2). Article 2A requires that a disclaimer of an implied warranty of merchantability mention merchantability, be in writing, and be conspicuous. Section 2A–214(2). For example, Bart wishes to buy a used refrigerator from Ben's Used Appliances Store for $100. Given the low purchase price, Ben is unwilling to guarantee the refrigerator's performance. Bart agrees to buy it with no warranty protection. To exclude the warranty, Ben writes conspicuously on the contract, "This refrigerator carries no warranties, including no warranty of MERCHANTABILITY." Ben has effectively disclaimed the implied warranty of merchantability. Some courts, however, do not require the disclaimer to be conspicuous where a *commercial* buyer has actual knowledge of the disclaimer. The Code's test for whether a provision is *conspicuous* is whether a reasonable person against whom the disclaimer is to operate ought to have noticed it. Section 1–201(10).

To exclude or to modify an **implied warranty of fitness** for the particular purpose of the buyer, the disclaimer must be in *writing* and *conspicuous.* Section 2–316(2); Section 2A–214(2).

*All implied warranties,* unless the circumstances indicate otherwise, are excluded by expressions like *as is, with all faults,* or other language plainly calling the buyer's attention to the exclusion of warranties. Section 2–316(3)(a); Section 2A–214(3)(a). Most courts require the "as is" clause to be conspicuous. Implied warranties also may be excluded by course of dealing, course of performance, or usage of trade. Section 2–316(3)(c); Section 2A–214(3)(c).

The courts will invalidate disclaimers they consider unconscionable. Sections 2–302 and 2A–108 of the Code, as discussed in Chapter 21, permit a court to limit the application of any contract or provision of a contract that it finds unconscionable.

 *See Case 24–3*

*Buyer's Examination or Refusal to Examine* If the buyer inspects the goods before entering into the contract, *implied warranties* do not apply to defects that are apparent upon examination. The particular buyer's skill and the normal method of examining goods in the circumstances determine what defects are excluded by examination. Section 2–316, Comment 8. Moreover, no implied warranty exists as to defects which an examination ought to have revealed, not only where the buyer has examined the goods as fully as she desired, but also where the buyer has *refused* to examine the goods. Section 2–316(3)(b); Section 2A–214(3)(b).

A mere failure or omission to examine the goods is not a refusal to examine them. It is not enough that the goods were available for inspection and the buyer did not see fit to inspect them. In order for the buyer to have "refused to examine the goods," the seller *must* first have demanded that the buyer examine them.

 *See Case 24–3*

## CISG

*If at the time of entering into the sales contract the buyer knew or could not have been unaware of the lack of conformity, the seller is not liable for the warranty of particular purpose, ordinary purpose, or sale by sample or model.*

*Federal Legislation Relating to Warranties of Consumer Goods* To protect purchasers of **consumer goods** (defined as "tangible personal property normally used for personal, family, or household purposes"), Congress enacted the **Magnuson-Moss Warranty Act**. The purpose of the act is to prevent deception and to make available to consumer purchasers adequate information with respect to warranties. Some courts have applied the act to leases.

The Federal Trade Commission administers and enforces the act. The commission's guidelines regarding the type of information a seller must set forth in warranties of consumer products are aimed at providing the consumer with clear and useful information. More significantly, the act provides that a seller who makes a written warranty cannot disclaim *any* implied warranty. For a complete discussion of the act, see Chapter 42.

◆ *See Figure 24–1*

## Limitation or Modification of Warranties

Sometimes a seller is willing to give some warranty protection but wishes to limit the scope or type of protection she gives. For example, a seller who is willing to repair or replace a defective product may not be willing to pay consequential damages, such as the buyer's lost profits, arising from any product defects. Sections 2–719 and 2A–503 of the Code permit a seller to *limit* or *modify* the buyer's remedies for breach of warranty. Two important exceptions to the seller's right are Sections 2–719(3) and 2A–503(3), which prohibit "unconscionable" limitations or exclusions of consequential damages. Specifically, the limitation of consequential damages for injury to the person in the case of consumer goods is prima facie unconscionable.

In some cases, a seller may choose not to limit the buyer's rights to seek damages for breach of warranty but to impose time limits within which the warranty is effective. Except for instances of unconscionability, the Code permits such clauses; it does not, however, permit any attempt to shorten to less than one year the time period for filing an action for personal injury.

## Privity of Contract

Because of the association of warranties with contracts, a principle of law in the nineteenth century established that a plaintiff could not recover for breach of warranty unless he was in a contractual relationship with the defendant. This relationship is known as privity of contract.

**Horizontal privity** pertains to noncontracting parties who are injured by the defective goods; this group would include users, consumers, and bystanders who are not the contracting purchaser. Horizontal privity determines who benefits from a warranty and who may, therefore, sue for its breach.

Under this rule, a warranty by seller Ingrid to buyer Sylvester, who resells the goods to purchaser Lyle under a similar warranty, gives Lyle no rights against Ingrid. There is no privity of contract between Ingrid and Lyle. In the event of breach of warranty, Lyle may recover only from his seller, Sylvester, who in turn may recover from Ingrid.

The Code relaxes the requirement of horizontal privity of contract by permitting recovery on a seller's warranty, at a minimum, to members of the buyer's family or household or to guests in his home. Section 2–318 of the Code provides three alternative sections from which the States may select. *Alternative A,* the least comprehensive and most widely adopted, provides that a seller's warranty, whether express or implied, extends to any natural person who is in the family or household of the buyer or who is a guest in his home, if it is reasonable to expect that such person may use, consume, or be affected by the goods, and who is injured in person by breach of the warranty. *Alternative B* extends Alternative A to any natural person who may reasonably be expected

**FIGURE 24–1** Warranties

| Type of Warranty | How Created | What Is Warranted | How Disclaimed |
|---|---|---|---|
| Title (Section 2–312)/ Use and Possession (2A–211) | Seller contracts to sell goods | • Good title<br>• Rightful transfer | • Specific language<br>• Circumstances giving buyer reason to know that seller does not claim title |
| Express (Section 2–313; Section 2A–210) | • Affirmation of fact<br>• Promise<br>• Description<br>• Sample or model | • Conform to affirmation<br>• Conform to promise<br>• Conform to description<br>• Conform to sample or model | • Specific language (extremely difficult) |
| Merchantability (Section 2–314; Section 2A–212*) | Merchant sells goods | • Fit for ordinary purpose<br>• Adequately contained, packaged, and labeled | • Must mention "merchantability"<br>• If in writing must be conspicuous/in lease must be in writing and conspicuous<br>• As-is sale<br>• Buyer examination<br>• Course of dealing, course of performance, usage of trade |
| Fitness for a particular purpose (Section 2–315; Section 2A–213*) | Seller knows buyer is relying upon seller to select goods suitable for buyer's particular purpose | Fit for particular purpose | • No buzzwords necessary<br>• Must be in writing and conspicuous<br>• As-is sale<br>• Buyer examination<br>• Course of dealing, course of performance, usage of trade |

*except in a finance lease

to use, consume, or be affected by the goods. *Alternative C* further expands the coverage of the section to any person, not just natural persons, and to property damage as well as personal injury. (A natural person would not include artificial entities such as corporations.) A seller may not exclude or limit the operation of this section for injury to a person. Section 2A–216 provides the same alternatives with slight modifications.

Nonetheless, the Code merely sets a minimum standard that the States may expand through case law. Most States have judicially accepted the Code's invitation to relax the requirements of horizontal privity and, for all practical purposes, have *eliminated* horizontal privity in warranty cases.

**Vertical privity**, in determining who is liable for breach of warranty, pertains to remote sellers within the chain of distribution, such as manufacturers and wholesalers, with whom the consumer purchaser has not entered into a contract. Although the Code adopts a neutral position regarding vertical privity, the courts in most States have eliminated the requirement of vertical privity in warranty actions.

## Notice of Breach of Warranty

When a buyer has accepted a tender of goods that are not as warranted by the seller, she is required to notify the seller of any breach of warranty within a reasonable time after she has discovered or should have discovered it. If the buyer fails to notify the seller of any breach within a reasonable time, she is barred from any remedy against the seller. Section 2–607(3)(a); Section 2A–516(3)(a).

The purpose of the reasonable notice requirement is (1) to enable the seller to cure the defect or to minimize the buyer's loss, (2) to provide the seller an opportunity to prepare for conflict resolution and litigation, and (3) to provide the seller with an end point to liability. In determining whether notice was provided within a reasonable time, commercial standards apply to a merchant buyer whereas standards designed to preserve a good faith consumer's right to his remedy apply to a retail consumer.

## Plaintiff's Conduct

Because warranty liability developed in the law of sales and contracts, in most States contributory negligence of the buyer is no defense to an action against the seller for breach of warranty. In some States, however, comparative negligence statutes apply to warranty actions. (Comparative negligence is discussed more fully later in this chapter.)

If the buyer discovers a defect in the goods that may cause injury and then proceeds to make use of the goods, he will not be permitted to recover damages from the seller for loss or injuries caused by such use. This is not contributory negligence but **voluntary assumption** of a known risk.

## STRICT LIABILITY IN TORT

The most recent and far-reaching development in the field of products liability is that of strict liability in tort. All but a very few States have now accepted the concept, which is embodied in **Section 402A** of the Restatement, Second, of Torts. A new Restatement of the Law, Third, Torts: Products Liability, has recently been promulgated. It is far more comprehensive than the second Restatement in dealing with the liability of commercial sellers and distributors of goods for harm caused by their products.

Section 402A imposes **strict liability in tort** on merchant sellers for both personal injuries and property damage resulting from selling a product in a **defective condition, unreasonably dangerous** to the user or consumer. Section 402A applies even though "the seller has exercised all possible care in the preparation and sale of his product." Thus, negligence is not the basis of liability in strict liability cases. The essential distinction between

the two doctrines is that actions in strict liability do not require the plaintiff to prove that the injury-producing defect resulted from any specific act of negligence of the seller. Strict liability actions focus on the product, not on the conduct of the manufacturer. Courts in strict liability cases are interested in the fact that a product defect arose—not in how it arose. Thus, even an "innocent" manufacturer—one who has not been negligent—may be liable if his product contains a defect that injures a consumer.

The reasons asserted in support of imposing strict liability in tort upon manufacturers and assemblers of products include the following: (1) consumers should be given maximum protection against dangerous defects in products; (2) manufacturers are in the best position to prevent or reduce the hazards to life and health in defective products; (3) manufacturers, who realize the most profit from the total sales of their goods, are best able to carry the financial burden of such liability by distributing it among the public as a cost of doing business; (4) manufacturers utilize wholesalers and retailers merely as conduits in the marketing of their products and should not be permitted to avoid liability simply because they have no contract with the user or consumer; and (5) because the manufacturer is liable to his purchaser who may be a wholesaler who in turn is liable to the retailer who in turn is liable to the ultimate purchaser, time and expense is saved by making liability direct rather than a chain reaction.

Although liability for personal injuries caused by a product in an unreasonably dangerous defective condition is usually associated with sales of goods, such liability also exists with respect to **leases** and **bailments** of defective goods. The extension of liability to lessors and bailors of goods is not surprising in view of the rationale the courts have developed in imposing strict liability in tort upon manufacturers and sellers of products. The danger to which the public is exposed by defectively manufactured cars and trucks traveling on the highways, for example, does not differ greatly from the hazards of defective cars and trucks leased to operators.

## *REQUIREMENTS OF STRICT LIABILITY*

Section 402A imposes strict liability in tort on merchant sellers for both personal injuries and property damage that result from selling a product in a defective condition unreasonably dangerous to the user or consumer. Specifically, this section provides:

1. One who sells any product in a defective condition unreasonably dangerous to the user or consumer or to his property is subject to liability for physical harm thereby caused to the ultimate user or consumer, or to his property, if (a) the seller is engaged in the business of selling such a product, and (b) it is expected to and does reach the user or consumer without substantial change in the condition in which it is sold.
2. The rule stated in Subsection (1) applies although (a) the seller has exercised all possible care in the preparation and sale of his product, and (b) the user or consumer has not bought the product from or entered into any contractual relation with the seller.

Negligence, as previously stated, is not the basis of this liability; it applies even though "the seller has exercised all possible care in the preparation and sale of his product." The seller is not an insurer of the goods which he manufactures or sells, however; and the essential requirements for strict product liability are that (1) the defendant was engaged in the business of selling such a product; (2) the defendant sold the product in a defective condition; (3) the defective condition was one which made the product unreasonably dangerous to the user or consumer or to his property; (4) the defect in the product existed at the time it left the hands of the defendant; (5) the plaintiff sustained physical harm or property damage by use or consumption of the product; and (6) the defective condition was the proximate cause of such injury or damage.

This liability is imposed by law as a matter of public policy and does not depend upon contract, either express or implied. It does not require reliance by the injured user or consumer upon any statements made by the manufacturer or seller. The liability is not limited to persons in a buyer-seller relationship; thus, neither vertical nor horizontal privity is required. No notice of the defect is required to have been given by the injured user or consumer. The liability, furthermore, is generally not subject to disclaimer, exclusion, or modification by contractual agreement. Rather, the liability is solely in tort and arises out of the common law; it is not governed by the provisions of the Uniform Commercial Code.

The majority of courts considering the question have held that Section 402A imposes liability for injury to person and damage to property (the economic loss doctrine) but not for commercial loss (such as loss of bargain or profits), which is recoverable in an action for breach of warranty. A minority of States have held, however, that commercial loss may be recovered in tort where the defect creates an unreasonable risk of personal injury or property damage, even though the only damage resulting is to the defective goods themselves.

## Merchant Sellers

Section 402A imposes liability only upon a person who is in the *business* of selling the product involved. It does *not* apply to an occasional seller, such as a person who trades in his used car or who sells his lawn mower to a neighbor. In this respect, the section is similar to the implied warranty of merchantability, which applies only to sales by a merchant with respect to goods of the type in which he deals. A growing number of jurisdictions recognize the applicability of strict liability in tort to merchant sellers of *used* goods.

## Defective Condition

In an action against a defendant manufacturer or other seller to recover damages under the rule of strict liability in tort, the plaintiff must prove a defective condition in the product, but she is not required to prove how or why the product became defective. In an action based on Section 402A, the reason for or cause of the defect is not material, although it would be in an action based on negligence. Under a strict liability approach, a manufacturer will be held liable even though it did not act negligently. For example, if the Quality Bottling Company, despite its having the most stringent quality control program in the industry, through no negligence of its own manufactures a bottle that explodes in the hands of a consumer, the company would be liable to the consumer under Section 402A. Whether or not Quality Bottling Company acted negligently is irrelevant. The plaintiff, however, must show that at the time she was injured the condition of the product was not substantially changed from the condition in which the manufacturer or seller sold it. In general, defects may arise through faulty manufacturing, faulty product design, or inadequate warning, labeling, packaging, or instructions.

*Manufacturing Defect* A **manufacturing defect** occurs when the product is not properly made; that is, it fails to meet its own manufacturing specifications. For instance, suppose a chair is manufactured with legs designed to be attached by four screws and glue. If such a chair were produced without the required screws, this would constitute a manufacturing defect.

*Design Defect* A product contains a design defect when, despite its being produced as specified, the product is dangerous or hazardous because of inadequate design. Design defects can result from a number of causes, including poor engineering and poor choice of materials. An example of a design defect that received great notoriety was the Ford Pinto. A number of courts found the car to be inadequately designed because its fuel tank had been placed too close to its rear axle, causing the tank to rupture upon impact from the rear.

Section 402A provides no guidance in determining which injury-producing designs should give rise to strict liability and which should not; consequently, the courts have adopted widely varying approaches in applying 402A to defective design cases.

At one extreme, a few courts have taken a very literal approach to Section 402A by ruling that a manufacturer is strictly liable for injuries caused by a design that a reasonable person would not have produced had he known of the design's harmful character at the time it was made. Whether the manufacturer did or could have known of the risk associated with the design, or of an alternative design that could have avoided the risk, is deemed irrelevant for purposes of strict liability. Manufacturers, in effect, are held liable for hazards that were unknowable at the time they manufactured their products.

A slightly larger number of courts, although still a minority, have taken the opposite approach: recognizing no difference between negligence and strict liability principles in defective design cases, they apply negligence principles to such cases. Unless the plaintiff can demonstrate that the manufacturer knew, or should have known, of a safer, cost-effective design, these courts will not hold the manufacturer liable.

The majority of courts have ostensibly adopted a middle-of-the-road approach, stating that strict liability cases should be viewed differently from negligence cases. Beyond reciting that strict liability cases focus on the product, not on the manufacturer's conduct, these courts have yet to clarify what the different view implies. Nevertheless, virtually none of them has upheld a judgment in a strict liability case in which the defendant demonstrated that the **"state of the art"** was such that the manufacturer (1) neither knew nor could have known of a product hazard, or (2) if he knew of the product hazard, could have designed a safer product given existing technology. Thus, almost all courts evaluate the design of a product on the basis of the dangers that could have been known when the product was produced or sold.

In deciding design defect cases, courts identify any government safety standards applicable to the design involved in the product liability lawsuit. If such a standard exists and the manufacturer's failure to follow it caused the plaintiff's injury, the courts tend to impose liability automatically. On the other hand, a manufacturer's compliance with safety standards does not equal automatic relief from liability. If a plaintiff can demonstrate that a safer, cost-effective design was available to the manufacturer, the plaintiff can still prevail in a product liability lawsuit even though the manufacturer complied with a government safety standard.

***Failure to Warn***  A seller is under a duty to provide adequate warning of possible danger, to provide appropriate directions for safe use, and to package the product safely. Warnings do not, however, always protect sellers from liability. A seller who could have designed or manufactured a product in a safe but cost-effective manner, but who instead chooses to produce the product cheaply and to provide a warning of the product's hazards, cannot escape liability simply through the warning. Warnings usually will avoid liability only if there are no cost-effective designs or manufacturing processes available to reduce a risk of injury.

The duty to give a warning arises out of a foreseeable danger of physical harm resulting from the normal or probable use of the product and out of the likelihood that, unless warned, the user or consumer will not ordinarily be aware of such danger or hazard. For example, a seller may reasonably assume that those with allergies to products such as eggs or strawberries will know of their allergies and therefore need not be warned of this risk. On the other hand, if a product contains an ingredient to which a substantial number of persons are allergic, and the ingredient is one whose danger is not generally known or, if known, is one which the consumer would not reasonably expect to find in the product, the seller is required to give a warning about it. Under strict liability principles, sellers are generally required to provide warnings against uses for which a product is not marketed, including certain instances of consumer misuse, if such uses are foreseeable by the manufacturer and the consumer is unlikely to recognize the hazard.

Section 402A imposes liability in failure-to-warn cases only where the seller "has knowledge, or by the application of reasonable, developed human skill and foresight should have knowledge, of the . . . danger." Comment j. In effect, the seller is held to the knowledge and skill of an expert in the field. Some courts have ruled that this means a manufacturer not only must keep abreast of scientific knowledge, discoveries, and advances, but also must conduct research to determine whether his product contains hazards. Most courts today require proof that the manufacturer knew, or could have known, of a product hazard before imposing liability for a failure to warn.

 *See Case 24–4*

## Unreasonably Dangerous

Section 402A liability applies only if the defective product is unreasonably dangerous to the user or consumer. An **unreasonably dangerous** product is one which contains a danger beyond that which the ordinary consumer, who purchases the product with common knowledge of its characteristics, would contemplate. Thus, "good whiskey is not unreasonably dangerous merely because it will make some people drunk, and is especially dangerous to alcoholics; but bad whiskey, containing a dangerous amount of fuel oil, is unreasonably dangerous. Good tobacco is not unreasonably dangerous merely because the effects of smoking may be harmful; but tobacco containing something like marijuana may be unreasonably dangerous. Good butter is not unreasonably dangerous merely because, if such be the case, it deposits cholesterol in the arteries and leads to heart attacks; but bad butter, contaminated with poisonous fish oil, is unreasonably dangerous." Comment i to Section 402A. Most courts have left the question of reasonable consumer expectations to the jury.

 *See Case 24–5*

## *OBSTACLES TO RECOVERY*

Few of the obstacles to recovery in warranty cases present serious problems to plaintiffs in strict liability actions brought pursuant to Section 402A because this section was drafted largely to avoid such obstacles.

## Disclaimers and Notice

Comment m to Section 402A provides that the basis of strict liability rests solely in tort and therefore is not subject to contractual defenses. The comment specifically states that strict product liability is not governed by the Code, that it is not affected by contractual limitations or disclaimers, and that it is not subject to any requirement that the injured party give notice to the seller within a reasonable time. Nevertheless, most courts have allowed clear and specific disclaimers of Section 402A liability in *commercial* transactions between merchants of relatively equal economic power.

## Privity

With respect to **horizontal privity,** the majority of States hold that the strict liability in tort of manufacturers and other sellers extends not only to buyers, users, and consumers, but also to injured bystanders. Bystanders to whom such liability has extended include the occupants of an automobile injured in a collision with another car due to the other car's having defective brakes; a golfer killed by a runaway golf cart that started due to a faulty transmission system; a bystander injured by a runaway truck started by a short circuit; a bystander injured by the explosion of a defective beer keg; a neighbor injured by the explosion of a propane gas tank; and a bystander injured by the explosion of a shotgun barrel caused by a defective shell. Some States, however, limit liability to foreseeable purchasers or users of the product.

In terms of **vertical privity,** strict liability in tort imposes liability on any seller who is engaged in the business of selling the product, including a wholesaler or distributor as well as the manufacturer and retailer. The rule of strict liability in tort also applies to the manufacturer of a defective component that has been incorporated into a larger product where the manufacturer of the finished product has made no essential change in the component.

## Plaintiff's Conduct

Many product liability defenses relate to the conduct of the plaintiff. The contention common to all of them is that the plaintiff's improper conduct so contributed to the plaintiff's injury that it would be unfair to blame the product or its seller.

*Contributory Negligence* Contributory negligence is conduct on the part of the plaintiff that falls below the standard to which he should conform for his own protection and that is the legal cause of the plaintiff's harm. Under traditional negligence law principles, if the negligence of the plaintiff together with that of the defendant proximately caused the plaintiff's injury, the plaintiff could not recover *any* damages from the defendant. It did not matter whether the plaintiff's contributory negligence was slight or extensive. Because strict liability is designed to assess liability without fault, Section 402A rejects contributory negligence as a defense. Thus, a seller cannot defend a strict liability lawsuit on the basis of a plaintiff's negligent failure to discover a defect or to guard against its possibility. But, as discussed below, contributory negligence in the form of an assumption of the risk can bar recovery under Section 402A.

***Comparative Negligence***  The harshness of the contributory negligence doctrine has caused all but a few States to reject the all-or-nothing rule of contributory negligence and to substitute the doctrine of comparative negligence. Under **comparative negligence,** damages are apportioned between the parties in proportion to the degree of fault or negligence found against them.

Despite Section 402A's bar of contributory negligence in strict liability cases, most courts apply comparative negligence to strict liability cases. (Some courts use the term *comparative responsibility* rather than *comparative negligence.*) There are two basic types of comparative negligence or comparative responsibility. One is **pure comparative responsibility,** which simply reduces the plaintiff's recovery in proportion to her fault, whatever that may be. Thus, the recovery of a plaintiff found to be 80 percent at fault in causing an accident in which she suffered a $100,000 loss would be limited to 20 percent of her damages, or $20,000. By comparison, under **modified comparative responsibility,** the plaintiff recovers according to the general principles of comparative responsibility *unless* she is more than 50 percent responsible for her injuries, in which case she recovers nothing. The majority of comparative negligence States follows the modified comparative responsibility approach.

***Voluntary Assumption of the Risk***  Assumption of risk is a defense in an action based on strict liability in tort. Basically, **assumption of risk** is the plaintiff's express or implied consent to encounter a known danger. The user or consumer who voluntarily uses goods in an unusual, inappropriate, or improper manner for which they were not intended, such use being, under the circumstances, unreasonable, assumes the risk of injuries that result from such use. Thus, a person who drives an automobile after realizing that the brakes are not working or an employee who attempts to remove a foreign object from a high-speed roller press without shutting off the power has assumed the risk of his own injury. In a comparative negligence or comparative responsibility State, assumption of the risk would either reduce or bar recovery, depending on the degree to which it contributed to the plaintiff's injury.

To establish such a defense, the defendant must show that (1) the plaintiff actually knew and appreciated the particular risk or danger the defect created, (2) the plaintiff voluntarily encountered the risk while realizing the danger, and (3) the plaintiff's decision to encounter the known risk was unreasonable.

***Misuse or Abuse of the Product***  Closely connected to voluntary assumption of the risk is the valid defense of misuse or abuse of the product by the injured party. **Misuse** or **abuse** occurs when the injured party knows, or should know, that he is using the product in a manner not contemplated by the seller. The major difference between misuse or abuse and assumption of the risk is that the former includes actions which the injured party does not know to be dangerous, whereas the latter does not. Instances of such misuse or abuse include standing on a rocking chair to change a lightbulb or using a lawn mower to trim hedges.

The courts, however, have significantly limited this defense by requiring that the misuse or abuse not be foreseeable by the seller. If a use is foreseeable, then the seller must take measures to guard against it. For example, if William stands on a rocking chair to change a lightbulb and is injured when the chair tilts and tips over, his misuse of the chair would bar his recovery. Similarly, if Jenny hammers a nail with a hair dryer and suffers an eye injury when a chip flies from the dryer, she will be unsuccessful in a claim against the manufacturer.

## Subsequent Alteration

Section 402A provides that liability exists only if the product reaches "the user or consumer without substantial change in the condition in which it is sold." Accordingly, most, but not all, courts would not hold a manufacturer liable for a faulty carburetor if a car dealer were to remove the part and make significant changes in it prior to reinstalling it in an automobile.

## Statute of Repose

Numerous lawsuits have been brought against manufacturers many years after a product was first sold. In one case, a manufacturer was successfully sued twenty-two years after a defective water meter was first purchased and fourteen years after it was installed in the plaintiff's home. In another case, Volkswagen of America was ordered to pay $1.8 million in damages in an accident case centering around a missing door latch costing 35 cents. The accident occurred ten years after the car had been manufactured and nine years after Volkswagen had informed its dealers about the defect.

In response, many States have adopted **statutes of repose.** These enactments limit the time period—typically to between six and twelve years—for which a manufacturer is liable for injury caused by a defective product. After the statutory period has elapsed, a manufacturer ceases to be liable for such harm.

◆ *See Figure 24–2*

**FIGURE 24–2** Products Liabilities

| Type of Warranty | Warranty of Merchantability* | Strict Liability in Tort |
|---|---|---|
| **Condition of Goods Creating Liability** | Not fit for ordinary purposes | Defective condition, unreasonably dangerous |
| **Type of Transaction Covered** | Sales and leases (except finance leases); some courts apply bailments of goods | Sales, leases, and bailments of goods |
| **Disclaimer** | Must mention "merchantability" If in writing, must be conspicuous (lease must be in writing) Must not be unconscionable Sales subject to Magnuson-Moss Act/leases may be subject | Not possible in consumer transactions; may be permitted in commercial transactions |
| **Notice to Seller** | Required within reasonable time | Not required |
| **Causation** | Required | Required |
| **Who May Sue** | In some States, buyer and the buyer's family or guests in home; in other States, any person who may be expected to use, consume, or be affected by goods | Any user or consumer of product; also, in most States, any bystander |
| **Compensable Harms** | Personal injury, property damage, economic loss | Personal injury, property damage |
| **Who May Be Sued** | Seller or lessor who is a merchant with respect to the goods sold | Seller who is a merchant with respect to the goods sold |

*The warranty of fitness for a particular purpose differs from the warranty of merchantability in the following respects: (1) the condition that triggers liability is the failure of the goods to perform according to the particular purpose of the warranty and (2) a disclaimer need not mention "fitness for a particular purpose but must be in writing."

 # Chapter Summary

## Warranties

| Types of Warranties | **Definition of Warranty** an obligation of the seller to the buyer concerning title, quality, characteristics, or condition of goods **Warranty of Title** the obligation of a seller to convey the right to ownership without any lien (in a lease the warranty protects the lessee's right to possess and use the goods) **Express Warranty** an affirmation of fact or promise about the goods or a description, including a sample, of the goods that becomes part of the basis of the bargain |
|---|---|

**Implied Warranty** a contractual obligation, arising out of certain circumstances of the sale, imposed by operation of law and not found in the language of the sales contract
- *Merchantability* warranty by a merchant seller that the goods are reasonably fit for the ordinary purpose for which they are manufactured or sold, pass without objection in the trade under the contract description, and are of fair, average quality
- *Fitness for Particular Purpose* warranty by any seller that goods are reasonably fit for a particular purpose if, at the time of contracting, the seller had reason to know the buyer's particular purpose and that the buyer was relying on the seller's skill and judgment to furnish suitable goods

**Obstacles to Warranty Actions**

**Disclaimers of Warranties** negations of warranties
- *Express Warranty* not usually possible to disclaim
- *Warranty of Title* may be excluded or modified by specific language or by certain circumstances, including judicial sale or a sale by a sheriff, executor, or foreclosing lienor
- *Implied Warranty of Merchantability* the disclaimer must mention "merchantability" and, in the case of a writing, must be conspicuous (in a lease the disclaimer must be in writing)
- *Implied Warranty of Fitness for a Particular Purpose* the disclaimer must be in writing and conspicuous
- *Other Disclaimers of Implied Warranties* the implied warranties of merchantability and fitness for a particular purpose may also be disclaimed (1) by expressions like "as is," "with all faults," or other similar language; (2) by course of dealing, course of performance, or usage of trade; or (3) as to defects an examination ought to have revealed where the buyer has examined the goods or where the buyer has refused to examine the goods
- *Federal Legislation Relating to Warranties of Consumer Goods* the Magnuson-Moss Warranty Act protects purchasers of consumer goods by providing that warranty information be clear and useful and that a seller who makes a written warranty cannot disclaim any implied warranty

**Limitation or Modification of Warranties** permitted as long as it is not unconscionable

**Privity of Contract** a contractual relationship between parties that was necessary at common law to maintain a lawsuit
- *Horizontal Privity* doctrine determining who benefits from a warranty and who therefore may bring a cause of action; the Code provides three alternatives
- *Vertical Privity* doctrine determining who in the chain of distribution is liable for a breach of warranty; the Code has not adopted a position on this

**Notice of Breach** if the buyer fails to notify the seller of any breach within a reasonable time, she is barred from any remedy against the seller

**Plaintiff's Conduct**
- *Contributory Negligence* is not a defense
- *Voluntary Assumption of the Risk* is a defense

# Strict Liability in Tort

**Nature**

**General Rule** imposes tort liability on merchant sellers for both personal injuries and property damage for selling a product in a defective condition unreasonably dangerous to the user or consumer

**Defective Condition**
- *Manufacturing Defect* by failing to meet its own manufacturing specifications, the product is not properly made

> - *Design Defect* the product, though made as designed, is dangerous because the design is inadequate
> - *Failure to Warn* failure to provide adequate warnings of possible danger or to provide appropriate directions for use of a product
>
> **Unreasonably Dangerous** contains a danger beyond that which would be contemplated by the ordinary consumer

| **Obstacles to Recovery** | **Contractual Defenses** defenses such as privity, disclaimers, and notice generally do not apply to tort liability<br>**Plaintiff's Conduct**<br>• *Contributory Negligence* not a defense in the majority of States<br>• *Comparative Negligence* most States have applied the rule of comparative negligence to strict liability in tort<br>• *Voluntary Assumption of the Risk* is a defense<br>• *Misuse or Abuse of the Product* is a defense<br>**Subsequent Alteration** liability exists only if the product reaches the user or consumer without substantial change in the condition in which it is sold<br>**Statute of Repose** limits the time period for which a manufacturer is liable for injury caused by its product |
|---|---|

 # Cases

### CASE 24–1
## Express Warranties
# *CIPOLLONE v. LIGGETT GROUP, INC.*
United States Court of Appeals, Third Circuit, 1990
893 F.2d 541, *aff'd* in part and *rev'd* in part 505 U.S. 504, 112 Ct. 2608, 120 L.Ed. 2d 407, 1992

BECKER, J.
[Between 1942 and her death in 1984, Rose Cipollone smoked between one and two packs of cigarettes a day. Upon her death in 1984 from lung cancer, Rose's husband Antonio Cipollone filed suit against the Liggett Group, Inc., Lorillard, Inc., and Philip Morris, Inc., three of the leading firms in the tobacco industry, for the wrongful death of his wife. Many theories of liability and defenses were asserted in this decidedly complex and protracted litigation.

One theory of liability claimed by Mr. Cipollone was breach of express warranty. It is uncontested that all three manufacturers ran multimedia ad campaigns that contained affirmations, promises, or innuendos

that smoking cigarettes was safe. For example, ads for Chesterfield cigarettes boasted that a medical specialist could find no adverse health effects in subjects after six months of smoking. Chesterfields were also advertised as being manufactured with "electronic miracle" technology which made them "better and safer for you." Another ad stated that Chesterfield ingredients were tested and approved by scientists from leading universities. Another brand, L&M, publicly touted the "miracle tip" filter, claiming it was "just what the doctor ordered."

At trial, the defendant tobacco companies were not permitted to try and prove that Mrs. Cipollone disbelieved or placed no reliance on the advertisements and their safety assurances. The jury returned a verdict for $400,000 on the breach of express warranty claim. The defendant tobacco companies appealed.]

\* \* \*

Authority on the question whether reliance is a necessary element of § 2–313 [express warranty] is divided. Although a few courts have held that reliance is not a necessary element of § 2–313, the more common view has been that it is, and that either a buyer must prove reliance in order to recover on an express warranty or the seller must be permitted to rebut a presumption of reliance in order to preclude recovery.

\* \* \*

Liggett argues that reliance must have some place in the "basis of the bargain" determination. Thus, even if reliance should be assumed, based on what "would reasonably induce the purchase of a product," a defendant must have an opportunity to prove non-reliance. This position finds some support in the U.C.C. comments. \* \* \* The plain language of these comments supports Liggett's position, at least to the extent it indicates that a defendant must be given some opportunity to show that the seller's statements were not meant to be part of the basis of the bargain.

\* \* \*

The above arguments notwithstanding, it is possible to read the "basis of the bargain" requirement as requiring some subjective inducement of the buyer, without requiring a reliance finding. Requiring that the buyer *rely* on an advertisement, whether by imposing this burden initially on the buyer bringing suit, or by allowing the seller to rebut a presumption of reliance, puts a heavy burden on the buyer—a burden that is arguably inconsistent with the U.C.C. as a whole, with other comments to § 2–313 in particular, and with several commentators' suggestions in this area.

\* \* \*

We believe that the most reasonable construction of § 2–313 is neither Liggett's reliance theory, which fails to explain how reliance can be relevant to "what a seller agreed to sell," or the district court's purely objective theory, which fails to explain how an advertisement that a buyer never even saw becomes part of the "basis of the bargain." Instead, we believe that the New Jersey Supreme Court would hold that a plaintiff effectuates

the "basis of the bargain" requirement of § 2–313 by proving that she read, heard, saw or knew of the advertisement containing the affirmation of fact or promise. Such proof will suffice "to weave" the affirmation of fact or promise "into the fabric of the agreement," U.C.C. Comment 3, and thus make it part of the basis of the bargain. We hold that once the buyer has become aware of the affirmation of fact or promise, the statements are presumed to be part of the "basis of the bargain" unless the defendant, by "clear affirmative proof," shows that the buyer knew that the affirmation of fact or promise was untrue.

\* \* \*

Applying our interpretation of § 2–313 to the case at bar, we conclude that the district court's jury instructions were erroneous for two reasons. First, they did not require the plaintiff to prove that Mrs. Cipollone had read, seen, or heard the advertisements at issue. Second, they did not permit the defendant to prove that although Mrs. Cipollone had read, seen, or heard the advertisements, she did not believe the safety assurances contained therein. We must therefore reverse and remand for a new trial on this issue.

\* \* \*

Liggett contends that it is entitled to judgment n.o.v. on the express warranty claim because the record contains insufficient evidence to support a jury verdict for Mr. Cipollone on this point. At the outset, we note that the express warranty provision of the Uniform Commercial Code, § 2–313, makes clear that no formality or magic words are required to create an express warranty. "It is not necessary to the creation of an express warranty that the seller use formal words such as 'warrant' or 'guarantee' or that he have a specific intention to make a warranty. . . ." § 2–313(2). The seller may be liable if its representation regarding the goods takes the form of newspaper, magazine, radio or television advertisements. [Citation.] Consequently, Mr. Cipollone was free to rely, as he did, on advertisements to prove the existence and scope of Liggett's warranty.

\* \* \*

Neither do we find, as Liggett contends, that there was insufficient evidence to prove that Mrs. Cipollone's smoking caused her cancer. \* \* \*

The statistical correlation between heavy smoking and lung cancer is well-documented. * * *

For the foregoing reasons we will: * * * remand for a new trial.

[Authors' note: this case was appealed on the issue of federal preemption of common law claims arising after January 1, 1966 and was reversed in part and affirmed in part by the U.S. Supreme Court.]

---

## CASE 24–2
### Express Warranties/Implied Warranties
### *IN RE L.B. TRUCKING, INC.*
United States Bankruptcy Court, D Del, February 3, 1994
163 BR 709, 23 UCC Rep Serv.2d 1092

BALICK, J.
Dudley B. Durham, Jr. and Barbara L. Durham, husband and wife, and their farming and trucking corporations, Double D Farms, Inc. and L.B. Trucking, Inc. filed Chapter 11 petitions on December 20, 1983. Later, these cases were consolidated. * * * On March 5, 1985, the Chapter 11 case of the consolidated debtors was converted to a Chapter 7 case. (James L. Patton was appointed Trustee of the Chapter 7 estate.)

At the time of trial this adversary proceeding involved a claim by Southern States Cooperative, Inc. (Southern States) for monies owed in connection with its sale and application of herbicides and other chemicals on the Durhams' farm fields. The Trustee was pursuing the Durhams' counterclaims contending that these herbicides were negligently misapplied and also breached the various UCC warranties which caused severe crop damage to the Durhams' 1983 harvest.

* * *

After consideration of the relevant facts and the applicable law, the court concludes that Southern States is not entitled to any recovery and that the Trustee, on behalf of the consolidated debtors' estate, is entitled to recover in full on its products liability claims, . . . .

## Background

Dudley Durham, Jr. has been a farmer most of his life and has been farming on his own since 1972. Durham leased most of the farmland he cultivated and handled most of the planting and other farming operations himself while his wife, Barbara Durham, maintained the farm business' books and records. * * *

The facts leading to this controversy arise from the Durhams' dealings with Southern States concerning the planting of their 1983 crops. Southern States is a farmers' cooperative that engages in the business of supplying farmers with various agricultural supplies like seed, fertilizer, feed, herbicides, and other farm products as well as certain services in connection with these products. * * * Durham had done business with Southern States before switching to Flo-N-Gro, Inc. as his supplier, but due in part to the substantial debt accumulated to Flo-N-Gro and other creditors, Durham approached Southern States once again prior to planting his 1983 corn and bean crops.

In April of 1983, Durham contacted Richard Thomas, the Southern States Middletown store manager, about arranging for the application of herbicides. Durham planned to use "no-till" farming for most of his 1983 crops. The "no-till" farming procedure does not require plowing or disking of the ground like the conventional plow mode of farming; instead, the farmer kills and controls weeds through the application of herbicides and then plants the seed with a special planter machine designed to plant in untilled soil. Durham apparently had done "no-till" farming in 1980, but did not personally apply the chemicals because he feared the potential health risks. * * * In any event, Durham explained to Thomas that he wanted to use "no-till" farming for most of his 1983 corn and bean crops and discussed credit terms generally regarding the chemicals. At this initial meeting, Thomas extended to Durham a $2,000 line of credit to purchase starter fertilizer known as "10–24–0" to begin his corn planting. Nevertheless, Thomas told Durham that a crop lien would be necessary for additional credit on the rest of the needed chemicals.

Subsequently, on May 5 or 6, 1983, Durham met Thomas again, this time accompanied by his father. The elder Durham signed a credit application with Southern States so that he might guarantee any credit extended to his son. During this meeting, the younger Durham told Thomas words to the effect of "Richard, you know I'm trying to pay, get straightened around and get all my stuff straightened around. I want it done the cheapest way, the best way it can be done." In response, Thomas replied, "Will do." The two Durhams and Thomas then went into a small room of the Middletown store where Thomas outlined with some specificity the herbicidal chemicals he proposed to use on Durham's fields. Thomas stated that water would be employed as a carrier for the herbicides with nitrogen being applied by drop nozzling at a rate of 150 lbs. per acre after the crops were standing. The alternative to using a water-based carrier for the chemicals would be to use a 30% nitrogen solution which was more expensive than using water as a carrier and violated the recommendations of the University of Delaware's Department of Agriculture. The junior Durham had no experience or expertise on herbicidal chemicals and relied on Thomas' briefing on the various herbicide mixtures in choosing which ones to apply. Yet, the younger Durham did emphasize to Thomas that a large number of acres per day would require spraying in order to keep up with Durham's heavy planting schedule. Thomas answered that the 1983 season was a normal year in terms of the number of acres to be sprayed by Southern States, and in most instances, Southern States was able to keep up with the farmers.

Durham actually began planting his crops a few days before his early May meeting with Thomas. Gilbert McClements, the principal Southern States herbicide applicator for Durham's fields, began spraying on May 8, 1983.

*  *  *

In sum, Durham's 1983 farming operations consisted of roughly 740 acres of corn, about 230 acres of beans, and a winter wheat crop.

As to the herbicidal chemical applications by McClements, spray tickets were issued by Southern States detailing the job date, location, approximate acreage, and the various chemicals used in each application. McClements received instructions concerning which chemicals to apply from his superiors at Southern States, namely, Mr. Thomas and Mr. Fox. McClements would mix the herbicides each day prior to spraying, but apparently did not make extensive prespraying inspections of the grass and weeds nor did he perform a "hands and knees" inspection of the planted corn prior to spraying.

After planting the corn and bean crop, Durham observed a significant number of weeds and grasses that had escaped the herbicidal treatment and the correspondingly low crop population. Durham promptly notified Southern States of these difficulties. On June 1, 1983, Thomas visited several of Durham's fields and indicated to Durham that Southern States would remedy the problem. As a result, numerous acres were resprayed by Southern States and fields with very low plant populations were replanted. Nevertheless, the 1983 corn and bean harvest was dismal and far below the County average.

*  *  *

## Discussion

The issues involved are: whether Southern States' herbicidal chemicals were negligently applied; [and] whether Southern States breached UCC warranties * * * . Collateral to the product liability claims, and asserted as an affirmative defense by the Trustee against Southern States' claim, is whether Southern States may recover payment for the chemicals and their application.

*  *  *

***Product Liability Claims Against Southern States For Alleged Harm Resulting from Use of Its Chemicals***  Delaware does not have strict products liability arising out of the sale of goods. [Citation.] (UCC warranty provisions on sales preempt judicial extension of strict liability in tort involving sale of goods.) Consequently, those claiming injury from defective products in Delaware must seek recovery under a negligence and/or warranty rubric rather than a theory premised on strict liability in tort. [Citations.]

*  *  *

***B. Warranty***  The Delaware version of the UCC provides for three types of warranties arising from the sale of goods: (1) express warranties, U.C.C. § 2–313, (2) implied warranties of merchantability U.C.C. § 2–314, and (3) implied warranties for a particular purpose, U.C.C. § 2–315. These warranties are mutually exclusive and independent of one another but each type of warranty may arise out of the sale of goods depending on the facts surrounding the sale. See U.C.C. § 2–102.

Southern States maintains that UCC warranties are inapplicable here since the contract between itself and

Durham was primarily a service contract for the application of herbicides. When a contract appears to be a mixed contract involving both goods and services, Delaware law requires the court to ascertain whether the contract is predominately one for the sale of goods or if it is mostly a services contract. [Citation.] In this case, the predominant purpose of the entire transaction was to purchase herbicides for Durham's no-till farming operations and, ancillary to this sale, Durham needed a trained herbicide applicator to spray the fields because he lacked the technical knowledge to competently do the job.

\* \* \*

**1. *Express Warranty*** An express warranty may be created by a seller through: (1) any affirmation of fact or promise to the buyer relating to the goods which becomes the basis of the bargain so that the goods conform to the affirmation or promise; (2) any description of the goods which is made part of the basis of the bargain so that the whole of the goods conform to the sample of model. U.C.C. § 2–313(1)(a)–(c). The question of whether an express warranty has been made in a particular transaction is for the trier of fact. [Citation.] In the case at bar, there are no written express warranties claimed, but instead, oral statements made principally by the Middletown store manager, Thomas, to Durham which the Trustee contends were express warranties.

The relevant testimony concerning Thomas' statements to Durham reveal several oral express warranties concerning the herbicides and their application which Southern States plainly breached. First, Thomas stated that water would be the carrier for the herbicides, especially since Durham wanted the job done inexpensively. In its application, Southern States used the nitrogen solution regardless of the University of Delaware recommendations dissuading its use and despite the fact that it is more expensive than using water as a carrier. Southern States' reference to the common trade usage of nitrogen in 1983 is inapposite in an action for breach of express warranty because it is the affirmation or promise—not the custom or trade usage—which becomes the standard against which a breach is determined. In addition, Thomas' statements were more than "seller's talk" or puffing in that they were product-specific and not overly broad or vague. Second, Thomas also made statements regarding the effectiveness of the herbicides in removing weeds and grass so as to promote successful no-till farming. The purchase of herbicides is characteristically the subject of express warranties because the buyer of the product cannot determine its effectiveness prior to use and evaluate its effectiveness in a given situation. Here, Thomas' statements in early May of 1983 were part of the basis of the bargain upon which Durham relied when purchasing the herbicides. Beyond this, Thomas had superior knowledge about the herbicides as opposed to Durham who had little or none. Consequently, Thomas' selection of herbicidal recipes combined with his statements as to their effectiveness amounted to an express warranty that the respective mixtures would do the job adequately. Thomas made at least two express warranties which formed the basis of Durham's purchase of the chemicals and were ultimately breached. The liability for breach of express warranty is a strict liability. No defect need be shown other than breach of the warranty itself which is the proximate cause of the property damage. [Citations.] Accordingly, the court finds that Southern States breached its express warranty to Durham and, thus, is liable for the Durham's crop damage. \* \* \*

**2. *Implied Warranties*** There are two theories of recovery for breach of implied warranty under the Delaware UCC: breach of implied warranty of merchantability under U.C.C. § 2–314 and breach of implied warranty of fitness for a particular purpose under U.C.C. § 2–315. The implied warranty of fitness for a particular purpose may, to some degree, overlap a seller's express warranty. [Citations.] Unless there is a valid disclaimer, these implied warranties are implied in every sales transaction involving goods and run not only to those in contractual privity with the seller but to third party beneficiaries as well. U.C.C. § 2–318; [Citation.]. Obviously, Durham was in direct privity with Southern States regarding the herbicides sale.

Turning first to the implied warranty of merchantability, there are five elements which the claimant must establish: (1) that a merchant sold goods, (2) which were not merchantable at the time of sale, (3) proximately causing by the defective nature of the goods, (4) injury and damages to the claimant or his property, and (5) notice to the seller of the injury. [Citation.] As to the element requiring the seller to be a merchant, there is no doubt that Southern States was a merchant as defined under the Delaware UCC because it "deals in goods of the kind or otherwise by his occupation holds himself out as having the knowledge or skill peculiar to the practices or goods involved in the transaction . . ." U.C.C. § 2–104(1). [Citations.] Southern States, as a farmers' co-op, regularly engaged in the sale of agricultural products and thereby is charged with the specialized knowledge or skill peculiar to those goods. It was plainly a merchant with respect to the type of goods sold to Durham.

Addressing the second element concerning whether the herbicides were "merchantable," the goods must pass without objection in the trade under the contract description *and* be fit for the ordinary purposes for which it was intended. U.C.C. § 2–314(2)(a) and (c). The facts show that Southern States sprayed (and in some instances resprayed) the various Durham farm tracts with herbicidal and other chemicals in order to increase the crop yields. Nevertheless, the farms' respective crop yields did not improve, but rather fell dramatically as the result of the chemical applications. Specifically, the herbicidal recipes were unfit for the ordinary purpose for which they were intended to be used, chemical agents that would kill weeds without damaging the primary crops. [Citation.] The chemicals did not operate for their ordinary purpose which was to promote no-till farming which is why Durham purchased them in the first place.

There is ample evidence to support the finding that the herbicides were not merchantable. Dr. Mitchell's unrebutted expert testimony indicates that Southern States incorrectly used liquid nitrogen as the herbicidal carrier rather than a water-based carrier. As a result, this created acidic soil conditions which inhibited operation of the herbicides. * * * In this case, the herbicides did not effectively control 85% of the weeds; instead, the weeds flourished and the crops died. Dr. Mitchell cited a number of other reasons for the crop failure, including: Southern States' improper selection of herbicides needed to control weeds based on the time of the crop planting, its failure to use a sufficient volume of carrier, and its applicator's failure to perform the necessary inspections (such as the "hands and knees" examination) to determine what herbicide recipe should be applied. * * * Based on this evidence, the court concludes that the herbicide and other chemicals were not merchantable since they neither could pass in the trade without objection nor were they fit for the ordinary purpose for which they were intended.

As for proximate cause and damages, the court finds that these elements have been met. * * *

Finally, the notice requirement for a breach of implied warranty of merchantability cause of action was plainly met. Durham notified Southern States as soon as he suspected that the herbicides were failing to work just a few weeks after their application. * * *

Southern States also breached the implied warranty that the herbicides were fit for their particular purpose. * * *

The breach of this warranty is the one most apparent on the facts. As indicated earlier, Durham relied on Thomas' skill and judgment in selecting suitable herbicides to conduct no-till farming on his farms. The chemicals were mixed by Southern States' herbicide applicator, McClements, before each job based on a formula or recipe provided by Thomas or some other Southern States official. The herbicides did not effectively do their job of keeping the fields clear of weeds and the crops died. Though thoroughly familiar with till farming, Durham had no experience with the no-till farming method and, therefore, was not a "sophisticated purchaser" who might have been able to recognize mistakes made by Southern States' personnel. As a result, the herbicides' failure to do their intended task coupled with Durham's reliance on Southern States' judgment and skill in formulating, mixing, and applying the herbicidal chemicals breached the implied warranty of fitness. [Citations.] Accordingly, Southern States is found to be liable under U.C.C. § 2–315.

* * *

## Order

And now, February 3, 1994, for the reasons stated in the attached Memorandum Opinion, it is ordered:

1. Judgment is entered in favor of James L. Patton, Jr., Trustee of the consolidated estate of Debtors, Dudley B. Durham, Jr., Barbara L. Durham, L.B. Trucking, Inc. and Double D Farms, Inc. against Southern States Cooperative, Incorporated, t/a Southern States Middletown Service Cooperative on the Trustee's counterclaim as follows:

| | | |
|---|---|---|
| Damages | $111,478.27 | |
| Less Credit for Items Unrelated to Herbicide Damages | 9,934.02 | |
| Judgment | $101,544.25 | with interest from February 3, 1994 and costs. |

## CASE 24–3
### Disclaimer of Warranties
# TRANS-AIRE INTERNATIONAL, INC. v. NORTHERN ADHESIVE CO., INC.

United States Court of Appeals, Seventh Circuit, 1989
882 F.2d 1254

**KANNE, J.**

Trans-Aire International, Inc. purchased a contact adhesive from Northern Adhesive Company, Inc. to laminate various materials during the process of converting standard automotive vans to recreational vehicles. The adhesive failed to perform during the summer months as Trans-Aire had hoped, and it sued Northern under a wide variety of legal theories. The district court entered summary judgment in favor of Northern, and Trans-Aire appeals. We affirm.

Trans-Aire International, Inc. converts ordinary automotive vans into recreational vehicles. Prior to October of 1982, Trans-Aire installed interior carpet and ceiling fabrics with an adhesive product, "3M 4500," manufactured by 3M Company. However, Trans-Aire experienced problems with that adhesive. Apparently, when the temperature rose inside a van, the adhesive often would fail to hold the fabrics in place.

Trans-Aire contacted Northern Adhesive Company, Inc., a manufacturer of a wide range of adhesive products, to find a replacement for the 3M product. Trans-Aire never requested a specific adhesive by name and instead merely informed Northern of the purposes for which Trans-Aire needed an adhesive. In response, Northern sent several adhesive samples to Trans-Aire for experimental purposes. Allegedly, Northern told Trans-Aire that one of their adhesives, Adhesive 7448, was a "match" for the 3M product which had failed previously.

Trans-Aire tested the sample adhesives by putting them into its application equipment and applying them in the same manner in which Trans-Aire had been applying the 3M adhesive. The tests were conducted in a cool plant, rather than under the warmer weather conditions which had caused the 3M product to fail. Nevertheless, Trans-Aire's chief engineer, Stephen Fribley, determined that Northern's Adhesive 7448 was better than the 3M product.

Fribley summarized the results of the various test applications to Robert Higgins, Trans-Aire's president. Fribley suggested to Higgins that they test Northern's adhesive under summer-like conditions. However, Higgins stated that he was satisfied that Adhesive 7448 was better than the 3M product.

When Higgins asked, Fribley told Higgins that to his knowledge Adhesive 7448 had no warranty. A Northern representative confirmed Fribley's belief, stating that "there was no warranty on [Adhesive 7448] other than that—what they would ship would be like the sample. It would be the same chemistry." Fribley informed Higgins of this conversation.

Between November of 1982 and May of 1983, Trans-Aire ordered several shipments of Adhesive 7448. Trans-Aire placed each order by telephone and subsequently confirmed its request by sending a written purchase order.

Trans-Aire began to use Adhesive 7448 in late 1982 after placing its initial order. Beginning sometime in the spring of 1983, Trans-Aire learned of numerous delamination problems in the interiors of the RVs in which Adhesive 7448 had been used—the same problems experienced previously with the 3M product. As a result, Trans-Aire was forced to repair well over 500 vans.

\* \* \*

**A. Implied Warranties of Fitness for a Particular Purpose and of Merchantability** Section 2–314 of the [Uniform] Commercial Code provides that every sale of goods by a merchant includes an implied warranty that the goods are fit for the ordinary purposes for which they are used unless the warranty is modified or excluded. Section 2–315 of the code states that a sale of goods also includes an implied warranty of fitness for a particular purpose if a seller knows of the buyer's particular purpose for the goods and the buyer relies upon the seller's skill or judgment to select suitable goods. However, § 2–316 of the code states that no implied warranties apply when a buyer examines the goods or a sample as fully as he desires, or refuses to examine the goods, prior to the purchase.

\* \* \*

Initially, we hold that the district court correctly concluded that no warranty of fitness for a particular purpose existed. We agree with the district court that Trans-Aire cannot demonstrate that it relied upon Northern's skill or judgment in deciding to purchase Adhesive 7448, even assuming that Northern knew of the purpose for which Trans-Aire needed the adhesive.

* * *

However, we need not dwell upon this issue because we agree with the district court that Trans-Aire excluded all implied warranties by its actions. Under § 2–316 of the [Uniform] Commercial Code, implied warranties are excluded when a party examines a product or sample "as fully as it desires" or "refuses to examine" the product or sample in a reasonable manner given the circumstances of the case. The undisputed facts and circumstances of this case preclude Trans-Aire's attempts to maintain an action based upon breaches of any existing implied warranties of fitness for a particular purpose or of merchantability.

* * *

Upon the facts, we must agree with the district court's finding that Trans-Aire clearly tested the samples as fully as it desired and refused to conduct further tests which would have confirmed a characteristic of contact adhesives which they already knew to be true, that they soften with heat. Trans-Aire attempts to argue that it did not have the means to discover the "latent defects" of the adhesive, because of the cool plant conditions at the time the tests were performed, and that § 2–316 does not exclude the implied warranties under these circumstances. See . . . Section 2–316 Comment 8 ("an examination under circumstances which do not permit chemical or other testing of the goods would not exclude defects which could be ascertained only by such testing"). We agree with the district court that this argument is without merit.

* * *

*B. Express Warranty* Trans-Aire next argues that the district court erroneously concluded that an express warranty was not created in this case. Trans-Aire contends that by sending specific adhesive samples to Trans-Aire in response to a general statement of need to find a new adhesive for the inadequate 3M product Northern expressly warranted that those samples would meet Trans-Aire's production needs. Trans-Aire apparently did not make this specific argument below, but it certainly would not have fared any better than it does here.

The record indicates that Trans-Aire requested product information from Northern and stated that it wished to purchase a "suitable" product. According to Fribley's undisputed testimony, a Northern representative did not state that any of its adhesives were "suitable" for Trans-Aire's purposes and instead merely commented that Northern manufactured various adhesives, one or more of which "might be applicable." At best (or perhaps worst), Northern stated that its Adhesive 7448 product was a "match" for the 3M product with which Trans-Aire had experienced lamination failures in warmer settings. Thereafter, Northern sent several adhesive samples to Trans-Aire for testing purposes in hopes that Trans-Aire would find an adhesive which it could use. With these facts, Trans-Aire cannot now claim that Northern provided a specific product in response to its needs which amounted to an "affirmation of fact" that the adhesive would meet Trans-Aire's manufacturing needs. See 2–313(1)(a).

* * *

The district court's decision is affirmed.

---

## CASE 24–4
## Failure to Warn
### *DUNNE v. WAL-MART STORES, INC.*
Court of Appeal of Louisiana, First Circuit, 1996
679 So.2d 1034

WHIPPLE, J.

Plaintiff, Judy Dunne [Dunne], appeals the judgment of the trial court in favor of defendants, Wal-Mart Stores, Incorporated (Wal-Mart) and Diversified Products Corporation (DP), dismissing her claim for damages. For the following reasons, we reverse. . . .

### Facts and Procedural History

On February 2, 1991, plaintiff's children purchased an Aero Cycle exercise bike for their mother to use in a weight loss program. The Aero Cycle bike was manufactured by DP and purchased from Wal-Mart, located in Slidell, Louisiana. When plaintiff received the bike, she rode it only for a moment. On August 16, 1991, plaintiff used the bike for the second time. She mounted the bike and pedaled for three or four rotations. The rear leg tubing and/or the connection between the rear leg tubing and the support strut failed and the bike collapsed under plaintiff. At the time of the accident, plaintiff weighed between 450 and 500 pounds. She fell off the bike backwards, struck her head on a nearby metal file cabinet and was knocked unconscious. When plaintiff regained consciousness, her mouth was bleeding and her neck, left shoulder, arm, leg, knee and ankle were injured.

Plaintiff was treated by a physician on the day of the accident. She was diagnosed as having a cervical strain and multiple contusions. She was given a prescription for a muscle relaxer and an analgesic. On August 22, 1991, she was also seen by her regular family physician with complaints of pain, dizziness, numbness and sensitivity to light. Although additional medical evaluation and therapy were suggested, plaintiff failed to seek additional medical care because she was unable to afford it until April 17, 1992. On that date, plaintiff was referred to Dr. Debra Burris, a neurologist, for further evaluation. Plaintiff was evaluated by Dr. Burris on May 21, 1992. She complained of neck pain and headaches. Dr. Burris prescribed physical therapy, a muscle relaxant and an anti-inflammatory and advised plaintiff to return for re-evaluation in six weeks. Plaintiff did not return.

Plaintiff filed suit against Wal-Mart and DP. At the time of the trial, plaintiff still had complaints of neck pain and tingling, numbness and spasms in her left arm and hand, with slight swelling and muscle spasms in her right hand. Following trial on the merits, the trial court found that plaintiff failed to carry her burden of proving that the product was unreasonably dangerous as the use of the bike by someone weighing 500 pounds was not a reasonably anticipated use of the product. From this judgment, plaintiff appeals * * * .

## Liability

On appeal, plaintiff contends that the trial court was manifestly erroneous in its finding that use of the Aero Cycle by an obese person like plaintiff was not a reasonably anticipated use of the product. We agree.

The Louisiana Products Liability Act (LPLA) * * * sets forth the threshold elements which must be proven by a claimant [in a product liability cause of action], providing as follows:

A. The manufacturer of a product shall be liable to a claimant for damage proximately caused by a characteristic of the product that renders the product unreasonably dangerous when such damage arose from a reasonably anticipated use of the product by the claimant or another person or entity.

A "reasonably anticipated use" means a use or handling of a product that the product's manufacturer should reasonably expect of an ordinary person in the same or similar circumstances. [Citation.] This definition is narrower in scope than its pre-LPLA counterpart,

"normal use," which included "all reasonable foreseeable uses and misuses of the product." [Citation]. Under the current definition contained in the LPLA, a manufacturer is not responsible for accounting for every conceivable foreseeable use of a product. [Citation.]

The trial court, * * * , concluded that "the use of this exercise bike by a woman of 500 pounds was not reasonably anticipated by [DP]." The trial court also cited the testimony of Mr. David Newton, the Consumer Affairs Manager for DP. Newton testified that DP manufactured the Aero Cycle to withstand use by adults weighing up to 250 pounds, as this encompasses greater than 98.5 percent of the United States adult population. Further, Newton stated that DP adheres to the American Society for Testing and Materials (ASTM) standards and that all DP products are tested and required to meet ASTM standards. He opined that because a prototype of the Aero Cycle was tested to a load of 440 pounds for five minutes without any resulting deflection * * * , a maximum load capacity warning was not required by the ASTM standards.

Initially, we note that DP is not automatically absolved of liability because it complied with the ASTM standards in not placing a maximum load capacity warning on the Aero Cycle. The ASTM standards, while relevant factors to be considered, are not determinative of the issue of liability. [Citation.]

More importantly, our review of the trial court's reasons for judgment convinces us that the trial court committed legal error. . . . Instead of considering whether plaintiff was engaged in a "reasonably anticipated use," the trial court considered whether plaintiff was a "reasonably anticipated user." In rejecting plaintiff's claim, the trial court [stated] that a manufacturer should not reasonably expect that an ordinary consumer will use a soft drink bottle for a hammer, attempt to drive an automobile across water or pour perfume on a candle to scent it. However, unlike these illustrations, there was no misuse of the product by plaintiff in this case. In fact, the record demonstrates that plaintiff used the product in a manner wholly consistent with its intended use. The Aero Cycle exercise bike was designed and marketed by DP primarily for use by overweight individuals. Plaintiff, an overweight person, was the type of consumer targeted by DP. The mere fact that plaintiff was considerably overweight does not place her in a category of persons for whom DP has no responsibility.

Accordingly, we find that the trial court's conclusion that the use of the Aero Cycle by plaintiff was not a reasonably anticipated use of the product was based on reversible legal error. The record shows that plaintiff's damages resulted from a reasonably anticipated use of the product.

* * *

It is undisputed that there was no maximum weight limit warning accompanying the Aero Cycle. The issue for our consideration at this point is whether * * * DP was required to warn. * * * In this case, according to David Newton, the Aero Cycle was not designed for use by individuals weighing over 250 pounds. The cover of the owner's manual contains other safety information and warnings and it was entirely feasible for DP to have included a statement or warning that the product should not be used by persons weighing over 250 pounds. Plaintiff had no reason to know that the Aero Cycle would not sustain her weight as she previously had used a similar exercise bike for several years without incident. Therefore, in light of DP's admission that the Aero Cycle was only intended to have a limited use, we find that plaintiff proved that DP failed to exercise reasonable care by failing to place a limited use warning on the Aero Cycle.

[T]here are two circumstances when the manufacturer does not have a duty to warn. A warning is not required when the danger would be obvious to an ordinary reasonable user of the product or when a claimant already knows or should know of the danger. [Citation.] Here, there is absolutely no evidence contained in the record that the danger was obvious or that plaintiff knew or should have known of the danger.

IT IS HEREBY ORDERED, ADJUDGED AND DECREED that there be judgment in favor of plaintiff-appellant, Judy Dunne, and against defendant-appellee, Diversified Products Corporation, in the amount of $10,469.72, plus interest from the date of judicial demand until paid. All trial costs and costs of this appeal are to be paid by defendant-appellee.

---

### CASE 24–5
## Unreasonably Dangerous
# GREENE v. BODDIE-NOELL ENTERPRISES, INC

United States District Court, W.D. Virginia, 1997
966 F.Supp. 416

JONES, J.
In this products liability case, the plaintiff contends that she was badly burned by hot coffee purchased from the drive-through window of a fast food restaurant, when the coffee spilled on her after it had been handed to her by the driver of the vehicle. The defendant restaurant operator moves for summary judgment on the ground that the plaintiff cannot show a *prima facie* case of liability. I agree, and dismiss the case.

* * *

[Plaintiff, Katherine] Greene was a passenger in a car driven by her boyfriend, Chris Blevins, on the morning of December 31, 1994, when he purchased food and drink [coffees] from the drive-through window of the Hardee's restaurant in Wise, Virginia, operated by the defendant. * * * He immediately handed the food and beverages to Greene. The food was on a plate, and the beverages were in cups. Greene placed the plate on her lap and held a cup in each hand. According to Greene, the Styrofoam coffee cup was comfortable to hold, and had a lid on the top, although she did not notice whether the lid was fully attached.

Blevins drove out of the restaurant parking lot, and over a "bad dip" at the point at which the lot meets the road. When the front tires of the car went slowly across the dip, the coffee "splashed out" on Greene, burning her legs through her clothes. Blevins remembers Greene exclaiming, "the lid came off." She did not look at the cup until the coffee burned her, and does not know whether the cup was tilted in one direction or another when the coffee spilled out.

As soon as the coffee burned her, Greene threw the food and drink to the floor of the car, and in the process stepped on the coffee cup. When the cup was later retrieved from the floor of the car, the bottom of the cup was damaged, and the lid was at least partially off of the top of the cup.

After Greene was burned by the coffee, Blevins drove her to the emergency room of a local hospital, where she was treated. She missed eleven days of work, and suffered permanent scarring to her thighs.

Both Greene and Blevins testified that they had heard of the "McDonalds' coffee case" prior to this incident* and Greene testified that while she was not a coffee drinker, she had been aware that if coffee spilled on her, it would burn her. After the accident, Greene gave a recorded statement to a representative of the defendant in which she stated, "I know the lid wasn't on there good. It came off too easy."

\* \* \*

To prove a case of liability in Virginia, a plaintiff must show that a product had a defect which rendered it unreasonably dangerous for ordinary or foreseeable use. [Citation]. In order to meet this burden, a plaintiff must offer proof that the product violated a prevailing safety standard, whether the standard comes from business, government or reasonable consumer expectation. [Citation.]

Here the plaintiff has offered no such proof. There is no evidence that either the heat of the coffee or the security of the coffee cup lid violated any applicable standard. Do other fast food restaurants serve coffee at a lower temperature, or with lids which will prevent spills even when passing over an obstruction in the road? Do customers expect cooler coffee, which may be less tasty, or cups which may be more secure, but harder to unfasten?

---

*On August 17, 1994, a state court jury in Albuquerque, New Mexico, awarded 81-year old Stella Liebeck $160,000 in compensatory damages and $2.7 million in punitive damages, after she was burned by coffee purchased from a drive-through window at a McDonalds restaurant. The trial judge later reduced the punitive damages to $480,000, and the parties settled the case before an appeal. According to news reports, Mrs. Liebeck contended that for taste reasons McDonalds served coffee about 20 degrees hotter than other fast food restaurants, and in spite of numerous complaints, had made a conscious decision not to warn customers of the possibility of serious burns. The jury's verdict received world-wide attention. See Andrea Gerlin, A Matter of Degree: How a Jury Decided That One Coffee Spill Is Worth $2.9 Million, Wall St. J.

In fact, the plaintiff testified that she knew, and therefore expected, that the coffee would be hot enough to burn her if it spilled. While she also expressed the opinion that the cup lid was too loose, that testimony does not substitute for evidence of a generally applicable standard or consumer expectation, since "[the plaintiff's] subjective expectations are insufficient to establish what degree of protection . . . society expects from [the product]." [Citation.]

The plaintiff argues that the mere fact that she was burned shows that the product was dangerously defective, either by being too hot or by having a lid which came off unexpectedly. But it is settled in Virginia that the happening of an accident is not sufficient proof of liability, even in products cases. [Citation.] This is not like the case of a foreign substance being found in a soft drink bottle, where a presumption of negligence arises. [Citation.]

To be merchantable, a product need not be foolproof, or perfect. As one noted treatise has expressed, "[i]t is the lawyer's challenging job to define the term 'merchantability' in [the] case in some objective way so that the court or jury can make a determination whether that standard has been breached." [Citation.]

In the present case, there has been no showing that a reasonable seller of coffee would not conclude that the beverage must be sold hot enough to be palatable to consumers, even though it is hot enough to burn other parts of the body. A reasonable seller might also conclude that patrons desire coffee lids which prevent spillage in ordinary handling, but are not tight enough to avert a spill under other circumstances, such as when driving over a bump. It was the plaintiff's obligation to demonstrate that she had proof that the defendant breached a recognizable standard, and that such proof is sufficient to justify a verdict in her favor at trial. She has not done so, and accordingly the motion for summary judgment must be granted.

---

|  | **Questions** |  |

1.   Identify and describe the types of warranties.
2.   Discuss the various defenses that may be successfully raised to a warranty action.
3.   Describe the elements of an action based upon strict liability in tort.
4.   Discuss the obstacles to an action based upon strict liability in tort.
5.   Compare strict liability in tort with the implied warranty of merchantability.

# Problems

**1.** At the advent of the social season, Aunt Lavinia purchased a hula skirt in Sadie's dress shop. The salesclerk told her, "This superior garment will do things for a person." Aunt Lavinia's houseguest, her niece, Florabelle, asked and obtained her aunt's permission to wear the skirt to a masquerade ball. In the midst of the festivity, at which there was much dancing, drinking, and smoking, the long skirt brushed against a glimmering cigarette butt. Unknown to Aunt Lavinia and Florabelle, its wearer, the garment was made of a fine unwoven fiber that is highly flammable. It burst into flames, and Florabelle suffered severe burns. Aunt Lavinia notified Sadie of the accident and of Florabelle's intention to recover from Sadie. Florabelle seeks to recover damages in an action against Sadie, the proprietor of the dress shop, and Exotic Clothes, Inc., the manufacturer from which Sadie purchased the skirt. Decision?

**2.** The Talent Company, manufacturer of a widely advertised and expensive perfume, sold a quantity of this product to Young, a retail druggist. Dentley and Bird visited Young's store and Dentley, desiring to make a gift to Bird, purchased from Young a bottle of this perfume, asking for it by its trade name. Young wrapped up the bottle and handed it directly to Bird. The perfume contained a foreign chemical which, upon the first use of the perfume by Bird, severely burned her face and caused a permanent facial disfigurement. What are the rights of Bird, if any, against Dentley, Young, and the Talent Company, respectively?

**3.** John Doe purchased a bottle of "Bleach-All," a well-known brand, from Roe's combination service station and grocery store. When John used the "Bleach-All," his clothes deteriorated due to an error in mixing the chemicals during the detergent's manufacture. John brings an action against Roe to recover damages. Decision?

**4.** A route salesperson for Ideal Milk Company delivered a one-half gallon glass jug of milk to Allen's home. The next day, when Allen grasped the milk container by its neck to take it out of his refrigerator, it shattered in his hand and caused serious injury. Allen paid Ideal on a monthly basis for the regular delivery of milk. Ideal's milk bottles each contained the legend "Property of Ideal—to be returned," and the route salesperson would pick up the empty bottles when he delivered milk. Allen brought an action against Ideal Milk Company. Decision?

**5.** While Butler and his wife, Wanda, were browsing through Sloan's used car lot, Butler told Sloan that he was looking for a safe but cheap family car. Sloan said, "That old Cadillac hearse ain't hurt at all, and I'll sell it to you for $3,950." Butler said, "I'll have to take your word for it because I don't know a thing about cars." Butler asked Sloan whether he would guarantee the car, and Sloan replied, "I don't guarantee used cars." Then Sloan added, "But I have checked that Caddy over, and it will run another 10,000 miles without needing any repairs." Butler replied, "It has to because I won't have an extra dime for any repairs." Butler made a down payment of $400 and signed a printed form contract furnished by Sloan which contained a provision, "Seller does not warrant the condition or performance of any used automobile."

As Butler drove the car out of Sloan's lot, the left rear wheel fell off, and Butler lost control of the vehicle. It veered over an embankment, causing serious injuries to Wanda. What is Sloan's liability to Butler and Wanda?

**6.** John purchased for cash a Revenge automobile manufactured by Japanese Motors, Ltd., from an authorized franchised dealer in the United States. The dealer told John that the car had a "24 month—24,000 mile warranty." Two days after John accepted delivery of the car, he received an eighty-page fine print manual which stated, among other things, on page 72:

The warranties herein are expressly in lieu of any other express or implied warranty, including any implied warranty of merchantability or fitness, and of any other obligation on the part of the company or the selling dealer.

Japanese Motors, Ltd., and the selling dealer warrant to the owner each part of this vehicle to be free under use and service from defects in material and workmanship for a period of twenty-four months from the date of original retail delivery of first use, or until it has been driven for 24,000 miles, whichever first occurs.

Within nine months after the purchase, John was forced to return the car for repairs to the dealer on thirty different occasions, and the car has been in the dealer's custody for more than seventy days during these nine months. The dealer has been forced to make major repairs to the engine, transmission, and steering assembly. The car is now in the custody of the dealer for further major repairs, and John has demanded that it keep the car and refund his entire purchase price. The dealer has refused on the ground that it has not breached its contract and is willing to continue repairing the car during the remainder of the "24–24" period. What are the rights and liabilities of the dealer and John?

**7.** Fred Lyon of New York, while on vacation in California, rented a new model Home Run automobile from Hart's Drive-A-Car. The car was manufactured by the Dumars Motor Company and was purchased by Hart's from Jammer, Inc., an automobile importer. Lyon was driving the car on a street in San Jose when, due to a defect in the steering mechanism, it suddenly became impossible to steer. The speed of the car at the time was thirty miles per hour, but before Lyon could bring it to a stop, the car jumped a low curb and struck Peter Wolf, who was standing on the sidewalk, breaking both of his legs and causing other injuries. Wolf sues Hart's, Dumars Motor Company, Jammer, and Lyon. Decisions?

8.    Plaintiff brings this cause of action against a manufacturer for the loss of one leg below the hip. The leg was lost when caught in the gears of a screw auger machine sold and installed by the defendant. Shortly before the accident, plaintiff's co-employees had removed a covering panel from the machine by use of sledgehammers and crowbars in order to do repair work. After finishing the repairs, they replaced the panel with a single piece of cardboard instead of restoring the equipment to its original condition. The plaintiff stepped on the cardboard in the course of his work and fell, catching his leg in the moving parts. Decision?

9.    The plaintiff, while driving a van manufactured by the defendant, was struck in the rear by another motor vehicle. Upon impact, the plaintiff's head was jarred backward against the rear window of the cab, causing the plaintiff serious injury. The van was not equipped with a headrest, and none was required at the time. Should the plaintiff prevail on a cause of action based upon strict liability in tort? Why?

10.    Plaintiff, while dining at defendant's restaurant, ordered a chicken pot pie. While she was eating, she swallowed a sliver of chicken bone which became lodged in her throat, causing her serious injury. Plaintiff brings a cause of action. Should she prevail? Why?

11.    Salem Supply Co. sells new and used gardening equipment. Ben Buyer purchased a slightly used, riding lawn mower for $1,500. The price was considerably less than that of comparable used mowers. The sale was clearly indicated to be "as is." Two weeks after Ben purchased the mower, the police arrived at his house with Owen Owner, the true owner of the lawn mower, which had been stolen from his yard, and reclaimed the mower. What recourse, if any, does Ben have?

12.    Seigel, a seventy-three-year-old man, was injured at one of Giant Food's retail food stores when a bottle of Coca-Cola exploded as he was placing a six-pack of Coke into his shopping cart. The explosion caused him to lose his balance and fall, injuring himself. Seigel brought suit against Giant Food for damages allegedly caused by Giant's breach of its implied warranty of merchantability. The trial court granted judgment in favor of Giant, and Seigel brought this appeal. Decision?

13.    Guarino and two others (plaintiffs) died of gas asphyxiation and five others were injured when they entered a sewer tunnel without masks to answer the cries for help of their crew leader, Rooney. Rooney had left the sewer shaft and entered the tunnel to fix a water leakage problem. Having corrected the problem, Rooney was returning to the shaft when he apparently was overcome by gas because of a defect in his oxygen mask, which was manufactured by Mine Safety Appliance Company (defendant). Plaintiffs brought this action against the defendant for breach of warranty, and defendant raised the defense of plaintiffs' voluntary assumption of the risk. Decision?

14.    Green Seed Company packaged, labeled, and marketed a quality tomato seed known as "Green's Pink Shipper" for commercial sale. Brown Seed Store, a retailer, purchased the seed from Green Seed and then sold it to Guy Jones, who was engaged in the business of growing tomato seedlings for sale to commercial tomato growers. Williams purchased the seedlings from Jones and then transplanted and raised them in accordance with accepted farming methods. The plants, however, produced not the promised "Pink Shipper" tomatoes but rather an inferior variety that spoiled in the field. Williams then brought an action against Green Seed for $900, claiming that his crop damage had been caused by Green Seed's breach of an express warranty. Green Seed argued in defense that its warranty did not extend to remote purchasers and that the company did not receive notice of the claimed breach of warranty. Decision?

15.    Shell Oil Company leased to Flying Tiger Line a gasoline tank truck with a movable ladder for refueling certain types of aircraft. Under the terms of the lease, Flying Tiger was to maintain the equipment in safe operating order, but Shell was obligated to make most of the repairs at Flying Tiger's request. Four years after the lease was entered, Shell, at Flying Tiger's request, replaced the original ladder with a new one built by an undisclosed manufacturer. Both Flying Tiger and Shell inspected the new ladder. Two years later, however, Price, an aircraft mechanic employed by Flying Tiger, was seriously injured when the ladder's legs split while he was climbing onto an airplane wing. Decision?

16.    A gasoline-powered lawn mower which had been used earlier to cut grass was left unattended next to a hot water heater which had been manufactured by Sears. Expert testimony was presented to demonstrate that vapors from the mower's gas tank accumulated under the hot water heater and resulted in an explosion. Three-year-old Shawn Toups was injured as a result. Evidence was also presented negating any claim that Shawn had been handling the gasoline can located nearby or the lawn mower. He was not burned on the soles of his feet or the palms of his hands, and, similarly, the gas can remained in an upright position even after the explosion. The Toups brought a strict product liability action against Sears. Decision?

17.    Mrs. Embs went into Stamper's Cash Market to buy soft drinks for her children. She removed five bottles from an upright soft drink cooler, placed them in a carton, and then turned to move away from the display when a bottle of Seven-Up in a carton at her feet exploded, cutting her leg. Apparently, several other bottles had exploded that same week. Stamper's Cash Market received its entire stock of Seven-Up from Arnold Lee Vice, the area distributor. Vice in turn received his entire stock of Seven-Up from Pepsi-Cola Bottling Co. Decision?

18.    Catania wished to paint the exterior of his house. He went to Brown, a local paint store owner, and asked him to recommend a paint for the job. Catania told Brown that the exterior walls were stucco and in a chalky, powdery condition. Brown suggested Pierce's shingle and shake paint. Brown then instructed Catania how to mix the paint and how to use a wire brush to prepare the surface. Five months later, the paint began to peel, flake, and blister. Catania brings an action against Brown. Decision?

**19.** Robinson, a truck driver for a moving company, decided to buy a used truck from the company. Branch, the owner, told Robinson that the truck was being repaired and that Robinson should wait and inspect the truck before signing the contract. Robinson, who had driven the truck before, felt that inspection was unnecessary. Again, Branch suggested Robinson wait to inspect the truck, and again Robinson declined. Branch then told Robinson he was buying the truck "as is." Robinson then signed the contract. After the truck broke down four times, Robinson sued. Decision?

**20.** Perfect Products manufactures balloons, which are then bought and resold by wholesale novelty distributors. Mego Corp. manufactures a doll called "Bubble Yum Baby." A balloon is inserted in the doll's mouth with a mouthpiece, and the doll's arm is pumped to inflate the balloon, simulating the blowing of a bubble. Mego Corp. used Perfect Products balloons in the dolls, bought through the independent distributors. Plaintiff's infant daughter died after swallowing a balloon removed from the doll. Plaintiff sues Perfect Products and others on a theory of strict liability. Decision?

**21.** Patient was injured when the footrest of an adjustable X-ray table collapsed, causing Patient to fall to the floor. G.E. manufactured the X-ray table and the footrest. At trial, evidence was introduced that G.E. had manufactured for several years another footrest model complete with safety latches. However, there was no evidence that the footrest involved was manufactured defectively. The action is based on a theory of strict liability. Who wins? Why?

**22.** Heckman, an employee of Clark Equipment Company, severely injured his left hand when he caught it in a power press that he was operating at work. The press was manufactured by Federal Press Company and sold to Clark. It could be operated either by hand controls that required the use of both hands away from the point of operation or by an optional foot pedal. When the foot pedal was used without a guard, nothing remained to keep the operator's hands from the point of operation. Federal Press did not provide safety appliances unless the customer requested them, but when it delivered the press to Clark with the optional pedal, it suggested that Clark install a guard. The press had a similar warning embossed on it. Clark did, in fact, purchase a guard for $100, but it was not mounted on the machine at the time of the injury; nor was it believed to be an effective safety device.

Heckman argued that one type of guard, if installed, would have made the press safe in 95 percent of its customary uses. Federal, in turn, argued that the furnishing of guards was not customary in the industry; that the machine's many uses made it impracticable to design and install any one guard as standard equipment; that Clark's failure to obey Federal's warning was a superseding cause of the injury; and that state regulations placed responsibility for the safe operation of presses on employers and employees. The jury awarded Heckman $750,000, and Federal appealed. Decision?

**23.** Raymond and Sandra Duford purchased a wood-burning stove from Sears. The stove was manufactured by Preway, Inc. At trial, it was shown that Raymond had inadvertently installed the section of the chimney pipe that went through the roof upside down; and all parties agreed that such improper installation caused a fire which had destroyed the Dufords' house.

At trial, the Dufords alleged, and Preway admitted, that there were no markings on the pipe to indicate "which end was up." An expert for the Dufords then testified that the simple precaution of an embossed marking would have been satisfactory. Later, to the amazement of all the parties, a witness for Preway pointed out that the actual pipe in question had been marked with embossed letters. The pipe in fact had tiny letters spelling "UP" with two arrows pointed in the proper direction. Since no one on either side had noticed the letters except the one witness, the Dufords hastily changed their claim to that of inadequacy of the marking. The trial court however issued a directed verdict for Preway and Sears, and the Dufords appealed. Decision?

**24.** Vlases, a coal miner who had always raised small flocks of chickens, spent two years building a new two-story chicken coop large enough to house 4,000 chickens. After its completion, he purchased 2,200 one-day-old chicks from Montgomery Ward for the purpose of producing eggs for sale. He had selected them from Ward's catalogue, which stated that these chicks, hybrid Leghorns, were noted for their excellent egg production. Vlases had equipped the coop with brand-new machinery and had taken further hygiene precautions for the chicks' health. Almost one month later, Vlases noticed that their feathers were beginning to fall off. A veterinarian's examination revealed signs of drug intoxication and hemorrhagic disease in a few of the chicks. Eight months later, it was determined that the chicks were suffering from visceral and ocular leukosis, or bird cancer, which reduced their egg-bearing capacity to zero. Avian leukosis may be transmitted either genetically or by unsanitary conditions. Subsequently, the disease infected the entire flock. Vlases then brought suit against Montgomery Ward for its breach of the implied warranties of merchantability and of fitness for a particular purpose. Ward claimed that there was no way to detect the disease in the one-day-old chicks, nor was there medication available to prevent this disease from occurring. Montgomery Ward brought this appeal from a judgment in favor of Vlases. Decision?

**WWW** **Internet Exercise** Find and review information about product liability reform.

# Remedies

A contract for the sale of goods may require total performance at one time or part performance in stages, according to the agreement of the parties. At any stage, one of the parties may repudiate the contract, may become insolvent, or may breach the contract by failing to perform his obligations under it. In a sales contract, breach may consist of the seller's delivering defective goods, too few goods, the wrong goods, or no goods. The buyer may breach by not accepting conforming goods or by failing to pay for conforming goods that he has accepted. Breach may occur when the goods are in the possession of the seller, in the possession of a bailee, in transit to the buyer, or in the possession of the buyer.

Remedies, therefore, need to address not only the type of breach of contract but also the situation with respect to the goods. Consequently, the Code provides distinct remedies for the seller and for the buyer, each specifically keyed to the factual situation.

In all events, the purpose of the Code is to put the aggrieved party in a position as good as the one he would have occupied, had the other party fully performed. To accomplish this purpose, the Code has provided that its remedies should be liberally administered. Moreover, damages do not have to be "calculable with mathematical precision": they need only be proved with "whatever definiteness and accuracy the facts permit, but no more." Comment 1 to Section 1–106. The purpose of remedies under the Code is compensation; therefore, punitive damages are generally not available.

Finally, the Code has rejected the doctrine of election of remedies, essentially providing that remedies for breach are cumulative in nature. Whether one remedy bars another depends entirely on the facts of the individual case.

## CISG

*Damages for breach of contract by one party consist of the loss, including loss of profit, suffered by the other party as a consequence of the breach. Such damages may not exceed the loss which the party in breach foresaw or should have foreseen at the time of the conclusion of the contract as a possible consequence of the breach of contract. The aggrieved party must take such measures as are reasonable in the circumstances to mitigate the loss, including loss of profit, resulting from the breach. If he fails to take such measures, the party in breach may claim a reduction in the damages in the amount by which the loss should have been mitigated.*

## REMEDIES OF THE SELLER

A buyer's default in performing any of his contractual obligations deprives the seller of the rights for which he bargained. Such default may consist of any of the following acts: wrongfully rejecting the goods, wrongfully revoking acceptance of the goods, failing to make a payment due on or before delivery, or repudiating (indicating an intention not to perform) the contract in whole or in part. Section 2–703; Section 2A–523(1). The Code catalogs the seller's remedies for each of these defaults. Section 2–703. (Section 2A–523(1) contains a comparable set of remedies for the lessor.) These remedies allow the seller to:

1. withhold delivery of the goods;
2. stop delivery of the goods by a carrier or other bailee;
3. identify to the contract conforming goods not already identified;
4. resell the goods and recover damages;
5. recover damages for nonacceptance of the goods or repudiation of the contract;
6. recover the price;
7. recover incidental damages;
8. cancel the contract; and
9. reclaim the goods on the buyer's insolvency (Section 2–702).

Under Article 2A a lessor also may recover compensation for any loss of or damage to the lessor's residual interest in the goods caused by the lessee's default. Section 2A–532.

It is useful to note that the first three and the ninth remedies indexed above are **goods-oriented**—that is, they relate to the seller's exercising control over the goods. The fourth through seventh remedies are **money-oriented** because they provide the seller with the opportunity to recover monetary damages. The eighth remedy is **obligation-oriented** because it allows the seller to avoid his obligation under the contract.

Moreover, if the seller delivers goods on credit and the buyer fails to pay the price when due, the seller's sole remedy, unless the buyer is insolvent, is to sue for the unpaid price. If, however, the buyer received the goods on credit while insolvent, the seller may be able to reclaim the goods. The Code defines **insolvency** to include both its equity meaning and its bankruptcy meaning. Section 1–201(23). The **equity** meaning of insolvency is the inability of a person to pay his debts in the ordinary course of business or as they become due. The **bankruptcy** meaning of insolvency is that total liabilities exceed the total value of all assets.

As noted above, the Code's remedies are *cumulative*. Thus, by way of example, an aggrieved seller may (1) identify goods to the contract; *and* (2) withhold delivery; *and* (3) resell or recover damages for nonacceptance or recover the price; *and* (4) recover incidental damages; *and* (5) cancel the contract.

---

## CISG

*If the buyer fails to perform any of his obligations, the seller may (1) require the buyer to pay the price or (2) may fix an additional period of time of reasonable length for performance by the buyer of his obligations. Unless the buyer notifies the seller that he will not perform within the period so fixed, the seller may not, during that period, resort to any remedy for breach of contract. Moreover, if the buyer's breach is fundamental or the buyer fails to perform within the additional time granted by the seller, the seller may avoid the contract. In addition to these remedies, the seller also has the right to damages.*

---

## To Withhold Delivery of the Goods

A seller may withhold delivery of goods to a buyer who has wrongfully rejected or revoked acceptance of the goods, who has failed to make a payment due on or before delivery, or who has repudiated the contract. Section 2–703; Section 2A–523(1). This right is essentially that of a seller to withhold or discontinue performance of her side of the contract because of the buyer's breach.

Where the contract calls for installments, any breach of an installment that impairs the value of the *whole* contract will permit the seller to withhold the entire undelivered balance of the goods. In addition, upon discovery of the buyer's insolvency, the seller may refuse to deliver the goods except for cash, including payment for all goods previously delivered under the contract. Section 2–702. (Section 2A–525(1) is similar.)

## To Stop Delivery of the Goods

An extension of the right to withhold delivery is the right of an aggrieved seller to stop the delivery of goods in transit to the buyer or in the possession of a bailee. A seller who discovers that the buyer is insolvent may stop *any* delivery. If the buyer is not insolvent but repudiates or otherwise breaches the contract, the seller may stop carload, truckload, planeload, or larger shipments. Section 2–705(1); Section 2A–526(1). To stop delivery, the seller must notify the carrier or other bailee soon enough for the bailee to prevent delivery of the goods. After this notification, the carrier or bailee must hold and deliver the goods according to the directions of the seller, who is liable to the carrier or bailee for any charges or damages incurred. If a negotiable document of title has been issued for the goods, the bailee need not obey a notification until the document is provided. Section 2–705(3).

The seller's right to stop delivery ceases when (1) the buyer receives the goods; (2) the bailee of the goods, except a carrier, acknowledges to the buyer that he holds them for the buyer; (3) the carrier acknowledges to the buyer that he holds them for the buyer by reshipment or as warehouseman; or (4) a negotiable document of title covering the goods is negotiated to the buyer. Section 2–705(2); Section 2A–526(2) is similar.

## To Identify Goods to the Contract

Upon a breach of the contract by the buyer, the seller may proceed to identify to the contract conforming goods in her possession or control that were not so identified at the time she learned of the breach. Section 2–704(1); Section 2A–524(1). This enables the seller to exercise the remedy of resale of goods (discussed below). Furthermore, the seller may resell any unfinished goods demonstrably intended to fulfill the particular contract. The seller may either complete the manufacture of unfinished goods and identify them to the contract or cease their manufacture and resell the unfinished goods for scrap or salvage value. Section 2–704(2); Section 2A–524(2). In so deciding, the seller must exercise reasonable commercial judgment to minimize her loss.

## To Resell the Goods and Recover Damages

Under the same circumstances that permit the seller to withhold delivery of goods to the buyer (i.e., wrongful rejection or revocation, repudiation, or failure to make timely payment), the seller may resell the goods or the undelivered balance. If the resale is made in good faith and is commercially reasonable, the seller may recover from the buyer the **difference between the contract price and the resale price**, together with any incidental damages (discussed below), less expenses saved because of the buyer's breach. Section 2–706(1). For example, Floyd agrees to sell goods to Beverly for a contract price of $8,000 due on delivery. Beverly wrongfully rejects the goods and refuses to pay Floyd anything. Floyd resells the goods in strict compliance with the Code for $6,000, incurring incidental damages for sales commissions of $500 but saving $200 in transportation costs. Floyd would recover from Beverly the difference between the contract price ($8,000) and the resale price ($6,000) plus incidental damages ($500) minus expenses saved ($200), which equals $2,300.

In a lease, the comparable recovery is the **difference between** the **present values** of the **old rent** due under the original lease and the **new rent** due under the new lease. More specifically, the lessor may recover (1) the accrued and unpaid rent as of the date of commencement of the new lease; (2) the present value as of that date of total rent for the then remaining term of the original lease minus the present value, as of the same date, of the rent under the new lease applicable to a comparable time period; and (3) any incidental damages, less expenses saved because of the lessee's breach. Section 2A–527(2).

The resale may be a public or private sale, and the goods may be sold as a unit or in parcels. The goods resold must be identified as those related to the contract, but where an anticipatory repudiation has occurred, for example, the goods need be neither in existence nor identified to the contract before the buyer's breach. Section 2–706(2).

Where the resale is at a private sale, the seller must give the buyer reasonable notice of his intention to resell.

Section 2–706(3). The seller or a broker may carry out a private sale by negotiations or solicitations. Where the resale is at a public sale (such as an auction), only identified goods can be sold, except where a recognized market exists for a public sale of future goods of the kind involved. The public sale must be made at a usual place or market for public sale, if one is reasonably available, and the seller must give the buyer reasonable notice of the time and place of the resale unless the goods are perishable or threaten to decline in value speedily. Prospective bidders must be given an opportunity for reasonable inspection of the goods before the sale. Moreover, the seller may be a purchaser of the goods at the public sale. Section 2–706(4). In choosing between a public and private sale, the seller must observe relevant trade practices and usages and take into account the character of the goods.

The seller is not accountable to the buyer for any profit made on any resale of the goods. Section 2–706(6); Section 2A–527(5). Moreover, a *bona fide* purchaser at a resale takes the goods free of any rights of the original buyer, even if the seller has failed to comply with one or more of the requirements of the Code in making the resale. Section 2–706(5); Section 2A–524(4).

Failure to act in good faith and in a commercially reasonable manner deprives the seller of this remedy and relegates him to the remedy of recovering damages for nonacceptance or repudiation (discussed below). Section 2–706, Comment 2; Section 2A–527(3).

## CISG

*If the contract is avoided and the seller has resold the goods in a reasonable manner and within a reasonable time after avoidance, he may recover the difference between the contract price and the resale price. In addition, he may recover consequential damages.*

## To Recover Damages for Nonacceptance or Repudiation

In the event of the buyer's wrongful rejection or revocation, repudiation, or failure to make timely payment, the seller may recover damages from the buyer equal to the **difference between the unpaid contract price and the market price** at the time and place of tender of the goods, plus incidental damages, less expenses saved because of the buyer's breach. Section 2–708(1). This remedy is an alternative to the remedy of reselling the goods.

In a lease the comparable recovery is the **difference between the present values** of the **old rent** due under the original lease and the **market rent**. Section 2A–528(1).

For example, Joan in Seattle agrees to sell goods to Nelson in Chicago for $20,000 F.O.B. Chicago, delivery on June 15. Nelson wrongfully rejects the goods. The market price would be ascertained as of June 15 in Chicago because F.O.B. Chicago is a destination contract in which the place of tender would be Chicago. The market price of the goods on June 15 in Chicago is $15,000. Joan, who incurred $1,000 in incidental expenses while saving $500 in expenses, would recover from Nelson the difference between the contract price ($20,000) and the market price ($15,000), plus incidental damages ($1,000), minus expenses saved ($500), which equals $5,500.

If the difference between the contract price and the market price will not place the seller in as good a position as performance would have, then the measure of damages is the **profit,** including reasonable overhead, which the seller would have realized from full performance by the buyer, plus any incidental damages, less expenses saved because of the buyer's breach. Section 2–708(2). For example, Green, an automobile dealer, enters into a contract to sell a large, fuel-inefficient luxury car to Holland for $22,000. The price of gasoline increases 20 percent, and Holland repudiates. The market value of the car is still $22,000, but because Green cannot sell as many cars as he can obtain, his sales volume has decreased by one as a result of Holland's breach. Therefore, Green would be permitted to recover the profits he lost on the sale to Holland (computed as the contract price minus what the car cost Green, plus an allocation of overhead), plus any incidental damages.

Article 2A has a comparable provision, except the profit is reduced to its present value as the lessor would have received it over the term of the lease. Section 2A–528(2).

## CISG

*If the contract is avoided and the seller has not made a resale, he may recover the difference between the contract price and the current price at the time of avoidance and at the place where delivery of the goods should have been made. In addition, he may recover consequential damages.*

⚖ *See Case 25–1*

## To Recover the Price

The Code permits the seller to recover the price plus incidental damages in only three situations: (1) where the buyer has accepted the goods; (2) where conforming goods have been lost or damaged after the risk of loss has passed to the buyer; and (3) where the goods have been identified to the contract and there is no ready market available for their resale at a reasonable price. Section 2–709(1). For example, Kelly, in accordance with her agreement with Sally, prints ten thousand letterheads and envelopes with Sally's name and address on them. Sally wrongfully rejects the stationery, which Kelly is unable to resell at a reasonable price. Kelly is entitled to recover the price plus incidental damages from Sally.

Article 2A has a similar provision except that the lessor is entitled to (1) accrued and unpaid rent as of the date of the judgment; (2) the present value as of the judgment date of the rent for the then remaining lease term; and (3) incidental damages less expenses saved. Section 2A–529(1).

A seller who sues for the price must hold for the buyer any goods identified to the contract that are still in her control. Section 2–709(2); Section 2A–529(2). If resale becomes possible, the seller may resell the goods at any time prior to the collection of the judgment, and the net proceeds of such resale must be credited to the buyer. Payment of the judgment entitles the buyer to any goods not resold. Section 2–709(2). In a lease, payment of the judgment entitles the lessee to the use and possession of the goods for the remaining lease term. Section 2A–529(4).

## CISG

*The seller may require the buyer to pay the price, take delivery or perform his other obligations, unless the seller has resorted to a remedy that is inconsistent with this requirement.*

## To Recover Incidental Damages

In addition to recovering damages for the difference between the contract price and the resale price, recovering damages for nonacceptance or repudiation, or recovering the price, the seller may in the same action recover her **incidental damages** in order to recoup expenses she reasonably incurred as a result of the buyer's breach. Section 2–710 defines a seller's incidental damages as follows:

> Incidental damages to an aggrieved seller include any commercially reasonable charges, expenses or commissions incurred in stopping delivery, in the transportation, care and custody of goods after the buyer's breach, in connection with return or resale of the goods or otherwise resulting from the breach.

Section 2A–530 has an analogous definition.

## To Cancel the Contract

Where the buyer wrongfully rejects or revokes acceptance of the goods, fails to make a payment due on or before delivery, or repudiates the contract in whole or in part, the seller may cancel the contract with respect to the goods directly affected. If the breach is of an installment contract and it substantially impairs the whole contract, the seller may cancel the entire contract. Section 2–703(f); Section 2A–523(1)(a).

The Code defines **cancellation** as one party's putting an end to the contract by reason of a breach by the other. Section 2–106(4); Section 2A–103(1)(b). The obligation of the canceling party for any future performance under the contract is discharged, although she retains any remedy for breach of the whole contract or any unperformed balance. Section 2–720; Section 2A–505(1). Thus, if the seller has the right to cancel, she may recover damages for breach without having to tender any further performance.

---

## CISG

*The seller may declare the contract avoided if (1) the buyer commits a fundamental breach or (2) the buyer does not, within the additional period of time fixed by the seller, perform his obligation to pay the price or take delivery of the goods. Avoidance of the contract releases both parties from their obligations under it, subject to any damages that may be due. Avoidance does not affect any provision of the contract for the settlement of disputes or any other provision of the contract governing the rights and obligations of the parties consequent upon the avoidance of the contract.*

---

## To Reclaim the Goods upon the Buyer's Insolvency

In addition to the right of an unpaid seller to withhold and stop delivery of the goods, he may reclaim them from an insolvent buyer by demand upon the buyer within ten days after the buyer has received the goods. Section 2–702(2). Where, however, the buyer has committed fraud by misrepresenting her solvency to the seller in writing within three months prior to delivery of the goods, the ten-day limitation does not apply.

The seller's right to reclaim the goods is subject to the rights of a buyer in the ordinary course of business or to the rights of any other good faith purchaser. Furthermore, upon reclaiming the goods from an insolvent buyer, the seller is excluded from all other remedies with respect to those goods. Section 2–702(3).

A lessor retains title to the goods and therefore has the right to recover possession of them upon default by the lessee. Section 2A–525(2).

◆ *See Figure 25–1*

## REMEDIES OF THE BUYER

Basically, a seller may default in three different ways: he may repudiate, he may fail to deliver the goods, or he may deliver or tender goods that do not conform to the contract. Section 2–711; Section 2A–508. The Code provides remedies for each of these breaches. Some remedies are available for all three types; others are not. Moreover, the availability of some remedies depends on the buyer's actions. For example, if the seller tenders nonconforming goods, the buyer may reject or accept them. If the buyer rejects them, he can choose from a number of remedies. On the other hand, if the buyer accepts the nonconforming goods and does not justifiably revoke his acceptance, he limits himself to recovering damages.

Where the seller fails to make delivery or repudiates, or where the buyer rightfully rejects or justifiably revokes acceptance, the buyer may, with respect to any goods involved, or with respect to the whole if the breach goes to the whole contract, (1) cancel *and* (2) recover payments made. In addition, the buyer may (3) "cover" and obtain damages *or* (4) recover damages for nondelivery. Where the seller fails to deliver or repudiates, the buyer, where appropriate, may also (5) recover identified goods if the seller is insolvent, *or* (6) replevy the goods, *or* (7) obtain specific performance. Moreover, upon rightful rejection or justifiable revocation of acceptance, the buyer (8) has

**FIGURE 25–1**  Remedies of the Seller

| Buyer's Breach | Obligation-oriented | Seller's Remedies Goods-oriented[1] | Money-oriented[2] |
|---|---|---|---|
| **Buyer wrongfully rejects goods** | Cancel | • Withhold delivery of goods <br> • Stop delivery of goods in transit <br> • Identify conforming goods to the contract | • Resell and recover damages <br> • Recover difference between unpaid contract and market prices *or* lost profits <br> • Recover price |
| **Buyer wrongfully revokes acceptance** | Cancel | • Withhold delivery of goods <br> • Stop delivery of goods in transit <br> • Identify conforming goods to the contract | • Resell and recover damages <br> • Recover difference between unpaid contract and market prices *or* lost profits <br> • Recover price |
| **Buyer fails to make payment** | Cancel | • Withhold delivery of goods <br> • Stop delivery of goods in transit <br> • Identify conforming goods to the contract <br> • Reclaim goods upon buyer's insolvency | • Resell and recover damages <br> • Recover difference between unpaid contract and market prices *or* lost profits <br> • Recover price |
| **Buyer repudiates** | Cancel | • Withhold delivery of goods <br> • Stop delivery of goods in transit <br> • Identify conforming goods to the contract | • Resell and recover damages <br> • Recover difference between unpaid contract and market prices *or* lost profits <br> • Recover price |

1. In a lease, the lessor has the right to recover possession of the goods upon default by the lessee.
2. In a lease, the lessor's recovery of damages for future rent payments is reduced to their present value.

a security interest in the goods. Where the buyer has accepted goods and notified the seller of their nonconformity, the buyer may (9) recover damages for breach of warranty. Finally, in addition to the remedies listed above, the buyer may, where appropriate, (10) recover incidental damages, and (11) recover consequential damages. Article 2A provides for essentially the same remedies for the lessee. Section 2A–508.

It may be observed that the first remedy catalogued above is **obligation-oriented;** the second through fourth and ninth through eleventh are **money-oriented;** and the fifth through eighth are **goods-oriented.**

The buyer may deduct from the price due any damages resulting from any breach of contract by the seller. The buyer must, however, give notice to the seller of her intention to withhold such damages from payment of the price due. Section 2–717; Section 2A–508(6).

## CISG

*If the seller fails to perform any of his obligations, the buyer may (1) require the seller to perform his contractual obligations or (2) may fix an additional period of time of reasonable length for performance by the seller of his obligations. Unless the seller notifies the buyer that he will not perform within the period so fixed, the buyer may not, during that period, resort to any remedy for breach of contract. Moreover, if the seller's breach is fundamental or the seller fails to perform within the additional time granted by the buyer, the buyer may avoid the contract. In addition to these remedies, the buyer also has the right to damages. If the goods do not conform with the contract, the buyer may reduce the price in the same proportion as the value that the goods actually delivered had at the time of the delivery bears to the value that conforming goods would have had at that time.*

## To Cancel the Contract

Where the seller fails to make delivery or repudiates the contract, or where the buyer rightfully rejects or justifiably revokes acceptance of goods tendered or delivered to him, the buyer may cancel the contract with respect to any goods involved; and if the breach by the seller concerns the whole contract, the buyer may cancel the entire contract. Section 2–711(1); Section 2A–508(1)(a). The buyer, who must give the seller notice of his cancellation, is excused from further performance or tender on his part. Section 2–106; Section 2A–505(1).

---

### CISG

*The buyer may declare the contract avoided if (1) the seller commits a fundamental breach or (2) the seller does not, within the additional period of time fixed by the buyer, deliver the goods. Avoidance of the contract releases both parties from their obligations under it, subject to any damages that may be due. Avoidance does not affect any provision of the contract for the settlement of disputes or any other provision of the contract governing the rights and obligations of the parties consequent upon the avoidance of the contract.*

---

## To Recover Payments Made

The buyer, upon the seller's breach, also may recover as much of the price as he has paid. Section 2–711(1). For example, Jonas and Sheila enter into a contract for a sale of goods for a contract price of $3,000, and Sheila, the buyer, has made a down payment of $600. Jonas delivers nonconforming goods to Sheila, who rightfully rejects them. Sheila may cancel the contract and recover the $600 plus whatever other damages she can prove. Under Article 2A, the lessee may recover so much of the rent and security as has been paid and is just under the circumstances. Section 2A–508(1)(b).

## To Cover

Upon the seller's breach, the buyer may protect himself by obtaining cover. **Cover** means that the buyer may in good faith and without unreasonable delay proceed to purchase needed goods or make a contract to purchase such goods in substitution for those due under the contract from the seller. Section 2–712(1). In a lease, the

lessee may purchase or lease substitute goods. Section 2A–518(1).

Upon making a reasonable contract of cover, the buyer may recover from the seller the **difference between the cost of cover and the contract price,** plus any incidental and consequential damages (discussed below), less expenses saved because of the seller's breach. Section 2–712(2). For example, Doug, whose factory is in Oakland, agrees to sell goods to Velda, in Atlanta, for $22,000 F.O.B. Oakland. Doug fails to deliver, and Velda covers by purchasing substitute goods in Atlanta for $25,000, incurring $700 in sales commissions but suffering no other damages as a consequence of Doug's breach. Shipping costs from Oakland to Atlanta for the goods are $1,300. Velda would recover the difference between the cost of cover ($25,000) and the contract price ($22,000), plus incidental damages ($700 in sales commissions), plus consequential damages ($0 in this example), minus expenses saved ($1,300 in shipping costs that Velda need not pay under the contract of cover), which equals $2,400.

In a lease, the comparable recovery is the **difference between the present values** of the **new rent** due under the new lease and the **old rent** due under the original lease. Section 2A–518(2).

The buyer is not required to obtain cover, and his failure to do so does not bar him from any other remedy the Code provides. Section 2–712(3); 2A–519(1). The buyer may not, however, recover consequential damages that he could have prevented by cover. Section 2–715(2)(a); Section 2A–520(2)(a).

---

### CISG

*If the contract is avoided and the buyer has bought goods in replacement in a reasonable manner and within a reasonable time after avoidance, he may recover the difference between the contract price and the price paid in the substitute transaction. In addition, he may recover consequential damages.*

---

 *See Case 25–2*

## To Recover Damages for Nondelivery or Repudiation

If the seller repudiates the contract or fails to deliver the goods, or if the buyer rightfully rejects or justifiably revokes acceptance of the goods, the buyer is entitled to recover damages from the seller equal to the **difference between** the **market price** at the time when the buyer learned of the breach and the **contract price**, together with incidental and consequential damages, less expenses saved because of the seller's breach. Section 2–713(1). This remedy is a complete alternative to the remedy of cover and, as such, is available only to the extent the buyer has not covered. As previously indicated, the buyer who elects this remedy may not recover consequential damages that she could have avoided by cover.

In a lease, the comparable recovery is the **difference between** the **present values** of the **market rent** and the **old rent** due under the original lease. Section 2A–519(1).

The market price is to be determined either as of the place for tender or, in the event that the buyer has rightfully rejected the goods or has justifiably revoked his acceptance of them, as of the place of arrival. Section 2–713(2). For example, Janet, in Portland, agrees to sell goods to Laura, in Minneapolis, for $7,000 C.O.D. with delivery by November 15. Janet fails to deliver. As a consequence, Laura suffers incidental damages of $1,500 and consequential damages of $1,000. In the case of nondelivery or repudiation, market price is determined as of the place of tender. Because C.O.D. is a shipment contract, the place of tender would be the seller's city. Therefore, the market price must be the market price in Portland, the seller's city, on November 15, the date when Laura learned of the breach. At this time and place the market price is $8,000. Laura would recover the difference between the market price ($8,000) and the contract price ($7,000), plus incidental damages ($1,500), plus consequential damages ($1,000), less expenses saved ($0 in this example), which equals $3,500.

In the example above, if Janet had instead delivered nonconforming goods that Laura rejected, then the market price would be determined at Laura's place of business in Minneapolis. If Janet had repudiated the contract on November 1 rather than November 15, then the market price would be determined as of November 1.

In a lease, market rent is to be determined as of the place for tender or, in cases of rejection after arrival or revocation of acceptance, as of the place of arrival. Section 2A–519(2).

## CISG

*If the contract is avoided and the buyer has not made a replacement purchase, he may recover the difference between the contract price and the current price at the time of avoidance and at the place where delivery of the goods should have been made. In addition, he may recover consequential damages.*

## To Recover Identified Goods upon the Seller's Insolvency

Where existing goods are identified to the contract of sale, the buyer acquires a *special property interest* in the goods. Section 2–501. This special property interest exists even though the goods are nonconforming, and the buyer therefore has the right to return or reject them. Either the buyer or the seller may identify the goods to the contract.

The Code gives the buyer a right, which does not exist at common law, to recover from an insolvent seller the goods in which the buyer has a special property interest and for which he has paid part or all of the price. This right exists where the seller, who is in possession or control of the goods, becomes insolvent within ten days after receiving the first installment of the price. To exercise it, the buyer must tender to the seller any unpaid portion of the price. If the special property interest exists by reason of an identification made by the buyer, he may recover the goods only if they conform to the contract for sale. Section 2–502; Section 2A–522.

## To Sue for Replevin

**Replevin** is an action at law to recover from a defendant's possession specific goods that are being unlawfully withheld from the plaintiff. Where the seller has repudiated or breached the contract, the buyer may maintain against the seller an action for replevin for goods that have been identified to the contract if the buyer after a reasonable effort is unable to effect cover for such goods. Section 2–716(3); Section 2A–521(3). Article 2 also provides the buyer with the right to replevin if the goods have been shipped under reservation of a security interest in the seller and satisfaction of this security interest has been made or tendered. Section 2–716(3).

## To Sue for Specific Performance

**Specific performance** is an equitable remedy compelling the party in breach to perform the contract according to its terms. At common law, specific performance is available only if legal remedies are inadequate. For example, where the contract is for the purchase of a unique item, such as a work of art, a famous racehorse, or an heirloom, money damages may not be an adequate remedy. In such a case, a court of equity has the discretion to order the seller specifically to deliver to the buyer the goods described in the contract upon payment of the price.

The Code not only has continued the availability of specific performance but also has sought to encourage a more liberal attitude toward its use. Accordingly, it does not expressly require that the remedy at law be inadequate. Instead, the Code states that specific performance may be granted where "the goods are unique or in other proper circumstances." Section 2–716(1); Section 2A–521(1). As the Comment to Section 2–716 explains, the test of uniqueness under the Code must be made in view of the total situation that characterizes the contract.

## CISG

*The buyer may require the seller to perform his contractual obligations. If the goods do not conform to the contract and the nonconformity constitutes a fundamental breach of contract, the buyer may require delivery of substitute goods. If the goods do not conform to the contract, the buyer may require the seller to remedy the lack of conformity by repair, unless this is unreasonable having regard to all the circumstances. Nevertheless, a court is not bound to enter a judgment for specific performance unless a court would do so under its own law in respect of similar contracts of sale not governed by the CISG.*

## To Enforce a Security Interest in the Goods

A buyer who has rightfully rejected or justifiably revoked acceptance of goods that remain in his possession or control has a security interest in these goods to the extent of any payment of the price that he has made and for any expenses he reasonably has incurred in their inspection, receipt, transportation, care, and custody. The buyer may hold such goods and resell them in the same manner as an aggrieved seller may resell goods. Section 2–711(3); Section 2A–508(5). In the event of resale the buyer is accountable to the seller for any amount of the net proceeds of the resale that exceeds the amount of his security interest. Section 2–706(6); Section 2A–527(5).

## To Recover Damages for Breach in Regard to Accepted Goods

Where the buyer has accepted nonconforming goods and has timely notified the seller of the breach of contract, the buyer is entitled to recover from the seller the damages resulting in the ordinary course of events from the seller's breach, as determined in any reasonable manner. Section 2–714(1); Section 2A–519(3). Where appropriate, incidental and consequential damages also may be recovered. Section 2–714(3); Section 2A–519(3). Nonconformity includes breaches of warranty as well as any failure of the seller to perform according to her obligations under the contract. Thus, even if a seller cures a nonconforming tender, the buyer may recover under this section for any injury he suffered because the original tender was nonconforming.

In the event of breach of warranty, the measure of damages is the **difference** at the time and place of acceptance **between** the **value of the goods which have been accepted and** the **value** that the goods would have had if they had been **as warranted,** unless special circumstances show proximate damages of a different amount. Section 2–714(2). Article 2A has a comparable provision, except the recovery is for the **present value** of the difference between the value of the use of the goods accepted and the value if they had been as warranted for the lease term. Section 2A–519(4).

The contract price of the goods does not figure in this computation because the buyer is entitled to the benefit of his bargain, which is to receive goods that are as warranted. For example, Max agrees to sell goods to Stanley for $1,000. The value of the goods accepted is only $800; had they been as warranted, their value would have been $1,200. Stanley's damages for breach of warranty are $400, which he may deduct from any unpaid balance due on the purchase price upon notice to Max of his intention to do so. Section 2–717; Section 2A–508(6).

## To Recover Incidental Damages

In addition to remedies such as covering, recovering damages for nondelivery or repudiation, or recovering damages for breach in regard to accepted goods, including breach of warranty, the buyer may recover incidental damages. A buyer's **incidental damages** provide reimbursement for the buyer who incurs reasonable expenses in handling rightfully rejected goods or in effecting cover. Section 2–715(1) of the Code defines the buyer's incidental damages as follows:

Incidental damages resulting from the seller's breach include expenses reasonably incurred in inspection, receipt, transportation and care and custody of goods rightfully rejected, any commercially reasonable charges, expenses or commissions in connection with effecting cover and any other reasonable expense incident to the delay or other breach.

Article 2A has an analogous definition. Section 2A–520(1).

For example, the buyer of a racehorse who justifiably revokes acceptance because the horse does not conform to the contract will be allowed to recover as incidental damages the cost of caring for the horse from the date the horse was delivered until the buyer returns it to the seller.

## To Recover Consequential Damages

In many cases, the remedies discussed above will not fully compensate the aggrieved buyer for her losses. For example, nonconforming goods that are accepted may in some way damage or destroy the buyer's warehouse and its contents, or undelivered goods may have been the subject of a lucrative contract of resale, the profits from which are now lost. The Code responds to this problem by providing the buyer with the opportunity to recover **consequential damages** resulting from the seller's breach, including (1) any loss resulting from the buyer's requirements and needs of which the seller at the time of contracting had reason to know and which the buyer could not reasonably prevent by cover or otherwise; and (2) injury to person or property proximately resulting from any breach of warranty. Section 2–715(2); Section 2A–520(2).

With respect to the first type of consequential damages, *particular* needs of the buyer usually must be made known to the seller, whereas *general* needs usually need not be. In the case of a buyer who is in the business of reselling goods, resale is one requirement of which the seller has reason to know. For example, Supreme Machine Co., a manufacturer, contracts to sell Allied Sales, Inc., a dealer in used machinery, a used machine that Allied plans to resell. When Supreme repudiates and Allied is unable to obtain a similar machine elsewhere, Allied's damages include the net profit that it would have made on resale of the machine. A buyer may not, however, recover consequential damages he could have prevented by cover. Section 2–715(2); Section 2A–520(2)(a). For instance, Supreme Machine Co. contracts for $10,000 to sell Capitol Manufacturing Co. a used machine to be delivered at Capitol's factory by June 1. Supreme repudiates the contract on May 1. By reasonable efforts, Capitol could buy a similar machine from United Machinery Inc. for $11,000 in time for a June 1 delivery. Capitol fails to do so, thereby losing a $5,000 profit that it would have made from the resale of the machine. Though Capitol can recover $1,000 from Supreme, its damages do not include the loss of the $5,000 profit.

An example of the second type of consequential damages would be the following: Federal Machine Co. sells a machine to Southern Manufacturing Co., warranting its suitability for Southern's purpose. The machine is not suitable for Southern's purpose, however, and causes $10,000 in damage to Southern's property and $15,000 in personal injuries. Southern can recover the $25,000 consequential damages in addition to any other loss suffered.

◆ *See Figure 25–2*

## CONTRACTUAL PROVISIONS AFFECTING REMEDIES

Within specified limits, the Code permits the parties to a sales contract to modify, exclude, or limit by agreement the remedies or damages that will be available for breach of that contract. Two basic types of contractual provisions affect remedies: (1) liquidation or limitation of damages and (2) modification or limitation of remedy.

## Liquidation or Limitation of Damages

The parties may provide for **liquidated damages** in their contract by specifying the amount or measure of damages that either party may recover in the event of a breach by the other. The amount of such damages must be reasonable in light of the anticipated or actual loss resulting from a breach, the difficulties of proof of loss, and the inconvenience or lack of feasibility of otherwise obtaining an adequate remedy. A contractual provision fixing unreasonably large liquidated damages is void as a penalty. Section 2–718(1). An unreasonably small amount, on the other hand, might be stricken on the grounds of unconscionability. Comment 1 to Section 2–718.

To illustrate, Sterling Cabinetry Company contracts to build and install shelves and cabinets for an office building being constructed by Baron Construction Company. The contract price is $120,000, and the contract provides that Sterling would be liable for $100 per day for every day's delay beyond the completion date specified in the contract. The stipulated sum of $100 per day is reasonable

FIGURE 25–2  Remedies of the Buyer

| Seller's Breach | Buyer's Remedies | | |
|---|---|---|---|
| | Obligation-oriented | Goods-oriented | Money-oriented* |
| **Buyer rightfully rejects goods** | Cancel | Have a security interest | • Recover payments made<br>• Cover and recover damages<br>• Recover damages for nondelivery |
| **Buyer justifiably revokes acceptance** | Cancel | Have a security interest | • Recover payments made<br>• Cover and recover damages<br>• Recover damages for nondelivery |
| **Seller fails to deliver** | Cancel | • Recover identified goods if seller is insolvent<br>• Replevy goods<br>• Obtain specific performance | • Recover payments made<br>• Cover and recover damages<br>• Recover damages for nondelivery |
| **Seller repudiates** | Cancel | • Recover identified goods if seller is insolvent<br>• Replevy goods<br>• Obtain specific performance | • Recover payments made<br>• Cover and recover damages<br>• Recover damages for nondelivery |
| **Buyer accepts nonconforming goods** | | | Recover damages for breach of warranty |

*In a lease, the lessee's recovery of damages for future rent payments is reduced to their present value.

and commensurate with the anticipated loss. Therefore, it is enforceable as liquidated damages. If, instead, the sum stipulated had been $5,000 per day, it would be unreasonably large and therefore void as a penalty.

Section 2A–504(1) authorizes liquidated damages payable by either party for default, or any other act or omission. The amount of, or formula for, liquidated damages must be reasonable in light of the then anticipated harm caused by default or other act or omission. Section 2A–504(1).

Where the seller justifiably withholds delivery of the goods because of the buyer's breach, and the buyer has made payments on the price, the buyer is entitled to restitution of the amount by which the sum of his payments exceeds the amount of liquidated damages to which the seller is entitled under the contract. In the absence of a provision for liquidated damages, the buyer may recover the difference between the amounts which he has paid on the price and 20 percent of the value of the total performance for which he is obligated under the contract, or $500, whichever is smaller. Section 2–718(2)(b). Article 2A has a comparable provision, except the $500 provision applies only to consumer leases. Section 2A–504(3)(b). The buyer's right to restitution

is offset by the seller's right to recover other damages provided in the Code and by the value of any benefits the buyer has received by reason of the contract. Section 2–718(3); Section 2A–504(4).

Thus, if a buyer, after depositing $1,500 with the seller on a $10,000 contract for goods, breaches the contract and the seller withholds delivery, in the absence of a provision for liquidated damages and in the absence of the seller's establishing greater actual damages resulting from the breach, the buyer is entitled to restitution of $1,000 ($1,500 less $500). If the deposit were $250 on a $500 contract, the buyer would be entitled to $150 ($250 less $100, which is 20 percent of the price).

 *See Case 25–3*

## Modification or Limitation of Remedy by Agreement

The contract between the seller and buyer may expressly provide for remedies in addition to or instead of those provided in the Code and may limit or change the measure of damages recoverable in the event of breach. Section 2–719(1); Section 2A–503(1). For instance, the contract may validly limit the buyer's remedy to a return of the goods and a refund of the price, or to the replacement of nonconforming goods or parts.

A contractual remedy is deemed optional, however, unless the parties expressly agree that it is to be exclusive of other remedies, in which event it becomes the sole remedy. Section 2–719(1)(b); Section 2A–503(2). Moreover, where circumstances cause an exclusive or limited remedy to fail in its essential purpose, the parties may resort to the remedies provided by the Code. Section 2–719(2); Section 2A–503(2).

The contract may expressly limit or exclude consequential damages unless such limitation or exclusion would be unconscionable. Limitation of consequential damages for personal injuries resulting from breach of warranty in the sale of consumer goods is *prima facie* unconscionable, whereas limitation of such damages for commercial loss is not. Section 2–719(3); Section 2A–503(3). For example, Ace Motors, Inc., sells a pickup truck to Brenda, a consumer. The contract of sale excludes liability for all consequential damages. The next day, the truck explodes, causing Brenda serious personal injury. Brenda would recover for her personal injuries

unless Ace could prove that the exclusion of consequential damages was not unconscionable.

 *See Case 25–4*

## Statute of Limitations

Any action for breach of a sales contract must be begun within four years after the cause of action has accrued. Section 2–725(1); Section 2A–506(1). The parties may reduce the period of limitation to not less than one year. Section 2–725(1); Section 2A–506(1). In a sale, they may not, however, extend the period. Article 2A does not include this limitation.

A cause of action accrues when the breach occurs without regard to the injured party's knowledge of the breach. Section 2–725(2). A breach of warranty occurs upon tender of delivery, except where the warranty extends to future performance. In that event, the cause of action occurs when the breach is or should have been discovered. In a lease, a cause of action for default accrues when the act or omission is discovered or should have been discovered by the aggrieved party, or when the default occurs, whichever is later. Section 2A–506(2).

---

                    # Chapter Summary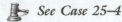

---

| **Remedies of the Seller** | **Buyer's Default**  the seller's remedies are triggered by the buyer's actions in wrongfully rejecting or revoking acceptance of the goods, in failing to make payment due on or before delivery, or in repudiating the contract |
|---|---|
| | **To Withhold Delivery** |
| | **To Stop Delivery**  if the buyer is insolvent (one who is unable to pay his debts as they become due or one whose total liabilities exceed his total assets), the seller may stop any delivery; if the buyer repudiates or otherwise breaches, the seller may stop carload, truckload, planeload, or larger shipments |
| | **To Identify Goods** |
| | **To Resell the Goods**  the seller may resell the goods concerned or the undelivered balance of the goods and recover the difference between the contract price and the resale price, together with any incidental damages, less expenses saved |
| | • *Type of Resale*  may be public or private |
| | • *Manner of Resale*  must be made in good faith and in a commercially reasonable manner |
| | **To Recover Damages for Nonacceptance or Repudiation** |
| | • *Market Price Differential*  the seller may recover damages from the buyer measured by the difference between the unpaid contract price and the market price at the time and place of tender of the goods, plus incidental damages, less expenses saved |
| | • *Lost Profit*  in the alternative, the seller may recover the lost profit, including reasonable overhead, plus incidental damages, less expenses saved |
| | **To Recover the Price**  the seller may recover the price |
| | • where the buyer has accepted the goods |

- where the goods have been lost or damaged after the risk of loss has passed to the buyer
- where the goods have been identified to the contract and there is no ready market available for their resale

**To Recover Incidental Damages**  incidental damages include any commercially reasonable charges, expenses, or commissions directly resulting from the breach

**To Cancel the Contract**

**To Reclaim the Goods upon the Buyer's Insolvency**  an unpaid seller may reclaim goods from an insolvent buyer under certain circumstances

## Remedies of the Buyer

**Seller's Default**  the buyer's remedies arise where the seller fails to make delivery or repudiates the contract, or where the buyer rightfully rejects or justifiably revokes acceptance of goods tendered or delivered

**To Cancel the Contract**

**To Recover Payments Made**

**To Cover**  the buyer may obtain cover by proceeding in good faith and without unreasonable delay to purchase substitute goods; the buyer may recover the difference between the cost of cover and the contract price, plus any incidental and consequential damages, less expenses saved

**To Recover Damages for Nondelivery or Repudiation**  the buyer may recover the difference between the market price at the time the buyer learned of the breach and the contract price, together with any incidental and consequential damages, less expenses saved

**To Recover Identified Goods on the Seller's Insolvency**  for which he has paid all or part of the price

**To Sue for Replevin**  the buyer may recover goods identified to the contract if (1) the buyer is unable to obtain cover or (2) the goods have been shipped under reservation of a security interest in the seller

**To Sue for Specific Performance**  the buyer may obtain specific performance where the goods are unique or in other proper circumstances

**To Enforce a Security Interest**  a buyer who has rightfully rejected or justifiably revoked acceptance of goods that remain in her possession has a security interest in these goods for any payments that she has made on their price and for any expenses she has reasonably incurred

**To Recover Damages for Breach in Regard to Accepted Goods**  the buyer may recover damages resulting in the ordinary course of events from the seller's breach; in the case of breach of warranty, such recovery is the difference between the value the goods would have had if they had been as warranted and the value of the nonconforming goods that have been accepted

**To Recover Incidental Damages**  the buyer may recover incidental damages, which include any commercially reasonable expenses connected with the delay or other breach

**To Recover Consequential Damages**  the buyer may recover consequential damages resulting from the seller's breach, including (1) any loss resulting from the buyer's requirements and needs of which the seller at the time of contracting had reason to know and which the buyer could not reasonably prevent by cover or otherwise, and (2) injury to person or property proximately resulting from any breach of warranty

## Contractual Provisions Affecting Remedies

**Liquidation or Limitation of Damages**  the parties may specify the amount or measure of damages that may be recovered in the event of a breach if the amount is reasonable

**Modification or Limitation of Remedy by Agreement**  the contract between the parties may expressly provide for remedies in addition to those in the Code, or it may limit or change the measure of damages recoverable for breach

# Cases

### CASE 25–1
### Seller's Damages for Nonacceptance or Repudiation
## *UNIQUE DESIGNS, INC. v. PITTARD MACHINERY COMPANY*
Court of Appeals of Georgia, 1991
200 Ga.App. 647, 409 S.E.2d 241

COOPER, J.

In January or February of 1988, Pittard Machinery Company ("Pittard"), a distributor of lathes, attempted to sell to Unique Designs, Inc. ("Unique") a "Mori Seiki" lathe; however, Unique instead purchased a less expensive "Mazak" lathe from one of Pittard's competitors. In June of 1988, Unique contacted Pittard and requested Pittard's assistance in disposing of the Mazak lathe because it had turned out to be incompatible with Unique's business. During the course of this conversation, Unique indicated that in return for Pittard's assistance in disposing of the Mazak lathe, Unique would replace the Mazak lathe by purchasing a Mori Seiki lathe from Pittard. Pittard proceeded to arrange for the resale of the Mazak lathe by putting Unique in contact with an international broker of machinery who quickly found a purchaser for the used lathe. Pittard never asked Unique to pay a commission on the sale of the Mazak lathe because of its expectation that Unique would be replacing the Mazak lathe with a Mori Seiki lathe purchased from Pittard. Thereafter, Unique and Pittard commenced negotiating the price of the Mori Seiki lathe and during the course of a telephone conversation, the parties finally agreed upon a price of either $104,000 or $104,850, and arrangements were made for the delivery of a lathe to Unique. It is undisputed that an oral agreement to purchase the lathe was made, although the amount of the purchase price is in dispute.

The day after the agreement was reached, Unique contacted Pittard and cancelled its order to purchase the lathe. Apparently, Unique had been negotiating all along with one of Pittard's competitors and had used its contract with Pittard as leverage to secure a reduced price on a different model lathe with the competitor. Shortly after Unique's repudiation of the contract, Pittard was able to resell the Mori Seiki lathe to one of its regular customers, Sieco, Inc. ("Sieco"), for $110,000.

Pittard brought suit against Unique seeking general damages and attorney fees for Unique's breach of its agreement to purchase the lathe. The trial court granted Pittard's motion for summary judgment on the issue of liability, ruling that the oral contract between the parties was valid pursuant to [U.C.C. §] 2–201(3)(b), and Pittard was a "high volume dealer," entitled to recover its lost profits pursuant to [U.C.C. §] 2–708(2), without having to offset the proceeds it received from the sale of the lathe to Sieco. The case proceeded to trial on the issue of damages, and the jury awarded Pittard $18,000 in general damages and $18,000 in attorney fees. Following the jury verdict, the trial court entered judgment in favor of Pittard for $18,000 in general damages but set aside the jury's award of attorney fees. Unique appeals from the trial court's grant of partial summary judgment to Pittard and the final judgment entered on the jury verdict for general damages. * * *

Unique contends . . . that the trial court erred in adopting the "lost volume dealer" rule, which allowed Pittard to recover its lost profits on the repudiated contract without offset for the proceeds received from the resale of the lathe to Sieco.

Both Pittard and Unique appear to be in agreement that [U.C.C. §] 2–708(2) sets forth the proper measure of damages in circumstances such as those presented by this appeal. Although there are no Georgia cases directly on point, this court has held that "[i]f the measure of damages under [U.C.C. §] 2–708(1) is inadequate to put the seller in as good a position as if the contract had been fully performed, then the damages are as prescribed by (2) . . ." [Citation.] Numerous authoritative writers and other jurisdictions agree that UCC § 2–708(2) is applicable under the present circumstances. See White & Summers, Uniform Commercial Code, § 7–9 (1988) (fn. 4). It is also the opinion of these authorities that the statutory history of the Uniform Commercial Code indicates that UCC

§ 2–708(2) was intended to provide an adequate remedy for the "lost volume dealer." "Lost volume dealer," sometimes referred to as a "lost volume seller," refers to a seller who due to the nature of its business, is damaged by a buyer's breach to the extent that it loses the entire profit from the sale.

When the seller is a dealer he is entitled to recover lost profits and incidental damages from a repudiating buyer, even though the seller has resold the goods to another buyer at the same price as the original buyer had contracted to pay, for the reason that if the original buyer had not repudiated, the seller would have been able to make two sales and thus obtain two profits.

The rationale for the rule for measuring damages in the case of a seller who is a middleman is that the breach by his buyer does not make possible a new sale which the seller could not have otherwise made in which new sale the profit lost upon the sale to the original buyer will be replaced; but rather, results in an irretrievable loss of profits. 4 Anderson, U.C.C., § 2–708:21 (1983).

In order for a seller to establish that he is a "lost volume dealer," he must prove that even though he later resold the repudiated contract goods, the sale to the third party would have been made regardless of the buyer's breach so that the seller would have realized two profits from two sales. "The key inquiry is the sellers' ability to provide the product to both the breaching buyer and the resale buyer." [Citations.]

In the case *sub judice* [under consideration], the record reveals that Pittard carries a large inventory of lathes; that the lathe to be delivered to Unique was a stock inventory item not specially ordered, made or adapted to any specifications on Unique's part; and that the sale of the Mori Seiki lathe to Sieco would have occurred even if Unique had not repudiated its contract. Thus, Pittard has clearly established itself as a "lost volume dealer," entitled to recover its lost profits pursuant to [U.C.C. §] 2–708(2).

[U.C.C. §] 2–708(2) provides: "If the measure of damages provided in subsection (1) of this Code section is inadequate to put the seller in as good a position as performance would have done then the measure of damages is the profit (including reasonable overhead) which the seller would have made from full performance by the buyer, together with any incidental damages provided in this article (Code section 2–710), due allowance for costs reasonably incurred and due credit for payments or proceeds of resale." Unique argues that the formula provided for in this code provision should be strictly applied so that Pittard should be required to give Unique due credit for the payments or proceeds from the resale of the lathe to Sieco. However, the overwhelming view of modern authority has concluded that the formula, if strictly applied, will not yield the correct recovery that a "lost volume dealer" deserves. See White & Summers, supra § 7–13 (fn. 3). As the court in [citation stated]:

Logically, lost volume status, which entitles the seller to the § 2–708(2) formula rather than the formula found in § 2–708(1), is inconsistent with a credit for the proceeds of resale. The whole concept of lost volume status is that the sale of the goods to the resale purchaser could have been made with other goods had there been no breach. In essence, the original sale and the second sale are independent events, becoming related only after breach, as the original sale goods are applied to the second sale. To require a credit for the proceeds of resale is to deny the essential element that entitles the lost volume seller to § 2–708(2) in the first place—the mutual independence of the contract and the resale.

Practically, if the 'due credit' clause is applied to the lost volume seller, his measure of damages is no different from his recovery under § 2–708(1). Under § 2–708(1) he recovers the contract/market differential and the profit he makes on resale. If the 'due credit' provision is applied, the seller recovers only the profit he makes on resale plus the difference between the resale price and the contract price, an almost identical measure to § 2–708(1). If the 'due credit' clause is applied to the lost volume seller, the damage measure of 'lost profits' is rendered nugatory, and he is not put in as good a position as if there had been performance.

* * *

[Citation. U.C.C. §] 1–106(1) provides that "[t]he remedies provided by [the Uniform Commercial Code] shall be liberally administered to the end that the aggrieved party may be put in as good a position as if the other party had fully performed. . ." The adoption of the "lost volume dealer" rule is inconsistent with the intent and purpose of the Uniform Commercial Code—to fairly compensate "lost profit dealers" so that they will be put in as good a position as if the other party had fully performed. Since Pittard clearly established that it was a "lost volume dealer," the trial court was correct to allow Pittard to recover its lost profits on its contract with Unique without having to offset profits it received on the resale to Sieco. Accordingly, appellant's [contentions] are without merit.

* * *

Judgment affirmed.

## CASE 25-2
## Buyer's Remedy of Cover
## *BIGELOW-SANFORD, INC. v. GUNNY CORP.*
United States Court of Appeals, Fifth Circuit, Unit B, 1981
649 F.2d 1060

KRAVITCH, J.

[The plaintiff, Bigelow-Sanford, Inc., contracted with defendant Gunny Corp. for the purchase of 100,000 linear yards of jute at $0.64 per yard. Gunny delivered 22,228 linear yards in January 1979. The February and March deliveries required under the contract were not made, though 8 rolls (each roll containing 66.7 linear yards) were delivered in April. With 72,265 linear yards undelivered, Gunny told Bigelow-Sanford that no more would be delivered. In mid-March, Bigelow-Sanford turned to the jute spot market to replace the balance of the order at a price of $1.21 per linear yard. Since several other companies had also defaulted on their jute contracts with Bigelow-Sanford, the plaintiff purchased a total of 164,503 linear yards on the spot market. Plaintiff sues defendant to recover losses sustained as a result of the breach of contract.]

\* \* \*

Gunny contends that appellee's [Bigelow-Sanford] alleged cover purchases should not have been used to measure damages in that they were not made in substitution for the contract purchases, were not made seasonably or in good faith and were not shown to be due to Gunny's breach. [W]e disagree. Again, we quote UCC § 2–711 providing in part for cover damages where the seller fails to make delivery or repudiates the contract:

(a) "cover" and have damages under the next section as to all the goods affected whether or not they have been identified to the contract; or

(b) recover damages for non-delivery as provided in this Article (2–713).

UCC § 2–712 defines cover:

(1) After a breach within the preceding section the buyer may "cover" by making in good faith and without unreasonable delay any reasonable purchase of or contract to purchase goods in substitution for those due from the seller.

(2) The buyer may recover from the seller as damages the difference between the cost of cover and the contract price together with any incidental or consequential damages as hereinafter defined (2–715), but less expenses saved in consequence of the seller's breach.

(3) Failure of the buyer to effect cover within this section does not bar him from any other remedy.

In addition, the purchaser may recover under 2–713:

(1) Subject to the provisions of this Article with respect to proof of market price (2–723), the measure of damages for non-delivery or repudiation by the seller is the difference between the market price at the time when the buyer learned of the breach and the contract price together with any incidental and consequential damages provided in this Article (2–715), but less expenses saved in consequence of the seller's breach.

(2) Market price is to be determined as of the place for tender or, in cases of rejection after arrival or revocation of acceptance, as of the place of arrival.

Most importantly, "whether a plaintiff has made his cover purchases in a reasonable manner poses a classic jury issue." [Citation.] The district court thus acted properly in submitting the question of cover damages to the jury, which found that Gunny had breached, appellee had covered, and had done so in good faith without unreasonable delay by making reasonable purchases, and was therefore entitled to damages under § 2–712. Gunny argues Bigelow is not entitled to such damages on the ground that it failed to make cover purchases without undue delay and that the jury should not have been permitted to average the cost of Bigelow's spot market purchases totalling 164,503 linear yards in order to arrive at the cost of cover for the 72,265 linear yards Gunny failed to deliver. Both arguments fail. Gunny notified Bigelow in February that no more jute would be forthcoming. Bigelow made its first spot market purchases in mid-March. Given that it is within the jury's province to decide the reasonableness of the manner in which cover purchases were made, we believe the jury could reasonably decide such purchases, made one month after the date the jury assigned to Gunny's breach, were made without undue delay. The same is true with respect to Gunny's second argument: Bigelow's spot market purchases were made to replace several vendors' shipments. Bigelow did not specifically allocate the spot market replacements to individual vendors' accounts, however, nor was there a requirement that they do so. The jury's method of averaging such costs and assigning them to Gunny in proportion to the amount of jute if [sic] failed to deliver would, therefore, seem not only fair but well within the jury's permissible bounds.

Gunny also argues that the court erroneously charged the jury regarding damages under both §§ 2–712 and 2–713. We disagree. Whether Bigelow covered was a question of fact submitted to the jury. In the event that it had not, alternative damages were available to Bigelow under § 2–713. [Citation.] The jury found that Bigelow had covered and awarded damages under § 2–712; § 2–713 then became irrelevant. Since either was applicable until that time, the court's charge as to both sections was not error.

\* \* \*

[Judgment for Bigelow is affirmed.]

---

## CASE 25–3
### Liquidation of Damages
# COASTAL LEASING CORPORATION v. T-BAR S CORPORATION
Court of Appeals of North Carolina, 1998
128 N.C.App. 379, 496 S.E.2d 795

WALKER, J.

Plaintiff entered into a lease agreement (lease) with defendant T-Bar S Corporation (T-Bar) in May of 1992, whereby plaintiff agreed to lease certain cash register equipment (equipment) to T-Bar. Under the lease, T-Bar agreed to monthly rental payments of $289.13 each for a total of 48 months. Defendants George and Sharon Talbott (appellants) were the officers of T-Bar and personally guaranteed payment of all amounts due under the lease.

After making 18 of the monthly payments, appellants and T-Bar defaulted on the lease in December of 1993. On 28 February 1994, plaintiff mailed a certified letter to appellants and T-Bar, return receipt requested, advising them that the lease was in default and, pursuant to the terms of the lease, plaintiff was accelerating the remaining payments due under the lease. They further advised appellants and T-Bar that if the entire amount due of $8,841.06 was not received within 7 days, plaintiff would seek to recover the balance due plus interest and reasonable attorneys' fees, as well as possession of the equipment. The record shows that appellants and T-Bar each received this letter on 1 March 1994.

On 10 March 1994, plaintiff mailed a certified letter and "Notice of Public Sale of Repossessed Leased Equipment" (notice of sale) to appellants and T-Bar at the same address, again return receipt requested. This letter advised appellants and T-Bar that plaintiff had taken possession of the equipment and was conducting a public sale pursuant to the terms of the lease. Although the date on the notice of sale stated that the sale was to be held on 23 March 1994, the sale was actually scheduled to be held on 25 March 1994. This letter and notice of sale were returned to plaintiffs "unclaimed" on 29 March 1994.

Plaintiffs conducted a public sale of the equipment on 25 March 1994 and no one appeared on behalf of appellants or T-Bar. There being no other bidders, plaintiff purchased the equipment at the sale for $2,000.00.

On 4 October 1994, plaintiff leased some of the same equipment to another company at a rate calculated to be $212.67 for 36 months. Plaintiff then filed this action on 6 October 1994 seeking to recover the balance due under the lease, minus the net proceeds from the 25 March 1994 public sale, plus interest and reasonable attorneys' fees. Appellants filed an answer and counterclaim on 27 July 1995. Plaintiff then filed a motion for summary judgment against appellants on 8 July 1996. When T-Bar failed to answer, a default judgment was entered against it on 30 December 1996.

After a hearing, the trial court entered summary judgment on 15 January 1997 in favor of plaintiff on its complaint and appellants' counterclaims and entered judgment against appellants for the sum of $7,223.56 plus interest and attorneys' fees of $1,083.54.

\* \* \*

Equipment leasing transactions are an ever increasing segment of commercial activity in North Carolina as well as in the rest of the United States. According to recent U.S. Department of Commerce statistics, "leasing transactions accounted for approximately $168.9 billion of new equipment installed in 1996, an expansion of 11.6% over 1995." [Citation.]

A threshold issue in this case is whether the transaction involved is a lease or a security interest disguised as a lease. If it is a security interest disguised as a lease, it will be governed by Article 9. However, if it is a lease, it will be governed by Article 2A. [Citation.]

By its terms, Article 2A "applies to any transaction, regardless of form, that creates a lease." [U.C.C. §]

2A–102. Further, a "lease" is defined as "a transfer of the right to possession and use of goods for a term in return for consideration, but a sale . . . is not a lease." [U.C.C. §] 2A–103(1)(j). In contrast, a transaction involves a security interest if it meets the general definition set forth in part 2 of Article 1. [U.C.C. §] 1–201(37)(a). Since both parties agree that the transaction at issue in this case is not a security interest, but rather is a lease, Article 2A controls.

Before addressing appellants' assignments of error, we should note that Article 2A did not become effective in this State until 1 October 1993. Therefore, there is an absence of case law interpreting this Article.

In their appeal, appellants contend that the trial court erred by granting summary judgment in favor of plaintiff because there exists a genuine issue of material fact as to whether: (1) the liquidated damages clause contained in Paragraph 13 of the lease is reasonable in light of the then-anticipated harm caused by default; * * *.

As to appellants' first contention, the official commentary to Article 2A states that "in recognition of the diversity of the transactions to be governed [and] the sophistication of many of the parties to these transactions . . ., freedom of contract has been preserved." [U.C.C. §] 2A–102 Official Comment. Also, under general contract principles, when the parties to a transaction deal with each other at arms length and without the exercise by one of the parties of superior bargaining power, the parties will be bound by their agreement. [Citation.]

Article 2A recognizes that "[m]any leasing transactions are predicated on the parties' ability to agree to an appropriate amount of damages or formula for damages in the event of default or other act or omission." [U.C.C. §] 2A–504 Official Comment. [U.C.C. §] 2A–504 states, in pertinent part:

(1) Damages payable by either party for default, or any other act or omission . . . may be liquidated in the lease agreement but only at an amount or by a formula that is reasonable in light of the then-anticipated harm caused by the default or other act or omission.

This liquidated damages provision is more flexible than that provided by its statutory analogue under Article 2, [U.C.C. §] 2–718. The Article 2 liquidated damages section provides, in pertinent part:

(1) Damages for breach by either party may be liquidated in the agreement but only at an amount which is reasonable in the light of the anticipated or actual harm caused by the breach, the difficulties of proof of loss, and the inconvenience or nonfeasibility of otherwise obtaining an adequate remedy. A term fixing unreasonably large liquidated damages is void as a penalty.

[U.C.C. §] 2–718(1) (emphasis added). A review of these statutes reveals two major differences.

First, the drafters of Article 2A chose not to incorporate the two tests which are required by Article 2, i.e., the difficulties of proof of loss and the inconvenience or nonfeasibility of otherwise obtaining an adequate remedy. In fact, the official commentary to [U.C.C. §] 2A–504 states that since "[t]he ability to liquidate damages is critical to modern leasing practice . . . [and] given the parties' freedom to contract at common law, the policy behind retaining these two additional requirements here was thought to be outweighed." [Citation.]

Secondly, the drafters of Article 2A recognized that in order to further promote freedom of contract, it was necessary to delete the last sentence of [U.C.C. §] 2–718(1), which provided that unreasonably large liquidated damages provisions were void as a penalty. As such, the parties to a lease transaction are free to negotiate the amount of liquidated damages, restrained only by the rule of reasonableness.

"The basic test of the reasonableness of an agreement liquidating damages is whether the stipulated amount or amount produced by the stipulated formula represents a reasonable forecast of the probable loss." [Citation.] However, "no court should strike down a reasonable liquidated damage agreement based on foresight that has proved on hindsight to have contained an inaccurate estimation of the probable loss. . . ." Id. And, "the fact that there is a difference between the actual loss, as determined at or about the time of the default, and the anticipated loss or stipulated amount or formula, as stipulated at the time the lease contract was entered into . . .," does not necessarily mean that the liquidated damage agreement is unreasonable. Id. This is so because "[t]he value of a lessor's interest in leased equipment depends upon 'the physical condition of the equipment and the market conditions at that time.'" [Citation.] Further, in determining whether a liquidated damages clause is reasonable:

[A] court should keep in mind that the clause was negotiated by the parties, who are familiar with the circumstances and practices with respect to the type of transaction involved, and the clause carries with it a consensual apportionment of the risks of the agreement that a court should be slow to overturn.

[Citation.]

In this case, Paragraph 13 of the lease (the liquidated damages clause) reads as follows:

13. REMEDIES. If an event of default shall occur, Lessor may, at its option, at any time (a) declare the entire amount of unpaid rental for the balance of the term of this lease immediately due and payable, whereupon Lessee shall become obligated to pay to Lessor forthwith the total amount of the said rental for the balance of the said term, and (b) without demand or legal process, enter into the premises where the equipment may be found and take possession of and remove the Equipment, without liability for suit, action or other proceeding, and all rights of Lessee in the Equipment so removed shall terminate absolutely. Lessee hereby waives notice of, or hearing with respect to, such retaking. Lessor may at its option, use, ship, store, repair or lease all Equipment so removed and sell or otherwise dispose of any such Equipment at a private or public sale. In the event Lessor takes possession of the Equipment, Lessor shall give Lessee credit for any sums received by Lessor from the sale or rental of the Equipment after deduction of the expenses of sale or rental and Lessor's residual interest in the Equipment. . . . Lessor and Lessee acknowledge the difficulty in establishing a value for the unexpired lease term and owing to such difficulty agree that the provisions of this paragraph represent an agreed measure of damages and are not to be deemed a forfeiture or penalty. . . .

All remedies of Lessor hereunder are cumulative, are in addition to any other remedies provided for by law, and may, to the extent permitted by law, be exercised concurrently or separately. The exercise of any one remedy shall not be deemed to be an election of such remedy or to preclude the exercise of any other remedy. No failure on the part of the Lessor to exercise and no delay in exercising any right or remedy shall operate as a waiver thereof or modify the terms of this lease.

After a careful review, we conclude the liquidated damages clause is a reasonable estimation of the then-anticipated damages in the event of default because it protects plaintiff's expectation interest. The liquidated damages clause places plaintiff in the position it would have occupied had the lease been fully performed by allowing it to accelerate the balance of the lease payments and repossess the equipment. Therefore, since there is no evidence that plaintiff exercised a superior bargaining position in the negotiation of the liquidated damages clause, no genuine issue of material fact exists as to its reasonableness, and the trial court did not err by enforcing its provisions.

---

## CASE 25–4
## Limitation of Remedy by Agreement
### *BISHOP LOGGING COMPANY v.*
### *JOHN DEERE INDUSTRIAL EQUIPMENT CO.*

Court of Appeals of South Carolina, 1995
317 S.C. 520, 455 S.E.2d 183

CURETON, J.

[Bishop Logging Company is a large, family owned logging contractor formed in 1980 in the low country of South Carolina. Bishop Logging has traditionally harvested pine timber. However, in 1988 Bishop Logging began investigating the feasibility of a fully mechanized hardwood swamp logging operation when its main customer, Stone Container Corporation, decided to expand hardwood production. In anticipating an increased demand for hardwood in conjunction with the operation of a new paper machine, Stone Container requested that Bishop Logging harvest and supply hardwood for processing at its mill. In South Carolina, most suitable hard-

wood is located deep in the swamplands. Because of the high accident risk in the swamp, Bishop Logging did not want to harvest hardwood by the conventional method of manual felling of trees. Since Bishop Logging had already been successful in its totally mechanized pine logging operation, it began a search for improved methods of hardwood swamp logging centered on mechanizing the process in order to reduce labor, minimize personal injury and insurance costs, and improve efficiency and productivity.

Bishop Logging ultimately purchased several pieces of John Deere equipment to comprise the system. The gross sales price of the machinery was $608,899. All the equipment came with a written John Deere "New Equipment Warranty," whereby John Deere agreed only to repair or replace the equipment during the warranty period and did not warrant the suitability of the equipment. In the "New Equipment Warranty," John Deere expressly provided: (1) John Deere would repair or replace parts which were defective in material or workmanship; (2) a disclaimer of any express warranties or implied warranties of merchantability or fitness for a particular purpose; (3) an exclusion of all incidental or consequential damages; and (4) no authority for the dealer to make any representations, promises, modifications, or limitations of John Deere's written warranty. Hoping to sell more equipment if the Bishop Logging system was successful, however, John Deere agreed to assume part of the risk of the new enterprise by extending its standard equipment warranties notwithstanding the unusual use and modifications to the equipment.

Soon after being placed in operation in the swamp, the machinery began to experience numerous mechanical problems. John Deere made over $110,000 in warranty repairs on the equipment. However, Bishop Logging contended the swamp logging system failed to operate as represented by John Deere and, as a result, it suffered a substantial financial loss. The jury returned a verdict for Bishop Logging against John Deere and awarded Bishop Logging $1,000,000 in actual damages.

John Deere appealed, claiming that the court erred in allowing Bishop Logging to receive lost profits and consequential damages for breach of express warranty because it effectively disclaimed express and implied warranties other than those contained in the John Deere "New Equipment Warranty," and those warranty provisions limited Bishop Logging's remedies for breach of the warranty to repair or replacement of defective parts, and explicitly excluded liability for consequential damages. Bishop Logging, on the other hand, maintained the exclusive remedy as limited failed of its essential purpose, thus entitling it to other remedies available under the Code, including consequential damages.]

Under the South Carolina Uniform Commercial Code (UCC), it is clear that the parties to a contract may establish exclusive, limited written warranties and limitation of damages as a remedy for breach thereof. [UCC] § 2–719. Section 2–719(1) of the Code provides that the agreement may limit the buyer's remedies to repair or replacement of nonconforming goods or parts, and if such remedy is expressly agreed to be exclusive, it is the sole remedy. Section 2–719(3) states that consequential damages may be limited or excluded unless the limitation or exclusion is unconscionable.

Despite the exclusive remedy provisions in § 2–719, in certain circumstances a party may nonetheless be entitled to the general remedies of the UCC. Section 2–719(2) states that when circumstances cause an exclusive remedy to "fail of its essential purpose, remedy may be had as provided in this Act." The official comments under § 2–719 further provide that "under subsection (2), where an apparently fair and reasonable clause because of circumstances fails in its purpose or operates to deprive either party of the substantial value of the bargain, it must give way to the general remedy provisions of this Article." [UCC] § 2–719, comment 1.

The purpose of the exclusive remedy of replacement or repair of defective parts from John Deere's viewpoint was to give it an opportunity to make the equipment conform with the contract while limiting the risks to which it was subject by excluding direct and consequential damages that might otherwise arise. From Bishop Logging's perspective, it was to insure that the equipment would be operable in the swamp application and if the equipment did not function properly, to insure John Deere would cure any defects within a reasonable time after they were discovered. Where a seller is given a reasonable chance to correct defects and the equipment still fails to function properly, the buyer is deprived of the benefits of the limited remedy and it therefore fails of its essential purpose. [Citation.] In such circumstances, § 2–719(2) permits the buyer to pursue the other remedies provided by the UCC if the defect substantially affects the value of the buyer's bargain. [UCC] § 2–719, comment 1; [citation].

* * *

The evidence at trial was clearly sufficient for the jury to determine that John Deere did not effectively perform its obligation to repair the equipment properly and within a reasonable time, and as a result, Bishop Logging was deprived of the substantial value of the equipment it contracted for. We therefore affirm the jury's verdict on the warranty claim implicitly finding that the limited warranty failed in its essential purpose so as to deprive Bishop Logging of the substantial value of the bargain, and, as a consequence, gave Bishop Logging the right to pursue other remedies provided by the UCC.

Notwithstanding Bishop Logging's ability to recover direct damages for breach of the warranty on the equipment due to the failure of its essential purposes, John Deere argues that the limitation of consequential damages expressed in the warranty has independent significance and should be effective to disclaim such damages under the facts of this case unless to do so would be unconscionable. In a purely commercial setting, as in this case, John Deere maintains that limitations on consequential damages are routinely upheld against challenges of unconscionability. [Citation.] Contrary to John Deere's assertion, Bishop Logging contends the premise of "certainty of repair" underlies the entire contract, and consequently "the exclusion of consequential damages logically refers to losses incurred only during a reasonable time before which repairs are successful." Since the attempted repairs never cured the defects in the equipment or made it operable as contemplated by the limited warranty, Bishop Logging argues the exclusion of consequential damages is inapplicable to those damages caused by John Deere's breach of its obligation to repair or replace the defective equipment.

The effect of the failure of a limited remedy under § 2–719(2) upon a clause excluding liability for consequential damages is a major issue that has not been resolved by the appellate courts of this State. [Citation.] One line of cases holds that the exclusion of consequential damages is part of the limited remedy which has failed and hence allows the buyer to recover consequential damages. A second line of cases holds that the clause excluding consequential damages is entitled to independent significance and remains enforceable despite a failure of essential purpose unless the buyer can establish that the clause is unconscionable. [Citation.]

* * *

* * * the parties in the present case assumed that any mechanical problems in the equipment could be corrected. In the context of the commercial nature of the transaction, John Deere's agent knew the equipment would be used in the swamp application and knew that regular, certain repair was promised and expected in order that all of the equipment could be used for its purpose. In negotiating the sale, John Deere's agent assured Bishop Logging that "those units would function properly in [the swamp] environment," and that he would have "at [his] beck and call . . . factory support to make sure that the equipment functioned properly." Therefore, we must interpret the exclusion of consequential damages in light of this premise of "certainty of repair" which underlies the entire contract. The parties obviously agreed to exclude consequential damages in the event that John Deere performed its obligation to repair or replace defects. However, Bishop Logging could reasonably have expected to recover consequential damages when, as here, the defects were never adequately corrected and the limited remedy proved ineffectual.

The failure of the limited remedy in this case materially altered the balance of risk set by the parties in the agreement. Therefore, we conclude that the court was correct in disregarding the other limitations and exclusions on John Deere's warranties, and allowing the full array of remedies provided by the UCC, including recovery of consequential damages and incidental losses under [UCC] §§ 2–714 and 2–715.

Section 2–714 sets forth the normal measure of direct damages for breach of warranty. The formula for calculating direct damages is the value of the goods as warranted less the value of the goods as accepted. [Citation.] In addition to the recovery of direct damages, § 2–714(3) also provides for the recovery of incidental and consequential damages. Incidental damages resulting from the sellers' breach include expenses reasonably incurred in inspection, receipt, transportation, and care and custody of goods rightfully rejected as well as expenses incident to effecting cover. See [UCC] § 2–715(1). Consequential damages include:

(a) any loss resulting from general or particular requirements and needs of which the seller at the time of contracting had reason to know and which could not reasonably be prevented by cover or otherwise; and

(b) injury to person or property proximately resulting from any breach of warranty.

See [UCC] § 2–715(2). Profits lost as a result of the breach are recoverable under this section as consequential damages. In [citation] the court indicated that consequential damages could also include additional operating expenses caused by the breach. The burden of proving the extent of loss incurred by way of consequential damages is on the buyer. [UCC] § 2–715, comment 4.

In the present case, the losses suffered by Bishop Logging were primarily lost anticipated profits. There was no personal injury and there was no injury to other property owned by Bishop Logging. According to Bishop Logging's expert witness who was hired to make a study of the economic loss in this case, the total financial loss to Bishop Logging was either $540,921 or $723,323 for the three year estimated life of the equipment. The difference depended upon the price Bishop Logging received per cord of wood logged by it. The one million dollar actual damage award recovered by Bishop Logging, however, was not only for lost profits from not meeting expected production schedules, but also other unspecified damages which the jury awarded. Although mathematical precision is not required in the proof of loss, we believe the jury's actual damage award lacked relation to the testimony in the record offered to establish damages and apparently included impermissible, noneconomic damages. To that extent, the actual damage award is reduced to the maximum total of economic damages claimed by Bishop Logging, $723,323.

# Questions

**1.** Identify and discuss the goods-oriented remedies of the seller and the buyer.

**2.** Identify and discuss the obligation-oriented remedies of the seller and the buyer.

**3.** Identify and discuss the money-oriented damages of the seller and the buyer.

**4.** Identify and discuss the "specific performance" remedies of the seller and the buyer.

**5.** Describe the basic types of contractual provisions affecting remedies and the limitations that the Code imposes upon these provisions.

# Problems

**1.** Mae contracted to sell one thousand bushels of wheat to Lloyd at $4 per bushel. Just before Mae was to deliver the wheat, Lloyd notified her that he would not receive or accept the wheat. Mae sold the wheat for $3.60 per bushel, the market price, and later sued Lloyd for the difference of $400. Lloyd claims he was not notified by Mae of the resale and, hence, is not liable. Decision?

**2.** On December 15, Judy wrote a letter to David stating that she would sell to David all of the mine-run coal that David might wish to buy during the next calendar year for use at David's factory, delivered at the factory at a price of $40 per ton. David immediately replied by letter to Judy, stating that he accepted the offer, that he would purchase all of his mine-run coal from Judy, and that he would need 200 tons of coal during the first week in January. During the months of January, February, and March, Judy delivered to David a total of 700 tons of coal, for all of which David made payment to Judy at the rate of $40 per ton. On April 10, David ordered 200 tons of mine-run coal from Judy, who replied to David on April 11 that she could not supply David with any more coal except at a price of $48 per ton delivered. David thereafter purchased elsewhere at the market price, namely $48 per ton, all of his factory's requirements of mine-run coal for the remainder of the year, amounting to a total of 2,000 tons of coal. David now brings an action against Judy to recover damages at the rate of $8 per ton for the coal thus purchased, amounting to $16,000. Decision?

**3.** On January 10, Betty, of Emanon, Missouri, visited the showrooms of the Forte Piano Company in St. Louis and selected a piano. A sales memorandum of the transaction signed both by Betty and by the salesperson of the Forte Piano Company read as follows: "Sold to Betty one new Andover piano, factory number 46832, price $3,300, to be shipped to the buyer at Emanon, Missouri, freight prepaid, before February 1. Prior to shipment, seller will stain the case a darker color in accordance with buyer's directions and will make the tone

more brilliant." On January 15, Betty repudiated the contract by letter to the Forte Piano Company. The company subsequently stained the case, made the tone more brilliant, and offered to ship the piano to Betty on January 26. Betty persisted in her refusal to accept the piano. The Forte Piano Company sued Betty to recover the contract price. Decision?

**4.** Sims contracted in writing to sell Blake 100 electric motors at a price of $100 each, freight prepaid to Blake's warehouse. By the contract of sale, Sims expressly warranted that each motor would develop 25-brake horsepower. The contract provided that the motors would be delivered in lots of twenty-five per week beginning January 2, and that Blake should pay for each lot of twenty-five motors as delivered, but that Blake was to have right of inspection upon delivery. Immediately upon delivery of the first lot of twenty-five motors on January 2, Blake forwarded Sims a check for $2,500, but upon testing each of the twenty-five motors Blake determined that none would develop more than 15-brake horsepower. State all of the remedies available to Blake.

**5.** Henry and Mary entered into a written contract whereby Henry agreed to sell and Mary agreed to buy a certain automobile for $3,500. Henry drove the car to Mary's residence and properly parked it on the street in front of her house, where he tendered it to Mary and requested payment of the price. Mary refused to take the car or pay the price. Henry informed Mary that he would hold her to the contract; but before Henry had time to enter the car and drive it away, a fire truck, answering a fire alarm and traveling at a high speed, crashed into the car and demolished it. Henry brings an action against Mary to recover the price of the car. Who is entitled to judgment? Would the result differ if Henry were a dealer in automobiles?

**6.** James sells and delivers to Gerald on June 1 certain goods and receives from Gerald at the time of delivery Gerald's check in the amount of $900 for the goods. The following day, Gerald is petitioned into bankruptcy, and the check is dishonored by Gerald's bank. On June 5, James serves notice upon Gerald and the trustee in bankruptcy that he reclaims the goods. The trustee is in possession of the goods and refuses to deliver them to James. What are the rights of the parties?

7.   The ABC Company, located in Chicago, contracted to sell a carload of television sets to Dodd in St. Louis, Missouri, on sixty days' credit. ABC Company shipped the carload to Dodd. Upon arrival of the car at St. Louis, Dodd paid the freight charges and reshipped the car to Hines of Little Rock, Arkansas, to whom he had previously contracted to sell the television sets. While the car was in transit to Little Rock, Dodd went bankrupt. ABC Company was informed of this at once and immediately telegraphed XYZ Railroad Company to withhold delivery of the television sets. What should the XYZ Railroad Company do?

8.   Robert in Chicago entered into a contract to sell certain machines to Terry in New York. The machines were to be manufactured by Robert and shipped F.O.B. Chicago not later than March 25. On March 24, when Robert is about to ship the machines, he receives a telegram from Terry wrongfully repudiating the contract. The machines cannot readily be resold for a reasonable price because they are a special kind used only in Terry's manufacturing processes. Robert sues Terry to recover the agreed price of the machines. What are the rights of the parties?

9.   Calvin purchased a log home construction kit manufactured by Boone Homes, Inc., from an authorized Boone dealer. The sales contract stated that Boone would repair or replace defective materials and that this was the exclusive remedy available against Boone. The dealer assembled the house, which was defective in several respects. The knotholes in the logs caused the walls and ceiling to leak. A support beam was too small and therefore cracked, causing the floor to crack also. These defects could not be completely cured by repair. Calvin sues Boone for breach of warranty to recover damages for the loss in value. Decision?

10.   Margaret contracted to buy a 1973 Rolls-Royce Corniche from Paragon Motors, Inc. Only 100 Corniches are built each year. She paid a $3,000 deposit on the car, but Paragon sold the car to Gluck. What remedy, if any, does Margaret have against Paragon?

11.   Technical Textile agreed by written contract to manufacture and sell 20,000 pounds of yarn to Jagger Brothers at a price of $2.15 per pound. After Technical had manufactured, delivered, and been paid for 3,723 pounds of yarn, Jagger Brothers by letter informed Technical that it was repudiating the contract and that it would refuse any further yarn deliveries. On August 12, the date of the letter, the market price of yarn was $1.90 per pound.

Technical was awarded $4,069.25 in damages by the trial court, an amount equal to 16,277 times the difference between the contract price ($2.15) and the market price ($1.90) of the yarn on the repudiation date. Jagger Brothers appealed, contending that the proper measure of damages was the difference between the contract price and the cost of manufacture and that, because no evidence was offered as to the cost of

manufacture, Technical was entitled only to nominal damages. Decision?

12.   Sherman Burrus, a job printer, purchased a printing press from the Itek Corporation for a price of $7,006.08. Before making the purchase, Burrus was assured by an Itek salesperson, Mr. Nessel, that the press was appropriate for the type of printing Burrus was doing. Burrus encountered problems in operating the press almost continuously from the time he received it. Burrus, his employees, and Itek representatives spent many hours in an unsuccessful attempt to get the press to operate properly. Burrus requested that the press be replaced, but Itek refused. Burrus then brought an action against Itek for (1) damages for breach of the implied warranty of merchantability and (2) consequential damages for losses resulting from the press's defective operation. The trial court awarded damages of $10,435 to Burrus, and Itek appealed. Decision?

13.   A farmer made a contract in April to sell a grain dealer 40,000 bushels of corn to be delivered in October. On June 3, the farmer unequivocally informed the grain dealer that he was not going to plant any corn, that he would not fulfill the contract, and that, if the buyer had commitments to resell the corn, he should make other arrangements. The grain dealer waited in vain until October for performance of the repudiated contract. Then he bought corn at a greatly increased price on the market in order to fulfill commitments to his purchasers. The grain dealer sued for damages. Decision?

14.   Through information provided by S-2 Yachts, Inc., the plaintiff, Barr located a yacht to his liking at the Crow's Nest marina and yacht sales company. When Barr asked the price, he was told that, although the yacht normally sold for $102,000, Crow's Nest was willing to sell this particular one for only $80,000 to make room for a new model from the manufacturer, S-2 Yachts, Inc. Barr was assured that the yacht in question came with full manufacturer's warranties. Barr asked if the yacht was new and if anything was wrong with it. Crow's Nest told him that nothing was wrong with the yacht and that there were only 20 hours of use on the engines.

Once the yacht had been delivered and Barr had taken it for a test run, he noticed several problems associated with saltwater damage, such as rusted screws, a rusted stove, and faulty electrical wiring. Barr was assured that Crow's Nest would pay for these repairs. However, as was later discovered, the yacht was in such a damaged condition that Barr experienced great personal hazard the two times that he used the boat. Examination by a marine expert revealed clearly that the boat had been sunk in saltwater prior to Barr's purchase. The engines were severely damaged, and there was significant structural and equipment damage as well. According to the expert, not only was the yacht not new, it was worth at most only one-half of the new value of $102,000. Barr sued both S-2 Yachts and Crow's Nest for breach of warranties. Decision?

15.   Lee Oldsmobile sells Rolls-Royce automobiles. Mrs. Kaiden sent Lee a $5,000 deposit on a $29,500 1973 Rolls-Royce. Although Lee informed Mrs. Kaiden that the car would

be delivered in November, the order form did not indicate the delivery date and contained a disclaimer for delay or failure to deliver due to circumstances beyond the dealer's control. On November 21, Mrs. Kaiden purchased another car from another dealer and canceled her car from Lee. When Lee attempted to deliver a Rolls-Royce to Mrs. Kaiden on November 29, Mrs. Kaiden refused to accept delivery. Lee later sold the car for $26,495.00. Mrs. Kaiden sued Lee for her $5,000 deposit plus interest. Lee counterclaims, based on the terms of the contract, for liquidated damages of $5,000 (the amount of the deposit) as a result of Mrs. Kaiden's breach of contract. Decision?

16. Servebest contracted to sell Emessee 200,000 pounds of 50 percent lean beef trimmings for $105,000. Upon a substantial fall in the market price, Emessee refused to pay the contract price and informed Servebest that the contract was canceled. Servebest sues Emessee for breach of contract including (a) damages for the difference between the contract price and the resale price of the trimmings and (b) incidental damages. Decision?

17. Mrs. French was the highest bidder on eight antique guns at an auction held by Sotheby & Company. When Sotheby's billed Mrs. French $24,886.27 for the guns, she refused to pay. Sotheby's sued Mrs. French for the price of the guns. Decision?

18. Teledyne Industries, Inc., entered into a contract with Teradyne, Inc., to purchase a T–347A transistor test system for the list and fair market price of $98,400 less a discount of $984. After the system was packed for shipment, Teledyne canceled the order, offering to purchase a Field Effects Transistor System for $65,000. Teradyne refused the offer and sold the T–347A to another purchaser pursuant to an order that was on hand prior to the cancellation. Teradyne then sued Teledyne for breach of contract. Judgment was entered in favor of Teradyne for lost profits, and Teledyne appealed. Decision?

19. Wilson Trading Corp. agreed to sell David Ferguson a specified quantity of yarn for use in making sweaters. The written contract provided that notice of defects, to be effective, had to be received by Wilson before knitting or within ten days of receipt of the yarn. When the knitted sweaters were washed, the color of the yarn "shaded" (i.e., variations in color from piece to piece appeared). David Ferguson immediately notified Wilson of the problem and refused to pay for the yarn, claiming that the defect made the sweaters unmarketable. Wilson brought suit against Ferguson. The trial court granted Wilson summary judgment for the contract price and the appellate court affirmed. Decision?

20. Daniel Martin and John Duke contracted with J & S Distributors, Inc. to purchase a KIS Magnum Speed printer for $17,000. The parties agreed that Martin and Duke would send one half of the money as a deposit and would pay the balance upon delivery. When the machine arrived five days late, Martin and Duke refused to accept it stating that they had purchased a substitute machine elsewhere. Martin and Duke requested the return of their deposit but J & S refused. Martin and Duke sued Jeff Sheffer and J & S for breach of contract, fraud, breach of good faith and unfair and deceptive trade practices. The defendants counterclaimed for full performance of the contract pursuant to a clause in the contract which provides:

In the event of non-payment of the balance of the purchase price reflected herein on due date and in the manner recorded or on such extended date which may be caused by late delivery on the part of [the seller], the Customer shall be liable for:

(1) immediate payment of the full balance recorded herein; and

(2) payment of interest at the rate of 12% per annum calculated on the balance due, when due, together with any attorney's fees, collection charges and other necessary expenses incurred by [the seller].

The trial court granted summary judgment to the defendants on both the claim against them and their counterclaim and ordered specific performance of the contract. Plaintiffs appeal. Decision?

WWW **Internet Exercise** Compare the remedies of the seller and buyer under the United Nations Convention on Contracts for the International Sale of Goods (Vienna, 1980) with their remedies under Article 2 of the Uniform Commercial Code.

# Negotiable Instruments

# CHAPTER 26

# Form and Content

In July 1990, the American Law Institute and the National Conference of Commissioners on Uniform Laws approved a Revised Article 3 to the Uniform Commercial Code (UCC). Named "Negotiable Instruments," the new Article, now adopted by nearly all of the States, maintains the basic scope and content of prior Article 3 ("Commercial Paper"). This part of the text will discuss Revised Article 3, but will also point out the major changes from prior Article 3. Revised Article 3 is presented in Appendix C.

Negotiable instruments, also referred to simply as instruments, include checks, promissory notes, drafts, and certificates of deposit. These instruments are crucial to the sale of goods and services as well as to the financing of most businesses. The use of negotiable instruments has increased to such an extent that payments made with these instruments, with checks in particular, are now many times greater than payments made with cash. In fact, currency now is used primarily for smaller transactions. Accordingly, the vital importance of negotiable instruments as a method of payment cannot be overstated.

To accomplish its social and economic objectives, the payment system must be quick, sure, and efficient. The use of cash can never satisfy all of these requirements because (1) it is inconvenient to maintain large quantities of cash; (2) the risk of loss or theft is far too great; (3) the risk in sending cash is likewise too high, as is the cost of postage and insurance in shipping cash over long distances; and (4) the costs to the Federal government of maintaining an adequate supply of currency would be prohibitive. In addition, negotiable instruments used for payment provide a convenient receipt as well as a record for accounting and tax purposes. Although negotiable instruments closely approximate cash for the purpose of payment, they are not exactly equivalent because, for example, negotiable instruments may be forged, they may be drawn on insufficient funds, payment may be

stopped, or the instrument may be materially altered. Nevertheless, these risks (which are real but very infrequent—more than 99 percent of all checks are paid) are slight compared with the advantages that negotiable instruments provide for payment. Consequently, a major objective of the law of negotiable instruments and the bank collection process is to reduce these risks by increasing the safety, soundness, and operating efficiency of the entire payment system.

Moreover, the credit function of negotiable instruments is indispensable. Promissory notes and drafts serve an important business purpose, not only in areas of high finance but also at the level of the small business and individual consumer. In recent years, individuals have increasingly used certificates of deposit instead of savings accounts.

## NEGOTIABILITY

**Negotiability** is a legal concept that makes written instruments more freely transferable and therefore a readily accepted form of payment in substitution for money.

### Development of Law of Negotiable Instruments

The starting point for an understanding of negotiable instruments is recognizing that four or five centuries ago in England a contract right to the payment of money was not assignable because a contractual promise ran to the promisee. The fact that performance could be rendered only to him constituted a hardship for the owner of the right because it prevented him from selling or disposing of it. Eventually, however, the law permitted recovery upon an assignment by the assignee against the obligor.

An innocent assignee bringing an action against the obligor was subject to all defenses available to the obligor. Such an action would result in the same outcome whether it was brought by the assignee or assignor. Thus, a contract right became assignable but not very marketable because merchants had little interest in buying paper that may be subject to a defense. This remains the law of **assignments**: *the assignee stands in the shoes of his assignor*. For a discussion of assignments, see Chapter 16.

With the flourishing of trade and commerce, it became essential to develop a more effective means of exchanging contractual rights for money. For example, a merchant who sold goods for cash might use the cash to buy more goods for resale. If he were to make a sale on credit in exchange for a promise to pay money, why should he not be permitted to sell that promise to someone else for cash with which to carry on his business? One difficulty was that the buyer of the goods gave the seller only a promise to pay money to him. The seller was the only person to whom performance or payment was promised. If, however, the seller obtained from the buyer a promise in writing to pay money to anyone in possession (a *bearer*) of the writing (the *paper* or *instrument*) or to anyone the seller (or *payee* in this case) designated, then the duty of performance would run directly to the holder (the bearer of the paper or to the person to whom the payee ordered payment to be made). This is one of the essential distinctions between negotiable and nonnegotiable instruments. Although a negotiable instrument has other formal requirements, this particular one eliminates the limitations of a promise to pay money only to a named promisee.

Moreover, if the promise to pay were not subject to all of the defenses available against the assignor, a transferee would not only be more willing to acquire the promise but also would pay more for it. Accordingly, the law of negotiable instruments developed the concept of the **holder in due course,** whereby certain good faith transferees who gave value acquired the right to be paid, free of most of the defenses to which an assignee would be subject. By reason of this doctrine, a transferee of a negotiable instrument could acquire *greater* rights than his transferor, whereas an assignee would acquire *only* the rights of his assignor. With these basic innovations, negotiable instruments enabled merchants to sell their contractual rights more readily and thereby keep their capital working.

## Assignment Compared with Negotiation

Negotiability invests negotiable instruments with a high degree of marketability and commercial utility. It allows negotiable instruments to be freely transferable and enforceable by a person with the rights of a holder in due course against any person obligated on the instrument, subject only to a limited number of defenses. To illustrate, assume that George sells and delivers goods to Elaine for $50,000 on sixty days' credit and that, a few days later, George assigns this account to Marsha. Unless Elaine is duly notified of this assignment, she may safely pay the $50,000 to George on the due date without incurring any liability to Marsha, the assignee. Assume next that the goods were defective and that Elaine, accordingly, has a defense against George to the extent of $20,000. Assume also that Marsha duly notified Elaine of the assignment. The result is that Marsha can recover only $30,000, not $50,000, from Elaine because Elaine's defense against George is equally available against George's assignee, Marsha. In other words, an assignee of contractual rights merely "steps into the shoes" of her assignor and, hence, acquires only the same rights as her assignor—and no more.

Assume, instead, that upon the sale by George to Elaine, Elaine executes and delivers her negotiable note to George for $50,000 payable to George's order in sixty days and that, a short time later, George duly negotiates (transfers) the note to Marsha. In the first place, Marsha is not required to notify Elaine that she has acquired the note from George, because one who issues a negotiable instrument is held to know that the instrument may be negotiated and is generally obligated to pay the holder of the instrument, whoever that may be. In the second place, Elaine's defense is not available against Marsha if Marsha acquired the note in good faith and for value and had no knowledge of Elaine's defense against George and took it without reason to question its authenticity. Marsha, therefore, is entitled to hold Elaine for the full face amount of the note at maturity, namely, $50,000. In other words, Marsha, by the negotiation of the negotiable note to her, acquired rights greater than those George had, because, by keeping the note, George could have recovered only $30,000 on it because Elaine successfully could have asserted her defense in the amount of $20,000 against him.

To have the full benefit of negotiability, negotiable instruments not only must meet the requirements of negotiability but also must be acquired by a holder in due course. This chapter discusses the formal requirements instruments must satisfy to be negotiable. Chapter 27 deals with the manner in which a negotiable instrument must be negotiated to preserve its advantages. Chapter 28 covers the requisites and rights of a holder in due course. Finally, Chapter 29 examines the liability of all the parties to a negotiable instrument.

## TYPES OF NEGOTIABLE INSTRUMENTS

There are four types of negotiable instruments: drafts, checks, notes, and certificates of deposit. Section 3–104. The first two contain **orders** or directions to pay money; the last two involve **promises** to pay money.

### Drafts

A **draft** involves three parties, each in a distinct capacity. One party, the **drawer,** *orders* a second party, the **drawee,** to pay a fixed amount of money to a third party, the payee. The drawee is ordinarily a person or entity who either is in possession of money belonging to the drawer or owes money to him. A sample draft is reproduced as Figure 26–2. The same party may appear in more than one capacity; for instance, the drawer may also be the payee.

Drafts may be either "time" or "sight." A **time draft** is one payable at a specified future date, whereas a **sight draft** is payable on demand (i.e., immediately upon presentation to the drawee). A form of time

draft known as a trade acceptance is frequently used as a credit device in commercial transactions. A **trade acceptance** is a time draft, drawn by the seller (drawer) on the buyer (drawee), that names the seller or some third party as the payee.

◆ *See Figures 26–1 and 26–2*

### Checks

A **check** is a specialized form of draft, namely, an order to pay money drawn on a *bank* and payable on *demand* (i.e., upon the payee's request for payment). Section 3–104(f). Once again, there are parties involved in three distinct capacities: the **drawer,** who orders the **drawee,** a bank, to pay the payee on demand. Checks are by far the most widely used form of negotiable instruments. Each year more than ten billion checks are written in the United States for a total of more than five trillion dollars.

A **cashier's check** is a check drawn by a bank upon itself to the order of a named payee. Section 3–104(g).

◆ *See Figure 26–3*

---

**FIGURE 26–1**  Order to Pay: Draft or Check

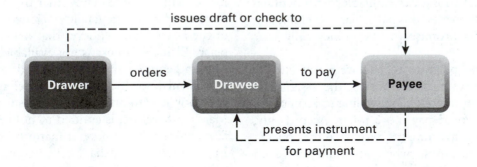

---

**FIGURE 26–2**  Draft

Two years from date pay to the order of                St. Louis, Missouri
Perry Payee                                             May 1, 1999
$50,000 Fifty Thousand . . . Dollars



To: DEBRA DRAWEE                                        (Signed) Donald Drawer
    50 Main St.                                         DONALD DRAWER
    Louisville, Kentucky

**FIGURE 26–3** Check

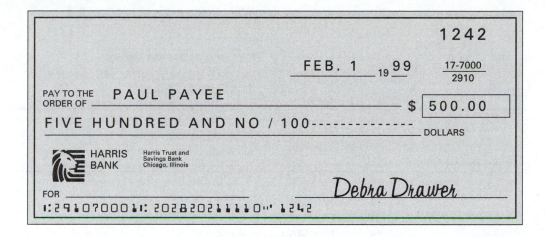

## Notes

A **promissory note** is an instrument involving two parties in two capacities. One party, the **maker,** promises to pay a second party, the payee, a stated sum of money, either on demand or at a stated future date. The note may range from a simple "I promise to pay $X to the order of Y" form to more complex legal instruments such as installment notes, collateral notes, mortgage notes, and judgment notes. Figure 26–5 is a note payable at a definite time—six months from the date of April 7, 1999—and hence is referred to as a **time note.** A note payable upon the request or demand of the payee or holder is a **demand note.**

◆ *See Figures 26–4 and 26–5*

## Certificates of Deposit

A certificate of deposit, or C.D. as it is frequently called, is a specialized form of *promise* to pay money given by a *bank.* A **certificate of deposit** is a written acknowledgment by a bank of the receipt of money that it promises to repay. Section 3–104(j). The issuing party, the **maker,** which is always a bank, promises to pay a second party, the payee, who is named in the C.D.

◆ *See Figure 26–6*

## *FORMAL REQUIREMENTS OF NEGOTIABLE INSTRUMENTS*

To perform its function in the business community effectively, negotiable instruments must be able to pass freely from person to person. The fact that *negotiability* is wholly a matter of form makes such freedom possible. The instrument must contain within its "four corners" all the information required to determine whether it is negotiable. No reference to any other source is permitted. For this reason, a negotiable instrument is called a

**FIGURE 26–4** Promise to Pay: Promissory Note or Certificate of Deposit

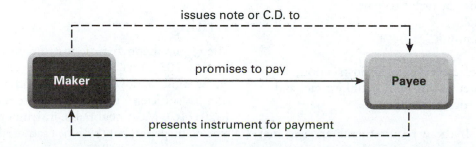

**FIGURE 26–5** Note

---

$10,000             Albany, N.Y.             April 7, 1999

Six months from date I promise to pay to the order of Pat Payee ten thousand dollars.

(signed) Matthew Maker

---

**FIGURE 26–6** Certificate of Deposit

---

NEGOTIABLE CERTIFICATE OF DEPOSIT

The Mountain Bank

No. 13900       Mountain, N.Y.       June 1, 1999

THIS CERTIFIES THAT THERE HAS BEEN DEPOSITED
with the undersigned the sum of             $200,000.00

Two hundred thousand ...............................................Dollars

Payable to the order of Pablo Payee on December 1, 2001 with
interest only to maturity at the rate of Seven percent (7%) per
annum upon surrender of this certificate properly indorsed.

The Mountain Bank

By (Signature) Malcolm Maker, Vice President

Authorized Signature

---

"courier without luggage." In addition, indorsements **cannot** create or destroy negotiability.

To be negotiable, the **instrument** must

1. be in writing,
2. be signed,
3. contain a promise or order to pay,
4. be unconditional,
5. be for a fixed amount,
6. be for money,
7. contain no other undertaking or instruction,
8. be payable on demand or at a definite time, and
9. be payable to order or to bearer.

Section 3–104(a). If these requirements are not met, the undertaking is not negotiable (nor is it a negotiable instrument or simply an instrument), and the rights of the parties are governed by the law of contract (assignment).

 *See Case 26–1*

## Writing

The requirement that the instrument be a writing (Sections 3–103(a)(6), (9)) is broadly construed. Printing, typewriting, handwriting, or any other tangible expression is sufficient to satisfy the requirement. Section 1–201(46). Most negotiable instruments, of course, are written on paper, but this is not required. In one instance, a check was reportedly written on a coconut.

## Signed

A note or certificate of deposit must be signed by the maker; a draft or check must be signed by the drawer. As in the case of a writing, extreme latitude is granted in determining what constitutes a **signature**, which is any symbol a party executes or adopts with the *intent* to validate a writing. Section 1–201(39). Moreover, it may consist of any word or mark used in place of a written signature, Section 3–401(b), such as initials, an X, or a thumbprint. It may be a trade name or an assumed name. Even the location of the signature on the document is unimportant. Normally, a maker or drawer signs in the lower right corner of the instrument, but this is not required. Negotiable instruments are frequently signed by an agent for her principal. For a discussion of the appropriate way in which an agent should sign a negotiable instrument, see Chapter 29.

## Promise or Order to Pay

A negotiable instrument must contain either a promise to pay money, in the case of a note or certificate of deposit, or an order to pay, in the case of a draft or check.

*Promise to Pay* A promise to pay is an undertaking and must be more than the mere acknowledgment or recognition of an existing obligation or debt. Section 3–103(a)(9). The so-called due bill or I.O.U. is not a promise but merely an acknowledgment of indebtedness. Accordingly, an instrument reciting "due Adam Brown $100" or "I.O.U., Adam Brown, $100" is not negotiable because it does not contain a promise to pay.

*Order to Pay* An order to pay is an instruction to pay. It must be more than an authorization or request and must identify with reasonable certainty the person to be paid. Section 3–103(a)(6). The usual way to express an order is by use of the word *pay:* "Pay to the order of John Jones" or "Pay bearer." The addition of words of courtesy, such as "please pay" or "kindly pay," will not destroy the negotiability. Nonetheless, caution should be exercised in employing words that modify the prototypically correct "Pay." For example, the use of the words "I wish you would pay" has been held to destroy the negotiability of an instrument and to render its transfer a contractual assignment.

## Unconditional

The requirement that the promise or order be unconditional is to prevent the inclusion of any term that could reduce the promisor's obligation to pay. Conditions limiting a promise would diminish the payment and credit functions of negotiable instruments by necessitating costly and time-consuming investigations to determine the degree of risk such conditions imposed. Moreover, if the holder (transferee) had to take an instrument subject to certain conditions, her risk factor would be substantial, and this would lead to limited transferability. Substitutes for money must be capable of rapid circulation at minimum risk.

A promise or order to pay is **unconditional** if it is absolute and not subject to any contingencies or qualifications. Thus, an instrument would not be negotiable if it stated that "ABC Corp. promises to pay $100,000 to the order of Johnson provided the helicopter sold meets all contractual specifications." On the other hand, suppose that upon delivering an instrument that provided, "ABC Corp. promises to pay $100,000 to the order of Johnson," Meeker, the president of ABC, stated that the money would be paid only if the helicopter met all contractual specifications. The instrument would be negotiable because negotiability is determined solely by examining the instrument itself and is not affected by matters beyond the instrument's face.

A promise or order is unconditional unless it states (a) that there is an express condition to payment, (b) that the promise or order is subject to or governed by another writing, or (c) that rights or obligations concerning the order or promise are stated in another writing. A mere reference to another writing, however, does not make the promise or order conditional. Section 3–106(a).

An instrument is not made conditional by the fact that it is subject to implied or constructive conditions; the condition must be expressed to destroy negotiability. Section 3–106(a). Implications of law or fact are not to be considered in deciding whether an instrument is negotiable. Thus, a statement in an instrument that it is given for an executory promise does not imply that the instrument is conditioned upon performance of that promise.

*Reference to Other Agreements* The restriction against reference to another agreement is to enable any person to determine the right to payment provided by the instrument without having to look beyond its four corners. If such right is made subject to the terms of another agreement, the instrument is nonnegotiable. Section 3–106(a)(ii).

A distinction is to be made between a mere recital of the *existence* of a separate agreement (this does not destroy negotiability) and a recital that makes the instrument *subject* to the terms of another agreement (this does destroy negotiability).

A statement in a note such as "This note is given in partial payment for a color TV set to be delivered two weeks from date in accordance with a contract of this date between the payee and the maker" does not impair negotiability. It merely describes the consideration and the transaction giving rise to the note. It does not place any restriction or condition on the maker's obligation to pay. The promise is not made subject to any other agreement.

Added words that would impair negotiability are "This note is subject to all terms of said contract." Such words make the promise to pay conditional upon the adequate performance of the television set in accordance with the terms of the contract and thus render the instrument nonnegotiable.

***The Particular Fund Doctrine*** Revised Article 3 eliminates the particular fund doctrine by providing that a promise or order is not made conditional because payment is to be made only out of a particular fund. Section 3–106(b)(ii).

Under prior Article 3 an order or promise to pay only out of a particular fund was conditional and destroyed negotiability because payment depended upon the existence and sufficiency of the particular fund. On the other hand, a promise or order to pay that merely indicated a particular fund out of which reimbursement was to be made or a particular account to be debited with the amount did not impair negotiability because the promise or order relied on the drawer's or maker's general credit and the notation charging a particular account was merely a bookkeeping entry to be followed after payment.

## Fixed Amount

The purpose of the requirement of a fixed amount in money is to enable the person entitled to enforce the instrument to determine from the instrument itself the amount that he is entitled to receive.

The requirement that payment be of a "fixed amount" must be considered from the point of view of the person entitled to enforce the instrument, not the maker or drawer. (Prior Article 3 used the term "sum certain," which means fundamentally the same as "fixed amount.") The holder must be assured of a determinable minimum payment, although provisions of the instrument may increase the recovery under certain circumstances. Revised Article 3, however, applies the fixed amount requirement only to the *principal*. Section 3–112, Comment 1. Thus, the fixed amount portion does not apply to interest or to other charges, such as collection fees or attorneys' fees.

Moreover, negotiability of an instrument is not affected by the inclusion or omission of a stated rate of interest. If the instrument does not state a rate of interest, it is payable without interest. Section 3–112(a). If the instrument states that it is payable "with interest" but does not specify a rate, the judgment rate of interest applies.

Most significantly, Revised Article 3 provides that "Interest may be stated in an instrument as a fixed or variable amount of money or it may be expressed as a fixed or variable rate or rates." Section 3–112(b). Moreover, determination of the rate of interest "may require reference to information not contained in the instrument." Section 3–112(b). Variable rate mortgages, therefore, may be negotiable; this result is consistent with the rule that the fixed amount requirement applies only to the principal.

Under prior Article 3, both principal and interest had to be determined from the face of the instrument. Thus, courts held that variable interest rate provisions destroyed negotiability because the interest rate was tied to a published index external to the instrument.

A sum payable is a fixed amount even though it is payable in installments or payable with a fixed discount, if paid before maturity, or with a fixed addition, if paid after maturity. This is because it is always possible to use the instrument itself to compute the amount due at any given time.

## Money

The term **money** means a medium of exchange authorized or adopted by a sovereign government as part of its currency. Section 1–201(24). Consequently, even though local custom may make gold or diamonds a medium of exchange, an instrument payable in such commodities would be nonnegotiable because of the lack of governmental sanction of such media as legal tender. On the other hand, an instrument paying a fixed amount in French francs, German marks, Italian lira, Japanese yen, or other foreign currency is negotiable. Section 3–107.

## No Other Undertaking or Instruction

A negotiable instrument must contain a promise or order to pay money, but it may not "state any other undertaking or instruction by the person promising or ordering payment to do any act in addition to the payment of money." Section 3–104(a)(3). Accordingly, an instrument containing an order or promise to do an act in addition to or in lieu of the payment of money is not negotiable. For example, a promise to pay $100 "and a ton of coal" would be nonnegotiable.

The Code sets out a list of terms and provisions that may be included in instruments without adversely affecting negotiability. Among these are (1) an undertaking or power to give, maintain, or protect collateral in order to secure payment, (2) an authorization or power to confess judgment (written authority by the debtor to allow the holder to enter judgment against the debtor in favor of the holder) on the instrument, (3) an authorization or power to sell or dispose of collateral upon default, and (4) a waiver of the benefit of any law intended for the advantage or protection of the obligor. It is important to note that the Code does not render any of these terms legal or effective; it merely provides that their inclusion will not affect negotiability.

## Payable on Demand or at a Definite Time

A negotiable instrument must "be payable on demand or at a definite time." Section 3–104. This requirement, like the other formal requirements of negotiability, is designed to promote certainty in determining the present value of a negotiable instrument.

*Demand* "Payable upon demand" means that the money owed under the instrument must be paid upon the holder's request. **Demand paper** always has been considered sufficiently certain as to time of payment to satisfy the requirements of negotiability because it is the person entitled to enforce the instrument who makes the demand and who thus sets the time for payment. Any instrument in which no time for payment is stated—a check, for example—is payable on demand. An instrument also qualifies as being payable on demand if it is payable at sight or on presentment. Section 3–108(a).

☞ *See Case 26–2*

*Definite Time* Instruments payable at a definite time are called **time paper**. A promise or order is payable at a definite time if it is payable:

1. at a fixed date or dates,
2. at a definite period of time after sight or acceptance, or

3. at a time readily ascertainable at the time the promise or order is issued.

Section 3–108(b). An instrument is payable at a definite time if it is payable "on or before" a stated date. The person entitled to enforce the instrument is thus assured that she will have her money by the maturity date at the latest, although she may receive it sooner. This right of anticipation enables the obligor, at his option, to pay before the stated maturity date (*prepayment*) and thereby stop the further accrual of interest or, if interest rates have gone down, to refinance at a lower rate of interest. Nevertheless, it constitutes sufficient certainty so as not to impair negotiability. Section 3–108(b)(i).

Frequently, instruments are made payable at a fixed period after a stated date. For example, the instrument may be made payable "thirty days after date." This means it is payable thirty days after the date of issuance, which is recited on the instrument. Such an instrument is payable at a definite time, for its exact maturity date can be determined by simple math.

An undated instrument payable "thirty days after date" is not payable at a definite time, because the date of payment cannot be determined from its face. It is therefore nonnegotiable until it is completed.

An instrument that by its terms is otherwise payable only upon an act or event whose time of occurrence is uncertain is *not* payable at a definite time. An example would be a note providing for payment to the order "when X dies." However, as previously stated, a time that is readily ascertainable at the time the promise or order is issued is a definite time. Section 3–108(b). This changes prior Article 3 and seemingly would permit a note reading "payable on the day of the next presidential election." As long as the scheduled event is certain to happen, Revised Article 3 appears to be satisfied.

The clause "at a fixed period after sight" is frequently used in drafts. Because a fixed period after sight means a fixed period after acceptance, a simple mathematical calculation makes the maturity date certain; and the instrument is, therefore, negotiable.

An instrument payable at a fixed time subject to **acceleration** by the holder also satisfies the requirement of being payable at a definite time. Section 3–108(b)(ii). Indeed, such an instrument would seem to have a more certain maturity date than a demand instrument because it at least states a definite maturity date. In addition, the acceleration may be contingent upon the happening of some act or event.

Finally, a provision in an instrument granting the holder an option to extend the maturity of the instrument for a definite or indefinite period does not impair its negotiability. Section 3–108(b)(iii). Nor does a provision permitting the obligor of an instrument to extend the maturity date to a further definite time. Section 3–108(b)(iv). For example, a provision in a note, payable one year from date, that the maker may extend the maturity date six months does not impair negotiability. If the obligor is given an option to extend the maturity of the instrument for an indefinite period, however, his promise is illusory; and there is no certainty regarding time of payment. Such an instrument is nonnegotiable. If the obligor's right to extend is limited to a definite time, the extension clause is no more indefinite than an acceleration clause with a time limitation.

In addition, extension may be made automatic upon or after a specified act or event, provided a definite time limit is stated. An example of such an extension clause is, "I promise to pay to the order of John Doe the sum of $2,000 on December 1, 1999, but it is agreed that if the crop of sections 25 and 26 of Twp. 145 is below eight bushels per acre for the 1999 season, this note shall be extended for one year."

### At a Definite Time and On Demand

If the instrument, payable at a fixed date, *also* provides that it is payable on demand made before the fixed date, it is still a negotiable instrument. Revised Article 3 provides that the instrument is payable on demand until the fixed date and, if demand is not made prior to the specified date, becomes payable at a definite time on the fixed date. Section 3–108(c).

## Payable to Order or to Bearer

A negotiable instrument must contain words indicating that the maker or drawer intends that it may pass into the hands of someone other than the payee. Although the "magic" **words of negotiability** typically are *to the order of* or *to bearer,* other clearly equivalent words also may fulfill this requirement. The use of synonyms, however, only invites trouble. Moreover, as noted above, indorsements cannot create or destroy negotiability, which must be determined from the "face" of the instrument. Words of negotiability must be present when the instrument is issued or first comes into possession of a holder. Section 3–104(a)(1).

Revised Article 3 provides that a *check* which meets all requirements of being a negotiable instrument except that it is not payable to bearer or order is nevertheless a negotiable instrument. Section 3–104(c). This rule does

*not* apply to instruments other than checks and does not exist under prior Article 3.

### Payable to Order

An instrument is payable to order if it is payable (a) to the order of an identified person or (b) to an identified person or order. Section 3–109(b). If an instrument is payable to bearer, it cannot be payable to order; an instrument that is ambiguous as to this point is payable to bearer. Prior Article 3 provided that use of the word *assigns* met the requirement of words of negotiability; Revised Article 3, however, does not so provide.

Moreover, in every instance the person to whose order the instrument is payable must be designated with reasonable certainty. Within this limitation a broad range of payees is possible, including an individual, two or more payees, an office, an estate, a trust or fund, a partnership or unincorporated association, and a corporation.

This requirement should not be confused with the requirement that the instrument contain an order or promise to pay. An order to pay is an instruction to a third party to pay the instrument as drawn. The word *order* in terms of an "order instrument," on the other hand, pertains to the transferability of the instrument rather than to instructions directing a specific party to pay.

A writing, other than a *check*, that names a specified person without indicating that it is payable to order—for example, "Pay to Justin Matthew"—is not payable to order or to bearer. Such a writing is not a negotiable instrument and is not covered by Article 3. On the other hand, a check that meets all of the requirements of a negotiable instrument, except that it does not provide the words of negotiability, is still a negotiable instrument and falls within the purview of Article 3. Section 3–104(c). Thus, a check payable to Justin Matthew is a negotiable check.

### Payable to Bearer

Section 3–109(a) of the Code states that an instrument fulfills the requirements of being **payable to bearer** if it (1) states it is payable to bearer or the order of bearer, (2) does not state a payee or (3) states it is payable to "cash" or to the order of "cash." Section 3–109(a). An instrument made payable both to order and to bearer, that is, "pay to the order of Mildred Courts or bearer," is payable to bearer. Section 3–109, Comment 2.

An instrument that does not state a payee is payable to bearer. Thus, if a drawer leaves blank the "pay to order of" line of a check or the maker of a notes writes "pay to _____," the instrument is a negotiable bearer instrument. Section 3–109(a)(2).

 *See Case 26–3*

## Terms and Omissions and Their Effect on Negotiability

The negotiability of an instrument may be questioned because of an omission of certain provisions or because of ambiguity. Problems may also arise in connection with the interpretation of an instrument, whether or not negotiability is called into question. Accordingly, the Code contains rules of construction that apply to every instrument.

**Dating of the Instrument**   The negotiability of an instrument is not affected by the fact that it is antedated, or postdated. Section 3–113(a). If the instrument is undated, its date is the date of its issuance. If it is unissued, its date is the date it first comes into the possession of a holder. Section 3–113(b).

**Incomplete Instruments**   Occasionally, a party will sign a paper that clearly is intended to become an instrument but that, either by intention or through oversight, is incomplete because of the omission of a necessary element such as a promise or order, a designated payee, an amount payable, or a time for payment. Section 3–115 provides that such an instrument is not negotiable until completed.

If, for example, an undated instrument is delivered on November 1, 1999, payable "thirty days after date," the payee has implied authority to fill in "November 1, 1999." Until he does so, however, the instrument is not negotiable because it is not payable at a definite time.

If the payee completes the instrument by inserting an erroneous date, the rules as to material alteration, covered in Chapter 29, apply.

**Ambiguous Instruments**   Rather than commit the parties to the use of parol evidence to establish the interpretation of an instrument, Article 3 establishes rules to resolve common ambiguities. This promotes negotiability by providing added certainty to the holder.

Where it is doubtful whether the instrument is a draft or note, the holder may treat it as either and present it for payment to the drawee or the person signing it. Section 3–104(e). For example, an instrument reading

To X: On demand I promise to pay $500 to the order of Y.

Signed, Z

may be presented for payment to X as a draft or to Z as a note.

An instrument naming no drawee but stating

On demand, pay $500 to the order of Y.

Signed, Z

although in the form of a draft, may be treated as a note and presented to Z for payment.

If a printed form of note or draft is used and the party signing it inserts handwritten or typewritten language that is inconsistent with the printed words, the handwritten words control the typewritten and the printed words, and the typewritten words control the printed words. Section 3–114.

If the amount payable is set forth on the face of the instrument in both figures and words and the amounts differ, the words control the figures. It is presumed that the maker or drawer would be more careful with words. If the words are ambiguous, however, then the figures control. Section 3–114.

# Chapter Summary

| | |
|---|---|
| **Negotiability** | **Rule** invests instruments with a high degree of marketability and commercial utility by conferring upon certain good faith transferees immunity from most defenses to the instrument<br>**Formal Requirements** negotiability is wholly a matter of form, and all the requirements for negotiability must be met within the four corners of the instrument |
| **Types of Negotiable Instruments** | **Orders to Pay**<br>• *Drafts* a draft involves three parties: the drawer orders the drawee to pay a fixed amount of money to the payee<br>• *Checks* a specialized form of draft that is drawn on a bank and payable on demand; the drawer orders the drawee (bank) to pay the payee on demand (upon the request of the holder)<br>**Promises to Pay**<br>• *Notes* a written promise by a maker (issuer) to pay a payee<br>• *Certificates of Deposit* a specialized form of note that is given by a bank or thrift association |
| **Formal Requirements of Negotiable Instruments** | **Writing** any reduction to tangible form is sufficient<br>**Signed** any symbol executed or adopted by a party with the intention to validate a writing<br>**Promise or Order to Pay**<br>• *Promise to Pay* an undertaking to pay, which must be more than a mere acknowledgment or recognition of an existing debt<br>• *Order to Pay* instruction to pay<br>**Unconditional** an absolute promise to pay that is not subject to any contingencies<br>• *Reference to Other Agreements* does not destroy negotiability unless the recital makes the instrument subject to or governed by the terms of another agreement<br>• *The Particular Fund Doctrine* an order or promise to pay only out of a particular fund no longer is conditional and does not destroy negotiability<br>**Fixed Amount** the holder must be assured of a determinable minimum principal payment although provisions in the instrument may increase the amount of recovery under certain circumstances<br>**Money** Legal tender authorized or adopted by a sovereign government as part of its currency<br>**No Other Promise or Order** a promise or order to do an act in addition to the payment of money destroys negotiability<br>**Payable on Demand or at a Definite Time** an instrument is demand paper if it must be paid upon request; an instrument is time paper if it is payable at a definite time<br>**Payable to Order or to Bearer** a negotiable instrument must contain words indicating that the maker or drawer intends that it pass into the hands of someone other than the payee<br>• *Payable to Order* payable to the "order of" (or other words which mean the same) a named person or anyone designated by that person<br>• *Payable to Bearer* payable to the holder of the instrument; includes instruments payable (1) payable to bearer or the order of bearer, (2) that do not specify a payee, or (3) payable to "cash" or to order of "cash" |

# Cases

### CASE 26–1
## Formal Requirements of Negotiable Instruments
## *YIN v. SOCIETY NATIONAL BANK INDIANA*
Court of Appeals of Indiana, 1996
665 N.E.2d 58

CHEZEM, J.

## Case Summary

Defendants-Appellants, Sam Yin ("Yin") and Sophia Kung ("Kung") appeal from the grant of partial summary judgment in favor of Plaintiff-Appellee, Society National Bank ("Society"). We reverse and remand for trial on the merits.

\* \* \*

## Facts and Procedural History

The undisputed facts are as follows. On January 2, 1991, Society agreed in a note to lend U.S.A. Diversified Products, Inc. ("USAD") up to $2,000,000.00 in the form of an operating line of credit. Paul Davis ("Davis") signed the note both personally and as the president of USAD. Yin, who jointly owns USAD with Davis, signed the note personally. Kung, who at that time was married to Yin, also signed the note personally. During negotiations regarding the note, Society directly dealt only with Davis. Once negotiations were finalized, Davis took the note, obtained Yin's and Kung's signatures, and returned it to Society. No party challenges the authenticity of any of the signatures on the 1991 note. The outstanding balance was to be paid on April 30, 1992, the note's expiration date.

\* \* \*

Some time prior to the end of April, 1992, Davis told Society that a 60-day extension of the original payment date was needed. Society agreed to the extension. Davis represented that he would obtain Yin's and Kung's signatures as he had for the 1991 document. However, for purposes of this partial summary judgment, the parties agree that Yin's and Kung's signatures were forged on the extension document.

As a result of USAD's default on the line of credit, Society filed a complaint against USAD, Davis, Yin, and

Kung on December 8, 1992. On May 27, 1994, the trial court granted partial summary judgment in favor of Society and against Yin and Kung in the amount of $2,160,331.73 including interest and attorney fees and expenses.

## Discussion and Decision

\* \* \*

**B. Is this line of credit a negotiable instrument?**
[Article 3] appl[ies] only to negotiable instruments. [Citation.] Non-negotiable agreements are governed by Indiana common law. [Citations.] Yin and Kung challenge the trial court's finding that their agreement for a line of credit is a negotiable instrument. \* \* \* We hold that it is not.

In determining the negotiability of an agreement, we apply the law in effect at the time of the execution of the agreement [Prior Article 3.]

\* \* \*

Yin and Kung assert that their line of credit meets neither the sum certain [fixed amount under Revised Article 3] nor the unconditional requirement. \* \* \*

Other courts have faced the issue or a situation quite similar to it and held that such an agreement is not a negotiable instrument. For example, in [Citation] the Fifth Circuit agreed with a district court's opinion that "[t]he note in this case does not contain an obligation to pay a 'sum certain,' but rather 'the sum of TWO MILLION AND NO/100 DOLLARS ($2,000,000) or so much thereof as may be advanced. . . .'". [Citation] The Fifth Circuit reasoned that the language employed by the note failed to disclose the exact amount to be repaid. [Citation.] That is, the amount advanced to the parties could not be determined with certainty absent an inquiry to other documents. Accordingly, the note did not facially demand payment of a sum certain [fixed amount], and hence was not negotiable. [Citations.]

The parties do not seriously dispute that the agreement in the present case is a line of credit upon which USAD could make draws of varying amounts. Indeed, the face of the note contains a notation regarding "draws." We note that although USAD did make various draws upon the line of credit, it was under no obligation to make any draws whatsoever. In fact, if USAD had never drawn upon the line of credit, it would have owed nothing when the agreement matured. The principal would have been zero. This is noteworthy because it illustrates an important feature of the line of credit: in order to ascertain the principal owed, one must look beyond the agreement itself. A current history of USAD's draws would also be necessary in order to calculate the amount USAD owed. Because of the potentially variable principal which results from such an arrangement, the line of credit contains no sum certain [fixed sum]. In addition, USAD's ability to make draws up to two million dollars was not unfettered. It was dependent upon the sufficiency of USAD's accounts receivable. That is, if USAD sold the accounts receivable (Society's security), then Society "in all likelihood . . . would put a hold on any further draws." Society conditioned USAD's access to the line of credit by tracking the company's collateral. Lacking an unconditional promise to pay a sum certain, the line of credit falls outside the definition of a negotiable instrument.* Thus, in addressing the parties' other issues regarding the line of credit, we apply Indiana common law.

* * *

Because the change must be a material and binding one, we cannot agree with Yin's and Kung's assertion that the forged extension note serves to discharge them from the potential liability they incurred upon signing the original 1991 agreement. They cannot be bound by a document (here, the extension note) which does not bear their signatures. In addition, by signing the 1991 note which contained a consent to future extensions provision, they explicitly gave prior consent to an extension. [Citation.] Accordingly, the extension note has no effect on their liability.

* * *

Reversed and remanded for trial on the merits.

---

*In reaching this conclusion, we distinguish between a variable principal and a variable interest rate. Unlike the former, the latter would not destroy the negotiability of an instrument. [Revised Article 3 holds] that variable interest rates do not affect negotiability. . . .

---

## CASE 26–2
### Demand
## *NATIONSBANK OF VIRGINIA, N.A. v. BARNES*

Virginia Circuit Court, Twentieth Circuit, 1994
24 U.C.C. Rep. Serv.2d 782

HORNE, J.

This matter is before the court on Plaintiff's Motion for Partial Summary Judgment. Defendants have filed a Grounds of Defense, asserting certain affirmative defenses to liability. Plaintiff argues that it is entitled to partial summary judgment. As discussed more fully below, Plaintiff's motion will be granted in part and denied in part. The court will address Defendant's affirmative defenses as they relate to each note specifically, and to both Notes in general.

* * *

The following facts are undisputed with respect to the 1991 Note which is the subject of Count II of the Motion for Judgment. Defendants Ad Barnes, Trustee, Ad Barnes and Elaine Barnes executed a . . . Note to Sovran Bank, N.A. on August 27, 1991, in the principal amount of $200,000. Plaintiff NationsBank is the successor by merger to Sovran and is now the holder of this Note. Under the terms of the Note, Plaintiff is entitled to collect all expenses, including court costs and attorney's fees, incurred in the enforcement of its rights under the Note. By letter dated February 17, 1993, NationsBank made demand on the 1991 Note.

The factual question still in dispute concerning the 1991 Note is whether it is a demand note. Plaintiff argues that the language of the note is unambiguous and is clearly a demand note. Defendants argue that the detailed enumeration of events constituting default is inconsistent with a demand note. Thus, a standard of good faith must be applied before a demand for accelerated repayment can be made.

[U.C.C.] § 1–203 establishes a general duty of good faith in every contract governed by the Commercial Code. Under any contract providing for accelerated payment at will, § 1–208 states that the option is to be exercised only in the good faith belief that the prospect of payment or performance is impaired. However, the Official Comment to this section indicates that it is not applicable to a demand instrument.

[U.C.C.] 3A–108(a) [U.C.C. Revised § 3–108(a)] states that a note is payable "on demand" if it says it is payable on demand or states no time for payment. In this case, the 1991 . . . Note is a standard form with different forms of repayment setout on the first page. The box marked payable "on demand" has been checked in this instance. There is no time set for repayment, only a provision requiring monthly payments of interest.

It is the court's opinion that the 1991 Note is unambiguous and is clearly a demand note. Thus, Plaintiff is under no obligation to show good faith before requesting payment on the note. Since demand has been made by Plaintiff, Defendants are liable. Thus, Plaintiff is entitled to summary judgment on the issue of liability under the 1991 Note.

As the question of the reasonableness of the attorney's fees and costs under the 1991 Note is still in dispute, summary judgment cannot be granted on this issue.

---

## CASE 26–3
### Payable to Order or to Bearer
# COOPERATIEVE CENTRALE RAIFFEISEN-BOERENLEENBANK
# B.A. v. BAILEY

United States District Court, Central District California, 1989
710 F.Supp. 737

REA, J.
This matter comes before the court on the motion of both parties to this action for partial summary adjudication and on plaintiff's motion for summary judgment.

* * *

This is an action for collection on a promissory note brought by plaintiff, Cooperatieve Centrale Raiffeisen-Boerenleenbank, B.A. ("the Bank"), against the maker of the note, William Bailey, M.D. ("Bailey"). Bailey executed the note in December, 1982, in favor of "California Dreamstreet," a joint venture which solicited investments in a cattle-breeding operation. California Dreamstreet negotiated the note in 1986 to the Bank, which in turn filed this action on August 29, 1988.

The note states in relevant part:

DR. WILLIAM H. BAILEY . . . hereby promises to pay to the order to CALIFORNIA DREAMSTREET . . . the sum of Three Hundred Twenty Nine Thousand Eight Hundred ($329,800.00) Dollars. . . .

* * *

By this motion for partial summary adjudication, the parties seek to determine, as a threshold matter, whether the subject promissory note is a negotiable instrument. * * * [The parties] agree that the sole issue is whether the unusual language in the note obliging Bailey to "pay to the order *to* California Dreamstreet" renders the note non-negotiable.

Whether an instrument is negotiable is a question of law to be determined solely from the face of the instrument, without reference to the intent of the parties. [Citation.] To be negotiable, an instrument must "be payable to order or bearer." Code § 3–104(1)(d) [Revised 3–104(a)(i)]. "Payable to order" is further defined by Code § 3–110(1), as follows:

(1) An instrument is payable to order when by its terms it is payable to the order or assigns of any person therein specified with reasonable certainty, or to him or his order, or when it is conspicuously designated on its face as 'exchange' or the like and names a payee.

[Compare Revised Section 3–109(b).]

It is well established that a promissory note is non-negotiable if it states only: "payable to (payee)," rather than "payable to the order of [payee]." [Citations.] Bailey claims that the instant note, which states "pay to the order to [payee]," falls between these two alternatives and should therefore be deemed non-negotiable.

The authorities are unhelpful. There is apparently no case on record in which a variance this small from the language of the Code has been called into question. Both parties direct the Court's attention to Official UCC Comment 5 to Code § 3–104, which states:

5. This Article omits the original Section 10, which provided that the instrument need not follow the language of the act if it 'clearly indicates an intention to conform'

to it. The provision has served no useful purpose, and it has been an encouragement to bad drafting and to liberality in holding questionable paper to be negotiable. The omission is not intended to mean that the instrument must follow the language of this section, or that one term may not be recognized as clearly the equivalent of another, as in the case of 'I undertake' instead of 'I promise,' or 'Pay to holder' instead of 'Pay to bearer.' It does mean that either the language of the section or a clear equivalent must be found, and that in doubtful cases the decision should be against negotiability.

In the court's opinion, the Comment fails to persuasively support either party's position. Rules of grammar belie the Bank's argument that the preposition "to" is an apt substitute for "of" since the resulting sentence, read literally, is not just ambiguous but incomplete. On the other hand, the Comment expressly disavows Bailey's argument that the Code drafters intended to set forth certain "magic words," the absence of which precludes negotiability.

What does emerge from the Comment is the need for certainty in determining negotiability. Though sensitive to this goal and to the potentially harsh result of such a finding, the court does not find the instant facts to present the kind of "doubtful" case which should be resolved against negotiability. In this context, the phrase "pay to the order to" can plausibly be construed only to mean "pay to the order of." While other explanations are possible, none are realistic. To hold otherwise would, in this court's opinion, set an overly technical standard that could unexpectedly frustrate legitimate expectations of negotiability in commercial transactions.

\* \* \*

For all the above reasons, It Is Hereby Adjudged that the promissory note which is the subject of this action is a negotiable instrument. It is further Ordered that plaintiff's motion for summary judgment is denied without prejudice to its being renewed upon the completion of discovery.

---

# Questions

**1.** Discuss the concept and importance of negotiability.

**2.** Identify and discuss the types of negotiable instruments involving an order to pay.

**3.** Identify and discuss the types of negotiable instruments involving a promise to pay.

**4.** List and discuss the formal requirements that an instrument must meet to be negotiable.

**5.** Discuss the effect on the negotiability of an instrument's (1) being undated, antedated, or postdated, (2) lack of completion, and (3) ambiguity.

---

# Problems

**1.** State whether the following provisions impair or preclude negotiability, the instrument in each instance being otherwise in proper form. Answer each statement with either the word "Negotiable" or "Nonnegotiable" and explain why.

(a) A note for $2,000 payable in twenty monthly installments of $100 each that provides the following: "In case of death of maker, all payments not due at date of death are canceled."

(b) A note stating "This note is secured by a mortgage of even date herewith on personal property located at 351 Maple Street, Smithton, Illinois."

(c) A certificate of deposit reciting "June 6, 1999, John Jones has deposited in the Citizens Bank of Emanon, Illinois, Two Thousand Dollars, to the credit of himself, payable upon the return of this instrument properly indorsed, with interest at the rate of 6 percent per annum from date of issue

upon ninety days' written notice. (Signed) Jill Crystal, President, Citizens Bank of Emanon."

(d) An instrument reciting "I.O.U., Mark Noble, $1,000.00."

(e) A note stating "In accordance with our contract of December 13, 1999, I promise to pay to the order of Sam Stone $100 on March 13, 2000."

(f) A draft drawn by Brown on the Acme Publishing Company for $500, payable to the order of the Sixth National Bank of Erehwon, directing the bank to "Charge this draft to my royalty account."

(g) A note executed by Pierre Janvier, a resident of Chicago, for $2,000, payable in Swiss francs.

(h) An undated note for $1,000 payable "six months after date."

(i)   A note for $500 payable to the order of Ray Rodes six months after the death of Albert Olds.

(j)   A note of $500 payable to the assigns of Levi Lee.

(k)   A check made payable "to Ketisha Johnson."

2.   State whether the following provisions in a note impair or preclude negotiability, the instrument in each instance being otherwise in proper form. Answer each statement with either the word "Negotiable" or "Nonnegotiable" and explain why.

(a)   A note signed by Henry Brown in the trade name of the Quality Store.

(b)   A note for $450, payable to the order of TV Products Company, "If, but only if, the color television set for which this note is given proves entirely satisfactory to me."

(c)   A note executed by Adams, Burton, and Cady Company, a partnership, for $1,000, payable to the order of Davis, payable only out of the assets of the partnership.

(d)   A note promising to pay $500 to the order of Leigh and to deliver ten tons of coal to Leigh.

(e)   A note for $10,000 executed by Eaton payable to the order of the First National Bank of Emanon in which Eaton promises to give additional collateral if the bank deems itself insecure and demands additional security.

(f)   A note reading, "I promise to pay to the order of Richard Roe $2,000 on January 31, 2001, but it is agreed that if the crop of Blackacre falls below ten bushels per acre for the 2000 season, this note shall be extended indefinitely."

(g)   A note payable to the order of Ray Rogers fifty years from date but providing that payment shall be accelerated by the death of Silas Hughes to a point of time four months after his death.

(h)   A note for $4,000 calling for payments of installments of $250 each and stating "In the event any installment hereof is not paid when due this note shall immediately become due at the holder's option."

(i)   An instrument dated September 17, 1999, in the handwriting of John Henry Brown, which reads in full: "Sixty days after date, I, John Henry Brown, promise to pay to the order of William Jones $500."

(j)   A note reciting "I promise to pay Ray Reed $100 on December 24, 1999."

3.   On March 10, Tolliver Tolles, also known as Thomas Towle, delivered to Alonzo Craig and Abigail Craig the following instrument, written by him in pencil:

For value received, I, Thomas Towle, promise to pay to the order of Alonzo Craig or Abigail Craig One Thousand Seventy-Five ($1,000.75) Dollars six months after my mother, Alma Tolles, dies with interest at the rate of 9 percent from date to maturity and after maturity at the rate of 9 3/4 percent. I hereby waive the benefit of all laws exempting real or personal property from levy or sale.

Is this instrument negotiable? Explain.

4.   Henry Hughes, who operates a department store, executed the following instrument:

$2,600                              Chicago, March 5, 1999
On July 1, 1999, I promise to pay Daniel Dalziel, or order, the sum of Twenty-Six Hundred Dollars for the privilege of one framed advertising sign, size 24 × 36 inches, at one end of each of two hundred sixty motor coaches of the New Omnibus Company for a term of three months from May 15, 1999.

                                   Henry Hughes

Is this instrument negotiable? Explain.

5.   Paul agreed to lend Marsha $500. Thereupon Marsha made and delivered her note for $500 payable to Paul or order "ten days after my marriage." Shortly thereafter Marsha was married. Is the instrument negotiable? Explain.

6.   For the balance due on the purchase of a tractor Henry Brown executed and delivered to Jane Jones his promissory note containing the following language:

January 1, 1999, I promise to pay to the order of Jane Jones the sum of $7,000 to be paid only out of my checking account at the XYZ National Bank in Pinckard, Illinois, in two installments of $3,500 each, payable on May 1, 1999, and on July 1, 1999, provided that if I fail to pay the first installment on the due date, the entire sum shall become immediately due. (Signed) Henry Brown

Is the note negotiable? Explain.

7.   Sam Sharpe executed and delivered to Don Dole the following instrument:

                              Knoxville, Tennessee
                              May 29, 1998
Thirty days after date I promise to pay Don Dole or order, Five Thousand Dollars. The holder of this instrument shall have the election to require the assignment and delivery to him of my 100 shares of Brookside Iron Works Corporation stock in lieu of the payment of Five Thousand Dollars in money.

                              (Signed) Sam Sharpe

Is this instrument negotiable? Explain.

8.   Is the following instrument negotiable?

                                   March 1, 1999
One month from date, I, James Jimson, hereby promise to pay Edmund Edwards: Six thousand, Seven hundred Fifty ($6,750.00) dollars, plus 8 3/4% interest. Payment for cutting machines to be delivered on March 15, 1999.

                                   James Jimson

9.   Broadway Management Corporation obtained a judgment against Briggs. The note on which the judgment was based reads in part: "Ninety Days after date, I, we, or either of us, promise to pay to the order of Three Thousand Four Hundred Ninety Eight and 45/100 ---------- Dollars." (The underlined words and symbols were typed in; the remainder was printed.) There are no blanks on the face of the instrument, any unused space having been filled in with hyphens. The note contains clauses permitting acceleration in the event the holder deems itself insecure and authorizes judgment "if this note is not paid at any stated or accelerated maturity." Briggs appeals, claiming that the note is not negotiable order paper. Decision?

10.    Sandra and Thomas McGuire entered into a purchase and sale agreement for "Becca's Boutique" with Pascal and Rebecca Tursi. The agreement provided that the McGuires would buy the store for $75,000, with a down payment of $10,000 and the balance of $65,000 to be paid at closing on October 5, 1999. The settlement clause stated that the sale was contingent upon the McGuires' obtaining a Small Business Administration loan of $65,000. On September 4, 1999, Mrs. McGuire signed a promissory note in which the McGuires promised to pay to the order of the Tursis and the Green Mountain Inn the sum of $65,000. The note specified that interest payments of $541.66 would become due and payable on the fifth days of October, November, and December 1999. The entire balance of the note, with interest, would become due and payable at the option of the holder if any installment of interest was not paid according to that schedule.

The Tursis had for several months been negotiating with Parker Perry for the purchase of the Green Mountain Inn in Stowe, Vermont. On September 7, 1999, the Tursis delivered to Perry a $65,000 promissory note payable to the order of Green Mountain Inn, Inc. This note was secured by transfer to the Green Mountain Inn of the McGuires' note to the Tursis. Subsequently, Mrs. McGuire learned that her Small Business Administration loan had been disapproved. On December 5, 1999, the Tursis defaulted on their promissory note to the Green Mountain Inn. On June 11, 2000, PP, Inc., formerly Green Mountain Inn, Inc., brought an action against the McGuires to recover on the note held as security for the Tursis' promissory note. Decision?

11.    On September 2, 1996, Levine executed a mortgage bond under which she promised to pay the Mykoffs a preexisting obligation of $54,000. On October 14, 1999, the Mykoffs transferred the mortgage to Bankers Trust Co., indorsing the instrument with the words "Pay to the Order of Bankers Trust Company Without Recourse." The Lincoln First Bank, N.A., brought this action asserting that the Mykoffs' mortgage is a nonnegotiable instrument because it is not payable to order or bearer; thus it is subject to Lincoln's defense that the mortgage was not supported by consideration as an antecedent debt is not consideration. Decision?

12.    Horne executed a $100,000 note in favor of R.C. Clark. On the back of the instrument was a restriction stating that the note could not be transferred, pledged, or otherwise assigned without Horne's written consent. As part of the same transaction between Horne and Clark, Horne gave Clark a separate letter authorizing Clark to pledge the note as collateral for a loan of $50,000 that Clark intended to secure from First State Bank. Clark did secure the loan and pledged the note, which was accompanied by Horne's letter authorizing Clark to use the note as collateral. First State contacted Horne and verified the agreement between Horne and Clark as to using the note as collateral. Clark defaulted on the loan. When First Bank later attempted to collect on the note, Horne refused to pay, arguing that the note was not negotiable as it could not be transferred without obtaining Horne's written consent. This suit was instituted. Decision?

13.    Holly Hill Acres, Ltd., executed and delivered a promissory note and a purchase money mortgage to Rogers and Blythe. The note provided that it was secured by a mortgage on certain real estate and that the terms of that mortgage "are by this reference made a part hereof." Rogers and Blythe then assigned the note to Charter Bank, and the bank sought to foreclose on the note and mortgage. Holly Hill Acres refused to pay, claiming that it was defrauded by Rogers and Blythe. Holly Hill appealed from a summary judgment entered in favor of plaintiff Charter Bank. Decision?

WWW   **Internet Exercise**   Find which version of the UCC Article 3 your State has adopted. (If your State's version is not available, choose that of another State.)

# CHAPTER 27

# Transfer

The primary advantage of negotiable instruments is their more ready acceptability. Nonetheless, although both negotiable instruments and non-negotiable undertakings are transferable by assignment, only negotiable instruments can result in the transferee becoming a holder. This distinction is highly significant. If the transferee of a negotiable instrument is entitled to payment by the terms of the instrument, he is a holder of the instrument. Only holders may be holders in due course and thus may be entitled to greater rights in the instrument than the transferor may have possessed. These rights, discussed in the next chapter, are the reason why negotiable instruments move freely in the marketplace. This chapter discusses the methods by which negotiable instruments may be transferred.

## NEGOTIATION

A **holder** is broadly defined in Section 1–201(20) as "a person who is in possession of . . . an instrument . . . drawn, issued, or indorsed to him or his order or to bearer or in blank." **Negotiation** is the transfer of possession, whether voluntary or involuntary, by a person other than the issuer of a negotiable instrument in such a manner that the transferee becomes a holder. Section 3–201(a). An instrument is transferred when a person other than its issuer delivers it for the purpose of giving the recipient the right to enforce the instrument. Section 3–203(a). Accordingly, to qualify as a holder a person must have possession of an instrument that runs to him. Thus, there are two ways in which a person can be a holder: (1) the instrument has been issued to that person, or (2) the instrument has been transferred to that person by negotiation.

The transfer of a nonnegotiable promise or order operates as an assignment, as does the transfer of a negotiable instrument by a means that does not render the transferee a holder. As discussed in Chapter 16, an **assignment** is

the voluntary transfer to a third party of the rights arising from a contract.

Whether a transfer is by assignment or by negotiation, the transferee acquires the rights his transferor had. Section 3–203(b). The transfer need not be for value: if the instrument is transferred as a gift, the donee acquires all the rights of the donor. If the transferor was a holder in due course, the transferee acquires the rights of a holder in due course, which rights he in turn may transfer. This rule, sometimes referred to as the *shelter rule*, existed at common law and still exists under the Uniform Commercial Code (UCC). The shelter rule is discussed more fully in Chapter 28.

The requirements for negotiation depend on whether the instrument is bearer paper or order paper.

### Negotiation of Bearer Paper

If an instrument is payable to bearer, it may be negotiated by transfer of possession alone. Section 3–201(b). Because bearer paper (an instrument payable to bearer) runs to whoever is in possession of it, a finder or a thief of bearer paper would be a holder even though he did not receive possession by voluntary transfer. Section 3–201(a). For example, P loses an instrument payable to bearer that I had issued to her. F finds it and delivers it to B, who thus receives it by negotiation and is a holder. F also qualified as a holder because he was in possession of bearer paper. As a holder, F had the power to negotiate the instrument, and B, the transferee, may be a holder in due course if he meets the Code's requirements for such a holder (discussed in Chapter 28). See Figure 27–1 for an illustration of this example. Because a bearer instrument is negotiated by mere *possession*, it is comparable to cash.

◆ *See Figure 27–1*

**FIGURE 27–1** Bearer Paper

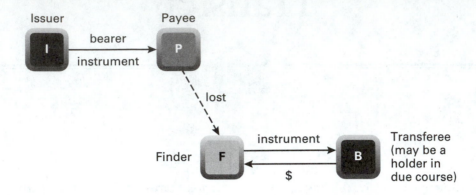

## Negotiation of Order Paper

If the instrument is **order paper** (an instrument payable to order), both (a) transfer of its *possession* and (b) its *indorsement* (signature) by the appropriate parties are necessary for the transferee to become a holder. Section 3–201(b). Figure 27–2 compares the negotiation of bearer and order paper.

Any transfer for *value* of order paper gives the transferee the specifically enforceable right to have the unqualified indorsement of the transferor, unless the parties agree otherwise. Section 3–203(c). The parties may agree that the transfer is to be an assignment rather than a negotiation, in which case no indorsement is required. Absent such agreement, the courts presume that negotiation was intended where value is given. Where a transfer is not for value (i.e., a gift), the transaction is normally noncommercial; thus, the courts do not presume the intent to negotiate.

Until the necessary indorsement has been supplied, the transferee has nothing more than the contract rights of an assignee. Negotiation takes effect only when a proper indorsement is made, at which time the transferee becomes a holder of the instrument.

If a customer deposits a check or other instrument for collection without properly indorsing the item, the depository bank becomes a holder when it accepts the item for deposit if the depositor is a holder. Section 4–205(i). It no longer needs to supply the customer's indorsement.

◆ *See Figure 27–2*

***The Impostor Rule*** Negotiation of an order instrument requires a valid indorsement by the person to whose order the instrument is payable. The impostor rule governing unauthorized signatures is an *exception* to this general rule. Usually, the impostor rule comes into play in situations involving a confidence man who impersonates a respected citizen and who deceives a third party into delivering a negotiable instrument to the impostor in the name of the respected citizen. For instance, John Doe, falsely representing himself as Richard Roe, a prominent citizen, induces Ray Davis to loan him $10,000. Davis draws a check payable to the order of Richard Roe and delivers it to Doe, who then forges Roe's name to the check and presents it to the drawee for payment. The drawee pays it. Subsequently, Davis, the drawer, denies the drawee's right of reimbursement upon the ground that the drawee did not pay in accordance with his order: Davis ordered payment to Roe or to Roe's order. Roe did not order payment to anyone; therefore, the drawee would not acquire a right of reimbursement against Davis. The general rule governing unauthorized signatures supports this argument in favor of the drawer.

Nevertheless, Section 3–404(c) provides that the indorsement of the impostor (Doe) or of any other person in the name of the named payee is **effective** as the indorsement of the payee if the impostor has induced the maker or drawer (Davis) to issue the instrument to him or his confederate using the name of the payee (Roe). It is as if the named payee had indorsed the instrument. The reason for this rule is that the drawer or maker is to blame for failing to detect the impersonation by the impostor. Thus, in the above example, the drawee would be able to debit the drawer's account. Moreover, Revised Article 3 expands the impostor rule by extending its coverage to include an impostor who is impersonating an agent. Section 3–404(a). Thus, if an impostor impersonates Jones and induces the drawer to draw a check

FIGURE 27–2   Negotiation of Bearer and Order Paper

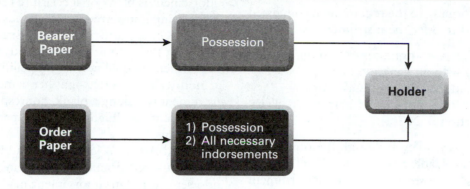

to the order of Jones, the impostor can negotiate the check. Moreover, under the Revision, if an impostor impersonates Jones, the president of Jones Corporation, and the check is to the order of Jones Corporation, the impostor can negotiate the check. Comment 1 to Section 3–404.

If the person paying the instrument fails to exercise ordinary care, the issuer may recover from the payor to the extent the payor's negligence contributed to the loss. If the issuer is also negligent, comparative negligence would apply.

***The Fictitious Payee Rule***  The rule just discussed also applies when a person who does not intend the payee to have an interest in the instrument signs as or on behalf of a maker or drawer. Section 3–404(b). In such a situation, any person's indorsement in the name of the named payee is **effective** if the person identified as the payee is a fictitious person. For instance, Palmer gives Albrecht, her employee, authority to write checks to pay Palmer's debts. Albrecht writes a check for $2,000 to Foushee, a fictitious payee, which Albrecht takes and indorses in Foushee's name to Albrecht. Albrecht cashes the check at Palmer's bank, which can debit Palmer's account because Albrecht's signature in Foushee's name is effective against Palmer. Palmer should bear the risk of her unscrupulous employees.

In a similar situation also involving a disloyal employee, a drawer's employee falsely tells the drawer that money is owed to Leon, and the drawer writes a check payable to the order of Leon and hands it to the agent for delivery to him. The agent forges Leon's name to the check and obtains payment from the drawee bank. The drawer then denies the bank's claim to reimbursement upon the ground that the bank did not comply with her order; that the drawer had ordered payment to

Leon or order; that the drawee did not make payment either to Leon or as ordered by him, inasmuch as the forgery of Leon's signature is wholly inoperative; and that the drawee paid in accordance with the scheme of the faithless agent and not in compliance with the drawer's order. Under Section 3–405, an employer has liability on the instrument when one of its employees, who is entrusted with responsibility with respect to such an instrument, makes a fraudulent indorsement if: (1) the instrument is payable to the employer and the employee forges the indorsement of the employer or (2) the instrument is issued by the employer and the employee forges the indorsement of the person identified as the payee. The example above falls under the second part of the rule just stated. Accordingly, the employee's indorsement is effective as that of the unintended payee, and the drawee bank will be able to debit the drawer's (employer's) account.

Section 3–405 also applies to a situation (number 1 in the paragraph above) not involving a fictitious payee: a fraudulent indorsement made by an employee entrusted with responsibility with respect to an instrument payable to the employer. For example, an employee, whose job involves posting amounts of checks payable to her employer, steals some of the checks and forges her employer's indorsement. The indorsement is effective as the employer's indorsement because the employee's duties included processing checks for bookkeeping purposes.

Section 3–405 provides, however, that the employer may recover from the drawee bank to the extent the loss resulted from the bank's failure to exercise ordinary care. If the employer is also negligent, a rule of comparative negligence applies.

*See Case 27–1*

## Negotiations Subject to Rescission

A negotiation conforming to the requirements discussed above is effective to transfer the instrument even if it is

1. made by an infant, a corporation exceeding its powers, or a person without capacity; or
2. obtained by fraud, duress, or mistake; or
3. made in breach of a duty or as part of an illegal transaction. Section 3–202(a).

Thus, a negotiation is valid even though the transaction in which it occurs is voidable or even void. In all of these instances, the transferor loses all rights in the instrument until he regains possession of it. His right to do so, determined by State law, is valid against the immediate transferee and all subsequent holders, but not against a subsequent holder in due course or a person paying the instrument in good faith and without notice. Section 3–202(b).

## *INDORSEMENTS*

An **indorsement** is "a signature, other than that of a signer as maker, drawer, or acceptor, that alone or accompanied by other words is made on an instrument for the purpose of (i) negotiating the instrument, (ii) restricting payment of the instrument, or (iii) incurring indorser's liability on the instrument, but regardless of the intent of the signer, a signature and its accompanying words is an indorsement unless the accompanying words, terms of the instrument, place of the signature, or other circumstances unambiguously indicate that the signature was made for a purpose other than indorsement." Section 3–204(a).

An indorsement may be complex or simple. It may be dated and may indicate where it is made, but neither date nor place is required to be shown. The simplest type is merely the signature of the indorser. The indorser undertakes certain obligations, as explained later, by merely signing her name. A forged or otherwise unauthorized signature necessary to negotiation is inoperative and thus breaks the chain of title to the instrument. Section 3–403(a).

The type of indorsement used in first negotiating an instrument affects its subsequent negotiation. Every indorsement is (1) either blank or special, (2) either restrictive or nonrestrictive, and (3) either qualified or unqualified. These categories are not mutually exclusive. Indeed, each indorsement may be placed within three of these six categories because all indorsements disclose three things: (1) the method to be employed in making

subsequent negotiations (this depends upon whether the indorsement is blank or special); (2) the kind of interest that is being transferred (this depends upon whether the indorsement is restrictive or nonrestrictive); and (3) the liability of the indorser (this depends upon whether the indorsement is qualified or unqualified). For instance, an indorser who merely signs her name on the back of an instrument is making a blank, nonrestrictive, unqualified indorsement. See Figure 27–3 on page 538 for further illustrations.

Revised Article 3 identifies an additional type of indorsement—an anomalous indorsement. An anomalous indorsement is "an indorsement made by a person that is not the holder of the instrument." Section 3–205(d). The only effect of an anomalous indorsement is to make the signer liable on the instrument as an indorser. Such an indorsement does not affect the manner in which the instrument may be negotiated.

The effectiveness of an indorsement as well as the rights of the transferee and transferor depend upon whether the indorsement meets certain formal requirements. This section will cover the different kinds of indorsements and the formal requirements of each.

◆ *See Figure 27–3*

## Blank Indorsements

A **blank indorsement,** which specifies no indorsee, may consist solely of the signature of the indorser or her authorized agent. Section 3–205(b). Such an indorsement converts order paper into bearer paper and leaves bearer paper as bearer paper. Thus, an instrument indorsed in blank may be negotiated by delivery alone without further indorsement. Hence, the holder should treat it with the same care as cash.

 *See Case 27–2*

## Special Indorsements

A **special indorsement** specifically identifies the person to whom or to whose order the instrument is to be payable. Section 3–205(a). Thus, if Peter, the payee of a note, indorses it "Pay to the order of Andrea," or even "Pay Andrea," the indorsement is special because it names the transferee. Words of negotiability—"pay to order or bearer"—are *not* required in an indorsement. Thus, an indorsement reading "Pay Edward" is interpreted as meaning "Pay to the order of Edward." Any further negotiation of the instrument would require Edward's indorsement.

Moreover, a holder of an instrument with a blank indorsement may protect himself by converting the blank indorsement to a special indorsement by writing over the signature of the indorser words identifying the person to whom the instrument is payable. Section 3–205(c). For example, on the back of a negotiable instrument appears the blank indorsement "Sally Seller." Harry Holder, who receives the instrument from Seller, may convert this bearer instrument into order paper by inserting above Seller's signature "Pay Harry Holder" or other similar words.

 *See Case 27–3*

## Restrictive Indorsements

As the term implies, a **restrictive indorsement** attempts to restrict the rights of the indorsee in some fashion. It limits the purpose for which the proceeds of the instrument can be applied. Section 3–206. The Code discusses four types of indorsements as restrictive: conditional indorsements, indorsements prohibiting further transfer, indorsements for deposit or collection, and indorsements in trust. Section 3–206. Only the last two are effective. An **unrestrictive indorsement,** in contrast, does not attempt to restrict the rights of the indorsee.

***Indorsements for Deposit or Collection*** The most frequently used form of restrictive indorsement is that designed to place the instrument in the banking system for deposit or collection. Indorsements of this type, collectively referred to as "collection indorsements," include "for collection," "for deposit," and "pay any bank." Such an indorsement *effectively limits* further negotiation to those consistent with its limitation and binds (1) all nonbanking persons, (2) a depositary bank that purchases the instrument or takes it for collection, and (3) a payor bank that is also the depositary bank or that takes the instrument for immediate payment over the counter from a person other than a collecting bank. Section 3–206(c). Thus, a collection indorsement binds all parties except an intermediary bank (discussed in Chapter 30) or a payor bank that is not also the depositary bank.

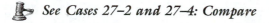 *See Cases 27–2 and 27–4: Compare*

***Indorsements in Trust*** Another common kind of restrictive indorsement is that in which the indorser creates a trust for the benefit of himself or others. If an instrument is indorsed "Pay Thelma in trust for Barbara," "Pay Thelma for Barbara," "Pay Thelma for account of Barbara," or "Pay Thelma as agent for Barbara," Thelma is a fiduciary, subject to liability for any breach of her obligation to Barbara. Trustees commonly and legitimately sell trust assets, and, consequently, a trustee has power to negotiate an instrument. The first taker under an indorsement to her in trust (in this case Thelma) is under a duty to pay or apply, in a manner consistent with the indorsement, all the funds she receives. Thelma's immediate transferee may safely pay Thelma for the instrument if he does not have *notice* of any breach of fiduciary duty. Section 3–206(d)(1). Subsequent indorsees or transferees are not bound by such indorsement unless they *know* that the trustee negotiated the instrument for her own benefit or otherwise in breach of her fiduciary duty. Section 3–206(d)(2).

***Indorsements with Ineffective Restrictions*** A **conditional indorsement** is one by which the indorser makes the rights of the indorsee subject to the happening or nonhappening of a specified event. Suppose Marcin makes a note payable to Parker's order. Parker indorses it "Pay Rodriguez, but only if the good ship Jolly Jack arrives in Chicago harbor by November 15, 1999." If Marcin had used this language in the instrument itself, it would be nonnegotiable because her promise to pay must be unconditional to satisfy the formal requisites of negotiability. Revised Article 3 makes such indorsements ineffective by providing that an indorsement stating a condition to the right of a holder to receive payment does not affect the right of the indorsee to enforce the instrument. Section 3–206(b).

An indorsement may by its express terms attempt to prohibit further transfer by stating "Pay [name] only" or language to similar effect. Such an indorsement, or any other purporting to prohibit further transfer, is designed to restrict the rights of the indorsee. To remove any doubt as to the effect of such a provision, the Code provides that *no* indorsement limiting payment to a particular person or otherwise prohibiting further transfer is effective. Section 3–206(a). As a result, an indorsement which purports to prohibit further transfer of the instrument is given the same effect as an unrestricted indorsement.

## Qualified and Unqualified Indorsements

**Unqualified** indorsers promise that they will pay the instrument according to its terms at the time of their indorsement to the holder or to any subsequent indorser who paid it. Section 3–415(a). In short, an unqualified indorser guarantees payment of the instrument if certain conditions are met.

An indorser may disclaim her liability on the contract of indorsement, but only if the indorsement so declares and the disclaimer is written on the instrument. The customary manner of disclaiming an indorser's liability is to add the words **"without recourse,"** either before or after her signature. Section 3–415(b). A "without recourse" indorsement, called a **qualified** indorsement, does not, however, eliminate all of an indorser's liability. As discussed in Chapter 29, a qualified indorsement disclaims contract liability but does not entirely remove the warranty liability of the indorser. A qualified indorsement and delivery is a negotiation and transfers legal title to the indorsee, but the indorser does not guarantee payment of the instrument. Furthermore, a qualified indorsement does not destroy negotiability or prevent further negotiation of the instrument. For example, assume that an attorney receives a check payable to her order in payment of a client's claim. She may indorse the check to the client without recourse, thereby disclaiming liability as a guarantor of payment of the check. The qualified indorsement plus delivery would transfer title to the client.

## Formal Requirements of Indorsements

*Place of Indorsement*   An indorsement must be written on the instrument or on a paper, called an **allonge,** affixed to the instrument. Section 3–204(a). An allonge may be used even if the instrument contains sufficient space for the indorsement.

Customarily, indorsements are made on the back or reverse side of the instrument, starting at the top and continuing down. Under Federal Reserve Board guidelines, indorsements of checks must be in ink of an appropriate color, such as blue or black, and must be made within 1 1/2 inches of the trailing (left) edge of the back of the check. The remaining space is reserved for bank indorsements. Nevertheless, failure to comply with the guidelines does not destroy negotiability, and there are no penalties for violating the standard.

Occasionally, however, a signature may appear on an instrument in such a way that it is impossible to tell with certainty the nature of the liability the signer intended to undertake. In such an event, the Code specifies that the signer is to be treated as an indorser. Section 3–204(a). In keeping with the rule that a transferee must be able to determine her rights from the face of the instrument, the person who signed in an ambiguous capacity may not introduce parol evidence to establish that she intended to be something other than an indorser.

◆ *See Figure 27–4*

*Incorrect or Misspelled Indorsements*   If an instrument is payable to a payee or indorsee under a misspelled name or a name different from that of the holder, the holder may require the indorsement in the name stated or in the holder's correct name or both. Section 3–204(d). Nevertheless, the person paying or taking the instrument for value may require the indorser to sign both names.

**FIGURE 27–3** Indorsements

| Indorsement | Type of Indorsement | Interest Transferred | Liability of Indorser |
|---|---|---|---|
| 1. "John Doe" | Blank | Nonrestrictive | Unqualified |
| 2. "Pay to Richard Roe, John Doe" | Special | Nonrestrictive | Unqualified |
| 3. "Without recourse, John Doe" | Blank | Nonrestrictive | Qualified |
| 4. "Pay to Richard Roe in trust for John Roe," without recourse, John Doe" | Special | Restrictive | Qualified |
| 5. "For collection only, without recourse, John Doe" | Blank | Restrictive | Qualified |
| 6. "Pay to XYZ Corp., on the condition that it delivers goods ordered this date, John Doe." | Special | Nonrestrictive | Unqualified |

**FIGURE 27–4** Placement of Indorsement

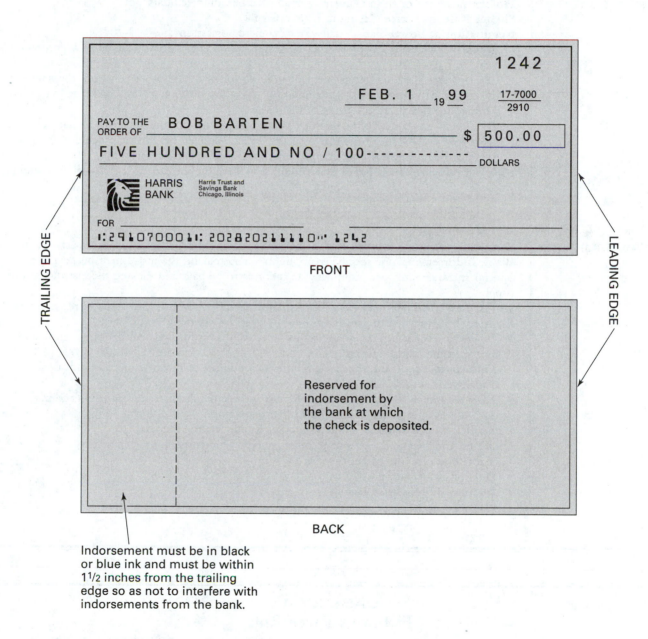

# Chapter Summary

**Negotiation**

**Holder**  possessor of an instrument with all necessary indorsements
**Shelter Rule**  transferee gets rights of transferor
**Negotiation of Bearer Paper**  transferred by mere possession
**Negotiation of Order Paper**  transferred by possession and indorsement by all appropriate parties
- *The Impostor Rule*  an indorsement of an impostor or of any other person in the name of the named payee is effective if the impostor has induced the maker or drawer to issue the instrument to him using the name of the payee
- *The Fictitious Payee Rule*  an indorsement by any person in the name of the named payee is effective if an agent of the maker or drawer has supplied her with the name of the payee for fraudulent purposes

**Negotiations Subject to Rescission**  negotiation is valid even though a transaction is void or voidable

**Indorsement**

**Definition**  signature (on the instrument) of a payee, drawee, accommodation party, or holder
**Blank Indorsement**  one specifying no indorsee and making the instrument bearer paper
**Special Indorsement**  one identifying an indorsee to be paid and making the instrument order paper
**Unrestrictive Indorsement**  one that does not attempt to restrict the rights of the indorsee
**Restrictive Indorsement**  one attempting to limit the rights of the indorsee
- *Indorsements for Deposit or Collection*  effectively limit further negotiation to those consistent with the indorsement
- *Indorsements in Trust*  effectively require the indorsee to pay or apply all funds in accordance with the indorsement
- *Indorsements with Ineffective Restrictions*  include conditional indorsements and indorsements attempting to prohibit further negotiation

**Unqualified Indorsement**  one that imposes liability on the indorser
**Qualified Indorsement**  without recourse, one that limits the indorser's liability
**Formal Requirements of Indorsements**
- *Place of Indorsement*
- *Incorrect or Misspelled Indorsement*

# Cases

### CASE 27–1
## Fictitious Payee Rule
### *SHEARSON LEHMAN BROTHERS, INC. v. WASATCH BANK*
United States District Court, D. Utah, C.D., 1992
788 F.Supp. 1184

ANDERSON, J.
Before the court is Defendant's Motion for Summary Judgment. The core issue presented by the motion is whether and to what extent a collecting or depositary bank will be liable to the drawer or the unintended payee of a check when the drawer's faithless employee induces

the drawer to issue checks, fraudulently indorses them in the name of the specified payee, and absconds with the funds. Because under the undisputed facts of the case, the "fictitious payee" defense as codified by section 3–405 [Revised § 3–404, 3–405] of the Uniform Commercial Code affords the defendant an absolute defense to all claims, summary judgment for the defendant is hereby granted.

The present litigation between plaintiff Shearson Lehman Brothers, Inc., ("Shearson") and defendant Wasatch Bank ("Wasatch") arises out of the activities of a former employee of Shearson, Stanley A. Erb ("Erb"). Erb began working as a financial consultant or broker at Shearson's Provo, Utah, branch office in 1984. By 1987, because of the volume of his sales, Erb had been given the cognomen of vice president. In 1987, Erb was contacted by McKay Matthews, the controller for the Orem, Utah, based WordPerfect Corporation, and its sister corporation, Utah Softcopy. On Matthews' request, Erb coordinated the establishment of three separate investment accounts at Shearson. The accounts were for the benefit of WordPerfect and Utah Softcopy as corporations and one account was established for the personal benefit of the WordPerfect principals, Allen C. Ashton, Bruce W. Bastian, and Willard E. Peterson. Thereafter, Erb assumed the responsibility for managing all three of the WordPerfect accounts at Shearson.

In March 1987, Erb personally accepted from Matthews a check drawn by Utah Softcopy and payable to the order of "ABP Investments." The amount of the check was $460,150.23. At that time, there was no ABP Investment account opened at Shearson, although the WordPerfect principals maintained accounts elsewhere in that name. Notwithstanding the absence of an account in the name of the payee, Erb accepted the check for deposit at Shearson. Matthews suggested that a substitute check be correctly drawn and submitted for deposit at Shearson. Erb responded by assuring Matthews that he would personally guarantee that the check was credited to the appropriate account. However, rather than depositing the check into one of the authorized WordPerfect accounts, Erb opened a new account at Shearson in the name of "ABP Investments." Erb apparently forged the signature of Bruce Bastian on the new account documents. No evidence in the record suggests that Bastian or any other WordPerfect or Utah Softcopy representative authorized or subsequently ratified the creation of the new account. Erb listed as the address of record for the ABP Investment account a post office box number in Orem, Utah, which was unknown to WordPerfect and

its principals and was different from the record address for the other three WordPerfect accounts.

Over the course of the next eleven months, Erb induced Shearson to draft checks on the ABP Investment account, payable to ABP Investments. Erb manipulated Shearson's procedure for making payments to clients by submitting to the Shearson cashier falsified payment request forms. Checks were drawn by Shearson in the requested amounts and were mailed to the Orem post office box. Erb then obtained the checks from the post office box, indorsed them in the name of ABP Investments, and took them to Wasatch for deposit into his personal account. In the course of his scheme, Erb fraudulently procured and negotiated approximately thirty-seven checks, totaling $504,295.30.

Wasatch accepted for deposit and subsequently allowed Erb to withdraw from his personal account all of the funds representing the thirty-seven checks Erb fraudulently procured from Shearson. Copies of those checks reveal that each was drawn payable to the order of ABP Investments and each was indorsed, in handwriting, in the name of ABP Investments and without Erb's personal indorsement or any other indication of Erb's authority to act on behalf of the payee. No ABP Investment account was maintained at Wasatch and therefore no signature card or other evidence on the premises of the bank could have been used to verify Erb's authority to deposit checks payable to ABP Investments. * * *

Erb's activities with respect to the ABP Investments account were not discovered until early 1989, by which time Erb had terminated his employment at Shearson. Lori Rogerson, the operations manager at the Provo Shearson office, testified that she had always been aware of the existence of the ABP Investment account, that she understood the initials "ABP" to represent the names of the WordPerfect principals, but that she also assumed the account was legitimately opened and managed by Erb. At a meeting with WordPerfect representatives in early 1989, Rogerson peripherally mentioned the ABP Investment account whereupon a WordPerfect representative informed her that neither WordPerfect nor its principals maintained such an account at Shearson. After this disclosure, Shearson requested an audit of the accounts managed by Erb and discovered the extent of his mishandling of the ABP Investment account as well as other unrelated mismanagement.

In June 1989, Shearson, WordPerfect and the WordPerfect principals entered a settlement agreement whereby all claims against Shearson arising out of Erb's mishandling of the WordPerfect and related accounts were settled for $1,208,903. Under the agreement,

Shearson acquired by assignment or was subrogated to all legal rights of WordPerfect, Ashton, Bastian and Peterson. Shearson subsequently initiated the present suit against Wasatch. Shearson's complaint alleges the following causes of action: (1) common law negligence, specifically, that the deposits were suspicious, Wasatch knew Erb was employed by the drawer of the checks he deposited into his personal account, and Wasatch made no reasonable attempt to determine the authenticity of endorsements; (2) breach of warranty of good title and implied covenant of good faith and fair dealing in that Wasatch failed to follow reasonable commercial banking practices; . . . .

Wasatch subsequently moved for summary judgment and asserts as the basis for that motion the following arguments: (1) the "fictitious payee defense," U.C.C. § 3–405(1)(c) [Revised § 3–405], bars all of Shearson's claims; . . . .

* * *

## Discussion

*I. Whether Shearson's Claims Are Barred by the "Fictitious Payee" Defense of U.C.C. 3–405(1)(c) [Revised § 3–405]* Wasatch acknowledges that, "[a]s a general rule, 'forged indorsements are ineffective to pass title or to authorize a drawee to pay.'" [Citations.] Consequently, when a collecting bank makes payment over a forged indorsement, it is generally liable for the amount paid. [Citations.]

Under this general rule, Wasatch clearly would be liable as the party that accepted checks over forged indorsements. Wasatch attempts to avoid such liability, however, by invoking what is known as the "fictitious payee" defense. The defense is an exception to the general rule that a party accepting or paying an instrument over a forged indorsement ultimately will be liable for the loss and is set forth in section 3–405 [3–405] of the Uniform Commercial Code:

* * *

The policy underlying section 3–405 [3–405] is thus to place the risk of loss of forgery on the party in the best position to avoid or insure against such loss. [Citations.]

As indicated by the language of section 3–405(1)(c) [3–405], if the defense applies to the facts of a given transaction, the result is to render the forged signature effective to transfer good title as if no forgery had occurred. [Citations.] * * *

For the defense to apply, an employee or agent of the drawer must "supply" the name of the payee to the drawer, and the faithless employee must intend that the payee have no interest in the instrument. [U.C.C.] § 3–405(1)(c) [3–405]. Although the defense commonly has been referred to as the "fictitious payee" defense, the payee named on the check need not be a fictitious person or entity. "'It is immaterial whether a person with the name of the payee actually exists or whether the name is in fact a wholly fictitious name.'" [Citations.] Moreover, courts applying the defense have liberally construed the term "supply." "An employee 'supplies' the name of the payee if he 'starts the wheels of normal business procedure in motion to produce a check for a nonauthorized transaction.'" [Citations.]

* * *

Thus Wasatch argues that the fictitious payee defense of section 3–405(1)(c) applies to the undisputed facts of the present case. Erb, an employee of the drawer of the check, "supplied" the name of the payee within the meaning of the statute and obviously intended that the named payee have no interest in the checks. He then procured the checks and fraudulently indorsed them for deposit into his account at Wasatch. Wasatch accordingly argues that the effect of Erb's actions was to validate the forged indorsements and to allow good title to pass to Wasatch thereby extinguishing Wasatch's liability for the transaction.

* * *

*II. Conclusion* The "fictitious payee" defense as articulated in section 3–405(1)(c) [3–405] of the Uniform Commercial Code operates under the facts of the present case to shield the collecting bank, Wasatch, from liability resulting from Erb's misconduct while in Shearson's employ. Erb deliberately induced the issuance of checks by Shearson. The payee named on those checks was never intended by Erb to take an interest in the checks. In such circumstances the mandate of the Code is clear—the drawer shall bear the loss resulting from the misdeeds of its employee. Wasatch's conduct in the relevant transactions raises serious questions about whether the bank discharged its duty to act in a commercially reasonable manner. Nevertheless, no fact has been alleged which would support the inference that Wasatch acted in bad faith so as to preclude the operation of the fictitious payee defense. [S]ummary judgment is hereby GRANTED in favor of Wasatch and all counts of Shearson's complaint are hereby dismissed with prejudice.

---

## CASE 27–2
### Blank Indorsements
# PALMER & RAY DENTAL SUPPLY OF ABILENE, INC. v. FIRST NAT'L BANK
Court of Civil Appeals of Texas, 1972
477 S.W.2d 954

---

WALTER, J.

. . . Palmer and Ray Dental Supply Company of Abilene, Inc. filed suit against First National Bank of Abilene for conversion of the proceeds of thirty-five checks presented to the Bank by its bookkeeper Mrs. Wilson on which she received cash. The court granted the Bank's motion for summary judgment and Palmer and Ray Dental Supply have appealed.

\* \* \*

James Frank Ray, President and manager of the dental supply company testified substantially as follows: Mrs. Wilson was employed as our office manager. In February 1970, our auditor found a discrepancy in our inventory and we started looking for the leak. After we had worked on it for about two weeks, Mrs. Wilson called me one Saturday night and told me she would like to talk to me. I met her at the office and she told me she had been stealing by cashing checks that she was supposed to deposit. She was employed to answer the phone, take orders, invoice merchandise, order merchandise and to perform the general office duties. She also made deliveries and looked after the internal workings of the office. We do a credit business and the customers pay by check. I generally take the checks from the mail and place them in Mrs. Wilson's desk and she deposited them. We try to do our banking business everyday. She made out the deposit slips in our office. At the time Mrs. Wilson was working for us we had a rubberstamp which we used to endorse our checks. The stamp read:

Palmer & Ray Dental Supply
Inc. of Abilene
Box 2894
3110 B N. 1st
Abilene, Texas 79603

I authorized and directed Mrs. Wilson to endorse the checks with this rubber stamp. During the time Mrs. Wilson worked for us this was the only endorsement stamp we used. We had no stamp which read "for deposit only."

Most of the time she would go to the bank in our van. All deposits were made at the First National Bank and she would bring the deposit slips back to the office. She made the deposits about 75% of the time.

\* \* \*

In its trial petition appellant alleges that Mrs. Wilson made the deposits for it at First National Bank but instead of depositing the thirty-five checks which are listed in appellant's petition as she was instructed to do, she drew cash on them and did not account to the company for such money. It further alleged: "and by means of an unauthorized endorsement by said Dinah Wilson, the defendant First National paid cash to the *plaintiff* (Mrs. Wilson?) for the amount of the checks." It further alleged that by giving Mrs. Wilson cash instead of depositing the checks to its account the Bank converted its funds. Its cause of action against the Bank was predicated on the theory of wrongful conversion.

Section 3–204 [Revised § 3–205] Tex. Uniform Commercial Code, defines a blank endorsement as one that specifies no particular endorsee and may consist of a mere signature. Section 3–205 [§ 3–206] of the U.C.C. defines a restrictive endorsement to include one that uses the words "for deposit." Section 1.201(43), U.C.C., defines an unauthorized signature or endorsement as one made without actual implied or apparent authority and includes a forgery.

The summary judgment proof establishes that each of the checks has affixed thereto the blank rubber stamp endorsement of the appellant. We hold that such blank endorsement constitutes an authorized endorsement. When the Bank delivered cash to Mrs. Wilson instead of depositing the proceeds from the checks to appellant's account, the Bank was not guilty of conversion [wrongdoing]. [Citation].

The judgment is affirmed.

## CASE 27–3
### Special Indorsements
### *CASAREZ v. GARCIA*
Court of Appeals of New Mexico, 1983
99 N.M. 508, 660 P.2d 598

DONNELLY, J.

The plaintiffs filed suit against the Garcias and the Estate of Oakley P. Guillory, deceased, alleging that the defendants had breached a written contract to properly construct a home for them in Jemez Springs. The first amended complaint asserted that Blas Garcia falsely represented he was acting through a licensed contractor, and that, after commencing the construction, defendants Blas Garcia and Guillory performed the work in a negligent and unworkmanlike manner so that the project was "red-tagged" and halted by state building inspectors.

* * *

The plaintiffs also alleged for their cause of action against the Bank that the defendants Garcia and Guillory conspired to defraud plaintiffs with a false loan for $25,000 and to wrongfully deprive plaintiffs of the loan proceeds. Plaintiffs alleged they specially indorsed a cashier's check owned by them to Albuquerque Fence Company and that Blas Garcia forged the company's name thereon. Plaintiffs further allege that the Bank wrongfully and negligently failed to make adequate inquiry or investigation before making payment of the cashier's check in the sum of $25,000. Plaintiffs allege the check was signed by Blas Garcia, without authorization, on behalf of Albuquerque Fence Company and the instrument was then fraudulently delivered to Cecil Garcia, who presented it to the Bank for payment.

* * *

Following a jury trial, the trial court granted the Bank's motion for directed verdict against the plaintiffs.

The single issue raised by the plaintiffs on appeal challenges the propriety of the trial court's order granting a directed verdict in favor of the Bank. The plaintiffs contend that the Bank negligently cashed a cashier's check in the sum of $25,000 without properly investigating the indorser and without requiring a proper indorsement.

* * *

Plaintiffs contend that Blas Garcia represented to them that he was a representative of Albuquerque Fence Company and that relying upon such representation they entered into a written contract dated July 4, 1979, with the company with the understanding that the company would construct a home for them in Jemez Springs for the sum of $48,875.66, plus tax. Blas Garcia later introduced the plaintiffs to Cecil Garcia who agreed to make a loan to plaintiffs to be used as a down payment under the construction contract.

George Martinez, Sr., the president of Albuquerque Fence Company, testified that his company was a domestic corporation and had never been licensed as a general contractor in New Mexico. He further testified that neither Blas Garcia nor Cecil Garcia were ever officers or directors of the corporation or in any way affiliated or employed by it. Albuquerque Fence Company makes no claim to the check.

As shown by the record, Cecil Garcia obtained a $25,000 loan from the Bank in the form of a $25,000 cashier's check payable to himself. Cecil Garcia took the check to a title company, arranged to loan $25,000 to the plaintiffs, and obtained a promissory note from them to evidence this indebtedness. Cecil Garcia then indorsed the cashier's check: "Pay to the order of Lucy N. Casarez, Cecil Garcia." Upon delivery of the check to Lucy Casarez, she indorsed the check: "Pay to the order of Albuquerque Fence Co., Lucy N. Casarez." Lucy Casarez then handed the check to Blas Garcia. Blas Garcia testified that after obtaining the check from Lucy Casarez, he followed the instructions of Cecil Garcia and indorsed the check: "Alb. Fence Co." Thereafter, Blas Garcia gave the check to Cecil Garcia, who signed his own name under the words "Alb. Fence Co." and later presented the check to the Bank in exchange for $5,000 in cash and four $5,000 cashier's checks.

The plaintiffs contend that the language placed on the check by Lucy Casarez, "Pay to the order of Albuquerque Fence Co.," preceding her signature constituted a special indorsement and that the check could be further negotiated only by a proper indorsement by an authorized representative of the company. Because of the special indorsement, plaintiffs argue, the action of the Bank in cashing the check without investigating or verifying the authority of Cecil Garcia to negotiate the check on behalf of Albuquerque Fence Company was sufficient to raise an issue as to negligence on the part of the Bank. The plaintiffs further assert that the writing of the words "Alb.

Fence Co." by Blas Garcia and the signature thereafter by Cecil Garcia amounted to an unauthorized signature or indorsement which invalidated the lawful negotiation of the check and rendered the Bank liable to the plaintiffs for the amount of the check.

\* \* \*

Since the plaintiff Lucy Casarez specially indorsed the cashier's check "Pay to the order of Albuquerque Fence Co., Lucy N. Casarez," and purportedly without authority, Blas Garcia placed the indorsement of "Alb. Fence Co." thereon, the indorsement, if unauthorized, was inoperative to pass title to the instrument to Cecil Garcia. A special indorsement specifies to whom or to whose order it makes the instrument payable; it becomes payable to the order of the special indorsee and may be further negotiated only by his indorsement. [U.C.C.] § 3–204 [Revised § 3–205]. As stated in the Official Comment to U.C.C. § 3–204, "The principle here adopted is that a special indorser, as the owner even of a bearer instrument, has the right to direct the payment and to require the indorsement of his indorsee as evidence of the satisfaction of his own obligation." Under the Uniform Commercial Code, a "person" includes an individual or an organization. § 1–201(30).

\* \* \*

As between the plaintiff Lucy Casarez, and Cecil Garcia, the plaintiff remained the owner of the check until the designated special indorsee indorsed the instrument. The unauthorized signature of the special indorsee rendered that signature inoperative under § 3–404(1) [§ 3–403(c)] and prevented the further negotiation of the check since negotiation requires the proper indorsement of all special indorsees.

As noted in [citation], "when a bank pays on an instrument bearing a forged indorsement, the owner of the instrument may sue the drawee . . . or drawer. . . ." The plaintiff as the true owner of the cashier's check had a right to bring an action for conversion or negligence against the Bank as drawee when it paid on the unauthorized indorsement of Albuquerque Fence Company. § 3–419(1)(c) [§ 3–420(a)] [citation].

\* \* \*

The order granting a directed verdict in favor of the Bank was error.

---

## CASE 27–4
## Indorsements for Deposit or Collection
### STATE OF QATAR v. FIRST AMERICAN BANK OF VIRGINIA

United States District Court, ED Va, 1995
885 F. Supp. 849

ELLIS, J.

At issue in this sequel to *State of Qatar v. First American Bank of Virginia* ("Qatar I") is the meaning and legal significance of the phrase "for deposit only" following an indorsement on the back of a check. More specifically, the question presented is whether a depositary bank complies with the restrictive indorsement "for deposit only" when it deposits a check bearing that restriction into *any* person's account, or whether that restriction requires a depositary bank to deposit the check's proceeds only into the account of the named payee. For the reasons that follow, the court holds that the unqualified language "for deposit only" following an indorsement on the back of a check requires a depositary bank to place the check's proceeds into the payee's account, and the bank violates that restrictive indorsement when it credits the check to any other account.

I

\* \* \*

Plaintiffs are the State of Qatar and certain of its agencies (collectively, "Qatar"). From approximately 1986 to 1992, one of Qatar's employees, Bassam Salous, defrauded his employer by having checks drawn on Qatar's account in purported payment of false or duplicated invoices that he had created. Although all of the unauthorized checks were made payable to individuals and entities other than Salous, he nonetheless successfully deposited the checks into his own personal accounts with Defendant First American Bank of Virginia ("First American") and Central Fidelity Banks, Inc. (collectively, "the depositary banks").

After Qatar discovered this fraudulent scheme in 1992, it brought suit against the depositary banks for conversion. \* \* \*

Only one category of checks remains in dispute. These checks all bear the forged indorsement of the payee named on the face of the check, followed by a stamped "for deposit only" restriction.

\* \* \*

## II

It is now established that First American may be liable to Qatar for handling a check's proceeds in violation of a restrictive indorsement. [Citation.] Under § 3–205(c) of the pre-1993 Uniform Commercial Code ("U.C.C." or "Code") [Virginia adopted Revised Article 3 in 1993] restrictive indorsements are defined to "include the words 'for collection,' 'for deposit,' 'pay any bank,' or like terms signifying a purpose of deposit or collection." Thus, the U.C.C. makes clear that the phrase "for deposit only" is, in fact, a restrictive indorsement. But the Code does not define "for deposit only" or specify what bank conduct would be inconsistent with that restriction. Nor does Virginia decisional law provide any guidance on this issue. As a result, reference to decisional law from other jurisdictions is appropriate.

Not surprisingly, most courts confronted with this issue have held that the restriction "for deposit only," without additional specification or directive, instructs depositary banks to deposit the funds only into the payee's account. In addition, commentators on commercial law uniformly agree that the function of such a restriction is to ensure that the checks' proceeds be deposited into the payee's account.

This construction of "for deposit only" is commercially sensible and is adopted here. The clear purpose of the restriction is to avoid the hazards of indorsing a check in blank. Pursuant to former § 3–204(2), a check indorsed in blank "becomes payable to bearer." It is, essentially, cash. Thus, a payee who indorses her check in blank runs the risk of having the check stolen and freely negotiated before the check reaches its intended destination. To protect against this vulnerability, the payee can add the restriction "for deposit only" to the indorsement, and the depositary bank is required to handle the check in a manner consistent with that restriction. § 3–206(3). And in so adding the restriction, the payee's intent plainly is to direct that the funds be deposited into her own account, not simply that the funds be deposited into some account. [Citation.] Any other construction of the phrase "for deposit only" is illogical and without commercial justification or utility. Indeed, it is virtually impossible to imagine a scenario in which a payee cared that her check be deposited, but was indifferent with respect to the particular account to which the funds would be credited.

\* \* \*

Finally, it is worth noting that the new revisions to the negotiable instruments provisions of the U.C.C., [Revised Article 3], support the result reached here. Although these revisions are inapplicable to this case, the commentary following § 3–206 states that the new subdivision dealing with "for deposit only" and like restrictions "continues previous law." § 3–206 comment 3. Shortly thereafter, the commentary provides an example in which a check bears the words "for deposit only" above the indorsement. In those circumstances, the commentary states, the depositary bank acts inconsistently with the restrictive indorsement where it deposits the check into an account other than that of the payee. Although the restriction in that example precedes the signature, whereas the restrictions on the checks at issue here follow the signature, this distinction is immaterial. The clear meaning of the restriction in both circumstances is that the funds should be placed into the payee's account.

Therefore, First American violated the restrictive indorsements in depositing into Bassam Salous' account checks made payable to others and restrictively indorsed "for deposit only." Pursuant to the holding in Qatar I, then, First American is liable to Qatar for conversion in the amount of the total face values of these checks.

---

#   Questions

1. Distinguish among (1) transfer, (2) negotiation, and (3) assignment.
2. Explain what is necessary to become a holder of an instrument.
3. Explain the imposter rule and the fictitious payee rule.

4. Distinguish among a blank indorsement, a special indorsement, a qualified indorsement, and an unqualified indorsement.
5. Discuss which types of restrictive indorsements are effective and ineffective.

# Problems

**1.** Roy Rand executed and delivered the following note to Sue Sims: "Chicago, Illinois, June 1, 1999; I promise to pay to Sue Sims or bearer, on or before July 1, 1999, the sum of $7,000. This note is given in consideration of Sims's transferring to the undersigned title to her 1996 Buick automobile. (signed) Roy Rand." Rand and Sims agreed to defer delivery of the car to July 1, 1999. On June 15, Sims sold and delivered the note, without indorsement, to Karl Kaye for $6,200. What rights, if any, has Kaye acquired?

**2.** Lavinia Lane received a check from Wilmore Enterprises, Inc., drawn on the Citizens Bank of Erehwon, in the sum of $10,000. Mrs. Lane indorsed the check "Mrs. Lavinia Lane for deposit only, Account of Lavinia Lane," placed it in a "Bank by Mail" envelope addressed to the First National Bank of Emanon, where she maintained a checking account, and placed the envelope over a tier of mailboxes in her apartment building along with other letters to be picked up by the postal carrier the next day.

Flora Fain stole the check, went to the Bank of Omaha, where Mrs. Lane was unknown, represented herself to be Lavinia Lane, and cashed the check. Has Bank of Omaha taken the check by negotiation? Why or why not?

**3.** What types of indorsements are the following:

    (a)   "Pay to Monseen without recourse."

    (b)   "Pay to Allinore for collection."

    (c)   "I hereby assign all my rights, title, and interest in this note to Fullilove in full."

    (d)   "Pay to the Southern Trust Company."

    (e)   "Pay to the order of the Farmers Bank of Nicholasville for deposit only."

Indicate whether the indorsement is (1) blank or special, (2) restrictive or nonrestrictive, and (3) qualified or unqualified.

**4.** Explain whether each of the following transactions results in a valid negotiation:

    (a)   Arnold gives a negotiable check payable to bearer to Betsy without indorsing it.

    (b)   Golden indorses a negotiable, promissory note payable to the order of Golden, "Pay to Chambers and Rambis, (signed) Golden."

    (c)   Porter lost a negotiable check payable to his order. Kersey found it and indorsed the back of the check as follows: "Pay to Drexler, (signed) Kersey."

    (d)   Thomas indorsed a negotiable promissory note payable to the order of Thomas, "(signed) Thomas," and delivered it to Sally. Sally then wrote above Thomas's signature, "Pay to Sally."

**5.** Alpha issues a negotiable check to Beta payable to the order of Beta in payment of an obligation Alpha owed Beta. Beta delivers the check to Gamma without indorsing it in exchange for 100 shares of General Motors stock owned by Gamma. How has Beta transferred the check? What rights, if any, does Gamma have against Beta?

**6.** Melvin executed and delivered to Dawkins a negotiable promissory note payable to the order of Dawkins as payment for 100 bushels of wheat Dawkins had sold to Melvin. Dawkins indorsed the note "Pay to Hersey only, (signed) Dawkins" and sold it to Hersey. Hersey then sold the note to Smith after indorsing it "Pay to Smith, (signed) Hersey." What rights, if any, does Smith acquire in the instrument?

**7.** Simon Sharpe executed and delivered to Ben Bates a negotiable promissory note payable to the order of Ben Bates for $500. Bates indorsed the note, "Pay to Carl Cady upon his satisfactorily repairing the roof of my house, (signed) Ben Bates," and delivered it to Cady as a down payment on the contract price of the roofing job. Cady then indorsed the note and sold it to Timothy Tate for $450. What rights, if any, does Tate acquire in the promissory note?

**8.** Debbie Dean issued a check to Betty Brown payable to the order of Cathy Cain and Betty Brown. Betty indorsed the check "Payable to Elizabeth East, (signed) Betty Brown." What rights, if any, does Elizabeth acquire in the check?

**9.** Triplett attempted to arrange a $2,850,000 loan through Meyer Rabin and his Consumer's Investment Company (CIC). CIC issued a commitment letter conditioned on the payment of a $14,250 commitment fee and the personal guarantee of C.D. Wyche. Triplett sought an additional loan from E.S. Tubin to cover the commitment fee. Tubin agreed to provide the $14,250 if the money would be "safe" pending the closing of the $2,850,000 loan and if he would receive $4,500 for the use of his money. Triplett agreed, and Tubin purchased a $14,250 cashier's check payable to Melvin Rueckhaus, his attorney. Rueckhaus typed the following indorsement on the back of the check: "PAY TO THE ORDER—CONSUMERS INVESTMENT CO. and CHARLES D. WYCHE, SR . . ."

Rabin presented the check to Fair Park National Bank for immediate credit to CIC's account. Not knowing that Wyche's signature had been forged by Rabin, the bank complied, and Rabin subsequently depleted CIC's account. The loan was never closed, and the $14,250 was never returned to Tubin. Tubin then brought this suit against Fair Park National Bank. Decision?

**10.** The drawer, Commercial Credit Corporation (Corporation), issued two checks payable to Rauch Motor Company. Rauch indorsed the checks in blank, deposited them to its account in University National Bank, and received a corresponding amount of money. The Bank stamped "pay any bank" on the checks and initiated collection. However, the checks were dishonored and returned to the Bank with the notation "payment stopped." Rauch, through subsequent deposits, repaid the bank. Later, to compromise a lawsuit, the Bank executed a special two-page indorsement of the two checks to Lamson. Lamson then sued the Corporation for the face value of the checks, plus interest. The Corporation contends that Lamson was not a holder of the checks because the indorsement was not in conformity with the U.C.C. in that it was stapled to the checks. Decision?

11.   Edmund Jezemski, estranged and living apart from his wife, Paula, was administrator and sole heir-at-law of his deceased mother's estate, one asset of which was real estate in Philadelphia. Without Edmund's knowledge or consent, and with the assistance of John M. McAllister, an attorney, and Anthony DiBenedetto, a real estate broker, Paula arranged for a mortgage on the property through Philadelphia Title Insurance Company. Shortly before settlement, Paula represented to McAllister and DiBenedetto that her husband would be unable to attend the closing on the mortgage. She appeared at McAllister's office in advance of the closing accompanied by a man whom she introduced to McAllister and DiBenedetto as her husband. She and this man, in the presence of McAllister and DiBenedetto, executed a deed conveying the property from the estate to her husband and herself as tenants by the entireties and also executed the mortgage. McAllister and DiBenedetto were witnesses. Thereafter, McAllister, DiBenedetto, and Paula met at the office of the Title Company on the closing date, produced the signed deed and mortgage, and Paula obtained from Title Company its check for the mortgage loan proceeds of $15,640.82, payable to the order of Edmund Jezemski and Paula Jezemski individually and to Edmund as administrator.

Paula cashed the check, bearing the purported indorsements of all the payees, at Penns Grove National Bank and Trust Company. Edmund received none of the proceeds, either individually or as administrator. His purported indorsements were forgeries. In the collection process the check was presented to and paid by the drawee bank, Fidelity-Philadelphia Trust Company, and charged against the drawer Title Company's account. Upon discovery of the existence of the mortgage, Edmund brought an action which resulted in the setting aside of the deed and mortgage and the repayment of the amount advanced by the mortgagee. Title Company thereupon sued the drawee bank (Fidelity) to recover the amount of the check, $15,640.82. Decision?

12.   Cole was supervisor of the shipping department of Machine Mfg. Inc. In February, Cole found herself in need of funds and, at the end of that month, submitted to Ames, the treasurer of the corporation, a payroll listing that showed as an employee, among others, "Ben Day," to whom was allegedly owed $800 for services rendered during February. Actually, there was no employee named Day. Relying upon the word of Cole, Ames drew and delivered to her a series of corporate payroll checks, drawn upon the corporate account in the Capital Bank, one of which was made payable to the order of "Ben Day" for $800. Cole took the check, indorsed on its back "Ben Day," cashed it at the Capital Bank, and pocketed the proceeds. She repeated the same procedure at the end of March, April, and May. In mid-June, Machine Mfg. Inc. learned of Cole's fraudulent conduct, fired her, and brought an appropriate action against Capital Bank, seeking a judgment for $3,200. Decision?

13.   While assistant treasurer of Travco Corporation, Frank Mitchell caused two checks, each payable to a fictitious company, to be drawn on Travco's account with Brown City Savings Bank. In each case, Mitchell indorsed the check in his own name and then cashed it at Citizens Federal Savings & Loan Association of Port Huron. Both checks were cleared through normal banking channels and charged against Travco's account with Brown City. Travco subsequently discovered the embezzlement, and after its demand for reimbursement was denied, it brought this suit against Citizens. Decision?

**WWW**   **Internet Exercise**  Compare the provisions governing transfer and negotiation contained in the United Nations Convention on International Bills of Exchange and International Promissory Notes with those of Article 3 of the Uniform Commercial Code.

# CHAPTER 28

# Holder in Due Course

The unique and most significant aspect of negotiability is the concept of the holder in due course. While a mere holder or assignee acquires a negotiable instrument subject to all claims and defenses to it, a holder in due course, except in consumer credit transactions, takes the instrument free of all claims of other parties and free of all defenses to the instrument except for a very limited number. The law has conferred this preferred position upon the holder in due course to encourage the free transferability of negotiable instruments by minimizing the risks assumed by an innocent purchaser of the instrument. The transferee of a negotiable instrument wants payment for it; he does not want to be subject to any dispute between the obligor and the obligee (generally the original payee). This chapter discusses the requirements of becoming a holder in due course and the benefits conferred upon a holder in due course.

## REQUIREMENTS OF A HOLDER IN DUE COURSE

To acquire the preferential rights of a holder in due course, a person either must meet the requirements of Section 3–302 of the Code or must "inherit" these rights under the shelter rule, Section 3–203(b) (discussed later in this chapter). To satisfy the requirements of Section 3–302, a transferee must

1. be a holder of a negotiable instrument;
2. take it for value;
3. take it in good faith; and
4. take it without notice
   (a) that it is overdue or has been dishonored, or
   (b) that the instrument contains an unauthorized signature or an alteration, or
   (c) that any person has any defense against or claim to it; and

5. take it without reason to question its authenticity due to apparent evidence of forgery, alteration, incompleteness, or other irregularity.

Figure 28–1 illustrates the various requirements of becoming a holder in due course and the consequence of meeting or not meeting these requirements.

◆ *See Figure 28–1*

## Holder

To become a holder in due course, the transferee must first be a holder. A holder, as discussed in Chapter 27, is a person who is in possession of a negotiable instrument that is "payable to bearer or, in the case of an instrument payable to an identified person, if the identified person is in possession." Section 1–201(20). In other words, a holder is a person who has both possession of an instrument and all indorsements necessary to it. Whether the holder is the owner of the instrument or not, he may transfer it, negotiate it, enforce payment of it (subject to valid claims and defenses), or, with certain exceptions, discharge it.

The following factual situation, illustrated in Figure 28–2, defines the significance of being a holder. Poe indorsed her paycheck in blank and cashed it at a hardware store where she was a well-known customer. Shortly thereafter, a burglar stole the check from the hardware store. The owner of the hardware store immediately notified Poe's employer, who gave the drawee bank a stop payment order (an order not to pay the instrument). The burglar indorsed the check in a false name and transferred it to a grocer who took it in good faith and for value. The check was dishonored (not paid) when presented to the drawee bank. The paycheck became bearer paper when Poe indorsed it in blank. It retained this character in the hands of the owner of the hardware store, in the hands of the burglar, and in the hands of

**FIGURE 28–1** Rights of Transferees

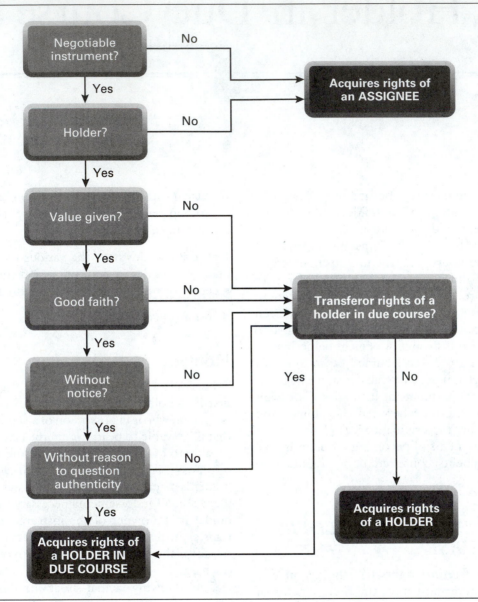

the grocer, who became a holder in due course even though he had received it from a thief who had indorsed it with a false name. Because an indorsement is not necessary to the negotiation of bearer paper, the fact that the indorsement was forged was immaterial. The thief was a "holder" of the check within the definition of Section 1–201(20) and may negotiate an instrument "whether or not he is the owner." Accordingly, one who, like the grocer, takes from a holder for value, in good faith, without notice, and without reason to question its authenticity, becomes a holder in due course. Furthermore, in the absence of a real defense, discussed later in this chapter, the grocer will be entitled to payment from the drawer.

This rule does not apply to a stolen order instrument. In the above example, assume that the thief had stolen the paycheck from Poe prior to indorsement. The thief then forged Poe's signature and transferred the check to the grocer, who again took it in good faith, for value, without notice, and without reason to question its authenticity. Negotiation of an order instrument requires a valid indorsement by the person to whose order the instrument is payable, in this case Poe. A forged indorsement is not valid. Consequently, the grocer has not taken the instrument with all necessary indorsements, and, therefore, he could not be a holder and, as a result, could not be a holder in due course. The grocer's only recourse would be to collect the amount of the check from the thief. Figure 28–3 illustrates this example.

In addition, certain other persons are entitled to enforce an instrument even though the person is not the owner of the instrument or is in wrongful possession of the instrument. Section 3–301. These other persons entitled to enforce an instrument include a nonholder in possession of the instrument who has the rights of a holder, and a person not in possession of the instrument who is entitled to enforce the instrument pursuant to special situations, such as where the instrument has been lost, destroyed, or stolen (Section 3–309) or where the instrument has been paid or accepted by mistake and the payor or acceptor has recovered the money or revoked acceptance (Section 3–418(d)).

◆ *See Figures 28–2 and 28–3*

 *See Case 28–1*

## Value

The law requires a holder in due course to give value. An obvious case of the failure to do so is where the holder makes a gift of the instrument to a third person.

The concept of value in the law of negotiable instruments is not the same as that of consideration under the law of contracts. **Value,** for purposes of negotiable instruments, is defined as (1) the actual *performing* of the agreed promise (executory promises are excluded because they have not been performed); (2) the acquiring of a security interest or other lien in the instrument other than a judicial lien; (3) the taking of the instrument in payment of or as security for an antecedent debt; (4) the giving of a negotiable instrument; and (5) the giving of an irrevocable obligation to a third party. Section 3–303(a).

*Executory Promise* An executory promise, though clearly valid consideration to support a contract, is *not* the giving of value to support holder in due course status because such a promise has yet to be performed. A purchaser of a note or draft who has not yet given value may rescind the transaction if she learns of a defense to the instrument. A person who has given value, however, cannot do this; to recover value, she needs the protection accorded a holder in due course.

For example, Mike executes and delivers a $1,000 note payable to the order of Pat, who negotiates it to Henry, who promises to pay Pat for it a month later. During the month, Henry learns that Mike has a defense against Pat. Henry can rescind the agreement with Pat and return or tender the note back to her. Because this makes him whole, Henry has no need to cut off Mike's defense. Assume, on the other hand, that Henry has paid Pat for the note before he learns of Mike's defense. Because he may be unable to recover his money from Pat, Henry needs holder in due course protection, which permits him to recover on the instrument from Mike.

**FIGURE 28–2**  Stolen Bearer Paper

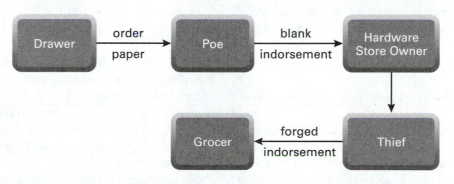

Grocer is a holder in due course because he
(1) Was a holder of a negotiable instrument,
(2) Gave value,
(3) Took in good faith,
(4) Took without notice, and
(5) Took without reason to question its authenticity.

**FIGURE 28–3** Stolen Order Paper

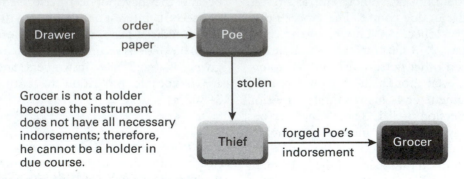

Grocer is not a holder because the instrument does not have all necessary indorsements; therefore, he cannot be a holder in due course.

A holder therefore takes an instrument for value to the extent that the agreed promise of performance has been performed provided the performance was given prior to the holder's learning of any defense or claim to the instrument. Assume that in the previous example Henry had agreed to pay Pat $900 for the note. If Henry had paid Pat $600, he could be a holder in due course to the extent of $666.67 ($\frac{600}{900} \times \$1000$), and if a defense were available, it would be valid against him only to the extent of the balance. Section 3–302(d). When Henry paid the $300 balance to Pat, he would become a holder in due course as to the full $1,000 face value of the note, provided payment was made prior to Henry's discovery of Mike's defense. If he made the $300 payment after discovering the defense or claim, Henry would be a holder in due course only to the extent of $666.67. A holder in due course, to give value, need pay only the amount he agreed to pay, not the face amount of the instrument.

The Code provides an exception to the executory promise rule in two situations: (1) the giving of a negotiable instrument and (2) the making of an irrevocable obligation to a third party. Section 3–303(a)(4), (5).

*Security Interest*   Where an instrument is given as security for an obligation, the lender is regarded as having given value to the extent of his security interest. Sections 3–302(e) and 3–303(a). For example, Pedro is the holder of a $1,000 note payable to his order, executed by Monica, and due in twelve months. Pedro uses the note as security for a $700 loan made to him by Larry. Larry has advanced $700; therefore, he has met the requirement of value to the extent of $700.

Likewise, a bank gives value when a depositor is allowed to withdraw funds against a deposited item. Sections 4–210 and 4–211. The provisional or temporary

crediting of a depositor's account (discussed in Chapter 30) is not sufficient. If a number of checks have been deposited, and some but not all of the funds have been withdrawn, the Code traces the deposit by following the "FIFO" or "first-in, first-out" method of accounting.

*Antecedent Debt*   Under general contract law, an antecedent debt (a preexisting obligation) is not consideration. Under Section 3–303(a)(3) of the Code, however, a holder gives value when she takes an instrument in payment of or as security for an antecedent debt. Thus, Martha makes and delivers a note for $1,000 to the order of Penny, who indorses the instrument and delivers it to Howard in payment of an outstanding debt of $970 which she owes him. Howard has given value.

 *See Case 28–2*

## Good Faith

Revised Article 3 defines **good faith** as "honesty in fact and the observance of reasonable commercial standards of fair dealing." Section 3–103(4). Thus, Revised Article 3 adopts a definition of good faith that has both a subjective and objective component. The subjective component ("honesty in fact") measures good faith by what the purchaser knows or believes. The objective component ("the observance of reasonable commercial standards of fair dealing") is comparable to the definition of good faith applicable to merchants under Article 2 in that it includes the requirement of the observance of reasonable commercial standards of fairness. Buying an instrument at a discounted price does not demonstrate lack of good faith.

# Lack of Notice

To become a holder in due course, a holder must also take the instrument without notice that it is (1) overdue, (2) dishonored, (3) forged or altered (see discussion of these later in the chapter), or (4) subject to any claim or defense. Notice of any of these matters should alert the purchaser that she may be buying a lawsuit and consequently, may not be accorded the favored position of a holder in due course. Section 1–201(25) defines *notice* as follows: "A person has 'notice' of a fact when (a) he has actual knowledge of it; or (b) he has received a notice or notification of it; or (c) from all the facts and circumstances known to him at the time in question he has reason to know that it exists." Whereas the first two clauses of this definition impose a wholly subjective standard, the last clause provides a partially objective one: the presence of suspicious circumstances does not adversely affect the purchaser, unless he has reason to recognize them as suspicious. Because the applicable standard is "actual notice," "notice received," or "reason to know," constructive notice through public filing or recording is not of itself sufficient notice to prevent a person from being a holder in due course.

To be effective, notice must be received at a time and in a manner that the recipient will have a reasonable opportunity to act on it. Section 3–302(f).

*Notice an Instrument Is Overdue* To be a holder in due course, the purchaser must take the instrument without notice that it is overdue. This requirement is based on the idea that overdue paper conveys a suspicion that something is wrong. **Time paper** is due on its stated due date if the stated date is a business day or, if not, on the next business day. It "becomes overdue on the day after the due date." Section 3–304(b)(2). Thus, if an instrument is payable on July 1, a purchaser cannot become a holder in due course by buying it on July 2, provided that July 1 was a business day. In addition, in the case of an installment note or of several notes issued as part of the same transaction with successive specified maturity dates, the purchaser has notice that an instrument is overdue if he has reason to know that any part of the principal amount is overdue or that there is an uncured default in payment of another instrument of the same series. Sections 3–302(a)(2) and 3–304(b).

**Demand paper** is overdue for purposes of preventing a purchaser from becoming a holder in due course if the purchaser has notice that she is taking the instrument on a day after demand has been made or after it has been outstanding for an unreasonably long time. Section

3–304(a). The Code provides that for checks a reasonable time is ninety days after its date. For all other demand instruments the reasonable period of time varies depending upon the facts of the particular case. Thus, the particular situation, business custom, and other relevant factors must be considered in determining whether an instrument is overdue: No hard-and-fast rules are possible.

Acceleration clauses have caused problems. If an instrument's maturity date has been accelerated, the instrument becomes overdue on the day after the accelerated due date even though the holder may be unaware that it is past due. Section 3–304(b)(3).

*Notice an Instrument Has Been Dishonored* **Dishonor** is the refusal to pay or accept an instrument when it becomes due. If a transferee has notice that an instrument has been dishonored, he cannot become a holder in due course. Section 3–302(a)(2)(iii). For example, a person who takes a check stamped "NSF" (not sufficient funds) or "no account" has notice of dishonor and will not be a holder in due course.

*Notice of a Claim or Defense* A purchaser of an instrument cannot become a holder in due course if he purchases it with notice of "any claim to the instrument described in Section 3–306" or "a defense or claim in recoupment described in Section 3–305(a)." Section 3–302(a)(2). A **defense** protects a person from liability on an instrument, whereas a **claim** to an instrument asserts ownership of it.

Claims covered by Section 3–306 "include not only claims to ownership but also any other claim of a property or possessory right. It includes the claim to a lien or the claim of a person in rightful possession of an instrument who was wrongfully deprived of possession." Section 3–306, Comment. Claims to instruments may be made against thieves, finders, or possessors with void or voidable title. In many instances, both a defense and claim will be involved. For example, Donna is fraudulently induced to issue a check to Pablo. Donna has a claim to ownership of the instrument as well as a defense to Pablo's demand for payment.

Section 3–305(a), which is more fully discussed later in this chapter, provides that personal defenses are valid against a holder, while real defenses are effective against both holders and holders in due course. In addition, a person without the rights of a holder in due course is subject to an obligor's claim in recoupment "against the original payee of the instrument if the claim arose from the transaction that gave rise to the instrument." Section

3–305(a)(3). For example, Buyer gives Seller a negotiable note in exchange for Seller's promise to deliver certain goods. Seller delivers nonconforming goods that Buyer elects to accept. Buyer has a cause of action under Article 2 for breach of warranty under the contract, which "claim may be asserted against Seller as a counterclaim or as a claim in recoupment to reduce the amount owing on the note. It is not relevant whether Seller knew or had notice that Buyer had the warranty claim." Section 3–305, Comment 3.

Buying an instrument at a discount or for a price less than face value does not mean that the buyer had notice of any defense or claim against the instrument. Nonetheless, a court may construe an unusually large discount as notice of a claim or defense.

## Without Reason to Question Its Authenticity

Under prior Article 3, a purchaser had notice of a claim or defense if the instrument was so incomplete, contained such visible evidence of forgery or alteration, or was otherwise so irregular as to call into question its validity. Courts differed greatly as to how irregular an instrument had to be for a holder to have notice. Revised Article 3 provides that a party may become a holder in due course only if the instrument issued or negotiated to the holder "does not bear such apparent evidence of forgery or alteration or is not otherwise so irregular or incomplete as to call into question its authenticity." Section 3–302(a)(1). According to the comments to this section, the term "authenticity" clarifies the idea that the irregularity or incompleteness must indicate that the instrument may not be what it purports to be. The Revision takes the position that persons who purchase such instruments do so at their own peril and should not be protected against defenses of the obligor or claims of prior owners. In addition, the Revision takes the position that it makes no difference if the holder does not have notice of such irregularity or incompleteness; it depends only on whether the instrument's defect is apparent and whether the taker should have reason to know of the problem.

*See Case 28–2*

## *HOLDER IN DUE COURSE STATUS*

A holder who meets the requirements discussed in the previous section obtains the preferred position of holder in due course status. This section discusses whether a payee may become a holder in due course. It also addresses the rights of a transferee from a holder in due course under the shelter rule. Finally, it identifies those special circumstances that prevent a transferee from acquiring holder in due course status.

## A Payee May Be a Holder in Due Course

A payee may be a holder in due course. Section 3–302, Comment 4. This does not mean that a payee automatically is a holder in due course but that he *may* be one if he satisfies the requirements for such status. For example, if a seller delivers goods to a buyer and accepts a current check in payment, the seller will be a holder in due course if he acted in good faith and had no notice of defenses or claims and no reason to question its authenticity. Nevertheless, the holder in due course doctrine is irrelevant when the issuer and payee are the only parties to the instrument. Section 3–302, Comment 4. In such a situation the seller/payee takes the instrument subject to all claims and defenses; the doctrine of the preferred position of a holder in due course "applies only to cases in which more than two parties are involved. Its essence is that the holder in due course does not have to suffer the consequences of a defense of the obligor on the instrument that arose from an occurrence with a third party." Section 3–305, Comment 2.

In some situations, the payee is not an immediate party to the transaction and therefore will not be subject to any claims and most defenses if he meets the requirements of a holder in due course. In such a situation, the transaction involves three parties, and the defense involves the parties other than the payee. For example, after purchasing goods from Punky, Robin fraudulently obtains a check from Clem payable to the order of Punky and forwards it to Punky. Punky takes it for value and without any knowledge that Robin had defrauded Clem into issuing the check. In such a case, the payee, Punky, is a holder in due course and takes the instrument free and clear of Clem's defense of fraud in the inducement.

## The Shelter Rule

Through operation of the **shelter rule,** the transferee of an instrument acquires the *same* rights in the instrument as the transferor had. Section 3–203(b). Therefore, even a holder who does not comply fully with the requirements for being a holder in due course nevertheless acquires all the rights of a holder in due course if some previous holder of the instrument had been a holder in due course. For example, Prosser induces Mundheim, by fraud in the inducement, to make a note payable to her order and then negotiates it to Henn, a holder in due course. After the note is overdue, Henn gives it to Corbin, who has notice of the fraud. Corbin is not a holder in due course, because he took the instrument when overdue, did not pay value, and had notice of Mundheim's defense. Nonetheless, through the operation of the shelter rule, Corbin acquires Henn's rights as a holder in due course, and Mundheim cannot successfully assert his defense against Corbin. The purpose of the shelter provision is not to benefit the transferee but to assure the holder in due course of a free market for the negotiable instruments he acquires.

The shelter rule, however, provides that a transferee who has been a party to any fraud or illegality affecting the instrument cannot subsequently acquire the rights of a holder in due course. For example, Parker induces Miles, by fraud in the inducement, to make an instrument payable to the order of Parker, who subsequently negotiates the instrument to Henson, a holder in due course. If Parker later reacquires it from Henson, Parker will not succeed to Henson's rights as a holder in due course and will remain subject to the defense of fraud.

 *See Case 28–3*

## THE PREFERRED POSITION OF A HOLDER IN DUE COURSE

In a **nonconsumer transaction** a holder in due course takes the instrument (1) free from all *claims* on the part of any person and (2) free from all *defenses* of any party with whom he has not dealt, except for a limited number of defenses that are available against anyone, including a holder in due course. Such defenses that are available against all parties are referred to as **real defenses**. In contrast, defenses that may not be asserted against a holder in due course are referred to as **personal** or **contractual defenses**.

### Real Defenses

The real defenses available against **all** holders, including holders in due course, are

1. infancy, to the extent that it is a defense to a simple contract, Section 3–305(a)(1)(i);
2. any other incapacity, duress, or illegality of the transaction that renders the obligation void, Section 3–305(a)(1)(ii);
3. fraud in the execution, Section 3–305(a)(1)(iii);

4. discharge in insolvency proceedings, Section 3–305(a)(1)(iv);
5. any other discharge of which the holder has notice when he takes the instrument, Section 3–601(b);
6. unauthorized signature, Section 3–401(a); and
7. fraudulent alteration, Section 3–407(b), (c).

***Infancy*** All States have a firmly entrenched public policy of protecting minors from persons who might take advantage of them through contractual dealings. The Code does not state when minority is available as a defense or the conditions under which it may be asserted. Rather, it provides that minority (infancy) is a defense available against a holder in due course to the extent that it is a defense to a contract under the laws of the State involved. See Chapter 14.

***Void Obligations*** Where the obligation on an instrument originates in such a way that it is *void* or null under the law of the State involved, the Code authorizes the use of this defense against a holder in due course. This follows from the idea that where the party was never obligated, it is unreasonable to permit an event over which he has no control—negotiation to a holder in due course—to convert a nullity into a valid claim against him.

Incapacity, duress, and the illegality of a transaction are defenses that may render the obligation of a party either voidable or void, depending upon the law of the State involved as applied to the facts of a given transaction. To the extent the obligation is rendered void (because of duress by physical force, because the party is a person under guardianship, or, in some cases, because the contract is illegal) the defense may be asserted against a holder in due course. To the extent it is voidable, which is generally the case, the defense (other than minority, discussed above) is not effective against a holder in due course.

 *See Case 28–4*

***Fraud in the Execution*** Fraud in the execution of the instrument renders the instrument void and therefore is a defense valid against a holder in due course. The Code describes this type of fraud as misrepresentation that induced the party to sign the instrument with neither knowledge nor reasonable opportunity to learn of its character or its essential terms. For example, Francis is asked to sign a receipt and does so without realizing or having the opportunity of learning that her signature is going on a promissory note cleverly concealed under the receipt. Because her signature has been obtained by fraud in the execution, Francis would have a valid defense against a holder in due course.

### Discharge in Insolvency Proceedings

If a party's obligation on an instrument is discharged in a proceeding for bankruptcy or for any other insolvency, he has a valid defense in any action brought against him on the instrument, including one brought by a holder in due course. Thus, a debtor whose obligation on a negotiable instrument is discharged in an insolvency proceeding (bankruptcy) is relieved of payment, even to a holder in due course.

### Discharge of Which the Holder Has Notice

Any holder, including a holder in due course, takes the instrument subject to *any* discharge of which she has notice at the time of taking. If only some, but not all, of the parties to the instrument have been discharged, the purchaser can still become a holder in due course. The discharged parties, however, have a real defense against a holder in due course who had notice of their discharge. For example, Harris, who is in possession of a negotiable instrument, strikes out the indorsement of Jones. The instrument is subsequently negotiated to Stephen, a holder in due course, against whom Jones has a real defense.

### Unauthorized Signature

A person's signature on an instrument is unauthorized when it is made without express, implied, or apparent authority. A person whose signature is unauthorized or forged cannot be held liable on the instrument in the absence of estoppel or ratification, even if the instrument is negotiated to a holder in due course. Similarly, if Joan's signature were forged on the back of an instrument, Joan could not be held as an indorser, because she has not made a contract. Thus, any unauthorized signature is totally invalid as that of the person whose name is signed unless she ratifies it or is precluded from denying it; the unauthorized signature operates only as the signature of the unauthorized signer. Section 3–403(a).

An unauthorized signature may be **ratified** and thereby become valid so far as its effect as a signature. Section 3–403(a). Thus, Kathy forges Laura's indorsement on a promissory note and negotiates it to Allison. Laura subsequently ratifies Kathy's act. As a result, Kathy is no longer liable to Allison on the note, although Laura is. Nonetheless, Laura's ratification does not relieve Kathy from civil liability to Laura; nor does it in any way affect Kathy's criminal liability for the forgery.

A party is precluded from denying the validity of his signature if his **negligence** substantially contributes to the making of the unauthorized signature. The most obvious case is that of a drawer who uses a mechanized or other automatic signing device and is negligent in safeguarding it. In such an instance, the drawer would not be permitted to assert an unauthorized signature as a defense against a holder in due course. Section 3–406(c). Under Revised Article 3, if the person seeking to enforce the instrument is also negligent, then comparative negligence applies. Section 3–406(b).

A person may also be precluded from asserting a defense by estoppel if his conduct in the matter has caused reliance by a third party to his loss or damage.

### Fraudulent Alteration

An alteration is (1) an unauthorized change that modifies the obligation of any party to the instrument or (2) an unauthorized addition or change to an incomplete instrument concerning the obligation of a party.

An alteration that is fraudulently made discharges a party whose obligation is affected by the alteration except where that party assents or is precluded by his own negligence from raising the defense. Section 3–407(b). All other alterations do not discharge any party, and the instrument may be enforced according to its original terms. Section 3–407(b). Thus, if an instrument has been nonfraudulently altered, it may be enforced, but only to the extent of its original tenor (that is, according to its initially written terms).

A discharge under Section 3–407(b) for fraudulent alteration, however, is not effective against a holder in due course who took the instrument without notice of the alteration. Such a subsequent holder in due course may always enforce the instrument according to its original terms and, in the case of an incomplete instrument, may enforce it as completed. Section 3–407(c). The following examples demonstrate the operation of these rules (Figure 28–5 illustrates these examples).

1. M executes and delivers a note to P for $2,000, which P subsequently indorses and transfers to A for $1,900. A intentionally and skillfully changes the figure on the note to $20,000 and then negotiates it to B, who takes it, in good faith, without notice of any wrongdoing and without reason to question its authenticity, for $19,000. B is a holder in due course and, therefore, can collect the original amount of the note ($2,000) from M or P and the full amount ($20,000) from A, less any amount paid by the other parties.

2. Assume the facts in (1) except that B is not a holder in due course. M and P are both discharged by A's fraudulent alteration. B's only recourse is against A for the full amount ($20,000).
3. M issues his blank check to P, who is to complete it when the exact amount is determined. Though the correct amount is set at $2,000, P fraudulently fills in $4,000 and then negotiates the check to T. If T is a holder in due course, she can collect the amount as completed ($4,000) from either M or P. If T is not a holder in due course, however, she has no recourse against M but may recover the full amount ($4,000) from P.
4. Assume the facts in (3) except that P filled in the $4,000 amount in good faith. No party is discharged from liability on the instrument because the alteration

was not fraudulent. If T is not a holder in due course, M is liable for the correct amount ($2,000). If T is a holder in due course, T is entitled to receive $4,000 from M because she can enforce an incomplete instrument as completed. Whether or not T is a holder in due course, T may recover $4,000 from P.

◆ *See Figures 28–4 and 28–5*

## Personal Defenses

Defenses to an instrument may arise in many ways, either when the instrument is issued or later. In general, the numerous defenses to liability on a negotiable instrument, which are similar to those that may be raised in an action for breach of contract, are available against any

**FIGURE 28–4** Effects of Alterations

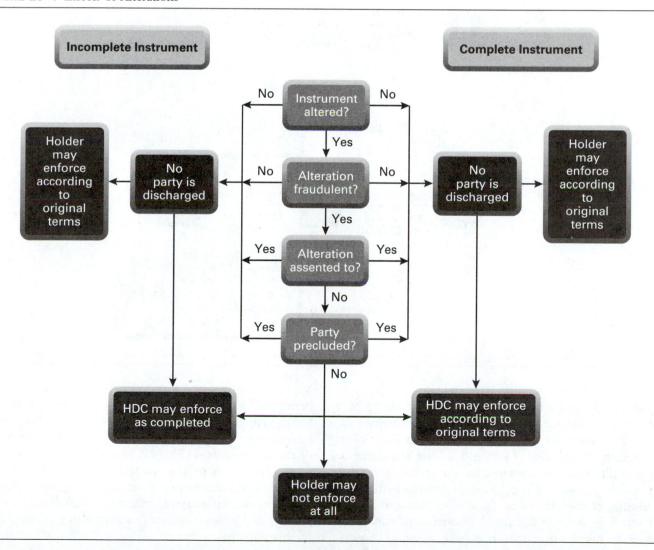

**FIGURE 28–5** Material Alteration

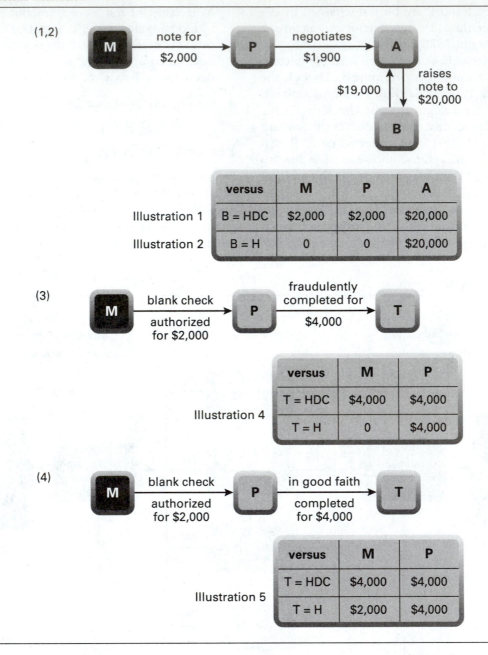

holder of the instrument unless he has the rights of a holder in due course. Among the personal defenses are (1) lack of consideration; (2) failure of consideration; (3) breach of contract; (4) fraud in the inducement; (5) illegality that does not render the transaction void; (6) duress, undue influence, mistake, misrepresentation, or incapacity that does not render the transaction void; (7) setoff or counterclaim; (8) discharge of which the holder in due course does not have notice; (9) non-delivery of an instrument, whether complete or incomplete; (10) unauthorized completion of an incomplete instrument; (11) payment without obtaining surrender of the instrument; (12) theft of a bearer instrument or of an instrument payable to the thief; and (13) lack of authority of a corporate officer, agent, or partner as to the particular instrument, where such officer, agent, or partner had general authority to issue negotiable paper for his principal or firm.

These situations are the most common examples, but others exist. Indeed, the Code does not attempt to detail defenses that may be cut off. It is content to state that a holder in due course takes the instrument free and clear of all claims and defenses, except those listed as real defenses.

◆ *See Figure 28–6*

## *LIMITATIONS UPON HOLDER IN DUE COURSE RIGHTS*

The preferential position enjoyed by a holder in due course has been severely limited by a Federal Trade Commission rule restricting the rights of a holder in due course of an instrument concerning a debt arising out of a **consumer credit contract,** which includes negotiable instruments. The rule, entitled "Preservation of Consumers' Claims and Defenses," applies to sellers and lessors of consumer goods, which are goods for personal, household, or family use. It also applies to lenders who advance money to finance a consumer's purchase of consumer goods or services. The rule is intended to prevent consumer purchase transactions from being financed in such a manner that the purchaser is legally obligated to make full payment of the price to a third party, even though the dealer from whom she bought the goods committed fraud or the goods were defective. Such obli-

gations arise when a purchaser executes and delivers to a seller a negotiable instrument that the seller negotiates to a holder in due course. The buyer's defense that the goods were defective or that the seller committed fraud, although valid against the seller, is not valid against the holder in due course.

To correct this situation, the Federal Trade Commission rule preserves claims and defenses of consumer buyers and borrowers against holders in due course. The rule states that no seller or creditor can take or receive a consumer credit contract unless the contract contains this conspicuous provision:

NOTICE: ANY HOLDER OF THIS CONSUMER CREDIT CONTRACT IS SUBJECT TO ALL CLAIMS AND DEFENSES WHICH THE DEBTOR COULD ASSERT AGAINST THE SELLER OF THE GOODS OR SERVICES OBTAINED PURSUANT HERETO OR WITH THE PROCEEDS HEREOF. RECOVERY HEREUNDER BY THE DEBTOR SHALL NOT EXCEED AMOUNTS PAID BY THE DEBTOR HEREUNDER.

The purpose of this notice is to inform any holder in due course of a paper or negotiable instrument that he takes the instrument subject to all claims and defenses that the buyer could assert against the seller. The effect of the rule is to place the holder in due course in the position of an assignee.

◆ *See Figure 28–7*

FIGURE 28–6   Availability of Defenses against Holders and Holders in Due Course

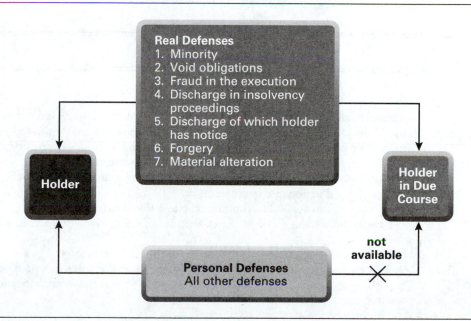

**FIGURE 28–7**  Rights of Holder in Due Course under FTC Rule

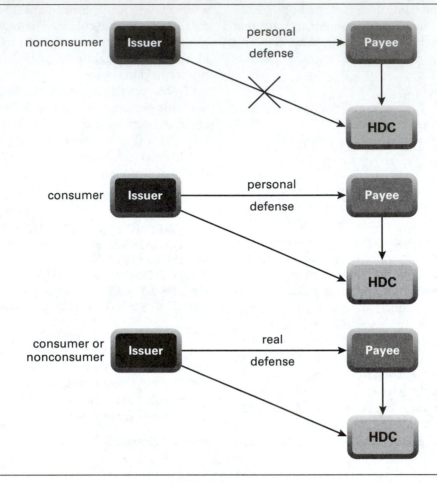

---

   **Chapter Summary**

| | |
|---|---|
| **Requirements of a Holder in Due Course** | **Holder**  a person who has both possession of an instrument and all indorsements necessary to it<br>**Value**  differs from contractual consideration and consists of any of the following:<br>• the timely performance of legal consideration (which excludes executory promises);<br>• the acquisition of a security interest in or a lien on the instrument;<br>• taking the instrument in payment of or as security for an antecedent debt;<br>• the giving of a negotiable instrument; or<br>• the giving of an irrevocable commitment to a third party<br>**Good Faith**  honesty in fact and the observance of reasonable commercial standards of fair dealing<br>**Lack of Notice**<br>• *Notice an Instrument Is Overdue*  time paper is overdue after its stated date; demand paper is overdue after demand has been made or after it has been outstanding for an unreasonable period of time |

* *Notice an Instrument Has Been Dishonored* dishonor is the refusal to pay or accept an instrument when it becomes due
* *Notice an Instrument Has Been Forged or Altered*
* *Notice of a Claim or Defense* a defense protects a person from liability, while a claim is an assertion of ownership

**Without Reason to Question Its Authenticity** instrument cannot bear such apparent evidence of forgery or alteration or otherwise be so irregular or incomplete as to call into question its authenticity

| | |
|---|---|
| **Holder in Due Course Status** | **A Payee May Be a Holder in Due Course** the payee's rights as a holder in due course are limited to defenses of persons with whom he has not dealt<br>**The Shelter Rule** the transferee of an instrument acquires the same rights that the transferor had in the instrument |

| | |
|---|---|
| **The Preferred Position of a Holder in Due Course** | **Real Defenses** real defenses are available against all holders, including holders in due course; such defenses are as follows:<br>• *Infancy*<br>• *Void Obligations*<br>• *Fraud in the Execution*<br>• *Discharge in Insolvency Proceedings*<br>• *Discharge of Which the Holder Has Notice*<br>• *Unauthorized Signature*<br>• *Fraudulent Alteration*<br>**Personal Defenses** all other defenses that might be asserted in the case of any action for breach of contract<br>**Limitations on Rights of Holder in Due Course** the preferential position of a holder in due course has been severely limited by a Federal Trade Commission rule that applies to consumer credit contracts: under this rule, a transferee of consumer credit contracts cannot take as a holder in due course |

 # Cases

### CASE 28–1
## Holder
## *TURMAN v. WARD'S HOME IMPROVEMENT, INC.*

Virginia Circuit Court, Fifteenth Judicial Circuit, 1995
26 U.C.C. Rep. Serv.2d 175

HALEY, J.

### I

The question here for resolution is whether an assignee of the payee of a negotiable instrument is a holder in due course, and as such immune to defenses that the makers might raise against the payee of the negotiable instrument.

### II

The pertinent facts can be concisely stated:

G. Michael Turman and Carolyn May Cash Turman (hereafter "Turman") executed a deed of trust note dated February 23, 1993 for $107,500.00 payable to Ward's Home Improvement, Inc. (hereafter "Ward"). The note was consideration for a contract by which Ward was to construct a home on property by Turman, and the note was secured by a deed of trust on that property. On that same date, Ward executed a separate written assignment of the note to Robert L. Pomerantz (hereafter "Pomerantz"). This document specifically uses the word "assigns." Ward did not endorse the note to Pomerantz or otherwise write upon the note. Ward apparently received $95,000.00 for the assignment from Pomerantz. Ward failed to complete the house and to do so will require the expenditure of an additional $42,000.00. Pomerantz maintains he is a holder in due course of the $107,500.00 note and has demanded payment.

### III

This matter comes before the court upon Turman's exception to the finding of the Commissioner that Pomerantz was a holder in due course immune from defenses Turman might raise against Ward.

* * *

[Revised] Code § 3–201(b) states that ". . . if an instrument is payable to an identified person, negotiation requires . . . its indorsement by the holder." [Citation.] An assignment is not an indorsement. [Revised] Code § 3–204(a). Accordingly such a transfer is not a negotiation. [Citations.] And the transferee is not a holder. [Citations.]

An assignment does, however, vest ". . . in the transferee any right of the transferor to enforce the instrument . . . (under [Revised] Code § 3–301) . . ." [Revised] Code § 3–203(b). The transferee's rights are derivative of the transferor's. Accordingly, and pursuant to [Revised] Code § 3–305(a)(2), a maker may assert a defense ". . . that would be available if the person entitled to enforce the instrument were enforcing a right to payment under a simple contract." In short, the assignee of a negotiable instrument is subject to defenses the maker can raise against the original payee/assignor. [Citation.] And such a defense is failure of consideration. [Citations.] [Revised] Code § 3–303(b). ". . . If an instrument is issued for a promise of performance, the issuer has a defense to the extent performance of the promise is due and the promise has not been performed . . ."

In light of the foregoing the above noted exception to the Commissioner's Report is sustained and the court holds Pomerantz is not a holder in due course and is subject to the defenses to payment of the $107,500.00 note that Turman could raise against Ward.

This cause is remanded to the Commissioner for such proceedings as he or the parties deem appropriate in consequence of the court's ruling.

---

### CASE 28–2
### Value/Notice

# ST. PAUL FIRE AND MARINE INSURANCE CO. v. STATE BANK OF SALEM

Court of Appeals of Indiana, First District, 1980
412 N.E.2d 103

NEAL, J.
On November 26, 1975, Stephens, a farmer, delivered and sold 184 bushels of corn to Aubrey for $478.23. Aubrey was engaged at the time in the sale and distribution of feed and grain in Louisville, Kentucky, under the name of Aubrey Feed Mills, Inc. The following day, Aubrey prepared its check payable to Stephens in payment for the corn and mailed it to Stephens. The check was prepared in the following fashion: the amount "478.23" was typewritten upon the line customarily used to express the amount of the check in numbers, abutting the printed dollar sign. On the line customarily used to express the amount in words there appeared "The sum of $100478 and 23 cts," which was imprinted in red by a checkwriting machine; the line ended with the printed word "Dollars."

On December 9, 1975, Stephens appeared at the Bank's branch in Hardinsburg, Indiana, and presented the Aubrey check and two other items totalling $5,604.51 to the branch manager Charles Anderson. Stephens told Anderson that he wished to apply these funds to the amount of his indebtedness to the Bank, to withdraw $2,000.00 in cash, and to deposit the balance in his checking account. During the interval between November 27, 1975, and December 9, 1975, someone had typed on the check the figures "100" immediately before the typed figures "478.23." This was rather crudely done, and involved typing the "100" in an uneven line; the second "0" was typed directly over the printed dollar sign on the check.

Anderson questioned Stephens about the Aubrey check since Stephens's prior dealings with the Bank had not involved transactions in the amount represented by the Aubrey check. Anderson also knew that Stephens had filed a voluntary petition in bankruptcy several months prior, but had subsequently reaffirmed his obligations to the Bank. Stephens explained that he had purchased a large quantity of corn in Northern Indiana and had sold it in Kentucky at a higher price. Evidently satisfied with his explanation, Anderson stamped nine promissory notes, of which Stephens was maker, "paid" and returned them to Stephens. Anderson then directed a teller at the Bank to fill out a deposit slip for the transaction. At that point, neither Anderson nor the teller noticed the typewritten modification on the check. The transaction consisted of applying the funds represented by the three items in the deposit ($106,082.74) to Stephens's debt represented by the nine promissory notes ($31,851.81), an installment payment of which Stephens was a joint obligor, of $27,559.27, accrued interest owed the Bank by Stephens in the amount of $5,265.65, and the $2,000 cash given to Stephens. The balance was credited to Stephens's account. Stephens then left the Bank.

Later that afternoon, Anderson began thinking about the transaction and examined the items in the deposit. He noted that Aubrey's check bore signs of possible tampering and contacted Aubrey's office in Louisville to inquire about the validity of the check. An Aubrey representative told Anderson that a check in that amount was suspicious, and Anderson then "froze" the transaction. The next day, Aubrey stopped payment on the check.

Thereafter, the Bank attempted to recover possession of the nine promissory notes from Stephens but was unsuccessful. Stephens subsequently left Hardinsburg and his present whereabouts are unknown.

After freezing Stephens's account, the Bank reversed the December 9, 1979, transaction by applying the $5,604.51 then on deposit in Stephens's account (said sum representing the amount of the two checks deposited on December 9, 1979 with Aubrey's check) against the $2,000 paid to Stephens in cash on December 9, 1979, and crediting the remaining $3,604.51 against the aggregate principal balance of the nine promissory notes delivered to Stephens on that date. As a result, the Bank claimed a loss of $28,193.91 and made demand therefor upon Aubrey. * * *

We think the only issue dispositive of Aubrey's appeal is whether the trial court could rightfully have found on the evidence that the Bank was a holder in due course of the Aubrey check under the Uniform Commercial Code (UCC) as adopted in Indiana * * *

The Bank's right to recover on the check is conditioned upon its status as a holder in due course of the check. * * *

* * *

There is no contention on appeal, and there was none at trial, that the Bank did not take the Aubrey check in good faith, which means honesty in fact in the transaction concerned. [Citation.] There is also no question that the Bank was a holder of the instrument, as it was in possession of the check indorsed by the payee Stephens in blank. See § 1–204(20).

We initially consider whether the Bank took the Aubrey check for value. The Bank contends that it gave value for the check to the extent that it (a) acquired a security interest in the instrument under §§ 3–303(a), 4–208 [Revised 4–210], and 4–209 [Revised 4–211] and (b) took the check in payment of an antecedent claim under § 3–303(b) [Revised 3–303(a)(3)]. Aubrey contends that the Bank did not take the check for value since it immediately froze Stephens's account upon appraisal that the validity of the check was suspect and cancelled the amounts it had credited against Stephens's debt. Aubrey considers that the Bank's action in crediting Stephens's debt on the notes merely constituted a bookkeeping procedure and the Bank did not change its position by doing so, particularly since the Bank could still maintain an action against Stephens on the notes. * * *

We are of the opinion that the Bank took the check for value. * * * The statute [U.C.C.] plainly states that value is given for an instrument when the instrument is taken in payment for an antecedent debt not yet due. * * *

While this section has not been construed in Indiana, an examination of authorities from other jurisdictions lends support to the Bank's position that the application of funds made available by the Aubrey check to Stephens's indebtedness and the surrender of the notes constituted taking the instrument for value.

Further, we believe that the Bank gave value for the check under §§ 4–208(1) [Revised 4–210] and 4–209 [Revised 4–211], in that it acquired a security interest in the check to the extent funds represented thereby were applied to Stephens's debt. * * *

We find no support for Aubrey's argument that the Bank did not give value since it did not change its position vis-a-vis Stephens and made a bookkeeping entry only of the credit given Stephens. . . . Official Comment 3 to

§ 3–303 states that it is not necessary to give holder in due course status to one who has not actually paid value, and cites as illustration "the bank credit not drawn upon, which can be and is revoked when a claim or defense appears." [Citation.] When the credit is drawn upon, however, value is given to that extent § 4–208(1)(a). Further, if the depositor's account is overdrawn at the time the check is taken, and funds represented thereby are applied to the overdrawal by way of set-off, value is given to that extent if the check is later dishonored. [Citation.]

\* \* \*

Aubrey vigorously contends the Bank was not a holder in due course of the check because, under the objective standard imposed upon the Bank by § 3–304(1) [compare to Revised 3–302(a)(1)], the Bank took the check with notice of a defense to the check on the part of Aubrey. Aubrey argues the evidence of alteration on the face of the check and the irregular circumstances attending the transaction were such as to put a reasonably prudent banker, exercising normal commercial standards, on notice. The circumstances alleged to have imparted notice to Bank include the small size of Stephens's farming operations, Stephens's banking history including frequent indebtedness and overdrawals, the Bank's knowledge of Stephens's petition in bankruptcy, the size of the Aubrey check in relation to typical transactions undertaken by the Bank, and the implausibility of Stephens's explanation to Anderson, himself familiar with farming, of the transaction underlying Stephens's receipt of the check. The Bank concedes the UCC imposed an objective standard of conduct upon it in the transaction. The essence of the Bank's contention is that the matter of the Bank's notice is a question of fact, and the trial court's implicit finding that the Bank took the check without notice of Aubrey's defense was not erroneous.

The general notice provision of the UCC is stated in § 1–201(25), which provides in part:

A person has 'notice' of a fact when (a) he has actual knowledge of it; or (b) he has received a notice or notification of it; or (c) from all the facts and circumstances known to him at the time in question he has reason to know that it exists.

Section 3–304 [Revised 3–302(a)(1)] titled "Notice to Purchasers," states in part:

(1) The purchaser has notice of a claim or defense if
  (a) the instrument is so incomplete, bears such visible evidence of forgery or alteration, or is otherwise so irregular as to call into question its validity, terms or ownership or to create an ambiguity as to the party to pay;
  . . .

The Bank is a "purchaser" within the meaning of § 3–304. [Citation.]

Section 1–201(25) imposes subjective and quasi-objective standards; § 3–304 imposes an objective standard. [Citation.] An irregularity on the face of an instrument is sufficient to import notice under § 3–304(1)(a) where,

A reasonably prudent person exercising normal commercial standards would immediately be put on notice that there was something very irregular about the terms of the [instrument.]

[Citation.]

The gist of Aubrey's argument is that the alleged "alteration" on the face of the check, i.e., the typed figure "100," was "such visible evidence" of alteration as to call into question its validity or terms.

We do not think that the trial court erred as a matter of law in finding that the Bank took the Aubrey check without notice of a defense. [Compare Revised 3–302(a)(1).]

The Bank's branch manager, Anderson, with whom Stephens dealt in the transaction, admitted that he took the check without comparing the amount expressed in typewritten figures; indeed, he testified that he did not even look at the figures. He relied, instead, upon the amount expressed by the checkwriter that was entered upon the line generally used to express the amount of a check in words.

Section 3–118 [Revised 3–114], captioned "Ambiguous terms and rules of construction," states in part:

The following rules apply to every instrument:
\* \* \*
(b) Handwritten terms control typewritten and printed terms, and typewritten control printed.
(c) Words control figures except that if the words are ambiguous figures control.

\* \* \*

As the section makes clear, in the event of an ambiguity between printed terms and typewritten terms, the latter would control. We do not consider the impressions made by the check imprinter to be "printed" terms under this section. [Citation.]

A conflict between the two amounts on a check would be resolved by § 3–118(c) [Revised 3–114] which states that words control figures. Arguably, the amount imprinted by the checkwriting machine upon the line customarily expressing the amount in words, is expressed in figures. (Recall that the entry reads: "The sum of $100478 and 23 cts.") We think, however, that the purposes of the UCC are best served by considering an amount imprinted by a checkwriting machine as "words" for the purpose of resolving an ambiguity between that amount and an amount entered upon the line usually used to express the amount in figures.

* * *

We cannot say as a matter of law that the bank acted unreasonably in relying upon the amount expressed by the checkwriting machine. Aubrey presented no evidence that customary banking standards require a bank to closely examine and compare the two amounts on the check, and it was Aubrey's burden to prove the existence of such custom. [Citation.] The issue of the Bank's constructive knowledge of any defense Aubrey may have had to the check, based on the alleged irregularity on the face of the check, was a question of fact for the trial court to determine. It was not error for the court to have determined that the Bank acted reasonably in relying on the amount imprinted by the checkwriting machine and took the check without notice, actual or constructive, of a defense thereto.

Aubrey further argues that the circumstances surrounding the transaction were so irregular as to put a reasonably prudent banker on notice of a defense to Aubrey's check. Aubrey directs us to no cases in which a holder was denied holder in due course status because of its knowledge of the questionable general financial position of the presenter of the instrument. Our research reveals such knowledge is not sufficient in itself to defeat holder in due course status. * * *

The only knowledge the Bank had concerning the transaction underlying the issue of the Aubrey check to Stephens, and thus the only knowledge relevant to the issue of Bank's notice of a possible defense to the check, grew out of Stephens's explanation to Anderson of how the check came into his hands. This was not sufficient to call into question the integrity of the Aubrey check.

We therefore hold that the evidence supports the trial court's determination that the Bank was a holder in due course of the Aubrey check. Since Aubrey has not shown a "real defense" under § 3–305(2) [Revised 3–305(a)(1)], the Bank may enforce the check against Aubrey to the extent it gave value therefor, and we shall not disturb the trial court's award of that amount.

---

## CASE 28–3
## The Shelter Rule
### TRIFFIN v. CIGNA INSURANCE

Superior Court of New Jersey, Appellate Division, 1997
687 A.2d 1045, 297 N.J.Super 199, 31 UCC Rep.Serv.2d 1040

DREIER, J.

Plaintiff, Robert J. Triffin, appeals from a . . . summary judgment dismissing his complaint for payment of a draft of defendant Cigna Insurance Company transferred to plaintiff by a holder in due course after Cigna had stopped payment on the instrument.

* * * The defaulting defendant, James Mills, received a draft in the amount of $484.12, dated July 7, 1993 from one of Cigna's constituent companies, Atlantic Employers Insurance Company. The draft had been issued for workers'compensation benefits. Mills falsely indicated to the issuer that he had not received the draft due to a change in his address and requested that payment be stopped and a new draft issued by defendant. The insurer complied and stopped payment on the initial draft. Mills nevertheless negotiated the initial draft to plaintiff's assignor, Sun Corp. t/a Sun's Market, before the stop payment notation was placed on the draft. All appear to agree that Sun Corp. was a holder in due course. Sun Corp. presented the draft for payment through depositary and collecting banks. The issuer's bank dishonored the draft in accordance with its customer's direction, stamped it "Stop Payment," and returned the draft to Sun Corp. There is no question that had Sun Corp. at that point pressed its claim against the insurer as the issuer of the instrument, Sun Corp. would have been entitled to a judgment because of its status as a holder in due course.

Thereafter, plaintiff, who apparently is in the business of purchasing dishonored instruments, obtained an assignment of Sun Corp.'s interests in this instrument and proceeded with this law suit. Plaintiff does not contend that he is a holder in due course of the instrument by virtue of it being negotiated to him for value, in good faith, without notice of dishonor, under the former holder in due course statute, UCC § 3–302, nor under the present statute, 3–302a(2).

Such negotiation is, of course, only one way for a holder to claim the status of a holder in due course. There exists a second method by which one may become a holder in due course. The shelter provisions of former UCC (§ 3–201), which was in effect when plaintiff obtained his assignment of this instrument, state clearly that "[t]ransfer of an instrument vests in the transferee such rights as the transferor has therein. . . ." Official Comment 3 to that section sets to rest any question of whether this section applies to the transfer by assignment of the rights of a holder in due course. The Comment reads: "A holder in due course may transfer his rights as such. . . . [The former Negotiable Instruments Law section's] policy is to assure the holder in due course a free market for the paper, and that policy is continued in this section." Example (a) following this comment could have been drawn from this case, but is even stronger because it adds an element of fraud and posits a gratuitous transfer rather than a purchase, as in our case:

(a) A [Mills] induces M [Cigna] by fraud to make an instrument payable to A. A negotiates it to B [Sun Corp.], who takes as a holder in due course. After the instrument is overdue B gives it to C [plaintiff], who has notice of the fraud. C succeeds to B's rights as a holder in due course, cutting off the defense.

If the 1995 amendments are to be given retroactive effect, the law governing the rights of a transferee who merely has accepted the transfer of the instrument is now found in Revised UCC [§ 3–203]. It restates the principle of the former Official Comment 3, example (a), as substantive law.

* * *

The Uniform Commercial Code Comment 2 to this [Revised] section similarly states:

Under subsection (b) a holder in due course that transfers an instrument transfers those rights as a holder in due course to the purchaser. The policy is to assure the holder in due course a free market for the instrument.

* * *

Also, both the old and new sections have exceptions where the transferee participated in the fraud or where the instrument is then reconveyed to the party who originally committed the fraud. Neither exception applies to this case.

These sections could not be clearer. Plaintiff received by [negotiation] the right of a holder in due course to this instrument, which apparently had been presented and then dishonored because of defendant's stop payment order. * * *

The summary judgment appealed from is reversed, and the matter is remanded with directions to enter judgment in favor of plaintiff, with interest.

---

**CASE 28–4**

## Void/Voidable Obligation
# *FEDERAL DEPOSIT INSURANCE CORPORATION v. MEYER*

United States District Court, District of Columbia, 1991
755 F.Supp. 10

PRATT, J.

### Background

The Federal Deposit Insurance Corporation ("FDIC") brings this action to collect on promissory notes signed by certain former partners of the law firm of Finley, Kumble, Wagner, Heine, Underberg, Manley, Myerson & Casey ("Finley Kumble"). The promissory notes secured loans that the National Bank of Washington ("NBW") made in 1986 to the Finley Partners to enable them to purchase stock in the Merchant Bank of California. After Finley Kumble declared bankruptcy, certain of the Finley Partners defaulted on their loans and NBW filed lawsuits in the Superior Court for the District of Columbia against defendants to collect on their promissory notes.

On August 10, 1990, the Office of the Comptroller of the Currency declared the NBW insolvent, closed the Bank, and appointed the Federal Deposit Insurance Corporation ("FDIC") as Receiver. The FDIC then removed these cases to federal court on September 7, 1990, and moved for summary judgment against each defendant on the grounds that the Federal Deposit Insurance Act of 1950, 12 U.S.C. § 1823(e) [places the FDIC in the position of a holder in due course and thus] provides special protections for the FDIC which bar all of the Finley Partners' defenses as a matter of law.

Twenty of the Finley Partners now oppose the FDIC's motion. * * *

## Discussion

*I. Defendants' Defense of Economic Duress*  The Finley Partners argue that the FDIC's motion for summary judgment should be denied because their defense of economic duress survives the effects of § 1823(e). They concede that § 1823(e) operates to place the FDIC in the position of a holder in due course, making promissory notes free of personal defenses. They argue, however, that § 1823(e) does not extinguish real defenses set forth in the Uniform Commercial Code ("UCC") and that their economic duress defense constitutes such a real defense.

Defendants are correct that § 1823(e) bars personal defenses but not real defenses. * * * As the Supreme Court explained in *Langley v. FDIC*, a real defense renders an instrument entirely void, leaving no interest that could be "'diminish[ed] or defeat[ed].'" [Citations.] In contrast, personal defenses render a note voidable but not void. * * *

Thus, if the Finley Partners' economic duress defense constitutes a real defense, then their promissory notes were void from the beginning. Asserting such a real defense could not "diminish or defeat" any interest of the FDIC because the FDIC did not have any interest to start with. On the other hand, if the Finley Partners' economic duress defense is a personal defense, then the FDIC received voidable title to the promissory notes from the NBW, which [defense would be cut off by the FDIC]. . . .

The main legal question, then, is whether economic duress is a personal defense that rendered NBW's title to the promissory notes voidable, or a real defense that rendered its title entirely void. The Finley Partners suggest that duress of any nature constitutes a real defense, citing UCC § 3–305(2)(b) [Revised 3–305(a)(1)] and several cases from outside of the District of Columbia. A careful reading of the UCC and its Official Commentary reveals that it does not make such a blanket classification.

First, § 3–305(2)(b) [Revised 3–305(a)(1)] provides that holders in due course take free of all defenses except for "(b) such other incapacity, or duress, or illegality of the transaction, as renders the obligation of the party a nullity." The words "such" and "as" indicate that the section is not stating that any type of duress renders an

obligation to be a nullity. Rather, it suggests that only those types of duress that are so severe as to render it a nullity stand as exceptions to the rule that holders in due course take free of defenses.

Of course, the question left open is what type of duress is severe enough to render it a nullity. Neither UCC § 3–305(2)(b) [Revised 3–305(a)(1)] nor the Official Comment attempt to establish a rule governing which types of duress render a transaction void as opposed to merely voidable. Instead, Official Comment 6 declares that "[a]ll such matters are therefore left to the local law." * * *

The Finley Partners do not cite any precedent from the District of Columbia that supports the view that economic duress renders a transaction void. In fact, they point out that [citation], the D.C. Court of Appeals quoted section 175 of the Restatement (Second) of Contracts which states that duress by threat (rather than by physical compulsion) renders a contract voidable rather than void. Although that case fails to distinguish between void and voidable contracts, it calls attention to the Restatement's distinction between the two categories:

Duress takes two forms. In one, a person physically compels conduct that appears to be a manifestation of assent by a party who has no intention of engaging in that conduct. The result of this type of duress is that the conduct is not effective to create a contract (§ 174). In the other, a person makes an improper threat that induces a party who has no reasonable alternative to manifesting his assent. The result of this type of duress is that the contract that is created is voidable by the victim (§ 175). [Citation.]

* * *

The Finley Partners do not allege that they were physically compelled to sign the promissory notes in question. They themselves labeled their defense as "economic" duress, and the substance of their allegations are that they signed the notes because of the threat that their wages and standing in the firm would decrease if they refused. Such economic duress does not reach the level of physical compulsion capable of rendering a transaction entirely void. Thus, NBW held at least voidable title to the promissory notes when the FDIC took over as Receiver. . . . Thus, defendants' economic defense duress is not valid against the FDIC.

* * *

## Conclusion

For the reasons discussed above, this Court finds that neither of the defendants' arguments has merit and that the FDIC is entitled to summary judgment as a matter of law. The defendants opposing the FDIC's motion for summary judgment are liable for the obligations they accepted when they signed the promissory notes. The FDIC is entitled to recover to the full extent of those obligations, as it requests in its motion for summary judgment.

# Questions

1. Discuss the requirements for becoming a holder in due course.
2. Discuss the shelter rule and when a payee can have the rights of a holder in due course.
3. Identify, define, and discuss the real defenses.
4. Define and discuss personal defenses.
5. Discuss the limitations the Federal Trade Commission imposes upon the rights of a holder in due course.

# Problems

1. Moore issues a negotiable promissory note payable to the order of Parish for the amount of $3,000. Parish raises the amount to $13,000 and negotiates it to Holton for $12,000.

  (a)  If Holton is a holder in due course, how much can she recover from Moore? How much from Parish? If Moore's negligence substantially contributed to the making of the alteration, how much can Holton recover from Moore and Parish, respectively?

  (b)  If Holton is not a holder in due course, how much can she recover from Moore? How much from Parish? If Moore's negligence substantially contributed to the making of the alteration, how much can Holton recover from Moore and Parish, respectively?

2. On December 2, 1999, Miles executed and delivered to Proctor a negotiable promissory note for $1,000, payable to Proctor or order, due March 2, 2000, with interest at 14 percent from maturity, in partial payment of a printing press. On January 3, 2000, Proctor, in need of ready cash, indorsed and sold the note to Hughes for $800. Hughes paid $600 in cash to Proctor on January 3 and agreed to pay the balance of $200 one week later, namely, on January 10. On January 6, Hughes learned that Miles claimed a breach of warranty by Proctor and, for this reason, intended to refuse to pay the note when it matured. On January 10, Hughes paid Proctor $200, in conformity with their agreement of January 3. Following Miles's refusal to pay the note on March 2, 2000, Hughes sues Miles for $1,000. Decision?

3. Thornton fraudulently represented to Daye that he would obtain for her a new car to be used in Daye's business for $7,800 from Pennek Motor Company. Daye thereupon executed her personal check for $7,800 payable to the order of Pennek Motor Company and delivered the check to Thornton, who immediately delivered it to the motor company in payment of his own prior indebtedness. The motor company had no knowledge of the representations made by Thornton to Daye. Pennek Motor Company now brings an action on the check against Daye, who defends on the ground of failure of consideration. Decision?

4. Adams, who reads with difficulty, arranged to borrow $200 from Bell. Bell prepared a note, which Adams read laboriously. As Adams was about to sign it, Bell diverted Adams's attention and substituted the following paper, which was identical to the note Adams had read except that the amounts were different:

On June 1, 1999, I promise to pay Ben Bell or order Two Thousand Dollars with interest from date at 16 percent. This note is secured by certificate No. 13 for 100 shares of stock of Brookside Mills, Inc.

Adams did not detect the substitution, signed as maker, handed the note and stock certificate to Bell, and received from Bell $200. Bell indorsed and sold the paper to Fore, a holder in due course, who paid him $1,800. Fore presented the note at maturity to Adams, who refused to pay. What are Fore's rights, if any, against Adams?

5. On January 2, 1999, Martin, seventeen years of age, as a result of Dealer's fraudulent misrepresentation, bought a used motorboat to use in his fishing business for $2,000 from Dealer, signed an installment contract for $1,500, and gave Dealer the following instrument as down payment:

Dated: _____1999
I promise to pay to the order of Dealer, six months after date, the sum of $500 without interest. This is given as a down payment on an installment contract for a motorboat.

(signed) Martin

Dealer, on July 1, sold his business to Henry and included this note in the transaction. Dealer indorsed the note in blank and handed it to Henry, who left the note in his office safe. On July 10, Sharpie, an employee of Henry, without authority stole the note and sold it to Bert for $300, indorsing the note "Sharpie." At the time, in Bert's presence, Sharpie filled in the date on the note as February 2, 1999. Bert demanded payment from Martin, who refused to pay.

What are Bert's rights against Martin?

6. McLaughlin borrowed $1,000 from Adler, who, apprehensive about McLaughlin's ability to pay, demanded security. McLaughlin indorsed and delivered to Adler a negotiable promissory note executed by Topping for $1,200 payable to McLaughlin's order in twelve equal monthly installments. The note did not contain an acceleration clause, but it recited that the consideration for the note was McLaughlin's promise to paint and shingle Topping's barn. At the time McLaughlin transferred the note to Adler, the first installment was overdue and unpaid. Adler was unaware that the installment had not been paid. Topping did not pay any of the installments on the note. When the last installment became due, Adler presented the note to Topping for payment. Topping refused upon the ground that McLaughlin had not painted or reshingled her barn.

What are Adler's rights, if any, against Topping on the note?

7. McEnally purchased a refrigerator for his home from Peircault Appliance Store for $700. McEnally paid $200 in cash and signed an installment contract for $500, which in its entirety stated:

January 15, 1999

I promise to pay to the order of Peircault Appliance Store the sum of $500 in ten equal monthly installments.

(Signed) McEnally

Peircault negotiated the installment contract to Hughes, who took the instrument for value, in good faith, without notice of any claim or defense of any party, and without question of the instrument's authenticity. After McEnally had paid two installments, the refrigerator ceased operating, and McEnally wishes to recover his down payment and first two monthly payments and to discontinue further payments. What outcome?

8. Adams, by fraudulent representations, induced Barton to purchase 100 shares of the capital stock of the Evermore Oil Company. The shares were worthless. Barton executed and delivered to Adams a negotiable promissory note for $5,000, dated May 5, in full payment for the shares, due six months after date. On May 20, Adams indorsed and sold the note to Cooper for $4,800. On October 21, Barton, having learned that Cooper now held the note, notified Cooper of the fraud and stated he would not pay the note. On December 1, Cooper negotiated the note to Davis who, while not a party, had full knowledge of the fraud perpetrated on Barton. Upon refusal of Barton to pay the note, Davis sues Barton for $5,000. Decision?

9. Donna gives Peter a check for $50,000 in return for a personal computer. The check is dated December 2. Peter transfers the check for value to Howard on December 14, and Howard deposits it in his bank on December 20. In the meantime, Donna has discovered that the personal computer is not what was promised and has stopped payment on the check. If Peter and Howard disappear, may the bank recover from Donna notwithstanding her defense of failure of consideration? What will be the bank's cause of action?

10. Eldon's Super Fresh Stores, Inc., is a corporation engaged in the retail grocery business. William Drexler was the attorney for and the corporate secretary of Eldon's and was also the personal attorney of Eldon Prinzing, the corporation's president and sole shareholder. From January 1998 through January 1999, Drexler maintained an active stock trading account in his name with Merrill Lynch. Eldon's had no such account. On August 12, 1998, Drexler purchased 100 shares of Clark Oil & Refining Company stock through his Merrill Lynch stockbroker. He paid for the stock with a check drawn by Eldon's made payable to Merrill Lynch and signed by Prinzing. On August 15, 1998, Merrill Lynch accepted the check as payment for Drexler's stock purchase. There was no communication between Eldon's and Merrill Lynch until November 1999, fifteen months after the issuance of the check. At that time, Eldon's asked Merrill Lynch about the whereabouts of the stock certificate and asserted a claim to its ownership. It then brought this action, claiming that it gave the check to Drexler to be delivered to Merrill Lynch for Eldon's benefit. Decision?

11. Consolidated Business Forms leased a Phillips business computer from Benchmark. Benchmark subsequently transferred the lease and promissory note to Exchange International Leasing Corporation. Consolidated stopped making rental payments when the computer malfunctioned, and Exchange International brought this suit to recover the payments due on the promissory note. Consolidated defends on the grounds that Benchmark prevented its agent, Mr. Spohn, from examining the contents of the agreement between the two companies and further represented that the computer would be removed with a complete refund if it failed to operate properly. Decision?

12. Litton decided to purchase photocopiers to use in its offices. Angelo Buquicchio, a Royal (a division of Litton) salesperson, recommended that Litton lease the machines from Regent. Regent was a company totally independent of Litton and had agreed to give Buquicchio "service fees" or, more appropriately, bribes. Regent borrowed money from Bankers Trust to finance purchases and transferred the Litton leases as security. A clause in the leases permitted transfer and provided that the transferee's rights would be independent of any claims or offsets of Litton as against Regent. Litton defaulted on the obligations, and the primary question was whether Regent's bribery of Royal's employee rendered Litton's obligations a nullity and a defense against the banks as holders in due course. Decision?

13. Supreme Radio, Inc., issued to Southern New England Distributing Corporation two notes worth $1,900. The two notes and others, all of a total face value of about $15,000, were transferred to Korzenik, an attorney, by his client Southern "as a retainer for services to be performed" by Korzenik. Although Korzenik was unaware of the fact,

Southern had obtained the notes by fraud. Southern retained Korzenik on October 25 in connection with certain antitrust litigation, and the notes were transferred on October 31. The value of the services performed by Korzenik during that time is unclear. Korzenik brought this action against Supreme Radio to recover $1,900 on the notes. Decision?

14.   Walter Duester purchased a John Deere combine from St. Paul Equipment. John Deere Co. was the lender and secured party under the agreement. The combine was pledged as collateral. Duester defaulted on his debt, and the manager of St. Paul, Hansen, was instructed to repossess the combine. Hansen went to Duester's farm to accomplish this. Duester told him that he had received some payments for custom combining and would immediately purchase a cashier's check to pay the John Deere debt. Hansen followed Duester to the Defendant, Boelus State Bank. Hansen remained outside, and Duester returned in a few minutes with a cashier's check in the amount of the balance of his indebtedness payable to John Deere. The check had been signed by an authorized bank employee. When John Deere, however, presented the check to the bank for payment shortly thereafter, the bank refused to pay. The trial court found for John Deere. Decision?

**Internet Exercise** Compare the provisions governing holders and protected holders contained in the United Nations Convention on International Bills of Exchange and International Promissory Notes with those governing holders and holders in due course under Article 3 of the Uniform Commercial Code.

# CHAPTER 29

# Liability of Parties

The preceding chapters discussed the requirements of negotiability, the transfer of negotiable instruments, and the preferred position of a holder in due course. When parties issue negotiable instruments they do so with the expectation that they, either directly or indirectly, will satisfy their obligation under the instrument. Likewise, when a person accepts, indorses, or transfers an instrument, he incurs liability for the instrument under certain circumstances. This chapter examines the liability of parties arising out of negotiable instruments and the ways in which liability may be terminated.

Two types of potential liability are associated with negotiable instruments: contractual liability and warranty liability. The law imposes **contractual liability** on those who **sign**, or have a representative agent sign, a negotiable instrument. Because some parties to a negotiable instrument never sign it, they never assume contractual liability. Section 3–401(a).

Warranty liability, on the other hand, is not based on signature; thus, it may be imposed on both signers and nonsigners. **Warranty liability** applies (1) to persons who transfer an instrument and (2) to persons who obtain payment or acceptance of an instrument.

## CONTRACTUAL LIABILITY

All parties whose signatures appear on a negotiable instrument incur certain contractual obligations, unless they disclaim liability. The *maker* of a promissory note and the *acceptor* of a draft assume primary, or unconditional, liability, subject to valid claims and defenses, to pay according to the terms of the instrument at the time they sign it or as completed according to the rules for incomplete instruments, discussed in Chapter 28. **Primary liability** means that a party is legally obligated to pay without the holder's having to resort first to another party. *Indorsers* of all instruments incur secondary, or conditional, liability if the instrument is not paid. **Secondary liability** means that a party is legally obligated to pay only after another party, who is expected to pay, fails to do so. The liability of drawers of drafts and checks is also conditional because it is generally contingent upon the drawee's dishonor of the instrument. A *drawee* has *no* liability on the instrument until he accepts it.

An **accommodation party** signs the instrument to lend her credit to another party to the instrument and is a direct beneficiary of the value received. Section 3–419(a). The liability of an accommodation party, who generally signs as a comaker, or anomalous indorser, is determined by the capacity in which she signs. Section 3–419(b). If she signs as a maker, she incurs primary liability; if she signs as an anomalous indorser, she incurs secondary liability.

## SIGNATURE

The word *signature,* as discussed in Chapter 26, is broadly defined to include any name, word, or mark, whether handwritten, typed, printed, or in any other form, made with the intention of authenticating an instrument. Sections 3–401(b) and 1–201(39). The signature may be made by the individual herself or on her behalf by the individual's authorized agent.

### Authorized Signatures

Authorized agents often execute negotiable instruments on behalf of their principals. The agent is not liable if she is authorized to execute the instrument and does so properly (e.g., "Prince, principal, by Adams, agent"). If these two conditions are met, then only the principal is liable on the instrument. (For a comprehensive discussion of the principal–agent relationship, see Chapters 19 and 20.)

Occasionally, however, the agent, although fully authorized, uses an inappropriate form of signature that may mislead holders or prospective holders as to the identity of the obligor. Although incorrect signatures by agents assume many forms, they can be conveniently sorted into three groups.

The first type occurs when an agent signs only his own name to an instrument, neither indicating that he is signing in a representative capacity nor stating the name of the principal. For example, Adams, the agent of Prince, makes a note on behalf of Prince but signs it "Adams." The signature does not indicate that Adams has signed in a representative capacity or that he has made the instrument on behalf of Prince. In this situation, only the agent is liable on the instrument; Prince is not liable because his name does not appear on the instrument. Prince may be liable to Adams or a third party, however, on the basis of contract or agency law.

The second type of incorrect form occurs when an authorized agent indicates that he is signing in a representative capacity but does not disclose the name of his principal. For example, Adams, executing an instrument on behalf of Prince, merely signs it "Adams, agent." In this situation, Prince is liable if the payee is an immediate party to the instrument and knows that Adams represents Prince. But as to any subsequent party, and as to the payee if he does not know that Adams represents Prince, Prince is not liable on the instrument; Adams alone is liable. As with the first situation, Prince may be liable to Adams or to a third party, based on contract or agency law.

The third type of inappropriate signature occurs when an agent reveals both her name and her principal's name, but does not indicate that she has signed in a representative capacity. For example, Adams, signing an instrument on behalf of Prince, signs it "Adams and Prince." Because a subsequent holder might reasonably believe that Adams and Prince were comakers, both are fully liable. But if the party who dealt with Adams knew or should have known that Adams was acting on behalf of Prince without intending to incur personal liability, Adams may prove this fact by parol evidence and avoid liability to this immediate party.

Under Revised Article 3, if a representative (an agent) signs his name as the drawer of a *check* without indicating his representative status and the check is payable from an account of the represented person (the principal) who is identified on the check, the representative is not liable on the check if he is an authorized agent. Some courts reached this result under prior Article 3.

 *See Case 29–1*

## Unauthorized Signatures

Unauthorized signatures include both forgeries and signatures made by an agent without authority. Though generally not binding on the person whose name appears on the instrument, the unauthorized signature is binding upon the unauthorized signer, whether her own name appears on the instrument or not, to any person who in good faith pays or gives value for the instrument. Section 3–403(a). Thus, if Adams, without authority, signed Prince's name to an instrument, Adams, not Prince, would be liable on the instrument. The rule, therefore, is an exception to the principle that only those whose names appear on a negotiable instrument can be liable on it.

***Ratification of Unauthorized Signature*** An unauthorized signature may be **ratified** by the person whose name appears on the instrument. Section 3–403(a). Although the ratification may relieve the actual signer from liability on the instrument, it does not of itself affect any rights the person ratifying the signature may have against the actual signer.

***Negligence Contributing to Forged Signature*** Any person who by his **negligence** substantially contributes to the making of an forged signature may *not* assert the lack of authority as a defense against a holder in due course or a person who in good faith pays the instrument or takes it for value or for collection. Section 3–406. For example, Ingrid employs a signature stamp to sign her checks and carelessly leaves it accessible to third parties. Lisa discovers the stamp and uses it to write a number of checks without Ingrid's authorization. Norman, a person who takes the instrument for value and in good faith, will not be subject to Ingrid's defense of unauthorized signature and will be able to recover the amount of the check from Ingrid, due to Ingrid's negligence in storing the signature stamp. Nevertheless, if the person asserting the preclusion also fails to exercise reasonable care, revised Section 3–406(b) adopts a comparative negligence standard.

## LIABILITY OF PRIMARY PARTIES

There is a primary party on every note: the *maker*. The maker's commitment is unconditional. Section 3–412. No one, however, is unconditionally liable on a draft or check as issued. A *drawee* is not liable on the instrument unless he accepts it. Section 3–408. If, however, the drawee accepts the draft, after which he is known as the *acceptor,* he becomes primarily liable on the instrument. **Acceptance** or, in the case of a check, certification is the drawee's signed promise to pay a draft as presented. Section 3–409(a), (d). Presentment (i.e., a demand for payment) is not a condition to the holder's right to recover from parties with primary liability.

## Makers

The maker of a note is obligated to pay the instrument according to its terms at the time of issuance or, if the instrument is incomplete, according to its terms when completed, as discussed in Chapter 28. Section 3–412. The obligation of the maker is owed to a person entitled to enforce the instrument or to an indorser who paid the instrument.

Primary liability also applies to issuers of cashier's checks and to issuers of drafts drawn on the drawer (i.e., where the issuer is both the drawee and the drawer). Section 3–412.

## Acceptors

A drawee has no liability on the instrument until she accepts it, at which time she becomes an acceptor and, like a maker, primarily liable. The acceptor becomes liable on the draft according to its terms at the time of acceptance or as completed according to the rules for incomplete instruments as discussed in Chapter 28. Section 3–413(a). Nevertheless, if the acceptor does not state the amount accepted and the amount of the draft is later raised, a subsequent holder in due course can enforce the instrument against the acceptor according to the terms at the time the holder in due course took possession. Section 3–413(b). Thus, an acceptor should always indicate on the instrument the amount that it is accepting. The acceptor owes the obligation to pay to a person entitled to enforce the instrument or to the drawer or an indorser who paid the draft under drawer's or indorser's liability. Section 3–413(a).

An acceptance must be written on the draft. Section 3–409(a). Having met this requirement, it may take many forms. It may be printed on the face of the draft, ready for the drawee's signature. It may consist of a rubber stamp, with the signature of the drawee added. It may be the drawee's signature, preceded by a word or phrase such as "Accepted," "Certified," or "Good." It may consist of nothing more than the drawee's signature. Normally, but by no means necessarily, an acceptance is written vertically across the face of the draft. It must not, however, contain any words indicating an intent to refuse to honor the draft. Furthermore, no writing separate from the draft and no oral statement or conduct of the drawee will convert the drawee into an acceptor.

Checks, when accepted, are said to be certified. **Certification** is a special type of acceptance consisting of the drawee bank's promise to pay the check when subsequently presented for payment. Section 3–409(d).

The drawee bank has no obligation to certify a check, and its refusal to certify does not constitute dishonor of the instrument. If the drawee refuses to accept or pay the instrument, he may be liable to the drawer for breach of contract.

## *LIABILITY OF SECONDARY PARTIES*

Parties with secondary (conditional) liability do not unconditionally promise to pay the instrument; rather, they engage to pay the instrument if the party expected to pay does not do so. The drawer is liable if the drawee dishonors the instrument. Indorsers (including the payee if he indorses) of an instrument are also conditionally liable; their liability is subject to the conditions of dishonor and notice of dishonor. If an instrument is *not* paid by the party expected to pay and the conditions precedent to the liability of a secondary party are satisfied, a secondary party is liable unless he has disclaimed his liability or he possesses a valid defense to the instrument.

## Drawers

A drawer of a draft orders the drawee to pay the instrument and does not expect to pay the draft personally. The drawer is obligated to pay the draft only if the drawee fails to pay the instrument. The drawer of an *unaccepted draft* is obligated to pay the instrument upon its dishonor according to its terms at the time it was issued or, in the case of an incomplete instrument, according to the rules discussed in Chapter 28. Under Revised Article 3, the drawer's liability is contingent only upon dishonor and does not require notice of dishonor. The drawer's obligation on an unaccepted draft is owed to a person entitled to enforce the instrument or to an indorser who paid the instrument under indorser's liability.

If the draft has been accepted and the acceptor is not a bank, the obligation of the drawer to pay the instrument is then contingent upon both dishonor of the instrument and notice of dishonor; the drawer's liability in this instance is equivalent to that of an indorser. Sections 3–414(d), 3–503.

 *See Case 29–2*

## Indorsers

An indorser promises that upon dishonor of the instrument *and* notice of dishonor she will pay the instrument according to the terms of the instrument at the time it was indorsed or, if an incomplete instrument when indorsed, according to its terms when completed, as discussed in Chapter 28. Sections 3–415, 3–503. Once again, this obligation is owed to a person entitled to enforce the instrument or to a subsequent indorser who paid the instrument under indorser's liability.

## Effect of Acceptance

Where a **draft** is accepted by a *bank*, the drawer and all prior indorsers are discharged. Sections 3–414(c), 3–415(d). The liability of indorsers subsequent to certification is not affected. When the bank accepts a draft, it should withhold from the drawer's account funds sufficient to pay the instrument. Because the bank is primarily liable on its acceptance and has the funds, whereas the drawer does not, the discharge is reasonable.

## Disclaimer of Liability by Secondary Parties

Both drawers and indorsers may disclaim their normal conditional liability by drawing or indorsing an instrument **"without recourse."** Sections 3–414(e), 3–415(b). However, drawers of *checks* may not disclaim contractual liability. Section 3–414(e). The use of the qualifying words *without recourse* is understood to place purchasers on notice that they may not rely on the credit of the person using this language. A person drawing or indorsing an instrument in this manner does not incur the normal contractual liability of a drawer or indorser to pay the instrument, but he may nonetheless be liable for breach of warranty.

## Conditions Precedent to Liability

A **condition precedent** is an event or events that must occur before liability arises. The condition precedent to

the liability of the drawer of an *unaccepted* draft is dishonor. Conditions precedent to the liability of any indorser or the drawer of an *accepted* draft by a nonbank are dishonor and notice of dishonor. If the conditions to secondary liability are not met, a party's conditional obligation on the instrument is discharged, unless the conditions are excused.

*Dishonor*   Dishonor generally involves the refusal to pay an instrument when it is presented. **Presentment** is a demand made by or on behalf of a person entitled to enforce the instrument for (1) **payment** by the drawee or other party obligated to pay the instrument or (2) **acceptance** by the drawee of a draft. Section 3–501(a). The return of any instrument for lack of necessary indorsements or for failure of the presentment to comply with the terms of the instrument, however, is not a dishonor. Section 3–501(b)(3).

What constitutes dishonor varies depending upon the type of instrument and whether presentment is required.

1. **Note**—A *demand note* is dishonored if the maker does not pay it on the day of presentment. Section 3–502(a)(1). If the note is payable at a *definite time* and (1) the terms of the note require presentment or (2) the note is payable at or through a bank, the note is dishonored if it is not paid on the date it is presented or its due date, whichever is later. Section 3–502(a)(2). All *other time notes* need not be presented and are dishonored if they are not paid on their due dates. Section 3–502(a)(3). Nevertheless, because makers are primarily liable on their notes, their liability is not affected by failure of proper presentment.

2. **Drafts**—An *unaccepted draft* (other than a check, discussed below) that is payable on *demand* is dishonored if presentment is made and it is not paid on the date presented. Section 3–502(b)(2). A *time draft* presented for *payment* is due on the due date or presentment date, whichever is later. Section 3–502(b)(3). A *time draft* presented for *acceptance* prior to its due date is dishonored if it is not accepted on the day presented. Section 3–502(b)(3). Refusal to accept a demand instrument is not a dishonor, although acceptance may be requested. Of course, if an instrument is payable at a certain time period after acceptance or sight, a refusal to accept the draft on the day presented is a dishonor. Section 3–502(b)(4).

   An accepted demand draft is dishonored if the acceptor (who is primarily liable on the instrument) does not pay it on the day presented for payment.

Section 3–502(d)(1). An accepted time draft is dishonored if it is not paid on the due date for payment or on the presentment date, whichever is later. Section 3–502(d)(2).

Drawers, with the exception of drafts accepted by a bank, are not discharged from liability by a delay in presentment. Once an instrument has been properly presented and dishonored, a drawer becomes liable to pay the instrument. As previously indicated, drawers and prior indorsers are discharged from liability when a draft is accepted by a bank. Sections 3–414, 3–415.

3. **Checks**—If a check is presented for payment directly to the payor/drawee bank for immediate payment, a refusal to pay the check on the day presented constitutes dishonor. Section 3–502(b)(2). In the more common situation of a check being presented through the normal collection process, a check is dishonored if the payor bank makes timely return of the check, sends timely notice of dishonor or nonpayment, or becomes accountable for the amount of the check (until that payment has been made the check is dishonored, Comment 4). Section 3–502(b)(1). As more fully explained in Chapter 30, under Article 4 a bank in most instances has a midnight deadline (before midnight of the next banking day) in which to decide whether to honor or dishonor an instrument. Thus, depending on the number of banks involved in the collection process, the time for dishonor can greatly vary.

*Delay* in presentment discharges an *indorser* only if the instrument is a check and it is not presented for payment or given to a depositary bank for collection within thirty days after the day the indorsement was made. Section 3–415(e). The same rule does not apply, however, to a drawer. If a person entitled to enforce a check fails to present a check within thirty days after its date, the drawer will be discharged only if the delay deprives the drawer of funds because of the suspension of payments by the drawee bank such as would result from a bank failure. Section 3–414(f). This discharge is quite unlikely because of Federal bank insurance but would be available where an account is not fully insured because it exceeds $100,000 or because the account doesn't qualify for deposit insurance. Section 3–414, Comment 6.

**Notice of Dishonor** The obligation of an indorser of any instrument and of a drawer of a draft accepted by a nonbank is not enforceable unless the indorser or drawer is given notice of dishonor or the notice is otherwise excused. Sections 3–503(a), 3–415(c). Thus, lack of proper notice discharges the liability of an indorser; for this purpose a drawer of a draft accepted by a party other than a bank is treated as an indorser. Notice of dishonor is *not* required to retain the liability of drawers of unaccepted drafts. In addition, as previously mentioned a drawer is discharged when a draft is accepted by a *bank*. Section 3–414. In short, a drawer's liability is usually not contingent upon receiving notice of dishonor, whereas an indorser's liability is.

Notice of dishonor is normally given by the holder or by an indorser who has himself received notice. For example, Michael makes a note payable to the order of Phyllis; Phyllis indorses it to Arthur; Arthur indorses it to Bambi; and Bambi indorses it to Henry, the last holder. Henry presents it to Michael within a reasonable time, but Michael refuses to pay. Henry may give notice of dishonor to all secondary parties: Phyllis, Arthur, and Bambi. If he is satisfied that Bambi will pay him or if he does not know how to contact Phyllis or Arthur, he may notify only Bambi, who then must see to it that Arthur or Phyllis is notified, or she will have no recourse. Bambi may notify either or both. If she notifies Arthur only, Arthur will have to see to it that Phyllis is notified, or Arthur will have no recourse. When properly given, notice benefits all parties who have rights on the instrument against the party notified. Section 3–503(b). Thus, Henry's notification to Phyllis operates as notice to Phyllis by both Arthur and Bambi. Likewise, if Henry notifies only Bambi and Bambi notifies Arthur and Phyllis, then Henry has the benefit of Bambi's notification of Arthur and Phyllis. Nonetheless, it would be advisable for Henry to give notice to all prior parties because Bambi may be insolvent and thus may not bother to notify Arthur or Phyllis.

If, in the above example, Henry were to notify Phyllis alone, Arthur and Bambi would be discharged. Because she has no claim against Arthur or Bambi, who indorsed after she did, Phyllis would have no ground for complaint. It cannot matter to Phyllis that she is compelled to pay Henry rather than Arthur. Therefore, subsequent parties are permitted to skip intermediate indorsers if they want to discharge them and are willing to look solely to prior indorsers for recourse.

Any necessary notice must be given by a **bank** before midnight on the *next* banking day following the banking day on which it receives notice of dishonor. Any **nonbank** with respect to an instrument taken for collection must give notice within thirty days following the day on which it received notice. In all other situations, notice of dishonor must be within thirty days following the day on which dishonor occurred. Section 3–503(c). For instance, Donna draws a check on Youngstown Bank payable to the order of Pablo; Pablo indorses it to Andrea; Andrea deposits it to her account in Second Chicago National Bank; Second Chicago National Bank properly presents it to Youngstown Bank, the drawee; and Youngstown dishonors it because the drawer, Donna, has insufficient funds on deposit to cover it. Youngstown has until midnight of the following day to notify Second Chicago National, Andrea, or Pablo of the dishonor. Second Chicago National then has until midnight on the day after receipt of notice of dishonor to notify Andrea or Pablo. That is, if Second Chicago National received the notice of dishonor on Monday, it would have until midnight on Tuesday to notify Andrea or Pablo. If it failed to notify Andrea, it could not charge the item back to her. Andrea, in turn, has thirty days after receipt of notice of dishonor to notify Pablo. Donna, a drawer of an unaccepted draft, is not discharged from liability for failure to receive notice of dishonor.

Frequently, notice of dishonor is given by returning the unpaid instrument with an attached stamp, ticket, or memorandum stating that the item was not paid and requesting that the recipient make good on it. But because the purpose of notice is to give knowledge of dishonor and to inform the secondary party that he may be held liable on the instrument, any kind of notice which informs the recipient of his potential liability is sufficient. No formal requisites are imposed—notice may be given by any commercially reasonable means, including oral, written, or electronic communication. Section 3–503(b). An oral notice, while sufficient, is inadvisable because it may be difficult to prove. Notice of dishonor must reasonably identify the instrument. Section 3–503(b).

***Presentment and Notice of Dishonor Excused*** The Code excuses *presentment* for payment or acceptance if (1) the person entitled to enforce the instrument cannot with reasonable diligence present the instrument, (2) the maker or acceptor of the instrument has repudiated the obligation to pay, is dead, or is in insolvency proceedings, (3) the terms of the instrument do not require presentment to hold the indorsers or drawer liable, (4) the drawer or indorser has waived the right of presentment, (5) the drawer instructed the drawee not to pay or accept the draft, or (6) the drawee was not obligated to the drawer to pay the draft. Section 3–504(a).

*Notice of dishonor* is excused if the terms of the instrument do not require notice to hold the party liable or if notice has been waived by the party whose obligation is being enforced. Moreover, a waiver of presentment is also a waiver of notice of dishonor. Section 3–504(b). Finally, delay in giving notice of dishonor is excused if the delay is caused by circumstances beyond the control of the person giving notice and that person exercised reasonable diligence in giving notice after the cause of the delay ceased to exist. Section 3–504(c).

◆ *See Figure 29–1*

## Liability for Conversion

Conversion is a **tort** by which a person becomes liable in damages because of his wrongful control over the personal property of another. The law applicable to conversion of personal property applies to instruments. Section 3–420(a). An instrument is so converted if the instrument "is taken by transfer, other than by negotiation, from a person *not* entitled to enforce the instrument or a bank makes or obtains payment with respect to

**FIGURE 29–1** Contractual Liability

| Party | Instrument | Liability | Conditions |
|-------|-----------|-----------|------------|
| **Maker** | Note | Unconditional | None |
| **Acceptor** | Draft | Unconditional | None |
| **Drawer** | Unaccepted draft | Conditional | Dishonor |
| | Draft accepted by a nonbank | Conditional | Dishonor and notice |
| | Cashier's check | Unconditional | None |
| | Draft drawn on drawer | Unconditional | None |
| | Draft accepted by a bank | None | |
| | Draft (not check) drawn without recourse | None | |
| **Indorser** | Note or draft | Conditional | Dishonor and notice |
| | Draft subsequently accepted by a bank | None | |
| | Note or draft indorsed without recourse | None | |
| **Drawee** | Draft | None | |

the instrument for a person *not* entitled to enforce the instrument or receive payment." Section 3–420(a) (emphasis added). Examples of conversion thus would include a drawee bank that pays an instrument containing a forged indorsement or a bank that pays an instrument containing only one of two required indorsements.

## TERMINATION OF LIABILITY

Eventually, every commercial transaction must end, terminating the potential liabilities of the parties to the instrument. The Code specifies the various methods by and extent to which the liability of *any* party, primary or secondary, is discharged. It also specifies when the liability of *all* parties is discharged. No discharge of a party is effective against a subsequent holder in due course, however, unless she has notice of the discharge when she takes the instrument. Section 3–601(b). In addition, discharge of liability is not always final; liability under certain circumstances (e.g., coming into possession of a subsequent holder in due course) can be revived.

### Payment

The most obvious and common way for a party to discharge liability on an instrument is to pay a party entitled to enforce the instrument. Section 3–602. An instrument is paid to the extent that payment is made by or for a person obligated to pay the instrument and to a person entitled to enforce the instrument. Section 3–602(a). Subject to three exceptions, such payment results in a discharge even though it is made with knowledge of another person's claim to the instrument, unless such other person either supplies adequate indemnity or obtains an injunction in a proceeding to which the holder is made a party.

The person making payment should, of course, take possession of the instrument or have it canceled—marked "paid" or "canceled"—so that it cannot pass to a subsequent holder in due course against whom his discharge would be ineffective.

### Tender of Payment

Any party liable on an instrument who makes proper tender of full payment to a person entitled to enforce the instrument when or after payment is due is discharged from liability for interest after the due date. Section 3–603(c). If her tender is refused, she is not discharged from liability for the face amount of the instrument or for any interest accrued until the time of tender. Moreover, if

an instrument requires presentment and the obligor is ready and able to pay the instrument when it is due at the place of payment specified in the instrument, such readiness is the equivalent of tender. Section 3–603(c).

Occasionally a person entitled to enforce an instrument will refuse a tender of payment for reasons known only to himself. It may be that he believes his rights exceed the amount of the tender or that he desires to enforce payment against another party. In any event, his refusal of the tender wholly discharges to the extent of the amount of tender every party who has a right of recourse against the party making tender. Section 3–603(b).

### Cancellation and Renunciation

Section 3–604 provides that a person entitled to enforce an instrument may discharge the liability of any party to an instrument by an intentional voluntary act, such as by canceling the instrument or the signature of the party or parties to be discharged, by mutilating or destroying the instrument, by obliterating a signature, or by adding words indicating a discharge. Section 3–604(a). A party entitled to enforce an instrument may also renounce his rights by a writing, signed and delivered, promising not to sue or otherwise renouncing rights against the party. Like other discharges, however, a written renunciation is of no effect against a subsequent holder in due course who takes without knowledge of the renunciation. Section 3–601(b).

Cancellation or renunciation is effective even without consideration.

## LIABILITY BASED ON WARRANTY

Article 3 imposes two types of implied warranties: (a) transferor's warranties and (b) presenter's warranties. Sections 3–416 and 3–417. Although these warranties are effective whether the transferor or presenter signs the instrument or not, the extension of the transferor's warranty to subsequent holders does depend on whether one or the other has indorsed the instrument. Like other warranties, these may be disclaimed by agreement between immediate parties. In the case of an indorser, his disclaimer of transfer warranties and presentment warranties must appear in the indorsement itself and is effective, except with respect to checks. Sections 3–416(c), 3–417(e). Such disclaimers must be specific, such as "without warranty." The use of "without recourse" will only disclaim contract liability, not warranty liability.

## WARRANTIES ON TRANSFER

Any person who transfers an instrument, whether by negotiation or assignment, and receives *consideration* makes certain **transferor's warranties.** Section 3–416. Any consideration sufficient to support a contract will support transfer warranties. If transfer is by delivery alone, warranties on transfer run only to the immediate transferee. If the transfer is made by indorsement, whether qualified or unqualified, the transfer warranty runs to "any subsequent transferee." *Transfer* means that the delivery of possession is voluntary. Sections 3–201(a), 1–201(14). The warranties of the transferor are as follows.

### Entitlement to Enforce

The first warranty that the Code imposes on a transferor is that the transferor is a person entitled to enforce the instrument. Section 3–416(a)(1). This warranty "is in effect a warranty that there are no unauthorized or missing indorsements that prevent the transferor from making the transferee a person entitled to enforce the instrument." Section 3–416, Comment 2. The following example illustrates this rule. Mitchell makes a note payable to the order of Penelope. A thief steals the note from Penelope, forges Penelope's indorsement, and sells the instrument to Aaron. Aaron is not entitled to enforce the instrument because the break in the indorsement chain prevents him from being a holder. If Aaron transfers the instrument to Judith for consideration, Judith can hold Aaron liable for breach of warranty. The warranty action is important to Judith because it enables her to hold Aaron liable, even if Aaron indorsed the note "without recourse."

### Authentic and Authorized Signatures

The second warranty imposed by the Code is that **all** signatures are authentic and authorized. In the example presented above, this warranty would also be breached. Section 3–416(a)(2). If, however, the signature of a maker, drawer, drawee, acceptor, or indorser not in the chain of title is unauthorized, there is a breach of this warranty but no breach of the warranty of entitlement to enforce.

### No Alteration

The third warranty is the warranty against alteration. Section 3–416(a)(3). Suppose that Maureen makes a note payable to the order of the payee in the amount of

$100. The payee, without authority, alters the note so that it appears to be drawn for $1,000 and negotiates the instrument to Lois, who buys it without knowledge of the alteration. Lois, indorsing "without recourse," negotiates the instrument to Kyle for consideration. Kyle presents the instrument to Maureen, who refuses to pay more than $100 on it. Kyle can collect the difference from Lois, for although her qualified indorsement saves Lois from liability to Kyle on the indorsement contract, she is liable to him for breach of warranty. If Lois had not qualified her indorsement, Kyle would be able to recover against her on the basis of either warranty or the indorsement contract.

### No Defenses

The fourth transferor's warranty imposed by the Code is that the instrument is not subject to a defense or claim in recoupment of any party. Section 3–416(a)(4). A claim in recoupment, as discussed in Chapter 28, is a counterclaim that arose from the transaction that gave rise to the instrument. Suppose that Madeline, a minor and a resident of a State where minors' contracts for non-necessaries are voidable, makes a note payable to bearer in payment of a motorcycle. Pierce, the first holder, negotiates it to Iola by mere delivery. Iola indorses it and negotiates it to Justin, who unqualifiedly indorses it to Hector. All negotiations are made for consideration. Because of Madeline's minority (a real defense), Hector cannot recover upon the instrument against Madeline. Hector therefore recovers against Justin or Iola on either the breach of warranty that no valid defenses exist to the instrument or the indorsement contract. Justin, if he is forced to pay Hector, can in turn recover against Iola on either a breach of warranty or the indorsement contract. Justin, however, cannot recover against Pierce. Pierce is not liable to Justin as an indorser because he did not indorse the instrument. Although Pierce, as a transferor, warrants that there are no defenses good against him, this warranty extends only to his immediate transferee, Iola. Therefore, Justin cannot hold Pierce liable. Iola, however, can recover from Pierce on a breach of warranty.

### No Knowledge of Insolvency

Any person who transfers a negotiable instrument warrants that he has no knowledge of any insolvency proceedings instituted with respect to the maker, acceptor, or drawer of an unaccepted instrument. Section 3–416(a)(5). Insolvency proceedings include bankruptcy and "any assignment for the benefit of creditors or other proceedings intended to liquidate or rehabilitate the estate of the person involved." Section 1–201(22). Thus, if Marcia makes a note payable to bearer, and the first holder, Taylor, negotiates it for consideration without indorsement to Ursula, who then negotiates it for consideration by qualified indorsement to Valerie, both Taylor and Ursula warrant that they do not know that Marcia is in bankruptcy. Valerie could not hold Taylor liable for breach of warranty, however, because Taylor's warranty runs only in favor of her immediate transferee, Ursula, because Taylor transferred the instrument without indorsement. If Valerie could hold Ursula liable on her warranty, Ursula could thereupon hold Taylor, her immediate transferor, liable.

◆ *See Figure 29–2*

## WARRANTIES ON PRESENTMENT

Any party who pays or accepts an instrument must do so in strict compliance with the orders that instrument contains. For example, the payment or acceptance must be made to a person entitled to receive payment or acceptance, the amount paid or accepted must be the correct amount, and the instrument must be genuine and unaltered. If the payment or acceptance is incorrect, the payor or acceptor potentially will incur a loss. In the case of a note, a maker who pays the wrong person will not be discharged from his obligation to pay the correct person. If the maker pays too much, the excess comes out of his pocket. If a drawee pays the wrong person, he generally cannot charge the drawer's account; if he pays too much, he generally cannot charge the drawer's account for the excess. Indorsers who pay an instrument may make similar incorrect payments.

After paying or accepting an instrument to the wrong person, for the wrong amount, or in some other incorrect way, does the person who incorrectly paid or accepted have any recourse against the person who received the payment or acceptance? Section 3–418 addresses this critical question by providing that "if an instrument has

**FIGURE 29–2**  Liability on Transfer

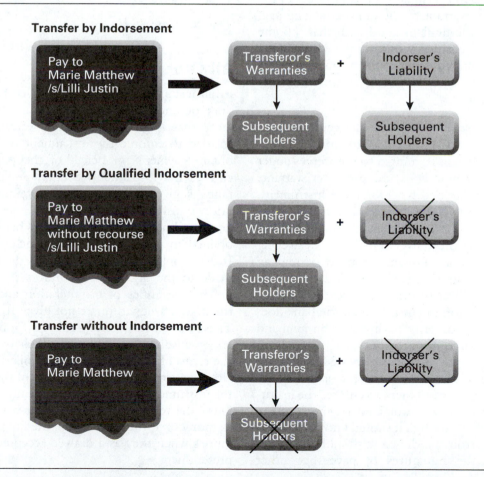

been paid or accepted by mistake . . . the person paying or accepting may, to the extent permitted by the law governing mistake and restitution, (i) recover the payment from the person to whom or for whose benefit payment was made or (ii) in the case of acceptance, may revoke the acceptance." Section 3–418(b). Nevertheless, this payment or acceptance is *final* and may not be asserted against a person who took the instrument in good faith and for value or who in good faith changed position in reliance on the payment or acceptance, unless there has been a breach of the implied **warranties on presentment.** Section 3–418(c). What warranties are given by presenters depend upon who is the payor or acceptor. The greatest protection is given to drawees of unaccepted drafts, while all other payors receive significantly less protection.

## Drawees of Unaccepted Drafts

A drawee of an unaccepted draft (including uncertified checks), who pays or accepts in good faith, receives a presentment warranty from the person obtaining payment or acceptance and from all prior transferors of the draft. These parties warrant to the drawee making payment or accepting the draft in good faith that: (1) the warrantor is a person entitled to enforce the draft, (2) the draft has not been altered, and (3) the warrantor has no knowledge that the drawer's signature is unauthorized. Section 3–417(a).

***Entitled to Enforce*** Presenters of unaccepted checks give the same warranty of entitlement to enforce to persons who pay or accept as is granted to transferees under the transferor's warranty. Thus, the presenter warrants that she is a person entitled to enforce the instrument. As explained above, this warranty extends to the genuineness and completeness of the indorser's signatures but not to the signature of the drawer or maker. It is "in effect a warranty that there are no unauthorized or missing indorsements." Section 3–417, Comment 2.

For example, if Donnese draws a check to Peter or order, and Peter's indorsement is forged, the bank does not follow Donnese's order in paying such an item and therefore cannot charge her account (except in the impostor or fictitious payee situations discussed in Chapter 27). The bank, however, can recover for breach of the presenter's warranty of entitlement to enforce the instrument from the person who obtained payment of the check from the bank. Although it should know the signatures of its own customers, the bank should not be expected to know the signatures of payees or other

indorsers of checks; the bank, therefore, should not have to bear this loss.

***No Alteration*** Presenters also give a warranty of no alteration. For example, if Dolores makes a check payable to Porter's order in the amount of $30, and the amount is fraudulently raised to $30,000, the drawee bank cannot charge to the drawer's account the $30,000 it pays out on the check. The drawee bank can charge the drawer's account only $30, because that is all the drawer ordered it to pay. Nonetheless, because the presenter's warranty of no alteration has been breached, the drawee bank can collect the difference from all warrantors. Section 3–417(a)(2), (b).

***Genuineness of Drawer's Signature*** Presenters lastly warrant that they have no knowledge that the signature of the drawer is unauthorized. Thus, unless the presenter has knowledge that the drawer's signature is unauthorized, the drawee bears the risk that the drawer's signature is unauthorized.

◆ *See Figure 29–3*

 *See Case 29–3*

## All Other Payors

In all instances other than a drawee of an unaccepted draft or uncertified check, the only presentment warranty that is given is that the warrantor is a person entitled to enforce the instrument or is authorized to obtain payment on behalf of the person entitled to enforce the instrument. Section 3–417(d). This warranty is given by the person obtaining payment and prior transferors and applies to the presentment of notes and accepted drafts for the benefit of any party obliged to pay the instrument, including an indorser. It also applies to presentment of dishonored drafts if made to the drawer or an indorser.

The warranties of no alteration and authenticity of the drawer's signature are not given to all other payors. These warranties are not necessary for makers and drawers because they should know their own signature and the terms of their instruments. Similarly, indorsers have already warranted the authenticity of signatures and that the instrument was not altered. Finally, acceptors should know the terms of the instrument when they accepted it; moreoever, they did receive the full presentment warranties when they as a drawee accepted the draft upon presentment.

**FIGURE 29–3** Liability Based on Warranty

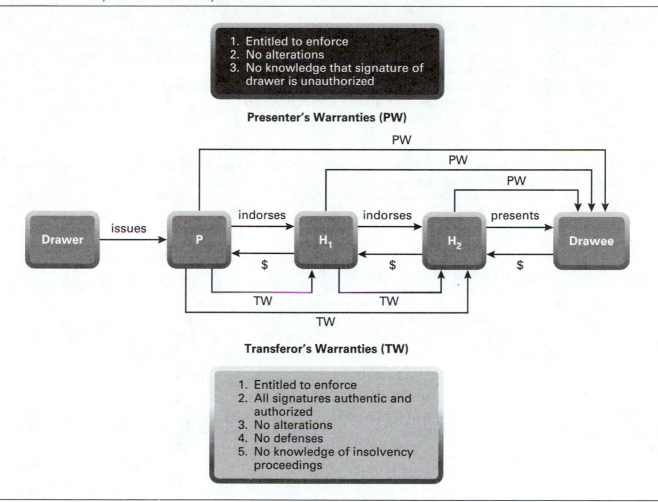

1. Entitled to enforce
2. No alterations
3. No knowledge that signature of drawer is unauthorized

**Presenter's Warranties (PW)**

**Transferor's Warranties (TW)**

1. Entitled to enforce
2. All signatures authentic and authorized
3. No alterations
4. No defenses
5. No knowledge of insolvency proceedings

 # Chapter Summary

## Contractual Liability

| General Principles | **Liability on the Instrument** no person has contractual liability on an instrument unless her signature appears on it<br>**Signature** a signature may be made by the individual herself or by her authorized agent<br>• *Authorized Signatures* an agent who executes a negotiable instrument on behalf of his principal is liable if the instrument is executed properly and as authorized<br>• *Unauthorized Signatures* include forgeries and signatures made by an agent without proper power; are generally not binding on the person whose name appears on the instrument but are binding on the unauthorized signer |
|---|---|

| **Liability of Primary Parties** | **Primary Liability** absolute obligation to pay a negotiable instrument<br>**Makers** the maker guarantees that he will pay the note according to its original terms<br>**Acceptors** a drawee has no liability on the instrument until she accepts it; she then becomes primarily liable<br>• *Acceptance* a drawee's signed engagement to honor the instrument<br>• *Certification* acceptance of a check by a bank |
|---|---|

| **Liability of Secondary Parties** | **Secondary (Conditional) Liability** obligation to pay a negotiable instrument that is subject to conditions precedent<br>**Indorsers and Drawers** if the instrument is not paid by a primary party and if the conditions precedent to the liability of secondary parties are satisfied, indorsers and drawers are secondarily (conditionally) liable unless they have disclaimed their liability or have a valid defense to the instrument<br>**Effect of Acceptance** when a draft is accepted by a bank the drawer and all prior indorsers are discharged from contractual liability<br>**Disclaimer by Secondary Parties** a drawer (except of a check) or indorser may disclaim liability by a qualified drawing or indorsing ("without recourse")<br>**Conditions Precedent to Liability**<br>• *Drawer* liability is generally only contingent upon dishonor and does not require notice<br>• *Indorser* liability is contingent upon dishonor and notice of dishonor |
|---|---|

| **Liability for Conversion** | **Tort Liability** conversion occurs (1) when a drawee refuses to return a draft that was presented for acceptance, (2) when any person refuses to return an instrument after he dishonors it, or (3) when an instrument is paid on a forged indorsement |
|---|---|

| **Termination of Liability** | **Effect of Discharge** potential liability of parties to the instrument is terminated<br>**Discharge**<br>• *Performance*<br>• *Tender of Payment* for interest, costs, and attorney's fees<br>• *Cancellation*<br>• *Renunciation* |
|---|---|

# Liability Based on Warranty

| **Warranties on Transfer** | **Parties**<br>• *Warrantor* any person who transfers an instrument and receives consideration gives the transferor's warranties<br>• *Beneficiary* if the transfer is by delivery, the warranties run only to the immediate transferee; if the transfer is by indorsement, the warranties run to any subsequent holder who takes the instrument in good faith<br>**Warranties**<br>• *Entitled to Enforce*<br>• *All Signatures Are Authentic and Authorized* |
|---|---|

- *No Alteration*
- *No Defenses*
- *No Knowledge of Insolvency*

| **Warranties on Presentment** | **Parties**<br>• *Warrantor* all people who obtain payment or acceptance of an instrument as well as all prior tranferors give the presenter's warranties<br>• *Beneficiary* the presenter's warranties run to any person who in good faith pays or accepts an instrument<br>**Warranties**<br>• *Entitled to Enforce*<br>• *No Alteration*<br>• *Genuineness of Drawer's Signature* |
| --- | --- |

 # Cases

## CASE 29–1
## Signature
### *COHEN v. DISNER*
California Court of Appeal, Second Appellate District, 1995
36 Cal. App. 4th 855, 42 Cal. Rptr. 2d 782, 27 U.C.C. Rep. Serv. 2d 540

ORTEGA, J.

Civil Code § 1719, subdivision (a) provides in part that any person who draws a check that is dishonored due to insufficient funds shall be liable to the payee for the amount owing upon the check and treble damages of at least $100, not to exceed $500.

In this § 1719 action, we conclude the [drawer] of a dishonored check may raise defenses under the Uniform Commercial Code ([UCC Revised 3] "UCC") to establish that the check is unenforceable. We affirm the summary judgment for defendants.

## Background

Attorney Eliot Disner was sued after serving as an intermediary for his clients, Irvin and Dorothea Kipnes, by tendering a check for a portion of the $961,000 settlement the Kipneses owed to Sidney and Lynne Cohen.

The Kipneses had made an initial $300,000 settlement payment to the Cohens on March 5, 1993, and their second payment of $100,100 was due on March 9, 1993.

Under the settlement agreement, a missed payment would entitle the Cohens to enter judgment against the Kipneses for $1.3 million less any partial payments.

The Kipneses gave Disner checks totalling $100,100 which he deposited into his professional corporation's client trust account on March 9, 1993. After confirming with the Kipneses' bank that their account held sufficient funds, Disner wrote and delivered a trust account check for $100,100 to the Cohens' attorney, with this note: "Please find $100,100 in settlement (partial) of *Cohen v. Kipnes*, et al[.] Per our agreement, delivery to you constitutes timely delivery to your clients." Also typed on the check was a notation identifying the underlying lawsuit.

Without Disner's knowledge, the Kipneses stopped payment on their checks to him, leaving him with insufficient funds in the trust account to cover the check to the Cohens. The trust account check bounced; the Kipneses declared bankruptcy; and the Cohens served Disner and his professional corporation (jointly, Disner) with the statutory demand for payment under

§ 1719. The Cohens sought the amount written on the check plus the $500 statutory penalty authorized under § 1719.

Both sides moved for summary judgment. The trial court denied the Cohens' motion and entered summary judgment for Disner, reasoning he is not liable on the check because he was a mere conduit or agent for transferring money from the Kipneses to the Cohens. The Cohens appealed from the judgment.

## Discussion

* * *

The Cohens do not dispute on appeal that Disner was a mere conduit or agent for transferring funds. They contend his representative status and motivations for transferring the funds are irrelevant. According to the Cohens, § 1719 imposes strict liability against the [drawer] of a check drawn on an account lacking sufficient funds.

Their contention of strict liability is based on legislative omission. While the UCC permits the [drawer] of a dishonored check to prove that he signed in a representative capacity and that the holder in due course took the check with notice of the representative's lack of liability (UCC, § 3–402, subd. (b)(2), sometimes hereinafter referred to as the "representative capacity" defense), § 1719 does not mention this defense.

* * *

The UCC recognizes the complexity of commercial transactions beyond the few good faith disputes mentioned in § 1719. For example, as against a holder in due course, the UCC permits the [drawer] to assert defenses of infancy, duress, lack of legal capacity, illegality of the contract, fraud in the inducement, or discharge in bankruptcy proceedings. (UCC, § 3–305, subd. (a)) If we were to accept the Cohens' position that § 1719 is a strict liability statute (with the sole exception of the stop payment defense), we would create a conflict with the pre-existing law of negotiable instruments. * * *

Nothing in § 1719 affirmatively supports the Cohens' contention that the "representative capacity" and other UCC defenses were written out of § 1719. On the contrary, the express language of subdivision (a) compels us to the opposite conclusion.

* * *

By acknowledging there must be an enforceable obligation to pay, § 1719 echoes the UCC, which precludes recovery where the payee has no "right to enforce the obligation of a party to pay an instrument." (UCC, § 3–305, subd. (a).) If the [drawer] has no enforceable obligation to pay a dishonored check, there is no amount "owing upon that check" under the plain language of § 1719.

* * *

We reject the Cohens' assertion in their reply brief that the "representative capacity" defense is inapplicable here because the conditions of UCC § 3–402, subdivision (c) have not been met. That subdivision provides: "If a representative signs the name of the representative as drawer of a check without indication of the representative status and the check is payable from an account of the representative person who is identified on the check, the signer is not liable on the check if the signature is an authorized signature of the represented person."

According to the official code comment on that subdivision: "Subdivision (c) is directed at the check cases. It states that if the check identifies the represented person, the agent who signs on the signature line does not have to indicate agency status. Virtually all checks used today are in personalized form which identify the person on whose account the check is drawn. In this case, nobody is deceived into thinking that the person signing the check is meant to be liable. . . ." [Citation.]

As we understand it, the Cohens' assertion is that because UCC § 3–402, subdivision (b)(2)'s "representative capacity" defense is "subject to" subdivision (c), Disner may not be relieved of liability unless he fulfills the requirements of the subdivision (c) defense. We do not read subdivisions (b)(2) and (c) in that restrictive manner. In our view, any finding of liability under UCC § 3–402, subdivision (b)(2) is subject to subdivision (c)'s additional exception that the representative is not liable if he signed his name on a personalized check identifying the account of the represented person. Subdivision (c) expands rather than contracts the representative's defenses.

We conclude that § 1719, by its clear and unambiguous language, permits the [drawer] of a dishonored check to prove he has no enforceable obligation to pay the check.

* * *

## Disposition

We affirm the summary judgment for defendants. Defendants are awarded costs on appeal.

---

## CASE 29–2
### Drawer's Liability
## *DAVIS v. WATSON BROTHERS PLUMBING, INC.*

Court of Civil Appeals of Texas, Dallas, 1981
615 S.W.2d 844

**AKIN, J.**

Defendant was the drawer of a check for $152.38 payable to its employee Arnett Lee. Lee, in turn, endorsed the check over to plaintiff, who operated a liquor store. After Lee endorsed the check to plaintiff and after plaintiff had placed cash on the counter, Lee stated that he wanted to buy a six-pack of beer and a bottle of scotch. When plaintiff turned to obtain the requested merchandise, a thief grabbed approximately $110.00 of the $150.88 ($152.38 less a $1.50 check cashing fee) for which plaintiff cashed the check. Lee took the remainder of the $150.88, approximately $40.88, and notified defendant of the theft. Defendant issued Lee a second check for $152.38 and stopped payment on the first check. Plaintiff sued defendant based on the dishonor of the first check.

The county court rendered judgment for plaintiff for the $40.88 that Lee actually received from plaintiff [after the robbery]. Plaintiff, as appellant, asserts that since he proved that he was the holder of the check and since defendant failed to raise any valid defenses, defendant was liable to him for the full face value of the check, $152.38. We agree.

"Holder" is defined in *Tex. Bus. & Com. Code Ann.* [U.C.C.] § 1–201(20) as: "[A] *person who is in possession of* a document of title or *an instrument* or an investment security drawn, issued or *indorsed to him* or to his order or to bearer or *in blank.*" Under the undisputed facts, Lee, the payee endorsed the check in blank to plaintiff, who is now in possession of the check. Thus, as a matter of law, plaintiff is a "holder" under the code [U.C.C.] § 3–413(2), Revised § 3–414(b)] which sets forth the rights of a holder, [and] provides, in pertinent part, that: "The drawer engages that upon dishonor of the draft . . . *he will pay the amount of the draft to the holder* or to any indorser who takes it up." Thus, the defendant is liable to the holder of the dishonored check unless the defendant has raised a valid defense against the holder.

The rights of a holder not in due course are subject to the defenses specified in § 3–306, [Revised § 3–305] which provides:

Unless he has the rights of a holder in due course any person takes the instrument subject to

**(1)** all valid claims to it on the part of any person; and

**(2)** all defenses of any party which would be available in an action on a simple contract; and

**(3)** *the defenses of want or failure of consideration,* nonperformance of any condition precedent, nondelivery, or delivery for a special purpose (Section 3–408); and

**(4)** the defense that he or a person through whom he holds the instrument acquired it by theft, or that payment or satisfaction to such holder would be inconsistent with the terms of a restrictive indorsement. *The claim of any third person to the instrument is not otherwise available as a defense to any party liable thereon unless the third person himself defends the action for such party.*

Defendant here asserts that it may raise want or failure of consideration in the transaction between *plaintiff and Lee,* its payee, as a defense to plaintiff's enforcement of the instrument against it. We disagree.

[U.C.C.] § 3–408 [Revised § 3–303(b), 3–305] provides, in pertinent part that: "Want or failure of consideration is a defense against any person not having the rights of a holder in due course . . ." The comments to § 3–408 provide that: "'Consideration' refers to what the obligor has received for his obligation, and is important only on the question of whether his obligation can be enforced against him." Thus, any holder can enforce the obligation of a draft against the drawer regardless of whether the holder gave anything in consideration for the draft to his endorser. The drawer can assert as a defense to enforcement of the draft want or failure of consideration only to the extent such defense lies against the payee of the draft. Thus, the fact that a holder remote to the drawer's transaction with the payee did not give full consideration for the draft is not a defense available to the drawer. [Citation.]

This is true because the drawer's sole obligation on the check is to pay it according to its tenor. Consequently, the fact that the transfer of the check by the payee to the transferee is without consideration is immaterial to the drawer's obligation and is not a defense available to the drawer against the holder. A similar conclusion was reached in [citation.] In that case the court held that a defendant maker was not the proper party to raise as a defense that the transfer of the note to the holder was void. Consequently, that court concluded that the maker could not assert the defense that the equitable ownership of the instrument was in someone other than the holder-plaintiff.

The rationale of this, and other decisions, reaching the same conclusion, is that the maker or drawer of an instrument admittedly owes the money and he should not be permitted to bring into the controversy equities of parties with which he has no connection. [Citation.] Furthermore, if the drawer or maker is permitted to assert the defense of another party such as the payee, the judgment on that issue would not be binding on the third party claimant who is not a party to the suit. [Citation.]

Because defendant here may not assert want or failure of consideration in the transaction between plaintiff and Lee, and because defendant has asserted no other defense against plaintiff, plaintiff is entitled to recover the full face value of the check under § 3–413(b) [Revised § 3–414] of the Texas Uniform Commercial Code. Accordingly, the judgment of the trial court is reversed and judgment is rendered that plaintiff recover judgment against defendant for $152.38 and all costs.

---

## CASE 29–3
### Warranties on Presentment
## *TRAVELERS INDEMNITY CO. v. STEDMAN*
United States District Court, ED Pa, 1995
895 F. Supp. 742

REED, J.

Currently pending before this court is the motion by defendant Main Line Federal Savings Bank ("Main Line") for judgment on the pleadings . . . or for partial summary judgment . . . on the crossclaim filed by codefendant Merrill, Lynch, Pierce, Fenner & Smith ("Merrill Lynch"). In dispute is the ultimate liability for pecuniary losses incurred by plaintiff The Travelers Indemnity Company ("Travelers") when defendants Main Line, as depositary and collecting bank, and Merrill Lynch, as drawee bank, honored seventeen checks unlawfully drawn on the account of the American Lung Association by codefendant Nancy Stedman. * * * In addition, Merrill Lynch advanced a claim for breach of presentment warranties against Main Line pursuant to [UCC] § 3–417. The instant motion by Main Line seeks judgment in its favor with regard to twelve of the seventeen checks. Merrill Lynch concedes that Main Line is entitled to judgment on the pleadings with regard to the six checks that were neither deposited nor cashed at Main Line, but Merrill Lynch argues that Main Line is not entitled to judgment on the pleadings with regard to the other six checks at issue.

## I. Factual Background and Procedural History

In November 1988, plaintiff Travelers issued a comprehensive crime insurance policy to the American Lung Association (the "ALA"), thereby insuring the ALA against financial losses due to employee fraud or dishonesty. Shortly thereafter, in October of 1989, the ALA hired defendant Nancy Stedman as the Director of Bureau Affairs. In her capacity as Director of Bureau Affairs, Stedman possessed the authority to draw checks on a Working Capital Management Account (the "WCMA"), an account established by the ALA with defendant Merrill Lynch for the sole purpose of paying the ALA's operating expenses. * * *

From approximately August 12, 1990 to March 13, 1992, Stedman embarked on a scheme of defalcation, misappropriating $129,624.23 of ALA funds from the WCMA. The ALA finally discovered the scheme in late April, 1992, and subsequently received compensation for its losses under the terms of its insurance policy with Travelers. Asserting its rights as the subrogee of the ALA, Travelers filed this civil action on July 9, 1993 against defendants Nancy Stedman, Merrill Lynch, and Main Line.

Merrill Lynch and Main Line agree that the seventeen checks misappropriated by Stedman can be divided into three groups based on the combination of forged or unauthorized [drawer] and payee signatures. Group One is comprised of six checks totalling $5,343.00, each bearing a forged cosignatory's signature, or [co-drawer's] signature, and forged indorsements. Main Line and Merrill Lynch agree that the Group One checks were neither deposited at nor cashed by defendant Main Line. * * *

Group Two is comprised of six checks totalling $85,241.01, each payable to either "American Lung Association" or "American Lung Association/Stedman." Each Group Two check bore two forged [drawer's] signatures and at least one forged indorsement. All Group Two checks were accepted for deposit into the personal checking account of Stedman by Main Line, and subsequently presented to and honored by Merrill Lynch. Finally, Group Three is comprised of five checks totalling $39,030.22, each payable to "American Lung Association" and bearing only a forged indorsement. * * * The Group Three checks are not the subject of the instant motion.

## II. Discussion

* * *

**B. Loss Allocation Under the Uniform Commercial Code** Liability, or loss allocation, under the Uniform Commercial Code ("UCC") for honoring negotiable instruments containing forged or unauthorized signatures is governed by whether the forgery at issue is that of a [drawer's] signature or of the indorsement of a payee or holder. [Citations.] Generally, a drawee bank is strictly liable to its customer, the drawer, for payment over either a forged [drawer's] signature or a forged indorsement. [Citation.] * * * Moreover, when a drawee bank honors an instrument bearing a forged [drawer's] signature, that payment is final in favor of a holder in due course or one who has in good faith changed his position in reliance on the payment. UCC § 3–418. As a result, where the only forgery is of the signature of the [drawer] and not of the indorsement, the negligence of a holder in taking the forged instrument will not allow a drawee bank to shift liability to a prior collecting or depositary bank, unless such negligence amounts to a lack of good faith, or unless the payee bank returns the instrument or sends notice of dishonor within the limited time provided by § 4–301 of the UCC. [Citation.] But where the only forged signature is an indorsement, the drawee normally may pass liability back through the collection chain to the depositary or collecting bank, or to the forger herself if she is available, by a claim for breach of presentment warranties. [Citation.]

Regrettably, the drafters of the UCC failed to address the allocation of liability for honoring instruments containing *both* a forged [drawer's] signature and a forged indorsement, so called "double forgeries." [Citation.]

Nor have the state courts of Pennsylvania addressed this issue. Based on a thorough examination of the rationales behind the allocation of liability in "single forgery" cases, however, the Court of Appeals for the Fifth Circuit concluded that double forgeries should be treated as though only containing forged [drawer's] signatures. [Citations.] * * * Therefore, this court concludes that under Pennsylvania's adoption of the UCC, checks containing both a forged [drawer's] signature and a forged indorsement should be treated, for loss allocation purposes, as though bearing only a forged [drawer's] signature. As a result, the negligence of a holder in taking a double forgery will not allow a drawee bank, such as Merrill Lynch, to shift liability to a prior collecting or depositary bank, such as Main Line, unless such negligence amounts to a lack of good faith, or unless the drawee bank returns the instrument or sends notice of dishonor within the limited time provided by § 4–301 of the Pennsylvania adoption of the UCC. [Citation.]

* * *

**3. Breach of Presentment Warranties** The final count of the crossclaim by Merrill Lynch is a claim for an alleged breach of presentment warranties under [UCC] § 3–417. As the court illustrated above, the loss allocation rules of the UCC permit a payee bank to shift liability to a depositary bank via a claim for breach of presentment warranties if, and only if, the checks at issue contain only forged indorsements. Should the checks in fact also bear forged [drawer's] signatures, then a depositary or collecting bank is immunized from liability for having honored such checks unless the depositary or collecting bank failed to meet the requirements of the final payment rule codified in [UCC] § 3–418. [Citation.] Moreover, checks bearing dual forgeries are treated as though containing only forged [drawer's] signatures. Thus, because it is uncontested that all Group Two checks bear forged [drawer's] signatures, liability for honoring these checks may only be assessed under the loss allocation rules relevant to checks bearing only forged [drawer's] signatures. See discussion supra part II.B. In other words, Merrill Lynch is precluded by the operation of law from asserting a claim for breach of presentment warranties under the loss allocation scheme of the UCC. As a matter of law, therefore, Merrill Lynch can prove no set of facts in support of this claim that would entitle it to the relief demanded, and this court will accordingly also grant judgment on the pleadings to Main Line on the claim for breach of presentment warranties as it relates to the Group Two checks.

# Questions

**1.** Discuss contractual liability, warranty liability, and liability for conversion.

**2.** Discuss the liability of makers, acceptors, drawees, drawers, indorsers, and accommodation parties.

**3.** Discuss the conditions precedent to the liability of secondary parties.

**4.** Discuss the methods by which liability on an instrument may be terminated.

**5.** Compare the warranties on transfer with the warranties on presentment.

# Problems

**1.**

| $900.00 | Smalltown, Illinois |
|---|---|
| **Maker** | November 15, 1999 |

The undersigned promises to pay to the order of John Doe, Nine Hundred Dollars with interest from date of note. Payment to be made in five monthly installments of One Hundred Eighty Dollars, plus accrued interest beginning on December 1, 1999. In the event of default in the payment of any installment or interest on installment date, the holder of this instrument may declare the entire obligation due and owing and proceed forthwith to collect the balance due on this instrument.

(Signed) Acton, agent

On December 18, no payment having been made on the note, Doe indorsed and delivered the instrument to Todd to secure a preexisting debt in the amount of $800.

On January 18, 2000, Todd brought an action against Acton and Phi Corporation, Acton's principal, to collect the full amount of the instrument with interest. Acton defended on the basis that he signed the instrument in a representative capacity and that Doe had failed to deliver the consideration for which the instrument had been issued. Phi Corporation defended on the basis that it did not sign the instrument and that its name does not appear on the instrument.

For what amount, if any, are Acton and Phi Corporation liable?

**2.** While employed as a night security guard at the place of business of A.B. Cate Trucking Company, Fred Fain observed that the office safe had been left unlocked. It contained fifty payroll checks, which were ready for distribution to employees two days later. The checks had all been signed by the sole proprietor, Cate. Fain removed five of these checks and two blank checks which were also in the safe. Fain forged the indorsements of the payees on the five payroll checks and cashed them at local supermarkets. He then filled out one of the blank checks, making himself payee, and forged Cate's signature as drawer. After cashing that check at a supermarket, Fain departed by airplane to Jamaica. The six checks were promptly presented for payment to the drawee bank, the Bank of Emanon, which paid each one. Shortly thereafter, Cate learned about the missing payroll checks and forgeries and demanded that the Bank of Emanon credit his account with the amount of the six checks.

Must the Bank comply with Cate's demand? What are the Bank's rights, if any, against the supermarkets? You may assume that the supermarkets cashed all of the checks in good faith.

**3.** A negotiable promissory note executed and delivered by B to C passed in due course to and was indorsed in blank by C, D, E, and F. G, the present holder, strikes out D's indorsement. What is the liability of D on her indorsement?

**4.** On June 15, 1994, Justin, for consideration, executed a negotiable promissory note for $10,000, payable to Reneé on or before June 15, 1999. Justin subsequently suffered financial reverses. In January of 1999, Reneé on two occasions told Justin that she knew he was having a difficult time; that she, Reneé, did not need the money; and that the debt should be considered completely canceled with no other act or payment being required. These conversations were witnessed by three persons, including Larry. On March 15, 1999, Reneé changed her mind and indorsed the note for value to Larry. The note was not paid by June 15, 1999, and Larry sued Justin for the amount of the note. Justin defended upon the ground that Reneé had canceled the debt and renounced all rights against Justin and that Larry had notice of this fact. Decision?

**5.** Tate and Fitch were longtime friends. Tate was a man of considerable means; Fitch had encountered financial difficulties. To bolster his failing business, Fitch desired to borrow $6,000 from Farmers Bank of Erehwon. To accomplish this, he persuaded Tate to aid him in the making of a promissory note by which it would appear that Tate had the responsibility of maker, but with Fitch's agreeing to pay the instrument when due. Accordingly, they executed the following instrument:

December 1, 1999

Thirty days after date and for value received, I promise to pay to the order of Frank Fitch the sum of $6,600.

/s/ Timothy Tate

On the back of the note, Fitch indorsed, "Pay to the order of Farmers Bank of Erehwon /s/ Frank Fitch" and delivered it to the bank in exchange for $6,000.

When the note was not paid at maturity, the bank, without first demanding payment by Fitch, brought an action on the note against Tate. (a) Decision? (b) If Tate voluntarily pays the note to the bank, may he then recover on the note against Fitch, who appears as an indorser?

6.   Alpha orally appointed Omega as his agent to find and purchase for him a 1930 Dodge automobile in good condition, and Omega located such a car. Its owner, Roe, agreed to sell and deliver the car on January 10, 1999, for $9,000. To evidence the purchase price, Omega mailed to Roe the following instrument:

                                                    December 1, 1998
$9,000.00
We promise to pay to the order of bearer Nine Thousand Dollars with interest from date of this instrument on or before January 10, 1999. This note is given in consideration of John Roe's transferring title to and possession of his 1930 Dodge automobile.
                                            (Signed) Omega, agent


Smith stole the note from Roe's mailbox, indorsed Roe's name on the note, and promptly discounted it with Sunset Bank for $8,700. Not having received the note, Roe sold the car to a third party. On January 10, the bank, having discovered all the facts, demanded payment of the note from Alpha and Omega. Both refused payment.

What are Sunset Bank's rights with regard to Omega? Its rights with regard to Roe and Smith?

7.   In payment of the purchase price of a used motorboat that had been fraudulently misrepresented, Young signed and delivered to Armstrong his negotiable note in the amount of $2,000 due October 1, with Selby as an accommodation comaker. Young intended to use the boat for his fishing business. Armstrong indorsed the note in blank preparatory to discounting it. Tillman stole the note from Armstrong and delivered it to McGowan on July 1 in payment of a past-due debt in the amount of $600 that he owed to McGowan, with McGowan making up the difference by giving Tillman his check for $800 and an oral promise to pay Tillman an additional $600 on October 1.

When McGowan demanded payment of the note on December 1, both Young and Selby refused to pay because the note had not been presented for payment on its due date and because Armstrong had fraudulently misrepresented the motorboat for which the note had been executed.

What are McGowan's rights, if any, against Young, Selby, Tillman, and Armstrong, respectively?

8.   On July 1, Anderson sold D'Aveni, a jeweler, a necklace containing imitation gems, which Anderson fraudulently represented to be diamonds. In payment for the necklace, D'Aveni executed and delivered to Anderson her promissory note for $25,000 dated July 1 and payable on December 1 to Anderson's order with interest at 12 percent per annum.

The note was thereafter successively indorsed in blank and delivered by Anderson to Bylinski, by Bylinski to Conrad, and by Conrad to Shearson, who became a holder in due course on August 10. On November 1, D'Aveni discovered Anderson's fraud and immediately notified Anderson, Bylinski, Conrad, and Shearson that she would not pay the note when it became due. Bylinski, a friend of Shearson, requested that Shearson release him from liability on the note, and Shearson, as a favor to Bylinski and for no other consideration, struck out Bylinski's indorsement.

On November 15, Shearson, who was solvent and had no creditors, indorsed the note to the order of Frederick, his father, and delivered it to Frederick as a gift. At the same time, Shearson told Frederick of D'Aveni's statement that D'Aveni would not pay the note when it became due. Frederick presented the note to D'Aveni for payment on December 1, but D'Aveni refused to pay. Thereafter, Frederick gave due notice of dishonor to Anderson, Bylinski, and Conrad.

What are Frederick's rights, if any, against Anderson, Bylinski, Conrad, and D'Aveni on the note?

9.   Saul sold goods to Bruce, warranting that the goods were of a specified quality. The goods were not of the quality warranted, however, and Saul knew this at the time of the sale. Bruce drew and delivered a check payable to Saul and drawn on Third National Bank in the amount of the purchase price. Bruce subsequently discovered the goods were faulty and stopped payment on the check. Saul brings a suit against Bruce. Decision?

10.   R&A Concrete Contractors, Inc., executed a promissory note that identifies both R&A Concrete and Grover Roberts as its makers. On the reverse side of the note, the following appears: "X John Ament Sec. & Treas." National Bank of Georgia, the payee, now sues both R&A Concrete and Ament on the note. Decision?

11.   On August 10, 1997, Theta Electronic Laboratories, Inc., executed a promissory note to George and Marguerite Thomson. Three other individuals, Gerald Exten, Emil O'Neil, and James Hane, and their wives also indorsed the note. The note was then transferred to Hane by the Thomsons on November 26, 1998. Although a default occurred at this time, it was not until April 2000, eighteen months later, that Hane gave notice of the dishonor and made a demand for payment on the Extens as indorsers. Hane appeals from a judgment in favor of the Extens. Decision?

**WWW** **Internet Exercise** Compare the provisions governing liability and discharge contained in the United Nations Convention on International Bill of Exchange and International Promissory Notes with those of Article 3 of the Uniform Commercial Code.

# Bank Deposits, Collections, and Funds Transfers

In today's society, most goods and services are bought and sold without a physical transfer of "money." Credit cards, charge accounts, and various deferred payment plans have made cash sales increasingly rare. But even credit sales must ultimately be settled—when they are, payment is usually made by check rather than with cash. If the parties to a sales transaction happen to have accounts at the same bank, a transfer of credit is easily accomplished. In the vast majority of cases, however, the parties do business at different banks. Then the buyer's check must journey from the seller-payee's bank (the depositary bank), where the check is deposited by the seller for credit to his account, to the buyer-drawer's bank (the payor bank) for payment. In this collection process, the check frequently passes through one or more other banks (intermediary banks), each of which must accurately record its passing, before it may be collected. Our banking system has developed a network to handle the collection of checks and other instruments.

In recent years, the amount of payment made by electronic funds transfers has increased at an astounding rate. The dollar volume of commercial payments made by wire transfer far exceeds the dollar amount made by checks or credit cards. In addition, electronic funds transfers have become exceedingly popular with consumers. Consumer electronic funds transfers are covered by the Federal Electronic Fund Transfer Act; nonconsumer (wholesale) electronic transfers are covered by Article 4A of the Uniform Commercial Code (UCC).

This chapter will cover both the bank deposit–collection system and electronic funds transfers.

## BANK DEPOSITS AND COLLECTIONS

Article 4 of the UCC, entitled "Bank Deposits and Collections," provides the principal rules governing the bank collection process. As items in the bank collection process are essentially those covered by Article 3, "Commercial Paper," and to a lesser extent by Article 8, "Investment Securities," these Articles often apply to a bank collection problem. In addition, Articles 3 and 4 are supplemented and, at times, preempted by Federal law: the Expedited Funds Availability Act and its implementing Federal Reserve Regulation (Regulation CC). This section will cover the collection of an item through the banking system and the relationship between the payor bank and its customer.

## COLLECTION OF ITEMS

When a person deposits a check in his bank (the **depositary bank**), the bank credits his account by the amount of the check. This initial crediting is **provisional.** Normally, a bank does not permit a customer to draw funds against a provisional credit; by permitting its customer to thus draw, the bank will have given *value* and, provided it meets the other requirements, will be a holder in due course. Under the customer's contract with his bank, the bank is obligated to make a reasonable effort to obtain payment of all checks deposited for collection. When the amount of the check has been collected from the payor bank (the drawee), the credit becomes a **final credit**.

The Competitive Equality Banking Act of 1987 has expedited the availability of funds by establishing maximum time periods for which a bank may hold (and thereby deny a customer access to the funds represented by) various types of instruments. Under the Act, (1) cash deposits, wire transfers, government checks, the first $100 of a day's check deposits, cashier's checks, and checks deposited in one branch of a depositary institution and drawn on the same or another branch of the same institution must clear by the next business day; (2) local checks must clear within one intervening business day;

and (3) nonlocal checks must clear in no more than four intervening business days.

If the payor bank (the drawee bank) does not pay the check for some reason, such as a stop payment order or insufficient funds in the drawer's account, the depositary bank reverses the provisional credit to the account, debits his account for that amount, and returns the check to him with a statement of the reason for nonpayment. If, in the meantime, the customer has been permitted to draw against the provisional credit, the bank may recover the payment from him.

In some cases, the bank involved is both the depositary bank and the payor bank. In most cases, however, the depositary and payor banks are different, in which event the bank collection aspects of Article 4 come into play. Where the depositary and payor banks differ, it is necessary for the item to pass from one to the other, either directly through a clearinghouse or through one or more **intermediary banks** (banks, other than the depositary payor bank, that are involved in the collection process, such as one of the twelve Federal Reserve Banks). A **clearinghouse** is an association, composed of banks or other payors, whose members settle accounts with each other on a daily basis. Each member of the clearinghouse forwards all deposited checks drawn on other members and receives from the clearinghouse all checks drawn on it. Balances are adjusted and settled each day.

◆ *See Figure 30–1*

## Collecting Banks

A **collecting bank** is any bank, other than the payor bank, handling an item for payment. In the usual situation, where the depositary and payor banks are different, the depositary bank gives a provisional credit to its customer, transfers the item to the next bank in the chain, and receives a provisional credit or "settlement" from it; the process repeats until the item reaches the payor bank, which gives a provisional settlement to its transferor. When the item is paid, all the provisional settlements given by the respective banks in the chain become final, and the particular transaction has been completed. Because this procedure simplifies bookkeeping by necessitating only one entry if the item is paid, no adjustment is necessary on the books of any of the banks involved.

If, however, the payor bank does not pay the check, it returns the item, and each intermediary or collecting

FIGURE 30–1  Bank Collections

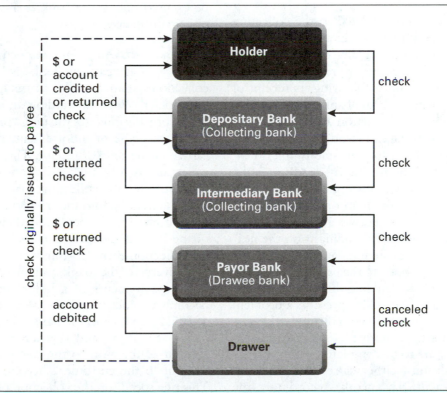

bank reverses the provisional settlement or credit it previously gave to its forwarding bank. Ultimately, the depositary bank will charge (remove the provisional credit from) the account of the customer who deposited the item. The customer must then seek recovery from the indorsers or the drawer.

A collecting bank is an **agent** or subagent of the owner of the item until the settlement becomes final. Section 4–201(a). Unless otherwise provided, any credit given for the item initially is provisional. Once settled, the agency relationship changes to one of **debtor-creditor.** The effects of this agency rule are that the risk of loss remains with the owner and any chargebacks go to her, not to the collecting bank.

All collecting banks have certain responsibilities and duties in collecting checks and other items. These will now be discussed.

*Duty of Care* A collecting bank must exercise ordinary care in handling an item transferred to it for collection. Section 4–202(a). The steps it takes in presenting an item or sending it for presentment are of particular importance. It must act within a reasonable time after receipt of the item and must choose a reasonable method of forwarding the item for presentment. It also is responsible for using care in routing and in selecting intermediary banks or other agents.

*Duty to Act Timely* Closely related to the collecting bank's duty of care is its duty to act in a timely manner. A collecting bank acts timely in any event if it takes proper action, such as forwarding or presenting an item before the "midnight deadline" following its receipt of the item, notice, or payment. If the bank adheres to this standard, the timeliness of its action cannot be challenged; should it, however, take a reasonably longer time, the bank bears the burden of proof in establishing timeliness. Section 4–202(b). The **midnight deadline** is the midnight of the banking day following the banking day on which the bank received the item or notice. Section 4–104(a)(10). Thus, if a bank receives a check on Monday, it must take proper action by midnight on the next banking day, or Tuesday. A banking day means the part of a day on which a bank is open to the public for carrying on substantially all of its banking functions. Section 4–104(a)(3). The midnight deadline presents a problem because it takes time to process an item through a bank—whether it be the depositary, intermediary, or payor bank. If a day's transactions are to be completed without overtime work, the bank must either close early or fix an earlier cutoff time for the day's work. Accordingly, the

Code provides that for the purpose of allowing time to process items, prove balances, and make the bookkeeping entries necessary to determine its position for the day, a bank may fix an afternoon hour of 2:00 PM or later as a cutoff point for handling money and items and for making entries on its books. Section 4–108. Items received after the cutoff hour fixed as the close of the banking day are considered to have been received at the opening of the next banking day, and the time for taking action and for determining the bank's midnight deadline begins to run from that point.

Recognizing that everyone involved will be greatly inconvenienced if an item is not paid, Section 4–109 provides that unless otherwise instructed, a collecting bank in a good faith effort to secure payment may, in the case of a specific item drawn on a payor other than a bank, waive, modify, or extend the time limits, but not in excess of two additional banking days. This extension may be made without the approval of the parties involved and without discharging drawers or indorsers. This section does not apply to checks and other drafts drawn on a bank. The Code also authorizes delay when communications or computer facilities are interrupted as a result of blizzard, flood, hurricane, or other disaster; the suspension of payments by another bank; war; emergency conditions; failure of equipment; or other circumstances beyond the bank's control. Nevertheless, such delay will be excused only if the bank exercises such diligence as the circumstances require.

*Indorsements* An item restrictively indorsed with words such as "pay any bank" is locked into the bank collection system, and only a bank may acquire the rights of a holder. When forwarding an item for collection, a bank normally indorses the item "pay any bank," regardless of the type of indorsement, if any, that the item carried at the time of receipt. This serves to protect the collecting bank by making it impossible for the item to stray from regular collection channels.

If the item had no indorsement when the depositary bank received it, the bank nonetheless becomes a holder of the item at the time it takes possession of the item for collection if the customer was a holder at the time of delivery to the bank and, if the bank satisfies the other requirements of a holder in due course, it will become a holder in due course in its own right. Section 4–205(1). In return, the bank warrants to the collecting banks, the payor, and the drawer that it has paid the amount of the item to the customer or deposited that amount to the customer's account. Section 4–205(2). This rule speeds up the collection process by eliminating the necessity of returning checks for indorsement when the depositary bank knows they came from its customers.

*Warranties* Customers and collecting banks give substantially the same warranties as those given by parties under Article 3 upon presentment and transfer, which were discussed in Chapter 29. In addition, under Article 4 customers and collecting banks may give encoding warranties. Each customer or collecting bank who transfers an item and receives a settlement or other consideration warrants to his transferee and any subsequent collecting bank that (1) he is a person entitled to enforce the item; (2) *all* signatures are authentic and authorized; (3) the item has not been altered; (4) he is not subject to any defense or claim in recoupment; and (5) he has no knowledge of any insolvency proceeding involving the maker or acceptor or the drawer of an unaccepted draft. Section 4–207(a). Moreover, each customer or collecting bank who obtains payment or acceptance from a drawee on a draft as well as each prior transferor warrants to the drawee who pays or accepts the draft in good faith that (1) she is a person entitled to enforce the draft; (2) the item has not been altered; and (3) she has no knowledge that the signature of the drawer is unauthorized. Section 4–208.

Processing of checks is now done by Magnetic Ink Character Recognition (MICR). When a check is deposited, the depositary bank magnetically encodes the check with the amount of the check (all checks are pre-encoded with the drawer's account number and the designation of the drawee bank), after which the processing occurs automatically, without further human involvement. Despite its efficiency, the magnetic encoding of checks has created several problems. The first is the problem a bank encounters when paying a postdated instrument prior to its date. The Revision changes prior law by providing that the drawee may debit the drawer's account, unless the drawer timely informs the drawee that the check is postdated. Section 4–401(c). A second difficulty arises when a depositing bank or its customer who encodes her own checks miscodes a check. Revised Article 4 provides that such an encoder **warrants** to any subsequent collecting bank and to the payor that information on a check is properly encoded. Section 4–209(a). If the encoding is done by the customer, the depositary bank also makes the warranty. Section 4–209(a).

*See Cases 30–1 and 30–2*

*Final Payment* The provisional settlements made in the collection chain are all directed toward final payment of the item by the payor bank. From this turnaround point in the collection process, the proceeds of the item begin their return flow, and provisional settlements become final. For example, a customer of the California Country State Bank may deposit a check drawn on the State of Maine Country National Bank. The check may then take a course such as follows: from the California Country State Bank to a correspondent bank in San Francisco, to the Federal Reserve Bank of San Francisco, to the Federal Reserve Bank of Boston, to the payor bank. Provisional settlements are made at each step. When the payor bank finally pays the item, the proceeds begin to flow back over the same course.

The critical question, then, is the point at which the payor bank has **paid** the item, as this not only commences the payment process but also affects questions of priority between the payment of an item and actions such as the filing of a stop payment order against it. Under the Code, *final payment* occurs when the payor bank first does any of the following: (1) pays an item in cash; (2) settles an item and does not have the right to revoke the settlement through statute, clearinghouse rule, or agreement; or (3) makes a provisional settlement and does not revoke it within the time and in the manner permitted by statute, clearinghouse rule, or agreement. Section 4–215(a).

## Payor Banks

The **payor** or drawee **bank,** under its contract of deposit with the drawer, agrees to pay to the payee or his order a check issued by the drawer, provided that the order is not countermanded and that there are sufficient funds in the drawer's account.

The tremendous increase in volume of bank collections has necessitated deferred posting procedures, whereby items are sorted and proved on the day of receipt but are not posted to customers' accounts or returned until the next banking day. The UCC not only approves such procedures but establishes specific standards to govern their application to the actions of payor banks.

When a payor bank that is not also a depositary bank receives a demand item other than for immediate payment over the counter, it must either return the item or give its transferor a provisional settlement before midnight of the banking day on which the item is received. Otherwise, the bank becomes liable to its transferor for the amount of the item, unless it has a valid defense, such as breach of a presentment warranty. Section 4–302.

If the payor bank gives the provisional settlement as required, it has until the midnight deadline to return the item or, if the item is held for protest or is otherwise unavailable for return, to send written notice of dishonor or nonpayment. Section 4–301(a). After doing this, the bank is entitled to revoke the settlement and recover any payment it has made. Should it fail to return the item or send notice before its midnight deadline, the payor bank will be accountable for the amount of the item unless it has a valid defense for its inaction.

There are innumerable reasons why a bank may dishonor an item and return it or send notice. The following situations are the most common: the drawer or maker may have no account or may have funds insufficient to cover the item; a signature on the item may be forged; or the drawer or maker may have stopped payment of the item.

If the funds in a customer's account are insufficient to pay all of the items that the bank receives on that account on any given day, the bank may charge them against the account in any order it deems convenient. The owner of the account from which the item was payable also has no basis for complaint when the bank pays one item rather than another. It is his responsibility to have enough funds on deposit to pay all of the items chargeable to his account at any time.

## RELATIONSHIP BETWEEN PAYOR BANK AND ITS CUSTOMER

The relationship between a payor bank and its checking account customer is primarily the product of their contractual arrangement. Although the parties have relatively broad latitude in establishing the terms of their agreement and in altering the provisions of the Code, a bank may not validly (1) disclaim responsibility for its lack of good faith, (2) disclaim responsibility for its failure to exercise ordinary care, or (3) limit its damages for a breach comprising such lack or failure. Section 4–103(a). The parties may by agreement, however, determine the standards by which the bank's responsibility is to be measured, if these standards are not clearly unreasonable.

### Payment of an Item

A payor bank owes a duty to its customer, the drawer, to pay checks properly drawn by him on an account having funds sufficient to cover the items. A check or draft, however, is not an assignment of the drawer's funds that are in the drawee's possession. Moreover, as

discussed in Chapter 29, the drawee is not liable on a check until it accepts the item. Section 3–408. Therefore, the *holder* of a check has no right to require the drawee bank to pay it, whether the drawer's account contains sufficient funds or not. But if a payor bank improperly refuses payment when presented with an item, it will incur a liability to the *customer* from whose account the item should have been paid. Section 4–402. If the customer has adequate funds on deposit, and there is no other valid basis for the refusal to pay, the bank is liable to its customer for damages proximately caused by the *wrongful dishonor*. Liability is limited to actual damages proved and may include damages for arrest, prosecution, or other consequential damages. Section 4–402.

When a payor bank receives an item properly payable from a customer's account but the funds in the account are insufficient to pay it, the bank may (1) dishonor the item and return it or (2) pay the item and charge its customer's account, even though the actions create an overdraft. Section 4–401(a). The item authorizes or directs the bank to make the payment and hence carries with it an enforceable implied promise to reimburse the bank. Furthermore, the customer may be liable to pay the bank a service charge for its handling of the overdraft or to pay interest on the amount of the overdraft. A customer, however, is not liable for an overdraft if the customer did not sign the item or benefit from the proceeds of the item. Section 4–401(b).

A payor bank is under no obligation to its customer to pay an uncertified check that is more than six months old. Section 4–404. This rule reflects the usual banking practice of consulting a depositor before paying a *"stale"* item (one more than six months old) on her account. The bank is not required to dishonor such an item, however; and if the bank makes payment in good faith, it may charge the amount of the item to its customers' account.

 *See Case 30–3*

### Stop Payment Orders

A check drawn on a bank is an order to pay a sum of money and an authorization to charge the amount to the drawer's account. The customer, or any person authorized to draw on the account, may countermand this order, however, by means of a **stop payment order.** Section 4–403. If the order does not come too late, the bank is bound by it. If the bank inadvertently pays a check over a valid stop order, it is *prima facie* liable to the customer, but only to the extent of the customer's loss resulting from the payment. The burden of establishing the fact and amount of loss is on the customer.

To be effective, a stop payment order must be received in time to provide the bank a reasonable opportunity to act on it. Section 4–403(a). An oral stop order is binding on the bank for only fourteen calendar days. Section 4–403(b). If the customer confirms an oral stop order in writing within the fourteen-day period, the order is effective for six months and may be renewed in writing for additional six-month periods.

The fact that a drawer has filed a stop payment order does not automatically relieve her of liability. If the bank honors the stop payment order and returns the check, the holder may bring an action against the drawer. If the holder qualifies as a holder in due course, personal defenses that the drawer might have to such an action would be of no avail.

 *See Case 30–3*

## Bank's Right to Subrogation on Improper Payment

If a payor bank pays an item over a stop payment order, after an account has been closed, or otherwise in violation of its contract with the drawer or maker, the payor bank is subrogated to (obtains) the rights of (1) any holder in due course on the item against the drawer or maker, (2) the payee or any other holder against the drawer or maker, and (3) the drawer or maker against the payee or any other holder. Section 4–407. For instance, over the drawer's stop payment order a bank pays a check presented to the bank by a holder in due course. The drawer's defense is that the check was obtained by fraud in the inducement. The drawee bank is subrogated to the rights of the holder in due course, who would not be subject to the drawer's personal defense, and thus can debit the drawer's account. Section 4–407(1). The same would be true if the presenter were the payee, against whom the drawer did not have a valid defense. Section 4–407(2).

## Disclosure Requirements

In 1992, Congress enacted the Truth in Savings Act, which requires all depositary institutions (including commercial banks, savings and loan associations, savings banks, and credit unions) to disclose in great detail to consumers the terms and conditions of their deposit accounts. The stated purpose of the Act is to allow consumers to make informed decisions regarding deposit accounts by mandating standardized disclosure of rates of interest and fees in order to facilitate meaningful comparison of different deposit products.

More specifically, the Act provides that the disclosures must be made in a clear and conspicuous writing and must be given to the consumer when an account is opened or service is provided. These disclosures must include the following: (1) the annual percentage yield (APY) and the percentage rate; (2) how variable rates are calculated and when the rates may be changed; (3) balance information (including how the balance is calculated); (4) when and how interest is calculated and credited; (5) the amount of fees that may be charged and how they are calculated; and (6) any limitation on the number or amount of withdrawals or deposits. In addition, the Act requires the depositary institution to disclose the following information with periodic statements it sends to its customers: (1) the APY earned; (2) any fees debited during the covered period; (3) the dollar amount of the interest earned during the covered period; and (4) the dates of the covered period.

## Customer's Death or Incompetence

The general rule is that death or incompetence revokes all agency agreements. Furthermore, adjudication of incompetency by a court is regarded as notice to the world of that fact. Actual notice is not required. Section 4–405 of the Code modifies these stringent rules in several ways with respect to bank deposits and collections.

First, if either a payor or collecting bank does not know that a customer has been adjudicated incompetent, the existence of such incompetence at the time an item is issued or its collection undertaken does not impair either bank's authority to accept, pay, or collect the item or to account for proceeds of its collection. The bank may pay the item without incurring any liability.

Second, neither death nor adjudication of incompetence of a customer revokes a payor or collecting bank's authority to accept, pay, or collect an item until the bank knows of the condition and has a reasonable opportunity to act on this knowledge.

Finally, even though a bank knows of the death of its customer, it may for ten days after the date of his death pay or certify checks drawn by the customer unless a person claiming an interest in the account, such as an heir, executor, or administrator, orders the bank to stop making such payments. Section 4–405(b).

## Customer's Duties

The Code imposes certain affirmative duties on bank customers and fixes time limits within which they must assert their rights. The duties arise and the time starts to run from the point at which the bank either sends or makes available to its customer a statement of account showing payment of items against the account. The statement of account will suffice provided it describes by item the number of the item, the amount, and the date of payment. The customer must exercise reasonable promptness in examining the bank statement or the items to discover whether any payment was unauthorized due to an *unauthorized signature* on or any *alteration* of an item. Section 4–406(c). Because he is not presumed to know the signatures of payees or indorsers, this duty of prompt and careful examination applies only to alterations and the customer's own signature, both of which he should be able to detect immediately. If he discovers an unauthorized signature or an alteration, he must notify the bank promptly. Section 4–406(c). A failure to fulfill these duties of prompt examination and notice precludes the customer from asserting against the bank his unauthorized signature or any alteration if the bank establishes that it suffered a loss by reason of such failure. Section 4–406(d).

Furthermore, the customer will lose his rights in a potentially more serious situation. Occasionally a forger, possibly an employee who has access to his employer's checkbook, carries out a series of transactions involving the account of the same individual. He may forge one or more checks each month until he is finally detected. The bank, noticing nothing suspicious, might pay one or more of the customer's checks bearing the false signatures before the customer detects the forgery, months or even years later. Section 4–406(d) of the Code deals with these situations by stating that once the statement and items become available to him, the customer must examine them within a reasonable period, which in no event may exceed thirty calendar days and which may, under certain circumstances, be less and notify the bank. Any instruments containing alterations or unauthorized signatures by the same wrongdoer that the bank pays during that period will be the bank's responsibility, but any paid thereafter but before the customer notifies the bank may not be asserted against it. This rule is based on the concept that the loss involved is directly traceable to the customer's negligence and that, as a result, he should stand the loss.

These rules depend, however, on the bank's exercising ordinary care in paying the items involved. If it does not, and that failure by the bank substantially contributed to the loss, the loss will be allocated between the bank and the customer based on their comparative negligence. Section 4–406(e). But whether the bank exercised due care or not, the customer must in all events report any alteration or his unauthorized signature within one year from the time the statement or items are made available to him or be barred from asserting them against the bank. Section 4–406(f). Any *unauthorized indorsement* must be asserted within three years under the Article's general Statute of Limitations provisions. Section 4–111.

Consistent with modern automated methods for processing checks, Articles 3 and 4 provide that "ordinary care" does not require a bank to examine every check if the failure to do so does not vary unreasonably from general banking usage. Section 3–103(7).

 *See Case 30–4*

# ELECTRONIC FUNDS TRANSFERS

As previously mentioned, the use of negotiable instruments for payment has transformed the United States into a virtually cashless society. The advent and technological advances of computers make it likely that in the foreseeable future electronic fund transfer systems (EFTS) will bring about a society that is virtually checkless as well. Financial institutions seek to substitute EFTS for checks for two principal reasons. The first is to eliminate the ever-increasing paperwork involved in processing the billions of checks issued annually. The second is to eliminate the "float" that a drawer of a check currently enjoys by maintaining the use of his funds during the processing period between the time at which he issues the check and final payment.

An electronic fund transfer (EFT) has been defined as "any transfer of funds, other than a transaction originated by check, draft, or similar paper instrument, which is initiated through an electronic terminal, telephonic instrument, or computer or magnetic tape so as to order, instruct or authorize a financial institution to debit or credit an account." For example, with an EFT, William in New York would be able to pay a debt he owes to Yvette in Illinois by entering into his computer an order to his bank to pay Yvette. The drawee bank would then instantly debit William's account and transfer the credit to Yvette's bank, where Yvette's account would immediately be credited in that amount. The entire transaction would be completed in minutes.

Although EFTs are still in their formative stages, their use has generated considerable confusion concerning the legal rights of customers and financial institutions. Congress provided a partial solution to these legal issues in 1978 by enacting the Electronic Fund Transfer Act (EFTA), discussed below. But significant and numerous legal problems remain. In an attempt to resolve some of these questions, the Permanent Editorial Board of the Uniform Commercial Code has promulgated Article 4A—Funds Transfer.

## TYPES OF ELECTRONIC FUNDS TRANSFERS

Although a number of new EFTs are likely to appear in the coming years, five main types of EFTs are currently in use: (1) automated teller machines, (2) point-of-sale systems, (3) direct deposit and withdrawal of funds, (4) pay-by-phone systems, and (5) wholesale electronic funds transfers.

### Automated Teller Machines

Now available throughout the country, automated teller machines (ATMs) permit customers to conduct various transactions with their bank through the use of electronic terminals. After activating an ATM with a plastic identification card and a personal identification number, or PIN, a customer can deposit and withdraw funds from her account, transfer funds between accounts, obtain cash advances, and make payments on loan accounts.

### Point-of-Sale Systems

Computerized point-of-sale (POS) systems permit consumers to transfer funds from their bank accounts to a merchant automatically. The POS machines, located within the merchant's store and activated by the consumer's identification card and code, instantaneously debit the consumer's account and credit the merchant's account.

### Direct Deposits and Withdrawals

Another type of EFT involves deposits, authorized in advance by a customer, that are made directly to his account through an electronic terminal. Examples include direct payroll deposits, deposits of Social Security payments, and deposits of pension payments. Conversely, automatic withdrawals are preauthorized electronic funds transfers from the customer's account for regular payments to some party other than the financial institution at which the funds are deposited. Automatic withdrawals to pay insurance premiums, utility bills, or automobile loan payments are common examples of this type of EFT.

### Pay-by-Phone Systems

Recently, some financial institutions have instituted a service that permits customers to pay bills by telephoning the bank's computer system and directing a transfer of funds to a designated third party. This service also permits customers to transfer funds between accounts.

### Wholesale Electronic Funds Transfers

Wholesale electronic funds transfers, commonly called wholesale wire transfers, involve the movement of funds between financial institutions, between financial institutions and businesses, and between businesses. More than one *trillion* dollars is transferred this way each business day over the two major transfer systems—the Federal Reserve wire transfer network system (Fedwire) and the New York Clearing House Interbank Payment System (CHIPS). In addition, a number of private wholesale wire systems exist among the large banks. Limited aspects of wholesale wire transfers are governed by uniform rules promulgated by the Federal Reserve, CHIPS, and the National Automated Clearing House Association.

## CONSUMER FUNDS TRANSFERS

In 1978, Congress determined that the use of electronic systems to transfer funds provided the potential for substantial benefits to consumers. Existing consumer protection legislation failed to account for the unique characteristics of such systems, however, leaving the rights and obligations of consumers and financial institutions undefined. Accordingly, Congress enacted Title IX of the Consumer Protection Act, called the Electronic Fund Transfer Act (EFTA), to "provide a basic framework establishing the rights, liabilities, and responsibilities of participants in electronic fund transfers" with primary emphasis on "the provision of individual consumer rights." Because the EFTA deals exclusively with the protection of **consumers**, it does not govern electronic transfers between financial institutions, between financial institutions and businesses, and between businesses. The act is similar in many respects to the Fair Credit Billing Act (see Chapter 42), which applies to credit card transactions. The Electronic Fund Transfer Act is administered by the Board of Governors of the Federal Reserve System, which is mandated to prescribe regulations to carry out the purposes of the act. Pursuant to this congressional mandate, the Federal Reserve has issued Regulation E.

## Disclosure

The EFTA is primarily a disclosure statute and as such requires that the terms and conditions of electronic funds transfers involving a consumer's account be disclosed in readily understandable language at the time the consumer contracts for such services. Included among the required disclosure are the consumer's liability for unauthorized transfers, the kinds of EFTs allowed, the charges for transfers or for the right to make transfers, the consumer's right to stop payment of preauthorized EFTs, the consumer's right to receive documentation of EFTs, rules concerning disclosure of information to third parties, procedures for correcting account errors, and the financial institution's liability to the consumer under the Act.

## Documentation and Periodic Statements

The Act requires the financial institution to provide the consumer with written documentation of each transfer made from an electronic terminal at the time of transfer—a receipt. The receipt must clearly state the amount involved, the date, the type of transfer, the identity of the account(s) involved, the identity of any third party involved, and the location of the terminal involved.

In addition, the financial institution must provide each consumer with a periodic statement for each account of the consumer that may be accessed by means of an EFT. The statement must describe the amount, date, and location for each transfer; the fee, if any, to be charged for the transaction; and an address and phone number for questions and information.

## Preauthorized Transfers

A preauthorized transfer from a consumer's account must be authorized in advance by the consumer in writing, and a copy of the authorization must be provided to the consumer when the transfer is made. Up to three business days before the scheduled date of the transfer, a consumer may stop payment of a preauthorized EFT by notifying the financial institution orally or in writing, though the financial institution may require the consumer to provide written confirmation of an oral notification within fourteen days.

## Error Resolution

The consumer has sixty days after the financial institution sends a periodic statement in which to notify the institution of any errors appearing on that statement. The financial institution is required to investigate alleged errors and report its findings within ten business days. If the financial institution needs more than ten days to investigate, it may take up to forty-five days, provided it recredits the consumer's account for the amount alleged to be in error. If it determines that an error did occur, it must properly correct the error. Failure to investigate in good faith makes the financial institution liable to the consumer for treble damages (three times the amount of provable damages).

## Consumer Liability

A consumer's liability for an unauthorized electronic fund transfer is limited to a maximum of $50 if the consumer notifies the financial institution within two days after he learns of the loss or theft. If the consumer does not report the loss or theft within two days, he is liable for losses up to $500. If the consumer fails to report the unauthorized use within sixty days of transmittal of a periodic statement, he is liable for losses resulting from any unauthorized EFT that appeared on the statement if the financial institution can show that the loss would not have occurred had the consumer reported the loss within sixty days.

## Liability of Financial Institution

A financial institution is liable to a consumer for all damages proximately caused by its failure to make an EFT in accordance with the terms and conditions of an account, in the correct amount, or in a timely manner when properly instructed to do so by the consumer. There are, however, exceptions to such liability. The financial institution will not be liable if

1. the consumer's account has insufficient funds through no fault of the financial institution,
2. the funds are subject to legal process,
3. the transfer would exceed an established credit limit,
4. an electronic terminal has insufficient cash, or
5. circumstances beyond the financial institution's control prevent the transfer.

The financial institution is also liable for failure to stop payment of a preauthorized transfer from a consumer's account when instructed to do so in accordance with the terms and conditions of the account.

## WHOLESALE FUNDS TRANSFERS

Article 4A, Funds Transfers, is designed to provide a statutory framework for a payment system that is not covered by existing Articles of the Uniform Commercial Code or by the Electronic Fund Transfer Act. The typical wholesale wire transfer involves sophisticated parties who desire great speed in transferring large sums of money. Article 4A has been universally adopted by the States and Territories.

Article 4A provides that the parties to a funds transfer generally may by agreement vary their rights and obligations. Moreover, funds-transfer system rules governing banks that use the system may be effective even if such rules conflict with Article 4A. Section 4A–501. Rights and obligations under Article 4A can also be changed by Federal Reserve regulations and operating circulars of Federal Reserve Banks. Section 4A–107.

### Scope of Article

Article 4A, which covers wholesale funds transfers, defines a funds transfer as a "series of transactions, beginning with the originator's payment order, made for the purpose of making payment to the beneficiary of the order. The term includes any payment order issued by the originator's bank or an intermediary bank intended to carry out the originator's payment order. A funds transfer is completed by acceptance by the beneficiary's bank of a payment order for the benefit of the beneficiary of the originator's payment order." Section 4A–104(a). The Article, therefore, covers the transfers of credit that move from an originator to a beneficiary through the banking system. If any step in the process is governed by the Electronic Fund Transfer Act, however, the entire transaction is excluded from the Article's coverage. Section 4A–108.

The following examples illustrate the coverage of the Article:

1. Johnson Co. instructs its bank, First National Bank (FNB), to pay $2 million to West Co., also a customer of FNB. FNB executes the payment order by crediting West's account with $2 million and notifying West that the credit has been made and is available.
2. Assume the same facts as those in the first example except that West's bank is Central Bank (CB). FNB will execute the payment order of Johnson Co. by issuing to CB its own payment order instructing CB to credit the account of West.
3. Assume the facts presented in the second example with the added fact that FNB does not have a correspondent relationship with CB. In this instance, FNB will have to issue its payment order to Northern Bank (NB), a bank that does have a correspondent relationship with CB, and NB will then issue its payment order to CB.

*Payment Order* A **payment order** is a sender's instruction to a receiving bank to pay, or to cause another bank to pay, a fixed or determinable amount of money to a beneficiary. Section 4A–103. The instruction may be communicated orally, electronically, or in writing. To be a payment order, the instruction must

1. contain no condition to payment other than the time of payment;
2. be sent to a receiving bank that is to be reimbursed either by debiting an account of the sender or by otherwise receiving payment from the sender; and
3. be transmitted by the sender directly to the receiving bank or indirectly through an agent, a funds-transfer system, or a communication system.

The payment order is issued when sent and, if more than one payment is to be made, each payment represents a separate payment order. Section 4A–104(b)(c). In the examples above, there is one payment order in the first example (from Johnson Co.), two in the second example (from Johnson Co. and from First National Bank), and three in the third example (from Johnson Co., from First National Bank, and from Northern Bank).

*Parties* The **originator** is either the sender of the payment order or, in a series of payment orders, the sender of the first payment order. Section 4A–104(c). A **sender** is the party who gives an instruction to the **receiving bank,** or the bank to which the sender's instruction is addressed. Section 4A–103(4). The receiving bank may be the originator's bank, an intermediary bank, or the beneficiary's bank. The **originator's bank** is either the bank that receives the original payment order or the originator if the originator is a bank. Section 4A–104(d). The **beneficiary's bank,** the last bank in the chain of a funds transfer, is the bank instructed in the payment order to credit the beneficiary's account. Section 4A–103(a)(3). The **beneficiary** is the person to be paid by the beneficiary bank. Section 4A–103(a)(2). An **intermediary bank** is any receiving bank, other than the originator's bank or the beneficiary's bank, that receives the payment order. Section 4A–104(b). Thus, in the above examples,

1. Johnson Co. is the *originator* in all three examples;
2. Johnson Co. is a *sender* in all three examples, FNB is a sender in examples 2 and 3, and NB is a sender in example 3;
3. FNB is the *receiving bank* of Johnson Co.'s payment order in all three examples; in example 2, CB is the receiving bank of FNB's payment order; and, in example 3, CB is the receiving bank of NB's payment order and NB is the receiving bank of FNB's payment order;
4. FNB is the *originator's bank* in all three examples;
5. FNB is the *beneficiary's bank* in example 1; CB is the beneficiary's bank in examples 2 and 3;
6. West is the *beneficiary* in all three examples;
7. NB is an *intermediary bank* in example 3.

See Figure 30–2 for a summary of the parties in these three examples. In some instances, the originator and the beneficiary may be the same party. For example, a corporation may wish to transfer funds from one account to another account that is in the same or a different bank.

◆ *See Figure 30–2*

***Excluded Transactions*** As previously mentioned, Section 4A–108 provides that if any part of a funds transfer is governed by the Electronic Fund Transfer Act, then the transfer is excluded from Article 4A coverage. In addition, Article 4A covers only credit transactions; it

therefore excludes debit transactions. If the person making the payment gives the instruction, the transfer is a credit transfer. If, however, the person receiving the payment gives the instruction, the transfer is a debit transfer. For example, a seller of goods obtains authority from the purchaser to debit the purchaser's account after the seller ships the goods. Article 4A does not cover this transaction because the instructions to make payment issue from the beneficiary (the seller), not from the party whose account is to be debited (the purchaser).

◆ *See Figure 30–3*

## Acceptance

Rights and obligations arise as a result of a receiving bank's acceptance of a payment order. The effect of acceptance depends upon whether the payment order was issued to the beneficiary's bank or to a receiving bank other than the beneficiary's bank.

If a receiving bank is not the beneficiary's bank, the receiving bank does not subject itself to any liability until it accepts the instrument. Acceptance by a receiving bank other than the beneficiary's bank occurs when the receiving bank executes the sender's order. Section 4A–209(a). Such execution occurs when the receiving bank "issues a payment order intended to carry out" the sender's payment order. Section 4A–301(a). When the receiving bank executes the sender's payment order, the bank is entitled to payment from the sender and can debit the sender's account. Section 4A–402(c).

**FIGURE 30–2**  Parties to a Funds Transfer

|  | Example 1 | Example 2 | Example 3 |
|---|---|---|---|
| **Originator** | Johnson Co. | Johnson Co. | Johnson Co. |
| **Sender(s)** | Johnson Co. | Johnson Co. FNB | Johnson Co. FNB NB |
| **Receiving Bank(s)** | FNB | FNB CB | FNB CB NB |
| **Originator's Bank** | FNB | FNB | FNB |
| **Beneficiary's Bank** | FNB | CB | CB |
| **Beneficiary** | West | West | West |
| **Intermediary Bank** | — | — | NB |

**FIGURE 30-3** Credit Transaction

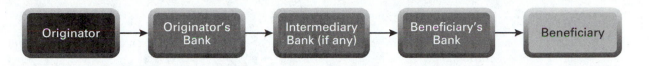

The beneficiary's bank may accept an order in any of three ways, and acceptance occurs at the earliest of these events: (1) when the bank (a) pays the beneficiary or (b) notifies the beneficiary that the bank has received the order or has credited the beneficiary's account with the funds; (2) when the bank receives payment of the sender's order; or (3) the opening of the next funds-transfer business day of the bank after the payment date of the order if the order was not rejected and funds are available for payment. Section 4A–209(b).

If a beneficiary's bank accepts a payment order, the bank is obliged to pay the beneficiary the amount of the order. Section 4A–404(a). The bank's acceptance of the payment order does not, however, create any obligation to either the sender or the originator.

### Erroneous Execution of Payment Orders

If a receiving bank mistakenly executes a payment order for an amount greater than the amount authorized, the bank is entitled to payment only in the amount of the sender's correct order. Section 4A–303(a). To the extent allowed by the law governing mistake and restitution, the receiving bank may then recover from the beneficiary of the erroneous order the amount in excess of the authorized amount. If the wrong beneficiary is paid, however, the bank that issued the erroneous payment order is entitled to payment neither from its sender nor from prior senders and has the burden of recovering the payment from the improper beneficiary. Section 4A–303(c).

### Unauthorized Payment Orders

If a bank wishing to prevent unauthorized transactions establishes commercially reasonable security measures, to which a customer agrees, and the bank properly follows the process it has established, the customer must pay an order even if it was unauthorized. Section 4A–202. The customer, however, can avoid liability by showing that the unauthorized order was not caused directly or indirectly by (1) a person with access to confidential security information who was acting for the customer or (2) a person who obtained such information from a source controlled by the customer. Section 4A–203.

# Chapter Summary

## Bank Deposits and Collections

| Collection of Items | |
|---|---|
| | **Depositary Bank** the bank in which the payee or holder deposits a check for credit |
| | **Provisional Credit** tentative credit for the deposit of an instrument until final credit is given |
| | **Final Credit** payment of the instrument by the payor bank; if the payor bank (drawee) does not pay the check, the depositary bank reverses the provisional credit |
| | **Intermediary Bank** a bank, other than the depositary or payor bank, involved in the collection process |
| | **Collecting Bank** any bank (other than the payor bank) handling the item for payment |
| | • *Agency* a collecting bank is an agent or subagent of the owner of the check until the settlement becomes final |
| | • *Duty of Care* a collecting bank must exercise ordinary care in handling an item |
| | • *Duty to Act Timely* a collecting bank acts timely if it takes proper action before its midnight deadline (midnight of the next banking day) |

- *Indorsements* if an item is restrictively indorsed "for deposit only," only a bank may be a holder
- *Warranties* customers and collecting banks give warranties on transfer, presentment, and encoding
- *Final Payment* occurs when the payor bank does any of the following, whichever happens first: (1) pays an item in cash; (2) settles and does not have the right to revoke the settlement; or (3) makes a provisional settlement and does not properly revoke it

**Payor Bank** under its contract with the drawer, the payor or drawee bank agrees to pay to the payee or his order checks that are issued by the drawer, provided the order is not countermanded by a stop payment order and provided there are sufficient funds in the drawer's account

## Relationship between Payor Bank and Its Customer

**Contractual Relationship** the relationship between a payor bank and its checking account customer is primarily the product of their contractual arrangement

**Payment of an Item** when a payor receives an item for which the funds in the account are insufficient, the bank may either dishonor the item and return it or pay the item and charge the customer's account even though an overdraft is created

**Stop Payment Orders** an oral stop payment order (a command from a drawer to a drawee not to pay an instrument) is binding for fourteen calendar days; a written order is effective for six months and may be renewed in writing

**Bank's Right to Subrogation on Improper Payment** if a payor bank pays an item over a stop payment order or otherwise in violation of its contract, the payor bank is subrogated to (obtains) the rights of (1) any holder in due course on the item against the drawer or maker; (2) the payee or any other holder against the drawer or maker; and (3) the drawer or maker against the payee or any other holder

**Disclosure Requirement** all depositary institutions must disclose in great detail to their consumers the terms and conditions of their deposit account

**Customers Death or Incompetence** a bank may pay an item if it does not know of the customer's incompetency or death

**Customer's Duties** the customer must examine bank statements and items carefully and promptly to discover any unauthorized signatures or alterations

# Electronic Funds Transfers

## Nature and Types of Electronic Funds Transfers

**Definition** any transfer of funds, other than a transaction originated by check, draft, or similar paper instrument, which is initiated through an electronic terminal, telephonic instrument, or computer or magnetic tape so as to order, instruct, or authorize a financial institution to debit or credit an account

**Purpose** to eliminate the paperwork involved in processing checks and the "float" available to a drawer of a check

**Types of Electronic Funds Transfers**
- *Automated Teller Machines*
- *Point-of-Sale Systems*
- *Direct Deposits and Withdrawals*
- *Pay-by-Phone Systems*
- *Wholesale Electronic Funds Transfers*

| Consumer Funds Transfers | **Electronic Fund Transfer Act** provides a basic framework establishing the rights, liabilities, and responsibilities of participants in consumer electronic fund transfers |
| | **Financial Institution Responsibility** liable to a consumer for all damage proximately caused by its failure to properly handle an EFT transaction |

| Wholesale Funds Transfers | **Scope**<br>• *Wholesale Funds Transfers* the movement of funds through the banking system; excludes all transactions governed by the Electronic Fund Transfer Act<br>• *Payment Order* an instruction of sender to a receiving bank to pay, or to cause another bank to pay, a fixed amount of money to a beneficiary<br>• *Parties* include originator, sender, receiving bank, originator's bank, beneficiary's bank, beneficiary, and intermediary banks<br>**Acceptance** rights and obligations that arise as a result of a receiving bank's acceptance of a payment order |

# Cases

## CASE 30–1
### Collecting Bank
## GREAT LAKES HIGHER EDUCATION CORPORATION v. AUSTIN BANK OF CHICAGO

United States District Court, N.D. Illinois, E.D., 1993
837 F.Supp. 892

**MAROVICH, J.**

[Authors' Note: Case applies revised Articles 3 and 4]

Plaintiffs Great Lakes Higher Education Corporation ("Great Lakes") and First Wisconsin National Bank of Milwaukee ("First Wisconsin") filed a five count complaint against Defendant Austin Bank of Chicago ("Austin") alleging breach of warranty ([UCC] 4–207), negligence in the presentment of certain checks [UCC] 4–202), breach of warranty to a third party beneficiary ([UCC] 4–207), conversion ([UCC] 3–420) and common law negligence. . . ., Austin filed a motion to dismiss. * * *

### Factual Background

Between October 1990 and January 1992, Great Lakes, as servicer, issued 224 checks (the "checks") drawn against lender's funds in the account of Great Lakes at First Wisconsin, payable to the order of various payees.

The checks were issued to the payees as loan proceeds pursuant to a student loan application submitted by each payee who was certified by the InterAmerican Business Institute ("IBI") located in Chicago, Illinois. Shortly after the issuance of each check, it was presented for payment to Austin Bank without the indorsement of the named payee. Austin Bank accepted each check for purposes of collection and forwarded each check to First Wisconsin for that purpose. Austin received payment from First Wisconsin in the face amount of each check even though the indorsement signature of the payee was not on any of the checks.

On February 27, 1992, First Wisconsin gave notice to Austin of its claim for breach of warranty by indicating that the checks lacked proper indorsement. First Wisconsin demanded that Austin refund to First Wisconsin the amount of the checks, a total of $273,152.88 plus interest. Austin failed to respond to this request for a refund, and Plaintiffs filed this suit.

# Discussion

* * *

*Count II: Negligence in the Presentment* In its second count, Great Lakes alleges that Austin was negligent and breached its duty to exercise ordinary care under [UCC] 4–202 by accepting the checks without proper indorsement and sending them for presentment to First Wisconsin. Austin contends that because the harm to Plaintiffs occurred in the acceptance of the checks by Austin without proper authorization, rather than in the presentment process, § 4–202 does not apply here.

Under the UCC, presentment means "a demand made by or on behalf of a person entitled to enforce an instrument (i) to pay the instrument made to the drawee or a party obliged to pay the instrument or, in the case of a note or accepted draft payable at a bank, to the bank or (ii) to accept a draft made to the drawee." § 3–501. Section 4–202 provides that: "A collecting bank must exercise ordinary care in . . . presenting an item or sending it for presentment." § 4–202(a)(1). Official Code Comment Two to this section states: "If the bank makes presentment itself, subsection (a)(1) requires ordinary care with respect both to the time and manner of presentment . . . If it forwards the item to be presented the subsection requires ordinary care with respect to routing (Section 4–204), and also in the selection of intermediary banks or other agents." [Citation.]

Under a plain reading of Official Comment Two, we hold that where, as here, Austin merely forwarded the item to First Wisconsin to be presented, it is only responsible for ordinary care under § 4–202 with respect to the routing and selection of intermediary banks or other agents. Because Austin displayed reasonable care in regard to these activities by immediately forwarding the checks to First Wisconsin, we hold that § 4–202 does not apply to the instant case.

The case cited by First Wisconsin, [citation], for the proposition that this Court should be flexible in applying § 4–202 claims is not persuasive. That case addressed wrongdoing in the presentment process where the defendant bank failed to timely return a fraudulent check or send notification of having received it unpaid within the applicable UCC time limits. [Citation.] By contrast, Great Lakes argues that the exercise of ordinary care in the presentment process set out in § 4–202 extends to the acceptance of unauthorized checks. We refuse to extend the ordinary care standard this far in light of the Official Comment and the fact that other relevant UCC remedies in breach of warranty exist that are more applicable to the instant situation. Because these alternative remedies exist, we are not, as First Wisconsin asserts, allowing Austin to completely avoid liability by refusing to allow a negligence claim against it.

## Count III: Common Law Negligence

* * *

Plaintiffs' argument is not persuasive that because the UCC clearly intended that it would be supplemented by common-law principles (§ 1–103), it follows that a claim for negligence may be asserted unless a specific provision of the UCC expressly overrules the common law. No section of the UCC expressly displaces any common law remedy. It is by implication that an alternative remedy under the UCC exists for such a factual situation that the common law is displaced on that same point. Here, First Wisconsin and Great Lakes have other remedies under the UCC which they have alternatively plead in their complaint, thus showing that a common law action for negligence is unnecessary and may not be alleged here.

* * *

*Count IV: Breach of Warranty Against Third Party* In Count IV, Great Lakes alleges that it is the third party beneficiary of a UCC § 4–207 transfer warranty owed by Austin to First Wisconsin, and thus Great Lakes is suing Austin for breach of warranty as a third party. Section 4–207 provides in relevant part that "a customer or collecting bank . . . warrants to the transferee and to any subsequent collecting bank that . . . all signatures on the item are authentic and authorized." § 4–207. Though Great Lakes is neither a customer nor a subsequent collecting bank, it relies upon a third party beneficiary theory of warranty owed by Austin to First Wisconsin. In this action, Great Lakes is the "drawer" of the checks from First Wisconsin, and First Wisconsin is the "drawee" of the checks.

Austin points to *Steinroe Income Trust v. Continental Bank N.A.,* [citation], in which the Illinois Appellate Court for the First District adopted the majority view that under Illinois law, a drawer may not maintain an action under UCC § 4–207. *Steinroe* specifically rejected *Sun'n Sand, Inc. v. United California Bank,* [citation], the California case representing the minority viewpoint that a drawer may maintain an action as a third party beneficiary. The *Steinroe* court based its decision in part upon the UCC Comment to newly amended UCC § 3–417 which explicitly rejected the *Sun'n Sand* case in favor of the majority view. § 3–417, UCC Comment 2.

Because *Steinroe* is the main case to address this issue under Illinois law, we accept its holding that a drawer, such as Great Lakes in the instant case, may not assert a third party beneficiary claim in order to maintain a breach of warranty under UCC § 4–207. Plaintiffs' fourth count must therefore be dismissed.

\* \* \*

## Conclusion

For the foregoing reasons, we dismiss with prejudice counts II, III, [and] IV, . . . of Plaintiff's complaint and give Plaintiffs leave to amend Count I by showing which party suffered damages in this suit.

---

## CASE 30–2
## Final Payment
## FIRST NATIONAL BANK OF BOSTON v. FIDELITY BANK, N.A.
United States District Court, E.D. Pennsylvania, 1989
724 F.Supp. 1168, *aff'd* 908 F.2d 962 (3rd Cir. 1990)

FULLAM, C.J.

This dispute between two banks over a mishandled check transaction requires the court to explore some of the consequences which automation has visited upon the respective legal liabilities of banks under Article 4 of the Uniform Commercial Code, which was enacted before the advent of computerized check-processing.

The method of processing checks now in universal use in the United States, Magnetic Ink Character Recognition (MICR) was first adopted by the American Bankers Association in 1956, and has been in common use since the mid-1960s. [Citation.] The form of each bank check is preprinted with magnetic characters, along the bottom of the check, toward the left-hand side. These characters designate the bank upon which the check is drawn, and the account number of the maker. When a check is presented to another bank (the "depositary bank"), that bank adds additional magnetic encoding, at the lower right-hand side of the check, specifying the amount of the check. From that point on, the check works its way through the bank clearing system to the bank on which the check is drawn (the "payor" bank) and is charged against the maker's account—all without further human intervention. Thus, the role of the encoder at the depositary bank (which then assumes the role of "collecting" bank as well), is crucial, since all subsequent steps in the processing of the check for payment depend upon the accuracy of the encoded information; ordinarily, no other human being actually examines the check from that point on. The development of this method of processing checks, it is generally agreed, has enabled the banking system to meet the needs of our ever-expanding economy. A bank such as the defendant, for example, routinely processes upwards of 300,000 checks daily.

The parties have stipulated the facts pertinent to their dispute. Plaintiff is the First National Bank of Boston (hereinafter "Boston"). The defendant is Fidelity Bank, National Association, . . . (hereinafter "Fidelity"). On or about September 22, 1986, one of defendant's customers, New York City Shoes ("NYC") issued a check in the amount of $100,000, to the Maxwell Shoe Company ("Maxwell"). The check was drawn on one of NYC's accounts at Fidelity in Philadelphia. Maxwell, a New England concern, deposited the check in its account at Boston, which credited Maxwell's account with the face amount of the check, and then proceeded to process the check through the Federal Reserve system. The check was properly encoded by Boston, and duly presented to Fidelity for payment. But NYC's account did not contain sufficient funds to cover the check, and Fidelity therefore returned the check to Boston for "non-sufficient funds."

Boston did not charge Maxwell's account because of the uncollectability of the check, but instead, at Maxwell's request, undertook to re-present the check to Fidelity. In order to re-process the check, Boston attached a "tape skirt" to the bottom of the check, and thereon re-encoded the check so that it could be processed through the Federal Reserve system. Unfortunately, however, Boston's encoder made an error, and encoded the amount of the check as $10,000, rather than $100,000. The computers which processed the check were, of course, unaware of the error and unable to appreciate it. When the check arrived at Fidelity, it was charged against NYC's account in the amount of $10,000, and that sum was duly forwarded to Boston. At that point, the error surfaced.

Boston made demand on Fidelity for the $90,000 difference between the face amount of the check and the amount which Fidelity had paid. The initial demands were made by telephone. On each occasion, Fidelity explained that it was unable to honor the request, because NYC's account continued to be insufficient to cover it. The first telephone demand was made by Boston on October 14, 1986. A second such demand was made on October 17, 1986. On both occasions, NYC's account lacked sufficient funds to honor the $90,000 request. On the latter occasion, Fidelity further explained that, under Fidelity's internal operating procedures, oral requests for "adjustments" could not be honored, and it would therefore be necessary for Boston to submit a written request for "adjustment."

On October 27, 1986, Boston submitted its written adjustment request, which was received by Fidelity's Adjustment Department on November 3, 1986. On that date, NYC's account showed a balance of $171,077.60, but $158,000 of that sum represented uncollected funds. The collected and available balance in the account was only $13,077.67. The following day, November 4, 1986, NYC's account was reduced by the payment of four other checks, totaling $155,148 (all of which were drawn against uncollected funds, but all of which were honored). By virtue of these checks and certain other transactions (a returned deposit and a charge against the account in an unrelated transaction), the ending balance in NYC's account on November 4, 1986 was $2,789.67.

* * *

Because of the unusual nature of several transactions in NYC's account—a large number of checks drawn against uncollected funds, and a large number of deposits which later proved to be uncollectible—the account had come to the attention of Fidelity's Security Division in July of 1986. As a result of the investigation, Mr. Donald Ebner, vice-president in charge of security at Fidelity, decided to end Fidelity's banking relationship with NYC. By agreement, all of NYC's accounts at Fidelity were closed, as of the end of business on November 21, 1986.

* * *

After [the] final rejection of Boston's adjustment request, Boston attempted to collect the $90,000 from NYC. An agreement was reached for NYC to pay off the balance in installments. NYC paid a total of $40,000 on account, but then defaulted and, on July 7, 1987, filed for bankruptcy.

In this action, Boston seeks to recover from Fidelity the $50,000 remaining unpaid, . . .

* * *

Boston's argument is straightforward: Fidelity did post the check against NYC's account on October 3, 1986, and is therefore, under the plain language of the statute, accountable to Boston "for the amount of the item." The fact that Fidelity listed the item in the wrong amount is irrelevant. * * *

The defendant, on the other hand, argues that, . . . the "amount of the item" for which the payor bank must account should be the encoded amount of the check, rather than its actual face amount.

* * *

* * * I reject the argument that the "amount of the item" . . . is the encoded amount, rather than the face amount, of the check. Stated that broadly, the argument is manifestly unacceptable, for if the encoded amount were greater than the face amount of the check, the error would produce a windfall for the collecting bank, and patently unjustifiable increases in the potential liability of the payor bank, the maker [sic], or both. Any such rule would have chaotic repercussions, and would be totally inconsistent with the scheme of the UCC.

A more narrowly stated rule—that the "amount of the item" . . . is the face amount of the check or the encoded amount, whichever is less—is merely another way of stating what I conceive to be the true thrust of defendant's argument in this case, namely, that as between the encoding bank and all other banks in the collecting process, including the payor bank, the encoder is estopped from claiming more than the encoded amount of the check.

* * *

The proposed ALI/NCCUSL revisions to Article 4 (specifically, revised § 4–207) would explicitly provide that an encoding bank warrants the accuracy of encoded amounts, and is liable for any resulting loss; this on the theory that the encoding bank is the party best able to avoid the loss. [Citations.]

In my view, most, if not all, of the reported decisions can readily be harmonized with the existence of the right of the payor bank to hold the encoding bank liable for any under-encoding error, if this equitable right is considered in conjunction with the obligation to mitigate damages. That is, the payor bank has the corollary obligation of attempting to avoid loss altogether, by recourse to the account of the maker [sic] of the check. If the maker's [sic] account, when the check is correctly presented, is insufficient to cover the item, the payor bank has a claim against the encoding bank, which it can offset against any claim made by the encoding bank under § 4–213(1). [Revised 4–215(a).]

I therefore conclude that Fidelity may not be held liable to plaintiff under § 4–213(1) [Revised 4–215(a).] of the UCC, the "final payment" rule.

* * *

---

## CASE 30–3
## Payment of an Item/Stop Payment Order
### *LEIBLING, P.C. v. MELLON PSFS (NJ) NATIONAL ASSOCIATION*
Superior Court of New Jersey, Law Division, Special Civil Part, Camden County, 1998
710 A.2d 1067, 311 N.J.Super. 651, 35 UCC Rep.Serv.2d 590

RAND, J.

### Facts

Mr. Scott D. Liebling, P.C. (hereinafter "Plaintiff") is an attorney at law. Plaintiff maintains an attorney trust account ("Account") at Mellon Bank (NJ) National Association ("Mellon"), * * * . Mellon uses a computerized system to process checks for payment.

Plaintiff represented, defendant, Fredy Winda Ramos ("Ramos") in a personal injury action which resulted in a settlement. On or about May 19, 1995, plaintiff issued Check No. 1031 in the amount of $8,483.06 to Ramos representing her net proceeds from the settlement. Mellon honored that check on May 26, 1995. On or about May 24, 1995, plaintiff mistakenly issued another check, Check No. 1043, to Ramos in the same amount of $8,483.06. Realizing his error, on or about May 30, 1995, Plaintiff called Ramos in Puerto Rico and advised her that the Check No. 1043 was issued by mistake and instructed her to destroy the check. Thereafter, Plaintiff called Mellon and ordered an oral stop payment on the check.

On December 21, 1996, some nineteen months after plaintiff issued the Check No. 1043, Ramos cashed the check from Puerto Rico.

Plaintiff filed this complaint against both Ramos and Mellon. Ramos was served and defaulted. Plaintiff's complaint against Mellon alleges breach of duty of good faith, negligence, breach of fiduciary duty, payment of a stale check, and breach of contract as a result of Mellon honoring the second check, Check No. 1043.

\* \* \*

### Issue

Whether the defendant bank acted in good faith when it honored a check that was presented for payment nineteen months after it was issued and subsequent to the expiration of an oral stop payment order?

### Discussion

It is important to consider the relevant New Jersey statute sections before discussing what actions constitute "good faith." Under [UCC] 4–403(b):

[a] stop-payment order is effective for six months, but it lapses after 14 calendar days if the original order was oral and was not confirmed in writing within that period. A stop-payment order may be renewed for additional six-month periods by a writing given to the bank within a period during which the stop-payment order is effective.

In addition, [UCC] 4–404 states:

A bank is under no obligation to a customer having a checking account to pay a check, other than a certified check, which is presented more than six months after its date, but it may charge its customer's account for a payment made thereafter in good faith.

Thus, the issue in the present case turns on whether Mellon acted in good faith when it honored plaintiff's check. Good faith under N.J. Uniform Commercial Code has been defined in [UCC] 3–103(a)(4) as "honesty in fact and the observance of reasonable commercial standards of fair dealing." Since there is no New Jersey case law directly on point, it is necessary to consider alternate sources. One law review article [citation] addressed the present issue. Specifically, the article explained that "Article 4 of the Uniform Commercial Code imposes on all banks the responsibility to act in good faith and to exercise ordinary care. The drafters of the Code chose not to provide an explicit definition of 'ordinary' care, stating only that the term is to be used 'with its normal tort meaning and not in any special sense relating to bank collections.'" [Citation.] In addition, the article suggested the appropriate standard of care in light of the widespread development of computerized check processing systems in banking industry. Specifically, the article explained a two-step analysis:

First, the court should determine whether the system is one in general banking usage not disapproved by the Code. If so, use of the system prima facie constitutes the exercise of ordinary care. The burden of proof then shifts to the party claiming that the bank has failed to use ordinary care to prove that selection or use of this system was unreasonable. If the system is so new that it is not yet in general use in the banking industry, the burden of proof would remain with the bank, and the analysis would involve determining whether the system is 'reasonable under the circumstances.' Once a bank has proven its prima facie case, the second step in this analysis involves a determination by the court that the particular system is reasonable under the specific circumstances of the case. At this stage, the court can examine a number of factors, including whether the computer procedure is reasonably related to the particular banking task, whether any increased accuracy from the use of another procedure or system outweighs the costs of implementing such a system, and whether the computer system is state of the art. If the bank succeeds [in proving its initial burden], then the burden shifts to the opposing party to prove that the system, although one in general banking usage, was not a reasonable one under the circumstances.

[Citation.]

The article explains that this analysis acknowledges that the Code was written before the era of computerized check processing.

In addition, the Third Circuit case of [citation] appears to be analogous to the present issue. In [that case], an insurance company brought a subrogation action against a payor bank to recover on an altered check that the bank had paid. On April 17, 1984, the plaintiff placed a written stop-payment order on a certain check, and under applicable state law the stop-payment order was good for six months. On December 26, 1984, two months after the stop payment order had expired, the bank honored the check. Before concluding that the payor bank had acted in good faith, the court analyzed the definition of "good faith." The court stated that "[UCC] § 1–201 defines good faith as 'honesty in fact.' This definition must be viewed subjectively; a finding of bad faith must be predicated on a showing of dishonesty. Likewise, mere negligence does not preclude a finding of good faith." [Citation.] In holding that the bank had acted in good faith, the court stated:

[a]s a result of the expiration of the order, [the bank] cannot be said to have the actual knowledge that would deny it the status of a good faith payor. . . . The obligations which a bank incurs as a result of its customer's imposing a stop order on a check do not continue in perpetuity. . . . [The bank] was neither negligent nor reckless and certainly cannot be said to have been subjectively dishonest. . . . A finding of bad faith requires actual knowledge on the part of the payor. An objective inquiry into what the circumstances should have revealed to [the bank] is simply not germane to the analysis.

[Citation.]

* * *

In contrast, plaintiff's argument centers on the proposition that the bank's duty of good faith required it to inquire or consult with plaintiff before honoring a stale check that had a previous oral stop payment order on it. * * *

However, in the Uniform Commercial Code Treatise, Mr. Hawkland stated that the above cases are not consistent with the Uniform Commercial Code, specifically, "[t]he duty [of inquiry] is inconsistent with the provisions of subsection 4–403(2) on the expiration of the 'effectiveness' of stop orders. Such a duty is hardly practical today." Moreover: "[t]o require that a payor bank check the date of every check received via the collection process would unreasonably increase the cost of processing every check written today."

* * *

The Commercial Code was initially adopted in November, 1961 in New Jersey. In 1990, Articles III and IV of the Code were substantially revised relating to, among other things, bank deposits and collections to become effective on June 1, 1995. The court is satisfied as pointed out by the defendant that those Amendments were enacted in order to address the effect of automated systems utilized by banks with the substantial increase in check usage after the original enactment of the Code. The Official Code Comment to the 1995 Amendments for § [UCC] 4–101, states as follows:

1. The great number of checks handled by banks and the country-wide nature of the bank collection process require uniformity in the law of bank collections. There is needed a uniform statement of the principal rules of the bank collection process with ample provision for flexibility to meet the needs of the large volume handled and the changing needs and conditions that are bound to come with the years. The Article meets that need.
2. . . . An important goal of the 1990 revision of Article 4 is to promote the efficiency of the check collection process by making the provisions of Article 4 more compatible with the needs of an automated system and, by doing so, increase the speed and lower the cost of check collection for those who write and receive checks. . . .

[Citation.]

* * *

Thus, in determining whether the defendant bank in the present action acted in good faith, the above cited material must be analyzed and applied. First, it appears clear that the Uniform Commercial Code acknowledges that computerized check processing systems are common and accepted banking procedures in the United States. [Citation.] Therefore, it can not be said that defendant bank acted in bad faith by using a computerized system when it honored plaintiff's "stale" check. Furthermore, it appears that the test for good faith is a subjective test. Thus, based on all of the foregoing material, as long as the defendant bank used an adequate computer system for processing checks (here there is no proof to the contrary), it appears to have acted in good faith even though it did not consult the Plaintiff before it honored the "stale" check that had an expired oral stop-payment order on it. * * * [T]he obligation of a bank to stop payment on a check does not continue in perpetuity once the stop payment order expires.

The bank's conduct was fair and in accordance with reasonable commercial standards. Accordingly, it appears that the defendant bank is not liable and should prevail. A finding of no liability is entered for the defendant bank.

---

### CASE 30-4
## Customer's Duties
### *MANSI v. GAINES*
Supreme Court, Appellate Division, Second Department, 1995
216 A.D.2d 536, 628 N.Y.S.2d 804

**MEMORANDUM BY THE COURT**

In an action, . . . , to recover damages for the payment of forged checks, the defendant Sterling National Bank & Trust Company of New York appeals from so much of an order of the Supreme Court, Queens County, . . . as denied its cross motion for summary judgment dismissing the complaint insofar as it is asserted against it.

ORDERED that the order is reversed insofar as appealed from, on the law, with costs, the cross motion is granted, the complaint is dismissed insofar as it is asserted against the appellant, and the action against the remaining defendants is severed.

In her complaint, the plaintiff alleged, . . . , that substantial sums of money were removed from her accounts with the appellant pursuant to a "fraudulent 'power of attorney'" and "divers" forged checks. * * *

The plaintiff moved for summary judgment and submitted an affidavit from a handwriting expert stating that the plaintiff's signature on 21 checks on accounts with the appellant were apparently forgeries. The appellant was unable to locate a copy of two of the disputed checks in its files, and the plaintiff failed to annex a copy of those checks to her motion papers. The plaintiff included a photocopy of a third check which, without explanation, she attributed to the appellant, but was drawn on the "American Express Centurion Bank."

The appellant cross-moved for a summary judgment, acknowledging that it honored the 18 remaining checks, but claiming that, pursuant to the bank's business practices, nine of those checks and the account statements with respect thereto were forwarded to the plaintiff more than one year before the commencement of the instant action. The appellant asserted that, since the plaintiff did not report the alleged fraud before she commenced the instant action against it, her claims with respect to those nine checks were barred by UCC 4-406(4) [Revised 4-406(f)].

With respect to the remaining nine checks, the appellant asserted that the plaintiff's claims were barred by UCC 4-406(2)(b) [Revised 4-406(d)(2)]. The appellant noted that the plaintiff stated at a deposition that she did not review her monthly bank statements. She acknowledged in her answer to interrogatories that she did not examine copies of the cancelled checks until the end of May or June 1989. The appellant submitted evidence that its practice was to check the signature on every check filed against the customer's signature card. The checks in question bore signatures which, according to the plaintiff's handwriting expert, were apparently "written by another person who attempted to simulate her signature," and thus were not obvious forgeries.

* * *

The plaintiff, in her motion papers, failed to identify a specific transaction in which the allegedly fraudulent power of attorney was used. Although the evidence in the record indicated that the appellant honored 18 checks which may have been forged, liability with respect to nine of those checks was barred by UCC 4-406(4) [Revised 4-406(f)] since the plaintiff did not report the alleged fraud within one year after those checks and the bank statements with respect thereto were made available to her [citations.]

With respect to the remaining nine checks, liability was barred by UCC 4-406(2)(b) [Revised 4-406(d)(2)] since it was established that the plaintiff failed to exercise reasonable care to examine her bank statements and the plaintiff failed to submit any evidence that the appellant failed to exercise ordinary care in paying the items [Citation.]

# Questions

1. Identify and explain the various stages and parties to the collection of a check.
2. Discuss the duties of collecting banks.
3. Discuss the relationship between a payor bank and its customers.

4. Define a consumer electronic fund transfer and outline the major provisions of the Electronic Fund Transfer Act.
5. Define a wholesale fund transfer and identify the parties to such a transfer.

# Problems

1. On December 9, Jane Jones writes a check for $500 payable to Ralph Rodgers in payment for goods to be received later in the month. Before the close of business on the ninth, Jane notifies the bank by telephone to stop payment on the check. On Monday, December 19, Ralph gives the check to Bill Briggs for value and without notice. On the twentieth, Bill deposits the check in his account at Bank A. On the twenty-first, Bank A sends the check to its correspondent, Bank B. On the twenty-second, Bank B presents the check through the clearinghouse to Bank C. On the twenty-third, Bank C presents the check to Bank P, the payor bank. On Wednesday, December 28, the payor bank makes payment of the check final. Jane Jones sues the payor bank. Decision?

2. Howard Harrison, a longtime customer of Western Bank, operates a small department store, Harrison's Store. Because his store has few experienced employees, Harrison frequently travels throughout the United States on buying trips, although he also runs the financial operations of the business. On one of his buying trips, Harrison purchased a gross of sport shirts from Well-Made Shirt Company and paid for the transaction with a check on his store account with Western Bank in the amount of $1,000. Adams, an employee of Well-Made who deposits its checks in Security Bank, sloppily raised the amount of the check to $10,000 and indorsed the check, "Pay to the order of Adams from Pension Plan Benefits, Well-Made Shirt Company by Adams." He cashed the check and cannot be found. Western Bank processed the check, paid it, and sent it to Harrison's Store with the monthly statement. After briefly examining the statement, Harrison left on another buying trip for three weeks.

(a) Assuming the bank acted in good faith and the alteration is not discovered and reported to the bank until an audit conducted thirteen months after the statement was received by Harrison's Store, who must bear the loss on the raised check?

(b) Assume that Harrison, who was unable to examine his statement promptly because of his buying trips, left instructions with the bank to carefully examine and to notify him of any item over $5,000 to be charged to his account; assume further that the bank nevertheless paid the item in his absence. Who bears the loss if the alteration is discovered one month after the statement was received by Harrison's Store? If the alteration is discovered thirteen months later?

3. Tom Jones owed Bank of Cleveland $10,000 on a note due November 17, with 1 percent interest due the bank for each day delinquent in payment. Jones issued a $10,000 check to Bank of Cleveland and deposited it in the night vault the evening of November 17. Several days later, he received a letter saying he owed one day's interest on the payment because of a one-day delinquency in payment. Jones refused because he said he had put the payment in the vault on November 17. Decision?

4. Assume that Dinah draws a check on Oxford Bank, payable to the order of Pam; that Pam indorses it to Amy; that Amy deposits it to her account in Houston Bank; that Houston Bank presents it to Oxford Bank, the drawee; and that Oxford Bank dishonors it because of insufficient funds. Houston Bank receives notification of the dishonor on Monday but, because of an interruption of communication facilities, fails to notify Amy until Wednesday. What result?

5. Jones, a food wholesaler whose company has an account with City Bank in New York City, is traveling in California on business. He finds a particularly attractive offer and decides to buy a carload of oranges for delivery in New York. He gives Saltin, the seller, his company's check for $25,000 to pay for the purchase. Saltin deposits the check, with others he received that day, with his bank, the Carrboro Bank. Carrboro Bank sends the check to Downs Bank in Los Angeles, which in turn deposits it with the Los Angeles Federal Reserve Bank. The L.A. Fed sends the check, with others, to the N.Y. Fed, which forwards the check to City Bank, Jones's bank, for collection.

(a)   Is City Bank a depositary bank? A collecting bank? A payor bank?

(b)   Is Carrboro Bank a depositary bank? A collecting bank?

(c)   Is the N.Y. Fed. an intermediary bank?

(d)   Is Downs Bank a collecting bank?

Explain.

**6.**   On April 1, Moore gave Pipkin a check properly drawn by Moore on Zebra Bank for $500 in payment of a painting to be framed and delivered the next day. Pipkin immediately indorsed the check and gave it to Yeager Bank as payment in full of his indebtedness to the bank on a note he previously had signed. Yeager Bank canceled the note and returned it to Pipkin.

On April 2, upon learning that the painting had been destroyed in a fire at Pipkin's studio, Moore promptly went to Zebra Bank, signed a printed form of stop payment order, and gave it to the cashier. Zebra Bank refused payment on the check upon proper presentment by Yeager Bank.

(a)   What are the rights of Yeager Bank against Zebra Bank?

(b)   What are the rights of Yeager Bank against Moore?

(c)   Assuming that Zebra Bank inadvertently paid the amount of the check to Yeager Bank and debited Moore's account, what are the rights of Moore against Zebra Bank?

**7.**   As payment in advance for services to be performed, Acton signed and delivered the following instrument:

December 1, 1999

LAST NATIONAL BANK
MONEYVILLE, STATE X

Pay to the order of Olaf Owen $1,500.00 _____

Fifteen Hundred Dollars _____ For services to be performed by Olaf Owen starting on December 6, 1999.

(signed) Arthur Acton

Owen requested and received Last National Bank's certification of the check even though Acton had only $900 on deposit. Owen indorsed the check in blank and delivered it to Dan Doty in payment of a preexisting debt.

When Owen failed to appear for work, Acton issued a written stop payment order ordering the bank not to pay the check. Doty presented the check to Last National Bank for payment. The bank refused payment.

What are the bank's rights and liabilities relating to the transactions described?

**8.**   Jones drew a check for $1,000 on The First Bank and mailed it to the payee, Thrift, Inc. Caldwell stole the check from Thrift, Inc., chemically erased the name of the payee, and inserted the name of Henderson as payee. Caldwell also increased the amount of the check to $10,000 and, by using the name of Henderson, negotiated the check to Willis. Willis then took the check to The First Bank, obtained its certification on the check, and negotiated the check to Griffin, who deposited the check in The Second National Bank for collection. The Second National Bank forwarded the check to the Detroit

Trust Company for collection from The First Bank, which honored the check. Griffin exhausted her account in the Second National Bank, and the account was closed. Shortly thereafter, The First Bank learned that it had paid an altered check.

What are the rights of each of the parties?

**9.**   Jason, who has extremely poor vision, went to an ATM to withdraw $200 on February 1. Joshua saw that Jason was having great difficulty reading the computer screen and offered to help. Joshua obtained Jason's personal identification number and secretly exchanged one of his old credit cards for Jason's ATM card. Between February 1 and February 15, Joshua withdrew $1,600 from Jason's account. On February 15, Jason discovered that his ATM card was missing and immediately notified his bank. The bank closed Jason's ATM account on February 16, by which time Joshua had withdrawn another $150. What is Jason's liability, if any, for the unauthorized use of his account?

**10.**   On July 21, Boehmer, a customer of Birmingham Trust, secured a loan from that bank for the principal sum of $5,500 to purchase a boat allegedly being built for him by A.C. Manufacturing Company, Inc. After Boehmer signed a promissory note, Birmingham Trust issued a cashier's check to Boehmer and A.C. Manufacturing Company as payees. The check was given to Boehmer, who then forged A.C. Manufacturing Company's indorsement and deposited the check in his own account at Central Bank. Central Bank credited Boehmer's account and then placed the legend "P.I.G.," meaning "Prior Indorsements Guaranteed," on the check. The check was presented to and paid by Birmingham Trust on July 22. When the loan became delinquent in March of the following year, Birmingham Trust contacted A.C. Manufacturing Company to learn the location of the boat. They were informed that it had never been purchased, and they soon after learned that Boehmer had died on January 24 of that year. On May 1, Birmingham Trust sought reimbursement from Central Bank under the latter's warranty of prior indorsements. Decision?

**11.**   Advanced Alloys, Inc., issued a check in the amount of $2,500 to Sergeant Steel Corporation. The check was presented for payment fourteen months later to the Chase Manhattan Bank, which made payment on the check and charged Advanced Alloy's account. Advanced Alloys now seeks to recover the payment made on the check. Decision?

**12.**   Laboratory Management deposited into its account at Pulaski Bank a check issued by Fairway Farms in the amount of $150,000. The date of deposit was February 5. Pulaski, the depositary bank, initiated the collection process immediately by forwarding the check to Worthen Bank on the sixth. Worthen sent the check on for collection to M Bank Dallas, and M Bank Dallas, still on February 6, delivered the check to M Bank Fort Worth. That same day, M Bank Fort Worth delivered the check to the Fort Worth Clearinghouse. Because TAB/West Side, the drawee/payor bank, was not a clearinghouse member, it had to rely on TAB/Fort Worth for further transmittal of the check. TASI, a processing center used by both TAB/Forth Worth and TAB/West Side, received the check on the sixth and processed it as a reject item because of insufficient funds. On the seventh, TAB/West Side determined to return the check unpaid. TASI gave M Bank Dallas telephone notice of the return on February 7 but physically misrouted the check. Because of this, M Bank Dallas did not physically receive the check until February 19. However, M Bank notified Worthen telephonically on the fifteenth of the dishonor and return of the check. Worthen received the check on the twenty-first and notified Pulaski by telephone on the twenty-second. Pulaski actually received the check from Worthen on the twenty-third. On February 22 and 23, Laboratory Management's checking account with Pulaski was $46,000. Pulaski did not freeze the account because it considered the return to be too late. The Laboratory Management account was finally frozen on April 30, 1985, when it had a balance of $1,400. Pulaski brings this suit against TAB/Fort Worth, TAB/Dallas, and TASI alleging their notice of dishonor was not timely relayed to Pulaski. The trial court found in favor of Pulaski but awarded a nominal amount of damages. Pulaski appeals, claiming that the liability of the collecting and payor banks was absolute. Decision?

13.    On Tuesday, June 11, Siniscalchi issued a $200 check on the drawee, Valley Bank. On Saturday morning, June 15, the check was cashed. This transaction, as well as others taking place on that Saturday morning, was not recorded or processed through the bank's bookkeeping system until Monday, June

17. On that date, Siniscalchi arrived at the bank at 9:00 AM and asked to place a stop payment order on the check. A bank employee checked the bank records, which at that time indicated the instrument had not cleared the bank. At 9:45 AM she gave him a printed notice confirming his request to stop payment. Siniscalchi sought to recover the $200 paid on the check. Decision?

14.    Morvarid Kashanchi and her sister, Firoyeh Paydar, held a savings account with Texas Commerce Medical Bank. An unauthorized withdrawal of $4,900 from the account was allegedly made by means of a telephone conversation between some other unidentified individual and a bank employee. Paydar learned of the transfer of funds when she received her bank statement and notified the bank that the withdrawal was unauthorized. The bank, however, declined to recredit the account for the $4,900 transfer. Kashanchi brought an action against the bank, claiming that the bank had violated the Electronic Fund Transfer Act. The district court dismissed the complaint for lack of subject matter jurisdiction, finding that the transaction in question was not governed by the act. Kashanchi appealed. Decision?

**WWW**   **Internet Exercise** Find and review information about (a) electronic banking, (b) the Federal Reserve System, and (c) the Federal Deposit Insurance Company.

# PART SIX

# Unincorporated Business Associations

# CHAPTER 31

# Formation and Dissolution of General Partnerships

A business enterprise may be operated or conducted as a sole proprietorship, an unincorporated business association (such as a general partnership, a limited partnership, or a limited liability company), or a corporation. The choice of the most appropriate form cannot be determined in a general way but depends on the particular circumstances of the owners. We will begin this chapter with a brief overview of the various types of business associations and the factors that are relevant to deciding which form to use. The rest of this chapter and the next chapter will examine general partnerships. Chapter 33 will cover other types of unincorporated business associations. Part seven (Chapters 34 through 37) will address corporations.

## CHOOSING A BUSINESS ASSOCIATION

The owners of an enterprise determine the form of business unit they wish to use based upon their specific circumstances. Corporations today outnumber unincorporated business associations (general partnerships, joint ventures, limited partnerships, and limited liability companies) by almost three to one and generate greater revenues by about twenty to one. Nevertheless, unincorporated business associations are common in a number of areas. General partnerships, for example, are used frequently in finance, insurance, accounting, real estate, law, and other service-related fields. Joint ventures have enjoyed popularity among major corporations planning to engage in cooperative research; in the exploitation of land and mineral rights; in the development, promotion, and sale of patents, trade names, and copyrights; and in manufacturing operations in foreign countries. Limited partnerships have been widely used for enterprises such as real estate investment and development, motion picture and theater productions, oil and gas ventures, and

equipment leasing. In the last few years the States have authorized the formation of limited liability companies. This form of business organization will probably appeal to a number of businesses including real estate ventures, high technology enterprises, businesses where transactions involve foreign investors, professional organizations, corporate joint ventures, start-up businesses, and venture capital projects.

First to be discussed are the most important factors to consider in choosing a form of business association. Then it will be explained how the various forms of business associations differ with respect to these factors.

◆ *See Figure 31–1*

## *FACTORS AFFECTING THE CHOICE*

In choosing the form in which to conduct business the owners should consider a number of factors, including ease of formation, Federal and State income tax laws, external liability, management and control, transferability of ownership interests, and continuity. The relative importance of each factor will vary with the specific needs and objectives of the owners.

### Ease of Formation

Business associations differ as to the formalities and expenses of formation. Some can be created with no formality, while others require the filing of documents with the State.

### Taxation

Some business associations are not considered to be separate taxable entities. In these cases, the income of the business is conclusively presumed to have been distributed to the owners, who must pay taxes on that income.

**FIGURE 31—1** General Partnership, Limited Partnership, Corporation, and Limited Liability Company

| | General Partnership | Limited Partnership | Corporation | Limited Liability Company |
|---|---|---|---|---|
| **Transferability** | Financial interest may be assigned; membership requires consent of all partners | Financial interest may be assigned, and assignee may become limited partner if all partners consent | Freely transferable unless shareholders agree otherwise | Financial interest may be assigned; membership requires consent of all members |
| **Liability** | Partners have unlimited liability* | General partners have unlimited liability**; limited partners have limited liability | Shareholders have limited liability | All members have limited liability |
| **Control** | By all partners | By general partners, not limited partners | By board of directors elected by shareholders | By all members |
| **Continuity** | Dissolved by death, bankruptcy, or withdrawal of a partner | Dissolved by death, bankruptcy, or withdrawal of a general partner | Unaffected by death, bankruptcy, or withdrawal of shareholder | Dissolved by death, bankruptcy, or withdrawal of member |
| **Taxation** | May elect that only partners are taxed | May elect that only partners are taxed | Corporation tax unless Subchapter S applies; shareholders taxed | May elect that only members are taxed |

*In an LLP, the partners' liability is limited for some or all of the partnership's obligations
**In an LLLP, the partners' liability is limited for some or all of the partnership's obligations

Losses receive comparable treatment and can be used to offset some of the owners' income. In contrast, some business forms, most significantly corporations, are considered separate tax entities and are directly taxed. When such an entity distributes income to the owners, that income is separately taxed to the recipients. Thus, these funds are taxed twice: once to the entity and once to the owners. Under a recent Internal Revenue Service regulation, unincorporated business entities can elect whether or not to be taxed as a separate entity.

## External Liability

External liability arises in a variety of ways, but the crucial and most commonly occurring are tort and contract liability. Owners of some business forms have unlimited liability for all of the obligations of the business. Thus, if the business does not have sufficient funds to pay its debts, each and every owner has personal liability to the creditors for the full amount of the debts. In brief, owners of interests in businesses with unlimited liability place their entire estate at risk. In some types of entities, the owners have unlimited liability for some but not all of

the entity's obligations. Finally, in some types of business associations, the owners enjoy limited liability, which means their liability is limited to the extent of their capital contribution. It should be noted, however, that creditors often require that the owners of small businesses guarantee personally loans made to the businesses.

## Management and Control

In some entities, the owners can fully share in the control of the business. In other types of business associations, the owners are restricted as to their right to take part in control.

## Transferability

An ownership interest in a business consists of a financial interest, which is the right to share in the profits of the business, and a management interest, which is the right to participate in control of the business. In some types of business associations, the owners may freely transfer their financial interest but may not transfer their management interest without the consent of all of the other owners. In other types of business associations, the entire ownership interest is freely transferable.

## Continuity

Some business associations have low continuity, which means that the death, bankruptcy, or withdrawal of an owner results in the dissolution of the association. Other types have high continuity and are not affected by the death, bankruptcy, or withdrawal of owners.

## FORMS OF BUSINESS ASSOCIATIONS

This section contains a brief description of the various types of business associations and how they differ with respect to the factors just discussed. In addition, general partnerships, limited partnerships, limited liability companies, limited liability partnerships, and corporations will be more extensively discussed in this and the next part of the book.

## Sole Proprietorship

A sole proprietorship is an unincorporated business consisting of one person who owns and completely controls the business. It is formed without any formality, and no documents need be filed. A sole proprietorship is not a separate taxable entity and only the sole proprietor is taxed. Sole proprietors have unlimited liability for the sole proprietorship's debts. The sole proprietor's interest in the business is freely transferable. The death of a sole proprietor dissolves the sole proprietorship.

## General Partnership

A general partnership is an unincorporated business association consisting of two or more persons who co-own a business for profit. It is formed without any formality and no documents need be filed. A partnership may elect not to be a separate taxable entity, in which case only the partners are taxed. Partners have unlimited liability for the partnership's debts. Each partner has an equal right to control of the partnership. Partners may assign their financial interest in the partnership, but the assignee may become a member of the partnership only if all of the members consent. The death, bankruptcy, or withdrawal of a partner dissolves a partnership.

## Joint Venture

A joint venture is an unincorporated business association composed of persons who combine their property, money, efforts, skill, and knowledge for the purpose of carrying out a particular business enterprise for profit. Usually, although not necessarily, it is of short duration. A joint venture, therefore, differs from a partnership, which is formed to carry on a business over a considerable or indefinite period of time. Nonetheless, except for a few differences, the law of partnerships generally governs a joint venture. An example of a joint venture is a securities underwriting syndicate or a syndicate formed to acquire a certain tract of land for subdivision and resale. Other common examples involve joint research conducted by corporations, the exploitation of mineral rights, and manufacturing operations in foreign countries.

## Limited Partnership

A limited partnership is an unincorporated business association consisting of at least one general partner and at least one limited partner. It is formed by filing a certificate of limited partnership with the State. A limited partnership may elect not to be a separate taxable entity, in which case only the partners are taxed. General partners have unlimited liability for the partnership's debts; limited partners have limited liability. Each general partner has an equal right to control of the partnership; limited partners have no right to participate in control. Partners may assign their financial interest in the partnership, but the assignee may become a limited partner only if all of the members consent. The death, bankruptcy, or withdrawal of a general partner dissolves a limited partnership; the limited partners have neither the right nor the power to dissolve the limited partnership.

## Limited Liability Company

A limited liability company (LLC) is an unincorporated business association that provides limited liability to all of its owners (members) and permits all of its members to participate in management of the business. It may elect not to be a separate taxable entity, in which case only the members are taxed. If an LLC has only one member, then it will be taxed as a sole proprietorship, unless separate entity tax treatment is elected. Thus, the LLC provides many of the advantages of a general partnership plus limited liability for all its members. Its benefits outweigh those of a limited partnership in that all members of an LLC not only enjoy limited liability but also may participate in management and control of the business. Members may assign their financial interest in the LLC, but the assignee may become a member of the LLC only if all of the members consent. The death, bankruptcy, or withdrawal of a member dissolves an LLC. Every State has adopted an LLC statute.

## Limited Liability Partnership

A registered limited liability partnership (LLP) is a general partnership that, by making the statutorily required filing, limits the liability of its partners for some or all of the partnership's obligations. To become an LLP, a general partnership must file with the State an application containing specified information. Nearly all of the States have enacted LLP statutes.

## Limited Liability Limited Partnership

A limited liability limited partnership (LLLP) is a limited partnership in which the liability of the general partners has been limited to the same extent as in an LLP. Where authorized, the general partners in an LLLP will obtain the same degree of liability limitation that general partners can achieve in LLPs. Where available, a limited partnership may register as an LLLP without having to form a new organization, as would be the case in converting to an LLC.

## Corporation

A corporation is a legal entity separate and distinct from its owners. It is formed by filing its articles of incorporation with the State. A corporation is taxed as a separate entity, and shareholders are taxed on corporate earnings that are distributed to them. (Some corporations are eligible to elect to be taxed as Subchapter S corporations, which results in only the shareholders being taxed.) The shareholders have limited liability for the corporation's obligations. The board of directors elected by the shareholders manages the corporation. Shares in a corporation are freely transferable. The death, bankruptcy, or withdrawal of a shareholder does not dissolve the corporation.

## Business Trusts

The business trust, sometimes called a Massachusetts trust, was devised to avoid the burdens of corporate regulation, particularly the formerly widespread prohibi-

tion denying to corporations the power to own and deal in real estate. Like an ordinary trust between natural persons, a business trust may be created by a voluntary agreement without any authorization or consent of the State. A business trust has three distinguishing characteristics: (1) the trust estate is devoted to the conduct of a business; (2) by the terms of the agreement, each beneficiary is entitled to a certificate evidencing his ownership of a beneficial interest in the trust, which he is free to sell or otherwise transfer; and (3) the trustees have the exclusive right to manage and control the business free from control of the beneficiaries. If the third condition is not met, the trust may fail; for the beneficiaries, by participating in control, would become personally liable as partners for the obligations of the business.

The trustees are personally liable for the debts of the business unless, in entering into contractual relations with others, it is expressly stated or definitely understood between the parties that the obligation is incurred solely upon the responsibility of the trust estate. To escape personal liability on the contractual obligations of the business, the trustee must obtain the agreement or consent of the other contracting party to look solely to the assets of the trust. The personal liability of the trustees for their own torts or the torts of their agents and servants employed in the operation of the business stands on a different footing. Although this liability cannot be avoided, the risk involved may be reduced substantially or eliminated altogether by insurance. In most jurisdictions, the beneficiaries of a business trust have no liability for obligations of the business trust.

# FORMATION OF GENERAL PARTNERSHIPS

The form of business association known as partnership can be traced to ancient Babylonia, classical Greece, and the Roman Empire. It was also used in Europe and England during the Middle Ages. Eventually the English common law recognized partnerships. In the nineteenth century, partnerships were widely used in England and the United States, and the common law of partnership developed considerably during this period. Partnerships are important in that they allow individuals with different expertise, backgrounds, resources, and interests to form a more competitive enterprise by combining their various skills. This part of the chapter will cover the nature of general partnerships and how they are formed.

# NATURE OF PARTNERSHIP

In 1914, the National Conference of Commissioners on Uniform State Laws promulgated the Uniform Partnership Act (UPA). Since then it has been adopted in all States (except Louisiana), as well as by the District of Columbia, the Virgin Islands, and Guam. (The UPA is reprinted in Appendix C.) Though fairly comprehensive, the UPA does not cover all legal issues concerning partnerships. Accordingly, Section 5 of the UPA provides that the rules of law and equity shall govern any situation for which the Act does not provide.

In August 1986, the UPA Revision Subcommittee of the Committee on Partnerships and Unincorporated Business Organizations of the American Bar Association's Section of Corporation, Banking and Business Law and the National Conference of Commissioners on Uniform State Laws decided to undertake a complete revision of the Uniform Partnership Act. The revision was approved in August 1992 and was amended in 1993, 1994, and 1996. More than twenty States have adopted the Revised Act. This chapter will discuss the original 1914 UPA and the significant changes made by the Revised Uniform Partnership Act, or RUPA. (References to provisions of the original UPA will state the section number only; references to the Revised Act will include the "RUPA" designation.)

## Definition

The UPA defines a **partnership** as "an association of two or more persons to carry on as co-owners a business for profit." Section 6. The UPA broadly defines "person" to include "individuals, partnerships, corporations, and other associations." Section 2. Also defined by Section 2, a business includes every trade, occupation, or profession.

## Entity Theory

A **legal entity** is a unit capable of possessing legal rights and of being subject to legal duties. A legal entity may acquire, own, and dispose of property. It may enter into contracts, commit wrongs, sue, and be sued. Each business corporation is a legal entity having a legal existence separate from that of its shareholders.

A partnership was regarded by the common law as a legal aggregate, a group of individuals having no legal existence apart from that of its members. The UPA has partially rejected the common law view by treating partnerships as legal entities for some purposes and as aggregates for others.

The Revised Act has greatly increased the extent to which partnerships are treated as entities. It applies aggregate treatment to very few aspects of partnerships, the most significant of which is that partners still have unlimited liability for the partnership's obligations.

***Partnership as a Legal Entity*** The UPA recognizes a partnership as an entity legally distinct from its members in several ways. (1) The assets of the firm are treated as those of the business and are considered to be distinct from the individual assets of the members. Section 25. (2) Title to real estate may be acquired by a partnership in the partnership name. Section 8(3). (3) A partner is accountable as a fiduciary to the partnership. Section 21. (4) Every partner is considered an agent of the partnership. Section 9(1). (5) Under the doctrine of marshaling of assets—which applies in cases of insolvency administered by a State court of equity—partnership creditors have a prior right to partnership assets, while creditors of the individual members have a prior right to the separate assets of their individual debtors. Section 40(h).

RUPA Section 201 states, "A partnership is an entity distinct from its partners." The Revised Act embraces the entity treatment of partnerships, particularly in matters concerning title to partnership property, legal actions by and against the partnership, and continuity of existence. The Revised Act, however, has abolished the marshaling of assets doctrine. RUPA Section 807.

***Partnership as a Legal Aggregate*** Because a partnership is considered an aggregate for some purposes, it can neither sue nor be sued in the firm name unless a statute specifically allows such an action. Similarly, the debts of the partnership are ultimately the debts of the individual partners, and any one partner may be held liable for the partnership's entire indebtedness. Section 15. Thus, if Meg and Mike enter into a partnership that becomes insolvent, as does Meg, making the debt uncollectible from the partnership and Meg, Mike is fully liable for the partnership's debts.

In addition, a partnership generally lacks continuity of existence: whenever any partner ceases to be associated with the partnership, it is dissolved. Section 29. Likewise, although a partner's interest in the partnership may be assigned, the assignee does not become a partner without the consent of all the partners. Section 18(g).

The Revised Act has retained the aggregate characteristic of a partner's unlimited liability for partnership obligations. RUPA Section 306. On the other hand, the RUPA has significantly changed the law regarding suing a partnership and continuity of existence. Under the

Revised Act, a partnership may sue and be sued in the name of the partnership. RUPA Section 307. Moreover, a partner's dissociation results in a dissolution only in limited circumstances. RUPA Section 801.

## Types of Partners

Partners can be classified as either general or limited. A partner may also be silent, secret, or dormant. In addition, nonpartners may be considered ostensible partners or subpartners.

A **general partner** is a partner of either a general or limited partnership whose liability for partnership indebtedness is unlimited, who has full management powers, and who shares in the profits. Most partnerships consist solely of general partners; such units are referred to as "general partnerships" or simply as "partnerships."

A special or **limited partner** is one who, as a member of a limited partnership, is liable for firm indebtedness only to the extent of the capital he has contributed or has agreed to contribute. Limited partnerships, discussed in Chapter 33, are formed through compliance with a number of statutory requirements.

A **silent partner** is a partner who elects to take no part in the partnership business.

A **secret partner** is a partner whose membership in the firm is not disclosed to the public.

A **dormant partner** is a partner who is both a silent and a secret partner.

An **ostensible partner** is one who has consented to be held out as a partner whether he is a real partner or not. The term more commonly describes one who is a partner by estoppel: although not an actual partner, he is liable to those who, in good faith, have extended credit on the reasonable assumption that he is a partner.

A **subpartner** is not a partner at all; rather, he has a contractual arrangement with a partner which entitles him to a share of that partner's profits. Maintaining the relationship requires neither continuous acts nor the performance of any duty by the subpartner.

## FORMATION OF A PARTNERSHIP

The formation of a partnership is relatively simple and may be done consciously or unconsciously. A partnership may result from an oral or written agreement between the parties, from an informal arrangement, or from the conduct of the parties, who become partners by associating themselves in a business as co-owners. Consequently, if two or more individuals share the control and profits of a business, the law may deem them partners without

regard to how they themselves characterize their relationship. Thus, associates frequently discover, to their chagrin, that they have inadvertently formed a partnership and have thereby subjected themselves to the duties and liabilities of partners. Whether their agreement is simple or elaborate, definite or indefinite, fully understood and fair or obscure and inequitable is of far less importance to the law than to the partners. The legal existence of the relationship depends merely upon the parties' explicit or implicit agreement and their association in business as co-owners, not upon the degree of care, intelligence, study, or investigation that preceded its formation.

## Articles of Partnership

To render their understanding more clear, definite, and complete, partners are advised, though not usually required, to put their agreement in writing. A written agreement creating a partnership is referred to as a partnership agreement or **articles of partnership.** Unless the agreement provides otherwise, the partners may amend it only by unanimous consent. Any partnership agreement should include

1. The firm name and the identity of the partners;
2. The nature and scope of the partnership business;
3. The duration of the partnership;
4. The capital contributions of each partner;
5. The division of profits and sharing of losses;
6. The managerial duties of each partner;
7. A provision for salaries, if desired;
8. Restrictions, if any, upon the authority of particular partners to bind the firm;
9. The right, if desired, of a partner to withdraw from the firm, and the terms, conditions, and notice required for such withdrawal; and
10. A provision by which the remaining partners, if they desire, may continue the business in the event of a partner's death or other dissolution, and a statement of the method or formula for appraising and paying the interest of the deceased or former partner.

A partnership agreement can provide almost any conceivable arrangement of capital investment, control sharing, and profit distribution that the partners desire. In addition, it can provide for the continuance of the partnership in the event of one member's death or retirement.

The RUPA gives almost total freedom to the partners to provide whatever provisions they agree upon in their partnership agreement. In essence, the RUPA is primarily a set of "default rules" that only apply when the partnership agreement does not address the issue.

◆ *See Figure 31–2*

***Statute of Frauds*** Because the statute of frauds does not apply expressly to a contract for the formation of a partnership, usually no writing is required to create the relationship. A contract to form a partnership to continue for a period longer than one year is within the statute, however, as is a contract for the transfer of an interest in real estate to or by a partnership; consequently, both of these contracts must be evidenced by a writing to be enforceable.

***Firm Name*** In the interest of acquiring and retaining goodwill, a partnership should have a firm name. Although the name selected by the partners may not be identical or deceptively similar to the name of any other existing business concern, it may be the name of the partners or of any one of them; or the partners may decide to operate the business under a fictitious or assumed name, such as "Peachtree Restaurant," "Globe Theater," or "Paradise Laundry." A partnership may not use a name that would be likely to indicate to the public that it is a corporation. Nearly all of the States have enacted statutes that require any person or persons conducting business under an assumed or fictitious name to file in a designated public office a certificate setting forth the name under which the business is conducted and the real names and addresses of all persons conducting the business as partners or proprietors.

## Tests of Partnership Existence

Partnerships can be formed without the slightest formality. Consequently, it is important that the law establish a test for determining whether or not a partnership has been formed. Two situations most often require this determination. The most common involves a creditor who has dealt only with one person but who wishes to hold another liable as well by asserting that the two were partners. Less frequently, a person seeks to share profits and property held by another by claiming that they are partners.

As previously mentioned, Section 6 of the UPA provides the basic definition of a partnership: an association of two or more persons to carry on as co-owners a business for profit. Thus, three components are essential to the existence of a partnership: (1) an association of two or more persons, (2) conducting a business for profit, (3) which they co-own.

◆ *See Figure 31–3*

***Association*** A partnership must consist of two or more persons who have agreed to become partners. Any natural person having full *capacity* may enter into a partnership. To the extent that a minor has capacity to act as a principal or agent, she may become a partner, although she has the right both to disaffirm the partnership agreement at any time before reaching majority and to avoid personal liability to partnership creditors. On disaffirmance and withdrawal from the partnership, a minor is entitled to the return of her capital contribution and her accrued and unpaid share of the profits, except to the extent that such funds are necessary to pay partnership creditors.

The position of a nonadjudicated incompetent is basically the same as that of a minor, except that his incompetency may afford his copartners a ground for seeking dissolution by court decree. Section 32. Because all contracts of an adjudicated incompetent are void, not voidable, a partnership agreement entered into by such an individual is void.

A corporation is defined as a "person" by Section 2 of the UPA and is, therefore, legally capable of entering into a partnership in those States whose incorporation statutes authorize a corporation to do so. Furthermore, a partnership may be a member of other partnerships. Section 2.

***Business for Profit*** The UPA provides that co-ownership does not in itself establish a partnership, even though the co-owners may share the profits derived from the use of the property. Section 7(2). For a partnership to exist, there must be co-ownership of a business. Moreover, to be a partnership, the business carried on by the association of two or more persons must be "for profit." This requirement excludes social clubs, fraternal orders, civic societies, and charitable organizations from being partnerships.

Nor does a partnership exist where persons associate for mutual financial gain on a temporary or limited basis involving a single transaction or a few isolated transactions: such persons are not engaged in the continuous series of commercial activities necessary to constitute a business. Co-ownership of the means or instrumentality of accomplishing a single business transaction or a limited series of transactions may result in a joint venture but not in a general partnership.

For example, Katherine and Edith have joint ownership of shares of the capital stock of a corporation, have a joint bank account, and have inherited or purchased real estate as joint tenants or tenants in common. They share the dividends paid on the stock, the interest on

**FIGURE 31–2** Sample Partnership Agreement under the UPA

## PARTNERSHIP AGREEMENT

This agreement, made and entered into as of the [*Date*], by and among [*Names*] (hereinafter collectively sometimes referred to as "Partners").

## WITNESSETH:

Whereas, the Parties hereto desire to form a General Partnership (hereinafter referred to as the "Partnership"), for the term and upon the conditions hereinafter set forth;

Now, therefore, in consideration of the mutual covenants hereinafter contained, it is agreed by and among the Parties hereto as follows:

### Article I
### BASIC STRUCTURE

#### § 1.1 Form

The Parties hereby form a General Partnership pursuant to the Laws of [*Name of State*].

#### § 1.2 Name

The business of the Partnership shall be conducted under the [*Name*].

#### § 1.3 Place of Business

The principal office and place of business of the Partnership shall be located at [*Describe*], or such other place as the Partners may from time to time designate.

#### § 1.4 Term

The Partnership shall commence on [*Date*], and shall continue for [*Number*] years, unless earlier terminated in the following manner:

(a) By the completion of the purpose intended, or

(b) Pursuant to this Agreement, or

(c) By applicable [*State*] law, or

(d) By death, insanity, bankruptcy, retirement, withdrawal, resignation, expulsion, or disability of all of the then Partners.

#### § 1.5 Purpose—General

The purpose for which the Partnership is organized is _____.

### Article II
### FINANCIAL ARRANGEMENTS

#### § 2.1 Initial Contributions of Partners

Each Partner has contributed to the initial capital of the Partnership property in the amount and form indicated on Schedule A attached hereto and made a part hereof. Capital contributions to the Partnership shall not earn interest. An individual capital account shall be maintained for each Partner.

#### § 2.2 Additional Capital Contribution

If at any time during the existence of the Partnership it shall become necessary to increase the capital with which the said Partnership is doing business, then (upon the vote of the Managing Partner(s)): Each party to this Agreement shall contribute to the capital of this Partnership within ____ days notice of such need in an amount according to his then Percentage Share of Capital as called for by the Managing Partner(s).

#### § 2.3 Percentage Share of Profits and Capital

(a) The Percentage Share of Profits Share of Profits and Capital of each Partnership shall be (unless otherwise modified by the terms of this Agreement) as follows:

| Names | Initial Percentage Share of Profits and Capital |
|-------|-------------------------------------------------|

**FIGURE 31-2** *(continued)*

### § 2.4 Interest

No interest shall be paid on any contribution to the capital of the Partnership.

### § 2.5 Return of Capital Contribution

No Partner shall have the right to demand the return of his capital contributions except as herein provided.

### § 2.6 Rights of Priority

Except as herein provided, the individual Partners shall have no right to any priority over each other as to the return of capital contributions except as herein provided.

### § 2.7 Distributions

Distributions to the Partners of net operating profits of the Partnership, as hereinafter defined, shall be made at (*lease monthly/at such times as the Managing Partner(s) shall reasonably agree.*) Such distributions shall be made to the Partners simultaneously.

### § 2.8 Compensation

No Partner shall be entitled to receive any compensation from the Partnership, nor shall any Partner receive any drawing account from the Partnership.

Article III

MANAGEMENT

### § 3. Managing Partners

The Managing Partner(s) shall be [*Names*] [*or* "all partners"].

### §3.2 Voting

The Managing Partner(s) shall have the right to vote as to the management and conduct of the business of the Partnership as follows:

**Names**                                                                 **Vote**

Article IV

DISSOLUTION

### §4.1 Dissolution

In the event that the Partnership shall hereafter be dissolved for any reason whatsoever, a full and general account of its assets, liabilities, and transactions shall at once be taken. Such assets may be sold and turned into cash as soon as possible and all debts and other amounts due the Partnership collected. The proceeds thereof shall thereupon be applied as follows:

(a) To discharge the debts and liabilities of the Partnership and the expenses of liquidation.
(b) To pay each Partner or his legal representative any unpaid salary, drawing account, interest or profits to which he shall then be entitled and in addition, to repay to any Partner his capital contributions in excess of his original capital contribution.
(c) To divide the surplus, if any, among the Partners or their representatives as follows:
    (1) First (to the extent of each Partner's then capital account) in proportion to their then capital accounts.
    (2) Then according to each Partner's the Percentage Share of *Capital/Income*.

### § 4.2 Right to Demand Property

No Partner shall have the right to demand and receive property in kind for his distribution.

**Witnesses**                                                                 **Partners**

**Dated:** _____

**FIGURE 31–3** Tests for Existence of a Partnership

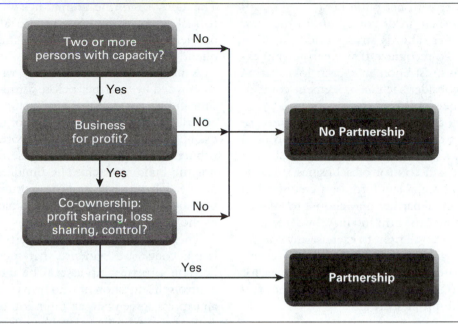

the bank account, and the net proceeds from the sale or lease of the real estate. Nevertheless, Katherine and Edith are not partners. Although they are co-owners and share profits, they are not engaged in carrying on a business; hence, no partnership exists. On the other hand, if Katherine and Edith continuously bought and sold real estate over a period of time and conducted a business of trading in real estate, a partnership relation would exist between them, regardless of whether they considered themselves partners or not.

To illustrate further: Alec, Laura, and Shirley each inherit an undivided one-third interest in a hotel and, instead of selling the property, decide by an informal agreement to continue operating the hotel. The operation of a hotel is a business; as co-owners of a hotel business, Alec, Laura, and Shirley are partners and are subject to all of the rights, duties, and incidents arising from the partnership relation.

*Co-ownership* Although the co-ownership of *property* used in a business is a condition neither necessary nor sufficient for the existence of a partnership, the co-ownership of a *business* is essential. In identifying business co-ownership, the two most important factors are the sharing of profits and the right to manage and control the business.

A person's receiving a share of the **profits** from a business is *prima facie* evidence that he is a partner in the business. Section 7(4) of the UPA, however, provides that the existence of a partnership relation shall not be inferred where such profits are received in payment

1. of a debt, by installments or otherwise;
2. of wages of an employee or rent to a landlord;
3. of an annuity to a widow or representative of a deceased partner;
4. of interest on a loan, though the amount of payment may vary with the profits of the business; or
5. as consideration for the sale of the goodwill of a business or other property, by installments or otherwise.

These transactions do not give rise to a presumption that the party is a partner because the law assumes that the creditor, employee, landlord, or other recipient of such profits is unlikely to be a co-owner. It is possible, nonetheless, to establish that such a person is a partner by proof of other facts and circumstances, such as the sharing of control.

The sharing of *gross returns*, in contrast to profits, does not of itself establish a partnership. Section 7(3). This is so whether or not the persons sharing the gross returns have a joint or common interest in any property from which the returns are derived. Thus, two brokers who share commissions are not necessarily partners, or even presumed to be. Similarly, an author who receives royalties (a share of gross receipts from the sales of a book) is not a partner with her publisher.

An agreement to share in or contribute to the *losses* of a business, however, affords strong evidence of an ownership interest. To recognize that a partnership exists, few jurisdictions insist upon an express loss-sharing agreement; but all consider such an agreement compelling proof of a partnership's existence.

By itself, evidence as to participation in the *management* or **control** of a business is not conclusive proof of a partnership relation, but it is persuasive. Limited voice in the management and control of a business may be accorded to an employee, a landlord, or a creditor. On the other hand, an actual partner may choose to take no active part in the affairs of the firm and may, by agreement with his copartners, forgo all right to exercise any control over the ordinary affairs of the business. In any event, the right to participate in control is an important factor considered by the courts in conjunction with other factors, particularly with profit sharing.

 *See Case 31–1*

## Partnership Capital and Property

The total money and property that the partners contribute and dedicate to use in the enterprise is the **partnership capital**. No minimum amount of capitalization is necessary before a partnership may commence business. Nonetheless, no partner may withdraw any part of his capital contribution without the consent of all the partners, except when the partnership is dissolved.

Whereas partnership capital is a fixed amount that may change only through amendment to the articles of partnership, **partnership property,** or the sum of the partnership's assets, may vary in amount. All property originally brought into the partnership or subsequently acquired by the partnership is partnership property. Section 8(1). Given no intention to the contrary, property acquired with partnership funds is partnership property. Section 8(2).

As discussed later, who owns the property—an individual partner or the partnership—determines (1) who gets it after dissolution of the partnership, (2) who shares in any loss or gain upon its sale, (3) who shares in income from it, (4) who may sell it or transfer it by will, and (5) whose creditors have a priority against it in satisfying their claims.

Title to real estate that is properly a partnership asset, such as that purchased with partnership funds or specifically made a capital contribution, may stand in the name of the partnership, an individual partner, or a third party. The UPA alters the common law by permitting title to real estate to be conveyed to a partnership in the partnership name. Section 8(3). Title so acquired subsequently may be conveyed only in the partnership name.

A question may arise regarding whether property that was owned by a partner before formation of the partnership and was used in the partnership business is a capital contribution and hence an asset of the partnership. For example, a partner who owns a store building may contribute to the partnership the use of the building but not the building itself. The building is, therefore, not partnership property, and the amount of capital contributed by this partner is the reasonable value of the rental of the building.

The fact that legal title to property remains unchanged is not conclusive evidence that such property has not become a partnership asset. The intent of the partners controls the question of who owns the property. Without an express agreement, an intention to consider property as partnership property may be inferred from any of the following facts: (1) the property was improved with partnership funds; (2) the property was carried on the books of the partnership as an asset; (3) taxes, liens, or expenses, such as insurance or repairs, were paid by the partnership; (4) income or proceeds of the property were treated as partnership funds; or (5) the partners declared or admitted the property to be partnership property.

 *See Case 31–2*

## Rights in Specific Partnership Property

A partner's ownership interest in any specific item of partnership property is that of a **tenant in partnership.** Section 25. This type of ownership, which exists only in a partnership, has the following principal characteristics:

1. Each partner has a right equal to that of his copartners to possess partnership property for partnership purposes, but he has no right to possess it for any other purpose without his copartners' consent.
2. A partner may not make an individual assignment of his right in specific partnership property.
3. A partner's interest in specific partnership property is not subject to attachment or execution by his individual creditors. It is subject to attachment or execution only on a claim against the partnership.
4. Upon the death of a partner, his right in specific partnership property vests in the surviving partner or partners. Upon the death of the last surviving partner,

his right in such property vests in his legal representative.

In adopting the entity theory, the Revised Act abolishes the UPA's concept of tenants in partnership: partnership property is owned by the partnership entity and not by the individual partners. RUPA Section 203. Moreover, RUPA Section 501 provides, "A partner is not a co-owner of partnership property and has no interest in partnership property which can be transferred, either voluntarily or involuntarily."

## Partner's Interest in the Partnership

In addition to owning as a tenant in partnership every specific item of partnership property, each partner has an **interest in the partnership,** which is defined as his share of the profits and surplus. This interest is expressly stated to be personal property. Section 26.

The Revised Act similarly provides that the only transferable interest of a partner in the partnership is the partner's share of the profits and losses of the partnership and the partner's right to receive distributions. This interest is personal property. RUPA Section 502.

*Assignability* A partner may sell or assign his interest in the partnership. The new owner, however, does not become a partner, does not succeed to the partner's rights to participate in the management, and does not have access to the information available to a member of the firm as a matter of right. She is merely entitled to receive upon liquidation the share of profits and rights to which the assigning partner would otherwise have been entitled. Section 27. The assigning partner remains a partner with all of a partner's other rights and duties. Although an assignment does not in itself dissolve the partnership, the other partners may rightfully dissolve the partnership by unanimous agreement. Moreover, the assignee may apply for a court-ordered dissolution. Dissolution is discussed later in this chapter.

The Revised Act is substantially the same but uses the term *transfer* instead of *assignment.* RUPA Section 503. Under RUPA Section 601(4)(ii), however, the other partners by a unanimous vote may expel a partner who has transferred substantially all of his partnership interest.

*Creditors' Rights* A partner's interest is subject to the claims of that partner's creditors, who may obtain a **charging order** (a type of judicial lien) against the partner's interest. Section 28. A creditor who has charged the interest of a partner with a judgment debt may apply

for the appointment of, and the court may then appoint, a receiver for the partner's interest who will receive and hold for the creditor's benefit the share of profits that ordinarily would be paid to the partner. Neither the judgment creditor nor the receiver becomes a partner, and neither is entitled to participate in the partnership's management or to have access to information.

Furthermore, neither the charging order nor its sale upon foreclosure causes a dissolution, though the other partners may dissolve the partnership or redeem the charged interest. Sections 32 and 28. The creditor has the same right to a court-ordered dissolution as an assignee has.

RUPA Section 601(4)(ii) provides that a partner may be expelled by a unanimous vote of the other partners upon foreclosure of a judicial lien charging a partner's interest.

◆ *See Figure 31–4*

# DISSOLUTION OF GENERAL PARTNERSHIPS

The extinguishment of a partnership consists of three stages: (1) dissolution, (2) winding up or liquidation, and (3) termination. Dissolution occurs when the partners cease to carry on the business together. Upon dissolution, the partnership is not terminated but continues until the winding up of its affairs is complete. During winding up, unfinished business is completed, receivables are collected, payments are made to creditors, and the remaining assets are distributed to the partners. Termination occurs when the process is finished.

In keeping with its adoption of entity treatment, the Revised Act significantly changes the law governing partnership breakups. The RUPA uses the term *dissociation*, instead of the UPA term *dissolution*, to denote the change in the relationship caused by a partner's ceasing to be associated in carrying on of the business. The Revised Act uses the term *dissolution* to refer to those situations when the Revised Act requires a partnership to wind up and terminate. Under the RUPA, a dissociation of a partner results in dissolution only in limited circumstances. In many instances, dissociation will result merely in a buyout of the withdrawing partner's interest rather than a winding up of the partnership. Those dissociations that require dissolution will be included with the discussion of dissolution under the UPA. Those dissociations that do not require dissolution will be covered with the

FIGURE 31–4  Partnership Property Compared with Partner's Interest

|  | Partnership Property | Partner's Interest |
|---|---|---|
| **Definition** | Tenant in partnership* | Share of profits and surplus |
| **Possession** | For partnership purposes, not individual ones | Intangible, personal property right |
| **Assignability** | If all other partners assign their rights in the property* | Assignee does not become a partner |
| **Attachment** | Only for a claim against the partnership | By a charging order |
| **Inheritance** | Goes to surviving partner(s)* | Passes to the personal representative of deceased partner |

*RUPA has changed these rules by providing that a partner is not a co-owner of partnership property and has no interest in partnership property which can be transferred, either voluntarily or involuntarily.

discussion of continuation after dissolution under the UPA.

## DISSOLUTION

The Uniform Partnership Act defines **dissolution** as the change in the relation of the partners caused by any partner's ceasing to be associated in the carrying on, as distinguished from the winding up, of the business. Section 29. The following sections discuss the causes and effects of dissolution.

### Causes of Dissolution

Dissolution may be brought about by (1) an act of the partners, (2) operation of law, or (3) court order. Section 31. A number of events that were considered causes of dissolution under the common law are no longer considered so under the UPA. For example, the assignment of a partner's interest, a creditor's charging order (judicial lien) on a partner's interest, and an accounting no longer trigger a dissolution.

*Dissolution by Act of the Partners* Because a partnership is a personal relationship, a partner always has the power to dissolve it by his actions, but whether he has the right to do so is determined by the partnership agreement. A partner who has withdrawn from the partnership in violation of the partnership agreement is liable to the remaining partners for damages resulting from the **wrongful dissolution.**

A partnership is **rightfully dissolved,** that is, dissolved in such a manner that the partner's or partners' act does not violate the partnership agreement

1. when all of those partners who have not assigned their interests or permitted their interests to be charged expressly agree to dissolve the partnership;
2. when the time period provided in the agreement has ended or the purpose for which the partnership was formed has been accomplished;
3. when a partner withdraws from a partnership at will, that is, a partnership with no definite term or specific undertaking; or
4. when a partner is expelled in accordance with a power to expel conferred by the partnership agreement. Section 31.

 *See Case 31–3*

*Dissolution by Operation of Law* A partnership is dissolved by operation of law upon (1) the death of a partner, (2) the bankruptcy of a partner or of the partnership, or (3) the subsequent illegality of the partnership, which includes any event that makes it unlawful for the partnership business to be carried on or for the members to carry on the business in partnership form. Section 31. For example, a partnership formed to manufacture liquor would be dissolved by a law prohibiting the production and sale of alcoholic beverages, whereas a partnership of lawyers would be dissolved if one of its members were disbarred from the practice of law.

*Dissolution by Court Order* Upon application by or for a partner, a court will order a dissolution if it finds that (1) a partner has been adjudicated mentally incompetent or suffers some other incapacity that prevents him from functioning as a partner; (2) a partner has engaged in conduct prejudicial to the business, has willfully or persistently breached the partnership agreement, or has conducted himself so that it is impracticable to carry on business; (3) the business can be carried on only at a loss; or (4) other circumstances render a dissolution equitable. Section 32.

An assignee of a partner's interest or a partner's personal creditor who has obtained a charging order against the partner's interest is entitled to a dissolution by court decree. If the partnership is not at will, however, the partnership will not be dissolved until the term or particular undertaking specified in the partnership agreement is complete.

*Dissolution under RUPA* As part of the Revised Act's according greater entity treatment to partnerships, RUPA Section 801 specifies the following, more limited, set of partner's dissociations that will result in dissolution of a partnership: (1) In a partnership at will, a partner gives notice of intent to withdraw. (2) In a partnership for a specific term or particular undertaking (a) the term of the partnership expires or the undertaking is complete; (b) upon the expiration of 90 days after a partner's dissociation by death, bankruptcy or similar financial impairment, a partner's incapacity, the distribution by a trust-partner of its entire partnership interest, the distribution by an estate-partner of its entire partnership interest, the termination of an entity-partner, or a partner's wrongful dissociation, *unless* before that time a majority in interest of the remaining partners agree to continue the partnership. A wrongful dissociation includes a partner's voluntary withdrawal in violation of the partnership agreement and the judicial expulsion of a partner; or (c) all of the partners expressly agree to dissolve. (3) An event occurs that was specified in the partnership agreement as resulting in dissolution. (4) An event occurs that makes it unlawful to carry on all or substantially all of the partnership's business. (5) On application by a partner, a court orders dissolution on grounds of another partner's misconduct or a finding that it is not reasonably practicable to carry on the business in conformity with the partnership agreement. (6) On application of a transferee of a partner's transferable interest or a purchaser at foreclosure of a charging order, a court determines that it is equitable to wind up the partnership business (a) at any time in a partnership at will or (b) after the term of a term partnership has expired. The partners may not by agreement vary or eliminate the last three grounds for dissolution. They may, however, by agreement modify or eliminate the other grounds.

## Effects of Dissolution

On dissolution, the partnership is not terminated but continues until the winding up of its affairs is complete. Section 30. Moreover, dissolution does not discharge the existing liability of any partner, though it does restrict her authority to act for the partnership.

*Authority* Upon dissolution, the *actual authority* of a partner to act for the partnership terminates, except so far as may be necessary to wind up partnership affairs. Section 33. Actual authority to wind up includes the authority to complete existing contracts, to collect debts, to sell partnership assets, and to pay partnership obligations.

Although actual authority terminates upon dissolution, *apparent authority* continues to bind the partnership for acts within the scope of the partnership business unless the third party is given notice of the dissolution. Section 35. A third party who extended credit to the partnership before dissolution may hold the partnership liable for any transaction that would have bound the partnership had dissolution not occurred, unless the third party had knowledge or actual notice of the dissolution. **Actual notice** requires a verbal statement to the third party or actual delivery of a written statement. Section 3(2). On the other hand, a third party who knew of or had dealt with the partnership but who had not extended credit to it before its dissolution can hold the partnership liable unless he had knowledge, actual notice, or constructive notice of the dissolution. **Constructive notice** consists of advertising a notice of dissolution in a newspaper of general circulation in the places at which the partnership regularly conducted its business. Section 35(1)(b)(II). No notice need be given to third parties who had no knowledge of the partnership before its dissolution.

The Revised Act continues the UPA's rule that a partner has actual authority to bind the partnership for acts after dissolution that are appropriate for winding up the partnership business. With respect to apparent authority, the partnership is bound in a transaction not appropriate for winding up only if the partner's act would have bound the partnership before dissolution and the other party to the transaction did not have notice of the dissolution. RUPA Section 804. A person has notice of a fact if the person (1) knows of it, (2) has received a notification of it, or (3) has reason to know it exists from all of the facts known to the person at the time in question. RUPA Section 102(b). Moreover, RUPA Section 805 provides that, after an event of dissolution, any partner who has not wrongfully dissociated may file a statement of dissolution on behalf of the partnership and that 90 days after the filing of the statement of dissolution nonpartners are deemed to have notice of the dissolution and the corresponding limitation on the authority of all partners. Thus, after 90 days the statement of dissolution operates as constructive notice conclusively limiting the apparent authority of partners to transactions that are appropriate for winding up the business. These provisions of the RUPA abolish the special protection the UPA extended to former creditors and the lesser special protection the UPA afforded to other parties who knew of the partnership before dissolution.

***Existing Liability*** The dissolution of the partnership does not of itself discharge the existing liability of any partner. Section 36(1). But in some instances the cause of dissolution may discharge an executory contract. For example, if a contract calls for the personal services of one of the partners, the death of that partner usually will discharge the contract and cause the dissolution of the partnership as well.

# WINDING UP

Whenever a dissolved partnership is not to be continued, the partnership must be liquidated. The process of liquidation, called **winding up,** involves completing unfinished business, collecting debts, taking inventory, reducing assets to cash, auditing the partnership books, paying creditors, and distributing the remaining assets to the partners. During this period, the fiduciary duties of the partners continue in effect.

The Revised Act is essentially the same, except after dissolution a partner may compete with the partnership unless the partnership agreement otherwise provides. RUPA Section 404.

## The Right to Wind Up

Upon dissolution any partner who has not wrongfully dissolved the partnership or been rightfully expelled according to the terms of the partnership agreement has the right to insist on the winding up of the partnership unless the partnership agreement provides otherwise. Unless otherwise agreed, all nonbankrupt partners who have not wrongfully dissolved the partnership have the right to wind up the partnership affairs. Section 37. A court, upon the petition of a partner, his legal representative, or his assignee, may appoint a receiver for all of the partnership's property and assets. The receiver has

authority to wind up the business under the court's direction. The appointment of a receiver is discretionary, based upon a showing of cause.

## Distribution of Assets

After all the partnership assets have been collected and reduced to cash, they are distributed to creditors and the partners. When the partnership has been profitable, the order of distribution is not critical; however, when liabilities exceed assets, the order of distribution has great importance.

Section 40 of the UPA sets forth the rules for settling accounts between the parties after dissolution. It states that the liabilities of a partnership are to be paid out of partnership assets in the following order:

1. amounts owing to nonpartner creditors
2. amounts owing to partners other than for capital and profits (loans or advances)
3. amounts owing to partners for capital
4. amounts owing to partners for profits

The partners may by agreement among themselves change the internal priorities of distribution (numbers 2, 3, and 4) but not the preferred position of third parties (number 1). The UPA defines partnership assets to include all partnership property as well as the contributions necessary for the payment of all partnership liabilities, which consist of numbers 1, 2, and 3. Section 40(a).

In addition, the UPA provides that, in the absence of any contrary agreement, each partner shall share equally in the profits and surplus remaining after all liabilities (numbers 1, 2, and 3) are satisfied and must contribute toward the partnership's losses, capital or otherwise, according to his share in the profits. Section 18(a). Thus, the proportion in which the partners bear losses depends not on their relative capital contributions but on their agreement. If no specific agreement exists, the partners bear losses in the same proportion in which they share profits.

If the partnership is insolvent, the partners individually must contribute their respective share of the losses to pay the creditors. Furthermore, if one or more of the partners is insolvent or bankrupt or is out of the jurisdiction and refuses to contribute, the other partners must contribute the additional amount necessary to pay the firm's liabilities in the relative proportions in which they share the profits. Section 40(d). Any partner who pays an amount in excess of his proper share of the losses has a right of contribution against the partners who have not paid their share. Section 40(f).

The RUPA has modified these rules. First, the partnership must apply its assets to discharge the obligations of partners who are creditors on parity with other creditors, subject to any other laws, such as fraudulent conveyance laws and voidable transfers under the Bankruptcy Act. Second, the RUPA's distribution does not distinguish between amounts owing to partners for capital and amounts owing to partners for profits. RUPA Section 807.

*Solvent Partnership* Assume that A, B, and C formed ABC Company, a partnership, with A contributing $6,000 capital, B contributing $4,000 capital, and C contributing services but no capital. A also loaned the partnership $3,000, which has not been repaid. No agreement describes the proportions in which profits and losses are to be shared. After a few years of operation, the partnership is liquidated. At this time, the assets of ABC Company are $54,000, and its liabilities to creditors are $26,000. The partnership is thus solvent and has enjoyed a profit of $15,000, calculated by subtracting the total liabilities ($39,000) from the total assets ($54,000). The total liabilities consist of the amount owed to creditors ($26,000), the amount owed to partners other than for capital and profits ($3,000 owed to A for his loan), and the capital contributions of the partners ($10,000: $6,000 from A and $4,000 from B). As A, B, and C have not explicitly agreed upon a profit-sharing ratio, they share the profits equally, in this case each receiving $5,000 ($15,000 ÷ 3). After the creditors have been paid in full, A will receive $14,000 ($3,000 for repayment of the loan, $6,000 for capital, and $5,000 for share of profits); B will receive $9,000 ($4,000 for capital and $5,000 for share of profits); and C will receive $5,000 (for share of profits).

*Insolvent Partnership* Assume that the same partnership had experienced financial adversity. It still owes its creditors $26,000, but its assets total only $12,000. In this case the partnership has sustained an aggregate loss of $27,000, calculated by subtracting the total liabilities ($39,000, calculated as in the example above) from the total assets ($12,000). In the absence of a contrary agreement, the losses are shared as the profits are, which in this case is equally. Accordingly, each partner's share of the loss will be $9,000 ($27,000 ÷ 3). After the creditors are paid ($26,000), A will receive nothing ($3,000 owed for the loan plus $6,000 for capital minus $9,000 for his share of losses); B must make an additional contribution of $5,000 to make good his share of the loss ($4,000 owed for capital minus $9,000 for his share of

losses); and C must contribute $9,000 (his share of losses).

| | Loans + | Capital Contributions − | Share of Loss = | Share of Assets or (Additional Contributions Owed) |
|---|---|---|---|---|
| A | $3,000 | $ 6,000 | − $ 9,000 | 0 |
| B | 0 | $ 4,000 | − $ 9,000 | $( 5,000) |
| C | 0 | 0 | − $ 9,000 | $( 9,000) |
| Total | $3,000 | $10,000 | − $27,000 | $(14,000) |

*Contribution of Partner upon Insolvency* In the insolvent partnership example above, if A were individually insolvent, the results would not change because A was not required to contribute any additional moneys. If A and B were solvent and C were individually insolvent, C would be unable to pay any of his share of the loss. A and B would then have to contribute equally, as that is the relative proportion in which they share profits, to make good the amount of C's share. Because C's share of the loss is $9,000, A and B would each contribute an additional $4,500. This means that, in total, A would have to contribute $4,500 and B $9,500 to satisfy the unpaid claims of partnership creditors. On the other hand, if A and C were individually insolvent and B were solvent, B would be required to pay the entire balance of $14,000 due to partnership creditors, representing his unpaid share of the loss plus a contribution of the full amount of C's unpaid share of the loss.

## Marshaling of Assets

The doctrine of marshaling of assets applies only where a court of equity is administering the assets of a partnership and of its members. **Marshaling of assets** means segregating and considering separately the assets and liabilities of the partnership and the respective assets and liabilities of the individual partners. Partnership creditors are entitled to be satisfied first out of partnership assets and may recover any deficiency out of the individually owned assets of the partners. This right is subordinate, however, to the rights of nonpartnership creditors to those assets. Conversely, the nonpartnership creditors have first claim to the individually owned assets of their respective debtors, whereas their claims to partnership assets are subordinate to the claims of partnership creditors. This approach is called the "dual priority" rule.

Finally, the assets of an insolvent partner are distributed in the following order: (1) debts and liabilities owing to her nonpartnership creditors, (2) debts and liabilities owing to partnership creditors, and (3) contributions owing to other partners who have paid more than their respective share of the firm's liabilities to partnership creditors. Section 40(i).

This rule, however, is no longer followed if the partnership is a debtor under the Bankruptcy Code. In a proceeding under the Federal bankruptcy law, a trustee is appointed to administer the estate of the debtor. If the partnership property is insufficient to pay all the claims against the partnership, the statute directs the trustee to seek recovery of the deficiency first from the general partners who are not bankrupt. The trustee may then seek recovery against the estates of bankrupt partners on the same basis as other creditors of the bankrupt partner. Bankruptcy Code, Section 723. This provision, although contrary to the UPA's doctrine of marshaling of assets, governs whenever partnership assets are being administered by a bankruptcy court.

The Revised Act also abolishes the marshaling of assets doctrine and the dual priority rule. RUPA Section 807.

# CONTINUATION AFTER DISSOLUTION

Dissolution produces one of two outcomes: either the partnership is liquidated or the remaining partners continue the partnership. Whereas liquidation sacrifices the value of a going concern, continuation of the partnership after dissolution avoids this loss. The UPA, nonetheless, gives each partner the right to have the partnership liquidated except in a few instances where the remaining partners have the right to continue the partnership. Section 37.

## Right to Continue Partnership

After dissolution, the remaining partners have the right to continue the partnership when (1) the partnership has been dissolved in contravention of the partnership agreement, (2) a partner has been expelled in accordance with the partnership agreement, or (3) all the partners agree to continue the business. Nevertheless, the noncontinuing partner, or his legal representative, has a right to an account of his interest against the person or partnership continuing the business as of the date of dissolution, unless otherwise agreed. Section 43. Moreover, when a partner dies or retires and the surviving partners continue the business, the retired partner or the legal representative of the deceased partner is entitled to be paid the value of his interest as of the date of the dissolution as an ordinary creditor of the partnership. In addition, he is entitled to receive interest on this amount or, at his option, in lieu of interest, the profits of the business attributable to the use of his right in the property of the dissolved partnership. His rights are subordinate, however, to those of creditors of the dissolved partnership. Section 42.

***Continuation after Wrongful Dissolution*** A partner who causes dissolution by wrongfully withdrawing cannot force the liquidation of the firm. The aggrieved partners may either liquidate the firm and recover damages for the breach of the partnership agreement or continue the partnership by buying out the withdrawing partner, who is entitled to realize his interest in the partnership less the amount of the damages that the other partners have sustained because of his breach. The withdrawing partner's interest is computed without considering the goodwill of the business. In addition, the remaining partners may use the capital contributions of the wrongdoing partner for the unexpired period of the partnership agreement. They must, however, indemnify the former partner against all present and future partnership liabilities. Section 38(2).

***Continuation after Expulsion*** A partner expelled pursuant to the partnership agreement cannot force the liquidation of the partnership. He is entitled only (1) to be discharged from all partnership liabilities either by payment or by a novation with the creditors and (2) to receive in cash the net amount due him from the partnership. Section 38(1).

***Continuation Agreement of the Partners*** By far the best and most reliable tool for preserving a partnership business after dissolution is through a continuation agreement. Frequently used to ensure continuity in the event of a partner's death or retirement, continuation agreements permit remaining partners to keep partnership property, carry on partnership business, and specify settlements for outgoing partners.

◆ *See Figure 31–5*

## Continuation after Dissociation under RUPA

As already mentioned, the RUPA uses the term *dissociation* instead of the UPA term *dissolution* to denote the

**FIGURE 31–5**  Causes and Effects of Dissolution under the UPA

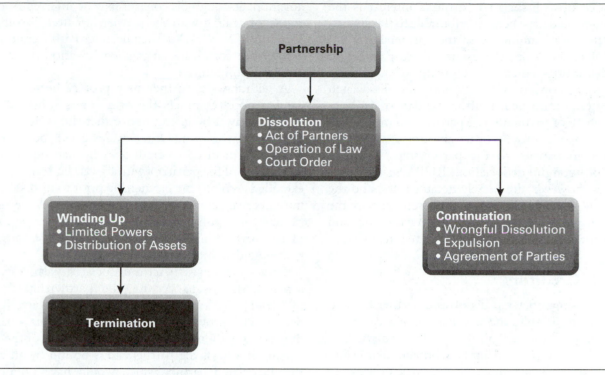

change in the relationship caused by a partner's ceasing to be associated in carrying on of the business. Under the RUPA, a dissociation of a partner results in dissolution only in limited circumstances, discussed above. In many instances, dissociation will result merely in a buyout of the withdrawing partner's interest rather than a winding up of the partnership. Those dissociations that do not require dissolution include the following.

In a *partnership at will* (one that is not for a definite term or particular undertaking), involving a partner's death, bankruptcy, or similar financial impairment; a partner's incapacity; the expulsion of a partner; the distribution by a trust-partner of its entire partnership interest; or the distribution by an estate-partner of its entire partnership interest, the termination of an entity-partner results in a dissociation of that partner but does not result in a dissolution. RUPA Sections 601 and 801. (As covered earlier, a partnership at will is *dissolved* upon notice of a partner's intent to withdraw.)

In a *term partnership*, if within 90 days after any of certain causes of dissolution occurs, a majority in interest of the remaining partners agree to continue a partnership that has been dissolved, then the partnership will not dissolve. These causes are the following: a partner's dissociation by death, bankruptcy, or similar financial impairment; a partner's incapacity; the distribution by a trust-partner of its entire partnership interest; the distribution by an estate-partner of its entire partnership interest; the termination of an entity-partner; or a partner's wrongful dissociation. (A wrongful dissociation includes a partner's voluntary withdrawal in violation of the partnership agreement and the judicial expulsion of a partner.) RUPA Section 801.

With three exceptions, the partners may by agreement modify or eliminate any of the grounds for dissolution. The three exceptions are carrying on an illegal business, a court-ordered dissolution on application of a partner, and a court-ordered dissolution on application of a transferee of a partner's interest. RUPA Section 103. Moreover, at any time after the dissolution of a partnership and before the winding up of its business is completed, all of the partners, including any dissociating partner other than a wrongfully dissociating partner, may waive the right to have the partnership's business wound up and the partnership terminated. In that event, the partnership resumes carrying on its business as if dissolution had never occurred, and any liability incurred by the partnership or a partner after the dissolution and before the waiver is determined as if dissolution had never occurred. RUPA Section 802(b).

If a partner is dissociated from a partnership without resulting in a dissolution, the partnership must purchase the dissociated partner's interest in the partnership. The buyout price of a dissociated partner's interest is the amount that would have been distributable to the dissociating partner in a winding up of the partnership if, on the date of dissociation, the assets of the partnership were sold at a price equal to the greater of liquidation value or going concern value without the dissociated partner. Interest must be paid from the date of dissociation to the date of payment. The partnership must offset against the buyout price all other amounts owing from the dissociated partner to the partnership, including damages for wrongful dissociation. RUPA Section 701. These rules, however, are merely default rules, and the partners may, in the partnership agreement, specify the method or formula for determining the buyout price and all of the other terms and conditions of the buyout right.

## Rights of Creditors

Any change in membership dissolves a partnership and forms a new one, despite the fact that the new combination may include a majority of the old partners. The creditors of the old partnership may pursue their claims against the new partnership and also may proceed to hold all of the members of the dissolved partnership personally liable. Section 41. Because the Revised Act adopts an entity approach to partnerships, generally the relationship between a partnership and its creditors is not affected by a change in membership of the partnership. If a withdrawing partner has made arrangements with those who continue the business whereby they assume and pay all debts and obligations of the firm, the partner is still liable to creditors whose claims arose before the dissolution. If compelled to pay such debts, the withdrawing partner nonetheless has a right of indemnity against her former partners, who agreed to pay the debts but failed to do so.

A retiring partner may be discharged from his existing liabilities by entering into a **novation** with the continuing partners and the creditors. A creditor must agree to a novation, although his consent may be inferred from his course of dealing with the partnership after dissolution. Section 36(2). Whether such dealings with a continuing partnership constitute an implied novation is a factual question of intent.

A withdrawing partner may protect herself against liability upon contracts the firm enters subsequent to her withdrawal by giving notice that she is no longer a member of the firm. Otherwise, she will be liable for debts thus incurred to creditors who had no notice or knowledge of the partner's withdrawal. Persons who had extended credit to the partnership prior to its dissolution must receive actual notice, whereas constructive notice by newspaper publication will suffice for those who knew of the partnership but had not extended credit to it before its dissolution. Section 35.

Under the Revised Act a dissociated partner has no actual authority to act for the partnership. RUPA 603(b)(1). With respect to apparent authority, RUPA Section 702 provides that for two years after a partner dissociates without resulting in a dissolution of the partnership business, the partnership is bound by an act of the dissociated partner which would have bound the partnership before dissociation but only if at the time of entering into the transaction the other party: (1) reasonably believed that the dissociated partner was then a partner; (2) did not have notice of the partner's dissociation; and (3) is not deemed to have had constructive notice under Section 704(c). RUPA Section 704(c) provides that 90 days after a statement of dissociation is filed, nonpartners are deemed to have constructive notice of the dissociation, thereby conclusively terminating a dissociated partner's apparent authority. The same rule applies to a dissociated partner's liability for transactions entered into within two years after he dissociates. RUPA Section 703.

 *See Case 31–4*

---

# Chapter Summary

## Formation of General Partnerships

| Nature | **Definition of Partnership** an association of two or more persons to carry on as co-owners a business for profit |
|---|---|

**Entity Theory**
- *Legal Entity* an organization having a legal existence separate from that of its members; the UPA considers a partnership a legal entity for some purposes
- *Legal Aggregate* a group of individuals not having a legal existence separate from that of its members; the UPA considers a partnership a legal aggregate for some purposes

**Types of Partners**
- *General Partner* member of either a general or a limited partnership with unlimited liability for its debts, full management powers, and a right to share profits
- *Limited Partner* member of a limited partnership with liability for its debts only to the extent of her capital contribution
- *Silent Partner* partner who takes no part in the partnership business
- *Secret Partner* partner whose membership in the partnership is not disclosed to the public
- *Dormant Partner* partner who is both a silent and a secret partner

## Formation

**Articles of Partnership** it is preferable, although not usually required, that the partners enter into a written partnership agreement (articles of partnership)

**Tests of Existence** the formation of a partnership requires all of the following:
- *Association* two or more persons with legal capacity who agree to become partners
- *Business for Profit*
- *Co-ownership* includes sharing of profits, losses, and control of the business

**Partnership Capital** total money and property contributed by the partners for permanent use by the partnership

**Partnership Property** sum of all of the partnership's assets, including all property brought into the partnership or subsequently acquired by it

**Tenancy in Partnership** type of joint ownership that determines partners' rights in specific partnership property

**Interest in Partnership** partner's share in the partnership's profits and surplus
- *Assignability* a partner may sell or assign his interest in the partnership; the new owner becomes entitled to the assigning partner's share of profits and surplus but does not become a partner
- *Creditors' Rights* a partner's interest is subject to the claims of creditors, who may obtain a charging order (judicial lien) against the partner's interest

# Dissolution of General Partnerships

## Dissolution

**Definition of Dissolution** the change in the relation of partners caused by any partner's ceasing to be associated with the carrying on of the business

**Causes of Dissolution**
- *Dissolution by Act of the Partners* a partner always has the power to dissolve a partnership, but the partnership agreement determines whether he has the right to do so
- *Dissolution by Operation of Law* a partnership is dissolved by operation of law upon (1) the death of a partner, (2) the bankruptcy of a partner or of the partnership, or (3) the subsequent illegality of the partnership
- *Dissolution by Court Order* a court will order dissolution of a partnership under certain conditions

**Effects of Dissolution** upon dissolution a partnership is not terminated but continues until the winding up is completed

- *Authority* a partner's actual authority to act for the partnership terminates, except so far as may be necessary to wind up partnership affairs; apparent authority continues unless notice of the dissolution is given to a third party
- *Existing Liability* dissolution does not in itself discharge the existing liability of any partner

## Winding Up

**Definition of Winding Up** completing unfinished business, collecting debts, and distributing assets to creditors and partners; also called liquidation

**Right to Wind Up** on dissolution, any partner has the right to insist on the winding up of the partnership unless the partnership agreement provides otherwise; however, a partner who has wrongfully dissolved the partnership or who has been properly expelled cannot force the liquidation of the partnership

**Distribution of Assets** the liabilities of a partnership are to be paid out of partnership assets in the following order: (1) amounts owing to nonpartner creditors, (2) amounts owing to partners other than for capital and profits, (3) amounts owing to partners for capital contributions, and (4) amounts owing to partners for profits

**Marshaling of Assets** only applies when a State court of equity administers the assets of a partnership and of its members; the process of segregating and considering separately the assets and liabilities of the partnership and the respective assets and liabilities of the individual partners

- *Partnership Creditors* are entitled to be first satisfied out of partnership assets
- *Nonpartnership Creditors* have first claim to the individually owned assets of their respective debtor-partners
- *Federal Bankruptcy* marshaling of assets is not followed if the partnership is a debtor

## Continuation after Dissolution

**Right to Continue Partnership** the remaining partners have the right to continue the partnership in the following situations:

- *Continuation after Wrongful Dissolution* the aggrieved partners can continue the firm by paying the withdrawing partner the value of his interest less the amount of damages they sustained as a result of the breach
- *Continuation after Expulsion* the expelled partner is entitled to be discharged from partnership liabilities and to receive cash in the net amount due him from the partnership
- *Continuation Agreement of the Partners* permits the remaining partners to keep partnership property and to carry on its business; provides a specified settlement to the departing partner

**Rights of Creditors** the creditors of the old partnership have claims against the continuing (new) partnership and may also proceed against all the members of the dissolved partnership

# Cases

## CASE 31–1
### Test of Partnership Existence
## *CHAIKEN v. EMPLOYMENT SECURITY COMMISSION*
Superior Court of Delaware, 1971
274 A.2d 707

STOREY, J.

[Chaiken entered into separate but nearly identical agreements with Strazella and Spitzer to operate a barber shop. Under the terms of the "partnership" agreements, Chaiken would provide barber chairs, supplies, and licenses, while the other two would provide tools of the trade. The agreements also stated that gross returns from the partnership were to be divided on a percentage basis among the three men and that Chaiken would decide all matters of partnership policy. Finally, the agreements stated hours of work and holidays for Strazella and Spitzer and required Chaiken to hold and distribute all receipts. The Delaware Employment Security Commission, however, determined that Strazella and Spitzer were not partners of Chaiken but rather were his employees. The commission then brought this action to assess unemployment compensation contributions against Chaiken for the two barbers. Chaiken contends that they are not employees but partners pursuant to written partnership agreements. As partners, Chaiken would not be liable for unemployment compensation contributions.]

* * *

Chaiken contends that he and his "partners":

(1) properly registered the partnership name and names of partners in the Prothonotary's office, in accordance with [citation],
(2) properly filed federal partnership information returns and paid federal taxes quarterly on an estimated basis, and
(3) duly executed partnership agreements.

Of the three factors, the last is most important. Agreements of "partnership" were executed between Chaiken and Mr. Strazella, a barber in the shop, and between Chaiken and Mr. Spitzer, similarly situated. The agreements were nearly identical. The first paragraph declared the creation of a partnership and the location of business. The second provided that Chaiken would provide barber chair, supplies, and licenses, while the other partner would provide tools of the trade. The para-

graph also declared that upon dissolution of the partnership, ownership of items would revert to the party providing them. The third paragraph declared that the income of the partnership would be divided 30% for Chaiken, 70% for Strazella; 20% for Chaiken and 80% for Spitzer. The fourth paragraph declared that all partnership policy would be decided by Chaiken, whose decision was final. The fifth paragraph forbade assignment of the agreement without permission of Chaiken. The sixth paragraph required Chaiken to hold and distribute all receipts. The final paragraph stated hours of work for Strazella and Spitzer and holidays.

The mere existence of an agreement labeled "partnership" agreement and the characterization of signatories as "partners" does not conclusively prove the existence of a partnership. Rather, the intention of the parties, as explained by the wording of the agreement, is paramount. [Citation.]

A partnership is defined as an association of two or more persons to carry on as co-owners a business for profit. [Citation.] As co-owners of a business, partners have an equal right in the decision making process. [Citation.] But this right may be abrogated by agreement of the parties without destroying the partnership concept, provided other partnership elements are present. [Citation.]

Thus, while paragraph four reserves for Chaiken all right to determine partnership policy, it is not standing alone, fatal to the partnership concept. Co-owners should also contribute valuable consideration for the creation of the business. Under paragraph two, however, Chaiken provides the barber chair (and implicitly the barber shop itself), mirror, licenses, and linen, while the other partners merely provide their tools and labor—nothing more than any barber-employee would furnish. Standing alone, however, mere contribution of work and skill can be valuable consideration for a partnership agreement. [Citations.]

Partnership interests may be assignable, although it is not a violation of partnership law to prohibit assignment in a partnership agreement. [Citation.] Therefore, paragraph five on assignment of partnership interests does not violate the partnership concept. On the other hand, distribution of partnership assets to the partners upon dissolution is only allowed after all partnership liabilities are satisfied. [Citation.] But paragraph two of the agreement, in stating the ground rules for dissolution, makes no declaration that the partnership assets will be utilized to pay partnership expenses before reversion to their original owners. This deficiency militates against a finding in favor of partnership intent since it is assumed Chaiken would have inserted such provision had he thought his lesser partners would accept such liability. Partners do accept such liability, employees do not.

Most importantly, co-owners carry on "a business for profit." The phrase has been interpreted to mean that partners share in the profits and the losses of the business. The intent to divide the profits is an indispensable requisite of partnership. [Citations.] Paragraph three of the agreement declares that each partner shall share in the income of the business. There is no sharing of the profits, and as the agreement is drafted, there are no profits. Merely sharing the gross returns does not establish a partnership. [Citation.] Nor is the sharing of profits prima facie evidence of a partnership where the profits received are in payment of wages. [Citation.]

The failure to share profits therefore, is fatal to the partnership concept here.

Evaluating Chaiken's agreement in the light of the elements implicit in a partnership, no partnership intent can be found. The absence of the important right of decision making or the important duty to share liabilities upon dissolution individually may not be fatal to a partnership. But when both are absent, coupled with the absence of profit sharing, they become strong factors in discrediting the partnership argument.  * * *

In addition, the total circumstances of the case taken together indicate the employer-employee relationship between Chaiken and his barbers. The agreement set forth the hours of work and days off—unusual subjects for partnership agreements. The barbers brought into the relationship only the equipment required of all barber shop operators. And each barber had his own individual "partnership" with Chaiken. Furthermore, Chaiken conducted all transactions with suppliers, and purchased licenses, insurance, and the lease for the business property in his own name. Finally, the name "Richard's Barber Shop" continued to be used after the execution of the so-called partnership agreements.


* * *


[Judgment for Commission.]

---

## CASE 31–2
## Partnership Property
### *STANDRING v. STANDRING*
Colorado Court of Appeals, 1990
794 P.2d 1089

**DAVIDSON, J.**

In this action seeking dissolution of a partnership and distribution of partnership assets, plaintiff, Stephen E. Standring, appeals the trial court's judgment insofar as the court held that one of the two parcels of real property under consideration was not a partnership asset and insofar as it ordered that the partnership assets be distributed to the partners consistent with their ownership percentages only after paying each party the amount in his capital account. Defendants, Frank E. Standring and Mountain Armory, cross-appeal the trial court's ruling that one parcel of real property was a partnership asset. We affirm.

Defendant Frank Standring and plaintiff are father and son. Before formation of the partnership giving rise to this litigation, the father owned two parcels of real property in Fort Collins: business property at 3842 South College Avenue, and a house at 1130 West Myrtle Street. On the South College Avenue property, the father ran a sole proprietorship known as Mountain Armory, for which he constructed a new building in 1972. The construction located on the South College Avenue property was financed with loans secured by both parcels of land.

In January 1975, the father entered into a partnership agreement concerning Mountain Armory with his son, Stephen, and a third-party, Dennis Combs. The purpose of the partnership was "to engage in the purchase, sale and maintenance of firearms and ammunition and other sporting goods." Stephen and Combs were to draw salaries from the business, and each acquired five percent ownership therein. At that time, Frank Standring maintained 90% ownership.

Combs eventually withdrew from the partnership, and Frank, as a Christmas present, raised Stephen's partnership interest to 49%, effective January 1, 1979. The partnership income included money from the rental of the Myrtle Street house, and Stephen testified that his duties included maintenance of both the shop and the house. Both parcels of real property were consistently listed as assets in partnership tax returns. Although title to both parcels remained in Frank Standring's name, Stephen testified that he understood them to belong to the partnership.

In October 1982, the retail business of Mountain Armory was converted into a corporation, but the partnership was not dissolved. Stephen continued working for Mountain Armory and testified that he continued to perform the maintenance on both parcels of real property until December 1986, when, after a dispute, his father told him that he never wanted to see him again.

Stephen subsequently brought this action to dissolve the partnership in accordance with the parties' 49%/51% ownership interests. The trial court, while granting dissolution, held that the business property was a partnership asset and that the residential property was not. It then ordered that the business property be sold, that amounts from the parties' capital accounts be deducted from the proceeds, and that any remaining partnership profits be distributed 49% to Stephen and 51% to his father.

Plaintiff first contends that the trial court erred in finding that the Myrtle Street property was not a partnership asset. Defendant Standring premises his allegation of error on the trial court's finding that the South College Avenue property was such an asset. We conclude that the trial court did not err in either respect.

As pertinent here, the Uniform Partnership Act, [§ 8(1)], provides that "all property originally brought into the partnership stock or subsequently acquired . . . on account of the partnership is partnership property." Partners have the right to contribute any property they wish to the partnership. [Citation.] Whether the property has been contributed to the partnership depends on whether the parties agreed to do so. [Citations.]

Thus, the determination whether real property purchased by and held in the name of a single partner is a private or partnership asset depends on the intent of the parties. [Citations.]

Some of the factors reflecting the parties' intent to contribute individually held property to a partnership include the language of any partnership agreement, [citation]; the use of the property in the partnership business, [citation]; the listing of the property as an asset and of its mortgage as a liability in the partnership books and tax returns, [citation]; the construction of improvements on the property at partnership expense, [citation]; payment of taxes and insurance premiums on the property out of partnership funds, [citation]; a party's declaration of intent, such as by letter or will, accompanying his act of entering the partnership, [citation]; and, generally, the parties' conduct with respect to the property. [Citations.]

The intent of the parties with respect to the issue of contribution of the property is a question of fact, [citations], and unless there is no competent evidence to support it, the trier of fact's determination thereof is binding on appeal. [Citations.]

Here, the trial court, as trier of fact, considered several of the above factors in determining that the South College Avenue property had become a partnership asset and that the Myrtle Street property had not. Although a few factors pertained to both parcels—both were listed as assets on the partnership's tax returns and the income and expenses of both were "run through the partnership"—several key factors also distinguish the parties' treatment of the two properties.

Only the College Street property was used in the partnership's business, as defined by the partnership agreement. Although Stephen testified that his work in renting and performing maintenance at the Myrtle Street property evidenced that the business extended to that property, the record also reflects that Stephen's wife was paid separately for managing rental of the property and that there is conflicting evidence as to whether Stephen, in fact, spent either time or partnership money to maintain it.

Finally, the record includes notes by the attorney who simultaneously formulated the partnership modification agreement and a will for the father which indicate that the father wanted to devise the Myrtle Street property through his will, while making no provision for devising the business property. This evidence supports an inference, as made by the trial court, that the father perceived the residential and business properties differently, with the latter belonging to the partnership.

Because the trial court's finding as to the parties' intent to dedicate one and only one parcel of real property to the partnership is supported by the record, we are bound by it on appeal. [Citation.]

## CASE 31-3
## Dissolution
### *RODGERS v. RAB INVESTMENTS, LTD.*

Court of Appeals of Texas, 1991
816 S.W.2d 543

**MALONEY, J.**

Stephen B. Rodgers and Newell E. Boughton, Jr. appeal from a judgment rendered for RAB Investments, Ltd. based on disputes arising out of a partnership. * * * We affirm the trial court's judgment.

RAB, a general partnership, and Rodgers and Boughton formed Viola Courts Partnership (Viola) to renovate an apartment complex known as Viola Courts. The partnership agreement required unanimous consent for dissolution of the partnership and transfers of partnership interests.

RAB invested $150,000 and received a fifty percent interest in the partnership. Rodgers and Boughton each received a twenty-five percent interest for originating the project. Viola obtained a $500,000 loan. Rodgers received a $15,000 sales commission at the closing of the loan. Viola purchased the apartments and began renovations. Rodgers and Boughton managed the project. Rodgers and Boughton each received $20,000 for their management efforts.

Cost overruns and delays occurred. The lender agreed to extend the maturity date of the original loan. In December 1984, Viola borrowed an additional $150,000. Because of the cost overruns and unexpected expenses, RAB formed a limited partnership, Viola Investors, Ltd. (Investors). On December 21, 1984, RAB purported to transfer its interest in Viola to Investors. Cost overruns continued. Rodgers and Boughton asked RAB for additional capital. When RAB refused to contribute more money, Rodgers and Boughton demanded additional capital and threatened to expel RAB from Viola. Rodgers and Boughton expelled RAB from Viola on April 11, 1985.

Shortly thereafter, the bank loans came due. The renovation was still unfinished. RAB agreed to a second $150,000 loan. The parties renewed all the bank loans and borrowed another $150,000 in May 1985.

Rodgers and Boughton sued RAB in May 1985. In addition to damages for RAB's breach of the partnership agreement, Rodgers and Boughton sought a declaratory judgment. They asked the court to (1) interpret the partnership agreement, (2) declare the expulsion of RAB legal, (3) establish the rights of the partners upon dissolution, and (4) award them attorney's fees. RAB counterclaimed alleging fraud, breach of contract, and breach of fiduciary duty. RAB sought actual and exemplary damages, dissolution of Viola, an accounting, and attorney's fees.

The bank loans again came due in August 1985. Rodgers and Boughton extended the existing loans and arranged for an additional $225,000 loan. RAB agreed to these acts on the condition that no funds be disbursed from the project except by unanimous consent of the parties or an order of the 95th Judicial District Court. Rodgers and Boughton agreed to RAB's conditions. Rodgers and Boughton later removed more than $40,000 from Viola as the commissions for the sale and lease of completed apartment units.

The jury found that RAB willfully breached the partnership agreement by transferring its partnership interest in Viola to Investors. Rodgers and Boughton did not ask the jury to determine any damages resulting from this breach. The jury also found that Rodgers and Boughton breached their fiduciary duty to RAB by expelling it on April 11, 1985 and by receiving commissions after entering into the last loan agreement.

The jury determined that $27,219.62 would compensate RAB for its damages resulting from the breach of fiduciary duty. The jury also assessed exemplary damages of $20,000 each against Rodgers and Boughton. Finally, the jury valued RAB's partnership interest in Viola as of April 11, 1985 at $613,400. The parties stipulated to the amount of their attorney's fees. The judgment awarded RAB the value of its partnership interest, damages for breach of fiduciary duty, exemplary damages, and attorney's fees. The trial court denied relief to Rodgers and Boughton.

* * *

RAB contends that a dissolution of the partnership occurred by operation of law on April 11, 1985, when Rodgers and Boughton purportedly expelled RAB.

Every partner has the inherent power to dissolve a partnership even though the dissolution would violate the partnership agreement. [Citations.] The dissolution may breach the partnership contract, but it may be accomplished nonetheless. [Citations.] A partner always has the power, although perhaps not the legal right, to dissolve the partnership. [Citation.] No partner has to continue in a partnership against his will. [Citation.]

An ouster of a partner is a sufficient expression of will to dissolve the partnership. [Citation.] The partnership continues to exist, at least for the purposes of winding up. Only on termination of the partnership does the relationship end. [Citation]; see TEX. UPA § 30. Section 42 of the Texas Uniform Partnership Act lists the rights of an outgoing partner when the remaining partners continue the partnership business after dissolution. The outgoing partner may claim the value of his interest at dissolution and either interest on that value from the date of dissolution or profits attributable to the use of his right in the partnership property from the date of dissolution. The outgoing partner's right to profits ends when he receives the value of his interest. [Citation]; see TEX. UPA § 42.

The partnership agreement prohibits dissolution except by a unanimous vote of the partners. The agreement also provides that: "[a] Partner may at any time be expelled by the unanimous vote of the other Partners for willful or persistent breach of this Agreement, or conduct which tends to affect prejudicially the carrying on of Partnership affairs." The letter notifying RAB of its expulsion invoked this provision. It stated that RAB's refusal to make contributions was conduct that prejudicially affected the carrying on of partnership affairs.

Although the provision allowing expulsion does not use the word "dissolution," we conclude that dissolution is the substantive effect of expulsion under the contract. Rodgers and Boughton's letter stated: "RAB Investments, Ltd. has officially been expelled from the partnership and all interest of RAB Investments, Ltd. in such partnership is henceforth terminated." This statement by Rodgers and Boughton is a clear expression of their will to accomplish a dissolution.

The jury valued RAB's interest in Viola at $613,400 as of the date of RAB's expulsion. The trial court apparently determined that Rodgers and Boughton caused a dissolution as a matter of law when they expelled RAB. We agree with this determination. The trial court properly awarded this amount to RAB. * * * We overrule Rodgers and Boughton's first point of error.

* * *

* * * We . . . affirm the trial court's judgment.

---

## CASE 31–4
### Rights of Creditors
## *VICTORIA AIR CONDITIONING, INC. v.*
## *SOUTHWEST TEXAS MECHANICAL INSULATION COMPANY*

Court of Appeals of Texas, 1993
850 S.W.2d 720

HINOJOSA, J.
Appellant, Victoria Air Conditioning, Inc., (VAC) * * * entered into a $225,000 subcontract in August, 1988, with Southwest Texas Mechanical Insulation Company (SWT), a partnership comprised of Nabors and Jupe. The contract was signed by Jupe on behalf of the partnership. Pursuant to the contract, SWT provided insulation services for VAC in San Antonio, Texas. The undisputed evidence shows that Jupe and Nabors were partners at the time of contract formation.

The primary issue in this case is whether an agreement to discharge Nabors from liability could be inferred from the course of dealing between VAC, Jupe and Nabors.

Jupe and Nabors served different functions in the partnership. Jupe was VAC's "contact person" and handled the financial and business affairs of SWT. Nabors was responsible for field operations, and SWT's equipment was warehoused at his residence in Somerset, Texas.

On February 28, 1989, Nabors and Jupe dissolved their partnership. Nabors entered into a buy-out agreement with Jupe in which he sold his interest in SWT to Jupe for $2,500. On the same day, Nabors filed a notice of abandonment of assumed name certificate with the Secretary of State's office, reflecting the disposition of his 50% interest in SWT. VAC did not receive a copy of this notice. Sometime later, SWT's insulation equipment was transferred from Nabors' premises to Jupe's possession. From then on, Nabors had no more involvement with SWT. Jupe continued the insulation project with VAC.

Approximately one month after dissolution, Nabors created his own insulation company, Navco Insulation.

Nabors testified that at this time he also told Frederick Von Behrenfeld, VAC's Project Manager, that he was no longer involved with SWT, but that he was interested in bidding on new jobs in his capacity as Navco Insulation. Because Jupe was SWT's contact person, Behrenfeld had only met Nabors three or four times. Nonetheless, Behrenfeld testified that he knew in February, 1989, that Nabors was "no longer involved in the company." Behrenfeld acknowledged that he had no subsequent contacts with Nabors with regard to SWT.

At trial, a series of letters and change orders were introduced into evidence by both parties on the subjects of VAC's knowledge of the dissolution of SWT's partnership, and the inferred agreement between VAC, Jupe and Nabors. The first letter, dated June 21, 1989, was the first warning of nonperformance of the contract. From Behrenfeld, the letter was addressed to Jupe at SWT's new address, "Highway 87 East," and the salutation read "Gentlemen." Nabors did not receive a copy of the letter.

After the first letter, VAC attempted to ensure compliance with the contract by negotiating with Jupe. Benjamin Heilker, Jr., President and owner of VAC, drove from the Victoria VAC office to the San Antonio VAC office to meet with Jupe, but never met with, nor attempted to contact, Nabors. Jupe promised to have the required materials on hand and to report daily to the San Antonio VAC office. VAC promised to fund SWT's payroll, and offered to permit the storage of SWT's insulation materials on VAC premises.

Two "change orders" resulted from this meeting. Both contained SWT's new address at Highway 87 East, San Antonio, and were authorized by Jupe, who signed his name and hand-wrote "Southwest Texas Mechanical Insulation Corp." above the signature. The evidence showed that a change order made prior to the dissolution of the partnership in February reflected SWT's old address at P.O. Box 512, Somerset, Texas. When authorizing this earlier change order, Jupe merely signed his name, without the reference to the company. Furthermore, the partnership's assumed name certificate on file at the Secretary of State's office referred to the partnership as "company" and not "corporation."

A second letter from VAC committed to writing the promises made during negotiations between Heilker and Jupe. The letter, dated June 29, 1989, was from Heilker and addressed to Jupe at SWT's old address at P.O. Box 512, Somerset, Texas. The salutation read "Dear Charlie." It had Jupe's notarized signature, and five copies were sent to VAC employees and officers. Nabors did not receive a copy of the letter.

A third letter was sent on August 28, 1989, to Jupe from Heilker. It was addressed to SWT's old address at P.O. Box 512, Somerset, Texas. The letter begins "Dear Charlie" and states that VAC "has attempted to contact you many, many times and you have failed to respond." Copies were sent to VAC employees and officers, but not to Nabors individually.

A week later, August 31, 1989, Heilker sent a default letter to Jupe at SWT's new address at Highway 87 East. The salutation read "Dear Mr. Jupe." The letter states that "We have been unable to locate you by any means," and that VAC would have preferred that SWT completed the job. As a final parenthetical, the letter states, "Come out from your hiding place." Copies were sent to VAC employees and officers and to "All Employees of Southwest Texas Mechanical Insulation Co.," but not to Nabors individually.

Behrenfeld and Heilker testified that VAC never tried to contact Nabors individually, but that they presumed that all correspondence was reviewed by Nabors. They testified that the references to "you" in the letters referred to both Jupe and Nabors as a partnership and not to Jupe individually.

[Court's footnote: We note that, assuming Mr. Behrenfeld and Mr. Heilker are born and bred Texas boys, they have been properly schooled in the etiquette and finesse of the Texas vernacular, and thus are fully cognizant of the fact that, when addressing more than one person, the term "ya'll" is used! Although we are not prepared to take judicial notice of this well-known fact (nor do we base our decision on it), we are compelled to point out this probable misuse of the term "you" when addressing more than one citizen of the sovereign State of Texas.]

VAC complains by its first two points of error that no evidence or insufficient evidence supports the jury's finding that VAC, Jupe and Nabors agreed to discharge Nabors from liability on the contract. VAC denies that the course of dealing between VAC and Jupe was the type from which one could infer such an agreement, arguing that, because a meeting of the minds did not exist, no implied agreement could have occurred.

* * *

The general rule is that the dissolution of a partnership does not of itself discharge any existing liabilities of a partner. [UPA §] 36(1). However, an exception to the general rule exists when the retired partner, the person continuing the partnership's business, and the partnership creditor agree that the retired partner will be discharged from liability.

[Court's footnote: Section 36 of the Texas Uniform Partnership Act provides as follows:

**(1)** The dissolution of the partnership does not of itself discharge the existing liability of any partner.

**(2)** A partner is discharged from any existing liability upon dissolution of the partnership by an agreement to that effect between himself, the partnership creditor and the person or partnership continuing the business; and such agreement may be inferred from the course of dealing between the creditor having knowledge of the dissolution and the person or partnership continuing the business.]

Furthermore, such an agreement may be inferred from the course of dealing between the creditor having knowledge of the dissolution and the person continuing the partnership's business. Id.

The general rule that a retired partner remains liable for those partnership obligations that existed prior to dissolution of the partnership has been reaffirmed. [Citations.] However, section 36(2) has not been interpreted by Texas or federal courts. As a consequence, we have little guidance regarding what type of evidence of "course of dealing" would suffice to "infer" an agreement between the parties to discharge liability.

This Court finds some guidance from the Colorado court of appeals. The pertinent section of Colorado's partnership act is virtually identical to section 36(2). It provides that an agreement to discharge a retired partner from liability "may be inferred from the course of dealing between the creditor having knowledge of the dissolution and the person or partnership continuing the business." [Citation.] In [*Nestle*], the Colorado court of appeals affirmed a trial court's finding of an inferred agreement based upon facts very similar to the case at hand. [Citation.] In that case, a landlord sued a retired partner on a partnership lease that was in default. The retired partner had assigned his interest in the partnership to the partner continuing the lease. Payment was not in default until after dissolution of the partnership. A copy of the assignment was sent to the landlord, and the partner continuing the lease introduced his new partner to the landlord. [Citation.] The court noted that the landlord did not object to a change in parties or request that the retired partner remain liable. Id. At trial, an affidavit of the landlord acknowledged that he knew the partner was retired, but he denied having knowledge of the dissolution until five months before the breach. The landlord also denied that he agreed to look to the remaining partners and the new partnership to satisfy its debts.

Applying [UPA § 36(2)], the trial court concluded, from the landlord's knowledge of the situation and the parties' course of dealings, that the landlord had consented to the retired partner's discharge from liability. [Citation.] The Colorado court of appeals affirmed the judgment of the trial court based on the inferential language in [UPA § 36(2)]. [Citation.] * * *

Turning to VAC's first point of error, we must determine whether the evidence is factually sufficient to support the jury's finding that there was an agreement between VAC, Jupe and Nabors to discharge Nabors from liability. The initial question is whether sufficient evidence exists for the jury to have found that VAC knew of the dissolution of the partnership. Unlike *Nestle*, Nabors did not send documents representing dissolution of the partnership to VAC. However, a conversation regarding Nabors' discontinuance with SWT did occur. Behrenfeld testified that as of February, 1989, he knew that Nabors was "no longer involved in the company." He acknowledged that he had no subsequent contacts with Nabors with regard to SWT. Furthermore, Nabors testified that he told Behrenfeld that he was interested in bidding on new jobs in his new capacity as Navco Insulation.

The letters and change orders support the contention that VAC was aware of SWT's change of address from Nabors' premises in Somerset to Highway 87 in San Antonio. Heilker testified that VAC offered to warehouse the insulation equipment on its premises. One of Nabors' functions in the partnership had been to warehouse the insulation equipment. After Heilker drove to San Antonio to meet with Jupe, the salutation in the letters changed from "Gentlemen" to "Dear Charlie" or "Dear Mr. Jupe." And, finally, Jupe hand-wrote "Southwest Texas Mechanical Insulation Corporation" above his signature on the final two change orders even though the partnership's name had been "Southwest Texas Mechanical Insulation Company." Jupe had not hand-written anything above his signature on the change order made prior to dissolution of the partnership.

Even though VAC asserts that it did not necessarily know of the actual dissolution of the partnership, we find that sufficient evidence exists for the jury to have found that VAC knew of the dissolution of the partnership. It is the jury's province to judge the credibility of witnesses and the weight to be given their testimony. [Citation.]

We now address the primary issue of whether sufficient evidence exists for the jury to have inferred that an agreement existed between VAC, Jupe and Nabors to discharge Nabors from liability. Such evidence is found in the course of dealing between Jupe and VAC. [UPA

§] 36(2). As in *Nestle*, VAC never objected to Nabors' absence from the project and it never requested that Nabors remain liable. This is true even though VAC and Jupe engaged in considerable negotiations from the time of dissolution until breach of the contract. Also, the record reflects that VAC not only continued to deal with Jupe, but also elected not to contact Nabors regarding default until suit was filed in this matter, even though Nabors was available at all times and his whereabouts were known and he had in fact communicated his wish to bid on new insulation jobs to Behrenfeld. After the breach, all demands were addressed to Jupe. The letters suggest that Jupe personally had "gone into hiding" to escape his responsibilities.

We hold that sufficient evidence of a course of dealing between VAC and Jupe exists in the record from which the jury could have inferred that an agreement existed between VAC, Jupe and Nabors to discharge Nabors from liability on the insulation contract. The evidence is conflicting, but it is within the jury's province to judge the credibility of the witnesses and the weight to be given their testimony. [Citation.] This Court may not interfere with the jury's resolution of conflicts in the evidence. Id. After considering all of the evidence, we do not find that the evidence supporting the jury verdict is so weak or that the finding is so against the great weight and preponderance of the evidence that the result is clearly wrong and unjust. [Citation.] * * *

# Questions

1. Identify the various types of business associations and explain the factors that are relevant to deciding which form to use.
2. Distinguish between a legal entity and a legal aggregate and identify those purposes for which a partnership is treated as a legal entity and those purposes for which it is treated as a legal aggregate.
3. Distinguish between a partner's rights in specific partnership property and a partner's interest in the partnership.
4. Identify the causes of dissolution of a partnership and the conditions under which partners have the right to continue the partnership after dissolution.
5. Explain the effect of dissolution upon the authority and liability of the partners and the order in which the assets of a partnership are distributed to creditors and partners.

# Problems

1. Lynn and Jack jointly own shares of stock of a corporation, have a joint bank account, and have purchased and own as tenants in common a piece of real estate. They share equally the dividends paid on the stock, the interest on the bank account, and the rent from the real estate. Without Lynn's knowledge, Jack makes a trip to inspect the real estate and on his way runs over Samuel. Samuel sues Lynn and Jack for his personal injuries, joining Lynn as defendant on the theory that Lynn was Jack's partner. Is Lynn liable as a partner of Jack?

2. James and Suzanne engaged in the grocery business as partners. In one year they earned considerable money, and at the end of the year they invested a part of the profits in oil land, taking title to the land in their names as tenants in common. The investment was fortunate, for oil was discovered near the land, and its value increased many times. Is the oil land partnership property? Why?

3. Sheila owned an old roadside building which she believed could be easily converted into an antique shop. She talked to her friend Barbara, an antique fancier, and they executed the following written agreement:

    (a) Sheila would supply the building, all utilities, and $10,000 capital for purchasing antiques.

    (b) Barbara would supply $3,000 for purchasing antiques, Sheila to repay her when the business terminated.

    (c) Barbara would manage the shop, make all purchases, and receive a salary of $100 per week plus 5 percent of the gross receipts.

    (d) Fifty percent of the net profits would go into the purchase of new stock. The balance of the net profits would go to Sheila.

    (e) The business would operate under the name "Roadside Antiques."

Business went poorly, and after one year a debt of $4,000 is owed to Old Fashioned, Inc., the principal supplier of antiques purchased by Barbara in the name of Roadside Antiques. Old Fashioned sues Roadside Antiques, and Sheila and Barbara as partners. Decision?

4. Clark, who owned a vacant lot, and Bird, who was engaged in building houses, entered into an oral agreement by which Bird was to erect a house on the lot. Upon the sale of

the house and lot, Bird was to have his money first. Clark was then to have the agreed value of the lot, and the profits were to be equally divided. Did a partnership exist?

5.   Grant, Arthur, and David formed a partnership for the purpose of betting on boxing matches. Grant and Arthur would become friendly with various boxers and offer them bribes to lose certain bouts. David would then place large bets, using money contributed by all three, and would collect the winnings. After David had accumulated a large sum of money, Grant and Arthur demanded their share, but David refused to make any split. Grant and Arthur then brought suit in a court of equity to compel David to account for the profits of the partnership. What decision?

6.   Teresa, Peter, and Walker were partners under a written agreement made in January that the partnership should continue for ten years. During the same year, Walker, being indebted to Smith, sold and conveyed his interest in the partnership to Smith. Teresa and Peter paid Smith $5,000 as Walker's share of the profits for that year but refused Smith permission to inspect the books or to come into the managing office of the partnership. Smith brings an action setting forth the above facts and asks for an account of partnership transactions and an order to inspect the books and to participate in the management of the partnership business.

(a)   Does Walker's action dissolve the partnership?

(b)   To what is Smith entitled with respect to (1) partnership profits, (2) inspection of partnership books, (3) an account of partnership transactions, and (4) participation in the partnership management?

7.   Horn's Crane Service furnished supplies and services under a written contract to a partnership engaged in operating a quarry and rock-crushing business. Horn brought this action against Prior and Cook, the individual members of the partnership, to recover a personal judgment against them for the partnership's liability under that contract. Horn has not sued the partnership itself, nor does he claim that the partnership property is insufficient to satisfy its debts. Decision?

8.   Cutler worked as a bartender for Bowen until they orally agreed that Bowen would have the authority and responsibility for the entire active management and operation of the tavern business known as the Havana Club. Each was to receive $100 per week plus half of the net profits. The business continued under this arrangement for four years until the building was taken over by the Salt Lake City Redevelopment Agency. The agency paid $10,000 to Bowen as compensation for disruption. The business, however, was terminated after Bowen and Cutler failed to find a new, suitable location. Cutler, alleging a partnership with Bowen, then brought this action against him to recover one-half of the $10,000. Bowen contends that he is entitled to the entire $10,000 because he was the sole owner of the business and that Cutler was merely his employee. Cutler argues that although Bowen owned the physical assets of the business, she, as a partner in the business, is entitled to one-half of the compensation that was paid for the business's goodwill and going-concern value. Decision?

9.   In 1966, Gauldin and Corn entered into a partnership for the purpose of raising cattle and hogs. The two men were to share equally all costs, labor, losses, and profits. The business was started on land owned initially by Corn's parents but later acquired by Corn and his wife. No rent was ever requested or paid for use of the land. Partnership funds were used to bulldoze and clear the land, to repair and build fences, and to seed and fertilize the land. In 1970, at a cost of $2,487.50, a machine shed was built on the land. In 1975, a Cargill unit was built on the land at a cost of $8,000. When the partnership dissolved in 1976, Gauldin paid Corn $7,500 for the "removable" assets; however, the two had no agreement regarding the distribution of the barn and the Cargill unit. Gauldin sues Corn, claiming he is entitled to one-half of the value of the two buildings. Decision?

10.   Simmons, Hoffman, and Murray were partners doing business under the firm name of Simmons & Co. The firm borrowed money from a bank and gave the bank the firm's note for the loan. In addition, each partner guaranteed the note individually. The firm became insolvent, and a receiver was appointed. The bank claims that it has a right to file its claim as a firm debt and also that it has a right to participate in the distribution of the assets of the individual partners before partnership creditors receive any payment from such assets.

(a)   Explain the principle involved in this case.

(b)   Is the bank correct?

11.   Lauren, Matthew, and Susan form a partnership, Lauren contributing $10,000; Matthew $5,000; and Susan her time and skill. Nothing is said regarding the division of profits. The firm becomes insolvent, and after payment of all firm debts, $6,000 is left. Lauren claims that she is entitled to the entire $6,000. Matthew contends that the distribution should be $4,000 to Lauren and $2,000 to Matthew. Susan claims the $6,000 should be divided equally among the partners. Who is correct? Explain.

12.   Martin, Mark, and Marvin formed a retail clothing partnership named M Clothiers and conducted a business for many years, buying most of their clothing from Hill, a wholesaler. On January 15, Marvin retired from the business, but Martin and Mark decided to continue it. As part of the retirement agreement, Martin and Mark agreed in writing with Marvin that Marvin would not be responsible for any of the partnership debts, either past or future. A news item concerning Marvin's retirement appeared in the local newspaper on January 15.

Before January 15, Hill was a creditor of M Clothiers to the extent of $10,000, and on January 30, he extended additional credit of $5,000. Hill was not advised and did not in fact know of Marvin's retirement and the change of the partnership. On January 30, Ray, a competitor of Hill, extended credit for the first time to M Clothiers in the amount of $3,000.

On February 1, Martin and Mark departed for parts unknown, leaving no partnership assets with which to pay the described debts. What is Marvin's liability, if any, (a) to Hill and (b) to Ray?

**13.** Ben, Dan, and Lilli were partners sharing profits in proportions of one-fourth, one-third, and five-twelfths, respectively. Their business failed, and the firm was dissolved. At the time of dissolution, no financial adjustments between the partners were necessary with reference to their respective capital contributions, but the firm's liabilities to creditors exceeded its assets by $24,000. Without contributing any amount toward the payment of the liabilities, Dan moved to a destination unknown. Ben and Lilli are financially responsible. How much must each contribute?

**14.** Ames, Bell, and Cole were equal partners in the ABC Construction Company. They had no formal or written partnership agreement. Cole died on June 30, and his widow, Cora Cole, qualified as executor of his will. Ames and Bell continued the business of the partnership until December 31, when they sold all of its assets. After paying all partnership debts, they distributed the balance equally among themselves and Mrs. Cole as executor.

Subsequently, Mrs. Cole learned that Ames and Bell had made and withdrawn a net profit of $20,000 from July 1 to December 31. The profit was made through new contracts using the partnership name and assets. Ames and Bell had concealed such contracts and profit from Mrs. Cole, and she learned about them from other sources. Immediately after acquiring this information, Mrs. Cole made demand upon Ames and Bell for one-third of the profit of $20,000. They rejected her demand. What are the rights and remedies, if any, of Cora Cole as executor?

**15.** The articles of partnership of the firm of Wilson and Company provide

William Smith to contribute $50,000; to receive interest thereon at 13 percent per annum and to devote such time as he may be able to give; to receive 30 percent of the profits.

John Jones to contribute $50,000; to receive interest on same at 13 percent per annum; to give all of his time to the business and to receive 30 percent of the profits.

Henry Wilson to contribute all of his time to the business and to receive 20 percent of the profits.

James Brown to contribute all of his time to the business and to receive 20 percent of the profits.

There is no provision for sharing losses. After six years of operation, the firm has assets of $400,000 and liabilities to creditors of $420,000. Upon dissolution and winding up, what are the rights and liabilities of the respective parties?

**16.** Adam, Stanley, and Rosalind formed a partnership in State X to distribute beer and wine. Their agreement provided that the partnership would continue until December 31, 2002. Which of the following events would cause the ABC partnership to dissolve? If so, when would the partnership be dissolved?

(a) Rosalind assigns her interest in the partnership to Mary on April 1, 2000.

(b) Stanley dies on June 1, 2002.

(c) Adam withdraws from the partnership on September 15, 2001.

(d) A creditor of Stanley obtains a charging order against Stanley's interest on October 9, 2000.

(e) In 2000, the legislature of State X enacts a statute making the sale or distribution of alcoholic beverages illegal.

(f) Stanley has a formal accounting of partnership affairs on September 19, 2000.

**17.** In 1971, Donald Petersen joined his father, William Petersen, in a chicken hatchery business William had previously operated as a sole proprietorship. When the partnership was formed, William contributed the assets of the proprietorship, which included cash, equipment, and inventory having a total value of $41,000. Donald contributed nothing. From 1971 until his death in 1999, Donald took over the operation of the hatchery. This suit was brought on behalf of Donald's estate when William refused to distribute any of the partnership assets to the estate. William contended that the total value of the partnership property at the time of Donald's death was $18,572. He claimed the full amount on the theory that he was entitled to the return of his capital investment of $41,000 before Donald's estate could recover anything. Decision?

**18.** Davis and Shipman founded a partnership in 1954 under the name of Shipman & Davis Lumber Company. On September 20, 1955, the partnership was dissolved by written agreement. Notice of the dissolution was published in a newspaper of general circulation in Merced County, where the business was conducted. No actual notice of dissolution was given to firms that had previously extended credit to the partnership. By the dissolution agreement, Shipman, who was to continue the business, was to pay all of the partnership's debts. He continued the business as a sole proprietorship for a short time until he formed a successor corporation, Shipman Lumber Servaes Co. After the partnership's dissolution, two firms that had previously done business with the partnership extended credit to Shipman for certain repair work and merchandise. The partnership also had a balance due to Valley Typewriter Company for the prior purchase of a calculator. In 1956, two checks were drawn by Shipman Lumber Servaes Co. and accepted by Valley Typewriter as partial payment on this debt. Credit Bureaus of Merced County, as assignee of these three accounts, sued the partnership as well as Shipman and Davis individually. Davis argued that the dissolution of the partnership relieved him of personal liability for the accounts. The trial court entered judgment in favor of the Credit Bureaus for all three accounts. Decision?

**WWW** **Internet Exercise** Find and review information about the selection of a form of business organization.

# CHAPTER 32

# Operation of General Partnerships

The operation and management of a partnership involves interactions among the partners as well as their interactions with third persons. This chapter will consider both of these relationships. The first part of the chapter focuses on the rights and duties of the partners among themselves, which are determined by the partnership agreement, the common law, and the Uniform Partnership Act (UPA). The second part of the chapter focuses on the relations between the partners and third persons who deal with the partnership, which are governed by the laws of agency, contracts, and torts as well as by the UPA.

## RELATIONSHIPS AMONG PARTNERS

When parties enter into a partnership, the law imposes certain obligations upon them and also grants them specific rights. The parties may, by agreement, vary these rights and obligations, so long as such variance recognizes the rights of third parties and maintains standards of fairness.

## *DUTIES AMONG PARTNERS*

The principal legal duties imposed upon partners in their relations with one another are (1) the fiduciary duty (the duty of loyalty), (2) the duty of obedience, and (3) the duty of care. In addition, each partner has a duty to inform his copartners and a duty to account to the partnership. (These additional duties are discussed later, in a section covering the rights of partners.) All of these duties correspond precisely with those duties owed by an agent to his principal and reflect the fact that much of the law of partnership is the law of agency.

## Fiduciary Duty

A fiduciary relationship exists among the members of a partnership, based on the high standards of trust and confidence that they place in one another. Each partner owes a duty of absolute good faith, fairness, and loyalty to his partners. So intimate a business relationship can function only upon such a basis.

The fiduciary duty requires that a partner make no profit other than his agreed compensation, not compete with the partnership, and not otherwise profit from the relationship at the partnership's expense. The UPA states that every partner must account to the partnership for any benefit he receives and must hold as trustee for it any profits he derives without the consent of the other partners from any transaction connected with the formation, conduct, or liquidation of the partnership or from any use he makes of its property. Section 21. A partner may not prefer himself over the firm, nor may he even deal at arm's length with his partners, to whom his duty is one of undivided and continuous loyalty. Thus, a partner committed a breach of fiduciary duty when he retained a secret discount on purchases of petroleum that he obtained through acquisition of a bulk plant, and the partnership was entitled to the entire amount of the discount. *Liggett v. Lester*, 237 Or. 52, 390 P.2d 351 (1964).

The extent of this fiduciary duty, which binds all fiduciaries, not just partners, has been most eloquently expressed by the often-quoted words of Judge (later Justice) Cardozo:

Joint adventurers, like copartners, owe to one another, while the enterprise continues, the duty of the *finest loyalty.* Many forms of conduct permissible in a workaday world for those acting at arm's length, are forbidden to those bound by fiduciary ties. A trustee is held to something stricter than the morals of the market place. *Not honesty alone, but the punctilio of an honor the most sensitive, is then the standard of behavior.* As to this there has developed a tradition that is unbending and inveterate. Uncompromising rigidity has been the attitude of courts of equity when petitioned to undermine the rule of undivided loyalty by the "disintegrating erosion" of particular exceptions. Only thus has the level of conduct for fiduciaries been kept at a level higher than that trodden by the crowd. It will not consciously be lowered by any judgment of this court. *Meinhard v. Salmon*, 249 N.Y. 458, 459, 164 N.E. 545, 546 (1928) [emphasis added].

Within the demands of the fiduciary duty, a partner cannot acquire for herself a partnership asset or opportunity without the consent of all the partners. Thus, a partner may not renew a partnership lease in her name alone. The fiduciary duty also applies to the purchase of a partner's interest from another partner. Each partner owes the highest duty of honesty and fair dealing to the other partners, including the obligation to disclose fully and accurately all material facts.

A partner cannot, without the permission of her partners, engage in any other business within the scope of the partnership enterprise. Should she participate in a competing or similar business, the disloyal partner not only must surrender any profit she has acquired from such business but must compensate the existing partnership for any damage it may have suffered as a result of the competition. A partner, however, may enter into any business neither in competition with nor within the scope of the partnership's business. For example, a partner in a law firm may, without violating her fiduciary duty, act as an executor or administrator of an estate. Furthermore, she need not account for her fees where it cannot be shown that her service in this other capacity impaired her duty to the partnership (e.g., by monopolizing her attention).

The Revised Act has made some significant changes to a partner's fiduciary duty. The RUPA provides that a partner owes the partnership and the other partners the duty of loyalty and the duty of care (the latter is discussed later in this chapter). The Act further provides that a partner's duty of loyalty is limited to the following: (1) to account to the partnership and hold as trustee for it any property, profit, or benefit derived by the partner in the conduct and winding up of the partnership business or derived from a use by the partner of partnership property, including the appropriation of a partnership opportunity; (2) to refrain from dealing with the partnership in the conduct or winding up of the partnership business as, or on behalf of, a party having an interest adverse to the partnership; and (3) to refrain from competing with the partnership in the conduct of the partnership business before the dissolution of the partnership. RUPA Section 404(b). The fiduciary duty does *not* extend to the formation of the partnership, when, according to the com-

ments to RUPA Section 404, the parties are really negotiating at arm's length.

The Revised Act imposes a duty of good faith and fair dealing when a partner discharges duties to the partnership and the other partners under the RUPA or under the partnership agreement and exercises any rights. RUPA Section 404(d). The comments to this section state: "The obligation of good faith and fair dealing is a contract concept, imposed on the partners because of the consensual nature of a partnership. . . . It is not characterized, in RUPA, as a fiduciary duty arising out of the partners' special relationship. Nor is it a separate and independent obligation. It is an ancillary obligation that applies whenever a partner discharges a duty or exercises a right under the partnership agreement or the Act."

The partnership agreement may not eliminate the duty of loyalty or the obligation of good faith and fair dealing. However, the partnership agreement may identify specific types or categories of activities that do not violate the duty of loyalty, if not clearly unreasonable. In addition, the other partners may consent to a specific act or transaction that otherwise violates the duty of loyalty, if there has been full disclosure of all material facts regarding the act or transaction as well as the partner's conflict of interest. Similarly, the partnership agreement may prescribe the standards by which the performance of the obligation of good faith and fair dealing is to be measured, if the standards are not clearly unreasonable. RUPA Section 103(b).

 *See Case 32–1*

## Duty of Obedience

A partner owes his partners a duty to act in obedience to the partnership agreement and to any business decisions properly made by the partnership. Any partner who violates this duty is liable individually to his partners for any resulting loss. For example, a partner who, in violation of a specific agreement not to extend credit to relatives, advances money from partnership funds and sells goods on credit to an insolvent relative, would be held personally liable to his partners for the unpaid debt.

## Duty of Care

Whereas under the fiduciary duty a partner "is held to something stricter than the morals of the market place," he is held to something less than the skill of the marketplace. Each partner owes the partnership a duty of faithful service to the best of his ability. Nonetheless, he need not possess the degree of knowledge and skill of an ordinary paid agent.

A partner must manage partnership affairs without culpable negligence. **Culpable negligence** is something more than ordinary negligence, yet short of gross negligence. Thus, a partner who makes honest errors of judgment or who fails to use ordinary skill in transacting partnership business does not breach the duty of care, so long as she is not culpably negligent. For example, a partner assigned to keep the partnership books uses an overly complicated bookkeeping system and consequently produces numerous mistakes. Because these errors result simply from poor judgment, not an intent to defraud, and are not intended to and do not operate to the personal advantage of the negligent bookkeeping partner, she is not liable to her copartners for any resulting loss.

Under the Revised Act a partner's duty of care to the partnership and the other partners in the conduct and winding up of the partnership business is limited to refraining from engaging in grossly negligent or reckless conduct, intentional misconduct, or a knowing violation of law. RUPA Section 404(c). The duty of care may not be eliminated entirely by agreement, but the standard may be reasonably reduced. Section 103(b)(4). The standard may be increased by agreement to one of ordinary care or an even higher standard of care. Comment 6 to RUPA Section 103.

## RIGHTS AMONG PARTNERS

The law provides partners with certain rights, which include (1) their right in specific partnership property, (2) their interest in the partnership, (3) their right to share in distributions, (4) their right to participate in management, (5) their right to choose associates, and (6) their enforcement rights. A partner's ownership of specific partnership property is that of a tenant in partnership. Section 25. In addition, each partner has an interest in the partnership, which is defined as her share of the profits and surplus. Section 26. These two rights were discussed in Chapter 31. The four remaining rights among partners are discussed in this section.

### Right to Share in Distributions

A **distribution** is a transfer of partnership property from the partnership to a partner. Distributions include a division of profits, a return of capital contributions, a repayment of a loan or advance made by a partner to the partnership, and a payment made to compensate a partner for services rendered to the partnership.

***Right to Share in Profits***   Because a partnership is an association to carry on a business for profit, each partner is entitled, unless otherwise agreed, to a share of the profits. Conversely, each partner must contribute toward any losses the partnership sustains. Section 18(a). In the absence of an agreement regarding the division of profits, the partners share the profits equally, regardless of the ratio of their financial contributions or the degree of their participation in management. Unless the partnership agreement provides otherwise, the partners bear losses in a proportion identical to that in which they share profits. The agreement may, however, validly provide for bearing losses in a proportion different from that in which profits are shared.

For example, Alice, Betty, and Carol form a partnership, with Alice contributing $10,000; Betty, $20,000; and Carol, $30,000. They could agree that Alice would receive 20 percent of the profits and assume 30 percent of the losses; that Betty would receive 30 percent of the profits and assume 50 percent of the losses; and that Carol would receive 50 percent of the profits and assume 20 percent of the losses. If their agreement is silent as to the sharing of profits and losses, however, each would have an equal one-third share of both profits and losses.

***Right to Return of Capital***   After all the partnership's creditors have been paid, each partner is entitled to repayment of his capital contribution during the winding up of the firm. Section 18(a). Unless otherwise agreed, a partner is not entitled to interest on his capital contribution; however, a delay in the return of his capital contribution entitles the partner to interest at the legal rate from the date when it should have been repaid. Section 18(d).

***Right to Return of Advances***   A partner who makes an advance (loan) over and above his agreed capital contribution is entitled to repayment of the loan plus interest on it. Section 18(c). His claim as a creditor of the firm, though subordinate to the claims of nonpartner creditors, is superior to the partners' rights to the return of capital. In addition, a partner who has reasonably and necessarily incurred personal liabilities in the ordinary and proper conduct of the firm's business or who has made payments on behalf of the partnership is entitled to indemnification or repayment on footing equal to that of partners who make advances. Section 18(b).

Under the Revised Act a loan from a partner to the partnership is treated the same as loans of a person not a partner, subject to other applicable law, such as fraudulent transfer law, the law of avoidable preferences under the Bankruptcy Act, and general debtor-creditor law. RUPA Section 404(f) and Comment 6.

***Right to Compensation***  The UPA provides that, unless otherwise agreed, no partner is entitled to remuneration (payment) for acting in the partnership business. Section 18(f). Even a partner who works disproportionately harder than the others to conduct the business is entitled to no salary but only to his share of the profits. A partner may, however, by agreement among all of the partners, receive a salary. Moreover, a surviving partner is entitled to reasonable compensation for his services in winding up the partnership affairs. Section 18(f).

## Right to Participate in Management

Each of the partners, unless otherwise agreed, has an equal voice in the management of the business. Section 18(e). The majority generally governs the actions and decisions of the partnership, with the exception that all the partners must consent to any acts in contravention of the partnership agreement. Section 18(h). In their partnership agreement, the partners may provide for unequal voting rights. For example, Jones, Smith, and Williams form a partnership, agreeing that Jones will have two votes, Smith four votes, and Williams five votes. Large partnerships commonly concentrate most or all management authority in a committee of a few partners or even in just one partner. Classes of partners with different management rights also may be created. This practice is common in accounting and law firms, which may have two classes (e.g., junior and senior partners) or three classes (e.g., junior, senior, and managing partners).

## Right to Choose Associates

No partner may be forced to accept as a partner any person of whom she does not approve. This is partly because of the fiduciary relationship between the partners and partly because each partner has a right to take part in the management of the business, to handle the partnership's assets for partnership purposes, and to act as an agent of the partnership. An ill-chosen partner, through negligence, poor judgment, or dishonesty, may bring financial loss or ruin to her copartners. Because of this danger and because of the close relationship among the members, partnerships must necessarily be founded on mutual trust and confidence. All this finds expression in the term *delectus personae* (literally, "choice of the person"), which indicates the right one has to choose her partners. This principle is embodied in Section 18(g) of the UPA, which provides: "No person can become a member of a partnership without the consent of *all* the partners." [Emphasis added.] It is because of *delectus personae* that a purchaser (assignee) of a partner's interest does not become a partner and is not entitled to participate in management. The partnership agreement may provide, however, for admission of a new partner by a less-than-unanimous vote.

## Enforcement Rights

As discussed, the partnership relationship creates a number of duties and rights among partners. Accordingly, partnership law provides partners with the means to enforce these rights and duties.

***Right to Information and Inspection of the Books***  Each partner may demand full information regarding all partnership matters, and, in turn, each partner has a duty to supply full and accurate information regarding all things that affect the partnership. Section 20. The right to demand information extends also to the legal representative of a deceased partner for a reasonable time following the dissolution of the partnership.

Unless the partners agree otherwise, the books of the partnership are to be kept at the principal place of business at all times, and each partner has a right to have access to inspect and to copy any of them. Section 19. This right may also be exercised by a duly authorized agent on behalf of a partner.

***Right to an Account***  A **formal account** is a complete review of all financial transactions of the partnership, including financial statements. The UPA grants to each partner the right to an account whenever (1) his copartners wrongfully exclude him from the partnership business or possession of its property, (2) the partnership agreement so provides, (3) a partner makes a profit in violation of his fiduciary duty, or (4) other circumstances render it just and reasonable. Section 22.

If a partner does not receive or is dissatisfied with a requested account, she may bring an enforcement action, called an accounting. Designed to produce and evaluate all testimony relevant to the various claims of the partners, an **accounting** is an equitable proceeding for a comprehensive and effective settlement of partnership affairs.

Under the Revised Act a partner may maintain an action against the partnership or another partner for legal or equitable relief, with or without an accounting as to partnership business, to enforce the partner's rights under the partnership agreement and the Act. RUPA Section 405(b). Thus, under the RUPA, an accounting is not a prerequisite to the availability of the other remedies a partner may have against the partnership or the other partners.

## RELATIONSHIP BETWEEN PARTNERS AND THIRD PARTIES

In the course of transacting business, partners also may acquire rights over and incur duties to third parties. For example, under the law of **agency**, a principal is liable upon contracts that his duly authorized agents make on his behalf and is liable in tort for the wrongful acts his employees commit in the course of their employment. Because much of the law of partnership is the law of agency, most problems arising between partners and third persons require the application of principles of agency law. The UPA makes this relationship explicit by stating that "[t]he law of agency shall apply under this act" and that "[e]very partner is an agent of the partnership for the purpose of its business." Sections 4(3) and 9(1). The law of agency is discussed in Chapters 19 and 20.

### CONTRACTS OF PARTNERSHIP

The act of every partner binds the partnership to transactions within the scope of the partnership business unless the partner does not have actual or apparent authority to so act. If the partnership is bound, then each general partner has **unlimited, personal liability** for that partnership obligation. The UPA provides that partners are jointly liable on all debts and contract obligations of the partnership. Section 15(b). Under **joint liability,** a creditor must bring suit against all of the partners as a group, and the judgment must be against all of the obligors. Therefore, any suit in contract against the partners must name all of them as defendants.

Under the Revised Act the partners are jointly and severally liable for all contract obligations of the partnership. RUPA Section 306(a). The Revised Act, in keeping with its entity treatment of partnerships, requires the judgment creditor to exhaust the partnership's assets before enforcing a judgment against the separate assets of a partner. RUPA Section 307(d).

◆ *See Figure 32–1*

## Authority to Bind Partnership

A partner may bind the partnership by her act if (1) she has actual authority, express or implied, to perform the act or (2) she has apparent authority to perform the act. If the act is not apparently within the scope of the partnership business, then the partnership is bound only where the partner has actual authority. In such a case, the third person dealing with the partner assumes the risk that such actual authority exists. Section 9(2). Where there is neither actual authority nor apparent authority, the partnership is bound only if it ratifies the act. Ratification is discussed in Chapter 20.

*Actual Express Authority* The actual express authority of partners may be written or oral; it may be specifically set forth in the partnership agreement or in an additional agreement between the partners. In addition, it may arise from decisions made by a majority of the partners regarding ordinary matters connected with the partnership business. Section 18(h).

Section 9(3) of the UPA provides that the following acts do not bind the partnership unless authorized by all of the partners:

1. assignment of partnership property for the benefit of its creditors;
2. disposal of the goodwill of the business;
3. any act which would make it impossible to carry on the ordinary business of the partnership;
4. confession of a judgment; or
5. submission of a partnership claim or liability to arbitration or reference.

In addition, a partner who does not have actual authority from all of her partners may not bind the partnership by any act that does not apparently relate to the usual conduct of the partnership business. Section 9(2). Such acts would include the following inasmuch as they are clearly outside the scope of the partnership under ordinary circumstances: (1) execution of contracts of guaranty or suretyship in the firm name, (2) sale of partnership property not held for sale in the usual course of business, and (3) payment of individual debts out of partnership assets.

The Revised Act omits the UPA's list of extraordinary acts that require unanimous consent, leaving it to the

**FIGURE 32–1**  Contract Liability

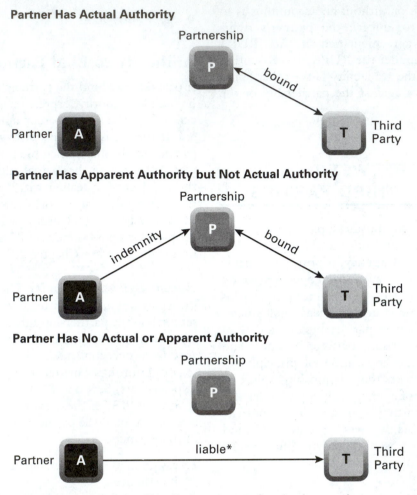

**Partner Has Actual Authority**

Partnership

P

*bound*

Partner   A

T   Third Party

**Partner Has Apparent Authority but Not Actual Authority**

Partnership

P

*indemnity*   *bound*

Partner   A

T   Third Party

**Partner Has No Actual or Apparent Authority**

Partnership

P

Partner   A   *liable\**   T   Third Party

*\*Partner is liable for breach of implied warranty of authority or misrepresentation*

courts to decide the outer limits of a partner's agency power. RUPA Section 301, Comment 4. The Revised Act also authorizes the optional, central filing of a statement of partnership authority specifying the names of the partners authorized to execute instruments transferring real property held in the name of the partnership. The statement may also grant supplementary authority to some or all the partners, or limit their authority, to enter into other transactions on behalf of the partnership. A filed statement is effective for up to five years. RUPA Section 303.

***Actual Implied Authority***  Actual implied authority is neither expressly granted nor expressly denied but is reasonably deduced from the nature of the partnership, the terms of the partnership agreement, or the relations

of the partners. For example, a partner has implied authority to hire and fire employees whose services are necessary to carry on the partnership business. In addition, a partner has implied authority to purchase property necessary for the business, to receive performance of obligations due to the partnership, and to bring legal actions to enforce claims of the partnership.

***Apparent Authority***  Apparent authority (which may or may not be actual) is authority that a third person, in view of the circumstances, the conduct of the parties, and a lack of knowledge or notice to the contrary, may reasonably believe to exist. For example, a partner has apparent authority to indorse checks and notes, to make representations and warranties in selling goods, and to enter into contracts for advertising. A third person, however, may not rely upon apparent authority in any situation where he is put on notice or already knows that the partner does not have actual authority. Sections 9(1) and 9(4).

 *See Case 32-2*

## Partnership by Estoppel

Partnership by estoppel imposes partnership duties and liabilities upon a nonpartner who has either represented himself or consented to be represented as a partner. It extends to a third person to whom such a representation is made and who justifiably relies upon the representation.

For example, Marks and Saunders are partners doing business as Marks and Company. Marks introduces Patterson to Taylor, describing Patterson as a member of the partnership. Patterson verbally confirms the statement made by Marks. Believing that Patterson is a member of the partnership and relying upon Patterson's good credit standing, Taylor sells goods on credit to Marks and Company. In an action by Taylor against Marks, Saunders, and Patterson as partners to recover the price of the goods, Patterson is liable although he is not a partner in Marks and Company. Taylor had justifiably relied upon the representation that Patterson was a partner in Marks and Company, to which Patterson actually consented. If, however, Taylor had known at the time of the sale that Patterson was not a partner, his reliance on the representation would not have been justified; and Patterson would not be liable.

Except where the representation of membership in a partnership has been made publicly, no person is entitled to rely upon a representation of partnership unless it is made directly to him. For example, Patterson falsely tells Dillon that he is a member of the partnership Marks and Company. Dillon casually relays this statement to Taylor, who in reliance sells goods on credit to Marks and Company. Taylor cannot hold Patterson liable, as he was not justified in relying on the representation made privately by Patterson to Dillon, which Patterson did not consent to have repeated to Taylor.

Where Patterson, however, knowingly permits his name to appear publicly in the firm name or in a list of partners, or to be used in public announcements or advertisements in a manner which indicates that he is a partner in the firm, Patterson is liable to any member of the public who deals with the partnership, whether or not the representations have been made or communicated to such person by or with the knowledge of Patterson. Section 16(1).

## TORTS AND CRIMES OF PARTNERSHIP

The UPA provides that a partnership is liable for the loss or injury any partner causes by any wrongful act or omission while acting within the ordinary course of the partnership business or with the authority of his copartners. Section 13. If the partnership is liable, each partner has **unlimited, personal liability** for the partnership obligation. The liability of partners for a tort or breach of trust committed by any partner or by an employee of the firm in the course of partnership business is joint and several. Section 15(a). **Joint and several liability** means that all of the partners may be sued jointly in one action based upon tort liability or that separate actions, leading to separate judgments, may be maintained against each of them. Judgments obtained are enforceable, however, only against property of the defendant or defendants named in the suit; and payment of any one of the judgments satisfies all of them.

This liability is comparable to the vicarious liability for the torts of an agent that the doctrine of *respondeat superior* imposes upon a principal. The partner who commits the tort is directly liable to the third party and must also **indemnify** the partnership for any damages it pays to the third party. Tort liability of the partnership may include not only the negligence of the partners but also trespass, fraud, defamation, and breach of fiduciary duty, so long as the tort is committed in the course of partnership business. Moreover, though the fact that a tort is intentional does not necessarily remove it from the course of business, it is a factor to be considered.

A partner is not criminally liable for the crimes of her partners unless she authorized or participated in them. Nor is a partnership criminally liable for the crimes of individual partners or employees unless a statute imposes vicarious liability. Even under such a statute, a partnership usually is liable only in those States that have adopted the entity theory or if the statute itself expressly imposes liability upon partnerships. Otherwise, the vicarious liability statute renders the partners liable as individuals.

As mentioned earlier, the Revised Act requires the judgment creditor to exhaust the partnership's assets before enforcing a judgment against the separate assets of a partner. RUPA Section 307(d).

◆ *See Figure 32–2*

⚖ *See Case 32–3*

## ADMISSIONS OF AND NOTICE TO A PARTNER

An admission or representation by any partner concerning partnership affairs within the scope of his authority may be used as evidence against the partnership. Section 11. An admission by one person that a partnership exists does not prove its existence. But once competent evidence establishes such existence, one partner's admission may be used against the partnership, provided the partner is acting within the scope of the partnership business.

A partnership is bound (1) by notice to any partner of any matter relating to partnership affairs; (2) by the knowledge of a partner acting in a particular matter, if he possessed or acquired such knowledge while he was a partner; and (3) by the knowledge of any other partner who reasonably could and should have communicated it to the acting partner. Section 12. Notice of a fact occurs when a person states or delivers a written statement of the fact to the partner. Section 3(2).

A demand upon one partner as representative of the firm constitutes a demand upon the partnership.

## LIABILITY OF INCOMING PARTNER

A person admitted as a partner into an existing partnership is as liable for all **antecedent debts** (partnership obligations that arose before his admission) as he would have been had he been a partner when such obligations were incurred, although this liability may be satisfied only out of partnership property. Section 17. This means that the liability of an incoming partner for antecedent debts and obligations of the firm is limited to his capital contribution. This restriction does not apply, of course, to **subsequent debts** (obligations arising after his admission into the partnership), for which obligations his liability is unlimited. For example, Nash is admitted to Higgins, Cooke, and White Co., a partnership. Nash's capital contribution is $7,500, which she paid in cash upon her admission to the partnership. A year later, when liabilities of the firm exceed its assets by $40,000, the partnership is dissolved. Porter had lent the firm $15,000 eight months before Nash was admitted; Skinner lent the firm $20,000 two months after Nash was admitted. Nash has no liability to Porter except to the extent of her capital contribution, but she is personally liable to Skinner.

⚖ *See Case 32–4*

---

**FIGURE 32–2** Tort Liability

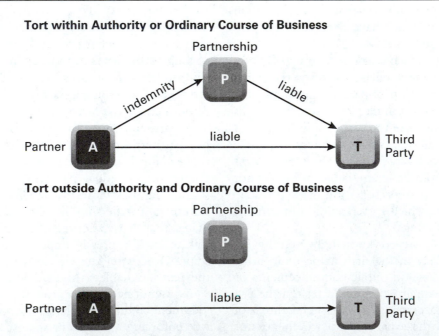

# Chapter Summary

## Relationships among Partners

| **Duties among Partners** | **Fiduciary Duty**  duty of utmost loyalty, fairness, and good faith owed by partners to each other and to the partnership<br>**Duty of Obedience**  duty to act in accordance with the partnership agreement and any business decisions properly made by the partners<br>**Duty of Care**  duty owed by partners to manage the partnership affairs without culpable negligence, which is greater than ordinary negligence but less than gross negligence |
|---|---|

| **Rights among Partners** | **Tenancy in Partnership**<br>**Interest in Partnership**<br>**Distributions**  transfer of partnership property from the partnership to a partner<br>• *Profits*  each partner is entitled to an equal share of the profits unless otherwise agreed<br>• *Capital*  after all partnership creditors have been paid, each partner is entitled to be repaid her capital contribution when the firm is terminated<br>• *Advances*  if a partner makes an advance (loan) to the firm, he is entitled to repayment of the advance plus interest; but his repayment is subordinate to that of nonpartner creditors<br>• *Compensation*  unless otherwise agreed, no partner is entitled to payment for acting in the partnership business<br>**Management**  each partner has an equal voice in management unless otherwise agreed<br>**Choice of Associates**  under the doctrine of *delectus personae,* no person can become a member of a partnership without the consent of all of the partners<br>**Enforcement Rights**<br>• *Information*  each partner may demand full information about all partnership matters, and each partner has a duty to supply other partners with full and accurate information<br>• *Formal Account*  complete review of all financial transactions of a partnership<br>• *Accounting*  equitable proceeding for a complete settlement of all partnership affairs |
|---|---|

## Relationship between Partners and Third Parties

| **Contracts** | **Partners' Liability**<br>• *Personal Liability*  if the partnership is contractually bound, each partner has joint, unlimited personal liability<br>• *Joint Liability*  a creditor must sue all of the partners as a group<br>**Authority to Bind Partnership**  a partner who has actual authority (express or implied) or apparent authority may bind the partnership<br>• *Actual Express Authority*  authority set forth in the partnership agreement, in additional agreements among the partners, or in decisions made by a majority of the partners regarding the ordinary business of the partnership<br>• *Actual Implied Authority*  authority that is reasonably deduced from the nature of the partnership, the terms of the partnership agreement, or the relations of the partners<br>• *Apparent Authority*  authority that a third person may reasonably assume to exist in light of the conduct of the parties, so long as that third person has no knowledge or notice of the lack of actual authority<br>**Partnership by Estoppel**  imposes partnership duties and liabilities on a nonpartner who has either represented himself or consented to be represented as a partner |
|---|---|

| | |
|---|---|
| **Torts and Crimes of Partnership** | ***Respondeat Superior*** the partnership is liable for loss or injury caused by any wrongful act or omission of any partner while acting within the ordinary course of the business or with the authority of her copartners<br>**Joint and Several Liability** the partners are jointly and severally liable for a tort or breach of trust committed by any partner or by an employee of the firm in the course of partnership business; under such liability, the creditors may sue the partners jointly as a group or separately as individuals<br>**Crimes** A partner is not criminally liable for the crimes of her partners unless she authorized or participated in them |
| **Other Powers** | **Admissions** an admission by one partner within the scope of his authority may be used as evidence against the partnership<br>**Notice** a partnership is bound by notice to and knowledge of a partner<br>**Demand** a demand on one partner is a demand on the partnership |
| **Liability of Incoming Partner** | **Antecedent Debts** the liability of an incoming partner for antecedent debts of the partnership is limited to her capital contribution<br>**Subsequent Debts** the liability of an incoming partner for subsequent debts of the partnership is unlimited |

 # Cases

### CASE 32–1
### Fiduciary Duty
## *CLEMENT v. CLEMENT*
Supreme Court of Pennsylvania, 1970
436 Pa. 466, 260 A.2d 728

**ROBERTS, J.**

Charles and L.W. Clement are brothers whose forty year partnership had ended in acrimonious litigation. The essence of the conflict lies in Charles' contention that L.W. has over the years wrongfully taken for himself more than his share of the partnership's profits. Charles discovered these misdeeds during negotiations with L.W. over the sale of Charles' interest in the partnership in 1964. He then filed an action in equity, asking for dissolution of the partnership, appointment of a receiver, and an accounting. Dissolution was ordered and a receiver appointed. After lengthy hearings on the issue of the accounting the chancellor decided that L.W., who was the brighter of the two and who kept the partnership books, had diverted partnership funds. The chancellor awarded Charles a one-half interest in several pieces of property owned by L.W. and in several insurance policies on L.W.'s life on the ground that these had been purchased with partnership assets.

The court en banc then heard the case and reversed the chancellor's decree in several material respects. The reversal was grounded on two propositions: that Charles' recovery could only be premised on a showing of fraud and that this burden was not met, and that the doctrine of laches [unreasonable delay] foreclosed Charles' right to complain about the bulk of the alleged misdeeds.

We disagree with the court en banc's statement of the applicable law and therefore reverse. Our theory is simple. There is a fiduciary relationship between partners. Where such a relationship exists actual fraud need not be shown. There was ample evidence of self-dealing and diversion of partnership assets on the part of L.W.—more than enough to sustain the chancellor's conclusion that several substantial investments made by L.W. over the years were bankrolled with funds improperly withdrawn from the partnership. Further, we are of the opinion that the doctrine of laches is inapplicable because Charles' delay in asserting his rights was as much a product of L.W.'s concealment and misbehavior as of any negligence on his part. In all this we are strongly motivated by the fact that the chancellor saw and heard the various witnesses for exhausting periods of time and was in a much better position than we could ever hope to be to taste the flavor of the testimony.

[UPA] § 21 very simply and unambiguously provides that partners owe a fiduciary duty one to another. [Citation.] One should not have to deal with his partner as though he were the opposite party in an arms-length transaction. One should be allowed to trust his partner, to expect that he is pursuing a common goal and not working at cross-purposes. * * *

It would be unduly harsh to require that one must prove actual fraud before he can recover for a partner's derelictions. Where one partner has so dealt with the partnership as to raise the probability of wrongdoing it ought to be his responsibility to negate that inference. It has been held that "where a partner fails to keep a record of partnership transactions, and is unable to account for them, every presumption will be made against him." [Citation.] Likewise, where a partner commingles partnership funds with his own assets he ought to have to shoulder the task of demonstrating the probity of his conduct.

In the instant case L.W. dealt loosely with partnership funds. At various times he made substantial investments in his own name. He was totally unable to explain where he got the funds to make these investments. The court en banc held that Charles had no claim on the fruits of these investments because he could not trace the money that was invested therein dollar for dollar from the partnership. Charles should not have had this burden. He did show that his brother diverted substantial sums from the partnership funds under his control. The inference that these funds provided L.W. with the wherewithal to make his investments was a perfectly reasonable one for the chancellor to make and his decision should have been allowed to stand.

* * *

The decree is vacated and the case remanded for further proceedings consistent with this opinion.

---

## CASE 32–2
## Authority to Bind Partnership
### *FIRST NATIONAL BANK AND TRUST COMPANY OF WILLISTON v. SCHERR*

Supreme Court of North Dakota, 1991
467 N.W.2d 427

MESCHKE, J.

The First National Bank & Trust Company of Williston appealed from a judgment that Albinus Scherr, a partner, and Scherr and Scherr, the partnership, were not liable on a $65,000 note to the Bank signed for the partnership by only one partner, Pius Scherr, contrary to a restriction in the partnership agreement known to the Bank. We affirm.

Pius Scherr and Albinus Scherr started a general partnership to construct and invest in buildings. On September 15, 1981, this new partnership, Scherr and Scherr, opened a checking account at the Bank. The Partnership Checking Account Signature Card, signed by each of the partners, authorized the Bank

to accept (whether or not payable to the partner who signs the same or to any other partner) checks, endorsements, notes, . . . mortgages or any other instruments for the deposit or withdrawal of funds, for borrowing money and pledging or mortgaging assets of the partnership as security for the payment thereof and for the transaction of any other business with it, when signed by any _____ of the undersigned.

A separate box adjacent to the partners' signatures on the signature card had in it printed instructions, "Number of Signatures Required," and was filled in with a typed "1." This signature card was kept in the checking account files, not the loan files, of the Bank.

Later a written partnership agreement was completed. It was dated, signed, and acknowledged by Pius on October 1, 1981, and by Albinus on December 21, 1981, when a copy was delivered to the Bank. This agreement included a clause restricting the authority of a single partner to engage in certain transactions for the partnership:

Neither partner shall, without the written consent of the other partner, endorse any note, or act as an accommodation party, or otherwise become surety for any person. Without the written consent of the other partner, neither partner shall on behalf of the partnership borrow or lend money, or make, deliver or accept any commercial paper, or execute any mortgage, security agreement, bond or lease, or purchase or contract to purchase, or sell or contract to sell any property for or of the partnership. Neither partner shall, except with the written consent of the other partner, assign, mortgage, grant a security interest [sic] in, or sell his share in the Partnership or in its capital assets or property, or enter into any agreement as a result of which any person shall become interested with him in the Partnership, or do any act detrimental to the best interests of the Partnership or which would make it impossible to carry on the ordinary business of the Partnership.

The signed copy of the partnership agreement was completed and delivered to the Bank at its request, and was kept in the Bank's loan file for the partnership.

Beginning in November 1981 and continuing into 1984, Scherr and Scherr borrowed large sums from the Bank to acquire property and to construct various buildings in Williston. One venture was construction of a building leased to a Famous Recipe Chicken fast-food franchisee. This project began with a mortgage, signed by both Pius and Albinus, to the Bank on April 29, 1983, for a construction advance of $100,000. Later, Pius alone signed the four notes to the Bank drawing on this short-term loan: One on May 2, 1983 for $10,000; another on June 2, 1983 for $20,000; the third on July 14, 1983 for $15,000; and the fourth note on August 1, 1983 for $55,000. This loan was soon converted to a $100,000 note secured by a long-term mortgage to the Bank, both dated October 26, 1983, and both signed by Pius and Albinus.

The next day, October 27, Pius Scherr alone signed another short-term partnership note to the Bank for $65,000. This note was filled in to say, "THE PURPOSE OF THIS LOAN IS: Final construction on Famous Recipe Chicken." The Bank repeatedly renewed this note through May 1985. Each renewal note was signed for the partnership by Pius alone.

The Scherrs defaulted on their Famous Recipe Chicken obligations to the Bank. The Bank foreclosed the $100,000 mortgage, and then sued the Scherrs to collect the $65,000 note. The trial court entered summary judgment for the Bank against Pius, Albinus, and the partnership for the balance due on the $65,000 note and interest. Pius, Albinus, and the partnership appealed. We affirmed the summary judgment against Pius but

reversed the summary judgment against Albinus and the partnership. *First National Bank and Trust Company of Williston v. Scherr*, 435 N.W.2d 704 (N.D. 1989) (Scherr I). We remanded for trial on the effect of the restriction in the partnership agreement on the liability of Albinus and the partnership to the Bank.

After trial on remand, the trial court determined that Pius was not authorized to sign the unsecured, $65,000 note for the partnership because the Bank "had written knowledge" about the specific restriction on his authority in the partnership agreement, and because the Bank "thereafter established a course of conduct of business with the partnership consistent with those restrictions." The trial court felt that it was "arguable but questionable" whether the signature card authorization bound the partnership to a promissory note signed by one partner. The trial court ruled that, "in any event, the restrictive language . . . in the Partnership Agreement . . . overrides and controls the signature card in the event of conflict." The court concluded that Albinus and the partnership were not liable on the note, and entered judgment dismissing the Bank's claim against them. The Bank appealed. This is Scherr III.

On appeal, the Bank argues that the signature card authorization was a controlling agreement between the Bank and the partnership, because Albinus thereby consented to Pius's lone signature on the $65,000 note. According to the Bank, any difference between the terms of that authorization and the terms of the later partnership agreement is immaterial. The Bank argues that the partnership's direct authorization to the Bank was not altered by the later restrictive agreement between the partners, even though the Bank knew about it.

In Scherr I, we recognized that statutes regulate the authority of a partner to act for the partnership. North Dakota has adopted the Uniform Partnership Act, as have nearly all states. [Citation.] [UPA § 9] says:

1. Every partner is an agent of the partnership for the purpose of its business, and the act of every partner, including the execution in the partnership name of any instrument, for apparently carrying on in the usual way the business of the partnership . . . binds the partnership, unless the partner so acting has in fact no authority to act for the partnership in the particular matter, and the person with whom he is dealing has knowledge of the fact that he has no such authority.

\* \* \*

4. No act of a partner in contravention of a restriction on authority shall bind the partnership to persons having knowledge of the restriction.

As this statute pronounces, a partner's liability to a third person is largely fixed by the law of agency. Restatement (Second) of Agency § 14A comment a (1958). Also, [UPA § 5] says, "[t]he law of agency applies under this title." Agency law, then, controls this case.

A partner, as an agent of the partnership, normally binds the partnership by executing any instrument that carries on the business of the partnership in the usual way. [UPA § 9(1).] But, as with any agent, that is not so if the partner's authority is restricted, and if the restriction is known to the person with whom the partner deals. Id. The repetition in [UPA § 9(4)] emphasizes that the law commands a different result when a partner acts "in contravention of a restriction on [his] authority" in dealing with someone "having knowledge of the restriction."

Many decisions by other courts have ruled that a person cannot recover from a second partner or the partnership for additional transactions with an acting partner after that person had notice of a later restriction on the acting partner's authority. [Citations.] These precedents demonstrate that knowledge of a restriction on, or revocation of, an individual partner's authority controls over a pre-existing arrangement with a creditor.

In this case, Pius had initial authority to act individually for the partnership in borrowing money from the Bank through the signature card authorization. Afterward, the partnership agreement restricted that authority. When a third person has "previously extended credit" to the principal through the agent "in reliance upon a manifestation from the principal of continuing authority in the agent," that authority can be restricted or revoked by notice to the third person. Restatement (Second) of Agency § 136(2)(a) (1958). N.D.C.C. 3–01–11 (part) says that, "[u]nless the power of an agent is coupled with an interest in the subject of the agency, it is terminated as to every person having notice thereof by: 1. Its revocation

by the principal. . . ." The question in this case is whether delivery of the written partnership's agreement to the Bank was effective notice that Pius's individual authorization had been restricted. The trial court found as a matter of fact that effective notice of restriction had been given.

One who claims that an agent acted within his authority has the burden of proving the scope of that authority. [Citation.] The scope of an agent's authority is a question of fact. Id. "If a person dealing with an agent has notice that the agent's authority is created or described in a writing which is intended for his inspection, he is affected by limitations upon the authority contained in the writing, unless misled by conduct of the principal." Restatement (Second) of Agency § 167 (1958). No question of fraud on the part of the partnership was raised in the trial court, or pursued on this appeal. "A person has 'notice' of a fact within the meaning of this title when the person who claims the benefit of the notice: . . . 2. Delivers through the mail, or by other means of communication, a written statement of the fact to such person or to a proper person at his place of business. . . ." [UPA § 3(2).] The trial court determined that notice of a restriction had been given to the Bank by delivery of the executed partnership agreement.

The signature card did not stand alone. After the signature card, the Bank sought, received, and knew about a later partnership agreement that restricted one partner's power to borrow for the partnership without the consent of the other partner. There is no claim, in this case, that the partnership subsequently ratified the $65,000 note to the Bank. [Citation.] Under agency principles and the Uniform Partnership Act, the trial court's factual determination that Pius acted in contravention of a restriction on his authority as a partner, known to the Bank, controls this case.

* * *

We affirm.

---

## CASE 32–3
### Torts of Partnership
### *HUSTED v. McCLOUD*
Supreme Court of Indiana, 1983
450 N.E.2d 491

PIVARNIK, J.
This cause comes to us on a Petition to Transfer from the First District Court of Appeals. Appeal was brought to the Court of Appeals by Edgar Husted from that portion of a judgment of the Montgomery Circuit Court awarding Herman McCloud punitive damages in an action involving the conversion of certain funds. The partnership of Husted & Husted also appealed contesting the

award of punitive damages and compensatory damages as against itself. The Court of Appeals, [citation], affirmed the trial court in its award of punitive damages against Edgar Husted and in its award of punitive and compensatory damages against Husted & Husted. We now find that the award of punitive damages against Edgar Husted was improper. While the award of compensatory damages against the partnership was proper, we now find that the award of punitive damages was not. Transfer is granted and the opinion of the Court of Appeals is accordingly vacated.

The facts as set out by the Court of Appeals are as follows:

Herman McCloud was the executor of his mother's estate. The firm of Husted and Husted was retained to act as attorneys for the estate. The partnership consisted of Selwyn and Edgar Husted. After the estate was closed, an Internal Revenue Service (IRS) audit and reappraisal of certain real estate resulted in an additional estate tax liability of $18,006.73. McCloud prepared a check payable to the IRS and a separate check for attorney fees. However, Edgar falsely represented that the exact amount of the tax liability was unknown. He instead took McCloud's check for $18,800.00, payable to the Husted and Husted Trust Account at Edgar's instance, and indicated that he would pay the liability upon exact determination and keep the remainder as his fee. There was no Husted and Husted Trust Account in existence. Edgar instead deposited the check into his own personal account and converted the funds to his own use.

Edgar Husted then induced officials of the First National Bank and Trust Company of Crawfordsville to issue a check from the estate of Walter Fletcher, deceased, in the exact amount needed to pay the additional estate tax liability on the estate of Maude McCloud. This check was credited to the McCloud estate by the IRS. Edgar advised McCloud that the additional taxes had been paid and delivered to McCloud a cash register receipt and computer transcript which purported to show payment. Although McCloud repeatedly asked therefor, Edgar never returned the cancelled check.

In December of 1978, Edgar Husted's misconduct was uncovered. Edgar entered into a plea agreement * * *

The IRS subsequently revoked the satisfaction of the estate tax liability of the McCloud estate, reassessed the additional tax due, and also assessed additional interest of $2,795.24. An additional penalty of $3,034.35 was later dropped. McCloud then paid the additional tax due from his savings and a loan he procured for that purpose.

Edgar pleaded guilty to the four felony charges as agreed and was convicted and sentenced to prison. McCloud subsequently filed a damages action when restitution was not forthcoming.

* * *

On the foregoing basis, the punitive damage award against Edgar Husted should be set aside. The public interest in punishing Husted and in deterring him from such misconduct was fully satisfied by the sentence Husted received. Accordingly, punitive damages are inappropriate. [Citation.] The award of punitive damages against Edgar Husted is set aside.

The trial court relied upon the provisions of Indiana's Uniform Partnership Act, [citation], when it entered judgment against the partnership for both punitive and compensatory damages. The trial court particularly relied upon the following sections of the Uniform Partnership Act which state:

[§]13. Partnership bound by partner's wrongful act.—Where, by any wrongful act or omission of any partner acting in the ordinary course of the business of the partnership or with the authority of his copartners, loss or injury is caused to any person, not being a partner in the partnership, or any penalty is incurred, the partnership is liable therefore to the same extent as the partner so acting or omitting to act.

[§]14. Partnership bound by partner's breach of trust.—The partnership is bound to make good the loss:

(a) Where one partner acting within the scope of his apparent authority receives money or property of a third person and misapplies it; and

(b) Where the partnership in the course of its business receives money or property of a third person and the money or property so received is misapplied by any partner while it is in the custody of the partnership.

The trial court and the Court of Appeals determined that § 13 required that the partnership be liable to the same extent as Edgar Husted for any civil penalty imposed in this case. The partnership claims that Edgar's criminal acts were not within the ordinary course of partnership business. Furthermore, the partnership claims that it never had possession of the certain funds converted and therefore the partnership cannot be held liable for Edgar's acts with respect to said funds. There were two partners in the partnership law firm, Edgar Husted and Selwyn Husted, Edgar's father. McCloud clearly was a client of the partnership since McCloud dealt with both Selwyn and Edgar on his estate case. In fact, Selwyn was the partner who first brought McCloud's case into the partnership's office. Edgar was acting within the ordinary course of the partnership's business and with apparent authority since Edgar's request for and acceptance of money from McCloud to pay McCloud's estate tax liability was well within the work parameters of an attorney properly handling a decedent's estate. We therefore find that even though fraud and conversion of a client's funds are not part of the ordinary course of a law partnership's business, the trial court correctly found pursuant to § 14 that the partnership was responsible for partner Edgar in taking money entrusted to him and misapplying it. We also find that the trial court was justified in finding that McCloud's money was in the partnership's possession when it was in Edgar's possession since Edgar deviated from McCloud's plan and converted the money to his own use only after he received it in the ordinary course of the partnership's business. Accordingly, the trial court did not err by holding the partnership responsible to McCloud for compensatory damages.

Whether Appellant partnership is liable for punitive damages, however, is another story. Husted & Husted argues that the cases decided under § 13 or its counterpart in other jurisdictions as well as the earlier cases decided under the common law of agency and partnership have generally held that where a partnership is sued for a partner's intentional tort, the partnership's liability turns on whether the purpose or effect of the tortious act was to benefit the partnership's business or whether the tort was so removed from the ordinary course of that business that it could not be considered within the implicit authorization of the copartners.
* * *

We accept Appellant's contention that § 13 is the only section by which punitive damages can be imposed against a partnership since § 14 merely limits a partnership's liability to restitution. We further agree with Appellant partnership that the rationale behind punitive damages in Indiana prohibits awarding such damages against an individual who is personally innocent of any wrongdoing. Punitive damages are not intended to compensate a plaintiff but rather are intended to punish the wrongdoer and thereby deter others from engaging in similar conduct in the future. [Citations.] Accordingly, we now hold that the trial court erred by adjudging the innocent partner in this case responsible for punitive damages.

---

## CASE 32–4
### Liability of Incoming Partner
## *CONKLIN FARM v. LEIBOWITZ*
Superior Court of New Jersey, Appellate Division, 1994
274 N.J.Super. 274, 525, 644 A.2d 687

**COHEN, J.**
A person admitted as a partner into an existing general partnership is liable for all partnership obligations arising before his admission, but, in the absence of contrary agreement, this liability may be satisfied only out of partnership property. [UPA § 17.] Partnership obligations arising after the new partner is admitted may be satisfied out of the personal assets of any partner, including the new one. [UPA §§ 18, 40(d).]

The question presented by this case is whether a new partner is liable to pay, out of personal assets, interest on a preexisting partnership promissory note accrued for periods of time after admission into the partnership. We hold that such personal liability exists, and we therefore reverse the summary judgment granted to defendant.

In 1986, a general partnership called Longview Estates was formed to purchase a piece of property from Conklin Farm and to develop it for residential condominiums. In connection with the purchase, Longview Estates executed a $9 million promissory note to Conklin Farm, secured by a mortgage bearing interest at agreed rates.

One of the partners in Longview Estates was Joel Leibowitz. On March 15, 1990, he transferred his thirty percent partnership share to his wife Doris, the defendant in this case. She owned the share until August 30, 1991, when she transferred it back to her husband. During the seventeen and one-half months of her participation, interest greater than $1 million accrued on the $9 million note and was not paid. The creditor sued the defendant late in 1991 for thirty percent of the interest, or more than $300,000. Longview Estates and the other partners have already been through bankruptcy, and the debt has been discharged as to them.

The question whether current interest on preexisting debt is part of the preexisting debt or is new debt for the purposes of [UPA § 17] has not been answered in a reported case in New Jersey or, to our knowledge, in any other jurisdiction. The reason may be either that the answer is clear, or that the problem is normally resolved by agreement in advance. For example, a financing party might reserve the authority to approve transfers of partnership shares or to require express assumptions of preexisting partnership debt as a price for release of a withdrawing partner.

The $9 million promissory note was a preexisting debt. As to that the parties agree. The whole outstanding principal of a partnership debt incurred before admission of a new partner is a partnership obligation arising before admission, no matter that some or all of the principal payments may not be due until after admission of the new partner. * * *

Here, the Law Division judge reasoned that interest was not a separate and distinct obligation, but rather arose from the note itself, [citation], and is therefore part of the preexisting obligation of the note. In our view, that conclusion does not comport with the purposes of Section 17 and the Uniform Partnership Act in general.

We have reviewed the Official Comments of the Commissioners on State Laws to both Section 17 and Section 41 of the Uniform Partnership Act. They are too long to set out in this opinion. They were written some time before 1914, the year in which the Commissioners adopted the Uniform Partnership Act and recommended it to the states for enactment. It is clear from the Official Comments that the purpose of the sections was to deal with the "doubt and confusion" in the common law of the time caused by the established concept that the addition of a partner dissolved the partnership and created a new one. General creditors rarely knew of the dissolution of the debtor partnership, and the creation of a new business firm. Unencumbered partnership assets were transferred from the old to the new partnership, and it continued the business. It was hard to conceive how the creditors of the old partnership automatically became creditors of the new partnership, or, if they did, what their standing was relative to the new partnership, the new partner, and new creditors. Did new creditors

have first claim on the assets of the business? Was the incoming partner in any way liable for the debts of the old firm?

The purpose of Section 17 and Sections 41(1) and 41(7) was to settle these questions and to deal fairly with the creditors of the old firm by giving them rights to transferred partnership property and the separate property of the old partners equivalent to the rights of new creditors. On the other hand, only the creditors of the new partnership would have rights against the new partner's separate property.

The primary thrust of Sections 17 and 41, then, was to fairly protect the rights of preexisting creditors in the assets of a newly created partnership. Only incidentally do the sections shield the new partner against the claims of preexisting creditors.

Creditors who had contributed to the wealth and operating viability of the old firm were put in one category. Only creditors who supplied new wealth and viability to the new firm were given the added security of resort to the new partner's personal assets. Thus viewed, the Act is best interpreted to treat as preexisting debt all unconditional obligations springing from contracts of the old partnership for which the old partnership has already received consideration, whether or not the payments on that obligation continue after the admission of the new partner. On the other hand, obligations for which consideration newly arises or continues to arise after the new firm opens are to be treated as new debt.

The only analogous reported cases we know of are those involving rent for current occupancy under preexisting partnership leases [Citations.] Those cases held essentially that current rent is compensation for current occupancy, and should thus be treated as new debt. From these cases, plaintiff draws the persuasive argument that interest is current rent for money and also should be treated as new debt.

We adopt this sound approach. A new partnership that pays rent for business premises under an old lease, or pays a supplier for new goods under an old contract to buy them secures a place to operate and inventory to sell, and thus incurs new debt. Just so, a new partnership that incurs interest for current periods on an old loan does so because it chooses to employ the capital borrowed for its enterprise instead of exercising its legal right to pay back the loan and thus cut off the interest obligation.

The summary judgment for defendant is reversed, and the matter is remanded for appropriate proceedings not inconsistent herewith.

## Questions

1. Discuss the duties owed by a partner to her copartners.

2. Identify and discuss the principal rights of partners (four are discussed in this chapter and two in the previous chapter).

3. Discuss the contract liability of a partnership and the partners.

4. Discuss the tort liability of a partnership and the partners.

5. Distinguish between the liability of an incoming partner for debts arising before his admission and those arising after his admission.

## Problems

1. Albert, Betty, and Carol own and operate the Roy Lumber Company. Each contributed one-third of the capital, and they share equally in the profits and losses. Their partnership agreement provides that all purchases over $500 must be authorized in advance by two partners and that only Albert is authorized to draw checks. Unknown to Albert or Carol, Betty purchases on the firm's account a $2,500 diamond bracelet and a $5,000 forklift and orders $2,000 worth of logs, all from Doug, who operates a jewelry store and is engaged in various activities connected with the lumber business. Before Betty made these purchases, Albert told Doug that Betty is not the log buyer. Albert refuses to pay Doug for Betty's purchases. Doug calls at the mill to collect, and Albert again refuses to pay him. Doug calls Albert an unprintable name, and Albert then punches Doug in the nose, knocking him out. While Doug is lying unconscious on the ground, an employee of Roy Lumber Company negligently drops a log on Doug's leg, breaking three bones. The firm and the three partners are completely solvent.

What are the rights of Doug?

2. Paula, Fred, and Stephanie agree that Paula and Fred will form and conduct a partnership business and that Stephanie will become a partner in two years. Stephanie agrees to lend the firm $5,000 and take 10 percent of the profits in lieu of interest. Without Stephanie's knowledge, Paula and Fred tell Harold that Stephanie is a partner, and Harold, relying on Stephanie's sound financial status, gives the firm credit. The firm later becomes insolvent, and Harold seeks to hold Stephanie liable as a partner. Should Harold succeed?

3. Anita and Duncan had been partners for many years in a mercantile business. Their relationship deteriorated to the point where Anita threatened to bring an action for an accounting and dissolution of the firm. Duncan then offered to buy Anita's interest in the partnership for $25,000. Anita refused the offer and told Duncan that she would take no less than $36,000. A short time later, James approached Duncan and informed him he had inside information that a proposed street change would greatly benefit the business and that he, James, would buy the entire business for $100,000 or buy a one-half interest for $50,000. Duncan made a final offer of $35,000 to Anita for her interest. Anita accepted this offer, and the transaction was completed. Duncan then sold the one-half interest to James for $50,000. Several months later, Anita learned for the first time of the transaction between Duncan and James.

What rights, if any, does Anita have against Duncan?

4. Anthony and Karen were partners doing business as the Petite Garment Company. Leroy owned a dye plant that did much of the processing for the company. Anthony and Karen decided to offer Leroy an interest in their company, in consideration for which Leroy would contribute his dye plant to the partnership. Leroy accepted the offer and was duly admitted as a partner. At the time he was admitted as a partner, Leroy did not know that the partnership was on the verge of insolvency. About three months after Leroy was admitted to the partnership, a textile firm obtained a judgment against the partnership in the amount of $50,000. This debt represented an unpaid balance that had existed before Leroy was admitted as a partner.

The textile firm brought an action to subject the partnership property, including the dye plant, to the satisfaction of its judgment. The complaint also requested that, in the event the judgment was unsatisfied by sale of the partnership property, Leroy's home be sold and the proceeds applied to the balance of the judgment. Anthony and Karen own nothing but their interest in the partnership property.

What should be the result (a) with regard to the dye plant and (b) with regard to Leroy's home?

5. Jones and Ray formed a partnership on January 1, known as JR Construction Co., to engage in the construction business, each partner owning a one-half interest. On February 10, while conducting partnership business, Jones negligently injured Ware, who brought an action against Jones, Ray, and JR Construction Co. and obtained judgment for $25,000 against them on March 1. On April 15, Muir joined the partnership by contributing $10,000 cash, and by agreement each partner was entitled to a one-third interest. In July, the partners agreed to purchase new construction equipment for the partnership, and Muir was authorized to obtain a loan from XYZ Bank in the partnership name for $20,000 to finance the purchase. On July 10, Muir signed a $20,000 note on behalf of the partnership, and the equipment was purchased. In November, the partnership was in financial difficulty, its total assets amounting to $5,000. The note was in default, with a balance

of $15,000 owing to XYZ Bank. Muir has substantial resources, while Jones and Ray each individually have assets of $2,000.

What is the extent of Muir's personal liability and the personal liability of Jones and Ray as to (a) the judgment obtained by Ware and (b) the debt owing to XYZ Bank?

6. ABCD Company is a general partnership organized under the UPA. It consists of Dianne, Greg, Knox, and Laura, whose capital contributions were as follows: Dianne = $5,000, Greg = $7,500, Knox = $10,000, and Laura = $5,000. The partnership agreement provided that the partnership would continue for three years and that no withdrawals of capital were to be made without the consent of all the partners. The agreement also provided that all advances would be entitled to interest at 10 percent per year. Six months after the partnership was formed, Dianne advanced $10,000 to the partnership. At the end of the first year, net profits totaled $11,000 before any moneys had been distributed to partners. How should the $11,000 be allocated to Dianne, Greg, Knox, and Laura? Explain.

7. Adams, a consulting engineer, entered into a partnership with three others for the practice of their profession. The only written partnership agreement is a brief document specifying that Adams is entitled to 55 percent of the profits and the others to 15 percent each. The venture is a total failure. Creditors are pressing for payment, and some have filed suit. The partners cannot agree on a course of action.

How many of the partners must agree to achieve each of the following objectives?

(a) To add Jones, also an engineer, as a partner, Jones being willing to contribute a substantial amount of new capital.

(b) To sell a vacant lot held in the partnership name, which had been acquired as a future office site for the partnership.

(c) To move the partnership's offices to less expensive quarters.

(d) To demand a formal accounting.

(e) To dissolve the partnership.

(f) To agree to submit certain disputed claims to arbitration, which Adams believes will prove less expensive than litigation.

(g) To sell all of the partnership's personal property, Adams having what he believes to be a good offer for the property from a newly formed engineering firm.

(h) To alter the respective interests of the parties in the profits and losses by decreasing Adams's share to 40 percent and increasing the others' shares accordingly.

(i) To assign all the partnership's assets to a bank in trust for the benefit of creditors, hoping to work out satisfactory arrangements without filing for bankruptcy.

8. Charles and Jack orally agreed to become partners in a small tool and die business. Charles, who had experience in tool and die work, was to operate the business. Jack was to take no active part but was to contribute the entire $50,000 capitalization. Charles worked ten hours a day at the plant, for which he was paid nothing. Nevertheless, despite Charles's best efforts, the business failed. The $50,000 capital was gone, and the partnership owed $50,000 in debts. Prior to the failure of the partnership business, Jack became personally insolvent; consequently, the creditors of the partnership collected the entire $50,000 indebtedness from Charles, who was forced to sell his home and farm to satisfy the indebtedness. Jack later regained his financial responsibility, and Charles brought an appropriate action against Jack for (a) one-half of the $50,000 Charles had paid to partnership creditors and (b) one-half of $18,000, the reasonable value of Charles's services during the operation of the partnership. Decision?

9. Glenn refuses an invitation to become a partner of Dorothy and Cynthia in a retail grocery business. Nevertheless, Dorothy inserts an advertisement in the local newspaper representing Glenn as their partner. Glenn takes no steps to deny the existence of a partnership between them. Ron, who extended credit to the firm, seeks to hold Glenn liable as a partner. Decision?

10. Hanover leased a portion of his farm to Brown and Black, doing business as the Colorite Hatchery. Brown went upon the premises to remove certain chicken sheds that he and Black had placed there for hatchery purposes. Thinking that Brown intended to remove certain other sheds, which were Hanover's property, Hanover accosted Brown, who willfully struck Hanover and knocked him down. Brown then ran to the Colorite truck, which he had previously loaded with chicken coops, and drove back to the hatchery. On the way, he picked up George, who was hitchhiking to the city to look for a job. Brown was driving at seventy miles an hour down the highway. At an open intersection with another highway, Brown in his hurry ran a stop sign, striking another vehicle. The collision caused severe injuries to George. Immediately thereafter, the partnership was dissolved, and Brown was insolvent. Hanover and George each bring separate actions against Black as copartner for the alleged tort committed by Brown against each.

What judgments as to each?

11. Phillips and Harris are partners in a used car business. Under their oral partnership, each has an equal voice in the conduct and management of the business. Because of their irregular business hours, the two further agreed that they could use any partnership vehicle as desired. This use includes transportation to and from work, even though the vehicles are for sale at all times. While driving a partnership vehicle home from the used car lot, Harris hit a car driven by Cook, who brought this action against Harris and Phillips individually and as copartners for his injuries. Decision?

12. Stroud and Freeman are general partners in Stroud's Food Center, a grocery store. Nothing in the articles of partnership restricts the power or authority of either partner to act in respect to the ordinary and legitimate business of the Food Center. In late 1955, however, Stroud informed National Biscuit that he would not be personally responsible for any more bread sold to the partnership. Then, in February 1956, at the request of Freeman, National Biscuit sold and delivered more

bread to the Food Center. When payment was refused, National Biscuit brought this action against Stroud and the partnership to recover the value of the bread delivered to the Food Center. Decision?

**13.**    Hodge and Voeller, the managing partner of the Pay-Out Drive-In Theatre, signed a contract for the sale of a small parcel of land belonging to the partnership. Except for the last twenty feet, which was necessary for the theatre's driveway, the parcel was not used in theatre operations. The agreement stated that it was between Hodge and the partnership, with Voeller signing for the partnership. Voeller claims that he told Hodge before signing that a plat plan would have to be approved by the other partners before the sale. Hodge denies this and sues for specific performance, claiming that Voeller had actual and apparent authority to bind the partnership. The partners argue that Voeller had no such authority and that Hodge knew this. Decision?

**14.**    L. G. and S. L. Patel, husband and wife, owned and operated the City Center Motel in Eureka. On April 16, 1986, Rajeshkumar, the son of L. G. and S. L., formed a partnership with his parents and became owner of 35 percent of the City Center Motel. The partnership agreement required that Rajeshkumar approve any sale of the motel. Record title to the motel was not changed, however, to reflect his interest. On April 21, L. G. and S. L. listed their motel for sale with a real estate broker. On May 2, P. V. and Kirit Patel made an offer on the motel, which L. G. and S. L. accepted. Neither the broker nor the purchasers knew of the son's interest in the motel. When L. G. and S. L. notified Rajeshkumar of their plans, to their surprise, he refused to sell his 35 percent of the motel. On May 4, L. G. and S. L. notified P. V. and Kirit that they wished to withdraw their acceptance. They offered to pay

$10,000 in damages and to give the purchasers a right of first refusal for five years. Rather than accept the offer, on May 29, P. V. and Kirit filed an action for specific performance and incidental damages. L. G., S. L., and Rajeshkumar responded that the contract could not lawfully be enforced. Decision?

**15.**    Wayne Taurman and Derrold Paige, employees of Felton Construction Company (FCC), were members of Felton Investment Group (FIG), a partnership of employee contributors to a retirement fund. The partnership agreement included a provision "that if a member ceases employment or is discharged for misconduct, his interest shall be returned in an amount equal to contributions paid into the fund plus 4% simple interest." In December 1978, Paige decided that his investment in FIG was in jeopardy and stopped contributing to the fund; however, he remained an employee of FCC. About a year later, Paige received a check from FIG, reflecting his contributions to the fund plus interest, in satisfaction of his claim in the partnership. He refused to indorse and cash the check. Taurman continued to invest in FIG until July 1980. At that time, FCC terminated both Taurman and Paige for refusing to accept nonunion work. Taurman was then offered by FIG an amount equal to his contribution plus interest in satisfaction of his claim in the partnership, but he too refused to indorse and cash the check. FIG filed a complaint requesting that Taurman and Paige be ordered to accept the amounts offered in satisfaction of their claims in the partnership. Taurman and Paige filed a complaint seeking the judicial dissolution of FIG, a formal accounting of the partnership, and *pro rata* shares in the partnership's assets. FIG appealed from a trial court judgment for Taurman and Paige. Decision?

**WWW** **Internet Exercise**  Examine sites that discuss and explain the duties of fiduciaries.

# CHAPTER 33

# Limited Partnerships and Limited Liability Companies

This chapter will consider other types of unincorporated business associations: limited partnerships, limited liability companies, limited liability partnerships, and limited liability limited partnerships. These organizations have developed to meet special business and investment needs. Consequently, each has characteristics that make it appropriate for certain purposes.

## LIMITED PARTNERSHIPS

The limited partnership has proved to be an attractive vehicle for a variety of investments because of its tax advantages and the limited liability it confers upon limited partners. Unlike general partnerships, limited partnerships are statutory creations. Before 1976, the governing statute in all States except Louisiana was the Uniform Limited Partnership Act (ULPA), which was promulgated in 1916. At that time, most limited partnerships were small and had only a few limited partners. Today, many limited partnerships are much larger, typically involving a small number of major investors and a relatively large group of widely distributed investors who purchase limited partnership interests. This type of organization has evolved to attract substantial amounts of investment capital. As a result, limited partnerships have been used to muster the sizable investments necessary in areas such as real estate, oil and gas, motion pictures, professional sports, and research and development. The large scale and multistate operations of the modern limited partnership, however, have severely burdened the framework established by the ULPA.

These shortcomings prompted the National Conference of Commissioners on Uniform State Laws to develop a Revised Uniform Limited Partnership Act (RULPA), which was promulgated in 1976. According to its preface, the RULPA is "intended to modernize the prior uniform law while retaining the special character of limited partnerships as compared with corporations."

In 1985, the National Conference revised the RULPA "for the purpose of more effectively modernizing, improving and establishing uniformity in the law of limited partnerships." The 1985 Act is substantially similar to the 1976 RULPA, preserving the philosophy of the older Act and making almost no change in its basic structure. Almost all the States have adopted either the 1976 Act or the 1985 Act with considerably more States adopting the 1985 version than the 1976 version.

This chapter will discuss the 1985 RULPA. The ULPA, the 1976 RULPA, and the 1985 RULPA are supplemented by the Uniform Partnership Act, which applies to limited partnerships in any case for which the Limited Partnership Act does not provide.

◆ *See Figure 31–1*

In addition, limited partnership interests are almost always considered to be securities, and their sale is therefore subject to State and Federal securities regulation, as discussed in Chapter 44.

## Definition

A **limited partnership** is a partnership formed by two or more persons under the laws of a State and having one or more general partners and one or more limited partners. Section 101(7). A *person* includes a natural person, partnership, limited partnership, trust, estate, association, or corporation. Section 101(11). A limited partnership differs from a general partnership in several respects, three of which are fundamental:

1. a statute providing for the formation of limited partnerships must be in effect;
2. the limited partnership must substantially comply with the requirements of that statute; and
3. the liability of a limited partner for partnership debts or obligations is limited to the extent of the capital he has contributed or has agreed to contribute.

# Formation

Although the formation of a general partnership calls for no special procedures, the formation of a limited partnership requires substantial compliance with the limited partnership statute. Failure to so comply may result in the limited partners' not obtaining limited liability.

*Filing of Certificate*  Section 201 of the RULPA provides that two or more persons desiring to form a limited partnership shall file in the office of the Secretary of State of the State in which the limited partnership is to have its principal office a signed certificate of limited partnership. The certificate must include the following information:

1. the name of the limited partnership;
2. the address of the office and the name and address of the agent for service of process;
3. the name and the business address of each general partner;
4. the latest date upon which the limited partnership is to dissolve; and
5. any other matters the general partners decide to include in the certificate.

The certificate of limited partnership must be amended if a new general partner is admitted, a general partner withdraws, or a general partner becomes aware that any statement in the certificate was or has become false. Section 202. In addition, the certificate may be amended at any time for any other purpose the general partners deem proper. As discussed later, false statements in a certificate or amendment that cause loss to third parties who rely on the statements may result in liability for the general partners.

*Name*  The inclusion of the surname of a limited partner in the partnership name is prohibited unless it is also the name of a general partner or unless the business had operated under that name before the admission of the limited partner. A limited partner who knowingly permits his name to be used in violation of this provision is liable to any creditor who did not know that he was a limited partner. Section 303(d). In addition, a limited partnership cannot use a name that is the same as, or deceptively similar to, the name of any corporation or other limited partnership. Section 102. Finally, the name of the limited partnership must contain the unabbreviated words "limited partnership."

*Contributions*  The contribution of a partner may be cash, property, services rendered, or a promissory note or other obligation to contribute cash or property or to perform services. Section 501. A promise by a limited partner to contribute to the limited partnership is not enforceable unless it is in a signed writing. Should a partner fail to make a required capital contribution described in a signed writing, the limited partnership may hold her liable to contribute the cash value of the stated contribution.

*Defective Formation*  A limited partnership is formed when a certificate of limited partnership that substantially complies with the requirements of the statute is filed. Therefore, the formation is defective if no certificate is filed or if the certificate filed does not substantially meet the statutory requirements. In either case, the limited liability of limited partners is jeopardized. The RULPA provides that a person who has contributed to the capital of a business (an "equity participant"), erroneously and in good faith believing that he has become a limited partner in a limited partnership, is not liable as a general partner, provided that on ascertaining the mistake he either (1) withdraws from the business and renounces future profits or (2) files a certificate or an amendment curing the defect. Section 304. The equity participant will be liable, however, to any third party who transacted business with the enterprise before the withdrawal or amendment and who in good faith believed that the equity participant was a general partner at the time of the transaction.

The 1985 Act does not require that the limited partners be named in the certificate. This greatly reduces the risk that an inadvertent omission of such information will expose a limited partner to liability.

*Foreign Limited Partnerships*  A limited partnership is considered "foreign" in any State other than the one in which it was formed. The laws of the State in which a foreign limited partnership is organized govern its organization, its internal affairs, and the liability of its limited partners. Section 901. In addition, the RULPA requires all foreign limited partnerships to register with the Secretary of State before transacting any business in a State. Section 902. Any foreign limited partnership transacting business without so registering may not bring enforcement actions in the State's courts until it registers, although it may defend itself in the State's courts. Section 907.

# Rights

Because limited partnerships are organized pursuant to statute, the rights of the parties are usually set forth in the certificate of limited partnership and the limited partnership agreement. Unless otherwise agreed or provided in the act, a general partner of a limited partnership has all the rights and powers of a partner in a partnership without limited partners. Section 403. A general partner also may be a limited partner; as such, he shares in profits, losses, and distributions both as a general partner and as a limited one. Section 404.

**Control**   The general partners of a limited partnership have almost exclusive control and management of the limited partnership. A limited partner, on the other hand, is not permitted to share in this management or control; if he does, he may forfeit his limited liability. Under the 1976 Act, a limited partner whose participation in control is substantially the same as the exercise of the powers of a general partner assumes the liability of a general partner to all third parties who transact business with the partnership. On the other hand, a limited partner whose participation in control of the business is not substantially the same as the exercise of the powers of a general partner is liable as a general partner for the obligations of the limited partnership only to those persons who transact business with the limited partnership with actual knowledge of his participation in control. Section 303(a).

The 1985 Act has eliminated the broader liability of a limited partner whose participation is substantially the same as that of a general partner and tightened the reliance test. Under the 1985 Act, a limited partner who participates in the control of the business is liable only to those persons who transact business with the limited partnership reasonably believing, based upon the limited partner's conduct, that the limited partner is a general partner.

In addition, Section 303(b) of the RULPA provides a "safe harbor" by enumerating activities that a limited partner may perform without being deemed to have taken part in control of the business. They are the following:

1. being a contractor for, or an agent or employee of, the limited partnership or of a general partner or being an officer, director, or shareholder of a general partner that is a corporation;
2. consulting with and advising a general partner with respect to the business of the limited partnership;
3. acting as surety for the limited partnership;
4. bringing a derivative action in the right of the limited partnership;
5. requesting or attending a meeting of partners;

6. voting on one or more of the following matters:
   (a) the dissolution and winding up of the limited partnership;
   (b) the sale, exchange, lease, mortgage, pledge, or other transfer of all or substantially all of the assets of the limited partnership;
   (c) the incurrence of indebtedness by the limited partnership other than in the ordinary course of its business;
   (d) a change in the nature of the business;
   (e) the admission or removal of a general partner;
   (f) the admission or removal of a limited partner;
   (g) a transaction involving an actual or potential conflict of interest between a general partner and the limited partnership or the limited partners;
   (h) an amendment to the partnership agreement or certificate of limited partnership; or
   (i) other matters related to the business of the limited partnership which the partnership agreement states in writing may be subject to the approval or disapproval of limited partners;
7. winding up the limited partnership;
8. exercising any other right or power permitted to limited partners under the Act.

 *See Case 33–1*

**Voting Rights**   The partnership agreement may grant to all or a specified group of general or limited partners the right to vote on any matter. Sections 302 and 405. If, however, the agreement grants limited partners voting powers beyond the safe harbor of Section 303, a court may hold that the limited partners have participated in control of the business. The RULPA does not require that limited partners have the right to vote on matters as a class separate from the general partners, although the partnership agreement may provide such a right.

**Choice of Associates**   After the formation of a limited partnership, the admission of additional limited partners requires the written consent of all partners, unless the partnership agreement provides otherwise. Section 301. The admission of the new limited partner is not effective until the records of the limited partnership have been amended to reflect that fact. Regarding the admission of additional general partners, the written partnership agreement determines the procedure for authorizing their admission. The written consent of all partners is required only if the partnership agreement fails to deal with this issue. Section 401.

***Withdrawal*** A general partner may withdraw from a limited partnership at any time by giving written notice to the other partners. Section 602. If the withdrawal violates the partnership agreement, the limited partnership may recover damages from the withdrawing general partner. A limited partner may withdraw as provided in the written partnership agreement. If the agreement does not specify when a limited partner may withdraw or a definite time for the limited partnership's dissolution, a limited partner may withdraw upon giving at least six months' prior written notice to each general partner. Section 603. Upon withdrawal, a withdrawing partner is entitled to receive any distribution to which she is entitled under the partnership agreement, subject to the restrictions on amount discussed below. If the partnership agreement makes no provision, the partner is entitled to receive the fair value of her interest in the limited partnership as of the date of withdrawal, based upon her right to share in distributions from the limited partnership. Section 604.

***Assignment of Partnership Interest*** A partnership interest is a partner's share of the profits and losses of a limited partnership and the right to receive distributions of partnership assets. Section 101(10). A partnership interest is personal property. Section 701. Unless otherwise provided in the partnership agreement, a partner may assign his partnership interest. An assignment does not dissolve the limited partnership. The assignee, who does not become a partner, may exercise none of the rights of a partner: the assignment entitles the assignee only to receive, to the extent of the assignment, the assigning partner's share of distributions. Except as otherwise provided in the partnership agreement, a partner ceases to be a partner upon assignment of all his partnership interest. Section 702.

An assignee of a partnership interest, including an assignee of a general partner, may, however, become a *limited* partner if all the other partners consent or if the assigning partner, having such power provided in the partnership agreement, grants the assignee this right. Section 704. An assignee who becomes a limited partner is liable for the obligation of his assignor to make or return contributions, except for those liabilities unknown to the assignee at the time he became a limited partner. Section 704(b). Upon the death of a partner, her executor or administrator has all the rights of the partner for the purpose of settling her estate, including any power the deceased partner had to make her assignee a substituted limited partner. Section 705.

A creditor of a partner may obtain a charging order against a partner's interest in the partnership. To the extent of the charging order, the creditor has the rights of an assignee of the partnership interest. Section 703.

***Profit and Loss Sharing*** Profits and losses are allocated among the partners as provided in the partnership agreement. If the agreement makes no such provision in writing, then the profits and losses are allocated on the basis of the value of the contributions each partner actually has made. Section 503. Nonetheless, limited partners usually are not liable for losses beyond their capital contribution. Section 303(a).

***Distributions*** The partners share distributions of cash or other assets of the limited partnership as provided in writing in the partnership agreement. The RULPA allows partners to share in distributions in a proportion different from that in which they share in profits. If the partnership agreement does not provide for allocation in writing, then distributions are based on the value of contributions each partner actually made. Section 504. Unless otherwise provided in writing, a partner has no right to demand a distribution in any form other than cash. Once a partner becomes entitled to a distribution, he has the status of a creditor with respect to that distribution. Section 606. A partner may not receive a distribution from a limited partnership unless the assets remaining after the distribution are sufficient to pay all partnership liabilities other than liabilities to partners on account of their partnership interests. Section 607.

***Loans*** Both general and limited partners may be secured or unsecured creditors of the partnership with the same rights as a person who is not a partner, subject to applicable State and Federal bankruptcy and fraudulent conveyance statutes. Section 107.

***Information*** The partnership must continuously maintain within the State an office at which it keeps basic organizational and financial records. Section 105. Each partner has the right to inspect and copy any of the partnership records. Each limited partner may obtain from the general partners upon reasonable demand (1) complete and accurate information regarding the business and financial condition of the limited partnership, (2) copies of the limited partnership's Federal, State, and local income tax returns for each year, and (3) any other reasonable information regarding the affairs of the limited partnership. Section 305.

***Derivative Actions***  A limited partner has the right to bring an action on behalf of a limited partnership to recover a judgment in its favor if the general partners having authority to bring the action have refused to do so. Section 1001. The act also establishes standing and pleading requirements similar to those imposed in shareholder's derivative actions and permits the court to award reasonable expenses, including attorneys' fees, to a successful plaintiff. Section 1002.

## Duties and Liabilities

The duties and liabilities of general partners in a limited partnership are quite different from those of limited partners. A general partner is subject to all the duties and restrictions of a partner in a partnership without limited partners, whereas a limited partner is subject to few, if any, duties and enjoys limited liability.

***Duties***  A *general partner* of a limited partnership owes a **fiduciary** duty to her general and limited partners. The existence of this duty is extremely important to the limited partners because of their circumscribed role in the control and management of the business enterprise. Conversely, whether a limited partner owes a fiduciary duty either to his general partners or to the limited partnership remains unclear. The very limited judicial authority on this question seems to indicate that the limited partner does not.

The RULPA does not distinguish between the duty of care owed by a general partner to a general partnership and that owed by a general partner to a limited partnership. Thus, although a general partner owes her partners a duty not to be culpably negligent (as discussed in Chapter 32), some courts have imposed upon general partners a higher duty of care toward *limited partners*. On the other hand, a limited partner owes no duty of care to a limited partnership as long as she remains a limited partner.

🔨 *See Case 33–2*

***Liabilities***  One of the most appealing features of a limited partnership is the limited personal liability it offers limited partners. **Limited liability** means that a limited partner who has paid her contribution has no further liability to the limited partnership or its creditors. Thus, if a limited partner buys a 25 percent share of a limited partnership for $50,000 and does not forfeit her limited liability, her liability is limited to the $50,000 she contributed, even if the limited partnership suffers losses of

$500,000. This protection is subject to three conditions discussed earlier:

1. that the partnership has substantially complied in good faith with the requirement that a certificate of limited partnership be filed;
2. that the surname of the limited partner does not appear in the partnership name; and
3. that the limited partner does not participate in control of the business.

In addition, if the certificate contains a false statement, anyone who suffers loss by reliance on that statement may hold liable any party to the certificate who knew the statement to be false when the certificate was executed. Section 207. As long as the limited partner abides by these conditions, his liability for any and all obligations of the partnership is limited to his capital contribution.

At the same time, the general partners of a limited partnership have unlimited external liability. Also, any general partner who knew or should have known that the limited partnership certificate contained a false statement is liable to anyone who suffers loss by reliance on that statement. Moreover, a general partner is liable if he knows or should know that a statement has become false and he does not amend the certificate within a reasonable time.

Any partner to whom any part of her contribution has been returned without violation of the partnership agreement or of the limited partnership act is liable for one year to the limited partnership, to the extent necessary to pay creditors who extended credit during the period the partnership held the contribution. Section 608. In contrast, any partner to whom any part of her contribution was returned in violation of the partnership agreement or the limited partnership act is liable to the limited partnership for six years for the amount of the contribution wrongfully returned.

◆ *See Figures 33–1 and 33–2*

## Dissolution

As with a general partnership, extinguishing a limited partnership involves three steps: (1) dissolution, (2) winding up or liquidation, and (3) termination. The causes of dissolution and the priorities for distributing the assets, however, differ somewhat from those in a general partnership.

***Causes***  In a limited partnership, the limited partners have no right or power to dissolve the partnership, except by court decree. The death or bankruptcy of a limited

**FIGURE 33–1** Liability of Limited Partners

| Activity | Consequences |
|---|---|
| **Defective formation** | Unlimited liability to third parties who transacted business before withdrawal or amendment and in good faith believed "equity participant" was a general partner |
| **Participation in control is substantially the same as powers of a general partner** | 1976 Act: Unlimited liability to all third parties who transact business with the partnership<br>1985 Act: Unlimited liability to third parties who transact business with reasonable belief, based on limited partner's conduct, that limited partner was a general partner |
| **Participation in control is *not* substantially the same as powers of a general partner** | 1976 Act: Unlimited liability to those persons who transacted business with actual knowledge of the limited partner's participation in control<br>1985 Act: Same as 1985 Act above, where participation in control is substantially the same as powers of a general partner |
| **Name used with permission** | Unlimited liability to third parties who did not have actual knowledge that she was a limited partner |

partner does not dissolve the partnership. Section 801 of the RULPA specifies those events that will trigger a dissolution, after which the affairs of the partnership must be liquidated:

1. the expiration of the time period specified in the certificate;
2. the happening of events specified in writing in the partnership agreement;
3. the unanimous written consent of all the partners;
4. the withdrawal of a general partner unless either (a) there is at least one other general partner and the written provisions of the partnership agreement permit the remaining general partners to continue the business or (b) within 90 days all partners agree in writing to continue the business; or
5. a decree of judicial dissolution, which may be granted whenever it is not reasonably practicable to carry on the business in conformity with the partnership agreement.

A general partner's withdrawal occurs upon his retirement, assignment of all his general partnership interest, removal, bankruptcy, death, or adjudication of incompetency.

A certificate of cancellation must be filed when the limited partnership dissolves and winding up commences. Section 203.

**FIGURE 33–2** Comparison of General and Limited Partners

| | General Partner | Limited Partner |
|---|---|---|
| **Control** | Has all the rights and powers of a partner in a partnership without limited partners | Has no right to take part in management or control |
| **Liability** | Unlimited | Limited, unless she takes part in control or her name is used |
| **Agency** | Is an agent of the partnership | Is not an agent of the partnership |
| **Fiduciary Duty** | Yes | No |
| **Duty of Care** | Yes | No |

***Winding Up*** Unless otherwise provided in the partnership agreement, the general partners who have not wrongfully dissolved the limited partnership may wind up its affairs. Section 803. The limited partners may wind up the limited partnership if all the general partners have wrongfully dissolved the partnership. But any partner, his legal representative, or his assignee may obtain a winding up by court if cause is shown.

***Distribution of Assets*** Section 804 sets forth the priorities in distributing the assets of a limited partnership:

1. to creditors, including partners who are creditors, except with respect to liabilities for distributions;
2. to partners and ex-partners in satisfaction of liabilities for unpaid distributions;
3. to partners for the return of their contributions, except as otherwise agreed; and
4. to partners for their partnership interests in the proportions in which they share in distributions, except as otherwise agreed.

General and limited partners rank equally unless the partnership agreement provides otherwise.

## LIMITED LIABILITY COMPANIES

A limited liability company (LLC) is another form of unincorporated business association. Prior to 1990, only two States had statutes permitting LLCs. Now all States have enacted LLC statutes. Until 1995, there was no uniform statute on which States might base their LLC legislation, and since its promulgation only a few States have adopted the uniform statute. Therefore, the enabling legislation varies from State to State. Nevertheless, the LLC statutes generally share certain characteristics.

A **limited liability company** is a noncorporate business organization that provides limited liability to *all* of its owners (members) and permits all of its members to participate in management of the business. It may elect not to be a separate taxable entity, in which case only the members are taxed. If an LLC has only one member, then it will be taxed as a sole proprietorship, unless separate entity tax treatment is elected. Thus, the LLC provides many of the advantages of a general partnership plus limited liability for all its members. Its benefits outweigh those of a limited partnership in that all members of a LLC not only enjoy limited liability but also may participate in management and control of the business. Ownership interests in a limited liability company may be considered to be securities, especially interests in those

LLCs operated by managers. If a particular LLC interest is considered a security, its sale would be subject to State and Federal securities regulation, as discussed in Chapter 44.

◆ *See Figure 31–1*

## Formation

The formation of a limited liability company requires substantial compliance with a State's limited liability company statute. Some of the statutes require an LLC to have at least two members. Once formed, an LLC is a separate legal entity that is distinct from its members, who are normally not liable for its debts and obligations. An LLC can contract in its own name and is generally empowered to carry on any lawful business, although some statutes restrict the permissible activities of LLCs.

***Filing*** The LLC statutes generally require the central filing of **articles of organization** in a designated State office. The States vary regarding the information they require the articles to include. Some LLC statutes limit LLCs to a duration of thirty years or less, while other statutes require the articles to specify the latest date on which the LLC is to dissolve.

***Name*** LLC statutes generally require the name of the LLC to include the words *limited liability company* or the abbreviation *LLC*. Some States also permit the use of the name *limited company* and the abbreviation *LC*.

***Contribution*** The contribution of a member to a limited liability company may be cash, property, services rendered, a promissory note, or other obligation to contribute cash, property, or to perform services. Members are liable to the LLC for failing to make an agreed contribution.

***Operating Agreement*** The members of an LLC adopt an **operating agreement,** which is the basic contract governing the affairs of a limited liability company and stating the various rights and duties of the members. Some States require the entire operating agreement to be in writing, while other States permit unwritten operating agreements to govern at least some of the relations among the members.

***Foreign Limited Liability Companies*** A limited liability company is considered "foreign" in any State other than that in which it was formed. LLC statutes typically provide that the laws of the State in which a foreign LLC is organized govern its organization, its internal affairs, and the liability of its members and managers. Foreign limited liability companies must register with the Secretary of State before transacting any business in a State. Any foreign limited liability company transacting business without so registering may not bring enforcement actions in the State's courts until it registers, although it may defend itself in the State's courts.

## Rights of Members

A member has no property interest in property owned by the LLC. On the other hand, a member does have an interest in the LLC, which is personal property. A member's interest in the LLC includes two components:

1. the **financial interest,** which is the right to distributions, and
2. the **management interest,** which consists of all other rights granted to a member by the LLC operating agreement and the LLC statute. The management interest typically includes the right to manage, vote, obtain information, and bring enforcement actions.

***Profit and Loss Sharing***  The LLC's operating agreement determines how the partners allocate the profits and losses. If the LLC's operating agreement makes no such provision, the profits and losses are typically allocated on the basis of the value of the members' contributions.

***Distributions***  The members share distributions of cash or other assets of a limited liability company as provided in the operating agreement. If the LLC's operating agreement does not allocate distributions, they are typically made on the basis of the contributions each member made.

***Withdrawal***  Most statutes permit a member to withdraw and demand payment of her interest upon giving the notice specified in the statute or the LLC's operating agreement. Some of the statutes permit the operating agreement to deny members the right to withdraw from the LLC.

***Management***  Most LLC statutes provide that, in the absence of a contrary agreement, each member has equal rights in the management of the LLC. All LLC statutes permit LLCs to be managed by one or more managers

who may, but need not, be members. In a member-managed LLC, the members have actual and apparent authority to bind the LLC. In a manager-managed LLC, the managers have this authority, while the members have no actual or apparent authority to bind the manager-managed LLC.

***Voting***  A number of the LLC statutes specify the voting rights of members, subject to a contrary provision in an LLC's operating agreement. Typically, members have the right to vote on proposals to (1) adopt or amend the operating agreement, (2) admit any person as a member, (3) sell all or substantially all of the LLC's assets prior to dissolution, and (4) merge the LLC with another LLC.

***Derivative Actions***  A member has the right to bring an action on behalf of a limited liability company to recover a judgment in its favor if the managers or members with authority to bring the action have refused to do so.

***Assignment of LLC Interest***  Unless otherwise provided in the LLC's operating agreement, a member may assign his financial interest in the LLC. An assignment does not dissolve the LLC. The assignee does not become a member and may not exercise any rights of a member. The assignment only entitles the assignee to receive, to the extent of the assignment, the assigning member's share of distributions. However, an assignee of a financial interest in an LLC may acquire the other rights by being admitted as a member of the company by all the remaining members. A judgment creditor of a member may obtain a charging order against the member's financial interest in the LLC.

## Duties

As with general partnerships and limited partnerships, the duties of care and loyalty also apply to LLCs. In a number of States, the LLC statute expressly imposes these duties. In other States, the common law imposes these duties. Who has these duties in a limited liability company depends upon whether the LLC is a manager-managed LLC or a member-managed LLC.

***Manager-managed LLCs***  Most LLC statutes impose upon the managers of an LLC a duty of care. In some States, this is a duty to refrain from grossly negligent, reckless, or intentional conduct; in other States, it is a duty to act as a prudent person would in similar circumstances. Managers also have a fiduciary duty, although the statutes vary in how they specify that duty. Usually, members of manager-managed LLCs have no duties to the LLC or its members by reason of being a member.

***Member-managed LLCs*** Members of member-managed LLCs have the same duties of care and loyalty that managers have in manager-managed LLCs.

◆ *See Figure 33–3*

## Liabilities

One of the most appealing features of a limited company is the limited personal liability it offers to all its members and managers. Statutes typically provide that no member or manager of a limited liability company shall be obligated personally for any debt, obligation, or liability of the limited liability company solely by reason of being a member or acting as a manager of the limited liability company.

As mentioned earlier, a member who fails to make an agreed contribution is liable to the limited liability company for the deficiency. Moreover, under the great majority of statutes, any member who receives a return of her contribution in violation of the LLC's operating agreement or the limited liability company act is liable to the limited liability company for the amount of the contribution wrongfully returned. Under a few of the statutes, even members who receive a return of their capital contribution without violating the LLC agreement or the limited liability company act remain liable to the limited liability company for a specified time to the extent necessary to pay creditors.

## Dissolution

Limited liability company statutes generally provide that an LLC will automatically dissolve upon

1. the dissociation of a member,
2. the expiring of the LLC's agreed duration or the happening of any of the events specified in the articles,
3. the unanimous written consent of all the members, or
4. a decree of judicial dissolution.

***Dissociation*** Dissociation means that a member has ceased to be associated with the company through voluntary withdrawal, death, incompetence, expulsion, or bankruptcy. Most statutes permit the nondissociating members by unanimous consent to continue the LLC after a member dissociates. Some allow continuation by majority vote.

 *See Case 33–3*

***Distribution of Assets*** Most statutes provide default rules for distributing the assets of a limited liability company as follows:

1. to creditors, including members and managers who are creditors, except with respect to liabilities for distributions;
2. to members and former members in satisfaction of liabilities for unpaid distributions, except as otherwise agreed;
3. to members for the return of their contributions, except as otherwise agreed; and
4. to members for their limited liability company interests in the proportions in which members share in distributions, except as otherwise agreed.

**FIGURE 33–3** Comparison of Member-Managed and Manager-Managed LLCs

| Activity | Member of Member-Managed LLC<br>Manager of Manager-Managed LLC | Member of Manager-Managed LLC |
| --- | --- | --- |
| **Control** | Full | None |
| **Liability** | Limited | Limited |
| **Agency** | Is an agent of the LLC | Is not an agent of the LLC |
| **Fiduciary Duty** | Yes | No |
| **Duty of Care** | Yes | No |

# OTHER TYPES OF UNINCORPORATED BUSINESS ASSOCIATIONS

## Limited Liability Partnerships

Nearly all of the States have enacted statutes enabling the formation of limited liability partnerships (LLPs). Until 1996 there was no uniform LLP statute, so the enabling statutes vary from State to State. In 1996 the Revised Uniform Partnership Act (RUPA) was amended to add provisions enabling general partnerships to elect to become limited liability partnerships, and a few States have adopted this version of the RUPA. A registered **limited liability partnership** is a general partnership that, by making the statutorily required filing, limits the liability of its partners for some or all of the partnership's obligations.

*Formalities*   To become an LLP, a general partnership must file with the Secretary of State an application containing specified information. The RUPA requires the partnership to file a statement of qualification. RUPA Section 1001(c). Most of the statutes require only a majority of the partners to authorize registration as an LLP; others require unanimous approval. The RUPA requires unanimity unless the partnership agreement provides otherwise. RUPA Section 1001(b). Some statutes require renewal of registrations annually; other statutes require periodic reports; and a few require no renewal. The RUPA requires filing annual reports. RUPA Section 1003. Some statutes require a new filing after any change in membership of the partnership, but a few of the statutes do not. The RUPA does not.

*Designation*   All statutes require LLPs to designate themselves as such. Most statutes require the name of the LLP to include the words *limited liability partnership* or *registered limited liability partnership,* or the abbreviation *LLP.* Most statutes provide that the laws of the jurisdiction under which a foreign LLP is registered shall govern its organization, internal affairs, and the liability and authority of its partners. Many, but not all, of the statutes require a foreign LLP to register or obtain a certificate of authenticity. The RUPA requires a foreign LLP to qualify and file annual reports. RUPA Sections 1102 and 1003.

*Liability Limitation*   LLP statutes have taken three different approaches to limiting the liability of partners for the partnership's obligations. The earliest statutes

limited liability only for negligent acts; they retained unlimited liability for all other obligations. The next generation of statutes extended limited liability to any partnership tort or contract obligation that arose from negligence, malpractice, wrongful acts, or misconduct committed by any partner, employee, or agent of the partnership. Unlimited liability remained for ordinary contract obligations, such as those owed to suppliers, lenders, and landlords. Some of the more recent statutes have provided limited liability for all debts and obligations of the partnership, including Section 306(c) of the RUPA.

The statutes, however, generally provide that the limitation on liability will not affect the liability of (1) a partner who committed the wrongful act giving rise to the liability and (2) a partner who supervised the partner, employee, or agent of the partnership who committed the wrongful act. The statutes also provide that the limitations on liability will apply only to claims that arise while the partnership was a registered limited liability partnership. Accordingly, partners would have unlimited liability for obligations that either arose before registration or after registration lapses.

Although limited liability company statutes provide greater protection against liability than most LLP statutes, the LLP form has attracted some businesses, especially professional firms. One advantage of the LLP is that an existing general partnership may become an LLP without forming a new organization or negotiating a new operating agreement.

◆ *See Figure 33–4*

## Limited Liability Limited Partnerships

A **limited liability limited partnership** (LLLP) is a limited partnership in which the liability of the general partners has been limited to the same extent as in an LLP. A few States have statutes expressly providing for LLLPs. In other States, by operation of the provision in the RULPA that a general partner in a limited partnership assumes the liabilities of a general partner in a general partnership, the LLP statute may provide limited liability to general partners in a limited partnership that registers as an LLLP under the LLP statute. Where authorized, the general partners in an LLLP will obtain the same degree of liability limitation that general partners can achieve in LLPs. Where available, a limited partnership may register as an LLLP without having to form a new organization, as would be the case in converting to an LLC.

**FIGURE 33–4** Liability Limitations in LLPs

| LLP Statutes | Limited Liability | Unlimited Liability |
|---|---|---|
| **First Generation** | Negligent acts | All other obligations<br>Wrongful partner<br>Supervising partner |
| **Second Generation** | Tort and contract obligations arising from wrongful acts | All other obligations<br>Wrongful partner<br>Supervising partner |
| **Third Generation** | All obligations | Wrongful partner<br>Supervising partner |

# Chapter Summary

**Limited Partnerships**

**Definition of a Limited Partnership** a partnership formed by two or more persons under the laws of a State and having one or more general partners and one or more limited partners

**Formation** a limited partnership can only be formed by substantial compliance with a State limited partnership statute

- *Filing of Certificate* two or more persons must file a signed certificate of limited partnership
- *Name* inclusion of a limited partner's surname in the partnership name in most instances will result in the loss of the limited partner's limited liability
- *Contributions* may be cash, property, services, or a promise to contribute cash, property, or services
- *Defective Formation* if no certificate is filed or if the one filed does not substantially meet the statutory requirements, the formation is defective and the limited liability of the limited partners is jeopardized
- *Foreign Limited Partnerships* a limited partnership is considered "foreign" in any State other than that in which it was formed

**Rights** a general partner in a limited partnership has all the rights and powers of a partner in a general partnership

- *Control* the general partners have almost exclusive control and management of the limited partnerships; a limited partner who participates in the control of the limited partnership may lose limited liability
- *Voting Rights* the partnership agreement may grant to all or a specified group of general or limited partners the right to vote on any matter
- *Choice of Associates* no person may be added as a general partner or a limited partner without the consent of all partners
- *Withdrawal* a general partner may withdraw from a limited partnership at any time by giving written notice to the other partners; a limited partner may withdraw as provided in the limited partnership certificate
- *Assignment of Partnership Interest* unless otherwise provided in the partnership agreement, a partner may assign his partnership interest; an assignee may become a substituted limited partner if all other partners consent

- *Profit and Loss Sharing* profits and losses are allocated among the partners as provided in the partnership agreement; if the partnership agreement has no such provision, then profits and losses are allocated on the basis of the contributions each partner actually made
- *Distributions* the partners share distributions of cash or other assets of a limited partnership as provided in the partnership agreement
- *Loans* both general and limited partners may be secured or unsecured creditors of the partnership
- *Information* each partner has the right to inspect and copy the partnership records
- *Derivative Actions* a limited partner may sue on behalf of a limited partnership if the general partners refuse to bring the action

**Duties and Liabilities**

- *Duties* general partners owe a duty of care and loyalty (fiduciary duty) to the general partners, the limited partners, and the limited partnership; limited partners do not
- *Liabilities* the general partners have unlimited liability; the limited partners have limited liability (liability for partnership obligations only to the extent of the capital that they contributed or agreed to contribute)

**Dissolution**

- *Causes* the limited partners have neither the right nor the power to dissolve the partnership, except by decree of the court; the following events trigger a dissolution: (1) the expiration of the time period; (2) the withdrawal of a general partner, unless all partners agree to continue the business; or (3) a decree of judicial dissolution
- *Winding Up* unless otherwise provided in the partnership agreement, the general partners who have not wrongfully dissolved the partnership may wind up its affairs
- *Distribution of Assets* the priorities for distribution are as follows: (1) creditors, including partners who are creditors; (2) partners and ex-partners in satisfaction of liabilities for unpaid distributions; (3) partners for the return of contributions, except as otherwise agreed; and (4) partners for their partnership interests in the proportions in which they share in distributions, except as otherwise agreed

## Limited Liability Companies

**Definition** a limited liability company is a noncorporate business organization that provides limited liability to all of its owners (members) and permits all of its members to participate in management of the business

**Formation** the formation of a limited liability company requires substantial compliance with a State's limited liability company statute

- *Filing* the LLC statutes generally require the central filing of articles of organization in a designated State office
- *Name* LLC statutes generally require the name of the LLC to include the words *limited liability company* or the abbreviation *LLC*
- *Contribution* the contribution of a member to a limited liability company may be cash, property, services rendered, a promissory note, or other obligation to contribute cash, property, or to perform services
- *Operating Agreement* the basic contract governing the affairs of a limited liability company and stating the various rights and duties of the members
- *Foreign Limited Liability Companies* a limited liability company is considered "foreign" in any State other than that in which it was formed

**Rights of Members** a member's interest in the LLC includes the financial interest (the right to distributions) and the management interest (which consists of all other rights granted to a member by the LLC operating agreement and the LLC statute)

- *Profit and Loss Sharing* the LLC's operating agreement determines how the partners allocate the profits and losses; if the LLC's operating agreement makes no such provision, the profits and losses are typically allocated on the basis of the value of the members' contributions
- *Distributions* the members share distributions of cash or other assets of a limited liability company as provided in the operating agreement; if the LLC's operating agreement does not allocate distributions, they are typically made on the basis of the contributions each member made
- *Withdrawal* a member may withdraw and demand payment of her interest upon giving the notice specified in the statute or the LLC's operating agreement
- *Management* in the absence of a contrary agreement, each member has equal rights in the management of the LLC, but LLCs may be managed by one or more managers who may be members
- *Voting* LLC statutes often specify the voting rights of members, subject to a contrary provision in a LLC's operating agreement
- *Derivative Actions* a member has the right to bring an action on behalf of a limited liability company to recover a judgment in its favor if the managers or members with authority to bring the action have refused to do so
- *Assignment of LLC Interest* Unless otherwise provided in the LLC's operating agreement, a member may assign his financial interest in the LLC; an assignee of a financial interest in an LLC may acquire the other rights by being admitted as a member of the company by all the remaining members

**Duties**

- *Manager-managed LLCs* the managers of a manager-managed LLC have a duty of care and loyalty; usually, members of a manager-managed LLC have no duties to the LLC or its members by reason of being members
- *Member-managed LLCs* members of member-managed LLCs have the same duties of care and loyalty that managers have in manager-managed LLCs

**Liabilities** no member or manager of a limited liability company is obligated personally for any debt, obligation, or liability of the limited liability company solely by reason of being a member or acting as a manager of the limited liability company

**Dissolution** an LLC will automatically dissolve upon (1) the dissociation of a member, (2) the expiration of the LLC's agreed duration or the happening of any of the events specified in the articles, (3) the unanimous written consent of all the members, or (4) a decree of judicial dissolution

- *Dissociation* means that a member has ceased to be associated with the company through voluntary withdrawal, death, incompetence, expulsion, or bankruptcy
- *Distribution of Assets* the default rules for distributing the assets of a limited liability company are (1) to creditors, including members and managers who are creditors, except with respect to liabilities for distributions; (2) to members and former members in satisfaction of liabilities for unpaid distributions, except as otherwise agreed; (3) to members for the return of their contributions, except as otherwise agreed; and (4) to members for their limited liability company interests in the proportions in which members share in distributions, except as otherwise agreed

| **Other Types of Unincorporated Business Associations** | **Limited Liability Partnership** a general partnership that, by making the statutorily required filing, limits the liability of its partners for some or all of the partnership's obligations |
|---|---|
| | • *Formalities* most statutes require only a majority of the partners to authorize registration as an LLP; others require unanimous approval |
| | • *Designation* the name of the LLP must include the words *limited liability partnership* or *registered limited liability partnership* or the abbreviation *LLP* |
| | • *Liability Limitation* some statutes limit liability only for negligent acts; others limit liability to any partnership tort or contract obligation that arose from negligence, malpractice, wrongful acts, or misconduct committed by any partner, employee, or agent of the partnership; some provide limited liability for all debts and obligations of the partnership |
| | **Limited Liability Limited Partnership** a limited partnership in which the liability of the general partners has been limited to the same extent as in an LLP |

 **Cases**

### CASE 33–1
## Control
# *ALZADO v. BLINDER, ROBINSON & CO., INC.*
Supreme Court of Colorado, 1988
752 P.2d 544

KIRSHBAUM, J.

In the spring of 1979, Alzado, Alzado's former accountant, Tinter, and Alzado's former agent, Ronald Kauffman (Kauffman), formed Combat Promotions, Inc. to promote an eight-round exhibition boxing match in Denver, Colorado, between Alzado and Ali. Alzado, Tinter and Kauffman were the directors and sole shareholders of the corporation. Ali had agreed to engage in the match on the condition that prior to the event his attorneys would receive an irrevocable letter of credit guaranteeing payment of $250,000 to Ali.

Combat Promotions, Inc. initially encountered difficulties in obtaining the letter of credit. Ultimately, however, Meyer Blinder (Blinder), President of Blinder-Robinson, expressed an interest in the event. Blinder anticipated that his company's participation would result in a positive public relations image for its recently opened Denver office. Blinder-Robinson ultimately agreed to provide the $250,000 letter of credit.

Blinder-Robinson insisted on several conditions to protect its investment. It required the formation of a limited partnership with specific provisions governing repayment to Blinder-Robinson of any sums drawn against the letter of credit. It also required Alzado's personal secured guarantee to reimburse Blinder-Robinson for any losses it might suffer. Alzado and Combat Promotions, Inc. accepted these conditions.

On June 25, 1979, an agreement was executed by Combat Promotions, Inc. and Blinder-Robinson creating a limited partnership, Combat Associates. Under the terms of the agreement, Combat Promotions, Inc. was the general partner and Blinder-Robinson was the sole limited partner. Blinder-Robinson contributed a $250,000 letter of credit to Combat Associates, and the partnership agreement provided expressly that the letter of credit was to be paid off as a partnership expense.

On the same day, June 25, 1979, Alzado executed a separate guaranty agreement with Blinder-Robinson. This agreement provided that if Ali drew the letter of credit, Alzado personally would reimburse Blinder-Robinson for any amount Blinder-Robinson was unable to recover from Combat Associates under the terms of the limited partnership agreement. As security for his agreement, Alzado placed a general warranty deed to his residence, an assignment of an investment account and a confession of judgment in escrow for the benefit of Blinder-Robinson. Thereafter, a separate agreement was apparently executed by Alzado and Combat Associates providing that Alzado would receive $100,000 in compensation for the exhibition match but subordinating any payment of that sum to the payment of expenses of the match, including, if drawn, the letter of credit.

Approximately one week before the date of the match, Alzado announced that he might not participate because he feared he might lose the assets he had pledged as security for the guaranty agreement. Alzado informed Blinder of this concern, and the two met the next day in Blinder-Robinson's Denver office. Tinter, Kauffman and Ali's representative, Greg Campbell, were also present. Subsequently, on July 14, 1979, the event occurred as scheduled.

Few tickets were sold, and the match proved to be a financial debacle. Ali drew the letter of credit and collected the $250,000 to which he was entitled. Combat Associates paid Blinder-Robinson only $65,000; it did not pay anything to Alzado or, apparently, to other creditors.

In January of 1980, Blinder-Robinson filed this civil action seeking $185,000 in damages plus costs and attorney fees from Alzado pursuant to the terms of the June 25, 1979, guaranty agreement. Alzado denied any liability to Blinder-Robinson and * * * also filed two counterclaims against Blinder-Robinson. The first alleged that because of its conduct Blinder-Robinson must be deemed a general partner of Combat Associates and, therefore, liable to Alzado under the agreement between Alzado and the partnership for Alzado's participation in the match. * * * [The jury returned a verdict of $92,500 in favor of Alzado on this counterclaim. The court of appeals reversed.]

* * *

Alzado next contends that the Court of Appeals erred in concluding that Blinder-Robinson's conduct in promoting the match did not constitute sufficient control of Combat Associates to justify the conclusion that the company must be deemed a general rather than a limited partner. We disagree.

A limited partner may become liable to partnership creditors as a general partner if the limited partner assumes control of partnership business. [Citations]; *see also* [RULPA] § 303, which provides that a limited partner does not participate in the control of partnership business solely by doing one or more of the following:

(a) Being a contractor for or an agent or employee of the limited partnership or of a general partner;
(b) Being an officer, director, or shareholder of a corporate general partner;
(c) Consulting with and advising a general partner with respect to the business of the limited partnership;
(d) Acting as surety for the limited partnership or guaranteeing or assuming one or more specific obligations of the

limited partnership or providing collateral for an obligation of the limited partnership;
(e) Bringing an action in the right of a limited partnership to recover a judgment in its favor pursuant to part 10 of this article;
(f) Calling, requesting, or participating in a meeting of the partners;
(g) Proposing or approving or disapproving, by voting or otherwise, one or more of the following matters:
   (I)     The dissolution and winding up or continuation of the limited partnership;
   (II)    The sale, exchange, lease, mortgage, pledge, or other transfer of any assets of the limited partnership;
   (III)   The incurrence of indebtedness by the limited partnership;
   (IV)    A change in the nature of the business;
   (V)     The admission or removal of a partner;
   (VI)    A transaction or other matter involving an actual or potential conflict of interest;
   (VII)   An amendment to the partnership agreement or certificate of limited partnership; or
   (VIII)  Such other matters as are stated in writing in the partnership agreement;
(h) Winding up the limited partnership; or
(i) Exercising any right or power permitted to limited partners under this article and not specifically enumerated in this subsection (2).

Early determinations regarding whether a limited partner's conduct constituted control of partnership business were largely fact-specific and did not attempt to state general standards for determining what acts evidence such control. [Citation.] More recent decisions construing section 7 of the Uniform Limited Partnership Act [predecessor to Section 303 of the RULPA] have also failed to provide definitive interpretations of what constitutes "control." [Citation.] One commentator has attributed this lack of definitive interpretation to the limited amount of litigation in this area and the tendency of courts to deal with section 7 control issues on an *ad hoc* basis. [Citation.] Any determination of whether a limited partner's conduct amounts to control over the business affairs of the partnership must be determined by consideration of several factors, including the purpose of the partnership, the administrative activities undertaken, the manner in which the entity actually functioned, and the nature and frequency of the limited partner's purported activities.

A judgment notwithstanding the verdict may be entered only if, when viewing the evidence in the light most favorable to the party against whom the motion is directed, reasonable persons could not reach the same conclusion as the jury. [Citations.] The record here reflects that Blinder-Robinson used its Denver office as a ticket outlet, gave two parties to promote the exhibition match and provided a meeting room for many of Combat Associates' meetings. Blinder personally appeared on a television talk show and gave television interviews to promote the match. Blinder-Robinson made no investment, accounting or other financial decisions for the partnership; all such fiscal decisions were made by officers or employees of Combat Promotions, Inc., the general partner. The evidence established at most that Blinder-Robinson engaged in a few promotional activities. It does not establish that it took part in the management or control of the business affairs of the partnership. Accordingly, we agree with the Court of Appeals that the trial court erred in denying Blinder-Robinson's motion for judgment notwithstanding the verdict with respect to Alzado's first counterclaim.

Alzado contends, in the alternative, that the actual management of the partnership's daily business activities is irrelevant to Blinder-Robinson's status for purposes of liability because Blinder-Robinson's power and authority over the partnership assets rendered it liable as a general partner. He finds this alleged unlimited authority in the expense distribution formula contained in section 4.4 of the limited partnership agreement. Alzado cites no authority, and we are aware of none, in support of the theory that provisions of a limited partnership agreement structuring expenses and establishing net profit and loss distribution formulae may themselves render a limited partner liable as a general partner for partnership debts. In theory it may be true that particular provisions of a limited partnership agreement might so circumscribe the general partners' ability to make management decisions as to constitute conclusive evidence of control by the challenged limited partner. We do not view the terms of the Combat Associates limited partnership agreement as constituting such conclusive evidence.

Alzado finally asserts that Blinder-Robinson fostered the appearance of being in control of Combat Associates, that such actions rendered Blinder-Robinson liable as a general partner and that this conduct allowed third parties to believe that Blinder-Robinson was in fact a general partner. The evidence does not support this argument. Certainly, as Vice President of Combat Promotions, Inc., the general partner of Combat Associates, Alzado had no misconception concerning the function and role of Blinder-Robinson as a limited partner only. The Court of Appeals concluded that the evidence failed to establish that Blinder-Robinson exercised control over the business affairs of Combat Associates. We agree with that conclusion.

\* \* \*

We . . . affirm the judgment of the Court of Appeals insofar as it reverses the judgments entered at trial in favor of Alzado on his first counterclaim against Blinder-Robinson.

---

## CASE 33–2
## Duties of General Partner
### *WYLER v. FEUER*
California Court of Appeal, Second District, Division 2, 1978
85 Cal.App.3d 392, 149 Cal.Rptr. 626

FLEMING, J.
Defendants Cy Feuer and Ernest Martin, associated as Feuer and Martin Productions, Inc. (FMPI), have been successful producers of Broadway musical comedies since 1948. Their first motion picture, "Cabaret," produced by Feuer in conjunction with Allied Artists and American Broadcasting Company, received eight Academy Awards in 1973. Plaintiff Wyler is president and largest shareholder of Tool Research and Engineering Corporation, a New York Stock Exchange Company based in Beverly Hills. Prior to 1972 Wyler had had no experience in the entertainment industry.

[In 1972, FMPI bought the motion picture and television rights to Simone Berteaut's best-selling books about her life with her half-sister Edith Piaf. To finance a movie based on this novel, FMPI sought a substantial private investment from Wyler. In July 1973, Wyler signed a final limited partnership agreement with FMPI. The agreement stated that Wyler would provide, interest free, 100 percent financing for the proposed $1.6 million project, in return for a certain portion of the profits, not to exceed 50 percent. In addition, FMPI would obtain $850,000 in production financing by September 30, 1973. The contract specifically provided that FMPI's failure to raise this amount by September 30, 1973, "shall not be deemed a breach of this agreement" and that Wyler's sole remedy would be a reduction in the producer's fee.]

Despite their acclaimed success in "Cabaret," defendants at the time of execution of the limited partnership agreement were experiencing difficulties in obtaining distributor commitments and knew it would be unlikely they could obtain any production financing by the September 30 deadline. Their difficulties arose from their overestimation of the attractiveness of the Piaf subject-matter, from the unknown leading actress, and from the scheduling of photography during the summer months when most Europeans go on vacation.

Filming of the motion picture began July 23 and ended October 9. By that time Wyler had advanced $1.25 million and defendants had failed to obtain any production financing. The completed cost of the picture was $1,512,000.

Early in October, Feuer met Wyler in Paris and requested an extension of the deadline for production financing to December 30, so that defendants could take advantage of distributor negotiations in process and recoup their profit percentage and their producer's fee. Wyler said he had already financed the picture and refused to extend the deadline, thereby maintaining his profit percentage at 50 percent.

[A year after its release in 1974, the motion picture proved less than an overwhelming success—costing $1.5 million but making only $478,000 in total receipts. From the receipts, Wyler received $313,500 for his investment. FMPI had failed to obtain an amount even close to the $850,000 required for production financing. Wyler then sued Feuer, Martin, and FMPI for mismanagement of the business of the limited partnership and to recover his $1.5 million as damages.]

A limited partnership affords a vehicle for capital investment whereby the limited partner restricts his liability to the amount of his investment in return for surrender of any right to manage and control the partnership business. [Citation.] In a limited partnership the general partner manages and controls the partnership business. [Citation.] In exercising his management functions the general partner comes under a fiduciary duty of good faith and fair dealing toward other members of the partnership. [Citations.]

These characteristics—limited investor liability, delegation of authority to management, and fiduciary duty owed by management to investors—are similar to those existing in corporate investment, where it has long been the rule that directors are not liable to stockholders for mistakes made in the exercise of honest business judgment [citations], or for losses incurred in the good faith performance of their duties when they have used such care as an ordinarily prudent person would use. [Citation.] By this standard a general partner may not be held liable for mistakes made or losses incurred in the good faith exercise of reasonable business judgment.

According all due inferences to plaintiff's evidence, as we do on review of a nonsuit, we agree with the trial court that plaintiff did not produce sufficient evidence to hold defendants liable for bad business management. Plaintiff's evidence showed that the Piaf picture did not make money, was not sought after by distributors, and did not live up to its producers' expectations. The same could be said of the majority of motion pictures made since the invention of cinematography. No evidence showed that defendants' decisions and efforts failed to conform to the general duty of care demanded of an ordinarily prudent person in like position under similar circumstances. The good faith business judgment and management of a general partner need only satisfy the standard of care demanded of an ordinarily prudent person, and will not be scrutinized by the courts with the cold clarity of hindsight.

[Judgment for Feuer, Martin, and FMPI affirmed.]

---

## CASE 33–3
## Limited Liability Company
### *IN THE MATTER OF DAUGHERTY CONSTRUCTION, INC.*

United States Bankruptcy Court, 1995
188 B.R. 607

MINAHAN, JR., J.
In this Chapter 11 case, the court must determine the validity of Nebraska statutory provisions dissolving a limited liability company upon the filing of a bankruptcy petition by one of its members. No cases are reported dealing with such a provision in a limited liability act in

any jurisdiction; it is a matter of first impression nationally. I conclude that Nebraska law is not enforceable in a Chapter 11 bankruptcy case to terminate the limited liability company and the debtor's membership therein. In addition, the debtor asserts that the automatic stay of section 362 was violated by actions taken by other members of the limited liability companies following the bankruptcy filing. I conclude that both sections 362 and 365(e) were violated and order that each of the limited liability companies be restored to the status existing at the time this bankruptcy case was commenced.

**Findings of Fact** The Chapter 11 debtor, Daugherty Construction, Inc. ("Debtor" or "DCI"), is a member of a number of Nebraska limited liability companies ("LLCs"), including Folsom Ridge Apartments, L.L.C., and Lakeview Park Apartments, L.L.C., which were formed to develop two apartment complexes in Lincoln, Nebraska. Debtor's membership capital contribution to each LLC was to provide general contractor services for construction of the apartment buildings. Lakeview Park Apartments, L.L.C., and Folsom Ridge Apartments, L.L.C., are LLCs organized pursuant to Nebraska's Limited Liability Companies Act. [Citation.] Section 21–2621 of the Nebraska statute is incorporated into the Articles of Organization and Operating Agreements of the two LLCs, and states that the bankruptcy of a member constitutes an act of dissolution, unless two-thirds of the remaining members vote to continue the LLC.

The non-debtor members of Lakeview Park Apartments, L.L.C., and Folsom Ridge Apartments, L.L.C., treated DCI's bankruptcy filing as an event of dissolution and voted to continue the respective LLCs and terminate debtor as general contractor on the respective LLC construction projects. In addition, the non-debtor members voted to remove Rick Daugherty (the President and sole shareholder of DCI) as general manager of each LLC. Highland Development Corporation, the only member of Folsom Ridge Apartments, L.L.C., other than DCI, added State Realty Company as a member of that LLC before voting to continue the business of Folsom Ridge Apartments, L.L.C., in order to comply with the Nebraska statute.

**Law** Section 21–2622 of Nebraska's Limited Liability Companies Act, which is incorporated into the Articles of Organization of Lakeview Part Apartments, L.L.C., and Folsom Ridge Apartments, L.L.C., states that an LLC shall be dissolved upon:

The death, retirement, resignation, expulsion, bankruptcy, or dissolution of a member or the occurrence of any other event which terminates the continued membership of a member in the limited liability company unless the business of the limited liability company is continued by the consent of the remaining members constituting at least a two-thirds majority in interest or such greater interest as otherwise provided in the articles of organization.

[Citation.]

Section 21–2605 provides, in part, that:

If the number of members of a limited liability company is reduced to less than two through the death, retirement, resignation, expulsion, bankruptcy, or dissolution of one or more members, the limited liability company may, through the remaining member, within ninety days of such event, admit one or more new members who shall have authority under section 21–2622 to consent to the continuation of the business of the limited liability company.

[Citation.]

Under section 21–2622, it is clear that an LLC dissolves upon the filing of a bankruptcy case by a member, unless the remaining members vote to continue the business. The reference to "remaining members" makes clear that the bankrupt member is not eligible to vote and infers that the bankrupt's membership is terminated. Section 21–2622 makes clear that the membership of the bankrupt member is terminated by stating that membership is reduced upon the bankruptcy. Section 21–2622 treats the bankruptcy of a member the same as the death or expulsion of a member.

The Nebraska Limited Liability Companies Act contains no other provisions addressing the issue of whether a member who has filed a Chapter 11 bankruptcy may continue to be a member of an LLC, when the LLC elects to continue business as allowed by statute. I conclude that, under the Nebraska Limited Liability Companies Act, bankruptcy of a member in an LLC causes the membership to terminate, and that if the remaining members vote to continue the business of the LLC, the bankruptcy debtor is not a member of the LLC.

\* \* \*

**Discussion** The Nebraska Limited Liability Companies Act was adopted in Nebraska in 1993, as a part of a growing national trend. Such a company is a hybrid business entity comprised of attributes from both the corporation and the partnership. The primary purpose is to provide the best aspects of both entities—the conduit taxation of a partnership in conjunction with the limited liability of a corporation.

To preserve conduit taxation attributes, limited liability acts contain provisions calculated to diminish the corporate attributes of an LLC enough for the LLC to qualify under Treasury Regulations for taxation as a partnership. One attribute of corporate existence sought to be avoided or diminished is continuity of LLC life.

With regard to continuity of life, one commentator noted:

> If the death, insanity, bankruptcy, retirement, resignation, or expulsion of any member will cause a dissolution of the organization, the entity does not possess continuity of life. (Citing Treasury Reg. § 301.7701–2(b) (1)). An agreement providing that the remaining members will continue the business in the event of the death or withdrawal of a member does not engender continuity of life if, under local law, the death or withdrawal of any member causes a dissolution of the organization.

[Citation.]

The provisions of Neb.Rev.Stat. § 21–2622 quoted above are referable to limiting continuity of life of an LLC upon occurrence of death, retirement, resignation, expulsion, bankruptcy or dissolution of a member.

Termination of an LLC upon bankruptcy of a member may also be in response to other concerns. Like a partnership, members of the LLC have voluntarily associated in a business enterprise and the relationship among members may be personal in character. Indeed, there are very strict limitations upon the transfer of a member's interest in the two LLCs involved in this case. These problems and concerns are addressed in LLC statutes by provisions that dissolve the LLC upon bankruptcy, and provide that if the non-bankrupt members of the LLC vote to continue the business of the LLC, the interest of the bankrupt member is terminated. However, Congress has also dealt with this problem in the context of bankruptcy cases, and has done so in a manner inconsistent with state law. Under the Supremacy Clause of the United States Constitution, federal law must prevail. The Nebraska Limited Liability Companies Act provisions dissolving a LLC upon a member filing a Chapter 11 bankruptcy case are not enforceable because they are in conflict with specific provisions of the Bankruptcy Code.

First, the debtor's interest in the LLCs constitutes property of the bankruptcy estate and state law purporting to terminate that interest is unenforceable under section 541(c). Second, under section 363, the debtor has the right to use, sell, or lease all property of the estate, including its membership interest in the LLC, notwithstanding state law to the contrary purporting to terminate the debtor's interest. See § 363(1). Third, the LLC Articles of Organization and the Operating Agreement among the LLC members (together the "LLC Articles and Agreements") constitute, on the facts of this case, executory contracts which the debtor may attempt to assume under section 365, notwithstanding provisions of the LLC Articles and Agreements which purport to terminate debtor's interest upon the commencement of a bankruptcy case.

* * *

Since DCI's membership interests in the LLCs constitute property of the bankruptcy estate and did not terminate upon the bankruptcy filing, and since the LLC Articles and Agreements constitute executory contracts, section 365(e)(1) applies to prevent termination or modification of the LLC Articles and Agreements at any time after the commencement of this case solely because of a provision in the LLC Articles and Agreements that is conditioned upon insolvency or the commencement of this bankruptcy case.

DCI has the right to attempt to assume the LLC Articles and Agreements and may do so upon fulfilling all the requirements of section 365(b). The requirement that the debtor in possession satisfy the requirements of section 365(b) fully assures that the legitimate expectation interest of the other members of the LLCs is fully protected and realized if the executory contracts are assumed. By separate order, I have established a deadline for the assumption or rejection of the debtor's interest in the LLCs.

* * *

My conclusions that an LLC and debtor's membership interest therein do not terminate upon commencement of a Chapter 11 case by a member and that the LLC Articles and Agreements constitute an executory contract are supported, in analogy, by bankruptcy court interpretations in the area of partnership law. Partnership agreements have been found to be assumable executory contracts in the case of a Chapter 11 debtor partner. [Citations.]

* * *

In summary, notwithstanding provisions of the Nebraska Limited Liability Companies Act to the contrary, the membership of DCI in Folsom Ridge Apartments, L.L.C., and Lakeview Park Apartments, L.L.C., did not terminate upon the commencement of this Chapter 11 bankruptcy case, the LLCs continued to exist and the LLC Articles and Agreements constitute an executory contract under section 365. Bankruptcy Code Sections 363(1), 365(e) and 541(c)(1) mandate this result and state law to the contrary is unenforceable under the Supremacy Clause. U.S. CONST. art. VI, cl. 2.

# Questions

1. Distinguish between a general partnership and a limited partnership.

2. Identify those activities in which a limited partner may engage without forfeiting limited liability.

3. Distinguish between a limited partnership and a limited liability company.

4. Distinguish between a member-managed limited liability company and a manager-managed limited liability company.

5. Distinguish between a limited liability partnership and a limited liability limited partnership.

# Problems

1. John Palmer and Henry Morrison formed the partnership of Palmer & Morrison for the management of the Huntington Hotel and filed an appropriate certificate in compliance with the limited partnership statute. The partnership agreement provided that Palmer would contribute $40,000 and be a general partner and that Morrison would contribute $30,000 and be a limited partner. Palmer was to manage the dining and cocktail rooms, and Morrison was to manage the rest of the hotel. Nanette, a popular French singer, who knew nothing of the partnership's affairs, appeared for four weeks in the Blue Room at the hotel and was not paid her fee of $8,000. Subsequently, Palmer and Morrison had a difference of opinion, and Palmer bought Morrison's interest in the partnership for $20,000. Palmer later went into bankruptcy. Nanette sued Morrison for $8,000. For how much, if anything, is Morrison liable?

2. A limited partnership was formed consisting of Webster as general partner and Stevens and Stewart as the limited partners. The limited partnership was organized in strict compliance with the limited partnership statute. Stevens was employed by the partnership as a purchasing agent. Stewart personally guaranteed a loan made to the partnership. Both Stevens and Stewart consulted with Webster with respect to partnership business, voted on a change in the nature of the partnership business, and disapproved an amendment to the partnership agreement proposed by Webster. The partnership experienced serious financial difficulties, and its creditors seek to hold Webster, Stevens, and Stewart personally liable for the debts of the partnership. Decision?

3. Fox, Dodge, and Gilbey agreed to become limited partners in Palatine Ventures, a limited partnership. The certificate of limited partnership stated that each would contribute $20,000. Fox's contribution consisted entirely of cash; Dodge contributed $12,000 in cash and gave the partnership her promissory note for $8,000; and Gilbey's contribution was his promise to perform 500 hours of legal services for the partnership. What liability, if any, do Fox, Dodge, and Gilbey have to the partnership by way of capital contribution?

4. Madison and Tilson agree to form a limited partnership with Madison as general partner and Tilson as the limited partner, each to contribute $12,500 as capital. No papers are ever filed, and after ten months the enterprise fails, its liabilities exceeding its assets by $30,000. Creditors of the partnership seek to hold Madison and Tilson personally liable for the $30,000. Decision?

5. Kraft is a limited partner of Johnson Enterprises, a limited partnership. As provided in the limited partnership agreement, Kraft decided to leave the partnership and demanded that her capital contribution of $20,000 be returned. At this time, the partnership assets were $150,000 and liabilities to all creditors totaled $140,000. The partnership returned to Kraft her capital contribution of $20,000. What liability, if any, does Kraft have to the creditors of Johnson Enterprises?

6. Gordon is the only limited partner in a limited partnership whose general partners are Daniels and McKenna. Gordon contributed $10,000 for his limited partnership interest and loaned the partnership $7,500. Daniels and McKenna each contributed $5,000 by way of capital. After a year, the partnership is dissolved, at which time it owes $12,500 to its only creditor, Dickel, and has assets of $30,000. How should these assets be distributed?

7. Discuss when a limited partner does or does not have the following rights or powers: (a) to assign his interest in the limited partnership, (b) to receive repayment of loans made to the partnership on a *pro rata* basis with general creditors, (c) to manage the affairs of the limited partnership, (d) to receive his share of the profits before the general partners receive their shares of the profits, and (e) to dissolve the partnership upon his withdrawing from the partnership.

8. In January, Dr. Vidricksen contributed $25,000 to become a limited partner in a Chevrolet car agency business with Thom, the general partner. Articles of limited partnership were drawn up, but no effort was made to comply with the State's statutory requirement of recording the certificate of limited partnership. In March, Vidricksen learned that because of the failure to file, he might not have formed a limited partnership.

At this time, the business developed financial difficulties and went into bankruptcy on September 11. Eight days later, Vidricksen filed a renunciation of the business's profits. The trustee in bankruptcy now seeks to have Dr. Vidricksen adjudged a general partner for bankruptcy purposes. Decision?

9.    Weil organized Diversified Properties as a limited partnership with varying degrees of ownership in several apartment complexes and other real estate located in Maryland. The parties signed a formal written agreement in July 1967, and the partnership was properly registered in the District of Columbia. Weil was the only general partner and managed the partnership's affairs until May 1, 1968. At that time, the partnership encountered cash flow problems, and to help matters, Weil gave up both his office and his salary. At a partnership meeting held the following week, the limited partners selected two third parties, Rubenstein and Tempchin, to manage the partnership properties on a commission basis in accordance with a proposal that Weil had advanced earlier. Weil began working for another real estate company as a vice president, but he remained a general partner of Diversified Properties. Creditors of the partnership, therefore, turned to him with demands for payment of the partnership debts that had not been met. Weil claims that after he surrendered his office and his salary, he remained as the general partner but that his directions were ignored. He also claims that the limited partners at various times gave direct orders to Rubenstein and Tempchin as to how to manage the partnership's affairs. Accordingly, he brings this action seeking to have the limited partners declared general partners. Decision?

10.    Dale Fullerton was chairman of the board of Envirosearch and the sole stockholder in Westover Hills Management. James Anderson was president of AGFC. Fullerton and Anderson agreed to form a limited partnership to purchase certain property from WYORCO, a joint venture of which Fullerton was a member. The parties intended to form a limited partnership with Westover Hills Management as the sole general partner and AGFC and Envirosearch as limited partners. The certificate filed with the Wyoming Secretary of State, however, listed all three companies as both general and limited partners of Westover Hills Ltd. Anderson and Fullerton later became aware of this error and filed an amended certificate of limited partnership, which correctly named Envirosearch and AGFC as limited partners only. When Westover Hills Ltd. became bankrupt, the court sought to determine whether the enterprise was a general or limited partnership for the purposes of determining eligibility of relief under the Bankruptcy Code. Decision?

WWW **Internet Exercise** Find and review information about (a) limited partnerships, (b) limited liability companies, and (c) limited liability partnerships.

## PART SEVEN

# Corporations

# CHAPTER 34

# Nature, Formation, and Powers

A corporation is an entity created by law whose existence is distinct from that of the individuals whose initiative, property, and control enable it to function. In the opinion of the Supreme Court in *Dartmouth College v. Woodward*, 17 U.S. (4 Wheat.) 518, 4 L.Ed. 629 (1819), Chief Justice Marshall stated,

A corporation is an artificial being, invisible, intangible, and existing only in contemplation of law. Being the mere creature of law, it possesses only those properties which the charter of its creation confers upon it, either expressly or as incidental to its very existence. These are such as are supposed best calculated to effect the object for which it was created. Among the most important are immortality, and, if the expression may be allowed, individuality; properties by which a perpetual succession of many persons are considered as the same, so that they may act as a single individual. A corporation manages its own affairs, and holds property without the hazardous and endless necessity of perpetual conveyances for the purpose of transmitting it from hand to hand.

The corporation is the dominant form of business organization in the United States, accounting for 90 percent of the gross revenues of all business entities. Around four million domestic corporations, with annual revenues and assets in the trillions of dollars, are currently doing business in the United States. More than 40 percent of American adults own stock directly or indirectly through institutional investors such as banks, insurance companies, pension funds, and investment companies. Corporations have achieved this dominance because their attributes of limited liability, free transferability of shares, and continuity have attracted great numbers of widespread investors. Moreover, the centralized management of corporations has facilitated the development of large organizations that employ great quantities of invested capital, thereby utilizing economies of scale.

Use of the corporation as an instrument of commercial enterprise has made possible the vast concentrations of wealth and capital that have largely transformed this country's economy from an agrarian to an industrial one. Due to its size, power, and impact, the business corporation is a key institution not only in the American economy but also in the world power structure.

In 1946, a committee of the American Bar Association, after careful study and research, submitted a draft of a Model Business Corporation Act (MBCA). The MBCA has been amended frequently since then. Although the provisions of the Act do not become law until enacted by a State, its influence has been widespread; and a majority of the States have adopted it in whole or in part.

In 1984, the Committee on Corporate Laws of the Section of Corporation, Banking, and Business Law of the American Bar Association approved a Revised Model Business Corporation Act (RMBCA). The Revised Act is the first complete revision of the Model Act in more than thirty years, although the Act had been amended frequently since it was first published. The Revised Act is "designed to be a convenient guide for revision of state business corporation statutes, reflecting current views as to the appropriate accommodation of the various commercial and social interests involved in modern business corporations." One of the tasks of the revision was to organize the provisions of the Model Act more logically and to revise the language to make the Act more consistent. In addition, substantive changes were made in a number of areas. Since 1984, several sections of the Revised Act have been amended. The Revised Act as amended will be used throughout the chapters on corporations in this text and will be referred to as the Revised Act or the RMBCA. Appendix D contains the RMBCA as amended.

## NATURE OF CORPORATIONS

To understand corporations, it is helpful to examine their common attributes and their various types. Both of these topics will be discussed in this section.

## CORPORATE ATTRIBUTES

The principal attributes of a corporation are as follows: (1) it is a legal entity; (2) it owes its existence to a State, which also regulates it; (3) it provides limited liability to its shareholders; (4) its shares of stock are freely transferable; (5) its existence may be perpetual; (6) its management is centralized; and it is considered, for some purposes, (7) a person and (8) a citizen.

◆ *See Figure 31–1*

## Legal Entity

A corporation is a legal entity separate from its shareholders, with rights and liabilities entirely distinct from theirs. It may sue or be sued by, as well as contract with, any other party, including any one of its shareholders. A transfer of stock in the corporation from one individual to another has no effect upon the legal existence of the corporation. Title to corporate property belongs not to the shareholders but to the corporation. Even where a single individual owns all of the stock of a corporation, the existence of the shareholder is distinct from that of the corporation.

## Creature of the State

A corporation may be formed only by substantial compliance with a State incorporation statute. Every State has a general incorporation statute authorizing the Secretary of State to issue a certificate of incorporation or charter upon compliance with its provisions.

A corporation's charter and the provisions of the statute under which it is formed constitute a contract between it and the State. Article I, Section 10, of the U.S. Constitution provides that no State shall pass any law "impairing the obligation of contracts," and this prohibition applies to contracts between a State and a corporation. See Chapter 4.

To avoid the impact of this provision, incorporation statutes reserve to the State the power to establish such regulations, provisions, and limitations as it deems advisable and to amend or repeal the statute at its pleasure. Section 1.02. This reservation is a material part of the contract between the State and a corporation formed under the statute; consequently, because the contract expressly permits them, amendments or modifications regulating or altering the structure of the corporation do not impair the obligation of contract.

## Limited Liability

A corporation is a legal entity and therefore is liable out of its own assets for its debts. Generally, the shareholders have **limited liability** for the corporation's debts—their liability does not extend beyond the amount of their investment—although, as discussed later in this chapter, under certain circumstances a shareholder may be personally liable.

## Free Transferability of Corporate Shares

In the absence of contractual restrictions, shares in a corporation may be freely transferred by way of sale, gift, or pledge. The ability to transfer shares is a valuable right and may enhance their market value. Transfers of shares of stock are governed by Article 8 of the Uniform Commercial Code, Investment Securities.

## Perpetual Existence

A corporation's existence is perpetual unless otherwise stated in its articles of incorporation. Section 3.02. Consequently, the death, withdrawal, or addition of a shareholder, director, or officer does not terminate the existence of a corporation.

## Centralized Management

The shareholders of a corporation elect a board of directors to manage the business of the corporation. The board in turn appoints officers to run the day-to-day operations of the business. As neither the directors nor the officers (collectively referred to as *management*) need be shareholders, it is entirely possible, and in large corporations quite typical, for ownership and management to be separate. The management structure of corporations is discussed in Chapter 36.

## As a Person

Whether a corporation is a "person" within the meaning of a constitution or statute is a matter of construction based upon the intent of the lawmakers in using the word. For example, a corporation is considered a person within the provision in the Fifth and Fourteenth Amendments to the U.S. Constitution that no "person" shall be "deprived of life, liberty, or property without due process of law"; and in the provision in the Fourteenth Amendment that no State shall "deny to any person within its jurisdiction the equal protection of the laws."

A corporation also enjoys the right of a person to be secure against unreasonable searches and seizures, as provided for in the Fourth Amendment. On the other hand, a corporation is not considered to be a person within the Fifth Amendment's clause that protects a "person" against self-incrimination.

## As a Citizen

A corporation is considered a citizen for some purposes but not for others. A corporation is not deemed to be a citizen as the term is used in the Fourteenth Amendment, which provides, "No State shall make or enforce any law which shall abridge the privileges or immunities of citizens of the United States."

A corporation is, however, regarded as a citizen of the State of its incorporation and of the State in which it has its principal office for the purpose of identifying diversity of citizenship between the parties to a lawsuit and thereby providing a basis for Federal court jurisdiction.

## CLASSIFICATION OF CORPORATIONS

Corporations may be classified as public or private, profit or nonprofit, domestic or foreign, publicly held or closely held, Subchapter S, and professional. As will be seen, these classifications are not mutually exclusive. For example, a corporation may be a closely held, professional, private, profit, domestic corporation.

## Public or Private

A **public corporation** is one that is created to administer a unit of local civil government, such as a county, city, town, village, school district or park district, or one created by the United States to conduct public business, such as the Tennessee Valley Authority or the Federal Deposit Insurance Corporation. A public corporation is usually created by specific legislation, which determines the corporation's purpose and powers. Many public corporations are also referred to as municipal corporations.

A **private corporation** is founded by and composed of private persons for private purposes and has no governmental duties. A private corporation may be for profit or nonprofit.

## Profit or Nonprofit

A **profit corporation** is one founded for the purpose of operating a business for profit from which payments are made to the corporation's shareholders in the form of dividends.

Although a **nonprofit** (or not-for-profit) **corporation** may make a profit, the profit may not be distributed to members, directors, or officers but must be used exclusively for the charitable, educational, or scientific purpose for which the corporation was organized. Examples of nonprofit corporations include private schools, library clubs, athletic clubs, fraternities, sororities, and hospitals. Most States have special incorporation statutes governing nonprofit corporations, most of which are patterned after the Model Nonprofit Corporation Act.

## Domestic or Foreign

A corporation is a **domestic corporation** in the State in which it is incorporated. It is a **foreign corporation** in every other State or jurisdiction. A corporation may not do business, except for acts in interstate commerce, in a State other than the State of its incorporation without the permission and authorization of the other State. Every State, however, provides for the issuance of certificates of authority that allow foreign corporations to do business within its borders and for the taxation of such foreign businesses. Obtaining a certificate (called "qualifying") usually involves filing certain information with the Secretary of State, paying prescribed fees, and designating a resident agent. Doing or transacting business within a particular State makes the corporation subject to local litigation, regulation, and taxation.

*Doing Business* The Revised Act does not attempt to fully define what constitutes the transaction of business. Instead, the Act provides a definition by exclusion by listing activities that do *not* constitute the transaction of business. Section 15.01. Generally, any conduct more regular, systematic, or extensive than that described in this section constitutes the transaction of business and requires a corporation to obtain a certificate of authority. Conduct typically requiring a certificate of authority includes maintaining an office to conduct local intrastate business, selling personal property not in interstate commerce, entering into contracts relating to local business or sales, and owning or using real estate for general corporate purposes. Section 15.01, Comment.

The Revised Act, as stated, provides a *nonexclusive* list of "safe harbors," that is activities in which a foreign corporation may engage without being considered to have transacted intrastate business. The list includes

1. maintaining bank accounts;

2. selling through independent contractors;

3. soliciting or obtaining orders, whether by mail or through employees or agents or otherwise, if such orders require acceptance outside the State before they become contracts;

4. owning, without more, real or personal property;

5. conducting an isolated transaction that is completed within thirty days and that is not one of a number of repeated transactions of like nature; and

6. transacting business in interstate commerce.

 *See Case 34–1*

***Scope of Regulation*** It is a common and accepted principle that local courts will not interfere with the internal affairs of a foreign corporation. To this end, the Revised Act states that "this Act does not authorize this state to regulate the organization or internal affairs of a foreign corporation." Section 15.05(c). Nevertheless, subjecting foreign corporations to reasonable regulation need not violate due process or constitute a burden on interstate commerce. A few States—most notably California and New York—regulate some of the internal affairs of foreign corporations that conduct a majority of their business in those States.

***Sanctions*** A foreign corporation that transacts business without having first qualified may be subject to a number of penalties. Most statutes provide that an unlicensed foreign corporation doing business in a State shall not be entitled to maintain a suit in the State's courts until such corporation obtains a certificate of authority to transact business in that State. Failure to obtain such a certificate does not, however, impair the validity of a contract entered into by the corporation or prevent such corporation from defending any action or proceeding brought against it in the State. Section 15.02. In addition, many States impose fines upon an unqualified corporation, while a few States also impose fines upon the corporation's officers and directors, as well as holding them personally liable on contracts made within the State.

## Publicly Held or Closely Held

A **publicly held corporation** is one whose shares are owned by a large number of people and are widely traded. There is no accepted minimum number of shareholders, but any corporation required to register under the Federal Securities and Exchange Act of 1934 is considered to be publicly held. In addition, corporations that have issued securities subject to a registered public distribution under the Federal Securities Act of 1933 are also usually considered publicly held. The Federal securities laws are discussed in Chapter 44.

A **corporation** is described as **closely held** when its outstanding shares of stock are held by a small number of persons who often are family, relatives, or friends. In most closely held corporations, the shareholders are active in the management and control of the business. Accordingly, they are concerned about the identities of their fellow shareholders, a concern that frequently leads shareholders to restrict the transfer of shares to prevent "outsiders" from obtaining stock in a closely held corporation. See the discussion of *Galler v. Galler* in Chapter 36. Although a vast majority of corporations in the United States are closely held, they account for only a small fraction of corporate revenues and assets.

In most States, closely held corporations are subject to the general incorporation statute that governs all corporations. The Revised Act includes a number of liberalizing provisions for closely held corporations. In addition, a number of States have enacted special legislation to accommodate the needs of such corporations, and a Statutory Close Corporation Supplement to the Model and Revised Acts (the Supplement) has been promulgated.

The Supplement applies only to those eligible corporations that elect statutory close corporation status. To be eligible, a corporation must have fewer than fifty shareholders. A corporation may voluntarily terminate statutory close corporation status. Other provisions of the Supplement will be discussed in this and other chapters.

## Subchapter S Corporation

Subchapter S of the Internal Revenue Code permits a corporation meeting specified requirements to elect to be taxed essentially as though it were a partnership. Under subchapter S, a corporation's income is taxed only once at the individual shareholder level.

## Professional Corporations

All of the States have professional association or corporation statutes that permit duly licensed individuals to practice their professions within the corporate form. Some statutes apply to all professions licensed to practice within the State, while others apply only to specified professions. There is a Model Professional Corporation Supplement to the MBCA.

# FORMATION OF A CORPORATION

The formation of a corporation under a general incorporation statute requires the action of various groups, individuals, and State officials. The procedure to organize a corporation begins with the promotion of the proposed corporation by its organizers, also known as promoters, who procure offers by interested persons, known as subscribers, to buy stock in the corporation, once created, and who prepare the necessary incorporation papers. The incorporators then execute the articles of incorporation and file them with the Secretary of State, who issues the charter or certificate of incorporation. Finally, an organizational meeting is held.

## *ORGANIZING THE CORPORATION*

### Promoters

A **promoter** is a person who brings about the "birth" of a corporation by arranging for capital and financing; assembling the necessary assets, equipment, licenses, personnel, leases, and services; and attending to the actual legal formation of the corporation. Upon incorporation, the promoter's organizational task is finished.

*Promoters' Contracts* In addition to procuring subscriptions and preparing the incorporation papers, promoters often enter into contracts in anticipation of the creation of the corporation. The contracts may be ordinary agreements necessary for the eventual operation of the business, such as leases, purchase orders, employment contracts, sales contracts, or franchises. If the promoter executes these contracts in her own name and there is no further action, the promoter is liable on such contracts; the corporation, when created, is not liable. Moreover, a preincorporation contract made by a promoter in the name of the corporation and on its behalf does not bind the corporation. The promoter, in executing such contracts, may do so in the corporate name even if incorporation has yet to occur. Before its formation, a corporation has no capacity to enter into contracts or to employ agents or representatives. After its formation, it is not liable at common law upon any prior contract, even one made in its name, unless it adopts the contract expressly, impliedly, or by knowingly accepting benefits under it.

A promoter who enters into a preincorporation contract in the name of the corporation usually remains liable on that contract even if the corporation adopts it. This liability results from the rule of agency law stating that to be able to ratify a contract, a principal must be in existence at the time the contract is made. A promoter will be relieved of liability, however, if the contract provides that adoption shall terminate the promoter's liability or if the promoter, the third party, and the corporation enter into a novation substituting the corporation for the promoter.

◆ *See Figure 34–1*

 *See Case 34–2*

*Promoters' Fiduciary Duty* The promoters of a corporation owe a fiduciary duty to one another as well as to the corporation, its subscribers, and its initial shareholders. This duty requires good faith, fair dealing, and full disclosure to an independent board of directors. If an independent board has not been elected, then full disclosure must be made to all shareholders. Accordingly, the promoters are under a duty to account for any *secret* profit they realize. Failure to disclose also may constitute a violation of Federal or State securities laws.

### Subscribers

A **preincorporation subscription** is an offer to purchase capital stock in a corporation yet to be formed. The offeror is called a "subscriber." Courts traditionally have viewed subscriptions in one of two ways. The majority regard a subscription as a continuing offer to purchase stock from a nonexisting entity, incapable of accepting the offer until it exists. Under this view, a subscription may be revoked at any time prior to its acceptance. In contrast, a minority of jurisdictions treat a subscription as a contract among the various subscribers, rendering the subscription irrevocable except with the subscribers' unanimous consent. Modern incorporation statutes, in turn, have adopted an intermediate position. The Revised Act provides that a preincorporation subscription is irrevocable for six months, unless the subscription agreement provides a different period or all of the subscribers consent to the revocation. Section 6.20. If the corporation accepts the subscription during the period of irrevocability, the subscription becomes a contract binding on both the subscriber and the corporation.

A **postincorporation subscription** is a subscription agreement entered into after incorporation. It is treated as a contract between the subscriber and the corporation. RMBCA Section 6.20(e). Unlike preincorporation subscriptions, the subscriber may withdraw her offer to enter

FIGURE 34–1   Promoters' Preincorporation Contracts

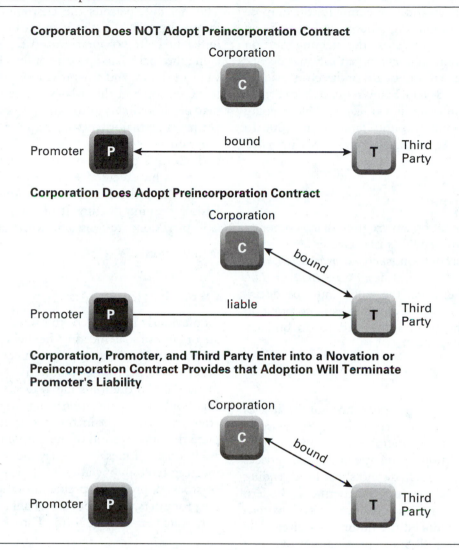

**Corporation Does NOT Adopt Preincorporation Contract**

**Corporation Does Adopt Preincorporation Contract**

**Corporation, Promoter, and Third Party Enter into a Novation or Preincorporation Contract Provides that Adoption Will Terminate Promoter's Liability**

into a post-incorporation subscription before the corporation accepts it. She cannot, however, withdraw the offer after the corporation has accepted it as the acceptance forms a contract.

## Selection of State for Incorporation

A corporation is usually incorporated in the State in which it intends to be located and to transact all or the principal part of its business. Nevertheless, a corporation may be formed in one State and have its principal place of business and conduct all or most of its operations in another State or States by duly qualifying and obtaining a certificate of authority to transact business in those States. The principal criteria in selecting a State for incorporation include the

flexibility accorded management, the rights granted to shareholders, the protection provided against takeovers, the limitations imposed upon the issuance of shares, the restrictions placed upon the payment of dividends, and organizational costs such as fees and taxes.

## FORMALITIES OF INCORPORATION

Although the procedure involved in organizing a corporation varies somewhat from State to State, typically the incorporators execute and deliver articles of incorporation to the Secretary of State or another designated official. The Revised Act provides that after incorporation, the board of directors named in the articles of incorporation shall hold an organizational meeting for the purpose of adopting bylaws, appointing officers, and carrying on any other business brought before the meeting. Section 2.05. After completion of these organizational details, the corporation's officers and board of directors manage its business and affairs. Several States require that a corporation have a minimum amount of capital before doing any business. Minimum amounts range from $300 to $1,000. The Revised Act and most States have eliminated this requirement.

## Selection of Name

Most general incorporation laws require that a corporate name contain a word or words that clearly identify the organization as a corporation, such as *corporation, company, incorporated, limited, Corp., Co., Inc.,* or *Ltd.* Section 4.01. Furthermore, the name must be distinguishable from the name of any domestic corporation or any foreign corporation authorized to do business within the State. Section 4.01.

## Incorporators

The **incorporators** are the persons who sign the articles of incorporation, which are filed with the Secretary of State of the State of incorporation. Although they perform a necessary function, in many States their services as incorporators are perfunctory and short-lived, ending with the organizational meeting. Furthermore, modern statutes have greatly relaxed the qualifications of incorporators and also have reduced the number required. The Revised Act and almost all States provide that only one person need act as the incorporator or incorporators, though more may do so. Section 2.01. The Revised Act and many States permit artificial entities to serve as incorporators. For example, the Revised Act defines a person to include individuals and entities, with an entity defined to include domestic and foreign corporations, not-for-profit corporations, profit and not-for-profit unincorporated associations, business trusts, estates, partnerships, and trusts. Section 1.40.

## Articles of Incorporation

The articles of incorporation, or **charter,** is generally a rather simple document that under the Revised Act must include the name of the corporation, the number of authorized shares, the street address of the registered office and the name of the registered agent, and the name and address of each incorporator. Section 2.02(a). The Act also permits the charter to include optional information such as the identities of the corporation's initial directors, corporate purposes, procedures for managing internal affairs, powers of the corporation, the par value of shares, and any provision required or permitted to be set forth in the bylaws. Some optional provisions may be elected *only* in the charter, including cumulative voting, supermajority voting requirements, and preemptive rights.

To form a corporation, the charter, once it is drawn up, must be executed and filed with the Secretary of State. The articles of incorporation then become the basic governing document of the corporation, so long as its provisions are consistent with State and Federal law.

◆ *See Figure 34–2*

## Organizational Meeting

As previously mentioned, the Revised Act requires that an organizational meeting be held to adopt the new corporation's bylaws, appoint officers, and carry on any other business brought before it. If the articles do not name the corporation's initial directors, the incorporators hold the organizational meeting to elect directors, after which either the incorporators or the directors complete the organization of the corporation. Section 2.05. Additional business that may be brought before the meeting typically includes authorization to issue shares of stock, approval of preincorporation contracts made by promoters, selection of a bank, and approval of a corporate seal and the form of stock certificates.

## Bylaws

The **bylaws** of a corporation are the rules and regulations that govern its internal management. Because bylaws are necessary to the organization of the corporation, their adoption is one of the first items of business at the organizational meeting held promptly after incorporation. Under the Revised Act, either the incorporators or the board of directors may adopt the bylaws. Section 2.06.

The bylaws may contain any provision for managing the business and regulating the affairs of the corporation that is not inconsistent with law or the articles of incorporation. Section 2.06. In contrast to the articles of incorporation, the bylaws do not have to be publicly filed. Under the Revised Act, the shareholders may amend or repeal the bylaws, as may the board of directors, unless

FIGURE 34-2  Sample Articles of Incorporation

**ARTICLES OF INCORPORATION OF [CORPORATE NAME]**

The undersigned, acting as incorporator(s) of a corporation under the _____ Business Corporation Act, adopt(s) the following Articles of Incorporation for such corporation:

*First:* The name of the corporation is _____

_____

*Second:* The period of its duration is _____

*Third:* The purpose or purposes for which the corporation is organized are _____

_____

*Fourth:* The aggregate number of shares which the corporation shall have authority to issue is _____

_____

*Fifth:* Provisions granting preemptive rights are _____

_____

*Sixth:* Provisions for the regulation of the internal affairs of the corporation are _____

*Seventh:* The address of the initial registered office of the corporation is, and the name of its initial registered agent at such address is _____

_____

*Eighth:* The number of directors constituting the initial board of directors of the corporation is _____, and the names and addresses of the persons who are to serve as directors until the first annual meeting of shareholders or until their successors are elected and shall qualify are

| **Name** | **Address** |
|---|---|
| _____ | _____ |
| _____ | _____ |
| _____ | _____ |

*Ninth:* The name and address of each incorporator is

| **Name** | **Address** |
|---|---|
| _____ | _____ |
| _____ | _____ |
| _____ | _____ |

Dated _____, 19____.

_____

_____

_____

Incorporator(s)

Source: Reprinted with permission from Henn & Alexander, *Corporations*, 3d ed. Copyright © 1983 by West Publishing Co.

the articles of incorporation or other sections of the RMBCA reserve that power exclusively to the shareholders in whole or in part. Section 10.20.

The Statutory Close Corporation Supplement (Section 22) permits close corporations bylaws to avoid the adoption of bylaws by including either in a shareholder agreement or in the articles of incorporation all information required in corporate bylaws. The comments to the Supplement explain this departure from tradition: "The highly structured formalities in typical bylaws, although necessary in larger corporations with numerous share-

holders, can be cumbersome when imposed on closely held corporations."

◆ *See Figure 34-3*

# RECOGNITION OR DISREGARD OF CORPORATENESS

Business associates choose to incorporate to obtain one or more corporate attributes—primarily limited liability

**FIGURE 34–3**   Comparison of Charter and Bylaws

| | Charter | Bylaws |
|---|---|---|
| **Filing** | Publicly | Not publicly |
| **Amendment** | Requires board and shareholder approval | Requires only board approval |
| **Availability** | Must include certain mandatory provisions; may include optional provisions although some optional provisions may be elected only in the charter | Must include certain provisions unless they are included in the charter |
| **Validity** | May include any provision not inconsistent with law | May include any provision not inconsistent with law and the charter |

and perpetual existence. Because a corporation is a creature of the State, such attributes are recognized when the enterprise complies with the State's requirements for incorporation. Although the formal procedures are relatively simple, errors or omissions sometimes occur. In some cases the mistakes may be trivial, such as incorrectly stating an incorporator's address; in other instances the error may be more significant, such as a complete failure to file the articles of incorporation. The consequences of procedural noncompliance depend upon the seriousness of the error. Conversely, even when a corporation has been formed in strict compliance with the incorporation statute, a court may disregard the corporateness of the enterprise if justice requires. This section addresses these two complementary issues.

## DEFECTIVE INCORPORATION

Although modern incorporation statutes have greatly simplified incorporation procedures, defective incorporations do occur. The possible consequences of a defective incorporation include the following: (1) the State brings an action against the association for involuntary dissolution, (2) the associates are held personally liable to a third party, (3) the association asserts that it is not liable on an obligation, or (4) a third party asserts that it is not liable to the association. Corporate statutes addressing this issue have taken an approach considerably different from that of the common law.

### Common Law Approach

Under the common law, a defectively formed corporation was, under certain circumstances, accorded corporate attributes. The courts developed a set of doctrines

granting corporateness to *de jure* (of right) corporations, *de facto* (of fact) corporations, and corporations by estoppel but denying corporateness to corporations that were too defectively formed.

***Corporation de Jure***   A corporation *de jure* is one that has been formed in substantial compliance with the incorporation statute and the required organizational procedure. Once such a corporation is formed, its existence may not be challenged by anyone, even by the State in a direct proceeding for this purpose.

***Corporation de Facto***   Though it fails to comply substantially with the incorporation statute (and therefore is not *de jure*), a corporation *de facto* nevertheless is recognized for most purposes as a corporation. A failure to form a *de jure* corporation may result in the formation of a *de facto* corporation if the following requirements are met: (1) the existence of a general corporation statute, (2) a *bona fide* attempt to comply with that law in organizing a corporation under the statute, and (3) the actual exercise of corporate power by conducting business in the belief that a corporation has been formed. If the corporation sues to collect a debt, the fact that the corporation is not *de jure* is not a defense. Furthermore, the existence of the *de facto* corporation can be challenged only by the State, though not even the State can question its existence collaterally (in a proceeding involving some other issue). The State must bring an independent suit against the corporation for this express purpose, known as an action of *quo warranto* ("by what right").

***Corporation by Estoppel***   The doctrine of corporation by estoppel is distinct from that of corporation *de facto*. Estoppel does not create a corporation. It operates only to prevent a person or persons under the facts and circumstances of a particular case from questioning a corporation's existence or its capacity to act or to own property. Corporation by estoppel requires a holding out by a purported corporation or its associates and reliance by a third party. In addition, application of the doctrine depends on equitable considerations. A person who has dealt with a defectively organized corporation may be precluded or estopped from denying its corporate existence where the necessary elements of holding out and reliance are present. The doctrine can be applied not only to third parties but also to the purported corporation and to the associates who held themselves out as a corporation.

**Defective Corporation** If the associates who purported to form a corporation so fail to comply with the requirements of the incorporation statute that neither a *de jure* nor a *de facto* corporation is formed and the circumstances do not justify applying the corporation by estoppel doctrine, the courts generally deny the associates the benefits of incorporation. This results in some or all of the associates being held unlimitedly liable for the obligations of the business.

## Statutory Approach

While the common law approach to defective incorporation is cumbersome both in theory and in application, the Revised Act provides simply that the *filing* of the articles of incorporation by the Secretary of State is conclusive proof that the incorporators have satisfied all conditions precedent to incorporation, except in a proceeding brought by the State. Section 2.03(b). This applies even if the articles of incorporation contain mistakes or omissions. The Revised Act imposes liability only on persons who purport to act as or on behalf of a corporation, knowing that there was no incorporation. Section 2.04.

The Model Act and many States provide that a "certificate of incorporation shall be conclusive evidence that all conditions precedent required to be performed by the incorporators have been complied with and that the corporation has been incorporated under this Act, except as against this State." Section 56. With respect to the attribute of limited liability, however, the Model Act provides that "[a]ll persons who assume to act as a corporation without authority so to do shall be jointly and severally liable for all debts and liabilities incurred or arising as a result thereof." Section 146.

Consider the following two illustrations: First, Smith had been shown executed articles of incorporation some months before he invested in the corporation and became an officer and director. He was also told by the corporation's attorney that the articles had been filed; however, because of confusion in the attorney's office, the filing had not in fact occurred. Under the Revised Act and many court decisions, Smith would not be held personally liable for the obligations of the defective corporation. Second, Jones represents that a corporation exists and enters into a contract in the corporate name when she knows that no corporation has been formed because no attempt has been made to file articles of incorporation. Jones would be held liable for the obligations of the defective corporation under the Model Act, the Revised Act, and most court decisions involving similar situations. RMBCA Section 2.04 and Comment.

♦ *See Figure 34–4*

⚖ *See Case 34–3*

## PIERCING THE CORPORATE VEIL

If substantial compliance with the incorporation statute results in a *de jure* or *de facto* corporation, the courts generally will recognize corporateness and its attendant

FIGURE 34–4   Recognition of Corporate Attributes: Statutory Approach

| | Nonrecognition of Corporateness | Recognition of Corporateness |
|---|---|---|
| **RMBCA Approach** | **No Filing of Articles of Incorporation**<br>No corporate attributes<br>Joint and several liability for those who act knowing that there was no incorporation | **Filing of Articles of Incorporation**<br>Corporate attributes<br>Limited liability<br>Insulation from collateral suits |
| **MBCA Approach** | **No Certificate Issued**<br>No corporate attributes<br>Joint and several liability for all who assume to act as a corporation | **Certificate Issued**<br>Corporate attributes<br>Limited liability<br>Insulation from collateral suits |

attributes, including limited liability. Nonetheless, the courts will disregard the corporate entity when it is used to defeat public convenience, commit a wrongdoing, protect fraud, or circumvent the law. Going behind the corporate entity to confront those seeking to insulate themselves from personal accountability and the consequences of their wrongdoing is known as piercing the corporate veil. Courts will pierce the corporate veil where they deem such action necessary to remedy wrongdoing. They have done so most frequently in regard to closely held corporations and parent-subsidiary relationships.

## Closely Held Corporations

The joint and active management by all the shareholders of closely held corporations frequently results in a tendency to forgo corporate formalities, such as holding meetings of the board and shareholders, while the small size of close corporations often renders creditors unable to fully satisfy their claims against the corporation. Such frustrated creditors often ask the court to disregard an organization's corporateness and to impose personal liability for the corporate obligations upon the shareholders. Courts have responded by piercing the corporate veil where the shareholders (1) have not conducted the business on a corporate basis, (2) have not provided an adequate financial basis for the business, or (3) have used the corporation to defraud. For example, in *D.I. Felsenthal Co. v. Northern Assurance Co.*, 284 Ill. 343, 120 N.E. 268 (1918), Felsenthal Company sued the Northern Assurance Company to collect on its fire insurance policy. Northern claimed that it was not liable under the policy because Felsenthal's property had been destroyed by a fire instigated by Fox, the president, director, creditor, and principal shareholder of Felsenthal. The court ruled in favor of Northern Assurance because the instigator of the fire, Fox, was the beneficial owner of almost all of Felsenthal's stock as well as the corporation's president and director. Under those circumstances, the corporation could not recover because to allow such a recovery would allow a wrongdoer to benefit from his own illegal act. The corporate form could not be used in this case to protect Fox and to aid him in his plan to defraud the insurance company.

Conducting the business on a corporate basis involves separately maintaining the corporation's funds and the shareholders' funds, maintaining separate financial records, holding regular directors' meetings, and generally observing corporate formalities. Adequate capitalization requires that the shareholders invest capital sufficient to meet the reasonably anticipated requirements of the enterprise.

The Statutory Close Corporation Supplement validates several arrangements whereby the shareholders may relax traditional corporate formalities. Section 25 of the Supplement provides: "The failure of a statutory close corporation to observe the usual corporate formalities or requirements relating to the exercise of its corporate powers or management of its business and affairs is not a ground for imposing personal liability on the shareholders for liabilities of the corporation." As the comments observe, the purpose of this section is to prevent a court from holding the shareholders in a statutory close corporation individually liable for the debts and torts of the business because the corporation does not follow the traditional corporate model. Courts may still pierce the corporate veil of a statutory close corporation if the same circumstances would justify imposing personal liability on the shareholders of a general business corporation. The Supplement simply prevents a court from piercing the corporate veil just because the corporation is a statutory close corporation.

 *See Case 34–4*

## Parent-Subsidiary Corporations

A corporation wishing to risk only a portion of its assets in a particular enterprise may choose to form a subsidiary corporation. A **subsidiary corporation** is one in which another corporation, the **parent corporation,** owns at least a majority of the shares and over which the other corporation therefore has control. Courts will pierce the corporate veil and hold the parent liable for the debts of its subsidiary if

1. both corporations are not adequately capitalized, *or*
2. the formalities of separate corporate procedures are not observed, *or*
3. each corporation is not held out to the public as a separate enterprise, *or*
4. the funds of the two corporations are commingled, *or*
5. the parent corporation completely dominates the subsidiary solely to advance its own interests.

So long as a parent and a subsidiary avoid these pitfalls, the courts generally will recognize the subsidiary as a separate entity, even if the parent owns all the subsidiary's stock and the two corporations share directors and officers.

# CORPORATE POWERS

Because a corporation derives its existence and all of its powers from its State of incorporation, it possesses only those powers that the State confers on it. These powers include those expressly set forth in the statute and articles of incorporation, as well as the powers reasonably implied from those documents.

## *SOURCES OF CORPORATE POWERS*

### Statutory Powers

Typical of the general powers granted by incorporation statutes are those provided by Section 3.02 of the Revised Act, which include the following:

1. to have perpetual succession;
2. to sue and be sued in the corporate name;
3. to have a corporate seal;
4. to make and amend bylaws for managing the business and regulating the affairs of the corporation;
5. to acquire, own, improve, use, and dispose of real or personal property;
6. to own, vote, and dispose of shares or other interests in, or obligations of, any other entity;
7. to make contracts and guarantees; incur liabilities; borrow money; issue notes, bonds, and other obligations; and secure any corporate obligations;
8. to lend money, invest and reinvest funds, and receive and hold real and personal property as security for repayment;
9. to be a promoter, partner, member, associate, or manager of any partnership, joint venture, trust, or other entity;
10. to conduct business, locate offices, and exercise the powers granted by the Act within or without the State of incorporation;
11. to elect directors and appoint officers, employees, and agents; define their duties; fix their compensation; and lend them money and credit;
12. to pay pensions and establish pension plans, pension trusts, profit sharing plans, share bonus plans, share option plans, and benefit or incentive plans for any or all current or former directors, officers, employees, and agents;
13. to make donations for the public welfare or for charitable, scientific, or educational purposes;
14. to transact any lawful business that will aid governmental policy; and
15. to make payments or donations or do any other act, not inconsistent with law, that furthers the business and affairs of the corporation.

The Revised Act also grants to all corporations the same powers as individuals have to do all things necessary or convenient to carry out their business and affairs. Section 3.02.

### Express Charter Powers

All State statutes provide that a corporation may be formed for any lawful purposes. Many State statutes, but not the RMBCA, require that the articles of incorporation specify the corporation's purposes. This serves (1) to advise the shareholders of the nature and kind of particular business activity in which their investment is being risked; (2) to advise the officers, directors, and management of the extent of the corporation's authority to act; and (3) to inform any person who may contemplate dealing with the corporation of the extent of its legally authorized power. The express powers must relate to a legitimate business activity or industry within the purview of the general statute.

### Implied Powers

A corporation may take any action necessary or convenient to and consistent with the execution of its express powers and the operation of the business that it was formed to conduct. This power exists by implication, depending not upon express language in the charter or statute but upon reasonable inference as to the proper scope and content of such language, given the facts and circumstances of the particular case.

## ULTRA VIRES *ACTS*

Because a corporation has authority to act only within its express and implied powers, any action or contract that is not within the scope and type of acts which the corporation is legally empowered to perform is *ultra vires*. The doctrine of *ultra vires* is less significant today because modern statutes permit incorporation for any lawful purpose, and most articles of incorporation do not limit corporate powers. Consequently, far fewer acts are *ultra vires*.

### Effect of *Ultra Vires* Acts

Traditionally, *ultra vires* contracts were unenforceable as null and void. Under the modern approach, courts allow the *ultra vires* defense where the contract is wholly executory on both sides. A corporation having received full performance from the other party to the contract is not permitted to escape liability by a plea of *ultra vires*. Conversely, the defense of *ultra vires* is unavailable to a corporation suing for breach of a contract which has been fully performed on its side.

Almost all statutes have abolished the defense of *ultra vires* in an action by or against a corporation. The Revised Act provides that "the validity of corporate action may not be challenged on the ground that the corporation lacks or lacked the power to act." Section 3.04. This section extends beyond contract actions to encompass any corporate action, including conveyances of property. Thus, under this section, persons dealing with a corporation need not examine its articles of incorporation for limitations upon its purposes or powers. The section does not, however, validate illegal corporate actions.

## Remedies for *Ultra Vires* Acts

Although *ultra vires* under modern statutes may no longer be used as a shield against liability, corporate activities that are *ultra vires* may be redressed in any of three ways, as provided by Section 3.04(b) of the Revised Act:

1. in a proceeding by a shareholder against the corporation to enjoin the Act, if such an injunction is equitable and if all affected persons are parties to the proceeding, and the court may award damages for loss suffered by the corporation or another party because of enjoining the unauthorized act;
2. in a proceeding by the corporation, or a shareholder derivatively, against the incumbent or former directors or officers for exceeding their authority; or

3. in a proceeding by the Attorney General of the State of incorporation to dissolve the corporation or to enjoin it from transacting unauthorized business.

## LIABILITY FOR TORTS AND CRIMES

A corporation is liable for the torts its agents commit in the course of their employment. The doctrine of *ultra vires*, even in those jurisdictions where it is permitted as a defense, does not apply to wrongdoing by the corporation. The doctrine of **respondeat superior** imposes full liability upon a corporation for the torts its agents and employees commit during the course of their employment. For example, Robert, a truck driver employed by the Webster Corporation, negligently runs over Pamela, a pedestrian, while on a business errand. Both Robert and the Webster Corporation are liable to Pamela in her action to recover damages for the injuries she sustained. A corporation also may be found liable for fraud, false imprisonment, malicious prosecution, libel, and other torts, though some States hold the corporation liable for *punitive* damages only if it authorized or ratified the agent's act.

Historically, corporations were not held criminally liable because, under the traditional view, a corporation could not possess the criminal intent requisite to committing a crime. Dramatic growth in the size and importance of corporations has changed this view. Under the modern approach, a corporation may be liable for violating statutes that impose liability without fault. In addition, a corporation may be liable for an offense perpetrated by a high corporate officer or by its board of directors. Punishment of a corporation for crimes is necessarily by fine, not imprisonment.

# Chapter Summary

## Nature of Corporations

**Corporate Attributes**     **Legal Entity** a corporation is an entity apart from its shareholders, with entirely distinct rights and liabilities

**Creature of the State** a corporation may be formed only by substantial compliance with a State incorporation statute

**Limited Liability**  a shareholder's liability is limited to the amount invested in the business enterprise

**Free Transferability of Corporate Shares**  unless otherwise specified in the charter

**Perpetual Existence**  unless the charter provides otherwise

**Centralized Management**  shareholders of a corporation elect the board of directors to manage its business affairs; the board appoints officers to run the day-to-day operations of the business

**As a Person**  a corporation is considered a person for some but not all purposes

**As a Citizen**  a corporation is considered a citizen for some but not all purposes

| | |
|---|---|
| **Classification of Corporations** | **Public or Private**<br>• *Public Corporation* one created to administer a unit of local civil government or one created by the United States to conduct public business<br>• *Private Corporation* one founded by and composed of private persons for private purposes; has no governmental duties<br>**Profit or Nonprofit**<br>• *Profit Corporation* one founded to operate a business for profit<br>• *Nonprofit Corporation* one whose profits must be used exclusively for charitable, educational, or scientific purposes<br>**Domestic or Foreign**<br>• *Domestic Corporation* one created under the laws of a given State<br>• *Foreign Corporation* one created under the laws of any other State or jurisdiction; it must obtain a certificate of authority from each State in which it does intrastate business<br>**Publicly Held or Closely Held**<br>• *Publicly Held Corporation* one whose shares are owned by a large number of people and are widely traded<br>• *Closely Held Corporation* one that is owned by few shareholders and whose shares are not actively traded<br>**Subchapter S Corporation** eligible corporation electing to be taxed as a partnership under the Internal Revenue Code<br>**Professional Corporations** corporate form under which duly licensed individuals may practice their professions |

# Formation of a Corporation

| | |
|---|---|
| **Organizing the Corporation** | **Promoter** person who takes the preliminary steps to organize a corporation<br>• *Promoters' Contracts* promoters remain liable on preincorporation contracts made in the name of the corporation unless the contract provides otherwise or unless a novation is effected<br>• *Promoters' Fiduciary Duty* promoters owe a fiduciary duty among themselves and to the corporation, its subscribers, and its initial shareholders<br>**Subscribers** persons who agree to purchase the initial stock in a corporation |

| | |
|---|---|
| **Formalities of Incorporation** | **Selection of Name** the name must clearly designate the entity as a corporation<br>**Incorporators** the persons who sign the articles of incorporation<br>**Articles of Incorporation** the charter or basic organizational document of a corporation |

**Organizational Meeting** the first meeting, held to adopt the bylaws and appoint officers
**Bylaws** rules governing a corporation's internal management

# Recognition or Disregard of Corporateness

## Defective Incorporation

**Common Law Approach**
- *Corporation de Jure* one formed in substantial compliance with the incorporation statute and having all corporate attributes
- *Corporation de Facto* one not formed in compliance with the statute but recognized for most purposes as a corporation
- *Corporation by Estoppel* prevents a person from raising the question of a corporation's existence
- *Defective Corporation* the associates are denied the benefits of incorporation

**Statutory Approach** the filing of the articles of incorporation is generally conclusive proof of proper incorporation
- *RMBCA* liability is imposed only on persons who act on behalf of a defectively formed corporation knowing that there was no incorporation
- *MBCA* unlimited personal liability is imposed on all persons who act on behalf of a defectively formed corporation

## Piercing the Corporate Veil

**General Rule** the courts will disregard the corporate entity when it is used to defeat public convenience, commit a wrongdoing, protect fraud, or circumvent the law
**Application** most frequently applied to
- *Closely Held Corporations*
- *Parent-Subsidiary Corporations*

# Corporate Powers

## Sources of Corporate Powers

**Statutory Powers** typically include perpetual existence, right to hold property in the corporate name, and all powers necessary or convenient to effect the corporation's purposes
**Express Charter Powers** those stated in the articles of incorporation
**Implied Powers** those necessary or convenient to and consistent with the express powers

## *Ultra Vires* Acts

**Definition of *Ultra Vires* Acts** any action or contract that goes beyond a corporation's express and implied powers
**Effect of *Ultra Vires* Acts** under RMBCA, *ultra vires* acts and conveyances are not invalid
**Remedies for *Ultra Vires* Acts** the RMBCA provides three possible remedies

## Liability for Torts and Crimes

**Torts** under the doctrine of *respondeat superior*, a corporation is liable for torts committed by its employees within the course of their employment
**Crimes** a corporation may be criminally liable for violations of statutes imposing liability without fault or for an offense perpetrated by a high corporate officer or its board of directors

# Cases

### CASE 34–1
### Foreign Corporation
## *TILLER CONSTRUCTION CORPORATION v. NADLER*
Court of Appeals of Maryland, 1994
334 Md. 1, 637 A.2d 1183

ORTH, JR., J.

In [a contract] action brought in the Circuit Court of Montgomery County, Tiller Construction Corporation sued Ronald Nadler, individually, and Glenmar Cinestate, Inc., a Maryland corporation. The case was called for trial on 20 April 1993. On the morning of trial Tiller filed an Amended Bill of Complaint. It alleged that Tiller was a New York corporation, registered and doing business in the State of New York. Ronald Nadler was a resident of the State of Maryland and the chief executive officer of Glenmar, as well as its principal, if not only, stockholder. To the best of Tiller's information and belief Glenmar leased certain space in the Westridge Square Shopping Center, located in Frederick, Maryland, and in Cranberry Mall, located in Westminster, Maryland. Tiller and Nadler entered into two contracts, one calling for Tiller to do "the work" for Nadler at Westridge for $637,000, and the other for Tiller to do "the work" for Nadler at Cranberry for $688,800. Ronald Nadler requested that Tiller send all bills to Glenmar, the lessee at both shopping malls. Ronald Nadler agreed to be personally liable to Tiller for the payment of both contracts. At the time of the suit, due to change orders and credits, there was a net balance due for the Cranberry project in the amount of $229,799.46, and on the Westridge project the sum of $264,273.85, which Nadler refused to pay, although it had approved all work, including change orders and their cost, and even though the work had been performed in a timely, good and workmanlike manner. The Amended Bill of Complaint contained two counts alleging breach of contract. Count I sought damages in the amount due under the Cranberry contract, and Count II sought damages in the amount due under the Westridge contract. Tiller demanded judgment against Ronald Nadler and Glenmar plus interest, costs, and attorney's fees.

Also on the morning of trial, Nadler handed to the court and to opposing counsel a Motion to Dismiss based on § 7–301. In his Motion Nadler asserted that Tiller was a New York Corporation "which has never qualified to transact business in the State of Maryland." * * *

Tiller's counsel conceded that the corporation had not qualified to do business in this State. His point, however, was that Tiller was not obliged to qualify because its activities did not mount up to doing business in Maryland in the contemplation of the statute. Tiller's counsel claimed that Tiller "just had occasional business" in Maryland. Nadler's counsel countered by asserting that there were two separate contracts to build movie theaters, each "in excess of one-half million dollars." The contracts involved the employment of a substantial number of subcontractors, most of whom were Maryland subcontractors, involved maintaining a supervisor on each job, as well as they opened Maryland bank accounts.

* * *

It was elicited from Mr. Tiller that on the Westridge and Cranberry projects Tiller and its superintendents "interacted not only with Mr. Nadler . . . but also interacted at times with the architect." The meetings were held on the job sites in Maryland. All but one of the dozen or so subcontractors on each job were from Maryland. Tiller opened a bank account in the Sovran Bank of Maryland and the Maryland subcontractors were paid by checks drawn on that account. Each project had a telephone for the duration of the jobs, listed with information in the name of Tiller Construction Corporation. Tiller billed the subcontractors for the work they did. The superintendent on the Cranberry project was an employee of Tiller and the superintendent on the Westridge job was an independent contractor hired by Tiller.

* * *

* * * Mr. Tiller testified that the supervisors on the construction jobs lived in a motel and their rooms were paid by Tiller as a business expense. Painters and clean-up men were brought in from New York and stayed in Maryland until the jobs were completed. Tiller did the "oversight. [It] saw how things got done." Liability insurance and workers' compensation insurance were obtained, covering each project in the name of Glenmar as

the insured. There was a sign at each project advertising Tiller as the contractor. A local construction permit was obtained. Subcontractors supplied all their own equipment from Maryland. Four or five months were spent on the projects.

As for Tiller's other business activities during the time it was engaged in construction work for Nadler, Mr. Tiller testified that the company was building a small hostel for the State of New York at a cost of $400,000 or $500,000 and a $300,000 project for AMC Theaters in Michigan. He added that Tiller might have been involved in a hospital project at that time, but he was not sure.

* * *

Nadler reiterated his contention that Tiller was required to qualify as a foreign corporation to do business in Maryland. Tiller had "pervasive activity in the State of Maryland," he argued. He said that he was relying on *Snavely, Inc. v. Wheeler*, 74 Md.App. 428, 538 A.2d 324 (1988) to support his Motion to Dismiss. Tiller countered that it was not engaged in so much business in Maryland as to bring it within the requirements of the foreign corporations statute. *Snavely*, it added, involved far more pervasive intrastate business than was represented by the Westridge and Cranberry construction projects.

In *Snavely, Inc. v. Wheeler*, the Court of Special Appeals * * * made a thorough analysis of the principles that have been applied to determine when a foreign corporation is doing intrastate business in Maryland. Judge Bell concluded:

The appellate decisions of this State make clear that "a foreign corporation is doing business within a state when it transacts some substantial part of its ordinary business therein." [Citations.]

Such a corporation is deemed "present" in the state when it does "a substantial amount of localized business in this State."

[Citation.] "Where," however,

the corporation does not engage in significant business activity in Maryland, § 7–301 has been interpreted to permit a corporation to maintain an action in the courts of this State even though it has neither registered nor qualified. [Citation.]

Judge Bell pointed out:

Mere solicitation, even if accompanied by activities directly related to the solicitation, including interstate delivery of the goods into the state, is not sufficient to constitute "doing

business"; however, solicitation, accompanied by the shipment of goods and an extensive set of activities or management functions in the state, is. [Citations.]

The resolution of "doing business" is on an ad hoc basis.

Whether the acts engaged in by the foreign corporation are sufficient to constitute "doing business" must be determined from the facts of each case, with particular emphasis on the nature and extent of the business and activities occurring in the forum state. [Citations.]

Among the factors to be considered are: (1) whether the foreign corporation pays state taxes; (2) whether it maintains property, an office, telephone listings, employees, agents, inventory, research and development facilities, advertising and bank accounts in the state; (3) whether it makes contracts in the state; and (4) whether its management functions in the state are pervasive. [Citation.]

* * *

The trial judge * * * said of § 7–301:

This is, to be sure, a real provision. . . . [F]oreign corporations who have failed to comply, regardless of the validity of their claim on the merits, have been denied access to our courts, period.

He explained.

It is not a matter of the court having special solicitude for people who are owed money. It is a question of whether our courts are, by legislative provision, open to parties to use our courts in the event they don't comply.

The judge recognized that the burden of proving that an unqualified foreign corporation is doing business in this State is upon the party presenting that defense, citing to [citation]. He observed that Maryland's foreign corporation is not unique to the State of Maryland. It is done all over the United States. Frankly, [Maryland's provisions] I think [are] based on the Model Business Corporation Act, . . . so there is nothing really unique about Maryland's statutes, either.

* * *

The trial judge looked at the facts in the light of the factors designated in *Snavely*, which may be considered in determining whether Tiller was doing business in Maryland, as he found those facts to be from the evidence before him. As to taxes:

To the extent that there were contracts made with local suppliers, that sales taxes were paid in this State.

[A]ll inventory was, in fact, local. According to Mr. Tiller, it was all bought locally and paid for locally, and the tax paid locally as well.

As to an office and telephones:

While there was no office maintained here, there was a motel room leased for a considerable period of time. There was presence of the corporation for up to five months. There was, while no, as I said, formal office, there was a sign on the job site and telephones listed in information.

As to management functions and bank accounts:

There was no substantial advertising in the State, although there was, in fact, a bank account that was maintained in the State. There were, in fact, fairly pervasive management functions in terms of these two projects. That, in fact, was what the general contractor was engaged to do.

As to the amount of Tiller's business which was conducted in Maryland:

The fact of the matter is that for the five-month period or so that Tiller Construction was on the job in Maryland, the value of the projects in question was far better than 50 percent of its income during that period of time based on the testimony given yesterday.

Mr. Tiller indicated that these two projects alone were in excess of $1 million. He mentioned a project in Detroit and another in New York State. Whatever it was, it was a substantial part, whatever the exact percentage, of the revenues of the corporation in that time frame.

The judge rejected Tiller's notion that "there must be a continuing course of conduct, and that coming in and even doing all these things is not sufficient to cause the corporation to be found to be doing business for purposes of having to qualify." The judge declared:

What we have here, essentially, is a builder coming in from a foreign jurisdiction to basically construct two projects of some substance over a five-month period, all aspects of the project. They contract for services, as defense counsel points out, to buy supplies here, to manage, to basically set up shop here, whether or not you have a desk and chair or office, but basically to do all the operations in this case.

* * *

Therefore, JUDGMENT OF THE CIRCUIT COURT FOR MONTGOMERY COUNTY AFFIRMED.

---

## CASE 34–2
## Promoters' Contracts
### COOPERS & LYBRAND v. FOX
Colorado Court of Appeals, Div. IV, 1988
758 P.2d 683

KELLY, C. J.

In an action based on breach of express and implied contracts, the plaintiff, Coopers & Lybrand (Coopers), appeals the judgment of the trial court in favor of the defendant, Garry J. Fox (Fox). Coopers contends that the trial court erred in ruling that Fox, a corporate promoter, could not be held liable on a pre-incorporation contract in the absence of an agreement that he would be so liable, and that Coopers had, and failed to sustain, the burden of proving any such agreement. We reverse.

On November 3, 1981, Fox met with a representative of Coopers, a national accounting firm, to request a tax opinion and other accounting services. Fox informed Coopers at this meeting that he was acting on behalf of a corporation he was in the process of forming, G. Fox and Partners, Inc. Coopers accepted the "engagement" with the knowledge that the corporation was not yet in existence.

G. Fox and Partners, Inc., was incorporated on December 4, 1981. Coopers completed its work by mid-December and billed "Mr. Garry R. (sic) Fox, Fox and Partners, Inc." in the amount of $10,827. When neither Fox nor G. Fox and Partners, Inc., paid the bill, Coopers sued Garry Fox, individually, for breach of express and implied contracts based on a theory of promoter liability.

Fox argued at trial that, although Coopers knew the corporation was not in existence when he engaged the firm's services, it either expressly or impliedly agreed to look solely to the corporation for payment. Coopers argued that its client was Garry Fox, not the corporation. The parties stipulated that Coopers had done the work, and Coopers presented uncontroverted testimony that the fee was fair and reasonable.

The trial court failed to make written findings of fact and conclusions of law. However, in its bench findings at the end of trial, the court found that there was no agreement, either express or implied, that would obligate

Fox, individually, to pay Coopers' fee, in effect, because Coopers had failed to prove the existence of any such agreement. The court entered judgment in favor of Fox.

As a preliminary matter, we reject Fox's argument that he was acting only as an agent for the future corporation. One cannot act as the agent of a nonexistent principal. [Citation.]

On the contrary, the uncontroverted facts place Fox squarely within the definition of a promoter. A promoter is one who, alone or with others, undertakes to form a corporation and to procure for it the rights, instrumentalities, and capital to enable it to conduct business. [Citations.]

When Fox first approached Coopers, he was in the process of forming G. Fox and Partners, Inc. He engaged Coopers' services for the future corporation's benefit. In addition, though not dispositive on the issue of his status as a promoter, Fox became the president, a director, and the principal shareholder of the corporation, which he funded, only nominally, with a $100 contribution. Under these circumstances, Fox cannot deny his role as a promoter.

Coopers asserts that the trial court erred in finding that Fox was under no obligation to pay Coopers' fee in the absence of an agreement that he would be personally liable. We agree.

As a general rule, promoters are personally liable for the contracts they make, though made on behalf of a corporation to be formed. [Citation.] The well-recognized exception to the general rule of promoter liability is that if the contracting party knows the corporation is not in existence but nevertheless agrees to look solely to the corporation and not to the promoter for payment, then the promoter incurs no personal liability. [Citations.] In the absence of an express agreement, the existence of an agreement to release the promoter from liability may be shown by circumstances making it reasonably certain that the parties intended to and did enter into the agreement. [Citations.]

Here, the trial court found there was no agreement, either express or implied, regarding Fox's liability. Thus, in the absence of an agreement releasing him from liability, Fox is liable.

Coopers also contends that the trial court erred in ruling, in effect, that Coopers had the burden of proving any agreement regarding Fox's personal liability for payment of the fee. We agree.

Release of the promoter depends on the intent of the parties. As the proponent of an alleged agreement to release the promoter from liability, the promoter has the burden of proving the release agreement. [Citations.]

Fox seeks to bring himself within the exception to the general rule of promoter liability. However, as the proponent of the exception, he must bear the burden of proving the existence of the alleged agreement releasing him from liability. The trial court found that there was no agreement regarding Fox's liability. Thus, Fox failed to sustain his burden of proof, and the trial court erred in granting judgment in his favor.

It is undisputed that the defendant, Garry J. Fox, engaged Coopers' services, that G. Fox and Partners, Inc., was not in existence at that time, that Coopers performed the work, and that the fee was reasonable. The only dispute, as the trial court found, is whether Garry Fox is liable for payment of the fee. We conclude that Fox is liable, as a matter of law, under the doctrine of promoter liability.

Accordingly, the judgment is reversed, and the cause is remanded with directions to enter judgment in favor of Coopers & Lybrand in the amount of $10,827, plus interest to be determined by the trial court pursuant to [citation].

---

## CASE 34–3
### Recognition of Corporateness
### HARRIS v. LOONEY
Court of Appeals of Arkansas, 1993
43 Ark.App. 127, 862 S.W.2d 282

PITTMAN, J.
On February 1, 1988, appellant, Robert L. Harris, sold his business and its assets to J & R Construction. The articles of incorporation for J & R Construction were signed by the incorporators on February 1, 1988, but were not filed with the Secretary of State's office until February 3, 1988. In 1991, J & R Construction defaulted on its contract and promissory note, and appellant sued the incorporators of J & R Construction, Joe Alexander and appellees, Avanell Looney and Rita Alexander, for

judgment jointly and severally on the corporation's debt of $49,696.21. In his amended complaint, appellant alleged that the incorporators were jointly and severally liable for the debt of J & R Construction because its articles of incorporation had not been filed with the Secretary of State's Office at the time Joe Alexander, on behalf of the corporation, entered into the contract with appellant. After a bench trial, the circuit court held that Joe Alexander was personally liable for the debts of J & R Construction because he was the contracting party who dealt on behalf of the corporation. The court refused, however, to hold appellees, Avanell Looney and Rita Alexander, liable, because neither of them had acted for or on behalf of the corporation pursuant to Ark. Code Ann. § 4–27–204.

On appeal, appellant contends that the trial court erred in not holding appellees jointly and severally liable, along with Joe Alexander. It was undisputed that the contract and promissory note were signed by Joe Alexander on behalf of J & R Construction and that J & R Construction had not yet been incorporated when the contract was executed. [Court's footnote: Arkansas Code Annotated § 4–27–203, which provides that, "[u]nless a delayed effective date is specified, the corporation's existence begins when the articles of incorporation are filed."] Appellant concludes that, because Arkansas law imposes joint and several liability on those purporting to act as or on behalf of a corporation knowing there is no incorporation, the trial court erred in not also awarding him judgment against appellees.

In support of his argument, appellant cites [citation], where the supreme court held that:

"[W]here an incorporator signs a contract or agreement in the name of the corporation before the corporation is actually formed and the other party to the agreement believes at the time of the signing that the corporation is already formed, then the incorporators are responsible as a partnership for the obligations contained in the contract or agreement, including damages resulting from any breach of the contract on their part. . . ."

[Citations.] These cases, however, were decided before the Arkansas General Assembly had specifically addressed the issue of liability of individuals for preincorporation debt.

In 1987, the Arkansas General Assembly passed Act 958 which adopted the Arkansas Business Corporation Act. Section 204 of this Act, Ark. Code Ann. § 4–27–204, concerns liability for pre-incorporation transactions and is identical to Section 2.04 of the Revised Model Business Corporation Act. It states: "All persons purporting to act as or on behalf of a corporation, knowing there was no incorporation under this Act, are jointly and severally liable for all liabilities created while so acting." The official comment to § 2.04 of the Revised Model Business Corporation Act explains:

Earlier versions of the Model Act, and the statutes of many states, have long provided that corporate existence begins only with the acceptance of articles of incorporation by the secretary of state. Many states also have statutes that provide expressly that those who prematurely act as or on behalf of a corporation are personally liable on all transactions entered into or liabilities incurred before incorporation. A review of recent case law indicates, however, that even in states with such statutes courts have continued to rely on common law concepts of *de facto* corporations, *de jure* corporations, and corporations by estoppel that provide uncertain protection against liability for preincorporation transactions. These cases caused a review of the underlying policies represented in earlier versions of the Model Act and the adoption of a slightly more flexible or relaxed standard.

Incorporation under modern statutes is so simple and inexpensive that a strong argument may be made that nothing short of filing articles of incorporation should create the privilege of limited liability. A number of situations have arisen, however, in which the protection of limited liability arguably should be recognized even though the simple incorporation process established by modern statutes has not been completed.

\* \* \*

\* \* \* [I]t seemed appropriate to impose liability only on persons who act as or on behalf of corporations "knowing" that no corporation exists. Analogous protection has long been accorded under the uniform limited partnership acts to limited partners who contribute capital to a partnership in the erroneous belief that a limited partnership certificate has been filed. UNIFORM LIMITED PARTNERSHIP ACT § 12 (1916); REVISED UNIFORM LIMITED PARTNERSHIP ACT § 3.04 (1976). Persons protected under § 3.04 of the latter are persons who "erroneously but in good faith" believe that a limited partnership certificate has been filed. The language of section 2.04 has essentially the same meaning.

While no special provision is made in section 2.04, the section does not foreclose the possibility that persons who urge defendants to execute contracts in the corporate name knowing that no steps to incorporate have been taken may be estopped to impose personal liability on individual defendants. This estoppel may be based on the inequity perceived when persons, unwilling or reluctant to enter into a commitment under their own name, are persuaded to use the name of a nonexistent corporation, and then are sought to be held personally liable under section 2.04 by the party advocating that form of execution. By contrast, persons who knowingly participate in a business under a corporate name are jointly and severally liable on "corporate" obligations under section 2.04 and may not argue that plaintiffs are "estopped" from holding them personally liable because all transactions were conducted on a corporate basis.

Model Business Corporation Act Ann. § 2.04 official cmt. at 130. 2–33 (3d ed. 1992).

In passing this Act, the Arkansas General Assembly adopted a heightened standard for imposing personal liability for transactions entered into before incorporation. The Act requires that, in order to find liability under § 4–27–204, there must be a finding that the persons sought to be charged acted as or on behalf of the corporation and knew there was no incorporation under the Act.

The evidence showed that the contract to purchase appellant's business and the promissory note were signed only by Joe Alexander on behalf of the corporation. The only evidence introduced to support appellant's allegation that appellees were acting on behalf of the corporation was Joe Alexander's and Avanell Looney's statements that they were present when the contract with

appellant was signed; however, these statements were disputed by appellant and his wife. Appellant testified that he, his wife, Kathryn Harris, and Joe Alexander were present when the documents were signed to purchase his business and he did not remember appellee Avanell Looney being present. Kathryn Harris testified that appellees were not present when the contract was signed.

The trial court denied appellant judgment against appellees because he found appellees had not acted for or on behalf of J & R Construction as required by § 4–27–204. The findings of fact of a trial judge sitting as the factfinder will not be disturbed on appeal unless the findings are clearly erroneous or clearly against the preponderance of the evidence, giving due regard to the opportunity of the trial court to assess the credibility of the witnesses. [Citation.] From our review of the records, we cannot say that the trial court's finding in this case is clearly against the preponderance of the evidence, and we find no error in the court's refusal to award appellant judgment against appellees.

Affirmed.

---

## CASE 34–4
### Disregard of Corporateness: Closely Held Corporation
### CRANE v. GREEN & FREEDMAN BAKING COMPANY, INC.
United States Court of Appeals, First Circuit, 1998
134 F.3d 17

CAMPBELL, J.
The terms of a collective bargaining agreement required Green & Freedman Baking Company, a Massachusetts corporation, to make periodic payments on behalf of its unionized drivers to the New England Teamsters and Baking Industry Health Benefits and Insurance Fund. After experiencing financial difficulties, Green & Freedman ceased to make the agreed-upon contributions and transferred all remaining assets to a successor entity named Boston Bakers, Inc. The Fund Manager of the Health Benefits and Insurance Fund (referred to hereinafter as the "Health Fund") thereupon sued Green & Freedman, Boston Bakers and the two corporations' principals, Richard Elman and Stanley Elman, in the district court to recover the payments owed by Green & Freedman with interest, costs and penalties.

Both corporate defendants conceded liability for the delinquent contributions owed by Green & Freedman to the Health Fund. The Elmans, however, denied they were personally liable for these corporate debts, and a jury trial took place to determine that issue. After the

presentation of evidence, and before submission to the jury, the district court entered judgment as a matter of law in favor of the Elmans, pursuant to Federal Rule of Civil Procedure 50(a). The Health Fund appeals. * * *

### I. Background

Defendant-Appellee Green & Freedman Baking Company ("Green & Freedman") was a family-owned Massachusetts corporation formed in 1934 that produced and sold baked goods until, on January 15, 1993, its remaining assets were transferred in bulk to Appellee Boston Bakers, Inc. ("Boston Bakers"). Boston Bakers operated essentially the same business as Green & Freedman until its demise in 1995.

Starting in 1975, responsibility for Green & Freedman's affairs rested with Defendants-Appellees Stanley Elman and Richard Elman, grandsons of one of the company founders. Stanley Elman started working for Green & Freedman in 1959 and by 1969 became its treasurer and a director, positions he occupied through the end of the corporation's and its successor's existence. Richard Elman began with Green & Freedman in 1964 and served as its President and a director from 1975.

Prior to transferring its assets to Boston Bakers as of January 15, 1993, Green & Freedman employed between 12 and 18 truck drivers who were members of the Bakery Drivers and Helpers Local 494. The union drivers' wages, hours, and conditions of employment were governed by a collective bargaining agreement between the Union and Green & Freedman, effective from May 5, 1991 to May 1, 1994. That agreement required Green & Freedman to contribute $88 per week for every covered worker to the New England Teamsters and Baking Industry Health Benefits and Insurance Fund. The Health Fund's contractual right to contribution was additionally protected by § 515 of the Employee Retirement Income Security Act ("ERISA"), [citation], which doubles the obligation of any employer who promises in a collective bargaining agreement to make contributions to a multiemployer benefits or pension plan.

From 1991, Green & Freedman began to suffer what the Elmans described as a serious, and ultimately irreversible, decline in sales and profits. Beginning in April 1992, and continuing until its business was terminated in January 15, 1993, Green & Freedman stopped making its required contributions to the Health Fund. Green & Freedman's unpaid contributions for this period, totaling $39,776, are the basis for the liability the Health Fund seeks to impose in this action.

By December 1992, the Elmans had decided to transfer all of Green & Freedman's assets to a newly-formed corporate shell entitled Boston Bakers, Inc., pursuant to the bulk transfer provisions of the Massachusetts Uniform Commercial Code. [Citation.]

Boston Bakers was simply a continuation of Green & Freedman's business. Its nominal and sole shareholder was Claire Lank, a long-time Green & Freedman employee installed by the Elmans. The Elmans were designated as the new corporation's officers and, along with their wives, as its directors. A voting trust with Lank enabled the Elmans to continue exercising complete control of Green & Freedman's assets, once transferred, in the form of Boston Bakers.

Boston Bakers thereafter carried on business in the same manner as Green & Freedman. Employing the same workers and equipment at the same plant, it produced the same kinds of baked goods for the same customers. Boston Bakers was as unprofitable as Green & Freedman. After two-and-a-half years of continued difficulties, U.S. Trust foreclosed, and Boston Bakers closed its doors in August 1995. According to Richard Elman's testimony, which was not contradicted, the Elmans personally received no distribution in settling the company's affairs.

Following the liquidation of Boston Bakers' assets, the Health Fund filed an amended complaint seeking recovery of the delinquent contributions from both corporations, and from Richard Elman and Stanley Elman as well. As Green & Freedman had done previously, Boston Bakers conceded liability for the contributions Green & Freedman failed to make to the Health Fund from April 1992 until the bulk transfer on January 15, 1993. With the assets of both Green & Freedman and Boston Bakers completely liquidated, the Health Fund looked to the Elmans personally for recovery of Green & Freedman's delinquent contributions. Count 3 of the Health Fund's Second Amended Complaint alleged that the Elmans were personally liable as the "'alter egos' of Green and Freedman." Count 4 premised the Elmans' personal liability on their disregard for Boston Bakers' corporate identity, alleging that the Elmans completely controlled Boston Bakers and created it with fraudulent intent. Both parties requested a trial by jury.

\* \* \*

At the close of the Health Fund's case-in-chief, the Elmans moved for judgment in their favor as a matter of law pursuant to Rule 50(a). \* \* \*

The Health Fund now appeals from the district court's grant of judgment as a matter of law.

## II. Standard of Review

\* \* \*

The legal standard for when it is proper to pierce the corporate veil is notably imprecise and fact-intensive. Leading commentators state that "no hard and fast rule as to the conditions under which the [corporate] entity may be disregarded can be stated as they vary according to the circumstances of each case," [citation], and, more skeptically, that "[t]here is a consensus that the whole area of limited liability, and conversely of piercing the corporate veil, is among the most confusing in corporate law," [citation].

Because a rigid test could not account for all the factual variety, the federal common law standard adopted in our Circuit for measuring an ERISA plaintiff's veil-piercing claim is somewhat open-ended. We said in *Alman* that courts should consider "the respect paid by the shareholders themselves to [the] separate corporate identity; the fraudulent intent of the [individual defendants]; and the degree of injustice that would be visited on the litigants by recognizing the corporate identity." *Alman*, [citation]. Of these three elements, "a finding of some fraudulent intent is a *sine qua non* to the remedy's availability." [Citation.]

\* \* \*

## III. Piercing the Corporate Veil: Green & Freedman

We hold that, on the record before the district court its decision to take from the jury the question of the Elmans' liability for Green & Freedman's delinquent contributions was erroneous and must be vacated. We find ample evidence to afford a reasonable jury, applying the *Alman* criteria, [citation], and exercising its broad authority over the veil-piercing issue, *supra*, a legally sufficient basis to reach beyond Green & Freedman's corporate identity and hold the Elmans liable for the corporation's unpaid contributions.

**A. Fraudulent Intent**   As previously noted, "the cases that permit veil piercing in the ERISA milieu all emphasize that a finding of some fraudulent intent is a *sine qua non* to the remedy's availability." [Citation.] We explained in that case that, in the ERISA veil-piercing sense, fraud need not reach the level needed for criminal or even independently actionable civil fraud. Still, it has to be more than "invisible." [Citation.]

There was evidence that the Elmans, through their domination of Green & Freedman, caused the corporation to make payments to themselves and their relatives at a time when the corporation was known to be failing and could be expected to default, or was already in default, on its obligations to the Health Fund. These payments could be found to lack any business justification. Courts have routinely viewed the wrongful diversion of corporate assets to or for controlling individuals at a time when the corporation is in financial distress as a fraud that can justify piercing the corporate veil. [Citations.]

The Health Fund introduced a series of checks that the Elmans made out to themselves from Green & Freedman's corporate accounts. These checks dated from January 1991 to January 1993, a period during which, according to Richard Elman, Green & Freedman "was in trouble," "los[ing] some money," and experiencing a "decline in profits and sales." In the last few months of this period, Green & Freedman ceased to be able to pay its debts including its required contributions to the Health Fund. It then transferred its assets to Boston Bakers.

Meanwhile, the Elmans had been writing themselves and their relatives checks for no business purpose that the Elmans could adequately explain. When questioned about one of these payments, Richard Elman testified that the corporation was repaying him an unrecorded loan—itself evidence weighing in favor of piercing the corporate veil, [citation] (piercing corporate veil on basis of repayment of shareholders' loan at time when corporation was failing)—before stating that he could not remember the purpose of the payment.

Particularly flagrant was the evidence of a personal vacation that the Elmans financed with corporate funds. In January 1991, the Elmans caused Green & Freedman to pay for them to travel to New Orleans, where they attended the Super Bowl. On direct examination, Stanley Elman testified that the checks in question represented "payment for expenses and conducting business." On cross-examination, however, Stanley Elman admitted that Green & Freedman had no customers in Louisiana and did no business in connection with the Super Bowl. Nothing in Stanley Elman's testimony rehabilitated his initial claim that he conducted business on the Super Bowl trip.

In addition, the Elmans caused Green & Freedman to pay Eleanor Elman, Stanley Elman's wife, three checks for a total of $4,500. Stanley Elman initially explained these payments as wages. However, the Elmans did not report this amount on their tax return and there was no evidence that Green & Freedman reported it as wages. Moreover, Green & Freedman's receptionist, Claire Lank, testified that Eleanor Elman did not work at Green & Freedman during 1992.

Finally, just days before Green & Freedman executed the bulk transfer to Boston Bakers, and at a time when the company had ceased to meet its obligations to the Health Fund, the Elmans caused the corporation to write an unexplained check for cash in the amount of $10,000, and a second check payable to Stanley Elman for $2,500.

The payments made by Green & Freedman to the Elmans and their relatives during 1991 and 1992 with no apparent business justification amounted to $30,109. In ruling on the Elmans' Rule 50(a) motion, the district court was required to draw all reasonable inferences and resolve credibility issues in favor of the non-movant Health Fund. Looked at in this light, the evidence was sufficient to support a jury determination that the Elmans had used corporate funds for personal purposes at times when they knew either that the company was inadequately capitalized to meet its obligations, or that, in fact, it had stopped doing so—and, in particular, had ceased to pay its Health Fund obligations. We add that the jury's ability to conclude that the Elmans had acted in a knowingly fraudulent manner would have been bolstered by inconsistencies in the Elmans' testimony about the payments, particularly their testimony that the Super Bowl trip and Eleanor Elman's "wages" had business purposes.

* * *

**B. Disregard of Corporate Identity** The fraudulent self-dealing just discussed was probative not only of fraudulent intent but also of another *Alman* element, disregard of corporate identity. On the latter score, there was additional evidence. For example, the Elmans appear to have mixed their own finances with those of Green & Freedman's. At a time that the Elmans owed the corporation $141,000 in loans, they also loaned it $170,000 through their real estate trust. These unexplained dealings suggest that money was being moved around with little or no regard for the corporate identity. There was no record of the terms of the purported loans nor of any agreement to repay. Undocumented and interest-free loans could be found to show a disregard for the corporate form. See, e.g., [citation] (treating unrecorded and interest-free loans from shareholders to the corporation as evidence of shareholders' disrespect for corporate form).

Beyond the undocumented loans, there was evidence of inadequate and, indeed, fraudulent record keeping. The Elmans admittedly falsified Green & Freedman's minutes to state that their wives, who served as nominal directors, attended and authorized corporate borrowing, when in fact their wives did neither.

We accept the Elmans' contention that a closely-held corporation need not hew to every corporate formality in order to maintain its shareholders' immunity from the corporation's debts. A veil-piercing plaintiff will not prevail if the evidence shows only that the closely-held defendant corporation was run without the strict formalities of its publicly-held counterpart. But the evidence adduced at trial, viewed most favorably to the Health Fund, could be found to show practices that went beyond mere informalities. Important transactions between the corporation and its controlling shareholders went undefined, and the Elmans appear to have created false minutes. These facts, when added to the financial self-dealing and when viewed in a light most favorable to the Health Fund, support a reasonable inference by a jury that the Elmans, in the two years before Green & Freedman's demise, did not treat Green & Freedman as a separate entity.

**C. Manifest Injustice** The evidence just described under the first two *Alman* factors could also allow a reasonable jury to conclude that sheltering the Elmans

from Green & Freedman's liability to the Health Fund would be manifestly unjust. As one commentator has explained, courts have found this prong met when "a corporation is so undercapitalized that it is unable to meet debts that may reasonably be expected to arise in the normal course of business." [Citation.] Thus, a jury would not be unreasonable in viewing as manifestly unjust the Elmans' decision to issue themselves payments for personal, non-corporate purposes, as well as other unexplained payments, at a time when the corporation could not meet its obligations to the Health Fund. Of course, the mere non-payment of debt is not, by itself, enough to justify piercing the corporate veil. However, a jury could reasonably conclude on the basis of the evidence below that the Elmans both placed their personal interests ahead of their corporation's responsibilities and did not themselves honor Green & Freedman's corporate form. As a result, it could be thought manifestly unjust to insist that the Health Fund be restricted by the corporate form.

## IV. Piercing the Corporate Veil: Boston Bakers

Whether the evidence sufficed for a jury to find the Elmans personally liable for Boston Bakers' successorship obligation to pay Green & Freedman's indebtedness for Health Fund contributions missed in April 1992, through January 1993, is more problematic. * * *

For the showing of fraud needed to pierce Boston Bakers' corporate veil, the Health Fund relies *inter alia* upon the Elmans' transfer of Green & Freedman's assets to Boston Bakers, a transaction said to be inherently fraudulent. Yet we can see nothing in the transfer itself that further disadvantaged the Health Fund in its ability to realize its claim for Green & Freedman's unpaid contributions.

* * *

Further undercutting the contention that the mere fact of the bulk transfer demonstrates the Elmans' fraudulent intent is the fact that they did not conceal the transfer. * * *

* * *

Besides the fact of the bulk transfer, the Health Fund points to other factors as a supposed basis for piercing Boston Bakers' veil. In its complaint it alleged that the nominal and sole shareholder, Claire Lank, was "unaware" of her obligations and rights as a shareholder and, instead of following her independent judgment, followed the Elmans' instructions. Also alleged was the Elmans' complete control over Boston Bakers, even though they owned no stock; the Elmans' disregard of corporate identity; and the incorporation of Boston Bakers with fraudulent intent. These allegations, however, to the extent legally material, must stand or fall on the existence in the record of some supporting evidence. Moreover, proof of corporate informalities, standing alone, are insufficient. Plaintiff may not prevail without some evidence of fraudulent intent material to the harm suffered.

There is no evidence of financial self-dealing in the case of Boston Bakers such as occurred with Green & Freedman. None of the checks introduced by the Health Fund as payable to or for the Elmans came from Boston Bakers' accounts.

* * *

Much is made of the fact that Richard Elman indicated ignorance as to how he was named president and director of Boston Bakers or whether Boston Bakers held an annual shareholders' meeting. Stanley Elman failed to recognize the firm's stock ledger. And Lank, the sole shareholder, appears to have been a straw for the Elmans, allegedly so as to make it harder for creditors to reach them personally. None of these items, however, singly or together, provide a sufficient evidentiary basis to pierce the corporate veil. While they may suggest a lack of attention to corporate formalities, they do not reflect fraudulent intent material to the harm alleged, nor is it clear how any of them, even slightly, disadvantaged the plaintiff.

There was also evidence that the Elmans' wives did not know they were directors; did not participate in board meetings, although corporate records falsely indicated they did; and did not know that Lank was the sole stockholder. But these snippets do little to demonstrate more than corporate informality. Even if the false corporate records concerning the wives' attendance at directors' meetings are characterized as a "fraud," there is no evidence the Health Fund knew or relied on this information to its detriment or sustained any injury whatever as a result. The "fraudulent intent of the individual defendants" mentioned in *Alman* requires some meaningful relationship between the intent and the harm visited upon plaintiff. We add that even the Health Fund itself does not argue that the incorrect records by themselves show fraudulent intent sufficient under *Alman*.

We conclude that the district court was correct in granting the Elmans' motion for judgment as a matter of law with respect to the Elmans' alleged personal liability for Boston Bakers' corporate obligation to make good Green & Freedman's delinquent payments to the Health Fund.

## V. Conclusion

The district court's grant of judgment as a matter of law is vacated with respect to Count 3 and affirmed with respect to Count 4. The case is remanded for a new trial and other proceedings consistent herewith.

---

# Questions

1. Identify the principal attributes and classifications of a corporation.
2. Discuss how a corporation is formed and the role, liability, and duties of promoters.
3. Distinguish between the statutory and common law approaches to defective formation of a corporation.

4. Explain how the doctrine of piercing the corporate veil applies to (a) closely held corporations and (b) parent-subsidiary corporations.
5. Identify the sources of corporate powers and explain the legal consequences of a corporation's exceeding its powers.

---

# Problems

1. After part of the shares of a proposed corporation had been successfully subscribed, one of the promoters hired a carpenter to repair a building that was to be conveyed to the proposed corporation. The promoters subsequently secured subscriptions to the balance of the shares and completed the organization, but the corporation, finding the building to be unsuitable for its purposes, declined to use the building or pay the carpenter. The carpenter brought suit against the corporation for the amount that the promoter agreed would be paid to him. Decision?

2. C.A. Nimocks was a promoter engaged in organizing the Times Printing Company. On September 12, on behalf of the proposed corporation, he made a contract with McArthur for her services as comptroller for a one-year period beginning

October 1. The Times Printing Company was incorporated October 16, and on that date McArthur commenced her duties as comptroller. Neither the board of directors nor any officer took formal action on her employment, but all the shareholders, directors, and officers knew of the contract made by Nimocks. On December 1, McArthur was discharged without cause. Has she a cause of action against the Times Printing Company?

3. Todd and Elaine obtained an option on a building that was used for manufacturing pianos. They acted as the promoters for a corporation and turned the building over to the new corporation for $500,000 worth of stock. In truth, their option on the building called for a purchase price of only $300,000. The other shareholders desire to have $200,000 of the common stock canceled. Can they succeed in this action?

4. Wayne signed a subscription agreement for ten shares of stock, having a value of $100 per share, of the proposed ABC Company. Two weeks later, the company was incorporated. A certificate was duly tendered to Wayne, but he refused to accept it. He was notified of all shareholders' meetings, but he never attended. A dividend check was sent to him, but he returned it. ABC Company brings a legal action against Wayne to recover $1,000. He defends upon the ground that his subscription agreement was an unaccepted offer and that he had done nothing to ratify it and was therefore not liable upon it. Decision?

5. Julian, Cornelia, and Sheila petitioned for a corporate charter for the purpose of conducting a retail shoe business. They met all of the statutory provisions, with the exception of having their charter recorded. This was simply an oversight on their part, and they felt that they had fully complied with the law. They operated the business for three years, after which time it became insolvent. The creditors desire to hold the members personally and individually liable. May they do so?

6. Arthur, Barbara, Carl, and Debra decided to form a corporation for bottling and selling apple cider. Arthur, Barbara, and Carl were to operate the business, and Debra was to supply the necessary capital but was to have no voice in the management. They went to Jane, a lawyer, who agreed to organize a corporation for them under the name A–B–C Inc., and paid her funds sufficient to accomplish the incorporation. Jane promised that the corporation would definitely be formed by May 3. On April 27, Arthur telephoned Jane to inquire how the incorporation was progressing, and Jane said she had drafted the articles of incorporation and would send them to the Secretary of State that very day. She assured Arthur that incorporation would occur before May 3.

Relying on Jane's assurance, Arthur, with the approval of Barbara and Carl, on May 4 entered into a written contract with Grower for the latter's entire apple crop. The contract was executed by Arthur on behalf of "A–B–C Inc." Grower delivered the apples as agreed. Unknown to Arthur, Barbara, Carl, Debra, or Grower, the articles of incorporation were never filed, through Jane's negligence. The business subsequently failed.

What are Grower's rights, if any, against Arthur, Barbara, Carl, and Debra as individuals?

7. The Pyro Corporation has outstanding 20,000 shares of common stock, of which 19,000 are owned by Peter B. Arson, 500 shares are owned by Elizabeth Arson, his wife, and 500 shares are owned by Joseph Q. Arson, his brother. These three individuals are the officers and directors of the corporation. The Pyro Corporation obtained a $250,000 fire insurance policy to cover a certain building it owned. Thereafter, Peter B. Arson set fire to the building, and it was totally destroyed. The corporation now brings an action against the fire insurance company to recover on the $250,000 fire insurance policy. What judgment?

8. A corporation formed for the purpose of manufacturing, buying, selling, and dealing in drugs, chemicals, and similar products contracted to purchase, under authority of its board of directors, the land and building it occupied as a factory and store. Collins, a shareholder, sues in equity to restrain the corporation from completing the contract, claiming that as the certificate of incorporation contained no provision authorizing the corporation to purchase real estate, the contract was *ultra vires*. Decision?

9. Amalgamated Corporation, organized under the laws of State S, sends traveling salespersons into State M to solicit orders, which are accepted only at the home office of Amalgamated Corporation in State S. Riley, a resident of State M, places an order which is accepted by Amalgamated Corporation in State S. The Corporation Act of State M provides that "no foreign corporation transacting business in this state without a certificate of authority shall be permitted to maintain an action in any court of this state until such corporation shall have obtained a certificate of authority." Riley fails to pay for the goods, and when Amalgamated Corporation sues Riley in a court of State M, Riley defends on the ground that Amalgamated Corporation does not possess a certificate of authority from State M. Result?

10. Dr. North, a surgeon practicing in Georgia, engaged an Arizona professional corporation consisting of twenty lawyers to represent him in a dispute with a Georgia hospital. West, a member of the law firm, flew to Atlanta and hired local counsel with Dr. North's approval. West represented Dr. North in two hearings before the hospital and in one court proceeding, as well as negotiating a compromise between Dr. North and the hospital. The total bill for the law firm's travel costs and professional services was $21,000, but Dr. North refused to pay $6,000 of it. When the law firm brought an action against Dr. North for the balance owed, he argued that the action should be dismissed because the law firm failed to register as a foreign corporation in accordance with the Georgia Corporation Statute. Decision?

11. An Arkansas statute provides that if any foreign corporation authorized to do business in the State should remove to the Federal court any suit brought against it by an Arkansas citizen or initiate any suit in the Federal court against a local citizen, without the consent of the other party, Arkansas's Secretary of

State should revoke all authority of the corporation to do business in the State. The Burke Construction Company, a Missouri corporation authorized to do business in Arkansas, has brought a suit in and has removed to the Federal Court a State suit brought against it. Burke now seeks to enjoin the Secretary of State from revoking its authority to do business in Arkansas, contending that the Arkansas statute is unconstitutional. Decision?

12.   Little Switzerland was incorporated on January 28, 1968. On February 18, Ellison and Oxley were made directors of the company after they purchased some stock. Then, on September 25, Ellison and Oxley signed stock subscription agreements to purchase 5,000 shares each. Under the agreement, they both issued a note which indicated that they would pay for the stock "at their discretion." In March 1970, the board of directors passed a resolution canceling the stock subscription agreements of Ellison and Oxley. The creditors of Little Switzerland brought suit against Ellison and Oxley to recover the money owed under the subscription agreements. Decision?

13.   Oahe Enterprises was formed by the efforts of Emmick, who acted as a promoter and contributed shares of Colonial Manors, Inc., (CM) stock in exchange for stock in Oahe. The CM stock had been valued by CM's directors for internal stock option purposes at $19 per share. One month prior to Emmick's incorporation of Oahe Enterprises, however, CM's board reduced the stock value to $9.50 per share. Although Emmick knew of this reduction before the meeting to form Oahe Enterprises, he did not disclose this information to the Morrises, the other shareholders of the new corporation. Oahe Enterprises then brought this action to recover the shortfall. Decision?

14.   On September 14, 1971, Healthwin-Midtown Convalescent Hospital, Inc., (Healthwin) was incorporated in California for the purpose of operating a health care facility. From that date until November 30, 1974, it participated as a provider of services under the Federal Medicare Act and received periodic payments from the United States Department of Health, Education and Welfare. Undisputed audits revealed that a series of overpayments had been made to Healthwin in the total amount of $30,481. The United States brought an action to recover this sum from the defendants, Healthwin and Israel Zide. Zide was a member of the board of directors of the Healthwin corporation, the administrator of its health care facility, its president, and owner of 50 percent of its stock. Only Zide could sign the corporation's checks without prior approval of another corporate officer. In addition, Zide had a 50 percent interest in a partnership that owned both the realty in which Healthwin's health care facility was located and the furnishings used at that facility. The corporation was initially undercapitalized, and its liabilities continued to exceed its assets substantially. Zide exercised control over Healthwin, causing its finances to become inextricably intertwined with both his personal finances and his other business holdings. The United States contends that the corporate veil should be pierced and that Zide should be held personally liable for the Medicare overpayments made to Healthwin. Decision?

15.   MPL Leasing Corporation is a California corporation that provides financing plans to dealers of Saxon Business Products. MPL invited Jay Johnson, a Saxon dealer in Alabama, to attend a sales seminar in Atlanta. MPL and Johnson entered into an agreement under which Johnson was to lease Saxon copiers with an option to buy. MPL shipped the equipment into Alabama and filed a financing statement with the Secretary of State. When Johnson became delinquent with his payments to MPL, MPL brought an action against Johnson in an Alabama court. Johnson moved to dismiss the action, claiming that MPL was not qualified to conduct business in Alabama and was thus barred from enforcing its contract with Johnson in an Alabama court. The trial court entered judgment in favor of MPL. Decision?

16.   In April 1961, Cranson was asked to invest in a new business corporation that was about to be created. He agreed to purchase stock and to become an officer and director. After his attorney advised him that the corporation had been formed under the laws of Maryland, Cranson paid for and received a stock certificate evidencing his ownership of shares. The business of the new venture was conducted as if it were a corporation. Cranson was elected president, and he conducted all of his corporate actions, including those with IBM, as an officer of the corporation. At no time did he assume any personal obligation or pledge his individual credit to IBM. As a result of an oversight of the attorney, of which Cranson was unaware, the certificate of incorporation, which had been signed and acknowledged prior to May 1, 1961, was not filed until November 24, 1961. Between May 1 and November 8, the "corporation" purchased eight typewriters from IBM. After the corporation made only partial payment, IBM brought suit against Cranson seeking to hold him personally liable for the $4,333.40 balance due. Decision?

17.   Berger was planning to produce a fashion show in Las Vegas. In April 1965, Berger entered into a written licensing agreement with CBS Films, Inc., a wholly owned subsidiary of CBS, for presentation of the show. In 1966, Stewart Cowley decided to produce a fashion show similar to Berger's and entered into a contract with CBS. CBS broadcast Cowley's show, but not Berger's; and Berger brought this action against CBS to recover damages for breach of his contract with CBS Films. Berger claimed that CBS was liable because CBS Films was its instrumentality or *alter ego,* and that the court should disregard the parent-subsidiary form. In support of this claim, Berger showed that CBS Films' directors were employees of CBS, that CBS's organizational chart included CBS Films, and that all lines of employee authority from CBS Films passed through CBS employees to the CBS chairman of the board. CBS, in turn, argued that Berger had failed to justify piercing the corporate veil and disregarding the corporate identity of CBS Films in order to hold CBS liable. Decision?

18.   Frank McAnarney and Joseph Lemon entered into an agreement to promote a corporation to engage in the manufacture of farm implements. Before the corporation was organized, McAnarney and Lemon solicited subscriptions to the stock of

the corporation and presented a written agreement for the subscribers to sign. The agreement provided that the subscribers would pay $100 per share for stock in the corporation in consideration of McAnarney and Lemon's agreement to organize the corporation and advance the preincorporation expenses. Thomas Jordan signed the agreement, making application for 100 shares of stock. After the articles of incorporation were filed with the Secretary of State, but before the charter was issued to the corporation, Jordan died. The administrator of Jordan's estate notified McAnarney and Lemon that the estate would not honor Jordan's subscription.

After the formation of the corporation, Franklin Adams signed a subscription agreement making application for 100 shares of stock. Before the corporation accepted the subscription, Adams informed the corporation that he was canceling it.

(a)   The corporation brings an appropriate action against Jordan's estate to enforce Jordan's stock subscription. Decision?

(b)   The corporation brings an appropriate action to enforce Adams's stock subscription. Decision?

**Internet Exercise**   Find samples of (a) articles of incorporation and (b) corporate bylaws.

# CHAPTER 35

# Financial Structure

Capital is necessary for any business to function. Two principal sources for corporate financing involve debt and equity investment securities. While equity securities represent an ownership interest in the corporation and include both common and preferred stock, corporations finance most of their operations through debt securities. Debt securities, which include notes and bonds, do not represent an ownership interest in the corporation but rather create a debtor-creditor relationship between the corporation and the bondholder. The third principal way in which a corporation may meet its financial needs is through retained earnings.

All States have statutes regulating the issuance and sale of corporate shares and other securities. Popularly known as **blue-sky laws,** these statutes typically have provisions prohibiting fraud in the sale of securities. In addition, a number of States require the registration of securities, and some States also regulate brokers, dealers, and others who engage in the securities business.

In 1933, Congress passed the first Federal statute for the regulation of securities offered for sale and sold through the use of the mails or otherwise in interstate commerce. The statute requires a corporation to disclose certain information about a proposed security in a registration statement and in its **prospectus** (an offer a corporation makes to interest people in buying securities). Although the Securities and Exchange Commission (SEC) does not examine the merits of the proposed security and although registration does not guarantee the accuracy of the facts presented in the registration statement or prospectus, the law does prohibit false and misleading statements under penalty of fine or imprisonment or both.

Under certain conditions, a corporation may receive an exemption from the requirement of registration under the blue-sky laws of most States and the Securities Act of 1933. If no exemption is available, a corporation offering for sale or selling its shares of stock or other securities,

as well as any person selling such securities, is subject to court injunction, possible criminal prosecution, and civil liability in damages to the persons to whom securities are sold in violation of the regulatory statute. A discussion of Federal regulation of securities appears in Chapter 44.

An investor has the right to transfer her investment securities by sale, gift, or pledge. The right to transfer is a valuable one, and easy transferability augments the value and marketability of investment securities. The availability of a ready market for any security affords liquidity and makes the security both attractive to investors and useful as collateral. The Uniform Commercial Code, Article 8, Investment Securities, contains the statutory rules applicable to transfers of investment securities; these rules are similar to those in Article 3, which concern negotiable instruments. In 1994 a revision to Article 8 was promulgated, and almost all of the States have adopted the revision. The Federal securities laws also regulate several aspects of the transfer of investment securities, as discussed in Chapter 44.

This chapter will discuss debt and equity securities as well as the payment of dividends and other distributions to shareholders.

## DEBT SECURITIES

Corporations frequently find it advantageous to use debt as a source of funds. **Debt securities** (also called **bonds**) generally involve the corporation's promise to repay the principal amount of a loan at a stated time and to pay interest, usually at a fixed rate, while the debt is outstanding. Thus, a debt security creates a debtor–creditor relationship between the corporation and the holder of the security. In addition to bonds, a corporation may finance its operations through other forms of debt, such as credit extended by its suppliers and short-term commercial paper. Some States, but not the Revised Act, permit the articles of incorporation to confer voting rights on debt security holders; a few States allow other shareholder rights to be conferred on bondholders.

## AUTHORITY TO ISSUE DEBT SECURITIES

The Revised Act provides that every corporation has the power "to make contracts and guarantees, incur liabilities, borrow money, issue its notes, bonds, and other obligations (which may be convertible into or include the option to purchase other securities of the corporation), and secure any of its obligations by mortgage or pledge of any of its property, franchises, or income." Section 3.02. The board of directors may issue bonds without the authorization or consent of the shareholders.

## TYPES OF DEBT SECURITIES

Debt securities can be classified into various types according to their characteristics. The variants and combinations possible within each type are limited only by a corporation's ingenuity. Debt securities are typically issued under an **indenture** or debt agreement, which specifies in great detail the terms of the loan.

 *See Case 35–1*

### Unsecured Bonds

Unsecured bonds, usually called **debentures,** have only the obligation of the corporation behind them. Debenture holders are thus unsecured creditors and rank equally with other general creditors. To protect the unsecured bondholders, indentures frequently impose limitations on the corporation's borrowing, its payment of dividends, and its redemption and reacquisition of its own shares. They also may require the corporation to maintain specified minimum reserves.

### Secured Bonds

A secured creditor is one whose claim not only is enforceable against the general assets of the corporation but also is a lien upon specific property. Thus, **secured** or mortgage **bonds** provide the security of specific corporate property in addition to the general obligation of the corporation. After resorting to the specified security, the holder of secured bonds becomes a general creditor for any unpaid amount of the debt.

### Income Bonds

Traditionally, debt securities bear a fixed interest rate that is payable without regard to the financial condition of the corporation. **Income bonds,** on the other hand, condition the payment of interest to some extent upon corporate earnings. This provision lessens the burden of the debt upon the issuer during periods of financial adversity. **Participating bonds** call for a stated percentage of return regardless of earnings, with additional payments dependent upon earnings.

### Convertible Bonds

**Convertible bonds** may be exchanged, usually at the option of the holder, for other securities of the corporation at a specified ratio. For example, a convertible bond may provide that the bondholder shall have the right for a specified time to exchange each bond for twenty shares of common stock.

### Callable Bonds

**Callable bonds** are bonds subject to a redemption provision that permits the corporation to redeem or call (pay off) all or part of the issue before maturity at a specified redemption price. This provision enables the corporation to reduce fixed costs, to improve its credit rating, to refinance at a lower interest rate, to free mortgaged property, or to reduce its proportion of debt.

## EQUITY SECURITIES

An **equity security** is a source of capital creating an ownership interest in the corporation. The holders of equity security, as owners of the corporation, occupy a position financially riskier than that of creditors; they, more than any other class of investor, bear the impact of changes in the corporation's fortunes and general economic conditions.

Though **shares** of equity securities describe a proportionate proprietary interest in a corporate enterprise, they do not in any way vest their owner with title to any of the corporation's property. Shares do, however, confer on their owner a threefold interest in the corporation: (1) the right to participate in control, (2) the right to participate in the earnings of the corporation, and (3) the right to participate in the residual assets of the corporation upon dissolution. The shareholder's interest is usually evidenced by a certificate of ownership and is recorded by the corporation.

## ISSUANCE OF SHARES

The State of incorporation regulates the issuance of shares by determining the type of shares that may be issued, the kinds and amount of consideration for which shares may be issued, and the rights of shareholders to purchase a proportionate part of additionally issued shares. Moreover, the Federal government and each State in which the shares are issued or sold regulate the issuance and sale of shares.

### Authority to Issue

The initial amount of shares to be issued is determined by the promoters or incorporators and is generally governed by practical business considerations and financial needs. A corporation is limited, however, to selling only the amount of shares that has been authorized in its articles of incorporation. Section 6.03. Unauthorized shares of stock that a corporation purportedly issues are void. The rights of parties entitled to these overissued shares are governed by Article 8 of the Uniform Commercial Code (UCC), which provides that the corporation must either obtain an identical security, if it is reasonably available, for the person entitled to the security or pay that person the price he (or the last purchaser for value) paid for it, with interest. UCC Section 8–104 (8–210 in Revised Article 8).

Once the amount of shares that the corporation is authorized to issue has been specified in the charter, it cannot be increased or decreased without amending the articles of incorporation. This means that the shareholders, who must approve any amendment to the articles of incorporation, have residual authority over increases in the amount of authorized capital stock. Consequently, articles of incorporation commonly specify more shares than are to be issued initially.

### Preemptive Rights

A shareholder's proportionate interest in a corporation can be changed by either a nonproportionate issuance of additional shares or a nonproportionate reacquisition of outstanding shares. In either transaction, management owes both the shareholder and the corporation a fiduciary duty. Moreover, when additional shares are issued, a shareholder may have the **preemptive right** to purchase a proportionate part of the new issue. Preemptive rights are used far more frequently in closely held corporations than in publicly traded corporations. Without such rights, a shareholder may be unable to prevent a dilution of his ownership interest in the corporation. For example, Leonard owns 200 shares of stock of the Fordham Company, which has a total of 1,000 shares outstanding. The company decides to increase its capital stock by issuing 1,000 additional shares of stock. If Leonard has preemptive rights, he and every other shareholder will be offered one share of the newly issued stock for every share they own. If he accepts the offer and buys the stock, he will have 400 shares out of a total of 2,000 outstanding, and his relative interest in the corporation will be unchanged. Without preemptive rights, however, he would have only 200 out of the 2,000 shares outstanding; instead of owning 20 percent of the stock, he would own 10 percent.

At common law, shareholders have preemptive rights to the issuance of additionally authorized shares. Such preemptive rights do not apply, however, to the reissue of previously issued shares, shares issued for noncash consideration, or shares issued in connection with a merger or consolidation. The jurisdictions are divided over whether preemptive rights apply to the issuance of unissued shares that were originally authorized.

Modern statutes expressly authorize articles of incorporation to deny or limit preemptive rights. In some States, preemptive rights exist unless denied by the charter; in others, they do not exist unless the charter so provides.

The Revised Act adopts the latter approach: preemptive rights are nonexistent unless the charter provides for them. Section 6.30. If the charter simply states that "the corporation elects to have preemptive rights," then the shareholders have a preemptive right to acquire proportional amounts of the corporation's unissued shares but they have no preemptive rights with respect to (1) shares issued as compensation to directors, officers, and employees, (2) shares issued within six months of incorporation, and (3) shares issued for consideration other than money. In addition, holders of nonvoting preferred stock have no preemptive rights with respect to *any* class of shares, and holders of voting common shares have no preemptive rights with respect to preferred stock unless the preferred stock is convertible into common stock. Section 6.30(b). The articles of incorporation may expressly render any or all of these limitations inapplicable.

### Amount of Consideration for Shares

The board of directors usually determines the price for which the corporation will issue shares, although the charter may reserve this power to the shareholders. Section 6.21. Shares are deemed fully paid and nonassessable when the corporation receives the consideration for which the board of directors authorized their issuance. Section 6.21(d). The amount of that consideration depends upon the kind of shares being issued.

**Par Value Stock**  Par value shares may be issued for any amount, not less than par, set by the board of directors or shareholders. The par value of a share of stock can be an arbitrary value selected by the corporation and may or may not reflect either the actual value of the share or the actual price paid to the corporation. It indicates only the *minimum price* that the corporation must receive for the share. The par value of stock must be stated in the articles of incorporation. The consideration received constitutes *stated capital* to the extent of the par value of the shares; any consideration in excess of par value constitutes *capital surplus*.

The Revised Act, the 1980 amendments to the MBCA, and about twenty-five States eliminate the concepts of par value, stated capital, and capital surplus. Under these acts, all shares may be issued for such consideration as authorized by the board of directors or, if the charter so provides, the shareholders. Section 6.21. A corporation may, however, elect to issue shares with par value. Section 2.02(b)(iv).

**No Par Value Stock**  Shares without par value may be issued for any amount set by the board of directors or shareholders. Under incorporation statutes recognizing par value, stated value, and capital surplus, the entire consideration the corporation receives for such stock constitutes stated capital unless the board of directors allocates a portion of the consideration to capital surplus. MBCA Section 21, repealed in 1980. (As noted above, the 1980 amendments to the Model Act and the Revised Act eliminated the concepts of par value, stated capital, and capital surplus.) The directors are free to allocate any or all of the consideration received, unless the no par stock has a liquidation preference. In that event, only the consideration in excess of the amount of liquidation preference may be allocated to capital surplus. No par shares provide the directors with great latitude in establishing capital surplus, which can, in some jurisdictions, provide greater flexibility in declaring subsequent distributions to shareholders.

**Treasury Stock**  Treasury stock consists of shares that the corporation has issued and subsequently reacquired. Treasury shares are issued *but not* outstanding, in contrast to shares owned by shareholders, which are issued *and* outstanding. A corporation may sell treasury shares for any amount the board of directors determines, even if the shares have a par value that is more than the sale price. Treasury shares provide neither voting rights nor preemptive rights; furthermore, no dividend may be paid upon them.

The Revised Act advances the 1980 amendments to the MBCA, which eliminated the concept of treasury shares. Under the Revised Act, all shares reacquired by a corporation constitute authorized but unissued shares, unless the articles of incorporation prohibit reissue, in which event the authorized shares are reduced by the number of shares reacquired. Section 6.31.

◆ *See Figure 35–1*

## Payment for Shares

Two major issues arise regarding payment for shares. First, what type of consideration may the corporation validly accept in payment for shares? Second, who shall determine the value to be placed upon the consideration the corporation receives in payment for shares?

**Type of Consideration**  In terms of the issuance of capital stock, consideration receives a more limited definition than it does under contract law. In about thirty States, cash, property, and services actually rendered to the corporation are generally acceptable as valid consideration, but promissory notes and promises regarding the performance of future services are not. Some States permit shares to be issued for preincorporation services; other States do not.

The Revised Act greatly liberalized these rules by specifically validating for the issuance of shares consideration consisting of any tangible or intangible property or *benefit* to the corporation, including cash, services performed, *contracts for future services,* and *promissory notes.* Section 6.21(b). To guard against possible abuse, the corporation may place the shares in escrow or otherwise restrict their transfer until the services are performed, the note is paid, or the benefits are received. If the services are not performed, the note is not paid, or the benefits are not received, the shares escrowed or restricted may be canceled. Section 6.21(e). Moreover, the Revised Act requires that corporations annually inform their shareholders in writing of all shares issued during the previous year for promissory notes or promises of future services. Section 16.21.

**FIGURE 35–1** Issuance of Shares

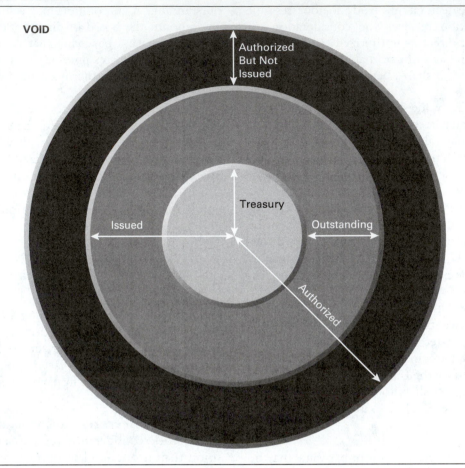

*Valuation of Consideration* Determining the value to be placed on the consideration that stock purchasers will exchange for shares is the responsibility of the directors. The majority of jurisdictions hold that this valuation is a matter of opinion and that, in the absence of fraud in the transaction, the judgment of the board of directors as to the value of the consideration actually or to be received for shares shall be conclusive. For example, assume that the directors of Elite Corporation authorize the issuance of 2,000 shares of common stock for $5 per share to Kramer for property that the directors purportedly value at $10,000. The valuation is fraudulent, however, and the property is actually worth only $5,000. Kramer is liable to Elite Corporation and its creditors for $5,000. If, on the other hand, the directors had made the valuation without fraud and in good faith, Kramer would not be liable, even though the property is actually worth less than $10,000.

Under the Revised Act, the directors simply determine whether or not the consideration received (or to be received) for shares is *adequate*. Their determination is "conclusive insofar as the adequacy of consideration for the issuance of shares relates to whether the shares are validly issued, fully paid, and nonassessable." Section 6.21(c). Under the Revised Act, the articles of incorporation may reserve to the shareholders the powers granted to the board regarding the issuance of shares. Section 6.21(a).

## Liability for Shares

A purchaser of shares has no liability to the corporation or its creditors with respect to the shares except to pay the corporation either the consideration for which the shares were authorized to be issued or the consideration specified in the preincorporation stock subscription. Section 6.22(a). When the corporation receives that consideration, the shares are fully paid and nonassessable. Section 6.21(d). A transferee who acquires these shares in good faith and without knowledge or notice that the full consideration had not been paid is not personally liable to the corporation or its creditors for the unpaid portion of the consideration.

## CLASSES OF SHARES

Corporations are generally authorized by statute to issue different classes of stock, which may vary with respect to their rights to dividends, their voting rights, and their right to share in the assets of the corporation upon liquidation. The usual classifications of stock are common and preferred shares. Although the Revised Act has eliminated the terms *preferred* and *common*, it permits the issuance of shares with different preferences, limitations, and relative rights. Section 6.01. The Revised Act explicitly requires that the charter authorize "(1) one or more classes of shares that together have unlimited voting rights, and (2) one or more classes of shares (which may be the same class or classes as those with voting rights) that together are entitled to receive the net assets of the corporation upon dissolution." Section 6.01(b). In most States, however, even nonvoting shares may vote on certain mergers, share exchanges, and other fundamental changes which affect that class of shares as a class. See Chapter 37.

### Common Stock

**Common stock** does not have any special contract rights or preferences. Often the only class of stock outstanding, it generally represents the greatest proportion of the corporation's capital structure and bears the greatest risk of loss, should the enterprise fail.

Common stock may be divided into one or more classes bearing designations, limitations, or relative rights stated in the articles of incorporation. Section 6.01. The Revised Act and some States permit common stock to be redeemable or convertible. Section 6.01(c)(2). The articles also may limit or deny the voting rights of classes of common shares, but at least one or more classes of shares must together have unlimited voting rights. Section 6.01(b). For example, Class A common may be entitled to three times the dividends per share to which Class B common is entitled. Or Class A common may be entitled to elect six directors while Class B common elects three directors. Or Class A common may have two votes per share while Class B common has no votes per share.

### Preferred Stock

Stock generally is considered **preferred stock** if it has contractual rights superior to those of common stock with regard to dividends, assets upon liquidation, or both. Other special rights or privileges generally do not remove stock from the common stock classification. The articles of incorporation must provide for the contractual rights and preferences of an issue of preferred stock. Section 6.01(c).

Notwithstanding the special rights and preferences that distinguish preferred from common stock, both represent a contribution of capital. Preferred stock is no more a debt than common, and until a dividend is declared, the holder of preferred shares is not a creditor of the corporation. Furthermore, the rights of preferred shareholders are subordinate to the rights of the corporation's creditors.

*Dividend Preferences*   Though the holders of an issue of preferred stock with a dividend preference will receive full dividends before any dividend may be paid to holders of common stock, no dividend is payable upon any class of stock, common or preferred, unless such dividend has been declared by the board of directors. The dividend preference may be described in terms of dollars per share ("$3.00 preferred") or as a percentage of par value ("ten percent preferred").

Preferred stock may provide that dividends are cumulative, noncumulative, or cumulative to the extent earned. For **cumulative** stock, if the board does not declare regular dividends on the preferred stock, such omitted dividends cumulate, and no dividend may be declared on common stock until all dividend arrearages on the preferred stock are declared and paid. For **non-cumulative** stock, regular dividends do not cumulate upon the board's failure to declare them, and all rights to a dividend for the period omitted are gone forever. Accordingly, noncumulative stock has a priority over common only during a fiscal period in which a dividend on common stock is declared. Unless the charter expressly makes the dividends on preferred stock noncumulative, the courts generally hold them to be cumulative. **Cumulative-to-the-extent-earned** stock cumulates unpaid dividends only to the extent that funds were legally available to pay such dividends during that fiscal period.

Preferred stock also may be **participating**, although generally it is not. The manner in which preferred stock participates in dividends with common stock must be specified in the articles of incorporation. For example, a class of participating preferred stock could be entitled to share at the same rate with the common stock in any additional distribution of earnings for a given year *after* provision has been made for paying the prior preferred dividend and for paying dividends on the common at a rate equal to the fixed rate of the preferred.

*Liquidation Preferences* After a corporation has been dissolved, its assets liquidated, and the claims of its creditors satisfied, the remaining assets are distributed *pro rata* among the shareholders according to their priority as provided in the articles of incorporation. In the event that a class of stock with a dividend preference does not expressly provide for a preference of any kind upon dissolution and liquidation, its holders share *pro rata* with the common shareholders.

When the articles provide a liquidation preference, preferred stock has priority over common to the extent the articles state. In addition, if specified, preferred shares may participate beyond the liquidation preference in a stated ratio with other classes of shares. Such shares are said to be participating preferred with reference to liquidation. Preferred shares not so specified do not participate beyond the liquidation preference.

*Additional Rights and Limitations* Preferred stock may have additional rights, designations, and limitations. For instance, it may be expressly denied voting rights if the statute so permits, or it may be redeemable by the corporation or convertible into shares of another class. Sections 6.01(c) and 7.21(a).

## Stock Rights

A corporation may issue stock rights or **stock options** entitling their holders to purchase from the corporation shares of a specified class or classes. A **stock warrant** is a type of stock option that typically has a longer term and is freely transferable. The board of directors determines the terms upon which stock rights, options, or warrants are issued; their form and content; and the consideration for which the shares are to be issued. Section 6.24. One use for share options or warrants is in incentive compensation plans for directors, officers, and employees. Another is to assist a corporation in raising capital by making one class of securities more attractive by including in it the right to purchase shares in another class.

◆ *See Figure 35–2*

## DIVIDENDS AND OTHER DISTRIBUTIONS

The board of directors, in its discretion, determines when and in what amount to declare distributions and dividends. The corporation's working capital requirements, shareholder expectations, tax consequences, and other factors influence the board as it creates distribution policy. In addition, the conditions under which the earnings of a business may be paid out in the form of dividends or other distributions of corporate assets will depend upon the contractual rights of those who hold the particular shares involved or shares having superior rights,

**FIGURE 35–2** Debt and Equity Securities

| | Debt | Equity Common | Equity Preferred |
|---|---|---|---|
| **Ownership Interest** | No | Yes | Yes |
| **Obligation to Repay Principal** | Yes | No | No |
| **Fixed Maturity** | Yes | No | No |
| **Obligation to Pay Income** | Yes | No | No |
| **Preference on Income** | Yes | No | Yes |
| **Preference on Liquidation** | Yes | No | Yes |
| **Voting Rights** | Some States | Yes, unless denied | Yes, unless denied |
| **Redeemable** | Yes | In some States | Yes |
| **Convertible** | Yes | In some States | Yes |

provisions in the charter and bylaws of the corporation, and provisions of the State incorporation statute that are designed to protect creditors and shareholders from the dissipation of corporate assets. Creditors receive more significant protection under contractual restrictions typically included in their loan agreements, as well as under State fraudulent conveyance laws and Federal bankruptcy law.

## TYPES OF DIVIDENDS AND OTHER DISTRIBUTIONS

The Revised Act defines a **distribution** as "a direct or indirect transfer of money or other property (except its own shares) or incurrence of indebtedness by a corporation to or for the benefit of its shareholders in respect of any of its shares. A distribution may be in the form of a declaration or payment of a dividend; a purchase, redemption, or other acquisition of shares; a distribution of indebtedness; or otherwise." Section 1.40(6). The comments to this section explain that the term *indirect* is intended to include any other transaction the substance of which is clearly the same as that of a typical dividend or share repurchase, without regard to how the transaction is labeled or structured. Stock dividends and stock splits, which are not included in this definition, will also be covered in this section.

### Cash Dividends

The most customary type of dividend is a cash dividend, declared and paid at regular intervals from legally available funds. These dividends may vary in amount, depending upon the policy of the board of directors and the earnings of the enterprise.

### Property Dividends

Although dividends are almost always paid in cash, shareholders occasionally receive a property dividend, a distribution of earnings in the form of property. On one occasion, a distillery declared and paid a dividend in bonded whiskey.

### Stock Dividends

A stock or share dividend is a ratable distribution of additional shares of the capital stock of a corporation to its shareholders. The practical and legal significance of a stock dividend differs greatly from that of a dividend payable in cash or property. Following the payment of a stock dividend, the assets of the corporation are no less than they were before, and the shareholder's relative interest in the net worth of the corporation is no greater than it was before, except possibly where the dividend is paid in shares of a different class. His shares will each represent a smaller proportionate interest in the corporation's assets, but by reason of the increase in the number of shares, his total investment will remain the same. Accordingly, a stock dividend is *not* considered a distribution. Under incorporation statutes recognizing par value and stated capital, a stock dividend results in the transfer from surplus to stated capital of an amount equal to the par value of the stock dividend.

### Stock Splits

In a stock split, the corporation simply breaks each of the issued and outstanding shares into a greater number of shares, each representing a proportionately smaller interest in the corporation. Under incorporation statutes recognizing par value and stated capital, the par value of the shares to be split is divided among the new shares. The usual purpose of a stock split is to lower the price per share to a more marketable price and thus increase the number of potential shareholders. Like a stock dividend, a stock split is not a distribution; unlike a stock dividend, a split entails no transfer of surplus to stated capital.

### Liquidating Dividends

Although dividends ordinarily are identified with the distribution of profits, a distribution of capital assets to shareholders is referred to as a liquidating dividend in some jurisdictions. Incorporation statutes usually require that the shareholder be informed when a distribution is a liquidating dividend.

### Redemption of Shares

Redemption is the repurchase by the corporation of its own shares, usually at its own option. The Model Act and the statutes of many States permit corporations to redeem preferred shares but not common stock; the Revised Act, in contrast, does not prohibit redeemable common stock. The articles of incorporation must expressly provide for the power of redemption.

## Acquisition of Shares

A corporation may acquire its own shares. Such shares, unless canceled, are referred to as treasury shares. Under the Revised Act, such shares are considered authorized but unissued. Section 6.31. As with redemption, the acquisition of shares constitutes a distribution to shareholders and has an effect similar to a dividend.

## LEGAL RESTRICTIONS ON DIVIDENDS AND OTHER DISTRIBUTIONS

Several legal restrictions limit the amount of distributions a board of directors may declare. Though all States have statutes restricting the funds that are legally available for dividends and other distributions of corporate assets, lender-imposed contractual restrictions often limit the declaration of dividends and distributions even more stringently.

States restrict the payment of dividends and other distributions to protect creditors. All States impose the **equity insolvency test,** which prohibits the payment of any dividend or other distribution when the corporation either is insolvent or would become so through the payment of the dividend or distribution. **Insolvent** indicates the inability of a corporation to pay its debts as they become due in the usual course of business. In addition, each State imposes further restrictions regarding the funds that are legally available to pay dividends and other distributions. These additional restrictions are based upon the corporation's assets or balance sheet, whereas the equity insolvency test is based upon the corporation's cash flow.

## Definitions

The legal, asset-based restrictions upon the payment of dividends or other distributions involve the concepts of earned surplus, surplus, net assets, stated capital, and capital surplus.

**Earned surplus** consists of the corporation's undistributed net profits, income, gains, and losses, computed from its date of incorporation.

**Surplus** is the amount by which the net assets of a corporation exceed its stated capital.

**Net assets** equal the amount by which the total assets of a corporation exceed its total debts.

**Stated capital** is the sum of the consideration the corporation has received for its issued stock, excepting the consideration properly allocated to capital surplus but including any amount transferred to stated capital when a stock dividend is declared. In the case of par value shares, the amount of stated capital is the total par value of all the issued shares. In the case of no par stock, it is the consideration the corporation has received for all the no par shares that it has issued, except that amount allocated to capital surplus or paid-in surplus.

**Capital surplus** means the entire surplus of a corporation other than its earned surplus. It may result from an allocation of part of the consideration received for no par shares, from any consideration in excess of par value received for par shares, or from a higher reappraisal of certain corporate assets.

◆ *See Figure 35–3*

## Legal Restrictions on Cash Dividends

Each State imposes an equity insolvency test on the payment of dividends. The States differ regarding the asset-based or balance sheet test they apply. Some apply the earned surplus test, others use the surplus test, and the Revised Act adopts a net assets test.

*Earned Surplus Test*  Unreserved and unrestricted earned surplus is available for dividends in all jurisdictions. Many States permit dividends to be paid only from earned surplus; corporations in these jurisdictions may not pay dividends out of capital surplus or stated capital. In addition, the corporation may not pay dividends if it is or would be rendered insolvent in the equity sense by the payment. The MBCA used this test until 1980.

*Surplus Test*  A number of less-restrictive States permit dividends to be paid out of any surplus—earned or capital. Some of these States express this test by prohibiting dividends that impair stated capital. Moreover, dividends may not be paid if the corporation is or would be rendered insolvent in the equity sense by the payment.

*Net Assets Test*  The MBCA, as amended in 1980, and the Revised Act have adopted a net assets test. Section 6.40 of the Revised Act as amended states,

(c) No distribution may be made if, after giving it effect:
   (1) the corporation would not be able to pay its debts as they become due in the usual course of business; or
   (2) the corporation's total assets would be less than the sum of its total liabilities plus (unless the articles of incorporation permit otherwise) the amount that

FIGURE 35–3   Key Concepts in Legal Restrictions upon Distributions

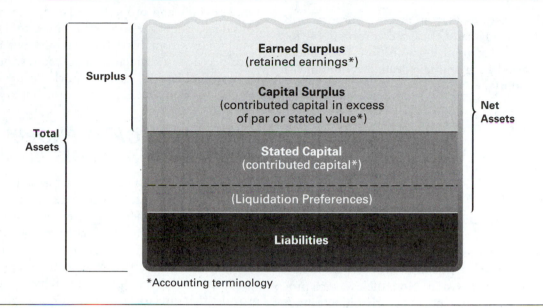

*Accounting terminology

would be needed, if the corporation were to be dissolved at the time of the distribution, to satisfy the preferential rights upon dissolution of shareholders whose preferential rights are superior to those receiving the distribution.

## Legal Restrictions on Liquidating Distributions

Even those States that do not permit cash dividends to be paid from capital surplus usually will permit distributions, or dividends, in partial liquidation from that source. Before 1980, the Model Act had such a provision. A distribution paid out of such surplus is a return to the shareholders of part of their investment.

The corporation may make no such distribution, however, when it is insolvent or when the distribution would render it so. Distributions from capital surplus are also restricted to protect the liquidation preference and cumulative dividend arrearages of preferred shareholders. Unless provided for in the articles of incorporation, a liquidating dividend must be authorized not only by the board of directors but also by the affirmative vote of the holders of a majority of the outstanding shares of stock of each class.

Because the Revised Act does not distinguish between cash and liquidating dividends, it therefore imposes upon

liquidating dividends the same limitations it imposes upon cash dividends, discussed above. Section 6.40.

## Legal Restrictions on Redemption and Acquisition of Shares

To protect creditors and holders of other classes of shares, most States place statutory restrictions upon redemption. A corporation may not redeem or purchase its redeemable shares when insolvent or when such redemption or purchase would render it insolvent or would reduce its net assets below the aggregate amount payable upon shares having prior or equal rights to the assets of the corporation upon involuntary dissolution.

A corporation may purchase its own shares only out of earned surplus or, if the articles of incorporation permit or if the shareholders approve, out of capital surplus. As with redemption, the corporation may make no purchase of shares when insolvent or when such purchase would make it insolvent.

The Revised Act permits a corporation to purchase, redeem, or otherwise acquire its own shares unless (1) the corporation's total assets after the distribution would be less than the sum of its total liabilities and the maximum amount that then would be payable for all outstanding shares having preferential rights in liquidation, or (2) the corporation would be unable to pay its debts as they become due in the usual course of its business. Section 6.40.

Additional restrictions may apply to a corporation's acquisition of its own shares. In close corporations, for example, courts may scrutinize acquisitions for compliance with the good faith and fair dealing requirements of the fiduciary duty.

 *See Cases 35–2 and 36–3*

## DECLARATION AND PAYMENT OF DISTRIBUTIONS

The declaration of dividends and other distributions is within the discretion of the board of directors and may not be delegated. If the charter clearly and expressly provides for mandatory dividends, however, the board must comply with the provision. Nonetheless, such provisions are extremely infrequent, and shareholders cannot usurp the board's power in any other way, although it is in their power to elect a new board. Moreover, the board cannot discriminate in its declaration of dividends among shareholders of the same class.

### Shareholders' Right to Compel a Dividend

Should the directors fail to declare a dividend, a shareholder may bring a suit in equity against them and the corporation to seek a mandatory injunction requiring the directors to declare a dividend. Courts of equity are reluctant to order an injunction of this kind, which involves substituting the business judgment of the court for that of the directors elected by the shareholders. Where the evidence shows noncorporate motives or personal animosity as the basis for a refusal to declare dividends, however, a court may require the directors to distribute an apparently reasonable portion of the earnings. This is not a frequent occurrence; *Dodge v. Ford Motor Co.* is a landmark example.

With respect to the directors' discretion regarding the declaration of dividends, a preferred shareholder having prior rights with respect to dividends occupies a position identical to that of a holder of common shares. In the absence of special contractual or statutory rights, the holder of preferred shares, like the holder of common ones, must abide by the directors' decision.

 *See Case 35–3*

### Effect of Declaration

Once lawfully and properly declared, a cash dividend is considered a debt the corporation owes to the shareholders. It follows from this debtor–creditor relationship that, once declared, a dividend cannot be rescinded without the shareholders' consent; a stock dividend, however, may be revoked unless actually distributed.

## LIABILITY FOR IMPROPER DIVIDENDS AND DISTRIBUTIONS

The Revised Act imposes personal liability upon the directors of a corporation who vote for or assent to the declaration of a dividend or other distribution of corporate assets contrary to the incorporation statute or the articles of incorporation. Section 8.33(a). Though directors generally are liable either to the corporation or to the corporation's creditors, the Revised Act expressly provides that directors who vote for or assent to an illegal dividend or distribution are liable to the corporation. Section 8.33(a). The measure of damages is the amount of the dividend or distribution in excess of the amount that the corporation lawfully may have paid.

A director is not liable if she acted in accordance with the relevant standard of conduct: in good faith, with reasonable care, and in a manner she reasonably believed to be in the best interests of the corporation. Sections 8.30 and 8.33. (This standard of conduct is discussed in the next chapter.) In discharging this duty, a director is entitled to rely in good faith upon financial statements presented by the corporation's officers, public accountants, or finance committee. Such statements must be prepared on the basis of "accounting practices and principles that are reasonable in the circumstances or on a fair valuation or other method that is reasonable in the circumstances." Section 6.40(d). According to the Comments to this section, generally accepted accounting principles are *always* reasonable in the circumstances; other accounting principles *may* be acceptable under a general standard of reasonableness.

A shareholder's obligation to repay an illegally declared dividend depends upon a variety of factors, which may include the good or bad faith in which the shareholder accepted the dividend, his knowledge of the facts, the solvency or insolvency of the corporation, and, in some instances, special statutory provisions. Statutory liability on the part of directors does not relieve shareholders of the duty to make repayment.

A shareholder who receives illegal dividends with knowledge of their illegality is under a duty to refund

**FIGURE 35–4** Liability for Improper Distributions

|  | Corporation Solvent | Corporation Insolvent |
| --- | :---: | :---: |
| **Nonbreaching Director** | No | No |
| **Breaching Director** | Yes | Yes |
| **Knowing Shareholder** | Yes | Yes |
| **Innocent Shareholder** | No | Yes |

them to the corporation. See Section 8.33(b). Where the corporation is insolvent, the shareholder may retain not even a dividend he received in good faith, as the assets of an insolvent corporation are regarded as a trust fund for its creditors. Where an unsuspecting shareholder receives an illegal dividend from a solvent corporation, however, the majority rule is that the corporation cannot compel a refund.

◆ *See Figure 35–4*

# Chapter Summary

## Debt Securities

| **Authority to Issue Debt Securities** | **Definitions**<br>• *Debt Security* source of capital creating no ownership interest and involving the corporation's promise to repay funds lent to it<br>• *Bond* a debt security<br>**Rule** each corporation has the power to issue debt securities as determined by the board of directors |
| --- | --- |
| **Types of Debt Securities** | **Unsecured Bonds** called debentures; have only the obligation of the corporation behind them<br>**Secured Bonds** are claims against a corporation's general assets and also liens on specific property<br>**Income Bonds** condition to some extent the payment of interest on corporate earnings<br>**Participating Bonds** call for a stated percentage of return regardless of earnings, with additional payments dependent upon earnings<br>**Convertible Bonds** may be exchanged for other securities<br>**Callable Bonds** bonds subject to redemption |

## Equity Securities

| **Issuance of Shares** | **Definitions**<br>• *Equity Security* source of capital creating an ownership interest in the corporation<br>• *Share* a proportionate ownership interest in a corporation<br>• *Treasury Stock* shares reacquired by a corporation |
| --- | --- |

**Authority to Issue**  only those shares authorized in the articles of incorporation may be issued

**Preemptive Rights**  right to purchase a *pro rata* share of new stock offerings

**Amount of Consideration for Shares**  shares are deemed fully paid and nonassessable when a corporation receives the consideration for which the board of directors authorized the issuance of the shares, which in the case of par value stock must be at least par

**Payment for Newly Issued Shares**  may be cash, property, and services actually rendered, as determined by the board of directors; under the Revised Act, promises to contribute cash, property, or services are also permitted

## Classes of Shares

**Common Stock**  stock not having any special contract rights

**Preferred Stock**  stock having contractual rights superior to those of common stock

- *Dividend Preferences*  must receive full dividends before any dividend may be paid on common stock
- *Liquidation Preferences*  priority over common stock in corporate assets upon liquidation

**Stock Rights**  contractual right to purchase stock from a corporation

# Dividends and Other Distributions

## Types of Dividends and Other Distributions

**Distributions**  transfers of property by a corporation to any of its shareholders with respect to its shares

**Cash Dividends**  the most common type of distribution

**Property Dividends**  distribution in form of property

**Stock Dividends**  a ratable distribution of additional shares of stock

**Stock Splits**  each of the outstanding shares is broken into a greater number of shares

**Liquidating Dividends**  a distribution of capital assets to shareholders

**Redemption of Shares**  a corporation's exercise of the right to purchase its own shares

**Acquisition of Shares**  a corporation's repurchase of its own shares

## Legal Restrictions on Dividends and Other Distributions

**Legal Restrictions on Cash Dividends**  dividends may be paid only if the cash flow and applicable balance sheet tests are satisfied

- *Cash Flow Test*  a corporation must not be or become insolvent (unable to pay its debts as they become due in the usual course of business)
- *Balance Sheet Test*  varies among the States and includes the earned surplus test (available in all States), the surplus test, and the net assets test (used by the Model and Revised Acts)

**Legal Restrictions on Liquidating Distributions**  States usually permit distribution in partial liquidation from capital surplus unless the company is insolvent

**Legal Restrictions on Redemptions of Shares**  in most States, a corporation may not redeem shares when insolvent or when such redemption would render it insolvent

**Legal Restrictions on Acquisition of Shares**  restrictions similar to those on cash dividends usually apply

| **Declaration and Payment of Distributions** | **Shareholders' Right to Compel a Distribution**  the declaration of distributions is within the discretion of the board of directors, and only rarely will a court substitute its business judgment for that of the board's<br>**Effect of Declaration**  once properly declared, a distribution is considered a debt the corporation owes to the shareholders |
| --- | --- |
| **Liability for Improper Dividends and Distributions** | **Directors**  the directors who assent to an improper dividend are liable for the unlawful amount of the dividend<br>**Shareholders**  a shareholder must return illegal dividends if he knew of the illegality, if the dividend resulted from his fraud, or if the corporation is insolvent |

  # Cases

### CASE 35–1
### Debt Securities
## *METROPOLITAN LIFE INSURANCE COMPANY v. RJR NABISCO, INC.*

United States District Court, S.D. New York, 1989
716 F.Supp. 1504

WALTER, J.

## I. Introduction

The corporate parties to this action are among the country's most sophisticated financial institutions, as familiar with the Wall Street investment community and the securities market as American consumers are with the Oreo cookies and Winston cigarettes made by defendant RJR Nabisco, Inc. (sometimes "the company" or "RJR Nabisco"). The present action traces its origins to October 20, 1988, when F. Ross Johnson, then the Chief Executive Officer of RJR Nabisco, proposed a $17 billion leveraged buy-out ("LBO") of the company's shareholders, at $75 per share. [Court's footnote: "A leveraged buy-out occurs when a group of investors, usually including members of a company's management team, buy the company under financial arrangements that include little equity and significant new debt. The necessary debt financing typically includes mortgages or high risk/high yield bonds, popularly known as "junk bonds." Additionally, a portion of this debt is generally secured by the company's assets. Some of the acquired company's assets are usually sold after the transaction is completed in order to reduce the debt incurred in the acquisition." (See Chapter 37.)] Within a few days, a bidding war developed among the investment group led by Johnson and the investment firm of Kohlberg Kravis Roberts & Co. ("KKR"), and others. On December 1, 1988, a special committee of RJR Nabisco directors, established by the company specifically to consider the competing proposals, recommended that the company accept the KKR proposal, a $24 billion LBO that called for the purchase of the company's outstanding stock at roughly $109 per share.

* * *

Plaintiffs . . . allege, in short, that RJR Nabisco's actions have drastically impaired the value of bonds previously issued to plaintiffs by, in effect, misappropriating the value of those bonds to help finance the LBO and to distribute an enormous windfall to the company's shareholders. As a result, plaintiffs argue, they have unfairly suffered a multimillion dollar loss in the value of their bonds.

* * *

Although the numbers involved in this case are large, and the financing necessary to complete the LBO unprecedented, the legal principles nonetheless remain discrete and familiar. Yet while the instant motions thus primarily require the Court to evaluate and apply traditional rules of equity and contract interpretation, plaintiffs do raise issues of first impression in the context of an LBO. At the heart of the present motions lies plaintiffs' claim that RJR Nabisco violated a restrictive covenant—not an explicit covenant found within the four corners of the relevant bond indentures, but rather an *implied* covenant of good faith and fair dealing—not to incur the debt necessary to facilitate the LBO and thereby betray what plaintiffs claim was the fundamental basis of their bargain with the company. The company, plaintiffs assert, consistently reassured its bondholders that it had a "mandate" from its Board of Directors to maintain RJR Nabisco's preferred credit rating. Plaintiffs ask this Court first to imply a covenant of good faith and fair dealing that would prevent the recent transaction, then to hold that this covenant has been breached, and finally to require RJR Nabisco to redeem their bonds.

RJR Nabisco defends the LBO by pointing to express provisions in the bond indentures that, *inter alia,* permit mergers and the assumption of additional debt. These provisions, as well as others that could have been included but were not, were known to the market and to plaintiffs, sophisticated investors who freely bought the bonds and were equally free to sell them at any time. Any attempt by this Court to create contractual terms *post hoc,* defendants contend, not only finds no basis in the controlling law and undisputed facts of this case, but also would constitute an impermissible invasion into the free and open operation of the marketplace.

For the reasons set forth below, this Court agrees with defendants. There being no express covenant between the parties that would restrict the incurrence of new debt, and no perceived direction to that end from covenants that are express, this Court will not imply a covenant to prevent the recent LBO and thereby create an indenture term that, while bargained for in other contexts, was not bargained for here and was not even within the mutual contemplation of the parties.

## II. Background

\* \* \*

**A. The Parties**  Metropolitan Life Insurance Co. ("MetLife"), incorporated in New York, is a life insurance company that provides pension benefits for 42 million individuals. According to its most recent annual report, MetLife's assets exceed $88 billion and its debt securities holdings exceed $49 billion. [Citation.] MetLife alleges that it owns $340,542,000 in principal amount of six separate RJR Nabisco debt issues, bonds allegedly purchased between July 1975 and July 1988. Some bonds become due as early as this year; others will not become due until 2017. The bonds bear interest rates of anywhere from 8 to 10.25 percent. MetLife also owned 186,000 shares of RJR Nabisco common stock at the time this suit was filed. [Citation.]

Jefferson–Pilot Life Insurance Co. ("Jefferson–Pilot") is a North Carolina company that has more than $3 billion in total assets, $1.5 billion of which are invested in debt securities. Jefferson–Pilot alleges that it owns $9.34 million in principal amount of three separate RJR Nabisco debt issues, allegedly purchased between June 1978 and June 1988. Those bonds, bearing interest rates of anywhere from 8.45 to 10.75 percent, become due in 1993 and 1998. [Citation.]

RJR Nabisco, a Delaware corporation, is a consumer products holding company that owns some of the country's best known product lines, including LifeSavers candy, Oreo cookies, and Winston cigarettes. The company was formed in 1985, when R.J. Reynolds Industries, Inc. ("R.J. Reynolds") merged with Nabisco Brands, Inc. ("Nabisco Brands"). In 1979, and thus before the R.J. Reynolds–Nabisco Brands merger, R.J. Reynolds acquired the Del Monte Corporation ("Del Monte"), which distributes canned fruits and vegetables. From January 1987 until February 1989, codefendant Johnson served as the company's CEO. KKR, a private investment firm, organizes funds through which investors provide pools of equity to finance LBOs. [Citation.]

**B. The Indentures**  The bonds implicated by this suit are governed by long, detailed indentures, which in turn are governed by New York contract law. No one disputes that the holders of public bond issues, like plaintiffs here, often enter the market after the indentures have been negotiated and memorialized. Thus, those indentures are often not the product of face-to-face negotiations between the ultimate holders and the issuing company. What remains equally true, however, is that underwriters ordinarily negotiate the terms of the indentures with the issuers. Since the underwriters must then sell or place the bonds, they necessarily negotiate in part with the interests of the buyers in mind. Moreover, these indentures were not secret agreements foisted upon unwitting participants in the bond market. No successive holder is required to accept or to continue to hold the bonds, governed by their accompanying indentures; indeed, plaintiffs readily admit that they could have sold their bonds right up until the announcement of the LBO. [Citation.] Instead, sophisticated investors like plaintiffs are well aware of the indenture terms and, presumably, review them carefully before lending hundreds of millions of dollars to any company.

Indeed, the prospectuses for the indentures contain a statement relevant to this action:

The Indenture contains no restrictions on the creation of unsecured short-term debt by [RJR Nabisco] or its subsidiaries, no restriction on the creation of unsecured Funded Debt by [RJR Nabisco] or its subsidiaries which are not Restricted Subsidiaries, and no restriction on the payment of dividends by [RJR Nabisco].

Further, as plaintiffs themselves note, the contracts at issue "[do] not impose debt limits, since debt is assumed to be used for productive purposes." [Citation.]

## III. Discussion

\* \* \*

The indentures at issue clearly address the eventuality of a merger. They impose certain related restrictions not at issue in this suit, but no restriction that would prevent the recent RJR Nabisco merger transaction. \* \* \*

\* \* \*

In contracts like bond indentures, "an implied covenant . . . derives its substance directly from the language of the Indenture, and 'cannot give the holders of Debentures any rights inconsistent with those set out in the Indenture.' *[Where] plaintiffs' contractual rights [have not been] violated, there can have been no breach of an implied covenant.*" [Citation.] (emphasis added).

\* \* \*

The appropriate analysis, then, is first to examine the indentures to determine "the fruits of the agreement" between the parties, and then to decide whether those "fruits" have been spoiled—which is to say, whether plaintiffs' contractual rights have been violated by defendants.

\* \* \*

A review of the parties' submissions and the indentures themselves satisfies the Court that the substantive "fruits" guaranteed by those contracts and relevant to the present motions include the periodic and regular payment of interest and the eventual repayment of principal. \* \* \*

It is not necessary to decide that indentures like those at issue could never support a finding of additional benefits, under different circumstances with different parties. Rather, for present purposes, it is sufficient to conclude what obligation is *not* covered, either explicitly or implicitly, by these contracts held by these plaintiffs. Accordingly, this Court holds that the "fruits" of these indentures do not include an implied restrictive covenant that would prevent the incurrence of new debt to facilitate the recent LBO. To hold otherwise would permit these plaintiffs to straightjacket the company in order to guarantee their investment. These plaintiffs do not invoke an implied covenant of good faith to protect a legitimate, mutually contemplated benefit of the indentures; rather, they seek to have this Court create an additional benefit for which they did not bargain.

\* \* \*

The sort of unbounded and one-sided elasticity urged by plaintiffs would interfere with and destabilize the market. And this Court, like the parties to these contracts, cannot ignore or disavow the marketplace in which the contract is performed. Nor can it ignore the expectations of that market—expectations, for instance, that the terms of an indenture will be upheld, and that a court will not, *sua sponte,* add new substantive terms to that indenture as it sees fit. The Court has no reason to believe that the market, in evaluating bonds such as those at issue here, did not discount for the possibility that any company, even one the size of RJR Nabisco, might engage in an LBO heavily financed by debt. That the bonds did not lose any of their value until the October 20, 1988 announcement of a possible RJR Nabisco LBO only suggests that the market had theretofore evaluated the risks of such a transaction as slight.

\* \* \*

[Judgment for defendant on count of breach of implied covenant.]

## CASE 35–2
## Legal Restrictions on Distributions
# KLANG v. SMITH'S FOOD & DRUG CENTERS, INC.
Supreme Court of Delaware, 1997
702 A.2d 150

**VEASEY, C.J.**

This appeal calls into question the actions of a corporate board in carrying out a merger and self-tender offer. Plaintiff in this purported class action alleges that a corporation's repurchase of shares violated the statutory prohibition against the impairment of capital. * * *

No corporation may repurchase or redeem its own shares except out of "surplus," as statutorily defined, or except as expressly authorized by provisions of the statute not relevant here. Balance sheets are not, however, conclusive indicators of surplus or a lack thereof. Corporations may revalue assets to show surplus, but perfection in that process is not required. Directors have reasonable latitude to depart from the balance sheet to calculate surplus, so long as they evaluate assets and liabilities in good faith, on the basis of acceptable data, by methods that they reasonably believe reflect present values, and arrive at a determination of the surplus that is not so far off the mark as to constitute actual or constructive fraud.

We hold that, on this record, the Court of Chancery was correct in finding that there was no impairment of capital * * *. Accordingly, we affirm.

## Facts

Smith's Food & Drug Centers, Inc. ("SFD") is a Delaware corporation that owns and operates a chain of supermarkets in the Southwestern United States. Slightly more than three years ago, Jeffrey P. Smith, SFD's Chief Executive Officer, began to entertain suitors with an interest in acquiring SFD. At the time, and until the transactions at issue, Mr. Smith and his family held common and preferred stock constituting 62.1% voting control of SFD. Plaintiff and the class he purports to represent are holders of common stock in SFD.

On January 29, 1996, SFD entered into an agreement with The Yucaipa Companies ("Yucaipa"), a California partnership also active in the supermarket industry. Under the agreement, the following would take place:

(1) Smitty's Supermarkets, Inc. ("Smitty's"), a wholly-owned subsidiary of Yucaipa that operated a supermarket chain in Arizona, was to merge into Cactus

Acquisition, Inc. ("Cactus"), a subsidiary of SFD, in exchange for which SFD would deliver to Yucaipa slightly over 3 million newly-issued shares of SFD common stock;

(2) SFD was to undertake a recapitalization, in the course of which SFD would assume a sizable amount of new debt, retire old debt, and offer to repurchase up to fifty percent of its outstanding shares (other than those issued to Yucaipa) for $36 per share; and

(3) SFD was to repurchase 3 million shares of preferred stock from Jeffrey Smith and his family.

SFD hired the investment firm of Houlihan Lokey Howard & Zukin ("Houlihan") to examine the transactions and render a solvency opinion. Houlihan eventually issued a report to the SFD Board replete with assurances that the transactions would not endanger SFD's solvency, and would not impair SFD's capital in violation of 8 Del.C. § 160. On May 17, 1996, in reliance on the Houlihan opinion, SFD's Board determined that there existed sufficient surplus to consummate the transactions, and enacted a resolution proclaiming as much. On May 23, 1996, SFD's stockholders voted to approve the transactions, which closed on that day. The self-tender offer was over-subscribed, so SFD repurchased fully fifty percent of its shares at the offering price of $36 per share.

* * *

## Plaintiff's Capital-Impairment Claim

A corporation may not repurchase its shares if, in so doing, it would cause an impairment of capital. [Citation.] A repurchase impairs capital if the funds used in the repurchase exceed the amount of the corporation's "surplus," defined by 8 Del.C. § 154 to mean the excess of net assets over the par value of the corporation's issued stock. [Citation.]

Plaintiff asked the Court of Chancery to rescind the transactions in question as violative of Section 160. As we understand it, plaintiff's position breaks down into two analytically distinct arguments. First, he contends that SFD's balance sheets constitute conclusive evidence of capital impairment. He argues that the negative net worth that appeared on SFD's books following the re-purchase compels us to find a violation of Section 160. Second, he suggests that even allowing the Board to "go behind the balance sheet" to calculate surplus does not save the transactions from violating Section 160. In connection with this claim, he attacks the SFD Board's off-balance-sheet method of calculating surplus on the theory that it does not adequately take into account all of SFD's assets and liabilities. * * * We hold that each of these claims is without merit.

## SFD's balance sheets do not establish a violation of 8 Del.C. § 160

In an April 25, 1996 proxy statement, the SFD Board released a pro forma balance sheet showing that the merger and self-tender offer would result in a deficit to surplus on SFD's books of more than $100 million. A balance sheet the SFD Board issued shortly after the transactions confirmed this result. Plaintiff asks us to adopt an interpretation of 8 Del.C. § 160 whereby balance-sheet net worth is controlling for purposes of determining compliance with the statute. [Citation.] Defendants do not dispute that SFD's books showed a negative net worth in the wake of its transactions with Yucaipa, but argue that corporations should have the presumptive right to revalue assets and liabilities to comply with Section 160.

Plaintiff advances an erroneous interpretation of Section 160. We understand that the books of a corporation do not necessarily reflect the current values of its assets and liabilities. Among other factors, unrealized appreciation or depreciation can render book numbers inaccurate. It is unrealistic to hold that a corporation is bound by its balance sheets for purposes of determining compliance with Section 160. Accordingly, we adhere to the principles of [citation] allowing corporations to revalue properly its assets and liabilities to show a surplus and thus conform to the statute.

It is helpful to recall the purpose behind Section 160. The General Assembly enacted the statute to prevent boards from draining corporations of assets to the detriment of creditors and the long-term health of the corporation. [Citation.] That a corporation has not yet realized or reflected on its balance sheet the appreciation of assets is irrelevant to this concern. Regardless of what a balance sheet that has not been updated may show, an actual, though unrealized, appreciation reflects real economic value that the corporation may borrow against or that creditors may claim or levy upon. Allowing corporations to revalue assets and liabilities to reflect current realities complies with the statute and serves well the policies behind this statute.

## The SFD Board appropriately revalued corporate assets to comply with 8 Del.C. § 160

\* \* \*

On May 17, 1996, Houlihan released its solvency opinion to the SFD Board, expressing its judgment that the merger and self-tender offer would not impair SFD's capital. Houlihan reached this conclusion by comparing SFD's "Total Invested Capital" of $1.8 billion—a figure Houlihan arrived at by valuing SFD's assets under the "market multiple" approach—with SFD's long-term debt of $1.46 billion. This comparison yielded an approximation of SFD's "concluded equity value" equal to $346 million, a figure clearly in excess of the outstanding par value of SFD's stock. Thus, Houlihan concluded, the transactions would not violate 8 Del.C. § 160.

\* \* \*

The record contains, in the form of the Houlihan opinion, substantial evidence that the transactions complied with Section 160. Plaintiff has provided no reason to distrust Houlihan's analysis. In cases alleging impairment of capital under Section 160, the trial court may defer to the board's measurement of surplus unless a plaintiff can show that the directors "failed to fulfill their duty to evaluate the assets on the basis of acceptable data and by standards which they are entitled to believe reasonably reflect present values." [Citation.] In the absence of bad faith or fraud on the part of the board, courts will not "substitute [our] concepts of wisdom for that of the directors." [Citation.] Here, plaintiff does not argue that the SFD Board acted in bad faith. Nor has he met his burden of showing that the methods and data that underlay the board's analysis are unreliable or that its determination of surplus is so far off the mark as to constitute actual or constructive fraud. [Court's footnote: We interpret 8 Del.C. § 172 to entitle boards to rely on experts such as Houlihan to determine compliance with 8 Del.C. § 160. Plaintiff has not alleged that the SFD Board failed to exercise reasonable care in selecting Houlihan, nor that rendering a solvency opinion is outside Houlihan's realm of competence. Compare 8 Del.C. § 141(e) (providing that directors may rely in good faith on records, reports, experts, etc.).] Therefore, we defer to the board's determination of surplus, and hold that SFD's self-tender offer did not violate 8 Del.C. § 160.

\* \* \*

The judgment of the Court of Chancery is affirmed.

## CASE 35-3
## Declaration of Dividends
### *DODGE v. FORD MOTOR CO.*
Supreme Court of Michigan, 1919
204 Mich. 459, 170 N.W. 668

OSTRANDER, J.

[Action in equity by John F. and Horace E. Dodge, plaintiffs, against the Ford Motor Company and its directors to compel the declaration of dividends and for an injunction restraining a contemplated expansion of the business. The complaint was filed in November 1916. Since 1909, the capital stock of the company has been $2,000,000, divided into 20,000 shares of a par value of $100 each, of which plaintiffs held 2,000. As of the close of business on July 31, 1916, the end of the company's fiscal year, the surplus above capital was $111,960,907.53 and the assets included cash on hand of $52,550,771.92.

For a number of years the company had regularly paid quarterly dividends equal to sixty percent annually on the capital stock of $2,000,000. In addition, from December 1911 to October 1915, inclusive, eleven special dividends totaling $41,000,000 had been paid, and in November 1916, after this action was commenced, a special dividend of $2,000,000 was paid.

Plaintiffs' complaint alleged that Henry Ford, president of the company and a member of its board of directors, had declared it to be the settled policy of the company not to pay any special dividends in the future but to put back into the business all future earnings in excess of the regular quarterly dividend. Plaintiffs sought an injunction restraining the carrying out of the alleged declared policy of Henry Ford and a decree requiring the directors to pay a dividend of at least seventy-five percent of the accumulated cash surplus.

In December 1917, the trial court entered a decree requiring the directors to declare and pay a dividend of $19,275,385.96 and enjoining the corporation from using its funds for a proposed smelting plant and certain other planned projects. From this decree, defendants have appealed.]

\* \* \*

The case for plaintiffs must rest upon the claim, and the proof in support of it, that the proposed expansion of the business of the corporation involving the further use of profits as capital, ought to be enjoined because inimical to the best interests of the company and its shareholders, and upon the further claim that in any event the withholding of the special dividend asked for by plaintiffs is arbitrary action of the directors requiring judicial interference.

The rule which will govern courts in deciding these questions is not in dispute. . . . In [citation], it is stated:

Profits earned by a corporation may be divided among its shareholders; but it is not a violation of the charter if they are allowed to accumulate and remain invested in the company's business. The managing agents of a corporation are impliedly invested with a discretionary power with regard to the time and manner of distributing its profits. They may apply profits in payment of floating or funded debts, or in development of the company's business; and so long as they do not abuse their discretionary powers, or violate the company's charter, the courts cannot interfere.

But it is clear that the agents of a corporation, and even the majority, cannot arbitrarily withhold profits earned by the company, or apply them to any use which is not authorized by the company's charter. The nominal capital of a company does not necessarily limit the scope of its operations; a corporation may borrow money for the purpose of enlarging its business, and in many instances it may use profits for the same purpose. . . .

When plaintiffs made their complaint and demand for further dividends the Ford Motor Company had concluded its most prosperous year of business. The demand for its cars at the price of the preceding year continued. It could make and could market in the year beginning August 1, 1916, more than 500,000 cars. Sales of parts and repairs would necessarily increase. The cost of materials was likely to advance, and perhaps the price of labor, but it reasonably might have expected a profit for the year of upwards of $60,000,000. It had assets of more than $132,000,000, a surplus of almost $112,000,000, and its cash on hand and municipal bonds were nearly $54,000,000. Its total liabilities, including capital stock, was a little over $20,000,000. It had declared no special dividend during the business year except the October, 1915, dividend. It had been the practice, under similar circumstances, to declare larger dividends. Considering only these facts, a refusal to declare and pay further dividends appears to be not an exercise of discretion on the part of the directors, but an arbitrary refusal to do what the circumstances required to be done. These facts and others call upon the directors to justify their action, or failure or refusal to act. In justification, the defendants have offered testimony tending to prove, and which does prove, the following facts. It had been the policy of the corporation for a considerable time to annually reduce the selling price of cars, while keeping up, or improving their quality. As early as in June 1915 a general plan for the expansion of the productive capacity of the concern by a practical duplication of its plant had been talked over by the executive officers and directors and agreed upon, not all of the details having been settled and no formal action of directors having been taken. The erection of a smelter was considered, and engineering and other data in connection therewith secured. In consequence, it was determined not to reduce the selling price of cars for the year beginning August 1, 1915, but to maintain the price and to accumulate a large surplus to pay for the proposed expansion of plant and equipment, and perhaps to build a plant for smelting ore. It is hoped, by Mr. Ford, that eventually 1,000,000 cars will be annually produced. The contemplated changes will permit the increased output.

The plan, as affecting the profits of the business for the year beginning August 1, 1916, and thereafter, calls for a reduction in the selling price of cars. . . . In short, the plan does not call for and is not intended to produce immediately a more profitable business but a less profitable one; not only less profitable than formerly but less profitable than it is admitted it might be made. The apparent immediate effect will be to diminish the value of shares and the return to shareholders.

It is the contention of plaintiffs that the apparent effect of the plan is intended to be the continued and continuing effect of it and that it is deliberately proposed, not of record and not by official corporate declaration, but nevertheless proposed, to continue the corporation henceforth as a semi-eleemosynary institution and not as a business institution. In support of this contention they point to the attitude and to the expressions of Mr. Henry Ford.

Mr. Henry Ford is the dominant force in the business of the Ford Motor Company. No plan of operations could be adopted unless he consented, and no board of directors can be elected whom he does not favor. One of the directors of the company has no stock. One share was assigned to him to qualify him for the position, but it is not claimed that he owns it. A business, one of the largest in the world, and one of the most profitable, has been built up. It employs many men, at good pay.

"My ambition," said Mr. Ford, "is to employ still more men, to spread the benefits of this industrial system to the greatest possible number, to help them build up their lives and their homes. To do this we are putting the greatest share of our profits back in the business." * * *

The record, and especially the testimony of Mr. Ford, convinces that he has to some extent the attitude towards shareholders of one who has dispensed and distributed to them large gains and that they should be content to take what he chooses to give. His testimony creates the impression, also, that he thinks the Ford Motor Company has made too much money, has had too large profits, and that although large profits might still be earned, a sharing of them with the public, by reducing the price of the output of the company, ought to be undertaken. We have no doubt that certain sentiments, philanthropic and altruistic, creditable to Mr. Ford, had large influence in determining the policy to be pursued by the Ford Motor Company—the policy which has been herein referred to. * * *

These cases, after all, like all others in which the subject is treated, turn finally upon the point, the question, whether it appears that the directors were not acting for the best interest of the corporation. . . . The difference between an incidental humanitarian expenditure of corporate funds for the benefit of the employees, like the building of a hospital for their use and the employment of agencies for the betterment of their condition, and a general purpose and plan to benefit mankind at the expense of others, is obvious. . . . A business corporation is organized and carried on primarily for the profit of the stockholders. The powers of the directors are to be employed for that end. The discretion of directors is to be exercised in the choice of means to attain that end and does not extend to a change in the end itself, to the reduction of profits or to the nondistribution of profits among stockholders in order to devote them to other purposes. * * *

We are not, however, persuaded that we should interfere with the proposed expansion of the business of the Ford Motor Company. In view of the fact that the selling price of products may be increased at any time, the ultimate results of the larger business cannot be certainly estimated. The judges are not business experts. It is recognized that plans must often be made for a long future, for expected competition, for a continuing as well as an immediately profitable venture. The experience of the Ford Motor Company is evidence of capable management of its affairs. * * *

Defendants say, and it is true, that a considerable cash balance must be at all times carried by such a concern. But, as has been stated, there was a large daily, weekly, monthly, receipt of cash. The output was practically continuous and was continuously, and within a few days, turned into cash. Moreover, the contemplated expenditures were not to be immediately made. The large sum appropriated for the smelter plant was payable over a considerable period of time. So that, without going further, it would appear that, accepting and approving the plan of the directors, it was their duty to distribute on or near the first of August, 1916, a very large sum of money to stockholders. * * *

The decree of the court below fixing and determining the specific amount to be distributed to stockholders is affirmed. In other respects, except as to the allowance of costs, the said decree is reversed.

# Questions

1. Distinguish between equity and debt securities.
2. Identify and describe the principal kinds of debt securities.
3. Identify and describe the principal kinds of equity securities.
4. Explain what type and amount of consideration a corporation may validly receive for the shares it issues.
5. Explain the legal restrictions imposed upon dividends and other distributions.

# Problems

1. Olympic National Agencies was organized with an authorized capitalization of preferred stock and common stock. The articles of incorporation provided for a 7 percent annual dividend for the preferred stock. The articles further stated that the preferred stock would be given priority interests in the corporation's assets up to the par value of the stock. Subsequently, the shareholders voted to dissolve Olympic. Because Olympic's assets greatly exceeded its liabilities, the liquidating trustee petitioned the court for instructions on the respective rights of the shareholders in the assets of the corporation upon dissolution. Decision?

2. The XYZ Corporation was duly organized on July 10. Its certificate of incorporation provides for total authorized capital of $100,000, consisting of 1,000 shares of common stock with a par value of $100 per share. The corporation issues for cash a total of 50 certificates, numbered 1 to 50 inclusive, representing various amounts of shares in the names of various individuals. The shares were all paid for in advance, so the certificates are all dated and mailed on the same day. The 50 certificates of stock represent a total of 1,050 shares. Certificate 49 for 30 shares was issued to Jane Smith. Certificate 50 for 25 shares was issued to William Jones. Is the validity of the stock thus issued in any way questionable? What are the rights of Smith and Jones?

3. Doris subscribed for 200 shares of 12 percent cumulative, participating, redeemable, convertible, preferred shares of the Ritz Hotel Company with a par value of $100 per share. The subscription agreement provided that she was to receive a bonus of one share of common stock of $100 par value for each share of preferred stock. Doris fully paid her subscription agreement of $20,000 and received the 200 shares of preferred and the bonus stock of 200 shares of the par value common. The Ritz Hotel Co. later becomes insolvent. Ronald, the receiver of the corporation, brings suit for $20,000, the par value of the common stock. What judgment?

4. The Hyperion Company has an authorized capital stock of 1,000 shares with a par value of $100 per share, of which 900 shares, all fully paid, are outstanding. Having an ample surplus, the Hyperion Company purchases from its shareholders 100 shares at par. Subsequently, the Hyperion Company, needing additional working capital, issues the 200 shares in question to Alexander at $80 per share. Two years later, the Hyperion Company is forced into bankruptcy. The trustee in bankruptcy now sues Alexander for $4,000. Decision?

5. For five years, Henry and James had been engaged as partners in building houses. They owned the equipment necessary to conduct the business and had an excellent reputation. In March, Joyce, who had previously been in the same kind of business, proposed that Henry, James, and Joyce form a corporation for the purpose of constructing medium-priced houses. They engaged attorney Portia, who did all the work required to incorporate the business under the name of Libra Corp.

The certificate of incorporation authorized 100 shares of $100 par value stock. At the organizational meeting of the incorporators, Henry, James, and Joyce were elected directors, and Libra Corp. issued a total of 65 shares for its stock. Henry and James each received 20 shares in consideration of transferring to Libra Corp. the equipment and goodwill of their partnership, which had a combined value of more than $4,000. Joyce received 20 shares in consideration for promising to work for Libra Corp. in the future, and Portia received 5 shares as compensation for the legal services she rendered in forming Libra Corp.

Later that year, Libra Corp. suffered several financial setbacks and in December ceased operations. What rights, if any, does Libra Corp. have against Henry, James, Joyce, and Portia in connection with the original issuance of its shares?

**6.** Paul Bunyan is the owner of noncumulative 8 percent preferred stock in the Broadview Corporation, which had no earnings or profits in 1997. In 1998, the corporation had large profits and a surplus from which it might properly have declared dividends. The directors refused to do so, however, instead using the surplus to purchase goods necessary for the corporation's expanding business. The corporation earned a small profit in 1999. The directors at the end of 1999 declared a 10 percent dividend on the common stock and an 8 percent dividend on the preferred stock without paying preferred dividends for 1998.

(a) Is Bunyan entitled to dividends for 1997? For 1998?

(b) Is Bunyan entitled to a dividend of 10 percent rather than 8 percent in 1999?

**7.** Alpha Corporation has outstanding 400 shares of $100 par value common stock, which has been issued and sold at $105 per share for a total of $42,000. Alpha is incorporated in State X, which has adopted the earned surplus test for all distributions. At a time when the assets of the corporation amount to $65,000 and the liabilities to creditors total $10,000, the directors learn that Rachel, who holds 100 of the 400 shares of stock, is planning to sell her shares on the open market for $10,500. Believing that this will not be in the best interest of the corporation, the directors enter into an agreement with Rachel to buy the shares for $10,500 from her. About six months later, when the assets of the corporation have decreased to $50,000 and its liabilities, not including its liability to Rachel, have increased to $20,000, the directors use $10,000 to pay a dividend to all of the shareholders. The corporation later becomes insolvent.

(a) Does Rachel have any liability to the corporation or its creditors in connection with the reacquisition by the corporation of the 100 shares?

(b) Was the payment of the $10,000 dividend proper?

**8.** Almega Corporation, organized under the laws of State S, has outstanding 20,000 shares of $100 par value nonvoting preferred stock calling for noncumulative dividends of $5 per year; 10,000 shares of voting preferred stock with $50 par value, calling for cumulative dividends of $2.50 per year; and 10,000 shares of no par common stock. State S has adopted the earned surplus test for all distributions. As of the end of 1994, the corporation had no earned surplus. In 1995, the corporation had net earnings of $170,000; in 1996, $135,000; in 1997, $60,000; in 1998, $210,000; and in 1999, $120,000. The board of directors passed over all dividends during the four years from 1995 to 1998, because the company needed working capital for expansion purposes. In 1999, however, the directors declared on the

noncumulative preferred shares a dividend of $5 per share, on the cumulative preferred stock a dividend of $12.50 per share, and on the common stock a dividend of $30 per share. The board submitted its declaration to the voting shareholders, and they ratified it. Before the dividends were paid, Payne, the record holder of 500 shares of the noncumulative preferred stock, brought an appropriate action to restrain any payment to the cumulative preferred or common shareholders until the company paid to noncumulative preferred shareholders a full dividend for the period from 1995 to 1998. Decision? What is the maximum lawful dividend that may be paid to each share of common stock?

**9.** Sayre learned that Adams, Boone, and Chase were planning to form a corporation for the purpose of manufacturing and marketing a line of novelties to wholesale outlets. Sayre had patented a self-locking gas tank cap but lacked the financial backing to market it profitably. He negotiated with Adams, Boone, and Chase, who agreed to purchase the patent rights for $5,000 in cash and 200 shares of $100 par value preferred stock in a corporation to be formed.

The corporation was formed and Sayre's stock issued to him, but the corporation has refused to make the cash payment. It has also refused to declare dividends, although the business has been very profitable because of Sayre's patent and has a substantial earned surplus with a large cash balance on hand. It is selling the remainder of the originally authorized issue of preferred shares, ignoring Sayre's demand to purchase a proportionate number of these shares. What are Sayre's rights, if any?

**10.** Wood, the receiver of Stanton Oil Company, sued Stanton's shareholders to recover dividends paid to them for three years, claiming that at the time these dividends were declared, Stanton was in fact insolvent. Wood did not allege that the present creditors were also creditors when the dividends were paid. Decision?

**11.** International Distributing Export Company (I.D.E.) was organized as a corporation on September 7, 1948, under the laws of New York and commenced business on November 1, 1948. I.D.E. formerly had been in existence as an individual proprietorship. On October 31, 1948, the newly organized corporation had liabilities of $64,084. Its only assets, in the sum of $33,042, were those of the former sole proprietorship. The corporation, however, set up an asset on its balance sheet in the amount of $32,000 for goodwill. As a result of this entry, I.D.E. had a surplus at the end of each of its fiscal years from 1949 until 1954. Cano, a shareholder, received $7,144 in dividends from I.D.E. during the period from 1950 to 1955. Fried, the trustee in bankruptcy of I.D.E., brought an action against Cano to recover the amount of these dividends, alleging that they had been paid when I.D.E. was insolvent or when its capital was impaired. Decision?

**12.** GM Sub Corporation ("GM Sub"), a subsidiary of Grand Metropolitan Limited, acquired all outstanding shares of Liggett Group, Inc., a Delaware corporation. Rothschild International Corporation ("Rothschild") was the owner of

650 shares of the 7 percent cumulative preferred stock of Liggett Group, Inc. According to Liggett's certificate of incorporation, the holders of the 7 percent preferred were to receive $100 per share "in the event of any liquidation of the assets of the Corporation." GM Sub had offered $70 per share for the 7 percent preferred, $158.63 for another class of preferred stock, and $69 for each common stock share. Liggett's board of directors approved the offer as fair and recommended acceptance by Liggett's shareholders. As a result, 39.8 percent of the 7 percent preferred shares was sold to GM Sub. In addition, GM Sub acquired 75.9 percent of the other preferred stock and 87.4 percent of the common stock. The acquisition of the overwhelming majority of these classes of stock—coupled with the fact that the 7 percent preferred shareholders could not vote as a class on the merger proposal—gave GM Sub sufficient voting power to approve a follow-up merger. As a result, all remaining shareholders other than GM Sub were eliminated in return for payment of cash for their shares. These shareholders received the same consideration ($70 per share) offered in the tender offer.

Rothschild brought suit against Liggett and Grand Metropolitan, charging each with a breach of its duty of fair dealing owed to the 7 percent preferred shareholders. Rothschild based both claims on the contention that the merger was a liquidation of Liggett insofar as the rights of the 7 percent preferred stockholders were concerned and that those preferred shareholders therefore were entitled to the liquidation preference of $100 per share, not $70 per share. Decision?

**Internet Exercise** Using the Securities and Exchange Commission's EDGAR database, find the Annual Report (Form 10-K) and, if necessary, the proxy statement (DEF 14A) of three companies of interest and determine with respect to their common stock: (a) on which exchanges it is listed, (b) earnings for the most recent quarter, (c) annual dividends, and (d) the high and low price for the stock over the previous 52-week period.

# CHAPTER 36

# Management Structure

The corporate management structure, as required by State incorporation statutes, is pyramidal. At the base of the pyramid are the *shareholders,* who are the residual owners of the corporation. Basic to their role in controlling the corporation is the right to elect representatives to manage the ordinary business matters of the corporation and the right to approve all extraordinary matters.

The *board of directors,* as the shareholders' elected representatives, are delegated the power to manage the business of the corporation. Directors exercise dominion and control over the corporation, hold positions of trust and confidence, and determine questions of operating policy. Because they are not expected to devote their time completely to the affairs of the corporation, directors have broad authority to delegate power to agents and to *officers* who hold their offices at the will of the board and who, in turn, hire and fire all necessary operating personnel and run the day-to-day affairs of the corporation.

◆ *See Figure 36–1*

## CORPORATE GOVERNANCE

The statutory model of corporate management, although required by most States, accurately describes the actual governance of only a few corporations. A great majority of corporations are closely held; they have a small number of stockholders and no ready market for their shares, and most of the shareholders actively participate in the management of the business. Typically, the shareholders of a closely held corporation are also its directors and officers.

Although the statutory model and the actual governance of closely held corporations diverge, in most States closely held corporations must adhere to the general corporate statutory model. One of the greatest burdens

conventional general business corporation statutes impose on closely held corporations is a set of rigid corporate formalities. Although these formalities may be necessary and desirable in publicly held corporations, where management and ownership are separate, in a closely held corporation, where the owners are usually the managers, many of these formalities are unnecessary and meaningless. Consequently, shareholders in closely held corporations tend to disregard corporate formalities, sometimes forfeiting their limited liability as a result. In response to this problem, the 1969 Amendments to the Model Business Corporation Act (MBCA) included several liberalizing provisions for closely held corporations. The amendments were carried over to the Revised Act. Moreover, a number of States have enacted special legislation to accommodate the needs of closely held corporations, and, as noted in Chapter 34, a Statutory Close Corporation Supplement (the Supplement) to the Model and Revised Acts has been promulgated.

The Supplement relaxes the most nonessential corporate formalities by permitting operation without a board of directors, authorizing broad use of shareholder agreements (including their use in place of bylaws), making annual meetings optional, and authorizing one person to execute documents in more than one capacity. Most important, it prevents courts from denying limited liability simply because the corporation is a statutory close corporation. The general incorporation statute applies to closely held corporations except to the extent that it is inconsistent with the Supplement.

In sharp contrast is the large, publicly held corporation with a vast market for its shares. These shares typically are widely dispersed, and very few are owned by management. Approximately one-half are held by institutional investors (such as insurance companies, pension funds, mutual funds, and trusts), which manage funds for individual investors; the remaining shares are owned directly by individual investors. Whereas a great majority of institutional investors exercise their right to vote their shares, most individual investors do not. Nonetheless, virtually all shareholders who vote for the directors do so through the use of a **proxy**—an authorization by a shareholder to an agent (usually the chief executive officer of the corporation) to vote his shares. The majority of shareholders who return their proxies vote as management advises. As a result, incumbent management prevails in nearly all elections and actually determines its own membership.

Thus, the 500 to 1,000 large, publicly held corporations—which own the great bulk of the industrial wealth of the United States—are controlled by a small group of corporate officers. This great concentration of control over wealth, and the power that results from it, raises social, policy, and ethical issues concerning the governance of these corporations and the accountability of their management. The actions (or inactions) of these powerful corporations greatly affect the national economy, employment policies, the health and safety of the workplace and the environment, product quality, and the effects of overseas operations.

Accordingly, the accountability of management is a critical issue. In particular, what obligations should the large, publicly held corporation and its management have to (1) the corporation's shareholders, (2) its employees, (3) its customers, (4) its suppliers, (5) the communities in which the corporation is located, and (6) the rest of society? These critical questions remain mostly unanswered. Some corporate statutes now provide that the board of directors, committees of the board, individual directors, and individual officers *may,* in determining the corporation's best interests, consider the effects of any action upon employees, suppliers, creditors, and customers of the corporation; the communities in which the corporation maintains offices or other establishments; the economy of the State and nation; societal considerations; and all other pertinent factors.

Nevertheless, the structure and governance of corporations must adhere to incorporation statute requirements. Therefore, this chapter will discuss the rights, duties, and liabilities of shareholders, directors, and officers under these statutes.

◆ *See Figures 36–2 and 36–3*

## ROLE OF SHAREHOLDERS

The role of the shareholders in managing the corporation is generally restricted to the election of directors, the approval of certain extraordinary matters, the approval of corporate transactions that are void or voidable unless ratified, and the right to bring suits to enforce these rights.

## *VOTING RIGHTS OF SHAREHOLDERS*

The shareholder's right to vote is fundamental both to the corporate concept and to the corporation's management structure. In most States today, a shareholder is entitled to one vote for each share of stock that she owns, unless the articles of incorporation provide otherwise. In addition, incorporation statutes generally permit the issuance of one or more classes of nonvoting stock, so long as at least one class of shares has voting rights. Section 6.01. The articles of incorporation may provide for more or less than one vote for any share. For example, in *Providence & Worcester Co. v. Baker,* 378 A.2d 121 (Del. 1977), the court upheld articles of incorporation which provided that each shareholder was entitled to one vote per share for each of fifty or fewer shares that he owned and one vote for every twenty shares in excess of fifty, but no shareholder was entitled to vote more than one-fourth of the whole number of outstanding shares.

### Shareholder Meetings

Shareholders may exercise their voting rights at both annual and special shareholder meetings. **Annual meetings** are required and must be held at a time fixed by the bylaws. Section 7.01. If the annual shareholder meeting is not held within the earlier of six months after the end of the corporation's fiscal year or fifteen months after its last annual meeting, any shareholder may petition and obtain a court order requiring such meeting to be held. Section 7.03. The Revised Act further provides that the failure to hold an annual meeting does not affect the validity of any corporate action. Section 7.01(c). In contrast, the Close Corporation Supplement provides that no annual meeting of shareholders need be held unless a shareholder makes a written request at least thirty days in advance of the date specified for the meeting. The date may be established in the articles of incorporation, in the bylaws, or in a shareholders' agreement.

**Special meetings** may be called by the board of directors, by holders of at least 10 percent of the shares, or by other persons authorized to do so in the articles of incorporation. Section 7.02.

Written notice, stating the date, time, and place of the meeting and, in the case of a special meeting, the purposes for which it is called, must be given in advance

**FIGURE 36–1**  Management Structure of Corporations: The Statutory Model

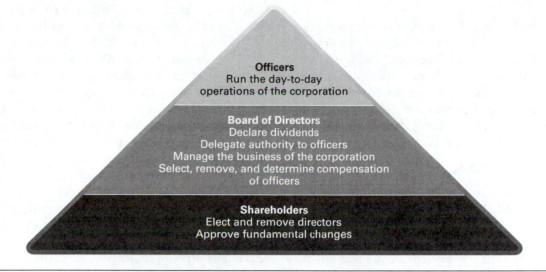

**Officers**
Run the day-to-day
operations of the corporation

**Board of Directors**
Declare dividends
Delegate authority to officers
Manage the business of the corporation
Select, remove, and determine compensation
of officers

**Shareholders**
Elect and remove directors
Approve fundamental changes

**FIGURE 36–2**  Management Structure of Typical Closely Held Corporation

**Shareholders = Directors = Officers**

**FIGURE 36–3**  Management Structure of Typical Publicly Held Corporation

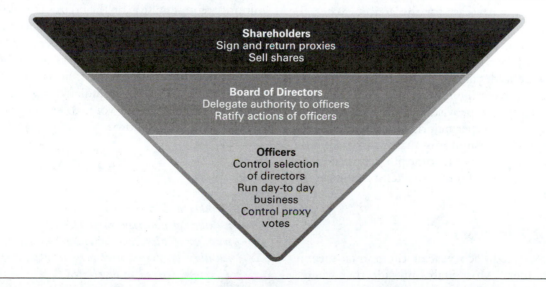

**Shareholders**
Sign and return proxies
Sell shares

**Board of Directors**
Delegate authority to officers
Ratify actions of officers

**Officers**
Control selection
of directors
Run day-to day
business
Control proxy
votes

of the meeting. Section 7.05. Notice, however, may be waived in writing by any shareholder entitled to notice. Section 7.06.

A number of States permit shareholders to conduct business without a meeting if they consent unanimously in writing to the action taken. Section 7.04. Some States have further relaxed the formalities of shareholder action by permitting shareholders to act without a meeting simply by obtaining the written consent of the number of shares required to act on the matter.

## Quorum and Voting

To effectuate corporate business, a quorum of shares must be represented at the meeting, either in person or by proxy. Unissued shares and treasury stock may not be voted or counted in determining whether a quorum exists. Once a quorum is present at a meeting, it is deemed present for the rest of the meeting, even if shareholders withdraw in an effort to break it. Unless the articles of incorporation otherwise provide, a majority of shares entitled to vote constitutes a **quorum.** In most States and under the Model Act, a quorum may not consist of less than one-third of the shares entitled to vote; the Revised Act and some States do not provide a statutory minimum for a quorum. State statutes do not impose an upper limit upon a quorum, so it may be set higher than a majority and may even require *all* the outstanding shares.

Most States require shareholder actions to be approved by a majority of shares represented at the meeting and entitled to vote. The Revised Act and some States, however, provide a different rule: if a quorum exists, a shareholder action (other than the election of directors) is approved if the votes cast for the action exceed the votes cast against it. Section 7.25(c). Moreover, virtually all States permit the articles of incorporation to increase the percentage of shares required to take any action that is subject to shareholder approval. Section 7.27. A provision that increases voting requirements is commonly called a "supermajority provision." Close corporations frequently have used supermajority shareholder voting requirements to protect minority shareholders from oppression by the majority, while some publicly held corporations recently have used them to defend against hostile takeover bids.

## Election of Directors

Directors are elected each year at the annual meeting of the shareholders. Most States provide that where a corporation's board consists of nine or more directors, the charter or bylaws may provide for a **classification** of directors, that is, a division into two or three classes to be as nearly equal in number as possible and to serve for staggered terms. Section 8.06. If the directors are divided into two classes, the members of each class are elected once a year in alternate years for a two-year term; if divided into three classes, they are elected for three-year terms. This permits one-half of the board to be elected every two years or one-third to be elected every three years, thus lending continuity to the board's membership. Moreover, where there are two or more classes of shares, the courts generally have held that each class may elect a specified number of directors, if the articles of incorporation so provide. The Revised Act makes this explicit. Section 8.04.

*Straight Voting* Normally, each shareholder has one vote for each share owned, and under the Revised Act and many State statutes directors are elected by a *plurality* of the votes. Section 7.28(a). The charter may increase the percentage of shares required for the election of directors.

*Cumulative Voting* In certain States shareholders have the right of cumulative voting when electing directors. In most of these States and under the Revised Act, cumulative voting is permissive, not mandatory. Section 7.28(b). **Cumulative voting** entitles the shareholders to multiply the number of votes they are entitled to cast by the number of directors for whom they are entitled to vote and to cast the product for a single candidate or distribute the product among two or more candidates. Cumulative voting permits a minority shareholder, or a group of minority shareholders acting together, to obtain minority representation on the board if they own a certain minimum number of shares. In the absence of cumulative voting, the holder or holders of 51 percent of the voting shares can elect all of the members of the board.

The formula for determining how many shares a minority shareholder with cumulative voting rights must own, or have proxies to vote, to secure representation on the board is as follows:

$$X = \frac{ac}{b+1} + 1$$

where
$a$ = *number of shares voting*
$b$ = *number of directors to be elected*
$c$ = *number of directors desired to be elected*
$X$ = *number of shares necessary to elect the number of directors desired to be elected*

For example, Gray Corporation has two shareholders, Stephanie with sixty-four shares and Thomas with thirty-six shares. The board of directors of Gray Corporation consists of three directors. Under "straight" or non-cumulative voting, Stephanie could cast sixty-four votes for each of her three candidates, and Thomas could cast thirty-six votes for his three candidates. As a result, all three of Stephanie's candidates would be elected. On the other hand, if cumulative voting were in force, Thomas could elect one director:

$$X = \frac{ac}{b+1} + 1$$

$$X = \frac{100(1)}{3+1} + 1 = 26 \text{ shares}$$

Because Thomas has the right to vote more than twenty-six shares, he would be able to elect one director. Stephanie, of course, with her sixty-four shares, could elect the remaining two directors.

The effect of cumulative voting for directors may be diluted by classification, by staggering elections, or by reducing the size of the board. For example, if nine directors are each elected annually, only 11 percent of the shares are needed to elect one director; if the nine directors' elections are staggered and three are elected annually, 26 percent of the shares are required to elect one director.

## Removal of Directors

By a majority vote, shareholders may remove any director or the entire board of directors, with or without cause, in a meeting called for that purpose. In the case of a corporation having cumulative voting, however, a director may be removed only if the number of votes opposing his removal would be insufficient to elect him. Section 8.08(c). Removal of directors is discussed more fully later in this chapter.

## Approval of Fundamental Changes

The board of directors manages the ordinary business affairs of the corporation. Extraordinary matters involving fundamental changes in the corporation require shareholder approval; such matters include amendments to the articles of incorporation, a sale or lease of all or substantially all of the corporate assets not in the regular course of business, most mergers, consolidations, compulsory share exchanges, and dissolution. Fundamental changes are discussed in Chapter 37.

## Concentrations of Voting Power

Certain devices enable groups of shareholders to combine their voting power for purposes such as obtaining or maintaining control or maximizing the impact of cumulative voting. The most important methods of concentrating voting power are proxies, voting trusts, and shareholder voting agreements.

◆ *See Figure 36–4*

*Proxies* A shareholder may vote either in person or by written proxy. Section 7.22(a). As mentioned earlier, a proxy is simply a shareholder's authorization to an agent to vote his shares at a particular meeting or on a particular question. Generally, proxies must be in writing to be

**FIGURE 36–4** Concentrations of Voting Power

|  | Proxy | Voting Trust | Shareholder Agreement |
|---|---|---|---|
| **Definition** | Authorization of an agent to vote shares | Conferral of voting rights on trustee | Agreement among shareholders on voting of shares |
| **Formalities** | Signed writing delivered to corporation | Signed writing delivered to corporation | Signed writing |
| **Duration** | Eleven months, unless otherwise agreed | Ten years; may be extended | No limit |
| **Revocability** | Yes, unless coupled with an interest | No | Only by unanimous agreement |
| **Prevalence** | Publicly held | Publicly and closely held | Closely held |

effective; furthermore, statutes typically limit the duration of proxies to no more than eleven months, unless the proxy specifically provides otherwise. Section 7.22(c). Some States limit all proxy appointments to a period of eleven months. Because a proxy is the appointment of an agent, it is revocable, as all agencies are, unless conspicuously stated to be irrevocable *and* coupled with an interest, such as shares held as collateral. Section 7.22(d). The solicitation of proxies by publicly held corporations is also regulated by the Securities Exchange Act of 1934, as discussed in Chapter 44.

*Voting Trusts* Voting trusts, which are designed to concentrate corporate control in one or more persons, have been used in both publicly held and closely held corporations. A voting trust is a device by which one or more shareholders separate the voting rights of their shares from the ownership of those shares. Under a voting trust, one or more shareholders confer on a trustee the right to vote or otherwise act for them by signing an agreement setting out the provisions of the trust and transferring their shares to the trustee. Section 7.30(a). In most States, voting trusts are permitted by statute but are usually limited in duration to ten years. The Revised Act and many States permit all or some of the parties to a voting trust to extend it for an additional term of up to ten years by signing an extension agreement and obtaining the voting trustee's written consent. Section 7.30(c). The extension runs from the time the first shareholder signs the agreement but binds only those shareholders who consent to it.

*Shareholder Voting Agreements* In most jurisdictions, shareholders may agree in writing to vote in a specified manner for the election or removal of directors or on any other matter subject to shareholder approval. Section 7.31(a). The Revised Act and some State statutes expressly provide that shareholder voting agreements are enforceable by a decree of specific performance. Section 7.31(b). Unlike voting trusts, shareholder voting agreements are usually not limited in duration. Shareholder voting agreements are used frequently in closely held corporations, especially in conjunction with restrictions on the transfer of shares, to provide each shareholder with greater control and *delectus personae* (the right to choose those who will become shareholders).

*Galler v. Galler*, 32 Ill.2d 16, 203 N.E.2d 577 (1964), provides a well-known example of the effect a shareholder agreement may have within a close corporation. In 1927, two brothers, Benjamin and Isadore Galler, incorporated the Galler Drug Co., a wholesale drug business that they had operated as equal partners since 1919. The company continued to grow, and in 1955 the two brothers and their wives, Emma and Rose Galler, entered into a written shareholder agreement to leave the corporation in equal control of each family after the death of either brother. Specifically, the agreement provided that the corporation would continue to provide income for the support and maintenance of their immediate families and that the parties would vote for directors so as to give the estate and heirs of a deceased shareholder the same representation as before. Benjamin died in 1957, and shortly thereafter his widow, Emma, requested that Isadore, the surviving brother, comply with the terms of the agreement. When he refused, instead proposing that certain changes be made in the agreement, Emma brought an action seeking specific performance of the agreement. Isadore and his wife, Rose, defended on the ground that the shareholder agreement was against public policy and the State's corporation law. The court decided in favor of Emma Galler, explaining that a close corporation is one in which the stock is held in a few hands and is rarely traded. In contrast to a shareholder in a public corporation, who may easily trade his shares on the open market when he disagrees with management over corporate policy, the shareholder of a closely held corporation often has no ready market in which to sell his shares should he wish to do so. Moreover, the shareholder in a closely held corporation often has most of his capital invested in the corporation and, therefore, views himself not only as an investor but also as a participant in the management of the business. Without a shareholder agreement subject to specific performance by the courts, the minority shareholder might find himself at the mercy of the controlling majority shareholder. In short, the detailed shareholder voting agreement is the only sound means by which the minority shareholder can protect himself. Therefore, the court concluded, because the agreement was reasonable in its scope and purpose of providing continuing support for the Galler brothers' families, it should be enforced.

## Restrictions on Transfer of Shares

In the absence of a specific agreement, shares of stock are freely transferable. Although free transferability of shares is usually considered an advantage of the corporate form, in some situations the shareholders may prefer to restrict the transfer of shares. In closely held corporations, for example, stock transfer restrictions are used to control who may become shareholders, thereby achieving the corporate equivalent of *delectus personae* (choice of the person). They are also used to maintain statutory close corporation status by restricting the number of persons who may become shareholders. In publicly held corporations, restrictions on the transfer of shares are used to preserve exemptions under State and Federal securities laws. (These are discussed in Chapter 44.)

Most incorporation statutes have no provisions governing share transfer restrictions. The common law validates such restrictions if they are adopted for a lawful purpose and do not unreasonably restrain or prohibit transferability. In addition, the Uniform Commercial Code (UCC) provides that an otherwise valid share transfer restriction is ineffective against a person without actual knowledge of it unless the restriction is conspicuously noted on the share certificate. Section 8–204.

The Revised Act and the statutes of several States permit the articles of incorporation, bylaws, or a shareholder agreement to impose transfer restrictions but require that the restriction be noted conspicuously on the stock certificate. The Revised Act authorizes restrictions for any reasonable purpose, including maintaining statutory close corporation status and preserving exemptions under Federal and State securities law. Section 6.27.

## ENFORCEMENT RIGHTS OF SHAREHOLDERS

To protect a shareholder's interests in the corporation, the law provides shareholders with certain enforcement rights, including the right to obtain information, the right to sue the corporation directly or to sue on the corporation's behalf, and the right to dissent.

## Right to Inspect Books and Records

Most States have enacted statutory provisions granting shareholders the right to inspect for a *proper purpose* books and records in person or through an agent and to make extracts from them. The Revised Act extends the right to copy records to include, if reasonable, the right to receive copies made by photographic, xerographic, or other means. Section 16.03. The Act provides that every shareholder is entitled to examine specified corporate records upon prior written request if the demand is made in good faith, for a proper purpose, and during regular business hours at the corporation's principal office. Section 16.02. Many States, however, limit this right to shareholders who own a minimum number of shares or to those who have been shareholders for a

specified minimum time. For example, the MBCA requires that a shareholder either must own 5 percent of the outstanding shares or must have owned his shares for at least six months; a court, however, may order an inspection even when neither condition is met.

A **proper purpose** for inspection is one that is reasonably relevant to a shareholder's interest in the corporation. Proper purposes include determining the financial condition of the corporation, the value of shares, the existence of mismanagement or improper transactions, or the names of other shareholders in order to communicate with them about corporate affairs. The right of inspection is subject to abuse and will be denied a shareholder who is seeking information for an improper purpose. Examples of improper purposes include obtaining information for use by a competing company or obtaining a list of shareholders in order to offer it for sale.

The Revised Act requires that a voting list of shareholders be prepared and that it be made available to shareholders upon request. Section 7.20. In addition, unlike most States, the Act requires every corporation to prepare and submit to its shareholders annual financial statements. Section 16.20.

 *See Case 36–1*

## Shareholder Suits

The ultimate recourse of a shareholder, short of selling her shares, is to bring suit against or on behalf of the corporation. Shareholder suits are essentially of two kinds: direct suits or derivative suits.

◆ *See Figure 36–5*

*Direct Suits* A shareholder may bring a direct suit to enforce a claim that he has *against* the corporation, based upon his ownership of shares. Any recovery in a direct suit goes to the shareholder plaintiff. Examples of direct suits include shareholder actions to compel payment of dividends properly declared, to enforce the right to inspect corporate records, to enforce the right to vote, to protect preemptive rights, and to compel dissolution. Shareholders also may bring a class suit or class action. A **class suit** is a direct suit in which one or more shareholders purport to represent a class of shareholders in order to recover for injuries to the entire class. Such a suit is a direct suit because the representative claims that all similarly situated shareholders were injured by an act that did not injure the corporation.

**FIGURE 36–5** Shareholder Suits

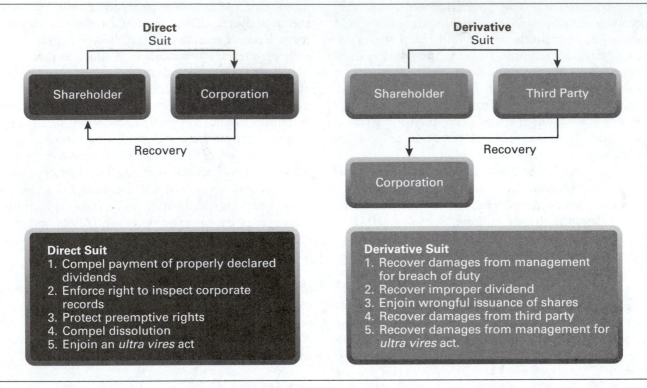

Direct Suit
- Shareholder → Corporation
- Recovery

**Direct Suit**
1. Compel payment of properly declared dividends
2. Enforce right to inspect corporate records
3. Protect preemptive rights
4. Compel dissolution
5. Enjoin an *ultra vires* act

Derivative Suit
- Shareholder → Third Party
- Recovery → Corporation

**Derivative Suit**
1. Recover damages from management for breach of duty
2. Recover improper dividend
3. Enjoin wrongful issuance of shares
4. Recover damages from third party
5. Recover damages from management for *ultra vires* act.

*Derivative Suits* A derivative suit is a cause of action brought by one or more shareholders *on behalf* of the corporation to enforce a right belonging to the corporation. Shareholders may bring such an action when the board of directors refuses to so act on the corporation's behalf. Recovery usually goes to the corporation's treasury, so that all shareholders can benefit proportionately. Examples of derivative suits are actions to recover damages from management for an *ultra vires* act, to recover damages for a managerial breach of duty, and to recover improper dividends. In such situations, the board of directors may well be hesitant to bring suit against the corporation's officers or directors. Consequently, a shareholder derivative suit is the only recourse.

In most States, a shareholder must have owned his shares at the time the complained-of transaction occurred in order to bring a derivative suit. Section 7.41. In addition, the shareholder must first make demand upon the board of directors to enforce the corporate right. The statutes of some States require a plaintiff to give security for reasonable expenses, including attorneys' fees, if his holdings of shares are not of a specified size or value.

See Case 36–2

## Shareholder's Right to Dissent

A shareholder has the right to dissent from certain corporate actions that require shareholder approval. These actions include most mergers, consolidations, compulsory share exchanges, and a sale or exchange of all or substantially all the assets of the corporation not in the usual and regular course of business. The shareholder's right to dissent is discussed in Chapter 37.

## ROLE OF DIRECTORS AND OFFICERS

Management of a corporation is vested by statute in its board of directors, which determines general corporate policy and appoints officers to execute that policy and to administer day-to-day corporate operations. Both the directors and the officers owe certain duties to the corporate entity as well as to the corporation's shareholders and are liable for breaching these duties.

The following sections will discuss the roles of corporate directors and officers. In some instances, controlling shareholders, or those owning a number of shares sufficient to allow them effective control over the corporation, are held to duties the same as those of directors and officers, which are discussed later in this chapter. Moreover, in close corporations, some courts impose upon *all* the shareholders a fiduciary duty similar to that imposed upon partners.

 *See Case 36–3*

## FUNCTION OF THE BOARD OF DIRECTORS

Although the directors are elected by the shareholders to manage the corporation, they are neither trustees nor agents of the shareholders or the corporation. They are, however, fiduciaries who must perform their duties in good faith, in the best interests of the corporation, and with due care.

The Revised Act and the statutes of many States provide that "[a]ll corporate powers shall be exercised by or under the authority of, and the business and affairs of the corporation managed under the direction of, its board of directors, subject to any limitation set forth in the articles of incorporation." Section 8.01(b). In some corporations, the members of the board all are actively involved in the management of the business. In these cases, the corporate powers are exercised *by* the board of directors. On the other hand, in publicly held corporations, most board members are unlikely to be actively involved in management. Here, the corporate powers are exercised *under* the authority of the board, which formulates major management policy but does not involve itself in day-to-day management.

In publicly held corporations, the directors who are also officers or employees of the corporation are **inside directors,** while the directors who are not officers or employees are **outside directors.** Outside directors who have no business contacts with the corporation are **unaffiliated directors;** outside directors who do have such contacts with the corporation—such as investment bankers, lawyers, or suppliers—are **affiliated directors.** Historically, the boards of many publicly held corporations consisted mainly or entirely of inside directors. During the past two decades, however, the number and influence of outside directors have increased substantially.

Under the Revised Act as originally enacted, a corporation having fifty or fewer shareholders may dispense with or limit the authority of a board of directors by describing in its articles of incorporation those who will perform some or all of the duties of a board. The Revised Act permits any corporation to dispense with a board of

directors by a written agreement executed by all of the shareholders. Sections 7.32 and 8.01.

The board determines corporate policy in a number of areas, including (1) selecting and removing officers, (2) determining the corporation's capital structure, (3) initiating fundamental changes, (4) declaring dividends, and (5) setting management compensation.

### Selection and Removal of Officers

In most States, the board of directors is responsible for choosing the corporation's officers and may remove any officer at any time. Sections 8.40 and 8.43. Officers are corporate agents who are delegated their responsibilities by the board of directors.

### Capital Structure

The board of directors determines the capital structure and financial policy of the corporation. For example, the board of directors has the power to

1. fix the selling price of newly issued shares unless the articles reserve this power to the shareholders;
2. determine the value of the consideration the corporation will receive in payment for the shares it issues;
3. purchase, redeem, or otherwise acquire shares of the corporation's equity securities;
4. borrow money; issue notes, bonds, and other obligations; and secure any of the corporation's obligations by mortgage or pledge of any or all of the corporation's property; and
5. sell, lease, or exchange assets of the corporation in the usual and regular course of business.

### Fundamental Changes

The board of directors has the power to amend or repeal the bylaws, unless the articles of incorporation reserve this power exclusively to the shareholders. Section 10.20. In a few States directors may not repeal or amend bylaws adopted by the shareholders. In addition, the board initiates certain actions that require shareholder approval. For instance, the board initiates proceedings to amend the articles of incorporation; to effect a merger, consolidation, compulsory share exchange, or the sale or lease of all or substantially all of the assets of the corporation other than in the usual and regular course of business; and to dissolve the corporation.

## Dividends

The board of directors declares the amount and type of dividends, subject to restrictions in the State incorporation statute, the articles of incorporation, and corporate loan and preferred stock agreements. Section 6.40. The board also fixes a record date for the purpose of determining the shareholders who are entitled to receive dividends. Section 6.40(b).

## Management Compensation

The board of directors usually determines the compensation of officers. Moreover, a number of States allow the board to fix the compensation of its members. Section 8.11. In addition to fixed salaries, executive compensation may include (1) cash bonuses, (2) share bonuses, (3) share options, (4) share purchase plans, (5) insurance benefits, (6) deferred compensation, (7) retirement plans, and (8) a variety of other fringe benefits.

## ELECTION AND TENURE OF DIRECTORS

The incorporation statute, articles of incorporation, and bylaws determine the qualifications essential for those who would be directors of the corporation. They also determine the election, number, tenure, and compensation of directors.

## Election, Number, and Tenure of Directors

The initial board of directors generally is named in the articles of incorporation and serves until the first meeting of the shareholders at which directors are elected. Section 8.05(a). Thereafter, directors are elected at annual meetings of the shareholders and hold office for one year unless their terms are staggered. If the shares represented at a meeting in person or by proxy are insufficient to constitute a quorum, however, or if the shareholders are deadlocked and unable to elect a new board, the incumbent directors continue in office as "holdover" directors until their successors are duly elected and qualified. Section 8.05(e). Although State statutes traditionally required each corporation to have three or more directors, most States permit the board to consist of one or more members. Section 8.03(a). Moreover, the number of directors may be increased or decreased, within statutory limits, by amendment to the bylaws or charter.

## Vacancies and Removal of Directors

The Revised Act provides that a vacancy in the board may be filled either by the shareholders or by the affirmative vote of a majority of the remaining directors, even if they constitute less than a quorum of the board. Section 8.10(a). When shareholders fill a vacant office which was held by a director elected by a class of shares, only the holders of that class of shares have the right to vote to fill that vacancy. The term of a director elected to fill a vacancy expires at the next shareholders' meeting at which directors are elected. Section 8.05(d).

Some States have no statutory provision for the removal of directors, although a common law rule permits removal for cause by action of the shareholders. The Revised Act and an increasing number of other statutes permit the shareholders to remove one or more directors or the entire board, with or without cause, at a special meeting called for that purpose, subject to cumulative voting rights, if applicable. Section 8.08. Nevertheless, the Revised Act permits the articles of incorporation to provide that directors may be removed only for cause. Section 8.08(a). In addition, however, the Revised Act and a number of States authorize a court to remove a director in a proceeding brought by the corporation or by shareholders who own at least 10 percent of the outstanding shares of any class of shares, if the court finds that (1) the director engaged in fraudulent or dishonest conduct or gross abuse of authority or discretion and (2) removal is in the best interests of the corporation. Section 8.09.

## Compensation of Directors

Traditionally, directors did not receive salaries for their directorial services, although they usually collected a fee or honorarium for attendance at meetings. The Revised Act and many incorporation statutes now specifically authorize the board of directors to fix the compensation of directors unless there is a contrary provision in the articles of incorporation or bylaws. Section 8.11.

## EXERCISE OF DIRECTORS' FUNCTIONS

Although they are powerless to bind the corporation when acting individually, directors can exert this power when acting as a board. Nevertheless, the board may act only through a meeting of the directors or with the written, unanimously signed consent of the directors, if written consent without a meeting is authorized by the statute and not contrary to the charter or bylaws. Section 8.21.

Meetings either are held at a regular time and place fixed in the bylaws or are called at special times. Notice of meetings must be given as prescribed in the bylaws. A director's attendance at any meeting is a waiver of such notice, unless the director attends only to object to the holding of the meeting or to the transacting of business at it and does not vote for or assent to action taken at the meeting. Section 8.23(b). Waiver of notice also may be given in a signed writing. Most modern statutes provide that meetings of the board may be held either in or outside the State of incorporation. Section 8.20(a).

## Quorum and Voting

A majority of board members constitutes a quorum (the minimum number of members that must be present at a meeting in order to transact business). Although most States do not permit a quorum to be set at less than a majority, the Revised Act allows the articles of incorporation or the bylaws to authorize a quorum consisting of as few as one-third of a board's members. Section 8.24(b). In contrast, however, the articles of incorporation or bylaws may require a number greater than a simple majority. If a quorum is present at any meeting, the act of a majority of the directors in attendance is the act of the board, unless the articles of incorporation or bylaws require the act of a greater number. Section 8.24(c).

Closely held corporations sometimes impose supermajority or unanimous quorum requirements. In addition, they may require a supermajority or unanimous vote of the board for some or all matters. The use of either or both of these provisions, however, creates the possibility of deadlock at the director level.

By requiring a quorum to be present when "a vote is taken," the Revised Act makes it clear that the board may act only when a quorum is present. Section 8.24(c) and Comment 2. This rule is in contrast to the rule governing shareholder meetings: once obtained, a quorum of shareholders cannot be broken by the withdrawal of shareholders. Many State statutes, however, do not have this provision. In any event, directors may not vote by proxy, although most States permit directors to participate in meetings through teleconference. See Section 8.20.

A director who is present at a board meeting at which action on any corporate matter is taken is deemed to have assented to such action unless, in addition to dissenting or abstaining from it, he (1) has his dissent or abstention entered in the minutes of the meeting, (2) files his written dissent or abstention to such action with the presiding officer before the meeting adjourns, or (3) delivers his written dissent or abstention to the corporation immediately after adjournment. Section 8.24(d).

## Action Taken without a Meeting

The Revised Act and most States provide that, unless the articles of incorporation or bylaws provide otherwise, any action the statute requires or permits to be taken at a meeting of the board may be taken without a meeting if consent in writing is signed by all of the directors. Section 8.21. Such consent has the same effect as a unanimous vote.

## Delegation of Board Powers

Unless otherwise provided by the articles of incorporation or bylaws, the board of directors may, by majority vote of the full board, appoint one or more committees, all of whose members must be directors. Section 8.25. Many State statutes, however, permit the board to form committees only if the charter or bylaws expressly authorize such action; furthermore, the Revised Act and many States require that the creation of a committee and appointment of members to it must be approved by the greater of (1) a majority of all the directors in office when the action is taken or (2) the number of directors required by the articles of incorporation or bylaws to take action. Section 8.25(b). The Revised Act and the statutes of many States require that a committee consist of at least two directors, although some statutes permit a committee to have as few as one member.

Committees may exercise all of the authority of the board, except with regard to certain matters specified in the incorporation statute, such as declaring dividends and other distributions, filling vacancies in the board or in any of its committees, amending the bylaws, recommending fundamental changes to the shareholder, approving a merger or charter amendment not requiring shareholder approval, and authorizing the sale or reacquisition of stock. Section 8.25(e). Delegating authority to a committee does not relieve any board member of his duties to the corporation. Commonly used committees include executive committees, audit committees (to recommend and oversee independent public accountants), compensation committees, finance committees, nominating committees, and investment committees.

## Directors' Inspection Rights

So that they can perform their duties competently and fully, directors have the right to inspect corporate books and records. This right is considerably broader than a shareholder's right to inspect. Nevertheless, it is subject to limitations.

## OFFICERS

In most States, the officers of a corporation are appointed by the board of directors to hold the offices provided in the bylaws, which set forth the respective duties of each officer. Statutes generally require as a minimum that the officers consist of a president, one or more vice presidents as prescribed by the bylaws, a secretary, and a treasurer. A person may hold more than one office, with the exception that the same person may not hold the office of president and secretary at the same time.

The Revised Act and other modern statutes permit every corporation to designate whatever officers it wants. Although the Act specifies no particular number of officers, one of them must be delegated responsibility for preparing the minutes of directors' and shareholders' meetings and authenticating corporate records. The Revised Act permits the same individual to hold *all* of the offices of a corporation. Section 8.40(d).

## Selection and Removal of Officers

Most State statutes provide that officers be appointed by the board of directors and that they serve at the pleasure of the board. Accordingly, the board may remove officers with or without cause. Section 8.43(b). Of course, if the officer has an employment contract that is valid for a specified time, removing the officer without cause before that time expires would constitute a breach of the employment contract. The board also determines the compensation of officers.

## Role of Officers

The officers are, like the directors, fiduciaries to the corporation. On the other hand, unlike the directors, they are agents of the corporation. The roles of officers are set forth in the corporate bylaws.

## Authority of Officers

The Revised Act provides that each officer has the authority provided in the bylaws or prescribed by the board of directors, to the extent that such prescribed authority is consistent with the bylaws. Section 8.41. Like that of other agents, the authority of an officer to bind the corporation may be (1) actual express, (2) actual implied, or (3) apparent.

*Actual Express Authority* Actual express authority results when the corporation manifests its assent to the officer that the officer should act on its behalf. Actual express authority arises from the incorporation statute, the articles of incorporation, the bylaws, and resolutions of the board of directors. The last represent the principal source of such authority.

*Actual Implied Authority* Officers, as agents of the corporation, have actual implied authority to do what is reasonably necessary to perform their actual, delegated authority. In addition, a common question is whether officers possess implied authority merely by virtue of their positions. The courts have been circumspect in granting such implied or inherent authority. Traditionally, the courts tended to hold that the president had no implied authority by virtue of his office, although more recent decisions tend to recognize his authority to bind the corporation in ordinary business transactions. Any act requiring board approval, such as issuing stock, however, is clearly beyond the implied authority of the president or any other officer. In most jurisdictions, implied authority of position does not extend to any officer other than the president.

*Apparent Authority* Apparent authority arises from acts of the corporation that lead third parties to believe reasonably and in good faith that an officer has the required authority. Apparent authority might arise when a third party relies on the fact that an officer has exercised the same authority in the past with the consent of the board of directors.

*Ratification* A corporation may ratify the unauthorized acts of its officers. Equivalent to the corporation's having granted the officer prior authority, ratification relates back to the original transaction and may either be express or implied from the corporation's acceptance of contractual benefits with full knowledge of the facts.

## DUTIES OF DIRECTORS AND OFFICERS

Generally, directors and officers owe the duties of obedience, diligence, and loyalty to the corporation. These duties are for the most part judicially imposed. State and Federal statutes supplement the common law by imposing liability upon directors and officers for specific acts, but the common law remains the most significant source of duties.

A corporation may not recover damages from its directors and officers for losses resulting from their poor business judgment or honest mistakes of judgment. Directors and officers are not insurers of business success. They are required only to be obedient, reasonably diligent, and completely loyal. In 1998 an amendment to the Revised Act was adopted refining the Act's standards of conduct and liability for directors.

## Duty of Obedience

Directors and officers must act within their respective authority. For any loss the corporation suffers because of their unauthorized acts, they are in some jurisdictions held strictly liable; in others, they are held liable only if they exceeded their authority intentionally or negligently.

## Duty of Diligence

In discharging their duties, directors and officers must exercise ordinary care and prudence. Some States interpret this standard to mean that directors and officers must exercise "the same degree of care and prudence that [those] promoted by self-interest generally exercise in their own affairs." *Hun v. Cary*, 82 N.Y. 65 (1880). Most States and the Revised Act, however, hold that the test requires a director or officer to discharge her duties

1. in good faith;
2. with the care an ordinarily prudent person in a like position would exercise under similar circumstances; and
3. in a manner she reasonably believes to be in the best interests of the corporation.

Sections 8.30 and 8.42. A director or officer who has performed the duties of his office in compliance with these requirements is liable neither for any action he has taken as a director or officer nor for any failure to act. Sections 8.30(d) and 8.42(d).

So long as the directors and officers act in good faith and with due care, the courts will not substitute their judgment for that of the board or officer—the so-called **business judgment rule.** Directors and officers will, nonetheless, be held liable for bad faith or negligent conduct. Moreover, they may be liable for failing to act.

In one instance, a bank director, who in the five-and-one-half years that he had been on the board had never attended a board meeting or made any examination of the books and records, was held liable for losses resulting from the unsupervised acts of the president and cashier, who had made various improper loans and had permitted large overdrafts.

 *See Case 37–4*

*Reliance upon Others* Directors and officers are, nevertheless, permitted to entrust important work to others, and if they have selected employees with care, they are not personally liable for the negligent acts or willful wrongs of those selected. A reasonable amount of supervision is required, however; and an officer or director who knew or should have known or suspected that an employee was incurring losses through carelessness, theft, or embezzlement will be held liable for such losses.

A director also may rely in good faith upon information provided him by officers and employees of the corporation; legal counsel, public accountants, or other persons as to matters the director reasonably believes are within the person's professional or expert competence; and a committee of the board of directors of which the director is not a member if the director reasonably believes the committee merits confidence. Section 8.30 of the Revised Act. A director is not acting in good faith if he has knowledge concerning the matter in question that makes reliance unwarranted.

An officer is also entitled to rely upon this information, but this right may, in many circumstances, be more limited than a director's right to so rely because of the officer's greater familiarity with the corporation's affairs. Section 8.42 and Comment.

*Business Judgment Rule* Directors and officers are continuously called upon to make decisions that require balancing benefits and risks to the corporation. Although hindsight may reveal that some of these decisions were less than optimal, the business judgment rule precludes imposing liability upon the directors or officers for honest mistakes of judgment. To subsequently benefit from the business judgment rule, a director or officer must make an informed decision, in good faith without any conflict of interests, and have a rational basis for believing it was in the best interests of the corporation. Moreover, when a director or officer fails to satisfy this standard of conduct, it must be shown that her action (or inaction) is the proximate cause of damage to the corporation.

Hasty or ill-advised action also can render directors liable. In a recent case, the Supreme Court of Delaware held directors liable for approving the terms of a cash-out merger. The court found that the directors did not adequately inform themselves of the company's intrinsic value and were grossly negligent in approving the terms of the merger upon two hours' consideration and without prior notice. *Smith v. Van Gorkom*, 488 A.2d 858 (1985).

## Duty of Loyalty

The officers and directors of a corporation owe a duty of loyalty (a **fiduciary duty**) to the corporation and to its shareholders. The essence of a fiduciary duty is the subordination of self-interest to the interest of the person or persons to whom the duty is owing. It requires officers and directors to be constantly loyal to the corporation, which they both serve and control.

An officer or director is required to disclose fully to the corporation any financial interest that he may have in any contract or transaction to which the corporation is a party. (This is a corollary to the rule that forbids fiduciaries from making secret profits.) He must eschew self-interest in his business conduct, and he may not advance his personal interests at the corporation's expense. Moreover, he may not represent conflicting interests; his duty is one of strict allegiance to the corporation.

The remedy for breach of fiduciary duty is a suit in equity by the corporation, or more often a derivative suit instituted by a shareholder, to require the fiduciary to pay to the corporation the profits that he obtained through breach of his fiduciary duty. It need not be shown that the corporation could otherwise have made the profits that the fiduciary has realized. The object of the rule is to discourage breaches of duty by taking from the fiduciary all of the profits he has made. Though enforcing the rule may result in a windfall to the corporation, this is incidental to the rule's deterrent objective. Whenever a director or officer breaches his fiduciary duty, he forfeits his right to compensation during the period he engaged in the breach.

*Conflict of Interests* A contract or other transaction between an officer or a director and the corporation inherently involves a conflict of interest. Contracts between officers and the corporation are covered under the law of agency. (See Chapter 19.) Early on, the common law viewed all director–corporation transactions as automatically void or voidable but eventually regarded this rule as unreasonable because it would prevent directors from entering into contracts beneficial to the corporation. Now, therefore, if such a contract is honest and fair, the courts will uphold it. In the case of contracts between corporations having an interlocking directorate (corporations whose boards of directors share one or more members), the courts subject the contracts to scrutiny and will set them aside unless the transaction is shown to have been entirely fair and entered in good faith.

Most States address these related problems by providing that such transactions are neither void nor voidable if, after full disclosure, they are approved by either the board of disinterested directors or the shareholders, or if they are fair and reasonable to the corporation.

The Revised Act has adopted a more specific approach to a director's conflict-of-interest transactions, which it defines as transactions between a corporation (or a subsidiary of it or an entity controlled by it) and one of the corporation's directors, a close relative of the director, or a person to whom the director owes a fiduciary duty. Section 8.60. The Revised Act establishes more clearly prescribed safe harbors to validate conflict-of-interest transactions. Section 8.61. The Revised Act provides two alternative safe harbors, each of which is available before or after the transaction: approval by the directors or approval by the shareholders. In either case, the interested director must make full disclosure to the approving group. Full disclosure requires the director to disclose both the existence of the conflicting interest and all material facts known to her regarding the subject matter of the transaction.

If neither of the safe harbor provisions is satisfied, then the transaction is subject to appropriate judicial action unless the transaction is fair to the corporation. The comments to Section 8.61 explain that fairness requires that (1) the terms of the transaction, including the price, are fair; (2) the transaction benefits the corporation; and (3) the course of dealing or process of the transaction is fair.

*Loans to Directors* The Model Act and some States permit a corporation to lend money to its directors only with its shareholders' authorization for each loan. The statutes in most States permit such loans either on a general or on a limited basis. The Revised Act initially permitted such loans if each was approved (1) by a majority of disinterested shareholders or (2) by the board of directors after its determination that the loan would benefit the corporation. Section 8.32. The 1988 amendments to the Revised Act deleted this section, instead subjecting director loans to the procedure that applies to a director's conflict-of-interest transactions.

***Corporate Opportunity*** Directors and officers may not usurp any corporate opportunity that in all fairness should belong to the corporation. A corporate opportunity is one in which the corporation has a right, property interest, or expectancy; whether or not such an opportunity exists depends on the facts and circumstances of each case.

A corporate opportunity must be promptly offered to the corporation, which, in turn, should promptly accept or reject it. Rejection may be based on one or more of several factors, such as the corporation's lack of interest in the opportunity, its financial inability to acquire the opportunity, legal restrictions on its ability to accept the opportunity, or a third party's unwillingness to deal with the corporation.

For instance, a party proposes a business arrangement to a corporation through its vice president, who personally accepts the arrangement without offering it to the corporation. The vice president has usurped a corporate opportunity. On the other hand, a corporate opportunity generally would not include one that the corporation was unable to accept or one that the corporation expressly rejected by a vote of disinterested directors after full disclosure. In both of these instances, a director or officer is free to take personal advantage of the opportunity.

 *See Case 36–5*

***Transactions in Shares*** The issuance of shares at favorable prices to management by excluding other shareholders normally will constitute a violation of the fiduciary duty. So might the issuance of shares to a director at a fair price if the purpose of the issuance is to perpetuate corporate control rather than to raise capital or to serve some other interest of the corporation.

Officers and directors have access to inside advance information, unavailable to the public, which may affect the future market value of the corporation's shares. Federal statutes have attempted to deal with this trading advantage by prohibiting officers and directors from purchasing or selling shares of their corporation's stock without adequately disclosing all material facts in their possession that may affect the stock's actual or potential value. See Chapter 44 for a discussion of these matters.

Although the imposition of liability upon officers and directors for secret, profitable use of inside information has been inconsistent under State law, the trend is toward holding them liable for breach of fiduciary duty to shareholders from whom they purchase stock without disclosing facts that give the stock added potential value. They are also held liable to the corporation for profits realized upon a sale of the stock when undisclosed conditions of the corporation make a substantial decline in value practically inevitable.

***Duty Not to Compete*** As fiduciaries, directors and officers owe to the corporation the duty of undivided loyalty, which means they may not compete with the corporation. A director or officer who breaches his fiduciary duty by competing with the corporation is liable for the damages he thus causes to the corporation. Although directors and officers may engage in their own business interests, courts will closely scrutinize any interest that competes with the corporation's business. Moreover, an officer or director may not use corporate personnel, facilities, or funds for her own benefit nor disclose trade secrets of the corporation to others.

## Indemnification of Directors and Officers

Directors and officers incur personal liability for breaching any of the duties they owe to the corporation and its shareholders. Under many modern incorporation statutes, a corporation *may* indemnify a director or officer for liability incurred if he acted in good faith and in a manner he reasonably believed to be in the best interests of the corporation, so long as he has not been adjudged negligent or liable for misconduct. The Revised Act provides for *mandatory* indemnification of directors and officers for reasonable expenses they incur in the wholly successful defense of any proceeding brought against them because they are or were directors or officers. Sections 8.52 and 8.56. These provisions, however, may be limited by the articles of incorporation. In addition, a corporation may purchase insurance to indemnify officers and directors for liability arising out of their corporate activities, including liabilities against which the corporation is not empowered to indemnify directly. Section 8.57.

## Liability Limitation Statutes

At least forty States have enacted legislation limiting the liability of directors. Most of these States, including Delaware, have authorized corporations—with shareholder approval—to limit or eliminate the liability of directors for some breaches of duty. A few States permit shareholders to limit the liability of officers. The Delaware statute provides that the articles of incorporation may contain a provision eliminating or limiting the personal liability of a director to the corporation or its stockholders for monetary damages for breach of her directorial duty, provided that such provision does not eliminate or limit the liability of a director (1) for any breach of the director's duty of loyalty to the corporation or its stockholders, (2) for acts or omissions lacking good faith or involving intentional misconduct or a knowing violation of law, (3) for liability for unlawful dividend payments or redemptions, or (4) for any transaction from which the director derived an improper personal benefit.

A handful of States have directly eliminated personal liability for money damages, subject to certain exceptions. For example, under the Indiana statute, a director is liable only if she has breached or failed to perform her duties in compliance with the statutory standard of care and the breach or failure to perform constitutes willful misconduct or recklessness. Other States adopt a third approach by limiting the amount of money damages that may be assessed against a director or officer.

The Revised Act authorizes the articles of incorporation to include a provision eliminating or limiting—with certain exceptions—the liability of a director to the corporation or its shareholders for any action that he, as a director, has taken or has failed to take. The exceptions, for which liability would be unaffected, are (1) the amount of any financial benefit the director receives to which he is not entitled, such as a bribe, kickback, or profits from a usurped corporate opportunity; (2) an intentional infliction of harm on the corporation or the shareholders; (3) liability under Section 8.33 for unlawful distributions; and (4) an intentional violation of the criminal law. Section 2.02(b)(4).

 # Chapter Summary

## Role of Shareholders

| **Voting Rights of Shareholders** | **Management Structure of Corporations** see Figures 36–1, 2, and 3 for illustrations of the statutory model of corporate governance, the structure of the typical closely held corporation, and the structure of the typical publicly held corporation<br>**Shareholder Meetings** shareholders may exercise their voting rights at both annual and special shareholder meetings<br>**Quorum** minimum number necessary to be present at a meeting in order to transact business<br>**Election of Directors** the shareholders elect the board at the annual meeting of the corporation<br>• *Straight Voting* directors are elected by a plurality of votes<br>• *Cumulative Voting* entitles shareholders to multiply the number of votes they are entitled to cast by the number of directors for whom they are entitled to vote and to cast the product for a single candidate or to distribute the product among two or more candidates<br>**Removal of Directors** the shareholders may by majority vote remove directors with or without cause, subject to cumulative voting rights<br>**Approval of Fundamental Changes** shareholder approval is required for charter amendments, most acquisitions, and dissolution<br>**Concentrations of Voting Power**<br>• *Proxy* authorization to vote another's shares at a shareholder meeting<br>• *Voting Trust* transfer of corporate shares' voting rights to a trustee<br>• *Shareholder Voting Agreement* used to provide shareholders with greater control over the election and removal of directors and other matters<br>**Restrictions on Transfer of Shares** must be reasonable and conspicuously noted on stock certificate |
|---|---|

| **Enforcement Rights of Shareholders** | **Right to Inspect Books and Records** if the demand is made in good faith and for a proper purpose<br>**Shareholder Suits**<br>• *Direct Suits* brought by a shareholder or a class of shareholders against the corporation based upon the ownership of shares<br>• *Derivative Suits* brought by a shareholder on behalf of the corporation to enforce a right belonging to the corporation<br>**Shareholder's Right to Dissent** a shareholder has the right to dissent from certain corporate actions that require shareholder approval |
|---|---|

# Role of Directors and Officers

| **Function of the Board of Directors** | **Selection and Removal of Officers**<br>**Capital Structure**<br>**Fundamental Changes** the directors have the power to make, amend, or repeal the bylaws, unless this power is exclusively reserved to the shareholders<br>**Dividends** directors declare the amount and type of dividends<br>**Management Compensation**<br>**Vacancies in the Board** may be filled by the vote of a majority of the remaining directors |
|---|---|
| **Exercise of Directors' Functions** | **Meeting** directors have the power to bind the corporation only when acting as a board<br>**Action Taken without a Meeting** permitted if a consent in writing is signed by all of the directors<br>**Delegation of Board Powers** committees may be appointed to perform some but not all of the board's functions<br>**Directors' Inspection Rights** directors have the right to inspect corporate books and records |
| **Officers** | **Role of Officers** officers are agents of the corporation<br>**Authority of Officers**<br>• *Actual Express Authority* arises from the incorporation statute, the charter, the bylaws, and resolutions of the directors<br>• *Actual Implied Authority* authority to do what is reasonably necessary to perform actual authority<br>• *Apparent Authority* acts of the principal that lead a third party to believe reasonably and in good faith that an officer has the required authority<br>• *Ratification* a corporation may ratify the unauthorized acts of its officers |
| **Duties of Directors and Officers** | **Duty of Obedience** must act within respective authority<br>**Duty of Diligence** must exercise ordinary care and prudence<br>**Duty of Loyalty** requires undeviating loyalty to the corporation<br>**Business Judgment Rule** precludes imposing liability on directors and officers for honest mistakes in judgment if they act with due care, in good faith, and in a manner reasonably believed to be in the best interests of the corporation |

**Indemnification** a corporation may indemnify a director or officer for liability incurred if he acted in good faith and was not adjudged negligent or liable for misconduct

**Liability Limitation Statutes** many States now authorize corporations—with shareholder approval—to limit or eliminate the liability of directors for some breaches of duty

# Cases

## CASE 36–1
### Right to Inspect Books and Records
## *COMPAQ COMPUTER CORPORATION v. HORTON*
Supreme Court of Delaware, 1993
631 A.2d 1

MOORE, J.

This is a stocklist case arising under 8 Del.C. § 220(b) of our General Corporation Law. The issue is whether a shareholder states a proper purpose for inspection under our statute in seeking to solicit the participation of other shareholders in legitimate non-derivative litigation against the defendant corporation. The Court of Chancery found that the litigation concerned alleged corporate wrongdoing that affected the value of the plaintiff's stock. Accordingly, the trial court concluded that plaintiff's desire to contact other stockholders, and solicit their involvement in the litigation, was a purpose reasonably related to one's interest as a stockholder. We agree and affirm.

### I

Compaq Computer Corporation ("Compaq") refused to permit Charles E. Horton ("Horton"), a Compaq stockholder, to inspect its stock ledger and other related materials. Horton has beneficially owned 112 shares of Compaq common stock continuously since December 6, 1990. Cede & Co., a nominal party to this action, is the record holder of these shares.

On July 22, 1991, Horton and seventy-eight other parties sued Compaq, fifteen of its advisors and certain management personnel (the "Texas litigation"). Horton and the other plaintiffs allege that Compaq and its co-defendants violated the Texas Security Act and the Texas Deceptive Trade Practices Consumer Protection Act. Plaintiffs also charge defendants with a continuing pattern of misconduct involving common law fraud, conspiracy, aiding and abetting, fraudulent concealment and

breach of fiduciary duty. All these claims arise from the contention that Compaq misled the public as to the true value of its stock at a time when members of management were selling their own shares. The plaintiffs seek individual damages.

On September 22, 1992, Horton, through counsel, delivered a letter demanding to inspect Compaq's stock ledger and related information for the period from October 1, 1990, to June 30, 1991, to the extent such information is available and in the possession or control of Compaq. The demand letter stated that the purpose of the request was:

[T]o enable Mr. Horton to communicate with other Compaq shareholders to inform them of the pending shareholders' suit of Charles E. Horton, *et al.* v. Compaq Computer Corporation and Joseph R. Canion and to ascertain whether any of them would desire to become associated with that suit or bring similar actions against Compaq, and assume a pro rata share of the litigated expenses.

On September 30, 1992, Compaq refused the demand, stating that the purpose described in the letter was not a "proper purpose" under Section 220(b) of the General Corporation Law of the State of Delaware. After this action was filed in the Court of Chancery, the parties presented cross-motions for summary judgment. Compaq conceded that Horton had met all of the technical requirements for making a demand under 8 Del. C. § 220, and that the only issue remaining for the trial court to resolve was whether Horton stated a proper purpose for inspecting the various documents.

On November 12, 1992, the Court of Chancery ordered Compaq to permit Horton and Cede to inspect and copy the stockholder lists and related stockholder information requested in their demand letter. The Vice Chancellor ruled that even though the Texas litigation is neither derivative, nor brought for the benefit of Compaq, it concerns alleged corporate wrongdoing that affected the value of Horton's Compaq stock. [Citation.] Accordingly, Horton stated a proper purpose reasonably related to his interest as a Compaq stockholder.

## II

The question of a "proper purpose" under Section 220(b) of our General Corporation Law is an issue of law and equity which this Court reviews de novo. [Citations.]

In Delaware, a shareholder's common law right to inspect the stock ledger is codified in 8 Del.C. § 220(b). It provides in pertinent part:

Any stockholder . . . shall, upon written demand under oath stating the purpose thereof, have the right during the usual hours for business to inspect for any proper purpose the corporation's stock ledger. . . . A proper purpose shall mean a purpose reasonably related to such person's interest as a stockholder. 8 Del.C. § 220(b) (emphasis added).

Under Section 220, when a stockholder complies with the statutory requirements as to form and manner of making a demand, then the corporation bears the burden of proving that the demand is for an improper purpose. 8 Del.C. § 220(c); [citation]. If there is any doubt, it must be resolved in favor of the statutory right of the stockholder to have an inspection. [Citation.]

Horton contends that this purpose is not only proper, but was earlier approved in *State ex rel. Foster v. Standard Oil Co. of Kansas* [citation]. The holding in *Standard Oil* has been interpreted by a number of authoritative treatises for the proposition Horton advances—that shareholders may inspect stocklists for the purpose of communicating with fellow shareholders, not only about pending litigation, but to solicit their interest in joining it. [Citations.] Most of the cases cited, however, involved derivative suits. Under the circumstances here, we consider that to be a distinction without a difference. [Citations.]

Essentially, Horton alleges that it is in the interests of Compaq's shareholders to know that acts of mismanagement and fraud are continuing and cannot be overlooked. Thus, it is assumed that the resultant filing of a large number of individual damage claims might well discourage further acts of misconduct by the defendants. In this specific context, the antidotal effect of the Texas litigation may indeed serve a purpose reasonably related to Horton's current interest as a Compaq stockholder.

We recognize that even though a purpose may be reasonably related to one's interest as a stockholder, it cannot be adverse to the interests of the corporation. [Citations.] In this respect, it becomes clear that a stockholder's right to inspect and copy a stockholder list is not absolute. Rather, it is a qualified right depending on the facts presented. [Citation.]

Horton's ultimate objective, to solicit additional parties to the Texas litigation, may impose substantial expenses upon the company. Compaq argues, therefore, that such a purpose is per se improper as adverse to the interests of the corporation. Significantly, however, Compaq conceded at oral argument that it could cite no authority in support of its proposition that the purpose behind a demand must benefit the defendant corporation.

Horton, as a current stockholder of Compaq, has nothing to gain by harming the legitimate interests of the company. Moreover, as he argues, the prospect of the Texas litigation poses no legitimate threat to Compaq's interests. The Texas litigation is already pending with seventy-nine plaintiffs. The inclusion of more plaintiffs will not substantially increase Compaq's costs of defending the action. The real risk to Compaq is that any additional plaintiffs, who may join the suit, potentially increase the damage award against the company. Yet, insofar as law and policy require corporations and their agents to answer for the breaches of their duties to shareholders, Compaq has no legitimate interest in avoiding the payment of compensatory damages which it, its management or advisors may owe to those who own the enterprise. [Citation.] Thus, common sense and public policy dictate that a proper purpose may be stated in these circumstances, notwithstanding the lack of a direct benefit flowing to the corporation.

Equally important is the fact that if damages are assessed against Compaq in the Texas litigation, the company is entitled to seek indemnification from its co-defendant managers and advisors or to pursue its own claims against them. The availability of this diminishes the possibility that Compaq will suffer any harm at all. It is well-settled that the mere prospect of harm to a corporate defendant is insufficient to deny relief under Section 220. [Citation.] Any doubt on the issue must be resolved in favor of the statutory right of the stockholder to an inspection. [Citation.] This is especially true where the burden is on the corporation to show an improper purpose. 8 Del.C. § 220(c); [citation]. Accordingly, we are satisfied that the purpose for which Horton seeks to inspect the stock ledger and related materials is not adverse to the legitimate interests of the company.

This conclusion does not suggest that Compaq's burden of showing an improper purpose is impossible to bear. Previous cases provide valuable examples of the degree to which a stated purpose is so indefinite, doubtful, uncertain or vexatious as to warrant denial of the right of inspection. In [citation], the trial court held that instituting annoying or harassing litigation against the corporation was an improper purpose. In [citation], the court ruled improper the stockholder's plan to use a stocklist in furtherance of a scheme to bring pressure on a third corporation. In [citation], it was recognized that obtaining a list for purposes of selling the stockholder's names was also improper. Finally, in [citation], the Court stated that neither conducting a "fishing expedition" nor satisfying idle curiosity were proper purposes to justify inspection. On the whole, a fair reading of these cases leads to the conclusion that where the person making demand is acting in bad faith or for reasons wholly unrelated to his or her role as a stockholder, access to the ledger will be denied. That simply is not the case here.

Horton seeks in good faith to solicit the support of other similarly situated Compaq stockholders, not only to seek monetary redress for their individual economic injuries, but also to prevent further acts of fraud or mismanagement from disrupting the fair market value of Compaq's stock. These goals are consistent with at least two different, but analogous purposes that have been previously upheld by our courts, regardless of whether the purpose benefitted the corporation or just the claimant alone.

First, in [citation], the Chancellor held that a stockholder's desire to contact other stockholders for the purpose of encouraging them to dissent from a merger and seek their appraisal rights was proper. [Citation] is analogous to this case insofar as both claimants seek to solicit other stockholders to bring actions against the corporation which may ultimately protect the value of its stock. Second, in [citation], this Court upheld a stockholder's right to inspect the ledger for the purposes of investigating allegedly improper transactions or mismanagement. [Citation] is similar to this case because Horton also seeks to curb managerial fraud and mismanagement.

# III

We find, therefore, that Compaq's arguments simply fail to meet the burden imposed on it by law to show that Horton acts from an improper purpose. First, Compaq's contention that Horton's demand is not connected to his status as a stockholder is unsubstantiated. Horton's demand is connected to his status as a stockholder because he seeks to bring an end to injuries sustained, past and present, that directly, and adversely, affect his stock ownership. Second, Compaq's complaint that Horton seeks an historical stocklist is inconsequential. Many cases recognize a stockholder's right to investigate past acts of mismanagement. Furthermore, Section 220(b) expressly grants the right to inspect not only a corporation's list of present stockholders, but also the stock ledger. Third, Compaq's accusation that Horton only seeks inspection for his personal gain is immaterial. So long as Horton establishes a single proper purpose related to his role as a stockholder, all other purposes are irrelevant. [Citation.]

Finally, Compaq's contention that Horton's purpose is contrary to the best interests of the corporation and its current stockholders is both speculative and specious. Any harm that may accrue to the corporation as a result of releasing the list is too remote and uncertain to warrant denial of the stockholder's statutory right to inspection. If anything, the corporation and its stockholders, as well as public policy, will best be served by exposure of the fraud, if that is the case, and restoration of the stock to a value set by a properly informed market.

The judgment of the Court of Chancery is AFFIRMED.

---

## CASE 36–2
## Shareholder Suits
# *RICHARDSON v. ARIZONA FUELS CORP.*
### Supreme Court of Utah, 1980
### 614 P.2d 636

STEWART, J.
Plaintiffs Donald J. Richardson, Grove L. Cook, and Wayne Weaver are stockholders of Major who brought this action individually and on behalf of all other stockholders of Major. * * *

* * *

* * * The amended complaint describes this action as one brought as a class action pursuant to Rule 23 and as a stockholders' derivative action pursuant to Rule 23.1. Plaintiffs moved for an order certifying this suit as

a class action . . . [The] motion [was] granted by the district court.

Defendants attack the order on the grounds . . . that certification of all the claims in the suit as a class action was improper * * *

* * *

A class action and a derivative action rest upon fundamentally different principles of substantive law; to ignore those differences is not a minor procedural solecism. A derivative action must necessarily be based on a claim for relief which is owned by the stockholders' corporation. Indeed, a prerequisite for filing a derivative action is the failure of the corporation to initiate the action in its own name. The stockholder, as a nominal party, has no right, title or interest whatsoever in the claim itself—whether the action is brought by the corporation or by the stockholder on behalf of the corporation.

A class action, on the other hand, is predicated on ownership of the claim for relief sued upon in the representative of the class and all other class members in their capacity *as individuals*. Shareholders of the corporation may, of course, have claims for relief directly against their corporation because the corporation itself has violated rights possessed by the shareholders, and a class action would be an appropriate means for enforcing their claims. A recovery in a class action is a recovery which belongs directly to the shareholders. However, in a derivative action, the plaintiff shareholder recovers nothing and the judgment runs in favor of the corporation.

The difference in the two procedures and their relationship to underlying substantive law has been stated as follows:

Suits which are said to be derivative, and therefore come within the rule, are those which seek to enforce any right which belongs to the corporation and is not being enforced, such as the liability of corporate officers or majority shareholders for mismanagement, to recover corporate assets and related claims, to enforce rights of the corporation by virtue of its contract with a third person, and to enjoin those in charge of the corporation from causing it to commit an ultra vires act. [Citation.]

On the other hand,

[i]f the injury is one to the plaintiff as a stockholder and to him individually, and not to the corporation, as where the action is based on a contract to which he is a party, or on a right belonging severally to him, or on a fraud affecting him directly, it is an individual action. [Citation.]

* * *

The amended complaint states twelve causes of action, the first eight of which allege some fraudulent appropriation of or scheme to appropriate Major's assets by defendants. These causes of action seek to require the defendants to disgorge and return to Major the assets wrongfully obtained. Of the remaining four causes, three seek compensatory or punitive damages for injury attributable to alleged breaches of fiduciary duty implicit in the fraudulent acts enumerated in the first eight causes. The final cause of action seeks appointment of a receiver.

There is no doubt that the first eight causes of action allege injury to the corporation only. The injury alleged can be asserted by plaintiffs only derivatively as stockholders on behalf of the corporation. This leaves the ninth, tenth and eleventh causes of action to be analyzed to determine if they state claims which may be pursued by the stockholders as a class to redress injuries to the stockholders as individuals.

The ninth cause of action alleges initially that the defendants "breached their fiduciary duties to Major Oil and to its stockholders. . . ." As a general rule, directors and other officers of a corporation stand in a fiduciary relation to the corporation. [Citation.] While the statement is made that directors and officers stand in a like relation to the stockholders of the corporation, [citation], in Utah it is clear that that relation is to the stockholders collectively. [Citations.] The distinction between a fiduciary duty owed to the corporation as a whole as opposed to the stockholders collectively does not appear to be one of substance in this case. There is no important issue as to whether the cause of action states a corporate claim. Although plaintiff frames this claim, in the alternative, as one belonging to the shareholders, the claim for relief belongs to the corporation.

The ninth cause of action then goes on to allege that the defendants "mismanaged the corporate and prudential affairs of Major Oil. . . ." The rule in Utah is that mismanagement of the corporation gives rise to a cause of action in the corporation, even if the mismanagement results in damage to stockholders by depreciating the value of the corporation's stock. [Citation.] Therefore, any compensatory damages which may be recovered on account of any breach by defendants of their fiduciary duty as directors and officers or arising as a result of mismanagement of the corporation by defendants belong to the corporation and not to the stockholders individually.

* * *

We therefore reverse the district court's certification of this suit as a class action and remand for further proceedings not inconsistent with this opinion.

## CASE 36–3
### Duties of Controlling Shareholders
## *DONAHUE v. RODD ELECTROTYPE CO., INC.*
Massachusetts Supreme Court, 1974
367 Mass. 578, 328 N.E.2d 505

TAURO, C. J.

The plaintiff, Euphemia Donahue, a minority stockholder in the Rodd Electrotype Company of New England, Inc. (Rodd Electrotype), a Massachusetts corporation, brings this suit against the directors of Rodd Electrotype, Charles H. Rodd, Frederick I. Rodd and Mr. Harold E. Magnuson, against Harry C. Rodd, a former director, officer, and controlling stockholder of Rodd Electrotype and against Rodd Electrotype (hereinafter called defendants). The plaintiff seeks to rescind Rodd Electrotype's purchase of Harry Rodd's shares in Rodd Electrotype and to compel Harry Rodd "to repay to the corporation the purchase price of said shares, $36,000, together with interest from the date of purchase." The plaintiff alleges that the defendants caused the corporation to purchase the shares in violation of their fiduciary duty to her, a minority stockholder of Rodd Electrotype.

* * * We deem a close corporation to be typified by: (1) a small number of stockholders; (2) no ready market for the corporate stock; and (3) substantial majority stockholder participation in the management, direction and operations of the corporation.

As thus defined, the close corporation bears striking resemblance to a partnership. Commentators and courts have noted that the close corporation is often little more than an "incorporated" or "chartered" partnership. . . . Just as in a partnership, the relationship among the stockholders must be one of trust, confidence and absolute loyalty if the enterprise is to succeed. Close corporations with substantial assets and with more numerous stockholders are no different from smaller close corporations in this regard. All participants rely on the fidelity and abilities of those stockholders who hold office. Disloyalty and self-seeking conduct on the part of any stockholder will engender bickering, corporate stalemates, and, perhaps, efforts to achieve dissolution. * * *

* * *

Although the corporate form provides . . . advantages for the stockholders (limited liability, perpetuity, and so forth), it also supplies an opportunity for the majority stockholders to oppress or disadvantage minority stockholders. The minority is vulnerable to a variety of oppressive devices, termed "freeze-outs," which the majority may employ. [Citation.] An authoritative study of such "freeze-outs" enumerates some of the possibilities: "The squeezers [those who employ the freeze-out techniques] may refuse to declare dividends; they may drain off the corporation's earnings in the form of exorbitant salaries and bonuses to the majority shareholder-officers and perhaps to their relatives, or in the form of high rent by the corporation for property leased from majority shareholders . . .; they may deprive minority shareholders of corporate offices and of employment by the company; they may cause the corporation to sell its assets at an inadequate price to the majority shareholders. . . ." [Citation.] In particular, the power of the board of directors, controlled by the majority, to declare or withhold dividends and to deny the minority employment is easily converted to a device to disadvantage minority stockholders.

* * *

The minority can, of course, initiate suit against the majority and their directors. Self-serving conduct by directors is proscribed by the director's fiduciary obligation to the corporation. [Citation.] However, in practice, the plaintiff will find difficulty in challenging dividend or employment policies. Such policies are considered to be within the judgment of the directors. This court has said: "The courts prefer not to interfere . . . with the sound financial management of the corporation by its directors, but declare as a general rule that the declaration of dividends rests within the sound discretion of the directors, refusing to interfere with their determination unless a plain abuse of discretion is made to appear." * * *

Thus, when these types of "freeze-outs" are attempted by the majority stockholders, the minority stockholders, cut off from all corporation-related revenues, must either suffer their losses or seek a buyer for their shares. Many minority stockholders will be unwilling or unable to wait for an alteration in majority policy. Typically, the minority stockholder in a close corporation has a substantial percentage of his personal assets invested in the corporation. [Citation.] The stockholder may have anticipated that his salary from his position with the corporation would be his livelihood. Thus, he cannot afford to wait passively. He must liquidate his investment in the close corporation in order to reinvest the funds in income-producing enterprises.

At this point, the true plight of the minority stockholder in a close corporation becomes manifest. He cannot easily reclaim his capital. In a large public corporation, the oppressed or dissident minority stockholder could sell his stock in order to extricate some of his invested capital. By definition, this market is not available for shares in the close corporation. In a partnership, a partner who feels abused by his fellow partners may cause dissolution by his "express will . . . at any time" [citation] and recover his share of partnership assets and accumulated profits. . . . To secure dissolution of the ordinary close corporation subject to [citation], the stockholder, in the absence of corporate deadlock, must own at least fifty per cent of the shares [citation] or have the advantage of a favorable provision in the articles of organization [citation]. The minority stockholder, by definition lacking fifty per cent of the corporate shares, can never "authorize" the corporation to file a petition for dissolution under [citation], by his own vote. He will seldom have at his disposal the requisite favorable provision in the articles of organization.

Thus, in a close corporation, the minority stockholders may be trapped in a disadvantageous situation. No outsider would knowingly assume the position of the disadvantaged minority. The outsider would have the same difficulties. To cut losses, the minority stockholder may be compelled to deal with the majority. This is the capstone of the majority plan. Majority "freeze-out" schemes which withhold dividends are designed to compel the minority to relinquish stock at inadequate prices. . . . When the minority stockholder agrees to sell out at less than fair value, the majority has won.

Because of the fundamental resemblance of the close corporation to the partnership, the trust and confidence which are essential to this scale and manner of enterprise, and the inherent danger to minority interests in the close corporation, we hold that stockholders in the close corporation owe one another substantially the same fiduciary duty in the operation of the enterprise that partners owe to one another. In our previous decisions, we have defined the standard of duty owed by partners to one another as the "utmost good faith and loyalty." [Citations.] Stockholders in close corporations must discharge their management and stockholder responsibilities in conformity with this strict good faith standard. They may not act out of avarice, expediency or self-interest in derogation of their duty of loyalty to the other stockholders and to the corporation.

We contrast this strict good faith standard with the somewhat less stringent standard of fiduciary duty to which directors and stockholders of all corporations must adhere in the discharge of their corporate responsibilities. Corporate directors are held to a good faith and inherent fairness standard of conduct [citation] and are not "permitted to serve two masters whose interests are antagonistic." [Citation.] "Their paramount duty is to the corporation, and their personal pecuniary interests are subordinate to that duty." [Citation.]

The more rigorous duty of partners and participants in a joint adventure, here extended to stockholders in a close corporation, was described by then Chief Judge Cardozo of the New York Court of Appeals in [citation]: "Joint adventurers, like co-partners, owe to one another, while the enterprise continues, the duty of the finest loyalty. Many forms of conduct permissible in a workaday world for those acting at arm's length, are forbidden to those bound by fiduciary ties. . . . Not honesty alone, but the punctilio of an honor the most sensitive, is then the standard of behavior."

Application of this strict standard of duty to stockholders in close corporations is a natural outgrowth of the prior case law. In a number of cases involving close corporations, we have held stockholders participating in management to a standard of fiduciary duty more exacting than the traditional good faith and inherent fairness standard because of the trust and confidence reposed in them by the other stockholders. * * *

* * *

Under settled Massachusetts law, a domestic corporation, unless forbidden by statute, has the power to purchase its own shares. When the corporation reacquiring its own stock is a close corporation, the purchase is subject to the additional requirement, in the light of our holding in this opinion, that the stockholders, who, as directors or controlling stockholders, caused the corporation to enter into the stock purchase agreement, must have acted with the utmost good faith and loyalty to the other stockholders.

To meet this test, if the stockholder whose shares were purchased was a member of the controlling group, the controlling stockholders must cause the corporation to offer each stockholder an equal opportunity to sell a ratable number of his shares to the corporation at an identical price. * * *

The benefits conferred by the purchase are two-fold: (1) provision of a market for shares; (2) access to corporate assets for personal use. By definition, there is no ready market for shares of a close corporation. The purchase creates a market for shares which previously had been unmarketable. It transforms a previously illiquid investment into a liquid one. If the close corporation purchases shares only from a member of the controlling group, the controlling stockholder can convert his shares into cash at a time when none of the other stockholders can. Consistent with its strict fiduciary duty, the controlling group may not utilize its control of the corporation to establish an exclusive market in previously unmarketable shares from which the minority stockholders are excluded. * * *

The purchase also distributes corporate assets to the stockholder whose shares were purchased. Unless an equal opportunity is given to all stockholders, the purchase of shares from a member of the controlling group operates as a *preferential* distribution of assets. In exchange for his shares, he receives a percentage of the contributed capital and accumulated profits of the enterprise. The funds he so receives are available for his personal use. The other stockholders benefit from no such access to corporate property and cannot withdraw their shares of the corporate profits and capital in this manner unless the controlling group acquiesces. Although the purchase price for the controlling stockholder's shares may seem fair to the corporation and other stockholders under the tests established in the prior case law, the controlling stockholder whose stock has been purchased has still received a relative advantage over his fellow stockholders, inconsistent with his strict fiduciary duty—an opportunity to turn corporate funds to personal use.

The rule of equal opportunity in stock purchases by close corporations provides equal access to these benefits for all stockholders. We hold that, in any case in which the controlling stockholders have exercised their power over the corporation to deny the minority such equal opportunity, the minority shall be entitled to appropriate relief. * * *

The strict standard of duty is plainly applicable to the stockholders in Rodd Electrotype. Rodd Electrotype is a close corporation. Members of the Rodd and Donahue families are the sole owners of the corporation's stock. In actual numbers, the corporation, immediately prior to the corporate purchase of Harry Rodd's shares, had six stockholders. The shares have not been traded, and no market for them seems to exist. Harry Rodd, Charles Rodd, Frederick Rodd, William G. Mason (Phyllis Mason's husband), and the plaintiff's husband all worked for the corporation. The Rodds have retained the paramount management positions.

Through their control of these management positions and of the majority of the Rodd Electrotype stock, the Rodds effectively controlled the corporation. In testing the stock purchase from Harry Rodd against the applicable strict fiduciary standard, we treat the Rodd family as a single controlling group. We reject the defendants' contention that the Rodd family cannot be treated as a unit for this purpose. From the evidence, it is clear that the Rodd family was a close-knit one with strong community of interest. [Citation.] Harry Rodd had hired his sons to work in the family business, Rodd Electrotype. As he aged, he transferred portions of his stock holdings to his children. Charles Rodd and Frederick Rodd were given positions of responsibility in the business as he withdrew from active management. In these circumstances, it is realistic to assume that appreciation, gratitude, and filial devotion would prevent the younger Rodds from opposing a plan which would provide funds for their father's retirement.

* * *

On its face, then, the purchase of Harry Rodd's shares by the corporation is a breach of the duty which the controlling stockholders, the Rodds, owed to the minority stockholders, the plaintiff and her son. The purchase distributed a portion of the corporate assets to Harry Rodd, a member of the controlling group, in exchange for his shares. The plaintiff and her son were not offered an equal opportunity to sell their shares to the corporation. In fact, their efforts to obtain an equal opportunity were rebuffed by the corporate representative. As the trial judge found, they did not, in any manner, ratify the transaction with Harry Rodd.

Because of the foregoing, we hold that the plaintiff is entitled to relief.

## CASE 36–4
## Duty of Diligence
## *FRANCIS v. UNITED JERSEY BANK*
Supreme Court of New Jersey, 1981
87 N.J. 15, 432 A.2d 814

**POLLOCK, J.**

[Pritchard & Baird was a reinsurance broker. A reinsurance broker arranges contracts between insurance companies so companies that have sold large policies may sell participations in these policies to other companies in order to share the risks. Pritchard & Baird was controlled for many years by Charles Pritchard, who died in December 1973. Prior to his death, he brought his two sons, Charles Jr. and William, into the business. The pair assumed an increasingly dominant role in the affairs of the business during the elder Charles's later years. Starting in 1970, Charles Jr. and William began to withdraw ever-increasing sums from the corporation account that were designated as "loans" on the balance sheet. These "loans," however, represented a significant misappropriation of funds belonging to the clients of the corporation. By late 1975, Charles Jr. and William had plunged the corporation into hopeless bankruptcy. A total of $12,333,514.47 in "loans" had accumulated by October of that year. Mrs. Lillian Pritchard, the widow of the elder Charles, was a member of the corporation's board of directors during this period until her resignation on December 3, 1975, the day before the corporation filed for bankruptcy. Francis, as trustee in the bankruptcy proceeding, brought suit against United Jersey Bank, the administrator of the estate of Charles Sr. He also charged that Lillian Pritchard, as a director of the corporation, was personally liable for the misappropriated funds on the basis of negligence in discharging her duties as director. The trial court found Lillian Pritchard liable and the appellate court affirmed.]

Individual liability of a corporate director for acts of the corporation is a prickly problem. Generally directors are accorded broad immunity and are not insurers of corporate activities. The problem is particularly nettlesome when a third party asserts that a director, because of nonfeasance, is liable for losses caused by acts of insiders, who in this case were officers, directors and shareholders. Determination of the liability of Mrs. Pritchard requires findings that she had a duty to the clients of Pritchard & Baird, that she breached that duty and that her breach was a proximate cause of their losses.

The New Jersey Business Corporation Act, which took effect on January 1, 1969, was a comprehensive revision of the statutes relating to business corporations. One section, [citation], concerning a director's general obligation had no counterpart in the old Act. That section makes it incumbent upon directors to

discharge their duties in good faith and with that degree of diligence, care and skill which ordinarily prudent men would exercise under similar circumstances in like positions.

* * *

As a general rule, a director should acquire at least a rudimentary understanding of the business of the corporation. Accordingly, a director should become familiar with the fundamentals of the business in which the corporation is engaged. [Citation.] Because directors are bound to exercise ordinary care, they cannot set up as a defense lack of the knowledge needed to exercise the requisite degree of care. If one "feels that he has not had sufficient business experience to qualify him to perform the duties of a director, he should either acquire the knowledge by inquiry, or refuse to act." [Citation.]

Directors are under a continuing obligation to keep informed about the activities of the corporation. Otherwise, they may not be able to participate in the overall management of corporate affairs. [Citations.] Directors may not shut their eyes to corporate misconduct, and then claim that because they did not see the misconduct, they did not have a duty to look. The sentinel asleep at his post contributes nothing to the enterprise he is charged to protect. [Citation.]

Directorial management does not require a detailed inspection of day-to-day activities, but rather a general monitoring of corporate affairs and policies. [Citation.] Accordingly, a director is well advised to attend board meetings regularly. Indeed, a director who is absent from a board meeting is presumed to concur in action taken on a corporate matter, unless he files a "dissent with the secretary of the corporation within a reasonable time after learning of such action." [Citation.] Regular attendance does not mean that directors must attend every meeting, but that directors should attend meetings as a matter of practice. A director of a publicly held corporation might be expected to attend regular monthly meetings, but a director of a small, family corporation might be asked to attend only an annual meeting. The point is that one of the responsibilities of a director is to attend meetings of the board of which he or she is a member. That burden is lightened by [citation], which permits board action without a meeting if all members of the board consent in writing.

While directors are not required to audit corporate books, they should maintain familiarity with the financial status of the corporation by a regular review of financial statements. * * *

* * *

The review of financial statements, however, may give rise to a duty to inquire further into matters revealed by those statements. [Citations.] Upon discovery of an illegal course of action, a director has a duty to object and, if the corporation does not correct the conduct, to resign. [Citations.]

In certain circumstances, the fulfillment of the duty of a director may call for more than mere objection and resignation. Sometimes a director may be required to seek the advice of counsel. * * *

* * *

As a director of a substantial reinsurance brokerage corporation, she should have known that it received annually millions of dollars of loss and premium funds which it held in trust for ceding and reinsurance companies. Mrs. Pritchard should have obtained and read the annual statements of financial condition of Pritchard & Baird. Although she had a right to rely upon financial statements prepared in accordance with [citation], such reliance would not excuse her conduct. The reason is that those statements disclosed on their face the misappropriation of trust funds.

From those statements, she should have realized that, as of January 31, 1970, her sons were withdrawing substantial trust funds under the guise of "Shareholders' Loans." The financial statements for each fiscal year commencing with that of January 31, 1970, disclosed that the working capital deficits and the "loans" were escalating in tandem. Detecting a misappropriation of funds would not have required special expertise or extraordinary diligence; a cursory reading of the financial statements

would have revealed the pillage. Thus, if Mrs. Pritchard had read the financial statements, she would have known that her sons were converting trust funds. When financial statements demonstrate that insiders are bleeding a corporation to death, a director should notice and try to stanch the flow of blood.

In summary, Mrs. Pritchard was charged with the obligation of basic knowledge and supervision of the business of Pritchard & Baird. Under the circumstances, this obligation included reading and understanding financial statements, and making reasonable attempts at detection and prevention of the illegal conduct of other officers and directors. She had a duty to protect the clients of Pritchard & Baird against policies and practices that would result in the misappropriation of money they had entrusted to the corporation. She breached that duty.

Nonetheless, the negligence of Mrs. Pritchard does not result in liability unless it is a proximate cause of the loss. . . . Thus, the plaintiff must establish not only a breach of duty, "but in addition that the performance by the director of his duty would have avoided loss, and the amount of the resulting loss." [Citation.]

* * *

Within Pritchard & Baird, several factors contributed to the loss of the funds: comingling of corporate and client monies, conversion of funds by Charles, Jr. and William and dereliction of her duties by Mrs. Pritchard. The wrongdoing of her sons, although the immediate cause of the loss, should not excuse Mrs. Pritchard from her negligence which also was a substantial factor contributing to the loss. [Citation.] Her sons knew that she, the only other director, was not reviewing their conduct; they spawned their fraud in the backwater of her neglect. Her neglect of duty contributed to the climate of corruption; her failure to act contributed to the continuation of that corruption. Consequently, her conduct was a substantial factor contributing to the loss.

Analysis of proximate cause is especially difficult in a corporate context where the allegation is that nonfeasance of a director is a proximate cause of damage to a third party. Where a case involves nonfeasance, no one can say "with absolute certainty what would have occurred if the defendant had acted otherwise." [Citation.] Nonetheless, where it is reasonable to conclude that the failure to act would produce a particular result and that result has followed, causation may be inferred. [Citation.] We conclude that even if Mrs. Pritchard's mere objection had not stopped the depredations of her sons, her consultation with an attorney and the threat of suit would have deterred them. That conclusion flows as a matter of common sense and logic from the record. Whether in other situations a director has a duty to do more than protest and resign is best left to case-by-case determinations. In this case, we are satisfied that there was a duty to do more than object and resign. Consequently, we find that Mrs. Pritchard's negligence was a proximate cause of the misappropriations.

To conclude, by virtue of her office, Mrs. Pritchard had the power to prevent the losses sustained by the clients of Pritchard & Baird. With power comes responsibility. She had a duty to deter the depredation of the other insiders, her sons. She breached that duty and caused plaintiffs to sustain damages.

[Judgment for Francis affirmed.]

---

## CASE 36–5
## Duty of Loyalty
### *KLINICKI v. LUNDGREN*
Supreme Court of Oregon, 1985
298 Or. 662, 695 P.2d 906

JONES, J.
The factual and legal background of this complicated litigation was succinctly set forth by Chief Judge Joseph in the Court of Appeals opinion as follows:

In January, 1977, plaintiff Klinicki conceived the idea of engaging in the air transportation business in Berlin, West Germany. He discussed the idea with his friend, defendant Lundgren. At that time, both men were furloughed Pan American pilots stationed in West Germany. They decided to enter the air transportation business, planning to begin operations with an air taxi service and later to expand into other service, such as regularly scheduled flights or charter flights. In April, 1977, they incorporated Berlinair, Inc., as a closely held Oregon corporation. Plaintiff was a vice-president and a director. Lundgren was the corporation's president and a director. Each man owned 33 percent of the company stock. Lelco, Inc., a corporation owned by Lundgren and members of his family, owned 33 percent of the stock. The corporation's attorney owned the remaining one percent of the stock. Berlinair obtained the necessary governmental licenses, purchased an aircraft and in November, 1977, began passenger service.

As president, Lundgren was responsible, in part, for developing and promoting Berlinair's transportation business. Plaintiff was in charge of operations and maintenance. In November, 1977, plaintiff and Lundgren, as representatives of Berlinair, met with representatives of the Berliner Flug Ring (BFR), a consortium of Berlin travel agents that contracts for charter flights to take sallow German tourists to sunnier climes. The BFR contract was considered a lucrative business opportunity by those familiar with the air transportation business, and plaintiff and defendant had contemplated pursuing the contract when they formed Berlinair. After the initial meeting, all subsequent contacts with BFR were made by Lundgren or other Berlinair employees acting under his directions.

During the early stages of negotiations, Lundgren believed that Berlinair could not obtain the contract because BFR was then satisfied with its carrier. In early June, 1978, however, Lundgren learned that there was a good chance that the BFR contract might be available. He informed a BFR representative that he would make a proposal on behalf of a new company. On July 7, 1978, he incorporated Air Berlin Charter Company (ABC) and was its sole owner. On August 20, 1978, ABC presented BFR with a contract proposal, and after a series of discussions it was awarded the contract on September 1, 1978. Lundgren effectively concealed from plaintiff his negotiations with BFR and his diversion of the BFR contract to ABC, even though he used Berlinair working time, staff, money and facilities.

Plaintiff, as a minority stockholder in Berlinair, brought a derivative action against ABC for usurping a corporate opportunity of Berlinair. He also brought an individual claim against Lundgren for compensatory and punitive damages based on breach of fiduciary duty.

The trial court found that ABC, acting through Lundgren, had wrongfully diverted the BFR contract, which was a corporate opportunity of Berlinair. The court imposed a constructive trust on ABC in favor of Berlinair, ordered an accounting by ABC and enjoined ABC from transferring its assets. The trial court also found that Lundgren, as an officer and director of Berlinair, had breached his fiduciary duties of good faith, fair dealing and full disclosure owed to plaintiff individually and to Berlinair. The court did not award plaintiff any actual damages on the breach of fiduciary duty claim. All the issues were tried to the court, except that a jury was empaneled to try the punitive damages issue. It returned a verdict in favor of plaintiff and assessed punitive damages against Lundgren in the amount of $750,000. Lundgren then moved to dismiss plaintiff's claim for punitive damages. The court granted the motion to dismiss and, *sua sponte,* entered judgment in favor of Lundgren notwithstanding the verdict on the punitive damages claim.

ABC appealed to the Court of Appeals contending that it did not usurp a corporate opportunity of Berlinair. * * *

ABC petitions for review to this court contending that the concealment and diversion of the BFR contract was not a usurpation of a corporate opportunity, because Berlinair did not have the financial ability to undertake that contract. ABC argues that proof of financial ability is a necessary part of a corporate opportunity case and that plaintiff had the burden of proof on that issue and did not carry that burden.

There is no dispute that the corporate opportunity doctrine precludes corporate fiduciaries from diverting to themselves business opportunities in which the corporation has an expectancy, property interest or right, or which in fairness should otherwise belong to the corporation. [Citation.] The doctrine follows from a corporate fiduciary's duty of undivided loyalty to the corporation. ABC agrees that, unless Berlinair's financial inability to undertake the contract makes a difference, the BFR contract was a corporate opportunity of Berlinair.

* * *

Where a director or principal senior executive of a close corporation wishes to take personal advantage of a "corporate opportunity," . . . the director or principal senior executive must comply strictly with the following procedure:

(1) the director or principal senior executive must promptly offer the opportunity and disclose all material facts known regarding the opportunity to the disinterested directors or, if there is no disinterested director, to the disinterested shareholders. If the director or principal senior executive learns of other material facts after such disclosure, the director or principal senior executive must disclose these additional facts in a like manner before personally taking the opportunity.

(2) The director or principal senior executive may take advantage of the corporate opportunity only after full disclosure and only if the opportunity is rejected by a majority of the disinterested directors or, if there are no disinterested directors, by a majority of the disinterested shareholders. If, after full disclosure, the disinterested directors or shareholders unreasonably fail to reject the offer, the interested director or principal senior executive may proceed to take the opportunity if he can prove the taking was otherwise "fair" to the corporation. Full disclosure to the appropriate corporate body is, however, an absolute condition precedent to the validity of any forthcoming rejection as well as to the availability to the director or principal senior executive of the defense of fairness.

(3) An appropriation of a corporate opportunity may be ratified by rejection of the opportunity by a majority of disinterested directors or a majority of disinterested shareholders, after full disclosure subject to the same rules as set out above for prior offer, disclosure and rejection. Where a director or principal senior executive of a close corporation appropriates a corporate opportunity without first fully disclosing the opportunity and offering it to the corporation, absent ratification, that director or principal senior executive holds the opportunity in trust for the corporation.

Applying these rules to the facts in this case, we conclude:

1. Lundgren, as director and principal executive officer of Berlinair, owed a fiduciary duty to Berlinair.
2. The BFR contract was a "corporate opportunity" of Berlinair.
3. Lundgren formed ABC for the purpose of usurping the opportunity presented to Berlinair by the BFR contract.
4. Lundgren did not offer Berlinair the BFR contract.
5. Lundgren did not attempt to obtain the consent of Berlinair to his taking of the BFR corporate opportunity.
6. Lundgren did not fully disclose to Berlinair his intent to appropriate the opportunity for himself and ABC.
7. Berlinair never rejected the opportunity presented by the BFR contract.
8. Berlinair never ratified the appropriation of the BFR contract.
9. Lundgren, acting for ABC, misappropriated the BFR contract.

Because of the above, the defendant may not now contend that Berlinair did not have the financial ability to successfully pursue the BFR contract. As stated in [citation]: "If the challenging party satisfies the burden of proving that a corporate opportunity was taken without being offered to the corporation, the challenging party will prevail."

[Judgment affirmed.]

# Questions

**1.** Compare the actual governance of closely held corporations, the actual governance of publicly held corporations, and the statutory model of corporate governance.

**2.** Explain the role of shareholders in the management of a corporation.

**3.** Explain the role of the board of directors in the management of a corporation.

**4.** Explain the role of officers in the management of a corporation.

**5.** Explain management's duties of loyalty, obedience, and diligence.

# Problems

**1.** Brown, the president and director of a corporation engaged in owning and operating a chain of motels, was advised, upon what seemed to be good authority, that a superhighway was to be constructed through the town of X, which would be a most desirable location for a motel. Brown presented these facts to the board of directors of the motel corporation and recommended that the corporation build a motel in the town of X at the location described. The board of directors agreed, and the new motel was constructed. The superhighway plans were changed, however, after the motel was constructed, and the highway was never built. Later, a packinghouse was built on property adjoining the motel, and the corporation sustained a considerable loss as a result. The shareholders brought an appropriate action against Brown, charging that his proposal had caused a substantial loss to the corporation and seeking recovery of that loss from Brown. Decision?

**2.** A, B, C, D, and E constituted the board of directors of the X Corporation. While D and E were out of town, A, B, and C held a special meeting of the board. Just as the meeting began, C became ill. He then gave a proxy to A and went home. A resolution was then adopted directing and authorizing X Corporation's purchase of an adjoining piece of land owned by S as a site for an additional factory building. As was known by S, the purchase required approval by the board of directors. A and B voted for the resolution, and A, as C's proxy, cast C's vote in favor of the resolution. X Corporation then made a contract with S for the purchase of the land. After the return of D and E, another special meeting of the board was held with all five directors present. A resolution was then unanimously adopted to cancel the contract with S. So notified, S now sues X Corporation for damages for breach of contract. Decision?

**3.** Bernard Koch was president of United Corporation, a closely held corporation. Koch, James Trent, and Henry Phillips made up the three-person board of directors. At a meeting of the board, Trent was elected president, replacing Koch. At the same meeting, Trent attempted to have the salary of the president increased. He was unable to obtain board approval of the increase because, although Phillips voted for the increase, Koch voted against it. Trent was disqualified from voting by the corporation's charter. As a result, the directors, by a two-to-one

vote, amended the bylaws to provide for the appointment of an executive committee composed of three reputable businesspersons to pass upon and fix all matters of salary for employees of the corporation. Subsequently, the executive committee, consisting of Jane Jones, James Black, and William Johnson, increased the salary of the president.

Koch brought an appropriate action against the corporation, Trent, and Phillips to enjoin them from paying compensation to the president above that fixed by the board of directors. What decision?

**4.** Zenith Steel Company operates a prosperous business. In January, its president, Roe, who is also a director, was voted a $100,000 bonus by the board of directors for the valuable services he provided to the company during the previous year. Roe receives an annual salary of $85,000 from the company. Black, a minority shareholder in Zenith Steel Company, brings an appropriate action to enjoin the company from paying the $100,000 bonus. Decision?

**5.** (a) Smith, a director of the Sample Corporation, sells a piece of vacant land to the Sample Corporation for $50,000. The land cost him $20,000.

(b) Jones, a shareholder of the Sample Corporation, sells a used truck to the Sample Corporation for $8,400, although the truck is worth $6,000.

Raphael, a minority shareholder of the Sample Corporation, claims that these sales are void and should be annulled. Is he correct? Why?

**6.** The X Corporation manufactures machine tools. The five directors of X Corporation are Black, White, Brown, Green, and Crimson. At a duly called meeting of the board of directors of X Corporation in January, all five directors were present. A contract for the purchase of $1 million worth of steel from the D Company, of which Black, White, and Brown are directors, was discussed and approved by a unanimous vote. The board also discussed at length entering into negotiations for the purchase of Q Corporation, which allegedly was about to be sold for around $15 million. By a three-to-two vote, it was decided not to open such negotiations.

Three months later, Green purchased Q Corporation for $15 million. Shortly thereafter, a new board of directors for

X Corporation took office. X Corporation now brings actions to rescind its contract with D Company and to compel Green to assign to X Corporation his contract for the purchase of Q Corporation. Decisions as to each action?

7.    Gore had been the owner of 1 percent of the outstanding shares of the Webster Company, a corporation, since its organization ten years ago. Ratliff, the president of the company, was the owner of 70 percent of the outstanding shares. Ratliff used the shareholders' list to submit to the shareholders an offer of $50 per share for their stock. Gore, upon receiving the offer, called Ratliff and told him that the offer was inadequate and advised that she was willing to offer $60 per share, and for that purpose demanded a shareholders' list. Ratliff knew that Gore was willing and able to supply the funds necessary to purchase the stock, but he nevertheless refused to supply the list to Gore. Further, he did not offer to transmit Gore's offer to the shareholders of record. Gore then brought an action to compel the corporation to make the shareholders' list available to her. Decision?

8.    Mitchell, Nelson, Olsen, and Parker, experts in manufacturing baubles, each owned fifteen out of one hundred authorized shares of Baubles, Inc., a corporation of State X, which does not permit cumulative voting. On July 7, 1989, the corporation sold forty shares to Quentin, an investor, for $1,500,000, which it used to purchase a factory building for $1,500,000. On July 8, 1989, Mitchell, Nelson, Olsen, and Parker contracted as follows:

All parties will act jointly in exercising voting rights as shareholders. In the event of a failure to agree, the question shall be submitted to George Yost, whose decision shall be binding upon all parties.

Until a meeting of shareholders on April 17, 1999, when a dispute arose, all parties to the contract had voted consistently and regularly for Nelson, Olsen, and Parker as directors. At that meeting, Yost considered the dispute and decided and directed that Mitchell, Nelson, Olsen, and Parker vote their shares for the latter three as directors. Nelson, Olsen, and Parker so voted. Mitchell and Quentin voted for themselves and Mrs. Quentin as directors.

   (a)   Is the contract of July 8, 1989, valid? If so, what is its effect?

   (b)   Who were elected directors of Baubles, Inc., at the meeting of its shareholders on April 17, 1999?

9.    Acme Corporation's articles of incorporation require cumulative voting for the election of its directors. The board of directors of Acme Corporation consists of nine directors, each elected annually.

   (a)   Smith owns 24 percent of the outstanding shares of Acme Corporation. How many directors can he elect with his votes?

   (b)   If Acme Corporation were to classify its board into three classes, each consisting of three directors elected every three years, how many directors would Smith be able to elect?

10.    Neese, trustee in bankruptcy for First Trust Company, brings a suit against the directors of the company for losses the company sustained as a result of the directors' failure to use due care and diligence in the discharge of their duties. The specific acts of negligence alleged are (1) failure to give as much time and attention to the affairs of the company as its business interests required; (2) abdication of their control of the corporation by turning its management entirely over to its president, Brown; (3) failure to keep informed as to the affairs, condition, and management of the corporation; (4) taking no action to direct or control the corporation's affairs; (5) permitting large, open, unsecured loans to affiliated but financially unsound companies that were owned and controlled by Brown; (6) failure to examine financial reports that would have shown illegal diversions and waste of the corporation's funds; and (7) failure to supervise properly the corporation's officers and directors. Decision?

11.    Minority shareholders of Midwest Technical Institute Development Corporation, a closed-end investment company owning assets consisting principally of securities of companies in technological fields, brought a shareholder derivative suit against officers and directors of Midwest, seeking to recover on Midwest's behalf profits that the officers and directors realized through dealings in stock held in Midwest's portfolio in breach of their fiduciary duty. Approximately three years after commencement of the action, a new corporation, Midtex, was organized to acquire Midwest's assets. The shareholders now seek to add Midtex as a party defendant to their suit. Decision?

12.    Litton, an officer and the dominant shareholder of Dixie Splint Coal Company, transferred the company's remaining assets to himself when the company came to the verge of bankruptcy. The transfer allegedly was in satisfaction of an accrued salary claim that Litton had not enforced until the company came into financial difficulty. The trustee in bankruptcy seeks to have Litton's claim disallowed. Decision?

13.    Riffe, while serving as an officer of Wilshire Oil Company, received a secret commission for work he did on behalf of a competing corporation. Wilshire Oil brings this action against Riffe to recover these secret profits and, in addition, to recover the compensation paid to Riffe by Wilshire Oil during the period that he acted on behalf of the competitor. Decision?

14.    Muller, a shareholder of SCM, brought an action against SCM over his unsuccessful negotiations to purchase some of SCM's assets overseas. He then formed a shareholder committee to challenge the position of SCM's management in that suit. To conduct a proxy battle for management control at the next election of directors, the committee sought to obtain the list of shareholders who would be eligible to vote. At the time, however, no member of the committee had owned stock in SCM for the six-month period required to gain access to such information. Then Lopez, a former SCM executive and a shareholder for more than one year, joined the committee and demanded to be allowed to inspect the minutes of SCM shareholder proceedings and to gain access to the current shareholder list. His stated reason for making the demand was to

solicit proxies in support of those the committee had nominated for positions as directors. Lopez brought this action after SCM rejected this demand. Decision?

**15.**   A bylaw of Betma Corporation provides that no shareholder can sell his shares unless he first offers them for sale to the corporation or its directors. The bylaw also states that this restriction shall be printed or stamped upon each stock certificate and shall bind all present or future owners or holders. Betma Corporation did not comply with this latter provision. Shaw, having knowledge of the bylaw restriction, nevertheless purchased twenty shares of the corporation's stock from Rice, without having Rice first offer them for sale to the corporation or its directors. When Betma Corporation refused to effectuate a transfer of the shares to her, Shaw sued to compel a transfer and the issuance of a new certificate to her. Decision?

**Internet Exercise** Using the Securities and Exchange Commission's EDGAR database, find the Annual Report (Form 10-K) and, if necessary, the proxy statement (DEF 14A) of three companies of interest and determine (a) the number of inside and outside directors, (b) what committees the board of directors has established, (c) the compensation for the three highest paid officers (including the value of stock options), and (d) whether any person owns more than 5 percent of the outstanding shares of common stock.

# CHAPTER 37

# Fundamental Changes

Certain extraordinary changes exert such a fundamental effect on a corporation by altering the corporation's basic structure that they fall outside the authority of the board of directors and require shareholder approval. Such fundamental changes include charter amendments, mergers, consolidations, compulsory share exchanges, dissolution, and the sale or lease of all or substantially all of the corporation's assets, other than those in the regular course of business. Although each of these actions is authorized by State incorporation statutes, which impose specific procedural requirements, they are also subject to equitable limitations imposed by the courts.

Because shareholder approval for fundamental changes usually does not need to be unanimous, such changes frequently will be approved despite opposition by minority shareholders. Shareholder approval means a majority (or some other specified fraction) of *all votes entitled* to be cast, rather than a majority (or other fraction) of votes represented at a shareholders' meeting at which a quorum is present. In some instances, minority shareholders have the right to dissent and to recover the fair value of their shares if they follow the prescribed procedure for doing so. This right is called the appraisal remedy. The legal aspects of fundamental changes will be discussed in this chapter.

## CHARTER AMENDMENTS

Shareholders do not have a vested property right resulting from any provision in the articles of incorporation. Section 10.01(b). Accordingly, corporate charters may be amended if proper procedures are followed. The amended articles of incorporation, however, may contain only those provisions that the articles of incorporation might lawfully contain at the time of the amendment. Section 10.01(a).

## Approval by Directors and Shareholders

Under modern statutes, the typical procedure for amending the articles of incorporation requires the board of directors to adopt a resolution setting forth the proposed amendment, which must then be approved by a majority vote of the shareholders entitled to vote, although some older statutes require a two-thirds shareholder vote. Moreover, a class of shares is entitled to vote as a class on certain proposed amendments, whether the articles of incorporation provide such entitlement or not.

After the shareholders approve the amendment, the corporation executes articles of amendment and delivers them to the Secretary of State for filing. Section 10.06. The amendment does not affect the existing rights of nonshareholders. Section 10.09.

Under Section 13.02(a)(4) of the Revised Act, dissenting shareholders may obtain the appraisal remedy only if an amendment materially and adversely affects their rights by

1. altering or abolishing a preferential right of the shares;
2. creating, altering, or abolishing a right involving the redemption of the shares;
3. altering or abolishing a preemptive right of the holder of the shares;
4. excluding or limiting the shareholder's right to vote on any matter or to cumulate his votes; or
5. reducing to a fraction of a share the number of shares the shareholder owns, if the fractional share is to be acquired for cash.

Under the Revised Act, the shareholder approval required for an amendment depends upon the nature of the amendment. An amendment that would give rise to dissenters' rights must be approved by a majority of all votes entitled to be cast on the amendment, unless the act, the charter, or the board of directors requires a greater vote. All other amendments must be approved by a majority of all votes cast on the amendment at a meeting where a quorum exists, unless the act, the charter, or the board of directors requires a greater vote. Sections 10.03, 7.25.

## Approval by Directors

The Revised Act permits the board of directors to adopt certain amendments without shareholder action, unless the articles of incorporation provide otherwise. Section 10.02. These amendments include (1) extending the duration of the corporation if it was incorporated when limited duration was required by law, (2) changing each issued and unissued authorized share of an outstanding class into a greater number of whole shares if the corporation has only one class of shares, and (3) making minor name changes.

## COMBINATIONS

Acquiring all or substantially all of the assets of another corporation or corporations may be both desirable and profitable. A corporation may accomplish this through (1) purchase or lease of other corporations' assets, (2) purchase of a controlling stock interest in other corporations, (3) merger with other corporations, or (4) consolidation with other corporations.

Any method of combination that involves the issuance of shares, proxy solicitations, or tender offers may be subject to Federal securities regulation, as discussed in Chapter 44. Moreover, a combination that is potentially detrimental to competition may be subject to Federal antitrust laws, as discussed in Chapter 41.

## Purchase or Lease of All or Substantially All of the Assets

When one corporation purchases or leases all or substantially all of the assets of another corporation, the legal personality of neither corporation changes. The purchaser or lessee corporation simply acquires ownership or control of additional physical assets. The selling or lessor corporation, in exchange for its physical properties, receives cash, other property, or a stipulated rental. Having altered only the form or extent of its assets, each corporation continues its separate existence.

Generally, a corporation that purchases the assets of another corporation does not assume the other's liabilities unless (1) the purchaser expressly or impliedly agrees to assume the seller's liabilities; (2) the transaction

amounts to a consolidation or merger of the two corporations; (3) the purchaser is a mere continuation of the seller; or (4) the sale is for the fraudulent purpose of avoiding the liabilities of the seller. Some courts recognize a fifth exception (called the "product line" exception), which imposes strict tort liability upon the purchaser for defects in products manufactured and distributed by the seller corporation when the purchaser corporation continues the product line.

***Regular Course of Business***  If the sale or lease of all or substantially all of its assets is in the selling or lessor corporation's usual and regular course of business, approval by its board of directors is required but shareholder authorization is not. Similarly, a mortgage or pledge of any or all of a corporation's property and assets—whether or not in the usual or regular course of business—requires only the approval of the board of directors. Section 12.01. The Revised Act considers a transfer of any or all of a corporation's assets to a wholly owned subsidiary to be a sale in the regular course of business. Section 12.01(a)(3). Under the Revised Act, a sale of assets in the regular course of business does not require shareholder approval unless the articles of incorporation provide otherwise. Section 12.01(b).

***Other Than in Regular Course of Business***  Shareholder approval is necessary *only if* a sale or lease of all or substantially all of its assets is *not* in the corporation's usual and regular course of business. The selling corporation, by liquidating its assets, or the lessor corporation, by placing its physical assets beyond its control, has significantly changed its position and perhaps its ability to carry on the type of business contemplated in its charter. For this reason, such sale or lease must be approved not only by action of the directors but also by the affirmative vote of the holders of a majority of the corporation's shares entitled to vote at a shareholders' meeting called for this purpose. Section 12.02. In most States, dissenting shareholders of the selling corporation are given an appraisal remedy. Section 13.02(a)(3).

## Purchase of Shares

An alternative to purchasing another corporation's assets is to purchase its stock. When one corporation acquires all of or a controlling interest in the stock of another corporation, the legal existence of neither corporation changes. The acquiring corporation acts through its board of directors, whereas the corporation that becomes a subsidiary does not act at all, because the decision to sell stock is made not by the corporation but by its individual shareholders. The capital structure of the subsidiary remains unchanged, and that of the parent is usually not altered unless financing the acquisition of the stock necessitates a change in capital. Because the action of neither corporation requires formal shareholder approval, there is no appraisal remedy.

***Sale of Control*** When a controlling interest is owned by one or a few shareholders, a privately negotiated transaction is possible, though the courts require that these sales be made with due care. The controlling shareholders must make a reasonable investigation so as not to transfer control to purchasers who wrongfully plan to steal or "loot" the corporation's assets or to act against its best interests. In addition, purchasers frequently are willing to pay a premium for a block of shares that conveys control. Although historically some courts have required that this so-called control premium inure to the benefit of the corporation, today virtually all courts permit the controlling shareholders to retain the full amount of the control premium.

***Tender Offer*** When a controlling interest is not held by one or a few shareholders, the acquisition of a corporation through the purchase of shares may take the form of a tender offer. A tender offer is a general invitation to all the shareholders of a target company to tender their shares for sale at a specified price. The offer may be for all of the target company's shares or for just a controlling interest. Tender offers for publicly held companies, which are subject to Federal securities regulation, are discussed in Chapter 44.

## Compulsory Share Exchange

The Revised Act and some States provide different procedures where a corporation acquires shares through a **compulsory share exchange,** a transaction by which the corporation becomes the owner of *all* the outstanding shares of one or more classes of another corporation by an exchange that is compulsory on all owners of the acquired shares. Section 11.02. The corporation may acquire the shares with its or any other corporation's shares, obligations, or other securities or for cash or other property. For example, if A corporation acquires all of the outstanding shares of B corporation through a compulsory exchange, then B becomes a wholly owned subsidiary of A. A compulsory share exchange affects the separate existence of neither corporate party to the transaction. Although they produce results similar to mergers,

as discussed below, compulsory share exchanges are used instead of mergers where preserving the existence of the acquired corporation is essential or desirable, as, for example, in the formation of holding company systems for insurance companies and banks.

A compulsory share exchange requires approval from the board of directors of each corporation and from the shareholders of the corporation whose shares are being acquired. Sections 11.02 and 11.03. Each included class of shares must vote separately on the exchange. The transaction need not be approved by the shareholders of the corporation acquiring the shares. Once the shareholders of the corporation whose shares are to be acquired have adopted and approved a compulsory share exchange plan, it is binding on all who hold shares of the class to be acquired. Dissenting shareholders are given an appraisal remedy. Section 13.02(a)(2).

## Merger

A **merger** of two or more corporations is the combination of all of their assets. One of the corporations, known as the **surviving corporation,** receives title to the combined assets. The other party or parties to the merger, known as the **merged corporation** or corporations, are merged into the surviving corporation and cease their separate existence. Thus, if A Corporation and B Corporation combine into the A Corporation, A is the surviving corporation and B the merged corporation. The shareholders of the merged corporation may receive stock or other securities issued by the surviving corporation or other consideration, as provided in the merger agreement. Moreover, the surviving corporation assumes all debts and other liabilities of the merged corporation. Section 11.06.

A merger requires the approval of each corporation's board of directors, as well as the affirmative vote of the holders of a majority of the shares of each corporation that are entitled to vote. Sections 11.01 and 11.03. A dissenting shareholder of any corporate party to the merger has an appraisal remedy if shareholder approval is required and the shareholder is entitled to vote on the merger. Section 13.02(a)(1).

In a **short-form merger,** a corporation that owns at least 90 percent of the outstanding shares of each class of a subsidiary may merge the subsidiary into itself without approval by the shareholders of either corporation. Section 11.04. Obtaining approval from the subsidiary's shareholders or from the subsidiary's board of directors is unnecessary because the parent's 90 percent ownership ensures approval of the merger plan. All the merger requires is a resolution by the board of directors of the parent corporation. The dissenting shareholders of the subsidiary have the right to obtain payment from the parent for their shares. Section 13.02(a)(1). The shareholders of the parent do not have this appraisal remedy because the transaction has not materially changed their rights. Instead of indirectly owning 90 percent of the subsidiary's assets, the parent now directly owns 100 percent of the same assets.

 *See Case 37–1*

## Consolidation

A **consolidation** of two or more corporations is the combination of all of their assets, the title to which is taken by a newly created corporation known as the **consolidated corporation.** Each constituent corporation ceases to exist, and all of its debts and liabilities are assumed by the new corporation. The shareholders of the constituent corporations receive stock or other securities, not necessarily of the same class, issued to them by the new corporation or other consideration provided in the plan of consolidation. A consolidation requires the approval of each corporation's board of directors, as well as the affirmative vote of the holders of a majority of the shares of each corporation that are entitled to vote. Dissenting shareholders have an appraisal remedy.

The Revised Act has deleted all references to consolidations, as explained by the comment to Section 11.01: "In modern corporate practice consolidation transactions are obsolete since it is nearly always advantageous for one of the parties in the transaction to be the surviving corporation."

## Going Private Transactions

Corporate combinations are sometimes used to take a publicly held corporation private in order to eliminate minority interests, to reduce the burdens of certain provisions of the Federal securities laws, or both. One method of going private is for the corporation or its majority shareholder to acquire the corporation's shares through purchases on the open market or through a tender offer for the shares. Other methods include a cash-out combination, a merger with or sale of assets to a corporation controlled by the majority shareholder. If the majority shareholder is a corporation, it may arrange a cash-out combination with itself or, if it owns enough shares, use a short-form merger. In recent years, a new

type of going private transaction—a management buyout—has become much more frequent. This section will examine cash-out combinations and management buyouts.

***Cash-out Combinations***  Cash-out combinations are used to eliminate minority shareholders by forcing them to accept cash or property for their shares. A cash-out combination often follows the acquisition, by a person, group, or company, of a large interest in a target company (T) through a tender offer. The tender offeror (TO) then seeks to eliminate all other shareholders, thereby achieving complete control of T. To do so, TO might form a new corporation (Corporation N) and take 100 percent of its stock. A cash-out merger of T into N is then arranged, with all the shareholders of T other than TO to receive cash for their shares. Because TO owns all the stock of N and a controlling interest in T, the shareholders of both companies will approve the merger. Alternatively, TO could purchase for cash or notes the assets of T, leaving the minority shareholders with only an interest in the proceeds of the sale. The use of cash-out combinations has raised questions concerning their purpose and their fairness to minority shareholders. Some States require that cash-out combinations have a valid business purpose and that they be fair to all concerned. Fairness, in this context, includes both fair dealing (which involves the procedural aspects of the transaction) and fair price (which involves the financial considerations of the merger). Other States require only the transaction to be fair.

 *See Case 37–2*

***Management Buyout***  A management buyout is a transaction by which existing management increases its ownership of a corporation while eliminating the entity's public shareholders. The typical procedure is as follows. The management of an existing company (Corporation A) forms a new corporation (Corporation B) in which the management owns some of the stock and institutional investors own the rest. Corporation B issues bonds to institutional investors to raise cash, with which it purchases the assets or stock of Corporation A. The assets of Corporation A are used as security for the bonds issued by Corporation B. (Because of the extensive use of borrowed funds, a management buyout is commonly called a **leveraged buyout** (LBO).) The result of this transaction is twofold: the public shareholders of Corporation A no longer have any proprietary interest in the assets of Corporation A, and management's equity interest in Corporation B is greater than its interest was in Corporation A.

A critical issue is the fairness of the management buyout to the shareholders of Corporation A. The transaction inherently presents a potential conflict of interest to those in management, who owe a fiduciary duty to represent the interests of the shareholders of Corporation A. As substantial shareholders of Corporation B, however, those in management are apt to have personal and probably adverse financial interests in the transaction.

## Dissenting Shareholders

The **shareholder's right to dissent,** a statutory right to obtain payment for shares, is accorded to shareholders who object to certain fundamental changes in the corporation. The Introductory Comment to Chapter 13 of the Revised Act explains the purpose of dissenters' rights:

Chapter 13 deals with the tension between the desire of the corporate leadership to be able to enter new fields, acquire new enterprises, and rearrange investor rights and the desire of investors to adhere to the rights and the risks on the basis of which they invested. Most contemporary corporation codes in the United States attempt to resolve this tension through a combination of two devices. On the one hand, the majority is given an almost unlimited power to change the nature and shape of the enterprise and the rights of its members. On the other hand, the members who dissent from these changes are given a right to withdraw their investment at a fair value.

### Transactions Giving Rise to Dissenters' Rights
Most States grant dissenters' rights to (1) dissenting shareholders of a corporation selling or leasing all or substantially all of its property or assets not in the usual or regular course of business; (2) dissenting shareholders of each corporate party to a merger, except in a short-form merger, where only the dissenting shareholders of the subsidiary have dissenters' rights; and (3) dissenting shareholders of each corporate party to a consolidation. In addition to these three fundamental changes, the Revised Act provides shareholders a right to dissent to (1) any plan of compulsory share exchange in which their corporation is to be the one acquired, (2) any amendment to the articles of incorporation that materially and adversely affects a dissenter's rights regarding her shares, and (3) any other corporate action taken pursuant to a shareholder vote with respect to which the articles of incorporation, the bylaws, or a resolution of the board of directors provides that shareholders shall have a right to dissent and obtain payment for their shares. Section 13.02.

Many States have a stock market exception to the appraisal remedy. Under these statutes, a shareholder has no right to dissent if an established market, such as the New York Stock Exchange, exists for the shares. The Revised Act does not contain this exception.

### Procedure
The corporation must notify the shareholders of the existence of dissenters' rights before taking the vote on the corporate action. A dissenting shareholder who strictly complies with the provisions of the statute is entitled to receive the fair value of his shares. Unless he makes written demand within the prescribed time, however, the dissenting shareholder is not entitled to payment for his shares.

### Appraisal Remedy
A dissenting shareholder who complies with all applicable requirements is entitled to an appraisal remedy, which is payment by the corporation of the fair value of his shares, plus accrued interest. The **fair value** is the value immediately preceding the effectuation of the corporate action to which the dissenter objects, excluding any appreciation or depreciation that occurs in anticipation of such corporate action, unless such exclusion would be inequitable.

A shareholder who has a right to obtain payment for his shares does not have the right to attack the validity of the corporate action that gives rise to his right to obtain payment or to have the action set aside or rescinded, except when the corporate action is unlawful or fraudulent with regard to the complaining shareholder or to the corporation. Section 13.02(b). Where the corporate action is not unlawful or fraudulent, the appraisal remedy is exclusive, and the shareholder may not challenge the action. Some States make the appraisal remedy exclusive in all cases; others make it nonexclusive in all cases.

## DISSOLUTION

Although a corporation may have perpetual existence, its life may be terminated in a number of ways. Incorporation statutes usually provide for both voluntary dissolution and involuntary dissolution. Dissolution does not in itself terminate the corporation's existence but does require that the corporation wind up its affairs and liquidate its assets.

## Voluntary Dissolution

Voluntary dissolution may be brought about through a board resolution approved by the affirmative vote of the holders of a majority of the corporation's shares entitled to vote at a shareholders' meeting duly called for this purpose. Section 14.02. Although shareholders who object to dissolution usually have no right to dissent and recover the fair value of their shares, the Revised Act grants dissenters' rights in connection with a sale or exchange of all or substantially all of a corporation's assets not made in the usual or regular course of business, including a sale in dissolution. Nevertheless, the Act excludes such rights in sales by court order and sales for cash on terms requiring that all or substantially all of the net proceeds be distributed to the shareholders within one year. Section 13.02(a)(3).

The Statutory Close Corporation Supplement gives the shareholders, if they elect such a right in the articles of incorporation, the power to dissolve the corporation. Unless the charter specifies otherwise, an amendment to include, modify, or delete a power to dissolve must be approved by *all* of the shareholders. The power to dissolve may be conferred upon any shareholder or holders of a specified number or percentage of shares of any class and may be exercised either at will or upon the occurrence of a specified event or contingency.

◆ *See Figure 37–1*

## Involuntary Dissolution

A corporation may be involuntarily dissolved by administrative dissolution or by judicial dissolution.

***Administrative Dissolution*** The Secretary of State may commence an administrative proceeding to dissolve a corporation if (1) the corporation does not pay within sixty days after they are due any franchise taxes or penalties; (2) the corporation does not deliver its annual report to the Secretary of State within sixty days after it is due; (3) the corporation is without a registered agent or registered office in the State for sixty days or more; (4) the corporation does not notify the Secretary of State within sixty days that it has changed its registered agent or registered office, that its registered agent has resigned, or that it has discontinued its registered office; or (5) the corporation's period of duration stated in its articles of incorporation expires. Section 14.20.

***Judicial Dissolution*** Judicial dissolution may be brought by the State, a shareholder, or a creditor. A court may dissolve a corporation in a proceeding brought

by the Attorney General if it is proved that the corporation obtained its charter through fraud or has continued to exceed or abuse the authority conferred upon it by law. Section 14.30(1).

A court may dissolve a corporation in a proceeding brought by a shareholder if it is established that (1) the directors are deadlocked in the management of the corporate affairs, the shareholders are unable to break the deadlock, and the corporation is threatened with or suffering irreparable injury; (2) the acts of the directors or those in control of the corporation are illegal, oppressive, or fraudulent; (3) the corporate assets are being misapplied or wasted; or (4) the shareholders are deadlocked and have failed to elect directors for at least two consecutive annual meetings. Section 14.30(2).

A creditor may bring a court action for dissolution upon a showing that the corporation has become unable to pay its debts and obligations as they mature in the regular course of its business and that either (a) the creditor has reduced his claim to a judgment and an execution issued on it has been returned unsatisfied or (b) the corporation has admitted in writing that the claim of the creditor is due and owing. Section 14.30(3).

 *See Case 37–3*

## Liquidation

Dissolution, as mentioned earlier, requires that the corporation devote itself to winding up its affairs and liquidating its assets. After dissolution, the corporation must cease carrying on its business except as is necessary to wind up. Section 14.05. When a corporation is dissolved, its assets are liquidated and used first to pay the expenses of liquidation and its creditors according to their respective contract or lien rights. Any remainder is distributed proportionately to shareholders according to their respective contract rights; stock with a liquidation preference has priority over common stock. Voluntary liquidation usually is carried out by the board of directors, who serve as trustees; involuntary liquidation may be conducted by a court-appointed receiver. Section 14.32.

## Protection of Creditors

The statutory provisions governing dissolution and liquidation usually prescribe procedures to safeguard the interests of the corporation's creditors. Such procedures typically include a required mailing of notice to known creditors, a general publication of notice, and the preservation of claims against the corporation. The Revised

**FIGURE 37–1** Fundamental Changes

| Change | Board of Director Resolution Required | Shareholder Approval Required | Shareholders' Appraisal Remedy Available |
|---|---|---|---|
| A amends its articles of incorporation | A: Yes | A: Yes | A: No, unless amendment materially and adversely affects rights of shares |
| B sells its assets in usual and regular course of business to A | B: Yes | B: No | B: No |
| B sells its assets not in usual and regular course of business to A | B: Yes | B: Yes | B: Yes |
| A voluntarily purchases shares of B | A: Yes<br>B: No | A: No<br>B: No, individual shareholders decide | A: No<br>B: No |
| A acquires shares of B through a compulsory exchange | A: Yes<br>B: Yes | A: No<br>B: Yes | A: No<br>B: Yes |
| A and B merge | A: Yes<br>B: Yes | A: Yes<br>B: Yes | A: Yes<br>B: Yes |
| A merges its 90 percent subsidiary B into A | A: Yes<br>B: No | A: No<br>B: No | A: No<br>B: Yes |
| A and B consolidate | A: Yes<br>B: Yes | A: Yes<br>B: Yes | A: Yes<br>B: Yes |
| A voluntarily dissolves | A: Yes | A: Yes | A: Not usually |

Act provides a five-year period within which an otherwise barred claim may be enforced for (1) a claimant who did not receive notice, (2) a claimant on whose timely claim the corporation failed to act, or (3) a claimant whose claim is contingent on an event occurring after dissolution. Section 14.07.

# Chapter Summary

**Charter Amendments**

**Authority to Amend** statutes permit charters to be amended
**Procedure** the board of directors adopts a resolution that must be approved by a majority vote of the shareholders

| **Combinations** | **Purchase or Lease of All or Substantially All of the Assets** results in no change in the legal personality of either corporation |
|---|---|
| | • *Regular Course of Business* approval by the selling corporation's board of directors is required, but shareholder authorization is not |
| | • *Other Than in Regular Course of Business* approval by the board of directors and shareholders of selling corporation is required |
| | **Purchase of Shares** a transaction by which one corporation acquires all of or a controlling interest in the stock of another corporation; no change occurs in the legal existence of either corporation, and no formal shareholder approval of either corporation is required |
| | **Compulsory Share Exchange** a transaction by which a corporation becomes the owner of all of the outstanding shares of one or more classes of stock of another corporation by an exchange that is compulsory on all owners of the acquired shares; the board of directors of each corporation and the shareholders of the corporation whose shares are being acquired must approve |
| | **Merger** the combination of the assets of two or more corporations into one of the corporations |
| | • *Procedure* requires approval by the board of directors and shareholders of each corporation |
| | • *Short-Form Merger* a corporation that owns at least 90 percent of the outstanding shares of a subsidiary may merge the subsidiary into itself without approval by the shareholders of either corporation |
| | • *Effect* the surviving corporation receives title to all of the assets of the merged corporation and assumes all of its liabilities; the merged corporation ceases to exist |
| | **Consolidation** the combination of two or more corporations into a new corporation |
| | • *Procedure* requires approval of the board of directors and shareholders of each corporation |
| | • *Effect* each constituent corporation ceases to exist; the new corporation assumes all of their debts and liabilities |
| | **Going Private Transactions** a combination that makes a publicly held corporation a private one; includes cash-out combinations and management buyouts |
| | **Dissenting Shareholder** one who opposes a fundamental change and has the right to receive the fair value of her shares |
| | • *Availability* dissenters' rights arise in (1) mergers, (2) consolidations, (3) sales or leases of all or substantially all of the assets of a corporation not in the regular course of business, (4) compulsory share exchanges, and (5) amendments that materially and adversely affect the rights of shares |
| | • *Appraisal Remedy* the right to receive the fair value of one's shares (the value of shares immediately before the corporate action to which the dissenter objects takes place, excluding any appreciation or depreciation in anticipation of such corporate action unless such exclusion would be inequitable) |

| **Dissolution** | **Voluntary Dissolution** may be brought about by a resolution of the board of directors that is approved by the shareholders |
|---|---|
| | **Involuntary Dissolution** may occur by administrative or judicial action taken (1) by the Attorney General, (2) by shareholders under certain circumstances, or (3) by a creditor on a showing that the corporation has become unable to pay its debts and obligations as they mature in the regular course of its business |
| | **Liquidation** when a corporation is dissolved, its assets are liquidated and used first to pay its liquidation expenses and its creditors according to their respective contract or lien rights; any remainder is proportionately distributed to shareholders according to their respective contract rights |

# Cases

### CASE 37–1
## Merger
## *SHELL PETROLEUM v. SMITH*
Supreme Court of Delaware, 1992
606 A.2d 112

**MOORE, J.**

Shell Petroleum, Inc., the successor to SPNV Holdings, Inc. ("Holdings"), appeals a decision of the Court of Chancery awarding the class plaintiffs, all former minority shareholders of Shell Oil Company ("Shell"), damages for material misstatements made to the latter in connection with a short form "freeze-out" merger initiated by Holdings. We agree that the misstatements were material and that Holdings must bear responsibility for them. Accordingly, we affirm.

## I

In early 1984, Royal Dutch Petroleum Company ("Royal Dutch"), through various subsidiaries, controlled approximately 70% of the outstanding common shares of Shell. On January 24, 1984, Royal Dutch announced its intention to merge Shell into Holdings (now Shell Petroleum, Inc.) by offering the minority $55 per share. However, Shell's board of directors rejected the offer as inadequate.

Royal Dutch then withdrew the merger proposal and initiated a tender offer at $58 per share. As a result of the tender offer, Holdings' ownership interest increased to 94.6% of Shell's outstanding stock. Holdings then initiated a short-form merger pursuant to 8 Del.C. § 253.

Under the terms of the short-form merger, Shell's minority stockholders were to receive $58 per share. However, if a shareholder waived his right to seek an appraisal before July 1, 1985, he would receive an extra $2 per share. In conjunction with the short-form merger, Holdings distributed several documents to the minority, including a document entitled "Certain Information About Shell" ("CIAS").

The CIAS included a table of discounted future net cash flows ("DCF") for Shell's oil and gas reserves. However, due to a computer programming error, the DCF failed to account for the cash flows from approximately 295 million barrel equivalents of U.S. proved oil and gas reserves. Shell's failure to include the reserves in its calculations resulted in an understatement of its discounted future net cash flows of approximately $993 million to $1.1 billion or $3.00 to $3.45 per share. Moreover, as a result of the error, Shell stated in the CIAS that there had been a slight decline in the value of its oil and gas reserves from 1984 to 1985. When properly calculated, the value of the reserves had actually increased over that time period.

Shell's minority shareholders sued in the Court of Chancery asserting that the error in the DCF along with other alleged disclosure violations constituted a breach of Holdings' fiduciary "duty of candor." After trial, the Court of Chancery held that the error in the DCF was both material and misleading. Moreover, the trial court concluded that Holdings, by virtue of its substantial role in preparing and distributing the disclosure materials, was liable to the minority shareholders for the error. The court then awarded the shareholder class $2 per share.

## II

We first consider Holdings' argument that the billion dollar understatement of Shell's oil and gas reserves was not material, and therefore, the Court of Chancery erred in finding a breach of fiduciary duty.

The question whether the disclosures to Shell's minority shareholders were adequate is a mixed one of law and fact, requiring an assessment of the inferences a reasonable shareholder would draw and the significance of those inferences to the individual shareholder. * * *

Holdings' duty with respect to disclosure is clear. As the majority shareholder, Holdings bears the burden of showing complete disclosure of all material facts relevant to a minority shareholders' decision whether to accept the short-form merger consideration or seek an appraisal. [Citation.] Thus, the question is one of materiality. [Citation.] A fact is considered material if there is a "substantial likelihood that the disclosure of the omitted fact would have been viewed by the reasonable investor as having significantly altered the 'total mix' of information made available." [Citation.] "While it need not be shown that an omission or distortion would have made an investor change his overall view of a proposed transaction, it must be shown that the fact in question would have been relevant to him." [Citation.]

The Court of Chancery concluded that "the understatement of Shell's oil and gas reserves by 294.6 million barrel equivalents, with a value of approximately $1 billion ($3.00–$3.45 per share) ... would have been viewed by a reasonable investor as significantly altering the 'total mix' of information available." [Citation.] It is clear from the Vice Chancellor's decision that he applied the proper legal standards and carefully considered the evidence presented. However, Holdings argues that the court's decision was incorrect because: 1) the error was insignificant when viewed in context; 2) the error was not significant enough to affect a shareholder's decision whether to seek an appraisal; and 3) the error was not material because the DCF was only an estimate.

Holdings contends that the billion dollar error was insignificant because it resulted in only a 5.5% understatement in the total discounted cash flows reported. However, the significance of the error is clearly demonstrated by the fact that a Shell executive vice president stated in *The Wall Street Journal* that a 220 million barrel discovery in the Gulf of Mexico was considered a major find. Thus, it is difficult to accept Holdings' argument that the failure to report cash flows from 295 million barrels was insignificant, when the discovery of 220 million barrels was considered important enough to merit coverage on the first page of *The Wall Street Journal*.

Holdings also argues that a $3 per share error was not significant enough to make a reasonable stockholder change his decision and seek an appraisal. However, the question is not whether the information would have changed the stockholder's decision to accept the merger consideration, but whether "the fact in question would have been relevant to him." [Citation.] "[T]he real worth of an oil company is centered in its reserves." [Citation.] We cannot agree that a billion dollar understatement of the value of Shell's reserves would have been anything but highly relevant and material to a reasonable stockholder.

Finally, Holdings contends that the DCF is only an estimate of future cash flows and, therefore, it would be unreasonable for a shareholder to conclude that Shell's oil and gas reserves were worth the amount presented in the DCF. In fact, according to Holdings, a reasonable shareholder should anticipate a certain margin of error simply due to the uncertainties inherent in the estimate process.

Although the DCF presents an estimate of future cash flows, a shareholder could reasonably conclude that the DCF was accurately prepared based on all available information. Moreover, a reasonable shareholder could conclude that the 1985 DCF was prepared in a manner consistent with the 1984 DCF. Thus, a comparison of the 1984 and 1985 DCFs should present an accurate indication of whether the value of Shell's reserves was increasing or decreasing. Such was not the case. A comparison of the 1984 and 1985 DCFs inevitably leads to the erroneous conclusion, as stated in the CIAS, that the value of Shell's reserves had declined. Most importantly, the misleading statement that the value of the reserves had declined was not based upon the inherent inaccuracies of the estimate process, but upon an error made by Shell. The fact that the error was included in a schedule which contained estimates does not diminish its materiality.

In the final analysis, the question is not whether this Court agrees or disagrees with the trial court's decision. Rather, the question is whether the Vice Chancellor's findings are "supported by the record and are the product of an orderly and logical deductive process." After reviewing the record, we conclude that the Vice Chancellor's decision was both supported by the record and well-reasoned.

---

## CASE 37–2
## Cash-out Combinations
### *ALPERT v. 28 WILLIAMS ST. CORP.*

New York Court of Appeals, 1984
63 N.Y.2d 557, 483 N.Y.S.2d 667, 473 N.E.2d 19

COOKE, C.J.
The subject of contention in this litigation is a valuable 17-story office building, located at 79 Madison Avenue in Manhattan. In dispute is the propriety of a complex series of transactions that had the net effect of permitting defendants, who were outside investors, to gain ownership of the property and to eliminate the ownership interests of plaintiffs, who were minority shareholders of the

corporation that formerly owned the building. This was achieved through what is commonly known as a "two-step" merger: (1) an outside investor purchases control of the majority shares of the target corporation by tender offer or through private negotiations; (2) this newly acquired control is used to arrange for the target and a second corporation controlled by the outside investor to merge, with one condition being the "freeze-out" of the minority shareholders of the target corporation by the forced cancellation of their shares, generally through a cash purchase. This accomplishes the investor's original goal of complete ownership of the target corporation.

Since 1955, the office building was owned by 79 Realty Corporation (Realty Corporation), which had no other substantial assets. About two-thirds of Realty Corporation's outstanding shares were held by two couples, the Kimmelmans and the Zauderers, who were also the company's sole directors and officers. Plaintiffs owned 26% of the outstanding shares. The remaining shares were owned by persons who are not parties to this litigation.

Defendants, a consortium of investors, formed a limited partnership, known as Madison 28 Associates (Madison Associates), for the purpose of purchasing the building. * * *

Madison Associates formed a separate, wholly owned company, 28 Williams Street Corporation (Williams Street), to act as the nominal purchaser and owner of the Kimmelman and Zauderer interests. * * *

[T]he partners of Madison Associates approved a plan to merge Realty Corporation with Williams Street, Realty Corporation being the surviving corporation. Together with a notice for a shareholders' meeting to vote on the proposed merger, a statement of intent was sent to all shareholders of Realty Corporation, explaining the procedural and financial aspects of the merger, as well as defendants' conflict of interest and the intended exclusion of the minority shareholders from the newly constituted Realty Corporation through a cash buy-out. Defendants also disclosed that they planned to dissolve Realty Corporation after the merger and thereafter to operate the business as a partnership. The merger plan did not require approval by any of the minority shareholders.

The merger proposed by the directors was approved at the shareholders meeting, held on November 7, 1980. As a result, the office building was owned by the "new" Realty Corporation, which, in turn, was wholly owned by Madison Associates. In accordance with the merger plan, Realty Corporation was dissolved within a month of the merger and its principal asset, title to the building, devolved to Madison Associates.

* * *

The plaintiffs instituted this action on October 31, 1980, initially seeking to enjoin the shareholders meeting called to approve the merger. Failing to temporarily enjoin the Realty Corporation's merger with Williams Street, plaintiffs later amended their complaint to include a request for equitable relief in the form of rescission of the merger.

The propriety of the merger was contested on several grounds. It was contended that the merger was unlawful because its sole purpose was to personally benefit the partners of Madison Associates and that the alleged purposes had no legitimate business benefit inuring to the corporation. Plaintiffs argue that the "business judgment" of the directors in assigning various purposes for the merger was indelibly tainted by a conflict of interest because they were committed to the merger prior to becoming directors and were on both sides of the merger transaction when consummated. Further, they assert that essential financial information was not disclosed and that the value offered for the minority's shares was understated and determined in an unfair manner.

* * *

On this appeal, the principal task facing this court is to prescribe a standard for evaluating the validity of a corporate transaction that forcibly eliminates minority shareholders by means of a two-step merger. It is concluded that the analysis employed by the courts below was correct: the majority shareholders' exclusion of minority interests through a two-step merger does not violate the former's fiduciary obligations so long as the transaction viewed as a whole is fair to the minority shareholders and is justified by an independent corporate business purpose. Accordingly, this court now affirms.

* * *

In New York, two or more domestic corporations are authorized to "merge into a single corporation which shall be one of the constituent corporations," known as the "surviving corporation" [citation]. The statute does not delineate substantive justifications for mergers, but only requires compliance with certain procedures: the adoption by the boards of each corporation of a plan of merger setting forth, among other things, the terms and conditions of the merger; a statement of any changes in the certificate of incorporation of the surviving corporation; the submission of the plan to a vote of shareholders pursuant to notice to all shareholders; and adoption of the plan by a vote of two-thirds of the shareholders entitled to vote on it [citation].

Generally, the remedy of a shareholder dissenting from a merger and the offered "cash-out" price is to obtain the fair value of his or her stock through an appraisal proceeding [citation]. This protects the minority shareholder from being forced to sell at unfair values imposed by those dominating the corporation while allowing the majority to proceed with its desired merger [citations]. The pursuit of an appraisal proceeding generally constitutes the dissenting stockholder's exclusive remedy [citations]. An exception exists, however, when the merger is unlawful or fraudulent as to that shareholder, in which event an action for equitable relief is authorized [citations]. Thus, technical compliance with the Business Corporation Law's requirements alone will not necessarily exempt a merger from further judicial review.

*  *  *

*  *  * In reviewing a freeze-out merger, the essence of the judicial inquiry is to determine whether the transaction, viewed as a whole, was "fair" as to all concerned. This concept has two principal components: the majority shareholders must have followed "a course of fair dealing toward minority holders" . . . and they must also have offered a fair price for the minority's stock. *  *  *

*  *  *

Fair dealing is also concerned with the procedural fairness of the transaction, such as its timing, initiation, structure, financing, development, disclosure to the independent directors and shareholders, and how the necessary approvals were obtained. . . . Basically, the courts must look for complete and candid disclosure of all the material facts and circumstances of the proposed merger known to the majority or directors, including their dual roles and events leading up to the merger proposal. *  *  *

The fairness of the transaction cannot be determined without considering the component of the financial remuneration offered the dissenting shareholders. *  *  *

In determining whether there was a fair price, the court need not ascertain the precise "fair value" of the shares as it would be determined in an appraisal proceeding. It should be noted, however, that the factors used in an appraisal proceeding are relevant here . . . This would include but would not be limited to net asset value, book value, earnings, market value, and investment value . . . Elements of future value arising from the accomplishment or expectation of the merger which are known or susceptible of proof as of the date of the merger and not the product of speculation may also be considered. *  *  *

*  *  *

In the context of a freeze-out merger, variant treatment of the minority shareholders—i.e., causing their removal—will be justified when related to the advancement of a general corporate interest. The benefit need not be great, but it must be for the corporation. For example, if the sole purpose of the merger is reduction of the number of profit sharers—in contrast to increasing the corporation's capital or profits, or improving its management structure—there will exist no "independent corporate interest" [citation]. All of these purposes ultimately seek to increase the individual wealth of the remaining shareholders. What distinguishes a proper corporate purpose from an improper one is that, with the former, removal of the minority shareholders furthers the objective of conferring some general gain upon the corporation. Only then will the fiduciary duty of good and prudent management of the corporation serve to override the concurrent duty to treat all shareholders fairly [citation]. We further note that a finding that there was an independent corporate purpose for the action taken by the majority will not be defeated merely by the fact that the corporate objective could have been accomplished in another way, or by the fact that the action chosen was not the best way to achieve the bona fide business objective.

In sum, in entertaining an equitable action to review a freeze-out merger, a court should view the transaction as a whole to determine whether it was tainted with fraud, illegality, or self-dealing, whether the minority shareholders were dealt with fairly, and whether there exists any independent corporate purpose for the merger.

*  *  *

Without passing on all of the business purposes cited by [the trial court] as underlying the merger, it is sufficient to note that at least one justified the exclusion of plaintiff's interests: attracting additional capital to effect needed repairs of the building. There is proof that there was a good-faith belief that additional, outside capital was required. Moreover, this record supports the conclusion that this capital would not have been available through the merger had not plaintiffs' interest in the corporation been eliminated. Thus, the approval of the merger, which would extinguish plaintiffs' stock, was supported by a bona fide business purpose to advance this general corporate interest of obtaining increased capital.

Accordingly, the order of the Appellate Division should be affirmed.

## CASE 37–3
### Involuntary Judicial Dissolution
## *MATTER OF KEMP & BEATLEY, INC.*
Court of Appeals of New York, 1984
64 N.Y.2d 63, 484 N.Y.S.2d 799, 473 N.E.2d 1173

COOKE, C.J.

The business concern of Kemp & Beatley, incorporated under the laws of New York, designs and manufactures table linens and sundry tabletop items. The company's stock consists of 1,500 outstanding shares held by eight shareholders. Petitioner Dissin had been employed by the company for 42 years when, in June 1979, he resigned. Prior to resignation, Dissin served as vice-president and a director of Kemp & Beatley. Over the course of his employment, Dissin had acquired stock in the company and currently owns 200 shares.

Petitioner Gardstein, like Dissin, had been a long-time employee of the company. Hired in 1944, Gardstein was for the next 35 years involved in various aspects of the business including material procurement, product design, and plant management. His employment was terminated by the company in December 1980. He currently owns 105 shares of Kemp & Beatley stock.

Apparent unhappiness surrounded petitioners' leaving the employ of the company. Of particular concern was that they no longer received any distribution of the company's earnings. Petitioners considered themselves to be "frozen out" of the company; whereas it had been their experience when with the company to receive a distribution of the company's earnings according to their stock-holdings, in the form of either dividends or extra compensation, that distribution was no longer forthcoming.

Gardstein and Dissin, together holding 20.33% of the company's outstanding stock, commenced the instant proceeding in June 1981, seeking dissolution of Kemp & Beatley pursuant to section 1104–a of the Business Corporation Law. Their petition alleged "fraudulent and oppressive" conduct by the company's board of directors such as to render petitioners' stock "a virtually worthless asset." Supreme Court referred the matter for a hearing, which was held in March 1982.

Upon considering the testimony of petitioners and the principals of Kemp & Beatley, the referee concluded that "the corporate management has by its policies effectively rendered petitioners' shares worthless, and . . . the only way petitioners can expect any return is by dissolution." Petitioners were found to have invested capital in the company expecting, among other things, to receive dividends or "bonuses" based upon their stock holdings. Also found was the company's "established buyout policy" by which it would purchase the stock of employee shareholders upon their leaving its employ.

The involuntary-dissolution statute (Business Corporation Law, § 1104–a) permits dissolution when a corporation's controlling faction is found guilty of "oppressive action" toward the complaining shareholders. The referee considered oppression to arise when "those in control" of the corporation "have acted in such a manner as to defeat those expectations of the minority stockholders which formed the basis of [their] participation in the venture." The expectations of petitioners that they would not be arbitrarily excluded from gaining a return on their investment and that their stock would be purchased by the corporation upon termination of employment, were deemed defeated by prevailing corporate policies. Dissolution was recommended in the referee's report, subject to giving respondent corporation an opportunity to purchase petitioners' stock.

Supreme Court confirmed the referee's report. It, too, concluded that due to the corporation's new dividend policy petitioners had been prevented from receiving any return on their investments. Liquidation of the corporate assets was found the only means by which petitioners would receive a fair return. The court considered judicial dissolution of a corporation to be "a serious and severe remedy." Consequently, the order of dissolution was conditioned upon the corporation's being permitted to purchase petitioners' stock. The Appellate Division affirmed, without opinion. [Citation.]

At issue in this appeal is the scope of section 1104–a of the Business Corporation Law. Specifically, this court must determine whether the provision for involuntary dissolution when the "directors or those in control of the corporation have been guilty of . . . oppressive actions toward the complaining shareholders" was properly applied in the circumstances of this case. We hold that it was, and therefore affirm.

\* \* \*

The statutory concept of "oppressive actions" can, perhaps, best be understood by examining the characteristics of close corporations and the Legislature's general purpose in creating this involuntary-dissolution statute. It is widely understood that, in addition to supplying capital to a contemplated or ongoing enterprise and expecting a fair and equal return, parties comprising the ownership of a close corporation may expect to be actively involved in its management and operation. . . . The small ownership cluster seeks to "contribute their capital, skills, experience and labor" toward the corporate enterprise. * * *

As a leading commentator in the field has observed: "Unlike the typical shareholder in a publicly held corporation, who may be simply an investor or a speculator and cares nothing for the responsibilities of management, the shareholder in a close corporation is a co-owner of the business and wants the privileges and powers that go with ownership. His participation in that particular corporation is often his principal or sole source of income. As a matter of fact, providing employment for himself may have been the principal reason why he participated in organizing the corporation. He may or may not anticipate an ultimate profit from the sale of his interest, but he normally draws very little from the corporation as dividends. In his capacity as an officer or employee of the corporation, he looks to his salary for the principal return on his capital investment, because earnings of a close corporation, as is well known, are distributed in major part in salaries, bonuses and retirement benefits." [Citation.]

Shareholders enjoy flexibility in memorializing these expectations through agreements setting forth each party's rights and obligations in corporate governance [citation]. In the absence of such an agreement, however, ultimate decision-making power respecting corporate policy will be reposed in the holders of a majority interest in the corporation [citation]. A wielding of this power by any group controlling a corporation may serve to destroy a stockholder's vital interests and expectations.

As the stock of closely held corporations generally is not readily salable, a minority shareholder at odds with management policies may be without either a voice in protecting his or her interests or any reasonable means of withdrawing his or her investment. This predicament may fairly be considered the legislative concern underlying the provision at issue in this case; inclusion of the criteria that the corporation's stock not be traded on securities markets and that the complaining shareholder be subject to oppressive actions supports this conclusion.

Defining oppressive conduct as distinct from illegality in the present context has been considered in other forums. The question has been resolved by considering

oppressive actions to refer to conduct that substantially defeats the "reasonable expectations" held by minority shareholders in committing their capital to the particular enterprise [citation]. This concept is consistent with the apparent purpose underlying the provision under review. A shareholder who reasonably expected that ownership in the corporation would entitle him or her to a job, a share of corporate earnings, a place in corporate management, or some other form of security, would be oppressed in a very real sense when others in the corporation seek to defeat those expectations and there exists no effective means of salvaging the investment.

Given the nature of close corporations and the remedial purpose of the statute, this court holds that utilizing a complaining shareholder's "reasonable expectations" as a means of identifying and measuring conduct alleged to be oppressive is appropriate. A court considering a petition alleging oppressive conduct must investigate what the majority shareholders knew, or should have known, to be the petitioner's expectations in entering the particular enterprise. Majority conduct should not be deemed oppressive simply because the petitioner's subjective hopes and desires in joining the venture are not fulfilled. Disappointment alone should not necessarily be equated with oppression.

Rather, oppression should be deemed to arise only when the majority conduct substantially defeats expectations that, objectively viewed, were both reasonable under the circumstances and were central to the petitioner's decision to join the venture. It would be inappropriate, however, for us in this case to delineate the contours of the courts' consideration in determining whether directors have been guilty of oppressive conduct. As in other areas of the law, much will depend on the circumstances in the individual case.

The appropriateness of an order of dissolution is in every case vested in the sound discretion of the court considering the application [citation]. Under the terms of this statute, courts are instructed to consider both whether "liquidation of the corporation is the only feasible means" to protect the complaining shareholder's expectation of a fair return on his or her investment and whether dissolution "is reasonably necessary" to protect "the rights or interests of any substantial number of shareholders" not limited to those complaining (Business Corporation Law, § 1104–a, subd. [b], pars. [1], [2]). Implicit in this direction is that once oppressive conduct is found, consideration must be given to the totality of circumstances surrounding the current state of corporate affairs and relations to determine whether some remedy short of or other than dissolution, constitutes a feasible means of satisfying both the petitioner's expectations and the rights and interests of any other substantial group of shareholders [citation].

* * *

One further observation is in order. The purpose of this involuntary dissolution statute is to provide protection to the minority shareholder whose reasonable expectations in undertaking the venture have been frustrated and who has no adequate means of recovering his or her investment. It would be contrary to this remedial purpose to permit its use by minority shareholders as merely a coercive tool [citation]. Therefore, the minority shareholder whose own acts, made in bad faith and undertaken with a view toward forcing an involuntary dissolution, give rise to the complained-of oppression should be given no quarter in the statutory protection [citation].

* * *

There was sufficient evidence presented at the hearing to support the conclusion that Kemp & Beatley had a long-standing policy of awarding *de facto* dividends based on stock ownership in the form of "extra compensation bonuses." Petitioners, both of whom had extensive experience in the management of the company, testified to this effect. Moreover, both related that receipt of this compensation, whether as true dividends or disguised as "extra compensation," was a known incident to ownership of the company's stock understood by all of the company's principals. Finally, there was uncontroverted proof that this policy was changed either shortly before or shortly after petitioners' employment ended. Extra compensation was still awarded by the company. The only difference was that stock ownership was no longer a basis for the payments;

it was asserted that the basis became services rendered to the corporation. It was not unreasonable for the fact finder to have determined that this change in policy amounted to nothing less than an attempt to exclude petitioners from gaining any return on their investment through the mere recharacterization of distributions of corporate income. Under the circumstances of this case, there was no error in determining that this conduct constituted oppressive action within the meaning of section 1104–a of the Business Corporation Law.

Nor may it be said that Supreme Court abused its discretion in ordering Kemp & Beatley's dissolution, subject to an opportunity for a buy-out of petitioners' shares. After the referee had found that the controlling faction of the company was, in effect, attempting to "squeeze-out" petitioners by offering them no return on their investment and increasing other executive compensation, respondents, in opposing the report's confirmation, attempted only to controvert the factual basis of the report. They suggested no feasible, alternative remedy to the forced dissolution. In light of an apparent deterioration in relations between petitioners and the governing shareholders of Kemp & Beatley, it was not unreasonable for the court to have determined that a forced buy-out of petitioners' shares or liquidation of the corporation's assets was the only means by which petitioners could be guaranteed a fair return on their investments.

Accordingly, the order of the Appellate Division should be modified, with costs to petitioners-respondents, by affirming the substantive determination of that court but extending the time for exercising the option to purchase petitioners-respondents' shares to 30 days following this court's determination.

---

 # Questions

**1.** Explain the procedure for amending the charter and identify which charter amendments give dissenting shareholders an appraisal remedy.

**2.** Which combinations (a) do not require shareholder approval and (b) give dissenting shareholders an appraisal remedy?

**3.** Distinguish between a tender offer and a compulsory share exchange.

**4.** Compare and contrast a cash-out combination and a management buyout.

**5.** Identify the ways by which involuntary and voluntary dissolution may occur.

---

 # Problems

**1.** The stock in Hotel Management, Inc., a hotel management corporation, was divided equally between two families.

For several years, the two families had been unable to agree on or cooperate in the management of the corporation. As a result, no meeting of shareholders or directors had been held for five years. There had been no withdrawal of profits for five years, and last year the hotel operated at a loss. Although the corporation was not insolvent, such a state was imminent because the business was poorly managed and its properties were in need of repair. As a result, the owners of half the stock brought an action in equity for dissolution of the corporation. What decision?

**2.** (a) When may a corporation sell, lease, exchange, mortgage, or pledge all or substantially all of its assets in the usual and regular course of its business?

(b) When may a corporation sell, lease, exchange, mortgage, or pledge all or substantially all of its assets other than in the usual and regular course of its business?

(c) What are the rights of a shareholder who dissents from a proposed sale or exchange of all or substantially all of the assets of a corporation other than in the usual and regular course of its business?

**3.** The Cutler Company was duly merged into the Stone Company. Yetta, a shareholder of the former Cutler Company, having paid only one-half of her subscription, is now sued by the Stone Company for the balance of the subscription. Yetta, who took no part in the merger proceedings, denies liability on the ground that, inasmuch as the Cutler Company no longer exists, all her rights and obligations in connection with the Cutler Company have been terminated. Decision?

**4.** Smith, while in the course of his employment with the Bee Corporation, negligently ran the company's truck into Williams, injuring him severely. Subsequently, the Bee Corporation and the Sea Corporation consolidated, forming the SeaBee Corporation. Williams filed suit against the SeaBee Corporation for damages, and the SeaBee Corporation asserted the defense that the injuries Williams sustained were not caused by any of SeaBee's employees, that SeaBee did not even exist at the time of the injury, and that the SeaBee Corporation was, therefore, not liable. What decision?

**5.** The Johnson Company, a corporation organized under the laws of State X, after proper authorization by the shareholders, sold its entire assets to the Samson Company, also a State X corporation. Ellen, an unpaid creditor of the Johnson Company, sues the Samson Company upon her claim. Decision?

**6.** Zenith Steel Company operates a prosperous business. The board of directors voted to spend $20 million of the company's surplus funds to purchase a majority of the stock of two other companies—the Green Insurance Company and the Blue Trust Company. The Green Insurance Company is a thriving business whose stock is an excellent investment at the price at which it will be sold to Zenith Steel Company. The principal reasons for Zenith's purchase of the Green Insurance stock are to invest surplus funds and to diversify its business. The Blue Trust Company owns a controlling interest in Zenith Steel Company. The main purpose for Zenith's purchase of the Blue Trust Company stock is to enable the present management and directors of Zenith Steel Company to perpetuate their management of the company. Jones, a minority share-

holder in Zenith Steel Company, brings an appropriate action to enjoin the purchase by Zenith Steel Company of the stock of either the Green Insurance Company or of the Blue Trust Company. Decision?

**7.** Mildred, Deborah, and Bob each own one-third of the stock of Nova Corporation. On Friday, Mildred received an offer to merge Nova into Buyer Corporation. Mildred, who agreed to call a shareholders' meeting to discuss the offer on the following Tuesday, telephoned Deborah and Bob and informed them of the offer and the scheduled meeting. Deborah agreed to attend. Bob, however, was unable to attend because he was leaving on a trip on Saturday and asked if the three of them could meet on Friday night instead. Mildred and Deborah agreed. The three shareholders met informally Friday night and agreed to accept the offer only if they received preferred stock of Buyer Corporation for their shares. Bob then left on his trip. On Tuesday, at the time and place appointed by Mildred, Mildred and Deborah convened the shareholders' meeting. After discussion, they concluded that the preferred stock payment limitation was unwise and passed a formal resolution to accept Buyer Corporation's offer without any such condition. Bob files suit to enjoin Mildred, Deborah, and the Nova Corporation from implementing this resolution. Decision?

**8.** Tretter alleged that his exposure over the years to asbestos products manufactured by Philip Carey Manufacturing Corporation caused him to contract asbestosis. Tretter brought an action against Rapid American Corporation, which was the surviving corporation of a merger between Philip Carey and Rapid American. Rapid American denied liability, claiming that immediately after the merger it had transferred its asbestos operations to a newly formed subsidiary corporation. Decision?

**9.** Wilcox was chief executive officer, chairman of the board of directors, and owner of 60 percent of the shares of Sterling Corporation. When the market price of Sterling's shares was $22 per share, Wilcox sold all of his shares in Sterling to Conrad for $29 per share. The minority shareholders of Sterling brought suit against Wilcox to demand a portion of the amount Wilcox received in excess of the market price. Decision?

**10.** All Steel Pipe and Tube is a closely held corporation engaged in the business of selling steel pipes and tubes. Leo and Scott Callier are its two equal shareholders. Scott, Leo's uncle, is one of the company's two directors and is president of the corporation. Scott is the general manager. Scott's father and Leo's grandfather, Felix, is the other director. Over the years, Scott and Leo have had differences of opinion regarding the operation of the business. Nevertheless, despite their deteriorating relationship, the company has flourished. When negotiations aimed at Leo's redemption of Scott's shares began, however, the parties could not reach an agreement. The discussion then turned to voluntary dissolution and liquidation of the corporation, but still no agreement could be reached. Finally, Leo fired Scott and began to wind down All Steel's business and to form a new corporation, Callier Steel Pipe and

Tube. Leo then brought this action seeking a dissolution and liquidation of All Steel. Decision?

**11.** The shareholders of Endicott Johnson who had dissented from a proposed merger of Endicott with McDonough Corporation brought a proceeding to fix the fair value of their stock. At issue was the proper weight to be given to the market price of the stock in fixing its fair value. The shareholders argued that the market value should not be considered because of McDonough's control of Endicott's stock and the stock's subsequent delisting from the New York Stock Exchange. Decision?

**12.** On March 24, 1969, Ray fell from a defective ladder while working for his employer. Ray brought suit in strict tort liability against the Alad Corporation (Alad II), which neither manufactured nor sold the ladder to Ray's employer. Prior to the accident, Alad II succeeded to the business of the ladder's manufacturer, the now-dissolved "Alad Corporation" (Alad I), through a purchase of Alad I's assets for an adequate cash consideration. Alad II acquired Alad I's plant, equipment, inventory, trade name, and goodwill and continued to manufacture the same line of ladders under the "Alad" name, using the same equipment, designs, and personnel. In addition, Alad II solicited through the same sales representatives with no outward indication of any change in the ownership of the business. The parties had no agreement, however, concerning Alad II's assumption of Alad I's tort liabilities. Ray appealed from a judgment for Alad II. Decision?

WWW **Internet Exercise** Find your State's incorporation statute and determine what kinds of fundamental changes it recognizes. (If your State's incorporation statute is not available, choose that of another State.

## PART EIGHT

# Debtor and Creditor Relations

# Secured Transactions and Suretyship

"Neither a borrower nor a lender be"—Shakespeare's well-known line in *Hamlet*—reflects an earlier view of debt, for today borrowed funds are both essential and honorable under our economic system. In fact, the absence of loans would severely restrict the availability of goods and services and would greatly limit consumers in the quantities they would be able to purchase.

The public policy and social issues created by today's enormous use of debt center on certain tenets, among which are the following:

1. The means by which debt is created and transferred should be as simple and as inexpensive as possible. The Official Comment to UCC Section 9–101 states, "The aim of this article is to provide a simple and unified structure within which the immense variety of present-day secured financing transactions can go forward with less cost and with greater certainty."
2. The risks to lenders should be minimized.
3. Lenders should have a way to collect unpaid debts. A lender typically incurs two basic collection risks: the borrower may be unwilling to repay the loan even though he is able to, or the borrower may prove to be unable to repay the loan. In addition to the remedies dealing with the first of these risks, the law has developed several devices to maximize the likelihood of repayment. These devices, which we will discuss in this chapter, include consensual security interests (also called secured transactions) and suretyships.

In addition, debtors of all sorts—wage earners, sole proprietorships, partnerships, and corporations—sometimes accumulate debts far in excess of their assets or suffer financial reverses that make it impossible for them to meet their obligations. In such an event, it is an important policy of the law to treat all creditors fairly and equitably and to provide the debtor with relief from these debts so that he may continue to contribute to

society. These are the two basic purposes of the federal bankruptcy law, which we will briefly discuss in this chapter and discuss more fully in Chapter 39.

## SECURED TRANSACTIONS IN PERSONAL PROPERTY

An obligation or debt can exist without security if the creditor deems adequate the integrity, reputation, and net worth of the debtor. Often, however, businesses or individuals cannot obtain credit without giving adequate security, or, in some cases, even if the borrower can obtain an unsecured loan, he can negotiate more favorable terms by giving security.

Transactions involving security in personal property are governed by Article 9 of the Uniform Commercial Code (UCC). This article provides a simple and unified structure within which a tremendous variety of secured financing transactions can take place with less cost and with greater certainty than was possible before the article's enactment. Moreover, the article's flexibility and simplified formalities allow new forms of secured financing to fit comfortably under its provisions.

### *ESSENTIALS OF SECURED TRANSACTIONS*

Article 9 governs a **secured transaction** in personal property in which the debtor *consents* to provide a security interest in personal property to secure the payment of a debt. Article 9 does *not* apply to nonconsensual security interests that arise by operation of law, such as mechanics' or landlords' liens. A common type of consensual secured transaction covered by Article 9 occurs when a person wanting to buy goods has neither the cash nor a sufficient credit standing to obtain the goods on open credit, and the seller, to secure payment of all or part of the price, obtains a security interest in the goods. Alternatively, the buyer may borrow the purchase price from a third party and pay the seller in cash. The third-party lender may then take a security interest in the goods to secure repayment of the loan.

Every consensual secured transaction involves a debtor, a secured party, collateral, a security agreement, and a security interest. As defined in Section 9–105(1) of the Code, a **debtor** is a person who owes payment or performance of an obligation. A **secured party** is the creditor (lender, seller, or other person) who owns the security interest in the collateral. **Collateral** is the property subject to the security interest. A **security agreement** is the agreement that creates or provides for a **security interest,** which Section 1–201(37) defines as "an interest in personal property or fixtures which secures payment or performance of an obligation." A seller who retains a security interest in goods by a security agreement has a **purchase money security interest** (PMSI). Similarly, a third-party lender who advances funds to enable the debtor to purchase goods has a purchase money security interest if she has a security agreement and the debtor in fact uses the funds to purchase the goods.

Thus, a security interest is created when an automobile dealer sells and delivers a car to an individual (the *debtor*) under a retail installment contract (a *security agreement*) that provides that the dealer (the *secured party*) obtains a *security interest* (a *purchase money security interest*) in the car (the *collateral*) until the price is paid. A security interest in property cannot exist apart from the debt it secures, and discharging the debt in any manner terminates the security interest in the property.

◆ *See Figure 38–1*

## CLASSIFICATION OF COLLATERAL

Although most of the provisions of Article 9 apply to all kinds of personal property, some provisions state special rules that apply only to particular kinds of collateral. Under the Code, collateral is classified according to its nature and its use. The classifications according to nature are (a) goods, (b) indispensable paper, and (c) intangibles.

### Goods

**Goods** are tangible personal property that can be moved when the security interest in them becomes enforceable. Section 9–105(1)(h). Goods are subdivided into (1) consumer goods, (2) farm products, (3) inventory, and (4) equipment. Goods that become affixed to real estate are called fixtures. Depending on its primary use or purpose, the same item of goods may fall into different classifications. For example, a refrigerator purchased by a physician to store medicines in his office is classified as equipment, while the same refrigerator would be classified as consumer goods if the physician purchased it for home use. In the hands of a refrigerator dealer or manufacturer, the refrigerator would be classified as inventory.

***Consumer Goods*** Goods used or bought for use primarily for personal, family, or household purposes are consumer goods. Section 9–109(1).

***Farm Products*** The Code defines farm products as "crops or livestock or supplies used or produced in farming operations or if they are products of crops or livestock in their unmanufactured states. . . ." Section 9–109(3). Thus, farm products would include wheat growing on

---

**FIGURE 38–1**  Fundamental Rights of Secured Party and Debtor

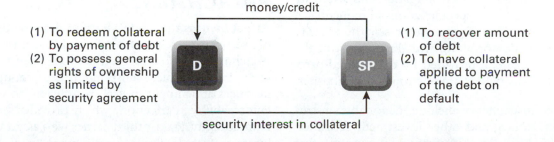

the farmer's land; the farmer's pigs, cows, and hens; and the hens' eggs. When such products become the possessions of a person not engaged in farming operations, they cease to be farm products.

*Inventory* The term *inventory* includes goods held for sale or lease and the raw materials, work in process, or materials used or consumed in a business. Section 9–109(4). Thus, a retailer's or wholesaler's merchandise as well as a manufacturer's materials are inventory.

*Equipment* Goods used or purchased for use primarily in business (including farming or a profession) are classified as equipment, provided they are not included in the definition of inventory, farm products, or consumer goods. Section 9–109(2). This category is broad enough to include a lawyer's library, a physician's office furniture, or machinery in a factory.

*Fixtures* Goods and personal property that have become so related to particular real property that an interest in them arises under real estate law are called fixtures. Section 9–313(1)(a). Thus, State law other than the Code determines whether and when goods become fixtures. In general terms, fixtures are goods so firmly affixed to real estate that they are considered part of such real estate. Examples are furnaces, central air-conditioning units, and plumbing fixtures. See Chapter 49 for a further discussion of fixtures. A security interest in fixtures may arise under Article 9, and, under certain circumstances, a perfected security interest in fixtures will have priority over a conflicting security interest or mortgage in the real property to which the goods are attached.

## Indispensable Paper

Three kinds of collateral involve rights evidenced by indispensable paper: (1) chattel paper, (2) instruments, and (3) documents.

*Chattel Paper* Chattel paper is a writing or writings that evidence both a monetary obligation and a security interest in or a lease of specific goods. Frequently, a secured party may borrow against or sell the security agreement of his debtor along with his interest in the collateral. The collateral provided by the secured party to his lender in this type of transaction is chattel paper.

*Instruments* Instruments include negotiable instruments, stocks, bonds, and other investment securities. Section 9–105(1)(i). An instrument is any writing that evidences a right to payment of money, that is transferable by delivery with any necessary indorsement or assignment, and that is not of itself a security agreement or lease.

*Documents* The term document includes documents of title, such as bills of lading and warehouse receipts, which may be either negotiable or nonnegotiable. Sections 9–105(1)(f), 1–201(15). A document of title is negotiable if by its terms the goods it covers are deliverable to bearer or to the order of a named person. Any other document is nonnegotiable. Documents of title are covered in Chapter 49.

## Intangibles

The Code also recognizes two kinds of collateral that are neither goods nor indispensable paper, namely, accounts and general intangibles. These types of intangible collateral are not evidenced by any indispensable paper, such as a stock certificate or a negotiable bill of lading.

*Accounts* The terms account and accounts receivable refer to the right to payment for goods sold or leased or for services rendered, whether or not such right has been earned by performance. Section 9–106. The 1972 Code deleted the term *contract right* but included contract rights in its expanded definition of account.

*General Intangibles* The term general intangibles applies to any personal property other than goods, accounts, chattel paper, documents, instruments, and money. Section 9–106. Except for those interests that Article 9 specifically excludes, this catchall category for interests not otherwise covered leaves room for the use of new kinds of collateral for financing purposes. General intangibles include goodwill, literary rights, and interests in patents, trademarks, and copyrights to the extent they are not regulated by Federal statute.

## *ATTACHMENT*

**Attachment** is the Code's term to describe the creation of a security interest that is enforceable against the *debtor*. Attachment is also a prerequisite to rendering a security interest enforceable against third parties, though in some instances attachment in itself is sufficient to create such enforceability. Perfection, which provides the greatest enforceability against third parties who assert competing interests in the collateral, is discussed below.

Until a security interest "attaches," it is *ineffective* against the debtor. Under Section 9–203 of the Code, the security interest created by a security agreement attaches to the described collateral once the following events have occurred:

1. the secured party has given value;
2. the debtor has acquired rights in the collateral; and
3. either the collateral is in the possession of the secured party pursuant to agreement or the security agreement is in a writing which contains a reasonable description of the collateral and is signed by the debtor.

The parties may, however, by explicit agreement postpone the time of attachment. Section 9–203(2).

## Value

The term **value** is broadly defined and includes consideration under contract law, a binding commitment to extend credit, and an antecedent debt. Section 1–201(44). For example, Buyer purchases equipment from Seller on credit. When Buyer fails to make timely payment, Seller and Buyer enter into a security agreement that grants Seller a security interest in the equipment. By entering the agreement, Seller has given value, even though he relies upon an antecedent debt—the original transfer of goods to Buyer—instead of providing new consideration. Moreover, Seller is not limited to acquiring a security interest in the equipment he sold to Buyer but also may obtain a security interest in other personal property of Buyer.

## Debtor's Rights in Collateral

The elusive concept of the debtor's rights in collateral is not specifically defined by the Code. Before the 1972 amendments, the UCC attempted to provide rules for determining when a debtor acquired rights in certain types of collateral. The 1972 amendments eliminated these provisions, which were considered unnecessary, arbitrary, and confusing, and left the question of a debtor's rights in collateral to the wisdom of the courts. As a general rule, the debtor is deemed to have **rights in collateral** that he owns or is in possession of as well as in those items that he is in the process of acquiring from the seller. For example, if Adrien borrows money from Richard and grants him a security interest in corporate stock that she owns, then Adrien had rights in the collateral before entering into the secured transaction. Likewise, if Sally sells goods to Benjamin on credit and he

provides Sally a security interest in the goods, Benjamin will acquire rights in the collateral upon identification of the goods to the contract.

 *See Case 38–1*

## Security Agreement

A security interest cannot attach unless an agreement between the debtor and creditor grants, creates, or provides the creditor with a security interest in the debtor's collateral. With the exception of pledges (discussed below), the agreement must (1) be in writing, (2) be signed by the debtor, and (3) contain a reasonable description of the collateral. Section 9–203(1)(a). In addition, if the collateral is crops growing or to be grown or timber to be cut, the agreement must contain a reasonable description of the land on which the collateral is or will be located.

Under the Code, no written security agreement is required when the collateral is pledged or in the possession of the secured party pursuant to an agreement. Section 9–203(1)(a). A **pledge** is the delivery of personal property to a creditor as security for the payment of a debt. A pledge requires that the secured party (the pledgee) and the debtor agree to the pledge of the collateral and that the collateral be *delivered* to the pledgee.

◆ *See Figure 38–2*

*See Case 38–2*

***Consumer Goods*** Federal regulation prohibits a credit seller or lender from obtaining a consumer's grant of a nonpossessory security interest in household goods. This rule does not apply to purchase money security interests or to pledges. Rather, it prevents a lender or seller from obtaining a nonpurchase money security interest covering the consumer's household goods, which are defined to include clothing, furniture, appliances, kitchenware, personal effects, one radio, and one television. The definition specifically excludes works of art, other electronic entertainment equipment, antiques, and jewelry.

***After-Acquired Property*** "[A] security agreement may provide that any or all obligations covered by the security agreement are to be secured by after-acquired collateral." Section 9–204(1). After-acquired property is property that the debtor presently does not own or have rights to but may acquire at some time. For example, an after-acquired property clause in a security agreement

**FIGURE 38–2** Sample Security Agreement

## SECURITY AGREEMENT

August 22, 1999

Daniel Debtor of 113 Hillsborough Street, City of Raleigh, County of Wake, State of North Carolina, hereinafter called the "Debtor," does hereby grant to S.P. & Assoc., Inc., of Raleigh, North Carolina, hereinafter called "S.P.," its successors and assigns, a security interest in the following described property, hereinafter called the "Collateral," to-wit:

One (1) Deluxe Personal Computer
Serial number VDL16794321
Manufacturer: Apex Mechanical Equipment Co.
Model 420A

to secure the payment of Debtor's note or notes of even date herewith in the aggregate principal or aggregate face amount of Seven Thousand Five Hundred Dollars ($7,500.00), together with interest and any renewal or extension thereof, in whole or in part, and any and all other debts, obligations, and liabilities of any kind of Debtor to S.P., however created, arising, or evidenced, whether direct or indirect, joint or several, whether as maker, indorser, surety, guarantor or otherwise, whether now or hereafter existing, whether due or not due, and however acquired by S.P. (all hereinafter called the "Obligations").

DEBTOR WARRANTS AND AGREES THAT:

1. Except for the security interest hereby granted, the Debtor will use the proceeds of advances made hereunder, which proceeds may be paid by the S.P. directly to the seller of the Collateral, to become the owner of marketable title to the Collateral free from any prior lien, security interest or encumbrance, and the Debtor will defend the Collateral against all claims and demands of all persons at any time claiming an interest therein.

2. The Collateral is and will be used primarily for personal, family, or household purposes, and the Debtor's residence is that shown at the beginning of this Agreement.

3. The Collateral will be kept at the Debtor's address shown at the beginning of this Agreement.

4. There are no financing statements covering any of the Collateral on file in any public office, and the Debtor has not executed in favor of other secured parties financing statements that could be placed on file prior to any of S.P.'s financing statements.

5. DEBTOR AGREES THAT:

   A. He will pay to S.P. all amounts due on the note or notes mentioned above and the other Obligations secured hereby as and when same shall be due and payable, whether by maturity, acceleration, or otherwise, and will pay to S.P. reasonable attorneys' fees incurred by S.P. in collection of said Obligations or enforcement of this Security Agreement.

   B. He will maintain all mechanical equipment and machinery hereby covered in sound and efficient operating condition, including the procurement and installation of such new parts, attachments, and replacements as may be necessary or desirable to maintain said Collateral in proper operating condition.

   C. He will maintain such insurance upon all of the Collateral as S.P. may require, payable to Debtor and S.P. as their interest may appear, in an amount not less than the actual value of the Collateral.

   D. He will pay all insurance premiums and taxes, licenses, or other charges assessed against the Collateral or required to be paid in connection with the use and ownership of the Collateral. If Debtor shall fail to pay such insurance premiums, taxes, licenses, or other charges when they are due, S.P. at its opinion, may pay the cost thereof, and the amounts so paid and advanced shall be added to the indebtedness secured hereby and shall bear interest at the maximum rate permitted by Law.

   E. He will not (a) permit any liens or security interest to attach to any of the Collateral; (b) permit any of the Collateral to be levied upon under any legal process; (c) sell or dispose of any of the Collateral without prior written consent of S.P.; (d) permit anything to be done that may impair the value of the Collateral or the security intended to be afforded by this Agreement.

   F. He will immediately notify S.P. in writing of any change of the Debtor's place or residence, place or places of business, or the location of the Collateral.

**FIGURE 38–2** *(continued)*

    **G.** He will not remove the Collateral from the State of North Carolina without prior written consent by S.P.

**6.** IT IS FURTHER AGREED THAT THE DEBTOR SHALL BE IN DEFAULT UNDER THIS AGREEMENT:

    **A.** If the Debtor uses any of the Collateral in violation of any statute or ordinance or the Debtor is found to have a record or reputation for violating the laws of the United States or any State relating to liquor or narcotics; or

    **B.** If the Debtor shall fail to perform any covenant or Agreement made by him herein; or

    **C.** If the Debtor shall fail to make due and punctual payment of any of the Obligations secured hereby when and as any part or all of such Obligation becomes due and payable; or

    **D.** If any warranty, representation, or statement made or furnished to S.P. by or on behalf of the Debtor in connection with this Agreement proves to have been false in any material respect when made or furnished; or

    **E.** If the Collateral suffers material damage or destruction; or

    **F.** If any bankruptcy or insolvency proceedings are commenced by or against the Debtor or any guarantor or surety for the Debtor; or

    **G.** If the Debtor dies, becomes incompetent, is dissolved, or the Debtor's existence otherwise terminates.

Upon the happening of any of the above events of default or in the event that S.P., in good faith, deems itself insecure, S.P. may at its option, declare all Obligations secured hereby due and payable immediately and have, in addition to other rights and remedies, the rights and remedies of a secured party upon default under the North Carolina Uniform Commercial Code.

The waiver of any particular default of the Debtor hereunder shall not be a waiver of any other or subsequent default of the Debtor.

Any requirement of the North Carolina Uniform Commercial Code of reasonable notification of time and place of public sale, or the time on or after which private sale may be held, may be met by sending written notice by registered or certified mail to the above address of the Debtor at least five (5) days prior to public sale or the date after which private sale may be made.

The Debtor shall be and remain liable for any deficiency remaining after applying the proceeds of disposition of the Collateral first to the reasonable expenses of re-taking, holding, preparing for sale, selling, and the like, including the reasonable attorneys' fees, incurred by S.P. in connection therewith, and then to satisfaction of the Obligations secured hereby.

This Agreement and all rights, remedies, and duties hereunder, including matters of construction, shall be governed by the laws of North Carolina.

This Agreement shall apply to, inure to the benefit of, and be binding upon the heirs, administrators, executors, and assigns of S.P. and the Debtor. This is the entire agreement of the parties, and no amendment, alteration, deletion, or addition hereto shall be effective and binding unless it is in writing and signed by the parties.

Debtor acknowledges that this Agreement is and shall be effective upon execution by the Debtor and delivery hereof to S.P., and it shall not be necessary for S.P. to execute or otherwise signify its acceptance hereof.

Signed and delivered on the day first above written.

                                                    _____ (SEAL)

                                                    Daniel Debtor

                                                     S.P. & Assoc., Inc.

                                                     (Secured Party)

                                                     By: _____

may include all present and subsequently acquired inventory, accounts, or equipment of the debtor. This clause would provide the secured party with a valid security interest not only in the typewriter, desk, and file cabinet that the debtor currently owns, but also in a personal computer she purchases later. Article 9 therefore accepts the concept of a "continuing general lien," or a *floating lien,* though the Code limits the operation of an after-acquired property clause against consumers and by providing that no such interest can be claimed as additional security in consumer goods, except accessions, if the goods are acquired more than ten days after the secured party gives value. Section 9–204(2). An *accession* is property installed in or affixed to other property. Section 9–314. For example, a new engine placed in an old automobile is an accession.

***Proceeds*** A secured party is necessarily interested in the use and control of proceeds, which include whatever is received from the sale, exchange, collection, or other disposition of the collateral. Section 9–306(1). These proceeds may be in the form of money, checks, deposit accounts, promissory notes, or other types of personal property. Unless otherwise agreed, a security agreement gives the secured party rights to proceeds. Section 9–203(3).

***Future Advances*** The obligations covered by a security agreement may include future advances. Section 9–204(3). Frequently, a debtor obtains a line of credit from a creditor for advances to be made at some later time. For instance, a manufacturer may provide a retailer with a $60,000 line of credit, only $20,000 of which the retailer initially uses. Nevertheless, the manufacturer and the retailer may enter a security agreement granting to the manufacturer a security interest in the retailer's inventory that covers not only the initial $20,000 advance but also any future advances.

## PERFECTION

To be effective against third parties who assert competing interests in the collateral (including other creditors of the debtor, the debtor's trustee in bankruptcy, and transferees of the debtor), the security interest must be perfected. **Perfection** of a security interest occurs when it has attached *and* when all the applicable steps required for perfection have been taken. Section 9–303(1). If these steps precede attachment, the security interest is perfected at the time it attaches. Once a security interest

becomes perfected, it "may still be or become subordinate to other interests but in general after perfection the secured party is protected against creditors and transferees of the debtor and in particular against any representative of creditors in insolvency proceedings instituted by or against the debtor." Section 9–303, Comment 1.

Depending on the type of collateral, a security interest may be perfected:

1. by the secured party filing a financing statement in the designated public office;
2. by the secured party taking or retaining possession of the collateral;
3. automatically, on the attachment of the security interest; or
4. temporarily, for a period specified by the Code.

◆ *See Figure 38–3*

## Filing a Financing Statement

Filing a financing statement is the general method of perfecting a security interest under Article 9. Filing may be used to perfect a security interest in any kind of collateral, with the *exception* of instruments. The form of the **financing statement,** which is filed to give public notice of the security interest, may vary from State to State. Though it need not be highly detailed, the financing statement must include the names and addresses of the secured party and the debtor, a reasonable description of the types or items of collateral, and the signature of the debtor. Section 9–402(1). Figure 38–4 shows a sample financing statement. If the financing statement substantially complies with these requirements, minor errors that do not seriously mislead will not render the financing statement ineffective. Section 9–402(8).

***Duration of Filing*** A financing statement that provides no maturity date is effective for five years from the date of filing. Section 9–403(2). A **continuation statement** filed by the secured party within six months prior to expiration will extend the effectiveness of the filing for another five years. Section 9–403(3).

In most States, security interests in **motor vehicles** must be perfected by making a notation on the certificate of title rather than by filing a financing statement. A **certificate of title** is an official representation of ownership. Nevertheless, in most States, certificate of title laws do not apply to motor vehicles that are held as inventory for sale by a dealer.

◆ *See Figure 38–4*

FIGURE 38–3  Requisites for Enforceability of Security Interests

| I. Attachment | II. Perfection |
|---|---|
| A. Agreement<br>  1. in writing (unless Secured Party has possession)<br>  2. providing a security interest<br>  3. in described collateral<br>  4. signed by debtor<br>B. Value given by secured party, and<br>C. Debtor has rights in collateral. | A. Secured Party files a financing statement, or<br>B. Secured Party takes possession, or<br>C. Automatically, or<br>D. Temporarily. |

***Place of Filing*** Section 9–401(1) of the Code provides three alternative provisions regarding the proper place at which to file a financing statement. The alternatives differ as to which types of collateral are to be filed *locally* (in the county) or *centrally* (with the Secretary of State or another designated State official).

The first alternative, which has been adopted in only a few States, provides that where the collateral is fixtures, timber to be cut, or minerals to be extracted, the financing statement should be filed locally in the office where a mortgage on real estate would be filed or recorded. All other filings should be made centrally with the Secretary of State or another designated State official.

The second alternative, which is the most widely adopted, stipulates local filing for fixtures, farm products, consumer goods, timber, minerals, and farming equipment. All other filings are to be made in the office of the Secretary of State or another designated State official.

The third alternative is the same as the second except that, where central filing is required, the secured party must *also* file locally if the debtor has a place of business in only one county or has no place of business in the State but resides in the State.

***Improper Filing*** If a secured party fails to file the financing statement in the proper location or fails to file it in all the required locations, the filing is ineffective, subject to two exceptions. First, a filing made in good faith is effective for any collateral for which the filing complies with the requirements of Article 9. Section 9–401(2). This exception applies when a filing covers several different kinds of collateral and is proper with respect to some but not all of them. Second, a filing made in good faith is also effective for collateral covered by the financing statement against any person who has knowledge of the contents of that financing statement. Section 9–401(2). This exception has been limited by

the 1972 amendments, which give a lien creditor priority over an unperfected security interest without regard to whether the lien creditor knew of the improperly perfected security interest. Section 9–301(1)(b).

***Subsequent Change of Information*** After a financing statement has been properly filed by a secured party, the debtor may change the place of his residence or business or the location or use of the collateral and thus render the information in the filing incorrect. In all the States, a change in the use of the collateral does not impair the effectiveness of the original filing. Most States also provide that the original filing made in the proper place continues to be effective despite any change of location, provided the change is **intrastate.** Section 9–401(3). A minority of States have adopted a second alternative provided by Section 9–401(3), which limits the effectiveness of a filing made in the proper county to four months after the debtor has moved his residence, place of business, or the collateral to another county. Under the second alternative, if the secured party does not file a financing statement in the new county within the four-month period, perfection ceases until a new filing is made.

With respect to **interstate** changes, two situations require a new filing: (1) the collateral is mobile goods, accounts, or general intangibles, and the debtor moves his residence or place of business to another State; or (2) the debtor moves the collateral to another State. Section 9–103. In either case, the security interest perfected in the former State remains in effect for four months or until perfection would have ceased under the laws of the first State, whichever occurs first. If the security interest is not perfected within the four-month period, it becomes unperfected, and such loss of perfection under the 1972 amendments is retroactive to the time at which the debtor or collateral changed location. For example, Davis purchases goods in Arizona and grants Sarah Penn a security interest in the goods, which Sarah

**FIGURE 38–4** Sample Financing Statement

## UNIFORM COMMERCIAL CODE—FINANCING STATEMENT APPROVED
## FOR USE IN NORTH CAROLINA AND THE FOLLOWING STATES

| | | | | | |
|---|---|---|---|---|---|
| Alabama | Delaware | Maine | New Jersey | Tennessee | |
| Alaska | Hawaii | Maryland | New Mexico | Virginia | |
| Arizona | Idaho | Massachusetts | North Dakota | West Virginia | UCC–1 |
| Arkansas | Indiana | Mississippi | Ohio | Wyoming | |
| Colorado | Kansas | Montana | Oklahoma | District of Columbia | |
| Connecticut | Kentucky | New Hampshire | South Carolina | | |

| | | |
|---|---|---|
| This FINANCING STATEMENT is presented to a Filing Officer for filing pursuant to the Uniform Commercial Code. | No. of Additional Sheets Presented: | |
| (1) Debtor(s) (Last Name First) and Address(es): | (2) Secured Party(ies) Name(s) and Address(es): | |
| (3) (a) ☐ Collateral is or includes fixtures<br><br>(b) ☐ Timber, Minerals or Accounts Subject to UCC 9–103(5) are covered<br><br>(c) ☐ Crops Are Growing Or To Be Grown On Real Property Described in Section (5). If either block 3(a) or block 3(b) applies, describe real estate, including record owner(s) in section (5). | (4) Assignee(s) of Secured Party, Address(es): | For<br>Filing<br>Officer |

(5)  This Financing Statement Covers the Following types [or items] of property.

☐ Products of the Collateral Are Also Covered.

(6)  Signatures: Debtor(s)                                    Secured Party(ies) [or Assignees]

(By) _____           (By) _____
Standard Form Approved by N.C. Sec. of State and          Signature of Secured Party Permitted in Lieu of Debtor's
   other states shown above.                  Signature:
   (1)  Filing Officer Copy—Numerical          (1)  Collateral is subject to Security Interest In Another Jurisdiction and ☐
                         ☐ Collateral Is Brought Into This State
                         ☐ Debtor's Location Changed To This State
   (2)  For Other Situations See: UCC 9–402(2)

                                                       UCC–1

perfects by filing. Davis then moves to Kansas and immediately sells the goods to Bruce. If Sarah refiles in Kansas within the four-month period, she would have priority over Bruce; however, if she fails to file within that time,

Bruce would prevail, because the loss of perfection dates back to the time of Davis's move from Arizona to Kansas.

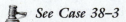 *See Case 38–3*

## Possession

Possession by the secured party perfects a security interest in goods (e.g., those in the possession of pawnbrokers), instruments, money, negotiable documents, or chattel paper. Section 9–305. Possession is *not* available, however, as a means of perfecting a security interest in accounts and general intangibles. With the limited exception of the twenty-one-day temporary period of perfection discussed later in this chapter, possession is the *only* way to perfect a security interest in instruments. Section 9–304. In addition, the usual and advisable method of perfecting a security interest in both negotiable documents and chattel paper is by possession. Although both of these types of collateral may be perfected by filing, this method of perfection is inadvisable because (a) the holder of a negotiable document of title which has been duly negotiated to him takes priority in the goods over an earlier security interest perfected by filing, Section 9–309; and (b) a good faith purchaser of chattel paper in the ordinary course of business takes priority over an earlier security interest perfected by filing. Section 9–308.

A pledge, which is a possessory security interest, is the delivery of personal property to a creditor, or to a third party acting as an agent or bailee for the creditor, as security for the payment of a debt. Perhaps the most common pledge is that of a borrower who pledges corporate stock by delivering the certificates to a bank in order to secure a loan. The delivery of the stock certificates (the collateral) to the bank (the secured party) is the essential element of the pledge. Because delivery is made, the security interest is "perfected" without filing. Section 9–302(1)(a). No pledge occurs where the debtor retains possession of the collateral. In making a pledge, the debtor is not legally required to sign a written security agreement; an oral agreement granting the secured party a security interest is sufficient. In any situation not involving a pledge, however, the Code requires a written security agreement. Section 9–203.

One type of pledge is the **field warehouse.** This common arrangement for financing inventory allows the debtor access to the pledged goods and provides the secured party with control over the pledged property at the same time. In this arrangement, a professional warehouseman generally establishes a warehouse on the debtor's premises—usually by enclosing a portion of those premises and posting appropriate signs—to store the debtor's unsold inventory. The warehouseman then typically issues nonnegotiable receipts for the goods to the secured party, who may then authorize the ware-houseman to release a portion of the goods to the debtor as the goods are sold, at a specified quantity per week, or at any rate on which the parties agree. Thus, the secured party legally possesses the goods while allowing the debtor easy access to her inventory.

## Automatic Perfection

In some situations, a security interest is automatically perfected on attachment. The most important situation to which automatic perfection applies is a purchase money security interest in consumer goods. Several States, however, either do not permit automatic perfection of purchase money security interests in consumer goods or impose limitations on the purchase price. A partial or isolated assignment of accounts that transfers a less-than-significant portion of the assignor's outstanding accounts is also automatically perfected. Section 9–302(1)(e).

A purchase money security interest in consumer goods, with the exception of motor vehicles, is perfected automatically upon attachment; filing a financing statement is unnecessary. Section 9–302(1)(d). For example, Doris purchases a refrigerator from Carol on credit for Doris's personal, family, or household use. Doris takes possession of the refrigerator and then grants Carol a security interest in the refrigerator pursuant to a written security agreement. Upon Doris's granting Carol the security interest, Carol's security interest attaches and is automatically perfected. The same would be true if Doris purchased the refrigerator for cash but borrowed the money from Logan, to whom Doris granted a security interest in the refrigerator pursuant to a written security agreement. Logan's security interest would attach and would be automatically perfected when she received the security agreement from Doris. Nevertheless, because an automatically perfected PMSI in consumer goods protects the secured party less fully than a filed PMSI, secured parties frequently file a financing statement, rather than rely solely on automatic perfection.

*See Case 39–3*

## Temporary Perfection

Depending on the type of collateral, certain security interests are automatically but only temporarily perfected. After the temporary period expires, the security interest becomes unperfected unless it is perfected by other means. A security interest in negotiable documents or instruments is automatically perfected, without filing or taking possession, for twenty-one days from the time it attaches, to the extent that it arises for new value given under a written security agreement. Section 9–304(4). The secured party, however, runs the risk of loss or impairment of his security interest during the twenty-one-day period; for although his interest is temporarily perfected, a holder in due course of a negotiable instrument or a holder to whom a document has been duly negotiated will take priority over the security interest. Sections 9–308 and 9–309.

The Code further provides that a security interest remains perfected for twenty-one days where a secured party, who already has a perfected security interest in an instrument, negotiable document, or goods in possession of a bailee (provided the secured party has not issued a negotiable document for the goods), under certain circumstances delivers the instrument to the debtor, releases the document to him, or makes the goods available to him. Section 9–304(5). Moreover, a security interest in proceeds is automatically perfected for ten days after receipt of the proceeds, if the security interest in the original collateral was perfected. Section 9–302(1)(b).

◆ *See Figure 38–5*

## PRIORITIES AMONG COMPETING INTERESTS

As previously noted, a security interest must be perfected to be most effective against the debtor's other creditors,

her trustee in bankruptcy, and her transferees. Nonetheless, perfection of a security interest does *not* provide the secured party with a **priority** over *all* third parties with an interest in the collateral. On the other hand, even an unperfected but attached security interest has priority over a limited number of third parties and is enforceable against the debtor. Article 9 establishes a complex set of rules that determine the relative priorities among these parties.

## Against Unsecured Creditors

Once a security interest *attaches,* it has priority over claims of other creditors who do not have a security interest or a lien. This priority does not depend upon perfection. If a security interest does not attach, the creditor is merely an unsecured or general creditor of the debtor.

## Against Other Secured Creditors

The rights of a secured creditor against other secured creditors depend upon the security interests perfected, when they are perfected, and the type of collateral. Notwithstanding the rules of priority, a secured party entitled to priority may subordinate her interest to that of another secured creditor. The parties may do this by agreement, and nothing need be filed.

**FIGURE 38–5** Methods of Perfecting Security Interests

| Collateral | Filing | Possession | Automatic | Temporary |
|---|---|---|---|---|
| **Goods** | • | • | PMSI | |
|   **Consumer** | • | • | | |
|   **Equipment** | • | • | | |
|   **Farm products** | • | • | | |
|   **Inventory** | • | • | | |
|   **Fixtures** | • | • | | |
| | | | | |
| **Indispensable Paper** | | | | |
|   **Chattel paper** | • | • | | |
|   **Instruments** | | • | | 21 days |
|   **Documents** | • | • | | 21 days |
| | | | | |
| **Intangibles** | • | | | |
|   **Account** | • | | Isolated Assignment | |
| | | | | |
| **General Intangibles** | • | | | |

***Perfected versus Unperfected*** A creditor with a perfected security interest has greater rights in the collateral than a creditor with an unperfected security interest, whether or not the unperfected security interest has attached.

***Perfected versus Perfected*** Two parties each having a perfected security interest rank according to priority in *time of filing or perfection*. This general rule is stated in Section 9–312(5)(a), which provides:

> Conflicting security interests rank according to priority in time of filing or perfection. Priority dates from the time a filing is first made covering the collateral or the time the security interest is first perfected, whichever is earlier, provided that there is no period thereafter when there is neither filing nor perfection.

This rule favors filing, as it can occur prior to attachment and thus grant priority from a time that may precede perfection.

For example, Debter Store and Leynder Bank enter into a loan agreement (assume there is no binding commitment to extend credit) under the terms of which Leynder agrees to lend $5,000 on the security of Debter's existing store equipment. A security agreement is executed and a financing statement is filed, but no funds are advanced. One week later, Debter enters into a loan agreement with Reserve Bank, and Reserve agrees to lend $5,000 on the security of the same store equipment. The funds are advanced, a security agreement is executed, and a financing statement is filed. One week later, Leynder Bank advances the agreed sum of $5,000. Debter Store defaults on both loans. Between Leynder Bank and Reserve Bank, Leynder has priority, because priority among security interests perfected by filing is determined by the order in which they were filed. Reserve Bank should have checked the financing statements on file. Had it done so, it would have discovered that Leynder Bank claimed a security interest in the equipment. Conversely, after filing its financing statement, with no prior secured party of record, Leynder had no need to check the files before advancing funds to Debter Store in accordance with its loan commitment.

To further illustrate, assume that Marc grants a security interest in a Chagall painting to Miro Bank and that the bank advances funds to Marc in accordance with the loan agreement. A financing statement is filed. Later, Marc wants more money and goes to Brague, an art dealer, who advances funds to Marc upon a pledge of the painting. Marc defaults on both loans. As between Miro and Brague, Miro has priority because its financing statement was filed before Brague's perfection by possession. By checking the financing statement on file, Brague would have discovered that Miro had a prior security interest in the painting.

Where there is a **purchase money security interest** in the collateral, the rules depend on whether the collateral is noninventory or inventory:

1. A purchase money security interest in **noninventory** collateral takes priority over a conflicting security interest if the purchase money security interest is perfected at the time the debtor receives possession of the collateral *or* within ten days of receipt. Section 9–312(4). Thus, the secured party has a ten-day grace period in which to perfect. Almost all of the States have extended the grace period to twenty days, although a few have extended the period to some other number of days (15, 20, or 30 days).

   For example, Dawkins Manufacturing Co. enters into a loan contract with Larkin Bank, which loans money to Dawkins on the security (as provided in the security agreement) of Dawkins's existing and future equipment and files a financing statement stating that the collateral is "all equipment presently owned and subsequently acquired" by Dawkins. At a later date, Dawkins buys new equipment from Parker Supply Co., paying 25 percent of the purchase price, with Parker retaining a security interest (as provided in the security agreement) in the equipment to secure the remaining balance. If Parker files a financing statement within ten days of Dawkins's obtaining possession of the equipment, Parker's purchase money security interest in the new equipment purchased from Parker has priority over Larkin's interest. If, however, Parker files one day beyond the statutory grace period, Parker's interest is subordinate to Larkin's.

2. A purchase money security interest in **inventory** has priority over conflicting security interests if the following requirements are met. The purchase money security holder must perfect his interest in the inventory at the time the debtor receives the inventory. He must also give written notification of his acquisition of a purchase money security interest and a description of the secured inventory to all holders of conflicting security interests who have filed financing statements covering the same type of inventory. Section 9–312(3).

   For example, Dodger Store and Lyons Bank enter into a loan agreement in which Lyons agrees to finance Dodger's entire inventory of stoves, refrigerators, and other kitchen appliances. A security agreement is executed and a financing statement is filed, and Lyons advances funds to Dodger. Subsequently, Dodger enters into an agreement under which Rodger Stove Co. will supply Dodger with stoves, retaining a purchase money security interest in this inventory. Rodger will have priority as to the inventory it supplies to Dodger, provided that Rodger files a financing statement by the time Dodger receives the goods and notifies Lyons that it is going to engage in this purchase money financing of the described stoves. If Rodger fails either to give the required notice or to file timely a financing statement, Lyons will have priority over Rodger as to the stoves Rodger supplies to Dodger. As noted, the Code adopts a system of notice filing, and secured parties who fail to check the financing statements on file proceed at their peril.

 *See Case 38–1*

**Unperfected versus Unperfected** If neither security interest is perfected, then the first to attach has priority. Section 9–312(5)(6). If neither attach, both of the creditors are general, unsecured creditors.

## Against Buyers

A security interest continues even in collateral that is sold, unless the secured party authorizes the sale. Thus, following a sale of collateral, a secured party who did not authorize the transaction does not have to file a new financing statement to continue her perfected interest. The security interest also continues in any identifiable proceeds from the sale. Section 9–306(2). In some instances, however, buyers of collateral sold without the secured party's authorization take it free of the security interest. Some of these purchasers take the collateral free of even a perfected security interest; others take it free of only an unperfected security interest.

**Buyers in the Ordinary Course of Business** A buyer in the ordinary course of business takes collateral free of any security interest created by *his* seller, even if the security interest is perfected and the buyer knows of its existence. Section 9–307(1). A buyer in the ordinary course of business is a person who, without knowledge that a sale will violate a security interest of a third party, buys in good faith from a person in the business of selling goods of that kind. Section 1–201(9). Thus, this rule applies primarily to purchasers of inventory. For example, a consumer who purchases a sofa from a furniture dealer and the dealer who purchases the sofa from another dealer are both buyers in the ordinary course of business. On the other hand, a person who purchases a sofa from a dentist who used the sofa in his waiting room or from an individual who used the sofa in his home is not a buyer in the ordinary course of business.

To illustrate further: A person who in the ordinary course of business buys an automobile from an automobile dealership will take free and clear of a security interest created by the dealer from whom she purchased the car. That same buyer in the ordinary course of business will not, however, take clear of a security interest created by any person who owned the automobile prior to the dealer. A leading case on this point is *National Shawmut Bank of Boston v. Jones*, 108 N.H. 386, 236 A.2d 484 (1967). In that case, Wever bought a 1964 Dodge Dart from Wentworth Motor Company for his own personal use and granted a security interest in the car to Wentworth. Wentworth later assigned the security interest to National Shawmut Bank, which properly perfected it. Without Shawmut's consent, Wever sold the car to Hanson-Rock, another automobile dealer. Hanson-Rock then sold the car to Jones. Even though Jones was a buyer in the ordinary course of business from Hanson-Rock, he took the automobile subject to Shawmut's security interest, as that interest had not been created by Jones's seller, Hanson-Rock.

**Buyers of Farm Products** Buyers in the ordinary course of business of **farm products,** although not protected by Section 9–307, are protected by the Federal Food Security Act. This Act defines a buyer in the ordinary course of business as "a person who, in the ordinary course of business, buys farm products from a person engaged in farming operations who is in the business of selling farm products." The Act provides that such a buyer shall take free of most security interests created by the seller, even if the security interest is perfected and the buyer knows of its existence. Nevertheless, three exceptions in the Act render a security interest effective against the buyer. Two of the exceptions depend upon the State's enacting a central filing system, as specified in the Act; the third applies if the creditor, in a form specified by the Act, gives the buyer written notice of her interest within one year before the sale.

**Buyers of Consumer Goods** In the case of consumer goods, a buyer who buys without knowledge of a security interest, for value, and for personal, family, or household use takes the goods free of any purchase money security interest *automatically* perfected, but takes the goods subject to a security interest perfected by filing. Section 9–307(2). For example, Ann purchases on credit a refrigerator from Sean for use in her home and grants Sean a security interest in the refrigerator. Sean does not file a financing statement but has a perfected security interest by attachment. Ann subsequently sells the refrigerator to her neighbor, Juwan, for use in his home. Juwan does not know of Sean's security interest and therefore takes the refrigerator free of that interest. If Sean had filed a financing statement, however, his security interest would continue in the collateral, even in Juwan's hands.

***Other Buyers*** An *unperfected* security interest is subordinated to the rights (1) in the case of goods, instruments, documents, and chattel paper, of a purchaser who gives value for the collateral and who takes it without knowledge of the existing security interest, before the interest is perfected, Section 9–301(1)(c); and (2) in the case of accounts and general intangibles, of a purchaser who, without knowledge of the security interest, takes for value before perfection. Section 9–301(1)(d). If either of these purchasers knows of the unperfected security interest, he takes the collateral subject to the interest.

A purchaser who gives new value for and takes possession of chattel paper or an instrument in the ordinary course of his business has priority over a perfected security interest in the chattel paper or instrument if he acts without knowledge that the specific paper or instrument is subject to a security interest. Section 9–308. A holder in due course of a negotiable instrument, a holder to whom a negotiable document of title has been duly negotiated, and a *bona fide* purchaser of an investment security take priority over an earlier security interest even though perfected. Filing under Article 9 does not constitute notice of the security interest to such holders or purchasers. Section 9–309.

## Against Lien Creditors

A **lien creditor** is a creditor who has acquired a lien in the property by judicial decree; such a creditor may be an assignee for the benefit of creditors, a receiver in equity, or a trustee in bankruptcy. Section 9–301(3). (A **trustee in bankruptcy** is a representative of an estate in bankruptcy who is responsible for collecting, liquidating, and distributing the debtor's assets.) Whereas a **perfected** security interest has priority over lien creditors who acquire their liens after perfection, an **unperfected** security interest is subordinate to the rights of one who becomes a lien creditor before its perfection. Section

9–301(1)(b). If a secured party files with respect to a *purchase money security interest* within ten days after the debtor receives possession of the collateral, however, the secured party takes priority over the rights of a lien creditor that arise between the time the security interest attaches and the time of filing. Section 9–301(2). Most of the States have expanded the ten-day grace period to twenty days (although a few have extended the period to either fifteen or twenty-one days).

Nonetheless, a lien securing claims arising from services or materials furnished in the ordinary course of a person's business with respect to goods (an artisan's or mechanic's lien) "takes priority over a perfected security interest unless the lien is statutory and the statute expressly provides otherwise." Section 9–310.

## Against Trustee in Bankruptcy

The Bankruptcy Act empowers a trustee in bankruptcy to invalidate secured claims in certain instances. It also imposes some limitations on the rights of secured parties. This section will examine the power of a trustee in bankruptcy to (a) take priority over an unperfected security interest and (b) avoid preferential transfers.

***Priority over Unperfected Security Interest*** A trustee in bankruptcy may invalidate any security interest that is voidable by a creditor who obtained a judicial lien on the date the bankruptcy petition was filed. Bankruptcy Act, Section 544. Under the Code and the Bankruptcy Act, the trustee, as a hypothetical **lien creditor,** has priority over a creditor whose security interest was not perfected when the bankruptcy petition was filed. A creditor with a purchase money security interest who files within the statutory grace period after the debtor receives the collateral will defeat the trustee, even if the bankruptcy petition is filed before the creditor perfects and after the security interest is created. For example, David borrowed $5,000 from Cynthia on September 1 and gave her a security interest in the equipment he purchased with the borrowed funds. On October 3, before Cynthia perfected her security interest, David filed for bankruptcy. The trustee in bankruptcy can invalidate Cynthia's security interest because it was unperfected when the bankruptcy petition was filed. If, however, David had filed for bankruptcy on September 8 and Cynthia had perfected the security interest within the statutorily provided grace period, Cynthia would prevail.

***Avoidance of Preferential Transfers*** Section 547 of the Bankruptcy Act provides that a trustee in bankruptcy may invalidate any transfer of property—including the granting of a security interest—from the debtor, provided that the transfer (1) was to or for the benefit of a creditor; (2) was made on account of an antecedent debt; (3) was made when the debtor was insolvent; (4) was made on the date of or within ninety days before the filing of the bankruptcy petition or, if made to an insider, was made within one year before the date of the filing; and (5) enabled the transferee to receive more than he would have received in bankruptcy. (An insider includes a relative or general partner of a debtor, as well as a partnership in which the debtor is a general partner or a corporation of which the debtor is a director, officer, or person in control.) In determining whether the debtor is insolvent, the Act establishes a rebuttable presumption of insolvency for the ninety days prior to the filing of the bankruptcy petition. To avoid a transfer to an insider that occurred more than one year before bankruptcy, the trustee must prove that the debtor was insolvent when the transfer was made. If a security interest is invalidated as a preferential transfer, the creditor may still make a claim for the unpaid debt, but the creditor's claim is unsecured.

To illustrate the operation of this rule, consider the following. On May 1, Debra bought and received merchandise from Stuart and gave him a security interest in the goods for the unpaid price of $20,000. On June 5, Stuart filed a financing statement. On August 1, Debra filed a petition for bankruptcy. The trustee in bankruptcy may avoid the perfected security interest as a preferential transfer because (1) the transfer of the perfected security interest on June 5 was to benefit a creditor (Stuart); (2) the transfer was on account of an antecedent debt (the $20,000 owed from the sale of the merchandise); (3) the debtor was insolvent at the time (the Act presumes that the debtor is insolvent for the ninety days preceding the date the bankruptcy petition was filed— August 1); (4) the transfer was made within ninety days of bankruptcy (June 5 is less than ninety days before August 1); and (5) the transfer enabled the creditor to receive more than he would have received in bankruptcy (Stuart would have a secured claim on which he would recover more than he would on an unsecured claim).

◆ *See Figure 38–6*

# DEFAULT

After default, the security agreement and the applicable provisions of the Code govern the rights and remedies of the parties. In general, the secured party may reduce his claim to judgment, foreclose, or otherwise enforce the security interest by available judicial procedure. Section 9–501. Unless the debtor has waived his rights in the collateral after default, he has a right of **redemption** (to free the collateral of the security interest by paying off the loan) at any time before the secured party has disposed of the collateral, has entered a contract to dispose of it, or has discharged the obligation by retaining the collateral. Sections 9–506 and 9–505(2). The rights and remedies of the creditor are cumulative.

## Repossession

Unless the parties have agreed otherwise, the secured party may take possession of the collateral on default. If it can be done without a breach of the peace, such taking may occur without judicial process. The Code leaves the term *breach of the peace* for the courts to define. Some States have defined such a breach to require either the use of violence or the threat of violence, while others require merely an entry without consent. Most States require permission for entry to a residence or garage. On the other hand, the courts do permit the repossession of motor vehicles from driveways or streets. Some courts, however, do not permit a creditor to repossess if the debtor has orally protested the repossession.

After default, instead of removing the collateral, the secured party may render it unusable and leave it on the debtor's premises until disposing of it. Section 9–503.

 *See Case 38–4*

## Sale of Collateral

The secured party may sell, lease, or otherwise dispose of any collateral in its existing condition at the time of default or following any commercially reasonable preparation or processing. Section 9–504(1). The debtor is entitled to any *surplus* and is liable for any *deficiency*, except in the case of a sale of accounts or chattel paper, where he is neither entitled nor liable unless the security agreement so provides. Section 9–504(2).

A purchaser for value of the collateral obtains all of the debtor's rights in the collateral and also discharges the security interest under which the sale occurred as well as all subordinate security interests and liens.

The collateral may be disposed of at public or private sale, so long as all aspects of the disposition, including its method, time, place, and terms, are "commercially reasonable." Section 9–504(3). The fact that the secured party could have received a better price "is not of itself sufficient to establish that the sale was not made in a

**FIGURE 38–6**  Priorities

| Vs. | Unsecured creditor | Creditor with unperfected security interest | Creditor with perfected security interest | Creditor with perfected purchase money security interest |
|---|---|---|---|---|
| **Unsecured creditor** | = | ↑ | ↑ | ↑ |
| **Creditor with unperfected security interest** | ← | first to attach | ↑ | ↑ |
| **Creditor with perfected security interest—noninventory** | ← | ← | first to file or perfect | ↑ if PMSI perfected within grace period |
| **Creditor with perfected security interest—inventory** | ← | ← | first to file or perfect | ↑ if PMSI gives notice and perfects by time debtor gets possession |
| **Buyer in ordinary course of business** | ← | ← | ← if created by immediate seller | ← |
| **Consumer buyer of consumer goods** | ← | ← | ↑ | ← if not filed |
| **Lien creditor (including trustee in bankruptcy)** | ← | ← | first in time | first in time but PMSI has grace period |
| **Trustee in bankruptcy—voidable preferences** | ← | ← | ↑ if secured party perfects within ten days | ↑ if PMSI perfects within grace period |

commercially reasonable manner." Section 9–507(2). Unless the collateral is perishable or threatens to decline speedily in value or is of a type customarily sold on a recognized market, both the debtor and, except in the case of consumer goods, other secured parties who have filed or who are known by the secured party to have security interests in the collateral must receive reasonable notice of a public sale or the time after which a private disposition will be made. The courts are divided over the effect of a commercially unreasonable disposition of collateral on the debtor's obligation to pay any deficiency. Three theories exist: one absolutely bars the creditor from recovering a deficiency, a second creates a rebuttable presumption that no deficiency exists, and the third provides that the debtor must establish that the unreasonable disposition caused him harm, which loss he may then set off against his debt.

The secured party may buy at a public sale and at a private sale if the collateral is customarily sold in a recognized market or is the subject of widely distributed standard price quotations. Section 9–504(3).

## Retention of Collateral

The secured party may, after default and repossession, send written notice to the debtor and, except in the case of consumer goods, to other secured parties that he proposes to retain the collateral in complete satisfaction of the obligation; and, if he receives no objection within twenty-one days, he may retain the collateral. If there is an objection, however, the secured party must dispose of the collateral as provided in the Code. Section 9–505(2). In the case of *consumer goods*, if the debtor has paid 60 percent or more of the obligation and has not, after default, signed a statement renouncing his rights, the secured party who has taken possession of the collateral must dispose of it by sale within ninety days after repossession or the debtor may recover, in conversion or under the Code, not less than the credit service charge, plus 10 percent of the principal amount of the debt or the time price differential, plus 10 percent of the cash price. Sections 9–505(1) and 9–507(1).

# SURETYSHIP

In many business transactions involving the extension of the credit, the creditor will require that someone in addition to the debtor promise to fulfill the obligation. This promisor generally is known as a surety. In a contract involving a minor, a surety commonly will act as a party with full contractual capacity who can be held responsible for the obligations arising from the contract. Sureties are often used in addition to security to further reduce the risks involved in the extension of credit and are used instead of security interests when security is unavailable or when the use of a secured transaction is too expensive or inconvenient. Employers frequently use sureties to protect against losses caused by employees' embezzlement, while property owners use sureties to bond the performance of contracts for the construction of commercial buildings. Similarly, statutes commonly require that contracts for work to be done for governmental entities have the added protection of a surety. Premiums for compensated sureties exceed $1 billion annually in the United States.

## *NATURE AND FORMATION*

A **surety** promises to answer for the payment of a debt or the performance of a duty owed to one person (called the **creditor**) by another (the **principal debtor**) upon the *failure* of the principal debtor to make payment or otherwise perform the obligation. Thus, the suretyship relationship involves three parties—the principal debtor, the creditor, and the surety—and three contractual obligations. Two or more persons bound for the same debt of a principal debtor are **cosureties.**

The creditor's rights against the principal debtor are determined by the contract between them. The creditor also may realize upon any collateral securing the principal debtor's performance that the creditor or the surety holds. In addition, the creditor may proceed against the surety if the principal debtor defaults. If the surety is an **absolute surety,** then the creditor may hold the surety liable as soon as the principal debtor defaults. The creditor need *not* proceed first against the principal debtor. In contrast, a surety who is a **conditional guarantor of collection** is liable only upon the creditor's first exhausting his legal remedies against the principal debtor. Thus, a conditional guarantor of collection is liable if the creditor first obtains, but is unable to collect, a judgment against the principal debtor.

A surety who is required to pay the creditor for the principal debtor's obligation is entitled to be exonerated (relieved of liability) and reimbursed by the principal debtor. In addition, the surety is subrogated to (assumes) the rights of the creditor and has a right of contribution from cosureties. These rights of sureties are discussed more fully later in this chapter.

Although in theory a surety and a guarantor are distinct entities, the two terms are nearly synonymous in common usage. Strictly speaking, a surety is bound with the principal debtor as a primary obligor, usually, although not necessarily, on the same instrument, whereas the guarantor is separately or collaterally bound to pay if the principal debtor does not. For convenience, and because the rights and duties of a surety are almost indistinguishable from those of a guarantor, the term *surety* will be used to include both terms.

◆ *See Figure 38–7*

⚖ *See Case 38–5*

## Types of Sureties

A suretyship arrangement is frequently used by creditors seeking to reduce the risk of default by their debtors. For example, Philco Developers, a closely held corporation, applies to Caldwell Bank, a lending institution, for a loan. After scrutinizing the assets and financial prospects of Philco, the lender refuses to extend credit unless Simpson, the sole shareholder of Philco, promises to repay the loan if Philco does not. Simpson agrees, and Caldwell Bank makes the loan. Simpson's undertaking is that of a surety. Similarly, Philco wishes to purchase goods on credit from Bird Enterprises, the seller, who agrees to extend credit only if Philco obtains an acceptable surety. Simpson agrees to pay Bird Enterprises for the goods if Philco does not. Simpson is a surety. In each of these examples, the surety's promise gives the creditor recourse for payment against two persons—the principal debtor and the surety—instead of one, thereby reducing the creditor's risk of loss.

Another common suretyship relation arises when an owner of property subject to a mortgage sells the property to a purchaser who expressly **assumes the mortgage.** Although by assuming the obligation the purchaser becomes the principal debtor and therefore personally obligated to pay the seller's debt to the lender, the seller

FIGURE 38—7  Suretyship Relationship

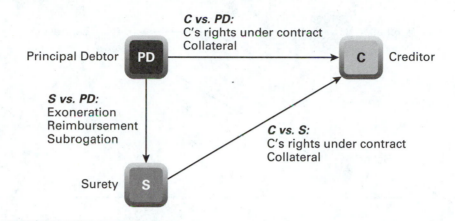

nevertheless remains liable to the lender and is a surety on the obligation the purchaser has assumed. If, however, the purchaser does not assume the mortgage but simply takes the property **"subject to"** the mortgage, he is neither personally liable for the mortgage nor a surety for the mortgage obligation. In this case, the purchaser's potential loss is limited to the value of the property; for although the mortgagee creditor may foreclose against the property, he may not hold the purchaser personally liable for the debt.

In addition to the more general types of sureties, there are numerous specialized kinds of suretyship, the most important of which are (1) fidelity, (2) performance, (3) official, and (4) judicial. A surety undertakes a **fidelity bond** to protect an employer against employee dishonesty. **Performance bonds** guarantee the performance of the terms and conditions of a contract. These bonds are used frequently in the construction industry to protect an owner from losses that may result from a contractor's failure to perform under a building contract. **Official bonds** arise from a common statutory requirement that public officers furnish bonds for the faithful performance of their duties. Such bonds obligate a surety for all losses that an officer causes through negligence or through nonperformance of her duties. **Judicial bonds** are provided on behalf of a party to a judicial proceeding to cover losses caused by delay or by deprivation of the use of property resulting from the institution of the action. In criminal proceedings, the purpose of a judicial bond, called a **bail bond,** is to ensure the appearance of the defendant in court.

◆ *See Figure 38–8*

## Formation

The suretyship relationship is contractual and must satisfy all the usual elements of a contract, including offer and acceptance, consideration, capacity of the parties, and legality of object. No particular words are required to constitute a contract of suretyship or guaranty.

As discussed in Chapter 15, the contractual promise of a surety to the creditor must be in writing to be enforceable under the statute of frauds. This requirement, which applies only to collateral promises, is subject to the exception known as the *main purpose doctrine.* Under this doctrine, if the leading object (main purpose) of the promisor (surety) is to obtain an economic benefit that he did not previously enjoy, the promise is not within the statute of frauds.

The promise of a surety is *not* binding without consideration. Because the surety generally makes her promise to induce the creditor to confer a benefit upon the principal debtor, the same consideration that supports the principal debtor's promise usually supports the surety's promise as well. Thus, if Constance lends money to Philip upon Sally's promise to act as a surety, Constance's extension of credit is the consideration to support not only Philip's promise to repay the loan but also Sally's suretyship undertaking. In contrast, a surety's promise made *subsequent* to the principal debtor's receipt of the creditor's consideration must be supported by new consideration. Accordingly, if Constance has already sold goods on credit to Philip, a subsequent guaranty by Sally will not be binding unless new consideration is given.

**FIGURE 38–8** Assumption of Mortgage

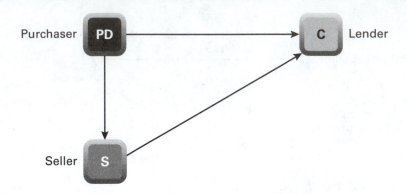

## RIGHTS OF SURETY

Upon the principal debtor's default, the surety has a number of rights against the principal debtor, third parties, and cosureties. These rights include (1) exoneration, (2) reimbursement, (3) subrogation, and (4) contribution. As discussed above, a surety or absolute guarantor has *no* right to compel the creditor to collect from the principal debtor or to realize upon collateral provided by the principal debtor. Nor is the creditor required to give the surety notice of the principal debtor's default unless the contract of suretyship provides otherwise. A conditional guarantor of collection, on the other hand, faces no liability until the creditor first exhausts his legal remedies of collection against the principal debtor.

### Exoneration

The ordinary expectation in a suretyship relation is that the principal debtor will perform the obligation and the surety will not be required to perform. Therefore, the surety has the right to require that her principal debtor pay the creditor when the obligation is due. This right of the surety against the principal debtor, called the right of **exoneration,** is enforceable at equity. If the principal debtor fails to pay the creditor when the debt is due, the surety may obtain a decree ordering the principal debtor to pay the creditor. The remedy of exoneration against the principal debtor does not, however, impair the creditor's right to proceed against the surety.

A surety also has a right of exoneration against his cosureties. When the principal debtor's obligation becomes due, each surety owes every other cosurety the duty to pay her proportionate share of the principal

debtor's obligation to the creditor. Accordingly, a surety may bring an action in equity to obtain an order requiring his cosureties to pay their share of the debt to the creditor.

### Reimbursement

When a surety pays the creditor upon the default of the principal debtor, the surety has the right of **reimbursement** (repayment) against the principal debtor. The surety, however, has no right to reimbursement until he actually has made payment, and then only to the extent of the payment. Thus, a surety who advantageously negotiates a defaulted obligation down to a compromise figure less than the original sum may recover from the principal debtor only the sum he actually paid, not the sum before negotiation.

### Subrogation

Upon payment of the principal debtor's *entire* obligation, the surety "steps into the shoes" of the creditor. This process of substitution, called **subrogation,** confers upon the surety all the rights the creditor has against or through the principal debtor. These include the creditor's rights

1. against the principal debtor, including the creditor's priorities in a bankruptcy proceeding;
2. in security of the principal debtor;
3. against third parties, such as co-makers, who are also obligated on the principal debtor's obligation; and
4. against cosureties.

## Contribution

Up to the amount of their individual undertakings, co-sureties are jointly and severally liable for the principal debtor's default. The creditor may proceed against any or all of the cosureties and collect from any of them the amount that the surety has agreed to guarantee, which may be the entire amount of the principal debtor's obligation.

A surety who pays her principal debtor's obligation may require her cosureties to pay her their proportionate shares of the obligation she has paid. This right of **contribution** arises when a surety has paid more than her proportionate share of a debt, even if the cosureties originally were unaware of each other or were bound on separate instruments. They need only be sureties for the same principal debtor and the same obligation. The right and extent of contribution is determined by contractual agreement among the cosureties. If no agreement exists, sureties obligated for equal amounts share equally; where they are obligated for varying amounts, the proportion of the debt that each surety must contribute is determined by proration according to each surety's undertaking. For example, if X, Y, and Z are cosureties for PD to C in the amounts of $5,000, $10,000, and $15,000 respectively, which totals $30,000, then X's contributive share is one-sixth ($5,000/$30,000), Y's share is one-third ($10,000/$30,000), and Z's share is one-half ($15,000/$30,000).

# DEFENSES OF SURETY AND PRINCIPAL DEBTOR

The obligations the principal debtor and the surety owe to the creditor arise out of contracts. Accordingly, those in surety relationships can assert the usual contractual defenses, such as those resulting from (1) the nonexistence of the principal debtor's obligation, (2) a discharge of the principal debtor's obligation, (3) a modification of the principal debtor's contract, or (4) a variation of the surety's risk. Some of these defenses are available only to the principal debtor, some only to the surety, and others are available to both parties.

◆ *See Figure 38–9*

## Personal Defenses of Principal Debtor

The defenses available only to a principal debtor are known as the personal defenses of the principal debtor. For example, the principal debtor's **incapacity** due to infancy or mental incompetency may serve as a defense

for the principal debtor but not for the surety. If, however, the principal debtor disaffirms the contract and returns the consideration he received from the creditor, then the surety is discharged from his liability. In contrast, a discharge of the principal debtor's obligation in **bankruptcy** does not in turn discharge the surety's liability to the creditor on that obligation. In addition, the surety may not use as a **setoff** any claim that the principal debtor has against the creditor.

## Personal Defenses of Surety

Those defenses that *only* the surety may assert are called personal defenses of the surety. The surety may use as a defense his own **incapacity,** noncompliance with the **statute of frauds,** and the absence of mutual assent or consideration to support his obligation. **Fraud** or **duress** practiced by the creditor upon the surety also is a defense. Although, as a general rule, nondisclosure of material facts by the creditor to the surety is not fraud, there are two important exceptions. First, if a prospective surety requests information, the creditor must disclose it; and the concealment of material facts will constitute fraud. Second, if the creditor knows, or should know, that the surety is being deceived, the creditor is under a duty to disclose this information; and nondisclosure is considered fraud on the surety. Fraud on the part of the principal debtor may not be asserted against the creditor if the creditor is unaware of such fraud. Similarly, duress exerted by the principal debtor upon the surety is not a defense against the creditor.

A surety is not liable if an intended cosurety, as named in the contract instrument, does not sign. Furthermore, a surety may **set off** his claims against a solvent creditor. Against an insolvent creditor, however, the surety may use his claim only if the principal debtor is also insolvent.

If the principal debtor and the creditor enter into a binding **modification** of their contract, the surety may be discharged unless he assents to the modification. The courts vary in their approach to modifications made without the surety's assent. Often, the courts will discharge an uncompensated surety (an **accommodation surety**) for any material modification, even one that does not prejudice his rights. In contrast, when contemplating the discharge of a compensated surety, a number of courts require the alteration to be both material and prejudicial to the interests of the surety.

Such modifications include valid and binding extensions of the time of payment unless the creditor expressly reserves his rights against the surety. An extension of time with reservation is construed only as an agreement

**FIGURE 38–9** Defenses of Surety and Principal Debtor

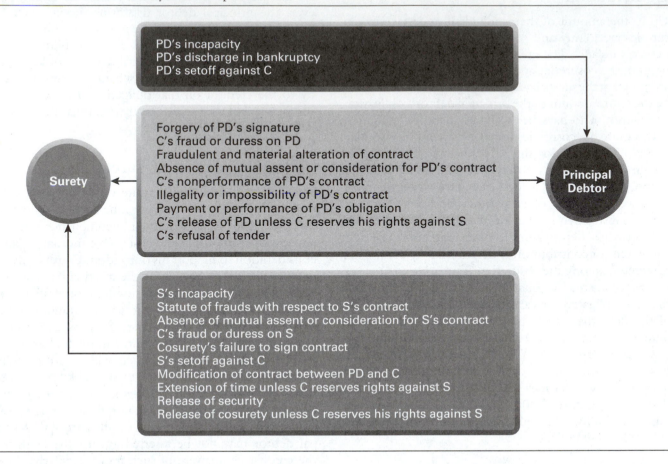

by the creditor not to sue the principal debtor for the period of the extension. Accordingly, the surety's rights of exoneration, reimbursement, and subrogation are not postponed. Thus, the surety's risk is not changed, and he is not discharged.

If the creditor releases or impairs the value of the security, the surety is discharged to the extent of the value of the security released or impaired. Similarly, if the creditor releases a cosurety, the other cosureties are discharged to the extent of the contributive share of the surety released. If the creditor reserves his rights against the remaining cosureties, however, the release is considered a promise not to sue. As a result, the remaining cosureties are not discharged.

## Defenses of Both Surety and Principal Debtor

A number of defenses are available to both the surety and the principal debtor. If the principal debtor's signature on an instrument is **forged** or if the creditor has exerted **fraud** or **duress** upon the principal debtor, neither the principal debtor nor the surety is liable. Likewise, if the creditor has fraudulently and **materially altered** the contract instrument, both the principal debtor and the surety are discharged.

The absence of mutual assent or consideration to support the principal debtor's obligation is a defense for both the principal debtor and the surety. In addition, both may assert as defenses the **illegality** and **impossibility** of performance of the principal debtor's contract.

Payment or **performance** of the principal debtor's obligation discharges both the principal debtor and the surety. If the principal debtor owes several debts to the creditor and makes a payment to the creditor without specifying the debt to which the payment should apply, the creditor is free to apply it to any one of them. For example, Pam owes Charles two debts, one for $5,000 and another for $10,000. Susan is a surety on the $10,000 debt. Pam sends Charles a payment in the amount of $3,500. If Pam directs Charles to apply the payment to the $10,000 debt, Charles must apply it accordingly. Otherwise, Charles may, if he pleases, apply the payment to the $5,000 debt.

If the creditor **releases** the principal debtor, then the surety is also discharged unless the surety consents to the release. If the creditor reserves his rights against the surety, however, the surety is not discharged, as the release with reservation is construed as a promise not to sue, which leaves the surety's rights against the principal debtor unimpaired.

The creditor's refusal to accept **tender** of payment or performance by either the principal debtor or the surety completely discharges the surety. The creditor's refusal of tender of payment by the principal debtor does not, however, discharge the principal debtor. Rather, such refusal stops further accrual of interest on the debt and deprives the creditor of court costs on a subsequent suit by him to recover the amount due.

---

  # Chapter Summary

## Secured Transactions in Personal Property

**Essentials of Secured Transactions**

**Definition of Secured Transaction** an agreement by which one party obtains a security interest in the personal property of another to secure the payment of a debt
- *Debtor* person who owes payment or performance of an obligation
- *Secured Party* creditor who possesses a security interest in collateral
- *Collateral* property subject to a security interest
- *Security Agreement* agreement that grants a security interest
- *Security Interest* right in personal property to ensure payment of an obligation
- *Purchase Money Security Interest* security interest in goods purchased; interest is retained either by the seller of the goods or by a lender who advances the purchase price
- *Financing Statement* document filed to provide notice of a security interest

**Fundamental Rights of Debtor** to redeem collateral by payment of the debt
  to possess general rights of ownership

**Fundamental Rights of Secured Party** to recover amount of debt
  to have collateral applied to payment of debt upon default

**Classification of Collateral**

**Goods** movable, tangible personal property
- *Consumer Goods* goods bought or used primarily for personal, family, or household purposes
- *Farm Products* crops, livestock, or supplies used or produced in farming
- *Inventory* goods held for sale or lease and raw materials used in business
- *Equipment* goods used primarily in business
- *Fixtures* goods that are so firmly attached to real property that they are considered part of the real estate

**Indispensable Paper**
- *Chattel Paper* writing that evidences both a debt and a security interest
- *Instruments* negotiable instruments and investment securities
- *Documents* documents of title

**Intangibles**
- *Account* right to payment for goods sold or leased or for services rendered
- *General Intangibles* catchall category of collateral not otherwise covered

| Attachment | **Definition** security interest that is enforceable against the debtor<br>**Value** consideration under contract law, a binding commitment to extend credit, or an antecedent debt<br>**Debtor's Rights in Collateral** personal property the debtor owns, possesses, or is in the process of acquiring<br>**Security Agreement** agreement between debtor and creditor creating a security interest (1) must be in writing, unless the secured party has possession of the collateral, (2) must be signed by the debtor, and (3) must contain a reasonable description of the collateral<br>• *Consumer Goods* Federal regulation prohibits a credit seller or lender from obtaining a consumer's grant of a nonpossessory security interest in household goods<br>• *After-Acquired Property* property the debtor may acquire in the future and may be covered by a security agreement<br>• *Proceeds* consideration received for the sale, exchange, or other disposition of the collateral; the secured party, unless the security agreement states otherwise, has rights to the proceeds<br>• *Future Advances* a security agreement may include future advances |
|---|---|
| Perfection | **Definition** attachment plus any steps required for perfection<br>**Effect** enforceable against third parties<br>**Methods of Perfecting**<br>• *Filing a Financing Statement* may be used for all collateral except instruments<br>• *Possession* by the secured party (a pledge); may be used for goods, instruments, documents, or chattel paper<br>• *Automatic Perfection* perfection upon attachment; applies to a purchase money security interest in consumer goods<br>• *Temporary Perfection* a security interest in certain collateral is automatically perfected for a limited time, depending upon the collateral |
| Priorities among Secured Parties | See Figure 38–6 for a summary of the priority rules |
| Default | **Repossession of Collateral** the secured party may take possession of the collateral on default without judicial process if it can be done without a breach of the peace<br>**Sale of Collateral** the secured party may sell, lease, or otherwise dispose of any collateral<br>**Retention of Collateral** the secured party, unless the debtor objects, may (with the exception of the compulsory disposition of some consumer goods) retain the collateral in satisfaction of the obligation |

# Suretyship

| Nature and Formation | **Definition of Surety** a person who promises to answer for the payment of a debt or the performance of a duty owed to the creditor by the principal debtor, upon the principal debtor's failure to perform |
|---|---|

- *Principal Debtor* the party primarily liable on the obligation
- *Cosurety* each of two or more sureties who are liable for the same debt of the principal debtor
- *Absolute Surety* surety liable to a creditor immediately upon the default of a principal debtor
- *Conditional Guarantor of Collection* surety liable to a creditor only after the creditor has exhausted the legal remedies against the principal debtor

**Types of Sureties**
- *Party Assuming a Mortgage*
- *Fidelity Bonds*
- *Performance Bonds*
- *Official Bonds*
- *Judicial Bonds*

**Formation** the promise of the surety must satisfy all the elements of a contract and must also be in writing

| | |
|---|---|
| **Rights of Surety** | **Exoneration** the right of a surety to be relieved of his obligation to the creditor by having the principal debtor perform the obligation<br><br>**Reimbursement** the right of a surety who has paid the creditor to be repaid by the principal debtor<br><br>**Subrogation** the right of a surety who has paid the creditor to assume all the rights the creditor has against the principal debtor<br><br>**Contribution** the right to payment from each cosurety of his proportionate share of the amount paid to the creditor |
| **Defenses of Surety and Principal Debtor** | **Personal Defenses of Principal Debtor** defenses available only to the principal debtor, including her incapacity, discharge in bankruptcy, and setoff<br><br>**Personal Defenses of Surety** defenses available only to the surety, including her own incapacity, the statute of frauds, contract defenses to her suretyship undertaking, setoff, modification of the contract between the creditor and the principal debtor, and the creditor's release of security or a cosurety<br><br>**Defenses of Both Surety and Principal Debtor** include contract defenses to the contract between the creditor and the principal debtor |

 **Cases**

### CASE 38–1
## Debtor's Rights in Collateral/Special Rights of PMSI
### *KUNKEL v. SPRAGUE NATIONAL BANK*
United States Court of Appeals, Eighth Circuit, 1997
128 F.3d 636

GIBSON, J.
In this appeal two creditors, Hoxie Feeders, Inc. and Sprague National Bank, both claim first priority security interests in the same cattle. The district court affirmed the bankruptcy court's summary judgment for Hoxie holding that Hoxie's purchase money security interest

had priority over Sprague's earlier security interest in the cattle. [Citation.] As an alternative holding for Hoxie, the district court held that Sprague did not have a security interest in the cattle because the debtor lacked "rights in the collateral," as required by the Uniform Commercial Code. [Citation.] * * * We reverse the district court's holding that Sprague did not have a security interest in the cattle but affirm its judgment for Hoxie because Hoxie's security interest is senior to Sprague's security interest.

Beginning in 1990, Sprague made a number of loans to John and Dorothy Morken pursuant to certain loan agreements and promissory notes. The Morkens executed a security agreement in favor of Sprague covering their inventory, farm products, equipment, and accounts receivable presently owned or thereafter acquired. Sprague filed with the Kansas Secretary of State a UCC–1 financing statement regarding the collateral located in Kansas. * * *

Hoxie is in the business of financing and selling cattle and operating a feedlot near Hoxie, Kansas. In five transactions between February and April 1994, John Morken purchased interests in approximately 1900 head of cattle from Hoxie. Hoxie financed Morken's cattle purchases. For each transaction, Morken executed a loan agreement and promissory note in favor of Hoxie and a security agreement granting Hoxie a purchase money security interest (PMSI) in the cattle, * * *

Hoxie did not file a UCC–1 financing statement with the Kansas Secretary of State but instead perfected its security interest by taking possession of the cattle pursuant to feedlot agreements between Morken and Hoxie. The feedlot agreements stated that the cattle belonged to "the Party of the First Part," meaning Morken, and acknowledged that Morken had delivered the cattle to Hoxie, although Morken never had physical possession of the cattle. Under the feedlot agreements, the cattle were to remain on Hoxie's feedlot for purposes of care and feeding. The feedlot and loan agreements authorized Hoxie to sell the cattle in its own name for slaughter, to receive direct payment from the packing house, and to deduct the feeding and purchase expenses from the sale proceeds and then remit the balance to Morken. Hoxie's general manager acknowledged, however, that he needed Morken's authority to sell the cattle, and that Morken determined at what price the cattle would be sold. The loan agreements recited that Morken bore all risk as to the profit or loss generated by feeding and selling the cattle.

On June 10, 1994, Morken and his wife filed a Chapter 11 bankruptcy case under Title 11 of the United States Bankruptcy Code. After the bankruptcy case was commenced, Hoxie sold the cattle to Iowa Beef Processors for slaughter. After deducting amounts owed to Hoxie for the care and feeding of the cattle, approximately $550,000 in sale proceeds remained. It is these funds which are the subject of competing claims by Sprague and Hoxie.

* * *

The issues on appeal are: (a) did Sprague have a perfected security interest in the cattle?; (b) did Hoxie have a "superpriority" purchase money security interest which had priority over Sprague's interest in the cattle?; and (c) was Hoxie entitled to the proceeds from the sale of the cattle to IBP?

# II

The district court held that Sprague did not have a security interest in the cattle because Morken did not have "rights in the collateral" sufficient for a security interest to attach. We reverse on this issue.

* * *

The phrase "rights in the collateral" is not defined in the UCC. "If the debtor owns the collateral outright, it is obvious that the security interest may attach. . . ." [Citation.] It is also well-settled, however, that "rights in the collateral" may be an interest less than outright ownership, but must be more than the mere right of possession. [Citation.] The concept of "title" is not determinative. [Citation.] "An agreement to purchase can give rise to sufficient rights in the debtor to allow a security interest to attach, regardless of whether the debtor has technically obtained title to the property." [Citation.] Courts consider factors such as the extent of the debtor's control over the property and whether the debtor bears the risk of ownership. [Citations.] The debtor need not have possession in order to pledge the property; the UCC expressly contemplates that the secured party may retain possession of the collateral. [Citation.]

A "sale" is the passing of title from buyer to seller for a price. [Citation.] Where delivery of the goods is made without moving the goods, title passes from buyer to seller at the time parties contracted if the goods are identified at that time. [Citation.] When identification occurs, the buyer acquires a "special property" and, importantly, any title interest retained by the seller is limited to the reservation of a security interest. [Citation.] Physical receipt of the goods by the debtor is not necessary; rather, a sale may take place if the goods are constructively delivered to the buyer through delivery to the buyer's agent or bailee. "Delivery is not required for a 'sale' to take place, and the buyer does not even need any right to possession of the goods in question." [Citation.] In this case, the cattle were identified in the invoices and other transaction documents, and the parties agreed that delivery would be made to Morken by delivering the cattle to Hoxie at its feedlot. The feedlot agreements recited that the cattle belonged to Morken. Morken solely bore the risk that the venture would not generate a profit. * * * Even though Hoxie had the right to deduct the costs of purchasing and caring for the cattle from the sale proceeds, the parties viewed Morken as owner of the cattle, and Morken determined when cattle would be sold and at what price. In sum, Morken became the owner of an interest in the cattle, and Hoxie's interest in the cattle was therefore limited to that of a bailee and secured party.

In similar circumstances, other courts have held that the debtor acquired "rights in the collateral" even though the debtor received only constructive delivery of the cattle to a feedlot. [Citations.]

* * *

Having determined that Sprague held a perfected security interest in the cattle, we now turn to the priority dispute between the two secured creditors, Sprague and Hoxie. We hold that Hoxie attained purchase money security interest "superpriority" under the Kansas UCC–9–312(3), and has priority over Sprague's interest.

Section 9–312 of the UCC sets forth rules for determining priorities among conflicting security interests in the same collateral. [UCC] 9–312. The general priority scheme is that the first creditor to perfect its security interest beats later perfected security interests. [UCC] 9–312(5)(a). There is an important exception to this "first-to-perfect" rule for a purchase money security interest. A PMSI in inventory has "superpriority" over an earlier perfected interest if: (a) the PMSI is perfected at the time the debtor receives possession of the inventory; (b) the PMSI creditor gives written notification to all holders of competing security interests which had UCC–1 financing statements on file when the PMSI creditor filed its UCC–1; * * * [UCC]–9–312(3).

Sprague contends that the Section 9–312(3)'s "superpriority" status cannot be attained by a creditor that has perfected its security interest in inventory by possession, rather than by filing a UCC–1 financing statement. It emphasizes language in this UCC section and its commentary that refers to perfection by filing and the debtor receiving possession of the inventory. [UCC]–9–312(3) & Official UCC comment. 3. We observe, however, that

there is no language expressly excluding a creditor that has perfected by possession from taking advantage of this UCC section. More importantly, there is no sound policy reason to distinguish between perfection by filing and possession, and to provide the former, but not the latter, the opportunity to attain "superpriority." The common law of pledge—perfection by possession—predates, and was incorporated by, the UCC. In addition, pre-UCC law afforded special priority to purchase money security interests, and this has been carried over into the UCC. [Citation.] Thus, the UCC, as it stands today, does not reflect any intent to penalize a PMSI creditor by depriving it of the opportunity to attain "superpriority" simply because of its means of perfection.

Having concluded that it was possible for Hoxie to use Section 9–312(3) to attain "superpriority," we must now decide whether it did so by fulfilling the statutory requirements. * * *

Sprague complains that the purpose of Section 9–312(3) is frustrated by granting "superpriority" to a PMSI without requiring pre-perfection notification to prior filed secured creditors. It contends that debtors on the brink of insolvency will now have the motive to create "secret liens" to the detriment of prior-perfected secured creditors. The notification requirement, however, was not intended to allow other secured creditors veto power over the extension of new credit because the notification does not have to be given before the PMSI is acquired. The notification is required to state "that the person giving the notice has or expects to acquire a purchase money security interest in inventory of the debtor, describing such inventory by item or type." 9–312(3)(d) Thus, the PMSI creditor can wait to notify competing secured creditors after it has acquired and perfected its security interest. The Official UCC Comment explains that the notification protects the inventory financier from making additional advances to the debtor in the mistaken belief that it is secured by inventory which, in fact, has been financed by a third party with a PMSI in that inventory. If the inventory financier "has received notification, he will presumably not make an advance; if he has not received notification (or if the other interest does not qualify as a purchase money interest), any advance he may make will have priority." 9–312 Official UCC cmt. 3.

Our holding is consistent with this purpose in the context of this case. Sprague did not extend further credit in reliance on the cattle serving as its collateral; in fact, Sprague had not made any loans to Morken since at least a year before Morken acquired an interest in these particular cattle. We stop short, however, of holding, as did the district court, that a PMSI creditor that perfects by possession of inventory does not ever have to send a statutory notification. It is not necessary to reach that issue because Hoxie timely sent its statutory notification.

* * *

In conclusion, we reverse the district court's holding that Sprague did not have a security interest in the cattle, but affirm its judgment that Hoxie's security interest has priority over Sprague's security interest.

---

## CASE 38–2
### Security Agreement
## *NEW WEST FRUIT CORPORATION v. COASTAL BERRY CORPORATION*
California Court of Appeal, Sixth District, 1991
1 Cal.App.4th 92, 1 Cal.Rptr.2d 664

CAPACCIOLI, J.

In this appeal we consider whether a contract that purports to grant a security interest to a creditor is enforceable if it fails to fully delineate the nature of the debtor's obligation. As we will explain below, we conclude that this fact alone does not preclude enforcement of a security agreement if the language of the agreement and circumstances of the transaction reveal an intent by the parties to grant a security interest to the creditor.

## Background

Both parties to this action, New West Fruit Corporation ("New West") and Coastal Berry Corporation ("Coastal Berry"), are brokers of fresh strawberries. In the second half of 1984 New West's predecessor, Monc's Consolidated Produce, Inc. ("Monc's"), made loans of money and strawberry plants to a group of strawberry growers known collectively as Cooperativa La Paz. In September 1984 Monc's and Cooperativa La Paz entered into a contract entitled "Sales and Marketing Agreement," which granted Monc's the exclusive right to market the strawberries grown by the collective during the 1984–85 season. The Agreement did not specifically refer to advances of money or plants either already made or contemplated.

Paragraph 18 of the Agreement provided the following: "In order to secure all of Grower's obligations under this agreement, Grower hereby gives to Shipper [Monc's] a security interest in all crops growing or to be grown on the above-described property in the crop year 1984–1985 and the proceeds thereof, and agrees to sign a financial statement and any other documents needed to perfect Shipper's security interest."

Matias Rosales, a representative of Cooperativa La Paz, signed both the Sales and Marketing Agreement and a commercial financing statement, which Monc's filed in order to perfect its security interest. (See Com. Code, §§ 9–401, 9–402.)

Monc's closed down in January 1985 and its assets were orally assigned to plaintiff New West Fruit Corporation. In April 1985 New West learned that Cooperativa La Paz had agreed to market its 1985 strawberry crop through its competitor, defendant Coastal Berry Corporation. New West representatives immediately arranged a meeting with the president and local manager of Coastal Berry. At the meeting, New West advised the Coastal Berry officers of its contract with the growers. According to the trial testimony of William Moncovich, president of New West, "we told them that [the growers] had a contract, that we had money lent out to these growers, that we basically wanted our money back if, in fact, they were planning on shipping through them. There was no way we could change our mind, that we did have a financing statement, we did have a contract with them that money was owed." Moncovich showed Coastal Berry representatives the Sales and Marketing Agreement and suggested that Coastal Berry either pay New West the amounts owed by the growers or allow New West to market the berries so it could recoup the money. New West received no response to its request.

After Coastal Berry began marketing the growers' berries, New West sent letters demanding payment of proceeds from the sale of the berries. In August 1985 New West filed suit against Coastal Berry, Cooperativa La Paz and its individual growers, and a berry freezing company that was accepting some of the growers' lower-quality berries. New West settled with all defendants except Coastal Berry before trial, leaving an outstanding claim of over $14,000.

At trial New West invoked the language of paragraph 18 of the Sales and Marketing Agreement, asserting that this provision had conveyed a security interest to Monc's in exchange for the advances Monc's had made to the growers. New West argued that Coastal Berry was not only on constructive notice of the security interest through the recorded financing statement, but also on actual notice through the direct information given to it at the April meeting and subsequent demand letters.

Coastal Berry responded, . . . , that the contract between Monc's and the growers was not an effective security agreement because it failed to identify precisely the debt to be secured.  * * *

The trial court found that the sales and marketing agreement was a "poorly drafted, but . . . adequate" security agreement which, when considered as a "routine business transaction" between the parties, was sufficient to memorialize the debt owed by Cooperativa La Paz to New West. Coastal Berry, the court reasoned, was put on actual notice of the debt when presented with this agreement, and consequently should have retained sufficient funds from its sales of the strawberries to cover New West's claim. The trial court accordingly granted judgment for New West in the amount of $14,269.86 plus interest.

## Discussion

* * *

The rules governing secured transactions are embodied in [Article] 9 of the California Uniform Commercial Code [citation]. These sections apply to any transaction, regardless of its form, which is intended to create a security interest in personal property or fixtures, including goods. (§ 9–102, subd. (1)(a).) "Security interest" is defined by section 1201, subdivision (37)(a), as "an interest in personal property or fixtures which secures payment or performance of an obligation."

A security interest becomes enforceable against the debtor when three conditions are met: (1) the debtor has signed a security agreement containing a description of the collateral and, when the security interest is in crops, a description of the land concerned; (2) value has been given; and (3) the debtor has rights in the collateral. (§ 9–203.) The filing of a financing statement perfects the security interest, thereby giving notice to and assuring priority over interested third parties. (§ 9–302.)

There is no dispute that the second and third conditions of section 9–203 were met in this case. Our focus is instead on the first requirement, in determining whether the document Matias Rosales signed on behalf of Cooperativa La Paz was a "security agreement." Coastal Berry argues that the Sales and Marketing Agreement was not a valid security agreement because it failed to describe the advances to the growers and their obligation to repay them.

A security agreement is simply defined by section (9–105, subdivision (1)(l), as "an agreement which creates or provides for a security interest." With specified exceptions, a security agreement is "effective according to its terms between the parties, against purchasers of the collateral and against creditors." (§ 9–201.) Section 9–102 does not limit the scope of secured obligations to pledges or loans of money, but can apply to any security interest created by contract. (§ 9–102, subd. (2))

[Article] 9 does not specifically require delineation of the debt owed to the secured party. Instead, the creation of a valid security interest turns on "whether the parties intended the transaction to have effect as security." (Cal.Code Comm. to § 9–102.) "No special form is necessary to create a security interest. [Citation.] It is sufficient if the parties use language that indicates the parties intended to create a security interest . . . and if the security agreement reasonably identifies the property subject to the agreement." [Citations.]

"Briefly stated, under section 9–201 alone the parties to a commercial security agreement can effectively secure the payment or performance of any past, present, or future legally enforceable obligation of the debtor to the creditor, and can do so with any of the debtor's existing or subsequently acquired personal property. Section 9–201 thus generally validates future advances and all obligations clauses against both debtors and third parties. Those agreements not meeting the formalities required by section 9–203 and those agreements running afoul of the common-law policing doctrines are the only commercially important exceptions." [Citations.]

Section 9–204, subdivision (3) further validates grants of security interests where, as in this case, the collateral secures "all obligations" or future advances: "Obligations covered by a security agreement may include future advances or other value whether or not the advances or value are [sic] given pursuant to commitment."

These provisions of the Commercial Code make it clear that to be enforceable, a security agreement need not specify the value of the loan or recite the debtor's obligation to repay it. As long as the formalities of section 9–203 have been met, any payment or performance obligation covered by the security agreement may be secured. [Citation.] The pivotal question, therefore, is whether the challenged obligation is covered by the security agreement. This question can be answered only by ascertaining the intent of the parties to the transaction.

* * *

* * * In summary, although the Sales and Marketing Agreement was, in the trial court's words, "not terribly artfully drafted," we agree with the court below that

it was adequate to convey the parties' intent to grant Monc's a security interest in the strawberries and the proceeds thereof. Furthermore, when considered together with the circumstances of its execution—including the financing statement, the past relationship between Monc's and the growers, and general practice in the strawberry production industry—this document should be read to encompass the growers' obligation to repay loans made by Monc's to assist them in financing production of their strawberry crop.

In view of this result, there is no justification for Coastal Berry's disregard of the growers' outstanding debt to New West. * * *

**Disposition**

The judgment is affirmed.

---

## CASE 38–3
### Automatic Perfection
### *KIMBRELL'S OF SANFORD, INC. v. KPS, INC.*

Court of Appeals of North Carolina, 1994
113 N.C.App. 830, 440 S.E.2d 329

MCCRODDEN, J.

This action arises out of plaintiff's attempt to recover from defendant KPS, Inc. a VCR which plaintiff had sold to defendant Burns and which Burns had immediately pawned at the Kendale Pawn Shop. Plaintiff filed a complaint in small claims court, and the magistrate, after a hearing on 17 February 1992, entered judgment denying plaintiff recovery of the VCR. Plaintiff appealed to the district court. Judge William A. Christian, sitting without a jury, entered judgment denying plaintiff recovery and dismissing the action. From this judgment, plaintiff appeals.

Plaintiff offers one argument raising the issue of whether it was entitled to recover from defendant pawn shop a VCR plaintiff had sold to defendant Burns under a purchase money security agreement. * * *

Plaintiff argues that the judgment denying it recovery of the VCR contravened Article 9 of the Uniform Commercial Code, [citation.] We agree.

At the time defendant Burns purchased the VCR from plaintiff, he signed a purchase money security agreement, thereby granting plaintiff a purchase money security interest in the VCR. [UCC] § 9–107. Since a VCR is a consumer good, [UCC] § 9–109(1), plaintiff did not have to file a financing statement in order to perfect its purchase money security interest in the VCR. [UCC] § 9–302(1)(d). Defendant Burns failed to make any further payments for the VCR and defaulted on the security agreement. Therefore, plaintiff was entitled to recover possession of the VCR when it filed its action in small claims court. [UCC] §§ 9–501, 9–503. Accordingly, we hold that the trial court erred in dismissing plaintiff's claim to recover possession of the VCR.

* * *

For the foregoing reasons, we reverse the judgment of the trial court and remand for entry of judgment in favor of plaintiff.

Reversed.

---

## CASE 38–4
### Repossession
### *CHRYSLER CREDIT CORPORATION v. KOONTZ*

Appellate Court of Illinois, 1996
214 Ill. Dec. 726, 661 N.E.2d 1171

MAAG, J.

Defendant, James Koontz, appeals from a deficiency judgment entered against him and in favor of the plaintiff, Chrysler Credit Corporation (Chrysler), in the amount of $4,439.92.

Koontz entered into an agreement with Chrysler to purchase a 1988 Plymouth Sundance in exchange for 60 monthly payments of $185.92. Koontz defaulted on the contract in early 1991. Chrysler notified Koontz that it would repossess the vehicle if Koontz did not make up the missed payments. Koontz notified Chrysler that he would make every effort to catch up on the payments, that he did not want the vehicle to be repossessed, and that Chrysler was not to enter onto his private property to repossess the car.

On the night of April 21, 1991, Chrysler sent the M & M Agency to repossess the vehicle pursuant to section 9–503 of the Commercial Code (the self-help repossession statute). The vehicle was parked outside of Koontz's home in his front yard when he heard the repossession in progress. Koontz, who was in his underwear, rushed outside and hollered, "Don't take it," to the repossessor. The repossessor did not respond and proceeded to take the vehicle.

Chrysler sold the vehicle and filed a complaint against Koontz seeking a deficiency judgment for the balance due on the loan. Koontz filed an affirmative defense alleging that Chrysler's repossession of the vehicle breached the peace, the remedy for which includes a denial of a deficiency judgment to the secured party.

The case was tried before the circuit court of Bond County in a bench trial on February 8, 1995. On March 6, 1995, the trial court entered its order finding "that Chrysler Credit Corporation's actions to repossess said vehicle did not constitute a breach of the peace." The court then entered the deficiency judgment on behalf of Chrysler in the amount of $4,439.92 plus costs and attorney fees of $950.00. Koontz appeals from this judgment.

Koontz raises only a single issue on appeal. He contends that the trial court erred in finding that Chrysler's repossession did not breach the peace because there was evidence that Koontz made an unequivocal oral protest to the repossession of his vehicle at the time of repossession. Koontz argues that when the vehicle was taken despite his protest, "Don't take it," a breach of the peace occurred, citing *Dixon v. Ford Motor Credit Co.* (1979), [citation.] In *Dixon*, the court, . . . stated that "[w]hen a creditor repossesses in disregard of the debtor's unequivocal oral protest, the repossession may be found to be in breach of the peace." [Citation.]

Chrysler contends that Koontz's oral protest did not breach the peace because "none of the elements of violence indicated in the decisions cited by the Defendant exists (sic) in this case." Chrysler argues by implication that without an element of violence there can be no breach of the peace. Chrysler also argues that if we find that an oral protest without an element of violence constitutes a breach of the peace, then we would be narrowing the self-help repossession statute to the point that it would be useless to a secured creditor.

We recognize that the self-help repossession statute extends a conditional self-help privilege to secured parties; however, we must apply the statute in a way that reduces the risk to the public associated with extrajudicial conflict resolution. It is apparent that the self-help remedy is efficient for secured creditors and results in reduced costs for both creditors and debtors. Efficiency and reduced litigation costs are desirable. Still, a debtor's private property interests and society's interest in tranquility must also be protected.

Because self-help repossession is statutory, we look to the language of section 9–503 to establish the parameters of the remedy that the statute offers to secured parties who seek to repossess collateral without judicial process. The statute provides in pertinent part: "Unless otherwise agreed a secured party has on default the right to take possession of the collateral. In taking possession a secured party may proceed without judicial process if this can be done without breach of the peace or may proceed by action." The key to whether a self-help repossession is permissible depends on whether the peace has been or is likely to be breached.

Section 9–503 does not define breach of the peace, and the phrase "breach of the peace" has never had a precise meaning in relation to specific conduct. The phrase has been construed on several occasions. In *Cantwell v. State of Connecticut* (1940), [citation], the [United States Supreme] court stated: "The offense known as breach of the public peace embraces a great variety of conduct destroying or menacing public order and tranquility. It includes not only violent acts but acts and words likely to produce violence in others." * * * The Restatement (Second) of Torts § 116, provides that "[a] breach of the peace is a public offense done by violence, or by one causing or likely to cause an immediate disturbance of public order." Threats and epithets directed at another may or may not constitute a breach of the peace, depending upon the likelihood that a disturbance will follow.

We therefore conclude that the term "breach of the peace" connotes conduct which incites or is likely to incite immediate public turbulence, or which leads to or is likely to lead to an immediate loss of public order and tranquility. Violent conduct is not a necessary element. The probability of violence at the time of or immediately prior to the repossession is sufficient. We now turn to Koontz's contention that Chrysler's repossession and the events at the time of and immediately prior to the repossession breached the peace.

After a thorough examination of the record, we find no abuse of discretion on the part of the trial court in ruling that Chrysler's repossession did not breach the peace. Whether a given act provokes a breach of the peace depends upon the accompanying circumstances of each particular case. In this case, Koontz testified that he only yelled, "Don't take it," and that the repossessor made no verbal or physical response. He also testified that although he was close enough to the repossessor to run over and get into a fight, he elected not to because he was in his underwear.

Furthermore, there was no evidence in the record that Koontz implied violence at the time of or immediately prior to the repossession by holding a weapon, clenching a fist, or even vehemently arguing toe-to-toe with the repossessor so that a reasonable repossessor would understand that violence was likely to ensue if he continued with the vehicle repossession. We think that the evidence, viewed as a whole, could lead a reasonable fact finder to determine that the circumstances of the repossession did not amount to a breach of the peace.

We note that to rule otherwise would be to invite the ridiculous situation whereby a debtor could avoid a deficiency judgment by merely stepping out of his house and yelling once at a nonreponsive repossessor. Such a narrow definition of the conduct necessary to breach the peace would, we think, render the self-help repossession statute useless. Therefore, we reject Koontz's invitation to define "an unequivocal oral protest," without more, as a breach of the peace.

Koontz also argues that Chrysler breached the peace by repossessing the vehicle under circumstances which would constitute a Class C misdemeanor, criminal trespass to real property, . . . . Koontz testified that he notified Chrysler prior to the date of the repossession that Chrysler did not have permission to enter onto his real property. Criminal trespass occurs when some person "enters upon the land * * * of another, after receiving, prior to such entry, notice from the owner or occupant that such entry is forbidden * * *." [Citation.] * * *

This is an issue of first impression in Illinois, so we turn to other jurisdictions for guidance. A review of the law in other jurisdictions reveals that in general, a mere trespass, standing alone, does not automatically constitute a breach of the peace. [Citations.] It is generally held that "simply going upon the private driveway of the debtor and taking possession of secured collateral, without more, does not constitute a breach of the peace." [Citations.]

In making this analysis, certain principles are clear and must be considered. When the collateral is located inside a fence or is otherwise enclosed, the secured creditor's privilege is considerably abridged. [Citation.] The creditor's privilege is most severely restricted when repossession can only be accomplished by the actual breaking or destruction of barriers designed to exclude trespassers. [Citations.] * * *

In this case, Koontz testified that he notified Chrysler prior to the repossession that it was not permitted to enter onto his property. He also testified that he pulled his vehicle into his front yard so that he could see it by the light of the front porch. This testimony was uncontroverted. There was no testimony, however, that Chrysler entered through any barricade or did anything other than simply enter onto the property and drive the car away. Viewing this evidence in the light most favorable to the prevailing party, we believe that Chrysler's entry upon the private real property of Koontz and taking possession of the secured collateral, without more, did not constitute a breach of the peace. Chrysler enjoyed a limited privilege to enter Koontz's property for the sole and exclusive purpose of effecting the repossession. So long as the entry was limited in purpose (repossession), and so long as no gates, barricades, doors, enclosures, buildings, or chains were breached or cut, no breach of the peace occurred by virtue of the entry onto his property.

* * *

Affirmed.

---

**CASE 38–5**
## Nature and Formation
### *UNITED STATES v. TILLERAAS*
United States Court of Appeals, Sixth Circuit, 1983
709 F.2d 1088

WELLFORD, J.
Defendant-appellant, Elizabeth Tilleraas, applied for and received three student loans totalling $3,500.00 under the Federal Insured Student Loan Program (FISLP) of the Higher Education Act of 1965, 20 U.S.C. § 1071, *et seq.* These loans were secured by three promissory

CHAPTER 38  Secured Transactions and Suretyship

notes executed, respectively, on September 4, 1969, June 18, 1970, and October 5, 1970, in favor of Dakota National Bank & Trust Co., Fargo, North Dakota. Under terms of these student loans, periodic payments were required commencing twelve months after Tilleraas ceased to carry at least one-half of a full-time academic workload at an eligible institution. 20 U.S.C. § 1077(a)(2)(B). Her student status terminated on January 28, 1971, and the first installment payment thus became due January 28, 1972. Appellant never made any payment on any of her loans. The United States insured to the lender bank the repayment in event of any failure to pay by the borrower under the terms of the FISLP.

Under 20 U.S.C. § 1080(e)(2)(B), it is provided:

the term "default" includes only such defaults as have existed for . . .

**(B)** one hundred eighty days in the case of a loan which is repayable in less frequent [than monthly] installments.

The first payment due on the loans was in "default" within the meaning of the law on or about July 27, 1972, one hundred and eighty days after the failure to make the first installment payment had continued to exist. It was not until December 17, 1973, that the Dakota National Bank sent notice of its election under the provisions of the loan to accelerate the maturity of the note. The Bank demanded payment in full of the full principal due by December 27, 1973. It then filed FISLP insurance claims against the United States on May 6, 1974, and assigned the three Tilleraas notes to the United States on May 10, 1974. The government, in turn, paid the Bank's claim in full on July 5, 1974. It was not until June 4, 1980, that the appellee government filed suit in Cleveland, Ohio, against the original borrower-recipient of this largess intended to assist students in obtaining a higher education.

The government's suit was met in the trial court by defendant-appellant's motion for a summary judgment based on her contention that the action of the United States was barred by the six year statute of limitations set forth in 28 U.S.C. § 2514(a). The complaint in the cause alleged that the government paid the Bank's insurance claim and was assigned title to the notes after default on the loan and payment by the government pursuant to 45 C.F.R. § 177.48.

* * *

The government argues, however, that it is not limited to assignee status, since it may also rely on its common law right as a surety to bring an action against the principal for reimbursement. Since a surety's or guarantor's cause of action for indemnity does not accrue until payment of the principal's liability [citations], the government claims that it *also* has a cause of action which accrued on the date it paid the lender, July 6, 1974, a cause which was timely when this action was filed.

* * *

The use of the word "insurance" in the statute is not determinative in light of the realities existing between the relevant parties. The nature of the substantive rights and duties among the parties clearly reflects a surety-principal-lender relationship. Insurance is a contract where one undertakes to indemnify another against loss, damage or liability caused by an unknown or contingent event. Since the insured pays the insurer for the promise of indemnity, the insurer benefits to the extent that a contingency never occurs. Where a contingency does occur, the insurer can still be made whole, by virtue of subrogation, to the extent that the insured would be able to recover damages from a third party. Despite the presence of this right of subrogation it is clear that *when the contract is formed* all legal rights and obligations flow between the insurer and the insured. At this initial stage, there is no legal obligation owing from the third party to the insurer. In fact, it is unknown at that stage whether such a third party obligation will ever arise and, if so, who that third party will be.

A surety, on the other hand, promises to assume the responsibility for the payment of a debt incurred by another should he or she fail to repay the creditor. The arrangement is made to induce the creditor to deal with the borrower where there might otherwise be a reluctance to do so. Under this arrangement, the nature, size, and source of the possible loss to the creditor is known from the start. In addition, there is no payment from the creditor to the surety or guarantor for this "insured" payment. Rather, a kind of tripartite relationship is formed. The consideration running from the creditor to the debtor is deemed sufficient to support the surety's promise to make the debt good. In turn, the benefit flowing to the debtor by virtue of the surety's promise places that debtor under an implied legal obligation to make good any loss incurred by any payment the surety must ultimately make to the creditor. [Citation.] It is clear then that the two contracts are materially distinguishable, as are the rights and duties of the parties involved. [Citations.]

Under the FISLP the student contracts to borrow money with no collateral and upon favorable interest and repayment terms. The lender, in turn, contracts with the

Department of Education to insure repayment should the student default. This has consistently been interpreted as creating a third-party surety contract, despite its nomenclature. [Citations.] The only possible "contingency" from which the government protects the lending institution is the possibility that the named student (in this case Tilleraas) may ultimately default on all or part of the designated loan amount. The interdependencies between the three parties, in this case the Dakota National Bank & Trust Co., Tilleraas, and the United States government, "are a situational adaptation of long-recognized principles of guaranty." [Citation.] At common law the nature of the relationship would have undoubtedly given rise to an implied obligation on the part of Tilleraas to make good the loss incurred by the government when forced to satisfy her debt, a loss arising when the monies were paid to the Dakota National Bank & Trust Co.

* * *

We conclude, therefore, that the United States in this instance stands in the position of a surety-guarantor, and therefore it may pursue its rights as a surety under FISLP. As pointed out, it was not until July of 1974 that the government paid the Bank's claim and obtained its right to sue the defaulting appellant on the underlying loan. Under the realities of the FISLP, the government is a surety of the borrower and is entitled to its rights as such. This is the position supported by the other Courts of Appeals that have considered the same issue under this law. [Citations.]

* * *

Accordingly, we affirm the thoughtful decision of the district court, concluding that the United States, as surety-guarantor, has six years after paying a claim under FISLP in which to institute suit against a defaulting borrower.

 # Questions

1.   Name and define the various kinds of collateral.

2.   Explain the purpose, methods, and requirements of attachment and perfection.

3.   Discuss the priorities among the various parties who may have competing interests in collateral and the rights and remedies of the parties to a security agreement after default by the debtor.

4.   Explain the requirements for the formation of a suretyship relationship.

5.   Explain the rights of a creditor against a surety and the rights of a surety, including those of a cosurety.

 # Problems

1.   Victor sells to Bonnie a refrigerator for $600 payable in monthly installments of $30 for twenty months. Bonnie signs a security agreement granting Victor a security interest in the refrigerator. The refrigerator is installed in the kitchen of Bonnie's apartment. There is no filing of any financing statement. Assume that after Bonnie has made the first three monthly payments:

   (a)   Bonnie moves from her apartment and sells the refrigerator in place to the new occupant for $350 cash. What are the rights of Victor?

   (b)   Bonnie is adjudicated bankrupt, and her trustee in bankruptcy claims the refrigerator. What are the rights of the parties?

2.   On January 2, Burt asked Logan to loan him money "against my diamond ring." Logan agreed to do so. To guard against intervening liens, Logan received permission to file a financing statement, and Burt and Logan signed a security agreement giving Logan an interest in the ring. Burt also signed

a financing statement which Logan properly filed on January 3. On January 4, Burt borrowed money from Tillo, pledging his ring to secure the debt. Tillo took possession of the ring and paid Burt the money on the same day. The next day, January 5, Logan loaned Burt the money under the assumption that Burt still had the ring.

   Who has priority, Logan or Tillo? Explain.

3.   Joanna takes a security interest in the equipment in Jason Store and files a financing statement claiming "equipment and all after-acquired equipment." Berkeley later sells Jason Store a cash register on conditional sale and (a) files nine days after Jason receives the register, or (b) files fifteen days after Jason receives the register. If Jason fails to pay both Joanna and Berkeley and they foreclose their security interests, who has priority on the cash register? What would occur if Jason was a consumer who purchased goods for personal use?

4.   Finley Motor Company sells an automobile to Sara and retains a security interest in it. The automobile is insured, and

Finley is named beneficiary. Three days after the automobile is totally destroyed in an accident, Sara files a petition in bankruptcy. As between Finley and Sara's trustee in bankruptcy, who is entitled to the insurance proceeds?

5. On September 5, Wanda, a widow who occasionally teaches piano and organ in her home, purchased an electric organ from Murphy's music store for $4,800, trading in her old organ for $1,200 and promising in writing to pay the balance at $120 per month and granting to Murphy a security interest in the property in terms consistent with and incorporating provisions of the UCC. A financing statement covering the transaction was also properly filled out and signed, and Murphy properly filed it. After Wanda failed to make the December or January payments, Murphy went to her home to collect the payments or take the organ. Finding no one home and the door unlocked, he went in and took the organ. Two hours later, Tia, a third party and the present occupant of the house, who had purchased the organ for her own use, stormed into Murphy's store, demanding the return of the organ. She showed Murphy a bill of sale from Wanda to her, dated December 15, that listed the organ and other furnishings in the house.

(a) What are the rights of Murphy, Tia, and Wanda?

(b) Would your answer change if Murphy had not filed a financing statement? Why?

(c) Would your answer change if the organ had been principally used to give lessons?

6. On May 1, Lincoln lends Donaldson $20,000 and receives from Donaldson his promissory note for this amount due in two years and takes a security interest in the machinery and equipment in Donaldson's factory. A proper financing statement is filed with respect to the security agreement. On August 1, upon Lincoln's request, Donaldson executes an addendum to the security agreement covering after-acquired machinery and equipment in Donaldson's factory. A second financing statement covering the addendum is filed. In September, Donaldson acquires $5,000 worth of new equipment from Thompson, which Donaldson installs in his factory. In December, Carter, a judgment creditor of Donaldson, causes an attachment to issue against the new equipment. What are the rights of Lincoln, Donaldson, Carter, and Thompson? What can the parties do to best protect themselves?

7. Anita bought a television set from Bertrum for her personal use. Bertrum, who was out of security agreement forms, showed Anita a form he had executed with Nathan, another consumer. Anita and Bertrum orally agreed to the terms of the form. Anita subsequently defaults on payment, and Bertrum seeks to repossess the television. Decision? Would the result differ if Bertrum had filed a financing statement?

8. Aaron bought a television set for personal use from Penny. Aaron properly signed a security agreement and paid Penny twenty-five dollars down, as their agreement required. Penny did not file, and subsequently Aaron sells the television for $300 to Clark, his neighbor, for use in Clark's hotel lobby.

(a) When Aaron fails to make the January and February payments, may Penny repossess the television from Clark?

(b) What if, instead of Aaron's selling the television set to Clark, a judgment creditor levied (sought possession) on the television? Who would prevail?

(c) What if Clark intended to use the television set in his home? Who would prevail?

9. Jones bought a used car from the A–Herts Car Rental System, which regularly sold its used equipment at the end of its fiscal year. First National Bank of Roxboro had previously obtained a perfected security interest in the car based upon its financing of A–Herts's automobiles. Upon A–Herts's failure to pay, First National is seeking to repossess the car from Jones. Decision?

10. Standridge purchased a 1965 Chevrolet automobile from Billy Deavers, an agent of Walker Motor Company. According to the sales contract, the balance due after the trade-in allowance was $282.50, to be paid in twelve weekly installments. Standridge claims that he was unable to make the second payment and that Billy Deavers orally agreed that he could make two payments the next week. The day after the double payment was due, Standridge still had not paid. That day, Ronnie Deavers, Billy's brother, went to Standridge's place of employment to repossess the car. Rather than consenting to the repossession, Standridge drove the car to the Walker Motor Company's place of business and tendered the overdue payments. The Deavers refused to accept the late payment and instead demanded the entire unpaid balance. Standridge could not pay it. The Deavers then blocked in Standridge's car with another car and told him he could just "walk his ____ home." Standridge brought suit, seeking damages for the Deavers's wrongful repossession of his car. The Deavers deny that they granted Standridge permission to make a double payment; that Standridge tendered the double payment; and that they rejected it. They claim that he made no payment and that, therefore, they were entitled to repossess the car. Decision?

11. National Cash Register Company (NCR), a manufacturer of cash registers, entered into a sales contract for a cash register with Edmund Carroll. On November 18, 1960, Firestone and Company made a loan to Carroll, who conveyed certain property to Firestone as collateral under a security agreement. The property outlined in the security agreement included "[a]ll contents of luncheonette including equipment such as * * *" twenty-five different listed items, " * * * together with all property and articles now, and which may hereafter be, used * * * with, [or] added * * * to * * * any of the foregoing described property." A similarly detailed description of the property conveyed as collateral appeared in Firestone's financing statement, but the financing statement made no mention of property to be acquired thereafter, and neither document made a specific reference to a cash register. NCR delivered the cash register to Carroll in Canton between November 19 and November 25 and filed a financing statement with the town clerk of Canton on December 20 and with the Secretary of State on December 21. Carroll subsequently defaulted both on the contract with NCR and on the security

agreement with Firestone. Firestone took possession of the cash register and sold it at auction. NCR brought an action against Firestone for conversion of the cash register. The trial court and the appellate court ruled in favor of NCR, and Firestone appealed. Decision?

**12.** National Acceptance Company loaned Ultra Precision Industries $692,000, and to secure repayment of the loan Ultra executed a chattel mortgage security agreement on National's behalf on March 7, 1997. National perfected the security interest by timely filing a financing statement. Although the security interest covered specifically described equipment of Ultra, both the security agreement and the financing statement contained an after-acquired property clause that did not refer to any specific equipment.

Later in 1997 and in 1998, Ultra placed three separate orders for machines from Wolf Machinery Company. In each case it was agreed that after the machines had been shipped to Ultra and installed, Ultra would be given an opportunity to test them in operation for a reasonable period. If the machines passed inspection, Wolf would then provide financing that was satisfactory to Ultra. In all three cases, financing was arranged with Community Bank (Bank) and accepted, and a security interest was given in the machines. Furthermore, in each case a security agreement was entered into, and a financing statement was then filed by the secured parties within ten days. Ultra became bankrupt on October 7, 1999. National claimed that its security interest in the after-acquired machines should take priority over those of Wolf and Bank because their interests were not perfected by timely filed financing statements. The district court affirmed the referee's ruling in favor of Wolf and Bank. National appealed. Decision?

**13.** Allen, Barker, and Cooper are cosureties on a $750,000 loan by Durham National Bank to Kingston Manufacturing Co., Inc. The maximum liability of the sureties is as follows: Allen—$750,000, Barker—$300,000, and Cooper—$150,000. If Kingston defaults on the entire $750,000 loan, what are the liabilities of Allen, Barker, and Cooper?

**14.** Peter Diamond owed Carter $500,000 secured by a first mortgage on Diamond's plant and land. Stephens was a surety on this obligation in the amount of $250,000. After Diamond defaulted on the debt, Carter demanded and received payment of $250,000 from Stephens. Carter then foreclosed upon the mortgage and sold the property for $375,000. What rights, if any, does Stephens have in the proceeds from the sale of the property?

**15.** Paula Daniels purchased an automobile from Carey on credit. At the time of the sale, Scott agreed to be a surety for Paula, who is sixteen years old. The automobile's odometer stated 52,000 miles, but Carey had turned it back from 72,000 miles. Paula refuses to make any payments due on the car. Carey proceeds against Paula and Scott. What defenses, if any, are available to (a) Paula and (b) Scott?

**16.** Stafford Surety Co. agreed to act as the conditional guarantor of collection on a debt owed by Preston Decker to Cole. Stafford was paid a premium by Preston to serve as

surety. Preston defaults on the obligation. What are Cole's rights against Stafford Surety Co.?

**17.** Campbell loaned Perry Dixon $7,000, which was secured by a possessory security interest in stock owned by Perry. The stock had a market value of $4,000. In addition, Campbell insisted that Perry obtain a surety. For a premium, Sutton Surety Co. agreed to act as a surety for the full amount of the loan. Prior to the due date of the loan, Perry convinced Campbell to return the stock because its value had increased and he wished to sell it to realize the gain. Campbell released the stock and Perry subsequently defaulted. Campbell proceeds against Sutton. Decision?

**18.** Pamela Darden owed Clark $5,000 on an unsecured loan. On May 1, Pamela approached Clark for an additional loan of $3,000. Clark agreed to make the loan only if Pamela could obtain a surety. On May 5, Simpson agreed to be a surety on the $3,000 loan, which was granted that day. Both loans were due on October 1. On June 15, Pamela sent $1,000 to Clark but did not provide any instructions.

   (a)   What are Clark's rights?

   (b)   What are Simpson's rights?

**19.** Patrick Dillon applied for a $10,000 loan from Carlton Savings & Loan. Carlton required him to obtain a surety. Patrick approached Sinclair Surety Co., which insisted that Patrick provide it with a financial statement. Patrick did so, but the statement was materially false. In reliance upon the financial statement and in return for a premium, Sinclair agreed to act as surety. Upon Sinclair's commitment to act as surety, Carlton loaned Patrick the $10,000. After one payment of $400, Patrick defaulted. He then filed a voluntary petition in bankruptcy. Carlton proceeds against Sinclair. Decision?

**20.** On June 1, Smith contracted with Martin d/b/a Martin Publishing Company to distribute Martin's newspapers and to account for the proceeds. As part of the contract, Smith agreed to furnish Martin a bond in the amount of $10,000 guaranteeing the payment of the proceeds. At the time the contract was executed and the credit extended, the bond was not furnished, and no mention was made as to the prospective sureties. On July 1, Smith signed the bond with Black and Blue signing as sureties. The bond recited the awarding of the contract for distribution of the newspapers as consideration for the bond.

On December 1, there was due from Smith to Martin the sum of $3,600 under the distributor's contract. Demand for payment was made, but Smith failed to make payment. As a result, Martin brought an appropriate action against Black and Blue to recover the $3,600. What decision?

**21.** Diggitt Construction Company was the low bidder on a well-digging job for the Village of Drytown. On April 15, Diggitt signed a contract with Drytown for the job at a price of $40,000. At the same time, pursuant to the notice of bidding, Diggitt prevailed upon Ace Surety Company to execute a performance bond indemnifying Drytown on the contract. On May 1, after Diggitt had put in three days on the job, the president of the company refigured his bid and realized that if his company were to complete the job it would lose $10,000. Accordingly, Diggitt notified Drytown that it was canceling the contract, effective immediately. What are the rights and duties of Ace Surety Company?

WWW **Internet Exercise** Find and examine (a) some surety and fidelity companies, and (b) the federal Small Business Administration's surety bond guarantee program.

# CHAPTER 39

# Bankruptcy

A debt is an obligation to pay money owed by a debtor to a creditor. Debts are created daily by countless purchasers of goods at the consumer level; by retailers of goods in buying merchandise from a manufacturer, wholesaler, or distributor; by borrowers of funds from various lending institutions; and through the issuance and sale of bonds and other types of debt securities. Multitudes of business transactions are entered into daily on a credit basis. Commercial activity would be restricted greatly if credit were not readily obtainable or if needed funds were unavailable for lending.

Fortunately, most debts are paid when due, thus justifying the extension of credit and encouraging its continuation. Although defaults may create credit and collection problems, the total amount in default normally represents a very small percentage of the total amount of outstanding indebtedness. Nevertheless, financial crises and business misfortune confront both individuals and businesses. Both may accumulate debts that exceed their total assets. Conversely, their assets may exceed their total indebtedness but be in such nonliquid form that these debtors are unable to pay their debts as they become due. For businesses as well as individuals, relief from overly burdensome debt and from the threat of impending lawsuits by creditors is frequently necessary for economic survival.

The conflict between creditor rights and debtor relief has engendered various solutions, such as voluntary adjustments and compromises requiring installment payments to creditors over a period of time during which they agree to withhold legal action. Other voluntary methods include compositions and assignments of assets by a debtor to a trustee or assignee for the benefit of creditors, who sometimes also file for equity receiverships or insolvency proceedings in a State court, pursuant to statute. Nonetheless, the most adaptable and frequently employed method of debtor relief—one which also affords protection to creditors—is a proceeding in a Federal court under Federal bankruptcy law.

## FEDERAL BANKRUPTCY LAW

The most important method of protecting creditor rights and granting debtor relief is Federal bankruptcy law, which is largely statutory and involves court supervision. Bankruptcy legislation serves a dual purpose: (1) to effect a quick, equitable distribution of the debtor's property among her creditors, and (2) to discharge the debtor from her debts, enabling her to rehabilitate herself and start afresh. Other purposes are to provide uniform treatment of similarly situated creditors, preserve existing business relations, and stabilize commercial usages.

The Constitution of the United States provides that "the Congress shall have power . . . to establish . . . uniform Laws on the subject of Bankruptcies throughout the United States." Article I, Section 8, clause 4. Federal bankruptcy law has generally superseded State insolvency laws.

The U.S. Bankruptcy Code consists of eight odd-numbered chapters and one even-numbered chapter (Chapter 12, which was added in 1986). Chapters 7, 9, 11, 12, and 13 provide five different types of proceedings; Chapters 1, 3, and 5 apply to all of those proceedings unless otherwise specified. **Straight,** or ordinary, **bankruptcy** (Chapter 7) provides for the liquidation of the debtor's property, whereas the other proceedings provide for the **reorganization** and adjustment of the debtor's debts and, in the case of a business debtor, the continuance of the debtor's business. In reorganization cases the creditors usually look to the debtor's future earnings, whereas in liquidation cases the creditors look to the debtor's property at the commencement of the bankruptcy proceeding. Chapters 7, 11, 12, and 13 have provisions governing conversion of a case under that chapter to another chapter.

Chapter 7 applies to *all* debtors, with the exception of railroads, insurance companies, banks, savings and loan associations, homestead associations, licensed small business investment companies, and credit unions. (More than 70 percent of bankruptcies are filed under Chapter 7.) Moreover, Chapter 7 has special provisions for liquidating the estates of stockbrokers and commodity brokers. Railroads and any person who may be a debtor under Chapter 7 (except a stockbroker or a commodity broker) may be a debtor under Chapter 11. (About one-half of one percent of bankruptcies are filed under Chapter 11.) Chapter 9, by comparison, applies only to municipalities that are generally authorized to be debtors under that chapter, that are insolvent, and that desire to effect plans to adjust their debts. Chapter 12 applies to individuals, or individuals and their spouses, who are engaged in farming if 50 percent of their gross income is from farming, their aggregate debts do not exceed $1.5 million, and at least 80 percent of their debts arise out of farming operations. (Less than one-tenth of one percent of bankruptcies are filed under Chapter 12.) Corporations or partnerships also may qualify for Chapter 12. Chapter 13 applies to individuals with regular income who owe liquidated unsecured debts of less than $269,250 and secured debts of less than $807,750. (Approximately 28 percent of bankruptcies are filed under Chapter 13.)

The 1994 amendments to the Bankruptcy Code require that every three years, beginning in 1998, the U.S. Judicial Conference adjust for inflation the dollar amounts of the following provisions: eligibility for Chapter 13, requirements for filing involuntary cases, priorities, exemptions, and exceptions to discharge. Section 104.

The Bankruptcy Code grants to U.S. district courts original and exclusive jurisdiction over all bankruptcy cases and original, but not exclusive, jurisdiction over civil proceedings arising under bankruptcy cases. The district court must, however, abstain from related matters that, except for their relationship to a bankruptcy, could not have been brought in a Federal court. The district court in which a bankruptcy case is commenced has exclusive jurisdiction over all of the debtor's property. In addition, within each Federal district court the Bankruptcy Code establishes a bankruptcy court staffed by bankruptcy judges. Bankruptcy courts are authorized to hear certain matters specified by the Bankruptcy Code and to enter appropriate orders and judgments subject to review by the district court or, where established, by a panel of three bankruptcy judges. The Federal Circuit Court of Appeals has jurisdiction over appeals from the district court or panel. In all other matters, unless the parties agree otherwise, only the district court may issue final order or judgment based upon proposed findings of fact and conclusions of law submitted to the court by the bankruptcy judge.

## CASE ADMINISTRATION— CHAPTER 3

Chapter 3 of the Bankruptcy Code contains provisions dealing with the commencement of a case in bankruptcy, the meetings of creditors, the officers who administer the case, and the administrative powers of those officers.

### Commencement of the Case

The filing of a voluntary or involuntary petition initiates the jurisdiction of the bankruptcy court and the operation of the bankruptcy laws.

*Voluntary Petitions* More than 99 percent of all bankruptcy petitions are filed voluntarily. Any person eligible to be a debtor under a given bankruptcy proceeding may file a voluntary petition under that chapter, and need *not* be insolvent to do so. Commencing a voluntary case by filing a petition constitutes an automatic **order for relief.** The petition must include a list of all creditors (secured and unsecured), a list of all property the debtor owns, a list of property that the debtor claims to be exempt, and a statement of the debtor's affairs.

*Involuntary Petitions* An involuntary petition in bankruptcy may be filed only under Chapter 7 (liquidation) or Chapter 11 (reorganization). It may be filed (1) by three or more creditors who have unsecured claims which total $10,775 or more, or (2) if the debtor has fewer than twelve creditors, by one or more creditors whose total unsecured claims equal $10,775 or more. Section 303(b). An involuntary petition may not be filed against a farmer or against a banking, insurance, or non-profit corporation. Section 303(a).

If the debtor does not contest the involuntary petition, the court will enter an order for relief against the debtor. If the debtor opposes the petition, however, the court may enter an order of relief only (1) if the debtor is generally not paying his undisputed debts as they become due, or (2) if, within 120 days before the filing of the petition, a custodian or receiver took possession of substantially all of the debtor's property to enforce a lien against that property. Section 303(h).

If an involuntary petition is contested successfully by the debtor and dismissed by the court, Section 303(i) empowers the court to grant a judgment in favor of the debtor against the petitioning creditors for (1) costs, (2) reasonable attorneys' fees, and (3) damages proximately caused by the trustee's taking possession of the debtor's property. Moreover, if the petition was filed in bad faith, the court may award damages proximately caused by the filing or punitive damages.

If the court orders relief, the debtor must provide the court with schedules the same as those provided by a voluntary petitioner.

## Dismissal

The court may dismiss a Chapter 7 case for cause after notice and a hearing. Section 707(a). In 1984, Congress amended the Bankruptcy Code to deal with abuses of Chapter 7 by consumer debtors who had the ability to pay their debts. The amendment empowers the court on its own motion, after notice and a hearing, to dismiss a case filed by an individual debtor whose debts are primarily consumer debts if the court finds that granting relief would be a substantial abuse of the provisions of Chapter 7. Section 707(b).

Under Chapter 11, the court may dismiss a case for cause after notice and a hearing. Section 1112(b). Under Chapters 12 and 13, the debtor has an absolute right to have his case dismissed. Under these chapters, if a motion to dismiss is filed by a party in interest other than the debtor, the court may dismiss the case only for cause after notice and a hearing.

## Automatic Stays

The filing of a voluntary or involuntary petition operates as a **stay** (i.e., restraint against ) all creditors beginning or continuing to recover claims against the debtor, or creating, perfecting, or enforcing liens against property of the debtor. Section 362. This stay applies to both secured and unsecured creditors, although a secured creditor may petition the court to terminate the stay as to her security upon showing that she lacks adequate protection in the secured property. An automatic stay ends when the bankruptcy case is closed or dismissed or when the debtor receives a discharge.

## Trustees

In a bankruptcy proceeding, the trustee represents the debtor's estate and has the capacity to sue and be sued on behalf of the estate. In proceedings under Chapter 7, trustees are selected by a vote of the creditors. The 1994 amendments allow the creditors to elect a trustee in a Chapter 11 proceeding if the court orders the appointment of a trustee for cause. In Chapters 12 and 13 the trustee is appointed. Under Chapter 7, the trustee is responsible for collecting, liquidating, and distributing the debtor's estate. Her duties and powers in fulfilling these responsibilities include the following: (1) to collect the property of the estate; (2) to challenge certain transfers of property of the estate; (3) to use, sell, or lease property of the estate; (4) to deposit or invest money of the estate; (5) to employ attorneys, accountants, appraisers, or auctioneers; (6) to assume or reject any executory contract or unexpired lease of the debtor; (7) to object to creditors' claims that are improper; and (8) to oppose, if advisable, the debtor's discharge. Trustees under Chapters 11, 12, and 13 perform some but not all of the duties of a Chapter 7 trustee.

## Meetings of Creditors

Within a reasonable time after relief is ordered, a meeting of creditors must be held. The court may not attend this meeting. The debtor must appear and submit to an examination by creditors and the trustee with respect to his financial situation. In a proceeding under Chapter 7, qualified creditors at this meeting elect a permanent trustee.

## CREDITORS, THE DEBTOR, AND THE ESTATE—CHAPTER 5

## Creditors

The Bankruptcy Code defines a **creditor** as any entity having a claim against the debtor that arose at the time of or before the order for relief. A **claim** means a "right to payment whether or not such right is reduced to judgment, liquidated, unliquidated, fixed, contingent, matured, unmatured, disputed, undisputed, legal, equitable, secured, or unsecured." Section 101(4).

*Proof of Claims* Creditors wishing to participate in the distribution of the debtor's estate may file a proof of claim. If a creditor does not do so in a timely manner, then the debtor or trustee may file a proof of such claim.

Section 501. The debtor thereby may prevent a claim from becoming nondischargeable. Filed claims are allowed unless a party in interest objects. If an objection is made, the court determines, after a hearing, the amount and validity of the claim. The court may not allow any claim that (1) is unenforceable against the debtor or his property, (2) is for unmatured interest, or (3) is for insider or attorney services in excess of the reasonable value of such services. Section 502. An **insider** includes a relative or general partner of a debtor as well as a partnership in which the debtor is a general partner or a corporation of which the debtor is a director, officer, or person in control. Section 101(28).

*Secured Claims* An allowed claim of a creditor who has a lien on property of the estate is a secured claim to the extent of the value of the creditor's interest in the property. The creditor's claim is unsecured to the extent of the difference between the value of his secured interest and the allowed amount of his claim. Thus, if Andrew has an allowed claim of $5,000 against the estate of debtor Barbara and has a security interest in property of the estate that is valued at $3,000, Andrew has a secured claim in the amount of $3,000 and an unsecured claim for $2,000.

*Priority of Claims* After secured claims have been satisfied, the remaining assets are distributed among creditors with unsecured claims. Certain classes of unsecured claims, however, have a **priority,** which means that they must be paid in full before any distribution is made to claims of lesser rank. Each claimant within a priority class shares *pro rata* if the assets are not sufficient to satisfy all claims in that class. The claims having a priority and the order of their priority, as provided in Section 507, are as follows:

1. **Expenses of administration** of the debtor's estate, including the filing fees paid by creditors in involuntary cases; the expenses of creditors in recovering concealed assets for the benefit of the bankrupt's estate; the trustee's necessary expenses; and reasonable compensation to receivers, trustees, and their attorneys, as allowed by the court.
2. Unsecured claims of **"gap" creditors**. These are claims in an involuntary case arising in the ordinary course of the debtor's business after the commencement of the case but before the earlier of either the appointment of the trustee or the entering of the order for relief.

3. Allowed, unsecured claims up to $4,300 for **wages, salaries, or commissions** earned within ninety days before the filing of the petition or before the date on which the debtor's business ceases, whichever comes first.
4. Allowed, unsecured claims for contributions to **employee benefit plans** arising from services rendered within 180 days before the filing of the petition or the cessation of the debtor's business, whichever occurs first, but limited to $4,300 multiplied by the number of employees covered by the plan, less the aggregate amount paid to such employees under number 3 above.
5. Allowed, unsecured claims up to $4,300 for **grain** or **fish producers** against a storage facility.
6. Allowed, unsecured claims up to $1,950 for **consumer deposits;** that is, moneys deposited in connection with the purchase, lease, or rental of property or the purchase of services for personal, family, or household use.
7. **Alimony** and **support** of a spouse or child.
8. Specified income, property, employment, or excise **taxes** owed to governmental units.

After creditors with secured claims and creditors with claims having a priority have been satisfied, creditors with allowed, unsecured claims share proportionately in any remaining assets.

*Subordination of Claims* A subordination agreement is enforceable under the Bankruptcy Code to the same extent that it is enforceable under nonbankruptcy law. Section 510. In addition to statutory and contract priorities, the bankruptcy court can, at its discretion in proper cases, apply equitable priorities. Section 510. The court accomplishes this through the doctrine of subordination of claims, whereby, assuming two claims of equal statutory priority, the court declares that one claim must be paid in full before the other claim can be paid anything. Subordination is applied in cases where allowing a claim in full would be unfair and inequitable to other creditors. (Allowing the inflated salary claims of officers in a closely held corporation would be an example.) In such cases, the court does not disallow the claim but merely orders that it be paid after all other claims are paid in full. For example, the claim of a parent corporation against its bankrupt subsidiary may be subordinated to the claims of other creditors of the subsidiary if the parent has so mismanaged the subsidiary to the detriment of its innocent creditors that this unconscionable conduct precludes the parent from seeking the aid of a bankruptcy court.

## Debtors

As previously indicated, the purpose of the Bankruptcy Code is to bring about an equitable distribution of the debtor's assets and to provide him a discharge. Accordingly, the Code explicitly subjects the debtor to specified duties while exempting some of his property and discharging most of his debts.

**Debtor's Duties**　Under the Bankruptcy Code, the debtor must file a list of creditors, a schedule of assets and liabilities, and a statement of her financial affairs. In any case in which a trustee is serving, the debtor must cooperate with the trustee and surrender to the trustee all property of the estate and all records relating to such property.

**Debtor's Exemptions**　Section 522 of the Bankruptcy Code exempts specified property of an individual debtor from bankruptcy proceedings, including the following:

1. up to $16,150 in equity in property used as a residence or burial plot;
2. up to $2,575 in equity in one motor vehicle;
3. up to $425 for any particular item, and not to exceed $8,625 in aggregate value, of household furnishings, household goods, wearing apparel, appliances, books, animals, crops, or musical instruments that are primarily for personal, family, or household use;
4. up to $1,075 in jewelry;
5. any property up to $850 plus up to $8,075 of any unused amount of the first exemption;
6. up to $1,625 in implements, professional books, or tools of the debtor's trade;
7. unmatured life insurance contracts owned by the debtor, other than a credit life insurance contract;
8. professionally prescribed health aids;
9. social security, veteran's, and disability benefits;
10. unemployment compensation;
11. alimony and support payments, including child support;
12. payments from pension, profit-sharing, and annuity plans; and
13. payments from an award under a crime victim's reparation law, a wrongful death award, and up to $16,150, not including compensation for pain and suffering or for actual pecuniary loss, from a personal injury award.

In addition, the debtor may avoid judicial liens on any exempt property and nonpossessory, nonpurchase money security interests on household goods, tools of the trade, and professionally prescribed health aids.

The debtor has the option of using either the exemptions provided by the Bankruptcy Code or those available under State law. Nevertheless, a State may by specific legislative action limit its citizens to the exemptions provided by State law. More than two-thirds of the States have enacted such "opt out" legislation.

**Discharge**　Discharge relieves the debtor from liability for all her dischargeable debts. Certain debts, however, are nondischargeable under the Code. A discharge of a debt voids any judgment obtained at any time with respect to that debt and operates as an injunction against commencing or continuing any action to recover that debt. A discharge does not, however, affect a secured creditor to the extent of his security.

No private employer may terminate the employment of, or discriminate with respect to employment against, an individual who is or has been a debtor under the Bankruptcy Code solely because such debtor (1) is or has been such a debtor; (2) has been insolvent before the commencement of a case or during the case; or (3) has not paid a debt that is dischargeable in a case under the Bankruptcy Code. Section 525(b).

An agreement between a debtor and a creditor permitting the creditor to enforce a discharged debt is enforceable to the extent State law permits but only if (1) the agreement was made before the discharge has been granted; (2) the agreement contains a clear and conspicuous statement which advises the debtor that the agreement may be rescinded; (3) the agreement has been filed with the court, accompanied, if applicable, by a declaration or an affidavit of the attorney who represented the debtor during the course of negotiating the agreement, which states that such agreement represents a fully informed and voluntary agreement by the debtor and imposes no undue hardship on her; (4) the debtor has not rescinded the agreement at any time prior to discharge or within sixty days after the agreement is filed with the court, whichever occurs later; (5) the court has informed a debtor who is an individual that he is not required to enter into such an agreement and has explained the legal effect of the agreement; and (6) in a case concerning an individual who was not represented by an attorney during the course of negotiating the agreement, the court has approved such agreement as imposing no undue hardship on the debtor and being in her best interests. Section 524.

Section 523 provides that certain debts of an individual are not dischargeable in bankruptcy. This section applies to individuals receiving discharges under Chapters 7, 11, 12, and, as discussed later in this chapter, the "hardship discharge" provision of Chapter 13. The nondischargeable debts include:

1. certain taxes and customs duties;
2. legal liabilities for obtaining money or property by false pretenses, false representations, or actual fraud;
3. legal liability for willful and malicious injuries to the person or property of another;
4. alimony and support of a spouse or a child;
5. debts not scheduled, unless the creditor knew of the bankruptcy;
6. debts the debtor created by fraud or defalcation while acting in a fiduciary capacity, embezzlement, or larceny;
7. student loans unless the debt would impose undue hardship;
8. debts that were or could have been listed in a previous bankruptcy in which the debtor waived or was denied a discharge;
9. consumer debts for luxury goods or services in excess of $1,075 per creditor if incurred by an individual debtor on or within sixty days before the order for relief;
10. cash advances aggregating more than $1,075 obtained by an individual debtor under an open end credit plan within sixty days before the order for relief;
11. liability for a court judgment based upon the debtor's operation of a motor vehicle while legally intoxicated; and
12. fines, penalties, or forfeitures owed to a governmental entity.

In Chapter 13 cases, usually the only debts *not* discharged are the above debts numbered: four, seven, eleven, and twelve.

The following illustrates the operation of discharge: Donaldson files a petition in bankruptcy. Donaldson owes Anders $1,500, Boynton $2,500, and Conroy $3,000. Assume that Anders's claim is not dischargeable in bankruptcy, whereas Boynton's and Conroy's claims are. Anders receives $180 from the liquidation of Donaldson's bankruptcy estate, Boynton receives $300, and Conroy receives $360. If Donaldson receives a bankruptcy discharge, Boynton and Conroy will be precluded from pursuing Donaldson for the remainder of their claims ($2,200 and $2,640 respectively). Anders, on the other hand, because his debt is not dischargeable, may pursue Donaldson for the remaining $1,320, subject to the applicable statute of limitations. If Donaldson does not receive a discharge, Anders, Boynton, and Conroy may all pursue Donaldson for the unpaid portions of their claims.

## The Estate

The commencement of a bankruptcy case creates an **estate** consisting of all legal and equitable interests of the debtor in nonexempt property at that time. The estate also includes property that the debtor acquires within 180 days after the filing of the petition by inheritance, by a property settlement, by a divorce decree, or as a beneficiary of a life insurance policy. In addition, the estate includes proceeds, rents, and profits from property of the estate and any interest in property that the estate acquires after the case commences. Finally, the estate includes property that the trustee recovers under her powers (1) as a lien creditor, (2) to avoid voidable preferences, (3) to avoid fraudulent transfers, and (4) to avoid statutory liens. While the estate does not include earnings from services an individual debtor performs after the case commences, in a Chapter 12 or 13 case, it does include wages the debtor earns and property she acquires after the case commences.

 *See Case 33–3*

***Trustee as Lien Creditor***  The trustee has, as of the commencement of the case, the rights and powers of any creditor with a judicial lien against the debtor or an execution that is returned unsatisfied, whether or not such a creditor exists. Section 544(a). Obtained by a judgment, a levy, or some other legal or equitable process, a **judicial lien** is a charge or interest in property to secure payment of a debt or performance of an obligation. The trustee is made an ideal creditor possessing every right and power that the State confers by law upon its most favored creditor who has acquired a lien through legal or equitable proceedings. By assuming the rights and powers of a purely hypothetical lien creditor, the trustee has no need to locate an actual existing lien creditor.

Thus, under the Uniform Commercial Code (UCC) and the Bankruptcy Code, the trustee, as a hypothetical lien creditor, has priority over a creditor with a security interest that was not perfected when the bankruptcy petition was filed. A creditor with a purchase money security interest who files within the grace period allowed under State law, which in most States is twenty days after the debtor receives the collateral, however, will defeat the trustee, even if the creditor gap-files the petition before perfecting and after the security interest is created. For example, Donald borrows $5,000 from Cathy on September 1 and gives her a security interest in the equipment he purchases with the borrowed funds. On October 3, before Cathy perfects her security interest, Donald files for bankruptcy. The trustee in bankruptcy can invalidate Cathy's security interest because it was unperfected when the bankruptcy petition was filed. Cathy would be able to assert a claim only as an unsecured creditor. If, however, Donald had filed for bankruptcy on September 18 and Cathy had perfected the security interest on September 19, Cathy would prevail because she perfected her purchase money security interest within twenty days after Donald received the equipment.

*Voidable Preferences* The Bankruptcy Code invalidates certain preferential transfers from the debtor to favored creditors before the date of bankruptcy. A creditor who has received a transfer invalidated as preferential still may make a claim for the unpaid debt, but the property he received under the preferential transfer becomes a part of the debtor's estate to be shared by all creditors. Under Section 547 the trustee may recover any transfer of the debtor's property

1. to or for the benefit of a creditor;
2. for or on account of an antecedent debt the debtor owed before such transfer was made;
3. made while the debtor was insolvent;
4. made on or within ninety days before the date of the filing of the petition or, if the creditor was an "insider" (as previously defined), made within one year of the date of the filing of the petition; *and*
5. that enables such creditor to receive more than he would have received under Chapter 7.

A **transfer** is any mode, direct or indirect, voluntary or involuntary, of disposing of property or an interest in property, including the retention of title as a security interest. Section 101(48). The debtor is presumed to have been insolvent on and during the ninety days immediately preceding the date on which the petition was filed. **Insolvency** is a financial condition of a debtor such that the sum of her debts exceeds the sum of all her property at fair valuation.

The policy behind the voidable preference provision is explained by the House report as follows:

The purpose of the preference section is two-fold. First, by permitting the trustee to avoid pre-bankruptcy transfers that

occur within a short period before bankruptcy, creditors are discouraged from racing to the courthouse to dismember the debtor during his slide into bankruptcy. The protection thus afforded the debtor often enables him to work his way out of a difficult financial situation through cooperation with all of his creditors. Second, and more important, the preference provisions facilitate the prime bankruptcy policy of equality of distribution among creditors of the debtor. Any creditor that received a greater payment than others of his class is required to disgorge so that all may share equally. *House of Representatives Report* 95–595 at 177–78 (1977).

For example, on March 3, David borrows $15,000 from Carla, promising to repay the loan on April 3. David repays Carla on April 3 as he promised. Then, on June 1, David files a petition in bankruptcy. His assets are sufficient to pay general creditors only 40 cents on the dollar. David's repayment of the loan is a voidable preference, which the trustee may recover from Carla. The transfer (repayment) on April 3 (1) was to a creditor (Carla); (2) was on account of an antecedent debt (the $15,000 loan made on March 3); (3) was made while the debtor was insolvent (a debtor is presumed insolvent for the ninety days preceding the filing of the bankruptcy petition—June 1); (4) was made within ninety days of bankruptcy (April 3 is less than ninety days before June 1); and (5) enabled the creditor to receive more than she would have received under Chapter 7 (Carla received $15,000; she would have received .40 × $15,000 = $6,000 in bankruptcy). After returning the property to the trustee, Carla would have an unsecured claim of $15,000 against David's estate in bankruptcy, for which she would receive $6,000.

To illustrate further, consider the following example. On May 1, Debra buys and receives merchandise from Stuart and gives him a security interest in the goods for the unpaid price of $20,000. On May 25, Stuart files a financing statement. On August 1, Debra files a petition for bankruptcy. The trustee in bankruptcy may avoid the perfected security interest as a preferential transfer because (1) the transfer of the perfected security interest on May 25 was to benefit a creditor (Stuart); (2) it was on account of an antecedent debt (the $20,000 owed from the sale of the merchandise); (3) the debtor was insolvent at the time (the debtor's insolvency is presumed for the ninety days preceding the filing of the bankruptcy petition—August 1); (4) the transfer was made within ninety days of bankruptcy (May 25 is less than ninety days before August 1); and (5) the transfer enabled the creditor to receive more than he would have received in bankruptcy (on his secured claim, Stuart would recover more than he would on an unsecured claim).

Nevertheless, not all transfers made within ninety days of bankruptcy are voidable. The Bankruptcy Code makes exceptions for certain pre-bankruptcy transfers, including

1. *Exchanges for new value.* If, for example, within ninety days before the petition is filed, the debtor purchases an automobile for $9,000, this transfer of property (i.e., the $9,000) is not voidable because it was not made for an antecedent debt but rather as a substantially contemporaneous exchange for new value.
2. *Enabling security interests.* If the creditor gives the debtor new value which the debtor uses to acquire property in which he grants the creditor a security interest, the security interest is not voidable if the creditor perfects it within twenty days after the debtor receives possession of the property. For example, if within ninety days of the filing of the petition, the debtor purchases a refrigerator on credit and grants the seller or lender a security interest in the refrigerator, the transfer of that interest is not voidable if the secured party perfects within twenty days after the debtor receives possession of the property.
3. *Payments in ordinary course.* The trustee may *not* avoid a transfer (1) in payment of a debt incurred in the ordinary course of business or financial affairs of the debtor and the transferee, (2) made in the ordinary course of business or financial affairs of the debtor and transferee, and (3) made according to ordinary business terms.
4. *Consumer debts.* This exception provides that if the debtor is an individual whose debts are primarily consumer debts, the trustee may not avoid any transfer of property valued at less than $600.
5. *Alimony and support.* This exception, added in 1994, provides that the trustee may not avoid any transfer that is a *bona fide* payment of a debt for alimony, maintenance, or support made to a spouse, former spouse, or a child of the debtor. Section 547(c).

*See Case 39–1*

**Fraudulent Transfers** The trustee may avoid fraudulent transfers made on or within one year before the date of the filing of the petition. Section 548. One type of fraudulent transfer consists of the debtor's transferring property with the actual intent to hinder, delay, or defraud any of her creditors. Another type of fraudulent transfer involves the debtor's transfer of property for less than a reasonably equivalent consideration when she is insolvent or when the transfer would render her so. For example, Dale, who is in debt, transfers title to her house to Tony, her father, without any payment by Tony to Dale and with the understanding that when the house is no longer in danger of seizure by creditors, Tony will reconvey it to Dale. The transfer of the house by Dale to Tony is a fraudulent transfer. A 1998 amendment to the Bankruptcy Code provides that a transfer of a charitable contribution to a qualified religious or charitable entity or organization will not be considered a fraudulent transfer if the amount of that contribution does not exceed 15 percent of the gross annual income of the debtor for the year in which the transfer is made. Transfers that exceed 15 percent are protected if they are "consistent with the practices of the debtor in making charitable contributions."

In addition, the trustee may avoid transfers by a creditor with an allowable, unsecured claim, when such transfers are voidable under State law. Section 544(b). This section empowers a trustee to avoid transfers that violate State fraudulent conveyance statutes. These statutes generally provide a three- to six-year limitations period, which the trustee can utilize under Section 544(b).

**Statutory Liens** A **statutory lien** arises solely by force of a statute and does not include a security interest or judicial lien. Section 101(45). The trustee may avoid a statutory lien on property of the debtor if the lien (1) first becomes effective when the debtor becomes insolvent, (2) is not perfected or enforceable on the date of the commencement of the case against a *bona fide* purchaser, or (3) is for rent. Section 545.

# LIQUIDATION—CHAPTER 7

To accomplish its dual goals of equitably distributing the debtor's property and providing the debtor with a fresh start, the Bankruptcy Code has established two approaches: liquidation and adjustment of debts. Chapter 7 uses liquidation, whereas Chapters 11, 12, and 13, discussed below, take the second approach, that of adjusting debts. Liquidation involves terminating the business of the debtor, distributing his nonexempt assets, and, usually, discharging all of his dischargeable debts.

## Proceedings

Proceedings under Chapter 7 apply to all debtors except railroads, insurance companies, banks, savings and loan associations, homestead associations, and credit unions. A petition commencing a case under Chapter 7 may be either voluntary or involuntary. After the order for relief, an interim trustee is appointed to serve until the creditors select a permanent trustee. If the creditors do not elect a trustee, the interim trustee becomes the permanent trustee. Under Chapter 7, the trustee collects and reduces to money the property of the estate; accounts for all property received; investigates the financial affairs of the debtor; examines and, if appropriate, challenges proofs of claims; opposes, if advisable, the discharge of the debtor; and makes a final report of the administration of the estate.

The creditors may also elect a committee of not fewer than three and not more than eleven unsecured creditors to consult with the trustee, to make recommendations to him, and to submit questions to the court.

## Distribution of the Estate

After the trustee has collected all the assets of the debtor's estate, she distributes them to the creditors and, if any assets remain, to the debtor, in the following order:

1. Secured creditors are paid on their security interests.
2. Creditors entitled to a priority are paid in the order provided.
3. Unsecured creditors who filed their claims on time (or tardily, if they did not have notice or actual knowledge of the bankruptcy) are paid.
4. Unsecured creditors who filed their claims late are paid.
5. Claims for fines and multiple, exemplary, or punitive damages are paid.
6. Interest at the legal rate from the date of the filing of the petition is paid to all of the above claimants.
7. Whatever property remains is distributed to the debtor.

Claims of the same rank are paid *pro rata*. For example: Donley has filed a petition for a Chapter 7 proceeding. The total value of Donley's estate after paying the expenses of administration is $25,000. Evans, who is owed $15,000, has a security interest in property valued at $10,000. Fishel has an unsecured claim of $6,000, which is entitled to a priority of $2,000. The United States has a claim for income taxes of $4,000. Green has an unsecured claim of $9,000 that was filed on time. Hiller has an unsecured claim of $12,000 that was filed on time. Jerdee has a claim of $8,000 that was filed late. The distribution would be as follows:

1. Evans receives $11,500
2. Fishel receives $3,200
3. United States receives $4,000
4. Green receives $2,700
5. Hiller receives $3,600
6. Jerdee receives $0

To analyze this distribution: Evans receives $10,000 as a secured creditor and has an unsecured claim of $5,000. Fishel receives $2,000 on the portion of his claim entitled to a priority and has an unsecured claim of $4,000. The United States has a priority of $4,000. After paying $10,000 to Evans, $2,000 to Fishel, and $4,000 to the United States, there remains $9,000 ($25,000 − $10,000 − $2,000 − $4,000) to be distributed *pro rata* to unsecured creditors who filed on time. Their claims total $30,000 (Evans = $5,000, Fishel = $4,000, Green = $9,000, and Hiller = $12,000). Therefore, each will receive $9,000/$30,000, or 30¢ on the dollar. Accordingly, Evans receives an additional $1,500, Fishel receives an additional $1,200, Green receives $2,700, and Hiller receives $3,600. Because the assets were insufficient to pay all unsecured claimants who filed on time, Jerdee, who filed tardily, receives nothing. If, however, Jerdee's late filing resulted from Donley's failure to schedule Jerdee's claim, then Donley's debts to Jerdee would not be discharged unless Jerdee knew or had notice of the bankruptcy.

◆ *See Figure 39–1*

## Discharge

A discharge under Chapter 7 relieves the debtor of all dischargeable debts that arose before the date of the order for relief. The discharge does not include those debts that are not dischargeable. After distribution of the estate, the court will grant the debtor a discharge unless the debtor

1. is not an individual (partnerships and corporations may not receive a discharge under Chapter 7);
2. has destroyed, falsified, concealed, or failed to keep records and account books;
3. has knowingly and fraudulently made a false oath or account, presented or used a false claim, or given or received bribes;
4. has transferred, removed, destroyed, or concealed any (a) of his property with intent to hinder, delay, or defraud his creditors within twelve months preceding the filing of the bankruptcy petition, or (b) property of the estate after the date of filing of the petition;
5. has within six years prior to bankruptcy been granted a discharge under Chapter 7 or 11. A debtor also will be denied a discharge under Chapter 7 if she received a discharge under Chapter 12 or 13 within

**FIGURE 39–1** Collection and Distribution of the Debtor's Estate

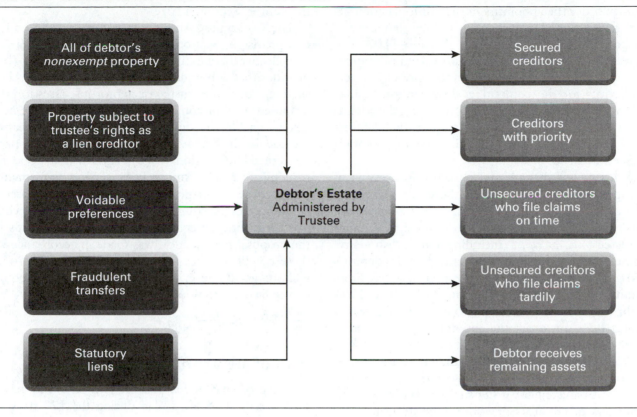

the past six years, unless payments under that chapter's plan totaled at least (1) 100 percent of the allowed unsecured claims or (2) 70 percent of such claims and the plan was the debtor's best effort;

6. refused to obey any lawful order of the court or to answer any question approved by the court;

7. has failed to explain satisfactorily, in terms of meeting his liabilities, any loss or deficiency of assets; or

8. has executed a written waiver of discharge approved by the court.

On the request of the trustee or a creditor and after notice and a hearing, the court may revoke within one year a discharge the debtor obtained through fraud.

## REORGANIZATION—CHAPTER 11

Reorganization is the process of correcting or eliminating factors responsible for the distress of a business enterprise, thereby preserving both the enterprise and its value as a going concern. Chapter 11 of the Bankruptcy Code governs reorganization of eligible debtors, including individuals, partnerships, and corporations, and permits the restructuring of their finances. A number of large

corporations have made use of Chapter 11, including Texaco, A H Robins, Johns-Manville, Allied Stores, and Eastern Airlines. The main objective of a reorganization proceeding is to develop and carry out a fair, equitable, and feasible plan of reorganization. After a plan has been prepared and filed, a hearing held before the court determines whether or not it will be confirmed.

### Proceedings

Any person who may be a debtor under Chapter 7 (except stockbrokers and commodity brokers) and railroads may be a debtor under Chapter 11. Petitions may be voluntary or involuntary.

The 1994 amendments permit small businesses to elect to be subject to streamlined procedures designed to expedite the administration of Chapter 11. The amendments define *small business* to include persons engaged in commercial or business activities whose aggregate, noncontingent, liquidated debts do not exceed $2 million.

As soon as practicable after the order for relief, a committee of unsecured creditors is appointed. This committee usually consists of persons holding the seven largest unsecured claims against the debtor. In addition, the court may order the appointment of additional committees of creditors or of equity security holders, if necessary, to ensure adequate representation. Section 1102. The committee may, with the court's approval, employ attorneys, accountants, and other agents to represent or perform services for the committee. The committee may consult with the debtor or trustee concerning the administration of the case and may investigate the debtor's affairs and participate in formulating a reorganization plan. Section 1103.

The debtor will manage and remain in possession of the property of the estate unless the court orders the appointment of a trustee, who may then operate the debtor's business. The court will order the appointment of a trustee *only for cause* (including fraud, dishonesty, incompetence, or gross mismanagement of the debtor's affairs) or if the appointment is in the interests of creditors or equity security holders. Section 1104. The 1994 amendments allow the creditors to elect the trustee. If the court does not order the appointment of a trustee upon the request of a party in interest, the court will order the appointment of an examiner to investigate allegations of fraud, dishonesty, incompetence, misconduct, or mismanagement if (1) such appointment is in the interests of creditors or equity security holders or (2) the debtor's fixed, liquidated, unsecured debts exceed $5 million.

The duties of a trustee in a case under Chapter 11 include the following:

1. to be accountable for all property received;
2. to examine proofs of claims;
3. to furnish information to all parties in interest;
4. to provide the court and taxing authorities with financial reports of the debtor's business operations;
5. to make a final report and account of the administration of the estate;
6. to investigate the financial condition of the debtor and determine the desirability of continuing the debtor's business; and
7. to file a plan, to file a report explaining why there will be no plan, or to recommend that the case be converted to Chapter 7.

At any time before confirmation of a plan, the court may terminate the trustee's appointment and restore the debtor to possession and management of the property of the estate and operation of the debtor's business. Section 1105.

When a trustee has not been appointed, the debtor in possession performs many of the functions and duties of a trustee, with the principal exception of investigating the debtor. Section 1107.

The Bankruptcy Amendments Act of 1984 added a new provision (Section 1113) dealing with the rejection of collective bargaining agreements. Subsection (b)(1) provides that subsequent to filing and prior to seeking such rejection, the trustee or debtor-in-possession must propose the labor contract modifications that are necessary to enable the debtor to reorganize and that will provide for the fair and equitable treatment of all parties concerned. Subsection (b)(2) requires that good faith meetings to reach a mutually satisfactory agreement be held between management and the union. Subsection (c) authorizes the court to approve rejection of the collective bargaining agreement only if the court finds that the proposal for rejection was made in accordance with these conditions, that the union refused the proposal without good cause, and that the balance of equities clearly favors rejection.

 *See Case 39–2*

## Plan of Reorganization

The debtor may file a plan at any time and has the exclusive right to file a plan during the 120 days after the order for relief, unless a trustee has been appointed. If the debtor has not filed a plan within 120 days or the plan has not been accepted within 180 days, then other parties in interest, including an appointed trustee or a creditors' committee, may file a plan. Section 1121. On request of a party in interest and after notice and a hearing, the court may reduce or increase the 120-day or 180-day periods.

A plan of reorganization must divide creditors' claims and shareholders' interests into classes, specify how each class will be treated, deal with claims within each class equally, and provide adequate means for implementing the plan. After a plan has been filed, the plan and a written disclosure statement approved by the court as containing adequate information must be transmitted to each holder of a claim before seeking acceptance or rejection of the plan. **Adequate information** is that which would enable a hypothetical, reasonable investor to make an informed judgment about the plan. Section 1125.

## Acceptance of Plan

Each class of claims and interests has the opportunity to accept or reject the proposed plan. To be accepted by a class of claims, a plan must be accepted by creditors that hold at least two-thirds in amount and more than one-half in number of the allowed claims of such class. Acceptance of a plan by a **class of interests,** such as shareholders, requires acceptance by holders of at least two-thirds in amount of the allowed interests of such class.

A class that is not impaired under a plan is conclusively presumed to have accepted the plan. Basically, a class is unimpaired if the plan leaves unaltered the legal, equitable, and contractual rights to which the holder of such claim or interest is entitled. Section 1124. A class that will receive no distribution under a plan is deemed not to have accepted the plan.

## Confirmation of Plan

Before a plan is binding on any parties, the court, after notice and a hearing, must confirm such plan. To be confirmed, the plan must meet all the requirements of Section 1129 of the Bankruptcy Code. The most important of these requirements are the following.

*Good Faith* The plan must have been proposed in good faith and not by any means forbidden by law. Section 1129(a)(3).

*Feasibility* The court must find that confirmation of the plan is not likely to be followed by the debtor's liquidation or by its need for further financial reorganization. Section 1129(a)(11). The essence of feasibility is that the reorganization entity will be able to operate economically and efficiently, will be able to compete upon fairly equal terms with other companies within the industry, and is not likely to require liquidation or a second reorganization within the foreseeable future.

*Cash Payments* Certain classes of creditors must have their allowed claims paid in full in cash immediately or, in some instances, on a deferred basis. Section 1129(a)(9). These classes include the expenses of administration, gap creditors, claims for wages and salaries, and employee benefits and consumer deposits.

*Acceptance by Creditors* To be confirmed, the plan must be accepted by at least *one* class of claims, and with respect to *each* class, each holder must either accept the plan *or* receive not less than the amount he would have received under Chapter 7. In addition, each class must accept the plan or be unimpaired by it. Nonetheless, under certain circumstances, the court may confirm a plan that is not accepted by all impaired classes, upon determining that the plan does not discriminate unfairly and that it is fair and equitable. Section 1129(b)(1). Under these circumstances, a class of claims or interests may, despite its objections, be subjected to the provisions of a plan.

"Fair and equitable" with respect to secured creditors requires that they either retain their security interest and receive deferred cash payments at least equal to their claims or that they realize the "indubitable equivalent" of their claims. Fair and equitable with respect to unsecured creditors means that such creditors are to receive property of value equivalent to the full amount of their claim or that no junior claim or interest is to receive anything. With respect to a class of interests, a plan is fair and equitable if the holders receive full value or if no junior interest receives anything at all.

## Effect of Confirmation

Once confirmed, the plan governs the debtor's performance obligations. The plan binds the debtor and any creditor, equity security holder, or general partner of the debtor. Upon the entry of a final decree closing the proceedings, the debtor is discharged from all of its debts and liabilities that arose before the date the plan was confirmed, except as otherwise provided in the plan, the order of confirmation, or the Bankruptcy Code. Section 1141. The confirmation of a plan does not discharge an *individual* debtor from debts that are not dischargeable under Section 523.

## ADJUSTMENT OF DEBTS OF A FAMILY FARMER—CHAPTER 12

In 1986, Congress amended the Bankruptcy Act by adding Chapter 12, which provides for the adjustment of the debts of a family farmer with regular annual income. Family farmers are defined as individuals, or individuals and their spouses, who are engaged in farming and who receive 50 percent of their gross income from farming. Their aggregate debts may not exceed $1.5 million, and at least 80 percent of those debts must arise from the farming operation. A corporation or partnership may also qualify as a family farmer if, in addition to meeting the requirements just mentioned, one family holds 50 percent of the stock or equity, and more than 80 percent of the assets of the corporation or partnership are related to the farming operation.

When this text went to press, Chapter 12 was due to expire on April 1, 1999 unless Congress reenacts or extends it.

The purpose of Chapter 12 is to provide a proceeding for family farmers who do not qualify for Chapter 13 and who find Chapter 11 proceedings overly burdensome. The provisions of Chapter 12 are based on and are substantially the same as those of Chapter 13.

## ADJUSTMENT OF DEBTS OF INDIVIDUALS—CHAPTER 13

To encourage debtors to pay their debts wherever possible, Congress enacted Chapter 13 of the Bankruptcy Code. This chapter permits an individual debtor to file a repayment plan which, if confirmed by the court, will discharge him from almost all of his debts when he completes his payments under the plan.

### Proceedings

Chapter 13 provides a procedure for adjusting the debts of an individual with regular income who owes liquidated, unsecured debts of less than $269,250 and secured debts of less than $807,750. Sole proprietorships meeting these debt limitations are also eligible; partnerships and corporations are not eligible. A case under Chapter 13 may be initiated only by a voluntary petition, and a trustee is appointed in every Chapter 13 case. Property of the estate in Chapter 13 includes wages earned and other property acquired by the debtor after the Chapter 13 filing. Section 1306.

### The Plan

The debtor files the plan and may modify it at any time before confirmation. The plan must meet three requirements under Section 1322:

1. It must require the debtor to submit all or any portion of her future earnings or income, as is necessary for the execution of the plan, to the trustee's supervision and control.
2. It must provide for full payment on a deferred basis of all claims entitled to a priority unless a holder of a claim agrees to a different treatment of such claim.
3. If the plan classifies claims, it must provide the same treatment for each claim in the same class.

In addition, the plan may modify the rights of unsecured and secured creditors, except those secured only by a security interest in the debtor's principal residence. The plan also may provide for payments on any unsecured claim to be made concurrently with payments on any secured claim. The plan may not provide for payments over a period longer than three years, unless the court approves, for cause, a longer period not to exceed five years.

### Confirmation

To be confirmed by the court, the plan must meet certain requirements. First, the plan must comply with applicable law and be proposed in good faith. Second, the value of the property to be distributed to unsecured creditors must be not less than the amount they would receive under Chapter 7. Third, either the secured creditors must accept the plan, the plan must provide that the debtor will surrender the collateral to the secured creditors, *or* the plan must permit the secured creditors to retain their security interest and the value of the property to be distributed to them is not less than the allowed amount of their claim. Fourth, the debtor must be able to make all payments and comply with the plan. Fifth, if the trustee or the holder of an unsecured claim objects to the plan's confirmation, then the plan must either provide for payment in full of that claim or provide that all of the debtor's disposable income for three years be applied to payments under the plan. For purposes of this provision, *disposable income* means income received by the debtor that is not reasonably necessary for the maintenance or support of the debtor or a dependent of the debtor or, if the debtor is engaged in business, for the payment of expenditures necessary for continuing, preserving, and operating the business.

 *See Case 39–3*

### Effect of Confirmation

The provisions of a confirmed plan bind the debtor and all of her creditors. The confirmation of a plan vests in the debtor all property of the estate free and clear of any creditor's claim or interest for which the plan provides, except as otherwise provided in the plan or in the order confirming the plan. Section 1327. A plan may be modified after confirmation at the request of the debtor, the trustee, or a holder of an unsecured claim. The modification may increase or decrease the amount of payments on claims of a particular class or extend or reduce the time for such payments. Section 1329.

### Discharge

After a debtor completes all payments under the plan, the court will grant him a discharge of all debts provided for by the plan, with the exception of nondischargeable debts for alimony, maintenance, and support; most student loans; liability for driving while intoxicated; governmental fines; and certain long-term obligations on which payments extend beyond the term of the plan. This discharge is considerably more extensive than that granted under Chapter 7. Moreover, a debtor who receives a discharge under Chapter 7 cannot obtain a discharge again under that chapter for six years; a debtor discharged under Chapter 13, however, is not subject to that limitation if payments under the plan totaled at least (1) 100 percent of unsecured claims or (2) 70 percent of such claims *and* the plan represented the debtor's best effort. Section 727(a)(9).

Even if the debtor fails to make all payments, the court may, after a hearing, grant a "hardship discharge" if the debtor's failure is due to circumstances for which the debtor is not justly accountable, the value of property actually distributed is not less than what the creditors would have received under Chapter 7, and modification of the plan is impracticable. Section 1328(b). This discharge is subject, however, to the same exceptions for nondischargeable debts as a discharge under Chapter 7.

◆ *See Figure 39–2*

## CREDITORS' RIGHTS AND DEBTOR'S RELIEF OUTSIDE OF BANKRUPTCY

The rights and remedies of debtors and creditors outside of bankruptcy are governed mainly by State law. Because of the expense and notoriety associated with bankruptcy, resolving claims outside of a bankruptcy proceeding is often in the best interests of both debtor and creditor. Accordingly, bankruptcy usually is considered a last resort.

The rights and remedies of creditors outside of bankruptcy are varied. The first part of this section examines the basic right of all creditors to pursue their overdue claims to judgment and to satisfy that judgment out of property belonging to the debtor. Other rights and remedies are discussed elsewhere in this book. The rights under Article 2 of the UCC of an unpaid credit seller to reclaim the goods sold are covered in Chapter 25. The right of a secured creditor to enforce a security interest in personal property is the subject of Chapter 38. Likewise, the right of a creditor to foreclose a mortgage on real property is discussed in Chapter 50. In addition, the right of a creditor to proceed against a surety on the debt is addressed in Chapter 38.

At the same time, the law attempts to protect debtors against overreaching by creditors. This goal has been pursued by a number of means. States have enacted usury laws, as discussed in Chapter 13. The Federal Trade Commission has limited the rights of a holder in due course against consumer debtors, as explained in Chapter 28. Congress has prohibited abusive, deceptive, and unfair debt collection practices employed by debt collection agencies, as discussed in Chapter 42. That chapter also covers other legal protection offered to *consumer* debtors. The second part of this section describes the various forms of nonbankruptcy compromises that provide relief to debtors who have become overextended and who are unable to pay all of their creditors.

**FIGURE 39–2**  Comparison of Bankruptcy Proceedings

| | Chapter 7 | Chapter 11 | Chapter 12 | Chapter 13 |
|---|---|---|---|---|
| **Objective** | Liquidation | Reorganization | Adjustment | Adjustment |
| **Eligible Debtors** | Most debtors | Most debtors, including railroads | Family farmer who meets certain debt limitations | Individual with regular income who meets certain debt limitations |
| **Type of Petition** | Voluntary or involuntary | Voluntary or involuntary | Voluntary | Voluntary |
| **Trustee** | Usually selected by creditors; otherwise appointed | Only if court orders appointment for cause; creditors then may select trustee | Appointed | Appointed |

# CREDITORS' RIGHTS

When a debtor fails to pay a debt, the creditor may file suit to collect the debt owed. The objective is to obtain a judgment against the debtor and ultimately to collect on that judgment.

## Prejudgment Remedies

Because litigation takes time, a creditor attempting to collect on a claim through the judicial process will almost always experience delay in obtaining judgment. To prevent the debtor from meanwhile disposing of his assets, the creditor may use, when available, certain prejudgment remedies. The most important of these is **attachment,** the process of seizing property, by virtue of a writ, summons, or other judicial order, and bringing the property into the custody of the court to secure satisfaction of the judgment ultimately to be entered in the action. At common law, the main objective of attachment was to coerce the defendant debtor into appearing in court; today the writ of attachment is statutory and is used primarily to seize the debtor's property in the event a judgment is rendered. Most States limit attachment to specified grounds and provide the debtor an opportunity for a hearing before a judge prior to the issuance of a writ of execution. Generally, attachment is limited to situations in which (a) the defendant cannot be personally served; (b) the claim is based upon fraud or the equivalent; or (c) the defendant has or is likely to transfer his property. In addition, the plaintiff generally must post a bond to compensate the defendant for loss should the plaintiff not prevail in the cause of action.

Similar in purpose is the remedy of prejudgment **garnishment,** which is a statutory proceeding directed at a third person who owes a debt to the debtor or who has property belonging to the debtor. Garnishment is most commonly used against the employer of the debtor and the bank in which the debtor has a savings or checking account. Property garnished remains in the hands of the third party pending the outcome of the suit. For example, Calvin brings an action against Daisy to collect a debt that is past due. Alvin has property belonging to Daisy. Calvin might garnish this property so that if he is successful in his action against Daisy, his judgment could be satisfied out of that property held by Alvin. If Alvin no longer had the property when Calvin obtained judgment, Calvin could recover from Alvin.

## Postjudgment Remedies

If the debtor still has not paid the claim, the creditor may proceed to trial and try to obtain a court judgment against the debtor. Though necessary, obtaining a judgment is, nevertheless, only the first step in collecting the debt. If the debtor does not voluntarily pay the judgment, the creditor will have to take additional steps to collect on it. These steps are called "postjudgment remedies."

First, the judgment creditor will have the court clerk issue a **writ of execution** demanding payment of the judgment, which is served by the sheriff upon the defendant/debtor. Upon return of the writ "unsatisfied," the judgment creditor may post bond or other security and order a levy on and sale of specified nonexempt property belonging to the defendant/debtor, which is then seized by the sheriff, advertised for sale, and sold at public sale under the writ of execution.

The writ of execution is limited to nonexempt property of the debtor. All States restrict creditors from recourse to certain property, the type and amount of which varies greatly from State to State.

If the proceeds of the sale do not produce funds sufficient to pay the judgment, the creditor may institute a **supplementary proceeding** in an attempt to locate money or other property belonging to the defendant. He also may proceed by **garnishment** against the debtor's employer or against a bank in which the debtor has an account.

# DEBTOR'S RELIEF

The creditor's pursuit of a judgment on which she can collect and the debtor's quest for relief inherently give rise to conflicts among (1) the right of diligent creditors to pursue their claims to judgment and to satisfy their judgments by sale of property of the debtor; (2) the right of unsecured creditors who have refrained from suing the debtor; and (3) the social policy of affording relief to a debtor who has contracted debts beyond his ability to pay and who therefore may bear a lifetime burden.

Various nonbankruptcy compromises provide relief to debtors. Certain compromises, such as those offered by credit agencies and adjustment bureaus, are relatively informal. Some, such as compositions and assignments, are founded in common law and involve simple contract and trust principles; others, such as statutory assignments, are statutory. Some, such as equity receiverships, involve the intervention of a court and its officers, while others do not.

## Compositions

A common law or nonstatutory **composition** is an ordinary contract or agreement between the debtor and her creditors, under which the creditors receive *pro rata* a part of their claims and the debtor is discharged from the balance of the claims. As a contract, it requires contractual formalities, such as offer, acceptance, and consideration. For example, debtor D, owing debts of $5,000 to A, $2,000 to B, and $1,000 to C, offers to settle these claims by paying a total of $4,000 to A, B, and C. If A, B, and C accept the offer, a composition results, with A receiving $2,500, B $1,000, and C $500. The consideration for the promise of A to forgive the balance of his claim consists of the promises of B and C to forgive the balance of their claims. By avoiding a race among themselves to obtain the debtor's limited assets, all the creditors benefit.

It should be noted, however, that the debtor in a composition is discharged from liability only regarding the claims of those creditors who voluntarily consent to the composition. If, in the illustration above, C had refused to accept the offer of composition and had refused to take the $500, he could attempt to collect his full $1,000 claim. Likewise, if D owed additional debts to X, Y, and Z, these creditors would not be bound by the agreement between D and A, B, and C. Another disadvantage of the composition is the fact that any creditor can attach the assets of the debtor during the negotiation period that usually precedes the execution of the composition agreement. For instance, once D advised A, B, and C that he was offering to compose the claims, any one of the creditors could seize D's property.

A variation of the composition is an extension agreement, developed by the debtor and her creditors, that provides for payment of her debts either in full or proportionally reduced over time.

## Assignments for Benefit of Creditors

A common law or nonstatutory assignment for the benefit of creditors, sometimes called a general assignment, is a voluntary transfer by the debtor of some or all of his property to a trustee who applies the property to the payment of all the debtor's debts. For instance, debtor D transfers title to his property to trustee T, who converts the property into money and pays it to all of the creditors on a *pro rata* basis.

The advantages of the assignment over the composition are that it protects the debtor's assets from attachment and execution and that it halts diligent creditors in their race to attach. On the other hand, although the common law assignment does not require the creditors' consent, payment by the trustee of part of the claims does not discharge the debtor from the balance of them. Thus, in the previous example, even after T pays A $2,500, B $1,000, and C $500 (and makes appropriate payments to all other creditors), A, B, and C and the other creditors still may attempt to collect the balance of their claims.

## Statutory Assignments

Because assignments benefit creditors by protecting the debtor's assets from attachment, many statutory enactments have endeavored to combine the idea of the assignment with a corresponding benefit that would discharge the debtor from the balance of his debts. But because the U.S. Constitution prohibits a State from impairing the contractual obligation between private citizens, it is impossible for a State to force all creditors to discharge a debtor upon a *pro rata* distribution of assets, although, as previously discussed, the Federal government *does* have such power and exercises it in the Bankruptcy Code. Accordingly, the States generally have enacted assignment statutes permitting the debtor to obtain *voluntary* releases of the balance of claims from creditors who accept partial payments, thus combining the advantages of common law compositions and assignments.

## Equity Receiverships

One of the oldest remedies in equity is the appointment of a receiver by the court. The receiver is a disinterested person who collects and preserves the debtor's assets and income and disposes of them at the direction of the court which appointed her. The court may instruct her (1) to liquidate the assets by public or private sale; (2) to operate the business as a going concern temporarily; or (3) to conserve the assets until final disposition of the matter before the court.

The court will appoint a receiver upon the petition (1) of a secured creditor seeking foreclosure of his security; (2) of a judgment creditor who has exhausted legal remedies to satisfy the judgment; or (3) of a shareholder of a corporate debtor whose assets will likely be dissipated by fraud or mismanagement. The appointment of a receiver always rests within the sound discretion of the court. Insolvency, in the equity sense of inability by the debtor to pay his debts as they mature, is one of the factors the court considers in appointing a receiver.

# Chapter Summary

## Federal Bankruptcy Law

| | |
|---|---|
| **Case Administration— Chapter 3** | **Commencement of the Case** the filing of a voluntary or involuntary petition begins jurisdiction of the bankruptcy court<br>• *Voluntary Petitions* available to any debtor even if solvent<br>• *Involuntary Petitions* may be filed only under Chapter 7 or 11 if the debtor is generally not paying his debts as they become due<br>**Dismissal** the court may dismiss a case for cause after notice and a hearing; under Chapters 12 and 13 the debtor has an absolute right to have his case dismissed<br>**Automatic Stay** prevents attempts by creditors to recover claims against the debtor<br>**Trustee** responsible for collecting, liquidating, and distributing the debtor's estate<br>**Meeting of Creditors** debtor must appear and submit to an examination of her financial situation |
| **Creditors, the Debtor, and the Estate— Chapter 5** | **Creditor** any entity that has a claim against the debtor<br>• *Claim* a right to payment<br>• *Secured Claim* claim with a lien on property of the debtor<br>• *Unsecured Claim* portion of a claim that exceeds the value of any property securing that claim<br>• *Priority of Claims* the right of certain claims to be paid before claims of lesser rank<br>**Debtors**<br>• *Debtor's Duties* the debtor must file specified information, cooperate with the trustee, and surrender all property of the estate<br>• *Debtor's Exemptions* determined by State or Federal law, depending upon the State<br>• *Discharge* relief from liability for all debts except those the Bankruptcy Code specifies as not dischargeable<br>**The Estate** all legal and equitable interests of the debtor in nonexempt property<br>• *Trustee as Lien Creditor* trustee gains the rights and powers of creditor with judicial lien (an interest in property, obtained by court action, to secure payment of a debt)<br>• *Voidable Preferences* Bankruptcy Code invalidates certain preferential transfers made before the date of bankruptcy from the debtor to favored creditors<br>• *Fraudulent Transfers* trustee may avoid fraudulent transfers made on or within one year before the date of bankruptcy<br>• *Statutory Liens* trustee may avoid statutory liens which first become effective on insolvency, are not perfected at commencement of case, or are for rent |
| **Liquidation— Chapter 7** | **Purpose** to distribute equitably the debtor's nonexempt assets and usually to discharge all dischargeable debts of the debtor<br>**Proceedings** apply to most debtors<br>**Distribution of the Estate** in the following order: (1) secured creditors, (2) creditors entitled to a priority, (3) unsecured creditors, and (4) the debtor<br>**Discharge** granted by the court unless the debtor has committed an offense under the Bankruptcy Code or has received a discharge within six years |

| Reorganization—Chapter 11 | **Purpose** to preserve a distressed entity and its value as a going concern<br>**Proceedings** debtor usually remains in possession of the property of the estate<br>**Acceptance of Plan** requires a specified proportion of creditors to approve the plan<br>**Confirmation of Plan** requires (1) good faith, (2) feasibility, (3) cash payments to certain creditors, and usually (4) acceptance by creditors<br>**Effect of Confirmation** binds the debtor and creditors and discharges the debtor |
|---|---|
| **Adjustment of Debts of a Family Farmer—Chapter 12** | **Purpose** to permit a family farmer to file a repayment plan that will discharge him from most debts<br>**Proceedings** available to a farmer who receives at least 50 percent of his income from farming and who meets certain debt limitations<br>**Confirmation of Plan** same as a Chapter 13 proceeding<br>**Discharge** after a debtor completes all payments under the plan |
| **Adjustment of Debts of Individuals—Chapter 13** | **Purpose** to permit an individual debtor to file a repayment plan which will discharge her from most debts<br>**Confirmation of Plan** requires (1) good faith, (2) that the value of property distributed to creditors be not less than the amount that would be paid them under Chapter 7, (3) that secured creditors accept the plan, and (4) that the debtor be able to make all payments and comply with the plan<br>**Discharge** after a debtor completes all payments under the plan |

# Creditors' Rights and Debtor's Relief Outside of Bankruptcy

| Creditors' Rights | **Prejudgment Remedies** include attachment and garnishment<br>**Postjudgment Remedies** include writ of execution and garnishment |
|---|---|
| **Debtor's Relief** | **Compositions** agreement between debtor and two or more of her creditors that each will take a portion of his claim as full payment<br>**Assignment for Benefit of Creditors** voluntary transfer by the debtor of some or all of his property to a trustee, who applies the property to the payment of all the debtor's debts<br>**Statutory Assignment** provides a voluntary release of balance of claims from creditors who accept partial payments made by the trustee for the debtor<br>**Equity Receivership** receiver is a disinterested person appointed by the court to collect and preserve the debtor's assets and income and to dispose of them at the direction of the court |

# Cases

### CASE 39–1
## Voidable Preferences
## *UNION BANK v. WOLAS*
Supreme Court of the United States, 1991
502 U.S. 151, 112 S.Ct. 527, 116 L.Ed.2d 514

STEVENS, J.
Section 547(b) of the Bankruptcy Code . . . authorizes a trustee to avoid certain property transfers made by a debtor within 90 days before bankruptcy. The Code makes an exception, however, for transfers made in the ordinary course of business, [Section 547(c)(2)]. The question presented is whether payments on long-term debt may qualify for that exception.

On December 17, 1986, ZZZZ Best Co., Inc. (Debtor) borrowed seven million dollars from petitioner, Union Bank (Bank). On July 8, 1987, the Debtor filed a voluntary petition under Chapter 7 of the Bankruptcy Code. During the preceding 90-day period, the Debtor had made two interest payments totalling approximately $100,000 and had paid a loan commitment fee of about $2,500 to the Bank. After his appointment as trustee of the Debtor's estate, respondent filed a complaint against the Bank to recover those payments pursuant to § 547(b).

The Bankruptcy Court found that the loans had been made "in the ordinary course of business or financial affairs" of both the Debtor and the Bank, and that both interest payments as well as the payment of the loan commitment fee had been made according to ordinary business terms and in the ordinary course of business. As a matter of law, the Bankruptcy Court concluded that the payments satisfied the requirements of § 547(c)(2) and therefore were not avoidable by the trustee. The District Court affirmed the Bankruptcy Court's summary judgment in favor of the Bank.

Shortly thereafter, in another case, the Court of Appeals held that the ordinary course of business exception to avoidance of preferential transfers was not available to long-term creditors. [Citation.] In reaching that conclusion, the Court of Appeals relied primarily on the policies underlying the voidable preference provisions and the state of the law prior to the enactment of the 1978 Bankruptcy Code and its amendment in 1984. Thus, the Ninth Circuit concluded, its holding in [citation] dictated a reversal in this case. [Citation.] The importance of the question of law decided by the Ninth Circuit, coupled with the fact that the Sixth Circuit had interpreted § 547(c)(2) in a contrary manner, [citation], persuaded us to grant the Bank's petition for certiorari. [Citation.]

We shall discuss the history and policy of § 547 after examining its text. In subsection (b), Congress broadly authorized bankruptcy trustees to "avoid any transfer of an interest of the debtor in property" if five conditions are satisfied and unless one of seven exceptions defined in subsection (c) is applicable. In brief, the five characteristics of a voidable preference are that it (1) benefit a creditor; (2) be on account of antecedent debt; (3) be made while the debtor was insolvent; (4) be within 90 days before bankruptcy; and (5) enable the creditor to receive a larger share of the estate than if the transfer had not been made. Section 547 also provides that the debtor is presumed to have been insolvent during the 90-day period preceding bankruptcy. [Citation.] In this case, it is undisputed that all five of the foregoing conditions were satisfied and that the interest and loan commitment fee payments were voidable preferences unless excepted by subsection (c)(2).

The most significant feature of subsection (c)(2) that is relevant to this case is the absence of any language distinguishing between long-term debt and short-term debt. That subsection provides:

The trustee may not avoid under this section a transfer—
(2) to the extent that such transfer was—

(A) in payment of a debt incurred by the debtor in the ordinary course of business or financial affairs of the debtor and the transferee;
(B) made in the ordinary course of business or financial affairs of the debtor and the transferee; and
(C) made according to ordinary business terms.

Instead of focusing on the term of the debt for which the transfer was made, subsection (c)(2) focuses on whether the debt was incurred, and payment made, in the "ordinary course of business or financial affairs" of the debtor and transferee. Thus, the text provides no support for respondent's contention that § 547(c)(2)'s coverage is limited to short-term debt, such as commercial paper or trade debt. Given the clarity of the statutory text, respondent's burden of persuading us that Congress intended to create or to preserve a special rule for long-term debt is exceptionally heavy. [Citation.] As did the Ninth Circuit, respondent relies on the history and the policies underlying the preference provision.

\* \* \*

The Bank and the trustee agree that § 547 is intended to serve two basic policies that are fairly described in the House Committee Report. The Committee explained:

A preference is a transfer that enables a creditor to receive payment of a greater percentage of his claim against the debtor than he would have received if the transfer had not been made and he had participated in the distribution of the assets of the bankrupt estate. The purpose of the preference section is two-fold. First, by permitting the trustee to avoid prebankruptcy transfers that occur within a short period before bankruptcy, creditors are discouraged from racing to the courthouse to dismember the debtor during his slide into bankruptcy. The protection thus afforded the debtor often enables him to work his way out of a difficult financial situation through cooperation with all of his creditors. Second, and more important, the preference provisions facilitate the prime bankruptcy policy of equality of distribution among creditors of the debtor. Any creditor that received a greater payment than others of his class is required to disgorge so that all may share equally. The operation of the preference section to deter 'the race of diligence' of creditors to dismember the debtor before bankruptcy furthers the second goal of the preference section—that of equality of distribution.

[Citation.] As this comment demonstrates, the two policies are not entirely independent. On the one hand, any exception for a payment on account of an antecedent debt tends to favor the payee over other creditors and therefore may conflict with the policy of equal treatment. On the other hand, the ordinary course of business exception may benefit all creditors by deterring the "race to the courthouse" and enabling the struggling debtor to continue operating its business.

\* \* \*

But the statutory text—which makes no distinction between short-term debt and long-term debt—precludes an analysis that divorces the policy of favoring equal distribution from the policy of discouraging creditors from racing to the courthouse to dismember the debtor. Long-term creditors, as well as trade creditors, may seek a head start in that race. Thus, even if we accept the Court of Appeals' conclusion that the availability of the ordinary business exception to long-term creditors does not directly further the policy of equal treatment, we must recognize that it does further the policy of deterring the race to the courthouse and, as the House Report recognized, may indirectly further the goal of equal distribution as well. Whether Congress has wisely balanced the sometimes conflicting policies underlying § 547 is not a question that we are authorized to decide.

In sum, we hold that payments on long-term debt, as well as payments on short-term debt, may qualify for the ordinary course of business exception to the trustee's power to avoid preferential transfers. \* \* \*

The judgment of the Court of Appeals is reversed and the case is remanded for further proceedings consistent with this opinion.

It is so ordered.

---

## CASE 39–2
## Proceedings in Chapter 11
### IN RE JOHNS—MANVILLE CORPORATION
United States Bankruptcy Court, Southern District of New York, 1984
36 B.R. 727

LIFLAND, BKRTCY. J.
Whether an industrial enterprise in the United States is highly successful is often gauged by its "membership" in what has come to be known as the "Fortune 500." Having attained this measure of financial achievement, Johns-Manville Corp. and its affiliated companies (collectively referred to as "Manville") were deemed a

paradigm of success in corporate America by the financial community. Thus, Manville's filing for protection under Chapter 11 . . . of the United States Code ("the Code or the Bankruptcy Code") on August 26, 1982 ("the filing date") was greeted with great surprise and consternation on the part of some of its creditors and other corporations that were being sued along with

Manville for injuries caused by asbestos exposure. As discussed at length herein, Manville submits that the sole factor necessitating its filing is the mammoth problem of uncontrolled proliferation of asbestos health suits brought against it because of its substantial use for many years of products containing asbestos which injured those who came into contact with the dust of this lethal substance. According to Manville, this current problem of approximately 16,000 lawsuits pending as of the filing date is compounded by the crushing economic burden to be suffered by Manville over the next 20–30 years by the filing of an even more staggering number of suits by those who had been exposed but who will not manifest the asbestos-related diseases until some time during this future period ("the future asbestos claimants"). Indeed, approximately 6,000 asbestos health claims are estimated to have arisen in only the first 16 months since the filing date. This burden is further compounded by the insurance industry's general disavowal of liability to Manville on policies written for this very purpose. * * *

It is the propriety of the filing by Manville which is the subject of the instant decision. Four separate motions to dismiss the petition . . . have been lodged before this Court.

* * *

Preliminarily, it must be stated that there is no question that Manville is eligible to be a debtor under the Code's statutory requirements.

* * *

Moreover, it should also be noted that [no] . . . provision relating to voluntary petitions by companies contains any insolvency requirement.

* * *

Accordingly, it is abundantly clear that Manville has met all of the threshold eligibility requirements for filing a voluntary petition under the Code. This Court will now turn to the issue of whether any of the movants have demonstrated sufficient "cause" . . . to warrant the dismissal of Manville's petition.

* * *

A "principal goal" of the Bankruptcy Code is to provide "open access" to the "bankruptcy process." [Citation.] The rationale behind this "open access" policy is to provide access to bankruptcy relief which is as "open" as "access to the credit economy." [Citation.] Thus, Congress intended that "there should be no legal barrier to voluntary petitions." [Citation.] Another major goal of the Code, that of "rehabilitation of debtors", requires that relief for debtors must be "timely." [Citation.]

* * *

Accordingly, the drafters of the Code envisioned that a financially beleaguered debtor with real debt and real creditors should not be required to wait until the economic situation is beyond repair in order to file a reorganization petition. The "Congressional purpose" in enacting the Code was to encourage resort to the bankruptcy process. [Citation.] This philosophy not only comports with the elimination of an insolvency requirement, but also is a corollary of the key aim of Chapter 11 of the Code, that of avoidance of liquidation. The drafters of the Code announced this goal, declaring that reorganization is more efficient than liquidation because "assets that are used for production in the industry for which they were designed are more valuable than those same assets sold for scrap." [Citation.] Moreover, reorganization also fosters the goals of preservation of jobs in the threatened entity. [Citation.]

In the instant case, not only would liquidation be wasteful and inefficient in destroying the utility of valuable assets of the companies as well as jobs, but, more importantly, liquidation would preclude just compensation of some present asbestos victims and all future asbestos claimants. This unassailable reality represents all the more reason for this Court to adhere to this basic potential liquidation avoidance aim of Chapter 11 and deny the motions to dismiss. Manville must not be required to wait until its economic picture has deteriorated beyond salvation to file for reorganization.

* * *

In [this case] it is undeniable that there has been no sham or hoax perpetrated on the Court in that Manville is a real business with real creditors in pressing need of economic reorganization. Indeed, the Asbestos Committee has belied its own contention that Manville has no debt and no real creditors by quantifying a benchmark settlement demand approaching one billion dollars for compensation of approximately 15,500 pre-petition asbestos claimants, during the course of negotiations pitched toward achieving a consensual plan. This huge asserted liability does not even take into account the estimated 6,000 new asbestos health claims which have arisen in only the first 16 months since the filing date. The number of post-filing claims increases each day as "future claims back into the present." * * *

Moreover, asbestos related property damage claims present another substantial contingent and unliquidated liability. Prior to the filing date, various schools initiated litigation seeking compensatory and punitive damages from . . . Manville for their unknowing use of asbestos-containing products in ceilings, walls, structural members, piping, ductwork and boilers in school buildings.

* * *

Accordingly, it is clear that Manville's liability for compensatory, if not punitive, damages to school authorities is not hypothetical, but real and massive debt. A range of $500 million to $1.4 billion is the total projected amount of Manville's real debt to the school creditors.

In addition, claims of $425 million of liquidated commercial debt have been filed in this proceeding. The filing also triggered the acceleration of more than $275 million in unsecured public and institutional debt which had not been due prior to the filing. Upon a dismissal of this petition, Manville may be liable in the amount of all of the above-described real debts, plus interest. Manville's present holdings of cash and liquid assets would be insufficient to pay these obligations and, as noted above, its insurance carriers have repeatedly expressed their unwillingness to contribute to the payment of this debt. Thus, upon dismissal, Manville would become a target for economic dismemberment, liquidation, and chaos, which would benefit no one except the few winners of the race to the courthouse. The economic reality of Manville's highly precarious financial position due to massive debt sustains its eligibility and candidacy for reorganization.

In short, there was justification for Manville to elect a course contemplating a viable court-supervised rehabilitation of the real debt owed by Manville to its real creditors. Manville's filing did not in the appropriate sense abuse the jurisdiction of this Court and it is indeed, like the debtor in (citation), a "once viable business supporting employees and unsecured creditors (which) has more recently been burdened with judgments (and suits) that threaten to put it out of existence." . . . [Citation.] Thus, its petition must be sustained.

* * *

In sum, Manville is a financially beseiged enterprise in desperate need of reorganization of its crushing real debt, both present and future. The reorganization provisions of the Code were drafted with the aim of liquidation avoidance by great access to Chapter 11. Accordingly, Manville's filing does not abuse the jurisdictional integrity of this Court, but rather presents the same kinds of reasons that were present in [citation], for awaiting the determination of Manville's good faith until it is considered . . . as a prerequisite to confirmation or as a part of the cadre of motions before me which are scheduled to be heard subsequently.

[Motions to dismiss the Manville petition denied.]

---

### CASE 39–3
## Confirmation of Chapter 13 Plan
### *ASSOCIATES COMMERCIAL CORPORATION v. RASH*

Supreme Court of the United States, 1997
_____ U.S. _____, 117 S.Ct. 1879, 138 L.Ed.2d 148

GINSBURG, J.
[In 1989, Elray Rash purchased for $73,700 a Kenworth tractor truck for use in his freight-hauling business. Rash made a downpayment on the truck, agreed to pay the seller the remainder in 60 monthly installments, and pledged the truck as collateral on the unpaid balance. The seller assigned the loan, and its lien on the truck, to Associates Commercial Corporation (ACC). In March 1992, Elray and Jean Rash filed a joint petition and a repayment plan under Chapter 13 of the Bankruptcy Code. At the time of the bankruptcy filing, the balance owed to ACC on the truck loan was $41,171. The Rashes' Chapter 13 plan invoked the cram down power. It proposed that the Rashes retain the truck for use in the freight-hauling business and pay ACC, over 58 months, an amount equal to the present value of the truck. That value, the Rashes' petition alleged, was $28,500. ACC objected to the plan and asked the Bankruptcy Court to lift the automatic stay so ACC could repossess the truck. ACC also filed a proof of claim alleging that its claim was fully secured in the amount of $41,171. The Rashes filed an objection to ACC's claim.

At an evidentiary hearing held to resolve the dispute, ACC maintained that the proper valuation was the price the Rashes would have to pay to purchase a like vehicle (the replacement-value standard), estimated to be $41,000. The Rashes, however, maintained that the proper valuation was the net amount ACC would realize upon foreclosure and sale of the collateral (the foreclosure-value standard), estimated to be $31,875. The Bankruptcy Court adopted the Rashes' valuation figure and approved the plan. The District Court and the Fifth Circuit affirmed.]

To qualify for confirmation under Chapter 13, the Rashes' plan had to satisfy the requirements set forth in § 1325(a) of the Code. The Rashes' treatment of

ACC's secured claim, in particular, is governed by subsection (a)(5). Under this provision, a plan's proposed treatment of secured claims can be confirmed if one of three conditions is satisfied: the secured creditor accepts the plan, the debtor surrenders the property securing the claim to the creditor, or the debtor invokes the so-called "cram down" power. Under the cram down option, the debtor is permitted to keep the property over the objection of the creditor; the creditor retains the lien securing the claim, and the debtor is required to provide the creditor with payments, over the life of the plan, that will total the present value of the allowed secured claim, i.e., the present value of the collateral. The value of the allowed secured claim is governed by § 506(a) of the Code.

\* \* \*

Courts of Appeals have adopted three different standards for valuing a security interest in a bankruptcy proceeding when the debtor invokes the cram down power to retain the collateral over the creditor's objection. In contrast to the Fifth Circuit's foreclosure-value standard, a number of Circuits have followed a replacement-value approach. [Citation.] Other courts have settled on the midpoint between foreclosure value and replacement value.

The Bankruptcy Code provision central to the resolution of this case is § 506(a), which states:

"An allowed claim of a creditor secured by a lien on property in which the estate has an interest . . . is a secured claim to the extent of the value of such creditor's interest in the estate's interest in such property, . . . and is an unsecured claim to the extent that the value of such creditor's interest . . . is less than the amount of such allowed claim. Such value shall be determined in light of the purpose of the valuation and of the proposed disposition or use of such property. . . ." [Citation.]

\* \* \*

We do not find in the § 506(a) first sentence words—"the creditor's interest in the estate's interest in such property"—the foreclosure-value meaning advanced by the Fifth Circuit. Even read in isolation, the phrase imparts no valuation standard: A direction simply to consider the "value of such creditor's interest" does not expressly reveal how that interest is to be valued.

Reading the first sentence of § 506(a) as a whole, we are satisfied that the phrase the Fifth Circuit considered key is not an instruction to equate a "creditor's interest" with the net value a creditor could realize through a foreclosure sale. The first sentence, in its entirety, tells us that a secured creditor's claim is to

be divided into secured and unsecured portions, with the secured portion of the claim limited to the value of the collateral. [Citation.] To separate the secured from the unsecured portion of a claim, a court must compare the creditor's claim to the value of "such property," i.e., the collateral. \* \* \* The full first sentence of § 506(a), in short, tells a court what it must evaluate, but it does not say more; it is not enlightening on how to value collateral.

The second sentence of § 506(a) does speak to the how question. "Such value," that sentence provides, "shall be determined in light of the purpose of the valuation and of the proposed disposition or use of such property." § 506(a). By deriving a foreclosure-value standard from § 506(a)'s first sentence, the Fifth Circuit rendered inconsequential the sentence that expressly addresses how "value shall be determined."

As we comprehend § 506(a), the "proposed disposition or use" of the collateral is of paramount importance to the valuation question. If a secured creditor does not accept a debtor's Chapter 13 plan, the debtor has two options for handling allowed secured claims: surrender the collateral to the creditor; or, under the cram down option, keep the collateral over the creditor's objection and provide the creditor, over the life of the plan, with the equivalent of the present value of the collateral. The "disposition or use" of the collateral thus turns on the alternative the debtor chooses—in one case the collateral will be surrendered to the creditor, and in the other, the collateral will be retained and used by the debtor. Applying a foreclosure-value standard when the cram down option is invoked attributes no significance to the different consequences of the debtor's choice to surrender the property or retain it. A replacement-value standard, on the other hand, distinguishes retention from surrender and renders meaningful the key words "disposition or use."

Tying valuation to the actual "disposition or use" of the property points away from a foreclosure-value standard when a Chapter 13 debtor, invoking cram down power, retains and uses the property. Under that option, foreclosure is averted by the debtor's choice and over the creditor's objection. From the creditor's perspective as well as the debtor's, surrender and retention are not equivalent acts.

When a debtor surrenders the property, a creditor obtains it immediately, and is free to sell it and reinvest the proceeds. We recall here that ACC sought that very advantage. [Citation.] If a debtor keeps the property and continues to use it, the creditor obtains at once neither the property nor its value and is exposed to double risks:

The debtor may again default and the property may deteriorate from extended use. * * *

Of prime significance, the replacement-value standard accurately gauges the debtor's "use" of the property. It values "the creditor's interest in the collateral in light of the proposed [repayment plan] reality: no foreclosure sale and economic benefit for the debtor derived from the collateral equal to . . . its [replacement] value." [Citation.] The debtor in this case elected to use the collateral to generate an income stream. That actual use, rather than a foreclosure sale that will not take place, is the proper guide under a prescription hinged to the property's "disposition or use."

* * *

Nor are we persuaded that the split-the-difference approach adopted by the Seventh Circuit provides the appropriate solution. [Citation.] Whatever the attractiveness of a standard that picks the midpoint between foreclosure and replacement values, there is no warrant for it in the Code. Section 506(a) calls for the value the property possesses in light of the "disposition or use" in fact "proposed," not the various dispositions or uses that might have been proposed. * * *

In sum, under § 506(a), the value of property retained because the debtor has exercised the § 1325(a)(5)(B) "cram down" option is the cost the debtor would incur to obtain a like asset for the same "proposed . . . use."

For the foregoing reasons, the judgment of the Court of Appeals is reversed, and the case is remanded for further proceedings consistent with this opinion.

# Questions

1. Explain (a) the requirements for voluntary and involuntary cases, (b) the priorities of creditors' claims, (c) the debtor's exemptions, and (d) the debts that are not dischargeable in bankruptcy.

2. Discuss the duties of a trustee and his rights (a) as a lien creditor, (b) to avoid preferential transfers, (c) to avoid fraudulent transfers, and (d) to avoid statutory liens.

3. Explain the procedure involved in distributing the debtor's estate under Chapter 7.

4. Compare the adjustment of debt proceedings under Chapters 11 and 13.

5. Identify and define the nonbankruptcy compromises between debtors and creditors.

# Problems

1. (a) Benson goes into bankruptcy. His estate has no assets. Are Benson's taxes discharged by the proceedings? Why or why not?

(b) Benson obtains property from Anderson on credit by representing that he is solvent when in fact he knows he is insolvent. Is Benson's debt to Anderson discharged by Benson's discharge in bankruptcy?

2. Bradley goes into bankruptcy owing $5,000 as wages to his four employees. There is enough in his estate to pay all costs of administration and enough to pay his employees, but nothing will be left for general creditors. Do the employees take all the estate? If so, under what conditions? If the general creditors received nothing, would these debts be discharged?

3. Jessica sold goods to Stacy for $2,500 and retained a security interest in them. Three months later, Stacy filed a petition in bankruptcy under Chapter 7. At this time, Stacy still owed Jessica $2,000 for the purchase price of the goods, whose value was $1,500.

(a) May the trustee invalidate Jessica's security interest? If so, under what provision?

(b) If the security interest is invalidated, what is Jessica's status in the bankruptcy proceeding?

(c) If the security interest is not invalidated, what is Jessica's status in the bankruptcy proceeding?

4. A debtor went through bankruptcy and received his discharge. Which of the following debts were completely discharged, and which will remain as future debts against him?

(a) A claim of $900 for wages earned within three months immediately prior to bankruptcy.

(b) A judgment of $3,000 against the debtor for breach of contract.

(c) $1,000 in past alimony and support money owed to his divorced wife for herself and their child.

(d) A judgment of $4,000 for injuries received because of the debtor's negligent operation of an automobile.

5. Rosinoff and his wife, who were business partners, entered bankruptcy. A creditor, Baldwin, objected to their discharge in bankruptcy on the grounds that

(a) the partners had obtained credit from Baldwin on the basis of a false financial statement;

(b)  the partners had failed to keep books of account and records from which their financial condition could be ascertained; and

(c)  Rosinoff had falsely sworn that he had taken $70 from the partnership account when the amount he took was actually $700.

Were the debtors entitled to a discharge?

**6.**  Ross Corporation is a debtor in a reorganization proceeding under Chapter 11 of the Bankruptcy Code. By fair and proper valuation, its assets are worth $100,000. The indebtedness of the corporation is $105,000, and it has outstanding $100 par value preferred stock in the amount of $20,000 and $30 par value common stock in the amount of $75,000. The plan of reorganization submitted by the trustees would give nothing to the common shareholders, bonds of the face amount of $5,000 to the creditors, and common stock in the ratio of 84 percent to the creditors and 16 percent to the preferred shareholders. Should this plan be confirmed?

**7.**  Alex is a wage earner with a regular income. He has unsecured debts of $42,000 and secured debts owing to Betty, Connie, David, and Eunice totaling $120,000. Eunice's debt is secured only by a mortgage on Alex's house. Alex files a petition under Chapter 13 and a plan providing payment as follows: (a) 60 percent of all taxes owed, (b) 35 percent of all unsecured debts, and (c) $100,000 in total to Betty, Connie, David, and Eunice. Should the court confirm the plan? If not, how must the plan be modified and/or what other conditions must be satisfied?

**8.**  John Bunker has assets of $130,000 and liabilities of $185,000 owed to nine creditors. Nonetheless, his cash flow is positive, and he is making payment on all of his obligations as they become due. I. M. Flintheart, who is owed $22,000 by Bunker, files an involuntary petition in bankruptcy against Bunker. Bunker contests the petition. Decision?

**9.**  Karen has filed a petition for a Chapter 7 proceeding. The total value of her estate is $35,000. Ben, who is owed $18,000, has a security interest in property valued at $12,000. Lauren has an unsecured claim of $9,000, which is entitled to a priority of $2,000. The United States has a claim for income taxes of $7,000. Steve has an unsecured claim of $10,000 that was filed on time. Sarah has an unsecured claim of $17,000 that was filed on time. Wally has a claim of $14,000 that he filed late, even though he was aware of the bankruptcy proceedings. What should each of the creditors receive in a distribution under Chapter 7?

**10.**  Landmark at Plaza Park, Ltd., filed a plan of reorganization under Chapter 11 of the Bankruptcy Code. Landmark is a limited partnership whose only substantial asset is a 200-unit garden apartment complex. City Federal holds the first mortgage on the property in the face amount of $2,250,000. The mortgage bears an interest rate of 9.5 percent and is due and payable six years from now.

Landmark has proposed a plan of reorganization under which the property now in possession of City Federal would be returned. Landmark will then deliver a nonrecourse note, payable in three years, in the face amount of $2,705,820.31 to City Federal in substitution of all of the partnership's existing liabilities. On the sixteenth month through the thirty-sixth month after the effective date of the plan, Landmark will make monthly interest payments at a rate of 12.5 percent computed on a property value of $2,260,000. Finally, the note will be secured by the existing mortgage. Landmark's theory is that the note will be paid off at the end of thirty-six months by a combination of refinancing and accumulation of cash from the project. The key is Landmark's proposal to obtain a new first mortgage in three years in the face amount of $2,400,000.

City Federal is a first mortgagee without recourse that has been collecting rents pursuant to a rent assignment agreement since the default on the mortgage eleven months ago. City Federal is impaired by the plan, has rejected the plan, and seeks to complete its foreclosure action. Decision?

**11.**  Freelin Conn filed a voluntary petition under Chapter 7 of the Bankruptcy Code on September 30, 1980. Conn listed BancOhio National Bank as having a claim incurred in October of 1979 in the amount of $4,000 secured by a 1978 Oldsmobile Omega. The car is listed as having a market value of $3,500. During the period from June 30, 1980, to September 30, 1980, Conn made three payments totaling $439.17 to BancOhio. The net payoff balance on the installment loan was $4,015.91 on September 30, the date on which the bankruptcy petition was filed. The trustee in bankruptcy now seeks to set aside those three payments as voidable preferences. Decision?

**12.**  On March 6, 1985, the debtor negotiated a loan with Interfirst Bank of Dallas (the Bank) and signed a promissory note for the purchase of a BMW from Howard Thornton Ford for his daughter. The daughter picked up the car on March 8, 1985, but the Bank did not perfect the purchase money security interest until March 19, 1985, which date was within the twenty-day limit for perfecting a purchase money security interest under Texas law. On May 23, 1985, the debtor filed a bankruptcy petition, and on August 25, 1985, the Bank repossessed the daughter's BMW. The bankruptcy trustee sought recovery of the BMW as an asset of the estate, arguing that the transfer of the collateral (the BMW) to the Bank was a voidable preference under the Bankruptcy Code because the Bank's security interest in the car was not perfected within the ten-day grace period then required by the Bankruptcy Code. The bankruptcy court held for the trustee, and the district court affirmed. The Bank appealed. Decision?

**13.**  Yolanda Christophe filed her Chapter 13 petition on April 19, 1992. Her scheduled debts consists of $11,100 of secured debt, $9,300 owed on an unsecured student loan, and $6,960 of other unsecured debt. Christophe asserts that the student loan is nondischargeable under § 23(a)(8), and that assertion has not been questioned. However, none of the details of this loan were presented as evidence before the Court. Christophe's proposed amended Chapter 13 Plan calls for 56 monthly payments of $440 a month. The questioned provision in that Plan is the division of the unsecured creditors into two classes. The general unsecured creditors would receive 32 percent, while the separately classified student loan creditor would receive 100 percent. Decision?

WWW **Internet Exercise** Using the American Bankruptcy Institute's site, find for the most recent year available (a) the total number of bankruptcy filings, (b) the number of nonbusiness filings according to chapter of the Bankruptcy Code, and (c) the number of business filings.

# CHAPTER 40

# Protection of Intellectual Property

The economic system in the United States is based upon free and fair competition. The law prevents businesses from taking unfair advantage of their competitors. Essential to this legal prevention is the protection of intellectual property, which includes trade secrets, trade symbols, copyrights, and patents. These interests are protected from **infringement,** or unauthorized use, by others. Such protection is essential to the conduct of business. For example, a business would be far less willing to invest considerable resources in research and development if the resulting discoveries, inventions, and processes were not protected by patents and trade secrets. Similarly, a company would not be secure in devoting time and money to marketing its products and services without laws that protect its trade symbols and trade names. Moreover, without copyright protection, the publishing, entertainment, and computer software industries would be vulnerable to piracy, both by corporate competitors and by the general public. This chapter will discuss the law protecting (1) trade secrets; (2) trade symbols, including trademarks, service marks, certification marks, collective marks, and trade names; (3) copyrights; and (4) patents.

## *TRADE SECRETS*

Every business has secret information. Such information may include customer lists or contracts with suppliers and customers; it also may comprise formulas, processes, and production methods that are vital to the successful operation of the business. A business may disclose a trade secret in confidence to an employee with the understanding that the employee will not reveal the information to others. To the extent the owner of the information obtains a patent on it, it is no longer a trade secret but is protected by patent law. Some businesses, however, choose not to obtain a patent because it provides protection for only a limited time, whereas State trade secret

law protects a trade secret as long as it is kept secret. Moreover, if the courts invalidate a patent, the information will have been disclosed to competitors without the owner of the information obtaining any benefit. The Uniform Trade Secrets Act, promulgated in 1979 and amended in 1985, has been adopted by more than forty States.

## Definition

A **trade secret** is commercially valuable information that is guarded from disclosure and is not general knowledge. The Uniform Trade Secrets Act defines a trade secret as

information, including a formula, pattern, compilation, program, device, method, technique, or process, that:

(i) derives independent economic value, actual or potential, from not being generally known to, and not being readily ascertainable by proper means by, other persons who can obtain economic value from its disclosure or use, and
(ii) is the subject of efforts that are reasonable under the circumstances to maintain its secrecy.

A famous example of a trade secret is the formula for Coca-Cola.

## Misappropriation

Misappropriation of a trade secret is the wrongful use of a trade secret. A person misappropriates a trade secret of another (1) by knowingly acquiring it through improper means or (2) by disclosing or using it without consent, if her knowledge of the trade secret came under circumstances giving rise to a duty to maintain secrecy or came from a person who used improper means or who owed the owner of the trade secret a duty to maintain secrecy. Trade secrets are most frequently misappropriated in two ways: (1) an employee wrongfully uses or discloses such information, or (2) a competitor wrongfully obtains it.

An employee is under a duty of loyalty to his employer, which, among other responsibilities, obligates the employee not to disclose trade secrets to competitors. It is wrongful, in turn, for a competitor to obtain vital secret trade information from an employee through bribery or other means. Besides breaching the duty of loyalty, the faithless employee who divulges secret trade information also commits a tort. In the absence of a contract restriction, an employee is under no duty upon termination of his employment to refrain either from competing with a former employer or from working for a competitor of that employer, but he may not use trade secrets or disclose them to third persons. The employee is entitled, however, to use the skill, knowledge, and general information he acquired during the previous employment relationship.

Another improper method of acquiring trade secrets is industrial espionage conducted through methods such as electronic surveillance or spying. Improper means of acquiring another person's trade secrets also include theft, bribery, fraud, unauthorized interception of communications, and inducement or knowing participation in a breach of confidence. In the broadest sense, discovering another's trade secrets by any means other than independent research or personal inspection of the publicly available finished product is improper unless the other party voluntarily discloses the secret or fails to take reasonable precautions to protect its secrecy.

## Remedies

Remedies for misappropriation of trade secrets are damages and, where appropriate, injunctive relief. Damages are awarded in the amount of either the pecuniary loss to the plaintiff caused by the misappropriation or the pecuniary gain to the defendant, whichever is greater. A court will grant an injunction to prevent a continuing or threatened misappropriation of a trade secret for as long as is necessary to protect the plaintiff from any harm attributable to the misappropriation and to deprive the defendant of any economic advantage attributable to the misappropriation.

 *See Case 40–1*

## Criminal Penalties

In 1996 Congress enacted the Economic Espionage Act of 1996 prohibiting the theft of trade secrets and providing criminal penalties for violations. (The statute does not provide any civil remedies.) The statute defines trade secrets to mean "all forms and types of financial, business, scientific, technical, economic, or engineering information, including patterns, plans, compilations, program devices, formulas, designs, prototypes, methods, techniques, processes, procedures, programs, or codes, whether tangible or intangible, and whether or how stored, compiled, or memorialized physically, electronically, graphically, photographically, or in writing if (A) the owner thereof has taken reasonable measures to keep such information secret; and (B) the information derives independent economic value, actual or potential, from not being generally known to, and not being readily ascertainable through proper means by the public."

The act broadly defines theft to include all types of conversion of trade secrets, including

1. stealing, obtaining by fraud, or concealing such information;
2. without authorization copying, duplicating, sketching, drawing, photographing, downloading, uploading, photocopying, or mailing such information;
3. purchasing or possessing a trade secret with knowledge that it had been stolen.

The act punishes thefts of trade secrets, as well as attempts and conspiracies to steal secrets, with fines of up to $500,000, imprisonment for up to 10 years, or both. Organizations that violate the act are subject to fines of up to $5 million.

## TRADE SYMBOLS

One of the earliest forms of unfair competition was the fraudulent marketing of one person's goods as those of another. Still common today, this unlawful practice is sometimes referred to as "passing off" or "palming off." Basically the process of "cashing in" on the goodwill, good name, and reputation of a competitor and of his products, this fraudulent marketing deceives the public and deprives honest businesses of trade. Section 43(a) of the Federal Trademark Act (the Lanham Act) prohibits businesses from using a false designation of origin in connection with any goods or services. This section also prohibits a business from falsely describing or representing its own goods and services. In 1988, this section was amended to prohibit the misrepresentations of *another* entity's goods, services, or commercial activities.

The Lanham Act also established Federal registration of trade symbols and protection against misuse or infringement by injunctive relief and a right of action for damages against the infringer. A form of passing off one's goods or services as those of the owner of the mark, an infringement deceives the public and constitutes unfair competition.

## Types of Trade Symbols

The Lanham Act recognizes four types of trade symbols or **marks.** A **trademark** is a distinctive mark, word, letter, number, design, picture, or combination in any arrangement that a person adopts or uses to identify goods that he manufactures or sells and to distinguish them from those manufactured or sold by others. Examples of trademarks include Kodak, Xerox, and the rainbow apple logo on Apple computers. A trademark can also consist of goods' "trade dress," which is the appearance or image of goods as presented to prospective purchasers. Trade dress would include the distinctive but nonfunctional design of packaging, labels, containers, and the product itself or its features. Examples include the Campbell Soup label and the shape of the Coca-Cola bottle. Internet domain names that are used to identify and distinguish the goods or services of one person from the goods or services of others and to indicate the source of the goods and services may be registered as trademarks. To qualify, an applicant must show that it offers services via the Internet and that it uses the Internet domain name as a source identifier.

Similar in function to the trademark, which identifies tangible goods and products, a **service mark** is used to identify and distinguish one person's services from those of others. For example, the titles, character names, and other distinctive features of radio and television shows may be registered as service marks. Service marks may also consist of trade dress such as the décor or shape of buildings in which services are provided. Examples include the Fotomart kiosk and Howard Johnson's orange roof.

A **certification mark** is used upon or in connection with goods or services to certify their regional or other origin, composition, mode of manufacture, quality, accuracy, or other characteristics or to certify that members of a union or other organization performed the work or labor in such goods or services. The marks "Good Housekeeping Seal of Approval" and "Underwriter's Laboratory" are examples of certification marks. The owner of the certification mark does *not* produce or provide the goods or services with which the mark is used.

A **collective mark** is a distinctive mark or symbol used to indicate either that the producer or provider is a member of a trade union, trade association, fraternal society, or other organization or that the goods or services are produced by members of a collective group. As in the case of a certification mark, the owner of a collective mark is not the producer or provider but rather is the group of which the producer or provider is a member. An example of a collective mark is the union mark attached to a product to indicate its manufacture by a unionized company.

## Registration

To be protected by the Lanham Act, a mark must be distinctive enough to identify clearly the origin of goods or services. A trade symbol may satisfy the distinctiveness requirement in either of two ways. First, it may be **"inherently distinctive"** if prospective purchasers are likely to associate it with the product or service it designates because of the nature of the designation and the context in which it is used. Fanciful or arbitrary marks satisfy the distinctiveness requirement. In contrast, a descriptive or geographic designation is *not* inherently distinctive. Such a designation is one that is likely to be perceived by prospective purchasers as merely descriptive of the nature, qualities, or other characteristics of the goods or service with which it is used. Thus, the word *Plow* cannot be a trademark for plows, although it may be a trademark for shoes.

Descriptive or geographic designations may, however, satisfy the distinctiveness requirement through the second method: acquiring distinctiveness through a "secondary meaning." A designation acquires a **secondary meaning** when a substantial number of prospective purchasers associate the designation with the product or service it identifies.

A **generic designation** is one that is understood by prospective purchasers to denominate the general category, type, or class of goods or services with which it is used. A user cannot acquire rights in a generic designation as a trade symbol. Moreover, a trade symbol will lose its eligibility for protection if prospective purchasers come to perceive a trade symbol primarily as a generic designation for the category, type, or class of goods or services with which it is used. Under the Lanham Act, the test for when this has occurred is "the primary significance of the registered mark to the relevant public rather than purchaser motivation." Examples of marks that have lost protection because they became generic include "aspirin," "thermos," and "cellophane."

Federal registration is denied to marks that are immoral, deceptive, or scandalous. Marks may not be registered if they disparage or falsely suggest a connection with persons, living or dead; institutions; beliefs; or national symbols. In addition, a trademark may not consist of the flag, coat of arms, or other insignia of the United States or of any State, municipality, or foreign nation.

To obtain Federal protection, which has a ten-year term with unlimited ten-year renewals, the mark must be registered with the Patent and Trademark Office. An applicant must either (1) have actually used the mark in commerce or (2) demonstrate a *bona fide* intent to use the mark in commerce and actually use it within six months.

Registration provides numerous advantages. It gives nationwide constructive notice of the mark to all later users. It permits the registrant to use the Federal courts to enforce the mark and constitutes *prima facie* evidence of the registrant's exclusive right to use the mark. This right becomes incontestable, subject to certain specified limitations, after five years. Finally, registration provides the registrant with Customs Bureau protection against imports that threaten to infringe upon the mark.

To retain trademark protection, the owner of a mark must not abandon it by failing to make *bona fide* use of it in the ordinary course of trade. Abandonment occurs when an owner does not use a mark and no longer intends to use it. Three years of nonuse raises a presumption of abandonment which the owner may rebut by proving her intent to resume use.

 *See Case 40–2*

## Infringement

Infringement of a mark occurs when a person without authorization uses an identical or substantially indistinguishable mark that is likely to cause confusion, to cause mistake, or to deceive. The intent to confuse purchasers is not required, nor is proof of actual confusion, although likelihood of confusion may be inferred from either. Infringement occurs if an appreciable number of ordinarily prudent purchasers are *likely* to be misled or confused as to the source of the goods or services. In deciding whether infringement has occurred, the courts consider various factors, including the strength of the mark, the intent of the unauthorized user, the degree of similarity between the two marks, the relation between the two products or services the marks identify, and the marketing channels through which the goods or services are purchased.

The Federal Trademark Dilution Act of 1995 amended the Lanham Act to protect famous marks from dilution of their distinctive quality. The term *dilution* means the lessening of the capacity of a famous mark to

identify and distinguish goods or services even if the other's use of the mark does not result in the likelihood of confusion, mistake, or deception. In determining whether a mark is distinctive and famous, a court may consider factors such as (1) the degree of inherent or acquired distinctiveness of the mark; (2) the degree of recognition of the mark; (3) the duration and extent of the use, advertising, and publicity of the mark; (4) the geographical extent of the trading area in which the mark is used; and (5) the channels of trade for the goods or services with which the mark is used. The amendment exempts fair use of a famous mark in comparative commercial advertising, noncommercial use of a mark, and mention of a famous mark in news reporting.

## Remedies

The Lanham Act provides several remedies for infringement: (1) injunctive relief, (2) an accounting for profits, (3) damages, (4) destruction of infringing articles, (5) attorneys' fees in exceptional cases, and (6) costs. In assessing profits, the plaintiff has to prove only the gross sales made by the defendant; the defendant has the burden of proving any costs to be deducted in determining profits. If the court finds that the amount of recovery based on profits is either inadequate or excessive, the court may, in its discretion, award an amount it determines to be just. In assessing damages, the court may award up to three times the actual damages, according to the circumstances of the case. When an infringement is knowing and intentional, the court in the absence of extenuating circumstances shall award attorneys' fees plus the greater of treble profits or treble damages. In an action brought under the Federal Trademark Dilution Act of 1995, the owner of the famous mark can obtain only injunctive relief unless the person against whom the injunction is sought willfully intended to trade on the owner's reputation or to cause dilution of the famous mark. If willful intent is proven, the owner of the famous mark may also obtain the other remedies discussed.

Where a counterfeit mark is intentionally and knowingly used, criminal sanctions may be imposed, and goods bearing the counterfeit mark may be destroyed. A **counterfeit mark** is a spurious mark that is identical with, or substantially indistinguishable from, a registered mark. Criminal sanctions include a fine of up to $250,000, imprisonment of up to five years, or both. For a repeat offense, the limits are $1 million and fifteen years, respectively. For a nonindividual offender, such as a corporation, the fine may be up to $1 million for a first offense and up to $5 million for a repeat offense.

## TRADE NAMES

A **trade name** is any name used to identify a business, vocation, or occupation. Descriptive and generic words, and personal and generic names, although not proper trademarks, may become protected as trade names upon acquiring a special significance in the trade. A name acquires such significance, frequently referred to as a "secondary meaning," through its continuing and extended use in connection with specific goods or services, whereby the acquired meaning eclipses the primary meaning of the name in the minds of a substantial number of purchasers or users of the goods or services. Although they are not eligible for Federal registration under the Lanham Act, trade names are protected, and a person who palms off her goods or services by using the trade name of another is liable in damages and also may be enjoined from doing so.

## COPYRIGHTS

**Copyright** is a form of protection provided by Federal law to authors of original works, which, under Section 102 of the Copyright Act, include literary, musical, and dramatic works; pantomimes; choreographic works; pictorial, graphic, and sculptural works; motion picture and other audiovisual works; sound recordings; and architectural works. This listing is illustrative, not exhaustive, as the act extends copyright protection to "original works of authorship in any tangible medium of expression, now known or later developed." Section 102(a). Moreover, in 1980, the Copyright Act was amended to extend copyright protection to computer programs. Furthermore, the Semiconductor Chip Protection Act of 1984 extended protection to safeguard works embodied in a semiconductor chip product.

On March 1, 1989, the United States joined the Berne Convention, an international treaty protecting copyrighted works. In 1998 Congress enacted the Digital Millennium Copyright Act, which amended the Copyright Act to implement the World Intellectual Property Organization (WIPO) Copyright Treaty and the WIPO Performances and Phonograms Treaty of 1996 by extending U.S. copyright protection to works required to be protected under these two treaties.

In no case does the copyright protection accorded an original work of authorship extend to any idea, procedure, process, system, method of operation, concept, principle, or discovery, regardless of the form in which it is described, explained, illustrated, or embodied in such work. Section 102(b). Copyright protection encompasses only an *original expression* of an idea. For example, the idea of interfamily feuding cannot be copyrighted, but a particular expression of that idea in the form of a novel, drama, movie, or opera may be copyrighted.

### Procedure

Copyright applications are filed with the Register of Copyrights in Washington, D.C. Although copyright registration is not required, because copyright protection begins as soon as the work is fixed in a tangible medium, registration is advisable, nonetheless, because it is a condition of certain remedies (statutory damages and attorneys' fees) for copyright infringement. When a work is published, it is advisable, though no longer required, to place a copyright notice on all publicly distributed copies so as to notify users about the copyright claim. If proper notice appears on the published copies to which a defendant in a copyright infringement case had access, then the defendant will be unable to mitigate actual or statutory damages by asserting a defense of innocent infringement. Section 401.

### Rights

As amended in 1998 by the Sonny Bono Copyright Extension Act, in most instances, copyright protection subsists for the duration of the author's life plus an additional 70 years. Section 106 of the Copyright Act gives the owner of the copyright the exclusive right to

1. reproduce the copyrighted work in copies or recordings;
2. prepare derivative works based upon the copyrighted work;
3. distribute copies or recordings of the copyrighted work to the public by sale or other transfer of ownership or by rental, lease, or lending;
4. perform the copyrighted work publicly, in the case of literary, musical, dramatic, choreographic, pantomime, motion picture, and other audiovisual works; and
5. display the copyrighted work publicly, in the case of literary, musical, dramatic, and choreographic works, pantomimes, and pictorial, graphic, or sculptural works, including the individual images of a motion picture or other audiovisual work.

These broad rights are subject, however, to several limitations, the most important of which are "compulsory licenses" and "fair use." **Compulsory licenses** permit certain limited uses of copyrighted material upon the payment of specified royalties and compliance with statutory conditions. Section 107 codifies the common law doctrine of **fair use** by providing that the fair use of a copyrighted work for purposes such as criticism, comment, news reporting, teaching (including multiple copies for classroom use), scholarship, or research is not an infringement of copyright. In determining whether the use made of a work in any particular case is fair, the courts consider the following factors: (1) the purpose and character of the use, including whether such use is of a commercial nature or is for nonprofit educational purposes; (2) the nature of the copyrighted work; (3) the amount and substantiality of the portion used in relation to the copyrighted work as a whole; and (4) the effect of the use upon the potential market for or value of the copyrighted work.

 *See Case 40–3*

## Ownership

The author of a creative work owns the entire copyright. Although the actual creator of a work is usually the author, in two situations under the doctrine of **works for hire,** she is not considered the author. Section 101. First, if an employee prepares a work within the scope of her employment, her employer is considered to be the author of the work. Second, if a work is specially ordered or commissioned for certain purposes specified in the copyright statute *and* the parties expressly agree in writing that the work shall be considered a work for hire, the person commissioning the work is deemed to be the author. The kinds of works subject to becoming works for hire by commission include contributions to collective works; parts of motion pictures or other audio-visual works; translations; supplementary works such as prefaces, illustrations, or afterwords; compilations; instructional texts; and tests.

The ownership of a copyright may be transferred in whole or in part by conveyance, will, or intestate succession. Section 201. A transfer of copyright ownership, other than by operation of law, is not valid, however, unless it is memorialized in a note or memorandum signed by the owner of the rights conveyed or by the owner's duly authorized agent. Section 204. An author may terminate any transfer of copyright ownership, other than that of a work for hire, during the five-year period beginning thirty-five years after the transfer was granted. Section 203.

Ownership of a copyright or of any of the exclusive rights under a copyright is distinct from the ownership

of any material object that embodies the work. Transferring the ownership of any material object, including the copy or recording in which the work was first fixed, does not in itself convey any rights in the copyrighted work embodied in the object; nor, in the absence of an agreement, does the transfer of copyright ownership or of any exclusive rights under a copyright convey property rights in any material object. Section 202. Thus, the purchase of this textbook neither affects the publisher's copyright nor authorizes the purchaser to make and sell copies of the book. The purchaser may, however, rent, lend, or resell the book.

## Infringement and Remedies

Infringement occurs whenever somebody exercises, without authorization, the rights exclusively reserved for the copyright owner. Infringement need not be intentional. To prove infringement, the plaintiff need only establish that he owns the copyright and that the defendant violated one or more of the plaintiff's exclusive rights under the copyright. Proof of infringement usually consists of showing that the allegedly infringing work is substantially similar to the copyrighted work and that the alleged infringer had access to the copyrighted work. The Digital Millennium Copyright Act of 1998 amended the Copyright Act to create limitations on the liability of on-line providers for copyright infringement when engaging in certain activities.

To be the subject of a suit for infringement, the copyright must be registered with the Copyright Office, unless the work is a Berne Convention work whose country of origin is not the United States. For an infringement occurring after registration, the following remedies are available: (1) injunction; (2) the impoundment and, possibly, destruction of infringing articles; (3) actual damages, plus profits made by the infringer that are additional to those damages, *or* statutory damages of at least $500 but no more than $20,000 ($100,000 if the infringement is willful), according to what the court determines to be just; (4) costs and, in the court's discretion, reasonable attorneys' fees to the prevailing party; and (5) criminal penalties of a fine of up to $10,000 or up to one year's imprisonment for willful infringement for purposes of commercial advantage or private financial gain. In 1997 Congress enacted the No Electronic Theft Act, increasing criminal penalties for certain copyright violations. Imprisonment for up to five years (ten years for subsequent offenses) may be imposed for willful infringement if at least ten copies or phonorecords with a total retail value of more than $2,500 in a 180-day period are reproduced or distributed.

## PATENTS

Through a **patent,** the Federal government grants an inventor a monopolistic right to make, use, or sell an invention to the absolute exclusion of others for the period of the patent. The patent owner may also profit by licensing others to use the patent on a royalty basis. The patent may not be renewed, however: upon expiration, the invention enters the "public domain," and anyone may use it.

### Patentability

The Patent Act specifies those inventions that may be patented as **utility patents**. Section 101 provides:

Whoever invents or discovers any new and useful process, machine, manufacture, or composition of matter, or any new and useful improvement thereof, may obtain a patent therefor, subject to the conditions and requirements of this title.

Thus, naturally occurring substances are not patentable, as the invention must be made or modified by humans. For example, the discovery of a bacterium with useful properties is not patentable, whereas the manufacture of a genetically engineered bacterium is. By the same token, laws of nature, principles, bookkeeping systems, fundamental truths, methods of calculation, and ideas are not patentable. Accordingly, as Chief Justice Burger noted in *Diamond, Commissioner of Patents and Trademarks v. Chakrabarty*, "Einstein could not patent his law that $E = mc^2$, nor could Newton have patented the law of gravity." Similarly, isolated computer programs are not patentable, although, as mentioned above, they may be copyrighted.

To be patentable as a utility patent, the process, machine, manufacture, or composition of matter must meet three criteria:

1. *Novelty.* The invention must not conflict with a prior pending application or a previously issued patent;
2. *Utility.* The invention must possess specific and substantial usefulness, which must be affirmatively disclosed by the application; and
3. *Nonobviousness.* The invention, in light of the prior art, must not be obvious to a person skilled in such prior art.

In addition to utility patents, the Patent Act provides for plant patents and design patents. A **plant patent** protects a new and distinctive variety of asexually reproducing plant. Plant patents require (1) novelty, (2) distinctiveness, and (3) nonobviousness. A **design patent** protects a new, original, ornamental design for an article of manufacture. Design patents require (1) novelty, (2) ornamentality, and (3) nonobviousness.

Utility and plant patents have a term that begins on the date of the patent's grant and ends twenty years from the date of application. Design patents have a term of fourteen years from the date of grant.

 *See Case 40–4*

### Procedure

The United States Patent and Trademark Office issues a patent upon the basis of a patent application containing a *specification,* which describes how the invention works, and *claims,* which describe the features that make the invention patentable. The applicant must be the inventor. Before granting a patent, the Patent Office thoroughly examines the prior art and determines whether the submitted invention is nonobvious and has novelty and utility (or distinctiveness or ornamentality, in the case of plant or design patents). An application for a patent is confidential, and the Patent Office will not divulge its contents. This confidentiality ends, however, upon the granting of the patent. Unlike rights under a copyright, no monopoly rights arise until the Patent Office actually issues a patent. Therefore, anyone is free to make, use, and sell an invention for which a patent application is filed until the patent has been granted.

An applicant whose application is rejected may apply for reexamination. If the application is again rejected, the applicant may appeal to the Patent and Trademark Office's Board of Appeals and from there to the Federal courts.

### Infringement

Anyone who, without permission, makes, uses, or sells a patented invention is a **direct infringer,** whereas a person who actively encourages another to make, use, offer to sell, or sell a patented invention without permission is an **indirect infringer.** A **contributory infringer** is one who knowingly sells or offers to sell a part or component of a patented invention, unless the component is a staple or commodity or is suitable for a substan-

**FIGURE 40–1** Intellectual Property

|  | Trade Secrets | Trade Symbols | Copyrights | Patents |
|---|---|---|---|---|
| **What is protected** | information | mark | work of authorship | invention |
| **Rights protected** | use or sell | use or sell | reproduce, prepare derivative works, distribute, perform, or display | make, use, or sell |
| **Duration** | until disclosed | until abandoned | usually author's life plus 70 years | for utility and plant patents, 20 years from application; 14 years for design patents |
| **Federally protected** | no | yes | yes | yes |
| **Requirements for protection** | valuable secret | distinctive | original and fixed | novel, useful, and nonobvious |

tial noninfringing use. While good faith and ignorance are defenses to contributory infringement, they are not defenses to direct infringement.

The rights under a patent do not extend beyond the first sale; that is, the purchaser of a patented item is permitted to use or resell that item. The right to use a purchased item includes the right to repair it so long as the repair does not constitute reconstruction, which would infringe upon the patent holder's exclusive right to make the invention.

## Remedies

The remedies for infringement under the Patent Act are (1) injunctive relief; (2) damages adequate to compensate the plaintiff but "in no event less than a reasonable royalty for the use made of the invention by the infringer"; (3) treble damages, when appropriate; (4) attorneys' fees in exceptional cases, such as those that involve knowing infringement; and (5) costs.

◆ *See Figure 40–1*

 # Chapter Summary

| **Trade Secrets** | **Definition** commercially valuable, secret information<br>**Protection** owner of a trade secret may obtain damages or injunctive relief when the secret is misappropriated (wrongfully used) by an employee or a competitor |
|---|---|

| **Trade Symbols** | **Types of Trade Symbols**<br>• *Trademark* distinctive symbol, word, or design that is used to identify the manufacturer<br>• *Service Mark* distinctive symbol, word, or design that is used to identify a provider's services<br>• *Certification Mark* distinctive symbol, word, or design used with goods or services to certify specific characteristics<br>• *Collective Mark* distinctive symbol used to indicate membership in an organization<br>**Registration** to be registered and thus protected by the Lanham Act, a mark must be distinctive and not immoral, deceptive, or scandalous |
|---|---|

**Infringement** occurs when a person without authorization uses a substantially indistinguishable mark that is likely to cause confusion, mistake, or deception

**Remedies** the Lanham Act provides the following remedies for infringement: injunctive relief, profits, damages, destruction of infringing articles, costs, and, in exceptional cases, attorneys' fees

## Trade Names

**Definition** any name used to identify a business, vocation, or occupation

**Protection** may not be registered under the Lanham Act, but infringement is prohibited

**Remedies** damages and injunctions are available if infringement occurs

## Copyrights

**Definition** exclusive right, usually for the author's life plus 70 years, to original works of authorship

**Procedure** registration is not required but provides additional remedies for infringement

**Rights** copyright protection provides the exclusive right to (1) reproduce the copyrighted work, (2) prepare derivative works based on the work, (3) distribute copies of the work, and (4) perform or display the work publicly

**Ownership** the author of the copyrighted work is usually the owner of the copyright, which may be transferred in whole or in part

**Infringement** occurs when someone exercises the copyright owner's rights without authorization

**Remedies** if infringement occurs after registration, the following remedies are available: (1) injunction, (2) impoundment and possible destruction of infringing articles, (3) actual damages plus profits or statutory damages, (4) costs, and (5) criminal penalties

## Patents

**Definition** the exclusive right to an invention for twenty years from the date of application for utility and plant patents; fourteen years from grant for design patents

**Patentability** to be patentable, the invention must be (1) novel, (2) useful, and (3) not obvious

**Procedure** patents are issued upon application to and after examination by the U.S. Patent and Trademark Office

**Infringement** occurs when anyone without permission makes, uses, or sells a patented invention

**Remedies** for infringement of a patent are (1) injunctive relief; (2) damages; (3) treble damages, where appropriate; (4) attorneys' fees; and (5) costs

# Cases

### CASE 40–1
## Trade Secrets
# B. C. ZIEGLER AND COMPANY v. EHREN
Court of Appeals of Wisconsin, 1987
141 Wis. 2d 19, 414 N.W. 2d 48

**BROWN, J.**

Lawrence P. Ehren appeals from a grant of summary judgment restraining him from using or disclosing information contained on business papers and records he bought from a scrap paper company but which originated with B. C. Ziegler and Company (Ziegler). The circuit court held that the information was entitled to common law trade secret protection and that Ehren did not acquire title to the information as a good faith purchaser. We affirm those rulings.

Ziegler is an underwriter of securities located in West Bend. Ehren is employed by a scrap dealer, Lynn's Waste Paper Co., Inc. (Lynn's), where his duties include determining the value for recycling purposes of scrap paper purchased by Lynn's. From 1981 to 1983, Ehren was a licensed securities salesman and worked for two brokerage firms which compete with Ziegler.

Ziegler considered its customer lists confidential and had developed policies for the disposal of scrap paper which were regularly communicated to its employees. Paper containing a customer name was to be burned or shredded on the Ziegler premises before disposal or was to be delivered for shredding to a commercial shredding concern in Appleton, in which case the employee delivering the paper was to wait while it was shredded. Under no circumstances was scrap paper containing names or information about Ziegler customers to leave the possession of its employees in readable form. Scrap paper not containing such information could be disposed of in unshredded form.

On several occasions in late 1985, boxes of scrap paper were delivered to Lynn's by Ziegler maintenance employees. Neither those employees nor Lynn's was aware that these batches of paper scrap contained Ziegler customer names, account summaries and other information on preaddressed envelopes bearing Ziegler's return address, a computer printout, monthly statements and other business records. Lynn's paid scrap rates for the paper. Ehren subsequently purchased from Lynn's six boxes of Ziegler materials in two transactions for a total of $16.75.

In the ensuing months, Ehren's daughter began sorting the Ziegler envelopes alphabetically and by zip code. In December of 1985, Ehren approached a former business associate, Thomas Thorson, a broker with a securities firm in competition with Ziegler, about using the names on the envelopes. There was some evidence that neither was sure of the value of the names, believing they might merely be the names of prospects rather than actual Ziegler customers. However, Ehren suggested compensation of one dollar per name.

Ehren delivered approximately 11,600 envelopes to Thorson. Thorson sent a mailing, soliciting securities sales, to some of the names and received responses at a rate of eight to ten percent, compared to a normal rate of two or three percent.

Ziegler learned that its customers were receiving solicitations and requested that the West Bend Police Department conduct a quiet investigation to determine whether customer information was being leaked from the company. After learning through the police investigation that Ehren possessed the customer information, Ziegler brought this action seeking injunctive relief and replevin. After granting Ziegler temporary relief, the circuit court granted Ziegler's motion for summary judgment, permanently enjoined Ehren from using or disclosing the information and ordered, subject to a stay pending appeal, that the Washington County Clerk of Courts . . . destroy the materials. * * * This appeal followed.

Ehren first claims the circuit court erred in finding that the information contained in the Ziegler materials was a trade secret belonging to Ziegler.

\* \* \*

Thus, we look to the common law of trade secrets. [The Abbott case (citation)], adopted a six-factor test based on language from the Restatement of Torts. These factors are: (1) the extent to which the information is known outside of the business of the party asserting trade secret status; (2) the extent to which it is known by employees and others involved in his business; (3) the extent or measures taken by him to guard the secrecy of the information; (4) the value of the information to him and to his competitors; (5) the amount of effort or money expended by him in developing the information; and (6) the ease or difficulty with which the information could be properly acquired or duplicated by others. [Citation.] Each of the six factors should indicate that a trade secret exists if the information is to be afforded protection. [Citation.]

* * *

The circuit court found, as essentially undisputed material facts, that: (1) the information was completely confidential and not known outside Ziegler; (2) the information was generally made available only to Ziegler employees who had reason to use it; (3) Ziegler had a policy, which was communicated to its employees, including maintenance personnel, of keeping confidential all material containing customer information; (4) Ziegler took reasonable measures to guard the confidentiality of information about the identity of its customers; (5) the information has substantial value to Ziegler, Ehren and Ziegler's competitors; (6) Ziegler's customer list has been developed through its substantial efforts over the last seventy-five years; (7) the papers in the six boxes contain information about Ziegler's transactions with its customers and contain the names and addresses of persons who have purchased securities from Ziegler in the past and are active prospects for future sales; and (8) the information contained in the six boxes cannot be acquired from sources other than Ziegler. We agree that these findings are not significantly disputed.

Applying these findings to the Abbott factors, we conclude that the Ziegler customer information qualifies for trade secret status.

* * *

Ehren next contends that even assuming trade secret status, this status does not survive an accidental or negligent disclosure. * * *

The rule that accidental disclosure negates trade secret protection has not been expressly adopted in Wisconsin. The determination whether to protect information in a particular case depends upon the circumstances and the nature of the information involved. [Citation.]

Trade secrets law has developed largely in an effort to balance two competing interests—the interest of an employer in precluding others from exploiting specialized knowledge developed in the course of an employment relationship and the interest of the former employee in the general use of his or her skills and training ("know-how"). [Citation.] Our supreme court has narrowly drawn the scope of trade secret protection "to effectuate the public policies of encouraging business competition and facilitating worker mobility." [Citation.]

In the present case, Ehren had no confidential or employment relationship with Ziegler. He purchased materials containing customer information for their scrap value and attempted to sell the information to a Ziegler competitor at an enormous profit. We are not persuaded that he may invoke the same policies which have led to the narrow scope of trade secret protection which applies as between an employer and a former employee. The circumstances are entirely different from those found in the employer-employee cases. No countervailing policy of worker mobility exists here to weigh against Ziegler's interest in the secrecy of extremely valuable and confidential information accidentally disposed of in readable form.

Essentially, we conclude that, even assuming and conceding that Ehren acquired the Ziegler materials through no wrongdoing on his part, it would be inequitable to allow him to make use of the information contained therein. We hold that the trade secret status of the customer information survived its inadvertent disclosure in the present case.

* * *

Judgment affirmed.

---

## CASE 40-2
### Trademarks
# QUALITEX CO. v. JACOBSON PRODUCTS CO., INC.
Supreme Court of the United States, 1995
514 U.S. 159, 115 S.Ct. 1300, 131 L.Ed.2d 248

BREYER, J.
The question in this case is whether the Lanham Trademark Act of 1946 (Lanham Act), [citation], permits the registration of a trademark that consists, purely and simply, of a color. We conclude that, sometimes, a color will meet ordinary legal trademark requirements. And,

when it does so, no special legal rule prevents color alone from serving as a trademark.

# I

The case before us grows out of petitioner Qualitex Company's use (since the 1950's) of a special shade of green-gold color on the pads that it makes and sells to dry cleaning firms for use on dry cleaning presses. In 1989 respondent Jacobson Products (a Qualitex rival) began to sell its own press pads to dry cleaning firms; and it colored those pads a similar green-gold. In 1991 Qualitex registered the special green-gold color on press pads with the Patent and Trademark Office as a trademark. [Citation.] Qualitex subsequently added a trademark infringement count, [citation], to an unfair competition claim, [citation], in a lawsuit it had already filed challenging Jacobson's use of the green-gold color.

Qualitex won the lawsuit in the District Court. [Citation.] But, the Court of Appeals for the Ninth Circuit set aside the judgment in Qualitex's favor on the trademark infringement claim because, in that Circuit's view, the Lanham Act does not permit Qualitex, or anyone else, to register "color alone" as a trademark. [Citation.]

The courts of appeals have differed as to whether or not the law recognizes the use of color alone as a trademark. [Citations.] We now hold that there is no rule absolutely barring the use of color alone, and we reverse the judgment of the Ninth Circuit.

# II

The Lanham Act gives a seller or producer the exclusive right to "register" a trademark, [citation], and to prevent his or her competitors from using that trademark, [citation]. Both the language of the Act and the basic underlying principles of trademark law would seem to include color within the universe of things that can qualify as a trademark. The language of the Lanham Act describes that universe in the broadest of terms. It says that trademarks "includ[e] any word, name, symbol, or device, or any combination thereof." [Citation.] Since human beings might use as a "symbol" or "device" almost anything at all that is capable of

carrying meaning, this language, read literally, is not restrictive. The courts and the Patent and Trademark Office have authorized for use as a mark a particular shape (of a Coca-Cola bottle), a particular sound (of NBC's three chimes), and even a particular scent (of plumeria blossoms on sewing thread). [Citation.] If a shape, a sound, and a fragrance can act as symbols why, one might ask, can a color not do the same?

A color is also capable of satisfying the more important part of the statutory definition of a trademark, which requires that a person "us[e]" or "inten[d] to use" the mark "to identify and distinguish his or her goods, including a unique product, from those manufactured or sold by others and to indicate the source of the goods, even if that source is unknown." [Citation.]

True, a product's color is unlike "fanciful," "arbitrary," or "suggestive" words or designs, which almost automatically tell a customer that they refer to a brand. [Citations.] The imaginary word "Suntost," or the words "Suntost Marmalade," on a jar of orange jam immediately would signal a brand or a product "source"; the jam's orange color does not do so. But, over time, customers may come to treat a particular color on a product or its packaging (say, a color that in context seems unusual, such as pink on a firm's insulating material or red on the head of a large industrial bolt) as signifying a brand. And, if so, that color would have come to identify and distinguish the goods—i.e. to "indicate" their "source"—much in the way that descriptive words on a product (say, "Trim" on nail clippers or "Car-Freshner" on deodorizer) can come to indicate a product's origin. [Citation.] In this circumstance, trademark law says that the word (e.g., "Trim"), although not inherently distinctive, has developed "secondary meaning." [Citation], ("secondary meaning" is acquired when "in the minds of the public, the primary significance of a product feature . . . is to identify the source of the product rather than the product itself"). Again, one might ask, if trademark law permits a descriptive word with secondary meaning to act as a mark, why would it not permit a color, under similar circumstances, to do the same?

We cannot find in the basic objectives of trademark law any obvious theoretical objection to the use of color alone as a trademark, where that color has attained "secondary meaning" and therefore identifies and distinguishes a particular brand (and thus indicates its "source"). In principle, trademark law, by preventing others from copying a source-identifying mark, "reduce[s] the customer's costs of shopping and making purchasing decisions, [citation], for it quickly and easily assures a potential customer that this item—the item with this mark—is made by the same producer as other similarly marked items that he or she liked (or disliked) in the past. At the same time, the law helps assure a producer that it (and not an imitating competitor) will reap the financial, reputation-related rewards associated with a desirable product. The law thereby "encourage[s] the production of quality products," and simultaneously discourages those who hope to sell inferior products by capitalizing on a consumer's inability quickly to evaluate the quality of an item offered for sale. [Citation.] It is the source-distinguishing ability of a mark—not its ontological status as color, shape, fragrance, word, or sign—that permits it to serve these basic purposes. [Citation.] And, for that reason, it is difficult to find, in basic trademark objectives, a reason to disqualify absolutely the use of a color as a mark.

Neither can we find a principled objection to the use of color as a mark in the important "functionality" doctrine of trademark law. The functionality doctrine prevents trademark law, which seeks to promote competition by protecting a firm's reputation, from instead inhibiting legitimate competition by allowing a producer to control a useful product feature. It is the province of patent law, not trademark law, to encourage invention by granting inventors a monopoly over new product designs or functions for a limited time, [citation], after which competitors are free to use the innovation. If a product's functional features could be used as trademarks, however, a monopoly over such features could be obtained without regard to whether they qualify as patents and could be extended forever (because trademarks may be renewed in perpetuity). [Citation], ("A functional characteristic is 'an important ingredient in the commercial success of the product,' and, after expiration of a patent, it is no more the property of the originator than the product itself"). Functionality doctrine therefore would require, to take an imaginary example, that even if customers have come to identify the special illumination-enhancing shape of a new patented light bulb with a particular manufacturer, the manufacturer may not use that shape as a trademark, for doing so, after the patent had expired, would impede competition—not by protecting the reputation of the original bulb maker, but by frustrating competitors' legitimate efforts to produce an equivalent illumination-enhancing bulb. [Citation.] This Court consequently has explained that, "[i]n general terms, a product feature is functional," and cannot serve as a trademark, "if it is essential to the

use or purpose of the article or if it affects the cost or quality of the article," that is, if exclusive use of the feature would put competitors at a significant non-reputation-related disadvantage. [Citation.] Although sometimes color plays an important role (unrelated to source identification) in making a product more desirable, sometimes it does not. And, this latter fact—the fact that sometimes color is not essential to a product's use or purpose and does not affect cost or quality—indicates that the doctrine of "functionality" does not create an absolute bar to the use of color alone as a mark. See Owens-Corning, [citation], (pink color of insulation in wall "performs no nontrademark function").

It would seem, then, that color alone, at least sometimes, can meet the basic legal requirements for use as a trademark. It can act as a symbol that distinguishes a firm's goods and identifies their source, without serving any other significant function. [Citation.] Indeed, the District Court, in this case, entered findings (accepted by the Ninth Circuit) that show Qualitex's green-gold press pad color has met these requirements. The green-gold color acts as a symbol. Having developed secondary meaning (for customers identified the green-gold color as Qualitex's), it identifies the press pads' source. And, the green-gold color serves no other function. (Although it is important to use some color on press pads to avoid noticeable stains, the court found "no competitive need in the press pad industry for the green-gold color, since other colors are equally usable." [Citation.] Accordingly, unless there is some special reason that convincingly militates against the use of color alone as a trademark, trademark law would protect Qualitex's use of the green-gold color on its press pads.

\* \* \*

Having determined that a color may sometimes meet the basic legal requirements for use as a trademark and that respondent Jacobson's arguments do not justify a special legal rule preventing color alone from serving as a trademark (and, in light of the District Court's here undisputed findings that Qualitex's use of the green-gold color on its press pads meets the basic trademark requirements), we conclude that the Ninth Circuit erred in barring Qualitex's use of color as a trademark.

## CASE 40–3
## Copyright
## *CAMPBELL v. ACUFF-ROSE MUSIC, INC.*
Supreme Court of the United States, 1994
510 U.S. 569, 114 S.Ct. 1164, 127 L.Ed.2d 500

SOUTER, J.

We are called upon to decide whether 2 Live Crew's commercial parody of Roy Orbison's song, "Oh, Pretty Woman," may be a fair use within the meaning of the Copyright Act of 1976, [citation]. Although the District Court granted summary judgment for 2 Live Crew, the Court of Appeals reversed, holding the defense of fair use barred by the song's commercial character and excessive borrowing. Because we hold that a parody's commercial character is only one element to be weighed in a fair use enquiry, and that insufficient consideration was given to the nature of parody in weighing the degree of copying, we reverse and remand.

### I

In 1964, Roy Orbison and William Dees wrote a rock ballad called "Oh, Pretty Woman" and assigned their rights in it to respondent Acuff-Rose Music, Inc. Acuff-Rose registered the song for copyright protection.

Petitioners Luther R. Campbell, Christopher Wongwon, Mark Ross, and David Hobbs, are collectively known as 2 Live Crew, a popular rap music group.

[Court's footnote: Rap has been defined as a "style of black American popular music consisting of improvised rhymes performed to a rhythmic accompaniment." * * * ]

In 1989, Campbell wrote a song entitled "Pretty Woman," which he later described in an affidavit as intended, "through comical lyrics, to satirize the original work. . . ." On July 5, 1989, 2 Live Crew's manager informed Acuff-Rose that 2 Live Crew had written a parody of "Oh, Pretty Woman," that they would afford all credit for ownership and authorship of the original song to Acuff-Rose, Dees, and Orbison, and that they were willing to pay a fee for the use they wished to make of it. Enclosed with the letter were a copy of the lyrics and a recording of 2 Live Crew's song. Acuff-Rose's agent refused permission, stating that "I am aware of the success enjoyed by 'The 2 Live Crews', but I must inform you that we cannot permit the use of a parody of 'Oh, Pretty Woman.'" Nonetheless, in June or July 1989, 2 Live Crew released records, cassette tapes, and compact discs of "Pretty Woman" in a collection of songs entitled "As Clean As They Wanna Be." The albums and compact discs identify the authors of "Pretty Woman" as Orbison and Dees and its publisher as Acuff-Rose.

Almost a year later, after nearly a quarter of a million copies of the recording had been sold, Acuff-Rose sued 2 Live Crew and its record company, Luke Skywalker Records, for copyright infringement. The District Court granted summary judgment for 2 Live Crew, reasoning that the commercial purpose of 2 Live Crew's song was no bar to fair use; that 2 Live Crew's version was a parody, which "quickly degenerates into a play on words, substituting predictable lyrics with shocking ones" to show "how bland and banal the Orbison song" is; that 2 Live Crew had taken no more than was necessary to "conjure up" the original in order to parody it; and that it was "extremely unlikely that 2 Live Crew's song would adversely affect the market for the original." The District Court weighed these factors and held that 2 Live Crew's song made fair use of Orbison's original. The Court of Appeals for the Sixth Circuit reversed and remanded.
* * *

We granted certiorari, [citation], to determine whether 2 Live Crew's commercial parody could be a fair use.

### II

It is uncontested here that 2 Live Crew's song would be an infringement of Acuff-Rose's rights in "Oh, Pretty Woman," under the Copyright Act of 1976, [citation], but for a finding of fair use through parody. From the infancy of copyright protection, some opportunity for fair use of copyrighted materials has been thought necessary to fulfill copyright's very purpose, "[t]o promote the Progress of Science and useful Arts. . . ." U.S. Const., Art. I, § 8, cl. 8. For as Justice Story explained, "[i]n truth, in literature, in science and in art, there are, and can be, few, if any, things which in an abstract sense, are strictly new and original throughout. Every book in literature, science and art, borrows, and must necessarily borrow, and use much which was well known and used before." * * *

＊　＊　＊

The fair use doctrine thus "permits [and requires] courts to avoid rigid application of the copyright statute when, on occasion, it would stifle the very creativity which that law is designed to foster." [Citation.]

＊　＊　＊

**A** The first factor in a fair use enquiry is "the purpose and character of the use, including whether such use is of a commercial nature or is for nonprofit educational purposes." § 107(1). ＊ ＊ ＊ The enquiry here may be guided by the examples given in the preamble to § 107, looking to whether the use is for criticism, or comment, or news reporting, and the like, see § 107. The central purpose of this investigation is to see, in Justice Story's words, whether the new work merely "supersede[s] the objects" of the original creation, [citation], or instead adds something new, with a further purpose or different character, altering the first with new expression, meaning, message; it asks, in other words, whether and to what extent the new work is "transformative." Although such transformative use is not absolutely necessary for a finding of fair use, [citation] the goal of copyright, to promote science and the arts, is generally furthered by the creation of transformative works.

[Court's footnote: The obvious statutory exception to this focus on transformative uses is the straight reproduction of multiple copies for classroom distribution.]

Such works thus lie at the heart of the fair use doctrine's guarantee of breathing space within the confines of copyright, [citation], and the more transformative the new work, the less will be the significance of other factors, like commercialism, that may weigh against a finding of fair use.

This Court has only once before even considered whether parody may be fair use, and that time issued no opinion because of the Court's equal division. [Citation.] Suffice it to say now that parody has an obvious claim to transformative value, as Acuff-Rose itself does not deny. Like less ostensibly humorous forms of criticism, it can provide social benefit, by shedding light on an earlier work, and, in the process, creating a new one. We thus line up with the courts that have held that parody, like other comment or criticism, may claim fair use under § 107. [Citations.]

＊ ＊ ＊ Parody needs to mimic an original to make its point, and so has some claim to use the creation of its victim's (or collective victims') imagination, whereas satire can stand on its own two feet and so requires justification for the very act of borrowing.

The fact that parody can claim legitimacy for some appropriation does not, of course, tell either parodist or judge much about where to draw the line. Like a book review quoting the copyrighted material criticized, parody may or may not be fair use, and petitioner's suggestion that any parodic use is presumptively fair has no more justification in law or fact than the equally hopeful claim that any use for news reporting should be presumed fair, [citation]. ＊ ＊ ＊ Accordingly, parody, like any other use, has to work its way through the relevant factors, and be judged case by case, in light of the ends of the copyright law.

Here, the District Court held, and the Court of Appeals assumed, that 2 Live Crew's "Pretty Woman" contains parody, commenting on and criticizing the original work, whatever it may have to say about society at large. ＊ ＊ ＊ [Citation.] Although the majority below had difficulty discerning any criticism of the original in 2 Live Crew's song, it assumed for purposes of its opinion that there was some. [Citation.]

We have less difficulty in finding that critical element in 2 Live Crew's song than the Court of Appeals did, although having found it we will not take the further step of evaluating its quality. The threshold question when fair use is raised in defense of parody is whether a parodic character may reasonably be perceived. Whether, going beyond that, parody is in good taste or bad does not and should not matter to fair use. As Justice Holmes explained, "[i]t would be a dangerous undertaking for persons trained only to the law to constitute themselves final judges of the worth of [a work], outside of the narrowest and most obvious limits. At the one extreme some works of genius would be sure to miss appreciation. Their very novelty would make them repulsive until the public had learned the new language in which their author spoke." [Citation.]

While we might not assign a high rank to the parodic element here, we think it fair to say that 2 Live Crew's song reasonably could be perceived as commenting on the original or criticizing it, to some degree. 2 Live Crew juxtaposes the romantic musings of a man whose fantasy comes true, with degrading taunts, a bawdy demand for sex, and a sigh of relief from paternal responsibility. The later words can be taken as a comment on the naivete of the original of an earlier day, as a rejection of its sentiment that ignores the ugliness of street life and the debasement that it signifies. It is this joinder of reference and ridicule that marks off the author's choice of parody from the other types of comment and criticism that traditionally have had a claim to fair use protection as transformative works.

* * *

* * * Rather, as we explained in [citation], *Sony* stands for the proposition that the "fact that a publication was commercial as opposed to nonprofit is a separate factor that tends to weigh against a finding of fair use." [Citation.] But that is all, and the fact that even the force of that tendency will vary with the context is a further reason against elevating commerciality to hard presumptive significance. The use, for example, of a copyrighted work to advertise a product, even in a parody, will be entitled to less indulgence under the first factor of the fair use enquiry, than the sale of a parody for its own sake, let alone one performed a single time by students in school.

*B* The second statutory factor, "the nature of the copyrighted work," § 107(2), * * * calls for recognition that some works are closer to the core of intended copyright protection than others, with the consequence that fair use is more difficult to establish when the former works are copied. [Citations.] We agree with both the District Court and the Court of Appeals that the Orbison original's creative expression for public dissemination falls within the core of the copyright's protective purposes. [Citations.] This fact, however, is not much help in this case, or ever likely to help much in separating the fair use sheep from the infringing goats in a parody case, since parodies almost invariably copy publicly known, expressive works.

*C* The third factor asks whether "the amount and substantiality of the portion used in relation to the copyrighted work as a whole, § 107(3) * * * are reasonable in relation to the purpose of the copying. Here, attention turns to the persuasiveness of a parodist's justification for the particular copying done, and the enquiry will harken back to the first of the statutory factors, for, as in prior cases, we recognize that the extent of permissible copying varies with the purpose and character of the use. [Citations.] The facts bearing on this factor will also tend to address the fourth, by revealing the degree to which the parody may serve as a market substitute for the original or potentially licensed derivatives. [Citation.]

* * *

We think the Court of Appeals was insufficiently appreciative of parody's need for the recognizable sight or sound when it ruled 2 Live Crew's use unreasonable as a matter of law. It is true, of course, that 2 Live Crew copied the characteristic opening bass riff (or musical phrase) of the original, and true that the words of the first line copy the Orbison lyrics. But if quotation of the opening riff and the first line may be said to go to the "heart" of the original, the heart is also what most readily conjures up the song for parody, and it is the heart at which parody takes aim. Copying does not become excessive in relation to parodic purpose merely because the portion taken was the original's heart. If 2 Live Crew had copied a significantly less memorable part of the original, it is difficult to see how its parodic character would have come through. [Citation.]

This is not, of course, to say that anyone who calls himself a parodist can skim the cream and get away scot free. In parody, as in news reporting, context is everything, and the question of fairness asks what else the parodist did besides go to the heart of the original.

* * *

Suffice it to say here, as to the lyrics, * * * we fail to see how the copying can be excessive in relation to its parodic purpose, even if the portion taken is the original's "heart." As to the music, we express no opinion whether repetition of the bass riff is excessive copying, and we remand to permit evaluation of the amount taken, in light of the song's parodic purpose and character, its transformative elements, and considerations of the potential for market substitution sketched more fully below.

* * *

*D* The fourth fair use factor is "the effect of the use upon the potential market for or value of the copyrighted work." § 107(4). It requires courts to consider not only the extent of market harm caused by the particular actions of the alleged infringer, but also "whether unrestricted and widespread conduct of the sort engaged in by the defendant . . . would result in a substantially adverse impact on the potential market" for the original. [Citations.] The enquiry "must take account not only of harm to the original but also of harm to the market for derivative works." [Citation.]

* * * In assessing the likelihood of significant market harm, the Court of Appeals quoted from language in *Sony* that "'[i]f the intended use is for commercial gain, that likelihood may be presumed. But if it is for a noncommercial purpose, the likelihood must be demonstrated.'" [Citation.] The court reasoned that because "the use of the copyrighted work is wholly commercial, . . . we presume a likelihood of future harm to Acuff-Rose exists." [Citation.] In so doing, the court resolved the fourth factor against 2 Live Crew, just as it had the first, by applying a presumption about the effect of commercial use, a presumption which as applied here we hold to be error.

No "presumption" or inference of market harm that might find support in *Sony* is applicable to a case involving something beyond mere duplication for commercial purposes. *Sony*'s discussion of a presumption contrasts a context of verbatim copying of the original in its entirety for commercial purposes, with the non-commercial context of *Sony* itself (home copying of television programming). In the former circumstances, what *Sony* said simply makes common sense: when a commercial use amounts to mere duplication of the entirety of an original, it clearly "supersede[s] the objects," [citation], of the original and serves as a market replacement for it, making it likely that cognizable market harm to the original will occur. [Citation.] But when, on the contrary, the second use is transformative, market substitution is at least less certain, and market harm may not be so readily inferred. Indeed, as to parody pure and simple, it is more likely that the new work will not affect the market for the original in a way cognizable under this factor, that is, by acting as a substitute for it ("supersed-[ing] [its] objects"). [Citation.] This is so because the parody and the original usually serve different market functions. [Citation.]

\* \* \*

## III

It was error for the Court of Appeals to conclude that the commercial nature of 2 Live Crew's parody of "Oh, Pretty Woman" rendered it presumptively unfair. No such evidentiary presumption is available to address either the first factor, the character and purpose of the use, or the fourth, market harm, in determining whether a transformative use, such as parody, is a fair one. The court also erred in holding that 2 Live Crew had necessarily copied excessively from the Orbison original, considering the parodic purpose of the use. We therefore reverse the judgment of the Court of Appeals and remand for further proceedings consistent with this opinion.

It is so ordered.

## APPENDIX A

"Oh, Pretty Woman" by Roy Orbison and William Dees

Pretty Woman, walking down the street,
Pretty Woman, the kind I like to meet,
Pretty Woman, I don't believe you, you're not the truth,
No one could look as good as you
Mercy
Pretty Woman, won't you pardon me,
Pretty Woman, I couldn't help but see,
Pretty Woman, that you look lovely as can be
Are you lonely just like me?
Pretty Woman, stop a while,
Pretty Woman, talk a while,
Pretty Woman give your smile to me
Pretty Woman, yeah, yeah, yeah
Pretty Woman, look my way,
Pretty Woman, say you'll stay with me
'Cause I need you, I'll treat you right
Come to me baby, Be mine tonight
Pretty Woman, don't walk on by,
Pretty Woman, don't make me cry,
Pretty Woman, don't walk away,
Hey, O.K.
If that's the way it must be, O.K.
I guess I'll go on home, it's late
There'll be tomorrow night, but wait!
What do I see
Is she walking back to me?
Yeah, she's walking back to me!
Oh, Pretty Woman.

## APPENDIX B

"Pretty Woman" as Recorded by 2 Live Crew

Pretty woman walkin' down the street
Pretty woman girl you look so sweet
Pretty woman you bring me down to that knee
Pretty woman you make me wanna beg please
Oh, pretty woman
Big hairy woman you need to shave that stuff
Big hairy woman you know I bet it's tough
Big hairy woman all that hair it ain't legit
'Cause you look like 'Cousin It'
Big hairy woman
Bald headed woman girl your hair won't grow
Bald headed woman you got a teeny weeny afro
Bald headed woman you know your hair could look nice
Bald headed woman first you get to roll it with rice
Bald headed woman here, let me get this hunk of biz for ya
Ya know what I'm saying you look better than rice a roni
Oh bald headed woman
Big hairy woman come on in
And don't forget your bald headed friend

Hey pretty woman let the boys
Jump in
Two timin' woman girl you know you ain't right
Two timin' woman you's out with my boy last night

Two timin' woman that takes a load off my mind
Two timin' woman now I know the baby ain't mine
Oh, two timin' woman
Oh pretty woman

---

## CASE 40–4
### Patents

# DIAMOND, COMMISSIONER OF PATENTS AND
# TRADEMARKS v. CHAKRABARTY

Supreme Court of the United States, 1980
447 U.S. 303, 100 S.Ct. 2204, 65 L.Ed.2d 144

BURGER, C.J.
We granted certiorari to determine whether a live, human-made micro-organism is patentable subject matter under § 101 [of the Patent Act].

* * *

In 1972, respondent Chakrabarty, a microbiologist, filed a patent application, assigned to the General Electric Co. The application asserted 36 claims related to Chakrabarty's invention of "a bacterium from the genus *Pseudomonas* containing therein at least two stable energy-generating plasmids, each of said plasmids providing a separate hydrocarbon degradative pathway." This human-made, genetically engineered bacterium is capable of breaking down multiple components of crude oil. Because of this property, which is possessed by no naturally occurring bacteria, Chakrabarty's invention is believed to have significant value for the treatment of oil spills.

Chakrabarty's patent claims were of three types: first, process claims for the method of producing the bacteria; second, claims for an inoculum comprised of a carrier material floating on water, such as straw, and the new bacteria; and third, claims to the bacteria themselves. The patent examiner allowed the claims falling into the first two categories, but rejected claims for the bacteria. His decision rested on two grounds: (1) that micro-organisms are "products of nature," and (2) that as living things they are not patentable subject matter under § 101 [of the Patent Act].

Chakrabarty appealed the rejection of these claims to the Patent Office Board of Appeals, and the Board affirmed the examiner on the second ground. Relying on the legislative history of the 1930 Plant Patent Act, in which Congress extended patent protection to certain asexually reproduced plants, the Board concluded that § 101 was not intended to cover living things such as these laboratory created micro-organisms.

The Court of Customs and Patent Appeals, by a divided vote, reversed on the authority of [citation], which held that "the fact that micro-organisms . . . are alive . . . [is] without legal significance" for purposes of the patent law. * * *

* * *

The Constitution grants Congress broad power to legislate to "promote the Progress of Science and useful Arts, by securing for limited Times to Authors and Inventors the exclusive Right to their respective Writings and Discoveries." Art. I, § 8, cl. 8. The patent laws promote this progress by offering inventors exclusive rights for a limited period as an incentive for their inventiveness and research efforts. [Citations.] The authority of Congress is exercised in the hope that "[t]he productive effort thereby fostered will have a positive effect on society through the introduction of new products and processes of manufacture into the economy, and the emanations by way of increased employment and better lives for our citizens." [Citation.]

The question before us in this case is a narrow one of statutory interpretation requiring us to construe § 101 [of the Patent Act], which provides:

Whoever invents or discovers any new and useful process, machine, manufacture, or composition of matter, or any new and useful improvement thereof, may obtain a patent therefor, subject to the conditions and requirements of this title.

Specifically, we must determine whether respondent's micro-organism constitutes a "manufacture" or "composition of matter" within the meaning of the statute.

* * *

In cases of statutory construction we begin, of course, with the language of the statute. [Citation.] And "unless otherwise defined, words will be interpreted as taking their ordinary, contemporary, common meaning." [Citation.] We have also cautioned that courts "should not read into the patent laws limitations and conditions which the legislature has not expressed." [Citation.]

Guided by these canons of construction, this Court has read the term "manufacture" in § 101 in accordance with its dictionary definition to mean "the production of articles for use from raw or prepared materials by giving to these materials new forms, qualities, properties, or combinations, whether by hand-labor or by machinery." [Citation.] Similarly, "composition of matter" has been construed consistent with its common usage to include "all compositions of two or more substances and . . . all composite articles, whether they be the results of chemical union, or of mechanical mixture, or whether they be gases, fluids, powders or solids." [Citation.] In choosing such expansive terms as "manufacture" and "composition of matter," modified by the comprehensive "any," Congress plainly contemplated that the patent laws would be given wide scope.

\* \* \*

This is not to suggest that § 101 has no limits or that it embraces every discovery. The laws of nature, physical phenomena, and abstract ideas have been held not patentable. [Citations.] Thus, a new mineral discovered in the earth or a new plant found in the wild is not patentable subject matter. Likewise, Einstein could not patent his celebrated law that $E = mc^2$; nor could Newton have patented the law of gravity. Such discoveries are "manifestations of . . . nature, free to all men and reserved exclusively to none." [Citation.]

Judged in this light, respondent's microorganism plainly qualifies as patentable subject matter. His claim is not to a hitherto unknown natural phenomenon, but to a non-naturally occurring manufacture or composition of matter—a product of human ingenuity "having a distinctive name, character [and] use." [Citation.] The point is underscored dramatically by comparison of the invention here with that in *Funk*. There, the patentee had discovered that there existed in nature certain species of root-nodule bacteria which did not exert a mutually inhibitive effect on each other. He used that discovery to produce a mixed culture capable of inoculating the seeds of leguminous plants. Concluding that the patentee had discovered "only some of the handiwork of nature," the Court ruled the product nonpatentable:

Each of the species of root-nodule bacteria contained in the package infects the same group of leguminous plants which it always infected. No species acquires a different use. The combination of species produces no new bacteria, no change in the six species of bacteria, and no enlargement of the range of their utility. Each species has the same effect it always had. The bacteria perform in their natural way. Their use in combination does not improve in any way their natural functioning. They serve the ends nature originally provided and act quite independently of any effort of the patentee. [Citation.]

Here, by contrast, the patentee has produced a new bacterium with markedly different characteristics from any found in nature and one having the potential for significant utility. His discovery is not nature's handiwork, but his own; accordingly it is patentable subject matter under § 101.

\* \* \*

We have emphasized in the recent past that "[o]ur individual appraisal of the wisdom or unwisdom of a particular [legislative] course . . . is to be put aside in the process of interpreting a statute." [Citation.] Our task, rather, is the narrow one of determining what Congress meant by the words it used in the statute; once that is done our powers are exhausted. Congress is free to amend § 101 so as to exclude from patent protection organisms produced by genetic engineering. Cf. 42 U.S.C. § 2181(a), exempting from patent protection inventions "useful solely in the utilization of special nuclear material or atomic energy in an atomic weapon." Or it may choose to craft a statute specifically designed for such living things. But, until Congress takes such action, this Court must construe the language of § 101 as it is. The language of that section fairly embraces respondent's invention.

Accordingly, the judgment of the Court of Customs and Patent Appeals is

Affirmed.

---

# Questions

1. Explain what trade secrets protect and how they may be infringed.
2. Distinguish among the various types of trade symbols.
3. Explain the extent to which trade names are protected.

4. Explain what copyrights protect and the remedies for infringement.
5. Explain what patents protect and the remedies for infringement.

# Problems

**1.** Keller, a professor of legal studies at Rhodes University, is a diligent instructor. Late one night while reading a newly published, copyrighted treatise of 1,800 pages written by Gilbert, he came across a three-page section discussing the subject matter he intended to cover in class the next day. Keller considered the treatment to be illuminating and therefore photocopied the three pages and distributed the copies to his class. One of Keller's students is a second cousin of Gilbert, the author of the treatise, and she showed Gilbert the copies. Instead of being flattered, Gilbert sued Keller for copyright infringement. Decision?

**2.** A conceived a secret process for the continuous freeze-drying of foodstuffs and related products and constructed a small pilot plant that practiced the process. A, however, lacked the financing necessary to develop the commercial potential of the process and, in hopes of obtaining a contract for its development and the payment of royalties, disclosed it in confidence to B, a coffee manufacturer, who signed an agreement not to disclose it to anyone else. At the same time, A signed an agreement not to disclose the process to any other person as long as A and B were considering a contract for its development. Upon A's disclosure of the process, B became extremely interested and offered to pay A the sum of $1,750,000 if, upon further development, the process proved to be commercially feasible. While negotiations between A and B were in progress, C, a competitor of B, learned of the process and requested a disclosure from A, who informed C that the process could not be disclosed to anyone unless negotiations with B were broken off. C offered to pay A $2,500,000 for the process, provided it met certain defined objective performance criteria. A contract was prepared and executed between A and C on this basis, without any prior disclosure of the process to C. Upon the making of this contract, A rejected B's offer. The process was thereupon disclosed to C, and demonstration runs of the pilot plant in the presence of representatives of C were conducted under varying conditions. After three weeks of conducting experimental demonstrations, compiling data, and analyzing results, C informed A that the process did not meet the performance criteria in the contract and that for this reason C was rejecting the process. Two years later, C placed on the market freeze-dried coffee that resembled in color, appearance, and texture the product of A's pilot plant. What are the rights of the parties?

**3.** B, a chemist, was employed by A, a manufacturer, to work on a secret process for A's product under an exclusive three-year contract. C, a salesperson, was employed by A on a week-to-week basis. B and C resigned their employment with A and accepted employment in their respective capacities with D, a rival manufacturer. C began soliciting patronage from A's former customers, whose names he had memorized. What are the rights of the parties in (a) a suit by A to enjoin B from

working for D and (b) a suit by A to enjoin C from soliciting A's customers?

**4.** Conrad and Darby were competitors in the business of dehairing raw cashmere, the fleece of certain Asiatic goats. Dehairing is the process of separating the commercially valuable soft down from the matted mass of raw fleece, which contains long coarse guard hairs and other impurities. Machinery for this process is not readily available on the open market. Each company in the business designed and built its own machinery and kept the nature of its process secret. Conrad contracted with Lawton, owner of a small machine shop, to build and install new improved dehairing machinery of increased efficiency for which Conrad furnished designs, drawings, and instructions. Lawton, who knew that the machinery design was confidential, agreed that he would manufacture the machinery exclusively for Conrad and that he would not reproduce the machinery or any of its essential parts for anyone else. Darby purchased from Lawton a copy of the dehairing machinery which Conrad had specially designed. Decision?

**5.** Jones, having filed locally an affidavit required under the assumed name statute, has been operating and advertising his exclusive toy store for twenty years in Centerville, Illinois. His advertising has consisted of large signs on his premises reading "The Toy Mart." Lewis, after operating a store in Chicago under the name of "The Chicago Toy Mart," relocated in Centerville, Illinois, and erected a large sign reading "TOY MART" with the word "Centerville" written underneath in substantially smaller letters. Thereafter, Jones's sales declined, and many of his customers patronized Lewis's store, thinking it to be a branch of Jones's business. What are the rights of the parties?

**6.** Ryan Corporation manufactures and sells a variety of household cleaning products in interstate commerce. On national television, Ryan falsely advertises that its laundry liquid is biodegradable. Has Ryan violated the Lanham Act?

**7.** Gibbons, Inc. and Marvin Corporation are manufacturers who sell a variety of household cleaning products in interstate commerce. On national television, Gibbons states that its laundry liquid is biodegradable and that Marvin's is not. In fact, both products are biodegradable. Has Gibbons violated the Lanham Act?

**8.** George McCoy of Florida has been manufacturing and distributing a cheesecake for more than five years, labeling his product with a picture of a cheesecake, which serves as a background for a Florida bathing beauty and under which is written the slogan "McCoy All Spice Florida Cheese Cake." George McCoy has not registered his trademark. Subsequently, Leo McCoy of California begins manufacturing a similar product on the West Coast using a label similar in appearance to that of George McCoy, containing a picture of a Hollywood star and the words "McCoy's All Spice Cheese Cake." Leo McCoy begins marketing his products in the eastern United

States, using labels with the word "Florida" added, as in George McCoy's label. Leo McCoy has registered his product under the Federal Trademark Act. To what relief, if any, is George McCoy entitled?

9. Sony Corporation manufactured and sold home video recorders, specifically Betamax videotape recorders (VTRs). Universal City Studios, Inc. (Universal), owned the copyrights on some programs aired on commercially sponsored television. Individual Betamax owners frequently used the device to record some of Universal's copyrighted television programs for their own noncommercial use. Universal brought suit, claiming that the sale of the Betamax VTRs to the general public violated its rights under the Copyright Act. It sought no relief against any Betamax consumer. Instead, Universal sued Sony for contributory infringement of its copyrights, seeking money damages, an equitable accounting of profits, and an injunction against the manufacture and sale of Betamax VTRs. Decision?

10. The Coca-Cola Company manufactures a carbonated beverage, Coke, made from coca leaves and cola nuts. The Koke Company of America introduced into the beverage market a similar product named Koke. The Coca-Cola Company brought a trademark infringement action against Koke. Coke claimed unfair competition within the beverage business due to Koke's imitation of the Coca-Cola product and Koke's attempt to reap the benefit of consumer identification with the Coke name. Decision?

11. Vuitton, a French corporation, manufactures high-quality handbags, luggage, and accessories. Crown Hand-bags, a New York corporation, manufactures and distributes ladies' handbags. Vuitton handbags are sold exclusively in expensive department stores, and distribution is strictly controlled to maintain a certain retail selling price. The Vuitton bags bear a registered trademark and a distinctive design. Crown's handbags appear identical to the Vuitton bags but are of inferior quality. Vuitton sues Crown for manufacturing counterfeit handbags and selling them at a discount. Decision?

12. T.G.I. Friday's, a New York corporation and registered service mark, entered into an exclusive licensing agreement with Tiffany & Co. which allowed Tiffany to open a Friday's restaurant in Jackson, Mississippi. International Restaurant Group, operated by the owners of Tiffany, applied for a license to open a Friday's in Baton Rouge, Louisiana, but was refused. In Baton Rouge, International then opened another restaurant, called E.L. Saturday's, or Ever Lovin' Saturday's, which had the same type of menu and decor as Friday's. Friday's sues International for trademark infringement. Decision?

13. As part of its business, Kinko's Graphics Corporation (Kinko's) copied excerpts from books, compiled them in "packets," and sold the packets to college students. Kinko's did this without permission from the owners of the copyrights to the books and without paying copyright fees or royalties. Kinko's has more than 200 stores nationwide and reported $15 million in assets and $3 million in profits for 1989. Basic Books, Harper & Row, John Wiley & Sons, and others (plaintiffs) sued Kinko's for violation of the Copyright Act of 1976. Plaintiffs owned copyrights to the works copied and sold by Kinko's and derived substantial income from royalties. They argued that Kinko's had infringed on their copyrights by copying excerpts from their books and selling the copies to college students for profit. Kinko's admitted that it had copied excerpts without permission and had sold them in packets to students, but it contended that its actions constituted a fair use of the works in question under the Copyright Act. Decision?

14. In 1967, a Chicago brewer, Meister Brau, Inc., began making and selling a reduced-calorie, reduced-carbohydrate beer under the name "LITE." Late in 1968, that company filed applications to register "LITE" as a trademark in the United States Patent Office, which ultimately approved three registrations of labels containing the name "LITE" for "beer with no available carbohydrates." In 1972, Meister Brau sold its interest in the "LITE" trademarks and the accompanying goodwill to Miller Brewing Company. Miller decided to expand its marketing of beer under the brand "LITE." It developed a modified recipe, which resulted in a beer lower in calories than Miller's regular beer but not without available carbohydrates. The label was revised, and one of the registrations was amended to show "LITE" printed rather than in script. In addition, Miller undertook an extensive advertising campaign. From 1973 through 1976, Miller expanded its annual sales of "LITE" from 50,000 barrels to 4,000,000 barrels and increased its annual advertising expenditures from $500,000 to more than $12,000,000.

Beginning in early 1975, a number of other brewers, including G. Heileman Brewing Company, introduced reduced-calorie beers labeled or described as "light." In response, Miller began filing trademark infringement actions against competitors to enjoin the use of the word "light." The District Court enjoined Heileman from continuing to sell, advertise, and distribute beer anywhere in the United States under a brand name incorporating the word "Light," and Heileman appealed. Decision?

WWW **Internet Exercise** Find information about the organization and procedures of (a) the United States Copyright Office and (b) the United States Patent and Trademark Office.

# CHAPTER 41

# Antitrust

The economic community is best served by free competition in trade and industry. It is in the public interest that quality, price, and service in an open, competitive market for goods and services be determining factors in the business rivalry for the customer's dollar. Nevertheless, in lieu of competing, businesses would prefer to eliminate their rivals and consequently gain a position from which they could dictate both the price of their goods and the quantity they produce. Although to eliminate competition by producing a better product is the goal of a business, some businesses try to effect this elimination through illegitimate means, such as fixing prices and allocating exclusive territories to certain competitors within an industry. The law of antitrust prohibits such activities and attempts to ensure free and fair competition in the marketplace.

The common law has traditionally favored competition and has held agreements and contracts in restraint of trade illegal and unenforceable. In addition, several States enacted antitrust statutes during the 1800s. The latter half of the nineteenth century, however, disclosed concentrations of economic power in the form of "trusts" and "combinations" that were too powerful and widespread to be effectively curbed by State action. In 1890, this awesome growth of corporate power prompted Congress to enact the Sherman Antitrust Act, which was the first Federal statute in this field. Since then, Congress has enacted other antitrust statutes, including the Clayton Act, the Robinson-Patman Act, and the Federal Trade Commission Act. These statutes prohibit anticompetitive practices and seek to prevent unreasonable concentrations of economic power that stifle or weaken competition.

## SHERMAN ACT

Section 1 of the Sherman Act prohibits contracts, combinations, and conspiracies that restrain trade, while Section 2 prohibits monopolies and attempts to monopolize. Failure to comply with either section is a criminal felony and subjects the offender to fine or imprisonment, or both. As amended by the 1990 Antitrust Amendments, the Act subjects individual offenders to imprisonment of up to three years and fines up to $350,000, while corporate offenders are subject to fines of up to $10 million per violation. Moreover, the Sherman Act empowers the Federal district courts to issue injunctions restraining violations, and anyone injured by a violation is entitled to recover in a civil action **treble damages,** that is, three times the amount of the actual loss sustained. In addition, State Attorneys General may bring suit for treble damages on behalf of citizens of their States. The United States Justice Department and the Federal Trade Commission have the duty to institute appropriate enforcement proceedings other than treble damage actions.

The Supreme Court stated the purpose of the Sherman Act as follows:

The Sherman Act was designed to be a comprehensive charter of economic liberty aimed at preserving free and unfettered competition as the rule of trade. It rests on the premise that the unrestrained interaction of competitive forces will yield the best allocation of our economic resources, the lowest prices, the highest quality and the greatest material progress, while at the same time providing an environment conducive to the preservation of our democratic political and social institutions. *Northern Pacific Railway Co. v. United States*, 356 U.S. 1 (1958).

In 1992, the Justice Department expanded its policy of enforcement regarding the Sherman Act to cover conduct by foreign companies that harms U.S. exports. Under the new policy, the department examines conduct to determine whether it would violate the law if it occurred within the borders of the United States. The department has indicated that it will focus primarily on boycotts and cartels that injure the export of U.S. products and services.

# Restraint of Trade

Section 1 of the Sherman Act provides that "[e]very contract, combination in the form of trust or otherwise, or conspiracy, in restraint of trade or commerce among the several states, or with foreign nations is hereby declared to be illegal." Because the language of the section is so broad, judicial interpretation has played a significant role in establishing the elements that constitute a violation.

**Standards** As noted above, Section 1 prohibits every contract, combination, or conspiracy in restraint of trade. Taken literally, this prohibition would invalidate every unperformed contract. For example, under a strict interpretation of the section, a contract in which a seller agrees to supply a buyer with 1,000 pounds of grapes, no one but the seller would be permitted to fulfill the buyer's need for those 1,000 pounds of grapes, and the seller would not be allowed to sell those grapes to any other buyer. This agreement would therefore restrain trade. To avoid such a broad and impractical application, the courts have interpreted this section to invalidate only *unreasonable* restraints of trade:

The true test of legality is whether the restraint imposed is such as merely regulates and perhaps thereby promotes competition or whether it is such as may suppress or even destroy competition. To determine that question the courts must ordinarily consider the facts peculiar to the business to which the restraint is applied; its condition before and after the restraint was imposed; the nature of the restraint and its effect, actual or probable. The history of the restraint, the evil believed to exist, the reason for adopting the particular remedy, the purpose or end sought to be attained, are all relevant facts. This is not because a good intention will save an otherwise objectionable regulation or the reverse; but because knowledge of intent may help the court to interpret facts and to predict consequences. *Chicago Board of Trade v. United States*, 246 U.S. 231 (1918).

This flexible standard, known as the **rule of reason test,** requires the courts, in determining whether a challenged practice unreasonably restricts competition, to consider a variety of factors, including the makeup of the relevant industry, the defendants' positions within that industry, the ability of the defendants' competitors to respond to the challenged practice, and the defendants' purpose in adopting the restraint. After reviewing the various factors, a court determines whether the challenged restraint unreasonably restricts competition. By requiring courts to balance the anticompetitive effects of every questioned restraint against its procompetitive effects, this standard

places a substantial burden upon the judicial system. The United States Supreme Court addressed this problem by declaring certain categories of restraints to be unreasonable by their very nature, that is, **illegal** *per se*:

[T]here are certain agreements or practices which because of their pernicious effect on competition and lack of any redeeming virtue are conclusively presumed to be unreasonable and therefore illegal without elaborate inquiry as to the precise harm they have caused or the business excuse for their use. This principle of *per se* unreasonableness not only makes the type of restraints which are proscribed by the Sherman Act more certain to the benefit of everyone concerned, but it also avoids the necessity for an incredibly complicated and prolonged economic investigation into the entire history of the industry involved, as well as related industries, in an effort to determine at large whether a particular restraint has been unreasonable—an inquiry so often wholly fruitless when undertaken. *Northern Pacific Railway Co. v. United States*, 356 U.S. 1 (1958).

Characterizing a type of restraint as *per se* illegal therefore has a significant effect on the prosecution of an antitrust suit. In such a case, the plaintiff need only show that the type of restraint occurred; she does not need to prove that the restraint limited competition. Furthermore, the defendants may not defend on the basis that the restraint is reasonable. Additionally, as noted in *Northern Pacific Railway*, the court is not required to conduct extensive, and often difficult, economic analysis. Not surprisingly, the ease of applying the *per se* rule has helped to deter those restraints subject to the rule.

 *See Case 41-1*

**Horizontal and Vertical Restraints** A restraint of trade may be classified as either horizontal or vertical. A **horizontal restraint** involves collaboration among competitors at the same level in the chain of distribution. For example, an agreement among manufacturers, among wholesalers, or among retailers would be horizontal.

On the other hand, an agreement made by parties that are not in direct competition at the same level of distribution is a **vertical restraint.** Thus, an agreement between a manufacturer and a wholesaler is vertical.

Although the distinction between horizontal and vertical restraints can become blurred, it often determines whether a restraint is illegal *per se* or should be judged by the rule of reason test. For instance, horizontal market allocations are illegal *per se,* whereas vertical market allocations are subject to the rule of reason test.

***Concerted Action*** Section 1 does not prohibit unilateral conduct; rather, it forbids **concerted action.** Thus, one person or business by itself cannot violate the section. An organization has the "right to deal, or refuse to deal, with whomever it likes, as long as it does so independently." *Monsanto Co. v. Spray-Rite Service Corporation*, 465 U.S. 752 (1984). For example, if a manufacturer announces its resale prices in advance and refuses to deal with those who disagree with the pricing, there is no violation of Section 1 because the manufacturer has acted alone. On the other hand, if a manufacturer and its retailers together agree that the manufacturer will sell only to those retailers who agree to sell at a specified price, there may be a violation of Section 1.

For purposes of the concerted action requirement, a firm and its employees are viewed as one entity. The same rule is also true for a corporation and its wholly owned subsidiaries; thus, the Sherman Act is not violated when a parent and its wholly owned subsidiary agree to a restraint in trade. *Copperwald Corp. v. Independence Tube Corp.*, 467 U.S. 752 (1984). The Supreme Court has yet to decide, however, whether a parent and its partially owned subsidiary may violate Section 1.

The concerted action requirement may be established by an express agreement. Not surprisingly, however, an express agreement often is nonexistent, leaving the court to infer an agreement between the parties from circumstantial evidence:

No formal agreement is necessary to constitute an unlawful conspiracy. Often crimes are a matter of inference deduced from the acts of the person accused and done in pursuance of a criminal purpose. Where the conspiracy is proved, as here, from the evidence of the action taken in concert by the parties to it, it is all the more convincing proof of an intent to exercise the power of exclusion acquired through the conspiracy. The essential combination or conspiracy in violation of the Sherman Act may be found in a course of dealings or other circumstances as well as in any exchange of words. * * * Where the circumstances are such as to warrant a jury in finding that the conspirators had a unity of purpose or a common design and understanding, or a meeting of minds in an unlawful arrangement, the conclusion that a conspiracy is established is justified. *American Tobacco Co. v. United States*, 328 U.S. 781 (1946).

Nonetheless, similar patterns of conduct among competitors, called **conscious parallelism,** are not sufficient in themselves to suggest a conspiracy in violation of Section 1. Actual conspiracy requires an additional factor, such as complex action that, to benefit the competitors, requires the participation of each or indications of a traditional conspiracy, such as identical sealed bids from each competitor.

Joint ventures, which are discussed in Chapter 31, are a form of business association organized to carry out a particular business enterprise. Competitors frequently will pool their resources to share costs and to eliminate wasteful redundancy. The validity under antitrust law of a joint venture generally depends on the competitors' primary purpose in forming it. A joint venture that was not formed to fix prices or divide markets will be judged under the rule of reason.

However, because uncertainty about the legality of joint ventures seemed to discourage their use for joint research and development, Congress passed the National Cooperative Research Act to facilitate such applications. The Act provides that joint ventures in the research and development of new technology are to be judged under the rule of reason test and that treble damages do not apply to ventures formed in violation of Section 1 if those forming the venture have notified the Justice Department and the Federal Trade Commission (FTC) of their intent to form the joint venture.

***Price Fixing*** Price fixing is an agreement with the purpose or effect of inhibiting price competition; such an agreement may attempt to raise, depress, fix, peg, or stabilize prices. Price fixing is the primary and most serious example of a *per se* violation under the Sherman Act. As held in *United States v. Socony-Vacuum Oil Co.*, 310 U.S. 150 (1940), all **horizontal** price-fixing agreements are illegal *per se*. This prohibition not only covers any agreement between sellers to establish the *maximum* prices at which certain commodities or services will be offered for sale but encompasses agreements establishing *minimum* prices as well.

The U.S. Supreme Court has condemned not only agreements among horizontal competitors that directly fix prices but also agreements whose effect on price is indirect. For example, in *Catalano, Inc. v. Target Sales, Inc.*, 446 U.S. 643 (1980), the Court held that an agreement among beer wholesalers to eliminate interest-free short-term credit on sales to beer retailers was illegal *per se*. The Court viewed the credit terms "as an inseparable part of price" and concluded that the agreement to eliminate interest-free short-term credit was equivalent to an agreement to eliminate discounts and was thus an agreement to fix prices.

Similarly, it is illegal *per se* for a seller to fix the price at which purchasers must resell its product. This **vertical** form of price fixing—usually called retail price maintenance—is considered a *per se* violation of Section 1.

Despite its early and consistent condemnation of resale price maintenance agreements, the U.S. Supreme Court has found no Section 1 violation when a manufacturer who announces in advance that it will not sell to dealers who cut prices then ceases to do business with dealers who actually do so. Not surprisingly, courts sometimes have difficulty distinguishing between an illegal resale price maintenance agreement and a manufacturer's legal refusal to deal with a retailer who refuses to charge the manufacturer's dictated minimum price.

In a recent case, *State Oil Company v. Khan* (Case 41–2), the U.S. Supreme Court dealt with whether manufacturers' restrictions on the maximum resale price violate the antitrust laws. Overruling a thirty-year-old precedent, the Court held that vertical maximum price fixing is not *per se* illegal but instead is to be judged by a rule of reason standard.

 *See Case 41–2*

**Market Allocations**  Direct price fixing is not the only way to control prices. Another method involves **market allocation,** whereby competitors agree not to compete with each other in specific markets, which may be defined by geographic area, customer type, or product class. All **horizontal** agreements to divide markets have been declared illegal *per se,* because they confer upon the firm remaining in the market a monopolistic control over price. Thus, if Suny and RGE, both manufacturers of color televisions, agree that Suny shall have the exclusive right to sell color televisions in Illinois and Iowa and that RGE shall have the exclusive right in Minnesota and Wisconsin, Suny and RGE have committed a *per se* violation of Section 1 of the Sherman Act. Likewise, if Suny and RGE agree that Suny shall have the exclusive right to sell color televisions to Sears and that RGE shall sell exclusively to J.C. Penney, or that Suny shall have the exclusive right to manufacture nineteen-inch color televisions while RGE alone manufactures fifteen-inch sets, they are also in *per se* violation of Section 1 of the Sherman Antitrust Act. Horizontal market allocations may be found not only on the manufacturing level but also on the wholesale or retail level.

No longer illegal *per se,* **vertical** territorial and customer restrictions are now judged by the rule of reason. This change in approach resulted from a U.S. Supreme Court decision that mandated the lower Federal courts to balance the positive effect of vertical market restrictions upon interbrand competition against the negative effects upon intrabrand competition. Consequently, in some situations, vertical market restrictions will be found legitimate if, on balance, they do not inhibit competition in the relevant market.

In 1985, the U.S. Department of Justice issued a "market structure screen," under which the Justice Department will not challenge restraints by a firm having less than 10 percent of the relevant market or a "Vertical Restraint Index" (a measure of relative market share) indicating that neither collusion nor exclusion is possible. The concept of relevant market is discussed later, in the section on monopolization.

**Boycotts**  As noted above, Section 1 of the Sherman Act applies not to unilateral action but only to agreements or combinations. Accordingly, a seller's refusal to deal with any particular buyer does not violate the act, and a manufacturer thus can refuse to sell to a retailer who persists in selling below the manufacturer's suggested retail price. On the other hand, when two or more firms agree not to deal with a third party, their agreement constitutes a **concerted refusal to deal,** or a group boycott, which may violate Section 1 of the Sherman Act. Such a boycott may be clearly anticompetitive, eliminating competition or reducing market entry.

Some group boycotts are illegal *per se,* while others are subject to the rule of reason. Group boycotts designed to eliminate a competitor or to force that competitor to meet a group standard are illegal *per se* if the group has market power. On the other hand, cooperative arrangements "designed to increase economic efficiency and render markets more, rather than less, competitive" are subject to the rule of reason.

Finally, most courts hold that the *per se* rule of illegality for concerted refusals to deal extends only to horizontal boycotts, not to vertical refusals to deal. Most courts have held that a rule of reason test should govern all nonprice vertical restraints, including concerted refusals to deal.

**Tying Arrangements**  A tying arrangement occurs when the seller of a product, service, or intangible (the "tying" product) conditions its sale on the buyer's purchasing a second product, service, or intangible (the "tied" product) from the seller. For example, assume that Xerox, a major manufacturer of photocopying equipment, were to require that all purchasers of its photocopiers also purchase from Xerox all of the paper they would use with the copiers. Xerox thereby would tie the sale of its photocopier—the *tying* product—to the sale of paper—the *tied* product.

Because tying arrangements limit buyers' freedom of choice and may exclude competitors, the law closely scrutinizes such agreements. A tying arrangement exists where a seller exploits its economic power in one market to expand its empire into another market. When the seller has considerable economic power in the tying product and more than an insubstantial amount of interstate commerce is affected in the tied product, the tying arrangement will be *per se* illegal. The courts may establish a seller's economic power by showing that (1) the seller occupied a dominant position in the tying market, (2) the seller's product enjoys an advantage not shared by its competitors in the tying market, or (3) a substantial number of customers have accepted the tying arrangement, and the sole explanation for their willingness to comply is the seller's economic power in the tying market. If the seller lacks economic power, the tying arrangement is judged by the rule of reason test.

Figure 41–1 summarizes how these restraints on trade are judged under Section 1.

◆  *See Figure 41–1*

⚖  *See Case 41–3*

## Monopolies

Economic analysis indicates that a monopolist will use its power to limit production and increase prices. Accordingly, a monopolistic market will produce fewer goods than a competitive market would and will sell those goods at higher prices. To address the problem of monopolization, Section 2 of the Sherman Act prohibits monopolies and all attempts or conspiracies to monopolize. Thus, Section 2 prohibits both agreements among businesses and, unlike Section 1, unilateral conduct by one firm.

*Monopolization*  Although the language of Section 2 appears to prohibit without exception *all* monopolization, the courts have required that in addition to merely possessing market power, a firm must have either attained the monopoly power unfairly or abused that power, once attained. Possession of monopoly power is not in itself considered a violation of Section 2 because a firm may have obtained such power through its skills in developing, marketing, and selling products; that is, through the very competitive conduct that the antitrust laws are designed to promote.

Because it is extremely rare to find an unregulated industry with only one firm, determining the presence of monopoly power involves defining the degree of market dominance that constitutes such power. **Monopoly power** is the ability to control prices or to exclude competitors from the marketplace. In grappling with this question of power, the courts have developed a number of criteria, but the prevalent test is market share. A market share greater than 75 percent generally indicates monopoly power, while a share less than 50 percent does not. A share between 50 percent and 75 percent share is inconclusive.

**Market share** is a firm's fractional share of the total relevant product and geographic markets, but defining these relevant markets is often a difficult and subjective task for the courts. The relevant *product market* includes products that are substitutable for the firm's product on the basis of price, quality, and elasticity. For example, although brick and wood siding are both used on building exteriors, they would not likely be considered part of the same product market. On the other hand, Coca-Cola and Pepsi are both soft drinks and would be considered part of the same product market.

The relevant *geographic market* is that territory in which the firm makes sales of its products or services.

**FIGURE 41–1**  Restraints of Trade under Sherman Act

| Type of Restraint | Standard | |
|---|---|---|
| | *Per Se* Illegal | Rule of Reason |
| **Price fixing** | Horizontal<br>Vertical (minimum) | Vertical (maximum) |
| **Market allocations** | Horizontal | Vertical |
| **Group boycotts or refusals to deal** | Horizontal, Vertical (minority) | Vertical (majority) |
| **Tying arrangements** | If seller has economic power in tying product and affects a not-insubstantial amount of interstate commerce in the tied product | If seller lacks economic power in tying product |

This may be at the local, regional, or national level. For instance, the relevant geographic market for the manufacture and sale of aluminum might be national whereas that of a taxicab operating company would be local. The scope of a geographic market depends upon factors such as transportation costs, the type of product or services, and the location of competitors and customers.

If sufficient monopoly power has been proved, the law then must show that the firm has engaged in **unfair conduct.** The courts, however, have yet to agree upon what constitutes such conduct. One judicial approach is to place upon a firm possessing monopoly power the burden of proving that it acquired such power passively or that the power was "thrust" upon it. An alternative view is that monopoly power, when coupled with conduct designed to exclude competitors, violates Section 2. A third approach requires monopoly power plus some type of predatory practice, such as pricing below marginal costs. For example, one case that adopted the third approach held that a firm does not violate Section 2 of the Sherman Act if it attained its market share through either (1) research, technical innovation, or a superior product, or (2) ordinary marketing methods available to all. *Telex Corp. v. IBM*, 510 F.2d 894 (10th Cir. 1975).

The U.S. Supreme Court decision in *Aspen Skiing Co. v. Aspen Highlands Skiing Corp.*, 472 U.S. 585 (1985), appears to combine these approaches. The Court held that "[i]f a firm has been attempting to exclude rivals on some basis other than efficiency, it is fair to characterize its behavior as predatory."

To date, however, the U.S. Supreme Court has yet to define the exact conduct, beyond the mere possession of monopoly power, that violates Section 2. To do so, the Court must resolve the complex and conflicting policies this most basic question regarding monopolies involves. On the one hand, condemning fairly acquired monopoly power—that acquired "merely by virtue of superior skill, foresight, and industry"—penalizes firms that compete effectively. On the other hand, permitting firms with monopoly power to continue provides them the opportunity to lower output and raise prices, thereby injuring consumers.

 *See Case 41–3*

***Attempts to Monopolize*** Section 2 also prohibits attempts to monopolize. As with monopolization, the courts have had difficulty developing a standard that distinguishes undesirable conduct likely to engender a monopoly from healthy competitive conduct. The standard test applied by the courts requires proof of a specific intent to monopolize plus a dangerous probability of success; however, this test neither defines an "intent" nor provides a standard of power by which to measure "success." Recent cases suggest that the greater the measure of market power a firm acquires, the less flagrant must its conduct be to constitute an attempt. These cases do not, however, specify any threshold level of market power.

***Conspiracies to Monopolize*** Section 2 also condemns conspiracies to monopolize. Few cases involve this offense alone, as any conspiracy to monopolize would also constitute a combination in restraint of trade in violation of Section 1. Because of the overlap between these two provisions, some scholars have stated that the offense of conspiracy to monopolize is "redundant."

## CLAYTON ACT

In 1914, Congress strengthened the Sherman Act by adopting the Clayton Act, which was expressly designed "to supplement existing laws against unlawful restraints and monopolies." The Act is intended to stop trade practices before they become restraints of trade or monopolies forbidden by the Sherman Act. The Clayton Act provides only for civil actions, not for criminal penalties. Private parties may bring civil actions in Federal court for treble damages and attorneys' fees. In addition, the Justice Department and the FTC are authorized to bring civil actions, including proceedings in equity, to prevent and restrict violations of the Act.

The substantive provisions of the Clayton Act deal with price discrimination, tying contracts, exclusive dealing, mergers, and interlocking directorates. Section 2, which deals with price discrimination, was amended and rewritten by the Robinson-Patman Act, discussed below. In addition, the Clayton Act exempts labor, agricultural, and horticultural organizations from all antitrust laws.

### Tying Contracts and Exclusive Dealing

Section 3 of the Clayton Act prohibits tying arrangements and exclusive dealing, selling, or leasing arrangements which prevent purchasers from dealing with the seller's competitors and which *may* substantially lessen competition or *tend* to create a monopoly. This section is intended to attack incipient anticompetitive practices before they ripen into violations of Section 1 or 2 of the Sherman Act. Unlike the Sherman Act, however, Section 3 applies only to practices involving commodities, not to those that involve services, intangibles, or land.

**Tying arrangements,** which were discussed in the sections covering the Sherman Act, have been labeled by the Supreme Court as serving "hardly any purpose beyond the suppression of competition." Although the Court at one time indicated that different standards applied under the Sherman Act and the Clayton Act, recent lower court cases suggest that the same rules now govern both types of actions.

**Exclusive dealing arrangements** are agreements by which the seller or lessor of a product conditions the agreement upon the buyer's or lessor's promise not to deal in the goods of a competitor. For example, a manufacturer of razors might require retailers wishing to sell its line of shaving equipment to agree not to carry competing merchandise. Such conduct, although treated more leniently than tying arrangements, violates Section 3 if it tends to create a monopoly or may substantially lessen competition. The courts regard exclusive dealing arrangements more tolerantly because such arrangements may be procompetitive to the extent that they benefit buyers, and thus, indirectly, ultimate consumers, by ensuring supplies, deterring price increases, and enabling long-term planning on the basis of known costs.

## Mergers

In the United States, corporate mergers have played a significant role in reshaping both the structure of corporations and our economic system. Mergers are horizontal, vertical, or conglomerate, depending upon the relationship between the acquirer and the acquired company. A **horizontal merger** involves the acquisition by a company of all or part of the stock or assets of a competing company. For example, if IBM were to acquire Apple, this would be a horizontal merger. A **vertical merger** is a company's acquisition of one of its customers or suppliers. A vertical merger is a *forward* merger if the acquiring company purchases a customer, such as the purchase of Revco Discount Drug Stores by Procter & Gamble. A vertical merger is a *backward* merger if the acquiring company purchases a supplier; for example, Circuit City's purchase of Maytag Appliance. The third type of merger, the **conglomerate merger,** is a catchall category that covers all acquisitions not involving a competitor, customer, or supplier.

Section 7 of the Clayton Act prohibits a corporation from merging or acquiring stock or assets of another corporation where such action would lessen competition substantially or would tend to create a monopoly.

Section 7 of the Clayton Act was intended to arrest the anticompetitive effects of market power in their incipiency.

The core question is whether a merger may substantially lessen competition, and necessarily requires a prediction of the merger's impact on competition, present and future. The section can deal only with probabilities, not with certainties. And there is certainly no requirement that the anticompetitive power manifest itself in anticompetitive action before § 7 can be called into play. If the enforcement of § 7 turned on the existence of actual anticompetitive practices, the congressional policy of thwarting such practices in their incipiency would be frustrated. *F.T.C. v. Procter & Gamble Co.*, 386 U.S. 568 (1967).

The principal objective of the antitrust law governing mergers is to maintain competition. Accordingly, horizontal mergers are scrutinized most stringently. Factors that the courts consider in reviewing the legality of a horizontal merger include the market share of each of the merging firms, the degree of industry concentration, the number of firms in the industry, entry barriers, market trends, the strength of other competitors in the industry, the character and history of the merging firms, market demand, and the extent of industry price competition. The leading Supreme Court cases on horizontal mergers date from the 1960s and early 1970s. Since then, lower Federal courts, the Department of Justice, and the FTC have emphasized antitrust's goal of promoting economic efficiency. Accordingly, while the Supreme Court cases remain the law of the land, recent lower court decisions reflect a greater willingness to tolerate industry concentrations. Nevertheless, the government continues to prosecute, and the courts continue to condemn, horizontal mergers that are likely to hurt consumers.

Though vertical mergers are far less likely to be challenged, the Justice Department and the FTC have attacked vertical mergers that threatened to raise entry barriers in the industry or to foreclose other firms in the acquiring firm's industry from competitively significant customers or suppliers. While the Supreme Court has not decided a vertical merger case since 1972, recent decisions indicate that at least some lower courts have been willing to condemn only those vertical mergers that clearly show anticompetitive effects.

Finally, conglomerate mergers have been challenged only (1) where one of the merging firms would be highly likely to enter the market of the other firm or (2) where the merged company would be disproportionately large as compared with the largest competitors in its industry.

The Justice Department and the FTC have both indicated that they will be primarily concerned with horizontal mergers in highly or moderately concentrated industries and that they question the benefits of challenging vertical and conglomerate mergers. Both the Justice

Department and the FTC have justified this policy on the basis that the latter two types of mergers are necessary to transfer assets to their most productive use and that any challenge to such mergers would impose costs on consumers without corresponding benefits.

Antitrust law, as currently applied, focuses on the size of the merged firm in relation to the relevant market, not on the resulting entity's absolute size. In 1992 (subsequently revised in 1997), the Justice Department and the FTC jointly issued new Horizontal Merger Guidelines to replace their earlier and separate guidelines. In doing so, the two agencies sought to prevent market power that results in "a transfer of wealth from buyers to sellers or a misallocation of resources." The guidelines are designed to provide an analytical framework to judge the impact of potential mergers:

The process of assessing market concentration, potential adverse competitive effects, entry, efficiency and failure is a tool that allows the Agency to answer the ultimate inquiry in merger analysis: whether the merger is likely to create or enhance market power or to facilitate its exercise.

Moreover, the guidelines clearly indicate that neither agency will apply them mechanically.

The 1992 and 1997 guidelines, like their earlier counterparts, quantify market concentration through the Herfindahl-Hirschman Index (HHI) and measure a horizontal merger's impact on the index. This concentration index is calculated by summing the squares of the individual market shares of all firms in the market. An industry with only one firm would have an HHI of 10,000 ($100^2$). With two firms of equal size, the index would be 5,000 ($50^2 + 50^2$); with five firms of equal size, the result would be 2,000 ($20^2 + 20^2 + 20^2 + 20^2 + 20^2$). The increase a merger would cause in the index is calculated by doubling the product of the merging firms' market shares. For example, the merger of two firms with market shares of 5 percent and 10 percent respectively would increase the index by 100 ($5 \times 10 \times 2 = 100$).

The guidelines use three categories of market concentration to analyze horizontal mergers and to determine the likelihood of governmental opposition, based on the increase the proposed merger would cause in the index. The three categories are classified according to the postmerger HHI. If the postmerger figure is below 1,000, the agencies are unlikely to challenge the merger without regard to the increase the merger would cause in the index. For postmerger HHIs between 1,000 and 1,800, the department will examine the increase in HHI due to the merger. Increases of less than 100 are unlikely to generate a challenge, but those greater than 100 raise

significant competitive concerns that mandate an examination of other factors. When the postmerger HHI is above 1,800, an increase of more than 50 points also will raise significant competitive concerns and thus force an examination of other factors; furthermore, the department is likely to challenge any merger contributing an increase of more than 100, for such a merger is presumed to enhance market power.

In 1987, the National Association of Attorneys General, composed of the Attorneys General of the fifty States and five U.S. territories and protectorates, promulgated its own set of guidelines for horizontal mergers. Intended to apply to enforcement actions brought by the State Attorneys General under Federal and State antitrust statutes, the State guidelines place a greater emphasis on preventing transfers of wealth from consumers to producers than do the Federal guidelines. Accordingly, the State Attorneys General would be more likely to challenge certain mergers than would the Federal government.

 *See Case 41–4*

## ROBINSON-PATMAN ACT

Section 2 of the Clayton Act originally prohibited only sellers from differentially pricing their products to injure local or regional competitors. In 1936, in an attempt to limit the power of large purchasers, Congress amended Section 2 of the Clayton Act by adopting the Robinson-Patman Act, which further prohibited **price discrimination** in interstate commerce involving commodities of like grade and quality. Thus, the Act prohibits buyers from inducing and sellers from granting discrimination in prices. To constitute a violation, the price discrimination must substantially lessen competition or tend to create a monopoly.

Under this Act, a seller of goods may not grant discounts to buyers, including allowances for advertisements, counter displays, and samples, unless the seller offers the same discounts to all other purchasers on proportionately equal terms. The Act also prohibits other types of discounts, rebates, and allowances and makes it unlawful to sell goods at unreasonably low prices for the purpose of destroying competition or eliminating a competitor. Furthermore, the Act makes it unlawful for a person knowingly to "induce or receive" an illegal discrimination in price, thus imposing liability on the buyer as well as the seller. Violation of the Robinson-Patman Act, with limited exceptions, is civil, not criminal, in nature. The Act does permit price differentials that are justified by proof of either a cost savings to the seller or a good-faith price reduction to meet the lawful price of a competitor.

## Primary-line Injury

In enacting Section 2 of the Clayton Act in 1914, Congress was concerned with sellers who sought to harm or eliminate their competitors through price discrimination. Injuries accruing to a seller's competitors are called "primary-line" injuries. Because the Act forbids price discrimination only where such discrimination may substantially lessen competition or tend to create a monopoly, the plaintiff in a Robinson-Patman primary-line injury case must either show that the defendant, with the intent to harm competition, has engaged in predatory pricing or present a detailed market analysis that demonstrates how the defendant's price discrimination actually harmed competition. To prove predatory intent, a plaintiff may rely either on direct evidence of such intent or, more commonly, on inferences drawn from the defendant's conduct, such as a significant period of below-cost or unprofitable pricing. A predatory pricing scheme also may be challenged under the Sherman Act.

## Secondary- and Tertiary-line Injury

In amending Section 2 of the Clayton Act in 1936 through the adoption of the Robinson-Patman Act, Congress was concerned primarily with small buyers, who were harmed by the discounts that sellers granted to large buyers. Injuries accruing to some buyers because of the lower prices granted to other buyers are called "secondary-line" injuries. To prove the required harm to competition, a plaintiff in a secondary-line injury case must either show substantial and sustained price differentials in a market or offer a detailed market analysis that demonstrates actual harm to competition. Because courts have been willing in secondary-line injury cases to infer harm to competition from a sustained and substantial price differential, proving a secondary-line injury generally is easier than proving a primary-line injury.

Tertiary-line injury occurs when the recipient of a favored price passes the benefits of the lower price on to the next level of distribution. Purchasers from other secondary-line sellers are injured in that they do not receive the benefits of the lower price; these purchasers may recover damages from the original discriminating seller.

## Cost Justification

If a seller can show that it costs less to sell a product to a particular buyer, the seller may lawfully pass along the cost savings. Section 2(a) provides that the Act does not "prevent differentials which make only due allowance for differences in the cost of manufacture, sale, or delivery resulting from the differing methods or quantities in which . . . commodities are . . . sold or delivered." For example, if Retailer A orders goods from Seller X by the carload, whereas Retailer B orders in small quantities, Seller X, who delivers F.O.B. buyer's warehouse, may pass along the transportation savings to Retailer A. Nonetheless, although it is possible to pass along transportation savings, it is extremely difficult to pass along alleged savings in manufacturing or distribution because of the complexity involved in calculating and proving such savings. Therefore, sellers rarely rely upon the defense of cost justification.

## Meeting Competition

A seller may lower his price in a good faith attempt to meet competition. To illustrate:

1. Manufacturer X sells its motor oil to retail outlets for 65 cents per can. Manufacturer Y approaches A, one of Manufacturer X's customers, and offers to sell a comparable type of motor oil for 60 cents per can. Manufacturer X will be permitted to lower its price to A to 60 cents per can and need not lower its price to its other retail customers—B, C, and D. Manufacturer X, however, may not lower its price to A to 55 cents unless it also offers this lower price to B, C, and D.
2. To allow A to meet the lower price that A's competitor, N, charges when selling Manufacturer Y's oil, Manufacturer X will not be permitted to lower its price to A without also lowering its price to B, C, and D.

A seller may beat its competitor's price, however, if it does not know the competitor's price, cannot reasonably determine the competitor's price, and acts reasonably in setting its own price.

◆ *See Figure 41–2*

## FEDERAL TRADE COMMISSION ACT

In 1914, through the enactment of the Federal Trade Commission Act, Congress created the Federal Trade

**FIGURE 41–2**  Meeting Competition Defense

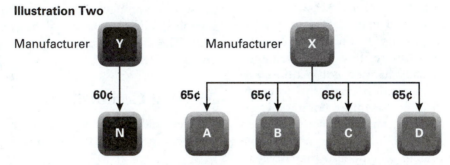

**Illustration One**

*Result:* Manufacturer **X** may lower its price to A to 60¢ without lowering its price to B, C, and D.

**Illustration Two**

*Result:* Manufacturer **X** may *not* lower its price to A to 60¢ without lowering its price to B, C, and D.

Commission and charged it with the duty to prevent "unfair methods of competition in commerce, and unfair or deceptive acts or practices in commerce." To this end, the five-member commission is empowered to conduct appropriate investigations and hearings and to issue against violators "cease and desist" orders enforceable in the Federal courts. Its broad power has been described by the U.S. Supreme Court:

The "unfair methods of competition," which are condemned by . . . the Act, are not confined to those that were illegal at common law or that were condemned by the Sherman Act. . . . It is also clear that the Federal Trade Commission Act was designed to supplement and bolster the Sherman Act and the Clayton Act . . . *to stop in their incipiency acts and practices which, when full blown, would violate those Acts. F.T.C. v. Motion Picture Advertising Service Co.,* 344 U.S. 392 (1953). (Emphasis supplied.)

Complaints may be instituted by the commission, which, after a hearing, "has wide latitude for judgment and the courts will not interfere except where the remedy selected has no reasonable relation to the unlawful practices found to exist." Although the commission most frequently enters a cease and desist order having the effect of an injunction, it may order other relief, such as affirmative disclosure, corrective advertising, and the granting of patent licenses on a reasonable royalty basis. Appeals may be taken from orders of the commission to the U.S. Courts of Appeals, which have exclusive jurisdiction to enforce, set aside, or modify orders of the commission.

In performing its duties, the FTC investigates not only possible violations of the antitrust laws but also unfair methods of competition, such as false and misleading advertisements, false or inadequate product labeling, the passing or palming off of goods as those of a competitor, lotteries, gambling schemes, discriminatory rebate or discount offers, false disparagement of a competitor's goods, false or misleading descriptive names of products, the use of false testimonials, and other unfair trade practices. For a more detailed discussion of the FTC and its powers, see Chapter 42.

# Chapter Summary

## Sherman Antitrust Act

**Restraint of Trade** Section 1 prohibits contracts, combinations, and conspiracies that restrain trade
- *Rule of Reason* standard that balances the anticompetitive effects against the procompetitive effects of the restraint
- **Per Se** *Violations* conclusively presumed unreasonable and therefore illegal
- *Horizontal Restraints* agreements among competitors
- *Vertical Restraints* agreements among parties at different levels in the chain of distribution

**Application of Section 1**
- *Price Fixing* an agreement with the purpose or effect of inhibiting price competition; both horizontal and minimum vertical agreements are *per se* illegal, while maximum vertical price fixing is judged by the rule of reason
- *Market Allocation* division of markets by customer type, geography, or products; horizontal agreements are *per se* illegal, while vertical agreements are judged by the rule of reason standard
- *Boycott* agreement among competitors not to deal with a supplier or customer; *per se* illegal
- *Tying Arrangement* conditioning a sale of a desired product (tying product) on the buyer's purchasing a second product (tied product); *per se* illegal if the seller has considerable power in the tying product or affects a not-insubstantial amount of interstate commerce in the tied product

**Monopolies** Section 2 prohibits monopolization, attempts to monopolize, and conspiracies to monopolize
- *Monopolization* requires market power (ability to control price or exclude others from the marketplace) plus either the unfair attainment of the power or the abuse of such power
- *Attempt to Monopolize* specific intent to monopolize, plus a dangerous probability of success
- *Conspiracies to Monopolize*

**Sanctions**
- *Treble Damages* three times actual loss
- *Criminal Penalties*

## Clayton Act

**Tying Arrangement** prohibited if it tends to create a monopoly or may substantially lessen competition

**Exclusive Dealing** arrangement by which a party has sole right to a market; prohibited if it tends to create a monopoly or may substantially lessen competition

**Merger** prohibited if it tends to create a monopoly or may substantially lessen competition
- *Horizontal Merger* one company's acquisition of a competing company
- *Vertical Merger* a company's acquisition of one of its suppliers or customers
- *Conglomerate Merger* the acquisition of a company that is not a competitor, customer, or supplier

**Sanctions** treble damages

| Robinson-Patman Act | **Price Discrimination** the act prohibits buyers from inducing or sellers from giving different prices to buyers of commodities of similar grade and quality<br>**Injury** plaintiff may prove injury to competitors of the seller (primary-line injury), to competitors of other buyers (secondary-line injury), or to purchasers from other secondary-line sellers (tertiary-line injury)<br>**Defenses** (1) cost justification, (2) meeting competition, and (3) functional discounts<br>**Sanctions** civil (treble damages); criminal in limited situations |
| --- | --- |

| Federal Trade Commission Act | **Purpose** to prevent unfair methods of competition and unfair or deceptive practices<br>**Sanctions** actions may be brought by the FTC, not by private individuals |
| --- | --- |

 **Cases**

### CASE 41–1
### Restraint of Trade: Standards
### *BCB ANESTHESIA CARE, LTD. v.*
### *PASSAVANT MEMORIAL AREA HOSPITAL ASSOCIATION*
United States Court of Appeals, Seventh Circuit, 1994
36 F.3d 664

MORAN, J.

Plaintiffs filed this complaint charging the defendants with violations of section 1 of the Sherman Act, [citation]. * * * They complain that their practice as nurse anesthetists at a central Illinois hospital has been unlawfully restricted. Defendants moved to dismiss on a variety of grounds and the district court did dismiss, concluding that plaintiffs had not alleged a sufficient nexus with interstate commerce to invoke Sherman Act jurisdiction. * * * We now affirm, but on different grounds.

According to the complaint, the three individual plaintiffs are certified registered nurse anesthetists (CRNAs) and the corporate plaintiff, BCB Anesthesia Care Ltd. (BCB), is a business equally owned by the three of them. CRNAs compete with physician anesthesiologists (MDAs) and provide anesthesia services at lower cost. The defendants are The Passavant Memorial Area Hospital Association (Passavant)—the only acute care general hospital in Jacksonville, Illinois; MDA Peter Roodhouse; Clarence Lay, the hospital's chief executive officer; and Dr. Eric Giebelhausen, a Jacksonville doctor with staff privileges at Passavant.

According to the complaint the individual plaintiffs were employed as anesthetists at the hospital prior to July 28, 1991. During the first half of that year they negotiated an agreement with Passavant, effective July 29, 1991, whereby BCB provided anesthesia services to hospital patients, and billed them directly at $35 per unit. The hospital billed separately at $11 per unit, which plaintiffs claim was a violation of the BCB contract. When the CRNAs were employees the hospital had billed at $17 per unit for a portion of such services. During that time Dr. Roodhouse also provided anesthesia services as an independent contractor, with the billing done separately at $28 per unit.

During the last five months of 1991, BCB and the hospital anesthetists (apparently there were other anesthetists on staff) performed all but three anesthesia procedures at Passavant. Dr. Roodhouse, however, plaintiffs allege, billed patients and third party payers for anesthesia services he had not performed, in an effort to injure BCB. This practice caused those billed to complain about double billing and, in some instances, to fail to pay legitimate BCB bills. Dr. Roodhouse also derided BCB's billing practices to local physicians, leading some to conclude that BCB billings were either too high or unethical. Dr. Giebelhausen had been opposed to the BCB contract even before its inception, and subsequently urged its cancellation on the ground that BCB's billings were unethical and supported the restoration of Dr. Roodhouse as the primary anesthesiologist.

Beginning in April 1992, Dr. Roodhouse scheduled anesthesia services so as to perform the majority of those services during that month. Then, on May 20, 1992, Clarence Lay, the hospital CEO, advised plaintiffs that Passavant was terminating the BCB contract. The hospital subsequently entered into a contract with Dr. Roodhouse and raised its separate charges to $17 per unit. The individual plaintiffs were given the option of returning to employee status, even though the supervision of an MDA was not required either by law or codes of professional responsibility. Dr. Roodhouse, plaintiffs charge, acted to destroy BCB's business and to maintain or increase his earnings. All this, they allege, was a conspiracy in restraint of trade to limit their practice, to initiate a tying agreement between Passavant and Dr. Roodhouse, to boycott the plaintiffs, and to fix prices illegally. * * *

The concept of interstate commerce under the Sherman Act has had a troubled history, . . . It has been marked by a disagreement over whether we should look to the concept of interstate commerce itself and the reach of congressional power, an expanding notion, [citation], or to the statutory prohibition against conspiracies that restrain interstate trade. [Citation.] In *McLain v. Real Estate Board of New Orleans, Inc.*, [1980 U.S. Supreme Court decision], the attention turned from whether or not the restraint, if successful, would have a substantial effect on interstate commerce, to whether or not activities allegedly infected by the restraint had a not insubstantial effect on interstate commerce.

* * *

Plaintiffs first alleged that Passavant derives substantial revenue from interstate insurance and federal Medicare and Medicaid payments, and that it purchased substantial quantities of supplies coming from other states. They further alleged that they provided services to patients and third party payers at lower cost than the charges of MDAs, with a change to MDA services resulting in higher costs for federal and third party payers. * * * [The plaintiffs further] alleged that Passavant and the plaintiffs treated out-of-state patients and that BCB billings were through a Minnesota agency. * * *

* * * [W]e conclude that they have alleged a not insubstantial effect on interstate commerce. * * *

But that does not end the inquiry. Defendants contended below, and continue to argue, that plaintiffs do not state a claim under section 1 of the Sherman Act, and with that we do agree. The Sherman Act is perhaps the quintessential delegation by the Congress to the courts of the task of fashioning a legal structure to govern conduct. From that delegation a number of judicially created principles have emerged. Only unreasonable restraints of trade are illegal. Some restraints, such as horizontal price-fixing, are so obviously anticompetitive that they are deemed, *per se*, illegal, without further elaboration. The anticompetitive effects of some conduct are problematic; we do not know whether or not the conduct is procompetitive or anticompetitive without a thorough exploration of its purpose and consequences in a competitive environment. We consider impact: does it potentially have a not insubstantial effect upon interstate commerce; and the nature of that impact: does it have an anticompetitive effect.

To be sure, an unlawful purpose and an anticompetitive effect are not alone sufficient. Two youngsters, not partners, who agree on prices for lemonade at stands on adjacent corners so as to eliminate price competition, have an unlawful purpose and their agreement is anticompetitive. That agreement does not, as a matter of practical economics, affect interstate commerce. We cannot say that those circumstances are comparable to those alleged here, but we can say, . . . that the interstate commerce threshold is relatively low.

But what if the conduct has a not insubstantial effect upon interstate commerce—but we do not know if it is pernicious without a thorough exploration of purpose and effect? Then we turn to the rule of reason; we seek an answer to that question of purpose and effect before we decide whether or not that conduct runs afoul of the Sherman Act, and that raises questions of market definition and market power. Indeed, pinning a label on conduct, such as "tying," or "boycott," is not enough if the conduct does not necessarily have the pernicious effect the label suggests. [Citation.]

This case involves one hospital's decisions about staff privileges and staffing patterns. The cases involving staffing at a single hospital are legion. * * * Those cases invariably analyze those circumstances under the rule of reason—there is nothing obviously anticompetitive about a hospital choosing one staffing pattern over another or in restricting the staffing to some rather than many, or all. [Citation.] A hospital has an unquestioned right to exercise some control over the identity and number to whom it accords staff privileges. [Citation.] * * *

Those hundreds or thousands of pages [of cases] almost always come to the same conclusion: the staffing decision at a single hospital was not a violation of section 1 of the Sherman Act. [Citations.]

The reasons advanced for that conclusion are varied. Insufficient nexus to interstate commerce, lack of standing, lack of antitrust injury, failure to show a detrimental effect on competition, the inability of a hospital to conspire with its staff, and insufficient market power in the relevant market are among the reasons relied upon for denying section 1 relief.

\* \* \*

A staffing decision does not itself constitute an antitrust injury. "If the law were otherwise, many a physician's workplace grievance with a hospital would be elevated to the status of an antitrust action. To keep the antitrust laws from becoming so trivialized, the reasonableness of a restraint is evaluated based on its impact on competition as a whole within the relevant market." [Citation.] Here we are given little reason to infer that there is an impact on competition within the relevant market defined by plaintiffs, and no reason to infer such an impact within the broader relevant market that we undoubtedly must consider.

The *per se* approach to antitrust law was a judicial creation—a belief that some conduct was so invariably anti-competitive that it did not justify a detailed examination of purpose and effect. We think the judicial concern with avoiding burdensome litigation unless there is an apparent justification for it applies with equal force here. How one hospital staffs its needs is so unlikely to be within the ambit of section 1 of the Sherman Act that it does not justify a detailed examination of purpose and effect unless plaintiffs give us far better reasons for that examination than they have here. "Although we hesitate to say that [a staffing decision at one hospital] . . . can never state an antitrust claim, we believe it is incumbent upon the plaintiff to plead some additional facts from which it can be inferred that the case falls within the ambit of the Sherman Act." [Citation.] \* \* \*

The judgment is affirmed.

---

## CASE 41–2
### Price Fixing
### *STATE OIL COMPANY v. KHAN*
Supreme Court of the United States, 1997
522 U.S. 3, 118 S.Ct. 275, 139 L.Ed.2d 199

O'CONNOR, J.

\* \* \*

### I

Respondents, Barkat U. Khan and his corporation, entered into an agreement with petitioner, State Oil Company, to lease and operate a gas station and convenience store owned by State Oil. The agreement provided that respondents would obtain the station's gasoline supply from State Oil at a price equal to a suggested retail price set by State Oil, less a margin of 3.25 cents per gallon. Under the agreement, respondents could charge any amount for gasoline sold to the station's customers, but if the price charged was higher than State Oil's suggested retail price, the excess was to be rebated to State Oil. Respondents could sell gasoline for less than State Oil's suggested retail price, but any such decrease would reduce their 3.25 cents-per-gallon margin.

About a year after respondents began operating the gas station, they fell behind in lease payments. State Oil then gave notice of its intent to terminate the agreement and commenced a state court proceeding to evict respondents. \* \* \*

Respondents sued State Oil in the United States District Court \* \* \* alleging in part that State Oil had engaged in price fixing in violation of § 1 of the Sherman Act by preventing respondents from raising or lowering retail gas prices. \* \* \*

The District Court found that the allegations in the complaint did not state a *per se* violation of the Sherman Act because they did not establish the sort of "manifestly anticompetitive implications or pernicious effect on competition" that would justify *per se* prohibition of State Oil's conduct. Subsequently, in ruling on cross-motions for summary judgment, the District Court concluded that respondents had failed to demonstrate antitrust injury or harm to competition. \* \* \* Accordingly, the District Court entered summary judgment for State Oil on respondents' Sherman Act claim.

The Court of Appeals for the Seventh Circuit reversed. [Citation.] The court first noted that the agreement between respondents and State Oil did indeed fix maximum gasoline prices by making it "worthless" for respondents to exceed the suggested retail prices. After reviewing legal and economic aspects of price fixing, the court concluded that State Oil's pricing scheme was a *per se* antitrust violation under *Albrecht v. Herald Co.*, [citation]. Although the Court of Appeals characterized *Albrecht* as "unsound when decided" and "inconsistent with later decisions" of this Court, it felt constrained to follow that decision. * * *

* * *

# II

Although the Sherman Act, by its terms, prohibits every agreement "in restraint of trade," this Court has long recognized that Congress intended to outlaw only unreasonable restraints. [Citations.] As a consequence, most antitrust claims are analyzed under a "rule of reason," according to which the finder of fact must decide whether the questioned practice imposes an unreasonable restraint on competition, taking into account a variety of factors, including specific information about the relevant business, its condition before and after the restraint was imposed, and the restraint's history, nature, and effect. [Citations.]

Some types of restraints, however, have such predictable and pernicious anticompetitive effect, and such limited potential for procompetitive benefit, that they are deemed unlawful *per se*. [Citation.] *Per se* treatment is appropriate "[o]nce experience with a particular kind of restraint enables the Court to predict with confidence that the rule of reason will condemn it." [Citations.] Thus, we have expressed reluctance to adopt *per se* rules with regard to "restraints imposed in the context of business relationships where the economic impact of certain practices is not immediately obvious." [Citation.]

A review of this Court's decisions leading up to and beyond *Albrecht* is relevant to our assessment of the continuing validity of the *per se* rule established in *Albrecht*.

* * * The Court [in *Albrecht*] acknowledged that "[m]aximum and minimum price fixing may have different consequences in many situations," but nonetheless condemned maximum price fixing for "substituting the perhaps erroneous judgment of a seller for the forces of the competitive market. [Citation.]

*Albrecht* was animated in part by the fear that vertical maximum price fixing could allow suppliers to discriminate against certain dealers, restrict the services that dealers could afford to offer customers, or disguise minimum price fixing schemes. * * *

* * *

We noted in [citation] that vertical restraints are generally more defensible than horizontal restraints. [Citation]. And we explained . . . that decisions such as [citation] "recognize the possibility that a vertical restraint imposed by a single manufacturer or wholesaler may stimulate interbrand competition even as it reduces intrabrand competition."

Thus, our reconsideration of *Albrecht's* continuing validity is informed by several of our decisions, as well as a considerable body of scholarship discussing the effects of vertical restraints. Our analysis is also guided by our general view that the primary purpose of the antitrust laws is to protect interbrand competition. [Citation] "Low prices," we have explained, "benefit consumers regardless of how those prices are set, and so long as they are above predatory levels, they do not threaten competition." [Citation]. Our interpretation of the Sherman Act also incorporates the notion that condemnation of practices resulting in lower prices to consumers is "especially costly" because "cutting prices in order to increase business often is the very essence of competition." [Citation.]

So informed, we find it difficult to maintain that vertically-imposed maximum prices could harm consumers or competition to the extent necessary to justify their *per se* invalidation.

* * *

The *Albrecht* Court also expressed the concern that maximum prices may be set too low for dealers to offer consumers essential or desired services. [Citation.]. But such conduct, by driving away customers, would seem likely to harm manufacturers as well as dealers and consumers, making it unlikely that a supplier would set such a price as a matter of business judgment. [Citations.] * * *

Finally, *Albrecht* reflected the Court's fear that maximum price fixing could be used to disguise arrangements to fix minimum prices [citation], which remain illegal *per se*. Although we have acknowledged the possibility that maximum pricing might mask minimum pricing, [citation], we believe that such conduct as with the other concerns articulated in *Albrecht* can be appropriately recognized and punished under the rule of reason. [Citation.]

* * *

After reconsidering *Albrecht's* rationale and the substantial criticism the decision has received, however, we conclude that there is insufficient economic justification for *per se* invalidation of vertical maximum price fixing.

* * *

\* \* \*

In overruling *Albrecht*, we of course do not hold that all vertical maximum price fixing is *per se* lawful. Instead, vertical maximum price fixing, like the majority of commercial arrangements subject to the antitrust laws, should be evaluated under the rule of reason. In our view, rule-of-reason analysis will effectively identify those situations in which vertical maximum price fixing amounts to anti-competitive conduct.

\* \* \*

We therefore vacate the judgment of the Court of Appeals and remand the case for further proceedings consistent with this opinion.

---

## CASE 41–3
### Tying Arrangements/Monopoly
# *EASTMAN KODAK CO. v. IMAGE TECHNICAL SERVICES, INC.*
Supreme Court of the United States, 1992
504 U.S. 451, 112 S.Ct. 2072, 119 L.Ed.2d 265

BLACKMUN, J.

\* \* \*

Kodak manufactures and sells complex business machines—as relevant here, high-volume photocopier and micrographics equipment. Kodak equipment is unique; micrographic software programs that operate on Kodak machines, for example, are not compatible with competitors' machines. Kodak parts are not compatible with other manufacturers' equipment, and vice versa. Kodak equipment, although expensive when new, has little resale value.

Kodak provides service and parts for its machines to its customers. It provides some of the parts itself; the rest are made to order for Kodak by independent original-equipment manufacturers (OEMs). Kodak does not sell a complete system of original equipment, lifetime service, and lifetime parts for a single price. Instead, Kodak provides service after the initial warranty period either through annual service contracts, which include all necessary parts, or on a per-call basis. It charges, through negotiations and bidding, different prices for equipment, service, and parts for different customers. Kodak provides 80% to 95% of the service for Kodak machines.

Beginning in the early 1980s, ISOs [independent service organizations] began repairing and servicing Kodak equipment. They also sold parts and reconditioned and sold used Kodak equipment. Their customers were federal, state, and local government agencies, banks, insurance companies, industrial enterprises, and providers of specialized copy and microfilming services. ISOs provide service at a price substantially lower than Kodak does.

Some customers found that the ISO service was of higher quality.

Some of the ISOs' customers purchase their own parts and hire ISOs only for service. Others choose ISOs to supply both service and parts. ISOs keep an inventory of parts, purchased from Kodak or other sources, primarily the OEMs.

In 1985 and 1986, Kodak implemented a policy of selling replacement parts for micrographic and copying machines only to buyers of Kodak equipment who use Kodak service or repair their own machines.

As part of the same policy, Kodak sought to limit ISO access to other sources of Kodak parts. Kodak and the OEMs agreed that the OEMs would not sell parts that fit Kodak equipment to anyone other than Kodak. Kodak also pressured Kodak equipment owners and independent parts distributors not to sell Kodak parts to ISOs. In addition, Kodak took steps to restrict the availability of used machines.

Kodak intended, through these policies, to make it more difficult for ISOs to sell service for Kodak machines. It succeeded. ISOs were unable to obtain parts from reliable sources, and many were forced out of business, while others lost substantial revenue. Customers were forced to switch to Kodak service even though they preferred ISO service.

In 1987, the [18] ISOs filed the present action in the District Court, alleging, inter alia, that Kodak had unlawfully tied the sale of service for Kodak machines to the sale of parts, in violation of § 1 of the Sherman Act, and had unlawfully monopolized and attempted to monopolize the sale of service for Kodak machines, in violation of § 2 of that Act.

\* \* \*

A tying arrangement is "an agreement by a party to sell one product but only on the condition that the buyer also purchases a different (or tied) product, or at least agrees that he will not purchase that product from any other supplier." [Citation.] Such an arrangement violates § 1 of the Sherman Act if the seller has "appreciable economic power" in the tying product market and if the arrangement affects a substantial volume of commerce in the tied market. [Citation.]

Kodak did not dispute that its arrangement affects a substantial volume of interstate commerce. It, however, did challenge whether its activities constituted a "tying arrangement" and whether Kodak exercised "appreciable economic power" in the tying market. We consider these issues in turn.

For the respondents to defeat a motion for summary judgment on their claim of a tying arrangement, a reasonable trier of fact must be able to find, first, that service and parts are two distinct products, and, second, that Kodak has tied the sale of the two products.

For service and parts to be considered two distinct products, there must be sufficient consumer demand so that it is efficient for a firm to provide service separately from parts. [Citation.] Evidence in the record indicates that service and parts have been sold separately in the past and still are sold separately to self-service equipment owners. Indeed, the development of the entire high-technology service industry is evidence of the efficiency of a separate market for service.

Kodak insists that because there is no demand for parts separate from service, there cannot be separate markets for service and parts. By that logic, we would be forced to conclude that there can never be separate markets, for example, for cameras and film, computers and software, or automobiles and tires. That is an assumption we are unwilling to make.

\* \* \*

Having found sufficient evidence of a tying arrangement, we consider the other necessary feature of an illegal tying arrangement: appreciable economic power in the tying market. Market power is the power "to force a purchaser to do something that he would not do in a competitive market." [Citation.] It has been defined as "the ability of a single seller to raise price and restrict output." [Citations.] The existence of such power ordinarily is inferred from the seller's possession of a predominant share of the market. [Citations.]

Respondents contend that Kodak has more than sufficient power in the parts market to force unwanted purchases of the tied market, service. Respondents provide evidence that certain parts are available exclusively through Kodak. Respondents also assert that Kodak has control over the availability of parts it does not manufacture. According to respondents' evidence, Kodak has prohibited independent manufacturers from selling Kodak parts to ISOs, pressured Kodak equipment owners and independent parts distributors to deny ISOs the purchase of Kodak parts, and taken steps to restrict the availability of used machines.

Respondents also allege that Kodak's control over the parts market has excluded service competition, boosted service prices, and forced unwilling consumption of Kodak service. Respondents offer evidence that consumers have switched to Kodak service even though they preferred ISO service, that Kodak service was of higher price and lower quality than the preferred ISO service, and that ISOs were driven out of business by Kodak's policies. Under our prior precedents, this evidence would be sufficient to entitle respondents to a trial on their claim of market power.

Kodak counters that even if it concedes monopoly share of the relevant parts market, it cannot actually exercise the necessary market power for a Sherman Act violation. This is so, according to Kodak, because competition exists in the equipment market. Kodak argues that it could not have the ability to raise prices of service and parts above the level that would be charged in a competitive market because any increase in profits from a higher price in the aftermarkets at least would be offset by a corresponding loss in profits from lower equipment sales as consumers began purchasing equipment with more attractive service costs.

\* \* \*

The extent to which one market prevents exploitation of another market depends on the extent to which consumers will change their consumption of one product in response to a price change in another, i.e., the "cross-elasticity of demand." See *du Pont*, [citations]. Kodak's proposed rule rests on a factual assumption about the cross-elasticity of demand in the equipment and aftermarkets: "If Kodak raised its parts or service prices above competitive levels, potential customers would simply stop buying Kodak equipment. Perhaps Kodak would be able to increase short term profits through such a strategy, but at a devastating cost to its long term interests." Kodak argues that the Court should accept, as a matter of law, this "basic economic realit[y]," that competition in the equipment market necessarily prevents market power in the aftermarkets.

\* \* \*

We conclude . . . that Kodak has failed to demonstrate that respondents' inference of market power in the service and parts markets is unreasonable, and that, consequently, Kodak is entitled to summary judgment. It is clearly reasonable to infer that Kodak has market power to raise prices and drive out competition in the aftermarkets, since respondents offer direct evidence that Kodak did so. It is also plausible, as discussed above, to infer that Kodak chose to gain immediate profits by exerting that market power where locked-in customers, high information costs, and discriminatory pricing limited and perhaps eliminated any long-term loss. Viewing the evidence in the light most favorable to respondents, their allegations of market power "mak[e] . . . economic sense." [Citation.]

\* \* \*

We need not decide whether Kodak's behavior has any procompetitive effects and, if so, whether they outweigh the anticompetitive effects. We note only that Kodak's service and parts policy is simply not one that appears always or almost always to enhance competition, and therefore to warrant a legal presumption without any evidence of its actual economic impact. In this case, when we weigh the risk of deterring procompetitive behavior by proceeding to trial against the risk that illegal behavior go unpunished, the balance tips against summary judgment. [Citations.]

\* \* \* We therefore affirm the denial of summary judgment on respondents' § 1 claim.

\* \* \*

Respondents also claim that they have presented genuine issues for trial as to whether Kodak has monopolized or attempted to monopolize the service and parts markets in violation of § 2 of the Sherman Act. "The offense of monopoly under § 2 of the Sherman Act has two elements: (1) the possession of monopoly power in the relevant market and (2) the willful acquisition or maintenance of that power as distinguished from growth or development as a consequence of a superior product, business acumen, or historic accident." [Citation.]

The existence of the first element, possession of monopoly power, is easily resolved. As has been noted, respondents have presented a triable claim that service and parts are separate markets, and that Kodak has the "power to control prices or exclude competition" in

service and parts. *Du Pont*, [citation]. Monopoly power under § 2 requires, of course, something greater than market power under § 1. [Citation.] Respondents' evidence that Kodak controls nearly 100% of the parts market and 80% to 95% of the service market, with no readily available substitutes, is, however, sufficient to survive summary judgment under the more stringent monopoly standard of § 2. [Citations.]

Kodak also contends that, as a matter of law, a single brand of a product or service can never be a relevant market under the Sherman Act. We disagree. The relevant market for antitrust purposes is determined by the choices available to Kodak equipment owners. [Citation.] Because service and parts for Kodak equipment are not interchangeable with other manufacturers' service and parts, the relevant market from the Kodak equipment owner's perspective is composed of only those companies that service Kodak machines. See du Pont, [citation] (the "market is composed of products that have reasonable interchangeability"). This Court's prior cases support the proposition that in some instances one brand of a product can constitute a separate market. [Citations.]

The second element of a § 2 claim is the use of monopoly power "to foreclose competition, to gain a competitive advantage, or to destroy a competitor." [Citation.] If Kodak adopted its parts and service policies as part of a scheme of willful acquisition or maintenance of monopoly power, it will have violated § 2. [Citations.]

As recounted at length above, respondents have presented evidence that Kodak took exclusionary action to maintain its parts monopoly and used its control over parts to strengthen its monopoly share of the Kodak service market. Liability turns, then, on whether "valid business reasons" can explain Kodak's actions. [Citations.] \* \* \*

\* \* \*

In the end, of course, Kodak's arguments may prove to be correct. It may be that its parts, service, and equipment are components of one unified market, or that the equipment market does discipline the aftermarkets so that all three are priced competitively overall, or that any anti-competitive effects of Kodak's behavior are outweighed by its competitive effects. But we cannot reach these conclusions as a matter of law on a record this sparse. Accordingly, the judgment of the Court of Appeals denying summary judgment is affirmed.

It is so ordered.

## CASE 41–4
## Horizontal Merger
# *HOSPITAL CORPORATION OF AMERICA v. FTC*

United States Court of Appeals, Seventh Circuit, 1986
807 F.2d 1381

POSNER, J.

Hospital Corporation of America, the largest proprietary hospital chain in the United States, asks us to set aside the decision by the Federal Trade Commission that it violated section 7 of the Clayton Act, [citation], by the acquisition in 1981 and 1982 of two corporations, Hospital Affiliates International, Inc. and Health Care Corporation. Before these acquisitions (which cost Hospital Corporation almost $700 million), Hospital Corporation had owned one hospital in Chattanooga, Tennessee. The acquisitions gave it ownership of two more. In addition, pursuant to the terms of the acquisitions it assumed contracts, both with four-year terms, that Hospital Affiliates International had made to manage two other Chattanooga-area hospitals. So after the acquisitions Hospital Corporation owned or managed 5 of the 11 hospitals in the area. Later one of the management contracts was cancelled; and one of the lesser issues raised by Hospital Corporation, which we might as well dispose of right now, is whether the Commission should have disregarded the assumption of that contract. We agree with the Commission that it was not required to take account of a post-acquisition transaction that may have been made to improve Hospital Corporation's litigating position. The contract was cancelled after the Commission began investigating Hospital Corporation's acquisition of Hospital Affiliates, and while the initiative in cancelling was taken by the managed hospital, Hospital Corporation reacted with unaccustomed mildness by allowing the hospital to withdraw from the contract. For it had sued three other hospitals that tried to get out of their management contracts—only none of these hospitals was in a market where Hospital Corporation's acquisition of Hospital Affiliates was likely to be challenged. Post-acquisition evidence that is subject to manipulation by the party seeking to use it is entitled to little or no weight. [Citation.] * * *

If all the hospitals brought under common ownership or control by the two challenged acquisitions are treated as a single entity, the acquisitions raised Hospital Corporation's market share in the Chattanooga area from 14 percent to 26 percent. This made it the second largest provider of hospital services in a highly concentrated market where the four largest firms together had a 91 percent market share compared to 79 percent before the acquisitions. These are the FTC's figures, and Hospital Corporation thinks they are slightly too high * * * but the discrepancy is too slight to make a legal difference. Nor would expressing the market shares in terms of the Herfindahl index alter the impression of a highly concentrated market.

* * *

The Commission may have made its task harder (and opinion longer) than strictly necessary, however, by studiously avoiding reliance on any of the [U.S.] Supreme Court's section 7 decisions from the 1960s except [citation], which took an explicitly economic approach to the interpretation of the statute. The other decisions in that decade * * * seemed, taken as a group, to establish the illegality of any nontrivial acquisition of a competitor, whether or not the acquisition was likely either to bring about or shore up collusive or oligopoly pricing. The elimination of a significant rival was thought by itself to infringe the complex of social and economic values conceived by a majority of the Court to inform the statutory words "may . . . substantially . . . lessen competition."

None of these decisions has been overruled. * * * The most important developments that cast doubt on the continued vitality of such [1960s] cases as [citations] are found in other cases, where the Supreme Court, echoed by the lower courts, has said repeatedly that the economic concept of competition, rather than any desire to preserve rivals as such, is the lodestar that shall guide the contemporary application of the antitrust laws, not excluding the Clayton Act. * * * Applied to cases brought under section 7, this principle requires the district court (in this case, the Commission) to make a judgment whether the challenged acquisition is likely to hurt consumers, as by making it easier for the firms in the market to collude, expressly or tacitly, and thereby force price above or farther above the competitive level. So it was prudent for the Commission, rather than resting on the very strict merger decisions of the 1960s, to inquire into the probability of harm to consumers. * * *

When an economic approach is taken in a section 7 case, the ultimate issue is whether the challenged acquisition is likely to facilitate collusion. In this perspective the acquisition of a competitor has no economic significance in itself; the worry is that it may enable the acquiring firm to cooperate (or cooperate better) with other leading competitors on reducing or limiting output, thereby pushing up the market price. * * * There is plenty of evidence to support the Commission's prediction of adverse competitive effect in this case. * * *

The acquisitions reduced the number of competing hospitals in the Chattanooga market from 11 to 7. * * *

The reduction in the number of competitors is significant in assessing the competitive vitality of the Chattanooga hospital market. The fewer competitors there are in a market, the easier it is for them to coordinate their pricing without committing detectable violations of section 1 of the Sherman Act, which forbids price fixing. This would not be very important if the four competitors eliminated by the acquisitions in this case had been insignificant, but they were not; they accounted in the aggregate for 12 percent of the sales of the market. As a result of the acquisitions the four largest firms came to control virtually the whole market, and the problem of coordination was therefore reduced to one of coordination among these four.

Moreover, both the ability of the remaining firms to expand their output should the big four reduce their own output in order to raise the market price (and, by expanding, to offset the leading firms' restriction of their own output), and the ability of outsiders to come in and build completely new hospitals, are reduced by Tennessee's certificate-of-need law. Any addition to hospital capacity must be approved by a state agency.

* * *

In showing that the challenged acquisitions gave four firms control over an entire market so that they would have little reason to fear a competitive reaction if they raised prices above the competitive level, the Commission went far to justify its prediction of probable anticompetitive effects. Maybe it need have gone no further. [Citations.] But it did. First it pointed out that the demand for hospital services by patients and their doctors is highly inelastic under competitive conditions. This is not only because people place a high value on their safety and comfort and because many of their treatment decisions are made for them by their doctor, who doesn't pay their hospital bills; it is also because most hospital bills are paid largely by insurance companies or the federal government rather than by the patient. The less elastic the demand for a good or service is, the greater are the profits that providers can make by raising price through collusion. * * *

Second, there is a tradition, well documented in the Commission's opinion, of cooperation between competing hospitals in Chattanooga. * * * But a market in which competitors are unusually disposed to cooperate is a market prone to collusion. * * *

Third, hospitals are under great pressure from the federal government and the insurance companies to cut costs. One way of resisting this pressure is by presenting a united front in negotiations with the third-party payors * * *. The fewer the independent competitors in a hospital market, the easier they will find it, by presenting an unbroken phalanx of representations and requests, to frustrate efforts to control hospital costs. This too is a form of collusion that the antitrust laws seek to discourage * * *.

All these considerations, taken together, supported * * * the Commission's conclusion that the challenged acquisitions are likely to foster collusive practices, harmful to consumers, in the Chattanooga hospital market. Section 7 does not require proof that a merger or other acquisition has caused higher prices in the affected market. All that is necessary is that the merger create an appreciable danger of such consequences in the future. A predictive judgment, necessarily probabilistic and judgmental rather than demonstrable [citation].

* * *

The Commission's order is affirmed and enforced.

---

# Questions

1. Discuss horizontal restraints of trade.
2. Discuss vertical restraints of trade.
3. Discuss monopolization, attempts to monopolize, and conspiracies to monopolize and explain why they are illegal.

4. Discuss the Clayton Act and its rules governing (a) tying contracts, (b) exclusive dealing, (c) vertical mergers, (d) horizontal mergers, and (e) conglomerate mergers.
5. Discuss (a) the Robinson-Patman Act and the various defenses to it and (b) the Federal Trade Commission Act.

# Problems

1. Discuss the validity and effect of each of the following:

(a) A, B, and C, manufacturers of stereos, orally agree that due to the disastrous, cutthroat competition in the market, they will establish a reasonable price to charge their purchasers.

(b) D, E, F, and G, newspaper publishers, agree not to charge their customers more than 30¢ per newspaper.

(c) H, a distiller of liquor, and I, H's retail distributor, agree that I should charge a price of five dollars per bottle.

2. Discuss the validity of the following:

(a) A territorial allocation agreement between two manufacturers of the same type of products, whereby neither will sell its products in the area allocated to the other.

(b) An agreement between manufacturer and distributor not to sell a dealer a particular product or parts necessary for repair of the product.

3. Universal Video sells $40 million worth of video recording equipment in the United States. The total sales of such equipment in the United States is $100 million. One-half of Universal's sales is to Giant Retailer, a company which possesses 50 percent of the retail market. Giant seeks (1) to obtain an exclusive dealing arrangement with Universal or (2) to acquire Universal. Please advise Giant as to the validity of its alternatives.

4. Z sells cameras to A, B, C, and D for $60 per camera. Y, one of Z's competitor's, sells a comparable camera to A for $58.50. Z, in response to this competitive pressure from Y, lowers its price to A to $58.50. B, C, and D insist that Z lower its price to them to $58.50, but Z refuses. B, C, and D sue Z for unlawful price discrimination. Decision? Would your answer differ if Z reduced its price to A to $58?

5. Discount is a discount appliance chain store that continually sells goods at a price below manufacturers' suggested retail prices. A, B, and C, the three largest manufacturers of appliances, agree that unless Discount ceases from its discount pricing, they will no longer sell to Discount. Discount refuses, and A, B, and C refuse to sell to Discount. Discount sues A, B, and C. Decision?

6. Magnum Company produces 77 percent of the coal utilized in the United States. Coal provides 25 percent of all of the energy used in the United States. In a suit brought by the United States against Magnum for violation of the antitrust laws, what result?

7. Justin Manufacturing Company sells high-fashion clothing under the prestigious "Justin" label. The company has a firm policy that it will not deal with any company that sells below its suggested retail price. Justin is informed by one of its customers, XYZ, that its competitor, Duplex, is selling the "Justin" line at a great discount. Justin now demands that Duplex comply with the agreement to not sell the "Justin" line below the suggested retail price. Discuss the implications of this situation.

8. Jay Corporation, the largest manufacturer of bicycles in the United States with 40 percent of the market, has recently entered into an agreement with Retail Bike, the largest retailer of bicycles in the United States with 37 percent of the market, under which Jay will furnish its bicycles only to Retail and Retail will sell only Jay's bicycles. The government is now questioning this agreement. Discuss.

9. Whirlpool Corporation manufactured vacuum cleaners under both its own name and under the Kenmore name. Oreck exclusively distributed the vacuum cleaners sold under the Whirlpool name. Sears, Roebuck & Co. exclusively distributed the Kenmore vacuum cleaners. Oreck alleged that its exclusive distributorship agreement with Whirlpool was not renewed because of the existence of an unlawful conspiracy between Whirlpool and Sears. Oreck further contended that a *per se* rule was applicable because the agreement was (a) price fixing or (b) a group boycott, or both. Decision?

10. Indian Coffee of Pittsburgh, Pennsylvania marketed vacuum-packed coffee under the Breakfast Cheer brand name in the Pittsburgh and Cleveland, Ohio, areas. That same year, Folger Coffee, a leading coffee seller, began selling coffee in Pittsburgh. To make inroads into the new territory, Folger sold its coffee at greatly reduced prices. At first, Indian Coffee met Folger's prices but could not continue operating at such a reduced price and was forced out of the market. Indian Coffee brings an antitrust action. Decision?

11. Von's Grocery, a large retail grocery chain in Los Angeles, sought to acquire Shopping Bag Food Stores, a direct competitor. At the time of the proposed merger, Von's sales ranked third in the Los Angeles area and Shopping Bag's ranked sixth. Both chains were increasing their number of stores. The merger would have resulted in the creation of the second largest grocery chain in Los Angeles, with total sales in excess of $170 million. Prior to the proposed merger, the number of owners operating single stores declined from 5,365 in 1950 to 3,590 by 1963. During this same period, the number of chains with two or more stores rose from 96 to 150. The United States brought suit against Von's to prevent the merger, claiming that the proposed merger violated Section 7 of the Clayton Act in that it could result in the substantial lessening of competition or could tend to create a monopoly. Decision?

12. Boise Cascade Corporation is a wholesaler and retailer of office products. The Federal Trade Commission issued a complaint charging that Boise had violated the Robinson-Patman Act by receiving a wholesaler's discount from certain suppliers on products that Boise resold at retail, in competition with other retailers that could not obtain wholesale discounts. Decision?

13. Zenith, an American manufacturer of television sets, and National Union Electric Corporation (NUE), the successor

company to an American television-manufacturing firm that had since withdrawn from the market, sued twenty-one Japanese-controlled corporations that manufactured or sold Consumer Electronic Products (CEP), claiming that these petitioners/defendants, over a twenty-year period, had legally conspired to drive American firms from the American CEP market by engaging in a scheme to fix and maintain artificially high prices for television sets sold by the petitioners in Japan, while simultaneously maintaining low prices for sets exported to and sold in the United States. The respondents claimed that such activity was concerted action in violation of Section 1 of the Sherman Act. The District Court held for petitioners, finding that the bulk of the evidence on which the respondents relied was inadmissible, that the admissible evidence did not raise a genuine issue of material fact as to the existence of the alleged conspiracy, and that any inference of conspiracy was unreasonable. The Court of Appeals reversed, holding that the District Court erred in granting summary judgment in that there was both direct and circumstantial admissible evidence of a conspiracy. Decision?

**14.**   Great Atlantic and Pacific Tea Company desired to achieve cost savings by switching to the sale of "private label" milk. A&P asked Borden company, its longtime supplier of "brand label" milk, to submit a bid to supply certain of A&P's private label dairy products. A&P was not satisfied with Borden's bid, however, and it solicited other offers. Bowman Dairy, a competitor of Borden's, submitted a lower bid. At this point, A&P contacted Borden and asked it to rebid on the private label contract. A&P included a warning that Borden would have to substantially lower its original bid in order to undercut Bowman's bid. Borden offered a bid that doubled A&P's potential annual cost savings. A&P accepted Borden's bid. The Federal Trade Commission then brought this action, charging that A&P had violated the Robinson-Patman Act by knowingly inducing or receiving illegal price discrimination from Borden. Decision?

**15.**   Clorox is the nation's leading manufacturer of household liquid bleach (accounting for 49 percent—$40 million—of sales annually) and is the only brand sold nationally. Clorox and its next largest competitor, Purex, hold 65 percent of national sales, and the top four bleach manufacturers control 80 percent of sales. As all bleach is chemically identical, Clorox spends over $5 million each year in advertising to attract and keep customers.

Procter & Gamble is the dominant national manufacturer of household cleaning products, with yearly sales of $1.1 billion. As with bleach, advertising is vital in the household cleaning products industry. Procter & Gamble spends over $127 million in advertising and promotions annually. Procter & Gamble decided to diversify into the bleach business, as its household cleaning products and bleach are both low-cost, high-turnover consumer goods; are dependent on mass advertising; and are sold to the same customers at the same stores through the same merchandising methods. Procter & Gamble decided to merge with Clorox, rather than start its own bleach

division, in order to secure the dominant position in the bleach market immediately. Should the FTC take action against this merger, and if so, what decision?

**16.**   The NCAA adopted a plan for televising college football games to reduce the adverse effect of TV coverage on spectator attendance. The plan limited the total number of televised intercollegiate football games and also limited the number of games any one school could televise. No member of the NCAA was permitted to sell any television rights except in accordance with the plan. As part of the plan, the NCAA had agreements with the American Broadcasting Company (ABC) and the Columbia Broadcasting System (CBS) to pay to each school at least a specified minimum price for televising football games. Several member universities now join to bring suit against the NCAA, claiming the new plan is a horizontal price fixing agreement and output limitation and as such is illegal *per se*. The NCAA counters that the existence of the product, college football, depends upon member compliance with restrictions and regulations. According to the NCAA, its restrictions, including the TV plan, have a procompetitive effect. Is the TV plan valid? Explain.

**17.**   The National Society of Professional Engineers (Society) had an ethics rule that prohibited member engineers from disclosing or discussing price/fee information with customers until after the customer had hired a particular engineer. This rule against competitive bidding was designed to maintain high standards in the field of engineering. The Society felt that competitive pressure to offer engineering services at the lowest possible price would encourage engineers to design and specify inefficient, unsafe, and unnecessarily expensive structures and construction methods. According to the Society, awarding engineering contracts to the lowest bidder, regardless of quality, would be dangerous to the public health, safety, and welfare. The Society emphasizes that the rule is not an agreement to fix prices. Rather, it claims the rule was drafted by experienced, highly trained professional engineers to prevent public harm and is therefore reasonable. The Government contends that the rule unreasonably restrains trade and thus violates § 1 of the Sherman Act. Decision?

**18.**   In the early 1930s, intense price competition characterized both the retail and the wholesale oil markets. At times, prices in the wholesale market fell below the manufacturer's cost. One cause of the volatile situation was the supply of "distress gasoline" placed on the market by seventeen independent refiners. These independent refiners had no retail sales outlets and little storage capacity, so they were forced to sell their product at "distress prices." In spite of their unprofitable operations, they could not afford to shut down, for if they did so, they would be apt to lose both their oil connections in the field and their regular customers.

In an attempt to remedy this problem, the major oil companies entered into an informal agreement whereby each selected as its "dancing partner" one or more independent refiners having distress gasoline. The major oil company would then assume responsibility for purchasing the independent's distress supply at the "fair going market price." As a result, the market price of oil rose for two consecutive years, and the spot market became stable. The United States then brought this criminal action against the major companies, charging them with horizontal price fixing in violation of the Sherman Act. Decision?

**19.**    As part of a corporate plan to stimulate sagging color television sales, GTE Sylvania began to phase out its wholesale distributors and began to sell its television sets directly to a smaller and more select group of franchised retailers. To this end, Sylvania limited the number of franchises granted for any given area and required each franchisee to sell Sylvania products only from the location or locations at which he was franchised. A franchise did not constitute an exclusive territory, and Sylvania retained sole discretion to increase the number of retailers in an area in light of the success or failure of existing retailers. The strategy apparently was successful, as Sylvania's national market share increased from less than 2 percent to 5 percent.

In the course of carrying out its plan, Sylvania franchised Young Brothers as a television retailer at a San Francisco location one mile from that of Continental T.V., Inc., one of Sylvania's most successful franchisees. A course of feuding began between Sylvania and Continental that reached a head when Continental requested permission to open a store in Sacramento, and Sylvania refused. Continental opened the Sacramento store anyway and began shipping merchandise there from its San Jose warehouse. Shortly thereafter, Sylvania terminated Continental's franchise.

Continental brought this action against Sylvania, claiming that the franchise location restriction is *per se* violative of the Sherman Act. The jury found for Continental and assessed damages at $591,505, which were trebled. On appeal, the Court of Appeals for the Ninth Circuit, sitting *en banc,* reversed the judgment. Decision?

**20.**    In 1923, du Pont was granted the exclusive right to make and sell cellophane in North America. In 1927, the company introduced a moisture-proof brand of cellophane that was ideal for various wrapping needs. Although more expensive than most competing wrapping, it offered a desired combination of transparency, strength, and cost. Except for its permeability to gases, however, cellophane had no qualities that a number of competing materials did not possess as well. Cellophane sales increased dramatically, and by 1950, du Pont produced almost 75 percent of the cellophane sold in the United States. Nevertheless, sales of the material constituted less than 20 percent of the sales of "flexible packaging materials."

The United States brought this action, contending that by so dominating cellophane production, du Pont had monopolized a part of trade or commerce in violation of the Sherman Act. Du Pont argued that it had not monopolized because it did not have the power to control the price of cellophane or to exclude competitors from the market for flexible wrapping materials. The government took a direct appeal from a ruling in favor of du Pont. Decision?

**Internet Exercise**  At the home pages for the Federal Trade Commission and the Department of Justice, explore the business and consumer issues these two agencies are currently examining.

# CHAPTER 42

# Consumer Protection

Consumer transactions have increased enormously since World War II, and today consumer debt amounts to more than one trillion dollars. Although the definition varies, a consumer transaction generally involves goods, credit, services, or land acquired for personal, household, or family purposes. Historically, consumers were subject to the rule of *caveat emptor*—let the buyer beware. In recent years, however, the law has largely abandoned this principle and now provides consumers greater protection. Most of this protection takes the form of statutory enactments at both the State and Federal levels, and a wide variety of governmental agencies are charged with enforcing these statutes. This enforcement varies enormously. In some cases, only government agencies may exercise enforcement rights, which they impose through criminal penalties, civil penalties, injunctions, and cease and desist orders. In other cases, in addition to the government's enforcement rights, consumers may privately seek the rescission of contracts and damages for harm resulting from violations of consumer protection laws. Finally, under certain consumer protection statutes such as State "lemon laws," consumers alone may exercise enforcement rights. This chapter examines State and Federal consumer protection agencies and consumer protection statutes.

## STATE AND FEDERAL CONSUMER PROTECTION AGENCIES

Through the enactment of laws and regulations, legislatures and administrative bodies at the Federal, State, and local levels all actively seek to shield consumers from an enormous range of harm. The most common abuses in consumer transactions involve the extension of credit, deceptive trade practices, unsafe products, and unfair pricing.

### State and Local Consumer Protection Agencies

The many consumer protection agencies at the State and local levels typically deal with fraudulent and deceptive trade practices and fraudulent sales practices, such as false statements about a product's value or quality. In most jurisdictions, consumer protection agencies also help to resolve consumer complaints about defective goods or poor service.

Most State Attorneys General play an active role in consumer protection by enforcing laws against consumer fraud through judicially imposed injunctions and restitution. In recent years, as the Federal government's role in consumer protection has diminished in response to the deregulatory movement, the States correspondingly have expanded their role. The National Association of Attorneys General (NAAG) has been active in coordinating lawsuits among the States. Under NAAG's guidance, several States often will simultaneously file lawsuits against a company that has been engaging in fraudulent acts involving more than one State.

In some instances, however, States have not coordinated their efforts and, as a consequence, have acted inconsistently with respect to consumer protection, especially in health and safety matters. This lack of coordination can present serious problems to companies that sell large numbers of products in interstate commerce. For example, assume that the Glueco Company, which makes and sells glue containing certain toxic chemicals, finds that Connecticut requires warning labels of a certain size and wording, while Indiana requires completely different labels. Glueco must incur the added expenses of placing different labels on different boxes and making sure that each State receives the correct label type. Should numerous States adopt inconsistent labeling requirements, the resulting increase in labeling costs could force Glueco to limit the number of States in which it sells or to raise its prices.

# The Federal Trade Commission

At the Federal level, the most significant consumer protection agency is the **Federal Trade Commission** (FTC). Established in 1914, the FTC has two major functions: (1) under its mandate to prevent "unfair methods of competition in commerce," it is responsible for roughly half of the antitrust enforcement at the Federal level (the FTC's role in antitrust enforcement is discussed in Chapter 41); and (2) under its mandate to prevent "unfair and deceptive" trade practices, it is responsible for stopping fraudulent sales techniques.

To address unfair and deceptive trade practices, the five-member commission (no more than three of whose members may be from the same political party) has the power to issue substantive "trade regulation rules" and to conduct appropriate investigations and hearings. Among the rules it has issued so far are those regulating used car sales, franchising and business opportunity ventures, funeral home services, and the issuance of consumer credit, as well as those requiring a "cooling-off" period for door-to-door sales (discussed later in this chapter).

When considering a deceptive trade practice, the agency often may seek a cease and desist order rather than issue a substantive trade rule. A **cease and desist order** directs a party to stop a certain practice or face punishment such as a fine. In a typical situation, the FTC staff discovers a potentially deceptive practice, investigates the matter, files a complaint against the alleged offender (usually referred to as the respondent), and after a hearing in front of an administrative law judge (ALJ) to determine whether a violation of the law has occurred, obtains a cease and desist order if the ALJ finds that one is necessary. The respondent may appeal to the FTC commissioners to reverse or modify the order. Appeals from orders issued by the commissioners go to the United States Courts of Appeals, which have exclusive jurisdiction to enforce, set aside, or modify orders of the commission.

*Standards* The FTC Act does not define the words *unfair* or *deceptive,* and for many years the Commission was criticized for its failure to do so. Partly in response to these criticisms and partly in response to congressional pressure, the Commission issued three policy statements. The first, which addresses the meaning of **unfairness,** provides the following:

To justify a finding of unfairness the injury must satisfy three tests. It must be substantial; it must not be outweighed by any countervailing benefits to consumers or competition that the practice produces; and it must be an injury that consumers themselves could not reasonably have avoided. The standard, therefore, applies a cost-benefit analysis to the issue of unfairness.

The second policy statement deals with the meaning of **deception**—the basis of most FTC consumer protection actions. The controversy that the formulation of this statement generated among the commissioners led to its approval by a narrow 3–2 vote and prompted the dissenting commissioners to issue a minority statement. It is generally accepted that the minority position reflected previous FTC policy, whereas the majority position established new policy.

The majority position provides that "the Commission will find deception if there is a misrepresentation, omission or practice that is likely to mislead the consumer acting reasonably in the circumstances, to the consumer's detriment." Thus, the Commission will find an act or practice deceptive if it meets a three-prong test:

First, there must be a representation, omission, or practice that is likely to mislead the consumer. Second, we examine the practice from the perspective of a consumer acting reasonably in the circumstances. Third, the representation, omission, or practice must be a "material" one. The basic question is whether the act or practice is likely to affect the consumer's conduct or decision with regard to a product or service. If so, the practice is material, and consumer injury is likely because consumers are likely to have chosen differently but for the deception.

Perhaps the most controversial feature of the new policy is the notion that deception can occur only with respect to "consumers acting reasonably."

Deception may occur through either false representation or material omission. Examples of deceptive practices have included advertising that a certain product will save consumers 25 percent on their automotive motor oil, when the product simply replaced a quart of oil in the engine (which normally contains four quarts of oil) and was, in fact, more expensive than the oil it replaced; placing marbles in a bowl of vegetable soup to displace the vegetables from the bottom of the bowl and therefore make the soup appear thicker; and claiming that one drug provides greater pain relief than another, when the evidence was insufficient to prove the claim to the medical community. On the other hand, the FTC will not take action against **puffery** (sales talk composed of general bragging or overstatement that makes no specific factual representation) if the consumer would recognize it as puffery and not be deceived. For example, a statement by a salesperson that "this is one terrific deal" would likely be considered puffery.

Deception can also occur through a failure to disclose important product information if such disclosure is necessary to correct a false and material expectation created in the consumer's mind by the product or by the circumstances of sale. For example, the FTC has insisted that the failure to disclose a product's country of origin constitutes a deceptive omission, based on the agency's view that consumers assume the United States to be the country of origin of a product bearing no other country's name.

The third policy statement issued by the commission involves **ad substantiation.** This policy requires advertisers to have a reasonable basis for their claims at the time they make such claims. Moreover, in determining the reasonableness of a claim, the commission places great weight upon the cost and benefits of substantiation.

*See Case 42–1*

*Remedies* In addition to the remedies discussed above, the FTC has employed three other potent remedies: (1) affirmative disclosure, (2) corrective advertising, and (3) multiple product orders.

**Affirmative disclosure,** a remedy frequently employed by the FTC, requires an offender to provide certain information in its advertisement to prevent the ad from being considered deceptive.

**Corrective advertising** goes beyond affirmative disclosure by requiring an advertiser who has made a deceptive claim to disclose in future advertisements that such prior claims were in fact untrue. The theory behind this remedy is that the effects of a previous deception will continue until expressly corrected.

A **multiple product order** requires a deceptive advertiser to cease and desist from any future deception not only in regard to the product in question but in regard to all products sold by the company. This remedy is particularly useful in dealing with companies that have violated the law repeatedly.

In addition to these traditional remedies, the FTC recently has turned to direct court action in lieu of administrative proceedings. Legislation enacted in 1973 gave the FTC the right to seek in a Federal district court a preliminary injunction, pending completion of administrative proceedings, whenever the agency had reason to believe that a person was violating FTC laws or rules. First used to stop mergers, this authority is now often invoked in consumer protection cases. The same provision also grants the agency authority to seek a permanent injunction "in proper cases" without a prior administrative finding that FTC law has been violated.

## The Consumer Product Safety Commission

In 1967, President Lyndon Johnson, in accordance with a joint resolution of Congress, appointed a study group to examine the level of product safety in the United States. In a report issued in 1970, the study group, known as the National Commission on Product Safety, disclosed the following:

Americans—20 million of them—are injured each year in the home as a result of incidents connected with consumer products. Of the total, 110,000 are permanently disabled and 30,000 are killed. A significant number could have been spared if more attention had been paid to hazard reduction. . . . The exposure of consumers to unreasonable consumer product hazards is excessive by any standard of measurement.

Two years later, Congress enacted the Consumer Product Safety Act (CPSA), which established an independent Federal regulatory agency, the Consumer Product Safety Commission (CPSC). The purposes of the CPSA were fourfold:

1. to protect the public against unreasonable risks of injury associated with consumer products;
2. to assist consumers in evaluating the comparative safety of consumer products;
3. to develop uniform safety standards for consumer products and to minimize conflicting State and local regulations; and
4. to promote research and investigation into the causes and prevention of product-related deaths, illnesses, and injuries.

Consisting of five commissioners, no more than three of whom can be from the same political party, the CPSC has authority to set safety standards for consumer products; ban unsafe products; issue administrative "recall" orders to compel repair, replacement, or refunds for products found to present substantial hazards; and seek court orders requiring the recall of "imminently hazardous" products. In addition, Congress requires businesses under CPSC jurisdiction to notify the agency of any information indicating that their products contain defects that "could create" substantial product hazards. By triggering investigations that may lead to product recalls, these reports play a major role in the agency's regulatory activities.

The CPSC also enforces four statutes previously enforced by other agencies. These acts, commonly referred to as the "transferred acts," are the Federal Hazardous Substances Act, the Flammable Fabrics Act, the Poison Prevention Packaging Act, and the Refrigerator Safety Act. Whenever the CPSC can regulate a product under one of these specific acts, rather than under the more general CPSA, the agency is directed to do so unless it finds specifically that regulating the product under the CPSA is in the public interest. Thus, many CPSC regulations, such as those for toys, children's flammable sleepwear, and hazard warnings on household chemical products, arise under the transferred acts rather than under the CPSA.

When first established, the CPSC promulgated a number of **mandatory safety standards;** manufacturers either must follow these rules, which regulate product design, packaging, and warning labels, or face legal sanctions. To save time and money, the agency began to rely on industry to establish **voluntary safety standards**—rules for which noncompliance does not violate the law—reserving mandatory standards for those instances in which voluntary standards proved inadequate. In 1981, Congress enacted legislation requiring the CPSC to rely on voluntary standards "whenever compliance with such voluntary standards would eliminate or adequately reduce the risk of injury addressed and there is substantial compliance with such voluntary standards." Although the 1981 amendments do not bar the CPSC from writing mandatory standards, the CPSC has promulgated few such standards since the law was amended.

## Other Federal Consumer Protection Agencies

Among the many other Federal agencies that play a major consumer protection role are the **National Highway Traffic Safety Administration (NHTSA)** and the **Food and Drug Administration (FDA)**.

Congress established the NHTSA to reduce the number of deaths and injuries resulting from automobile accidents. Highway crashes kill approximately 45,000 Americans each year (equal to 121 fatalities per day) and inflict disabling injuries on 1.6 million others. Under authority similar to that of the CPSC, the NHTSA sets motor vehicle safety standards that promote crash prevention (e.g., rules for safer tires and brakes) and crashworthiness (e.g., interior padding, safety belts, and collapsible steering columns). As with the CPSC, manufacturers are required to report possible safety defects,

and the agency may seek a recall if it determines that a particular automobile model presents a sufficiently great hazard. The NHTSA also is authorized to provide grants-in-aid for State highway safety programs and to conduct research on improving highway safety.

The Food and Drug Administration is the oldest Federal consumer protection agency, dating back to 1906. The FDA enforces the Food, Drug and Cosmetic Act, enacted in 1938, which authorizes the agency to regulate "adulterated and misbranded" products. The agency uses two basic methods of enforcement: it sets standards for products or requires their premarket approval. The products most often subject to premarket approval are drugs. Since 1976, the agency also has had the authority to require the premarket approval of medical devices such as pacemakers and intrauterine devices; the number of such devices required to undergo this approval process is large and increasing.

Although the FTC, CPSC, NHTSA, and FDA are perhaps the best known Federal consumer protection agencies, numerous other agencies also play important roles in this area. For example, the United States Postal Service (USPS) brings many cases every year to close down mail fraud operations; the Interstate Commerce Commission (ICC) enforces rules to prevent unfair business practices by interstate moving companies; and the Securities and Exchange Commission (SEC) protects consumers against fraud in the sale of securities. (The SEC is discussed in Chapter 44.) In addition, many other agencies assist consumers with specific types of problems that fall within the agency's scope.

## *CONSUMER PURCHASES*

Whenever a consumer purchases a product or obtains a service, certain rights and obligations arise. The extent to which these rights and obligations apply to all contracts is discussed more fully in Chapters 9 through 18; the extent to which they apply to a sale of goods under the Uniform Commercial Code (UCC) is discussed in Chapters 21 through 25. Although a number of consumer protection laws have been enacted in recent years, they still leave large areas of a consumer's rights and duties to State contract law. In particular, Article 2 of the UCC provides the basic rules governing when a contract for the sale of goods is formed, what constitutes a breach of contract, and what rights an innocent party has against a party who commits a breach. While many consumer protection laws provide for rights the UCC does not address, they still use its principles as building blocks. For example, the

Magnuson-Moss Warranty Act builds upon the perceived inadequacy of the UCC in permitting sellers to disclaim or modify warranties. Similarly, many States have passed so-called "lemon laws" to provide additional contract cancellation rights to dissatisfied automobile purchasers.

## Federal Warranty Protection

A **warranty** creates a duty on the part of the seller to ensure that the goods or services she sells will conform to certain qualities, characteristics, or conditions. A seller, however, is not required to warrant what she sells; and in general she may, by appropriate words, disclaim (exclude) or modify a particular warranty or all warranties. Because a seller's power to disclaim or modify is so flexible, consumer protection laws have been enacted to ensure that consumers understand the warranty protection provided them.

To protect buyers and to prevent deception in selling, Congress enacted the **Magnuson-Moss Warranty Act**, which requires sellers of consumer products to provide adequate information about written warranties. The FTC administers and enforces the Act, which was enacted to alleviate certain reported warranty problems: (1) most warranties were not understandable; (2) most warrantors disclaimed implied warranties; (3) most warranties were unfair; and (4) in some instances the warrantors did not live up to their warranties. Through the Magnuson-Moss Warranty Act, Congress attempted to make consumer product warranties more comprehensible and to facilitate the satisfactory enforcement of consumer remedies. To accomplish these purposes, the Act provides for

1. clear and understandable disclosure of the warranty that is to be offered,
2. a description of the warranty as either "full" or "limited,"
3. a prohibition against disclaiming implied warranties if a written warranty is given, and
4. an optional informal settlement mechanism.

The Act applies to consumer products with **written warranties.** A consumer product is any item of tangible personal property that is normally used for family, household, or personal use and is distributed in commerce. The Act does not protect commercial purchasers, who are considered sufficiently knowledgeable, in terms of contracting, to protect themselves; better able to retain attorneys for their ongoing protection, and able to spread the cost of their injuries in the marketplace.

*Presale Disclosure*  The Act contains presale disclosure provisions, which are calculated to avert confusion and deception and to enable purchasers to make educated product comparisons. A warrantor must, "to the extent required by the rules of the [Federal Trade] Commission, fully and conspicuously disclose in simple and readily understood language the terms and conditions of such warranty." When it implemented this requirement, the FTC adopted a rule requiring that the text of a warranty be accessible to the consumer. Under that rule, the warranty could be attached to the package, placed on a visible sign, or maintained in a binder. In 1986, the FTC relaxed the rule by permitting stores simply to make warranties available to consumers upon request. Retailers using this option, however, must post signs informing the consumer that the warranties are available. Separate rules apply to mail order, catalog, and door-to-door sales.

*Labeling Requirements*  The second major part of the Act provides for labeling requirements by first dividing written warranties into two categories—limited and full—one of which, for any product costing more than ten dollars, must be designated on the written warranty itself. The purpose of this provision is to enable the consumer to make an initial comparison of her legal rights under certain warranties. The Act provides that under a **full warranty** the warrantor must agree to repair the product to conform with the warranty, without charge; no limitation may be placed on the duration of any implied warranty; the consumer must be given the option of a refund or replacement if repair is unsuccessful; and consequential damages may be excluded only if the warranty conspicuously notes their exclusion. A **limited warranty** is any warranty not designated as full.

*Limitations on Disclaimers*  Most significantly, the Act provides that a written warranty, whether full or limited, cannot disclaim any implied warranty. This provision strikes at the heart of the problems plaguing warranty protection, for, as revealed in an earlier presidential task force report, most written warranties provided limited protection but in return nullified the more valuable implied warranties. Hence, consumers believed—often mistakenly—that the warranties they received and the warranty registration cards they promptly returned to the manufacturer were to their benefit. The Act, on the other hand, provides that a full warranty must not disclaim, modify, or limit any implied warranty and that a limited warranty cannot disclaim or modify any implied warranty but can limit its duration to that of the written warranty, provided that such limitation is reasonable, conscionable, and conspicuously displayed. Some States, however, do not allow limitations in the duration of implied warranties.

For example, GE sells consumer goods to Barry for $150 and provides a written warranty regarding the quality of the goods. GE must designate the warranty as full or limited, depending on its characteristics, and cannot disclaim or modify any implied warranty. On the other hand, if GE had not provided Barry with a written warranty, the Magnuson-Moss Warranty Act would not apply, and GE could then disclaim any and all implied warranties.

◆ *See Figure 42-1*

## State "Lemon Laws"

With the enactment of the Magnuson-Moss Warranty Act, many consumers assumed that automobile manufacturers would feel compelled to offer full warranties to buyers of new cars, thereby giving such buyers the option to obtain a refund or replacement without charge for a defective automobile or defective parts. Automobile sellers, however, opted for limited warranties. In response, virtually all of the State legislatures enacted **"lemon laws"** that attempt to provide new car purchasers with rights that are similar to full warranties under the Magnuson-Moss Warranty Act. Some States have broadened their laws to cover used cars; some also cover motorcycles. There are many different lemon laws, but most define a *lemon* as a car that continues to have a defect that substantially impairs its use, value, or safety,

even after the manufacturer has made reasonable attempts to correct the problem. In most States, the opportunity to repair a defect is considered sufficient if the manufacturer made four unsuccessful attempts to fix the problem or the car was out of service for more than thirty days during the year it was sold. If a consumer can prove that her car is a lemon, most lemon laws require the manufacturer either to replace the car or to refund its retail price, less an allowance for the consumer's use of the car. In addition, most lemon laws provide that the consumer may recover attorneys' fees and expenses if the case goes to litigation.

## Consumer Right of Rescission

In most cases, a consumer is legally obligated once he has signed a contract. In many States, however, a consumer has by statute a brief time—generally two or three days—during which he may **rescind** an otherwise binding credit obligation if the sale was solicited in his home. Moreover, the FTC has promulgated a trade regulation applicable to door-to-door sales, leases, or rentals of goods and services for twenty-five dollars or more, whether the sale is for cash or on credit. The regulation permits a consumer to rescind a contract within three days of signing. To make the rule effective, the FTC requires sellers to provide a buyer with written notice of her cancellation rights. If the buyer properly cancels, she must make available to the seller, in a condition substantially as good as that in which they were received, any goods the seller has delivered. The seller in turn

**FIGURE 42-1**    Magnuson-Moss Act

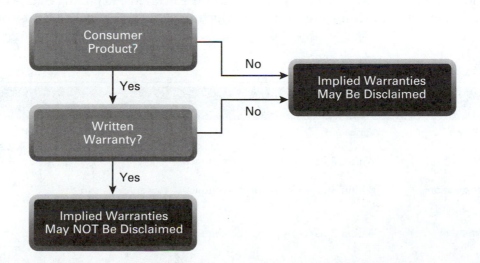

must, within ten business days of receiving notice of rescission, return any money paid or any negotiable instrument (such as a personal check or a promissory note) executed by the buyer and cancel any security interest arising out of the transaction. If the seller fails to comply, the FTC will consider the noncompliance to be a violation of the Federal Trade Commission Act and will seek appropriate sanctions, such as a cease and desist order and civil penalties. To the extent that State laws on door-to-door sales are directly inconsistent with the FTC rule (e.g., if a State provides only two days for rescission) they are unenforceable.

The right of rescission also exists under the **Federal Consumer Credit Protection Act** (discussed more fully below), which allows a consumer three days during which he may withdraw from any credit obligation secured by a mortgage on his home, unless the extension of credit was made to acquire the dwelling. This right of rescission exists whether the contract was the result of a door-to-door sale or not. If the consumer rescinds, the creditor has twenty days to return any money or property he has received from the consumer.

The **Interstate Land Sales Full Disclosure Act** applies to sales or leases of 100 or more lots of unimproved land as part of a common promotional plan in interstate commerce. The Act requires a developer to file a detailed "statement of record" containing specified information about the subdivision and the developer with the Department of Housing and Urban Development (HUD) before offering the lots for sale or lease. The developer must provide a property report, which is a condensed version of the statement of record, to each prospective purchaser or lessee. The Act provides that a purchaser or lessee may revoke any contract or agreement for sale or lease at her option within seven days of signing the contract and that the contract must clearly provide this right. A purchaser or lessee who does not receive a property report before signing a contract may revoke the contract within two years from the date of signing.

◆ *See Figure 42–2*

## CONSUMER CREDIT TRANSACTIONS

A **consumer credit transaction** is customarily defined as any credit transaction involving subject matter to be used by one of the parties for personal, household, or family purposes. The following are illustrative: Atkins borrows $600 from a bank to pay a dentist bill or to take a vacation; Bevins buys a refrigerator for her home from a department store and agrees to pay the purchase price in twelve equal monthly installments; Carpenter has an oil company credit card that he uses to purchase gasoline and tires for his family car.

Regulation of consumer credit has increased considerably because of the dramatic expansion of consumer credit since World War II and the numerous abuses in credit transactions, including misleading credit disclosures, unfair marketing practices, and oppressive collection methods. In 1968, in response to concerns about consumer credit, Congress passed the **Federal Consumer Credit Protection Act (FCCPA)**, which requires creditors to disclose finance charges (including interest and other charges) and credit extension charges, and sets limits on garnishment proceedings. Since 1968, Congress has added additional titles to this law. Today, it includes the following laws: (1) the Truth-in-Lending Act (including the Fair Credit Billing Act and the Consumer Leasing Act), (2) the Restriction on Garnishment, (3) the Fair Credit Reporting Act, (4) the Equal Credit Opportunity Act, (5) the Fair Debt Collection Practices

FIGURE 42–2   Consumer Rescission Rights

| Law | Rescission Period | Door-to-Door Solicitation Required? | Credit or Cash |
|-----|-------------------|-------------------------------------|----------------|
| **State "cooling-off" laws** | Varies | Yes | Varies |
| **FTC trade regulation** | Within 3 days of signing the contract | Yes | Both |
| **Consumer Credit Protection Act (CCPA)** | Within 3 days of signing the contract | No | Credit only |
| **Interstate Land Sales Full Disclosure Act** | Within 7 days of signing the contract | No | Both |

Act, and (6) the Electronic Fund Transfer Act. Also in 1968, the National Conference of Commissioners on Uniform State Laws (the group that drafted the UCC) promulgated the **Uniform Consumer Credit Code (UCCC)**, which integrated into one recommended law the regulation of all consumer credit transactions—loans and purchases on credit. Though the UCCC has been adopted in only nine States, its impact on the development of consumer credit has extended well beyond their borders.

## Access to the Market

The **Equal Credit Opportunity Act**, enacted by Congress in 1974 and subsequently revised on a number of occasions, prohibits all businesses that regularly extend credit from discriminating against any applicant for credit on the basis of sex, marital status, race, color, religion, national origin, or age. A major congressional goal in passing the Act was to eliminate the lenders' practice of refusing credit to women of childbearing age under the assumption that such women were apt to quit work to have children and thereby reduce their ability to repay credit. Under **Regulation B**, issued by the Federal Reserve Board to implement the Act, and the Women's Business Ownership Act of 1988, creditors who are determining an applicant's creditworthiness cannot inquire into or use information about the applicant's marital status or her likelihood of having children.

Under the Act, a creditor has thirty days after receiving a credit application to notify the applicant of action taken, and the creditor must give specific reasons for a denial of credit. Several Federal agencies administer and enforce the Act, under the overall enforcement authority of the FTC. Credit applicants aggrieved by a violation of the Act may recover actual and punitive damages plus attorneys' fees.

The **Home Mortgage Disclosure Act** (HMDA) was enacted by Congress along with the **Community Reinvestment Act** (CRA) to emphasize to financial institutions the importance of their reinvesting funds in the communities that they serve. Through the HMDA, Congress outlawed geographic discrimination, or *redlining*, the process by which financial institutions refuse to provide reasonable home financing terms to qualified applicants whose homes are located in geographic areas of declining value. In addition, the HMDA requires public disclosure of the financial institution's geographic pattern of mortgage lending. The CRA, by comparison, was intended to encourage financial institutions to meet the credit needs of their local communities. In 1989,

Congress adopted a major banking bailout bill, the **Financial Institutions Reform, Recovery, and Enforcement Act** (FIRREA), which included amendments to the HMDA and the CRA. The amendments expanded the disclosure and reporting requirements for all mortgage lenders and mandated that Federal regulating agencies evaluate and rate CRA performance reports.

## Disclosure Requirements

Title One of the FCCPA, also known as the **Truth-in-Lending Act**, has superseded State disclosure requirements relating to credit terms for both consumer loans and credit sales under $25,000. The Act does not cover credit transactions for business, commercial, or agricultural purposes. Creditors in every State not specifically exempted by the Federal Reserve Board must comply with Federal disclosure standards. The board exempts only those States that have disclosure requirements substantially the same as the Federal requirements and that ensure enforcement of their requirements. The FCCPA does not, however, excuse creditors from compliance with State requirements not covered by, or more stringent than, the FCCPA requirements, so long as the State-required disclosure is not inconsistent with the FCCPA.

Before a consumer formally incurs a contractual obligation for credit, both State and Federal statutes require a creditor to present to the consumer a written statement containing certain information about contract terms. Generally, the required disclosure concerns the cost of credit, such as interest, sales charges, finder's fees, mortgage guarantee insurance, or any mandatory credit life insurance. An important requirement in the Truth-in-Lending Act is that sales finance charges and interest rates must be quoted in terms of an **annual percentage rate (APR)** and must be calculated on a uniform basis. Congress required disclosure of this information to encourage consumers to compare credit terms, to increase competition among financial institutions, and to facilitate economic stability. Enforcement and interpretation of the Truth-in-Lending Act was assigned to several agencies, the two most important being the FTC and the Federal Reserve Board, which issued **Regulation Z** to carry out this responsibility.

Many individuals have claimed that the interest rates charged for credit cards are unfairly excessive and should be limited by legislation. In 1988, statutes for this purpose were proposed in Congress, but none was enacted. Instead, Congress passed the **Fair Credit and Charge**

**Card Disclosure Act** of 1988. The Act, which is consistent with other legislation in the field in that it emphasizes the disclosure of key items, adds to the Truth-in-Lending Act a new section requiring all credit and charge card applications and solicitations to include extensive disclosures whose requirements depend upon the type of card involved and whether the application or solicitation is by mail, telephone, or other means.

*Credit Accounts*   In addition to the cost of the credit, under the Truth-in-Lending Act a creditor must inform consumers who open revolving or open-end credit accounts about how the finance charge is computed and when it is charged, what other charges may be imposed, and whether the creditor retains or acquires a security interest. An **open-end** credit account is one that permits the debtor to enter into a series of credit transactions that he may pay off either in installments or in a lump sum. Examples of this type of credit include most department store credit cards, most gasoline credit cards, VISA cards, and MasterCards. With this type of credit, the creditor is also required to provide a statement of account for each billing period.

**Closed-end** credit is credit extended for a specified time, during which the debtor generally makes periodic payments in an amount and at a time agreed upon in advance. Examples of this type of credit include most automobile financing agreements, most real estate mortgages, and numerous other major purchases. For nonrevolving or closed-end credit accounts, the creditor must provide the consumer with information about the total amount financed; the cash price; the number, amount, and due date of installments; delinquency charges; and a description of the security, if any.

*ARMs*   In 1987, the Federal Reserve Board amended Regulation Z to deal with variable or adjustable rate mortgages (ARMs). The *ARM disclosure rules* apply to any loan that is (1) a closed-end consumer transaction, (2) secured by the consumer's principal residence, (3) longer than one year in duration, and (4) subject to interest rate variation. This coverage excludes open-end lines of credit secured by the consumer's principal dwelling. A creditor must make the disclosures when he furnishes an application to a prospective borrower or before the creditor receives payment of a nonrefundable fee, whichever occurs first. The ARM disclosure rules require that the creditor provide the consumer with a consumer handbook on ARMs and a loan program disclosure statement covering the terms of each ARM that the creditor offers.

*Home Equity Loans*   In recent years a popular method of consumer borrowing has been the home equity loan. To regulate the disclosures and advertising of these loans, in 1988 Congress enacted the **Home Equity Loan Consumer Protection Act (HELCPA)**. HELCPA amends the Truth-in-Lending Act to require that lenders provide a disclosure statement and consumer pamphlet at (or, in some limited instances, within three days of) the time they provide an application to a prospective consumer borrower. HELCPA applies to all open-end credit plans for consumer loans that are secured by the consumer's principal dwelling. Unlike other Truth-in-Lending statutes, HELCPA defines a principal dwelling to include second or vacation homes. The disclosure statement must include a statement that (1) a default on the loan may result in the consumer's loss of the dwelling, (2) certain conditions must be met, such as a time by which an application must be submitted to obtain the specified terms, and (3) the creditor, under certain circumstances, may terminate the plan and accelerate the outstanding balance, prohibit the further extension of credit, reduce the plan's credit limit, or impose fees upon the termination of the account. In addition, if the plan contains a fixed interest rate, the creditor must disclose each APR imposed. If the plan involves an ARM, it must include how the rate is computed, the manner in which rates will be changed, the initial rate and how it was determined, the maximum rate change that may occur in any one year, the maximum rate that can be charged under the plan, the earliest time at which the maximum interest can be reached, and an itemization of all fees imposed by the plan. Regulation Z provides the consumer with the right to rescind such a plan until midnight of the third day following the opening of the plan, until delivery of a notice of the right to rescind, or until delivery of all material disclosures, whichever comes last.

*Billing Errors*   The **Fair Credit Billing Act** went into effect to relieve some of the problems and abuses associated with credit card billing errors. The Act establishes procedures for the consumer to follow in making complaints about specified billing errors and requires the creditor to explain or correct such errors. Billing errors include (1) credit extensions that were never made or were not made in the amount indicated on the billing statement; (2) undelivered or unaccepted goods or services; (3) incorrect recording of payments or credits; and (4) accounting or computational errors. Until the creditor responds to the complaint, it may not take any action to collect the disputed amount, restrict the use of an open-ended credit account because the disputed amount is unpaid, or report the disputed amount as delinquent.

*Settlement Charges* Congress enacted the **Real Estate Settlement Procedures Act (RESPA)** to provide consumers who purchase a home with greater and more timely information on the nature and costs of the settlement process and to protect them from unnecessarily high settlement charges. The Act, which applies to all Federally related mortgage loans, requires advance disclosure to homebuyers and sellers of all settlement costs, including attorneys' fees, credit reports, title insurance, and, if relevant, an initial escrow account statement. Nearly all first mortgage loans fall within the scope of the Act. RESPA prohibits kickbacks and referral fees and limits the amount homebuyers must place in escrow accounts to insure payment of real estate taxes and insurance. RESPA was amended in 1990 by the National Affordable Housing Act of 1990 to require an annual analysis of escrow accounts. The Act is administered and enforced by the Secretary of Housing and Urban Development.

## Contract Terms

Consumer credit is marketed on a mass basis. Frequently, contract documents are printed forms containing blank spaces to accommodate the contractual details the creditor usually will negotiate at the time she extends credit. Standardization and uniformity of contract terms facilitate the transfer of the creditor's rights (in most situations, those of a seller) to a third party, usually a bank or finance company.

Almost all the States impose statutory ceilings on the amount that creditors may charge for the extension of consumer credit. Statutes regulating rates also specify what other charges may be made. For example, charges for insurance, official fees, and taxes usually are not considered part of the finance charge, whereas charges incidental to the extension of credit, such as a service charge or a commission for extending credit, usually are. Any charge that does not qualify as an authorized additional charge is treated as part of the finance charge and is subject to the statutory rate ceiling. Other special permitted charges include delinquency and default charges, charges incurred in connection with storing and repairing repossessed goods for sale, reasonable fees for a lawyer who is not a salaried employee of the creditor, and court costs.

Most statutes require a creditor to permit the debtor to pay her obligation in full at any time prior to the maturity date of the final installment. If the interest charge for the loan period was computed in advance and added to the principal of the loan, a debtor who prepays in full is entitled to a refund of the unearned interest already paid.

Aside from provisions relating to cost, the balance of a credit contract deals with repayment terms and the remedies available to the creditor if payments are delinquent. Usually, payments must be periodic and substantially equal in amount. Balloon payments (loans in which the final payment is much larger than the regular payments; for example, where the monthly installments are $50 and the final installment is $1,000) may be prohibited. Where they are not prohibited, the creditor may be required to refinance the loan at the same rate and with installments in the same amount as the original loan without penalty to the borrower.

In the past, certain purchases involving consumer goods were financed in such a manner that the consumer was legally obligated to make full payment of the price to a third party, even though the dealer from whom she bought the goods had committed fraud or the goods were defective. This occurred when the purchaser executed and delivered to the seller a negotiable promissory note which the seller negotiated to a holder in due course, a third party who purchased the note for value, in good faith, and without notice of its being overdue or of any defenses or claims to it. Though valid against the seller, the buyer's defense that the goods were defective or that the seller had committed fraud was not valid against a holder in due course of the note. To preserve the claims and defenses of consumer buyers and borrowers and to make such claims and defenses available against holders in due course, the FTC adopted a rule that limits the rights of a holder in due course of an instrument that evidences a debt arising out of a consumer credit contract. The rule applies to sellers and lessors of goods. A discussion of the rule is in Chapter 28.

A similar rule applies to credit card issuers under the Fair Credit Billing Act. The Act preserves a consumer's defenses against the issuer (provided the consumer has made a good faith attempt to resolve the dispute with the seller), but only if (1) the seller is controlled by the card issuer or is under common control with the issuer; (2) the issuer has included the seller's promotional literature in the monthly billing statements sent to the card holder; or (3) the sale involves more than fifty dollars and the consumer's billing address is in the same State as, or within 100 miles of, the seller's place of business.

## Consumer Credit Card Fraud

Consumer credit card fraud has become an increasingly serious problem and now totals approximately $200 million per year. In 1984, Congress enacted the **Credit Card Fraud Act**, which closed many of the loopholes in prior law. The Act prohibits the following practices: (1) possessing unauthorized cards, (2) counterfeiting or altering credit cards, (3) using account numbers alone, and (4) using cards obtained from a third party with his consent, even if the third party conspires to report the cards as stolen. It also imposes stiffer, criminal penalties for violation.

The FCCPA protects the credit card holder from loss by limiting to fifty dollars the card holder's liability for another's unauthorized use of the holder's card. The card issuer may collect up to that amount for unauthorized use only if (1) the holder has accepted the card; (2) the issuer has furnished adequate notice of potential liability to the card holder; (3) the issuer has provided the card holder with a statement describing the means by which the holder may notify the card issuer of the loss or theft of the credit card; (4) the unauthorized use occurs before the card holder has notified the card issuer of the loss or theft; and (5) the card issuer has provided a method by which the person using the card can be identified as the person authorized to use the card.

## Fair Reportage

Whenever an individual applies for credit, the lender is likely to run a credit check on the applicant, commonly by purchasing a credit report from a credit bureau—a private company that keeps files on consumers and their skill at paying their debts. An applicant whose file indicates that he fails to repay loans or pays them delinquently may have difficulty obtaining credit.

Before passage of the Fair Credit Reporting Act, certain unscrupulous creditors coerced consumers into paying questionable claims by preying on their fears of bad credit ratings. For example, if today Barry bought an overpriced, malfunctioning vacuum cleaner from the Ajax Vacuum Company based on the false representations of Ajax's salesperson, Barry would have the right to rescind the sale and refuse to pay Ajax. Before the Act, however, if Barry withheld payments, Ajax might have threatened to report him to the credit bureau as being delinquent on his account. This would have been a significant threat because such a report might have ruined Barry's ability to obtain other credit. Accordingly, Barry might have paid Ajax simply to avoid future credit

problems. Consumers faced other problems with credit bureaus. In some instances, a credit bureau might simply have made a mistake, such as listing Harry Jones instead of Larry Jones as delinquent, but then have no procedure for, or interest in, correcting the error. In other cases, outdated information concerning a consumer's conduct formed the basis for the denial of credit. These and other perceived credit abuses led Congress to enact the **Fair Credit Reporting Act**, which sets guidelines for credit reports used to secure employment, insurance, and credit.

The Act prohibits consumer reporting agencies from including inaccurate or obsolete information in consumer reports (most information is obsolete after seven years; bankruptcy information becomes obsolete after ten years) and requires consumer reporting agencies to give consumers written, advance notice before making investigative reports. Consumers may request and receive from any consumer reporting agency information regarding (1) the nature and substance of all information on the consumer in the agency's files, (2) the sources of the information, and (3) the names of all recipients to whom the agency has furnished the information for employment purposes within the preceding two years and for other purposes within the preceding six months.

If the consumer believes that the information in the file is inaccurate or incomplete, and so notifies the agency, the agency must then reinvestigate the matter within a reasonable period of time unless the complaint is frivolous or irrelevant. If reinvestigation proves that the information is inaccurate, it must be promptly deleted. If the dispute remains unresolved after reinvestigation, the consumer may submit a brief statement setting forth the nature of the dispute, which the agency must incorporate into the report.

In 1997, Congress amended the Act to restrict the use of credit reports by employers. An employer must now notify the job applicant or current employee that a report may be used and must obtain the applicant's consent prior to requesting an individual's credit report from a credit bureau. In addition, prior to taking an adverse action (refusal to hire, reassignment or termination, or denial of a promotion) against the applicant or employee, the employer must provide the individual with a "pre-adverse action disclosure," which must contain the credit report and a copy of the FTC's "A Summary of Your Rights Under the Fair Credit Reporting Act."

*See Case 42-2*

# CREDITORS' REMEDIES

A primary concern of creditors involves their rights should a debtor default or become tardy in payment. When the credit charge is precomputed, the creditor may impose a delinquency charge for late payments, subject to statutory limits for such charges. If, instead of being delinquent, the consumer defaults, the creditor may declare the entire balance of the debt immediately due and payable and may sue on the debt. The other courses of action to which the creditor may turn depend upon his security. Security provisions included in consumer credit contracts may require a cosigner, an assignment of wages, a security interest in the goods sold, a security interest in other real or personal property of the debtor, and a confession of judgment clause (i.e., an agreement by the debtor giving the creditor the authority to enter judgment against the debtor).

## Wage Assignments and Garnishment

Wage assignments are prohibited by some States. In most States and under the FCCPA, a limitation is imposed on the amount that may be deducted from an individual's wages during any pay period. In addition, the FCCPA prohibits an employer from discharging an employee solely because of a creditor's exercise of an assignment of wages in connection with any one debt.

Even where wage assignments are prohibited, the creditor may still reach a consumer's wages through garnishment. But garnishment is only available in a court proceeding to enforce the collection of a judgment. The FCCPA and State statutes contain exemption provisions which limit the amount of wages subject to garnishment.

## Security Interests

In the case of credit sales, the seller may retain a security interest in the goods sold. Many States impose restrictions on other security the creditor may obtain. Where the debt is secured by property as collateral, the creditor, upon default by the debtor, may take possession of the property and, subject to the provisions of the UCC, either retain it in full satisfaction of the debt or sell it and, if the proceeds are less than the outstanding debt, sue the debtor for the balance and obtain a deficiency judgment. The UCC provides that where a buyer of goods has paid 60 percent of the purchase price or 60 percent of a loan secured by consumer goods, the secured creditor may not retain the property in full satisfaction but must sell the goods and pay to the buyer that part

of the sale proceeds in excess of the balance due. In addition, Federal regulation prohibits a credit seller or lender from obtaining a consumer's grant of a nonpossessory security interest in household goods. Household goods include clothing, furniture, appliances, kitchenware, personal effects, one radio, and one television; such goods specifically exclude works of art, other electronic entertainment equipment, antiques, and jewelry. This rule, which does not apply to purchase money security interests or to pledges, prevents a lender or seller from obtaining a nonpurchase money security interest covering the consumer's household goods. Secured transactions are discussed in Chapter 38.

## Debt Collection Practices

Abuses by some collection agencies led Congress in 1977 to pass the **Fair Debt Collection Practices Act**, which makes abusive, deceptive, and unfair practices by debt collectors in collecting consumer debts illegal. The Act does not apply to creditors who use their own names in trying to collect debts themselves. Rather, it applies only to those who collect debts for others. This does not mean that creditors are free to use improper methods to collect debts. Most States have laws or common law decisions that prohibit unfair debt collection practices.

Before the Act, many debt collectors contacted third parties, such as relatives, neighbors, or employers, to inquire about the whereabouts or financial condition of the debtor. In doing so, the collectors made sure to tell the third parties who they were and why they were calling. To avoid the embarrassment resulting from such contacts, many debtors would hasten to pay their debts, even questionable ones. To prevent these often unfair and unnecessary disclosures, the Act bars, except in certain narrow circumstances, debt collectors from communicating with third parties about a consumer's debt. The Act does permit debt collectors to contact a third party to ascertain the location of the consumer, but it prohibits them from disclosing that they are debt collectors and from stating that the consumer owes any debt.

The Act forbids other abusive collection practices, including (1) communication with the consumer at unusual or inconvenient hours; (2) communication with the consumer if he is represented by an attorney; (3) harassing, oppressive, or abusive conduct, such as threats of violence or the use of obscene language; (4) false, deceptive, or misleading representations, such as false claims that the debt collector is an attorney or a government official, or that the consumer has committed a crime; or (5) other unfair or unconscionable means to collect or attempt to collect a debt, such as a false threat of a lawsuit.

The Act requires a debt collector, within five days of the initial communication with a consumer, to provide the consumer with a written notice that includes (1) the amount of the debt; (2) the name of the current creditor; and (3) a statement informing the consumer that she can request verification of the alleged debt.

The Act gives consumers one extremely powerful right in dealing with debt collectors. If a consumer notifies a debt collector in writing that the consumer refuses to pay a debt or that the consumer wishes the debt collector to cease further communication with the consumer, the debt collector must stop further communication except to notify the consumer that the creditor or collector may invoke specified remedies such as filing a lawsuit to collect the debt. Consumers have the right to seek damages from debt collectors for violations of the Act. In addition, the FTC has authority for administrative enforcement of its provisions.

 *See Case 42–4*

---

# Chapter Summary

| **Federal Trade Commission** | **Purpose** to prevent unfair methods of competition and unfair or deceptive acts or practices<br>**Standards**<br>• *Unfairness* requires injury to be (1) substantial, (2) not outweighed by any countervailing benefit, and (3) unavoidable by reasonable consumer action<br>• *Deception* misrepresentation, omission, or practice that is likely to mislead the consumer acting reasonably in the circumstances<br>• *Ad Substantiation* requires advertisers to have a reasonable basis for their claims<br>**Remedies**<br>• *Cease and Desist Order* command to stop doing the act in question<br>• *Affirmative Disclosure* requires an advertiser to include certain information in its ad so that the ad is not deceptive<br>• *Corrective Advertising* requires an advertiser to disclose that previous ads were deceptive<br>• *Multiple Product Order* requires an advertiser to cease and desist from deceptive statements regarding all products it sells |
|---|---|
| **Consumer Health and Safety** | **Consumer Product Safety Act** Federal statute enacted to<br>• *Protect public against unsafe products*<br>• *Assist consumers in evaluating products*<br>• *Develop uniform safety standards*<br>• *Promote safety research*<br>**Other Federal Consumer Protection Agencies** |
| **Consumer Purchases** | **Federal Warranty Protection** applies to sellers of consumer goods who give written warranties<br>• *Presale Disclosure* requires terms of warranty to be simple and readily understood and to be made available before the sale<br>• *Labeling Requirement* requires warrantor to inform consumers of their legal rights under a warranty (full or limited)<br>• *Disclaimer Limitation* prohibits a written warranty from disclaiming any implied warranty<br>**State "Lemon Laws"** State laws that attempt to provide new car purchasers with rights similar to full warranties under the Magnuson-Moss Warranty Act |

| | |
|---|---|
| | **Consumer Right of Rescission** in certain instances a consumer is granted a brief period of time during which she may rescind (cancel) an otherwise binding obligation |
| **Consumer Credit Transactions** | **Definition** any credit transaction involving goods, services, or land for personal, household, or family purposes<br>**Access to the Market** discrimination in extending credit on the basis of gender, marital status, race, color, religion, national origin, or age is prohibited<br>**Truth-in-Lending Act** requires creditor to provide certain information about contract terms, including annual percentage rate (APR), to the consumer before he formally incurs the obligation<br>**Contract Terms** statutory and judicial limitations have been imposed on consumer obligations<br>**Consumer Credit Card Fraud Act** prohibits certain fraudulent practices and limits a card holder's liability for unauthorized use of a credit card to $50<br>**Fair Credit Reporting** consumer credit reports are prohibited from containing inaccurate or obsolete information |
| **Creditors' Remedies** | **Wage Assignments and Garnishment** most States limit the amount that may be deducted from an individual's wages through either assignment or garnishment<br>**Security Interest** seller may retain a security interest in goods sold or other collateral of the buyer, although some restrictions are imposed<br>**Debt Collection Practices** abusive, deceptive, and unfair practices by debt collectors in collecting consumer debts are prohibited by the Fair Debt Collection Practices Act |

# Cases

## CASE 42–1
## FTC: Standards
## *FEDERAL TRADE COMMISSION v. PANTRON I CORPORATION*

United States Court of Appeals, Ninth Circuit, 1994
33 F.3d 1088

REINHARDT, J.

These consolidated appeals require us to decide a previously unresolved question of federal consumer protection law: Whether it is lawful for a seller to represent a product as "effective" when its efficacy results solely from a "placebo effect."[1] We conclude that the answer is no

---

[1]The term "placebo effect" refers to the fact that even a product of no inherent merit whatsoever will often have some degree of effectiveness in treating the condition for which it is employed, for psychological or other reasons. For example, a patient who ingests sugar pills while believing that they are strong pain relievers may well experience some pain relief, even though sugar pills are themselves inherently worthless in treating pain. In this example, the sugar pill is a "placebo" and the relief experienced by the patient is the "placebo effect."

and that the representation constitutes a "false advertisement" under the Federal Trade Commission Act.

\* \* \*

### I

Pantron I Corporation and Hal Z. Lederman market a product known as the Helsinki Formula. This product supposedly arrests hair loss and stimulates hair regrowth in baldness sufferers. The Formula consists of a conditioner and a shampoo, and it sells at a list price of $49.95 for a three-month supply. The ingredients which allegedly cause the advertised effects are polysorbate 60 and polysorbate 80. Pantron offers a full money-back guarantee for those who are not satisfied with the product.

This case involves the F.T.C.'s challenge to Pantron's advertisements promoting the Helsinki Formula. These advertisements (including late-night infomercials hosted by the "Man from U.N.C.L.E.," Robert Vaughn) feature both the hair loss claim and the claim that the Formula promotes growth of new hair in baldness sufferers. They also represent that recognized scientific studies support these claims. * * *

The district court conducted a 5-day bench trial in November of 1989. The F.T.C. presented a variety of evidence which tended to show that the Helsinki Formula had no effectiveness (other than its placebo effect) in arresting hair loss or promoting hair regrowth. The Commission introduced the expert testimony of Dr. Karl Kramer, a dermatologist who stated that, based on his knowledge and review of the medical literature, there was "no reason to believe" that the Helsinki Formula would be in any way useful in treating hair loss. He also stated that his opinion was in accord with the consensus view of the medical community.

Dr. Kramer's testimony was corroborated by two other experts. * * *

Finally, the F.T.C. introduced evidence of two studies which had determined that polysorbate-based products were ineffective in stopping hair loss and promoting hair regrowth. * * *

In response, Pantron introduced evidence that users of the Helsinki Formula were satisfied that it was effective. It offered the live and deposition testimony of 18 users who had experienced hair regrowth or a reduction in hair loss after using the Formula. It also introduced evidence of a "consumer satisfaction survey" it conducted in late 1988. * * * Pantron also introduced evidence that over half of its orders come from repeat purchasers, that it had received very few written complaints, and that very few of Pantron's customers (less than 3%) had exercised their rights under the money-back guarantee.

Pantron also introduced several clinical studies of its own. First, it offered the results of Finnish studies, for which the Helsinki Formula was named, performed by Dr. Ilona Schreck-Purola. Her uncontrolled, unblinded, unrandomized, un-peer-reviewed study concluded that a polysorbate-based product was effective in arresting excessive hair loss within two to four weeks, and that it led to new hair growth in 60% of the subjects within four months. Although Dr. Schreck-Purola acknowledged that "the medical community remains of the opinion that polysorbates are not effective in treating male pattern baldness," she nonetheless stated that, in her opinion, polysorbates help alleviate baldness by destroying the cholesterol in the testosterone that destroys hair follicles.

Pantron also introduced the testimony of * * *, a French dermatologist who conducted an uncontrolled, unblinded study of a polysorbate product's effectiveness.

* * *

[T]he district court issued findings of fact and conclusions of law. It found that Pantron had made the representations of efficacy and scientific support that the F.T.C. had alleged. Turning to the question whether these representations were false, the district court determined that "[t]here is no evidence in the record to support a contention that the Helsinki Formula is wholly ineffective." The district court found that the studies and anecdotal evidence offered by Pantron "support[ed] the proposition that the compound works for some people some of the time." Thus, it concluded that the F.T.C. had failed to carry its burden of showing that Pantron made a false claim when it represented that the Helsinki Formula was effective.

However, the district court found "no scientifically valid evidence that polysorbate 60 is effective for treatment of hair loss or for inducing growth." * * * Accordingly, it entered an injunction, which barred Pantron and Lederman from making any express or explicit representations that scientific evidence establishes that the Helsinki Formula "is effective in any way in the treatment of baldness or hair loss." However, the order specifically allowed the defendants to

state that the Helsinki Formula (or a product similar thereto) was the subject of medical investigative work by responsible European physicians, if such statement is accompanied by clear and conspicuous disclosure that the work did not conform to recognized standards in the United States for medical/scientific studies.

Another provision of the injunction prohibited "any misrepresentation . . . regarding the effectiveness of such product or program in the treatment of baldness," but it allowed Pantron and Lederman to

state that the Helsinki Formula is effective to some extent for some people in dealing with male pattern baldness, if such statement is accompanied by clear and conspicuous disclosure that the product's effectiveness (1) is more likely to involve arrest of hair loss than growth of new hair, and (2) is not explained or supported by scientific studies recognized under standards in use in the United States.

* * *

## II

* * * The Commission [FTC] also claims that the district court applied an incorrect legal standard in evalu-

ating the evidence of effectiveness. We agree that the district court used an erroneous legal standard and hold that the parts of the order challenged by the F.T.C. must be modified.

## A

The Federal Trade Commission brought this suit pursuant to sections 5(a) and 12 of the Federal Trade Commission Act, [Citation]. Section 5(a) of the Act declares unlawful "unfair or deceptive acts or practices in or affecting commerce" and empowers the Commission to prevent such acts or practices. [Citation.] Section 12 of the Act is specifically directed to false advertising. That section prohibits the dissemination of "any false advertisement" in order to induce the purchase of "food, drugs, devices, or cosmetics." * * *

In its own adjudications, the F.T.C. has to some extent clarified the legal standards which apply in section 12 cases. In *Cliffdale Associates,* [Citation], the Commission announced a three-part test for determining whether an advertisement is misleading and deceptive in violation of section 12. Under this test,

the Commission will find an act or practice deceptive if, first, there is a representation, omission, or practice that, second, is likely to mislead consumers acting reasonably under the circumstances, and third, the representation, omission, or practice is material.

* * * [W]e believe that the general outlines of the *Cliffdale Associates* test set forth the appropriate general principles for determining whether advertising is deceptive. * * *

In this case, there is no question that Pantron represented that the Helsinki Formula was effective. * * * There is also no question that these claims are material. * * * Therefore, the only question before us is whether Pantron's representations regarding the product's effectiveness were likely to deceive or mislead consumers.

There are a number of ways in which a representation, omission, or practice can mislead consumers within the meaning of section 12. In particular, the Commission has identified two theories on which the government can and often does rely in section 12 cases involving objective product claims. First, the government can assert a so-called "falsity" theory. To prevail on such a theory, the government must "carry the burden of proving that the express or implied message conveyed by the ad is false." [Citation.] Alternatively, the government can rely on a so-called "reasonable basis" theory. To prevail on this theory, the government must "show that the advertiser lacked a reasonable basis for asserting that the message was true." * * *

Although the district court conducted both a "falsity" and a "reasonable basis" analysis, the F.T.C clearly and expressly abandoned the reasonable basis theory, both in the district court and in this court.[23] Accordingly, we discuss only the falsity theory.

## B

The district court concluded that the F.T.C. failed to carry its burden of proving that Pantron's efficacy representations were false. It held that "[t]o prevail on its charge that defendant has misrepresented the efficacy of the 'Helsinki Formula,' the F.T.C. must prove that the product is wholly ineffective; i.e., that it does not work at all." * * *

We hold that the district court erred in concluding that Pantron's representations regarding the Helsinki Formula's efficacy did not amount to false advertising. Although there was sufficient evidence in the record to support the district court's finding that use of the Helsinki Formula might arrest hair loss in some of the people some of the time, the overwhelming weight of the proof at trial made clear that any effectiveness is due solely to the product's placebo effect. * * *, [W]e conclude that a claim of product effectiveness is "false" for purposes of section 12 of the Federal Trade Commission Act if evidence developed under accepted standards of scientific research demonstrates that the product has no force beyond its placebo effect.

* * *

Yet Pantron did not present any evidence which rebutted the consensus of the medical community that polysorbate-based products such as the Helsinki Formula are inherently ineffective. All of the evidence of effectiveness adduced by Pantron can be explained by the placebo effect. * * *

None of Pantron's evidence of effectiveness takes the placebo effect into account. Pantron's evidence of consumer satisfaction is the most obviously flawed. The substantial placebo effect indicates that consumers simply cannot tell whether over-the-counter baldness cures are effective, inherently or otherwise. * * * Much of Pantron's "consumer satisfaction" evidence is suspect on other grounds as well. Pantron's so-called "consumer satisfaction survey" was conducted by its own sales staff

---

[23]This abandonment is puzzling, to say the least, because it is difficult to imagine how the Commission could fail to prevail on a reasonable basis theory. * * *

"as we did our follow ups to offer additional product."
No record of the questions was kept. In addition, Pantron's low refund rate may not represent satisfaction.

* * *

C

* * *

However, neither scientific standards on the one hand,
nor the broadest possible definition of "truth" on the
other, can determine what constitutes a "false advertisement" under section 12 of the Federal Trade Commission Act. Indeed, a "false advertisement" need not even
be "false"; it need only be "misleading in a material
respect." [Citation.] We must read this definition of
"false advertis[ing]" in light of the overriding purpose
of the F.T.C. Act: "to protect the consumer from being
misled by governing the conditions under which goods
and services are advertised and sold to individual purchasers." [Citations.] The question we must face, then, is not
whether Pantron's claims were "true" in some abstract
epistemological sense, nor even whether they could conceivably be described as "true" in ordinary parlance.
Rather, we must determine whether or not efficacy representations based solely on the placebo effect are "misleading in a material respect," and hence prohibited as
"false advertis[ing]" under the Act.

Taking account of these principles, we hold that the
Federal Trade Commission is not required to prove that
a product is "wholly ineffective" in order to carry its
burden of showing that the seller's representations of
product efficacy are "false." Where, as here, a product's
effectiveness arises solely as a result of the placebo effect,
a representation that the product is effective constitutes
a "false advertisement" even though some consumers
may experience positive results. In such circumstances,
the efficacy claim "is 'misleading' because the [product]

is not inherently effective, its results being attributable
to the psychosomatic effect produced by the advertising
and marketing of the [product]," * * *

* * *

The evidence before the district court made clear that
there is no reason to believe that the Helsinki Formula
is at all effective outside of its placebo effect. Accordingly,
it was materially "misleading" under *Cliffdale Associates*
for Pantron to represent that the Formula is effective in
combatting male pattern baldness. * * *

* * * On remand, the district court shall modify its
injunction to prohibit the company from making any
representations that the Helsinki Formula is effective in
arresting hair loss or promoting hair regrowth.

* * *

III

The F.T.C. argues that the district court erred in refusing
to order Pantron or Lederman to pay restitution to consumers or disgorge their profits. Because the district
court's refusal to award monetary equitable relief was
based on the application of erroneous legal principles,
we reverse. [We conclude that an application of the correct legal principles requires the district court to order
monetary relief in this case, especially in light of our
conclusion, set forth in the previous Part, that the F.T.C.
fully proved its falsity case.

* * *

IV

The judgment of the district court is REVERSED in
part and AFFIRMED in part. On remand, the district
court is directed to modify the injunction as set forth in
this opinion, and to order both Pantron and Lederman
to pay monetary equitable relief.

---

**CASE 42–2**
Fair Reporting
*HENSON v. CSC CREDIT SERVICES*
United States Court of Appeals, Seventh Circuit, 1994
29 F.3d 280

KANNE, J.
This case has its origin in an earlier suit filed in an Indiana
state court by the Cosco Federal Credit Union against
one of the plaintiffs, Greg Henson, and his brother Jeff.

In that action, the state court clerk erroneously noted
in the Judgment Docket that a money judgment had
been entered against Greg. Two credit reporting agencies, CSC Credit Services and Trans Union Corporation,

relied on the state court Judgment Docket and indicated in Greg's credit report that he owed the money judgment. Greg and Mary Henson subsequently brought this suit against Cosco, CSC, and Trans Union. They sought recovery against CSC and Trans Union for violating various provisions of the Fair Credit Reporting Act ("FCRA"), [citation] * * *. The district court dismissed the Henson's second amended complaint for failure to state a claim for which relief can be granted. We affirm in part and reverse in part.

*Background* In June of 1986, Greg Henson purchased a 1980 Chevrolet Camaro Z-28 from an unknown party. He financed the purchase by executing a note with Irwin Union Bank of Columbus, Indiana. In March of 1990, Greg's brother, Jeff, filed a loan application with Cosco so that he could purchase the Camaro from Greg. Cosco loaned Jeff enough money to purchase the car and paid off Greg's note with Irwin. Soon thereafter, the Camaro was stolen and Jeff stopped making payments to Cosco.

On February 7, 1990, Cosco filed suit against Jeff and Greg in the Bartholomew Circuit Court in Columbus, Indiana. Cosco alleged in its complaint that Jeff had defaulted on his loan obligation. Cosco sought possession of the Camaro and a 1978 Ford Mustang, so that they could be sold and the proceeds applied to Jeff's outstanding loan balance. Cosco stated in the complaint that "Greg Henson, may claim some interest in the 1980 Chevy Camaro Z-28 . . . and he is made a party to this litigation to answer as to any ownership interest in or other claim that he may have to said automobile, if any."

On April 7, 1990, Cosco filed a Motion for Default Judgment and Judgment of Foreclosure against Jeff and Greg. The motion was prepared by Cosco's attorney, James K. Voelz, and contained proposed findings of fact and law. Cosco proposed the following finding, which the state court adopted: "the Court further finds that the Defendant, Greg Henson, has no ownership of or interest in the 1980 Chevy Camaro Z-28 . . . and the Plaintiff may sell said automobile free and clear of any claim or right of Greg Henson." After Cosco took possession of the Camaro and sold it for $850, it asked the court to render a deficiency judgment against Jeff. The court rendered this judgment against Jeff on July 18, 1990. Shortly thereafter, the Clerk of the Bartholomew Circuit Court incorrectly noted the judgment in the Judgment Docket. The Judgment Docket listed Jeff and Greg together and erroneously indicated that a money judgment was entered against both of them in the amount of $4,075.54.

\* \* \*

In [their] complaint, Greg and [his wife,] Mary allege that CSC and Trans Union violated the FCRA by "erroneously report[ing] in its credit reports that Greg owed a money/civil judgment in the amount of $4,076." According to the Henson's complaint, the erroneously reported money/civil judgment arose out of the earlier Indiana state court action. The Hensons also allege that they "contacted Trans twice, in writing, to correct the horrible injustice. However, nobody at Trans would correct the injustice." The Henson's complaint does not allege that they ever contacted CSC concerning the alleged error in Greg's credit report.

\* \* \*

After the Hensons filed their . . . complaint, all the defendants reasserted previously filed motions to dismiss. The district court granted the defendants' motions and dismissed the Hensons' complaint for failure to state a claim. * * * In reaching its decision, the district court noted that a consumer must allege that a credit reporting agency prepared a credit report containing inaccurate information to state a claim under the FCRA. * * *

[T]he district court found that "requiring Trans Union and CSC to have discovered the clerk's erroneous entry of judgment against Greg is overly burdensome. . . ." [Citation.] Thus, the court held that "Trans Union's and CSC's reporting of the recorded default judgment was not 'inaccurate' under FCRA" and granted their motions to dismiss.

\* \* \*

*Duty to Use Reasonable Procedures Under the FCRA* Under the FCRA, a consumer reporting agency is required to follow "reasonable procedures to assure maximum possible accuracy" of the information contained in a consumer's credit report. [Citation.] A credit reporting agency that negligently violates the provisions of the FCRA, is potentially liable for actual damages, costs, and attorney's fees. [Citation.] A credit reporting agency that willfully violates the Act may be liable for punitive damages as well. [Citation.]

In order to state a claim under [FCRA], a consumer must sufficiently allege "that a credit reporting agency prepared a report containing 'inaccurate' information." [Citation.] However, the credit reporting agency is not automatically liable even if the consumer proves that it prepared an inaccurate credit report because the FCRA "does not make reporting agencies strictly liable for all inaccuracies." [Citation.] A credit reporting agency is not liable under the FCRA if it followed "reasonable procedures to assure maximum possible accuracy," but nonetheless reported inaccurate information in the consumer's credit report.

The parties initially dispute whether the information contained in Greg's credit report was inaccurate. Greg argues that the information was inaccurate because his credit report indicated that he owed a money judgment in the amount of $4,075.74. Greg has shown that he owes no such money judgment. Trans Union and CSC, on the other hand, state that they simply reported that "a judgment against [Greg] in the amount of $4,076 had been entered in the public records of the Bartholomew Superior Court." According to Trans Union and CSC, this was true—a judgment had been entered against Greg by the Clerk of the Bartholomew Superior Court.

Trans Union and CSC argue that the Judgment Docket conclusively establishes that a money judgment was entered against Greg. They are wrong. * * *

The court documents in question conclusively establish that no money judgment was rendered against Greg. * * * The documents do conclusively establish, however, that the clerk erroneously noted in the Judgment Docket that a money judgment had been entered against Greg.

Thus, even if we were to accept CSC and Trans Union's position that they only reported that a money judgment had been entered against Greg, we would still conclude that this information was inaccurate. * * *

Our finding that the information contained in Greg's credit report was inaccurate does not end our inquiry. CSC and Trans Union are not liable under the FCRA if they followed "reasonable procedures to assure maximum possible accuracy" of the information reported. CSC and Trans Union argue that they followed "reasonable procedures" by obtaining the information from the Judgment Docket, a presumptively reliable source. We agree and hold that, as a matter of law, a credit reporting agency is not liable under the FCRA for reporting inaccurate information obtained from a court's Judgment Docket, absent prior notice from the consumer that the information may be inaccurate.

* * *

*Duty to Reinvestigate* In their complaint, the Hensons also allege that "Greg by his wife Mary, contacted, Trans [Union] twice, in writing, to correct the horrible injustice. However, nobody at Trans would correct the injustice." * * *

If the completeness or accuracy of any item of information contained in his file is disputed by the consumer, and such dispute is directly conveyed to the consumer reporting agency by the consumer, the consumer reporting agency shall within a reasonable period of time reinvestigate and record the current status of that information unless it has reasonable grounds to believe that the dispute by the consumer is frivolous or irrelevant. If after such reinvestigation such information is found to be inaccurate or can no longer be verified, the consumer reporting agency shall promptly delete such information.

* * *

Trans Union argues that it did not violate a duty to reinvestigate because it had no duty, as a matter of law, to go beyond the Judgment Docket in conducting its reinvestigation. We disagree. A credit reporting agency that has been notified of potentially inaccurate information in a consumer's credit report is in a very different position than one who has no such notice. As we indicated earlier, a credit reporting agency may initially rely on public court documents, because to require otherwise would be burdensome and inefficient. However, such exclusive reliance may not be justified once the credit reporting agency receives notice that the consumer disputes information contained in his credit report. When a credit reporting agency receives such notice, it can target its resources in a more efficient manner and conduct a more thorough investigation.

Accordingly, a credit reporting agency may be required, in certain circumstances, to verify the accuracy of its initial source of information, in this case the Judgment Docket. [Citation.]

Whether the credit reporting agency has a duty to go beyond the original source will depend, in part, on whether the consumer has alerted the reporting agency to the possibility that the source may be unreliable or the reporting agency itself knows or should know that the source is unreliable. The credit reporting agency's duty will also depend on the cost of verifying the accuracy of the source versus the possible harm inaccurately reported information may cause the consumer.

* * *

## CASE 42–3
## Creditors' Remedies
# MILLER v. PAYCO-GENERAL AMERICAN CREDITS, INC.

United States Court of Appeals, Fourth Circuit, 1991
943 F.2d 482

WILKINSON, J.

This case examines whether a form letter used by a debt collection agency observed the rights of consumers under the Fair Debt Collection Practices Act, [citation]. We hold that the collection agency did not effectively convey certain statutorily required information to the consumer and therefore reverse the judgment of the district court.

Lenvil Miller owed $2,501.61 to the Star Bank of Cincinnati. Star Bank referred collection of Miller's account to Payco—General American Credits, Inc. ("Payco"), a debt collection agency. Payco then sent to Miller the collection form which is the source of the controversy.

Across the top of the one page form is the title, "DE-MAND FOR PAYMENT," in large, red, boldface type. After the title follows information as to the creditor, the amount owed, and Payco's address. In the middle of the page, again in large, red, boldface type, is the statement, "THIS IS A DEMAND FOR IMMEDIATE FULL PAYMENT OF YOUR DEBT." That statement is followed by these sentences in black boldface type: YOUR SERIOUSLY PAST DUE ACCOUNT HAS BEEN GIVEN TO US FOR IMMEDIATE ACTION. YOU HAVE HAD AMPLE TIME TO PAY YOUR DEBT, BUT YOU HAVE NOT. IF THERE IS A VALID REA-SON, PHONE US AT [telephone number] TODAY. IF NOT, PAY US—NOW. The bottom third of the document is almost completely filled by the single word, "NOW," in white letters nearly two inches tall against a red background.

At the very bottom of the page, in the smallest type to appear on the form (letters one-eighth of an inch high), is the statement, "NOTICE: SEE RE-VERSE SIDE FOR IMPORTANT INFORMATION." The notice is printed in white against a red background. On the reverse of the document are four paragraphs printed in gray ink. The last three paragraphs contain the validation notice—that is, statements required by the Fair Debt Collection Practices Act (FDCPA) that inform the consumer how to obtain verification of the debt. [Citation.]

Miller brought suit against Payco in the United States District Court for the District of Maryland . . . on the ground that the validation notice did not comply with the FDCPA. Miller did not dispute that Payco included all the debt validation information required by the FDCPA. Rather, Miller charged that the validation notice was contradicted by other parts of the collection letter, that it was overshadowed by the demands for immediate payment, and that it was not effectively conveyed to the consumer. The district court granted summary judgment for Payco, concluding that the company had complied with the FDCPA by printing the validation notice on the back of the document and referring to it on the front.

Miller now appeals.

[The FDCPA] requires a debt collector to send a consumer, either in its initial communication or within five days of its initial communication, a written notice containing: 1) the debt amount; 2) the name of the current creditor; 3) a statement that if the consumer disputes the debt in writing within thirty days, the collector will send verification of the debt to the consumer; 4) a statement that if the consumer does not dispute the debt within thirty days, the collector will assume the debt to be valid; 5) a statement that the collector will send the name of the original creditor, upon written request within thirty days. [Citation.] If the consumer, in writing, disputes the debt or requests the name of the original creditor, then the collector must halt all collection efforts until it mails verification of the debt or the creditor's name to the consumer. [Citation.]

In interpreting the demands of the FDCPA, we bear in mind that the statute was enacted "to eliminate abusive debt collection practices" which "contribute to the number of personal bankruptcies, to marital instability, to the loss of jobs, and to invasions of individual privacy." [Citation.] Congress included the debt validation provisions in order to guarantee that consumers would receive adequate notice of their legal rights. [Citation.] Thus, a debt collector does not comply with [the Act] "merely by inclusion of the required debt validation notice; the notice Congress required must be conveyed effectively to the debtor." [Citation.] * * * Furthermore, in order to be effective, "the notice must not be overshad-owed or contradicted by other messages or notices appearing on the initial communication from the collection agency." [Citation.]

We agree with Miller that the form he received from Payco both contradicted and overshadowed the required validation notice, preventing the notice's effective communication. The front of the Payco form demands "IMMEDIATE FULL PAYMENT" and commands the consumer to "PHONE US TODAY," emphasized by the word "NOW" emblazoned in white letters nearly two inches tall against a red background. The message conveyed by those statements on the face of the form flatly contradicts the information contained on the back.

A consumer who wished to obtain validation of his debt could lose his rights under the statute if he followed the commands to telephone. [The Act] guarantees that validation will be sent and collection activities will cease only when the consumer disputes the debt in writing. If a consumer attempted to exercise his statutory rights by making the requested telephone call, Payco would be under no obligation to comply with [the Act's] directives to verify the debt and to cease collection efforts. The language on the front of the form emphatically instructs consumers to dispute their debt by telephone, in opposition to the statutory requirements.

The emphasis on immediate action also stands in contradiction to the FDCPA, which provides consumers a thirty day period to decide to request validation. A consumer who received Payco's form could easily be confused between the commands to respond "immediately," "now," and "today," and the thirty day response time contemplated by the statute.

\* \* \*

For the foregoing reasons, we reverse the judgment of the district court and remand for further proceedings. REVERSED AND REMANDED.

---

 **Questions**

1.   Discuss the role of the Federal Trade Commission (FTC) and the major enforcement sanctions that it may use.
2.   Discuss the role and workings of the Consumer Product Safety Commission (CPSC).
3.   Discuss the principal provisions of the Magnuson-Moss Warranty Act and distinguish between a full and a limited warranty.

4.   Discuss what information a creditor must provide a consumer before the consumer incurs the obligation. Distinguish between open-end and closed-end credit.
5.   Outline the major remedies that are available to a creditor.

---

 **Problems**

1.   The Federal Trade Commission (FTC) brings a deceptive trade practice action against Beneficial Finance Company based on Beneficial's use of its "instant tax refund" slogan. The FTC argues that Beneficial's advertising a tax refund loan or instant tax refund is deceptive in that the loan is not in any way connected with a tax refund but is merely Beneficial's everyday loan based on the applicant's creditworthiness. Decision?
2.   Barnes borrows $1,000 from Linda for one year, agreeing to pay Linda $200 in interest on the loan and to repay the loan in twelve monthly installments of $100. The contract which Linda provides and Barnes signs specifies that the annual percentage rate is 20 percent. Barnes now contends that the contract violates the Federal Consumer Credit Protection Act (FCCPA). Decision?
3.   A consumer entered into an agreement with Rent-It Corporation for the rental of a television set at a charge of seventeen dollars per week. The agreement also provides that if the renter chooses to rent the set for seventy-eight consecutive weeks,

title would be transferred. The consumer now contends that the agreement was really a sales agreement, not a lease, and therefore is a credit sale subject to the Truth-in-Lending Act. Decision?
4.   Central Adjustment Bureau allegedly threatened Consumer with a lawsuit, service at his office, and attachment and sale of his property to collect a debt when it did not intend to take such actions and when it did not have the authority to commence litigation. On some notices sent to Consumer, Central failed to disclose that it was attempting to collect a debt. In addition, Consumer claims that Central sent notices demanding payment that purported to be from attorneys but that were in fact written, signed, and sent by Central. Decision?
5.   The Giant Development Company undertakes a massive real estate venture to sell 9,000 one-acre unimproved lots in Utah. The company advertises the project nationally. Arrington, a resident of New York, learns of the opportunity and requests information about the project. The company provides

Arrington with a small advertising brochure that is devoid of information about the developer and the land. The brochure consists of vague descriptions of the joys of homeownership and nothing else. Arrington purchases a lot. Two weeks after entering into the agreement, Arrington wishes to rescind the contract. Will Arrington prevail?

6.   Jane Jones, a married woman, applies for a credit card from Exxon but is refused credit. Jane is bewildered as to why she was turned down. What are her legal rights in this situation?

7.   On a beautiful Saturday in October, Francie decides to take the twenty-mile ride from her home in New Jersey into New York City to do some shopping. Francie finds that Brown's Retail Sales, Inc., has a terrific sale on television sets and decides to surprise her husband with a new color TV. She purchases the set from Brown's on her American Express credit card for $450. When the set is delivered, Francie discovers that it does not work. Brown's refuses to repair or replace it or to credit Francie's charge account. Francie, therefore, refuses to pay American Express for the television. American Express brings this suit against Francie. Decision?

8.   Frank finds Thomas's wallet, which contains numerous credit cards and Thomas's identification. By using Thomas's identification and VISA card, Frank goes on a shopping spree and runs up $5,000 in charges. Thomas does not discover that he has lost his wallet until the following day, when he promptly notifies his VISA bank. How much can VISA collect from Thomas?

9.   Robert applies to Northern National Bank for a loan. Prior to granting the loan, Northern requests that Callis Credit Agency provide it with a credit report on Robert. Callis reports that three years previously, Robert had embezzled money from his employer. Based on this report, Northern rejects Robert's loan application.

   (a)   Robert demands to know why, but Northern refuses to divulge the information, arguing that it is privileged. Is Robert entitled to the information?

   (b)   Assume that Robert obtains the information and alleges that it is inaccurate. What recourse does Robert have?

10.   Colgate-Palmolive Co. produced a television advertisement that dramatically demonstrated the effectiveness of its Rapid Shave shaving cream. The ad purported to show the shaving cream being used to shave sandpaper. But because actual sandpaper appeared on television to be regular colored paper, Colgate substituted a sheet of Plexiglas with sand sprinkled on it. The FTC brought an action against Colgate, claiming that Colgate's ad was deceptive. Colgate defended on the ground that the consumer was merely being shown a representation of the actual test. Decision?

11.   In 1982, several manufacturers introduced into the American market a product known as all-terrain vehicles (ATVs). ATVs are motorized bikes that sit on three or four low-pressure balloon tires and are meant to be driven off paved roads. Almost immediately, the Consumer Product Safety Commission (CPSC) began receiving reports of deaths and serious injuries. As the number of injuries and deaths increased,

the CPSC began investigating ATV hazards. According to CPSC staff, children under the age of sixteen accounted for roughly half the deaths and injuries associated with this product.

What type of rule, if any, may the CPSC issue for ATVs?

12.   In the early 1970s, Sears formulated a plan to increase sales of its top-of-the-line "Lady Kenmore" brand dishwasher. Sears's plan sought to change the Lady Kenmore's image without reengineering or making any mechanical improvements in the dishwasher itself. To accomplish this, Sears undertook a four-year, $8 million advertising campaign that claimed that the Lady Kenmore completely eliminated the need to prerinse and prescrape dishes. As a result of this campaign, sales rose by more than 300 percent. The "no scraping, no prerinsing" claim was not true, however, and Sears had no reasonable basis for asserting the claim. In addition, the owner's manual that customers received after they purchased the dishwasher contradicted the claim.

After a thorough investigation, the Federal Trade Commission (FTC), in 1977, filed a complaint against Sears, alleging that the advertisements were false and misleading. The final FTC order required Sears to stop making the no prescraping, no prerinsing claim. The order also prevented Sears from (1) making any "performance claims" for "major home appliances" without first establishing a reasonable basis consisting of substantiating tests or other evidence; (2) misrepresenting any test, survey, or demonstration regarding "major home appliances"; and (3) making any advertising statements not consistent with statements in postpurchase materials supplied to purchasers of "major home appliances." Sears contends the order is too broad, as it covers appliances other than dishwashers and includes "performance claims" as well. Decision?

13.   Onondaga Bureau of Medical Economics (OBME), a collection agency for physicians, sent plaintiff Seabrook a letter demanding payment for a $198 physicians' bill. In addition to demanding payment, the letter stated that legal action resulting in a garnishment of his wages could be commenced against the plaintiff. Plaintiff sued OBME, alleging that the letter violated the Fair Debt Collection Practices Act in that it did not give him required notice and that it threatened legal action against him. Decision?

14.   William Thompson was denied credit based on an inaccurate credit report compiled by the San Antonio Retail Merchant's Association. The Association confused Thompson's credit history with that of another William Thompson and failed to use social security numbers to distinguish the two men. The second Mr. Thompson had a poor credit history. Thompson made numerous attempts to have the Association correct its mistake, but the error was never corrected. Thompson sued the Association for violation of the Fair Credit Reporting Act. Decision?

15.   Thompson Medical Company manufactures and sells Aspercreme, a topical analgesic. Aspercreme is a pain reliever that contains no aspirin. Thompson's advertisements strongly

suggest that Aspercreme is related to aspirin, however, by claiming that it provides "the strong relief of aspirin right where you hurt." The Federal Trade Commission brought a complaint against Thompson for false and misleading advertising of Aspercreme. Decision?

16.   Mary Smith bought a car from Doug Chapman under an installment sales contract. Smith carried the insurance on the car, as required by the contract. Shortly after Smith purchased the car, it was wrecked in an accident. Smith's insurance company paid Chapman the installments still owed on the car as well as Smith's equity in the car. Smith requested a new car from Chapman under an installment plan the same as the one under which she purchased the first car. Chapman refused, claiming that the contract for the first car allowed him to retain the equity amount as security interest and that Smith understood this as a term of the contract. The provision relating to the security interest appeared on the back of the contract, although the Truth-in-Lending Act required it to be on the front side. The front side had a notice referring to provisions on the back side. Smith sued Chapman for violation of the Truth-in-Lending Act. Decision?

17.   The FTC ordered Warner-Lambert to cease and desist from advertising that its product, Listerine antiseptic mouthwash, prevents, cures, or alleviates the common cold and sore throats. The order further required Warner-Lambert to disclose in future advertisements that "[c]ontrary to prior advertising, Listerine will not help prevent colds or sore throats or lessen their severity." Warner-Lambert contended that even if its past advertising claims were false, the corrective advertising portion of the order exceeded the FTC's statutory power. The FTC claimed that corrective advertising was necessary in light of Warner-Lambert's 100 years of false claims and the resulting persistence of erroneous consumer beliefs. Decision?

**WWW**   **Internet Exercise**  Learn about the consumer protection activities of (a) the Federal Trade Commission, (b) the Consumer Product Safety Commission, (c) the National Highway Traffic Safety Administration, (d) the Food and Drug Administration, and (e) the Federal Reserve.

# CHAPTER 43

# Employment Law

Though in general the common law governs the relationship between employer and employee in terms of tort and contract duties (rules that are part of the law of agency; see Chapter 19), this common law has been supplemented—and in some instances replaced—by statutory enactments, principally at the Federal level. In fact, government regulation now affects the balance and working relationship between employers and employees in three areas. First, the general framework in which management and labor negotiate the terms of employment is regulated by Federal statutes designed to promote both labor-management harmony and the welfare of society at large. Second, Federal law prohibits employment discrimination based upon race, sex, religion, age, disability, or national origin. Finally, Congress, in response to the changing nature of American industry and the tremendous number of industrial accidents, has mandated that employers provide their employees with a safe and healthy work environment. Moreover, all of the States have adopted workers' compensation acts to provide compensation to employees injured during the course of employment.

This chapter will focus upon these three categories of government regulation of the employment relationship: (1) labor law, (2) employment discrimination law, and (3) employee protection.

## LABOR LAW

Traditionally, labor law opposed concerted activities by workers, such as strikes, picketing, and refusals to deal, to obtain higher wages and better working conditions. At various times, such activities were found to constitute criminal conspiracy, tortious conduct, and violation of antitrust law. As subjecting union workers to criminal sanctions became publicly unpopular, employers began to resort to civil remedies in an attempt to halt unionization. The primary tool in this campaign was the injunc-

tion. Eventually, public pressure opposing such action forced Congress to intervene.

## Norris–La Guardia Act

Congress enacted the Norris–La Guardia Act in 1932 in response to the growing criticism of the use of injunctions in peaceful labor disputes. The Act withdrew from the Federal courts the power to issue injunctions in nonviolent labor disputes. Section 1. The term **labor dispute** was broadly defined to include any controversy concerning terms or conditions of employment or union representation, regardless of whether the parties stood in an employer-employee relationship or not. Section 13(c). More significantly, the Act declared it to be United States policy that labor was to have full freedom to form unions without employer interference. Section 2. Accordingly, the Act prohibited the so-called yellow dog contracts through which employers coerced their employees into promising that they would not join a union.

## National Labor Relations Act

Enacted in 1935, the National Labor Relations Act (NLRA), or the **Wagner Act**, embodied the Federal government's effort to support collective bargaining and unionization. The Act provides that "the right to self-organization, to form, join or assist labor organizations, to bargain collectively through representatives of their own choosing, and to engage in concerted activities for the purpose of collective bargaining or other mutual aid or protection" is, for workers, a Federally protected right. Thus, the Act gave employees the right to union representation when negotiating employment terms with their employer. Section 7. The Supreme Court upheld the Act against constitutional challenge in *NLRB v. Jones & Laughlin Steel Corp.*, 301 U.S. 1 (1937).

[The right of employees to bargain collectively] is a fundamental right. Employees have as clear a right to organize and select their representatives for lawful purposes as the respondent [employer] has to organize its business and select its own officers and agents. Discrimination and coercion to prevent the free exercise of the right of employees to self-organization and representation is a proper subject for condemnation by competent legislative authority. Long ago we stated the reason for labor organizations. We said that they were organized out of the necessities of the situation; that a single employee was helpless in dealing with an employer; that he was dependent ordinarily on his daily wage for the maintenance of himself and family; that if the employer refused to pay him the wages that he thought fair, he was nevertheless unable to leave the employ and resist arbitrary and unfair treatment; that union was essential to give laborers opportunity to deal on an equality with their employer. . . . Fully recognizing the legality of collective action on the part of employees in order to safeguard their proper interests, we said that Congress was not required to ignore this right but could safeguard it. Congress could seek to make appropriate collective action of employees an instrument of peace rather than of strife. We said that such collective action would be a mockery if representation were made futile by interference with freedom of choice. Hence the prohibition by Congress of interference with the selection of representatives for the purpose of negotiation and conference between employers and employees, "instead of being an invasion of the constitutional right of either, was based on the recognition of the rights of both." *NLRB v. Jones & Laughlin Steel Corp.*, 301 U.S. 1 (1937).

The Act sought to enforce the collective bargaining right by prohibiting certain employer conduct deemed to constitute unfair labor practices. Under the Act, the following employer activities are **unfair labor practices:** (1) to interfere with the employees' rights to unionize and bargain collectively; (2) to dominate the union; (3) to discriminate against union members; (4) to discriminate against an employee who has filed charges or testified under the NLRA; and (5) to refuse to bargain in good faith with duly established employee representatives. Section 8(a). The U.S. Supreme Court has interpreted this section to include as an unfair labor practice employer conduct that improves employment conditions or benefits in an attempt to undermine a union's efforts to organize:

The danger inherent in well-timed increases in benefits is the suggestion of a fist inside the velvet glove. Employees are not likely to miss the inference that the source of benefits now conferred is also the source from which future benefits must flow and which may dry up if it is not obliged. *NLRB v. Exchange Parts Co.*, 375 U.S. 405 (1964).

Moreover, the Act established the **National Labor Relations Board** (NLRB) to monitor and administer these employee rights. The NLRB is empowered to order employers to remedy their unfair labor practices and to supervise elections by secret ballot so that employees can freely select a representative organization.

## Labor-Management Relations Act

Following the passage of the National Labor Relations Act, union membership and labor unrest increased tremendously in the United States. In response to this trend, Congress passed the Labor-Management Relations Act (the **LMRA**, or **Taft-Hartley Act**) in 1947. The Act prohibits certain unfair union practices and separates the NLRB's prosecutorial and adjudicative functions. More specifically, the Act amended the NLRA by declaring the following seven *union* activities to be **unfair labor practices:** (1) coercing an employee to join a union, (2) causing an employer to discharge or discriminate against a nonunion employee, (3) refusing to bargain in good faith, (4) levying excessive or discriminatory dues or fees, (5) causing an employer to pay for work not performed ("featherbedding"), (6) picketing an employer to require it to recognize an uncertified union, and (7) engaging in secondary activities. NLRA Section 8(b). A **secondary activity** is a boycott, strike, or picketing of an employer with whom a union has no labor dispute to persuade the employer to cease doing business with the company that is the target of the labor dispute. For example, assume that a union is engaged in a labor dispute with Adams Company. To coerce Adams into resolving the dispute in the union's favor, the union organizes a strike against Brookings Company, with which the union has no labor dispute. The union agrees to cease striking Brookings Company if Brookings agrees to cease doing business with Adams. The strike against Brookings Company is a secondary activity prohibited as an unfair labor practice.

In addition to prohibiting unfair union practices, the Act also fosters employer free speech by declaring that no *employer* unfair labor practice could be based on any statement of opinion or argument that contains no threat of reprisal. NLRA Section 8(c).

The LMRA also prohibits the closed shop, although it permits union shops if such are not prohibited by a State right-to-work law. A **closed shop** contract requires the employer to hire only union members. A **union shop** contract permits the employer to hire nonunion members but requires them to become union members within a specified time and to remain members in good standing as a condition of employment. Although a State may prohibit union shop contracts through a **right-to-work** law, most States permit the existence of union shops.

Finally, the Act reinstates the availability of civil injunctions in labor disputes, if requested of the NLRB to prevent an unfair labor practice. The Act also empowers the president of the United States to obtain an injunction for an eighty-day cooling-off period for a strike that is likely to endanger the national health or safety.

♦ *See Figure 43–1*

## Labor-Management Reporting and Disclosure Act

The Labor-Management Reporting and Disclosure Act, also known as the **Landrum-Griffin Act**, is aimed at eliminating corruption in labor unions. Section 2(b) of the Act provides the following statement in support of the passage of the Act:

The Congress further finds, from recent investigations in the labor and management fields, that there have been a number of instances of breach of trust, corruption, disregard of the rights of individual employees, and other failures to observe high standards of responsibility and ethical conduct which require further and supplementary legislation that will afford necessary protection of the rights and interests of employees and the public generally as they relate to the activities of labor organizations, employers, labor relations consultants, and their officers and representatives.

The Act attempts to eradicate corruption through an elaborate reporting system and a union "bill of rights" designed to make unions more democratic. Section 101. The latter provides union members with the right to nominate candidates for union offices, to vote in elections, to attend membership meetings, to participate in union business, to express themselves freely at union meetings and conventions, and to be accorded a full and fair hearing before the union takes any disciplinary action against them.

## EMPLOYMENT DISCRIMINATION LAW

A number of Federal statutes prohibit discrimination in employment on the basis of race, sex, religion, national origin, age, and disability. The cornerstone of Federal employment discrimination law is Title VII of the 1964 Civil Rights Act, but other statutes and regulations also are significant, including two recently enacted discrimination laws: the Civil Rights Act of 1991 and the Americans with Disabilities Act of 1990. In addition, most States have enacted similar laws prohibiting discrimination based on race, sex, religion, national origin, and disability. The Civil Rights Act of 1991 extended the coverage of both Title VII and the Americans with Disabilities Act to include United States citizens working for U.S.-owned or controlled companies in foreign countries.

## Equal Pay Act

The **Equal Pay Act** prohibits an employer from discriminating between employees on the basis of sex by paying unequal wages for the same work. The Act forbids an employer from paying wages at a rate less than the rate at which he pays wages to employees of the opposite sex for equal work at the same establishment. Most courts define *equal work* to mean "substantially equal" rather than identical. The burden of proof is on the claimant to make a *prima facie* showing that the employer pays unequal wages for work requiring equal skill, effort, and responsibility under similar working conditions. Once the employee has demonstrated that the employer pays members of the opposite sex unequal wages for equal

**FIGURE 43–1** Unfair Labor Practices

| Unfair Employer Practices | Unfair Union Practices |
|---|---|
| • Interfering with right to unionize | • Coercing an employee to joining the union |
| • Refusing to bargain in good faith | • Refusing to bargain in good faith |
| • Discriminating against union members | • Causing employer to discriminate against a nonunion employee |
| • Dominating the union | • Featherbedding |
| • Discriminating against an employee | • Picketing an employer to require recognition of an uncertified union |
| | • Engaging in secondary activity |
| | • Levying excessive or discriminatory dues |

work, the burden shifts to the employer to prove that the pay differential is based on

1. a seniority system,
2. a merit system,
3. a system that measures earnings by quantity or quality of production, or
4. any factor except sex.

Remedies include the recovery of back pay, an award of liquidated damages (an additional amount equal to back pay), and enjoining the employer from further unlawful conduct. Although the Department of Labor is the Federal agency designated by the statute to interpret and enforce the Act, these functions were transferred to the Equal Employment Opportunity Commission in 1979.

## Civil Rights Act of 1964

Title VII of the **Civil Rights Act of 1964** prohibits **employment discrimination** on the basis of race, color, sex, religion, or national origin in hiring, firing, compensating, promoting, training, and other employment-related processes. The definition of *religion* includes all aspects of religious observance and practice, and the statute provides that an employer must make reasonable efforts to accommodate an employee's religious belief. The Act applies to employers engaged in an industry affecting commerce and having fifteen or more employees.

When Congress passed the **Pregnancy Discrimination Act of 1978**, it extended the benefits of Title VII to pregnant women. Under the Act, an employer cannot refuse to hire a pregnant woman, fire her, or force her to take maternity leave unless the employer can establish a *bona fide* occupational qualification defense (discussed later in this chapter). The Act, which protects the job reinstatement rights of women returning from maternity leave, requires employers to treat pregnancy like any other temporary disability.

The enforcement agency for Title VII is the **Equal Employment Opportunity Commission (EEOC)**. The EEOC is empowered (1) to file legal actions in its own name or to intervene in actions filed by third parties; (2) to attempt to resolve alleged violations through informal means prior to bringing suit; (3) to investigate all charges of discrimination; and (4) to issue guidelines and regulations concerning enforcement policy.

⚖ *See Case 43–1*

◆ *See Figure 43–2*

***Proving Discrimination*** Each of the following constitutes discriminatory conduct prohibited by the Act:

1. **Disparate Treatment.** An individual shows that an employer used a prohibited criterion in making an employment decision. The Supreme Court held in *McDonnell Douglas Corp. v. Green*, 411 U.S. 792 (1973), that a *prima facie* case of discrimination would be shown if the plaintiff (a) is within a protected class, (b) applied for an open position, (c) was qualified for the position, (d) was denied the job, and (e) the employer continued to try to fill the position from a pool of applicants with the complainant's qualifications. Once the plaintiff establishes a *prima facie* case, the burden shifts to the defendant to "articulate legitimate and nondiscriminatory reasons for the plaintiff's rejection." If the defendant so rebuts, the plaintiff then has the opportunity to demonstrate that the employer's stated reason was merely a pretext.
2. **Present Effects of Past Discrimination.** An employer engages in conduct that on its face is "neutral," that is, nondiscriminatory, but that actually perpetuates past discriminatory practices. For example, it has

**FIGURE 43–2** Charges Filed in 1995 with the EEOC

| Category | Number of Charges | Percent |
|---|---|---|
| Race | 29,986 | 34.3 |
| Religion | 1,582 | 1.8 |
| National Origin | 7,035 | 8.0 |
| Sex | 26,181 | 29.9 |
| Retaliation | 15,342 | 17.5 |
| Disability | 19,778 | 22.6 |
| Equal Pay | 1,273 | 1.5 |

Source: Equal Employment Opportunity Commission National Database, March 10, 1997

been held illegal for a union that had previously limited its membership to whites to adopt a requirement that new members be related to or recommended by existing members. *Local 53 of International Association of Heat and Frost Insulators and Asbestos Workers v. Vogler*, 407 F.2d 1047 (5th Cir. 1969).

3. **Disparate Impact.** An employer adopts "neutral" rules that adversely affect a protected class and that are not justified as being necessary to the business. Despite the employee's proof of disparate impact, the employer may prevail if it can demonstrate that the challenged practice is "job related for the position in question and consistent with business necessity." *Wards Cove Packing Co. v. Antonio*, 490 U.S. 642, 109 S.Ct. 2115 (1989). Thus, all requirements that might have a disparate impact upon women, such as height and weight requirements, must be shown to be job related. Nevertheless, under the **Civil Rights Act of 1991**, even if the employer can demonstrate the business necessity of the questioned practice, the complainant will still prevail if she shows that a non-discriminatory alternative practice exists.

 *See Case 43–2*

**Defenses** The Act provides three basic defenses: (1) a *bona fide* seniority or merit system; (2) a professionally developed ability test; and (3) a *bona fide* occupational qualification (BFOQ). The BFOQ defense does not apply to discrimination based on race. A fourth defense, business necessity, is available in a disparate impact case.

*See Case 43–1*

**Remedies** Remedies for violation of the Act include enjoining the employer from engaging in the unlawful behavior, appropriate affirmative action, and reinstatement of employees to their rightful place (which may include promotion) and award of back pay from a date not more than two years prior to the filing of the charge with the EEOC. First employed by Executive Order, as discussed below, **affirmative action** generally means the active recruitment of minority applicants, although courts also have used the remedy to impose numerical hiring ratios (quotas) and hiring goals based on race and sex. In 1985, the EEOC defined affirmative action in employment as "actions appropriate to overcome the effects of past or present practices, policies, or other barriers to equal employment opportunity."

Prior to 1991, only victims of *racial* discrimination could recover compensatory and punitive damages from the courts. Today, however, under the Civil Rights Act of 1991, *all* victims of *intentional* discrimination—whether based on race, sex, religion, national origin, or disability—can recover compensatory and punitive damages, except in cases involving disparate impact. In cases not involving race, the Act limits the amount of recoverable damages according to the number of persons the defendant employs. Companies with 15 to 100 employees are required to pay no more than $50,000; companies with 101 to 200 employees, no more than $100,000; those with 201 to 500 employees, no more than $200,000; and those with 501 or more employees, no more than $300,000. Either party may demand a jury trial. Victims of racial discrimination are still entitled to recover unlimited compensatory and punitive damages.

*Reverse Discrimination* A major controversy has arisen over the use of reverse discrimination in achieving affirmative action. In this context, **reverse discrimination** refers to affirmative action that directs an employer to remedy the underrepresentation of a given race or sex in a traditionally segregated job by considering an individual's race or gender when hiring or promoting. An example would be an employer who discriminates against white males to increase the proportion of females or members of a racial minority in a company's workforce. This question was presented in *United Steelworkers of America v. Weber*, 443 U.S. 193 (1979). In *Weber*, the employer and union were implementing a collectively bargained affirmative action plan that granted preference to blacks even though the employer had engaged in no proven racial discrimination. There was, however, a conspicuous racial imbalance in the employer's skilled labor force. The Supreme Court upheld the affirmative action plan against a challenge under Title VII, even though the plan favored black employees with less seniority than white employees. The Court held,

We need not today define in detail the line of demarcation between permissible and impermissible affirmative action plans [under Title VII]. It suffices to hold that the challenged Kaiser-USWA affirmative action plan falls on the permissible side of the line. The purposes of the plan mirror those of the statute. Both were designed to break down old patterns of racial segregation and hierarchy. Both were structured to "open employment opportunities for Negroes in occupations which have been traditionally closed to them." [Citation.]

At the same time, the plan does not unnecessarily trammel the interests of the white employees. The plan does not require the discharge of white workers and their replacement with new black hires. [Citation.] Nor does the plan create an absolute bar to the advancement of white employees; half of those trained in the program will be white.

Moreover, the plan is a temporary measure; it is not intended to maintain racial balance, but simply to eliminate a manifest racial imbalance.

Due to the absence of State action, challenges to affirmative action plans adopted by private employers—those that are not governmental units at the local, State, or Federal level—are tested under Title VII of the Civil Rights Act of 1964, not under the Equal Protection Clause of the U.S. Constitution.

In *Johnson v. Transportation Agency*, 480 U.S. 616 (1987), also an action under Title VII, the Supreme Court upheld the employer's right to promote a female employee rather than a white male employee who had scored higher on a qualifying examination:

In making our decision, we find that the employment decision was justified by the existence of a "manifest imbalance" that reflected underrepresentation of women in "traditionally segregated job categories." The Agency's [employer's] Plan did not authorize such blind hiring but expressly directed that numerous factors be taken into account in making employment decisions. Furthermore, the Plan did not trammel male employee's rights or create a bar to their advancement as it set aside no positions for women. Substantial evidence shows that the Agency has sought to take a moderate, gradual approach to eliminating the imbalance in its work force, one which establishes realistic guidance for employment decisions. Given this fact, as well as the Agency's express commitment to "attain" a balanced work force, there is ample assurance that the Agency does not seek to use its Plan to "maintain" a permanent racial and sexual balance. Thus, we do not find the Agency in violation of Title VII.

When a State or local government adopts an affirmative action plan that is challenged as constituting illegal reverse discrimination, the plan is subject to strict scrutiny under the **Equal Protection Clause** of the Fourteenth Amendment. Under the strict scrutiny test, the subject classification must (1) be justified by a compelling governmental interest and (2) be the least intrusive means available. (For a fuller discussion of the Equal Protection Clause and the standards of review, see Chapter 4.) With regard to racial discrimination, the U.S. Supreme Court, in 1995, placed significant constraints upon the ability of governments to create programs favoring minorities over whites: benign and invidious discrimination are both held to the standard under which the government must show a compelling interest that is as narrowly tailored as feasible. Following this decision, the EEOC issued a statement which provided that "affirmative action is lawful only when it is designed to respond to a demonstrated and serious imbalance in the work force, is flexible, time-limited, applies only to qualified workers, and respects the rights of non-minorities and men."

***Sexual Harassment***   In 1980, the EEOC issued a definition of sexual harassment:

Unwelcome sexual advances, requests for sexual favors, and other verbal or physical conduct of a sexual nature constitute sexual harassment when

**(1)** submission to such conduct is made either explicitly or implicitly a term or condition of an individual's employment,
**(2)** submission to or rejection of such conduct by an individual is used as the basis for employment decisions affecting such individual, or
**(3)** such conduct has the purpose or effect of reasonably interfering with an individual's work performance or creating an intimidating, hostile or offensive working environment.

The courts, including the Supreme Court, have held that sexual harassment may constitute illegal sexual discrimination in violation of Title VII. Moreover, an employer will be held liable for sexual harassment committed by one of its employees if it does not take reasonable action when it knows or should have known of the harassment. When the employee engaging in sexual harassment is an agent of the employer or holds a supervisory position over the victim, the employer may be liable without knowledge or reason to know.

In 1998, the U.S. Supreme Court held that sex discrimination consisting of same-sex harassment is actionable under Title VII.

 *See Case 43-3*

***Comparable Worth***   Industrial statistics indicate that women earn approximately two-thirds as much as men do. Studies have suggested that between one-third and one-half of this disparity in earnings results from sexual discrimination. Other probable causes for the gap include (1) the differing educational backgrounds and job skills of males and females, (2) the tendency for females to be employed in lower-paying occupations, and (3) the idea that females are more likely to interrupt their careers to raise families.

Because the Equal Pay Act only requires equal pay for equal work, it does not apply to different jobs even if they are comparable. Thus, that statute provides no remedy for women who have been systematically undervalued and underpaid in "traditional" occupations, such as secretary, teacher, or nurse. As a result, women have sought redress under Title VII by arguing that the failure to pay comparable worth is discrimination on the basis of sex. The concept of **comparable worth** provides that employers should measure the relative values of different jobs through a job evaluation rating system that is free of any potential sex bias. Theoretically, the consistent application of objective criteria (including factors such as skill, effort, working conditions, responsibility, and mental demands) across job categories will ensure fair payment for all employees. For example, if under such a system the jobs of truck driver and nurse were evaluated at the same level, then workers in both jobs would receive the same pay.

In 1981, the Supreme Court held that a claim of discriminatory undercompensation based on sex may be brought under Title VII, even where the plaintiffs (women, in the 1981 case) were performing jobs different from those of their opposite-sex counterparts. As the Court noted, however, the case involved a situation in which the defendant intentionally discriminated in wages; and the defendant, not the courts, had compared the jobs in terms of value. *County of Washington v. Gunther*, 452 U.S. 161 (1981). The Court also held that the four defenses available under the Equal Pay Act would apply to a Title VII claim. Since *Gunther*, the concept of comparable worth has met with limited success in the courts. Nonetheless, a number of States have adopted legislation requiring public and private employers to pay equally for comparable work.

## Executive Order

In 1965, President Johnson issued an executive order that prohibits discrimination by Federal contractors on the basis of race, color, sex, religion, or national origin in employment on any work the contractor performs during the period of the Federal contract. Federal contractors are also required to implement affirmative action in recruiting. The Secretary of Labor, **Office of Federal Contract Compliance Programs** (OFCCP), enforces compliance with the program.

The program applies to all contractors (and all of their subcontractors in excess of $10,000) who enter into a Federal contract to be performed in the United States. Compliance with the affirmative action requirement differs for construction and nonconstruction contractors. All **nonconstruction** contractors with fifty or more employees or with contracts for more than $50,000 must have a written affirmative action plan to be in compliance. The plan must include a workforce analysis; planned

corrective action, if necessary, with specific goals and timetables; and procedures for auditing and reporting. The Director of the OFCCP periodically issues goals and timetables for each segment of the construction industry for each region of the country. As a condition precedent to bidding on a Federal contract, a contractor must agree to make a good faith effort to achieve current published goals.

## Age Discrimination in Employment Act of 1967

The **Age Discrimination in Employment Act** (ADEA) prohibits discrimination in hiring, firing, compensating, or other employment-related processes on the basis of age when the employee or applicant is over forty years old. The Act applies to private employers having twenty or more employees and to all governmental units regardless of size. The Act also prohibits the mandatory retirement of most employees, no matter what their age, though it provides employers a limited exception regarding *bona fide* executives and high policymaking employees.

The major statutory defenses include (1) a *bona fide* occupational qualification; (2) a *bona fide* seniority system; and (3) any other reasonable action. Remedies include back pay, injunctive relief, affirmative action, and liquidated damages equal to the amount of the award for "willful" violations. Furthermore, an ADEA claimant is entitled to a jury trial.

## Disability Law

The **Rehabilitation Act of 1973** attempts to assist the handicapped in obtaining rehabilitation training, access to public facilities, and employment. The Act requires Federal contractors and Federal agencies to take affirmative action to hire qualified handicapped persons. It also prohibits discrimination on the basis of handicap in Federal programs and programs receiving Federal financial assistance.

A **handicapped person** is defined as an individual who (1) has a physical or mental impairment that substantially affects one or more of her major life activities; (2) has a history of major life activity impairment; *or* (3) is regarded as having such an impairment. Major life activities include such functions as caring for oneself, seeing, speaking, or walking. Alcohol and drug abuses are not considered handicapping conditions for the purposes of this statute.

The **Americans with Disabilities Act (ADA) of 1990** forbids an employer from discriminating against any person with a disability with regard to "hiring or discharge . . . , employee compensation, advancement, job training and other terms, conditions and privileges of employment." In addition, businesses must make special accommodations, such as installing wheelchair-accessible bathrooms, for handicapped workers and customers unless the cost is unduly burdensome. An employer may use qualification standards, tests, or selection criteria that screen out handicapped workers if these measures are job related and consistent with business necessity *and* if no reasonable accommodation is possible. The ADA took effect on July 26, 1992, for employers with twenty-five or more employees and on July 26, 1994, for employers with fifteen or more employees. Remedies for violation of the ADA are those generally allowed under Title VII and include injunctive relief, reinstatement, back pay, and, for intentional discrimination, compensatory and punitive damages (capped according to company size by the Civil Rights Act of 1991).

In addition, the **Vietnam Veterans Readjustment Act of 1974** requires firms having $10,000 or more in Federal contracts to take affirmative action regarding handicapped veterans and Vietnam era veterans.

◆ *See Figure 43–3*

⚖ *See Case 43–4*

## EMPLOYEE PROTECTION

Employees are accorded a number of job-related protections. These include a limited right not to be unfairly dismissed, a right to a safe and healthy workplace, compensation for injuries sustained in the workplace, and some financial security upon retirement or loss of employment. This section discusses (1) employee termination at will, (2) occupational safety and health, (3) employee privacy, (4) workers' compensation, (5) Social Security and unemployment insurance, (6) the Fair Labor Standards Act, (7) employee notice of termination or layoff, and (8) family and health leave.

### Employee Termination at Will

Under the common law, a contract of employment for other than a definite term is terminable at will by either party. Accordingly, under the common law, employers may "dismiss their employees at will for good cause, for no cause or even for cause morally wrong, without being thereby guilty of legal wrong." In recent years, however, the courts have delineated a growing number of judicial exceptions to the rule, based on implied contract, tort, and public policy. A number of Federal and State statutes enacted in the last fifty years further limit the rule, which also may be restricted by contractual agreement between employer and employee. In particular, most collective bargaining agreements negotiated through union representatives contain a provision prohibiting dismissal "without cause."

*Statutory Limitations* In 1934, as previously discussed, Congress enacted the National Labor Relations Act, which provided employees with the right to unionize free of intimidation or coercion from their employers, including freedom from dismissal for engaging in union activities. Since the enactment of the NLRA, additional Federal legislation has limited the employer's right to discharge. These statutes fall into three categories: (1) those protecting certain employees from discriminatory discharge; (2) those protecting certain employees in their exercise of statutory rights; and (3) those protecting certain employees from discharge without cause.

At the State level, statutes protect workers from discriminatory discharge for filing workers' compensation claims. Also, many State statutes parallel Federal legislation. Some States have adopted statutes similar to the NLRA, and many States prohibit discrimination in employment on the basis of factors such as race, creed, nationality, sex, or age. In addition, some States have statutes prohibiting employers from discharging employees or taking other punitive actions in order to influence voting or, in some States, political activity.

*Judicial Limitations* Judicial limitations on the employment-at-will doctrine have been based on contract law, tort law, and public policy. Cases founded in contract theory have relied on arguments contending, among other things, (1) that the dismissal was improper because the employee had detrimentally relied on the employer's promise of work for a reasonable time; (2) that the employment was not at will because of implied-in-fact promises of employment for a specific duration, which meant that the employer could not terminate the employee without just cause; (3) that the employment contract implied or provided expressly that the employee would not be dismissed so long as he satisfactorily performed his work; (4) that the employer had assured the employee that he would not be dismissed except for cause; or (5) that, upon entering into the employment contract, the employee gave consideration

**FIGURE 43–3** Federal Employment Discrimination Laws

| | Protected Characteristics | Prohibited Conduct | Defenses | Remedies |
|---|---|---|---|---|
| **Equal Pay Act** | Sex | Wages | Seniority<br>Merit<br>Quality or quantity measures<br>Any factor other than sex | Back pay<br>Injunction<br>Liquidated damages<br>Attorneys' fees |
| **Title VII of Civil Rights Acts** | Race<br>Color<br>Sex<br>Religion<br>National origin | Terms, conditions, or privileges of employment | Seniority<br>Ability test<br>BFOQ (except for race)<br>Business necessity (disparate impact only) | Back pay<br>Injunction<br>Reinstatement<br>Compensatory and punitive damages for intentional discrimination<br>• unlimited for race<br>• limited for all others |
| **Age Discrimination in Employment Act** | Age | Terms, conditions, or privileges of employment | Seniority<br>BFOQ<br>Any other reasonable act | Attorneys' fees<br>Back pay<br>Injunction<br>Reinstatement<br>Liquidated damages for willful violation |
| **Americans with Disabilities Act** | Disability | Terms, conditions, or privileges of employment | Undue hardship<br>Job-related criteria and business necessity<br>Risk to public health and safety | Attorneys' fees<br>Back pay<br>Injunction<br>Reinstatement<br>Compensatory and punitive damages for intentional discrimination (limited)<br>Attorneys' fees |

over and above the performance of services to support a promise of job security.

Some courts have circumvented the common law at-will doctrine under implied contract theories by finding that employment contracts contain an implied promise to deal in good faith, including a duty on the part of the employer to terminate only in good faith. These cases provide a remedy for an employee whose discharge was motivated by bad faith, malice, or retaliation.

Courts have also created exceptions to the employment-at-will doctrine by imposing tort obligations on employers, particularly the torts of intentional infliction of emotional distress and of interference with employment relations.

The most common basis for designating a discharge as wrongful is its violation of statutory or other established public policy. In general, a wrongful discharge involves dismissal for (1) refusing to violate a statute, (2) exercising a statutory right, (3) performing a statutory obligation, or (4) reporting an alleged violation of a statute that is of public interest.

 *See Case 43–5*

## Occupational Safety and Health Act

In 1970, Congress enacted the Occupational Safety and Health Act to ensure, as far as possible, a safe and healthful working environment for every worker. The Act established the **Occupational Safety and Health Administration** (OSHA) to develop standards, conduct inspections, monitor compliance, and institute enforcement actions against those who are not in compliance.

Upon each employer engaged in a business affecting interstate commerce, the Act imposes a general duty to provide a work environment that is "free from recognized hazards that are causing or likely to cause death or serious physical harm to his employees." Section 119. In addition to this general duty, the employer must comply with specific OSHA-promulgated safety rules. The Act also requires employees to comply with all OSHA rules and regulations. Finally, the Act prohibits any employer from discharging or discriminating against an employee who exercises her rights under the Act. Section 11(c)(1).

Enforcing the Act generally involves OSHA inspections and citations of employers, as appropriate, for (1) breach of the general duty obligation; (2) breach of specific safety and health standards; or (3) failure to keep records, make reports, or post notices required by the Act.

When a violation is discovered, the offending employer receives a written citation, a proposed penalty, and a date by which the employer must remedy the breach. A citation may be contested, in which case the Occupational Safety and Health Review Commission assigns an administrative law judge to hold a hearing. The commission, at its discretion, may grant review of an administrative law judge's decision; review is not a matter of right. If no such review occurs, the judge's decision becomes the final order of the commission thirty days after its receipt by the aggrieved party, who then may appeal the order to the appropriate United States Circuit Court of Appeals.

Penalties for violations are both civil and criminal. In cases involving civil penalties, serious violations require that a penalty be proposed; in contrast, for nonserious violations, penalties are discretionary and rarely proposed. The Act further empowers the Secretary of Labor to obtain temporary restraining orders when regular OSHA procedures are insufficient to halt imminently hazardous or deadly business operations.

One stated purpose of the Act is to encourage State participation in regulating safety and health. The Act therefore permits a State to regulate the safety and health of the work environment within its borders, provided that OSHA approves the plan. The Act sets minimum acceptable standards for the States to impose, but it does not require that a State plan be identical to OSHA guidelines. More than half of the States regulate workplace health and safety through State-promulgated plans.

## Employee Privacy

Over the last decade, employee privacy has become a major issue. The fundamental right to privacy is a product of common-law protection, discussed in Chapter 7. Thus, employee protection from unwanted searches, electronic monitoring and other forms of surveillance, and disclosure of confidential records is safeguarded by the tort of invasion of privacy, which actually consists of four different torts: (1) unreasonable intrusion into the seclusion of another; (2) unreasonable public disclosure of private facts; (3) unreasonable publicity that places another in a false light; and (4) appropriation of a person's name or likeness. In addition, the Federal government and some States have legislatively supplemented the common law in certain areas.

*Drug and Alcohol Testing* Although no Federal legislation deals comprehensively with drug and alcohol tests, legislation in a number of States either prohibits such tests altogether or prescribes certain scientific and procedural standards for conducting them. In the absence of a State statute, *private* sector employees have little or no protection from such tests. The NLRB has held, however, that drug and alcohol testing in a union setting is a mandatory subject of collective bargaining.

In 1989, the U.S. Supreme Court ruled that the employer of a *public* sector employee whose position involved public health or safety or national security could subject the employee to a drug or alcohol test without either first obtaining a search warrant or having reasonable grounds to believe the individual had engaged in any wrongdoing. Based on Supreme Court and lower court decisions, it appears that a government employer may use (1) random or universal testing where the public health or safety or national security is involved and (2) selective drug testing where there is sufficient cause to believe an employee has a drug problem.

*Lie Detector Tests* The **Federal Employee Polygraph Protection Act of 1988** prohibits private employers from requiring employees or prospective employees to undergo a lie detector test, inquiring about the results of such a test, or using the results of such a test or the refusal to be thus tested as grounds for an adverse employment decision. The Act exempts government employers and, in certain situations, Energy Department contractors or persons providing consulting services for Federal intelligence agencies. In addition, security firms and manufacturers of controlled substances may use a polygraph to test prospective employees. Moreover, an employer, as part of an ongoing investigation of economic loss or injury to its business, may utilize a polygraph test. Nevertheless, the use of the test must meet the following requirements: (1) it must be designed to investigate a specific incident or activity, not to document a chronic problem; (2) the employee to be tested must have had access to the property that is the subject of the investigation; and (3) the employer must have reason to suspect the particular employee.

Employees and prospective employees tested under any of these exemptions cannot be terminated, disciplined, or denied employment solely as a result of the test. The Act further provides that those subjected to a polygraph test (1) cannot be asked intrusive or degrading questions regarding topics such as their religious beliefs, opinions as to racial matters, political views, or sexual preferences or behaviors; (2) must be given the right to review all questions before the test and to terminate the test at any time; and (3) must receive a complete copy of the test results.

## Workers' Compensation

At common law, the basis of most actions by an injured employee against his employer was the employer's failure to use reasonable care under the circumstances to ensure the employee's safety. In such an action, however, the employer could make use of several well-established defenses, including the fellow servant rule, contributory negligence on the part of the employee, and the doctrine of assumption of risk by the employee. By establishing any of these defenses, the employer was not liable to the injured employee.

The **fellow servant rule** relieved an employer from liability for injuries an employee sustained through the negligence of a fellow employee. Under the common law defense of **contributory negligence,** if an employer established that an employee's negligence contributed to the injury he sustained in the course of his employment, in many jurisdictions the employee could not recover damages from the employer. Additionally, at common law, an employer was not liable to an employee for harm or injury caused by the unsafe condition of the premises if the employee, with knowledge of the facts and an understanding of the risks involved, voluntarily entered into or continued in the employment. This was regarded as a **voluntary assumption of risk** by the employee.

To provide speedier and more certain relief to injured employees, all States have adopted statutes providing for workers' compensation. (Several States, however, exempt specified employers from such statutes.) Workers' compensation statutes create commissions or boards that determine whether an injured employee is entitled to receive compensation and, if so, how much. The basis of recovery under workers' compensation is strict liability: the employee does not have to prove that the employer was negligent. The common law defenses discussed above are not available to employers in proceedings under these statutes. Such defenses are abolished. The only requirement is that the employee be injured and that the injury arises out of and in the course of his employment. The amounts recoverable are fixed by statute for each type of injury and are lower than the amounts a court or jury would probably award in an action at common law. The courts, therefore, do not have jurisdiction over such cases, except to review decisions of the board or commission; even then, the courts may only determine whether such decisions are in accordance with the statute. If a third party causes the injury, however, the employee may bring a tort action against that third party.

Early workers' compensation laws did not provide coverage for occupational disease, and most courts held that occupational injury did not include disease. Today, virtually all States provide general compensation coverage for occupational diseases, although the coverage varies greatly from State to State.

## Social Security and Unemployment Insurance

Social Security was enacted in 1935 in an attempt to provide limited retirement and death benefits to certain employees. Since then, the benefits have increased greatly; the Federal Social Security system, which has expanded to cover almost all employees, now contains four major benefit programs: (1) Old-Age and Survivors Insurance (OASI) (providing retirement and survivor benefits), (2) Disability Insurance (DI), (3) Hospitalization Insurance (Medicare), and (4) Supplemental Security Income (SSI).

The system is financed by contributions (taxes) paid by employers, employees, and self-employed individuals. Employees and employers pay matching contributions. These contributions are calculated by multiplying the Social Security tax (a fixed percentage) times the employee's wages up to a specified maximum. Both the base tax rate and the maximum dollar amount are subject to change by Congress. It is the employer's responsibility to withhold the employee's contribution and to forward the full amount of the tax to the Internal Revenue Service. Contributions made by the employee are not tax deductible by the employee, while those made by the employer are tax deductible.

The Federal **unemployment insurance** system was initially created by Title IX of the Social Security Act of 1935. Subsequently, Title IX was supplemented by the Federal Unemployment Tax Act and by numerous other Federal statutes. This complex system depends upon cooperation between State and Federal entities. Federal law provides the general guidelines, standards, and requirements for the program, while the States administer the program through their employment laws. The system is funded by employer taxes: Federal taxes generally pay the administrative costs of the program, and State contributions pay for the actual benefits.

Under the Federal Unemployment Tax Act, unemployment compensation is provided to workers who have lost their jobs, usually through no fault of their own. The Act is meant to help workers who are temporarily out of work and who need to support themselves while they search for a job. Unemployed workers usually receive weekly payments in an amount based on each State's particular formula. Employees who voluntarily quit without good cause, who have been dismissed for misconduct, or who fail to look for or who refuse suitable work are not eligible for unemployment benefits.

## Fair Labor Standards Act

The **Fair Labor Standards Act** (FLSA) regulates the employment of child labor outside of agriculture. The Act prohibits the employment of anyone under fourteen years of age in all nonfarm work except newspaper delivery and acting. Fourteen- and fifteen-year-olds may work for a limited number of hours outside of school hours, under specific conditions, in certain nonhazardous occupations. Sixteen- and seventeen-year-olds may work in any nonhazardous job, while persons eighteen years old or older may work in any job, whether it is hazardous or not. The Secretary of Labor determines which occupations are considered hazardous.

In addition, the FLSA imposes wage and hour requirements upon covered employers. With certain exceptions, the Act provides for a minimum hourly wage and overtime pay of time-and-a-half for hours worked in excess

of forty hours per week; those workers exempted from both the FLSA's minimum wage and overtime provisions include professionals, managers, and outside salespersons.

## Worker Adjustment and Retraining Notification Act

The Worker Adjustment and Retraining Notification Act (WARN) requires an employer to provide sixty days' advance notice of a plant closing or mass layoff. A "plant closing" is defined as the permanent or temporary shutting down of a single site or units within a site if the shutdown results in fifty or more employees losing employment during any thirty-day period. A "mass layoff" is defined as a loss of employment during a thirty-day period either for 500 employees or for at least one-third of the employees at a given site, if that one-third equals or exceeds fifty employees. WARN requires that notification be given to specified State and local officials as well as to the affected employees or their union representatives. The Act, which reduces the notification period with regard to failing companies and emergency situations, applies to employers with a total of 100 or more employees who in the aggregate work at least 2,000 hours per week, not including overtime.

## Family and Medical Leave Act of 1993

The **Family and Medical Leave Act of 1993** requires employers with fifty or more employees and governments at the Federal, State, and local levels to grant employees up to twelve weeks of leave during any twelve-month period for the birth of a child; adopting or gaining foster care of a child; or the care of a spouse, child, or parent who suffers from a serious health condition. A "serious health condition" is defined as an "illness, injury, impairment or physical or mental condition" that involves inpatient medical care at a hospital, hospice, or residential care facility or continuing medical treatment by a health care provider. Employees are eligible for such leave if they have been employed by their present employer for at least twelve months and have worked at least 1,250 hours for their employer during the twelve months preceding the leave request. The requested leave may be paid, unpaid, or a combination of both.

# Chapter Summary

**Labor Law**

**Purpose** to provide the general framework in which management and labor negotiate terms of employment

**Norris–La Guardia Act** established as United States policy the full freedom of labor to form labor unions without employer interference and withdrew from the Federal courts the power to issue injunctions in nonviolent labor disputes (any controversy concerning terms or conditions of employment or union representation)

**National Labor Relations Act**

- *Right to Unionize* declares it a Federally protected right of employees to unionize and to bargain collectively
- *Prohibits Unfair Employer Practices* the Act identifies five unfair labor practices by an employer
- *National Labor Relations Board (NLRB)* created to administer these rights

**Labor-Management Relations Act**

- *Prohibits Unfair Union Practices* the Act identifies seven unfair labor practices by a union
- *Prohibits Closed Shops* which are agreements that mandate that employers can hire only union members
- *Allows Union Shops* an employer can hire nonunion members, but the employee must join the union

**Labor-Management Reporting and Disclosure Act** aimed at eliminating corruption in labor unions

**Employment Discrimination Law**

**Equal Pay Act** prohibits an employer from discriminating between employees on the basis of gender by paying unequal wages for the same work

**Civil Rights Act of 1964** prohibits employment discrimination on the basis of race, color, gender, religion, or national origin

- *Pregnancy Discrimination Act of 1978* extends the benefits of the Civil Rights Act to pregnant women
- *Equal Employment Opportunity Commission (EEOC)* enforcement agency for the Act
- *Affirmative Action* the active recruitment of a designated group of applicants
- *Discrimination* prohibited by the Act; includes (1) using proscribed criteria to produce disparate treatment, (2) engaging in nondiscriminatory conduct that perpetuates past discrimination, and (3) adopting neutral roles that have a disparate impact
- *Reverse Discrimination* affirmative action that directs an employer to consider an individual's race or gender when hiring or promoting for the purpose of remedying underrepresentation of that race or gender in traditionally segregated jobs
- *Defenses* three defenses are provided by the Act (1) a *bona fide* seniority or merit system, (2) a professionally developed ability test, and (3) a *bona fide* occupational qualification
- *Remedies* remedies for violation of the Act include injunctions, affirmative action, reinstatement, back pay, and compensatory and punitive damages
- *Sexual Harassment* an illegal form of sexual discrimination that includes unwelcome sexual advances, requests for sexual favors, and other verbal or physical conduct of a sexual nature
- *Comparable Worth* equal pay for jobs that are of equal value to the employer

**Executive Order** prohibits discrimination by Federal contractors on the basis of race, color, gender, religion, or national origin on any work the contractors perform during the period of the Federal contract

**Age Discrimination in Employment Act of 1967** prohibits discrimination on the basis of age in hiring, firing, or compensating

**Disability Law** several Federal acts, including the Americans with Disabilities Act, provide assistance to the disabled in obtaining rehabilitation training, access to public facilities, and employment

**Employee Protection**

**Employee Termination at Will** under the common law, a contract of employment for other than a definite term is terminable at will by either party
- *Statutory Limitations* have been enacted by the Federal government and some States
- *Judicial Limitations* based on contract law, tort law, or public policy
- *Limitations Imposed by Union Contract*

**Occupational Safety and Health Act** enacted to assure workers of a safe and healthful work environment

**Employee Privacy**
- *Drug and Alcohol Testing* some States either prohibit such tests or prescribe certain scientific and procedural safeguards
- *Lie Detector Tests* Federal statute prohibits private employers from requiring employees or prospective employees to take such tests

**Workers' Compensation** compensation awarded to an employee who is injured in the course of his employment

**Social Security** measures by which the government provides economic assistance to disabled or retired employees and their dependents

**Unemployment Compensation** compensation awarded to workers who have lost their jobs and cannot find other employment

**Fair Labor Standards Act** regulates the employment of child labor outside of agriculture

**Worker Adjustment and Retraining Notification Act** Federal statute that requires an employer to provide sixty days' advance notice of a plant closing or mass layoff

**Family and Medical Leave Act of 1993** requires some employers to grant employees leave for serious health conditions or certain other events

---

 # Cases

### CASE 43–1
## Civil Rights Act of 1964 and Pregnancy Discrimination Act: Defenses
## *INTERNATIONAL UNION, UNITED AUTOMOBILE, AEROSPACE AND AGRICULTURAL IMPLEMENT WORKERS OF AMERICA, UAW v. JOHNSON CONTROLS, INC.*
U.S. Supreme Court, 1991
499 U.S. 187, 111 S.Ct. 1196, 113 L.Ed.2d 158

BLACKMUN, J.

In this case we are concerned with an employer's gender-based fetal-protection policy. May an employer exclude a fertile female employee from certain jobs because of its concern for the health of the fetus the woman might conceive?

Respondent Johnson Controls, Inc., manufactures batteries. In the manufacturing process, the element lead is a primary ingredient. Occupational exposure to lead entails health risks, including the risk of harm to any fetus carried by a female employee.

Before the Civil Rights Act of 1964, [citation], became law, Johnson Controls did not employ any woman in a battery-manufacturing job. In June 1977, however, it announced its first official policy concerning its employment of women in lead-exposure work:

[P]rotection of the health of the unborn child is the immediate and direct responsibility of the prospective parents. While the medical profession and the company can support them in the exercise of this responsibility, it cannot assume it for them without simultaneously infringing their rights as persons.

* * *

. . . Since not all women who can become mothers wish to become mothers (or will become mothers), it would appear to be illegal discrimination to treat all who are capable of pregnancy as though they will become pregnant.

Consistent with that view, Johnson Controls "stopped short of excluding women capable of bearing children from lead exposure," but emphasized that a woman who expected to have a child should not choose a job in which she would have such exposure. The company also required a woman who wished to be considered for employment to sign a statement that she had been advised of the risk of having a child while she was exposed to lead. The statement informed the woman that although there was evidence "that women exposed to lead have a higher rate of abortion," this evidence was "not as clear . . . as the relationship between cigarette smoking and cancer," but that it was, "medically speaking, just good sense not to run that risk if you want children and do not want to expose the unborn child to risk, however small. . . ."

Five years later, in 1982, Johnson Controls shifted from a policy of warning to a policy of exclusion. Between 1979 and 1983, eight employees became pregnant while maintaining blood lead levels in excess of 30 micrograms per deciliter. This appeared to be the critical level noted by the Occupational Health and Safety Administration (OSHA) for a worker who was planning to have a family. The company responded by announcing a broad exclusion of women from jobs that exposed them to lead:

. . . [I]t is [Johnson Controls'] policy that women who are pregnant or who are capable of bearing children will not be placed into jobs involving lead exposure or which could expose them to lead through the exercise of job bidding, bumping, transfer or promotion rights.

* * *

In April 1984, petitioners filed in the United States District Court for the Eastern District of Wisconsin a class action challenging Johnson Controls' fetal-protection policy as sex discrimination that violated Title VII of the Civil Rights Act of 1964. Among the individual plaintiffs were petitioners Mary Craig, who had chosen to be sterilized in order to avoid losing her job, Elsie Nason, a 50-year-old divorcee, who had suffered a loss in compensation when she was transferred out of a job where she was exposed to lead, and Donald Penney, who had been denied a request for a leave of absence for the purpose of lowering his lead level because he intended to become a father. * * *

The District Court granted summary judgment for defendant-respondent Johnson Controls. Applying a three-part business necessity defense . . . Court concluded that while "there is a disagreement among the experts regarding the effect of lead on the fetus," the hazard to the fetus through exposure to lead was established by "a considerable body of opinion"; . . . and that petitioners had "failed to establish that there is an acceptable alternative policy which would protect the fetus." The court stated that, in view of this disposition of the business necessity defense, it did not "have to undertake a bona fide occupational qualification's (BFOQ) analysis."

The Court of Appeals for the Seventh Circuit, sitting en banc, affirmed the summary judgment by a 7-to-4 vote. The majority held that the proper standard for evaluating the fetal-protection policy was the defense of business necessity; that Johnson Controls was entitled to summary judgment under that defense; and that even if the proper standard was a BFOQ, Johnson Controls still was entitled to summary judgment.

* * *

The bias in Johnson Controls' policy is obvious. Fertile men, but not fertile women, are given a choice as to whether they wish to risk their reproductive health for a particular job. [T]he Civil Rights Act of 1964, [citation], prohibits sex-based classifications in terms and conditions of employment, in hiring and discharging decisions, and in other employment decisions that adversely affect an employee's status. Respondent's fetal-protection policy explicitly discriminates against women on the basis of their sex. The policy excludes women with childbearing capacity from lead-exposed jobs and so creates a facial classification based on gender.

* * *

We concluded above that Johnson Controls' policy is not neutral because it does not apply to the reproductive capacity of the company's male employees in the same way as it applies to that of the females. Moreover, the absence of a malevolent motive does not convert a facially discriminatory policy into a neutral policy with a discriminatory effect. Whether an employment practice involves disparate treatment through explicit facial discrimination does not depend on why the employer discriminates but rather on the explicit terms of the discrimination. * * *

In sum, Johnson Controls' policy "does not pass the simple test of whether the evidence shows 'treatment of a person in a manner which but for that person's sex would be different.'" [Citation.] We hold that Johnson Controls' fetal-protection policy is sex discrimination forbidden under Title VII unless respondent can establish that sex is a "bona fide occupational qualification."

Under Title VII, an employer may discriminate on the basis of "religion, sex, or national origin in those certain instances where religion, sex, or national origin is a bona fide occupational qualification reasonably necessary to the normal operation of that particular business or enterprise." * * *

The BFOQ defense is written narrowly, and this Court has read it narrowly. [Citations.]

* * *

The wording of the BFOQ defense contains several terms of restriction that indicate that the exception reaches only special situations. The statute thus limits the situations in which discrimination is permissible to "certain instances" where sex discrimination is "reasonably necessary" to the "normal operation" of the "particular" business. Each one of these terms—certain, normal, particular—prevents the use of general subjective standards and favors an objective, verifiable requirement. But the most telling term is "occupational"; this indicates that these objective, verifiable requirements must concern job-related skills and aptitudes.

* * *

Our case law, therefore, makes clear that the safety exception is limited to instances in which sex or pregnancy actually interferes with the employee's ability to perform the job. This approach is consistent with the language of the BFOQ provision itself, for it suggests that permissible distinctions based on sex must relate to ability to perform the duties of the job. Johnson Controls suggests, however, that we expand the exception to allow fetal-protection policies that mandate particular standards for pregnant or fertile women. We decline to do so. Such an expansion contradicts not only the language of the BFOQ and the narrowness of its exception but the plain language and history of the Pregnancy Discrimination Act.

The PDA's amendment to Title VII contains a BFOQ standard of its own: unless pregnant employees differ from others "in their ability or inability to work," they must be "treated the same" as other employees "for all employment-related purposes."

* * *

We conclude that the language of both the BFOQ provision and the PDA which amended it, as well as the legislative history and the case law, prohibit an employer from discriminating against a woman because of her capacity to become pregnant unless her reproductive potential prevents her from performing the duties of her job. * * *

We have no difficulty concluding that Johnson Controls cannot establish a BFOQ. Fertile women, as far as appears in the record, participate in the manufacture of batteries as efficiently as anyone else. Johnson Controls' professed moral and ethical concerns about the welfare of the next generation do not suffice to establish a BFOQ of female sterility. Decisions about the welfare of future children must be left to the parents who conceive, bear, support, and raise them rather than to the employers who hire those parents. Congress has mandated this choice through Title VII, as amended by the Pregnancy Discrimination Act.

* * *

Johnson Controls argues that it must exclude all fertile women because it is impossible to tell which women will become pregnant while working with lead. This argument is somewhat academic in light of our conclusion that the company may not exclude fertile women at all; it perhaps is worth noting, however, that Johnson Controls has shown no "factual basis for believing that all or substantially all women would be unable to perform safely and efficiently the duties of the job involved." [Citation.] Even on this sparse record, it is apparent that Johnson Controls is concerned about only a small minority of women. Of the eight pregnancies reported among the female employees, it has not been shown that any of the babies have birth defects or other abnormalities. The record does not reveal the birth rate for Johnson Controls' female workers but national statistics show that approximately nine percent of all fertile women become pregnant each year. The birthrate drops to two percent for blue collar workers over age 30. [Citation.] Johnson Controls' fear of prenatal injury, no matter how sincere, does not begin to show that substantially all of its fertile women employees are incapable of doing their jobs.

A word about tort liability and the increased cost of fertile women in the workplace is perhaps necessary. One of the dissenting judges in this case expressed concern about an employer's tort liability and concluded that liability for a potential injury to a fetus is a social cost that Title VII does not require a company to ignore. It is correct to say that Title VII does not prevent the employer from having a conscience. The statute, however, does prevent sex-specific fetal-protection policies. These two aspects of Title VII do not conflict.

\* \* \*

If state tort law furthers discrimination in the workplace and prevents employers from hiring women who are capable of manufacturing the product as efficiently as men, then it will impede the accomplishment of Congress' goals in enacting Title VII. Because Johnson Controls has not argued that it faces any costs from tort liability, not to mention crippling ones, the pre-emption question is not before us. We therefore say no more than that the concurrence's speculation [about potential tort liability] appears unfounded as well as premature.

The tort-liability argument reduces to two equally unpersuasive propositions. First, Johnson Controls attempts to solve the problem of reproductive health hazards by resorting to an exclusionary policy. Title VII plainly forbids illegal sex discrimination as a method of diverting attention from an employer's obligation to police the workplace. Second, the spectre of an award of damages reflects a fear that hiring fertile women will cost more. The extra cost of employing members of one sex, however, does not provide an affirmative Title VII defense for a discriminatory refusal to hire members of that gender. [Citation.] Indeed, in passing the PDA, Congress considered at length the considerable cost of providing equal treatment of pregnancy and related conditions, but made the "decision to forbid special treatment of pregnancy despite the social costs associated therewith." [Citations.]

We, of course, are not presented with, nor do we decide, a case in which costs would be so prohibitive as to threaten the survival of the employer's business. We merely reiterate our prior holdings that the incremental cost of hiring women cannot justify discriminating against them.

\* \* \*

The judgment of the Court of Appeals is reversed and the case is remanded for further proceedings consistent with this opinion.

---

## CASE 43–2
### Discrimination
## EQUAL EMPLOYMENT OPPORTUNITY COMMISSION v. STEAMSHIP CLERKS UNION, LOCAL 1066

United States Court of Appeals, First Circuit, 1995
48 F.3d 594

SELYA, J.

Labor unions have historically been instruments of solidarity, forged in an ostensible effort to counterbalance the weight of concentrated industrial power. It is, therefore, ironic—but not unprecedentedly so, inasmuch as "irony is no stranger to the law," [citation]—that unions themselves sometimes engage in exclusionary membership practices. The court below detected such an elitist strain in the operation of the Steamship Clerks Union, Local 1066 (the Union), determining that the Union's policy requiring prospective members to be "sponsored" by existing members—all of whom, from time immemorial, have been white—constituted race-based discrimination. [Citation.]

\* \* \*

### I. Background

The relevant facts are not disputed. The Union is "a labor organization engaged in an industry affecting commerce," [citation]. It has approximately 124 members, 80 of whom are classified as active. The members serve as steamship clerks who, during the loading and unloading of vessels in the port of Boston, check cargo against inventory lists provided by shippers and consignees. The work is not taxing; it requires little in the way of particular skills.

On October 1, 1980, the Union formally adopted the membership sponsorship policy (the MSP) around which this suit revolves. The MSP provided that any applicant for membership in the Union (other than an injured longshoreman) had to be sponsored by an existing member in order for his application to be considered. The record reveals, without contradiction, that (1) the Union had no African American or Hispanic members when it adopted the MSP; (2) blacks and Hispanics constituted from 8% to 27% of the relevant labor pool in the Boston area; (3) the Union welcomed at least 30 new members between 1980 and 1986, and then closed the membership rolls; (4) all the "sponsored" applicants during this period and, hence, all the new members, were Caucasian; and (5) every recruit was related to—usually the son or brother of—a Union member.

After conducting an investigation and instituting administrative proceedings, the EEOC brought suit on June 7, 1991, alleging that the Union had discriminated against African-Americans and Hispanics by means of the MSP.

\* \* \*

On the very same date, the district judge, presumably unaware of the EEOC's letter, issued his decision. Judge Stearns granted the EEOC's motion for partial summary judgment, holding that the MSP evinced unlawful discrimination on the basis of race. \* \* \*

Nothing significant occurred until April 10, 1994, when the court, without awaiting further motions or soliciting any input from the parties, entered final judgment. Among other things, it ordered the Union to (1) scrap the MSP; (2) open its membership "to enable admission of at least one new member for each listed member who, since the books were closed in 1986, has died, retired or [become inactive]"; (3) submit a plan for publicizing membership opportunities, taking special cognizance of the need to recruit minority applicants; (4) periodically submit membership information to the EEOC; and (5) comply with the EEOC's record-keeping requirements \* \* \*. These appeals followed.

## II. Liability

We begin with the liability issue. The EEOC's allegations against the Union find their genesis in Title VII of the Civil Rights Act of 1964, [citation]. Broadly speaking, Title VII outlaws discrimination based on race, color, religion, gender, or national origin. In so doing, the law forbids both "overt discrimination" in the form of disparate treatment, *Griggs v. Duke Power Co.*, [citation], and more subtle forms of discrimination, known as disparate impact discrimination, arising from "the consequences of employment practices, not simply the motivation." [Citation]. In this instance, we limit our

inquiry to whether the court below supportably determined that the MSP resulted in race-based disparate impact discrimination during the years 1980 through 1986.

**A. The Disparate Impact Approach** It has long been understood that discrimination, whether measured quantitatively or qualitatively, is not always a function of a pernicious motive or malign intent. Discrimination may also result from otherwise neutral policies and practices that, when actuated in real-life settings, operate to the distinct disadvantage of certain classes of individuals. [Citation.] Within the world of Title VII, this understanding is reflected in the concept of disparate impact discrimination—a concept born of a perceived need to ensure that Title VII's proscriptive sweep encompasses "not only overt discrimination but also practices that are fair in form, but discriminatory in operation." *Griggs*, [citation]. Thus, the disparate impact approach roots out "employment policies that are facially neutral in their treatment of different groups but that in fact fall more harshly on one group than another and cannot be justified by business necessity." [Citations.] \* \* \*

Under the legal framework that applies in this case, see supra note 5, it is incumbent upon the plaintiff to demonstrate a *prima facie* case of discrimination. [Citations.] In the disparate impact milieu, the *prima facie* case consists of three elements: identification, impact, and causation. First, the plaintiff must identify the challenged employment practice or policy, and pinpoint the defendant's use of it. [Citation.] Second, the plaintiff must demonstrate a disparate impact on a group characteristic, such as race, that falls within the protective ambit of Title VII. [Citation.] Third, the plaintiff must demonstrate a causal relationship between the identified practice and the disparate impact. [Citations.]

When the plaintiff rests, declaring herself satisfied that she has established a *prima facie* case of disparate impact discrimination, the ball bounces into the defendant's court. At that point, the defendant has several options. First, it may attack the plaintiff's proof head-on, \* \* \*.

Alternatively, the defendant may confess and avoid, acknowledging the legal sufficiency of the *prima facie* case but endeavoring to show either that the challenged practice is job-related and consistent with business necessity, see *Griggs*, [citation], or that it fits within one or more of the explicit statutory exceptions covering bona fide seniority systems, veterans' preferences, and the like. [Citations.] In all events, however, a defendant's good faith is not a defense to a disparate impact claim. See *Griggs,* [citation].

If the defendant fails in its efforts to counter the plaintiff's *prima facie* case, then the factfinder is entitled—though not necessarily compelled, [citations] to enter judgment for the plaintiff. On the other hand, even if the defendant stalemates the *prima facie* case by elucidating a legitimate, nondiscriminatory rationale for utilizing the challenged practice, the plaintiff may still prevail if she is able to establish that the professed rationale is pretextual. [Citations.] The plaintiff might demonstrate, for example, that some other practice, without a similarly undesirable side effect, was available and would have served the defendant's legitimate interest equally well. [Citation.] Such an exhibition constitutes competent evidence that the defendant was using the interdicted practice "merely as a 'pretext' for discrimination." [Citation.]

* * *

**C. Application of the Law**   In this case, the district court adroitly applied the substantive law and concluded that the Union's sponsorship-based membership policy constituted disparate impact discrimination. [Citation.] We descry no error.

1. The *Prima Facie* Case. We agree with the district court that the EEOC carried its burden of producing facts sufficient to limn the three elements essential to its *prima facie* case. The first element—identification—requires no elaboration. We start, therefore, with the element of disparate impact and then move to causation. In both instances, the relevant facts are not disputed.

*a* Population statistics for the Boston area, proffered by the EEOC and unchallenged by the Union, show that in the relevant time frame African-Americans comprised 21%, and Hispanics 6%, of the available labor force. Although there are no known statistics on the racial composition of the steamship clerk industry—if such an "industry" exists—"Census Bureau statistics that merge the transportation industry's employment statistics with similar statistics for public utilities . . . show that blacks and Hispanics participate in the labor force as clerical/clerks at a rate of 7% and 1% of the total, respectively." Despite the fact that the combined pool of potential black and Hispanic applicants for union membership ranged between 8% and 27% of the overall pool of potential applicants, no African-American or Hispanic was granted Union membership. Finally, during the MSP's heyday—the six-year period from 1980 through 1986—the Union admitted 30 new members. Based on a comparison of these figures with the profile of the newly minted Union members—0 of 30, or zero percent—the district court found that the EEOC adequately demonstrated a race-based disparate impact.

The utility of statistical evidence "depends on all of the surrounding facts and circumstances." [Citation.] In this instance, the sample, though small, is telling. * * *

*b* Reluctant to raise a white flag, the Union further contends that, even if the EEOC established a significant racial disparity, its prima facie case misfired on the element of causation. * * *

In sum, it was not error for the lower court to conclude, on the idiosyncratic facts of this case, that the MSP, though neutral on its face, proximately caused the exclusion of minorities between 1980 and 1986.

2. The Union's Response. Once the EEOC demonstrated a prima facie case of discrimination, the burden of production shifted. In the absence of any applicable statutory exemption, it became incumbent upon the Union either to mount a satisfactory empirical rebuttal or to show that the challenged practice was job-related and consistent with business necessity. For all intents and purposes, the Union travels only the second path. Its sojourn is unavailing.

The Union suggests that the MSP is job-related and consistent with business necessity because it represents an important vehicle for continuing family traditions. Most of the 30 new members, according to the Union, "joined simply because their fathers had been members and because they wanted to maintain a family tradition. . . ." We approach the task of evaluating this rationale mindful that the meaning and scope of the "business necessity" concept are blurred at the edges. [Citation.] In the case at bar, however, such potential indeterminacy is of no consequence, for the Union's "family tradition" thesis falls hopelessly short of limning a business necessity, and, thus, does not require us to explore *terra incognita*.

We will not tarry. Here, the Union has not shown even the glimmerings of a business necessity defense. * * *

The finish line looms. Because the Union neither rebutted the EEOC's prima facie case nor articulated a legitimate, nondiscriminatory justification for its membership policy, we uphold the grant of partial summary judgment in the EEOC's favor.

## CASE 43–3
### Sexual Harassment
## *FARAGHER v. CITY OF BOCA RATON*
Supreme Court of the United States, 1998
118 S.Ct. 2275, 141 L.Ed.2d 662

SOUTER, J.
This case calls for identification of the circumstances under which an employer may be held liable under Title VII of the Civil Rights Act of 1964, [citation], for the acts of a supervisory employee whose sexual harassment of subordinates has created a hostile work environment amounting to employment discrimination. We hold that an employer is vicariously liable for actionable discrimination caused by a supervisor, but subject to an affirmative defense looking to the reasonableness of the employer's conduct as well as that of a plaintiff victim.

## I

Between 1985 and 1990, while attending college, petitioner Beth Ann Faragher worked part time and during the summers as an ocean lifeguard for the Marine Safety Section of the Parks and Recreation Department of respondent, the City of Boca Raton, Florida (City). During this period, Faragher's immediate supervisors were Bill Terry, David Silverman, and Robert Gordon. In June 1990, Faragher resigned.

\* \* \*

In February 1986, the City adopted a sexual harassment policy, which it stated in a memorandum from the City Manager addressed to all employees. [Citation.]. In May 1990, the City revised the policy and reissued a statement of it. Although the City may actually have circulated the memos and statements to some employees, it completely failed to disseminate its policy among employees of the Marine Safety Section, with the result that Terry, Silverman, Gordon, and many lifeguards were unaware of it. [Citation.]

From time to time over the course of Faragher's tenure at the Marine Safety Section, between 4 and 6 of the 40 to 50 lifeguards were women. During that 5-year period, Terry repeatedly touched the bodies of female employees without invitation, [citation], would put his arm around Faragher, with his hand on her buttocks, [citation], and once made contact with another female lifeguard in a motion of sexual simulation, [citation]. He made crudely demeaning references to women generally, and once commented disparagingly on Faragher's shape, [citation]. During a job interview with a woman he hired as a lifeguard, Terry said that the female lifeguards had sex with their male counterparts and asked whether she would do the same. [Citation.]

Silverman behaved in similar ways. He once tackled Faragher and remarked that, but for a physical characteristic he found unattractive, he would readily have had sexual relations with her. [Citation.] Another time, he pantomimed an act of oral sex. [Citation.] Within earshot of the female lifeguards, Silverman made frequent, vulgar references to women and sexual matters, commented on the bodies of female lifeguards and beachgoers, and at least twice told female lifeguards that he would like to engage in sex with them. [Citation.]

Faragher did not complain to higher management about Terry or Silverman. Although she spoke of their behavior to Gordon, she did not regard these discussions as formal complaints to a supervisor but as conversations with a person she held in high esteem. [Citation.] Other female lifeguards had similarly informal talks with Gordon, but because Gordon did not feel that it was his place to do so, he did not report these complaints to Terry, his own supervisor, or to any other city official. [Citation.] Gordon responded to the complaints of one lifeguard by saying that "the City just [doesn't] care." [Citation.]

In April 1990, however, two months before Faragher's resignation, Nancy Ewanchew, a former lifeguard, wrote to Richard Bender, the City's Personnel Director, complaining that Terry and Silverman had harassed her and other female lifeguards. Following investigation of this complaint, the City found that Terry and Silverman had behaved improperly, reprimanded them, and required them to choose between a suspension without pay or the forfeiture of annual leave. [Citation.]

On the basis of these findings, the District Court concluded that the conduct of Terry and Silverman was discriminatory harassment sufficiently serious to alter the conditions of Faragher's employment and constitute an abusive working environment. [Citation.] The District Court then ruled that there were three justifications for holding the City liable for the harassment of its supervisory employees. First, the court noted that the harassment was pervasive enough to support an inference that the City had "knowledge, or constructive knowledge" of it. [Citation.] Next, it ruled that the City was liable under traditional agency principles because Terry and Silverman were acting as its agents when they committed the harassing acts. [Citation.] Finally, the court observed that Gordon's knowledge of the harassment, combined with his inaction, "provides a further basis for imputing liability on [sic] the City." [Citation.] The District Court then awarded Faragher one dollar in nominal damages on her Title VII claim. [Citation.]

A panel of the Court of Appeals for the Eleventh Circuit reversed the judgment against the City. [Citation.] Although the panel had "no trouble concluding that Terry's and Silverman's conduct . . . was severe and pervasive enough to create an objectively abusive work environment," [citation], it overturned the District Court's conclusion that the City was liable. The panel ruled that Terry and Silverman were not acting within the scope of their employment when they engaged in the harassment, that they were not aided in their actions by the agency relationship, [citation], and that the City had no constructive knowledge of the harassment by virtue of its pervasiveness or Gordon's actual knowledge, [citation].

In a 7-to-5 decision, the full Court of Appeals, sitting en banc, adopted the panel's conclusion. [Citation.]

* * *

## II

### A

Thus, in *Meritor* we held that sexual harassment so "severe or pervasive" as to "'alter the conditions of [the victim's] employment and create an abusive working environment'" violates Title VII. [Citation.]

In thus holding that environmental claims are covered by the statute, we drew upon earlier cases recognizing liability for discriminatory harassment based on race and national origin, [citations], just as we have also followed the lead of such cases in attempting to define the severity of the offensive conditions necessary to constitute actionable sex discrimination under the statute. [Citations.]

So, in *Harris,* we explained that in order to be actionable under the statute, a sexually objectionable environment must be both objectively and subjectively offensive, one that a reasonable person would find hostile or abusive, and one that the victim in fact did perceive to be so. [Citation.] We directed courts to determine whether an environment is sufficiently hostile or abusive by "looking at all the circumstances," including the "frequency of the discriminatory conduct; its severity; whether it is physically threatening or humiliating, or a mere offensive utterance; and whether it unreasonably interferes with an employee's work performance." [Citation.] Most recently, we explained that Title VII does not prohibit "genuine but innocuous differences in the ways men and women routinely interact with members of the same sex and of the opposite sex." *Oncale,* [citation]. A recurring point in these opinions is that "simple teasing," [citation], offhand comments, and isolated incidents (unless extremely serious) will not amount to discriminatory changes in the "terms and conditions of employment."

These standards for judging hostility are sufficiently demanding to ensure that Title VII does not become a "general civility code." [Citation.] Properly applied, they will filter out complaints attacking "the ordinary tribulations of the workplace, such as the sporadic use of abusive language, gender-related jokes, and occasional teasing." [Citations.]

While indicating the substantive contours of the hostile environments forbidden by Title VII, our cases have established few definite rules for determining when an employer will be liable for a discriminatory environment that is otherwise actionably abusive.  * * * There have, for example, been myriad cases in which District Courts and Courts of Appeals have held employers liable on account of actual knowledge by the employer, or high-echelon officials of an employer organization, of sufficiently harassing action by subordinates, which the employer or its informed officers have done nothing to stop. * * *

Nor was it exceptional that standards for binding the employer were not in issue in *Harris.* In that case of discrimination by hostile environment, the individual charged with creating the abusive atmosphere was the president of the corporate employer, [citation], who was indisputably within that class of an employer organization's officials who may be treated as the organization's proxy. [Citations.]

Finally, there is nothing remarkable in the fact that claims against employers for discriminatory employment actions with tangible results, like hiring, firing, promotion, compensation, and work assignment, have resulted in employer liability once the discrimination was shown. [Citations.]

* * *

The soundness of the results in these cases (and their continuing vitality), in light of basic agency principles, was confirmed by this Court's only discussion to date of standards of employer liability, in *Meritor,* which involved a claim of discrimination by a supervisor's sexual harassment of a subordinate over an extended period. In affirming the Court of Appeals's holding that a hostile atmosphere resulting from sex discrimination is actionable under Title VII, we also anticipated proceedings on remand by holding agency principles relevant in assigning employer liability and by rejecting three *per se* rules of liability or immunity. * * *

We then proceeded to reject two limitations on employer liability, while establishing the rule that some limitation was intended. We held that neither the existence of a company grievance procedure nor the absence of actual notice of the harassment on the part of upper management would be dispositive of such a claim; while either might be relevant to the liability, neither would result automatically in employer immunity.

* * *

## B

The Court of Appeals identified, and rejected, three possible grounds drawn from agency law for holding the City vicariously liable for the hostile environment created by the supervisors.

* * *

We therefore agree with Faragher that in implementing Title VII it makes sense to hold an employer vicariously liable for some tortious conduct of a supervisor made possible by abuse of his supervisory authority, and that the aided-by-agency-relation principle embodied in § 219(2)(d) of the Restatement provides an appropriate starting point for determining liability for the kind of harassment presented here.

* * *

There is certainly some authority for requiring active or affirmative, as distinct from passive or implicit, misuse of supervisory authority before liability may be imputed.

* * *

In order to accommodate the principle of vicarious liability for harm caused by misuse of supervisory authority, as well as Title VII's equally basic policies of encouraging forethought by employers and saving action by objecting employees, we adopt the following holding in this case and in *Burlington Industries, Inc. v. Ellerth,* [citation], also decided today. An employer is subject to

vicarious liability to a victimized employee for an actionable hostile environment created by a supervisor with immediate (or successively higher) authority over the employee. When no tangible employment action is taken, a defending employer may raise an affirmative defense to liability or damages, subject to proof by a preponderance of the evidence, see [citation]. The defense comprises two necessary elements: (a) that the employer exercised reasonable care to prevent and correct promptly any sexually harassing behavior, and (b) that the plaintiff employee unreasonably failed to take advantage of any preventive or corrective opportunities provided by the employer or to avoid harm otherwise. While proof that an employer had promulgated an antiharassment policy with complaint procedure is not necessary in every instance as a matter of law, the need for a stated policy suitable to the employment circumstances may appropriately be addressed in any case when litigating the first element of the defense. And while proof that an employee failed to fulfill the corresponding obligation of reasonable care to avoid harm is not limited to showing an unreasonable failure to use any complaint procedure provided by the employer, a demonstration of such failure will normally suffice to satisfy the employer's burden under the second element of the defense. No affirmative defense is available, however, when the supervisor's harassment culminates in a tangible employment action, such as discharge, demotion, or undesirable reassignment. [Citation.]

Applying these rules here, we believe that the judgment of the Court of Appeals must be reversed. The District Court found that the degree of hostility in the work environment rose to the actionable level and was attributable to Silverman and Terry. It is undisputed that these supervisors "were granted virtually unchecked authority" over their subordinates, "directly controll[ing] and supervis[ing] all aspects of [Faragher's] day-to-day activities." [Citation.] It is also clear that Faragher and her colleagues were "completely isolated from the City's higher management." [Citation.] The City did not seek review of these findings.

While the City would have an opportunity to raise an affirmative defense if there were any serious prospect of its presenting one, it appears from the record that any such avenue is closed. The District Court found that the City had entirely failed to disseminate its policy against sexual harassment among the beach employees and that its officials made no attempt to keep track of the conduct of supervisors like Terry and Silverman. The record also makes clear that the City's policy did not include any assurance that the harassing supervisors could be bypassed in registering complaints. Under such circumstances, we hold as a matter of law that the City could not be found to have exercised reasonable care to prevent the supervisors' harassing conduct. Unlike the employer of a small workforce, who might expect that sufficient care to prevent tortious behavior could be exercised informally, those responsible for city operations could not reasonably have thought that precautions against hostile environments in any one of many departments in far-flung locations could be effective without communicating some formal policy against harassment, with a sensible complaint procedure.

**3** The Court of Appeals also rejected the possibility that it could hold the City liable for the reason that it knew of the harassment vicariously through the knowledge of its supervisors. We have no occasion to consider whether this was error, however. We are satisfied that liability on the ground of vicarious knowledge could not be determined without further factfinding on remand, whereas the reversal necessary on the theory of supervisory harassment renders any remand for consideration of imputed knowledge entirely unjustifiable (as would be any consideration of negligence as an alternative to a theory of vicarious liability here).

## III

The judgment of the Court of Appeals for the Eleventh Circuit is reversed, and the case is remanded for reinstatement of the judgment of the District Court.

---

**CASE 43–4**
## Discrimination Based on Disability
### *BRAGDON v. ABBOTT*
Supreme Court of the United States, 1998
118 S.Ct. 2196, 141 L.Ed.2d 540

**KENNEDY, J.**
We address in this case the application of the Americans with Disabilities Act of 1990 (ADA), [citation], to persons infected with the human immunodeficiency virus (HIV). We granted certiorari to review, first, whether HIV infection is a disability under the ADA when the infection has not yet progressed to the so-called symptomatic phase; and, second, whether the Court of Appeals, in affirming a grant of summary judgment, cited sufficient material in the record to determine, as a matter of law, that respondent's infection with HIV posed no direct threat to the health and safety of her treating dentist.

### I

Respondent Sidney Abbott has been infected with HIV since 1986. When the incidents we recite occurred, her infection had not manifested its most serious symptoms. On September 16, 1994, she went to the office of petitioner Randon Bragdon in Bangor, Maine, for a dental appointment. She disclosed her HIV infection on the patient registration form. Petitioner completed a dental examination, discovered a cavity, and informed respondent of his policy against filling cavities of HIV-infected patients. He offered to perform the work at a hospital with no added fee for his services, though respondent would be responsible for the cost of using the hospital's facilities. Respondent declined.

Respondent sued petitioner * * * alleging discrimination on the basis of her disability. * * * Section 302 of the ADA provides:

No individual shall be discriminated against on the basis of disability in the full and equal enjoyment of the goods, services, facilities, privileges, advantages, or accommodations of any place of public accommodation by any person who . . . operates a place of public accommodation. § 12182(a).

The term "public accommodation" is defined to include the "professional office of a health care provider." § 12181(7)(F).

A later subsection qualifies the mandate not to discriminate. It provides:

Nothing in this subchapter shall require an entity to permit an individual to participate in or benefit from the goods, services, facilities, privileges, advantages and accommodations of such entity where such individual poses a direct threat to the health or safety of others. § 12182(b)(3).

* * *

## II

We first review the ruling that respondent's HIV infection constituted a disability under the ADA. The statute defines disability as:

(A) a physical or mental impairment that substantially limits one or more of the major life activities of such individual;
(B) a record of such an impairment; or
(C) being regarded as having such impairment. § 12102(2).

We hold respondent's HIV infection was a disability under subsection (A) of the definitional section of the statute. In light of this conclusion, we need not consider the applicability of subsections (B) or (C).

\* \* \*

## A

**1** The first step in the inquiry under subsection (A) requires us to determine whether respondent's condition constituted a physical impairment.

\* \* \*

HIV infection is not included in the list of specific disorders constituting physical impairments, in part because HIV was not identified as the cause of AIDS until 1983. [Citations.] HIV infection does fall well within the general definition set forth by the regulations, however.

In light of the immediacy with which the virus begins to damage the infected person's white blood cells and the severity of the disease, we hold it is an impairment from the moment of infection. As noted earlier, infection with HIV causes immediate abnormalities in a person's blood, and the infected person's white cell count continues to drop throughout the course of the disease, even when the attack is concentrated in the lymph nodes. In light of these facts, HIV infection must be regarded as a physiological disorder with a constant and detrimental effect on the infected person's hemic and lymphatic systems from the moment of infection. HIV infection satisfies the statutory and regulatory definition of a physical impairment during every stage of the disease.

**2** The statute is not operative, and the definition not satisfied, unless the impairment affects a major life activity. Respondent's claim throughout this case has been that the HIV infection placed a substantial limitation on her ability to reproduce and to bear children. [Citation.] Given the pervasive, and invariably fatal, course of the disease, its effect on major life activities of many sorts might have been relevant to our inquiry. Respondent

and a number of amici [those filing friends-of-the-court briefs] make arguments about HIV's profound impact on almost every phase of the infected person's life. In light of these submissions, it may seem legalistic to circumscribe our discussion to the activity of reproduction. We have little doubt that had different parties brought the suit they would have maintained that an HIV infection imposes substantial limitations on other major life activities.

From the outset, however, the case has been treated as one in which reproduction was the major life activity limited by the impairment. \* \* \*

We have little difficulty concluding that it is. As the Court of Appeals held, "[t]he plain meaning of the word 'major' denotes comparative importance" and "suggest[s] that the touchstone for determining an activity's inclusion under the statutory rubric is its significance." [Citation.] Reproduction falls well within the phrase "major life activity." Reproduction and the sexual dynamics surrounding it are central to the life process itself.

While petitioner concedes the importance of reproduction, he claims that Congress intended the ADA only to cover those aspects of a person's life which have a public, economic, or daily character. [Citations.] The argument founders on the statutory language. Nothing in the definition suggests that activities without a public, economic, or daily dimension may somehow be regarded as so unimportant or insignificant as to fall outside the meaning of the word "major." The breadth of the term confounds the attempt to limit its construction in this manner.

\* \* \*

**3** The final element of the disability definition in subsection (A) is whether respondent's physical impairment was a substantial limit on the major life activity she asserts. \* \* \*

Our evaluation of the medical evidence leads us to conclude that respondent's infection substantially limited her ability to reproduce in two independent ways. First, a woman infected with HIV who tries to conceive a child imposes on the man a significant risk of becoming infected. The cumulative results of 13 studies collected in a 1994 textbook on AIDS indicates that 20% of male partners of women with HIV became HIV-positive themselves, with a majority of the studies finding a statistically significant risk of infection. [Citations.]

Second, an infected woman risks infecting her child during gestation and childbirth, i.e., perinatal transmission. Petitioner concedes that women infected with HIV face about a 25% risk of transmitting the virus to their children.

* * *

The Act addresses substantial limitations on major life activities, not utter inabilities. Conception and childbirth are not impossible for an HIV victim but, without doubt, are dangerous to the public health. This meets the definition of a substantial limitation. * * *

* * * Respondent's HIV infection is a physical impairment which substantially limits a major life activity, as the ADA defines it. In view of our holding, we need not address the second question presented, i.e., whether HIV infection is a per se disability under the ADA.

* * *

## III

The petition for certiorari presented * * * other questions for review. The questions stated:

3. When deciding under title III of the ADA whether a private health care provider must perform invasive procedures on an infectious patient in his office, should courts defer to the health care provider's professional judgment, as long as it is reasonable in light of then-current medical knowledge?

* * *

The existence, or nonexistence, of a significant risk must be determined from the standpoint of the person who refuses the treatment or accommodation, and the risk assessment must be based on medical or other objective evidence. [Citations.] As a health care professional, petitioner had the duty to assess the risk of infection based on the objective, scientific information available to him and others in his profession. His belief that a significant risk existed, even if maintained in good faith, would not relieve him from liability. To use the words of the question presented, petitioner receives no special deference simply because he is a health care professional. * * *

Our conclusion that courts should assess the objective reasonableness of the views of health care professionals without deferring to their individual judgments does not answer the implicit assumption in the question presented, whether petitioner's actions were reasonable in light of the available medical evidence. * * *

* * *

We conclude the proper course is to give the Court of Appeals the opportunity to determine whether our analysis of some of the studies cited by the parties would change its conclusion that petitioner presented neither objective evidence nor a triable issue of fact on the question of risk. In remanding the case, we do not foreclose the possibility that the Court of Appeals may reach the same conclusion it did earlier. A remand will permit a full exploration of the issue through the adversary process.

The determination of the Court of Appeals that respondent's HIV infection was a disability under the ADA is affirmed. The judgment is vacated, and the case is remanded for further proceedings consistent with this opinion.

---

**CASE 43–5**
## Termination at Will
### *HUNGER v. GRAND CENTRAL SANITATION*
Superior Court of Pennsylvania, 1996
670 A.2d 173

HESTER, J.
Mark Hunger appeals from the December 9, 1994 grant of summary judgment to appellees, Grand Central Sanitation and Gary Perin. We are constrained to affirm under current precedent of this court.

Appellant instituted this action on January 26, 1993, against his former employer and Mr. Perin, who terminated appellant. The action is based upon wrongful discharge, . . .

* * *

Appellant was employed by Grand Central Sanitation ("Grand Central") on June 28, 1990, as the company's safety director. Mr. Perin is the vice-president and owner of Grand Central. On September 7, 1991, appellant "became aware" that hazardous materials consisting of blasting caps were being deposited into garbage containers at Shu-Deb Inc. ("Shu-Deb"). * * * Grand Central picked up garbage for Shu-Deb and dumped it at a dump site. Appellant knew that Grand Central was not licensed to dispose of hazardous materials at any of its dump sites and believed that it would be a violation of federal law, state law, or both if the company transported or disposed of hazardous materials. Appellant also became concerned about the safety of company employees from the danger of transporting blasting caps.

On September 9, 1991, appellant told Mr. Perin about the information he received that blasting caps were being dumped into the containers at Shu-Deb. The next day, he contacted state and local police asking for a description of blasting caps, which he never had seen. He also made arrangements to search Shu-Deb's garbage container.

On September 12, 1991, appellant, accompanied by Pennsylvania State Police and members of the federal Bureau of Alcohol, Tobacco, and Firearms, went to search the contents of the garbage container. When appellant and police arrived at Shu-Deb, the garbage had been collected, so police located the garbage truck that had the garbage and searched it. "No hazardous materials were found." On October 4, 1991, appellant was discharged as a result of the incident.

Appellant first alleges that his wrongful discharge claim was dismissed improperly due to the public policy exception to the doctrine of at-will employment. We examine the applicable law:

In Pennsylvania, as a general rule, no common law cause of action exists against an employer for termination of an at-will employment relationship. [Citation.] Moreover, "exceptions to this rule have been recognized in only the most limited of circumstances, where discharges of at-will employees would threaten the clear mandates of public policy." [Citation.]

The public policy exception to the at-will doctrine was recognized by our Supreme Court in *Geary v. United States Steel Corp.,* [citation], a case remarkably similar to the one at bar. There, the plaintiff was a salesman for the defendant and criticized to company officials above his immediate supervisors the quality of the steel being produced. He was discharged even though the product later was determined to be substandard and withdrawn from the market. Geary alleged that his termination fell within a public policy exception to the at-will doctrine since he was acting in the interest of the safety of the general public.

While the Supreme Court recognized that a public policy exception may exist under appropriate conditions, it rejected plaintiff's argument that his allegations fell within its ambit on two grounds. First, the plaintiff was not obligated statutorily to report defective products. Second, on its face, the complaint offered the existence of a plausible reason for discharge in that the plaintiff had bypassed his immediate supervisors to make the complaint.

To state a public policy exception to the at-will-employment doctrine, the employee must point to a clear public policy articulated in the constitution, in legislation, an administrative regulation, or a judicial decision. [Citation.] Furthermore, the stated mandate of public policy, as articulated in the constitution, statute, or judicial decision, must be applicable directly to the employee and the employee's actions. It is not sufficient that the employer's actions toward the employee are unfair. [Citations.]

We have recognized a public policy exception only in extremely limited circumstances. If an employee is fired for performing a function that he is required to perform by law, an action for wrongful discharge on public policy grounds will be allowed. See e.g., [citation] (employee fired for reporting a nuclear safety violation that he was required to report under federal law); [citation] (employer fired an employee for serving on a jury; public policy was violated since people are required by law to serve on jury and since service on jury has constitutional implications).

A public policy exception to the at-will doctrine also will be found when the firing itself is a criminal activity * * *.

Herein, appellant notes that it is illegal to transport hazardous materials without a license. We agree. However, appellant admitted in his complaint that no blasting caps were discovered. Thus, appellees did not violate the law. If appellant had observed a deliberate violation of the law, reported it to proper authorities, and was fired, then the reasoning of [citation] may have been applicable. There is no indication that this occurred herein.

In this case, appellant's actions were premature. He provides no specifics about how he "became aware" that blasting caps were being dumped. He fails to indicate the capacity of the person who informed him of this, the nature of his investigation into substantiating the reliability of the information, and why it was necessary to inform state and federal law enforcement officials about the situation immediately.

Our disposition of this case may have been different if appellant discovered that his employer was deliberately transporting hazardous materials after being told of the situation. That is not what occurred, regardless of appellant's concern with the public safety. The source of appellant's "awareness" of the alleged illegal activities is completely unsubstantiated. Furthermore, his employer's criminal intent is not established. At most, one of the employer's customers allegedly was dumping illegal explosives.

* * *

# Questions

**1.** List and briefly discuss the major labor law statutes.

**2.** List and describe the major laws prohibiting employment discrimination.

**3.** Discuss the defenses available to an employer under the various laws prohibiting discrimination in employment.

**4.** Discuss the doctrine of employment at will and the laws protecting employee privacy.

**5.** Discuss (a) the Occupational Safety and Health Administration (OSHA) and the Occupational Safety and Health Act, (b) workers' compensation, (c) unemployment compensation, (d) social security, (e) the Fair Labor Standards Act, (f) the Worker Adjustment and Retraining Notification Act, and (g) the Family and Medical Leave Act.

# Problems

**1.** Gooddecade manufactures and sells automobile parts throughout the eastern United States. Among its full-time employees are 220 fourteen- and fifteen-year-olds. These teenagers are employed throughout the company and are paid an hourly wage rate of $3 per hour. Discuss the legality of this arrangement.

**2.** Janet, a twenty-year-old woman, applied for a position driving a truck for Federal Trucking, Inc. Janet, who is 5'4" tall and weighs 135 lbs., was denied the job because the company requires that all employees be at least 5'6" tall and weigh at least 150 lbs. Federal justifies this requirement on the basis that its drivers frequently are forced to move heavy loads when making pickups and deliveries. Janet brings a cause of action. Decision?

**3.** N.I.S. promoted John, a 42-year-old employee, to a foreman's position while passing over James, a 58-year-old employee. N.I.S. told James he was too old for the job and that the company preferred to have a younger man in the position. James brings a cause of action. Decision?

**4.** Anthony was employed as a forklift operator for Blackburn Construction Company. While on the job, Anthony operated the forklift in a careless manner and in direct violation of Blackburn's procedure manual. As a result, he caused himself severe injury. Blackburn denies liability based on Anthony's (a) gross negligence, (b) disobedience of the procedure manual, and (c) written waiver of liability. Anthony now brings a cause of action. Decision?

**5.** Hazelwood School District, located in Sleepy Hollow Township, is being sued by several teachers who applied for teaching positions within the school district but were rejected. The plaintiffs, who are all African American, produce the following evidence:

    (a)    1.8 percent of the Hazelwood School District's teachers are African American, whereas 15.4 percent of the teachers in Sleepy Hollow Township are African American; and

    (b)    the hiring decisions by Hazelwood School District are based solely on subjective criteria.

Will the plaintiffs prevail? Explain.

**6.** T.W.E., a large manufacturer, prohibited its employees from distributing union leaflets to other employees while on the company's property. Richard, an employee of T.W.E., disregarded the prohibition and passed out the leaflets before his work shift began. T.W.E. discharged Richard for his actions. Has T.W.E. committed an unfair labor practice?

**7.** Erwick was dismissed from her job at the C & T Steel Company because she was "an unsatisfactory employee." At the time, Erwick was active in an effort to organize a union at C & T. Is the dismissal valid?

**8.** Johnson, president of the First National Bank of A, believes that it is appropriate to employ only female tellers. Hence, First National refuses to employ Ken Baker as a teller but does offer him a maintenance position at the same salary. Baker brings a cause of action against First National Bank. Decision?

**9.** Section 103 of the Federal Public Works Employment Act of 1977 establishes the MBE (Minority Business Enterprise) program and requires that, absent a waiver by the Secretary of Commerce, 10 percent of all Federal grants given by the Economic Development Administration must be used to purchase services or supplies from businesses owned and controlled by U.S. citizens belonging to one of six minority groups: African American, Spanish-speaking, Oriental, Native American, Eskimo, and Aleut. White owners of businesses contend that the Act constitutes illegal reverse discrimination. Discuss.

**10.** Worth H. Percivil, a mechanical engineer, was first employed by General Motors in 1947 and remained in their employment until he was discharged in 1973. At the time his employment was terminated, Percivil was head of GM's Mechanical Development department. Percivil sued GM for wrongful discharge. He contends that he was discharged as a result of a conspiracy among his fellow executives to force him out of his employment because of his age, because he had legitimately complained about certain deceptive practices of GM, because he had refused to give the government false information although urged to do so by his superiors, and because he had, on the contrary, undertaken to correct certain alleged misrepresentations made to the government. General Motors claims that Percivil's employment was terminable at the will of GM for any reason and with or without cause, provided that the discharge was not prohibited by statute. Decision?

11.    On May 26, the trial examiner issued his Intermediate Report finding that the respondent (Sailers' Union) had not engaged in unfair union practices under Section 8(b) in its dispute with Samsoc. With respect to the unfair labor practices, the complaint alleged that the respondent induced and encouraged employees of Moore Dry Dock Company to engage in a strike or concerted refusal in the course of their employment to perform services for Moore in connection with the conversion into a bulk gypsum carrier of the SS *Phopho,* a vessel owned by Samsoc, the object being to force Moore to cease doing business with Samsoc and thus force Samsoc to resolve its dispute with the respondent. The General Counsel and Moore appealed. Decision?

12.    The defendant, Berger Transfer and Storage, operated a national moving and transfer business employing approximately forty persons. In May and June, Local 705 of the International Brotherhood of Teamsters spoke with a number of Berger employees, obtaining twenty-eight cards signed in support of the union. The management of Berger, unwilling to work with the union, attempted to prevent it from representing Berger employees. The company first assigned all work to those with high seniority, in effect temporarily laying off low-seniority employees. The management then threatened to lay off permanently those with low seniority and threatened all employees with a total shutdown of the plant. The management interrogated several employees about their union involvement and attempted to extract information about other employees' activities. When the union presented the company the signed cards and recognition agreement, Berger refused to acknowledge the union's existence or its right to bargain on behalf of the employees. The union then called a strike, with employees picketing the Berger warehouse. During the picketing, the company threatened to terminate the picketers if they did not return to work. Later, one manager on two occasions recklessly drove a truck through the picket line, striking employees. Finally, the company contacted several of the employees and offered them the "grievance procedures and job security" the union would provide. The employees refused the offer. On June 15, the strike ended, with most of the picketers returning to work. Local 705 filed a complaint with the National Labor Relations Board, alleging that Berger had committed unfair labor practices in violation of the National Labor Relations Act. Decision?

13.    Appellant, City of Richmond, Virginia, adopted a Minority Business Utilization Plan requiring prime contractors awarded city construction contracts to subcontract at least 30 percent of the dollar amount of each contract to one or more Minority Business Enterprises (MBEs). The Plan defined an MBE to include a business from anywhere in the country that is at least 51 percent owned and controlled by African American, Spanish-speaking, Oriental, Native American, Eskimo, or Aleut citizens. Although the Plan declared that it was "remedial" in nature, it was adopted after a public hearing at which no direct evidence was presented that the City had discriminated on the basis of race in letting contracts or that its prime contractors had discriminated against minority subcontractors. The evidence introduced in support of the Plan included a statistical study indicating that, although the City's population was 50 percent African American, less than 1 percent of its prime construction contracts had been awarded to minority businesses in recent years. Additional evidence showed that a variety of local contractors' trade associations had virtually no MBE members. Appellee, J.A. Crosen Co., the sole bidder on a city contract, was denied a waiver and lost its contract because of the Plan. Appellee brought suit alleging that the Plan was unconstitutional under the Fourteenth Amendment's Equal Protection Clause. Decision?

14.    Burdine, a female, was hired by the Texas Department of Community Affairs as a clerk in the Public Service Careers Division (PSC). The PSC provides training and employment opportunities for unskilled workers. At the time she was hired, Burdine already had several years' experience in employment training. She was soon promoted, and later, when her supervisor resigned, she performed additional duties that usually had been assigned to the supervisor. Burdine applied for the position of supervisor, but the position remained unfilled for six months until a male employee from another division was brought in to fill it. Burdine alleges discrimination violating Title VII of the 1964 Civil Rights Act. The defendant, Texas Department of Community Affairs, responds that nondiscriminatory evaluation criteria were used to choose the new supervisor. To comply with Title VII, must the Texas Department of Community Affairs hire Burdine as supervisor if she and the male candidate are equally qualified? Explain.

15.    Ms. Wise was fired from her job at the Mead Corporation after she was involved in a fight with a coworker. On four other unrelated occasions, fights occurred between male coworkers. Only one of the males was fired, but this was after his second fight, in which he seriously injured another employee. There is no dispute that Ms. Wise was qualified and performed her duties adequately. Ms. Wise successfully establishes a *prima facie* case of discrimination; however, defendant Mead Corporation meets its burden to "articulate legitimate and nondiscriminatory reasons" for firing Ms. Wise. Can she prevail? Explain.

16.    The United Steelworkers of America and Kaiser Aluminum entered into a master collective bargaining agreement covering terms and conditions of employment at fifteen Kaiser plants. The agreement contained an affirmative action plan designed to eliminate conspicuous racial imbalances in Kaiser's then almost exclusively white craftwork forces. African American craft-hiring goals were set for each Kaiser plant equal to the percentage of African Americans in the respective local labor forces. To meet these goals, on-the-job training programs were established to teach unskilled production workers—

African Americans and whites—the skills necessary to become craftworkers. The plan reserved for African American employees 50 percent of the openings in these newly created in-plant training programs.

Pursuant to the national agreement, Kaiser altered its craft-hiring practice in its Gramercy, Louisiana, plant by establishing a program to train its production workers to fill craft openings. Selection of craft trainees was made on the basis of seniority. At least 50 percent of the new trainees were to be African American until the percentage of African American skilled craftworkers in the Gramercy plant approximated the percentage of African Americans in the local labor force. During this affirmative action plan's first year of operation, thirteen craft trainees (seven African American, six white) were selected from Gramercy's productions workforce. The most senior African American selected had less seniority than several white production workers who were denied admission to the program. Weber, one of these white employees, brought suit claiming that the affirmative action plan discriminated against white employees and therefore violated the Civil Rights Act of 1964. Decision?

17.    At Whirlpool's manufacturing plant in Ohio, overhead conveyors transported household appliance components throughout the plant. A wire mesh screen was positioned below the conveyors to catch falling components and debris. Maintenance employees frequently had to stand on the screens to clean them. Whirlpool began installing heavier wire because several employees had fallen partly through the old screens, and one had fallen completely through to the plant floor. At this time, the company warned workers to walk only on the frames beneath the wire but not on the wire itself. Before the heavier wire had been completely installed, a worker fell to his death through the old screen. A short time after this incident, Deemer and Cornwell, two plant employees, met with the plant safety director to discuss the mesh, to voice their concerns, and to obtain the name, address, and telephone number of the local Occupational Safety and Health Administration (OSHA) representative. The next day, the two employees refused to clean a portion of the old screen. They were then ordered to punch out for the remainder of the shift without pay and also received written reprimands, which were placed in their employment files. Secretary of Labor Marshall brought suit, claiming that Whirlpool's actions against Deemer and Cornwell constituted discrimination in violation of the Occupational Safety and Health Act. Decision?

18.    John Novosel was employed by Nationwide Insurance for fifteen years. Novosel had been a model employee and, at the time of discharge, was a district claims manager and a candidate for the position of division claims manager. Just prior to his dismissal, Nationwide circulated a memorandum requesting the participation of all employees in an effort to lobby the Pennsylvania state legislature for the passage of a certain bill before the body. Novosel, who had privately indicated his disagreement with Nationwide's political views, refused to lend his support to the lobby, and his employment

with Nationwide was terminated. Novosel brought two separate claims against Nationwide, arguing, first, that his discharge for refusing to lobby the state legislature on behalf of Nationwide constituted the tort of wrongful discharge in that it was arbitrary, malicious, and contrary to public policy. Novosel also contended that Nationwide breached an implied contract guaranteeing continued employment so long as his job performance was satisfactory. The district court dismissed both claims, and Novosel appealed. Decision?

19.    During the years prior to the passage of the Civil Rights Act of 1964, Duke Power openly discriminated against African Americans by allowing them to work only in the labor department of the plant's five departments. The highest paying job in the labor department paid less than the lowest paying jobs in the other four "operating" departments in which only whites were employed. In 1955, the company began requiring a high school education for initial assignment to any department except labor. However, when Duke Power stopped restricting African Americans to the labor department in 1965, it made completion of high school a prerequisite to transfer from labor to any other department. White employees hired before the high school education requirement was adopted continued to perform satisfactorily and to achieve promotions in the "operating" departments.

In 1965, the company also began requiring new employees in the departments other than labor to register satisfactory scores on two professionally prepared aptitude tests, in addition to having a high school education. In September 1965, Duke Power began to permit employees to qualify for transfer to another department from labor by passing two tests, neither of which was directed or intended to measure the ability to learn to perform a particular job or category of jobs. Griggs brought suit against Duke Power, claiming that the high school education and testing requirements were discriminatory and therefore prohibited by the Civil Rights Act of 1964. The district court held that Title VII was prospective only and that Duke's earlier policy of racial discrimination was thus beyond the reach of the Act. The Court of Appeals rejected the district court's holding that residual discrimination from previous employment practices was beyond the scope of the Act, but it held the district court was correct in its conclusion that there was no showing of a racial purpose or invidious intent in the promulgation of the new hiring requirements. The Court of Appeals, therefore, held that the use of such standards was not prohibited by the Act. Decision?

20.    Mechelle Vinson was an employee of Meritor Savings Bank for approximately four years. Beginning as a teller-trainee, she ultimately advanced to the position of assistant branch manager. Her promotions were based solely upon merit. Sidney Taylor, a vice president of the bank and manager of the branch office in which Vinson worked, was Vinson's supervisor throughout her employment with the bank. After the bank fired Vinson for her abusive use of sick leave, Vinson brought an action against Taylor and the bank, alleging that during her employment she had "constantly been subjected to sexual

harassment" by Taylor in violation of Title VII of the Civil Rights Act of 1964. At trial, Vinson stated that Taylor repeatedly demanded sexual favors from her, fondled her in front of other employees, and forcibly raped her on a number of occasions. Taylor and the bank categorically denied Vinson's allegations. The district court denied relief to Vinson, finding that any sexual relationship between Vinson and Taylor "was a voluntary one having nothing to do with her continued employment * * * or her advancement or promotions at that institution." Notwithstanding this conclusion, the district court went on to determine that "the bank was without notice [of Taylor's alleged conduct] and cannot be held liable for the alleged actions of Taylor." The Court of Appeals reversed. Decision?

**Internet Exercise** Find the Occupational Safety and Health Administration's home page and (a) explore "what's new," (b) determine what OSHA is doing about workplace violence and injury, (c) examine the Occupational Injury and Illness Incidence rates, and (d) review the latest news releases.

# CHAPTER 44

# Securities Regulation

T he primary purpose of Federal securities regulation is to foster public confidence in the securities market by preventing fraudulent practices in the sale of securities. Federal securities law consists principally of two statutes: the Securities Act of 1933, which focuses on the issuance of securities, and the Securities Exchange Act of 1934, which deals mainly with trading in issued securities. These "secondary" transactions greatly exceed in number and dollar value the original offerings by issuers.

Both statutes are administered by the Securities and Exchange Commission (SEC), an independent, quasi-judicial agency consisting of five commissioners. The SEC has the power to seek in a Federal district court civil injunctions against violations of the statutes, to recommend that the Justice Department bring criminal prosecutions, and to issue orders censuring, suspending, or expelling broker-dealers, investment advisers, and investment companies. The Securities Enforcement Remedies and Penny Stock Reform Act of 1990 granted the SEC the power to issue cease-and-desist orders and to impose administrative, civil penalties up to $550,000. Congress enacted the Private Securities Litigation Reform Act of 1995 (Reform Act), which amends both the 1933 Act and the 1934 Act. One of its provisions grants authority to the SEC to bring civil actions for specified violations of the 1934 Act against aiders and abettors (those who knowingly provide substantial assistance to a person who violates the statute).

The Reform Act sought to prevent abuses in private securities fraud lawsuits. To prevent certain State private securities class action lawsuits alleging fraud from being used to frustrate the objectives of the Reform Act, Congress enacted the Securities Litigation Uniform Standards Act of 1998. The act sets national standards for securities class action lawsuits involving nationally traded securities, while preserving the appropriate enforcement powers of State securities regulators and leaving unchanged the current treatment of individual lawsuits. The act amends both the 1933 Act and the 1934 Act by prohibiting any private class action suit in State or Federal court by any private party based upon State statutory or common law alleging: (1) an untrue statement or omission in connection with the purchase or sale of a covered security; or (2) that the defendant used any manipulative or deceptive device in connection with such a transaction.

The 1933 Act has two basic objectives: (1) to provide investors with material information concerning securities offered for sale to the public and (2) to prohibit misrepresentation, deceit, and other fraudulent acts and practices in the sale of securities generally, whether or not they are required to be registered.

The 1934 Act extends protection to investors trading in securities that are already issued and outstanding. The 1934 Act also imposes disclosure requirements on publicly held corporations and regulates tender offers and proxy solicitations.

Effective October 6, 1995, the SEC provided interpretative guidance for the use of electronic media for the delivery of information required by the Federal securities laws. The SEC defined *electronic media* to include audiotapes, videotapes, facsimiles, CD-ROM, electronic mail, bulletin boards, Internet Web sites, and computer networks. Basically, electronic delivery must provide notice, access, and evidence of delivery comparable to that provided by paper delivery.

The SEC has established the EDGAR (Electronic Data Gathering, Analysis, and Retrieval) computer system which performs automated collection, validation, indexing, acceptance, and dissemination of reports required to be filed with the SEC. Its primary purpose is to increase the efficiency and fairness of the securities market for the benefit of investors, corporations, and the economy by speeding up the receipt, acceptance, dissemination, and analysis of corporate information filed with the SEC. After a phase-in period, the SEC now requires all public domestic companies to make their filings on EDGAR, except filings exempted for hardship. EDGAR filings are posted at the SEC's Web site 24 hours after the date of filing.

In addition to the Federal laws regulating the sale of securities, each State has its own laws regulating such sales within its borders. Commonly called **blue sky laws,** these statutes all contain provisions prohibiting fraud in the sale of securities. In addition, most States require the registration of securities and also regulate brokers and dealers.

Any person who sells securities must comply with the Federal securities laws as well as with the securities laws of each State in which he intends to offer his securities. However, in 1996 Congress enacted the National Securities Markets Improvements Act, preempting State regulation of the offerings of certain securities. Because the State securities laws vary greatly, this chapter will discuss only the 1933 Act and the 1934 Act.

# SECURITIES ACT OF 1933

The 1933 Act, also called the "Truth in Securities Act," requires that a registration statement be filed with the Securities and Exchange Commission and that it become effective before any securities may be offered for sale to the public, unless either the securities or the transaction in which they are offered is exempt from registration. The purpose of registration is to disclose financial and other information about the issuer and those who control it, so that potential investors may appraise the merits of the securities. The 1933 Act also requires that potential investors be furnished with a **prospectus** (a document offering the securities for sale) containing the important data set forth in the registration statement. The 1933 Act prohibits fraud in all sales of securities involving interstate commerce or the mails, even if the securities are exempt from the registration and disclosure requirements of the 1933 Act. Civil and criminal liability may be imposed for violations of the 1933 Act.

The National Securities Markets Improvements Act of 1996 broadly authorized the SEC to issue regulations or rules exempting any person, security, or transaction from any of the provisions of the 1933 Act or the SEC's rules promulgated under that act. This authorization extends so far as such exemption is necessary or appropriate in the public interest and is consistent with the protection of investors.

## DEFINITION OF A SECURITY

Section 2(1) of the 1933 Act defines a **security** as

any note, stock, treasury stock, bond, debenture, evidence of indebtedness, certificate of interest or participation in any profit-sharing agreement, collateral-trust certificate, preorganization certificate or subscription, transferable share, investment contract, voting-trust certificate, certificate of deposit for a security, fractional undivided interest in oil, gas, or other mineral rights, any put, call, straddle, option, or privilege on any security . . . or, in general, any interest or instrument commonly known as a "security," or any certificate of interest or participation in, temporary or interim certificate for, receipt for, guarantee of, or warrant or right to subscribe to or purchase, any of the foregoing.

This definition broadly incorporates the many types of instruments that fall within the concept of a security. Furthermore, the courts generally have interpreted the statutory definition to include nontraditional forms of investments. In *Landreth Timber Co. v. Landreth*, 471 U.S. 681 (1985), the Supreme Court adopted a two-tier analysis of what constitutes a security. Under this analysis, the Court will presumptively treat as a security a financial instrument designated as a note, stock, bond, or other instrument specifically named in the Act.

 *See Case 44–1*

On the other hand, if a financial transaction lacks the traditional characteristics of an instrument specifically named in the statute, the Court has used a three-part test, derived from *Securities and Exchange Commission v. W.J. Howey Co.*, 328 U.S. 293 (1946), to determine whether that financial transaction constitutes an investment contract and thus a security. Under the *Howey* test, a financial instrument or transaction that involves (1) an investment in a common venture (2) premised on a reasonable expectation of profit (3) to be derived from the entrepreneurial or managerial efforts of others constitutes an investment contract. In certain circumstances, investments in limited partnership interests, citrus groves, whiskey warehouse receipts, real estate condominiums, cattle, franchises, and pyramid schemes have been held to be securities under this test.

## REGISTRATION OF SECURITIES

The 1933 Act prohibits the offer or sale of any security through the use of the mails or any means of interstate commerce unless a registration statement for that security is in effect or the issuer secures an exemption from registration. Section 5. The purpose of registration is to adequately and accurately disclose financial and other information upon which investors may appraise the merits of the securities. Registration does not, however, insure investors against loss—the SEC does not judge the financial merits of any security. Moreover, the SEC does not guarantee the accuracy of the information presented in a registration statement.

## Disclosure Requirements

In general, registration (Form S–1) calls for disclosure of such information as (1) a description of the registrant's properties and business, (2) a description of the significant provisions of the security to be offered for sale and its relationship to the registrant's other capital securities, (3) information about the management of the registrant, and (4) financial statements certified by independent public accountants. In 1992, the SEC imposed new disclosure requirements regarding compensation paid to senior executives and directors. The registration statement must be signed by the issuer, its chief executive officer, its chief financial officer, its chief accounting officer, and a majority of its board of directors.

A registration statement and prospectus become public immediately on filing with the SEC. The effective date of a registration statement is the twentieth day after filing, although the commission, at its discretion, may advance the effective date or require an amendment to the filing, which will begin a new twenty-day period.

Before the filing of the registration statement, it is unlawful to sell, offer to sell, or offer to buy the securities, though the issuer may give notice that it proposes to make a public offer. Furthermore, although it is unlawful to sell the securities until the effective date, the issuer may, after filing the registration statement, *offer* the securities (1) orally; (2) by certain summaries of the information in the registration statement, as permitted by SEC rules; (3) by a "tombstone advertisement" that identifies the security, its price, and by whom orders will be executed; or (4) by a preliminary prospectus, called a "red herring," which may contain substantially the same information as a final prospectus but must bear a legend in red ink stating that the registration statement has not become effective. After the effective date, the issuer may make sales, provided the purchaser has received a final prospectus.

◆ *See Figure 44–1*

In 1998 the SEC issued a rule requiring issuers to write and design the cover page, summary, and risk factors section of their prospectuses in plain English. In these sections issuers must use short sentences; definite, concrete, everyday language; tabular presentation of complex information; no legal or business jargon; and no multiple negatives. Issuers will also have to design these sections to make them inviting to the reader and free from legalese and repetition that blur important information.

## Integrated Disclosure

The disclosure system under the 1933 Act developed independently of that required by the 1934 Act, which is discussed later in this chapter. As a result, issuers subject to both statutes were compelled to provide duplicative or overlapping disclosure. In an effort to reduce or

**FIGURE 44–1** Permissible Sales Activities

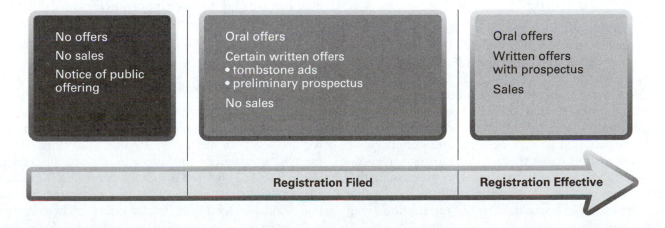

eliminate unnecessary duplication of corporate reporting, the SEC in 1982 adopted an integrated system that provides for three levels of disclosure, depending on the issuer's reporting history and market following. All issuers may use the detailed form (S–1) described previously. Corporations that have reported continuously under the 1934 Act for at least three years are permitted to disclose less detailed information in the 1933 Act registration statement (S–2) and to incorporate by reference certain information from reports filed under the 1934 Act. Those corporations that have filed continuously under the 1934 Act for at least one year and that have a minimum market value of publicly held voting and nonvoting stock of $75 million are permitted to disclose even less detail in the 1933 Act registration (S–3) and to incorporate even more information by reference to 1934 Act reports.

In 1992, the SEC issued new rules establishing an integrated registration and reporting system for small business issuers. These rules are intended to facilitate access to the public financial markets for start-up and developing companies and to reduce costs for small business issuers wishing to have their securities traded in public markets. The rules define a small business issuer as a noninvestment company whose annual revenues total less than $25 million and whose voting stock has a market value of less than $25 million. A new form (SB–2) has been designated as the registration form for small business issuers, although, if eligible, they may use Forms S–2 or S–3. Form SB–2 has no dollar limit. In 1993 the SEC adopted another new form (SB–1), which small business issuers may use to sell up to $10 million of securities in any twelve-month period. Form SB–1 is a streamlined disclosure document permitting either a narrative or a question-and-answer format.

## Shelf Registrations

Shelf registrations permit certain qualified issuers to register securities that are to be offered and sold "off the shelf" on a delayed or continuous basis in the future. This is a departure from the requirement that an issuer must file a registration for *every* new distribution of nonexempt securities. **Rule 415** of the SEC, which governs shelf registrations, requires that the information in the original registration be kept accurate and current. Only companies eligible to use the S–3 short form for registration qualify for shelf registrations. The issuer must reasonably expect that the securities will be sold within two years of the effective date of the registration. Shelf registrations allow issuers to respond more quickly to

market conditions such as changes in stock prices and interest rates.

## EXEMPT SECURITIES

The 1933 Act exempts a number of specific securities from its registration requirements. Because these exemptions apply to the securities themselves, the securities also may be resold without registration.

### Short-Term Commercial Paper

The Act exempts any note, draft, or bankers' acceptance (a draft accepted by a bank) issued for working capital that has a maturity of not more than nine months when issued. Section 3(a)(3). This exemption is not available, however, if the proceeds are to be used for permanent purposes, such as the acquisition of a plant, or if the paper is of a type not ordinarily purchased by the general public.

### Other Exempt Securities

The 1933 Act also exempts the following kinds of securities from registration:

1. securities issued or guaranteed by domestic governmental organizations, such as municipal bonds;
2. securities of domestic banks and savings and loan associations;
3. securities of not-for-profit, charitable organizations;
4. certain securities issued by Federally regulated common carriers; and
5. insurance policies and annuity contracts issued by State-regulated insurance companies.

In addition, the Bankruptcy Act exempts securities issued by a debtor if they are offered under a reorganization plan in exchange for a claim or interest in the debtor. Bankruptcy Act, Section 1145(a).

## EXEMPT TRANSACTIONS FOR ISSUERS

In addition to exempting specific types of securities, the 1933 Act also exempts *issuers* from the registration requirements for certain kinds of transactions. These exempt transactions include (1) private placements (Rule 506), (2) limited offers not exceeding $5 million (Rule 505), (3) limited offers not exceeding $1 million (Rule 504), and (4) limited offers solely to accredited investors (Section 4(6)). Except for Rule 504, these exemptions from registration apply only to the transaction in which the securities are issued; therefore, any resale must be made by registration, unless the resale qualifies as an exempt transaction.

In addition, the 1933 Act provides a number of securities exemptions that are in effect transaction exemptions. These include intrastate issues, exchanges between an issuer and its security holders, and reorganization securities issued and exchanged with court or other governmental approval. These exemptions apply only to the original issuance; resales may be made only by registration unless the resale qualifies as an exempt transaction.

Another transaction exemption is Regulation A, which permits an issuer to sell a limited amount of securities in an unregistered public offering if certain conditions are met. Unlike other transaction exemptions, Regulation A places no restrictions upon the resale of securities issued pursuant to it.

◆ *See Figure 44–2*

## Limited Offers

The 1933 Act exempts, or authorizes the SEC to exempt, transactions that do not require the protection of regis-

tration because they either involve a small amount of money or are made in a limited manner. Sections 3(b) and 4(2). Promulgated in 1982 to simplify and clarify the transaction exemptions relating to small issues and small issuers, Regulation D contains three separate exemptions (Rules 504, 505, and 506), each involving limited offers. Section 4(6), also aimed at small issues, is a companion section to the exemptions under Regulation D.

Securities sold pursuant to these exemptions (with the exception of those sold pursuant to Rule 504) are considered **restricted securities** and may be resold only by registration or in another transaction exempt from registration. An issuer who uses these exemptions must take reasonable care to prevent nonexempt, unregistered resales of restricted securities. Reasonable care includes, but is not limited to, the following: (a) making a reasonable inquiry to determine if the purchaser is acquiring the securities for herself or for other persons; (b) providing written disclosure prior to the sale to each purchaser that the securities have not been registered and therefore cannot be resold unless they are registered or unless an exemption from registration is available; and (c) placing a legend on the securities certificate stating that the securities have not been registered and that they are restricted securities.

**FIGURE 44–2**  Registration and Exemptions under the 1933 Act

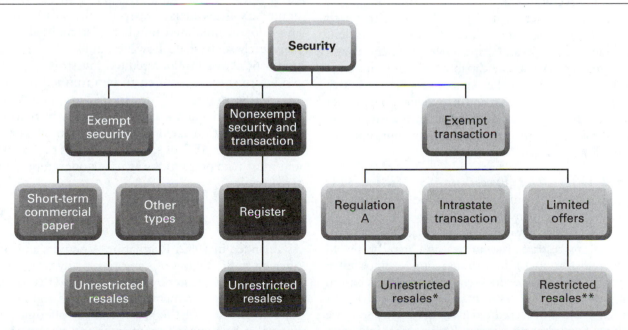

\* Under intrastate exemption, resales to nonresidents may only be made nine months after the last sale in the initial issuance.

\*\* Except under Rule 504.

*Private Placements* The most important transaction exemption for issuers is the so-called private placement provision of the Act, which exempts "transactions by an issuer not involving any public offering." Section 4(2). SEC **Rule 506** establishes a nonexclusive safe harbor for limited offers and sales without regard to the dollar amount of the offering. While compliance with the rule ensures the exemption, the exemption is not presumed to be unavailable for noncomplying transactions.

Securities sold under this exemption are restricted securities and may be resold only by registration or in a transaction exempt from registration. General advertising or general solicitation is not permitted. The issue may be purchased by an unlimited number of "accredited investors" and by no more than thirty-five other purchasers. **Accredited investors** include banks, insurance companies, investment companies, executive officers or directors of the issuer, savings and loan associations, registered broker-dealers, certain employee benefit plans with total assets in excess of $5 million, any person whose net worth exceeds $1 million, and any person whose income exceeded $200,000 in each of the two preceding years and who reasonably expects an income in excess of $200,000 in the current year. Before a sale involving any nonaccredited investors, such purchasers must receive specified material information about the issuer, its business, and the securities being offered. If the sale involves only accredited investors, such disclosure is not mandatory. The issuer must reasonably believe that each purchaser who is not an accredited investor has sufficient knowledge regarding and experience in financial and business matters to evaluate capably the merits and risks of the investment or has the services of a representative possessing such knowledge and experience. The issuer must notify the SEC of sales made under the exemption and must take precautions against nonexempt, unregistered resales.

*Limited Offers Not Exceeding $5 Million* SEC **Rule 505** exempts from registration those offerings by noninvestment company issuers that do not exceed $5 million over twelve months. Securities sold under this exemption are restricted securities and may be resold only by registration or in a transaction exempt from registration. General advertising or general solicitation is not permitted. The issue may be purchased by an unlimited number of accredited investors and by no more than thirty-five other purchasers. Before a sale involving any nonaccredited investors, such purchasers must receive specified material information about the issuer, its

business, and the securities being offered; in the absence of nonaccredited investors, such disclosure is unnecessary. Unlike the issuer under Rule 506, however, the issuer under Rule 505 is *not* required to believe reasonably that each nonaccredited investor, either alone or with his representative, has sufficient knowledge and experience regarding financial matters to be capable of evaluating the merits and risks of the investment. Like its counterpart under Rule 506, the issuer must take precautions against nonexempt, unregistered resales and must notify the SEC of sales made under the exemption.

*Limited Offers Not Exceeding $1 Million* As amended in 1992, SEC **Rule 504** provides private, noninvestment company issuers with an unconditional exemption from registration for small issues not exceeding $1 million within twelve months. Issuers required to report under the 1934 Act and investment companies may not use Rule 504. The issuer is to notify the SEC of sales under the rule, which permits sales to an unlimited number of investors and does not require the issuer to furnish any information to them. The exemption does not forbid general solicitations, and acquired shares are freely transferable.

*Limited Offers Solely to Accredited Investors* In 1980, Congress added **Section 4(6)**, which provides an exemption for offers and sales of $5 million made by an issuer solely to accredited investors. General advertising or public solicitation is not permitted. As with Rules 505 and 506, an unlimited number of accredited investors may purchase the issue; however, unlike these rules, Section 4(6) allows no unaccredited investors to purchase. No information is required to be furnished to the purchasers. Securities sold under this exemption are restricted securities and may be resold only by registration or in a transaction exempt from registration. The issuer must notify the SEC of sales made under the exemption and must take precautions against nonexempt, unregistered resales.

## Regulation A

As amended in 1992, Regulation A permits an issuer to offer up to $5 million of securities in any twelve-month period without registering them, provided that the issuer files an offering statement with the SEC's regional office prior to the sale of the securities. An offering circular must also be provided to offerees and purchasers. The issuer may make offers upon filing the offering statement but may make sales only after the SEC has qualified it. Issuers required to report under the 1934 Act and investment companies may not use Regulation A. Regulation A filings are less detailed and time-consuming than full registration statements, and the required financial statements are simpler and need not be audited unless the issuer is a reporting company under the 1934 Act. Issuers now may use an optional, simplified question-and-answer disclosure document.

Regulation A sets no restrictions regarding the number or qualifications of investors who may purchase securities under its provisions. Furthermore, securities sold under Regulation A may be resold freely after they are issued.

## Intrastate Issues

The 1933 Act also exempts from registration any security that is part of an issue offered and sold only to persons resident within a single State where the issuer of such security is resident and doing business. Section 3(a)(11). This exemption is intended to apply to local issues representing local financing carried out by local persons through local investments. The exemption does not apply if *any* offeree, who need not become a purchaser, is not a resident of the State in which the issuer is resident.

The courts and the SEC have interpreted the exemption narrowly. **Rule 147**, promulgated by the SEC, provides a nonexclusive safe harbor for securing the intrastate exemption. Rule 147 requires that

1. the issuer be incorporated or organized in the State in which the issuance occurs;

2. the issuer be principally doing business in that State, which means that the issuer must derive 80 percent of its gross revenues from that State, 80 percent of its assets must be located in that State, and 80 percent of its net proceeds from the issue must be used in that State;

3. all of the *offerees* and purchasers be residents of that State;

4. no resales to nonresidents be made during the period of sale and for nine months after the last sale; and

5. the issuer take precautions against interstate distributions. Such precautions include (a) placing on the security certificate a legend stating that the securities have not been registered and that resales can be made only to residents of the State and (b) obtaining a written statement of residence from each purchaser.

◆ *See Figure 44–3*

## EXEMPT TRANSACTIONS FOR NON-ISSUERS

The 1933 Act requires registration for any sale by any person (including non-issuers) of any nonexempt security unless a statutory exemption can be found for the transaction. The Act, however, provides a transaction exemption for any person other than an issuer, underwriter, or dealer. Section 4(1). In addition, the Act exempts most transactions by dealers and brokers. Sections 4(3) and 4(4). These three provisions exempt from the registration requirements of the 1933 Act most secondary transactions; that is, the numerous resales that occur on an exchange or in the over-the-counter market.

**FIGURE 44–3** Exempt Transactions for Issuers under the 1933 Act

| Exemption | Price Limitation | Information Required | Limitations on Purchasers | Resales |
|---|---|---|---|---|
| **Regulation A** | $5 million | Offering circular | None | Unrestricted |
| **Intrastate Rule 147** | None | None | Intrastate only | Only to residents before 9 months |
| **Rule 506** | None | Material information to unaccredited purchasers | Unlimited accredited; 35 unaccredited | Restricted |
| **Rule 505** | $5 million | Material information to unaccredited purchasers | Unlimited accredited; 35 unaccredited | Restricted |
| **Rule 504** | $1 million | None | None | Unrestricted |
| **Section 4(6)** | $5 million | None | Only accredited | Restricted |

Nevertheless, these exemptions do not extend to some situations involving resales by non-issuers, in particular to (1) resales of restricted securities acquired under Regulation D (Rules 506 or 505) or Sections 4(6) and (2) sales of restricted *or* nonrestricted securities by affiliates. Such sales must be made pursuant to registration, Rule 144, or Regulation A. An **affiliate** is a person who controls, is controlled by, or is under common control with the issuer. **Control** is the direct or indirect possession of the power to direct the management and policies of a person through ownership of securities, by contract, or otherwise. Rule 405.

## Rule 144

Rule 144 of the SEC sets forth conditions that, if met by an affiliate or any person selling restricted securities, exempt her from registering those securities. The rule requires that there be adequate current public information about the issuer, that the person selling under the rule have owned the securities for at least one year, that she sell them only in limited amounts in unsolicited brokers' transactions, and that notice of the sale be provided to the SEC. A person who is not an affiliate of the issuer when the restricted securities are sold and who has owned the securities for at least two years may, however, sell them in unlimited amounts and is not subject to any of the other requirements of Rule 144. Sales by an affiliate are subject to Rule 144 whether the securities are restricted or nonrestricted; however, an affiliate who sells nonrestricted securities need not comply with the one-year holding period.

## Rule 144A

While Rule 144 permits sales of restricted securities, the requirements of the rule have hampered the liquidity of privately placed securities. To improve the liquidity of such securities, in 1990 the SEC adopted Rule 144A, which provides an additional, nonexclusive safe harbor from registration for resales of restricted securities. Only securities that at the time of issue are not of the same class as securities listed on a national securities exchange or quoted in a U.S. automated interdealer quotation system ("nonfungible securities") may be sold under Rule 144A. Such nonfungible securities may be sold only to a qualified institutional buyer, defined generally as an institution that in the aggregate owns and invests on a discretionary basis at least $100 million in securities. Rule 144A also requires the seller of the nonfungible securities to take reasonable steps to ensure that the buyer knows that the seller is relying on Rule 144A. In addition, special requirements apply to securities issued by foreign companies. Securities acquired pursuant to Rule 144A are restricted securities.

## Regulation A

In addition to providing issuers an exemption from registration for securities up to $5 million, Regulation A provides an exemption for non-issuers. Use of this exemption, which places a $1.5 million limit on the total amount of securities sold in any twelve-month period by all non-issuers, requires compliance with all of the conditions Regulation A imposes upon issuers, as discussed above.

## *LIABILITY*

To implement the statutory objectives of providing full disclosure and preventing fraud in the sale of securities, the 1933 Act imposes a number of sanctions for noncompliance with its requirements. These sanctions include administrative remedies by the SEC, civil liability to injured investors, and criminal penalties.

The Reform Act provides "forward-looking" statements (predictions) a "safe harbor" under the 1933 Act from civil liability based on an untrue statement of material fact or an omission of a material fact necessary to make the statement not misleading. The safe harbor applies only to issuers required to report under the 1934 Act. The safe harbor eliminates civil liability if a forward-looking statement is (1) immaterial, (2) made without actual knowledge that it was false or misleading, or (3) identified as a forward-looking statement and is accompanied by meaningful cautionary statements identifying important factors that could cause actual results to differ materially from those predicted. "Forward-looking statements" include projections of revenues, income, earnings per share, capital expenditures, dividends, or capital structure; management's plans and objectives for future operations; and statements of future economic performance. The safe harbor provision, however, does not cover statements made in connection with an initial public offering, a tender offer, a going private transaction, or offerings by a partnership or a limited liability company.

## Unregistered Sales

The Act imposes express civil liability for the sale of an unregistered security that is required to be registered, the sale of a registered security without delivery of a prospectus, the sale of a security by use of an outdated prospectus, or the offer of a sale prior to the filing of the registration statement. **Section 12(a)(1).** Liability is strict or absolute because there are no defenses. The person who purchases a security sold in violation of this provision has the right to tender it back to the seller and recover the purchase price. If the purchaser no longer owns the security, he may recover monetary damages from the seller.

## False Registration Statements

When securities have been sold subject to a registration statement, **Section 11** of the Act imposes express liability upon those who have included any untrue statement in the registration statement or who omit from the statement any material fact. **Material** matters are those to which a reasonable investor would be substantially likely to attach importance in determining whether to purchase the security registered. SEC Rule 405. Usually, proof of reliance upon the misstatement or omission is not required. The section imposes liability upon (1) the issuer; (2) all persons who signed the registration statement, including the principal executive officer, principal financial officer, and principal accounting officer; (3) every person who was a director or partner; (4) every accountant, engineer, appraiser, or expert who prepared or certified any part of the registration statement; and (5) all underwriters. These persons are generally jointly and severally liable for the amount paid for the security, less either its value at the time of suit or the price for which it was sold, to any person who acquires the security without knowledge of the untruth or omission. A defendant is not liable for any or the entire amount otherwise recoverable under Section 11 that the defendant proves was caused by something other than the defective disclosure. The court may award attorneys' fees against any party who brings suit or asserts a defense without merit.

An expert is liable only for misstatements or omissions in the portion of the registration that he prepared or certified. Moreover, any defendant, other than the issuer (who has strict liability), may assert the affirmative defense of due diligence. This **due diligence** defense generally requires the defendant to show that she had reasonable grounds to believe, and did believe, that there were no untrue statements or material omissions. In some instances, due diligence requires a reasonable investigation to determine grounds for belief. The standard of reasonableness for such investigation and such grounds

is that required of a prudent person in the management of his own property. Section 11(c).

 **See Case 44–2**

## Antifraud Provisions

The 1933 Act also contains two antifraud provisions: Section 12(a)(2) and Section 17(a). In addition, Rule 10b–5 of the 1934 Act applies to the issuance or sale of all securities, even those exempted by the 1933 Act. Rule 10b–5 is discussed later in this chapter.

*Section 12(a)(2)* Section 12(a)(2) imposes express liability upon any person who offers or sells a security by means of a prospectus or oral communication that contains an untrue statement of material fact or omits a material fact. That liability extends only to the immediate purchaser, provided she did not know of the untruth or omission. The seller may avoid liability by proving that he did not know and in the exercise of reasonable care could not have known of the untrue statement or omission. The seller is liable to the purchaser for the amount paid upon tender of the security. If the purchaser no longer owns the security, she may recover damages from the seller. A defendant is not liable for any or the entire amount otherwise recoverable under Section 12(a)(2) that the defendant proves was caused by something other than the defective disclosure.

*Section 17(a)* Section 17(a) makes it unlawful for any person in the offer or sale of any securities, whether registered or not, to do any of the following when using any means of transportation or communication in interstate commerce or the mails:

1. employ any device, scheme, or artifice to defraud;
2. obtain money or property by means of any untrue statement of a material fact or any statement that omits a material fact, without which the information is misleading; or
3. engage in any transaction, practice, or course of business that operates or would operate as a fraud or deceit upon the purchaser.

There is some doubt whether the courts may imply a private right of action for persons injured by violations of this section. The Supreme Court has reserved this question, and the lower courts are divided on the issue. The SEC may, however, bring enforcement actions under Section 17(a).

## Criminal Sanctions

The 1933 Act imposes criminal sanctions upon any person who willfully violates any of its provisions or the rules and regulations the SEC promulgates pursuant to the Act. Section 24. Conviction may carry a fine of not more than $10,000 or imprisonment of not more than five years, or both.

◆ *See Figure 44–4*

# SECURITIES EXCHANGE ACT OF 1934

The Securities Exchange Act of 1934 deals principally with the secondary distribution (resale) of securities. The definition of a security in the 1934 Act is substantially the same as the definition in the 1933 Act. The 1934 Act seeks to ensure fair and orderly securities markets by prohibiting fraudulent and manipulative practices and by establishing rules for market operations. It provides protection for holders of all securities listed on national exchanges, as well as for those holders of equity securities of companies traded over the counter whose corporate assets exceed $10 million and whose equity securities include a class with five hundred or more shareholders. Companies must register such securities and are also subject to the 1934 Act's periodic reporting requirements, short-swing profits provision, tender offer provisions, and proxy solicitation provisions, as well as the internal control and recordkeeping requirements of the Foreign Corrupt Practices Act. An over-the-counter issuer may terminate its registration when the holders of its registered equity securities number fewer than three hundred or when the issuer has had fewer than five hundred shareholders *and* assets totaling less than $10 million on the last day of each of the past three years. In addition, issuers of securities, whether registered under the 1934 Act or not, must comply with the antifraud and antibribery provisions of the Act.

◆ *See Figure 44–5*

**FIGURE 44–4**  Registration and Liability Provisions of the 1933 Act

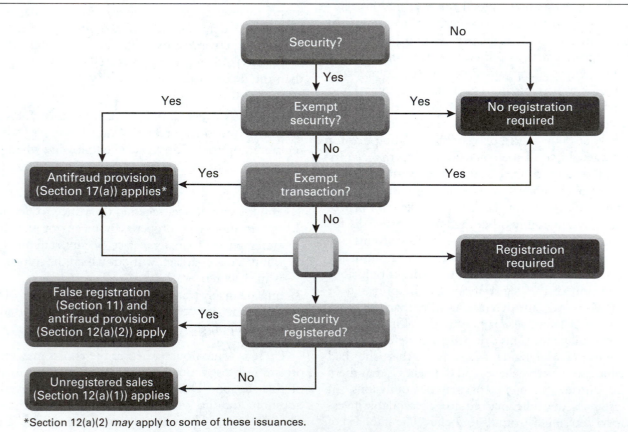

*Section 12(a)(2) *may* apply to some of these issuances.

**FIGURE 44–5** Applicability of the 1934 Act

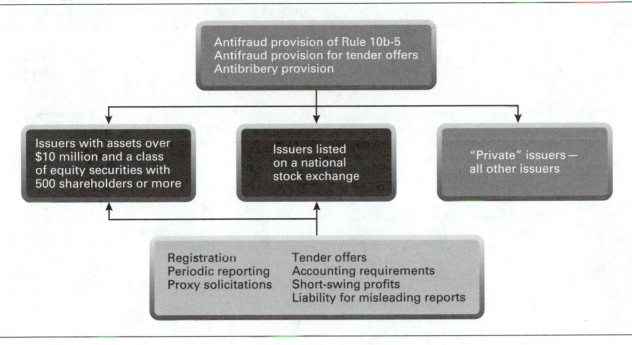

The National Securities Markets Improvements Act of 1996 broadly authorized the SEC to issue regulations, rules, or orders exempting any person, security, or transaction from any of the provisions of the 1934 Act or the SEC's rules promulgated under that act. This authorization extends so far as such exemption is necessary or appropriate in the public interest and is consistent with the protection of investors. This exemptive authority does not, however, extend to the regulation of government securities broker-dealers.

## DISCLOSURE

The 1934 Act imposes significant disclosure requirements upon reporting companies. These include the filing of securities registrations, periodic reports, disclosure statements for proxy solicitations, and disclosure statements for tender offers, as well as compliance with the accounting requirements imposed by the Foreign Corrupt Practices Act. As part of its integrated registration and reporting system for small business issuers, in 1992 the SEC developed a new series of forms for qualifying issuers to use for registration and periodic reporting under the 1934 Act. Also in 1992, the SEC imposed new disclosure requirements for registration statements, periodic reports, and proxy statements that contain information regarding the compensation paid to senior

executives and directors. The compensation disclosure rules are designed to provide shareholders with a lucid presentation of both annual and long-term compensation for senior executives over the previous three years. In addition, the issuer must inform the shareholders of their cumulative return over the previous five years and how that figure compares with the Standard and Poor's 500 Composite Stock Price Index *and* any recognized industry index.

◆ *See Figure 44–6*

## Registration Requirements for Securities

The 1934 Act requires all regulated publicly held companies to register with the SEC. Section 12. These one-time registrations apply to an entire class of securities. Thus, they differ from registrations under the Securities Act of 1933, which relate only to the securities involved in a specific offering. Registration requires disclosure of information such as the organization, financial structure, and nature of the business; the terms, positions, rights, and privileges of the different classes of outstanding securities; the names of the directors, officers, and underwriters and of each security holder owning more than 10 percent of any class of nonexempt equity security; bonus and profit-sharing arrangements; and balance sheets and

**FIGURE 44–6** Disclosure under the 1934 Act

| | Initial Registration | Periodic Reporting | Insider Reporting | Proxy Statement | Tender Offer |
|---|---|---|---|---|---|
| **Registrant** | Issuer if regulated, publicly held company | Issuer if regulated, publicly held company | Statutory insiders (directors, officers, and principal stockholders) | Issuer and other persons soliciting proxies | 5 percent stockholder, tender offeror, or issuer |
| **Information** | Nature of business; Financial structure; Directors and executive officers; Financial statements | Annual, quarterly, or current report updating information in initial registration | Initial statement of beneficial ownership of equity securities; Changes in beneficial ownership | Details of solicitation; Legal terms of proxy; Annual report (if directors to be elected) | Identity and background; Terms of transaction; Source of funds; Intentions |
| **Filing Date** | Within 120 days after becoming a reporting company | Annual: within 90 days after year's end; Quarterly: within 45 days after quarter's end; Current: within 15 days after any material change | Within 10 days of (1) becoming a statutory insider or (2) the end of a month in which a change in ownership takes place | 10 days before final proxy statement is distributed | 5 percent stockholder: within 10 days after acquiring more than 5 percent of a class of registered securities; Tender offeror: before tender offer is made; Issuer: before offer to repurchase |
| **Purpose of Disclosure** | Adequate and accurate disclosure of material facts regarding securities listed on a national exchange or traded publicly over the counter | Update information contained in initial registration | Prevent unfair use of information which may have been obtained by statutory insider | Full disclosure of material information; Facilitation of shareholder proposals | Adequate and accurate disclosure of material facts; Opportunity to reach uncoerced decision |

profit-and-loss statements for the three preceding fiscal years.

## Periodic Reporting Requirements

Following registration, an issuer must file specified annual (10–K) and periodic (10–Q and 8–K) reports to update the information contained in the original registration. Also subject to the periodic reporting requirements are issuers who have filed a 1933 Act registration statement with respect to any security. Section 15. This duty is suspended, however, in any subsequent year during which the securities registered under the 1933 Act are held by fewer than three hundred persons. The Act also requires that each director, officer, and any person who owns more than 10 percent of a registered equity security

file reports with the SEC for any month during which changes in his ownership of such equity securities have occurred.

## Proxy Solicitations

A **proxy** is a writing signed by a shareholder authorizing a named person to vote his shares of stock at a specified shareholders' meeting. To ensure that shareholders have adequate information with which to vote, the 1934 Act regulates the proxy solicitation process. The Act makes it unlawful for any person to solicit any proxy with respect to any registered security "in contravention of such rules and regulations as the Commission may prescribe." Section 14. **Solicitation** includes any request for a proxy, any request not to execute a proxy, or any request to revoke a proxy.

**Proxy Statements**   Rule 14a–3 prohibits the solicitation of a proxy unless each person solicited has been furnished with a written proxy statement containing specified information. An issuer making solicitations must furnish security holders with a *proxy statement* describing all material facts concerning the matters being submitted to their vote, together with a *proxy form* on which the security holders can indicate their approval or disapproval of each proposal to be presented. Even a company that submits a matter to a shareholder vote rather than solicit proxies must provide its shareholders with information substantially equivalent to what would appear in a proxy statement. With few exceptions, the issuer must file preliminary copies of a proxy statement and proxy form with the SEC at least ten days prior to the first date they are to be sent. In addition, in an election of directors, solicitations of proxies by a person other than the issuer are subject to similar disclosure requirements. The issuer in such an election also must include an annual report with the proxy statement.

**Shareholder Proposals**   Where management makes a solicitation, any security holder entitled to vote has the opportunity to communicate with other security holders. Upon written request, the corporation must mail the communication at the security holder's expense or, at its option, promptly furnish to that security holder a current list of security holders.

If an eligible security holder entitled to vote submits a timely proposal for action at a forthcoming meeting, management must include the proposal in its proxy statement and provide security holders with an opportunity to vote for or against it. To be eligible, the holder must own the lesser of 1 percent or $2,000 in market value of the security for at least one year prior to submitting the proposal. If management opposes the proposal, it must include in its proxy materials a statement by the security holder in support of the proposal. The aggregate length of the proposal and the supporting statement may not exceed five hundred words. A security holder is limited to submitting one proposal to an issuer each year.

Management may omit a proposal if, among other things, (1) under State law it is not a proper subject for shareholder action, (2) it would require the company to violate any law, (3) it is beyond the issuer's power to effectuate, (4) it relates to the conduct of the ordinary business operations of the issuer, or (5) it relates to an election to office.

## Tender Offers

A **tender offer** is a general invitation by a buyer (bidder) to the shareholders of a target company to tender their shares for sale at a specified price for a specified time. In 1968, Congress enacted the Williams Act, which amended the 1934 Act to extend reporting and disclosure requirements to tender offers and other block acquisitions. The purpose of the Williams Act is to provide public shareholders with full disclosure by both the bidder and the target company, so that the shareholders may make an informed decision.

**Disclosure Requirements**   The 1934 Act imposes disclosure requirements in three situations: (1) when a person or group acquires more than 5 percent of a class of voting securities registered under the 1934 Act, (2) when a person makes a tender offer for more than 5 percent of a class of registered equity securities, or (3) when the issuer makes an offer to repurchase its own registered shares. Although each situation is governed by different rules, the disclosure required is substantially the same. A statement must be filed with the SEC containing (1) the acquisitor's background; (2) the source of the funds used to acquire the securities; (3) the purpose of the acquisition, including any plans to liquidate the company or to make major changes in the corporate structure; (4) the number of shares owned; and (5) any relevant contracts, arrangements, or understandings. Sections 13(d) and 14(d). This disclosure is also required of anyone soliciting shareholders to accept or reject a tender offer. A copy of the statement must be furnished to each offeree and sent to the issuer.

The target company has ten days in which to respond to the bidder's tender offer by (1) recommending acceptance or rejection, (2) expressing no opinion and remaining neutral, or (3) stating that it is unable to take a position. The target company's response must include the reasons for the position taken.

**Required Practices**   A tender offer by either a third party or the issuer is subject to the following rules. The tender offer must be kept open for at least twenty business days and for at least ten days after any change in terms. Shareholders who tender their shares may withdraw them at any time during the offering period. The tender offer must be open to all holders of the class of shares subject to the offer, and all shares tendered must be purchased for the same price; thus, if an offering price is increased, both those who have tendered and those who have yet to tender will receive the benefit of the increase. A tender offeror who offers to purchase less than all of the outstanding securities of the target must accept, on a *pro rata* basis, securities tendered during the offer. During the tender offer, the bidder may buy shares of the target only through that tender offer.

*Defensive Tactics* When confronted by an uninvited takeover bid—or by a potential, uninvited bid—management of the target company may decide either to oppose the bid or seek to prevent it. The defensive tactics management employs to prevent or defend against undesired tender offers have developed (and are still evolving) into a highly ingenious, and metaphorically named, set of maneuvers, some of which require considerable planning and several of which are of questionable legality.

*State Regulation* More than two-thirds of the States have enacted statutes regulating tender offers. Although they vary greatly, most of these statutes tend to protect a target company from an unwanted tender offer. Some empower the State to review the merits of an offer or the adequacy of disclosure. Many impose waiting periods before the tender offer becomes effective. The State statutes generally require disclosures more detailed than those the Williams Act requires, and many of them exempt tender offers supported by the target company's management. A number of States have adopted fair price statutes, which require the acquisitor to pay to all shareholders the highest price paid to any shareholder. Some States have enacted business combination statutes prohibiting transactions with an acquisitor for a specified time after change in control, unless disinterested shareholders approve.

## Foreign Corrupt Practices Act

In 1977, Congress enacted the Foreign Corrupt Practices Act (FCPA) as an amendment to the 1934 Act. Amended in 1988, the Act imposes internal control requirements upon companies with securities registered under the 1934 Act and, as discussed later in this chapter, prohibits all domestic concerns from bribing foreign governmental or political officials.

The accounting requirements of the FCPA reflect the ideas that accurate recordkeeping is essential to managerial responsibility and that investors should be able to rely on the financial reports they receive. Accordingly, the accounting requirements were enacted (1) to assure that an issuer's books accurately reflect financial transactions, (2) to protect the integrity of independent audits of financial statements, and (3) to promote the reliability of financial information required by the 1934 Act.

The FCPA requires every issuer that has a class of registered securities to

1. make and keep books, records, and accounts which, in reasonable detail, accurately and fairly reflect the transactions and disposition of the assets of the issuer, and
2. devise and maintain a system of internal controls to assure that transactions are executed as authorized and recorded in conformity with generally accepted accounting principles, thereby establishing accountability with regard to assets and assuring that access to those assets is permitted only with management's authorization. Section 13(b).

## LIABILITY

To implement its objectives, the 1934 Act imposes a number of sanctions for noncompliance with its disclosure and antifraud requirements. These sanctions include civil liability to injured investors and issuers, civil penalties, and criminal penalties.

The Reform Act contains several provisions that affect civil liability under the 1934 Act. First, the Reform Act imposes on a plaintiff in any private action under the 1934 Act the burden of proving that the defendant's alleged violation of the 1934 Act caused the loss for which the plaintiff seeks to recover damages. Second, the Reform Act imposes a limit on the amount of damages a plaintiff can recover in any private action under the 1934 Act based on a material misstatement or omission in which she seeks to establish damages by reference to the market price of a security. The plaintiff may not recover damages in excess of the difference between the purchase or sale price she paid or received for the security and the mean trading price of that security during the ninety-day period beginning on the date when the information correcting the misstatement or omission is disseminated to the market. Third, the Reform Act provides a "safe harbor" under the 1934 Act from civil liability based on an untrue statement of material fact or an omission of a material fact necessary to make the statement not misleading. The safe harbor applies to issuers required to report under the 1934 Act and who make "forward-looking" statements (predictions) if the statements meet specified requirements. The requirements of the safe harbor and the transactions to which it does not apply were discussed earlier in this chapter.

## Misleading Statements in Reports

Section 18 imposes express civil liability upon any person who makes or causes to be made any false or misleading statement with respect to any material fact in any application, report, document, or registration filed with the SEC under the 1934 Act. Any person who purchased or sold a security in reliance upon a false or misleading statement without knowing that it was false or misleading may recover under Section 18. Nevertheless, a person who made such a statement or who caused one to be made is not liable if she proves that she acted in good faith and had no knowledge that such statement was false or misleading. The court may award attorneys' fees against either the plaintiff or the defendant.

## Short-Swing Profits

**Section 16(b)** of the 1934 Act imposes express liability upon insiders—directors, officers, and any person owning more than 10 percent of the stock of a corporation listed on a national stock exchange or registered with the SEC—for all profits resulting from their "short-swing" trading in such stock. If any insider sells such stock within six months from the date of its purchase or purchases such stock within six months from the date of a sale of the stock, the corporation is entitled to recover any and all profit the insider realizes from these transactions. The "profit" recoverable is calculated by matching the highest sale price against the lowest purchase price within the relevant six-month period. Losses cannot be offset against profits. Suit to recover such profit may be brought by the issuer or by the owner of any security of the issuer in the name and on behalf of the issuer if the issuer fails or refuses to bring such suit within sixty days of the owner's request.

## Antifraud Provision

**Section 10(b)** of the 1934 Act and SEC **Rule 10b–5** make it unlawful for any person to do any of the following when using the mails or facilities of interstate commerce in connection with the purchase or sale of any security:

1. employ any device, scheme, or artifice to defraud;
2. make any untrue statement of a material fact;
3. omit to state a material fact without which the information is misleading; or

4. engage in any act, practice, or course of business that operates or would operate as a fraud or deceit upon any person.

Rule 10b–5 applies to any purchase or sale of any security, whether it is registered under the 1934 Act or not, whether it is publicly traded or closely held, whether it is listed on an exchange or sold over the counter, or whether it is part of an initial issuance or a secondary distribution. There are *no* exemptions. The implied liability under Rule 10b–5 applies to purchaser as well as seller misconduct and allows both defrauded sellers and buyers to recover.

***Requisites of Rule 10b–5***   Recovery of damages under Rule 10b–5 requires proof of (1) a misstatement or omission (2) that is material, (3) made with *scienter,* and (4) relied upon (5) in connection with the purchase or sale of a security. This rule differs from common law fraud in that Rule 10b–5 imposes an affirmative duty of disclosure. A misstatement or omission is material if there is a substantial likelihood that a reasonable investor would consider it important in deciding whether to purchase or sell the security. Examples of material facts include substantial changes in dividends or earnings, significant misstatements of asset value, and the fact that the issuer is about to become a target of a tender offer. In an action for damages under Rule 10b–5, it must be shown that the violation was committed with **scienter**, or intentional misconduct. Negligence is not sufficient. Although the Supreme Court has yet to decide whether reckless conduct is sufficient to satisfy the requirement of *scienter,* a great majority of circuit and district courts have held recklessness to be sufficient.

Direct reliance may be difficult to prove in a 10b–5 action because the buyer and seller usually do not negotiate their deal face-to-face. Recognizing the special nature of securities market transactions, the Supreme Court adopted the fraud-on-the-market theory, which establishes a rebuttable presumption of reliance based on the premise that the market price of a stock reflects any misstatement or omission and that the fraudulently affected market price has injured the plaintiff.

Remedies for violations of Rule 10b–5 include rescission, damages, and injunctions. The courts are divided over the measure of damages to impose.

***Insider Trading***   Rule 10b–5 applies to sales or purchases of securities made by an "insider" who possesses material information that is not available to the general public. An insider who fails to disclose the material, nonpublic information before trading on the information will be liable under Rule 10b–5 unless he waits for the information to become public. **Insiders,** for the purpose of Rule 10b–5, include directors, officers, employees, and agents of the security issuer, as well as those with whom the issuer has entrusted information solely for corporate purposes, such as underwriters, accountants, lawyers, and consultants. In some instances, the rule also precludes persons who receive material, nonpublic information from insiders—tippees—from trading on that information. A tippee who knows or should know that an insider has breached his fiduciary duty to the shareholders by disclosing inside information to the tippee is under a duty not to trade on such information.

◆ *See Figure 44–7*

The U.S. Supreme Court has upheld the misappropriation theory as an additional and complementary basis for imposing liability for insider trading. Under this theory, a person may be held liable for insider trading under Rule 10b–5 if she trades in securities for personal profit using confidential information misappropriated in breach of a fiduciary duty to the source of the information. This liability applies even though the source of information is not the issuer of the securities that were traded.

 *See Case 44–3*

Although both Section 16(b) and Rule 10b–5 address the problem of insider trading and both may apply to the same transaction, they differ in several respects. First, Section 16(b) applies only to transactions involving registered equity securities; Rule 10b–5 applies to all securities. Second, the definition of *insider* under Rule 10b–5 extends beyond directors, officers, and owners of more than 10 percent of a company's stock, whereas the definition under Section 16(b) is limited to these persons. Third, Section 16(b) does not require that the insider possess material, nonpublic information; liability is strict. Rule 10b–5 applies to insider trading only where such information is not disclosed. Fourth, Section 16(b) applies only to transactions occurring within six months of each other; Rule 10b–5 has no such limitation. Fifth, under Rule 10b–5, injured investors may recover damages on their own behalf; under Section 16(b), although shareholders may bring suit, any recovery is on behalf of the corporation.

## Express Insider Trading Liability

In 1988, Congress amended the 1934 Act by adding **Section 20A,** which imposes express civil liability upon any person who violates the Act by purchasing or selling a security while in possession of material, nonpublic information. Any person who contemporaneously sold or purchased securities of the same class as those

**FIGURE 44–7** Parties Forbidden to Trade on Inside Information

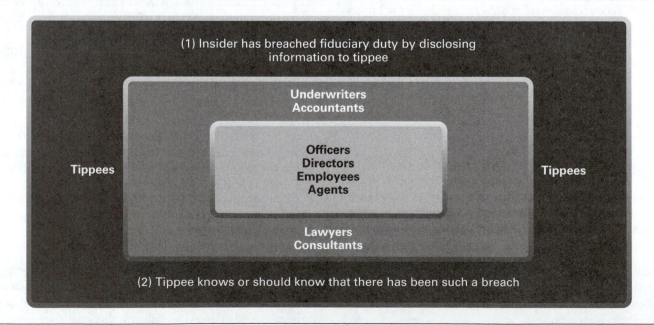

improperly traded may bring a private action against the traders to recover damages for the violation. The total amount of damages may not exceed the profit gained or loss avoided by the violation, diminished by any amount the violator disgorges to the SEC pursuant to a court order. The action must be brought within five years after the date of the last transaction that is the subject of the violation. Tippers are jointly and severally liable with tippees who commit a violation by trading on the inside information.

## Civil Penalties for Insider Trading

In addition to the remedies discussed above, the SEC is authorized by legislation enacted in 1984 and 1988 to bring an action in a U.S. district court to have a civil penalty imposed upon any person who purchases or sells a security while in possession of material, nonpublic information. Liability also extends to any person who by communicating material, nonpublic information aids and abets another in committing such a violation. Liability may also be imposed on any person who directly or indirectly controlled a person who ultimately committed a violation if the controlling person knew or recklessly disregarded the fact that the controlled person was likely to commit a violation and consequently failed to take appropriate steps to prevent the transgression. The violating transaction must be on or through the facilities of a national securities exchange or from or through a broker or dealer. Purchases that are part of a public offering by an issuer of securities are not subject to this provision.

The civil penalty for a person who trades on inside information is determined by the court in light of the facts and circumstances but may not exceed three times the profit gained or loss avoided as a result of the unlawful purchase or sale. The maximum amount that may be imposed upon a controlling person is the greater of $1.1 million or three times the profit gained or loss avoided as a result of the controlled person's violation. If that violation consists of tipping inside information, the court measures the controller's liability by the profit gained or loss avoided by the person to whom the controlled person directed the tip. For the purpose of this provision, "profit gained" or "loss avoided" is "the difference between the purchase or sale price of the security and the value of that security as measured by the trading price of the security a reasonable period after public dissemination of the nonpublic information."

Civil penalties for insider trading are payable into the United States Treasury. The SEC is authorized to award bounties of up to 10 percent of a recovered penalty to informants who provide information leading to the imposition of the penalty. An action to recover a penalty must be brought within five years after the date of the purchase or sale.

## Misleading Proxy Statements

Any person who distributes a materially false or misleading proxy statement may be liable to a shareholder who relies upon the statement in purchasing or selling a security and thereby suffers a loss. In this context, a misstatement or omission is material if there is a substantial likelihood that a reasonable shareholder would consider it important in deciding how to vote. A number of courts have held that negligence is sufficient for an action under the proxy rule's antifraud provisions. In addition, when the proxy disclosure or filing requirement has been violated, a court may, if appropriate, enjoin a shareholder meeting or any action taken at that meeting. Other remedies are rescission, damages, and attorneys' fees.

## Fraudulent Tender Offers

It is unlawful for any person to make any untrue statement of material fact, to omit to state any material fact, or to engage in any fraudulent, deceptive, or manipulative practices in connection with any tender offer. Section 14(e). This provision applies even if the target company is not subject to the 1934 Act's reporting requirements. Insider trading during a tender offer is prohibited by Rule 14e–3.

Some courts have implied civil liability for violations of Section 14(e). Because relatively few cases have involved such violations, however, the requirements for such an action are not entirely clear. At present, a target company may seek an injunction, and a shareholder of the target may be able to recover damages or obtain rescission. Furthermore, it appears likely that the courts will require *scienter*.

 *See Case 44–4*

◆ *See Figure 44–8*

## Antibribery Provision of FCPA

The FCPA makes it unlawful for any domestic concern or any of its officers, directors, employees, or agents to offer or give anything of value directly or indirectly to any foreign official, political party, or political official for the purpose of (1) influencing any act or decision of that

**FIGURE 44–8** Civil Liability under the 1933 and 1934 Acts

| Provision | Conduct | Plaintiffs | Defendants | Standard of Culpability | Reliance Required | Type of Liability | Remedies |
|---|---|---|---|---|---|---|---|
| Section 12(1) 1933 Act | Unregistered sale or sale without prospectus | Purchasers from a violator | Sellers in violation | Strict liability | No | Express | Rescission Damages |
| Section 11 1933 Act | Registration statement containing material misstatement or omission | Purchasers of registered security | Issuer Directors Signers Underwriters Experts | Strict liability for issuer; Negligence for others | No | Express | Damages Attorneys' fees |
| Section 12(2) 1933 Act | Material misstatement or omission | Purchasers from violator | Sellers in violation | Negligence | No | Express | Rescission Damages |
| Section 18 1934 Act | False or misleading statements in a document filed with SEC | Purchasers or sellers | Persons making filing in violation | Knowledge or bad faith | Yes | Express | Damages Attorneys' fees |
| Section 16(b) 1934 Act | Short-swing profit by insider | Issuer; Shareholder of issuer | Directors; Officers; 10 percent shareholders | Strict liability | No | Express | Damages |
| Rule 10b–5 1934 Act | Deception or material misstatement or omission | Purchasers or sellers | Purchasers or sellers in violation | *Scienter* | Yes | Implied | Rescission Damages Injunction |
| Section 20A 1934 Act | Insider trading | Contemporaneous purchasers or sellers | Inside traders | *Scienter* | No | Express | Damages |
| Section 14(a) 1934 Act | Materially false or misleading proxy solicitation | Shareholders | Persons making proxy solicitation in violation | Negligence (probably) | Probably | Implied | Rescission Damages Injunction Attorneys' fees |
| Section 14(e) 1934 Act | Tender offer with: Deception or Manipulation or Material misstatement or omission | Target company; Shareholders of target | Persons making tender offer in violation | *Scienter* (probably) | Probably | Implied | Rescission Damages Injunction |

person or party in his or its official capacity, (2) inducing an act or omission in violation of his or its lawful duty, or (3) inducing such person or party to use his or its influence to affect a decision of a foreign government in order to assist the domestic concern in obtaining or retaining business. An offer or promise to make a prohibited payment is a violation even if the offer is not accepted or the promise is not performed. The 1988 amendments to the Act explicitly excluded routine governmental actions not involving the official's discretion, such as obtaining permits or processing applications. They also added an affirmative defense for payments that are lawful under the written laws or regulations of the foreign official's country.

Violations can result in fines of up to $2 million for companies; individuals may be fined a maximum of $100,000 or be imprisoned for up to five years, or both. Section 32(c). Fines imposed upon individuals may not be paid directly or indirectly by the domestic concern on whose behalf they acted. In addition, the courts may impose civil penalties of up to $11,000.

In 1997 the United States and thirty-three other nations signed the Organization for Economic Cooperation and Development Convention on Combating Bribery of Foreign Public Officials in International Business Transactions (OECD Convention). In 1998 Congress enacted the International Anti-Bribery and Fair Competition Act of 1998 to conform the FCPA to the Convention. The 1998 Act expands the FCPA to include (1) payments made to "secure any improper advantage" from foreign officials, (2) all foreign persons who commit an act in furtherance of a foreign bribe while in the United States, and (3) officials of public international organizations within the definition of a "foreign official." A public international organization is defined as either an organization designated by executive order pursuant to the International Organizations Immunities Act, or any other international organization designated by executive order of the president.

## Criminal Sanctions

Section 32 of the 1934 Act imposes criminal sanctions on any person who willfully violates any provision of the Act (except the antibribery provision) or the rules and regulations the SEC promulgates pursuant to the Act. For individuals, conviction may carry a fine of not more than $1 million or imprisonment for not more than ten years, or both, with one exception: a person who proves she had no knowledge of the rule or regulation is not subject to imprisonment. If the person, however, is not a natural person (e.g., a corporation), a fine not exceeding $2.5 million may be imposed.

---

 # Chapter Summary

## Securities Act of 1933

| | |
|---|---|
| **Definition of a Security** | **Security** includes any note, stock, bond, preorganization subscription, and investment contract<br>**Investment Contract** any investment of money or property made in expectation of receiving a financial return solely from the efforts of others |
| **Registration of Securities** | **Disclosure Requirements** disclosure of accurate material information required in all public offerings of nonexempt securities unless offering is an exempt transaction<br>**Integrated Disclosure and Shelf Registrations** permitted for certain qualified issuers |
| **Exempt Securities** | **Definition** securities not subject to the registration requirements of the 1933 Act<br>**Types** exempt securities include short-term commercial paper, municipal bonds, and certain insurance policies and annuity contracts |

| **Exempt Transactions for Issuers** | **Definition** issuance of securities not subject to the registration requirements of the 1933 Act<br>**Types** exempt transactions include limited offers under Regulation D and Section 4(6), Regulation A, and intrastate issues |
| --- | --- |

| **Exempt Transactions for Non-issuers** | **Definition** resales by persons other than the issuer that are exempted from the registration requirements of the 1933 Act<br>**Types** exempt transactions include Rule 144, Regulation A, and Rule 144A |
| --- | --- |

| **Liability** | **Unregistered Sales** Section 12(a)(1) imposes absolute civil liability as there are no defenses<br>**False Registration Statements** Section 11 imposes liability on the issuer, all persons who signed the statement, every director or partner, experts who prepared or certified any part of the statement, and all underwriters; defendants other than issuer may assert the defense of due diligence<br>**Antifraud Provisions** Section 12(a)(2) imposes liability upon the seller to the immediate purchaser, provided the purchaser did not know of the untruth or omission, but the seller is not liable if he did not know and, in the exercise of reasonable care could not have known, of the untrue statement or omission; Section 17(a) broadly prohibits fraud in the sale of securities<br>**Criminal Sanctions** willful violations are subject to a fine of not more than $10,000 and/or imprisonment of not more than five years |
| --- | --- |

# Securities Exchange Act of 1934

| **Disclosure** | **Registration and Periodic Reporting Requirements** apply to all regulated publicly held companies and include one-time registration as well as annual, quarterly, and monthly reports<br>**Proxy Solicitations**<br>• *Definition of a Proxy* a signed writing by a shareholder authorizing a named person to vote her stock at a specified meeting of shareholders<br>• *Proxy Statements* proxy disclosure statements are required when proxies are solicited or an issuer submits a matter to a shareholder vote<br>**Tender Offers**<br>• *Definition of a Tender Offer* a general invitation to shareholders to purchase their shares at a specified price for a specified time<br>• *Disclosure Requirements* a statement disclosing specified information must be filed with the SEC and furnished to each offeree<br>**Foreign Corrupt Practices Act** imposes internal control requirements on companies with securities registered under the 1934 Act |
| --- | --- |

| **Liability** | **Misleading Statements in Reports** Section 18 imposes civil liability for any false or misleading statement made in a registration or report filed with the SEC<br>**Short-Swing Profits** Section 16(b) imposes liability on certain insiders (directors, officers, and shareholders owning more than 10 percent of the stock of a corporation) for all profits made on sales and purchases within six months of each other, with any recovery going to the issuer |
| --- | --- |

**Antifraud Provision** Rule 10b–5 makes it unlawful to (1) employ any device, scheme, or artifice to defraud; (2) make any untrue statement of a material fact; (3) omit to state a material fact; or (4) engage in any act that operates as a fraud

- *Requisites of Rule 10b–5* recovery requires (1) a misstatement or omission, (2) materiality, (3) *scienter* (intentional and knowing conduct), (4) reliance, and (5) connection with the purchase or sale of a security
- *Insider Trading* "insiders" are liable under Rule 10b–5 for failing to disclose material, nonpublic information before trading on the information

**Express Insider Trading Liability** is imposed on any person who sells or buys a security while in possession of inside information

**Civil Penalties for Inside Trading** may be imposed on inside traders in an amount up to three times the gains they made or losses they avoided

**Misleading Proxy Statements** any person who distributes a false or misleading proxy statement is liable to injured investors

**Fraudulent Tender Offers** Section 14(e) imposes civil liability for false and material statements or omissions or fraudulent, deceptive, or manipulative practices in connection with any tender offer

**Antibribery Provision of FCPA** prohibited bribery can result in fines and imprisonment

**Criminal Sanctions** individuals who willfully violate the 1934 Act are subject to a fine of not more than $1 million and/or imprisonment of not more than ten years

 # Cases

### CASE 44–1
## Definition of a Security
### *REVES v. ERNST & YOUNG*
Supreme Court of the United States, 1990
494 U.S. 56, 110 S.Ct. 945, 108 L.Ed.2d 47

**MARSHALL, J.**
This case presents the question whether certain demand notes issued by the Farmer's Cooperative of Arkansas and Oklahoma are "securities" within the meaning of § 3(a)(10) of the Securities Exchange Act of 1934. We conclude that they are.

### I

The Co-Op is an agricultural cooperative that, at the time relevant here, had approximately 23,000 members. In order to raise money to support its general business operations, the Co-Op sold promissory notes payable on demand by the holder. Although the notes were uncollateralized and uninsured, they paid a variable rate of interest that was adjusted monthly to keep it higher than the rate paid by local financial institutions. The Co-Op offered the notes to both members and nonmembers,

marketing the scheme as an "Investment Program." Advertisements for the notes, which appeared in each Co-Op newsletter, read in part: "YOUR CO-OP has more than $11,000,000 in assets to stand behind your investments. The Investment is not Federal [*sic*] insured but it is . . . Safe . . . Secure . . . and available when you need it." [Citation] (ellipses in original). Despite these assurances, the Co-Op filed for bankruptcy in 1984. At the time of the filing, over 1,600 people held notes worth a total of $10 million.

After the Co-Op filed for bankruptcy, petitioners, a class of holders of the notes, filed suit against Arthur Young & Co., the firm that had audited the Co-Op's financial statements (and the predecessor to respondent Ernst & Young). Petitioners alleged, *inter alia*, that Arthur Young had intentionally failed to follow generally accepted accounting principles in its audit, specifically with respect to the valuation of one of the Co-Op's major assets, a gasohol plant. Petitioners claimed that Arthur

Young violated these principles in an effort to inflate the assets and net worth of the Co-Op. Petitioners maintained that, had Arthur Young properly treated the plant in its audits, they would not have purchased demand notes because the Co-Op's insolvency would have been apparent. On the basis of these allegations, petitioners claimed that Arthur Young had violated the antifraud provisions of the 1934 Act as well as Arkansas' securities laws.

Petitioners prevailed at trial on both their federal and state claims, receiving a $6.1 million judgment. Arthur Young appealed, claiming that the demand notes were not "securities" under either the 1934 Act or Arkansas law, and that the statutes' antifraud provisions therefore did not apply. A panel of the Eighth Circuit, agreeing with Arthur Young on both the state and federal issues, reversed. [Citation.] We granted certiorari to address the federal issue, [citation], and now reverse the judgment of the Court of Appeals.

# II

This case requires us to decide whether the note issued by the Co-Op is a "security" within the meaning of the 1934 Act. * * *

The fundamental purpose undergirding the Securities Acts is "to eliminate serious abuses in a largely unregulated securities market." [Citation.] In defining the scope of the market that it wished to regulate, Congress painted with a broad brush. It recognized the virtually limitless scope of human ingenuity, especially in the creation of "countless and variable schemes devised by those who seek the use of the money of others on the promise of profits," *SEC v. W.J. Howey Co.*, [citation], and determined that the best way to achieve its goal of protecting investors was "to define 'the term "security" in sufficiently broad and general terms so as to include within that definition the many types of instruments that in our commercial world fall within the ordinary concept of a security.'" [Citation.] Congress therefore did not attempt precisely to cabin the scope of the Securities Acts. [Court's footnote: We have consistently held that "[t]he definition of a security in § 3(a)(10) of the 1934 Act, is virtually identical [to the 1933 Act's definition] and, for present purposes, the coverage of the two Acts may be considered the same." [Citation.] We reaffirm that principle here.] Rather, it enacted a definition of "security" sufficiently broad to encompass virtually any instrument that might be sold as an investment.

Congress did not, however, "intend to provide a broad federal remedy for all fraud." [Citation.] Accordingly, "[t]he task has fallen to the Securities and Exchange Commission (SEC), the body charged with administering the Securities Acts, and ultimately to the federal courts to decide which of the myriad financial transactions in our society come within the coverage of these statutes." [Citation.] In discharging our duty, we are not bound by legal formalisms, but instead take account of the economics of the transaction under investigation. [Citation.] Congress' purpose in enacting the securities laws was to regulate *investments*, in whatever form they are made and by whatever name they are called.

\* \* \*

* * * While common stock is the quintessence of a security, *Landreth Timber*, [citation], and investors therefore justifiably assume that a sale of stock is covered by the Securities Acts, the same simply cannot be said of notes, which are used in a variety of settings, not all of which involve investments. Thus, the phrase "any note" should not be interpreted to mean literally "any note," but must be understood against the backdrop of what Congress was attempting to accomplish in enacting the Securities Acts.

\* \* \*

* * * First, we examine the transaction to assess the motivations that would prompt a reasonable seller and buyer to enter into it. If the seller's purpose is to raise money for the general use of a business enterprise or to finance substantial investments and the buyer is interested primarily in the profit the note is expected to generate, the instrument is likely to be a "security." If the note is exchanged to facilitate the purchase and sale of a minor asset or consumer good, to correct for the seller's cash-flow difficulties, or to advance some other commercial or consumer purpose, on the other hand, the note is less sensibly described as a "security." [Citation.] Second, we examine the "plan of distribution" of the instrument, [citation], to determine whether it is an instrument in which there is "common trading for speculation or investment," [citation]. Third, we examine the reasonable expectations of the investing public: The Court will consider instruments to be "securities" on the basis of such public expectations, even where an economic analysis of the circumstances of the particular transaction might suggest that the instruments are not "securities" as used in that transaction. [Citations.] Finally, we examine whether some factor such as the existence of another regulatory scheme significantly reduces the risk of the

instrument, thereby rendering application of the Securities Acts unnecessary. [Citation.]

* * *

Applying [this] approach to this case, we have little difficulty in concluding that the notes at issue here are "securities." * * * The Co-Op sold the notes in an effort to raise capital for its general business operations, and purchasers bought them in order to earn a profit in the form of interest. Indeed, one of the primary inducements offered purchasers was an interest rate constantly revised to keep it slightly above the rate paid by local banks and savings and loans. From both sides, then, the transaction is most naturally conceived as an investment in a business enterprise rather than as a purely commercial or consumer transaction.

As to the plan of distribution, the Co-Op offered the notes over an extended period to its 23,000 members, as well as to non-members, and more than 1,600 people held notes when the Co-Op filed for bankruptcy. To be sure, the notes were not traded on an exchange. They were, however, offered and sold to a broad segment of the public, and that is all we have held to be necessary to establish the requisite "common trading" in an instrument. [Citations.]

The third factor—the public's reasonable perceptions—also supports a finding that the notes in this case are "securities." We have consistently identified the fundamental essence of a "security" to be its character as an "investment." [Citation.] . . . The advertisements for the notes here characterized them as "investments," [Citation] . . . and there were no countervailing factors that would have led a reasonable person to question this characterization. In these circumstances, it would be reasonable for a prospective purchaser to take the Co-Op at its word.

Finally, we find no risk-reducing factor to suggest that these instruments are not in fact securities. The notes are uncollateralized and uninsured. Moreover, . . . the notes here would escape federal regulation entirely if the Acts were held not to apply.

* * *

For the foregoing reasons, we conclude that the demand notes at issue here fall under the "note" category of instruments that are "securities" under the 1933 and 1934 Acts. * * * Accordingly, we reverse the judgment of the Court of Appeals and remand the case for further proceedings consistent with this opinion.

So ordered.

---

**CASE 44–2**
## Liability for False Registration Statements
### ESCOTT v. BARCHRIS CONSTRUCTION CORP.
United States District Court, Southern District of New York, 1968
283 F.Supp. 643

McLEAN, J.
This is an action by purchasers of 5 1/2 per cent convertible subordinated fifteen year debentures of BarChris Construction Corporation (BarChris). * * *

The action is brought under Section 11 of the Securities Act of 1933. Plaintiffs allege that the registration statement with respect to these debentures filed with the Securities and Exchange Commission, which became effective on May 16, 1961, contained material false statements and material omissions.

Defendants fall into three categories: (1) the persons who signed the registration statement; (2) the underwriters, consisting of eight investment banking firms, led by Drexel & Co. (Drexel); and (3) BarChris's auditors, Peat, Marwick, Mitchell & Co. (Peat, Marwick).

* * *

Defendants, in addition to denying that the registration statement was false, have pleaded the defense open to them under Section 11 of the Act, . . . . On the main issue of liability, the questions to be decided are (1) did the registration statement contain false statements of fact, or did it omit to state facts which should have been stated in order to prevent it from being misleading; (2) if so, were the facts which were falsely stated or omitted "material" within the meaning of the Act; (3) if so, have defendants established their affirmative defenses?

* * *

In December 1959, BarChris sold 560,000 shares of common stock to the public at $3.00 per share. This issue was underwritten by Peter Morgan & Company, one of the present defendants.

By early 1961, BarChris needed additional working capital. The proceeds of the sale of the debentures involved in this action were to be devoted, in part at least, to fill that need.

The registration statement of the debentures, in preliminary form, was filed with the Securities and Exchange Commission on March 30, 1961. A first amendment was filed on May 11 and a second on May 16. The registration statement became effective on May 16. The closing of the financing took place on May 24. On that day BarChris received the net proceeds of the financing.

By that time BarChris was experiencing difficulties in collecting amounts due from some of its customers. Some of them were in arrears in payments due to factors on their discounted notes. As time went on those difficulties increased. Although BarChris continued to build [bowling] alleys in 1961 and 1962, it became increasingly apparent that the industry was overbuilt. Operators of alleys, often inadequately financed, began to fail. Precisely when the tide turned is a matter of dispute, but at any rate, it was painfully apparent in 1962.

In May of that year BarChris made an abortive attempt to raise more money by the sale of common stock. It filed with the Securities and Exchange Commission a registration statement for the stock issue which it later withdrew. In October 1962 BarChris came to the end of the road. On October 29, 1962, it filed in this court a petition for an arrangement under Chapter XI of the Bankruptcy Act.

[The court found that the registration statement contained material false statements.]

* * *

## The "Due Diligence" Defenses

Section 11(b) of the Act provides that:

. . . no person, other than the issuer, shall be liable . . . who shall sustain the burden of proof—

* * *

"(3) that (A) as regards any part of the registration statement not purporting to be made on the authority of an expert . . . he had, after reasonable investigation, reasonable ground to believe and did believe, at the time such part of the registration statement became effective, that the statements therein were true and that there was no omission to state a material fact required to be stated therein or necessary to make the statements therein not misleading; . . . and (C) as regards any part of the registration statement purporting to be made on the authority of an expert (other than himself) . . . he had no reasonable ground to believe and did not believe, at the time such part of the registration statement became effective, that the statements therein were untrue or that there was an omission to state a material fact

required to be stated therein or necessary to make the statements therein not misleading. . . .

Section 11(c) defines "reasonable investigation" as follows:

In determining, for the purposes of paragraph (3) of subsection (b) of this section, what constitutes reasonable investigation and reasonable ground for belief, the standard of reasonableness shall be that required of a prudent man in the management of his own property.

Every defendant, except BarChris itself, to whom, as the issuer, these defenses are not available, and except Peat, Marwick, whose position rests on a different statutory provision, has pleaded these affirmative defenses.

* * *

* * *

I turn now to the question of whether defendants have proved their due diligence defenses. The position of each defendant will be separately considered.

* * *

***Kircher*** Kircher was treasurer of BarChris and its chief financial officer. He is a certified public accountant and an intelligent man. He was thoroughly familiar with BarChris's financial affairs. * * *

Moreover, as a member of the executive committee, Kircher was kept informed as to those branches of the business of which he did not have direct charge.

* * *

Knowing the facts, Kircher had reason to believe that the expertised portion of the prospectus, *i.e.,* the 1960 figures, was in part incorrect. He could not shut his eyes to the facts and rely on Peat, Marwick for that portion.

As to the rest of the prospectus, knowing the facts, he did not have a reasonable ground to believe it to be true. On the contrary, he must have known that in part it was untrue. * * *

Kircher has not proved his due diligence defenses.

* * *

***Birnbaum*** Birnbaum was a young lawyer, admitted to the bar in 1957, who, after brief periods of employment by two different law firms and an equally brief period of practicing in his own firm, was employed by BarChris as house counsel and assistant secretary in October 1960. Unfortunately for him, he became secretary and a director of BarChris on April 17, 1961, after the first version of the registration statement had been filed with the Securities and Exchange Commission. He signed the later amendments, thereby becoming responsible for the accuracy of the prospectus in its final form.

Although the prospectus, in its description of "management," lists Birnbaum among the "executive officers" and devotes several sentences to a recital of his career, the fact seems to be that he was not an executive officer in any real sense. He did not participate in the management of the company. As house counsel, he attended to legal matters of a routine nature.

* * *

One of Birnbaum's more important duties, first as assistant secretary and later as full-fledged secretary, was to keep the corporate minutes of BarChris and its subsidiaries. This necessarily informed him to a considerable extent about the company's affairs. * * *

It seems probable that Birnbaum did not know of many of the inaccuracies in the prospectus. He must, however, have appreciated some of them. In any case, he made no investigation and relied on the others to get it right. . . . As a lawyer, he should have known his obligations under the statute. He should have known that he was required to make a reasonable investigation of the truth of all the statements in the unexpertised portion of the document which he signed. Having failed to make such an investigation, he did not have reasonable ground to believe that all these statements were true. Birnbaum has not established his due diligence defenses except as to the audited 1960 figures.

*Auslander* Auslander was an "outside" director, *i.e.,* one who was not an officer of BarChris. He was chairman of the board of Valley Stream National Bank. * * *

* * *

In considering Auslander's due diligence defenses, a distinction is to be drawn between the expertised and non-expertised portions of the prospectus. As to the former, Auslander knew that Peat, Marwick had audited the 1960 figures. He believed them to be correct because he had confidence in Peat, Marwick. He had no reasonable ground to believe otherwise.

As to the non-expertised portions, however, Auslander is in a different position. He seems to have been under the impression that Peat, Marwick was responsible for all the figures. This impression was not correct, as he would have realized if he had read the prospectus carefully. Auslander made no investigation of the accuracy of the prospectus. * * *

It is true that Auslander became a director on the eve of the financing. He had little opportunity to familiarize himself with the company's affairs. The question is whether, under such circumstances, Auslander did enough to establish his due diligence defense with respect to the non-expertised portions of the prospectus.

* * *

Section 11 imposes liability in the first instance upon a director, no matter how new he is. He is presumed to know his responsibility when he becomes a director. He can escape liability only by using that reasonable care to investigate the facts which a prudent man would employ in the management of his own property. In my opinion, a prudent man would not act in an important matter without any knowledge of the relevant facts, in sole reliance upon representations of persons who are comparative strangers and upon general information which does not purport to cover the particular case. To say that such minimal conduct measures up to the statutory standard would to all intents and purposes, absolve new directors from responsibility merely because they are new. This is not a sensible construction of Section 11, when one bears in mind its fundamental purpose of requiring full and truthful disclosures for the protection of investors.

* * *

*The Underwriters* The underwriters other than Drexel made no investigation of the accuracy of the prospectus. * * * They all relied upon Drexel as the "lead" underwriter.

Drexel did make an investigation. The work was in charge of Coleman, a partner of the firm, assisted by Casperson, an associate. Drexel's attorneys acted as attorneys for the entire group of underwriters. Ballard did the work, assisted by Stanton.

* * *

The underwriters say that the prospectus is the company's prospectus, not theirs. Doubtless this is the way they customarily regard it. But the Securities Act makes no such distinction. The underwriters are just as responsible as the company if the prospectus is false. And prospective investors rely upon the reputation of the underwriters in deciding whether to purchase the securities.

* * *

The purpose of Section 11 is to protect investors. To that end the underwriters are made responsible for the truth of the prospectus. If they may escape that responsibility by taking at face value representations made to them by the company's management, then the inclusion of underwriters among those liable under Section 11 affords the investors no additional protection. To effectuate the statute's purpose, the phrase "reasonable investigation" must be construed to require more effort on the part of the underwriters than the mere accurate reporting in the prospectus of "data presented" to them by the company. It should make no difference that this data is elicited by questions addressed to the company officers by the underwriters, or that the underwriters at the time believe that the company's officers are truthful and reliable. In order to make the underwriters' participation in this enterprise of any value to the investors, the underwriters must make some reasonable attempt to verify the data submitted to them. They may not rely solely on the company's officers or on the company's counsel. A prudent man in the management of his own property would not rely on them.

It is impossible to lay down a rigid rule suitable for every case defining the extent to which such verification must go. It is a question of degree, a matter of judgment in each case. In the present case, the underwriters' counsel made almost no attempt to verify management's representations. I hold that that was insufficient.

On the evidence in this case, I find that the underwriters' counsel did not make a reasonable investigation of the truth of those portions of the prospectus which were not made on the authority of Peat, Marwick as an expert. Drexel is bound by their failure. It is not a matter of relying upon counsel for legal advice. Here the attorneys were dealing with matters of fact. Drexel delegated to them, as its agent, the business of examining the corporate minutes and contracts. It must bear the consequences of their failure to make an adequate examination.

The other underwriters, who did nothing and relied solely on Drexel and on the lawyers, are also bound by it. It follows that although Drexel and the other underwriters believed that those portions of the prospectus were true, they had no reasonable ground for that belief, within the meaning of the statute. Hence, they have not established their due diligence defense, except as to the 1960 audited figures.

---

## CASE 44–3
### Insider Trading
## *UNITED STATES v. O'HAGAN*

Supreme Court of the United States, 1997
521 U.S. 642, 117 S.Ct. 2199, 138 L.Ed.2d 724

GINSBURG, J.
Respondent James Herman O'Hagan was a partner in the law firm of Dorsey & Whitney in Minneapolis, Minnesota. In July 1988, Grand Metropolitan PLC (Grand Met), a company based in London, England, retained Dorsey & Whitney as local counsel to represent Grand Met regarding a potential tender offer for the common stock of the Pillsbury Company, headquartered in Minneapolis. Both Grand Met and Dorsey & Whitney took precautions to protect the confidentiality of Grand Met's tender offer plans. O'Hagan did no work on the Grand Met representation. Dorsey & Whitney withdrew from representing Grand Met on September 9, 1988. Less than a month later, on October 4, 1988, Grand Met publicly announced its tender offer for Pillsbury stock.

On August 18, 1988, while Dorsey & Whitney was still representing Grand Met, O'Hagan began purchasing call options for Pillsbury stock. Each option gave him the right to purchase 100 shares of Pillsbury stock by a specified date in September 1988. Later in August and in September, O'Hagan made additional purchases of Pillsbury call options. By the end of September, he owned 2,500 unexpired Pillsbury options, apparently more than any other individual investor. [Citation.] O'Hagan also

purchased, in September 1988, some 5,000 shares of Pillsbury common stock, at a price just under $39 per share. When Grand Met announced its tender offer in October, the price of Pillsbury stock rose to nearly $60 per share. O'Hagan then sold his Pillsbury call options and common stock, making a profit of more than $4.3 million.

[The Securities and Exchange Commission initiated an investigation into O'Hagan's transactions, culminating in an indictment alleging that O'Hagan defrauded his law firm and its client, Grand Met, by using for his own trading purposes material, nonpublic information regarding Grand Met's planned tender offer in violation of § 10(b) of the Securities Exchange Act of 1934 and SEC Rule 10b–5. A jury convicted O'Hagan and he was sentenced to a 41-month term of imprisonment. A divided panel of the Court of Appeals for the Eighth Circuit reversed O'Hagan's conviction holding that liability under § 10(b) and Rule 10b–5 may not be grounded on the "misappropriation theory" of securities fraud on which the prosecution relied.]

We address . . . the Court of Appeals' reversal of O'Hagan's convictions under § 10(b) and Rule 10b–5. Following the Fourth Circuit's lead, see [citation], the

Eighth Circuit rejected the misappropriation theory as a basis for § 10(b) liability. We hold, in accord with several other Courts of Appeals, that criminal liability under § 10(b) may be predicated on the misappropriation theory.

Under the "traditional" or "classical theory" of insider trading liability, § 10(b) and Rule 10b–5 are violated when a corporate insider trades in the securities of his corporation on the basis of material, nonpublic information. Trading on such information qualifies as a "deceptive device" under § 10(b), we have affirmed, because "a relationship of trust and confidence [exists] between the shareholders of a corporation and those insiders who have obtained confidential information by reason of their position with that corporation." [Citation.] That relationship, we recognized, "gives rise to a duty to disclose [or to abstain from trading] because of the 'necessity of preventing a corporate insider from . . . tak[ing] unfair advantage of . . . uninformed . . . stockholders.'" [Citation.] The classical theory applies not only to officers, directors, and other permanent insiders of a corporation, but also to attorneys, accountants, consultants, and others who temporarily become fiduciaries of a corporation. [Citation.]

The "misappropriation theory" holds that a person commits fraud "in connection with" a securities transaction, and thereby violates § 10(b) and Rule 10b–5, when he misappropriates confidential information for securities trading purposes, in breach of a duty owed to the source of the information. [Citation.] Under this theory, a fiduciary's undisclosed, self-serving use of a principal's information to purchase or sell securities, in breach of a duty of loyalty and confidentiality, defrauds the principal of the exclusive use of that information. In lieu of premising liability on a fiduciary relationship between company insider and purchaser or seller of the company's stock, the misappropriation theory premises liability on a fiduciary-turned-trader's deception of those who entrusted him with access to confidential information.

The two theories are complementary, each addressing efforts to capitalize on nonpublic information through the purchase or sale of securities. The classical theory targets a corporate insider's breach of duty to shareholders with whom the insider transacts; the misappropriation theory outlaws trading on the basis of nonpublic information by a corporate "outsider" in breach of a duty owed not to a trading party, but to the source of the information. The misappropriation theory is thus designed to "protec[t] the integrity of the securities markets against abuses by 'outsiders' to a corporation who have access to confidential information that will affect th[e] corpora-tion's security price when revealed, but who owe no fiduciary or other duty to that corporation's shareholders." [Citation.]

In this case, the indictment alleged that O'Hagan, in breach of a duty of trust and confidence he owed to his law firm, Dorsey & Whitney, and to its client, Grand Met, traded on the basis of nonpublic information regarding Grand Met's planned tender offer for Pillsbury common stock. [Citation.] This conduct, the Government charged, constituted a fraudulent device in connection with the purchase and sale of securities. [Court's footnote: The Government could not have prosecuted O'Hagan under the classical theory, for O'Hagan was not an "insider" of Pillsbury, the corporation in whose stock he traded. Although an "outsider" with respect to Pillsbury, O'Hagan had an intimate association with, and was found to have traded on confidential information from, Dorsey & Whitney, counsel to tender offeror Grand Met.]

We agree with the Government that misappropriation, as just defined, satisfies § 10(b)'s requirement that chargeable conduct involve a "deceptive device or contrivance" used "in connection with" the purchase or sale of securities. We observe, first, that misappropriators, as the Government describes them, deal in deception. A fiduciary who "[pretends] loyalty to the principal while secretly converting the principal's information for personal gain," [citation], "dupes" or defrauds the principal. [Citation.]

* * *

The misappropriation theory advanced by the Government is consistent with *Santa Fe Industries, Inc. v. Green*, [citation], a decision underscoring that § 10(b) is not an all-purpose breach of fiduciary duty ban; rather, it trains on conduct involving manipulation or deception. [Citation.] In contrast to the Government's allegations in this case, in *Santa Fe Industries*, all pertinent facts were disclosed by the persons charged with violating § 10(b) and Rule 10b–5, see [citation]; therefore, there was no deception through nondisclosure to which liability under those provisions could attach, see [citation]. Similarly, full disclosure forecloses liability under the misappropriation theory: Because the deception essential to the misappropriation theory involves feigning fidelity to the source of information, if the fiduciary discloses to the source that he plans to trade on the nonpublic information, there is no "deceptive device" and thus no § 10(b) violation—although the fiduciary-turned-trader may remain liable under state law for breach of a duty of loyalty.

We turn next to the § 10(b) requirement that the misappropriator's deceptive use of information be "in connection with the purchase or sale of [a] security." This element is satisfied because the fiduciary's fraud is consummated, not when the fiduciary gains the confidential information, but when, without disclosure to his principal, he uses the information to purchase or sell securities. The securities transaction and the breach of duty thus coincide. This is so even though the person or entity defrauded is not the other party to the trade, but is, instead, the source of the nonpublic information. [Citation.] A misappropriator who trades on the basis of material, nonpublic information, in short, gains his advantageous market position through deception; he deceives the source of the information and simultaneously harms members of the investing public. [Citation.]

\* \* \*

The misappropriation theory comports with § 10(b)'s language, which requires deception "in connection with the purchase or sale of any security," not deception of an identifiable purchaser or seller. The theory is also well-tuned to an animating purpose of the Exchange Act: to insure honest securities markets and thereby promote investor confidence. [Citation.] Although informational disparity is inevitable in the securities markets, investors likely would hesitate to venture their capital in a market where trading based on misappropriated nonpublic information is unchecked by law. An investor's informational disadvantage vis-a-vis a misappropriator with material, nonpublic information stems from contrivance, not luck; it is a disadvantage that cannot be overcome with research or skill. [Citation.]

In sum, considering the inhibiting impact on market participation of trading on misappropriated information, and the congressional purposes underlying § 10(b), it makes scant sense to hold a lawyer like O'Hagan a § 10(b) violator if he works for a law firm representing the target of a tender offer, but not if he works for a law firm representing the bidder. The text of the statute requires no such result. The misappropriation at issue here was properly made the subject of a § 10(b) charge because it meets the statutory requirement that there be "deceptive" conduct "in connection with" securities transactions.

\* \* \*

The judgment of the Court of Appeals for the Eighth Circuit is reversed, and the case is remanded for further proceedings consistent with this opinion.

---

## CASE 44–4
### Fraudulent Tender Offers
### *SCHREIBER v. BURLINGTON NORTHERN, INC.*

Supreme Court of the United States, 1985
472 U.S. 1, 105 S.Ct. 2458, 86 L.Ed.2d 1

BURGER, C. J.

On December 21, 1982, Burlington Northern, Inc., made a hostile tender offer for El Paso Gas Co. Through a wholly owned subsidiary, Burlington proposed to purchase 25.1 million El Paso shares at $24 per share. Burlington reserved the right to terminate the offer if any of several specified events occurred. El Paso management initially opposed the takeover, but its shareholders responded favorably, fully subscribing the offer by the December 30, 1982 deadline.

Burlington did not accept those tendered shares; instead, after negotiations with El Paso management, Burlington announced on January 10, 1983, the terms of a new and friendly takeover agreement. Pursuant to the new agreement, Burlington undertook, *inter alia*, to (1) rescind the December tender offer, (2) purchase 4,166,667 shares from El Paso at $24 per share, (3) substitute a new tender offer for only 21 million shares at $24 per share, (4) provide procedural protections against a squeeze-out merger of the remaining El Paso shareholders, and (5) recognize "golden parachute" contracts between El Paso and four of its senior officers. By February 8, more than 40 million shares were tendered in response to Burlington's January offer, and the takeover was completed.

The rescission of the first tender offer caused a diminished payment to those shareholders who had tendered during the first offer. The January offer was greatly oversubscribed and consequently those shareholders who re-tendered were subject to substantial proration. Petitioner Barbara Schreiber filed suit on behalf of herself and similarly situated shareholders, alleging that Burlington, El Paso, and members of El Paso's board violated § 14(e)'s prohibition of "fraudulent, deceptive or manipulative acts or practices . . . in connection with any tender offer." [Citation.] She claimed that Burlington's withdrawal of the December tender offer coupled with the substitution of the January tender offer was a "manipulative" distortion of the market for El Paso stock. Schreiber also alleged that Burlington violated § 14(e) by failing in the January offer to disclose the "golden parachutes" offered to four of El Paso's managers. She claims that this January non-disclosure was a deceptive act forbidden by § 14(e).

The District Court dismissed the suit for failure to state a claim. * * *

* * *

We are asked in this case to interpret § 14(e) of the Securities Exchange Act, [citation]. The starting point is the language of the statute. Section 14(e) provides:

It shall be unlawful for any person to make any untrue statement of a material fact or omit to state any material fact necessary in order to make the statements made, in the light of the circumstances under which they are made, not misleading, or to engage in any fraudulent, deceptive or manipulative acts or practices, in connection with any tender offer or request or invitation for tenders, or any solicitation of security holders in opposition to or in favor of any such offer, request, or invitation. The Commission shall, for the purposes of this subsection, by rules and regulations define, and prescribe means reasonably designed to prevent, such acts and practices as are fraudulent, deceptive, or manipulative.

[Citation.]

Petitioner relies on a construction of the phrase, "fraudulent, deceptive or manipulative acts or practices." Petitioner reads the phrase "fraudulent, deceptive or manipulative acts or practices" to include acts which, although fully disclosed, "artificially" affect the price of the takeover target's stock. Petitioner's interpretation relies on the belief that § 14(e) is directed at purposes broader than providing full and true information to investors.

Petitioner's reading of the term "manipulative" conflicts with the normal meaning of the term. We have held in the context of an alleged violation of § 10(b) of the Securities Exchange Act:

Use of the word 'manipulative' is especially significant. It is and was virtually a term of art when used in connection

with the securities markets. It connotes intentional or willful conduct *designed to deceive or defraud* investors by controlling or artificially affecting the price of securities.

*Ernst & Ernst v. Hochfelder*, [see Chapter 45].

* * * The meaning the Court has given the term "manipulative" is consistent with the use of the term at common law, and with its traditional dictionary definition.

* * *

Our conclusion that "manipulative" acts under § 14(e) require misrepresentation or nondisclosure is buttressed by the purpose and legislative history of the provision. Section 14(e) was originally added to the Securities Exchange Act as part of the Williams Act, [citation]. "The purpose of the Williams Act is to insure that public shareholders who are confronted by a cash tender offer for their stock will not be required to respond without adequate information." [Citation.]

* * *

Nowhere in the legislative history is there the slightest suggestion that § 14(e) serves any purpose other than disclosure, or that the term "manipulative" should be read as an invitation to the courts to oversee the substantive fairness of tender offers; the quality of any offer is a matter for the marketplace.

* * *

We hold that the term "manipulative" as used in § 14(e) requires misrepresentation or nondisclosure. It connotes "conduct designed to deceive or defraud investors by controlling or artificially affecting the price of securities." *Ernst & Ernst v. Hochfelder*, [see Chapter 45]. Without misrepresentation or nondisclosure, § 14(e) has not been violated.

Applying that definition to this case, we hold that the actions of respondents were not manipulative. The amended complaint fails to allege that the cancellation of the first tender offer was accompanied by any misrepresentation, nondisclosure or deception. The District Court correctly found, "All activity of the defendants that could have conceivably affected the price of El Paso shares was done openly." [Citation.]

* * *

The judgment of the Court of Appeals is affirmed.

 **Questions**

1.   Explain the disclosure requirements of the 1933 Act including which securities and transactions are exempt from these disclosure requirements.

2.   Discuss the potential civil liabilities under the 1933 Act.

3.   Distinguish between publicly held companies under the 1934 Act and those that are not publicly held. Which provisions

of the 1934 Act apply only to publicly held companies and which apply to all companies?

**4.** Discuss the disclosure requirements of the 1934 Act.

**5.** Discuss the potential civil liabilities under the 1934 Act.

# Problems

**1.** Acme Realty, a real estate development company, is a limited partnership organized in Georgia. It is planning to develop a 200-acre parcel of land for a regional shopping center and needs to raise $1,250,000. As part of its financing, Acme plans to offer $1,250,000 worth of limited partnership interests to about one hundred prospective investors in the southeastern United States. It anticipates that about forty to fifty private investors will purchase the limited partnership interests.

    (a)   Must Acme register this offering? Why or why not?

    (b)   If Acme must register but fails to do so, what are the legal consequences?

**2.** Bigelow Corporation has total assets of $850,000, sales of $1,350,000, and one class of common stock with 375 shareholders, and a class of preferred stock with 250 shareholders, both of which are traded over the counter. Which provisions of the Securities Exchange Act of 1934 apply to Bigelow Corporation?

**3.** Capricorn, Inc. is planning to "go public" by offering its common stock, which previously had been owned by only three shareholders. The company intends to limit the number of purchasers to twenty-five persons resident in the State of its incorporation. All of Capricorn's business and all of its assets are located in its State of incorporation. Based upon these facts, what exemptions from registration, if any, are available to Capricorn, and what conditions would each of these available exemptions impose upon the terms of the offer?

**4.** The boards of directors of DuMont Corp. and Epsot, Inc. agreed to enter into a friendly merger, with DuMont to be the surviving entity. The stock of both corporations was listed on a national stock exchange. In connection with the merger, both corporations distributed to their shareholders proxy statements seeking approval of the proposed merger. The shareholders of both corporations voted to approve the merger. About three weeks after the merger was consummated, the price of DuMont stock fell from $25 to $13 as a result of the discovery that Epsot, had entered into several unprofitable long-term contracts two months before the merger had been proposed. The contracts will result in substantial losses from Epsot's operations for at least the next four years. The existence and effect of these contracts, although known to both corporations at the time of the proposed merger, were not disclosed in the proxy statements of either corporation. Shareholders of DuMont bring suit against DuMont under the 1934 Act. Decision?

**5.** Farthing is a director and vice president of Garp, Inc., whose common stock is listed on the New York Stock Exchange. Farthing engaged in the following transactions in the same calendar year: on January 1, Farthing sold 500 shares at $30 per share; on January 15, she purchased 300 shares at $30 per share; on February 1, she purchased 200 shares at $45 per share; on March 1, she purchased 300 shares at $60 per share; on March 15, she sold 200 shares at $55 per share; and on April 1, she sold 100 shares at $40 per share. Howell brings suit on behalf of Garp, alleging that Farthing has violated the Securities Exchange Act of 1934. Farthing defends on the ground that she lost money on the transactions in question. Decision?

**6.** Intercontinental Widgets, Inc. had applied for a patent for a new state-of-the-art widget which, if patented, would significantly increase the value of Intercontinental's shares. On September 1, the Patent Office notified Jackson, the attorney for Intercontinental, that the patent application had been approved. After informing Kingsley, the president of Intercontinental, of the good news, Jackson called his broker and purchased 1,000 shares of Intercontinental at $18 per share. He also told his partner, Lucas, who immediately proceeded to purchase 500 shares at $19 per share. Lucas then called his brother-in-law, Mammon, and told him the news. On September 3, Mammon bought 4,000 shares at $21 per share. On September 4, Kingsley issued a press release which accurately reported that a patent had been granted to Intercontinental. The next day Intercontinental's stock soared to $38 per share. A class action suit is brought against Jackson, Lucas, Mammon, and Intercontinental for violations of Rule 10b–5. Who, if anyone, is liable?

**7.** Nova, Inc. sought to sell a new issue of common stock. It registered the issue with the Securities and Exchange Commission but included false information in both the registration statement and the prospectus. The issue was underwritten by Omega & Sons and was sold in its entirety by Periwinkle, Ramses, and Sheffield, Inc., a securities broker-dealer. Telford purchased 500 shares at $6 per share. Three months later, the falsity of the information contained in the prospectus was made public, and the price of the shares fell to $1 per share. The following week Telford brought suit against Nova, Inc., Omega & Sons, and Periwinkle, Ramses and Sheffield, Inc. under the Securities Act of 1933.

    (a)   Who, if anyone, is liable under the Act?

    (b)   What defenses, if any, are available to the various defendants?

**8.** Tanaka, a director and officer of Deep Hole Oil Company, approached Romani for the purpose of buying 200 shares of Deep Hole Company stock owned by Romani. During the period of negotiations, Tanaka concealed his identity and did not disclose the fact that earlier in the day he had received a report of two rich oil strikes on the oil company's property.

Romani sold his 200 shares to Tanaka for $10 per share. Taking into consideration the new strikes, the fair value of the stock was approximately $20 per share. Romani sues Tanaka to recover damages. Decision?

9. Venable Corporation has 750,000 shares of common stock outstanding, which are owned by 640 shareholders. The assets of Venable Corporation are valued at more than $10 million. In March, Underhill began purchasing shares of Venable's common stock in the open market. By April, he had acquired 40,000 shares at prices ranging from $12 to $14. Upon discovering Underhill's activities in late April, the directors of Venable had the corporation purchase the 40,000 shares from Underhill for $18 per share. Which provisions of the 1934 Act, if any, have been violated?

10. In 1973, Dirks was an officer of a New York broker-dealer firm that specialized in providing investment analysis of insurance company securities to institutional investors. On March 6, Dirks received information from Ronald Secrist, a former officer of Equity Funding of America. Secrist alleged that the assets of Equity Funding, a diversified corporation primarily engaged in selling life insurance and mutual funds, were vastly overstated as the result of fraudulent corporate practices. Dirks decided to investigate the allegations. He visited Equity Funding's headquarters in Los Angeles and interviewed several officers and employees of the corporation. The senior management denied any wrongdoing, but certain corporation employees corroborated the charges of fraud. Neither Dirks nor his firm owned or traded any Equity Funding stock, but throughout his investigation he openly discussed the information he had obtained with a number of clients and investors. Some of these persons sold their holdings of Equity Funding securities, including five investment advisers who liquidated holdings of more than $16 million.

While Dirks was in Los Angeles, he was in touch regularly with William Blundell, *The Wall Street Journal's* Los Angeles bureau chief. Dirks urged Blundell to write a story on the fraud allegations. Blundell did not believe, however, that such a massive fraud could go undetected and declined to write the story. He feared that publishing such damaging hearsay might be libelous.

During the two-week period in which Dirks pursued his investigation and spread word of Secrist's charges, the price of Equity Funding stock fell from $26 per share to less than $15 per share. This led the New York Stock Exchange to halt trading on March 27. Shortly thereafter, California insurance authorities impounded Equity Funding's records and uncovered evidence of the fraud. Only then did the Securities and Exchange Commission (SEC) file a complaint against Equity Funding.

The SEC began an investigation into Dirks's role in the exposure of the fraud. After a hearing by an administrative law judge, the SEC found that Dirks had aided and abetted violations of Section 10(b) of the Securities Exchange Act of 1934 and SEC Rule 10b–5 by repeating the allegations of fraud to members of the investment community who later sold their Equity Funding stock. Recognizing, however, that Dirks "played an important role in bringing Equity Funding's massive fraud to light," the SEC only censured him. Dirks appealed. Decision?

11. Texas Gulf Sulphur Company (TGS) was a corporation engaged in exploring for and mining certain minerals. A particular tract of Canadian land looked very promising as a source of desired minerals, and Texas Gulf drilled a test hole on November 8, 1963. Because the core sample of the hole contained minerals of amazing quality, Texas Gulf began to acquire surrounding tracts of land. Stevens, the president of Texas Gulf, instructed all on-site personnel to keep the find a secret. Because subsequent test drillings were performed, the amount of activity surrounding the drilling gave rise to rumors regarding the size and quality of the find. To counteract these rumors, Stevens authorized a press release denying the validity of the rumors and describing them as excessively optimistic. The release was issued on April 12, 1964, though drilling continued through April 15. In the meantime, several officers, directors, and employees had purchased or accepted options to purchase additional Texas Gulf stock on the basis of the information concerning the drilling. They also recommended similar purchases to outsiders without divulging the inside information to the public. At 10 AM on April 16, an accurate report on the find was finally released to the American financial press. The SEC brought this action against Texas Gulf Sulphur and several of its officers, directors, and employees to enjoin conduct alleged to violate Section 10(b) of the Securities Act of 1934 and to compel rescission by the individual defendants of securities transactions assertedly conducted in violation of Rule 10b–5. Decision?

12. W. J. Howey Company and Howey-in-the-Hills Service, Inc. were Florida corporations under direct common control and management. Howey Company owned large tracts of citrus acreage in Florida. The service company cultivated, harvested, and marketed the crops. For several years, Howey Company offered one-half of its planted acreage to the public to help it "finance additional development." Each prospective customer was offered both a land sales contract and a service contract with Howey-in-the-Hills after being told that it was not feasible to invest in the grove without a service arrangement. Upon payment of the purchase price, the land was conveyed by warranty deed. The service company was given full discretion over cultivating and marketing the crop. The purchaser had no right of entry to market the crop. The service company also was accountable only for an allocation of the net profits after the companies pooled the produce. The purchasers were predominantly nonresident businesspersons attracted by the expectation of substantial profits. Contending that this arrangement was an investment contract within the coverage of the Securities Act of 1933, the Securities and Exchange Commission brought this action against the two companies to restrain them from using the mails and instrumentalities of interstate commerce in the offer and sale of unregistered and nonexempt securities. Decision?

**13.**   Prior to December 20, 1978, Basic Inc. was a publicly traded company engaged in the business of manufacturing chemical refractories for the steel industry. Beginning in September 1976, Combustion Engineering, Inc., and Basic began discussions concerning the possibility of a merger of the two companies. Nevertheless, during 1977 and 1978, Basic made three public statements denying that it was engaged in merger negotiations. On December 18, 1978, Basic asked the New York Stock Exchange to suspend trading in its shares and issued a statement saying that it had been "approached" by another company concerning a merger. On December 20, Basic publicly announced its approval of Combustion's offer for all its outstanding shares. Plaintiffs were former owners of Basic stock who sold their shares after Basic publicly denied that it was engaged in merger negotiations. Plaintiffs brought a class action suit against Basic and its directors, alleging that they had released false or misleading information in violation of Section 10(b) of the 1934 Act and in violation of Rule 10b–5. Plaintiffs claimed that they were injured by selling their shares at prices which were artificially depressed as a consequence of Basic's misleading public statements. The Court of Appeals held that the plaintiffs had carried their burden of proof. Defendants appealed, claiming that the plaintiffs had not proven that they had, in fact, relied upon the misleading statements in selling their stock. Decision?

**Internet Exercise**   Find the Securities and Exchange Commission Web site and learn about the agency's (a) structure, (b) functions, and (c) current activities.

# CHAPTER 45

# Accountants' Legal Liability

Accountants perform a number of important roles in our business society. One such role is to provide reliable financial information to facilitate the effective and efficient allocation of resources in the economy. As Harold M. Williams, former chair of the Securities and Exchange Commission, has observed, "Obviously, if users of financial data, who often may have little or no contact with the business in question, could not trust in its financial statements, capital formation and lending could not be carried on as they are today."

An accountant is subject to potential civil liability arising from the professional services he provides to his clients and third parties. This legal liability is imposed both by the common law at the State level and by securities laws at the Federal level. In addition, an accountant may violate Federal or State criminal law through the performance of his professional activities. This chapter will deal with accountants' legal liability under both State and Federal law.

## COMMON LAW

An accountant's legal responsibility under State law may be based upon (1) contract law, (2) tort law, or (3) criminal law. In addition, the common law provides accountants with certain rights and privileges: in particular, the ownership of their working papers and, in some States, a limited accountant–client privilege.

### Contract Liability

The employment contract between an accountant and her client is subject to the general principles of contract law. For the contract to be binding, therefore, it must meet all of the requirements of a common law contract, including offer and acceptance, capacity, consideration, legality, and a writing if, as is often the case, the

agreement falls within the one-year provision of the statute of frauds.

Upon entering into a contract (frequently referred to as an *engagement* letter), the accountant is bound to perform all the duties she **explicitly** agrees to provide under the contract. For example, if an accountant agrees to complete her audit of a client by October 15 so that the client may release its annual report on time, the accountant is under a contractual obligation to do so. Likewise, an accountant who contractually promises to conduct an audit to detect possible embezzlement is under a contractual obligation to provide for her client an expanded audit *beyond* Generally Accepted Auditing Standards (GAAS).

By entering into a contract, an accountant also **implicitly** agrees to perform the contract in a competent and professional manner. His agreement to render professional services holds an accountant to those standards that are generally accepted by the accounting profession, such as GAAS and Generally Accepted Accounting Practices (GAAP). Although accountants need not ensure the absolute accuracy of their work, they must exercise the care of reasonably skilled professionals.

An accountant who breaches his contract incurs liability not only to his client but also to certain third-party contract beneficiaries. A **third-party beneficiary** is a noncontracting party whom the contracting parties *intend* to receive the primary benefit under the contract. For example, Otis Manufacturing Co. hires Adler, an accountant, to prepare a financial statement for Otis to use in obtaining a loan from Chemical Bank. Chemical Bank is a third-party beneficiary of the contract between Otis and Adler. Another example of a potential third party is an investor considering the purchase of part or all of a particular company. For a more detailed discussion of third-party beneficiaries, see Chapter 16.

Pursuant to general contract principles, an accountant who *materially breaches* his contract is entitled to no compensation (i.e., the client is discharged from his obligations under the contract because of the material breach). Thus, if an accountant does not perform an audit on time when time is of the essence, or completes only 60 percent of the audit, she has committed a material breach. On the other hand, an accountant who *substantially performs* his contractual duties is generally entitled to be compensated for the contractually agreed-upon fee, less any damages or loss his nonmaterial breach has caused the client. (See Chapter 18.)

## Tort Liability

In performing his professional services, an accountant may incur tort liability to his client or third parties for negligence or fraud. A tort, as discussed in Chapters 7 (intentional torts, including fraud) and 8 (negligence), is a private or civil wrong or injury, other than a breach of contract, for which the courts will provide a remedy in the form of an action for damages.

*Negligence*  An accountant is negligent if she does not exercise the degree of care a reasonably competent accountant would exercise under the circumstances. For example, Arthur, an accountant, is engaged to audit the books of Zebra Corporation. During the course of Arthur's investigation, Olivia, an officer of Zebra, notifies Arthur that she suspects that Terrence, Zebra's treasurer, is engaged in a scheme to embezzle from the corporation. Previously informed that Olivia and Terrence are on bad terms with each other, Arthur does not pursue the matter. Terrence is, in fact, engaged in a common embezzlement scheme. Arthur is negligent for failing to conduct a reasonable investigation of the alleged defalcation. Nonetheless, an accountant is *not* liable for honest inaccuracies or errors of judgment so long as she exercised reasonable care in performing her duties. Moreover, as previously mentioned, an accountant need *not* guarantee the accuracy of her reports, provided she acted in a reasonably competent and professional manner.

Most courts do not permit an accountant to raise the defense of the plaintiff's contributory (or comparative) negligence. Nevertheless, a few courts do permit the defense of contributory or comparative negligence despite the fact that they recognize "that professional malpractice actions pose peculiar problems and that the comparison of fault between a layperson and a professional should be approached with caution." *Halla Nursery, Inc. v. Baumann-Furrie & Co.*, 454 N.W.2d 905 (Minn. 1990).

Historically, an accountant's liability for negligence extended only to the client and to third-party beneficiaries. Under this view, **privity** of contract was a requirement for a cause of action based upon negligence. This approach was established by the landmark case *Ultramares Corporation v. Touche*, 255 N.Y. 170, 170 N.E. 441 (1931):

The defendants owed to their employer a duty imposed by law to make their certificate without fraud, and a duty growing out of contract to make it with the care and caution proper to their calling. Fraud includes the pretense of knowledge when knowledge there is none. To creditors and investors to whom the employer exhibited the certificate, the defendants owed a like duty to make it without fraud, since there was notice in the circumstances of its making that the employer did not intend to keep it to himself. [Citations.] A different question develops when we ask whether they owed a duty to these to make it without negligence. If liability for negligence exists, a thoughtless slip or blunder, the failure to detect a theft or forgery beneath the cover of deceptive entries, may expose accountants to a liability in an indeterminate amount for an indeterminate time to an indeterminate class. The hazards of a business conducted on these terms are so extreme as to enkindle doubt whether a flaw may not exist in the implication of a duty that exposes to these consequences.

\* \* \*

Our holding does not emancipate accountants from the consequences of fraud. It does not relieve them if their audit has been so negligent as to justify a finding that they had no genuine belief in its adequacy, for this again is fraud. It does no more than say that, if less than this is proved, if there has been neither reckless misstatement nor insincere profession of an opinion, but only honest blunder, the ensuing liability for negligence is one that is bounded by the contract and is to be enforced between the parties by whom the contract has been made. We doubt whether the average business man receiving a certificate without paying for it, and receiving it merely as one among a multitude of possible investors, would look for anything more.

Today, the courts apply three different tests to determine accountants' liability for negligence to third parties. Several States follow the *Ultramares* test, which has evolved into a **primary-benefit** test, explained in *Credit Alliance Corp. v. Arthur Andersen & Co.*, 65 N.Y.2d 536 (1985), as follows:

Before accountants may be held liable in negligence to noncontractual parties who rely to their detriment on inaccurate financial reports, certain prerequisites must be satisfied: (1) the accountants must have been aware that the financial reports were to be used for a particular purpose or purposes; (2) in the furtherance of which a known party or parties was intended to rely; and (3) there must have been some conduct on the part of the accountants linking them to that party or parties, which evinces the accountants' understanding of that party or parties' reliance.

In recent years, a majority of the States has adopted a **foreseen users** or **foreseen class of users** test. This test expands the class of protected individuals to include those whom the accountant knew would use the work product *or* those who use the accountant's work for a purpose for which the accountant knew the work would be used. For instance, an accountant knows that her client will use a work product to try to obtain a loan from a particular bank. Even if the client uses the audited financial statements to obtain a loan from a different bank, the auditor would be liable to that second bank for any negligent misrepresentations in the financial statements. This class of protected individuals does not, however, include potential investors and the general public.

This approach has also been adopted by the Restatement of Torts. Section 552 provides:

(1) One who, in the course of his business, profession or employment, or in any other transaction in which he has a pecuniary interest, supplies false information for the guidance of others in their business transactions, is subject to liability for pecuniary loss caused to them by their justifiable reliance upon the information, if he fails to exercise reasonable care or competence in obtaining or communicating the information.

(2) Except as stated in Subsection (3), the liability stated in Subsection (1) is limited to loss suffered
   (a) by the person or one of a limited group of persons for whose benefit and guidance he intends to supply the information or knows that the recipient intends to supply it; and
   (b) through reliance upon it in a transaction that he intends the information to influence or knows that the recipient so intends or in a substantially similar transaction.

(3) The liability of one who is under a public duty to give the information extends to loss suffered by any of the class of persons for whose benefit the duty is created, in any of the transactions in which it is intended to protect them.

See *Bily v. Arthur Young & Co.* (Case 45–1), which adopts the Restatement position for negligent misrepresentation and the privity standard for other types of negligence.

Some courts have extended liability to benefit an even broader group: reasonably **foreseeable plaintiffs** who are neither known to the accountant nor members of a class of intended recipients. A few States have adopted this test, which requires only that the accountant reasonably foresee that such individuals might use the financial statements. The rationale behind the foreseeability standard of the law of negligence is that a tort-feasor should be fully liable for all reasonably foreseeable consequences of her conduct.

◆ *See Figure 45–1*

 *See Case 45–1*

*Fraud* An accountant who commits a fraudulent act is liable to any person whom the accountant reasonably should have foreseen would be injured through justifiable reliance on the misrepresentation. The requisite elements of fraud, which are more fully discussed in Chapter 11, are (1) a false representation (2) of fact (3) that is material and (4) is made with knowledge of its falsity and with the intention to deceive, (5) is justifiably relied upon, and (6) causes injury to the plaintiff. An accountant who commits fraud may be held liable for both compensatory and punitive damages.

In recent years, accountants also have been subject to a number of civil lawsuits based on the Racketeer Influenced and Corrupt Organizations Act (RICO). For a discussion of this Act, see Chapter 6.

## Criminal Liability

An accountant's potential criminal liability in rendering professional services is based primarily on the Federal law of securities regulation (discussed below) and taxation. Nonetheless, an accountant would violate State criminal law if she knowingly and willfully certified false documents, altered or tampered with accounting records, used false financial reports, gave false testimony under oath, or committed forgery.

Criminal sanctions may be imposed under the Internal Revenue Code for knowingly preparing false or fraudulent tax returns or documents used in connection with a tax return. Such liability also extends to willfully assisting or advising a client or others to prepare a false return. Penalties for tax fraud may be a fine not to exceed $100,000 ($500,000 for a corporation) or three years' imprisonment, or both.

## Client Information

In providing services for his client, an accountant necessarily obtains information concerning the client's business affairs. Two legal issues concerning this client

**FIGURE 45–1** Accountants' Liability to Third Parties for Negligent Misrepresentation

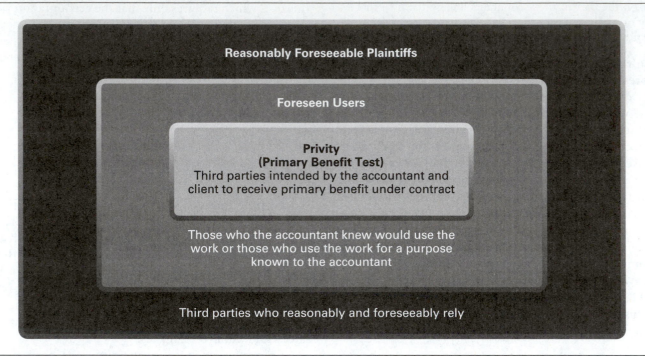

Reasonably Foreseeable Plaintiffs

Foreseen Users

**Privity**
**(Primary Benefit Test)**
Third parties intended by the accountant and
client to receive primary benefit under contract

Those who the accountant knew would use the
work or those who use the work for a purpose
known to the accountant

Third parties who reasonably and foreseeably rely

information involve (1) the ownership of the working papers generated by the accountant and (2) the question of whether or not client information is privileged.

***Working Papers*** Audit working papers include an auditor's records of the procedures she followed, the tests she performed, the information she obtained, and the conclusions she reached in connection with an audit. All relevant information pertaining to the examination should be included in the working papers. Because an accountant is held to be the owner of his working papers, he need not surrender them to his client. Nevertheless, the accountant may not disclose the contents of these papers unless either (1) the client consents or (2) a court orders the disclosure.

***Accountant–Client Privilege*** Because information considered to be privileged may not be admitted into evidence over the objection of the person possessing the privilege, an accountant must endeavor to maintain confidentiality regarding her communications with her client. The question of a possible accountant–client privilege frequently arises in tax disputes, criminal prosecution, and civil litigation.

Neither the common law nor Federal law recognizes a general privilege. Nevertheless, a number of States have

adopted statutes granting some form of accountant–client privilege. Most of these statutes grant the privilege to the client, although a few extend the privilege to the accountant. In addition, the IRS Restructuring and Reform Act of 1998 grants accountants authorized under Federal law to practice before the IRS the privilege of confidentiality for tax advice given their client-taxpayers with respect to Internal Revenue Code matters. Regardless of whether the privilege exists, it is generally considered to be professionally unethical for an accountant to disclose confidential communications from a client unless the disclosure is in accordance with (1) American Institute of Certified Public Accountants (AICPA) or GAAS requirements, (2) a court order, or (3) the client's request.

 *See Case 45–2*

# FEDERAL SECURITIES LAW

Accountants may be both civilly and criminally liable under provisions of the Securities Act of 1933 and the Securities Exchange Act of 1934. This liability is more extensive and has fewer limitations than liability under the common law. Securities and Exchange Commission (SEC) regulations require that public accounting firms and their members not have, or commit to acquire, any direct or material indirect financial interest in their audit clients or their clients' parents, subsidiaries, or other affiliates. Rule 2–01(b) of SEC Regulation S-X defines the term *member* to mean (1) all partners, shareholders, and other principals of the firm; (2) any professional employee involved in providing any professional service to the client, its parents, subsidiaries, or other affiliates; and (3) any professional employee having managerial responsibilities and located in the engagement office or other office of the firm which participates in a significant portion of the audit.

## Securities Act of 1933

Accountants are subject to express **civil** liability under Section 11 if the financial statements they prepare or certify for inclusion in a registration statement contain any untrue statement or omit any material fact. This liability extends to anyone who acquires the security without knowledge of the untruth or omission. Not only does such liability require no proof of privity between the accountant and the purchasers, but proof of reliance upon the financial statements is also usually not required under Section 11. An accountant will not be liable, however, if he can prove his "due diligence defense." **Due diligence** requires that the accountant had, after reasonable investigation, reasonable ground to believe and did believe, at the time the registration statement became effective, that the financial statements were true, complete, and accurate. The standard of reasonableness is that required of a prudent person in the management of her own property. Thus, Section 11 imposes liability upon accountants for **negligence** in the conduct of an audit or in the presentation of information in financial statements.

Moreover, an accountant who *willfully* violates this section may be held criminally liable for a fine of not more than $10,000 or imprisonment of not more than five years, or both. Section 24.

## Securities Exchange Act of 1934

*Civil Liability* Section 18 imposes express civil liability upon an accountant who makes or causes to be made any false or misleading statement with respect to any material fact in any application, report, document, or registration filed with the SEC under the 1934 Act. Liability extends to any person who purchased or sold a security in reliance upon that statement without knowing that it was false or misleading. An accountant is not liable, however, if she proves that she acted in good faith and had no knowledge that such statement was false or misleading. Thus, an accountant is not liable for false or misleading statements resulting from good faith negligence.

Accountants also may be held civilly liable for violations of **Rule 10b–5**. Rule 10b–5, as discussed in Chapter 44, is extremely broad in that it applies to both oral and written misstatements or omissions of material fact and to all securities. An accountant may be liable for a violation of the rule to those who rely upon the misstatement or omission of material fact when purchasing or selling a security. Nevertheless, liability is imposed only if the accountant acted with *scienter*, or intentional or knowing conduct. Therefore, accountants are not liable under Rule 10b–5 for mere negligence, although most courts have held that reckless disregard of the truth is sufficient.

◆ *See Figure 45–2*

FIGURE 45–2 Accountants' Liability under Federal Securities Law

| | Section 11 1933 Act | Section 18 1934 Act | Rule 10b–5 1934 Act |
|---|---|---|---|
| **Conduct** | Registration statement containing material misstatement or omission | False or misleading statements in a document filed with SEC | Deception or material misstatement or omission |
| **Fault** | Negligence | Knowledge or bad faith | *Scienter* |
| **Plaintiff's knowledge is a defense** | Yes | Yes | Yes |
| **Reliance required** | No | Yes | Yes |
| **Privity required** | No | No | No |

 *See Case 45–3*

***Criminal Liability*** Accountants may also be held **criminally** liable for any willful violation of Section 18 or Rule 10b–5. Conviction may carry a fine of not more than $1 million or imprisonment for not more than ten years, or both. An accounting firm may be fined up to $2.5 million. Section 32.

***Audit Requirements*** The Private Securities Litigation Reform Act of 1995 (Reform Act) imposed a significant set of obligations upon independent public accountants who audit financial statements required by the 1934 Act. The Reform Act authorizes the SEC to adopt rules that modify or supplement the practices or procedures followed by auditors in the conduct of an audit. Moreover, the Act requires auditors to establish procedures capable of detecting material illegal acts, identifying material related party transactions, and evaluating whether there is a substantial doubt about the issuer's ability to continue as a going concern during the next fiscal year.

If the auditor becomes aware of information indicating an illegal act, the auditor must determine whether an illegal act occurred and the illegal act's possible effect on the issuer's financial statements. Then the auditor must inform the issuer's management about any illegal activity and make sure that the audit committee or the board of directors is adequately informed. If the auditor concludes that (1) the illegal act has a material effect on the issuer's financial statements, (2) neither senior management nor the board has taken timely and appropriate remedial actions, *and* (3) the failure to take remedial action is reasonably expected to warrant departure from a standard auditor report or warrant resignation from the auditor's engagement, then the auditor promptly must report these conclusions to the issuer's board.

Within one day of receiving such report, the issuer must notify the SEC and furnish the auditor with a copy of that notice. If the auditor does not receive such notice, then the auditor must either resign or furnish the SEC with the auditor's report to the board. If the auditor resigns, the auditor must furnish the SEC with a copy of the auditor's report.

The Reform Act provides that an auditor shall not be held liable in a private action for any finding, conclusion, or statement expressed in the report the Act requires the auditor to make to the SEC. The SEC can impose civil penalties against an auditor who willfully violates the Reform Act by failing to resign or to furnish a report to the SEC.

---

 **Chapter Summary**

---

| **Common Law** | **Contract Liability** the employment contract between an accountant and her client is subject to the general principles of contract law |
|---|---|

- ***Explicit Duties*** the accountant is bound to perform all the duties she expressly agrees to provide
- ***Implicit Duties*** the accountant impliedly agrees to perform the contract in a competent and professional manner
- ***Beneficiaries*** contract liability extends to the client/contracting party and to third-party beneficiaries (noncontracting parties intended by the contracting parties to receive the primary benefit under the contract)
- ***Breach of Contract*** general contract law principles apply

**Tort Liability** a tort is a private or civil wrong or injury other than a breach of contract

- ***Negligence*** an accountant is liable for failing to exercise the degree of care a reasonably competent accountant would exercise under the circumstances; most courts have extended an accountant's liability for negligence beyond the client and third-party beneficiaries to foreseen third parties
- ***Fraud*** an accountant who commits a fraudulent act is liable for both compensatory and punitive damages to any person who he should have reasonably foreseen would be injured; a fraudulent act is a false representation of fact that is material, is made with knowledge of its falsity and with the intention to deceive, and is justifiably relied on

**Criminal Liability** State law imposes criminal liability on accountants for willfully certifying false documents, altering or tampering with accounting records, using false financial reports, giving false testimony, and committing forgery

**Client Information**

* *Working Papers* an accountant is considered the owner of his working papers but may not disclose their contents unless the client agrees or a court orders the disclosure
* *Accountant–Client Privilege* not recognized generally by the common law or Federal law, although some States have adopted statutes granting some form of privilege; accountants authorized to pracice before the IRS have privilege for tax advice given their client-taxpayers with respect to Internal Revenue Code matters

**Federal Securities Law**

**1933 Act**

* *Civil Liability* Section 11 imposes express civil liability upon accountants if the financial statements they prepare or certify for a registration statement contain any untrue statement or omit any material fact, unless the accountant proves her due diligence defense, which requires that the accountant had, after reasonable investigation, reasonable grounds to believe and did believe that the financial statements were true, complete, and accurate
* *Criminal Liability* a willful violator of Section 11 is subject to fines of not more than $10,000 and/or imprisonment of not more than five years

**1934 Act**

* *Section 18* imposes express civil liability on an accountant who knowingly makes any false or misleading statement about any material fact in any report, document, or registration filed with the SEC
* *Rule 10b–5* an accountant is civilly liable under this rule if he acts with *scienter* in making oral or written misstatements or omissions of material fact in connection with the purchase or sale of a security
* *Criminal Liability* a willful violator of either Section 18 or Rule 10b–5 is subject to fines of not more than $1 million and/or imprisonment of not more than ten years
* *Audit Requirements* auditors must establish procedures capable of detecting material illegal acts, identifying material related party transactions, and evaluating whether there is a substantial doubt about the issuer's ability to continue as a going concern during the next fiscal year

# Cases

### CASE 45–1

## Tort Liability

## *BILY v. ARTHUR YOUNG & CO.*

Supreme Court of California, In Bank, 1992
3 Cal.4th 370, 11 Cal. Rptr.2d 51, 834 P.2d 745

LUCAS, C.J.

[Osborne Computer Corporation manufactured the first portable personal computer for the mass market. Shipments began in 1981, and by fall 1982, sales of the company's sole product, the Osborne I, had reached $10 million per month. In late 1982, the company began planning for an early 1983 initial public offering of its stock. In order to obtain the financing it needed to meet its capital requirements until the offering, the company issued warrants to investors, in exchange for direct loans or letters of credit, to secure bank loans to the company. The warrants entitled their holders to purchase blocks of the company's stock at favorable prices that were expected to yield a sizable profit when the public offering took place. The company retained Arthur Young & Company, which issued unqualified or "clean" audit opinions on the company's 1981 and 1982 financial statements. Each opinion appeared on Arthur Young's letterhead and stated that (1) Arthur Young had examined the accompanying financial statements in accordance with the accounting profession's Generally Accepted Auditing Standards (GAAS); (2) the statements had been prepared in accordance with Generally Accepted Accounting Principles (GAAP); and (3) the statements "presented fairly" the company's financial position. The 1981 financial statement showed a net operating loss of approximately $1 million on sales of $6 million. The 1982 financial statement revealed a modest net operating profit of $69,000 on sales of more than $68 million. As the warrant transaction closed on April 8, 1983, the company's financial performance began to falter, and the company later filed for bankruptcy. Investors who had purchased Osborne stock and warrants (plaintiffs) brought suit against Arthur Young, claiming that they had made their investments in reliance on Arthur Young's unqualified audit. The plaintiffs presented evidence that Arthur Young's audit was not performed in accordance with GAAS and that, as a result, Osborne's financial statements had overstated the company's profits by $3 million. The plaintiffs also presented evidence that Arthur Young had discovered material weaknesses in the company's accounting controls but had failed to report these weaknesses to management.

The court instructed the jury on fraud, negligent misrepresentation, and professional negligence. With respect to third parties, the negligence instructions stated that "[a]n accountant owes a further duty of care to those third parties who reasonably and foreseeably rely on an audited financial statement prepared by the accountant. A failure to fulfill any such duty is negligence." The jury found Arthur Young liable only for professional negligence and awarded the plaintiffs $4.3 million. The Court of Appeals affirmed.]

## Approaches to the Problem of Auditor Liability to Third Persons

The complex nature of the audit function and its economic implications has resulted in different approaches to the question whether CPA auditors should be subjected to liability to third parties who read and rely on audit reports. Although three schools of thought are commonly recognized, there are some variations within each school and recent case law suggests a possible trend toward merger of two of the three approaches.

\* \* \*

### A. Privity of Relationship

\* \* \*

From the cases cited by the parties, it appears at least nine states purport to follow privity or near privity rules restricting the liability of auditors to parties with whom they have a contractual or similar relationship. \* \* \* Federal court decisions have held that the rule represents the law of three additional states whose highest courts have not expressly considered the question. \* \* \*

### B. Foreseeability

Arguing that accountants should be subject to liability to third persons on the same basis as other tortfeasors, Justice Howard Wiener advocated rejection of the rule of Ultramares in a 1983 law review article. [Citation.] In its place, he proposed a rule based on foreseeability of injury to third persons. Criticizing what he called the "anachronistic protection" given to accountants by the traditional rules limiting third person liability, he concluded: "Accountant liability based on foreseeable injury would serve the dual functions of compensation for injury and deterrence of negligent conduct. Moreover, it is a just and rational judicial policy that the same criteria govern the imposition of negligence liability, regardless of the context in which it arises." [Citation.]

\* \* \*

In the nearly 10 years since it was formally proposed, the foreseeability approach has not attracted a substantial following. And at least four state supreme courts have explicitly rejected the foreseeability approach in favor of the Restatement's "intended beneficiary" approach. . . .

\* \* \*

### C. The Restatement: Intent to Benefit Third Persons

Section 552 of the Restatement Second of Torts covers "Information Negligently Supplied for the Guidance of Others." It states a general principle that one who negligently supplies false information "for the guidance of others in their business transactions" is liable for economic loss suffered by the recipients in justifiable reliance on the information. But the liability created by the general principle is expressly limited to loss suffered: "(a) [B]y the person or one of a limited number of persons for whose benefit and guidance he intends to supply the information or knows that the recipient intends to supply it; and (b) [T]hrough reliance upon it in a transaction that he intends the information to influence or knows that the recipient so intends or in a substantially similar transaction." To paraphrase, a supplier of information is liable for negligence to a third party only if he or she intends to supply the information for the benefit of one or more third parties in a specific transaction or type of transaction identified to the supplier.

\* \* \*

Although the parties debate precisely how many states follow the Restatement rule, a review of the cases reveals the rule has somewhat more support than the privity of relationship rule and much more support than the foreseeability rule. At least 17 state and federal decisions have endorsed the rule in this and related contexts. Whatever the exact number of states that have endorsed it, the Restatement rule has been for many, if not most, courts a satisfactory compromise between their discomfort with the traditional privity approach and the "specter of unlimited liability." [Citation.]

\* \* \*

## Analysis of Auditor's Liability to Third Persons for Audit Opinions

\* \* \*

**A. Negligence** "[N]egligence is conduct which falls below the standard established by law for the protection of others." (Rest.2d Torts, § 282.) "Every one is responsible, not only for the result of his willful acts, but also for an injury occasioned to another by his want of ordinary care or skill in the management of his property or person, except so far as the latter has, willfully or by want of ordinary care, brought the injury upon himself." [Citation.]

\* \* \*

Viewing the problem before us . . . , we decline to permit all merely foreseeable third party users of audit reports to sue the auditor on a theory of professional negligence. Our holding is premised on three central concerns:

(1) Given the secondary "watchdog" role of the auditor, the complexity of the professional opinions rendered in audit reports, and the difficult and potentially tenuous causal relationships between audit reports and economic losses from investment and credit decisions, the auditor exposed to negligence claims from all foreseeable third parties faces potential liability far out of proportion to its fault;

(2) The generally more sophisticated class of plaintiffs in auditor liability cases (e.g., business lenders and investors) permits the effective use of contract rather than tort liability to control and adjust the relevant risks through "private ordering"; and

(3) The asserted advantages of more accurate auditing and more efficient loss spreading relied upon by those who advocate a pure foreseeability approach are unlikely to occur; indeed, dislocations of resources, including increased expense and decreased availability of auditing services in some sectors of the economy, are more probable consequences of expanded liability.

\* \* \*

The sole client of Arthur Young in the audit engagements involved in this case was the company. None of the plaintiffs qualify as clients. Under the rule we adopt, they are not entitled to recover on a pure negligence theory. Therefore, the verdict and judgment in their favor based on that theory are reversed.

**B. Negligent Misrepresentation** One difficulty in considering the problem before us is that neither the courts (ourselves included), the commentators, nor the authors of the Restatement Second of Torts have made clear or careful distinctions between the tort of negligence and the separate tort of negligent misrepresentation. The distinction is important not only because of the different statutory bases of the two torts, but also because it has practical implications for the trial of cases in complex areas such as the one before us.

Negligent misrepresentation is a separate and distinct tort, a species of the tort of deceit. "Where the defendant makes false statements, honestly believing that they are true, but without reasonable ground for such belief, he may be liable for negligent misrepresentation, a form of deceit." [Citation.]

Under certain circumstances, expressions of professional opinion are treated as representations of fact. When a statement, although in the form of an opinion, is "not a casual expression of belief" but "a deliberate affirmation of the matters stated," it may be regarded as a positive assertion of fact. [Citation.] Moreover, when a party possesses or holds itself out as possessing superior knowledge or special information or expertise regarding the subject matter and a plaintiff is so situated that it may reasonably rely on such supposed knowledge, information, or expertise, the defendant's representation may be treated as one of material fact. [Citations.] There is no dispute that Arthur Young's statements in audit opinions fall within these principles.

\* \* \*

Of the approaches we have reviewed, Restatement Second of Torts section 552, subdivision (b) is most consistent with the elements and policy foundations of the tort of negligent misrepresentation. The rule expressed there attempts to define a narrow and circumscribed class of persons to whom or for whom representations are made. In this way, it recognizes commercial realities by avoiding both unlimited and uncertain liability for economic losses in cases of professional mistake and exoneration of the auditor in situations where it clearly intended to undertake the responsibility of influencing particular business transactions involving third persons. The Restatement rule thus appears to be a sensible and moderate approach to the potential consequences of imposing unlimited negligence liability which we have identified.

\* \* \*

Having determined that intended beneficiaries of an audit report are entitled to recovery on a theory of negligent misrepresentation, we must consider whether they may also recover on a general negligence theory. We conclude they may not. Nonclients of the auditor are connected with the audit only through receipt of and express reliance on the audit report. Similarly, the gravamen of the cause of action for negligent misrepresenta-

tion in this context is actual, justifiable reliance on the representations in that report. Without such reliance, there is no recovery regardless of the manner in which the audit itself was conducted. [Citation.]

By allowing recovery for negligent misrepresentation (as opposed to mere negligence), we emphasize the indispensability of justifiable reliance on the statements contained in the report. \* \* \* Because the audit report, not the audit itself, is the foundation of the third person's claim, negligent misrepresentation more precisely captures the gravamen of the cause of action and more clearly conveys the elements essential to a recovery. [Citation.]

\* \* \*

Arthur Young has requested that we remand this case to the Court of Appeal with instructions to enter judgment in its favor. With one exception, we accede to the request. As explained above, plaintiffs' verdict for general negligence must be reversed. The jury also rejected plaintiffs' causes of action for negligent misrepresentation and intentional fraud. Although it was not instructed in accordance with the rules we have announced here, the jury was told Arthur Young could be held liable for misrepresentation to "plaintiff or a particular class of persons to which plaintiff belonged." If anything, these general instructions are more favorable to plaintiffs than the ones required by our decision, which more narrowly and specifically defines the "class of persons" entitled to recover.

\* \* \*

---

## CASE 45–2
### Accountant–Client Privilege
## *UNITED STATES v. ARTHUR YOUNG & COMPANY*
Supreme Court of the United States, 1984
465 U.S. 805, 104 S.Ct. 1495, 79 L.Ed.2d 826

BURGER, C. J.
We granted certiorari to consider whether tax accrual workpapers prepared by a corporation's independent certified public accountant in the course of regular financial audits are protected from disclosure in response to an Internal Revenue Service summons issued under [citation].

\* \* \*

Respondent Arthur Young & Co. is a firm of certified public accountants. As the independent auditor for

respondent Amerada Hess Corp., Young is responsible for reviewing the financial statements prepared by Amerada as required by the federal securities laws. In the course of its review of these financial statements, Young verified Amerada's statement of its contingent tax liabilities, and, in so doing, prepared the tax accrual workpapers at issue in this case. Tax accrual workpapers are documents and memoranda relating to Young's evaluation of Amerada's reserves for contingent tax liabilities. Such workpapers sometimes contain information pertaining to Amerada's financial transactions, identify questionable positions Amerada may have taken on its tax returns, and reflect Young's opinions regarding the validity of such positions.

In 1975 the Internal Revenue Service began a routine audit to determine Amerada's corporate income tax liability for the tax years 1972 through 1974. When the audit revealed that Amerada had made questionable payments of $7830 from a "special disbursement account," the IRS instituted a criminal investigation of Amerada's tax returns as well. In that process, pursuant to § 7602, the IRS issued an administrative summons to Young, which required Young to make available to the IRS all its Amerada files, including its tax accrual workpapers. Amerada instructed Young not to comply with the summons.

The IRS then commenced this enforcement action against Young in the United States District Court for the Southern District of New York. Amerada intervened, as permitted by [citation]. The District Court found that Young's tax accrual workpapers were relevant to the IRS investigation within the meaning of § 7602 and refused to recognize an accountant–client privilege that would protect the workpapers. [Citation.] Accordingly, the District Court ordered the summons enforced.

\* \* \*

A divided United States Court of Appeals for the Second Circuit affirmed in part and reversed in part. . . . [T]he Court of Appeals fashioned a work-product immunity doctrine for tax accrual workpapers prepared by independent auditors in the course of compliance with the federal securities laws. Because the IRS had not demonstrated a sufficient showing of need to overcome the immunity and was not seeking to prove fraud on Amerada's part, the Court of Appeals refused to enforce the summons insofar as it sought Young's tax accrual workpapers.

\* \* \*

We now turn to consider whether tax accrual workpapers prepared by an independent auditor in the course of a routine review of corporate financial statements should be protected by some form of work-product immunity from disclosure under § 7602. Based upon its evaluation of the competing policies of the federal tax and securities laws, the Court of Appeals found it necessary to create a so-called privilege for the independent auditor's workpapers.

Our complex and comprehensive system of federal taxation, relying as it does upon self-assessment and reporting, demands that all taxpayers be forthright in the disclosure of relevant information to the taxing authorities. Without such disclosure, and the concomitant power of the Government to compel disclosure, our national tax burden would not be fairly and equitably distributed. In order to encourage effective tax investigations, Congress has endowed the IRS with expansive information-gathering authority; . . .

While § 7602 is "subject to the traditional privileges and limitations," [citation], any other restrictions upon the IRS summons power should be avoided "absent unambiguous directions from Congress." [Citation.] We are unable to discern the sort of "unambiguous directions from Congress" that would justify a judicially created work-product immunity for tax accrual workpapers summoned under § 7602. Indeed, the very language of § 7602 reflects precisely the opposite: a congressional policy choice in favor of disclosure of all information relevant to a legitimate IRS inquiry. In light of this explicit statement by the Legislative Branch, courts should be chary in recognizing exceptions to the broad summons authority of the IRS or in fashioning new privileges that would curtail disclosure under § 7602. [Citation.] If the broad latitude granted to the IRS by § 7602 is to be circumscribed, that is a choice for Congress, and not this Court, to make. [Citation.]

\* \* \*

The Court of Appeals nevertheless concluded that "substantial countervailing policies," [citation], required the fashioning of a work-product immunity for an independent auditor's tax accrual workpapers. To the extent that the Court of Appeals, in its concern for the "chilling effect" of the disclosure of tax accrual workpapers, sought to facilitate communication between independent auditors and their clients, its remedy more closely resembles a testimonial accountant–client privilege than a work-product immunity for accountants' workpapers. But as this Court stated in [citation], "no confidential accountant-client privilege exists under federal law, and no state-created privilege has been recognized in federal cases." In light of [citation], the Court of Appeals' effort to foster candid communication between accountant and client by creating a self-styled work-product privilege was misplaced, and conflicts with what we see as the clear intent of Congress.

Nor do we find persuasive the argument that a work-product immunity for accountants' tax accrual workpapers is a fitting analogue to the attorney work-product doctrine established in [citation]. The . . . work-product doctrine was founded upon the private attorney's role as the client's confidential advisor and advocate, a loyal representative whose duty it is to present the client's case in the most favorable possible light. An independent certified public accountant performs a different role. By certifying the public reports that collectively depict a corporation's financial status, the independent auditor assumes a public responsibility transcending any employment relationship with the client. The independent public accountant performing this special function owes ultimate allegiance to the corporation's creditors and stockholders, as well as to the investing public. This "public watchdog" function demands that the accountant maintain total independence from the client at all times and requires complete fidelity to the public trust. To insulate from disclosure a certified public accountant's interpretations of the client's financial statements would be to ignore the significance of the accountant's role as a disinterested analyst charged with public obligations.

We cannot accept the view that the integrity of the securities markets will suffer absent some protection for accountants' tax accrual workpapers. The Court of Appeals apparently feared that, were the IRS to have access to tax accrual workpapers, a corporation might be tempted to withhold from its auditor certain information relevant and material to a proper evaluation of its financial statements. But the independent certified public accountant cannot be content with the corporation's representations that its tax accrual reserves are adequate; the auditor is ethically and professionally obligated to ascertain for himself as far as possible whether the corporation's contingent tax liabilities have been accurately stated. If the auditor were convinced that the scope of the examination had been limited by management's reluctance to disclose matters relating to the tax accrual reserves, the auditor would be unable to issue an unqualified opinion as to the accuracy of the corporation's financial statements. Instead, the auditor would be required to issue a qualified opinion, an adverse opinion, or a disclaimer of opinion, thereby notifying the investing public of possible potential problems inherent in the corporation's financial reports. Responsible corporate management would not risk a qualified evaluation of a corporate taxpayer's financial posture to afford cover for questionable positions reflected in a prior tax return. Thus, the independent auditor's obligation to serve the public interest assures that the integrity of the securities markets will be preserved, without the need for a work-product immunity for accountants' tax accrual workpapers.

We also reject respondents' position that fundamental fairness precludes IRS access to accountants' tax accrual workpapers. Respondents urge that the enforcement of an IRS summons for accountants' tax accrual workpapers permits the Government to probe the thought processes of its taxpayer citizens, thereby giving the IRS an unfair advantage in negotiating and litigating tax controversies. But if the SEC itself, or a private plaintiff in securities litigation, sought to obtain the tax accrual workpapers at issue in this case, they would surely be entitled to do so. In light of the broad congressional command of § 7602, no sound reason exists for conferring lesser authority upon the IRS than upon a private litigant suing with regard to transactions concerning which the public has no interest.

Congress has granted to the IRS "broad latitude to adopt enforcement techniques helpful in the performance of (its) tax collection and assessment responsibilities." [Citation.] Recognizing the intrusiveness of demands for the production of tax accrual workpapers, the IRS has demonstrated administrative sensitivity to the concerns expressed by the accounting profession by tightening its internal requirements for the issuance of such summonses. [Citation.] Although these IRS guidelines were not applicable during the years at issue in this case, their promulgation further refutes respondents' fairness argument and reflects an administrative flexibility that reinforces our decision not to reduce irrevocably the § 7602 summons power.

* * *

Beyond question it is desirable and in the public interest to encourage full disclosures by corporate clients to their independent accountants; if it is necessary to balance competing interests, however, the need of the Government for full disclosure of all information relevant to tax liability must also weigh in that balance. This kind of policy choice is best left to the Legislative Branch. Accordingly, the judgment of the Court of Appeals is affirmed in part and reversed in part, and the case is remanded for proceedings consistent with this opinion.

It is so ordered.

---

## CASE 45–3
### Liability under the 1934 Act: Rule 10b–5
## ERNST & ERNST v. HOCHFELDER
Supreme Court of the United States, 1976
425 U.S. 185, 96 S.Ct. 1375, 47 L.Ed.2d 668

POWELL, J.

The issue in this case is whether an action for civil damages may lie under § 10(b) of the Securities Exchange Act of 1934 (1934 Act), . . . , and Securities and Exchange Commission Rule 10b–5, . . . in the absence of an allegation of intent to deceive, manipulate, or defraud on the part of the defendant.

Petitioner, Ernst & Ernst, is an accounting firm. From 1946 through 1967 it was retained by First Securities Company of Chicago (First Securities), a small brokerage firm and member of the Midwest Stock Exchange and of the National Association of Securities Dealers, to perform periodic audits of the firm's books and records. In connection with these audits Ernst & Ernst prepared for filing with the Securities and Exchange Commission (Commission) the annual reports required of First Securities under § 17(a) of the 1934 Act. It also prepared for First Securities responses to the financial questionnaires of the Midwest Stock Exchange (Exchange).

Respondents were customers of First Securities who invested in a fraudulent securities scheme perpetrated by Leston B. Nay, president of the firm and owner of 92% of its stock. * * *

This fraud came to light in 1968 when Nay committed suicide, leaving a note that described First Securities as bankrupt and the escrow accounts as "spurious." Respondents subsequently filed this action for damages against Ernst & Ernst in the United States District Court for the Northern District of Illinois under § 10(b) of the 1934 Act. The complaint charged that Nay's escrow scheme violated § 10(b) and Commission Rule 10b–5, and that Ernst & Ernst had "aided and abetted" Nay's violations by its "failure" to conduct proper audits of First Securities. As revealed through discovery, respondents' cause of action rested on a theory of negligent nonfeasance. The premise was that Ernst & Ernst had failed to utilize "appropriate auditing procedures" in its audits of First Securities, thereby failing to discover internal practices of the firm said to prevent an effective audit.

* * *

Federal regulation of transactions in securities emerged as part of the aftermath of the market crash in 1929. The Securities Act of 1933 (1933 Act), [citation] was designed to provide investors with full disclosure of material information concerning public offerings of securities in commerce, to protect investors against fraud and, through the imposition of specified civil liabilities, to promote ethical standards of honesty and fair dealing. [Citation.] The 1934 Act was intended principally to protect investors against manipulation of stock prices through regulation of transactions upon securities exchanges and in over-the-counter markets, and to impose regular reporting requirements on companies whose stock is listed on national securities exchanges. [Citation.] Although the Acts contain numerous carefully drawn express civil remedies and criminal penalties, Congress recognized that efficient regulation of securities trading could not be accomplished under a rigid statutory program. As part of the 1934 Act Congress created the Commission, which is provided with an arsenal of flexible enforcement powers. [Citations.]

Section 10 of the 1934 Act makes it "unlawful for any person . . . (b) [t]o use or employ, in connection with the purchase or sale of any security . . . any manipulative or deceptive device or contrivance in contravention of such rules and regulations as the Commission may prescribe as necessary or appropriate in the public interest or for the protection of investors." [Citation.] In 1942, acting pursuant to the power conferred by § 10(b), the Commission promulgated Rule 10b–5.

* * *

Although § 10(b) does not by its terms create an express civil remedy for its violation, and there is no indication that Congress, or the Commission when adopting Rule 10b–5, contemplated such a remedy, the existence of a private cause of action for violations of the statute and the Rule is now well established. [Citation.] During the 30-year period since a private cause of action was first implied under § 10(b) and Rule 10b–5, a substantial body of case law and commentary has developed as to its elements. Courts and commentators long have differed with regard to whether scienter is a necessary element of such a cause of action, or whether negligent conduct alone is sufficient.

* * *

Although the extensive legislative history of the 1934 Act is bereft of any explicit explanation of Congress' intent, we think the relevant portions of that history support our conclusion that § 10(b) was addressed to practices that involve some element of scienter and cannot be read to impose liability for negligent conduct alone.

* * *

The section was described rightly as a "catchall" clause to enable the Commission "to deal with new manipulative [or cunning] devices." It is difficult to believe that any lawyer, legislative draftsman, or legislator would use these words if the intent was to create liability for merely negligent acts or omissions. Neither the legislative history nor the briefs supporting respondents identify any usage or authority for construing "manipulative [or cunning] devices" to include negligence.

* * *

The Commission argues that Congress has been explicit in requiring willful conduct when that was the standard of fault intended. * * *

* * *

The structure of the Acts does not support the Commission's argument. In each instance that Congress created express civil liability in favor of purchasers or sellers of securities it clearly specified whether recovery was to be premised on knowing or intentional conduct, negligence, or entirely innocent mistake. [Citations.] For example, § 11 of the 1933 Act unambiguously creates a private action for damages when a registration statement includes untrue statements of material facts or fails to state material facts necessary to make the statements therein not misleading. Within the limits specified by § 11(e), the issuer of the securities is held absolutely liable for any damages resulting from such misstatement or omission. But experts such as accountants who have prepared portions of the registration statement are accorded a "due diligence" defense. In effect, this is a negligence standard. An expert may avoid civil liability with respect to the portions of the registration statement for which he was responsible by showing that "after reasonable investigation" he had "reasonable ground[s] to believe" that the statements for which he was responsible were true and there was no omission of a material fact. § 11(b)(3)(B)(i). See e.g., *Escott v. BarChris Const. Corp.* [citation]. The express recognition of a cause of action premised on negligent behavior in § 11 stands in sharp contrast to the language of § 10(b), and significantly undercuts the Commission's argument.

We also consider it significant that each of the express civil remedies in the 1933 Act allowing recovery for negligent conduct, see §§ 11, 12(2), 15, [citations] is subject to significant procedural restrictions not applicable under § 10(b). * * *

* * *

We have addressed, to this point, primarily the language and history of § 10(b). The Commission contends, however, that subsections (b) and (c) of Rule 10b–5 are cast in language which—if standing alone— could encompass both intentional and negligent behavior. These subsections respectively provide that it is unlawful "[t]o make any untrue statement of a material fact or to omit to state a material fact necessary in order to make the statements made, in the light of the circumstances under which they were made, not misleading . . ." and "[t]o engage in any act, practice, or course of business which operates or would operate as a fraud or deceit upon any person. . . ."

Viewed in isolation the language of subsection (b), and arguably that of subsection (c), could be read as proscribing, respectively, any type of material misstatement or omission, and any course of conduct, that has the effect of defrauding investors, whether the wrongdoing was intentional or not.

We note first that such a reading cannot be harmonized with the administrative history of the Rule, a history making clear that when the Commission adopted the Rule it was intended to apply only to activities that involved scienter. More importantly, Rule 10b–5 was adopted pursuant to authority granted the Commission under § 10(b). The rulemaking power granted to an administrative agency charged with the administration of a federal statute is not the power to make law. Rather, it is "'the power to adopt regulations to carry into effect the will of Congress as expressed by the statute.'" [Citations.] . . . When a statute speaks so specifically in terms of manipulation and deception, and of implementing devices and contrivances—the commonly understood terminology of intentional wrongdoing—and when its history reflects no more expansive intent, we are quite unwilling to extend the scope of the statute to negligent conduct.

* * *

The judgment of the Court of Appeals is reversed.

# Questions

1. Explain the contract liability of an accountant to her client.
2. For what and to whom does an accountant have tort liability?
3. Explain who owns the working papers an accountant generates and whether client information is privileged.

4. Discuss the potential civil and criminal liability of an accountant under the 1933 Act.
5. Discuss the potential civil and criminal liability of an accountant under the 1934 Act.

# Problems

1. Baldwin Corporation made a public offering of $25 million of convertible debentures and registered the offering with the SEC. The registration statement contained financial statements certified by Adams and Allen, CPAs. The financial statements overstated Baldwin's net income and assets by 20 percent while understating the company's liability by 15 percent. Because Adams and Allen did not carefully follow GAAS, it failed to detect these inaccuracies, the discovery of which has caused the bond prices to drop from their original selling price of $1,000 per bond to $720. Conrad, who purchased $10,000 of the debentures, has brought suit against Adams and Allen. Decision?

2. Ingram is a CPA employed by Jordan, Keller and Lane, CPAs, to audit Martin Enterprises, Inc., a fast-growing service firm that went public two years ago. The financial statements Ingram audited were included in a proxy statement proposing a merger with several other firms. The proxy statement was filed with the SEC and included several inaccuracies. First, approximately $1 million, or more than 20 percent, of the previous year's "net sales originally reported" had proven nonexistent by the time the proxy statement was filed and had been written off on Martin's own books. This was not disclosed in the proxy statement, in violation of Accounting Board Opinion Number 9. Second, Martin's net sales for the current year were stated as $11,300,000 when in fact they were less than $10,500,000. Third, Martin's net profits for the current year were reported as $700,000, when the firm actually had no earnings at all.

   (a) What civil liability, if any, does Ingram have?
   (b) What criminal liability, if any, does Ingram have?

3. Girard & Company, CPAs, audited the financial statements included in the annual report submitted by PMG Enterprises, Inc., to the SEC. The audit failed to detect numerous false and misleading statements contained in the financial statements.

   (a) Investors who subsequently purchased PMG stock have brought suit against Girard under Section 18 of the 1934 Act. What defenses, if any, are available to Girard?
   (b) The SEC has initiated criminal proceedings under the 1934 Act against Girard. What must be proven for Girard to be held criminally liable?

4. Dryden, a certified public accountant, audited the books of Elixir, Inc., and certified incorrect financial statements in a form that was filed with the SEC. Shortly thereafter, Elixer, Inc., went bankrupt. Investigation into the bankruptcy disclosed that through an intricate and clever embezzlement scheme Kraft, the president of Elixir, had siphoned off substantial sums of money that now support Kraft in a luxurious lifestyle in South America. Investors who purchased shares of Elixir have brought suit against Dryden under Rule 10b–5. At trial, Dryden produces evidence demonstrating that his failure to discover the embezzlement resulted merely from negligence on his part and that he had no knowledge of the fraudulent conduct. Decision?

5. Johnson Enterprises, Inc., contracted with the accounting firm of P, A & E to perform an audit of Johnson. The accounting firm performed its duty in a nonnegligent, competent manner but failed to discover a novel embezzlement scheme perpetrated by Johnson's treasurer. Shortly thereafter, Johnson's treasurer disappeared with $75,000 of the company's money. Johnson now refuses to pay P, A & E its $20,000 audit fee and is seeking to recover $75,000 from P, A & E.

   (a) What are the rights and liabilities of P, A & E and Johnson? Explain.
   (b) Would your answer to (a) differ if the scheme were a common embezzlement scheme that GAAS should have disclosed? Explain.

6. The accounting firm of T, W & S was engaged to perform an audit of Progate Manufacturing Company. During the course of the audit, T, W & S discovered that the company had overvalued its inventory by carrying the inventory on its books at the previous year's prices, which were significantly higher than current prices. When T, W & S approached Progate's president, Lehman, about the improper valuation of inventory, Lehman became enraged and told T, W & S that unless the firm accepted the valuation, Progate would sue T, W & S. Although T, W & S knew that Progate's suit was frivolous and unfounded, it wished to avoid the negative publicity that would arise from any suit brought against it. Therefore, on the assumption that the overvaluation would not harm anybody, T, W & S accepted Progate's

inflated valuation of inventory. Progate subsequently went bankrupt, and T, W & S is now being sued by (1) First National Bank, a bank that relied upon T, W & S's statement to loan money to Progate, and (2) Thomas, an investor who purchased 20 percent of Progate's stock after receiving T, W & S's statement. What are the rights and liabilities of First National Bank, Thomas, and T, W & S?

7.   J, B & J, CPAs, has audited the Highcredit Corporation for the past five years. Recently, the SEC has commenced an investigation of Highcredit for possible violations of Federal securities law. The SEC has subpoenaed all of J, B & J's working papers pertinent to the audit of Highcredit. Highcredit insists that J, B & J not turn over the documents to the SEC. What action should J, B & J take? Why?

8.   On February 1, the Gazette Corporation hired Susan Sharp to conduct an audit of its books and to prepare financial statements for the corporation's annual meeting on July 1. Sharp made every reasonable attempt to comply with the deadline but could not finish the report on time due to delays in receiving needed information from Gazette. Gazette now refuses to pay Sharp for her audit and is threatening to bring a cause of action against Sharp. What course of action should Sharp pursue? Why?

9.   John P. Butler Accountancy Corporation agreed to audit the financial statements of Westside Mortgage, Inc., a mortgage company that arranged financing for real property, for the year ending December 31, 1978. On March 22, 1979, after completing the audit, Butler issued unqualified audited financial statements listing Westside's corporate net worth as $175,036. The primary asset on the balance sheet was a $100,000 note receivable that had, in reality, been rendered worthless in August 1977 when the trust deed on real property securing the note was wiped out by a prior foreclosure of a superior deed of trust. The note constituted 57 percent of Westside's net worth and was thus material to an accurate representation of Westside's financial position. In October 1979, International Mortgage Company (IMC) approached Westside for the purpose of buying and selling loans on the secondary market. IMC signed an agreement with Westside in December after reviewing Westside's audited financial statements. In June 1980, Westside issued a $475,293 promissory note to IMC, on which it ultimately defaulted. IMC brought an action against Westside, its owners, principals, and Butler. IMC alleged negligence and negligent misrepresentation against Butler in auditing and issuing without qualification the defective financial statements on which IMC relied in deciding to do business with Westside. Butler moved for summary judgment, claiming that it owed no duty of care to IMC, a third party who was not specifically known to Butler as an intended recipient of the audited financial statements. The trial court granted Butler's motion, and IMC appealed. Decision?

**WWW**   **Internet Exercise**  Find information about the structure and mission of the Financial Accounting Standards Board and examine its recent announcements and documents.

# CHAPTER 46

# Environmental Law

As technology has advanced and people have become more urbanized, their effect on the environment has increased. Our air has become dirtier; our waters have become more polluted. While individuals and environmental groups have brought private actions against some polluters, the common law has proved unable to control environmental damage. Because of this inadequacy, the Federal and State governments have enacted a variety of statutes designed to promote environmental concerns and prevent environmental harm. Although in recent years certain developed countries, such as the United States, have made significant progress in controlling pollutants, such is not the case worldwide. Moreover, even as we have enjoyed some success in controlling some pollutants, a new generation of environmental problems has arisen. In this chapter, we will discuss both common law causes of action for environmental damage and Federal regulation of the environment.

## COMMON LAW ACTIONS FOR ENVIRONMENTAL DAMAGE

Private tort actions may be used to recover for harm to the environment. For example, if Alice's land is polluted by the mill next door, Alice may sue the mill in tort for the damage to her land. In suing to recover for environmental damage, plaintiffs generally have relied on the theories of nuisance, trespass, and strict liability.

### NUISANCE

The term *nuisance* encompasses two distinct types of wrong: private nuisance and public nuisance. A private nuisance involves an interference with a person's use and enjoyment of his land, while a public nuisance is an act that interferes with a public right.

### Private Nuisance

To establish a **private nuisance,** a plaintiff must show that the defendant has substantially and unreasonably interfered with the use and enjoyment of the plaintiff's land. In an action for damages, the plaintiff need not prove that the defendant's conduct was unreasonable, only that the interference was unreasonable. Thus, assuming all other requirements are met, the question in a private nuisance suit for damages is whether the defendant should pay for the harm it caused the plaintiff, even if the defendant's action was not unreasonable. For example, in one case, an electric utility using a coal-burning electric generator which employed the latest scientific methods for reducing emissions was held liable for the harm it caused its neighbor's alfalfa crops, even though the utility was performing the socially useful function of creating electric power.

Although a plaintiff need not prove the defendant's conduct is unreasonable to recover in a private nuisance action for damages, such reasonableness is an issue when the plaintiff sues for an injunction. In determining whether an injunction against a nuisance is appropriate, a court will "balance the equities" by considering a number of factors, including the gravity of the harm to the plaintiff, the social value of the defendant's activity that is causing the harm, the feasibility and costs of avoiding the harm, and the public interest, if any.

The need to balance the equities has meant that courts often deny injunctions when the defendant is engaged in a socially useful activity. Additionally, injunctions are frequently denied because the defendant successfully raises an equitable defense. Consequently, private nuisance actions have been of limited value in controlling environmental damage.

## Public Nuisance

To be treated as a **public nuisance,** an activity must somehow interfere with the health, safety, or comfort of the public. For example, the actions of an industrial plant in polluting a stream will be treated as a private nuisance if such actions inconvenience only the owners of land downstream but will be treated as a public nuisance if they kill the stream's marine life. Generally, only a public representative, such as the attorney general, may sue to stop a public nuisance. If, however, the nuisance inflicts upon an individual some unique harm that the general populace does not suffer, that individual may also sue to halt the nuisance. Out of concern about the economic impact of closing an industrial operation, public representatives frequently are unwilling to sue to abate a public nuisance. Consequently, because these representatives often will not, and private parties may not, sue, relatively few public nuisance actions have been brought against polluters.

## TRESPASS TO LAND

To establish **trespass to land,** a plaintiff must show an invasion that interferes with the plaintiff's right of exclusive possession of the property and that is the direct result of an action by the defendant. For example, entering or throwing trash on someone else's land without permission constitutes a trespass. Trespass differs from private nuisance in that trespass requires an interference with the plaintiff's possession of the land. Thus, sending smoke or gas onto another's property may constitute a private nuisance but does not constitute a trespass.

Trespass often is difficult to establish in actions for environmental damage, either because the plaintiff is not in possession of the property or because the injury does not stem from an invasion of the property. Trespass actions have thus been of limited benefit in halting environmental damage. For a more complete discussion of trespass, see Chapter 7.

## STRICT LIABILITY FOR ABNORMALLY DANGEROUS ACTIVITIES

While they generally base tort liability on fault, the courts may hold **strictly liable,** that is, liable without fault, a person engaged in an abnormally dangerous activity. To establish such strict liability, a plaintiff must show that the defendant is carrying on an unduly dangerous activity in an inappropriate location and that the plaintiff has suffered damage because of this activity. For example, a person who operates an oil refinery in a densely populated area may be held strictly liable for any damage the refinery causes. The requirement that the activity engaged in be (1) ultrahazardous and (2) inappropriate for its locale has limited the number of strict liability actions brought against polluters.

## PROBLEMS COMMON TO PRIVATE CAUSES OF ACTION

In addition to the shortcomings of each tort theory discussed above, using a private cause of action to control environmental damage presents its own problems. The costs associated with private litigation (including the payment of one's own legal fees) are high, and although overall the environmental damage may be considerable, the extent of any particular injury may not warrant pursuing a private lawsuit. Furthermore, tort actions generally do not provide relief for aesthetic, as opposed to physical, injury. Additionally, in many tort actions a significant issue of causation arises. For example, if a landowner lives near several plants, each of which emits pollution and none of which, by itself, would cause the amount of damage the landowner's property has suffered, the landowner may have difficulty recovering from any of the plant owners. Finally, even if a private plaintiff is successful, her recovery may be limited to monetary damages, leaving the defendant free to continue to pollute.

## FEDERAL REGULATION OF THE ENVIRONMENT

Because private causes of action have proved inadequate to recompense and prevent environmental damage, the Federal, State, and some local governments have enacted statutes designed to protect the environment. In this chapter, we will consider some of the more important Federal environmental laws. In addition, the Environmental Protection Agency (EPA) has encouraged companies to conduct voluntary environmental audits. One of the key issues surrounding such self-audits is whether these audits are discoverable by State or Federal prosecutors.

# THE NATIONAL ENVIRONMENTAL POLICY ACT

In 1969, Congress enacted the National Environmental Policy Act (NEPA) to establish environmental protection as a goal of Federal policy. The NEPA's declaration of national environmental policy states the following:

The Congress, recognizing the profound impact of man's activity on the interrelations of all components of the natural environment, particularly the profound influences of population growth, high-density urbanization, industrial expansion, resource exploitation, and new and expanding technological advances, and recognizing further the critical importance of restoring and maintaining environmental quality to the overall welfare and development of man, declares that it is the continuing policy of the Federal Government, in cooperation with State and local governments * * * to use all practicable means and measures * * * in a manner calculated to foster and promote the general welfare, to create and maintain conditions under which man and nature can exist in productive harmony, and fulfill the social, economic and other requirements of present and future generations of Americans.

The NEPA has two major substantive sections, one creating the Council on Environmental Quality (CEQ) and the other requiring that each Federal agency, when recommending or reporting on proposals for legislation or other major Federal action, prepare an **environmental impact statement** (EIS) if the legislation or Federal action will have a significant environmental effect.

## The Council on Environmental Quality

The Council on Environmental Quality (CEQ), a three-member advisory group, is not a separate administrative agency but rather is part of the Executive Office of the President; as such, it makes recommendations to the president on environmental matters and prepares annual reports on the condition of the environment. Although not expressly authorized to do so by statute, the CEQ, acting under a series of executive orders, has issued regulations regarding the content and preparation of environmental impact statements. The Federal courts generally have deferred to these regulations.

## Environmental Impact Statements

Unlike most Federal environmental statutes, the NEPA does not focus on a particular type of environmental damage or harmful substance but instead expresses the Federal government's continuing concern with protection of the environment. The NEPA's promotion of environmental considerations is effected through the EIS requirement.

***Procedure for Preparing an EIS*** When proposing legislation or considering a major Federal action, the CEQ regulations require that a Federal agency initially make an "environmental assessment," which is a short analysis of the need for an EIS. If the agency decides that no EIS is required, it must make this decision available to the public. If, on the other hand, the agency concludes that an EIS is required, the agency must engage in "scoping," which consists of consulting other relevant Federal agencies and the public to determine the significant issues the EIS will address and the statement's appropriate scope. After scoping, the agency prepares a draft EIS, for which there is a comment period. After the comment period ends and revisions, if necessary, are made, a final EIS is published.

***Scope of EIS Requirement*** The EIS requirement of the NEPA applies to a broad range of projects:

[T]here is "Federal action" within the meaning of the statute not only when an agency proposes to build a facility itself, but also whenever an agency makes a decision which permits action by other parties which will affect the quality of the environment. NEPA's impact statement procedure has been held to apply where a federal agency approves a lease of land to private parties, grants licenses and permits to private parties, or approves and funds state highway projects. In each of these instances the federal agency took action affecting the environment in the sense that the agency made a decision which permitted some other party—private or governmental—to take action affecting the environment.

The NEPA's EIS requirement applies not only to a broad range of projects but also to a broad range of environmental effects. The NEPA has been held to apply not only to the natural environment but also to the urban environment.

The Act [NEPA] must be construed to include protection of the quality of life for city residents. Noise, traffic, overburdened mass transportation systems, crime, congestion and even availability of drugs all affect the urban "environment" and are surely results of the "profound influences of * * * high-density urbanization [and] industrial expansion."

While effects on health, including psychological health, are considered environmental effects under the NEPA, the Supreme Court has held that an effect is environmental only if it has a reasonably close causal relation to an impact on the physical environment.

**Content of an EIS** The NEPA requires that an EIS describe in detail the environmental impact of a proposed action, any adverse environmental effects which could not be avoided if the proposal were implemented, alternatives to the proposed action, the relationship between local short-term uses of the environment and the maintenance and enhancement of long-term productivity, and any irreversible and irretrievable commitments of resources the proposed action would involve if it were implemented. Impact statements provide a basis for evaluating the benefits of a proposed project in light of its environmental risks and for comparing its environmental risks with those of alternatives. The Supreme Court has held that a Federal agency is required to consider only all *reasonable* alternatives in its EIS.

**Nature of EIS Requirement** Whether the NEPA was solely procedural or whether it had a substantive component was initially unclear. The Supreme Court resolved the issue by holding that the NEPA's requirements are primarily procedural and that the NEPA does not require that the relevant Federal agency attempt to mitigate the adverse effects of a proposed Federal action.

## THE CLEAN AIR ACT

Initially, the Federal government's role in controlling air pollution was quite limited. The States had primary responsibility for air pollution control, and the Federal government merely supervised their efforts and offered technical and financial assistance. When State efforts proved inadequate to alleviate the problem, Congress enacted the Clean Air Act Amendments of 1970, greatly expanding the Federal role in antipollution efforts. Major revisions to the Clean Air Act were enacted in 1977 and 1990.

The Act establishes two regulatory schemes, one for existing sources and one for new stationary sources. The States retain primary responsibility for regulating existing stationary sources and motor vehicles then in use (i.e., in use when the Act, or its subsequently enacted amendments, took effect), while the Federal government regulates new sources, new vehicles, and hazardous air pollutants.

Under the Act, the Environmental Protection Agency (EPA) may impose civil penalties of up to $25,000 per day of violation. Criminal penalties, which depend on the type of violation, vary greatly, providing for a maximum fine of $1 million per violation and/or fifteen years' imprisonment for a knowing violation that endangers a person. For repeat convictions, the Act doubles the maximum punishments.

## Existing Stationary Sources and Motor Vehicles Then in Use

Because the States had not managed adequately to control air pollution, the 1970 amendments provided that, with respect to existing stationary sources and motor vehicles then in use, the Federal government would set national air quality standards that the States would be primarily responsible for achieving.

**National Ambient Air Quality Standards** Under the Act, the EPA administrator is required to establish **national ambient air quality standards (NAAQSs)** for air pollutants that endanger the public health and welfare. The EPA administrator must establish "primary" standards to protect the public health, allowing for an adequate safety margin, and "secondary" standards to protect elements relating to the public welfare, such as animals, crops, and structures. The NAAQS for a particular pollutant specifies the concentration of that pollutant that will be allowed in the outside air over designated periods of time.

The EPA administrator established quality standards for seven major classes of pollutants—carbon monoxide, particulates, sulfur dioxide, nitrogen dioxide, hydrocarbons, ozone, and lead, although the hydrocarbon NAAQS was subsequently withdrawn as no longer being necessary. Recognizing that many areas would not meet the 1977 NAAQS deadline, Congress, in the 1977 amendments to the Act, extended the deadline to December 1982 and further provided that States demonstrating the impossibility of meeting the 1982 deadline "despite the implementation of all reasonably available measures" could obtain an extension until December 1987. In 1987, Congress extended the deadline for another eight months. The August 1988 deadline expired without extension, but the EPA has not vigorously enforced it.

The 1990 amendments sought to hasten attainment of the standards and provided that the EPA must establish new standards for major pollutants every five years. The amendments also imposed tighter standards with regard to ozone pollution, due to the lack of progress in this area.

***State Implementation Plans*** Once the EPA promulgates a new NAAQS, each State must submit to the agency a **State implementation plan (SIP)** detailing how the State will implement and maintain the NAAQS within the State. If the State adopted the SIP after public hearings and the SIP meets certain statutory conditions, the EPA is required to approve it. Foremost among the statutory conditions is the requirement that under the SIP the State will attain primary standards as soon as practicable but in any case within three years after the EPA approves the SIP. If the EPA determines that under an SIP a State will not attain an NAAQS within the designated time and the State fails to make the necessary amendments, the EPA is authorized to make amendments that will be binding on the State.

Under the 1990 amendments, the EPA also must decide whether an SIP is complete. If it is not, the EPA may treat the plan as a nullity in whole or in part. If it is complete, the EPA must approve or disapprove the plan within a year. Once the EPA approves an SIP, the plan is regarded as both State and Federal law, enforceable by either its State of implementation or the Federal government.

***Prevention of Significant Deterioration Areas*** Prior to the 1977 amendments, an issue arose as to whether air that was cleaner than required by an applicable NAAQS would be allowed to deteriorate to the NAAQS level. This issue was significant because much of the United States, particularly land in the Southwest, had air whose quality was higher than that required by applicable standards. Responding to this issue, Congress, in the 1977 amendments, established a policy to prevent the quality of such air from deteriorating. To effectuate this policy, Congress established rules for areas whose air quality was higher than the applicable NAAQS required it to be or for which information was insufficient to determine the air quality (so-called **prevention of significant deterioration [PSD] areas**). Because the rules classified an area on a pollutant-by-pollutant basis, a particular area might be a PSD area with respect to one pollutant and an area that had not met the applicable NAAQS with respect to another pollutant.

In PSD areas, only limited increases in air pollution are allowed. Before a major stationary source in a PSD area may be constructed or modified, the owner or operator of the source must receive a permit from the applicable State regulator. To receive a permit, the owner/operator must demonstrate that the source will not increase pollution beyond permitted levels and must show that the source will utilize the best control technology available.

***Nonattainment Areas*** The 1977 and 1990 amendments also established special rules for areas that did not meet applicable NAAQSs, so-called **nonattainment areas.** Before a major stationary source may be constructed or modified in a nonattainment area, the owner/operator of the source must receive a permit from the applicable State regulator. To receive a permit, the owner/operator must show that the source will comply with the lowest achievable emission rate, which is the more stringent of either the most stringent emission limitation contained in any SIP or the most stringent emission limitation actually achieved. Additionally, total emissions from existing stationary sources and the proposed new or modified source together must be less than the total emissions allowed from existing sources at the time the permit is sought. Thus, to obtain a permit in a nonattainment area, an owner/operator must in some way reduce total emissions from all sources (existing and new/modified). Under the 1990 amendments, the reduction required varies with the severity of the area's nonattainment problem. One way to reduce total emissions from all sources is to pay the owner/operator of another source to reduce its emissions by either installing more advanced emission control technology or closing its source. Alternatively, an owner/operator may reduce its own total emissions by altering the mix of emission controls at its plant. Under the EPA's **"bubble concept,"** an entire plant is viewed as one source; consequently, the permit process applies only if total emissions from the plant increase. If, instead, the EPA treated each unit at a plant as a separate source, the owner/operator would be required to obtain a permit whenever it made a change to one unit. The bubble concept thus enables an owner/operator to bypass the permit process in some instances. Though environmental groups challenged the concept on this basis, in 1984 the Supreme Court upheld the bubble concept, finding the regulation to be a reasonable exercise of the EPA's discretion.

## New Source Standards

The scheme of Federal NAAQSs and State SIPs applies to existing stationary sources and to motor vehicles then in use. In contrast, the Clean Air Act authorizes the Federal government to establish national emission standards for new stationary sources, new vehicles, and hazardous air pollutants.

*New Stationary Sources* The Act requires the EPA administrator to establish performance standards for stationary sources that are constructed or modified after the publication of applicable regulations. The standard of performance must "reflect the degree of emission limitation and percentage reduction achievable through application of the best technological system of continuous emission reduction which * * * has been adequately demonstrated." As Case 46–1 indicates, the standard governing new sources is more stringent than the standard governing existing sources; accordingly, it is, from industry's perspective, better to be considered an existing source than a new or modified one.

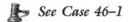 *See Case 46–1*

*New Vehicles* The Clean Air Act requires the EPA administrator to establish emission standards for new motor vehicles and new motor vehicle engines. The Act also requires the use of reformulated automotive fuels to reduce ozone and carbon monoxide pollution. The reformulated gasoline must contain more oxygen and less in terms of volatile organic compounds.

*Hazardous Air Pollutants* The Act authorizes the EPA administrator to establish national emission standards for hazardous or toxic air pollutants, defined as "air pollutant[s] * * * caus[ing], or contribut[ing] to, air pollution which may reasonably be anticipated to result in an increase in mortality or an increase in serious irreversible, or incapacitating reversible, illness." The standard must be set at a level that "provides an ample margin of safety to protect the public health."

*Acid Rain* The 1990 amendments attempt to halt environmental destruction caused by **acid rain**: precipitation that contains high levels of sulfuric or nitric acid. Because sulfur dioxide (which forms sulfuric acid in the atmosphere and comes back as acid rain) is released into the atmosphere primarily by electric utilities, the 1990 amendments regulate such utilities by allotting them emission allowances with regard to the amount of sulfur dioxide they may release into the atmosphere, based upon past emissions and fuel consumption. The amendments establish an allowance schedule that will significantly reduce emissions of sulfur dioxide and nitrous oxides by the year 2000. The amendments also permit each utility to bank or sell its emission allowances.

## THE CLEAN WATER ACT

As with air pollution control, the primary responsibility for controlling water pollution fell initially to the States. When their efforts proved inadequate, Congress fundamentally revised the nation's water pollution laws in its 1972 amendments to the Federal Water Pollution Control Act (subsequently renamed the Clean Water Act). Substantially amended again in 1977, 1981, and 1987, the Act attempts comprehensively to restore and maintain the chemical, physical, and biological integrity of the nation's waters.

The EPA may impose civil penalties of up to $25,000 per day for each violation. Maximum criminal penalties for knowing violations are $50,000 per day of violation and/or three years' imprisonment. For repeat convictions, the maximum punishments are doubled.

Like the Clean Air Act, the Clean Water Act establishes different schemes for existing sources and new sources. Additionally, the Act provides different programs for point and nonpoint sources of pollution. A **point source** is "any discernible, confined and discrete conveyance * * * from which pollutants are or may be discharged." A **nonpoint source,** in contrast, is a land use that causes pollution, such as a pesticide runoff from farming operations.

The scope of the Act is extremely broad, applying not only to all navigable waters in the United States but also to tributaries of navigable waters, interstate waters and their tributaries, the use of nonnavigable intrastate waters, if their misuse could affect interstate commerce, and freshwater wetlands.

### Point Sources

The Act mandates that the EPA administrator establish effluent limitations for categories of existing point sources. An **effluent limitation** is a technology-based standard that limits the amount of a pollutant that a point source may discharge into a body of water. The Act effectuates such limitations through the **National Pollutant Discharge Elimination System (NPDES)**, a permit system.

*Effluent Limitations* Under the 1972 amendments, effluent limitations for existing point sources, other than publicly owned treatment works, required application of the **best practicable control technology (BPT)** currently available by 1977 and application of the **best available technology (BAT)** economically achievable by 1983. According to the EPA, BPT is "the average of the best existing performance by well-operated plants within each industrial category or subcategory," while BAT is "the very best control and treatment measures that have been or are capable of being achieved." Somewhat different standards apply to publicly owned treatment works.

***The National Pollutant Discharge Elimination System***   The National Pollutant Discharge Elimination System (NPDES), the permit system through which effluent limitations are to be achieved, requires that any person responsible for the discharge from a point source of a pollutant into U.S. waters must obtain a discharge permit from the EPA, the Army Corps of Engineers, or, in some circumstances, the relevant State. An NPDES permit incorporates the applicable effluent limitations and establishes a schedule for compliance. The holder of an NPDES permit is required to notify the appropriate authority if the holder will not meet its obligations under the permit. A discharge not in compliance with a permit is unlawful. With limited exceptions, new permits for existing facilities cannot be less stringent than current permits.

 *See Case 46–2*

***The 1977 Amendments***   Recognizing that the application deadlines it had set in the 1972 amendments would not be met, Congress extended and modified the deadlines in 1977. The 1977 amendments to the Clean Water Act divided pollutants into three categories—toxic, conventional, and nonconventional (any pollutants that are neither toxic nor conventional)—and established different deadlines and standards for each category. For toxic pollutants, the 1983 BAT deadline was extended to 1984; for nonconventional pollutants, this standard was to be achieved by 1984 or within three years after the effluent limitation was established, whichever was later. For conventional pollutants, a new standard, **best conventional pollution control technology (BCT),** was to be achieved by 1984. These deadlines were subsequently extended to 1989.

## Nonpoint Source Pollution

Controlling nonpoint source pollution—such as agricultural and urban runoff—is inherently more difficult than controlling point source pollution.

There is no effective way as yet, other than land use control, by which you can intercept that runoff and control it in a way that you do a point source. We have not yet developed technology to deal with that kind of a problem. We need to find ways to deal with it, because a great quantity of pollutants [are] discharged by runoff, not only from agriculture but from construction sites, from streets, from parking lots, and so on, and we have to be concerned with developing controls for them.

Although Congress tried to address the problem of nonpoint source pollution in the 1972 amendments, little effective control of nonsource pollution occurred before 1987. The 1987 amendments require States to identify State waters that will not meet the Act's requirements without the management of nonpoint sources of pollution and to institute "best management practices" to control such sources. The EPA must approve each State's management plan.

## New Source Performance Standards

The Act requires the EPA administrator to establish Federal performance standards for new sources. A performance standard should "reflect the greatest degree of effluent reduction * * * achievable through application of the best available demonstrated control technology." The preferred standard for new sources is one "permitting no discharge of pollutants." Violation of a standard by an owner/operator of a new source is unlawful.

# *HAZARDOUS SUBSTANCES*

Technological advances have enabled human beings to produce numerous artificial substances, some of which have proven extremely hazardous to health. As the potential and actual harm from these latter substances became clear, Congress responded by enacting various hazardous substances-related statutes. In this section, we will consider some of the most important Federal statutes governing hazardous substances: the Federal Insecticide, Fungicide and Rodenticide Act (FIFRA), the Toxic Substances Control Act (TSCA), the Resource Conservation and Recovery Act (RCRA), the Comprehensive Environmental Response, Compensation and Liability Act (CERCLA, or the Superfund), and the Superfund Amendments and Reauthorization Act of 1986 (SARA).

## The Federal Insecticide, Fungicide and Rodenticide Act

The Federal government began regulating pesticides in 1910 and greatly expanded its control over such substances in 1947 with the passage of the Federal

Insecticide, Fungicide and Rodenticide Act (FIFRA). Concern about pesticides increased dramatically after the publication in 1962 of *Silent Spring,* by Rachel Carson, and Congress has amended the FIFRA several times in the last thirty years.

The FIFRA requires that a pesticide be registered with the EPA before any person in any State may distribute it. Such registration is legal only if the pesticide's composition warrants the claims its manufacturer proposes for it, the pesticide will perform its intended function without "unreasonable adverse effects on the environment," the pesticide generally will not cause unreasonably adverse environmental effects when used in accordance with widespread and commonly recognized practice, and the pesticide complies with FIFRA labeling requirements. The FIFRA defines "unreasonable adverse effects on the environment" as any unreasonable risk to humans or the environment, taking into account the economic, social, and environmental costs and benefits of the use of any pesticide. Thus, unlike many environmental statutes, the FIFRA expressly requires the EPA to consider the costs of the action it takes under the statute.

If a pesticide is registered and subsequent data reveals additional hazards, the EPA may cancel the registration after an administrative hearing. The 1988 amendments placed upon industry the cost of disposing of canceled pesticides. Cancellation proceedings typically take years, both because of the numerous stages of the administrative process and because of the required use of a scientific advisory committee. While the cancellation process is in progress, the pesticide may be manufactured and sold. If additional hazard is imminent, however, the product's registration may be suspended until the cancellation proceeding is completed. Once its registration has been suspended, the pesticide may not be manufactured or distributed.

Until recently, the FIFRA did not adequately address the problem of old pesticides that had been registered under earlier and less strict standards. Concerned that these pesticides did not meet current standards, Congress in 1988 amended the FIFRA to require the reregistration of pesticides registered before 1984. U.S. exports are not subject to most of the act's requirements, though an exported pesticide not registered under the FIFRA must bear a label stating "Not Registered for Use in the United States of America."

The EPA may impose civil penalties of up to $5,000 for each offense. Maximum criminal penalties for knowing violations are a $50,000 fine and/or one year imprisonment.

## The Toxic Substances Control Act

Congress passed the Toxic Substances Control Act (TSCA) in 1976 in an effort to provide a comprehensive scheme for regulating toxic substances. The TSCA contains provisions on the manufacture of new chemicals, the testing of suspect chemicals, the regulation of chemicals that present an unreasonable risk of injury to health and the environment, and the inventorying of all chemicals.

Under the Act, a manufacturer must notify the EPA before it manufactures a new chemical or makes a significant new use of an existing chemical. If the EPA administrator concludes that the information submitted is insufficient to permit a reasoned evaluation of the health and environmental effects of the chemical and the chemical may present an unreasonable risk of injury to health or the environment, the administrator may limit or prohibit the chemical's manufacture or distribution.

The Act authorizes the EPA to require the testing of any substance, whether existing or new, if (1) the manufacture or distribution of the substance may present an unreasonable risk of injury to health or the environment, (2) the data on the effects of the substance on health and the environment is insufficient, and (3) testing is necessary to develop such data.

Because of the many substances that might be subject to testing under the statutory standard, the TSCA mandates that the EPA establish a priority list for testing that contains no more than fifty substances at any time. This list is established by a committee whose members come from eight specified agencies.

Once the EPA determines, either through its testing program or through the premanufacturing notice process, that a substance "presents or will present an unreasonable risk of injury to health or the environment," the agency may restrict or prohibit use of the substance.

If the EPA administrator believes that a substance presents an imminent hazard, he is authorized to bring an action in Federal district court for seizure of the substance or other appropriate relief. The statute defines an "imminently hazardous chemical substance or mixture" as one that presents an unreasonable risk of serious or widespread injury to health or the environment.

The TSCA requires the EPA to compile and keep current a list of each chemical substance manufactured or processed in the United States. The EPA's initial inventory of existing chemicals, completed in 1980, listed approximately 55,000 substances. A chemical not listed on the inventory is subject to premanufacture review, even if it was in fact previously manufactured. Although not explicitly required to do so by the TSCA, the EPA reviews the substances on the inventory to determine their safety.

The EPA may impose civil penalties of up to $20,000 per day for a violation of the TSCA. Maximum criminal penalties for knowing violations are $25,000 fines for each day of violation and/or one year's imprisonment.

## The Resource Conservation and Recovery Act

In 1976, Congress enacted the Resource Conservation and Recovery Act (RCRA) to provide a comprehensive scheme for the treatment of solid waste, particularly hazardous waste. The statute provides that the States are primarily responsible for nonhazardous waste, while the EPA regulates all phases of hazardous waste: generation, transportation, and disposal. Under the Act, the Federal government must establish criteria for identifying hazardous waste, taking into account factors that include toxicity, persistence, degradability, flammability, and corrosiveness.

The Act prescribes for generators (entities that produce hazardous waste) standards concerning record-keeping, labeling, the use of appropriate containers, and reporting. The statute requires the EPA to establish a **manifest system** to be used by generators. A manifest is a form on which the generator must specify the quantity, composition, origin, routing, and destination of hazardous waste. On the manifest the generator also must certify that the volume and toxicity of the waste have been reduced to the greatest degree economically practicable and that the method of treatment, storage, and disposal minimizes the threat to health and the environment.

Transporters must maintain records and properly label the waste they transport. Furthermore, they must comply with manifests and may transport hazardous waste only to facilities holding an RCRA hazardous waste facility permit.

Owners/operators of hazardous waste treatment, storage, and disposal sites must maintain records and comply with generator manifests. Facilities for hazardous waste treatment, storage, and disposal must obtain an RCRA hazardous waste facility permit. To obtain a permit, a facility must comply with relevant EPA standards. Failure to comply may subject the owner/operator to civil or criminal penalties.

The Act authorizes the EPA administrator to sue in Federal court for an injunction if the administrator has evidence that "the past or present handling, storage, treatment, transportation or disposal of any solid waste or hazardous waste may present an imminent and substantial endangerment to health or the environment." Moreover, the EPA may impose civil penalties of up to $25,000 per day of violation. Maximum criminal penalties for knowing violations are $50,000 for each day of violation and/or five years' imprisonment. Where a knowing violation endangers a person, the maximum criminal penalty is a $1 million fine and/or fifteen years' imprisonment.

## The Superfund

Although the RCRA regulates current and future generation, transportation, and disposal of hazardous waste, the Act provides only limited authority for the cleanup of abandoned or inactive hazardous waste sites. To fill this gap, Congress in 1980 enacted the Comprehensive Environmental Response, Compensation and Liability Act (CERCLA, or the Superfund). By 1986, the EPA, working under the Act, had spent $1.6 billion and had begun the cleanup of only eight sites. This record and other problems with the initial legislation prompted Congress to amend the CERCLA by enacting the Superfund Amendments and Reauthorization Act of 1986 (SARA). As of early 1998, the EPA had cleaned up 509 National Priorities List sites and had 470 still under construction. Nevertheless, it is predicted that if Congress does not provide additional funds the Superfund will run out of money during the year 2000.

CERCLA requires the Federal government to establish a National Contingency Plan (NCP) prescribing procedures and standards for responding to hazardous substance releases. The NCP specifies criteria for determining the priority of sites to be cleaned. The plan also identifies, on at least an annual basis, the sites that most require immediate cleanup.

Under the Act, the Federal government has authority to take either removal or remedial actions in response to a release or threatened release of hazardous substances, as long as such removal or remedial actions are consistent with the NCP. Removal typically is an immediate response to control a specific release of a hazardous substance. Remedial actions, on the other hand, consist of efforts to prevent or reduce the release of hazardous substances; such actions are intended to be long-term solutions. The president may impose a civil penalty of up to $25,000 per day of violation; for repeat violations, the penalty may reach up to $75,000 per day of violation.

States and private parties also may engage in response actions, although such actions must meet certain conditions for the responder to recover its costs from either the governmental trust fund or the parties responsible under CERCLA for the release or threatened release of hazardous substances.

CERCLA establishes a trust fund to pay for hazardous waste removal and other remedial actions. The trust fund is financed in part by a surtax on businesses with annual incomes over $2 million, a tax on petroleum, and a tax on chemical feedstocks. An additional part of the trust fund comes from money recovered from persons responsible for the release of hazardous substances. These parties include the owners and operators of a hazardous waste disposal facility from which there has been a release, as well as any generator of hazardous wastes that were disposed of at that facility.

Because CERCLA initially imposed liability on all owners of contaminated property, some parties were held liable even though they had acquired the land either involuntarily or without knowledge of the hazardous wastes stored there. For example, after foreclosing on a mortgage of $335,000 and taking title to a piece of property, a bank was held liable for Superfund costs of more than $555,000. Responding to the inequity of such situations, Congress in SARA established a new defense to CERCLA liability for "innocent landowners." To qualify as an innocent landowner, one "must have undertaken, at the time of acquisition, all appropriate inquiry into the previous ownership and uses of the property consistent with good commercial or customary practice in an effort to minimize liability."

◆ *See Figure 46–1*

⚖ *See Case 46–3*

## INTERNATIONAL PROTECTION OF THE OZONE LAYER

In 1987, the United States and twenty-three other countries entered into the Montreal Protocol on Substances that Deplete the Ozone Layer, a treaty designed to prevent pollution that harms the ozone layer. The treaty requires all signatories to reduce their production and consumption of all chemicals, in particular chlorofluorocarbons (CFCs, more commonly called freon), that deplete the ozone layer by 50 percent. Although excessive ozone in the air we breathe can be hazardous, the ozone layer in the stratosphere helps to protect the earth from harmful ultraviolet radiation. By 1985, scientists believed that the release of CFCs into the atmosphere had caused a hole to develop in the ozone layer over Antarctica.

Chlorofluorocarbons, halocarbons, carbon dioxide, methane, and nitrous oxide are extremely potent "greenhouse gases," which trap heat and thereby warm the earth. Human activities, however, have increased the release of greenhouse gases, resulting in the serious threat of global warming. Scientists warn that the earth's temperature could rise by as much as 6 degrees over the next century due to global warming. If this occurs, the levels of the seas will rise and the climate will change over most of the earth, causing severe flooding and disruptions of agricultural production.

To combat this predicted climate change, 165 nations in 1992 negotiated a treaty at the UN Convention on Climate Change (FCCC) in Rio de Janeiro. The treaty's ultimate objective was to stabilize the "greenhouse gas concentration in the atmosphere at a level that would prevent dangerous anthropogenic [human-induced] interference with the climate system." More than 160 countries eventually ratified the treaty, which went into effect on March 21, 1994. The FCCC calls for all signatory countries to develop and update national inventories of all greenhouse gases not otherwise covered by the Montreal Protocol. The treaty, however, is voluntary, and most nations, including the United States, will not meet its objectives. At a subsequent FCCC, held in Kyoto, Japan in December 1997, the participating nations proposed the Kyoto Protocol, which is a set of binding emission targets for developed nations. Under this Protocol, the United States is to reduce by the years 2008–2012 its emissions of greenhouse gases (carbon dioxide, methane, nitrous oxide, and synthetic substitutes for CFCs) to a level 7 percent below 1990 emission standards. Japan agreed to reduce its level to 6 percent below 1990 levels, and the European Union agreed to a level 8 percent below 1990 emission levels.

**FIGURE 46–1**  Major Federal Environmental Statutes

| Act | Major Purpose | Maximum Civil Penalty | Maximum Criminal Penalty |
|---|---|---|---|
| **National Environmental Policy Act (NEPA)** | • Establish environmental protection as a major national goal<br>• Mandate environmental impact statements prepared prior to Federal action having a significant environmental effect | None | None |
| **Clean Air Act** | • Control and reduce air pollution<br>• Establish National Ambient Air Quality Standards | $25,000 per day of violation | $1,000,000 fine per violation and/or 15 years' imprisonment* |
| **Clean Water Act** | • Protect against water pollution<br>• Establish effluent limitations | $25,000 per day of violation | $50,000 per day of violation and/or 3 years' imprisonment* |
| **Federal Insecticide, Fungicide and Rodenticide Act (FIFRA)** | • Regulate the sale and distribution of pesticides<br>• Prevent pesticides having an unreasonably adverse effect on the environment | $5,000 per offense | $50,000 fine and/or 1 year's imprisonment |
| **Toxic Substances Control Act (TSCA)** | • Regulate toxic substances<br>• Prevent unreasonable risk of injury to health and the environment from toxic substances | $20,000 per day of violation | $25,000 fine per day of violation and/or 1 year's imprisonment |
| **Resource Conservation and Recovery Act (RCRA)** | • Regulate the disposal of solid waste<br>• Establish standards to protect human health and the environment from hazardous wastes | $25,000 per day of violation | $1,000,000 fine and/or 15 years' imprisonment |
| **Comprehensive Environmental Response, Compensation and Liability Act (CERCLA, or the Superfund) and Superfund Amendments and Reauthorization Act (SARA)** | • Establish a national contingency plan for responding to releases of hazardous substances<br>• Establish a trust fund to pay for removal of hazardous waste and other remedial actions | $25,000 per day of violation; $75,000 for repeat violations | None |

*Doubled for repeat convictions.

# Chapter Summary

## Common Law Actions for Environmental Damage

| | |
|---|---|
| **Nuisance** | **Private Nuisance** substantial and unreasonable interference with the use and enjoyment of a person's land<br>**Public Nuisance** interference with the health, safety, or comfort of the public |

| | |
|---|---|
| **Other Common Law Actions** | **Trespass** an invasion of land that interferes with the right of exclusive possession of the property<br>**Strict Liability for Abnormally Dangerous Activities** liability without fault for an individual who engages in an unduly dangerous activity in an inappropriate location |

## Federal Regulation of the Environment

| | |
|---|---|
| **National Environmental Policy Act (NEPA)** | **Purpose** to establish environmental protection as a goal of Federal policy<br>**Council on Environmental Quality** three-member advisory group in the Executive Office of the President that makes recommendations to the president on environmental matters<br>**Environmental Impact Statement** a detailed statement concerning the environmental impact of a proposed Federal action<br>• *Scope* NEPA applies to a broad range of activities, including direct action by a Federal agency as well as any action by a Federal agency that permits action by other parties that will affect the quality of the environment<br>• *Content* the EIS must contain, among other items, a detailed statement of the environmental impact of the proposed action, any adverse environmental effects that cannot be avoided, and alternative proposals |

| | |
|---|---|
| **Clean Air Act** | **Purpose** to control and reduce air pollution<br>**Existing Sources**<br>• *National Ambient Air Quality Standards (NAAQSs)* the EPA administrator must establish NAAQSs for air pollutants that endanger the public health and welfare<br>• *State Implementation Plan* each State must submit a plan for each NAAQS detailing how the State will implement and maintain the standard<br>**New Sources**<br>• *New Stationary Sources* owner/operator must employ the best technological system of continuous emission reduction that has been adequately demonstrated<br>• *New Vehicles* extensive emission standards are established<br>• *Hazardous Air Pollutants* to protect the public health, the EPA administrator must establish for hazardous air pollutants standards that provide ample safety margins<br>• *Acid Rain* standards are established to protect against acid rain (precipitation that contains high levels of sulfuric or nitric acid) |

| Clean Water Act | **Purpose** protect against water pollution<br>**Point Sources** Act establishes the National Pollutant Discharge Elimination System (NPDES), a permit system, to control the amounts of pollutants that may be discharged by point sources into U.S. waters<br>**Nonpoint Sources** Act requires the States to use best management practices to control water runoff from agricultural and urban areas |
|---|---|
| **Hazardous Substances** | **FIFRA** the Federal Insecticide, Fungicide and Rodenticide Act regulates the sale and distribution of pesticides<br>**TSCA** the Toxic Substances Control Act provides a comprehensive scheme for regulation of toxic substances<br>**RCRA** the Resource Conservation and Recovery Act provides a comprehensive scheme for treatment of solid waste, particularly hazardous waste<br>**Superfund** the Comprehensive Environmental Response, Compensation and Liability Act (CERCLA) establishes (1) a national contingency plan for responding to releases of hazardous substances and (2) a trust fund to pay for removal and cleanup of hazardous waste |
| **International Protection of the Ozone Layer** | **Montreal Protocol** treaty by which countries agreed to cut production of chlorofluorocarbons (CFCs) by 50 percent<br>**Kyoto Protocol** reduction of greenhouse gases |

 **Cases**

### CASE 46–1
### New Source Standards: Stationary Sources
## *NATIONAL-SOUTHWIRE ALUMINUM CO. v. U.S. EPA*
United States Court of Appeals, Sixth Circuit, 1988
838 F.2d 835

Guy, J.

National-Southwire Aluminum Company (NSA) petitions this court for review of a determination by the United States Environmental Protection Agency (EPA) that the turning off of certain pollution control equipment (i.e., wet scrubbers) at NSA's aluminum reduction plant in Hawesville, Kentucky, would constitute a "modification" of a stationary source within the meaning . . . of the Clean Air Act, [citation]. If turning off the equipment is such a modification, the plant would be subject to the New Source Performance Standards (NSPS) . . . , which, NSA claims, could only be met by tearing out the wet scrubbers and installing a new system utilizing dry scrubbers at a prohibitive expense.

\* \* \* The standard of review of an EPA determination of NSPS applicability is specified in the Administra-

tive Procedure Act, [citation], which provides that agency action may be set aside only if it is found to be "arbitrary, capricious, an abuse of discretion, or otherwise not in accordance with law." Because we do not find the EPA's determination here to have been arbitrary or capricious, the petition will be denied.

### I

NSA owns and operates a primary aluminum reduction plant which emits fluoride in both gaseous and particulate forms. The EPA has determined that fluoride air pollution presents a serious threat to public welfare by injuring natural vegetation, herbivorous animals, and agricultural crops. [Citation.]

* * *

The EPA promulgated NSPS for fluoride emissions from new and modified primary aluminum reduction plants on October 23, 1974. [Citation.] Kentucky was then required, . . . , to adopt state standards to limit fluoride emissions from existing, unmodified plants, which included NSA. At the time of construction of the plant in 1969, before passage of the Clean Air Act, NSA equipped the plant with wet scrubbers, which represented the best known technology at that time for the control of emission of gaseous fluoride. Kentucky adopted its standards in 1981 and the EPA approved Kentucky's standards in 1982. These standards did not require NSA to reduce the gaseous fluoride emissions from its Hawesville plant but simply required the same level of emission control that NSA had been achieving with its wet scrubbers since 1969.

In 1982, during a routine maintenance-related shutdown of the wet scrubbers, NSA observed that its ambient air monitors did not detect any appreciable change in ambient fluoride levels as a result of not scrubbing the exhaust gases. Because of the substantial cost of operating the wet scrubbers, NSA sought and obtained from Kentucky a relaxation of the state's . . . standard by a factor of thirteen, from 1.0 pounds of fluoride emitted per ton of aluminum produced to 290 pounds of fluoride emitted per hour, the equivalence of 13.18 pounds of fluoride per ton of aluminum. This action results in increasing gaseous fluoride emissions from the plant by 1,174 tons per year. This relaxation is not effective, however, unless and until it is approved by the EPA. [Citation.]

* * *

On August 27, 1986, the EPA received NSA's request for a formal determination of whether the turning off of the wet scrubbers would be a modification that would trigger application of the NSPS. In making its request, NSA argued that such change should not be considered a modification because (1) pollution control equipment is not part of a "stationary source," and therefore turning off such equipment is not a modification of such a source, and (2) NSA's plant is an existing facility subject to state regulation . . . and therefore cannot be subject to the NSPS.

On September 22, 1986, the EPA issued the determination which is the subject of this appeal. The Agency concluded that, under the plain words of the statute, pollution control equipment is part of a stationary source, and changes in such equipment that cause increases in emissions are modifications of the source. . . . It also determined that, under the plain words of both the statute and the EPA's regulations, an existing facility becomes subject to the NSPS when it undergoes a modification.

* * *

NSA claims that a "stationary source" consists only of pollution generating equipment, and does not include attached air pollution control equipment. Therefore, it argues, the turning off of its wet scrubbers would not constitute a "modification" of a "stationary source." Under this theory, the existence of a modification would depend on the amount of pollutant created by the pollution-generating equipment, without regard to the amount of pollution actually emitted into the atmosphere after the pollution-control equipment has done its work.

Section 111(a)(4) of the Act, [citation] provides:

The term "modification" means any physical change in, or change in the method of operation of, a stationary source which increases the amount of any air pollutant emitted by such source or which results in the emission of any air pollutant not previously emitted.

Section 111(a)(3), [citation], defines the term "stationary source" as "any building, structure, facility, or installation which emits or may emit any air pollutant." Clearly, while the statutory definition does not specifically reference or include pre-existing pollution control equipment, it certainly does not exclude it either. Moreover, the EPA explicitly considered and rejected NSA's theory when the agency amended the applicable regulations in 1975. The current regulations define "modification" to include any change in the method of operation of "an existing facility which increases the amount of any air pollutant . . . emitted into the atmosphere. . . ." [Citation.] As the EPA explained at the time it proposed the amendments:

The new phrase ('emitted into the atmosphere') clarifies that for an existing facility to undergo a modification there must be an increase in actual emissions. . . . The Administrator considered defining "modification" so that increases in pre-controlled (potential) emissions would be modifications. However, the proposed definition of modification is limited to increases in actual emissions.

[Citation.] As the agency further explained:

If any increase in emissions that would result from a physical or operational change to an existing facility can be offset by improving an existing control system for that facility, such a change would not be considered a modification because there would be no increase in emissions to the atmosphere.

[Citation.] It is clear from the foregoing that the agency considered such a definition to be a limiting one which would allow a facility to change or add to its operation such that increased pollution would be generated but would not constitute a modification provided such increase were offset by a corresponding increase in the effectiveness of its pollution control mechanisms. * * * We find the agency's interpretation of the term "stationary source" as including a structure's pollution control equipment to be reasonable and not inconsistent with the statutory language.

NSA next argues that its proposed change in operations falls within the following regulatory exception to the definition of "modification":

The following shall not, by themselves, be considered modifications under this part:

* * *

(5) The addition or use of any system or device whose primary function is the reduction of air pollutants, except when an emission control system is removed or is replaced by a system which the Administrator determines to be less environmentally beneficial. [Citation.]

* * *

NSA's proposal to turn off a portion of its air pollution control equipment does not fit within the delineated exception. By its terms, the regulation does not apply to the removal of such a system, nor to the replacement of such a system with one that is "less environmentally beneficial." The purpose of this de minimis exception is to permit a source to install a pollution control system that would bring about a major decrease in emissions of one pollutant while causing a smaller incidental increase in emissions of another pollutant. * * * Rather than an "addition or use" of a pollution control system, NSA's proposal contemplates the non-use, or subtraction of a pollution control device, i.e., the wet scrubbers.

It should be noted that this "replacement" system would leave gaseous fluorides virtually uncontrolled. Such result would be incompatible with a major purpose of the Clean Air Act—to prevent or minimize any increases in existing levels of pollution. * * *

It is inconsistent with the Congressional purpose of maximum feasible control to have existing, functional air pollution control equipment sitting idle while the pollution that the equipment could be preventing escapes into the atmosphere. The turning off of NSA's wet scrubbers would result in an increase of 1,174 tons per year of fluoride emissions with no decrease whatsoever in the emission of any other pollutant. It is apparent that such a changed system would be substantially "less environmentally beneficial" and cannot be deemed so de minimis as to qualify it for exemption under [citation].

* * *

The EPA's determination will require NSA either to continue operating its existing wet scrubbers (and thereby avoid application of the NSPS) or to install new control equipment. If, as NSA claims, the latter option is prohibitively expensive, then presumably the company will choose the former option. In contrast to NSA's proposed plan permitting vastly increased fluoride emissions, either of the above options will further the Act's stated purpose of protecting and enhancing the quality of the nation's air by virtue of increased federal participation. [Citation.]

---

## CASE 46–2
## Point Source: NPDES
### ARKANSAS v. OKLAHOMA

Supreme Court of the United States, 1992
503 U.S. 91, 112 S.Ct. 1046, 117 L.Ed.2d 239

STEVENS, J.
Pursuant to the Clean Water Act, [citation], the Environmental Protection Agency (EPA) issued a discharge permit to a new point source in Arkansas, about 39 miles upstream from the Oklahoma state line. The question presented in this litigation is whether the EPA's finding that discharges from the new source would not cause a detectable violation of Oklahoma's water quality standards satisfied the EPA's duty to protect the interests of the downstream State. Disagreeing with the Court of Appeals, we hold that the Agency's action was authorized by the statute.

### I

In 1985, the City of Fayetteville, Arkansas, applied to the EPA, seeking a permit for the City's new sewage treatment plant under the National Pollution Discharge Elimination System (NPDES). After the appropriate procedures, the EPA, . . . issued a permit authorizing the plant to discharge up to half of its effluent (to a limit of 6.1 million gallons per day) into an unnamed stream in northwestern Arkansas. That flow passes through a series of three creeks for about 17 miles, and then enters the Illinois River at a point 22 miles upstream from the Arkansas-Oklahoma border.

The permit imposed specific limitations on the quantity, content, and character of the discharge and also included a number of special conditions, including a provision that if a study then underway indicated that more stringent limitations were necessary to ensure compliance with Oklahoma's water quality standards, the permit would be modified to incorporate those limits.

Respondents challenged this permit before the EPA, alleging, . . . , that the discharge violated the Oklahoma water quality standards. Those standards provide that "no degradation [of water quality] shall be allowed" in the upper Illinois River, including the portion of the River immediately downstream from the state line.

Following a hearing, the Administrative Law Judge (ALJ) concluded that the Oklahoma standards would not be implicated unless the contested discharge had 'something more than a mere *de minimis* impact' on the State's waters. He found that the discharge would not have an 'undue impact' on Oklahoma's water and, accordingly, affirmed the issuance of the permit.

On a petition for review, the EPA's Chief Judicial Officer first ruled that 301(b)(1)(c) of the Clean Water Act 'requires an NPDES permit to impose any effluent limitations necessary to comply with applicable state water quality standards.' He then held that the Act and EPA regulations offered greater protection for the downstream State than the ALJ's 'undue impact' standard suggested.

* * *

On remand, the ALJ made detailed findings of fact and concluded that the City had satisfied the standard set forth by the Chief Judicial Officer. Specifically, the ALJ found that there would be no detectable violation of any of the components of Oklahoma's water quality standards. The Chief Judicial Officer sustained the issuance of the permit.

Both the petitioners . . . (collectively Arkansas) and the respondents in this litigation sought judicial review. Arkansas argued that the Clean Water Act did not require an Arkansas point source to comply with Oklahoma's water quality standards. Oklahoma challenged the EPA's determination that the Fayetteville discharge would not produce a detectable violation of the Oklahoma standards.

The Court of Appeals did not accept either of these arguments. The court agreed with the EPA that the statute required compliance with Oklahoma's water quality standards, [citation], and did not disagree with the Agency's determination that the discharges from the Fayetteville plant would not produce a detectable violation of those standards. Nevertheless, relying on a theory that neither party had advanced, the Court of Appeals reversed the Agency's issuance of the Fayetteville permit. The court first ruled that the statute requires that "where a proposed source would discharge effluents that would contribute to conditions currently constituting a violation of applicable water quality standards, such [a] proposed source may not be permitted." [Citation.] Then the court found that the Illinois River in Oklahoma was "already degraded," that the Fayetteville effluent would reach the Illinois River in Oklahoma, and that that effluent could "be expected to contribute to the ongoing deterioration of the scenic [Illinois R]iver" in Oklahoma even though it would not detectably affect the River's water quality. [Citation.]

The importance and the novelty of the Court of Appeals' decision persuaded to grant certiorari. [Citation.] We now reverse.

The parties have argued three analytically distinct questions concerning the interpretation of the Clean Water Act. First, does the Act require the EPA, in crafting and issuing a permit to a point source in one State, to apply the water quality standards of downstream States? Second, even if the Act does not require as much, does the Agency have the statutory authority to mandate such compliance? Third, does the Act provide, as the Court of Appeals held, that once a body of water fails to meet water quality standards no discharge that yields effluent that reach the degraded waters will be permitted?

In this case, it is neither necessary nor prudent for us to resolve the first of these questions. In issuing the Fayetteville permit, the EPA assumed it was obligated by both the Act and its own regulations to ensure that the Fayetteville discharge would not violate Oklahoma's standards. As we discuss below, this assumption was permissible and reasonable and therefore there is no need for us to address whether the Act requires as much. * * * Our decision not to determine at this time the scope of the Agency's statutory obligations does not affect our resolution of the second question, which concerns the Agency's statutory authority. Even if the Clean Water Act itself does not require the Fayetteville discharge to comply with

Oklahoma's water quality standards, the statute clearly does not limit the EPA's authority to mandate such compliance.

Since 1973, EPA regulations have provided that an NPDES permit shall not be issued "[w]hen the imposition of conditions cannot ensure compliance with the applicable water quality requirements of all affected States." [Citations.] Those regulations—relied upon by the EPA in the issuance of the Fayetteville permit—constitute a reasonable exercise of the Agency's statutory authority.

Congress has vested in the Administrator broad discretion to establish conditions for NPDES permits. Section 402(a)(2) provides that for EPA-issued permits "[t]he Administrator shall prescribe conditions for such permits to assure compliance with the requirements of [§ 402(a)(1)] and such other requirements as he deems appropriate." [Citation.]

Similarly, Congress preserved for the Administrator broad authority to oversee state permit programs:

\* \* \*

The regulations relied on by the EPA were a perfectly reasonable exercise of the Agency's statutory discretion. The application of state water quality standards in the interstate context is wholly consistent with the Act's broad purpose, "to restore and maintain the chemical, physical, and biological integrity of the Nation's waters." [Citation.] Moreover, as noted above, [the Act] expressly identifies the achievement of state water quality standards as one of the Act's central objectives. The Agency's regulations conditioning NPDES permits are a well-tailored means of achieving this goal.

Notwithstanding this apparent reasonableness, Arkansas argues that our description in *Ouellette* of the role of affected States in the permit process and our characterization of the affected States' position as "subordinate," [citation], indicates that the EPA's application of the Oklahoma standards was error. We disagree. Our statement in *Ouellette* concerned only an affected State's input into the permit process; that input is clearly limited by the plain language of § 402(b). Limits on an affected State's direct participation in permitting decisions, however, do not in any way constrain the EPA's authority to require a point source to comply with downstream water quality standards.

\* \* \*

Similarly, we agree with Arkansas that in the Clean Water Act Congress struck a careful balance among competing policies and interests, but do not find the EPA regulations concerning the application of downstream water quality standards at all incompatible with that balance. \* \* \*

For these reasons, we find the EPA's requirement that the Fayetteville discharge comply with Oklahoma's water quality standards to be a reasonable exercise of the Agency's substantial statutory discretion. [Citation.]

The Court of Appeals construed the Clean Water Act to prohibit any discharge of effluent that would reach waters already in violation of existing water quality standards. We find nothing in the Act to support this reading.

---

## CASE 46–3
## The Superfund
### *UNITED STATES v. BESTFOODS*
Supreme Court of the United States, 1998
118 S.Ct. 1876, 141 L.Ed.2d 43

SOUTER, J.
The United States brought this action for the costs of cleaning up industrial waste generated by a chemical plant. The issue before us, under the Comprehensive Environmental Response, Compensation, and Liability Act of 1980 (CERCLA), [citation], is whether a parent corporation that actively participated in, and exercised control over, the operations of a subsidiary may, without more, be held liable as an operator of a polluting facility owned or operated by the subsidiary. We answer no, unless the corporate veil may be pierced. But a corporate parent that actively participated in, and exercised control over, the operations of the facility itself may be held directly liable in its own right as an operator of the facility.

**I**

In 1980, CERCLA was enacted in response to the serious environmental and health risks posed by industrial pollution. [Citation.] "As its name implies, CERCLA is a comprehensive statute that grants the President broad power to command government agencies and private parties to clean up hazardous waste sites." [Citation.] If it satisfies certain statutory conditions, the United States may, for instance, use the "Hazardous Substance Superfund" to finance cleanup efforts, [citation], which it may then replenish by suits brought under § 107 of the Act against, among others, "any person who at the time of disposal of any hazardous substance owned or operated any facility." [Citation.] So, those actually "responsible for any damage, environmental harm, or injury from chemical poisons [may be tagged with] the cost of their actions," * * *

## II

In 1957, Ott Chemical Co. (Ott I) began manufacturing chemicals at a plant near Muskegon, Michigan, and its intentional and unintentional dumping of hazardous substances significantly polluted the soil and ground water at the site. In 1965, respondent CPC International Inc. incorporated a wholly owned subsidiary to buy Ott I's assets in exchange for CPC stock. The new company, also dubbed Ott Chemical Co. (Ott II), continued chemical manufacturing at the site, and continued to pollute its surroundings. CPC kept the managers of Ott I, including its founder, president, and principal shareholder, Arnold Ott, on board as officers of Ott II. Arnold Ott and several other Ott II officers and directors were also given positions at CPC, and they performed duties for both corporations.

In 1972, CPC sold Ott II to Story Chemical Company, which operated the Muskegon plant until its bankruptcy in 1977. Shortly thereafter, when respondent Michigan Department of Natural Resources (MDNR) examined the site for environmental damage, it found the land littered with thousands of leaking and even exploding drums of waste, and the soil and water saturated with noxious chemicals. MDNR sought a buyer for the property who would be willing to contribute toward its cleanup, and after extensive negotiations, respondent Aerojet-General Corp. arranged for transfer of the site from the Story bankruptcy trustee in 1977. Aerojet created a wholly owned California subsidiary, Cordova Chemical Company (Cordova/California), to purchase the property, and Cordova/California in turn created a wholly owned Michigan subsidiary, Cordova Chemical Company of Michigan (Cordova/Michigan), which manufactured chemicals at the site until 1986.

By 1981, the federal Environmental Protection Agency had undertaken to see the site cleaned up, and

its long-term remedial plan called for expenditures well into the tens of millions of dollars. To recover some of that money, the United States filed this action under § 107 in 1989, naming five defendants as responsible parties: CPC, Aerojet, Cordova/California, Cordova/Michigan, and Arnold Ott. (By that time, Ott I and Ott II were defunct.) After the parties (and MDNR) had launched a flurry of contribution claims, counterclaims, and cross-claims, the District Court consolidated the cases for trial in three phases: liability, remedy, and insurance coverage. So far, only the first phase has been completed; in 1991, the District Court held a 15-day bench trial on the issue of liability. [T]he trial focused on the issues of whether CPC and Aerojet, as the parent corporations of Ott II and the Cordova companies, had "owned or operated" the facility within the meaning of § 107(a)(2).

The District Court said that operator liability may attach to a parent corporation both directly, when the parent itself operates the facility, and indirectly, when the corporate veil can be pierced under state law. * * * [T]he District Court held both CPC and Aerojet liable under § 107(a)(2) as operators. As to CPC, the court found it particularly telling that CPC selected Ott II's board of directors and populated its executive ranks with CPC officials, and that a CPC official, G.R.D. Williams, played a significant role in shaping Ott II's environmental compliance policy.

* * *

Applying Michigan veil-piercing law, the Court of Appeals decided that neither CPC nor Aerojet was liable for controlling the actions of its subsidiaries, since the parent and subsidiary corporations maintained separate personalities and the parents did not utilize the subsidiary corporate form to perpetrate fraud or subvert justice.

* * *

## III

It is a general principle of corporate law deeply "ingrained in our economic and legal systems" that a parent corporation (so-called because of control through ownership of another corporation's stock) is not liable for the acts of its subsidiaries. [Citations.] * * * The Government has indeed made no claim that a corporate parent is liable as an owner or an operator under § 107 simply because its subsidiary is subject to liability for owning or operating a polluting facility.

But there is an equally fundamental principle of corporate law, applicable to the parent-subsidiary relationship as well as generally, that the corporate veil may be pierced and the shareholder held liable for the corporation's conduct when the corporate form would otherwise be misused to accomplish certain wrongful purposes, most notably fraud, on the shareholder's behalf. [Citations.] Nothing in CERCLA purports to rewrite this well-settled rule, either. * * * The Court of Appeals was accordingly correct in holding that when (but only when) the corporate veil may be pierced, may a parent corporation be charged with derivative CERCLA liability for its subsidiary's actions.

# IV

## A

If the act rested liability entirely on ownership of a polluting facility, this opinion might end here; but CERCLA liability may turn on operation as well as ownership, and nothing in the statute's terms bars a parent corporation from direct liability for its own actions in operating a facility owned by its subsidiary. As Justice (then-Professor) Douglas noted almost 70 years ago, derivative liability cases are to be distinguished from those in which "the alleged wrong can seemingly be traced to the parent through the conduit of its own personnel and management" and "the parent is directly a participant in the wrong complained of." [Citation.] In such instances, the parent is directly liable for its own actions. [Citation.] The fact that a corporate subsidiary happens to own a polluting facility operated by its parent does nothing, then, to displace the rule that the parent "corporation is [itself] responsible for the wrongs committed by its agents in the course of its business," [Citations.] It is this direct liability that is properly seen as being at issue here.

Under the plain language of the statute, any person who operates a polluting facility is directly liable for the costs of cleaning up the pollution. [Citation.] This is so regardless of whether that person is the facility's owner, the owner's parent corporation or business partner, or even a saboteur who sneaks into the facility at night to discharge its poisons out of malice. If any such act of operating a corporate subsidiary's facility is done on behalf of a parent corporation, the existence of the parent-subsidiary relationship under state corporate law is simply irrelevant to the issue of direct liability. [Citations.]

This much is easy to say; the difficulty comes in defining actions sufficient to constitute direct parental "operation." * * * So, under CERCLA, an operator is simply someone who directs the workings of, manages, or conducts the affairs of a facility. To sharpen the definition for purposes of CERCLA's concern with environmental contamination, an operator must manage, direct, or conduct operations specifically related to pollution, that is, operations having to do with the leakage or disposal of hazardous waste, or decisions about compliance with environmental regulations.

## B

With this understanding, we are satisfied that the Court of Appeals correctly rejected the District Court's analysis of direct liability. But we also think that the appeals court erred in limiting direct liability under the statute to a parent's sole or joint venture operation, so as to eliminate any possible finding that CPC is liable as an operator on the facts of this case.

**1** By emphasizing that "CPC is directly liable under section 107(a)(2) as an operator because CPC actively participated in and exerted significant control over Ott II's business and decision-making," [citation], the District Court applied the "actual control" test of whether the parent "actually operated the business of its subsidiary," [citation].

* * *

In imposing direct liability on these grounds, the District Court failed to recognize that "it is entirely appropriate for directors of a parent corporation to serve as directors of its subsidiary, and that fact alone may not serve to expose the parent corporation to liability for its subsidiary's acts." [citations] ("Control through the ownership of shares does not fuse the corporations, even when the directors are common to each"); [citation] (noting that it is "normal" for a parent and subsidiary to "have identical directors and officers").

This recognition that the corporate personalities remain distinct has its corollary in the "well established principle [of corporate law] that directors and officers holding positions with a parent and its subsidiary can and do 'change hats' to represent the two corporations separately, despite their common ownership." * * * The Government would have to show that, despite the general presumption to the contrary, the officers and directors were acting in their capacities as CPC officers and directors, and not as Ott II officers and directors, when they committed those acts. The District Court made no such enquiry here, however, disregarding entirely this time-honored common law rule.

* * *

**2** We accordingly agree with the Court of Appeals that a participation-and-control test looking to the parent's supervision over the subsidiary, especially one that assumes that dual officers always act on behalf of the parent, cannot be used to identify operation of a facility resulting in direct parental liability. Nonetheless, a return to the ordinary meaning of the word "operate" in the organizational sense will indicate why we think that the Sixth Circuit stopped short when it confined its examples of direct parental operation to exclusive or joint ventures, and declined to find at least the possibility of direct operation by CPC in this case.

In our enquiry into the meaning Congress presumably had in mind when it used the verb "to operate," we recognized that the statute obviously meant something more than mere mechanical activation of pumps and valves, and must be read to contemplate "operation" as including the exercise of direction over the facility's activities. The Court of Appeals recognized this by indicating that a parent can be held directly liable when the parent operates the facility in the stead of its subsidiary or alongside the subsidiary in some sort of a joint venture. We anticipated a further possibility above, however, when we observed that a dual officer or director might depart so far from the norms of parental influence exercised through dual officeholding as to serve the parent, even when ostensibly acting on behalf of the subsidiary in operating the facility. Yet another possibility, suggested by the facts of this case, is that an agent of the parent with no hat to wear but the parent's hat might manage or direct activities at the facility.

Identifying such an occurrence calls for line drawing yet again, since the acts of direct operation that give rise to parental liability must necessarily be distinguished from the interference that stems from the normal relationship between parent and subsidiary. Again norms of corporate behavior (undisturbed by any CERCLA provision) are crucial reference points. * * * The critical question is whether, in degree and detail, actions directed to the facility by an agent of the parent alone are eccentric under accepted norms of parental oversight of a subsidiary's facility.

There is, in fact, some evidence that CPC engaged in just this type and degree of activity at the Muskegon plant. The District Court's opinion speaks of an agent of CPC alone who played a conspicuous part in dealing with the toxic risks emanating from the operation of the plant. G.R.D. Williams worked only for CPC; he was not an employee, officer, or director of Ott II, and thus, his actions were of necessity taken only on behalf of CPC. The District Court found that "CPC became directly involved in environmental and regulatory matters through the work of . . . Williams, CPC's governmental and environmental affairs director. Williams . . . became heavily involved in environmental issues at Ott II." He "actively participated in and exerted control over a variety of Ott II environmental matters," and he "issued directives regarding Ott II's responses to regulatory inquiries."

We think that these findings are enough to raise an issue of CPC's operation of the facility through Williams's actions, though we would draw no ultimate conclusion from these findings at this point.

## V

The judgment of the Court of Appeals for the Sixth Circuit is vacated, and the case is remanded with instructions to return it to the District Court for further proceedings consistent with this opinion.

---

 # Questions

**1.** Discuss the common law actions for environmental damage and the difficulties involved in prevailing in such actions.
**2.** Discuss the major substantive provisions of the National Environmental Policy Act.
**3.** Discuss the regulatory schemes of the Clean Air Act.

**4.** Discuss the regulation of both point and nonpoint sources of pollution by the Clean Water Act.
**5.** Discuss (a) the Federal Insecticide, Fungicide and Rodenticide Act; (b) the Toxic Substances Control Act; (c) the Resource Conservation and Recovery Act; (d) the Superfund; (e) the Montreal Protocol; and (f) the Kyoto Protocol.

# Problems

**1.** Atlantic Cement operated a large cement plant. Neighboring landowners sued for damages and an injunction, claiming that their properties were injured by the dirt, smoke, and vibrations coming from the plant. The lower court found that the plant constituted a nuisance and granted temporary damages but refused to grant an injunction because the benefits of operating the plant outweighed the harm to the plaintiffs' properties. The landowners appealed. Decision?

**2.** Seindenberg and Hutchinson (the site owners) leased a four-acre tract of land (the Bluff Road site) to a chemical manufacturing corporation (COCC). While the lease initially was for the sole purpose of allowing COCC to store raw materials and finished products in a warehouse on the land, COCC later expanded its business to include the brokering and recycling of chemical waste generated by third parties. COCC's owners subsequently formed a new corporation, South Carolina Recycling and Disposal, Inc. (SCRDI) for the purpose of taking over COCC's waste-handling business. The site owners accepted rent from SCRDI. The waste stored at Bluff Road contained many chemical substances that Federal law defines as hazardous. In 1980, the EPA concluded that the site was a major fire hazard. The Federal government contracted with a third party to perform a partial cleanup of the site. South Carolina completed the cleanup. The Federal government and South Carolina sued SCRDI, COCC, the site owners, and three third-party generators as responsible parties under RCRA and CERCLA. Decision?

**3.** The State of Y submits a plan under the Clean Air Act to attain national ambient air quality standards. Can the EPA administrator deny approval of the State plan because it is (a) less stringent or (b) more stringent than the agency believes is feasible? Explain.

**4.** Kennecott Copper Corp. brings this challenge to an EPA order that rejected a portion of the State of Nevada's implementation plan dealing with the control of stationary sources of sulfur dioxide ($SO_2$). All of the $SO_2$ emissions come from a single source—the Kennecott copper smelter at McGill. The EPA based its decision on the belief that the Clean Air Act NAAQS must be met by continuous emission limitations to the maximum extent possible and that the Act permits the intermittent use of emission controls only when continuous controls are not economically feasible. Kennecott contends that the EPA must approve any State implementation plan that will attain and maintain an NAAQS within the statutory time period. Decision?

**5.** The EPA administrator issued an order suspending the registration of the pesticides heptachlor and chlordane under the FIFRA. Velsicol Chemical Corp., the sole manufacturer

of these pesticides, brings this action, contending that the evidence does not support the administrator's contention that the continued use of these chemicals poses an imminent hazard to human health. Velsicol and the U.S. Department of Agriculture (USDA) contend (1) that the EPA's laboratory tests on mice and rats do not "conclusively" show that either chemical is carcinogenic; (2) that mice are too prone to tumors to be reliable test subjects; and (3) that human exposure to these chemicals is insufficient to create a risk. Nonetheless, human epidemiology studies on both chemicals provide no basis for concluding that either pesticide is safe. The administrator based part of his claim on residues of these chemicals found in soil, air, and the aquatic ecosystem over long periods of time and on the presence of these chemicals in the human diet and human tissue. Decision?

**6.** The U.S. Department of the Interior filed an environmental impact statement with regard to its proposal to lease approximately eighty tracts of submerged land, primarily located off the coast of Louisiana, for oil and gas exploration. Adjacent to the proposed area is the greatest estuarine coastal marsh in the United States. This marsh provides rich nutrients for the Gulf of Mexico, the most productive fishing region of the country. The EIS focused primarily on oil pollution and its negative environmental effect. Three conservation groups contend that the EIS is insufficient in that it does not properly discuss alternatives. The government contends that (a) it need only provide a detailed statement of the alternatives, not a discussion of their environmental impact, and (b) the only alternatives the NEPA requires it to discuss are those which can be adopted and implemented by the agency issuing the impact statement. Decision?

**7.** When considering an application for a special use permit to develop and operate a ski resort at Sandy Butte, a mountain in Washington that is part of a national forest, the Forest Service prepared an EIS. The EIS recommend the issuance of a special use permit for what was to be a sixteen-lift ski area, and the regional forest issued the permit as recommended. Four organizations sued, claiming that the EIS was inadequate. The lower court held that the EIS was adequate, but the Court of Appeals reversed, concluding that the NEPA required that actions be taken to mitigate the adverse effects of a major federal action and that the EIS contain a detailed mitigation plan. Decision?

**Internet Exercise** Find information about the United States Environmental Protection Agency, then choose a State and determine if it has a State environmental agency and, if so, what its responsibilities are.

# CHAPTER 47

# International Business Law

Today every aspect of business, including business law, requires some understanding of international business practices. Since World War II, the global economy has become increasingly interconnected. Many U.S. corporations now have investments or manufacturing facilities in other countries, while an increasing number of foreign corporations are conducting business operations in the United States. Furthermore, whether a domestic corporation exports goods or not, it competes with imports from many other countries. For example, U.S. firms face competition from Japanese electronics and automobiles, French wines and fashions, German machinery, and Taiwanese textiles. To compete effectively, U.S. firms need to be aware of international business practices and developments.

Laws vary greatly from country to country: what one nation requires by law, another may forbid. To complicate matters, there is no single authority in international law that can compel countries to act. When the laws of two or more nations conflict, or when one party has violated an agreement and the other party wishes to enforce it or recover damages, establishing who will adjudicate the matter, which laws will be applied, what remedies will be available, or where the matter will be decided often is very confusing. Nonetheless, given the growing impact of the global economy, a basic understanding of international business law is essential.

## THE INTERNATIONAL ENVIRONMENT

**International law** deals with the conduct and relations between nation-states and international organizations, as well as some of their relations with persons. Unlike domestic law, international law generally cannot be enforced. Nevertheless, although international courts do not have compulsory jurisdiction to resolve international disputes, they do have authority to resolve an international dispute if the parties to the dispute *accept* the court's jurisdiction over the matter. Furthermore, a sovereign nation that has adopted an international law will enforce that law to the same extent as all of its domestic laws. This section of the chapter examines some of the sources and institutions of international law.

## International Court of Justice

The United Nations, which is probably the most famous international organization, has a judiciary branch called the International Court of Justice (ICJ). The ICJ consists of fifteen judges, no two of whom may be from the same sovereign state, elected for nine-year terms by a majority of both the U.N. General Assembly and the U.N. Security Council. The usefulness of the ICJ is limited, however, because only nations (not private individuals or corporations) may be parties to an action before the court. Furthermore, the ICJ has contentious jurisdiction only over nation-parties who agree not only to allow the ICJ to decide the case but also to be bound by its decision. Moreover, because the ICJ cannot enforce its rulings, countries displeased with an ICJ decision may simply ignore it. Consequently, few nations submit their disputes to the ICJ.

The ICJ also has advisory jurisdiction if requested by a U.N. organ or specialized U.N. agency. Neither sovereign states nor individuals may request an advisory opinion. These opinions are nonbinding, and the U.N. agency requesting the opinion usually decides by vote whether to follow it.

## Regional Trade Communities

Of much greater significance are international organizations, conferences, and treaties that focus on business and trade regulation. Regional trade communities, such as the European Union (EU), promote common trade policies among member nations. Other important regional trade communities include the Central American Common Market (CACM), the Caribbean Community (CARICOM), the Association of Southeast Asian Nations (ASEAN), the Andean Common Market (ANCOM), the Common Market for Eastern and Southern Africa (COMESA), the Asian Pacific Economic Cooperation (APEC), Mercado Comun del Cono Sur (Latin American Trading Group, MERCO-SUR), and the Economic Community of West African States (ECOWAS).

*European Union (EU)* The European Community (EC), the predecessor to the European Union, was formed in 1967 through a merger between the European Economic Community (better known as the Common Market), the European Coal and Steel Community, and the European Atomic Energy Community (Euratom). The EC worked to remove trade barriers between its member nations and to unify their economic policies. The EC had the power to make rules that bound member nations and that preempted their domestic laws.

In 1993 the Treaty on European Union (popularly called the Maastricht Treaty) took effect. It changed the name of the EC to the European Union (EU) and stated the Union's objectives to include (1) promoting economic and social progress by creating an area without internal borders and by establishing an economic and monetary union; (2) asserting its identity on the international scene by implementing a common foreign and security policy; (3) strengthening the protection of the rights and interests of citizens of its member states; and (4) developing close cooperation on justice and home affairs. The EU currently has fifteen full members: Austria, Belgium, Denmark, Finland, France, Germany, Greece, Ireland, Italy, Luxembourg, the Netherlands, Portugal, Spain, Sweden, and the United Kingdom.

*NAFTA* The North American Free Trade Agreement, which took effect in 1994, established a free trade area among the United States, Canada, and Mexico. Its objectives are to (1) eliminate trade barriers to the movement of goods and services across the borders, (2) promote conditions of fair competition in the free trade area, (3) increase investment opportunities in the area, and (4) provide adequate and effective enforcement of intellectual property rights. Over fifteen years, the treaty will gradually eliminate all tariffs between the three countries.

## International Treaties

A **treaty** is an agreement between or among independent nations. As discussed in Chapter 1, the U.S. Constitution authorizes the president to enter into treaties with the advice and consent of the Senate "providing two-thirds of the Senators present concur." The Constitution provides that all valid treaties are "the law of the land," having the legal force of a Federal statute.

Nations have entered into bilateral and multilateral treaties to facilitate and regulate trade and to protect their national interests. In addition, treaties have been used to serve as constitutions of international organizations, to establish general international law, to transfer territory, to settle disputes, to secure human rights, and to protect investments. The Treaty Section of the Office of Legal Affairs within the United Nations Secretariat is responsible for registering and publishing treaties and agreements among member nations. Since its inception in 1946, the U.N. Secretariat has registered and published more than 30,000 treaties that expressly or indirectly concern international business.

Probably the most important multilateral trade treaty is the General Agreement on Tariffs and Trade (GATT). The basic purpose of GATT (now called the World Trade Organization [WTO] with more than 120 members) is to facilitate the flow of trade by establishing agreements on potential trade barriers such as import quotas, customs, export regulations, antidumping restrictions (the prohibition against selling goods for less than their fair market value), subsidies, and import fees. Such agreements arise under GATT's **most-favored nation provision,** which states that all signatories must treat each other as favorably as they treat any other country. Thus, any privilege, immunity, or favor given to one country must be given to all. Nevertheless, nations may give preferential treatment to developing nations and also may enter into free trade areas with one or more other nations. A free trade area permits countries to discriminate in favor of their free trade partners, provided that the agreement covers substantially all trade among the partners. A second important principle adopted by GATT is that the protection accorded domestic industries should take the form of a customs tariff, rather than other more trade-inhibiting measures.

The most recent set of accords, adopted in 1994, included agreements on such matters as agricultural products, textiles and clothing, technical barriers to trade, trade-related investment measures, customs valuation, subsidies and countervailing measures, trade in services, antidumping measures, and protection of intellectual property rights. It also created the Dispute Settlement Body and increased the scope of GATT's dispute resolution process.

# JURISDICTION OVER ACTIONS OF FOREIGN GOVERNMENTS

This section will focus on the power, and the limits on that power, of a sovereign nation to exercise jurisdiction over a foreign nation or to take over property owned by foreign citizens. More specifically, it will examine state immunities (the principle of sovereign immunity and the act of state doctrine) and the power of a state to take foreign investment property.

## Sovereign Immunity

One of the oldest concepts in international law is that each nation has absolute authority over the events occurring within its territory. It also has been long recognized, however, that to maintain international relations and trade, a host country must refrain from imposing its laws on a foreign sovereign nation present within its borders. This absolute immunity from the courts of a host country is known as **sovereign immunity.** Originally, all acts of a foreign sovereign nation within a host country were considered immune from the host country's laws. In modern times, however, international law distinguishes between the public and commercial acts of a foreign nation. Only public acts, such as those concerning diplomatic activity, internal administration, or armed forces, will be granted sovereign immunity. When engaging in trade or commercial activities, a foreign nation subjects itself to the jurisdiction of the host country's courts with respect to disputes arising out of those commercial activities.

In 1976, Congress enacted the Foreign Sovereign Immunities Act in order to establish the circumstances under which the United States would extend immunity to foreign nations. The Act specifically provides that a foreign state shall be immune from neither Federal nor State court jurisdiction if the suit is based upon (1) a commercial activity conducted in the United States by the foreign state, (2) an act that the foreign state performed in the United States in connection with a commercial activity it carried on elsewhere, or (3) a commercial activity performed outside U.S. borders that directly affects the United States. If an activity is one that a private party could normally carry on, it is commercial and a foreign government engaging in that activity

is not immune. On the other hand, if the activity is one that only governments can undertake, it is noncommercial under the Act. Examples of commercial activities include a contract by a foreign government to buy provisions or equipment for its armed forces; a contract by a foreign government to construct or repair a government building; and a sale of a service or a product by a foreign government or its leasing of property, borrowing of money, or investing in a security of a U.S. corporation. Examples of public (noncommercial) activities to which sovereign immunity would extend include nationalizing a corporation, determining limitations upon the use of natural resources, and granting licenses to export a natural resource.

 *See Case 47–1*

## Act of State Doctrine

The **act of state doctrine** provides that a nation's judicial branch should not question the validity of the actions a foreign government takes within its own borders. In 1897, the U.S. Supreme Court described the act of state doctrine in terms that remain valid today: "Every sovereign State is bound to respect the independence of every other sovereign State, and the courts of one country will not sit in judgment on the acts of the government of another done within its own territory."

In the United States, there are several possible exceptions to the act of state doctrine. Some courts hold (1) that a sovereign may waive its right to raise the act of state defense and (2) that the doctrine may be inapplicable to commercial activities of a foreign sovereign. In addition, by Federal statute, the courts will not apply the act of state doctrine to claims to property based on the assertion that a foreign state confiscated the property in violation of the principles of international law, unless the president of the United States determines that the doctrine should be applied in a particular case.

## Taking of Foreign Investment Property

Investing in foreign states involves the risk that the host nation's government may take the investment property. An **expropriation** or nationalization occurs when a government seizes foreign-owned property or assets for a public purpose and pays the owner just compensation for what is taken. In contrast, **confiscation** occurs when a government offers no payment (or a highly inadequate payment) in exchange for seized property or seizes it for a nonpublic purpose. Confiscations violate generally observed principles of international law, whereas expropriations do not. In either case, few remedies are available to injured parties.

One precaution that U.S. firms can take is to obtain insurance from a private insurer or from the Overseas Private Investment Corporation (OPIC), an agency of the U.S. government. The World Bank established the Multilateral Investment Guarantee Agency (MIGA) to encourage increased investment in developing nations. The MIGA Convention has been signed by more than 150 nations. It offers foreign investment risk insurance for noncommercial risks including deprivation of ownership or control by governmental actions, breach of contract by a government where there is no judicial recourse, and loss from military action or civil disturbance.

## TRANSACTING BUSINESS ABROAD

Transacting business abroad may involve activities such as selling goods, information, or services; investing capital; or arranging for the movement of labor. Because these transactions may affect the national security, economy, foreign policy, and interests of both the exporting and importing countries, nations have imposed measures to restrict or encourage such transactions. This section examines the legal controls imposed upon the flow of trade, labor, and capital across national borders.

### Flow of Trade

Advances in modern technology, communication, transportation, and production methods have greatly increased the flow of goods across national boundaries. The governments within each country thereby face a dilemma. On the one hand, they wish to protect and stimulate domestic industry. On the other hand, they want to provide their citizens with the best quality goods at the lowest possible prices and to encourage exports from their own countries.

Governments have used a variety of trade barriers to protect domestic businesses and to achieve other social and political goals. A frequently applied device is the **tariff,** which is a duty or tax imposed on goods moving into or out of a country. Tariffs raise the price of imported goods, prompting some consumers to purchase less expensive, domestically produced items. Governments can also use **nontariff barriers** to give local industries a competitive advantage. Examples of nontariff barriers include unilateral or bilateral import quotas; import bans;

overly restrictive safety, health, or manufacturing standards; environmental laws; complicated and time-consuming customs procedures; and subsidies to local industry.

Dumping is the sale of exported goods from one country to another country at less than normal value. Under the WTO's Antidumping Code, "normal value" is the price that would be charged for the same or a similar product in the ordinary course of trade for domestic consumption in the exporting country. Dumping violates the GATT "if it causes or threatens material injury to an established industry in the territory of a contracting party or materially retards the establishment of a domestic industry."

Governments also control the flow of goods out of their countries by imposing quotas, tariffs, or total prohibitions. **Export controls** or restrictions usually result from important policy considerations, such as national defense, foreign policy, or the protection of scarce national resources. For example, the United States passed the Export Administration Act of 1979, amended in 1985 and 1988, which restricts the flow of technologically advanced goods and data from the United States to other countries. Nonetheless, to assist domestic businesses, countries generally encourage exports through the use of **export incentives** and **export subsidies.**

### Flow of Labor

The flow of labor across national borders generates policy questions involving the employment needs of local workers. Each country has immigration policies and regulations. Almost all countries require that foreigners obtain valid passports before entering their borders; citizens, in turn, often must have passports to leave or reenter the country. In addition, a country may issue foreign citizens visas that permit them to enter the country for identified purposes or for specific periods of time. For example, the U.S. Immigration and Naturalization Service issues various types of visas to persons who are temporarily visiting the United States for pleasure or business, to persons who enter the United States to perform services that the unemployed in this country cannot perform, and to persons who are transferred to the United States by their employers.

### Flow of Capital

Multinational businesses frequently need to transfer funds to, and receive money from, operations in other countries. Because there is no international currency, nations have sought to ease the flow of capital among themselves. In 1945, the International Monetary Fund (IMF) was established to facilitate the expansion and balanced growth of international trade, to assist in the elimination of foreign exchange restrictions that hamper such growth, and to shorten the duration and lessen the disequilibrium in the international balance of payments between the members of the fund. Currently, more than 150 countries are members of the IMF.

Many nations have laws regulating foreign investment. Restrictions on the establishment of foreign investment tend to limit the amount of equity and the amount of control allowed foreign investors. They may also restrict the way in which the investment is created, such as limiting or prohibiting investment by acquiring an existing locally owned business. Approximately 100 nations have become parties to the Convention on the Settlement of Investment Disputes Between States and Nationals of Other States. The Convention created the International Centre for the Settlement of Investment Disputes, which offers a form of arbitration for investment disputes.

Nations also have joined to form international and regional banks to facilitate the flow of capital and trade. Such banks include the International Bank for Reconstruction and Development (part of the World Bank), the African Development Bank, the Asian Development Bank, the European Investment Bank, and the Inter-American Development Bank.

## International Contracts

The legal issues inherent in domestic commercial contracts also arise in international contracts. Moreover, certain additional issues, such as differences in language, customs, legal systems, and currency, are peculiar to international contracts. Such a contract should specify its official language and define all of the significant legal terms it incorporates. In addition, it should specify the acceptable currency (or currencies) and payment method. The contract should include a choice of law clause designating what law will govern any breach or dispute regarding the contract, and a choice of forum clause designating whether the parties will resolve disputes through one nation's court system or through third-party arbitration. Finally, the contract should include a *force majeure* (unavoidable superior force) clause apportioning the liabilities and responsibilities of the parties in the event of an unforeseeable occurrence, such as a typhoon, tornado, flood, earthquake, war, or nuclear disaster.

*CISG* The United Nations Convention on Contracts for the International Sales of Goods (CISG), which has been ratified by the United States and more than forty other countries, governs all contracts for the international sales of goods between parties located in different nations that have ratified the CISG. Because treaties are Federal law, the CISG supersedes the Uniform Commercial Code in any situation to which either could apply. The CISG includes provisions dealing with interpretation, trade usage, contract formation, obligations and remedies of sellers and buyers, and risk of loss. Parties to an international sales contract may, however, expressly exclude CISG governance from their contract. The CISG specifically excludes sales of (1) goods bought for personal, family, or household use; (2) ships or aircraft; and (3) electricity. In addition, it does not apply to contracts in which the primary obligation of the party furnishing the goods consists of supplying labor or services. The CISG is discussed in Chapters 21 through 25.

*Letters of Credit* International trade involves a number of risks not usually encountered in domestic trade, particularly the threat of governmental controls over the export or import of goods and currency. The most effective means of managing these risks—as well as the ordinary trade risks of nonperformance by seller and buyer—is the irrevocable documentary letter of credit. Most international letters of credit are governed by the Uniform Customs and Practices for Documentary Credits, a document drafted by commercial law experts from many countries and adopted by the International Chamber of Commerce. A **letter of credit** is a promise by a buyer's bank to pay the seller, provided certain conditions are met. The letter of credit transaction involves three or four different parties and three underlying contracts. To illustrate: a U.S. business wishes to sell computers to a Belgian company. The U.S. and Belgian firms enter into a sales agreement that includes details such as the number of computers, the features they will have, and the date they will be shipped. The buyer then enters into a second contract with a local bank, called an **issuer,** committing the bank to pay the agreed price upon receiving specified documents. These documents normally include a bill of lading (proving that the seller has delivered the goods for shipment), a commercial invoice listing the purchase terms, proof of insurance, and a customs certificate indicating that customs officials have cleared the goods for export. The buyer's bank's commitment to pay is the irrevocable letter of credit. Typically, a **correspondent** or **paying bank** located in the seller's country makes payment to the seller. Here, the Belgian issuing bank arranges to pay the U.S. correspondent bank the agreed sum of money in exchange for the documents. The issuer then sends the U.S. computer firm the letter of credit. When the U.S. firm obtains all the necessary documents, it presents them to the U.S. correspondent bank, which verifies the documents, pays the computer company in U.S. dollars, and sends the documents to the Belgian issuing bank. Upon receiving the required documents, the issuing bank pays the correspondent bank and then presents the documents to the buyer. In our example, the Belgian buyer pays the issuing bank in Belgian francs for the letter of credit when the buyer receives the specified documents from the bank.

## Antitrust Laws

Section 1 of the Sherman Act provides that U.S. antitrust laws shall have a broad, extraterritorial reach. As discussed in Chapter 41, contracts, combinations, or conspiracies that restrain trade with foreign nations, as well as among the domestic States, are deemed illegal. Therefore, agreements among competitors to increase the cost of imports, as well as arrangements to exclude imports from U.S. domestic markets in exchange for agreements not to compete in other countries, clearly violate U.S. antitrust laws. The antitrust provisions are also designed to protect U.S. exports from privately imposed restrictions seeking to exclude U.S. competitors from foreign markets. Amendments to the Sherman Act and the Federal Trade Commission Act limit their application to unfair methods of competition that have a direct, substantial, and reasonably foreseeable effect on U.S. domestic commerce, U.S. import commerce, or U.S. export commerce.

 *See Case 47–2*

## Securities Regulation

The securities markets have become increasingly internationalized, thereby raising questions regarding which country's law governs a particular transaction in securities. (U.S. Federal securities laws are discussed in Chapter 44.) Foreign issuers who issue securities in the United States must register them under the 1933 Act unless an exemption is available. Foreign issuers whose securities are sold in the secondary market in the United States must register under the 1934 Act unless the issuer is exempt. Some nonexempt foreign issuers may avoid registration under the 1934 Act by providing the Securities and Exchange Commission (SEC) with copies of all information material to investors that they have made public in their home country. Regulation S provides a safe harbor from the 1993 Act registration requirements for offshore sales of equity securities of U.S. issuers. The antifraud provisions of the U.S. securities laws apply to securities sold by the use of any means or instrumentality of interstate commerce. In determining the extraterritorial application of these provisions, the courts have generally found jurisdiction where there is either *conduct* or *effects* in the United States relating to a violation of the Federal securities laws.

 *See Case 47–3*

## Protection of Intellectual Property

The U.S. laws protecting intellectual property (discussed in Chapter 40) do not apply to transactions in other countries. Generally, the owner of an intellectual property right must comply with each country's requirements to obtain from that country whatever protection is available. The requirements vary substantially from country to country, as does the degree of protection. The United States belongs to multinational treaties that try to coordinate the application of member nations' intellectual property laws. The principal treaties for patent protection are the Paris Convention for the Protection of Industrial Property and the Patent Cooperation Treaty. International treaties protecting trademarks are the Paris Convention, the Arrangement of Nice Concerning the International Classification of Goods and Services, and the Vienna Trademark Registration Treaty. Copyrights are covered by the Universal Copyright Convention and the Berne Convention for the Protection of Literary and Artistic Works. The Trade-Related Aspects of Intellectual Property Rights (TRIPS) portion of the World Trade Organization Agreement covers the range of intellectual property.

## Foreign Corrupt Practices Act

In 1977, Congress enacted the Foreign Corrupt Practices Act (FCPA), prohibiting all domestic concerns from bribing foreign governmental or political officials. The FCPA makes it unlawful for any domestic concern or any of its officers, directors, employees, or agents to offer or give anything of value directly or indirectly to any foreign official, political party, or political official for the purpose of (1) influencing any act or decision of that person or party in his or its official capacity, (2) inducing an act or omission in violation of his or its lawful duty, or (3) inducing such person or party to use his or its influence to affect a decision of a foreign government to assist the domestic concern in obtaining or retaining business. An offer or promise to make a prohibited payment is a violation even if the offer is not accepted or the promise is not performed. The 1988 amendments to the FCPA explicitly excluded routine governmental actions not involving the discretion of the official, such as obtaining permits or processing applications. This exclusion does *not* cover any decision by a foreign official whether, or on what terms, to award new business or to continue business with a particular party. The amendments also added an affirmative defense for payments that are lawful under the written laws or regulations of the foreign officials' country.

Violations can result in fines of up to $2 million for companies; individuals may be fined a maximum of $100,000 or imprisoned up to five years, or both. Section 32(c). Fines imposed upon individuals may not be paid directly or indirectly by the domestic concern on whose behalf they acted. In addition, the courts may impose civil penalties of up to $11,000.

In 1997 the United States and thirty-three other nations signed the Organization for Economic Cooperation and Development Convention on Combating Bribery of Foreign Public Officials in International Business Transactions (OECD Convention). In 1998 Congress enacted the International Anti-Bribery and Fair Competition Act of 1998 to conform the FCPA to the Convention. The 1998 Act expands the FCPA to include (1) payments made to "secure any improper advantage" from foreign officials, (2) all foreign persons who commit an act in furtherance of a foreign bribe while in the United States, and (3) officials of public international organizations within the definition of a "foreign official." A public international organization is defined as either an organization designated by executive order pursuant to the International Organizations Immunities Act, or any other international organization designated by executive order of the president.

## Employment Discrimination

Title VII of the Civil Rights Act of 1964, the Americans with Disabilities Act, and the Age Discrimination in Employment Act, discussed in Chapter 43, apply to U.S. citizens employed abroad by U.S. employers or by foreign companies controlled by U.S. employers. Employers, however, are not required to comply with these employment discrimination laws if compliance would violate the law of the foreign country in which the workplace is located.

## FORMS OF MULTINATIONAL ENTERPRISES

The term **multinational enterprise** refers to any business that engages in transactions involving the movement of goods, information, money, people, or services across national borders. Such an enterprise may conduct its business in any of several forms: direct sales, foreign agents, distributorships, licensing, joint ventures, and wholly owned subsidiaries. A number of considerations determine the form of business organization that would be best for conducting international transactions. These factors include financing, tax consequences, legal restrictions imposed by the host country, and the degree to which the multinational enterprise wishes to control the business.

 *See Case 47–4*

### Direct Export Sales

Under a direct export sale, the seller contracts directly with the buyer in the other country. This is the simplest and least involved multinational enterprise.

### Foreign Agents

An agency relationship often is used by multinational enterprises seeking limited involvement in an international market. The principal firm will appoint a local agent, who may be empowered to enter into contracts in the agent's country on behalf of the principal or who may be authorized only to solicit and take orders. The agent generally does not take title to the merchandise.

### Distributorships

A commonly used form of multinational enterprise is the distributorship, in which a producer of goods appoints a foreign distributor. Unlike an agent, a distributor takes title to the merchandise it receives; consequently, the distributor, not the producer, bears many of the risks connected with commercial sales. By its very format, the distributorship is especially susceptible to antitrust violations. Therefore, both the producer and the distributor must take special care to ensure that the arrangement does not violate the antitrust laws of their respective governments.

## Licensing

A multinational enterprise wishing to exploit an intellectual property right, such as a patent, trademark, trade secret, or an unpatented but innovative production technology, may choose to sell the right to use such property to a foreign company rather than enter the foreign market itself. The sale of such rights, called licensing, is one of the major means by which technology and information are transferred among nations. Normally, the foreign firm will pay royalties in exchange for the information, technology, or patent. Franchising is a form of licensing in which the owner of intellectual property grants permission to a foreign business under carefully specified conditions.

## Joint Ventures

In a joint venture, two or more independent businesses from different countries agree to coordinate their efforts to achieve a common result. The sharing of profits and liabilities, as well as the delegation of responsibilities, is fixed by contract. One advantage of the joint venture is that each company can be assigned responsibility for that which it does best. To promote local ownership of investments, a number of developing nations and regional groups have enacted legislation that prohibits foreign businesses from owning more than 49 percent of any business enterprise in those countries. In addition, each country may require that its citizens comprise a majority of the management of an enterprise.

## Wholly Owned Subsidiaries

By far, wholly owned subsidiaries require the most active participation by a parent firm. Nevertheless, creating a foreign wholly owned subsidiary corporation can offer a business numerous advantages, most significantly the ability to retain authority and control over all phases of operation. This is especially attractive to businesses wishing to safeguard their technology.

---

 # Chapter Summary

| The International Environment | **International Law** includes law that deals with the conduct and relations of nation-states and international organizations as well as some of their relations with persons; such law is enforceable by the courts of a nation that has adopted the international law as domestic law<br>**International Court of Justice** judicial branch of the United Nations having voluntary jurisdiction over nations<br>**Regional Trade Communities** international organizations, conferences, and treaties focusing on business and trade regulation; the EU (European Union) is the most prominent of these<br>**International Treaties** agreements between or among independent nations, such as the General Agreement on Tariffs and Trade (GATT), now called the World Trade Organization |
|---|---|
| Jurisdiction over Actions of Foreign Governments | **Sovereign Immunity** foreign country's freedom from a host country's laws<br>**Act of State Doctrine** rule that a court should not question the validity of actions taken by a foreign government in its own country<br>**Taking of Foreign Investment Property**<br>• *Expropriation* governmental taking of foreign-owned property for a public purpose and with payment of just compensation<br>• *Confiscation* governmental taking of foreign-owned property without payment (or for a highly inadequate payment) or for a nonpublic purpose |

## Transacting Business Abroad

**Flow of Trade** controlled by trade barriers on imports and exports
- *Tariff* duty or tax imposed on goods moving into or out of a country
- *Nontariff Barriers* include quotas, bans, safety standards, and subsidies

**Flow of Labor** controlled through passport, visa, and immigration regulations

**Flow of Capital** International Monetary Fund facilitates the expansion and balanced growth of international trade, assists in eliminating foreign exchange restrictions, and smooths the international balance of payments

**International Contracts** involve additional issues beyond those in domestic contracts, such as differences in language, legal systems, and currency
- *CISG* United Nations Convention on Contracts for the International Sales of Goods governs all contracts for international sales of goods between parties located in different nations that have ratified the CISG
- *Letter of Credit* bank's promise to pay the seller, provided certain conditions are met; used to manage the payment risks in international trade

**Antitrust Laws** U.S. antitrust laws apply to unfair methods of competition that have a direct, substantial, and reasonably foreseeable effect on the domestic, import, or export commerce of the United States

**Securities Regulation** foreign issuers who issue securities, or whose securities are sold in the secondary market, in the United States must register them unless an exemption is available; the antifraud provisions apply where there is either *conduct* or *effects* in the United States relating to a violation of the Federal securities laws

**Protection of Intellectual Property** the owner of an intellectual property right must comply with each country's requirement to obtain from that country whatever protection is available

**Foreign Corrupt Practices Act** prohibits all U.S. companies from bribing foreign governmental or political officials

**Employment Discrimination** Title VII of the Civil Rights Act of 1964, the Americans with Disabilities Act, and the Age Discrimination in Employment Act apply to U.S. citizens employed in foreign countries by U.S.-owned or -controlled companies

## Forms of Multinational Enterprises (MNE)

**Definition** any business that engages in transactions involving the movement of goods, information, money, people, or services across national borders

**Forms of MNE** the choice of form depends on a number of factors including financing considerations, tax consequences, and degree of control
- *Direct Export Sales* seller contracts directly with the buyer in the other country
- *Foreign Agents* a local agent in the host country is used to provide limited involvement for an MNE
- *Distributorship* MNE sells to a foreign distributor who takes title to the merchandise
- *Licensing* MNE sells a foreign company the right to use technology or information
- *Joint Ventures* two independent businesses from different countries share profits, liabilities, and duties
- *Wholly Owned Subsidiary* enables an MNE to retain control and authority over all phases of operation

# Cases

### CASE 47–1
## Sovereign Immunity
### *SAUDI ARABIA v. NELSON*
Supreme Court of the United States, 1993
507 U.S. 349, 113 S.Ct. 1471, 123 L.Ed.2d 47

SOUTER, J.
* * * Petitioner Kingdom of Saudi Arabia owns and operates petitioner King Faisal Specialist Hospital in Riyadh, as well as petitioner Royspec Purchasing Services, the Hospital's corporate purchasing agent in the United States. [Citation.] The Hospital Corporation of America, Ltd. (HCA), an independent corporation existing under the laws of the Cayman Islands, recruits Americans for employment at the Hospital under an agreement signed with Saudi Arabia in 1973. [Citation.]

In its recruitment effort, HCA placed an advertisement in a trade periodical seeking applications for a position as a monitoring systems engineer at the Hospital. The advertisement drew the attention of respondent Scott Nelson in September 1983, while Nelson was in the United States. After interviewing for the position in Saudi Arabia, Nelson returned to the United States, where he signed an employment contract with the Hospital, [citation], satisfied personnel processing requirements, and attended an orientation session that HCA conducted for Hospital employees. In the course of that program, HCA identified Royspec as the point of contact in the United States for family members who might wish to reach Nelson in an emergency. [Citation.]

In December 1983, Nelson went to Saudi Arabia and began work at the Hospital, monitoring all "facilities, equipment, utilities and maintenance systems to insure the safety of patients, hospital staff, and others." [Citation.] He did his job without significant incident until March 1984, when he discovered safety defects in the Hospital's oxygen and nitrous oxide lines that posed fire hazards and otherwise endangered patients' lives. [Citation.] Over a period of several months, Nelson repeatedly advised Hospital officials of the safety defects and reported the defects to a Saudi Government commission as well. [Citation.] Hospital officials instructed Nelson to ignore the problems. [Citation.]

The Hospital's response to Nelson's reports changed, however, on September 27, 1984, when certain Hospital employees summoned him to the Hospital's security office where agents of the Saudi Government arrested him.

The agents transported Nelson to a jail cell, in which they "shackled, tortured and bea[t]" him, [citation], and kept him four days without food. [Citation.] Although Nelson did not understand Arabic, Government agents forced him to sign a statement written in that language, the content of which he did not know; a Hospital employee who was supposed to act as Nelson's interpreter advised him to sign "anything" the agents gave him to avoid further beatings. [Citation.] Two days later, Government agents transferred Nelson to the Al Sijan Prison "to await trial on unknown charges." [Citation.]

At the Prison, Nelson was confined in an overcrowded cell area infested with rats, where he had to fight other prisoners for food and from which he was taken only once a week for fresh air and exercise. [Citation.] Although police interrogators repeatedly questioned him in Arabic, [citation], Nelson did not learn the nature of the charges, if any, against him. [Citation.] For several days, the Saudi Government failed to advise Nelson's family of his whereabouts, though a Saudi official eventually told Nelson's wife, respondent Vivian Nelson, that he could arrange for her husband's release if she provided sexual favors. [Citation.]

Although officials from the United States Embassy visited Nelson twice during his detention, they concluded that his allegations of Saudi mistreatment were "not credible" and made no protest to Saudi authorities. [Citation.] It was only at the personal request of a United States Senator that the Saudi Government released Nelson, 39 days after his arrest, on November 5, 1984. [Citation.] Seven days later, after failing to convince him to return to work at the Hospital, the Saudi Government allowed Nelson to leave the country. [Citation.]

In 1988, Nelson and his wife filed this action against petitioners in the United States District Court for the Southern District of Florida seeking damages for personal injury. * * *

The District Court dismissed for lack of subject-matter jurisdiction under the Foreign Sovereign Immunities Act of 1976, [citation]. It rejected the Nelsons' argument that jurisdiction existed, under the first clause of

§ 1605(a)(2), because the action was one "based upon a commercial activity" that petitioners had "carried on in the United States." * * *

The Court of Appeals reversed. [Citation.] It concluded that Nelson's recruitment and hiring were commercial activities of Saudi Arabia and the Hospital, carried on in the United States for purposes of the Act, [citation], and that the Nelsons' action was "based upon" these activities within the meaning of the statute. * * * We now reverse.

The Foreign Sovereign Immunities Act "provides the sole basis for obtaining jurisdiction over a foreign state in the courts of this country." [Citation.] Under the Act, a foreign state is presumptively immune from the jurisdiction of United States courts; unless a specified exception applies, a federal court lacks subject-matter jurisdiction over a claim against a foreign state. [Citations.]

Only one such exception is said to apply here. The first clause of § 1605(a)(2) of the Act provides that a foreign state shall not be immune from the jurisdiction of United States courts in any case "in which the action is based upon a commercial activity carried on in the United States by the foreign state." The Act defines such activity as "commercial activity carried on by such state and having substantial contact with the United States," [citation], and provides that a commercial activity may be "either a regular course of commercial conduct or a particular commercial transaction or act," the "commercial character of [which] shall be determined by reference to" its "nature," rather than its "purpose." [Citation.]

* * *

In this case, the Nelsons have alleged that petitioners recruited Scott Nelson for work at the Hospital, signed an employment contract with him, and subsequently employed him. While these activities led to the conduct that eventually injured the Nelsons, they are not the basis for the Nelsons' suit. Even taking each of the Nelsons' allegations about Scott Nelson's recruitment and employment as true, those facts alone entitle the Nelsons to nothing under their theory of the case. The Nelsons have not, after all, alleged breach of contract, [citation], but personal injuries caused by petitioners' intentional wrongs and by petitioners' negligent failure to warn Scott Nelson that they might commit those wrongs. Those torts, and not the arguably commercial activities that preceded their commission, form the basis for the Nelsons' suit.

* * *

We took up the task [of defining commercial activity for purposes of the Act] just last Term in [*Republic of*

*Argentina v.*] *Weltover*, [citation], which involved Argentina's unilateral refinancing of bonds it has issued under a plan to stabilize its currency. Bondholders sued Argentina in federal court, asserting jurisdiction under the third clause of § 1605(a)(2). In the course of holding the refinancing to be a commercial activity for purposes of the Act, we observed that the statute "largely codifies the so-called 'restrictive' theory of foreign sovereign immunity first endorsed by the State Department in 1952." [Citation.] We accordingly held that the meaning of "commercial" for purposes of the Act must be the meaning Congress understood the restrictive theory to require at the time it passed the statute. [Citation.]

Under the restrictive, as opposed to the "absolute," theory of foreign sovereign immunity, a state is immune from the jurisdiction of foreign courts as to its sovereign or public acts (*jure imperii*), but not as to those that are private or commercial in character (*jure gestionis*). [Citations.] We explained in *Weltover*, [citation], that a state engages in commercial activity under the restrictive theory where it exercises "'only those powers that can also be exercised by private citizens,'" as distinct from those "'powers peculiar to sovereigns.'" Put differently, a foreign state engages in commercial activity for purposes of the restrictive theory only where it acts "in the manner of a private player within" the market. [Citation.]

We emphasized in *Weltover* that whether a state acts "in the manner of" a private party is a question of behavior, not motivation: "[B]ecause the Act provides that the commercial character of an act is to be determined by reference to its 'nature' rather than its 'purpose,' the question is not whether the foreign government is acting with a profit motive or instead with the aim of fulfilling uniquely sovereign objectives. Rather, the issue is whether the particular actions that the foreign state performs (whatever the motive behind them) are the type of actions by which a private party engages in 'trade and traffic or commerce.'" [Citation.] We did not ignore the difficulty of distinguishing "'purpose' (i.e., the reason why the foreign state engages in the activity) from 'nature' (i.e., the outward form of the conduct that the foreign state performs or agrees to perform)," but recognized that the Act "unmistakably commands" us to observe the distinction. [Citation.] Because Argentina had merely dealt in the bond market in the manner of a private player, we held, its refinancing of the bonds qualified as a commercial activity for purposes of the Act despite the apparent governmental motivation. [Citation.]

Unlike Argentina's activities that we considered in *Weltover*, the intentional conduct alleged here (the Saudi Government's wrongful arrest, imprisonment, and torture of Nelson) could not qualify as commercial under the restrictive theory. The conduct boils down to abuse of the power of its police by the Saudi Government, and however monstrous such abuse undoubtedly may be, a foreign state's exercise of the power of its police has long been understood for purposes of the restrictive theory as peculiarly sovereign in nature. [Citations.] Exercise of

the powers of police and penal officers is not the sort of action by which private parties can engage in commerce. "[S]uch acts as legislation, or the expulsion of an alien, or a denial of justice, cannot be performed by an individual acting in his own name. They can be performed only by the state acting as such." [Citation.]

\* \* \*

---

## CASE 47–2
## Antitrust
# UNITED STATES v. NIPPON PAPER INDUSTRIES CO., LTD.
United States Court of Appeals, First Circuit, 1997
109 F.3d 1

---

SELYA, J.

This case raises an important, hitherto unanswered question. In it, the United States attempts to convict a foreign corporation under the Sherman Act, a federal antitrust statute, alleging that price-fixing activities which took place entirely in Japan are prosecutable because they were intended to have, and did in fact have, substantial effects in this country. The district court, declaring that a criminal antitrust prosecution could not be based on wholly extraterritorial conduct, dismissed the indictment. [Citation.] We reverse.

## I. Just the Fax

\* \* \*

In 1995, a federal grand jury handed up an indictment naming as a defendant Nippon Paper Industries Co., Ltd. (NPI), a Japanese manufacturer of facsimile paper. The indictment alleges that in 1990 NPI and certain unnamed coconspirators held a number of meetings in Japan which culminated in an agreement to fix the price of thermal fax paper throughout North America. NPI and other manufacturers who were privy to the scheme purportedly accomplished their objective by selling the paper in Japan to unaffiliated trading houses on condition that the latter charge specified (inflated) prices for the paper when they resold it in North America. The trading houses then shipped and sold the paper to their subsidiaries in the United States who in turn sold it to American consumers at swollen prices. The indictment further relates that, in 1990 alone, NPI sold thermal fax paper worth approximately $6,100,000 for eventual import into the United States; and that in order to ensure the

success of the venture, NPI monitored the paper trail and confirmed that the prices charged to end users were those that it had arranged. These activities, the indictment posits, had a substantial adverse effect on commerce in the United States and unreasonably restrained trade in violation of Section One of the Sherman Act, [citation].

\* \* \*

## II. Analysis

\* \* \*

**A. An Historical Perspective**  Our law has long presumed that "legislation of Congress, unless a contrary intent appears, is meant to apply only within the territorial jurisdiction of the United States." [Citation.] In this context, the Supreme Court has charged inquiring courts with determining whether Congress has clearly expressed an affirmative desire to apply particular laws to conduct that occurs beyond the borders of the United States. [Citation.]

\* \* \*

\* \* \* [in] the Supreme Court's most recent exploration of the Sherman Act's extraterritorial reach, *Hartford Fire Ins. Co. v. California*, [citation], the Justices endorsed [citation]'s core holding, permitting civil antitrust claims under Section One to go forward despite the fact that the actions which allegedly violated Section One occurred entirely on British soil. \* \* \* the *Hartford Fire* Court deemed it "well established by now that the Sherman Act applies to foreign conduct that was meant to produce and did in fact produce some substantial effect in the United States." [Citation.] The conduct alleged, a London-based conspiracy to alter the American insurance market, met that benchmark. [Citation.]

To sum up, the case law now conclusively establishes that civil antitrust actions predicated on wholly foreign conduct which has an intended and substantial effect in the United States come within Section One's jurisdictional reach. * * *

**B. The Merits**   Were this a civil case, our journey would be complete. But here the United States essays a criminal prosecution for solely extraterritorial conduct rather than a civil action. This is largely uncharted terrain; we are aware of no authority directly on point, and the parties have cited none.

Be that as it may, one datum sticks out like a sore thumb: in both criminal and civil cases, the claim that Section One applies extraterritorially is based on the same language in the same section of the same statute: "Every contract, combination in the form of trust or otherwise, or conspiracy, in restraint of trade or commerce among the several States, or with foreign nations, is declared to be illegal." [Citation.] Words may sometimes be chameleons, possessing different shades of meaning in different contexts, [citation], but common sense suggests that courts should interpret the same language in the same section of the same statute uniformly, regardless of whether the impetus for interpretation is criminal or civil.

Common sense is usually a good barometer of statutory meaning. Here, however, we need not rely on common sense alone; accepted canons of statutory construction point in the same direction. It is a fundamental interpretive principle that identical words or terms used in different parts of the same act are intended to have the same meaning. [Citation.] * * *

* * *

* * * The words of Section One have not changed since the *Hartford Fire* Court found that they clearly evince Congress' intent to apply the Sherman Act extraterritorially in civil actions, and it would be disingenuous for us to pretend that the words had lost their clarity simply because this is a criminal proceeding. Thus, unless some special circumstance obtains in this case, there is no principled way in which we can uphold the order of dismissal.

* * *

NPI and the district court, [citation], both sing the praises of the Restatement (Third) of Foreign Relations Law (1987), claiming that it supports a distinction between civil and criminal cases on the issue of extraterritoriality. The passage to which they pin their hopes states:

[I]n the case of regulatory statutes that may give rise to both civil and criminal liability, such as the United States antitrust and securities laws, the presence of substantial foreign elements will ordinarily weigh against application of criminal law. In such cases, legislative intent to subject conduct outside the state's territory to its criminal law should be found only on the basis of express statement or clear implication.

Id. at § 403 cmt. f. We believe that this statement merely reaffirms the classic presumption against extraterritoriality—no more, no less. After all, nothing in the text of the Restatement proper contradicts the government's interpretation of Section One. See, e.g., id. at § 402(1)(c) (explaining that, subject only to a general requirement of reasonableness, a state has jurisdiction to proscribe "conduct outside its territory that has or is intended to have substantial effect within its territory"); id. at § 415(2) ("Any agreement in restraint of United States trade that is made outside of the United States . . . [is] subject to the jurisdiction to prescribe of the United States, if a principal purpose of the conduct or agreement is to interfere with the commerce of the United States, and the agreement or conduct has some effect on that commerce."). What is more, other comments indicate that a country's decision to prosecute wholly foreign conduct is discretionary. See, e.g., id. at § 403 rep. n. 8.

* * *

International comity is a doctrine that counsels voluntary forbearance when a sovereign which has a legitimate claim to jurisdiction concludes that a second sovereign also has a legitimate claim to jurisdiction under principles of international law. [Citation.] Comity is more an aspiration than a fixed rule, more a matter of grace than a matter of obligation. In all events, its growth in the antitrust sphere has been stunted by *Hartford Fire*, in which the Court suggested that comity concerns would operate to defeat the exercise of jurisdiction only in those few cases in which the law of the foreign sovereign required a defendant to act in a manner incompatible with the Sherman Act or in which full compliance with both statutory schemes was impossible. See *Hartford Fire*, [citations]. Accordingly, the *Hartford Fire* Court gave short shrift to the defendants' entreaty that the conduct leading to antitrust liability was perfectly legal in the United Kingdom. [Citation.]

In this case the defendant's comity-based argument is even more attenuated. The conduct with which NPI is charged is illegal under both Japanese and American laws, thereby alleviating any founded concern about NPI being whipsawed between separate sovereigns. And, moreover, to the extent that comity is informed by general principles of reasonableness, see Restatement (Third) of Foreign Relations Law § 403, the indictment lodged against NPI is well within the pale. In it, the government charges that the defendant orchestrated a conspiracy with the object of rigging prices in the United States. If the government can prove these charges, we see no tenable reason why principles of comity should shield NPI from prosecution. We live in an age of international commerce, where decisions reached in one corner of the world can reverberate around the globe in less time than it takes to tell the tale. Thus, a ruling in NPI's favor would create perverse incentives for those who would use nefarious means to influence markets in the United States,

rewarding them for erecting as many territorial firewalls as possible between cause and effect.

We need go no further. *Hartford Fire* definitively establishes that Section One of the Sherman Act applies to wholly foreign conduct which has an intended and substantial effect in the United States. We are bound to accept that holding. Under settled principles of statutory construction, we also are bound to apply it by interpreting Section One the same way in a criminal case. The combined force of these commitments requires that we accept the government's cardinal argument, reverse the order of the district court, reinstate the indictment, and remand for further proceedings.

Reversed and remanded.

## CASE 47–3
## Securities Regulation
### *ITOBA LIMITED v. LEP GROUP PLC*
United States Court of Appeals, Second Circuit, 1995
54 F.3d 118

**VAN GRAAFEILAND, J.**
Itoba Limited appeals from a judgment of the United States District Court for the District of Connecticut dismissing its securities fraud action against Lep Group PLC, . . . for lack of subject matter jurisdiction. For the reasons stated below, we reverse and remand for further proceedings.

The corporate defendant in this case, Lep Group PLC, is a London-based holding company with some fifty subsidiaries operating in thirty countries. It is a true conglomerate, owning businesses in freight forwarding, home security systems, biotechnology, travel services, and real estate speculation. Lep's "ordinary shares," the British equivalent of common stock, are registered in the United Kingdom, obligating the company to comply with United Kingdom securities laws. The primary trading market for Lep's ordinary shares is the International Stock Exchange of the United Kingdom and the Republic of Ireland Ltd. (the "London Exchange").

To create a United States market for its ordinary shares, Lep deposited 12,842,850 of its approximately 136 million shares in an American depository in 1988. The depository in turn issued an American Depository Receipt (ADR) for each five ordinary shares of Lep on

deposit. Because these ADRs trade in the form of American Depository Shares (ADSs) on the National Association of Securities Dealers Automated Quotation System ("NASDAQ"), Lep is subject to the reporting and disclosure requirements of United States securities law.

A.D.T. Limited ("ADT") is a transnational holding company based in Bermuda. Its shares are listed on the New York Stock Exchange and approximately fifty percent of its shareholders of record reside in the United States. Itoba, a Channel Islands company, is a wholly-owned subsidiary of ADT. ADT also is the corporate parent of A.D.T. Securities Systems, Inc., a Delaware-based firm and one of America's largest suppliers of security and protection services.

In mulling over expansion plans for A.D.T. Securities Systems, ADT considered the possible acquisition of one of A.D.T. Securities Systems' largest competitors in the American security market, National Guardian. ADT already owned a small interest in that corporation through shares it held of Lep, the parent company of National Guardian. Because ownership of Lep would lead to control of National Guardian, ADT considered increasing its Lep holdings.

At the same time, Canadian Pacific was interested in expanding into the freight forwarding business and also was pondering a sizeable investment in Lep. Learning of their mutual interest, the companies agreed to explore a joint purchase of Lep. Canadian Pacific hired S.G. Warburg, a London investment bank, to evaluate Lep's business operations. Nicholas Wells, ADT's in-house financial analyst, was directed by Michael Ashcroft, ADT's chairman, to perform a valuation of Lep.

In December 1989, S.G. Warburg issued an extensive report assessing Lep's prospects. The analysis in this report was based on Lep's U.K. annual reports, the Form 20–F that Lep filed with the United States Securities and Exchange Commission for the year ended December 31, 1988, Lep's shareholder register, and broker reports. Shortly after the Warburg report was issued, Canadian Pacific abandoned the proposed joint venture.

ADT's interest, on the other hand, did not diminish. Wells continued his examination of Lep, relying heavily on the Warburg report. To supplement his research, he obtained from Canadian Pacific a copy of Lep's Form 20–F for 1988. Wells frequently discussed his analyses of these documents with David Hammond, ADT's vice chairman and the person in charge of acquisitions.

Based on Wells' analyses and their own review of the Warburg report, Hammond and Ashcroft decided to acquire Lep. Soon thereafter, Hammond formulated a plan to increase ADT's Lep holdings by making anonymous purchases on the market through one of ADT's offshore companies, in this case Itoba. Hammond contacted the board members of Itoba and recommended that they approve his purchase plan.

As expected, Itoba's board approved the plan. Itoba's board then requested one of ADT's employees to commence share purchases in Itoba's name; these purchases were made according to Hammond's plan and paid for by ADT. During the second half of 1990, Itoba executed a number of significant purchases on the London Exchange pursuant to the plan. By November 1990, Itoba had acquired over 37 million Lep ordinary shares for approximately $114 million.

Before ADT could complete its planned acquisition, however, Lep disclosed a series of business reversals that decimated its share value; Lep's stock price plummeted 97% and the value of Itoba's Lep holdings declined by nearly $111 million. Lep wrote off approximately $522 million from its books for the fiscal year ended December 31, 1991.

Itoba sued Lep and its officers in the District of Connecticut, asserting violations of sections 10(b) and 20 of the Securities Exchange Act of 1934 (the "Act")

and of Rule 10b–5. According to Itoba, the defendants were subject to liability because they failed to disclose material matters in statements filed with the SEC. Specifically, Itoba alleged that Lep made high risk investments and engaged in speculative business ventures without informing the investment public. Itoba claimed that had these matters been properly disclosed, it would not have purchased Lep's stock at artificially inflated prices.

\* \* \*

Defendants moved to dismiss Itoba's claims for lack of subject matter jurisdiction, and Magistrate Judge Jean Margolis, to whom the matter was referred for recommendation and report, issued a report that recommended dismissing Itoba's action on jurisdictional grounds. The district court adopted the magistrate judge's recommendations in toto. It dismissed Itoba's action on [jurisdictional] grounds in a short-form order. This, we conclude, was error.

It is well recognized that the Securities Exchange Act is silent as to its extraterritorial application. [Citation.] However, in determining whether Congress intended that the "precious resources of United States courts" be devoted to a specific transnational securities fraud claim, we are not without guidance. Two jurisdictional tests have emerged under this Court's decisions: the "conduct test," as announced in [citation], and the "effects test," as announced in [citation]. There is no requirement that these two tests be applied separately and distinctly from each other. Indeed, an admixture or combination of the two often gives a better picture of whether there is sufficient United States involvement to justify the exercise of jurisdiction by an American court. It is in this manner that we address the issue of jurisdiction in the instant case. Because we believe that the allegations are sufficient to support jurisdiction, we reverse.

Under the conduct test, a federal court has subject matter jurisdiction if (1) the defendant's activities in the United States were more than "merely preparatory" to a securities fraud conducted elsewhere, [citation], and (2) these activities or culpable failures to act within the United States "directly caused" the claimed losses, [citation]. Inherent in the conduct test is the principle that Congress does not want "'the United States to be used as a base for manufacturing fraudulent security devices for export, even when these are peddled only to foreigners.'" [Citation].

* * *

The magistrate judge's first finding—that ADT and Itoba did not read and rely on the SEC filing in making their purchase decision—must be rejected in view of the clearly-established fact that the executives of Itoba and ADT based their investment decision on the Warburg report. The analyses and conclusions in this report were predicated on information found in the Form 20–F that Lep filed with the SEC. Nicholas Wells, the ADT executive responsible for assessing investment prospects, made the Warburg report the centerpiece of his Lep valuation. Moreover, he not only relied on the discussion of the SEC filing as contained in the Warburg report, he also used his own copy of the 1988 Form 20–F to formulate his purchase recommendations. According to the affidavit of ADT's vice chairman, the decision to acquire Lep was based upon these recommendations.

* * *

The magistrate judge's second reason for denying jurisdiction, i.e., that the SEC filings were made in connection with Lep's ADSs and ADRs, not its ordinary shares, is only fifty percent correct and therefore is one hundred percent wrong. The ADRs were simply a grouping into one security of five ordinary shares. Inevitably, there was a direct linkage between the price of the ADRs representing five ordinary shares and the prices of the single ordinary shares themselves. If the ordinary share price fell on the London Exchange, the market price of an ADR would decrease in similar manner, and vice versa.

Finally, a Rule 10b–5 action is not barred because a false and misleading statement in an SEC filing pertains to a security that is not the security purchased. [Citation.] So long as the fraudulent device employed is of the type that would cause reasonable investors to rely thereon and, so relying, cause them to purchase or sell the corporation's securities, a Rule 10b–5 action may lie. [Citation.] SEC filings generally are the type of "devices" that a reasonable investor would rely on in purchasing securities of the filing corporation. When these United States filings include substantial misrepresentations, they may be a predicate for subject matter jurisdiction. [Citation.]

The fact that the Lep ordinary shares were issued and purchased in England does not change our conclusion. "The conduct test does not center its inquiry on whether domestic investors or markets are affected, but on the nature of conduct within the United States as it relates to carrying out the alleged fraudulent scheme. . . ."

Moreover, the making of the allegedly false and misleading filings with the SEC was not "merely preparatory to the fraud." * * *

* * *

* * * A material fact that is undisclosed in an SEC filing remains undisclosed absent public enlightenment. This may bring into play a concomitant duty, i.e., the duty to correct. [Citation.] Lep's uncorrected nondisclosure played as much a role in Itoba's purchases as the price listings on the London Exchange and NASDAQ. In view of the deleterious effect this continued nondisclosure had on the thousands of ADT shareholders in the United States, it cannot be described correctly as incidental or preparatory.

This argument, of course, combines pertinent principles of both the conduct and effects tests, the latter one being based on fraud which takes place abroad which impacts on "stock registered and listed on [an American] national securities exchange and [is] detrimental to the interests of American investors." [Citation.] Here, we have fraud occurring on an American exchange and persisting abroad that has impacted detrimentally upon thousands of United States shareholders in the defrauded company, i.e., over $100 million lost in the shareholders' corporate equity.

The magistrate judge held that "if ADT were the plaintiff, the 'effects test' would be met, in that ADT's stock is traded on the New York Stock Exchange and approximately fifty percent (50%) of its shares are held in this country." [Citations.] We believe this reasoning applies with equal effect where, although Itoba, ADT's wholly-owned subsidiary, was the nominal purchaser and owner of the Lep stock, it was ADT which financed the deal and which, with its shareholders, ultimately must bear the loss. This is not a case in which Lep's acts "simply [had] an adverse affect [sic] on the American economy or American investors generally." [Citation.] In short, we hold that a sufficient combination of ingredients of the conduct and effects tests is present in the instant case to justify the exercise of jurisdiction by the district court. [Citation.]

---

## CASE 47–4
### Forms of Multinational Enterprises
# *BULOVA WATCH COMPANY, INC. v. K. HATTORI & CO.*

United States District Court, Eastern District of New York, 1981

508 F.Supp. 1322

---

**WEINSTEIN, C. J.**

This motion to dismiss for lack of personal jurisdiction (F.R.Civ.P. 12(b)(2)), presents a classic problem in adjudicating claims against a multinational corporation using subsidiaries to penetrate the American market.

\* \* \*

Plaintiff Bulova Watch Co., Inc. charges K. Hattori & Co., Ltd. and . . . others with unfair competition and disparagement and with engaging in a conspiracy to raid plaintiff's marketing staff in order to appropriate plaintiff's trade secrets.

Bulova is a New York corporation with its principal place of business in Flushing, New York. It manufactures and sells watches and claims to have the largest direct sales marketing system in the watch business.

Hattori is a company incorporated under the laws of Japan with its principal offices in Tokyo. It owns all the stock of Seiko Corporation of America (SCA), a New York corporation. SCA owns all the stock of Seiko Time Corp., Pulsar Time, Inc. and SPD Precision, Inc., all New York corporations. Hattori contracts in Japan for the manufacture of its watches and sells them under the Seiko, Pulsar and other brand names to its three American sub-subsidiaries. The Japanese parent's annual sales in 1978 were in excess of $1 billion. While the "Hattori group" manufactures many products including computers, measuring instruments, industrial robots, spectacle lenses and electric shavers . . . , watches and clocks account for approximately ninety percent of Hattori's sales. . . . A very substantial amount of its total revenue is derived from exports of watches and timepieces, the United States being its largest foreign market. In 1980 over four million Hattori timepieces were sold in this country at prices to the consumer of one hundred twenty-five dollars and higher—far more than half a billion dollars at retail. [Citation.]

Hattori sells products to distributors in over one hundred countries around the world. Wholly-owned subsidiaries of Hattori handle distribution of Hattori's products in about ten of those countries, including the United States. In the rest, or the great majority of the countries in which Hattori's products are sold, sales are made by Hattori or its subsidiaries to independent distributors who conduct their own advertising and other marketing activities and maintain their own repair centers pursuant to agreement or arrangements with Hattori. . . . Hattori has never directly marketed its products in any country except Japan.

Hattori's United States subsidiaries sold Seiko-branded products totalling over $50,000,000 in wholesale dollars in 1979 to retail customers and wholesale distributors in the Caribbean, South America and Europe. SCA has also made substantial investments in third countries to assist Hattori in selling its Japanese manufactured timepieces. It owns one hundred percent of the capital stock of Pulsar subsidiaries which it has established in Canada and Europe during the past two years. Seiko Time Canada, Ltd., in 1979, represented an investment of $5,000,000 and accounted for Canadian sales of Hattori products in excess of $35,000,000 in wholesale dollars. In 1980, Seiko Corporation of America also acquired one hundred percent of the stock of a Brazilian corporation, Seiko Time, Ltd., which in turn acquired all the stock of Hase, S.A., a company which sells Hattori's Seiko-branded products in Brazil. [Citation.]

\* \* \*

Between July and December of 1978, six members of Bulova's staff—three regional sales managers and three more senior executive personnel—left Bulova to join either a Seiko subsidiary or a Seiko distributor. During December, 1978 four Bulova salesmen joined SPD Precision's Pulsar division which in January, 1979 was separately incorporated as Pulsar Time, Inc. Sometime during 1979 a number of Bulova salesmen were hired by Pulsar Time. What sharply divides plaintiff from defendant is the question of whether these hirings were the result of a conspiracy among defendants to appropriate Bulova's trade secrets and marketing system and to damage Bulova and destroy its business and reputation.

\* \* \*

[The N.Y. statute] permits the exercise of such jurisdiction over "persons, property, or status as might have been exercised heretofore." It confers personal jurisdiction over unlicensed foreign corporations that are "doing business" in New York. [Citations.]

The definition of "doing business" has been variously stated, but the common denominator is that the corporation is operating within the state "not occasionally or casually, but with a fair measure of permanence and continuity." [Citations.]

It is no longer a matter of doubt that a foreign corporation can do business in New York through its employees, [citations].

Equally settled is the concept that a corporation may be amenable to New York personal jurisdiction when the systematic activities of a subsidiary in this state may fairly be attributed to the parent. [Citations.]

\* \* \*

When Cardozo enunciated the standard for doing business in New York, [citation], there would have been little need to consider how, or whether, a foreign-based multinational enterprise would be found to be doing business in New York. For one thing, the term "multinational firm," so common in today's parlance, was first used only in 1960. [Citation.] For another, it was not until after World War II that the phenomenon of the multinational enterprise, as we now know it, became a major factor in the world scene. [Citation.] Since then tens of thousands of subsidiaries have been created or acquired by parent enterprises located in other countries. [Citation.] By 1972 it was estimated that in a world that produced about $3,000 billion of goods and services a year, something like one-eighth of the output moved across international boundaries. [Citation.] In that same year the value of American investments abroad was $94 billion. [Citation.]

After the Second World War investment in the United States by foreign parent companies also expanded tremendously so that by the early 1970s non-United States corporations owned more than seven hundred "major manufacturing enterprises" in this country. [Citation.] Direct foreign investment, defined as ownership by foreign parents of at least ten percent of the equity of an American enterprise, was $3.4 billion at the start of the 1950s, $6.6 billion in 1959 and $26.5 billion by 1974. [Citation.] Total assets of foreign-owned affiliates in the United States in 1974 were $174.3 billion, of which more than one-fifth was Japanese-owned. [Citation.] These trends have accelerated.

The vehicles of this modern international economic growth were and are the multinational enterprises. Their size is often awesome: the annual sales of General Motors exceeded the gross national products of Switzerland, Pakistan, or South Africa. [Citation.]

The phenomenon of penetration into the economies of distant areas can be traced through artifacts back into pre-history. But the current situation is in many respects quite different in the sophisticated organizational and legal techniques utilized from even that of earlier periods in American history when foreign financing made so much of our industrial and commercial expansion possible and when American companies like Singer, the American sewing machine company, established manufacturing plants abroad. [Citations.] Aside from their magnitude, today's multinationals are unique in the way vast investments in myriad locations are made to serve the interests of a single organization. Large advantages lie in the possibility of making centralized management and investment decisions on the basis of the situations and opportunities prevailing in various host countries. [Citations.] Such an organization has the resources and scope to plan and to utilize world-wide markets and resources. [Citations.]

The profit motivation for international expansion is common to multinationals. [Citations.] Nevertheless, the means by which the multinational exercises control over its far-flung elements vary. The degree and nature of control may depend upon the nationality of the corporate parent. [Citations.] The formal structure of the parent's form of ownership also has control implications. Choice among the various corporate modes of entering a market, e.g., by means of licensing arrangement, joint venture, minority-, majority- or wholly-owned subsidiary, has very significant implications for the control exercised by the parent. [Citation.] Utilization of a wholly-owned marketing-based subsidiary is found where "the . . . retention of unambiguous control of foreign operations is critical to the firm's strategy." [Citation.] The decision of marketing-oriented firms to choose wholly-owned subsidiaries means that they can exercise more control over their foreign operation in subtle, indirect ways as well as directly. [Citation.]

Another criterion that will determine the "corporate intimacy" joining a parent and its subsidiary, [citation], is the type and range of products being sold. Enterprises with narrow product lines tend to organize their operations on a highly integrated basis, linking production and marketing into tight strategic patterns. [Citation.] While Hattori manufactures a number of products, the overwhelming concern of its American marketing operation is with its timepieces—constituting ninety percent of its total production by value.

Thus sales subsidiaries tend to be under especially close control where a company produces a limited number of products. In such a case the company has a higher stake in the maintenance of quality standards, a higher sense of risk in sharing its technology with others, a higher need for a centralized marketing strategy. . . . The strategy of [these] firms, therefore, requires relatively tight controls.

[Citation.]

Finally, a crucial factor in the degree of control over the subsidiary is the age of the subsidiary and the extent to which the subsidiary has been able to develop independently of its parent. A leading scholar of international trade distinguishes multinational firms from national firms with foreign operations: "A multinational firm starts out like a national firm with foreign operations, but after time each national operation takes on a life of its own." [Citation.] The history of modern international business enterprise is largely the history of just this development from a national firm with foreign sales operations, to the truly multinational firm with quasi-independent component entities. [Citation.]

An important question in assessing presence for jurisdictional purposes is whether a multinational has reached a state in its evolution when it can be said that its sales and marketing subsidiaries truly have a "life of their own." [Citation.]   *   *   *

The expanding multinational generally traverses a number of stages. At first it exports its goods to markets abroad, next it establishes sales organizations abroad, then it may license the use of its patents, and finally it may establish foreign manufacturing facilities. At a later stage it may "multinationalize its management and, ultimately, multinationalize the ownership of its stock." [Citation.] While many thousands of corporations are at the first, export stage, only a handful have developed into advanced multinational enterprises each of whose elements can be said to be significant in its own right.

After World War II, foreign companies gained familiarity with the United States market "by first exporting to this country; then, after achieving acceptance for their products, foreign firms set up manufacturing or assembly plants here." [Citation.] As these later stages were reached, the businesses established came to have lives of their own. The "monocentric" enterprise gradually gave way to a polycentric one, with more autonomy in the different elements. Wilkins detects three stages: in the first stage, the firm "reached out to sell or to obtain and in doing so felt the necessity or saw the opportunity to cross over domestic boundaries." [Citation.] The relationship was "monocentric" with the center of operations clearly in the parent's home country. The external activities in a monocentric relationship were "spokes on a wheel, with the parent company at the hub." [Citation.] In stage two, the functions of the branches broadened.

There might, for example, be investment by the subsidiary in a plant for local production or the subsidiary might sell products in third-country markets. "What characterizes stage two is the presence of foreign units that have developed their own separate histories and their own satellite activities." [Citation.] The final, third, stage is characteristic of the most advanced of these entities:

It garbles any chart's attempt to delineate international trade and control lines. The parent company comes to have a number of foreign multifunctional centers, serving overlapping geographical areas with various products. Supply and market lines cross international boundaries in . . . chaotic confusion. . . .

[Citation.]

Over time, certain foreign subsidiaries and affiliates have become full-fledged, fully integrated, multiprocess, multiproduct enterprises, with engineering, product planning and research staffs, with a continuity of employee, supplier, dealer, consumer and banking relationships with their own prominent role in foreign industries, with their own dealings with foreign governments and with their own third-country investments.

[Citation.] At this final stage, complicated, many-faceted relationships have replaced simple bilateral connections. [Citation.]

*   *   *

It is apparent that Hattori's international activities, large as they may be in terms of sales figures and associated product lines, are essentially akin to Wilkins' stage one "monocentric" export model and not to the much more complex multinationals to which defendants point. What is involved here is a series of relatively young sales and marketing subsidiaries abroad, whose purpose is to market a single product—timepieces. There is no manufacturing or product research done by any of these subsidiaries. They do not seem to have developed third-country trade except for the purpose of selling Hattori's Japanese manufactured goods. Only very recently have they begun to make some investments in third countries, again to produce further outlets for Hattori's factories in Japan. The use of the wholly-owned subsidiary form here reflects the desire for "unambiguous control" over sales and marketing subsidiaries to insure uniform quality and promotion of the product sold. [Citations.]

Hattori and its American subsidiaries do maintain some independence—about as much as the egg and vegetables in a western omelette. Just as, from a culinary point of view, we focus on the ultimate omelette and not its ingredients, so, too, from a jurisdictional standpoint, it is the integrated international operation of Hattori affecting activities in New York that is the primary focus of our concern.

Although with time the Hattori subsidiaries might well evolve, along with their parent, into the later stages of multinational development, today Hattori is a highly effective export manufacturer and not a fully developed multinational. It is monocentric more than polycentric. Large and sophisticated as it may be, it is very much the hub of a wheel with many spokes. It is appropriate, therefore, to look to the center of the wheel in Japan when the spokes violate substantive rights in other countries.

\* \* \*

What is decisive is that at the time this complaint was filed, Hattori, through its American subsidiaries, continued to engage in the market penetration and expansion that are its corporate *raison d'être* and that are the grounds underlying this action. We have no doubt about

the validity of an "inference as to the broad scope of the agency" linking Hattori to the activities of its subsidiaries in New York. [Citation.]

\* \* \*

A court might well find substantial unfairness were it to drag a foreign parent into court to defend itself against actions completely unrelated to the subsidiary corporation's purposive activities on behalf of its parent. The holding in this case is simply that while a subsidiary establishes and expands a parent's market position then, so long as that activity is being conducted, and with respect to those activities furthering the parent's ends, the parent is doing business in New York. This is particularly true as to activities directly related to primary steps taken to ensure a place for its subsidiaries, as where action is taken to raid an established competitor's personnel in penetrating the American market.

[Motion to dismiss denied.]

# Questions

1. Discuss the purpose and major features of regional trade communities (especially the European Union and NAFTA) and the World Trade Organization (GATT).

2. Discuss sovereign immunity, the act of state doctrine, expropriation, and confiscation.

3. Discuss the legal controls imposed on the flow of trade, labor, and capital across national borders.

4. Explain the international dimensions of antitrust law, securities regulation, the protection of intellectual property, and employment discrimination.

5. List and describe the various forms in which a multinational enterprise may conduct its business in a foreign country.

# Problems

1. Three banks that are wholly owned by the Republic of Costa Rica had issued promissory notes, payable in U.S. dollars in New York City. The notes are now in default due solely to actions of the Costa Rican government, which had suspended all payments of external debt because of escalating economic problems. Efforts by Costa Rica to curb foreign debt payment difficulties conflicted with U.S. policy for debt resolution procedure as conducted under the auspices of the International Monetary Fund. A syndicate of U.S. banks brought suit to recover on the promissory notes. The three Costa Rican banks assert the act of state doctrine as a defense. Decision?

2. Six U.S. manufacturers of broad-spectrum antibiotics derived a large percentage of their sales from overseas markets, including India, Iran, the Philippines, Spain, South Korea, Germany, Colombia, and Kuwait. The manufacturers agreed

to a common plan of marketing, whereby territories were divided and prices for products were set. The members of the plan also agreed not to grant foreign producers licenses to the manufacturing technology of any of their "big money" drugs. The above foreign countries bring suit for treble damages for violation of the U.S. antitrust laws. Decision?

3. After reading attractive brochures advertising a package tour of the Dominican Republic, a U.S. family decided to purchase tickets for the family vacation plan. The tour was a product of four different business entities, two domestic (U.S.) and two foreign. Sheraton Hotels & Inns, World Corporation, was to provide food and lodging; Dominicana Airlines, wholly owned by the government of the Dominican Republic, which routinely flew into Miami International Airport and sold tickets within the United States, was to provide round-trip air transportation and "tourist cards"

necessary for entry into the Dominican Republic; and two U.S. firms organized and sold the tour. Problems for the family began when their Dominicana flight landed in the Dominican Republic, and immigration officials denied them entry. Forced to leave, the family was shuttled first to Puerto Rico and then to Haiti, where they had to secure their own passage back to the United States at additional expense. The family brings suit against all four different business entities. Decision?

4.   A privately owned business in a developing country determines that current computer technology could solve many of the problems faced by its country's private and public sectors. This business, however, lacks the capital resources necessary for research and development to acquire such computer technology, even if trained personnel were available. Furthermore, despite a sense of patriotism, the business concludes that its national government could not efficiently or effectively handle such a development project. What business forms are available to this business for acquiring sophisticated computer technology? What are the advantages and problems inherent in the various options?

5.   King Faisal II of Iraq was killed on July 14, 1958, in the midst of a revolution in that country which led to the establishment of a republic subsequently recognized by the U.S. government. On July 19, 1958, the new republic issued a decree that all property of the former ruling dynasty, regardless of location, should be confiscated. Subsequently, the Republic of Iraq brought suit in the United States to obtain possession of money and stocks deposited in the deceased king's U.S. bank account in New York City. Decision?

6.   A business entity incorporated under the laws of one of the EU member nations contracts with the government of a developing nation to form a joint venture for the mining and refining of a scarce raw material used by several developed nations in the manufacture of highly sensitive weapons systems. The contract calls for the EU-based corporation to invest money and technology that will be used to build permanent refinery plants that eventually will revert to the developing nation. The developing nation also reserves the right to set quotas on sales of this scarce resource and to choose the destination of exports. Due to political conflicts, the developing nation refuses to allow any exports of the scarce material to the United States. This causes a sharp price increase in exports to the United States by other suppliers. The United States asserts antitrust violations against the EU-based corporation for the effects produced within the United States. Decision?

7.   A Panamanian corporation lends money to a Turkish enterprise, which issues a promissory note. The loan contract specifies that payment on the interest and principal shall be made to the Chemical Bank of New York City, where both parties maintain accounts. The loan contract contains no choice of law designation, but the Panamanian and Turkish companies have referred to the Chemical Bank in New York as their "legal address." As a result of a contractual performance dispute,

the Turkish company suspends payments on the loan. The Panamanian corporation then brings suit in the United States to recover the balance of the payments due. What possible options for choice of law apply?

8.   New England Petroleum Corporation (NEPCO), a New York corporation, was in the business of selling fuel oil in the United States. PETCO, a refinery incorporated in the Bahamas, was a wholly owned subsidiary of NEPCO. In 1968, PETCO entered into a long-term contract to purchase crude oil from Chevron Oil Trading (COT), which held 50 percent of an oil concession in Libya. In 1973, Libya nationalized COT and several other foreign-owned oil concessions, thereby forcing COT to terminate its contract with PETCO. To secure needed oil supplies, PETCO entered into a new contract with National Oil Corporation (NOC), which was wholly owned by the Libyan government. This contract was at a substantially higher price than the original contract with COT. The following month, Libya declared an oil embargo on exports to the United States, the Netherlands, and the Bahamas. Accordingly, NOC canceled its contracts with PETCO. After oil prices rose dramatically, NOC accepted bids for new contracts to replace the ones inactivated by the embargo. NEPCO brought suit against the Libyan government and NOC, alleging breach of contract. The district court dismissed the case for lack of jurisdiction, and the plaintiff appealed. Decision?

9.   Nigeria, experiencing an economic boom due to exports of high-grade oil, embarked on an infrastructure development plan. Accordingly, Nigeria entered into at least 109 contracts with 68 suppliers for the purchase of cement at a price of almost $1 billion. Among the contracting suppliers were four American corporations, including Texas Trading & Milling Corporation. Nigeria misjudged the cement market (having anticipated only a 20 percent fulfillment rate) and was forced to repudiate most of the contracts. Texas Trading & Milling Corporation and three other American companies brought suit, alleging anticipatory breach of contract. Nigeria claimed immunity under the Foreign Sovereign Immunities Act of 1976. In three of the cases, the district court held jurisdiction to be present and proceeded to trial. In one of the cases, the district court dismissed for lack of jurisdiction. Decision?

10.   Prior to 1918, a Russian corporation had deposited sums of money with August Belmont, a private banker doing business in New York City. In 1918, the Soviet government nationalized the corporation and appropriated all of the corporation's property and assets, including the deposit account with Belmont. The deposit became the property of the Soviet government until 1933, when it was released and assigned to the U.S. government as part of an international compact between the United States and the Soviet Union. The purpose of this arrangement was to bring about a final settlement of the claims and counterclaims between the two countries. The United States brought an action to recover the deposit from Belmont. The district court held against the United States because the act of nationalization by the

Soviets was a confiscation prohibited by the Fifth Amendment to the U.S. Constitution and was also a violation of New York public policy. The Court of Appeals affirmed, and the United States appealed. Decision?

WWW **Internet Exercise** Find information about (a) the United Nations, (b) the International Court of Justice, (c) the World Trade Organization (GATT), (d) NAFTA, and (e) the European Union.

# PART TEN

# Property

# CHAPTER 48

# Introduction to Property and Property Insurance

In our democratic and free enterprise society, the importance of the concept of property is second only to that of liberty. Although many of our rules of property stem directly from English law, in the United States property occupies a unique status because of the protection expressly granted it by the U.S. Constitution and by most State constitutions as well. The Fifth Amendment to the Constitution provides that "No person shall be . . . deprived of life, liberty, or property, without due process of law; nor shall private property be taken for public use, without just compensation." The Fourteenth Amendment contains a similar requirement: "No State shall . . . deprive any person of life, liberty, or property, without due process of law." Under the police power, however, this protection afforded to property owners is subject to regulation for the public good. The first part of this chapter will provide a general introduction to the law governing real and personal property. The second part of this chapter deals specifically with personal property; the last part covers property insurance.

By property we mean an exclusive right to control an economic good.

By private property we mean the exclusive right of a private person to control an economic good.

By public property we mean the exclusive right of a political unit (city, state, nation, etc.) to control an economic good.

\* \* \*

Speaking accurately, then, property is not a thing but the rights which extend over a thing. A less strict use of the word property makes property include the things over which the right extends. We say of a farm, this is my property, meaning the land and improvements on it and not merely the right, or rather, the land and its improvements together with the right. But, strictly speaking, property is the right, and not the object over which the right extends. R. Ely, *Property and Contract in their Relation to the Distribution of Wealth,* 101–2, 108.

In either sense of the word—the right over the object or the object itself—there is an enormous quantity of property in the United States today.

## INTRODUCTION TO PROPERTY

In spite of the unique place accorded property in our society, the term *property* is not easily defined. Given the fact that property includes almost every right, exclusive of personal liberty, that the law will protect, this uncertainty is not surprising. Property is valuable only because our law provides that certain consequences follow from the ownership of it. The right to use property, sell it, and control to whom it shall pass on the death of the owner are all included within the term *property*. Accordingly, **property** is a legally protected interest or group of interests. More specifically, property consists of a set of *rights* entitling one person to use and enjoy exclusively some item:

## *KINDS OF PROPERTY*

Property may be classified as (1) tangible or intangible property and (2) real or personal property, but these classifications are not mutually exclusive.

◆ *See Figure 48–1*

### Tangible and Intangible

A forty-acre farm, a chair, and a household pet are tangible property. Each of these physical objects embodies the group of rights or interests known as "title" to or "ownership" of **tangible property. Intangible property,** in contrast, does not exist in a physical form. For example, the rights represented by a stock certificate, a

**FIGURE 48–1** Kinds of Property

|  | Personal | Real |
| --- | --- | --- |
| **Tangible** | Goods | Land<br>Buildings<br>Fixtures |
| **Intangible** | Commercial paper<br>Stock certificates<br>Contract rights<br>Copyrights<br>Patents | Leases<br>Easements<br>Mortgages |

promissory note, and a deed granting Jones a right-of-way over Smith's land are intangible property. Each represents certain rights that defy reduction to physical possession but have a legal reality in that the courts will protect them.

The same item may be the object of both tangible and intangible property rights. Suppose Ann purchases a book published by Brown & Sons. On the first page is the statement "Copyright 1993 by Brown & Sons." Ann owns the volume she has purchased. She has the right to exclusive physical possession and use of that particular copy. It is a tangible piece of property of which she is the owner. Brown & Sons, however, has the exclusive right to publish copies of the book, a right granted the publisher by the copyright laws. The courts will protect this intangible property of Brown & Sons, as well as Ann's right to her particular volume.

## Real and Personal

The most significant practical distinction between types of property is the classification into real and personal property. To define this distinction simply: land and all interests in it are **real property** (also called realty), and every other thing or interest identified as property is **personal property** (also called **chattel**). This easy description encompasses most property, with the exception of certain physical objects that are personal property under most circumstances but that may, because of their attachment to land or their use in connection with land, become a form of real property called fixtures.

## Fixtures

A **fixture** is an article or piece of property that was formerly treated as personal property but has been attached in such a manner to land or a building that it is now designated as real property even though it retains its original identity. The intent of the parties to convert the property to real property from personal property is usually shown by the permanent manner of affixation or the adaptation of the affixed object to the property. For example, building materials are clearly personal property; but when worked into a building as its construction progresses, they become real property, as buildings are a part of the land they occupy. Thus, clay in its natural state is, of course, real property; when made into bricks, it becomes personal property; and if the bricks are then built into the wall of a house, the "clay" once again becomes real property.

Although determining whether various items are personal property or real property may be difficult, making such a determination may represent the sole manner of settling conflicting ownership claims. Unless otherwise provided by agreement, personal property remains the property of the person who placed it on the real estate. On the other hand, property that has been affixed so as to become a fixture (an actual part of the real estate) becomes the property of the real estate owner.

These considerations affect many persons. The apartment dweller who puts a new chandelier or a bathroom cabinet in his landlord's apartment and the shoe repairman who attaches equipment to the floor of his leased premises will not be entitled to remove them when their respective leases expire if the added objects are held to have become part of the real estate.

In determining whether personal property has become a fixture, the **intention** of the parties, as expressed in their agreement, will control the settlement of conflicting claims. In the absence of an agreement, the following factors are relevant in determining whether any particular item is a fixture:

1. the intention of the person who attached the item to the land or building;

2. the physical relationship of the item to the land or building;

3. the purpose served by the item in relation to the land or building and in relation to the person who brought it there; and

4. the interest of that person in the land or building at the time of the item's attachment.

Although physical attachment is significant, a more important test is whether the item can be removed without material injury to the land or building on the land. If it cannot be so removed, the item is generally held to have become part of the realty. The converse is also true but to a lesser degree. Where the item may be removed without material injury to the land or building, it is generally held not to be part of the realty. This test, however, is inconclusive.

Rather, the courts have sought the answer in the intention of the person who attached the item to the realty. The tests of intention are objective. One such test examines the purpose or use of the item in relation to the land and in relation to the person who brought it there.

Moreover, an item is not regarded as part of the realty merely because its use or purpose is usual for the kind of realty involved. For example, it is usual to have beds and dressers in bedrooms and dining tables in dining rooms, but these items are not ordinarily part of the realty. The test of purpose or use applies only if the item (1) is affixed to the realty in some way but (2) can be removed without material injury to the realty. In such a situation, if the use or purpose of the item is peculiar to a particular owner or occupant of the premises, the courts will tend to let him remove the item when he leaves. Accordingly, in the law of landlord and tenant, the tenant may remove **trade fixtures** (i.e., items used in connection with a trade but not intended to become part of the realty), provided that she can accomplish this without material injury to the realty. On the other hand, doors may be removed without injury to the structure; yet, because they are necessary to the ordinary use of the building and are not peculiar to the use of the occupant, they are considered to be fixtures and thus part of the real property.

*See Case 48-1*

## INCIDENTS OF PROPERTY OWNERSHIP

Practical and important legal consequences stem from the distinction between real and personal property. These consequences involve the transfer of property and its taxation.

## Transfer of Property

As will be explained in Chapter 51, the transfer of title to real property during life can be accomplished only by certain formalities, including the execution and delivery of a written instrument known as a deed. Title to personal property, on the other hand, may be transferred with relative simplicity and informality.

## Taxation

While most States levy taxes on the ownership of both real property and personal property, the applicable tax rate usually varies dramatically, depending on whether the property is classified as real or personal.

# PERSONAL PROPERTY

The law concerning personal property has been largely codified. The Uniform Commercial Code (UCC) includes the law of sales of goods (Article 2), as well as the law governing the transfer and negotiation of negotiable instruments (Article 3) and of investment securities (Article 8). Nonetheless, the Code does not cover a number of issues (addressed in the remainder of this chapter) involving the ownership and transfer of title to personal property. In addition, personal property may be, and often is, acquired by producing the item, rather than by selling or transferring it.

## TRANSFER OF TITLE

The transfer of title to real property is generally a formal affair. In contrast, title to personal property may be acquired and transferred with relative ease and with a minimum of formality. Such facility with regard to the transfer of personal property is essential within a society whose trade and industry are based principally upon transactions in personal property. In a free economy, stocks, bonds, merchandise, and intellectual property must be sold with minimal delay. It is only natural that the law will reflect these needs.

## By Sale

By definition, a **sale** of *tangible* personal property (goods) is a transfer of title to specified existing goods for a consideration known as the price. Title passes when the parties intend it to pass, and transfer of possession is not required for a transfer of title. For a discussion of this manner of transfer of title, see Chapter 23.

Sales of *intangible* personal property also involve the transfer of title. Many of these sales also are governed by UCC provisions, while some, such as sales of copyrights and patents, are governed by specialized Federal legislation.

## By Gift

A **gift** is a transfer of title to property from one person to another without consideration. This lack of consideration is the basic distinction between a gift and a sale. Because a gift involves no consideration or compensation, it must be completed by delivery of the gift to be effective. A gratuitous promise to make a gift is not binding. In addition, there must be intent on the part of the maker (the **donor**) of the gift to make a present transfer, and there must be acceptance by the recipient (the **donee**) of the gift.

*Delivery*   Delivery is essential to a valid gift. The term *delivery* has a very special meaning that includes, but is not limited to, the manual transfer of the item to the donee. A donor may effect an irrevocable delivery by, for example, turning an item over to a third person with instructions to give it to the donee. Frequently, an item, because of its size, location, or intangibility, is incapable of immediate manual delivery. In such cases, an irrevocable gift may be effected through the delivery of something that symbolizes dominion over the item. This is referred to as **constructive delivery.** For example, if Joanne declares that she gives an antique desk and all its contents to Barry and hands Barry the key to the desk, in many States a valid gift has been made.

⚖ *See Case 48–2*

*Intent*   The law also provides clearly that the donor must intend to make a present gift of the property. Thus, if Jack leaves a packet of stocks and bonds with Joan, her acquiring good title to them depends on whether Jack intended to make a gift of them or simply intended to place them in Joan's hands for safekeeping. A voluntary, uncompensated delivery made with the intent to give the recipient title constitutes a gift when the donee accepts the delivery. If these conditions are met, the donor has no further claim to the property.

Gifts, therefore, cannot be conditional. There is, however, one major exception to this rule: an engagement gift given in anticipation of marriage. If the marriage does not take place, the donor generally can recover the gift unless the donor broke the engagement without justification. But the courts will not apply the exception when a marriage is called off due to the death of one of the engaged parties.

*Acceptance*   The final requirement of a valid gift is acceptance by the donee. In most instances, of course, the donee will accept the gift with gratitude. Accordingly, the law usually presumes that the donee has accepted. But there are situations in which acceptance is objectionable, such as when a gift would impose a burden upon the donee. In such cases, the law will not require the recipient to accept an unwanted gift. For example, a donee may prudently reject a gift of an elephant or a wrecked car in need of extensive repairs.

*Classification*   Gifts may be either *inter vivos* or *causa mortis*. An *inter vivos* gift is a gift made by a donor during her lifetime. A gift *causa mortis* is a gift made by a donor in contemplation of her imminent death. A gift *causa mortis* is a conditional gift and is contingent upon (1) the donor's death as she anticipated, (2) the donor's not revoking the gift prior to her death, and (3) the donee's surviving the donor.

## By Will or Descent

Title to personal property is frequently acquired by inheritance from a person who dies, either with or without a will. This method of acquiring title is discussed in Chapter 52.

## By Accession

Many of the practical problems surrounding the right to title to personal property stem from its principal characteristic—movability. One general solution to the problem of movability is identified by the phrase "title by accession." **Accession,** in its strict sense, means the right of the owner of property to any increase in it, whether natural or human made. For example, the owner of a cow acquires title by accession to any calves born to that cow.

## By Confusion

The basic problem of confusion is somewhat similar to problems involving title by accession. **Confusion** arises when identical goods belonging to different people are so *commingled* (mixed) that the owners cannot identify their own property. For example, Hereford cattle belonging to Benton are mixed with Hereford cattle belonging to Armstrong, and neither can specifically identify his herd; or grain owned by Courts is combined with similar grain owned by Reichel. Confusion may result from accident, mistake, willful act, or agreement of the parties. If the goods can be apportioned, each owner who can prove his proportion of the whole is entitled to receive his share. If, however, the confusion results from the willful and wrongful act of one of the parties, he will lose his entire interest if he cannot prove his share. Frequently, problems arise not because the owners cannot prove their original interests but because there is not enough left to distribute a full share to each. In such cases, if the confusion was due to mistake, accident, or agreement, each owner will bear the loss in proportion to his share. If the confusion resulted from an intentional and unauthorized act, the wrongdoer will first bear any loss.

## By Possession

In some instances a person may acquire title to movable personal property by taking possession of it. If the property has been intentionally **abandoned** (intentionally disposed of), a *finder* is entitled to the property. Moreover, under the general rule, a finder is entitled to **lost** (unintentionally left) property against everyone except the true *owner*. Suppose Zenner, the owner of an apartment complex, leases a kitchenette apartment to Terrell. One night, Waters, Terrell's mother-in-law, is invited to sleep in the convertible bed in the living room. In the course of preparing the bed, Waters finds an emerald ring caught on the springs under the mattress. The ring is turned over to the police, but diligent inquiry fails to ascertain the true owner. As the finder, Waters will be entitled to the ring.

A different rule applies when the lost property is in the ground. Here, the owner of the land has a claim superior to that of the finder. For example, Josephs employs Kasarda to excavate a lateral sewer. Kasarda uncovers ancient Native American artifacts. Josephs, not Kasarda, has the superior claim.

A further exception to the rule gives the finder first claim against all but the true owner. If property is intentionally placed somewhere by the owner, who then unintentionally leaves it, it becomes **mislaid property.** Most courts hold that if property has been mislaid, not lost, then the owner of the premises, not the finder, has first claim if the true owner is not discovered. This doctrine is frequently invoked in cases involving items found in restaurants or on trains, buses, or airplanes.

Another category of property is the **treasure trove,** which consists of coins or currency concealed by the owner. To be classified as treasure trove, the property must have been hidden or concealed for such a length of time that the owner is probably dead or undiscoverable. Treasure trove belongs to the finder as against all but the true owner.

Many States now have statutes that provide a means of vesting title to lost property in the finder where a prescribed search for the owner proves fruitless. Under these statutes, a finder generally may assert the right to possession against any party other than the true owner.

 *See Case 48–3*

# CONCURRENT OWNERSHIP

Real or personal property may be owned by one individual or by two or more persons concurrently. Those who hold title concurrently are generally referred to as **co-tenants,** each entitled to an undivided interest in the entire item and neither having a claim to any specific portion of it. Their undivided interests may be equal, or one may have a larger undivided share than the other.

There are four ways in which personal property may be owned concurrently: (1) joint tenancy, (2) tenancy in common, (3) tenancy by the entireties, and (4) community property. The forms of concurrent ownership are discussed in Chapter 50.

# PROPERTY INSURANCE

Insurance covers a vast range of contracts, each of which distributes *risk* among a large number of members (the **insureds**) through an insurance company (the **insurer**). **Insurance** is a contractual undertaking by the insurer to pay a sum of money or give something of value to the insured or a beneficiary upon the happening of a contingency or fortuitous event that is beyond the control of the contracting parties.

It is impossible to name a commercial activity not affected by insurance coverage of one form or another. Through insurance, a business can safeguard its tangible assets against almost any form of damage or destruction, whether resulting from natural causes or from the accidental or improper actions of individuals. Insurance may also protect a business from tort liability, including assertions involving strict liability, negligence, or the intentional acts of its representatives. A business may procure credit insurance to guard against losses from poor credit risks and fidelity bonds to secure it against losses incurred through employee defalcations. If a business hires a famous pianist, it may insure the latter's hands; if it decides to present an outdoor concert, it may insure against the possibility of rain. A business may purchase life insurance on its key executives to reimburse it for financial losses arising from their deaths, or it may purchase such life insurance payable to the families of executives as part of their compensation. An additional development of growing importance is the use of insurance to carry out pension commitments arising from agreements with employees. Nonetheless, the remaining sections of this chapter will focus on the insurance of property.

The McCarran-Ferguson Act, enacted by Congress in 1945, left the regulation of insurance to the States. Statutes in each State regulate domestic insurance companies and establish standards for foreign (out-of-State) insurance companies wishing to do business within the State. Most State legislation relates to the incorporation, licensing, supervision, and liquidation of insurers and to the licensing and supervision of agents and brokers.

Because the insurance relationship arises from a contract of insurance between the insurer and the insured, the law of insurance is a branch of contract law. For this reason, the doctrines of offer and acceptance, consideration, and other rules applicable to contracts in general are equally applicable to insurance contracts. Beyond that, however, insurance law, like the law of sales, bailments, negotiable instruments, or other specialized types of contracts, contains numerous modifications of fundamental contract law, with which the following sections are concerned.

## FIRE AND PROPERTY INSURANCE

**Fire and property insurance** protects the owner (or another person with an insurable interest, such as a secured creditor or mortgagee) of real or personal property against loss resulting from damage to or destruction of the property by fire and certain related perils. Most fire insurance policies also cover damage caused by lightning, explosion, earthquake, water, wind, rain, collision, and riot.

Fire insurance policies are standardized in the United States, either by statute or by order of the State insurance departments, but their coverage is frequently enlarged through an "endorsement" or "rider" to include other perils or to benefit the insured in ways the provisions in the standard form do not. These policies are normally written for periods of one or three years.

## Types of Fire

Fire insurance policies are generally held to cover damage from "hostile" fires but do not cover losses caused by "friendly" fires. A **friendly fire** is one that is contained in its intended location, for instance, a fire in a fireplace, furnace, or stove. A **hostile fire** is any other fire—all fires outside their intended or usual locales. Thus, a friendly fire will be hostile once it escapes from its usual confines. A standard insurance policy therefore will not cover heat or soot damage to a fireplace resulting from its continual use or damage done to personal property accidentally thrown into a stove. Damages caused by smoke, soot, water, and heat from a hostile fire are covered by the standard fire insurance policy, whereas such damages caused by a friendly fire generally are not. Moreover, a policy usually will not cover recovery for business interruption unless it contains a special endorsement covering such loss.

## Co-insurance Clauses

An arrangement common in property insurance, **co-insurance** is a means of sharing the risk between insurer and insured. For example, under the typical 80 percent co-insurance clause, the insured may recover the full amount of loss, not to exceed the face amount of the policy, provided the policy is for an amount not less than 80 percent of the insurable value of the property. If the policy is for less than 80 percent, the insured recovers that proportion of the loss that the amount of the policy bears, up to 80 percent of the insurable value. The formula for recovery is as follows:

$$\text{Recovery} = \frac{\text{Face Value of Policy}}{\text{Fair Market Value of Property} \times \text{Co-insurance \%}} \times \text{Loss}$$

Thus, if the co-insurance percentage is 80 percent, the value of the property is $100,000, and the policy is for $80,000 or more, the insured is fully protected against loss not to exceed the amount of the policy. If the policy amount is less than 80 percent of the property value, however, the insured receives only the proportion of the loss amount as determined in the formula above. Thus, in the above example, if the fire policy was for $60,000 and the property was 50 percent destroyed, the loss would be $50,000, of which the insurer would pay $37,500, which is $60,000/(100,000 \times 80\%)$ of $50,000. On a total loss, the recovery could not, of course, exceed the face amount of the policy. Some States do not favor co-insurance clauses and strictly construe the applicable statute against their validity. In addition, property insurance is not held to be co-insurance unless the policy specifically so provides.

## Other Insurance Clauses

Recovery under property insurance policies typically is also limited by other insurance clauses. These clauses generally require that liability be distributed *pro rata* among the various insurers. For example, Alexander insures his $150,000 building with Hamilton Insurance Co. for $60,000 and Jefferson Insurance Co. for $90,000. Alexander's building is partially destroyed by fire, causing Alexander $20,000 in damages. Alexander will collect two-fifths (60,000/150,000) of his damages from Hamilton ($8,000) and three-fifths (90,000/150,000) from Jefferson ($12,000).

 *See Case 48–4*

## Types of Policies

Property insurance may be either a valued policy or an open policy. A **valued policy** is one providing for the full value of the property, upon which the insured and the insurer specifically agree at the time the policy is issued. Should total loss occur, the insurer must pay this amount, not the actual or fair market value of the property. By comparison, an **open policy** contains no agreement as to the specific value of the property; instead, the insurer pays the fair market value of the property calculated immediately prior to its loss. Thus, if Latrisha insures her building for $650,000 and at the time of its loss the property is valued at $600,000, under an open policy Latrisha would recover $600,000, while under a valued policy she would recover $650,000. If she insured the building for $700,000 and it was valued at that amount just prior to being blown apart by a tornado, under both types of policies Latrisha would recover $700,000.

Insurance of property under a marine policy (insurance covering marine vessels and cargo) is generally considered to be valued, whereas nonmarine property insurance is presumed to be unvalued or open.

## NATURE OF INSURANCE CONTRACTS

The basic principles of **contract** law apply to insurance policies. Furthermore, because insurance companies engage in a large volume of business over wide areas, they tend to standardize their policies. In some States, standardization is required by statute. This usually means that the insured must accept a given policy or do without the desired insurance.

## Offer and Acceptance

No matter how many stories tell of insurance agents aggressively soliciting would-be insureds to take out policies, the applicant is generally the one who makes the offer, and the contract is created when the insurance company accepts that offer. The company's acceptance may be conditioned, for instance, upon payment of the premium. The company may, however, write a policy that differs from the application, thereby making a counteroffer that the applicant may or may not choose to accept.

In fire and casualty insurance, agents often have authority to make the insurance effective immediately, when needed, by means of a **binder.** Should a loss occur before the company has actually issued a policy, the binder will be effective on the same terms and conditions the policy would have had if it had been issued.

In general, insurance contracts have not been held to be subject to the statute of frauds; thus, oral contracts for insurance have been held to be enforceable. As a practical matter, however, oral contracts for insurance are very infrequent.

## Insurable Interest

The concept of insurable interest has been developed over many years, primarily to eliminate gambling and to lessen the moral hazard. If a person could obtain an enforceable fire insurance policy on property that he did not own or in which he had no interest, he would be in a position to profit by the destruction of property which represented no loss to him. An **insurable interest** is a relationship which a person has with respect to certain property such that the happening of a possible, specific, damage-causing contingency would result in direct loss or injury to her. The purpose of insurance is protection against the risk of loss that would result from such a happening, not the realization of gain or profit.

Whether sole or concurrent, ownership obviously creates an insurable interest in property. Moreover, a right deriving from a contract concerning the property also gives rise to an insurable interest. For instance, shareholders in a closely held corporation have been held to have an insurable interest in the corporation's property to the extent of their interest. Likewise, lessees of property have insurable interests, as do holders of security interests, such as mortgagees or sellers with a purchase money security interest. Most courts have gone beyond the requirement of a legally recognized interest and apply a factual expectancy test. Under this test, the determinative question is whether the insured will obtain a benefit from the continued existence of the property or suffer a loss from its destruction. Thus, an individual who buys and insures a stolen automobile without knowledge that the automobile is stolen has an insurable interest in the automobile.

The insurable interest must exist at the time the property loss occurs, although some courts speak in terms of having the insurable interest at the time of insuring *and* at the time of loss. Property insurance policies are freely assignable after, but not before, a loss occurs.

 *See Case 48–4*

## Premiums

Premiums are the consideration paid for an insurance policy. Property insurance policies are written only for periods lasting a few years at most. Long, continued liability on this type of policy is the exception rather than the rule. The rates that may be charged for fire and various kinds of casualty insurance are regulated by State law. The regulatory authorities are under a duty to require that the companies' rates be reasonable, not unfairly discriminatory, and neither excessively high nor inordinately low.

## Defenses of the Insurer

An insurer may assert the ordinary defenses available to any contract. In addition, the terms of the insurance contract may provide specific defenses such as the subject matter of the policy, types of perils covered, amount of coverage, and period of coverage. Moreover, the insurer may assert the defenses of misrepresentation, breach of warranty, and concealment, which are closely related to each other.

*Misrepresentation* A representation is a statement made by or on behalf of an applicant for insurance to induce an insurer to enter into a contract. The representation is not a part of the insurance contract, but if the application containing the representation is incorporated by reference into the contract, the representation becomes a warranty. For a **misrepresentation** to have legal consequences, it must be material, the insurer must have relied on it as an inducement to enter into the contract, and it must either have been substantially false when the insured made it or have become so, to the insured's knowledge, before the contract was created. The principal remedy of the insurer on discovery of the material misrepresentation is rescission of the contract. To rescind the contract, the insurer must tender to the insured all premiums that have been paid, unless the misrepresentation was fraudulent. To be effective, rescission must be made as soon as possible after discovery of the misrepresentation.

*Breach of Warranty* Warranties are of great importance in insurance contracts because they operate as conditions that *must* exist before the contract is effective or before the insurer's promise to pay is enforceable. If such is the case, the insurer does not merely have a defense against payment of the policy, but can void the policy.

Failure of the condition to exist or to occur relieves the insurer from any obligation to perform its promise. Broadly speaking, a condition is simply an event whose happening or failure to happen either precedes the existence of a legal relationship or terminates one previously existing. Conditions are either precedent or subsequent. For example, payment of the premium is a condition precedent to the enforcement of the insurer's promise, as is the happening of the insured event. A condition subsequent is an operative event the happening of which terminates an existing, matured legal obligation. A provision in a policy to the effect that the insured shall not be liable unless suit is brought within twelve months from the date on which the loss occurs is an example of a condition subsequent.

To be a warranty, the provision must be expressly included in the insurance contract or clearly incorporated by reference. Usually, the policy statements that the insurer considers to be express warranties can be identified by the use of such words as *warrant, on condition that, provided that,* or words of similar import. Other statements important to the risk assumed, such as the address of a building in a case where personal property at a particular location is insured against fire, are sometimes held to be informal warranties.

Generally, it is becoming more difficult for an insurer to avoid liability on a policy when an insured breaches a warranty. For example, a number of States now require a breach to be material before the insurer may avoid liability.

***Concealment*** Concealment is the failure of an applicant for insurance to disclose material facts that the insurer does not know. The nondisclosure normally must be fraudulent as well as material to invalidate the policy; the applicant must have had reason to believe the fact was material; and its disclosure must have affected the insurer's acceptance of the risk.

## Waiver and Estoppel

In certain instances, an insurer who normally would be entitled to deny liability under a policy because of a misrepresentation, breach of condition, or concealment, is "estopped" from taking advantage of the defense or else is said to have "waived" the right to rely on it because of other facts.

The terms *waiver* and *estoppel* are used interchangeably, although by definition they are not synonymous. As generally defined, **waiver** is the intentional relinquishment of a known right; **estoppel** means that a person is prevented by his own conduct from asserting a position inconsistent with such conduct, on which another person has justifiably relied.

Because a corporation such as an insurance company can act only through agents, situations involving waiver invariably are based on an agent's conduct. The higher the agent's position in the company's organization, the more likely his conduct is to bind the company, as an agent acting within the scope of his authority binds his principal. Insureds have the right to rely on representations made by the insurer's employees, and where such representations reasonably induce or cause a change of position by the insured or prevent the insured from causing a condition to occur, the insurer may not assert as a defense the failure of the condition to occur, whether the term applied to his situation be waiver or estoppel. Companies have tried with little success to limit the authority of local selling agents to bind the company through waiver or estoppel.

## Termination

Most contracts of insurance are performed according to their terms, and due **performance** terminates the insurer's obligation. Normally, the insurer pays the principal sum due, and the contract is thereby performed and discharged.

**Cancellation** by mutual consent is another way of terminating an insurance contract. Cancellation by the insurer alone means that the insurer remains liable, according to the terms of the policy, until such time as the cancellation is effective. To cancel a policy, the insurer must tender the unearned portion of the premium to the insured.

---

 **Chapter Summary**

## Introduction to Property and Personal Property

| Kinds of Property | **Definition** interest, or group of interests, that is legally protected<br>**Tangible Property** physical objects<br>**Intangible Property** property that does not exist in a physical form<br>**Real Property** land and interests in land<br>**Personal Property** all property that is not real property<br>**Fixture** personal property so firmly attached to real property that an interest in it arises under real property law |
|---|---|

| **Transfer of Title to Personal Property** | **Sale**  transfer of property for consideration (price) |
|---|---|
| | **Gift**  transfer of property without consideration |
| | • *Delivery* includes both manual transfer of the item and constructive delivery (delivery of something that symbolizes control over the item) |
| | • *Intent* |
| | • *Acceptance* |
| | • *Classification* |
| | **Will**  right to property acquired upon death of the owner |
| | **Accession**  right of a property owner to any increase in such property |
| | **Confusion**  intermixing of goods belonging to two or more owners such that they can identify their individual property only as part of a mass of like goods |
| | • If due to mistake, accident, or agreement, loss shared proportionately |
| | • If caused by an intentional or unauthorized act, wrongdoer bears loss |
| | **Possession**  a person may acquire title by taking possession of property |
| | • *Abandoned Property* intentionally disposed of by the owner; the finder is entitled to the property |
| | • *Lost Property* unintentionally left by the owner; the finder is generally entitled to the property |
| | • *Mislaid Property* intentionally placed by the owner but unintentionally left; the owner of the premises is generally entitled to the property |
| | • *Treasure Trove* coins or currency hidden or concealed by the owner for such a length of time that the owner is probably dead or undiscoverable |

# Property Insurance

| **Fire and Property Insurance** | **General Definition of Insurance**  contractual arrangement that distributes risk of loss among a large number of members (the insureds) through an insurance company (the insurer) |
|---|---|
| | **Coverage**  of fire and property insurance provides protection against loss due to fire or related perils |
| | **Types of Fire** |
| | • *Friendly Fire* fire contained in its intended location |
| | • *Hostile Fire* any fire outside its intended or usual location |
| | **Co-insurance**  insurance in which a person insures property for less than its full or stated value and agrees to share the risk of loss |
| | **Other Insurance Clauses**  if multiple insurers are involved, liability is distributed *pro rata* |
| | **Types of Policies** |
| | • *Valued Policy* covers full value of property as agreed upon by the parties at the time the policy is issued |
| | • *Open Policy* covers fair market value of property as calculated immediately prior to the loss |

| **Nature of Insurance Contracts** | **General Contract Law**  basic principles of contract law apply |
|---|---|
| | **Insurable Interest**  a financial interest or a factual expectancy interest in someone's property that justifies insuring the property; the interest must exist at the time the property loss occurs |
| | **Premium**  amount to be paid for an insurance policy |
| | **Defenses of the Insurer** |
| | • *Misrepresentation* false representation of a material fact made by the insured that is justifiably relied upon by the insurer; enables the insurer to rescind the contract within a specified time |

- *Breach of Warranty* the failure of a required condition; generally an insurer may avoid liability for a breach of warranty only if the breach is material
- *Concealment* fraudulent failure of an applicant for insurance to disclose material facts that the insurer does not know; allows the insurer to rescind the contract
- *Waiver* an insurer intentionally relinquishes the right to deny liability
- *Estoppel* an insurer is prevented by its own conduct from asserting a defense

**Termination** an insurance contract may be terminated by due performance or cancellation

 # Cases

### CASE 48–1
### Fixtures

## *NEW ENGLAND TELEPHONE AND TELEGRAPH CO.*
## *v. CITY OF FRANKLIN*

Supreme Court of New Hampshire, 1996
141 N.H. 449, 685 A.2d 913

HORTON, J.

Following consolidation of various tax abatement proceedings, the Superior Court (Nadeau, C.J.) granted summary judgment to plaintiffs New England Telephone and Telegraph Company (NET), Merrimack County Telephone Company (MCT), and Contoocook Valley Telephone Company (CVT), holding that their communications equipment was personal, not real, property and therefore not subject to taxation by the municipal defendants. [Citation.] The defendants appeal. We affirm.

The plaintiffs are public utilities providing telecommunications services in New Hampshire. NET commenced separate actions for abatement of real estate taxes against the City of Franklin and fifteen other municipalities. NET disputed the defendants' treatment of its communications equipment as real estate, thereby challenging their authority to tax its equipment. The communications equipment at issue involves two basic categories: (1) distribution plant, which includes telephone poles, wires, and underground conduits, and (2) central office equipment, consisting of frames, switches, and other power equipment. The superior court consolidated NET's various actions, as well as a similar action brought by MCT and CVT against the Town of Hopkinton. The plaintiffs jointly moved for summary judgment, arguing that their communications equipment was personal property not subject to municipal taxation.

In support of the summary judgment motion, the plaintiffs submitted affidavits setting forth the following facts. All of the plaintiffs' poles, wires, and underground conduits located in the municipalities are placed either on public rights of way or on private property owned by third parties. Approximately ninety percent of the poles are located on public rights of way pursuant to licenses issued by the State or the municipalities. [Citation.] The remaining ten percent of the poles are placed on private property either by consent of the property owner or pursuant to an easement. The poles, wires, and underground conduits are installed in a manner that permits and facilitates their removal and relocation. Consequently, removal of that equipment is neither complicated nor time-consuming, and does not harm the underlying land or change its usefulness. The plaintiffs remove and relocate their poles, wires, and underground conduits at the request of the State or the applicable private landowner or municipality. In obtaining the licenses, consents, or easements for their poles, wires, and underground conduits, the plaintiffs insist on maintaining ownership of that equipment and refuse any requests to make the equipment a permanent part of the realty. The plaintiffs' central office equipment, most of which is located in buildings owned by the plaintiffs, is both portable and designed to permit removal and relocation. The plaintiffs' practice and policy is to move pieces of central office equipment among buildings in response to changes in technology or system use. Although certain frames are bolted to the buildings, their removal is achieved without affecting the usefulness of the buildings or the frames themselves. When the plaintiffs ultimately vacate a building used as a central office, they remove all of their equipment and merely transfer the building "as a shell." The vacated building, though devoid of central office equipment, retains utility for other commercial or professional uses.

In opposition to the motion for summary judgment, the defendants did not dispute the specific facts set forth by the plaintiffs. Moreover, the defendants' affidavits acknowledged the general removability and transportability of the communications equipment. The defendants, however, produced the following additional facts regarding the equipment at issue. Installation of telephone poles typically involves placing them six feet into the ground. Telephone poles often have a life expectancy or replacement cycle exceeding forty years, and must be sufficiently sturdy to withstand harsh weather and vehicle collisions. Based on these additional facts and on the asserted importance to the plaintiffs of providing reliable and uninterrupted service, the defendants contended that the telephone poles and related equipment were "permanent."

\* \* \*

Accordingly, if the items of communications equipment "are real estate \* \* \*, they are taxable unless exempted by some other provision." [Citation.]

## I. Communications Equipment as Fixtures

The defendants primarily argue that the superior court erred by refusing to characterize the communications equipment as fixtures and, therefore, by failing to treat the equipment as realty. "A chattel loses its character as personalty and becomes a fixture and part of the realty when there exists an actual or constructive annexation to the realty with the intention of making it a permanent accession to the freehold, and an appropriation or adaptation to the use or purpose of that part of the realty with which it is connected." [Citation.] A mixed question of law and fact, [citation] whether an item of property is properly classified as either personalty or a fixture turns on several factors, including: the item's nature and use; the intent of the party making the annexation; the degree and extent to which the item is specially adapted to the realty; the degree and extent of the item's annexation to the realty; and the relationship between the realty's owner and the person claiming the item. [Citations.]

\* \* \*

In this case, the items of communications equipment did not constitute fixtures. Each of the relevant factors supports the superior court's holding that the property remained personalty. The poles, wires, and central office equipment, though placed in the ground or bolted to the buildings, were readily removable and transportable without affecting the utility of the underlying land, the buildings, or the equipment itself. Because removal of the equipment would not render the land or buildings "incomplete and unfit for use," and because the equipment could be "equally useful and adapted for general use elsewhere," the communications equipment did not constitute fixtures. [Citations.] In addition, the very nature of telephone poles and wires, as well as their use by the plaintiffs in connection with integrated telecommunications systems, belies the proposition that the equipment became a permanent and essential part of the underlying realty so as to pass by conveyance with it. [Citation.] Furthermore, the statute governing the licensing of telephone poles and wires on public ways specifically provides for their removal on ten days' notice and therefore establishes, as a matter of law, their impermanence. [Citation.] Finally, the defendants never challenged the plaintiffs' asserted intent to maintain the communications equipment as personalty.

The defendants' other arguments on the fixtures issue are not persuasive. First, the defendants' evidence concerning the installation, durability, and longevity of the distribution equipment failed to raise a genuine issue of material fact regarding the status of the property under our law of fixtures in light of the defendants' failure to contradict the specific facts in the plaintiffs' affidavits. [Citations.] Similarly, the defendants' conclusory assertions concerning the "permanent" nature of the communications equipment did not satisfy their burden in opposing the summary judgment motion. [Citation.]

\* \* \*

\* \* \*

Affirmed.

---

## CASE 48–2
## Delivery of Gift
### *ESTATE OF ROSS v. ROSS*
Supreme Court of Utah, 1981
626 P.2d 489

**HOWE, J.**

This action was initiated by the personal representative of decedent David E. Ross to determine whether the decedent had made completed *inter vivos* gifts of certain shares of corporate stock to his son E. Roderick Ross (hereinafter called Rod) or whether the shares were a part of the decedent's estate and should be distributed equally among his three children, who are his heirs under his will. The District Court held that the decedent had made valid *inter vivos* gifts of the stock to Rod. David E. Ross II and Betsy Louise Ross Rapps (hereinafter called David and Betsy), the brother and sister of Rod, appeal.

Decedent was the secretary and treasurer of Equitable Life and Casualty Insurance Company and also served as one of its directors and as stock transfer agent. The entire stock was owned by the decedent and his two brothers and their families. Decedent also served in the same capacities in four other family-owned companies, namely, Ross Brothers Corporation, National Housing and Finance Syndicate, Insurance Investment Company, and Equitable Investment Company.

In 1972 Rod began working for Equitable Life. David and Betsy lived out of the state and were not involved in the operations of the various companies. Between 1974 and 1978, decedent told several persons of his desire to reward Rod for his work with Equitable Life by giving him stock which would be in addition to the stock he would later inherit. A number of stock transfers were subsequently made on the corporate books by the decedent. In November 1974 decedent cancelled a stock certificate representing his ownership of 2440.87 shares of Equitable Life. In its place a certificate for 2210.70 shares was issued in Rod's name and another for 230.17 shares was issued to decedent. These transfers were shown by appropriate entries on the stock ledger sheet of the company. The certificate issued to Rod was placed in an envelope on which was typed his name, the certificate number, the number of shares it represented, and the date. The envelope was placed in a bank safety deposit box with other envelopes that contained stock certificates belonging to other stockholders.

In December 1974 a 25 percent share dividend was declared and paid to all shareholders of record of Equit-

able Life. A certificate for 552.67 shares of common stock was issued in Rod's name and was placed in the envelope containing the other certificate already issued to him. A notation on the envelope identified the second certificate. Cash dividends were paid to shareholders in November 1976 and May 1977 and Rod received the amounts of $276.33 and $276.34. He also attended and voted at shareholders' meetings.

In May 1977 Ray Ross, decedent's brother and business associate, died. At that time the decedent and his surviving brother, Galen, transferred the contents of the safety deposit box where the stock certificates of various family members had been kept to a safe located in the company offices. Only the decedent and the president and vice president of Equitable Life had the combination to the safe.

The Ross Brothers Corporation was organized at a meeting held in December 1977 for the purpose of distributing the assets of a former partnership involving the three brothers. Galen Ross issued stock certificates in the new corporation. A certificate for 250 shares, which represented 25 percent of the shares allotted to his father, was issued in Rod's name and handed to him personally. He delivered the certificate to his father, and it was placed in an envelope identified by his name and kept with the other family stock certificates.

In February 1978 there were several transactions in which stock certificates were issued in Rod's name. These certificates represented shares in Equitable Investment Company, Insurance Investment Company, and the National Housing and Finance Syndicate Corporation. The trial court found that "[a]ll actions necessary to complete the transfer on the books and records of each of the corporations for each of the shares of stock in question were completed. . . ." The certificates were placed in a single envelope with the name of Rod Ross and the certificate numbers written upon it. The envelope was placed with the others in the office safe.

The shares transferred to Rod represented one-fourth of the stock holdings of his father. There was testimony that the decedent had expressed his intention that Rod should receive one-fourth of his stock through lifetime gifts, and that the remaining three-quarters would pass by will and be equally divided among Rod, David and Betsy. This would result in Rod's receiving a total of one-half of his father's stock, and his brother and sister each receiving one-fourth.

A will prepared for the decedent by his brother Galen and dated February 1978 divided the estate equally among the three surviving children. There was no reference in the will to prior gifts of stock to Rod.

After their father's death, on April 19, 1978, David and Betsy challenged the validity of the inter vivos stock transfers. Their position before the trial court was that there had been no completed gifts because Rod did not have possession of the stock certificates issued in his name, he did not know where the certificates were or have access to the safe where they were kept, and no gift tax returns were ever filed by the decedent with respect to the transfers.

* * *

Appellants assert that three elements must be proven for a person to claim valid title to property by *inter vivos* gift: a clear and unmistakable intention on the part of the donor to pass immediate ownership, an irrevocable delivery, and acceptance. They concede that there is substantial evidence in the record to support the lower court's conclusion that there was the necessary intent on the part of decedent to make a gift and that Rod "accepted" the stock transfer. They contend, however, that the court's decision was erroneous in that the element of irrevocable delivery was not established by clear and convincing evidence.

An important purpose of the delivery requirement is to avoid the hedging of a would-be donor who wishes to retain certain benefits of ownership, including the control of the gift property, while designating another as the recipient of the property during the donor's lifetime. If a gift is not completed before one's death, of course, it is subject to the formalities of testamentary disposition. In the instant case, therefore, the finding of a gift must be based on the decedent's voluntary parting with the control of the stock during his lifetime.

It is appellants' position that decedent should have parted with his dominion over the certificates by physically delivering them to Rod and that the transfer of ownership on the corporate records was insufficient to meet the requirement of delivery. Other courts have split on this issue, and the question has not been ruled on by this Court.

* * *

We . . . hold that manual delivery of the stock certificates personally to Rod was not a prerequisite to a valid gift.

Viewing the facts of this case in light of the requirements of inter vivos gifts, we find the gifts of stock to Rod were complete and valid. Evidence of decedent's intention that Rod be made the owner of the stock in question during his lifetime was uncontroverted. Appellants do not challenge the sufficiency of the evidence as to donative intent nor the finding of the trial court that the change in ownership was recorded on the corporate books. New certificates were issued in Rod's name. The decedent did not thereafter exercise control over the stocks. On the contrary, Rod voted the stock as its legal owner and received cash and stock dividends.

The fact that the stock certificates were kept in a safe to which decedent, but not Rod, had access is not fatal to the finding of a completed gift. The decedent had physical possession of stock certificates belonging to a number of other Ross family members. There was no assertion or evidence that he exerted control or possessory rights over any of that stock. His custody of Rod's stock was simply consistent with the practice within the family businesses of keeping the stock certificates in a central location clearly identified as to the owners of the shares. Individual envelopes carried owners' names, stock certificate numbers, and the number of shares represented by the certificates.

We find no error in the trial court's interpretation of the evidence or its application of Utah law in reaching the conclusion that the *inter vivos* gifts to Rod were valid.

* * *

Affirmed.

---

## CASE 48–3
### Title to Lost or Misplaced Personal Property
### *BENJAMIN v. LINDNER AVIATION, INC.*

Supreme Court of Iowa, 1995
534 N.W.2d 400

TERNUS, J.
Appellant [plaintiff], Heath Benjamin, found over $18,000 in currency inside the wing of an airplane. At the time of this discovery, appellee, State Central Bank, owned the plane and it was being serviced by appellee, Lindner Aviation, Inc. All three parties claimed the

money as against the true owner. After a bench trial, the district court held that the currency was mislaid property and belonged to the owner of the plane. The court awarded a finder's fee to Benjamin. Benjamin appealed and Lindner Aviation and State Central Bank cross-appealed. * * *

## I. Background Facts and Proceedings

* * *

As part of the inspection, Benjamin removed panels from the underside of the wings. Although these panels were to be removed annually as part of the routine inspection, a couple of the screws holding the panel on the left wing were so rusty that Benjamin had to use a drill to remove them. Benjamin testified that the panel probably had not been removed for several years.

Inside the left wing Benjamin discovered two packets approximately four inches high and wrapped in aluminum foil. He removed the packets from the wing and took off the foil wrapping. Inside the foil was paper currency, tied in string and wrapped in handkerchiefs. The currency was predominately twenty-dollar bills with mint dates before the 1960s, primarily in the 1950s. The money smelled musty.

Benjamin took one packet to his jeep and then reported what he had found to his supervisor, offering to divide the money with him. However, the supervisor reported the discovery to the owner of Lindner Aviation, William Engle. Engle insisted that they contact the authorities and he called the Department of Criminal Investigation. The money was eventually turned over to the Keokuk police department.

Two days later, Benjamin filed an affidavit with the county auditor claiming that he was the finder of the currency under the provisions of Iowa Code [citation]. Lindner Aviation and the bank also filed claims to the money. * * * No one came forward within twelve months claiming to be the true owner of the money. [Citation.]

* * *

Benjamin * * * claims that [Iowa Code] governs the disposition of all found property and any common law distinctions between various types of found property are no longer valid. He asserts alternatively that even under the common law classes of found property, he is entitled to the money he discovered. He claims that the trial court should have found that the property was treasure trove or was lost or abandoned rather than mislaid, thereby entitling the finder to the property.

* * *

## III. Does Chapter 644 Supersede the Common Law Classifications of Found Property?

Benjamin argues that [Iowa Statute] Chapter 644 governs the rights of finders of property and abrogates the common law distinctions between types of found property. As he points out, lost property statutes are intended "to encourage and facilitate the return of property to the true owner, and then to reward a finder for his honesty if the property remains unclaimed." [Citations.] These goals, Benjamin argues, can best be achieved by applying such statutes to all types of found property.

* * *

Although a few courts have adopted an expansive view of lost property statutes, we think Iowa law is to the contrary. * * * As recently as 1991, we stated that "[t]he rights of finders of property vary according to the characterization of the property found." [Citation.]. We went on to define and apply the common law classifications of found property in deciding the rights of the parties. [Citation.] As our prior cases show, we have continued to use the common law distinctions between classes of found property despite the legislature's enactment of chapter 644 and its predecessors.

* * *

In summary, chapter 644 applies only if the property discovered can be categorized as "lost" property as that term is defined under the common law. Thus, the trial court correctly looked to the common law classifications of found property to decide who had the right to the money discovered here.

## IV. Classification of Found Property

Under the common law, there are four categories of found property: (1) abandoned property, (2) lost property, (3) mislaid property, and (4) treasure trove. [Citation.] The rights of a finder of property depend on how the found property is classified. [Citation.]

**A. Abandoned Property**  Property is abandoned when the owner no longer wants to possess it. [Citation.] Abandonment is shown by proof that the owner intends to abandon the property and has voluntarily relinquished all right, title and interest in the property. [Citations.] Abandoned property belongs to the finder of the property against all others, including the former owner. [Citation.]

**B. Lost Property** "Property is lost when the owner unintentionally and involuntarily parts with its possession and does not know where it is." [Citations.] Stolen property found by someone who did not participate in the theft is lost property. [Citations]. Under chapter 644, lost property becomes the property of the finder once the statutory procedures are followed and the owner makes no claim within twelve months. [Citation.]

**C. Mislaid Property** Mislaid property is voluntarily put in a certain place by the owner who then overlooks or forgets where the property is. [Citation.] It differs from lost property in that the owner voluntarily and intentionally places mislaid property in the location where it is eventually found by another. [Citation.] In contrast, property is not considered lost unless the owner parts with it involuntarily. [Citations.]

The finder of mislaid property acquires no rights to the property. [Citation.] The right of possession of mislaid property belongs to the owner of the premises upon which the property is found, as against all persons other than the true owner. [Citation.]

**D. Treasure Trove** Treasure trove consists of coins or currency concealed by the owner. [Citation.] It includes an element of antiquity. Id. To be classified as treasure trove, the property must have been hidden or concealed for such a length of time that the owner is probably dead or undiscoverable. [Citations.]. Treasure trove belongs to the finder as against all but the true owner. [Citation.]

## V. Is There Substantial Evidence to Support the Trial Court's Finding That the Money Found by Benjamin Was Mislaid?

We think there was substantial evidence to find that the currency discovered by Benjamin was mislaid property. * * *

The place where Benjamin found the money and the manner in which it was hidden are also important here. The bills were carefully tied and wrapped and then concealed in a location that was accessible only by removing screws and a panel. These circumstances support an inference that the money was placed there intentionally. This inference supports the conclusion that the money was mislaid. [Citations.]

The same facts that support the trial court's conclusion that the money was mislaid prevent us from ruling as a matter of law that the property was lost. Property is not considered lost unless considering the place where and the conditions under which the property is found, there is an inference that the property was left there unintentionally. [Citations.] Contrary to Benjamin's position the circumstances here do not support a conclusion that the money was placed in the wing of the airplane unintentionally. * * *

We also reject Benjamin's assertion that as a matter of law this money was abandoned property. Both logic and common sense suggest that it is unlikely someone would voluntarily part with over $18,000 with the intention of terminating his ownership. The location where this money was found is much more consistent with the conclusion that the owner of the property was placing the money there for safekeeping. * * *

Finally, we also conclude that the trial court was not obligated to decide that this money was treasure trove. Based on the dates of the currency, the money was no older than thirty-five years.

* * *

## VI. Is the Airplane Or the Hangar the "Premises" Where the Money Was Discovered?

Because the money discovered by Benjamin was properly found to be mislaid property, it belongs to the owner of the premises where it was found. Mislaid property is entrusted to the owner of the premises where it is found rather than the finder of the property because it is assumed that the true owner may eventually recall where he has placed his property and return there to reclaim it. [Citation.]

We think that the premises where the money was found is the airplane, not Lindner Aviation's hangar where the airplane happened to be parked when the money was discovered. The policy behind giving ownership of mislaid property to the owner of the premises where the property was mislaid supports this conclusion. If the true owner of the money attempts to locate it, he would initially look for the plane; it is unlikely he would begin his search by contacting businesses where the airplane might have been inspected. Therefore, we affirm the trial court's judgment that the bank, as the owner of the plane, has the right to possession of the property as against all but the true owner.

## VIII. Summary

We conclude that the district court's finding that the money discovered by Benjamin was mislaid property is supported by substantial evidence. Therefore, we affirm the district court's judgment that the bank has the right to the money as against all but the true owner. This decision makes it unnecessary to decide whether Benja- min or Lindner Aviation was the finder of the property. We reverse the court's decision awarding a finder's fee to Benjamin.

---

## CASE 48–4
### *Pro Rata* Clauses/Insurable Interest
## ALBERICI v. SAFEGUARD MUTUAL INSURANCE COMPANY
Superior Court of Pennsylvania, 1995
444 Pa.Super. 351, 664 A.2d 110

WIEAND, J.

On or about May 9, 1977, Joseph Alberici entered an agreement to purchase a theatre property in Aston, Delaware County, for a price of $210,000.00. The named purchaser was Joseph Alberici or his nominee. A down payment of $21,000.00 was made by withdrawing funds from a savings account owned jointly by Joseph Alberici and Theresa Alberici, husband and wife. On August 6, 1977, prior to closing, the theatre was seriously damaged by fire. After the fire, Joseph and Theresa Alberici mortgaged other real estate which they owned, and these proceeds were used to close on the theatre property. Title was taken in the name of La Casa Mia.

After signing the agreement to purchase the theatre, Alberici had purchased fire insurance as follows:

| Insurer | Property | Amount | Insured |
|---|---|---|---|
| 1. Safeguard Mutual | building | 100,000 | Joseph Alberici |
| 2. Safeguard Mutual | contents | 25,000 | Joseph & Theresa Alberici |
| 3. General Accident | building | 125,000 | Joseph & Theresa Alberici |
| 4. Insurance Placement | building | 100,000 | Joseph Alberici |
| 5. Quaker State Mutual | building contents | 62,500 12,500 | Joseph & Theresa Alberici |
| 6. Home Mutual Ins. | building contents | 62,500 12,000 | Joseph & Theresa Alberici |

Joseph Alberici subsequently came under suspicion for arson, and he was ultimately convicted of mail fraud in connection with the submission of fire loss claims to the insurers. Because of this, summary judgment was entered in favor of the insurers in an action brought against them by Joseph and Theresa Alberici. On appeal, the Superior Court affirmed the judgment on Joseph's claim, but determined that a possibility existed that Theresa could show an insurable interest entitling her to recover under fire policies issued to her. On remand and following a trial without jury, the trial court found that Theresa Alberici did have an insurable interest in the real estate and, therefore, could recover under the terms of policies in which she was a named insured. From this aspect of the case, both insurer and insured appealed.

\* \* \*

Before Theresa could recover on the policies in which she had been named as an insured, it had to be shown that she possessed an insurable interest in the property. [Citations.] To determine whether a party has an insurable interest in property, it is necessary to focus upon the facts as they existed at the time the policy was issued and at the time the loss occurred. [Citation.] Generally, whether a person has an insurable interest is an issue to be decided by the finder of fact. [Citations.]

A policy that insures against loss by fire is a contract for indemnity which protects the insured's interest in the property, not the property itself. [Citation.] One who "derives pecuniary benefit or advantage from the preservation or continued existence of [ ] property or who will suffer pecuniary loss from its destruction" has an insurable interest in the property. [Citation.] Upon execution of an agreement of sale, a purchaser of real estate has an equitable title to property and may insure his or her interest therein. [Citation.] A purchaser's insurable interest is in the entire property, not merely the extent to which he or she has made payments towards the purchase price. [Citation.]

After reviewing the testimony and evidence, the trial court concluded that appellant had an insurable interest in the theatre property at 247 Concord Avenue from the date of the agreement of sale. Although the agreement did not specifically identify appellant as a purchaser, it designated the "buyer" as "Joseph Alberici or his nominee." The trial court concluded that Joseph Alberici and Theresa Alberici, husband and wife, were intended nominees. The court observed that appellant and her husband had always purchased property together in the past, she had accompanied her husband to inspect the property prior to the purchase, and the monies to pay for the property had been taken from marital assets. Both appellant and her husband, the court concluded, had approached the purchase in a manner which indicated that they were purchasing it jointly. Because appellant was a purchaser of the property, she had an insurable interest therein. Her interest was in the value of the entire property and not merely her contribution toward the down payment. We find no basis for disturbing the trial court's findings.

We must next determine whether the trial court correctly apportioned liability solely among the carriers who insured the interest of Joseph and Theresa Alberici. In Pennsylvania, [citation], [the law] requires that every policy of fire insurance include a proration clause. A "pro rata clause" in an insurance policy allows the liability of one insurer to be measured by the proportion that its policy bears to the total insurance on the property. [Citations.] A purpose of a proration clause is to "relieve the insurer from the burden of litigating with the insured as to the validity of other policies." [Citation.]

In the case [before us], each of the policies on the theatre property contained the following clause:

This company shall not be liable for a greater proportion of any loss than the amount hereby insured shall bear to the whole insurance covering the property against the peril involved, whether collectible or not.

In order for proration to apply, there must be two or more policies covering the same risk, the same subject matter and the same interest. [Citations.] Here, it is agreed that the policies naming Joseph Alberici as the sole insured and those naming Joseph and Theresa Alberici as coinsureds covered the same risk and the same subject matter. Appellant contends, however, that the policies issued to Joseph Alberici individually did not apply to the same interest as those in which she and her husband were named jointly as co-insureds. The trial court disagreed and pro rated liability on the basis of all policies insuring either Joseph Alberici or Joseph and Theresa Alberici. Appellant contends that this was error.

Two or more policies of insurance cover the same interest where there is a potential for the insured to experience a double recovery. "Since fire insurance is only a contract of indemnity and its object is not to permit a gain by the insured but only to compensate him [or her] for a loss, it is obvious that he [or she] cannot recover insurance in an amount greater than the loss which he [or she] sustained." * * * [Citation.]

In a policy for fire insurance, the right of indemnity is provided to the insured according to the terms of the policy; it is not necessarily payable to all the owners of the property. [Citation.] Whether a policy covers separately the interests of a husband and a wife must be determined by reference to the policy language. [Citations.]

In the instant case, the buyer of the theatre named in the agreement of sale was Joseph Alberici or his nominee. The evidence is clear that it was Alberici who also purchased fire insurance to protect the interest of the purchaser. In two policies, which he purchased from Safeguard Mutual and Insurance Placement, he caused himself to be named as the insured. In four other policies which he purchased from Safeguard Mutual, General Accident, Quaker State Mutual and Home Mutual, the nominee which he named in the policies was himself and his wife. The trial court found that Theresa had acquired an interest in the real estate which was insurable and which would support the issuance of a policy of insurance to protect that interest. That interest, however, was the interest of a purchaser. Joseph's interest in the real estate was also that of a purchaser. If both Joseph Alberici and his nominee were paid the full purchase price, there clearly would be a double recovery. Or to put it another way, there could be only one recovery for the fire loss by the purchaser. That purchaser was either Joseph Alberici or his nominee. There could not be a full recovery by both. Under these circumstances, it seems clear that all policies insured a single interest, i.e., the interest of the purchaser. Therefore, the trial court properly calculated the pro rata apportionment among all policies insuring the interest of the buyer or buyers under the terms of the sales agreement.

# Questions

**1.** Distinguish between (a) tangible and intangible property, and (b) real and personal property.

**2.** Define and give three examples of a fixture.

**3.** Explain: (a) the ways to transfer title to personal property; (b) the three elements of a valid gift; and (c) the difference in the law's treatment of abandoned property, lost property, mislaid property, and treasure trove property.

**4.** With respect to property insurance contracts, explain (a) co-insurance clauses, (b) an insurable interest, (c) the different types of fires, (d) other insurance clauses, and (e) valued and open policies.

**5.** Compare the defenses of misrepresentation, concealment, breach of warranty, waiver, and estoppel.

# Problems

**1.** In January, Roger Burke loaned his favorite nephew, Jimmy White, his valuable Picasso painting. Knowing that Jimmy would celebrate his twenty-first birthday on May 15, Burke sent a letter to Jimmy on April 14 stating:

Dear Jimmy,
Tomorrow I leave on my annual trip to Europe, and I want to make you a fitting birthday gift, which I do by sending you my enclosed promissory note. Also I want you to keep the Picasso, which I loaned you last January, and you may now consider it yours. Happy birthday!

Affectionately,
/s/ Uncle Roger

The negotiable promissory note for $5,000 sent with the letter was signed by Roger Burke, payable to Jimmy White or bearer, and dated May 15. On May 21, Burke was killed in an automobile accident while motoring in France.

First Bank was appointed administrator of Burke's estate. Jimmy presented the note to the administrator and demanded payment, which was refused. Jimmy brought an action against First Bank as administrator, seeking recovery on the note. The administrator in turn brought an action against Jimmy, seeking the return of the Picasso.

(a) What decision in the action on the note?

(b) What decision in the action to recover the painting?

**2.** Several years ago, Pierce purchased a tract of land on which stood an old, vacant house. Recently, Pierce employed Fried, a carpenter, to repair and remodel the house. While Fried was tearing out a partition to enlarge one of the rooms, he found a metal box hidden in the wall. After breaking open the box and discovering that it contained $2,000 in gold and silver coins and old-style bills, Fried took the box and its contents to Pierce and told her where he had found it. When Fried handed the box and the money over to Pierce, he said, "If you do not find the owner, I claim the money." Pierce placed the money in an envelope and deposited it in her safe deposit box, where it presently remains. No one has ever claimed the money, but Pierce refuses to give it to Fried.

Fried brings an action against Pierce to recover the money. Decision?

**3.** Gable, the owner of a lumber company, was cutting trees over the boundary line between his property and property owned by Lane. Although he realized he had crossed onto Lane's property, Gable continued to cut trees of the same kind as those he had cut on his own land. While on Lane's property, he found a diamond ring on the ground, which he took home. All of the timber Gable cut that day was commingled.

What are Lane's rights, if any, (a) in the timber and (b) in the ring?

**4.** Decide each of the following problems.

(a) A chimney sweep found a jewel and took it to a goldsmith, whose apprentice removed the stone and refused to return it. The chimney sweep sues the goldsmith.

(b) One of several boys walking along a railroad track found an old stocking. All started playing with it until it burst in the hands of its discoverer, revealing several hundred dollars. The original discoverer claims all of the money; the other boys claim it should be divided equally.

(c) A traveling salesperson leaving a store notices a parcel of bank notes on the floor. He picks them up and gives them to the owner of the store to keep for the true owner. After three years, they have not been reclaimed, and the salesperson sues the storekeeper.

(d) Frank is hired to clean the swimming pool at the country club. He finds a diamond ring on the bottom of the pool. The true owner cannot be found. The country club sues Frank for possession of the ring.

(e) A customer found a pocketbook lying on a barber's table. He gave it to the barber to hold for the true owner, who failed to appear. The customer sues the barber.

**5.** Jones had 50 crates of oranges equally divided between grades A, B, and C, grade A being the highest quality and C being the lowest. Smith had 1,000 crates of oranges, about 90 percent of which were grade A, but some of which were grades B and C, the exact percentage of each being unknown. Smith willfully mixed Jones's crates with his own so that it was impossible to identify any particular crate. Jones seized the whole lot. Smith demanded 900 crates of grade A and 50 crates each of grades B and C. Jones refused to give them up unless Smith could identify particular crates. This Smith could not do. Smith brought an action against Jones to recover what he demanded or its value. Judgment for whom, and why?

**6.** Barnes, the owner and operator of Blackacre, decided to cease farming operations and liquidate his holdings. Barnes sold fifty head of yearling Merino sheep to Billing and then sold Blackacre to Clifton. He executed and delivered to Billing a bill of sale for the sheep and was paid for them. It was understood that Billing would send a truck for the sheep within a few days. At the same time, Barnes executed a warranty deed conveying Blackacre to Clifton. Clifton took possession of the farm and brought along one hundred head of his yearling Merino sheep and turned them into the pasture, not knowing the sheep Barnes sold Billing were still in the pasture. After the sheep were mixed, it was impossible to identify the fifty head belonging to Billing. After proper demand, Billing sued Clifton to recover the fifty head of sheep. Decision?

**7.** Susan permitted Kevin to take her very old grandfather clock on the basis of Kevin's representations that he was skilled at repairing such clocks and restoring them to their original condition and could do the job for $60. The clock had been badly damaged for years. Kevin immediately sold the clock to Fixit Shop for $30. Fixit Shop was in the business of repairing a large variety of items and also sold used articles. Three months later, Susan was in the Fixit Shop and clearly identified a grandfather clock Fixit Shop had for sale as the one she had given Kevin to repair. Fixit Shop had replaced more than half of the moving parts by having exact duplicates custom-made; the clock's exterior had been restored by a skilled cabinetmaker; and the clock's face had been replaced by a duplicate. All materials belonged to Fixit Shop, and the work was accomplished by its employees. Fixit Shop asserts it bought the clock in the normal course of business from Kevin, who represented that it belonged to him. The fair market value of the clock in its damaged condition was $30, and the value of repairs made is $220.

Susan sued Fixit Shop for return of the clock. Fixit Shop defended that it now had title to the clock and, in the alternative, that Susan must pay the value of the repairs if she is entitled to regain possession. Decision?

**8.** Hyer rented a vacant lot from Bateman for a filling station under an oral agreement and placed on it a lightly constructed building bolted to a concrete slab and storage tanks laid on the ground in a shallow excavation. Later, Hyer prepared a lease providing that he might remove the equipment at the termination of the lease. This lease was not executed, having been rejected by Bateman because of a renewal clause it contained; but several years later another lease was prepared, which both Hyer and Bateman did sign. This lease did not mention removal of the equipment. At the termination of this lease, Hyer removed the equipment, and Bateman brought an action to recover possession of the equipment. What judgment?

**9.** Elvers sold a parcel of real estate, describing it by its legal description and making no mention of any improvements or fixtures on it. The land had upon it a residence, a barn, a rail fence, a stack of hay, some growing corn, and a windmill. The residence had a mirror built into the west wall of the living room and a heating system consisting of a furnace, steam pipes, and coils. In the house were chairs, beds, tables, and other furniture. On the house was a lightning rod. In the basement were screens for the windows. Which of these things passed by the deed and which did not?

**10.** John Swan rented a safety deposit box at the Tenth Citizens Bank of Emanon, State of X. On December 17, 1993, Swan went to the bank with stock certificates to place in the safety deposit box. After he was admitted to the vault and had placed the stock certificates in the box, Swan found lying on the floor of the vault a $5,000 negotiable bearer bond issued by the State of Wisconsin with coupons attached, due June 30, 1999. Swan picked up the bond and, observing that it did not carry the name of the owner, left the vault and went to the office of the president of the bank. He told the president what had occurred and delivered the bond to the president only after obtaining his promise that, should the owner not call for the bond or become known to the bank by June 30, 1994, the bank would redeliver the bond to Swan. On July 1, 1994, Swan learned that the owner of the bond had not called for it; nor was his identity known to the bank. Swan then asked that the bond be returned to him. The bank refused, stating that it would continue to hold the bond until the owner claimed it. Swan brings an action against the bank to recover possession of the bond. Decision?

**11.** Lile, an insurance broker who handled all insurance for Tempo Co., purchased a fire policy from Insurance Company insuring Tempo Co.'s factory against fire in the amount of $150,000. Before the policy was delivered to Tempo and while it was still in Lile's hands, Tempo advised Lile to cancel the policy. Prior to cancellation, however, Tempo suffered a loss. Tempo now makes a claim against Insurance Company on the policy. The premium had been billed to Lile but was unpaid at the time of loss. In an action by Tempo Co. against Insurance Company, what judgment?

**12.** On July 15, Adler purchased in Chicago a Buick sedan, intending to drive it that day to St. Louis, Missouri. He telephoned a friend, Maruchek, who was in the insurance business, and told him that he wanted liability insurance on the automobile, limited in amount to $50,000 for injuries to one person and to $100,000 for any one accident. Maruchek took the order and told Adler over the telephone that he was covered and that his policy would be written by the Young Insurance Company. Later that same day and before Maruchek had informed the Young Insurance Company of Adler's application, Adler negligently operated the automobile and seriously injured Brown, who brings suit against Adler. Is Adler covered by liability insurance?

**13.** Graham owns a building having a fair market value of $120,000. She takes out a fire insurance policy from the Bentley Insurance Company for $72,000; the policy contains an 80 percent co-insurance clause. The building is damaged by fire to the extent of $48,000. How much insurance is Graham entitled to collect?

**14.** Scarola purchased an automobile for value and without knowledge that it was stolen. After he insured the car with Insurance Company of North America (INA), the car was stolen once again. When INA refused to reimburse Scarola for the loss, contending that he did not have an insurable interest in the car, Scarola brought an action. Decision?

**15.** Sears had sold to and installed in Seven Palms Motor Inn a number of furnishings, including drapes and bedspreads, in connection with the construction of a motel on land Seven Palms owned. Sears did not receive payment in full for the materials and labor and brought suit to recover $8,357.49, with interest, and to establish a mechanic's lien on the motel and land for the unpaid portion of the furnishings. Seven Palms asserted that neither the drapes nor bedspreads were fixtures and that, thus, Sears could not obtain a mechanic's lien on them. The trial court decided that Sears was entitled to recover $8,357.49, with interest, and that it did have a mechanic's lien. The court of appeals affirmed the money judgment but reversed the mechanic's lien, holding that the bedspreads were not lienable items and that their inclusion would void the entire lien. Decision?

**16.** When Richard Rothchild became engaged to Carol Cohen, he gave her a diamond engagement ring valued at $1,000. Shortly before the wedding date, however, Richard was killed in an automobile accident. His estate then instituted this action to recover the ring. Decision?

**17.** While in the examination booth in the safety deposit vault of Old Orchard Bank, Brenice Paset found $6,235 in currency in the seat of a chair that was partially under the table. She notified the bank officials and turned the money over to them. They told her that they would try to locate the owner but that, if they failed to locate the owner within one year, she, Brenice, could have the money. The bank then sent a notice to all of its safety deposit box customers asking if they had lost some property. Though it received no response within a year, the bank still refused to turn over the money, contending that it had to hold the money for the true owner. Brenice then brought this action to establish herself as the owner of the money by her compliance with the requirements of the applicable state statute. The bank argued that the money was mislaid and that therefore the statute was not applicable. The trial court adopted the bank's argument, and the plaintiff appealed. Decision?

**WWW**   **Internet Exercise** Find information about (a) business insurance, (b) homeowner's insurance, and (c) the ten largest home insurers and their market share.

# CHAPTER 49

# Bailments and Documents of Title

A bailment is the relationship created when one person (called the bailor) transfers the possession of personal property by delivery, without transfer of title, to another (called the bailee) for the accomplishment of a certain purpose, after which the bailee is to return the property to the bailor or dispose of it according to the bailor's directions. Unlike such well-known legal terms as contract, agent, sale, partnership, corporation, and insurance, the term *bailment* has not passed into common usage and so is not familiar to many people. Nonetheless, the word bailment denotes a transaction that not only is of considerable antiquity but also is one of the most common occurrences in everyday life. It is not an exaggeration to say that practically every person, whether carrying on a business or not, becomes a party to a bailment. This will be readily understood from the following common examples of bailments: keeping a car in a public garage; leaving a car, a watch, or any other article to be repaired; renting a car or truck; checking a hat or coat at a theatre or restaurant; leaving clothes to be laundered; storing goods in a warehouse; and shipping goods by public or private transportation.

Bailments are not only common, but are of great commercial importance as well. As the above examples indicate, bailments include the transportation, storage, repair, and rental of goods, which together involve billions of dollars in transactions each year.

Documents of title are commonly used in bailment transactions. The most frequently used documents of title are the warehouse receipts issued by warehousers and the bills of lading issued by carriers.

## BAILMENTS

A **bailment**, as previously mentioned, is the temporary transfer of possession, without title, of personal property by one party (the **bailor**) to another (the **bailee**). The benefit of a bailment may, by its terms, accrue solely to the bailor, solely to the bailee, or to both parties. A bailment may be with or without compensation. On these bases, bailments are classified as follows:

1. *Bailments for the bailor's sole benefit* include the gratuitous custody of personal property and the gratuitous services that involve custody of personal property, such as repairs or transportation. For example, if Ed stores, repairs, or transports Francis's goods without compensation, this is a bailment for the sole benefit of the bailor, Francis.
2. *Bailments for the bailee's sole benefit* are usually limited to the gratuitous loan of personal property for use by the bailee, as where Francis, without compensation, lends his car, lawn mower, or book to Edith for her use.
3. *Bailments for the benefit of both parties* include ordinary commercial bailments, such as goods delivered to a person for repair, jewels to a pawnbroker, or an automobile to a parking lot attendant.

## ESSENTIAL ELEMENTS OF A BAILMENT

The basic elements of a bailment are (1) the delivery of possession from a bailor to a bailee; (2) the delivery of personal, not real, property; (3) possession without ownership by the bailee for a determinable period of time; and (4) an absolute duty on the bailee to return the property to the bailor or to dispose of it according to the bailor's directions.

In the great majority of cases, the existence of a bailment can be determined by two simple tests: (1) a separation of ownership and possession of the property (possession without ownership) and (2) a duty on the party in possession to redeliver the identical property to the owner or to dispose of it according to the owner's directions. Because a bailment need not be a contract, consideration is not required.

 *See Case 49–1*

## Delivery of Possession

The term *bailment* is derived from the French word *baillier,* meaning "to deliver." Possession by a bailee in a bailment relationship involves (1) the bailee's power to control the personal property and (2) her intention to control it. Thus, for example, where a restaurant customer hangs his hat or coat on a hook furnished for that purpose, the hat or coat is within an area under the physical control of the restaurant owner. But the restaurant owner is not a bailee of the hat or coat unless he clearly signifies an intention to exercise control over the hat or coat. On the other hand, where a clerk in a store helps a customer to remove her coat in order to try on a new one, the owner of the store generally is held to become a bailee of the old coat through the clerk, his employee. Here, the clerk has signified an intention to control the coat by taking it from the customer, and a bailment results.

Leaving a car in a commercial parking lot may be a bailment. Parking lot cases fall generally into three categories:

1. Where an owner parks his car in a parking lot, pays a charge, and receives a claim check, but locks the car and takes the keys away. This class of cases generally is held to be a license (a right to use the space).
2. Where an owner leaves her car with an attendant who assumes control of the car and parks it, and the owner pays a charge and receives a ticket as a means of identifying the car on redelivery. This class is held to be a bailment.
3. Where the status of the parties falls between the first two categories and is determined by the circumstances. This class covers cases where, even though the owner parks his car and keeps the keys, the parking lot operator maintains control sufficient to constitute a bailment. In analyzing this third class of cases, the amount of free access the parking lot operator permits the owner and the amount of control the parking lot operator exercises, according to her representations to the public, are crucial.

## Personal Property

No bailment results from the delivery of possession of real property by the owner to another; rather, the bailment relationship can exist only with respect to personal property. The bailed property need not be tangible. Intangible property, such as the rights represented by promissory notes, corporate bonds, shares of stock, documents of title, and life insurance policies that are evidenced by written instruments and are thus capable of delivery, may be and frequently are the subject matter of bailments.

## Possession for a Determinable Time

To establish a bailment relationship, the person receiving possession must be under a duty to return the personal property and must not obtain title to it. The particular situation dictates whether a transaction constitutes a bailment or a sale. A sale always involves a transfer of *title* to specific property to the buyer. If the identical property transferred is to be returned, even in an altered form, the transaction is a bailment; however, if other property of equal value or the money value of the original property may be returned, title has transferred, and the transaction is a sale.

## Restoration of Possession to the Bailor

The bailee is legally obligated to restore possession of the property when the bailment period ends. A bailment for the mutual benefit of the parties ordinarily terminates when the purpose of the bailment is fully accomplished or when the time for which the bailment was created expires. The parties may, of course, terminate the bailment earlier by mutual consent. A breach by the bailee of any of his obligations entitles the bailor to terminate the bailment. A bailment also terminates upon the destruction of the bailed property, because the relation cannot exist without the subject personal property.

Normally, the bailee is required to return the identical goods bailed, though their condition may be changed due to the work that the bailee was required to perform on them. An exception to this rule involves **fungible goods,** such as grain, every particle of which is, for all practical purposes, the equivalent of every other particle and which are expected to be mingled with like goods during a bailment. Given such subject matter, a bailee obviously cannot be required to return the identical goods bailed. His obligation is simply to return goods of the same quality and quantity.

## *RIGHTS AND DUTIES OF BAILOR AND BAILEE*

The bailment relationship creates rights and duties on the part of the bailor and the bailee. The bailee is under a duty to exercise due care for the safety of the property and to return it to the right person; in return, he has the exclusive right to possess the property for the term of the bailment. In addition, depending on the nature of the transaction, a bailee may have the right to limit his liability and to receive compensation. With respect to the condition of the bailed goods, the bailor also has certain duties.

## Bailee's Duty to Exercise Due Care

The bailee must exercise due care not to injure or destroy the property or to permit third parties to do so. The degree of care necessary depends on the nature of the bailment relationship and the character of the property. Ordinarily, a bailee does not insure the subject of the bailment. Because his liability rests on his failure to exercise due care for the property or on his intentional wrongdoing, in the absence of fault, the bailee is not liable when property is lost, stolen, or destroyed.

In the context of a **commercial bailment,** from which the parties derive a mutual benefit, the law requires the bailee to exercise the care that a reasonably prudent person would exercise under the same circumstances. Where the bailment benefits the bailee alone, as in the case of one who gratuitously borrows a motor vehicle from another, the law requires more than reasonable care of him. On the other hand, where the bailee accepts the property for the sole benefit of the bailor, the law requires a lesser degree of care.

Nevertheless, the amount of care required to satisfy any of the standards will vary with the character of the property. A bailee required to take only slight care under the general rules mentioned above may be liable if he does not treat a $10,000 bracelet with care greater than that with which he would treat a $20 watch. In practice, therefore, a bailee must look beyond the degree of care required in the abstract and assess the magnitude of the consequences that she reasonably ought to have foreseen, were the property to be lost or destroyed.

When property is lost, damaged, or destroyed while in the possession of a bailee, it is often impossible for the bailor to obtain enough information to show that the loss or damage was due to the bailee's failure to exercise the required care. Nevertheless, the law aids the bailor by *presuming* that the bailee was at fault. The bailor is merely required to show that certain property was delivered by way of bailment and that the bailee either has failed to return it or has returned it in a damaged condition. The burden then rests upon the bailee to prove that he exercised the degree of care required of him.

◆ *See Figure 49–1*

## Bailee's Absolute Liability to Return Property

As discussed earlier, the bailee is free from liability if she has exercised the degree of care required of her under the particular bailment while the property was within her control. This general rule has certain important exceptions that impose an absolute duty upon the bailee to return the property undamaged to the proper person.

Where the bailee has an obligation by express *agreement* with the bailor or by *custom* to insure the property against certain risks but fails to do so, and the property is destroyed or damaged through such risks, she is liable for the damage or nondelivery, even though she has exercised due care.

Where the bailee uses the bailed property in a manner not authorized by the bailor or by the character of the bailment, and during the course of such use the property is damaged or destroyed, without fault on the part of the bailee, the bailee is absolutely (strictly) liable for the damage or destruction. The wrongful use by the bailee automatically terminates her lawful possession: she becomes a trespasser as to the property and, as such, is liable for whatever harm befalls it.

A bailee has a duty to return the property to the right person. If the bailee, by mistake or intent, *misdelivers*

FIGURE 49–1   Duties in a Bailment

| Type of Bailment | Bailee's Duty of Care | Bailor's Duty |
| --- | --- | --- |
| **For sole benefit of bailor** | Slight care | To warn of defects of which she knew or should have known |
| **For sole benefit of bailee** | Utmost care | To warn of known defects |
| **For mutual benefit** | Ordinary care | To warn of defects of which she knew or should have known |

the property to someone who has no right to its possession, she is guilty of conversion and is liable to the bailor, even when the bailor has caused the mistake through his own negligence.

## Bailee's Right to Limit Liability

Certain bailees—common carriers, public warehousers, and innkeepers—may limit their liability for breach of their duties to a bailor only as provided by statute. Other bailees, however, may vary their duties and liabilities by contract with the bailor. Where liability may be limited by contract, the law requires that any such limitation be properly brought to the bailor's attention before she bails the property. This is especially true of bailments involving "professional bailees," or those who make it their principal business to act as bailees and who deal with the public on a uniform rather than an individual basis. Thus, a variation or limitation in writing, contained, for example, in a check or stub given to the bailor or posted on the walls of the bailee's place of business, will not ordinarily bind the bailor unless (a) the bailee draws the bailor's attention to the writing and (b) informs the bailor that it contains a limitation or variation of liability and (c) the limitation is not the result of unequal bargaining power. Some States do not permit professional bailees (who commonly include warehousers, garagers, and parking lot owners) to disclaim liability for their own negligence.

 *See Case 49-2*

## Bailee's Right to Compensation

A bailee who by express or implied agreement undertakes to perform work on or render services in connection with the bailed goods is entitled to reasonable compensation for those services or that work and to reimbursement for his expenses. In most cases, the agreement between bailor and bailee fixes the amount of compensation and provides how it shall be paid. In the absence of a contrary agreement, the compensation is payable upon the bailee's completion of the work or performance of the services. If, after such completion or performance, and before the goods are redelivered to the bailor, the goods are lost or damaged through no fault of the bailee, the bailee is still entitled to compensation for his work and services.

Most bailees who are entitled to compensation for work and services performed in connection with bailed goods acquire a possessory lien upon the goods to secure the payment of such compensation. In most jurisdictions,

the bailee has a statutory right to obtain a judicial foreclosure of his lien and a sale of the goods. Many statutes also provide that the bailee does not lose his lien upon redelivery of the goods to the bailor, as is the case at common law. Instead, the lien will continue for a specified period after redelivery, if the bailee timely records with the proper authorities an instrument claiming such a lien.

## Bailor's Duties

In a bailment for the sole benefit of the bailee, the bailor warrants that she is unaware of any defects in the bailed property. In all other instances, the bailor has a duty to warn the bailee of all defects she knows of or should have discovered upon a reasonable inspection of the bailed property. A number of courts have extended strict liability in tort and the implied warranties under Article 2 of the Uniform Commercial Code (UCC) to leases and bailments. Article 2A, discussed in Chapter 21, imposes implied warranties on the lease of goods.

◆ *See Figure 49-1*

## SPECIAL TYPES OF BAILMENTS

Although pledgees, warehousers, and safe deposit companies are governed by the general principles that apply to all ordinary bailees, certain special features about the transactions in which they respectively engage subject them to further consideration. In addition, innkeepers and common carriers may be identified as *extraordinary bailees*, whereas all other bailees are *ordinary bailees*. This distinction is based on the character and extent of the liability of these two classes of bailees for the loss of or any injury to bailed goods. As has been seen, an **ordinary bailee** is liable only for loss or injury that results from his failure to exercise ordinary or reasonable care. The liability of the **extraordinary bailee,** on the other hand, is, in general, **absolute.** In other words, the extraordinary bailee is liable to the bailor for any loss or injury to the goods without regard to his care or negligence as to their safety. It is frequently said that an extraordinary bailee insures the safety of the goods. This simply means that just as an insurer, in general, becomes automatically liable to the insured upon the happening of the hazard insured against, regardless of the cause, the extraordinary bailee becomes liable to the bailor for any loss or injury to the goods, regardless of the cause.

## Pledges

A **pledge** is a bailment for security in which the owner gives possession of her personal property to another (the secured party) to secure a debt or the performance of some obligation. The secured party does not have title to the property involved but merely a possessory security interest. Pledges of most types of personal property for security purposes are governed by Article 9 of the UCC, which is discussed in Chapter 38. In most respects, the secured party's duties and liabilities are the same as those of a bailee for compensation.

## Warehousing

A **warehouser** is a bailee who, for compensation, receives goods to be stored in a warehouse. His duties and liabilities under the common law were in all ways the same as those of the ordinary bailee for compensation. Today, because a strong public interest affects their activities, warehousers are subject to extensive State and Federal regulation. Warehousers also must be distinguished from ordinary bailees in that the receipts they issue for storage have acquired a special status in commerce. Regarded as documents of title, these receipts are governed by Article 7 of the UCC, discussed later in this chapter.

## Safe Deposit Boxes

A majority of States hold that a person who rents a safe deposit box from a bank enters into a bailment relationship. As this constitutes a bailment for the parties' mutual benefit, the bailee bank owes the customer the duty to act with ordinary due care and is liable only if negligent.

## Carriers of Goods

In the broadest sense, anyone who transports goods from one place to another, either gratuitously or for compensation, is a **carrier.** Normally, however, a carrier engages in the business of transportation for hire or reward. The delivery of goods to a carrier for shipment creates a bailment; the carrier has exclusive possession of the goods without ownership and is under a duty to deliver them to the person designated by the shipper. Carriers of goods are by far the most important of all bailees. Not only are their transactions the most numerous and the largest in volume, but their function in the movement of raw materials and the distribution of manufactured and other goods of every description is of enormous importance in our economic system.

Carriers are classified primarily as common carriers and private carriers. A **common carrier** offers its services and facilities to the public upon terms and under circumstances indicating that the offering is made to all persons. Stated somewhat differently, the criteria that denote a common carrier are as follows: (1) the carriage must be part of its business; (2) the carriage must be for remuneration; and (3) the carrier must represent to the general public that it is willing to serve the public in the transportation of property. Common carriers of goods include railroad, ship, aircraft, public trucking, and pipeline companies. In contrast, a **private** or **contract carrier** is one who carries the goods of another on isolated occasions or who serves a limited number of customers under individual contracts without offering the same or similar contracts to the public at large.

The person who delivers goods to a carrier for shipment is known as the **consignor** or **shipper.** The person to whom the carrier is to deliver the goods is known as the **consignee.** The instrument containing the terms of the contract of transportation, which the carrier issues to the shipper, is called a *bill of lading* (discussed later in this chapter).

***Duty to Carry*** A common carrier is under a duty to serve the public to the limits of its capacity and, within those limits, to accept for carriage goods of the kind that it normally transports. A private carrier, by comparison, has no duty to accept goods for carriage except where it agrees to do so by contract.

***Duty to Deliver to the Right Person*** Whether common or private, a carrier is under an absolute duty to deliver the goods to the person to whom they are consigned by the shipper. Essentially, this is the duty that renders an ordinary bailee liable for misdelivery. The form of the bill of lading or other contract of carriage determines the person to whom delivery must be made.

***Liability for Loss or Damage*** A private carrier, in the absence of special contract terms, is liable as a bailee for the goods it undertakes to carry. The liability of a common carrier, on the other hand, approaches that of one who insures the safety of the goods, except where loss or damage is caused by an act of God, an act of a public enemy, the acts or fault of the shipper, the inherent nature of or a defect in the goods, or an act of public authority.

The carrier, however, is permitted to limit its liability through its contract with the shipper, provided the carrier gives the shipper notice of this limitation and the opportunity to declare a higher value for the goods. UCC Section 7–309.

 *See Case 49–3*

## Innkeepers

With regard to their guests' belongings, at common law **innkeepers** (today better known as hotel owners or operators) are held to **strict liability** or **absolute liability** the same as that to which common carriers are held with regard to the goods they carry. This rule of strict liability applies only to those who furnish lodging to the public for compensation as a regular business and extends only to the belongings of lodgers who are guests.

Today, in almost all jurisdictions, the old common law strict liability of the innkeeper has been substantially modified by case law and statute. Although the statutes vary as to detail, they share certain features. All provide, for example, that the innkeeper may avoid strict liability for loss of his guests' valuables or money by providing a safe where such items may be kept and by posting adequate notice of its availability. For articles that are not placed in a safe provided for this purpose, or that are not articles of the kind normally kept in a safe, the statutes often limit recovery to a maximum figure that, although varying from State to State, is generally insubstantial. These statutory limitations do not apply, however, where the loss is due to the fault of the innkeeper or his employees, in which case the innkeeper is liable for the full value of the lost property.

## DOCUMENTS OF TITLE

A **document of title** is a warehouse receipt, bill of lading, or other document evidencing a right to receive, hold, and dispose of the document *and* the goods it covers. To be a document of title, a document must be issued by or addressed to a bailee and must cover goods in the bailee's possession that either are identified or are fungible portions of an identified mass. UCC Section 1–201(15).

Briefly, a document of title symbolizes ownership of the goods it describes. Because of the legal characteristics of a document of title, its ownership is equivalent to the ownership or control of the goods it represents, without the necessity of actual or physical possession of the goods. Likewise, its transfer passes the ownership or control of the goods without necessitating the physical transfer of the goods themselves. For these reasons, documents of title are a convenient means of handling the billions of dollars' worth of goods transported by carriers or stored with warehousers. Documents of title also facilitate the transfer of title to goods and the creation of a security interest in goods. **Article 7** of the UCC governs documents of title.

## TYPES OF DOCUMENTS OF TITLE

### Warehouse Receipts

A **warehouse receipt** is a receipt issued by a person engaged in the business of storing goods for hire. Section 1–201(45).

*Duties of Warehousers* A warehouser is liable for damages for loss or injury to the goods caused by his failure to exercise such care in regard to them as a reasonably careful person would exercise under the circumstances. Section 7–204(1). The States and the Federal government may impose more rigid standards of responsibility. Section 7–204(2). Several States have so elected.

The warehouser must deliver the goods to the person entitled to receive them under the terms of the warehouse receipt. If he has already delivered the goods to another, the burden is on him to establish that such delivery was rightful as against the holder of the document. Similarly, if the goods have become damaged, lost, or destroyed, the burden is on the warehouser to prove by evidence the facts and circumstances which establish her nonliability. Section 7–403(1).

The warehouser may limit her liability by a provision in the warehouse receipt fixing a specific maximum liability per article or item or unit of weight. This limitation does not apply, however, when a warehouser converts goods to her own use. Section 7–204(2).

A warehouser is not required to keep goods indefinitely. Upon termination of the storage period stated in the document, the warehouser may notify the person on whose account the goods are held to pay storage charges and remove the goods. If no period is stated in the document, the warehouser is required to give thirty days' notice to pay charges and remove the goods. A shorter time, which must be reasonable, is permitted if the goods are about to deteriorate or decline in value to less than the amount of the warehouser's lien, or if the quality or condition of the goods makes them hazardous to other property or to persons. Section 7–206.

 *See Case 49-4*

***Lien of Warehouser*** To enforce the payment of his charges and necessary expenses in connection with keeping and handling the goods, a warehouser has a lien on the goods that enables him to sell them at public or private sale after notice and to apply the net proceeds of the sale to the amount of his charges. The Code, moreover, provides the warehouser a definite procedure for enforcing his lien against the goods stored and in his possession. Section 2–710.

Against the holder of a negotiable warehouse receipt to whom it has been duly negotiated, the courts limit this lien to charges at the rate specified in the receipt; if no rate is specified, the lien is limited to a reasonable charge for storage of the goods subsequent to the date of the receipt. Section 7–209(1).

## Bills of Lading

A **bill of lading** is a document issued by a carrier upon receipt of goods for transportation. It serves (1) as a receipt for the goods, (2) as evidence of the contract of carriage, and (3) as a document of title. A bill of lading is negotiable if, by its terms, the goods are deliverable to bearer or to the order of a named person. Any other document is nonnegotiable. Section 7–104.

Under the Code, bills of lading may be issued not only by common carriers but also by contract carriers, freight forwarders, or any person engaged in the business of transporting or forwarding goods. Section 1–201(6).

***Duties of Issuer of Bill of Lading*** The carrier must deliver the goods to the person entitled to receive them under the terms of the bill of lading. The carrier's duty in this respect is similar to that of the warehouser. Article 7 does not affect any State or Federal law imposing liability upon a common carrier for damages not caused by its negligence. Section 7–309(1). Common carriers are extraordinary bailees under the law of many States and consequently are subject to greater liability than ordinary bailees.

The Code allows a carrier to limit its liability by contract in all cases where its rates depend on the value of the goods and the carrier provides the shipper an opportunity to declare a higher value. The limitation does not apply, however, where the carrier converts the goods to its own use. Section 7–309(2).

 *See Case 49-3*

***Through Bills of Lading*** A bill of lading may provide that the issuer deliver the goods to a connecting carrier for further transportation to a destination. A bill of lading that specifies one or more connecting carriers is called a **through bill of lading.**

The initial or originating carrier, which receives the goods from the shipper and issues a through bill of lading, is liable to the holder of the document for loss or damage to the goods caused by any connecting or delivering carrier. Section 7–302(1). A carrier is not, however, required to issue through bills of lading; furthermore, an initial carrier has a right of reimbursement from the connecting or delivering carrier in possession of the goods when the loss or damage occurred.

Unlike the liability of the initial carrier, the liability of a connecting carrier is limited to the period during which the goods are in its possession.

***Lien of Carrier*** Upon goods in its possession that are covered by a bill of lading, the carrier has a lien for the charges and expenses it necessarily incurs in preserving such goods. Against a purchaser for value of a negotiable bill of lading, this lien is limited to charges stated in the bill or in the applicable published tariff or, if no charges are so stated, to a reasonable charge. Section 7–307(1).

The carrier may enforce its lien by public or private sale of the goods after providing notice to all persons known by the carrier to claim an interest in them. The sale must be on "commercially reasonable" terms and must be conducted in a "commercially reasonable manner." Section 7–308(1).

A purchaser in good faith of goods sold to enforce the lien takes free of any rights of persons against whom the lien was valid, even if the enforcement of the lien does not comply with Code requirements. This rule applies to both carrier's and warehouser's liens. Sections 7–308(4) and 7–310(5).

## NEGOTIABILITY OF DOCUMENTS OF TITLE

The concept of negotiability has long been established in law. It is important not only in connection with documents of title but also in connection with commercial paper and investment securities, topics treated in other chapters of this book.

The law confers negotiability upon instruments and documents that comply with certain statutory criteria. The magic words are *bearer* or *order*. A promise to deliver goods to a named person is manifestly different from a promise to deliver the goods to bearer or to the order of a named person. The promisor may safely perform the first promise delivering the goods to the person named in the promise. This is typical of a straight bill of lading; that is, one issued by a carrier that undertakes to deliver the goods to a named consignee at a specific destination. In this case, the carrier need not obtain the bill of lading upon delivering the goods at their destination. The carrier's only concern is to make sure that the person to whom it delivers the goods at the specified destination is the person named in the straight bill of lading as the consignee. Such a bill of lading is **nonnegotiable.**

If, on the other hand, the carrier promises in the bill of lading to deliver the goods to **bearer** or to the **order** of a person named in the bill, the carrier may not safely deliver the goods to anyone at the destination without obtaining surrender of the original bill of lading. Anyone in possession of a bearer form document is entitled to receive the goods from the carrier. Anyone in possession of an order form document, properly indorsed, is likewise entitled to receive possession of the goods from the carrier. A bearer or order form document of title is **negotiable.** By the terms of the promise contained on its face, it was intended to go to market, to pass from hand to hand, and to circulate freely through the channels of commerce.

The Code provides that a warehouse receipt, bill of lading, or other document of title is negotiable if, by its terms, the goods are to be delivered to bearer or to the order of a named person or where, in overseas trade, it runs to a named person or assigns. Any other document is nonnegotiable. Section 7–104.

A nonnegotiable document, such as a straight bill of lading or a warehouse receipt under which the goods are deliverable only to a person named in the bill, not to the order of any person or to bearer, may be transferred by assignment but may not be negotiated. Only a negotiable document or instrument may be negotiated.

## Due Negotiation

The manner in which a negotiable document of title may be negotiated and the requirements of due negotiation are set forth in Section 7–501 of the Code. An order form negotiable document of title running to the order of a named person is negotiated by her indorsement and delivery. After such indorsement in blank or to bearer, the document may be negotiated by delivery alone. A special indorsement, by which the document is indorsed over to a specified person, requires the indorsement of the special indorsee as well as delivery to accomplish a further negotiation.

The naming in a negotiable document of a person to be notified upon the arrival of the goods neither limits the negotiability of the bill of lading nor serves as notice to any purchaser of the document that such person has any interest in the goods.

**Due negotiation,** a term peculiar to Article 7, requires not only that the purchaser of the negotiable document take it in good faith, without notice of any adverse claim or defense, and pay value, but also that she take it in the regular course of business or financing, not in settlement or payment of a money obligation (in essence, a holder by due negotiation). Thus, a transfer for value of a negotiable document of title to a nonbanker or to a person not in business, such as a college professor or student, would not be a due negotiation.

*Rights Acquired by Due Negotiation* Negotiation is a form of transfer in which the transferee acquires not only the rights that the transferor had but also rights set forth directly in the language of the instrument or document. Where a property right is merely assigned, the assignee takes only those rights that the assignor had. He stands in the shoes of the assignor, and his rights are subject to all defects and infirmities in the title of the assignor. Where a document is negotiable and is transferred by due negotiation, however, the transferee is one to whom the promise of the issuer runs to the transferee, who thereby acquires the issuer's direct obligation. Thus, if Keith issues a warehouse receipt to Donna in which he promises to deliver the goods to bearer, and subsequently Gail presents the document to Keith and demands the goods, Gail is the bearer and therefore the very person to whom Keith promised to deliver the goods. The same is true for a properly indorsed order form warehouse receipt or bill of lading.

Due negotiation creates new rights in the holder of the document. On due negotiation, the transferee does not stand in the shoes of his transferor; in other words, the defects and defenses available against the transferor are not available against the new holder. Newly created by the negotiation, his rights are free of such defects and defenses. This enables bankers and businesspersons to extend credit upon documents of title without concern about possible adverse claims or the rights of third parties.

The rights of a holder of a negotiable document of title to whom it has been duly negotiated include (1) title to the document; (2) title to the goods; (3) all rights accruing under the law of agency or estoppel, including rights to goods delivered to the bailee after the document was issued; and (4) the direct obligation of the issuer to hold or deliver the goods according to the terms of the document. Section 7–502.

If an order form document of title is transferred without a requisite indorsement, the transferee has the right to compel his transferor to supply any necessary indorsement. This right is specifically enforceable in a court of equity. The transfer becomes a negotiation only as of the time the indorsement is supplied. Section 7–506.

***Rights Acquired in the Absence of Due Negotiation***  If a nonnegotiable document is transferred or a negotiable document is transferred without due negotiation, the transferee acquires all of the title and rights that the transferor had or had actual authority to convey. Prior to the bailee's receiving notification of the transfer, the rights of the transferee may be defeated (1) by the creditors of the transferor, who could treat the sale as void; (2) by a buyer from the transferor in the ordinary course of business, if the bailee has delivered the goods to the buyer; or (3) against the bailee through good faith dealings between the bailee and the transferor. Section 7–504.

## Warranties

A person, other than a collecting bank or other intermediary, who either negotiates or transfers a document of title for value incurs certain warranty obligations unless otherwise agreed. Section 7–507. Such transferor warrants to her immediate purchaser (1) that the document is genuine; (2) that she had no knowledge of any fact that would impair its validity or worth; and (3) that her negotiation or transfer is rightful and fully effective with respect to the title to the document and the goods it represents.

## Ineffective Documents of Title

It is fundamental that a thief or finder of goods may not deliver them to a warehouser or carrier in return for a negotiable document of title and thus defeat the rights of the owner by a negotiation of the document. Although such a document would be genuine and its indorsement by the thief or finder would not be a forgery, it would not represent title to the goods.

For a person to obtain title to goods by a negotiation to him of a document, the goods must have been delivered to the issuer of the document by the owner of the goods, by one to whom the owner has delivered the goods, or by one whom she has entrusted with actual or apparent authority to ship, store, or sell them. Section 7–503(1). A warehouser or carrier, however, may deliver goods according to the terms of the document which it has issued or otherwise dispose of the goods as provided in the Code without incurring liability, even if the document does not represent title to the goods. The warehouser or carrier need only act in good faith and comply with reasonable commercial standards in both the receipt and delivery or other disposition of the goods. The bailee has no liability, even if the person from whom it received the goods had no authority to obtain the issuance of the document or to dispose of the goods and the person to whom it delivered the goods had no authority to receive them. Section 7–404.

Thus, a carrier or warehouser who receives goods from a thief or finder and later delivers them to a person to whom the thief or finder ordered them to be delivered is not liable to the true owner of the goods. Even a sale of the goods by the carrier or warehouser to enforce a lien for transportation or storage charges and expenses would not subject it to liability.

## Lost or Missing Documents of Title

If a document of title has been lost, stolen, or destroyed, a claimant of the goods may apply to a court for an order directing the carrier or warehouser to deliver the goods or to issue a substitute document. Compliance with the court order relieves the carrier or warehouser of liability. Section 7–601(1). The claimant must provide security approved by the court if the missing document is negotiable.

If the carrier or warehouser delivers goods to a person claiming them under a missing negotiable document without a court order, it is liable to any person who is thereby injured. Nevertheless, delivery to such person in good faith is not a conversion of the goods if the claimant has posted security in an amount at least double the value of the goods to indemnify any person who is injured by the delivery and who files notice of claim within one year. Section 7–601(2).

# Chapter Summary

## Bailments

**Definition** the temporary transfer of personal property by one party (the bailor) to another (the bailee)

**Classification of Bailments**
- *For the Bailor's Sole Benefit*
- *For the Bailee's Sole Benefit*
- *For Mutual Benefit* includes ordinary commercial bailments

**Essential Elements**
- *Delivery of Possession*
- *Personal Property*
- *Possession, but Not Ownership, for a Determinable Time*
- *Restoration of Possession to the Bailor*

**Rights and Duties**
- *Bailee's Duty to Exercise Due Care* the bailee must exercise reasonable care to protect the safety of the property and to return it to the proper person
- *Bailee's Absolute Liability* occurs when (1) the parties so agree; (2) the custom of the industry requires the bailee to insure the property against the risk in question, but he fails to do so; or (3) the bailee uses the bailed property in an unauthorized manner
- *Bailee's Right to Limit Liability* certain bailees are not permitted to limit their liability for breach of their duties, except as provided by statute
- *Bailee's Right to Compensation* bailee is entitled to reasonable compensation for work or services performed on the bailed goods
- *Bailor's Duties* in bailment for sole benefit of bailee, the bailor warrants that she is unaware of any defects; in all other bailments, the bailor has a duty to warn of all known defects and all defects she should discover upon a reasonable inspection

**Special Types**
- *Pledge* security interest by possession
- *Warehouser* storer of goods for compensation; warehouser must exercise reasonable care to protect the safety of the stored goods and to deliver them to the proper person
- *Safe Deposit Boxes*
- *Carrier of Goods* transporter of goods; a common carrier is an extraordinary bailee, while a private carrier is an ordinary bailee
- *Innkeeper* hotel or motel operator; is an extraordinary bailee except as limited by statute or case law

## Documents of Title

**Definition** an instrument evidencing ownership of the document and the goods it covers

**Types**
- *Warehouse Receipt* receipt issued by person storing goods
- *Bill of Lading* document issued to the shipper by the carrier (1) as a receipt for the goods, (2) as evidence of their carriage contract, and (3) as a document of title

**Negotiability** a document of title is negotiable if, by its terms, the goods are to be delivered to bearer or to the order of a named person
- *Due Negotiation* transfer of a negotiable document in the regular course of business to a holder, who takes in good faith, for value, and without notice of any defense or claim
- *Rights Acquired in the Absence of Due Negotiation* transferee acquires all the rights the transferor had

> - **Warranties** a person who negotiates or transfers a document of title for value, other than a collecting bank or other intermediary, incurs certain warranty obligations unless otherwise agreed
> - **Ineffective Documents** for a person to obtain title to goods by negotiation of a document, the goods must have been delivered to the issuer of the document by the owner of the goods or by one to whom actual or apparent authority has been entrusted by the owner
> - **Lost or Missing Documents of Title** claimant may apply to a court for issuance of a substitute document

 **Cases**

## CASE 49–1
### Essential Elements of a Bailment
### *LITTLE, BROWN AND COMPANY v.*
### *AMERICAN PAPER RECYCLING CORP.*
United States District Court, D. Massachusetts, 1993
824 F.Supp. 11

COLLINGS, J.

\* \* \*

## II. The Undisputed Facts

Little, Brown and APR [American Paper Recycling Corp.] had an arrangement whereby APR would pick up books from Little, Brown for purposes of recycling said books. After the books were destroyed, APR paid Little, Brown ten dollars ($10.00) per ton for the usable weight of each shipment which was determined by weighing the paper after the books had been debound, i.e., once the book covers and bindings had been removed. The parties understood that, upon a request from Little, Brown, APR was required to provide a certificate of destruction with respect to any shipment, confirming that in fact the books in that shipment had been destroyed.

\* \* \*

The instant litigation concerns books which APR picked up from Little, Brown, on or about October 31, 1990, November 6, 1990, November 7, 1990 and November 14, 1990. Among the books consigned to APR by Little, Brown on these dates were copies of the novels *Vineland* and *Masquerade* which were published by Little, Brown with notices of copyright on their title pages and which were registered with the copyright office. \* \* \* APR did not destroy these four shipments of books; rather it sold them to Advantage Paper Stock,

Inc./Viking Fibres, Inc. (hereafter "Advantage"). Prior to October of 1990, APR had never before used Advantage to process books.

Advantage faxed a purchase confirmation to APR on or about October 29, 1990, therein agreeing to buy "books for cutting" at the price of thirty dollars ($30.00) per ton. APR did in fact receive thirty dollars ($30.00) per ton from Advantage for the sale of the four shipments of Little, Brown books. There is no evidence that Little, Brown knew at any time prior to the initiation of this lawsuit that APR intended to sell or had sold to Advantage any books consigned to APR by Little, Brown, or that APR had shipped any such books to Advantage.

Rather than destroying the Little, Brown books, Advantage sold them to Perkins Recycling Corp. (hereinafter "Perkins") for a price of forty dollars ($40.00) per ton. In turn, Perkins sold two truckloads of the Little, Brown books to Diversified Business Enterprises, Inc. (hereinafter "Diversified") for two hundred forty dollars ($240.00) per ton. NBE West, Inc. acquired some of the Little, Brown books sold to Diversified and thereafter resold some of them to other entities including Sea Span Publications, Inc. and New England Mobile Book Fair, Inc.

The parties have stipulated there is no evidence that APR knew that Advantage had sold the Little, Brown books to Perkins, or that any entity or entities had come into possession of the books prior to receiving notice of the instant lawsuit from counsel for Little, Brown.

Further, there is no evidence that APR participated in the activities of any entity or entities that came into possession of the Little, Brown books after APR sold them to Advantage. Finally, the parties agree that Little, Brown never expressly authorized APR's sale of Little, Brown books to other recyclers for the purpose of recycling and, on the other hand, never expressly restricted APR's sale of Little, Brown books to other recyclers for the purpose of recycling.

## III. Legal Analysis

There is no written contract incorporating the terms of the parties' agreement. Little, Brown takes the position that it did not sell books to APR but rather sold the usable weight of paper remaining after the covers and bindings of the books had been removed. The plaintiff characterizes the arrangement between itself and APR as a contract for services, i.e., recycling, with the parties in a bailor/bailee relationship. APR, as the bailee, was responsible for destroying the books. After discharge of the duty to destroy, the contract price based on the remaining usable weight of paper was established and the sale of the paper consummated. Little, Brown argues that APR's sale of the books to Advantage constituted a breach of the bailment contract.

APR, conversely, avers that pursuant to their arrangement, Little, Brown sold the books to APR with the restriction that they be recycled. In APR's view, the provisions of the Uniform Commercial Code are applicable to this transaction such that upon delivery of the books by Little, Brown to APR title to the books passed to the defendant. [Citations.] APR argues that is was entitled to sell the books to Advantage. Moreover, having sold the books to Advantage under the specific terms "for cutting," APR contends that it complied with the terms of its contract with Little, Brown and, consequently, cannot be held liable for the actions of any other entities that later come into possession of the books.

* * *

Thus, it is undisputed that APR paid Little, Brown not for the value of the books as books, or for books with the restriction to recycle, but rather for the usable weight of each shipment after the books were destroyed. Indeed, the contract price could not be ascertained until after certain services had been rendered, i.e., once the book covers and bindings had been removed. It has also been stipulated that the shipments of books that APR sold to Advantage had been "consigned to APR by Little, Brown." * * *

These stipulated facts are more indicative of a bailment for mutual benefit than they are of an outright sale of the books. By definition, a bailment is:

. . . the delivery of personal property by one person to another in trust for a specific purpose, with a contract, express or implied, that the trust shall be faithfully executed, and the property returned or duly accounted for when the special purpose is accomplished, or kept until the bailor reclaims it.

[Citation.]

The arrangement between Little, Brown and APR appears to fall squarely within the quoted description. This interpretation is buttressed by other considerations.

* * *

APR conceded during oral argument that the duty to provide a certificate of destruction was nondelegable. There is a distinction to be made between the duty to provide the certificate of destruction and the duty actually to destroy. APR argues that having received certificates of destruction from entities other than APR, Little, Brown was on notice that APR had previously sold books consigned to it by Little, Brown. None of these certificates of destruction reflect a sale of books by APR to the certifying entity. Thus, it is equally plausible to infer from these documents that APR had delegated its responsibility to recycle the subject books. Such a delegation is perfectly consistent with a bailment. [Citation.] While a bailee properly may delegate to another the performance of the services required with respect to the bailed property, the bailee remains accountable to the bailor to demonstrate that the specific purpose of the trust was faithfully executed. [Citation.]

* * *

## IV. Conclusions of Law

Based upon the stipulated facts and documentary evidence, as well as the reasonable inferences to be drawn therefrom, I find that the arrangement between Little, Brown and APR pursuant to which APR would pick up books from Little, Brown for purposes of recycling was not a contract for the sale of books, but rather a contract for services. * * *

* * *

Based on all the facts and circumstances, I find that from the time APR picked up the books at Little, Brown until such time that the sale of the paper after destruction of the books was consummated, APR had possession of the books as a bailee, it being ". . . universally agreed that a bailment for hire, or for mutual benefit, arises when a chattel is delivered by its owner to another for repairs, service, or alteration." [Citation.] In this instance, APR took possession of the books in order to recycle them. Delegation of the duty to destroy is not inconsistent with a bailment in that the personal skill of APR was not necessary to perform the services. [Citation.] Others could, and in fact did, render Little, Brown books unusable. However, the fact that APR was ultimately responsible to Little, Brown for the purposes of the bailment, i.e., debinding the books, is underscored by the parties' understanding that, upon request, APR was required to provide certificates of destruction.

The law is clear that:

On creation of the ordinary bailment, the general property remains in the bailor, and the bailee has only a special interest for the express or implied objects of the bailment. Where one with legal title to property becomes the bailor thereof, the contract of bailment does not contemplate any change in that title, and it remains in the bailor.

[Citation.]

In the present case, Little, Brown as the bailor of the books retained ownership of and title to the books; APR, as the bailee, had the right to possession.

I conclude that in selling the four shipments of books to Advantage, APR breached its contract with Little, Brown.

* * *

---

## CASE 49–2
### Bailee's Right to Limit Liability
# *AMERICAN NURSERY PRODUCTS, INC. v. INDIAN WELLS ORCHARDS*

Supreme Court of Washington, 1990
115 Wash.2d 217, 707 P.2d 477

**DOLLIVER, J.**
In the fall of 1983 defendant Indian Wells Orchards decided to acquire apple trees for development of a 500-acre orchard. After contacting various commercial nurseries to grow the trees, Indian Wells entered negotiations with plaintiff American Nursery Products, Inc., doing business as Mount Arbor Nurseries (Mt. Arbor). Pursuant to preliminary discussions between the parties, Mt. Arbor drafted a proposed contract for approval by Indian Wells. After discussing the proposed contract, a revised contract was delivered to the general manager of Indian Wells during December 1983. On January 18, 1984, after reading the revised contract and reviewing it with other Indian Wells representatives, the general manager executed the contract on behalf of Indian Wells.

The entire contract consists of six pages, the last of which is exclusively devoted to signatures and arrangements on financing. It is written in normal size type and double spaced between paragraphs. The terms of the agreement include the duties of the parties, the allocation of risk, guidelines for acceptance and rejection of deliveries, and the available remedies. Under the terms of the agreement, Mt. Arbor was to grow 200,000 grafted apple trees and 500,000 budded apple trees for Indian Wells. Indian Wells was to provide the 700,000 trees for growing and Mt. Arbor was to provide up to 65,000 understocks for grafting and budding as necessary to compensate for mortality during the nursery phase. Trees produced by grafting were to be delivered in the fall of 1984 or spring of 1985, and trees produced by budding were to be delivered in the fall of 1985 or spring of 1986. By agreement of the parties, the deliveries took place in the spring of 1985 and 1986.

The parties agreed they were entering into a service agreement and no warranties, express or implied, were given which extended beyond the conditions and services in the contract. Mt. Arbor did warrant, however, that at least 88 percent of the delivered trees would have a caliper size greater than five-sixteenths of an inch. Any trees not meeting this standard could be rejected by Indian Wells.

The contract provided for a 15-day period within which Indian Wells could inspect and count the delivered trees and give notice of rejection of the delivery or adjustment to the bill of lading. In the event of rejection by Indian Wells, paragraph 5.2 provided for a limited remedy whereby "Grower [Mt. Arbor], at its option, shall replace the nonconforming Trees or reduce the purchase price."

Once the trees were accepted, the contract placed the risk of loss upon Indian Wells. Paragraph 3.4 provided:

All Trees shall be maintained by Grower in a moist condition between the time of harvest and the time of delivery to Owner [Indian Wells], after which delivery Owner accepts all maintenance responsibility for, and risk of loss to, the Trees.

The contract in section 9 entitled "Default; Remedies" further provided in paragraph 9.3:

The party declaring default shall have all rights provided under the Washington Uniform Commercial Code and other applicable laws of the State of Washington and the terms and provisions of this Agreement; provided that in no event shall Grower be subject to or liable for incidental or consequential damages. All rights and remedies of either party may be exercised consecutively, successively and cumulatively. The prevailing party shall be entitled to reimbursement for any expenses incurred by it in enforcing and protecting its rights under this Agreement, including but not limited to reasonable attorney fees and expenses.

Pursuant to the contract, the rootstocks and the budding and grafting wood were delivered by Indian Wells to Mt. Arbor. Prior to planting the grafted and the to-be-budded rootstocks in 1984, Mt. Arbor dipped the rootstocks in various fungicides and bactericides, including Ridomil 2E. Ridomil 2E is considered by its manufacturer to be an extremely erratic chemical which can, and does, cause damage to rootstocks at lesser concentrations than those used by Mt. Arbor. After the dipping in Ridomil, many of the grafted rootstocks broke and died and many of the to-be-budded rootstocks died prior to budding or failed to grow in a normal manner. Consequently, Mt. Arbor delivered only 108,158 of the 200,000 grafted trees and 372,360 of the 500,000 budded trees anticipated under the contract. Of those trees delivered, approximately 32,750 were rightfully rejected by Indian Wells. Of those accepted and planted, 89,983 later died. Indian Wells was able to cover 190,790 of the 342,215 trees short under the contract. Of the trees covered, 73,164 are 1 year behind in production.

In April 1986, Mt. Arbor brought suit against Indian Wells in the Superior Court for Yakima County to recover the sums due under the contract. Indian Wells counterclaimed alleging breach of contract and negligence.

The trial court, sitting without a jury, found the dipping of the rootstocks in Ridomil proximately caused over $2.3 million in direct and consequential damages and constituted negligence per se and a breach of contract. Over $1.7 million of these damages resulted from production losses. The damages, plus attorney fees and costs of $147,198.01, were reduced by the $383,528.44 still due under the contract, and a judgment of $2,081,854.10 was awarded to Indian Wells. In awarding these damages, the trial court held the provision in the agreement which excluded incidental and consequential damages was unconscionable, unenforceable and against public policy. We granted Mt. Arbor's appeal. We affirm in part and reverse in part.

* * *

The trial court held the exclusionary clause invalid on public policy grounds because bailees for mutual benefit are not permitted to disclaim or limit liability for negligence. The trial court, however, does not make any distinction between professional bailees and bailees for mutual benefit.

The general rule is that a party to a contract can limit liability for damages resulting from negligence. [Citation.] However, historically there are specific exceptions where limitations on liability are void as against public policy. [Citation.] One such exception prohibits professional bailees from limiting their liability for negligence. [Citation.]

It is well settled in Washington that professional bailees may not limit their liability for negligence. [Citation.] However, the scope of this exception needs delineation. The distinction between bailees for mutual benefit and professional bailments has been blurred by two Court of Appeals cases. [Citations.] These cases held that bailees for mutual benefit may not disclaim liability for negligence. However, the precedent cited for this proposition neither supports that rule nor is it the rule in this state. In [citation], we stated that Washington had adopted the general rule . . . that professional bailees cannot disclaim liability for their own negligence. The cited annotation defines professional bailees as persons who make it their principal business to act as bailees and who deal with the public on a uniform rather than on an individual basis, including primarily owners of parcel checkrooms, owners of parking places, garagemen, and warehousemen. [Citations.] Professional bailees are treated differently than other bailees because the equality of bargaining power of the two parties to the [professional bailment] contract is largely theoretical in nature while actually the bailor, being in need of the services to be rendered by the bailee and usually being in no position to take his trade elsewhere, is compelled to agree to the terms stipulated by the bailee. [Citation.] The rule in this state continues to be that professional bailees may not limit their liability for negligence; in every instance where a disclaimer of liability has been invalidated, a professional bailee was involved. [Citations.]

While professional bailments are necessarily bailments for mutual benefit, not all bailments for mutual benefit are professional bailments. [Citation.] Bailments for mutual benefit include all nongratuitous bailments and arise when both parties to the contract receive a benefit flowing from the bailment. [Citation.] The benefit to the bailee need not be in the form of cash. Rather, the benefit may derive from a bailment [which] is a mere incident to the performance of services for which the bailee receives compensation or to the conduct of a business from which the bailee derives profit, or where the bailment is motivated by the bailor's desire to promote a sale [citation].

Thus, bailments arising from a service transaction are bailments for mutual benefit. These bailees are not professional bailees and may validly contract to limit their liability for negligence.

Mt. Arbor is a large commercial nursery which contracted with Indian Wells individually to grow apple trees from rootstocks. Mt. Arbor was to receive compensation for the service performed upon the bailed goods, the rootstocks. Mt. Arbor and Indian Wells had equal bargaining strength, and Indian Wells was free to choose another commercial nursery for the needed service. Mt. Arbor was not a professional bailee; rather the bailment was an incident to the performance of services for which Mt. Arbor was to receive compensation. There is no rule prohibiting Mt. Arbor, as a bailee for mutual benefit, from contractually limiting its liability for negligence.

The question whether this exclusionary clause violates public policy is properly analyzed under the . . . standards recently set forth [in [citation]:]

[An] invalid exemption involves a transaction which exhibits some or all of the following characteristics. It concerns a business of a type generally thought suitable for public regulation. The party seeking exculpation is engaged in performing a service of great importance to the public, which is often a matter of practical necessity for some members of the public. The party holds himself out as willing to perform this service for any member of the public who seeks it, or at least for any member coming within certain established standards. As a result of the essential nature of the service, in the economic setting of the transaction, the party invoking exculpation possesses a decisive advantage of bargaining strength against any member of the public who seeks his services. In exercising a superior bargaining power the party confronts the public with a standardized adhesion contract of exculpation, and makes no provision whereby a purchaser may pay additional reasonable fees and obtain protection against negligence. Finally, as a result of the transaction, the person or property of the purchaser is placed under the control of the seller, subject to the risk of carelessness by the seller or his agents. [Citation.]

Under this test, the exclusionary clause in question is not void as a matter of public policy. Mt. Arbor did not possess a "decisive advantage of bargaining strength." [Citation.] Nor did Mt. Arbor present Indian Wells with a standard adhesion contract. Although nurseries are an important business in this state, individual members of the public do not normally require such services as a matter of practical necessity. In addition, while this transaction may put the property of Indian Wells under the control of Mt. Arbor, this characteristic is involved in every bailment and, alone, is not sufficient to void a contracted for limitation on public policy grounds. [Citation.]

* * *

We uphold the contract between American Nursery Products, Inc. and Indian Wells Orchards and affirm those damages assessed by the trial court under the terms of the contract. We find the exclusionary clause validly excludes incidental and consequential damages and reverse the award by the trial court of those damages. We remand to the trial court for further proceedings consistent with this opinion, . . . .

---

## CASE 49–3
### Liability of Carrier/Duties of Issuer of Bill of Lading
### CALVIN KLEIN LTD. v. TRYLON TRUCKING CORP.

United States Court of Appeals, Second Circuit, 1989
892 F.2d 191

MINER, J.

Defendant-appellant Trylon Trucking Corp. ("Trylon") appeals from a judgment entered on April 10, 1989 in the United States District Court for the Southern District of New York (Brieant, Ch.J.) in favor of plaintiff-appellee Calvin Klein Ltd. ("Calvin Klein") for the full value of a lost shipment of clothing. The appeal presents a novel issue under New York law: whether a limitation of liability agreement between a shipper and a carrier is enforceable when the shipment is lost as a result of the carrier's gross negligence.

The district court held that the parties' customary limitation of liability agreement did not extend to the shipment at issue, due to the absence of assent and consideration. The court observed that, had there been such an agreement, the liability of the carrier for its gross negligence would be limited. For the reasons that follow, we reverse the judgment of the district court, find that the parties agreed to the limitation of liability, and determine that the agreement limits Trylon's liability for its gross negligence.

* * *

Calvin Klein, a New York clothing company, had used the services of Trylon for at least three years, involving hundreds of shipments, prior to the lost shipment at issue. In past deliveries Calvin Klein, through its customs broker, would contact Trylon to pick up the shipment from the airport for delivery to Calvin Klein's facility. After completing the carriage, Trylon would forward to Calvin Klein an invoice, which contained a limitation of liability provision as follows:

In consideration of the rate charged, the shipper agrees that the carrier shall not be liable for more than $50.00 on any shipment accepted for delivery to one consignee unless a greater value is declared, in writing, upon receipt at time of shipment and charge for such greater value paid, or agreed to be paid, by the shipper.

A shipment of 2,833 blouses from Hong Kong arrived at John F. Kennedy International Airport for Calvin Klein on March 27, 1986. Calvin Klein arranged for Trylon to pick up the shipment and deliver it to Calvin Klein's New Jersey warehouse. On April 2, Trylon dispatched its driver, Jamahl Jefferson, to pick up this shipment. Jefferson signed a receipt for the shipment from Calvin Klein's broker. By April 2, the parties discovered that Jefferson had stolen Trylon's truck and its shipment. The shipment never was recovered. Calvin Klein sent a claim letter to Trylon for the full value of the lost blouses.

* * *

In their stipulation in lieu of a jury trial, the parties agreed that Trylon is liable to Calvin Klein for the loss of the shipment and that Trylon was grossly negligent in the hiring and supervision of Jefferson. They also agreed that "[t]he terms and conditions of [Trylon]'s carriage [were] that liability for loss or damage to cargo is limited to $50 in accordance with the legend on Trylon's invoice forms." Calvin Klein conceded that it was aware of this limitation of liability, and that it did not declare a value on the blouses at the time of shipment.

The parties left at issue whether the limitation of liability clause was valid and enforceable. Calvin Klein argued in the district court, as it does here, that the limitation clause was not enforceable for two reasons: no agreement existed between Calvin Klein and Trylon as to the limita-

tion of liability; and, if such an agreement existed, public policy would prevent its enforcement because of Trylon's gross negligence.

* * *

A common carrier, [citation], under New York law is strictly liable for the loss of goods in its custody. "Where the loss is not due to the excepted causes [that is, an act of God or of a public enemy, the inherent nature of the goods, or the shipper's fault], it is immaterial whether the carrier was negligent or not. . . ." [Citations.] Even in the case of loss from theft by third parties, liability may be imposed upon a negligent common carrier. [Citation.]

A shipper and a common carrier may contract to limit the carrier's liability in cases of loss to an amount agreed to by the parties, [citation], so long as the language of the limitation is clear, the shipper is aware of the terms of the limitation, and the shipper can change the terms by indicating the true value of the goods being shipped. U.C.C. § 7–309(2); [citations.] Such a limitation agreement is generally valid and enforceable despite carrier negligence. [Citation.] The limitation of liability provision involved here clearly provides that, at the time of delivery, the shipper may increase the limitation by written notice of the value of the goods to be delivered and by payment of a commensurately higher fee.

The parties stipulated to the fact that the $50 limitation of liability was a term and condition of carriage and that Calvin Klein was aware of that limitation. This stipulated fact removes the first issue, namely whether an agreement existed as to a liability limitation between the parties, from this case. Calvin Klein's argument that it never previously acknowledged this limitation by accepting only $50 in settlement of a larger loss does not alter this explicit stipulation. * * *

The remaining issue concerns the enforceability of the limitation clause in the light of Trylon's conceded gross negligence. The district court considered that, assuming an agreement between the parties as to Trylon's liability, Trylon's gross negligence would not avoid the enforcement of a limitation clause.

The district court found that New York law, as opposed to federal interstate commerce law, applies in this case.

* * *

Since carriers are strictly liable for loss of shipments in their custody and are insurers of these goods, the degree of carrier negligence is immaterial. [Citation.] The common carrier must exercise reasonable care in relation to the shipment in its custody. U.C.C. § 7–309(1). Carriers can contract with their shipping customers on the amount of liability each party will bear for the loss of a shipment, regardless of the degree of carrier negligence. See U.C.C. § 7–309(2) (allowing limitation of liability for losses from any cause save carrier conversion). . . . [T]he shipper can calculate the specific amount of its potential damages in advance, declare the value of the shipment based on that calculation, and pay a commensurately higher rate to carry the goods, in effect buying additional insurance from the common carrier.

In this case, Calvin Klein and Trylon were business entities with an on-going commercial relationship involving numerous carriages of Calvin Klein's goods by Trylon. Where such entities deal with each other in a commercial setting, and no special relationship exists between the parties, clear limitations between them will be enforced. [Citation.] Here, each carriage was under the same terms and conditions as the last, including a limitation of Trylon's liability. [Citation.] This is not a case in which the shipper was dealing with the common

carrier for the first time or contracting under new or changed terms. Calvin Klein was aware of the terms and was free to adjust the limitation upon a written declaration of the value of a given shipment, but failed to do so with the shipment at issue here. Since Calvin Klein failed to adjust the limitation, the limitation applies here, and no public policy that dictates otherwise can be identified.

Calvin Klein now argues that the limitation is so low as to be void. * * * This amount is immaterial because Calvin Klein had the opportunity to negotiate the amount of coverage by declaring the value of the shipment. [Citation.] Commercial entities can easily negotiate the degree of risk each party will bear and which party will bear the cost of insurance.

* * *

We reverse and remand to the district court with instructions to enter judgment against defendant in the sum of $50.

---

## CASE 49–4
### Duties of Warehousers
## I.C.C. METALS, INC. v. MUNICIPAL WAREHOUSE CO.
Court of Appeals of New York, 1980
50 N.Y.2d 657, 431 N.Y.S.2d 372, 409 N.E.2d 849

GABRIELLI, J.
[In the fall of 1974, I.C.C. Metals, Inc., delivered three lots of indium, an industrial metal, to Municipal Warehouse Company for safekeeping. The indium had an aggregate weight of 845 pounds and was worth $100,000. The warehouse supplied I.C.C. with receipts for each lot. Printed on the back of these receipts were the terms and conditions of the bailment, including an exculpatory clause limiting the liability of the warehouse to a maximum of $50.00. For two years, the warehouse billed I.C.C. for storage of the indium, and I.C.C. paid each invoice. In 1976, I.C.C. requested the return of the indium. For the first time, the warehouse told I.C.C. it was unable to locate any of the indium. I.C.C. brought an action in conversion to recover the full value of the indium. The warehouse defended on the grounds that the metal had been stolen through no fault of its own and that its liability was limited to $50.00 in accordance with the terms of the warehouse receipts.]

Absent an agreement to the contrary, a warehouse is not an insurer of goods and may not be held liable for any injury to or loss of stored property not due to some

fault upon its part (Uniform Commercial Code, § 7–204, subd. [1]). As a bailee, however, a warehouse is required both to exercise reasonable care so as to prevent loss of or damage to the property [citation] and, a fortiori, to refrain from itself converting materials left in its care [citation]. If a warehouse does not convert the goods to its own use and does exercise reasonable care, it may not be held liable for any loss of or damage to the property unless it specifically agrees to accept a higher burden. If, however, the property is lost or damaged as a result of negligence upon the part of the warehouse, it will be liable in negligence. Similarly, should a warehouse actually convert stored property to its own use, it will be liable in conversion. Hence, a warehouse which fails to redeliver goods to the person entitled to their return upon a proper demand, may be liable for either negligence or conversion, depending upon the circumstances. [Citation.]

A warehouse unable to return bailed property either because it has lost the property as a result of its negligence or because it has converted the property will be liable for the full value of the goods at the time of the loss or conversion [citations], unless the parties have agreed to limit the warehouse's potential liability. It has long been the law in this State that a warehouse, like a common carrier, may limit its liability for loss of or damage to stored goods even if the injury or loss is the result of the warehouse's negligence, so long as it provides the bailor with an opportunity to increase that potential liability by payment of a higher storage fee. [Citations.] If the warehouse converts the goods, however, strong policy considerations bar enforcement of any such limitation upon its liability. [Citations.] This rule, which has now been codified in subdivision (2) of section 7–204 of the Uniform Commercial Code, is premised on the distinction between an intentional and an unintentional tort. Although public policy will in many situations countenance voluntary prior limitations upon that liability which the law would otherwise impose upon one who acts carelessly [citations], such prior limitations may not properly be applied so as to diminish one's liability for injuries resulting from an affirmative and intentional act of misconduct (see, generally, Restatement, Torts 2d, § 500; Restatement, Contracts 2d, Tent. Draft No. 12, § 337) such as a conversion. Any other rule would encourage wrongdoing by allowing the converter to retain the difference between the value of the converted property and the limited amount of liability provided in the agreement of storage. That result would be absurd. To avoid such an anomaly, the law provides that when a warehouse converts bailed property, it thereby ceases to function as a warehouse and thus loses its entitlement to the protections afforded by the agreement of storage. [Citation.] In short, although the merely careless bailee remains a bailee and is entitled to whatever limitations of liability the bailor has agreed to, the converter forsakes his status as bailee completely and accordingly forfeits the protections of such limitations. Hence, in the instant case, whether defendant is entitled to the benefit of the liability limiting provision of the warehouse receipt turns upon whether plaintiff has proven conversion or merely negligence.

Plaintiff [I.C.C.] has proffered uncontroverted proof of delivery of the indium to defendant [Warehouse], of a proper demand for its return, and of defendant's failure to honor that demand. Defendant has failed to make a sufficient showing in support of its suggested explanation of the loss. . . . [Defendant's] unsupported claim that the metal was stolen does not suffice to raise any issue of fact on this point. Upon this record, it is beyond cavil that plaintiff would be entitled to judgment had it elected to sue defendant in negligence. [Citations.] We now hold that such a record also suffices to sustain plaintiff's action in conversion, thereby rendering inapplicable the contractual limitation upon defendant's liability.

[Judgment for I.C.C.]

## Questions

1. Discuss the essential elements of a bailment.
2. Discuss the rights and duties of the bailor and bailee.
3. Discuss the duties of an (a) warehouser, (b) common carrier, and (c) innkeeper.

4. Define a document of title. Identify and discuss the various types of documents of title.
5. Discuss the negotiability of documents of title, the rights acquired by due negotiation, and the rights acquired in the absence of due negotiation.

## Problems

1. Mercer was the owner of a herd of twenty highly bred dairy cows. He was a prosperous farmer, but his health was very poor. On the advice of his doctor, Mercer decided to winter in Arizona. Before he left, he made an agreement with Freya under which Freya was to keep the cows on her farm through the winter, pay Mercer the sum of $800, and return to Mercer the twenty cows at the close of the winter. For reasons that Freya thought made good farming sense, she sold six of the cows and replaced them with six other cows. After winter was over, Mercer returned from Arizona. When he saw that Freya had replaced six of his cows, he sued Freya for the conversion of the original six cows. Decision?

2. Hines stored her furniture, including a grand piano, in Arnett's warehouse. Needing more space, Arnett stored Hines's piano in Butler's warehouse next door. As a result of a fire, which occurred without any fault of Arnett or Butler, both warehouses and their contents were destroyed. Hines sues Arnett for the value of her piano and furniture. Decision?

3. Curtis rented a safe deposit box from Reliable Safe Deposit Company, in which he deposited valuable securities and

$4,000 in cash. Subsequently, upon opening the box and discovering that $1,000 was missing, Curtis brought an action against Reliable. At trial, the company showed that its customary procedure was as follows: that there were two keys for each box furnished to each renter; that if a key were lost, the lock was changed; that new keys were provided for each lock each time a box was rented; that there were two clerks in charge of the vault; and that one of the clerks was always present to open the box. Reliable Safe Deposit Company also proved that two keys were given to Curtis at the time he rented his box, that his box could not be opened without the use of one of the keys in his possession, and that the company had issued no other keys to Curtis's box. Decision?

**4.**   A, B, and C each stored 5,000 bushels of yellow corn in the same bin in X's warehouse. X wrongfully sold 10,000 bushels of this corn to Y. A contends that inasmuch as his 5,000 bushels of corn were placed in the bin first, the remaining 5,000 bushels belong to him. What are the rights of the parties?

**5.**   (a)   On April 1, Mary Rich, at the solicitation of Super Fur Company, delivered a $3,000 mink coat to the company at its place of business for storage in its vaults until November 1. On the same day, she paid the company its customary charge of $20 for such storage. After Mary left the store, the general manager of the company, upon finding that its storage vaults were already filled to capacity, delivered Mary's coat to Swift Trucking Company for shipment to Fur Storage Company. En route, the truck in which Mary's coat was being transported was totally damaged by fire caused by negligence on the part of the truck driver, and Mary's coat was destroyed. Is Super Fur Company liable to Mary for the value of her coat? Why?

   (b)   Would your answer be the same if Mary's coat had been safely delivered to Fur Storage Company and had been stolen from its storage vaults without negligence on its part? Why?

**6.**   Rich, a club member, left his golf clubs with Bogan, the pro at the Happy Hours Country Club, to be refinished at Bogan's pro shop. The refinisher employed by Bogan suddenly left town, taking Rich's clubs with him. The refinisher had previously been above suspicion, although Bogan had never checked on the man's character references. A valuable sand wedge, which Bogan had borrowed from another member, Smith, for his own use in an important tournament, was also stolen by the refinisher, as well as several pairs of golf shoes that Bogan had checked for members without charge as an accommodation. The club members concerned each made claims against Bogan for their losses. Can (a) Rich, (b) Smith, and (c) the other members compel Bogan to make good their respective losses?

**7.**   Bert left his automobile at Tanya's garage for repairs he and Tanya agreed would cost $125. Bert never returned to reclaim the automobile, and two months later Caldwell saw it in Tanya's garage. Caldwell claimed it as his own, asserting that it had been stolen from him. Tanya told Caldwell that he could have the automobile if he paid for the repairs and storage. Caldwell paid her, took the automobile, and disappeared. One week later, Owens appeared and proved that the automobile was hers, that it had been stolen from her, and that neither Bert nor Caldwell had any rights in it.

Owens brings an action against Tanya for conversion of the automobile. Decision?

**8.**   On June 1, Cain delivered his automobile to Barr, the operator of a repair shop, for necessary repairs. Barr put the car in his lot on Main Street. The lot, which was fenced on all sides except along Main Street, accommodated one hundred cars and was unguarded at night, although the police made periodic checks. The lot was well lighted. The cars did not have the keys in them when left out overnight. At some time during the night of June 4, the hood, starter, alternator, and gearshift were stolen from Cain's car. The car remained on the lot, and during the evening of June 5, the transmission was stolen from the car. The cost of replacing the parts stolen in the first theft was $600 and in the second theft $500.

Cain sued Barr to recover $1,100. Decision?

**9.**   Arlington in Phoenix, pursuant to a contract with Rider in New York, ships to Rider goods conforming to the contract and takes from the carrier a shipper's order bill of lading. Arlington indorses the bill of lading in blank and forwards it by mail to Clemson, his agent in New York, with instructions to deliver the bill of lading to Rider upon receipt of payment of the price for the goods. Forest, a thief, steals the bill of lading from Clemson and transfers it for value to Pace, a *bona fide* purchaser. Before the goods arrive in New York, Rider is petitioned into bankruptcy. What are the rights of the parties?

**10.**   Rutger, a Philadelphia merchant, purchased merchandise from Waters in Chicago. The contract of sale provided that the merchandise was sold F.O.B. Chicago, payment to be made sixty days after delivery. Waters delivered the goods to the railroad carrier in Chicago, took an order bill of lading in the name of Rutger, and forwarded it to Rutger. Before the goods arrived in Philadelphia, Waters learned that Rutger had become insolvent and exercised a right of stoppage in transit by proper notice to the railroad company. Thereafter, and before the shipment reached Philadelphia, Rutger indorsed and delivered the bill of lading to Lee, an innocent purchaser for value. Lee claimed the goods by reason of holding the bill of lading. To whom should the goods be awarded?

**11.**   Mrs. Laval was a patient of Dr. Leopold, a practicing psychiatrist. Dr. Leopold shared an office with two associates practicing in the same field. No receptionist or other employee attended the office. Mrs. Laval placed her coat in the clothes closet in the office reception room. Later, when she returned to retrieve the coat to leave, she found it missing. Mrs. Laval then brought this action to recover $1,725, the value of her coat. Decision? Explain.

**12.**   Robert L. Moore, a United States Army sergeant stationed at Fort Benning, Georgia, rented a fourteen-foot aluminum boat from the Fort Benning Morale Support Activities Division, Outdoor Rentals. The manager of the rentals section gave Moore general instructions concerning the use of the craft and provided Moore with a copy of the Fort Benning Boating Safety Rules. He also followed the routine procedure of examining the fuel line of the boat and starting the motor to ensure its serviceability. Three days later, while Moore was operating the boat on the Chattahoochee River, the motor stalled, forcing Moore to row the boat back to shore. Later that same day, Moore took six minor children out in the boat to give them a ride on the river. At the time, Moore's blood alcohol level was 0.29 percent, a level that would have made it "extremely difficult to do it [operate a boat] with any type of proficiency." Moore recklessly moved into the swift current and headed toward a concrete dam and spillway. When he finally reversed course, the motor stalled again, the boat was swept over the dam, and the children were drowned. Juanita Craine and Nancy Brown, parents of four of the drowned children, brought an action against the United States, claiming that the government breached its duty to warn Moore and that the government is liable as the owner of a vessel that was negligently operated. Decision?

13.    Mr. Sewall left his car in a parking lot owned by Fitz-Inn Auto Parks, Inc. The lot was approximately 100 by 200 feet in size and had a chain link fence along the rear boundary to separate the lot from a facility of the Massachusetts Bay Transportation Authority. Although the normal entrance and exit were located at the front of the lot, it was also possible to leave by way of small side streets on either side of the lot. Upon entering the lot, the driver would pay the attendant on duty a fee of twenty-five cents to park. The attendant's duties were limited to collecting money from patrons and directing them to parking spaces. Ordinarily, the attendant remained on duty until 11:00 AM, after which time the lot was left unattended. Furthermore, a patron could remove his car from the lot at any time without interference by any employee of the parking lot.

On the morning of April 15, Sewall entered the lot, paid the twenty-five cent fee, parked his car in a space designated by the attendant, locked it, and took the keys with him. This was a routine he had followed for several years. When he returned to the unattended lot that evening, however, he found that his car was gone, apparently having been stolen by an unidentified third person. He then brought this action against Fitz-Inn, the owner of the lot, to recover the value of the car. Decision?

14.    Mrs. Mieske delivered thirty-two fifty-foot reels of developed movie film to the Bartell Drug Company to be spliced together into four reels for viewing convenience. She placed the films, which contained irreplaceable pictures of her family's activities over a period of years, into the order in which they were to be spliced and then delivered them to the manager of Bartell. The manager placed a film processing packet on the bag of films and gave Mrs. Mieske a receipt that stated, "We assume no responsibility beyond retail cost of film unless otherwise agreed in writing." Although the disclaimer was not discussed, Mrs. Mieske's parting words to the store manager were "Don't lose these. They are my life."

Bartell sent the film to its processing agent, GAF Corporation, which intended to send them to another processing lab for splicing. While at the GAF laboratory, however, the film was accidentally placed in the garbage dumpster and was never recovered. Upon learning of the loss of their film, the Mieskes brought this action to recover damages from Bartell and GAF. The defendants argued that their liability was limited to the cost of the unexposed film. A jury verdict was entered for the Mieskes for $7,500, and the defendants appealed. Decision?

**Internet Exercise**  Renting an automobile and shipping a package by express transportation are both examples of a bailment. Find and compare the rates and contract provisions of (a) three automobile rental companies and (b) two express package transportation companies.

# CHAPTER 50

# Interests in Real Property

Interests in real property may be classified as possessory or nonpossessory interests. Possessory interests in real property, called **estates,** are classified to indicate the quantity, nature, and extent of the rights they involve. The two major categories are freehold estates (those existing for an indefinite time or for the life of a person) and estates less than freehold (those that exist for a predetermined time), called leasehold estates. Both freehold estates and leasehold estates are regarded as possessory interests in property. In addition, there are several nonpossessory interests in property, including easements and *profits à prendre*. In addition, a person may have a privilege or a license to go on the property for a certain purpose. The ownership of an interest in property may be held by one individual or concurrently by two or more persons, each of whom is entitled to an undivided interest in the entire property. This chapter will consider these topics.

## FREEHOLD ESTATES

As stated above, a **freehold estate** is a right of ownership of real property for an indefinite time or for the life of a person. Of all the estates in real property, the most valuable usually are those estates that combine the enjoyment of immediate possession with ownership at least for life. These estates are either some form of fee estates or estates for life. In addition, either type of estate may be created without immediate right to possession; such an estate is known as a future interest.

### Fee Estates

**Fee estates** include the right to immediate possession for an indefinite time and the right to transfer the interest by deed or will. Fee estates include both fee simple and qualified fee estates.

*Fee Simple* When a person says that he has "bought" a house or a corporation informs its shareholders that it has "purchased" an industrial site, the property generally is held in fee simple. **Fee simple** means that the property is owned absolutely and can be sold or passed on at will. The absolute rights to transfer ownership and to transmit that ownership through inheritance are basic characteristics of a fee simple estate. The estate signifies full control over the property, which can be sold or disposed of as desired. Fee simple is the most extensive and comprehensive estate in land; all other estates are derived from it.

A fee simple is created by any words that indicate an intent to convey absolute ownership. "To B in fee simple" will accomplish this, as will "To B forever." The general presumption is that a conveyance is intended to convey full and absolute title in the absence of a clear intent to the contrary. The grantor must possess, or have the right to transfer, a fee simple interest in order to transfer such an interest.

*Qualified or Base Fee* It is possible to convey or will property to a person to enjoy absolutely, subject to its being taken away at a later date should a certain event occur. The estate thus created is known as a **qualified fee,** base fee, conditional fee, or fee simple defeasible. For example, Abe may provide in his will that his daughter is to have his house and lot in "fee simple forever so long as she does not use it to sell alcoholic beverages, in which case the house shall revert to Abe's estate." If his daughter dies without using the house to sell alcoholic beverages, the property is transferred to her heirs as though she owned it absolutely. If, however, Abe's daughter uses the house to sell alcoholic beverages, the daughter would lose her title to the land, and it would revert to Abe's heirs.

The holder of a qualified fee interest may transfer the property by deed or will, and the property will pass by intestate succession. All transferees, however, take the property subject to the initial condition imposed upon the interest.

## Life Estates

A grant or a devise (grant by will) "to Alex for life" creates in Alex an estate that terminates on his death. Such a provision may stand alone, in which case the property will revert to the grantor and his heirs; or, as is more likely, it will be followed by a subsequent grant to another party, such as "to Alex for life and then to Benjamin and his heirs." Alex is the **life tenant,** and Benjamin is generally described as the **remainderman.** Alex's life, however, need not be the measure of his life estate, as where an estate is granted "to Alex for the life of Dale." Upon Dale's death, Alex's interest terminates; if Alex dies before Dale, Alex's interest passes to his heirs or as he directs in his will for the remainder of Dale's life. Thus, a **life estate** is an ownership right in property for the life of a designated individual, while a **remainder** is the ownership estate that takes effect when a prior life estate terminates.

No particular words are necessary to create a life estate, so long as the words chosen clearly reflect the intent of the grantor. Life estates arise most frequently in connection with the creation of trusts, a subject considered in Chapter 52.

Generally, a life tenant may make reasonable use of the property as long as he does not commit "waste." Any act or omission that permanently injures the realty or unreasonably changes its characteristics or value constitutes **waste.** For example, failing to repair a building, cutting timber excessively without replanting, or neglecting to observe adequate conservation techniques may subject the life tenant to an action by the remainderman to recover damages for waste.

A conveyance by the life tenant passes only her interest. The life tenant and the remainderman may, however, join in a conveyance to pass the entire fee to the property, or the life tenant may terminate her interest by conveying it to the remainderman.

## Future Interests

Not every interest in property carries the right to immediate possession, even though the right and title to the interest are absolute. Thus, where property is conveyed or devised by will "to Anderson during his life and then to Brown and her heirs," Brown has a definite presently existing *interest* in the property, but she is not entitled to immediate *possession.* This right and similar rights, generically referred to as **future interests,** are of two principal types: reversions and remainders.

*Reversions* If Anderson conveys property "to Brown for life" and makes no disposition of the remainder of the estate, Anderson holds the **reversion**—the grantor's right to the property upon the death of the life tenant. Thus, Anderson would regain ownership to the property when Brown dies. Furthermore, because the grantor has only to allow his grantee's estate to expire before he may regain ownership, a reversion in Anderson also is created if he conveys property "to Caldwell for ten years." Reversions may be transferred by deed or will and pass by intestate succession.

A **possibility of reverter,** or a conditional reversionary interest, exists where property *may* return to the grantor or his successor in interest because an event upon which a fee simple estate was to terminate has occurred. This potential for reversion is present in the grant of a base or qualified fee, previously discussed in this chapter. Thus, Ellen has a possibility of reverter if she dedicates property to a public use "so long as it is used as a park" and indicates that if it is not so used it will revert to her heirs. If, in one hundred years, the city ceases to use the property for a park, Ellen's heirs would be entitled to the property. A possibility of a reverter may pass by will or intestate succession. In some States, it may be transferred by deed.

*Remainders* A remainder, as discussed earlier, is an estate in property that, like a reversion, will take effect in possession, if at all, upon the termination of a prior estate created by the *same instrument.* Unlike a reversion, a remainder is held by a person other than the grantor or his successors. A grant from Gwen to "William for his life and then to Charles and his heirs" creates a remainder in Charles. Upon the termination of the life estate, Charles will be entitled to possession as remainderman, taking his title not from William but from the original grantor, Gwen. Remainders are of two kinds: vested remainders and contingent remainders.

A **vested remainder** is one in which the only contingency to possession by the remainderman is the termination of all preceding estates created by the transferor. When Jalen has a remainder in fee, subject only to a life estate in Carol, the only obstacle to the right of immediate possession by Jalen or his heirs is Carol's life. Carol's death is sufficient and necessary to place Jalen in possession. The law considers this unconditional or vested remainder as a fixed, present interest to be enjoyed in the future. Such an interest in property is just as transferable as the life estate that precedes it, and it is characteristic of a vested remainder that the owner of the preceding estate can do nothing to defeat the remainder.

A **contingent remainder,** by comparison, is one in which the right to possession is dependent or conditional on the happening of some event in addition to the termination of the preceding estates. The contingent remainder may be conditioned on the existence of some person not yet born or on the happening of an event that may never occur. A provision in a will "to Sandy for life and then to her children, but if she has no children then to Douglas" creates contingent remainders both as to the children and as to Douglas. If Sandy marries and has a child, the remainder then vests in that child, and Douglas's expectancy is closed out. If Sandy dies without having had a child, then and only then will an estate vest in Douglas. It is, of course, possible for a contingent remainder to become vested while possession is still in the preceding life estate, as evidenced by the birth of a child to Sandy in the above example. In most States, a contingent remainder is transferable by deed. It also is inheritable, unless by limitation it terminates before the death of the remainderman.

◆ *See Figure 50–1*

## LEASEHOLD ESTATES

A lease is both a contract and a conveyance of an estate in land. It is a contract by which the owner of the land, the **landlord,** grants to another, the **tenant,** an exclusive right to use and possession of the land for a definite or ascertainable time, or term. The possessory term thus granted is an estate in land called a **leasehold.** The landlord retains an interest in the property, called a *reversion*. A leasehold estate has two principal characteristics: it continues for a definite or ascertainable term and carries with it the tenant's obligation to pay rent to the landlord. Thus, if Linda, the owner of a house and lot, rents both to Ted for a year, Linda, of course, retains the title to the property, but she has sold to Ted the right to occupy it. During the term of the lease, Ted's right to occupy the property is superior to that of Linda, and as long as he occupies in accordance with the lease contract, he has, as a practical matter, exclusive possession against all the world as though he were the actual owner.

The law of leasehold estates has changed considerably over the past few decades. Traditionally, the common law viewed a leasehold estate less as a contract than as a conveyance of the use of land. Today, the landlord–tenant relationship is primarily viewed as a contract and therefore subject to the contract doctrines of unconscionability, implied warranties, and constructive conditions.

**FIGURE 50–1** Freehold Estates

| Interest | Complementary Estate | Duration | Transfer by Deed | Transfer by Will or Intestacy |
|---|---|---|---|---|
| **Fee Simple** | None | Perpetual | Yes | Yes |
| **Qualified Fee** | Possibility of a reverter | Until contingency occurs | Yes | Yes |
| **Life Estate** | Reversion or remainder | Life of indicated person | Yes | No, unless measuring life is not life tenant's |
| **Reversion** | Life estate | Perpetual | Yes | Yes |
| **Possibility of Reverter** | Qualified fee | Perpetual if contingency occurs | In some States | Yes |
| **Vested Remainder** | Life estate | Perpetual | Yes | Yes |
| **Contingent Remainder** | Life estate | Perpetual if contingency occurs | In most States | Yes, unless by limitation it terminates before the death of the remainderman |

Moreover, numerous ordinances and statutes, such as the Uniform Residential Landlord and Tenant Act enacted by a number of States, now protect tenants' rights, thereby further modifying the landlord–tenant relationship.

## Creation and Duration

Because they are created by contract, the usual requirements for contract formation apply to leaseholds. In most jurisdictions, leases for a term longer than a statutorily specified period, generally fixed at either one or three years, must be in writing. A few States require that all leases be in writing.

*Definite Term* A lease for a definite term automatically expires at the end of the term. Such a lease is frequently termed an estate for years, even though its duration may be one year or less. No notice to terminate is required.

*Periodic Tenancy* A **periodic tenancy** is a lease of indefinite duration that continues for successive periods unless one party terminates it by notice to the other. For example, a lease to Ted "from month to month" or "from year to year" creates a periodic tenancy. Periodic tenancies arise frequently by implication. If Laura leases to Ted without stating any term in the lease, this creates a tenancy at will. If, moreover, Ted pays rent to Laura at the beginning of each month and Laura accepts such payments, most courts would hold that the tenancy at will has been transformed into a tenancy from month to month.

Either party may terminate a periodic tenancy at the expiration of any one period, but only upon adequate notice to the other party. In the absence of an express agreement in the lease, the common law requires six months' notice in tenancies from year to year. In most jurisdictions, this period has been shortened by statute to periods ranging between thirty and ninety days. In periodic tenancies involving periods of less than one year, the notice required at common law is one full period in advance, but, again, this requirement may be subject to statutory regulation.

*Tenancy at Will* A lease containing a provision that either party may terminate at any time creates a tenancy at will. A lease that does not specify duration likewise creates a tenancy at will. At common law, such tenancies were terminable without any prior notice, but many jurisdictions now have statutes requiring a period of notice before termination, usually thirty days.

*Tenancy at Sufferance* A tenancy at sufferance arises when a tenant fails to vacate the premises at the expiration of the lease and thereby becomes a holdover tenant. The common law gives the landlord the right to elect either to dispossess such tenant or to hold her for another term. Until the landlord makes this election, a tenancy at sufferance exists.

## Transfer of Interests

Both the tenant's possessory interest in the leasehold and the landlord's reversionary interest in the property may be freely transferred in the absence of contractual or statutory prohibition. This general rule is subject to one major exception: the tenancy at will. Any attempt by either party to transfer her interest is usually considered an expression of the intent to terminate the tenancy.

*Transfers by Landlord* After conveying the leasehold interest, a landlord is left with a reversionary interest in the property plus the right to rent and other benefits acquired under the lease. The landlord may transfer either or both of these interests. The party to whom the reversion is transferred takes the property subject to the tenant's leasehold interest, if the transferee has actual *or* constructive notice of the lease. For example, Linda leases Whiteacre to Tina for five years, and Tina records the lease with the register of deeds. Linda then sells Whiteacre to Arthur. Tina's lease is still valid and enforceable against Arthur, whose right to possession of Whiteacre begins only after the lease expires.

*Transfers by Tenant* A tenant may dispose of his interest either by (1) assignment or (2) sublease, and in the absence of a lease provision, she may do both. As a result, most standard leases expressly require the consent of the landlord to an assignment or subletting of the premises. Under the majority view, a covenant against assignment of a lease does not prohibit the tenant from subleasing the premises. Conversely, a prohibition against subleasing is not considered a restriction upon the right to assign the lease.

If a tenant transfers *all* his interest in a leasehold, thereby forfeiting his reversionary rights, he has made an **assignment.** Many leases prohibit assignment without the landlord's written consent.

If the tenant assigns the lease without consent, the assignment is not void, but it may be avoided by the landlord. In other words, the prohibition of assignment in a lease is solely for the landlord's benefit; the assignor, therefore, cannot rely upon the prohibition in attempting to terminate an otherwise valid assignment on the ground that the landlord did not consent. If, however, the landlord accepts rent from the assignee, he will be held to have waived the restriction.

The tenant's agreement to pay rent and other contractual **covenants** (express promises) pass to and obligate the assignee of the lease as long as the assignee remains in possession of the leasehold estate. Although the assignee is thus bound to pay rent, the original tenant is not thereby relieved of his contractual obligation to do so. If the assignee fails to pay the stipulated rent, the original tenant will have to pay, though he will have a right to be reimbursed by the assignee. Thus, after an assignment of a tenant's interest, both the original tenant and the assignee are liable to the landlord for failure to pay rent.

A **sublease** differs from an assignment in that the tenant transfers *less* than all of her rights in the lease and thereby retains a reversion in the leasehold. For example, Mary is a tenant under a lease from Leon which is to terminate on December 31, 1999. If Mary leases the premises to Tony for a period shorter than that covered by her own lease, e.g., until November 30, 1999, Mary has subleased the premises because she has transferred less than her whole interest in the lease.

The legal effects of a sublease are entirely different from those of an assignment. In a sublease, the sublessee (Tony, in the example above) has no obligation to Mary's landlord, Leon. Tony's obligations run solely to Mary, the original tenant, and Mary is not relieved of any of her obligations under the lease. Thus, Leon has no right of action against Mary's sublessee, Tony, under any covenants contained in the original lease between him and Mary because that lease has not been assigned to Tony. Mary, of course, remains liable to Leon for the rent and for all other covenants in the original lease.

◆ *See Figure 50–2*

## Tenant's Obligations

While the leasehold estate carries with it only an implied obligation on the part of the tenant to pay reasonable rent, the lease contract almost always contains an express promise or covenant by the tenant to pay rent in specified amounts at specified times. In the absence of a specific covenant providing the amount of rental and the times for payment, the rent will be a *reasonable* amount *payable only at the end of the term.*

Most leases provide that if the tenant breaches any of the covenants in the lease, the landlord may declare the lease at an end and regain possession of the premises. The tenant's express undertaking to pay rent thus becomes one of the covenants upon which this provision

**FIGURE 50–2** Assignment Compared with Sublease

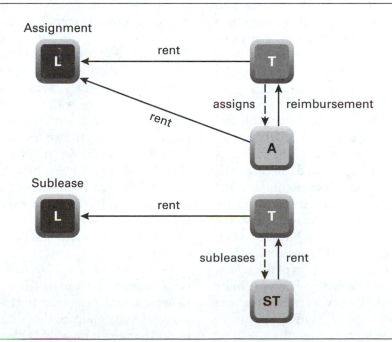

can operate. Where the lease makes no such provision, at common law the tenant's failure to pay rent when due gives the landlord only the right to recover a judgment for the amount of such rent; it gives him no right to oust the tenant from the premises. In most jurisdictions, however, the common law rule has been changed by statute to entitle the landlord to dispossess the tenant for nonpayment of rent, even if the lease does not provide for such action.

Unless the lease contains express provisions to the contrary, a tenant is under no duty to make any repairs to the leased premises. He is not obliged to repair or restore substantial or extraordinary damage occurring without his fault, nor must he repair damage caused by ordinary wear and tear. The tenant is obliged, however, to use the premises in a manner that causes them no substantial injury. The law imposes this duty; it need not be expressly stipulated in the lease. For example, a tenant who overloads an electrical connection, thereby damaging a wiring system, is liable to the landlord.

### Destruction of the Premises

The dual character of a lease as a contract and as a grant of an estate in land is particularly evident with regard to the common law rule governing the destruction of premises by fire or other cause. Where the tenant leases land together with a building, and the building is destroyed by fire or some other adverse cause, the common law neither relieves him of his obligation to pay rent nor permits him to terminate the lease. In most States, however, the common law rule has been modified by statute to exclude tenants who occupy only a portion of a building and who have no interest in the building as a whole, such as apartment tenants. Most leases contain clauses covering the accidental destruction of the premises.

### Eviction

When the tenant breaches one of the covenants in her lease, such as the covenant to pay rent, and the landlord evicts or dispossesses her pursuant to an express provision in the lease or under a statute authorizing her to do so, the lease is terminated. Because the breach of the covenant to pay rent does not involve any injury to the premises and because the landlord's action in evicting the tenant terminates the lease, the evicted tenant is not liable to the landlord for any future installments of rent. Most long-term leases, however, contain a *survival clause* providing that the eviction of the tenant for nonpayment of rent will not relieve her of liability for damages equal to the difference between the rent reserved in the lease and the rent the landlord is able to obtain when reletting the premises.

If the landlord wrongfully evicts the tenant, the tenant's obligations under the lease are terminated, and, as discussed below, the landlord is liable for breach of the tenant's right of quiet enjoyment.

### Abandonment

If the tenant wrongfully abandons the premises before the term of the lease expires, and the landlord reenters the premises or relets them to another, a majority of the courts hold that the tenant's obligation to pay rent after reentry terminates. The landlord, if he desires to hold the tenant to his obligation to pay rent, either must leave the premises vacant or must have in the lease another "survival clause" that covers this situation.

## Landlord's Obligations

Under the Fair Housing Act, a landlord cannot discriminate against a tenant with regard to race, color, sex, religion, national origin, or familial status (except under the housing for older persons exception). Nevertheless, absent express provisions in the lease, the landlord, under the common law, has few obligations to her tenant. Under the majority (American) rule, at the beginning of the lease, she has only to give the tenant the right to possession. In a minority of States (the English rule), she has to give actual possession. Thus, in States following the American rule, if the previous tenant refuses to move out when his lease terminates, the landlord must bring dispossession proceedings to oust him; she is not responsible to the new tenant for the delay thus brought about, and the new tenant is not relieved of the obligation to pay rent from the starting date of the lease.

### Quiet Enjoyment

The landlord may not interfere with the tenant's right to physical possession, use, and enjoyment of the premises. Rather, the landlord is bound to provide the tenant with quiet and peaceful enjoyment, a duty known as the covenant of **quiet enjoyment.** The landlord breaches this covenant, which arises by implication, whenever he wrongfully evicts the tenant. He is also regarded as having breached this covenant if the tenant is evicted by someone having better title to the property than the landlord has. The landlord is not responsible, however, for the wrongful acts of third parties unless they are done with his assent and under his direction.

Eviction need not be actual. Under the doctrine of **constructive eviction,** a failure by the landlord in any of her undertakings under the lease that causes a substantial and lasting injury to the tenant's beneficial enjoyment of the premises is regarded as being, in effect, an eviction of the tenant. Under such circumstances, the courts permit the tenant to abandon the premises and terminate the lease. The tenant must abandon possession within a reasonable time, however, in order to claim that a constructive eviction occurred.

 *See Case 50–1*

**Fitness for Use** Historically, as the primary value of the lease to the tenant was the land, the landlord, under the common law, is under no obligation to provide or maintain the premises in a tenantable (livable) condition or to make them fit for any purpose, unless there is a specific provision in the lease. Most States, however, have abandoned this rule in residential leases by imposing an **implied warranty of habitability** that requires the leased premises to be fit for ordinary residential purposes. These courts also have held that the covenant to pay rent is conditioned upon the landlord's performance of this implied warranty of habitability. Courts reaching these results have emphasized that the tenant's interest is in a place to live, not merely in land. The common law assumption that the value of the leasehold is the land may have been valid in an agricultural society and may continue to be valid with regard to certain farm leases, but it is not applicable in the case of a modern apartment rental.

A number of States have statutes requiring landlords to keep residential premises fit for occupation. Zoning ordinances, health and safety regulations, and building and housing codes may also impose certain duties upon the landlord.

If the landlord violates the warranty of habitability, the tenant may terminate the lease and avoid further liability for rent and in some States withhold rent and sue for damages.

 *See Case 50–2*

**Repair** Under the common law, in the absence of an express provision in the lease or a statutory duty to do so, the landlord has no obligation to repair or restore the premises. The landlord does, however, have a duty to maintain, repair, and keep in safe condition those portions of the premises that remain under her control. For example, an apartment house owner who controls the lobbies, stairways, elevators, and other common areas of the building is liable for their maintenance and repair and is responsible for injuries that occur as a result of her failure to do so. With respect to apartment buildings, the courts presume that any portion of the premises that is not expressly leased to the tenants remains under the

landlord's control. Thus, the landlord, in such cases, is liable to make external repairs, including repairs to the roof.

While at common law in a number of States the landlord is under no duty to repair, restore, or keep the premises in a tenantable condition, she may and often does assume those duties in the lease. Her breach of any such undertakings does not, however, entitle the tenant to abandon the premises and refuse to pay rent. Unless an express provision in the lease gives the tenant this right, the common law allows him only an action for damages. As mentioned above, a number of States now have statutes that require the landlord to keep residential premises fit for occupancy and accordingly have imposed upon the landlord a duty to repair those items.

**Landlord's Liability for Injury Caused by Third Parties** Chapter 7 discusses the duties and tort liabilities of a landlord to a tenant for defects in common areas and for failure to disclose hidden defects in the rented premises of which the landlord knew or should have known. Under the common law, a landlord also was liable if he did not exercise reasonable care in repairing such defects. Today, by statute or judicial decision, many States are requiring landlords to maintain leased premises in good repair and are holding them liable for a negligent failure to do so.

Some States hold landlords liable for injuries their tenants and others suffer as a result of the foreseeable criminal conduct of third parties. Although landlords cannot be insurers of their tenants' safety, courts have held landlords liable for failure "to take minimal precautions to protect members of the public from the reasonably foreseeable criminal acts of third persons." *Ianelli v. Powers*, 498 N.Y.S.2d 377 (N.Y. App. Div. 1986).

## CONCURRENT OWNERSHIP

Property may be owned by one individual or by two or more persons concurrently. Two or more persons who hold title concurrently are generally referred to as **co-tenants**. Each is entitled to an undivided interest in the entire property, and neither has a claim to any specific portion of it. Each may have equal undivided interests, or one may have a larger undivided share than the other. Regardless of the particular relationships between the co-tenants, this form of ownership is distinct from the separate ownership of specific parts of property by different persons. Thus, Anne, Barbara, and Carol each may own separate parts of Blackstone Manor, or each may own, as a co-tenant, an undivided one-third interest in all of Blackstone Manor. Their being co-tenants or the owners of specific portions depends on the manner and form in which they acquired their interests.

The two major types of concurrent ownership are tenancy in common and joint tenancy. Both provide an undivided interest in the whole, the right of both tenants to possession, and the right of either to sell his interest during life and thus terminate the original relationship. Other forms of co-ownership of real estate are tenancy by the entireties, community property, condominiums, and cooperatives.

## Tenancy in Common

Under a **tenancy in common,** the most frequently used form of concurrent ownership, each co-owner has both an undivided interest in the property and the right to possession and use, but none claims any specific portion of the property. Tenants in common need not have acquired their interests at the same time or by the same instrument, and their interests may differ as to duration and scope. Because there is no right of survivorship, the interests of tenants in common may be devised by will or pass by intestate succession. By statute in all States, a transfer of title to two or more persons is presumed to create a tenancy in common. Tenants in common may terminate their tenancy either by transferring all of their co-interests to one person or by partitioning the property among themselves. **Partition** is the act of physically dividing the property and thereby changing undivided interests into smaller parcels that each person owns individually. The size of an individual parcel is based upon the size of the owner's prior share of the undivided interest. If physical division of the property (e.g., a house) is not practicable, the property will be sold and the proceeds divided.

## Joint Tenancy

The most significant feature of joint tenancy is the right of *survivorship*: upon the death of a joint tenant, title to the entire property passes by operation of law to the survivor or survivors. Neither the heirs of the deceased joint tenant nor his general creditors have a claim to his interest after his death, and a joint tenant cannot transfer his interest by executing a will. Nevertheless, a joint tenant may sever the tenancy by conveying or mortgaging his interest to a third party. Further, the interest of either co-tenant is subject to levy and sale upon execution. To sever a joint tenancy is to forfeit the right of survivorship: following severance, the tenancy becomes

a tenancy in common among the remaining joint tenants and the transferee. A joint tenancy may be terminated by partitioning the property among the tenants, making each the exclusive owner of a specific part of the entire property.

To sustain a **joint tenancy,** the common law requires the presence of what are known as the *four unities* of time, title, interest, and possession.

1. The unity of time means that the interests of all tenants must vest at the same time;
2. the unity of title means that all tenants must acquire title by the same instrument;
3. the unity of interest means that the tenants' interests must be identical in duration and scope; and
4. the unity of possession means that the tenants have identical rights of possession and enjoyment.

While the absence of any unity will prevent the creation of a joint tenancy, the presence of the fourth unity and any two of the others will result in the creation of a tenancy in common, because the only unity required of a tenancy in common is the unity of possession.

 *See Case 50–3*

## Tenancy by the Entireties

**Tenancy by the entireties,** which is recognized in some States, is created only by a conveyance to a *husband and wife*. It is distinguished from joint tenancy by the inability of either spouse to convey separately his or her interest during life and thus destroy the right of survivorship. Likewise, the interest of either spouse cannot be attached by creditors. By the nature of the tenancy, divorce would terminate the relationship, and partition would then be available as a method of creating separate interests in the property.

◆ *See Figure 50–3*

## Community Property

In Arizona, California, Idaho, Louisiana, Nevada, New Mexico, Puerto Rico, Texas, Washington, and Wisconsin, one-half of any property acquired by either a husband or wife belongs to each spouse. Originating in the civil law of continental Europe, this system, known as **community property**, has been modified by United States common law and by statutes as well.

In most instances, the only property belonging separately to either spouse is that acquired prior to the marriage or acquired subsequent to it by gift or devise. Upon

FIGURE 50–3  Rights of Concurrent Owners

| | Undivided Interest | Right to Possession | Right to Sell | Right to Mortgage | Levy by Creditors | Right to Will | Right of Survivorship |
|---|---|---|---|---|---|---|---|
| **Joint Tenancy** | Yes | Yes | Yes | Yes | Yes | No | Yes |
| **Tenancy in Common** | Yes | Yes | Yes | Yes | Yes | Yes | No |
| **Tenancy by Entireties** | Yes | Yes | No | No | No | No | Yes |

the death of either spouse, one-half of the community property belongs outright to the survivor, and the interest of the deceased spouse in the other half may go to the heirs of the decedent or as directed by will. Under certain conditions in a few jurisdictions, however, the surviving spouse may also claim an interest in the decedent's one-half share of the property.

## Condominiums

Condominiums embody a form of co-ownership now widely utilized in the United States. All States have enacted statutes authorizing this form of ownership. The purchaser of a condominium acquires separate ownership to the unit and becomes a tenant in common with respect to its common facilities, such as the land upon which the project is built, recreational facilities, hallways, parking areas, and spaces between the units. The common elements are maintained by a condominium association funded by assessments levied on each unit. The transfer of a condominium conveys both the separate ownership of the unit and the share in the common elements.

## Cooperatives

Cooperatives involve an indirect form of common ownership. A cooperative, usually a corporation, purchases or constructs the dwelling units and then leases the units to its shareholders as tenants, who acquire the right to use and occupy their units.

## *NONPOSSESSORY INTERESTS*

Although a nonpossessory interest in land entitles the holder to use the land or to take something from it, the interest does not give him the right to possess the land. Nonpossessory interests include easements, *profits à prendre,* and licenses.

## Definition of Easements

An **easement** is a limited right to use the land of another in a manner specified by the acts of the parties or by operation of law and possessing all the attributes of an estate in the land itself. For example, a typical easement exists where Liz sells part of her land to Neal and expressly provides in the same or a separate document that Neal, as the adjoining landowner, shall have a right-of-way over a strip of Liz's remaining parcel of land. Neal's land is said to be the **dominant** parcel (land whose owner has rights in other land), and Liz's land, which is subject to the easement, is the **servient** parcel. Easements may, of course, involve a multitude of different uses, as, for example, a right to run a ditch across another's land, to lay pipe under the surface, to erect power lines, or, in the case of adjacent buildings, to use a stairway or a common or "party" wall.

Because the owner of the entire servient tract retains the title to the servient parcel, she may make any use of or allow others the use of the tract as long as this use does not interfere with the easement. Thus, crops may be grown over an easement for a pipeline, but livestock cannot be pastured on an easement for a driveway. Although the owner of the servient parcel is under a duty not to interfere with the use of the easement, the owner of the dominant parcel generally is responsible for maintaining the easement and keeping it in repair.

## Types of Easements

Easements fall into two classes: appurtenant easements and easements in gross. **Appurtenant easements** are by far the more common type; the rights and duties they create pertain to the land itself, not to the individuals who have created such easements. Therefore, the easement usually stays with the land when it is sold. For example, if Liz (from the previous example) sells her servient parcel to Kyle, who has actual notice of the easement for the benefit of Neal's land or constructive notice by means of the local recording act, Kyle takes the parcel subject to the easement. Likewise, if Neal conveys his dominant parcel to Daniel, the deed from Neal to Daniel need contain no specific reference to the easement to give to Daniel, as the dominant parcel's new owner, the right to use the right-of-way over the servient parcel. As Neal does not then own the dominant parcel, he has no further right to use the right-of-way. Neal could not, however, transfer the benefit of the easement to a party who did not acquire an interest in the dominant parcel of land. Most frequently, a deed conveying certain land "together with all appurtenances" is sufficient to transfer an easement. This characteristic of an appurtenant easement is described by the statement that both the burden and the benefit of an appurtenant easement pass with the land.

The second type of easement is an **easement in gross,** which is personal to the particular individual who receives the right. It, in effect, amounts to little more than an irrevocable personal right to use.

 *See Case 50–4*

## Creation of Easements

Easements may be created by (1) express grant or reservation, (2) implied grant or reservation, (3) necessity, (4) dedication, and (5) prescription.

*Express Grant or Reservation*  The most common way to create an easement is to convey it by deed. For example, when Amy conveys part of her land to Robert, she may, in the same deed, expressly grant him an easement over her remaining property. Alternatively, Amy may grant an easement to Robert in a separate document. This document must comply with all the formalities of a deed. An easement is an interest in land subject to the statute of frauds.

In other instances, when an owner transfers land, she may wish to retain certain rights in it. In the example given, Amy may want to "reserve" over the land she grants to Robert an easement in favor of the land she retains. Amy may reserve this right by express words in the deed of conveyance to Robert.

*Implied Grant or Reservation*  Easements by implied grant or implied reservation arise whenever an owner of adjacent properties establishes an *apparent* and *permanent* use in the nature of an easement and then conveys one of the properties without mention of any easement. For example, suppose that Andrew owns two adjacent lots, Nos. 1 and 2. There is a house on each lot. Behind each house is a garage. Andrew has constructed a driveway along the boundary between the two lots, partly on lot 1 and partly on lot 2, which leads from the street in front of the houses to the two garages in the rear. Andrew conveys lot 2 to Michael without any mention of the driveway. Andrew is held to have *impliedly granted* an easement to Michael over the portion of the driveway that lies on Andrew's lot 1, and he is held to have *impliedly reserved* an easement over the portion of the driveway that lies on Michael's lot 2.

*Necessity*  If Sharon conveys part of her land to Terry, and the part conveyed to Terry is so situated that he would have no access to it except across Sharon's remaining land, the law implies a grant by Sharon to Terry of an easement by necessity across her remaining land. An easement by necessity usually will not arise if an alternative, albeit circuitous, approach to the land is available.

An easement by necessity may also arise by implied reservation. This would be the case where Sharon conveys part of her land to Terry, and her remaining property would be wholly landlocked unless she were given a right-of-way across the land conveyed to Terry.

*Dedication*  When an owner of land subdivides it into lots and records the plan or plat of the subdivision, she is held, both by common law and now more frequently by statute, to have dedicated *to the public* all of the streets, alleys, parks, playgrounds, and beaches shown on the plat. In addition, when the subdivider sells the lots by reference to the plat, it is now generally recognized that the purchasers acquire easements by implication over the areas shown to be dedicated to the public.

*Prescription*  An easement may arise by prescription in most States if certain required conditions are met. To obtain an easement by prescription, a person must use a portion of land owned by another in a way (1) that is adverse to the rightful owner's use, (2) that is open and notorious, and (3) that continues, uninterrupted, for a specific period that varies from State to State. The claimant acquires no easement by prescription, however, if given the owner's permission to use the land.

## Profits à Prendre

The French phrase *profit à prendre* describes the right to remove the produce of another's land. An example would be the grant by Jack to Roger, an adjoining landowner, of the right to remove coal, fish, or timber from

Jack's land or to graze his cattle on Jack's land. Like an easement, a *profit à prendre* may arise by prescription, but if it comes about through an act of the parties, it must be created with all the formalities accorded the grant of an estate in real property. Unless the right is clearly designated as exclusive, the owner of the land is entitled to exercise it as well. Furthermore, even one who does not own adjacent land may hold the right to take profits. Thus, Norman may have a right to remove crushed gravel from John's acreage even though Norman lives in another part of the county.

## Licenses

Real interests in property such as easements or *profits à prendre* are considered interests in land. On the other hand, a license, which is created by a contract granting permission to make use of an owner's land, does not create an interest in the property. A license is usually exercised only at the will of the owner and subject to revocation by him at any time. For example, if Carter tells Karen she may cut across Carter's land to pick hickory nuts, Karen has nothing but a license subject to revocation at any time. It is possible that, upon the basis of a license, Karen may expend funds to exercise the right, and the courts may prevent Carter from revoking the license simply because it would be unfair to penalize Karen under the circumstances. In such a case, Karen's interest is practically indistinguishable from an easement.

A common example of a license is a theatre ticket or the use of a hotel room. No interest is acquired in the premises; there is simply a right of use for a given length of time, subject to good behavior. No formality is required to create a license; a shopkeeper licenses persons to enter his establishment merely by being open for business.

 **Chapter Summary**

| **Freehold Estates** | **Fee Estates** right to immediate possession of real property for an indefinite time |
|---|---|
| | • *Fee Simple* absolute ownership of property |
| | • *Qualified Fee* ownership subject to its being taken away upon the happening of an event |
| | **Life Estates** ownership right in property for the life of a designated person, while remainder is the ownership estate that takes effect when the prior estate terminates |
| | **Future Interests** |
| | • *Reversion* grantor's right to property upon termination of another estate |
| | • *Remainders* are of two kinds: vested remainders (unconditional remainder that is a fixed, present interest to be enjoyed in the future) and contingent remainders (remainder interest conditional upon the happening of an event in addition to the termination of the preceding estate) |

| **Leasehold Estates** | **Lease** both (1) a contract for use and possession of land and (2) a grant of an estate in land |
|---|---|
| | • *Landlord* owner of land who grants a leasehold interest to another while retaining a reversionary interest in the property |
| | • *Tenant* possessor of the leasehold interest in the land |
| | **Duration of Leases** |
| | • *Definite Term* lease that automatically expires at the end of the term |
| | • *Periodic Tenancy* lease consisting of specific terms that continue in indefinite succession |
| | • *Tenancy at Will* lease that is terminable at any time |
| | • *Tenancy at Sufferance* possession of real property without a lease |

**Transfer of Tenant's Interest**
- *Assignment* transfer of all of the tenant's interest in the leasehold
- *Sublease* transfer of less than all of the tenant's interest in the leasehold

**Tenant's Obligations** the tenant has an obligation to pay a specified rent at specified times or, if none is specified, to pay a reasonable amount at the end of the term
- *Destruction of the Premises* under the common law, if the premises are destroyed the tenant is not relieved of his obligation to pay rent and cannot terminate the lease
- *Eviction* if the tenant breaches one of the covenants of her lease, the landlord may terminate the lease and evict (remove) her from the premises
- *Abandonment* if tenant abandons property and the landlord reenters or relets it, tenant's obligation to pay rent terminates

**Landlord's Obligations**
- *Quiet Enjoyment* the right of the tenant to have physical possession of the premises free of landlord interference
- *Fitness for Use* most courts impose for residential leases an implied warranty of habitability that the leased premises are fit for ordinary residential purposes
- *Repair* unless there is a statute or a specific provision in the lease, the landlord has no duty to repair or restore the premises

## Concurrent Ownership

**Tenancy in Common** co-ownership in which each tenant holds an undivided interest with no right of survivorship

**Joint Tenancy** co-ownership with the right of survivorship; requires the presence of the four unities (time, title, interest, and possession)

**Tenancy by the Entireties** co-ownership by spouses in which neither may convey his or her interest during life

**Community Property** spouses' rights in property acquired by the other during their marriage

**Condominium** separate ownership of an individual unit with tenancy in common with respect to common areas

**Cooperative** the corporate owner of the property leases units to its shareholders as tenants

## Nonpossessory Interests

**Easement** limited right to use the land of another in a specified manner
- *Appurtenant* rights and duties created by the easement pertain to and run with the land of the owner of the easement (dominant parcel) and the land subject to the easement (servient parcel)
- *In Gross* rights and duties created by the easement are personal to the individual who received the right
- *Creation of Easements* easements may be created by (1) express grant or reservation, (2) implied grant or reservation, (3) necessity, (4) dedication, and (5) prescription (adverse use)

**Profits à Prendre** right to remove produce from the land of another

**Licenses** permission to use the land of another

# Cases

### CASE 50–1
## Constructive Eviction
## *HOME RENTALS CORP. v. CURTIS*
Appellate Court of Illinois, Fifth District, 1992
236 Ill.App.3d 994, 176 Ill.Dec. 913

HARRISON, J.

Plaintiff, Home Rentals Corporation (Home Rentals), appeals from a judgment of the circuit court of Jackson County which denied its claim for money damages for breach of a residential lease and awarded defendants, Chris Curtis, Ed Domaracki, Mike Fraser, and Carson Flugstad, the sum of $1980 plus costs on their counterclaim for constructive eviction. We affirm.

The record . . . established that Home Rentals owns approximately 300 rental properties, including a single-family residence located at 512 S. Beveridge near Southern Illinois University in Carbondale. Home Rentals agreed to rent the Beveridge house to the four defendants in this action, each of whom was a student at SIU. The terms of the agreement were governed by a written lease signed on behalf of Home Rentals by its president, Henry Fisher, in February of 1989. The lease was to commence on August 17, 1989, and to expire on August 13, 1990. Rent was fixed at $740 per month, and a $500 damage deposit was required. By payments made in April, May and June, defendants gave Home Rentals a total of $1980 to cover the damage deposit plus advance rent for the last two months of the lease term.

Under the lease defendants were to receive the premises "in good order and repair." While there is no dispute that the house was in acceptable condition when the lease was signed in February, the record established that the situation had changed drastically by the time defendants attempted to take possession six months later. The first to reach the scene was Mike Fraser, who arrived in Carbondale from his home in northern Illinois on August 15. At that time the electricity had not yet been turned on, and he was not able to view the premises during daylight hours until Wednesday, August 16. What Fraser found then was a house that was not fit for human habitation.

Roaches had overrun the rooms. The kitchen was so filthy and so infested by bugs that food could not be stored there. The living room carpet smelled, and one could actually see outside through holes in the wall around the frame of the front door. The bathrooms were unsanitary, and when the water was turned on the following day, August 17, Fraser discovered that not one of the toilets in the building worked. He also discovered that one of the bathtubs did not drain at all, while another drained only slowly, and that bathroom waste water drained directly onto the floor of the basement. In attempting to explain this open drain at trial, Henry Fisher tried to assert that it was simply part of the washing machine hookup. As evidence that this was laundry-related, he pointed to white matter on the basement floor by the drain which he claimed was spilled laundry detergent. Other evidence indicated, however, that the white matter was, in fact, a mass of roach eggs.

As the remaining defendants began to arrive for the start of school, they found the same conditions discovered by Fraser. They and their friends described those conditions to the court at trial, and photographs depicting the squalid conditions were admitted into evidence. Fraser testified that he spoke with Fisher at Home Rentals on the 16th and told him that the place was uninhabitable because of the filth and the roaches. Fisher's response was to suggest that the students buy roach bombs and cleaning supplies to take care of the problems themselves, although he did offer to reimburse them for those items and represented that he would arrange to have an exterminator spray.

Fraser contacted Home Rentals again the following day after discovering the plumbing problems. Fraser notified the company of those problems, complained again about the overall dirtiness of the house, and reported that the roach problem was even more severe than originally thought. This time he was told by the secretary that someone would be sent to "check it out." By the time the lease term commenced the following day, however, defendants were still waiting for a Home Rentals representative to visit.

Hopeful that the situation might somehow be salvaged, defendants spent several days attempting on their own to make the house liveable. Although an exterminator finally appeared on Friday, August 18, or Saturday, August 19, the problem of roach infestation continued, and Home Rentals did nothing about the dirt or plumbing problems. The condition of the house was so bad that defendants were never able to spend the night there. Henry Fisher himself admitted that he would not have moved in either, at least not until after the exterminator had sprayed and the dead roaches were removed. The closest defendants came to occupying the premises was when they unloaded some of their personal property from the rental truck they were using so that the truck could be returned on time.

On Monday, August 21, defendants finally gave up. They packed up their property and sought housing elsewhere. While this was happening, someone from Home Rentals appeared at last with a plunger, presumably to work on the toilets, but by this time defendants' patience was exhausted. They went to the Home Rentals office, advised that they would not be living in the house, and returned the keys. They also reported the condition of the house to the City of Carbondale's Code Enforcement Division.

Following an inspection on August 23, 1989, the Code Enforcement Division notified Home Rentals that it had found numerous violations of the City's codes and ordinances. These included open sewers in the basement, the open waste water drain from the upstairs bathroom, unclean and unsanitary conditions in the first and second floor kitchens and bathrooms, severe roach infestation, a "stopped up" lavatory basin, no smoke detectors, a broken window, a large hole in the wall, a structurally unsound handrail by the steps to the second floor, and various exterior surfaces which were in need of painting. The notice of violations, dated August 25, 1989, warned Home Rentals that "due to the severe nature of the violations * * * and the potential hazard they create to the health, safety and welfare of anyone occupying the structure in its present condition," the house would be deemed "unfit for human habitation" pursuant to the Carbondale Revised Code and would be posted "occupancy prohibited" unless all cited violations were corrected within 72 hours.

By August 28, 1989, 11 days after defendant's lease was to have commenced, Home Rentals finally remedied all of the violations found by the City, with the exception of the exterior painting. Although the City apparently then withdrew its threat to prohibit further occupancy, Home Rentals did not rent the property out to anyone else. Instead, it brought this action against defendants for breach of the lease. For its damages, Home Rentals claimed the sum of $6900, representing the rent due for all 12 months under the lease, less the two months' advance rent defendants had already paid as part of their deposit. Home Rentals also asked for its costs and attorney fees of $2300.

Defendants denied Home Rentals' allegations and raised as affirmative defenses breach of implied warranty of habitability and constructive eviction. Based on the theory of constructive eviction, they also asserted a counterclaim seeking return of the $500 damage deposit and $1480 in advance rent they had previously paid to Home Rentals. * * *

* * *

A constructive eviction occurs where a landlord has done "something of a grave and permanent character with the intention of depriving the tenant of enjoyment of the premises." [Citation.] Because persons are presumed to intend the natural and probable consequences of their acts, constructive eviction does not require a finding that the landlord had the express intention to compel a tenant to leave the demised premises or to deprive him of their beneficial enjoyment. All that is necessary is that the landlord committed acts or omissions which rendered the leased premises useless to the tenant or deprived the tenant of the possession and enjoyment of the premises, in whole or part, making it necessary for the tenant to move. * * *

At oral argument, counsel for Home Rentals asserted that defendants did what they did simply because "the premises did not meet their expectations." The inference, of course, was that defendants were overly particular and that their expectations were unrealistic. It is scarcely unreasonable, however, for tenants paying $740 per month to expect flushing toilets, sewage-free basements, and kitchens that are not overrun with roaches. These are things that Home Rentals failed to provide. What Home Rentals did provide was a house that was clearly and unquestionably unfit for people to live in. As a result, defendants had no alternative but to vacate the premises.

Home Rentals correctly points out that a tenant may not abandon premises under the theory of constructive eviction without first affording the lessor a reasonable opportunity to correct the defects in the property [citation], but such an opportunity existed here. Home Rentals' president, Henry Fisher, admitted that he actually inspected the premises as early as August 13. * * *

Considering the magnitude of the problems, four days was opportunity enough for Home Rentals to act. Constructive eviction has been found in analogous circumstances where an even shorter period was involved. [Citation.] We note, moreover, that there is no indication that giving Home Rentals additional time would have made any difference. In the four days before defendants left, the only action the company took at all was to send someone out to spray for bugs, which did not work, and to dispatch a man with a plunger. In the end, it was only because of the intervention by the City of Carbondale that Home Rentals implemented the necessary remedial measures.

* * *

For the foregoing reasons, the judgment of the circuit court of Jackson County is affirmed.

Affirmed.

---

### CASE 50–2
## Warranty of Habitability
# *JAVINS v. FIRST NATIONAL REALTY CORP.*

United States Court of Appeals, District of Columbia Circuit, 1970
428 F.2d 1071

WRIGHT, J.

These cases present the question whether housing code violations which arise during the term of a lease have any effect upon the tenant's obligation to pay rent. The Landlord and Tenant Branch of the District of Columbia Court of General Sessions ruled proof of such violations inadmissible when proffered as a defense to an eviction action for nonpayment of rent. The District of Columbia Court of Appeals upheld this ruling. [Citation.]

Because of the importance of the question presented, we granted appellants' petitions for leave to appeal. We now reverse and hold that a warranty of habitability, measured by the standards set out in the Housing Regulations for the District of Columbia, is implied by operation of law into leases of urban dwelling units covered by those Regulations and that breach of this warranty gives rise to the usual remedies for breach of contract.

The facts revealed by the record are simple. By separate written leases, each of the appellants rented an apartment in a three-building apartment complex in Northwest Washington known as Clifton Terrace. The landlord, First National Realty Corporation, filed separate actions in the Landlord and Tenant Branch of the Court of General Sessions on April 8, 1966, seeking possession on the ground that each of the appellants had defaulted in the payment of rent due for the month of April. The tenants, appellants here, admitted that they had not paid the landlord any rent for April. However, they alleged numerous violations of the Housing Regulations as "an equitable defense of [a] claim by way of recoupment or set-off in an amount equal to the rent claim," as provided in the rules of the Court of General Sessions. They offered to prove

[t]hat there are approximately 1500 violations of the Housing Regulations of the District of Columbia in the building

at Clifton Terrace, where Defendant resides some affecting the premises of this Defendant directly, others indirectly, and all tending to establish a course of conduct of violation of the Housing Regulations to the damage of Defendants. . . .

[Citation.] Appellants conceded at trial, however, that this offer of proof reached only violations which had arisen since the term of the lease had commenced.

* * *

Since, in traditional analysis, a lease was the conveyance of an interest in land, courts have usually utilized the special rules governing real property transactions to resolve controversies involving leases. However, as the Supreme Court has noted in another context, "the body of private property law . . . , more than almost any other branch of law, has been shaped by distinctions whose validity is largely historical." Courts have a duty to reappraise old doctrines in the light of the facts and values of contemporary life—particularly old common law doctrines which the courts themselves created and developed. * * *

The assumption of landlord-tenant law, derived from feudal property law, that a lease primarily conveyed to the tenant an interest in land may have been reasonable in a rural, agrarian society; it may continue to be reasonable in some leases involving farming or commercial land. In these cases, the value of the lease to the tenant is the land itself. But in the case of the modern apartment dweller, the value of the lease is that it gives him a place to live. The city dweller who seeks to lease an apartment on the third floor of a tenement has little interest in the land 30 or 40 feet below, or even in the bare right to possession within the four walls of his apartment. When American city dwellers, both rich and poor, seek "shelter" today, they seek a well known package of goods and services—a package which includes not merely walls and ceilings, but also adequate heat, light and ventilation, serviceable plumbing facilities, secure windows and doors, proper sanitation, and proper maintenance.

\* \* \*

Ironically, however, the rules governing the construction and interpretation of "predominantly contractual" obligations in leases have too often remained rooted in old property law.

Some courts have realized that certain of the old rules of property law governing leases are inappropriate for today's transactions. In order to reach results more in accord with the legitimate expectations of the parties and the standard of the community, courts have been gradually introducing more modern precepts of contract law in interpreting leases. \* \* \*

In our judgment the trend toward treating leases as contracts is wise and well considered. \* \* \*

Modern contract law has recognized that the buyer of goods and services in an industrialized society must rely upon the skill and honesty of the supplier to assure that goods and services purchased are of adequate quality. In interpreting most contracts, courts have sought to protect the legitimate expectations of the buyer and have steadily widened the seller's responsibility for the quality of goods and services through implied warranties of fitness and merchantability.

\* \* \*

The rigid doctrines of real property law have tended to inhibit the application of implied warranties to transactions involving real estate. Now, however, courts have begun to hold sellers and developers of real property responsible for the quality of their product. For example, builders of new homes have recently been held liable to purchasers for improper construction on the ground that the builders had breached an implied warranty of fitness. In other cases courts have held builders of new homes liable for breach of an implied warranty that all local building regulations had been complied with. And following the developments in other areas, very recent decisions and commentary suggest the possible extension of liability to parties other than the immediate seller for improper construction of residential real estate.

Despite this trend in the sale of real estate, many courts have been unwilling to imply warranties of quality, specifically a warranty of habitability, into leases of apartments. Recent decisions have offered no convincing explanation for their refusal; rather they have relied without discussion upon the old common law rule that the lessor is not obligated to repair unless he covenants to do so in the written lease contract. \* \* \* In our judgment,

the old no-repair rule cannot coexist with the obligations imposed on the landlord by a typical modern housing code, and must be abandoned in favor of an implied warranty of habitability. In the District of Columbia, the standards of this warranty are set out in the Housing Regulations.

In our judgment the common law itself must recognize the landlord's obligation to keep his premises in a habitable condition.

\* \* \*

Today's urban tenants, the vast majority of whom live in multiple dwelling houses, are interested, not in the land, but solely in "a house suitable for occupation." Furthermore, today's city dweller usually has a single, specialized skill unrelated to maintenance work; he is unable to make repairs, like the "jack-of-all-trades" farmer who was the common law's model of the lessee. Further, unlike his agrarian predecessor who often remained on one piece of land for his entire life, urban tenants today are more mobile than ever before. A tenant's tenure in a specific apartment will often not be sufficient to justify efforts at repairs. In addition, the increasing complexity of today's dwellings renders them much more difficult to repair than the structures of earlier times. In a multiple dwelling, repair may require access to equipment and areas in control of the landlord. Low and middle income tenants, even if they were interested in making repairs, would be unable to obtain any financing for major repairs since they have no long-term interest in the property.

\* \* \*

Since a lease contract specifies a particular period of time during which the tenant has a right to use his apartment for shelter, he may legitimately expect that the apartment will be fit for habitation for the time period for which it is rented. We point out that in the present cases there is no allegation that appellants' [lessees'] apartments were in poor condition or in violation of the housing code at the commencement of the leases. Since the lessees continue to pay the same rent, they were entitled to expect that the landlord would continue to keep the premises in their beginning condition during the lease term. It is precisely such expectations that the law now recognizes as deserving of formal, legal protection.

\* \* \*

We follow the Illinois court in holding that the housing code must be read into housing contracts—a holding also required by the purposes and the structure of the code itself. The duties imposed by the Housing Regulations may not be waived or shifted by agreement if the Regulations specifically place the duty upon the lessor.

\* \* \*

In the present cases, the landlord sued for possession for nonpayment of rent. Under contract principles, however, the tenant's obligation to pay rent is dependent upon the landlord's performance of his obligations, including his warranty to maintain the premises in habitable condition.

\* \* \*

The judgment of the District of Columbia Court of Appeals is reversed and the cases are remanded for further proceedings consistent with this opinion.

---

## CASE 50–3
## Concurrent Ownership
## *ESTATE OF GULLEDGE*
District of Columbia Court of Appeals, 1996
673 A.2d 1278

SCHWELB, J.

The issue in these related appeals is whether the unilateral transfer by one of two joint tenants of his interest to a third party, without the consent of the other joint tenant, converts the joint tenancy into a tenancy in common. We hold that it does.

### I

The dispositive facts are undisputed. Clayton and Margie Gulledge owned a house at 532 Somerset Place, N.W. (the Somerset property) as tenants by the entirety. They had three children—Bernis Gulledge, Johnsie Walker, and Marion Watkins. Margie Gulledge died in 1970. Clayton Gulledge remarried the following year, but his second marriage was apparently unsuccessful.

In order to avert the possible loss, in any divorce proceedings, of the Somerset property, Bernis Gulledge advanced to his father the funds necessary to satisfy the second Mrs. Gulledge's financial demands. In exchange, Clayton Gulledge created a joint tenancy in the Somerset property, naming Bernis and himself as joint tenants. Bernis evidently expected that his father would predecease him, and that the right of survivorship which is the essence of a joint tenancy would enable him to acquire the entire property upon his father's death.

In 1988, however, Clayton Gulledge conveyed his interest in the Somerset property to his daughter, Marion Watkins, "in fee simple tenants in common." In 1991, Clayton Gulledge died, and he was survived by his three children. Bernis Gulledge died in 1993 and Johnsie B. Walker died in 1994. In the now consolidated proceedings relating to the estates of Clayton Gulledge, Bernis Gulledge, and Johnsie Walker, appellant Deborah Walker, Bernis' personal representative, claims that when Clayton died, Bernis, as the surviving joint tenant, became the sole owner of the Somerset property. Ms. Watkins, on the other hand, contends that Clayton Gulledge's earlier conveyance of his interest to her severed the joint tenancy, thereby destroying Clayton's right of survivorship, and that Ms. Watkins and Bernis became tenants in common. The trial court agreed with Ms. Watkins. We affirm.

### II

The parties agree that Clayton Gulledge's interest in the joint tenancy was alienable. They disagree only as to the nature of the interest which Clayton transferred to Ms. Watkins. The Estate of Bernis Gulledge (the Estate) argues that an owner cannot convey to a third party a greater interest than his own, [citation], and that because Clayton Gulledge's interest was subject to Bernis' right of survivorship, the interest which Ms. Watkins received from Clayton must be similarly restricted. Ms. Watkins contends, on the other hand, that Clayton's conveyance to her converted the joint tenancy into a tenancy in common by operation of law, and that she received from Clayton an undivided one-half interest in the property.

The question whether a joint tenant severs a joint tenancy by ultimately conveying his interest to a third party without the consent of the other joint tenant has not been squarely decided in the District of Columbia. \* \* \* The applicable rule in a large majority of jurisdictions is that either party to a joint tenancy may sever that tenancy by unilaterally disposing of his interest, that the consent of the other tenant is not required, and that the transfer converts the estate into a tenancy in common. [Citations.]

Although no decision by a court in this jurisdiction is directly on point, the discussion of joint tenancy that can be found in District of Columbia cases is consistent with the majority approach. In [citation], the court explained that "[j]oint tenancy cannot exist unless there be present unity of interest, title, time and possession; that is to say, the interests must be identical, they must accrue by the same conveyance, they must commence at the same time and the estate must be held by the same undivided possession." The interests of Bernis Gulledge and Marion Watkins were not created by the same conveyance, nor did they commence at the same time; the conveyance to Ms. Watkins thus destroyed the unities of title and time. [Citation.]

* * *

Although the foregoing authorities do not conclusively settle the question before us, they provide no support for the notion that this court should reject the majority rule. Moreover, "[b]ecause District of Columbia law is derived from Maryland law, decisions of the Court of Appeals of Maryland, and particularly those relating to the law of property, are accorded the most respectful consideration by our courts." [Citation.] Under Maryland law, the transfer of an interest in a joint tenancy by either joint tenant "will sever the joint tenancy and cause the share conveyed to become property held as tenants in common with the other co-tenants." [Citation.] We adopt the same rule here.

* * *

Affirmed.

---

## CASE 50–4
## Types of Easements
### BORTON v. FOREST HILLS COUNTRY CLUB
Missouri Court of Appeals, Eastern District, Division Five, 1996
926 S.W. 232

AHRENS, J.
Plaintiffs, Gene and Deborah Borton, appeal from the trial court's grant of summary judgment in favor of defendant, Forest Hills Country Club on plaintiffs' claims for injunctive relief and money damages due to golf balls hit onto their property from defendant's golf course. Plaintiffs also appeal from the summary judgment in favor of defendant on its counterclaim asserting it had gained an easement allowing its members to hit errant golf balls onto plaintiffs' property. We reverse and remand.

The developer of defendant's golf course began to sell lots for residential use adjacent to the golf course in 1963. The developer filed and recorded a set of deed restrictions on all the residential lots adjacent to the golf course in November, 1963. Paragraph 11 of these deed restrictions recites:

All owners and occupants of any lot in the Forest Hills Club Estates Subdivision shall extend to one person, in a group of members or guests playing a normal game of golf on the Forest Hills Golf and Country Club, or their caddy, the courtesy of allowing such person or caddy the privilege of retrieving any and all errant golf balls which may have landed or remained on any lot in the subdivision. However, care shall be exercised in the retrieving of such golf ball to prevent damage to any lawn, flowers, shrubbery, or other improvement on the lot.

Plaintiffs purchased a residence adjacent to the fairway on the eleventh hole on defendant's golf course in March, 1994. The general warranty deed to plaintiffs provided that the property was subject to the set of deed restrictions and covenants. Because of the proximity of the tee boxes on the eleventh hole to plaintiffs' home, thousands of errant golf balls have been hit onto plaintiffs' property since they purchased their residence.

* * *

Plaintiffs concede that paragraph 11 of the deed restriction gives defendant and its members some right with respect to retrieving errant golf balls. Plaintiffs argue, however, that the right created in paragraph 11 is simply a license. Defendant contends it has an easement over the Borton's property, either by express grant via paragraph 11 in the deed restriction or by prescription.

Both a license and easement give the grantee the right to go onto the grantor's property for a limited use. [Citations.] A license is a personal right and as such, may be revoked at the will of the licensor. [Citation.] An easement, by contrast, gives the grantee an interest in the property of the grantor and thus runs with the land and is binding upon successive landowners. [Citations.]

In the instant case, since the original developer of the property properly recorded and filed the deed restrictions, those restrictions created property interests that run with the land and are binding on successive landowners. [Citations.] Thus, plaintiffs do not have the power to revoke or modify the rights granted to defendant in paragraph 11 of the deed restrictions. Therefore, the deed restrictions in paragraph 11 are in the nature of an easement in favor of defendant and its members to retrieve errant golf balls hit onto plaintiffs' property during a normal game of golf.

\* \* \*

Since the terms of paragraph 11 are binding upon the parties and run with the land, we hold that defendant was granted an express easement by paragraph 11 of the deed restrictions.

\* \* \*

Plaintiffs may recover \* \* \* if they can demonstrate that defendant's current use of the easement constitutes a greater burden to their land than what was contemplated or intended. [Citations.] The defendant did not address plaintiffs' [claims] in its cross motion for summary judgment, and did not submit summary judgment facts to demonstrate that there is no material issue of fact in dispute as to this issue. Thus, the trial court's dismissal of plaintiffs' [claim] was premature and must be reversed.

The trial court's judgment granting defendant an easement over plaintiffs' property is reversed with instructions to enter judgment that defendant was granted an express easement by paragraph 11 of the deed restrictions. The trial court's dismissal of plaintiffs' [claim] is reversed and remanded for further proceedings.

---

# Questions

1.  Define and discuss the following freehold interests: (a) fee simple, (b) qualified fee, (c) life estate, (d) remainder interest, and (e) reversionary interest.
2.  Distinguish between a vested and a contingent remainder.
3.  Discuss the primary rights and obligations of landlords and tenants.

4.  Identify and discuss the various forms of concurrent ownership of real property.
5.  Identify and discuss the various ways in which an easement may be created.

---

# Problems

1.  Kirkland conveyed a farm to Adland to have and to hold for and during his life and upon his death to Rubin. Some years thereafter, oil was discovered in the vicinity. Adland thereupon made an oil and gas lease, and the oil company set up its machinery to commence drilling operations. Rubin thereupon filed suit to enjoin the operations. Assuming an injunction to be the proper form of remedy, what decision?
2.  Smith owned Blackacre in fee simple absolute. In section 3 of a properly executed will, Smith devised Blackacre as follows: "I devise my farm Blackacre to my son Darwin so long as it is used as a farm." Sections 5 and 6 of the will made gifts to persons other than Darwin. The last and residuary clause of Smith's will provided: "All the residue of my real and personal property not disposed of heretofore in this will, I devise and bequeath to Stanford University."

Smith died in 1999, survived by her son Darwin. Smith's estate has been administered. Darwin has been offered $100,000 for Blackacre if he can convey title to it in fee simple. What interests in Blackacre were created by Smith's will?
3.  Panessi leased to Barnes for a term of ten years beginning May 1 certain premises located at 527–529 Main Street in Cleveland. The premises were improved with a three-story building, the first floor being occupied by stores and the upper stories by apartments. On May 1 of the following year, Barnes leased one of the apartments to Charles for one year. On July 5, a fire destroyed the second and third floors of the building. The first floor was not burned but was rendered untenantable. Neither the lease from Panessi to Barnes nor the lease from Barnes to Charles contained any provision in regard to the fire loss. Discuss the liability of Barnes and Charles to continue to pay rent.
4.  Ames leased an apartment to Boor at $200 a month, payable the last day of each month. The term of the written lease was from January 1, 1998 through April 30, 1999. On March 15, 1998, Boor moved out, telling Ames that he disliked all the other tenants. Ames replied, "Well, you're no prize as a tenant; I probably can get more rent from someone more agreeable." Ames and Boor then had a minor physical altercation in which neither was injured. Boor sent the apartment keys to Ames by mail. Ames wrote Boor, "It will be my pleasure to hold you for every penny you owe me. I am renting the apartment on your behalf to Clay until April 30, 1999 at $175

a month." Boor had paid his rent through February 28, 1998. Clay entered the premises on April 1, 1998.

How much rent, if any, may Ames recover from Boor?

**5.** Jay signed a two-year lease containing a clause that expressly prohibited subletting. After six months, Jay asked the landlord for permission to sublet the apartment for one year. The landlord refused. This angered Jay, and he immediately assigned his right under the lease to Kay. Kay was a distinguished gentleman, and Jay knew that everyone would consider him a desirable tenant. Is Jay's assignment of his lease to Kay valid?

**6.** In 1990, Roy Martin and his wife, Alice, their son, Hiram, and Hiram's wife, Myrna acquired title to a 240-acre farm. The deed ran to Roy Martin and Alice Martin, the father and mother, as joint tenants with the right of survivorship, and to Hiram Martin and Myrna Martin, the son and his wife, as joint tenants with the right of survivorship. Alice Martin died in 1995, and in 1998, Roy Martin married Agnes Martin. By his will, Roy Martin bequeathed and devised his entire estate to Agnes Martin. When Roy Martin died in 2000, Hiram and Myrna Martin assumed complete control of the farm.

State the interest in the farm, if any, of Agnes, Hiram, and Myrna Martin immediately upon the death of Roy Martin.

**7.** In her will, Teressa granted a life estate to Ames in certain real estate, with remainder to Brenda and Clive in joint tenancy. All the residue of Teressa's estate was left to Hillman College. While going to Teressa's funeral, the car in which Ames, Brenda, and Clive were driving was wrecked. Brenda was killed instantly, Clive died a few minutes later, and Ames died on his way to the hospital. Who is entitled to the real estate in question?

**8.** Otis Olson, the owner of two adjoining city lots, A and B, built a house on each. He laid a drainpipe from lot B across lot A to the main sewer pipe under the alley beyond lot A. Olson then sold and conveyed lot A to Fred Ford. The deed, which made no mention of the drainpipe, was promptly recorded. Ford had no actual knowledge or notice of the drainpipe, although it would have been apparent to anyone inspecting the premises because it was only partially buried. Later, Olson sold and conveyed lot B to Luke Lane. This deed also made no reference to the drainpipe and was promptly recorded.

A few weeks thereafter Ford discovered the drainpipe across lot A and removed it. Did he have the right to do so?

**9.** At the time of his marriage to Ann, Robert owned several parcels of real estate in joint tenancy with his brother, Sam. During his marriage, Robert purchased a house and put the title in his name and his wife's name as joint tenants, not as tenants in common. Robert died; within a month of his death, Smith obtained a judgment against the estate of Robert. What are the relative rights of Sam, Smith, and Ann?

**10.** In 1972, Ogle was the owner of two adjoining lots numbered 6 and 7 fronting at the north on a city street. In that year, she laid out and built a concrete driveway along and two feet in front of what she erroneously believed to be the west boundary of lot 7. Ogle used the driveway for access to buildings situated at the southern end of both lots. Later in 1972, she conveyed lot 7 to Dale, and thereafter in the same year she conveyed lot 6 to Pace. Neither deed made any reference to the driveway, and after the conveyance, Dale used it exclusively for access to lot 7. In 2000, a survey by Pace established that the driveway encroached six inches on lot 6, and he brought an appropriate action to establish his lawful ownership of the strip upon which the driveway approaches, to enjoin its use by Dale, and to require Dale to remove the overlap. Decision?

**11.** Temco, Inc., conveyed to the Wynns certain property adjoining an apartment complex being developed by Sonnett Realty Company. Although nothing to this effect was contained in the deed, the sales contract gave the purchaser of the property use of the apartment's swimming pool. Temco's sales agent also emphasized that use of the pool would be a desirable feature in the event that the Wynns decided to sell the property.

Seven years later, the Bunns contracted to buy the property from the Wynns through the latter's agent, Sonnett Realty. Although both the Wynns and Sonnett Realty's agent told the Bunns that the use of the apartment's pool went with the purchased property, neither the contract nor the deed subsequently conveyed to the Bunns so provided. When the Bunns requested pool access passes from Temco and Offutt, the company that owned the apartments, their request was refused. The Bunns then brought this action. Decision?

**12.** On January 1, Mrs. Irene Kern leased an apartment from Colonial Court Apartments, Inc., for a one-year term. When the lease was entered into, Mrs. Kern asked for a quiet apartment, and Colonial assured her that the assigned apartment was in a quiet, well-insulated building. In fact, however, the apartment above Mrs. Kern's was occupied by a young couple, the Lindgrens. From the start of her occupancy, Mrs. Kern complained of their twice-weekly parties and other actions that so disturbed her sleep that she had to go elsewhere for rest. After Mrs. Kern had lodged several complaints, Colonial terminated the Lindgrens' lease effective February 28. The termination of the lease was prolonged, however, and Mrs. Kern vacated her apartment, claiming that she was no longer able to endure the continued disturbances. Colonial then brought this action to recover rent owed by Mrs. Kern. Decision?

**13.** On June 30, 1989, Martin Hendrickson and Solveig Hendrickson were married, and on January 3, 1990, a home previously owned by Martin was conveyed to them as joint tenants and not as tenants in common. No part of the consideration for the premises was paid by Mrs. Hendrickson.

On August 3, 1997, Martin Hendrickson duly executed a Declaration of Election to Sever Survivorship of Joint Tenancy by which he endeavored to preserve an interest in the premises for Ruth Halbert, appellant, his daughter by a previous marriage. On the same day, he executed his last will and testament, by the terms of which he directed that his wife, Solveig M. Hendrickson, receive the minimum amount to which she was entitled under the laws of the State of Minnesota. Mr. Hendrickson died testate on October 9, 1997. Decision?

**14.** In 1955 a deed for land in Pitt County was executed and delivered by Joel and Louisa Tyson "unto M. H. Jackson and wife Maggie Jackson, for and during the term of their natural lives and after their death to the children of the said M. H. Jackson and Maggie Jackson that shall be born to their inter-marriage as shall survive them to them and their heirs and assigns in fee simple forever." Thelma Jackson Vester, a daughter of M. H. and Maggie Jackson, died in 1997, survived by three children. M. H. Jackson, who survived his wife, Maggie Jackson, died in 1998, survived by four sons. The children of Thelma Jackson Vester brought this action against M. P. Jackson, a son of and executor of the will of M. H. Jackson. The children of Vester contended that through their deceased mother they were entitled to one-fifth interest in the land conveyed by the deed of 1955. The executor contended that the deed conveyed a contingent remainder and only those children who survived the parents took an interest in the land. The trial court granted the executor's demurrer to the complaint for its failure to state a cause of action. Decision?

**15.** Robert and Majorie Wake owned land that they used as both a cattle ranch and a farm. Each spring and autumn, the Wakes would drive their cattle from the ranch portion of the operation across an access road on the farmland to Butler Springs, which was also on the farmland.

In December 1976, the Wakes sold the farm to Jesse and Maud Hess but retained for themselves a right-of-way over the farm access road and the right to use Butler Springs for watering their livestock. In 1983, the Hesses sold the farm to the Johnsons, granting them uninterrupted possession of the property "excepting only that permissive use of the premises" owned by the Wakes.

The Wakes continued to use the access road and Butler Springs until 1984, when they sold their ranch and granted the new owners "their rights to the water of Butler Springs," but they said nothing about the access road. The ranch was subsequently sold several times and all the owners used the access road and watering hole. In 1998, the Nelsons purchased the ranch. Shortly thereafter, the Johnsons notified the Nelsons that they had revoked the Nelsons' right to use the access road and Butler Springs. In 1999, the Johnsons closed the access road by locking the gates across the road. The Nelsons brought this action, claiming easements to both the access road and Butler Springs. The trial court ruled in favor of the Nelsons, and the Johnsons appealed. Decision?

**WWW** **Internet Exercise** Find and explore information about the rights of residential tenants.

# CHAPTER 51

# Transfer and Control of Real Property

The law has always been, and still is, extremely cautious about the transfer of title to real estate. Personal property may, for the most part, be passed from owner to owner easily and informally, but real property can be transferred only through compliance with a variety of formalities. Such protocol is apparent in the transfer of property at death, where strict formalities are relaxed only with respect to personal property; it is most evident in a transfer of land during the owner's lifetime.

Title to land may be transferred in three principal ways: (1) by deed; (2) by will or by the law of descent upon the death of the owner; and (3) by open, continuous, and adverse possession by a nonowner for a statutorily prescribed period of years. This chapter will discuss the first and third methods of transfer—transfer by deed and adverse possession. The second method is covered in Chapter 52.

In addition to the legal restrictions placed on the transfer of real property, a number of other controls apply to the use of privately owned property. Some of these, including zoning and the taking of property by eminent domain, are imposed by governmental units. Others are imposed by private parties through restrictive covenants. These three controls are considered in the second part of this chapter.

## TRANSFER OF REAL PROPERTY

The most common way in which real property is transferred is by deed. Such transfers usually involve a contract for the sale of the land, the subsequent delivery of the deed, and payment of the agreed consideration. The transfer of real estate by deed, however, does not require consideration to be valid; it may be made as a gift. In most cases, the real estate purchaser must borrow part of the purchase price, using the real property as security.

A far less usual method of transferring title, called *adverse possession,* requires no contract, deed, or other formality.

## CONTRACT OF SALE

As indicated in the chapter on contracts, general contract law governs the sale of real property. In addition, the Fair Housing Act (Title VIII of the Civil Rights Act, as amended) prohibits discrimination in the real estate market on the basis of race, color, religion, sex, national origin, disability, or familial status. The Act exempts the sale or rental of a single-family house owned by a private individual who owns fewer than four houses, provided that the owner does not use a broker or discriminatory advertising. Nevertheless, these exemptions do not apply to discrimination based on race or color; in the sale or rental of property, the Act prohibits all discrimination based on these factors.

### Formation

Because an oral agreement for the sale of an interest in land is not enforceable under the statute of frauds, the buyer and seller must reduce the agreement to writing and have it signed by the other party to be able to enforce the agreement against that party. The simplest agreement should contain (1) the names and addresses of the parties, (2) a description of the property to be conveyed, (3) the time for the conveyance (called the *closing*), (4) the type of deed to be given, and (5) the price and manner of payment. To avoid dispute and to protect the rights of both parties, a properly drawn contract for the sale of land will cover many other points as well.

A majority of jurisdictions adhere to the common law rule that the risk of loss or destruction of the property, not caused through the fault of the seller, rests with the purchaser after the contract is formed. The contract of sale may, of course, provide that such risk shall remain with the seller until she conveys the deed to the purchaser, that the seller must obtain insurance for the benefit of the purchaser, or that the risk is allocated in some other manner on which the parties have agreed.

## Marketable Title

The law of conveyancing has firmly established that a contract for the sale of land carries with it an implied obligation on the part of the seller to transfer marketable title. **Marketable title** means that the title is free from (a) encumbrances (such as mortgages, easements, liens, leases, and restrictive covenants); (b) defects in the chain of title appearing in the land records (such as a prior recorded conveyance of the same property by the seller); and (c) events depriving the seller of title, such as adverse possession or eminent domain. The seller's obligation to convey marketable title is significant, for if a title search reveals any flaw not specifically excepted in the contract, the seller has materially breached the contract. The buyer's remedies for breach include specific performance with a price reduction, rescission and restitution, or damages for loss of bargain.

There are two important exceptions to this rule. First, most courts hold that the seller's implied or express obligation to convey marketable title does not include the obligation to convey title free from existing zoning restrictions. Second, some courts also hold that the seller's implied or express obligation to convey marketable title does not require him to convey title free from open and visible public rights-of-way or easements, such as public roads and sewers.

Before title to the property passes, the buyer should ensure that she is receiving good title by having the title searched. A title search involves examining prior transfers of and encumbrances to the property. Such an examination does not guarantee rightful ownership, however; consequently, most buyers purchase title insurance as well. Issued in the amount of the purchase price of the property, **title insurance** indemnifies the owner against any loss due to defects in the title to the property or due to liens or encumbrances, except for those stated in the policy as existing at the time the policy is issued. Such policies also may be issued to protect the interests of mortgagees or tenants of property.

## Implied Warranty of Habitability

Because the obligation of marketable title involves only the title to the property conveyed, such an obligation does not apply to the quality of any improvements to the land. The traditional common law rule is *caveat emptor*—let the buyer beware. Under this rigid maxim, the buyer must inspect the property thoroughly before completing the sale, as any defect discovered only after the transaction is complete would not be the seller's responsibility. The seller is liable only for any misrepresentation or express warranty he may have made about the property.

A majority of States have relaxed the harshness of the common law in sales made by one who builds and then sells residential dwellings. In such a sale, the builder-seller impliedly warrants a newly constructed house to be free of latent defects, that is, those defects not apparent upon a reasonable inspection of the house at the time of sale. In some States, this implied warranty of habitability benefits only the original purchaser. In other States, the warranty has been extended to subsequent purchasers for a reasonable time. In addition, many jurisdictions now require *all* sellers to disclose hidden defects that materially affect the property's value and that would remain undetected following a reasonable examination. See Chapter 11 for a discussion of misrepresentation.

 *See Case 51–1*

## DEEDS

A **deed** is a formal document transferring any interest in land upon delivery and acceptance. The party who transfers property by a deed is called the **grantor;** the transferee of the property is the **grantee.**

## Types of Deeds

The rights conveyed by a deed vary, depending on the type of deed used. Deeds are of three basic types: warranty, special warranty, and quitclaim.

*Warranty* By a warranty deed (also called a general warranty deed), the grantor promises the grantee that the grantor has a valid title to the property. In addition, under a warranty deed, the grantor, either expressly or impliedly, obliges herself to make the grantee whole for any damage the grantee might suffer should the grantor's title prove to be defective. Aside from rendering the grantor liable for any defects in her title, the general warranty deed is distinct in that it will convey after-acquired title. For example, on January 30, Andrea conveys Blackacre by warranty deed to Bob. On January 30, Andrea's title to Blackacre is defective, but by February 14, Andrea has acquired a good title. Without more,

Bob has acquired Andrea's good title under the January 30 warranty deed.

**Special Warranty** Whereas a warranty deed contains a general warranty of title, a special warranty deed warrants only that the title has not been impaired, encumbered, or rendered defective because of any act or omission of the grantor. The grantor merely warrants the title so far as his acts or omissions are concerned. He does not warrant the title to be free of defects caused by the acts or omissions of others.

**Quitclaim** By a quitclaim deed, the grantor, in effect, says no more than "I make no promise as to what interest I have in this land, but whatever it is I convey it to you." Quitclaim deeds most commonly are used as a means for persons apparently having an interest in land to release their interest.

## Formal Requirements

As previously noted, any transfer of an interest in land that is of more than a limited duration falls within the statute of frauds and must therefore be in writing. The wording of nearly all deeds, whatever the type, follows substantially the same pattern, though the words used will vary, depending upon whether the instrument is a warranty deed, a special warranty deed, or a quitclaim deed. Moreover, statutes in most States suggest that certain words of conveyance be used to make the deed effective. A common phrase for a warranty deed is "convey and warrant," although in a number of States the phrase "grant, bargain, and sell" is used together with a covenant by the seller later in the deed that she will "warrant and defend the title." A quitclaim deed generally will provide that the grantor "conveys and quitclaims" or, more simply, "quitclaims all interest" in the property.

**Description of the Land** The description must be sufficiently clear to permit identification of the property conveyed. A common test of clarity is to ask whether a subsequent purchaser or a surveyor employed by him could mark off the land using the description.

**Quantity of the Estate** After describing the property, the deed usually will describe the quantity of estate conveyed to the grantee. Thus, either "to have and to hold to himself and his heirs forever" or "to have and to hold in fee simple" would vest the grantee with absolute title to the land. A deed conveying title to "George for life and to Elliott upon George's death," by comparison, would grant a life estate to George and a remainder interest to Elliott.

**Covenants of Title** Customarily, in making a deed, the grantor makes certain promises concerning her title to the land. Such promises or covenants, the most usual of which are **title** *(seisen)*, **against encumbrances, quiet enjoyment,** and **warranty,** ensure that the grantee will have undisturbed possession of the land and will, in turn, be able to transfer it free of the adverse claims of third parties. For the grantor's breach of covenant, the grantee is, moreover, entitled to be indemnified. In many States, all or many of these covenants are implied from the words of conveyance themselves—for example, "warrants" or "grant, bargain, and sell."

**Execution** Deeds generally end with the signature of the grantor, a seal, and an acknowledgment before a notary public or other official authorized to attest to the authenticity of documents. The grantor's signature can be made by an agent having written authority from the grantor in a form required by law. Today the seal has lost most of its former significance, and in those few jurisdictions where it is required, the seal is sufficient if the word *Seal* or the letters *L.S.* appear next to the signature.

## Delivery of Deeds

A deed does not transfer title to land until it is delivered. **Delivery** consists of the grantor's *intent* that the deed shall take effect, as evidenced by his acts or statements. Indispensable to delivery is the grantor's parting with control of the deed with the intention that it immediately will become operative to convey the estate it describes. Physical transfer of the deed is usually the best evidence of this intent, but it is not necessary. For example, the act of the grantor in placing a deed in a safe deposit box may or may not constitute delivery, depending on such facts as whether the grantee did or did not have access to the box and whether the grantor acts as if the property were the grantee's. A deed conceivably may be "delivered" even when kept in the grantor's possession; just as conceivably, physical delivery of a deed to a grantee may fail to transfer title. Frequently, in a transfer known as an escrow, a grantor will turn a deed over to a third party, the escrow agent, to hold until the grantee performs certain conditions. Upon the performance of the condition, the escrow agent must turn the deed over to the grantee.

## Recordation

In almost all States, recording a deed is not necessary to pass title from grantor to grantee. Unless the grantee has the deed recorded, however, a subsequent good faith purchaser for value of the property will acquire title superior to that of the grantee. Recordation consists of delivering a duly executed and acknowledged deed to the recorder's office in the county where the property is located. There, a copy of the instrument is inserted in the current deed book and indexed.

In some States, called **notice** States, unrecorded instruments are invalid against any subsequent purchaser without notice. In **notice-race** States, an unrecorded deed is invalid against any subsequent purchaser without notice who records first. Finally, in a few States, known as **race** States, an unrecorded deed is invalid against any deed recorded before it.

## SECURED TRANSACTIONS

The purchase of real estate usually involves a relatively large outlay of money, and few people pay cash for a house or business real estate. Most people must borrow part of the purchase price or defer payment over time. In these cases, the real estate itself is used to secure the obligation, which is evidenced by a note and either a mortgage or a deed of trust. The debtor is referred to as the **mortgagor** and the creditor as the **mortgagee.**

A secured transaction includes two elements: (1) a debt or obligation to pay money and (2) the creditor's interest in specific property that secures performance of the obligation. A security interest in property cannot exist apart from the debt it secures; consequently, discharging the debt in any manner terminates the interest. Transactions involving the use of real estate as security for a debt are subject to real estate law, which consists of statutes and rules developed by the common law of mortgages and trust deeds. The Uniform Commercial Code (UCC) does *not* apply to real estate mortgages or deeds of trust.

## Form of Mortgages

The instrument creating a mortgage is in the form of a conveyance from the mortgagor to the mortgagee and must meet all the requirements for such documents: it must be in writing, it must contain an adequate description of the property, and it must be executed and delivered. The usual mortgage, however, differs from an outright conveyance of property by providing, in a condition referred to as a "defeasance," that, upon the performance of the promise by the mortgagor, the conveyance is void and of no effect. Although the defeasance normally appears on the face of the mortgage, it may be in a separate document.

The concept of a **mortgage** as a lien upon real property for the payment of a debt applies with equal force to transactions having the same purpose but possessing a different name and form. A **deed of trust** is fundamentally identical to a mortgage, the most striking difference being that, under a deed of trust, the property is conveyed not to the creditor as security but to a third person who acts as trustee for the creditor's benefit. The deed of trust creates rights substantially similar to those created by a mortgage. In some States, it is customary to use a deed of trust in lieu of the ordinary form of mortgage.

As with all interests in realty, the mortgage or deed of trust should be promptly recorded to protect the mortgagee's rights against third persons who acquire an interest in the mortgaged property without knowledge of the mortgage.

## Rights and Duties

The rights and duties of the parties to a mortgage may depend upon whether it is viewed as creating a lien or as transferring legal title to the mortgagee. Most States have adopted the **lien** theory. The mortgagor retains title and, even in the absence of any stipulation in the mortgage, is entitled to possession of the premises to the exclusion of the mortgagee, even if the mortgagor defaults. Only through foreclosure or sale or through the court appointment of a receiver can the right of possession be taken from the mortgagor. A minority of States have adopted the common law **title** theory, which gives the mortgagee the right of ownership and possession. In most cases, as a practical matter, the mortgagor retains possession simply because the mortgagee has little interest in possession unless the mortgagor defaults.

Even though the mortgagor is generally entitled to possession and to many of the advantages of unrestricted ownership, he has a responsibility to deal with the property in a manner that will not impair the security. In most instances, *waste* (impairment of the security) results from the mortgagor's failure to prevent the actual or threatened action of third parties against the land. Thus, the debtor's failure to pay taxes or to discharge a prior lien may seriously impair the security of the mortgagee. In such cases, the courts generally permit the mortgagee to pay the obligation and add it to his claim against the mortgagor.

The mortgagor has the right to relieve his mortgaged property from the lien of a mortgage by paying the debt that it secures. Characteristic of a mortgage, this right of **redemption** can be extinguished only by operation of law. The right to redeem carries with it the obligation to pay the debt, and payment in full, with interest, is prerequisite to redemption.

◆ *See Figure 51–1*

## Transfer of Mortgage Interests

The original mortgagor and mortgagee can transfer their interests to assignees whose rights and obligations will depend primarily upon (1) the agreement of the parties to the assignment and (2) the legal rules protecting the interest of one who is party to the mortgage but not to the transfer.

*By Mortgagor*  If the mortgagor conveys the land, the purchaser is not personally liable for the mortgage debt unless she expressly assumes the mortgage. If she **assumes the mortgage,** she is personally obligated to pay the debt the mortgagor owes to the mortgagee, who can also hold the mortgagor on his promise to pay. A transfer of mortgaged property **subject to the mortgage** does not personally obligate the transferee to pay the mortgage debt. In such a case, the transferee's risk of loss is limited to the realty.

*By Mortgagee*  A mortgagee has the right to assign the mortgage to another person without the consent of the mortgagor. An assignee of a mortgage is well advised to protect her rights against persons who subsequently acquire an interest in the mortgaged property without

knowledge of the assignment by obtaining the assignment in a writing duly executed by the mortgagee and recording it promptly with the proper public official. Failure to record an assignment may cause an assignee of a mortgage note to lose her security. For example, Dylan buys land from Owen, relying upon a release executed and recorded by the mortgagee, Kristi. Kristi, however, had previously assigned the mortgage to Ali, who failed to have her assignment recorded. In the absence of Dylan's actual knowledge of the assignment by Kristi, Ali has no claim against the property.

## Foreclosure

The right to foreclose usually arises upon default by the mortgagor. Foreclosure is an action through which the mortgage holder takes the property from the mortgagor, ends the mortgagor's rights in the property, and sells the property to pay the mortgage debt. The mortgagor's failure to perform other promises in the mortgage also may give the mortgagee this right. Thus, a mortgage may provide that the mortgagor's failure to pay taxes constitutes a default that permits foreclosure. Mortgages also commonly provide that default in the payment of an installment makes the entire unpaid balance of the debt immediately due and payable, permitting foreclosure for the entire amount.

Whether foreclosure is by sale under judicial proceeding or by grant of power in the mortgage itself, the transaction is still a procedure to obtain satisfaction of a debt. If the proceeds are insufficient to satisfy the debt in full, the debtor-mortgagor remains liable for paying the balance. Generally, the mortgagee will obtain a *deficiency judgment* for any unsatisfied balance of the debt and may proceed to enforce the payment of this amount out of the mortgagor's other assets.

FIGURE 51–1  Fundamental Rights of Mortgagor and Mortgagee

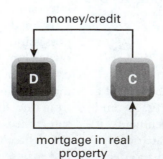

money/credit

**Debtor/Mortgagor (D)**

(1) To redeem property by payment of debt

(2) To possess general rights of ownership as limited by mortgage

**Creditor/Mortgagee (C)**

(1) To recover amount of debt

(2) To foreclose the mortgaged property upon default to satisfy debt

mortgage in real property

## ADVERSE POSSESSION

It is possible, although very rare, for title to land to be transferred **involuntarily,** without deed or other formality, by "adverse possession." In most States, a person who openly and continuously occupies the land of another for a statutorily prescribed time, typically ten to twenty years, will gain title to the land. The possession must be actual, not merely constructive. Courts have held that living on land, farming it, building on it, or maintaining structures on it are sufficient to constitute possession. Possession, however, must be adverse. This means that any act of dominion by the true owner, such as her entry on the land or assertion of ownership, will stop the period from running. In such event, the period will commence anew from the point at which the owner interrupted it.

By statute, some jurisdictions have established shorter periods of adverse possession where possession is accompanied by some other claim, such as the payment of taxes or an apparent, even if invalid, claim of title.

# PUBLIC AND PRIVATE CONTROLS

As discussed in Chapter 7, the law of nuisance imposes controls upon a landowner's use of her property. In exercising its police power for the benefit of the community, the State also can and does place controls upon the use of privately owned land. Moreover, the State does not compensate an owner for loss or damage he sustains by reason of such legitimate controls. The enforcement of zoning laws, which is a proper exercise of the police power, is not a taking of property but a regulation of its use. The taking of private property for a public use or purpose under the State's power of eminent domain is not, however, an exercise of the police power; and the owners of the property so taken are entitled to be paid its fair and reasonable value. In addition, private owners are entitled to control the use of privately owned property by means of restrictive covenants. This section will address these various methods of State and private control of property.

## ZONING

**Zoning** is the principal method of public control over land use. The validity of zoning is rooted in the police power of the State, the inherent power of government to provide for the public health, safety, morals, and welfare. Police power can be used only to regulate private property, never to "take" it. It is firmly established that regulation which has no reasonable relation to public health,

safety, morals, or welfare is unconstitutional as a denial of due process of law.

### Enabling Acts and Zoning Ordinances

The power to zone is generally delegated to local authorities by statutes known as enabling statutes. A typical enabling statute grants municipalities the following powers: (1) to regulate and limit the height and bulk of buildings to be erected; (2) to establish, regulate, and limit the building or setback lines on or along any street, trafficway, drive, or parkway; (3) to regulate and limit the intensity of the use of lot areas and to regulate and determine the area of open spaces within and around buildings; (4) to classify, regulate, and restrict the location of trades and industries and the location of buildings designated for specified industrial, business, residential, and other uses; (5) to divide the entire municipality into districts of such number, shape, area, and class (or classes) as may be deemed best suited to carry out the purposes of the statute; and (6) to fix standards to which buildings or structures must conform.

Under these powers, the local authorities may enact zoning ordinances consisting of a map and correlating descriptive text. The map divides the municipality into districts, which are designated principally as industrial, commercial, or residential, with possible subclassifications. A well-drafted zoning ordinance will carefully define the uses permitted in each area.

### Variance

Enabling statutes empower zoning authorities to grant variances where the application of a zoning ordinance to specific property would cause its owner "particular hardship" unique or peculiar to the property. A **variance** permits a deviation from the zoning ordinance. Special circumstances applicable to particular property might include its unusual shape, topography, size, location, or surroundings. A variance is not available, however, if the hardship is caused by conditions general to the neighborhood or by the actions of the property owner. It must affirmatively appear that the property as presently zoned cannot yield a reasonable return upon the owner's investment.

### Nonconforming Uses

A zoning ordinance may not immediately terminate a lawful use that existed before it was enacted. Rather, such a nonconforming use must be permitted to continue—at least for a reasonable time. Most ordinances provide that nonconforming use may be eliminated (1) when the use is discontinued, (2) when a nonconforming structure is destroyed or substantially damaged, or (3) when a nonconforming structure has been permitted to exist for the period of its useful life as fixed by municipal authorities.

## Judicial Review of Zoning

Although the zoning process is traditionally viewed as legislative, it is subject to judicial review on a number of grounds, including claims that the zoning ordinance is invalid or amounts to a taking of property.

*Invalidity of Zoning Ordinance* A zoning ordinance may be invalid as a whole either because it bears no reasonable relation to public health, safety, morals, or welfare; because it involves the exercise of powers not granted to the municipality by the enabling act; or because it violates the State or U.S. Constitution.

 *See Case 51–2*

*Zoning Amounts to a Taking* Another form of attack is to show that zoning restrictions amount to confiscation or a "taking." It is not sufficient that the property owner will sustain a financial loss if the restrictions are not lifted. But when the owner can show that the restrictions make it impracticable for him to use the property for *any* beneficial purpose, he should prevail. Deprivation of all beneficial use is confiscation.

## Subdivision Master Plans

A growing municipality has a special interest in regulating new housing developments so that they will harmonize with the rest of the community; so that streets within the development are integrated with existing streets or planned roads; and so that adequate provision is made for water, drainage, and sanitary facilities, as well as for traffic, recreation, light, and air. Accordingly, most States have legislation enabling local authorities to require municipal approval of every land subdivision plat. These enabling statutes provide penalties for failure to secure such approval where required by local ordinance. Some statutes provide that selling lots by reference to unrecorded plats is a criminal offense and provide further that such plats may not be recorded unless approved by the local planning board. Other statutes provide that building permits will not be issued unless the plat is approved and recorded.

## EMINENT DOMAIN

The power to take private property for public use, known as the power of **eminent domain,** is recognized as one of the inherent powers of government both in the U.S. Constitution and in the constitutions of the States. At the same time, however, the power is carefully circumscribed and controlled. The Fifth Amendment to the U.S. Constitution provides, "[N]or shall private property be taken for public use, without just compensation." Similar or identical provisions are found in the constitutions of the States. There is, therefore, a direct constitutional prohibition against taking private property without just compensation and an implicit prohibition against taking private property for other than public use. Moreover, under both Federal and State constitutions, the individual from whom property is to be taken is entitled to due process of law.

 *See Case 51–3*

## Public Use

As noted, there is an implicit constitutional prohibition against taking private property for other than public use. Most States interpret public use to mean "public advantage." Thus, the power of eminent domain may be delegated to railroad and public utility companies. Because it enables such companies to offer continued and improved service to the public, the reasonable exercise of this power is upheld as being for a public advantage. As society grows more complex, other public purposes become legitimate grounds for exercising the power of eminent domain. One such use is in the area of urban renewal. Most States have legislation permitting the establishment of housing authorities with the power to condemn slum, blighted, and vacant areas and to finance, construct, and maintain housing projects. Some States recently have gone further by permitting private companies to exercise the power of eminent domain, provided the use is primarily for a public benefit, such as the alleviation of unemployment or economic decay within the community.

## Just Compensation

When the power of eminent domain is exercised, just compensation must be made to the owners of the property taken. The measure of compensation is the fair market value of the property as of the time of taking. The compensation goes to holders of vested interests in the condemned property.

◆ *See Figure 51–2*

**FIGURE 51–2** Eminent Domain

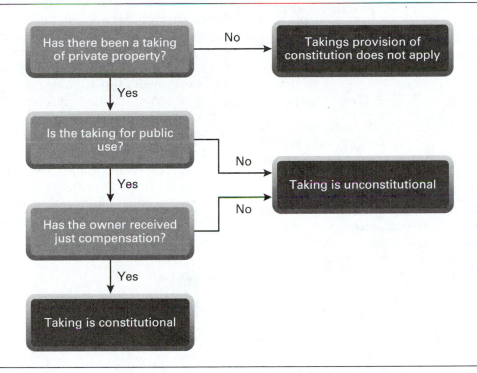

## PRIVATE RESTRICTIONS UPON LAND USE

Owners of real property may impose private restrictions, called **restrictive covenants** (or negative covenants), on the use of land. Historically, two types of private restrictions developed—real covenants and equitable servitudes. The two had different, although overlapping, requirements. Today, equitable servitudes have nearly replaced real covenants. Accordingly, this section will cover only equitable servitudes, which will be referred to by the more general term *restrictive covenant*.

### Requirements for Covenants Running with the Land

If certain conditions are satisfied, a restrictive covenant will bind not only the original parties to it but also remote parties who subsequently acquire the property. A restrictive covenant that binds remote parties is said to "run with the land." To run with the land, the restrictive covenant must involve promises that are enforceable under the law of contracts. A majority of courts hold that the covenant must be in writing. The parties who agree to the restrictive covenant must intend that the covenant bind their successors. Moreover, the covenant

must "touch and concern" the land by affecting its use, utility, or value. Finally, a restrictive covenant will bind only those successors who have actual or constructive notice of the covenant.

### Restrictive Covenants in Subdivisions

Restrictive covenants are widely used in subdivisions. The owners of lots are subject to restrictive covenants which, if actually brought to the attention of subsequent purchasers or recorded either by original deed or by means of a recorded plat or separate agreement, bind purchasers of lots in the subdivision as though the restrictions had been inserted in their own deeds. If the entire subdivision has been subjected to a general building plan designed to benefit all of the lots, any lot owner in the subdivision has the right to enforce the restriction against a purchaser whose title descends from a common grantor. If a restriction clearly is intended to benefit an entire tract, the covenant will be enforced against a subsequent purchaser of one of the lots in the tract if (1) the restriction apparently was intended to benefit the purchaser of any lot in the tract and (2) the restriction appears somewhere in the chain of title to which the lot is subject.

Subdivisions may involve many types of restrictive covenants. The more common ones limit the use of property to residential purposes, restrict the area of the lot on which a structure can be built, or provide for a special type of architecture. Frequently a subdivider will specify a minimum size for each house in an attempt to maintain structural unity in a neighborhood.

## Termination of Restrictive Covenants

A restrictive covenant may end by the terms of the original agreement. For example, the developer of a subdivision may provide that the restrictive covenant will terminate after thirty-five years unless a specified majority of the property owners reaffirm the covenant. In addition, a court will not enforce a restrictive covenant if changed circumstances make enforcement inequitable and oppressive. Evidence of changed conditions may be found either within the tract covered by the original covenant or within the area adjacent to or surrounding the tract.

## Validity of Restrictive Covenants

Although restrictions upon land use have never been popular in the law, the courts will enforce a restriction that apparently will operate to the general benefit of the owners of all the land the restriction is intended to affect. The usual method of enforcing such agreements is by an injunction restraining violation.

The law for many years has held, however, that under the Fourteenth Amendment to the U.S. Constitution, a State or municipality cannot impose any racial restrictions by statute or ordinance. In 1947, the U.S. Supreme Court held that because State courts are an arm of State government, such courts cannot enforce private racial restrictive covenants. This effectively invalidated private racial restrictive covenants.

 *See Case 51–4*

---

# Chapter Summary

## Transfer of Real Property

| **Contract of Sale** | **Formation** a contract to transfer any interest in land must be in writing to be enforceable<br>**Marketable Title** the seller must transfer marketable title, which is a title free from any defects or encumbrances<br>**Quality of Improvements**<br>• *Common Law Rule* under *caveat emptor* ("let the buyer beware") the seller is not liable for any undiscovered defects<br>• *Implied Warranty of Habitability* in a number of States, the builder-seller of a dwelling impliedly warrants that a newly constructed house is free from latent defects |
|---|---|
| **Deeds** | **Definition** a formal document transferring any type of interest in land<br>**Types**<br>• *Warranty Deed* the grantor (seller) promises the grantee (buyer) that she has valid title to the property without defect<br>• *Special Warranty Deed* the seller promises that he has not impaired the title<br>• *Quitclaim Deed* the seller transfers whatever interest she has in the property<br>**Requirements** the deed must (1) be written, (2) contain certain words of conveyance and a description of the property, (3) end with the signature of the grantor, a seal, and an acknowledgment before a notary public, and (4) be delivered<br>**Delivery** intent that the deed take effect, as evidenced by acts or statements of the grantor<br>**Recordation** required to protect the buyer's interest against third parties; consists of delivery of a duly executed and acknowledged deed to the appropriate recorder's office |

| Secured Transactions | **Elements** a secured transaction involves (1) a debt or obligation to pay money, (2) an interest of the creditor in specific property that secures performance, and (3) the debtor's right to redeem the property (remove the security interest) by paying the debt<br>**Mortgage** interest in land created by a written document that provides security to the mortgagee (secured party) for payment of the mortgagor's debt<br>**Deed of Trust** an interest in real property which is conveyed to a third person as trustee for the benefit of the creditor<br>**Transfer of Mortgage Interests**<br>• *Assumes the Mortgage* the purchaser of mortgaged property becomes personally liable to pay the debt<br>• *Subject to the Mortgage* purchaser is not personally liable to pay the debt, but the property remains subject to the mortgage<br>**Foreclosure** upon default, sale of the mortgaged property to satisfy the debt |
|---|---|
| Adverse Possession | **Definition** acquisition of title to land by open, continuous, and adverse occupancy for a statutorily prescribed period<br>**Possession** must be actual and without intervening domination by true owner |

# Public and Private Controls

| Zoning | **Definition** principal method of public control over private land use; involves regulation of land but may not constitute a taking of the property<br>**Authority** the power to zone is generally delegated to local authorities by statutes known as *enabling acts*<br>**Variance** a use differing from that provided in the zoning ordinance and granted to avoid undue hardship<br>**Nonconforming Use** a use not in accordance with, but existing prior to, a zoning ordinance; permitted to continue for at least a reasonable time<br>**Judicial Review** zoning ordinances may be reviewed to determine if they are invalid or a confiscation of property |
|---|---|
| Eminent Domain | **Definition** the power of a government to take (buy) private land for public use<br>**Public Use** public advantage<br>**Just Compensation** the owner of the property taken by eminent domain must be paid the fair market value of the property |
| Restrictive Covenants | **Definition** private restrictions on property contained in a conveyance<br>**Covenants Running with the Land** covenants that bind not only the original parties but also subsequent owners of the property<br>**Covenants in Subdivision** bind purchasers of lots in the subdivision as if the restrictions had been inserted in their own deeds |

# Cases

## Implied Warranty of Habitability
### VonHOLDT v. BARBA & BARBA CONSTRUCTION, INC.
Supreme Court of Illinois, 1997
175 Ill.2d 426, 677 N.E.2d 836, 222 Ill.Dec. 302

MILLER, J.

The plaintiff, John W. VonHoldt, Jr., brought the present action in the circuit court of Cook County against defendant, Barba & Barba Construction, Inc. The complaint alleged that defendant breached an implied warranty of habitability in its construction of a structural addition to an existing residence. * * *

## I. Background

In August 1982, defendant constructed a multilevel addition to a single family residence in Glenview, Illinois. Before the addition, the residence consisted of approximately 2,300 square feet. After the addition, the residence consisted of approximately 3,200 square feet. More than 11 years later, on November 5, 1993, plaintiff purchased the residence.

Shortly after taking occupancy, plaintiff noticed a deflection of the wood flooring at the partition wall separating the master bedroom from an adjoining bathroom. This deflection created a depression in the floor plane. Plaintiff maintained that, due to the thickness of the carpet, the depression was nearly concealed. An investigation revealed that the addition was not constructed in accordance with the architectural plans approved by the Village of Glenview or the Glenview Building Code. Specifically, the partition wall between the master bedroom and the bathroom was constructed as a bearing element supporting a portion of both the roof and ceiling construction. This variance resulted in excessive stress on the floor joists and inadequate support for a portion of the roof and ceiling causing a greater than expected floor deflection.

The plaintiff instituted the present action on March 28, 1994, by filing a complaint in the circuit court of Cook County. Plaintiff sought recovery from the defendant for breach of an implied warranty of habitability. Defendant moved to dismiss the complaint * * * for failure to state a claim upon which relief could be granted. On September 29, 1994, the trial judge dismissed plaintiff's amended complaint without prejudice.

* * * Plaintiff subsequently appealed.

The appellate court affirmed the judgment of the circuit court. * * * Thus, it refused to extend protection under the doctrine to a construction setting not involving a builder-vendor of a new residence. [Citation.] We allowed plaintiff's petition for leave to appeal.

## II. Discussion

### A. The Implied Warranty's Applicability to Additions

On appeal to this court, plaintiff contends that the appellate court erred in rejecting his claim of breach of an implied warranty of habitability. Plaintiff asks us to extend the implied warranty of habitability to a cause of action by a subsequent purchaser for damages against a builder constructing a later addition to a house. Defendant argues that the protection of the implied warranty of habitability should be limited to actions against builder-vendors and that plaintiff's action, if any exists, is time-barred. For the reasons expressed below, we find that the implied warranty of habitability extends to cases brought by subsequent purchasers involving subsequent additions to homes.

The implied warranty of habitability is a judicially created doctrine designed to avoid the unjust results of *caveat emptor* and the doctrine of merger. [Citation.]. Initially, Illinois courts applied the doctrine to the sale of new homes to protect innocent purchasers who did not possess the ability to determine whether the house they purchased contained latent defects. [Citation.]

* * * [T]he owner needs this protection because he is making a major investment, in many instances the largest single investment of his life. [Citation.]. Additionally, the owner usually relies on the integrity and skill of the builder, who is in the business of building houses. [Citation.]. Finally, the owner has a right to expect to receive a house that is reasonably fit for use as a residence. [Citation.]

* * * Illinois courts have [subsequently] defined and extended the circumstances under which claims

based on an implied warranty of habitability can be recognized. [Citation] (builder-vendor need not be mass producer, just one engaged in the business of building such that the sale is of a commercial nature); [Citation] (house built upon foundation of an old house still qualified as a "new" home); [Citation] (doctrine applies to person who erected a house manufactured by another company and built on the plaintiff's land); [Citation] (latent defect in common land can affect habitability); [Citation] (innocent purchaser could bring an action against a subcontractor when he had no recourse to the builder-vendor and he had sustained a loss in his home due to a latent defect); [Citation] (doctrine applies against developer-seller of new condominium unit).

Plaintiff claims that the implied warranty of habitability should now be extended to include actions against a builder brought by a subsequent purchaser for latent defects in a later addition to a home. In [citation], this court held that the defendants were not subject to the implied warranty of habitability for a condominium-conversion project. The court held that the doctrine of implied warranty of habitability did not apply because the refurbishing and renovation of the project had not been significant. [Citation.] In the present case, the builder made a major addition to an existing home. We now hold that, when a builder makes a significant addition to a previously built home, an action for damages resulting from latent defects affecting habitability exists under the doctrine of implied warranty of habitability.

An owner claiming that latent defects exist in a major addition to a structure should be provided the same protection for the addition as that given to the [original] owners * * *. In both cases, the owner of the house usually has little knowledge regarding the construction.

The purchaser of both a completed home and an addition places the same trust in the builder that the structure being erected is suitable for living. Further, the ordinary buyer is not in a position to discover hidden defects in a structure even through the exercise of ordinary and reasonable care.

We must next determine whether the plaintiff can bring this action even though he is a subsequent purchaser. In [citation], this court extended the implied warranty of habitability to subsequent purchasers of a new home, finding that there was no need for privity of contract because the warranty of habitability exists independently of the contract for sale. Because the doctrine of implied warranty of habitability has been extended to actions by subsequent purchasers of new homes, we can see no reason why the doctrine should not be extended to actions by subsequent purchasers of a home for latent defects in a significant addition to the home made prior to the time of sale.

* * *

## III. Conclusion

For the foregoing reasons, we hold that actions for damages from latent defects in the construction of a significant structural addition to an existing residence can be brought against the builder by subsequent purchasers under the doctrine of implied warranty of habitability. However, because here the action was time-barred * * * plaintiff's complaint was properly dismissed. We therefore affirm the judgment of the appellate court.

Affirmed.

---

CASE 51–2
# Zoning
## CITY OF RENTON v. PLAYTIME THEATRES, INC.
Supreme Court of the United States, 1986
475 U.S. 41

REHNQUIST, J.
This case involves a constitutional challenge to a zoning ordinance, enacted by appellant city of Renton, Washington, that prohibits adult motion picture theaters from locating within 1,000 feet of any residential zone, single-

or multiple-family dwelling, church, park, or school. Appellees, Playtime Theatres, Inc., and Sea-First Properties, Inc., filed an action in the United States District Court for the Western District of Washington seeking a declaratory judgment that the Renton ordinance violated the

First and Fourteenth Amendments and a permanent injunction against its enforcement. The District Court ruled in favor of Renton and denied the permanent injunction * * *.

* * *

The Court of Appeals for the Ninth Circuit reversed. The Court of Appeals first concluded, contrary to the finding of the District Court, that the Renton ordinance constituted a substantial restriction on First Amendment interests. Then, using the standards set forth in [citation], the Court of Appeals held that Renton had improperly relied on the experiences of other cities in lieu of evidence about the effects of adult theaters on Renton, that Renton had thus failed to establish adequately the existence of a substantial governmental interest in support of its ordinance, and that in any event Renton's asserted interests had not been shown to be unrelated to the suppression of expression. The Court of Appeals remanded the case to the District Court for reconsideration of Renton's asserted interests.

In our view, the resolution of this case is largely dictated by our decision in [citation]. There, although five Members of the Court did not agree on a single rationale for the decision, we held that the city of Detroit's zoning ordinance, which prohibited locating an adult theater within 1,000 feet of any two other "regulated uses" or within 500 feet of any residential zone, did not violate the First and Fourteenth Amendments. [Citation.] The Renton ordinance, ... does not ban adult theaters altogether, but merely provides that such theaters may not be located within 1,000 feet of any residential zone, single- or multiple-family dwelling, church, park, or school. The ordinance is therefore properly analyzed as a form of time, place, and manner regulation. [Citation.]

* * *

The District Court's finding as to "predominate" intent, left undisturbed by the Court of Appeals, is more than adequate to establish that the city's pursuit of its zoning interests here was unrelated to the suppression of free expression. The ordinance by its terms is designed to prevent crime, protect the city's retail trade, maintain property values, and generally "protec[t] and preserv[e] the quality of [the city's] neighborhoods, commercial districts, and the quality of urban life," not to suppress the expression of unpopular views. [Citation.] As Justice POWELL observed in [citation], "[i]f [the city] had been concerned with restricting the message purveyed by adult theaters, it would have tried to close them or restrict their number rather than circumscribe their choice as to location." [Citation.]

In short, the Renton ordinance is completely consistent with our definition of "content-neutral" speech regulations as those that "are *justified* without reference to the content of the regulated speech." [Citations.] The ordinance does not contravene the fundamental principle that underlies our concern about "content-based" speech regulations: that "government may not grant the use of a forum to people whose views it finds acceptable, but deny use to those wishing to express less favored or more controversial views." [Citation.]

It was with this understanding in mind that, [citation], a majority of this Court decided that, at least with respect to businesses that purvey sexually explicit materials, zoning ordinances designed to combat the undesirable secondary effects of such businesses are to be reviewed under the standards applicable to "content-neutral" time, place, and manner regulations.

* * *

The appropriate inquiry in this case, then, is whether the Renton ordinance is designed to serve a substantial governmental interest and allows for reasonable alternative avenues of communication. [Citations.] It is clear that the ordinance meets such a standard. As a majority of this Court recognized in [citation], a city's "interest in attempting to preserve the quality of urban life is one that must be accorded high respect." [Citation.] Exactly the same vital governmental interests are at stake here.

The Court of Appeals ruled, however, that because the Renton ordinance was enacted without the benefit of studies specifically relating to "the particular problems or needs of Renton," the city's justifications for the ordinance were "conclusory and speculative." [Citation.] We think the Court of Appeals imposed on the city an unnecessarily rigid burden of proof. The record in this case reveals that Renton relied heavily on the experience of, and studies produced by, the city of Seattle. In Seattle, as in Renton, the adult theater zoning ordinance was aimed at preventing the secondary effects caused by the presence of even one such theater in a given neighborhood.

* * *

We also find no constitutional defect in the method chosen by Renton to further its substantial interests. Cities may regulate adult theaters by dispersing them, as in Detroit, or by effectively concentrating them, as in Renton. "It is not our function to appraise the wisdom of [the city's] decision to require adult theaters to be separated rather than concentrated in the same areas. . . . [T]he city must be allowed a reasonable opportunity to experiment with solutions to admittedly serious problems." [Citation.]

* * *

Finally, turning to the question whether the Renton ordinance allows for reasonable alternative avenues of communication, we note that the ordinance leaves some 520 acres, or more than five percent of the entire land area of Renton, open to use as adult theater sites. The District Court found, and the Court of Appeals did not dispute the finding, that the 520 acres of land consists of "[a]mple, accessible real estate," including "acreage in all stages of development from raw land to developed, industrial, warehouse, office, and shopping space that is criss-crossed by freeways, high-ways, and roads." [Citation.]

* * *

In sum, we find that the Renton ordinance represents a valid governmental response to the "admittedly serious problems" created by adult theaters. [Citation.] Renton has not used "the power to zone as a pretext for suppressing expression," [citation], but rather has sought to make some areas available for adult theaters and their patrons, while at the same time preserving the quality of life in the community at large by preventing those theaters from locating in other areas. This, after all, is the essence of zoning. Here, as in [citation], the city has enacted a zoning ordinance that meets these goals while also satisfying the dictates of the First Amendment. The judgment of the Court of Appeals is therefore

Reversed.

---

## CASE 51–3
## Eminent Domain
# LUCAS v. SOUTH CAROLINA COASTAL COUNCIL

Supreme Court of the United States, 1992
505 U.S. 1003, 112 S.Ct. 2886, 120 L.Ed.2d 798

SCALIA, J.

In 1986, petitioner David H. Lucas paid $975,000 for two residential lots on the Isle of Palms in Charleston County, South Carolina, on which he intended to build single-family homes. In 1988, however, the South Carolina Legislature enacted the Beachfront Management Act, [citation], which had the direct effect of barring petitioner from erecting any permanent habitable structures on his two parcels. [Citation.] A state trial court found that this prohibition rendered Lucas's parcels "valueless." This case requires us to decide whether the Act's dramatic effect on the economic value of Lucas's lots accomplished a taking of private property under the Fifth and Fourteenth Amendments requiring the payment of "just compensation." [Citation.]

South Carolina's expressed interest in intensively managing development activities in the so-called "coastal zone" dates from 1977 when, in the aftermath of Congress's passage of the federal Coastal Zone Management Act of 1972, [citation], the legislature enacted a Coastal Zone Management Act of its own. [Citation.] In its original form, the South Carolina Act required owners of coastal zone land that qualified as a "critical area" (defined in the legislation to include beaches and immediately adjacent sand dunes, [citation] to obtain a permit from the newly created South Carolina Coastal Council (respondent here) prior to committing the land to a "use other than the use the critical area was devoted to on [September 28, 1977]." [Citation.]

In the late 1970s, Lucas and others began extensive residential development of the Isle of Palms, a barrier island situated eastward of the City of Charleston. Toward the close of the development cycle for one residential subdivision known as "Beachwood East," Lucas in 1986 purchased the two lots at issue in this litigation for his own account. No portion of the lots, which were located approximately 300 feet from the beach, qualified as a "critical area" under the 1977 Act; accordingly, at the time Lucas acquired these parcels, he was not legally obliged to obtain a permit from the Council in advance of any development activity. His intention with respect to the lots was to do what the owners of the immediately adjacent parcels had already done: erect single-family residences. He commissioned architectural drawings for this purpose.

The Beachfront Management Act brought Lucas's plans to an abrupt end. Under that 1988 legislation, the Council was directed to establish a "baseline" connecting the landward-most "point[s] of erosion . . . during the past forty years" in the region of the Isle of Palms that includes Lucas's lots. [Citation.] In action not challenged here, the Council fixed this baseline landward of Lucas's parcels. . . . The Act provided no exceptions.

Lucas promptly filed suit in the South Carolina Court of Common Pleas, contending that the Beachfront Management Act's construction bar effected a taking of his property without just compensation. Lucas did not take issue with the validity of the Act as a lawful exercise of

South Carolina's police power, but contended that the Act's complete extinguishment of his property's value entitled him to compensation regardless of whether the legislature had acted in furtherance of legitimate police power objectives. Following a bench trial, the court agreed. Among its factual determinations was the finding that "at the time Lucas purchased the two lots, both were zoned for single-family residential construction and . . . there were no restrictions imposed upon such use of the property by either the State of South Carolina, the County of Charleston, or the Town of the Isle of Palms." The trial court further found that the Beachfront Management Act decreed a permanent ban on construction insofar as Lucas's lots were concerned, and that this prohibition "deprive[d] Lucas of any reasonable economic use of the lots, . . . eliminated the unrestricted right of use, and render[ed] them valueless." The court thus concluded that Lucas's properties had been "taken" by operation of the Act, and it ordered respondent to pay "just compensation" in the amount of $1,232,387.50.

The Supreme Court of South Carolina reversed. It found dispositive what it described as Lucas's concession "that the Beachfront Management Act [was] properly and validly designed to preserve . . . South Carolina's beaches." [Citation.] Failing an attack on the validity of the statute as such, the court believed itself bound to accept the "uncontested . . . findings" of the South Carolina legislature that new construction in the coastal zone—such as petitioner intended—threatened this public resource. [Citation.] The Court ruled that when a regulation respecting the use of property is designed "to prevent serious public harm," [citation], no compensation is owing under the Takings Clause regardless of the regulation's effect on the property's value.

* * *

Prior to Justice Holmes' exposition in *Pennsylvania Coal Co. v. Mahon*, [citation], it was generally thought that the Takings Clause reached only a "direct appropriation" of property, [citation], or the functional equivalent of a "practical ouster of [the owner's] possession." [Citations.] Justice Holmes recognized . . . that, "while property may be regulated to a certain extent, if regulation goes too far it will be recognized as a taking." [Citation.]

Nevertheless, our decision in Mahon offered little insight into when, and under what circumstances, a given regulation would be seen as going "too far" for purposes of the Fifth Amendment. In 70-odd years of succeeding "regulatory takings" jurisprudence, we have generally eschewed any "'set formula'" for determining how far is too far, preferring to "engag[e] in . . . essentially ad hoc, factual inquiries," [citations.] We have, however,

described at least two discrete categories of regulatory action as compensable without case-specific inquiry into the public interest advanced in support of the restraint. The first encompasses regulations that compel the property owner to suffer a physical "invasion" of his property. In general (at least with regard to permanent invasions), no matter how minute the intrusion, and no matter how weighty the public purpose behind it, we have required compensation. * * *

The second situation in which we have found categorical treatment appropriate is where regulation denies all economically beneficial or productive use of land. [Citations.] As we have said on numerous occasions, the Fifth Amendment is violated when land-use regulation "does not substantially advance legitimate state interests or denies an owner economically viable use of his land." [Citation.]

* * *

Where the State seeks to sustain regulation that deprives land of all economically beneficial use, we think it may resist compensation only if the logically antecedent inquiry into the nature of the owner's estate shows that the proscribed use interests were not part of his title to begin with. This accords, we think, with our "takings" jurisprudence, which has traditionally been guided by the understandings of our citizens regarding the content of, and the State's power over, the "bundle of rights" that they acquire when they obtain title to property. It seems to us that the property owner necessarily expects the uses of his property to be restricted, from time to time, by various measures newly enacted by the State in legitimate exercise of its police powers; "[a]s long recognized, some values are enjoyed under an implied limitation and must yield to the police power." [Citation.] And in the case of personal property, by reason of the State's traditionally high degree of control over commercial dealings, he ought to be aware of the possibility that new regulation might even render his property economically worthless (at least if the property's only economically productive use is sale or manufacture for sale), [citation]. In the case of land, however, we think the notion pressed by the Council that title is somehow held subject to the "implied limitation" that the State may subsequently eliminate all economically valuable use is inconsistent with the historical compact recorded in the Takings Clause that has become part of our constitutional culture.

Where "permanent physical occupation" of land is concerned, we have refused to allow the government to decree it anew (without compensation), no matter how weighty the asserted "public interests" involved, [citation]—though we assuredly would permit the government to assert a permanent easement that was a pre-existing limitation upon the landowner's title. [Citations.] We believe similar treatment must be accorded confiscatory regulations, i.e., regulations that prohibit all economically beneficial use of land: Any limitation so severe cannot be newly legislated or decreed (without compensation), but must inhere in the title itself, in the restrictions that background principles of the State's law of property and nuisance already place upon land ownership. A law or decree with such an effect must, in other words, do no more than duplicate the result that could have been achieved in the courts—by adjacent landowners (or other uniquely affected persons) under the State's law of private nuisance, or by the State under its complementary power to abate nuisances that affect the public generally, or otherwise.

\* \* \*

The "total taking" inquiry we require today will ordinarily entail (as the application of state nuisance law ordinarily entails) analysis of, among other things, the degree of harm to public lands and resources, or adjacent private property, posed by the claimant's proposed activities, see, e.g., Restatement (Second) of Torts [citation], the social value of the claimant's activities and their suitability to the locality in question, [citation], and the relative ease with which the alleged harm can be avoided through measures taken by the claimant and the government (or adjacent private landowners) alike, [citation]. The fact that a particular use has long been engaged in by similarly situated owners ordinarily imports a lack of

any common-law prohibition (though changed circumstances or new knowledge may make what was previously permissible no longer so, see Restatement (Second) of Torts, [citation]. So also does the fact that other landowners, similarly situated, are permitted to continue the use denied to the claimant.

It seems unlikely that common-law principles would have prevented the erection of any habitable or productive improvements on petitioner's land; they rarely support prohibition of the "essential use" of land, [citation]. The question, however, is one of state law to be dealt with on remand. We emphasize that to win its case South Carolina must do more than proffer the legislature's declaration that the uses Lucas desires are inconsistent with the public interest, or the conclusory assertion that they violate a common-law maxim. . . . As we have said, a "State, . . . may not transform private property into public property without compensation. . . ." [Citation.] Instead, as it would be required to do if it sought to restrain Lucas in a common-law action for public nuisance, South Carolina must identify background principles of nuisance and property law that prohibit the uses he now intends in the circumstances in which the property is presently found. Only on this showing can the State fairly claim that, in proscribing all such beneficial uses, the Beachfront Management Act is taking nothing.

\* \* \*

The judgment is reversed and the cause remanded for proceedings not inconsistent with this opinion.

So ordered.

---

### CASE 51–4
### Restrictive Covenants
## *CORNER v. MILLS*
Court of Appeals of Indiana, 1995
650 N.E.2d 712

HOFFMAN, J.
Appellants-plaintiffs Marie H. Corner, et al. (plaintiffs), appeal from a judgment granted in favor of appellees-defendants Patrick D. Mills, et al. (defendants), in an action to declare certain restrictive covenants to real estate unenforceable. The relevant facts are summarized below.

In 1937, Perry and Florence Shupert purchased a tract of land located in Elkhart, Indiana. The tract was divided into 32 individual residential lots and named "Christiana Acres." Between 1939 and 1941, four of the lots were

sold to purchasers without restrictions. However, in 1942, Lot No. 11 was sold with the following restrictions attached:

(a) All lots shall be known and described as residential lots, except residential building lots other than one detached single family.

(b) No building shall be erected on any residential building plot nearer than forty (40) [feet] to the front lot line, not nearer than six feet to any side set line.

(c) No residential structure shall be erected or placed on any building lot, which tract has an area of less than

10,000 square feet or a width of less than forty feet at the front of the building set back line, except that a residence may be erected or placed on a lot of odd size and constructed according to the City building ordinance.

(d) No noxious or offensive trade or activity shall be carried on upon any lot nor shall anything be done thereon which may be or become an annoyance or nuisance to the neighborhood.

(e) No persons of any race other than the white race shall use or occupy any building or any lot, except that this covenant shall not prevent occupancy by domestic servants of a different race domiciled with an owner or tenant.

(f) No trailer, basement, tent, shack, garage, barn or other outbuilding erected in the tract shall at anytime be used as a residence temporarily or permanently, nor shall any structure of a temporary character be used as a residence.

(g) No dwelling costing less than $3500.00 shall be permitted on any lot in the tract. The ground floor area of the main structure exclusive of one story open porches, and garages shall be not less than 480 square feet in the case of a one and one half two or two and one half story structure.

In the following years, two additional lots were sold, one with the above restriction attached and the other without it.

In 1946, the Christiana Acres tract was recorded. At that time, all owners of the lots were using their properties for residential use only. Also, every lot owner joined in the recording. However, no restrictions were included in the tract record.

Thereafter, the next 13 lots were conveyed. Some of these lots included restrictions similar to the ones above. Others had certain residential restrictions but no racial covenants. Also, one lot was conveyed "subject to restrictions of record." Another was conveyed with restrictions against conducting "noxious or offensive trade[s] or activities."

Currently, there are two vacant lots in Christiana Acres. The remaining lots are being used and have been used since the initial recording for residential purposes only. At all times relevant to this dispute, every lot in Christiana Acres has been zoned by the City of Elkhart as R–1 Single Family Residential.

* * * In March 1993, the plaintiffs decided their properties would be more valuable if used commercially. Hence, they filed a complaint in the Elkhart Superior Court for declaratory relief seeking to have the restrictive covenants on their properties lifted. Defendants responded and filed a counterclaim seeking enforcement of the covenants. After conducting a hearing, the trial

court entered findings of facts and conclusions of law and upheld the residential restrictions on Christiana Acres. This appeal ensued.

The sole consolidated issue on appeal is whether the trial court erred in enforcing the restrictions attached to the properties in Christiana Acres.

* * *

In its findings, the trial court found the racial covenants to be unenforceable and redacted [removed] them from the deeds. However, it enforced the remaining restrictions as part of a general scheme or plan of development for residential use. The plaintiffs contend this was in error. Specifically, they claim the racial covenants cannot be redacted without disturbing the underlying intent of the grantors. Plaintiffs further argue that because the inclusion of the unenforceable covenants within several of the deeds poison the remaining covenants, no restrictions on Christiana Acres should be upheld because they violate public policy.

Restrictive covenants which restrict use of land based on race are unconstitutional. [Citation.] Thus, indisputably, the racial restriction contained in the deeds are invalid. However, as the defendants point out, restrictive covenants are express contracts between a grantor and a grantee. [Citation.] Accordingly, as in other contracts, illegal covenants may be removed if to do so will not affect the intent or symmetry of the remaining covenants. [Citation.]

Racial restrictions aside, it is evident that the other residential covenants seek to independently ensure the residential quality of Christiana Acres. They do this by setting forth very specific set-back and minimum value requirements, by prohibiting certain commercial and trade behavior, and by imposing restrictions against certain temporary residential structures. As the trial court noted in its findings, severing the illegal racial covenants only destroys a small portion of the covenants' intent. It does not affect the prevailing and apparent intent to have Christiana Acres remain residential. Consequently, the trial court did not err in redacting the illegal covenants while allowing the others to remain intact.

Plaintiffs next contend the trial court erred in finding a general scheme or plan of residential development to exist in Christiana Acres. In support of their argument, plaintiffs argue that some of the covenants are ambiguous, and point out that many of the deeds are not identical in their restrictions, that some properties do not have restrictions on them at all, and that several lots were conveyed without restrictions before the plat was recorded.

However, the lack of uniformity in restrictions in a subdivision does not conclusively prove the nonexistence of a general plan or scheme for residential development. [Citation.] Nor does the fact that some of the lots contain no restrictions, that a few lots were conveyed before the plat was recorded, or that the recorded plat itself contains no restrictions, conclusively show the nonexistence of such a plan. [Citations.]

Instead, in determining whether a general scheme or plan of development exists, the pertinent focus is on whether the circumstances and facts of the case, including the language of the deeds and the grantors' actions, reveal an intent by them to create such a plan or scheme. [Citation.]

\* \* \*

In 1946, the plat was recorded. At that time, all the owners maintained their properties strictly for residential use. Also, each property owner joined in the recording. In doing so, it is reasonable to infer that the owners all intended to combine in their efforts to develop Christiana Acres as a residential neighborhood. By making Christiana Acres exclusively residential, it is also inferable that the common grantors wished to enhance the value of their lots to the benefit of all others in the subdivision.

At present, every owner can trace their properties to this common source beginning in 1946. Moreover, a review of the deeds in aggregate reveals an unmistakable intent to place residential restrictions on the properties and the subdivision as a whole. [Citation.] After the initial recording, although not identical, lots were consistently transferred with various residential restrictions.

\* \* \*

Next, plaintiffs complain that because there has been significant commercial development [next to Christiana Acres] in recent years, the continued residential nature of Christiana Acres is no longer feasible. The facts, however, indicate a conclusion to the contrary.

It is only where the use of the property and the surrounding area has so radically changed from what was originally envisioned making the covenants no longer sustainable, that they will be lifted as unenforceable. [Citation.] In this analysis, the equities must be viewed to determine if they favor dismantling the neighborhood restrictions.

Plaintiffs' unilateral speculation that their properties are worth more if developed commercially is insufficient by itself to nullify the otherwise valid covenants for residential use. [Citation.] \* \* \*

Affirmed.

---

# Questions

1. Explain (a) the essential elements of a contract for sale of an interest in real property, (b) the meaning and importance of marketable title, and (c) the concept of implied warranty of habitability.

2. Describe the fundamental requirements of a valid deed and distinguish among warranty, special warranty, and quitclaim deeds.

3. Explain (a) the elements of a secured transaction, (b) the difference between a mortgage and a deed of trust, and (c) the difference between an assumption of a mortgage and buying subject to a mortgage.

4. Define and give an example of (a) adverse possession, (b) a variance, (c) a nonconforming use, and (d) eminent domain.

5. Describe the nature and types of restrictive covenants.

---

# Problems

1. A was the father of B, C, and D and the owner of Redacre, Blackacre, and Greenacre.

A made and executed a warranty deed conveying Redacre to B. The deed provided that "this deed shall only become effective upon the death of the grantor." A retained possession of the deed and died leaving the deed in his safe deposit box.

A made and executed a warranty deed conveying Blackacre to C. This deed also provided that "this deed shall only become effective upon the death of the grantor." A delivered the deed to C. After A died, C recorded the deed.

A made and executed a warranty deed conveying Greenacre to D. The deed was delivered by A to X with specific instructions to deliver the deed to D upon A's death. Upon the death of A, X duly delivered the deed to D.

    (a)    What is the interest of B in Redacre, if any?

    (b)    What is the interest of C in Blackacre, if any?

    (c)    What is the interest of D in Greenacre, if any?

**2.** Arkin, the owner of Redacre, executed a real estate mortgage to the Shawnee Bank and Trust Company for $10,000. After the mortgage was executed and recorded, Arkin constructed a dwelling on the premises and planted a corn crop. After Arkin defaulted in the payment of the mortgage debt, the bank proceeded to foreclose the mortgage. At the time of the foreclosure sale, the corn crop was mature and unharvested. Arkin contends that the mortgage should not apply to (a) the dwelling and (b) the corn crop. Decision?

**3.** Robert and Stanley held legal title of record to adjacent tracts of land, each consisting of eighty acres. Stanley fenced his eighty acres in 1975. He placed his east fence fifteen feet onto Robert's property. Thereafter, he was in possession of this fifteen-foot strip of land and kept it fenced and cultivated continuously until he sold his tract of land to Nathan on March 1, 1981. Nathan took possession under deed from Stanley and continued possession and cultivation of the fifteen-foot strip until May 27, 2000, when Robert, having on several occasions strenuously objected to Nathan's possession, brought suit against Nathan for trespass. Decision?

**4.** Marcia executed a mortgage on Blackacre to secure her indebtedness to Ajax Savings and Loan Association in the amount of $25,000. Later, Marcia sold Blackacre to Morton. The deed contained the following provision: "This deed is subject to the mortgage executed by the Grantor herein to Ajax Savings and Loan Association."

The sale price of Blackacre to Morton was $50,000. Morton paid $25,000 in cash, deducting the $25,000 mortgage debt from the purchase price. Upon default in the payment of the mortgage debt, Ajax brings an action against Marcia and Morton to recover a judgment for the amount of the mortgage debt and to foreclose the mortgage. Decision?

**5.** On January 1, 1999, Davis and Hershey owned Blackacre as tenants in common. On July 1, 1999, Davis made a written contract to sell Blackacre to Grigg for $25,000. Pursuant to this contract, Grigg paid Davis $25,000 on August 1, 1999, and Davis executed and delivered to Grigg a warranty deed to Blackacre. On May 1, 2000, Hershey quitclaimed his interest in Blackacre to Davis. Grigg brings an action against Davis for breach of warranty of title. What judgment?

**6.** John Doe, for valuable consideration, agreed to convey to Richard Roe eighty acres of land. He delivered a deed, the material portions of which read:

"I, John Doe, grant and convey to Richard Roe eighty acres of land [legal description]: To have and to hold unto Richard Roe, his heirs, and assigns forever.

"I, John Doe, covenant to warrant and defend the premises hereby conveyed against all persons claiming the same or any part thereof by or through me."

Thereafter, Roe conveyed "all my right, title, and interest" in the eighty acres to Paul Poe. It develops that Doe had no title to the land when he conveyed it to Roe. Subsequently, Doe inherited an undivided one-half interest in the property.

What rights, if any, does Poe have against Doe and Roe?

**7.** Barker operated a retail bakery, Davidson a drugstore, Farrell a food store, Gibson a gift shop, and Harper a hardware store in adjoining locations along one side of a single suburban village block. As the population grew, the business section developed at the other end of the village, and the establishments of Barker, Davidson, Farrell, Gibson, and Harper were surrounded for at least a mile in each direction solely by residences. The village adopted a typical zoning ordinance, the provisions of which declared the area including the five stores to be a "residential district for single-family dwellings." Thereafter, Barker tore down the frame building which housed the bakery and began to construct a modern brick bakery. Davidson found her business increasing to such an extent that she began to build an addition that would extend the drugstore to the rear alley. Farrell's building was destroyed by fire, and he started to reconstruct it with the intention of restoring it to its former condition. Gibson changed the gift shop into a sporting goods store and after six months of operation decided to go back into the gift shop business. Harper sold his hardware store to Hempstead.

The village building commissioner brings an action under the zoning ordinance to enjoin the construction work of Barker, Davidson, and Farrell and to enjoin the carrying on of any business by Gibson and Hempstead. Assume the ordinance is valid. What result?

**8.** Alda and Mattingly are residents of phase I of the Chimney Hills subdivision. The lots owned by Alda and Mattingly are subject to the following restrictive covenant: "Lots shall be for single-family residence purposes only." Alda intends to convert her carport into a beauty shop, and Mattingly brings suit against Alda to enjoin her from doing so. Alda argues that the covenant restricts only the type of building that can be constructed, not the incidental use to which residential structures are put. Decision?

**9.** The city of Boston sought to condemn land in fee simple for use in constructing an entrance to an underground terminal for a subway. The owners of the land contend that no more than surface and subsurface easements are necessary for the terminal entrance and seek to retain air rights above thirty-six feet. The city argues that any building utilizing this airspace would require structural supports that would interfere with the city's plan for the terminal. The city concedes that the properties around the condemned property could be assembled and structures could be designed to span over the condemned property, in which case the air rights would be quite valuable. Decision?

**10.** In May 1988, Fred Parramore executed four deeds, each conveying a life estate in his land to him and his wife and a remainder interest in one-fourth of his land to each of his four children: Alney, Eudell, Bernice, and Iris. Although Fred executed and acknowledged the four deeds as part of his plan to distribute his estate at his death, he did not deliver them to his children at this time. Instead, he placed the deeds with his will in a safe deposit box and instructed the children to pick up their deeds at his death. Fred later conveyed Alney's deed to Alney, thereby vesting Alney's interest in that parcel, but Eudell, Bernice, and Iris's deeds were never handed over to them during Fred's lifetime. Fred, however, acted as if the land were beyond his control, and on one occasion told a prospective buyer that the land had already been deeded away. When Fred died in November 1999, Alney brought this action, claiming that the deeds to Eudell, Bernice, and Iris were ineffective because they had never been handed over during Fred's lifetime. Accordingly, Alney argued, the remaining land should pass in equal shares to each of the four children under the residuary clause of Fred's will. Decision?

11. The Gerwitz family resides on a piece of land known as Lot #24 of the Belleville tract, which they acquired by deed in 1980. Shortly thereafter, the Gerwitzes began to use the adjacent vacant Lot #25. At various times they planted grass seed, flowers, and shrubs on the land and used it for picnics and cookouts. In 2000, Gelsomin acquired Lot #25 and constructed a foundation on it so that he could place a house there. The Gerwitzes then brought this action to stop him, claiming title to Lot #25 by adverse possession. Decision?

12. Leo owned a one-story, one-family dwelling in a single-family residential zoning district in Detroit. He attempted to sell the house with its adjoining lot for $38,500. Houses in the neighborhood generally sold for $20,000 to $25,000. Immediately to the west of Leo's property was a gasoline service station. In addition, Leo's property was located on a corner frequented with heavy traffic. Having received no offers from residence-use buyers during the period of over a year that the property was listed and offered for sale, Leo applied to the board of zoning appeals for a variance to permit the use of the property as a dental and medical clinic and to use the side yard for off-street parking. The variance would be subject to certain conditions, including the preservation of the building's exterior as that of a one-family dwelling. Puritan-Greenfield Improvement Association, a nonprofit corporation, filed a complaint against Leo's variance request. Decision?

13. The Glendale Church purchased a twenty-one-acre parcel of land in a canyon along the banks of Mill Creek in Angeles National Forest. The church used the twelve flat acres next to the stream to operate a campground for disabled children. This area had a number of improved buildings located on it. In July, a forest fire destroyed all ground cover upstream from the church's campground, and a subsequent flood destroyed all the buildings. In response, the county of Los Angeles enacted an interim ordinance which temporarily prohibited the church from constructing new buildings. At trial, the question presented was whether the church was as entitled to compensation for a temporary taking of its property as it would have been in a formal eminent domain proceeding. Decision?

14. Robert V. Gross owned certain land on which he proposed to construct an eighty-three-unit apartment house. The land, however, was subject to a restriction imposed by a 1947 deed to a predecessor in title that provided that no part of the premises could be used for business purposes other than raising, growing, and selling live bait, fishing tackle, and sporting goods. Gross sought a decree stating that the restriction did not prohibit the construction and operation of an apartment house. Decision?

15. For seven years, Desford Potts had owned a six-acre tract of land within the corporate limits of the city of Franklin. The tract contained a livestock barn in which Potts stored lumber and other building materials. Bricks were also stored in stacks four or five feet high outside and behind the barn. Franklin passed a zoning ordinance by virtue of which Potts's lot was classified as residential property. Soon afterward, Potts moved some saw logs onto his back lot, and the city complained that Potts's use of his property for storage of building materials was a "nonconforming use." Potts then brought an action to enjoin interference by the city of Franklin. Decision?

16. Sam and Eleanor Gaito purchased a home from Howard Frank Auman, Jr., in the spring of 1978. Auman had completed the construction of the house in November 1973. In the interim, three different parties had lived in the house for brief periods, but Auman had retained ownership. The last tenants, the Ashleys, experienced difficulties with the home's air conditioning system. Repairs were attempted, but no effort was made to change the capacity of the air conditioning unit.

When the Gaitos moved into the house in June 1978, they too had problems with the air conditioning. The system created only a ten-degree difference between the outside and inside temperatures. The Gaitos complained to Auman on a number of occasions, but extensive repairs failed to correct the cooling problem. In May 1981, the Gaitos brought an action against Auman, alleging that the purchase price of the home included central air conditioning and that Auman had breached the implied warranty of habitability. At trial, an expert in the field of heating and air conditioning testified that a four-ton air conditioning system, rather than the three-and-one-half-ton system originally installed, was appropriate for the Gaitos' house. The jury returned a verdict in favor of the Gaitos in the amount of $3,655, and the court of appeals affirmed. Decision?

**WWW** **Internet Exercise** Find and compare the rates among mortgage providers on (a) thirty-year mortgages, (b) fifteen-year mortgages, and (c) adjustable rate mortgages.

# CHAPTER 52

# Trusts and Decedents' Estates

In previous chapters, we have seen that real and personal property may be transferred in a number of ways, including by sale and by gift. Another important way in which a person may convey property or allow others to use or benefit from it is through trusts and wills. Trusts may take effect during the transferor's lifetime or, when used in a will, they may become effective upon his death. Wills enable individuals to control the transfer of their property at their death. Upon a person's death, his or her property must pass to someone, and individuals are well advised to decide how their property should be distributed. Except for statutory or common law rights of spouses, the law permits individuals to make such distributions by sale, gift, trust, and will. If, however, an individual dies without a will—that is, intestate—State law prescribes who shall be entitled to the property that individual owned at death. This chapter will examine both trusts and wills, as well as the manner in which property descends when a person dies without leaving a will.

## TRUSTS

A **trust** is a *fiduciary relationship* in which one or more persons hold *legal title* to property while its use, enjoyment, and benefit (*equitable title*) belong to another. A trust may be created for any purpose that is not against the law or public policy and may be established by agreement of the parties, by bequest in a will, or by a court decree. However created, the relationship is known as a trust. The party creating the trust is the **creator** or **settlor,** the party holding the legal title to the property is the **trustee** of the trust, and the person who receives the benefit of the trust is the **beneficiary.**

◆ *See Figure 52–1*

## TYPES OF TRUSTS

Although they are of many varieties, all trusts may be divided into two major groups: express and implied. Implied trusts, which are imposed upon property by court order, are categorized as either "constructive" or "resulting" trusts.

### Express Trusts

An express trust is, as the name indicates, a trust established by voluntary action and is represented by a written document, an oral statement, or conduct of the settlor. In a majority of jurisdictions, an express trust of real property must be in writing to meet the requirements of the statute of frauds. Trusts of personal property and implied trusts do not fall within the requirements of the statute of frauds.

No particular words are necessary to create a trust, provided that the intent of the settlor to establish a trust is unmistakable. Sometimes a settlor will offer a gift accompanied by words of request or recommendation implying or expressing the settlor's hope that the gift should or will be used for a particular purpose. Thus, instead of clearly creating a trust by leaving property "to X for the benefit and use of Y," a settlor may leave property to X "in full confidence and with hope that he will care for Y." Such a **"precatory expression"** (words of request) may be so definite as to impose a trust upon the property for the benefit of Y. Whether it creates a trust or is considered nothing more than a gratuitous wish will depend on whether the court concludes from all the facts that the settlor genuinely intended a trust. Generally, courts hold that words such as *request, hope,* and *rely* place no legal obligation upon the recipient of a gift and therefore do not create a trust.

*Testamentary Trust* Trusts employed in wills are known as **testamentary trusts** because they become effective after the settlor's death.

**FIGURE 52–1** Trusts

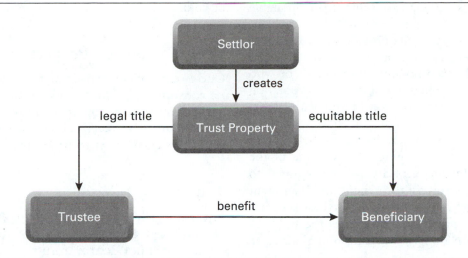

---

*Inter Vivos Trust* A trust established during the settlor's lifetime is referred to as an *inter vivos* or "between the living" trust.

*Charitable Trusts* Almost any trust that has for its purpose a benefit for the public or a sizeable segment of the public is classified as a **charitable trust,** unless it is so vague that it cannot be enforced. Gifts for public museums, for park maintenance, and for the dissemination of a particular political doctrine or religious belief have been upheld as charitable.

*Spendthrift Trusts* Often, believing that a beneficiary cannot be relied on to preserve even the limited rights granted her as beneficiary, a settlor may provide in the trust instrument that the beneficiary cannot, by assignment or otherwise, impair her rights to receive principal or income in the future and that creditors of the beneficiary cannot attach the fund or the income. The term *spendthrift,* as used in connection with the relationship known as a **spendthrift trust,** refers to a provision in a trust instrument under which the trust estate is removed both from the beneficiary's control and disposition and from liability for her individual debts. Spendthrift provisions are valid in most States. Once the beneficiary actually receives income from the trust, however, creditors may seize the income or the beneficiary may use it as she pleases.

*Totten Trusts* A **totten trust** or **savings account trust** involves a bank account opened by the settlor of the trust. For example, Joanne deposits a sum of money into a savings account in the name of "Joanne, in trust for Justin." The settlor, Joanne, may make additional deposits in the account from time to time and may withdraw money from it whenever she pleases. Because the settlor may revoke the totten trust by withdrawing the funds or by changing the form of the account, the courts have held such a trust to be tentative. Usually the transfer of ownership becomes complete only upon the depositor's death, when the beneficiary is entitled to the balance of the account.

## Implied Trusts

In some cases, the courts, in the absence of any express intent to create a trust, will impose a trust upon property because the acts of the parties appear to warrant such a construction. An implied trust owes its existence to the law. As previously stated, implied trusts generally are divided into two classes: constructive trusts and resulting trusts.

*Constructive Trusts* A court of equity creates a **constructive trust** to rectify misconduct or to prevent unjust enrichment. Misconduct includes abuse of a confidential relationship, actual fraud, undue influence, and duress. Justice Cardozo referred to a constructive trust as "the formula through which the conscience of equity finds expression. When property has been acquired in such circumstances that the holder of the legal title may not in good conscience retain the beneficial interest, equity converts him into a trustee." *Beatty v. Guggenheim Exploration Co.*, 225 N.Y. 380, 122 N.E. 378 (1919). Rather than reflect the intent of the parties, a constructive trust represents a court's attempt to achieve an equitable result.

Business and personal affairs provide many examples of constructive trusts. A director of a corporation who takes advantage of a "corporate opportunity" or who makes an undisclosed profit in a deal with the corporation will be treated as a trustee for the corporation with respect to the property or profits he acquires. Likewise, a trustee under an express trust who permits a lease held by the trust to expire and then acquires a new lease of the property in his individual capacity will be required to hold the new lease in trust for the beneficiary. If an agent who is given money by his principal to purchase property in the name of the principal instead uses the funds to acquire title in himself, courts will treat him as a trustee for the principal.

As previously indicated, the courts also invoke constructive trusts in situations involving those who use positions of friendship or marriage to their unjust advantage.

 *See Case 52–1*

*Resulting Trusts* A resulting trust serves to effect the inferred or presumed intent of parties who have inadequately expressed their actual wishes. A resulting trust does not depend on contract or agreement and, as it is created by implication and by operation of law, it does not need to be evidenced in writing. The most common example of a resulting trust is where Joel pays the purchase price for property and takes title in the name of Ann. The presumption here is that the parties intended Ann to hold the property for Joel's benefit, and Ann will be treated as a trustee. The presumption, however, may be rebutted by evidence that Joel intended to make a gift to Ann.

## CREATION OF TRUSTS

Each trust has (1) a creator or settlor, (2) a "corpus" or trust property, (3) a trustee, and (4) a beneficiary. As previously mentioned, no particular words are necessary to create a trust, provided that the settlor's intent to establish a trust is unmistakable. Consideration is not essential to an enforceable trust.

### Settlor

Any person legally capable of making a contract may create a trust. But if the settlor's contract would be voidable or void because of infancy, incompetency, or some

other reason, her declaration of trust is also voidable or void.

## Trust Corpus or Property

One essential characteristic of a trust is a trust corpus or *res* consisting of definite and specific property. The *res* may be any type of property that exists and is assignable. A trust cannot be effective immediately for property not yet in existence or yet to be acquired.

## Trustee

Anyone legally capable of holding title to the trust property may be a trustee. Furthermore, the lack of a trustee will not destroy a trust. If the settlor neglects to appoint one, if the named trustee does not qualify, or if the named trustee declines to serve, the court will appoint an individual or institution to act as trustee. A trustee can, of course, decline to serve, and before the property will vest in her it is necessary that she accept the trust.

*Duties of the Trustee* A trustee has three primary duties:

1. to carry out the purposes of the trust,
2. to act with prudence and care in the administration of the trust, and
3. to exercise a high degree of loyalty toward the beneficiary.

Under ordinary circumstances, no special skills are required of a trustee, who is required simply to act with the same degree of care that a **prudent person** would exercise with respect to his personal affairs. The trustee has a duty to make the trust property productive and thus to invest it in income-producing assets. Given the myriad circumstances that may affect any particular case, what constitutes the care of a "prudent person" is, of course, not easy to generalize.

The duty of loyalty arises from and illustrates the fiduciary character of the relationship between the trustee and the beneficiary. In all his dealings with the trust property, the beneficiary, and third parties, the trustee must act exclusively in the interest of the beneficiary. A failure to so act may arise from obvious self-dealing, or it may be entirely innocent; in either event, the trustee can be charged with lack of loyalty.

 *See Case 52–2*

*Powers of the Trustee* The powers of a trustee are determined by (1) the authority granted him by the settlor in the instrument creating the trust and (2) the rules of law in the jurisdiction in which the trust is established. State laws affecting the powers of trustees have their greatest impact upon the investments a trustee may make with trust funds. Most States have adopted a prudent investor rule. Some States, however, still follow the historical test, which prescribes a list of types of securities qualified for trust investment. In some jurisdictions, this list is permissive; in others, it is mandatory. If the list is permissive, the trustee may invest in types of securities not listed but carries the burden of showing that he made a prudent choice. The trust instrument may give the trustee wide discretion as to investments; in such an event, the trustee need not adhere to the list deemed advisable under the statute.

*Allocation of Principal and Income* Trusts often settle a life estate in the trust corpus on one beneficiary and a remainder interest on another beneficiary. For example, on his death, a man leaves his property to a trustee who is instructed to pay the income from the property to his widow during her life and to distribute the property to his children upon her death. In these instances, the trustee must distribute the principal to one party (the remainderman) and the income to another (the life tenant or income beneficiary). The trustee also must allocate receipts and charge expenses between the income beneficiary and the remainderman. If the trust agreement does not specify how the funds should be allocated, the trustee is provided statutory guidance, derived in most States from the **Uniform Principal and Income Act**. A trustee who fails to comply with the trust agreement or the statute is personally liable for any loss.

The general rule in allocating benefits and burdens between income beneficiaries and remaindermen is that *ordinary* or current receipts and expenses are chargeable to the income beneficiary, whereas *extraordinary* receipts and expenses are allocated to the remainderman. Ordinary income is money paid for the use of trust property and any gain from the use of the trust property, while property received as a substitute for or a change in the form of the trust *res* is allocated to the trust principal.

◆ *See Figure 52–2*

## Beneficiary

There are very few restrictions on who (or what) may be a beneficiary. Charitable uses are a common purpose of trusts, and if the settlor's object does not outrage public policy or morals, the courts will uphold almost any purpose that happens to strike a settlor's fancy.

A person named as a beneficiary of a trust may accept or reject the trust. In the absence of restrictive provisions in the trust instrument, such as a spendthrift clause, a beneficiary's interest may be reached by his creditors, or the beneficiary may sell or dispose of his interest. Upon his death, if the beneficiary held more than a life estate in the trust, the beneficiary's interest, unless disposed of by his will, passes to his heirs or personal representatives.

## TERMINATION OF A TRUST

Unless the settlor reserves a power of revocation, the general rule is that a trust, once validly created, is irrevocable. If subject to such reservation, the trust may be terminated at the settlor's discretion.

FIGURE 52–2  Allocation of Principal and Income

| | Receipts | Expenses |
|---|---|---|
| **Ordinary—Income Beneficiary** | Rents<br>Royalties<br>Cash dividends (regular and extraordinary)<br>Interest | Interest payments<br>Insurance<br>Ordinary taxes<br>Ordinary repairs<br>Depreciation |
| **Extraordinary—Remainderman** | Stock dividends<br>Stock splits<br>Proceeds from sale or exchange of corpus<br>Settlement of claims for injury to corpus | Extraordinary repairs<br>Long-term improvements<br>Principal amortization<br>Costs incurred in the sale or purchase of corpus |

Normally, the instrument creating a trust establishes the date on which the trust will terminate. The instrument may specify a period of years for which the trust is to endure, or the settlor may provide that the trust shall continue during the life of a named individual. The death of the trustee or beneficiary does not terminate the trust if neither of their lives delimits the duration of the trust.

If the purpose for which a trust has been established is fulfilled before the specified termination date, a court may decree the trust terminated. Most courts will not order the termination of a trust, even at the request of all the beneficiaries, if any of its purposes remain unfulfilled. The purposes the settlor set forth in the trust instrument, not the beneficiaries' wishes, will govern the court's actions. If the trustee acquires both the equitable and legal title to the trust *res,* the *merger doctrine* applies, and the trust terminates as the trustee and beneficiary must be different persons for a trust to exist.

# DECEDENTS' ESTATES

When a person dies, the title to his property must pass to someone. If the decedent leaves a valid will, his property will pass as he directs, subject only to certain limitations imposed by the State. If, however, no valid will has been executed, the decedent is said to have died "intestate," and the State prescribes who shall be entitled to the property. If a decedent dies leaving a valid will that disposes of less than all of her net probate estate, intestacy laws govern the portion not effectively devised by the will. If a person dies without a will and leaves no heirs or next of kin, her property *escheats* (reverts) to the State. Nonetheless, not all of a decedent's property will pass through the probate estate (the distribution of a decedent's estate to her successors). Certain property will pass outside of the estate, through arrangements unaffected by the distribution of the decedent's estate. For instance, a decedent's life insurance policy or pension plan will pass to the beneficiary of the policy or plan, property the decedent jointly owned with a right of survivorship will pass to the survivor, and property subject to a trust will be governed by the trust instrument.

## *WILLS*

A **will** is a written instrument, executed according to statutorily imposed formalities, whereby a person makes a disposition of his property which is to take effect after

his death. A will is also called a **testament;** the maker of the will is called a testator; and gifts made in a will are called devises or bequests. A **bequest** or **legacy** is a gift by will of personal property; a **devise** is a gift by will of real property.

One major characteristic of a will sets it apart from other transactions such as deeds and contracts: a will is revocable at any time during life. There is no such thing as an irrevocable will. A document binding during life (such as a promise to make a will) may be a contract or a deed (conveying, for instance, a vested remainder after a life estate in the grantor), but it is not a will. Even a testator who, by executing a joint or mutual will, contractually promises not to revoke her will retains the power to revoke. Nonetheless, such a testator may be liable for breach of contract, and the courts may impose a constructive trust upon the beneficiaries of her estate. A will takes effect only on the death of the testator.

In 1969, the National Conference of Commissioners on Uniform State Laws and the American Bar Association approved the Uniform Probate Code (UPC), an attempt to encourage throughout the United States the adoption of a uniform, flexible, speedy, efficient, and, in most cases, less expensive system of settling a decedent's estate. The UPC, which has been updated a number of times, is based on the major premise that the probate court's appropriate role in the settlement of an estate is to offer assistance as requested or required, not to impose supervision or pointlessly detailed formality upon completely noncontentious settlements. The following discussion summarizes the general principles and procedures applicable to decedents' estates and notes the parallel principles and procedures under the UPC.

## Mental Capacity

To make a valid will, the testator must have both the "power" and the "capacity" to do so. The requisite testamentary intent must always be present to create a valid will.

***Testamentary Power and Capacity*** The State grants the *power* to make a will to persons who are of a class believed generally able to handle their affairs without regard to the personal limitations of individual members of that class. Thus, in most States, children under a certain age cannot make valid wills.

The *capacity* to make a will refers to the measures by which the courts determine whether a particular person in the class generally granted the power to make wills is, in fact, mentally capable of doing so. Testamentary capacity generally requires that the testator be of sound mind and that she know the nature and extent of her property and the objects of her bounty. Underlying the notion of capacity is the premise that, for a will to be valid, a testator must *intend* a document to be his will. This requisite intent is considered absent if the testator is mentally incompetent or suffers from delusions. Nevertheless, because capacity is an individual matter, devising a universal test to measure this qualification is not easy. A person adjudicated incompetent can, in a lucid period, make a valid will. An aged and enfeebled octogenarian may have the capacity to execute a will. Meeting the test of capacity to make a will takes less in the way of mental ability than does independently managing one's affairs during her lifetime.

Under the UPC, any person eighteen or more years of age who is of sound mind may make a will. Section 2–501.

See Case 52–3

**Conduct Invalidating a Will** Any document that purports to be a will but has been induced by misconduct negating the testator's voluntary intent is not a valid will. This is the basis for the rule that a will resulting from *duress, undue influence,* or *fraud* is no will at all.

**Undue influence** is influence that destroys the testator's free will and substitutes another person's will for that of the testator. A general influence over the testator is not sufficient to prove improper pressure. The influence must be directed specifically to the act of making the will. A wife urges her husband to leave all his property to her; this influence is not "undue." Most frequently, the charge of undue influence arises when a testator leaves her property to one who is not a blood relative, such as a friend who took care of the testator in her last illness or during her last years. Evidence demonstrating that the beneficiary under the will was in close contact with the testator and that the natural objects of the testator's bounty are ignored in the will may imply undue influence.

**Fraud** is a misrepresentation of material fact that is made by a beneficiary of a will with the intent to deceive the decedent and that causes the decedent to write or change her will in reliance upon it. The charge of fraud can also be used to invalidate a will. For example, Brian dies, leaving all his property to Mark upon Mark's representation that he is Brian's long-lost son. Mark in fact is not Brian's son. In such a case, the will may be set aside because the misrepresentation was made with the intent to deceive, and Brian justifiably relied upon it.

See Chapter 11 for a more complete discussion of duress, undue influence, and fraud.

 See Case 52–1

## Formal Requirements of a Will

By statute in all jurisdictions, a will must comply with certain formalities to be valid. These formalities are intended both to ensure that the testator understood what she was doing and to help prevent fraud. As discussed later, some States permit specific types of wills that do not meet all of these requirements to be enforced with respect to testamentary dispositions of certain property.

**Writing** A basic requirement of a valid will is that it be in writing. UPC, Section 2–502. The writing may be informal, as long as it substantially meets the basic statutory requirements. Pencil, ink, typewriting, and photocopy are equally valid media, and valid wills have been made on scratch paper and on an envelope.

It is also valid to incorporate into a will by reference another document which in itself is not a will for lack of proper execution. For a memorandum to be thus incorporated, the following four conditions must exist: (1) the memorandum must be in writing; (2) it must be in existence when the will is executed; (3) it must be adequately described in the will; and (4) in some States it must be described in the will as being in existence. UPC, Section 2–510.

**Signature** A will must be signed by the testator or in the testator's name by some other individual in the testator's presence and at the testator's direction. UPC, Section 2–502. A fundamental requirement in almost all jurisdictions, the signature verifies that the will has been executed. The testator's initials, a single word, such as "father," or a mark at the end of a will in the testator's handwriting are adequate if intended as an execution.

Most statutes require the signature to be at the end of the will. Even in jurisdictions that do not so require, placing the signature at the end will preclude the charge that the portions of a will that follow the signature were written subsequent to its execution and are therefore invalid.

**Attestation** A written will must be attested (witnessed or certified) by witnesses, who serve to acknowledge that the testator did execute the will and that she had the requisite intent and capacity. The number and qualifications of witnesses and the manner of attestation are generally specified by statute. Usually two or three witnesses are required. Section 2–502 of the UPC requires that at least two persons, each of whom witnessed either the signing or the testator's acknowledgment of the will, act as witnesses to the will.

The most common restriction on the ability to act as a witness is that a witness must not have any interest under the will. This requirement takes at least two forms under statutes. One type of statute disqualifies a witness who is also a beneficiary under the will. The other type voids the bequest or devise to the interested witness, thus making him a disinterested and thereby qualified witness. Defining what constitutes an "interest" sufficient to disqualify a witness is not always easy. The spouse of a beneficiary under a will has been held to be "interested" and thus not qualified. Usually, though, the courts will not disqualify a person simply because he is named as executor in the will. The attorney who drafts the will generally is a qualified witness. Under the UPC, attestation by an interested witness does not invalidate a will or any provision thereof. Section 2–505(b).

## Revocation of a Will

A will is revocable by the testator, and, under certain circumstances, a will may be revoked by operation of law. Most jurisdictions specify by statute the methods by which a will may be revoked. The three generally accepted methods for revoking a will are as follows:

***Destruction or Alteration***  Tearing, burning, or otherwise destroying a will is an effective way of revoking a will, unless such destruction is shown to be inadvertent or without intent. UPC, Section 2–507. In some States, partial revocation may be accomplished by erasing or obliterating a part of the will. In no case, however, will a substituted or additional bequest by interlineation be effective without re-execution and re-attestation.

Courts occasionally face the difficult question of determining whether a will was revoked by destruction or simply mislaid.

👨‍⚖️ *See Case 52–4*

***Subsequent Will***  The execution of a second will does not in itself constitute a revocation of an earlier will. The first will is revoked to the extent that the second will is inconsistent with the first. UPC, Section 2–507. The most certain manner of revocation is the execution of a later will containing a declaration that all former wills are revoked. In some but not all jurisdictions, a testator may revoke a will by a written declaration to this effect in a subsequent document, such as a letter, even though the document does not meet the formal requirements of a will.

***Operation of Law***  A *marriage* generally revokes a will executed prior to the marriage. Divorce, on the other hand, under the general rule, does not revoke a provision in the will of one party for the benefit of the other. Section 2–508 of the UPC takes a different position by providing that a divorce or annulment occurring after the execution of a will revokes any disposition of property the will made to the former spouse. No change of circumstances, however, other than divorce, annulment, or the testator's homicide by a devisee, revokes a will. Thus, a subsequent marriage does not revoke a will. Nonetheless, a spouse who marries the testator after the execution of the will is entitled only to the share she would receive if the testator were to die without a will. UPC, Section 2–301.

The *birth* of a child after execution of a will may revoke a will at least as far as that child is concerned if it appears that the testator omitted to make a provision for the child. In some jurisdictions and under the UPC, the subsequent birth of a child will not revoke the will; rather, unless it appears from the will that the omission was intentional, the child is entitled to a share the same as the one he would receive were the testator to die without a will. Section 2–302.

## Effectiveness of Testamentary Provisions

***Renunciation by the Surviving Spouse***  Statutes generally provide a surviving spouse the right to renounce a will and set forth the method by which the spouse may do so. Such statutory provisions enable the spouse to decide which method of taking—under the will or under intestate succession—would be most advantageous. Only those whom the statute designates may exercise the right to renounce a will, and the right conferred on the surviving spouse is personal. Upon renunciation of the will, the law of intestate succession determines the share of the estate taken by the surviving spouse.

***Abatement and Ademption of a Bequest***  Abatement is the reduction or elimination of gifts by category upon the reduction in the value of the estate of the testator after the execution of his will. It can have serious implications. The first items to abate in a will are the **residue,** or those items remaining after provisions for specific and general gifts. **Specific gifts,** which must be satisfied first, involve particular or uniquely identifiable items; **general gifts** do not. For example, if John, a widower, after making specific gifts, leaves "all the rest, residue, and remainder of my estate to my daughter, Mary," Mary may receive a great deal less than her deceased father intended. Suppose at the time John executes his will, he estimates his worth at $150,000. He leaves $20,000 to his church, $10,000 to the Salvation Army, and his car, worth $10,000, to his business partner and assumes that Mary will receive approximately $110,000. Having suffered substantial business and market reverses, John dies five years later without having changed his will. His executor reports that there is only $50,000 in the estate. Mary will receive only $10,000 because the specific devise of the car and the general devises of the $20,000 and $10,000 will abate only after the residue is depleted.

Ademption, or the removal or extinction of a gift by act of the testator, occurs when a testator neglects to change his will after changed circumstances have made the performance of a provision in the will impossible. For example, Hope buys a farm, Blackacre, wishing it to go on her death to a favorite nephew who is studying agriculture at college. After so providing in her will, she sells Blackacre and uses the money to buy Greenacre. The general rule is that the nephew will not be entitled to Greenacre. Nonetheless, the courts sometimes have modified this doctrine to reflect the perceived intent of the decedent. Under the "modified intention theory," through which a court attempts to effectuate the decedent's presumed intent, no ademption occurs where the property in question is missing from the estate because of some involuntary act of the decedent or some event over which he had no control.

## Special Types of Wills

There are a number of special types of wills, including nuncupative wills, holographic wills, soldiers' and sailors' wills, conditional wills, joint and reciprocal wills, and living wills.

*Nuncupative Wills* A **nuncupative will** is an unwritten oral declaration made before witnesses. In the few jurisdictions that authorize them, such declarations usually can be made only when the testator is in his last illness. Under most statutes permitting nuncupative wills, only limited amounts of personal property, generally under $1,000, may be passed by such wills. Under the UPC, all wills must be in writing. Section 2–502.

*Holographic Wills* In approximately one-half of the jurisdictions, a signed will *entirely* in the handwriting of the testator is a valid testamentary document even if the will is not witnessed. Under the UPC, Section 2–503, the signature and *material* provisions must be in the testator's handwriting. Such an instrument, referred to as a **holographic will,** must comply strictly with the statutory requirements for such wills.

*Soldiers' and Sailors' Wills* For soldiers on active duty and sailors at sea, most statutes relax the formal requirements for a will and permit a testamentary disposition to be valid regardless of the informality of the document. In most jurisdictions, however, such a will cannot pass title to real estate.

*Conditional Wills* A contingent or conditional will is one that takes effect only on the happening of a specified contingency, which is a condition precedent to the operation of the will.

*Joint and Mutual or Reciprocal Wills* A joint will consists of a single instrument that is made the will of two or more persons and is signed by them jointly. By comparison, in making mutual or reciprocal wills, two or more persons execute separate instruments with reciprocal terms in which each testator makes a testamentary disposition in favor of the other.

*Living Wills* Almost all States have adopted statutes that permit an individual to execute a living will. A **living will** is a document by which an individual states that she does not wish to receive extraordinary medical treatment to preserve her life. Such a document, which must comply with applicable statutory requirements, allows an individual to reject the use of life-prolonging procedures that artificially delay the dying process and to die naturally should she suffer an incurable illness or injury.

## Codicils

A **codicil** is a subsequent will, executed with all the formal requirements of a will, that augments or revises a prior will. The most frequent problem such an instrument raises involves the extent to which its terms, if not absolutely clear, revoke or alter provisions in the will. For the purpose of determining the testator's intent, the codicil and the will are regarded as a single instrument.

# INTESTATE SUCCESSION

Property not effectively disposed of before death or by will passes in accordance with the law of intestate succession. The rules set forth in statutes for determining, in case of intestacy, to whom the decedent's property shall be distributed not only ensure an orderly transfer of title to property but also purport to effect what would probably be the wishes of the decedent. Nonetheless, the intestacy statute will govern the distribution of the estate even if such distribution is contrary to the clear intention of the decedent.

The rules of descent vary widely from State to State, but as a general rule and except for the specific statutory or dower rights of the widow, the intestate property passes in equal shares to each child of the decedent living at the time of his death, with the share of any predeceased child to be divided equally among the children of such predeceased child. For example, if Arthur dies intestate leaving a widow and children, his widow generally will receive one-third of his real estate and personal property, and the remainder will pass to his children in the manner stated above. If his wife does not survive Arthur, his entire estate passes to their children. If Arthur dies leaving two surviving children, Belinda and Carl, and two grandchildren, Donna and David, the children of a predeceased child Darwin, the estate will go one-third to Belinda, one-third to Carl, and one-sixth each to Donna and David, the grandchildren, who divide equally their parent's one-third share. This result is described legally by the statement that *lineal descendants* of predeceased children take **per stirpes,** or by representation of their parent. If Arthur had executed a will, he may have provided that all his lineal descendants, regardless of generation, would share equally. In that case, Arthur's estate would be divided into four equal parts, and his descendants would be said to take **per capita.**

If only the widow and relatives other than his children survive the decedent, a larger share is generally allotted the widow. She may receive all the decedent's personal property and one-half his real estate or, in some States, his entire estate.

At common law, property could not ascend lineally; parents of an intestate decedent did not share in his estate. Today, in many States, if a decedent has no lineal descendants or a surviving spouse, the statute provides that parents are the next to share.

Most statutes make some provision for brothers and sisters in the event no spouse, parents, or children survive the decedent. Brothers and sisters, together with nieces, nephews, aunts, and uncles, are termed *collateral heirs.*

Beyond these limits, most statutes provide that, if there are no survivors in the named classes, the property shall be distributed equally among the next of kin in equal degree.

The common law did not consider a stepchild as an heir or next of kin, that is, as one to whom property would descend by operation of law, and this rule prevails today. Legally adopted children are, however, recognized as lawful heirs of their adoptive parents.

These generalities should be accepted as such; few fields of the law of property are so strictly a matter of statute, and the rights of heirs cannot reasonably be predicted without a knowledge of the exact terms of the applicable statute.

Under the UPC, if the decedent dies without a will, (1) if there is no descendant and no parent surviving or if all surviving children are children of the decedent and the spouse, the surviving spouse is entitled to the entire estate; (2) if there is a parent surviving but no descendants, the spouse is entitled to the first $200,000 plus three-quarters of the remaining estate; (3) if the decedent is survived by one or more descendants who are also descendants of the surviving spouse and also by descendants who are not descendants of the surviving spouse, the spouse is entitled to the first $150,000 plus one-half of the remaining estate; and (4) if the decedent is survived by descendants who are not also descendants of the surviving spouse, the spouses is entitled to the first $100,000 plus one-half of the remaining estate.

◆ *See Figure 52–3*

🔨 *See Case 52–5*

# ADMINISTRATION OF ESTATES

Because they are statutory, the rules and procedures controlling the management of a decedent's estate vary somewhat from State to State. In all jurisdictions, the estate is managed and finally disbursed under the supervision of a court. The procedure for managing the distribution of decedents' estates is known as **probate**, and the court that supervises the procedure is often designated the probate court.

The first legal step after death is usually to determine whether or not the deceased left a will. If a will exists, the testator likely has named her executor in it. If there is no will or if a will exists but fails to name an executor, the court will, upon petition, appoint an administrator. The closest adult relative who is a resident of the State is entitled to such appointment.

FIGURE 52–3   *Per Stirpes* and *Per Capita*

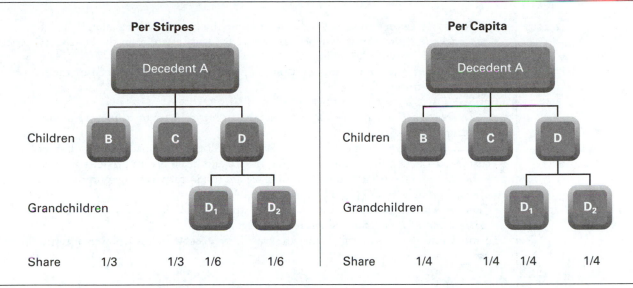

Once approved or appointed by the court, the **executor** or **administrator** holds title to all the personal property of the deceased and is accountable to the creditors and the beneficiaries. The estate is his responsibility.

If there is a will, the witnesses must prove it before the court by testifying to the signing of the will by all signatories and by confirming the mental condition of the testator at the time she executed the will. If the witnesses are dead, proof of their handwriting is necessary. If satisfied that the will is proved, the court will enter a formal decree admitting the will to probate.

Soon after the admission of the will to probate, the decedent's personal representative—the executor or administrator—must file an inventory of the estate. The personal representative will then commence her duties

of collecting the assets, paying the debts, and disbursing the remainder. The executor or administrator occupies a fiduciary position not unlike that of a trustee, and his responsibility for investing proceeds and otherwise managing the estate is equally demanding.

The administration of every estate involves probate expenses as well as fees to be paid to the executor or administrator and to the attorney who handles the estate. In addition, taxes are imposed at death by both the Federal and State governments. The Federal government imposes an **estate tax** on the transfer of property at death, while most State governments impose an **inheritance tax** on the privilege of an heir or beneficiary to receive the property. These taxes are separate from the basic income tax that the estate must pay on income received during estate administration.

 # Chapter Summary

| **Trusts** | **Definition** a trust is a fiduciary relationship in which legal title to property (trust corpus) is held by one or more parties (the trustee) for the use, enjoyment, and benefit of another (the beneficiary)<br>**Express Trust** a trust established by voluntary action by the creator (settlor); usually in writing, although it may be oral<br>• *Testamentary Trust* a trust employed in a will; it becomes effective after the settlor's death<br>• **Inter Vivos** *Trust* a trust established during the settlor's lifetime |
| --- | --- |

- *Charitable Trust* a trust that has as its purpose the benefit of humankind
- *Spendthrift Trust* a trust designed to remove the trust estate from the beneficiary's control and from liability for his individual debts
- *Totten Trust* a tentative trust consisting of a joint bank account opened by the settlor (creator of the trust)

**Implied Trust** a trust created by operation of law

- *Constructive Trust* an implied trust imposed to rectify fraud or to prevent unjust enrichment
- *Resulting Trust* an implied trust imposed to fulfill the presumed intent of the settlor

**Trustee** anyone legally capable of holding title to and dealing with property may be a trustee

- *Duties* the three primary duties of a trustee are to (1) carry out the purposes of the trust, (2) act prudently, and (3) act with utmost loyalty
- *Powers* generally established by the trust instrument and State law
- *Allocation of Principal and Income* see Figure 52–2

**Termination** the general rule is that the trust is irrevocable unless a power of revocation is reserved in the trust instrument

## Wills

**Definition** a will (or testament) is a written instrument, executed with the formalities required by statute, whereby a person makes a disposition of his property to take effect after his death

**Mental Capacity**

- *Testamentary Capacity* for a will to be valid the testator must be sufficiently competent to intend the document to be her will
- *Conduct Invalidating a Will* a will that is the product of duress, undue influence, or fraud is invalid and of no effect

**Formal Requirements** a will must be (1) in writing, (2) signed, and (3) attested to by witnesses

**Revocation** a will is revocable by the testator and under certain circumstances may be revoked by operation of law

- *Destruction or Alteration* revokes a will
- *Subsequent Will* revokes prior wills to the extent they are inconsistent
- *Codicil* an addition to or revision of a will executed with all the formalities of a will
- *Marriage* generally revokes a will executed before the marriage
- *Birth of a Child* may revoke a will at least as far as that child is concerned
- *Renunciation by Surviving Spouse* surviving spouse may elect to take under laws of descent

**Special Types of Wills** generally binding only in specific situations and may have limitations upon their use

## Intestate Succession

**Intestate** condition of person who dies without a valid will

**Course of Descent** each State prescribes rules for the passage of property not governed by a valid will; as a general rule the property passes in equal shares to each child after the widow's statutory or dower rights have been settled

| **Administration of Estates** | **Probate**  the court's supervision of the management and distribution of the estate<br>**Executor or Administrator**  a person who is responsible for collecting the assets, paying the debts, and disbursing the remainder according to the will or intestate statute<br>• **_Executor_**  the person named in the will and appointed by the court to administer the will<br>• **_Administrator_**  a person appointed by the court to administer the estate when there is no will or when the person named in the will fails to qualify |
| --- | --- |

# Cases

### CASE 52–1
## Constructive Trusts/Undue Influence
### *IN RE ESTATE OF WELCH*
Court of Appeals of Iowa, 1995
534 N.W.2d 109

CADY, J.

This is an appeal by plaintiff, Patricia Fisher, from the district court's refusal to establish a constructive trust over certain inter vivos transfers of property by her father to his wife. On . . . review, we reverse.

George W. Welch died testate on April 25, 1991. He was sixty-nine years old. He was survived by his third wife, Dorothy Welch, and his daughter from his first marriage, Patricia Fisher. George and Dorothy had been married for eight months prior to George's death. George was very wealthy.

Although George and Dorothy executed a prenuptial agreement, George made a new will during the month preceding his death. Dorothy was the sole beneficiary under the will if she survived George. Patricia was the sole beneficiary under George's former will.

George owned property valued at nearly one million dollars prior to his death. Of this amount, approximately $400,000 was owned with Patricia in joint tenancy. During the eight-month marriage to Dorothy, George transferred over $330,000 of assets, annuities, and insurance to Dorothy, either as joint tenant or as sole owner. George also asked Patricia to transfer a portion of their jointly-owned assets back to him. Dorothy assisted in the transfer of George's assets and often completed checks and other papers for George's signature. During the last month of George's life, Dorothy wrote checks totaling over $36,000. Dorothy received approximately sixty percent, or $570,000, of George's estate, either by his will or through [the inter vivos] transfer of assets during the marriage.

Patricia sought to set aside the will and the inter vivos transfers based on undue influence. She also claimed the premarital agreement precluded the inter vivos transfers.

The will contest was submitted to a jury, and the trial court heard the claim involving the inter vivos transfers. The jury found undue influence and set aside the will, while the trial court found no undue influence to support a constructive trust over the inter vivos transfers. The trial court determined that a confidential relationship did not exist between George and Dorothy and found Patricia failed to meet her burden of showing Dorothy exercised a dominating influence over George.

\* \* \*

## II. Constructive Trust

A constructive trust is a remedial device by which the holder of legal title is held to be a trustee for the benefit of another who in good conscience is entitled to the beneficial interest. [Citation.] It is an equitable doctrine applied for purposes of restitution, to prevent unjust enrichment. [Citation.]

Constructive trusts fall into three categories: "(1) those arising from actual fraud; (2) those arising from constructive fraud (appropriation of property by fiduciaries or others in confidential relationships); and (3) those based on equitable principles other than fraud." [Citation.] Other circumstances supporting imposition of equitable principles include bad faith, duress, coercion, undue influence, abuse of confidence, or any form of unconscionable conduct or questionable means by which one obtains the legal right to property which they should not in equity and good conscience hold. [Citations.]

* * *

Patricia seeks imposition of a constructive trust on two alternative bases. First she asserts a constructive trust should be created because a confidential relationship existed between Dorothy and George, and Dorothy abused this relationship. Second, she claims even if a confidential relationship did not exist, a constructive trust should be established on the basis that Dorothy unduly influenced George.

Undue influence is unfair persuasion of a party who is under the domination of the person exercising the persuasion or who by virtue of the relation between them is justified in assuming that the person will not act in a manner inconsistent with his or her welfare. [Citation.] The ultimate question is whether the result was produced by means that seriously impaired the free and competent exercise of judgment. [Citation.] There are four elements necessary to sustain a finding of undue influence. They are: (1) the grantor's susceptibility to undue influence; (2) opportunity to exercise such influence and effect the wrongful purpose; (3) disposition to influence unduly for the purpose of procuring an improper favor; and (4) a result clearly the effect of undue influence. [Citation.]

On our review of the record, we find it unnecessary to determine the existence of a confidential relationship or to determine the effect of the prenuptial agreement. We find clear and convincing evidence that Dorothy acted unconscionably by exercising undue influence over George in order to gain title to his property. Under the circumstances of this case, allowing Dorothy to retain the property gained in this manner would be inequitable.

George was in very poor health at the time of his marriage to Dorothy in August 1990. He suffered a crippling heart attack in 1988 and was told by doctors he would only live a few more years. After the heart attack, George was not permitted to drive and could not live alone. There was evidence that the damage to his heart might have affected the flow of blood to his brain. George suffered from severe depression and was suicidal. He was also an alcoholic.

Dorothy was a friend of George and his previous wife, Betty. Betty died in May 1988. Within a few days after Betty's death, Dorothy told George she had always loved him and wanted to marry him. She later threatened to commit suicide if George did not marry her. George asked other women to marry him before he married Dorothy. He was lonely and desperately looking for companionship.

After George and Dorothy married, George became isolated from his family and medical assistance. He stopped seeing his cardiologist and psychiatrist. His physical and medical condition deteriorated. There was medical testimony that George was very vulnerable and susceptible to undue influence during the last year of his life. He was dependent upon Dorothy for transportation, to remind him to take his medicine, for care when he had angina attacks, and for emotional support.

Dorothy was aware of George's wealth and knew George had a limited time to live due to his heart condition. * * * The transfer of assets into joint tenancy began shortly after the marriage and continued until shortly before George's death. Dorothy even removed George's name from their joint bank account within a month before his death. When George died she had all the locks changed on the house and allegedly informed Patricia of George's death by stating the money was put in joint accounts, the wills were changed, and your father has died. We do not share the trial court's view that the various financial arrangements between George and Dorothy were normal transactions between a husband and wife.

We conclude that a fair and pragmatic review of all the evidence clearly shows undue influence. Dorothy positioned herself as a dominant influence over George during the last months of his life. At the same time, George became particularly susceptible to being influenced due to his advancing age, impending death, deteriorating physical condition, and unstable emotional health. Furthermore, the manner in which George and Dorothy conducted their business, and even Dorothy's actions after George died, reveal a pattern of unfair persuasion or influence. George was isolated from family, friends, and complete medical care. The efforts to transfer his property were rushed and the transactions were done at unusual times. Upon our review of all the facts and circumstances, we find: George was susceptible; Dorothy had an opportunity to exercise undue influence, as well as the disposition to wrongfully influence George for the purpose of obtaining money and assets; and the assets she received resulted from the undue influence.

* * *

REVERSED AND REMANDED.

## CASE 52–2
# Duties of the Trustee
## *STURGIS v. STINSON*

Supreme Court of Virginia, 1991
241 Va. 531, 404 S.E.2d 56

LACY, J.

In this will construction case, we determine whether the testator placed restrictions on the amount of income which the income beneficiary was to receive and, if not, whether the executor was required to administer the assets of the trust created by the will in a manner which did not discriminate between successive beneficiaries and which produced a reasonable level of income in relation to the value of the trust assets.

Dr. William J. Sturgis, Jr., died testate in 1986, leaving an estate valued at $1,140,462, consisting of an automobile, approximately $300,000 in various stocks and bonds, and two parcels of real estate—Bush Hill Farm (the farm), valued in the estate inventory at $708,500, and a one-third undivided interest in another parcel of land with a value of $126,000. His will provided that his widow, Anne Sturgis, receive all the income from his estate for her lifetime. At her death, or if she were to renounce the income, the residue of the estate was to pass to his children, Susan Sturgis Stinson and Christopher S. Sturgis (the remaindermen).

The testator named his wife and Robert C. Oliver, Jr., as co-executors. Upon the wife's election not to serve, Oliver qualified as executor of the estate. In 1989, he filed a bill of complaint stating that the income beneficiary, Mrs. Sturgis, had complained that "the income derived from the estate is insufficient based upon the value of the assets of the estate" and asked that property of the trust be sold and so reinvested as to derive greater income. The remaindermen opposed the sale of the property and maintained that the trust assets could not be sold without their consent. The executor sought the guidance of the chancellor. . . . [T]he court entered a final decree holding that the will "created a trust"; that the executor had the obligation to deliver all the net income of the trust to Mrs. Sturgis and to invade the trust corpus when he determined the income therefrom was insufficient to meet the needs of the income beneficiary; that the executor had the "authority, but not the obligation, to convert assets of the estate . . . including real estate, to forms other than those in which he received them, so long as he behaves consistently with the 'prudent man' rule"; and that the executor "has performed

properly under the terms of the will." We awarded Mrs. Sturgis, the income beneficiary, an appeal from this decree.

The primary controversy here revolves around a single, but valuable, asset of the trust—Bush Hill Farm. This farm constitutes approximately 75 percent of the corpus of the trust and, at the time of trial, had a fair market value of $1.5 million. The maximum annual net income generated by this asset and paid to Mrs. Sturgis was $1,265.99 in 1988.

Mrs. Sturgis asserts that this return on the property, representing eighty-four one-thousandths of one percent of its fair market value, classifies this property as an unproductive asset and that, under general trust principles, the executor has an obligation to sell it and reinvest the proceeds. The executor and remaindermen contest Mrs. Sturgis' assertion that selling the farm is required in this case.

Under general trust law principles, where, as here, a trust is created for successive beneficiaries, the trustee has a duty to deal impartially with them. [Citations.] The parties agree that the executor's duties in relation to trust assets set out in the Restatement (Second) of Trusts embody sound and appropriate principles: The trustee is under a duty to the beneficiary to use reasonable care and skill to make the trust property productive. [Citation.] Unless it is otherwise provided by the terms of the trust, if property held in trust to pay the income to a beneficiary for a designated period and thereafter to pay the principal to another beneficiary produces no income or an income substantially less than the current rate of return on trust investments, and is likely to continue unproductive or underproductive, the trustee is under a duty to the beneficiary entitled to the income to sell such property within a reasonable time. [Citation.]

The executor and remaindermen assert that the trial court was correct in declining to apply these principles and require sale of the farm because the disposition and management of the farm and other trust assets were "otherwise provided by the terms of the" will. The remaindermen argue that the testator intended that the farm not be sold unless necessary to meet the needs of the income beneficiary. The executor argues that as long as the income beneficiary is receiving income sufficient to meet her needs, his discretion as to the management of trust assets should not be disturbed.

In contrast, Mrs. Sturgis argues that the will places no condition or limitation on the amount of income she is to receive and contains nothing to support the inference drawn by the chancellor that the testator wished to retain the farm as a family heritage.

* * *

Paragraph Four of the will consists of three sections. The first declares that Mrs. Sturgis is to receive "[a]ll of the income of my estate, of every nature and wheresoever situate," during her lifetime.

The second section of Paragraph Four provides that:

If at any time, . . . in the opinion of my Co-Executor, . . . the income of my estate together with such other income available to my wife is insufficient to meet any unusual expense . . . or to provide for her comfortable maintenance and welfare, then such Co-Executor may pay to my wife . . . such amounts from the principal or corpus of my estate as such Co-Executor deems necessary for such purposes.

* * *

Contrary to the argument advanced by the executor and the remaindermen, the second section of Paragraph Four imposes no limitation on the first section of that paragraph. Indeed, the second section confers a separate benefit upon the widow; in the event the income otherwise available to her "is insufficient to meet any unusual expense . . . or to provide for her comfortable maintenance and welfare," the executor is empowered to invade and deplete the corpus of the trust for her benefit. Consideration of the widow's need is of concern to the executor and a precondition to his actions only for depletion of the trust corpus. The power to deplete the corpus for that purpose is irrelevant to the issues framed in this appeal.

The power of the executor to convert and reinvest corpus assets is granted by Paragraph Six, in which the executor is given the right to dispose of property and to exercise all powers and rights afforded a fiduciary under general law. . . . The will does not specify any criteria of need or other preconditions for the executor's exercise of these powers. Nor is there any indication that the income beneficiary would receive anything less than all the net income, regardless of amount, and irrespective of need, generated from the executor's exercise of his investment and management authority.

* * *

Furthermore, there is nothing in the will or the record to suggest that the executor was required to treat Bush Hill Farm in a different manner than other trust assets. Although the testator easily could have addressed the disposition of the farm, he did not. Indeed, the will does not even refer to the farm specifically. While Bush Hill Farm had been in the Sturgis family for many years, neither the remaindermen, Dr. Sturgis, nor his parents had ever lived on the property. The only dwellings on the property were tenant farmers' shacks which had burned prior to Dr. Sturgis' death. This record does not reflect any connection the testator had with this piece of property which would support the conclusion that the testator intended to distinguish its treatment from that to be accorded other real or personal property in the trust.

We conclude, therefore, that the testator intended that Mrs. Sturgis, the income beneficiary, receive unconditionally all the income generated by the trust's assets. Additionally, if, in the opinion of the executor, the income from the trust and any other income available to her should become insufficient to meet her needs, the executor would be required to provide payments to her directly by depleting the corpus of the trust. Furthermore, we conclude that the testator did not intend to, and did not, direct or restrict the executor's management of the trust's assets, including Bush Hill Farm, except as provided under general law.

We have not previously addressed the duty of a fiduciary regarding the level of productivity of trust assets in circumstances where there are successive beneficiaries and no explicit instruction by the testator concerning that duty. [Citation.] We agree with the parties that the trust principles expressed in the Restatement and quoted above are appropriate, and we adopt them here.

* * * The Restatement principles adopted . . . define a trustee's obligations under the "prudent man rule" regarding productivity of trust assets. These principles are applicable to the executor in this case as the return generated by Bush Hill Farm is so disproportionate to its value, the farm is rendered an unproductive asset.

* * *

Reversed and remanded.

---

## CASE 52–3
## Testamentary Capacity and Power
### *In the Matter of the GUARDIANSHIP AND*
### *CONSERVATORSHIP OF LANNING*
Supreme Court of South Dakota, 1997
565 N.W.2d 794, 1997 S.D. 81

GILBERTSON, J.

The Cathey children appeal from an order denying the petition of their mother, Ursula Lanning, to make a new will and to amend her existing trust, and finding lack of testamentary capacity and undue influence. We affirm.

### Facts and Procedure

Ursula Lanning had 12 children from two marriages. Ten children were born of her first marriage to John Cathey, but one child predeceased her. She has two children from her current marriage to Edward Lanning. Mrs. Lanning did not raise the youngest Cathey children. The older Cathey children petitioned for custody and raised the youngest children themselves.

In January, 1996, at the time of the hearing for guardianship and conservatorship, Mrs. Lanning was 87 years old. She lived with her husband in a mobile home one mile outside Belle Fourche. Neither of the Lannings was in good health; Mrs. Lanning was recovering from colon cancer surgery, and Mr. Lanning was suffering from congestive heart failure. A housekeeper was paid to come in 40 hours a week to see to the daily needs of the couple. The Lannings' daughter, Sherry, lived nearby.

Mrs. Lanning and her first husband raised sheep on their ranch in Montana. Upon his death, each of the Cathey children inherited a share of the ranch from their father's estate. Mrs. Lanning eventually gifted the widow's share she received to the children of her second marriage.

Edward Lanning owned a ranch in Montana where the couple lived until ill health forced them to move to South Dakota to be near their daughter. The Lannings received royalties for oil on the property in Montana, and at the time of the hearing in this matter, the value of their combined assets was in the neighborhood of $2 million.

In 1984, Mrs. Lanning had executed a will leaving the bulk of her estate to the Lanning children. In 1993, due to the size of their assets and upon the advice of their accountant, the Lannings began estate tax planning. Edward Lanning gifted property to his wife in an attempt to equalize their estates for federal estate tax purposes. The property was placed into trust. Testimony at hearing indicated that the Lannings were aware that Edward Lanning could have placed restrictions on Mrs. Lanning's right to convey the property to the children of her first marriage, but no such restrictions were imposed. Nonetheless, Mrs. Lanning's 1984 will and the 1994 trust contained identical dispositive provisions: upon Mrs. Lanning's death, each Cathey child would receive $1,000, and the rest of the estate would be divided equally between the two Lanning children.

In November 1995, Danny Lanning petitioned for temporary guardianship of his mother. Pioneer Bank & Trust, which had been the Lannings' bank for some 40 years, was named as temporary conservator of Mrs. Lanning's estate. In January 1996, during the pendency of the proceedings for appointment of a permanent guardian and conservator, Mrs. Lanning executed a new will which was a 180-degree reversal of her former will. The new will gave each of the Lanning children $1,000, and gave the remainder of her $1 million estate in equal shares to the Cathey children.

Following its appointment as permanent conservator, Pioneer Bank moved to revoke the January 1996 will. In April 1996, Mrs. Lanning had a third attorney prepare a new will and petition the court to allow her to amend the provisions of her trust to conform to the testamentary disposition in the new will. Under this proposal, all of Mrs. Lanning's children would get an equal share of the estate. Following a hearing, the trial court determined that the January 1996 will was invalid and the petition to execute a new will and amend the trust should be denied because Mrs. Lanning lacked testamentary capacity and had been subjected to undue influence. The Cathey children appeal. * * *.

### Legal Analysis and Decision

**1. Whether the trial court erred in finding that Mrs. Lanning lacked the testamentary capacity to make the proposed April 1996 will and amendments to the trust?** Under our law, anyone over the age of 18 years who is of sound mind may make a will. [Citation.]. We have defined "sound mind" for purposes of testamentary capacity as follows: "One has a sound mind, for the purposes of making a will, if, without prompting, he is able 'to comprehend the nature and extent of his property, the persons who are the natural objects of his bounty and the disposition that he desires to make of such property.' [Citation]. Soundness of mind, for the purpose of executing a will, does not mean 'that degree of intellectual vigor which one has in youth or that is usually enjoyed by one in perfect health.' [Citation.] Mere physical weakness is not determinative of the soundness of mind, [citation], and it is not necessary that a person desiring to make a will 'should have sufficient capacity to make contracts and do business generally nor to engage in complex and intricate business matters.'" [Citation.]

[Citation.]

Testamentary capacity cannot be determined based on a single moment in time, but rather is based on consideration of the condition of the testator's mind a reasonable length of time before and after the making of the will. [Citation.]

Our review of the record supports the trial court's finding that Mrs. Lanning did not know the natural objects of her bounty. She could not, without prompting, name all 12 of the children born to her. The first time she was asked, by her own attorney at a January 19, 1996 hearing, Mrs. Lanning testified she thought she had six children born of the Cathey marriage. The second time she testified, four months later, she named 11 of her 12 children (seven of whom apparently were in attendance at the hearing). However, the transcripts indicate that following a discussion the morning of trial, one of the Cathey children had provided Mrs. Lanning with a written list of the children, which Mrs. Lanning took to the stand with her.

Mrs. Lanning also was unable to understand the nature and extent of her property. When asked about her assets, Mrs. Lanning testified she was "not right on top of this" and did not know "what everything is and where it's at." * * * The attorney testified that, in 1993, Mrs. Lanning was assertive in expressing her estate planning desires, but after watching her testimony at the 1996 hearing, he testified that she appeared to be vague and that he would be "on inquiry" as to her competence if she now came to him to change her estate plan.

Mrs. Lanning's testimony regarding her disposition of property was conflicting. She testified she wanted to change her plan to be "fair" to all her children "alike," which is the general effect of the plan in her petition. Nevertheless, when asked if the petition disposed of her property as she wanted, she stated she hadn't made a decision on the disposal of her property yet. When presented with a copy of the 1994 trust agreement, she could not identify it or figure out what it did.

* * *

We affirm.

---

## CASE 52–4
### Revocation of a Will
## *GOLINI v. BOLTON*
Court of Appeals of South Carolina, 1997
326 S.C. 333, 482 S.E.2d 784

HOWARD, J.
Mary Lou Golini appeals the circuit court's affirmance of a probate court order admitting a copy of Willie Mae Arant's last will to formal probate and appointing Melvin R. Bolton personal representative under the will. Because we find evidence which reasonably supports the factual findings of the probate court, we affirm.

### Facts

Willie Mae Arant executed her Last Will and Testament on August 5, 1992. Arant executed her will, which had been drafted by an attorney, in her home with two witnesses present. The original will could not be found after Arant's death, so a copy of the will was filed in Calhoun County Probate Court. The probate court issued an order of informal probate and appointed Melvin R. Bolton personal representative under the will. The will left the bulk of the estate to Bolton, Arant's nephew, and Kent Sutcliffe, Arant's grandson. Mary Lou Golini, Arant's only surviving daughter, filed suit challenging the probate of the will on the ground that because the original will could not be found, it had been destroyed *animo revocandi* (with the intent to revoke).

The probate court found Arant's will had not been revoked because it was returned to her attorney's office after it was executed and it was lost some time after that. Furthermore, the probate court found Arant thought she had the original in her possession, but did not. The probate court found that Arant always indicated where her will was located and copies of her will were found in those locations after her death. The probate court admitted the will to formal probate and appointed and qualified Bolton as personal representative of Arant's estate.

Golini appealed to circuit court. The circuit court affirmed the probate court and stated the preponderance of evidence showed Arant was not in possession of her will after its execution. The circuit court based this conclusion on the fact that before the factual presumption of *animo revocandi* arises in a lost will situation, it must be proven the testator had possession of the will.

\* \* \*

All parties agree Arant properly executed her will. The dispute arises over what happened to the original will after its execution. Golini claims the evidence proves Arant was the last person to have possession of her will because the will was executed in Arant's home and the witnesses to the will testified they left the will with Arant after it was executed. Bolton claims, and the lower courts agreed, the evidence tended to show the last verifiable location of the will was in Arant's attorney's office, and therefore, the presumption of *animo revocandi* did not apply.

\* \* \*

"A will or any part thereof is revoked . . . by being burned, torn, canceled, obliterated, or destroyed, with the intent and for the purpose of revoking it by the testator or by another person in his presence and by his direction." [Citation.] Revocation by an act or by a subsequent instrument must be accompanied by an intention to revoke, and, without the intention, revocation does not take place. [Citation.]

Generally, contestants of a will have the burden of establishing revocation. [Citation.]. However, when the testator takes possession of his will and it cannot be found at his death, the law presumes that the testator destroyed the will *animo revocandi*. [Citations.]

"This is merely a presumption of fact and may be rebutted by showing by the evidence that the will existed at the time of his death, was lost subsequent thereto, or had been destroyed by another without authority to do so." [Citation.]

If the testator was known to have her last will in her possession or had ready access to it, and it cannot be found on her death, it is presumed, rebuttably, that she destroyed it and thereby revoked it. \* \* \* [T]he evidence to rebut the presumption must be clear and convincing. \* \* \*

From a review of the record, this court finds evidence which reasonably supports the factual findings of the probate court including the fact Arant was not in possession of her will. Both witnesses to the will's execution testified they were the only ones present when Arant signed her will and Arant had possession of the will when they left her home. Arant told the witnesses to the will she intended to have the will taken to her attorney's office.

Attorney Thomas Culclasure drafted two wills for Arant. He prepared the first will, which also excluded Golini, in 1988. He prepared the second will in 1992 after Arant's daughter, Sally, died. The second will Culclasure drafted was picked up from his office. After it was executed, Culclasure testified the will was returned to his office. However, Culclasure said he "can only assume that the original made it back" to his office because he had a copy of the executed will. Culclasure stated "I did not give her the original Will, nor did I receive the original Will back, personally."

Culclasure maintained a card file for all wills he drafted in his practice. The card for Arant states that Arant signed her will August 5, 1992, and that "Mrs. Arant has the original." This handwritten notation was written by Culclasure's secretary. Culclasure's practice was to put any original wills he kept in his lock-box at the bank. He searched the lock-box and all his office files but was unable to locate Arant's original will. Culclasure did not know who may have picked up the will from his office but he thought the will had been given to someone.

Kent Sutcliffe, Arant's grandson, testified Arant kept her important papers in a little chest and that she kept a sealed envelope in there which he thought contained her will. Sutcliffe's stepmother, Beth, testified Arant was a very organized person and kept her important papers in a little desk in her dining room. \* \* \* After Arant's death, Bolton retrieved the two sealed envelopes from the two locations and took them to the probate court judge to have them opened. Only then did he discover the envelopes contained copies of Arant's will but neither contained the original. Bolton also checked Arant's personal lock-box at the bank but the original will was not there.

"Proof that a testator, whose will cannot be found after his death, entertained a kindly or loving feeling toward the beneficiaries under the will carries weight and tends toward the conclusion of nonrevocation of the will by the testator." [Citations.] Numerous witnesses testified as to the love and affection that existed between Arant and Bolton and Bolton's daily visits with Arant as well as his cooking her meals and running her errands.

Even Golini testified Bolton was "like a son" to Arant. Before she died, Arant gave Bolton her Power of Attorney.

Numerous witnesses also testified that Arant and Golini did not get along and that Arant stated on numerous occasions she intended to leave Golini out of her will.

\* \* \*

AFFIRMED.

---

## CASE 52–5
### Intestate Succession
## *FERGUSON v. CROOM*
Court of Appeals of North Carolina, 1985
73 N.C.App. 316, 326 S.E.2d 373

ARNOLD, J.

On 21 June 1983, George Washington Croom died testate. In his will Croom left various bequests of real and personal property to his children and a grandchild. In Item Eight of his will Croom stated "I leave nothing whatsoever to my daughter Kathryn Elizabeth Turner, and my son Ernest Edward Croom." At his death, Croom also left three optional share certificates in Carolina Savings & Loan Association issued to George W. Croom or Kimberly Joyce Croom, the deceased's minor daughter. Each of these certificates had attached to it an "Agreement Concerning Stock in Carolina Savings and Loan Association" which purported to create a joint account with a right of survivorship. Two of these agreements were signed by George Croom only and the third agreement was not signed at all. None of these certificates were specifically devised by Croom's will and the will contained no residuary clause. The plaintiff by this action seeks a determination as to who is entitled to share in these assets. [Kimberly Croom contends the certificates pass to her by right of survivorship.]

\* \* \*

By their appeal, Ernest Edward Croom and Kathryn Elizabeth Turner contend the court erred by concluding that they were not to share in the property which passed by partial intestacy because the deceased's will evidenced an intent that they should be disinherited. We agree, therefore, we reverse.

[North Carolina statute] states: "If part but not all of the estate of a decedent is validly disposed of by his will, the part not disposed of by such will *shall* descend and *be distributed as intestate property.*" [This statute] creates a mandatory plan for disposing of a decedent's property which does not pass by will. It directs that the property pass by intestate succession without regard to the intent expressed by a testator in a will. The statute, which was adopted in 1959, was a codification of our common law. [Citation] (where our Supreme Court held that property not disposed of by will passes as directed by the law regardless of attempts by the testator to disinherit the lawful takers). The rule adopted by [the Statute] is also in accordance with the rule followed by a majority of our sister states. [Citation.]

Under the Intestate Succession Act each of testator's children is entitled to take an equal share of the property not disposed of by his will. [Citation.] Thus, the trial court erred in excluding Kathryn Elizabeth Turner and Ernest Edward Croom from taking a share of the intestate property. The judgment of the court is reversed and the case is remanded for the entry of judgment consistent with this opinion.

Reversed.

---

 # Questions

**1.** Define the following types of trusts: (a) express, (b) testamentary, (c) *inter vivos*, (d) charitable, (e) spendthrift, (f) totten, (g) implied, (h) constructive, and (i) resulting.

**2.** Describe the powers and duties of a trustee.

**3.** Discuss the formal requirements of making a valid will and the various ways in which a will may be revoked.

**4.** Define the following types of wills: (a) nuncupative, (b) holographic, (c) soldiers' and sailors', (d) conditional, (e) joint, (f) reciprocal, and (g) living.

**5.** Discuss intestate succession and the administration of decedents' estate.

# Problems

**1.** State whether or not a trust is created in each of the following situations:

(a) A declares herself trustee of "the bulk of my securities" in trust for B.

(b) A, the owner of Blackacre, purports to convey to B in trust for C "a small part" of Blackacre.

(c) A orders B, a stockbroker, to buy 2,000 shares of American Steel or any part thereof at $20 per share. After the broker has bought 500 shares but before A knows whether any shares have been bought for him, A declares himself trustee for C of such shares of American Steel as B has bought.

(d) A owns ten bonds. He declares himself trustee for B of such five of the bonds as B may select at any time within a month.

(e) A deposits $1,000 in a savings bank. He declares himself trustee of the deposit in trust to pay B $500 out of the deposit, reserving the power to withdraw from the deposit any amounts not in excess of $500.

**2.** Testator gives property to Tim in trust for Barney's benefit, providing that Barney cannot anticipate the income by assignment or pledge. Barney borrows money from Linda, assigning his future income under the trust for a stated period. Can Linda obtain any judicial relief to prevent Barney from collecting this income?

**3.** Collins was trustee for Indolent under the will of Indolent's father. Indolent, a middle-aged doctor, gave little concern to the management of the trust fund, contenting himself with receiving the income paid him by the trustee. Among the assets of the trust were 100 shares of ABC Corporation and 100 shares of XYZ Corporation. About two years before the termination of the trust, Collins, at a fair price and after full explanation to Indolent, purchased from the trust the ABC stock. At the same time but without saying anything to Indolent, he purchased the XYZ stock at a price in excess of its then market value. At the termination of the trust, both stocks had advanced in market value well beyond the prices paid by Collins, and Indolent demanded that Collins either account for this advance in the value of both stocks or replace the stocks. What are Indolent's rights?

**4.** On September 1, 1990, Joe Brown gave to his wife, Mary Brown, $35,000 with which to buy real property. They orally agreed that title to the real property should be taken in the name of Mary Brown but that she should hold the property in trust for Joe Brown. There were two witnesses to the oral agreement, both of whom are still living. Mary purchased the property on September 2, and a deed to it with Mary Brown as the grantee was delivered.

Mary died on October 5, 2000, without a will. The real property is now worth $100,000. Joe Brown is claiming the property as the beneficiary of a trust. Mary's children are claiming that the property belongs to Mary's estate and have pleaded the statute of limitations and the statute of frauds as defenses to the claim of Joe. There is no evidence to prove whether Mary would or would not have conveyed the property to Joe during her lifetime if she had been requested to do so.

What are Joe's ownership rights to this particular real property?

**5.** On March 10, 1999, John Carver executed his will, which was witnessed by William Hobson and Sam Witt. By his will, Carver devised his farm, Stonecrest, to his nephew, Roy White. The residue of his estate was given to his sister, Florence Carver.

A codicil to his will executed April 15, 1999, provided that $5,000 be given to Carver's niece, Mary Jordan, and $5,000 to Wanda White, Roy White's wife. The codicil was witnessed by Roy White and Harold Brown. John Carver died September 1, 1999, and the will and codicil were admitted to probate.

How should Carver's estate be distributed?

**6.** Edwin Fuller, a bachelor, prepared his will in his office. The will, which contained no residuary clause, provided that one-third of his estate would go to his nephew, Tom Fuller, one-third to the city of Emanon to be used for park improvements, and one-third to his brother, Kurt.

He signed the will in his office and then went to the office of his nephew, Tom Fuller, who, at Edwin's request, signed the will as a witness. As no other persons were available in Tom's office, Edwin then went to the bank, where Frank Cash, the cashier, at Edwin's request, also signed as a witness. In each instance, Edwin stated that he had signed the document but did not state that it was his will.

Edwin returned to his office and placed the will in his safe. Subsequently, Edwin died, survived by Kurt, his only heir-at-law. How should the estate be distributed?

**7.** Arnold executed a one-page will, in which he devised his farm to Burton. Later, as the result of a quarrel with Burton, Arnold wrote the words, "I hereby cancel and revoke this will /s/Arnold," in the margin of the will but did not destroy the will. Arnold then executed a deed to the farm, naming Connie as grantee, and placed the deed and will in his safe. Shortly afterwards, Arnold married Donna, with whom he had one child, Ernest. Thereafter, Arnold died, and the deed and will were found in his safe. Burton, Connie, and Ernest claim the farm, and Donna claims dower. Discuss the validity of each claim.

**8.** John Walker, a widower, died testate. His will, in part, provided:

"I give and bequeath my piano to my daughter Nancy. I give and bequeath to my daughter Jennifer the sum of $1,000. I give and bequeath to my son John the sum of $1,000 to be paid out of my account at the Tenth National Bank in the city of Erehwon. All the rest and residue of my estate I give to Nancy, Jennifer, and John, share and share alike."

After the will was executed, Walker sold his piano for $2,300 and deposited the proceeds in the Citizens Bank of Erehwon. He withdrew the money he had on deposit in the Tenth National Bank and purchased a new automobile.

At the time of his death, Walker had no debts. The account in the Citizens Bank of Erehwon had a balance of $2,300, which constituted his entire net estate after all expenses of administration were paid. How should Walker's estate be distributed?

9. The validly executed will of John Dane contained the following provision: "I give and devise to my daughter, Mary, Redacre for and during her natural life and, at her death, the remainder to go to Wilmore College." The will also provided that the residue of his estate should go to Wilmore College. Thereafter, Dane sold Redacre and then added a validly executed codicil to his will, "Due to the fact that I have sold Redacre which I previously gave to my daughter, Mary, I now give and devise Blackacre to Mary in place and instead of Redacre."

Another clause of the codicil provided: "I give to my son, Henry, my one-half interest in the oil business, which I own in common with William Steele." Subsequently, Dane acquired all of the interest in the oil business from his partner, Steele, and, at the time of his death, Dane owned the entire oil business. The will and codicil have been admitted to probate.

(a) What interest, if any, does Mary acquire in Blackacre?

(b) What interest, if any, does Henry acquire in the oil business?

10. Leonard Wolfe was killed in an automobile accident while driving his 1994 Buick Century. The car was rendered a total loss, and Wolfe's insurance carrier paid his estate $8,550 for damage to the vehicle. Under the terms of Wolfe's will, any car owned at his death was to be given to his brother, David. Wolfe's daughter, Carol, however, brought an action, claiming that the gift of the car to David was adeemed by its total destruction and that she, as the residuary legatee under the will, was entitled to the insurance proceeds. Decision?

11. In April 1994, Grace Peterson, a spinster then aged seventy-four, asked Chester Gustafson, a Minneapolis attorney, to draw a will for her. Gustafson, who had also probated Peterson's sister's estate, drew this first will and six subsequent wills and codicils free of charge because he claimed that she had no money to pay for his services. Over the five-year period during which Gustafson redrew Peterson's will, an increasing amount of property was devised to Gustafson's children, until, finally, the seventh will so devised Peterson's entire estate. Peterson, however, hardly knew the children except from several chance encounters ten years before. She died on February 1, 1999, without ever having changed the seventh will, and Gustafson, who was named as executor, now seeks to have the will admitted to probate. Decision?

12. Rodney Sharp was a fifty-six-year-old dairy farmer whose education did not go beyond the eighth grade. Upon the death of his wife of thirty-two years, Sharp developed a very close relationship with Jean Kosmalski, a schoolteacher sixteen years his junior. Sharp eventually proposed to Kosmalski, but when she refused, he continued to make gifts to her in hopes of changing her mind. He also gave her access to his bank account, from which she withdrew substantial amounts of money; made a will naming her as sole beneficiary; and executed a deed naming her as a joint owner of his farm. Then, in September 1997, Sharp transferred his remaining joint interest in the farm to Kosmalski. In February 1999, Kosmalski ordered Sharp to move out of his home and to vacate the farm. She then took possession of both, leaving Sharp with assets of $300. Sharp brought this action to impose a constructive trust on the property transferred to Kosmalski. The trial court dismissed the plaintiff's complaint, and the decision was affirmed by the appellate court. Decision?

13. John Hobelsberger lived alone on his farm near Kranzburg, South Dakota. A grandniece, Phyllis Raml, and her husband, Ralph, lived on and operated a farm about two miles away. Hobelsberger and the Ramls had a friendly and cordial relationship. The Ramls visited him rather frequently and largely cared for him during his later years. Hobelsberger was hospitalized on October 23, 1998, and his condition was diagnosed as intermittent cerebral insufficiency. During his hospitalization, he requested that the Ramls send an attorney to see him about the preparation of a will. Thomas Green, an attorney, interviewed the testator on or about November 10 and prepared a will in compliance with his instructions.

Hobelsberger was transferred to a nursing home on November 19. On November 22, Green and a secretary went to the nursing home and witnessed his signing of the will. Hobelsberger was then eighty years old. He subscribed the will with a mark because he was having trouble with his hands. Hobelsberger died on July 19, 1999, survived by twenty-seven nieces and nephews and seven grandnieces and grandnephews. The will, after providing for the payment of debts and funeral expenses, left Hobelsberger's entire estate to Phyllis Raml. Nine of the nieces and nephews contested the will, claiming lack of testamentary capacity, undue influence by the Ramls, and improper execution. The county court admitted the will to probate, the circuit court affirmed, and the contestants appealed. Decision?

14. Mamie Henry, a widow, died on October 18, 1999. She had no children, but was survived by several nieces and nephews. At first no will was found, and Joe Barksdale, a nephew, was appointed administrator of Mrs. Henry's estate. Later, Rita Pendergrass produced a copy of a will allegedly made by Mrs. Henry. The will left all of Mrs. Henry's property to Mrs. Pendergrass and appointed her as executrix. When Mrs. Pendergrass sought to have the will admitted to probate, Joe Barksdale and Olen Barksdale filed a contest on the grounds that the purported will was never duly executed, or, if executed, was destroyed by Mrs. Henry prior to her death. The jury found in favor of Rita Pendergrass, and judgment was entered ordering the admission of the will to probate. Decision?

**WWW**   **Internet Exercise** Find the last will and testament of three celebrities.

# Appendices

# The Constitution of the United States of America

We the People of the United States, in Order to form a more perfect Union, establish Justice, insure domestic Tranquility, provide for the common defense, promote the general Welfare, and secure the Blessings of Liberty to ourselves and our Posterity, do ordain and establish this Constitution for the United States of America.

## ARTICLE I

### Section 1

All legislative Powers herein granted shall be vested in a Congress of the United States, which shall consist of a Senate and House of Representatives.

### Section 2

The House of Representatives shall be composed of Members chosen every second Year by the People of the several States, and the Electors in each State shall have the Qualifications requisite for Electors of the most numerous Branch of the State Legislature.

No Person shall be a Representative who shall not have attained to the Age of twenty five Years, and been seven Years a Citizen of the United States, and who shall not, when elected, be an Inhabitant of that State in which he shall be chosen.

Representatives and direct Taxes shall be apportioned among the several States which may be included within this Union, according to their respective Numbers, which shall be determined by adding to the whole Number of free Persons, including those bound to Service for a Term of Years, and excluding Indians not taxed, three fifths of all other Persons. The actual Enumeration shall be made within three Years after the first Meeting of the Congress of the United States, and within every subsequent Term of ten Years, in such Manner as they shall by Law direct. The number of Representatives shall not exceed one for every thirty Thousand, but each State shall have at Least one Representative; and until such enumeration shall be made, the State of New Hampshire shall be entitled to chuse three, Massachusetts eight, Rhode Island and Providence Plantations one, Connecticut five, New-York six, New Jersey four, Pennsylvania eight, Delaware one, Maryland six, Virginia ten, North Carolina five, South Carolina five, and Georgia three.

When vacancies happen in the Representation from any State, the Executive Authority thereof shall issue Writs of Election to fill such vacancies.

The House of Representatives shall chuse their Speaker and other Officers; and shall have the sole Power of Impeachment.

### Section 3

The Senate of the United States shall be composed of two Senators from each State, chosen by the Legislature thereof, for six Years; and each Senator shall have one Vote.

Immediately after they shall be assembled in Consequence of the first Election, they shall be divided as equally as may be into three Classes. The Seats of the Senators of the first Class shall be vacated at the Expiration of the second Year, of the second Class at the Expiration of the fourth Year, and of the third Class at the Expiration of the sixth Year, so that one third may be chosen every second Year; and if Vacancies happen by Resignation or otherwise, during the Recess of the Legislature of any State, the Executive thereof may make temporary Appointments until the next Meeting of the Legislature, which shall then fill such Vacancies.

No Person shall be a Senator who shall not have attained to the Age of thirty Years, and been nine Years a Citizen of the United States, and who shall not, when elected, be an Inhabitant of that State for which he shall be chosen.

The Vice President of the United States shall be President of the Senate, but shall have no Vote, unless they be equally divided.

The Senate shall chuse their other Officers, and also a President pro tempore, in the Absence of the Vice President, or when he shall exercise the Office of President of the United States.

The Senate shall have the sole power to try all Impeachments. When sitting for that Purpose, they shall be an Oath or Affirmation. When the President of the United States is tried, the Chief Justice shall preside: And no Person shall be convicted without the Concurrence of two thirds of the Members present.

Judgment in Cases of Impeachment shall not extend further than to removal from Office, and disqualification to hold and enjoy any Office of honor, Trust or Profit under the United States: but the Party convicted shall nevertheless be liable and subject to Indictment, Trial, Judgment and Punishment, according to Law.

### Section 4

The Times, Places and Manner of holding Elections for Senators and Representatives, shall be prescribed in each State by the Legislature thereof: but the Congress may at any time by Law make or alter such Regulations, except as to the Places of chusing Senators.

The Congress shall assemble at least once in every Year, and such Meeting shall be on the first Monday in December, unless they shall by Law appoint a different Day.

### Section 5

Each House shall be the Judge of the Elections, Returns and Qualifications of its own Members, and a Majority of each shall constitute a

Quorum to do Business; but a smaller Number may adjourn from day to day, and may be authorized to compel the Attendance of absent Members, in such Manner, and under such Penalties as each House may provide.

Each House may determine the Rules of its Proceedings, punish its Members for disorderly Behaviour, and, with the Concurrence of two thirds, expel a Member.

Each House shall keep a Journal of its Proceedings, and from time to time publish the same, excepting such Parts as may in their Judgment require Secrecy; and the Yeas and Nays of the Members of either House on any question shall, at the Desire of one fifth of those Present, be entered on the Journal.

Neither House, during the Session of Congress, shall, without the Consent of the other, adjourn for more than three days, nor to any other Place than that in which the two Houses shall be sitting.

## Section 6

The Senators and Representatives shall receive a Compensation for their Services, to be ascertained by Law, and paid out of the Treasury of the United States. They shall in all Cases, except Treason, Felony and Breach of the Peace, be privileged from Arrest during their Attendance at the Session of their respective Houses, and in going to and returning from the same; and for any Speech or Debate in either House, they shall not be questioned in any other Place.

No Senator or Representative shall, during the Time for which he was elected, be appointed to any civil Office under the Authority of the United States, which shall have been created, or the Emoluments whereof shall have been encreased during such time; and no Person holding any Office under the United States, shall be a Member of either House during his Continuance in Office.

## Section 7

All Bills for raising Revenue shall originate in the House of Representatives; but the Senate may propose or concur with Amendments as on other Bills.

Every Bill which shall have passed the House of Representatives and the Senate, shall, before it become a Law, be presented to the President of the United States; If he approve he shall sign it, but if not he shall return it, with his Objections to that House in which it shall have originated, who shall enter the Objections at large on their Journal, and proceed to reconsider it. If after such Reconsideration two thirds of that House shall agree to pass the Bill, it shall be sent, together with the Objections, to the other House, by which it shall likewise be reconsidered, and if approved by two thirds of that House, it shall become a Law. But in all such Cases the Votes of both Houses shall be determined by Yeas and Nays, and the Names of the Persons voting for and against the Bill shall be entered on the Journal of each House respectively. If any Bill shall not be returned by the President within ten Days (Sundays excepted) after it shall have been presented to him, the Same shall be a Law, in like Manner as if he had signed it, unless the Congress by their Adjournment prevent its Return, in which Case it shall not be a Law.

Every Order, Resolution, or Vote to which the Concurrence of the Senate and House of Representatives may be necessary (except on a question of Adjournment) shall be presented to the President of the United States; and before the Same shall take Effect, shall be approved by him, or being disapproved by him, shall be repassed by two thirds of the Senate and House of Representatives, according to the Rules and Limitations prescribed in the Case of a Bill.

## Section 8

The Congress shall have Power to lay and collect Taxes, Duties, Imposts and Excises, to pay the Debts and provide for the common Defence and general Welfare of the United States; but all Duties, Imposts and Excises shall be uniform throughout the United States;

To borrow Money on the credit of the United States;

To regulate Commerce with foreign Nations, and among the several States, and with the Indian Tribes;

To establish an uniform Rule of Naturalization, and uniform Laws on the subject of Bankruptcies throughout the United States;

To coin Money, regulate the Value thereof, and of foreign Coin, and fix the Standard of Weights and Measures;

To provide for the Punishment of counterfeiting the Securities and current Coin of the United States;

To establish Post Offices and post Roads;

To promote the Progress of Science and useful Arts, by securing for limited Times to Authors and Inventors the exclusive Right to their respective Writings and Discoveries;

To constitute Tribunals inferior to the supreme Court;

To define and punish Piracies and Felonies committed on the high Seas, and Offenses against the Law of Nations;

To declare War, grant Letters of Marque and Reprisal, and make Rules concerning Captures on Land and Water;

To raise and support Armies, but no Appropriation of Money to that Use shall be for a longer Term than two Years;

To provide and maintain a Navy;

To make Rules for the Government and Regulation of the land and naval Forces;

To provide for calling forth the Militia to execute the Laws of the Union, suppress Insurrections and repel Invasions;

To provide for organizing, arming, and disciplining, the Militia, and for governing such Part of them as may be employed in the Service of the United States, reserving to the States respectively, the Appointment of the Officers, and the Authority of training the Militia according to the discipline described by Congress;

To exercise exclusive Legislation in all Cases whatsoever, over such District (not exceeding ten Miles square) as may, by Cession of particular States, and the Acceptance of Congress, become the Seat of the Government of the United States, and to exercise like Authority over all Places purchased by the Consent of the Legislature of the State in which the Same shall be, for the Erection of Forts, Magazines, Arsenals, dock-Yards, and other needful Buildings;—And

To make all Laws which shall be necessary and proper for carrying into Execution the foregoing Powers, and all other Powers vested by this Constitution in the Government of the United States, or in any Department or Officer thereof.

## Section 9

The Migration or Importation of such Persons as any of the States now existing shall think proper to admit, shall not be prohibited by the Congress prior to the Year one thousand eight hundred and eight, but a Tax or Duty may be imposed on such Importation, not exceeding ten dollars for each Person.

The Privilege of the Writ of Habeas Corpus shall not be suspended, unless when in Cases of Rebellion or Invasion the public Safety may require it.

No Bill of Attainder or ex post facto Law shall be passed.

No Capitation, or other direct, Tax shall be laid, unless in Proportion to the Census or Enumeration herein before directed to be taken.

No Tax or Duty shall be laid on Articles exported from any State.

No Preference shall be given by any Regulation of Commerce or Revenue to the Ports of one State over those of another; nor shall Vessels bound to, or from, one State, be obliged to enter, clear, or pay Duties in another.

No Money shall be drawn from the Treasury, but in Consequence of Appropriations made by Laws; and a regular Statement and Account of the Receipts and Expenditures of all public Money shall be published from time to time.

No Title of Nobility shall be granted by the United States: And no Person holding any Office of Profit or Trust under them, shall, without the Consent of the Congress, accept of any present, Emolument, Office, or Title, of any kind whatever, from any King, Prince, or foreign State.

## Section 10

No State shall enter into any Treaty, Alliance, or Confederation; grant Letters of Marque and Reprisal; coin Money; emit Bills of Credit; make any Thing but gold and silver Coin a Tender in Payment of Debts; pass any Bill of Attainder, ex post facto Law, or Law impairing the Obligation of Contracts, or grant any Title of Nobility.

No State shall, without the Consent of the Congress, lay any Imposts or Duties on Imports or Exports, except what may be absolutely necessary for executing its inspection Laws: and the net Produce of all Duties and Imposts, laid by any State on Imports or Exports, shall be for the Use of the Treasury of the United States; and all such Laws shall be subject to the Revision and Controul of the Congress.

No State shall, without the Consent of Congress, lay any Duty of Tonnage, keep Troops, or Ships of War in time of Peace, enter into any Agreement or Compact with another State, or with a foreign Power, or engage in War, unless actually invaded, or in such imminent Danger as will not admit of delay.

## ARTICLE II

### Section 1

The executive Power shall be vested in a President of the United States of America. He shall hold his Office during the Term of four Years, and, together with the Vice President, chosen for the same Term, be elected, as follows:

Each State shall appoint, in such Manner as the Legislature thereof may direct, a Number of Electors, equal to the whole Number of Senators and Representatives to which the State may be entitled in the Congress: but no Senator or Representative, or Person holding an Office of Trust or Profit under the United States, shall be appointed an Elector.

The Electors shall meet in their respective States, and vote by Ballot for two Persons, of whom one at least shall not be an Inhabitant of the same State with themselves. And they shall make a list of all the Persons voted for, and of the Number of Votes for each; which List they shall sign and certify, and transmit sealed to the Seat of the Government of the United States, directed to the President of the Senate. The President of the Senate shall, in the presence of the Senate and House of Representatives, open all the Certificates, and the Votes shall be counted. The Person having the greatest Number of Votes shall be the President, if such Number be a Majority of the whole Number of Electors appointed; and if there be more than one who have such Majority, and have an equal Number of Votes, then the House of Representatives shall immediately chuse by Ballot one of them for President; and if no Person have a Majority, then from the five highest on the List the said House shall in like Manner chuse the

President. But in chusing the President, the Votes shall be taken by States, the Representation from each State having one Vote; A quorum for this Purpose shall consist of a Member or Members from two thirds of the States, and a Majority of all the States shall be necessary to a Choice. In every Case, after the Choice of the President, the Person having the greatest Number of Votes of the Electors shall be the Vice President. But if there should remain two or more who have equal Votes, the Senate shall chuse from them by Ballot the Vice President.

The Congress may determine the Time of Chusing the Electors, and the Day on which they shall give their Votes; which Day shall be the same throughout the United States.

No Person except a natural born Citizen, or a Citizen of the United States, at the time of the Adoption of this Constitution, shall be eligible to the Office of President; neither shall any Person be eligible to that Office who shall not have attained to the Age of thirty five Years, and been fourteen Years a Resident within the United States.

In Case of the Removal of the President from Office, or of his Death, Resignation, or Inability to discharge the Powers and Duties of the said Office, the Same shall devolve on the Vice President, and the Congress may by Law provide for the Case of Removal, Death, Resignation or Inability, both of the President and Vice President, declaring what Officer shall then act as President, and such Officer shall act accordingly, until the Disability be removed, or a President shall be elected.

The President shall, at stated Times, receive for his Services, a Compensation, which shall neither be encreased nor diminished during the Period for which he shall have been elected, and he shall not receive within that Period any other Emolument from the United States, or any of them.

Before he enter on the Execution of his Office, he shall take the following Oath or Affirmation:—"I do solemnly swear (or affirm) that I will faithfully execute the Office of President of the United States, and will to the best of my Ability, preserve, protect and defend the Constitution of the United States."

### Section 2

The President shall be Commander in Chief of the Army and Navy of the United States, and of the Militia of the several States, when called into the actual Service of the United States; he may require the Opinion, in writing, of the principal Officer in each of the executive Departments, upon any Subject relating to the Duties of their respective Offices, and he shall have Power to grant Reprieves and Pardons for Offenses against the United States, except in Cases of Impeachment.

He shall have Power, by and with the Advice and Consent of the Senate, to make Treaties, providing two thirds of the Senators present concur; and he shall nominate, and by and with the Advice and Consent of the Senate, shall appoint Ambassadors, other public Ministers and Consuls, Judges of the supreme Court, and all other Officers of the United States, whose Appointments are not herein otherwise provided for, and which shall be established by Law: but the Congress may by Law vest the Appointment of such inferior Officers, as they think proper, in the President alone, in the Courts of Law, or in the Heads of Departments.

The President shall have Power to fill up all Vacancies that may happen during the Recess of the Senate, by granting Commissions which shall expire at the End of their next Session.

### Section 3

He shall from time to time give to the Congress Information of the State of the Union, and recommend to their Consideration such

Measures as he shall judge necessary and expedient; he may, on extraordinary Occasions, convene both Houses, or either of them, and in Case of Disagreement between them, with Respect to the Time of Adjournment, he may adjourn them to such Time as he shall think proper, he shall receive Ambassadors and other public Ministers; he shall take Care that the Laws be faithfully executed, and shall Commission all the Offices of the United States.

## Section 4

The President, Vice President and all civil Officers of the United States, shall be removed from Office on Impeachment for, and Conviction of, Treason, Bribery, or other high Crimes and Misdemeanors.

# ARTICLE III

## Section 1

The judicial Power of the United States, shall be vested in one supreme Court, and in such inferior Courts as the Congress may from time to time ordain and establish. The Judges, both of the supreme and inferior Courts, shall hold their Offices during good Behaviour, and shall, at Times, receive for their Services, a Compensation, which shall not be diminished during their Continuance in Office.

## Section 2

The judicial Power shall extend to all Cases, in Law and Equity, arising under this Constitution, the Laws of the United States, and Treaties made, or which shall be made, under their Authority;—to all Cases affecting Ambassadors, other public Ministers and Consuls;—to all Cases of admiralty and maritime Jurisdiction;—to Controversies to which the United States shall be a Party;—to controversies between two or more States;—between a State and Citizens of another State;—between Citizens of different States;—between Citizens of the same State claiming Lands under Grants of different States; and between a State, or the Citizens thereof, and foreign States, Citizens or Subjects.

In all Cases affecting Ambassadors, other public Ministers and Consuls, and those in which a State shall be Party, the supreme Court shall have original Jurisdiction. In all the other Cases before mentioned, the supreme Court shall have appellate Jurisdiction, both as to Law and Fact, with such Exceptions, and under such Regulations as the Congress shall make.

The Trial of all Crimes, except in Cases of Impeachment, shall be by Jury; and such Trial shall be held in the State where the said Crimes shall have been committed; but when not committed within any State, the Trial shall be at such Place or Places as the Congress may by Law have directed.

## Section 3

Treason against the United States, shall consist only in levying War against them, or in adhering to their Enemies, giving them Aid and Comfort. No Person shall be convicted of Treason unless on the Testimony of two Witnesses to the same overt Act, or on Confession in open Court.

The Congress shall have Power to declare the Punishment of Treason, but no Attainder of Treason shall work Corruption of Blood, or Forfeiture except during the Life of the Person attainted.

# ARTICLE IV

## Section 1

Full Faith and Credit shall be given in each State to the public Acts, Records, and judicial Proceedings of every other State. And the Congress may by general Laws prescribe the Manner in which such Acts, Records and Proceedings shall be proved, and the Effect thereof.

## Section 2

The Citizens of each State shall be entitled to all Privileges and Immunities of Citizens in the several States.

A Person charged in any State with Treason, Felony, or other Crime, who shall flee from Justice, and be found in another State, shall on Demand of the executive Authority of the State from which he fled, be delivered up, to be removed to the State having Jurisdiction of the Crime.

No Person held to Service or Labour in one State, under the Laws thereof, escaping into another, shall, in Consequence of any Law or Regulation therein, be discharged from such Service or Labour, but shall be delivered up on Claim of the Party to whom such Service or Labour may be due.

## Section 3

New States may be admitted by the Congress into this Union; but no new State shall be formed or erected within the Jurisdiction of any other State; nor any State be formed by the Junction of two or more States, or Parts of States, without the Consent of the Legislatures of the States concerned as well as the Congress.

The Congress shall have Power to dispose of and make all needful Rules and Regulations respecting the Territory or other Property belonging to the United States; and nothing in this Constitution shall be so construed as to Prejudice any Claims of the United States, or of any particular State.

## Section 4

The United States shall guarantee to every State in this Union a Republican Form of Government, and shall protect each of them against Invasion; and on Application of the Legislature, or of the Executive (when the Legislature cannot be convened) against domestic Violence.

# ARTICLE V

The Congress, whenever two thirds of both Houses shall deem it necessary, shall propose Amendments to this Constitution, or, on the Application of the Legislatures of two thirds of the several States, shall call a Convention for proposing Amendments, which, in either Case, shall be valid to all Intents and Purposes, as Part of this Constitution, when ratified by the Legislatures of three fourths of the several States, or by Conventions in three fourths thereof, as the one or the other Mode of Ratification may be proposed by the Congress; Provided that no Amendment which may be made prior to the Year One thousand eight hundred and eight shall in any Manner affect the first and fourth Clauses in the Ninth Section of the first Article; and that no State, without its Consent, shall be deprived of its equal Suffrage in the Senate.

## ARTICLE VI

All Debts contracted and Engagements entered into, before the Adoption of this Constitution, shall be as valid against the United States under this Constitution, as under the Confederation.

This Constitution, and the Laws of the United States which shall be made in Pursuance thereof; and all Treaties made, or which shall be made, under the Authority of the United States, shall be the supreme Law of the Land; and the Judges in every State shall be bound thereby, any Thing in the Constitution or Laws of any State to the Contrary notwithstanding.

The Senators and Representatives before mentioned, and the Members of the several State Legislatures, and all executive and judicial Officers, both of the United States and of the Several States, shall be bound by Oath or Affirmation, to support this Constitution; but no religious Test shall ever be required as a Qualification to any Office or public Trust under the United States.

## ARTICLE VII

The Ratification of the Conventions of nine States, shall be sufficient for the Establishment of this Constitution between the States so ratifying the Same.

### Amendment I [1791]

Congress shall make no law respecting an establishment of religion, or prohibiting the free exercise thereof; or abridging the freedom of speech, or the press; or the right of the people peaceably to assemble, and to petition the Government for a redress of grievances.

### Amendment II [1791]

A well regulated Militia, being necessary to the security for a free State, the right of the people to keep and bear Arms, shall not be infringed.

### Amendment III [1791]

No Soldier shall, in time of peace be quartered in any house, without the consent of the Owner, nor in time of war, but in a manner to be prescribed by law.

### Amendment IV [1791]

The right of the people to be secure in their persons, houses, papers, and effects, against unreasonable searches and seizures, shall not be violated, and no Warrants shall issue, but upon probable cause, supported by Oath or Affirmation, and particularly describing the place to be searched, and the persons or things to be seized.

### Amendment V [1791]

No person shall be held to answer for a capital, or otherwise infamous crime, unless on a presentment or indictment of a Grand Jury, except in cases arising in the land or naval forces, or in the Militia, when in actual service in time of War or public danger; nor shall any person be subject for the same offense to be twice put in jeopardy of life or limb; nor shall be compelled in any criminal case to be a witness against himself, nor be deprived of life, liberty, or property, without due process of law; nor shall private property be taken for public use, without just compensation.

### Amendment VI [1791]

In all criminal prosecutions, the accused shall enjoy the right to a speedy and public trial, by an impartial jury of the State and district wherein the crime shall have been committed, which district shall have been previously ascertained by law, and to be informed of the nature and cause of the accusation; to be confronted with the Witnesses against him; to have compulsory process for obtaining witnesses in his favor, and to have the Assistance of counsel for his defence.

### Amendment VII [1791]

In suits at common law, where the value in controversy shall exceed twenty dollars, the right of trial by jury shall be preserved, and no fact tried by a jury, shall be otherwise re-examined in any Court of the United States, than according to the rules of the common law.

### Amendment VIII [1791]

Excessive bail shall not be required, no excessive fines imposed, nor cruel and unusual punishments inflicted.

### Amendment IX [1791]

The enumeration in the Constitution, of certain rights, shall not be construed to deny or disparage others retained by the people.

### Amendment X [1791]

The powers not delegated to the United States by the Constitution, nor prohibited by it to the States, are reserved to the States respectively, or to the people.

### Amendment XI [1798]

The judicial power of the United States shall not be construed to extend to any suit in law or equity, commenced or prosecuted against one of the United States by Citizens of another State, or by Citizens or Subjects of any Foreign State.

### Amendment XII [1804]

The Electors shall meet in their respective states and vote by ballot for President and Vice-President, one of whom, at least, shall not be an inhabitant of the same state with themselves; they shall name in their ballots the person voted for as President, and in distinct ballots the person voted for as Vice-President, and they shall make distinct lists of all persons voted for as President, and of all persons voted for as Vice-President, and of the number of votes for each, which lists they shall sign and certify, and transmit sealed to the seat of the government of the United States, directed to the President of the Senate;—The President of the Senate shall, in the presence of the Senate and House of Representatives, open all the certificates and the votes shall then be counted;—The person having the greatest number of votes for President, shall be the President, if such number be a majority of the whole number of Electors appointed; and if no person have such majority, then from the persons having the highest numbers not exceeding three on the list of those voted for as President, the House of Representatives shall choose immediately, by ballot, the President. But in choosing the President, the votes shall be taken by states, the representation from each state having one vote; a quorum for this purpose shall consist of a member or members from two-thirds of the states, and a majority of all the states shall be necessary to a choice. And if the House of Representatives shall not choose a President whenever the right of choice shall devolve upon them, before the fourth day of March next following, then the Vice-President shall act as President, as in the case of the death or other constitutional disability of the President. The person having the greatest number of votes as Vice-President, shall be the Vice-President, if such number be a majority of the whole number of Electors appointed, and if no person have a majority, then from the two highest numbers on the list, the Senate shall choose the Vice-President; a quorum for the purpose shall consist of two-thirds of the whole number of Senators, and a majority of the whole number shall be necessary to a choice. But no person constitutionally ineligible to the office of President shall be eligible to that of the Vice-President of the United States.

## Amendment XIII [1865]

### Section 1

Neither slavery nor involuntary servitude, except as a punishment for crime whereof the party shall have been duly convicted, shall exist within the United States, or any place subject to their jurisdiction.

### Section 2

Congress shall have power to enforce this article by appropriate legislation.

## Amendment XIV [1868]

### Section 1

All persons born or naturalized in the United States, and subject to the jurisdiction thereof, are citizens of the United States and of the State wherein they reside. No State shall make or enforce any law which shall abridge the privileges or immunities of citizens of the United States; nor shall any State deprive any person of life, liberty, or property, without due process of law; nor deny to any person within its jurisdiction the equal protection of the laws.

### Section 2

Representatives shall be appointed among the several States according to their respective numbers, counting the whole number of persons in each State, excluding Indians not taxed. But when the right to vote at any election for the choice of electors for President and Vice President of the United States, Representatives in Congress, the Executive and Judicial officers of a State, or the members of the Legislature thereof, is denied to any of the male inhabitants of such State, being twenty-one years of age, and citizens of the United States, or in any way abridged, except for participation in rebellion, or other crime, the basis of representation therein shall be reduced in the proportion which the number of such male citizens shall bear the whole number of male citizens twenty-one years of age in such State.

### Section 3

No person shall be a Senator or Representative in Congress, or elector of President and Vice President, or hold any office, civil or military, under the United States, or under any State, who, having previously taken an oath, as a member of Congress, or as an officer of the United States, or as a member of any State legislature, or as an executive or judicial officer of any State, to support the Constitution of the United States, shall have engaged in insurrection or rebellion against the same, or given aid or comfort to the enemies thereof. But Congress may by a vote of two-thirds of each House, remove such disability.

### Section 4

The validity of the public debt of the United States, authorized by law, including debts incurred for payment of pensions and bounties for services in suppressing insurrection or rebellion, shall not be questioned. But neither the United States nor any State shall assume or pay any debt or obligation incurred in aid of insurrection of rebellion

against the United States, or any claim for the loss or emancipation of any slave; but all such debts, obligations and claims shall be held illegal and void.

### Section 5

The Congress shall have power to enforce, by appropriate legislation, the provisions of this article.

## Amendment XV [1870]

### Section 1

The right of citizens of the United States to vote shall not be denied or abridged by the United States or by any State on account of race, color, or previous condition of servitude.

### Section 2

The Congress shall have power to enforce this article by appropriate legislation.

## Amendment XVI [1913]

The Congress shall have power to lay and collect taxes on incomes, from whatever source derived, without apportionment among the several States, and without regard to any census or enumeration.

## Amendment XVII [1913]

The Senate of the United States shall be composed of two Senators from each State, elected by the people thereof, for six years; and each Senator shall have one vote. The electors in each State shall have the qualifications requisite for electors of the most numerous branch of the State legislatures.

When vacancies happen in the representation of any State in the Senate, the executive authority of each State shall issue writs of election to fill such vacancies; *Provided*, That the legislature of any State may empower the executive thereof to make temporary appointments until the people fill the vacancies by election as the legislature may direct.

This amendment shall not be construed as to affect the election or term of any Senator chosen before it becomes valid as part of the Constitution.

## Amendment XVIII [1919]

### Section 1

After one year from the ratification of this article the manufacture, sale, or transportation of intoxicating liquors within, the importation thereof into, or the exportation thereof from the United States and all territory subject to the jurisdiction thereof for beverage purposes is hereby prohibited.

### Section 2

The Congress and the several States shall have concurrent power to enforce this article by appropriate legislation.

### Section 3

This article shall be inoperative unless it shall have been ratified as an amendment to the Constitution by the legislatures of the several States, as provided in the Constitution, within seven years from the date of the submission hereof to the States by the Congress.

## Amendment XIX [1920]

The right of citizens of the United States to vote shall not be denied or abridged by the United States or by any State on account of sex.

Congress shall have power to enforce this article by appropriate legislation.

## Amendment XX [1933]

### Section 1
The terms of the President and Vice President shall end at noon on the 20th day of January, and the terms of Senators and Representatives at noon on the 3d day of January, of the years in which such terms would have ended if this article had not been ratified; and the terms of their successors shall then begin.

### Section 2
The Congress shall assemble at least once in every year, and such meeting shall begin at noon on the 3d day of January, unless they shall by law appoint a different day.

### Section 3
If, at the time fixed for the beginning of the term of the President, the President elect shall have died, the Vice President elect shall become President. If a President shall not have been chosen before the time fixed for the beginning of his term, or if the President elect shall have failed to qualify, then the Vice President elect shall act as President until a President shall have qualified; and the Congress may by law provide for the case wherein neither a President elect nor a Vice President elect shall have qualified, declaring who shall then act as President, or the manner in which one who is to act shall be selected, and such person shall act accordingly until a President or Vice President shall have qualified.

### Section 4
The Congress may by law provide for the case of the death of any of the persons from whom the House of Representatives may choose a President whenever the right of choice shall have devolved upon them, and for the case of the death of any of the persons from whom the Senate may choose a Vice President whenever the right of choice shall have devolved upon them.

### Section 5
Sections 1 and 2 shall take effect on the 15th day of October following the ratification of this article.

### Section 6
This article shall be inoperative unless it shall have been ratified as an amendment to the Constitution by the legislatures of three-fourths of the several States within seven years from the date of its submission.

## Amendment XXI [1933]

### Section 1
The eighteenth article of amendment to the Constitution of the United States is hereby repealed.

### Section 2
The transportation or importation into any State, Territory, or possession of the United States for delivery or use therein of intoxicating liquors, in violation of the laws thereof, is hereby prohibited.

### Section 3
This article shall be inoperative unless it shall have been ratified as an amendment to the Constitution by conventions in the several States, as provided in the Constitution, within seven years from the date of the submission hereof to the States by the Congress.

## Amendment XXII [1951]

### Section 1
No person shall be elected to the office of the President more than twice, and no person who has held the office of President, or acted as President, for more than two years of a term to which some other person was elected President shall be elected to the office of the President more than once. But this Article shall not apply to any person holding the office of President when this Article was proposed by the Congress, and shall not prevent any person who may be holding the office of President, or acting as President, during the term within which this Article becomes operative from holding the office of President, or acting as President during the remainder of such term.

### Section 2
This article shall be inoperative unless it shall have been ratified as an amendment to the Constitution by the legislatures of three-fourths of the several States within seven years from the date of its submission to the States by the Congress.

## Amendment XXIII [1961]

### Section 1
The District constituting the seat of Government of the United States shall appoint in such manner as the Congress may direct:

A number of electors of President and Vice President equal to the whole number of Senators and Representatives in Congress to which the District would be entitled if it were a State, but in no event more than the least populous State; they shall be in addition to those appointed by the States, but they shall be considered, for the purposes of the election of President and Vice President, to be electors appointed by a State; and they shall meet in the District and perform such duties as provided by the twelfth article of amendment.

### Section 2
The Congress shall have power to enforce this article by appropriate legislation.

## Amendment XXIV [1964]

### Section 1
The right of citizens of the United States to vote in any primary or other election for President or Vice President, for electors for President or Vice President, or for Senator or Representative in Congress, shall not be denied or abridged by the United States or any State by reason of failure to pay any poll tax or other tax.

### Section 2
The Congress shall have power to enforce this article by appropriate legislation.

## Amendment XXV [1967]

### Section 1
In case of the removal of the President from office or of his death or resignation, the Vice President shall become President.

### Section 2
Whenever there is a vacancy in the office of the Vice President, the President shall nominate a Vice President who shall take office upon confirmation by a majority vote of both Houses of Congress.

### Section 3
Whenever the President transmits to the President pro tempore of the Senate and the Speaker of the House of Representatives his written declaration that he is unable to discharge the powers and duties of his office, and until he transmits to them a written declaration to the contrary, such powers and duties shall be discharged by the Vice President as Acting President.

**Section 4**

Whenever the Vice President and a majority of either the principal officers of the executive departments or of such other body as Congress may by law provide, transmit to the President pro tempore of the Senate and the Speaker of the House of Representatives their written declaration that the President is unable to discharge the powers and duties of his office, the Vice President shall immediately assume the powers and duties of the office as Acting President.

Thereafter, when the President transmits to the President pro tempore of the Senate and the Speaker of the House of Representatives his written declaration that no inability exists, he shall resume the powers and duties of his office unless the Vice President and a majority of either the principal officers of the executive department or of such other body as Congress may by law provide, transmit within four days to the President pro tempore of the Senate and the Speaker of the House of Representatives their written declaration that the President is unable to discharge the powers and duties of his office. Thereupon Congress shall decide the issue, assembling within forty-eight hours for that purpose if not in session. If the Congress, within twenty-one days after receipt of the latter written declaration, or, if Congress is not in session, within twenty-one days after Congress is required to assemble, determines by two-thirds vote of both Houses that the President shall continue to discharge the same as Acting President; otherwise, the President shall resume the powers and duties of his office.

## Amendment XXVI [1971]

**Section 1**

The right of citizens of the United States, who are eighteen years of age or older, to vote shall not be denied or abridged by the United States or by any State on account of age.

**Section 2**

The Congress shall have power to enforce this article by appropriate legislation.

## Amendment XXVII [1992]

No law, varying the compensation for the services of the Senators and Representatives, shall take effect, until an election of Representatives shall have intervened.

# Uniform Commercial Code*

The Code consists of thirteen Articles as follows:
1. General Provisions
2. Sales
2A. Leases
3. Negotiable Instruments
4. Bank Deposits and Collections
4A. Funds Transfers
5. Letters of Credit
6. Bulk Transfers
7. Warehouse Receipts, Bills of Lading and Other Documents of Title
8. Investment Securities
9. Secured Transactions: Sales of Accounts, Contract Rights and Chattel Paper
10. Effective Date and Repealer
11. Effective Date and Transition Provisions

## ARTICLE 1: GENERAL PROVISIONS

### Part 1—Short Title, Construction, Application and Subject Matter of the Act

#### § 1–101. Short Title.
This Act shall be known and may be cited as Uniform Commercial Code.

#### § 1–102. Purposes; Rules of Construction; Variation by Agreement.
(1) This Act shall be liberally construed and applied to promote its underlying purposes and policies.
(2) Underlying purposes and policies of this Act are
    (a) to simplify, clarify and modernize the law governing commercial transactions;
    (b) to permit the continued expansion of commercial practices through custom, usage and agreement of the parties;
    (c) to make uniform the law among the various jurisdictions.
(3) The effect of provisions of this Act may be varied by agreement, except as otherwise provided in this Act and except that the obligations of good faith, diligence, reasonableness and care prescribed by this Act may not be disclaimed by agreement but the parties may by agreement determine the standards by which the performance of such

obligations is to be measured if such standards are not manifestly unreasonable.
(4) The presence in certain provisions of this Act of the words "unless otherwise agreed" or words of similar import does not imply that the effect of other provisions may not be varied by agreement under subsection (3).
(5) In this Act unless the context otherwise requires
    (a) words in the singular number include the plural, and in the plural include the singular;
    (b) words of the masculine gender include the feminine and the neuter, and when the sense so indicates words of the neuter gender may refer to any gender.

#### § 1–103. Supplementary General Principles of Law Applicable.
Unless displaced by the particular provisions of this Act, the principles of law and equity, including the law merchant and the law relative to capacity to contract, principal and agent, estoppel, fraud, misrepresentation, duress, coercion, mistake, bankruptcy, or other validating or invalidating cause shall supplement its provisions.

#### § 1–104. Construction Against Implicit Repeal.
This Act being a general act intended as a unified coverage of its subject matter, no part of it shall be deemed to be impliedly repealed by subsequent legislation if such construction can reasonably be avoided.

#### § 1–105. Territorial Application of the Act; Parties' Power to Choose Applicable Law.
(1) Except as provided hereafter in this section, when a transaction bears a reasonable relation to this state and also to another state or nation the parties may agree that the law either of this state or of such other state or nation shall govern their rights and duties. Failing such agreement this Act applies to transactions bearing an appropriate relation to this state.
(2) Where one of the following provisions of this Act specifies the applicable law, that provision governs and a contrary agreement is effective only to the extent permitted by the law (including the conflict of laws rules) so specified:
    Rights of creditors against sold goods. Section 2–402.
    Applicability of the Article on Leases. Sections 2A–105 and 2A–106.
    Applicability of the Article on Bank Deposits and Collections. Section 4–102.
    Governing law in the Article on Funds Transfers. Section 4A–507.

*[Publisher's Editorial Note: If a state adopts the repealer of Article 6—Bulk Transfers (Alternative A), there should not be any item relating to bulk transfers. If, however, a state adopts Revised Article 6—Bulk*

*Sales (Alternative B), then the item relating to bulk sales should read as follows:]*

Bulk sales subject to the Article on Bulk Sales. Section 6–103.

Applicability of the Article on Investment Securities. Section 8–110.

Perfection provisions of the Article on Secured Transactions. Section 9–103.

## § 1–106. Remedies to Be Liberally Administered.

(1) The remedies provided by this Act shall be liberally administered to the end that the aggrieved party may be put in as good a position as if the other party had fully performed but neither consequential or special nor penal damages may be had except as specifically provided in this Act or by other rule of law.

(2) Any right or obligation declared by this Act is enforceable by action unless the provision declaring it specifies a different and limited effect.

## § 1–107. Waiver or Renunciation of Claim or Right After Breach.

Any claim or right arising out of an alleged breach can be discharged in whole or in part without consideration by a written waiver or renunciation signed and delivered by the aggrieved party.

## § 1–108. Severability.

If any provision or clause of this Act or application thereof to any person or circumstances is held invalid, such invalidity shall not affect other provisions or applications of the Act which can be given effect without the invalid provision or application, and to this end the provisions of this Act are declared to be severable.

## § 1–109. Section Captions.

Section captions are parts of this Act.

## Part 2—General Definitions and Principles of Interpretation

## § 1–201. General Definitions.

Subject to additional definitions contained in the subsequent Articles of this Act which are applicable to specific Articles or Parts thereof, and unless the context otherwise requires, in this Act:

(1) "Action" in the sense of a judicial proceeding includes recoupment, counterclaim, set-off, suit in equity and any other proceedings in which rights are determined.

(2) "Aggrieved party" means a party entitled to resort to a remedy.

(3) "Agreement" means the bargain of the parties in fact as found in their language or by implication from other circumstances including course of dealing or usage of trade or course of performance as provided in this Act (Sections 1–205, 2–208, and 2A–207). Whether an agreement has legal consequences is determined by the provisions of this Act, if applicable; otherwise by the law of contracts (Section 1–103). (Compare "Contract".)

(4) "Bank" means any person engaged in the business of banking.

(5) "Bearer" means the person in possession of an instrument, document of title, or certificated security payable to bearer or indorsed in blank.

(6) "Bill of lading" means a document evidencing the receipt of goods for shipment issued by a person engaged in the business of transporting or forwarding goods, and includes an airbill. "Airbill" means a document serving for air transportation as a bill of lading does for marine or rail transportation, and includes an air consignment note or air waybill.

(7) "Branch" includes a separately incorporated foreign branch of a bank.

(8) "Burden of establishing" a fact means the burden of persuading the triers of fact that the existence of the fact is more probable than its non-existence.

(9) "Buyer in ordinary course of business" means a person who in good faith and without knowledge that the sale to him is in violation of the ownership rights or security interest of a third party in the goods buys in ordinary course from a person in the business of selling goods of that kind but does not include a pawnbroker. All persons who sell minerals or the like (including oil and gas) at wellhead or minehead shall be deemed to be persons in the business of selling goods of that kind. "Buying" may be for cash or by exchange of other property or on secured or unsecured credit and includes receiving goods or documents of title under a pre-existing contract for sale but does not include a transfer in bulk or as security for or in total or partial satisfaction of a money debt.

(10) "Conspicuous": A term or clause is conspicuous when it is so written that a reasonable person against whom it is to operate ought to have noticed it. A printed heading in capitals (as: NON-NEGOTIABLE BILL OF LADING) is conspicuous. Language in the body of a form is "conspicuous" if it is in larger or other contrasting type or color. But in a telegram any stated term is "conspicuous". Whether a term or clause is "conspicuous" or not is for decision by the court.

(11) "Contract" means the total legal obligation which results from the parties' agreement as affected by this Act and any other applicable rules of law. (Compare "Agreement".)

(12) "Creditor" includes a general creditor, a secured creditor, a lien creditor and any representative of creditors, including an assignee for the benefit of creditors, a trustee in bankruptcy, a receiver in equity and an executor or administrator of an insolvent debtor's or assignor's estate.

(13) "Defendant" includes a person in the position of defendant in a cross-action or counterclaim.

(14) "Delivery" with respect to instruments, documents of title, chattel paper, or certificated securities means voluntary transfer of possession.

(15) "Document of title" includes bill of lading, dock warrant, dock receipt, warehouse receipt or order for the delivery of goods, and also any other document which in the regular course of business or financing is treated as adequately evidencing that the person in possession of it is entitled to receive, hold and dispose of the document and the goods it covers. To be a document of title a document must purport to be issued by or addressed to a bailee and purport to cover goods in the bailee's possession which are either identified or are fungible portions of an identified mass.

(16) "Fault" means wrongful act, omission or breach.

(17) "Fungible" with respect to goods or securities means goods or securities of which any unit is, by nature or usage of trade, the equivalent of any other like unit. Goods which are not fungible shall be deemed fungible for the purposes of this Act to the extent that under a particular agreement or document unlike units are treated as equivalents.

(18) "Genuine" means free of forgery or counterfeiting.

(19) "Good faith" means honesty in fact in the conduct or transaction concerned.

(20) "Holder," with respect to a negotiable instrument, means the person in possession if the instrument is payable to bearer or, in the case of an instrument payable to an identified person, if the identified

person is in possession. "Holder" with respect to a document of title means the person in possession if the goods are deliverable to bearer or to the order of the person in possession.

(21) To "honor" is to pay or to accept and pay, or where a credit so engages to purchase or discount a draft complying with the terms of the credit.

(22) "Insolvency proceedings" includes any assignment for the benefit of creditors or other proceedings intended to liquidate or rehabilitate the estate of the person involved.

(23) A person is "insolvent" who either has ceased to pay his debts in the ordinary course of business or cannot pay his debts as they become due or is insolvent within the meaning of the federal bankruptcy law.

(24) "Money" means a medium of exchange authorized or adopted by a domestic or foreign government and includes a monetary unit of account established by an intergovernmental organization or by agreement between two or more nations.

(25) A person has "notice" of a fact when
    (a) he has actual knowledge of it; or
    (b) he has received a notice or notification of it; or
    (c) from all the facts and circumstances known to him at the time in question he has reason to know that it exists.
A person "knows" or has "knowledge" of a fact when he has actual knowledge of it. "Discover" or "learn" or a word or phrase of similar import refers to knowledge rather than to reason to know. The time and circumstances under which a notice or notification may cease to be effective are not determined by this Act.

(26) A person "notifies" or "gives" a notice or notification to another by taking such steps as may be reasonably required to inform the other in ordinary course whether or not such other actually comes to know of it. A person "receives" a notice or notification when
    (a) it comes to his attention; or
    (b) it is duly delivered at the place of business through which the contract was made or at any other place held out by him as the place for receipt of such communications.

(27) Notice, knowledge or a notice or notification received by an organization is effective for a particular transaction from the time when it is brought to the attention of the individual conducting that transaction, and in any event from the time when it would have been brought to his attention if the organization had exercised due diligence. An organization exercises due diligence if it maintains reasonable routines for communicating significant information to the person conducting the transaction and there is reasonable compliance with the routines. Due diligence does not require an individual acting for the organization to communicate information unless such communication is part of his regular duties or unless he has reason to know of the transaction and that the transaction would be materially affected by the information.

(28) "Organization" includes a corporation, government or governmental subdivision or agency, business trust, estate, trust, partnership or association, two or more persons having a joint or common interest, or any other legal or commercial entity.

(29) "Party", as distinct from "third party", means a person who has engaged in a transaction or made an agreement within this Act.

(30) "Person" includes an individual or an organization (See Section 1–102).

(31) "Presumption" or "presumed" means that the trier of fact must find the existence of the fact presumed unless and until evidence is introduced which would support a finding of its non-existence.

(32) "Purchase" includes taking by sale, discount, negotiation, mortgage, pledge, lien, issue or re-issue, gift or any other voluntary transaction creating an interest in property.

(33) "Purchaser" means a person who takes by purchase.

(34) "Remedy" means any remedial right to which an aggrieved party is entitled with or without resort to a tribunal.

(35) "Representative" includes an agent, an officer of a corporation or association, and a trustee, executor or administrator of an estate, or any other person empowered to act for another.

(36) "Rights" includes remedies.

(37) "Security interest" means an interest in personal property or fixtures which secures payment or performance of an obligation. The retention or reservation of title by a seller of goods notwithstanding shipment or delivery to the buyer (Section 2–401) is limited in effect to a reservation of a "security interest". The term also includes any interest of a buyer of accounts or chattel paper which is subject to Article 9. The special property interest of a buyer of goods on identification of those goods to a contract for sale under Section 2–401 is not a "security interest", but a buyer may also acquire a "security interest" by complying with Article 9. Unless a consignment is intended as security, reservation of title thereunder is not a "security interest", but a consignment in any event is subject to the provisions on consignment sales (Section 2–326).

Whether a transaction creates a lease or security interest is determined by the facts of each case; however, a transaction creates a security interest if the consideration the lessee is to pay the lessor for the right to possession and use of the goods is an obligation for the term of the lease not subject to termination by the lessee, and
    (a) the original term of the lease is equal to or greater than the remaining economic life of the goods,
    (b) the lessee is bound to renew the lease for the remaining economic life of the goods or is bound to become the owner of the goods,
    (c) the lessee has an option to renew the lease for the remaining economic life of the goods for no additional consideration or nominal additional consideration upon compliance with the lease agreement, or
    (d) the lessee has an option to become the owner of the goods for no additional consideration or nominal additional consideration upon compliance with the lease agreement.

A transaction does not create a security interest merely because it provides that
    (a) the present value of the consideration the lessee is obligated to pay the lessor for the right to possession and use of the goods is substantially equal to or is greater than the fair market value of the goods at the time the lease is entered into,
    (b) the lessee assumes risk of loss of the goods, or agrees to pay taxes, insurance, filing, recording, or registration fees, or service or maintenance costs with respect to the goods,
    (c) the lessee has an option to renew the lease or to become the owner of the goods,
    (d) the lessee has an option to renew the lease for a fixed rent that is equal to or greater than the reasonably predictable fair market rent for the use of the goods for the term of the renewal at the time the option is to be performed, or
    (e) the lessee has an option to become the owner of the goods for a fixed price that is equal to or greater than the reasonably predictable fair market value of the goods at the time the option is to be performed.

For purposes of this subsection (37):
    (x) Additional consideration is not nominal if (i) when the option to renew the lease is granted to the lessee the rent is stated to be the fair market rent for the use of the goods for the term of

the renewal determined at the time the option is to be performed, or (ii) when the option to become the owner of the goods is granted to the lessee the price is stated to be the fair market value of the goods determined at the time the option is to be performed. Additional consideration is nominal if it is less than the lessee's reasonably predictable cost of performing under the lease agreement if the option is not exercised;

(y) "Reasonably predictable" and "remaining economic life of the goods" are to be determined with reference to the facts and circumstances at the time the transaction is entered into; and

(z) "Present value" means the amount as of a date certain of one or more sums payable in the future, discounted to the date certain. The discount is determined by the interest rate specified by the parties if the rate is not manifestly unreasonable at the time the transaction is entered into; otherwise, the discount is determined by a commercially reasonable rate that takes into account the facts and circumstances of each case at the time the transaction was entered into.

(38) "Send" in connection with any writing or notice means to deposit in the mail or deliver for transmission by any other usual means of communication with postage or cost of transmission provided for and properly addressed and in the case of an instrument to an address specified thereon or otherwise agreed, or if there be none to any address reasonable under the circumstances. The receipt of any writing or notice within the time at which it would have arrived if properly sent has the effect of a proper sending.

(39) "Signed" includes any symbol executed or adopted by a party with present intention to authenticate a writing.

(40) "Surety" includes guarantor.

(41) "Telegram" includes a message transmitted by radio, teletype, cable, any mechanical method of transmission, or the like.

(42) "Term" means that portion of an agreement which relates to a particular matter.

(43) "Unauthorized" signature means one made without actual, implied, or apparent authority and includes a forgery.

(44) "Value". Except as otherwise provided with respect to negotiable instruments and bank collections (Sections 3–303, 4–210 and 4–211) a person gives "value" for rights if he acquires them

(a) in return for a binding commitment to extend credit or for the extension of immediately available credit whether or not drawn upon and whether or not a charge-back is provided for in the event of difficulties in collection; or

(b) as security for or in total or partial satisfaction of a pre-existing claim; or

(c) by accepting delivery pursuant to a pre-existing contract for purchase; or

(d) generally, in return for any consideration sufficient to support a simple contract.

(45) "Warehouse receipt" means a receipt issued by a person engaged in the business of storing goods for hire.

(46) "Written" or "writing" includes printing, typewriting or any other intentional reduction to tangible form.

### § 1–202.  Prima Facie Evidence by Third Party Documents.

A document in due form purporting to be a bill of lading, policy or certificate of insurance, official weigher's or inspector's certificate, consular invoice, or any other document authorized or required by the contract to be issued by a third party shall be prima facie evidence of its own authenticity and genuineness and of the facts stated in the document by the third party.

### § 1–203.  Obligation of Good Faith.

Every contract or duty within this Act imposes an obligation of good faith in its performance or enforcement.

### § 1–204.  Time; Reasonable Time; "Seasonably".

(1) Whenever this Act requires any action to be taken within a reasonable time, any time which is not manifestly unreasonable may be fixed by agreement.

(2) What is a reasonable time for taking any action depends on the nature, purpose and circumstances of such action.

(3) An action is taken "seasonably" when it is taken at or within the time agreed or if no time is agreed at or within a reasonable time.

### § 1–205.  Course of Dealing and Usage of Trade.

(1) A course of dealing is a sequence of previous conduct between the parties to a particular transaction which is fairly to be regarded as establishing a common basis of understanding for interpreting their expressions and other conduct.

(2) A usage of trade is any practice or method of dealing having such regularity of observance in a place, vocation or trade as to justify an expectation that it will be observed with respect to the transaction in question. The existence and scope of such a usage are to be proved as facts. If it is established that such a usage is embodied in a written trade code or similar writing the interpretation of the writing is for the court.

(3) A course of dealing between parties and any usage of trade in the vocation or trade in which they are engaged or of which they are or should be aware give particular meaning to and supplement or qualify terms of an agreement.

(4) The express terms of an agreement and an applicable course of dealing or usage of trade shall be construed wherever reasonable as consistent with each other, but when such construction is unreasonable express terms control both course of dealing and usage of trade and course of dealing controls usage of trade.

(5) An applicable usage of trade in the place where any part of performance is to occur shall be used in interpreting the agreement as to that part of the performance.

(6) Evidence of a relevant usage of trade offered by one party is not admissible unless and until he has given the other party such notice as the court finds sufficient to prevent unfair surprise to the latter.

### § 1–206.  Statute of Frauds for Kinds of Personal Property Not Otherwise Covered.

(1) Except in the cases described in subsection (2) of this section a contract for the sale of personal property is not enforceable by way of action or defense beyond five thousand dollars in amount or value of remedy unless there is some writing which indicates that a contract for sale has been made between the parties at a defined or stated price, reasonably identifies the subject matter, and is signed by the party against whom enforcement is sought or by his authorized agent.

(2) Subsection (1) of this section does not apply to contracts for the sale of goods (Section 2–201) nor of securities (Section 8–113) nor to security agreements (Section 9–203).

### § 1–207.  Performance or Acceptance Under Reservation of Rights.

A party who with explicit reservation of rights performs or promises performance or assents to performance in a manner demanded or offered by the other party does not thereby prejudice the rights reserved. Such words as "without prejudice", "under protest" or the like are sufficient.

## § 1–208. Option to Accelerate at Will.

A term providing that one party or his successor in interest may accelerate payment or performance or require collateral or additional collateral "at will" or "when he deems himself insecure" or in words of similar import shall be construed to mean that he shall have power to do so only if he in good faith believes that the prospect of payment or performance is impaired. The burden of establishing lack of good faith is on the party against whom the power has been exercised.

## § 1–209. Subordinated Obligations.

An obligation may be issued as subordinated to payment of another obligation of the person obligated, or a creditor may subordinate his right to payment of an obligation by agreement with either the person obligated or another creditor of the person obligated. Such a subordination does not create a security interest as against either the common debtor or a subordinated creditor. This section shall be construed as declaring the law as it existed prior to the enactment of this section and not as modifying it. Added 1966.

Note: *This new section is proposed as an optional provision to make it clear that a subordination agreement does not create a security interest unless so intended.*

# ARTICLE 2: SALES

## Part 1—Short Title, Construction and Subject Matter

### § 2–101. Short Title.

This Article shall be known and may be cited as Uniform Commercial Code—Sales.

### § 2–102. Scope; Certain Security and Other Transactions Excluded From This Article.

Unless the context otherwise requires, this Article applies to transactions in goods; it does not apply to any transaction which although in the form of an unconditional contract to sell or present sale is intended to operate only as a security transaction nor does this Article impair or repeal any statute regulating sales to consumers, farmers or other specified classes of buyers.

### § 2–103. Definitions and Index of Definitions.

(1) In this Article unless the context otherwise requires
    (a) "Buyer" means a person who buys or contracts to buy goods.
    (b) "Good faith" in the case of a merchant means honesty in fact and the observance of reasonable commercial standards of fair dealing in the trade.
    (c) "Receipt" of goods means taking physical possession of them.
    (d) "Seller" means a person who sells or contracts to sell goods.
(2) Other definitions applying to this Article or to specified Parts thereof, and the sections in which they appear are:
    "Acceptance". Section 2–606.
    "Banker's credit". Section 2–325.
    "Between merchants". Section 2–104.
    "Cancellation". Section 2–106(4).
    "Commercial unit". Section 2–105.
    "Confirmed credit". Section 2–325.
    "Conforming to contract". Section 2–106.
    "Contract for sale". Section 2–106.
    "Cover". Section 2–712.
    "Entrusting". Section 2–403.
    "Financing agency". Section 2–104.
    "Future goods". Section 2–105.
    "Goods". Section 2–105.
    "Identification". Section 2–501.
    "Installment contract". Section 2–612.
    "Letter of Credit". Section 2–325.
    "Lot". Section 2–105.
    "Merchant". Section 2–104.
    "Overseas". Section 2–323.
    "Person in position of seller". Section 2–707.
    "Present sale". Section 2–106.
    "Sale". Section 2–106.
    "Sale on approval". Section 2–326.
    "Sale or return". Section 2–326.
    "Termination". Section 2–106.
(3) The following definitions in other Articles apply to this Article:
    "Check". Section 3–104.
    "Consignee". Section 7–102.
    "Consignor". Section 7–102.
    "Consumer goods". Section 9–109.
    "Dishonor". Section 3–502.
    "Draft". Section 3–104.
(4) In addition Article 1 contains general definitions and principles of construction and interpretation applicable throughout this Article.

### § 2–104. Definitions: "Merchant"; "Between Merchants"; "Financing Agency".

(1) "Merchant" means a person who deals in goods of the kind or otherwise by his occupation holds himself out as having knowledge or skill peculiar to the practices or goods involved in the transaction or to whom such knowledge or skill may be attributed by his employment of an agent or broker or other intermediary who by his occupation holds himself out as having such knowledge or skill.
(2) "Financing agency" means a bank, finance company or other person who in the ordinary course of business makes advances against goods or documents of title or who by arrangement with either the seller or the buyer intervenes in ordinary course to make or collect payment due or claimed under the contract for sale, as by purchasing or paying the seller's draft or making advances against it or by merely taking it for collection whether or not documents of title accompany the draft. "Financing agency" includes also a bank or other person who similarly intervenes between persons who are in the position of seller and buyer in respect to the goods (Section 2–707).
(3) "Between merchants" means in any transaction with respect to which both parties are chargeable with the knowledge or skill of merchants.

### § 2–105. Definitions: Transferability; "Goods"; "Future" Goods; "Lot"; "Commercial Unit".

(1) "Goods" means all things (including specially manufactured goods) which are movable at the time of identification to the contract for sale other than the money in which the price is to be paid, investment securities (Article 8) and things in action. "Goods" also includes the unborn young of animals and growing crops and other identified things attached to realty as described in the section on goods to be severed from realty (Section 2–107).
(2) Goods must be both existing and identified before any interest in them can pass. Goods which are not both existing and identified are "future" goods. A purported present sale of future goods or of any interest therein operates as a contract to sell.
(3) There may be a sale of a part interest in existing identified goods.
(4) An undivided share in an identified bulk of fungible goods is sufficiently identified to be sold although the quantity of the bulk is

not determined. Any agreed proportion of such a bulk or any quantity thereof agreed upon by number, weight or other measure may to the extent of the seller's interest in the bulk be sold to the buyer who then becomes an owner in common.

(5) "Lot" means a parcel or a single article which is the subject matter of a separate sale or delivery, whether or not it is sufficient to perform the contract.

(6) "Commercial unit" means such a unit of goods as by commercial usage is a single whole for purposes of sale and division of which materially impairs its character or value on the market or in use. A commercial unit may be a single article (as a machine) or a set of articles (as a suite of furniture or an assortment of sizes) or a quantity (as a bale, gross, or carload) or any other unit treated in use or in the relevant market as a single whole.

### § 2–106.  Definitions: "Contract"; "Agreement"; "Contract for Sale"; "Sale"; "Present Sale"; "Conforming" to Contract; "Termination"; "Cancellation".

(1) In this Article unless the context otherwise requires "contract" and "agreement" are limited to those relating to the present or future sale of goods. "Contract for sale" includes both a present sale of goods and a contract to sell goods at a future time. A "sale" consists in the passing of title from the seller to the buyer for a price (Section 2–401). A "present sale" means a sale which is accomplished by the making of the contract.

(2) Goods or conduct including any part of a performance are "conforming" or conform to the contract when they are in accordance with the obligations under the contract.

(3) "Termination" occurs when either party pursuant to a power created by agreement or law puts an end to the contract otherwise than for its breach. On "termination" all obligations which are still executory on both sides are discharged but any right based on prior breach or performance survives.

(4) "Cancellation" occurs when either party puts an end to the contract for breach by the other and its effect is the same as that of "termination" except that the cancelling party also retains any remedy for breach of the whole contract or any unperformed balance.

### § 2–107.  Goods to Be Severed From Realty: Recording.

(1) A contract for the sale of minerals or the like (including oil and gas) or a structure or its materials to be removed from realty is a contract for the sale of goods within this Article if they are to be severed by the seller but until severance a purported present sale thereof which is not effective as a transfer of an interest in land is effective only as a contract to sell.

(2) A contract for the sale apart from the land of growing crops or other things attached to realty and capable of severance without material harm thereto but not described in subsection (1) or of timber to be cut is a contract for the sale of goods within this Article whether the subject matter is to be severed by the buyer or by the seller even though it forms part of the realty at the time of contracting, and the parties can by identification effect a present sale before severance.

(3) The provisions of this section are subject to any third party rights provided by the law relating to realty records, and the contract for sale may be executed and recorded as a document transferring an interest in land and shall then constitute notice to third parties of the buyer's rights under the contract for sale.

## Part 2—Form, Formation and Readjustment of Contract

### § 2–201.  Formal Requirements; Statute of Frauds.

(1) Except as otherwise provided in this section a contract for the sale of goods for the price of $500 or more is not enforceable by way

of action or defense unless there is some writing sufficient to indicate that a contract for sale has been made between the parties and signed by the party against whom enforcement is sought or by his authorized agent or broker. A writing is not insufficient because it omits or incorrectly states a term agreed upon but the contract is not enforceable under this paragraph beyond the quantity of goods shown in such writing.

(2) Between merchants if within a reasonable time a writing in confirmation of the contract and sufficient against the sender is received and the party receiving it has reason to know its contents, it satisfies the requirements of subsection (1) against such party unless written notice of objection to its contents is given within ten days after it is received.

(3) A contract which does not satisfy the requirements of subsection (1) but which is valid in other respects is enforceable

    (a) if the goods are to be specially manufactured for the buyer and are not suitable for sale to others in the ordinary course of the seller's business and the seller, before notice of repudiation is received and under circumstances which reasonably indicate that the goods are for the buyer, has made either a substantial beginning of their manufacture or commitments for their procurement; or

    (b) if the party against whom enforcement is sought admits in his pleading, testimony or otherwise in court that a contract for sale was made, but the contract is not enforceable under this provision beyond the quantity of goods admitted; or

    (c) with respect to goods for which payment has been made and accepted or which have been received and accepted (Sec. 2–606).

### § 2–202.  Final Written Expression: Parol or Extrinsic Evidence.

Terms with respect to which the confirmatory memoranda of the parties agree or which are otherwise set forth in a writing intended by the parties as a final expression of their agreement with respect to such terms as are included therein may not be contradicted by evidence of any prior agreement or of a contemporaneous oral agreement but may be explained or supplemented

    (a) by course of dealing or usage of trade (Section 1–205) or by course of performance (Section 2–208); and

    (b) by evidence of consistent additional terms unless the court finds the writing to have been intended also as a complete and exclusive statement of the terms of the agreement.

### § 2–203.  Seals Inoperative.

The affixing of a seal to a writing evidencing a contract for sale or an offer to buy or sell goods does not constitute the writing a sealed instrument and the law with respect to sealed instruments does not apply to such a contract or offer.

### § 2–204.  Formation in General.

(1) A contract for sale of goods may be made in any manner sufficient to show agreement, including conduct by both parties which recognizes the existence of such a contract.

(2) An agreement sufficient to constitute a contract for sale may be found even though the moment of its making is undetermined.

(3) Even though one or more terms are left open a contract for sale does not fail for indefiniteness if the parties have intended to make a contract and there is a reasonably certain basis for giving an appropriate remedy.

### § 2–205.  Firm Offers.

An offer by a merchant to buy or sell goods in a signed writing which by its terms gives assurance that it will be held open is not revocable, for lack of consideration, during the time stated or if no time is stated for reasonable time, but in no event may such period of irrevocability exceed three months; but any such term of assurance on a form supplied by the offeree must be separately signed by the offeror.

### § 2–206.  Offer and Acceptance in Formation of Contract.
(1) Unless other unambiguously indicated by the language or circumstances

    (a) an offer to make a contract shall be construed as inviting acceptance in any manner and by any medium reasonable in the circumstances;

    (b) an order or other offer to buy goods for prompt or current shipment shall be construed as inviting acceptance either by a prompt promise to ship or by the prompt or current shipment of conforming or nonconforming goods, but such a shipment of non-conforming goods does not constitute an acceptance if the seller seasonably notifies the buyer that the shipment is offered only as an accommodation to the buyer.

(2) Where the beginning of a requested performance is a reasonable mode of acceptance an offeror who is not notified of acceptance within a reasonable time may treat the offer as having lapsed before acceptance.

### § 2–207.  Additional Terms in Acceptance or Confirmation.
(1) A definite and seasonable expression of acceptance or a written confirmation which is sent within a reasonable time operates as an acceptance even though it states terms additional to or different from those offered or agreed upon, unless acceptance is expressly made conditional on assent to the additional or different terms.

(2) The additional terms are to be construed as proposals for addition to the contract. Between merchants such terms become part of the contract unless:

    (a) the offer expressly limits acceptance to the terms of the offer;

    (b) they materially alter it; or

    (c) notification of objection to them has already been given or is given within a reasonable time after notice of them is received.

(3) Conduct by both parties which recognizes the existence of a contract is sufficient to establish a contract for sale although the writings of the parties do not otherwise establish a contract. In such case the terms of the particular contract consist of those terms on which the writings of the parties agree, together with any supplementary terms incorporated under any other provisions of this Act.

### § 2–208.  Course of Performance or Practical Construction.
(1) Where the contract for sale involves repeated occasions for performance by either party with knowledge of the nature of the performance and opportunity for objection to it by the other, any course of performance accepted or acquiesced in without objection shall be relevant to determine the meaning of the agreement.

(2) The express terms of the agreement and any such course of performance, as well as any course of dealing and usage of trade, shall be construed whenever reasonable as consistent with each other; but when such construction is unreasonable, express terms shall control course of performance and course of performance shall control both course of dealing and usage of trade (Section 1–205).

(3) Subject to the provisions of the next section on modification and waiver, such course of performance shall be relevant to show a waiver or modification of any term inconsistent with such course of performance.

### § 2–209.  Modification, Rescission and Waiver.
(1) An agreement modifying a contract within this Article needs no consideration to be binding.

(2) A signed agreement which excludes modification or rescission except by a signed writing cannot be otherwise modified or rescinded, but except as between merchants such a requirement on a form supplied by the merchant must be separately signed by the other party.

(3) The requirements of the statute of frauds section of this Article (Section 2–201) must be satisfied if the contract as modified is within its provisions.

(4) Although an attempt at modification or rescission does not satisfy the requirements of subsection (2) or (3) it can operate as a waiver.

(5) A party who has made a waiver affecting an executory portion of the contract may retract the waiver by reasonable notification received by the other party that strict performance will be required of any term waived, unless the retraction would be unjust in view of a material change of position in reliance on the waiver.

### § 2–210.  Delegation of Performance; Assignment of Rights.
(1) A party may perform his duty through a delegate unless otherwise agreed or unless the other party has a substantial interest in having his original promisor perform or control the acts required by the contract. No delegation of performance relieves the party delegating of any duty to perform or any liability for breach.

(2) Unless otherwise agreed all rights of either seller or buyer can be assigned except where the assignment would materially change the duty of the other party, or increase materially the burden or risk imposed on him by his contract, or impair materially his chance of obtaining return performance. A right to damages for breach of the whole contract or a right arising out of the assignor's due performance of his entire obligation can be assigned despite agreement otherwise.

(3) Unless the circumstances indicate the contrary a prohibition of assignment of "the contract" is to be construed as barring only the delegation to the assignee of the assignor's performance.

(4) An assignment of "the contract" or of "all my rights under the contract" or an assignment in similar general terms is an assignment of rights and unless the language or the circumstances (as in an assignment for security) indicate the contrary, it is a delegation of performance of the duties of the assignor and its acceptance by the assignee constitutes a promise by him to perform those duties. This promise is enforceable by either the assignor or the other party to the original contract.

(5) The other party may treat any assignment which delegates performance as creating reasonable grounds for insecurity and may without prejudice to his rights against the assignor demand assurances from the assignee (Section 2–609).

## Part 3—General Obligation and Construction of Contract

### § 2–301.  General Obligations of Parties.
The obligation of the seller is to transfer and deliver and that of the buyer is to accept and pay in accordance with the contract.

### § 2–302.  Unconscionable Contract or Clause.
(1) If the court as a matter of law finds the contract or any clause of the contract to have been unconscionable at the time it was made the court may refuse to enforce the contract, or it may enforce the remainder of the contract without the unconscionable clause, or it may so limit the application of any unconscionable clause as to avoid any unconscionable result.

(2) When it is claimed or appears to the court that the contract or any clause thereof may be unconscionable the parties shall be afforded a reasonable opportunity to present evidence as to its commercial

setting, purpose and effect to aid the court in making the determination.

### § 2–303.  Allocation or Division of Risks.

Where this Article allocates a risk or a burden as between the parties "unless otherwise agreed", the agreement may not only shift the allocation, but may also divide the risk or burden.

### § 2–304.  Price Payable in Money, Goods, Realty, or Otherwise.

(1)  The price can be made payable in money or otherwise. If it is payable in whole or in part in goods each party is a seller of the goods which he is to transfer.

(2)  Even though all or part of the price is payable in an interest in realty the transfer of the goods and the seller's obligations with reference to them are subject to this Article, but not the transfer of the interest in realty or the transferor's obligations in connection therewith.

### § 2–305.  Open Price Term.

(1)  The parties if they so intend can conclude a contract for sale even though the price is not settled. In such a case the price is a reasonable price at the time for delivery if
    (a)  nothing is said as to price; or
    (b)  the price is left to be agreed by the parties and they fail to agree; or
    (c)  the price is to be fixed in terms of some agreed market or other standard as set or recorded by a third person or agency and it is not so set or recorded.

(2)  A price to be fixed by the seller or by the buyer means a price for him to fix in good faith.

(3)  When a price left to be fixed otherwise than by agreement of the parties fails to be fixed through fault of one party the other may at his option treat the contract as cancelled or himself fix a reasonable price.

(4)  Where, however, the parties intend not to be bound unless the price be fixed or agreed and it is not fixed or agreed there is no contract. In such a case the buyer must return any goods already received or if unable so to do must pay their reasonable value at the time of delivery and the seller must return any portion of the price paid on account.

### § 2–306.  Output, Requirements and Exclusive Dealings.

(1)  A term which measures the quantity by the output of the seller or the requirements of the buyer means such actual output or requirements as may occur in good faith, except that no quantity unreasonably disproportionate to any stated estimate or in the absence of a stated estimate to any normal or otherwise comparable prior output or requirements may be tendered or demanded.

(2)  A lawful agreement by either the seller or the buyer for exclusive dealing in the kind of goods concerned imposes unless otherwise agreed an obligation by the seller to use best efforts to supply the goods and by the buyer to use best efforts to promote their sale.

### § 2–307.  Delivery in Single Lot or Several Lots.

Unless otherwise agreed all goods called for by a contract for sale must be tendered in a single delivery and payment is due only on such tender but where the circumstances give either party the right to make or demand delivery in lots the price if it can be apportioned may be demanded for each lot.

### § 2–308.  Absence of Specified Place for Delivery.

Unless otherwise agreed
    (a)  the place for delivery of goods is the seller's place of business or if he has none his residence; but

    (b)  in a contract for sale of identified goods which to the knowledge of the parties at the time of contracting are in some other place, that place is the place for their delivery; and
    (c)  documents of title may be delivered through customary banking channels.

### § 2–309.  Absence of Specific Time Provisions; Notice of Termination.

(1)  The time for shipment or delivery or any other action under a contract if not provided in this Article or agreed upon shall be a reasonable time.

(2)  Where the contract provides for successive performances but is indefinite in duration it is valid for a reasonable time but unless otherwise agreed may be terminated at any time by either party.

(3)  Termination of a contract by one party except on the happening of an agreed event requires that reasonable notification be received by the other party and an agreement dispensing with notification is invalid if its operation would be unconscionable.

### § 2–310.  Open Time for Payment or Running of Credit; Authority to Ship Under Reservation.

Unless otherwise agreed
    (a)  payment is due at the time and place at which the buyer is to receive the goods even though the place of shipment is the place of delivery; and
    (b)  if the seller is authorized to send the goods he may ship them under reservation, and may tender the documents of title, but the buyer may inspect the goods after their arrival before payment is due unless such inspection is inconsistent with the terms of the contract (Section 2–513); and
    (c)  if delivery is authorized and made by way of documents of title otherwise than by subsection (b) then payment is due at the time and place at which the buyer is to receive the documents regardless of where the goods are to be received; and
    (d)  where the seller is required or authorized to ship the goods on credit the credit period runs from the time of shipment but post-dating the invoice or delaying its dispatch will correspondingly delay the starting of the credit period.

### § 2–311.  Options and Cooperation Respecting Performance.

(1)  An agreement for sale which is otherwise sufficiently definite (subsection (3) of Section 2–204) to be a contract is not made invalid by the fact that it leaves particulars of performance to be specified by one of the parties. Any such specification must be made in good faith and within limits set by commercial reasonableness.

(2)  Unless otherwise agreed specifications relating to assortment of the goods are at the buyer's option and except as otherwise provided in subsections (1)(c) and (3) of Section 2–319 specifications or arrangements relating to shipment are at the seller's option.

(3)  Where such specification would materially affect the other party's performance but is not seasonably made or where one party's cooperation is necessary to the agreed performance of the other but is not seasonably forthcoming, the other party in addition to all other remedies
    (a)  is excused for any resulting delay in his own performance; and
    (b)  may also either proceed to perform in any reasonable manner or after the time for a material part of his own performance treat the failure to specify or to cooperate as a breach by failure to deliver or accept the goods.

## § 2–312. Warranty of Title and Against Infringement; Buyer's Obligation Against Infringement.

(1) Subject to subsection (2) there is in a contract for sale a warranty by the seller that

    (a) the title conveyed shall be good, and its transfer rightful; and

    (b) the goods shall be delivered free from any security interest or other lien or encumbrance of which the buyer at the time of contracting has no knowledge.

(2) A warranty under subsection (1) will be excluded or modified only by specific language or by circumstances which give the buyer reason to know that the person selling does not claim title in himself or that he is purporting to sell only such right or title as he or a third person may have.

(3) Unless otherwise agreed a seller who is a merchant regularly dealing in goods of the kind warrants that the goods shall be delivered free of the rightful claim of any third person by way of infringement or the like but a buyer who furnishes specifications to the seller must hold the seller harmless against any such claim which arises out of compliance with the specifications.

## § 2–313. Express Warranties by Affirmation, Promise, Description, Sample.

(1) Express warranties by the seller are created as follows:

    (a) Any affirmation of fact or promise made by the seller to the buyer which relates to the goods and becomes part of the basis of the bargain creates an express warranty that the goods shall conform to the affirmation or promise.

    (b) Any description of the goods which is made part of the basis of the bargain creates an express warranty that the goods shall conform to the description.

    (c) Any sample or model which is made part of the basis of the bargain creates an express warranty that the whole of the goods shall conform to the sample or model.

(2) It is not necessary to the creation of an express warranty that the seller use formal words such as "warrant" or "guarantee" or that he have a specific intention to make a warranty, but an affirmation merely of the value of the goods or a statement purporting to be merely the seller's opinion or commendation of the goods does not create a warranty.

## § 2–314. Implied Warranty: Merchantability; Usage of Trade.

(1) Unless excluded or modified (Section 2–316), a warranty that the goods shall be merchantable is implied in a contract for their sale if the seller is a merchant with respect to goods of that kind. Under this section the serving for value of food or drink to be consumed either on the premises or elsewhere is a sale.

(2) Goods to be merchantable must be at least such as

    (a) pass without objection in the trade under the contract description; and

    (b) in the case of fungible goods, are of fair average quality within the description; and

    (c) are fit for the ordinary purpose for which such goods are used; and

    (d) run, within the variations permitted by the agreement, of even kind, quality and quantity within each unit and among all units involved; and

    (e) are adequately contained, packaged, and labeled as the agreement may require; and

    (f) conform to the promises or affirmations of fact made on the container or label if any.

(3) Unless excluded or modified (Section 2–316) other implied warranties may arise from course of dealing or usage of trade.

## § 2–315. Implied Warranty: Fitness for Particular Purpose.

Where the seller at the time of contracting has reason to know any particular purpose for which the goods are required and that the buyer is relying on the seller's skill or judgment to select or furnish suitable goods, there is unless excluded or modified under the next section an implied warranty that the goods shall be fit for such purpose.

## § 2–316. Exclusion or Modification of Warranties.

(1) Words or conduct relevant to the creation of an express warranty and words or conduct tending to negate or limit warranty shall be construed wherever reasonable as consistent with each other, but subject to the provisions of this Article on parol or extrinsic evidence (Section 2–202) negation or limitation is inoperative to the extent that such construction is unreasonable.

(2) Subject to subsection (3), to exclude or modify the implied warranty of merchantability or any part of it the language must mention merchantability and in case of a writing must be conspicuous, and to exclude or modify any implied warranty of fitness the exclusion must be by a writing and conspicuous. Language to exclude all implied warranties of fitness is sufficient if it states, for example, that "There are no warranties which extend beyond the description on the face hereof."

(3) Notwithstanding subsection (2)

    (a) unless the circumstances indicate otherwise, all implied warranties are excluded by expressions like "as is", "with all faults" or other language which in common understanding calls the buyer's attention to the exclusion of warranties and makes plain that there is no implied warranty; and

    (b) when the buyer before entering into the contract has examined the goods or the sample or model as fully as he desired or has refused to examine the goods there is no implied warranty with regard to defects which an examination ought in the circumstances to have revealed to him; and

    (c) an implied warranty can also be excluded or modified by course of dealing or course of performance or usage of trade.

(4) Remedies for breach of warranty can be limited in accordance with the provisions of this Article on liquidation or limitation of damages and on contractual modification of remedy (Sections 2–718 and 2–719).

## § 2–317. Cumulation and Conflict of Warranties Express or Implied.

Warranties whether express or implied shall be construed as consistent with each other and as cumulative, but if such construction is unreasonable the intention of the parties shall determine which warranty is dominant. In ascertaining that intention the following rules apply:

    (a) Exact or technical specifications displace an inconsistent sample or model or general language of description.

    (b) A sample from an existing bulk displaces inconsistent general language of description.

    (c) Express warranties displace inconsistent implied warranties other than an implied warranty of fitness for a particular purpose.

## § 2–318. Third Party Beneficiaries of Warranties Express or Implied.

Note: *If this Act is introduced in the Congress of the United States this section should be omitted. (States to select one alternative.)*

**Alternative A** A seller's warranty whether express or implied extends to any natural person who is in the family or household of his buyer or who is a guest in his home if it is reasonable to expect that such person may use, consume or be affected by the goods and who is injured in person by breach of the warranty. The seller may not exclude or limit the operation of this section.

**Alternative B**  A seller's warranty whether express or implied extends to any natural person who may reasonably be expected to use, consume or be affected by the goods and who is injured in person by breach of the warranty. A seller may not exclude or limit the operation of this section.

**Alternative C**  A seller's warranty whether express or implied extends to any person who may reasonably be expected to use, consume or be affected by the goods and who is injured by breach of the warranty. A seller may not exclude or limit the operation of this section with respect to injury to the person of an individual to whom the warranty extends. As amended 1966.

### § 2–319. F.O.B. and F.A.S. Terms.

(1)  Unless otherwise agreed the term F.O.B. (which means "free on board") at a named place, even though used only in connection with the stated price, is a delivery term under which

    (a)  when the term is F.O.B. the place of shipment, the seller must at that place ship the goods in the manner provided in this Article (Section 2–504) and bear the expense and risk of putting them into the possession of the carrier; or

    (b)  when the term is F.O.B. the place of destination, the seller must at his own expense and risk transport the goods to that place and there tender delivery of them in the manner provided in this Article (Section 2–503);

    (c)  when under either (a) or (b) the term is also F.O.B. vessel, car or other vehicle, the seller must in addition at his own expense and risk load the goods on board. If the term is F.O.B. vessel the buyer must name the vessel and in an appropriate case the seller must comply with the provisions of this Article on the form of bill of lading (Section 2–323).

(2)  Unless otherwise agreed the term F.A.S. vessel (which means "free alongside") at a named port, even though used only in connection with the stated price, is a delivery term under which the seller must

    (a)  at his own expense and risk deliver the goods alongside the vessel in the manner usual in that port or on a dock designated and provided by the buyer; and

    (b)  obtain and tender a receipt for the goods in exchange for which the carrier is under a duty to issue a bill of lading.

(3)  Unless otherwise agreed in any case falling within subsection (1)(a) or (c) or subsection (2) the buyer must seasonably give any needed instructions for making delivery, including when the term is F.A.S. or F.O.B. the loading berth of the vessel and in an appropriate case its name and sailing date. The seller may treat the failure of needed instructions as a failure of cooperation under this Article (Section 2–311). He may also at his option move the goods in any reasonable manner preparatory to delivery or shipment.

(4)  Under the term F.O.B. vessel or F.A.S. unless otherwise agreed the buyer must make payment against tender of the required documents and the seller may not tender nor the buyer demand delivery of the goods in substitution for the documents.

### § 2–320. C.I.F. and C. & F. Terms.

(1)  The term C.I.F. means that the price includes in a lump sum the cost of the goods and the insurance and freight to the named destination. The term C. & F. or C.F. means that the price so includes cost and freight to the named destination.

(2)  Unless otherwise agreed and even though used only in connection with the stated price and destination, the term C.I.F. destination or its equivalent requires the seller at his own expense and risk to

    (a)  put the goods into the possession of a carrier at the port for shipment and obtain a negotiable bill or bills of lading covering the entire transportation to the named destination; and

    (b)  load the goods and obtain a receipt from the carrier (which may be contained in the bill of lading) showing that the freight has been paid or provided for; and

    (c)  obtain a policy or certificate of insurance, including any war risk insurance, of a kind and on terms then current at the port of shipment in the usual amount, in the currency of the contract, shown to cover the same goods covered by the bill of lading and providing for payment of loss to the order of the buyer or for the account of whom it may concern; but the seller may add to the price the amount of premium for any such war risk insurance; and

    (d)  prepare an invoice of the goods and procure any other documents required to effect shipment or to comply with the contract; and

    (e)  forward and tender with commercial promptness all the documents in due form and with any indorsement necessary to perfect the buyer's rights.

(3)  Unless otherwise agreed the term C. & F. or its equivalent has the same effect and imposes upon the seller the same obligations and risks as a C.I.F. term except the obligation as to insurance.

(4)  Under the term C.I.F. or C. & F. unless otherwise agreed the buyer must make payment against tender of the required documents and the seller may not tender nor the buyer demand delivery of the goods in substitution for the documents.

### § 2–321. C.I.F. or C. & F.: "Net Landed Weights"; "Payment on Arrival"; Warranty of Condition on Arrival.

Under a contract containing a term C.I.F. or C. & F.

(1)  Where the price is based on or is to be adjusted according to "net landed weights", "delivered weights", "out turn" quantity or quality or the like, unless otherwise agreed the seller must reasonably estimate the price. The payment due on tender of the documents called for by the contract is the amount so estimated, but after final adjustment of the price a settlement must be made with commercial promptness.

(2)  An agreement described in subsection (1) or any warranty of quality or condition of the goods on arrival places upon the seller the risk of ordinary deterioration, shrinkage and the like in transportation but has no effect on the place or time of identification to the contract for sale or delivery or on the passing of the risk of loss.

(3)  Unless otherwise agreed where the contract provides for payment on or after arrival of the goods the seller must before payment allow such preliminary inspection as is feasible; but if the goods are lost delivery of the documents and payment are due when the goods should have arrived.

### § 2–322. Delivery "Ex-Ship".

(1)  Unless otherwise agreed a term for delivery of goods "ex-ship" (which means from the carrying vessel) or in equivalent language is not restricted to a particular ship and requires delivery from a ship which has reached a place at the named port of destination where goods of the kind are usually discharged.

(2)  Under such a term unless otherwise agreed

    (a)  the seller must discharge all liens arising out of the carriage and furnish the buyer with a direction which puts the carrier under a duty to deliver the goods; and

(b) the risk of loss does not pass to the buyer until the goods leave the ship's tackle or are otherwise properly unloaded.

### § 2–323. Form of Bill of Lading Required in Overseas Shipment; "Overseas".

(1) Where the contract contemplates overseas shipment and contains a term C.I.F. or C. & F. or F.O.B. vessel, the seller unless otherwise agreed must obtain a negotiable bill of lading stating that the goods have been loaded on board or, in the case of a term C.I.F. or C. & F., received for shipment.

(2) Where in a case within subsection (1) a bill of lading has been issued in a set of parts, unless otherwise agreed if the documents are not to be sent from abroad the buyer may demand tender of the full set; otherwise only one part of the bill of lading need be tendered. Even if the agreement expressly requires a full set

(a) due tender of a single part is acceptable within the provisions of this Article on cure of improper delivery (subsection (1) of Section 2–508); and

(b) even though the full set is demanded, if the documents are sent from abroad the person tendering an incomplete set may nevertheless require payment upon furnishing an indemnity which the buyer in good faith deems adequate.

(3) A shipment by water or by air or a contract contemplating such shipment is "overseas" insofar as by usage of trade or agreement it is subject to the commercial, financing or shipping practices characteristic of international deep water commerce.

### § 2–324. "No Arrival, No Sale" Term.

Under a term "no arrival, no sale" or terms of like meaning, unless otherwise agreed,

(a) the seller must properly ship conforming goods and if they arrive by any means he must tender them on arrival but he assumes no obligation that the goods will arrive unless he has caused the non-arrival; and

(b) where without fault of the seller the goods are in part lost or have so deteriorated as no longer to conform to the contract or arrive after the contract time, the buyer may proceed as if there had been casualty to identified goods (Section 2–613).

### § 2–325. "Letter of Credit" Term; "Confirmed Credit".

(1) Failure of the buyer seasonably to furnish an agreed letter of credit is a breach of the contract for sale.

(2) The delivery to seller of a proper letter of credit suspends the buyer's obligation to pay. If the letter of credit is dishonored, the seller may on seasonable notification to the buyer require payment directly from him.

(3) Unless otherwise agreed the term "letter of credit" or "banker's credit" in a contract for sale means an irrevocable credit issued by a financing agency of good repute and, where the shipment is overseas, of good international repute. The term "confirmed credit" means that the credit must also carry the direct obligation of such an agency which does business in the seller's financial market.

### § 2–326. Sale on Approval and Sale or Return; Consignment Sales and Rights of Creditors.

(1) Unless otherwise agreed, if delivered goods may be returned by the buyer even though they conform to the contract, the transaction is

(a) a "sale on approval" if the goods are delivered primarily for use, and

(b) a "sale or return" if the goods are delivered primarily for resale.

(2) Except as provided in subsection (3), goods held on approval are not subject to the claims of the buyer's creditors until acceptance; goods held on sale or return are subject to such claims while in the buyer's possession.

(3) Where goods are delivered to a person for sale and such person maintains a place of business at which he deals in goods of the kind involved, under a name other than the name of the person making delivery, then with respect to claims of creditors of the person conducting the business the goods are deemed to be on sale or return. The provisions of this subsection are applicable even though an agreement purports to reserve title to the person making delivery until payment or resale or uses such words as "on consignment" or "on memorandum". However, this subsection is not applicable if the person making delivery

(a) complies with an applicable law providing for a consignor's interest or the like to be evidenced by a sign, or

(b) establishes that the person conducting the business is generally known by his creditors to be substantially engaged in selling the goods of others, or

(c) complies with the filing provisions of the Article on Secured Transactions (Article 9).

(4) Any "or return" term of a contract for sale is to be treated as a separate contract for sale within the statute of frauds section of this Article (Section 2–201) and as contradicting the sale aspect of the contract within the provisions of this Article on parol or extrinsic evidence (Section 2–202).

### § 2–327. Special Incidents of Sale on Approval and Sale or Return.

(1) Under a sale on approval unless otherwise agreed

(a) although the goods are identified to the contract the risk of loss and the title do not pass to the buyer until acceptance; and

(b) use of the goods consistent with the purpose of trial is not acceptance but failure seasonably to notify the seller of election to return the goods is acceptance, and if the goods conform to the contract acceptance of any part is acceptance of the whole; and

(c) after due notification of election to return, the return is at the seller's risk and expense but a merchant buyer must follow any reasonable instructions.

(2) Under a sale or return unless otherwise agreed

(a) the option to return extends to the whole or any commercial unit of the goods while in substantially their original condition, but must be exercised seasonably; and

(b) the return is at the buyer's risk and expense.

### § 2–328. Sale by Auction.

(1) In a sale by auction if goods are put up in lots each lot is the subject of a separate sale.

(2) A sale by auction is complete when the auctioneer so announces by the fall of the hammer or in other customary manner. Where a bid is made while the hammer is falling in acceptance of a prior bid the auctioneer may in his discretion reopen the bidding or declare the goods sold under the bid on which the hammer was falling.

(3) Such a sale is with reserve unless the goods are in explicit terms put up without reserve. In an auction with reserve the auctioneer may withdraw the goods at any time until he announces completion of the sale. In an auction without reserve, after the auctioneer calls for bids on an article or lot, that article or lot cannot be withdrawn unless no bid is made within a reasonable time. In either case a bidder may retract his bid until the auctioneer's announcement of completion of the sale, but a bidder's retraction does not revive any previous bid.

(4) If the auctioneer knowingly receives a bid on the seller's behalf or the seller makes or procures such a bid, and notice has not been given that liberty for such bidding is reserved, the buyer may at his option avoid the sale or take the goods at the price of the last good faith bid prior to the completion of the sale. This subsection shall not apply to any bid at a forced sale.

## Part 4—Title, Creditors and Good Faith Purchasers

### § 2–401. Passing of Title; Reservation for Security; Limited Application of This Section.

Each provision of this Article with regard to the rights, obligations and remedies of the seller, the buyer, purchasers or other third parties applies irrespective of title to the goods except where the provision refers to such title. Insofar as situations are not covered by the other provisions of this Article and matters concerning title became material the following rules apply:

(1) Title to goods cannot pass under a contract for sale prior to their identification to the contract (Section 2–501), and unless otherwise explicitly agreed the buyer acquires by their identification a special property as limited by this Act.

Any retention or reservation by the seller of the title (property) in goods shipped or delivered to the buyer is limited in effect to a reservation of a security interest. Subject to these provisions and to the provisions of the Article on Secured Transactions (Article 9), title to goods passes from the seller to the buyer in any manner and on any conditions explicitly agreed on by the parties.

(2) Unless otherwise explicitly agreed title passes to the buyer at the time and place at which the seller completes his performance with reference to the physical delivery of the goods, despite any reservation of a security interest and even though a document of title is to be delivered at a different time or place; and in particular and despite any reservation of a security interest by the bill of lading

(a) if the contract requires or authorizes the seller to send the goods to the buyer but does not require him to deliver them at destination, title passes to the buyer at the time and place of shipment; but

(b) if the contract requires delivery at destination, title passes on tender there.

(3) Unless otherwise explicitly agreed where delivery is to be made without moving the goods,

(a) if the seller is to deliver a document of title, title passes at the time when and the place where he delivers such documents; or

(b) if the goods are at the time of contracting already identified and no documents are to be delivered, title passes at the time and place of contracting.

(4) A rejection or other refusal by the buyer to receive or retain the goods, whether or not justified, or a justified revocation of acceptance revests title to the goods in the seller. Such revesting occurs by operation of law and is not a "sale".

### § 2–402. Rights of Seller's Creditors Against Sold Goods.

(1) Except as provided in subsections (2) and (3), rights of unsecured creditors of the seller with respect to goods which have been identified to a contract for sale are subject to the buyer's rights to recover the goods under this Article (Sections 2–502 and 2–716).

(2) A creditor of the seller may treat a sale or an identification of goods to a contract for sale as void if as against him a retention of possession by the seller is fraudulent under any rule of law of the state where the goods are situated, except that retention of possession in good faith and current course of trade by a merchant-seller for a commercially reasonable time after a sale or identification is not fraudulent.

(3) Nothing in this Article shall be deemed to impair the rights of creditors of the seller

(a) under the provisions of the Article on Secured Transactions (Article 9); or

(b) where identification to the contract or delivery is made not in current course of trade but in satisfaction of or as security for a pre-existing claim for money, security or the like and is made under circumstances which under any rule of law of the state where the goods are situated would apart from this Article constitute the transaction a fraudulent transfer or voidable preference.

### § 2–403. Power to Transfer; Good Faith Purchase of Goods; "Entrusting".

(1) A purchaser of goods acquires all title which his transferor had or had power to transfer except that a purchaser of a limited interest acquires rights only to the extent of the interest purchased. A person with voidable title has power to transfer a good title to a good faith purchaser for value. When goods have been delivered under a transaction of purchase the purchaser has such power even though

(a) the transferor was deceived as to the identity of the purchaser, or

(b) the delivery was in exchange for a check which is later dishonored, or

(c) it was agreed that the transaction was to be a "cash sale", or

(d) the delivery was procured through fraud punishable as larcenous under the criminal law.

(2) Any entrusting of possession of goods to a merchant who deals in goods of that kind gives him power to transfer all rights of the entruster to a buyer in ordinary course of business.

(3) "Entrusting" includes any delivery and any acquiescence in retention of possession regardless of any condition expressed between the parties to the delivery or acquiescence and regardless of whether the procurement of the entrusting or the possessor's disposition of the goods have been such as to be larcenous under the criminal law.

(4) The rights of other purchasers of goods and of lien creditors are governed by the Articles on Secured Transactions (Article 9), Bulk Transfers (Article 6) and Documents of Title (Article 7).

## Part 5—Performance

### § 2–501. Insurable Interest in Goods; Manner of Identification of Goods.

(1) The buyer obtains a special property and an insurable interest in goods by identification of existing goods as goods to which the contract refers even though the goods so identified are nonconforming and he has an option to return or reject them. Such identification can be made at any time and in any manner explicitly agreed to by the parties. In the absence of explicit agreement identification occurs

(a) when the contract is made if it is for the sale of goods already existing and identified;

(b) if the contract is for the sale of future goods other than those described in paragraph (c), when goods are shipped, marked or otherwise designated by the seller as goods to which the contract refers;

(c) when the crops are planted or otherwise become growing crops or the young are conceived if the contract is for the sale of unborn young to be born within twelve months after contracting or for the sale of crops to be harvested within twelve months or the next normal harvest season after contracting whichever is longer.

(2) The seller retains an insurable interest in goods so long as title to or any security interest in the goods remains in him and where the identification is by the seller alone he may until default or insolvency or notification to the buyer that the identification is final substitute other goods for those identified.

(3) Nothing in this section impairs any insurable interest recognized under any other statute or rule of law.

### § 2–502.  Buyer's Right to Goods on Seller's Insolvency.

(1) Subject to subsection (2) and even though the goods have not been shipped a buyer who has paid a part or all of the price of goods in which he has a special property under the provisions of the immediately preceding section may on making and keeping good a tender of any unpaid portion of their price recover them from the seller if the seller becomes insolvent within ten days after receipt of the first installment on their price.

(2) If the identification creating his special property has been made by the buyer he acquires the right to recover the goods only if they conform to the contract for sale.

### § 2–503.  Manner of Seller's Tender of Delivery.

(1) Tender of delivery requires that the seller put and hold conforming goods at the buyer's disposition and give the buyer any notification reasonably necessary to enable him to take delivery. The manner, time and place for tender are determined by the agreement and this Article, and in particular

(a) tender must be at a reasonable hour, and if it is of goods they must be kept available for the period reasonably necessary to enable the buyer to take possession; but

(b) unless otherwise agreed the buyer must furnish facilities reasonably suited to the receipt of the goods.

(2) Where the case is within the next section respecting shipment tender requires that the seller comply with its provisions.

(3) Where the seller is required to deliver at a particular destination tender requires that he comply with subsection (1) and also in any appropriate case tender documents as described in subsections (4) and (5) of this section.

(4) Where goods are in the possession of a bailee and are to be delivered without being moved

(a) tender requires that the seller either tender a negotiable document of title covering such goods or procure acknowledgment by the bailee of the buyer's right to possession of the goods; but

(b) tender to the buyer of a non-negotiable document of title or of a written direction to the bailee to deliver is sufficient tender unless the buyer seasonably objects, and receipt by the bailee of notification of the buyer's rights fixes those rights as against the bailee and all third persons; but risk of loss of the goods and of any failure by the bailee to honor the non-negotiable document of title or to obey the direction remains on the seller until the buyer has had a reasonable time to present the document or direction, and a refusal by the bailee to honor the document or to obey the direction defeats the tender.

(5) Where the contract requires the seller to deliver documents

(a) he must tender all such documents in correct form, except as provided in this Article with respect to bills of lading in a set (subsection (2) of Section 2–323); and

(b) tender through customary banking channels is sufficient and dishonor of a draft accompanying the documents constitutes non-acceptance or rejection.

### § 2–504.  Shipment by Seller.

Where the seller is required or authorized to send the goods to the buyer and the contract does not require him to deliver them at a particular destination, then unless otherwise agreed he must

(a) put the goods in the possession of such a carrier and make such a contract for their transportation as may be reasonable having regard to the nature of the goods and other circumstances of the case; and

(b) obtain and promptly deliver or tender in due form any document necessary to enable the buyer to obtain possession of the goods or otherwise required by the agreement or by usage of trade; and

(c) promptly notify the buyer of the shipment.

Failure to notify the buyer under paragraph (c) or to make a proper contract under paragraph (a) is a ground for rejection only if material delay or loss ensues.

### § 2–505.  Seller's Shipment Under Reservation.

(1) Where the seller has identified goods to the contract by or before shipment:

(a) his procurement of a negotiable bill of lading to his own order or otherwise reserves in him a security interest in the goods. His procurement of the bill to the order of a financing agency or of the buyer indicates in addition only the seller's expectation of transferring that interest to the person named.

(b) a non-negotiable bill of lading to himself or his nominee reserves possession of the goods as security but except in a case of conditional delivery (subsection (2) of Section 2–507) a non-negotiable bill of lading naming the buyer as consignee reserves no security interest even though the seller retains possession of the bill of lading.

(2) When shipment by the seller with reservation of a security interest is in violation of the contract for sale it constitutes an improper contract for transportation within the preceding section but impairs neither the rights given to the buyer by shipment and identification of the goods to the contract nor the seller's powers as a holder of a negotiable document.

### § 2–506.  Rights of Financing Agency.

(1) A financing agency by paying or purchasing for value a draft which relates to a shipment of goods acquires to the extent of the payment or purchase and in addition to its own rights under the draft and any document of title securing it any rights of the shipper in the goods including the right to stop delivery and the shipper's right to have the draft honored by the buyer.

(2) The right to reimbursement of a financing agency which has in good faith honored or purchased the draft under commitment to or authority from the buyer is not impaired by subsequent discovery of defects with reference to any relevant document which was apparently regular on its face.

### § 2–507.  Effect of Seller's Tender; Delivery on Condition.

(1) Tender of delivery is a condition to the buyer's duty to accept the goods and, unless otherwise agreed, to his duty to pay for them. Tender entitles the seller to acceptance of the goods and to payment according to the contract.

(2) Where payment is due and demanded on the delivery to the buyer of goods or documents of title, his right as against the seller to retain or dispose of them is conditional upon his making the payment due.

### § 2–508. Cure by Seller of Improper Tender or Delivery; Replacement.

(1) Where any tender or delivery by the seller is rejected because non-conforming and the time for performance has not yet expired, the seller may seasonally notify the buyer of his intention to cure and may then within the contract time make a conforming delivery.

(2) Where the buyer rejects a non-conforming tender which the seller had reasonable grounds to believe would be acceptable with or without money allowance the seller may if he seasonably notifies the buyer have a further reasonable time to substitute a conforming tender.

### § 2–509. Risk of Loss in the Absence of Breach.

(1) Where the contract requires or authorizes the seller to ship the goods by carrier

(a) if it does not require him to deliver them at a particular destination, the risk of loss passes to the buyer when the goods are duly delivered to the carrier even though the shipment is under reservation (Section 2–505); but

(b) if it does require him to deliver them at a particular destination and the goods are there duly tendered while in the possession of the carrier, the risk of loss passes to the buyer when the goods are there duly so tendered as to enable the buyer to take delivery.

(2) Where the goods are held by a bailee to be delivered without being moved, the risk of loss passes to the buyer

(a) on his receipt of a negotiable document of title covering the goods; or

(b) on acknowledgment by the bailee of the buyer's right to possession of the goods; or

(c) after his receipt of a non-negotiable document of title or other written direction to deliver, as provided in subsection (4)(b) of Section 2–503.

(3) In any case not within subsection (1) or (2), the risk of loss passes to the buyer on his receipt of the goods if the seller is a merchant; otherwise, the risk passes to the buyer on tender of delivery.

(4) The provisions of this section are subject to contrary agreement of the parties and to the provisions of this Article on sale on approval (Section 2–327) and on effect of breach on risk of loss (Section 2–510).

### § 2–510. Effect of Breach on Risk of Loss.

(1) Where a tender or delivery of goods so fails to conform to the contract as to give a right of rejection the risk of their loss remains on the seller until cure or acceptance.

(2) Where the buyer rightfully revokes acceptance he may to the extent of any deficiency in his effective insurance coverage treat the risk of loss as having rested on the seller from the beginning.

(3) Where the buyer as to conforming goods already identified to the contract for sale repudiates or is otherwise in breach before risk of their loss has passed to him, the seller may to the extent of any deficiency in his effective insurance coverage treat the risk of loss as resting on the buyer for a commercially reasonable time.

### § 2–511. Tender of Payment by Buyer; Payment by Check.

(1) Unless otherwise agreed tender of payment is a condition to the seller's duty to tender and complete any delivery.

(2) Tender of payment is sufficient when made by any means or in any manner current in the ordinary course of business unless the seller demands payment in legal tender and gives any extension of time reasonably necessary to procure it.

(3) Subject to the provisions of this Act on the effect of an instrument on an obligation (Section 3–310), payment by check is conditional and is defeated as between the parties by dishonor of the check on due presentment.

### § 2–512. Payment by Buyer Before Inspection.

(1) Where the contract requires payment before inspection non-conformity of the goods does not excuse the buyer from so making payment unless

(a) the non-conformity appears without inspection; or

(b) despite tender of the required documents the circumstances would justify injunction against honor under the provisions of this Act (Section 5–114).

(2) Payment pursuant to subsection (1) does not constitute an acceptance of goods or impair the buyer's right to inspect or any of his remedies.

### § 2–513. Buyer's Right to Inspection of Goods.

(1) Unless otherwise agreed and subject to subsection (3), where goods are tendered or delivered or identified to the contract for sale, the buyer has a right before payment or acceptance to inspect them at any reasonable place and time and in any reasonable manner. When the seller is required or authorized to send the goods to the buyer, the inspection may be after their arrival.

(2) Expenses of inspection must be borne by the buyer but may be recovered from the seller if the goods do not conform and are rejected.

(3) Unless otherwise agreed and subject to the provisions of this Article on C.I.F. contracts (subsection (3) of Section 2–321), the buyer is not entitled to inspect the goods before payment of the price when the contract provides

(a) for delivery "C.O.D." or on other like terms; or

(b) for payment against documents of title, except where such payment is due only after the goods are to become available for inspection.

(4) A place or method of inspection fixed by the parties is presumed to be exclusive but unless otherwise expressly agreed it does not postpone identification or shift the place for delivery or for passing the risk of loss. If compliance becomes impossible, inspection shall be as provided in this section unless the place or method fixed was clearly intended as an indispensable condition failure of which avoids the contract.

### § 2–514. When Documents Deliverable on Acceptance; When on Payment.

Unless otherwise agreed documents against which a draft is drawn are to be delivered to the drawee on acceptance of the draft if it is payable more than three days after presentment; otherwise, only on payment.

### § 2–515. Preserving Evidence of Goods in Dispute.

In furtherance of the adjustment of any claim or dispute

(a) either party on reasonable notification to the other and for the purpose of ascertaining the facts and preserving evidence has the right to inspect, test and sample the goods including such of them as may be in the possession or control of the other; and

(b) the parties may agree to a third party inspection or survey to determine the conformity or condition of the goods and may agree that the findings shall be binding upon them in any subsequent litigation or adjustment.

## Part 6—Breach, Repudiation and Excuse

### § 2–601.  Buyer's Rights on Improper Delivery.

Subject to the provisions of this Article on breach in installment contracts (Section 2–612) and unless otherwise agreed under the sections on contractual limitations of remedy (Sections 2–718 and 2–719), if the goods or the tender of delivery fail in any respect to conform to the contract, the buyer may

    (a) reject the whole; or

    (b) accept the whole; or

    (c) accept any commercial unit or units and reject the rest.

### § 2–602.  Manner and Effect of Rightful Rejection.

(1) Rejection of goods must be within a reasonable time after their delivery or tender. It is ineffective unless the buyer seasonably notifies the seller.

(2) Subject to the provisions of the two following sections on rejected goods (Sections 2–603 and 2–604),

    (a) after rejection any exercise of ownership by the buyer with respect to any commercial unit is wrongful as against the seller; and

    (b) if the buyer has before rejection taken physical possession of goods in which he does not have a security interest under the provisions of this Article (subsection (3) of Section 2–711), he is under a duty after rejection to hold them with reasonable care at the seller's disposition for a time sufficient to permit the seller to remove them; but

    (c) the buyer has no further obligations with regard to goods rightfully rejected.

(3) The seller's rights with respect to goods wrongfully rejected are governed by the provisions of this Article on seller's remedies in general (Section 2–703).

### § 2–603.  Merchant Buyer's Duties as to Rightfully Rejected Goods.

(1) Subject to any security interest in the buyer (subsection (3) of Section 2–711), when the seller has no agent or place of business at the market of rejection a merchant buyer is under a duty after rejection of goods in his possession or control to follow any reasonable instructions received from the seller with respect to the goods and in the absence of such instructions to make reasonable efforts to sell them for the seller's account if they are perishable or threaten to decline in value speedily. Instructions are not reasonable if on demand indemnity for expenses is not forthcoming.

(2) When the buyer sells goods under subsection (1), he is entitled to reimbursement from the seller or out of the proceeds for reasonable expenses of caring for and selling them, and if the expenses include no selling commission then to such commission as is usual in the trade or if there is none to a reasonable sum not exceeding ten per cent on the gross proceeds.

(3) In complying with this section the buyer is held only to good faith and good faith conduct hereunder is neither acceptance nor conversion nor the basis of an action for damages.

### § 2–604.  Buyer's Options as to Salvage of Rightfully Rejected Goods.

Subject to the provisions of the immediately preceding section on perishables if the seller gives no instructions within a reasonable time after notification of rejection the buyer may store the rejected goods for the seller's account or reship them to him or resell them for the seller's account with reimbursement as provided in the preceding section. Such action is not acceptance or conversion.

### § 2–605.  Waiver of Buyer's Objections by Failure to Particularize.

(1) The buyer's failure to state in connection with rejection a particular defect which is ascertainable by reasonable inspection precludes him from relying on the unstated defect to justify rejection or to establish breach

    (a) where the seller could have cured it if stated seasonably; or

    (b) between merchants when the seller has after rejection made a request in writing for a full and final written statement of all defects on which the buyer proposes to rely.

(2) Payment against documents made without reservation of rights precludes recovery of the payment for defects apparent on the face of the documents.

### § 2–606.  What Constitutes Acceptance of Goods.

(1) Acceptance of goods occurs when the buyer

    (a) after a reasonable opportunity to inspect the goods signifies to the seller that the goods are conforming or that he will take or retain them in spite of their nonconformity; or

    (b) fails to make an effective rejection (subsection (1) of Section 2–602), but such acceptance does not occur until the buyer has had a reasonable opportunity to inspect them; or

    (c) does any act inconsistent with the seller's ownership; but if such act is wrongful as against the seller it is an acceptance only if ratified by him.

(2) Acceptance of a part of any commercial unit is acceptance of that entire unit.

### § 2–607.  Effect of Acceptance; Notice of Breach; Burden of Establishing Breach After Acceptance; Notice of Claim or Litigation to Person Answerable Over.

(1) The buyer must pay at the contract rate for any goods accepted.

(2) Acceptance of goods by the buyer precludes rejection of the goods accepted and if made with knowledge of a non-conformity cannot be revoked because of it unless the acceptance was on the reasonable assumption that the non-conformity would be seasonably cured but acceptance does not of itself impair any other remedy provided by this Article for non-conformity.

(3) Where a tender has been accepted

    (a) the buyer must within a reasonable time after he discovers or should have discovered any breach notify the seller of breach or be barred from any remedy; and

    (b) if the claim is one for infringement or the like (subsection (3) of Section 2–312) and the buyer is sued as a result of such a breach he must so notify the seller within a reasonable time after he receives notice of the litigation or be barred from any remedy over for liability established by the litigation.

(4) The burden is on the buyer to establish any breach with respect to the goods accepted.

(5) Where the buyer is sued for breach of a warranty or other obligation for which his seller is answerable over

    (a) he may give his seller written notice of the litigation. If the notice states that the seller may come in and defend and that if the seller does not do so he will be bound in any action against him by his buyer by any determination of fact common to the two litigations, then unless the seller after seasonable receipt of the notice does come in and defend he is so bound.

    (b) if the claim is one for infringement or the like (subsection (3) of Section 2–312) the original seller may demand in writing that his buyer turn over to him control of the litigation including settlement or else be barred from any remedy over and if he also agrees to bear all expense and to satisfy any adverse judgment, then unless the buyer after seasonable receipt of the demand does turn over control the buyer is so barred.

(6) The provisions of subsections (3), (4) and (5) apply to any obligation of a buyer to hold the seller harmless against infringement or the like (subsection (3) of Section 2–312).

### § 2–608.  Revocation of Acceptance in Whole or in Part.

(1) The buyer may revoke his acceptance of a lot or commercial unit whose non-conformity substantially impairs its value to him if he has accepted it

    (a)  on the reasonable assumption that its non-conformity would be cured and it has not been seasonably cured; or

    (b)  without discovery of such non-conformity if his acceptance was reasonably induced either by the difficulty of discovery before acceptance or by the seller's assurances.

(2) Revocation of acceptance must occur within a reasonable time after the buyer discovers or should have discovered the ground for it and before any substantial change in condition of the goods which is not caused by their own defects. It is not effective until the buyer notifies the seller of it.

(3) A buyer who so revokes has the same rights and duties with regard to the goods involved as if he had rejected them.

### § 2–609.  Right to Adequate Assurance of Performance.

(1) A contract for sale imposes an obligation on each party that the other's expectation of receiving due performance will not be impaired. When reasonable grounds for insecurity arise with respect to the performance of either party the other may in writing demand adequate assurance of due performance and until he receives such assurance may if commercially reasonable suspend any performance for which he has not already received the agreed return.

(2) Between merchants the reasonableness of grounds for insecurity and the adequacy of any assurance offered shall be determined according to commercial standards.

(3) Acceptance of any improper delivery or payment does not prejudice the aggrieved party's right to demand adequate assurance of future performance.

(4) After receipt of a justified demand failure to provide within a reasonable time not exceeding thirty days such assurance of due performance as is adequate under the circumstances of the particular case is a repudiation of the contract.

### § 2–610.  Anticipatory Repudiation.

When either party repudiates the contract with respect to a performance not yet due the loss of which will substantially impair the value of the contract to the other, the aggrieved party may

    (a)  for a commercially reasonable time await performance by the repudiating party; or

    (b)  resort to any remedy for breach (Section 2–703 or Section 2–711), even though he has notified the repudiating party that he would await the latter's performance and has urged retraction; and

    (c)  in either case suspend his own performance or proceed in accordance with the provisions of this Article on the seller's right to identify goods to the contract notwithstanding breach or to salvage unfinished goods (Section 2–704).

### § 2–611.  Retraction of Anticipatory Repudiation.

(1) Until the repudiating party's next performance is due he can retract his repudiation unless the aggrieved party has since the repudiation cancelled or materially changed his position or otherwise indicated that he considers the repudiation final.

(2) Retraction may be by any method which clearly indicates to the aggrieved party that the repudiating party intends to perform, but must include any assurance justifiably demanded under the provisions of this Article (Section 2–609).

(3) Retraction reinstates the repudiating party's rights under the contract with due excuse and allowance to the aggrieved party for any delay occasioned by the repudiation.

### § 2–612.  "Installment Contract"; Breach.

(1) An "installment contract" is one which requires or authorizes the delivery of goods in separate lots to be separately accepted, even though the contract contains a clause "each delivery is a separate contract" or its equivalent.

(2) The buyer may reject any installment which is non-conforming if the non-conformity substantially impairs the value of that installment and cannot be cured or if the non-conformity is a defect in the required documents; but if the non-conformity does not fall within subsection (3) and the seller gives adequate assurance of its cure the buyer must accept that installment.

(3) Whenever non-conformity or default with respect to one or more installments substantially impairs the value of the whole contract there is a breach of the whole. But the aggrieved party reinstates the contract if he accepts a non-conforming installment without seasonably notifying of cancellation or if he brings an action with respect only to past installments or demands performance as to future installments.

### § 2–613.  Casualty to Identified Goods.

Where the contract requires for its performance goods identified when the contract is made, and the goods suffer casualty without fault of either party before the risk of loss passes to the buyer, or in a proper case under a "no arrival, no sale" term (Section 2–324) then

    (a)  if the loss is total the contract is avoided; and

    (b)  if the loss is partial or the goods have so deteriorated as no longer to conform to the contract the buyer may nevertheless demand inspection and at his option either treat the contract as avoided or accept the goods with due allowance from the contract price for the deterioration or the deficiency in quantity but without further right against the seller.

### § 2–614.  Substituted Performance.

(1) Where without fault of either party the agreed berthing, loading, or unloading facilities fail or an agreed type of carrier becomes unavailable or the agreed manner of delivery otherwise becomes commercially impracticable but a commercially reasonable substitute is available, such substitute performance must be tendered and accepted.

(2) If the agreed means or manner of payment fails because of domestic or foreign governmental regulation, the seller may withhold or stop delivery unless the buyer provides a means or manner of payment which is commercially a substantial equivalent. If delivery has already been taken, payment by the means or in the manner provided by the regulation discharges the buyer's obligation unless the regulation is discriminatory, oppressive or predatory.

### § 2–615.  Excuse by Failure of Presupposed Conditions.

Except so far as a seller may have assumed a greater obligation and subject to the preceding section on substituted performance:

    (a)  Delay in delivery or non-delivery in whole or in part by a seller who complies with paragraphs (b) and (c) is not a breach of his duty under a contract for sale if performance as agreed has been made impracticable by the occurrence of a contingency the non-occurrence of which was a basic assumption on which the contract was made or by compliance in good faith with any applicable foreign or domestic governmental regulation or order whether or not it later proves to be invalid.

(b) Where the causes mentioned in paragraph (a) affect only a part of the seller's capacity to perform, he must allocate production and deliveries among his customers but may at his option include regular customers not then under contract as well as his own requirements for further manufacture. He may so allocate in any manner which is fair and reasonable.

(c) The seller must notify the buyer seasonably that there will be delay or non-delivery and, when allocation is required under paragraph (b), of the estimated quota thus made available for the buyer.

### § 2–616.  Procedure on Notice Claiming Excuse.

(1) Where the buyer receives notification of a material or indefinite delay or an allocation justified under the preceding section he may by written notification to the seller as to any delivery concerned, and where the prospective deficiency substantially impairs the value of the whole contract under the provisions of this Article relating to breach of installment contracts (Section 2–612), then also as to the whole,

(a) terminate and thereby discharge any unexecuted portion of the contract; or

(b) modify the contract by agreeing to take his available quota in substitution.

(2) If after receipt of such notification from the seller the buyer fails so to modify the contract within a reasonable time not exceeding thirty days the contract lapses with respect to any deliveries affected.

(3) The provisions of this section may not be negated by agreement except in so far as the seller has assumed a greater obligation under the preceding section.

## Part 7—Remedies

### § 2–701.  Remedies for Breach of Collateral Contracts Not Impaired.

Remedies for breach of any obligation or promise collateral or ancillary to a contract for sale are not impaired by the provisions of this Article.

### § 2–702.  Seller's Remedies on Discovery of Buyer's Insolvency.

(1) Where the seller discovers the buyer to be insolvent he may refuse delivery except for cash including payment for all goods theretofore delivered under the contract, and stop delivery under this Article (Section 2–705).

(2) Where the seller discovers that the buyer has received goods on credit while insolvent he may reclaim the goods upon demand made within ten days after the receipt, but if misrepresentation of solvency has been made to the particular seller in writing within three months before delivery the ten day limitation does not apply. Except as provided in this subsection the seller may not base a right to reclaim goods on the buyer's fraudulent or innocent misrepresentation of solvency or of intent to pay.

(3) The seller's right to reclaim under subsection (2) is subject to the rights of a buyer in ordinary course or other good faith purchaser under this Article (Section 2–403). Successful reclamation of goods excludes all other remedies with respect to them.

### § 2–703.  Seller's Remedies in General.

Where the buyer wrongfully rejects or revokes acceptance of goods or fails to make a payment due on or before delivery or repudiates with respect to a part or the whole, then with respect to any goods directly affected and, if the breach is of the whole contract (Section 2–612), then also with respect to the whole undelivered balance, the aggrieved seller may

(a) withhold delivery of such goods;

(b) stop delivery by any bailee as hereafter provided (Section 2–705);

(c) proceed under the next section respecting goods still unidentified to the contract;

(d) resell and recover damages as hereafter provided (Section 2–706);

(e) recover damages for non-acceptance (Section 2–708) or in a proper case the price (Section 2–709);

(f) cancel.

### § 2–704.  Seller's Right to Identify Goods to the Contract Notwithstanding Breach or to Salvage Unfinished Goods.

(1) An aggrieved seller under the preceding section may

(a) identify to the contract conforming goods not already identified if at the time he learned of the breach they are in his possession or control;

(b) treat as the subject of resale goods which have demonstrably been intended for the particular contract even though those goods are unfinished.

(2) Where the goods are unfinished an aggrieved seller may in the exercise of reasonable commercial judgment for the purposes of avoiding loss and of effective realization either complete the manufacture and wholly identify the goods to the contract or cease manufacture and resell for scrap or salvage value or proceed in any other reasonable manner.

### § 2–705.  Seller's Stoppage of Delivery in Transit or Otherwise.

(1) The seller may stop delivery of goods in the possession of a carrier or other bailee when he discovers the buyer to be insolvent (Section 2–702) and may stop delivery of carload, truckload, planeload or larger shipments of express or freight when the buyer repudiates or fails to make a payment due before delivery or if for any other reason the seller has a right to withhold or reclaim the goods.

(2) As against such buyer the seller may stop delivery until

(a) receipt of the goods by the buyer; or

(b) acknowledgment to the buyer by any bailee of the goods except a carrier that the bailee holds the goods for the buyer; or

(c) such acknowledgment to the buyer by a carrier by reshipment or as warehouseman; or

(d) negotiation to the buyer of any negotiable document of title covering the goods.

(3) (a) To stop delivery the seller must so notify as to enable the bailee by reasonable diligence to prevent delivery of the goods.

(b) After such notification the bailee must hold and deliver the goods according to the directions of the seller but the seller is liable to the bailee for any ensuing charges or damages.

(c) If a negotiable document of title has been issued for goods the bailee is not obliged to obey a notification to stop until surrender of the document.

(d) A carrier who has issued a non-negotiable bill of lading is not obliged to obey a notification to stop received from a person other than the consignor.

### § 2–706.  Seller's Resale Including Contract for Resale.

(1) Under the conditions stated in Section 2–703 on seller's remedies, the seller may resell the goods concerned or the undelivered balance thereof. Where the resale is made in good faith and in a commercially reasonable manner the seller may recover the difference between the

resale price and the contract price together with any incidental damages allowed under the provisions of this Article (Section 2–710), but less expenses saved in consequence of the buyer's breach.

(2)  Except as otherwise provided in subsection (3) or unless otherwise agreed resale may be at public or private sale including sale by way of one or more contracts to sell or of identification to an existing contract of the seller. Sale may be as a unit or in parcels and at any time and place and on any terms but every aspect of the sale including the method, manner, time, place and terms must be commercially reasonable. The resale must be reasonably identified as referring to the broken contract, but it is not necessary that the goods be in existence or that any or all of them have been identified to the contract before the breach.

(3)  Where the resale is at private sale the seller must give the buyer reasonable notification of his intention to resell.

(4)  Where the resale is at public sale

(a)  only identified goods can be sold except where there is a recognized market for a public sale of futures in goods of the kind; and

(b)  it must be made at a usual place or market for public sale if one is reasonably available and except in the case of goods which are perishable or threaten to decline in value speedily the seller must give the buyer reasonable notice of the time and place of the resale; and

(c)  if the goods are not to be within the view of those attending the sale the notification of sale must state the place where the goods are located and provide for their reasonable inspection by prospective bidders; and

(d)  the seller may buy.

(5)  A purchaser who buys in good faith at a resale takes the goods free of any rights of the original buyer even though the seller fails to comply with one or more of the requirements of this section.

(6)  The seller is not accountable to the buyer for any profit made on any resale. A person in the position of a seller (Section 2–707) or a buyer who has rightfully rejected or justifiably revoked acceptance must account for any excess over the amount of his security interest, as hereinafter defined (subsection (3) of Section 2–711).

## § 2–707.  "Person in the Position of a Seller".

(1)  A "person in the position of a seller" includes as against a principal an agent who has paid or become responsible for the price of goods on behalf of his principal or anyone who otherwise holds a security interest or other right in goods similar to that of a seller.

(2)  A person in the position of a seller may as provided in this Article withhold or stop delivery (Section 2–705) and resell (Section 2–706) and recover incidental damages (Section 2–710).

## § 2–708.  Seller's Damages for Non-Acceptance or Repudiation.

(1)  Subject to subsection (2) and to the provisions of this Article with respect to proof of market price (Section 2–723), the measure of damages for non-acceptance or repudiation by the buyer is the difference between the market price at the time and place for tender and the unpaid contract price together with any incidental damages provided in this Article (Section 2–710), but less expenses saved in consequence of the buyer's breach.

(2)  If the measure of damages provided in subsection (1) is inadequate to put the seller in as good a position as performance would have done then the measure of damages is the profit (including reasonable overhead) which the seller would have made from full performance by the buyer, together with any incidental damages provided in this

Article (Section 2–710), due allowance for costs reasonably incurred and due credit for payments or proceeds of resale.

## § 2–709.  Action for the Price.

(1)  When the buyer fails to pay the price as it becomes due the seller may recover, together with any incidental damages under the next section, the price

(a)  of goods accepted or of conforming goods lost or damaged within a commercially reasonable time after risk of their loss has passed to the buyer; and

(b)  of goods identified to the contract if the seller is unable after reasonable effort to resell them at a reasonable price or the circumstances reasonably indicate that such effort will be unavailing.

(2)  Where the seller sues for the price he must hold for the buyer any goods which have been identified to the contract and are still in his control except that if resale becomes possible he may resell them at any time prior to the collection of the judgment. The net proceeds of any such resale must be credited to the buyer and payment of the judgment entitles him to any goods not resold.

(3)  After the buyer has wrongfully rejected or revoked acceptance of the goods or has failed to make a payment due or has repudiated (Section 2–610), a seller who is held not entitled to the price under this section shall nevertheless be awarded damages for non-acceptance under the preceding section.

## § 2–710.  Seller's Incidental Damages.

Incidental damages to an aggrieved seller include any commercially reasonable charges, expenses or commissions incurred in stopping delivery, in the transportation, care and custody of goods after the buyer's breach, in connection with return or resale of the goods or otherwise resulting from the breach.

## § 2–711.  Buyer's Remedies in General; Buyer's Security Interest in Rejected Goods.

(1)  Where the seller fails to make delivery or repudiates or the buyer rightfully rejects or justifiably revokes acceptance then with respect to any goods involved, and with respect to the whole if the breach goes to the whole contract (Section 2–612), the buyer may cancel and whether or not he has done so may in addition to recovering so much of the price as has been paid

(a)  "cover" and have damages under the next section as to all the goods affected whether or not they have been identified to the contract; or

(b)  recover damages for non-delivery as provided in this Article (Section 2–713).

(2)  Where the seller fails to deliver or repudiates the buyer may also

(a)  if the goods have been identified recover them as provided in this Article (Section 2–502); or

(b)  in a proper case obtain specific performance or replevy the goods as provided in this Article (Section 2–716).

(3)  On rightful rejection or justifiable revocation of acceptance a buyer has a security interest in goods in his possession or control for any payments made on their price and any expenses reasonably incurred in their inspection, receipt, transportation, care and custody and may hold such goods and resell them in like manner as an aggrieved seller (Section 2–706).

## § 2–712.  "Cover"; Buyer's Procurement of Substitute Goods.

(1)  After a breach within the preceding section the buyer may "cover" by making in good faith and without unreasonable delay any reasonable purchase of or contract to purchase goods in substitution for those due from the seller.

(2) The buyer may recover from the seller as damages the difference between the cost of cover and the contract price together with any incidental or consequential damages as hereinafter defined (Section 2–715), but less expenses saved in consequence of the seller's breach.
(3) Failure of the buyer to effect cover within this section does not bar him from any other remedy.

### § 2–713.  Buyer's Damages for Non-Delivery or Repudiation.
(1) Subject to provisions of this Article with respect to the proof of market price (Section 2–723), the measure of damages for non-delivery or repudiation by the seller is the difference between the market price at the time when the buyer learned of the breach and the contract price together with any incidental and consequential damages provided in this Article (Section 2–715), but less expenses saved in consequence of the seller's breach.
(2) Market price is to be determined as of the place for tender or, in cases of rejection after arrival or revocation of acceptance, as of the place of arrival.

### § 2–714.  Buyer's Damages for Breach in Regard to Accepted Goods.
(1) Where the buyer has accepted goods and given notification (subsection (3) of Section 2–607) he may recover as damages for any non-conformity of tender the loss resulting in the ordinary course of events from the seller's breach as determined in any manner which is reasonable.
(2) The measure of damages for breach of warranty is the difference at the time and place of acceptance between the value of the goods accepted and the value they would have had if they had been as warranted, unless special circumstances show proximate damages of a different amount.
(3) In a proper case any incidental and consequential damages under the next section may be recovered.

### § 2–715.  Buyer's Incidental and Consequential Damages.
(1) Incidental damages resulting from the seller's breach include expenses reasonably incurred in inspection, receipt, transportation and care and custody of goods rightfully rejected, any commercially reasonable charges, expenses or commissions in connection with effecting cover and any other reasonable expense incident to the delay or other breach.
(2) Consequential damages resulting from the seller's breach include
    (a) any loss resulting from general or particular requirements and needs of which the seller at the time of contracting had reason to know and which could not reasonably be prevented by cover or otherwise; and
    (b) injury to person or property proximately resulting from any breach of warranty.

### § 2–716.  Buyer's Right to Specific Performance or Replevin.
(1) Specific performance may be decreed where the goods are unique or in other proper circumstances.
(2) The decree for specific performance may include such terms and conditions as to payment of the price, damages, or other relief as the court may deem just.
(3) The buyer has a right of replevin for goods identified to the contract if after reasonable effort he is unable to effect cover for such goods or the circumstances reasonably indicate that such effort will be unavailing or if the goods have been shipped under reservation and satisfaction of the security interest in them has been made or tendered.

### § 2–717.  Deduction of Damages From the Price.
The buyer on notifying the seller of his intention to do so may deduct all or any part of the damages resulting from any breach of the contract from any part of the price still due under the same contract.

### § 2–718.  Liquidation or Limitation of Damages; Deposits
(1) Damages for breach by either party may be liquidated in the agreement but only at an amount which is reasonable in the light of the anticipated or actual harm caused by the breach, the difficulties of proof of loss, and the inconvenience or nonfeasibility of otherwise obtaining an adequate remedy. A term fixing unreasonably large liquidated damages is void as a penalty.
(2) Where the seller justifiably withholds delivery of goods because of the buyer's breach, the buyer is entitled to restitution of any amount by which the sum of his payments exceeds
    (a) the amount to which the seller is entitled by virtue of terms liquidating the seller's damages in accordance with subsection (1), or
    (b) in the absence of such terms, twenty per cent of the value of the total performance for which the buyer is obligated under the contract or $500, whichever is smaller.
(3) The buyer's right to restitution under subsection (2) is subject to offset to the extent that the seller establishes
    (a) a right to recover damages under the provisions of this Article other than subsection (1), and
    (b) the amount or value of any benefits received by the buyer directly or indirectly by reason of the contract.
(4) Where a seller has received payment in goods their reasonable value or the proceeds of their resale shall be treated as payments for the purposes of subsection (2); but if the seller has notice of the buyer's breach before reselling goods received in part performance, his resale is subject to the conditions laid down in this Article on resale by an aggrieved seller (Section 2–706).

### § 2–719.  Contractual Modification or Limitation of Remedy.
(1) Subject to the provisions of subsection (2) and (3) of this section and of the preceding section on liquidation and limitation of damages,
    (a) the agreement may provide for remedies in addition to or in substitution for those provided in this Article and may limit or alter the measure of damages recoverable under this Article, as by limiting the buyer's remedies to return of the goods and repayment of the price or to repair and replacement of non-conforming goods or parts; and
    (b) resort to a remedy as provided is optional unless the remedy is expressly agreed to be exclusive, in which case it is the sole remedy.
(2) Where circumstances cause an exclusive or limited remedy to fail of its essential purpose, remedy may be had as provided in this Act.
(3) Consequential damages may be limited or excluded unless the limitation or exclusion is unconscionable. Limitation of consequential damages for injury to the person in the case of consumer goods is prima facie unconscionable but limitation of damages where the loss is commercial is not.

### § 2–720.  Effect of "Cancellation" or "Rescission" on Claims for Antecedent Breach.
Unless the contrary intention clearly appears, expressions of "cancellation" or "rescission" of the contract or the like shall not be construed as a renunciation or discharge of any claim in damages for an antecedent breach.

**§ 2–721. Remedies for Fraud.**
Remedies for material misrepresentation or fraud include all remedies available under this Article for non-fraudulent breach. Neither rescission or a claim for rescission of the contract for sale nor rejection or return of the goods shall bar or be deemed inconsistent with a claim for damages or other remedy.

**§ 2–722. Who Can Sue Third Parties for Injury to Goods.**
Where a third party so deals with goods which have been identified to a contract for sale as to cause actionable injury to a party to that contract

(a) a right of action against the third party is in either party to the contract for sale who has title to or a security interest or a special property or an insurable interest in the goods; and if the goods have been destroyed or converted a right of action is also in the party who either bore the risk of loss under the contract for sale or has since the injury assumed that risk as against the other;

(b) if at the time of the injury the party plaintiff did not bear the risk of loss as against the other party to the contract for sale and there is no arrangement between them for disposition of the recovery, his suit or settlement is subject to his own interest, as a fiduciary for the other party to the contract;

(c) either party may with the consent of the other sue for the benefit of whom it may concern.

**§ 2–723. Proof of Market Price: Time and Place.**
(1) If an action based on anticipatory repudiation comes to trial before the time for performance with respect to some or all of the goods, any damages based on market price (Section 2–708 or Section 2–713) shall be determined according to the price of such goods prevailing at the time when the aggrieved party learned of the repudiation.

(2) If evidence of a price prevailing at the times or places described in this Article is not readily available the price prevailing within any reasonable time before or after the time described or at any other place which in commercial judgment or under usage of trade would serve as a reasonable substitute for the one described may be used, making any proper allowance for the cost of transporting the goods to or from such other place.

(3) Evidence of a relevant price prevailing at a time or place other than the one described in this Article offered by one party is not admissible unless and until he has given the other party such notice as the court finds sufficient to prevent unfair surprise.

**§ 2–724. Admissibility of Market Quotations.**
Whenever the prevailing price or value of any goods regularly bought and sold in any established commodity market is in issue, reports in official publications or trade journals or in newspapers or periodicals of general circulation published as the reports of such market shall be admissible in evidence. The circumstances of the preparation of such a report may be shown to affect its weight but not its admissibility.

**§ 2–725. Statute of Limitations in Contracts for Sale.**
(1) An action for breach of any contract for sale must be commenced within four years after the cause of action has accrued. By the original agreement the parties may reduce the period of limitation to not less than one year but may not extend it.

(2) A cause of action occurs when the breach occurs, regardless of the aggrieved party's lack of knowledge of the breach. A breach of warranty occurs when tender of delivery is made, except that where a warranty explicitly extends to future performance of the goods and discovery of the breach must await the time of such performance the cause of action accrues when the breach is or should have been discovered.

(3) Where an action commenced within the time limited by subsection (1) is so terminated as to leave available a remedy by another action for the same breach such other action may be commenced after the expiration of the time limited and within six months after the termination of the first action unless the termination resulted from voluntary discontinuance or from dismissal for failure or neglect to prosecute.

(4) This section does not alter the law on tolling of the statute of limitations nor does it apply to causes of action which have accrued before this Act becomes effective.

# ARTICLE 2A: LEASES

## Part 1—General Provisions

**§ 2A–101. Short Title.**
This Article shall be known and may be cited as the Uniform Commercial Code—Leases.

**§ 2A–102. Scope.**
This Article applies to any transaction, regardless of form, that creates a lease.

**§ 2A–103. Definitions and Index of Definitions.**
(1) In this Article unless the context otherwise requires:

(a) "Buyer in ordinary course of business" means a person who in good faith and without knowledge that the sale to him [or her] is in violation of the ownership rights or security interest or leasehold interest of a third party in the goods buys in ordinary course from a person in the business of selling goods of that kind but does not include a pawnbroker. "Buying" may be for cash or by exchange of other property or on secured or unsecured credit and includes receiving goods or documents of title under a pre-existing contract for sale but does not include a transfer in bulk or as security for or in total or partial satisfaction of a money debt.

(b) "Cancellation" occurs when either party puts an end to the lease contract for default by the other party.

(c) "Commercial unit" means such a unit of goods as by commercial usage is a single whole for purposes of lease and division of which materially impairs its character or value on the market or in use. A commercial unit may be a single article, as a machine, or a set of articles, as a suite of furniture or a line of machinery, or a quantity, as a gross or carload, or any other unit treated in use or in the relevant market as a single whole.

(d) "Conforming" goods or performance under a lease contract means goods or performance that are in accordance with the obligations under the lease contract.

(e) "Consumer lease" means a lease that a lessor regularly engaged in the business of leasing or selling makes to a lessee who is an individual and who takes under the lease primarily for a personal, family, or household purpose [, if the total payments to be made under the lease contract, excluding payments for options to renew or buy, do not exceed $].

(f) "Fault" means wrongful act, omission, breach, or default.

(g) "Finance lease" means a lease with respect to which:
(i) the lessor does not select, manufacture, or supply the goods;
(ii) the lessor acquires the goods or the right to possession and use of the goods in connection with the lease; and

(iii) one of the following occurs:

   (A) the lessee receives a copy of the contract by which the lessor acquired the goods or the right to possession and use of the goods before signing the lease contract;

   (B) the lessee's approval of the contract by which the lessor acquired the goods or the right to possession and use of the goods is a condition to effectiveness of the lease contract;

   (C) the lessee, before signing the lease contract, receives an accurate and complete statement designating the promises and warranties, and any disclaimers of warranties, limitations or modifications of remedies, or liquidated damages, including those of a third party, such as the manufacturer of the goods, provided to the lessor by the person supplying the goods in connection with or as part of the contract by which the lessor acquired the goods or the right to possession and use of the goods; or

   (D) if the lease is not a consumer lease, the lessor, before the lessee signs the lease contract, informs the lessee in writing (a) of the identity of the person supplying the goods to the lessor, unless the lessee has selected that person and directed the lessor to acquire the goods or the right to possession and use of the goods from that person, (b) that the lessee is entitled under this Article to the promises and warranties, including those of any third party, provided to the lessor by the person supplying the goods in connection with or as part of the contract by which the lessor acquired the goods or the right to possession and use of the goods, and (c) that the lessee may communicate with the person supplying the goods to the lessor and receive an accurate and complete statement of those promises and warranties, including any disclaimers and limitations of them or of remedies.

(h) "Goods" means all things that are movable at the time of identification to the lease contract, or are fixtures (Section 2A–309), but the term does not include money, documents, instruments, accounts, chattel paper, general intangibles, or minerals or the like, including oil and gas, before extraction. The term also includes the unborn young of animals.

(i) "Installment lease contract" means a lease contract that authorizes or requires the delivery of goods in separate lots to be separately accepted, even though the lease contract contains a clause "each delivery is a separate lease" or its equivalent.

(j) "Lease" means a transfer of the right to possession and use of goods for a term in return for consideration, but a sale, including a sale on approval or a sale or return, or retention or creation of a security interest is not a lease. Unless the context clearly indicates otherwise, the term includes a sublease.

(k) "Lease agreement" means the bargain, with respect to the lease, of the lessor and the lessee in fact as found in their language or by implication from other circumstances including course of dealing or usage of trade or course of performance as provided in this Article. Unless the context clearly indicates otherwise, the term includes a sublease agreement.

(l) "Lease contract" means the total legal obligation that results from the lease agreement as affected by this Article and any other applicable rules of law. Unless the context clearly indicates otherwise, the term includes a sublease contract.

(m) "Leasehold interest" means the interest of the lessor or the lessee under a lease contract.

(n) "Lessee" means a person who acquires the right to possession and use of goods under a lease. Unless the context clearly indicates otherwise, the term includes a sublessee.

(o) "Lessee in ordinary course of business" means a person who in good faith and without knowledge that the lease to him [or her] is in violation of the ownership rights or security interest or leasehold interest of a third party in the goods, leases in ordinary course from a person in the business of selling or leasing goods of that kind but does not include a pawnbroker. "Leasing" may be for cash or by exchange of other property or on secured or unsecured credit and includes receiving goods or documents of title under a pre-existing lease contract but does not include a transfer in bulk or as security for or in total or partial satisfaction of a money debt.

(p) "Lessor" means a person who transfers the right to possession and use of goods under a lease. Unless the context clearly indicates otherwise, the term includes a sublessor.

(q) "Lessor's residual interest" means the lessor's interest in the goods after expiration, termination, or cancellation of the lease contract.

(r) "Lien" means a charge against or interest in goods to secure payment of a debt or performance of an obligation, but the term does not include a security interest.

(s) "Lot" means a parcel or a single article that is the subject matter of a separate lease or delivery, whether or not it is sufficient to perform the lease contract.

(t) "Merchant lessee" means a lessee that is a merchant with respect to goods of the kind subject to the lease.

(u) "Present value" means the amount as of a date certain of one or more sums payable in the future, discounted to the date certain. The discount is determined by the interest rate specified by the parties if the rate was not manifestly unreasonable at the time the transaction was entered into; otherwise, the discount is determined by a commercially reasonable rate that takes into account the facts and circumstances of each case at the time the transaction was entered into.

(v) "Purchase" includes taking by sale, lease, mortgage, security interest, pledge, gift, or any other voluntary transaction creating an interest in goods.

(w) "Sublease" means a lease of goods the right to possession and use of which was acquired by the lessor as a lessee under an existing lease.

(x) "Supplier" means a person from whom a lessor buys or leases goods to be leased under a finance lease.

(y) "Supply contract" means a contract under which a lessor buys or leases goods to be leased.

(z) "Termination" occurs when either party pursuant to a power created by agreement or law puts an end to the lease contract otherwise than for default.

(2) Other definitions applying to this Article and the sections in which they appear are:

   "Accessions". Section 2A–310(1).
   "Construction mortgage". Section 2A–309(1)(d).
   "Encumbrance". Section 2A–309(1)(e).
   "Fixtures". Section 2A–309(1)(a).
   "Fixture filing". Section 2A–309(1)(b).
   "Purchase money lease". Section 2A–309(1)(c).

(3) The following definitions in other Articles apply to this Article:
   "Account". Section 9–106.

"Between merchants". Section 2–104(3).
"Buyer". Section 2–103(1)(a).
"Chattel paper". Section 9–105(1)(b).
"Consumer goods". Section 9–109(1).
"Document". Section 9–105(1)(f).
"Entrusting". Section 2–403(3).
"General intangibles". Section 9–106.
"Good faith". Section 2–103(1)(b).
"Instrument". Section 9–105(1)(i).
"Merchant". Section 2–104(1).
"Mortgage". Sect 9–105(1)(j).
"Pursuant to commitment". Section 9–105(1)(k).
"Receipt". Section 2–103(1)(c).
"Sale". Section 2–106(1).
"Sale on approval". Section 2–326.
"Sale or return". Section 2–326.
"Seller". Section 2–103(1)(d).

(4) In addition Article 1 contains general definitions and principles of construction and interpretation applicable throughout this Article. As amended in 1990.

### § 2A–104. Leases Subject to Other Law.

(1) A lease, although subject to this Article, is also subject to any applicable:

(a) certificate of title statute of this State: (list any certificate of title statutes covering automobiles, trailers, mobile homes, boats, farm tractors, and the like);

(b) certificate of title statute of another jurisdiction (Section 2A–105); or

(c) consumer protection statute of this State, or final consumer protection decision of a court of this State existing on the effective date of this Article.

(2) In case of conflict between this Article, other than Sections 2A–105, 2A–304(3), and 2A–305(3), and a statute or decision referred to in subsection (1), the statute or decision controls.

(3) Failure to comply with an applicable law has only the effect specified therein.

As amended in 1990.

### § 2A–105. Territorial Application of Article to Goods Covered by Certificate of Title.

Subject to the provisions of Sections 2A–304(3) and 2A–305(3), with respect to goods covered by a certificate of title issued under a statute of this State or of another jurisdiction, compliance and the effect of compliance or noncompliance with a certificate of title statute are governed by the law (including the conflict of laws rules) of the jurisdiction issuing the certificate until the earlier of (a) surrender of the certificate, or (b) four months after the goods are removed from that jurisdiction and thereafter until a new certificate of title is issued by another jurisdiction.

### § 2A–106. Limitation on Power of Parties to Consumer Lease to Choose Applicable Law and Judicial Forum.

(1) If the law chosen by the parties to a consumer lease is that of a jurisdiction other than a jurisdiction in which the lessee resides at the time the lease agreement becomes enforceable or within 30 days thereafter or in which the goods are to be used, the choice is not enforceable.

(2) If the judicial forum chosen by the parties to a consumer lease is a forum that would not otherwise have jurisdiction over the lessee, the choice is not enforceable.

### § 2A–107. Waiver or Renunciation of Claim or Right After Default.

Any claim or right arising out of an alleged default or breach of warranty may be discharged in whole or in part without consideration by a written waiver or renunciation signed and delivered by the aggrieved party.

### § 2A–108. Unconscionability.

(1) If the court as a matter of law finds a lease contract or any clause of a lease contract to have been unconscionable at the time it was made the court may refuse to enforce the lease contract, or it may enforce the remainder of the lease contract without the unconscionable clause, or it may so limit the application of any unconscionable clause as to avoid any unconscionable result.

(2) With respect to a consumer lease, if the court as a matter of law finds that a lease contract or any clause of a lease contract has been induced by unconscionable conduct or that unconscionable conduct has occurred in the collection of a claim arising from a lease contract, the court may grant appropriate relief.

(3) Before making a finding of unconscionability under subsection (1) or (2), the court, on its own motion or that of a party, shall afford the parties a reasonable opportunity to present evidence as to the setting, purpose, and effect of the lease contract or clause thereof, or of the conduct.

(4) In an action in which the lessee claims unconscionability with respect to a consumer lease:

(a) If the court finds unconscionability under subsection (1) or (2), the court shall award reasonable attorney's fees to the lessee.

(b) If the court does not find unconscionability and the lessee claiming unconscionability has brought or maintained an action he [or she] knew to be groundless, the court shall award reasonable attorney's fees to the party against whom the claim is made.

(c) In determining attorney's fees, the amount of the recovery on behalf of the claimant under subsections (1) and (2) is not controlling.

### § 2A–109. Option to Accelerate at Will.

(1) A term providing that one party or his [or her] successor in interest may accelerate payment or performance or require collateral or additional collateral "at will" or "when he [or she] deems himself [or herself] insecure" or in words of similar import must be construed to mean that he [or she] has power to do so only if he [or she] in good faith believes that the prospect of payment or performance is impaired.

(2) With respect to a consumer lease, the burden of establishing good faith under subsection (1) is on the party who exercised the power; otherwise the burden of establishing lack of good faith is on the party against whom the power has been exercised.

## Part 2—Formation and Construction of Lease Contract

### § 2A–201. Statute of Frauds.

(1) A lease contract is not enforceable by way of action or defense unless:

(a) the total payments to be made under the lease contract, excluding payments for options to renew or buy, are less than $1,000; or

(b) there is a writing, signed by the party against whom enforcement is sought or by that party's authorized agent, sufficient to indicate that a lease contract has been made between the parties and to describe the goods leased and the lease term.

(2) Any description of leased goods or of the lease term is sufficient and satisfies subsection (1)(b), whether or not it is specific, if it reasonably identifies what is described.

(3) A writing is not insufficient because it omits or incorrectly states a term agreed upon, but the lease contract is not enforceable under subsection (1)(b) beyond the lease term and the quantity of goods shown in the writing.

(4) A lease contract that does not satisfy the requirements of subsection (1), but which is valid in other respects, is enforceable:

(a) if the goods are to be specially manufactured or obtained for the lessee and are not suitable for lease or sale to others in the ordinary course of the lessor's business, and the lessor, before notice of repudiation is received and under circumstances that reasonably indicate that the goods are for the lessee, has made either a substantial beginning of their manufacture or commitments for their procurement;

(b) if the party against whom enforcement is sought admits in that party's pleading, testimony or otherwise in court that a lease contract was made, but the lease contract is not enforceable under this provision beyond the quantity of goods admitted; or

(c) with respect to goods that have been received and accepted by the lessee.

(5) The lease term under a lease contract referred to in subsection (4) is:

(a) if there is a writing signed by the party against whom enforcement is sought or by that party's authorized agent specifying the lease term, the term so specified;

(b) if the party against whom enforcement is sought admits in that party's pleading, testimony, or otherwise in court a lease term, the term so admitted; or

(c) a reasonable lease term.

### § 2A–202.  Final Written Expression: Parol or Extrinsic Evidence.

Terms with respect to which the confirmatory memoranda of the parties agree or which are otherwise set forth in a writing intended by the parties as a final expression of their agreement with respect to such terms as are included therein may not be contradicted by evidence of any prior agreement or of a contemporaneous oral agreement but may be explained or supplemented:

(a) by course of dealing or usage of trade or by course of performance; and

(b) by evidence of consistent additional terms unless the court finds the writing to have been intended also as a complete and exclusive statement of the terms of the agreement.

### § 2A–203.  Seals Inoperative.

The affixing of a seal to a writing evidencing a lease contract or an offer to enter into a lease contract does not render the writing a sealed instrument and the law with respect to sealed instruments does not apply to the lease contract or offer.

### § 2A–204.  Formation in General.

(1) A lease contract may be made in any manner sufficient to show agreement, including conduct by both parties which recognizes the existence of a lease contract.

(2) An agreement sufficient to constitute a lease contract may be found although the moment of its making is undetermined.

(3) Although one or more terms are left open, a lease contract does not fail for indefiniteness if the parties have intended to make a lease contract and there is a reasonably certain basis for giving an appropriate remedy.

### § 2A–205.  Firm Offers.

An offer by a merchant to lease goods to or from another person in a signed writing that by its terms gives assurance it will be held open is not revocable, for lack of consideration, during the time stated or, if no time is stated, for a reasonable time, but in no event may the period of irrevocability exceed 3 months. Any such term of assurance on a form supplied by the offeree must be separately signed by the offeror.

### § 2A–206.  Offer and Acceptance in Formation of Lease Contract.

(1) Unless otherwise unambiguously indicated by the language or circumstances, an offer to make a lease contract must be construed as inviting acceptance in any manner and by any medium reasonable in the circumstances.

(2) If the beginning of a requested performance is a reasonable mode of acceptance, an offeror who is not notified of acceptance within a reasonable time may treat the offer as having lapsed before acceptance.

### § 2A–207.  Course of Performance or Practical Construction.

(1) If a lease contract involves repeated occasions for performance by either party with knowledge of the nature of the performance and opportunity for objection to it by the other, any course of performance accepted or acquiesced in without objection is relevant to determine the meaning of the lease agreement.

(2) The express terms of a lease agreement and any course of performance, as well as any course of dealing and usage of trade, must be construed whenever reasonable as consistent with each other; but if that construction is unreasonable, express terms control course of performance, course of performance controls both course of dealing and usage of trade, and course of dealing controls usage of trade.

(3) Subject to the provisions of Section 2A–208 on modification and waiver, course of performance is relevant to show a waiver or modification of any term inconsistent with the course of performance.

### § 2A–208.  Modification, Rescission and Waiver.

(1) An agreement modifying a lease contract needs no consideration to be binding.

(2) A signed lease agreement that excludes modification or rescission except by a signed writing may not be otherwise modified or rescinded, but, except as between merchants, such a requirement on a form supplied by a merchant must be separately signed by the other party.

(3) Although an attempt at modification or rescission does not satisfy the requirements of subsection (2), it may operate as a waiver.

(4) A party who has made a waiver affecting an executory portion of a lease contract may retract the waiver by reasonable notification received by the other party that strict performance will be required of any term waived, unless the retraction would be unjust in view of a material change of position in reliance on the waiver.

### § 2A–209.  Lessee Under Finance Lease as Beneficiary of Supply Contract.

(1) The benefit of a supplier's promises to the lessor under the supply contract and of all warranties, whether express or implied, including those of any third party provided in connection with or as part of the supply contract, extends to the lessee to the extent of the lessee's leasehold interest under a finance lease related to the supply contract, but is subject to the terms of the warranty and of the supply contract and all defenses or claims arising therefrom.

(2) The extension of the benefit of a supplier's promises and of warranties to the lessee (Section 2A–209(1)) does not: (i) modify the rights and obligations of the parties to the supply contract, whether

arising therefrom or otherwise, or (ii) impose any duty or liability under the supply contract on the lessee.

(3) Any modification or rescission of the supply contract by the supplier and the lessor is effective between the supplier and the lessee unless, before the modification or rescission, the supplier has received notice that the lessee has entered into a finance lease related to the supply contract. If the modification or rescission is effective between the supplier and the lessee, the lessor is deemed to have assumed, in addition to the obligations of the lessor to the lessee under the lease contract, promises of the supplier to the lessor and warranties that were so modified or rescinded as they existed and were available to the lessee before modification or rescission.

(4) In addition to the extension of the benefit of the supplier's promises and of warranties to the lessee under subsection (1), the lessee retains all rights that the lessee may have against the supplier which arise from an agreement between the lessee and the supplier or under other law.

As amended in 1990.

### § 2A–210. Express Warranties.

(1) Express warranties by the lessor are created as follows:

(a) Any affirmation of fact or promise made by the lessor to the lessee which relates to the goods and becomes part of the basis of the bargain creates an express warranty that the goods will conform to the affirmation or promise.

(b) Any description of the goods which is made part of the basis of the bargain creates an express warranty that the goods will conform to the description.

(c) Any sample or model that is made part of the basis of the bargain creates an express warranty that the whole of the goods will conform to the sample or model.

(2) It is not necessary to the creation of an express warranty that the lessor use formal words, such as "warrant" or "guarantee," or that the lessor have a specific intention to make a warranty, but an affirmation merely of the value of the goods or a statement purporting to be merely the lessor's opinion or commendation of the goods does not create a warranty.

### § 2A–211. Warranties Against Interference and Against Infringement; Lessee's Obligation Against Infringement.

(1) There is in a lease contract a warranty that for the lease term no person holds a claim to or interest in the goods that arose from an act or omission of the lessor, other than a claim by way of infringement or the like, which will interfere with the lessee's enjoyment of its leasehold interest.

(2) Except in a finance lease there is in a lease contract by a lessor who is a merchant regularly dealing in goods of the kind a warranty that the goods are delivered free of the rightful claim of any person by way of infringement or the like.

(3) A lessee who furnishes specifications to a lessor or a supplier shall hold the lessor and the supplier harmless against any claim by way of infringement or the like that arises out of compliance with the specifications.

### § 2A–212. Implied Warranty of Merchantability.

(1) Except in a finance lease, a warranty that the goods will be merchantable is implied in a lease contract if the lessor is a merchant with respect to goods of that kind.

(2) Goods to be merchantable must be at least such as

(a) pass without objection in the trade under the description in the lease agreement;

(b) in the case of fungible goods, are of fair average quality within the description;

(c) are fit for the ordinary purposes for which goods of that type are used;

(d) run, within the variation permitted by the lease agreement, of even kind, quality, and quantity within each unit and among all units involved;

(e) are adequately contained, packaged, and labeled as the lease agreement may require; and

(f) conform to any promises or affirmations of fact made on the container or label.

(3) Other implied warranties may arise from course of dealing or usage of trade.

### § 2A–213. Implied Warranty of Fitness for Particular Purpose.

Except in a finance lease, if the lessor at the time the lease contract is made has reason to know of any particular purpose for which the goods are required and that the lessee is relying on the lessor's skill or judgment to select or furnish suitable goods, there is in the lease contract an implied warranty that the goods will be fit for that purpose.

### § 2A–214. Exclusion or Modification of Warranties.

(1) Words or conduct relevant to the creation of an express warranty and words or conduct tending to negate or limit a warranty must be construed wherever reasonable as consistent with each other; but, subject to the provisions of Section 2A–202 on parol or extrinsic evidence, negation or limitation is inoperative to the extent that the construction is unreasonable.

(2) Subject to subsection (3), to exclude or modify the implied warranty of merchantability or any part of it the language must mention "merchantability", be by a writing, and be conspicuous. Subject to subsection (3), to exclude or modify any implied warranty of fitness the exclusion must be by a writing and be conspicuous. Language to exclude all implied warranties of fitness is sufficient if it is in writing, is conspicuous and states, for example, "There is no warranty that the goods will be fit for a particular purpose".

(3) Notwithstanding subsection (2), but subject to subsection (4),

(a) unless the circumstances indicate otherwise, all implied warranties are excluded by expressions like "as is," or "with all faults," or by other language that in common understanding calls the lessee's attention to the exclusion of warranties and makes plain that there is no implied warranty, if in writing and conspicuous;

(b) if the lessee before entering into the lease contract has examined the goods or the sample or model as fully as desired or has refused to examine the goods, there is no implied warranty with regard to defects that an examination ought in the circumstances to have revealed; and

(c) an implied warranty may also be excluded or modified by course of dealing, course of performance, or usage of trade.

(4) To exclude or modify a warranty against interference or against infringement (Section 2A–211) or any part of it, the language must be specific, be by a writing, and be conspicuous, unless the circumstances, including course of performance, course of dealing, or usage of trade, give the lessee reason to know that the goods are being leased subject to a claim or interest of any person.

### § 2A–215. Cumulation and Conflict of Warranties Express or Implied.

Warranties, whether express or implied, must be construed as consistent with each other and as cumulative, but if that construction is unreasonable, the intention of the parties determines which warranty is dominant. In ascertaining that intention the following rules apply:

(a) Exact or technical specifications displace an inconsistent sample or model or general language of description.

(b) A sample from an existing bulk displaces inconsistent general language of description.

(c) Express warranties displace inconsistent implied warranties other than an implied warranty of fitness for a particular purpose.

## § 2A–216.  Third-Party Beneficiaries of Express and Implied Warranties.

**Alternative A** A warranty to or for the benefit of a lessee under this Article, whether express or implied, extends to any natural person who is in the family or household of the lessee or who is a guest in the lessee's home if it is reasonable to expect that such person may use, consume, or be affected by the goods and who is injured in person by breach of the warranty. This section does not displace principles of law and equity that extend a warranty to or for the benefit of a lessee to other persons. The operation of this section may not be excluded, modified, or limited, but an exclusion, modification, or limitation of the warranty, including any with respect to rights and remedies, effective against the lessee is also effective against any beneficiary designated under this section.

**Alternative B** A warranty to or for the benefit of a lessee under this Article, whether express or implied, extends to any natural person who may reasonably be expected to use, consume, or be affected by the goods and who is injured in person by breach of the warranty. This section does not displace principles of law and equity that extend a warranty to or for the benefit of a lessee to other persons. The operation of this section may not be excluded, modified, or limited, but an exclusion, modification, or limitation of the warranty, including any with respect to rights and remedies, effective against the lessee is also effective against the beneficiary designated under this section.

**Alternative C** A warranty to or for the benefit of a lessee under this Article, whether express or implied, extends to any person who may reasonably be expected to use, consume, or be affected by the goods and who is injured by breach of the warranty. The operation of this section may not be excluded, modified, or limited with respect to injury to the person of an individual to whom the warranty extends, but an exclusion, modification, or limitation of the warranty, including any with respect to rights and remedies, effective against the lessee is also effective against the beneficiary designated under this section.

## § 2A–217.  Identification.

Identification of goods as goods to which a lease contract refers may be made at any time and in any manner explicitly agreed to by the parties. In the absence of explicit agreement, identification occurs:

(a) when the lease contract is made if the lease contract is for a lease of goods that are existing and identified;

(b) when the goods are shipped, marked, or otherwise designated by the lessor as goods to which the lease contract refers, if the lease contract is for a lease of goods that are not existing and identified; or

(c) when the young are conceived, if the lease contract is for a lease of unborn young of animals.

## § 2A–218.  Insurance and Proceeds.

(1) A lessee obtains an insurable interest when existing goods are identified to the lease contract even though the goods identified are nonconforming and the lessee has an option to reject them.

(2) If a lessee has an insurable interest only by reason of the lessor's identification of the goods, the lessor, until default or insolvency or notification to the lessee that identification is final, may substitute other goods for those identified.

(3) Notwithstanding a lessee's insurable interest under subsections (1) and (2), the lessor retains an insurable interest until an option to buy has been exercised by the lessee and risk of loss has passed to the lessee.

(4) Nothing in this section impairs any insurable interest recognized under any other statute or rule of law.

(5) The parties by agreement may determine that one or more parties have an obligation to obtain and pay for insurance covering the goods and by agreement may determine the beneficiary of the proceeds of the insurance.

## § 2A–219.  Risk of Loss.

(1) Except in the case of a finance lease, risk of loss is retained by the lessor and does not pass to the lessee. In the case of a finance lease, risk of loss passes to the lessee.

(2) Subject to the provisions of this Article on the effect of default on risk of loss (Section 2A–220), if risk of loss is to pass to the lessee and the time of passage is not stated, the following rules apply:

(a) If the lease contract requires or authorizes the goods to be shipped by carrier

(i) and it does not require delivery at a particular destination, the risk of loss passes to the lessee when the goods are duly delivered to the carrier; but

(ii) if it does require delivery at a particular destination and the goods are there duly tendered while in the possession of the carrier, the risk of loss passes to the lessee when the goods are there duly so tendered as to enable the lessee to take delivery.

(b) If the goods are held by a bailee to be delivered without being moved, the risk of loss passes to the lessee on acknowledgment by the bailee of the lessee's right to possession of the goods.

(c) In any case not within subsection (a) or (b), the risk of loss passes to the lessee on the lessee's receipt of the goods if the lessor, or, in the case of a finance lease, the supplier, is a merchant; otherwise the risk passes to the lessee on tender of delivery.

## § 2A–220.  Effect of Default on Risk of Loss.

(1) Where risk of loss is to pass to the lessee and the time of passage is not stated:

(a) If a tender or delivery of goods so fails to conform to the lease contract as to give a right of rejection, the risk of their loss remains with the lessor, or, in the case of a finance lease, the supplier, until cure or acceptance.

(b) If the lessee rightfully revokes acceptance, he [or she], to the extent of any deficiency in his [or her] effective insurance coverage, may treat the risk of loss as having remained with the lessor from the beginning.

(2) Whether or not risk of loss is to pass to the lessee, if the lessee as to conforming goods already identified to a lease contract repudiates or is otherwise in default under the lease contract, the lessor, or, in the case of a finance lease, the supplier, to the extent of any deficiency in his [or her] effective insurance coverage may treat the risk of loss as resting on the lessee for a commercially reasonable time.

## § 2A–221.  Casualty to Identified Goods.

If a lease contract requires goods identified when the lease contract is made, and the goods suffer casualty without fault of the lessee, the lessor or the supplier before delivery, or the goods suffer casualty before risk of loss passes to the lessee pursuant to the lease agreement or Section 2A–219, then:

(a) if the loss is total, the lease contract is avoided; and

(b) if the loss is partial or the goods have so deteriorated as to no longer conform to the lease contract, the lessee may nevertheless demand inspection and at his [or her] option either treat the lease contract as avoided or, except in a finance lease that is not a consumer lease, accept the goods with due allowance from the rent payable for the balance of the lease term for the deterioration or the deficiency in quantity but without further right against the lessor.

## Part 3—Effect of Lease Contract

### § 2A–301.  Enforceability of Lease Contract.

Except as otherwise provided in this Article, a lease contract is effective and enforceable according to its terms between the parties, against purchasers of the goods and against creditors of the parties.

### § 2A–302.  Title to and Possession of Goods.

Except as otherwise provided in this Article, each provision of this Article applies whether the lessor or a third party has title to the goods, and whether the lessor, the lessee, or a third party has possession of the goods, notwithstanding any statute or rule of law that possession or the absence of possession is fraudulent.

### § 2A–303.  Alienability of Party's Interest Under Lease Contract or of Lessor's Residual Interest in Goods; Delegation of Performance; Transfer of Rights.

(1) As used in this section, "creation of a security interest" includes the sale of a lease contract that is subject to Article 9, Secured Transactions, by reason of Section 9–102(1)(b).

(2) Except as provided in subsections (3) and (4), a provision in a lease agreement which (i) prohibits the voluntary or involuntary transfer, including a transfer by sale, sublease, creation or enforcement of a security interest, or attachment, levy, or other judicial process, of an interest of a party under the lease contract or of the lessor's residual interest in the goods, or (ii) makes such a transfer an event of default, gives rise to the rights and remedies provided in subsection (5), but a transfer that is prohibited or is an event of default under the lease agreement is otherwise effective.

(3) A provision in a lease agreement which (i) prohibits the creation or enforcement of a security interest in an interest of a party under the lease contract or in the lessor's residual interest in the goods, or (ii) makes such a transfer an event of default, is not enforceable unless, and then only to the extent that, there is an actual transfer by the lessee of the lessee's right of possession or use of the goods in violation of the provision or an actual delegation of a material performance of either party to the lease contract in violation of the provision. Neither the granting nor the enforcement of a security interest in (i) the lessor's interest under the lease contract or (ii) the lessor's residual interest in the goods is a transfer that materially impairs the prospect of obtaining return performance by, materially changes the duty of, or materially increases the burden or risk imposed on, the lessee within the purview of subsection (5) unless, and then only to the extent that, there is an actual delegation of a material performance of the lessor.

(4) A provision in a lease agreement which (i) prohibits a transfer of a right to damages for default with respect to the whole lease contract or of a right to payment arising out of the transferor's due performance of the transferor's entire obligation, or (ii) makes such a transfer an event of default, is not enforceable, and such a transfer is not a transfer that materially impairs the prospect of obtaining return performance by, materially changes the duty of, or materially increases the burden

or risk imposed on, the other party to the lease contract within the purview of subsection (5).

(5) Subject to subsections (3) and (4):

(a) if a transfer is made which is made an event of default under a lease agreement, the party to the lease contract not making the transfer, unless that party waives the default or otherwise agrees, has the rights and remedies described in Section 2A–501(2);

(b) if paragraph (a) is not applicable and if a transfer is made that (i) is prohibited under a lease agreement or (ii) materially impairs the prospect of obtaining return performance by, materially changes the duty of, or materially increases the burden or risk imposed on, the other party to the lease contract, unless the party not making the transfer agrees at any time to the transfer in the lease contract or otherwise, then, except as limited by contract, (i) the transferor is liable to the party not making the transfer for damages caused by the transfer to the extent that the damages could not reasonably be prevented by the party not making the transfer and (ii) a court having jurisdiction may grant other appropriate relief, including cancellation of the lease contract or an injunction against the transfer.

(6) A transfer of "the lease" or of "all my rights under the lease", or a transfer in similar general terms, is a transfer of rights and, unless the language or the circumstances, as in a transfer for security, indicate the contrary, the transfer is a delegation of duties by the transferor to the transferee. Acceptance by the transferee constitutes a promise by the transferee to perform those duties. The promise is enforceable by either the transferor or the other party to the lease contract.

(7) Unless otherwise agreed by the lessor and the lessee, a delegation of performance does not relieve the transferor as against the other party of any duty to perform or of any liability for default.

(8) In a consumer lease, to prohibit the transfer of an interest of a party under the lease contract or to make a transfer an event of default, the language must be specific, by a writing, and conspicuous.
As amended in 1990.

### § 2A–304.  Subsequent Lease of Goods by Lessor.

(1) Subject to Section 2A–303, a subsequent lessee from a lessor of goods under an existing lease contract obtains, to the extent of the leasehold interest transferred, the leasehold interest in the goods that the lessor had or had power to transfer, and except as provided in subsection (2) and Section 2A–527(4), takes subject to the existing lease contract. A lessor with voidable title has power to transfer a good leasehold interest to a good faith subsequent lessee for value, but only to the extent set forth in the preceding sentence. If goods have been delivered under a transaction of purchase, the lessor has that power even though:

(a) the lessor's transferor was deceived as to the identity of the lessor;

(b) the delivery was in exchange for a check which is later dishonored;

(c) it was agreed that the transaction was to be a "cash sale"; or

(d) the delivery was procured through fraud punishable as larcenous under the criminal law.

(2) A subsequent lessee in the ordinary course of business from a lessor who is a merchant dealing in goods of that kind to whom the goods were entrusted by the existing lessee of that lessor before the interest of the subsequent lessee became enforceable against that lessor obtains, to the extent of the leasehold interest transferred, all of that lessor's and the existing lessee's rights to the goods, and takes free of the existing lease contract.

(3) A subsequent lessee from the lessor of goods that are subject to an existing lease contract and are covered by a certificate of title issued under a statute of this State or of another jurisdiction takes no greater rights than those provided both by this section and by the certificate of title statute.
As amended in 1990.

## § 2A–305.  Sale or Sublease of Goods by Lessee.

(1) Subject to the provisions of Section 2A–303, a buyer or sublessee from the lessee of goods under an existing lease contract obtains, to the extent of the interest transferred, the leasehold interest in the goods that the lessee had or had power to transfer, and except as provided in subsection (2) and Section 2A–511(4), takes subject to the existing lease contract. A lessee with a voidable leasehold interest has power to transfer a good leasehold interest to a good faith buyer for value or a good faith sublessee for value, but only to the extent set forth in the preceding sentence. When goods have been delivered under a transaction of lease the lessee has that power even though:

   (a)  the lessor was deceived as to the identity of the lessee;
   (b)  the delivery was in exchange for a check which is later dishonored; or
   (c)  the delivery was procured through fraud punishable as larcenous under the criminal law.

(2) A buyer in the ordinary course of business or a sublessee in the ordinary course of business from a lessee who is a merchant dealing in goods of that kind to whom the goods were entrusted by the lessor obtains, to the extent of the interest transferred, all of the lessor's and lessee's rights to the goods, and takes free of the existing lease contract.

(3) A buyer or sublessee from the lessee of goods that are subject to an existing lease contract and are covered by a certificate of title issued under a statute of this State or of another jurisdiction takes no greater rights than those provided both by this section and by the certificate of title statute.

## § 2A–306.  Priority of Certain Liens Arising by Operation of Law.

If a person in the ordinary course of his [or her] business furnishes services or materials with respect to goods subject to a lease contract, a lien upon those goods in the possession of that person given by statute or rule of law for those materials or services takes priority over any interest of the lessor or lessee under the lease contract or this Article unless the lien is created by statute and the statute provides otherwise or unless the lien is created by rule of law and the rule of law provides otherwise.

## § 2A–307.  Priority of Liens Arising by Attachment or Levy on, Security Interests in, and Other Claims to Goods.

(1) Except as otherwise provided in Section 2A–306, a creditor of a lessee takes subject to the lease contract.

(2) Except as otherwise provided in subsections (3) and (4) and in Sections 2A–306 and 2A–308, a creditor of a lessor takes subject to the lease contract unless:

   (a)  the creditor holds a lien that attached to the goods before the lease contract became enforceable;
   (b)  the creditor holds a security interest in the goods and the lessee did not give value and receive delivery of the goods without knowledge of the security interest; or
   (c)  the creditor holds a security interest in the goods which was perfected (Section 9–303) before the lease contract became enforceable.

(3) A lessee in the ordinary course of business takes the leasehold interest free of a security interest in the goods created by the lessor even though the security interest is perfected (Section 9–303) and the lessee knows of its existence.

(4) A lessee other than a lessee in the ordinary course of business takes the leasehold interest free of a security interest to the extent that it secures future advances made after the secured party acquires knowledge of the lease or more than 45 days after the lease contract becomes enforceable, whichever first occurs, unless the future advances are made pursuant to a commitment entered into without knowledge of the lease and before the expiration of the 45-day period.
As amended in 1990.

## § 2A–308.  Special Rights of Creditors.

(1) A creditor of a lessor in possession of goods subject to a lease contract may treat the lease contract as void if as against the creditor retention of possession by the lessor is fraudulent under any statute or rule of law, but retention of possession in good faith and current course of trade by the lessor for a commercially reasonable time after the lease contract becomes enforceable is not fraudulent.

(2) Nothing in this Article impairs the rights of creditors of a lessor if the lease contract (a) becomes enforceable, not in current course of trade but in satisfaction of or as security for a pre-existing claim for money, security, or the like, and (b) is made under circumstances which under any statute or rule of law apart from this Article would constitute the transaction a fraudulent transfer or voidable preference.

(3) A creditor of a seller may treat a sale or an identification of goods to a contract for sale as void if as against the creditor retention of possession by the seller is fraudulent under any statute or rule of law, but retention of possession of the goods pursuant to a lease contract entered into by the seller as lessee and the buyer as lessor in connection with the sale or identification of the goods is not fraudulent if the buyer bought for value and in good faith.

## § 2A–309.  Lessor's and Lessee's Rights When Goods Become Fixtures.

(1) In this section:

   (a)  goods are "fixtures" when they become so related to particular real estate that an interest in them arises under real estate law;
   (b)  a "fixture filing" is the filing, in the office where a mortgage on the real estate would be filed or recorded, of a financing statement covering goods that are or are to become fixtures and conforming to the requirements of Section 9–402(5);
   (c)  a lease is a "purchase money lease" unless the lessee has possession or use of the goods or the right to possession or use of the goods before the lease agreement is enforceable;
   (d)  a mortgage is a "construction mortgage" to the extent it secures an obligation incurred for the construction of an improvement on land including the acquisition cost of the land, if the recorded writing so indicates; and
   (e)  "encumbrance" includes real estate mortgages and other liens on real estate and all other rights in real estate that are not ownership interests.

(2) Under this Article a lease may be of goods that are fixtures or may continue in goods that become fixtures, but no lease exists under this Article of ordinary building materials incorporated into an improvement on land.

(3) This Article does not prevent creation of a lease of fixtures pursuant to real estate law.

(4) The perfected interest of a lessor of fixtures has priority over a conflicting interest of an encumbrancer or owner of the real estate if:

   (a)  the lease is a purchase money lease, the conflicting interest of the encumbrancer or owner arises before the goods become fixtures, the interest of the lessor is perfected by a fixture filing before the goods become fixtures or within ten days thereafter, and the lessee has an interest of record in the real estate or is in possession of the real estate; or

(b) the interest of the lessor is perfected by a fixture filing before the interest of the encumbrancer or owner is of record, the lessor's interest has priority over any conflicting interest of a predecessor in title of the encumbrancer or owner, and the lessee has an interest of record in the real estate or is in possession of the real estate.

(5) The interest of a lessor of fixtures, whether or not perfected, has priority over the conflicting interest of an encumbrancer or owner of the real estate if:

(a) the fixtures are readily removable factory or office machines, readily removable equipment that is not primarily used or leased for use in the operation of the real estate, or readily removable replacements of domestic appliances that are goods subject to a consumer lease, and before the goods become fixtures the lease contract is enforceable; or

(b) the conflicting interest is a lien on the real estate obtained by legal or equitable proceedings after the lease contract is enforceable; or

(c) the encumbrancer or owner has consented in writing to the lease or has disclaimed an interest in the goods as fixtures; or

(d) the lessee has a right to remove the goods as against the encumbrancer or owner. If the lessee's right to remove terminates, the priority of the interest of the lessor continues for a reasonable time.

(6) Notwithstanding subsection (4)(a) but otherwise subject to subsections (4) and (5), the interest of a lessor of fixtures, including the lessor's residual interest, is subordinate to the conflicting interest of an encumbrancer of the real estate under a construction mortgage recorded before the goods become fixtures if the goods become fixtures before the completion of the construction. To the extent given to refinance a construction mortgage, the conflicting interest of an encumbrancer of the real estate under a mortgage has this priority to the same extent as the encumbrancer of the real estate under the construction mortgage.

(7) In cases not within the preceding subsections, priority between the interest of a lessor of fixtures, including the lessor's residual interest, and the conflicting interest of an encumbrancer or owner of the real estate who is not the lessee is determined by the priority rules governing conflicting interests in real estate.

(8) If the interest of a lessor of fixtures, including the lessor's residual interest, has priority over all conflicting interests of all owners and encumbrancers of the real estate, the lessor or the lessee may (i) on default, expiration, termination, or cancellation of the lease agreement but subject to the agreement and this Article, or (ii) if necessary to enforce other rights and remedies of the lessor or lessee under this Article, remove the goods from the real estate, free and clear of all conflicting interests of all owners and encumbrancers of the real estate, but the lessor or lessee must reimburse any encumbrancer or owner of the real estate who is not the lessee and who has not otherwise agreed for the cost of repair of any physical injury, but not for any diminution in value of the real estate caused by the absence of the goods removed or by any necessity of replacing them. A person entitled to reimbursement may refuse permission to remove until the party seeking removal gives adequate security for the performance of this obligation.

(9) Even though the lease agreement does not create a security interest, the interest of a lessor of fixtures, including the lessor's residual

interest, is perfected by filing a financing statement as a fixture filing for leased goods that are or are to become fixtures in accordance with the relevant provisions of the Article on Secured Transactions (Article 9).
As amended in 1990.

### § 2A–310. Lessor's and Lessee's Rights When Goods Become Accessions.

(1) Goods are "accessions" when they are installed in or affixed to other goods.

(2) The interest of a lessor or a lessee under a lease contract entered into before the goods became accessions is superior to all interests in the whole except as stated in subsection (4).

(3) The interest of a lessor or a lessee under a lease contract entered into at the time or after the goods became accessions is superior to all subsequently acquired interests in the whole except as stated in subsection (4) but is subordinate to interests in the whole existing at the time the lease contract was made unless the holders of such interests in the whole have in writing consented to the lease or disclaimed an interest in the goods as part of the whole.

(4) The interest of a lessor or a lessee under a lease contract described in subsection (2) or (3) is subordinate to the interest of

(a) a buyer in the ordinary course of business or a lessee in the ordinary course of business of any interest in the whole acquired after the goods became accessions; or

(b) a creditor with a security interest in the whole perfected before the lease contract was made to the extent that the creditor makes subsequent advances without knowledge of the lease contract.

(5) When under subsections (2) or (3) and (4) a lessor or a lessee of accessions holds an interest that is superior to all interests in the whole, the lessor or the lessee may (a) on default, expiration, termination, or cancellation of the lease contract by the other party but subject to the provisions of the lease contract and this Article, or (b) if necessary to enforce his [or her] other rights and remedies under this Article, remove the goods from the whole, free and clear of all interests in the whole, but he [or she] must reimburse any holder of an interest in the whole who is not the lessee and who has not otherwise agreed for the cost of repair of any physical injury but not for any diminution in value of the whole caused by the absence of the goods removed or by any necessity for replacing them. A person entitled to reimbursement may refuse permission to remove until the party seeking removal gives adequate security for the performance of this obligation.

### § 2A–311. Priority Subject to Subordination.
Nothing in this Article prevents subordination by agreement by any person entitled to priority.
As added in 1990.

## Part 4—Performance of Lease Contract: Repudiated, Substituted and Excused

### § 2A–401. Insecurity: Adequate Assurance of Performance.
(1) A lease contract imposes an obligation on each party that the other's expectation of receiving due performance will not be impaired.
(2) If reasonable grounds for insecurity arise with respect to the performance of either party, the insecure party may demand in writing adequate assurance of due performance. Until the insecure party receives that assurance, if commercially reasonable the insecure party may suspend any performance for which he [or she] has not already received the agreed return.

(3) A repudiation of the lease contract occurs if assurance of due performance adequate under the circumstances of the particular case is not provided to the insecure party within a reasonable time, not to exceed 30 days after receipt of a demand by the other party.

(4) Between merchants, the reasonableness of grounds for insecurity and the adequacy of any assurance offered must be determined according to commercial standards.

(5) Acceptance of any nonconforming delivery or payment does not prejudice the aggrieved party's right to demand adequate assurance of future performance.

## § 2A–402. Anticipatory Repudiation.

If either party repudiates a lease contract with respect to a performance not yet due under the lease contract, the loss of which performance will substantially impair the value of the lease contract to the other, the aggrieved party may:

(a) for a commercially reasonable time, await retraction of repudiation and performance by the repudiating party;

(b) make demand pursuant to Section 2A–401 and await assurance of future performance adequate under the circumstances of the particular case; or

(c) resort to any right or remedy upon default under the lease contract or this Article, even though the aggrieved party has notified the repudiating party that the aggrieved party would await the repudiating party's performance and assurance and has urged retraction. In addition, whether or not the aggrieved party is pursuing one of the foregoing remedies, the aggrieved party may suspend performance or, if the aggrieved party is the lessor, proceed in accordance with the provisions of this Article on the lessor's right to identify goods to the lease contract notwithstanding default or to salvage unfinished goods (Section 2A–524).

## § 2A–403. Retraction of Anticipatory Repudiation.

(1) Until the repudiating party's next performance is due, the repudiating party can retract the repudiation unless, since the repudiation, the aggrieved party has cancelled the lease contract or materially changed the aggrieved party's position or otherwise indicated that the aggrieved party considers the repudiation final.

(2) Retraction may be by any method that clearly indicates to the aggrieved party that the repudiating party intends to perform under the lease contract and includes any assurance demanded under Section 2A–401.

(3) Retraction reinstates a repudiating party's rights under a lease contract with due excuse and allowance to the aggrieved party for any delay occasioned by the repudiation.

## § 2A–404. Substituted Performance.

(1) If without fault of the lessee, the lessor and the supplier, the agreed berthing, loading, or unloading facilities fail or the agreed type of carrier becomes unavailable or the agreed manner of delivery otherwise becomes commercially impracticable, but a commercially reasonable substitute is available, the substitute performance must be tendered and accepted.

(2) If the agreed means or manner of payment fails because of domestic or foreign governmental regulation:

(a) the lessor may withhold or stop delivery or cause the supplier to withhold or stop delivery unless the lessee provides a means or manner of payment that is commercially a substantial equivalent; and

(b) if delivery has already been taken, payment by the means or in the manner provided by the regulation discharges the lessee's

obligation unless the regulation is discriminatory, oppressive, or predatory.

## § 2A–405. Excused Performance.

Subject to Section 2A–404 on substituted performance, the following rules apply:

(a) Delay in delivery or nondelivery in whole or in part by a lessor or a supplier who complies with paragraphs (b) and (c) is not a default under the lease contract if performance as agreed has been made impracticable by the occurrence of a contingency the nonoccurrence of which was a basic assumption on which the lease contract was made or by compliance in good faith with any applicable foreign or domestic governmental regulation or order, whether or not the regulation or order later proves to be invalid.

(b) If the causes mentioned in paragraph (a) affect only part of the lessor's or the supplier's capacity to perform, he [or she] shall allocate production and deliveries among his [or her] customers but at his [or her] option may include regular customers not then under contract for sale or lease as well as his [or her] own requirements for further manufacture. He [or she] may so allocate in any manner that is fair and reasonable.

(c) The lessor seasonably shall notify the lessee and in the case of a finance lease the supplier seasonably shall notify the lessor and the lessee, if known, that there will be delay or nondelivery and, if allocation is required under paragraph (b), of the estimated quota thus made available for the lessee.

## § 2A–406. Procedure on Excused Performance.

(1) If the lessee receives notification of a material or indefinite delay or an allocation justified under Section 2A–405, the lessee may by written notification to the lessor as to any goods involved, and with respect to all of the goods if under an installment lease contract the value of the whole lease contract is substantially impaired (Section 2A–510):

(a) terminate the lease contract (Section 2A–505(2)); or

(b) except in a finance lease that is not a consumer lease, modify the lease contract by accepting the available quota in substitution, with due allowance from the rent payable for the balance of the lease term for the deficiency but without further right against the lessor.

(2) If, after receipt of a notification from the lessor under Section 2A–405, the lessee fails so to modify the lease agreement within a reasonable time not exceeding 30 days, the lease contract lapses with respect to any deliveries affected.

## § 2A–407. Irrevocable Promises: Finance Leases.

(1) In the case of a finance lease that is not a consumer lease the lessee's promises under the lease contract become irrevocable and independent upon the lessee's acceptance of the goods.

(2) A promise that has become irrevocable and independent under subsection (1):

(a) is effective and enforceable between the parties, and by or against third parties including assignees of the parties; and

(b) is not subject to cancellation, termination, modification, repudiation, excuse, or substitution without the consent of the party to whom the promise runs.

(3) This section does not affect the validity under any other law of a covenant in any lease contract making the lessee's promises irrevocable and independent upon the lessee's acceptance of the goods.
As amended in 1990.

# Part 5—Default

## A. In General

### § 2A–501. Default: Procedure.

(1) Whether the lessor or the lessee is in default under a lease contract is determined by the lease agreement and this Article.

(2) If the lessor or the lessee is in default under the lease contract, the party seeking enforcement has rights and remedies as provided in this Article and, except as limited by this Article, as provided in the lease agreement.

(3) If the lessor or the lessee is in default under the lease contract, the party seeking enforcement may reduce the party's claim to judgment, or otherwise enforce the lease contract by self-help or any available judicial procedure or nonjudicial procedure, including administrative proceeding, arbitration, or the like, in accordance with this Article.

(4) Except as otherwise provided in Section 1–106(1) or this Article or the lease agreement, the rights and remedies referred to in subsections (2) and (3) are cumulative.

(5) If the lease agreement covers both real property and goods, the party seeking enforcement may proceed under this Part as to the goods, or under other applicable law as to both the real property and the goods in accordance with that party's rights and remedies in respect of the real property, in which case this Part does not apply. As amended in 1990.

### § 2A–502. Notice After Default.

Except as otherwise provided in this Article or the lease agreement, the lessor or lessee in default under the lease contract is not entitled to notice of default or notice of enforcement from the other party to the lease agreement.

### § 2A–503. Modification or Impairment of Rights and Remedies.

(1) Except as otherwise provided in this Article, the lease agreement may include rights and remedies for default in addition to or in substitution for those provided in this Article and may limit or alter the measure of damages recoverable under this Article.

(2) Resort to a remedy provided under this Article or in the lease agreement is optional unless the remedy is expressly agreed to be exclusive. If circumstances cause an exclusive or limited remedy to fail of its essential purpose, or provision for an exclusive remedy is unconscionable, remedy may be had as provided in this Article.

(3) Consequential damages may be liquidated under Section 2A–504, or may otherwise be limited, altered, or excluded unless the limitation, alteration, or exclusion is unconscionable. Limitation, alteration, or exclusion of consequential damages for injury to the person in the case of consumer goods is prima facie unconscionable but limitation, alteration, or exclusion of damages where the loss is commercial is not prima facie unconscionable.

(4) Rights and remedies on default by the lessor or the lessee with respect to any obligation or promise collateral or ancillary to the lease contract are not impaired by this Article. As amended in 1990.

### § 2A–504. Liquidation of Damages.

(1) Damages payable by either party for default, or any other act or omission, including indemnity for loss or diminution of anticipated tax benefits or loss or damage to lessor's residual interest, may be liquidated in the lease agreement but only at an amount or by a formula that is reasonable in light of the then anticipated harm caused by the default or other act or omission.

(2) If the lease agreement provides for liquidation of damages, and such provision does not comply with subsection (1), or such provision is an exclusive or limited remedy that circumstances cause to fail of its essential purpose, remedy may be had as provided in this Article.

(3) If the lessor justifiably withholds or stops delivery of goods because of the lessee's default or insolvency (Section 2A–525 or 2A–526), the lessee is entitled to restitution of any amount by which the sum of his [or her] payments exceeds:

   (a) the amount to which the lessor is entitled by virtue of terms liquidating the lessor's damages in accordance with subsection (1); or

   (b) in the absence of those terms, 20 percent of the then present value of the total rent the lessee was obligated to pay for the balance of the lease term, or, in the case of a consumer lease, the lesser of such amount or $500.

(4) A lessee's right to restitution under subsection (3) is subject to offset to the extent the lessor establishes:

   (a) a right to recover damages under the provisions of this Article other than subsection (1); and

   (b) the amount or value of any benefits received by the lessee directly or indirectly by reason of the lease contract.

### § 2A–505. Cancellation and Termination and Effect of Cancellation, Termination, Rescission, or Fraud on Rights and Remedies.

(1) On cancellation of the lease contract, all obligations that are still executory on both sides are discharged, but any right based on prior default or performance survives, and the cancelling party also retains any remedy for default of the whole lease contract or any unperformed balance.

(2) On termination of the lease contract, all obligations that are still executory on both sides are discharged but any right based on prior default or performance survives.

(3) Unless the contrary intention clearly appears, expressions of "cancellation," "rescission," or the like of the lease contract may not be construed as a renunciation or discharge of any claim in damages for an antecedent default.

(4) Rights and remedies for material misrepresentation or fraud include all rights and remedies available under this Article for default.

(5) Neither rescission nor a claim for rescission of the lease contract nor rejection or return of the goods may bar or be deemed inconsistent with a claim for damages or other right or remedy.

### § 2A–506. Statute of Limitations.

(1) An action for default under a lease contract, including breach of warranty or indemnity, must be commenced within 4 years after the cause of action accrued. By the original lease contract the parties may reduce the period of limitation to not less than one year.

(2) A cause of action for default accrues when the act or omission on which the default or breach of warranty is based is or should have been discovered by the aggrieved party, or when the default occurs, whichever is later. A cause of action for indemnity accrues when the act or omission on which the claim for indemnity is based is or should have been discovered by the indemnified party, whichever is later.

(3) If an action commenced within the time limited by subsection (1) is so terminated as to leave available a remedy by another action for the same default or breach of warranty or indemnity, the other action may be commenced after the expiration of the time limited and within 6 months after the termination of the first action unless the termination resulted from voluntary discontinuance or from dismissal for failure or neglect to prosecute.

(4) This section does not alter the law on tolling of the statute of limitations nor does it apply to causes of action that have accrued before this Article becomes effective.

### § 2A–507.  Proof of Market Rent: Time and Place.

(1) Damages based on market rent (Section 2A–519 or 2A–528) are determined according to the rent for the use of the goods concerned for a lease term identical to the remaining lease term of the original lease agreement and prevailing at the times specified in Sections 2A–519 and 2A–528.

(2) If evidence of rent for the use of the goods concerned for a lease term identical to the remaining lease term of the original lease agreement and prevailing at the times or places described in this Article is not readily available, the rent prevailing within any reasonable time before or after the time described or at any other place or for a different lease term which in commercial judgment or under usage of trade would serve as a reasonable substitute for the one described may be used, making any proper allowance for the difference, including the cost of transporting the goods to or from the other place.

(3) Evidence of a relevant rent prevailing at a time or place or for a lease term other than the one described in this Article offered by one party is not admissible unless and until he [or she] has given the other party notice the court finds sufficient to prevent unfair surprise.

(4) If the prevailing rent or value of any goods regularly leased in any established market is in issue, reports in official publications or trade journals or in newspapers or periodicals of general circulation published as the reports of that market are admissible in evidence. The circumstances of the preparation of the report may be shown to affect its weight but not its admissibility.
As amended in 1990.

### B.  Default by Lessor

### § 2A–508.  Lessee's Remedies.

(1) If a lessor fails to deliver the goods in conformity to the lease contract (Section 2A–509) or repudiates the lease contract (Section 2A–402), or a lessee rightfully rejects the goods (Section 2A–509) or justifiably revokes acceptance of the goods (Section 2A–517), then with respect to any goods involved, and with respect to all of the goods if under an installment lease contract the value of the whole lease contract is substantially impaired (Section 2A–510), the lessor is in default under the lease contract and the lessee may:

    (a) cancel the lease contract (Section 2A–505(1));

    (b) recover so much of the rent and security as has been paid and is just under the circumstances;

    (c) cover and recover damages as to all goods affected whether or not they have been identified to the lease contract (Sections 2A–518 and 2A–520), or recover damages for nondelivery (Sections 2A–519 and 2A–520);

    (d) exercise any other rights or pursue any other remedies provided in the lease contract.

(2) If a lessor fails to deliver the goods in conformity to the lease contract or repudiates the lease contract, the lessee may also:

    (a) if the goods have been identified, recover them (Section 2A–522); or

    (b) in a proper case, obtain specific performance or replevy the goods (Section 2A–521).

(3) If a lessor is otherwise in default under a lease contract, the lessee may exercise the rights and pursue the remedies provided in the lease contract, which may include a right to cancel the lease, and in Section 2A–519(3).

(4) If a lessor has breached a warranty, whether express or implied, the lessee may recover damages (Section 2A–519(4)).

(5) On rightful rejection or justifiable revocation of acceptance, a lessee has a security interest in goods in the lessee's possession or control for any rent and security that has been paid and any expenses reasonably incurred in their inspection, receipt, transportation, and care and custody and may hold those goods and dispose of them in good faith and in a commercially reasonable manner, subject to Section 2A–527(5).

(6) Subject to the provisions of Section 2A–407, a lessee, on notifying the lessor of the lessee's intention to do so, may deduct all or any part of the damages resulting from any default under the lease contract from any part of the rent still due under the same lease contract.
As amended in 1990.

### § 2A–509.  Lessee's Rights on Improper Delivery; Rightful Rejection.

(1) Subject to the provisions of Section 2A–510 on default in installment lease contracts, if the goods or the tender or delivery fail in any respect to conform to the lease contract, the lessee may reject or accept the goods or accept any commercial unit or units and reject the rest of the goods.

(2) Rejection of goods is ineffective unless it is within a reasonable time after tender or delivery of the goods and the lessee seasonably notifies the lessor.

### § 2A–510.  Installment Lease Contracts: Rejection and Default.

(1) Under an installment lease contract a lessee may reject any delivery that is nonconforming if the nonconformity substantially impairs the value of that delivery and cannot be cured or the nonconformity is a defect in the required documents; but if the nonconformity does not fall within subsection (2) and the lessor or the supplier gives adequate assurance of its cure, the lessee must accept that delivery.

(2) Whenever nonconformity or default with respect to one or more deliveries substantially impairs the value of the installment lease contract as a whole there is a default with respect to the whole. But, the aggrieved party reinstates the installment lease contract as a whole if the aggrieved party accepts a nonconforming delivery without seasonably notifying of cancellation or brings an action with respect only to past deliveries or demands performance as to future deliveries.

### § 2A–511.  Merchant Lessee's Duties as to Rightfully Rejected Goods.

(1) Subject to any security interest of a lessee (Section 2A–508(5)), if a lessor or a supplier has no agent or place of business at the market of rejection, a merchant lessee, after rejection of goods in his [or her] possession or control, shall follow any reasonable instructions received from the lessor or the supplier with respect to the goods. In the absence of those instructions, a merchant lessee shall make reasonable efforts to sell, lease, or otherwise dispose of the goods for the lessor's account if they threaten to decline in value speedily. Instructions are not reasonable if on demand indemnity for expenses is not forthcoming.

(2) If a merchant lessee (subsection (1)) or any other lessee (Section 2A–512) disposes of goods, he [or she] is entitled to reimbursement either from the lessor or the supplier or out of the proceeds for reasonable expenses of caring for and disposing of the goods and, if the expenses include no disposition commission, to such commission as is usual in the trade, or if there is none, to a reasonable sum not exceeding 10 percent of the gross proceeds.

(3) In complying with this section or Section 2A–512, the lessee is held only to good faith. Good faith conduct hereunder is neither acceptance or conversion nor the basis of an action for damages.

(4) A purchaser who purchases in good faith from a lessee pursuant to this section or Section 2A–512 takes the goods free of any rights of the lessor and the supplier even though the lessee fails to comply with one or more of the requirements of this Article.

### § 2A–512. Lessee's Duties as to Rightfully Rejected Goods.

(1) Except as otherwise provided with respect to goods that threaten to decline in value speedily (Section 2A–511) and subject to any security interest of a lessee (Section 2A–508(5)):

    (a) the lessee, after rejection of goods in the lessee's possession, shall hold them with reasonable care at the lessor's or the supplier's disposition for a reasonable time after the lessee's seasonable notification of rejection;

    (b) if the lessor or the supplier gives no instructions within a reasonable time after notification of rejection, the lessee may store the rejected goods for the lessor's or the supplier's account or ship them to the lessor or the supplier or dispose of them for the lessor's or the supplier's account with reimbursement in the manner provided in Section 2A–511; but

    (c) the lessee has no further obligations with regard to goods rightfully rejected.

(2) Action by the lessee pursuant to subsection (1) is not acceptance or conversion.

### § 2A–513. Cure by Lessor of Improper Tender or Delivery; Replacement.

(1) If any tender or delivery by the lessor or the supplier is rejected because nonconforming and the time for performance has not yet expired, the lessor or the supplier may seasonably notify the lessee of the lessor's or the supplier's intention to cure and may then make a conforming delivery within the time provided in the lease contract.

(2) If the lessee rejects a nonconforming tender that the lessor or the supplier had reasonable grounds to believe would be acceptable with or without money allowance, the lessor or the supplier may have a further reasonable time to substitute a conforming tender if he [or she] seasonably notifies the lessee.

### § 2A–514. Waiver of Lessee's Objections.

(1) In rejecting goods, a lessee's failure to state a particular defect that is ascertainable by reasonable inspection precludes the lessee from relying on the defect to justify rejection or to establish default:

    (a) if, stated seasonably, the lessor or the supplier could have cured it (Section 2A–513); or

    (b) between merchants if the lessor or the supplier after rejection has made a request in writing for a full and final written statement of all defects on which the lessee proposes to rely.

(2) A lessee's failure to reserve rights when paying rent or other consideration against documents precludes recovery of the payment for defects apparent on the face of the documents.

### § 2A–515. Acceptance of Goods.

(1) Acceptance of goods occurs after the lessee has had a reasonable opportunity to inspect the goods and

    (a) the lessee signifies or acts with respect to the goods in a manner that signifies to the lessor or the supplier that the goods are conforming or that the lessee will take or retain them in spite of their nonconformity; or

    (b) the lessee fails to make an effective rejection of the goods (Section 2A–509(2)).

(2) Acceptance of a part of any commercial unit is acceptance of that entire unit.

### § 2A–516. Effect of Acceptance of Goods; Notice of Default; Burden of Establishing Default After Acceptance; Notice of Claim or Litigation to Person Answerable Over.

(1) A lessee must pay rent for any goods accepted in accordance with the lease contract, with due allowance for goods rightfully rejected or not delivered.

(2) A lessee's acceptance of goods precludes rejection of the goods accepted. In the case of a finance lease, if made with knowledge of a nonconformity, acceptance cannot be revoked because of it. In any other case, if made with knowledge of a nonconformity, acceptance cannot be revoked because of it unless the acceptance was on the reasonable assumption that the nonconformity would be seasonably cured. Acceptance does not of itself impair any other remedy provided by this Article or the lease agreement for nonconformity.

(3) If a tender has been accepted:

    (a) within a reasonable time after the lessee discovers or should have discovered any default, the lessee shall notify the lessor and the supplier, if any, or be barred from any remedy against the party not notified;

    (b) except in the case of a consumer lease, within a reasonable time after the lessee receives notice of litigation for infringement or the like (Section 2A–211) the lessee shall notify the lessor or be barred from any remedy over for liability established by the litigation; and

    (c) the burden is on the lessee to establish any default.

(4) If a lessee is sued for breach of a warranty or other obligation for which a lessor or a supplier is answerable over the following apply:

    (a) The lessee may give the lessor or the supplier, or both, written notice of the litigation. If the notice states that the person notified may come in and defend and that if the person notified does not do so that person will be bound in any action against that person by the lessee by any determination of fact common to the two litigations, then unless the person notified after seasonable receipt of the notice does come in and defend that person is so bound.

    (b) The lessor or the supplier may demand in writing that the lessee turn over control of the litigation including settlement if the claim is one for infringement or the like (Section 2A–211) or else be barred from any remedy over. If the demand states that the lessor or the supplier agrees to bear all expense and to satisfy any adverse judgment, then unless the lessee after seasonable receipt of the demand does turn over control the lessee is so barred.

(5) Subsections (3) and (4) apply to any obligation of a lessee to hold the lessor or the supplier harmless against infringement or the like (Section 2A–211).

As amended in 1990.

### § 2A–517. Revocation of Acceptance of Goods.

(1) A lessee may revoke acceptance of a lot or commercial unit whose nonconformity substantially impairs its value to the lessee if the lessee has accepted it:

    (a) except in the case of a finance lease, on the reasonable assumption that its nonconformity would be cured and it has not been seasonably cured; or

    (b) without discovery of the nonconformity if the lessee's acceptance was reasonably induced either by the lessor's assurances or, except in the case of a finance lease, by the difficulty of discovery before acceptance.

(2) Except in the case of a finance lease that is not a consumer lease, a lessee may revoke acceptance of a lot or commercial unit if the lessor defaults under the lease contract and the default substantially impairs the value of that lot or commercial unit to the lessee.

(3) If the lease agreement so provides, the lessee may revoke acceptance of a lot or commercial unit because of other defaults by the lessor.

(4) Revocation of acceptance must occur within a reasonable time after the lessee discovers or should have discovered the ground for it and before any substantial change in condition of the goods which is not caused by the nonconformity. Revocation is not effective until the lessee notifies the lessor.

(5) A lessee who so revokes has the same rights and duties with regard to the goods involved as if the lessee had rejected them.
As amended in 1990.

## § 2A–518.  Cover; Substitute Goods.

(1) After a default by a lessor under the lease contract of the type described in Section 2A–508(1), or, if agreed, after other default by the lessor, the lessee may cover by making any purchase or lease of or contract to purchase or lease goods in substitution for those due from the lessor.

(2) Except as otherwise provided with respect to damages liquidated in the lease agreement (Section 2A–504) or otherwise determined pursuant to agreement of the parties (Sections 1–102(3) and 2A–503), if a lessee's cover is by a lease agreement substantially similar to the original lease agreement and the new lease agreement is made in good faith and in a commercially reasonable manner, the lessee may recover from the lessor as damages (i) the present value, as of the date of the commencement of the term of the new lease agreement, of the rent under the new lease agreement applicable to that period of the new lease term which is comparable to the then remaining term of the original lease agreement minus the present value as of the same date of the total rent for the then remaining lease term of the original lease agreement, and (ii) any incidental or consequential damages, less expenses saved in consequence of the lessor's default.

(3) If a lessee's cover is by lease agreement that for any reason does not qualify for treatment under subsection (2), or is by purchase or otherwise, the lessee may recover from the lessor as if the lessee had elected not to cover and Section 2A–519 governs.
As amended in 1990.

## § 2A–519.  Lessee's Damages for Non-delivery, Repudiation, Default, and Breach of Warranty in Regard to Accepted Goods.

(1) Except as otherwise provided with respect to damages liquidated in the lease agreement (Section 2A–504) or otherwise determined pursuant to agreement of the parties (Sections 1–102(3) and 2A–503), if a lessee elects not to cover or a lessee elects to cover and the cover is by lease agreement that for any reason does not qualify for treatment under Section 2A–518(2), or is by purchase or otherwise, the measure of damages for non-delivery or repudiation by the lessor or for rejection or revocation of acceptance by the lessee is the present value, as of the date of the default, of the then market rent minus the present value as of the same date of the original rent, computed for the remaining lease term of the original lease agreement, together with incidental and consequential damages, less expenses saved in consequence of the lessor's default.

(2) Market rent is to be determined as of the place for tender or, in cases of rejection after arrival or revocation of acceptance, as of the place of arrival.

(3) Except as otherwise agreed, if the lessee has accepted goods and given notification (Section 2A–516(3)), the measure of damages for non-conforming tender or delivery or other default by a lessor is the loss resulting in the ordinary course of events from the lessor's default as determined in any manner that is reasonable together with incidental and consequential damages, less expenses saved in consequence of the lessor's default.

(4) Except as otherwise agreed, the measure of damages for breach of warranty is the present value at the time and place of acceptance of the difference between the value of the use of the goods accepted and the value if they had been as warranted for the lease term, unless special circumstances show proximate damages of a different amount, together with incidental and consequential damages, less expenses saved in consequence of the lessor's default or breach of warranty.
As amended in 1990.

## § 2A–520.  Lessee's Incidental and Consequential Damages.

(1) Incidental damages resulting from a lessor's default include expenses reasonably incurred in inspection, receipt, transportation, and care and custody of goods rightfully rejected or goods the acceptance of which is justifiably revoked, any commercially reasonable charges, expenses or commissions in connection with effecting cover, and any other reasonable expense incident to the default.

(2) Consequential damages resulting from a lessor's default include:
   (a) any loss resulting from general or particular requirements and needs of which the lessor at the time of contracting had reason to know and which could not reasonably be prevented by cover or otherwise; and
   (b) injury to person or property proximately resulting from any breach of warranty.

## § 2A–521.  Lessee's Right to Specific Performance or Replevin.

(1) Specific performance may be decreed if the goods are unique or in other proper circumstances.

(2) A decree for specific performance may include any terms and conditions as to payment of the rent, damages, or other relief that the court deems just.

(3) A lessee has a right of replevin, detinue, sequestration, claim and delivery, or the like for goods identified to the lease contract if after reasonable effort the lessee is unable to effect cover for those goods or the circumstances reasonably indicate that the effort will be unavailing.

## § 2A–522.  Lessee's Right to Goods on Lessor's Insolvency.

(1) Subject to subsection (2) and even though the goods have not been shipped, a lessee who has paid a part or all of the rent and security for goods identified to a lease contract (Section 2A–217) on making and keeping good a tender of any unpaid portion of the rent and security due under the lease contract may recover the goods identified from the lessor if the lessor becomes insolvent within 10 days after receipt of the first installment of rent and security.

(2) A lessee acquires the right to recover goods identified to a lease contract only if they conform to the lease contract.

## C.  Default by Lessee

## § 2A–523.  Lessor's Remedies.

(1) If a lessee wrongfully rejects or revokes acceptance of goods or fails to make a payment when due or repudiates with respect to a part or the whole, then, with respect to any goods involved, and with respect to all of the goods if under an installment lease contract the value of the whole lease contract is substantially impaired (Section 2A–510), the lessee is in default under the lease contract and the lessor may:

(a) cancel the lease contract (Section 2A–505(1));

(b) proceed respecting goods not identified to the lease contract (Section 2A–524);

(c) withhold delivery of the goods and take possession of goods previously delivered (Section 2A–525);

(d) stop delivery of the goods by any bailee (Section 2A–526);

(e) dispose of the goods and recover damages (Section 2A–527), or retain the goods and recover damages (Section 2A–528), or in a proper case recover rent (Section 2A–529);

(f) exercise any other rights or pursue any other remedies provided in the lease contract.

(2) If a lessor does not fully exercise a right or obtain a remedy to which the lessor is entitled under subsection (1), the lessor may recover the loss resulting in the ordinary course of events from the lessee's default as determined in any reasonable manner, together with incidental damages, less expenses saved in consequence of the lessee's default.

(3) If a lessee is otherwise in default under a lease contract, the lessor may exercise the rights and pursue the remedies provided in the lease contract, which may include a right to cancel the lease. In addition, unless otherwise provided in the lease contract:

(a) if the default substantially impairs the value of the lease contract to the lessor, the lessor may exercise the rights and pursue the remedies provided in subsections (1) or (2); or

(b) if the default does not substantially impair the value of the lease contract to the lessor, the lessor may recover as provided in subsection (2).

As amended in 1990.

## § 2A–524. Lessor's Right to Identify Goods to Lease Contract.

(1) After default by the lessee under the lease contract of the type described in Section 2A–523(1) or 2A–523(3)(a) or, if agreed, after other default by the lessee, the lessor may:

(a) identify to the lease contract conforming goods not already identified if at the time the lessor learned of the default they were in the lessor's or the supplier's possession or control; and

(b) dispose of goods (Section 2A–527(1)) that demonstrably have been intended for the particular lease contract even though those goods are unfinished.

(2) If the goods are unfinished, in the exercise of reasonable commercial judgment for the purposes of avoiding loss and of effective realization, an aggrieved lessor or the supplier may either complete manufacture and wholly identify the goods to the lease contract or cease manufacture and lease, sell, or otherwise dispose of the goods for scrap or salvage value or proceed in any other reasonable manner.

As amended in 1990.

## § 2A–525. Lessor's Right to Possession of Goods.

(1) If a lessor discovers the lessee to be insolvent, the lessor may refuse to deliver the goods.

(2) After a default by the lessee under the lease contract of the type described in Section 2A–523(1) or 2A–523(3)(a) or, if agreed, after other default by the lessee, the lessor has the right to take possession of the goods. If the lease contract so provides, the lessor may require the lessee to assemble the goods and make them available to the lessor at a place to be designated by the lessor which is reasonably convenient to both parties. Without removal, the lessor may render unusable any goods employed in trade or business, and may dispose of goods on the lessee's premises (Section 2A–527).

(3) The lessor may proceed under subsection (2) without judicial process if it can be done without breach of the peace or the lessor may proceed by action.

As amended in 1990.

## § 2A–526. Lessor's Stoppage of Delivery in Transit or Otherwise.

(1) A lessor may stop delivery of goods in the possession of a carrier or other bailee if the lessor discovers the lessee to be insolvent and may stop delivery of carload, truckload, planeload, or larger shipments of express or freight if the lessee repudiates or fails to make a payment due before delivery, whether for rent, security or otherwise under the lease contract, or for any other reason the lessor has a right to withhold or take possession of the goods.

(2) In pursuing its remedies under subsection (1), the lessor may stop delivery until

(a) receipt of the goods by the lessee;

(b) acknowledgment to the lessee by any bailee of the goods, except a carrier, that the bailee holds the goods for the lessee; or

(c) such an acknowledgment to the lessee by a carrier via reshipment or as warehouseman.

(3) (a) To stop delivery, a lessor shall so notify as to enable the bailee by reasonable diligence to prevent delivery of the goods.

(b) After notification, the bailee shall hold and deliver the goods according to the directions of the lessor, but the lessor is liable to the bailee for any ensuing charges or damages.

(c) A carrier who has issued a nonnegotiable bill of lading is not obliged to obey a notification to stop received from a person other than the consignor.

## § 2A–527. Lessor's Rights to Dispose of Goods.

(1) After a default by a lessee under the lease contract of the type described in Section 2A–523(1) or 2A–523(3)(a) or after the lessor refuses to deliver or takes possession of goods (Section 2A–525 or 2A–526), or, if agreed, after other default by a lessee, the lessor may dispose of the goods concerned or the undelivered balance thereof by lease, sale, or otherwise.

(2) Except as otherwise provided with respect to damages liquidated in the lease agreement (Section 2A–504) or otherwise determined pursuant to agreement of the parties (Sections 1–102(3) and 2A–503), if the disposition is by lease agreement substantially similar to the original lease agreement and the new lease agreement is made in good faith and in a commercially reasonable manner, the lessor may recover from the lessee as damages (i) accrued and unpaid rent as of the date of the commencement of the term of the new lease agreement, (ii) the present value, as of the same date, of the total rent for the then remaining lease term of the original lease agreement minus the present value, as of the same date, of the rent under the new lease agreement applicable to that period of the new lease term which is comparable to the then remaining term of the original lease agreement, and (iii) any incidental damages allowed under Section 2A–530, less expenses saved in consequence of the lessee's default.

(3) If the lessor's disposition is by lease agreement that for any reason does not qualify for treatment under subsection (2), or is by sale or otherwise, the lessor may recover from the lessee as if the lessor had elected not to dispose of the goods and Section 2A–528 governs.

(4) A subsequent buyer or lessee who buys or leases from the lessor in good faith for value as a result of a disposition under this section takes the goods free of the original lease contract and any rights of the original lessee even though the lessor fails to comply with one or more of the requirements of this Article.

(5) The lessor is not accountable to the lessee for any profit made on any disposition. A lessee who has rightfully rejected or justifiably revoked acceptance shall account to the lessor for any excess over the amount of the lessee's security interest (Section 2A–508(5)).
As amended in 1990.

## § 2A–528.  Lessor's Damages for Non-acceptance, Failure to Pay, Repudiation, or Other Default.

(1) Except as otherwise provided with respect to damages liquidated in the lease agreement (Section 2A–504) or otherwise determined pursuant to agreement of the parties (Sections 1–102(3) and 2A–503), if a lessor elects to retain the goods or a lessor elects to dispose of the goods and the disposition is by lease agreement that for any reason does not qualify for treatment under Section 2A–527(2), or is by sale or otherwise, the lessor may recover from the lessee as damages for a default of the type described in Section 2A–523(1) or 2A–523(3)(a), or, if agreed, for other default of the lessee, (i) accrued and unpaid rent as of the date of default if the lessee has never taken possession of the goods, or, if the lessee has taken possession of the goods, as of the date the lessor repossesses the goods or an earlier date on which the lessee makes a tender of the goods to the lessor, (ii) the present value as of the date determined under clause (i) of the total rent for the then remaining lease term of the original lease agreement minus the present value as of the same date of the market rent at the place where the goods are located computed for the same lease term, and (iii) any incidental damages allowed under Section 2A–530, less expenses saved in consequence of the lessee's default.

(2) If the measure of damages provided in subsection (1) is inadequate to put a lessor in as good a position as performance would have, the measure of damages is the present value of the profit, including reasonable overhead, the lessor would have made from full performance by the lessee, together with any incidental damages allowed under Section 2A–530, due allowance for costs reasonably incurred and due credit for payments or proceeds of disposition.
As amended in 1990.

## § 2A–529.  Lessor's Action for the Rent.

(1) After default by the lessee under the lease contract of the type described in Section 2A–523(1) or 2A–523(3)(a) or, if agreed, after other default by the lessee, if the lessor complies with subsection (2), the lessor may recover from the lessee as damages:

   (a) for goods accepted by the lessee and not repossessed by or tendered to the lessor, and for conforming goods lost or damaged within a commercially reasonable time after risk of loss passes to the lessee (Section 2A–219), (i) accrued and unpaid rent as of the date of entry of judgment in favor of the lessor, (ii) the present value as of the same date of the rent for the then remaining lease term of the lease agreement, and (iii) any incidental damages allowed under Section 2A–530, less expenses saved in consequence of the lessee's default; and

   (b) for goods identified to the lease contract if the lessor is unable after reasonable effort to dispose of them at a reasonable price or the circumstances reasonably indicate that effort will be unavailing, (i) accrued and unpaid rent as of the date of entry of judgment in favor of the lessor, (ii) the present value as of the same date of the rent for the then remaining lease term of the lease agreement, and (iii) any incidental damages allowed under Section 2A–530, less expenses saved in consequence of the lessee's default.

(2) Except as provided in subsection (3), the lessor shall hold for the lessee for the remaining lease term of the lease agreement any goods that have been identified to the lease contract and are in the lessor's control.

(3) The lessor may dispose of the goods at any time before collection of the judgment for damages obtained pursuant to subsection (1). If the disposition is before the end of the remaining lease term of the lease agreement, the lessor's recovery against the lessee for damages is governed by Section 2A–527 or Section 2A–528, and the lessor will cause an appropriate credit to be provided against a judgment for damages to the extent that the amount of the judgment exceeds the recovery available pursuant to Section 2A–527 or 2A–528.

(4) Payment of the judgment for damages obtained pursuant to subsection (1) entitles the lessee to the use and possession of the goods not then disposed of for the remaining lease term of and in accordance with the lease agreement.

(5) After default by the lessee under the lease contract of the type described in Section 2A–523(1) or Section 2A–523(3)(a) or, if agreed, after other default by the lessee, a lessor who is held not entitled to rent under this section must nevertheless be awarded damages for non-acceptance under Section 2A–527 or Section 2A–528.
As amended in 1990.

## § 2A–530.  Lessor's Incidental Damages.

Incidental damages to an aggrieved lessor include any commercially reasonable charges, expenses, or commissions incurred in stopping delivery, in the transportation, care and custody of goods after the lessee's default, in connection with return or disposition of the goods, or otherwise resulting from the default.

## § 2A–531.  Standing to Sue Third Parties for Injury to Goods.

(1) If a third party so deals with goods that have been identified to a lease contract as to cause actionable injury to a party to the lease contract (a) the lessor has a right of action against the third party, and (b) the lessee also has a right of action against the third party if the lessee:

   (i) has a security interest in the goods;
   (ii) has an insurable interest in the goods; or
   (iii) bears the risk of loss under the lease contract or has since the injury assumed that risk as against the lessor and the goods have been converted or destroyed.

(2) If at the time of the injury the party plaintiff did not bear the risk of loss as against the other party to the lease contract and there is no arrangement between them for disposition of the recovery, his [or her] suit or settlement, subject to his [or her] own interest, is as a fiduciary for the other party to the lease contract.

(3) Either party with the consent of the other may sue for the benefit of whom it may concern.

## § 2A–532.  Lessor's Rights to Residual Interest.

In addition to any other recovery permitted by this Article or other law, the lessor may recover from the lessee an amount that will fully compensate the lessor for any loss of or damage to the lessor's residual interest in the goods caused by the default of the lessee.
As added in 1990.

# ARTICLE 3: NEGOTIABLE INSTRUMENTS

## Part 1—General Provisions and Definitions

### § 3–101.  Short Title.

This Article may be cited as Uniform Commercial Code—Negotiable Instruments.

## § 3–102. Subject Matter.

(a)  This Article applies to negotiable instruments. It does not apply to money or to payment orders governed by Article 4A. A negotiable instrument that is also a certificated security under Section 8–102(1)(a) is subject to Article 8 and to this Article.

(b)  In the event of conflict between the provisions of this Article and those of Article 4, Article 8, or Article 9, the provisions of Article 4, Article 8 and Article 9 prevail over those of this Article.

(c)  Regulations of the Board of Governors of the Federal Reserve System and operating circulars of the Federal Reserve Banks supersede any inconsistent provision of this Article to the extent of the inconsistency.

## § 3–103. Definitions.

(a)  In this Article:

(1)  "Acceptor" means a drawee that has accepted a draft.

(2)  "Drawee" means a person ordered in a draft to make payment.

(3)  "Drawer" means a person that signs a draft as a person ordering payment.

(4)  "Good faith" means honesty in fact and the observance of reasonable commercial standards of fair dealing.

(5)  "Maker" means a person that signs a note as promisor of payment.

(6)  "Order" means a written instruction to pay money signed by the person giving the instruction. The instruction may be addressed to any person, including the person giving the instruction, or to one or more persons jointly or in the alternative but not in succession. An authorization to pay is not an order unless the person authorized to pay is also instructed to pay.

(7)  "Ordinary care" in the case of a person engaged in business means observance of reasonable commercial standards, prevailing in the area in which that person is located, with respect to the business in which that person is engaged. In the case of a bank that takes an instrument for processing for collection or payment by automated means, reasonable commercial standards do not require the bank to examine the instrument if the failure to examine does not violate the bank's prescribed procedures and the bank's procedures do not vary unreasonably from general banking usage not disapproved by this Article or Article 4.

(8)  "Party" means party to an instrument.

(9)  "Promise" means a written undertaking to pay money signed by the person undertaking to pay. An acknowledgment of an obligation by the obligor is not a promise unless the obligor also undertakes to pay the obligation.

(10)  "Prove" with respect to a fact means to meet the burden of establishing the fact (Section 1–201(8)).

(11)  "Remitter" means a person that purchases an instrument from its issuer if the instrument is payable to an identified person other than the purchaser.

(b)  Other definitions applying to this Article and the sections in which they appear are:

"Acceptance" Section 3–409.
"Accommodated party" Section 3–419.
"Accommodation indorsement" Section 3–205.
"Accommodation party" Section 3–419.
"Alteration" Section 3–407.
"Blank indorsement" Section 3–205.
"Cashier's check" Section 3–104.
"Certificate of deposit" Section 3–104.
"Certified check" Section 3–409.

"Check" Section 3–104.
"Consideration" Section 3–303.
"Draft" Section 3–104.
"Fiduciary" Section 3–307.
"Guarantor" Section 3–417.
"Holder in due course" Section 3–302.
"Incomplete instrument" Section 3–115.
"Indorsement" Section 3–204.
"Indorser" Section 3–204.
"Instrument" Section 3–104.
"Issue" Section 3–105.
"Issuer" Section 3–105.
"Negotiable instrument" Section 3–104.
"Negotiation" Section 3–201.
"Note" Section 3–104.
"Payable at a definite time" Section 3–108.
"Payable on demand" Section 3–108.
"Payable to bearer" Section 3–109.
"Payable to order" Section 3–110.
"Payment" Section 3–603.
"Person entitled to enforce" Section 3–301.
"Presentment" Section 3–501.
"Reacquisition" Section 3–207.
"Represented person" Section 3–307.
"Special indorsement" Section 3–205.
"Teller's check" Section 3–104.
"Traveler's check" Section 3–104.
"Value" Section 3–303.

(c)  The following definitions in other Articles apply to this Article:

"Bank" Section 4–105.
"Banking day" Section 4–104.
"Clearing house" Section 4–104.
"Collecting bank" Section 4–105.
"Customer" Section 4–104.
"Depositary bank" Section 4–105.
"Documentary draft" Section 4–104.
"Intermediary bank" Section 4–105.
"Item" Section 4–104.
"Midnight deadline" Section 4–104.
"Payor bank" Section 4–105.
"Suspends payments" Section 4–104.

(d)  In addition, Article 1 contains general definitions and principles of construction and interpretation applicable throughout this Article.

## § 3–104. Negotiable Instrument.

(a)  "Negotiable instrument" means an unconditional promise or order to pay a fixed amount of money, with or without interest or other charges described in the promise or order, if it:

(1)  is payable to bearer or to order at the time it is issued or first comes into possession of a holder;

(2)  is payable on demand or at a definite time; and

(3)  does not state any other undertaking or instruction by the person promising or ordering payment to do any act in addition to the payment of money except that the promise or order may contain (i) an undertaking or power to give, maintain, or protect collateral to secure payment, (ii) an authorization or power to the holder to confess judgment or realize on or dispose of collateral, or (iii) a waiver of the benefit of any law intended for the advantage or protection of any obligor.

(b) "Instrument" means negotiable instrument.

(c) An order that meets all of the requirements of subsection (a) except subparagraph (1) and otherwise falls within the definition of "check" in subsection (f) is a negotiable instrument and a check.

(d) Notwithstanding subsection (a), a promise or order other than a check is not an instrument if, at the time it is issued or first comes into possession of a holder, it contains a conspicuous statement, however expressed, indicating that the writing is not an instrument governed by this Article.

(e) An instrument is a "note" if it is a promise, and is a "draft" if it is an order. If an instrument falls within the definition of both "note" and "draft," the person entitled to enforce the instrument may treat it as either.

(f) "Check" means (i) a draft, other than a documentary draft, payable on demand and drawn on a bank or (ii) a cashier's check or teller's check. An instrument may be a check even though it is described on its face by another term such as "money order."

(g) "Cashier's check" means a draft with respect to which the drawer and drawee are the same bank or branches of the same bank.

(h) "Teller's check" means a draft drawn by a bank (i) on another bank, or (ii) payable at or through a bank.

(i) "Traveler's check" means an instrument that (i) is payable on demand, (ii) is drawn on or payable at or through a bank, (iii) is designated by the term "traveler's check" or by a substantially similar term, and (iv) requires, as a condition to payment, a countersignature by a person whose specimen signature appears on the instrument.

(j) "Certificate of deposit" means an instrument containing an acknowledgment by a bank that a sum of money has been received by the bank, and a promise by the bank to repay the sum of money. A certificate of deposit is a note of the bank.

## § 3–105.  Issue of Instrument.

(a) "Issue" means the first delivery of an instrument by the maker or drawer, whether to a holder or nonholder, for the purpose of giving rights on the instrument to any person.

(b) An unissued instrument, or an unissued incomplete instrument (Section 3–115) that is completed, is binding on the maker or drawer, but nonissuance is a defense. An instrument that is conditionally issued or is issued for a special purpose is binding on the maker or drawer, but failure of the condition or special purpose to be fulfilled is a defense.

(c) "Issuer" applies to issued and unissued instruments and means any person that signs an instrument as maker or drawer.

## § 3–106.  Unconditional Promise or Order.

(a) Except as provided in subsections (b) and (c), for the purposes of Section 3–104(a), a promise or order is unconditional unless it states (i) an express condition to payment or (ii) that the promise or order is subject to or governed by another writing, or that rights or obligations with respect to the promise or order are stated in another writing; however, a mere reference to another writing does not make the promise or order conditional.

(b) A promise or order is not made conditional (i) by a reference to another writing for a statement of rights with respect to collateral, prepayment, or acceleration, or (ii) because payment is limited to resort to a particular fund or source.

(c) If a promise or order requires, as a condition to payment, a countersignature by a person whose specimen signature appears on the promise or order, the condition does not make the promise or order conditional for the purposes of Section 3–104(a). If the person whose specimen signature appears on an instrument fails to countersign the instrument, the failure to countersign is a defense to the obligation of the issuer, but the failure does not prevent a transferee of the instrument from becoming a holder of the instrument.

(d) If a promise or order at the time it is issued or first comes into possession of a holder contains a statement, required by applicable statutory or administrative law, to the effect that the rights of a holder or transferee are subject to claims or defenses that the issuer could assert against the original payee, the promise or order is not thereby made conditional for the purposes of Section 3–104(a), but there cannot be a holder in due course of the promise or order.

## § 3–107.  Instrument Payable in Foreign Money.

Unless the instrument otherwise provides, an instrument that states the amount payable in foreign money may be paid in the foreign money or in an equivalent amount in dollars calculated by using the current bank-offered spot rate at the place of payment for the purchase of dollars on the day on which the instrument is paid.

## § 3–108.  Payable on Demand or at a Definite Time.

(a) A promise or order is "payable on demand" if (i) it states that it is payable on demand or at sight, or otherwise indicates that it is payable at the will of the holder, or (ii) it does not state any time of payment.

(b) A promise or order is "payable at a definite time" if it is payable on elapse of a definite period of time after sight or acceptance or at a fixed date or dates or at a time or times readily ascertainable at the time the promise or order is issued, subject to rights of (i) prepayment, (ii) acceleration, or (iii) extension at the option of the holder or (iv) extension to a further definite time at the option of the maker or acceptor or automatically upon or after a specified act or event.

(c) If an instrument, payable at a fixed date, is also payable upon demand made before the fixed date, the instrument is payable on demand until the fixed date and, if demand for payment is not made before that date, becomes payable at a definite time on the fixed date.

## § 3–109.  Payable to Bearer or to Order.

(a) A promise or order is payable to bearer if it:

(1) states that it is payable to bearer or to the order of bearer or otherwise indicates that the person in possession of the promise or order is entitled to payment,

(2) does not state a payee, or

(3) states that it is payable to or to the order of cash or otherwise indicates that it is not payable to an identified person.

(b) A promise or order that is not payable to bearer is payable to order if it is payable (i) to the order of an identified person or (ii) to an identified person or order. A promise or order that is payable to order is payable to the identified person.

(c) An instrument payable to bearer may become payable to an identified person if it is specially indorsed as stated in Section 3–205(a). An instrument payable to an identified person may become payable to bearer if it is indorsed in blank as stated in Section 3–205(b).

## § 3–110.  Identification of Person to Whom Instrument Is Payable.

(a) A person to whom an instrument is payable is determined by the intent of the person, whether or not authorized, signing as, or in the name or behalf of, the maker or drawer. The instrument is payable to the person intended by the signer even if that person is identified in the instrument by a name or other identification that is not that of the intended person. If more than one person signs in the name or behalf of the maker or drawer and all the signers do not intend the same person as payee, the instrument is payable to any person intended by one or more of the signers.

(b) If the signature of the maker or drawer of an instrument is made by automated means such as a check-writing machine, the payee of the instrument is determined by the intent of the person who supplied the name or identification of the payee, whether or not authorized to do so.

(c) A person to whom an instrument is payable may be identified in any way including by name, identifying number, office, or account number. For the purpose of determining the holder of an instrument, the following rules apply:

(1) If an instrument is payable to an account and the account is identified only by number, the instrument is payable to the person to whom the account is payable. If an instrument is payable to an account identified by number and by the name of a person, the instrument is payable to the named person, whether or not that person is the owner of the account identified by number.

(2) If an instrument is payable to:

(i) a trust, estate, or a person described as trustee or representative of a trust or estate, the instrument is payable to the trustee, the representative, or a successor of either, whether or not the beneficiary or estate is also named;

(ii) a person described as agent or similar representative of a named or identified person, the instrument is payable either to the represented person, the representative, or a successor of the representative;

(iii) a fund or organization that is not a legal entity, the instrument is payable to a representative of the members of the fund or organization; or

(iv) an office or to a person described as holding an office, the instrument is payable to the named person, the incumbent of the office, or a successor to the incumbent.

(d) If an instrument is payable to two or more persons alternatively, it is payable to any of them and may be negotiated, discharged, or enforced by any of them in possession of the instrument. If an instrument is payable to two or more persons not alternatively, it is payable to all of them and may be negotiated, discharged, or enforced only by all of them. If an instrument payable to two or more persons is ambiguous as to whether it is payable to the persons alternatively, the instrument is payable to the persons alternatively.

### § 3–111. Place of Payment.

Except as otherwise provided for items in Article 4, an instrument is payable at the place of payment stated in the instrument. If no place of payment is stated, an instrument is payable at the address of the drawee or maker stated in the instrument. If no address is stated, the place of payment is the place of business of the drawee or maker. If a drawee or maker has more than one place of business, the place of payment is any place of business of the drawee or maker chosen by the person entitled to enforce the instrument. If the drawee or maker has no place of business, the place of payment is the residence of the drawee or maker.

### § 3–112. Interest.

(a) Unless otherwise provided in the instrument, (i) an instrument is not payable with interest, and (ii) interest on an interest-bearing instrument is payable from the date of the instrument.

(b) Interest may be stated in an instrument as a fixed or variable amount of money or it may be expressed as a fixed or variable rate or rates. The amount or rate of interest may be stated or described in the instrument in any manner and may require reference to information not contained in the instrument. If an instrument provides for interest but the amount of interest payable cannot be ascertained from the description, interest is payable at the judgment rate in effect at the place of payment of the instrument and at the time interest first accrues.

### § 3–113. Date of Instrument.

(a) An instrument may be antedated or postdated. The date stated determines the time of payment if the instrument is payable at a fixed period after date. Except as provided in Section 4–401(3), an instrument payable on demand is not payable before the date of the instrument.

(b) If an instrument is undated, its date is the date of its issue or, in the case of an unissued instrument, the date it first comes into possession of a holder.

### § 3–114. Contradictory Terms of Instrument.

If an instrument contains contradictory terms, typewritten terms prevail over printed terms, handwritten terms prevail over both, and words prevail over numbers.

### § 3–115. Incomplete Instrument.

(a) "Incomplete instrument" means a signed writing, whether or not issued by the signer, the contents of which show at the time of signing that it is incomplete but that the signer intended it to be completed by the addition of words or numbers.

(b) Subject to subsection (c), if an incomplete instrument is an instrument under Section 3–104, it may be enforced (i) according to its terms if it is not completed, or (ii) according to its terms as augmented by completion. If an incomplete instrument is not an instrument under Section 3–104 but, after completion, the requirements of Section 3–104 are met, the instrument may be enforced according to its terms as augmented by completion.

(c) If words or numbers are added to an incomplete instrument without authority of the signer, there is an alteration of the incomplete instrument governed by Section 3–407.

(d) The burden of establishing that words or numbers were added to an incomplete instrument without authority of the signer is on the person asserting the lack of authority.

### § 3–116. Joint and Several Liability; Contribution.

(a) Except as otherwise provided in the instrument, two or more persons who have the same liability on an instrument as makers, drawers, acceptors, indorsers who are indorsing joint payees, or anomalous indorsers, are jointly and severally liable in the capacity in which they sign.

(b) Except as provided in Section 3–417(e) or by agreement of the affected parties, a party with joint and several liability that pays the instrument is entitled to receive from any party with the same joint and several liability contribution in accordance with applicable law.

(c) Discharge of one party with joint and several liability by a person entitled to enforce the instrument does not affect the right under subsection (b) of a party with the same joint and several liability to receive contribution from the party discharged.

### § 3–117. Other Agreements Affecting an Instrument.

Subject to applicable law regarding exclusion of proof of contemporaneous or prior agreements, the obligation of a party to an instrument to pay the instrument may be modified, supplemented, or nullified by a separate agreement of the obligor and a person entitled to enforce the instrument if the instrument is issued or the obligation is incurred in reliance on the agreement or as part of the same transaction giving rise to the agreement. To the extent an obligation is modified, supplemented, or nullified by an agreement under this section, the agreement is a defense to the obligation.

## § 3–118.  Statute of Limitations.

(a)  Except as provided in subsection (e), an action to enforce the obligation of a party to pay a note payable at a definite time must be commenced within six years after the payment date or dates stated in the note or, if a payment date is accelerated, within six years after the accelerated payment date.

(b)  Except as provided in subsection (d) or (e), if demand for payment is made to the maker of a note payable on demand, an action to enforce the obligation of a party to pay the note must be commenced within six years after the demand. If no demand for payment is made to the maker, an action to enforce the note is barred if neither principal nor interest on the note has been paid for a continuous period of 10 years.

(c)  Except as provided in subsection (d), an action to enforce the obligation of a party to an unaccepted draft to pay the draft must be commenced within six years after dishonor of the draft or 10 years after the date of the draft, whichever period expires first.

(d)  An action to enforce the obligation of the acceptor of a certified check or the issuer of a teller's check, cashier's check, or traveler's check must be commenced within six years after demand for payment is made to the acceptor or issuer, as the case may be.

(e)  An action to enforce the obligation of a party to a certificate of deposit to pay the instrument must be commenced within six years after demand for payment is made to the maker, but if the instrument states a maturity date and the maker is not required to pay before that date, the six-year period begins when a demand for payment is in effect and the maturity date has passed.

(f)  This subsection applies to an action to enforce the obligation of a party to pay an accepted draft, other than a certified check. If the obligation of the acceptor is payable at a definite time, the action must be commenced within six years after the payment date or dates stated in the draft or acceptance. If the obligation of the acceptor is payable on demand, the action must be commenced within six years after the date of the acceptance.

(g)  Unless governed by other law regarding claims for indemnity or contribution, an action (i) for conversion of an instrument, for money had and received, or like action based on conversion, (ii) for breach of warranty, or (iii) to enforce an obligation, duty, or right arising under this Article and not governed by this section must be commenced within three years after the cause of action accrues.

## § 3–119.  Notice of Right to Defend Action.

In an action for breach of an obligation for which a third person is answerable over pursuant to this Article or Article 4, the defendant may give the third person written notice of the litigation, and the person notified may then give similar notice to any other person who is answerable over. If the notice states (i) that the person notified may come in and defend and (ii) that failure to do so will bind the person notified in an action later brought by the person giving the notice as to any determination of fact common to the two litigations, the person notified is so bound unless after seasonable receipt of the notice the person notified does come in and defend.

## Part 2—Negotiation, Transfer and Indorsement

## § 3–201.  Negotiation.

(a)  "Negotiation" means a transfer of possession, whether voluntary or involuntary, of an instrument to a person who thereby becomes its holder if possession is obtained from a person other than the issuer of the instrument.

(b)  Except for a negotiation by a remitter, if an instrument is payable to an identified person, negotiation requires transfer of possession of the instrument and its indorsement by the holder. If an instrument is payable to bearer, it may be negotiated by transfer of possession alone.

## § 3–202.  Negotiation Subject to Rescission.

(a)  Negotiation is effective even if obtained (i) from an infant, a corporation exceeding its powers, or a person without capacity, or (ii) by fraud, duress, or mistake, or in breach of duty or as part of an illegal transaction.

(b)  To the extent permitted by law, negotiation may be rescinded or may be subject to other remedies, but those remedies may not be asserted against a subsequent holder in due course or a person paying the instrument in good faith and without knowledge of facts that are a basis for rescission or other remedy.

## § 3–203.  Rights Acquired by Transfer.

(a)  An instrument is transferred when it is delivered by a person other than its issuer for the purpose of giving to the person receiving delivery the right to enforce the instrument.

(b)  Transfer of an instrument, regardless of whether the transfer is a negotiation, vests in the transferee any right of the transferor to enforce the instrument, including any right as a holder in due course, but the transferee cannot acquire rights of a holder in due course by a transfer, directly or indirectly, from a holder in due course if the purchaser engaged in fraud or illegality affecting the instrument.

(c)  Unless otherwise agreed, if an instrument is transferred for value and the transferee does not become a holder because of lack of indorsement by the transferor, the transferee has a specifically enforceable right to the unqualified indorsement of the transferor, but negotiation of the instrument does not occur until the indorsement is made.

(d)  If a transferor purports to transfer less than the entire instrument, negotiation of the instrument does not occur. The transferee obtains no rights under this Article and has only the rights of a partial assignee.

## § 3–204.  Indorsement.

(a)  "Indorsement" means a signature, other than that of a maker, drawer, or acceptor, that alone or accompanied by other words, is made on an instrument for the purpose of (i) negotiating the instrument, (ii) restricting payment of the instrument, or (iii) incurring indorser's liability on the instrument, but regardless of the intent of the signer, a signature and its accompanying words is an indorsement unless the accompanying words, the terms of the instrument, the place of the signature, or other circumstances unambiguously indicate that the signature was made for a purpose other than indorsement. For the purpose of determining whether a signature is made on an instrument, a paper affixed to the instrument is a part of the instrument.

(b)  "Indorser" means a person who makes an indorsement.

(c)  For the purpose of determining whether the transferee of an instrument is a holder, an indorsement that transfers a security interest in the instrument is effective as an unqualified indorsement of the instrument.

(d)  If an instrument is payable to a holder under a name that is not the name of the holder, indorsement may be made by the holder in the name stated in the instrument or in the holder's name or both, but signature in both names may be required by a person paying or taking the instrument for value or collection.

## § 3–205. Special Indorsement; Blank Indorsement; Anomalous Indorsement.

(a) If an indorsement is made by the holder of an instrument, whether payable to an identified person or payable to bearer, and the indorsement identifies a person to whom it makes the instrument payable, it is a "special indorsement." When specially indorsed, an instrument becomes payable to the identified person and may be negotiated only by the indorsement of that person. The principles stated in Section 3–110 apply to special indorsements.

(b) If an indorsement is made by the holder of an instrument and it is not a special indorsement, it is a "blank indorsement." When indorsed in blank, an instrument becomes payable to bearer and may be negotiated by transfer of possession alone until specially indorsed.

(c) The holder may convert a blank indorsement that consists only of a signature into a special indorsement by writing, above the signature of the indorser, words identifying the person to whom the instrument is made payable.

(d) "Anomalous indorsement" means an indorsement made by a person that is not the holder of the instrument. An anomalous indorsement does not affect the manner in which the instrument may be negotiated.

## § 3–206. Restrictive Indorsement.

(a) An indorsement limiting payment to a particular person or otherwise prohibiting further transfer or negotiation of the instrument is not effective to prevent further transfer or negotiation of the instrument.

(b) An indorsement stating a condition to the right of the indorsee to receive payment does not affect the right of the indorsee to enforce the instrument. A person paying the instrument or taking it for value or collection may disregard the condition, and the rights and liabilities of that person are not affected by whether the condition has been fulfilled.

(c) The following rules apply to an instrument bearing an indorsement (i) described in Section 4–201(2), or (ii) in blank or to a particular bank using the words "for deposit," "for collection," or other words indicating a purpose of having the instrument collected for the indorser or for a particular account:

    (1) A person, other than a bank, that purchases the instrument when so indorsed converts the instrument unless the proceeds of the instrument are received by the indorser or are applied consistently with the indorsement.

    (2) A depositary bank that purchases the instrument or takes it for collection when so indorsed converts the instrument unless the proceeds of the instrument are received by the indorser or applied consistently with the indorsement.

    (3) A payor bank that is also the depositary bank or that takes the instrument for immediate payment over the counter from a person other than a collecting bank converts the instrument unless the proceeds of the instrument are received by the indorser or applied consistently with the indorsement.

    (4) Except as otherwise provided in paragraph (3), a payor bank or intermediary bank may disregard the indorsement and is not liable if the proceeds of the instrument are not received by the indorser or applied consistently with the indorsement.

(d) Except for an indorsement covered by subsection (c), the following rules apply to an instrument bearing an indorsement using words to the effect that payment is to be made to the indorsee as agent, trustee, or other fiduciary for the benefit of the indorser or another person:

    (1) Unless there is notice of breach of fiduciary duty as provided in Section 3–307, a person that purchases the instrument from the indorsee or takes the instrument from the indorsee for collection or payment may pay the proceeds of payment or the value given for the instrument to the indorsee without regard to whether the indorsee violates a fiduciary duty to the indorser.

    (2) A later transferee of the instrument or person that pays the instrument is neither given notice nor otherwise affected by the restriction in the indorsement unless the transferee or payor knows that the fiduciary dealt with the instrument or its proceeds in breach of fiduciary duty.

(e) Purchase of an instrument bearing an indorsement to which this section applies does not prevent the purchaser from becoming a holder in due course of the instrument unless the purchaser is a converter under subsection (c).

(f) In an action to enforce the obligation of a party to pay the instrument, the obligor has a defense if payment would violate an indorsement to which this section applies and the payment is not permitted by this section.

## § 3–207. Reacquisition.

Reacquisition of an instrument occurs if it is transferred, by negotiation or otherwise, to a former holder. A former holder that reacquires the instrument may cancel indorsements made after the reacquirer first became a holder of the instrument. If the cancellation causes the instrument to be payable to the reacquirer or to bearer, the reacquirer may negotiate the instrument. An indorser whose indorsement is canceled is discharged, and the discharge is effective against any later holder.

## Part 3—Enforcement of Instruments

### § 3–301. Person Entitled to Enforce Instrument.

"Person entitled to enforce" an instrument means (i) the holder of the instrument, (ii) a nonholder in possession of the instrument who has the rights of a holder, or (iii) a person not in possession of the instrument who is entitled to enforce the instrument pursuant to Section 3–309. A person may be a person entitled to enforce the instrument even though the person is not the owner of the instrument or is in wrongful possession of the instrument.

### § 3–302. Holder in Due Course.

(a) Subject to subsection (c) and Section 3–106(d), "holder in due course" means the holder of an instrument if:

    (1) the instrument when issued or negotiated to the holder does not bear such apparent evidence of forgery or alteration or is not otherwise so irregular or incomplete as to call into question its authenticity, and

    (2) the holder took the instrument (i) for value, (ii) in good faith, (iii) without notice that the instrument is overdue or has been dishonored or that there is an uncured default with respect to payment of another instrument issued as part of the same series, (iv) without notice that the instrument contains an unauthorized signature or has been altered, (v) without notice of any claim to the instrument stated in Section 3–306, and (vi) without notice that any party to the instrument has any defense or claim in recoupment stated in Section 3–305(a).

(b) Notice of discharge of a party to the instrument, other than discharge in an insolvency proceeding, is not notice of a defense under subsection (a), but discharge is effective against a person who became a holder in due course with notice of the discharge. Public filing or recording of a document does not of itself constitute notice of a defense, claim in recoupment, or claim to the instrument.

(c) Except to the extent a transferor or predecessor in interest has rights as a holder in due course, a person does not acquire rights of a holder in due course of an instrument taken (i) by legal process or by purchase at an execution, bankruptcy, or creditor's sale or similar proceeding, (ii) by purchase as part of a bulk transaction not in ordinary course of business of the transferor, or (iii) as the successor in interest to an estate or other organization.

(d) If, under Section 3–303(a)(1), the promise of performance that is the consideration for an instrument has been partially performed, the holder may assert rights as a holder in due course of the instrument only to the fraction of the amount payable under the instrument equal to the value of the partial performance divided by the value of the promised performance.

(e) If (i) the person entitled to enforce an instrument has only a security interest in the instrument and (ii) the person obliged to pay the instrument has a defense, claim in recoupment or claim to the instrument that may be asserted against the person who granted the security interest, the person entitled to enforce the instrument may assert rights as a holder in due course only to an amount payable under the instrument which, at the time of enforcement of the instrument, does not exceed the amount of the unpaid obligation secured.

(f) To be effective, notice must be received at such time and in such manner as to give a reasonable opportunity to act on it.

(g) This section is subject to any law limiting status as a holder in due course in particular classes of transactions.

## § 3–303. Value and Consideration.

(a) An instrument is issued or transferred for value if:

(1) the instrument is issued or transferred for a promise of performance, to the extent the promise has been performed;

(2) the transferee acquires a security interest or other lien in the instrument other than a lien obtained by judicial proceedings;

(3) the instrument is issued or transferred as payment of, or as security for, an existing obligation of any person, whether or not the obligation is due;

(4) the instrument is issued or transferred in exchange for a negotiable instrument; or

(5) the instrument is issued or transferred in exchange for the incurring of an irrevocable obligation to a third party by the person taking the instrument.

(b) "Consideration" means any consideration sufficient to support a simple contract. The drawer or maker of an instrument has a defense if the instrument is issued without consideration. If an instrument is issued for a promise of performance, the drawer or maker has a defense to the extent performance of the promise is due and the promise has not been performed. If an instrument is issued for value as stated in subsection (a), the instrument is also issued for consideration.

## § 3–304. Overdue Instrument.

(a) An instrument payable on demand becomes overdue at the earliest of the following times:

(1) on the day after the day demand for payment is duly made;

(2) if the instrument is a check, 90 days after its date; or

(3) if the instrument is not a check, when the instrument has been outstanding for a period of time after its date which is unreasonably long under the circumstances of the particular case in light of the nature of the instrument and trade usage.

(b) With respect to an instrument payable at a definite time the following rules apply: (1) If the principal is payable in installments and a due date has not been accelerated, the instrument becomes overdue upon default under the instrument for nonpayment of an installment, and the instrument remains overdue until the default is cured. (2) If the principal is not payable in installments and the due date has not been accelerated, the instrument becomes overdue on the day after the due date. (3) If a due date with respect to principal has been accelerated, the instrument becomes overdue on the day after the accelerated due date.

(c) Unless the due date of principal has been accelerated, an instrument does not become overdue if there is default in payment of interest but no default in payment of principal.

## § 3–305. Defenses and Claims in Recoupment.

(a) Except as stated in subsection (b), the right to enforce the obligation of a party to pay the instrument is subject to the following:

(1) A defense of the obligor based on (i) infancy of the obligor to the extent it is a defense to a simple contract, (ii) duress, lack of legal capacity, or illegality of the transaction that nullifies the obligation of the obligor, (iii) fraud that induced the obligor to sign the instrument with neither knowledge nor reasonable opportunity to learn of its character or its essential terms, or (iv) discharge of the obligor in insolvency proceedings.

(2) A defense of the obligor stated in another section of this Article or a defense of the obligor that would be available if the person entitled to enforce the instrument were enforcing a right to payment under a simple contract.

(3) A claim in recoupment of the obligor against the original payee of the instrument if the claim arose from the transaction that gave rise to the instrument. The claim of the obligor may be asserted against a transferee of the instrument only to reduce the amount owing on the instrument at the time the action is brought.

(b) The right of a holder in due course to enforce the obligation of a party to pay the instrument is subject to defenses of the obligor stated in subsection (a)(1), but is not subject to defenses of the obligor stated in subsection (a)(2) or claims in recoupment stated in subsection (a)(3) against a person other than the holder.

(c) Except as stated in subsection (d), in an action to enforce the obligation of a party to pay the instrument, the obligor may not assert against the person entitled to enforce the instrument a defense, claim in recoupment, or claim to the instrument (Section 3–306) of another person, but the other person's claim to the instrument may be asserted by the obligor if the other person is joined in the action and personally asserts the claim against the person entitled to enforce the instrument. An obligor is not obliged to pay the instrument if the person seeking enforcement of the instrument does not have rights of a holder in due course and the obligor proves that the instrument is a lost or stolen instrument.

(d) In an action to enforce the obligation of an accommodation party to pay an instrument, the accommodation party may assert against the person entitled to enforce the instrument any defense or claim in recoupment under subsection (a) that the accommodated party could assert against the person entitled to enforce the instrument, except the defenses of discharge in insolvency proceedings, infancy, or lack of legal capacity.

## § 3–306. Claims to an Instrument.

A person taking an instrument, other than a person having rights of a holder in due course, is subject to a claim of a property or possessory right in the instrument or its proceeds, including a claim to rescind a negotiation and to recover the instrument or its proceeds. A person having rights of a holder in due course takes free of the claim to the instrument.

## § 3–307.  Notice of Breach of Fiduciary Duty.

(a)  This section applies if (i) an instrument is taken from a fiduciary for payment or collection or for value, (ii) the taker has knowledge of the fiduciary status of the fiduciary, and (iii) the represented person makes a claim to the instrument or its proceeds on the basis that the transaction of the fiduciary is a breach of fiduciary duty. Notice of breach of fiduciary duty by the fiduciary is notice of the claim of the represented person. "Fiduciary" means an agent, trustee, partner, corporation officer or director, or other representative owing a fiduciary duty with respect to the instrument. "Represented person" means the principal, beneficiary, partnership, corporation, or other person to whom the duty is owed.

(b)  If the instrument is payable to the fiduciary, as such, or to the represented person, the taker has notice of the breach of fiduciary duty if the instrument is (i) taken in payment of or as security for a debt known by the taker to be the personal debt of the fiduciary, (ii) taken in a transaction known by the taker to be for the personal benefit of the fiduciary, or (iii) deposited to an account other than an account of the fiduciary, as such, or an account of the represented person.

(c)  If the instrument is made or drawn by the fiduciary, as such, payable to the fiduciary personally, the taker does not have notice of the breach of fiduciary duty unless the taker knows of the breach of fiduciary duty.

(d)  If the instrument is made or drawn by or on behalf of the represented person to the taker as payee, the taker has notice of the breach of fiduciary duty if the instrument is (i) taken in payment of or as security for a debt known by the taker to be the personal debt of the fiduciary, (ii) taken in a transaction known by the taker to be for the personal benefit of the fiduciary, or (iii) deposited to an account other than an account of the fiduciary, as such, or an account of the represented person.

## § 3–308.  Proof of Signatures and Status as Holder in Due Course.

(a)  In an action with respect to an instrument, the authenticity of, and authority to make, each signature on the instrument is admitted unless specifically denied in the pleadings. If the validity of a signature is denied in the pleadings, the burden of establishing validity is on the person claiming validity, but the signature is presumed to be authentic and authorized unless the action is to enforce the liability of the purported signer and the signer is dead or incompetent at the time of trial of the issue of validity of the signature. If an action to enforce the instrument is brought against a person as the undisclosed principal of a person who signed the instrument as a party to the instrument, the plaintiff has the burden of establishing that the defendant is liable on the instrument as a represented person pursuant to Section 3–402(a).

(b)  If the validity of signatures is admitted or proved and there is compliance with subsection (a), a plaintiff producing the instrument is entitled to payment if the plaintiff proves entitlement to enforce the instrument under Section 3–301, unless the defendant proves a defense or claim in recoupment. If a defense or claim in recoupment is proved, the right to payment of the plaintiff is subject to the defense or claim except to the extent the plaintiff proves that the plaintiff has rights of a holder in due course which are not subject to the defense or claim.

## § 3–309.  Enforcement of Lost, Destroyed, or Stolen Instrument.

(a)  A person not in possession of an instrument is entitled to enforce the instrument if (i) that person was in rightful possession of the instrument and entitled to enforce it when loss of possession occurred, (ii) the loss of possession was not the result of a voluntary transfer by that person or a lawful seizure, and (iii) that person cannot reasonably obtain possession of the instrument because the instrument was destroyed, its whereabouts cannot be determined, or it is in the wrongful possession of an unknown person or a person that cannot be found or is not amenable to service of process.

(b)  A person seeking enforcement of an instrument pursuant to subsection (a) must prove the terms of the instrument and the person's right to enforce the instrument. If that proof is made, Section 3–308 applies to the case as though the person seeking enforcement had produced the instrument. The court may not enter judgment in favor of the person seeking enforcement unless it finds that the person required to pay the instrument is adequately protected against loss that might occur by reason of a claim by another person to enforce the instrument. Adequate protection may be provided by any reasonable means.

## § 3–310.  Effect of Instrument on Obligation for Which Taken.

(a)  Unless otherwise agreed, if a certified check, cashier's check, or teller's check is taken for an obligation, the obligation is discharged to the same extent discharge would result if an amount of money equal to the amount of the instrument were taken in payment of the obligation. Discharge of the obligation does not affect any liability that the obligor may have as an indorser of the instrument.

(b)  Unless otherwise agreed and except as provided in subsection (a), if a note or an uncertified check is taken for an obligation, the obligation is suspended to the same extent the obligation would be discharged if an amount of money equal to the amount of the instrument were taken.

(1)  In the case of an uncertified check, suspension of the obligation continues until dishonor of the check or until it is paid or certified. Payment or certification of the check results in discharge of the obligation to the extent of the amount of the check.

(2)  In the case of a note, suspension of the obligation continues until dishonor of the note or until it is paid. Payment of the note results in discharge of the obligation to the extent of the payment.

(3)  If the check or note is dishonored and the obligee of the obligation for which the instrument was taken has possession of the instrument, the obligee may enforce either the instrument or the obligation. In the case of an instrument of a third person which is negotiated to the obligee by the obligor, discharge of the obligor on the instrument also discharges the obligation.

(4)  If the person entitled to enforce the instrument taken for an obligation is a person other than the obligee, the obligee may not enforce the obligation to the extent the obligation is suspended. If the obligee is the person entitled to enforce the instrument but no longer has possession of it because it was lost, stolen, or destroyed, the obligation may not be enforced to the extent of the amount payable on the instrument, and to that extent the obligee's rights against the obligor are limited to enforcement of the instrument.

(c)  If an instrument other than one described in subsection (a) or (b) is taken for an obligation, the effect is (i) that stated in subsection (a) if the instrument is one on which a bank is liable as maker or acceptor, or (ii) that stated in subsection (b) in any other case.

## § 3–311.  Accord and Satisfaction by Use of Instrument.

(a)  This section applies if a person against whom a claim is asserted proves that (i) that person in good faith tendered an instrument to the claimant as full satisfaction of the claim, (ii) the amount of the claim was unliquidated or subject to a bona fide dispute, and (iii) the claimant obtained payment of the instrument.

(b) Unless subsection (c) applies, the claim is discharged if the person against whom the claim is asserted proves that the instrument or an accompanying written communication contained a conspicuous statement to the effect that the instrument was tendered as full satisfaction of the claim.

(c) Subject to subsection (d), a claim is not discharged under subsection (b) if the claimant is an organization and proves that within a reasonable time before the tender, the claimant sent a conspicuous statement to the person against whom the claim is asserted that communications concerning disputed debts, including an instrument tendered as full satisfaction of a debt, are to be sent to a designated person, office or place, and the instrument or accompanying communication was not received by that designated person, office, or place.

(d) Notwithstanding subsection (c), a claim is discharged under subsection (b) if the person against whom the claim is asserted proves that within a reasonable time before collection of the instrument was initiated, an agent of the claimant having direct responsibility with respect to the disputed obligation knew that the instrument was tendered in full satisfaction of the claim, or received the instrument and any accompanying written communication.

## Part 4—Liability of Parties

### § 3–401. Signature.

(a) A person is not liable on an instrument unless (i) the person signed the instrument, or (ii) the person is represented by an agent or representative who signed the instrument and the signature is binding on the represented person under Section 3–402.

(b) A signature may be made (i) manually or by means of a device or machine, and (ii) by the use of any name, including any trade or assumed name, or by any word, mark, or symbol executed or adopted by a person with present intention to authenticate a writing.

### § 3–402. Signature by Representative.

(a) If a person acting, or purporting to act, as a representative signs an instrument by signing either the name of the represented person or the name of the signer, the represented person is bound by the signature to the same extent the represented person would be bound if the signature were on a simple contract. If the represented person is bound, the signature of the representative is the "authorized signature of the represented person" and the represented person is liable on the instrument, whether or not identified in the instrument.

(b) If a representative signs the name of the representative to an instrument and that signature is an authorized signature of the represented person, the following rules apply:

(1) If the form of the signature shows unambiguously that the signature is made on behalf of the represented person who is identified in the instrument, the representative is not liable on the instrument.

(2) Subject to subsection (c), if (i) the form of the signature does not show unambiguously that the signature is made in a representative capacity or (ii) the represented person is not identified in the instrument, the representative is liable on the instrument to a holder in due course that took the instrument without notice that the representative was not intended to be liable on the instrument. With respect to any other person, the representative is liable on the instrument unless the representative proves that the original parties to the instrument did not intend the representative to be liable on the instrument.

(c) If a representative signs the name of the representative as drawer of a check without indication of the representative status and the check is payable from an account of the represented person who is identified on the check, the signer is not liable on the check if the signature is an authorized signature of the represented person.

### § 3–403. Unauthorized Signature.

(a) Except as otherwise provided in this Article, an unauthorized signature is ineffective except as the signature of the unauthorized signer in favor of a person who in good faith pays the instrument or takes it for value. An unauthorized signature may be ratified for all purposes of this Article.

(b) If the signature of more than one person is required to constitute the authorized signature of an organization, the signature of the organization is unauthorized if one of the required signatures is missing.

(c) The civil or criminal liability of a person who makes an unauthorized signature is not affected by any provision of this Article that makes the unauthorized signature effective for the purposes of this Article.

### § 3–404. Impostors; Fictitious Payees.

(a) If an impostor by use of the mails or otherwise induces the maker or drawer of an instrument to issue the instrument to the impostor, or to a person acting in concert with the impostor, by impersonating the payee of the instrument or a person authorized to act for the payee, an indorsement of the instrument by any person in the name of the payee is effective as the indorsement of the payee in favor of any person that in good faith pays the instrument or takes it for value or for collection.

(b) If (i) a person whose intent determines to whom an instrument is payable (Section 3–110(a) or (b)) does not intend the person identified as payee to have any interest in the instrument, or (ii) the person identified as payee of the instrument is a fictitious person, the following rules apply until the instrument is negotiated by special indorsement:

(1) Any person in possession of the instrument is its holder.

(2) An indorsement by any person in the name of the payee stated in the instrument is effective as the indorsement of the payee in favor of any person that in good faith pays the instrument or takes it for value or for collection.

(c) Under subsection (a) or (b) an indorsement is made in the name of a payee if (i) it is made in a name substantially similar to that of the payee or (ii) the instrument, whether or not indorsed, is deposited in a depositary bank to an account in a name substantially similar to that of the payee.

(d) With respect to an instrument to which subsection (a) or (b) applies, if a person paying the instrument or taking it for value or for collection fails to exercise ordinary care in paying or taking the instrument and that failure substantially contributes to loss resulting from payment of the instrument, the person bearing the loss may recover from the person failing to exercise ordinary care to the extent the failure to exercise ordinary care contributed to the loss.

### § 3–405. Employer Responsibility for Fraudulent Indorsement by Employee.

(a) This section applies to fraudulent indorsements of instruments with respect to which an employer has entrusted an employee with responsibility as part of the employee's duties. The following definitions apply to this section:

(1) "Employee" includes, in addition to an employee of an employer, an independent contractor and employee of an independent contractor retained by the employer.

(2) "Fraudulent indorsement" means (i) in the case of an instrument payable to the employer, a forged indorsement purporting to be that of the employer, or (ii) in the case of an instrument with respect to which the employer is drawer or maker, a forged indorsement purporting to be that of the person identified as payee.

(3) "Responsibility" with respect to instruments means authority (i) to sign or indorse instruments on behalf of the employer, (ii) to process instruments received by the employer for bookkeeping purposes, for deposit to an account, or for other disposition, (iii) to prepare or process instruments for issue in the name of the employer, (iv) to supply information determining the names or addresses of payees of instruments to be issued in the name of the employer, (v) to control the disposition of instruments to be issued in the name of the employer, or (vi) to otherwise act with respect to instruments in a responsible capacity. "Responsibility" does not include the assignment of duties that merely allow an employee to have access to instruments or blank or incomplete instrument forms that are being stored or transported or are part of incoming or outgoing mail, or similar access.

(b) For the purpose of determining the rights and liabilities of a person who, in good faith, pays an instrument or takes it for value or for collection, if an employee entrusted with responsibility with respect to the instrument or a person acting in concert with the employee makes a fraudulent indorsement to the instrument, the indorsement is effective as the indorsement of the person to whom the instrument is payable if it is made in the name of that person. If the person paying the instrument or taking it for value or for collection fails to exercise ordinary care in paying or taking the instrument and that failure substantially contributes to loss resulting from the fraud, the person bearing the loss may recover from the person failing to exercise ordinary care to the extent the failure to exercise ordinary care contributed to the loss.

(c) Under subsection (b) an indorsement is made in the name of the person to whom an instrument is payable if (i) it is made in a name substantially similar to the name of that person or (ii) the instrument, whether or not indorsed, is deposited in a depositary bank to an account in a name substantially similar to the name of that person.

## § 3–406. Negligence Contributing to Forged Signature or Alteration of Instrument.

(a) A person whose failure to exercise ordinary care substantially contributes to an alteration of an instrument or to the making of a forged signature on an instrument is precluded from asserting the alteration or the forgery against a person that, in good faith, pays the instrument or takes it for value.

(b) If the person asserting the preclusion fails to exercise ordinary care in paying or taking the instrument and that failure substantially contributes to loss, the loss is allocated between the person precluded and the person asserting the preclusion according to the extent to which the failure of each to exercise ordinary care contributed to the loss.

(c) Under subsection (a) the burden of proving failure to exercise ordinary care is on the person asserting the preclusion. Under subsection (b) the burden of proving failure to exercise ordinary care is on the person precluded.

## § 3–407. Alteration.

(a) "Alteration" means (i) an unauthorized change in an instrument that purports to modify in any respect the obligation of a party to the instrument, or (ii) an unauthorized addition of words or numbers or other change to an incomplete instrument relating to the obligation of any party to the instrument.

(b) Except as provided in subsection (c), an alteration fraudulently made by the holder discharges any party to whose obligation the alteration applies unless that party assents or is precluded from asserting the alteration. No other alteration discharges any party, and the instrument may be enforced according to its original terms.

(c) If an instrument that has been fraudulently altered is acquired by a person having rights of a holder in due course, it may be enforced by that person according to its original terms. If an incomplete instrument is completed and is then acquired by a person having rights of a holder in due course, it may be enforced by that person as completed, whether or not the completion is a fraudulent alteration.

## § 3–408. Drawee Not Liable on Unaccepted Draft.

A check or other draft does not of itself operate as an assignment of funds in the hands of the drawee available for its payment, and the drawee is not liable on the instrument until the drawee accepts it.

## § 3–409. Acceptance of Draft; Certified Check.

(a) "Acceptance" means the drawee's signed agreement to pay a draft as presented. It must be written on the draft and may consist of the drawee's signature alone. Acceptance may be made at any time and becomes effective when notification pursuant to instructions is given or the accepted draft is delivered for the purpose of giving rights on the acceptance to any person.

(b) A draft may be accepted although it has not been signed by the drawer, is otherwise incomplete, is overdue, or has been dishonored.

(c) If a draft is payable at a fixed period after sight and the acceptor fails to date the acceptance, the holder may complete the acceptance by supplying a date in good faith.

(d) "Certified check" means a check accepted by the bank on which it is drawn. Acceptance may be made as stated in subsection (a) or by a writing on the check which indicates that the check is certified. The drawee of a check has no obligation to certify the check, and refusal to certify is not dishonor of the check.

## § 3–410. Acceptance Varying Draft.

(a) If the terms of a drawee's acceptance vary from the terms of the draft as presented, the holder may refuse the acceptance and treat the draft as dishonored. In that case, the drawee may cancel the acceptance.

(b) The terms of a draft are not varied by an acceptance to pay at a particular bank or place in the United States, unless the acceptance states that the draft is to be paid only at that bank or place.

(c) If the holder assents to an acceptance varying the terms of a draft, the obligation of each drawer and indorser that does not expressly assent to the acceptance is discharged.

## § 3–411. Refusal to Pay Cashier's Checks, Teller's Checks, and Certified Checks.

(a) In this section, "obligated bank" means the acceptor of a certified check or the issuer of a cashier's check or teller's check bought from the issuer.

(b) If the obligated bank wrongfully (i) refuses to pay a cashier's check or certified check, (ii) stops payment of a teller's check, or (iii) refuses to pay a dishonored teller's check, the person asserting the right to enforce the check is entitled to compensation for expenses and loss of interest resulting from the nonpayment and may recover consequential damages if the obligated bank refused to pay after receiving notice of particular circumstances giving rise to the damages.

(c) Expenses or consequential damages under subsection (b) are not recoverable if the refusal of the obligated bank to pay occurs because (i) the bank suspends payments, (ii) the obligated bank is asserting a claim or defense of the bank that it has reasonable grounds to believe is available against the person entitled to enforce the instrument, (iii) the obligated bank has a reasonable doubt whether the person demanding payment is the person entitled to enforce the instrument, or (iv) payment is prohibited by law.

## § 3–412. Obligation of Maker.

A maker of a note is obliged to pay the note (i) according to its terms at the time it was issued or, if not issued, at the time it first came into possession of a holder, or (ii) if the maker signed an incomplete instrument, according to its terms when completed as stated in Sections 3–115 and 3–407. The obligation is owed to a person entitled to enforce the note or to an indorser that paid the note pursuant to Section 3–415.

## § 3–413. Obligation of Acceptor.

(a) An acceptor of a draft is obliged to pay the draft (i) according to its terms at the time it was accepted, even though the acceptance states that the draft is payable "as originally drawn" or equivalent terms, (ii) if the acceptance varies the terms of the draft, according to the terms of the draft as varied, or (iii) if the acceptance is of a draft that is an incomplete instrument, according to its terms when completed as stated in Sections 3–115 and 3–407. The obligation is owed to a person entitled to enforce the draft or to the drawer or an indorser that paid the draft pursuant to Section 3–414 or 3–415.

(b) If the certification of a check or other acceptance of a draft states the amount certified or accepted, the obligation of the acceptor is that amount. If (i) the certification or acceptance does not state an amount, (ii) the instrument is subsequently altered by raising its amount, and (iii) the instrument is then negotiated to a holder in due course, the obligation of the acceptor is the amount of the instrument at the time it was negotiated to the holder in due course.

## § 3–414. Obligation of Drawer.

(a) If an unaccepted draft is dishonored, the drawer is obliged to pay the draft (i) according to its terms at the time it was issued or, if not issued, at the time it first came into possession of a holder, or (ii) if the drawer signed an incomplete instrument, according to its terms when completed as stated in Sections 3–115 and 3–407. The obligation is owed to a person entitled to enforce the draft or to an indorser that paid the draft pursuant to Section 3–415.

(b) If a draft is accepted by a bank and the acceptor dishonors the draft, the drawer has no obligation to pay the draft because of the dishonor, regardless of when or by whom acceptance was obtained.

(c) If a draft is accepted and the acceptor is not a bank, the obligation of the drawer to pay the draft if the draft is dishonored by the acceptor is the same as the obligation of an indorser stated in Section 3–415(a) and (c).

(d) Words in a draft indicating that the draft is drawn without recourse are effective to disclaim all liability of the drawer to pay the draft if the draft is not a check or a teller's check, but they are not effective to disclaim the obligation stated in subsection (a) if the draft is a check or a teller's check.

(e) If (i) a check is not presented for payment or given to a depositary bank for collection within 30 days after its date, (ii) the drawee suspends payments after expiration of the 30-day period without paying the check, and (iii) because of the suspension of payments the drawer is deprived of funds maintained with the drawee to cover payment of the check, the drawer to the extent deprived of funds may discharge its obligation to pay the check by assigning to the person entitled to enforce the check the rights of the drawer against the drawee with respect to the funds.

## § 3–415. Obligation of Indorser.

(a) Subject to subsections (b), (c) and (d) and to Section 3–419(d), if an instrument is dishonored, an indorser is obliged to pay the amount due on the instrument (i) according to the terms of the instrument at the time it was indorsed, or (ii) if the indorser indorsed an incomplete instrument, according to its terms when completed as stated in Sections 3–115 and 3–407. The obligation of the indorser is owed to a person entitled to enforce the instrument or to a subsequent indorser that paid the instrument pursuant to this section.

(b) If an indorsement states that it is made "without recourse" or otherwise disclaims liability of the indorser, the indorser is not liable under subsection (a) to pay the instrument.

(c) If notice of dishonor of an instrument is required by Section 3–503 and notice of dishonor complying with that section is not given to an indorser, the liability of the indorser under subsection (a) is discharged.

(d) If a draft is accepted by a bank after an indorsement was made and the acceptor dishonors the draft, the indorser is not liable under subsection (a) to pay the instrument.

(e) If an indorser of a check is liable under subsection (a) and the check is not presented for payment, or given to a depositary bank for collection, within 30 days after the day the indorsement was made, the liability of the indorser under subsection (a) is discharged.

## § 3–416. Transfer Warranties.

(a) A person that transfers an instrument for consideration warrants to the transferee and, if the transfer is by indorsement, to any subsequent transferee that:

  (1) the warrantor is a person entitled to enforce the instrument,

  (2) all signatures on the instrument are authentic and authorized,

  (3) the instrument has not been altered,

  (4) the instrument is not subject to a defense or claim in recoupment stated in Section 3–305(a) of any party that can be asserted against the warrantor, and

  (5) the warrantor has no knowledge of any insolvency proceeding commenced with respect to the maker or acceptor or, in the case of an unaccepted draft, the drawer.

(b) A person to whom the warranties under subsection (a) are made and who took the instrument in good faith may recover from the warrantor as damages for breach of warranty an amount equal to the loss suffered as a result of the breach, but not more than the amount of the instrument plus expenses and loss of interest incurred as a result of the breach.

(c) The warranties stated in subsection (a) cannot be disclaimed with respect to checks. Unless notice of a claim for breach of warranty is given to the warrantor within 30 days after the claimant has reason to know of the breach and the identity of the warrantor, the warrantor is discharged to the extent of any loss caused by the delay in giving notice of the claim.

(d) A cause of action for breach of warranty under this section accrues when the claimant has reason to know of the breach.

## § 3–417. Presentment Warranties.

(a) If an unaccepted draft is presented to the drawee for payment or acceptance and the drawee pays or accepts the draft, (i) the person obtaining payment or acceptance, at the time of presentment, and (ii) a previous transferor of the draft, at the time of transfer, warrant to the drawee making payment or accepting the draft in good faith that:

(1) the warrantor is or was, at the time the warrantor transferred the draft, a person entitled to enforce the draft or authorized to obtain payment or acceptance of the draft on behalf of a person entitled to enforce the draft;

(2) the draft has not been altered; and

(3) the warrantor has no knowledge that the signature of the purported drawer of the draft is unauthorized.

(b) A drawee making payment may recover from any warrantor damages for breach of warranty equal to the amount paid by the drawee less the amount the drawee received or is entitled to receive from the drawer because of payment of the draft. In addition the drawee is entitled to compensation for expenses and loss of interest resulting from the breach. The right of the drawee to recover damages under this subsection is not affected by any failure of the drawee to exercise ordinary care in making payment. If the drawee accepts the draft (i) breach of warranty is a defense to the obligation of the acceptor, and (ii) if the acceptor makes payment with respect to the draft, the acceptor is entitled to recover from any warrantor for breach of warranty the amounts stated in the first two sentences of this subsection.

(c) If a drawee asserts a claim for breach of warranty under subsection (a) based on an unauthorized indorsement of the draft or an alteration of the draft, the warrantor may defend by proving that the indorsement is effective under Section 3–404 or 3–405 or the drawer is precluded under Section 3–406 or 4–406 from asserting against the drawee the unauthorized indorsement or alteration.

(d) This subsection applies if (i) a dishonored draft is presented for payment to the drawer or an indorser or (ii) any other instrument is presented for payment to a party obliged to pay the instrument, and payment is received. The person obtaining payment and a prior transferor of the instrument warrant to the person making payment in good faith that the warrantor is or was, at the time the warrantor transferred the instrument, a person entitled to enforce the instrument or authorized to obtain payment on behalf of a person entitled to enforce the instrument. The person making payment may recover from any warrantor for breach of warranty an amount equal to the amount paid plus expenses and loss of interest resulting from the breach.

(e) The warranties stated in subsections (a) and (d) cannot be disclaimed with respect to checks. Unless notice of a claim for breach of warranty is given to the warrantor within 30 days after the claimant has reason to know of the breach and the identity of the warrantor, the warrantor is discharged to the extent of any loss caused by the delay in giving notice of the claim.

(f) A cause of action for breach of warranty under this section accrues when the claimant has reason to know of the breach.

### § 3–418.  Payment or Acceptance by Mistake.

(a) Except as provided in subsection (c), if the drawee of a draft pays or accepts the draft and the drawee acted on the mistaken belief that (i) payment of the draft had not been stopped under Section 4–403, (ii) the signature of the purported drawer of the draft was authorized, or (iii) the balance in the drawer's account with the drawee represented available funds, the drawee may recover the amount paid from the person to whom or for whose benefit payment was made or, in the case of acceptance, may revoke the acceptance. Rights of

the drawee under this subsection are not affected by failure of the drawee to exercise ordinary care in paying or accepting the draft.

(b) Except as provided in subsection (c), if an instrument has been paid or accepted by mistake and the case is not covered by subsection (a), the person paying or accepting may recover the amount paid or revoke acceptance to the extent allowed by the law governing mistake and restitution.

(c) The remedies provided by subsection (a) or (b) may not be asserted against a person who took the instrument in good faith and for value. This subsection does not limit remedies provided by Section 3–417 for breach of warranty.

### § 3–419.  Instruments Signed for Accommodation.

(a) If an instrument is issued for value given for the benefit of a party to the instrument ("accommodated party") and another party to the instrument ("accommodation party") signs the instrument for the purpose of incurring liability on the instrument without being a direct beneficiary of the value given for the instrument, the instrument is signed by the accommodation party "for accommodation."

(b) An accommodation party may sign the instrument as maker, drawer, acceptor, or indorser and, subject to subsection (d), is obliged to pay the instrument in the capacity in which the accommodation party signs. The obligation of an accommodation party may be enforced notwithstanding any statute of frauds and regardless of whether the accommodation party receives consideration for the accommodation.

(c) A person signing an instrument is presumed to be an accommodation party and there is notice that the instrument is signed for accommodation if the signature is an anomalous indorsement or is accompanied by words indicating that the signer is acting as surety or guarantor with respect to the obligation of another party to the instrument. Except as provided in Section 3–606, the obligation of an accommodation party to pay the instrument is not affected by the fact that the person enforcing the obligation had notice when the instrument was taken by that person that the accommodation party signed the instrument for accommodation.

(d) If the signature of a party to an instrument is accompanied by words indicating unambiguously that the party is guaranteeing collection rather than payment of the obligation of another party to the instrument, the signer is obliged to pay the amount due on the instrument to a person entitled to enforce the instrument only if (i) execution of judgment against the other party has been returned unsatisfied, (ii) the other party is insolvent or in an insolvency proceeding, (iii) the other party cannot be served with process, or (iv) it is otherwise apparent that payment cannot be obtained from the party whose obligation is guaranteed.

(e) An accommodation party that pays the instrument is entitled to reimbursement from the accommodated party and is entitled to enforce the instrument against the accommodated party. An accommodated party that pays the instrument has no right of recourse against, and is not entitled to contribution from, an accommodation party.

### § 3–420.  Conversion of Instrument.

(a) The law applicable to conversion of personal property applies to instruments. An instrument is also converted if the instrument lacks an indorsement necessary for negotiation and it is purchased or taken for collection or the drawee takes the instrument and makes payment to a person not entitled to receive payment. An action for conversion of an instrument may not be brought by (i) the maker, drawer, or acceptor of the instrument or (ii) a payee or indorsee who did not receive delivery of the instrument either directly or through delivery to an agent or a co-payee.

(b) In an action under subsection (a), the measure of liability is presumed to be the amount payable on the instrument, but recovery may not exceed the amount of the plaintiff's interest in the instrument.

(c) A representative, other than a depositary bank, that has in good faith dealt with an instrument or its proceeds on behalf of one who was not the person entitled to enforce the instrument is not liable in conversion to that person beyond the amount of any proceeds that it has not paid out.

## Part 5—Dishonor

### § 3–501. Presentment.

(a) "Presentment" means a demand (i) to pay an instrument made to the maker, drawee, or acceptor or, in the case of a note or accepted draft payable at a bank, to the bank, or (ii) to accept a draft made to the drawee, by a person entitled to enforce the instrument.

(b) Subject to Article 4, agreement of the parties, clearing house rules and the like,

(1) presentment may be made at the place of payment of the instrument and must be made at the place of payment if the instrument is payable at a bank in the United States; may be made by any commercially reasonable means, including an oral, written, or electronic communication; is effective when the demand for payment or acceptance is received by the person to whom presentment is made; is effective if made to any one of two or more makers, acceptors, drawees or other payors; and

(2) without dishonoring the instrument, the party to whom presentment is made may (i) treat presentment as occurring on the next business day after the day of presentment if the party to whom presentment is made has established a cut-off hour not earlier than 2 p.m. for the receipt and processing of instruments presented for payment or acceptance and presentment is made after the cut-off hour, (ii) require exhibition of the instrument, (iii) require reasonable identification of the person making presentment and evidence of authority to make it if made on behalf of another person, (iv) require a signed receipt on the instrument for any payment made or surrender of the instrument if full payment is made, (v) return the instrument for lack of a necessary indorsement, or (vi) refuse payment or acceptance for failure of the presentment to comply with the terms of the instrument, an agreement of the parties, or other law or applicable rule.

### § 3–502. Dishonor.

(a) Dishonor of a note is governed by the following rules:

(1) If the note is payable on demand, the note is dishonored if presentment is duly made and the note is not paid on the day of presentment.

(2) If the note is not payable on demand and is payable at or through a bank or the terms of the note require presentment, the note is dishonored if presentment is duly made and the note is not paid on the day it becomes payable or the day of presentment, whichever is later.

(3) If the note is not payable on demand and subparagraph (2) does not apply, the note is dishonored if it is not paid on the day it becomes payable.

(b) Dishonor of an unaccepted draft other than a documentary draft is governed by the following rules:

(1) If a check is presented for payment otherwise than for immediate payment over the counter, the check is dishonored if the payor bank makes timely return of the check or sends timely notice of dishonor or nonpayment under Section 4–301 or 4–302, or becomes accountable for the amount of the check under Section 4–302.

(2) If the draft is payable on demand and subparagraph (1) does not apply, the draft is dishonored if presentment for payment is duly made and the draft is not paid on the day of presentment.

(3) If the draft is payable on a date stated in the draft, the draft is dishonored if (i) presentment for payment is duly made and payment is not made on the day the draft becomes payable or the day of presentment, whichever is later, or (ii) presentment for acceptance is duly made before the day the draft becomes payable and the draft is not accepted on the day of presentment.

(4) If the draft is payable on elapse of a period of time after sight or acceptance, the draft is dishonored if presentment for acceptance is duly made and the draft is not accepted on the day of presentment.

(c) Dishonor of an unaccepted documentary draft occurs according to the rules stated in subparagraphs (2), (3), and (4) of subsection (b) except that payment or acceptance may be delayed without dishonor until no later than the close of the third business day of the drawee following the day on which payment or acceptance is required by those subparagraphs.

(d) Dishonor of an accepted draft is governed by the following rules:

(1) If the draft is payable on demand, the draft is dishonored if presentment for payment is duly made and the draft is not paid on the day of presentment.

(2) If the draft is not payable on demand, the draft is dishonored if presentment for payment is duly made and payment is not made on the day it becomes payable or the day of presentment, whichever is later.

(e) In any case in which presentment is otherwise required for dishonor under this section and presentment is excused under Section 3–504, dishonor occurs without presentment if the instrument is not duly accepted or paid.

(f) If a draft is dishonored because timely acceptance of the draft was not made and the person entitled to demand acceptance consents to a late acceptance, from the time of acceptance the draft is treated as never having been dishonored.

### § 3–503. Notice of Dishonor.

(a) The obligation of an indorser stated in Section 3–415(a) and the obligation of a drawer stated in Section 3–414(c) may not be enforced unless (i) the indorser or drawer is given notice of dishonor of the instrument complying with this section or (ii) notice of dishonor is excused under Section 3–504(c).

(b) Notice of dishonor may be given by any person; may be given by any commercially reasonable means including an oral, written, or electronic communication; is sufficient if it reasonably identifies the instrument and indicates that the instrument has been dishonored or has not been paid or accepted. Return of an instrument given to a bank for collection is a sufficient notice of dishonor.

(c) Subject to Section 3–504(d), with respect to an instrument taken for collection by a collecting bank, notice of dishonor must be given (i) by the bank before midnight of the next banking day following the banking day on which the bank receives notice of dishonor of the instrument, and (ii) by any other person within 30 days following the day on which the person receives notice of dishonor. With respect to any other instrument, notice of dishonor must be given within 30 days following the day on which dishonor occurs.

### § 3–504. Excused Presentment and Notice of Dishonor.

(a) Presentment for payment or acceptance of an instrument is excused if (i) the person entitled to present the instrument cannot with reasonable diligence make presentment, (ii) the maker or acceptor has repudiated an obligation to pay the instrument or is dead or in insolvency proceedings, (iii) by the terms of the instrument presentment is not necessary to enforce the obligation of indorsers or the drawer, or (iv) the drawer or indorser whose obligation is being enforced waived presentment or otherwise had no reason to expect or right to require that the instrument be paid or accepted.

(b) Presentment for payment or acceptance of a draft is also excused if the drawer instructed the drawee not to pay or accept the draft or the drawee was not obligated to the drawer to pay the draft.

(c) Notice of dishonor is excused if (i) by the terms of the instrument notice of dishonor is not necessary to enforce the obligation of a party to pay the instrument, or (ii) the party whose obligation is being enforced waived notice of dishonor. A waiver of presentment is also a waiver of notice of dishonor.

(d) Delay in giving notice of dishonor is excused if the delay was caused by circumstances beyond the control of the person giving the notice and the person giving the notice exercised reasonable diligence after the cause of the delay ceased to operate.

### § 3–505. Evidence of Dishonor.

(a) The following are admissible as evidence and create a presumption of dishonor and of any notice of dishonor stated:

(1) a document regular in form as provided in subsection (b) which purports to be a protest;

(2) a purported stamp or writing of the drawee, payor bank, or presenting bank on or accompanying the instrument stating that acceptance or payment has been refused unless reasons for the refusal are stated and the reasons are not consistent with dishonor;

(3) a book or record of the drawee, payor bank, or collecting bank, kept in the usual course of business which shows dishonor, even if there is no evidence of who made the entry.

(b) A protest is a certificate of dishonor made by a United States consul or vice consul, or a notary public or other person authorized to administer oaths by the law of the place where dishonor occurs. It may be made upon information satisfactory to that person. The protest must identify the instrument and certify either that presentment has been made or, if not made, the reason why it was not made, and that the instrument has been dishonored by nonacceptance or nonpayment. The protest may also certify that notice of dishonor has been given to some or all parties.

## Part 6—Discharge and Payment

### § 3–601. Discharge and Effect of Discharge.

(a) The obligation of a party to pay the instrument is discharged as stated in this Article or by an act or agreement with the party which would discharge an obligation to pay money under a simple contract.

(b) Discharge of the obligation of a party is not effective against a person acquiring rights of a holder in due course of the instrument without notice of the discharge.

### § 3–602. Payment.

(a) Subject to subsection (b), an instrument is paid to the extent payment is made (i) by or on behalf of a party obliged to pay the instrument, and (ii) to a person entitled to enforce the instrument. To the extent of the payment, the obligation of the party obliged to pay the instrument is discharged even though payment is made with knowledge of a claim to the instrument under Section 3–306 by another person.

(b) The obligation of a party to pay the instrument is not discharged under subsection (a) if:

(1) a claim to the instrument under Section 3–306 is enforceable against the party receiving payment and (i) payment is made with knowledge by the payor that payment is prohibited by injunction or similar process of a court of competent jurisdiction, or (ii) in the case of an instrument other than a cashier's check, teller's check, or certified check, the party making payment accepted, from the person having a claim to the instrument, indemnity against loss resulting from refusal to pay the person entitled to enforce the instrument, or

(2) the person making payment knows that the instrument is a stolen instrument and pays a person that it knows is in wrongful possession of the instrument.

### § 3–603. Tender of Payment.

(a) If tender of payment of an obligation of a party to an instrument is made to a person entitled to enforce the obligation, the effect of tender is governed by principles of law applicable to tender of payment of an obligation under a simple contract.

(b) If tender of payment of an obligation to pay the instrument is made to a person entitled to enforce the instrument and the tender is refused, there is discharge, to the extent of the amount of the tender, of the obligation of an indorser or accommodation party having a right of recourse against the obligor making the tender.

(c) If tender of payment of an amount due on an instrument is made by or on behalf of the obligor to the person entitled to enforce the instrument, the obligation of the obligor to pay interest after the due date on the amount tendered is discharged. If presentment is required with respect to an instrument and the obligor is able and ready to pay on the due date at every place of payment stated in the instrument, the obligor is deemed to have made tender of payment on the due date to the person entitled to enforce the instrument.

### § 3–604. Discharge by Cancellation or Renunciation.

(a) A person entitled to enforce an instrument may, with or without consideration, discharge the obligation of a party to pay the instrument (i) by an intentional voluntary act such as surrender of the instrument to the party, destruction, mutilation, or cancellation of the instrument, cancellation or striking out of the party's signature, or the addition of words to the instrument indicating discharge, or (ii) by agreeing not to sue or otherwise renouncing rights against the party by a signed writing.

(b) Cancellation or striking out of an indorsement pursuant to subsection (a) does not affect the status and rights of a party derived from the indorsement.

### § 3–605. Discharge of Indorsers and Accommodation Parties.

(a) For the purposes of this section, the term "indorser" includes a drawer having the obligation stated in Section 3–414(c).

(b) Discharge of the obligation of a party to the instrument under Section 3–605 does not discharge the obligation of an indorser or accommodation party having a right of recourse against the discharged party.

(c) If a person entitled to enforce an instrument agrees, with or without consideration, to a material modification of the obligation of a party to the instrument, including an extension of the due date, there is discharge of the obligation of an indorser or accommodation party having a right of recourse against the person whose obligation is modified to the extent the modification causes loss to the indorser or accommodation party with respect to the right of recourse. The indorser or accommodation party is deemed to have suffered loss as a result of the modification equal to the amount of the right of recourse unless the person enforcing the instrument proves that no loss was caused by the modification or that the loss caused by the modification was less than the amount of the right of recourse.

(d) If the obligation of a party to an instrument is secured by an interest in collateral and impairment of the value of the interest is caused by a person entitled to enforce the instrument, there is discharge of the obligation of an indorser or accommodation party having a right of recourse against the obligor to the extent of the impairment. The value of an interest in collateral is impaired to the extent (i) the value of the interest is reduced to an amount less than the amount of the right of recourse of the party asserting discharge, or (ii) the reduction in value of the interest causes an increase in the amount by which the amount of the right of recourse exceeds the value of the interest. The burden of proving impairment is on the party asserting discharge.

(e) If the obligation of a party to an instrument is secured by an interest in collateral not provided by an accommodation party and the value of the interest is impaired by a person entitled to enforce the instrument, the obligation of any party who is jointly and severally liable with respect to the secured obligation is discharged to the extent the impairment causes the party asserting discharge to pay more than that party would have been obliged to pay, taking into account rights of contribution, if impairment had not occurred. If the party asserting discharge is an accommodation party not entitled to discharge under subsection (d), the party is deemed to have a right to contribution based on joint and several liability rather than a right to reimbursement. The burden of proving impairment is on the party asserting discharge.

(f) Under subsection (d) or (e) causation of impairment includes (i) failure to obtain or maintain perfection or recordation of the interest in collateral, (ii) release of collateral without substitution of collateral of equal value, (iii) failure to perform a duty to preserve the value of collateral owed, under Article 9 or other law, to a debtor or surety or other person secondarily liable, or (iv) failure to comply with applicable law in disposing of collateral.

(g) An accommodation party is not discharged under subsection (c) or (d) unless the person agreeing to the modification or causing the impairment knows of the accommodation or has notice under Section 3–419(c) that the instrument was signed for accommodation. There is no discharge of any party under subsection (c), (d), or (e) if (i) the party asserting discharge consents to the event or conduct that is the basis of the discharge, or (ii) the instrument or a separate agreement of the party provides for waiver of discharge under this section either specifically or by general language indicating that parties to the instrument waive defenses based on suretyship or impairment of collateral.

# ARTICLE 4: BANK DEPOSITS AND COLLECTIONS

## Part 1—General Provisions and Definitions

### § 4–101.  Short Title.
This Article may be cited as Uniform Commercial Code—Bank Deposits and Collections.

### § 4–102.  Applicability.
(a) To the extent that items within this Article are also within Articles 3 and 8, they are subject to those Articles. If there is conflict, this Article governs Article 3, but Article 8 governs this Article.

(b) The liability of a bank for action or non-action with respect to an item handled by it for purposes of presentment, payment, or collection is governed by the law of the place where the bank is located. In the case of action or non-action by or at a branch or separate office of a bank, its liability is governed by the law of the place where the branch or separate office is located.

### § 4–103.  Variation by Agreement; Measure of Damages; Action Constituting Ordinary Care.
(a) The effect of the provisions of this Article may be varied by agreement, but the parties to the agreement cannot disclaim a bank's responsibility for its lack of good faith or failure to exercise ordinary care or limit the measure of damages for the lack or failure. However, the parties may determine by agreement the standards by which the bank's responsibility is to be measured if those standards are not manifestly unreasonable.

(b) Federal Reserve regulations and operating circulars, clearing-house rules, and the like have the effect of agreements under subsection (a), whether or not specifically assented to by all parties interested in items handled.

(c) Action or non-action approved by this Article or pursuant to Federal Reserve regulations or operating circulars is the exercise of ordinary care and, in the absence of special instructions, action or non-action consistent with clearing-house rules and the like or with a general banking usage not disapproved by this Article, is prima facie the exercise of ordinary care.

(d) The specification or approval of certain procedures by this Article is not disapproval of other procedures that may be reasonable under the circumstances.

(e) The measure of damages for failure to exercise ordinary care in handling an item is the amount of the item reduced by an amount that could not have been realized by the exercise of ordinary care. If there is also bad faith it includes any other damages the party suffered as a proximate consequence.

### § 4–104.  Definitions and Index of Definitions.
(a) In this Article, unless the context otherwise requires:

(1) "Account" means any deposit or credit account with a bank, including a demand, time, savings, passbook, share draft, or like account, other than an account evidenced by a certificate of deposit;

(2) "Afternoon" means the period of a day between noon and midnight;

(3) "Banking day" means the part of a day on which a bank is open to the public for carrying on substantially all of its banking functions;

(4) "Clearing house" means an association of banks or other payors regularly clearing items;

(5) "Customer" means a person having an account with a bank or for whom a bank has agreed to collect items, including a bank that maintains an account at another bank;

(6) "Documentary draft" means a draft to be presented for acceptance or payment if specified documents, certificated securities (Section 8–102) or instructions for uncertificated securities (Section 8–102), or other certificates, statements, or the like are to be received by the drawee or other payor before acceptance or payment of the draft;

(7) "Draft" means a draft as defined in Section 3–104 or an item, other than an instrument, that is an order;

(8) "Drawee" means a person ordered in a draft to make payment;

(9) "Item" means an instrument or a promise or order to pay money handled by a bank for collection or payment. The term does not include a payment order governed by Article 4A or a credit or debit card slip;

(10) "Midnight deadline" with respect to a bank is midnight on its next banking day following the banking day on which it receives the relevant item or notice or from which the time for taking action commences to run, whichever is later;

(11) "Settle" means to pay in cash, by clearing-house settlement, in a charge or credit or by remittance, or otherwise as agreed. A settlement may be either provisional or final;

(12) "Suspends payments" with respect to a bank means that it has been closed by order of the supervisory authorities, that a public officer has been appointed to take it over, or that it ceases or refuses to make payments in the ordinary course of business.

(b) Other definitions applying to this Article and the sections in which they appear are:

| | |
|---|---|
| "Agreement for electronic presentment" | Section 4–110. |
| "Bank" | Section 4–105. |
| "Collecting bank" | Section 4–105. |
| "Depository bank" | Section 4–105. |
| "Intermediary bank" | Section 4–105. |
| "Payor bank" | Section 4–105. |
| "Presenting bank" | Section 4–105. |
| "Presentment notice" | Section 4–110. |

(c) The following definitions in other Articles apply to this Article:

| | |
|---|---|
| "Acceptance" | Section 3–409. |
| "Alteration" | Section 3–407. |
| "Cashier's check" | Section 3–104. |
| "Certificate of deposit" | Section 3–104. |
| "Certified check" | Section 3–109. |
| "Check" | Section 3–104. |
| "Good faith" | Section 3–103. |
| "Holder in due course" | Section 3–302. |
| "Instrument" | Section 3–104. |
| "Notice of dishonor" | Section 3–503. |
| "Order" | Section 3–103. |
| "Ordinary care" | Section 3–103. |
| "Person entitled to enforce" | Section 3–301. |
| "Presentment" | Section 3–501. |
| "Promise" | Section 3–103. |
| "Prove" | Section 3–103. |
| "Teller's check" | Section 3–104. |
| "Unauthorized signature" | Section 3–403. |

(d) In addition, Article 1 contains general definitions and principles of construction and interpretation applicable throughout this Article. As amended in 1990 and 1994.

### § 4–105. "Bank"; "Depository Bank"; "Payor Bank"; "Intermediary Bank"; "Collecting Bank"; "Presenting Bank".

In this Article:

(1) "Bank" means a person engaged in the business of banking, including a savings bank, savings and loan association, credit union, or trust company;

(2) "Depository bank" means the first bank to take an item even though it is also the payor bank, unless the item is presented for immediate payment over the counter;

(3) "Payor bank" means a bank that is the drawee of a draft;

(4) "Intermediary bank" means a bank to which an item is transferred in course of collection except the depositary or payor bank;

(5) "Collecting bank" means a bank handling an item for collection except the payor bank;

(6) "Presenting bank" means a bank presenting an item except a payor bank.

### § 4–106. Payable Through or Payable at Bank: Collecting Bank.

(a) If an item states that it is "payable through" a bank identified in the item, (i) the item designates the bank as a collecting bank and does not by itself authorize the bank to pay the item, and (ii) the item may be presented for payment only by or through the bank.

**Alternative A**

(b) If an item states that it is "payable at" a bank identified in the item, the item is equivalent to a draft drawn on the bank.

**Alternative B**

(b) If an item states that it is "payable at" a bank identified in the item, (i) the item designates the bank as a collecting bank and does not by itself authorize the bank to pay the item, and (ii) the item may be presented for payment only by or through the bank.

(c) If a draft names a nonbank drawee and it is unclear whether a bank named in the draft is a co-drawee or a collecting bank, the bank is a collecting bank.

### § 4–107. Separate Office of Bank.

A branch or separate office of a bank is a separate bank for the purpose of computing the time within which and determining the place at or to which action may be taken or notices or orders shall be given under this Article and under Article 3.

### § 4–108. Time of Receipt of Items.

(a) For the purpose of allowing time to process items, prove balances, and make the necessary entries on its books to determine its position for the day, a bank may fix an afternoon hour of 2 P.M. or later as a cutoff hour for the handling of money and items and the making of entries on its books.

(b) An item or deposit of money received on any day after a cutoff hour so fixed or after the close of the banking day may be treated as being received at the opening of the next banking day.

### § 4–109. Delays.

(a) Unless otherwise instructed, a collecting bank in a good faith effort to secure payment of a specific item drawn on a payor other than a bank, and with or without the approval of any person involved, may waive, modify, or extend time limits imposed or permitted by this [Act] for a period not exceeding two additional banking days without discharge of drawers or indorsers or liability to its transferor or a prior party.

(b) Delay by a collecting bank or payor bank beyond time limits prescribed or permitted by this [Act] or by instructions is excused if (i) the delay is caused by interruption of communication or computer facilities, suspension of payments by another bank, war, emergency conditions, failure of equipment, or other circumstances beyond the control of the bank, and (ii) the bank exercises such diligence as the circumstances require.

### § 4–110. Electronic Presentment.

(a) "Agreement for electronic presentment" means an agreement, clearing-house rule, or Federal Reserve regulation or operating circular, providing that presentment of an item may be made by transmission of an image of an item or information describing the item ("presentment notice") rather than delivery of the item itself. The agreement may provide for procedures governing retention, presentment, payment, dishonor, and other matters concerning items subject to the agreement.

(b) Presentment of an item pursuant to an agreement for presentment is made when the presentment notice is received.

(c) If presentment is made by presentment notice, a reference to "item" or "check" in this Article means the presentment notice unless the context otherwise indicates.

### § 4–111.  Statute of Limitations.

An action to enforce an obligation, duty, or right arising under this Article must be commenced within three years after the [cause of action] accrues.

## Part 2—Collection of Items: Depositary and Collecting Banks

### § 4–201.  Status of Collecting Bank as Agent and Provisional Status of Credits; Applicability of Article; Item Indorsed "Pay Any Bank".

(a) Unless a contrary intent clearly appears and before the time that a settlement given by a collecting bank for an item is or becomes final, the bank, with respect to an item, is an agent or sub-agent of the owner of the item and any settlement given for the item is provisional. This provision applies regardless of the form of indorsement or lack of indorsement and even though credit given for the item is subject to immediate withdrawal as of right or is in fact withdrawn; but the continuance of ownership of an item by its owner and any rights of the owner to proceeds of the item are subject to rights of a collecting bank, such as those resulting from outstanding advances on the item and rights of recoupment or setoff. If an item is handled by banks for purposes of presentment, payment, collection, or return, the relevant provisions of this Article apply even though action of the parties clearly establishes that a particular bank has purchased the item and is the owner of it.

(b) After an item has been indorsed with the words "pay any bank" or the like, only a bank may acquire the rights of a holder until the item has been:

(1) returned to the customer initiating collection; or

(2) specially indorsed by a bank to a person who is not a bank.

### § 4–202.  Responsibility for Collection or Return; When Action Timely.

(a) A collecting bank must exercise ordinary care in:

(1) presenting an item or sending it for presentment;

(2) sending notice of dishonor or nonpayment or returning an item other than a documentary draft to the bank's transferor after learning that the item has not been paid or accepted, as the case may be;

(3) settling for an item when the bank receives final settlement; and

(4) notifying its transferor of any loss or delay in transit within a reasonable time after discovery thereof.

(b) A collecting bank exercises ordinary care under subsection (a) by taking proper action before its midnight deadline following receipt of an item, notice, or settlement. Taking proper action within a reasonably longer time may constitute the exercise of ordinary care, but the bank has the burden of establishing timeliness.

(c) Subject to subsection (a)(1), a bank is not liable for the insolvency, neglect, misconduct, mistake, or default of another bank or person or for loss or destruction of an item in the possession of others or in transit.

### § 4–203.  Effect of Instructions.

Subject to Article 3 concerning conversion of instruments (Section 3–420) and restrictive indorsements (Section 3–206), only a collecting bank's transferor can give instructions that affect the bank or constitute notice to it, and a collecting bank is not liable to prior parties for any action taken pursuant to the instructions or in accordance with any agreement with its transferor.

### § 4–204.  Methods of Sending and Presenting; Sending Directly to Payor Bank.

(a) A collecting bank shall send items by a reasonably prompt method, taking into consideration relevant instructions, the nature of the item, the number of those items on hand, the cost of collection involved, and the method generally used by it or others to present those items.

(b) A collecting bank may send:

(1) an item directly to the payor bank;

(2) an item to a nonbank payor if authorized by its transferor; and

(3) an item other than documentary drafts to a nonbank payor, if authorized by Federal Reserve regulation or operating circular, clearing-house rule, or the like.

(c) Presentment may be made by a presenting bank at a place where the payor bank or other payor has requested that presentment be made.

### § 4–205.  Depositary Bank Holder of Unindorsed Item.

If a customer delivers an item to a depositary bank for collection:

(1) the depositary bank becomes a holder of the item at the time it receives the item for collection if the customer at the time of delivery was a holder of the item, whether or not the customer indorses the item, and, if the bank satisfies the other requirements of Section 3–302, it is a holder in due course; and

(2) the depositary bank warrants to collecting banks, the payor bank or other payor, and the drawer that the amount of the item was paid to the customer or deposited to the customer's account.

### § 4–206.  Transfer Between Banks.

Any agreed method that identifies the transferor bank is sufficient for the item's further transfer to another bank.

### § 4–207.  Transfer Warranties.

(a) A customer or collecting bank that transfers an item and receives a settlement or other consideration warrants to the transferee and to any subsequent collecting bank that:

(1) the warrantor is a person entitled to enforce the item;

(2) all signatures on the item are authentic and authorized;

(3) the item has not been altered;

(4) the item is not subject to a defense or claim in recoupment (Section 3–305(a)) of any party that can be asserted against the warrantor; and

(5) the warrantor has no knowledge of any insolvency proceeding commenced with respect to the maker or acceptor or, in the case of an unaccepted draft, the drawer.

(b) If an item is dishonored, a customer or collecting bank transferring the item and receiving settlement or other consideration is obliged to pay the amount due on the item (i) according to the terms of the item at the time it was transferred, or (ii) if the transfer was of an incomplete item, according to its terms when completed as stated in Sections 3–115 and 3–407. The obligation of a transferor is owed to the transferee and to any subsequent collecting bank that takes the item in good faith. A transferor cannot disclaim its obligation under this subsection by an indorsement stating that it is made "without recourse" or otherwise disclaiming liability.

(c) A person to whom the warranties under subsection (a) are made and who took the item in good faith may recover from the warrantor as damages for breach of warranty an amount equal to the loss suffered as a result of the breach, but not more than the amount of the item plus expenses and loss of interest incurred as a result of the breach.

(d) The warranties stated in subsection (a) cannot be disclaimed with respect to checks. Unless notice of a claim for breach of warranty is given to the warrantor within 30 days after the claimant has reason to know of the breach and the identity of the warrantor, the warrantor is discharged to the extent of any loss caused by the delay in giving notice of the claim.

(e) A cause of action for breach of warranty under this section accrues when the claimant has reason to know of the breach.

### § 4–208. Presentment Warranties.

(a) If an unaccepted draft is presented to the drawee for payment or acceptance and the drawee pays or accepts the draft, (i) the person obtaining payment or acceptance, at the time of presentment, and (ii) a previous transferor of the draft, at the time of transfer, warrant to the drawee that pays or accepts the draft in good faith that:

(1) the warrantor is, or was, at the time the warrantor transferred the draft, a person entitled to enforce the draft or authorized to obtain payment or acceptance of the draft on behalf of a person entitled to enforce the draft;

(2) the draft has not been altered; and

(3) the warrantor has no knowledge that the signature of the purported drawer of the draft is unauthorized.

(b) A drawee making payment may recover from a warrantor damages for breach of warranty equal to the amount paid by the drawee less the amount the drawee received or is entitled to receive from the drawer because of the payment. In addition, the drawee is entitled to compensation for expenses and loss of interest resulting from the breach. The right of the drawee to recover damages under this subsection is not affected by any failure of the drawee to exercise ordinary care in making payment. If the drawee accepts the draft (i) breach of warranty is a defense to the obligation of the acceptor, and (ii) if the acceptor makes payment with respect to the draft, the acceptor is entitled to recover from a warrantor for breach of warranty the amounts stated in this subsection.

(c) If a drawee asserts a claim for breach of warranty under subsection (a) based on an unauthorized indorsement of the draft or an alteration of the draft, the warrantor may defend by proving that the indorsement is effective under Section 3–404 or 3–405 or the drawer is precluded under Section 3–406 or 4–406 from asserting against the drawee the unauthorized indorsement or alteration.

(d) If (i) a dishonored draft is presented for payment to the drawer or an indorser or (ii) any other item is presented for payment to a party obliged to pay the item, and the item is paid, the person obtaining payment and a prior transferor of the item warrant to the person making payment in good faith that the warrantor is, or was, at the time the warrantor transferred the item, a person entitled to enforce the item or authorized to obtain payment on behalf of a person entitled to enforce the item. The person making payment may recover from any warrantor for breach of warranty an amount equal to the amount paid plus expenses and loss of interest resulting from the breach.

(e) The warranties stated in subsections (a) and (d) cannot be disclaimed with respect to checks. Unless notice of a claim for breach of warranty is given to the warrantor within 30 days after the claimant has reason to know of the breach and the identity of the warrantor, the warrantor is discharged to the extent of any loss caused by the delay in giving notice of the claim.

(f) A cause of action for breach of warranty under this section accrues when the claimant has reason to know of the breach.

### § 4–209. Encoding and Retention Warranties.

(a) A person who encodes information on or with respect to an item after issue warrants to any subsequent collecting bank and to the payor bank or other payor that the information is correctly encoded. If the customer of a depositary bank encodes, that bank also makes the warranty.

(b) A person who undertakes to retain an item pursuant to an agreement for electronic presentment warrants to any subsequent collecting bank and to the payor bank or other payor that retention and presentment of the item comply with the agreement. If a customer of a depositary bank undertakes to retain an item, that bank also makes this warranty.

(c) A person to whom warranties are made under this section and who took the item in good faith may recover from the warrantor as damages for breach of warranty an amount equal to the loss suffered as a result of the breach, plus expenses and loss of interest incurred as a result of the breach.

### § 4–210. Security Interest of Collecting Bank in Items, Accompanying Documents and Proceeds.

(a) A collecting bank has a security interest in an item and any accompanying documents or the proceeds of either:

(1) in case of an item deposited in an account, to the extent to which credit given for the item has been withdrawn or applied;

(2) in case of an item for which it has given credit available for withdrawal as of right, to the extent of the credit given, whether or not the credit is drawn upon or there is a right of charge-back; or

(3) if it makes an advance on or against the item.

(b) If credit given for several items received at one time or pursuant to a single agreement is withdrawn or applied in part, the security interest remains upon all the items, any accompanying documents or the proceeds of either. For the purpose of this section, credits first given are first withdrawn.

(c) Receipt by a collecting bank of a final settlement for an item is a realization on its security interest in the item, accompanying documents, and proceeds. So long as the bank does not receive final settlement for the item or give up possession of the item or accompanying documents for purposes other than collection, the security interest continues to that extent and is subject to Article 9, but:

(1) no security agreement is necessary to make the security interest enforceable (Section 9–203 (1)(a));

(2) no filing is required to perfect the security interest; and

(3) the security interest has priority over conflicting perfected security interests in the item, accompanying documents, or proceeds.

### § 4–211. When Bank Gives Value for Purposes of Holder in Due Course.

For purposes of determining its status as a holder in due course, a bank has given value to the extent it has a security interest in an item, if the bank otherwise complies with the requirements of Section 3–302 on what constitutes a holder in due course.

### § 4–212. Presentment by Notice of Item Not Payable by, Through, or at Bank; Liability of Drawer or Indorser.

(a) Unless otherwise instructed, a collecting bank may present an item not payable by, through, or at a bank by sending to the party to accept or pay a written notice that the bank holds the item for acceptance or payment. The notice must be sent in time to be received on or before the day when presentment is due and the bank must meet any requirements of the party to accept or pay under Section 3–501 by the close of the bank's next banking day after it knows of the requirement.

(b) If presentment is made by notice and payment, acceptance, or request for compliance with a requirement under Section 3–501 is not received by the close of business on the day after maturity or, in the case of demand items, by the close of business on the third banking day after notice was sent, the presenting bank may treat the item as dishonored and charge any drawer or indorser by sending it notice of the facts.

### § 4–213. Medium and Time of Settlement by Bank.

(a) With respect to settlement by a bank, the medium and time of settlement may be prescribed by Federal Reserve regulations or circulars, clearing-house rules, and the like, or agreement. In the absence of such prescription:

(1) the medium of settlement is cash or credit to an account in a Federal Reserve bank of or specified by the person to receive settlement; and

(2) the time of settlement, is:

(i) with respect to tender of settlement by cash, a cashier's check, or teller's check, when the cash or check is sent or delivered;

(ii) with respect to tender of settlement by credit in an account in a Federal Reserve Bank, when the credit is made;

(iii) with respect to tender of settlement by a credit or debit to an account in a bank, when the credit or debit is made or, in the case of tender of settlement by authority to charge an account, when the authority is sent or delivered; or

(iv) with respect to tender of settlement by a funds transfer, when payment is made pursuant to Section 4A–406(a) to the person receiving settlement.

(b) If the tender of settlement is not by a medium authorized by subsection (a) or the time of settlement is not fixed by subsection (a), no settlement occurs until the tender of settlement is accepted by the person receiving settlement.

(c) If settlement for an item is made by cashier's check or teller's check and the person receiving settlement, before its midnight deadline:

(1) presents or forwards the check for collection, settlement is final when the check is finally paid; or

(2) fails to present or forward the check for collection, settlement is final at the midnight deadline of the person receiving settlement.

(d) If settlement for an item is made by giving authority to charge the account of the bank giving settlement in the bank receiving settlement, settlement is final when the charge is made by the bank receiving settlement if there are funds available in the account for the amount of the item.

### § 4–214. Right of Charge—Back or Refund; Liability of Collecting Bank: Return of Item.

(a) If a collecting bank has made provisional settlement with its customer for an item and fails by reason of dishonor, suspension of payments by a bank, or otherwise to receive settlement for the item which is or becomes final, the bank may revoke the settlement given by it, charge back the amount of any credit given for the item to its customer's account, or obtain refund from its customer, whether or not it is able to return the item, if by its midnight deadline or within a longer reasonable time after it learns the facts it returns the item or sends notification of the facts. If the return or notice is delayed beyond the bank's midnight deadline or a longer reasonable time after it learns the facts, the bank may revoke the settlement, charge back the credit, or obtain refund from its customer, but it is liable for any loss resulting from the delay. These rights to revoke, charge back, and obtain refund terminate if and when a settlement for the item received by the bank is or becomes final.

(b) A collecting bank returns an item when it is sent or delivered to the bank's customer or transferor or pursuant to its instructions.

(c) A depositary bank that is also the payor may charge back the amount of an item to its customer's account or obtain refund in accordance with the section governing return of an item received by a payor bank for credit on its books (Section 4–301).

(d) The right to charge back is not affected by:

(1) previous use of a credit given for the item; or

(2) failure by any bank to exercise ordinary care with respect to the item, but a bank so failing remains liable.

(e) A failure to charge back or claim refund does not affect other rights of the bank against the customer or any other party.

(f) If credit is given in dollars as the equivalent of the value of an item payable in foreign money, the dollar amount of any charge-back or refund must be calculated on the basis of the bank-offered spot rate for the foreign money prevailing on the day when the person entitled to the charge-back or refund learns that it will not receive payment in ordinary course.

As amended in 1990.

### § 4–215. Final Payment of Item by Payor Bank; When Provisional Debits and Credits Become Final; When Certain Credits Become Available for Withdrawal.

(a) An item is finally paid by a payor bank when the bank has first done any of the following:

(1) paid the item in cash;

(2) settled for the item without having a right to revoke the settlement under statute, clearing-house rule, or agreement; or

(3) made a provisional settlement for the item and failed to revoke the settlement in the time and manner permitted by statute, clearing-house rule, or agreement.

(b) If provisional settlement for an item does not become final, the item is not finally paid.

(c) If provisional settlement for an item between the presenting and payor banks is made through a clearing house or by debits or credits in an account between them, then to the extent that provisional debits or credits for the item are entered in accounts between the presenting and payor banks or between the presenting and successive prior collecting banks seriatim, they become final upon final payment of the item by the payor bank.

(d) If a collecting bank receives a settlement for an item which is or becomes final, the bank is accountable to its customer for the amount of the item and any provisional credit given for the item in an account with its customer becomes final.

(e) Subject to (i) applicable law stating a time for availability of funds and (ii) any right of the bank to apply the credit to an obligation of the customer, credit given by a bank for an item in a customer's account becomes available for withdrawal as of right:

(1) if the bank has received a provisional settlement for the item, when the settlement becomes final and the bank has had a reasonable time to receive return of the item and the item has not been received within that time;

(2) if the bank is both the depositary bank and the payor bank, and the item is finally paid, at the opening of the bank's second banking day following receipt of the item.

(f) Subject to applicable law stating a time for availability of funds and any right of a bank to apply a deposit to an obligation of the depositor, a deposit of money becomes available for withdrawal as of right at the opening of the bank's next banking day after receipt of the deposit.

### § 4–216. Insolvency and Preference.

(a) If an item is in or comes into the possession of a payor or collecting bank that suspends payment and the item has not been finally paid, the item must be returned by the receiver, trustee, or agent in charge of the closed bank to the presenting bank or the closed bank's customer.

(b) If a payor bank finally pays an item and suspends payments without making a settlement for the item with its customer or the presenting bank which settlement is or becomes final, the owner of the item has a preferred claim against the payor bank.

(c) If a payor bank gives or a collecting bank gives or receives a provisional settlement for an item and thereafter suspends payments, the suspension does not prevent or interfere with the settlement's becoming final if the finality occurs automatically upon the lapse of certain time or the happening of certain events.

(d) If a collecting bank receives from subsequent parties settlement for an item, which settlement is or becomes final and the bank suspends payments without making a settlement for the item with its customer which settlement is or becomes final, the owner of the item has a preferred claim against the collecting bank.

## Part 3—Collection of Items: Payor Banks

### § 4–301. Deferred Posting; Recovery of Payment by Return of Items; Time of Dishonor; Return of Items by Payor Bank.

(a) If a payor bank settles for a demand item other than a documentary draft presented otherwise than for immediate payment over the counter before midnight of the banking day of receipt, the payor bank may revoke the settlement and recover the settlement if, before it has made final payment and before its midnight deadline, it

    (1) returns the item; or

    (2) sends written notice of dishonor or nonpayment if the item is unavailable for return.

(b) If a demand item is received by a payor bank for credit on its books, it may return the item or send notice of dishonor and may revoke any credit given or recover the amount thereof withdrawn by its customer, if it acts within the time limit and in the manner specified in subsection (a).

(c) Unless previous notice of dishonor has been sent, an item is dishonored at the time when for purposes of dishonor it is returned or notice sent in accordance with this section.

(d) An item is returned:

    (1) as to an item presented through a clearing house, when it is delivered to the presenting or last collecting bank or to the clearing house or is sent or delivered in accordance with clearing-house rules; or

    (2) in all other cases, when it is sent or delivered to the bank's customer or transferor or pursuant to instructions.

### § 4–302. Payor Bank's Responsibility for Late Return of Item.

(a) If an item is presented to and received by a payor bank, the bank is accountable for the amount of:

    (1) a demand item, other than a documentary draft, whether properly payable or not, if the bank, in any case in which it is not also the depositary bank, retains the item beyond midnight of the banking day of receipt without settling for it or, whether or not it is also the depositary bank, does not pay or return the item or send notice of dishonor until after its midnight deadline; or

    (2) any other properly payable item unless, within the time allowed for acceptance or payment of that item, the bank either accepts or pays the item or returns it and accompanying documents.

(b) The liability of a payor bank to pay an item pursuant to subsection (a) is subject to defenses based on breach of a presentment warranty (Section 4–208) or proof that the person seeking enforcement of the liability presented or transferred the item for the purpose of defrauding the payor bank.

### § 4–303. When Items Subject to Notice, Stop-Payment Order, Legal Process, or Setoff; Order in Which Items May Be Charged or Certified.

(a) Any knowledge, notice, or stop-payment order received by, legal process served upon, or setoff exercised by a payor bank comes too late to terminate, suspend, or modify the bank's right or duty to pay an item or to charge its customer's account for the item if the knowledge, notice, stop-payment order, or legal process is received or served and a reasonable time for the bank to act thereon expires or the setoff is exercised after the earliest of the following:

    (1) the bank accepts or certifies the item;

    (2) the bank pays the item in cash;

    (3) the bank settles for the item without having a right to revoke the settlement under statute, clearing-house rule, or agreement;

    (4) the bank becomes accountable for the amount of the item under Section 4–302 dealing with the payor bank's responsibility for late return of items; or

    (5) with respect to checks, a cutoff hour no earlier than one hour after the opening of the next banking day after the banking day on which the bank received the check and no later than the close of that next banking day or, if no cutoff hour is fixed, the close of the next banking day after the banking day on which the bank received the check.

(b) Subject to subsection (a), items may be accepted, paid, certified, or charged to the indicated account of its customer in any order.

## Part 4—Relationship Between Payor Bank and Its Customer

### § 4–401. When Bank May Charge Customer's Account.

(a) A bank may charge against the account of a customer an item that is properly payable from the account even though the charge creates an overdraft. An item is properly payable if it is authorized by the customer and is in accordance with any agreement between the customer and bank.

(b) A customer is not liable for the amount of an overdraft if the customer neither signed the item nor benefited from the proceeds of the item.

(c) A bank may charge against the account of a customer a check that is otherwise properly payable from the account, even though payment was made before the date of the check, unless the customer has given notice to the bank of the postdating describing the check with reasonable certainty. The notice is effective for the period stated in Section 4–403(b) for stop-payment orders, and must be received at such time and in such manner as to afford the bank a reasonable opportunity to act on it before the bank takes any action with respect to the check described in Section 4–303. If a bank charges against the account of a customer a check before the date stated in the notice of postdating, the bank is liable for damages for the loss resulting from its act. The loss may include damages for dishonor of subsequent items under Section 4–402.

(d) A bank that in good faith makes payment to a holder may charge the indicated account of its customer according to:

(1) the original terms of the altered item; or

(2) the terms of the completed item, even though the bank knows the item has been completed unless the bank has notice that the completion was improper.

## §4–402. Bank's Liability to Customer for Wrongful Dishonor; Time of Determining Insufficiency of Account.

(a) Except as otherwise provided in this Article, a payor bank wrongfully dishonors an item if it dishonors an item that is properly payable, but a bank may dishonor an item that would create an overdraft unless it has agreed to pay the overdraft.

(b) A payor bank is liable to its customer for damages proximately caused by the wrongful dishonor of an item. Liability is limited to actual damages proved and may include damages for an arrest or prosecution of the customer or other consequential damages. Whether any consequential damages are proximately caused by the wrongful dishonor is a question of fact to be determined in each case.

(c) A payor bank's determination of the customer's account balance on which a decision to dishonor for insufficiency of available funds is based may be made at any time between the time the item is received by the payor bank and the time that the payor bank returns the item or gives notice in lieu of return, and no more than one determination need be made. If, at the election of the payor bank, a subsequent balance determination is made for the purpose of reevaluating the bank's decision to dishonor the item, the account balance at that time is determinative of whether a dishonor for insufficiency of available funds is wrongful.

As amended in 1990.

See Appendix IX for material relating to changes made in text in 1990.

## § 4–403. Customer's Right to Stop Payment; Burden of Proof of Loss.

(a) A customer or any person authorized to draw on the account if there is more than one person may stop payment of any item drawn on the customer's account or close the account by an order to the bank describing the item or account with reasonable certainty received at a time and in a manner that affords the bank a reasonable opportunity to act on it before any action by the bank with respect to the item described in Section 4–303. If the signature of more than one person is required to draw on an account, any of these persons may stop payment or close the account.

(b) A stop-payment order is effective for six months, but it lapses after 14 calendar days if the original order was oral and was not confirmed in writing within that period. A stop-payment order may be renewed for additional six-month periods by a writing given to the bank within a period during which the stop-payment order is effective.

(c) The burden of establishing the fact and amount of loss resulting from the payment of an item contrary to a stop-payment order or order to close an account is on the customer. The loss from payment of an item contrary to a stop-payment order may include damages for dishonor of subsequent items under Section 4–402.

## § 4–404. Bank Not Obliged to Pay Check More Than Six Months Old.

A bank is under no obligation to a customer having a checking account to pay a check, other than a certified check, which is presented more than six months after its date, but it may charge its customer's account for a payment made thereafter in good faith.

## § 4–405. Death or Incompetence of Customer.

(a) A payor or collecting bank's authority to accept, pay, or collect an item or to account for proceeds of its collection, if otherwise effective, is not rendered ineffective by incompetence of a customer of either bank existing at the time the item is issued or its collection is undertaken if the bank does not know of an adjudication of incompetence. Neither death nor incompetence of a customer revokes the authority to accept, pay, collect, or account until the bank knows of the fact of death or of an adjudication of incompetence and has reasonable opportunity to act on it.

(b) Even with knowledge, a bank may for 10 days after the date of death pay or certify checks drawn on or before that date unless ordered to stop payment by a person claiming an interest in the account.

## § 4–406. Customer's Duty to Discover and Report Unauthorized Signature or Alteration.

(a) A bank that sends or makes available to a customer a statement of account showing payment of items for the account shall either return or make available to the customer the items paid or provide information in the statement of account sufficient to allow the customer reasonably to identify the items paid. The statement of account provides sufficient information if the item is described by item number, amount, and date of payment.

(b) If the items are not returned to the customer, the person retaining the items shall either retain the items or, if the items are destroyed, maintain the capacity to furnish legible copies of the items until the expiration of seven years after receipt of the items. A customer may request an item from the bank that paid the item, and that bank must provide in a reasonable time either the item or, if the item has been destroyed or is not otherwise obtainable, a legible copy of the item.

(c) If a bank sends or makes available a statement of account or items pursuant to subsection (a), the customer must exercise reasonable promptness in examining the statement or the items to determine whether any payment was not authorized because of an alteration of an item or because a purported signature by or on behalf of the customer was not authorized. If, based on the statement or items provided, the customer should reasonably have discovered the unauthorized payment, the customer must promptly notify the bank of the relevant facts.

(d) If the bank proves that the customer failed, with respect to an item, to comply with the duties imposed on the customer by subsection (c), the customer is precluded from asserting against the bank:

(1) the customer's unauthorized signature or any alteration on the item, if the bank also proves that it suffered a loss by reason of the failure; and

(2) the customer's unauthorized signature or alteration by the same wrong-doer on any other item paid in good faith by the bank if the payment was made before the bank received notice from the customer of the unauthorized signature or alteration and after the customer had been afforded a reasonable period of time, not exceeding 30 days, in which to examine the item or statement of account and notify the bank.

(e) If subsection (d) applies and the customer proves that the bank failed to exercise ordinary care in paying the item and that the failure substantially contributed to loss, the loss is allocated between the customer precluded and the bank asserting the preclusion according to the extent to which the failure of the customer to comply with subsection (c) and the failure of the bank to exercise ordinary care contributed to the loss. If the customer proves that the bank did not pay the item in good faith, the preclusion under subsection (d) does not apply.

(f) Without regard to care or lack of care of either the customer or the bank, a customer who does not within one year after the statement or items are made available to the customer (subsection (a)) discover and report the customer's unauthorized signature on or any alteration on the item is precluded from asserting against the bank the unauthorized signature or alteration. If there is a preclusion under this subsection, the payor bank may not recover for breach or warranty under Section 4–208 with respect to the unauthorized signature or alteration to which the preclusion applies.

### § 4–407.  Payor Bank's Right to Subrogation on Improper Payment.

If a payor bank has paid an item over the order of the drawer or maker to stop payment, or after an account has been closed, or otherwise under circumstances giving a basis for objection by the drawer or maker, to prevent unjust enrichment and only to the extent necessary to prevent loss to the bank by reason of its payment of the item, the payor bank is subrogated to the rights

> (1) of any holder in due course on the item against the drawer or maker;
> (2) of the payee or any other holder of the item against the drawer or maker either on the item or under the transaction out of which the item arose; and
> (3) of the drawer or maker against the payee or any other holder of the item with respect to the transaction out of which the item arose.

### Part 5—Collection of Documentary Drafts

### § 4–501.  Handling of Documentary Drafts; Duty to Send for Presentment and to Notify Customer of Dishonor.

A bank that takes a documentary draft for collection shall present or send the draft and accompanying documents for presentment and, upon learning that the draft has not been paid or accepted in due course, shall seasonably notify its customer of the fact even though it may have discounted or bought the draft or extended credit available for withdrawal as of right.

### § 4–502.  Presentment of "On Arrival" Drafts.

If a draft or the relevant instructions require presentment "on arrival", "when goods arrive" or the like, the collecting bank need not present until in its judgment a reasonable time for arrival of the goods has expired. Refusal to pay or accept because the goods have not arrived is not dishonor; the bank must notify its transferor of the refusal but need not present the draft again until it is instructed to do so or learns of the arrival of the goods.

### § 4–503.  Responsibility of Presenting Bank for Documents and Goods; Report of Reasons for Dishonor; Referee in Case of Need.

Unless otherwise instructed and except as provided in Article 5, a bank presenting a documentary draft:

> (1) must deliver the documents to the drawee on acceptance of the draft if it is payable more than three days after presentment; otherwise, only on payment; and
> (2) upon dishonor, either in the case of presentment for acceptance or presentment for payment, may seek and follow instructions from any referee in case of need designated in the draft or, if the presenting bank does not choose to utilize the referee's

services, it must use diligence and good faith to ascertain the reason for dishonor, must notify its transferor of the dishonor and of the results of its effort to ascertain the reasons therefor, and must request instructions.

However the presenting bank is under no obligation with respect to goods represented by the documents except to follow any reasonable instructions seasonably received; it has a right to reimbursement for any expense incurred in following instructions and to prepayment of or indemnity for those expenses.

### § 4–504.  Privilege of Presenting Bank to Deal With Goods; Security Interest for Expenses.

(a) A presenting bank that, following the dishonor of a documentary draft, has seasonably requested instructions but does not receive them within a reasonable time may store, sell, or otherwise deal with the goods in any reasonable manner.

(b) For its reasonable expenses incurred by action under subsection (a) the presenting bank has a lien upon the goods or their proceeds, which may be foreclosed in the same manner as an unpaid seller's lien.

## ARTICLE 4A:  FUNDS TRANSFERS

### Part 1—Subject Matter and Definitions

### § 4A–101.  Short Title.

This Article may be cited as Uniform Commercial Code—Funds Transfers.

### § 4A–102.  Subject Matter.

Except as otherwise provided in Section 4A–108, this Article applies to funds transfers defined in Section 4A–104.

### § 4A–103.  Payment Order—Definitions.

(a) In this Article:

> (1) "Payment order" means an instruction of a sender to a receiving bank, transmitted orally, electronically, or in writing, to pay, or to cause another bank to pay, a fixed or determinable amount of money to a beneficiary if:
>> (i) the instruction does not state a condition to payment to the beneficiary other than time of payment,
>> (ii) the receiving bank is to be reimbursed by debiting an account of, or otherwise receiving payment from, the sender, and
>> (iii) the instruction is transmitted by the sender directly to the receiving bank or to an agent, funds-transfer system, or communication system for transmittal to the receiving bank.
> (2) "Beneficiary" means the person to be paid by the beneficiary's bank.
> (3) "Beneficiary's bank" means the bank identified in a payment order in which an account of the beneficiary is to be credited pursuant to the order or which otherwise is to make payment to the beneficiary if the order does not provide for payment to an account.
> (4) "Receiving bank" means the bank to which the sender's instruction is addressed.
> (5) "Sender" means the person giving the instruction to the receiving bank.

(b) If an instruction complying with subsection (a)(1) is to make more than one payment to a beneficiary, the instruction is a separate payment order with respect to each payment.

(c) A payment order is issued when it is sent to the receiving bank.

### § 4A–104. Funds Transfer—Definitions.

In this Article:

(a) "Funds transfer" means the series of transactions, beginning with the originator's payment order, made for the purpose of making payment to the beneficiary of the order. The term includes any payment order issued by the originator's bank or an intermediary bank intended to carry out the originator's payment order. A funds transfer is completed by acceptance by the beneficiary's bank of a payment order for the benefit of the beneficiary of the originator's payment order.

(b) "Intermediary bank" means a receiving bank other than the originator's bank or the beneficiary's bank.

(c) "Originator" means the sender of the first payment order in a funds transfer.

(d) "Originator's bank" means (i) the receiving bank to which the payment order of the originator is issued if the originator is not a bank, or (ii) the originator if the originator is a bank.

### § 4A–105. Other Definitions.

(a) In this Article:

(1) "Authorized account" means a deposit account of a customer in a bank designated by the customer as a source of payment orders issued by the customer to the bank. If a customer does not so designate an account, any account of the customer is an authorized account if payment of a payment order from that account is not inconsistent with a restriction on the use of that account.

(2) "Bank" means a person engaged in the business of banking and includes a savings bank, savings and loan association, credit union, and trust company. A branch or separate office of a bank is a separate bank for purposes of this Article.

(3) "Customer" means a person, including a bank, having an account with a bank or from whom a bank has agreed to receive payment orders.

(4) "Funds-transfer business day" of a receiving bank means the part of a day during which the receiving bank is open for the receipt, processing, and transmittal of payment orders and cancellations and amendments of payment orders.

(5) "Funds-transfer system" means a wire transfer network, automated clearing house, or other communication system of a clearing house or other association of banks through which a payment order by a bank may be transmitted to the bank to which the order is addressed.

(6) "Good faith" means honesty in fact and the observance of reasonable commercial standards of fair dealing.

(7) "Prove" with respect to a fact means to meet the burden of establishing the fact (Section 1–201(8)).

(b) Other definitions applying to this Article and the sections in which they appear are:

"Acceptance" Section 4A–209
"Beneficiary" Section 4A–103
"Beneficiary's bank" Section 4A–103
"Executed" Section 4A–301
"Execution date" Section 4A–301
"Funds transfer" Section 4A–104
"Funds-transfer system rule" Section 4A–501
"Intermediary bank" Section 4A–104
"Originator" Section 4A–104
"Originator's bank" Section 4A–104

"Payment by beneficiary's bank to beneficiary" Section 4A–405
"Payment by originator to beneficiary" Section 4A–406
"Payment by sender to receiving bank" Section 4A–403
"Payment date" Section 4A–401
"Payment order" Section 4A–103
"Receiving bank" Section 4A–103
"Security procedure" Section 4A–201
"Sender" Section 4A–103

(c) The following definitions in Article 4 apply to this Article:

"Clearing house" Section 4–104
"Item" Section 4–104
"Suspends payments" Section 4–104

(d) In addition Article 1 contains general definitions and principles of construction and interpretation applicable throughout this Article.

### § 4A–106. Time Payment Order Is Received.

(a) The time of receipt of a payment order or communication cancelling or amending a payment order is determined by the rules applicable to receipt of a notice stated in Section 1–201(27). A receiving bank may fix a cut-off time or times on a funds-transfer business day for the receipt and processing of payment orders and communications cancelling or amending payment orders. Different cut-off times may apply to payment orders, cancellations, or amendments, or to different categories of payment orders, cancellations, or amendments. A cut-off time may apply to senders generally or different cut-off times may apply to different senders or categories of payment orders. If a payment order or communication cancelling or amending a payment order is received after the close of a funds-transfer business day or after the appropriate cut-off time on a funds-transfer business day, the receiving bank may treat the payment order or communication as received at the opening of the next funds-transfer business day.

(b) If this Article refers to an execution date or payment date or states a day on which a receiving bank is required to take action, and the date or day does not fall on a funds-transfer business day, the next day that is a funds-transfer business day is treated as the date or day stated, unless the contrary is stated in this Article.

### § 4A–107. Federal Reserve Regulations and Operating Circulars.

Regulations of the Board of Governors of the Federal Reserve System and operating circulars of the Federal Reserve Banks supersede any inconsistent provision of this Article to the extent of the inconsistency.

### § 4A–108. Exclusion of Consumer Transactions Governed by Federal Law.

This Article does not apply to a funds transfer any part of which is governed by the Electronic Fund Transfer Act of 1978 (Title XX, Public Law 95–630, 92 Stat. 3728, 15 U.S.C. § 1693 et seq.) as amended from time to time.

## Part 2—Issue and Acceptance of Payment Order

### § 4A–201. Security Procedure.

"Security procedure" means a procedure established by agreement of a customer and a receiving bank for the purpose of (i) verifying that a payment order or communication amending or cancelling a payment order is that of the customer, or (ii) detecting error in the transmission or the content of the payment order or communication. A security procedure may require the use of algorithms or other codes, identifying words or numbers, encryption, callback procedures, or similar security devices. Comparison of a signature on a payment order or communication with an authorized specimen signature of the customer is not by itself a security procedure.

## § 4A–202.  Authorized and Verified Payment Orders.

(a)  A payment order received by the receiving bank is the authorized order of the person identified as sender if that person authorized the order or is otherwise bound by it under the law of agency.

(b)  If a bank and its customer have agreed that the authenticity of payment orders issued to the bank in the name of the customer as sender will be verified pursuant to a security procedure, a payment order received by the receiving bank is effective as the order of the customer, whether or not authorized, if (i) the security procedure is a commercially reasonable method of providing security against unauthorized payment orders, and (ii) the bank proves that it accepted the payment order in good faith and in compliance with the security procedure and any written agreement or instruction of the customer restricting acceptance of payment orders issued in the name of the customer. The bank is not required to follow an instruction that violates a written agreement with the customer or notice of which is not received at a time and in a manner affording the bank a reasonable opportunity to act on it before the payment order is accepted.

(c)  Commercial reasonableness of a security procedure is a question of law to be determined by considering the wishes of the customer expressed to the bank, the circumstances of the customer known to the bank, including the size, type, and frequency of payment orders normally issued by the customer to the bank, alternative security procedures offered to the customer, and security procedures in general use by customers and receiving banks similarly situated. A security procedure is deemed to be commercially reasonable if (i) the security procedure was chosen by the customer after the bank offered, and the customer refused, a security procedure that was commercially reasonable for that customer, and (ii) the customer expressly agreed in writing to be bound by any payment order, whether or not authorized, issued in its name and accepted by the bank in compliance with the security procedure chosen by the customer.

(d)  The term "sender" in this Article includes the customer in whose name a payment order is issued if the order is the authorized order of the customer under subsection (a), or it is effective as the order of the customer under subsection (b).

(e)  This section applies to amendments and cancellations of payment orders to the same extent it applies to payment orders.

(f)  Except as provided in this section and in Section 4A–203(a)(1), rights and obligations arising under this section or Section 4A–203 may not be varied by agreement.

## § 4A–203.  Unenforceability of Certain Verified Payment Orders.

(a)  If an accepted payment order is not, under Section 4A–202(a), an authorized order of a customer identified as sender, but is effective as an order of the customer pursuant to Section 4A–202(b), the following rules apply:

(1)  By express written agreement, the receiving bank may limit the extent to which it is entitled to enforce or retain payment of the payment order.

(2)  The receiving bank is not entitled to enforce or retain payment of the payment order if the customer proves that the order was not caused, directly or indirectly, by a person (i) entrusted at any time with duties to act for the customer with respect to payment orders or the security procedure, or (ii) who obtained access to transmitting facilities of the customer or who obtained, from a source controlled by the customer and without authority of the receiving bank, information facilitating breach of the security procedure, regardless of how the information was obtained

or whether the customer was at fault. Information includes any access device, computer software, or the like.

(b)  This section applies to amendments of payment orders to the same extent it applies to payment orders.

## § 4A–204.  Refund of Payment and Duty of Customer to Report with Respect to Unauthorized Payment Order.

(a)  If a receiving bank accepts a payment order issued in the name of its customer as sender which is (i) not authorized and not effective as the order of the customer under Section 4A–202, or (ii) not enforceable, in whole or in part, against the customer under Section 4A–203, the bank shall refund any payment of the payment order received from the customer to the extent the bank is not entitled to enforce payment and shall pay interest on the refundable amount calculated from the date the bank received payment to the date of the refund. However, the customer is not entitled to interest from the bank on the amount to be refunded if the customer fails to exercise ordinary care to determine that the order was not authorized by the customer and to notify the bank of the relevant facts within a reasonable time not exceeding 90 days after the date the customer received notification from the bank that the order was accepted or that the customer's account was debited with respect to the order. The bank is not entitled to any recovery from the customer on account of a failure by the customer to give notification as stated in this section.

(b)  Reasonable time under subsection (a) may be fixed by agreement as stated in Section 1–204(1), but the obligation of a receiving bank to refund payment as stated in subsection (a) may not otherwise be varied by agreement.

## § 4A–205.  Erroneous Payment Orders.

(a)  If an accepted payment order was transmitted pursuant to a security procedure for the detection of error and the payment order (i) erroneously instructed payment to a beneficiary not intended by the sender, (ii) erroneously instructed payment in an amount greater than the amount intended by the sender, or (iii) was an erroneously transmitted duplicate of a payment order previously sent by the sender, the following rules apply:

(1)  If the sender proves that the sender or a person acting on behalf of the sender pursuant to Section 4A–206 complied with the security procedure and that the error would have been detected if the receiving bank had also complied, the sender is not obliged to pay the order to the extent stated in paragraphs (2) and (3).

(2)  If the funds transfer is completed on the basis of an erroneous payment order described in clause (i) or (iii) of subsection (a), the sender is not obliged to pay the order and the receiving bank is entitled to recover from the beneficiary any amount paid to the beneficiary to the extent allowed by the law governing mistake and restitution.

(3)  If the funds transfer is completed on the basis of a payment order described in clause (ii) of subsection (a), the sender is not obliged to pay the order to the extent the amount received by the beneficiary is greater than the amount intended by the sender. In that case, the receiving bank is entitled to recover from the beneficiary the excess amount received to the extent allowed by the law governing mistake and restitution.

(b)  If (i) the sender of an erroneous payment order described in subsection (a) is not obliged to pay all or part of the order, and (ii) the sender receives notification from the receiving bank that the order was accepted by the bank or that the sender's account was debited with respect to the order, the sender has a duty to exercise ordinary care, on the basis of information available to the sender, to discover the error with respect to the order and to advise the bank of the relevant facts within a reasonable time, not exceeding 90 days, after the bank's notification was received by the sender. If the bank proves that the sender failed to perform that duty, the sender is liable to the bank for the loss the bank proves it incurred as a result of the failure, but the liability of the sender may not exceed the amount of the sender's order.

(c) This section applies to amendments to payment orders to the same extent it applies to payment orders.

### § 4A–206.  Transmission of Payment Order Through Funds-Transfer or Other Communication System.

(a) If a payment order addressed to a receiving bank is transmitted to a funds-transfer system or other third-party communication system for transmittal to the bank, the system is deemed to be an agent of the sender for the purpose of transmitting the payment order to the bank. If there is a discrepancy between the terms of the payment order transmitted to the system and the terms of the payment order transmitted by the system to the bank, the terms of the payment order of the sender are those transmitted by the system. This section does not apply to a funds-transfer system of the Federal Reserve Banks.

(b) This section applies to cancellations and amendments of payment orders to the same extent it applies to payment orders.

### § 4A–207.  Misdescription of Beneficiary.

(a) Subject to subsection (b), if, in a payment order received by the beneficiary's bank, the name, bank account number, or other identification of the beneficiary refers to a nonexistent or unidentifiable person or account, no person has rights as a beneficiary of the order and acceptance of the order cannot occur.

(b) If a payment order received by the beneficiary's bank identifies the beneficiary both by name and by an identifying or bank account number and the name and number identify different persons, the following rules apply:

(1) Except as otherwise provided in subsection (c), if the beneficiary's bank does not know that the name and number refer to different persons, it may rely on the number as the proper identification of the beneficiary of the order. The beneficiary's bank need not determine whether the name and number refer to the same person.

(2) If the beneficiary's bank pays the person identified by name or knows that the name and number identify different persons, no person has rights as beneficiary except the person paid by the beneficiary's bank if that person was entitled to receive payment from the originator of the funds transfer. If no person has rights as beneficiary, acceptance of the order cannot occur.

(c) If (i) a payment order described in subsection (b) is accepted, (ii) the originator's payment order described the beneficiary inconsistently by name and number, and (ii) the beneficiary's bank pays the person identified by number as permitted by subsection (b)(1), the following rules apply:

(1) If the originator is a bank, the originator is obliged to pay its order.

(2) If the originator is not a bank and proves that the person identified by number was not entitled to receive payment from the originator, the originator is not obliged to pay its order unless the originator's bank proves that the originator, before acceptance of the originator's order, had notice that payment of a payment order issued by the originator might be made by the beneficiary's bank on the basis of an identifying or bank account

number even if it identifies a person different from the named beneficiary. Proof of notice may be made by any admissible evidence. The originator's bank satisfies the burden of proof if it proves that the originator, before the payment order was accepted, signed a writing stating the information to which the notice relates.

(d) In a case governed by subsection (b)(1), if the beneficiary's bank rightfully pays the person identified by number and that person was not entitled to receive payment from the originator, the amount paid may be recovered from that person to the extent allowed by the law governing mistake and restitution as follows:

(1) If the originator is obliged to pay its payment order as stated in subsection (c), the originator has the right to recover.

(2) If the originator is not a bank and is not obliged to pay its payment order, the originator's bank has the right to recover.

### § 4A–208.  Misdescription of Intermediary Bank or Beneficiary's Bank.

(a) This subsection applies to a payment order identifying an intermediary bank or the beneficiary's bank only by an identifying number.

(1) The receiving bank may rely on the number as the proper identification of the intermediary or beneficiary's bank and need not determine whether the number identifies a bank.

(2) The sender is obliged to compensate the receiving bank for any loss and expenses incurred by the receiving bank as a result of its reliance on the number in executing or attempting to execute the order.

(b) This subsection applies to a payment order identifying an intermediary bank or the beneficiary's bank both by name and an identifying number if the name and number identify different persons.

(1) If the sender is a bank, the receiving bank may rely on the number as the proper identification of the intermediary or beneficiary's bank if the receiving bank, when it executes the sender's order, does not know that the name and number identify different persons. The receiving bank need not determine whether the name and number refer to the same person or whether the name refers to a bank. The sender is obliged to compensate the receiving bank for any loss and expenses incurred by the receiving bank as a result of its reliance on the number in executing or attempting to execute the order.

(2) If the sender is not a bank and the receiving bank proves that the sender, before the payment order was accepted, had notice that the receiving bank might rely on the number as the proper identification of the intermediary or beneficiary's bank even if it identifies a person different from the bank identified by name, the rights and obligations of the sender and the receiving bank are governed by subsection (b)(1), as though the sender were a bank. Proof of notice may be made by any admissible evidence. The receiving bank satisfies the burden of proof if it proves that the sender, before the payment order was accepted, signed a writing stating the information to which the notice relates.

(3) Regardless of whether the sender is a bank, the receiving bank may rely on the name as the proper identification of the intermediary or beneficiary's bank if the receiving bank, at the time it executes the sender's order, does not know that the name and number identify different persons. The receiving bank need not determine whether the name and number refer to the same person.

(4) If the receiving bank knows that the name and number identify different persons, reliance on either the name or the

number in executing the sender's payment order is a breach of the obligation stated in Section 4A–302(a)(1).

## § 4A–209.  Acceptance of Payment Order.

(a)  Subject to subsection (d), a receiving bank other than the beneficiary's bank accepts a payment order when it executes the order.

(b)  Subject to subsections (c) and (d), a beneficiary's bank accepts a payment order at the earliest of the following times:

(1)  when the bank (i) pays the beneficiary as stated in Section 4A–405(a) or 4A–405(b), or (ii) notifies the beneficiary of receipt of the order or that the account of the beneficiary has been credited with respect to the order unless the notice indicates that the bank is rejecting the order or that funds with respect to the order may not be withdrawn or used until receipt of payment from the sender of the order;

(2)  when the bank receives payment of the entire amount of the sender's order pursuant to Section 4A–403(a)(1) or 4A–403(a)(2); or

(3)  the opening of the next funds-transfer business day of the bank following the payment date of the order if, at that time, the amount of the sender's order is fully covered by a withdrawable credit balance in an authorized account of the sender or the bank has otherwise received full payment from the sender, unless the order was rejected before that time or is rejected within (i) one hour after that time, or (ii) one hour after the opening of the next business day of the sender following the payment date if that time is later. If notice of rejection is received by the sender after the payment date and the authorized account of the sender does not bear interest, the bank is obliged to pay interest to the sender on the amount of the order for the number of days elapsing after the payment date to the day the sender receives notice or learns that the order was not accepted, counting that day as an elapsed day. If the withdrawable credit balance during that period falls below the amount of the order, the amount of interest payable is reduced accordingly.

(c)  Acceptance of a payment order cannot occur before the order is received by the receiving bank. Acceptance does not occur under subsection (b)(2) or (b)(3) if the beneficiary of the payment order does not have an account with the receiving bank, the account has been closed, or the receiving bank is not permitted by law to receive credits for the beneficiary's account.

(d)  A payment order issued to the originator's bank cannot be accepted until the payment date if the bank is the beneficiary's bank, or the execution date if the bank is not the beneficiary's bank. If the originator's bank executes the originator's payment order before the execution date or pays the beneficiary of the originator's payment order before the payment date and the payment order is subsequently canceled pursuant to Section 4A–211(b), the bank may recover from the beneficiary any payment received to the extent allowed by the law governing mistake and restitution.

## § 4A–210.  Rejection of Payment Order.

(a)  A payment order is rejected by the receiving bank by a notice of rejection transmitted to the sender orally, electronically, or in writing. A notice of rejection need not use any particular words and is sufficient if it indicates that the receiving bank is rejecting the order or will not execute or pay the order. Rejection is effective when the notice is given if transmission is by a means that is reasonable in the circumstances. If notice of rejection is given by a means that is not reasonable, rejection is effective when the notice is received. If an agreement of the sender and receiving bank establishes the means to be used to reject a payment order, (i) any means complying with the agreement is reasonable and (ii) any means not complying is not reasonable unless no significant delay in receipt of the notice resulted from the use of the noncomplying means.

(b)  This subsection applies if a receiving bank other than the beneficiary's bank fails to execute a payment order despite the existence on the execution date of a withdrawable credit balance in an authorized account of the sender sufficient to cover the order. If the sender does not receive notice of rejection of the order on the execution date and the authorized account of the sender does not bear interest, the bank is obliged to pay interest to the sender on the amount of the order for the number of days elapsing after the execution date to the earlier of the day the order is canceled pursuant to Section 4A–211(d) or the day the sender receives notice or learns that the order was not executed, counting the final day of the period as an elapsed day. If the withdrawable credit balance during that period falls below the amount of the order, the amount of interest is reduced accordingly.

(c)  If a receiving bank suspends payments, all unaccepted payment orders issued to it are deemed rejected at the time the bank suspends payments.

(d)  Acceptance of a payment order precludes a later rejection of the order. Rejection of a payment order precludes a later acceptance of the order.

## § 4A–211.  Cancellation and Amendment of Payment Order.

(a)  A communication of the sender of a payment order cancelling or amending the order may be transmitted to the receiving bank orally, electronically, or in writing. If a security procedure is in effect between the sender and the receiving bank, the communication is not effective to cancel or amend the order unless the communication is verified pursuant to the security procedure or the bank agrees to the cancellation or amendment.

(b)  Subject to subsection (a), a communication by the sender cancelling or amending a payment order is effective to cancel or amend the order if notice of the communication is received at a time and in a manner affording the receiving bank a reasonable opportunity to act on the communication before the bank accepts the payment order.

(c)  After a payment order has been accepted, cancellation or amendment of the order is not effective unless the receiving bank agrees or a funds-transfer system rule allows cancellation or amendment without agreement of the bank.

(1)  With respect to a payment order accepted by a receiving bank other than the beneficiary's bank, cancellation or amendment is not effective unless a conforming cancellation or amendment of the payment order issued by the receiving bank is also made.

(2)  With respect to a payment order accepted by the beneficiary's bank, cancellation or amendment is not effective unless the order was issued in execution of an unauthorized payment order, or because of a mistake by a sender in the funds transfer which resulted in the issuance of a payment order (i) that is a duplicate of a payment order previously issued by the sender, (ii) that orders payment to a beneficiary not entitled to receive payment from the originator, or (iii) that orders payment in an amount greater than the amount the beneficiary was entitled to receive from the originator. If the payment order is canceled or amended, the beneficiary's bank is entitled to recover from the beneficiary any amount paid to the beneficiary to the extent allowed by the law governing mistake and restitution.

(d)  An unaccepted payment order is canceled by operation of law at the close of the fifth funds-transfer business day of the receiving bank after the execution date or payment date of the order.

(e) A canceled payment order cannot be accepted. If an accepted payment order is canceled, the acceptance is nullified and no person has any right or obligation based on the acceptance. Amendment of a payment order is deemed to be cancellation of the original order at the time of amendment and issue of a new payment order in the amended form at the same time.

(f) Unless otherwise provided in an agreement of the parties or in a funds-transfer system rule, if the receiving bank, after accepting a payment order, agrees to cancellation or amendment of the order by the sender or is bound by a funds-transfer system rule allowing cancellation or amendment without the bank's agreement, the sender, whether or not cancellation or amendment is effective, is liable to the bank for any loss and expenses, including reasonable attorney's fees, incurred by the bank as a result of the cancellation or amendment or attempted cancellation or amendment.

(g) A payment order is not revoked by the death or legal incapacity of the sender unless the receiving bank knows of the death or of an adjudication of incapacity by a court of competent jurisdiction and has reasonable opportunity to act before acceptance of the order.

(h) A funds-transfer system rule is not effective to the extent it conflicts with subsection (c)(2).

## § 4A–212.  Liability and Duty of Receiving Bank Regarding Unaccepted Payment Order.

If a receiving bank fails to accept a payment order that it is obliged by express agreement to accept, the bank is liable for breach of the agreement to the extent provided in the agreement or in this Article, but does not otherwise have any duty to accept a payment order or, before acceptance, to take any action, or refrain from taking action, with respect to the order except as provided in this Article or by express agreement. Liability based on acceptance arises only when acceptance occurs as stated in Section 4A–209, and liability is limited to that provided in this Article. A receiving bank is not the agent of the sender or beneficiary of the payment order it accepts, or of any other party to the funds transfer, and the bank owes no duty to any party to the funds transfer except as provided in this Article or by express agreement.

## Part 3—Execution of Sender's Payment Order by Receiving Bank

### § 4A–301.  Execution and Execution Date.

(a) A payment order is "executed" by the receiving bank when it issues a payment order intended to carry out the payment order received by the bank. A payment order received by the beneficiary's bank can be accepted but cannot be executed.

(b) "Execution date" of a payment order means the day on which the receiving bank may properly issue a payment order in execution of the sender's order. The execution date may be determined by instruction of the sender but cannot be earlier than the day the order is received and, unless otherwise determined, is the day the order is received. If the sender's instruction states a payment date, the execution date is the payment date or an earlier date on which execution is reasonably necessary to allow payment to the beneficiary on the payment date.

### § 4A–302.  Obligations of Receiving Bank in Execution of Payment Order.

(a) Except as provided in subsections (b) through (d), if the receiving bank accepts a payment order pursuant to Section 4A–209(a), the bank has the following obligations in executing the order:

(1) The receiving bank is obliged to issue, on the execution date, a payment order complying with the sender's order and to follow the sender's instructions concerning (i) any intermediary bank or funds-transfer system to be used in carrying out the funds transfer, or (ii) the means by which payment orders are to be transmitted in the funds transfer. If the originator's bank issues a payment order to an intermediary bank, the originator's bank is obliged to instruct the intermediary bank according to the instruction of the originator. An intermediary bank in the funds transfer is similarly bound by an instruction given to it by the sender of the payment order it accepts.

(2) If the sender's instruction states that the funds transfer is to be carried out telephonically or by wire transfer or otherwise indicates that the funds transfer is to be carried out by the most expeditious means, the receiving bank is obliged to transmit its payment order by the most expeditious available means, and to instruct any intermediary bank accordingly. If a sender's instruction states a payment date, the receiving bank is obliged to transmit its payment order at a time and by means reasonably necessary to allow payment to the beneficiary on the payment date or as soon thereafter as is feasible.

(b) Unless otherwise instructed, a receiving bank executing a payment order may (i) use any funds-transfer system if use of that system is reasonable in the circumstances, and (ii) issue a payment order to the beneficiary's bank or to an intermediary bank through which a payment order conforming to the sender's order can expeditiously be issued to the beneficiary's bank if the receiving bank exercises ordinary care in the selection of the intermediary bank. A receiving bank is not required to follow an instruction of the sender designating a funds-transfer system to be used in carrying out the funds transfer if the receiving bank, in good faith, determines that it is not feasible to follow the instruction or that following the instruction would unduly delay completion of the funds transfer.

(c) Unless subsection (a)(2) applies or the receiving bank is otherwise instructed, the bank may execute a payment order by transmitting its payment order by first class mail or by any means reasonable in the circumstances. If the receiving bank is instructed to execute the sender's order by transmitting its payment order by a particular means, the receiving bank may issue its payment order by the means stated or by any means as expeditious as the means stated.

(d) Unless instructed by the sender, (i) the receiving bank may not obtain payment of its charges for services and expenses in connection with the execution of the sender's order by issuing a payment order in an amount equal to the amount of the sender's order less the amount of the charges, and (ii) may not instruct a subsequent receiving bank to obtain payment of its charges in the same manner.

### § 4A–303.  Erroneous Execution of Payment Order.

(a) A receiving bank that (i) executes the payment order of the sender by issuing a payment order in an amount greater than the amount of the sender's order, or (ii) issues a payment order in execution of the sender's order and then issues a duplicate order, is entitled to payment of the amount of the sender's order under Section 4A–402(c) if that subsection is otherwise satisfied. The bank is entitled to recover from the beneficiary of the erroneous order the excess payment received to the extent allowed by the law governing mistake and restitution.

(b) A receiving bank that executes the payment order of the sender by issuing a payment order in an amount less than the amount of the sender's order is entitled to payment of the amount of the sender's order under Section 4A–402(c) if (i) that subsection is otherwise satisfied and (ii) the bank corrects its mistake by issuing an additional payment order for the benefit of the beneficiary of the sender's order. If the error is not corrected, the issuer of the erroneous order is entitled to receive or retain payment from the sender of the order it accepted only to the extent of the amount of the erroneous order. This subsection does not apply if the receiving bank executes the sender's payment order by issuing a payment order in an amount less than the amount of the sender's order for the purpose of obtaining payment of its charges for services and expenses pursuant to instruction of the sender.

(c) If a receiving bank executes the payment order of the sender by issuing a payment order to a beneficiary different from the beneficiary of the sender's order and the funds transfer is completed on the basis of that error, the sender of the payment order that was erroneously executed and all previous senders in the funds transfer are not obliged to pay the payment orders they issued. The issuer of the erroneous order is entitled to recover from the beneficiary of the order the payment received to the extent allowed by the law governing mistake and restitution.

### § 4A–304. Duty of Sender to Report Erroneously Executed Payment Order.

If the sender of a payment order that is erroneously executed as stated in Section 4A–303 receives notification from the receiving bank that the order was executed or that the sender's account was debited with respect to the order, the sender has a duty to exercise ordinary care to determine, on the basis of information available to the sender, that the order was erroneously executed and to notify the bank of the relevant facts within a reasonable time not exceeding 90 days after the notification from the bank was received by the sender. If the sender fails to perform that duty, the bank is not obliged to pay interest on any amount refundable to the sender under Section 4A–402(d) for the period before the bank learns of the execution error. The bank is not entitled to any recovery from the sender on account of a failure by the sender to perform the duty stated in this section.

### § 4A–305. Liability for Late or Improper Execution or Failure to Execute Payment Order.

(a) If a funds transfer is completed but execution of a payment order by the receiving bank in breach of Section 4A–302 results in delay in payment to the beneficiary, the bank is obliged to pay interest to either the originator or the beneficiary of the funds transfer for the period of delay caused by the improper execution. Except as provided in subsection (c), additional damages are not recoverable.

(b) If execution of a payment order by a receiving bank in breach of Section 4A–302 results in (i) noncompletion of the funds transfer, (ii) failure to use an intermediary bank designated by the originator, or (iii) issuance of a payment order that does not comply with the terms of the payment order of the originator, the bank is liable to the originator for its expenses in the funds transfer and for incidental expenses and interest losses, to the extent not covered by subsection (a), resulting from the improper execution. Except as provided in subsection (c), additional damages are not recoverable.

(c) In addition to the amounts payable under subsections (a) and (b), damages, including consequential damages, are recoverable to the extent provided in an express written agreement of the receiving bank.

(d) If a receiving bank fails to execute a payment order it was obliged by express agreement to execute, the receiving bank is liable to the sender for its expenses in the transaction and for incidental expenses and interest losses resulting from the failure to execute. Additional damages, including consequential damages, are recoverable to the

extent provided in an express written agreement of the receiving bank, but are not otherwise recoverable.

(e) Reasonable attorney's fees are recoverable if demand for compensation under subsection (a) or (b) is made and refused before an action is brought on the claim. If a claim is made for breach of an agreement under subsection (d) and the agreement does not provide for damages, reasonable attorney's fees are recoverable if demand for compensation under subsection (d) is made and refused before an action is brought on the claim.

(f) Except as stated in this section, the liability of a receiving bank under subsections (a) and (b) may not be varied by agreement.

## Part 4—Payment

### § 4A–401. Payment Date.

"Payment date" of a payment order means the day on which the amount of the order is payable to the beneficiary by the beneficiary's bank. The payment date may be determined by instruction of the sender but cannot be earlier than the day the order is received by the beneficiary's bank and, unless otherwise determined, is the day the order is received by the beneficiary's bank.

### § 4A–402. Obligation of Sender to Pay Receiving Bank.

(a) This section is subject to Sections 4A–205 and 4A–207.

(b) With respect to a payment order issued to the beneficiary's bank, acceptance of the order by the bank obliges the sender to pay the bank the amount of the order, but payment is not due until the payment date of the order.

(c) This subsection is subject to subsection (e) and to Section 4A–303. With respect to a payment order issued to a receiving bank other than the beneficiary's bank, acceptance of the order by the receiving bank obliges the sender to pay the bank the amount of the sender's order. Payment by the sender is not due until the execution date of the sender's order. The obligation of that sender to pay its payment order is excused if the funds transfer is not completed by acceptance by the beneficiary's bank of a payment order instructing payment to the beneficiary of that sender's payment order.

(d) If the sender of a payment order pays the order and was not obliged to pay all or part of the amount paid, the bank receiving payment is obliged to refund payment to the extent the sender was not obliged to pay. Except as provided in Sections 4A–204 and 4A–304, interest is payable on the refundable amount from the date of payment.

(e) If a funds transfer is not completed as stated in subsection (c) and an intermediary bank is obliged to refund payment as stated in subsection (d) but is unable to do so because not permitted by applicable law or because the bank suspends payments, a sender in the funds transfer that executed a payment order in compliance with an instruction, as stated in Section 4A–302(a)(1), to route the funds transfer through that intermediary bank is entitled to receive or retain payment from the sender of the payment order that it accepted. The first sender in the funds transfer that issued an instruction requiring routing through that intermediary bank is subrogated to the right of the bank that paid the intermediary bank to refund as stated in subsection (d).

(f) The right of the sender of a payment order to be excused from the obligation to pay the order as stated in subsection (c) or to receive refund under subsection (d) may not be varied by agreement.

### § 4A–403. Payment by Sender to Receiving Bank.

(a) Payment of the sender's obligation under Section 4A–402 to pay the receiving bank occurs as follows:

(1) If the sender is a bank, payment occurs when the receiving bank receives final settlement of the obligation through a Federal Reserve Bank or through a funds-transfer system.

(2) If the sender is a bank and the sender (i) credited an account of the receiving bank with the sender, or (ii) caused an account of the receiving bank in another bank to be credited, payment occurs when the credit is withdrawn or, if not withdrawn, at midnight of the day on which the credit is withdrawable and the receiving bank learns of that fact.

(3) If the receiving bank debits an account of the sender with the receiving bank, payment occurs when the debit is made to the extent the debit is covered by a withdrawable credit balance in the account.

(b) If the sender and receiving bank are members of a funds-transfer system that nets obligations multilaterally among participants, the receiving bank receives final settlement when settlement is complete in accordance with the rules of the system. The obligation of the sender to pay the amount of a payment order transmitted through the funds-transfer system may be satisfied, to the extent permitted by the rules of the system, by setting off and applying against the sender's obligation the right of the sender to receive payment from the receiving bank of the amount of any other payment order transmitted to the sender by the receiving bank through the funds-transfer system. The aggregate balance of obligations owed by each sender to each receiving bank in the funds-transfer system may be satisfied, to the extent permitted by the rules of the system, by setting off and applying against that balance the aggregate balance of obligations owed to the sender by other members of the system. The aggregate balance is determined after the right of setoff stated in the second sentence of this subsection has been exercised.

(c) If two banks transmit payment orders to each other under an agreement that settlement of the obligations of each bank to the other under Section 4A–402 will be made at the end of the day or other period, the total amount owed with respect to all orders transmitted by one bank shall be set off against the total amount owed with respect to all orders transmitted by the other bank. To the extent of the setoff, each bank has made payment to the other.

(d) In a case not covered by subsection (a), the time when payment of the sender's obligation under Section 4A–402(b) or 4A–402(c) occurs is governed by applicable principles of law that determine when an obligation is satisfied.

## § 4A–404.  Obligation of Beneficiary's Bank to Pay and Give Notice to Beneficiary.

(a) Subject to Sections 4A–211(e), 4A–405(d), and 4A–405(e), if a beneficiary's bank accepts a payment order, the bank is obliged to pay the amount of the order to the beneficiary of the order. Payment is due on the payment date of the order, but if acceptance occurs on the payment date after the close of the funds-transfer business day of the bank, payment is due on the next funds-transfer business day. If the bank refuses to pay after demand by the beneficiary and receipt of notice of particular circumstances that will give rise to consequential damages as a result of nonpayment, the beneficiary may recover damages resulting from the refusal to pay to the extent the bank had notice of the damages, unless the bank proves that it did not pay because of a reasonable doubt concerning the right of the beneficiary to payment.

(b) If a payment order accepted by the beneficiary's bank instructs payment to an account of the beneficiary, the bank is obliged to notify the beneficiary of receipt of the order before midnight of the next funds-transfer business day following the payment date. If the payment order does not instruct payment to an account of the beneficiary, the bank is required to notify the beneficiary only if notice is required by the order. Notice may be given by first class mail or any other means reasonable in the circumstances. If the bank fails to give the required notice, the bank is obliged to pay interest to the beneficiary on the amount of the payment order from the day notice should have been given until the day the beneficiary learned of receipt of the payment order by the bank. No other damages are recoverable. Reasonable attorney's fees are also recoverable if demand for interest is made and refused before an action is brought on the claim.

(c) The right of a beneficiary to receive payment and damages as stated in subsection (a) may not be varied by agreement or a funds-transfer system rule. The right of a beneficiary to be notified as stated in subsection (b) may be varied by agreement of the beneficiary or by a funds-transfer system rule if the beneficiary is notified of the rule before initiation of the funds transfer.

## § 4A–405.  Payment by Beneficiary's Bank to Beneficiary.

(a) If the beneficiary's bank credits an account of the beneficiary of a payment order, payment of the bank's obligation under Section 4A–404(a) occurs when and to the extent (i) the beneficiary is notified of the right to withdraw the credit, (ii) the bank lawfully applies the credit to a debt of the beneficiary, or (iii) funds with respect to the order are otherwise made available to the beneficiary by the bank.

(b) If the beneficiary's bank does not credit an account of the beneficiary of a payment order, the time when payment of the bank's obligation under Section 4A–404(a) occurs is governed by principles of law that determine when an obligation is satisfied.

(c) Except as stated in subsections (d) and (e), if the beneficiary's bank pays the beneficiary of a payment order under a condition to payment or agreement of the beneficiary giving the bank the right to recover payment from the beneficiary if the bank does not receive payment of the order, the condition to payment or agreement is not enforceable.

(d) A funds-transfer system rule may provide that payments made to beneficiaries of funds transfers made through the system are provisional until receipt of payment by the beneficiary's bank of the payment order it accepted. A beneficiary's bank that makes a payment that is provisional under the rule is entitled to refund from the beneficiary if (i) the rule requires that both the beneficiary and the originator be given notice of the provisional nature of the payment before the funds transfer is initiated, (ii) the beneficiary, the beneficiary's bank and the originator's bank agreed to be bound by the rule, and (iii) the beneficiary's bank did not receive payment of the payment order that it accepted. If the beneficiary is obliged to refund payment to the beneficiary's bank, acceptance of the payment order by the beneficiary's bank is nullified and no payment by the originator of the funds transfer to the beneficiary occurs under Section 4A–406.

(e) This subsection applies to a funds transfer that includes a payment order transmitted over a funds-transfer system that (i) nets obligations multilaterally among participants, and (ii) has in effect a loss-sharing agreement among participants for the purpose of providing funds necessary to complete settlement of the obligations of one or more participants that do not meet their settlement obligations. If the beneficiary's bank in the funds transfer accepts a payment order and the system fails to complete settlement pursuant to its rules with respect to any payment order in the funds transfer, (i) the acceptance by the beneficiary's bank is nullified and no person has any right or obligation based on the acceptance, (ii) the beneficiary's bank is entitled to recover payment from the beneficiary, (iii) no payment by the originator to the beneficiary occurs under Section 4A–406, and (iv) subject to Section 4A–402(e), each sender in the funds transfer is excused from its obligation to pay its payment order under Section 4A–402(c) because the funds transfer has not been completed.

## § 4A–406.  Payment by Originator to Beneficiary; Discharge of Underlying Obligation.

(a)  Subject to Sections 4A–211(e), 4A–405(d), and 4A–405(e), the originator of a funds transfer pays the beneficiary of the originator's payment order (i) at the time a payment order for the benefit of the beneficiary is accepted by the beneficiary's bank in the funds transfer and (ii) in an amount equal to the amount of the order accepted by the beneficiary's bank, but not more than the amount of the originator's order.

(b)  If payment under subsection (a) is made to satisfy an obligation, the obligation is discharged to the same extent discharge would result from payment to the beneficiary of the same amount in money, unless (i) the payment under subsection (a) was made by a means prohibited by the contract of the beneficiary with respect to the obligation, (ii) the beneficiary, within a reasonable time after receiving notice of receipt of the order by the beneficiary's bank, notified the originator of the beneficiary's refusal of the payment, (iii) funds with respect to the order were not withdrawn by the beneficiary or applied to a debt of the beneficiary, and (iv) the beneficiary would suffer a loss that could reasonably have been avoided if payment had been made by a means complying with the contract. If payment by the originator does not result in discharge under this section, the originator is subrogated to the rights of the beneficiary to receive payment from the beneficiary's bank under Section 4A–404(a).

(c)  For the purpose of determining whether discharge of an obligation occurs under subsection (b), if the beneficiary's bank accepts a payment order in an amount equal to the amount of the originator's payment order less charges of one or more receiving banks in the funds transfer, payment to the beneficiary is deemed to be in the amount of the originator's order unless upon demand by the beneficiary the originator does not pay the beneficiary the amount of the deducted charges.

(d)  Rights of the originator or of the beneficiary of a funds transfer under this section may be varied only by agreement of the originator and the beneficiary.

## Part 5—Miscellaneous Provisions

### § 4A–501.  Variation by Agreement and Effect of Funds-Transfer System Rule.

(a)  Except as otherwise provided in this Article, the rights and obligations of a party to a funds transfer may be varied by agreement of the affected party.

(b)  "Funds-transfer system rule" means a rule of an association of banks (i) governing transmission of payment orders by means of a funds-transfer system of the association or rights and obligations with respect to those orders, or (ii) to the extent the rule governs rights and obligations between banks that are parties to a funds transfer in which a Federal Reserve Bank, acting as an intermediary bank, sends a payment order to the beneficiary's bank. Except as otherwise provided in this Article, a funds-transfer system rule governing rights and obligations between participating banks using the system may be effective even if the rule conflicts with this Article and indirectly affects another party to the funds transfer who does not consent to the rule. A funds-transfer system rule may also govern rights and obligations of parties other than participating banks using the system to the extent stated in Sections 4A–404(c), 4A–405(d), and 4A–507(c).

### § 4A–502.  Creditor Process Served on Receiving Bank; Setoff by Beneficiary's Bank.

(a)  As used in this section, "creditor process" means levy, attachment, garnishment, notice of lien, sequestration, or similar process issued by or on behalf of a creditor or other claimant with respect to an account.

(b)  This subsection applies to creditor process with respect to an authorized account of the sender of a payment order if the creditor process is served on the receiving bank. For the purpose of determining rights with respect to the creditor process, if the receiving bank accepts the payment order the balance in the authorized account is deemed to be reduced by the amount of the payment order to the extent the bank did not otherwise receive payment of the order, unless the creditor process is served at a time and in a manner affording the bank a reasonable opportunity to act on it before the bank accepts the payment order.

(c)  If a beneficiary's bank has received a payment order for payment to the beneficiary's account in the bank, the following rules apply:

(1)  The bank may credit the beneficiary's account. The amount credited may be set off against an obligation owed by the beneficiary to the bank or may be applied to satisfy creditor process served on the bank with respect to the account.

(2)  The bank may credit the beneficiary's account and allow withdrawal of the amount credited unless creditor process with respect to the account is served at a time and in a manner affording the bank a reasonable opportunity to act to prevent withdrawal.

(3)  If creditor process with respect to the beneficiary's account has been served and the bank has had a reasonable opportunity to act on it, the bank may not reject the payment order except for a reason unrelated to the service of process.

(d)  Creditor process with respect to a payment by the originator to the beneficiary pursuant to a funds transfer may be served only on the beneficiary's bank with respect to the debt owed by that bank to the beneficiary. Any other bank served with the creditor process is not obliged to act with respect to the process.

### § 4A–503.  Injunction or Restraining Order With Respect to Funds Transfer.

For proper cause and in compliance with applicable law, a court may restrain (i) a person from issuing a payment order to initiate a funds transfer, (ii) an originator's bank from executing the payment order of the originator, or (iii) the beneficiary's bank from releasing funds to the beneficiary or the beneficiary from withdrawing the funds. A court may not otherwise restrain a person from issuing a payment order, paying or receiving payment of a payment order, or otherwise acting with respect to a funds transfer.

### § 4A–504.  Order in Which Items and Payment Orders May Be Charged to Account; Order of Withdrawals From Account.

(a)  If a receiving bank has received more than one payment order of the sender or one or more payment orders and other items that are payable from the sender's account, the bank may charge the sender's account with respect to the various orders and items in any sequence.

(b)  In determining whether a credit to an account has been withdrawn by the holder of the account or applied to a debt of the holder of the account, credits first made to the account are first withdrawn or applied.

### § 4A–505.  Preclusion of Objection to Debit of Customer's Account.

If a receiving bank has received payment from its customer with respect to a payment order issued in the name of the customer as sender and accepted by the bank, and the customer received notification reasonably identifying the order, the customer is precluded from asserting that the bank is not entitled to retain the payment unless the customer notifies the bank of the customer's objection to the payment within one year after the notification was received by the customer.

### § 4A–506.  Rate of Interest.

(a)  If, under this Article, a receiving bank is obliged to pay interest with respect to a payment order issued to the bank, the amount payable may be determined (i) by agreement of the sender and receiving bank, or (ii) by a funds-transfer system rule if the payment order is transmitted through a funds-transfer system.

(b)  If the amount of interest is not determined by an agreement or rule as stated in subsection (a), the amount is calculated by multiplying the applicable Federal Funds rate by the amount on which interest is payable, and then multiplying the product by the number of days for which interest is payable. The applicable Federal Funds rate is the average of the Federal Funds rates published by the Federal Reserve Bank of New York for each of the days for which interest is payable divided by 360. The Federal Funds rate for any day on which a published rate is not available is the same as the published rate for the next preceding day for which there is a published rate. If a receiving bank that accepted a payment order is required to refund payment to the sender of the order because the funds transfer was not completed, but the failure to complete was not due to any fault by the bank, the interest payable is reduced by a percentage equal to the reserve requirement on deposits of the receiving bank.

### § 4A–507.  Choice of Law.

(a)  The following rules apply unless the affected parties otherwise agree or subsection (c) applies:

(1)  The rights and obligations between the sender of a payment order and the receiving bank are governed by the law of the jurisdiction in which the receiving bank is located.

(2)  The rights and obligations between the beneficiary's bank and the beneficiary are governed by the law of the jurisdiction in which the beneficiary's bank is located.

(3)  The issue of when payment is made pursuant to a funds transfer by the originator to the beneficiary is governed by the law of the jurisdiction in which the beneficiary's bank is located.

(b)  If the parties described in each paragraph of subsection (a) have made an agreement selecting the law of a particular jurisdiction to govern rights and obligations between each other, the law of that jurisdiction governs those rights and obligations, whether or not the payment order or the funds transfer bears a reasonable relation to that jurisdiction.

(c)  A funds-transfer system rule may select the law of a particular jurisdiction to govern (i) rights and obligations between participating banks with respect to payment orders transmitted or processed through the system, or (ii) the rights and obligations of some or all parties to a funds transfer any part of which is carried out by means of the system. A choice of law made pursuant to clause (i) is binding on participating banks. A choice of law made pursuant to clause (ii) is binding on the originator, other sender, or a receiving bank having notice that the funds-transfer system might be used in the funds transfer and of the choice of law by the system when the originator, other sender, or receiving bank issued or accepted a payment order. The beneficiary of a funds transfer is bound by the choice of law if, when the funds transfer is initiated, the beneficiary has notice that the funds-transfer system might be used in the funds transfer and of the choice of law by the system. The law of a jurisdiction selected pursuant to this subsection may govern, whether or not that law bears a reasonable relation to the matter in issue.

(d)  In the event of inconsistency between an agreement under subsection (b) and a choice-of-law rule under subsection (c), the agreement under subsection (b) prevails.

(e)  If a funds transfer is made by use of more than one funds-transfer system and there is inconsistency between choice-of-law rules of the systems, the matter in issue is governed by the law of the selected jurisdiction that has the most significant relationship to the matter in issue.

## ARTICLE 5: LETTERS OF CREDIT

### § 5–101.  Short Title.

This Article shall be known and may be cited as Uniform Commercial Code—Letters of Credit.

### § 5–102.  Scope.

(1)  This Article applies

(a)  to a credit issued by a bank if the credit requires a documentary draft or a documentary demand for payment; and

(b)  to a credit issued by a person other than a bank if the credit requires that the draft or demand for payment be accompanied by a document of title; and

(c)  to a credit issued by a bank or other person if the credit is not within subparagraphs (a) or (b) but conspicuously states that it is a letter of credit or is conspicuously so entitled.

(2)  Unless the engagement meets the requirements of subsection (1), this Article does not apply to engagements to make advances or to honor drafts or demands for payment, to authorities to pay or purchase, to guarantees or to general agreements.

(3)  This Article deals with some but not all of the rules and concepts of letters of credit as such rules or concepts have developed prior to this act or may hereafter develop. The fact that this Article states a rule does not by itself require, imply or negate application of the same or a converse rule to a situation not provided for or to a person not specified by this Article.

### § 5–103.  Definitions.

(1)  In this Article unless the context otherwise requires

(a)  "Credit" or "letter of credit" means an engagement by a bank or other person made at the request of a customer and of a kind within the scope of this Article (Section 5–102) that the issuer will honor drafts or other demands for payment upon compliance with the conditions specified in the credit. A credit may be either revocable or irrevocable. The engagement may be either an agreement to honor or a statement that the bank or other person is authorized to honor.

(b)  A "documentary draft" or a "documentary demand for payment" is one honor of which is conditioned upon the presentation of a document or documents. "Document" means any paper including document of title, security, invoice, certificate, notice of default and the like.

(c)  An "issuer" is a bank or other person issuing a credit.

(d)  A "beneficiary" of a credit is a person who is entitled under its terms to draw or demand payment.

(e)  An "advising bank" is a bank which gives notification of the issuance of a credit by another bank.

(f)  A "confirming bank" is a bank which engages either that it will itself honor a credit already issued by another bank or that such a credit will be honored by the issuer or a third bank.

(g) A "customer" is a buyer or other person who causes an issuer to issue a credit. The term also includes a bank which procures issuance or confirmation on behalf of that bank's customer.

(2) Other definitions applying to this Article and the sections in which they appear are:

"Notation of Credit". Section 5–108.

"Presenter". Section 5–112(3).

(3) Definitions in other Articles applying to this Article and the sections in which they appear are:

"Accept" or "Acceptance". Section 3–409.

"Contract for sale". Section 2–106.

"Draft". Section 3–104.

"Holder in due course". Section 3–302.

"Midnight deadline". Section 4–104.

"Security". Section 8–102.

(4) In addition, Article 1 contains general definitions and principles of construction and interpretation applicable throughout this Article.

## § 5–104.  Formal Requirements; Signing.

(1) Except as otherwise required in subsection (1)(c) of Section 5–102 on scope, no particular form of phrasing is required for a credit. A credit must be in writing and signed by the issuer and a confirmation must be in writing and signed by the confirming bank. A modification of the terms of a credit or confirmation must be signed by the issuer or confirming bank.

(2) A telegram may be a sufficient signed writing if it identifies its sender by an authorized authentication. The authentication may be in code and the authorized naming of the issuer in an advice of credit is a sufficient signing.

## § 5–105.  Consideration.

No consideration is necessary to establish a credit or to enlarge or otherwise modify its terms.

## § 5–106.  Time and Effect of Establishment of Credit.

(1) Unless otherwise agreed a credit is established.

(a) as regards the customer as soon as a letter of credit is sent to him or the letter of credit or an authorized written advice of its issuance is sent to the beneficiary; and

(b) as regards the beneficiary when he receives a letter of credit or an authorized written advice of its issuance.

(2) Unless otherwise agreed once an irrevocable credit is established as regards the customer it can be modified or revoked only with the consent of the customer and once it is established as regards the beneficiary it can be modified or revoked only with his consent.

(3) Unless otherwise agreed after a revocable credit is established it may be modified or revoked by the issuer without notice to or consent from the customer or beneficiary.

(4) Notwithstanding any modification or revocation of a revocable credit any person authorized to honor or negotiate under the terms of the original credit is entitled to reimbursement for or honor of any draft or demand for payment duly honored or negotiated before receipt of notice of the modification or revocation and the issuer in turn is entitled to reimbursement from its customer.

## § 5–107.  Advice of Credit; Confirmation; Error in Statement of Terms.

(1) Unless otherwise specified an advising bank by advising a credit issued by another bank does not assume any obligation to honor drafts drawn or demands for payment made under the credit but it does assume obligation for the accuracy of its own statement.

(2) A confirming bank by confirming a credit becomes directly obligated on the credit to the extent of its confirmation as though it were its issuer and acquires the rights of an issuer.

(3) Even though an advising bank incorrectly advises the terms of a credit it has been authorized to advise the credit is established as against the issuer to the extent of its original terms.

(4) Unless otherwise specified the customer bears as against the issuer all risks of transmission and reasonable translation or interpretation of any message relating to a credit.

## § 5–108.  "Notation Credit"; Exhaustion of Credit.

(1) A credit which specifies that any person purchasing or paying drafts drawn or demands for payment made under it must note the amount of the draft or demand on the letter or advice of credit is a "notation credit".

(2) Under a notation credit

(a) a person paying the beneficiary or purchasing a draft or demand for payment from him acquires a right to honor only if the appropriate notation is made and by transferring or forwarding for honor the documents under the credit such a person warrants to the issuer that the notation has been made; and

(b) unless the credit or a signed statement that an appropriate notation has been made accompanies the draft or demand for payment the issuer may delay honor until evidence of notation has been procured which is satisfactory to it but its obligation and that of its customer continue for a reasonable time not exceeding thirty days to obtain such evidence.

(3) If the credit is not a notation credit

(a) the issuer may honor complying drafts or demands for payment presented to it in the order in which they are presented and is discharged pro tanto by honor of any such draft or demand;

(b) as between competing good faith purchasers of complying drafts or demands the person first purchasing has priority over a subsequent purchaser even though the later purchased draft or demand has been first honored.

## § 5–109.  Issuer's Obligation to Its Customer.

(1) An issuer's obligation to its customer includes good faith and observance of any general banking usage but unless otherwise agreed does not include liability or responsibility

(a) for performance of the underlying contract for sale or other transaction between the customer and the beneficiary; or

(b) for any act or omission of any person other than itself or its own branch or for loss or destruction of a draft, demand or document in transit or in the possession of others; or

(c) based on knowledge or lack of knowledge of any usage of any particular trade.

(2) An issuer must examine documents with care so as to ascertain that on their face they appear to comply with the terms of the credit but unless otherwise agreed assumes no liability or responsibility for the genuineness, falsification or effect of any document which appears on such examination to be regular on its face.

(3) A non-bank issuer is not bound by any banking usage of which it has no knowledge.

## § 5–110.  Availability of Credit in Portions; Presenter's Reservation of Lien or Claim.

(1) Unless otherwise specified a credit may be used in portions in the discretion of the beneficiary.

(2) Unless otherwise specified a person by presenting a documentary draft or demand for payment under a credit relinquishes upon its

honor all claims to the documents and a person by transferring such draft or demand or causing such presentment authorizes such relinquishment. An explicit reservation of claim makes the draft or demand non-complying.

## § 5-111. Warranties on Transfer and Presentment.

(1) Unless otherwise agreed the beneficiary by transferring or presenting a documentary draft or demand for payment warrants to all interested parties that the necessary conditions of the credit have been complied with. This is in addition to any warranties arising under Articles 3, 4, 7 and 8.

(2) Unless otherwise agreed a negotiating, advising, confirming, collecting or issuing bank presenting or transferring a draft or demand for payment under a credit warrants only the matters warranted by a collecting bank under Article 4 and any such bank transferring a document warrants only the matters warranted by an intermediary under Articles 7 and 8.

## § 5-112. Time Allowed for Honor or Rejection; Withholding Honor or Rejection by Consent; "Presenter".

(1) A bank to which a documentary draft or demand for payment is presented under a credit may without dishonor of the draft, demand or credit

    (a) defer honor until the close of the third banking day following receipt of the documents; and

    (b) further defer honor if the presenter has expressly or impliedly consented thereto.

Failure to honor within the time here specified constitutes dishonor of the draft or demand and of the credit [except as otherwise provided in subsection (4) of Section 5-114 on conditional payment].

Note: *The bracketed language in the last sentence of subsection (1) should be included only if the optional provisions of Section 5-114(4) and (5) are included.*

(2) Upon dishonor the bank may unless otherwise instructed fulfill its duty to return the draft or demand and the documents by holding them at the disposal of the presenter and sending him an advice to that effect.

(3) "Presenter" means any person presenting a draft or demand for payment for honor under a credit even though that person is a confirming bank or other correspondent which is acting under an issuer's authorization.

## § 5-113. Indemnities.

(1) A bank seeking to obtain (whether for itself or another) honor, negotiation or reimbursement under a credit may give an indemnity to induce such honor, negotiation or reimbursement.

(2) An indemnity agreement inducing honor, negotiation or reimbursement

    (a) unless otherwise explicitly agreed applies to defects in the documents but not in the goods; and

    (b) unless a longer time is explicitly agreed expires at the end of ten business days following receipt of the documents by the ultimate customer unless notice of objection is sent before such expiration date. The ultimate customer may send notice of objection to the person from whom he received the documents and any bank receiving such notice is under a duty to send notice to its transferor before its midnight deadline.

## § 5-114. Issuer's Duty and Privilege to Honor; Right to Reimbursement.

(1) An issuer must honor a draft or demand for payment which complies with the terms of the relevant credit regardless of whether the goods or documents conform to the underlying contract for sale or other contract between the customer and the beneficiary. The issuer is not excused from honor of such a draft or demand by reason of an additional general term that all documents must be satisfactory to the issuer, but an issuer may require that specified documents must be satisfactory to it.

(2) Unless otherwise agreed when documents appear on their face to comply with the terms of a credit but a required document does not in fact conform to the warranties made on negotiation or transfer of a document of title (Section 7-507) or of a certificated security (Section 8-306) or is forged or fraudulent or there is fraud in the transaction:

    (a) the issuer must honor the draft or demand for payment if honor is demanded by a negotiating bank or other holder of the draft or demand which has taken the draft or demand under the credit and under circumstances which would make it a holder in due course (Section 3-302) and in an appropriate case would make it a person to whom a document of title has been duly negotiated (Section 7-502) or a bona fide purchaser of a certificated security (Section 8-302); and

    (b) in all other cases as against its customer, an issuer acting in good faith may honor the draft or demand for payment despite notification from the customer of fraud, forgery or other defect not apparent on the face of the documents but a court of appropriate jurisdiction may enjoin such honor.

(3) Unless otherwise agreed an issuer which has duly honored a draft or demand for payment is entitled to immediate reimbursement of any payment made under the credit and to be put in effectively available funds not later than the day before maturity of any acceptance made under the credit.

[(4) When a credit provides for payment by the issuer on receipt of notice that the required documents are in the possession of a correspondent or other agent of the issuer

    (a) any payment made on receipt of such notice is conditional; and

    (b) the issuer may reject documents which do not comply with the credit if it does so within three banking days following its receipt of the documents; and

    (c) in the event of such rejection, the issuer is entitled by charge back or otherwise to return of the payment made.]

[(5) In the case covered by subsection (4) failure to reject documents within the time specified in sub-paragraph (b) constitutes acceptance of the documents and makes the payment final in favor of the beneficiary.] Amended in 1977.

Note: *Subsections (4) and (5) are bracketed as optional. If they are included the bracketed language in the last sentence of Section 5-112(1) should also be included.*

## § 5-115. Remedy for Improper Dishonor or Anticipatory Repudiation.

(1) When an issuer wrongfully dishonors a draft or demand for payment presented under a credit the person entitled to honor has with respect to any documents the rights of a person in the position of a seller (Section 2-707) and may recover from the issuer the face amount of the draft or demand together with incidental damages under Section 2-710 on seller's incidental damages and interest but less any amount realized by resale or other use or disposition of the subject matter of the transaction. In the event no resale or other utilization is made the documents, goods or other subject matter involved in the transaction must be turned over to the issuer on payment of judgment.

(2)  When an issuer wrongfully cancels or otherwise repudiates a credit before presentment of a draft or demand for payment drawn under it the beneficiary has the rights of a seller after anticipatory repudiation by the buyer under Section 2–610 if he learns of the repudiation in time reasonably to avoid procurement of the required documents. Otherwise the beneficiary has an immediate right of action for wrongful dishonor.

### § 5–116.  Transfer and Assignment.
(1)  The right to draw under a credit can be transferred or assigned only when the credit is expressly designated as transferable or assignable.
(2)  Even though the credit specifically states that it is nontransferable or nonassignable the beneficiary may before performance of the conditions of the credit assign his right to proceeds. Such an assignment is an assignment of an account under Article 9 on Secured Transactions and is governed by that Article except that

    (a)  the assignment is ineffective until the letter of credit or advice of credit is delivered to the assignee which delivery constitutes perfection of the security interest under Article 9; and

    (b)  the issuer may honor drafts or demands for payment drawn under the credit until it receives a notification of the assignment signed by the beneficiary which reasonably identifies the credit involved in the assignment and contains a request to pay the assignee; and

    (c)  after what reasonably appears to be such a notification has been received the issuer may without dishonor refuse to accept or pay even to a person otherwise entitled to honor until the letter of credit or advice of credit is exhibited to the issuer.

(3)  Except where the beneficiary has effectively assigned his right to draw or his right to proceeds, nothing in this section limits his right to transfer or negotiate drafts or demands drawn under the credit.

### § 5–117.  Insolvency of Bank Holding Funds for Documentary Credit.
(1)  Where an issuer or an advising or confirming bank or a bank which has for a customer procured issuance of a credit by another bank becomes insolvent before final payment under the credit and the credit is one to which this Article is made applicable by paragraphs (a) or (b) of Section 5–102(1) on scope, the receipt or allocation of funds or collateral to secure or meet obligations under the credit shall have the following results:

    (a)  to the extent of any funds or collateral turned over after or before the insolvency as indemnity against or specifically for the purpose of payment of drafts or demands for payment drawn under the designated credit, the drafts or demands are entitled to payment in preference over depositors or other general creditors of the issuer or bank; and

    (b)  on expiration of the credit or surrender of the beneficiary's rights under it unused any person who has given such funds or collateral is similarly entitled to return thereof; and

    (c)  a charge to a general or current account with a bank if specifically consented to for the purpose of indemnity against or payment of drafts or demands for payment drawn under the designated credit falls under the same rules as if the funds had been drawn out in cash and then turned over with specific instructions.

(2)  After honor or reimbursement under this section the customer or other person for whose account the insolvent bank has acted is entitled to receive the documents involved.

## ARTICLE 6: BULK TRANSFERS

### § 6–101.  Short Title.
This Article shall be known and may be cited as Uniform Commercial Code—Bulk Transfers.

### § 6–102.  "Bulk Transfer"; Transfers of Equipment; Enterprises Subject to This Article; Bulk Transfers Subject to This Article.
(1)  A "bulk transfer" is any transfer in bulk and not in the ordinary course of the transferor's business of a major part of the materials, supplies, merchandise or other inventory (Section 9–109) of an enterprise subject to this Article.
(2)  A transfer of a substantial part of the equipment (Section 9–109) of such an enterprise is a bulk transfer if it is made in connection with a bulk transfer of inventory, but not otherwise.
(3)  The enterprises subject to this Article are all those whose principal business is the sale of merchandise from stock, including those who manufacture what they sell.
(4)  Except as limited by the following section all bulk transfers of goods located within this state are subject to this Article.

### § 6–103.  Transfers Excepted From This Article.
The following transfers are not subject to this Article:
(1)  Those made to give security for the performance of an obligation;
(2)  General assignments for the benefit of all the creditors of the transferor, and subsequent transfers by the assignee thereunder;
(3)  Transfers in settlement or realization of a lien or other security interest;
(4)  Sales by executors, administrators, receivers, trustees in bankruptcy, or any public officer under judicial process;
(5)  Sales made in the course of judicial or administrative proceedings for the dissolution or reorganization of a corporation and of which notice is sent to the creditors of the corporation pursuant to order of the court or administrative agency;
(6)  Transfers to a person maintaining a known place of business in this State who becomes bound to pay the debts of the transferor in full and gives public notice of that fact, and who is solvent after becoming so bound;
(7)  A transfer to a new business enterprise organized to take over and continue the business, if public notice of the transaction is given and the new enterprise assumes the debts of the transferor and he receives nothing from the transaction except an interest in the new enterprise junior to the claims of creditors;
(8)  Transfers of property which is exempt from execution.
Public notice under subsection (6) or subsection (7) may be given by publishing once a week for two consecutive weeks in a newspaper of general circulation where the transferor had its principal place of business in this state an advertisement including the names and addresses of the transferor and transferee and the effective date of the transfer.

### § 6–104.  Schedule of Property, List of Creditors.
(1)  Except as provided with respect to auction sales (Section 6–108), a bulk transfer subject to this Article is ineffective against any creditor of the transferor unless:

    (a)  The transferee requires the transferor to furnish a list of his existing creditors prepared as stated in this section; and

    (b)  The parties prepare a schedule of the property transferred sufficient to identify it; and

    (c)  The transferee preserves the list and schedule for six months next following the transfer and permits inspection of either or both and copying therefrom at all reasonable hours by any creditor of the transferor, or files the list and schedule in *(a public office to be here identified)*.

(2) The list of creditors must be signed and sworn to or affirmed by the transferor or his agent. It must contain the names and business addresses of all creditors of the transferor, with the amounts when known, and also the names of all persons who are known to the transferor to assert claims against him even though such claims are disputed. If the transferor is the obligor of an outstanding issue of bonds, debentures or the like as to which there is an indenture trustee, the list of creditors need include only the name and address of the indenture trustee and the aggregate outstanding principal amount of the issue.

(3) Responsibility for the completeness and accuracy of the list of creditors rests on the transferor, and the transfer is not rendered ineffective by errors or omissions therein unless the transferee is shown to have had knowledge.

## § 6–105.  Notice to Creditors.

In addition to the requirements of the preceding section, any bulk transfer subject to this Article except one made by auction sale (Section 6–108) is ineffective against any creditor of the transferor unless at least ten days before he takes possession of the goods or pays for them, whichever happens first, the transferee gives notice of the transfer in the manner and to the persons hereafter provided (Section 6–107).

## [§ 6–106.  Application of the Proceeds

In addition to the requirements of the two preceding sections:

(1) Upon every bulk transfer subject to this Article for which new consideration becomes payable except those made by sale at auction it is the duty of the transferee to assure that such consideration is applied so far as necessary to pay those debts of the transferor which are either shown on the list furnished by the transferor (Section 6–104) or filed in writing in the place stated in the notice (Section 6–107) within thirty days after the mailing of such notice. This duty of the transferee runs to all the holders of such debts, and may be enforced by any of them for the benefit of all.

(2) If any of said debts are in dispute the necessary sum may be withheld from distribution until the dispute is settled or adjudicated.

(3) If the consideration payable is not enough to pay all of the said debts in full distribution shall be made pro rata.]

Note: *This section is bracketed to indicate division of opinion as to whether or not it is a wise provision, and to suggest that this is a point on which State enactments may differ without serious damage to the principal of uniformity. In any State where this section is omitted, the following parts of sections, also bracketed in the text, should also be omitted, namely:*

> *Section 6–107(2)(e).*
> *6–108(3)(c).*
> *6–109(2).*
> *In any State where this section is enacted, these other provisions should be also.*

## Optional Subsection (4)

[[(4) The transferee may within ten days after he takes possession of the goods pay the consideration into the (specify court) in the county where the transferor had its principal place of business in this state and thereafter may discharge his duty under this section by giving notice by registered or certified mail to all the persons to whom the duty runs that the consideration has been paid into that court and that they should file their claims there. On motion of any interested party, the court may order the distribution of the consideration to the persons entitled to it.]

Note: *Optional subsection (4) is recommended for those states which do not have a general statute providing for payment of money into court.*

## § 6–107.  The Notice.

(1) The notice to creditors (Section 6–105) shall state:

> (a) that a bulk transfer is about to be made; and
>
> (b) the names and business addresses of the transferor and transferee, and all other business names and addresses used by the transferor within three years last past so far as known to the transferee; and
>
> (c) whether or not all the debts of the transferor are to be paid in full as they fall due as a result of the transaction, and if so, the address to which creditors should send their bills.

(2) If the debts of the transferor are not to be paid in full as they fall due or if the transferee is in doubt on that point then the notice shall state further:

> (a) the location and general description of the property to be transferred and the estimated total of the transferor's debts;
>
> (b) the address where the schedule of property and list of creditors (Section 6–104) may be inspected;
>
> (c) whether the transfer is to pay existing debts and if so the amount of such debts and to whom owing;
>
> (d) whether the transfer is for new consideration and if so the amount of such consideration and the time and place of payment; [and]
>
> [(e) if for new consideration the time and place where creditors of the transferor are to file their claims.]

(3) The notice in any case shall be delivered personally or sent by registered or certified mail to all the persons shown on the list of creditors furnished by the transferor (Section 6–104) and to all other persons who are known to the transferee to hold or assert claims against the transferor.

## § 6–108.  Auction Sales; "Auctioneer".

(1) A bulk transfer is subject to this Article even though it is by sale at auction, but only in the manner and with the results stated in this section.

(2) The transferor shall furnish a list of his creditors and assist in the preparation of a schedule of the property to be sold, both prepared as before stated (Section 6–104).

(3) The person or persons other than the transferor who direct, control or are responsible for the auction are collectively called the "auctioneer". The auctioneer shall:

> (a) receive and retain the list of creditors and prepare and retain the schedule of property for the period stated in this Article (Section 6–104);
>
> (b) give notice of the auction personally or by registered or certified mail at least ten days before it occurs to all persons shown on the list of creditors and to all other persons who are known to him to hold or assert claims against the transferor; [and]
>
> [(c) assure that the net proceeds of the auction are applied as provided in this Article (Section 6–106).]

(4) Failure of the auctioneer to perform any of these duties does not affect the validity of the sale or the title of the purchasers, but if the auctioneer knows that the auction constitutes a bulk transfer such failure renders the auctioneer liable to the creditors of the transferor as a class for the sums owing to them from the transferor up to but not exceeding the net proceeds of the auction. If the auctioneer consists of several persons their liability is joint and several.

## § 6–109. What Creditors Protected; [Credit for Payment to Particular Creditors].

(1) The creditors of the transferor mentioned in this Article are those holding claims based on transactions or events occurring before the bulk transfer, but creditors who become such after notice to creditors is given (Sections 6–105 and 6–107) are not entitled to notice.

[(2) Against the aggregate obligation imposed by the provisions of this Article concerning the application of the proceeds (Section 6–106 and subsection (3)(c) of 6–108) the transferee or auctioneer is entitled to credit for sums paid to particular creditors of the transferor, not exceeding the sums believed in good faith at the time of the payment to be properly payable to such creditors.]

## § 6–110. Subsequent Transfers.

When the title of a transferee to property is subject to a defect by reason of his non-compliance with the requirements of this Article, then:

(1) a purchaser of any such property from such transferee who pays no value or who takes with notice of such noncompliance takes subject to such defect, but

(2) a purchaser for value in good faith and without such notice takes free of such defect.

## § 6–111. Limitation of Actions and Levies.

No action under this Article shall be brought nor levy made more than six months after the date on which the transferee took possession of the goods unless the transfer has been concealed. If the transfer has been concealed, actions may be brought or levies made within six months after its discovery.

Note to Article 6: *Section 6–106 is bracketed to indicate division of opinion as to whether or not it is a wise provision, and to suggest that this is a point on which State enactments may differ without serious damage to the principle of uniformity. In any State where Section 6–106 is not enacted, the following parts of sections, also bracketed in the text, should also be omitted, namely:*

> *Sec. 6–107(2)(e).*
> *6–108(3)(c).*
> *6–109(2).*
> *In any State where Section 6–106 is enacted, these other provisions should be also.*

# ARTICLE 7: WAREHOUSE RECEIPTS, BILLS OF LADING AND OTHER DOCUMENTS OF TITLE

## Part 1—General

### § 7–101. Short Title.

This Article shall be known and may be cited as Uniform Commercial Code—Documents of Title.

### § 7–102. Definitions and Index of Definitions.

(1) In this Article, unless the context otherwise requires:

(a) "Bailee" means the person who by a warehouse receipt, bill of lading or other document of title acknowledges possession of goods and contracts to deliver them.

(b) "Consignee" means the person named in a bill to whom or to whose order the bill promises delivery.

(c) "Consignor" means the person named in a bill as the person from whom the goods have been received for shipment.

(d) "Delivery order" means a written order to deliver goods directed to a warehouseman, carrier or other person who in the ordinary course of business issues warehouse receipts or bills of lading.

(e) "Document" means document of title as defined in the general definitions in Article 1 (Section 1–201).

(f) "Goods" means all things which are treated as movable for the purposes of a contract of storage or transportation.

(g) "Issuer" means a bailee who issues a document except that in relation to an unaccepted delivery order it means the person who orders the possessor of goods to deliver. Issuer includes any person for whom an agent or employee purports to act in issuing a document if the agent or employee has real or apparent authority to issue documents, notwithstanding that the issuer received no goods or that the goods were misdescribed or that in any other respect the agent or employee violated his instructions.

(h) "Warehouseman" is a person engaged in the business of storing goods for hire.

(2) Other definitions applying to this Article or to specified Parts thereof, and the sections in which they appear are:

> "Duly negotiate". Section 7–501.
> "Person entitled under the document". Section 7–403(4).

(3) Definitions in other Articles applying to this Article and the sections in which they appear are:

> "Contract for sale". Section 2–106.
> "Overseas". Section 2–323.
> "Receipt" of goods. Section 2–103.

(4) In addition Article 1 contains general definitions and principles of construction and interpretation applicable throughout this Article.

### § 7–103. Relation of Article to Treaty, Statute, Tariff, Classification or Regulation.

To the extent that any treaty or statute of the United States, regulatory statute of this State or tariff, classification or regulation filed or issued pursuant thereto is applicable, the provisions of this Article are subject thereto.

### § 7–104. Negotiable and Non-Negotiable Warehouse Receipt, Bill of Lading or Other Document of Title.

(1) A warehouse receipt, bill of lading or other document of title is negotiable

(a) if by its terms the goods are to be delivered to bearer or to the order of a named person; or

(b) where recognized in overseas trade, if it runs to a named person or assigns.

(2) Any other document is non-negotiable. A bill of lading in which it is stated that the goods are consigned to a named person is not made negotiable by a provision that the goods are to be delivered only against a written order signed by the same or another named person.

### § 7–105. Construction Against Negative Implication.

The omission from either Part 2 or Part 3 of this Article of a provision corresponding to a provision made in the other Part does not imply that a corresponding rule of law is not applicable.

## Part 2—Warehouse Receipts: Special Provisions

### § 7–201. Who May Issue a Warehouse Receipt; Storage Under Government Bond.

(1) A warehouse receipt may be issued by any warehouseman.

(2) Where goods including distilled spirits and agricultural commodities are stored under a statute requiring a bond against withdrawal or a license for the issuance of receipts in the nature of warehouse receipts, a receipt issued for the goods has like effect as a warehouse receipt

even though issued by a person who is the owner of the goods and is not a warehouseman.

## § 7–202. Form of Warehouse Receipt; Essential Terms; Optional Terms.

(1) A warehouse receipt need not be in any particular form.

(2) Unless a warehouse receipt embodies within its written or printed terms each of the following, the warehouseman is liable for damages caused by the omission to a person injured thereby:

(a) the location of the warehouse where the goods are stored;

(b) the date of issue of the receipt;

(c) the consecutive number of the receipt;

(d) a statement whether the goods received will be delivered to the bearer, to a specified person, or to a specified person or his order;

(e) the rate of storage and handling charges, except that where goods are stored under a field warehousing arrangement a statement of that fact is sufficient on a non-negotiable receipt;

(f) a description of the goods or of the packages containing them;

(g) the signature of the warehouseman, which may be made by his authorized agent;

(h) if the receipt is issued for goods of which the warehouseman is owner, either solely or jointly or in common with others, the fact of such ownership; and

(i) a statement of the amount of advances made and of liabilities incurred for which the warehouseman claims a lien or security interest (Section 7–209). If the precise amount of such advances made or of such liabilities incurred is, at the time of the issue of the receipt, unknown to the warehouseman or to his agent who issues it, a statement of the fact that advances have been made or liabilities incurred and the purpose thereof is sufficient.

(3) A warehouseman may insert in his receipt any other terms which are not contrary to the provisions of this Act and do not impair his obligation of delivery (Section 7–403) or his duty of care (Section 7–204). Any contrary provisions shall be ineffective.

## § 7–203. Liability for Non-Receipt or Misdescription.

A party to or purchaser for value in good faith of a document of title other than a bill of lading relying in either case upon the description therein of the goods may recover from the issuer damages caused by the non-receipt or misdescription of the goods, except to the extent that the document conspicuously indicates that the issuer does not know whether any part or all of the goods in fact were received or conform to the description, as where the description is in terms of marks or labels or kind, quantity or condition, or the receipt or description is qualified by "contents, condition and quality unknown", "said to contain" or the like, if such indication be true, or the party or purchaser otherwise has notice.

## § 7–204. Duty of Care; Contractual Limitation of Warehouseman's Liability.

(1) A warehouseman is liable for damages for loss of or injury to the goods caused by his failure to exercise such care in regard to them as a reasonably careful man would exercise under like circumstances but unless otherwise agreed he is not liable for damages which could not have been avoided by the exercise of such care.

(2) Damages may be limited by a term in the warehouse receipt or storage agreement limiting the amount of liability in case of loss or damage, and setting forth a specific liability per article or item, or value per unit of weight, beyond which the warehouseman shall not be liable; provided, however, that such liability may on written request

of the bailor at the time of signing such storage agreement or within a reasonable time after receipt of the warehouse receipt be increased on part or all of the goods thereunder, in which event increased rates may be charged based on such increased valuation, but that no such increase shall be permitted contrary to a lawful limitation of liability contained in the warehouseman's tariff, if any. No such limitation is effective with respect to the warehouseman's liability for conversion to his own use.

(3) Reasonable provisions as to the time and manner of presenting claims and instituting actions based on the bailment may be included in the warehouse receipt or tariff.

(4) This section does not impair or repeal...

Note: *Insert in subsection (4) a reference to any statute which imposes a higher responsibility upon the warehouseman or invalidates contractual limitations which would be permissible under this Article.*

## § 7–205. Title Under Warehouse Receipt Defeated in Certain Cases.

A buyer in the ordinary course of business of fungible goods sold and delivered by a warehouseman who is also in the business of buying and selling such goods takes free of any claim under a warehouse receipt even though it has been duly negotiated.

## § 7–206. Termination of Storage at Warehouseman's Option.

(1) A warehouseman may on notifying the person on whose account the goods are held and any other person known to claim an interest in the goods require payment of any charges and removal of the goods from the warehouse at the termination of the period of storage fixed by the document, or, if no period is fixed, within a stated period not less than thirty days after the notification. If the goods are not removed before the date specified in the notification, the warehouseman may sell them in accordance with the provisions of the section on enforcement of a warehouseman's lien (Section 7–210).

(2) If a warehouseman in good faith believes that the goods are about to deteriorate or decline in value to less than the amount of his lien within the time prescribed in subsection (1) for notification, advertisement and sale, the warehouseman may specify in the notification any reasonable shorter time for removal of the goods and in case the goods are not removed, may sell them at public sale held not less than one week after a single advertisement or posting.

(3) If as a result of a quality or condition of the goods of which the warehouseman had no notice at the time of deposit the goods are a hazard to other property or to the warehouse or to persons, the warehouseman may sell the goods at public or private sale without advertisement on reasonable notification to all persons known to claim an interest in the goods. If the warehouseman after a reasonable effort is unable to sell the goods he may dispose of them in any lawful manner and shall incur no liability by reason of such disposition.

(4) The warehouseman must deliver the goods to any person entitled to them under this Article upon due demand made at any time prior to sale or other disposition under this section.

(5) The warehouseman may satisfy his lien from the proceeds of any sale or disposition under this section but must hold the balance for delivery on the demand of any person to whom he would have been bound to deliver the goods.

## § 7–207. Goods Must Be Kept Separate; Fungible Goods.

(1) Unless the warehouse receipt otherwise provides, a warehouseman must keep separate the goods covered by each receipt so as to permit at all times identification and delivery of those goods except that different lots of fungible goods may be commingled.

(2) Fungible goods so commingled are owned in common by the persons entitled thereto and the warehouseman is severally liable to each owner for that owner's share. Where because of overissue a mass of fungible goods is insufficient to meet all the receipts which the warehouseman has issued against it, the persons entitled include all holders to whom overissued receipts have been duly negotiated.

## § 7–208. Altered Warehouse Receipts.

Where a blank in a negotiable warehouse receipt has been filled in without authority, a purchaser for value and without notice of the want of authority may treat the insertion as authorized. Any other unauthorized alteration leaves any receipt enforceable against the issuer according to its original tenor.

## § 7–209. Lien of Warehouseman.

(1) A warehouseman has a lien against the bailor on the goods covered by a warehouse receipt or on the proceeds thereof in his possession for charges for storage or transportation (including demurrage and terminal charges), insurance, labor, or charges present or future in relation to the goods, and for expenses necessary for preservation of the goods or reasonably incurred in their sale pursuant to law. If the person on whose account the goods are held is liable for like charges or expenses in relation to other goods whenever deposited and it is stated in the receipt that a lien is claimed for charges and expenses in relation to other goods, the warehouseman also has a lien against him for such charges and expenses whether or not the other goods have been delivered by the warehouseman. But against a person to whom a negotiable warehouse receipt is duly negotiated a warehouseman's lien is limited to charges in an amount or at a rate specified on the receipt or if no charges are so specified then to a reasonable charge for storage of the goods covered by the receipt subsequent to the date of the receipt.

(2) The warehouseman may also reserve a security interest against the bailor for a maximum amount specified on the receipt for charges other than those specified in subsection (1), such as for money advanced and interest. Such a security interest is governed by the Article on Secured Transactions (Article 9).

(3) (a) A warehouseman's lien for charges and expenses under subsection (1) or a security interest under subsection (2) is also effective against any person who so entrusted the bailor with possession of the goods that a pledge of them by him to a good faith purchaser for value would have been valid but is not effective against a person as to whom the document confers no right in the goods covered by it under Section 7–503.

(b) A warehouseman's lien on household goods for charges and expenses in relation to the goods under subsection (1) is also effective against all persons if the depositor was a legal possessor of the goods at the time of deposit. "Household goods" means furniture, furnishings and personal effects used by the depositor in a dwelling.

(4) A warehouseman loses his lien on any goods which he voluntarily delivers or which he unjustifiably refuses to deliver.

## § 7–210. Enforcement of Warehouseman's Lien.

(1) Except as provided in subsection (2), a warehouseman's lien may be enforced by public or private sale of the goods in bloc or in parcels, at any time or place and on any terms which are commercially reasonable, after notifying all persons known to claim an interest in the goods. Such notification must include a statement of the amount due, the nature of the proposed sale and the time and place of any public sale. The fact that a better price could have been obtained by a sale at a different time or in a different method from that selected by the warehouseman is not of itself sufficient to establish that the sale was not made in a commercially reasonable manner. If the warehouseman either sells the goods in the usual manner in any recognized market therefor, or if he sells at the price current in such market at the time of his sale, or if he has otherwise sold in conformity with commercially reasonable practices among dealers in the type of goods sold, he has sold in a commercially reasonable manner. A sale of more goods than apparently necessary to be offered to insure satisfaction of the obligation is not commercially reasonable except in cases covered by the preceding sentence.

(2) A warehouseman's lien on goods other than goods stored by a merchant in the course of his business may be enforced only as follows:

(a) All persons known to claim an interest in the goods must be notified.

(b) The notification must be delivered in person or sent by registered or certified letter to the last known address of any person to be notified.

(c) The notification must include an itemized statement of the claim, a description of the goods subject to the lien, a demand for payment within a specified time not less than ten days after receipt of the notification, and a conspicuous statement that unless the claim is paid within the time the goods will be advertised for sale and sold by auction at a specified time and place.

(d) The sale must conform to the terms of the notification.

(e) The sale must be held at the nearest suitable place to that where the goods are held or stored.

(f) After the expiration of the time given in the notification, an advertisement of the sale must be published once a week for two weeks consecutively in a newspaper of general circulation where the sale is to be held. The advertisement must include a description of the goods, the name of the person on whose account they are being held, and the time and place of the sale. The sale must take place at least fifteen days after the first publication. If there is no newspaper of general circulation where the sale is to be held, the advertisement must be posted at least ten days before the sale in not less than six conspicuous places in the neighborhood of the proposed sale.

(3) Before any sale pursuant to this section any person claiming a right in the goods may pay the amount necessary to satisfy the lien and the reasonable expenses incurred under this section. In that event the goods must not be sold, but must be retained by the warehouseman subject to the terms of the receipt and this Article.

(4) The warehouseman may buy at any public sale pursuant to this section.

(5) A purchaser in good faith of goods sold to enforce a warehouseman's lien takes the goods free of any rights of persons against whom the lien was valid, despite noncompliance by the warehouseman with the requirements of this section.

(6) The warehouseman may satisfy his lien from the proceeds of any sale pursuant to this section but must hold the balance, if any, for delivery on demand to any person to whom he would have been bound to deliver the goods.

(7) The rights provided by this section shall be in addition to all other rights allowed by law to a creditor against his debtor.

(8) Where a lien is on goods stored by a merchant in the course of his business the lien may be enforced in accordance with either subsection (1) or (2).

(9) The warehouseman is liable for damages caused by failure to comply with the requirements for sale under this section and in case of willful violation is liable for conversion.

## Part 3—Bills of Lading: Special Provisions

### § 7–301. Liability for Non-Receipt or Misdescription; "Said to Contain"; "Shipper's Load and Count"; Improper Handling.

(1) A consignee of a non-negotiable bill who has given value in good faith or a holder to whom a negotiable bill has been duly negotiated relying in either case upon the description therein of the goods, or upon the date therein shown, may recover from the issuer damages caused by the misdating of the bill or the non-receipt or misdescription of the goods, except to the extent that the document indicates that the issuer does not know whether any part of all of the goods in fact were received or conform to the description, as where the description is in terms of marks or labels or kind, quantity, or condition or the receipt or description is qualified by "contents or condition of contents of packages unknown", "said to contain", "shipper's weight, load and count" or the like, if such indication be true.

(2) When goods are loaded by an issuer who is a common carrier, the issuer must count the packages of goods if package freight and ascertain the kind and quantity if bulk freight. In such cases "shipper's weight, load and count" or other words indicating that the description was made by the shipper are ineffective except as to freight concealed by packages.

(3) When bulk freight is loaded by a shipper who makes available to the issuer adequate facilities for weighing such freight, an issuer who is a common carrier must ascertain the kind and quantity within a reasonable time after receiving the written request of the shipper to do so. In such cases "shipper's weight" or other words of like purport are ineffective.

(4) The issuer may by inserting in the bill the words "shipper's weight, load and count" or other words of like purport indicate that the goods were loaded by the shipper; and if such statement be true the issuer shall not be liable for damages caused by the improper loading. But their omission does not imply liability for such damages.

(5) The shipper shall be deemed to have guaranteed to the issuer the accuracy at the time of shipment of the description, marks, labels, number, kind, quantity, condition and weight, as furnished by him; and the shipper shall indemnify the issuer against damage caused by inaccuracies in such particulars. The right of the issuer to such indemnity shall in no way limit his responsibility and liability under the contract of carriage to any person other than the shipper.

### § 7–302. Through Bills of Lading and Similar Documents.

(1) The issuer of a through bill of lading or other document embodying an undertaking to be performed in part by persons acting as its agents or by connecting carriers is liable to anyone entitled to recover on the document for any breach by such other persons or by a connecting carrier of its obligation under the document but to the extent that the bill covers an undertaking to be performed overseas or in territory not contiguous to the continental United States or an undertaking including matters other than transportation this liability may be varied by agreement of the parties.

(2) Where goods covered by a through bill of lading or other document embodying an undertaking to be performed in part by persons other than the issuer are received by any such person, he is subject with respect to his own performance while the goods are in his possession to the obligation of the issuer. His obligation is discharged by delivery of the goods to another such person pursuant to the document, and does not include liability for breach by any other such persons or by the issuer.

(3) The issuer of such through bill of lading or other document shall be entitled to recover from the connecting carrier or such other person

in possession of the goods when the breach of the obligation under the document occurred, the amount it may be required to pay to anyone entitled to recover on the document therefor, as may be evidenced by any receipt, judgment, or transcript thereof, and the amount of any expense reasonably incurred by it in defending any action brought by anyone entitled to recover on the document therefor.

### § 7–303. Diversion; Reconsignment; Change of Instructions.

(1) Unless the bill of lading otherwise provides, the carrier may deliver the goods to a person or destination other than that stated in the bill or may otherwise dispose of the goods on instructions from

(a) the holder of a negotiable bill; or

(b) the consignor on a non-negotiable bill notwithstanding contrary instructions from the consignee; or

(c) the consignee on a non-negotiable bill in the absence of contrary instructions from the consignor, if the goods have arrived at the billed destination or if the consignee is in possession of the bill; or

(d) the consignee on a non-negotiable bill if he is entitled as against the consignor to dispose of them.

(2) Unless such instructions are noted on a negotiable bill of lading, a person to whom the bill is duly negotiated can hold the bailee according to the original terms.

### § 7–304. Bills of Lading in a Set.

(1) Except where customary in overseas transportation, a bill of lading must not be issued in a set of parts. The issuer is liable for damages caused by violation of this subsection.

(2) Where a bill of lading is lawfully drawn in a set of parts, each of which is numbered and expressed to be valid only if the goods have not been delivered against any other part, the whole of the parts constitute one bill.

(3) Where a bill of lading is lawfully issued in a set of parts and different parts are negotiated to different persons, the title of the holder to whom the first due negotiation is made prevails as to both the document and the goods even though any later holder may have received the goods from the carrier in good faith and discharged the carrier's obligation by surrender of his part.

(4) Any person who negotiates or transfers a single part of a bill of lading drawn in a set is liable to holders of that part as if it were the whole set.

(5) The bailee is obliged to deliver in accordance with Part 4 of this Article against the first presented part of a bill of lading lawfully drawn in a set. Such delivery discharges the bailee's obligation on the whole bill.

### § 7–305. Destination Bills.

(1) Instead of issuing a bill of lading to the consignor at the place of shipment a carrier may at the request of the consignor procure the bill to be issued at destination or at any other place designated in the request.

(2) Upon request of anyone entitled as against the carrier to control the goods while in transit and on surrender of any outstanding bill of lading or other receipt covering such goods, the issuer may procure a substitute bill to be issued at any place designated in the request.

### § 7–306. Altered Bills of Lading.

An unauthorized alteration or filling in of a blank in a bill of lading leaves the bill enforceable according to its original tenor.

## § 7–307.  Lien of Carrier.

(1) A carrier has a lien on the goods covered by a bill of lading for charges subsequent to the date of its receipt of the goods for storage or transportation (including demurrage and terminal charges) and for expenses necessary for preservation of the goods incident to their transportation or reasonably incurred in their sale pursuant to law. But against a purchaser for value of a negotiable bill of lading a carrier's lien is limited to charges stated in the bill or the applicable tariffs, or if no charges are stated then to a reasonable charge.

(2) A lien for charges and expenses under subsection (1) on goods which the carrier was required by law to receive for transportation is effective against the consignor or any person entitled to the goods unless the carrier had notice that the consignor lacked authority to subject the goods to such charges and expenses. Any other lien under subsection (1) is effective against the consignor and any person who permitted the bailor to have control or possession of the goods unless the carrier had notice that the bailor lacked such authority.

(3) A carrier loses his lien on any goods which he voluntarily delivers or which he unjustifiably refuses to deliver.

## § 7–308.  Enforcement of Carrier's Lien.

(1) A carrier's lien may be enforced by public or private sale of the goods, in bloc or in parcels, at any time or place and on any terms which are commercially reasonable, after notifying all persons known to claim an interest in the goods. Such notification must include a statement of the amount due, the nature of the proposed sale and the time and place of any public sale. The fact that a better price could have been obtained by a sale at a different time or in a different method from that selected by the carrier is not of itself sufficient to establish that the sale was not made in a commercially reasonable manner. If the carrier either sells the goods in the usual manner in any recognized market therefor or if he sells at the price current in such market at the time of his sale or if he has otherwise sold in conformity with commercially reasonable practices among dealers in the type of goods sold he has sold in a commercially reasonable manner. A sale of more goods than apparently necessary to be offered to ensure satisfaction of the obligation is not commercially reasonable except in cases covered by the preceding sentence.

(2) Before any sale pursuant to this section any person claiming a right in the goods may pay the amount necessary to satisfy the lien and the reasonable expenses incurred under this section. In that event the goods must not be sold, but must be retained by the carrier subject to the terms of the bill and this Article.

(3) The carrier may buy at any public sale pursuant to this section.

(4) A purchaser in good faith of goods sold to enforce a carrier's lien takes the goods free of any rights of persons against whom the lien was valid, despite noncompliance by the carrier with the requirements of this section.

(5) The carrier may satisfy his lien from the proceeds of any sale pursuant to this section but must hold the balance, if any, for delivery on demand to any person to whom he would have been bound to deliver the goods.

(6) The rights provided by this section shall be in addition to all other rights allowed by law to a creditor against his debtor.

(7) A carrier's lien may be enforced in accordance with either subsection (1) or the procedure set forth in subsection (2) of Section 7–210.

(8) The carrier is liable for damages caused by failure to comply with the requirements for sale under this section and in case of willful violation is liable for conversion.

## § 7–309.  Duty of Care; Contractual Limitation of Carrier's Liability.

(1) A carrier who issues a bill of lading whether negotiable or non-negotiable must exercise the degree of care in relation to the goods which a reasonably careful man would exercise under like circumstances. This subsection does not repeal or change any law or rule of law which imposes liability upon a common carrier for damages not caused by its negligence.

(2) Damages may be limited by a provision that the carrier's liability shall not exceed a value stated in the document if the carrier's rates are dependent upon value and the consignor by the carrier's tariff is afforded an opportunity to declare a higher value or a value as lawfully provided in the tariff, or where no tariff is filed he is otherwise advised of such opportunity; but no such limitation is effective with respect to the carrier's liability for conversion to its own use.

(3) Reasonable provisions as to the time and manner of presenting claims and instituting actions based on the shipment may be included in a bill of lading or tariff.

## Part 4—Warehouse Receipts and Bills of Lading: General Obligations

### § 7–401.  Irregularities in Issue of Receipt or Bill or Conduct of Issuer.

The obligations imposed by this Article on an issuer apply to a document of title regardless of the fact that

    (a) the document may not comply with the requirements of this Article or of any other law or regulation regarding its issue, form or content; or

    (b) the issuer may have violated laws regulating the conduct of his business; or

    (c) the goods covered by the document were owned by the bailee at the time the document was issued; or

    (d) the person issuing the document does not come within the definition of warehouseman if it purports to be a warehouse receipt.

### § 7–402.  Duplicate Receipt or Bill; Overissue.

Neither a duplicate nor any other document of title purporting to cover goods already represented by an outstanding document of the same issuer confers any right in the goods, except as provided in the case of bills in a set, overissue of documents for fungible goods and substitutes for lost, stolen or destroyed documents. But the issuer is liable for damages caused by his overissue or failure to identify a duplicate document as such by conspicuous notation on its face.

### § 7–403.  Obligation of Warehouseman or Carrier to Deliver; Excuse.

(1) The bailee must deliver the goods to a person entitled under the document who complies with subsections (2) and (3), unless and to the extent that the bailee establishes any of the following:

    (a) delivery of the goods to a person whose receipt was rightful as against the claimant;

    (b) damage to or delay, loss or destruction of the goods for which the bailee is not liable [, but the burden of establishing negligence in such cases is on the person entitled under the document];

Note: *The brackets in (1)(b) indicate that State enactments may differ on this point without serious damage to the principle of uniformity.*

    (c) previous sale or other disposition of the goods in lawful enforcement of a lien or on warehouseman's lawful termination of storage;

(d) the exercise by a seller of his right to stop delivery pursuant to the provisions of the Article on Sales (Section 2–705);

(e) a diversion, reconsignment or other disposition pursuant to the provisions of this Article (Section 7–303) or tariff regulating such right;

(f) release, satisfaction or any other fact affording a personal defense against the claimant;

(g) any other lawful excuse.

(2) A person claiming goods covered by a document of title must satisfy the bailee's lien where the bailee so requests or where the bailee is prohibited by law from delivering the goods until the charges are paid.

(3) Unless the person claiming is one against whom the document confers no right under Sec. 7–503(1), he must surrender for cancellation or notation of partial deliveries any outstanding negotiable document covering the goods, and the bailee must cancel the document or conspicuously note the partial delivery thereon or be liable to any person to whom the document is duly negotiated.

(4) "Person entitled under the document" means holder in the case of a negotiable document, or the person to whom delivery is to be made by the terms of or pursuant to written instructions under a non-negotiable document.

## § 7–404. No Liability for Good Faith Delivery Pursuant to Receipt or Bill.

A bailee who in good faith including observance of reasonable commercial standards has received goods and delivered or otherwise disposed of them according to the terms of the document of title or pursuant to this Article is not liable therefor. This rule applies even though the person from whom he received the goods had no authority to procure the document or to dispose of the goods and even though the person to whom he delivered the goods had no authority to receive them.

## Part 5—Warehouse Receipts and Bills of Lading: Negotiation and Transfer

### § 7–501. Form of Negotiation and Requirements of "Due Negotiation".

(1) A negotiable document of title running to the order of a named person is negotiated by his indorsement and delivery. After his indorsement in blank or to bearer any person can negotiate it by delivery alone.

(2) (a) A negotiable document of title is also negotiated by delivery alone when by its original terms it runs to bearer.

(b) When a document running to the order of a named person is delivered to him the effect is the same as if the document had been negotiated.

(3) Negotiation of a negotiable document of title after it has been indorsed to a specified person requires indorsement by the special indorsee as well as delivery.

(4) A negotiable document of title is "duly negotiated" when it is negotiated in the manner stated in this section to a holder who purchases it in good faith without notice of any defense against or claim to it on the part of any person and for value, unless it is established that the negotiation is not in the regular course of business or financing or involves receiving the document in settlement or payment of a money obligation.

(5) Indorsement of a non-negotiable document neither makes it negotiable nor adds to the transferee's rights.

(6) The naming in a negotiable bill of a person to be notified of the arrival of the goods does not limit the negotiability of the bill nor constitute notice to a purchaser thereof of any interest of such person in the goods.

### § 7–502. Rights Acquired by Due Negotiation.

(1) Subject to the following section and to the provisions of Section 7–205 on fungible goods, a holder to whom a negotiable document of title has been duly negotiated acquires thereby:

(a) title to the document;

(b) title to the goods;

(c) all rights accruing under the law of agency or estoppel, including rights to goods delivered to the bailee after the document was issued; and

(d) the direct obligation of the issuer to hold or deliver the goods according to the terms of the document free of any defense or claim by him except those arising under the terms of the document or under this Article. In the case of a delivery order the bailee's obligation accrues only upon acceptance and the obligation acquired by the holder is that the issuer and any indorser will procure the acceptance of the bailee.

(2) Subject to the following section, title and rights so acquired are not defeated by any stoppage of the goods represented by the document or by surrender of such goods by the bailee, and are not impaired even though the negotiation or any prior negotiation constituted a breach of duty or even though any person has been deprived of possession of the document by misrepresentation, fraud, accident, mistake, duress, loss, theft or conversion, or even though a previous sale or other transfer of the goods or document has been made to a third person.

### § 7–503. Document of Title to Goods Defeated in Certain Cases.

(1) A document of title confers no right in goods against a person who before issuance of the document had a legal interest or a perfected security interest in them and who neither

(a) delivered or entrusted them or any document of title covering them to the bailor or his nominee with actual or apparent authority to ship, store or sell or with power to obtain delivery under this Article (Section 7–403) or with power of disposition under this Act (Sections 2–403 and 9–307) or other statute or rule of law; nor

(b) acquiesced in the procurement by the bailor or his nominee of any document of title.

(2) Title to goods based upon an unaccepted delivery order is subject to the rights of anyone to whom a negotiable warehouse receipt or bill of lading covering the goods has been duly negotiated. Such a title may be defeated under the next section to the same extent as the rights of the issuer or a transferee from the issuer.

(3) Title to goods based upon a bill of lading issued to a freight forwarder is subject to the rights of anyone to whom a bill issued by the freight forwarder is duly negotiated; but delivery by the carrier in accordance with Part 4 of this Article pursuant to its own bill of lading discharges the carrier's obligation to deliver.

### § 7–504. Rights Acquired in the Absence of Due Negotiation; Effect of Diversion; Seller's Stoppage of Delivery.

(1) A transferee of a document, whether negotiable or non-negotiable, to whom the document has been delivered but not duly negotiated, acquires the title and rights which his transferor had or had actual authority to convey.

(2) In the case of a non-negotiable document, until but not after the bailee receives notification of the transfer, the rights of the transferee may be defeated

    (a) by those creditors of the transferor who could treat the sale as void under Section 2–402; or

    (b) by a buyer from the transferor in ordinary course of business if the bailee has delivered the goods to the buyer or received notification of his rights; or

    (c) as against the bailee by good faith dealings of the bailee with the transferor.

(3) A diversion or other change of shipping instructions by the consignor in a non-negotiable bill of lading which causes the bailee not to deliver to the consignee defeats the consignee's title to the goods if they have been delivered to a buyer in ordinary course of business and in any event defeats the consignee's rights against the bailee.

(4) Delivery pursuant to a non-negotiable document may be stopped by a seller under Section 2–705, and subject to the requirement of due notification there provided. A bailee honoring the seller's instructions is entitled to be indemnified by the seller against any resulting loss or expense.

## § 7–505. Indorser Not a Guarantor for Other Parties.

The indorsement of a document of title issued by a bailee does not make the indorser liable for any default by the bailee or by previous indorsers.

## § 7–506. Delivery Without Indorsement: Right to Compel Indorsement.

The transferee of a negotiable document of title has a specifically enforceable right to have his transferor supply any necessary indorsement but the transfer becomes a negotiation only as of the time the indorsement is supplied.

## § 7–507. Warranties on Negotiation or Transfer of Receipt or Bill.

Where a person negotiates or transfers a document of title for value otherwise than as a mere intermediary under the next following section, then unless otherwise agreed he warrants to his immediate purchaser only in addition to any warranty made in selling the goods

    (a) that the document is genuine; and

    (b) that he has no knowledge of any fact which would impair its validity or worth; and

    (c) that his negotiation or transfer is rightful and fully effective with respect to the title to the document and the goods it represents.

## § 7–508. Warranties of Collecting Bank as to Documents.

A collecting bank or other intermediary known to be entrusted with documents on behalf of another or with collection of a draft of other claim against delivery of documents warrants by such delivery of the documents only its own good faith and authority. This rule applies even though the intermediary has purchased or made advances against the claim or draft to be collected.

## § 7–509. Receipt or Bill: When Adequate Compliance With Commercial Contract.

The question whether a document is adequate to fulfill the obligations of a contract for sale or the conditions of a credit is governed by the Articles on Sales (Article 2) and on Letters of Credit (Article 5).

## Part 6—Warehouse Receipts and Bills of Lading: Miscellaneous Provisions

### § 7–601. Lost and Missing Documents.

(1) If a document has been lost, stolen or destroyed, a court may order delivery of the goods or issuance of a substitute document and the bailee may without liability to any person comply with such order. If the document was negotiable the claimant must post security approved by the court to indemnify any person who may suffer loss as a result of non-surrender of the document. If the document was not negotiable, such security may be required at the discretion of the court. The court may also in its discretion order payment of the bailee's reasonable costs and counsel fees.

(2) A bailee who without court order delivers goods to a person claiming under a missing negotiable document is liable to any person injured thereby, and if the delivery is not in good faith becomes liable for conversion. Delivery in good faith is not conversion if made in accordance with a filed classification or tariff or, where no classification or tariff is filed, if the claimant posts security with the bailee in an amount at least double the value of the goods at the time of posting to indemnify any person injured by the delivery who files a notice of claim within one year after the delivery.

### § 7–602. Attachment of Goods Covered by a Negotiable Document.

Except where the document was originally issued upon delivery of the goods by a person who had no power to dispose of them, no lien attaches by virtue of any judicial process to goods in the possession of a bailee for which a negotiable document of title is outstanding unless the document be first surrendered to the bailee or its negotiation enjoined, and the bailee shall not be compelled to deliver the goods pursuant to process until the document is surrendered to him or impounded by the court. One who purchases the document for value without notice of the process or injunction takes free of the lien imposed by judicial process.

### § 7–603. Conflicting Claims; Interpleader.

If more than one person claims title or possession of the goods, the bailee is excused from delivery until he has had a reasonable time to ascertain the validity of the adverse claims or to bring an action to compel all claimants to interplead and may compel such interpleader, either in defending an action for non-delivery of the goods, or by original action, whichever is appropriate.

## REVISED (1994) ARTICLE 8 INVESTMENT SECURITIES

## PART 1. SHORT TITLE AND GENERAL MATTERS

### § 8–101. Short Title.

This Article may be cited as Uniform Commercial Code—Investment Securities.

### § 8–102. Definitions.

(a) In this Article:

    (1) "Adverse claim" means a claim that a claimant has a property interest in a financial asset and that it is a violation of the rights of the claimant for another person to hold, transfer, or deal with the financial asset.

    (2) "Bearer form," as applied to a certificated security, means a form in which the security is payable to the bearer of the security

certificate according to its terms but not by reason of an indorsement.

(3) "Broker" means a person defined as a broker or dealer under the federal securities laws, but without excluding a bank acting in that capacity.

(4) "Certificated security" means a security that is represented by a certificate.

(5) "Clearing corporation" means:

(i) a person that is registered as a "clearing agency" under the federal securities laws;

(ii) a federal reserve bank; or

(iii) any other person that provides clearance or settlement services with respect to financial assets that would require it to register as a clearing agency under the federal securities laws but for an exclusion or exemption from the registration requirement, if its activities as a clearing corporation, including promulgation of rules, are subject to regulation by a federal or state governmental authority.

(6) "Communicate" means to:

(i) send a signed writing; or

(ii) transmit information by any mechanism agreed upon by the persons transmitting and receiving the information.

(7) "Entitlement holder" means a person identified in the records of a securities intermediary as the person having a security entitlement against the securities intermediary. If a person acquires a security entitlement by virtue of Section 8–501(b)(2) or (3), that person is the entitlement holder.

(8) "Entitlement order" means a notification communicated to a securities intermediary directing transfer or redemption of a financial asset to which the entitlement holder has a security entitlement.

(9) "Financial asset," except as otherwise provided in Section 8–103, means:

(i) a security;

(ii) an obligation of a person or a share, participation, or other interest in a person or in property or an enterprise of a person, which is, or is of a type, dealt in or traded on financial markets, or which is recognized in any area in which it is issued or dealt in as a medium for investment; or

(iii) any property that is held by a securities intermediary for another person in a securities account if the securities intermediary has expressly agreed with the other person that the property is to be treated as a financial asset under this Article.

As context requires, the term means either the interest itself or the means by which a person's claim to it is evidenced, including a certificated or uncertificated security, a security certificate, or a security entitlement.

(10) "Good faith," for purposes of the obligation of good faith in the performance or enforcement of contracts or duties within this Article, means honesty in fact and the observance of reasonable commercial standards of fair dealing.

(11) "Indorsement" means a signature that alone or accompanied by other words is made on a security certificate in registered form or on a separate document for the purpose of assigning, transferring, or redeeming the security or granting a power to assign, transfer, or redeem it.

(12) "Instruction" means a notification communicated to the issuer of an uncertificated security which directs that the transfer of the security be registered or that the security be redeemed.

(13) "Registered form," as applied to a certificated security, means a form in which:

(i) the security certificate specifies a person entitled to the security; and

(ii) a transfer of the security may be registered upon books maintained for that purpose by or on behalf of the issuer, or the security certificate so states.

(14) "Securities intermediary" means:

(i) a clearing corporation; or

(ii) a person, including a bank or broker, that in the ordinary course of its business maintains securities accounts for others and is acting in that capacity.

(15) "Security," except as otherwise provided in Section 8–103, means an obligation of an issuer or a share, participation, or other interest in an issuer or in property or an enterprise of an issuer:

(i) which is represented by a security certificate in bearer or registered form, or the transfer of which may be registered upon books maintained for that purpose by or on behalf of the issuer;

(ii) which is one of a class or series or by its terms is divisible into a class or series of shares, participations, interests, or obligations; and

(iii) which:

(A) is, or is of a type, dealt in or traded on securities exchanges or securities markets; or

(B) is a medium for investment and by its terms expressly provides that it is a security governed by this Article.

(16) "Security certificate" means a certificate representing a security.

(17) "Security entitlement" means the rights and property interest of an entitlement holder with respect to a financial asset specified in Part 5.

(18) "Uncertificated security" means a security that is not represented by a certificate.

(b) Other definitions applying to this Article and the sections in which they appear are:

Appropriate person. Section 8–107.

Control. Section 8–106.

Delivery. Section 8–301.

Investment company security. Section 8–103.

Issuer. Section 8–201.

Overissue. Section 8–210.

Protected purchaser. Section 8–303.

Securities account. Section 8–501.

(c) In addition, Article 1 contains general definitions and principles of construction and interpretation applicable throughout this Article.

(d) The characterization of a person, business, or transaction for purposes of this Article does not determine the characterization of the person, business, or transaction for purposes of any other law, regulation, or rule.

### § 8–103. Rules for Determining Whether Certain Obligations and Interests Are Securities or Financial Assets.

(a) A share or similar equity interest issued by a corporation, business trust, joint stock company, or similar entity is a security.

(b) An "investment company security" is a security. "Investment company security" means a share or similar equity interest issued by an entity that is registered as an investment company under the federal investment company laws, an interest in a unit investment trust that is so registered, or a face-amount certificate issued by a face-amount certificate company that is so registered. Investment company security does not include an insurance policy or endowment policy or annuity contract issued by an insurance company.

(c) An interest in a partnership or limited liability company is not a security unless it is dealt in or traded on securities exchanges or in securities markets, its terms expressly provide that it is a security governed by this Article, or it is an investment company security. However, an interest in a partnership or limited liability company is a financial asset if it is held in a securities account.

(d) A writing that is a security certificate is governed by this Article and not by Article 3, even though it also meets the requirements of that Article. However, a negotiable instrument governed by Article 3 is a financial asset if it is held in a securities account.

(e) An option or similar obligation issued by a clearing corporation to its participants is not a security, but is a financial asset.

(f) A commodity contract, as defined in Section 9–115, is not a security or a financial asset.

### § 8–104.   Acquisition of Security or Financial Asset or Interest Therein.

(a) A person acquires a security or an interest therein, under this Article, if:

(1) the person is a purchaser to whom a security is delivered pursuant to Section 8–301; or

(2) the person acquires a security entitlement to the security pursuant to Section 8–501.

(b) A person acquires a financial asset, other than a security, or an interest therein, under this Article, if the person acquires a security entitlement to the financial asset.

(c) A person who acquires a security entitlement to a security or other financial asset has the rights specified in Part 5, but is a purchaser of any security, security entitlement, or other financial asset held by the securities intermediary only to the extent provided in Section 8–503.

(d) Unless the context shows that a different meaning is intended, a person who is required by other law, regulation, rule, or agreement to transfer, deliver, present, surrender, exchange, or otherwise put in the possession of another person a security or financial asset satisfies that requirement by causing the other person to acquire an interest in the security or financial asset pursuant to subsection (a) or (b).

### § 8–105.   Notice of Adverse Claim.

(a) A person has notice of an adverse claim if:

(1) the person knows of the adverse claim;

(2) the person is aware of facts sufficient to indicate that there is a significant probability that the adverse claim exists and deliberately avoids information that would establish the existence of the adverse claim;  or

(3) the person has a duty, imposed by statute or regulation, to investigate whether an adverse claim exists, and the investigation so required would  establish the existence of the adverse claim.

(b) Having knowledge that a financial asset or interest therein is or has been transferred by a representative imposes no duty of inquiry into the rightfulness of a transaction and is not notice of an adverse claim.  However, a person who knows that a representative has transferred a financial asset or interest therein in a transaction that is, or whose proceeds are being used, for the individual benefit of the representative or otherwise in breach of duty has notice of an adverse claim.

(c) An act or event that creates a right to immediate performance of the principal obligation represented by a security certificate or sets a date on or after which the certificate is to be presented or surrendered for redemption or exchange does not itself constitute notice of an adverse claim except in the case of a transfer more than:

(1) one year after a date set for presentment or surrender for redemption or exchange;  or

(2) six months after a date set for payment of money against presentation or surrender of the certificate, if money was available for payment on that date.

(d) A purchaser of a certificated security has notice of an adverse claim if the security certificate:

(1) whether in bearer or registered form, has been indorsed "for collection"  or "for surrender" or for some other purpose not involving transfer;  or

(2) is in bearer form and has on it an unambiguous statement that it is the property of a person other than the transferor, but the mere writing of a name on the certificate is not such a statement.

(e) Filing of a financing statement under Article 9 is not notice of an adverse claim to a financial asset.

### § 8–106.   Control.

(a) A purchaser has "control" of a certificated security in bearer form if the certificated security is delivered to the purchaser.

(b) A purchaser has "control" of a certificated security in registered form if the certificated security is delivered to the purchaser, and:

(1) the certificate is indorsed to the purchaser or in blank by an effective indorsement;  or

(2) the certificate is registered in the name of the purchaser, upon original  issue or registration of transfer by the issuer.

(c) A purchaser has "control" of an uncertificated security if:

(1) the uncertificated security is delivered to the purchaser;  or

(2) the issuer has agreed that it will comply with instructions originated by the purchaser without further consent by the registered owner.

(d) A purchaser has "control" of a security entitlement if:

(1) the purchaser becomes the entitlement holder;  or

(2) the securities intermediary has agreed that it will comply with entitlement orders originated by the purchaser without further consent by the entitlement holder.

(e) If an interest in a security entitlement is granted by the entitlement holder to the entitlement holder's own securities intermediary, the securities intermediary has control.

(f) A purchaser who has satisfied the requirements of subsection (c)(2) or (d)(2) has control even if the registered owner in the case of subsection (c)(2) or the entitlement holder in the case of subsection (d)(2) retains the right to make substitutions for the uncertificated security or security entitlement, to originate instructions or entitlement orders to the issuer or securities intermediary, or otherwise to deal with the uncertificated security or security entitlement.

(g) An issuer or a securities intermediary may not enter into an agreement of the kind described in subsection (c)(2) or (d)(2) without the consent of the registered owner or entitlement holder, but an issuer or a securities intermediary is not required to enter into such an agreement even though the registered owner or entitlement holder so directs.  An issuer or securities intermediary that has entered into such an agreement is not required to confirm the existence of the agreement to another party unless requested to do so by the registered owner or entitlement holder.

### § 8–107.   Whether Indorsement, Instruction, or Entitlement Order Is Effective.

(a) "Appropriate person" means:

(1) with respect to an indorsement, the person specified by a security certificate or by an effective special indorsement to be entitled to the security;

(2) with respect to an instruction, the registered owner of an uncertificated security;

(3) with respect to an entitlement order, the entitlement holder;

(4) if the person designated in paragraph (1), (2), or (3) is deceased, the designated person's successor taking under other law or the designated person's personal representative acting for the estate of the decedent; or

(5) if the person designated in paragraph (1), (2), or (3) lacks capacity, the designated person's guardian, conservator, or other similar representative who has power under other law to transfer the security or financial asset.

(b) An indorsement, instruction, or entitlement order is effective if:

(1) it is made by the appropriate person;

(2) it is made by a person who has power under the law of agency to transfer the security or financial asset on behalf of the appropriate person, including, in the case of an instruction or entitlement order, a person who has control under Section 8–106(c)(2) or (d)(2); or

(3) the appropriate person has ratified it or is otherwise precluded from asserting its ineffectiveness.

(c) An indorsement, instruction, or entitlement order made by a representative is effective even if:

(1) the representative has failed to comply with a controlling instrument or with the law of the State having jurisdiction of the representative relationship, including any law requiring the representative to obtain court approval of the transaction; or

(2) the representative's action in making the indorsement, instruction, or entitlement order or using the proceeds of the transaction is otherwise a breach of duty.

(d) If a security is registered in the name of or specially indorsed to a person described as a representative, or if a securities account is maintained in the name of a person described as a representative, an indorsement, instruction, or entitlement order made by the person is effective even though the person is no longer serving in the described capacity.

(e) Effectiveness of an indorsement, instruction, or entitlement order is determined as of the date the indorsement, instruction, or entitlement order is made, and an indorsement, instruction, or entitlement order does not become ineffective by reason of any later change of circumstances.

### § 8–108. Warranties in Direct Holding.

(a) A person who transfers a certificated security to a purchaser for value warrants to the purchaser, and an indorser, if the transfer is by indorsement, warrants to any subsequent purchaser, that:

(1) the certificate is genuine and has not been materially altered;

(2) the transferor or indorser does not know of any fact that might impair the validity of the security;

(3) there is no adverse claim to the security;

(4) the transfer does not violate any restriction on transfer;

(5) if the transfer is by indorsement, the indorsement is made by an appropriate person, or if the indorsement is by an agent, the agent has actual authority to act on behalf of the appropriate person; and

(6) the transfer is otherwise effective and rightful.

(b) A person who originates an instruction for registration of transfer of an uncertificated security to a purchaser for value warrants to the purchaser that:

(1) the instruction is made by an appropriate person, or if the instruction is by an agent, the agent has actual authority to act on behalf of the appropriate person;

(2) the security is valid;

(3) there is no adverse claim to the security; and

(4) at the time the instruction is presented to the issuer:

(i) the purchaser will be entitled to the registration of transfer;

(ii) the transfer will be registered by the issuer free from all liens, security interests, restrictions, and claims other than those specified in the instruction;

(iii) the transfer will not violate any restriction on transfer; and

(iv) the requested transfer will otherwise be effective and rightful.

(c) A person who transfers an uncertificated security to a purchaser for value and does not originate an instruction in connection with the transfer warrants that:

(1) the uncertificated security is valid;

(2) there is no adverse claim to the security;

(3) the transfer does not violate any restriction on transfer; and

(4) the transfer is otherwise effective and rightful.

(d) A person who indorses a security certificate warrants to the issuer that:

(1) there is no adverse claim to the security; and

(2) the indorsement is effective.

(e) A person who originates an instruction for registration of transfer of an uncertificated security warrants to the issuer that:

(1) the instruction is effective; and

(2) at the time the instruction is presented to the issuer the purchaser will be entitled to the registration of transfer.

(f) A person who presents a certificated security for registration of transfer or for payment or exchange warrants to the issuer that the person is entitled to the registration, payment, or exchange, but a purchaser for value and without notice of adverse claims to whom transfer is registered warrants only that the person has no knowledge of any unauthorized signature in a necessary indorsement.

(g) If a person acts as agent of another in delivering a certificated security to a purchaser, the identity of the principal was known to the person to whom the certificate was delivered, and the certificate delivered by the agent was received by the agent from the principal or received by the agent from another person at the direction of the principal, the person delivering the security certificate warrants only that the delivering person has authority to act for the principal and does not know of any adverse claim to the certificated security.

(h) A secured party who redelivers a security certificate received, or after payment and on order of the debtor delivers the security certificate to another person, makes only the warranties of an agent under subsection (g).

(i) Except as otherwise provided in subsection (g), a broker acting for a customer makes to the issuer and a purchaser the warranties provided in subsections (a) through (f). A broker that delivers a security certificate to its customer, or causes its customer to be registered as the owner of an uncertificated security, makes to the customer the warranties provided in subsection (a) or (b), and has the rights and privileges of a purchaser under this section. The warranties of and in favor of the broker acting as an agent are in addition to applicable warranties given by and in favor of the customer.

### § 8–109. Warranties in Indirect Holding.

(a) A person who originates an entitlement order to a securities intermediary warrants to the securities intermediary that:

(1) the entitlement order is made by an appropriate person, or if the entitlement order is by an agent, the agent has actual authority to act on behalf of the appropriate person; and

(2) there is no adverse claim to the security entitlement.

(b) A person who delivers a security certificate to a securities intermediary for credit to a securities account or originates an instruction with respect to an uncertificated security directing that the uncertificated security be credited to a securities account makes to the securities intermediary the warranties specified in Section 8–108(a) or (b).

(c) If a securities intermediary delivers a security certificate to its entitlement holder or causes its entitlement holder to be registered as the owner of an uncertificated security, the securities intermediary makes to the entitlement holder the warranties specified in Section 8–108(a) or (b).

## § 8–110. Applicability; Choice of Law.

(a) The local law of the issuer's jurisdiction, as specified in subsection (d), governs:

(1) the validity of a security;

(2) the rights and duties of the issuer with respect to registration of transfer;

(3) the effectiveness of registration of transfer by the issuer;

(4) whether the issuer owes any duties to an adverse claimant to a security; and

(5) whether an adverse claim can be asserted against a person to whom transfer of a certificated or uncertificated security is registered or a person who obtains control of an uncertificated security.

(b) The local law of the securities intermediary's jurisdiction, as specified in subsection (e), governs:

(1) acquisition of a security entitlement from the securities intermediary;

(2) the rights and duties of the securities intermediary and entitlement holder arising out of a security entitlement;

(3) whether the securities intermediary owes any duties to an adverse claimant to a security entitlement; and

(4) whether an adverse claim can be asserted against a person who acquires a security entitlement from the securities intermediary or a person who purchases a security entitlement or interest therein from an entitlement holder.

(c) The local law of the jurisdiction in which a security certificate is located at the time of delivery governs whether an adverse claim can be asserted against a person to whom the security certificate is delivered.

(d) "Issuer's jurisdiction" means the jurisdiction under which the issuer of the security is organized or, if permitted by the law of that jurisdiction, the law of another jurisdiction specified by the issuer. An issuer organized under the law of this State may specify the law of another jurisdiction as the law governing the matters specified in subsection (a)(2) through (5).

(e) The following rules determine a "securities intermediary's jurisdiction" for purposes of this section:

(1) If an agreement between the securities intermediary and its entitlement holder specifies that it is governed by the law of a particular jurisdiction, that jurisdiction is the securities intermediary's jurisdiction.

(2) If an agreement between the securities intermediary and its entitlement holder does not specify the governing law as provided in paragraph (1), but expressly specifies that the securities account is maintained at an office in a particular jurisdiction, that jurisdiction is the securities intermediary's jurisdiction.

(3) If an agreement between the securities intermediary and its entitlement holder does not specify a jurisdiction as provided in paragraph (1) or (2), the securities intermediary's jurisdiction is the jurisdiction in which is located the office identified in an account statement as the office serving the entitlement holder's account.

(4) If an agreement between the securities intermediary and its entitlement holder does not specify a jurisdiction as provided in paragraph (1) or (2) and an account statement does not identify an office serving the entitlement holder's account as provided in paragraph (3), the securities intermediary's jurisdiction is the jurisdiction in which is located the chief executive office of the securities intermediary.

(f) A securities intermediary's jurisdiction is not determined by the physical location of certificates representing financial assets, or by the jurisdiction in which is organized the issuer of the financial asset with respect to which an entitlement holder has a security entitlement, or by the location of facilities for data processing or other record keeping concerning the account.

## § 8–111. Clearing Corporation Rules.

A rule adopted by a clearing corporation governing rights and obligations among the clearing corporation and its participants in the clearing corporation is effective even if the rule conflicts with this [Act] and affects another party who does not consent to the rule.

## § 8–112. Creditor's Legal Process.

(a) The interest of a debtor in a certificated security may be reached by a creditor only by actual seizure of the security certificate by the officer making the attachment or levy, except as otherwise provided in subsection (d). However, a certificated security for which the certificate has been surrendered to the issuer may be reached by a creditor by legal process upon the issuer.

(b) The interest of a debtor in an uncertificated security may be reached by a creditor only by legal process upon the issuer at its chief executive office in the United States, except as otherwise provided in subsection (d).

(c) The interest of a debtor in a security entitlement may be reached by a creditor only by legal process upon the securities intermediary with whom the debtor's securities account is maintained, except as otherwise provided in subsection (d).

(d) The interest of a debtor in a certificated security for which the certificate is in the possession of a secured party, or in an uncertificated security registered in the name of a secured party, or a security entitlement maintained in the name of a secured party, may be reached by a creditor by legal process upon the secured party.

(e) A creditor whose debtor is the owner of a certificated security, uncertificated security, or security entitlement is entitled to aid from a court of competent jurisdiction, by injunction or otherwise, in reaching the certificated security, uncertificated security, or security entitlement or in satisfying the claim by means allowed at law or in equity in regard to property that cannot readily be reached by other legal process.

## § 8–113. Statute of Frauds Inapplicable.

A contract or modification of a contract for the sale or purchase of a security is enforceable whether or not there is a writing signed or record authenticated by a party against whom enforcement is sought, even if the contract or modification is not capable of performance within one year of its making.

## § 8–114. Evidentiary Rules Concerning Certificated Securities.

The following rules apply in an action on a certificated security against the issuer:

(1) Unless specifically denied in the pleadings, each signature on a security certificate or in a necessary indorsement is admitted.

(2) If the effectiveness of a signature is put in issue, the burden of establishing effectiveness is on the party claiming under the signature, but the signature is presumed to be genuine or authorized.

(3) If signatures on a security certificate are admitted or established, production of the certificate entitles a holder to recover on it unless the defendant establishes a defense or a defect going to the validity of the security.

(4) If it is shown that a defense or defect exists, the plaintiff has the burden of establishing that the plaintiff or some person under whom the plaintiff claims is a person against whom the defense or defect cannot be asserted.

## § 8–115. Securities Intermediary and Others Not Liable to Adverse Claimant.

A securities intermediary that has transferred a financial asset pursuant to an effective entitlement order, or a broker or other agent or bailee that has dealt with a financial asset at the direction of its customer or principal, is not liable to a person having an adverse claim to the financial asset, unless the securities intermediary, or broker or other agent or bailee:

(1) took the action after it had been served with an injunction, restraining order, or other legal process enjoining it from doing so, issued by a court of competent jurisdiction, and had a reasonable opportunity to act on the injunction, restraining order, or other legal process; or

(2) acted in collusion with the wrongdoer in violating the rights of the adverse claimant; or

(3) in the case of a security certificate that has been stolen, acted with notice of the adverse claim.

## § 8–116. Securities Intermediary as Purchaser for Value.

A securities intermediary that receives a financial asset and establishes a security entitlement to the financial asset in favor of an entitlement holder is a purchaser for value of the financial asset. A securities intermediary that acquires a security entitlement to a financial asset from another securities intermediary acquires the security entitlement for value if the securities intermediary acquiring the security entitlement establishes a security entitlement to the financial asset in favor of an entitlement holder.

# PART 2. ISSUE AND ISSUER

## § 8–201. Issuer.

(a) With respect to an obligation on or a defense to a security, an "issuer" includes a person that:

(1) places or authorizes the placing of its name on a security certificate, other than as authenticating trustee, registrar, transfer agent, or the like, to evidence a share, participation, or other interest in its property or in an enterprise, or to evidence its duty to perform an obligation represented by the certificate;

(2) creates a share, participation, or other interest in its property or in an enterprise, or undertakes an obligation, that is an uncertificated security;

(3) directly or indirectly creates a fractional interest in its rights or property, if the fractional interest is represented by a security certificate; or

(4) becomes responsible for, or in place of, another person described as an issuer in this section.

(b) With respect to an obligation on or defense to a security, a guarantor is an issuer to the extent of its guaranty, whether or not its obligation is noted on a security certificate.

(c) With respect to a registration of a transfer, issuer means a person on whose behalf transfer books are maintained.

## § 8–202. Issuer's Responsibility and Defenses; Notice of Defect or Defense.

(a) Even against a purchaser for value and without notice, the terms of a certificated security include terms stated on the certificate and terms made part of the security by reference on the certificate to another instrument, indenture, or document or to a constitution, statute, ordinance, rule, regulation, order, or the like, to the extent the terms referred to do not conflict with terms stated on the certificate. A reference under this subsection does not of itself charge a purchaser for value with notice of a defect going to the validity of the security, even if the certificate expressly states that a person accepting it admits notice. The terms of an uncertificated security include those stated in any instrument, indenture, or document or in a constitution, statute, ordinance, rule, regulation, order, or the like, pursuant to which the security is issued.

(b) The following rules apply if an issuer asserts that a security is not valid:

(1) A security other than one issued by a government or governmental subdivision, agency, or instrumentality, even though issued with a defect going to its validity, is valid in the hands of a purchaser for value and without notice of the particular defect unless the defect involves a violation of a constitutional provision. In that case, the security is valid in the hands of a purchaser for value and without notice of the defect, other than one who takes by original issue.

(2) Paragraph (1) applies to an issuer that is a government or governmental subdivision, agency, or instrumentality only if there has been substantial compliance with the legal requirements governing the issue or the issuer has received a substantial consideration for the issue as a whole or for the particular security and a stated purpose of the issue is one for which the issuer has power to borrow money or issue the security.

(c) Except as otherwise provided in Section 8–205, lack of genuineness of a certificated security is a complete defense, even against a purchaser for value and without notice.

(d) All other defenses of the issuer of a security, including nondelivery and conditional delivery of a certificated security, are ineffective against a purchaser for value who has taken the certificated security without notice of the particular defense.

(e) This section does not affect the right of a party to cancel a contract for a security "when, as and if issued" or "when distributed" in the event of a material change in the character of the security that is the subject of the contract or in the plan or arrangement pursuant to which the security is to be issued or distributed.

(f) If a security is held by a securities intermediary against whom an entitlement holder has a security entitlement with respect to the security, the issuer may not assert any defense that the issuer could not assert if the entitlement holder held the security directly.

## § 8–203. Staleness as Notice of Defect or Defense.

After an act or event, other than a call that has been revoked, creating a right to immediate performance of the principal obligation represented by a certificated security or setting a date on or after which the security is to be presented or surrendered for redemption or exchange, a purchaser is charged with notice of any defect in its issue or defense of the issuer, if the act or event:

(1) requires the payment of money, the delivery of a certificated security, the registration of transfer of an uncertificated security, or any of them on presentation or surrender of the security certificate, the money or security is available on the date set for payment or exchange, and the purchaser takes the security more than one year after that date; or

(2) is not covered by paragraph (1) and the purchaser takes the security more than two years after the date set for surrender or presentation or the date on which performance became due.

### § 8–204.  Effect of Issuer's Restriction on Transfer.

A restriction on transfer of a security imposed by the issuer, even if otherwise lawful, is ineffective against a person without knowledge of the restriction unless:

(1) the security is certificated and the restriction is noted conspicuously on the security certificate; or

(2) the security is uncertificated and the registered owner has been notified of the restriction.

### § 8–205.  Effect of Unauthorized Signature on Security Certificate.

An unauthorized signature placed on a security certificate before or in the course of issue is ineffective, but the signature is effective in favor of a purchaser for value of the certificated security if the purchaser is without notice of the lack of authority and the signing has been done by:

(1) an authenticating trustee, registrar, transfer agent, or other person entrusted by the issuer with the signing of the security certificate or of similar security certificates, or the immediate preparation for signing of any of them; or

(2) an employee of the issuer, or of any of the persons listed in paragraph (1), entrusted with responsible handling of the security certificate.

### § 8–206.  Completion or Alteration of Security Certificate.

(a) If a security certificate contains the signatures necessary to its issue or transfer but is incomplete in any other respect:

(1) any person may complete it by filling in the blanks as authorized; and

(2) even if the blanks are incorrectly filled in, the security certificate as completed is enforceable by a purchaser who took it for value and without notice of the incorrectness.

(b) A complete security certificate that has been improperly altered, even if fraudulently, remains enforceable, but only according to its original terms.

### § 8–207.  Rights and Duties of Issuer With Respect to Registered Owners.

(a) Before due presentment for registration of transfer of a certificated security in registered form or of an instruction requesting registration of transfer of an uncertificated security, the issuer or indenture trustee may treat the registered owner as the person exclusively entitled to vote, receive notifications, and otherwise exercise all the rights and powers of an owner.

(b) This Article does not affect the liability of the registered owner of a security for a call, assessment, or the like.

### § 8–208.  Effect of Signature of Authenticating Trustee, Registrar, or Transfer Agent.

(a) A person signing a security certificate as authenticating trustee, registrar, transfer agent, or the like, warrants to a purchaser for value of the certificated security, if the purchaser is without notice of a particular defect, that:

(1) the certificate is genuine;

(2) the person's own participation in the issue of the security is within the person's capacity and within the scope of the authority received by the person from the issuer; and

(3) the person has reasonable grounds to believe that the certificated security is in the form and within the amount the issuer is authorized to issue.

(b) Unless otherwise agreed, a person signing under subsection (a) does not assume responsibility for the validity of the security in other respects.

### § 8–209.  Issuer's Lien.

A lien in favor of an issuer upon a certificated security is valid against a purchaser only if the right of the issuer to the lien is noted conspicuously on the security certificate.

### § 8–210.  Overissue.

(a) In this section, "overissue" means the issue of securities in excess of the amount the issuer has corporate power to issue, but an overissue does not occur if appropriate action has cured the overissue.

(b) Except as otherwise provided in subsections (c) and (d), the provisions of this Article which validate a security or compel its issue or reissue do not apply to the extent that validation, issue, or reissue would result in overissue.

(c) If an identical security not constituting an overissue is reasonably available for purchase, a person entitled to issue or validation may compel the issuer to purchase the security and deliver it if certificated or register its transfer if uncertificated, against surrender of any security certificate the person holds.

(d) If a security is not reasonably available for purchase, a person entitled to issue or validation may recover from the issuer the price the person or the last purchaser for value paid for it with interest from the date of the person's demand.

## PART 3.  TRANSFER OF CERTIFICATED AND UNCERTIFICATED SECURITIES

### § 8–301.  Delivery.

(a) Delivery of a certificated security to a purchaser occurs when:

(1) the purchaser acquires possession of the security certificate;

(2) another person, other than a securities intermediary, either acquires possession of the security certificate on behalf of the purchaser or, having previously acquired possession of the certificate, acknowledges that it holds for the purchaser; or

(3) a securities intermediary acting on behalf of the purchaser acquires possession of the security certificate, only if the certificate is in registered form and has been specially indorsed to the purchaser by an effective indorsement.

(b) Delivery of an uncertificated security to a purchaser occurs when:

(1) the issuer registers the purchaser as the registered owner, upon original issue or registration of transfer; or

(2) another person, other than a securities intermediary, either becomes the registered owner of the uncertificated security on behalf of the purchaser or, having previously become the registered owner, acknowledges that it holds for the purchaser.

### § 8–302. Rights of Purchaser.

(a) Except as otherwise provided in subsections (b) and (c), upon delivery of a certificated or uncertificated security to a purchaser, the purchaser acquires all rights in the security that the transferor had or had power to transfer.

(b) A purchaser of a limited interest acquires rights only to the extent of the interest purchased.

(c) A purchaser of a certificated security who as a previous holder had notice of an adverse claim does not improve its position by taking from a protected purchaser.

### § 8–303. Protected Purchaser.

(a) "Protected purchaser" means a purchaser of a certificated or uncertificated security, or of an interest therein, who:

   (1) gives value;

   (2) does not have notice of any adverse claim to the security; and

   (3) obtains control of the certificated or uncertificated security.

(b) In addition to acquiring the rights of a purchaser, a protected purchaser also acquires its interest in the security free of any adverse claim.

### § 8–304. Indorsement.

(a) An indorsement may be in blank or special. An indorsement in blank includes an indorsement to bearer. A special indorsement specifies to whom a security is to be transferred or who has power to transfer it. A holder may convert a blank indorsement to a special indorsement.

(b) An indorsement purporting to be only of part of a security certificate representing units intended by the issuer to be separately transferable is effective to the extent of the indorsement.

(c) An indorsement, whether special or in blank, does not constitute a transfer until delivery of the certificate on which it appears or, if the indorsement is on a separate document, until delivery of both the document and the certificate.

(d) If a security certificate in registered form has been delivered to a purchaser without a necessary indorsement, the purchaser may become a protected purchaser only when the indorsement is supplied. However, against a transferor, a transfer is complete upon delivery and the purchaser has a specifically enforceable right to have any necessary indorsement supplied.

(e) An indorsement of a security certificate in bearer form may give notice of an adverse claim to the certificate, but it does not otherwise affect a right to registration that the holder possesses.

(f) Unless otherwise agreed, a person making an indorsement assumes only the obligations provided in Section 8–108 and not an obligation that the security will be honored by the issuer.

### § 8–305. Instruction.

(a) If an instruction has been originated by an appropriate person but is incomplete in any other respect, any person may complete it as authorized and the issuer may rely on it as completed, even though it has been completed incorrectly.

(b) Unless otherwise agreed, a person initiating an instruction assumes only the obligations imposed by Section 8–108 and not an obligation that the security will be honored by the issuer.

### § 8–306. Effect of Guaranteeing Signature, Indorsement, or Instruction.

(a) A person who guarantees a signature of an indorser of a security certificate warrants that at the time of signing:

   (1) the signature was genuine;

   (2) the signer was an appropriate person to indorse, or if the signature is by an agent, the agent had actual authority to act on behalf of the appropriate person; and

   (3) the signer had legal capacity to sign.

(b) A person who guarantees a signature of the originator of an instruction warrants that at the time of signing:

   (1) the signature was genuine;

   (2) the signer was an appropriate person to originate the instruction, or if the signature is by an agent, the agent had actual authority to act on behalf of the appropriate person, if the person specified in the instruction as the registered owner was, in fact, the registered owner, as to which fact the signature guarantor does not make a warranty; and

   (3) the signer had legal capacity to sign.

(c) A person who specially guarantees the signature of an originator of an instruction makes the warranties of a signature guarantor under subsection (b) and also warrants that at the time the instruction is presented to the issuer:

   (1) the person specified in the instruction as the registered owner of the uncertificated security will be the registered owner; and

   (2) the transfer of the uncertificated security requested in the instruction will be registered by the issuer free from all liens, security interests, restrictions, and claims other than those specified in the instruction.

(d) A guarantor under subsections (a) and (b) or a special guarantor under subsection (c) does not otherwise warrant the rightfulness of the transfer.

(e) A person who guarantees an indorsement of a security certificate makes the warranties of a signature guarantor under subsection (a) and also warrants the rightfulness of the transfer in all respects.

(f) A person who guarantees an instruction requesting the transfer of an uncertificated security makes the warranties of a special signature guarantor under subsection (c) and also warrants the rightfulness of the transfer in all respects.

(g) An issuer may not require a special guaranty of signature, a guaranty of indorsement, or a guaranty of instruction as a condition to registration of transfer.

(h) The warranties under this section are made to a person taking or dealing with the security in reliance on the guaranty, and the guarantor is liable to the person for loss resulting from their breach. An indorser or originator of an instruction whose signature, indorsement, or instruction has been guaranteed is liable to a guarantor for any loss suffered by the guarantor as a result of breach of the warranties of the guarantor.

### § 8–307. Purchaser's Right to Requisites for Registration of Transfer.

Unless otherwise agreed, the transferor of a security on due demand shall supply the purchaser with proof of authority to transfer or with any other requisite necessary to obtain registration of the transfer of the security, but if the transfer is not for value, a transferor need not comply unless the purchaser pays the necessary expenses. If the transferor fails within a reasonable time to comply with the demand, the purchaser may reject or rescind the transfer.

## PART 4. REGISTRATION

### § 8–401. Duty of Issuer to Register Transfer.

(a) If a certificated security in registered form is presented to an issuer with a request to register transfer or an instruction is presented to an issuer with a request to register transfer of an uncertificated security, the issuer shall register the transfer as requested if:

(1) under the terms of the security the person seeking registration of transfer is eligible to have the security registered in its name;

(2) the indorsement or instruction is made by the appropriate person or by an agent who has actual authority to act on behalf of the appropriate person;

(3) reasonable assurance is given that the indorsement or instruction is genuine and authorized (Section 8–402);

(4) any applicable law relating to the collection of taxes has been complied with;

(5) the transfer does not violate any restriction on transfer imposed by the issuer in accordance with Section 8–204;

(6) a demand that the issuer not register transfer has not become effective under Section 8–403, or the issuer has complied with Section 8–403(b) but no legal process or indemnity bond is obtained as provided in Section 8–403(d); and

(7) the transfer is in fact rightful or is to a protected purchaser.

(b) If an issuer is under a duty to register a transfer of a security, the issuer is liable to a person presenting a certificated security or an instruction for registration or to the person's principal for loss resulting from unreasonable delay in registration or failure or refusal to register the transfer.

## § 8–402. Assurance That Indorsement or Instruction Is Effective.

(a) An issuer may require the following assurance that each necessary indorsement or each instruction is genuine and authorized:

(1) in all cases, a guaranty of the signature of the person making an indorsement or originating an instruction including, in the case of an instruction, reasonable assurance of identity;

(2) if the indorsement is made or the instruction is originated by an agent, appropriate assurance of actual authority to sign;

(3) if the indorsement is made or the instruction is originated by a fiduciary pursuant to Section 8–107(a)(4) or (a)(5), appropriate evidence of appointment or incumbency;

(4) if there is more than one fiduciary, reasonable assurance that all who are required to sign have done so; and

(5) if the indorsement is made or the instruction is originated by a person not covered by another provision of this subsection, assurance appropriate to the case corresponding as nearly as may be to the provisions of this subsection.

(b) An issuer may elect to require reasonable assurance beyond that specified in this section.

(c) In this section:

(1) "Guaranty of the signature" means a guaranty signed by or on behalf of a person reasonably believed by the issuer to be responsible. An issuer may adopt standards with respect to responsibility if they are not manifestly unreasonable.

(2) "Appropriate evidence of appointment or incumbency" means:

(i) in the case of a fiduciary appointed or qualified by a court, a certificate issued by or under the direction or supervision of the court or an officer thereof and dated within 60 days before the date of presentation for transfer; or

(ii) in any other case, a copy of a document showing the appointment or a certificate issued by or on behalf of a person reasonably believed by an issuer to be responsible or, in the absence of that document or certificate, other evidence the issuer reasonably considers appropriate.

## § 8–403. Demand That Issuer Not Register Transfer.

(a) A person who is an appropriate person to make an indorsement or originate an instruction may demand that the issuer not register transfer of a security by communicating to the issuer a notification that identifies the registered owner and the issue of which the security is a part and provides an address for communications directed to the person making the demand. The demand is effective only if it is received by the issuer at a time and in a manner affording the issuer reasonable opportunity to act on it.

(b) If a certificated security in registered form is presented to an issuer with a request to register transfer or an instruction is presented to an issuer with a request to register transfer of an uncertificated security after a demand that the issuer not register transfer has become effective, the issuer shall promptly communicate to (i) the person who initiated the demand at the address provided in the demand and (ii) the person who presented the security for registration of transfer or initiated the instruction requesting registration of transfer a notification stating that:

(1) the certificated security has been presented for registration of transfer or the instruction for registration of transfer of the uncertificated security has been received;

(2) a demand that the issuer not register transfer had previously been received; and

(3) the issuer will withhold registration of transfer for a period of time stated in the notification in order to provide the person who initiated the demand an opportunity to obtain legal process or an indemnity bond.

(c) The period described in subsection (b)(3) may not exceed 30 days after the date of communication of the notification. A shorter period may be specified by the issuer if it is not manifestly unreasonable.

(d) An issuer is not liable to a person who initiated a demand that the issuer not register transfer for any loss the person suffers as a result of registration of a transfer pursuant to an effective indorsement or instruction if the person who initiated the demand does not, within the time stated in the issuer's communication, either:

(1) obtain an appropriate restraining order, injunction, or other process from a court of competent jurisdiction enjoining the issuer from registering the transfer; or

(2) file with the issuer an indemnity bond, sufficient in the issuer's judgment to protect the issuer and any transfer agent, registrar, or other agent of the issuer involved from any loss it or they may suffer by refusing to register the transfer.

(e) This section does not relieve an issuer from liability for registering transfer pursuant to an indorsement or instruction that was not effective.

## § 8–404. Wrongful Registration.

(a) Except as otherwise provided in Section 8–406, an issuer is liable for wrongful registration of transfer if the issuer has registered a transfer of a security to a person not entitled to it, and the transfer was registered:

(1) pursuant to an ineffective indorsement or instruction;

(2) after a demand that the issuer not register transfer became effective under Section 8–403(a) and the issuer did not comply with Section 8–403(b);

(3) after the issuer had been served with an injunction, restraining order, or other legal process enjoining it from registering the transfer, issued by a court of competent jurisdiction, and the issuer had a reasonable opportunity to act on the injunction, restraining order, or other legal process; or

(4) by an issuer acting in collusion with the wrongdoer.

(b) An issuer that is liable for wrongful registration of transfer under subsection (a) on demand shall provide the person entitled to the security with a like certificated or uncertificated security, and any payments or distributions that the person did not receive as a result of the wrongful registration. If an overissue would result, the issuer's liability to provide the person with a like security is governed by Section 8–210.

(c) Except as otherwise provided in subsection (a) or in a law relating to the collection of taxes, an issuer is not liable to an owner or other person suffering loss as a result of the registration of a transfer of a security if registration was made pursuant to an effective indorsement or instruction.

### § 8–405. Replacement of Lost, Destroyed, or Wrongfully Taken Security Certificate.

(a) If an owner of a certificated security, whether in registered or bearer form, claims that the certificate has been lost, destroyed, or wrongfully taken, the issuer shall issue a new certificate if the owner:

(1) so requests before the issuer has notice that the certificate has been acquired by a protected purchaser;

(2) files with the issuer a sufficient indemnity bond; and

(3) satisfies other reasonable requirements imposed by the issuer.

(b) If, after the issue of a new security certificate, a protected purchaser of the original certificate presents it for registration of transfer, the issuer shall register the transfer unless an overissue would result. In that case, the issuer's liability is governed by Section 8–210. In addition to any rights on the indemnity bond, an issuer may recover the new certificate from a person to whom it was issued or any person taking under that person, except a protected purchaser.

### § 8–406. Obligation to Notify Issuer of Lost, Destroyed, or Wrongfully Taken Security Certificate.

If a security certificate has been lost, apparently destroyed, or wrongfully taken, and the owner fails to notify the issuer of that fact within a reasonable time after the owner has notice of it and the issuer registers a transfer of the security before receiving notification, the owner may not assert against the issuer a claim for registering the transfer under Section 8–404 or a claim to a new security certificate under Section 8–405.

### § 8–407. Authenticating Trustee, Transfer Agent, and Registrar.

A person acting as authenticating trustee, transfer agent, registrar, or other agent for an issuer in the registration of a transfer of its securities, in the issue of new security certificates or uncertificated securities, or in the cancellation of surrendered security certificates has the same obligation to the holder or owner of a certificated or uncertificated security with regard to the particular functions performed as the issuer has in regard to those functions.

## PART 5.  SECURITY ENTITLEMENTS

### § 8–501.  Securities Account; Acquisition of Security Entitlement From Securities Intermediary.

(a) "Securities account" means an account to which a financial asset is or may be credited in accordance with an agreement under which the person maintaining the account undertakes to treat the person for whom the account is maintained as entitled to exercise the rights that comprise the financial asset.

(b) Except as otherwise provided in subsections (d) and (e), a person acquires a security entitlement if a securities intermediary:

(1) indicates by book entry that a financial asset has been credited to the person's securities account;

(2) receives a financial asset from the person or acquires a financial asset for the person and, in either case, accepts it for credit to the person's securities account; or

(3) becomes obligated under other law, regulation, or rule to credit a financial asset to the person's securities account.

(c) If a condition of subsection (b) has been met, a person has a security entitlement even though the securities intermediary does not itself hold the financial asset.

(d) If a securities intermediary holds a financial asset for another person, and the financial asset is registered in the name of, payable to the order of, or specially indorsed to the other person, and has not been indorsed to the securities intermediary or in blank, the other person is treated as holding the financial asset directly rather than as having a security entitlement with respect to the financial asset.

(e) Issuance of a security is not establishment of a security entitlement.

### § 8–502.  Assertion of Adverse Claim Against Entitlement Holder.

An action based on an adverse claim to a financial asset, whether framed in conversion, replevin, constructive trust, equitable lien, or other theory, may not be asserted against a person who acquires a security entitlement under Section 8–501 for value and without notice of the adverse claim.

### § 8–503.  Property Interest of Entitlement Holder in Financial Asset Held by Securities Intermediary.

(a) To the extent necessary for a securities intermediary to satisfy all security entitlements with respect to a particular financial asset, all interests in that financial asset held by the securities intermediary are held by the securities intermediary for the entitlement holders, are not property of the securities intermediary, and are not subject to claims of creditors of the securities intermediary, except as otherwise provided in Section 8–511.

(b) An entitlement holder's property interest with respect to a particular financial asset under subsection (a) is a pro rata property interest in all interests in that financial asset held by the securities intermediary, without regard to the time the entitlement holder acquired the security entitlement or the time the securities intermediary acquired the interest in that financial asset.

(c) An entitlement holder's property interest with respect to a particular financial asset under subsection (a) may be enforced against the securities intermediary only by exercise of the entitlement holder's rights under Sections 8–505 through 8–508.

(d) An entitlement holder's property interest with respect to a particular financial asset under subsection (a) may be enforced against a purchaser of the financial asset or interest therein only if:

(1) insolvency proceedings have been initiated by or against the securities intermediary;

(2) the securities intermediary does not have sufficient interests in the financial asset to satisfy the security entitlements of all of its entitlement holders to that financial asset;

(3) the securities intermediary violated its obligations under Section 8–504 by transferring the financial asset or interest therein to the purchaser; and

(4) the purchaser is not protected under subsection (e).

The trustee or other liquidator, acting on behalf of all entitlement holders having security entitlements with respect to a particular financial asset, may recover the financial asset, or interest therein, from the purchaser. If the trustee or other liquidator elects not to pursue that right, an entitlement holder whose security entitlement remains unsatisfied has the right to recover its interest in the financial asset from the purchaser.

(e) An action based on the entitlement holder's property interest with respect to a particular financial asset under subsection (a), whether framed in conversion, replevin, constructive trust, equitable lien, or other theory, may not be asserted against any purchaser of a financial asset or interest therein who gives value, obtains control, and does not act in collusion with the securities intermediary in violating the securities intermediary's obligations under Section 8–504.

## § 8–504. Duty of Securities Intermediary to Maintain Financial Asset.

(a) A securities intermediary shall promptly obtain and thereafter maintain a financial asset in a quantity corresponding to the aggregate of all security entitlements it has established in favor of its entitlement holders with respect to that financial asset. The securities intermediary may maintain those financial assets directly or through one or more other securities intermediaries.

(b) Except to the extent otherwise agreed by its entitlement holder, a securities intermediary may not grant any security interests in a financial asset it is obligated to maintain pursuant to subsection (a).

(c) A securities intermediary satisfies the duty in subsection (a) if:

(1) the securities intermediary acts with respect to the duty as agreed upon by the entitlement holder and the securities intermediary; or

(2) in the absence of agreement, the securities intermediary exercises due care in accordance with reasonable commercial standards to obtain and maintain the financial asset.

(d) This section does not apply to a clearing corporation that is itself the obligor of an option or similar obligation to which its entitlement holders have security entitlements.

## § 8–505. Duty of Securities Intermediary With Respect to Payments and Distributions.

(a) A securities intermediary shall take action to obtain a payment or distribution made by the issuer of a financial asset. A securities intermediary satisfies the duty if:

(1) the securities intermediary acts with respect to the duty as agreed upon by the entitlement holder and the securities intermediary; or

(2) in the absence of agreement, the securities intermediary exercises due  care in accordance with reasonable commercial standards to attempt to obtain the payment or distribution.

(b) A securities intermediary is obligated to its entitlement holder for a payment or distribution made by the issuer of a financial asset if the payment or distribution is received by the securities intermediary.

## § 8–506. Duty of Securities Intermediary to Exercise Rights as Directed by Entitlement Holder.

A securities intermediary shall exercise rights with respect to a financial asset if directed to do so by an entitlement holder. A securities intermediary satisfies the duty if:

(1) the securities intermediary acts with respect to the duty as agreed upon by the entitlement holder and the securities intermediary; or

(2) in the absence of agreement, the securities intermediary either places  the entitlement holder in a position to exercise the rights directly or exercises due care in accordance with reasonable commercial standards to follow the direction of the entitlement holder.

## § 8–507. Duty of Securities Intermediary to Comply With Entitlement Order.

(a) A securities intermediary shall comply with an entitlement order if the entitlement order is originated by the appropriate person, the securities intermediary has had reasonable opportunity to assure itself that the entitlement order is genuine and authorized, and the securities intermediary has had reasonable opportunity to comply with the entitlement order. A securities intermediary satisfies the duty if:

(1) the securities intermediary acts with respect to the duty as agreed upon by the entitlement holder and the securities intermediary; or

(2) in the absence of agreement, the securities intermediary exercises due care in accordance with reasonable commercial standards to comply with the entitlement order.

(b) If a securities intermediary transfers a financial asset pursuant to an ineffective entitlement order, the securities intermediary shall reestablish a security entitlement in favor of the person entitled to it, and pay or credit any payments or distributions that the person did not receive as a result of the wrongful transfer.  If the securities intermediary does not reestablish a security entitlement, the securities intermediary is liable to the entitlement holder for damages.

## § 8–508. Duty of Securities Intermediary to Change Entitlement Holder's Position to Other Form of Security Holding.

A securities intermediary shall act at the direction of an entitlement holder to change a security entitlement into another available form of holding for which the entitlement holder is eligible, or to cause the financial asset to be transferred to a securities account of the entitlement holder with another securities intermediary. A securities intermediary satisfies the duty if:

(1) the securities intermediary acts as agreed upon by the entitlement holder  and the securities intermediary; or

(2) in the absence of agreement, the securities intermediary exercises due care in accordance with reasonable commercial standards to follow the direction of the entitlement holder.

## § 8–509. Specification of Duties of Securities Intermediary by Other Statute or Regulation; Manner of Performance of Duties of Securities Intermediary and Exercise of Rights of Entitlement Holder.

(a) If the substance of a duty imposed upon a securities intermediary by Sections 8–504 through 8–508 is the subject of other statute, regulation, or rule, compliance with that statute, regulation, or rule satisfies the duty.

(b) To the extent that specific standards for the performance of the duties of a securities intermediary or the exercise of the rights of an entitlement holder are not specified by other statute, regulation, or rule or by agreement between the securities intermediary and entitlement holder, the securities intermediary shall perform its duties and the entitlement holder shall exercise its rights in a commercially reasonable manner.

(c) The obligation of a securities intermediary to perform the duties imposed by Sections 8–504 through 8–508 is subject to:

(1) rights of the securities intermediary arising out of a security interest under a security agreement with the entitlement holder or otherwise;  and

(2) rights of the securities intermediary under other law, regulation, rule, or agreement to withhold performance of its duties as a result of unfulfilled obligations of the entitlement holder to the securities intermediary.

(d) Sections 8–504 through 8–508 do not require a securities intermediary to take any action that is prohibited by other statute, regulation, or rule.

### § 8–510. Rights of Purchaser of Security Entitlement From Entitlement Holder.

(a) An action based on an adverse claim to a financial asset or security entitlement, whether framed in conversion, replevin, constructive trust, equitable lien, or other theory, may not be asserted against a person who purchases a security entitlement, or an interest therein, from an entitlement holder if the purchaser gives value, does not have notice of the adverse claim, and obtains control.

(b) If an adverse claim could not have been asserted against an entitlement holder under Section 8–502, the adverse claim cannot be asserted against a person who purchases a security entitlement, or an interest therein, from the entitlement holder.

(c) In a case not covered by the priority rules in Article 9, a purchaser for value of a security entitlement, or an interest therein, who obtains control has priority over a purchaser of a security entitlement, or an interest therein, who does not obtain control. Purchasers who have control rank equally, except that a securities intermediary as purchaser has priority over a conflicting purchaser who has control unless otherwise agreed by the securities intermediary.

### § 8–511. Priority Among Security Interests and Entitlement Holders.

(a) Except as otherwise provided in subsections (b) and (c), if a securities intermediary does not have sufficient interests in a particular financial asset to satisfy both its obligations to entitlement holders who have security entitlements to that financial asset and its obligation to a creditor of the securities intermediary who has a security interest in that financial asset, the claims of entitlement holders, other than the creditor, have priority over the claim of the creditor.

(b) A claim of a creditor of a securities intermediary who has a security interest in a financial asset held by a securities intermediary has priority over claims of the securities intermediary's entitlement holders who have security entitlements with respect to that financial asset if the creditor has control over the financial asset.

(c) If a clearing corporation does not have sufficient financial assets to satisfy both its obligations to entitlement holders who have security entitlements with respect to a financial asset and its obligation to a creditor of the clearing corporation who has a security interest in that financial asset, the claim of the creditor has priority over the claims of entitlement holders.

## PART 6. TRANSITION PROVISIONS FOR REVISED ARTICLE 8

### § 8–601. Effective Date.
This [Act] takes effect ....

### § 8–602. Repeals.
This [Act] repeals ....

### § 8–603. Savings Clause.
(a) This [Act] does not affect an action or proceeding commenced before this [Act] takes effect.

(b) If a security interest in a security is perfected at the date this [Act] takes effect, and the action by which the security interest was perfected would suffice to perfect a security interest under this [Act], no further action is required to continue perfection. If a security interest in a security is perfected at the date this [Act] takes effect but the action by which the security interest was perfected would not suffice to perfect a security interest under this [Act], the security interest remains perfected for a period of four months after the effective date and continues perfected thereafter if appropriate action to perfect under this [Act] is taken within that period. If a security interest is perfected at the date this [Act] takes effect and the security interest can be perfected by filing under this [Act], a financing statement signed by the secured party instead of the debtor may be filed within that period to continue perfection or thereafter to perfect.

## ARTICLE 9: SECURED TRANSACTIONS; SALES OF ACCOUNTS AND CHATTEL PAPER

Note: *The adoption of this Article should be accompanied by the repeal of existing statutes dealing with conditional sales, trust receipts, factor's liens where the factor is given a non-possessory lien, chattel mortgages, crop mortgages, mortgages on railroad equipment, assignment of accounts and generally statutes regulating security interests in personal property.*

*Where the state has a retail installment selling act or small loan act, that legislation should be carefully examined to determine what changes in those acts are needed to conform them to this Article. This Article primarily sets out rules defining rights of a secured party against persons dealing with the debtor; it does not prescribe regulations and controls which may be necessary to curb abuses arising in the small loan business or in the financing of consumer purchases on credit. Accordingly there is no intention to repeal existing regulatory acts in those fields by enactment or re-enactment of Article 9. See Section 9–203(4) and the Note thereto.*

### Part 1—Short Title, Applicability and Definitions

### § 9–101. Short Title.
This Article shall be known and may be cited as Uniform Commercial Code—Secured Transactions.

### § 9–102. Policy and Subject Matter of Article.
(1) Except as otherwise provided in Section 9–104 on excluded transactions, this Article applies
   (a) to any transaction (regardless of its form) which is intended to create a security interest in personal property or fixtures including goods, documents, instruments, general intangibles, chattel paper or accounts; and also
   (b) to any sale of accounts or chattel paper.

(2) This Article applies to security interests created by contract including pledge, assignment, chattel mortgage, chattel trust, trust deed, factor's lien, equipment trust, conditional sale, trust receipt, other lien or title retention contract and lease or consignment intended as security. This Article does not apply to statutory liens except as provided in Section 9–310.

(3) The application of this Article to a security interest in a secured obligation is not affected by the fact that the obligation is itself secured by a transaction or interest to which this Article does not apply.

### § 9–103. Perfection of Security Interest in Multiple State Transactions.
(1) Documents, instruments and ordinary goods.
   (a) This subsection applies to documents and instruments and to goods other than those covered by a certificate of title described in subsection (2), mobile goods described in subsection (3), and minerals described in subsection (5).

(b) Except as otherwise provided in this subsection, perfection and the effect of perfection or non-perfection of a security interest in collateral are governed by the law of the jurisdiction where the collateral is when the last event occurs on which is based the assertion that the security interest is perfected or unperfected.

(c) If the parties to a transaction creating a purchase money security interest in goods in one jurisdiction understand at the time that the security interest attaches that the goods will be kept in another jurisdiction, then the law of the other jurisdiction governs the perfection and the effect of perfection or non-perfection of the security interest from the time it attaches until thirty days after the debtor receives possession of the goods and thereafter if the goods are taken to the other jurisdiction before the end of the thirty-day period.

(d) When collateral is brought into and kept in this state while subject to a security interest perfected under the law of the jurisdiction from which the collateral was removed, the security interest remains perfected, but if action is required by Part 3 of this Article to perfect the security interest,

> (i) if the action is not taken before the expiration of the period of perfection in the other jurisdiction or the end of four months after the collateral is brought into this state, whichever period first expires, the security interest becomes unperfected at the end of that period and is thereafter deemed to have been unperfected as against a person who became a purchaser after removal;

> (ii) if the action is taken before the expiration of the period specified in subparagraph (i), the security interest continues perfected thereafter;

> (iii) for the purpose of priority over a buyer of consumer goods (subsection (2) of Section 9–307), the period of the effectiveness of a filing in the jurisdiction from which the collateral is removed is governed by the rules with respect to perfection in subparagraphs (i) and (ii).

(2) Certificate of title.

(a) This subsection applies to goods covered by a certificate of title issued under a statute of this state or of another jurisdiction under the law of which indication of a security interest on the certificate is required as a condition of perfection.

(b) Except as otherwise provided in this subsection, perfection and the effect of perfection or non-perfection of the security interest are governed by the law (including the conflict of laws rules) of the jurisdiction issuing the certificate until four months after the goods are removed from that jurisdiction and thereafter until the goods are registered in another jurisdiction, but in any event not beyond surrender of the certificate. After the expiration of that period, the goods are not covered by the certificate of title within the meaning of this section.

(c) Except with respect to the rights of a buyer described in the next paragraph, a security interest, perfected in another jurisdiction otherwise than by notation on a certificate of title, in goods brought into this state and thereafter covered by a certificate of title issued by this state is subject to the rules stated in paragraph (d) of subsection (1).

(d) If goods are brought into this state while a security interest therein is perfected in any manner under the law of the jurisdiction from which the goods are removed and a certificate of title is issued by this state and the certificate does not show that the goods are subject to the security interest or that they may be subject to security interests not shown on the certificate, the security interest is subordinate to the rights of a buyer of the goods who is not in the business of selling goods of that kind to the extent that he gives value and receives delivery of the goods after issuance of the certificate and without knowledge of the security interest.

(3) Accounts, general intangibles and mobile goods.

(a) This subsection applies to accounts (other than an account described in subsection (5) on minerals) and general intangibles (other than uncertificated securities) and to goods which are mobile and which are of a type normally used in more than one jurisdiction, such as motor vehicles, trailers, rolling stock, airplanes, shipping containers, road building and construction machinery and commercial harvesting machinery and the like, if the goods are equipment or are inventory leased or held for lease by the debtor to others, and are not covered by a certificate of title described in subsection (2).

(b) The law (including the conflict of laws rules) of the jurisdiction in which the debtor is located governs the perfection and the effect of perfection or non-perfection of the security interest.

(c) If, however, the debtor is located in a jurisdiction which is not a part of the United States, and which does not provide for perfection of the security interest by filing or recording in that jurisdiction, the law of the jurisdiction in the United States in which the debtor has its major executive office in the United States governs the perfection and the effect of perfection or non-perfection of the security interest through filing. In the alternative, if the debtor is located in a jurisdiction which is not a part of the United States or Canada and the collateral is accounts or general intangibles for money due or to become due, the security interest may be perfected by notification to the account debtor. As used in this paragraph, "United States" includes its territories and possessions and the Commonwealth of Puerto Rico.

(d) A debtor shall be deemed located at his place of business if he has one, at his chief executive office if he has more than one place of business, otherwise at his residence. If, however, the debtor is a foreign air carrier under the Federal Aviation Act of 1958, as amended, it shall be deemed located at the designated office of the agent upon whom service of process may be made on behalf of the foreign air carrier.

(e) A security interest perfected under the law of the jurisdiction of the location of the debtor is perfected until the expiration of four months after a change of the debtor's location to another jurisdiction, or until perfection would have ceased by the law of the first jurisdiction, whichever period first expires. Unless perfected in the new jurisdiction before the end of that period, it becomes unperfected thereafter and is deemed to have been unperfected as against a person who became a purchaser after the change.

(4) Chattel paper.

The rules stated for goods in subsection (1) apply to a possessory security interest in chattel paper. The rules stated for accounts in subsection (3) apply to a non-possessory security interest in chattel paper, but the security interest may not be perfected by notification to the account debtor.

(5) Minerals.

Perfection and the effect of perfection or non-perfection of a security interest which is created by a debtor who has an interest in minerals or the like (including oil and gas) before extraction and which attaches thereto as extracted, or which attaches to an account resulting from the sale thereof at the wellhead or minehead are governed by the law (including the conflict of laws rules) of the jurisdiction wherein the wellhead or minehead is located.

(6) Uncertificated securities.

The law (including the conflict of laws rules) of the jurisdiction of organization of the issuer governs the perfection and the effect of perfection or non-perfection of a security interest in uncertificated securities.

## § 9–104.  Transactions Excluded From Article.

This Article does not apply

(a) to a security interest subject to any statute of the United States, to the extent that such statute governs the rights of parties to and third parties affected by transactions in particular types of property; or

(b) to a landlord's lien; or

(c) to a lien given by statute or other rule of law for services or materials except as provided in Section 9–310 on priority of such liens; or

(d) to a transfer of a claim for wages, salary or other compensation of an employee; or

(e) to a transfer by a government or governmental subdivision or agency; or

(f) to a sale of accounts or chattel paper as part of a sale of the business out of which they arose, or an assignment of accounts or chattel paper which is for the purpose of collection only, or a transfer of a right to payment under a contract to an assignee who is also to do the performance under the contract or a transfer of a single account to an assignee in whole or partial satisfaction of a preexisting indebtedness; or

(g) to a transfer of an interest in or claim in or under any policy of insurance, except as provided with respect to proceeds (Section 9–306) and priorities in proceeds (Section 9–312); or

(h) to a right represented by a judgment (other than a judgment taken on a right to payment which was collateral); or

(i) to any right of set-off; or

(j) except to the extent that provision is made for fixtures in Section 9–313, to the creation or transfer of an interest in or lien on real estate, including a lease or rents thereunder; or

(k) to a transfer in whole or in part of any claim arising out of tort; or

(l) to a transfer of an interest in any deposit account (subsection (1) of Section 9–105), except as provided with respect to proceeds (Section 9–306) and priorities in proceeds (Section 9–312).

## § 9–105.  Definitions and Index of Definitions.

(1) In this Article unless the context otherwise requires:

(a) "Account debtor" means the person who is obligated on an account, chattel paper or general intangible;

(b) "Chattel paper" means a writing or writings which evidence both a monetary obligation and a security interest in or a lease of specific goods, but a charter or other contract involving the use or hire of a vessel is not chattel paper. When a transaction is evidenced both by such a security agreement or a lease and by an instrument or a series of instruments, the group of writings taken together constitutes chattel paper;

(c) "Collateral" means the property subject to a security interest, and includes accounts and chattel paper which have been sold;

(d) "Debtor" means the person who owes payment or other performance of the obligation secured, whether or not he owns or has rights in the collateral, and includes the seller of accounts or chattel paper. Where the debtor and the owner of the collateral are not the same person, the term "debtor" means the owner of the collateral in any provision of the Article dealing with the collateral, the obligor in any provision dealing with the obligation, and may include both where the context so requires;

(e) "Deposit account" means a demand, time, savings, passbook or like account maintained with a bank, savings and loan association, credit union or like organization, other than an account evidenced by a certificate of deposit;

(f) "Document" means document of title as defined in the general definitions of Article 1 (Section 1–201), and a receipt of the kind described in subsection (2) of Section 7–201;

(g) "Encumbrance" includes real estate mortgages and other liens on real estate and all other rights in real estate that are not ownership interests;

(h) "Goods" includes all things which are movable at the time the security interest attaches or which are fixtures (Section 9–313), but does not include money, documents, instruments, accounts, chattel paper, general intangibles, or minerals or the like (including oil and gas) before extraction. "Goods" also includes standing timber which is to be cut and removed under a conveyance or contract for sale, the unborn young of animals, and growing crops;

(i) "Instrument" means a negotiable instrument (defined in Section 3–104), or a certificated security (defined in Section 8–102) or any other writing which evidences a right to the payment of money and is not itself a security agreement or lease and is of a type which is in ordinary course of business transferred by delivery with any necessary indorsement or assignment;

(j) "Mortgage" means a consensual interest created by a real estate mortgage, a trust deed on real estate, or the like;

(k) An advance is made "pursuant to commitment" if the secured party has bound himself to make it, whether or not a subsequent event of default or other event not within his control has relieved or may relieve him from his obligation;

(l) "Security agreement" means an agreement which creates or provides for a security interest;

(m) "Secured party" means a lender, seller or other person in whose favor there is a security interest, including a person to whom accounts or chattel paper have been sold. When the holders of obligations issued under an indenture of trust, equipment trust agreement or the like are represented by a trustee or other person, the representative is the secured party;

(n) "Transmitting utility" means any person primarily engaged in the railroad, street railway or trolley bus business, the electric or electronics communications transmission business, the transmission of goods by pipeline, or the transmission or the production and transmission of electricity, steam, gas or water, or the provision of sewer service.

(2) Other definitions applying to this Article and the sections in which they appear are:

"Account". Section 9–106.
"Attach". Section 9–203.
"Construction mortgage". Section 9–313(1).
"Consumer goods". Section 9–109(1).
"Equipment". Section 9–109(2).
"Farm products". Section 9–109(3).
"Fixture". Section 9–313(1).
"Fixture filing". Section 9–313(1).
"General intangibles". Section 9–106.

"Inventory". Section 9–109(4).
"Lien creditor". Section 9–301(3).
"Proceeds". Section 9–306(1).
"Purchase money security interest". Section 9–107.
"United States". Section 9–103.

(3) The following definitions in other Articles apply to this Article:
"Check". Section 3–104.
"Contract for sale". Section 2–106.
"Holder in due course". Section 3–302.
"Note". Section 3–104.
"Sale". Section 2–106.

(4) In addition Article 1 contains general definitions and principles of construction and interpretation applicable throughout this Article.

### § 9–106. Definitions: "Account"; "General Intangibles".

"Account" means any right to payment for goods sold or leased or for services rendered which is not evidenced by an instrument or chattel paper, whether or not it has been earned by performance. "General intangibles" means any personal property (including things in action) other than goods, accounts, chattel paper, documents, instruments, and money. All rights to payment earned or unearned under a charter or other contract involving the use or hire of a vessel and all rights incident to the charter or contract are accounts.

### § 9–107. Definitions: "Purchase Money Security Interest".

A security interest is a "purchase money security interest" to the extent that it is

(a) taken or retained by the seller of the collateral to secure all or part of its price; or

(b) taken by a person who by making advances or incurring an obligation gives value to enable the debtor to acquire rights in or the use of collateral if such value is in fact so used.

### § 9–108. When After-Acquired Collateral Not Security for Antecedent Debt.

Where a secured party makes an advance, incurs an obligation, releases a perfected security interest, or otherwise gives new value which is to be secured in whole or in part by after-acquired property his security interest in the after-acquired collateral shall be deemed to be taken for new value and not as security for an antecedent debt if the debtor acquires his rights in such collateral either in the ordinary course of his business or under a contract of purchase made pursuant to the security agreement within a reasonable time after new value is given.

### § 9–109. Classification of Goods; "Consumer Goods"; "Equipment"; "Farm Products"; "Inventory".

Goods are

(1) "consumer goods" if they are used or bought for use primarily for personal, family or household purposes;

(2) "equipment" if they are used or bought for use primarily in business (including farming or a profession) or by a debtor who is a non-profit organization or a governmental subdivision or agency or if the goods are not included in the definitions of inventory, farm products or consumer goods;

(3) "farm products" if they are crops or livestock or supplies used or produced in farming operations or if they are products of crops or livestock in their unmanufactured states (such as ginned cotton, wool-clip, maple syrup, milk and eggs), and if they are in the possession of a debtor engaged in raising, fattening, grazing or other farming operations. If goods are farm products they are neither equipment nor inventory;

(4) "inventory" if they are held by a person who holds them for sale or lease or to be furnished under contracts of service or if he has so furnished them, or if they are raw materials, work in process or materials used or consumed in a business. Inventory of a person is not to be classified as his equipment.

### § 9–110. Sufficiency of Description.

For purposes of this Article any description of personal property or real estate is sufficient whether or not it is specific if it reasonably identifies what is described.

### § 9–111. Applicability of Bulk Transfer Laws.

The creation of a security interest is not a bulk transfer under Article 6 (see Section 6–103).

### § 9–112. Where Collateral Is Not Owned by Debtor.

Unless otherwise agreed, when a secured party knows that collateral is owned by a person who is not the debtor, the owner of the collateral is entitled to receive from the secured party any surplus under Section 9–502(2) or under Section 9–504(1), and is not liable for the debt or for any deficiency after resale, and he has the same right as the debtor.

(a) to receive statements under Section 9–208;

(b) to receive notice of and to object to a secured party's proposal to retain the collateral in satisfaction of the indebtedness under Section 9–505;

(c) to redeem the collateral under Section 9–506;

(d) to obtain injunctive or other relief under Section 9–507(1); and

(e) to recover losses caused to him under Section 9–208(2).

### § 9–113. Security Interests Arising Under Article on Sales.

A security interest arising solely under the Article on Sales (Article 2) is subject to the provisions of this Article except that to the extent that and so long as the debtor does not have or does not lawfully obtain possession of the goods

(a) no security agreement is necessary to make the security interest enforceable; and

(b) no filing is required to perfect the security interest; and

(c) the rights of the secured party on default by the debtor are governed by the Article on Sales (Article 2).

### § 9–114. Consignment.

(1) A person who delivers goods under a consignment which is not a security interest and who would be required to file under this Article by paragraph (3)(c) of Section 2–326 has priority over a secured party who is or becomes a creditor of the consignee and who would have a perfected security interest in the goods if they were the property of the consignee, and also has priority with respect to identifiable cash proceeds received on or before delivery of the goods to a buyer, if

(a) the consignor complies with the filing provision of the Article on Sales with respect to consignments (paragraph (3)(c) of Section 2–326) before the consignee receives possession of the goods; and

(b) the consignor gives notification in writing to the holder of the security interest if the holder has filed a financing statement covering the same types of goods before the date of the filing made by the consignor; and

(c) the holder of the security interest receives the notification within five years before the consignee receives possession of the goods; and

(d) the notification states that the consignor expects to deliver goods on consignment to the consignee, describing the goods by item or type.

(2) In the case of a consignment which is not a security interest and in which the requirements of the preceding subsection have not been met, a person who delivers goods to another is subordinate to a person who would have a perfected security interest in the goods if they were the property of the debtor.

## Part 2—Validity of Security Agreement and Rights of Parties Thereto

### § 9–201.  General Validity of Security Agreement.

Except as otherwise provided by this Act a security agreement is effective according to its terms between the parties, against purchasers of the collateral and against creditors. Nothing in this Article validates any charge or practice illegal under any statute or regulation thereunder governing usury, small loans, retail installment sales, or the like, or extends the application of any such statute or regulation to any transaction not otherwise subject thereto.

### § 9–202.  Title to Collateral Immaterial.

Each provision of this Article with regard to rights, obligations and remedies applies whether title to collateral is in the secured party or in the debtor.

### § 9–203.  Attachment and Enforceability of Security Interest; Proceeds; Formal Requisites.

(1) Subject to the provisions of Section 4–210 on the security interest of a collecting bank, Section 8–321 on security interests in securities and Section 9–113 on a security interest arising under the Articles on Sales and Leases, a security interest is not enforceable against the debtor or third parties with respect to the collateral and does not attach unless:

    (a) the collateral is in the possession of the secured party pursuant to agreement, or the debtor has signed a security agreement which contains a description of the collateral and in addition, when the security interest covers crops growing or to be grown or timber to be cut, a description of the land concerned;

    (b) value has been given; and

    (c) the debtor has rights in the collateral.

(2) A security interest attaches when it becomes enforceable against the debtor with respect to the collateral. Attachment occurs as soon as all of the events specified in subsection (1) have taken place unless explicit agreement postpones the time of attaching.

(3) Unless otherwise agreed a security agreement gives the secured party the rights to proceeds provided by Section 9–306.

(4) A transaction, although subject to this Article, is also subject to . . .*, and in the case of conflict between the provisions of this Article and any such statute, the provisions of such statute control. Failure to comply with any applicable statute has only the effect which is specified therein.

Note: *At * in subsection (4) insert reference to any local statute regulating small loans, retail installment sales and the like.*

*The foregoing subsection (4) is designed to make it clear that certain transactions, although subject to this Article, must also comply with other applicable legislation.*

*This Article is designed to regulate all the "security" aspects of transactions within its scope. There is, however, much regulatory legislation, particularly in the consumer field, which supplements this Article and should not be repealed by its enactment. Examples are small loan acts, retail installment selling acts and the like. Such acts may provide for licensing and rate regulation and may prescribe particular forms of contract. Such provisions should remain in force despite the enactment of this Article. On the other hand if a retail installment selling act*

*contains provisions on filing, rights on default, etc., such provisions should be repealed as inconsistent with this Article except that inconsistent provisions as to deficiencies, penalties, etc., in the Uniform Consumer Credit Code and other recent related legislation should remain because those statutes were drafted after the substantial enactment of the Article and with the intention of modifying certain provisions of this Article as to consumer credit.*

### § 9–204.  After-Acquired Property; Future Advances.

(1) Except as provided in subsection (2), a security agreement may provide that any or all obligations covered by the security agreement are to be secured by after-acquired collateral.

(2) No security interest attaches under an after-acquired property clause to consumer goods other than accessions (Section 9–314) when given as additional security unless the debtor acquires rights in them within ten days after the secured party gives value.

(3) Obligations covered by a security agreement may include future advances or other value whether or not the advances or value are given pursuant to commitment (subsection (1) of Section 9–105).

### § 9–205.  Use or Disposition of Collateral Without Accounting Permissible.

A security interest is not invalid or fraudulent against creditors by reason of liberty in the debtor to use, commingle or dispose of all or part of the collateral (including returned or repossessed goods) or to collect or compromise accounts or chattel paper, or to accept the return of goods or make repossessions, or to use, commingle or dispose of proceeds, or by reason of the failure of the secured party to require the debtor to account for proceeds or replace collateral. This section does not relax the requirements of possession where perfection of a security interest depends upon possession of the collateral by the secured party or by a bailee.

### § 9–206.  Agreement Not to Assert Defenses Against Assignee; Modification of Sales Warranties Where Security Agreement Exists.

(1) Subject to any statute or decision which establishes a different rule for buyers or lessees of consumer goods, an agreement by a buyer or lessee that he will not assert against an assignee any claim or defense which he may have against the seller or lessor is enforceable by an assignee who takes his assignment for value, in good faith and without notice of a claim or defense, except as to defenses of a type which may be asserted against a holder in due course of a negotiable instrument under the Article on Negotiable Instruments (Article 3). A buyer who as part of one transaction signs both a negotiable instrument and a security agreement makes such an agreement.

(2) When a seller retains a purchase money security interest in goods the Article on Sales (Article 2) governs the sale and any disclaimer, limitation or modification of the seller's warranties.

### § 9–207.  Rights and Duties When Collateral Is in Secured Party's Possession.

(1) A secured party must use reasonable care in the custody and preservation of collateral in his possession. In the case of an instrument or chattel paper reasonable care includes taking necessary steps to preserve rights against prior parties unless otherwise agreed.

(2) Unless otherwise agreed, when collateral is in the secured party's possession

    (a) reasonable expenses (including the cost of any insurance and payment of taxes or other charges) incurred in the custody, preservation, use or operation of the collateral are chargeable to the debtor and are secured by the collateral;

(b) the risk of accidental loss or damage is on the debtor to the extent of any deficiency in any effective insurance coverage;

(c) the secured party may hold as additional security any increase or profits (except money) received from the collateral, but money so received, unless remitted to the debtor, shall be applied in reduction of the secured obligation;

(d) the secured party must keep the collateral identifiable but fungible collateral may be commingled;

(e) the secured party may repledge the collateral upon terms which do not impair the debtor's right to redeem it.

(3) A secured party is liable for any loss caused by his failure to meet any obligation imposed by the preceding subsections but does not lose his security interest.

(4) A secured party may use or operate the collateral for the purpose of preserving the collateral or its value or pursuant to the order of a court of appropriate jurisdiction or, except in the case of consumer goods, in the manner and to the extent provided in the security agreement.

### § 9–208.  Request for Statement of Account or List of Collateral.

(1) A debtor may sign a statement indicating what he believes to be the aggregate amount of unpaid indebtedness as of a specified date and may send it to the secured party with a request that the statement be approved or corrected and returned to the debtor. When the security agreement or any other record kept by the secured party identifies the collateral a debtor may similarly request the secured party to approve or correct a list of the collateral.

(2) The secured party must comply with such a request within two weeks after receipt by sending a written correction or approval. If the secured party claims a security interest in all of a particular type of collateral owned by the debtor he may indicate that fact in his reply and need not approve or correct an itemized list of such collateral. If the secured party without reasonable excuse fails to comply he is liable for any loss caused to the debtor thereby; and if the debtor has properly included in his request a good faith statement of the obligation or a list of the collateral or both the secured party may claim a security interest only as shown in the statement against persons misled by his failure to comply. If he no longer has an interest in the obligation or collateral at the time the request is received he must disclose the name and address of any successor in interest known to him and he is liable for any loss caused to the debtor as a result of failure to disclose. A successor in interest is not subject to this section until a request is received by him.

(3) A debtor is entitled to such a statement once every six months without charge. The secured party may require payment of a charge not exceeding $10 for each additional statement furnished.

## Part 3—Rights of Third Parties; Perfected and Unperfected Security Interests; Rules of Priority

### § 9–301.  Persons Who Take Priority Over Unperfected Security Interests; Rights of "Lien Creditor".

(1) Except as otherwise provided in subsection (2), an unperfected security interest is subordinate to the rights of

(a) persons entitled to priority under Section 9–312;

(b) a person who becomes a lien creditor before the security interest is perfected;

(c) in the case of goods, instruments, documents, and chattel paper, a person who is not a secured party and who is a transferee in bulk or other buyer not in ordinary course of business or is a buyer of farm products in ordinary course of business, to the extent that he gives value and receives delivery of the collateral without knowledge of the security interest and before it is perfected;

(d) in the case of accounts and general intangibles, a person who is not a secured party and who is a transferee to the extent that he gives value without knowledge of the security interest and before it is perfected.

(2) If the secured party files with respect to a purchase money security interest before or within ten days after the debtor receives possession of the collateral, he takes priority over the rights of a transferee in bulk or of a lien creditor which arise between the time the security interest attaches and the time of filing.

(3) A "lien creditor" means a creditor who has acquired a lien on the property involved by attachment, levy or the like and includes an assignee for benefit of creditors from the time of assignment, and a trustee in bankruptcy from the date of the filing of the petition or a receiver in equity from the time of appointment.

(4) A person who becomes a lien creditor while a security interest is perfected takes subject to the security interest only to the extent that it secures advances made before he becomes a lien creditor or within 45 days thereafter or made without knowledge of the lien or pursuant to a commitment entered into without knowledge of the lien.

### § 9–302.  When Filing Is Required to Perfect Security Interest; Security Interests to Which Filing Provisions of This Article Do Not Apply.

(1) A financing statement must be filed to perfect all security interests except the following:

(a) a security interest in collateral in possession of the secured party under Section 9–305;

(b) a security interest temporarily perfected in instruments or documents without delivery under Section 9–304 or in proceeds for a 10 day period under Section 9–306;

(c) a security interest created by an assignment of a beneficial interest in a trust or a decedent's estate;

(d) a purchase money security interest in consumer goods; but filing is required for a motor vehicle required to be registered; and fixture filing is required for priority over conflicting interests in fixtures to the extent provided in Section 9–313;

(e) an assignment of accounts which does not alone or in conjunction with other assignments to the same assignee transfer a significant part of the outstanding accounts of the assignor;

(f) a security interest of a collecting bank (Section 4–210) or in securities (Section 8–321) or arising under the Articles on Sales and Leases (see Section 9–113) or covered in subsection (3) of this section;

(g) an assignment for the benefit of all the creditors of the transferor, and subsequent transfers by the assignee thereunder.

(2) If a secured party assigns a perfected security interest, no filing under this Article is required in order to continue the perfected status of the security interest against creditors of and transferees from the original debtor.

(3) The filing of a financing statement otherwise required by this Article is not necessary or effective to perfect a security interest in property subject to

(a) a statute or treaty of the United States which provides for a national or international registration or a national or international certificate of title or which specifies a place of filing different from that specified in this Article for filing of the security interest; or

(b) the following statutes of this state; [list any certificate of title statute covering automobiles, trailers, mobile homes, boats, farm tractors, or the like, and any central filing statute]; but during any period in which collateral is inventory held for sale by a person who is in the business of selling goods of that kind, the filing provisions of this Article (Part 4) apply to a security interest in that collateral created by him as debtor; or

(c) a certificate of title statute of another jurisdiction under the law of which indication of a security interest on the certificate is required as a condition of perfection (subsection (2) of Section 9–103).

(4) Compliance with a statute or treaty described in subsection (3) is equivalent to the filing of a financing statement under this Article, and a security interest in property subject to the statute or treaty can be perfected only by compliance therewith except as provided in Section 9–103 on multiple state transactions. Duration and renewal of perfection of a security interest perfected by compliance with the statute or treaty are governed by the provisions of the statute or treaty; in other respects the security interest is subject to this Article. Amended in 1972 and 1977.

## § 9–303. When Security Interest Is Perfected; Continuity of Perfection.

(1) A security interest is perfected when it has attached and when all of the applicable steps required for perfection have been taken. Such steps are specified in Sections 9–302, 9–304, 9–305 and 9–306. If such steps are taken before the security interest attaches, it is perfected at the time when it attaches.

(2) If a security interest is originally perfected in any way permitted under this Article and is subsequently perfected in some other way under this Article, without an intermediate period when it was unperfected, the security interest shall be deemed to be perfected continuously for the purposes of this Article.

## § 9–304. Perfection of Security Interest in Instruments, Documents, and Goods Covered by Documents; Perfection by Permissive Filing; Temporary Perfection Without Filing or Transfer of Possession.

(1) A security interest in chattel paper or negotiable documents may be perfected by filing. A security interest in money or instruments (other than certificated securities or instruments which constitute part of chattel paper) can be perfected only by the secured party's taking possession, except as provided in subsections (4) and (5) of this section and subsections (2) and (3) of Section 9–306 on proceeds.

(2) During the period that goods are in the possession of the issuer of a negotiable document therefor, a security interest in the goods is perfected by perfecting a security interest in the document, and any security interest in the goods otherwise perfected during such period is subject thereto.

(3) A security interest in goods in the possession of a bailee other than one who has issued a negotiable document therefor is perfected by issuance of a document in the name of the secured party or by the bailee's receipt of notification of the secured party's interest or by filing as to the goods.

(4) A security interest in instruments (other than certificated securities) or negotiable documents is perfected without filing or the taking of possession for a period of 21 days from the time it attaches to the extent that it arises for new value given under a written security agreement.

(5) A security interest remains perfected for a period of 21 days without filing where a secured party having a perfected security interest in an instrument (other than a certificated security), a negotiable document or goods in possession of a bailee other than one who has issued a negotiable document therefor

(a) makes available to the debtor the goods or documents representing the goods for the purpose of ultimate sale or exchange or for the purpose of loading, unloading, storing, shipping, transshipping, manufacturing, processing or otherwise dealing with them in a manner preliminary to their sale or exchange, but priority between conflicting security interests in the goods is subject to subsection (3) of Section 9–312; or

(b) delivers the instrument to the debtor for the purpose of ultimate sale or exchange or of presentation, collection, renewal or registration of transfer.

(6) After the 21 day period in subsections (4) and (5) perfection depends upon compliance with applicable provisions of this Article.

## § 9–305. When Possession by Secured Party Perfects Security Interest Without Filing.

A security interest in letters of credit and advices of credit (subsection (2)(a) of Section 5–116), goods, instruments (other than certificated securities), money, negotiable documents, or chattel paper may be perfected by the secured party's taking possession of the collateral. If such collateral other than goods covered by a negotiable document is held by a bailee, the secured party is deemed to have possession from the time the bailee receives notification of the secured party's interest. A security interest is perfected by possession from the time possession is taken without a relation back and continues only so long as possession is retained, unless otherwise specified in this Article. The security interest may be otherwise perfected as provided in this Article before or after the period of possession by the secured party.

## § 9–306. "Proceeds"; Secured Party's Rights on Disposition of Collateral.

(1) "Proceeds" includes whatever is received upon the sale, exchange, collection or other disposition of collateral or proceeds. Insurance payable by reason of loss or damage to the collateral is proceeds, except to the extent that it is payable to a person other than a party to the security agreement. Money, checks, deposit accounts, and the like are "cash proceeds". All other proceeds are "non-cash proceeds".

(2) Except where this Article otherwise provides, a security interest continues in collateral notwithstanding sale, exchange or other disposition thereof unless the disposition was authorized by the secured party in the security agreement or otherwise, and also continues in any identifiable proceeds including collections received by the debtor.

(3) The security interest in proceeds is a continuously perfected security interest if the interest in the original collateral was perfected but it ceases to be a perfected security interest and becomes unperfected ten days after receipt of the proceeds by the debtor unless

(a) a filed financing statement covers the original collateral and the proceeds are collateral in which a security interest may be perfected by filing in the office or offices where the financing statement has been filed and, if the proceeds are acquired with cash proceeds, the description of collateral in the financing statement indicates the types of property constituting the proceeds; or

(b) a filed financing statement covers the original collateral and the proceeds are identifiable cash proceeds; or

(c) the security interest in the proceeds is perfected before the expiration of the ten day period.

Except as provided in this section, a security interest in proceeds can be perfected only by the methods or under the circumstances permitted in this Article for original collateral of the same type.

(4) In the event of insolvency proceedings instituted by or against a debtor, a secured party with a perfected security interest in proceeds has a perfected security interest only in the following proceeds:

(a) in identifiable non-cash proceeds and in separate deposit accounts containing only proceeds;

(b) in identifiable cash proceeds in the form of money which is neither commingled with other money nor deposited in a deposit account prior to the insolvency proceedings;

(c) in identifiable cash proceeds in the form of checks and the like which are not deposited in a deposit account prior to the insolvency proceedings; and

(d) in all cash and deposit accounts of the debtor in which proceeds have been commingled with other funds, but the perfected security interest under this paragraph (d) is

(i) subject to any right to set-off; and

(ii) limited to an amount not greater than the amount of any cash proceeds received by the debtor within ten days before the institution of the insolvency proceedings less the sum of (I) the payments to the secured party on account of cash proceeds received by the debtor during such period and (II) the cash proceeds received by the debtor during such period to which the secured party is entitled under paragraphs (a) through (c) of this subsection (4).

(5) If a sale of goods results in an account or chattel paper which is transferred by the seller to a secured party, and if the goods are returned to or are repossessed by the seller or the secured party, the following rules determine priorities:

(a) If the goods were collateral at the time of sale, for an indebtedness of the seller which is still unpaid, the original security interest attaches again to the goods and continues as a perfected security interest if it was perfected at the time when the goods were sold. If the security interest was originally perfected by a filing which is still effective, nothing further is required to continue the perfected status; in any other case, the secured party must take possession of the returned or repossessed goods or must file.

(b) An unpaid transferee of the chattel paper has a security interest in the goods against the transferor. Such security interest is prior to a security interest asserted under paragraph (a) to the extent that the transferee of the chattel paper was entitled to priority under Section 9–308.

(c) An unpaid transferee of the account has a security interest in the goods against the transferor. Such security interest is subordinate to a security interest asserted under paragraph (a).

(d) A security interest of an unpaid transferee asserted under paragraph (b) or (c) must be perfected for protection against creditors of the transferor and purchasers of the returned or repossessed goods.

## § 9–307.  Protection of Buyers of Goods.

(1) A buyer in ordinary course of business (subsection (9) of Section 1–201) other than a person buying farm products from a person engaged in farming operations takes free of a security interest created by his seller even though the security interest is perfected and even though the buyer knows of its existence.

(2) In the case of consumer goods, a buyer takes free of a security interest even though perfected if he buys without knowledge of the security interest, for value and for his own personal, family or household purposes unless prior to the purchase the secured party has filed a financing statement covering such goods.

(3) A buyer other than a buyer in ordinary course of business (subsection (1) of this section) takes free of a security interest to the extent that it secures future advances made after the secured party acquires knowledge of the purchase, or more than 45 days after the purchase, whichever first occurs, unless made pursuant to a commitment entered into without knowledge of the purchase and before the expiration of the 45 day period.

## § 9–308.  Purchase of Chattel Paper and Instruments.

A purchaser of chattel paper or an instrument who gives new value and takes possession of it in the ordinary course of his business has priority over a security interest in the chattel paper or instrument

(a) which is perfected under Section 9–304 (permissive filing and temporary perfection) or under Section 9–306 (perfection as to proceeds) if he acts without knowledge that the specific paper or instrument is subject to a security interest; or

(b) which is claimed merely as proceeds of inventory subject to a security interest (Section 9–306) even though he knows that the specific paper or instrument is subject to the security interest.

## § 9–309.  Protection of Purchasers of Instruments, Documents and Securities.

Nothing in this Article limits the rights of a holder in due course of a negotiable instrument (Section 3–302) or a holder to whom a negotiable document of title has been duly negotiated (Section 7–501) or a bona fide purchaser of a security (Section 8–302) and the holders or purchasers take priority over an earlier security interest even though perfected. Filing under this Article does not constitute notice of the security interest to such holders or purchasers.

## § 9–310.  Priority of Certain Liens Arising by Operation of Law.

When a person in the ordinary course of his business furnishes services or materials with respect to goods subject to a security interest, a lien upon goods in the possession of such person given by statute or rule of law for such materials or services takes priority over a perfected security interest unless the lien is statutory and the statute expressly provides otherwise.

## § 9–311.  Alienability of Debtor's Rights: Judicial Process.

The debtor's rights in collateral may be voluntarily or involuntarily transferred (by way of sale, creation of a security interest, attachment, levy, garnishment or other judicial process) notwithstanding a provision in the security agreement prohibiting any transfer or making the transfer constitute a default.

## § 9–312.  Priorities Among Conflicting Security Interests in the Same Collateral.

(1) The rules of priority stated in other sections of this Part and in the following sections shall govern when applicable: Section 4–208 with respect to the security interests of collecting banks in items being collected, accompanying documents and proceeds; Section 9–103 on security interests related to other jurisdictions; Section 9–114 on consignments.

(2) A perfected security interest in crops for new value given to enable the debtor to produce the crops during the production season and given not more than three months before the crops become growing crops by planting or otherwise takes priority over an earlier perfected security interest to the extent that such earlier interest secures obligations due more than six months before the crops become growing crops by planting or otherwise, even though the person giving new value had knowledge of the earlier security interest.

(3) A perfected purchase money security interest in inventory has priority over a conflicting security interest in the same inventory and also has priority in identifiable cash proceeds received on or before the delivery of the inventory to a buyer if

    (a) the purchase money security interest is perfected at the time the debtor receives possession of the inventory; and

    (b) the purchase money secured party gives notification in writing to the holder of the conflicting security interest if the holder had filed a financing statement covering the same types of inventory (i) before the date of the filing made by the purchase money secured party, or (ii) before the beginning of the 21 day period where the purchase money security interest is temporarily perfected without filing or possession (subsection (5) of Section 9–304); and

    (c) the holder of the conflicting security interest receives the notification within five years before the debtor receives possession of the inventory; and

    (d) the notification states that the person giving the notice has or expects to acquire a purchase money security interest in inventory of the debtor, describing such inventory by item or type.

(4) A purchase money security interest in collateral other than inventory has priority over a conflicting security interest in the same collateral or its proceeds if the purchase money security interest is perfected at the time the debtor receives possession of the collateral or within ten days thereafter.

(5) In all cases not governed by other rules stated in this section (including cases of purchase money security interests which do not qualify for the special priorities set forth in subsections (3) and (4) of this section), priority between conflicting security interests in the same collateral shall be determined according to the following rules:

    (a) Conflicting security interests rank according to priority in time of filing or perfection. Priority dates from the time a filing is first made covering the collateral or the time the security interest is first perfected, whichever is earlier, provided that there is no period thereafter when there is neither filing nor perfection.

    (b) So long as conflicting security interests are unperfected, the first to attach has priority.

(6) For the purposes of subsection (5) a date of filing or perfection as to collateral is also a date of filing or perfection as to proceeds.

(7) If future advances are made while a security interest is perfected by filing, the taking of possession, or under Section 8–321 on securities, the security interest has the same priority for the purposes of subsection (5) with respect to the future advances as it does with respect to the first advance. If a commitment is made before or while the security interest is so perfected, the security interest has the same priority with respect to advances made pursuant thereto. In other cases a perfected security interest has priority from the date the advance is made.

## § 9–313. Priority of Security Interests in Fixtures.

(1) In this section and in the provisions of Part 4 of this Article referring to fixture filing, unless the context otherwise requires

    (a) goods are "fixtures" when they become so related to particular real estate that an interest in them arises under real estate law

    (b) a "fixture filing" is the filing in the office where a mortgage on the real estate would be filed or recorded of a financing statement covering goods which are or are to become fixtures and conforming to the requirements of subsection (5) of Section 9–402

    (c) a mortgage is a "construction mortgage" to the extent that it secures an obligation incurred for the construction of an improvement on land including the acquisition cost of the land, if the recorded writing so indicates.

(2) A security interest under this Article may be created in goods which are fixtures or may continue in goods which become fixtures, but no security interest exists under this Article in ordinary building materials incorporated into an improvement on land.

(3) This Article does not prevent creation of an encumbrance upon fixtures pursuant to real estate law.

(4) A perfected security interest in fixtures has priority over the conflicting interest of an encumbrancer or owner of the real estate where

    (a) the security interest is a purchase money security interest, the interest of the encumbrancer or owner arises before the goods become fixtures, the security interest is perfected by a fixture filing before the goods become fixtures or within ten days thereafter, and the debtor has an interest of record in the real estate or is in possession of the real estate; or

    (b) the security interest is perfected by a fixture filing before the interest of the encumbrancer or owner is of record, the security interest has priority over any conflicting interest of a predecessor in title of the encumbrancer or owner, and the debtor has an interest of record in the real estate or is in possession of the real estate; or

    (c) the fixtures are readily removable factory or office machines or readily removable replacements of domestic appliances which are consumer goods, and before the goods become fixtures the security interest is perfected by any method permitted by this Article; or

    (d) the conflicting interest is a lien on the real estate obtained by legal or equitable proceedings after the security interest was perfected by any method permitted by this Article.

(5) A security interest in fixtures, whether or not perfected, has priority over the conflicting interest of an encumbrancer or owner of the real estate where

    (a) the encumbrancer or owner has consented in writing to the security interest or has disclaimed an interest in the goods as fixtures; or

    (b) the debtor has a right to remove the goods as against the encumbrancer or owner. If the debtor's right terminates, the priority of the security interest continues for a reasonable time.

(6) Notwithstanding paragraph (a) of subsection (4) but otherwise subject to subsections (4) and (5), a security interest in fixtures is subordinate to a construction mortgage recorded before the goods become fixtures if the goods become fixtures before the completion of the construction. To the extent that it is given to refinance a construction mortgage, a mortgage has this priority to the same extent as the construction mortgage.

(7) In cases not within the preceding subsections, a security interest in fixtures is subordinate to the conflicting interest of an encumbrancer or owner of the related real estate who is not the debtor.

(8) When the secured party has priority over all owners and encumbrancers of the real estate, he may, on default, subject to the provisions of Part 5, remove his collateral from the real estate but he must reimburse any encumbrancer or owner of the real estate who is not the debtor and who has not otherwise agreed for the cost of repair of any physical injury, but not for any diminution in value of the real estate caused by the absence of the goods removed or by any necessity of replacing them. A person entitled to reimbursement may refuse permission to remove until the secured party gives adequate security for the performance of this obligation.

## § 9–314. Accessions.

(1) A security interest in goods which attaches before they are installed in or affixed to other goods takes priority as to the goods installed or affixed (called in this section "accessions") over the claims of all persons to the whole except as stated in subsection (3) and subject to Section 9–315(1).

(2) A security interest which attaches to goods after they become part of a whole is valid against all persons subsequently acquiring interests in the whole except as stated in subsection (3) but is invalid against any person with an interest in the whole at the time the security interest attaches to the goods who has not in writing consented to the security interest or disclaimed an interest in the goods as part of the whole.

(3) The security interests described in subsections (1) and (2) do not take priority over

    (a) a subsequent purchaser for value of any interest in the whole; or

    (b) a creditor with a lien on the whole subsequently obtained by judicial proceedings; or

    (c) a creditor with a prior perfected security interest in the whole to the extent that he makes subsequent advances

if the subsequent purchase is made, the lien by judicial proceedings obtained or the subsequent advance under the prior perfected security interest is made or contracted for without knowledge of the security interest and before it is perfected. A purchaser of the whole at a foreclosure sale other than the holder of a perfected security interest purchasing at his own foreclosure sale is a subsequent purchaser within this section.

(4) When under subsections (1) or (2) and (3) a secured party has an interest in accessions which has priority over the claims of all persons who have interests in the whole, he may on default subject to the provisions of Part 5 remove his collateral from the whole but he must reimburse any encumbrancer or owner of the whole who is not the debtor and who has not otherwise agreed for the cost of repair of any physical injury but not for any diminution in value of the whole caused by the absence of the goods removed or by any necessity for replacing them. A person entitled to reimbursement may refuse permission to remove until the secured party gives adequate security for the performance of this obligation.

## § 9–315. Priority When Goods Are Commingled or Processed.

(1) If a security interest in goods was perfected and subsequently the goods or a part thereof have become part of a product or mass, the security interest continues in the product or mass if

    (a) the goods are so manufactured, processed, assembled or commingled that their identity is lost in the product or mass; or

    (b) a financing statement covering the original goods also covers the product into which the goods have been manufactured, processed or assembled.

In a case to which paragraph (b) applies, no separate security interest in that part of the original goods which has been manufactured, processed or assembled into the product may be claimed under Section 9–314.

(2) When under subsection (1) more than one security interest attaches to the product or mass, they rank equally according to the ratio that the cost of the goods to which each interest originally attached bears to the cost of the total product or mass.

## § 9–316. Priority Subject to Subordination.

Nothing in this Article prevents subordination by agreement by any person entitled to priority.

## § 9–317. Secured Party Not Obligated on Contract of Debtor.

The mere existence of a security interest or authority given to the debtor to dispose of or use collateral does not impose contract or tort liability upon the secured party for the debtor's acts or omissions.

## § 9–318. Defenses Against Assignee; Modification of Contract After Notification of Assignment; Term Prohibiting Assignment Ineffective; Identification and Proof of Assignment.

(1) Unless an account debtor has made an enforceable agreement not to assert defenses or claims arising out of a sale as provided in Section 9–206 the rights of an assignee are subject to

    (a) all the terms of the contract between the account debtor and assignor and any defense or claim arising therefrom; and

    (b) any other defense or claim of the account debtor against the assignor which accrues before the account debtor receives notification of the assignment.

(2) So far as the right to payment or a part thereof under an assigned contract has not been fully earned by performance, and notwithstanding notification of the assignment, any modification of or substitution for the contract made in good faith and in accordance with reasonable commercial standards is effective against an assignee unless the account debtor has otherwise agreed but the assignee acquires corresponding rights under the modified or substituted contract. The assignment may provide that such modification or substitution is a breach by the assignor.

(3) The account debtor is authorized to pay the assignor until the account debtor receives notification that the amount due or to become due has been assigned and that payment is to be made to the assignee. A notification which does not reasonably identify the rights assigned is ineffective. If requested by the account debtor, the assignee must seasonably furnish reasonable proof that the assignment has been made and unless he does so the account debtor may pay the assignor.

(4) A term in any contract between an account debtor and an assignor is ineffective if it prohibits assignment of an account or prohibits creation of a security interest in a general intangible for money due or to become due or requires the account debtor's consent to such assignment or security interest.

## Part 4—Filing

## § 9–401. Place of Filing; Erroneous Filing; Removal of Collateral.

**First Alternative Subsection (1)**

(1) The proper place to file in order to perfect a security interest is as follows:

    (a) when the collateral is timber to be cut or is minerals or the like (including oil and gas) or accounts subject to subsection (5) of Section 9–103, or when the financing statement is filed as a fixture filing (Section 9–313) and the collateral is goods which are or are to become fixtures, then in the office where a mortgage on the real estate would be filed or recorded;

    (b) in all other cases, in the office of the [Secretary of State].

**Second Alternative Subsection (1)**

(1) The proper place to file in order to perfect a security interest is as follows:

    (a) when the collateral is equipment used in farming operations, or farm products, or accounts or general intangibles arising from or relating to the sale of farm products by a farmer, or consumer goods, then in the office of the _____ in the county of the debtor's residence or if the debtor is not a resident of this state then in the office of the _____ in the county where the goods are kept, and in addition when the collateral is crops growing or to be grown in the office of the _____ in the county where the land is located;

(b) when the collateral is timber to be cut or is minerals or the like (including oil and gas) or accounts subject to subsection (5) of Section 9–103, or when the financing statement is filed as a fixture filing (Section 9–313) and the collateral is goods which are or are to become fixtures, then in the office where a mortgage on the real estate would be filed or recorded;

(c) in all other cases, in the office of the [Secretary of State].

## Third Alternative Subsection (1)

(1) The proper place to file in order to perfect a security interest is as follows:

(a) when the collateral is equipment used in farming operations, or farm products, or accounts or general intangibles arising from or relating to the sale of farm products by a farmer, or consumer goods, then in the office of the _____ in the county of the debtor's residence or if the debtor is not a resident of this state then in the office of the _____ in the county where the goods are kept, and in addition when the collateral is crops growing or to be grown in the office of the _____ in the county where the land is located;

(b) when the collateral is timber to be cut or is minerals or the like (including oil and gas) or accounts subject to subsection (5) of Section 9–103, or when the financing statement is filed as a fixture filing (Section 9–313) and the collateral is goods which are or are to become fixtures, then in the office where a mortgage on the real estate would be filed or recorded;

(c) in all other cases, in the office of the [Secretary of State] and in addition, if the debtor has a place of business in only one county of this state, also in the office of _____ of such county, or, if the debtor has no place of business in this state, but resides in the state, also in the office of _____ of the county in which he resides.

Note: *One of the three alternatives should be selected as subsection (1).*

(2) A filing which is made in good faith in an improper place or not in all of the places required by this section is nevertheless effective with regard to any collateral as to which the filing complied with the requirements of this Article and is also effective with regard to collateral covered by the financing statement against any person who has knowledge of the contents of such financing statement.

(3) A filing which is made in the proper place in this state continues effective even though the debtor's residence or place of business or the location of the collateral or its use, whichever controlled the original filing, is thereafter changed.

## Alternative Subsection (3)

[(3) A filing which is made in the proper county continues effective for four months after a change to another county of the debtor's residence or place of business or the location of the collateral, whichever controlled the original filing. It becomes ineffective thereafter unless a copy of the financing statement signed by the secured party is filed in the new county within said period. The security interest may also be perfected in the new county after the expiration of the four-month period; in such case perfection dates from the time of perfection in the new county. A change in the use of the collateral does not impair the effectiveness of the original filing.]

(4) The rules stated in Section 9–103 determine whether filing is necessary in this state.

(5) Notwithstanding the preceding subsections, and subject to subsection (3) of Section 9–302, the proper place to file in order to perfect a security interest in collateral, including fixtures, of a transmitting utility is the office of the [Secretary of State]. This filing constitutes a fixture filing (Section 9–313) as to the collateral described therein which is or is to become fixtures.

(6) For the purposes of this section, the residence of an organization is its place of business if it has one or its chief executive office if it has more than one place of business.

Note: *Subsection (6) should be used only if the state chooses the Second or Third Alternative Subsection (1).*

## § 9–402. Formal Requisites of Financing Statement; Amendments; Mortgage as Financing Statement.

(1) A financing statement is sufficient if it gives the names of the debtor and the secured party, is signed by the debtor, gives an address of the secured party from which information concerning the security interest may be obtained, gives a mailing address of the debtor and contains a statement indicating the types, or describing the items, of collateral. A financing statement may be filed before a security agreement is made or a security interest otherwise attaches. When the financing statement covers crops growing or to be grown, the statement must also contain a description of the real estate concerned. When the financing statement covers timber to be cut or covers minerals or the like (including oil and gas) or accounts subject to subsection (5) of Section 9–103, or when the financing statement is filed as a fixture filing (Section 9–313) and the collateral is goods which are or are to become fixtures, the statement must also comply with subsection (5). A copy of the security agreement is sufficient as a financing statement if it contains the above information and is signed by the debtor. A carbon, photographic or other reproduction of a security agreement or a financing statement is sufficient as a financing statement if the security agreement so provides or if the original has been filed in this state.

(2) A financing statement which otherwise complies with subsection (1) is sufficient when it is signed by the secured party instead of the debtor if it is filed to perfect a security interest in

(a) collateral already subject to a security interest in another jurisdiction when it is brought into this state, or when the debtor's location is changed to this state. Such a financing statement must state that the collateral was brought into this state or that the debtor's location was changed to this state under such circumstances; or

(b) proceeds under Section 9–306 if the security interest in the original collateral was perfected. Such a financing statement must describe the original collateral; or

(c) collateral as to which the filing has lapsed; or

(d) collateral acquired after a change of name, identity or corporate structure of the debtor (subsection (7)).

(3) A form substantially as follows is sufficient to comply with subsection (1):

Name of debtor (or assignor) _____

Address _____

Name of secured party (or assignee) _____

Address _____

1. This financing statement covers the following types (or items) of property:

(Describe) _____

2. (If collateral is crops) The above described crops are growing or are to be grown on:
(Describe Real Estate) _____

3. (If applicable) The above goods are to become fixtures on*
*Where appropriate substitute either "The above timber is standing on _____" or "The above minerals or the like (including oil and gas) or accounts will be financed at the wellhead or minehead of the well or mine located on _____"
(Describe Real Estate) _____ and this financing statement is to be filed [for record] in the real estate records. (If the debtor does not have an interest of record) The name of a record owner is _____

4. (If products of collateral are claimed) Products of the collateral are also covered.

| (use | _____ |
| whichever | Signature of Debtor (or Assignor) |
| is | _____ |
| applicable) | Signature of Secured Party (or Assignee) |

(4) A financing statement may be amended by filing a writing signed by both the debtor and the secured party. An amendment does not extend the period of effectiveness of a financing statement. If any amendment adds collateral, it is effective as to the added collateral only from the filing date of the amendment. In this Article, unless the context otherwise requires, the term "financing statement" means the original financing statement and any amendments.

(5) A financing statement covering timber to be cut or covering minerals or the like (including oil and gas) or accounts subject to subsection (5) of Section 9–103, or a financing statement filed as a fixture filing (Section 9–313) where the debtor is not a transmitting utility, must show that it covers this type of collateral, must recite that it is to be filed [for record] in the real estate records, and the financing statement must contain a description of the real estate [sufficient if it were contained in a mortgage of the real estate to give constructive notice of the mortgage under the law of this state]. If the debtor does not have an interest of record in the real estate, the financing statement must show the name of a record owner.

(6) A mortgage is effective as a financing statement filed as a fixture filing from the date of its recording if
 (a) the goods are described in the mortgage by item or type; and
 (b) the goods are or are to become fixtures related to the real estate described in the mortgage; and
 (c) the mortgage complies with the requirements for a financing statement in this section other than a recital that it is to be filed in the real estate records; and
 (d) the mortgage is duly recorded.
No fee with reference to the financing statement is required other than the regular recording and satisfaction fees with respect to the mortgage.

(7) A financing statement sufficiently shows the name of the debtor if it gives the individual, partnership or corporate name of the debtor, whether or not it adds other trade names or names of partners. Where the debtor so changes his name or in the case of an organization its name, identity or corporate structure that a filed financing statement becomes seriously misleading, the filing is not effective to perfect a security interest in collateral acquired by the debtor more than four months after the change, unless a new appropriate financing statement is filed before the expiration of that time. A filed financing statement remains effective with respect to collateral transferred by the debtor even though the secured party knows of or consents to the transfer.

(8) A financing statement substantially complying with the requirements of this section is effective even though it contains minor errors which are not seriously misleading.
Note: *Language in brackets is optional.*
Note: *Where the state has any special recording system for real estate other than the usual grantor-grantee index (as, for instance, a tract system or a title registration or Torrens system) local adaptations of subsection (5) and Section 9–403(7) may be necessary. See Mass.Gen. Laws Chapter 106, Section 9–409.*

## § 9–403.  What Constitutes Filing; Duration of Filing; Effect of Lapsed Filing; Duties of Filing Officer.

(1) Presentation for filing of a financing statement and tender of the filing fee or acceptance of the statement by the filing officer constitutes filing under this Article.

(2) Except as provided in subsection (6) a filed financing statement is effective for a period of five years from the date of filing. The effectiveness of a filed financing statement lapses on the expiration of the five year period unless a continuation statement is filed prior to the lapse. If a security interest perfected by filing exists at the time insolvency proceedings are commenced by or against the debtor, the security interest remains perfected until termination of the insolvency proceedings and thereafter for a period of sixty days or until expiration of the five year period, whichever occurs later. Upon lapse the security interest becomes unperfected, unless it is perfected without filing. If the security interest becomes unperfected upon lapse, it is deemed to have been unperfected as against a person who became a purchaser or lien creditor before lapse.

(3) A continuation statement may be filed by the secured party within six months prior to the expiration of the five year period specified in subsection (2). Any such continuation statement must be signed by the secured party, identify the original statement by file number and state that the original statement is still effective. A continuation statement signed by a person other than the secured party of record must be accompanied by a separate written statement of assignment signed by the secured party of record and complying with subsection (2) of Section 9–405, including payment of the required fee. Upon timely filing of the continuation statement, the effectiveness of the original statement is continued for five years after the last date to which the filing was effective whereupon it lapses in the same manner as provided in subsection (2) unless another continuation statement is filed prior to such lapse. Succeeding continuation statements may be filed in the same manner to continue the effectiveness of the original statement. Unless a statute on disposition of public records provides otherwise, the filing officer may remove a lapsed statement from the files and destroy it immediately if he has retained a microfilm or other photographic record, or in other cases after one year after the lapse. The filing officer shall so arrange matters by physical annexation of financing statements to continuation statements or other related filings, or by other means, that if he physically destroys the financing statements of a period more than five years past, those which have been continued by a continuation statement or which are still effective under subsection (6) shall be retained.

(4) Except as provided in subsection (7) a filing officer shall mark each statement with a file number and with the date and hour of filing and shall hold the statement or a microfilm or other photographic copy thereof for public inspection. In addition the filing officer shall index the statement according to the name of the debtor and shall note in the index the file number and the address of the debtor given in the statement.

(5) The uniform fee for filing and indexing and for stamping a copy furnished by the secured party to show the date and place of filing for an original financing statement or for a continuation statement shall be $_____ if the statement is in the standard form prescribed by the [Secretary of State] and otherwise shall be $_____, plus in each case, if the financing statement is subject to subsection (5) of Section 9–402, $. The uniform fee for each name more than one required to be indexed shall be $_____. The secured party may at his option show a trade name for any person and an extra uniform indexing fee of $_____ shall be paid with respect thereto.

(6) If the debtor is a transmitting utility (subsection (5) of Section 9–401) and a filed financing statement so states, it is effective until a termination statement is filed. A real estate mortgage which is effective as a fixture filing under subsection (6) of Section 9–402 remains effective as a fixture filing until the mortgage is released or satisfied of record or its effectiveness otherwise terminates as to the real estate.

(7) When a financing statement covers timber to be cut or covers minerals or the like (including oil and gas) or accounts subject to subsection (5) of Section 9–103, or is filed as a fixture filing, [it shall be filed for record and] the filing officer shall index it under the names of the debtor and any owner of record shown on the financing statement in the same fashion as if they were the mortgagors in a mortgage of the real estate described, and, to the extent that the law of this state provides for indexing of mortgages under the name of the mortgagee, under the name of the secured party as if he were the mortgagee thereunder, or where indexing is by description in the same fashion as if the financing statement were a mortgage of the real estate described.

Note: *In states in which writings will not appear in the real estate records and indices unless actually recorded the bracketed language in subsection (7) should be used.*

## § 9–404. Termination Statement.

(1) If a financing statement covering consumer goods is filed on or after _____, then within one month or within ten days following written demand by the debtor after there is no outstanding secured obligation and no commitment to make advances, incur obligations or otherwise give value, the secured party must file with each filing officer with whom the financing statement was filed, a termination statement to the effect that he no longer claims a security interest under the financing statement, which shall be identified by file number. In other cases whenever there is no outstanding secured obligation and no commitment to make advances, incur obligations or otherwise give value, the secured party must on written demand by the debtor send the debtor, for each filing officer with whom the financing statement was filed, a termination statement to the effect that he no longer claims a security interest under the financing statement, which shall be identified by file number. A termination statement signed by a person other than the secured party of record must be accompanied by a separate written statement of assignment signed by the secured party of record complying with subsection (2) of Section 9–405, including payment of the required fee. If the affected secured party fails to file such a termination statement as required by this subsection, or to send such a termination statement within ten days after proper demand therefor, he shall be liable to the debtor for one hundred dollars, and in addition for any loss caused to the debtor by such failure.

(2) On presentation to the filing officer of such a termination statement he must note it in the index. If he has received the termination statement in duplicate, he shall return one copy of the termination statement to the secured party stamped to show the time of receipt thereof. If the filing officer has a microfilm or other photographic record of the financing statement, and of any related continuation statement, statement of assignment and statement of release, he may remove the originals from the files at any time after receipt of the termination statement, or if he has no such record, he may remove them from the files at any time after one year after receipt of the termination statement.

(3) If the termination statement is in the standard form prescribed by the [Secretary of State], the uniform fee for filing and indexing the termination statement shall be $, and otherwise shall be $_____, plus in each case an additional fee of $_____ for each name more than one against which the termination statement is required to be indexed.

Note: *The date to be inserted should be the effective date of the revised Article 9.*

## § 9–405. Assignment of Security Interest; Duties of Filing Officer; Fees.

(1) A financing statement may disclose an assignment of a security interest in the collateral described in the financing statement by indication in the financing statement of the name and address of the assignee or by an assignment itself or a copy thereof on the face or back of the statement. On presentation to the filing officer of such a financing statement the filing officer shall mark the same as provided in Section 9–403(4). The uniform fee for filing, indexing and furnishing filing data for a financing statement so indicating an assignment shall be $_____ if the statement is in the standard form prescribed by the [Secretary of State] and otherwise shall be $_____, plus in each case an additional fee of $_____ for each name more than one against which the financing statement is required to be indexed.

(2) A secured party may assign of record all or part of his rights under a financing statement by the filing in the place where the original financing statement was filed of a separate written statement of assignment signed by the secured party of record and setting forth the name of the secured party of record and the debtor, the file number and the date of filing of the financing statement and the name and address of the assignee and containing a description of the collateral assigned. A copy of the assignment is sufficient as a separate statement if it complies with the preceding sentence. On presentation to the filing officer of such a separate statement, the filing officer shall mark such separate statement with the date and hour of the filing. He shall note the assignment on the index of the financing statement, or in the case of a fixture filing, or a filing covering timber to be cut, or covering minerals or the like (including oil and gas) or accounts subject to subsection (5) of Section 9–103, he shall index the assignment under the name of the assignor as grantor and, to the extent that the law of this state provides for indexing the assignment of a mortgage under the name of the assignee, he shall index the assignment of the financing statement under the name of the assignee. The uniform fee for filing, indexing and furnishing filing data about such a separate statement of assignment shall be $_____ if the statement is in the standard form prescribed by the [Secretary of State] and otherwise shall be $_____, plus in each case an additional fee of $_____ for each name more than one against which the statement of assignment is required to be indexed. Notwithstanding the provisions of this subsection, an assignment of record of a security interest in a fixture contained in a mortgage effective as a fixture filing (subsection (6) of Section 9–402) may be made only by an assignment of the mortgage in the manner provided by the law of this state other than this Act.

(3) After the disclosure or filing of an assignment under this section, the assignee is the secured party of record.

## § 9–406. Release of Collateral; Duties of Filing Officer; Fees.

A secured party of record may by his signed statement release all or a part of any collateral described in a filed financing statement. The statement of release is sufficient if it contains a description of the collateral being released, the name and address of the debtor, the name and address of the secured party, and the file number of the financing statement. A statement of release signed by a person other than the secured party of record must be accompanied by a separate written statement of assignment signed by the secured party of record and complying with subsection (2) of Section 9–405, including payment of the required fee. Upon presentation of such a statement of release to the filing officer he shall mark the statement with the hour and date of filing and shall note the same upon the margin of the index of the filing of the financing statement. The uniform fee for filing and noting such a statement of release shall be $_____ if the statement is in the standard form prescribed by the [Secretary of State] and otherwise shall be $_____, plus in each case an additional fee of $_____ for each name more than one against which the statement of release is required to be indexed.

## [§ 9–407. Information From Filing Officer].

[(1) If the person filing any financing statement, termination statement, statement of assignment, or statement of release, furnishes the filing officer a copy thereof, the filing officer shall upon request note upon the copy the file number and date and hour of the filing of the original and deliver or send the copy to such person.]

[(2) Upon request of any person, the filing officer shall issue his certificate showing whether there is on file on the date and hour stated therein, any presently effective financing statement naming a particular debtor and any statement of assignment thereof and if there is, giving the date and hour of filing of each such statement and the names and addresses of each secured party therein. The uniform fee for such a certificate shall be $_____ if the request for the certificate is in the standard form prescribed by the [Secretary of State] and otherwise shall be $_____. Upon request the filing officer shall furnish a copy of any filed financing statement or statement of assignment for a uniform fee of $_____ per page.]

Note: *This section is proposed as an optional provision to require filing officers to furnish certificates. Local law and practices should be consulted with regard to the advisability of adoption.*

## § 9–408. Financing Statements Covering Consigned or Leased Goods.

A consignor or lessor of goods may file a financing statement using the terms "consignor," "consignee," "lessor," "lessee" or the like instead of the terms specified in Section 9–402. The provisions of this Part shall apply as appropriate to such a financing statement but its filing shall not of itself be a factor in determining whether or not the consignment or lease is intended as security (Section 1–201(37)). However, if it is determined for other reasons that the consignment or lease is so intended, a security interest of the consignor or lessor which attaches to the consigned or leased goods is perfected by such filing.

## Part 5—Default

## § 9–501. Default; Procedure When Security Agreement Covers Both Real and Personal Property.

(1) When a debtor is in default under a security agreement, a secured party has the rights and remedies provided in this Part and except as limited by subsection (3) those provided in the security agreement. He may reduce his claim to judgment, foreclose or otherwise enforce the security interest by any available judicial procedure. If the collateral is documents the secured party may proceed either as to the documents or as to the goods covered thereby. A secured party in possession has the rights, remedies and duties provided in Section 9–207. The rights and remedies referred to in this subsection are cumulative.

(2) After default, the debtor has the rights and remedies provided in this Part, those provided in the security agreement and those provided in Section 9–207.

(3) To the extent that they give rights to the debtor and impose duties on the secured party, the rules stated in the subsections referred to below may not be waived or varied except as provided with respect to compulsory disposition of collateral (subsection (3) of Section 9–504 and Section 9–505) and with respect to redemption of collateral (Section 9–506) but the parties may by agreement determine the standards by which the fulfillment of these rights and duties is to be measured if such standards are not manifestly unreasonable:

(a) subsection (2) of Section 9–502 and subsection (2) of Section 9–504 insofar as they require accounting for surplus proceeds of collateral;

(b) subsection (3) of Section 9–504 and subsection (1) of Section 9–505 which deal with disposition of collateral;

(c) subsection (2) of Section 9–505 which deals with acceptance of collateral as discharge of obligation;

(d) Section 9–506 which deals with redemption of collateral; and

(e) subsection (1) of Section 9–507 which deals with the secured party's liability for failure to comply with this Part.

(4) If the security agreement covers both real and personal property, the secured party may proceed under this Part as to the personal property or he may proceed as to both the real and the personal property in accordance with his rights and remedies in respect of the real property in which case the provisions of this Part do not apply.

(5) When a secured party has reduced his claim to judgment the lien of any levy which may be made upon his collateral by virtue of any execution based upon the judgment shall relate back to the date of the perfection of the security interest in such collateral. A judicial sale, pursuant to such execution, is a foreclosure of the security interest by judicial procedure within the meaning of this section, and the secured party may purchase at the sale and thereafter hold the collateral free of any other requirements of this Article.

## § 9–502. Collection Rights of Secured Party.

(1) When so agreed and in any event on default the secured party is entitled to notify an account debtor or the obligor on an instrument to make payment to him whether or not the assignor was theretofore making collections on the collateral, and also to take control of any proceeds to which he is entitled under Section 9–306.

(2) A secured party who by agreement is entitled to charge back uncollected collateral or otherwise to full or limited recourse against the debtor and who undertakes to collect from the account debtors or obligors must proceed in a commercially reasonable manner and may deduct his reasonable expenses of realization from the collections. If the security agreement secures an indebtedness, the secured party must account to the debtor for any surplus, and unless otherwise agreed, the debtor is liable for any deficiency. But, if the underlying transaction was a sale of accounts or chattel paper, the debtor is entitled to any surplus or is liable for any deficiency only if the security agreement so provides.

## § 9–503. Secured Party's Right to Take Possession After Default.

Unless otherwise agreed a secured party has on default the right to take possession of the collateral. In taking possession a secured party may proceed without judicial process if this can be done without breach of the peace or may proceed by action. If the security agreement so provides the secured party may require the debtor to assemble the collateral and make it available to the secured party at a place to be designated by the secured party which is reasonably convenient to both parties. Without removal a secured party may render equipment unusable, and may dispose of collateral on the debtor's premises under Section 9–504.

### § 9–504.  Secured Party's Right to Dispose of Collateral After Default; Effect of Disposition.

(1) A secured party after default may sell, lease or otherwise dispose of any or all of the collateral in its then condition or following any commercially reasonable preparation or processing. Any sale of goods is subject to the Article on Sales (Article 2). The proceeds of disposition shall be applied in the order following to

(a) the reasonable expenses of retaking, holding, preparing for sale or lease, selling, leasing and the like and, to the extent provided for in the agreement and not prohibited by law, the reasonable attorneys' fees and legal expenses incurred by the secured party;

(b) the satisfaction of indebtedness secured by the security interest under which the disposition is made;

(c) the satisfaction of indebtedness secured by any subordinate security interest in the collateral if written notification of demand therefor is received before distribution of the proceeds is completed. If requested by the secured party, the holder of a subordinate security interest must seasonably furnish reasonable proof of his interest, and unless he does so, the secured party need not comply with his demand.

(2) If the security interest secures an indebtedness, the secured party must account to the debtor for any surplus, and, unless otherwise agreed, the debtor is liable for any deficiency. But if the underlying transaction was a sale of accounts or chattel paper, the debtor is entitled to any surplus or is liable for any deficiency only if the security agreement so provides.

(3) Disposition of the collateral may be by public or private proceedings and may be made by way of one or more contracts. Sale or other disposition may be as a unit or in parcels and at any time and place and on any terms but every aspect of the disposition including the method, manner, time, place and terms must be commercially reasonable. Unless collateral is perishable or threatens to decline speedily in value or is of a type customarily sold on a recognized market, reasonable notification of the time and place of any public sale or reasonable notification of the time after which any private sale or other intended disposition is to be made shall be sent by the secured party to the debtor, if he has not signed after default a statement renouncing or modifying his right to notification of sale. In the case of consumer goods no other notification need be sent. In other cases notification shall be sent to any other secured party from whom the secured party has received (before sending his notification to the debtor or before the debtor's renunciation of his rights) written notice of a claim of an interest in the collateral. The secured party may buy at any public sale and if the collateral is of a type customarily sold in a recognized market or is of a type which is the subject of widely distributed standard price quotations he may buy at private sale.

(4) When collateral is disposed of by a secured party after default, the disposition transfers to a purchaser for value all of the debtor's rights therein, discharges the security interest under which it is made and any security interest or lien subordinate thereto. The purchaser takes free of all such rights and interests even though the secured

party fails to comply with the requirements of this Part or of any judicial proceedings

(a) in the case of a public sale, if the purchaser has no knowledge of any defects in the sale and if he does not buy in collusion with the secured party, other bidders or the person conducting the sale; or

(b) in any other case, if the purchaser acts in good faith.

(5) A person who is liable to a secured party under a guaranty, indorsement, repurchase agreement or the like and who receives a transfer of collateral from the secured party or is subrogated to his rights has thereafter the rights and duties of the secured party. Such a transfer of collateral is not a sale or disposition of the collateral under this Article.

### § 9–505.  Compulsory Disposition of Collateral; Acceptance of the Collateral as Discharge of Obligation.

(1) If the debtor has paid sixty per cent of the cash price in the case of a purchase money security interest in consumer goods or sixty per cent of the loan in the case of another security interest in consumer goods, and has not signed after default a statement renouncing or modifying his rights under this Part a secured party who has taken possession of collateral must dispose of it under Section 9–504 and if he fails to do so within ninety days after he takes possession the debtor at his option may recover in conversion or under Section 9–507(1) on secured party's liability.

(2) In any other case involving consumer goods or any other collateral a secured party in possession may, after default, propose to retain the collateral in satisfaction of the obligation. Written notice of such proposal shall be sent to the debtor if he has not signed after default a statement renouncing or modifying his rights under this subsection. In the case of consumer goods no other notice need be given. In other cases notice shall be sent to any other secured party from whom the secured party has received (before sending his notice to the debtor or before the debtor's renunciation of his rights) written notice of a claim of an interest in the collateral. If the secured party receives objection in writing from a person entitled to receive notification within twenty-one days after the notice was sent, the secured party must dispose of the collateral under Section 9–504. In the absence of such written objection the secured party may retain the collateral in satisfaction of the debtor's obligation.

### § 9–506.  Debtor's Right to Redeem Collateral.

At any time before the secured party has disposed of collateral or entered into a contract for its disposition under Section 9–504 or before the obligation has been discharged under Section 9–505(2) the debtor or any other secured party may unless otherwise agreed in writing after default redeem the collateral by tendering fulfillment of all obligations secured by the collateral as well as the expenses reasonably incurred by the secured party in retaking, holding and preparing the collateral for disposition, in arranging for the sale, and to the extent provided in the agreement and not prohibited by law, his reasonable attorneys' fees and legal expenses.

### § 9–507.  Secured Party's Liability for Failure to Comply With This Part.

(1) If it is established that the secured party is not proceeding in accordance with the provisions of this Part disposition may be ordered or restrained on appropriate terms and conditions. If the disposition has occurred the debtor or any person entitled to notification or whose security interest has been made known to the secured party prior to the disposition has a right to recover from the secured party any loss

caused by a failure to comply with the provisions of this Part. If the collateral is consumer goods, the debtor has a right to recover in any event an amount not less than the credit service charge plus ten per cent of the principal amount of the debt or the time price differential plus 10 per cent of the cash price.

(2) The fact that a better price could have been obtained by a sale at a different time or in a different method from that selected by the secured party is not of itself sufficient to establish that the sale was not made in a commercially reasonable manner. If the secured party either sells the collateral in the usual manner in any recognized market therefor or if he sells at the price current in such market at the time of his sale or if he has otherwise sold in conformity with reasonable commercial practices among dealers in the type of property sold he has sold in a commercially reasonable manner. The principles stated in the two preceding sentences with respect to sales also apply as may be appropriate to other types of disposition. A disposition which has been approved in any judicial proceeding or by any bona fide creditors' committee or representative of creditors shall conclusively be deemed to be commercially reasonable, but this sentence does not indicate that any such approval must be obtained in any case nor does it indicate that any disposition not so approved is not commercially reasonable.

## ARTICLE 10: EFFECTIVE DATE AND REPEALER

### § 10–101.  Effective Date.

This Act shall become effective at midnight on December 31st following its enactment. It applies to transactions entered into and events occurring after that date.

### § 10–102.  Specific Repealer; Provision for Transition.

(1) The following acts and all other acts and parts of acts inconsistent herewith are hereby repealed: (Here should follow the acts to be specifically repealed including the following:

Uniform Negotiable Instruments Act
Uniform Warehouse Receipts Act
Uniform Sales Act
Uniform Bills of Lading Act
Uniform Stock Transfer Act
Uniform Conditional Sales Act
Uniform Trust Receipts Act
Also any acts regulating:
Bank collections
Bulk sales
Chattel mortgages
Conditional sales
Factor's lien acts
Farm storage of grain and similar acts
Assignment of accounts receivable)

(2) Transactions validly entered into before the effective date specified in Section 10–101 and the rights, duties and interests flowing from them remain valid thereafter and may be terminated, completed, consummated or enforced as required or permitted by any statute or other law amended or repealed by this Act as though such repeal or amendment had not occurred.

Note: *Subsection (1) should be separately prepared for each state. The foregoing is a list of statutes to be checked.*

### § 10–103.  General Repealer.

Except as provided in the following section, all acts and parts of acts inconsistent with this Act are hereby repealed.

### § 10–104.  Laws Not Repealed.

(1) The Article on Documents of Title (Article 7) does not repeal or modify any laws prescribing the form or contents of documents of title or the services or facilities to be afforded by bailees, or otherwise regulating bailees' businesses in respects not specifically dealt with herein; but the fact that such laws are violated does not affect the status of a document of title which otherwise complies with the definition of a document of title (Section 1–201).

[(2) This Act does not repeal _____*, cited as the Uniform Act for the Simplification of Fiduciary Security Transfers, and if in any respect there is any inconsistency between that Act and the Article of this Act on investment securities (Article 8) the provisions of the former Act shall control.]

Note: *At * in subsection (2) insert the statutory reference to the Uniform Act for the Simplification of Fiduciary Security Transfers if such Act has previously been enacted. If it has not been enacted, omit subsection (2).*

## ARTICLE 11: (REPORTERS' DRAFT) EFFECTIVE DATE AND TRANSITION PROVISIONS

This material has been numbered Article 11 to distinguish it from Article 10, the transition provision of the 1962 Code, which may still remain in effect in some states to cover transition problems from pre-Code law to the original Uniform Commercial Code. Adaptation may be necessary in particular states. The terms "[old Code]" and "[new Code]" and "[old U.C.C.]" and "[new U.C.C.]" are used herein, and should be suitably changed in each state.

Note: *This draft was prepared by the Reporters and has not been passed upon by the Review Committee, the Permanent Editorial Board, the American Law Institute, or the National Conference of Commissioners on Uniform State Laws. It is submitted as a working draft which may be adapted as appropriate in each state.*

### § 11–101.  Effective Date.

This Act shall become effective at 12:01 A.M. on _____, 19_____.

### § 11–102.  Preservation of Old Transition Provision.

The provisions of [here insert reference to the original transition provision in the particular state] shall continue to apply to [the new U.C.C.] and for this purpose the [old U.C.C. and new U.C.C.] shall be considered one continuous statute.

### § 11–103.  Transition to [New Code]—General Rule.

Transactions validly entered into after [effective date of old U.C.C.] and before [effective date of new U.C.C.], and which were subject to the provisions of [old U.C.C.] and which would be subject to this Act as amended if they had been entered into after the effective date of [new U.C.C.] and the rights, duties and interests flowing from such transactions remain valid after the latter date and may be terminated, completed, consummated or enforced as required or permitted by the [new U.C.C.]. Security interests arising out of such transactions which are perfected when [new U.C.C.] becomes effective shall remain perfected until they lapse as provided in [new U.C.C.], and may be continued as permitted by [new U.C.C.], except as stated in Section 11–105.

## § 11–104.  Transition Provision on Change of Requirement of Filing.

A security interest for the perfection of which filing or the taking of possession was required under [old U.C.C.] and which attached prior to the effective date of [new U.C.C.] but was not perfected shall be deemed perfected on the effective date of [new U.C.C.] if [new U.C.C.] permits perfection without filing or authorizes filing in the office or offices where a prior ineffective filing was made.

## § 11–105.  Transition Provision on Change of Place of Filing.

(1)  A financing statement or continuation statement filed prior to [effective date of new U.C.C.] which shall not have lapsed prior to [the effective date of new U.C.C.] which shall remain effective for the period provided in the [old Code], but not less than five years after the filing.

(2)  With respect to any collateral acquired by the debtor subsequent to the effective date of [new U.C.C.], any effective financing statement or continuation statement described in this section shall apply only if the filing or filings are in the office or offices that would be appropriate to perfect the security interests in the new collateral under [new U.C.C.].

(3)  The effectiveness of any financing statement or continuation statement filed prior to [effective date of new U.C.C.] may be continued by a continuation statement as permitted by [new U.C.C.], except that if [new U.C.C.] requires a filing in an office where there was no previous financing statement, a new financing statement conforming to Section 11–106 shall be filed in that office.

(4)  If the record of a mortgage of real estate would have been effective as a fixture filing of goods described therein if [new U.C.C.] had been in effect on the date of recording the mortgage, the mortgage shall be deemed effective as a fixture filing as to such goods under subsection (6) of Section 9–402 of the [new U.C.C.] on the effective date of [new U.C.C.].

## § 11–106.  Required Refilings.

(1)  If a security interest is perfected or has priority when this Act takes effect as to all persons or as to certain persons without any filing or recording, and if the filing of a financing statement would be required for the perfection or priority of the security interest against those persons under [new U.C.C.], the perfection and priority rights of the security interest continue until 3 years after the effective date of [new U.C.C.]. The perfection will then lapse unless a financing statement is filed as provided in subsection (4) or unless the security interest is perfected otherwise than by filing.

(2)  If a security interest is perfected when [new U.C.C.] takes effect under a law other than [U.C.C.] which requires no further filing, refiling or recording to continue its perfection, perfection continues until and will lapse 3 years after [new U.C.C.] takes effect, unless a financing statement is filed as provided in subsection (4) or unless the security interest is perfected otherwise than by filing, or unless under subsection (3) of Section 9–302 the other law continues to govern filing.

(3)  If a security interest is perfected by a filing, refiling or recording under a law repealed by this Act which required further filing, refiling or recording to continue its perfection, perfection continues and will lapse on the date provided by the law so repealed for such further filing, refiling, or recording unless a financing statement is filed as provided in subsection (4) or unless the security interest is perfected otherwise than by filing.

(4)  A financing statement may be filed within six months before the perfection of a security interest would otherwise lapse. Any such financing statement may be signed by either the debtor or the secured party. It must identify the security agreement, statement or notice (however denominated in any statute or other law repealed or modified by this Act), state the office where and the date when the last filing, refiling or recording, if any, was made with respect thereto, and the filing number, if any, or book and page, if any, of recording and further state that the security agreement, statement or notice, however denominated, in another filing office under the [U.C.C.] or under any statute or other law repealed or modified by this Act is still effective. Section 9–401 and Section 9–103 determine the proper place to file such a financing statement. Except as specified in this subsection, the provisions of Section 9–403(3) for continuation statements apply to such a financing statement.

## § 11–107.  Transition Provisions as to Priorities.

Except as otherwise provided in [Article 11], [old U.C.C.] shall apply to any questions of priority if the positions of the parties were fixed prior to the effective date of [new U.C.C.]. In other cases questions of priority shall be determined by [new U.C.C.].

## § 11–108.  Presumption that Rule of Law Continues Unchanged.

Unless a change in law has clearly been made, the provisions of [new U.C.C.] shall be deemed declaratory of the meaning of the [old U.C.C.].

# Uniform Partnership Act

The Act consists of seven Parts as follows:

I. Preliminary Provisions
II. Nature of Partnership
III. Relations of Partners to Persons Dealing with the Partnership
IV. Relations of Partners to One Another
V. Property Rights of a Partner
VI. Dissolution and Winding Up
VII. Miscellaneous Provisions
An Act to make uniform the Law of Partnerships
Be it enacted, etc.:

## Part I.   Preliminary Provisions

### § 1.   Name of Act
This act may be cited as Uniform Partnership Act.

### § 2.   Definition of Terms
In this act, "Court" includes every court and judge having jurisdiction in the case.

"Business" includes every trade, occupation, or profession.

"Person" includes individuals, partnerships, corporations, and other associations.

"Bankrupt" includes bankrupt under the Federal Bankruptcy Act or insolvent under any state insolvent act.

"Conveyance" includes every assignment, lease, mortgage, or encumbrance.

"Real property" includes land and any interest or estate in land.

### § 3.   Interpretation of Knowledge and Notice
(1)  A person has "knowledge" of a fact within the meaning of this act not only when he has actual knowledge thereof, but also when he has knowledge of such other facts as in the circumstances shows bad faith.

(2)  A person has "notice" of a fact within the meaning of this act when the person who claims the benefit of the notice

(a)  States the fact to such person, or

(b)  Delivers through the mail, or by other means of communication, a written statement of the fact to such person or to a proper person at his place of business or residence.

### § 4.   Rules of Construction
(1)  The rule that statutes in derogation of the common law are to be strictly construed shall have no application to this act.

(2)  The law of estoppel shall apply under this act.

(3)  The law of agency shall apply under this act.

(4)  This act shall be so interpreted and construed as to effect its general purpose to make uniform the law of those states which enact it.

(5)  This act shall not be construed so as to impair the obligations of any contract existing when the act goes into effect, nor to affect any action or proceedings begun or right accrued before this act takes effect.

### § 5.   Rules for Cases Not Provided for in This Act
In any case not provided for in this act the rules of law and equity, including the law merchant, shall govern.

## Part II.   Nature of Partnership

### § 6.   Partnership Defined
(1)  A partnership is an association of two or more persons to carry on as co-owners a business for profit.

(2)  But any association formed under any other statute of this state, or any statute adopted by authority, other than the authority of this state, is not a partnership under this act, unless such association would have been a partnership in this state prior to the adoption of this act; but this act shall apply to limited partnerships except in so far as the statutes relating to such partnerships are inconsistent herewith.

### § 7.   Rules for Determining the Existence of a Partnership
In determining whether a partnership exists, these rules shall apply:

(1)  Except as provided by Section 16 persons who are not partners as to each other are not partners as to third persons.

(2)  Joint tenancy, tenancy in common, tenancy by the entireties, joint property, common property, or part ownership does not of itself establish a partnership, whether such co-owners do or do not share any profits made by the use of the property.

(3)  The sharing of gross returns does not of itself establish a partnership, whether or not the persons sharing them have a joint or common right or interest in any property from which the returns are derived.

(4)  The receipt by a person of a share of the profits of a business is prima facie evidence that he is a partner in the business, but no such inference shall be drawn if such profits were received in payment:

(a)  As a debt by installments or otherwise,

(b)  As wages of an employee or rent to a landlord,

(c)  As an annuity to a widow or representative of a deceased partner,

(d)  As interest on a loan, though the amount of payment vary with the profits of the business,

(e)  As the consideration for the sale of a good-will of a business or other property by installments or otherwise.

### § 8.   Partnership Property
(1)  All property originally brought into the partnership stock or subsequently acquired by purchase or otherwise, on account of the partnership, is partnership property.

(2) Unless the contrary intention appears, property acquired with partnership funds is partnership property.

(3) Any estate in real property may be acquired in the partnership name. Title so acquired can be conveyed only in the partnership name.

(4) A conveyance to a partnership in the partnership name, though without words of inheritance, passes the entire estate of the grantor unless a contrary intent appears.

## Part III.  Relations of Partners to Persons Dealing with the Partnership

### § 9.  Partner Agent of Partnership as to Partnership Business

(1) Every partner is an agent of the partnership for the purpose of its business, and the act of every partner, including the execution in the partnership name of any instrument, for apparently carrying on in the usual way the business of the partnership of which he is a member binds the partnership, unless the partner so acting has in fact no authority to act for the partnership in the particular matter, and the person with whom he is dealing has knowledge of the fact that he has no such authority.

(2) An act of a partner which is not apparently for the carrying on of the business of the partnership in the usual way does not bind the partnership unless authorized by the other partners.

(3) Unless authorized by the other partners or unless they have abandoned the business, one or more but less than all the partners have no authority to:

(a) Assign the partnership property in trust for creditors or on the assignee's promise to pay the debts of the partnership,

(b) Dispose of the good-will of the business,

(c) Do any other act which would make it impossible to carry on the ordinary business of a partnership,

(d) Confess a judgment,

(e) Submit a partnership claim or liability to arbitration or reference.

(4) No act of a partner in contravention of a restriction on authority shall bind the partnership to persons having knowledge of the restriction.

### § 10.  Conveyance of Real Property of the Partnership

(1) Where title to real property is in the partnership name, any partner may convey title to such property by a conveyance executed in the partnership name; but the partnership may recover such property unless the partner's act binds the partnership under the provisions of paragraph (1) of section 9 or unless such property has been conveyed by the grantee or a person claiming through such grantee to a holder for value without knowledge that the partner, in making the conveyance, has exceeded his authority.

(2) Where title to real property is in the name of the partnership, a conveyance executed by a partner, in his own name, passes the equitable interest of the partnership, provided the act is one within the authority of the partner under the provisions of paragraph (1) of section 9.

(3) Where title to real property is in the name of one or more but not all the partners, and the record does not disclose the right of the partnership, the partners in whose name the title stands may convey title to such property, but the partnership may recover such property if the partners' act does not bind the partnership under the provisions of paragraph (1) of section 9, unless the purchaser or his assignee, is a holder for value, without knowledge.

(4) Where the title to real property is in the name of one or more or all the partners, or in a third person in trust for the partnership, a conveyance executed by a partner in the partnership name, or in his own name, passes the equitable interest of the partnership, provided the act is one within the authority of the partner under the provisions of paragraph (1) of section 9.

(5) Where the title to real property is in the names of all the partners a conveyance executed by all the partners passes all their rights in such property.

### § 11.  Partnership Bound by Admission of Partner

An admission or representation made by any partner concerning partnership affairs within the scope of his authority as conferred by this act is evidence against the partnership.

### § 12.  Partnership Charged with Knowledge of or Notice to Partner

Notice to any partner of any matter relating to partnership affairs, and the knowledge of the partner acting in the particular matter, acquired while a partner or then present to his mind, and the knowledge of any other partner who reasonably could and should have communicated it to the acting partner, operate as notice to or knowledge of the partnership, except in the case of a fraud on the partnership committed by or with the consent of that partner.

### § 13.  Partnership Bound by Partner's Wrongful Act

Where, by any wrongful act or omission of any partner acting in the ordinary course of the business of the partnership or with the authority of his co-partners, loss or injury is caused to any person, not being a partner in the partnership, or any penalty is incurred, the partnership is liable therefor to the same extent as the partner so acting or omitting to act.

### § 14.  Partnership Bound by Partner's Breach of Trust

The partnership is bound to make good the loss:

(a) Where one partner acting within the scope of his apparent authority receives money or property of a third person and misapplies it; and

(b) Where the partnership in the course of its business receives money or property of a third person and the money or property so received is misapplied by any partner while it is in the custody of the partnership.

### § 15.  Nature of Partner's Liability

All partners are liable

(a) Jointly and severally for everything chargeable to the partnership under sections 13 and 14.

(b) Jointly for all other debts and obligations of the partnership; but any partner may enter into a separate obligation to perform a partnership contract.

### § 16.  Partner by Estoppel

(1) When a person, by words spoken or written or by conduct, represents himself, or consents to another representing him to any one, as a partner in an existing partnership or with one or more persons not actual partners, he is liable to any such person to whom such representation has been made, who has, on the faith of such representation, given credit to the actual or apparent partnership, and if he has made such representation or consented to its being made in a public manner he is liable to such person, whether the representation has or has not been made or communicated to such person so giving credit by or with the knowledge of the apparent partner making the representation or consenting to its being made.

(a) When a partnership liability results, he is liable as though he were an actual member of the partnership.

(b) When no partnership liability results, he is liable jointly with the other persons, if any, so consenting to the contract or representation as to incur liability, otherwise separately.

(2) When a person has been thus represented to be a partner in an existing partnership, or with one or more persons not actual partners, he is an agent of the persons consenting to such representation to bind them to the same extent and in the same manner as though he were a partner in fact, with respect to persons who rely upon the representation. Where all the members of the existing partnership consent to the representation, a partnership act or obligation results; but in all other cases it is the joint act or obligation of the person acting and the persons consenting to the representation.

## § 17.  Liability of Incoming Partner

A person admitted as a partner into an existing partnership is liable for all the obligations of the partnership arising before his admission as though he had been a partner when such obligations were incurred, except that this liability shall be satisfied only out of partnership property.

## Part IV.   Relations of Partners to One Another

## § 18.  Rules Determining Rights and Duties of Partners

The rights and duties of the partners in relation to the partnership shall be determined, subject to any agreement between them, by the following rules:

(a) Each partner shall be repaid his contributions, whether by way of capital or advances to the partnership property and share equally in the profits and surplus remaining after all liabilities, including those to partners, are satisfied; and must contribute towards the losses, whether of capital or otherwise, sustained by the partnership according to his share in the profits.

(b) The partnership must indemnify every partner in respect of payments made and personal liabilities reasonably incurred by him in the ordinary and proper conduct of its business, or for the preservation of its business or property.

(c) A partner, who in aid of the partnership makes any payment or advance beyond the amount of capital which he agreed to contribute, shall be paid interest from the date of the payment or advance.

(d) A partner shall receive interest on the capital contributed by him only from the date when repayment should be made.

(e) All partners have equal rights in the management and conduct of the partnership business.

(f) No partner is entitled to remuneration for acting in the partnership business, except that a surviving partner is entitled to reasonable compensation for his services in winding up the partnership affairs.

(g) No person can become a member of a partnership without the consent of all the partners.

(h) Any difference arising as to ordinary matters connected with the partnership business may be decided by a majority of the partners; but no act in contravention of any agreement between the partners may be done rightfully without the consent of all the partners.

## § 19.  Partnership Books

The partnership books shall be kept, subject to any agreement between the partners, at the principal place of business of the partnership, and every partner shall at all times have access to and may inspect and copy any of them.

## § 20.  Duty of Partners to Render Information

Partners shall render on demand true and full information of all things affecting the partnership to any partner or the legal representative of any deceased partner or partner under legal disability.

## § 21.  Partner Accountable as a Fiduciary

(1) Every partner must account to the partnership for any benefit, and hold as trustee for it any profits derived by him without the consent of the other partners from any transaction connected with the formation, conduct, or liquidation of the partnership or from any use by him of its property.

(2) This section applies also to the representatives of a deceased partner engaged in the liquidation of the affairs of the partnership as the personal representatives of the last surviving partner.

## § 22.  Right to an Account

Any partner shall have the right to a formal account as to partnership affairs:

(a) If he is wrongfully excluded from the partnership business or possession of its property by his co-partners,

(b) If the right exists under the terms of any agreement,

(c) As provided by section 21,

(d) Whenever other circumstances render it just and reasonable.

## § 23.  Continuation of Partnership Beyond Fixed Term

(1) When a partnership for a fixed term or particular undertaking is continued after the termination of such term or particular undertaking without any express agreement, the rights and duties of the partners remain the same as they were at such termination, so far as is consistent with a partnership at will.

(2) A continuation of the business by the partners or such of them as habitually acted therein during the term, without any settlement or liquidation of the partnership affairs, is prima facie evidence of a continuation of the partnership.

## Part V.  Property Rights of a Partner

## § 24.  Extent of Property Rights of a Partner

The property rights of a partner are (1) his rights in specific partnership property, (2) his interest in the partnership, and (3) his right to participate in the management.

## § 25.  Nature of a Partner's Right in Specific Partnership Property

(1) A partner is co-owner with his partners of specific partnership property holding as a tenant in partnership.

(2) The incidents of this tenancy are such that:

(a) A partner, subject to the provisions of this act and to any agreement between the partners, has an equal right with his partners to possess specific partnership property for partnership purposes; but he has no right to possess such property for any other purpose without the consent of his partners.

(b) A partner's right in specific partnership property is not assignable except in connection with the assignment of rights of all the partners in the same property.

(c) A partner's right in specific partnership property is not subject to attachment or execution, except on a claim against the partnership. When partnership property is attached for a partnership debt the partners, or any of them, or the representatives of a deceased partner, cannot claim any right under the homestead or exemption laws.

(d) On the death of a partner his right in specific partnership property vests in the surviving partner or partners, except where the deceased was the last surviving partner, when his right in such property vests in his legal representative. Such surviving partner or partners, or the legal representative of the last surviving partner, has no right to possess the partnership property for any but a partnership purpose.

(e) A partner's right in specific partnership property is not subject to dower, curtesy, or allowances to widows, heirs, or next of kin.

## § 26. Nature of Partner's Interest in the Partnership

A partner's interest in the partnership is his share of the profits and surplus, and the same is personal property.

## § 27. Assignment of Partner's Interest

(1) A conveyance by a partner of his interest in the partnership does not of itself dissolve the partnership, nor, as against the other partners in the absence of agreement, entitle the assignee, during the continuance of the partnership to interfere in the management or administration of the partnership business or affairs, or to require any information or account of partnership transactions, or to inspect the partnership books; but it merely entitles the assignee to receive in accordance with his contract the profits to which the assigning partner would otherwise be entitled.

(2) In case of a dissolution of the partnership, the assignee is entitled to receive his assignor's interest and may require an account from the date only of the last account agreed to by all the partners.

## § 28. Partner's Interest Subject to Charging Order

(1) On due application to a competent court by any judgment creditor of a partner, the court which entered the judgment, order, or decree, or any other court, may charge the interest of the debtor partner with payment of the unsatisfied amount of such judgment debt with interest thereon; and may then or later appoint a receiver of his share of the profits, and of any other money due or to fall due to him in respect of the partnership, and make all other orders, directions, accounts and inquiries which the debtor partner might have made, or which the circumstances of the case may require.

(2) The interest charged may be redeemed at any time before foreclosure, or in case of a sale being directed by the court may be purchased without thereby causing a dissolution:

(a) With separate property, by any one or more of the partners, or

(b) With partnership property, by any one or more of the partners with the consent of all the partners whose interests are not so charged or sold.

(3) Nothing in this act shall be held to deprive a partner of his right, if any, under the exemption laws, as regards his interest in the partnership.

## Part VI. Dissolution and Winding Up

### § 29. Dissolution Defined

The dissolution of a partnership is the change in the relation of the partners caused by any partner ceasing to be associated in the carrying on as distinguished from the winding up of the business.

### § 30. Partnership Not Terminated by Dissolution

On dissolution the partnership is not terminated, but continues until the winding up of partnership affairs is completed.

### § 31. Causes of Dissolution

Dissolution is caused:

(1) Without violation of the agreement between the partners,

(a) By the termination of the definite term or particular undertaking specified in the agreement,

(b) By the express will of any partner when no definite term or particular undertaking is specified,

(c) By the express will of all the partners who have not assigned their interests or suffered them to be charged for their separate debts, either before or after the termination of any specified term or particular undertaking,

(d) By the expulsion of any partner from the business bona fide in accordance with such a power conferred by the agreement between the partners;

(2) In contravention of the agreement between the partners, where the circumstances do not permit a dissolution under any other provision of this section, by the express will of any partner at any time;

(3) By any event which makes it unlawful for the business of the partnership to be carried on or for the members to carry it on in partnership;

(4) By the death of any partner;

(5) By the bankruptcy of any partner or the partnership;

(6) By decree of court under section 32.

### § 32. Dissolution by Decree of Court

(1) On application by or for a partner the court shall decree a dissolution whenever:

(a) A partner has been declared a lunatic in any judicial proceeding or is shown to be of unsound mind,

(b) A partner becomes in any other way incapable of performing his part of the partnership contract,

(c) A partner has been guilty of such conduct as tends to affect prejudicially the carrying on of the business,

(d) A partner wilfully or persistently commits a breach of the partnership agreement, or otherwise so conducts himself in matters relating to the partnership business that it is not reasonably practicable to carry on the business in partnership with him,

(e) The business of the partnership can only be carried on at a loss,

(f) Other circumstances render a dissolution equitable.

(2) On the application of the purchaser of a partner's interest under sections 27 or 28:

(a) After the termination of the specified term or particular undertaking,

(b) At any time if the partnership was a partnership at will when the interest was assigned or when the charging order was issued.

### § 33. General Effect of Dissolution on Authority of Partner

Except so far as may be necessary to wind up partnership affairs or to complete transactions begun but not then finished, dissolution terminates all authority of any partner to act for the partnership,

(1) With respect to the partners,

(a) When the dissolution is not by the act, bankruptcy or death of a partner; or

(b) When the dissolution is by such act, bankruptcy or death of a partner, in cases where section 34 so requires.

(2) With respect to persons not partners, as declared in section 35.

### § 34. Right of Partner to Contribution from Copartners after Dissolution

Where the dissolution is caused by the act, death or bankruptcy of a partner, each partner is liable to his copartners for his share of any liability created by any partner acting for the partnership as if the partnership had not been dissolved unless

(a) The dissolution being by act of any partner, the partner acting for the partnership had knowledge of the dissolution, or

(b) The dissolution being by the death or bankruptcy of a partner, the partner acting for the partnership had knowledge or notice of the death or bankruptcy.

## § 35.  Power of Partner to Bind Partnership to Third Persons after Dissolution

(1) After dissolution a partner can bind the partnership except as provided in Paragraph (3)

(a) By any act appropriate for winding up partnership affairs or completing transactions unfinished at dissolution;

(b) By any transaction which would bind the partnership if dissolution had not taken place, provided the other party to the transaction

(I) Had extended credit to the partnership prior to dissolution and had no knowledge or notice of the dissolution; or

(II) Though he had not so extended credit, had nevertheless known of the partnership prior to dissolution, and, having no knowledge or notice of dissolution, the fact of dissolution had not been advertised in a newspaper of general circulation in the place (or in each place if more than one) at which the partnership business was regularly carried on.

(2) The liability of a partner under paragraph (1b) shall be satisfied out of partnership assets alone when such partner had been prior to dissolution

(a) Unknown as a partner to the person with whom the contract is made; and

(b) So far unknown and inactive in partnership affairs that the business reputation of the partnership could not be said to have been in any degree due to his connection with it.

(3) The partnership is in no case bound by any act of a partner after dissolution

(a) Where the partnership is dissolved because it is unlawful to carry on the business, unless the act is appropriate for winding up partnership affairs; or

(b) Where the partner has become bankrupt; or

(c) Where the partner has no authority to wind up partnership affairs; except by a transaction with one who

(I) Had extended credit to the partnership prior to dissolution and had no knowledge or notice of his want of authority; or

(II) Had not extended credit to the partnership prior to dissolution, and, having no knowledge or notice of his want of authority, the fact of his want of authority has not been advertised in the manner provided for advertising the fact of dissolution in paragraph (1bII).

(4) Nothing in this section shall affect the liability under section 16 of any person who after dissolution represents himself or consents to another representing him as a partner in a partnership engaged in carrying on business.

## § 36.  Effect of Dissolution on Partner's Existing Liability

(1) The dissolution of the partnership does not of itself discharge the existing liability of any partner.

(2) A partner is discharged from any existing liability upon dissolution of the partnership by an agreement to that effect between himself, the partnership creditor and the person or partnership continuing the business; and such agreement may be inferred from the course of dealing between the creditor having knowledge of the dissolution and the person or partnership continuing the business.

(3) Where a person agrees to assume the existing obligations of a dissolved partnership, the partners whose obligations have been assumed shall be discharged from any liability to any creditor of the partnership who, knowing of the agreement, consents to a material alteration in the nature or time of payment of such obligations.

(4) The individual property of a deceased partner shall be liable for all obligations of the partnership incurred while he was a partner but subject to the prior payment of his separate debts.

## § 37.  Right to Wind Up

Unless otherwise agreed the partners who have not wrongfully dissolved the partnership or the legal representative of the last surviving partner, not bankrupt, has the right to wind up the partnership affairs; provided, however, that any partner, his legal representative or his assignee, upon cause shown, may obtain winding up by the court.

## § 38.  Rights of Partners to Application of Partnership Property

(1) When dissolution is caused in any way, except in contravention of the partnership agreement, each partner as against his co-partners and all persons claiming through them in respect of their interests in the partnership, unless otherwise agreed, may have the partnership property applied to discharge its liabilities, and the surplus applied to pay in cash the net amount owing to the respective partners. But if dissolution is caused by expulsion of a partner, bona fide under the partnership agreement and if the expelled partner is discharged from all partnership liabilities, either by payment or agreement under section 36(2), he shall receive in cash only the net amount due him from the partnership.

(2) When dissolution is caused in contravention of the partnership agreement the rights of the partners shall be as follows:

(a) Each partner who has not caused dissolution wrongfully shall have,

(I) All the rights specified in paragraph (1) of this section, and

(II) The right, as against each partner who has caused the dissolution wrongfully, to damages for breach of the agreement.

(b) The partners who have not caused the dissolution wrongfully, if they all desire to continue the business in the same name, either by themselves or jointly with others, may do so, during the agreed term for the partnership and for that purpose may possess the partnership property, provided they secure the payment by bond approved by the court, or pay to any partner who has caused the dissolution wrongfully, the value of his interest in the partnership at the dissolution, less any damages recoverable under clause (2aII) of the section, and in like manner indemnify him against all present or future partnership liabilities.

(c) A partner who has caused the dissolution wrongfully shall have:

(I) If the business is not continued under the provisions of paragraph (2b) all the rights of a partner under paragraph (1), subject to clause (2aII), of this section,

(II) If the business is continued under paragraph (2b) of this section the right as against his copartners and all claiming through them in respect of their interests in the partnership, to have the value of his interest in the partnership, less any damages caused to his co-partners by the dissolution, ascertained and paid to him in cash, or the payment secured by bond approved by the court, and to be released from all existing liabilities of the partnership; but in ascertaining the value of the partner's interest the value of the good-will of the business shall not be considered.

## § 39. Rights Where Partnership is Dissolved for Fraud or Misrepresentation

Where a partnership contract is rescinded on the ground of the fraud or misrepresentation of one of the parties thereto, the party entitled to rescind is, without prejudice to any other right, entitled,

(a) To a lien on, or right of retention of, the surplus of the partnership property after satisfying the partnership liabilities to third persons for any sum of money paid by him for the purchase of an interest in the partnership and for any capital or advances contributed by him; and

(b) To stand, after all liabilities to third persons have been satisfied, in the place of the creditors of the partnership for any payments made by him in respect of the partnership liabilities; and

(c) To be indemnified by the person guilty of the fraud or making the representation against all debts and liabilities of the partnership.

## § 40. Rules for Distribution

In settling accounts between the partners after dissolution, the following rules shall be observed, subject to any agreement to the contrary:

(a) The assets of the partnership are:

(I) The partnership property,

(II) The contributions of the partners necessary for the payment of all the liabilities specified in clause (b) of this paragraph.

(b) The liabilities of the partnership shall rank in order of payment, as follows:

(I) Those owing to creditors other than partners,

(II) Those owing to partners other than for capital and profits,

(III) Those owing to partners in respect of capital,

(IV) Those owing to partners in respect of profits.

(c) The assets shall be applied in the order of their declaration in clause (a) of this paragraph to the satisfaction of the liabilities.

(d) The partners shall contribute, as provided by section 18(a) the amount necessary to satisfy the liabilities; but if any, but not all, of the partners are insolvent, or, not being subject to process, refuse to contribute, the other parties shall contribute their share of the liabilities, and, in the relative proportions in which they share the profits, the additional amount necessary to pay the liabilities.

(e) An assignee for the benefit of creditors or any person appointed by the court shall have the right to enforce the contributions specified in clause (d) of this paragraph.

(f) Any partner or his legal representative shall have the right to enforce the contributions specified in clause (d) of this paragraph, to the extent of the amount which he has paid in excess of his share of the liability.

(g) The individual property of a deceased partner shall be liable for the contributions specified in clause (d) of this paragraph.

(h) When partnership property and the individual properties of the partners are in possession of a court for distribution, partnership creditors shall have priority on partnership property and separate creditors on individual property, saving the rights of lien or secured creditors as heretofore.

(i) Where a partner has become bankrupt or his estate is insolvent the claims against his separate property shall rank in the following order:

(I) Those owing to separate creditors,

(II) Those owing to partnership creditors,

(III) Those owing to partners by way of contribution.

## § 41. Liability of Persons Continuing the Business in Certain Cases

(1) When any new partner is admitted into an existing partnership, or when any partner retires and assigns (or the representative of the deceased partner assigns) his rights in partnership property to two or more of the partners, or to one or more of the partners and one or more third persons, if the business is continued without liquidation of the partnership affairs, creditors of the first or dissolved partnership are also creditors of the person or partnership so continuing the business.

(2) When all but one partner retire and assign (or the representative of a deceased partner assigns) their rights in partnership property to the remaining partner, who continues the business without liquidation of partnership affairs, either alone or with others, creditors of the dissolved partnership are also creditors of the person or partnership so continuing the business.

(3) When any partner retires or dies and the business of the dissolved partnership is continued as set forth in paragraphs (1) and (2) of this section, with the consent of the retired partners or the representative of the deceased partner, but without any assignment of his right in partnership property, rights of creditors of the dissolved partnership and of the creditors of the person or partnership continuing the business shall be as if such assignment had been made.

(4) When all the partners or their representatives assign their rights in partnership property to one or more third persons who promise to pay the debts and who continue the business of the dissolved partnership, creditors of the dissolved partnership are also creditors of the person or partnership continuing the business.

(5) When any partner wrongfully causes a dissolution and the remaining partners continue the business under the provisions of section 38(2b), either alone or with others, and without liquidation of the partnership affairs, creditors of the dissolved partnership are also creditors of the person or partnership continuing the business.

(6) When a partner is expelled and the remaining partners continue the business either alone or with others, without liquidation of the partnership affairs, creditors of the dissolved partnership are also creditors of the person or partnership continuing the business.

(7) The liability of a third person becoming a partner in the partnership continuing the business, under this section, to the creditors of the dissolved partnership shall be satisfied out of partnership property only.

(8) When the business of a partnership after dissolution is continued under any conditions set forth in this section the creditors of the dissolved partnership, as against the separate creditors of the retiring or deceased partner or the representative of the deceased partner, have a prior right to any claim of the retired partner or the representative of the deceased partner against the person or partnership continuing the business, on account of the retired or deceased partner's interest in the dissolved partnership or on account of any consideration promised for such interest or for his right in partnership property.

(9) Nothing in this section shall be held to modify any right of creditors to set aside any assignment on the ground of fraud.

(10) The use by the person or partnership continuing the business of the partnership name, or the name of a deceased partner as part thereof, shall not of itself make the individual property of the deceased partner liable for any debts contracted by such person or partnership.

## § 42.  Rights of Retiring or Estate of Deceased Partner When the Business is Continued

When any partner retires or dies, and the business is continued under any of the conditions set forth in section 41(1, 2, 3, 5, 6), or section 38(2b), without any settlement of accounts as between him or his estate and the person or partnership continuing the business, unless otherwise agreed, he or his legal representative as against such persons or partnership may have the value of his interest at the date of dissolution ascertained, and shall receive as an ordinary creditor an amount equal to the value of his interest in the dissolved partnership with interest, or, at his option or at the option of his legal representative, in lieu of interest, the profits attributable to the use of his right in the property of the dissolved partnership; provided that the creditors of the dissolved partnership as against the separate creditors, or the representative of the retired or deceased partner, shall have priority on any claim arising under this section, as provided by section 41(8) of this act.

## § 43.  Accrual of Actions

The right to an account of his interest shall accrue to any partner, or his legal representative, as against the winding up partners or the surviving partners or the person or partnership continuing the business, at the date of dissolution, in the absence of any agreement to the contrary.

# Part VII.  Miscellaneous Provisions

## § 44.  When Act Takes Effect

This act shall take effect on the _____ day of _____ one thousand nine hundred and _____.

## § 45.  Legislation Repealed

All acts or parts of acts inconsistent with this act are hereby repealed.

# Revised Model Business Corporation Act

## CHAPTER 1. GENERAL PROVISIONS

### Subchapter A. Short Title and Reservation of Power

#### § 1.01 Short Title

This Act shall be known and may be cited as the "[name of state] Business Corporation Act."

#### § 1.02 Reservation of Power to Amend or Repeal

The [name of state legislature] has power to amend or repeal all or part of this Act at any time and all domestic and foreign corporations subject to this Act are governed by the amendment or repeal.

### Subchapter B. Filing Documents

#### § 1.20 Filing Requirements

(a) A document must satisfy the requirements of this section, and of any other section that adds to or varies these requirements, to be entitled to filing by the secretary of state.

(b) This Act must require or permit filing the document in the office of the secretary of state.

(c) The document must contain the information required by this Act. It may contain other information as well.

(d) The document must be typewritten or printed.

(e) The document must be in the English language. A corporate name need not be in English if written in English letters or Arabic or Roman numerals, and the certificate of existence required of foreign corporations need not be in English if accompanied by a reasonably authenticated English translation.

(f) The document must be executed:

    (1) by the chairman of the board of directors of a domestic or foreign corporation, by its president, or by another of its officers;

    (2) if directors have not been selected or the corporation has not been formed, by an incorporator; or

    (3) if the corporation is in the hands of a receiver, trustee, or other court-appointed fiduciary, by that fiduciary.

(g) The person executing the document shall sign it and state beneath or opposite his signature his name and the capacity in which he signs. The document may but need not contain: (1) the corporate seal, (2) an attestation by the secretary or an assistant secretary, (3) an acknowledgement, verification, or proof.

(h) If the secretary of state has prescribed a mandatory form for the document under section 1.21, the document must be in or on the prescribed form.

(i) The document must be delivered to the office of the secretary of state for filing and must be accompanied by one exact or conformed copy (except as provided in sections 5.03 and 15.09), the correct filing fee, and any franchise tax, license fee, or penalty required by this Act or other law.

#### § 1.21 Forms

(a) The secretary of state may prescribe and furnish on request forms for: (1) an application for a certificate of existence, (2) a foreign corporation's application for a certificate of authority to transact business in this state, (3) a foreign corporation's application for a certificate of withdrawal, and (4) the annual report. If the secretary of state so requires, use of these forms is mandatory.

(b) The secretary of state may prescribe and furnish on request forms for other documents required or permitted to be filed by this Act but their use is not mandatory.

#### § 1.22 Filing, Service and Copying Fees

[Text omitted.]

#### § 1.23 Effective Time and Date of Document

(a) Except as provided in subsection (b) and section 1.24(c), a document accepted for filing is effective:

    (1) at the time of filing on the date it is filed, as evidenced by the secretary of state's date and time endorsement on the original document; or

    (2) at the time specified in the document as its effective time on the date it is filed.

(b) A document may specify a delayed effective time and date, and if it does so the document becomes effective at the time and date specified. If a delayed effective date but no time is specified, the document is effective at the close of business on that date. A delayed effective date for a document may not be later than the 90th day after the date it is filed.

#### § 1.24 Correcting Filed Document

(a) A domestic or foreign corporation may correct a document filed by the secretary of state if the document (1) contains an incorrect statement or (2) was defectively executed, attested, sealed, verified, or acknowledged.

(b) A document is corrected:

    (1) by preparing articles of correction that (i) describe the document (including its filing date) or attach a copy of it to the articles, (ii) specify the incorrect statement and the reason it is incorrect or the manner in which the execution was defective, and (iii) correct the incorrect statement or defective execution; and

    (2) by delivering the articles to the secretary of state for filing.

(c) Articles of correction are effective on the effective date of the document they correct except as to persons relying on the uncorrected document and adversely affected by the correction. As to those persons, articles of correction are effective when filed.

### § 1.25 Filing Duty of Secretary of State

(a) If a document delivered to the office of the secretary of state for filing satisfies the requirements of section 1.20, the secretary of state shall file it.

(b) The secretary of state files a document by stamping or otherwise endorsing "Filed," together with his name and official title and the date and time of receipt, on both the original and the document copy and on the receipt for the filing fee. After filing a document, except as provided in sections 5.03 and 15.10, the secretary of state shall deliver the document copy, with the filing fee receipt (or acknowledgement of receipt if no fee is required) attached, to the domestic or foreign corporation or its representative.

(c) If the secretary of state refuses to file a document, he shall return it to the domestic or foreign corporation or its representative within five days after the document was delivered, together with a brief, written explanation of the reason for his refusal.

(d) The secretary of state's duty to file documents under this section is ministerial. His filing or refusing to file a document does not:

(1) affect the validity or invalidity of the document in whole or part;

(2) relate to the correctness or incorrectness of information contained in the document;

(3) create a presumption that the document is valid or invalid or that information contained in the document is correct or incorrect.

### § 1.26 Appeal From Secretary of State's Refusal to File Document

(a) If the secretary of state refuses to file a document delivered to his office for filing, the domestic or foreign corporation may appeal the refusal to the [name or describe] court [of the county where the corporation's principal office (or, if none in this state, its registered office) is or will be located] [of _____ county]. The appeal is commenced by petitioning the court to compel filing the document and by attaching to the petition the document and the secretary of state's explanation of his refusal to file.

(b) The court may summarily order the secretary of state to file the document or take other action the court considers appropriate.

(c) The court's final decision may be appealed as in other civil proceedings.

### § 1.27 Evidentiary Effect of Copy of Filed Document

A certificate attached to a copy of the document filed by the secretary of state, bearing his signature (which may be in facsimile) and the seal of this state, is conclusive evidence that the original document is on file with the secretary of state.

### § 1.28 Certificate of Existence

(a) Anyone may apply to the secretary of state to furnish a certificate of existence for a domestic corporation or a certificate of authorization for a foreign corporation.

(b) A certificate of existence or authorization sets forth:

(1) the domestic corporation's corporate name or the foreign corporation's corporate name used in this state;

(2) that (i) the domestic corporation is duly incorporated under the law of this state, the date of its incorporation, and the period of its duration if less than perpetual; or (ii) that the foreign corporation is authorized to transact business in this state;

(3) that all fees, taxes, and penalties owed to this state have been paid, if (i) payment is reflected in the records of the secretary of state and (ii) nonpayment affects the existence or authorization of the domestic or foreign corporation;

(4) that its most recent annual report required by section 16.22 has been delivered to the secretary of state;

(5) that articles of dissolution have not been filed; and

(6) other facts of record in the office of the secretary of state that may be requested by the applicant.

(c) Subject to any qualification stated in the certificate, a certificate of existence or authorization issued by the secretary of state may be relied upon as conclusive evidence that the domestic or foreign corporation is in existence or is authorized to transact business in this state.

### § 1.29 Penalty for Signing False Document

(a) A person commits an offense if he signs a document he knows is false in any material respect with intent that the document be delivered to the secretary of state for filing.

(b) An offense under this section is a [_____] misdemeanor [punishable by a fine of not to exceed $____].

## Subchapter C. Secretary of State

### § 1.30 Powers

The secretary of state has the power reasonably necessary to perform the duties required of him by this Act.

## Subchapter D. Definitions

### § 1.40 Act Definitions

In this Act:

(1) "Articles of incorporation" include amended and restated articles of incorporation and articles of merger.

(2) "Authorized shares" means the shares of all classes a domestic or foreign corporation is authorized to issue.

(3) "Conspicuous" means so written that a reasonable person against whom the writing is to operate should have noticed it. For example, printing in italics or boldface or contrasting color, or typing in capitals or underlined, is conspicuous.

(4) "Corporation" or "domestic corporation" means a corporation for profit, which is not a foreign corporation, incorporated under or subject to the provisions of this Act.

(5) "Deliver" includes mail.

(6) "Distribution" means a direct or indirect transfer of money or other property (except its own shares) or incurrence of indebtedness by a corporation to or for the benefit of its shareholders in respect of any of its shares. A distribution may be in the form of a declaration or payment of a dividend; a purchase, redemption, or other acquisition of shares; a distribution of indebtedness; or otherwise.

(7) "Effective date of notice" is defined in section 1.41.

(8) "Employee" includes an officer but not a director. A director may accept duties that make him also an employee.

(9) "Entity" includes corporation and foreign corporation; not-for-profit corporation; profit and not-for-profit unincorporated association; business trust, estate, partnership, trust, and two or more persons having a joint or common economic interest; and state, United States, and foreign government.

(10) "Foreign corporation" means a corporation for profit incorporated under a law other than the law of this state.

(11) "Governmental subdivision" includes authority, county, district, and municipality.

(12) "Includes" denotes a partial definition.

(13) "Individual" includes the estate of an incompetent or deceased individual.

(14) "Means" denotes an exhaustive definition.

(15) "Notice" is defined in section 1.41.

(16) "Person" includes individual and entity.

(17) "Principal office" means the office (in or out of this state) so designated in the annual report where the principal executive offices of a domestic or foreign corporation are located.

(18) "Proceeding" includes civil suit and criminal, administrative, and investigatory action.

(19) "Record date" means the date established under chapter 6 or 7 on which a corporation determines the identity of its shareholders and their shareholdings for purposes of this Act. The determinations shall be made as of the close of business on the record date unless another time for doing so is specified when the record date is fixed.

(20) "Secretary" means the corporate officer to whom the board of directors has delegated responsibility under section 8.40(c) for custody of the minutes of the meetings of the board of directors and of the shareholders and for authenticating records of the corporation.

(21) "Share" means the unit into which the proprietary interests in a corporation are divided.

(22) "Shareholder" means the person in whose name shares are registered in the records of a corporation or the beneficial owner of shares to the extent of the rights granted by a nominee certificate on file with a corporation.

(23) "State," when referring to a part of the United States, includes a state and commonwealth (and their agencies and governmental subdivisions) and a territory, and insular possession (and their agencies and governmental subdivisions) of the United States.

(24) "Subscriber" means a person who subscribes for shares in a corporation, whether before or after incorporation.

(25) "United States" includes district, authority, bureau, commission, department, and any other agency of the United States.

(26) "Voting group" means all shares of one or more classes or series that under the articles of incorporation or this Act are entitled to vote and be counted together collectively on a matter at a meeting of shareholders. All shares entitled by the articles of incorporation or this Act to vote generally on the matter are for that purpose a single voting group.

## § 1.41  Notice

(a) Notice under this Act shall be in writing unless oral notice is reasonable under the circumstances.

(b) Notice may be communicated in person; by telephone, telegraph, teletype, or other form of wire or wireless communication; or by mail or private carrier. If these forms of personal notice are impracticable, notice may be communicated by a newspaper of general circulation in the area where published; or by radio, television, or other form of public broadcast communication.

(c) Written notice by a domestic or foreign corporation to its shareholder, if in a comprehensible form, is effective when mailed, if mailed postpaid and correctly addressed to the shareholder's address shown in the corporation's current record of shareholders.

(d) Written notice to a domestic or foreign corporation (authorized to transact business in this state) may be addressed to its registered agent at its registered office or to the corporation or its secretary at its principal office shown in its most recent annual report or, in the case of a foreign corporation that has not yet delivered an annual report, in its application for a certificate of authority.

(e) Except as provided in subsections (c) and (d), written notice, if in a comprehensible form, is effective at the earliest of the following:

(1) when received;

(2) five days after its deposit in the United States Mail, as evidenced by the postmark, if mailed postpaid and correctly addressed;

(3) on the date shown on the return receipt, if sent by registered or certified mail, return receipt requested, and the receipt is signed by or on behalf of the addressee.

(f) Oral notice is effective when communicated if communicated in a comprehensible manner.

(g) If this Act prescribes notice requirements for particular circumstances, those requirements govern. If articles of incorporation or bylaws prescribe notice requirements, not inconsistent with this section or other provisions of this Act, those requirements govern.

## § 1.42  Number of Shareholders

(a) For purposes of this Act, the following identified as a shareholder in a corporation's current record of shareholders constitutes one shareholder:

(1) three or fewer co-owners;

(2) a corporation, partnership, trust, estate, or other entity;

(3) the trustees, guardians, custodians, or other fiduciaries of a single trust, estate, or account.

(b) For purposes of this Act, shareholdings registered in substantially similar names constitute one shareholder if it is reasonable to believe that the names represent the same person.

# CHAPTER 2.  INCORPORATION

## § 2.01  Incorporators

One or more persons may act as the incorporator or incorporators of a corporation by delivering articles of incorporation to the secretary of state for filing.

## § 2.02  Articles of Incorporation

(a) The articles of incorporation must set forth:

(1) a corporate name for the corporation that satisfies the requirements of section 4.01;

(2) the number of shares the corporation is authorized to issue;

(3) the street address of the corporation's initial registered office and the name of its initial registered agent at that office; and

(4) the name and address of each incorporator.

(b) The articles of incorporation may set forth:

(1) the names and addresses of the individuals who are to serve as the initial directors;

(2) provisions not inconsistent with law regarding:

(i) the purpose or purposes for which the corporation is organized;

(ii) managing the business and regulating the affairs of the corporation;

(iii) defining, limiting, and regulating the powers of the corporation, its board of directors, and shareholders;

(iv) a par value for authorized shares or classes of shares;

(v) the imposition of personal liability on shareholders for the debts of the corporation to a specified extent and upon specified conditions;

(3) any provision that under this Act is required or permitted to be set forth in the bylaws; and

(4) a provision eliminating or limiting the liability of a director to the corporation or its shareholders for money damages for any action taken, or any failure to take any action, as a director, except liability for (A) the amount of a financial benefit received by a director to which he is not entitled; (B) an intentional infliction of harm on the corporation or the shareholders; (C) a violation of section 8.33; or (D) an intentional violation of criminal law.

(c) The articles of incorporation need not set forth any of the corporate powers enumerated in this Act.

### § 2.03  Incorporation

(a) Unless a delayed effective date is specified, the corporate existence begins when the articles of incorporation are filed.

(b) The secretary of state's filing of the articles of incorporation is conclusive proof that the incorporators satisfied all conditions precedent to incorporation except in a proceeding by the state to cancel or revoke the incorporation or involuntarily dissolve the corporation.

### § 2.04  Liability for Preincorporation Transactions

All persons purporting to act as or on behalf of a corporation, knowing there was no incorporation under this Act, are jointly and severally liable for all liabilities created while so acting.

### § 2.05  Organization of Corporation

(a) After incorporation:

(1) if initial directors are named in the articles of incorporation, the initial directors shall hold an organizational meeting, at the call of a majority of the directors, to complete the organization of the corporation by appointing officers, adopting bylaws, and carrying on any other business brought before the meeting;

(2) if initial directors are not named in the articles, the incorporator or incorporators shall hold an organizational meeting at the call of a majority of the incorporators:

(i) to elect directors and complete the organization of the corporation; or

(ii) to elect a board of directors who shall complete the organization of the corporation.

(b) Action required or permitted by this Act to be taken by incorporators at an organizational meeting may be taken without a meeting if the action taken is evidenced by one or more written consents describing the action taken and signed by each incorporator.

(c) An organizational meeting may be held in or out of this state.

### § 2.06  Bylaws

(a) The incorporators or board of directors of a corporation shall adopt initial bylaws for the corporation.

(b) The bylaws of a corporation may contain any provision for managing the business and regulating the affairs of the corporation that is not inconsistent with law or the articles of incorporation.

### § 2.07  Emergency Bylaws

(a) Unless the articles of incorporation provide otherwise, the board of directors of a corporation may adopt bylaws to be effective only in an emergency defined in subsection (d). The emergency bylaws, which are subject to amendment or repeal by the shareholders, may make all provisions necessary for managing the corporation during the emergency, including:

(1) procedures for calling a meeting of the board of directors;

(2) quorum requirements for the meeting; and

(3) designation of additional or substitute directors.

(b) All provisions of the regular bylaws consistent with the emergency bylaws remain effective during the emergency. The emergency bylaws are not effective after the emergency ends.

(c) Corporate action taken in good faith in accordance with the emergency bylaws:

(1) binds the corporation; and

(2) may not be used to impose liability on a corporate director, officer, employee, or agent.

(d) An emergency exists for purposes of this section if a quorum of the corporation's directors cannot readily be assembled because of some catastrophic event.

## CHAPTER 3.  PURPOSES AND POWERS

### § 3.01  Purposes

(a) Every corporation incorporated under this Act has the purpose of engaging in any lawful business unless a more limited purpose is set forth in the articles of incorporation.

(b) A corporation engaging in a business that is subject to regulation under another statute of this state may incorporate under this Act only if permitted by, and subject to all limitations of, the other statute.

### § 3.02  General Powers

Unless its articles of incorporation provide otherwise, every corporation has perpetual duration and succession in its corporate name and has the same powers as an individual to do all things necessary or convenient to carry out its business and affairs, including without limitation power:

(1) to sue and be sued, complain and defend in its corporate name;

(2) to have a corporate seal, which may be altered at will, and to use it, or a facsimile of it, by impressing or affixing it or in any other manner reproducing it;

(3) to make and amend bylaws, not inconsistent with its articles of incorporation or with the laws of this state, for managing the business and regulating the affairs of the corporation;

(4) to purchase, receive, lease, or otherwise acquire, and own, hold, improve, use, and otherwise deal with, real or personal property, or any legal or equitable interest in property, wherever located;

(5) to sell, convey, mortgage, pledge, lease, exchange, and otherwise dispose of all or any part of its property;

(6) to purchase, receive, subscribe for, or otherwise acquire; own, hold, vote, use, sell, mortgage, lend, pledge, or otherwise dispose of; and deal in and with shares or other interests in, or obligations of, any other entity;

(7) to make contracts and guarantees, incur liabilities, borrow money, issue its notes, bonds, and other obligations, (which may be convertible into or include the option to purchase other securities of the corporation), and secure any of its obligations by mortgage or pledge of any of its property, franchises, or income;

(8) to lend money, invest and reinvest its funds, and receive and hold real and personal property as security for repayment;

(9) to be a promoter, partner, member, associate, or manager of any partnership, joint venture, trust, or other entity;

(10) to conduct its business, locate offices, and exercise the powers granted by this Act within or without this state;

(11) to elect directors and appoint officers, employees, and agents of the corporation, define their duties, fix their compensation, and lend them money and credit;

(12) to pay pensions and establish pension plans, pension trusts, profit sharing plans, share bonus plans, share option plans, and benefit or incentive plans for any or all of its current or former directors, officers, employees, and agents;

(13) to make donations for the public welfare or for charitable, scientific, or educational purposes;

(14) to transact any lawful business that will aid governmental policy;

(15) to make payments or donations, or do any other act, not inconsistent with law, that furthers the business and affairs of the corporation.

## § 3.03  Emergency Powers

(a) In anticipation of or during an emergency defined in subsection (d), the board of directors of a corporation may:

(1) modify lines of succession to accommodate the incapacity of any director, officer, employee, or agent; and

(2) relocate the principal office, designate alternative principal offices or regional offices, or authorize the officers to do so.

(b) During an emergency defined in subsection (d), unless emergency bylaws provide otherwise:

(1) notice of a meeting of the board of directors need be given only to those directors whom it is practicable to reach and may be given in any practicable manner, including by publication and radio; and

(2) one or more officers of the corporation present at a meeting of the board of directors may be deemed to be directors for the meeting, in order of rank and within the same rank in order of seniority, as necessary to achieve a quorum.

(c) Corporate action taken in good faith during an emergency under this section to further the ordinary business affairs of the corporation:

(1) binds the corporation; and

(2) may not be used to impose liability on a corporate director, officer, employee, or agent.

(d) An emergency exists for purposes of this section if a quorum of the corporation's directors cannot readily be assembled because of some catastrophic event.

## § 3.04  Ultra Vires

(a) Except as provided in subsection (b), the validity of corporate action may not be challenged on the ground that the corporation lacks or lacked power to act.

(b) A corporation's power to act may be challenged:

(1) in a proceeding by a shareholder against the corporation to enjoin the act;

(2) in a proceeding by the corporation, directly, derivatively, or through a receiver, trustee, or other legal representative, against an incumbent or former director, officer, employee, or agent of the corporation; or

(3) in a proceeding by the Attorney General under section 14.30.

(c) In a shareholder's proceeding under subsection (b)(1) to enjoin an unauthorized corporate act, the court may enjoin or set aside the act, if equitable and if all affected persons are parties to the proceeding, and may award damages for loss (other than anticipated profits) suffered by the corporation or another party because of enjoining the unauthorized act.

## CHAPTER 4.  NAME

### § 4.01  Corporate Name

(a) A corporate name:

(1) must contain the word "corporation," "incorporated," "company," or "limited," or the abbreviation "corp.," "inc.," "co.," or "ltd.," or words or abbreviations of like import in another language; and

(2) may not contain language stating or implying that the corporation is organized for a purpose other than that permitted by section 3.01 and its articles of incorporation.

(b) Except as authorized by subsections (c) and (d), a corporate name must be distinguishable upon the records of the secretary of state from:

(1) the corporate name of a corporation incorporated or authorized to transact business in this state;

(2) a corporate name reserved or registered under section 4.02 or 4.03;

(3) the fictitious name adopted by a foreign corporation authorized to transact business in this state because its real name is unavailable; and

(4) the corporate name of a not-for-profit corporation incorporated or authorized to transact business in this state.

(c) A corporation may apply to the secretary of state for authorization to use a name that is not distinguishable upon his records from one or more of the names described in subsection (b). The secretary of state shall authorize use of the name applied for if:

(1) the other corporation consents to the use in writing and submits an undertaking in form satisfactory to the secretary of state to change its name to a name that is distinguishable upon the records of the secretary of state from the name of the applying corporation; or

(2) the applicant delivers to the secretary of state a certified copy of the final judgment of a court of competent jurisdiction establishing the applicant's right to use the name applied for in this state.

(d) A corporation may use the name (including the fictitious name) of another domestic or foreign corporation that is used in this state if the other corporation is incorporated or authorized to transact business in this state and the proposed user corporation:

(1) has merged with the other corporation;

(2) has been formed by reorganization of the other corporation; or

(3) has acquired all or substantially all of the assets, including the corporate name, of the other corporation.

(e) This Act does not control the use of fictitious names.

### § 4.02  Reserved Name

(a) A person may reserve the exclusive use of a corporate name, including a fictitious name for a foreign corporation whose corporate name is not available, by delivering an application to the secretary of state for filing. The application must set forth the name and address of the applicant and the name proposed to be reserved. If the secretary of state finds that the corporate name applied for is available, he shall reserve the name for the applicant's exclusive use for a nonrenewable 120-day period.

(b) The owner of a reserved corporate name may transfer the reservation to another person by delivering to the secretary of state a signed notice of the transfer that states the name and address of the transferee.

### § 4.03  Registered Name

(a) A foreign corporation may register its corporate name, or its corporate name with any addition required by section 15.06, if the name is distinguishable upon the records of the secretary of state from the corporate names that are not available under section 4.01(b)(3).

(b)  A foreign corporation registers its corporate name, or its corporate name with any addition required by section 15.06, by delivering to the secretary of state for filing an application:

>(1)  setting forth its corporate name, or its corporate name with any addition required by section 15.06, the state or country and date of its incorporation, and a brief description of the nature of the business in which it is engaged; and

>(2)  accompanied by a certificate of existence (or a document of similar import) from the state or country of incorporation.

(c)  The name is registered for the applicant's exclusive use upon the effective date of the application.

(d)  A foreign corporation whose registration is effective may renew it for successive years by delivering to the secretary of state for filing a renewal application, which complies with the requirements of subsection (b), between October 1 and December 31 of the preceding year. The renewal application renews the registration for the following calendar year.

(e)  A foreign corporation whose registration is effective may thereafter qualify as a foreign corporation under that name or consent in writing to the use of that name by a corporation thereafter incorporated under this Act or by another foreign corporation thereafter authorized to transact business in this state. The registration terminates when the domestic corporation is incorporated or the foreign corporation qualifies or consents to the qualification of another foreign corporation under the registered name.

## CHAPTER 5.  OFFICE AND AGENT

### § 5.01  Registered Office and Registered Agent

Each corporation must continuously maintain in this state:

>(1)  a registered office that may be the same as any of its places of business; and

>(2)  a registered agent, who may be:

>>(i)  an individual who resides in this state and whose business office is identical with the registered office;

>>(ii)  a domestic corporation or not-for-profit domestic corporation whose business office is identical with the registered office; or

>>(iii)  a foreign corporation or not-for-profit foreign corporation authorized to transact business in this state whose business office is identical with the registered office.

### § 5.02  Change of Registered Office or Registered Agent

(a)  A corporation may change its registered office or registered agent by delivering to the secretary of state for filing a statement of change that sets forth:

>(1)  the name of the corporation,

>(2)  the street address of its current registered office;

>(3)  if the current registered office is to be changed, the street address of the new registered office;

>(4)  the name of its current registered agent;

>(5)  if the current registered agent is to be changed, the name of the new registered agent and the new agent's written consent (either on the statement or attached to it) to the appointment; and

>(6)  that after the change or changes are made, the street addresses of its registered office and the business office of its registered agent will be identical.

(b)  If a registered agent changes the street address of his business office, he may change the street address of the registered office of any corporation for which he is the registered agent by notifying the corporation in writing of the change and signing (either manually or in facsimile) and delivering to the secretary of state for filing a statement that complies with the requirements of subsection (a) and recites that the corporation has been notified of the change.

### § 5.03  Resignation of Registered Agent

(a)  A registered agent may resign his agency appointment by signing and delivering to the secretary of state for filing the signed original and two exact or conformed copies of a statement of resignation. The statement may include a statement that the registered office is also discontinued.

(b)  After filing the statement the secretary of state shall mail one copy to the registered office (if not discontinued) and the other copy to the corporation at its principal office.

(c)  The agency appointment is terminated, and the registered office discontinued if so provided, on the 31st day after the date on which the statement was filed.

### § 5.04  Service on Corporation

(a)  A corporation's registered agent is the corporation's agent for service of process, notice, or demand required or permitted by law to be served on the corporation.

(b)  If a corporation has no registered agent, or the agent cannot with reasonable diligence be served, the corporation may be served by registered or certified mail, return receipt requested, addressed to the secretary of the corporation at its principal office. Service is perfected under this subsection at the earliest of:

>(1)  the date the corporation receives the mail;

>(2)  the date shown on the return receipt, if signed on behalf of the corporation; or

>(3)  five days after its deposit in the United States Mail, if mailed postpaid and correctly addressed.

(c)  This section does not prescribe the only means, or necessarily the required means, of serving a corporation.

## CHAPTER 6.  SHARES AND DISTRIBUTIONS

### Subchapter A.  Shares

### § 6.01  Authorized Shares

(a)  The articles of incorporation must prescribe the classes of shares and the number of shares of each class that the corporation is authorized to issue. If more than one class of shares is authorized, the articles of incorporation must prescribe a distinguishing designation for each class, and prior to the issuance of shares of a class the preferences, limitations, and relative rights of that class must be described in the articles of incorporation. All shares of a class must have preferences, limitations, and relative rights identical with those of other shares of the same class except to the extent otherwise permitted by section 6.02.

(b)  The articles of incorporation must authorize: (1) one or more classes of shares that together have unlimited voting rights, and (2) one or more classes of shares (which may be the same class or classes as those with voting rights) that together are entitled to receive the net assets of the corporation upon dissolution.

(c)  The articles of incorporation may authorize one or more classes of shares that:

>(1)  have special, conditional, or limited voting rights, or no right to vote, except to the extent prohibited by this Act;

(2) are redeemable or convertible as specified in the articles of incorporation (i) at the option of the corporation, the shareholder, or another person or upon the occurrence of a designated event; (ii) for cash, indebtedness, securities, or other property; (iii) in a designated amount or in an amount determined in accordance with a designated formula or by reference to extrinsic data or events;

(3) entitle the holders to distributions calculated in any manner, including dividends that may be cumulative, noncumulative, or partially cumulative;

(4) have preference over any other class of shares with respect to distributions, including dividends and distributions upon the dissolution of the corporation.

(d) The description of the designations, preferences, limitations, and relative rights of share classes in subsection (c) is not exhaustive.

### § 6.02  Terms of Class or Series Determined by Board of Directors

(a) If the articles of incorporation so provide, the board of directors may determine, in whole or part, the preferences, limitations, and relative rights (within the limits set forth in section 6.01) of (1) any class of shares before the issuance of any shares of that class or (2) one or more series within a class before the issuance of any shares of that series.

(b) Each series of a class must be given a distinguishing designation.

(c) All shares of a series must have preferences, limitations, and relative rights identical with those of other shares of the same series and, except to the extent otherwise provided in the description of the series, of those of other series of the same class.

(d) Before issuing any shares of a class or series created under this section, the corporation must deliver to the secretary of state for filing articles of amendment, which are effective without shareholder action, that set forth:

(1) the name of the corporation;

(2) the text of the amendment determining the terms of the class or series of shares;

(3) the date it was adopted; and

(4) a statement that the amendment was duly adopted by the board of directors.

### § 6.03  Issued and Outstanding Shares

(a) A corporation may issue the number of shares of each class or series authorized by the articles of incorporation. Shares that are issued are outstanding shares until they are reacquired, redeemed, converted, or cancelled.

(b) The reacquisition, redemption, or conversion of outstanding shares is subject to the limitations of subsection (c) of this section and to section 6.40.

(c) At all times that shares of the corporation are outstanding, one or more shares that together have unlimited voting rights and one or more shares that together are entitled to receive the net assets of the corporation upon dissolution must be outstanding.

### § 6.04  Fractional Shares

(a) A corporation may:

(1) issue fractions of a share or pay in money the value of fractions of a share;

(2) arrange for disposition of fractional shares by the shareholders;

(3) issue scrip in registered or bearer form entitling the holder to receive a full share upon surrendering enough scrip to equal a full share.

(b) Each certificate representing scrip must be conspicuously labeled "scrip" and must contain the information required by section 6.25(b).

(c) The holder of a fractional share is entitled to exercise the rights of a shareholder, including the right to vote, to receive dividends, and to participate in the assets of the corporation upon liquidation. The holder of scrip is not entitled to any of these rights unless the scrip provides for them.

(d) The board of directors may authorize the issuance of scrip subject to any condition considered desirable, including:

(1) that the scrip will become void if not exchanged for full shares before a specified date; and

(2) that the shares for which the scrip is exchangeable may be sold and the proceeds paid to the scripholders.

## Subchapter B.  Issuance of Shares

### § 6.20  Subscription for Shares Before Incorporation

(a) A subscription for shares entered into before incorporation is irrevocable for six months unless the subscription agreement provides a longer or shorter period or all the subscribers agree to revocation.

(b) The board of directors may determine the payment terms of subscriptions for shares that were entered into before incorporation, unless the subscription agreement specifies them. A call for payment by the board of directors must be uniform so far as practicable as to all shares of the same class or series, unless the subscription agreement specifies otherwise.

(c) Shares issued pursuant to subscriptions entered into before incorporation are fully paid and nonassessable when the corporation receives the consideration specified in the subscription agreement.

(d) If a subscriber defaults in payment of money or property under a subscription agreement entered into before incorporation, the corporation may collect the amount owed as any other debt. Alternatively, unless the subscription agreement provides otherwise, the corporation may rescind the agreement and may sell the shares if the debt remains unpaid more than 20 days after the corporation sends written demand for payment to the subscriber.

(e) A subscription agreement entered into after incorporation is a contract between the subscriber and the corporation subject to section 6.21.

### § 6.21  Issuance of Shares

(a) The powers granted in this section to the board of directors may be reserved to the shareholders by the articles of incorporation.

(b) The board of directors may authorize shares to be issued for consideration consisting of any tangible or intangible property or benefit to the corporation, including cash, promissory notes, services performed, contracts for services to be performed, or other securities of the corporation.

(c) Before the corporation issues shares, the board of directors must determine that the consideration received or to be received for shares to be issued is adequate. That determination by the board of directors is conclusive insofar as the adequacy of consideration for the issuance of shares relates to whether the shares are validly issued, fully paid, and nonassessable.

(d) When the corporation receives the consideration for which the board of directors authorized the issuance of shares, the shares issued therefor are fully paid and nonassessable.

(e) The corporation may place in escrow shares issued for a contract for future services or benefits or a promissory note, or make other arrangements to restrict the transfer of the shares, and may credit distributions in respect of the shares against their purchase price, until the services are performed, the note is paid, or the benefits received. If the services are not performed, the note is not paid, or the benefits are not received, the shares escrowed or restricted and the distributions credited may be cancelled in whole or part.

### § 6.22  Liability of Shareholders

(a)  A purchaser from a corporation of its own shares is not liable to the corporation or its creditors with respect to the shares except to pay the consideration for which the shares were authorized to be issued (section 6.21) or specified in the subscription agreement (section 6.20).

(b)  Unless otherwise provided in the articles of incorporation, a shareholder of a corporation is not personally liable for the acts or debts of the corporation except that he may become personally liable by reason of his own acts or conduct.

### § 6.23  Share Dividends

(a)  Unless the articles of incorporation provide otherwise, shares may be issued pro rata and without consideration to the corporation's shareholders or to the shareholders of one or more classes or series. An issuance of shares under this subsection is a share dividend.

(b)  Shares of one class or series may not be issued as a share dividend in respect of shares of another class or series unless (1) the articles of incorporation so authorize, (2) a majority of the votes entitled to be cast by the class or series to be issued approve the issue, or (3) there are no outstanding shares of the class or series to be issued.

(c)  If the board of directors does not fix the record date for determining shareholders entitled to a share dividend, it is the date the board of directors authorizes the share dividend.

### § 6.24  Share Options

A corporation may issue rights, options, or warrants for the purchase of shares of the corporation. The board of directors shall determine the terms upon which the rights, options, or warrants are issued, their form and content, and the consideration for which the shares are to be issued.

### § 6.25  Form and Content of Certificates

(a)  Shares may but need not be represented by certificates. Unless this Act or another statute expressly provides otherwise, the rights and obligations of shareholders are identical whether or not their shares are represented by certificates.

(b)  At a minimum each share certificate must state on its face:

   (1)  the name of the issuing corporation and that it is organized under the law of this state;
   (2)  the name of the person to whom issued; and
   (3)  the number and class of shares and the designation of the series, if any, the certificate represents.

(c)  If the issuing corporation is authorized to issue different classes of shares or different series within a class, the designations, relative rights, preferences, and limitations applicable to each class and the variations in rights, preferences, and limitations determined for each series (and the authority of the board of directors to determine variations for future series) must be summarized on the front or back of each certificate. Alternatively, each certificate may state conspicuously on its front or back that the corporation will furnish the shareholder this information on request in writing and without charge.

(d)  Each share certificate (1) must be signed (either manually or in facsimile) by two officers designated in the bylaws or by the board of directors and (2) may bear the corporate seal or its facsimile.

(e)  If the person who signed (either manually or in facsimile) a share certificate no longer holds office when the certificate is issued, the certificate is nevertheless valid.

### § 6.26  Shares Without Certificates

(a)  Unless the articles of incorporation or bylaws provide otherwise, the board of directors of a corporation may authorize the issue of some or all of the shares of any or all of its classes or series without certificates. The authorization does not affect shares already represented by certificates until they are surrendered to the corporation.

(b)  Within a reasonable time after the issue or transfer of shares without certificates, the corporation shall send the shareholder a written statement of the information required on certificates by section 6.25(b) and (c), and, if applicable, section 6.27.

### § 6.27  Restriction on Transfer or Registration of Shares and Other Securities

(a)  The articles of incorporation, bylaws, an agreement among shareholders, or an agreement between shareholders and the corporation may impose restrictions on the transfer or registration of transfer of shares of the corporation. A restriction does not affect shares issued before the restriction was adopted unless the holders of the shares are parties to the restriction agreement or voted in favor of the restriction.

(b)  A restriction on the transfer or registration of transfer of shares is valid and enforceable against the holder or a transferee of the holder if the restriction is authorized by this section and its existence is noted conspicuously on the front or back of the certificate or is contained in the information statement required by section 6.26(b). Unless so noted, a restriction is not enforceable against a person without knowledge of the restriction.

(c)  A restriction on the transfer or registration of transfer of shares is authorized:

   (1)  to maintain the corporation's status when it is dependent on the number or identity of its shareholders;
   (2)  to preserve exemptions under federal or state securities law;
   (3)  for any other reasonable purpose.

(d)  A restriction on the transfer or registration of transfer of shares may:

   (1)  obligate the shareholder first to offer the corporation or other persons (separately, consecutively, or simultaneously) an opportunity to acquire the restricted shares;
   (2)  obligate the corporation or other persons (separately, consecutively, or simultaneously) to acquire the restricted shares;
   (3)  require the corporation, the holders of any class of its shares, or another person to approve the transfer of the restricted shares, if the requirement is not manifestly unreasonable;
   (4)  prohibit the transfer of the restricted shares to designated persons or classes of persons, if the prohibition is not manifestly unreasonable.

(e)  For purposes of this section, "shares" includes a security convertible into or carrying a right to subscribe for or acquire shares.

### § 6.28  Expense of Issue

A corporation may pay the expenses of selling or underwriting its shares, and of organizing or reorganizing the corporation, from the consideration received for shares.

## Subchapter C.  Subsequent Acquisition of Shares by Shareholders and Corporation

### § 6.30  Shareholders' Preemptive Rights

(a)  The shareholders of a corporation do not have a preemptive right to acquire the corporation's unissued shares except to the extent the articles of incorporation so provide.

(b)  A statement included in the articles of incorporation that "the corporation elects to have preemptive rights" (or words of similar import) means that the following principles apply except to the extent the articles of incorporation expressly provide otherwise:

(1) The shareholders of the corporation have a preemptive right, granted on uniform terms and conditions prescribed by the board of directors to provide a fair and reasonable opportunity to exercise the right, to acquire proportional amounts of the corporation's unissued shares upon the decision of the board of directors to issue them.

(2) A shareholder may waive his preemptive right. A waiver evidenced by a writing is irrevocable even though it is not supported by consideration.

(3) There is no preemptive right with respect to:

(i) shares issued as compensation to directors, officers, agents, or employees of the corporation, its subsidiaries or affiliates;

(ii) shares issued to satisfy conversion or option rights created to provide compensation to directors, officers, agents, or employees of the corporation, its subsidiaries or affiliates;

(iii) shares authorized in articles of incorporation that are issued within six months from the effective date of incorporation;

(iv) shares sold otherwise than for money.

(4) Holders of shares of any class without general voting rights but with preferential rights to distributions or assets have no preemptive rights with respect to shares of any class.

(5) Holders of shares of any class with general voting rights but without preferential rights to distributions or assets have no preemptive rights with respect to shares of any class with preferential rights to distributions or assets unless the shares with preferential rights are convertible into or carry a right to subscribe for or acquire shares without preferential rights.

(6) Shares subject to preemptive rights that are not acquired by shareholders may be issued to any person for a period of one year after being offered to shareholders at a consideration set by the board of directors that is not lower than the consideration set for the exercise of preemptive rights. An offer at a lower consideration or after the expiration of one year is subject to the shareholders' preemptive rights.

(c) For purposes of this section, "shares" includes a security convertible into or carrying a right to subscribe for or acquire shares.

### § 6.31 Corporation's Acquisition of Its Own Shares

(a) A corporation may acquire its own shares and shares so acquired constitute authorized but unissued shares.

(b) If the articles of incorporation prohibit the reissue of acquired shares, the number of authorized shares is reduced by the number of shares acquired, effective upon amendment of the articles of incorporation.

(c) Articles of amendment may be adopted by the board of directors without shareholder action, shall be delivered to the secretary of state for filing, and shall set forth:

(1) the name of the corporation;

(2) the reduction in the number of authorized shares, itemized by class and series; and

(3) the total number of authorized shares, itemized by class and series, remaining after reduction of the shares.

### Subchapter D. Distributions

### § 6.40 Distributions to Shareholders

(a) A board of directors may authorize and the corporation may make distributions to its shareholders subject to restriction by the articles of incorporation and the limitation in subsection (c).

(b) If the board of directors does not fix the record date for determining shareholders entitled to a distribution (other than one involving a purchase, redemption, or other acquisition of the corporation's shares), it is the date the board of directors authorizes the distribution.

(c) No distribution may be made if, after giving it effect:

(1) the corporation would not be able to pay its debts as they become due in the usual course of business; or

(2) the corporation's total assets would be less than the sum of its total liabilities plus (unless the articles of incorporation permit otherwise) the amount that would be needed, if the corporation were to be dissolved at the time of the distribution, to satisfy the preferential rights upon dissolution of shareholders whose preferential rights are superior to those receiving the distribution.

(d) The board of directors may base a determination that a distribution is not prohibited under subsection (c) either on financial statements prepared on the basis of accounting practices and principles that are reasonable in the circumstances or on a fair valuation or other method that is reasonable in the circumstances.

(e) Except as provided in subsection (g), the effect of a distribution under subsection (c) is measured:

(1) in the case of distribution by purchase, redemption, or other acquisition of the corporation's shares, as of the earlier of (i) the date money or other property is transferred or debt incurred by the corporation or (ii) the date the shareholder ceases to be a shareholder with respect to the acquired shares;

(2) in the case of any other distribution of indebtedness, as of the date the indebtedness is distributed;

(3) in all other cases, as of (i) the date the distribution is authorized if the payment occurs within 120 days after the date of authorization or (ii) the date the payment is made if it occurs more than 120 days after the date of authorization.

(f) A corporation's indebtedness to a shareholder incurred by reason of a distribution made in accordance with this section is at parity with the corporation's indebtedness to its general, unsecured creditors except to the extent subordinated by agreement.

(g) Indebtedness of a corporation, including indebtedness issued as a distribution, is not considered a liability for purposes of determinations under subsection (c) if its terms provide that payment of principal and interest are made only if and to the extent that payment of a distribution to shareholders could then be made under this section. If the indebtedness is issued as a distribution, each payment of principal or interest is treated as a distribution, the effect of which is measured on the date the payment is actually made.

## CHAPTER 7.  SHAREHOLDERS

### Subchapter A.  Meetings

### § 7.01 Annual Meeting

(a) A corporation shall hold annually at a time stated in or fixed in accordance with the bylaws a meeting of shareholders.

(b) Annual shareholders' meetings may be held in or out of this state at the place stated in or fixed in accordance with the bylaws. If no place is stated in or fixed in accordance with the bylaws, annual meetings shall be held at the corporation's principal office.

(c) The failure to hold an annual meeting at the time stated in or fixed in accordance with a corporation's bylaws does not affect the validity of any corporate action.

## § 7.02 Special Meeting

(a) A corporation shall hold a special meeting of shareholders:

    (1) on call of its board of directors or the person or persons authorized to do so by the articles of incorporation or bylaws; or

    (2) if the holders of at least 10 percent of all the votes entitled to be cast on any issue proposed to be considered at the proposed special meeting sign, date, and deliver to the corporation's secretary one or more written demands for the meeting describing the purpose or purposes for which it is to be held.

(b) If not otherwise fixed under sections 7.03 or 7.07, the record date for determining shareholders entitled to demand a special meeting is the date the first shareholder signs the demand.

(c) Special shareholders' meetings may be held in or out of this state at the place stated in or fixed in accordance with the bylaws. If no place is stated or fixed in accordance with the bylaws, special meetings shall be held at the corporation's principal office.

(d) Only business within the purpose or purposes described in the meeting notice required by section 7.05(c) may be conducted at a special shareholders' meeting.

## § 7.03 Court-Ordered Meeting

(a) The [name or describe] court of the county where a corporation's principal office (or, if none in this state, its registered office) is located may summarily order a meeting to be held:

    (1) on application of any shareholder of the corporation entitled to participate in an annual meeting if an annual meeting was not held within the earlier of 6 months after the end of the corporation's fiscal year or 15 months after its last annual meeting; or

    (2) on application of a shareholder who signed a demand for a special meeting valid under section 7.02 if:

        (i) notice of the special meeting was not given within 30 days after the date the demand was delivered to the corporation's secretary; or

        (ii) the special meeting was not held in accordance with the notice.

(b) The court may fix the time and place of the meeting, determine the shares entitled to participate in the meeting, specify a record date for determining shareholders entitled to notice of and to vote at the meeting, prescribe the form and content of the meeting notice, fix the quorum required for specific matters to be considered at the meeting (or direct that the votes represented at the meeting constitute a quorum for action on those matters), and enter other orders necessary to accomplish the purpose or purposes of the meeting.

## § 7.04 Action Without Meeting

(a) Action required or permitted by this Act to be taken at a shareholders' meeting may be taken without a meeting if the action is taken by all the shareholders entitled to vote on the action. The action must be evidenced by one or more written consents describing the action taken, signed by all the shareholders entitled to vote on the action, and delivered to the corporation for inclusion in the minutes or filing with the corporate records.

(b) If not otherwise determined under sections 7.03 or 7.07, the record date for determining shareholders entitled to take action without a meeting is the date the first shareholder signs the consent under subsection (a).

(c) A consent signed under this section has the effect of a meeting vote and may be described as such in any document.

(d) If this Act requires that notice of proposed action be given to nonvoting shareholders and the action is to be taken by unanimous consent of the voting shareholders, the corporation must give its nonvoting shareholders written notice of the proposed action at least 10 days before the action is taken. The notice must contain or be accompanied by the same material that, under this Act, would have been required to be sent to nonvoting shareholders in a notice of meeting at which the proposed action would have been submitted to the shareholders for action.

## § 7.05 Notice of Meeting

(a) A corporation shall notify shareholders of the date, time, and place of each annual and special shareholders' meeting no fewer than 10 nor more than 60 days before the meeting date. Unless this Act or the articles of incorporation require otherwise, the corporation is required to give notice only to shareholders entitled to vote at the meeting.

(b) Unless this Act or the articles of incorporation require otherwise, notice of an annual meeting need not include a description of the purpose or purposes for which the meeting is called.

(c) Notice of a special meeting must include a description of the purpose or purposes for which the meeting is called.

(d) If not otherwise fixed under sections 7.03 or 7.07, the record date for determining shareholders entitled to notice of and to vote at an annual or special shareholders' meeting is the day before the first notice is delivered to shareholders.

(e) Unless the bylaws require otherwise, if an annual or special shareholders' meeting is adjourned to a different date, time, or place, notice need not be given of the new date, time, or place if the new date, time, or place is announced at the meeting before adjournment. If a new record date for the adjourned meeting is or must be fixed under section 7.07, however, notice of the adjourned meeting must be given under this section to persons who are shareholders as of the new record date.

## § 7.06 Waiver of Notice

(a) A shareholder may waive any notice required by this Act, the articles of incorporation, or bylaws before or after the date and time stated in the notice. The waiver must be in writing, be signed by the shareholder entitled to the notice, and be delivered to the corporation for inclusion in the minutes or filing with the corporate records.

(b) A shareholder's attendance at a meeting:

    (1) waives objection to lack of notice or defective notice of the meeting, unless the shareholder at the beginning of the meeting objects to holding the meeting or transacting business at the meeting;

    (2) waives objection to consideration of a particular matter at the meeting that is not within the purpose or purposes described in the meeting notice, unless the shareholder objects to considering the matter when it is presented.

## § 7.07 Record Date

(a) The bylaws may fix or provide the manner of fixing the record date for one or more voting groups in order to determine the shareholders entitled to notice of a shareholders' meeting, to demand a special meeting, to vote, or to take any other action. If the bylaws do not fix or provide for fixing a record date, the board of directors of the corporation may fix a future date as the record date.

(b) A record date fixed under this section may not be more than 70 days before the meeting or action requiring a determination of shareholders.

(c) A determination of shareholders entitled to notice of or to vote at a shareholders' meeting is effective for any adjournment of the meeting unless the board of directors fixes a new record date, which it must do if the meeting is adjourned to a date more than 120 days after the date fixed for the original meeting.

(d) If a court orders a meeting adjourned to a date more than 120 days after the date fixed for the original meeting, it may provide that the original record date continues in effect or it may fix a new record date.

## Subchapter B. Voting

### § 7.20 Shareholders' List for Meeting

(a) After fixing a record date for a meeting, a corporation shall prepare an alphabetical list of the names of all its shareholders who are entitled to notice of a shareholders' meeting. The list must be arranged by voting group (and within each voting group by class or series of shares) and show the address of and number of shares held by each shareholder.

(b) The shareholders' list must be available for inspection by any shareholder, beginning two business days after notice of the meeting is given for which the list was prepared and continuing through the meeting, at the corporation's principal office or at a place identified in the meeting notice in the city where the meeting will be held. A shareholder, his agent, or attorney is entitled on written demand to inspect and, subject to the requirements of section 16.02(c), to copy the list, during regular business hours and at his expense, during the period it is available for inspection.

(c) The corporation shall make the shareholders' list available at the meeting, and any shareholder, his agent, or attorney is entitled to inspect the list at any time during the meeting or any adjournment.

(d) If the corporation refuses to allow a shareholder, his agent, or attorney to inspect the shareholders' list before or at the meeting (or copy the list as permitted by subsection (b)), the [name or describe] court of the county where a corporation's principal office (or, if none in this state, its registered office) is located, on application of the shareholder, may summarily order the inspection or copying at the corporation's expense and may postpone the meeting for which the list was prepared until the inspection or copying is complete.

(e) Refusal or failure to prepare or make available the shareholders' list does not affect the validity of action taken at the meeting.

### § 7.21 Voting Entitlement of Shares

(a) Except as provided in subsections (b) and (c) or unless the articles of incorporation provide otherwise, each outstanding share, regardless of class, is entitled to one vote on each matter voted on at a shareholders' meeting. Only shares are entitled to vote.

(b) Absent special circumstances, the shares of a corporation are not entitled to vote if they are owned, directly or indirectly, by a second corporation, domestic or foreign, and the first corporation owns, directly or indirectly, a majority of the shares entitled to vote for directors of the second corporation.

(c) Subsection (b) does not limit the power of a corporation to vote any shares, including its own shares, held by it in a fiduciary capacity.

(d) Redeemable shares are not entitled to vote after notice of redemption is mailed to the holders and a sum sufficient to redeem the shares has been deposited with a bank, trust company, or other financial institution under an irrevocable obligation to pay the holders the redemption price on surrender of the shares.

### § 7.22 Proxies

(a) A shareholder may vote his shares in person or by proxy.

(b) A shareholder may appoint a proxy to vote or otherwise act for him by signing an appointment form, either personally or by his attorney-in-fact.

(c) An appointment of a proxy is effective when received by the secretary or other officer or agent authorized to tabulate votes. An appointment is valid for 11 months unless a longer period is expressly provided in the appointment form.

(d) An appointment of a proxy is revocable by the shareholder unless the appointment form conspicuously states that it is irrevocable and the appointment is coupled with an interest. Appointments coupled with an interest include the appointment of:

   (1) a pledgee;
   (2) a person who purchased or agreed to purchase the shares;
   (3) a creditor of the corporation who extended it credit under terms requiring the appointment;
   (4) an employee of the corporation whose employment contract requires the appointment; or
   (5) a party to a voting agreement created under section 7.31.

(e) The death or incapacity of the shareholder appointing a proxy does not affect the right of the corporation to accept the proxy's authority unless notice of the death or incapacity is received by the secretary or other officer or agent authorized to tabulate votes before the proxy exercises his authority under the appointment.

(f) An appointment made irrevocable under subsection (d) is revoked when the interest with which it is coupled is extinguished.

(g) A transferee for value of shares subject to an irrevocable appointment may revoke the appointment if he did not know of its existence when he acquired the shares and the existence of the irrevocable appointment was not noted conspicuously on the certificate representing the shares or on the information statement for shares without certificates.

(h) Subject to section 7.24 and to any express limitation on the proxy's authority appearing on the face of the appointment form, a corporation is entitled to accept the proxy's vote or other action as that of the shareholder making the appointment.

### § 7.23 Shares Held by Nominees

(a) A corporation may establish a procedure by which the beneficial owner of shares that are registered in the name of a nominee is recognized by the corporation as the shareholder. The extent of this recognition may be determined in the procedure.

(b) The procedure may set forth:

   (1) the types of nominees to which it applies;
   (2) the rights or privileges that the corporation recognizes in a beneficial owner;
   (3) the manner in which the procedure is selected by the nominee;
   (4) the information that must be provided when the procedure is selected;
   (5) the period for which selection of the procedure is effective; and
   (6) other aspects of the rights and duties created.

### § 7.24 Corporation's Acceptance of Votes

(a) If the name signed on a vote, consent, waiver, or proxy appointment corresponds to the name of a shareholder, the corporation if acting in good faith is entitled to accept the vote, consent, waiver, or proxy appointment and give it effect as the act of the shareholder.

(b) If the name signed on a vote, consent, waiver, or proxy appointment does not correspond to the name of its shareholder, the corporation if acting in good faith is nevertheless entitled to accept the vote, consent, waiver, or proxy appointment and give it effect as the act of the shareholder if:

(1) the shareholder is an entity and the name signed purports to be that of an officer or agent of the entity;

(2) the name signed purports to be that of an administrator, executor, guardian, or conservator representing the shareholder and, if the corporation requests, evidence of fiduciary status acceptable to the corporation has been presented with respect to the vote, consent, waiver, or proxy appointment;

(3) the name signed purports to be that of a receiver or trustee in bankruptcy of the shareholder and, if the corporation requests, evidence of this status acceptable to the corporation has been presented with respect to the vote, consent, waiver, or proxy appointment;

(4) the name signed purports to be that of a pledgee, beneficial owner, or attorney-in-fact of the shareholder and, if the corporation requests, evidence acceptable to the corporation of the signatory's authority to sign for the shareholder has been presented with respect to the vote, consent, waiver, or proxy appointment;

(5) two or more persons are the shareholder as cotenants or fiduciaries and the name signed purports to be the name of at least one of the coowners and the person signing appears to be acting on behalf of all the coowners.

(c) The corporation is entitled to reject a vote, consent, waiver, or proxy appointment if the secretary or other officer or agent authorized to tabulate votes, acting in good faith, has reasonable basis for doubt about the validity of the signature on it or about the signatory's authority to sign for the shareholder.

(d) The corporation and its officer or agent who accepts or rejects a vote, consent, waiver, or proxy appointment in good faith and in accordance with the standards of this section are not liable in damages to the shareholder for the consequences of the acceptance or rejection.

(e) Corporate action based on the acceptance or rejection of a vote, consent, waiver, or proxy appointment under this section is valid unless a court of competent jurisdiction determines otherwise.

### § 7.25  Quorum and Voting Requirements for Voting Groups

(a) Shares entitled to vote as a separate voting group may take action on a matter at a meeting only if a quorum of those shares exists with respect to that matter. Unless the articles of incorporation or this Act provide otherwise, a majority of the votes entitled to be cast on the matter by the voting group constitutes a quorum of that voting group for action on that matter.

(b) Once a share is represented for any purpose at a meeting, it is deemed present for quorum purposes for the remainder of the meeting and for any adjournment of that meeting unless a new record date is or must be set for that adjourned meeting.

(c) If a quorum exists, action on a matter (other than the election of directors) by a voting group is approved if the votes cast within the voting group favoring the action exceed the votes cast opposing the action, unless the articles of incorporation or this Act require a greater number of affirmative votes.

(d) An amendment of articles of incorporation adding, changing, or deleting a quorum or voting requirement for a voting group greater than specified in subsection (b) or (c) is governed by section 7.27.

(e) The election of directors is governed by section 7.28.

### § 7.26  Action by Single and Multiple Voting Groups

(a) If the articles of incorporation or this Act provide for voting by a single voting group on a matter, action on that matter is taken when voted upon by that voting group as provided in section 7.25.

(b) If the articles of incorporation or this Act provide for voting by two or more voting groups on a matter, action on that matter is taken only when voted upon by each of those voting groups counted separately as provided in section 7.25. Action may be taken by one voting group on a matter even though no action is taken by another voting group entitled to vote on the matter.

### § 7.27  Greater Quorum or Voting Requirements

(a) The articles of incorporation may provide for a greater quorum or voting requirement for shareholders (or voting groups of shareholders) than is provided for by this Act.

(b) An amendment to the articles of incorporation that adds, changes, or deletes a greater quorum or voting requirement must meet the same quorum requirement and be adopted by the same vote and voting groups required to take action under the quorum and voting requirements then in effect or proposed to be adopted, whichever is greater.

### § 7.28  Voting for Directors; Cumulative Voting

(a) Unless otherwise provided in the articles of incorporation, directors are elected by a plurality of the votes cast by the shares entitled to vote in the election at a meeting at which a quorum is present.

(b) Shareholders do not have a right to cumulate their votes for directors unless the articles of incorporation so provide.

(c) A statement included in the articles of incorporation that "[all] [a designated voting group of] shareholders are entitled to cumulate their votes for directors" (or words of similar import) means that the shareholders designated are entitled to multiply the number of votes they are entitled to cast by the number of directors for whom they are entitled to vote and cast the product for a single candidate or distribute the product among two or more candidates.

(d) Shares otherwise entitled to vote cumulatively may not be voted cumulatively at a particular meeting unless:

(1) the meeting notice or proxy statement accompanying the notice states conspicuously that cumulative voting is authorized; or

(2) a shareholder who has the right to cumulate his votes gives notice to the corporation not less than 48 hours before the time set for the meeting of his intent to cumulate his votes during the meeting, and if one shareholder gives this notice all other shareholders in the same voting group participating in the election are entitled to cumulate their votes without giving further notice.

## Subchapter C.  Voting Trusts and Agreements

### § 7.30  Voting Trusts

(a) One or more shareholders may create a voting trust, conferring on a trustee the right to vote or otherwise act for them, by signing an agreement setting out the provisions of the trust (which may include anything consistent with its purpose) and transferring their shares to the trustee. When a voting trust agreement is signed, the trustee shall prepare a list of the names and addresses of all owners of beneficial interests in the trust, together with the number and class of shares each transferred to the trust, and deliver copies of the list and agreement to the corporation's principal office.

(b) A voting trust becomes effective on the date the first shares subject to the trust are registered in the trustee's name. A voting trust is valid for not more than 10 years after its effective date unless extended under subsection (c).

(c) All or some of the parties to a voting trust may extend it for additional terms of not more than 10 years each by signing an extension agreement and obtaining the voting trustee's written consent to the extension. An extension is valid for 10 years from the date the first shareholder signs the extension agreement. The voting trustee must deliver copies of the extension agreement and list of beneficial owners to the corporation's principal office. An extension agreement binds only those parties signing it.

### § 7.31 Voting Agreements

(a) Two or more shareholders may provide for the manner in which they will vote their shares by signing an agreement for that purpose. A voting agreement created under this section is not subject to the provisions of section 7.30.

(b) A voting agreement created under this section is specifically enforceable.

### § 7.32 Shareholder Agreements

(a) An agreement among the shareholders of a corporation that complies with this section is effective among the shareholders and the corporation even though it is inconsistent with one or more other provisions of this Act in that it:

    (1) eliminates the board of directors or restricts the discretion or powers of the board of directors;

    (2) governs the authorization or making of distributions whether or not in proportion to ownership of shares, subject to the limitations in section 6.40;

    (3) establishes who shall be directors or officers of the corporation, or their terms of office or manner of selection or removal;

    (4) governs, in general or in regard to specific matters, the exercise or division of voting power by or between the shareholders and directors or by or among any of them, including use of weighted voting rights or director proxies;

    (5) establishes the terms and conditions of any agreement for the transfer or use of property or the provision of services between the corporation and any shareholder, director, officer or employee of the corporation or among any of them;

    (6) transfers to one or more shareholders or other persons all or part of the authority to exercise the corporate powers or to manage the business and affairs of the corporation, including the resolution of any issue about which there exists a deadlock among directors or shareholders;

    (7) requires dissolution of the corporation at the request of one or more of the shareholders or upon the occurrence of a specified event or contingency; or

    (8) otherwise governs the exercise of the corporate powers or the management of the business and affairs of the corporation or the relationship among the shareholders, the directors and the corporation, or among any of them, and is not contrary to public policy.

(b) An agreement authorized by this section shall be:

    (1) set forth (A) in the articles of incorporation or bylaws and approved by all persons who are shareholders at the time of the agreement or (B) in a written agreement that is signed by all persons who are shareholders at the time of the agreement and is made known to the corporation;

    (2) subject to amendment only by all persons who are shareholders at the time of the amendment, unless the agreement provides otherwise; and

    (3) valid for 10 years, unless the agreement provides otherwise.

(c) The existence of an agreement authorized by this section shall be noted conspicuously on the front or back of each certificate for outstanding shares or on the information statement required by section 6.26(b). If at the time of the agreement the corporation has shares outstanding represented by certificates, the corporation shall recall the outstanding certificates and issue substitute certificates that comply with this subsection. The failure to note the existence of the agreement on the certificate or information statement shall not affect the validity of the agreement or any action taken pursuant to it. Any purchaser of shares who, at the time of purchase, did not have knowledge of the existence of the agreement shall be entitled to rescission of the purchase. A purchaser shall be deemed to have knowledge of the existence of the agreement if its existence is noted on the certificate or information statement for the shares in compliance with this subsection and, if the shares are not represented by a certificate, the information statement is delivered to the purchaser at or prior to the time of purchase of the shares. An action to enforce the right of rescission authorized by this subsection must be commenced within the earlier of 90 days after discovery of the existence of the agreement or two years after the time of purchase of the shares.

(d) An agreement authorized by this section shall cease to be effective when shares of the corporation are listed on a national securities exchange or regularly traded in a market maintained by one or more members of a national or affiliated securities association. If the agreement ceases to be effective for any reason, the board of directors may, if the agreement is contained or referred to in the corporation's articles of incorporation or bylaws, adopt an amendment to the articles of incorporation or bylaws, without shareholder action, to delete the agreement and any references to it.

(e) An agreement authorized by this section that limits the discretion or powers of the board of directors shall relieve the directors of, and impose upon the person or persons in whom such discretion or powers are vested, liability for acts or omissions imposed by law on directors to the extent that the discretion or powers of the directors are limited by the agreement.

(f) The existence or performance of an agreement authorized by this section shall not be a ground for imposing personal liability on any shareholder for the acts or debts of the corporation even if the agreement or its performance treats the corporation as if it were a partnership or results in failure to observe the corporate formalities otherwise applicable to the matters governed by the agreement.

(g) Incorporators or subscribers for shares may act as shareholders with respect to an agreement authorized by this section if no shares have been issued when the agreement is made.

## Subchapter D.  Derivative Proceedings

### § 7.40 Subchapter Definitions

In this subchapter:

    (1) "Derivative proceeding" means a civil suit in the right of a domestic corporation or, to the extent provided in section 7.47, in the right of a foreign corporation.

    (2) "Shareholder" includes a beneficial owner whose shares are held in a voting trust or held by a nominee on the beneficial owner's behalf.

### § 7.41 Standing

A shareholder may not commence or maintain a derivative proceeding unless the shareholder:

    (1) was a shareholder of the corporation at the time of the act or omission complained of or became a shareholder through transfer by operation of law from one who was a shareholder at that time; and

    (2) fairly and adequately represents the interests of the corporation in enforcing the right of the corporation.

## § 7.42 Demand

No shareholder may commence a derivative proceeding until:

(1) a written demand has been made upon the corporation to take suitable action; and

(2) 90 days have expired from the date the demand was made unless the shareholder has earlier been notified that the demand has been rejected by the corporation or unless irreparable injury to the corporation would result by waiting for the expiration of the 90 day period.

## § 7.43 Stay of Proceedings

If the corporation commences an inquiry into the allegations made in the demand or complaint, the court may stay any derivative proceeding for such period as the court deems appropriate.

## § 7.44 Dismissal

(a) A derivative proceeding shall be dismissed by the court on motion by the corporation if one of the groups specified in subsections (b) or (f) has determined in good faith after conducting a reasonable inquiry upon which its conclusions are based that the maintenance of the derivative proceeding is not in the best interests of the corporation.

(b) Unless a panel is appointed pursuant to subsection (f), the determination in subsection (a) shall be made by:

(1) a majority vote of independent directors present at a meeting of the board of directors if the independent directors constitute a quorum; or

(2) a majority vote of a committee consisting of two or more independent directors appointed by majority vote of independent directors present at a meeting of the board of directors, whether or not such independent directors constituted a quorum.

(c) None of the following shall by itself cause a director to be considered not independent for purposes of this section:

(1) the nomination or election of the director by persons who are defendants in the derivative proceeding or against whom action is demanded;

(2) the naming of the director as a defendant in the derivative proceeding or as a person against whom action is demanded; or

(3) the approval by the director of the act being challenged in the derivative proceeding or demand if the act resulted in no personal benefit to the director.

(d) If a derivative proceeding is commenced after a determination has been made rejecting a demand by a shareholder, the complaint shall allege with particularity facts establishing either (1) that a majority of the board of directors did not consist of independent directors at the time the determination was made or (2) that the requirements of subsection (a) have not been met.

(e) If a majority of the board of directors does not consist of independent directors at the time the determination is made, the corporation shall have the burden of proving that the requirements of subsection (a) have been met. If a majority of the board of directors consists of independent directors at the time the determination is made, the plaintiff shall have the burden of proving that the requirements of subsection (a) have not been met.

(f) The court may appoint a panel of one or more independent persons upon motion by the corporation to make a determination whether the maintenance of the derivative proceeding is in the best interests of the corporation. In such case, the plaintiff shall have the burden of proving that the requirements of subsection (a) have not been met.

## § 7.45 Discontinuance or Settlement

A derivative proceeding may not be discontinued or settled without the court's approval. If the court determines that a proposed discontinuance or settlement will substantially affect the interests of the corporation's shareholders or a class of shareholders, the court shall direct that notice be given to the shareholders affected.

## § 7.46 Payment of Expenses

On termination of the derivative proceeding the court may:

(1) order the corporation to pay the plaintiff's reasonable expenses (including counsel fees) incurred in the proceeding if it finds that the proceeding has resulted in a substantial benefit to the corporation;

(2) order the plaintiff to pay any defendant's reasonable expenses (including counsel fees) incurred in defending the proceeding if it finds that the proceeding was commenced or maintained without reasonable cause or for an improper purpose; or

(3) order a party to pay an opposing party's reasonable expenses (including counsel fees) incurred because of the filing of a pleading, motion or other paper, if it finds that the pleading, motion or other paper was not well grounded in fact, after reasonable inquiry, or warranted by existing law or a good faith argument for the extension, modification or reversal of existing law and was interposed for an improper purpose, such as to harass or to cause unnecessary delay or needless increase in the cost of litigation.

## § 7.47 Applicability to Foreign Corporations

In any derivative proceeding in the right of a foreign corporation, the matters covered by this subchapter shall be governed by the laws of the jurisdiction of incorporation of the foreign corporation except for sections 7.43, 7.45 and 7.46.

# CHAPTER 8.  DIRECTORS AND OFFICERS

## Subchapter A.  Board of Directors

### § 8.01  Requirements for and Duties of Board of Directors

(a) Except as provided is section 7.32, each corporation must have a board of directors.

(b) All corporate powers shall be exercised by or under the authority of, and the business and affairs of the corporation managed under the direction of, its board of directors, subject to any limitation set forth in the articles of incorporation or in an agreement authorized under section 7.32.

### § 8.02  Qualifications of Directors

The articles of incorporation or bylaws may prescribe qualifications for directors. A director need not be a resident of this state or a shareholder of the corporation unless the articles of incorporation or bylaws so prescribe.

### § 8.03  Number and Election of Directors

(a) A board of directors must consist of one or more individuals, with the number specified in or fixed in accordance with the articles of incorporation or bylaws.

(b) If a board of directors has power to fix or change the number of directors, the board may increase or decrease by 30 percent or less the number of directors last approved by the shareholders, but only the shareholders may increase or decrease by more than 30 percent the number of directors last approved by the shareholders.

(c) The articles of incorporation or bylaws may establish a variable range for the size of the board of directors by fixing a minimum and maximum number of directors. If a variable range is established, the number of directors may be fixed or changed from time to time, within the minimum and maximum, by the shareholders or the board of directors. After shares are issued, only the shareholders may change the range for the size of the board or change from a fixed to a variable-range size board or vice versa.

(d) Directors are elected at the first annual shareholders' meeting and at each annual meeting thereafter unless their terms are staggered under section 8.06.

## § 8.04  Election of Directors by Certain Classes of Shareholders

If the articles of incorporation authorize dividing the shares into classes, the articles may also authorize the election of all or a specified number of directors by the holders of one or more authorized classes of shares. Each class (or classes) of shares entitled to elect one or more directors is a separate voting group for purposes of the election of directors.

## § 8.05  Terms of Directors Generally

(a) The terms of the initial directors of a corporation expire at the first shareholders' meeting at which directors are elected.

(b) The terms of all other directors expire at the next annual shareholders' meeting following their election unless their terms are staggered under section 8.06.

(c) A decrease in the number of directors does not shorten an incumbent director's term.

(d) The term of a director elected to fill a vacancy expires at the next shareholders' meeting at which directors are elected.

(e) Despite the expiration of a director's term, he continues to serve until his successor is elected and qualifies or until there is a decrease in the number of directors.

## § 8.06  Staggered Terms for Directors

If there are nine or more directors, the articles of incorporation may provide for staggering their terms by dividing the total number of directors into two or three groups, with each group containing one-half or one-third of the total, as near as may be. In that event, the terms of directors in the first group expire at the first annual shareholders' meeting after their election, the terms of the second group expire at the second annual shareholders' meeting after their election, and the terms of the third group, if any, expire at the third annual shareholders' meeting after their election. At each annual shareholders' meeting held thereafter, directors shall be chosen for a term of two years or three years, as the case may be, to succeed those whose terms expire.

## § 8.07  Resignation of Directors

(a) A director may resign at any time by delivering written notice to the board of directors, its chairman, or to the corporation.

(b) A resignation is effective when the notice is delivered unless the notice specifies a later effective date.

## § 8.08  Removal of Directors by Shareholders

(a) The shareholders may remove one or more directors with or without cause unless the articles of incorporation provide that directors may be removed only for cause.

(b) If a director is elected by a voting group of shareholders, only the shareholders of that voting group may participate in the vote to remove him.

(c) If cumulative voting is authorized, a director may not be removed if the number of votes sufficient to elect him under cumulative voting is voted against his removal. If cumulative voting is not authorized, a director may be removed only if the number of votes cast to remove him exceeds the number of votes cast not to remove him.

(d) A director may be removed by the shareholders only at a meeting called for the purpose of removing him and the meeting notice must state that the purpose, or one of the purposes, of the meeting is removal of the director.

## § 8.09  Removal of Directors by Judicial Proceeding

(a) The [name or describe] court of the county where a corporation's principal office (or, if none in this state, its registered office) is located may remove a director of the corporation from office in a proceeding commenced either by the corporation or by its shareholders holding at least 10 percent of the outstanding shares of any class if the court finds that (1) the director engaged in fraudulent or dishonest conduct, or gross abuse of authority or discretion, with respect to the corporation and (2) removal is in the best interest of the corporation.

(b) The court that removes a director may bar the director from reelection for a period prescribed by the court.

(c) If shareholders commence a proceeding under subsection (a), they shall make the corporation a party defendant.

## § 8.10  Vacancy on Board

(a) Unless the articles of incorporation provide otherwise, if a vacancy occurs on a board of directors, including a vacancy resulting from an increase in the number of directors:

   (1) the shareholders may fill the vacancy;
   (2) the board of directors may fill the vacancy; or
   (3) if the directors remaining in office constitute fewer than a quorum of the board, they may fill the vacancy by the affirmative vote of a majority of all the directors remaining in office.

(b) If the vacant office was held by a director elected by a voting group of shareholders, only the holders of shares of that voting group are entitled to vote to fill the vacancy if it is filled by the shareholders.

(c) A vacancy that will occur at a specific later date (by reason of a resignation effective at a later date under section 8.07(b) or otherwise) may be filled before the vacancy occurs but the new director may not take office until the vacancy occurs.

## § 8.11  Compensation of Directors

Unless the articles of incorporation or bylaws provide otherwise, the board of directors may fix the compensation of directors.

# Subchapter B.  Meetings and Action of the Board

## § 8.20  Meetings

(a) The board of directors may hold regular or special meetings in or out of this state.

(b) Unless the articles of incorporation or bylaws provide otherwise, the board of directors may permit any or all directors to participate in a regular or special meeting by, or conduct the meeting through the use of, any means of communication by which all directors participating may simultaneously hear each other during the meeting. A director participating in a meeting by this means is deemed to be present in person at the meeting.

## § 8.21  Action Without Meeting

(a) Unless the articles of incorporation or bylaws provide otherwise, action required or permitted by this Act to be taken at a board of directors' meeting may be taken without a meeting if the action is taken by all members of the board. The action must be evidenced by one or more written consents describing the action taken, signed by each director, and included in the minutes or filed with the corporate records reflecting the action taken.

(b) Action taken under this section is effective when the last director signs the consent, unless the consent specifies a different effective date.

(c) A consent signed under this section has the effect of a meeting vote and may be described as such in any document.

### § 8.22  Notice of Meeting

(a) Unless the articles of incorporation or bylaws provide otherwise, regular meetings of the board of directors may be held without notice of the date, time, place, or purpose of the meeting.

(b) Unless the articles of incorporation or bylaws provide for a longer or shorter period, special meetings of the board of directors must be preceded by at least two days' notice of the date, time, and place of the meeting. The notice need not describe the purpose of the special meeting unless required by the articles of incorporation or bylaws.

### § 8.23  Waiver of Notice

(a) A director may waive any notice required by this Act, the articles of incorporation, or bylaws before or after the date and time stated in the notice. Except as provided by subsection (b), the waiver must be in writing, signed by the director entitled to the notice, and filed with the minutes or corporate records.

(b) A director's attendance at or participation in a meeting waives any required notice to him of the meeting unless the director at the beginning of the meeting (or promptly upon his arrival) objects to holding the meeting or transacting business at the meeting and does not thereafter vote for or assent to action taken at the meeting.

### § 8.24  Quorum and Voting

(a) Unless the articles of incorporation or bylaws require a greater number, a quorum of a board of directors consists of:

(1) a majority of the fixed number of directors if the corporation has a fixed board size; or

(2) a majority of the number of directors prescribed, or if no number is prescribed the number in office immediately before the meeting begins, if the corporation has a variable-range size board.

(b) The articles of incorporation or bylaws may authorize a quorum of a board of directors to consist of no fewer than one-third of the fixed or prescribed number of directors determined under subsection (a).

(c) If a quorum is present when a vote is taken, the affirmative vote of a majority of directors present is the act of the board of directors unless the articles of incorporation or bylaws require the vote of a greater number of directors.

(d) A director who is present at a meeting of the board of directors or a committee of the board of directors when corporate action is taken is deemed to have assented to the action taken unless: (1) he objects at the beginning of the meeting (or promptly upon his arrival) to holding it or transacting business at the meeting; (2) his dissent or abstention from the action taken is entered in the minutes of the meeting; or (3) he delivers written notice of his dissent or abstention to the presiding officer of the meeting before its adjournment or to the corporation immediately after adjournment of the meeting. The right of dissent or abstention is not available to a director who votes in favor of the action taken.

### § 8.25  Committees

(a) Unless the articles of incorporation or bylaws provide otherwise, a board of directors may create one or more committees and appoint members of the board of directors to serve on them. Each committee may have two or more members, who serve at the pleasure of the board of directors.

(b) The creation of a committee and appointment of members to it must be approved by the greater of (1) a majority of all the directors in office when the action is taken or (2) the number of directors required by the articles of incorporation or bylaws to take action under section 8.24.

(c) Sections 8.20 through 8.24, which govern meetings, action without meetings, notice and waiver of notice, and quorum and voting requirements of the board of directors, apply to committees and their members as well.

(d) To the extent specified by the board of directors or in the articles of incorporation or bylaws, each committee may exercise the authority of the board of directors under section 8.01.

(e) A committee may not, however:

(1) authorize distributions;

(2) approve or propose to shareholders action that this Act requires to be approved by shareholders;

(3) fill vacancies on the board of directors or on any of its committees;

(4) amend articles of incorporation pursuant to section 10.02;

(5) adopt, amend, or repeal bylaws;

(6) approve a plan of merger not requiring shareholder approval;

(7) authorize or approve reacquisition of shares, except according to a formula or method prescribed by the board of directors; or

(8) authorize or approve the issuance or sale or contract for sale of shares, or determine the designation and relative rights, preferences, and limitations of a class or series of shares, except that the board of directors may authorize a committee (or a senior executive officer of the corporation) to do so within limits specifically prescribed by the board of directors.

(f) The creation of, delegation of authority to, or action by a committee does not alone constitute compliance by a director with the standards of conduct described in section 8.30.

## Subchapter C.  Standards of Conduct

### § 8.30  General Standards for Directors

(a) A director shall discharge his duties as a director, including his duties as a member of a committee:

(1) in good faith;

(2) with the care an ordinarily prudent person in a like position would exercise under similar circumstances; and

(3) in a manner he reasonably believes to be in the best interests of the corporation.

(b) In discharging his duties a director is entitled to rely on information, opinions, reports, or statements, including financial statements and other financial data, if prepared or presented by:

(1) one or more officers or employees of the corporation whom the director reasonably believes to be reliable and competent in the matters presented;

(2) legal counsel, public accountants, or other persons as to matters the director reasonably believes are within the person's professional or expert competence; or

(3) a committee of the board of directors of which he is not a member if the director reasonably believes the committee merits confidence.

(c) A director is not acting in good faith if he has knowledge concerning the matter in question that makes reliance otherwise permitted by subsection (b) unwarranted.

(d) A director is not liable for any action taken as a director, or any failure to take any action, if he performed the duties of his office in compliance with this section.

## § 8.31 Director Conflict of Interest*

(a) A conflict of interest transaction is a transaction with the corporation in which a director of the corporation has a direct or indirect interest. A conflict of interest transaction is not voidable by the corporation solely because of the director's interest in the transaction if any one of the following is true:

(1) the material facts of the transaction and the director's interest were disclosed or known to the board of directors or a committee of the board of directors and the board of directors or committee authorized, approved, or ratified the transaction;

(2) the material facts of the transaction and the director's interest were disclosed or known to the shareholders entitled to vote and they authorized, approved, or ratified the transaction; or

(3) the transaction was fair to the corporation.

(b) For purposes of this section, a director of the corporation has an indirect interest in a transaction if (1) another entity in which he has a material financial interest or in which he is a general partner is a party to the transaction or (2) another entity of which he is a director, officer, or trustee is a party to the transaction and the transaction is or should be considered by the board of directors of the corporation.

(c) For purposes of subsection (a)(1), a conflict of interest transaction is authorized, approved, or ratified if it receives the affirmative vote of a majority of the directors on the board of directors (or on the committee) who have no direct or indirect interest in the transaction, but a transaction may not be authorized, approved, or ratified under this section by a single director. If a majority of the directors who have no direct or indirect interest in the transaction vote to authorize, approve, or ratify the transaction, a quorum is present for the purpose of taking action under this section. The presence of, or a vote cast by, a director with a direct or indirect interest in the transaction does not affect the validity of any action taken under subsection (a)(1) if the transaction is otherwise authorized, approved, or ratified as provided in that subsection.

(d) For purposes of subsection (a)(2), a conflict of interest transaction is authorized, approved, or ratified if it receives the vote of a majority of the shares entitled to be counted under this subsection. Shares owned by or voted under the control of a director who has a direct or indirect interest in the transaction, and shares owned by or voted under the control of an entity described in subsection (b)(1), may not be counted in a vote of shareholders to determine whether to authorize, approve, or ratify a conflict of interest transaction under subsection (a)(2). The vote of those shares, however, shall be counted in determining whether the transaction is approved under other sections of this Act. A majority of the shares, whether or not present, that are entitled to be counted in a vote on the transaction under this subsection constitutes a quorum for the purpose of taking action under this section.

## § 8.32 Loans to Directors*

(a) Except as provided by subsection (c), a corporation may not lend money to or guarantee the obligation of a director of the corporation unless:

---

*[Editors' Note: *In 1989, the Revised Model Business Corporation Act was amended by deleting Sections 8.31 and 8.32 and replacing them with a new Subchapter F, consisting of Sections 8.60 – 8.63. Because of the relatively short period of time since the adoption of Subchapter F, this volume retains the deleted sections as well as the new material.*]

(1) the particular loan or guarantee is approved by a majority of the votes represented by the outstanding voting shares of all classes, voting as a single voting group, except the votes of shares owned by or voted under the control of the benefited director; or

(2) the corporation's board of directors determines that the loan or guarantee benefits the corporation and either approves the specific loan or guarantee or a general plan authorizing loans and guarantees.

(b) The fact that a loan or guarantee is made in violation of this section does not affect the borrower's liability on the loan.

(c) This section does not apply to loans and guarantees authorized by statute regulating any special class of corporations.

## § 8.33 Liability for Unlawful Distributions

(a) A director who votes for or assents to a distribution made in violation of section 6.40 or the articles of incorporation is personally liable to the corporation for the amount of the distribution that exceeds what could have been distributed without violating section 6.40 or the articles of incorporation if it is established that he did not perform his duties in compliance with section 8.30. In any proceeding commenced under this section, a director has all of the defenses ordinarily available to a director.

(b) A director held liable under subsection (a) for an unlawful distribution is entitled to contribution:

(1) from every other director who could be held liable under subsection (a) for the unlawful distribution; and

(2) from each shareholder for the amount the shareholder accepted knowing the distribution was made in violation of section 6.40 or the articles of incorporation.

(c) A proceeding under this section is barred unless it is commenced within two years after the date on which the effect of the distribution was measured under section 6.40(e) or (g).

## Subchapter D.  Officers

### § 8.40 Required Officers

(a) A corporation has the officers described in its bylaws or appointed by the board of directors in accordance with the bylaws.

(b) A duly appointed officer may appoint one or more officers or assistant officers if authorized by the bylaws or the board of directors.

(c) The bylaws or the board of directors shall delegate to one of the officers responsibility for preparing minutes of the directors' and shareholders' meetings and for authenticating records of the corporation.

(d) The same individual may simultaneously hold more than one office in a corporation.

### § 8.41 Duties of Officers

Each officer has the authority and shall perform the duties set forth in the bylaws or, to the extent consistent with the bylaws, the duties prescribed by the board of directors or by direction of an officer authorized by the board of directors to prescribe the duties of other officers.

### § 8.42 Standards of Conduct for Officers

(a) An officer with discretionary authority shall discharge his duties under that authority:

(1) in good faith;

(2) with the care an ordinarily prudent person in a like position would exercise under similar circumstances; and

(3) in a manner he reasonably believes to be in the best interests of the corporation.

(b) In discharging his duties an officer is entitled to rely on information, opinions, reports, or statements, including financial statements and other financial data, if prepared or presented by:

(1) one or more officers or employees of the corporation whom the officer reasonably believes to be reliable and competent in the matters presented; or

(2) legal counsel, public accountants, or other persons as to matters the officer reasonably believes are within the person's professional or expert competence.

(c) An officer is not acting in good faith if he has knowledge concerning the matter in question that makes reliance otherwise permitted by subsection (b) unwarranted.

(d) An officer is not liable for any action taken as an officer, or any failure to take any action, if he performed the duties of his office in compliance with this section.

### § 8.43  Resignation and Removal of Officers

(a) An officer may resign at any time by delivering notice to the corporation. A resignation is effective when the notice is delivered unless the notice specifies a later effective date. If a resignation is made effective at a later date and the corporation accepts the future effective date, its board of directors may fill the pending vacancy before the effective date if the board of directors provides that the successor does not take office until the effective date.

(b) A board of directors may remove any officer at any time with or without cause.

### § 8.44  Contract Rights of Officers

(a) The appointment of an officer does not itself create contract rights.

(b) An officer's removal does not affect the officer's contract rights, if any, with the corporation. An officer's resignation does not affect the corporation's contract rights, if any, with the officer.

## Subchapter E.  Indemnification

### § 8.50  Subchapter Definitions

In this subchapter:

(1) "Corporation" includes any domestic or foreign predecessor entity of a corporation in a merger or other transaction in which the predecessor's existence ceased upon consummation of the transaction.

(2) "Director" means an individual who is or was a director of a corporation or an individual who, while a director of a corporation, is or was serving at the corporation's request as a director, officer, partner, trustee, employee, or agent of another foreign or domestic corporation, partnership, joint venture, trust, employee benefit plan, or other enterprise. A director is considered to be serving an employee benefit plan at the corporation's request if his duties to the corporation also impose duties on, or otherwise involve services by, him to the plan or to participants in or beneficiaries of the plan. "Director" includes, unless the context requires otherwise, the estate or personal representative of a director.

(3) "Expenses" include counsel fees.

(4) "Liability" means the obligation to pay a judgment, settlement, penalty, fine (including an excise tax assessed with respect to an employee benefit plan), or reasonable expenses incurred with respect to a proceeding.

(5) "Official capacity" means: (i) when used with respect to a director, the office of director in a corporation; and (ii) when used with respect to an individual other than a director, as contemplated in section 8.56, the office in a corporation held by the officer or the employment or agency relationship undertaken by the employee or agent on behalf of the corporation. "Official capacity" does not include service for any other foreign or domestic corporation or any partnership, joint venture, trust, employee benefit plan, or other enterprise.

(6) "Party" includes an individual who was, is, or is threatened to be made a named defendant or respondent in a proceeding.

(7) "Proceeding" means any threatened, pending, or completed action, suit, or proceeding, whether civil, criminal, administrative, or investigative and whether formal or informal.

### § 8.51  Authority to Indemnify

(a) Except as provided in subsection (d), a corporation may indemnify an individual made a party to a proceeding because he is or was a director against liability incurred in the proceeding if:

(1) he conducted himself in good faith; and

(2) he reasonably believed:

(i) in the case of conduct in his official capacity with the corporation, that his conduct was in its best interests; and

(ii) in all other cases, that his conduct was at least not opposed to its best interests; and

(3) in the case of any criminal proceeding, he had no reasonable cause to believe his conduct was unlawful.

(b) A director's conduct with respect to an employee benefit plan for a purpose he reasonably believed to be in the interests of the participants in and beneficiaries of the plan is conduct that satisfies the requirement of subsection (a)(2)(ii).

(c) The termination of a proceeding by judgment, order, settlement, conviction, or upon a plea of nolo contendere or its equivalent is not, of itself, determinative that the director did not meet the standard of conduct described in this section.

(d) A corporation may not indemnify a director under this section:

(1) in connection with a proceeding by or in the right of the corporation in which the director was adjudged liable to the corporation; or

(2) in connection with any other proceeding charging improper personal benefit to him, whether or not involving action in his official capacity, in which he was adjudged liable on the basis that personal benefit was improperly received by him.

(e) Indemnification permitted under this section in connection with a proceeding by or in the right of the corporation is limited to reasonable expenses incurred in connection with the proceeding.

### § 8.52  Mandatory Indemnification

Unless limited by its articles of incorporation, a corporation shall indemnify a director who was wholly successful, on the merits or otherwise, in the defense of any proceeding to which he was a party because he is or was a director of the corporation against reasonable expenses incurred by him in connection with the proceeding.

### § 8.53  Advance for Expenses

(a) A corporation may pay for or reimburse the reasonable expenses incurred by a director who is a party to a proceeding in advance of final disposition of the proceeding if:

(1) the director furnishes the corporation a written affirmation of his good faith belief that he has met the standard of conduct described in section 8.51;

(2) the director furnishes the corporation a written undertaking, executed personally or on his behalf, to repay the advance if it is ultimately determined that he did not meet the standard of conduct; and

(3) a determination is made that the facts then known to those making the determination would not preclude indemnification under this subchapter.

(b) The undertaking required by subsection (a)(2) must be an unlimited general obligation of the director but need not be secured and may be accepted without reference to financial ability to make repayment.

(c) Determinations and authorizations of payments under this section shall be made in the manner specified in section 8.55.

### § 8.54 Court-Ordered Indemnification

Unless a corporation's articles of incorporation provide otherwise, a director of the corporation who is a party to a proceeding may apply for indemnification to the court conducting the proceeding or to another court of competent jurisdiction. On receipt of an application, the court after giving any notice the court considers necessary may order indemnification if it determines:

(1) the director is entitled to mandatory indemnification under section 8.52, in which case the court shall also order the corporation to pay the director's reasonable expenses incurred to obtain court-ordered indemnification; or

(2) the director is fairly and reasonably entitled to indemnification in view of all the relevant circumstances, whether or not he met the standard of conduct set forth in section 8.51 or was adjudged liable as described in section 8.51(d), but if he was adjudged so liable his indemnification is limited to reasonable expenses incurred.

### § 8.55 Determination and Authorization of Indemnification

(a) A corporation may not indemnify a director under section 8.51 unless authorized in the specific case after a determination has been made that indemnification of the director is permissible in the circumstances because he has met the standard of conduct set forth in section 8.51.

(b) The determination shall be made:

(1) by the board of directors by majority vote of a quorum consisting of directors not at the time parties to the proceeding;

(2) if a quorum cannot be obtained under subdivision (1), by majority vote of a committee duly designated by the board of directors (in which designation directors who are parties may participate), consisting solely of two or more directors not at the time parties to the proceeding;

(3) by special legal counsel:

(i) selected by the board of directors or its committee in the manner prescribed in subdivision (1) or (2); or

(ii) if a quorum of the board of directors cannot be obtained under subdivision (1) and a committee cannot be designated under subdivision (2), selected by majority vote of the full board of directors (in which selection directors who are parties may participate); or

(4) by the shareholders, but shares owned by or voted under the control of directors who are at the time parties to the proceeding may not be voted on the determination.

(c) Authorization of indemnification and evaluation as to reasonableness of expenses shall be made in the same manner as the determination that indemnification is permissible, except that if the determination is made by special legal counsel, authorization of indemnification and evaluation as to reasonableness of expenses shall be made by those entitled under subsection (b)(3) to select counsel.

### § 8.56 Indemnification of Officers, Employees, and Agents

Unless a corporation's articles of incorporation provide otherwise:

(1) an officer of the corporation who is not a director is entitled to mandatory indemnification under section 8.52, and is entitled

to apply for court-ordered indemnification under section 8.54, in each case to the same extent as a director;

(2) the corporation may indemnify and advance expenses under this subchapter to an officer, employee, or agent of the corporation who is not a director to the same extent as to a director; and

(3) a corporation may also indemnify and advance expenses to an officer, employee, or agent who is not a director to the extent, consistent with public policy, that may be provided by its articles of incorporation, bylaws, general or specific action of its board of directors, or contract.

### § 8.57 Insurance

A corporation may purchase and maintain insurance on behalf of an individual who is or was a director, officer, employee, or agent of the corporation, or who, while a director, officer, employee, or agent of the corporation, is or was serving at the request of the corporation as a director, officer, partner, trustee, employee, or agent of another foreign or domestic corporation, partnership, joint venture, trust, employee benefit plan, or other enterprise, against liability asserted against or incurred by him in that capacity or arising from his status as a director, officer, employee, or agent, whether or not the corporation would have power to indemnify him against the same liability under section 8.51 or 8.52.

### § 8.58 Application of Subchapter

(a) A provision treating a corporation's indemnification of or advance for expenses to directors that is contained in its articles of incorporation, bylaws, a resolution of its shareholders or board of directors, or in a contract or otherwise, is valid only if and to the extent the provision is consistent with this subchapter. If articles of incorporation limit indemnification or advance for expenses, indemnification and advance for expenses are valid only to the extent consistent with the articles.

(b) This subchapter does not limit a corporation's power to pay or reimburse expenses incurred by a director in connection with his appearance as a witness in a proceeding at a time when he has not been made a named defendant or respondent to the proceeding.

## Subchapter F. Directors' Conflicting Interest Transactions*

### § 8.60 Subchapter Definitions

In this subchapter:

(1) "Conflicting interest" with respect to a corporation means the interest a director of the corporation has respecting a transaction effected or proposed to be effected by the corporation (or by a subsidiary of the corporation or any other entity in which the corporation has a controlling interest) if

(i) whether or not the transaction is brought before the board of directors of the corporation for action, the director knows at the time of commitment that he or a related person is a party to the transaction or has a beneficial financial interest in or so closely linked to the transaction and of such financial significance to the director or a related person that the interest would reasonably be expected to exert an

*[Editors' Note: *In 1989, the Revised Model Business Corporation Act was amended by deleting Sections 8.31 and 8.32 and replacing them with a new Subchapter F, consisting of Sections 8.60 – 8.63. Because of the relatively short period of time since the adoption of Subchapter F, this volume retains the deleted sections as well as the new material.*]

influence on the director's judgment if he were called upon to vote on the transaction; or

(ii) the transaction is brought (or is of such character and significance to the corporation that it would in the normal course be brought) before the board of directors of the corporation for action, and the director knows at the time of commitment that any of the following persons is either a party to the transaction or has a beneficial financial interest in or so closely linked to the transaction and of such financial significance to the person that the interest would reasonably be expected to exert an influence on the director's judgment if he were called upon to vote on the transaction: (A) an entity (other than the corporation) of which the director is a director, general partner, agent, or employee; (B) a person that controls one or more of the entities specified in subclause (A) or an entity that is controlled by, or is under common control with, one or more of the entities specified in subclause (A); or (C) an individual who is a general partner, principal, or employer of the director.

(2) "Director's conflicting interest transaction" with respect to a corporation means a transaction effected or proposed to be effected by the corporation (or by a subsidiary of the corporation or any other entity in which the corporation has a controlling interest) respecting which a director of the corporation has a conflicting interest.

(3) "Related person" of a director means (i) the spouse (or a parent or sibling thereof) of the director, or a child, grandchild, sibling, parent (or spouse of any thereof) of the director, or an individual having the same home as the director, or a trust or estate of which an individual specified in this clause (i) is a substantial beneficiary; or (ii) a trust, estate, incompetent, conservatee, or minor of which the director is a fiduciary.

(4) "Required disclosure" means disclosure by the director who has a conflicting interest of (i) the existence and nature of his conflicting interest, and (ii) all facts known to him respecting the subject matter of the transaction that an ordinarily prudent person would reasonably believe to be material to a judgment about whether or not to proceed with the transaction.

(5) "Time of commitment" respecting a transaction means the time when the transaction is consummated or, if made pursuant to contract, the time when the corporation (or its subsidiary or the entity in which it has a controlling interest) becomes contractually obligated so that its unilateral withdrawal from the transaction would entail significant loss, liability, or other damage.

## § 8.61   Judicial Action

(a) A transaction effected or proposed to be effected by a corporation (or by a subsidiary of the corporation or any other entity in which the corporation has a controlling interest) that is not a director's conflicting interest transaction may not be enjoined, set aside, or give rise to an award of damages or other sanctions, in a proceeding by a shareholder or by or in the right of the corporation, because a director of the corporation, or any person with whom or which he has a personal, economic, or other association, has an interest in the transaction.

(b) A director's conflicting interest transaction may not be enjoined, set aside, or give rise to an award of damages or other sanctions, in a proceeding by a shareholder or by or in the right of the corporation, because the director, or any person with whom or which he has

a personal, economic, or other association, has an interest in the transaction, if:

(1) directors' action respecting the transaction was at any time taken in compliance with section 8.62;

(2) shareholders' action respecting the transaction was at any time taken in compliance with section 8.63; or

(3) the transaction, judged according to the circumstances at the time of commitment, is established to have been fair to the corporation.

## § 8.62   Directors' Action

(a) Directors' action respecting a transaction is effective for purposes of section 8.61(b)(1) if the transaction received the affirmative vote of a majority (but no fewer than two) of those qualified directors on the board of directors or on a duly empowered committee of the board who voted on the transaction after either required disclosure to them (to the extent the information was not known by them) or compliance with subsection (b); provided that action by a committee is so effective only if:

(1) all its members are qualified directors; and

(2) its members are either all the qualified directors on the board or are appointed by the affirmative vote of a majority of the qualified directors on the board.

(b) If a director has a conflicting interest respecting a transaction, but neither he nor a related person of the director specified in section 8.60(3)(i) is a party to the transaction, and if the director has a duty under law or professional canon, or a duty of confidentiality to another person, respecting information relating to the transaction such that the director may not make the disclosure described in section 8.60(4)(ii), then disclosure is sufficient for purposes of subsection (a) if the director (1) discloses to the directors voting on the transaction the existence and nature of his conflicting interest and informs them of the character and limitations imposed by that duty before their vote on the transaction, and (2) plays no part, directly or indirectly, in their deliberations or vote.

(c) A majority (but no fewer than two) of all the qualified directors on the board of directors, or on the committee, constitutes a quorum for purposes of action that complies with this section. Directors' action that otherwise complies with this section is not affected by the presence or vote of a director who is not a qualified director.

(d) For purposes of this section, "qualified director" means, with respect to a director's conflicting interest transaction, any director who does not have either (1) a conflicting interest respecting the transaction, or (2) a familial, financial, professional, or employment relationship with a second director who does have a conflicting interest respecting the transaction, which relationship would, in the circumstances, reasonably be expected to exert an influence on the first director's judgment when voting on the transaction.

## § 8.63   Shareholders' Action

(a) Shareholders' action respecting a transaction is effective for purposes of section 8.61(b)(2) if a majority of the votes entitled to be cast by the holders of all qualified shares were cast in favor of the transaction after (1) notice to shareholders describing the director's conflicting interest transaction, (2) provision of the information referred to in subsection (d), and (3) required disclosure to the shareholders who voted on the transaction (to the extent the information was not known by them).

(b) For purposes of this section, "qualified shares" means any shares entitled to vote with respect to the director's conflicting interest transaction except shares that, to the knowledge, before the vote, of the secretary (or other officer or agent of the corporation authorized to tabulate votes), are beneficially owned (or the voting of which is controlled) by a director who has a conflicting interest respecting the transaction or by a related person of the director, or both.

(c) A majority of the votes entitled to be cast by the holders of all qualified shares constitutes a quorum for purposes of action that complies with this section. Subject to the provisions of subsections (d) and (e), shareholders' action that otherwise complies with this section is not affected by the presence of holders, or the voting, of shares that are not qualified shares.

(d) For purposes of compliance with subsection (a), a director who has a conflicting interest respecting the transaction shall, before the shareholders' vote, inform the secretary (or other office or agent of the corporation authorized to tabulate votes) of the number, and the identity of persons holding or controlling the vote, of all shares that the director knows are beneficially owned (or the voting of which is controlled) by the director or by a related person of the director, or both.

(e) If a shareholders' vote does not comply with subsection (a) solely because of a failure of a director to comply with subsection (d), and if the director establishes that his failure did not determine and was not intended by him to influence the outcome of the vote, the court may, with or without further proceedings respecting section 8.61(b)(3), take such action respecting the transaction and the director, and give such effect, if any, to the shareholders' vote, as it considers appropriate in the circumstances.

# CHAPTER 9.  [RESERVED]

# CHAPTER 10.  AMENDMENT OF ARTICLES OF INCORPORATION AND BYLAWS

## Subchapter A.  Amendment of Articles of Incorporation

### § 10.01  Authority to Amend

(a) A corporation may amend its articles of incorporation at any time to add or change a provision that is required or permitted in the articles of incorporation or to delete a provision not required in the articles of incorporation. Whether a provision is required or permitted in the articles of incorporation is determined as of the effective date of the amendment.

(b) A shareholder of the corporation does not have a vested property right resulting from any provision in the articles of incorporation, including provisions relating to management, control, capital structure, dividend entitlement, or purpose or duration of the corporation.

### § 10.02  Amendment by Board of Directors

Unless the articles of incorporation provide otherwise, a corporation's board of directors may adopt one or more amendments to the corporation's articles of incorporation without shareholder action:

(1) to extend the duration of the corporation if it was incorporated at a time when limited duration was required by law;

(2) to delete the names and addresses of the initial directors;

(3) to delete the name and address of the initial registered agent or registered office, if a statement of change is on file with the secretary of state;

(4) to change each issued and unissued authorized share of an outstanding class into a greater number of whole shares if the corporation has only shares of that class outstanding;

(5) to change the corporate name by substituting the word "corporation," "incorporated," "company," "limited," or the abbreviation "corp.," "inc.," "co.," or "ltd.," for a similar word or abbreviation in the name, or by adding, deleting, or changing a geographical attribution for the name; or

(6) to make any other change expressly permitted by this Act to be made without shareholder action.

### § 10.03  Amendment by Board of Directors and Shareholders

(a) A corporation's board of directors may propose one or more amendments to the articles of incorporation for submission to the shareholders.

(b) For the amendment to be adopted:

(1) the board of directors must recommend the amendment to the shareholders unless the board of directors determines that because of conflict of interest or other special circumstances it should make no recommendation and communicates the basis for its determination to the shareholders with the amendment; and

(2) the shareholders entitled to vote on the amendment must approve the amendment as provided in subsection (e).

(c) The board of directors may condition its submission of the proposed amendment on any basis.

(d) The corporation shall notify each shareholder, whether or not entitled to vote, of the proposed shareholders' meeting in accordance with section 7.05. The notice of meeting must also state that the purpose, or one of the purposes, of the meeting is to consider the proposed amendment and contain or be accompanied by a copy or summary of the amendment.

(e) Unless this Act, the articles of incorporation, or the board of directors (acting pursuant to subsection (c)) require a greater vote or a vote by voting groups, the amendment to be adopted must be approved by:

(1) a majority of the votes entitled to be cast on the amendment by any voting group with respect to which the amendment would create dissenters' rights; and

(2) the votes required by sections 7.25 and 7.26 by every other voting group entitled to vote on the amendment.

### § 10.04  Voting on Amendments by Voting Groups

(a) The holders of the outstanding shares of a class are entitled to vote as a separate voting group (if shareholder voting is otherwise required by this Act) on a proposed amendment if the amendment would:

(1) increase or decrease the aggregate number of authorized shares of the class;

(2) effect an exchange or reclassification of all or part of the shares of the class into shares of another class;

(3) effect an exchange or reclassification, or create the right of exchange, of all or part of the shares of another class into shares of the class;

(4) change the designation, rights, preferences, or limitations of all or part of the shares of the class;

(5) change the shares of all or part of the class into a different number of shares of the same class;

(6) create a new class of shares having rights or preferences with respect to distributions or to dissolution that are prior, superior, or substantially equal to the shares of the class;

(7) increase the rights, preferences, or number of authorized shares of any class that, after giving effect to the amendment, have rights or preferences with respect to distributions or to

dissolution that are prior, superior, or substantially equal to the shares of the class;

(8) limit or deny an existing preemptive right of all or part of the shares of the class; or

(9) cancel or otherwise affect rights to distributions or dividends that have accumulated but not yet been declared on all or part of the shares of the class.

(b) If a proposed amendment would affect a series of a class of shares in one or more of the ways described in subsection (a), the shares of that series are entitled to vote as a separate voting group on the proposed amendment.

(c) If a proposed amendment that entitles two or more series of shares to vote as separate voting groups under this section would affect those two or more series in the same or a substantially similar way, the shares of all the series so affected must vote together as a single voting group on the proposed amendment.

(d) A class or series of shares is entitled to the voting rights granted by this section although the articles of incorporation provide that the shares are nonvoting shares.

### § 10.05  Amendment Before Issuance of Shares

If a corporation has not yet issued shares, its incorporators or board of directors may adopt one or more amendments to the corporation's articles of incorporation.

### § 10.06  Articles of Amendment

A corporation amending its articles of incorporation shall deliver to the secretary of state for filing articles of amendment setting forth:

(1) the name of the corporation;

(2) the text of each amendment adopted;

(3) if an amendment provides for an exchange, reclassification, or cancellation of issued shares, provisions for implementing the amendment if not contained in the amendment itself;

(4) the date of each amendment's adoption;

(5) if an amendment was adopted by the incorporators or board of directors without shareholder action, a statement to that effect and that shareholder action was not required;

(6) if an amendment was approved by the shareholders:

(i) the designation, number of outstanding shares, number of votes entitled to be cast by each voting group entitled to vote separately on the amendment, and number of votes of each voting group indisputably represented at the meeting;

(ii) either the total number of votes cast for and against the amendment by each voting group entitled to vote separately on the amendment or the total number of undisputed votes cast for the amendment by each voting group and a statement that the number cast for the amendment by each voting group was sufficient for approval by that voting group.

### § 10.07  Restated Articles of Incorporation

(a) A corporation's board of directors may restate its articles of incorporation at any time with or without shareholder action.

(b) The restatement may include one or more amendments to the articles. If the restatement includes an amendment requiring shareholder approval, it must be adopted as provided in section 10.03.

(c) If the board of directors submits a restatement for shareholder action, the corporation shall notify each shareholder, whether or not entitled to vote, of the proposed shareholders' meeting in accordance with section 7.05. The notice must also state that the purpose, or one of the purposes, of the meeting is to consider the proposed restatement and contain or be accompanied by a copy of the restatement that identifies any amendment or other change it would make in the articles.

(d) A corporation restating its articles of incorporation shall deliver to the secretary of state for filing articles of restatement setting forth the name of the corporation and the text of the restated articles of incorporation together with a certificate setting forth:

(1) whether the restatement contains an amendment to the articles requiring shareholder approval and, if it does not, that the board of directors adopted the restatement; or

(2) if the restatement contains an amendment to the articles requiring shareholder approval, the information required by section 10.06.

(e) Duly adopted restated articles of incorporation supersede the original articles of incorporation and all amendments to them.

(f) The secretary of state may certify restated articles of incorporation, as the articles of incorporation currently in effect, without including the certificate information required by subsection (d).

### § 10.08  Amendment Pursuant to Reorganization

(a) A corporation's articles of incorporation may be amended without action by the board of directors or shareholders to carry out a plan of reorganization ordered or decreed by a court of competent jurisdiction under federal statute if the articles of incorporation after amendment contain only provisions required or permitted by section 2.02.

(b) The individual or individuals designated by the court shall deliver to the secretary of state for filing articles of amendment setting forth:

(1) the name of the corporation;

(2) the text of each amendment approved by the court;

(3) the date of the court's order or decree approving the articles of amendment;

(4) the title of the reorganization proceeding in which the order or decree was entered; and

(5) a statement that the court had jurisdiction of the proceeding under federal statute.

(c) Shareholders of a corporation undergoing reorganization do not have dissenters' rights except as and to the extent provided in the reorganization plan.

(d) This section does not apply after entry of a final decree in the reorganization proceeding even though the court retains jurisdiction of the proceeding for limited purposes unrelated to consummation of the reorganization plan.

### § 10.09  Effect of Amendment

An amendment to articles of incorporation does not affect a cause of action existing against or in favor of the corporation, a proceeding to which the corporation is a party, or the existing rights of persons other than shareholders of the corporation. An amendment changing a corporation's name does not abate a proceeding brought by or against the corporation in its former name.

## Subchapter B.  Amendment of Bylaws

### § 10.20  Amendment by Board of Directors or Shareholders

(a) A corporation's board of directors may amend or repeal the corporation's bylaws unless:

(1) the articles of incorporation or this Act reserve this power exclusively to the shareholders in whole or part; or

(2) the shareholders in amending or repealing a particular bylaw provide expressly that the board of directors may not amend or repeal that bylaw.

(b) A corporation's shareholders may amend or repeal the corporation's bylaws even though the bylaws may also be amended or repealed by its board of directors.

### § 10.21  Bylaw Increasing Quorum or Voting Requirement for Shareholders

(a) If expressly authorized by the articles of incorporation, the shareholders may adopt or amend a bylaw that fixes a greater quorum or voting requirement for shareholders (or voting groups of shareholders) than is required by this Act. The adoption or amendment of a bylaw that adds, changes, or deletes a greater quorum or voting requirement for shareholders must meet the same quorum requirement and be adopted by the same vote and voting groups required to take action under the quorum and voting requirement then in effect or proposed to be adopted, whichever is greater.

(b) A bylaw that fixes a greater quorum or voting requirement for shareholders under subsection (a) may not be adopted, amended, or repealed by the board of directors.

### § 10.22  Bylaw Increasing Quorum or Voting Requirement for Directors

(a) A bylaw that fixes a greater quorum or voting requirement for the board of directors may be amended or repealed:

(1) if originally adopted by the shareholders, only by the shareholders;

(2) if originally adopted by the board of directors, either by the shareholders or by the board of directors.

(b) A bylaw adopted or amended by the shareholders that fixes a greater quorum or voting requirement for the board of directors may provide that it may be amended or repealed only by a specified vote of either the shareholders or the board of directors.

(c) Action by the board of directors under subsection (a)(2) to adopt or amend a bylaw that changes the quorum or voting requirement for the board of directors must meet the same quorum requirement and be adopted by the same vote required to take action under the quorum and voting requirement then in effect or proposed to be adopted, whichever is greater.

## CHAPTER 11.  MERGER AND SHARE EXCHANGE

### § 11.01  Merger

(a) One or more corporations may merge into another corporation if the board of directors of each corporation adopts and its shareholders (if required by section 11.03) approve a plan of merger.

(b) The plan of merger must set forth:

(1) the name of each corporation planning to merge and the name of the surviving corporation into which each other corporation plans to merge;

(2) the terms and conditions of the merger; and

(3) the manner and basis of converting the shares of each corporation into shares, obligations, or other securities of the surviving or any other corporation or into cash or other property in whole or part.

(c) The plan of merger may set forth:

(1) amendments to the articles of incorporation of the surviving corporation; and

(2) other provisions relating to the merger.

### § 11.02  Share Exchange

(a) A corporation may acquire all of the outstanding shares of one or more classes or series of another corporation if the board of directors of each corporation adopts and its shareholders (if required by section 11.03) approve the exchange.

(b) The plan of exchange must set forth:

(1) the name of the corporation whose shares will be acquired and the name of the acquiring corporation;

(2) the terms and conditions of the exchange;

(3) the manner and basis of exchanging the shares to be acquired for shares, obligations, or other securities of the acquiring or any other corporation or for cash or other property in whole or part.

(c) The plan of exchange may set forth other provisions relating to the exchange.

(d) This section does not limit the power of a corporation to acquire all or part of the shares of one or more classes or series of another corporation through a voluntary exchange or otherwise.

### § 11.03  Action on Plan

(a) After adopting a plan of merger or share exchange, the board of directors of each corporation party to the merger, and the board of directors of the corporation whose shares will be acquired in the share exchange, shall submit the plan of merger (except as provided in subsection (g)) or share exchange for approval by its shareholders.

(b) For a plan of merger or share exchange to be approved:

(1) the board of directors must recommend the plan of merger or share exchange to the shareholders, unless the board of directors determines that because of conflict of interest or other special circumstances it should make no recommendation and communicates the basis for its determination to the shareholders with the plan; and

(2) the shareholders entitled to vote must approve the plan.

(c) The board of directors may condition its submission of the proposed merger or share exchange on any basis.

(d) The corporation shall notify each shareholder, whether or not entitled to vote, of the proposed shareholders' meeting in accordance with section 7.05. The notice must also state that the purpose, or one of the purposes, of the meeting is to consider the plan of merger or share exchange and contain or be accompanied by a copy or summary of the plan.

(e) Unless this Act, the articles of incorporation, or the board of directors (acting pursuant to subsection (c)) require a greater vote or a vote by voting groups, the plan of merger or share exchange to be authorized must be approved by each voting group entitled to vote separately on the plan by a majority of all the votes entitled to be cast on the plan by that voting group.

(f) Separate voting by voting groups is required:

(1) on a plan of merger if the plan contains a provision that, if contained in a proposed amendment to articles of incorporation, would require action by one or more separate voting groups on the proposed amendment under section 10.04;

(2) on a plan of share exchange by each class or series of shares included in the exchange, with each class or series constituting a separate voting group.

(g) Action by the shareholders of the surviving corporation on a plan of merger is not required if:

(1) the articles of incorporation of the surviving corporation will not differ (except for amendments enumerated in section 10.02) from its articles before the merger;

(2) each shareholder of the surviving corporation whose shares were outstanding immediately before the effective date of the merger will hold the same number of shares, with identical designations, preferences, limitations, and relative rights, immediately after;

(3) the number of voting shares outstanding immediately after the merger, plus the number of voting shares issuable as a result of the merger (either by the conversion of securities issued pursuant to the merger or the exercise of rights and warrants issued pursuant to the merger), will not exceed by more than 20 percent the total number of voting shares of the surviving corporation outstanding immediately before the merger; and

(4) the number of participating shares outstanding immediately after the merger, plus the number of participating shares issuable as a result of the merger (either by the conversion of securities issued pursuant to the merger or the exercise of rights and warrants issued pursuant to the merger), will not exceed by more than 20 percent the total number of participating shares outstanding immediately before the merger.

(h) As used in subsection (g):

(1) "Participating shares" means shares that entitle their holders to participate without limitation in distributions.

(2) "Voting shares" means shares that entitle their holders to vote unconditionally in elections of directors.

(i) After a merger or share exchange is authorized, and at any time before articles of merger or share exchange are filed, the planned merger or share exchange may be abandoned (subject to any contractual rights), without further shareholder action, in accordance with the procedure set forth in the plan of merger or share exchange or, if none is set forth, in the manner determined by the board of directors.

## § 11.04  Merger of Subsidiary

(a) A parent corporation owning at least 90 percent of the outstanding shares of each class of a subsidiary corporation may merge the subsidiary into itself without approval of the shareholders of the parent or subsidiary.

(b) The board of directors of the parent shall adopt a plan of merger that sets forth:

(1) the names of the parent and subsidiary; and

(2) the manner and basis of converting the shares of the subsidiary into shares, obligations, or other securities of the parent or any other corporation or into cash or other property in whole or part.

(c) The parent shall mail a copy or summary of the plan of merger to each shareholder of the subsidiary who does not waive the mailing requirement in writing.

(d) The parent may not deliver articles of merger to the secretary of state for filing until at least 30 days after the date it mailed a copy of the plan of merger to each shareholder of the subsidiary who did not waive the mailing requirement.

(e) Articles of merger under this section may not contain amendments to the articles of incorporation of the parent corporation (except for amendments enumerated in section 10.02).

## § 11.05  Articles of Merger or Share Exchange

(a) After a plan of merger or share exchange is approved by the shareholders, or adopted by the board of directors if shareholder approval is not required, the surviving or acquiring corporation shall deliver to the secretary of state for filing articles of merger or share exchange setting forth:

(1) the plan of merger or share exchange;

(2) if shareholder approval was not required, a statement to that effect;

(3) if approval of the shareholders of one or more corporations party to the merger or share exchange was required:

(i) the designation, number of outstanding shares, and number of votes entitled to be cast by each voting group entitled to vote separately on the plan as to each corporation; and

(ii) either the total number of votes cast for and against the plan by each voting group entitled to vote separately on the plan or the total number of undisputed votes cast for the plan separately by each voting group and a statement that the number cast for the plan by each voting group was sufficient for approval by that voting group.

(b) Unless a delayed effective date is specified, a merger or share exchange takes effect when the articles of merger or share exchange are filed.

## § 11.06  Effect of Merger or Share Exchange

(a) When a merger takes effect:

(1) every other corporation party to the merger merges into the surviving corporation and the separate existence of every corporation except the surviving corporation ceases;

(2) the title to all real estate and other property owned by each corporation party to the merger is vested in the surviving corporation without reversion or impairment;

(3) the surviving corporation has all liabilities of each corporation party to the merger;

(4) a proceeding pending against any corporation party to the merger may be continued as if the merger did not occur or the surviving corporation may be substituted in the proceeding for the corporation whose existence ceased;

(5) the articles of incorporation of the surviving corporation are amended to the extent provided in the plan of merger; and

(6) the shares of each corporation party to the merger that are to be converted into shares, obligations, or other securities of the surviving or any other corporation or into cash or other property are converted and the former holders of the shares are entitled only to the rights provided in the articles of merger or to their rights under chapter 13.

(b) When a share exchange takes effect, the shares of each acquired corporation are exchanged as provided in the plan, and the former holders of the shares are entitled only to the exchange rights provided in the articles of share exchange or to their rights under chapter 13.

## § 11.07  Merger or Share Exchange With Foreign Corporation

(a) One or more foreign corporations may merge or enter into a share exchange with one or more domestic corporations if:

(1) in a merger, the merger is permitted by the law of the state or country under whose law each foreign corporation is incorporated and each foreign corporation complies with that law in effecting the merger;

(2) in a share exchange, the corporation whose shares will be acquired is a domestic corporation, whether or not a share exchange is permitted by the law of the state or country under whose law the acquiring corporation is incorporated;

(3) the foreign corporation complies with section 11.05 if it is the surviving corporation of the merger or acquiring corporation of the share exchange; and

(4) each domestic corporation complies with the applicable provisions of sections 11.01 through 11.04 and, if it is the surviving corporation of the merger or acquiring corporation of the share exchange, with section 11.05.

(b) Upon the merger or share exchange taking effect, the surviving foreign corporation of a merger and the acquiring foreign corporation of a share exchange is deemed:

(1) to appoint the secretary of state as its agent for service of process in a proceeding to enforce any obligation or the rights of dissenting shareholders of each domestic corporation party to the merger or share exchange; and

(2) to agree that it will promptly pay to the dissenting shareholders of each domestic corporation party to the merger or share exchange the amount, if any, to which they are entitled under chapter 13.

(c) This section does not limit the power of a foreign corporation to acquire all or part of the shares of one or more classes or series of a domestic corporation through a voluntary exchange or otherwise.

## CHAPTER 12.  SALE OF ASSETS

### § 12.01  Sale of Assets in Regular Course of Business and Mortgage of Assets

(a) A corporation may, on the terms and conditions and for the consideration determined by the board of directors:

(1) sell, lease, exchange, or otherwise dispose of all, or substantially all, of its property in the usual and regular course of business,

(2) mortgage, pledge, dedicate to the repayment of indebtedness (whether with or without recourse), or otherwise encumber any or all of its property whether or not in the usual and regular course of business, or

(3) transfer any or all of its property to a corporation all the shares of which are owned by the corporation.

(b) Unless the articles of incorporation require it, approval by the shareholders of a transaction described in subsection (a) is not required.

### § 12.02  Sale of Assets Other Than in Regular Course of Business

(a) A corporation may sell, lease, exchange, or otherwise dispose of all, or substantially all, of its property (with or without the good will), otherwise than in the usual and regular course of business, on the terms and conditions and for the consideration determined by the corporation's board of directors, if the board of directors proposes and its shareholders approve the proposed transaction.

(b) For a transaction to be authorized:

(1) the board of directors must recommend the proposed transaction to the shareholders unless the board of directors determines that because of conflict of interest or other special circumstances it should make no recommendation and communicates the basis for its determination to the shareholders with the submission of the proposed transaction; and

(2) the shareholders entitled to vote must approve the transaction.

(c) The board of directors may condition its submission of the proposed transaction on any basis.

(d) The corporation shall notify each shareholder, whether or not entitled to vote, of the proposed shareholders' meeting in accordance with section 7.05. The notice must also state that the purpose, or one of the purposes, of the meeting is to consider the sale, lease, exchange, or other disposition of all, or substantially all, the property of the corporation and contain or be accompanied by a description of the transaction.

(e) Unless the articles of incorporation or the board of directors (acting pursuant to subsection (c)) require a greater vote or a vote by voting groups, the transaction to be authorized must be approved by a majority of all the votes entitled to be cast on the transaction.

(f) After a sale, lease, exchange, or other disposition of property is authorized, the transaction may be abandoned (subject to any contractual rights) without further shareholder action.

(g) A transaction that constitutes a distribution is governed by section 6.40 and not by this section.

## CHAPTER 13.  DISSENTERS' RIGHTS

### Subchapter A.  Right to Dissent and Obtain Payment for Shares

#### § 13.01  Definitions

In this chapter:

(1) "Corporation" means the issuer of the shares held by a dissenter before the corporate action, or the surviving or acquiring corporation by merger or share exchange of that issuer.

(2) "Dissenter" means a shareholder who is entitled to dissent from corporate action under section 13.02 and who exercises that right when and in the manner required by sections 13.20 through 13.28.

(3) "Fair value," with respect to a dissenter's shares, means the value of the shares immediately before the effectuation of the corporate action to which the dissenter objects, excluding any appreciation or depreciation in anticipation of the corporate action unless exclusion would be inequitable.

(4) "Interest" means interest from the effective date of the corporate action until the date of payment, at the average rate currently paid by the corporation on its principal bank loans or, if none, at a rate that is fair and equitable under all the circumstances.

(5) "Record shareholder" means the person in whose name shares are registered in the records of a corporation or the beneficial owner of shares to the extent of the rights granted by a nominee certificate on file with a corporation.

(6) "Beneficial shareholder" means the person who is a beneficial owner of shares held in a voting trust or by a nominee as the record shareholder.

(7) "Shareholder" means the record shareholder or the beneficial shareholder.

#### § 13.02  Right to Dissent

(a) A shareholder is entitled to dissent from, and obtain payment of the fair value of his shares in the event of, any of the following corporate actions:

(1) consummation of a plan of merger to which the corporation is a party (i) if shareholder approval is required for the merger by section 11.03 or the articles of incorporation and the shareholder is entitled to vote on the merger or (ii) if the corporation is a subsidiary that is merged with its parent under section 11.04;

(2) consummation of a plan of share exchange to which the corporation is a party as the corporation whose shares will be acquired, if the shareholder is entitled to vote on the plan;

(3) consummation of a sale or exchange of all, or substantially all, of the property of the corporation other than in the usual and regular course of business, if the shareholder is entitled to vote on the sale or exchange, including a sale in dissolution, but not including a sale pursuant to court order or a sale for cash

pursuant to a plan by which all or substantially all of the net proceeds of the sale will be distributed to the shareholders within one year after the date of sale;

(4) an amendment of the articles of incorporation that materially and adversely affects rights in respect of a dissenter's shares because it:

(i) alters or abolishes a preferential right of the shares;

(ii) creates, alters, or abolishes a right in respect of redemption, including a provision respecting a sinking fund for the redemption or repurchase, of the shares;

(iii) alters or abolishes a preemptive right of the holder of the shares to acquire shares or other securities;

(iv) excludes or limits the right of the shares to vote on any matter, or to cumulate votes, other than a limitation by dilution through issuance of shares or other securities with similar voting rights; or

(v) reduces the number of shares owned by the shareholder to a fraction of a share if the fractional share so created is to be acquired for cash under section 6.04; or

(5) any corporate action taken pursuant to a shareholder vote to the extent the articles of incorporation, bylaws, or a resolution of the board of directors provides that voting or nonvoting shareholders are entitled to dissent and obtain payment for their shares.

(b) A shareholder entitled to dissent and obtain payment for his shares under this chapter may not challenge the corporate action creating his entitlement unless the action is unlawful or fraudulent with respect to the shareholder or the corporation.

### § 13.03 Dissent by Nominees and Beneficial Owners

(a) A record shareholder may assert dissenters' rights as to fewer than all the shares registered in his name only if he dissents with respect to all shares beneficially owned by any one person and notifies the corporation in writing of the name and address of each person on whose behalf he asserts dissenters' rights. The rights of a partial dissenter under this subsection are determined as if the shares as to which he dissents and his other shares were registered in the names of different shareholders.

(b) A beneficial shareholder may assert dissenters' rights as to shares held on his behalf only if:

(1) he submits to the corporation the record shareholder's written consent to the dissent not later than the time the beneficial shareholder asserts dissenters' rights; and

(2) he does so with respect to all shares of which he is the beneficial shareholder or over which he has power to direct the vote.

## Subchapter B. Procedure for Exercise of Dissenters' Rights

### § 13.20 Notice of Dissenters' Rights

(a) If proposed corporate action creating dissenters' rights under section 13.02 is submitted to a vote at a shareholders' meeting, the meeting notice must state that shareholders are or may be entitled to assert dissenters' rights under this chapter and be accompanied by a copy of this chapter.

(b) If corporate action creating dissenters' rights under section 13.02 is taken without a vote of shareholders, the corporation shall notify in writing all shareholders entitled to assert dissenters' rights that the action was taken and send them the dissenters' notice described in section 13.22.

### § 13.21 Notice of Intent to Demand Payment

(a) If proposed corporate action creating dissenters' rights under section 13.02 is submitted to a vote at a shareholders' meeting, a shareholder who wishes to assert dissenters' rights (1) must deliver to the corporation before the vote is taken written notice of his intent to demand payment for his shares if the proposed action is effectuated and (2) must not vote his shares in favor of the proposed action.

(b) A shareholder who does not satisfy the requirements of subsection (a) is not entitled to payment for his shares under this chapter.

### § 13.22 Dissenters' Notice

(a) If proposed corporate action creating dissenters' rights under section 13.02 is authorized at a shareholders' meeting, the corporation shall deliver a written dissenters' notice to all shareholders who satisfied the requirements of section 13.21.

(b) The dissenters' notice must be sent no later than 10 days after the corporate action was taken, and must:

(1) state where the payment demand must be sent and where and when certificates for certificated shares must be deposited;

(2) inform holders of uncertificated shares to what extent transfer of the shares will be restricted after the payment demand is received;

(3) supply a form for demanding payment that includes the date of the first announcement to news media or to shareholders of the terms of the proposed corporate action and requires that the person asserting dissenters' rights certify whether or not he acquired beneficial ownership of the shares before that date;

(4) set a date by which the corporation must receive the payment demand, which date may not be fewer than 30 nor more than 60 days after the date the subsection (a) notice is delivered; and

(5) be accompanied by a copy of this chapter.

### § 13.23 Duty to Demand Payment

(a) A shareholder sent a dissenters' notice described in section 13.22 must demand payment, certify whether he acquired beneficial ownership of the shares before the date required to be set forth in the dissenter's notice pursuant to section 13.22(b)(3), and deposit his certificates in accordance with the terms of the notice.

(b) The shareholder who demands payment and deposits his shares under section (a) retains all other rights of a shareholder until these rights are cancelled or modified by the taking of the proposed corporate action.

(c) A shareholder who does not demand payment or deposit his share certificates where required, each by the date set in the dissenters' notice, is not entitled to payment for his shares under this chapter.

### § 13.24 Share Restrictions

(a) The corporation may restrict the transfer of uncertificated shares from the date the demand for their payment is received until the proposed corporate action is taken or the restrictions released under section 13.26.

(b) The person for whom dissenters' rights are asserted as to uncertificated shares retains all other rights of a shareholder until these rights are cancelled or modified by the taking of the proposed corporate action.

### § 13.25 Payment

(a) Except as provided in section 13.27, as soon as the proposed corporate action is taken, or upon receipt of a payment demand, the corporation shall pay each dissenter who complied with section 13.23 the amount the corporation estimates to be the fair value of his shares, plus accrued interest.

(b) The payment must be accompanied by:
    (1) the corporation's balance sheet as of the end of a fiscal year ending not more than 16 months before the date of payment, an income statement for that year, a statement of changes in shareholders' equity for that year, and the latest available interim financial statements, if any;
    (2) a statement of the corporation's estimate of the fair value of the shares;
    (3) an explanation of how the interest was calculated;
    (4) a statement of the dissenter's right to demand payment under section 13.28; and
    (5) a copy of this chapter.

### § 13.26  Failure to Take Action

(a) If the corporation does not take the proposed action within 60 days after the date set for demanding payment and depositing share certificates, the corporation shall return the deposited certificates and release the transfer restrictions imposed on uncertificated shares.

(b) If after returning deposited certificates and releasing transfer restrictions, the corporation takes the proposed action, it must send a new dissenters' notice under section 13.22 and repeat the payment demand procedure.

### § 13.27  After-Acquired Shares

(a) A corporation may elect to withhold payment required by section 13.25 from a dissenter unless he was the beneficial owner of the shares before the date set forth in the dissenters' notice as the date of the first announcement to news media or to shareholders of the terms of the proposed corporate action.

(b) To the extent the corporation elects to withhold payment under subsection (a), after taking the proposed corporate action, it shall estimate the fair value of the shares, plus accrued interest, and shall pay this amount to each dissenter who agrees to accept it in full satisfaction of his demand. The corporation shall send with its offer a statement of its estimate of the fair value of the shares, an explanation of how the interest was calculated, and a statement of the dissenter's right to demand payment under section 13.28.

### § 13.28  Procedure if Shareholder Dissatisfied With Payment or Offer

(a) A dissenter may notify the corporation in writing of his own estimate of the fair value of his shares and amount of interest due, and demand payment of his estimate (less any payment under section 13.25), or reject the corporation's offer under section 13.27 and demand payment of the fair value of his shares and interest due, if:
    (1) the dissenter believes that the amount paid under section 13.25 or offered under section 13.27 is less than the fair value of his shares or that the interest due is incorrectly calculated;
    (2) the corporation fails to make payment under section 13.25 within 60 days after the date set for demanding payment; or
    (3) the corporation, having failed to take the proposed action, does not return the deposited certificates or release the transfer restrictions imposed on uncertificated shares within 60 days after the date set for demanding payment.

(b) A dissenter waives his right to demand payment under this section unless he notifies the corporation of his demand in writing under subsection (a) within 30 days after the corporation made or offered payment for his shares.

## Subchapter C.  Judicial Appraisal of Shares

### § 13.30  Court Action

(a) If a demand for payment under section 13.28 remains unsettled, the corporation shall commence a proceeding within 60 days after receiving the payment demand and petition the court to determine the fair value of the shares and accrued interest. If the corporation does not commence the proceeding within the 60-day period, it shall pay each dissenter whose demand remains unsettled the amount demanded.

(b) The corporation shall commence the proceeding in the [name or describe] court of the county where a corporation's principal office (or, if none in this state, its registered office) is located. If the corporation is a foreign corporation without a registered office in this state, it shall commence the proceeding in the county in this state where the registered office of the domestic corporation merged with or whose shares were acquired by the foreign corporation was located.

(c) The corporation shall make all dissenters (whether or not residents of this state) whose demands remain unsettled parties to the proceeding as in an action against their shares and all parties must be served with a copy of the petition. Nonresidents may be served by registered or certified mail or by publication as provided by law.

(d) The jurisdiction of the court in which the proceeding is commenced under subsection (b) is plenary and exclusive. The court may appoint one or more persons as appraisers to receive evidence and recommend decision on the question of fair value. The appraisers have the powers described in the order appointing them, or in any amendment to it. The dissenters are entitled to the same discovery rights as parties in other civil proceedings.

(e) Each dissenter made a party to the proceeding is entitled to judgment (1) for the amount, if any, by which the court finds the fair value of his shares, plus interest, exceeds the amount paid by the corporation or (2) for the fair value, plus accrued interest, of his after-acquired shares for which the corporation elected to withhold payment under section 13.27.

### § 13.31  Court Costs and Counsel Fees

(a) The court in an appraisal proceeding commenced under section 13.30 shall determine all costs of the proceeding, including the reasonable compensation and expenses of appraisers appointed by the court. The court shall assess the costs against the corporation, except that the court may assess costs against all or some of the dissenters, in amounts the court finds equitable, to the extent the court finds dissenters acted arbitrarily, vexatiously, or not in good faith in demanding payment under section 13.28.

(b) The court may also assess the fees and expenses of counsel and experts for the respective parties, in amounts the court finds equitable:
    (1) against the corporation and in favor of any or all dissenters if the court finds the corporation did not substantially comply with the requirements of sections 13.20 through 13.28; or
    (2) against either the corporation or a dissenter, in favor of any other party, if the court finds that the party against whom the fees and expenses are assessed acted arbitrarily, vexatiously, or not in good faith with respect to the rights provided by this chapter.

(c) If the court finds that the services of counsel for any dissenter were of substantial benefit to other dissenters similarly situated, and that the fees for those services should not be assessed against the corporation, the court may award to these counsel reasonable fees to be paid out of the amounts awarded the dissenters who were benefited.

# CHAPTER 14.  DISSOLUTION

## Subchapter A.  Voluntary Dissolution

### § 14.01  Dissolution by Incorporators or Initial Directors

A majority of the incorporators or initial directors of a corporation that has not issued shares or has not commenced business may dissolve the corporation by delivering to the secretary of state for filing articles of dissolution that set forth:

    (1)  the name of the corporation;

    (2)  the date of its incorporation;

    (3)  either (i) that none of the corporation's shares has been issued or (ii) that the corporation has not commenced business;

    (4)  that no debt of the corporation remains unpaid;

    (5)  that the net assets of the corporation remaining after winding up have been distributed to the shareholders, if shares were issued; and

    (6)  that a majority of the incorporators or initial directors authorized the dissolution.

### § 14.02  Dissolution by Board of Directors and Shareholders

(a)  A corporation's board of directors may propose dissolution for submission to the shareholders.

(b)  For a proposal to dissolve to be adopted:

    (1)  the board of directors must recommend dissolution to the shareholders unless the board of directors determines that because of conflict of interest or other special circumstances it should make no recommendation and communicates the basis for its determination to the shareholders; and

    (2)  the shareholders entitled to vote must approve the proposal to dissolve as provided in subsection (e).

(c)  The board of directors may condition its submission of the proposal for dissolution on any basis.

(d)  The corporation shall notify each shareholder, whether or not entitled to vote, of the proposed shareholders' meeting in accordance with section 7.05. The notice must also state that the purpose, or one of the purposes, of the meeting is to consider dissolving the corporation.

(e)  Unless the articles of incorporation or the board of directors (acting pursuant to subsection (c)) require a greater vote or a vote by voting groups, the proposal to dissolve to be adopted must be approved by a majority of all the votes entitled to be cast on that proposal.

### § 14.03  Articles of Dissolution

(a)  At any time after dissolution is authorized, the corporation may dissolve by delivering to the secretary of state for filing articles of dissolution setting forth:

    (1)  the name of the corporation;

    (2)  the date dissolution was authorized;

    (3)  if dissolution was approved by the shareholders:

        (i)  the number of votes entitled to be cast on the proposal to dissolve; and

        (ii)  either the total number of votes cast for and against dissolution or the total number of undisputed votes cast for dissolution and a statement that the number cast for dissolution was sufficient for approval.

    (4)  If voting by voting groups is required, the information required by subparagraph (3) shall be separately provided for each voting group entitled to vote separately on the plan to dissolve.

(b)  A corporation is dissolved upon the effective date of its articles of dissolution.

### § 14.04  Revocation of Dissolution

(a)  A corporation may revoke its dissolution within 120 days of its effective date.

(b)  Revocation of dissolution must be authorized in the same manner as the dissolution was authorized unless that authorization permitted revocation by action by the board of directors alone, in which event the board of directors may revoke the dissolution without shareholder action.

(c)  After the revocation of dissolution is authorized, the corporation may revoke the dissolution by delivering to the secretary of state for filing articles of revocation of dissolution, together with a copy of its articles of dissolution, that set forth:

    (1)  the name of the corporation;

    (2)  the effective date of the dissolution that was revoked;

    (3)  the date that the revocation of dissolution was authorized;

    (4)  if the corporation's board of directors (or incorporators) revoked the dissolution, a statement to that effect;

    (5)  if the corporation's board of directors revoked a dissolution authorized by the shareholders, a statement that revocation was permitted by action by the board of directors alone pursuant to that authorization; and

    (6)  if shareholder action was required to revoke the dissolution, the information required by section 14.03(3) or (4).

(d)  Unless a delayed effective date is specified, revocation of dissolution is effective when articles of revocation of dissolution are filed.

(e)  When the revocation of dissolution is effective, it relates back to and takes effect as of the effective date of the dissolution and the corporation resumes carrying on its business as if dissolution had never occurred.

### § 14.05  Effect of Dissolution

(a)  A dissolved corporation continues its corporate existence but may not carry on any business except that appropriate to wind up and liquidate its business and affairs, including:

    (1)  collecting its assets;

    (2)  disposing of its properties that will not be distributed in kind to its shareholders;

    (3)  discharging or making provision for discharging its liabilities;

    (4)  distributing its remaining property among its shareholders according to their interests; and

    (5)  doing every other act necessary to wind up and liquidate its business and affairs.

(b)  Dissolution of a corporation does not:

    (1)  transfer title to the corporation's property;

    (2)  prevent transfer of its shares or securities, although the authorization to dissolve may provide for closing the corporation's share transfer records;

    (3)  subject its directors or officers to standards of conduct different from those prescribed in chapter 8;

    (4)  change quorum or voting requirements for its board of directors or shareholders; change provisions for selection, resignation, or removal of its directors or officers or both; or change provisions for amending its bylaws;

    (5)  prevent commencement of a proceeding by or against the corporation in its corporate name;

    (6)  abate or suspend a proceeding pending by or against the corporation on the effective date of dissolution; or

    (7)  terminate the authority of the registered agent of the corporation.

## § 14.06  Known Claims Against Dissolved Corporation

(a)  A dissolved corporation may dispose of the known claims against it by following the procedure described in this section.

(b)  The dissolved corporation shall notify its known claimants in writing of the dissolution at any time after its effective date. The written notice must:

(1)  describe information that must be included in a claim;

(2)  provide a mailing address where a claim may be sent;

(3)  state the deadline, which may not be fewer than 120 days from the effective date of the written notice, by which the dissolved corporation must receive the claim; and

(4)  state that the claim will be barred if not received by the deadline.

(c)  A claim against the dissolved corporation is barred:

(1)  if a claimant who was given written notice under subsection (b) does not deliver the claim to the dissolved corporation by the deadline;

(2)  if a claimant whose claim was rejected by the dissolved corporation does not commence a proceeding to enforce the claim within 90 days from the effective date of the rejection notice.

(d)  For purposes of this section, "claim" does not include a contingent liability or a claim based on an event occurring after the effective date of dissolution.

## § 14.07  Unknown Claims Against Dissolved Corporation

(a)  A dissolved corporation may also publish notice of its dissolution and request that persons with claims against the corporation present them in accordance with the notice.

(b)  The notice must:

(1)  be published one time in a newspaper of general circulation in the county where the dissolved corporation's principal office (or, if none in this state, its registered office) is or was last located;

(2)  describe the information that must be included in a claim and provide a mailing address where the claim may be sent; and

(3)  state that a claim against the corporation will be barred unless a proceeding to enforce the claim is commenced within five years after the publication of the notice.

(c)  If the dissolved corporation publishes a newspaper notice in accordance with subsection (b), the claim of each of the following claimants is barred unless the claimant commences a proceeding to enforce the claim against the dissolved corporation within five years after the publication date of the newspaper notice:

(1)  a claimant who did not receive written notice under section 14.06;

(2)  a claimant whose claim was timely sent to the dissolved corporation but not acted on;

(3)  a claimant whose claim is contingent or based on an event occurring after the effective date of dissolution.

(d)  A claim may be enforced under this section:

(1)  against the dissolved corporation, to the extent of its undistributed assets; or

(2)  if the assets have been distributed in liquidation, against a shareholder of the dissolved corporation to the extent of his pro rata share of the claim or the corporate assets distributed to him in liquidation, whichever is less, but a shareholder's total liability for all claims under this section may not exceed the total amount of assets distributed to him.

## Subchapter B.  Administrative Dissolution

### § 14.20  Grounds for Administrative Dissolution

The secretary of state may commence a proceeding under section 14.21 to administratively dissolve a corporation if:

(1)  the corporation does not pay within 60 days after they are due any franchise taxes or penalties imposed by this Act or other law;

(2)  the corporation does not deliver its annual report to the secretary of state within 60 days after it is due;

(3)  the corporation is without a registered agent or registered office in this state for 60 days or more;

(4)  the corporation does not notify the secretary of state within 60 days that its registered agent or registered office has been changed, that its registered agent has resigned, or that its registered office has been discontinued; or

(5)  the corporation's period of duration stated in its articles of incorporation expires.

## § 14.21  Procedure for and Effect of Administrative Dissolution

(a)  If the secretary of state determines that one or more grounds exist under section 14.20 for dissolving a corporation, he shall serve the corporation with written notice of his determination under section 5.04.

(b)  If the corporation does not correct each ground for dissolution or demonstrate to the reasonable satisfaction of the secretary of state that each ground determined by the secretary of state does not exist within 60 days after service of the notice is perfected under section 5.04, the secretary of state shall administratively dissolve the corporation by signing a certificate of dissolution that recites the ground or grounds for dissolution and its effective date. The secretary of state shall file the original of the certificate and serve a copy on the corporation under section 5.04.

(c)  A corporation administratively dissolved continues its corporate existence but may not carry on any business except that necessary to wind up and liquidate its business and affairs under section 14.05 and notify claimants under sections 14.06 and 14.07.

(d)  The administrative dissolution of a corporation does not terminate the authority of its registered agent.

## § 14.22  Reinstatement Following Administrative Dissolution

(a)  A corporation administratively dissolved under section 14.21 may apply to the secretary of state for reinstatement within two years after the effective date of dissolution. The application must:

(1)  recite the name of the corporation and the effective date of its administrative dissolution;

(2)  state that the ground or grounds for dissolution either did not exist or have been eliminated;

(3)  state that the corporation's name satisfies the requirements of section 4.01; and

(4)  contain a certificate from the [taxing authority] reciting that all taxes owed by the corporation have been paid.

(b)  If the secretary of state determines that the application contains the information required by subsection (a) and that the information is correct, he shall cancel the certificate of dissolution and prepare a certificate of reinstatement that recites his determination and the effective date of reinstatement, file the original of the certificate, and serve a copy on the corporation under section 5.04.

(c)  When the reinstatement is effective, it relates back to and takes effect as of the effective date of the administrative dissolution and the corporation resumes carrying on its business as if the administrative dissolution had never occurred.

## § 14.23  Appeal From Denial of Reinstatement

(a)  If the secretary of state denies a corporation's application for reinstatement following administrative dissolution, he shall serve the corporation under section 5.04 with a written notice that explains the reason or reasons for denial.

(b) The corporation may appeal the denial of reinstatement to the [name or describe] court within 30 days after service of the notice of denial is perfected. The corporation appeals by petitioning the court to set aside the dissolution and attaching to the petition copies of the secretary of state's certificate of dissolution, the corporation's application for reinstatement, and the secretary of state's notice of denial.

(c) The court may summarily order the secretary of state to reinstate the dissolved corporation or may take other action the court considers appropriate.

(d) The court's final decision may be appealed as in other civil proceedings.

## Subchapter C.  Judicial Dissolution

### § 14.30  Grounds for Judicial Dissolution

The [name or describe court or courts] may dissolve a corporation:

    (1) in a proceeding by the attorney general if it is established that:

        (i) the corporation obtained its articles of incorporation through fraud; or

        (ii) the corporation has continued to exceed or abuse the authority conferred upon it by law;

    (2) in a proceeding by a shareholder if it is established that:

        (i) the directors are deadlocked in the management of the corporate affairs, the shareholders are unable to break the deadlock, and irreparable injury to the corporation is threatened or being suffered, or the business and affairs of the corporation can no longer be conducted to the advantage of the shareholders generally, because of the deadlock;

        (ii) the directors or those in control of the corporation have acted, are acting, or will act in a manner that is illegal, oppressive, or fraudulent;

        (iii) the shareholders are deadlocked in voting power and have failed, for a period that includes at least two consecutive annual meeting dates, to elect successors to directors whose terms have expired; or

        (iv) the corporate assets are being misapplied or wasted;

    (3) in a proceeding by a creditor if it is established that:

        (i) the creditor's claim has been reduced to judgment, the execution on the judgment returned unsatisfied, and the corporation is insolvent; or

        (ii) the corporation has admitted in writing that the creditor's claim is due and owing and the corporation is insolvent; or

    (4) in a proceeding by the corporation to have its voluntary dissolution continued under court supervision.

### § 14.31  Procedure for Judicial Dissolution

(a) Venue for a proceeding by the attorney general to dissolve a corporation lies in [name the county or counties]. Venue for a proceeding brought by any other party named in section 14.30 lies in the county where a corporation's principal office (or, if none in this state, its registered office) is or was last located.

(b) It is not necessary to make shareholders parties to a proceeding to dissolve a corporation unless relief is sought against them individually.

(c) A court in a proceeding brought to dissolve a corporation may issue injunctions, appoint a receiver or custodian pendente lite with all powers and duties the court directs, take other action required to preserve the corporate assets wherever located, and carry on the business of the corporation until a full hearing can be held.

(d) Within 10 days of the commencement of a proceeding under section 14.30(2) to dissolve a corporation that has no shares listed on a national securities exchange or regularly traded in a market maintained by one or more members of a national securities exchange, the corporation must send to all shareholders, other than the petitioner, a notice stating that the shareholders are entitled to avoid the dissolution of the corporation by electing to purchase the petitioner's shares under section 14.34 and accompanied by a copy of section 14.34.

### § 14.32  Receivership or Custodianship

(a) A court in a judicial proceeding brought to dissolve a corporation may appoint one or more receivers to wind up and liquidate, or one or more custodians to manage, the business and affairs of the corporation. The court shall hold a hearing, after notifying all parties to the proceeding and any interested persons designated by the court, before appointing a receiver or custodian. The court appointing a receiver or custodian has exclusive jurisdiction over the corporation and all its property wherever located.

(b) The court may appoint an individual or a domestic or foreign corporation (authorized to transact business in this state) as a receiver or custodian. The court may require the receiver or custodian to post bond, with or without sureties, in an amount the court directs.

(c) The court shall describe the powers and duties of the receiver or custodian in its appointing order, which may be amended from time to time. Among other powers:

    (1) the receiver (i) may dispose of all or any part of the assets of the corporation wherever located, at a public or private sale, if authorized by the court; and (ii) may sue and defend in his own name as receiver of the corporation in all courts of this state;

    (2) the custodian may exercise all of the powers of the corporation, through or in place of its board of directors or officers, to the extent necessary to manage the affairs of the corporation in the best interests of its shareholders and creditors.

(d) The court during a receivership may redesignate the receiver a custodian, and during a custodianship may redesignate the custodian a receiver, if doing so is in the best interests of the corporation, its shareholders, and creditors.

(e) The court from time to time during the receivership or custodianship may order compensation paid and expense disbursements or reimbursements made to the receiver or custodian and his counsel from the assets of the corporation or proceeds from the sale of the assets.

### § 14.33  Decree of Dissolution

(a) If after a hearing the court determines that one or more grounds for judicial dissolution described in section 14.30 exist, it may enter a decree dissolving the corporation and specifying the effective date of the dissolution, and the clerk of the court shall deliver a certified copy of the decree to the secretary of state, who shall file it.

(b) After entering the decree of dissolution, the court shall direct the winding up and liquidation of the corporation's business and affairs in accordance with section 14.05 and the notification of claimants in accordance with sections 14.06 and 14.07.

### § 14.34  Election to Purchase in Lieu of Dissolution

(a) In a proceeding under section 14.30(2) to dissolve a corporation that has no shares listed on a national securities exchange or regularly traded in a market maintained by one or more members of a national or affiliated securities association, the corporation may elect or, if it fails to elect, one or more shareholders may elect to purchase all shares owned by the petitioning shareholder at the fair value of the shares. An election pursuant to this section shall be irrevocable unless the court determines that it is equitable to set aside or modify the election.

(b) An election to purchase pursuant to this section may be filed with the court at any time within 90 days after the filing of the petition under section 14.30(2) or at such later time as the court in its discretion may allow. If the election to purchase is filed by one or more shareholders, the corporation shall, within 10 days thereafter, give written notice to all shareholders, other than the petitioner. The notice must state the name and number of shares owned by the petitioner and the name and number of shares owned by each electing shareholder and must advise the recipients of their right to join in the election to purchase shares in accordance with this section. Shareholders who wish to participate must file notice of their intention to join in the purchase no later than 30 days after the effective date of the notice to them. All shareholders who have filed an election or notice of their intention to participate in the election to purchase thereby become parties to ownership of shares as of the date the first election was filed, unless they otherwise agree or the court otherwise directs. After an election has been filed by the corporation or one or more shareholders, the proceeding under section 14.30(2) may not be discontinued or settled, nor may the petitioning shareholder sell or otherwise dispose of his shares, unless the court determines that it would be equitable to the corporation and the shareholders, other than the petitioner, to permit such discontinuance, settlement, sale, or other disposition.

(c) If, within 60 days of the filing of the first election, the parties reach agreement as to the fair value and terms of purchase of the petitioner's shares, the court shall enter an order directing the purchase of petitioner's shares upon the terms and conditions agreed to by the parties.

(d) If the parties are unable to reach an agreement as provided for in subsection (c), the court, upon application of any party, shall stay the section 14.30(2) proceedings and determine the fair value of the petitioner's shares as of the day before the date on which the petition under section 14.30(2) was filed or as of such other date as the court deems appropriate under the circumstances.

(e) Upon determining the fair value of the shares, the court shall enter an order directing the purchase upon such terms and conditions as the court deems appropriate, which may include payment of the purchase price in installments, where necessary in the interests of equity, provision for security to assure payment of the purchase price and any additional costs, fees, and expenses as may have been awarded, and, if the shares are to be purchased by shareholders, the allocation of shares among them. In allocating petitioner's shares among holders of different classes of shares, the court should attempt to preserve the existing distribution of voting rights among holders of different classes insofar as practicable and may direct that holders of a specific class or classes shall not participate in the purchase. Interest may be allowed at the rate and from the date determined by the court to be equitable, but if the court finds that the refusal of the petitioning shareholder to accept an offer of payment was arbitrary or otherwise not in good faith, no interest shall be allowed. If the court finds that the petitioning shareholder had probable grounds for relief under paragraphs (ii) or (iv) of section 14.30(2), it may award to the petitioning shareholder reasonable fees and expenses of counsel and of any experts employed by him.

(f) Upon entry of an order under subsections (c) or (e), the court shall dismiss the petition to dissolve the corporation under section 14.30, and the petitioning shareholder shall no longer have any rights or status as a shareholder of the corporation, except the right to receive the amounts awarded to him by the order of the court which shall be enforceable in the same manner as any other judgment.

(g) The purchase ordered pursuant to subsection (e), shall be made within 10 days after the date the order becomes final unless before that time the corporation files with the court a notice of its intention to adopt articles of dissolution pursuant to sections 14.02 and 14.03, which articles must then be adopted and filed within 50 days thereafter. Upon filing of such articles of dissolution, the corporation shall be dissolved in accordance with the provisions of sections 14.05 through 07, and the order entered pursuant to subsection (e) shall no longer be of any force or effect, except that the court may award the petitioning shareholder reasonable fees and expenses in accordance with the provisions of the last sentence of subsection (e) and the petitioner may continue to pursue any claims previously asserted on behalf of the corporation.

(h) Any payment by the corporation pursuant to an order under subsections (c) or (e), other than an award of fees and expenses pursuant to subsection (e), is subject to the provisions of section 6.40.

## Subchapter D. Miscellaneous

### § 14.40 Deposit With State Treasurer

Assets of a dissolved corporation that should be transferred to a creditor, claimant, or shareholder of the corporation who cannot be found or who is not competent to receive them shall be reduced to cash and deposited with the state treasurer or other appropriate state official for safekeeping. When the creditor, claimant, or shareholder furnishes satisfactory proof of entitlement to the amount deposited, the state treasurer or other appropriate state official shall pay him or his representative that amount.

# CHAPTER 15. FOREIGN CORPORATIONS

## Subchapter A. Certificate of Authority

### § 15.01 Authority to Transact Business Required

(a) A foreign corporation may not transact business in this state until it obtains a certificate of authority from the secretary of state.

(b) The following activities, among others, do not constitute transacting business within the meaning of subsection (a):

    (1) maintaining, defending, or settling any proceeding;

    (2) holding meetings of the board of directors or shareholders or carrying on other activities concerning internal corporate affairs;

    (3) maintaining bank accounts;

    (4) maintaining offices or agencies for the transfer, exchange, and registration of the corporation's own securities or maintaining trustees or depositaries with respect to those securities;

    (5) selling through independent contractors;

    (6) soliciting or obtaining orders, whether by mail or through employees or agents or otherwise, if the orders require acceptance outside this state before they become contracts;

    (7) creating or acquiring indebtedness, mortgages, and security interests in real or personal property;

    (8) securing or collecting debts or enforcing mortgages and security interests in property securing the debts;

    (9) owning, without more, real or personal property;

    (10) conducting an isolated transaction that is completed within 30 days and that is not one in the course of repeated transactions of a like nature;

(11) transacting business in interstate commerce.

(c) The list of activities in subsection (b) is not exhaustive.

## § 15.02 Consequences of Transacting Business Without Authority

(a) A foreign corporation transacting business in this state without a certificate of authority may not maintain a proceeding in any court in this state until it obtains a certificate of authority.

(b) The successor to a foreign corporation that transacted business in this state without a certificate of authority and the assignee of a cause of action arising out of that business may not maintain a proceeding based on that cause of action in any court in this state until the foreign corporation or its successor obtains a certificate of authority.

(c) A court may stay a proceeding commenced by a foreign corporation, its successor, or assignee until it determines whether the foreign corporation or its successor requires a certificate of authority. If it so determines, the court may further stay the proceeding until the foreign corporation or its successor obtains the certificate.

(d) A foreign corporation is liable for a civil penalty of $ for each day, but not to exceed a total of $ _____ for each year, it transacts business in this state without a certificate of authority. The attorney general may collect all penalties due under this subsection.

(e) Notwithstanding subsections (a) and (b), the failure of a foreign corporation to obtain a certificate of authority does not impair the validity of its corporate acts or prevent it from defending any proceeding in this state.

## § 15.03 Application for Certificate of Authority

(a) A foreign corporation may apply for a certificate of authority to transact business in this state by delivering an application to the secretary of state for filing. The application must set forth:

(1) the name of the foreign corporation or, if its name is unavailable for use in this state, a corporate name that satisfies the requirements of section 15.06;

(2) the name of the state or country under whose law it is incorporated;

(3) its date of incorporation and period of duration;

(4) the street address of its principal office;

(5) the address of its registered office in this state and the name of its registered agent at that office; and

(6) the names and usual business addresses of its current directors and officers.

(b) The foreign corporation shall deliver with the completed application a certificate of existence (or a document of similar import) duly authenticated by the secretary of state or other official having custody of corporate records in the state or country under whose law it is incorporated.

## § 15.04 Amended Certificate of Authority

(a) A foreign corporation authorized to transact business in this state must obtain an amended certificate of authority from the secretary of state if it changes:

(1) its corporate name;

(2) the period of its duration; or

(3) the state or country of its incorporation.

(b) The requirements of section 15.03 for obtaining an original certificate of authority apply to obtaining an amended certificate under this section.

## § 15.05 Effect of Certificate of Authority

(a) A certificate of authority authorizes the foreign corporation to which it is issued to transact business in this state subject, however, to the right of the state to revoke the certificate as provided in this Act.

(b) A foreign corporation with a valid certificate of authority has the same but no greater rights and has the same but no greater privileges as, and except as otherwise provided by this Act is subject to the same duties, restrictions, penalties, and liabilities now or later imposed on, a domestic corporation of like character.

(c) This Act does not authorize this state to regulate the organization or internal affairs of a foreign corporation authorized to transact business in this state.

## § 15.06 Corporate Name of Foreign Corporation

(a) If the corporate name of a foreign corporation does not satisfy the requirements of section 4.01, the foreign corporation to obtain or maintain a certificate of authority to transact business in this state:

(1) may add the word "corporation," "incorporated," "company," or "limited," or the abbreviation "corp.," "inc.," "co.," or "ltd.," to its corporate name for use in this state; or

(2) may use a fictitious name to transact business in this state if its real name is unavailable and it delivers to the secretary of state for filing a copy of the resolution of its board of directors, certified by its secretary, adopting the fictitious name.

(b) Except as authorized by subsections (c) and (d), the corporate name (including a fictitious name) of a foreign corporation must be distinguishable upon the records of the secretary of state from:

(1) the corporate name of a corporation incorporated or authorized to transact business in this state;

(2) a corporate name reserved or registered under section 4.02 or 4.03;

(3) the fictitious name of another foreign corporation authorized to transact business in this state; and

(4) the corporate name of a not-for-profit corporation incorporated or authorized to transact business in this state.

(c) A foreign corporation may apply to the secretary of state for authorization to use in this state the name of another corporation (incorporated or authorized to transact business in this state) that is not distinguishable upon his records from the name applied for. The secretary of state shall authorize use of the name applied for if:

(1) the other corporation consents to the use in writing and submits an undertaking in form satisfactory to the secretary of state to change its name to a name that is distinguishable upon the records of the secretary of state from the name of the applying corporation; or

(2) the applicant delivers to the secretary of state a certified copy of a final judgment of a court of competent jurisdiction establishing the applicant's right to use the name applied for in this state.

(d) A foreign corporation may use in this state the name (including the fictitious name) of another domestic or foreign corporation that is used in this state if the other corporation is incorporated or authorized to transact business in this state and the foreign corporation:

(1) has merged with the other corporation;

(2) has been formed by reorganization of the other corporation; or

(3) has acquired all or substantially all of the assets, including the corporate name, of the other corporation.

(e) If a foreign corporation authorized to transact business in this state changes its corporate name to one that does not satisfy the requirements of section 4.01, it may not transact business in this state under the changed name until it adopts a name satisfying the requirements of section 4.01 and obtains an amended certificate of authority under section 15.04.

## § 15.07 Registered Office and Registered Agent of Foreign Corporation

Each foreign corporation authorized to transact business in this state must continuously maintain in this state:

(1) a registered office that may be the same as any of its places of business; and

(2) a registered agent, who may be:

(i) an individual who resides in this state and whose business office is identical with the registered office;

(ii) a domestic corporation or not-for-profit domestic corporation whose business office is identical with the registered office; or

(iii) a foreign corporation or foreign not-for-profit corporation authorized to transact business in this state whose business office is identical with the registered office.

## § 15.08 Change of Registered Office or Registered Agent of Foreign Corporation

(a) A foreign corporation authorized to transact business in this state may change its registered office or registered agent by delivering to the secretary of state for filing a statement of change that sets forth:

(1) its name;

(2) the street address of its current registered office;

(3) if the current registered office is to be changed, the street address of its new registered office;

(4) the name of its current registered agent;

(5) if the current registered agent is to be changed, the name of its new registered agent and the new agent's written consent (either on the statement or attached to it) to the appointment; and

(6) that after the change or changes are made, the street addresses of its registered office and the business office of its registered agent will be identical.

(b) If a registered agent changes the street address of his business office, he may change the street address of the registered office of any foreign corporation for which he is the registered agent by notifying the corporation in writing of the change and signing (either manually or in facsimile) and delivering to the secretary of state for filing a statement of change that complies with the requirements of subsection (a) and recites that the corporation has been notified of the change.

## § 15.09 Resignation of Registered Agent of Foreign Corporation

(a) The registered agent of a foreign corporation may resign his agency appointment by signing and delivering to the secretary of state for filing the original and two exact or conformed copies of a statement of resignation. The statement of resignation may include a statement that the registered office is also discontinued.

(b) After filing the statement, the secretary of state shall attach the filing receipt to one copy and mail the copy and receipt to the registered office if not discontinued. The secretary of state shall mail the other copy to the foreign corporation at its principal office address shown in its most recent annual report.

(c) The agency appointment is terminated, and the registered office discontinued if so provided, on the 31st day after the date on which the statement was filed.

## § 15.10 Service on Foreign Corporation

(a) The registered agent of a foreign corporation authorized to transact business in this state is the corporation's agent for service of process, notice, or demand required or permitted by law to be served on the foreign corporation.

(b) A foreign corporation may be served by registered or certified mail, return receipt requested, addressed to the secretary of the foreign corporation at its principal office shown in its application for a certificate of authority or in its most recent annual report if the foreign corporation:

(1) has no registered agent or its registered agent cannot with reasonable diligence be served;

(2) has withdrawn from transacting business in this state under section 15.20; or

(3) has had its certificate of authority revoked under section 15.31.

(c) Service is perfected under subsection (b) at the earliest of:

(1) the date the foreign corporation receives the mail;

(2) the date shown on the return receipt, if signed on behalf of the foreign corporation; or

(3) five days after its deposit in the United States Mail, as evidenced by the postmark, if mailed postpaid and correctly addressed.

(d) This section does not prescribe the only means, or necessarily the required means, of serving a foreign corporation.

## Subchapter B.  Withdrawal

### § 15.20 Withdrawal of Foreign Corporation

(a) A foreign corporation authorized to transact business in this state may not withdraw from this state until it obtains a certificate of withdrawal from the secretary of state.

(b) A foreign corporation authorized to transact business in this state may apply for a certificate of withdrawal by delivering an application to the secretary of state for filing. The application must set forth:

(1) the name of the foreign corporation and the name of the state or country under whose law it is incorporated;

(2) that it is not transacting business in this state and that it surrenders its authority to transact business in this state;

(3) that it revokes the authority of its registered agent to accept service on its behalf and appoints the secretary of state as its agent for service of process in any proceeding based on a cause of action arising during the time it was authorized to transact business in this state;

(4) a mailing address to which the secretary of state may mail a copy of any process served on him under subdivision (3); and

(5) a commitment to notify the secretary of state in the future of any change in its mailing address.

(c) After the withdrawal of the corporation is effective, service of process on the secretary of state under this section is service on the foreign corporation. Upon receipt of process, the secretary of state shall mail a copy of the process to the foreign corporation at the mailing address set forth under subsection (b).

## Subchapter C.  Revocation of Certificate of Authority

### § 15.30 Grounds for Revocation

The secretary of state may commence a proceeding under section 15.31 to revoke the certificate of authority of a foreign corporation authorized to transact business in this state if:

(1) the foreign corporation does not deliver its annual report to the secretary of state within 60 days after it is due;

(2) the foreign corporation does not pay within 60 days after they are due any franchise taxes or penalties imposed by this Act or other law;

(3) the foreign corporation is without a registered agent or registered office in this state for 60 days or more;

(4) the foreign corporation does not inform the secretary of state under section 15.08 or 15.09 that its registered agent or registered office has changed, that its registered agent has resigned, or that its registered office has been discontinued within 60 days of the change, resignation, or discontinuance;

(5) an incorporator, director, officer, or agent of the foreign corporation signed a document he knew was false in any material respect with intent that the document be delivered to the secretary of state for filing;

(6) the secretary of state receives a duly authenticated certificate from the secretary of state or other official having custody of corporate records in the state or country under whose law the foreign corporation is incorporated stating that it has been dissolved or disappeared as a result of a merger.

## § 15.31  Procedure for and Effect of Revocation

(a)  If the secretary of state determines that one or more grounds exist under section 15.30 for revocation of a certificate of authority, he shall serve the foreign corporation with written notice of his determination under section 15.10.

(b)  If the foreign corporation does not correct each ground for revocation or demonstrate to the reasonable satisfaction of the secretary of state that each ground determined by the secretary of state does not exist within 60 days after service of the notice is perfected under section 15.10, the secretary of state may revoke the foreign corporation's certificate of authority by signing a certificate of revocation that recites the ground or grounds for revocation and its effective date. The secretary of state shall file the original of the certificate and serve a copy on the foreign corporation under section 15.10.

(c)  The authority of a foreign corporation to transact business in this state ceases on the date shown on the certificate revoking its certificate of authority.

(d)  The secretary of state's revocation of a foreign corporation's certificate of authority appoints the secretary of state the foreign corporation's agent for service of process in any proceeding based on a cause of action which arose during the time the foreign corporation was authorized to transact business in this state. Service of process on the secretary of state under this subsection is service on the foreign corporation. Upon receipt of process, the secretary of state shall mail a copy of the process to the secretary of the foreign corporation at its principal office shown in its most recent annual report or in any subsequent communication received from the corporation stating the current mailing address of its principal office, or, if none are on file, in its application for a certificate of authority.

(e)  Revocation of a foreign corporation's certificate of authority does not terminate the authority of the registered agent of the corporation.

## § 15.32  Appeal From Revocation

(a)  A foreign corporation may appeal the secretary of state's revocation of its certificate of authority to the [name or describe] court within 30 days after service of the certificate of revocation is perfected under section 15.10. The foreign corporation appeals by petitioning the court to set aside the revocation and attaching to the petition copies of its certificate of authority and the secretary of state's certificate of revocation.

(b)  The court may summarily order the secretary of state to reinstate the certificate of authority or may take any other action the court considers appropriate.

(c)  The court's final decision may be appealed as in other civil proceedings.

# CHAPTER 16.  RECORDS AND REPORTS

## Subchapter A.  Records

### § 16.01  Corporate Records

(a)  A corporation shall keep as permanent records minutes of all meetings of its shareholders and board of directors, a record of all actions taken by the shareholders or board of directors without a meeting, and a record of all actions taken by a committee of the board of directors in place of the board of directors on behalf of the corporation.

(b)  A corporation shall maintain appropriate accounting records.

(c)  A corporation or its agent shall maintain a record of its shareholders, in a form that permits preparation of a list of the names and addresses of all shareholders, in alphabetical order by class of shares showing the number and class of shares held by each.

(d)  A corporation shall maintain its records in written form or in another form capable of conversion into written form within a reasonable time.

(e)  A corporation shall keep a copy of the following records at its principal office:

(1)  its articles or restated articles of incorporation and all amendments to them currently in effect;

(2)  its bylaws or restated bylaws and all amendments to them currently in effect;

(3)  resolutions adopted by its board of directors creating one or more classes or series of shares, and fixing their relative rights, preferences, and limitations, if shares issued pursuant to those resolutions are outstanding;

(4)  the minutes of all shareholders' meetings, and records of all action taken by shareholders without a meeting, for the past three years;

(5)  all written communications to shareholders generally within the past three years, including the financial statements furnished for the past three years under section 16.20;

(6)  a list of the names and business addresses of its current directors and officers; and

(7)  its most recent annual report delivered to the secretary of state under section 16.22.

### § 16.02  Inspection of Records by Shareholders

(a)  Subject to section 16.03(c), a shareholder of a corporation is entitled to inspect and copy, during regular business hours at the corporation's principal office, any of the records of the corporation described in section 16.01(e) if he gives the corporation written notice of his demand at least five business days before the date on which he wishes to inspect and copy.

(b)  A shareholder of a corporation is entitled to inspect and copy, during regular business hours at a reasonable location specified by the corporation, any of the following records of the corporation if the shareholder meets the requirements of subsection (c) and gives the corporation written notice of his demand at least five business days before the date on which he wishes to inspect and copy:

(1)  excerpts from minutes of any meeting of the board of directors, records of any action of a committee of the board of directors while acting in place of the board of directors on behalf of the corporation, minutes of any meeting of the shareholders, and records of action taken by the shareholders or board of directors without a meeting, to the extent not subject to inspection under section 16.02(a);

(2) accounting records of the corporation; and

(3) the record of shareholders.

(c) A shareholder may inspect and copy the records identified in subsection (b) only if:

(1) his demand is made in good faith and for a proper purpose;

(2) he describes with reasonable particularity his purpose and the records he desires to inspect; and

(3) the records are directly connected with his purpose.

(d) The right of inspection granted by this section may not be abolished or limited by a corporation's articles of incorporation or bylaws.

(e) This section does not affect:

(1) the right of a shareholder to inspect records under section 7.20 or, if the shareholder is in litigation with the corporation, to the same extent as any other litigant;

(2) the power of a court, independently of this Act, to compel the production of corporate records for examination.

(f) For purposes of this section, "shareholder" includes a beneficial owner whose shares are held in a voting trust or by a nominee on his behalf.

## § 16.03 Scope of Inspection Right

(a) A shareholder's agent or attorney has the same inspection and copying rights as the shareholder he represents.

(b) The right to copy records under section 16.02 includes, if reasonable, the right to receive copies made by photographic, xerographic, or other means.

(c) The corporation may impose a reasonable charge, covering the costs of labor and material, for copies of any documents provided to the shareholder. The charge may not exceed the estimated cost of production or reproduction of the records.

(d) The corporation may comply with a shareholder's demand to inspect the record of shareholders under section 16.02(b)(3) by providing him with a list of its shareholders that was compiled no earlier than the date of the shareholder's demand.

## § 16.04 Court-Ordered Inspection

(a) If a corporation does not allow a shareholder who complies with section 16.02(a) to inspect and copy any records required by that subsection to be available for inspection, the [name or describe court] of the county where the corporation's principal office (or, if none in this state, its registered office) is located may summarily order inspection and copying of the records demanded at the corporation's expense upon application of the shareholder.

(b) If a corporation does not within a reasonable time allow a shareholder to inspect and copy any other record, the shareholder who complies with section 16.02(b) and (c) may apply to the [name or describe court] in the county where the corporation's principal office (or, if none in this state, its registered office) is located for an order to permit inspection and copying of the records demanded. The court shall dispose of an application under this subsection on an expedited basis.

(c) If the court orders inspection and copying of the records demanded, it shall also order the corporation to pay the shareholder's costs (including reasonable counsel fees) incurred to obtain the order unless the corporation proves that it refused inspection in good faith because it had a reasonable basis for doubt about the right of the shareholder to inspect the records demanded.

(d) If the court orders inspection and copying of the records demanded, it may impose reasonable restrictions on the use or distribution of the records by the demanding shareholder.

## Subchapter B.  Reports

### § 16.20  Financial Statements for Shareholders

(a) A corporation shall furnish its shareholders annual financial statements, which may be consolidated or combined statements of the corporation and one or more of its subsidiaries, as appropriate, that include a balance sheet as of the end of the fiscal year, an income statement for that year, and a statement of changes in shareholders' equity for the year unless that information appears elsewhere in the financial statements. If financial statements are prepared for the corporation on the basis of generally accepted accounting principles, the annual financial statements must also be prepared on that basis.

(b) If the annual financial statements are reported upon by a public accountant, his report must accompany them. If not, the statements must be accompanied by a statement of the president or the person responsible for the corporation's accounting records:

(1) stating his reasonable belief whether the statements were prepared on the basis of generally accepted accounting principles and, if not, describing the basis of preparation; and

(2) describing any respects in which the statements were not prepared on a basis of accounting consistent with the statements prepared for the preceding year.

(c) A corporation shall mail the annual financial statements to each shareholder within 120 days after the close of each fiscal year. Thereafter, on written request from a shareholder who was not mailed the statements, the corporation shall mail him the latest financial statements.

### § 16.21  Other Reports to Shareholders

(a) If a corporation indemnifies or advances expenses to a director under section 8.51, 8.52, 8.53, or 8.54 in connection with a proceeding by or in the right of the corporation, the corporation shall report the indemnification or advance in writing to the shareholders with or before the notice of the next shareholders' meeting.

(b) If a corporation issues or authorizes the issuance of shares for promissory notes or for promises to render services in the future, the corporation shall report in writing to the shareholders the number of shares authorized or issued, and the consideration received by the corporation, with or before the notice of the next shareholders' meeting.

### § 16.22  Annual Report for Secretary of State

(a) Each domestic corporation, and each foreign corporation authorized to transact business in this state, shall deliver to the secretary of state for filing an annual report that sets forth:

(1) the name of the corporation and the state or country under whose law it is incorporated;

(2) the address of its registered office and the name of its registered agent at that office in this state;

(3) the address of its principal office;

(4) the names and business addresses of its directors and principal officers;

(5) a brief description of the nature of its business;

(6) the total number of authorized shares, itemized by class and series, if any, within each class; and

(7) the total number of issued and outstanding shares, itemized by class and series, if any, within each class.

(b) Information in the annual report must be current as of the date the annual report is executed on behalf of the corporation.

(c) The first annual report must be delivered to the secretary of state between January 1 and April 1 of the year following the calendar year in which a domestic corporation was incorporated or a foreign corporation was authorized to transact business. Subsequent annual reports must be delivered to the secretary of state between January 1 and April 1 of the following calendar years.

(d) If an annual report does not contain the information required by this section, the secretary of state shall promptly notify the reporting domestic or foreign corporation in writing and return the report to it for correction. If the report is corrected to contain the information required by this section and delivered to the secretary of state within 30 days after the effective date of notice, it is deemed to be timely filed.

## CHAPTER 17. TRANSITION PROVISIONS

### § 17.01 Application to Existing Domestic Corporations

This Act applies to all domestic corporations in existence on its effective date that were incorporated under any general statute of this state providing for incorporation of corporations for profit if power to amend or repeal the statute under which the corporation was incorporated was reserved.

### § 17.02 Application to Qualified Foreign Corporations

A foreign corporation authorized to transact business in this state on the effective date of this Act is subject to this Act but is not required to obtain a new certificate of authority to transact business under this Act.

### § 17.03 Saving Provisions

(a) Except as provided in subsection (b), the repeal of a statute by this Act does not affect:

(1) the operation of the statute or any action taken under it before its repeal;

(2) any ratification, right, remedy, privilege, obligation, or liability acquired, accrued, or incurred under the statute before its repeal;

(3) any violation of the statute, or any penalty, forfeiture, or punishment incurred because of the violation, before its repeal;

(4) any proceeding, reorganization, or dissolution commenced under the statute before its repeal, and the proceeding, reorganization, or dissolution may be completed in accordance with the statute as if it had not been repealed.

(b) If a penalty or punishment imposed for violation of a statute repealed by this Act is reduced by this Act, the penalty or punishment if not already imposed shall be imposed in accordance with this Act.

### § 17.04 Severability

If any provision of this Act or its application to any person or circumstance is held invalid by a court of competent jurisdiction, the invalidity does not affect other provisions or applications of the Act that can be given effect without the invalid provision or application, and to this end the provisions of the Act are severable.

### § 17.05 Repeal

The following laws and parts of laws are repealed: [to be inserted].

### § 17.06 Effective Date

This Act takes effect _____.

# Dictionary of Legal Terms

**abatement**  Reduction or elimination of gifts by category upon the reduction in value of the estate.

**absolute surety**  Surety liable to a creditor immediately upon the default of the principal debtor.

**acceptance**  *Commercial paper*  Acceptance is the drawee's signed engagement to honor the draft as presented. It becomes operative when completed by delivery or notification. U.C.C. § 3–410.

*Contracts*  Compliance by offeree with terms and conditions of offer

*Sale of goods*  U.C.C. § 2–606 provides three ways a buyer can accept goods: (1) by signifying to the seller that the goods are conforming or that he will accept them in spite of their nonconformity, (2) by failing to make an effective rejection, and (3) by doing an act inconsistent with the seller's ownership.

**acceptor**  Drawee who has accepted an instrument.

**accession**  An addition to one's property by increase of the original property or by production from such property. *E.g.*, A innocently converts the wheat of B into bread. U.C.C. § 9–315 changes the common law where a perfected security interest is involved.

**accident and health insurance**  Provides protection from losses due to accident or sickness.

**accommodation**  An arrangement made as a favor to another, usually involving a loan of money or commercial paper. While a party's intent may be to aid a maker of note by lending his credit, if he seeks to accomplish thereby legitimate objects of his own, and not simply to aid the maker, the act is not for accommodation.

**accommodation indorser**  Signer not in the chain of title.

**accommodation party**  A person who signs commercial paper in any capacity for the purpose of lending his name to another party to an instrument. U.C.C. § 3–415.

**accord and satisfaction**  A method of discharging a claim whereby the parties agree to accept something in settlement, the "accord" being the agreement and the "satisfaction" its execution or performance. It is a new contract that is substituted for an old contract, which is thereby discharged, or for an obligation or cause of action and that must have all of the elements of a valid contract.

**account**  Any account with a bank, including a checking, time, interest or savings account. U.C.C. § 4–194. Also, any right to payment, for goods or services, that is not evidenced by an instrument or chattel paper. *E.g.*, account receivable.

**accounting**  Equitable proceeding for a complete settlement of all partnership affairs.

**act of state doctrine**  Rule that a court should not question the validity of actions taken by a foreign government in its own country.

**actual authority**  Power conferred upon agent by actual consent given by principal.

**actual express authority**  Actual authority derived from written or spoken words of principal.

**actual implied authority**  Actual authority inferred from words or conduct manifested to agent by principal.

**actual notice**  Knowledge actually and expressly communicated.

**actus reas**  Wrongful or overt act.

**ademption**  The removal or extinction of a devise by act of the testator.

**adequacy of consideration**  Not required where parties have freely agreed to the exchange.

**adhesion contract**  Standard "form" contract, usually between a large retailer and a consumer, in which the weaker party has no realistic choice or opportunity to bargain.

**adjudication**  The giving or pronouncing of a judgment in a case; also the judgment given.

**administrative agency**  Governmental entity (other than courts and legislatures) having authority to affect the rights of private parties.

**administrative law**  Law dealing with the establishment, duties and powers of agencies in the executive branch of government.

**administrative process**  Entire set of activities engaged in by administrative agencies while carrying out their rulemaking, enforcement, and adjudicative functions.

**administrator**  A person appointed by the court to manage the assets and liabilities of an intestate (person dying without a will). A person who is named in the will by testator (person dying with a will) is called the executor. Female designations are administratrix and executrix.

**adversary system**  System in which opposing parties initiate and present their case.

**adverse possession**  A method of acquisition of title to real property by possession for a statutory period under certain conditions. There may be different periods of time, depending on whether the adverse possessor has color of title.

---

Many of the definitions are abridged and adapted from *Black's Law Dictionary*, 5th edition, West Publishing Company, 1979.

**affidavit**  A written statement of facts, made voluntarily, confirmed by oath or affirmation of party making it, and taken before an authorized officer.

**affiliate**  Person who controls, is controlled by, or is under common control with the issuer.

**affirm**  Uphold the lower court's judgment.

**affirmative action**  Active recruitment of minority applicants.

**affirmative defense**  A response that attacks the plaintiff's legal right to bring an action as opposed to attacking the truth of the claim. *E.g.*, accord and satisfaction; assumption of risk; contributory negligence; duress; estoppel.

**affirmative disclosure**  Requirement that an advertiser include certain information in its advertisement so that it is not deceptive.

**after acquired property**  Property the debtor may acquire at some time after the security interest attaches.

**agency**  Relation in which one person acts for or represents another by the latter's authority.
   *Actual agency*  Exists where the agent is really employed by the principal.
   *Agency by estoppel*  One created by operation of law and established by proof of such acts of the principal as reasonably lead to the conclusion of its existence.
   *Implied agency*  One created by acts of parties and deduced from proof of other facts.

**agent**  Person authorized to act on another's behalf.

**allegation**  A statement of a party setting out what he expects to prove.

**allonge**  Piece of paper firmly affixed to the instrument.

**annuity contract**  Agreement to pay periodic sums to insured upon reaching a designated age.

**annul**  To annul a judgment or judicial proceeding is to deprive it of all force and operation.

**answer**  The answer is the formal written statement made by a defendant setting forth the ground of his defense.

**antecedent debt**  Preexisting obligation.

**anticipatory breach of contract**  (or **anticipatory repudiation**)  The unjustified assertion by a party that he will not perform an obligation that he is contractually obligated to perform at a future time. See U.C.C. §§ 610 & 611.

**apparent authority**  Such principal power that a reasonable person would assume an agent has in light of the principal's conduct.

**appeal**  Resort to a superior (appellate) court to review the decision of an inferior (trial) court or administrative agency.

**appeal by right**  Mandatory review by a higher court.

**appellant**  A party who takes an appeal from one court to another. He may be either the plaintiff or defendant in the original court proceeding.

**appellee**  The party in a cause against whom an appeal is taken; that is, the party who has an interest adverse to setting aside or reversing the judgment. Sometimes also called the "respondent."

**appropriation**  Unauthorized use of another person's name or likeness for one's own benefit.

**appurtenances**  Things appurtenant pass as incident to the principal thing. Sometimes an easement consisting of a right of way over one piece of land will pass with another piece of land as being appurtenant to it.

**APR**  Annual percentage rate.

**arbitration**  The reference of a dispute to an impartial (third) person chosen by the parties who agree in advance to abide by the arbitrator's award issued after a hearing at which both parties have an opportunity to be heard.

**arraignment**  Accused is informed of the crime against him and enters a plea.

**articles of incorporation**  (or **certificate of incorporation**)  The instrument under which a corporation is formed. The contents are prescribed in the particular state's general incorporation statute.

**articles of partnership**  A written agreement by which parties enter into a partnership, to be governed by the terms set forth therein.

**as is**  Disclaimer of implied warranties.

**assault**  Unlawful attempted battery; intentional infliction of apprehension of immediate bodily harm or offensive contact.

**assignee**  Party to whom contract rights are assigned.

**assignment**  A transfer of the rights to real or personal property, usually intangible property such as rights in a lease, mortgage, sale agreement or partnership.

**assignment of rights**  Voluntary transfer to a third party of the rights arising from a contract.

**assignor**  Party making an assignment.

**assumes**  Delegatee agrees to perform the contractual obligation of the delegator.

**assumes the mortgage**  Purchaser of mortgaged property becomes personally liable to pay the debt.

**assumption of risk**  Plaintiff's express or implied consent to encounter a known danger.

**attachment**  The process of seizing property, by virtue of a writ, summons, or other judicial order, and bringing the same into the custody of the court for the purpose of securing satisfaction of the judgment ultimately to be entered in the action. While formerly the main objective was to coerce the defendant debtor to appear in court, today the writ of attachment is used primarily to seize the debtor's property in the event a judgment is rendered.
   *Distinguished from execution*  See **execution**.
   Also, the process by which a security interest becomes enforceable. Attachment may occur upon the taking of possession or upon the signing of a security agreement by the person who is pledging the property as collateral.

**authority**  Power of an agent to change the legal status of his principal.

**authorized means**  Any reasonable means of communication.

**automatic perfection**  Perfection upon attachment.

**award**  The decision of an arbitrator.

**bad checks**  Issuing a check with insufficient funds to cover the check.

**bailee**  The party to whom personal property is delivered under a contract of bailment.
   *Extraordinary bailee*  Absolutely liable for the safety of the bailed property without regard to the cause of the loss.
   *Ordinary bailee*  Must exercise due care.

**bailment** A delivery of personal property in trust for the execution of a special object in relation to such goods, beneficial either to the bailor or bailee or both, and upon a contract to either redeliver the goods to the bailor or otherwise dispose of the same in conformity with the purpose of the trust.

**bailor** The party who delivers goods to another in the contract of bailment.

**Bankruptcy Code** A Federal law for the benefit and relief of creditors and their debtors in cases in which the latter are unable or unwilling to pay their debts. Straight bankruptcy is in the nature of a liquidation proceeding and involves the collection and distribution to creditors of all the bankrupt's non-exempt property by the trustee in the manner provided by the Code. The debtor rehabilitation provisions of the Code (Chapters 11, 12, and 13) differ however from straight bankruptcy in that the debtor looks to rehabilitation and reorganization, rather than liquidation, and the creditor looks to future earnings of the bankrupt, rather than property held by the bankrupt to satisfy their claims.

**bargain** Negotiated exchange.

**bargained exchange** Mutually agreed upon exchange.

**basis of the bargain** Part of the buyer's assumption underlying the sale.

**battery** Unlawful touching of another; intentional infliction of harmful or offensive bodily contact.

**bearer** Person in possession of an instrument.

**bearer paper** Payable to holder of the instrument.

**beneficiary** One who benefits from act of another. See also **third party beneficiary**.

*Incidental* A person who may derive benefit from performance of a contract, though he is neither the promisee nor the one to whom performance is to be rendered. Since the incidental beneficiary is not a donee or creditor beneficiary (see **third party beneficiary**), he has no right to enforce the contract.

*Intended beneficiary* Third party intended by the two contracted parties to receive a benefit from their contract.

*Trust* As it relates to trust beneficiaries, includes a person who has any present or future interest, vested or contingent, and also includes the owner of an interest by assignment or other transfer and, as it relates to a charitable trust, includes any person entitled to enforce the trust.

**beyond a reasonable doubt** Proof that is entirely convincing, satisfied to a moral certainty; criminal law standard.

**bilateral contract** Contract in which both parties exchange promises.

**bill of lading** Document evidencing receipt of goods for shipment issued by person engaged in business of transporting or forwarding goods and it includes air-bill. U.C.C. § 1–201(6).

*Through bill of lading* A bill of lading which specifies at least one connecting carrier.

**bill of sale** A written agreement, formerly limited to one under seal, by which one person assigns or transfers his right to or interest in goods to another.

**binder** A written memorandum of the important terms of contract of insurance which gives temporary protection to insured pending investigation of risk by insurance company or until a formal policy is issued.

**blue law** Prohibition of certain types of commercial activity on Sunday.

**blue sky laws** A popular name for State statutes providing for the regulation and supervision of securities offerings and sales, for the protection of citizen-investors from investing in fraudulent companies.

**bona fide** Latin. In good faith.

**bond** A certificate or evidence of a debt on which the issuing company or governmental body promises to pay the bondholders a specified amount of interest for a specified length of time, and to repay the loan on the expiration date. In every case a bond represents debt—its holder is a creditor of the corporation and not a part owner as is the shareholder.

**boycott** Agreement among parties not to deal with a third party.

**breach** Wrongful failure to perform the terms of a contract.

*Material breach* Nonperformance which significantly impairs the aggrieved party's rights under the contract.

**bribery** Offering property to a public official to influence the official's decision.

**bulk transfer** Transfer not in the ordinary course of the transferor's business of a major part of his inventory.

**burglary** Breaking and entering the home of another at night with intent to commit a felony.

**business judgment rule** Protects directors from liability for honest mistakes of judgment.

**business trust** A trust (managed by a trustee for the benefit of a beneficiary) established to conduct a business for a profit.

**but for rule** Conduct is a cause of an event if the event would not have occurred in the absence of the person's negligent conduct.

**buyer in ordinary course of business** Person who buys in ordinary course, in good faith, and without knowledge that the sale to him is in violation of anyone's ownership rights or of a security interest.

**by-laws** Regulations, ordinances, rules of laws adopted by an association or corporation for its government.

**callable bond** Bond that is subject to redemption (reacquisition) by the corporation.

**cancellation** Putting an end to a contract by one party because of a breach by another party.

**capital** Accumulated goods, possessions, and assets, used for the production of profits and wealth. Owners' equity in a business. Often used equally correctly to mean the total assets of a business. Sometimes used to mean capital assets.

**capital surplus** Surplus other than earned surplus.

**carrier** Transporter of goods.

**casualty insurance** Covers property loss due to causes other than fire or the elements.

**cause of action** The ground on which an action may be sustained.

**caveat emptor** Latin. Let the buyer beware. This maxim is more applicable to judicial sales, auctions, and the like, than to sales of consumer goods where strict liability, warranty, and other laws protect.

**certificate of deposit** A written acknowledgment by a bank or banker of a deposit with promise to pay to depositor, to his order, or to some other person or to his order. U.C.C. § 3–104(2)(c).

**certificate of title**  Official representation of ownership.

**certification**  Acceptance of a check by a drawee bank.

**certification of incorporation**  See **articles of incorporation**.

**certification mark**  Distinctive symbol, word, or design used with goods or services to certify specific characteristics.

**certiorari**  Latin. To be informed of. A writ of common law origin issued by a superior to an inferior court requiring the latter to produce a certified record of a particular case tried therein. It is most commonly used to refer to the Supreme Court of the United States, which uses the writ of certiorari as a discretionary device to choose the cases it wishes to hear.

**chancery**  Equity; equitable jurisdiction; a court of equity; the system of jurisprudence administered in courts of equity.

**charging order**  Judicial lien against a partner's interest in the partnership.

**charter**  An instrument emanating from the sovereign power, in the nature of a grant. A charter differs from a constitution in that the former is granted by the sovereign, while the latter is established by the people themselves.

*Corporate law*  An act of a legislature creating a corporation, or creating and defining the franchise of a corporation. Also a corporation's constitution or organic law; that is to say, the articles of incorporation taken in connection with the law under which the corporation was organized.

**chattel mortgage**  A pre-Uniform Commercial Code security device whereby a security interest was taken by the mortgagee in personal property of the mortgagor. Such security device has generally been superseded by other types of security agreements under U.C.C. Article 9 (Secured Transactions).

**chattel paper**  Writings that evidence both a debt and a security interest.

**check**  A draft drawn upon a bank and payable on demand, signed by the maker or drawer, containing an unconditional promise to pay a sum certain in money to the order of the payee. U.C.C. § 3–104(2)(b).

*Cashier's check*  A bank's own check drawn on itself and signed by the cashier or other authorized official. It is a direct obligation of the bank.

**C. & F.**  Cost and freight; a shipping contract.

**C.I.F.**  Cost, insurance, and freight; a shipping contract.

**civil law**  Laws concerned with civil or private rights and remedies, as contrasted with criminal laws.

The system of jurisprudence administered in the Roman empire, particularly as set forth in the compilation of Justinian and his successors, as distinguished from the common law of England and the canon law. The civil law (Civil Code) is followed by Louisiana.

**claim**  A right to payment.

**clearing house**  An association of banks for the purpose of settling accounts on a daily basis.

**close corporation**  See **corporation**.

**closed-ended credit**  Credit extended to debtor for a specific period of time.

**closed shop**  Employer can only hire union members.

**C.O.D.**  Collect on delivery; generally a shipping contract.

**code**  A compilation of all permanent laws in force consolidated and classified according to subject matter. Many States have published official codes of all laws in force, including the common law and statutes as judicially interpreted, which have been compiled by code commissions and enacted by the legislatures.

**codicil**  A supplement or an addition to a will; it may explain, modify, add to, subtract from, qualify, alter, restrain or revoke provisions in existing will. It must be executed with the same formalities as a will.

**cognovit judgment**  Written authority by debtor for entry of judgment against him in the event he defaults in payment. Such provision in a debt instrument on default confers judgment against the debtor.

**collateral**  Secondarily liable, only liable if the party with primary liability does not perform.

**collateral (security)**  Personal property subject to a security interest.

*Banking*  Some form of security in addition to the personal obligation of the borrower.

**collateral promise**  Undertaking to be secondarily liable, that is, liable if the principal debtor does not perform.

**collecting bank**  Any bank handling the item for collection except the payor bank. U.C.C. § 4–105(d).

**collective mark**  Distinctive symbol used to indicate membership in an organization.

**collision insurance**  Protects the owner of an automobile against damage due to contact with other vehicles or objects.

**commerce power**  Exclusive power granted by the U.S. Constitution to the Federal government to regulate commerce with foreign countries and among the States.

**commercial bailment**  Bailment in which both parties derive a mutual benefit.

**commercial impracticability**  Performance can only be accomplished with unforeseen and unjust hardship.

**commercial law**  A phrase used to designate the whole body of substantive jurisprudence (*e.g.*, Uniform Commercial Code; Truth in Lending Act) applicable to the rights, intercourse, and relations of persons engaged in commerce, trade, or mercantile pursuits. See **Uniform Commercial Code**.

**commercial paper**  Bills of exchange (*i.e.*, drafts), promissory notes, bank-checks, and other negotiable instruments for the payment of money, which, by their form and on their face, purport to be such instruments. U.C.C. Article 3 is the general law governing commercial paper.

**commercial reasonableness**  Judgment of reasonable persons familiar with the business transaction.

**commercial speech**  Expression related to the economic interests of the speaker and its audience.

**common carrier**  Carrier open to the general public.

**common law**  Body of law originating in England and derived from judicial decisions. As distinguished from statutory law created by the enactment of legislatures, the common law comprises the judgments and decrees of the courts recognizing, affirming, and enforcing usages and customs of immemorial antiquity.

**community property**  Rights by spouses in property acquired by the other during marriage.

**comparable worth**  Equal pay for jobs of equal value to the employer.

**comparative negligence**  Under comparative negligence statutes or doctrines, negligence is measured in terms of percentage, and any damages allowed shall be diminished in proportion to amount of negligence attributable to the person for whose injury, damage or death recovery is sought.

**complainant**  One who applies to the courts for legal redress by filing complaint (*i.e.,* plaintiff).

**complaint**  The pleading which sets forth a claim for relief. Such complaint (whether it be the original claim, counterclaim, cross-claim, or third-party claim) shall contain: (1) a short and plain statement of the grounds upon which the court's jurisdiction depends, unless the court already has jurisdiction and the claim needs no new grounds of jurisdiction to support it, (2) a short and plain statement of the claim showing that the pleader is entitled to relief, and (3) a demand for judgment for the relief to which he deems himself entitled. The complaint, together with the summons, is required to be served on the defendant.

**composition**  Agreement between debtor and two or more of her creditors that each will take a portion of his claim as full payment.

**compulsory arbitration**  Arbitration required by statute for specific types of disputes.

**computer crime**  Crime by, with, or at a computer.

**concealment**  Fraudulent failure to disclose a material fact.

**conciliation**  Nonbinding process in which a third party acts as an intermediary between the disputing parties.

**concurrent jurisdiction**  Authority of more than one court to hear the same case.

**condition**  An uncertain event which affects the duty of performance.
   *Concurrent conditions*  Mutual duties of performance are to occur simultaneously.
   *Express condition*  Performance is contingent on the happening or nonhappening of a stated event.

**condition precedent**  An event which must occur or not occur before performance is due; event or events (presentment, dishonor, notice of dishonor) which must occur to hold a secondary party liable to commercial paper.

**condition subsequent**  An event which terminates a duty of performance.

**conditional acceptance**  An acceptance of an offer contingent upon the acceptance of an additional or different term.

**conditional contract**  Obligations are contingent upon a stated event.

**conditional guarantor of collection**  Surety liable to creditor only after creditor exhausts his legal remedies against the principal debtor.

**confession of judgment**  Written agreement by debtor authorizing creditor to obtain a court judgment in the event debtor defaults. See also **cognovit judgment**.

**confiscation**  Governmental taking of foreign-owned property without payment.

**conflict of laws**  That branch of jurisprudence, arising from the diversity of the laws of different nations, States or jurisdictions, that reconciles the inconsistency, or decides which law is to govern in the particular case.

**confusion**  Results when goods belonging to two or more owners become intermixed to the point where the property of any of them no longer can be identified except as part of a mass of like goods.

**consanguinity**  Kinship; blood relationship; the connection or relation of persons descended from the same stock or common ancestor.

**consensual arbitration**  Arbitration voluntarily entered into by the parties.

**consent**  Voluntary and knowing willingness that an act should be done.

**conservator**  Appointed by court to manage affairs of incompetent or to liquidate business.

**consideration**  The cause, motive, price, or impelling influence which induces a contracting party to enter into a contract. Some right, interest, profit or benefit accruing to one party, or some forbearance, detriment, loss, or responsibility, given, suffered, or undertaken by the other.

**consignee**  One to whom a consignment is made. Person named in bill of lading to whom or to whose order the bill promises delivery. U.C.C. § 7–102(b).

**consignment**  Ordinarily implies an agency and denotes that property is committed to the consignee for care or sale.

**consignor**  One who sends or makes a consignment; a shipper of goods. The person named in a bill of lading as the person from whom the goods have been received for shipment. U.C.C. § 7–102(c).

**consolidation**  In *corporate law,* the combination of two or more corporations into a newly created corporation. Thus, A Corporation and B Corporation combine to form C Corporation.

**constitution**  Fundamental law of a government establishing its powers and limitations.

**constructive**  That which is established by the mind of the law in its act of *construing* facts, conduct, circumstances, or instruments. That which has not the character assigned to it in its own essential nature, but acquires such character in consequence of the way in which it is regarded by a rule or policy of law; hence, inferred, implied, or made out by legal interpretation; the word "legal" being sometimes used here in lieu of "constructive."

**constructive assent**  An assent or consent imputed to a party from a construction or interpretation of his conduct; as distinguished from one which he actually expresses.

**constructive conditions**  Conditions in contracts which are neither expressed nor implied but are rather imposed by law to meet the ends of justice.

**constructive delivery**  Term comprehending all those acts which, although not truly conferring a real possession of the vendee, have been held by construction of law to be the equivalent to acts of real delivery.

**constructive eviction**  Failure by the landlord in any obligation under the lease that causes a substantial and lasting injury to the tenant's enjoyment of the premises.

**constructive notice**  Knowledge imputed by law.

**constructive trust**  Arising by operation of law to prevent unjust enrichment. See also **trustee**.

**consumer goods**  Goods bought or used for personal, family, or household purposes.

**consumer product**  Tangible personal property normally used for family, household, or personal purposes.

**contingent remainder**  Remainder interest, conditional upon the happening of an event in addition to the termination of the preceding estate.

**contract** An agreement between two or more persons which creates an obligation to do or not to do a particular thing. Its essentials are competent parties, subject matter, a legal consideration, mutuality of agreement, and mutuality of obligation.

*Destination contract* Seller is required to tender delivery of the goods at a particular destination; seller bears the expense and risk of loss.

*Executed contract* Fully performed by all of the parties.

*Executory contract* Contract partially or entirely unperformed by one or more of the parties.

*Express contract* Agreement of parties that is expressed in words either in writing or orally.

*Formal contract* Agreement which is legally binding because of its particular form or mode of expression.

*Implied in fact contract* Contract where agreement of the parties is inferred from their conduct.

*Informal contract* All oral or written contracts other than formal contracts.

*Installment contract* Goods are delivered in separate lots.

*Integrated contract* Complete and total agreement.

*Output contract* A contract in which one party agrees to sell his entire output and the other agrees to buy it; it is not illusory, though it may be indefinite.

*Quasi contract* Obligation not based upon contract that is imposed to avoid injustice.

*Requirements contract* A contract in which one party agrees to purchase his total requirements from the other party and hence it is binding and not illusory.

*Substituted contract* An agreement between the parties to rescind their old contract and replace it with a new contract.

*Unconscionable contract* One which no sensible man not under delusion, duress, or in distress would make, and such as no honest and fair man would accept. A contract the terms of which are excessively unreasonable, overreaching and one-sided.

*Unenforceable contract* Contract for the breach of which the law does not provide a remedy.

*Unilateral and bilateral* A unilateral contract is one in which one party makes an express engagement or undertakes a performance, without receiving in return any express engagement or promise of performance from the other. Bilateral (or reciprocal) contracts are those by which the parties expressly enter into mutual engagements.

**contract clause** Prohibition against the States' retroactively modifying public and private contracts.

**contractual liability** Obligation on a negotiable instrument, based upon signing the instrument.

**contribution** Payment from cosureties of their proportionate share.

**contributory negligence** The act or omission amounting to want of ordinary care on part of complaining party, which, concurring with defendant's negligence, is proximate cause of injury.

The defense of contributory negligence is an absolute bar to any recovery in some States; because of this, it has been replaced by the doctrine of comparative negligence in many other States.

**conversion** Unauthorized and wrongful exercise of dominion and control over another's personal property, to exclusion of or inconsistent with rights of the owner.

**convertible bond** Bond that may be exchanged for other securities of the corporation.

**copyright** Exclusive right granted by Federal government to authors of original works including literary, musical, dramatic, pictorial, graphic, sculptural, and film works.

**corporation** A legal entity ordinarily consisting of an association of numerous individuals. Such entity is regarded as having a personality and existence distinct from that of its several members and is vested with the capacity of continuous succession, irrespective of changes in its membership, either in perpetuity or for a limited term of years.

*Closely held* or *close corporation* Corporation that is owned by few shareholders and whose shares are not actively traded.

*Corporation de facto* One existing under color of law and in pursuance of an effort made in good faith to organize a corporation under the statute. Such a corporation is not subject to collateral attack.

*Corporation de jure* That which exists by reason of full compliance with requirements of an existing law permitting organization of such corporation.

*Domestic corporation* Corporation created under the laws of a given State.

*Foreign corporation* Corporation created under the laws of any other State, government, or country.

*Subchapter S corporation* A small business corporation which, under certain conditions, may elect to have its undistributed taxable income taxed to its shareholders. I.R.C. § 1371 *et seq.* Of major significance is the fact that Subchapter S status usually avoids the corporate income tax, and corporate losses can be claimed by the shareholders.

*Subsidiary and parent corporation* Subsidiary corporation is one in which another corporation (called parent corporation) owns at least a majority of the shares, and thus has control.

**corrective advertising** Disclosure in an advertisement that previous ads were deceptive.

**costs** A pecuniary allowance, made to the successful party (and recoverable from the losing party), for his expenses in prosecuting or defending an action or a distinct proceeding within an action. Generally, "costs" do not include attorney fees unless such fees are by a statute denominated costs or are by statute allowed to be recovered as costs in the case.

**cosureties** Two or more sureties bound for the same debt of a principal debtor.

**co-tenants** Persons who hold title concurrently.

**counter offer** A statement by the offeree which has the legal effect of rejecting the offer and of proposing a new offer to the offeror. However, the provisions of U.C.C. § 2–207(2) modifies this principle by providing that the "additional terms are to be construed as proposals for addition to the contract."

**counterclaim** A claim presented by a defendant in opposition to or deduction from the claim of the plaintiff.

**course of dealing** A sequence of previous acts and conduct between the parties to a particular transaction which is fairly to be regarded as establishing a common basis of understanding for interpreting their expressions and other conduct. U.C.C. § 1–205(1).

**course of performance** Conduct between the parties concerning performance of the particular contract.

**court above—court below** In appellate practice, the "court above" is the one to which a cause is removed for review, whether by appeal, writ of error, or certiorari; while the "court below" is the one from which the case is being removed.

**covenant** Used primarily with respect to promises in conveyances or other instruments dealing with real estate.

*Covenants against encumbrances* A stipulation against all rights to or interests in the land which may subsist in third persons to the diminution of the value of the estate granted.

*Covenant appurtenant* A covenant which is connected with land of the grantor, and not in gross. A covenant running with the land and binding heirs, executors and assigns of the immediate parties.

*Covenant for further assurance* An undertaking, in the form of a covenant, on the part of the vendor of real estate to do such further acts for the purpose of perfecting the purchaser's title as the latter may reasonably require.

*Covenant for possession* A covenant by which the grantee or lessee is granted possession.

*Covenant for quiet enjoyment* An assurance against the consequences of a defective title, and of any disturbances thereupon.

*Covenants for title* Covenants usually inserted in a conveyance of land, on the part of the grantor, and binding him for the completeness, security, and continuance of the title transferred to the grantee. They comprise covenants for seisin, for right to convey, against encumbrances, or quiet enjoyment, sometimes for further assurance, and almost always of warranty.

*Covenant in gross* Such as do not run with the land.

*Covenant of right to convey* An assurance by the covenantor that the grantor has sufficient capacity and title to convey the *estate* which he by his deed undertakes to convey.

*Covenant of seisin* An assurance to the purchaser that the grantor has the very estate in quantity and quality which he purports to convey.

*Covenant of warranty* An assurance by the grantor of an estate that the grantee shall enjoy the same without interruption by virtue of paramount title.

*Covenant running with land* A covenant which goes with the land, as being annexed to the estate, and which cannot be separated from the land, and transferred without it. A covenant is said to run with the land when not only the original parties or their representatives, but each successive owner of the land, will be entitled to its benefit, or be liable (as the case may be) to its obligation. Such a covenant is said to be one which "touches and concerns" the land itself, so that its benefit or obligation passes with the ownership. Essentials are that the grantor and grantee must have intended that the covenant run with the land, the covenant must affect or concern the land with which it runs, and there must be privity of estate between party claiming the benefit and the party who rests under the burden.

**covenant not to compete** Agreement to refrain from entering into a competing trade, profession, or business.

**cover** Buyer's purchase of goods in substitution for those not delivered by breaching seller.

**credit beneficiary** See **third party beneficiary**.

**creditor** Any entity having a claim against the debtor.

**crime** An act or omission in violation of a public law and punishable by the government.

**criminal duress** Coercion by threat of serious bodily injury.

**criminal intent** Desired or virtually certain consequences of one's conduct.

**criminal law** The law that involves offenses against the entire community.

**cure** The right of a seller under U.C.C. to correct a non-conforming delivery of goods to buyer within the contract period. U.C.C. § 2–508.

**curtsey** Husband's estate in the real property of his wife.

**cy-pres** As near as (possible). Rule for the construction of instruments in equity, by which the intention of the party is carried out *as near as may be,* when it would be impossible or illegal to give it literal effect.

**damage** Loss, injury, or deterioration, caused by the negligence, design, or accident of one person to another, in respect of the latter's person or property. The word is to be distinguished from its plural, "damages," which means a compensation in money for a loss or damage.

**damages** Money sought as a remedy for breach of contract or for tortious acts.

*Actual damages* Real, substantial, and just damages, or the amount awarded to a complainant in compensation for his actual and real loss or injury, as opposed on the one hand to "nominal" damages, and on the other to "exemplary" or "punitive" damages. Synonymous with "compensatory damages" and with "general damages."

*Benefit-of-the-bargain damages* Difference between the value received and the value of the fraudulent party's performance as represented.

*Compensatory damages* Compensatory damages are such as will compensate the injured party for the injury sustained, and nothing more; such as will simply make good or replace the loss caused by the wrong or injury.

*Consequential damages* Such damage, loss or injury as does not flow directly and immediately from the act of the party, but only from some of the consequences or results of such act. Consequential damages resulting from a seller's breach of contract include any loss resulting from general or particular requirements and needs of which the seller at the time of contracting had reason to know and which could not reasonably be prevented by cover or otherwise, and injury to person or property proximately resulting from any breach of warranty. U.C.C. § 2–715(2).

*Exemplary or punitive damages* Damages other than compensatory damages which may be awarded against a person to punish him for outrageous conduct.

*Expectancy damages* Calculable by subtracting the injured party's actual dollar position as a result of the breach from that party's projected dollar position had performance occurred.

*Foreseeable damages* Loss that the party in breach had reason to know of when the contract was made.

*Incidental damages* Under U.C.C. § 2–710, such damages include any commercially reasonable charges, expenses or commissions incurred in stopping delivery, in the transportation, care and custody of goods after the buyer's breach, in connection with the return or resale of the goods or otherwise resulting from the breach. Also, such damages, resulting from a seller's breach of contract, include expenses reasonably incurred in inspection, receipt, transportation and care and custody of goods rightfully rejected, any commercially reasonable charges, expenses or commissions in connection with effecting cover and any other reasonable expense incident to the delay or other breach. U.C.C. § 2–715(1).

*Irreparable damages* In the law pertaining to injunctions, damages for which no certain pecuniary standard exists for measurement.

*Liquidated damages and penalties* Damages for breach by either party may be liquidated in the agreement but only at an amount which is reasonable in the light of the anticipated or actual harm caused by the breach, the difficulties of proof of loss, and the inconvenience or nonfeasibility of otherwise obtaining an adequate remedy. A term fixing unreasonably large liquidated damages is void as a penalty. U.C.C. § 2–718(1).

*Mitigation of damages*  A plaintiff may not recover damages for the effects of an injury which reasonably could have been avoided or substantially ameliorated. This limitation on recovery is generally denominated as "mitigation of damages" or "avoidance of consequences."

*Nominal damages*  A small sum awarded where a contract has been breached but the loss is negligible or unproven.

*Out-of-pocket damages*  Difference between the value received and the value given.

*Reliance damages*  Contract damages placing the injured party in as good a position as he would have been in had the contract not been made.

*Treble damages*  Three times actual loss.

**de facto**  In fact, in deed, actually. This phrase is used to characterize an officer, a government, a past action, or a state of affairs which must be accepted for all practical purposes, but is illegal or illegitimate. See also **corporation**, *corporation de facto*.

**de jure**  Descriptive of a condition in which there has been total compliance with all requirements of law. In this sense it is the contrary of *de facto*. See also **corporation**, *corporation de jure*.

**de novo**  Anew; afresh; a second time.

**debenture**  Unsecured bond.

**debt security**  Any form of corporate security reflected as debt on the books of the corporation in contrast to equity securities such as stock; *e.g.*, bonds, notes, and debentures are debt securities.

**debtor**  Person who owes payment or performance of an obligation.

**deceit**  A fraudulent and cheating misrepresentation, artifice, or device, used to deceive and trick one who is ignorant of the true facts, to the prejudice and damage of the party imposed upon. See also **fraud**; **misrepresentation**.

**decree**  Decision of a court of equity.

**deed**  A conveyance of realty; a writing signed by grantor, whereby title to realty is transferred from one to another.

**deed of trust**  Interest in real property which is conveyed to a third person as trustee for the creditor.

**defamation**  Injury of a person's reputation by publication of false statements.

**default judgment**  Judgment against a defendant who fails to respond to a complaint.

**defendant**  The party against whom legal action is sought.

**definite term**  Lease that automatically expires at end of the term.

**delectus personae**  Partner's right to choose who may become a member of the partnership.

**delegatee**  Third party to whom the delegator's duty is delegated.

**delegation of duties**  Transferring all or part of one's duties arising under a contract to another.

**delegator**  Party delegating his duty to a third party.

**delivery**  The physical or constructive transfer of an instrument or of goods from the hands of one person to those of another. See also **constructive delivery**.

**demand**  Request for payment made by the holder of the instrument.

**demand paper**  Payable on request.

**demurrer**  An allegation of a defendant that, even if the facts as stated in the pleading to which objection is taken be true, yet their legal consequences are not such as to put the demurring party to the necessity of answering them or proceeding further with the cause.

**deposition**  The testimony of a witness taken upon interrogatories, not in court, but intended to be used in court. See also **discovery**.

**depository bank**  The first bank to which an item is transferred for collection even though it may also be the payor bank. U.C.C. § 4–105(a).

**descent**  Succession to the ownership of an estate by inheritance, or by any act of law, as distinguished from "purchase."

Descents are of two sorts, *lineal* and *collateral*. Lineal descent is descent in a direct or right line, as from father or grandfather to son or grandson. Collateral descent is descent in a collateral or oblique line, that is, up to the common ancestor and then down from him, as from brother to brother, or between cousins.

**design defect**  Inadequate plans or specifications to insure the products' safety.

**devise**  A testamentary disposition of land or realty; a gift of real property by the last will and testament of the donor. When used as a noun, means a testamentary disposition of real or personal property and when used as a verb, means to dispose of real or personal property by will.

**dictum**  Generally used as an abbreviated form of *obiter dictum*,"a remark by the way"; that is, an observation or remark made by a judge which does not embody the resolution or determination of the court and which is made without argument or full consideration of the point.

**directed verdict**  In a case in which the party with the burden of proof has failed to present a prima facie case for jury consideration, the trial judge may order the entry of a verdict without allowing the jury to consider it, because, as a matter of law, there can be only one such verdict.

**disaffirmance**  Avoidance of the contract.

**discharge**  Termination of certain allowed claims against a debtor.

**disclaimer**  Negation of warranty.

**discount**  A discount by a bank means a drawback or deduction made upon its advances or loans of money, upon negotiable paper or other evidences of debt payable at a future day, which are transferred to the bank.

**discovery**  The pre-trial devices that can be used by one party to obtain facts and information about the case from the other party in order to assist the party's preparation for trial. Discovery includes: depositions upon oral and written questions, written interrogatories, production of documents or things, permission to enter upon land or other property, physical and mental examinations and requests for admission.

**dishonor**  To refuse to accept or pay a draft or to pay a promissory note when duly presented. U.C.C. § 3–507(1); § 4–210. See also **protest**.

**disparagement**  Publication of false statements resulting in harm to another's monetary interests.

**disputed debt**  Obligation whose existence or amount is contested.

**dissenting shareholder**  One who opposes a fundamental change and has the right to receive the fair value of her shares.

**dissolution**  The dissolution of a partnership is the change in the relation of the partners caused by any partner ceasing to be associated in the carrying on as distinguished from the winding up of the business. See also **winding up**.

**distribution**  Transfer of partnership property from the partnership to a partner; transfer of property from a corporation to any of its shareholders.

**dividend**  The payment designated by the board of directors of a corporation to be distributed pro rata among a class or classes of the shares outstanding.

**document**  Document of title.

**document of title**  Instrument evidencing ownership of the document and the goods it covers.

**domicile**  That place where a person has his true, fixed, and permanent home and principal establishment, and to which whenever he is absent he has the intention of returning.

**dominant**  Land whose owner has rights in other land.

**donee**  Recipient of a gift.

**donee beneficiary**  See **third party beneficiary**.

**donor**  Maker of a gift.

**dormant partner**  One who is both a silent and a secret partner.

**dower**  A species of life-estate which a woman is, by law, entitled to claim on the death of her husband, in the lands and tenements of which he was seised in fee during the marriage, and which her issue, if any, might by possibility have inherited.

Dower has been abolished in the majority of the states and materially altered in most of the others.

**draft**  A written order by the first party, called the drawer, instructing a second party, called the drawee (such as a bank) to pay a third party, called the payee. An order to pay a sum certain in money, signed by a drawer, payable on demand or at a definite time, and to order or bearer. U.C.C. § 3–104.

**drawee**  A person to whom a bill of exchange or draft is directed, and who is requested to pay the amount of money therein mentioned. The drawee of a check is the bank on which it is drawn.

When drawee accepts, he engages that he will pay the instrument according to its tenor at the time of his engagement or as completed. U.C.C. § 3–413(1).

**drawer**  The person who draws a bill or draft. The drawer of a check is the person who signs it.

The drawer engages that upon dishonor of the draft and any necessary notice of dishonor or protest, he will pay the amount of the draft to the holder or to any indorser who takes it up. The drawer may disclaim this liability by drawing without recourse. U.C.C. § 3–413(2).

**due negotiation**  Transfer of a negotiable document in the regular course of business to a holder, who takes in good faith, without notice of any defense or claim, and for value.

**duress**  Unlawful constraint exercised upon a person, whereby he is forced to do some act against his will.

*Physical duress*  Coercion involving physical force or the threat of physical force.

**duty**  Legal obligation requiring a person to perform or refrain from performing an act.

**earned surplus**  Undistributed net profits, income, gains and losses.

**earnest**  The payment of a part of the price of goods sold, or the delivery of part of such goods, for the purpose of binding the contract.

**easement**  A right in the owner of one parcel of land, by reason of such ownership, to use the land of another for a special purpose not inconsistent with a general property in the owner. This right is distinguishable from a "license" which merely confers personal privilege to do some act on the land.

*Affirmative easement*  One where the servient estate must permit something to be done thereon, as to pass over it, or to discharge water on it.

*Appurtenant easement*  An incorporeal right which is attached to a superior right and inheres in land to which it is attached and is in the nature of a covenant running with the land.

*Easement by necessity*  Such arises by operation of law when land conveyed is completely shut off from access to any road by land retained by grantor or by land of grantor and that of a stranger.

*Easement by prescription*  A mode of acquiring title to property by immemorial or long-continued enjoyment, and refers to personal usage restricted to claimant and his ancestors or grantors.

*Easement in gross*  An easement in gross is not appurtenant to any estate in land or does not belong to any person by virtue of ownership of estate in other land but is mere personal interest in or right to use land of another; it is purely personal and usually ends with death of grantee.

*Easement of access*  Right of ingress and egress to and from the premises of a lot owner to a street appurtenant to the land of the lot owner.

**ejectment**  An action of which the purpose is to determine whether the title to certain land is in the plaintiff or is in the defendant.

**electronic fund transfer**  A transaction with a financial institution by means of computer, telephone, or electronic instrument.

**emancipation**  The act by which an infant is set at liberty from the control of parent or guardian and made his own master.

**embezzlement**  The taking in violation of a trust the property of one's employer.

**emergency**  Sudden, unexpected event calling for immediate action.

**eminent domain**  Right of the people or government to take private property for public use upon giving of a fair consideration.

**employment discrimination**  Hiring, firing, compensating, promoting, or training of employees based on race, color, sex, religion, or national origin.

**employment relationship**  One in which employer has right to control the physical conduct of employee.

**endowment contract**  Agreement to pay insured a lump sum upon reaching a specified age or in event of death.

**entirety**  Used to designate that which the law considers as one whole, and not capable of being divided into parts.

**entrapment**  Induced into committing a crime by a government official.

**entrusting**  Transfer of possession of goods to a merchant who deals in goods of that kind and who may in turn transfer valid title to a buyer in the ordinary course of business.

**equal pay**  Equivalent pay for the same work.

**equal protection**  Requirement that similarly situated persons be treated similarly by government action.

**equipment**  Goods used primarily in business.

**equitable**  Just, fair, and right. Existing in equity; available or sustainable only in equity, or only upon the rules and principles of equity.

**equity**  Justice administered according to fairness as contrasted with the strictly formulated rules of common law. It is based on a system of rules and principles which originated in England as an alternative to the harsh rules of common law and which were based on what was fair in a particular situation.

**equity of redemption**  The right of the mortgagor of an estate to redeem the same after it has been forfeited, at law, by a breach of the condition of the mortgage, upon paying the amount of debt, interest, and costs.

**equity securities**  Stock or similar security, in contrast to debt securities such as bonds, notes, and debentures.

**error**  A mistake of law, or false or irregular application of it, such as vitiates the proceedings and warrants the reversal of the judgment.

*Harmless error*  In appellate practice, an error committed in the progress of the trial below which was not prejudicial to the rights of the party assigning it and for which, therefore, the court will not reverse the judgment.

*Reversible error*  In appellate practice, such an error as warrants the appellate court in reversing the judgment before it.

**escrow**  A system of document transfer in which a deed, bond, or funds is delivered to a third person to hold until all conditions in a contract are fulfilled; *e.g.,* delivery of deed to escrow agent under installment land sale contract until full payment for land is made.

**estate**  The degree, quantity, nature, and extent of interest which a person has in real and personal property. An estate in lands, tenements, and hereditaments signifies such interest as the tenant has therein.

Also, the total property of whatever kind that is owned by a decedent prior to the distribution of that property in accordance with the terms of a will, or, when there is no will, by the laws of inheritance in the State of domicile of the decedent.

*Future estate*  An estate which is not now vested in the grantee, but is to commence in possession at some future time. Examples include reversions and remainders.

**estoppel**  A bar or impediment raised by the law, which precludes a man from alleging or from denying a certain fact or state of facts, in consequence of his previous allegation or denial or conduct or admission, or in consequence of a final adjudication of the matter in a court of law. See also **waiver**.

**eviction**  Dispossession by process of law; the act of depriving a person of the possession of lands which he has held, in pursuance of the judgment of a court.

**evidence**  Any species of proof, or probative matter, legally presented at the trial of an issue, by the act of the parties and through the medium of witnesses, records, documents, concrete objects, etc., for the purpose of inducing belief in the minds of the court or jury as to their contention.

**exception**  A formal objection to the action of the court, during the trial of a cause, in refusing a request or overruling an objection; implying that the party excepting does not acquiesce in the decision of the court, but will seek to procure its reversal, and that he means to save the benefit of his request or objection in some future proceeding.

**exclusionary rule**  Prohibition of illegally obtained evidence.

**exclusive dealing**  Sole right to sell goods in a defined market.

**exclusive jurisdiction**  Such jurisdiction that permits only one court (State or Federal) to hear a case.

**exculpatory clause**  Excusing oneself from fault or liability.

**execution**  *Execution of contract* includes performance of all acts necessary to render it complete as an instrument and imports idea that nothing remains to be done to make a complete and effective contract.

*Execution upon a money judgment*  is the legal process of enforcing the judgment, usually by seizing and selling property of the debtor.

**executive order**  Legislation issued by the President or a governor.

**executor**  A person appointed by a testator to carry out the directions and requests in his will, and to dispose of the property according to his testamentary provisions after his decease. The female designation is executrix. A person appointed by the court in an intestacy situation is called the administrator(rix).

**executory**  That which is yet to be executed or performed; that which remains to be carried into operation or effect; incomplete; depending upon a future performance or event. The opposite of executed.

**executory contract**  See **contracts**.

**executory promise**  Unperformed obligation.

**exemplary damages**  See **damages**.

**exoneration**  Relieved of liability.

**express**  Manifested by direct and appropriate language, as distinguished from that which is inferred from conduct. The word is usually contrasted with "implied."

**express warranty**  Explicitly made contractual promise regarding property or contract rights transferred; in a sale of goods affirmation of fact or promise about the goods or a description, including sample, of goods which becomes part of the basis of the bargain.

**expropriation**  Governmental taking of foreign-owned property for a public purpose and with payment.

**ex-ship**  Risk of loss passes to buyer upon the goods leaving the ship. See U.C.C. § 2–322. See also **F.A.S.**

**extortion**  Making threats to obtain property.

**fact**  An event that took place or a thing that exists.

**false imprisonment**  Intentional interference with a person's freedom of movement by unlawful confinement.

**false light**  Offensive publicity placing another in a false light.

**false pretenses**  Intentional misrepresentation of fact for purpose to cheat.

**farm products**  Crops, livestock, or stock used or produced in farming.

**F.A.S.**  Free alongside. Term used in sales price quotations, indicating that the price includes all costs of transportation and delivery of the goods alongside the ship. See U.C.C. § 2–319(2).

**Federal preemption**  First right of the Federal government to regulate matters within its powers to the possible exclusion of State regulation.

**Federal question**  Any case arising under the Constitution, statutes, or treaties of the United States.

**fee simple**  An estate of inheritance.

*Absolute*  A fee simple absolute is an estate that is unlimited as to duration, disposition, and descendibility. It is the largest estate and most extensive interest that can be enjoyed in land.

*Conditional* Type of transfer in which grantor conveys fee simple on condition that something be done or not done.

*Defeasible* Type of fee grant which may be defeated on the happening of an event. An estate which may last forever, but which may end upon the happening of a specified event, is a "fee simple defeasible."

*Determinable* Created by conveyance which contains words effective to create a fee simple and, in addition, a provision for automatic expiration of estate on occurrence of stated event.

**fee tail** An estate of inheritance, descending only to a certain class or classes or heirs; *e.g.,* an estate is conveyed or devised "to A. and the heirs of his body," or "to A. and the heirs male of his body," or "to A., and the heirs female of his body." State statutes have dealt variously with estates tail, some converting them into estates in fee simple.

**fellow servant rule** Common law defense relieving employer for liability to an employee for injuries caused by negligence of fellow employee.

**felony** Serious crime.

**fiduciary** A person or institution who manages money or property for another and who must exercise a standard of care in such management activity imposed by law or contract; *e.g.,* executor of estate; receiver in bankruptcy; trustee.

**fiduciary duty** Duty of utmost loyalty and good faith owed by a fiduciary such as an agent owes to her principal.

**field warehouse** Secured party takes possession of the goods but the debtor has access to the goods.

**final credit** Payment of the instrument by the payor bank.

**financing statement** Under the Uniform Commercial Code, a financing statement is used under Article 9 to reflect a public record that there is a security interest or claim to the goods in question to secure a debt. The financing statement is filed by the security holder with the Secretary of State, or similar public body, and as such becomes public record. See also **secured transaction.**

**fire (property) insurance** Provides protection against loss due to fire or other related perils.

**firm offer** Irrevocable offer to sell or buy goods by a merchant in a signed writing which gives assurance that it will not be rescinded for up to three months.

**fitness for a particular purpose** Goods are fit for a stated purpose provided the seller selects the product knowing the buyer's intended use and that the buyer is relying on the seller's judgment.

**fixture** An article in the nature of personal property which has been so annexed to realty that it is regarded as a part of the land. Examples include a furnace affixed to a house or other building, counters permanently affixed to the floor of a store, a sprinkler system installed in a building. U.C.C. § 9–313(1)(a).

*Trade fixtures* Such chattels as merchants usually possess and annex to the premises occupied by them to enable them to store, handle, and display their goods, which are generally removable without material injury to the premises.

**F.O.B.** Free on board some location (for example, F.O.B. shipping point; F.O.B. destination); the invoice price includes delivery at seller's expense to that location. Title to goods usually passes from seller to buyer at the F.O.B. location. U.C.C. § 2–319(1).

**foreclosure** Procedure by which mortgaged property is sold on default of mortgagor in satisfaction of mortgage debt.

**forgery** Intentional falsification of a document with intent to defraud.

**four unities** Time, title, interest, and possession.

**franchise** A privilege granted or sold, such as to use a name or to sell products or services. The right given by a manufacturer or supplier to a retailer to use his name and name on terms and conditions mutually agreed upon.

**fraud** Elements include: false representation; of a present or past fact; made by defendant; action in reliance thereon by plaintiff; damage resulting to plaintiff from such misrepresentation.

**fraud in the execution** Misrepresentation that deceives the other party as to the nature of a document evidencing the contract.

**fraud in the inducement** Misrepresentation regarding the subject matter of a contract and inducing the other party to enter into it.

**fraudulent misrepresentation** False statement made with knowledge of its falsity and intent to mislead.

**freehold** An estate for life or in fee. It must possess two qualities: (1) immobility, that is, the property must be either land or some interest issuing out of or annexed to land; and (2) indeterminate duration.

**friendly fire** Fire contained where it is intended to be.

**frustration of purpose doctrine** Excuses a promisor in certain situations when the objectives of contract have been utterly defeated by circumstances arising after formation of agreement, and performance is excused under this rule even though there is no impediment to actual performance.

**full warranty** One under which warrantor will repair the product and, if unsuccessful, will replace or refund.

**fungibles** With respect to goods or securities, those of which any unit is, by nature or usage of trade, the equivalent of any other like unit. U.C.C. § 1–201(17); *e.g.,* a bushel of wheat or other grain.

**future estate** See **estate.**

**garnishment** A statutory proceeding whereby a person's property, money, or credits in the possession or control of another are applied to payment of the former's debt to a third person.

**general intangible** Catchall category of collateral not otherwise covered.

**general partner** Member of either a general or limited partnership with unlimited liability for its debts, full management powers, and a right to share in the profits.

**gift** A voluntary transfer of property to another made gratuitously and without consideration. Essential requisites of "gift" are capacity of donor, intention of donor to make gift, completed delivery to or for donee, and acceptance of gift by donee.

**gift causa mortis** A gift in view of death is one which is made in contemplation, fear, or peril of death, and with intent that it shall take effect only in case of the death of the giver.

**good faith** Honesty in fact in conduct or a transaction.

**good faith purchaser** Buyer who acts honestly, gives value, and takes the goods without notice or knowledge of any defect in the title of his transferor.

**goods** A term of variable content and meaning. It may include every species of personal property or it may be given a very restricted meaning. Sometimes the meaning of "goods" is extended to include all tangible items, as in the phrase "goods and services."

All things (including specially manufactured goods) which are movable at the time of identification to the contract for sale other than the money in which the price is to be paid, investment securities and things in action. U.C.C. § 2–105(1).

**grantee** Transferee of property.

**grantor** A transferor of property. The creator of a trust is usually designated as the grantor of the trust.

**gratuitous promise** Promise made without consideration.

**group insurance** Covers a number of individuals.

**guaranty** A promise to answer for the payment of some debt, or the performance of some duty, in case of the failure of another person, who, in the first instance, is liable to such payment or performance

The terms *guaranty* and *suretyship* are sometimes used interchangeably; but they should not be confounded. The distinction between contract of suretyship and contract of guaranty is whether or not the undertaking is a joint undertaking with the principal or a separate and distinct contract; if it is the former it is one of "suretyship," and if the latter, it is one of "guaranty." See also **surety**.

**guardianship** The relationship under which a person (the guardian) is appointed by a court to preserve and control the property of another (the ward).

**heir** A person who succeeds, by the rules of law, to an estate in lands, tenements, or hereditaments, upon the death of his ancestor, by descent and right of relationship.

**holder** Person who is in possession of a document of title or an instrument or an investment security drawn, issued or endorsed to him or to his order, or to bearer or in blank. U.C.C. § 1–201(20).

**holder in due course** A holder who takes an instrument for value, in good faith, and without notice that it is overdue or has been dishonored or of any defense against or claim to it on the part of any person.

**holograph** A will or deed written entirely by the testator or grantor with his own hand and not witnessed (attested). State laws vary with respect to the validity of the holographic will.

**homicide** Unlawful taking of another's life.

**horizontal privity** Who may bring a cause of action.

**horizontal restraints** Agreements among competitors.

**hostile fire** Any fire outside its intended or usual place.

**identified goods** Designated goods as part of a particular contract.

**illegal per se** Conclusively presumed unreasonable and therefore illegal.

**illusory promise** Promise imposing no obligation on the promisor.

**implied-in-fact condition** Contingencies understood but not expressed by the parties.

**implied-in-law condition** Contingency that arises from operation of law.

**implied warranty** Obligation imposed by law upon the transferor of property or contract rights; implicit in the sale arising out of certain circumstances.

**implied warranty of habitability** Leased premises are fit for ordinary residential purposes.

**impossibility** Performance that cannot be done.

**in personam** Against the person. Action seeking judgment against a person involving his personal rights and based on jurisdiction of his person, as distinguished from a judgment against property (*i.e.,* in rem).

**in personam jurisdiction** Jurisdiction based on claims against a person in contrast to jurisdiction over his property.

**in re** In the affair; in the matter of; concerning; regarding. This is the usual method of entitling a judicial proceeding in which there are not adversary parties, but merely some *res* concerning which judicial action is to be taken, such as a bankrupt's estate, an estate in the probate court, a proposed public highway, etc.

**in rem** A technical term used to designate proceedings or actions instituted *against the thing*, in contradistinction to personal actions, which are said to be *in personam*.

*Quasi in rem* A term applied to proceedings which are not strictly and purely *in rem*, but are brought against the defendant personally, though the real object is to deal with particular property or subject property to the discharge of claims asserted; for example, foreign attachment, or proceedings to foreclose a mortgage, remove a cloud from title, or effect a partition.

**in rem jurisdiction** Jurisdiction based on claims against property.

**incidental beneficiary** Third party whom the two parties to a contract have no intention of benefitting by their contract.

**income bond** Bond that conditions payment of interest on corporate earnings.

**incontestability clause** The prohibition of an insurer to avoid an insurance policy after a specified period of time.

**indemnification** Duty owed by principal to agent to pay agent for losses incurred while acting as directed by principal.

**indemnify** To reimburse one for a loss already incurred.

**indenture** A written agreement under which bonds and debentures are issued, setting forth maturity date, interest rate, and other terms.

**independent contractor** Person who contracts with another to do a particular job and is not subject to the control of the other.

**indicia** Signs; indications. Circumstances which point to the existence of a given fact as probable, but not certain.

**indictment** Grand jury charge that the defendant should stand trial.

**indispensable paper** Chattel paper, instruments, and documents.

**indorsee** The person to whom a negotiable instrument, promissory note, bill of lading, etc., is assigned by indorsement.

**indorsement** The act of a payee, drawee, accommodation indorser, or holder of a bill, note, check, or other negotiable instrument, in writing his name upon the back of the same, with or without further or qualifying words, whereby the property in the same is assigned and transferred to another. U.C.C. § 3–202 *et seq.*

*Blank indorsement* No indorsee is specified.

*Qualified indorsement* Without recourse, limiting one's liability of the instrument.

*Restrictive indorsement* Limits the rights of the indorser in some manner.

*Special indorsement* Designates an indorsee to be paid.

**infliction of emotional distress** Extreme and outrageous conduct intentionally or recklessly causing severe emotional distress.

**information** Formal accusation of a crime brought by a prosecutor.

**infringement** Unauthorized use.

**injunction** An equitable remedy forbidding the party defendant from doing some act which he is threatening or attempting to commit, or restraining him in the continuance thereof, such act being unjust and inequitable, injurious to the plaintiff, and not such as can be adequately redressed by an action at law.

**innkeeper** Hotel or motel operator.

**inquisitorial system** System in which the judiciary initiates, conducts, and decides cases.

**insider** Relative or general partner of debtor, partnership in which debtor is a partner, or corporation in which debtor is an officer, director, or controlling person.

**insiders** Directors, officers, employees, and agents of the issuer as well as those the issuer has entrusted with information solely for corporate purposes.

**insolvency** Under U.C.C., a person is insolvent who either has ceased to pay his debts in the ordinary course of business or cannot pay his debts as they fall due or is insolvent within the meaning of the Federal Bankruptcy Law. U.C.C. § 1–201(23).

*Insolvency (bankruptcy)* Total liabilities exceed total value of assets.

*Insolvency (equity)* Inability to pay debts in ordinary course of business or as they become due.

**inspection** Examination of the goods to determine whether they conform to the contract.

**instrument** Negotiable instruments, stocks, bonds, and other investment securities.

**insurable interest** Exists where insured derives pecuniary benefit or advantage by preservation and continued existence of property or would sustain pecuniary loss from its destruction.

**insurance** A contract whereby, for a stipulated consideration, one party undertakes to compensate the other for loss on a specified subject by specified perils. The party agreeing to make the compensation is usually called the "insurer" or "underwriter"; the other, the "insured" or "assured"; the written contract, a "policy"; the events insured against, "risks" or "perils"; and the subject, right, or interest to be protected, the "insurable interest." Insurance is a contract whereby one undertakes to indemnify another against loss, damage, or liability arising from an unknown or contingent event.

*Co-insurance* A form of insurance in which a person insures property for less than its full or stated value and agrees to share the risk of loss.

*Life insurance* Payment of a specific sum of money to a designated beneficiary upon the death of the insured.

*Ordinary life* Life insurance with a savings component that runs for the life of the insured.

*Term life* Life insurance issued for a limited number of years that does not have a savings component.

**intangible property** Protected interests that are not physical.

**intangibles** Accounts and general intangibles.

**intent** Desire to cause the consequences of an act or knowledge that the consequences are substantially certain to result from the act.

**inter alia** Latin. Among other things.

**inter se** or **inter sese** Latin. Among or between themselves; used to distinguish rights or duties between two or more parties from their rights or duties to others.

**interest in land** Any right, privilege, power, or immunity in real property.

**interest in partnership** Partner's share in the partnership's profits and surplus.

**interference with contractual relations** Intentionally causing one of the parties to a contract not to perform the contract.

**intermediary bank** Any bank to which an item is transferred in the course of collection except the depositary or payor bank. U.C.C. § 4–105(c).

**intermediate test** Requirement that legislation have a substantial relationship to an important governmental objective.

**international law** Deals with the conduct and relations of nation-states and international organizations.

**interpretation** Construction or meaning of the contract.

**interpretative rules** Statements issued by an administrative agency indicating its construction of its governing statute.

**intestate** A person is said to die intestate when he dies without making a will. The word is also often used to signify the person himself. *Compare* **testator**.

**intrusion** Unreasonable and highly offensive interference with the seclusion of another.

**inventory** Goods held for sale or lease or consumed in a business.

**invitee** A person is an "invitee" on land of another if (1) he enters by invitation, express or implied, (2) his entry is connected with the owner's business or with an activity the owner conducts or permits to be conducted on his land and (3) there is mutuality of benefit or benefit to the owner.

**joint and several liability** Liability where creditor may sue partners jointly as a group or separately as individuals.

**joint liability** Liability where creditor must sue all of the partners as a group.

**joint stock company** A general partnership with some corporate attributes.

**joint tenancy** See **tenancy**.

**joint venture** An association of two or more persons to carry on a single business transaction for profit.

**judgment** The official and authentic decision of a court of justice upon the respective rights and claims of the parties to an action or suit therein litigated and submitted to its determination.

**judgment in personam** A judgment against a particular person, as distinguished from a judgment against a thing or a right or *status*.

**judgment in rem** An adjudication pronounced upon the status of some particular thing or subject matter, by a tribunal having competent authority.

**judgment n. o. v.** Judgment non obstante verdicto in its broadest sense is a judgment rendered in favor of one party notwithstanding the finding of a verdict in favor of the other party.

**judgment notwithstanding the verdict** A final binding determination on the merits made by the judge after and contrary to the jury's verdict.

**judgment on the pleadings** Final binding determination on the merits made by the judge after the pleadings.

**judicial lien** Interest in property that is obtained by court action to secure payment of a debt.

**judicial review** Power of the courts to determine the constitutionality of legislative and executive acts.

**jurisdiction** The right and power of a court to adjudicate concerning the subject matter in a given case.

**jurisdiction over the parties** Power of a court to bind the parties to a suit.

**jury** (From the Latin jurare, to swear.) A body of persons selected and summoned by law and sworn to try the facts of a case and to find according to the law and the evidence. In general, the province of the jury is to find the facts in a case, while the judge passes upon pure questions of law. As a matter of fact, however, the jury must often pass upon mixed questions of law and fact in determining the case, and in all such cases the instructions of the judge as to the law become very important.

**justifiable reliance** Reasonably influenced by the misrepresentation.

**labor dispute** Any controversy concerning terms or conditions of employment or union representation.

**laches** Based upon maxim that equity aids the vigilant and not those who slumber on their rights. It is defined as neglect to assert right or claim which, taken together with lapse of time and other circumstances causing prejudice to adverse party, operates as bar in court of equity.

**landlord** The owner of an estate in land, or a rental property, who has leased it to another person, called the "tenant." Also called "lessor."

**larceny** Trespassory taking and carrying away the goods of another with the intent to permanently deprive.

**last clear chance** Final opportunity to avoid an injury.

**lease** Any agreement which gives rise to relationship of landlord and tenant (real property) or lessor and lessee (real or personal property)
The person who conveys is termed the "lessor," and the person to whom conveyed, the "lessee"; when the lessor conveys land or tenements to a lessee, he is said to lease, demise, or let them.
*Sublease, or underlease* One executed by the lessee of an estate to a third person, conveying the same estate for a shorter term than that for which the lessee holds it.

**leasehold** An estate in realty held under a lease. The four principal types of leasehold estates are the estate for years, periodic tenancy, tenancy at will, and tenancy at sufferance.

**leasehold estate** Right to possess real property.

**legacy** "Legacy" is a gift or bequest by will of personal property, whereas a "devise" is a testamentary disposition of real estate.
*Demonstrative legacy* A bequest of a certain sum of money, with a direction that it shall be paid out of a particular fund. It differs from a specific legacy in this respect: that, if the fund out of which it is payable fails for any cause, it is nevertheless entitled to come on the estate as a general legacy. And it differs from a general legacy in this: that it does not abate in that class, but in the class of specific legacies.
*General legacy* A pecuniary legacy, payable out of the general assets of a testator.
*Residuary legacy* A bequest of all the testator's personal estate not otherwise effectually disposed of by his will.
*Specific legacy* One which operates on property particularly designated. A legacy or gift by will of a particular specified thing, as of a horse, a piece of furniture, a term of years, and the like.

**legal aggregate** A group of individuals not having a legal existence separate from its members.

**legal benefit** Obtaining something one had no legal right to.

**legal detriment** Doing an act not legally obligated to do or not doing an act which one has a legal right to do.

**legal entity** An organization having a separate legal existence from its members.

**legal sufficiency** Benefit to promisor or detriment to promisee.

**legislative rules** Substantive rules issued by an administrative agency under the authority delegated to it by the legislature.

**letter of credit** An engagement by a bank or other person made at the request of a customer that the issuer will honor drafts or other demands for payment upon compliance with the conditions specified in the credit.

**letters of administration** Formal document issued by probate court appointing one an administrator of an estate.

**letters testamentary** The formal instrument of authority and appointment given to an executor by the proper court, empowering him to enter upon the discharge of his office as executor. It corresponds to letters of administration granted to an administrator.

**levy** To assess; raise; execute; exact; tax; collect; gather; take up; seize. Thus, to levy (assess, exact, raise, or collect) a tax; to levy an execution, *i.e.*, to levy or collect a sum of money on an execution.

**liability insurance** Covers liability to others by reason of damage resulting from injuries to another's person or property.

**liability without fault** Crime to do a specific act or cause a certain result without regard to the care exercised.

**libel** Defamation communicated by writing, television, radio, or the like.

**liberty** Ability of individuals to engage in freedom of action and choice regarding their personal lives.

**license** License with respect to real property is a privilege to go on premises for a certain purpose, but does not operate to confer on, or vest in, licensee any title, interest, or estate in such property.

**licensee** Person privileged to enter or remain on land by virtue of the consent of the lawful possessor.

**lien** A qualified right of property which a creditor has in or over specific property of his debtor, as security for the debt or charge or for performance of some act.

**lien creditor** A creditor who has acquired a lien on the property by attachment.

**life estate** An estate whose duration is limited to the life of the party holding it, or some other person. Upon the death of the life tenant, the property will go to the holder of the remainder interest or to the grantor by reversion.

**limited liability** Liability limited to amount invested in a business enterprise.

**limited partner** Member of a limited partnership with liability for its debts only to the extent of her capital contribution.

**limited partnership** See **partnership**.

**limited partnership association** A partnership which closely resembles a corporation.

**liquidated** Ascertained; determined; fixed; settled; made clear or manifest. Cleared away; paid; discharged.

**liquidated damages** See **damages**.

**liquidated debt** Obligation that is certain in amount.

**liquidation** The settling of financial affairs of a business or individual, usually by liquidating (turning to cash) all assets for distribution to creditors, heirs, etc. It is to be distinguished from dissolution.

**loss of value** Value of promised performance minus value of actual performance.

**lost property** Property which the owner has involuntarily parted with and does not know where to find or recover it, not including property which he has intentionally concealed or deposited in a secret place for safekeeping. Distinguishable from mislaid property which has been deliberately placed somewhere and forgotten.

**McNaughton test** Right/wrong test for criminal insanity.

**main purpose rule** Where object of promisor/ surety is to provide an economic benefit for herself, the promise is considered outside of the statute of frauds.

**maker** One who makes or executes; as the maker of a promissory note. One who signs a check; in this context, synonymous with drawer. See **draft**.

**mala in se** Latin. Morally wrong.

**mala prohibita** Latin. Wrong by law.

**mandamus** Latin, we command. A legal writ compelling the defendant to do an official duty.

**manslaughter** Unlawful taking of another's life without malice.

　*Involuntary manslaughter* Taking the life of another by criminal negligence or during the course of a misdemeanor.

　*Voluntary manslaughter* Intentional killing of another under extenuating circumstances.

**manufacturing defect** Not produced according to specifications.

**mark** Trade symbol.

**market allocations** Division of market by customers, geographic location, or products.

**marketable title** Free from any defects, encumbrances, or reasonable objections to one's ownership.

**marshaling of assets** Segregating the assets and liabilities of the partnership separately from the assets and liabilities of the individual partners.

**master** See **principal**.

**material** Matters to which a reasonable investor would attach importance in deciding whether to purchase a security.

**material alteration** Any change that changes the contract of any party to the instrument.

**maturity** The date at which an obligation, such as the principal of a bond or a note, becomes due.

**maxim** A general legal principle.

**mechanic's lien** A claim created by State statutes for the purpose of securing priority of payment of the price or value of work performed and materials furnished in erecting or repairing a building or other structure, and as such attaches to the land as well as buildings and improvements erected thereon.

**mediation** Nonbinding process in which a third party acts as an intermediary between the disputing parties and proposes solutions for them to consider.

**mens rea** Criminal intent.

**mentally incompetent** Unable to understand the nature and effect of one's acts.

**mercantile law** An expression substantially equivalent to commercial law. It designates the system of rules, customs, and usages generally recognized and adopted by merchants and traders, and which, either in its simplicity or as modified by common law or statutes, constitutes the law for the regulation of their transactions and the solution of their controversies. The Uniform Commercial Code is the general body of law governing commercial or mercantile transactions.

**merchant** A person who deals in goods of the kind or otherwise by his occupation holds himself out as having knowledge or skill peculiar to the practices or goods involved in the transaction or to whom such knowledge or skill may be attributed by his employment of an agent or broker or other intermediary who by his occupation holds himself out as having such knowledge or skill. U.C.C. § 2–104(1).

**merchantability** Merchant seller guarantees that the goods are fit for their ordinary purpose.

**merger** The fusion or absorption of one thing or right into another. In corporate law, the absorption of one company by another, latter retaining its own name and identity and acquiring assets, liabilities, franchises, and powers of former, and absorbed company ceasing to exist as separate business entity. It differs from a consolidation wherein all the corporations terminate their existence and become parties to a new one.

　*Conglomerate merger* An acquisition by one company of another which is not horizontal or vertical.

　*Horizontal merger* Merger between business competitors, such as manufacturers of the same type products or distributors selling competing products in the same market area.

　*Short-form merger* Merger of a 90 percent subsidiary into its parent.

　*Vertical merger* Union with corporate customer or supplier.

**midnight deadline** Midnight of the next banking day after receiving an item.

**mining partnership** A specific type of partnership for the purpose of extracting raw minerals.

**minor** Under full legal age (usually eighteen).

**mirror image rule** An acceptance cannot deviate from the terms of the offer.

**misdemeanor** Less serious crime.

**mislaid property** Property which an owner has put deliberately in a certain place but owner is unable to remember where he put it, as distinguished from lost property which the owner leaves unwittingly in a place, forgetting its location. See also **lost property**.

**misrepresentation** Any manifestation by words or other conduct by one person to another that, under the circumstances, amounts to an assertion not in accordance with the facts. A "misrepresentation" that justifies the rescission of a contract is a false statement of a substantive fact, or any conduct which leads to a belief of a substantive fact material to proper understanding of the matter in hand. See also **deceit; fraud**.

*Fraudulent misrepresentation* False statement made with knowledge of its falsity and intent to mislead.

*Innocent misrepresentation* Misrepresentation made without knowledge of its falsity but with due care.

*Negligent misrepresentation* Misrepresentation made without due care in ascertaining its falsity.

**modify** Change the lower court's judgment.

**money** Medium of exchange issued by government body.

**monopoly** Ability to control price or exclude others from the marketplace.

**mortgage** A mortgage is an interest in land created by a written instrument providing security for the performance of a duty or the payment of a debt.

**mortgagor** Debtor who uses real estate to secure an obligation.

**multinational enterprise** Business that engages in transactions involving the movement of goods, information, money, people, or services across national borders.

**multiple product order** Order requiring an advertiser to cease and desist from deceptive statements on all products it sells.

**murder** Unlawful and premeditated taking of another's life.

**mutual mistake** Where both parties have a common but erroneous belief forming the basis of a contract.

**necessary** Items needed to maintain a person's station in life.

**negligence** The omission to do something which a reasonable man, guided by those ordinary considerations which ordinarily regulate human affairs, would do, or the doing of something which a reasonable and prudent man would not do.

*Culpable negligence* Greater than ordinary negligence but less than gross negligence.

**negligence per se** Conclusive on the issue of negligence (duty of care and breach).

**negotiable** Legally capable of being transferred by endorsement or delivery. Usually said of checks and notes and sometimes of stocks and bearer bonds.

**negotiable instrument** Signed document (such as a check or promissory note) containing an unconditional promise or order to pay a fixed amount of money at demand or a definite time to order or bearer.

**negotiation** Transferee becomes a holder.

**net assets** Total assets minus total debts.

**no arrival, no sale** A destination contract, but if goods do not arrive, seller is excused from liability unless it is due to the seller's fault.

**no-fault insurance** Compensates victims of automobile accidents regardless of fault.

**nonconforming use** Pre-existing use not in accordance with the zoning ordinance.

**nonprofit corporation** One whose profits must be used exclusively for the charitable, educational, or scientific purpose for which it was formed.

**nonsuit** Action in form of a judgment taken against a plaintiff who has failed to appear to prosecute his action or failed to prove his case.

**note** See **promissory note**.

**novation** A novation substitutes a new party and discharges one of the original parties to a contract by agreement of all three parties. A new contract is created with the same terms as the original one but only the parties are changed.

**nuisance** Nuisance is that activity which arises from unreasonable, unwarranted or unlawful use by a person of his own property, working obstruction or injury to right of another, or to the public, and producing such material annoyance, inconvenience, and discomfort that law will presume resulting damage.

**obiter dictum** See **dictum**.

**objective fault** Gross deviation from reasonable conduct.

**objective manifestation** What a reasonable man under the circumstances would believe.

**objective satisfaction** Approval based upon whether a reasonable person would be satisfied.

**objective standard** What a reasonable man under the circumstances would reasonably believe or do.

**obligee** Party to whom a duty of performance is owed (by delegator and delegatee).

**obligor** Party owing a duty (to the assignor).

**offer** A manifestation of willingness to enter into a bargain, so made as to justify another person in understanding that his assent to that bargain is invited and will conclude it. Restatement, Second, Contracts, § 24.

**offeree** Recipient of the offer.

**offeror** Person making the offer.

**open-ended credit** Credit arrangement under which debtor has rights to enter into a series of credit transactions.

**opinion** Belief in the existence of a fact or a judgment as to value.

**option** Contract that provides that an offer will stay open for a specified period of time.

**order** A final disposition made by an agency.

**order paper** Payable to a named person or anyone designated by that person.

**order to pay** Direction or command to pay.

**original promise** Promise to become primarily liable.

**output contract** See **contracts**.

**palpable unilateral mistake** Erroneous belief by one party that is recognized by the other.

**parent corporation** Corporation which controls another corporation.

**parol evidence** Literally oral evidence, but now includes prior to and contemporaneous, oral and written evidence.

**parol evidence rule**   Under this rule, when parties put their agreement in writing, all previous oral agreements merge in the writing and a contract as written cannot be modified or changed by parol evidence, in the absence of a plea of mistake or fraud in the preparation of the writing. But rule does not forbid a resort to parol evidence not inconsistent with the matters stated in the writing. Also, as regards sales of goods, such written agreement may be explained or supplemented by course of dealing or usage of trade or by course of conduct, and by evidence of consistent additional terms unless the court finds the writing to have been intended also as a complete and exclusive statement of the terms of the agreement. U.C.C. § 2–202.

**part performance**   In order to establish part performance taking an oral contract for the sale of realty out of the statute of frauds, the acts relied upon as part performance must be of such a character that they can reasonably be naturally accounted for in no other way than that they were performed in pursuance of the contract, and they must be in conformity with its provisions. See U.C.C. § 2–201(3).

**partial assignment**   Transfer of a portion of contractual rights to one or more assignees.

**partition**   The dividing of lands held by joint tenants, copartners, or tenants in common, into distinct portions, so that they may hold them in severalty.

**partnership**   An association of two or more persons to carry on, as co-owners, a business for profit.

Partnerships are treated as a conduit and are, therefore, not subject to taxation. The various items of partnership income, gains, and losses, etc., flow through to the individual partners and are reported on their personal income tax returns.

*Limited partnership*   Type of partnership comprised of one or more general partners who manage business and who are personally liable for partnership debts, and one or more limited partners who contribute capital and share in profits but who take no part in running business and incur no liability with respect to partnership obligations beyond contribution.

*Partnership at will*   One with no definite term or specific undertaking.

**partnership capital**   Total money and property contributed by partners for permanent use by the partnership.

**partnership property**   Sum of all of the partnership's assets.

**past consideration**   An act done before the contract is made.

**patent**   Exclusive right to an invention.

**payee**   The person in whose favor a bill of exchange, promissory note, or check is made or drawn.

**payer, or payor**   One who pays, or who is to make a payment; particularly the person who is to make payment of a check, bill or note. Correlative to "payee."

**payor bank**   A bank by which an item is payable as drawn or accepted. U.C.C. § 4–105(b). Drawee bank.

**per capita**   This term, derived from the civil law, is much used in the law of descent and distribution, and denotes that method of dividing an intestate estate by which an equal share is given to each of a number of persons, all of whom stand in equal degree to the decedent, without reference to their stocks or the right of representation. It is the opposite of *per stirpes*.

**per stirpes**   This term, derived from the civil law, is much used in the law of descents and distribution, and denotes that method of dividing an intestate estate where a class or group of distributees take the share which their deceased would have been entitled to, taking thus by their right of representing such ancestor, and not as so many individuals. It is the opposite of *per capita*.

**perfect tender rule**   Seller's tender of delivery must conform exactly to the contract.

**perfection of security interest**   Acts required of a secured party in the way of giving at least constructive notice so as to make his security interest effective at least against lien creditors of the debtor. See U.C.C. §§ 9–302 through 9–306. In most cases, the secured party may obtain perfection either by filing with Secretary of State or by taking possession of the collateral.

**performance**   Fulfillment of one's contractual obligations. See also **part performance; specific performance**.

**periodic tenancy**   Lease with a definite term that is to be continued.

**personal defenses**   Contractual defenses which are good against holders but not holders in due course.

**personal property**   Any property other than an interest in land.

**petty crime**   Misdemeanor punishable by imprisonment of six months or less.

**plaintiff**   The party who initiates a civil suit.

**pleadings**   The formal allegations by the parties of their respective claims and defenses. Under rules of civil procedure the pleadings consist of a complaint, an answer, a reply to a counterclaim, an answer to a cross-claim, a third party complaint, and a third party answer.

**pledge**   A bailment of goods to a creditor as security for some debt or engagement.

Much of the law of pledges has been replaced by the provisions for secured transactions in Article 9 of the U.C.C.

**possibility of reverter**   The interest which remains in a grantor or testator after the conveyance or devise of a fee simple determinable and which permits the grantor to be revested automatically of his estate on breach of the condition.

**possibility test**   Under the statute of frauds the one year test is satisfied if performance possibly could be completed within one year.

**power of appointment**   A power of authority conferred by one person by deed or will upon another (called the "donee") to appoint, that is, to select and nominate, the person or persons who are to receive and enjoy an estate or an income therefrom or from a fund, after the testator's death, or the donee's death, or after the termination of an existing right or interest.

**power of attorney**   An instrument authorizing a person to act as the agent or attorney of the person granting it.

**power of termination**   The interest left in the grantor or testator after the conveyance or devise of a fee simple on condition subsequent or conditional fee.

**precatory**   Expressing a wish.

**precedent**   An adjudged case or decision of a court, considered as furnishing an example or authority for an identical or similar case afterwards arising or a similar question of law. See also **stare decisis**.

**preemptive right**   The privilege of a stockholder to maintain a proportionate share of ownership by purchasing a proportionate share of any new stock issues.

**preference**   The act of an insolvent debtor who, in distributing his property or in assigning it for the benefit of his creditors, pays or secures to one or more creditors the full amount of their claims or a larger amount than they would be entitled to receive on a *pro rata* distribution.

**preliminary hearing** Determine whether there is probable cause.

**premium** The price for insurance protection for a specified period of exposure.

**preponderance of the evidence** Greater weight of the evidence; standard used in civil cases.

**prescription** Acquisition of a personal right to use a way, water, light, and air by reason of continuous usage. See also **easement**.

**presenter's warranty** Warranties given to any payor or acceptor of an instrument.

**presentment** The production of a negotiable instrument to the drawee for his acceptance, or to the drawer or acceptor for payment; or of a promissory note to the party liable, for payment of the same. U.C.C. § 3–504(1).

**presumption** A presumption is a rule of law, statutory or judicial, by which finding of a basic fact gives rise to existence of presumed fact, until presumption is rebutted. A presumption imposes on the party against whom it is directed the burden of going forward with evidence to rebut or meet the presumption, but does not shift to such party the burden of proof in the sense of the risk of nonpersuasion, which remains throughout the trial upon the party on whom it was originally cast.

**price discrimination** Price differential.

**price fixing** Any agreement for the purpose and effect of raising, depressing, fixing, pegging, or stabilizing prices.

**prima facie** Latin. At first sight; on the first appearance; on the face of it; so far as can be judged from the first disclosure; presumably; a fact presumed to be true unless disproved by some evidence to the contrary.

**primary liability** Absolute obligation to pay the negotiable instrument.

**principal** *Law of agency* The term "principal" describes one who has permitted or directed another (*i.e.,* agent or servant) to act for his benefit and subject to his direction and control. Principal includes in its meaning the term "master" or employer, a species of principal who, in addition to other control, has a right to control the physical conduct of the species of agents known as servants or employees, as to whom special rules are applicable with reference to harm caused by their physical acts.

*Disclosed principal* One whose existence and identity is known.

*Partially disclosed principal* One whose existence is known but whose identity is not known.

*Undisclosed principal* One whose existence and identity are not known.

**principal debtor** Person whose debt is being supported by a surety.

**priority** Precedence in order of right.

**private carrier** Carrier which limits its service and is not open to the general public.

**private corporation** One organized to conduct either a privately owned business enterprise for profit or a nonprofit corporation.

**private law** The law involving relationships among individuals and legal entities.

**privilege** Immunity from tort liability.

**privity** Contractual relationship.

**privity of contract** That connection or relationship which exists between two or more contracting parties. The absence of privity as a defense in actions for damages in contract and tort actions is generally no longer viable with the enactment of warranty statutes (*e.g.,* U.C.C. § 2–318), acceptance by States of doctrine of strict liability and court decisions which have extended the right to sue to third party beneficiaries and even innocent bystanders.

**probable cause** Reasonable belief of the offense charged.

**probate** Court procedure by which a will is proved to be valid or invalid; though in current usage this term has been expanded to generally include all matters and proceedings pertaining to administration of estates, guardianships, etc.

**procedural due process** Requirement that governmental action depriving a person of life, liberty, or property be done through a fair procedure.

**procedural law** Rules for enforcing substantive law.

**procedural rules** Rules issued by an administrative agency establishing its organization, method of operation, and rules of conduct for practice before it.

**procedural unconscionability** Unfair or irregular bargaining.

**proceeds** Consideration for the sale, exchange, or other disposition of the collateral.

**process** *Judicial process* In a wide sense, this term may include all the acts of a court from the beginning to the end of its proceedings in a given cause; but more specifically it means the writ, summons, mandate, or other process which is used to inform the defendant of the institution of proceedings against him and to compel his appearance, in either civil or criminal cases.

*Legal process* This term is sometimes used as equivalent to "lawful process." Thus, it is said that legal process means process not merely fair on its face, but in fact valid. But properly it means a summons, writ, warrant, mandate, or other process issuing from a court.

**profit à prendre** Right to make some use of the soil of another, such as a right to mine metals, and it carries with it the right of entry and the right to remove.

**profit corporation** One founded for the purpose of operating a business for profit.

**promise to pay** Undertaking to pay an existing obligation.

**promisee** Person to whom a promise is made.

**promisor** Person making a promise.

**promissory estoppel** Arises where there is a promise which promisor should reasonably expect to induce action or forbearance on part of promisee and which does induce such action or forbearance, and where injustice can be avoided only by enforcement of the promise.

**promissory note** An unconditional written promise to pay a specified sum of money on demand or at a specified date. Such a note is negotiable if signed by the maker and containing an unconditional promise to pay a sum certain in money either on demand or at a definite time and payable to order or bearer. U.C.C. § 3–104.

**promoters** In the law relating to corporations, those persons are called the "promoters" of a company who first associate themselves together for the purpose of organizing the company, issuing its prospectus, procuring subscriptions to the stock, securing a charter, etc.

**property** Interest that is legally protected.

*Abandoned property* Intentionally disposed of by the owner.

*Lost property* Unintentionally left by the owner.

*Mislaid property* Intentionally placed by the owner but unintentionally left.

**prosecute** To bring a criminal proceeding.

**protest** A formal declaration made by a person interested or concerned in some act about to be done, or already performed, whereby he expresses his dissent or disapproval, or affirms the act against his will. The object of such a declaration is generally to save some right which would be lost to him if his implied assent could be made out, or to exonerate himself from some responsibility which would attach to him unless he expressly negatived his assent.

*Notice of protest* A notice given by the holder of a bill or note to the drawer or indorser that the bill has been protested for refusal of payment or acceptance. U.C.C. § 3–509.

**provisional credit** Tentative credit for the deposit of an instrument until final credit is given.

**proximate cause** Where the act or omission played a substantial part in bringing about or actually causing the injury or damage and where the injury or damage was either a direct result or a reasonably probable consequence of the act or omission.

**proxy** (Contracted from procuracy.) Written authorization given by one person to another so that the second person can act for the first, such as that given by a shareholder to someone else to represent him and vote his shares at a shareholders' meeting.

**public corporation** One created to administer a unit of local civil government or one created by the United States to conduct public business.

**public disclosure of private facts** Offensive publicity given to private information about another person.

**public law** The law dealing with the relationship between government and individuals.

**puffery** Sales talk that is considered general bragging or overstatement.

**punitive damages** Damages awarded in excess of normal compensation to punish a defendant for a serious civil wrong.

**purchase money security interest** A seller of goods who retains a security interest in goods purchased with the loaned money.

**qualified fee** Ownership subject to its being taken away upon the happening of an event.

**quantum meruit** Expression "quantum meruit" means "as much as he deserves" and it is an expression that describes the extent of liability on a contract implied by law. Essential elements of recovery under quantum meruit are: (1) valuable services were rendered or materials furnished, (2) for person sought to be charged, (3) which services and materials were accepted by person sought to be charged, used, and enjoyed by him, and (4) under such circumstances as reasonably notified person sought to be charged that plaintiff, in performing such services, was expected to be paid by person sought to be charged.

**quasi** Latin. As if; almost as it were; analogous to. It negatives idea of identity, but points out that the conceptions are sufficiently similar for one to be classed as the equal of the other.

**quasi contract** Legal fiction invented by common law courts to permit recovery by contractual remedy in cases where, in fact, there is no contract, but where circumstances are such that justice warrants a recovery as though there had been a promise.

**quasi in rem** See *in rem*.

**quasi in rem jurisdiction** Jurisdiction over property not based on claims against it.

**quiet enjoyment** Right of a tenant not to have his physical possession of premises interfered with by the landlord.

**quitclaim deed** A deed of conveyance operating by way of release; that is, intended to pass any title, interest, or claim which the grantor may have in the premises, but not professing that such title is valid, nor containing any warranty or covenants for title.

**quorum** When a committee, board of directors, meeting of shareholders, legislature, or other body of persons cannot act unless a certain number at least of them are present.

**rape** Unlawful and unconsented to sexual intercourse.

**ratification** In a broad sense, the confirmation of a previous act done either by the party himself or by another; as, confirmation of a voidable act.

In the law of principal and agent, the adoption and confirmation by one person with knowledge of all material facts, of an act or contract performed or entered into in his behalf by another who at the time assumed without authority to act as his agent.

**rational relationship test** Requirement that legislation bear a rational relationship to a legitimate governmental interest.

**real defenses** Defenses that are valid against all holders, including holders in due course.

**real property** Land, and generally whatever is erected or growing upon or affixed to land. Also rights issuing out of, annexed to, and exercisable within or about land. See also **fixture**.

**reasonable man standard** Duty of care required to avoid being negligent; one who is careful, diligent, and prudent.

**receiver** A fiduciary of the court, appointed as an incident to other proceedings wherein certain ultimate relief is prayed. He is a trustee or ministerial officer representing court, and all parties in interest in litigation, and property or fund intrusted to him.

**recognizance** Formal acknowledgment of indebtedness made in court.

**redemption** The realization of a right to have the title of property restored free and clear of the mortgage; performance of the mortgage obligation being essential for that purpose

Repurchase by corporation of its own shares.

**reformation** Equitable remedy used to reframe written contracts to reflect accurately real agreement between contracting parties when, either through mutual mistake or unilateral mistake coupled with actual or equitable fraud by other party, the writing does not embody contract as actually made.

**regulatory license** Requirement to protect the public interest.

**reimbursement** Duty owed by principal to pay back authorized payments agent has made on principal's behalf. Duty owed by a principal debtor to repay surety who pays principal debtor's obligation.

**rejection** The refusal to accept an offer; manifestation of an unwillingness to accept the goods (sales).

**release** The relinquishment, concession, or giving up of a right, claim, or privilege, by the person in whom it exists or to whom it accrues, to the person against whom it might have been demanded or enforced.

**remainder** An estate limited to take effect and be enjoyed after another estate is determined.

**remand** To send back. The sending by the appellate court of the cause back to the same court out of which it came, for purpose of having some further action taken on it there.

**remedy** The means by which the violation of a right is prevented, redressed, or compensated. Though a remedy may be by the act of the party injured, by operation of law, or by agreement between the injurer and the injured, we are chiefly concerned with one kind of remedy, the judicial remedy, which is by action or suit.

**rent** Consideration paid for use or occupation of property. In a broader sense, it is the compensation or fee paid, usually periodically, for the use of any property, land, buildings, equipment, etc.

**replevin** An action whereby the owner or person entitled to repossession of goods or chattels may recover those goods or chattels from one who has wrongfully taken or who wrongfully detains such goods or chattels.

**reply** Plaintiff's pleading in response to the defendant's answer.

**repudiation** Repudiation of a contract means refusal to perform duty or obligation owed to other party.

**requirements contract** See **contracts**.

*res ipsa loquitur* "The thing speaks for itself"; permits the jury to infer both negligent conduct and causation.

**rescission** An equitable action in which a party seeks to be relieved of his obligations under a contract on the grounds of mutual mistake, fraud, impossibility, etc.

**residuary** Pertaining to the residue; constituting the residue; giving or bequeathing the residue; receiving or entitled to the residue. See also **legacy**, *residuary legacy*.

**respondeat superior** Latin. Let the master answer. This maxim means that a master or employer is liable in certain cases for the wrongful acts of his servant or employee, and a principal for those of his agent.

**respondent** In equity practice, the party who makes an answer to a bill or other proceeding in equity. In appellate practice, the party who contends against an appeal; *i.e.*, the appellee. The party who appeals is called the "appellant."

**restitution** An equitable remedy under which a person who has rendered services to another seeks to be reimbursed for the costs of his acts (but not his profits) even though there was never a contract between the parties.

**restraint on alienation** A provision in an instrument of conveyance which prohibits the grantee from selling or transferring the property which is the subject of the conveyance. Many such restraints are unenforceable as against public policy and the law's policy of free alienability of land.

**restraint of trade** Agreement that eliminates or tends to eliminate competition.

**restrictive covenant** Private restriction on property contained in a conveyance.

**revenue license** Measure to raise money.

**reverse** An appellate court uses the term "reversed" to indicate that it annuls or avoids the judgment, or vacates the decree, of the trial court.

**reverse discrimination** Employment decisions taking into account race or gender in order to remedy past discrimination.

**reversion** The term reversion has two meanings, first, as designating the estate left in the grantor during the continuance of a particular estate and also the residue left in grantor or his heirs after termination of particular estate. It differs from a remainder in that it arises by act of the law, whereas a remainder is by act of the parties. A reversion, moreover, is the remnant left in the grantor, while a remainder is the remnant of the whole estate disposed of, after a preceding part of the same has been given away.

**revocation** The recall of some power, authority, or thing granted, or a destroying or making void of some deed that had existence until the act of revocation made it void.

**revocation of acceptance** Rescission of one's acceptance of goods based upon the nonconformity of the goods which substantially impairs their value.

**right** Legal capacity to require another person to perform or refrain from performing an act.

**right of entry** The right of taking or resuming possession of land by entering on it in a peaceable manner.

**right of redemption** The right (granted by statute only) to free property from the encumbrance of a foreclosure or other judicial sale, or to recover the title passing thereby, by paying what is due, with interest, costs, etc. Not to be confounded with the "equity of redemption," which exists independently of statute but must be exercised before sale. See also **equity of redemption**.

**right to work law** State statute that prohibits union shop contracts.

**rights in collateral** Personal property the debtor owns, possesses, or is in the process of acquiring.

**risk of loss** Allocation of loss between seller and buyer where the goods have been damaged, destroyed, or lost.

**robbery** Larceny from a person by force or threat of force.

**rule** Agency statement of general or particular applicability designed to implement, interpret, or process law or policy.

**rule against perpetuities** Principle that no interest in property is good unless it must vest, if at all, not later than 21 years, plus period of gestation, after some life or lives in being at time of creation of interest.

**rule of reason** Balancing the anticompetitive effects against procompetitive effects of the restraint.

**sale** Transfer of title to goods from seller to buyer for a price.

**sale on approval** Transfer of possession without title to buyer for trial period.

**sale or return** Sale where buyer has option to return goods to seller.

**sanction** Means of enforcing legal judgments.

**satisfaction** The discharge of an obligation by paying a party what is due to him (as on a mortgage, lien, or contract) or what is awarded to him, by the judgment of a court or otherwise. Thus, a judgment is satisfied by the payment of the amount due to the party who has recovered such judgment, or by his levying the amount. See also **accord and satisfaction**.

**scienter** Latin. Knowingly.

**seal** Symbol that authenticates a document.

**secondary liability** Obligation to pay is subject to the conditions of presentment, dishonor, notice of dishonor, and sometimes protest.

**secret partner** Partner whose membership in the partnership is not disclosed.

**Section 402A** Strict liability in tort.

**secured bond** A bond having a lien on specific property.

**secured claim** Claim with a lien on property of the debtor.

**secured party** Creditor who possesses a security interest in collateral.

**secured transaction** A transaction which is founded on a security agreement. Such agreement creates or provides for a security interest. U.C.C. § 9–105(h).

**securities** Stocks, bonds, notes, convertible debentures, warrants, or other documents that represent a share in a company or a debt owed by a company.
  *Certificated security* Security represented by a certificate.
  *Exempt security* Security not subject to registration requirements of 1933 Act.
  *Exempt transaction* Issuance of securities not subject to the registration requirements of 1933 Act.
  *Restricted securities* Securities issued under an exempt transaction.
  *Uncertificated security* Security not represented by a certificate.

**security agreement** Agreement that grants a security interest.

**security interest** Right in personal property securing payment or performance of an obligation.

**seisin** Possession with an intent on the part of him who holds it to claim a freehold interest.

**self-defense** Force to protect oneself against attack.

**separation of powers** Allocation of powers among the legislative, executive, and judicial branches of government.

**service mark** Distinctive symbol, word, or design that is used to identify the services of a provider.

**servient** Land subject to an easement.

**set-off** A counterclaim demand which defendant holds against plaintiff, arising out of a transaction extrinsic of plaintiff's cause of action.

**settlor** Creator of the trust.

**severance** The destruction of any one of the unities of a joint tenancy. It is so called because the estate is no longer a joint tenancy, but is severed.
  Term may also refer to cutting of the crops, such as corn, wheat, etc., or the separating of anything from the realty.

**share** A proportionate ownership interest in a corporation.

**Shelley's case, rule in** Where a person takes an estate of freehold, legally, or equitably, under a deed, will, or other writing, and in the same instrument there is a limitation by way of remainder of any interest of the same legal or equitable quality to his heirs, or heirs of his body, as a class of persons to take in succession from generation to generation, the limitation to the heirs entitles the ancestor to the whole estate.
  The rule was adopted as a part of the common law of this country, though it has long since been abolished by most States.

**shelter rule** Transferee gets rights of transferor.

**shipment contract** Seller is authorized or required only to bear the expense of placing goods with the common carrier and bears the risk of loss only up to such point.

**short swing profits** Profits made by insider through sale or other disposition of the corporate stock within six months after purchase.

**sight draft** An instrument payable on presentment.

**signature** Any symbol executed with intent to validate a writing.

**silent partner** Partner takes no part in the partnership business.

**slander** Oral defamation.

**small claims courts** Inferior civil courts with jurisdiction limited by dollar amount.

**social security** Measures by which the government provides economic assistance to disabled or retired employees and their dependents.

**sole proprietorship** A form of business in which one person owns all the assets of the business in contrast to a partnership and corporation.

**sovereign immunity** Foreign country's freedom from the host country's laws.

**special warranty deed** Seller promises that he has not impaired title.

**specific performance** The doctrine of specific performance is that, where damages would be an inadequate compensation for the breach of an agreement, the contractor or vendor will be compelled to perform specifically what he has agreed to do; *e.g.,* ordered to execute a specific conveyance of land.
  With respect to sale of goods, specific performance may be decreed where the goods are unique or in other proper circumstances. The decree for specific performance may include such terms and conditions as to payment of the price, damages, or other relief as the court may deem just. U.C.C. §§ 2–711(2)(b), 2–716.

**standardized business form** A preprinted contract.

**stare decisis** Doctrine that, when court has once laid down a principle of law as applicable to a certain state of facts, it will adhere to that principle, and apply it to all future cases, where facts are substantially the same; regardless of whether the parties and property are the same.

**state action** Actions by governments as opposed to actions taken by private individuals.

**state of the art** Made in accordance with the level of technology at the time the product is made.

**stated capital** Consideration received for issued stock other than that allocated to capital surplus.

**statute of frauds** A celebrated English statute, passed in 1677, and which has been adopted, in a more or less modified form, in nearly all of the United States. Its chief characteristic is the provision that no action shall be brought on certain contracts unless there be a note or memorandum thereof in writing, signed by the party to be charged or by his authorized agent.

**statute of limitation** A statute prescribing limitations to the right of action on certain described causes of action; that is, declaring that no suit shall be maintained on such causes of action unless brought within a specified period after the right accrued.

**statutory lien** Interest in property to secure payment of a debt that arises solely by statute.

**stock** "Stock" is distinguished from "bonds" and, ordinarily, from "debentures," in that it gives right of ownership in part of assets of corporation and right to interest in any surplus after payment of debt. "Stock" in a corporation is an equity, and it represents an ownership interest, and it is to be distinguished from obligations such as notes or bonds which are not equities and represent no ownership interest.

*Capital stock* See **capital**.

*Common stock* Securities which represent an ownership interest in a corporation. If the company has also issued preferred stock, both common and preferred have ownership rights. Claims of both common and preferred stockholders are junior to claims of bondholders or other creditors of the company. Common stockholders assume the greater risk, but generally exercise the greater control and may gain the greater reward in the form of dividends and capital appreciation.

*Convertible stock* Stock which may be changed or converted into common stock.

*Cumulative preferred* A stock having a provision that if one or more dividends are omitted, the omitted dividends must be paid before dividends may be paid on the company's common stock.

*Preferred stock* A separate portion or class of the stock of a corporation, which is accorded, by the charter or by-laws, a preference or priority in respect to dividends, over the remainder of the stock of the corporation, which in that case is called *common stock*.

*Stock warrant* A certificate entitling the owner to buy a specified amount of stock at a specified time(s) for a specified price. Differs from a stock option only in that options are granted to employees and warrants are sold to the public.

*Treasury stock* Shares reacquired by a corporation.

**stock option** Contractual right to purchase stock from a corporation.

**stop payment** Order for a drawee not to pay an instrument.

**strict liability** A concept applied by the courts in product liability cases in which a seller is liable for any and all defective or hazardous products which unduly threaten a consumer's personal safety. This concept applies to all members involved in the manufacturing and selling of any facet of the product.

**strict scrutiny test** Requirement that legislation be necessary to promote a compelling governmental interest.

**subagent** Person appointed by agent to perform agent's duties.

**subject matter jurisdiction** Authority of a court to decide a particular kind of case.

**subject to the mortgage** Purchaser is not personally obligated to pay the debt, but the property remains subject to the mortgage.

**subjective fault** Desired or virtually certain consequences of one's conduct.

**subjective satisfaction** Approval based upon a party's honestly held opinion.

**sublease** Transfer of less than all of the tenant's interest in the leasehold.

**subpoena** A subpoena is a command to appear at a certain time and place to give testimony upon a certain matter. A subpoena duces tecum requires production of books, papers, and other things.

**subrogation** The substitution of one thing for another, or of one person into the place of another with respect to rights, claims, or securities.

Subrogation denotes putting a third person who has paid a debt in the place of the creditor to whom he has paid it, so that he may exercise against the debtor all the rights which the creditor, if unpaid, might have done.

**subscribe** Literally to write underneath, as one's name. To sign at the end of a document. Also, to agree in writing to furnish money or its equivalent, or to agree to purchase some initial stock in a corporation.

**subscriber** Person who agrees to purchase initial stock in a corporation.

**subsidiary corporation** Corporation controlled by another corporation.

**substantial performance** Equitable doctrine protects against forfeiture for technical inadvertence or trivial variations or omissions in performance.

**substantive due process** Requirement that governmental action be compatible with individual liberties.

**substantive law** The basic law of rights and duties (contract law, criminal law, tort law, law of wills, etc.) as opposed to procedural law (law of pleading, law of evidence, law of jurisdiction, etc.).

**substantive unconscionability** Oppressive or grossly unfair contractual terms.

**sue** To begin a lawsuit in a court.

**suit** "Suit" is a generic term, of comprehensive signification, and applies to any proceeding in a court of justice in which the plaintiff pursues, in such court, the remedy which the law affords him for the redress of an injury or the recovery of a right.

*Derivative suit* Suit brought by a shareholder on behalf of the corporation to enforce a right belonging to the corporation.

*Direct suit* Suit brought by a shareholder against the corporation based upon his ownership of shares.

**summary judgment** Any party to a civil action may move for a summary judgment on a claim, counterclaim, or cross-claim when he believes that there is no genuine issue of material fact and that he is entitled to prevail as a matter of law.

**summons** Writ or process directed to the sheriff or other proper officer, requiring him to notify the person named that an action has been commenced against him in the court from where the process issues, and that he is required to appear, on a day named, and answer the complaint in such action.

**superseding cause** Intervening event that occurs after the defendant's negligent conduct and relieves him of liability.

**supreme law** Law that takes precedence over all conflicting laws.

**surety** One who undertakes to pay money or to do any other act in event that his principal debtor fails therein.

**suretyship** A guarantee of debts of another.

**surplus** Excess of net assets over stated capital.

**tangible property** Physical objects.

**tariff** Duty or tax imposed on goods moving into or out of the country.

**tenancy** Possession or occupancy of land or premises under lease.

*Joint tenancy* Joint tenants have one and the same interest, accruing by one and the same conveyance, commencing at one and the same time, and held by one and the same undivided possession. The primary incident of joint tenancy is survivorship, by which the entire tenancy on the decease of any joint tenant remains to the survivors, and at length to the last survivor.

*Tenancy at sufferance*  Only naked possession which continues after tenant's right of possession has terminated.

*Tenancy at will*  Possession of premises by permission of owner or landlord, but without a fixed term.

*Tenancy by the entirety*  A tenancy which is created between a husband and wife and by which together they hold title to the whole with right of survivorship so that, upon death of either, other takes whole to exclusion of deceased heirs. It is essentially a "joint tenancy," modified by the common law theory that husband and wife are one person.

*Tenancy for a period*  A tenancy for years or for some fixed period.

*Tenancy in common*  A form of ownership whereby each tenant (*i.e.,* owner) holds an undivided interest in property. Unlike a joint tenancy or a tenancy by the entirety, the interest of a tenant in common does not terminate upon his or her prior death (*i.e.,* there is no right of survivorship).

**tenancy in partnership**  Type of joint ownership that determines partners' rights in specific partnership property.

**tenant**  Possessor of the leasehold interest.

**tender**  An offer of money; the act by which one produces and offers to a person holding a claim or demand against him the amount of money which he considers and admits to be due, in satisfaction of such claim or demand, without any stipulation or condition.

Also, there may be a tender of performance of a duty other than the payment of money.

**tender of delivery**  Seller makes available to buyer goods conforming to the contract and so notifies the buyer.

**tender offer**  General invitation to all shareholders to purchase their shares at a specified price.

**testament**  Will.

**testator**  One who makes or has made a testament or will; one who dies leaving a will.

**third party beneficiary**  One for whose benefit a promise is made in a contract but who is not a party to the contract.

*Creditor beneficiary*  Where performance of a promise in a contract will benefit a person other than the promisee, that person is a creditor beneficiary if no purpose to make a gift appears from the terms of the promise in view of the accompanying circumstances and performance of the promise will satisfy an actual or supposed or asserted duty of the promisee to the beneficiary.

*Donee beneficiary*  The person who takes the benefit of the contract even though there is no privity between him and the contracting parties. A third party beneficiary who is not a creditor beneficiary. See also **beneficiary**.

**time paper**  Payable at definite time.

**time-price doctrine**  Permits sellers to have different prices for cash sales and credit sales.

**title**  The means whereby the owner of lands or of personalty has the just possession of his property.

**title insurance**  Provides protection against defect in title to real property.

**tort**  A private or civil wrong or injury, other than breach of contract, for which the court will provide a remedy in the form of an action for damages.

Three elements of every tort action are: Existence of legal duty from defendant to plaintiff, breach of duty, and damage as proximate result.

**tort-feasor**  One who commits a tort.

**trade acceptance**  A draft drawn by a seller which is presented for signature (acceptance) to the buyer at the time goods are purchased and which then becomes the equivalent of a note receivable of the seller and the note payable of the buyer.

**trade name**  Name used in trade or business to identify a particular business or manufacturer.

**trade secrets**  Private business information.

**trademark**  Distinctive insignia, word, or design of a good that is used to identify the manufacturer.

**transferor's warranty**  Warranties given by any person who transfers an instrument and receives consideration.

**treaty**  An agreement between or among independent nations.

**treble damages**  Three times actual loss.

**trespass**  At common law, trespass was a form of action brought to recover damages for any injury to one's person or property or relationship with another.

*Trespass to chattels or personal property*  An unlawful and serious interference with the possessory rights of another to personal property.

*Trespass to land*  At common law, every unauthorized and direct breach of the boundaries of another's land was an actionable trespass. The present prevailing position of the courts finds liability for trespass only in the case of intentional intrusion, or negligence, or some "abnormally dangerous activity" on the part of the defendant. Compare **nuisance**.

**trespasser**  Person who enters or remains on the land of another without permission or privilege to do so.

**trust**  Any arrangement whereby property is transferred with intention that it be administered by trustee for another's benefit.

*Charitable trust*  To benefit humankind.

*Constructive trust*  Wherever the circumstances of a transaction are such that the person who takes the legal estate in property cannot also enjoy the beneficial interest without necessarily violating some established principle of equity, the court will immediately raise a *constructive trust,* and fasten it upon the conscience of the legal owner, so as to convert him into a trustee for the parties who in equity are entitled to the beneficial enjoyment.

*Intervivos trust*  Established during the settlor's lifetime.

*Resulting trust*  One that arises by implication of law, where the legal estate in property is disposed of, conveyed, or transferred, but the intent appears or is inferred from the terms of the disposition, or from the accompanying facts and circumstances, that the beneficial interest is not to go or be enjoyed with the legal title.

*Spendthrift trust*  Removal of the trust's estate from the beneficiary's control.

*Testamentary trust*  Established by a will.

*Totten trust*  A tentative trust which is a joint bank account opened by the settlor.

*Voting trust*  A trust which holds the voting rights to stock in a corporation. It is a useful device when a majority of the shareholders in a corporation cannot agree on corporate policy.

**trustee**  In a strict sense, a "trustee" is one who holds the legal title to property for the benefit of another, while, in a broad sense, the term is sometimes applied to anyone standing in a fiduciary or confidential relation to another, such as agent, attorney, bailee, etc.

**trustee in bankruptcy** Representative of the estate in bankruptcy who is responsible for collecting, liquidating, and distributing the debtor's assets.

**tying arrangements** Conditioning a sale of a desired product (tying product) on the buyer's purchasing a second product (tied product).

**ultra vires** Acts beyond the scope of the powers of a corporation, as defined by its charter or laws of state of incorporation. By doctrine of ultra vires a contract made by a corporation beyond the scope of its corporate powers is unlawful.

**unconscionable** Unfair or unduly harsh.

**unconscionable contract** See **contracts**.

**underwriter** Any person, banker, or syndicate that guarantees to furnish a definite sum of money by a definite date to a business or government in return for an issue of bonds or stock. In insurance, the one assuming a risk in return for the payment of a premium.

**undisputed debt** Obligation whose existence and amount is not contested.

**undue influence** Term refers to conduct by which a person, through his power over mind of testator, makes the latter's desires conform to his own, thereby overmastering the volition of the testator.

**unemployment compensation** Compensation awarded to workers who have lost their jobs and cannot find other employment.

**unenforceable** Neither party can recover under the contract.

**unfair employer practice** Conduct in which an employer is prohibited from engaging.

**unfair labor practice** Conduct in which an employer or union is prohibited from engaging.

**unfair union practice** Conduct in which a union is prohibited from engaging.

**Uniform Commercial Code** One of the Uniform Laws drafted by the National Conference of Commissioners on Uniform State Laws governing commercial transactions (sales of goods, commercial paper, bank deposits and collections, letters of credit, bulk transfers, warehouse receipts, bills of lading, investment securities, and secured transactions).

**unilateral mistake** Erroneous belief on the part of only one of the parties to a contract.

**union shop** Employer can hire nonunion members, but the employee must join the union.

**universal life** Ordinary life divided into two components, a renewable term insurance policy and an investment portfolio.

**unliquidated debt** Obligation that is uncertain or contested in amount.

**unqualified indorsement** (see **Indorsement**) One that imposes liability upon the indorser.

**unreasonably dangerous** Danger beyond that which the ordinary consumer contemplates.

**unrestrictive indorsement** (see **Indorsement**) One that does not attempt to restrict the rights of the indorsee.

**usage of trade** A usage of trade is any practice or method of dealing having such regularity of observance in a place, vocation, or trade as to justify an expectation that it will be observed with respect to the transaction in question.

**usury** Collectively, the laws of a jurisdiction regulating the charging of interest rates. A usurious loan is one whose interest rates are determined to be in excess of those permitted by the usury laws.

**value** The performance of legal consideration, the forgiveness of an antecedent debt, the giving of a negotiable instrument, or the giving of an irrevocable commitment to a third party. U.C.C. § 1–201(44).

**variance** A use differing from that provided in the zoning ordinance in order to avoid undue hardship.

**vendee** A purchaser or buyer; one to whom anything is sold. See also **vendor**.

**vendor** The person who transfers property by sale, particularly real estate; "seller" being more commonly used for one who sells personalty. See also **vendee**.

**venue** "Jurisdiction" of the court means the inherent power to decide a case, whereas "venue" designates the particular county or city in which a court with jurisdiction may hear and determine the case.

**verdict** The formal and unanimous decision or finding of a jury, impaneled and sworn for the trial of a cause, upon the matters or questions duly submitted to them upon the trial.

**vertical privity** Who is liable to the plaintiff.

**vertical restraints** Agreements among parties at different levels of the distribution chain.

**vested** Fixed; accrued; settled; absolute. To be "vested," a right must be more than a mere expectation based on an anticipation of the continuance of an existing law; it must have become a title, legal or equitable, to the present or future enforcement of a demand, or a legal exemption from the demand of another.

**vested remainder** Unconditional remainder that is a fixed, present interest to be enjoyed in the future.

**vicarious liability** Indirect legal responsibility; for example, the liability of an employer for the acts of an employee, or, a principal for torts and contracts of an agent.

**void** Null; ineffectual; nugatory; having no legal force or binding effect; unable, in law, to support the purpose for which it was intended.

There is this difference between the two words "void" and "voidable": *void* in the strict sense means that an instrument or transaction is nugatory and ineffectual so that nothing can cure it; *voidable* exists when an imperfection or defect can be cured by the act or confirmation of him who could take advantage of it.

Frequently the word "void" is used and construed as having the more liberal meaning of "voidable."

**voidable** Capable of being made void. See also **void**.

**voir dire** Preliminary examination of potential jurors.

**voluntary** Resulting from free choice. The word, especially in statutes, often implies knowledge of essential facts.

**voting trust** Transfer of corporate shares voting rights to a trustee.

**wager (gambling)** Agreement that one party will win or lose depending upon the outcome of an event in which the only interest is the gain or loss.

**waiver** Terms "estoppel" and "waiver" are not synonymous; "waiver" means the voluntary, intentional relinquishment of a known right, and "estoppel" rests upon principle that, where anyone has done an act, or made a statement, which would be a fraud on his part to controvert or impair, because other party has acted upon it in belief that what was done or said was true, conscience and honest dealing require that he not be permitted to repudiate his act or gainsay his statement. See also **estoppel**.

**ward** An infant or insane person placed by authority of law under the care of a guardian.

**warehouse receipt** Receipt issued by a person storing goods.

**warehouser** Storer of goods for compensation.

**warrant,** *v.* In contracts, to engage or promise that a certain fact or state of facts, in relation to the subject-matter, is, or shall be, as it is represented to be.

In conveyancing, to assure the title to property sold, by an express covenant to that effect in the deed of conveyance.

**warranty** A warranty is a statement or representation made by seller of goods, contemporaneously with and as a part of contract of sale, having reference to character, quality, or title of goods, and by which seller promises or undertakes to insure that certain facts are or shall be as he then represents them.

The general statutory law governing warranties on sales of goods is provided in U.C.C. § 2–312 *et seq.* The three main types of warranties are: (1) express warranty; (2) implied warranty of fitness; (3) implied warranty of merchantability.

**warranty deed** Deed in which grantor warrants good clear title. The usual covenants of title are warranties of seisin, quiet enjoyment, right to convey, freedom from encumbrances, and defense of title as to all claims.

*Special warranty deed* Seller warrants that he has not impaired title.

**warranty liability** Applies to persons who transfer an instrument or receive payment or acceptance.

**warranty of title** Obligation to convey the right to ownership without any lien.

**waste** Any act or omission that does permanent injury to the realty or unreasonably changes its value.

**white collar crime** Corporate crime.

**will** A written instrument executed with the formalities required by statutes, whereby a person makes a disposition of his property to take effect after his death.

**winding up** To settle the accounts and liquidate the assets of a partnership or corporation, for the purpose of making distribution and terminating the concern.

**without reserve** Auctioneer may not withdraw the goods from the auction.

**workers' compensation** Compensation awarded to an employee who is injured when the injury arose out of and in the course of his employment.

**writ of certiorari** Discretionary review by a higher court. See also **certiorari**.

**writ of execution** Order served by sheriff upon debtor demanding payment of a court judgment against debtor.

**zoning** Public control over land use.

# Index

Page numbers in *italic* denote illustrations.